The

American

Book of Days

The
American
Book of Days

FOURTH EDITION

Compiled and Edited by
Stephen G. Christianson

The H.W. Wilson Company
New York • Dublin
2000

The American Book of Days
Fourth Edition
Copyright © 2000
By the H. W. Wilson Company

Third Edition Copyright 1978

Revised Edition Copyright 1948
By Helen Douglas Compton
Copyright renewed 1976
By Richard D. Forrest

First Edition
Copyright 1937
By George William Douglas
Copyright renewed 1965
By Helen Douglas Compton and Gertrude W. Douglas

Library of Congress Cataloging-in-Publication Data

Christianson, Stephen G.
    The American book of days.--4th ed. / by Stephen G. Christianson
        p. cm.
    Rev. ed. of: The American book of days / compiled and edited by Jane M. Hatch. 3rd ed. 1978.
    Includes index.
    ISBN 0-8242-0954-0 (alk. paper)
    1. Holidays--United States. 2. Fasts and feasts--United States. 3. Festivals--United States.
    I. Hatch, Jane M. American book of days. II. Title.

GT4803 .D6 2000
394.26973--dc21   99-086611

The excerpts from the speech "I Have a Dream" are reprinted by arrangement with The Heirs to the Estate of Martin Luther King, Jr., c/o Writers House, Inc., as agent for the proprietor. Copyright 1963 by Martin Luther King, Jr., copyright renewed 1991 by Coretta Scott King.

Printed in the United States of America

Visit H.W. Wilson's Web site: www.hwwilson.com

Contents

Preface

TO THE FOURTH EDITION

The Fourth Edition of *The American Book of Days* continues the work by George W. Douglas first published in 1937. His daughter Helen Douglas Compton revised and updated the book in a Second Edition, published in 1948. Jane M. Hatch oversaw the compilation and editing of the Third Edition, which was published in 1978.

The American Book of Days is a unique record of American history. For each of the 366 days of the year (including February 29), several substantial essays explore significant events through their anniversaries or through the birthdays of the individuals involved. Religious and secular holidays are included, but this book goes far beyond recording the well-known history of celebrations and festivals. Here the reader will find in-depth treatments of a wide variety of events of military, scientific, ethnic, political, or cultural significance. This completely updated and revised Fourth Edition of *The American Book of Days* expands the coverage of American history by substantially increasing the number of articles that were published in the 1978 Third Edition. The new essays serve a dual purpose: They keep the reader informed of the most important events in American history during the past years, and they apprise the student or researcher of significant developments that occurred prior to 1978 but were not included in the Third Edition, such as the life of Malcolm X.

The Fourth Edition retains the special emphasis given to the admission of new states to the Union, the birthdays of all of the American presidents, and the birthdays of chief justices of the Supreme Court. New features in the Fourth Edition include additional appendixes comprising such significant historical documents as the Constitution and the Declaration of Independence. Cross-referencing and an extensive index facilitate research and help readers trace specific themes throughout several articles.

Some events are "movable events," meaning they do not occur on the same calendar day every year. For example, the first Monday in September is Labor Day and the fourth Thursday in November is Thanksgiving. *See "A Note on Movable Events" on page xxvi.*

This book is dedicated to the authors and editors of the previous editions of this work, George W. Douglas, Helen Douglas Compton, and Jane M. Hatch. I have been fortunate enough to inherit the benefit of their labors, which spanned many decades, and no writer who contributes to the preservation of history and the passage of knowledge should ever be forgotten. I hope my successor, many years from now, will take these words to heart.

I would also like to thank two people at The H. W. Wilson Company who made this book possible, namely Michael P. Schulze, former vice president and director of General Reference, and Hilary Claggett, former senior editor.

STEPHEN G. CHRISTIANSON

List of Days and Events

January

February

June

July

September

December

A NOTE ON MOVABLE EVENTS

The dates of certain festivals, holidays, observances, and events change from year to year. These movable events, as they are called, include all Christian holy days whose dates depend on the movable feast of Easter; Jewish holy days, which fall on fixed days of the Hebrew calendar; and the festivals and observances that are scheduled for such shifting times as the first Monday in September (Labor Day) or the fourth Thursday in November (Thanksgiving).

Each movable event described in *The American Book of Days* is so designated at the beginning of the article. For the sake of consistency, articles from the 1978 Third Edition of this work are still listed under the date on which they took place in 1970. Movable events added to this Fourth Edition of the work are listed under the date on which they took place in 1997.

January

January is the first month in the modern, or Gregorian, calendar and consists of 31 days. The name (*Januarius* in Latin) derives from the two-faced Roman god Janus. Some scholars have claimed that the derivation of the name Janus is from the Latin *ianua*, meaning "door." Others have explained the name as the masculine form of Diana, which would be Dianus or Ianus.

There are many conflicting theories about Janus and his role in the Roman religion. He apparently figured prominently as the god of all beginnings. As the god of spatial beginnings, he watched over gates and doorways, which were generally under his protection; as the god of temporal beginnings, he presided over the first hour of the day. The first day of the month and the first month of the year were also sacred to him. Of all the gods, including Jupiter, his name was invoked first at the start of important undertakings, perhaps with the idea that his intervention as the "janitor" of all avenues would speed prayers directly to the immortals. As the deity of all beginnings, Janus was also entitled Consivius or "sower," in reference to his role as the beginner, or originator, of agriculture.

The worship of Janus existed as a local cult on the Janiculan Hill (variously interpreted as "door hill" or "city of Janus") west of Rome, on the banks of the Tiber River. Traditionally, this cult went back to Romulus or even to the period before the putative founding of Rome in 753 B.C. In addition, a festival in honor of Janus, called the *Agonalia*, was celebrated on January 9. The officiating priest, in this case the *rex sacrorum*, who represented the ancient king in his role as head of the state religion, sacrificed a ram on the occasion. Later Romans, intrigued by the lofty character of this ceremony, proposed various additional interpretations about the possible nature of Janus: perhaps he was a cosmic deity, sky god, or god of water crossings. Discovering in the name Janus the same Latin root as in the name of Diana, the moon goddess, they even imagined him to be a moon deity.

As the animistic spirit of doorways (*ianuae*) and arches (*iani*), Janus guarded the numerous ceremonial gateways in Rome. These freestanding structures were used especially for noteworthy entrances and exits on state occasions. Numa Pompilius, the legendary second king of Rome (roughly 715–672 B.C.), probably dedicated the famous *Ianus geminus*, the arcade or covered passage facing east and west which was located at the northeast end of the Roman Forum. A simple, rectangular, bronze edifice, it had double doors at each end that were traditionally opened in time of war and closed in peace. This highly symbolic arcade, sometimes described simply as an arch, was undoubtedly connected with a type of war magic, a superstitious belief that passage through it brought luck to outgoing and incoming armies. The Romans were so often at war, however, that it is said the doors of the structure were closed only twice during the seven centuries between the reigns of Numa and Augustus. Janus was also honored by a less well-known archway, located near the theater of Marcellus in the *forum holitorium* (where vegetables were sold). It was probably erected by the Roman general and consul Gaius Duilius, about 260 B.C., following his victory over the Carthaginian fleet off Mylae.

Janus was closely connected with early Roman coinage. He was represented as a deity with two faces on the ancient *as*, which often had on its reverse side a representation of a ship's prow. An ancient source says that Roman boys liked to toss these coins and bet *capita aut navia* ("heads or ships"), in much the same way that today's children play "heads or tails."

Although Janus was usually depicted with two bearded faces looking in opposite directions, representing the future and the past, the number of faces shown gradually increased to four. Emperor Domitian (A.D. 81–96), for example, dedicated a temple to Janus Quadrifrons, or "four-faced Janus." In his role as porter, or doorkeeper, the god was sometimes pictured as holding a staff in his right hand and a key or keys in his left. As such, he was termed Patulcius, meaning "opener," and Clusius, or "closer". In the late Roman Empire, he was portrayed as both a bearded and unbearded figure; in place of the staff and keys, the fingers of his right hand sometimes showed the number CCC, or 300, and those of his left LXV, or 65, for the total 365 days of the year.

The earliest calendars, such as the Egyptian, Jewish, and Greek, did not place the beginning of the year in January. The early Romans originally began the calendar year with Martius (see March), and January did not even appear among their ten months. Numa Pompilius supposedly decreed that two new months should be added at the end of the ten previous ones. He called the first of these additions Januarius in honor of Janus, the cult god of the doorways. In 153 B.C., the Roman state proclaimed January 1 to be New Year's Day, thus turning the 11th month, Januarius, into the first month of the year. For a long time, however, older traditions prevailed and most Romans still considered the year to start in March. Moreover, by the end of the Roman republic, the entire calendar had become highly inaccurate and confused, since state officials were constantly making changes in it for political purposes. In 46 B.C., Julius Caesar instituted a much-needed calendar reform (see Appendix A: The Calendar). The resulting Julian calendar—now also known as the Old Style calendar—which became effective in 45 B.C., reinstated January as the first month and January 1 as the first day of the year. In later centuries, however, from the fall of the Roman Empire through the Middle Ages, there was widespread diversity as to the date on which the year began in different areas. Contributing to the diversity were political fragmentation, meager communications, and the hostility of the Catholic Church to pagan traditions. Experimentation with a return to the January 1 new year of ancient Roman times was attempted as early as the 13th century in present-day Germany, and continued sporadically throughout western Europe into the 16th century. The Gregorian, or New Style, calendar instituted by Pope Gregory XIII in 1582 also employed this innovation, decreeing January 1 as the beginning of the new year for all Catholic countries. By degrees Protestant countries fell into line as they adopted the new calendar over the next 170 years. Thus, at the brink of the modern era, January 1 reassumed its former place as the start of the new year.

Among non-Roman peoples, the names of the months often stemmed from a natural phenomenon or a seasonal occupation peculiar to the particular month. Such series of month names have been found in all parts of the world with the exception of South America and Australia. In western Europe, for example, the Anglo-Saxons called January Wulf-monath, in allusion to the hunger of the wolves at that time of year, which made them bold enough to leave the forests and enter villages in search of food. The name Aefter-Yule was also used to designate the month after the great feast of Christmas. Charlemagne, the early medieval Frankish emperor, appropriately called January Wintarmanoth, or "wintermonth."

In ancient and modern times, particular stones have been connected with the various months. The lucky gem or birthstone often associated with January is the garnet, which symbolizes constancy.

January 1

New Year's Day

So fundamental to everyday life are ways of marking the passage of time that most people feel their own calendar customs have been virtually ordained by nature (see Appendix A: The Calendar). The Gregorian, or New Style, calendar now used throughout most of the world starts the year on January 1. Although that date has been recognized as New Year's Day in more and more countries since the "new" calendar was first introduced in 1582, it is actually a rather unnatural day for beginning the year, since it has no special place in the sun's cycle. January 1 is connected with neither the winter nor the summer solstice, nor with the spring or autumn equinox—four dates that do relate to the change of the seasons and which historically related to significant festivities and religious rites. The ancient Egyptians, Phoenicians, and Persians, for example, began their year with the autumn equinox (on or about September 21 in the Gregorian calendar), and the Greeks for many centuries used the winter solstice (December 21 or 22 in the Gregorian calendar). Other societies, such as the Chinese, base the new year on the lunar cycle rather than the solar cycle. Chinese New Year, for example, takes place any time between January 21 and February 19, inclusive, and always on the new moon.

The United States inherited January 1 as the beginning of the new year from the English and other European settlers, who themselves came to embrace that date over the course of roughly two thousand years. The ancient Romans, under a very old and inaccurate calendar, had originally taken Martius (see March) as the first month of the year. But in 153 B.C., the Roman state declared January 1 thenceforth to be New Year's Day, turning the 11th month, Januarius (see January), into a new first month. In a pattern that would often be repeated, however, the common people remembered their old traditions and for a long time still considered the year to end with the celebration of the *Terminalia* on February 23, after which intercalation (the insertion of a varying number of days) was made to offset errors in the calendar and so complete the year.

By the end of the Roman republic, the calendar was once more highly confused, since officials had tampered with it to cut short or extend magistrates' terms of office. In 46 B.C., Julius Caesar, as *pontifex maximus* and dictator, instituted necessary reforms. Under his new calendar, subsequently named the Julian calendar (see Appendix A: The Calendar), January 1 was reinstituted as New Year's Day. The new calendar became effective the following year, 45 B.C.

The Romans traditionally celebrated the Feast of Janus, the god of doorways and of beginnings who is depicted as looking both forward to the future and backward to the past, on the first of January. This deity was certainly suitable to the New Year, and to begin the year auspiciously the Romans offered sacrifices to him. They also exchanged greetings with kin and acquaintances and gave New Year's gifts, called *strenae*, after Strenia, the goddess of strength. According to tradition, the custom of giving *strenae* originated in the eighth century B.C., when the Romans presented the king of the Sabines with branches from the trees consecrated to Strenia, as tokens of good omen. *Strenae* also means "omens" in Latin, and this semantic link captures the superstition and expectancy with which most peoples have greeted the New Year. As with the Romans and Sabines, New Year's festivities throughout the world still tend to be occasions for smoothing over quarrels and reaffirming human ties.

In time, the Romans replaced with more elaborate gifts the branches of bay and palm traditionally gathered on the first day of the year. During the days of the Roman Empire, courtiers and others gave the emperor New Year's presents of great value, which enriched his personal coffers and became a source of political corruption. Aware of the burden that these traditional gifts placed on the people, the Emperor Claudius issued a decree limiting the amounts to be given. In addition, the New Year's Feast of Janus was also marked by masquerades and public entertainments, not to mention the occasional Roman orgy.

After their conversion to Christianity in the fourth century, the Roman emperors continued for some time the pagan traditions of New Year's. The young church, however, increasingly condemned these observances as scandalous and forbade Christians to participate. Much of the struggle between the growing faith and the old pagan culture centered around such public observances. As it gained strength, the church purposely planned Christian festivals in competition with pagan ones. It established Christmas on December 25 (then the winter solstice) in counterpoint to the Mithraic rites and the Roman *Saturnalia*, for example. Following the biblical account, the Feast of the Circumcision of the infant Jesus then fell eight days later, on January 1, competing conveniently with the Feast of Janus and New Year's Day. Saint Ambrose declared, "We fast on this day [Circumcision] that the heathen may know we condemn their pleasures." Even in modern times, some branches of the Christian church celebrate January 1 as the Feast of the Circumcision or as the Solemnity of Mary.

The church remained strongly hostile to the old pagan New Year throughout the Middle Ages. As a result, January 1 was weakened and its observance as New Year's Day may have disappeared for some centuries in parts of Western Europe. Certainly, political fragmentation and poor communications after the collapse of Rome encouraged diversity concerning the beginning of the calendar year. Between the 9th and the late 11th centuries, Christmas gained wide acceptance as the date for changing the year. Gradually, December 25 thus replaced such earlier New Year dates as January 1, the Franks' March 1, and the late Roman Empire's September 1, which also continued in use in the Byzantine Empire for many centuries. From Anglo-Saxon times until the reign of Henry II in the mid-12th century, the new year began on Christmas in England, although William the Conqueror briefly tried to institute January 1.

In the High Middle Ages, growing veneration of the Virgin Mary made March 25, the Feast of the Annunciation, or Lady Day (the supposed date of Jesus' conception), an increasingly great church festival, and in some lands attention focused on this day as an appropriate beginning for the year. The practice of starting the new calendar year from the Feast of the Annunciation spread from the early 11th century on. In England, March 25 became established as the beginning of the calendar year from the late 12th century, and this was also the practice in most domains of the French king and in Florence and Pisa. December 25, however, continued to begin the year in much of the Holy Roman Empire and in Scandinavia. Only on the Iberian Peninsula did January 1 begin the year through the Middle Ages, and even there the dating was changed to December 25 in the 14th century. By contrast, from the reign of Philip II, king of France, in the early 13th century, the French court began the new year on the movable feast of Easter. With all its inconveniences, this usage spread to districts bordering France on the north and east. However, in folk tradition throughout these areas, the New Year usually continued to be Lady Day or Christmas.

Although scattered attempts to revive the practice of starting the year on January 1 were made as early as the mid-13th century, little came of such efforts until the 16th century. Then, at the threshold of the modern period, a really significant movement developed to restore the ancient civil New Year of January 1. The interest of humanists and their patrons in the literature of antiquity during this period encouraged rulers to imitate the ancient Roman New Year. The increasing administration of government by laymen instead of by priests may also have encouraged detachment of the civil New Year from the festivals of the church. As early as 1532, the Estates of Holland declared January 1 New Year's Day. In 1556 the king of Spain issued a similar decree for his lands; in 1558, the Holy Roman Emperor did the same for the Empire; and in 1563 King Charles IX of France followed suit, though the reform did not take effect until it was registered by the Parlement of Paris in 1567. In 1575, Protestant Geneva also declared January 1 as the beginning of the New Year.

By this time, however, the whole Julian calendar was seen to be badly in need of reform. The most pressing of the difficulties was that over the approximately 1,600 years that the Julian calendar had been in use, a small discrepancy between the actual length of the solar year and the length of the year by the Julian calendar had added up to approximately ten days. With the advice of astronomers, Pope Gregory XIII promulgated the needed changes in 1582, rectifying the above discrepancy by ordering ten calendar days to be dropped. Among other things, his New Style, or Gregorian, calendar also caused the year to begin on January 1 wherever the new calendar was adopted (except in a few Italian cities).

Although the calendar reformers made this change on ecclesiastical grounds related to the church's reckoning of Easter, its effect was to strengthen the revival of the ancient pagan date of January 1 for the New Year. Where January 1 had already become New Year's Day (as in Holland, Spain, Portugal, France, and the Holy Roman Empire), adoption of the Gregorian calendar simply caused the year to begin ten days earlier, on January 1, New Style, instead of on January 1, Old Style. General acceptance of the Gregorian calendar was complicated, however, by the fact that by 1582 many European governments no longer acknowledged papal authority. In predominantly Roman Catholic states and provinces, and in the Protestant provinces of Holland and Zeeland as well, the new calendar was instituted rapidly between 1582 and 1584, but most Protestant states would not comply. In 1599 the king of Scotland ordered that thenceforth January 1 should begin the year in his realm, but the Scots celebrated New Year's Day on January 1, Old Style, through 1752, in which year the Gregorian calendar was instituted for all Great Britain by act of Parliament. Denmark and Norway, the Protestant states of Germany, the provinces of the United Netherlands, and the Protestant cantons of Switzerland all introduced the new calendar in 1700 or 1701, and presumably thereafter celebrated New Year's Day on January 1, New Style, although there are indications that the Swiss may not have used that date to begin their calendar year before 1740.

England, Ireland, and the American colonies began the calendar year on March 25, Old Style, up through 1751, a period extending nearly a century and a half beyond the first permanent English settlement in the New World. By act of Parliament, however, the year 1751 was shortened to 282 days (March 25 to December 31), and the year 1752 was ordered to begin on January 1, Old Style. Thus, the dates January 1 to March 24, 1751, were nonexistent in England and the colonies. To complete the Gregorian reform for Great Britain, the by then requisite 11 days were dropped from the calendar between September 2 and 14, 1752, so that New Year's Day in 1753 was January 1, New Style. Curiously, there were more than a few violent riots in London due to this changeover, started by crowds of people who were convinced that the 11 days being dropped from the calendar were in effect 11 days by which their lives were being shortened. Sweden's first January 1 New Year, New Style, came in 1754, the reformed calendar having been introduced there in 1753. The maverick cities of Florence and Pisa adopted January 1 as the beginning of the year after 1749, but the Republic of Venice held out for its unique date of March 1 until its demise in 1797. Peter the Great, in a *ukase* of 1699, ordered that in Russia the new year begin thenceforth on January 1, Old Style, but the Gregorian calendar was not introduced into Russia until 1918, after the Russian Revolution. Thus the Russians' first January 1 New Year to be observed under the New Style calendar was in 1919. Greece and Greek Orthodox communities made the change to the Gregorian, New Style, calendar in 1924. However, some of the Eastern Orthodox national churches resisted the change much longer, with the result that their New Year observances, on what the old Julian calendar said was January 1, fell on what the Gregorian calendar in the 20th century regarded as January 14. Tenacious adherence to the Julian calendar was particularly notable among Russian Orthodox churches. Not until the beginning of the 1970s, for instance, did the change to the new calendar become really widespread among Russian Orthodox churches in the United States.

This involved history of the beginnings of the year suggests the relative unimportance of coordinated timing for medieval and early modern European societies. Political rivalries also contributed to the variations, for styling the year in a particular way was an indication of political independence.

During the centuries when Christmas began the calendar year, the old Roman New Year of January 1 may have been retained in some manner in the Christmas festivities, which lasted at least for the following week through January 1. Scattered evidence indeed suggests that for many centuries when it did not begin the calendar year, January 1 was nonetheless referred to as New Year's Day by the English. The Roman custom of lavish New Year's gifts to rulers would seem to have given kings a particular stake in keeping January 1 alive as New Year's Day, even when they styled their calendars otherwise. Queen Elizabeth I was able to obtain almost her entire wardrobe and jewels from such gifts, and British rulers before and after her benefited from the custom of New Year's gifts until about the end of the 18th century.

Gift-giving among the people at New Year's rather than at Christmas has varied with the centuries. The custom in England is thought to have originated in earliest British history, with the Celtic druids' distribution of branches of the sacred mistletoe as New Year's gifts to the people. The invading Saxons are also believed to have exchanged gifts at New Year's. Certainly under the Tudor and Stuart monarchs it was the custom for all classes to give New Year's presents to friends and relatives. Among ordinary folk, favorite gifts were multicolored eggs, nuts, apples or oranges studded with cloves, special cakes of mincemeat, and plain or gilded nutmegs. Women in the wealthier classes were given books, ornamented gloves, or brooches, and from the practice of sometimes giving a monetary equivalent of the article came the term "pin money" for the little bit of cash that women were allowed to spend as they pleased during the centuries when they lacked economic rights. By the mid-19th century, however, the New Year's gift-giving had died out in England and of course is very rare in the United States today. There are other countries, however, such as Japan, where gift-giving or the exchange of greeting cards as part of New Year's is the common practice.

As today, New Year's festivities in the past often lasted from late on New Year's Eve to the early hours of New Year's Day, with celebrators bidding the old year farewell and welcoming the new at midnight in one combined set of gestures. One of the most dramatic Old World customs, which was carried to the Americas, was to toll the passing of the year just before midnight. Remnants of this custom can still be seen in such events as the countdown from Times Square in New York City on New Year's Eve that is typically broadcast live on American television.

From colonial Dutch practice, the presidents of the United States followed a long-observed custom of welcoming the New Year by holding an open house on January 1. George Washington began the tradition with the first presidential reception on New Year's Day, January 1, 1791, in New York (then the capital of the country), and John and Abigail Adams carried it to the new capital of Washington, D.C. Their first reception was held when the White House was still unfinished. Thomas Jefferson, the first president of the opposing party, later continued the custom. The presidential New Year's reception remained a major social event in the capital through January 1, 1933, under President Herbert Hoover. But in 1934, because his physical condition made it difficult to stand in a long receiving line, President Franklin Delano Roosevelt discontinued the custom. It has never been revived in any significant way, at least not as an annual ritual, although of course the president and the first lady frequently hold such social functions (private and otherwise) as their personal schedules and the affairs of state permit.

The custom of paying New Year's calls has generally declined in the United States during the 20th century. This practice reached its greatest height in the latter decades of the 19th century. Those who intended to receive their friends and acquaintances sent their names to the newspapers with the hours when they would be at home, so that callers might know which homes would welcome them. These lists filled many columns and included the names of famous socialites and ordinary citizens alike. However, the tradition was eventually absorbed into the practice of holding

January 1

New Year's Eve parties, and the invention of the telephone made personal house calls more and more of an anachronism.

Today, Americans are primarily event-oriented rather than tradition-oriented about New Year's Day. While gift-giving and important family gatherings still prevail in other lands, many Americans devote at least part of New Year's Day to watching, in person or on television, a choice of spectacles. These events include college football bowl games and parades such as the Tournament of Roses Parade (see below).

The first of January is a legal holiday in every state of the Union, the District of Columbia, and in all U.S. territories and possessions. It begins the fiscal year for most U.S. taxpayers and is the civil New Year for all U.S. citizens. But certain groups celebrate additional versions of the New Year, in keeping with their ancestral and religious traditions. The Chinese New Year falls in either January or February; the Jewish New Year, Rosh Hashanah, in either September or October; and the Islamic New Year is on the first day of the month of Muharram (all according to lunar reckonings).

The Emancipation Proclamation

During the Civil War, President Abraham Lincoln issued his historic Emancipation Proclamation on January 1, 1863. In it the president declared that all slaves within those states and parts of states then in rebellion against the authority of the federal government "are, and henceforward shall be, free." The president had announced his intention to issue such a proclamation the previous fall, in the ill-founded hope that some of the slaveholding Confederate states would have laid down their arms before the January 1 deadline.

Since the Emancipation Proclamation applied only to areas not controlled by the federal government, it had little immediate practical effect. Its long-range effects, however, were major. It broadened the purpose of the war, which the federal government previously saw purely as a struggle to preserve the federal Union. Now the fighting was viewed as not only for union, but also for human freedom. The broadened goal enlisted the ardor of those who opposed slavery and won friends abroad for the Union cause. Britain and France, both wavering earlier, were deterred from recognizing the Confederacy.

Any lingering doubts about the constitutionality of the Emancipation Proclamation, which had been put forward by the president as a war measure, were removed on December 18, 1865, when the 13th Amendment to the Constitution, abolishing slavery throughout the United States, became effective through ratification by 27 states (the necessary three-fourths). The text of the proclamation that preceded it on January 1, 1863 (with the introductory section omitted), is as follows:

Now, therefore, I, Abraham Lincoln, President of the United States, by virtue of the power in me vested as Commander-in-Chief of the Army and Navy of the United States in time of actual armed rebellion against the authority and government of the United States, and as a fit and necessary war measure for suppressing said rebellion, do, on this first day of January, A.D. 1863, and in accordance with my purpose so to do, publicly proclaim for the full period of one hundred days from [September 22, 1862] . . . order and designate as the States and parts of States wherein the people thereof, respectively, are this day in rebellion against the United States the following, to wit:

Arkansas, Texas, Louisiana (except the parishes of St. Bernard, Plaquemines, Jefferson, St. John, St. Charles, St. James, Ascension, Assumption, Terrebonne, Lafourche, St. Mary, St. Martin and Orleans, including the city of New Orleans), Mississippi, Alabama, Florida, Georgia, South Carolina, North Carolina and Virginia (except the forty-eight counties designated as West Virginia and also the counties of Berkeley, Accomac, Northhampton, Elizabeth City, York, Princess Anne and Norfolk, including the cities of Norfolk and Portsmouth) and which excepted parts are for the present left precisely as if this proclamation were not issued.

And by virtue of the power and for the purpose aforesaid, I do order and declare that all persons held as slaves within said designated States and parts of States are, and henceforward shall be, free; and that the Executive Government of the United States, including the military and naval authorities thereof, will recognize and maintain the freedom of said persons.

And I hereby enjoin upon the people so declared to be free to abstain from all violence, unless in necessary self-defense; and I recommend to them that, in all cases when allowed, they labor faithfully for reasonable wages.

And I further declare and make known that such persons of suitable condition will be received into the armed service of the United States to garrison forts, positions, stations, and other places, and to man vessels of all sorts in said service.

Lincoln presents the Emancipation Proclamation.

And upon this act, sincerely believed to be an act of justice, warranted by the Constitution upon military necessity, I invoke the considerate judgment of mankind and the gracious favor of Almighty God.

January 1, the anniversary of Lincoln's final Emancipation Proclamation, is the date that generally has been regarded as Emancipation Day. Sometimes September 22, the anniversary of Lincoln's preliminary Emancipation Proclamation, is marked instead. In various parts of the country certain other days have been observed as Emancipation Day. African American citizens in Texas, for example, celebrate June 19, the date in 1865 when General Robert S. Granger, in command of the military district of Texas, issued a proclamation notifying the slaves that they were free. Emancipation Day has been noted in some states on the anniversary of their adoption of the 13th Amendment to the Constitution; in others, on the date when they abolished slavery. Thus the anniversary of emancipation has been marked, from time to time, on such varying dates as May 22, May 29, May 30, June 19, August 2, August 4, August 8, September 12, September 22, and October 15, as well as on January 1.

In an effort to achieve for everyone those "certain unalienable Rights" of which the Declaration of Independence had spoken, advocates of civil rights began in the mid-1950s to utilize picketing, sit-ins, freedom bus rides, mass meetings, boycotts, prayer demonstrations, protest marches, and other forms of nonviolent demonstration to fight discrimination and hasten desegregation. The chief (though far from only) spokesman for the movement in this early phase was the Reverend Martin Luther King Jr., who borrowed heavily from the precepts of civil disobedience enunciated by Henry David Thoreau and Mahatma Gandhi. The protests brought a measure of success, including the desegregation of a number of public facilities, and incidents of police brutality against the protesters (such as in Birmingham, Alabama) served only to ignite more demonstrations.

The summer of protest in 1963, which marked the 100th anniversary year of the Emancipation Proclamation, came to a climax on August 28, 1963, when 200,000 persons joined in a multiracial March on Washington for Jobs and Freedom. With the rallying cry "Freedom Now!" and the theme song "We Shall Overcome," the march had the support of civil rights, religious, labor, and other groups. One of its aims was to garner support for what became the 1964 Civil Rights Act, then just a bill under consideration by Congress. The marchers' destination was the Lincoln Memorial. There before the likeness of the man who had penned the Emancipation Proclamation 100 years before, Martin Luther King Jr. capped the day's other addresses with what is remembered as his "I Have a Dream" speech, telling how much remained to be done before emancipation was complete.

January 1

First National Flag

See also Flag Day, June 14.

In an act crucial to the cause of American independence, the Second Continental Congress on June 15, 1775, chose George Washington as general and commander in chief of the Continental army. Although the actual nomination of Washington was made by Thomas Johnson of Maryland, the idea originated with an earlier speech by John Adams. The delegate from Massachusetts urged the Congress to accept as an army the colonial forces then besieging the British at Boston, and to name without further delay a general who might preserve the colonists' precarious hope of obtaining redress for their grievances against the British motherland.

For that high command, as Adams recalled in his autobiography, he hinted unmistakably to the Congress that he "had but one gentleman in . . . mind . . . a gentleman from Virginia . . . well known to all of us, a gentleman whose skill and experience as an officer, whose . . . great talents, and excellent universal character would command the approbation of all America, and unite the cordial exertions of all the Colonies better than any other person in the Union."

The suggestion was direct enough to send Washington, who was attending the Congress as a delegate from Virginia, scurrying from the room while the matter was discussed. After the Congress had voted to adopt the besieging army and unanimously approved Washington as general and commander in chief, the Virginian accepted "the momentous duty" with thanks, but he added characteristically, "lest some unlucky event should happen, I beg it may be remembered . . . that I this day declare with the utmost sincerity, I do not think myself equal to the Command I am honoured with."

Washington left Philadelphia, where the Congress was meeting, on June 23. Arriving at Cambridge, Massachusetts, just across the Charles River from Boston, he officially took command of his ragged force of some 16,000 men on July 3, 1775. In the ensuing months, most of his energies were devoted to equipping and training this raw force, strengthening discipline, and securing longer enlistments than the initial brief commitments, which had resulted in recruits departing inopportunely.

As the months went by, Washington acquired weapons and ammunition and shaped his unseasoned militiamen into something that resembled a coordinated fighting force. Finally, on January 1, 1776, he was ready to officially proclaim the for-

mation of the Continental army, issuing this announcement from his headquarters at Cambridge. The occasion called for a flag that would serve as the Continental colors, and one of Washington's choosing (which he referred to as the Union Flag) accordingly was hoisted. The flag had 13 horizontal stripes of alternating red and white, representing the 13 colonies, with the corner (now occupied by 50 stars) bearing a blue canton with the crosses of St. George and St. Andrew. Although Washington had called his army's flag the Union Flag, others would refer to it by other names: the Great (or Grand) Union Flag, the Continental Flag, the Congress Flag, and, misleadingly, the Cambridge Flag.

Although Revolutionary soldiers would march under a variety of colonial, regimental, and company flags, this first flag of Washington's army gained rapidly in popularity and appeared throughout the colonies during 1776 and 1777. It was, in effect, the first national American flag, even though there is no record that the Congress ever designated it so officially.

On June 14, 1777 (see also Flag Day, June 14), the Continental Congress adopted a flag with 13 alternating red and white stripes, with 13 white stars in a blue field to represent the 13 colonies. Set forth below is a brief chronology of the evolution of the modern American flag from these Revolutionary predecessors.

1795: After Vermont and Kentucky are admitted to the Union, a new flag with 15 stars and 15 stripes is adopted.

1818: After five more states are admitted to the Union (Indiana, Louisiana, Mississippi, Ohio, and Tennessee), a flag with 20 stars is adopted, but the new design reverts to 13 stripes. The flag has remained at 13 stripes ever since, to honor the 13 original colonies of the American Revolution. Congress provided that henceforth one star would be added to the flag when a new state is admitted to the Union, to take place on the Fourth of July following the formal date of admission.

1819, 1820, 1822, 1836, 1837, 1845, 1846, 1847, 1848, 1851, 1858, 1859, 1861, 1863, 1865, 1867, 1877, 1890, 1891, 1896, 1908, 1912: The flag goes from 20 stars to 48 stars as 28 more states are admitted to the Union. No stars were removed from the flag during the Civil War when 11 southern states seceded from the Union, since their secession was not recognized, and in fact one star was added to the flag in 1863 when West Virginia was admitted to the Union from territory formerly belonging to Confederate Virginia.

1960: The modern flag of 50 stars is adopted after Alaska and Hawaii are admitted to the Union.

1969: Astronaut Neil Armstrong places an American flag on the Moon. The flag is specially constructed from self-supporting material so that it will unfurl in an airless environment, the first instance of a flag designed for use off the planet Earth.

Barry Goldwater's Birthday

Barry Morris Goldwater was born on January 1, 1909, in Phoenix, Territory of Arizona, to Baron Goldwater and Josephine (Williamson) Goldwater. His surname came from his paternal grandfather, Michael Goldwasser, a Polish Jew and successful merchant whose name was Americanized to Goldwater.

As a youth, Goldwater was more interested in having fun than in studying, and so his parents sent him to Staunton Military Academy in Lexington, Virginia, for his high school education and to instill some discipline. Goldwater managed to finish high school, but when he returned to Arizona in 1928 to attend the University of Arizona at Tucson, he dropped out after only one year. Goldwater later characterized his decision to drop out as "the worst mistake I ever made." He went to work in the family's retail trade business and prospered, starting out as a junior clerk and eventually working his way up to president in 1937. By then Goldwater had married the wealthy Margaret Johnson, on September 22, 1934. The couple would have four children: Joanne, Barry Jr., Michael, and Margaret.

During World War II, Goldwater flew cargo planes in both the European and Pacific theaters. He left the service in 1945 with the rank of lieutenant colonel. He returned to Arizona, and entered politics in 1949 when he ran for the Phoenix city council on a nonpartisan ticket. Although by now Goldwater was a registered Republican, his family's ties were with the Democrats, which may have explained his decision to run on a neutral slate. He won the election handily, and went on to serve in Republican Howard Pyle's successful campaign for governor in 1950.

Encouraged by his fellow Republicans, in 1952 Goldwater ran for the United States Senate, taking on a formidable Democratic opponent in the form of Senate majority leader Ernest W. McFarland. Since Arizona was still largely Democratic, Goldwater campaigned as "not a me-too Republican . . . but a Republican opposed to the superstate and to gigantic bureaucratic, centralized authority." Thanks to a well-run campaign, and to the Re-

publican victory in the 1952 presidential election which helped give Goldwater some momentum, Goldwater was able to defeat McFarland by approximately 7,000 votes.

In the Senate, Goldwater showed himself to be a true conservative, voting against most federal spending proposals for domestic social programs, although he was more of a moderate when it came to social security. Not coincidentally, Arizona was experiencing an influx of retirees, who tended to be politically conservative and vote Republican but who were dependent on social security. Goldwater also became one of the intellectual spokesmen for the Republican Party and for American conservatism. His 1960 book, *The Conscience of a Conservative*, was an eloquent expression of his conservative ideals:

> My aim is not to pass laws, but to repeal them. It is not to inaugurate new programs, but to cancel old ones that do violence to the Constitution . . . and if I should be attacked for neglecting my constituents' "interests," I shall reply that I was informed that their main interest is liberty and that in that cause I am doing the very best that I can.

In 1962 Goldwater published another book, entitled *Why Not Victory?*, in which he strongly criticized the supporters of accommodation with the Soviet Union. Goldwater had always been staunchly anti-Communist. He was one of the few senators to vote against the censure of Joseph McCarthy in 1954, he supported the "appropriate use of nuclear weapons" against Communist enemies, and he voted against the 1963 Nuclear Test Ban Treaty with the Soviet Union.

In the early 1960s, the Republican Party was on the defensive politically. Its presidential candidate, Richard M. Nixon, had lost to John F. Kennedy in the 1960 presidential campaign. Kennedy was a popular president, and the Democrats were taking the initiative on issues such as civil rights. Many Republicans turned to Goldwater for leadership, attracted by his intellectual abilities and conservative puritanism. Goldwater was also an active fund-raiser, and helped campaign for his fellow Republicans. Although for a time Goldwater denied that he was interested in seeking the 1964 Republican nomination for president, by 1963 a Goldwater campaign organization had emerged.

In his presidential campaign, Goldwater benefited from the fact that other leading Republicans, such as former candidate Nixon, stayed out of the race. There was a minor challenge by Pennsylvania governor William W. Scranton, but by the time of the Republican National Convention in July

1964, Goldwater had locked up the primaries and won the nomination on the first ballot. For his running mate, Goldwater chose New York congressman William E. Miller. During his acceptance speech, Goldwater summarized his puritanical conservatism with two phrases that would become famous: "extremism in the defense of liberty is no vice" and "moderation in pursuit of justice is no virtue."

Goldwater's stance made many people nervous. During the Cuban missile crisis of October 1962, the country had been at the brink of nuclear war, and it was a sobering experience not soon forgotten. Goldwater's tacit endorsement of the selective use of nuclear weapons was unpopular, and many Republicans distanced themselves from the Goldwater candidacy. The phrase "extremism in the defense of liberty is no vice" helped to cement Goldwater's image as a warmonger. These facts were not lost on the incumbent president, Democrat Lyndon Baines Johnson, who had risen to the presidency when Kennedy was assassinated on November 22, 1963. In one of the most effective pieces of political advertising in history, the Johnson campaign ran a television advertisement featuring a little girl picking petals from a flower in a field during a nuclear countdown, which ended in a mushroom-cloud explosion and a somber message from President Johnson that "we must all learn to love one another or die."

The ad was broadcast only once, but it was devastating for the Goldwater campaign. Further, Johnson had the advantage of popular sympathy in the wake of the Kennedy assassination. On November 3, 1964, Goldwater lost by a landslide, taking only 38.7 percent of the electorate compared to Johnson's 61.3 percent.

Goldwater left the Senate and returned to Arizona, where he was treated like a pariah by his fellow Republicans. He would never again be a contender for the presidency, but he did reemerge on the national political scene in 1968, when he successfully ran once again for the Senate. Predictably, Goldwater supported the Vietnam War in his third term. Surprisingly, he also supported President Nixon's initiative with Communist China, a move that shocked other conservative Republicans. Goldwater was not just a Nixon yes-man, however. During the Watergate affair he criticized the administration and told Nixon to come clean and "get rid of the smell." It was Goldwater who eventually led the congressional Republicans to the White House and told the president that impeachment was inevitable, a move that helped seal Nixon's decision to resign.

Goldwater's performance during Watergate restored his credibility in the public eye and his stature with conservative Republicans. Reelected to a fourth term in 1974, he continued to be a "cold warrior," voting in favor of military buildup and against withdrawals of American power such as President Jimmy Carter's Panama Canal treaty. By the early 1980s, however, Goldwater—despite his reelection in 1980—had been eclipsed by new conservative leaders such as Ronald Reagan, who was elected president in 1980. In 1986, now well into his 70s, Goldwater decided to retire from the Senate. He was not inactive in retirement, however. Ironically for the proponent of conservative "extremism," Goldwater came to believe that his fellow Republicans were going too far. Goldwater broke from the party over its opposition to abortion, supporting a woman's right to choose, and also supported President Clinton's "don't ask, don't tell" policy toward gays in the military.

Goldwater died at the age of 89 on May 29th, 1998, at his home in Paradise Valley, a suburb of Phoenix.

J. Edgar Hoover's Birthday

John Edgar Hoover, or more popularly J. Edgar Hoover, was born in Washington, D.C., on January 1, 1895, the son of Dickerson Naylor and Annie Marie (Scheitlin) Hoover. From the beginning he was ambitious and hardworking. He put himself through college, working by day and going to school at night, and graduated from the George Washington University Law School in 1916 at the age of only 21. After being admitted to the bar, he went to work for the Department of Justice in 1917, where he was to remain in one role or another for the rest of his working life.

Hoover rose quickly in the Justice Department bureaucracy, impressing his superiors with his intelligence and administrative abilities. In 1917, the same year he was hired, he was placed in charge of the Enemy Alien Registration Section of the Bureau of Investigation. In 1919 he was appointed special assistant to the attorney general, and during the "red scare" of that same year he served Attorney General A. Mitchell Palmer as head of the General Intelligence Division. Hoover's job was to investigate radicals and other possible "reds," which often led to their deportation. Hoover continued as special assistant until 1921, when he was named assistant director. In 1924 Attorney General Harlan F. Stone promoted Hoover to active director of the whole Bureau of Investigation. At the time, the administration of President Warren G. Harding was reeling from several scandals, and so Hoover was able to successfully negotiate for a degree of autonomy when he accepted the job. Hoover argued that the bureau should be free from political influence, and once he achieved independence, Hoover promptly established within the bureau his own bureaucracy, which was loyal only to him. In 1935 the bureau became the Federal Bureau of Investigation, today's FBI.

The 1930s made Hoover a national figure. The FBI pursued such well-known public enemies as Ma Barker, John Dillinger, Machine Gun Kelly, and Baby Face Nelson. It was during the 1930s that the "Ten Most Wanted List" was created, and that Congress gave the FBI jurisdiction over federal offenses such as bank robbery and interstate kidnapping. Under Hoover's direction, the FBI created the first modern crime labs, systematized the record-keeping of fingerprints, and established the National Police Academy to assist in the training of local law enforcement officers.

During World War II, Hoover's FBI was actively involved in counter-espionage activities against Axis agents, but Hoover's real interest was in bringing the bureau to bear against Communism. Hoover's fixation on Communism, which went back to his red scare days, was fanned by the cold war hysteria that engulfed the nation after World War II and by the Soviet military and ideological threat to American power. For example, his FBI was intimately involved in the prosecutions of Julius and Ethel Rosenberg, who were ultimately executed for allegedly spying for the Soviets, and of former State Department official Alger Hiss, who was imprisoned for perjury. In 1956, Hoover initiated the infamous Counter Intelligence Program (COINTELPRO), whose motto was "do unto others as they are doing unto you." Ostensibly, the program's mission was to keep an eye on American Communists and Communist sympathizers, but in fact any political activity deemed "subversive" was targeted.

In the 1960s Hoover entered a period of conflict. The election of John F. Kennedy to the presidency in 1960 brought the president's brother Robert Kennedy into the Justice Department as attorney general, Hoover's legal superior. Relations between Hoover and Kennedy were strained from the beginning, and the two men disliked each other immensely. Robert Kennedy had spent many years investigating organized crime, but Hoover refused to admit that the "Mafia" existed, since the existence of a Mafia implied a failure of federal law enforcement and thus of the FBI. Further, Hoover was convinced that the budding civil rights rights movement led by Rev. Martin Luther King Jr. had Communist connections. Despite Kennedy's orders to the contrary, Hoover had King and other civil rights leaders wiretapped on a regular basis. Legend has it that when President Kennedy was assassinated, Hoover promptly had the phone link between Hoover's office and Robert Kennedy's office terminated.

Hoover was not entirely anti–civil rights, however. When in the summer of 1964 civil rights volunteers Michael Schwerner, Andrew Goodman, and James Chaney were murdered near Philadelphia, Mississippi, the FBI conducted a vigorous investigation. After years of litigation, seven men were found guilty. By the late 1960s, the FBI was actively enforcing the federal laws that were now intended to guarantee African Americans their civil liberties, and whether through political prudence or personal conviction, Hoover oversaw that effort.

Under presidents Lyndon B. Johnson and Richard M. Nixon, Hoover also initiated the oversight of groups and individuals opposed to the Vietnam War. Hoover considered the political dissent over policy in Southeast Asia to be a threat to the American nation. In a magazine interview, he stated that the anti–Vietnam War movement represented something very ominous:

> A new style in conspiracy—conspiracy that is extremely subtle and devious and hence difficult to understand . . . a conspiracy reflected by questionable moods and attitudes, by unrestrained individualism, by nonconformism in dress and speech, even by obscene language, rather than by formal membership in specific organizations.

Both Johnson and Nixon harbored doubts about Hoover, who had become almost imperial in his rule of the FBI and refused to surrender his office to younger men, but Hoover's public approval rating was strong. After so many decades, Hoover and the all-American image of the FBI had become linked in the popular imagination. Neither president forced the issue of resignation on Hoover, especially since Hoover was rumored to have extensive background files on the personal lives of many men in public office. On May 1, 1972, during the first Nixon administration, Hoover died at the age of 77 in his home. His body was laid in state in the Capitol Rotunda, an honor given to very few people, and Nixon appointed L. Patrick Gray to succeed Hoover as FBI director.

Notwithstanding the controversy surrounding his methods and style, Hoover was certainly an exceptional individual. Thanks to his leadership, the FBI has become the world's foremost law enforcement agency, and the bureau still sets the standard in modern forensic and investigative techniques.

January 1

College Football Bowl Games

As every sports enthusiast knows, New Year's Day is the occasion for a series of college football matchups known as bowl games. College football teams play roughly a dozen games every fall, and the best of these teams are invited to participate in matchups with other outstanding teams in the bowl games. Who are the "best" teams is determined by national polls of sportswriters and coaches, whose opinions are based on such factors as the win-loss record, the points-scored record, and the points-scored-by-opposing-teams record. This system differs from professional football, where a series of playoffs pits the best teams against each other in a succession of games that ultimately culminates in the Super Bowl. The winners of the various college bowl games held around the country do not go on to play each other in further bowl games to determine the one best team through actual matchups.

What happens instead is that the very cream of the college football teams go to the most prestigious bowl games: either the Rose Bowl in Pasadena, the Sugar Bowl in New Orleans, the Orange Bowl in Miami, or the Cotton Bowl in Dallas. In previous years the two best teams traditionally went to the Rose Bowl, because the Rose Bowl is the oldest bowl game, dating back to 1902 when Stanford University played the University of Michigan in Pasadena, California, on New Year's Day. However, that tradition has faded as the Sugar Bowl, Orange Bowl, and Cotton Bowl have risen in prominence and attracted wealthy corporate sponsors. Other teams that place high in the rankings but not at the very top may be invited to one of the other bowl games: for example, the Gator Bowl, the Fiesta Bowl, the Citrus Bowl, and so forth. Being invited to a bowl game is not only prestigious, but very lucrative for the sponsors and the teams involved, since the television advertising dollars are enormous, increasing with the prestige of the particular bowl game in question.

Bowl games are important for another reason: They are an opportunity for players to demonstrate their abilities and generate interest from the professional teams. When a player graduates or otherwise leaves college, he can enter the National Football League draft, a system whereby teams are permitted to make offers to rookie players. A good bowl performance raises the odds of getting drafted and drafted early, and signing a lucrative contract.

Tournament of Roses

The Pasadena, California, Tournament of Roses has been called the world's greatest parade. Since the late 1960s, roughly a million people have attended the event in person each year, and millions more have watched the event live on television. The tournament is perhaps most famous for its dozens of floats, of the most intricate design, which are completely covered with flowers, not to mention celebrities and what a less politically correct generation would have called "beauty queens." The floats are interspersed with marching bands invited to participate in the event.

Traditionally, the elaborate floats have been keyed to some sort of central theme established by the parade's organizers. In keeping with the bicentennial of the American Revolution, for example, the themes in 1976 and 1975 were America, Let's Celebrate! and Heritage of America, respectively. In 1975 the individual floats represented everything from such symbols of liberty as the flag, the Declaration of Independence, and the Liberty Bell to noted historic figures such as Washington, Lincoln, and the Pilgrims, not to mention historically significant events and places such as the first Thanksgiving, the Lewis and Clark expedition, the California gold rush, and the Oregon Trail.

Today's event is a far cry from the first Tournament of Roses, held in Pasadena by the Valley Hunt Club on January 1, 1890, at the suggestion of Charles Frederick Holder, a naturalist and author of many books on natural history. Holder was born in Lynn, Massachusetts, in 1851. He served for five years as associate curator of zoology at the American Museum of Natural History in New York and in 1885 went to Pasadena to become a teacher of zoology. Among other things he was a traveler and lecturer. In 1886, Holder's travels included southern France, where he saw the renowned Battle of Flowers, one of the French Riviera's extravagant celebrations, and well calculated to remind a newcomer that the southern California climate also produced flowers in midwinter. After his return to Pasadena, he suggested to the members of the Valley Hunt Club that on January 1 they decorate their carriages with flowers and drive them over a prearranged route, and that this parade be followed by athletic events. In a letter, Holder wrote that the first parade "consisted of a long line of carriages beautifully decorated with natural flowers, and . . . I am told, [it] was the finest thing of the kind ever seen . . . in this country or in Europe."

The Valley Hunt Club had charge of the tournament for several years and bore the cost of it, but when it became so elaborate that the cost was burdensome to the members, the Tournament of Roses Association was formed to take charge of the celebration. Holder's original intention was to arrange an artistic celebration of the ripening of the oranges at about the beginning of the year, and New Year's Day was chosen as a date when people were free to celebrate.

The tournament passed through several stages in the course of its development. At first it was merely a parade of decorated private carriages, followed by athletic events. Then floral floats were entered for a parade in the morning, with a chariot race or football game in the afternoon, and a ball in the evening. Prizes for floats and for chariot race winners were presented at the ball, over which a queen of the tournament presided. On January 1, 1902, the afternoon program consisted of a football game between the University of Michigan and Stanford University. Interest in the chariot races gradually died out, and they were abandoned by 1916 in favor of the afternoon football game. With the increase in population of the city, the annual parade grew larger from year to year. In 1920 it was two and a half miles long, and it was estimated that more than 1.5 million blossoms were used to decorate the floats. By 1935 the floats had come to stretch for more than four miles, and although no one any longer tried to estimate how many millions of blossoms were used, the Russian Firebird (the float of the Tournament of Roses Association, on which the queen of the tournament rode) was said to contain 250,000 blossoms. With the increase in popularity of televised sports after World War II, however, the college football Rose Bowl began to eclipse the tournament in popularity. Today, the Rose Bowl and the other college bowl games (see below) dominate the public's attention, but the Tournament still has a loyal following (particularly in southern California) and is still carried live by most television stations on New Year's Day.

Paul Revere's Birthday

Paul Revere, craftsman, industrialist, and patriot of the American Revolution, was born in Boston on January 1, 1735, the son of the French Huguenot refugee Apollos De Revoire (or Rivoire). From his father, who anglicized the family name, young Revere learned the silversmith's craft. He read the books on metallurgy of his time, turned out superior work, and was regarded by at least one visiting authority as the only American then knowledgeable in his field. His silver, including the famous Revere bowl, which is widely copied today, is still admired as art. But Revere, a man of apparently prodigious energies, also manufac-

tured surgical instruments and false teeth, sold spectacles, and carved frames for the portraits of John Singleton Copley.

Revere was a member of the politically influential North End Caucus Club, and the acknowledged leader of Boston's mechanic class, from which he was able to supply enthusiastic volunteers in the colonies' budding efforts to shake off British rule. His patriotism was also revealed in his work as an engraver, including the cartoons and drawings that made him a leading anti-British propagandist. One of these, his inaccurate but politically effective drawing of the Boston Massacre of 1770, has been described as probably the most famous print in America. In 1773 Revere was one of a committee of three chosen to suggest what form the protest against local sale of British tea should take. The result, a spectacular rebuff to the British, in which Revere participated with 50 other workingmen disguised as Native Americans, went down in history as the Boston Tea Party.

These and other political activities brought him into close contact with such pre-Revolutionary leaders as Samuel Adams and John Hancock. Revere played an important role as the Boston Committee of Safety's main express rider and as official courier for the defiant Massachusetts Provincial Assembly. Soon after the Boston Tea Party he was in New York, apprising local Sons of Liberty of the event. In the spring of 1774, he went by horseback to New York and Philadelphia with an appeal for help in protesting the Boston Port Bill, which threatened ruin for North America's second-largest port. He also carried to the Continental Congress, meeting in Philadelphia, the Suffolk Resolves, a stirring declaration on American rights, subsequently endorsed by the Congress, which outlined measures for defiance of the Intolerable Acts of 1774. In December of the same year, he rode off for New Hampshire, where he warned local patriots of British plans for removing a valuable store of munitions from Portsmouth's Fort William and Mary. His message precipitated the colonists' first aggressive act, a raid in which John Sullivan and his men captured the fort's arms and gunpowder. As things turned out, the captured munitions were used six months later against the British at the battle of Bunker Hill.

During the years of agitation that preceded the American Revolution, Revere's stocky figure was seen galloping across the countryside so frequently that his name even began to appear in London newspapers. This was before his most famous ride of all, however, on April 18, 1775, to warn of an impending British march on Lexington, Massachusetts (where John Hancock and Samuel Adams were staying), and Concord, Massachusetts (where the colonists had stored military supplies). William Dawes and Samuel Prescott rode with Revere, who was captured by the British before reaching Concord, but it was Revere who was memorialized by Henry Wadsworth Longfellow, who also described Revere's arrangement with confederates to signal the British approach by hanging lanterns in Boston's North Church steeple: "One if by land, and two if by sea; / And I on the opposite shore will be, / Ready to ride and spread the alarm / Through every Middlesex village and farm. . . ." With this forewarning, the colonists were not surprised by the arrival of British troops the next day. The resulting incident marked the beginning of the American Revolution.

Revere served the Revolution by building a powder mill that helped supply colonial troops with ammunition. More actively, he also served as a lieutenant colonel, but his military career (most notably the command of strategic Castle William in Boston Harbor) was pale beside some of his other endeavors. After the Revolution, Revere turned back to business and became a prosperous industrialist. He established a large sheet-copper mill, worked with inventor Robert Fulton in making copper boilers for steamboats, and, with his sons, he cast hundreds of church bells. Revere spent the rest of his life in Boston, where he died on May 10, 1818.

January 2

Georgia Ratifies the Constitution

On January 2, 1788, Georgia became the fourth state to ratify the U.S. Constitution. Like Delaware and New Jersey before it, Georgia sanctioned the new form of government by the unanimous vote of a specially elected convention. Georgia, founded in 1733, was the youngest of the colonies, and its action was not so crucial to the Constitution's viability as the ratification of such states as Pennsylvania (which had been second to ratify) or Massachusetts (which would be sixth); but it did mark another important step along the path to stronger national government.

When the Continental Congress called for a Constitutional Convention to meet in May 1787, the Georgia legislature appointed six delegates to represent its interests at the Philadelphia meeting. George Walton and Nathaniel Pendleton either declined to serve or failed to attend the Philadelphia caucus, and their absence reduced the size of the contingent to four: Abraham Baldwin, William Few, William Houstoun, and William Pierce. These men had commissions that authorized them to take whatever steps appeared necessary to render the Articles of Confederation adequate to meet the requirements of Georgia.

Abraham Baldwin was the son of a Connecticut blacksmith who went heavily into debt in order to educate his children. The young Baldwin graduated from Yale in 1772, studied theology, and taught divinity at his alma mater until 1779. He then entered the army and served as a chaplain until the conclusion of the War for Independence. Baldwin, who studied law during his military service, moved to Augusta, Georgia, in 1784, won a seat in the state legislature, and served two terms in the Continental Congress. Baldwin sponsored a bill to establish Franklin College, now the University of Georgia, and became the first president of that institution.

William Few was the son of a poor Maryland farmer who moved to North Carolina during William's early years. Debts eventually destroyed the family farm, and William Few moved to Georgia in 1776. After the American Revolution, Few began educating himself in the study of the law, and he won a seat in the state legislature as well as election to two terms in the Continental Congress.

William Houstoun was a young member of Georgia's emerging planter aristocracy. Some of his relatives had been high royal officials during Georgia's colonial period, and William Houstoun attended the Inner Temple in London to study law. At the outbreak of the American Revolution, Houstoun returned to Georgia and became a staunch patriot. Houstoun, who combined the practice of law with the ownership of a plantation, was the wealthiest member of the Georgia delegation, but he lacked liquid capital and had heavy debts. William Pierce said of Houstoun that "Nature seems to have done more for his corporeal than mental powers. His person is striking, but his mind very little improved with useful or elegant knowledge."

William Pierce was the fourth member of the Georgia delegation. Born, probably in Georgia, about 1740, he served with distinction in the Revolution and emerged from the army in 1783 as a major with special citations and a sword from Congress. After the war Pierce became a merchant engaged in the import-export business. Pierce, who was a member of the Continental Congress, created a series of witty and perceptive character sketches of the members of the convention, but declined to describe himself. Instead he left evaluation of his personality to "those who may choose to speculate on it, to consider it in any light their fancy or imagination may depict." Pierce left the convention in mid-July to go to New York in a futile attempt to save his sagging business fortunes;

he went bankrupt in 1788 and died in debt in 1789.

Georgia was a prosperous state during the 1780s. Its population doubled during the decade, as did the volume of exports from its port at Savannah. Georgia owned a large expanse of western territory, and in the convention usually aligned itself with the larger states. Not surprisingly, Georgia, as a state in which black slaves formed an important element of the labor force and of the population, voted against any constitutional interference with the slave trade and suggested in vain that blacks be counted equally with whites for purposes of allotting representatives.

Abraham Baldwin, the most able member of the Georgia delegation, perhaps saved the convention from collapse during the heated debate over the nature of representation in the upper and lower houses of the national legislature. On July 2 the delegates voted on a proposal to give each state equal representation in the upper house. Initially five states voted in the affirmative, and six states, including Georgia, voted in the negative. Baldwin, who feared that the small states might leave the convention in protest, decided to change his ballot to produce a tie vote with five states in favor of the proposal, five states opposed to it, and the Georgia delegation equally divided. Faced with this situation, the convention named a committee, which eventually worked out a compromise acceptable to both large and small states.

The Constitutional Convention ended on September 17, 1787. In October, a copy of the proposed form of government reached Georgia for its consideration. The legislature, in emergency session to prepare the state for imminent attack by the Creek Indians, called for a ratifying convention to meet in Augusta on Christmas Day. In the elections for delegates to the convention, which took place in the first week of December, supporters of the Constitution won a sweeping victory. Georgians looked upon the proposed new government as the best hope of assistance in their continuing frontier Indian wars, which threatened the very existence of the state.

Georgia's ratifying convention met as scheduled on December 25, 1787. The delegates, who included two physicians, two lawyers, three merchants, ten planters, three small farmers, three frontiersmen, one full-time public officeholder, and two other delegates about whom little is known, spent approximately one week in formal proceedings. On January 2, 1788, the convention voted unanimously to adopt the Constitution. To celebrate the occasion, there was a cannon salute of 13 shots, one for each of the 13 states.

Georgia, like the other colonies that separated from Great Britain, became a part of the United States in 1776 with the issuance of the Declaration of Independence. As a matter of convenience, however, historians have established the chronology in which states entered the Union in terms of the order of their ratification of the Constitution. They accordingly describe Georgia as the fourth state to join the Union.

Speed Limit of 55 Miles an Hour Is Imposed

Few things epitomize the American way of life more than the automobile. Until the early 1970s, however, one of the lowest priorities in automobile design was fuel efficiency. America had abundant petroleum reserves, and gasoline was cheap and abundant, so Americans drove cars that were not only big but wasteful. Low fuel efficiency, such as 13 or 14 miles per gallon, was common. Over time, however, America increasingly relied on imported petroleum as demand rose while domestic production peaked. Without realizing it, America had become dependent on the vast oil production of the Mideast, where the oil fields were located in Arab countries that had banded together in the Organization of Petroleum Exporting Countries (OPEC).

When the United States chose to support Israel in the October 1973 Middle East conflict, OPEC supported Israel's Arab enemies and suspended oil exports to the United States. The embargo resulted in long gas lines and measures such as gas rationing. In order to help conserve gasoline, on January 2, 1974, President Nixon signed a bill that imposed a national speed limit of 55 miles per hour. The measure was applauded by highway safety advocates, who pointed to statistics showing that 55 miles per hour not only conserved gas but saved thousands of lives in traffic accidents. Thus, after the oil embargo was lifted and the gasoline crisis ended, the 55-mile-per-hour limit remained in place.

By the late 1980s, some organized opposition to the 55-mile-per-hour limit had arisen. In western states and rural areas, the speed limit seemed harsh for people traveling long distances in sparsely populated areas, so a 65-mile-per-hour exception was enacted for highways in regions with low population density. When the Republicans took control of Congress after the 1994 elections, a bill was introduced to repeal the 55-mile-per-hour speed limit altogether. On November 28, 1995, President Clinton signed the bill, which returned control over speed limits to the states. Most states limited the increase in the speed limit to 65 or 75 miles per hour, although Montana decided to repeal the speed limit altogether for daytime driving.

As of this writing in the late 1990s, it appears that highway fatalities have in fact risen once again in response to the repeal of the 55-mile-per-hour limit. However, the original impetus for the national speed limit, namely gasoline conservation, has largely disappeared. Modern automobiles get much better gas mileage than their 1970s counterparts, thanks in large part to federal fuel efficiency legislation, and OPEC's control over oil production ended with the discovery of vast new reserves in Alaska, Mexico, the North Sea, and other sites.

Senator John F. Kennedy Announces His Candidacy for the 1960 Democratic Presidential Nomination

See also May 29, John F. Kennedy's Birthday.

John F. Kennedy's presidential ambitions first surfaced during the 1956 election, in which the young and promising senator from Massachusetts was considered for the vice-presidential slot in the presidential campaign of Adlai Stevenson, but lost to Senator Estes Kefauver of Tennessee. However, Kennedy's popularity convinced his father, the wealthy and powerful Joseph Kennedy, that JFK could make a serious bid for the presidency. With a personal fortune estimated to be in the hundreds of millions, derived from bootlegging, movie-making, and stock market speculations, "Joe" Kennedy was certainly in a position to bankroll his son.

In 1958 JFK was reelected as senator, but almost immediately began to maneuver for the 1960 Democratic presidential primaries. Like most politicians throughout American history, Kennedy declined to publicly acknowledge his interest in the presidency until his campaign was organized. In fact, the Kennedy campaign faced several formidable obstacles. First, he was a Roman Catholic, and this religious difference was still important in a country that had a Protestant majority and had never elected a Catholic president. Second, he was young and inexperienced. Third, he had sustained a serious back injury during World War II, requiring the frequent use of a back brace and medication, which cast doubt on his ability to take on the rigors of a national campaign.

Kennedy was ambitious, however. Joe Kennedy, who had once served as ambassador to Great Britain, had also once held political ambitions for himself but had never been able to capitalize on them. Now he could realize these ambitions through his son, and so he encouraged JFK to enter the race. On January 2, 1960, JFK formally announced his intention to seek the Democratic Party's presidential nomination for the upcoming November 1960 presidential elections. For more information, see the Kennedy biography at May 29, and also the biography of his 1960 opponent Richard Nixon at January 9.

January 3

Alaska Admitted to the Union

Alaska, the region once known as Russian America (see October 18, Alaska Day) and then derisively tagged as "Seward's folly" before its riches were glimpsed (see March 30, Seward's Day), became a state on January 3, 1959. More than twice the size of Texas, which had long enjoyed its rank as the nation's largest state, the country's new giant and northernmost outpost was the 49th state to be admitted to the Union.

The region, long a stepchild of absentee governments (first of Russia and then of the United States, which purchased it in 1867), was hampered in its development by the remoteness of those who controlled it even after it achieved territorial status in 1912. It was difficult for the Congress in Washington to keep in the forefront of its collective mind the day-to-day realities of survival in Alaska.

In 1916, when the first bill for statehood was introduced; in the 27 succeeding years, when emphasis shifted to attempts to strengthen Alaska's territorial government; and after 1943, when a bill for statehood was again presented to Congress, there were attempts to form a government more responsive to local needs. The idea of statehood, which Congress debated exhaustively in 1950, was kept alive throughout the following decade.

In 1956 a constitutional convention was called by Alaska's territorial legislature. The resulting draft constitution was approved by a vote of the populace in April 1956. Statehood followed after another period of long discussion between proponents, who favored local control, and opponents, who thought that higher taxes or loss of federal subsidies might result. Finally, after the U.S. Senate gave an overwhelming 64 to 20 vote in favor of admission on June 30, 1958, President Dwight D. Eisenhower signed the Alaskan statehood bill on July 7, and it was declared that he would release a formal proclamation announcing Alaska's admission sometime during the next year. The official recognition of Alaskan statehood came with Eisenhower's declaration of January 3, 1959. This declaration was immediately followed by an executive order directing the addition of a 49th star to a new U.S. flag that was to become official on Independence Day, July 4, 1959. But the new 49-star flag had already become obsolete by July 4, 1960, for by then Hawaii had been admitted as the nation's 50th state.

Battle of Princeton

During the American Revolution, after the defeat of the British at Trenton, New Jersey, in December 1776, Washington returned to the Pennsylvania side of the Delaware River. On the night of December 30–31, however, he moved his men back to the New Jersey side, determined to strike the enemy again. Meanwhile, Lord Charles Cornwallis, the British commander in New Jersey, had his own ideas for smashing the Americans. With a superior force of almost 8,000 men and with more expected from Princeton, he took up a position confronting Washington. The American commander, with a smaller force of some 5,000 patriots, stood with his back to the river, prevented from retreating across it both by a lack of sufficient boats and by ice in the river.

To both the British and the American officers, the situation of Washington's Continentals on the night of January 2 looked desperate. Cornwallis, convinced that the American rebels were cut off from escape, delayed action until morning. Washington and his fellow officers looked for a way out of their trap. At an emergency council of war, they made a daring decision. Instead of attempting to retreat, and instead of waiting for Cornwallis's impending attack, they would move forward, slipping north of the enemy lines to attack the British strongholds of Princeton and, they hoped, New Brunswick.

Leaving their campfires burning, with a few brave men to stoke them and keep up a clangor of activity during the night, the main American force, with gun wheels muffled, silently set forth on its desperate trek at 1:00 A.M. on January 3, 1777. In the darkness, it was as much a stumble as a march over a barely cleared, stump-studded, newly opened back road, but it led them, undetected, around and behind the British left. After they reached a point not far from the Stony Brook bridge on the outskirts of Princeton at about sunrise on January 3, Washington sent General Hugh Mercer with about 400 men to destroy the bridge, a vital link on the main road from Princeton to Trenton. Near their goal, Mercer and his men were sighted by two British regiments under Lieutenant Colonel Charles Mawhood, en route from Princeton to Trenton, where they were to join Cornwallis's main force. In the ensuing bloody melee, the Americans relied on their slow-loading rifles and the British on a devastating bayonet

charge. General Mercer was fatally wounded and his men thrown into panic, fleeing in all directions with the British in hot pursuit.

However, Washington, mounted on a white horse and careless of his own safety, dashed from group to frightened group, encouraging, bolstering, urging. Thus rallied, his force of regulars and militia, supplemented now by new arrivals, routed the British. Some of the enemy survivors fled by a roundabout way to Trenton, although most made for the British supply headquarters at New Brunswick. Entering Princeton, the Americans quickly subdued a small British detachment occupying Princeton University's Nassau Hall. There was no time for delay, however, especially since Cornwallis, with his main force at Trenton, undoubtedly realized what had happened and could be expected to arrive in Princeton at any moment. Casting a regretful eye in the direction of the tempting British stores at New Brunswick, Washington abandoned his hopes of taking that center and withdrew abruptly, out of the probable British path. When Cornwallis did arrive, furious at being outwitted, it was too late for pursuit of the vanished Americans.

The battle of Princeton is regarded as being of strategic importance. Together with the patriot success at Trenton a week earlier, it had a galvanizing effect on American morale. Restoring hope in a cause that had seemed almost lost, it stimulated enlistments and, as the British pulled back their farthest outposts, left New Jersey largely free of British troops. Washington, for his part, moved inland to a position of strength on the high ground of Morristown, where his ragged army rested and was replenished over the rest of the winter.

Lucretia C. Mott's Birthday

Lucretia Coffin Mott, a leader in both the abolitionist and women's suffrage movements, was born on January 3, 1793, on Nantucket Island, Massachusetts. She was a descendant of Tristram Coffin, an English immigrant who was one of the original purchasers and settlers of Nantucket Island. Her father, Thomas Coffin, was originally a ship's captain but relocated the family to Boston in 1803 to become a businessman.

The Coffins were members of the Society of Friends, popularly known as the Quakers, so the young Lucretia was raised in the Quaker religion. In Boston she went to public school, and then at 13 was sent to a Quaker boarding school called Nine Partners, located near Poughkeepsie, New York. She spent two years there and then returned to her family, which had in the meantime moved to Philadelphia. During her stay at Nine Partners, she met a fellow student named James Mott, and the two were married in 1811.

The couple had six children, five of whom lived into adulthood. A boy, however, died as an infant in 1817. The grieving Lucretia now turned to religion for solace. She began to be active in Society of Friends meetings, and achieved the rank of "acknowledged minister" within the society. However, her views were too liberal even for the tolerant Quakers. In the 1820s she became a follower of Elias Hicks, the radical Quaker teacher who separated from the society in 1827 and formed his own following of "Hicksites." Lucretia gained a reputation as one of Philadelphia's most eloquent preachers, and traveled extensively to speak at Hicksite meetings across the country. In her talks, she spoke in favor of a number of ideas that were very controversial for that time: the ending of slavery ("abolition"), equal rights for women ("suffrage"), and making alcoholic beverages illegal ("temperance").

Lucretia's talks made her increasingly famous. In 1833 she and her husband helped organize the American Anti-Slavery Society, and they personally organized the Philadelphia Female Anti-Slavery Society, which she headed as president. In 1840 she traveled to London to attend the World Anti-Slavery Convention, where she was an influential figure even though she was refused formal admission because of her gender. The Motts were also active in the Underground Railroad, which helped African American slaves escape to Canada and freedom, activities that violated the Fugitive Slave Law of 1850.

Lucretia Mott's interest in the suffrage movement originated from a childhood sense of being wronged solely because she was female, namely when at the Nine Partners school she was a student teacher but was paid only half as much as the male student teachers for doing the same work. Further, she was incensed when the World Anti-Slavery Convention refused to admit her because she was a woman. One of Lucretia's fellow delegates to the convention had been Elizabeth Cady Stanton, another activist in the suffrage movement. Mott and Stanton became leading organizers of the first women's rights convention, held on July 19 and 20, 1848, in Seneca Falls, New York. The Seneca Falls Convention was the seminal event in launching the movement that eventually secured the right to vote for women in the 20th century.

The Motts retired to a country estate called Roadside outside Philadelphia in 1857. They were far from inactive, however. Lucretia's husband was one of the founders of Swarthmore College in 1864. Lucretia continued to travel and speak, and

lent her support to the budding Prohibition movement. As late as May 1880 she was still giving speeches to Quaker meeting groups. On November 11, 1880, she died at Roadside.

Congress Meets

Every two years there are elections for the Congress of the United States. These elections take place in November, and on the following January 3 the new Congress convenes. The January 3 meeting date took over a century and a half to evolve, however.

When the first Congress went into session on March 4, 1789, the members lived in a day and age when winter was a time for staying at home. There were no railroads or airplanes; most roads were not paved, and travel by ship could take months. Thus, a person elected to Congress in the November election needed time to travel to Washington, D.C., bring family and personal possessions by ship or wagon, and establish a household. Therefore, the March 4 date for the meeting of Congress was a convenient one. Further, since communications were slow, there was no reason why a new Congress should be in any particular hurry to meet: Even serious matters such as a declaration of war could take months to be conveyed.

By the early 20th century, however, the situation had changed. Now there were telephones and telegraphs, so both news and events moved much faster than in 1789. And with the development of modern roads, railroads, ships, and airplanes, traveling to Washington, D.C., in the winter was much less onerous. Therefore, it began to seem archaic for Congress to meet in March. The result was the Twentieth Amendment to the Constitution, which became effective on October 15, 1933, during the 73rd Congress:

> Section 1. . . . the terms of Senators and Representatives [shall end] at noon on the 3d day of January . . . and the terms of their successors shall then begin.
> Section 2. The Congress shall assemble at least once in every year, and such meeting shall begin at noon on the 3d day of January, unless they shall by law appoint a different day.

Therefore, the 73rd Congress was two months shorter than usual, since it began on March 4, 1933, before the Twentieth Amendment became effective, but ended on the new date of January 3, 1935.

Joseph Rauh's Birthday

Joseph Louis Rauh Jr. was born in Cincinnati, Ohio, on January 3, 1911. As a youth he showed exceptional academic ability, and in 1928 went to Harvard University, where he majored in economics and graduated *magna cum laude* in 1932. He went on to attend Harvard Law School, where in 1935 he also graduated *magna cum laude*. After graduation, he went to work as a law clerk for Supreme Court Justice Benjamin Cardozo. During World War II he served as a military legal expert on Lend-Lease, and in 1946 he returned to Washington, D.C.

Rauh had long been active in the Democratic Party. Upon returning to Washington, he helped form the organization known as Americans for Democratic Action, which had a liberal domestic agenda but was strongly anti-communist. The ADA continues today to work for liberal causes. Rauh also opened a law firm in Washington, Rauh & Levy, which represented a number of unions and helped fight for the rights of organized labor. Rauh's other clients included playwright Arthur Miller, whom he represented when the House Un-American Activities Committee charged Miller with contempt for refusing to name other writers who might have "communist sympathies."

Rauh continued to be active in the Democratic Party, and beginning in 1948 was an influential participant in the Democratic national conventions that select presidential candidates every four years and establish the party platform. For example, Rauh inserted civil rights positions into the party plank, despite opposition from some Southerners. He was also a member of the executive board of the NAACP, a prominent opponent of the Vietnam War, and a leader in the fight for home rule in the District of Columbia. In 1976, however, he was notably absent from the Democratic Convention, and was unenthusiastic about Jimmy Carter.

By the 1980s, Rauh's era had passed. Labor unions and civil rights groups were on the defensive in the Reagan era. Nevertheless, Rauh, once described as "the personal embodiment of American liberalism," continued to stay active and guide his law firm's vigorous litigation practice. On September 3, 1992, at the age of 81, he died after a massive heart attack.

January 4

Feast of St. Elizabeth Ann Seton

Elizabeth Ann Seton, a 19th-century pioneer in providing parochial education and charity for the sick and poor, was the first native-born American declared a saint. She was canonized during 1975, which was being observed as a Holy Year by the Roman Catholic Church, according to the Catholic tradition of marking such a year once each quarter century. Canonization of the new saint, whose feast day is January 4, coincided with the UN-designated observance of 1975 as International Women's Year, and with the Vatican's designation of September 14 (the day she was declared a saint) as Woman's Day. Although not by official design, the canonization of the first American-born saint also coincided with the 1975–76 celebration of the bicentennial of the American Revolution.

The elevation of Mother Seton to sainthood was the culmination of a long process, including acceptance by church authorities of claims of miraculous cures. The effort originated in the order of nuns she founded and was taken up by James Cardinal Gibbons, who lent his advocacy to her cause in 1882 and began the organized effort on behalf of her sainthood. Following decades of biographical and other investigation by church authorities, Pope Pius XII in 1940 formally requested that the Vatican pursue her cause. After further preliminary actions she was beatified, that is, declared blessed (the step preceding canonization) by Pope John XXIII on St. Patrick's Day, March 17, 1963. Since a vote of the National Conference of Catholic Bishops in November 1971, her feast day has been included in the liturgical calendar for all Roman Catholic dioceses in the United States, to be celebrated as a memorial on January 4, the date of her death in 1821.

In her lifetime, "the mother of the American Church," as she sometimes was called, founded the first native religious community for women in the United States, laid the foundation of the American Catholic parochial school system, and opened orphan asylums, which were the forerunners of hundreds of modern foundling homes and child-care centers. Although Mother Seton died before she could start the hospital she had long dreamed of establishing, her order of nuns accomplished her dream a few years after her death. Today there are hundreds of such hospitals, many of them run by her Sisters of Charity. The order specializes in teaching as well as in nursing and orphan care.

Elizabeth Ann Bayley was born in New York City to Episcopalian parents on August 28, 1774. Her father, Dr. Richard Bayley, was a respected physician who became the first professor of anatomy at Columbia University (then King's College) and the first health officer of New York City. Her mother was Catherine Charlton Bayley, daughter of the rector of St. Andrew's Episcopal Church on Staten Island. Related by birth and marriage to socially prominent New York families, Elizabeth Bayley was to meet many important and famous people in the course of her lifetime, among them George Washington, Alexander Hamilton, and John Jay. But New York City at the time had a population of only about 20,000, and the social circle in which her family moved was small and tightly knit. Her parents' second daughter, she was not yet three when her mother died. After the traditional year of mourning, her father married Charlotte Amelia Barclay, daughter of Andrew Barclay and the former Helena Roosevelt, whose father established the Roosevelt dynasty in America. The second Mrs. Bayley bore her husband seven children and indulged them to the neglect of his two older daughters. From the time she was eight, Elizabeth Bayley and her sister Mary accordingly lived often with relatives and friends, especially when their father was studying or working abroad, as he sometimes did for years at a time.

From her earliest years, Elizabeth Bayley showed deeply religious inclinations, which grew stronger with the passing years. In 1794, she married William Magee Seton. Her husband was the son of William Seton, an extremely successful businessman who, in 1784, had been appointed to the influential position of cashier of the Bank of New York. The marriage of Elizabeth and William M. Seton was a happy and affectionate union, although he was afflicted from the beginning by tuberculosis. They had many good friends and a glittering social life. Elizabeth Seton flowered amid the affection and security she had lacked as a child. Even in this happy period, however, her dedication to the poor was a force in her life, and she helped organize the Widows' Society of New York for the aid of widows and orphans in the New York area.

In 1798, the Seton family's fortunes changed for the worse when the elder William Seton died in June. Elizabeth's husband contracted yellow fever during an epidemic, and Elizabeth, together with her infant son, were sickly as well. Her father died in 1801. As tragedies multiplied, Seton ships were seized by pirates and the firm's business interests in Germany and England failed. During this dismal period, Elizabeth Seton drew daily strength from her religion and eagerly anticipated Sunday worship services, which she attended at Trinity Episcopal Church. In 1803, the Setons took a trip to Italy to visit some old friends, the influential Filicchi family. Unfortunately, William's health continued to deteriorate, and he died on December 27, 1803, in Pisa and was buried in Leghorn, Italy. During her stay with the Filicchis, Elizabeth converted to Catholicism, and she formally joined the Roman Catholic Church when she returned to New York despite the unpopularity of this decision with her remaining family and with her New York society friends.

By 1808 Elizabeth Seton's situation in New York City had worsened, and she was literally desperate. Providentially she was then invited to open a school for girls in Baltimore, where more than half of all American Catholics then lived. This meant that she would have a means of livelihood and could be with her three daughters and near her sons. In addition, it was a step closer to the religious life that she had been contemplating for some time. When Elizabeth started her school, she had a total of seven students: her own three daughters and four other girls. Soon, however, other students came and young women volunteered to assist in the school duties. In June 1809 Elizabeth was appointed Mother of the community and school she had founded. Living according to a religious rule given her by Bishop Carroll, she moved with her daughters as well as other followers to Emmitsburg, a village in northwestern Maryland about 50 miles from Baltimore. There, in 1812, the women adapted the religious rule which had been given to the first Sisters of Charity by St. Vincent de Paul in France in the 17th century and became the first native religious community of women founded in the United States.

Once settled in Emmitsburg, Mother Seton trained her band of nun-teachers, and she herself prepared textbooks for use in her schools. Her plans and accomplishments laid the foundation for the American parochial school system. The number of girls in her community grew, and for their religious guidance and training Mother Seton translated religious books from French and wrote several spiritual treatises. Retaining her dedication to the sick and poor, she visited the needy and afflicted in the area and converted many to Catholicism. She sent her Sisters of Charity to open an orphanage in Philadelphia in 1814 and one in New York City in 1817. Today, many hundreds of Mother Seton's Sisters of Charity, under separate provinces or motherhouses, serve in both North and South America and in foreign missions.

After a long illness, Mother Seton died on January 4, 1821, at the age of 47. She was buried in Emmitsburg, near the 15 sisters and novices who had died during the early years of her young community. She was survived by more than 50 sister-members of the community and by her two sons and one daughter. The oldest and youngest of her three daughters had died before her in 1812 and 1816, respectively.

Once beatified by Pope John XXIII, who referred to her as the "flower of American piety," Mother Seton became Blessed Elizabeth Ann Seton. With the canonization ceremonies held in Rome on September 14, 1975, she became known as Saint Elizabeth Ann Seton. The first church named in her honor is in Shrub Oak, Westchester County, New York.

Utah Admitted to the Union

On January 4, 1896, Utah became the 45th state to enter the Union. Its settlement by members of the Church of Jesus Christ of Latter-Day Saints, unofficially known as the Mormons, contributed greatly to the uniqueness of Utah's history.

Utah was originally settled by the Ute, Paiute, and Shoshone tribes. Before the 19th century, present-day Utah, like most of the southwestern United States, was claimed by Spain. The incomplete and often vague records left by Spanish explorers indicate that a few men from Francisco Vásquez de Coronado's expedition may have crossed southern Utah in 1540. It was only in 1776, however, that the Spanish missionaries Silvestre Vélez de Escalante and Francisco Atanasio Domínguez made the first large-scale explorations. A section of their route later became part of the Old Spanish Trail, which stretched from Santa Fe in present New Mexico to Monterey in Alta, California.

Since Meriwether Lewis and William Clark passed north of Utah during their famous expedition of 1804–1806, the first Americans to enter Utah probably were four members of the 1811–1812 overland expedition sponsored by John Jacob Astor. By the early 1820s, fur traders, lured by reports of rich beaver streams, had found their way over the rugged terrain, and they rapidly depleted the fur supply between 1824 and 1830. Starting in the 1840s, California-bound emigrant trains made their way across the great salt desert. In 1846 the Donner party struggled through the mountains east of the Great Salt Lake and plodded across the desert only to fall victim to heavy snows and starvation farther west. Shortly before 1847, Miles Goodyear set up the first trading post, Fort Buenaventura, at the site of present-day Ogden, thus becoming Utah's first settler.

Farther east, meanwhile, the Mormons were suffering the persecution that had already driven them from New York State to the Midwest. After the murder of their founder and prophet, Joseph Smith, at Nauvoo, Illinois, on June 27, 1844, the Mormons turned to Brigham Young, and under his leadership they sought refuge far beyond the country's western frontier. In 1847, after a harrowing overland trek, they arrived in the parched and barren basin of the Great Salt Lake, where they laid out their new city. As the Latter-Day Saints assembled, and emigrants from this country and abroad swelled their ranks, Mormon communities spread along the western slopes of the Wasatch Range, where irrigation techniques helped to support the rapid growth in population.

Utah was ceded to the United States in the Treaty of Guadalupe Hidalgo of 1848, which ended the Mexican War. As spokesman for the approximately 11,000 Mormons who had settled in and near Salt Lake City by 1849, Brigham Young held a convention to organize the Latter-Day Saints' aggressive theocracy into a state under the name of Deseret. He claimed a far-flung empire, including the present states of Utah and Nevada and parts of Arizona, New Mexico, Colorado, Wyoming, Idaho, Oregon, and California. Petitioning Congress for statehood, Young established a provisional government on March 10, 1849, and became governor in the first election.

The petition for statehood failed, however, and Deseret as originally conceived was short-lived. Congress even refused to accept its name. The bill setting up the geographically smaller Territory of Utah was signed by President Millard Fillmore on September 9, 1850. The newly established territory consisted of what is now Utah, western Colorado, most of Nevada, and a slice of Wyoming. Brigham Young was appointed territorial governor. The first official census in 1850 listed 11,380 persons. Almost immediately the Mormons were in conflict with the federal authorities, who were suspicious of Mormon ways and the autocratic rule of Brigham Young. In the summer of 1857, President James Buchanan ordered army troops, commanded by Colonel Albert Sidney Johnston, to proceed to the Utah Territory and occupy Salt Lake City. The Mormons organized a guerrilla force of militiamen that successfully resisted the federal troops, and when the Civil War broke out the Lincoln administration quietly decided to leave the Mormons alone.

After the Civil War, America's westward expansion resumed and the issue of Utah's status in general and statehood in particular resurfaced. Brigham Young's final years before his death on August 29, 1877, were marked by two struggles:

the attempt to preserve Mormon polygamy and the attempt to achieve statehood for Utah. The two were closely connected, for much of the outside opposition to the Mormons came as a consequence of polygamy, and it was this very vocal opposition that prevented the government from admitting Utah to the Union with Brigham as its governor.

The Mormon practice of polygamy derived from a divine revelation sanctioning the practice that the prophet Joseph Smith claimed to have received on July 12, 1843. Although there was little concealment of the practice either in Nauvoo, Illinois, or later on in Utah, Smith's controversial revelation was not officially proclaimed until August 1852, when Brigham Young judged the community strong enough and sufficiently isolated to prevent serious consequences. But reformers such as Harriet Beecher Stowe soon linked polygamy with slavery as those "twin relics of barbarism" that must be swept from the face of the earth. After Young's death in 1877, the Reverend De Witt Talmage of Brooklyn, New York, even paused in the midst of a church service to offer a suggestion to the national government: "Now, my friends, now at the death of the Mormon chieftain, is the time for the United States government to strike. . . . Give Phil Sheridan enough troops, and he will teach all Utah that 40 wives is 39 too many."

However, polygamy raised difficult legal problems for those legislators who desired its prohibition. The Constitution does not prevent a man from having as many wives as he wants (or, in fact, a woman from having as many husbands as she wants, although that twist to polygamy was not part of Joseph Smith's revelation). Moreover, legislation against polygamy might conceivably be interpreted as an infringement upon the constitutional guarantees of religious liberty.

Nevertheless, antipolygamy laws were passed: The first, in 1862, was later supplemented in 1882 and 1887. Under these statutes not only was polygamy forbidden, but the Mormon church was disincorporated and much of its property temporarily confiscated. Vigorous prosecution was carried on in Utah, where polygamists caught in surprise raids were heavily fined and given prison sentences. Many frustrated the investigators by seeking refuge in the winding foothills of the territory or by making two-family houses out of single dwellings by means of camouflaged twin-entrance doors. The elderly John Taylor, who had succeeded Brigham Young as president of the church, went into hiding in 1884 and directed church affairs from seclusion until his death in 1887.

On September 25, 1890, following a Supreme Court decision affirming the constitutionality of the antipolygamy laws, the president of the Church of Jesus Christ of Latter-Day Saints, Wilford Woodruff, issued a statement known as The Manifesto. It was not a revelation, or even an explicit retraction of the Mormons' belief in plural marriage, but merely a declaration of expediency, which read in part:

> To Whom It May Concern: Inasmuch as laws have been enacted by Congress forbidding plural marriages, which laws have been pronounced constitutional by the court of last resort, I hereby declare my intention to submit to those laws, and to use my influence with the members of the Church over which I preside, to have them do likewise.

A general church conference held in October supported this move and laid the ban of excommunication on persons continuing to practice polygamy. On January 4, 1893, President Benjamin Harrison granted amnesty to all husbands who repudiated their extra wives and to all polygamists who had married before November 1, 1890.

The renunciation of polygamy cleared the way for Utah's statehood, although by the 1890s the once vast Territory of Utah had been whittled down by the establishment of the territories of Nevada and Colorado in 1861 and Wyoming in 1868. Congress passed the enabling act in 1893; the state constitution was framed and approved in 1895, and Utah entered the Union on January 4, 1896.

Don Shula's Birthday

Donald "Don" Francis Shula, "the winningest coach in the history of the National Football League," was born on January 4, 1930, in Grand River, Ohio. He was the fourth of seven children, and was raised in Painesville, Ohio. From an early age he showed exceptional athletic ability, lettering in no less than four sports at Harvey High School (football, baseball, basketball, and track). After high school, he went to John Carroll University in Cleveland, where he played on the college football team and majored in sociology.

After graduating from John Carroll in 1951, Shula was drafted by the Cleveland Browns as a defensive back. During the 1950s, Shula also played for the Baltimore Colts and the Washington Redskins, and briefly coached college football. His professional football coaching career began in 1960, when the Detroit Lions hired him as defensive coordinator. In 1963, he returned to the Baltimore Colts, this time as head coach even though he was only 33.

Shula coached the Colts through the 1969 season. His record was 71 wins, 21 losses, and four ties, better than any other coach during that time period. However, Shula never won a championship for the Colts. He took the team to Super Bowl III on January 12, 1969, but lost to the New York Jets 16–7. After the Fall 1969 season, he left the Colts to become the head coach for the Miami Dolphins.

Under Shula's leadership, the Dolphins went to their first Super Bowl in January 1972, but lost to the Cowboys. Then, in the Fall 1972 regular season, Shula coached the Dolphins through football's legendary "perfect season." The Dolphins won all of their regular season games (14 at that time), both playoff games, and finally the January 1973 Super Bowl for a perfect 17–0 record. In 1974, the Dolphins returned to the Super Bowl and won again. The Dolphins went to the Super Bowl in 1983 and 1985 but were not victorious.

Nevertheless, Shula's Dolphins achieved a 65.8 percent winning record during his tenure, the best in professional football. During his coaching career, Shula amassed 347 victories, the best record of any NFL coach. By the 1990s, however, his age was beginning to show. Despite extraordinary talent on the team, such as quarterback Dan Marino, the Dolphins were lucky if they got to the first round in the playoffs. After the 1995 regular season, Shula decided to retire. His sons have carried on the Shula coaching tradition. Dave Shula has coached for the Cincinnati Bengals and Mike Shula for the Tampa Bay Buccaneers.

January 5

Twelfth Night, or Epiphany Eve

The last evening of the traditional Twelve Days of Christmas is known as the Twelfth Night, or Epiphany Eve. Twelfth Night observances gained popularity in Europe during the Middle Ages and spread to America, although today the custom has fallen into obscurity in the popular culture. January 5 is also referred to as Old Christmas Eve. According to the Old Style or Julian calendar, Christmas, celebrating Christ's Nativity, fell on what is now January 6 according to the New Style or Gregorian calendar in common use today.

The Christian observance of the Twelve Days of Christmas, culminating with Twelfth Night, may have developed from the pagan custom of marking the natural phenomenon of the winter solstice for a number of days. The tradition was firmly embedded in Europe, especially in England, from the 11th century onwards, but reached its height during the reign of the Tudor monarchs Henry VIII (1509–1547) and Elizabeth I (1558–1603). Elaborate pageants, processions, and song-fests, combined with feasting and dancing, were planned for the pleasure of the nobility and royalty under the direction of a mock official known as the Lord of Misrule. The Elizabethan period saw the introduction of magnificent Twelfth Night dramatic productions. For a number of centuries, miracle plays about the Three Kings had traditionally been performed at this time of year. Staged at first in church sanctuaries to illustrate the religious meaning of the coming of the Wise Men, the dramas later became so secular in tone that they were eventually banned in churches. However, not only did the custom of presenting religious dramas continue to flourish outside church confines, but the staging of secular tragedies, comedies, and historical chronicles also became a Twelfth Night feature, notably in court circles. William Shakespeare's *Twelfth Night* was probably first presented as a command performance for Queen Elizabeth I at Whitehall Palace on January 6, 1601; her successor, James I (1603–1625), had seven of Shakespeare's plays and two of Ben Johnson's performed to celebrate his second Christmas season (1604/1605) as king of England. In the 18th century the lavish celebration of Twelfth Night began to lose its appeal, especially in the more elevated social circles. By the 19th century, extensive observance of the occasion had practically died out, although scattered remnants of the ancient festivities survived.

Several of the Twelfth Night customs were introduced into the American colonies. The feasting and revelry flourished especially in the South, where the Christmas season was a time for joy and merriment. In 1759, for example, George Washington regarded Twelfth Night as an appropriate date for his wedding to Martha Custis. The event was marked with a yule log, firecrackers, greenery, and a sumptuous banquet. In the 19th and early 20th centuries, there were many secular observances of Twelfth Night throughout the United States, but the custom has rapidly dwindled. One exception is with respect to Mardi Gras, which traditionally represents the end of a carnival season that began at Twelfth Night.

Feast of St. John Neumann, the First American Male Saint

On June 19, 1977, a century after his death, John Nepomucene Neumann, "The Little Bishop of Philadelphia," was canonized in Rome by Pope Paul VI, becoming the first American male saint. Tens of thousands gathered for the outdoor ceremony in St. Peter's Square to pay homage to a man who had spent his life in quiet dedication to the church.

Born in Prachatitz, Bohemia, on March 28, 1811, John Neumann was one of six children of Philip and Agnes Neumann. From early childhood he displayed an avid interest in religion and the priesthood, and despite his parents' later urgings that he go into the medical profession, he entered the seminary of Budweis in 1831. An intense student, he eagerly absorbed knowledge of canon law and the scriptures. After completing his courses at Budweis, he went on to the University of Prague. Although he was fluent in many Slavic dialects and at least eight modern languages, he studied English at Prague with the hope of going on to become an American missionary. After graduating with honors from the seminary in Prague in August 1835, he returned to Budweis for ordination. However, because of an overabundance of priests, he was unable to be ordained in his native diocese.

Undismayed, he decided to sail to America in April 1836. Arriving in New York City on June 2, he was received by Bishop John DuBois and was ordained on June 25 in St. Patrick's Cathedral. Because of Father Neumann's fluency in German, DuBois assigned him to Williamsville, New York, where he was to attend a number of frontier missions. During the next four years he journeyed on foot and by wagon, ministering to the poor German immigrant congregations scattered throughout the upstate area. Being of small stature (5 feet 4 inches tall), he began to be fondly called "little priest" by his charges.

In 1840 his self-sacrificing work was brought to the attention of the Redemptorist Fathers, who were establishing a monastery in Pittsburgh. Esteeming their rigorous rule, he joined the congregation. After a period of probation, he made his profession of vows in St. James's Church in Baltimore on January 16, 1842, becoming the first person to be received into the Redemptorist order in the United States. While a Redemptorist, he continued to preach and minister to the impoverished and sick throughout the Northeast. In 1844, he was called upon to head the Redemptorist missions at Pittsburgh. His appointment as superior of the community was a heavy burden for Neumann. Not only did he continue to visit missionary territory in addition to his parish work, but he became instrumental in the building of the elaborate Gothic church of St. Philomena.

Neumann's labors were received with gratitude by the Redemptorist order, and in 1846, at the age of 35, he was made vice provincial of the Redemptorists in America and left Pittsburgh for their headquarters in Baltimore. For the next five years

Neumann worked as diligently as he had in the past, establishing many parishes and schools and encouraging religious vocations. In 1851 he was appointed pastor of the unfinished church of St. Alphonsus in Baltimore. This position was much more to his liking because it allowed him to step out of the limelight and afforded him the seclusion he desired. However, this respite from worldly influence was brief, for in 1852 he was selected to succeed Francis P. Kenrick as bishop of Philadelphia. Although reluctant to accept the post, once consecrated under the rule of obedience, Bishop Neumann applied the same energy and dedication to his new duties that he had to his earlier ones.

During his tenure as Philadelphia's fourth bishop, he was responsible for the establishment of 80 new parishes and the building of hundreds of parochial schools. The schools were staffed by various teaching sisterhoods, some of which he helped bring from Europe. Among those were the Sisters of Notre Dame of Munich and the Sisters of the Holy Cross from France. When Neumann was consecrated as a bishop there were only 500 children in Philadelphia parochial schools, but within three years enrollment had increased to 9,000. Because of his work in the Catholic school system, he has been referred to by many as the Father of the American Parochial School System.

After serving faithfully for eight years as bishop, Neumann collapsed and died on a Philadelphia street on January 5, 1860, at the age of 48. The cause of his sudden death is uncertain. The sad news was announced at all masses in the diocese the following day. In 1866, six years after his death, the question of beatification arose. Certain miracles were said to have occurred at his tomb in St. Peter the Apostle Church in Philadelphia. A commission was formed to inquire into his life and give testimony to the Vatican. In 1896 the church pronounced Neumann Venerable, and in 1963 he was proclaimed Blessed. This level of sanctity was one step away from sainthood, for which there would have to be proof that three miracles had taken place through Neumann's intercession. Accounts of three miraculous cures of hopelessly ill young people were accepted by the church: one in Italy in 1923; one in Villanova, Pennsylvania, in 1949; and the third in West Philadelphia in 1963. All three who were cured were present in Rome at the canonization ceremony in 1977. The canonization was observed in the United States in Philadelphia at St. Peter's, where the bishop's body was on display behind glass in the altar.

Henry Ford Institutes the $5.00 a Day Minimum Wage

See also July 30, Henry Ford's Birthday.

In 1903, Henry Ford established the Ford Motor Company. Ford revolutionized the young automobile industry by adopting the assembly line method, in which workers used standard interchangeable parts in a continuous process, with each worker performing one precise task on the line. Previously, most cars had been custom-made, meaning that they were expensive to purchase and expensive to repair. Ford Motor became the industry leader, making quality automobiles available to the general public at affordable prices.

The assembly line method had its drawbacks, however. The work was repetitious and boring, and workers had to keep up with the fast-moving production line or be fired. Not surprisingly, the labor turnover rate was high, often as much as 50 percent a month. This constant turnover was a drain on efficiency, since new employees had to be continuously hired and trained. Further, the unhappy work force was fertile ground for union organizers, something that Ford dreaded. Therefore, on January 5, 1914, he announced that henceforth the minimum wage for Ford employees would be $5 for an eight-hour day, more than doubling the previous Ford minimum wage of $2.34 for a nine-hour day. At first the five-dollar day only applied to male employees, but it was extended to cover women in October 1916.

Ford gambled that for high wages, workers would both tolerate the conditions of the assembly line and lose interest in unionizing. He was right. The labor force became more stable; the higher wages were offset by a reduction in operating costs; and Ford Motor's profits doubled from 1914 to 1916. Ford also instituted another revolutionary measure: a profit sharing plan, which began to distribute 10 million to 30 million dollars a year to Ford employees. In 1922 Ford raised the daily minimum wage to $6 a day, and he raised it again in 1929 to $7 a day, although the Depression forced him to bring it back to $6 a day.

Ford shocked his contemporaries with the novel proposition that a well-paid work force with benefits would be more loyal and in the long run more profitable for the company. Although his motives were hardly pure, Ford was truly a pioneer in labor-management relations.

Walter Mondale's Birthday

U.S. Senate Historical Office

Walter Mondale

Walter Frederick "Fritz" Mondale was born in Ceylon, Minnesota, on January 5, 1928. His parents were Theodore Sigvaard Mondale, a farmer who later became a Methodist minister, and Claribel Hope Mondale. The last name Mondale was originally "Mundal" when the family came to Minnesota from Norway, but it was Americanized to Mondale. Walter graduated from high school in 1946 and entered Macalester College in St. Paul, Minnesota. He dropped out of school briefly and transferred to the University of Minnesota, where he graduated in 1951. During his school years, Mondale was active in student political organizations, and he helped Minneapolis mayor Hubert Humphrey win his campaign for the United States Senate in 1948.

After graduating from college, Mondale enlisted in the army, which had the effect of preventing him from being drafted and having to serve in the Korean War. From 1951 until 1953, Mondale served at Fort Knox, Kentucky, reaching the rank of corporal, and then entered the University of Minnesota Law School on the G.I. Bill. He graduated in 1956 and practiced law until 1960. That year, Minnesota attorney general Orville Freeman resigned and appointed Mondale his successor. Mondale successfully pursued various civil rights causes, including the case of Clarence Earl Gideon, a Florida prisoner who established the right to free counsel for indigent criminal defendants. Attorney General Mondale not only filed a brief with the Supreme Court on Gideon's behalf, but convinced colleagues from 23 other states to co-sign and lend their support.

When Mondale's mentor Hubert Humphrey was elected vice president in 1964, the governor of Minnesota chose Mondale to complete Humphrey's term in the Senate. Mondale went back to the Senate in 1966 and 1972, where he supported Great Society programs and most other liberal causes, and came to oppose the Vietnam War in 1968 after some earlier hesitation. In 1972 Mondale turned down the opportunity to be Senator George McGovern's running mate in the presidential campaign against Richard Nixon, which was probably a wise move given McGovern's crushing defeat. He briefly tested the waters for his own presidential bid in the 1976 campaign, but dropped out early in the Democratic Party process. On July 15, 1976, he agreed to be Jimmy Carter's running mate in the election, adding an important Northern element to the Georgia governor's presidential campaign.

After Carter was defeated in 1980 by Republican Ronald Reagan, Mondale temporarily returned to practicing law, but entered the Democratic presidential primaries in 1984. He became the first candidate of a major party to choose a female for the vice-presidential slot, namely Geraldine Ferraro. Mondale's liberal views were no longer popular, however, and he was soundly defeated by incumbent President Reagan. After this defeat, Mondale continued to be active in Democratic Party politics, and his loyalty earned him the ambassadorship to Japan in 1993 after Democrat Bill Clinton retook the White House in the 1992 elections.

Stephen Decatur's Birthday

Stephen Decatur, a prominent naval officer in the nation's early years, was born on January 5, 1779, in Sinepuxent, Maryland. He grew up in Philadelphia, and after attending the Episcopal Academy went to the University of Pennsylvania, but dropped out to join the navy in 1798 when the United States entered an unofficial sea war with France. His abilities impressed his superiors, and he rose quickly in rank, despite his somewhat pugnacious personality. At this point in history, duels over "matters of honor" were still rather common, and Decatur was not only quick to fight over such matters but would eventually die over one.

In the early 1800s, the United States was a budding mercantile nation, but was harassed in its trade with Europe by the pirate colonies in north-

ern Africa along the Mediterranean (the "Barbary Coast"). The largest colony was centered in the city of Tripoli, where the ruler tacitly encouraged the pirates' activities. When the United States decided to take on the Barbary pirates and Tripoli, Decatur served with distinction, notably by destroying the captured American frigate *Philadelphia* before it could be used by the enemy. Decatur also distinguished himself in the War of 1812, during which he fought and captured the British frigate *Macedonian*.

After the War of 1812, Decatur was sent back to the Barbary Coast for more anti-piracy operations against Tripoli and the other pirate states of Tunis and Algiers. After a successful mission, he returned in 1815 to the United States, where he made a famous toast at a dinner party in his honor: "Our country! In her intercourse with foreign nations may she always be in the right; but our country, right or wrong." Having accumulated a significant personal fortune, Decatur retired to private life, but kept a position on the Board of Navy Commissioners. As a commissioner, Decatur questioned the service record of a certain Captain James Barron, who challenged Decatur to a duel.

On March 22, 1820, the two met at Bladensburg, Maryland, outside of Washington, D.C. During their duel, Decatur shot Barron in the thigh, but Barron shot Decatur through the body. Decatur was carried home and died the same day.

January 6

Sam Rayburn's Birthday

Samuel Taliaferro Rayburn, known as "Sam" or even "Mr. Sam" in his later years, was born on January 6, 1882, in Roane County, Tennessee. The Rayburn family moved to Texas in 1887, and young Sam grew up on the family farm. In 1900, Rayburn entered the Mayo Normal School, now part of the Texas State University system, in Commerce, Texas. He worked his way through college, graduating in 1903 with a B.S. in education, and then went on to be a small-town schoolteacher.

In 1906, Rayburn decided to leave teaching for politics, and successfully ran for the Texas state House of Representatives. He was of course a Democrat, since in that day and age there were practically no Republicans (the "party of Lincoln") in the old Confederacy. In his free time, he studied law at the University of Texas, and passed his bar exam in 1908. He stayed in politics, however, and his political shrewdness led to his election as speaker of the Texas House in 1911. This was quite an accomplishment for a man not yet out of his twenties in the rough and tumble world of Texas politics. He proved to be a strong speaker, but left the position in 1912 when he went into national politics and was elected to the U.S. House of Representatives.

Rayburn was a leader among his fellow southern Democrats in the House, supporting states' rights, agricultural aid, and limits on the power of big business. He served on the Committee on Interstate and Foreign Commerce until he was elected speaker of the House in 1940, and contributed to such measures as the Esch-Cummins Act of 1920, which imposed new regulations on railroad securities. Rayburn's ascendancy was helped by his friendship with fellow Texan and congressman John Nance Garner, who was speaker of the House from 1931 to 1933 and vice president from 1933 to 1941.

During the Roosevelt administration, Rayburn loyally supported the New Deal and swallowed any doubts he may have had about controversial proposals such as the Supreme Court "court packing" plan of 1937. He worked on such New Deal legislative achievements as the securities reform acts of 1933 and 1934, the Public Utility Holding Company Act of 1935, and the Rural Electrification Act of 1936. Rayburn first tried for the speakership in 1934 but lost to Joseph Byrns (D., Tennessee), and he lost again in 1936 to William Bankhead (D., Alabama). However, Bankhead's rise to the speakership gave Rayburn the chance to take Bankhead's old job as the House majority leader. With some exceptions, the majority leader is traditionally next in line for the speakership, so Rayburn was content to take the job and bide his time.

When Bankhead died in September 1940, the Democrats elected Rayburn as the next speaker, a position that he would hold for the rest of his life except for 1947–1949 and 1953–1955, which were those periods when the Republicans briefly held the majority in the House. During World War II, he shepherded the administration's war measures through the House. After the war, he supported the Truman administration's cold war policies, but as a congressman from an oil producing state he opposed Truman's "Northern" policy of keeping the price of energy low. Initially he resisted both Truman's and Eisenhower's tentative initiatives in the area of civil rights, this being anathema for a Southern politician, but he was sensitive enough to the shifting moods in the Democratic Party and the national electorate to quietly drop his opposition by the late 1950s.

During his speakership, Rayburn became the mentor of another Texas congressman, Lyndon Baines Johnson. Johnson would eventually go on to the Senate and become Senate majority leader,

then Kennedy's vice president, and finally president. Johnson continued to rely on Rayburn's advice when Johnson went to the Senate, although he did accept the position of vice president on Kennedy's 1960 ticket over Rayburn's objection. After Kennedy's victory, Rayburn used the Democrats' momentum to reform the House Rules Committee, which had become a conservative bastion and was blocking measures on issues such as civil rights that Rayburn now reluctantly supported.

The genial "Mr. Sam" Rayburn was a true politician, dedicated to the House and the political process over ideology. His favorite expression was, "If you want to get along, go along." Such views may be unfashionable today, but party feuding never caused a government shutdown in Rayburn's day. As a moderate, he got along equally well with liberals and conservatives, and he succeeded in holding the speakership for most of 20 years. In 1961, now nearly 80, he returned to his ranch in Bonham, Texas, for health reasons. He was diagnosed with cancer, which proved to be terminal, and died on November 16, 1961. His support and advice were sorely missed by the Democrats, especially Lyndon Johnson, since Rayburn would have been a significant ally in the approaching era of civil rights and Great Society legislation.

Carl Sandburg's Birthday

Carl August Sandburg, the famous writer and poet, was born on January 6, 1878, in Galesburg, Illinois, to a working class family of Swedish immigrants. He developed literary interests early in his childhood, but had to leave school after the eighth grade in 1891 to work. He held a variety of odd jobs, often riding the freight trains to find work as a farmhand. In 1898 he returned to Galesburg and joined the army as a private, just in time to serve in the Spanish-American War. He was in Puerto Rico for six months but saw no combat, and after the war he came home and entered Lombard College.

Sandburg dropped out of school again, and briefly went back to a life on the road. When he returned to Galesburg, he went to work for the local *Evening Mail*, and began his literary career when in 1904 his first book of poems, *In Reckless Ecstasy*, was published. In 1905 he moved to Chicago, where he wrote poems for the magazine *Tomorrow*. Now in the big city, Sandburg was exposed to and attracted by various liberal causes, joining the Socialist Party and campaigning for Socialist Eugene V. Debs in his 1908 presidential campaign. Also that year, Sandburg married fellow Socialist Lilian Stelchen. After Debs's unsuccessful campaign, Sandburg worked for Emil Seidel, the Socialist mayor of Milwaukee, and wrote articles for several progressive-leaning magazines.

In March 1914, Sandburg's poem "Chicago" was published. The work attracted national attention and gave Chicago the nickname "City of the big shoulders." Sandburg won a poetry prize, and although the reviews were not always favorable due to his unconventional use of colloquialisms, the publicity made him famous. By 1916 he had written enough material to justify publishing a book called *Chicago Poems*. The book was well-received, and Sandburg followed with *Cornhuskers* in 1918, *Smoke and Steel* in 1920, and *Slabs of the Sunburnt West* in 1922. Sandburg's political views manifested themselves in the gritty urban realism of his poetry. He also did a series of articles on the July 1919 Chicago race riots, published collectively later that year as *The Chicago Race Riots*, with a foreword by Walter Lippmann.

Sandburg continued to pursue his Socialist affiliations, taking an interest in the Bolshevik Revolution and the social experiments of the Soviet Union. At one point he smuggled a missive by Soviet leader V. I. Lenin, entitled "Letter to American Workingmen," into the United States. He also developed an interest in the life of Abraham Lincoln, which was to give him his credentials as a serious historian. He published a two-volume series entitled *Abraham Lincoln: The Prairie Years* in 1926 that was well-reviewed and became very popular. With his earnings he bought property on the southern shore of Lake Michigan, where he moved in 1928 and began writing the rest of his Lincoln biography. In 1939 he published the four-volume *Abraham Lincoln: The War Years*, which won him the Pulitzer Prize in 1940. During the term of this massive project he also found time to write a book on Lincoln's spouse, which was published in 1932 as *Mary Lincoln: Wife and Widow*.

In 1945, Sandburg moved from Michigan to North Carolina, where he lived for the rest of his life. He won another Pulitzer Prize in 1951 for his 1950 publication of *Complete Poems*. Sandburg's other works during his lifetime include *The American Songbag* in 1927, *Steichen the Photographer* in 1929, *Home Front Memo* in 1943, the novel *Remembrance Rock* in 1948, *Always the Young Strangers* in 1953, and some children's books such as *Rootabaga Stories* in 1922. His works earned him the Presidential Medal of Freedom in 1964 from President Lyndon Johnson.

During his remaining years, Sandburg worked on a variety of projects, including revisions to his earlier books. He died on July 22, 1967. Some excellent material that was never published during his lifetime was published posthumously. *Breath-*

ing Tokens, a collection of poems, was published in 1978, and *Billy Sunday and Other Poems*, was published in 1993. Sandburg's collected letters were published in 1968, and an uncompleted work titled *Ever the Winds of Chance* was published in 1983.

The Feast of the Epiphany

The Feast of the Epiphany, older than Christmas, is observed in varying degrees by all branches of the Christian church on January 6. The term, from the Greek word *epiphaneia*, refers to the manifestations of the divinity of Jesus Christ.

According to biblical accounts, these manifestations occurred when the Three Wise Men from the East (variously known as the Magi or as the Three Kings) came to worship Jesus at the manger in Bethlehem; during his baptism in the River Jordan by John the Baptist, when the Holy Spirit descended upon Jesus in the form of a dove and a voice proclaimed him the Son of God; and when he performed his first miracle by changing water into wine during the wedding feast at Cana. This multiple anniversary is the occasion for the Feast of the Epiphany. Historically, Eastern Orthodox churches focused on the event of the baptism, while the Roman Catholic and Protestant churches focused on the visit of the Three Wise Men.

The existence of a feast on January 6 was first mentioned by the early church father Clement of Alexandria at the end of the second century. He wrote in the *Stromata* (I, 21) that the Basilidians, followers of Basilides, who founded a heretical sect of Gnostics in Alexandria, kept an all-night vigil on either January 6 or January 10 to commemorate the baptism of Jesus. The more widely based Christian Feast of the Epiphany, which had the approval of church authorities, probably also originated in Egypt and in the East in the very early Christian period. It was celebrated on January 6 to coincide with, and therefore combat, a pagan feast on that date. The ancient Egyptians, for example, observed the winter solstice and a ritual in honor of the sun god on January 6; and on the previous night, January 5, Alexandrian pagans marked the birth of their god Aeon (Aion) from the virgin Kore, which means "the Maiden."

By the fourth century, Christians throughout most of the East celebrated the Feast of the Epiphany in a multiple sense as the anniversary of the physical birth of Jesus Christ, of the adoration of the Magi, of Christ's baptism, and of the miracle at Cana. From the East, the feast entered Europe sometime in the fourth century. In Gaul, Spain, and northern Italy, it was observed primarily as the commemoration of Christ's birth. However,

Christmas, celebrated at Rome on December 25 by the mid-fourth century, soon became universally recognized throughout western Christendom as the occasion for celebrating the birth of Christ. Between 380 and 430, the eastern church also embraced December 25 as the date for the Feast of the Nativity.

As a result, the Epiphany underwent a major transformation liturgically, although it continued to be numbered among the great feasts of the Christian calendar. In the West, its significance centered about the visit of the Magi and the symbolic spreading of the gospel to non-Christians. In the East, where the Adoration of the Magi was celebrated together with Christmas, Christians placed stress on the Epiphany as the feast of Christ's baptism.

In western Europe, the Feast of the Epiphany was from the first an occasion of great religious solemnity. In the year 400, the Roman emperor of the West, Honorius, forbade attendance at horse races and the circus on January 6 lest Christians be diverted from church services. In 565 the Byzantine emperor Justinian proclaimed the feast a civil holy day. During the Middle Ages, the Epiphany, like all the major ancient feasts, had its own vigil with strict fast and abstinence regulations. There were also, however, festivities associated with the event. For example, on January 6, 1601, William Shakespeare's *Twelfth Night* was first presented in a command court performance at Whitehall Palace for Queen Elizabeth I.

Most of the pageantry attached to the Feast of the Epiphany in the past has long since disappeared in the United States, although there are still "Three Kings' Day" celebrations in Puerto Rico and the Virgin Islands. The Epiphany is also observed as Three Kings' Day in some New Mexico Native American pueblos, where the Spanish and Roman Catholic missionaries' influence persists.

New Mexico Admitted to the Union

On January 6, 1912, New Mexico entered the Union as the 47th state. The area now known as the State of New Mexico has a long and varied history extending back to pre-Columbian times. Ancient southwestern Indian civilizations antedated the flourishing culture of the Pueblo Indians found by the early 16th-century Spanish explorers along the Rio Grande basin. Spanish interest in the area began in 1528, when Nuño de Guzman, the governor of New Spain, heard about the supposed hoards of gold and silver in seven towns so large that they could be compared in size to Mexico.

Determined to reach these settlements, vaguely described as being northward between the two seas and across a grassy desert for 40 days, Guzman assembled an army of 400 Spanish soldiers and some native auxiliaries. He set out in December 1529 to find what became known as the fabled Seven Cities of Cíbola, but lost his way. In 1539, a new viceroy, Antonio de Mendoza, outfitted an exploration party under the direction of the Franciscan missionary Fray Marcos de Niza. A full-scale expedition headed by Captain General Francisco Vásquez de Coronado followed in 1540–1542. Since none of these groups had discovered the legendary golden cities or even gold deposits, further Spanish government-sponsored expeditions north of Mexico were suspended by royal ordinance. However, the Southwest remained an attractive field for missionary activity among the Pueblo peoples.

In 1582, Antonio de Espejo led an expedition to rescue some Franciscan friars. His reports about the great mineral wealth and good grazing lands in much of the Pueblo country led in 1598 to Don Juan de Oñate's founding of the first permanent colony in New Mexico at San Juan de los Caballeros, 30 miles north of present-day Santa Fe. It was the second oldest permanent settlement in what is now the United States, the first having been made at St. Augustine, Florida, in 1565. In the winter of 1609–1610, Santa Fe, the new capital of the Province of New Mexico, was founded.

Colonization in the 17th century proceeded at a slow pace. Having failed as a source of easy gold, New Mexico was of interest to the Spanish authorities only as a frontier buffer for northern Mexico and as a mission field. Santa Fe was the only major city, although sparsely populated Spanish settlements had spread along the Rio Grande from Taos in the north to Isleta south of the capital. Friction between Spanish civil and religious authorities and conflicts with the Native Americans further hindered the development of Spanish New Mexico. The exploitation of native peoples through forced labor and the exaction of tribute, as well as the suppression of their religion, led to a series of sporadic uprisings beginning as early as 1640. The unrest culminated in the Apache revolt of 1676 and the Great Pueblo Revolt of 1680, which forced the Spaniards to abandon their holdings in New Mexico and retreat back to Mexico for 13 years. A campaign led by Captain General Don Diego de Vargas Zapata Lujan Ponce de León restored Spanish rule in 1692.

In the 19th century, the Spanish became alarmed at the westward expansion of the Americans, especially after the United States acquired the huge Louisiana Territory in 1803. The Spanish undertook measures, which ultimately proved unsuccessful, to prevent American penetration of Spanish-held Texas and New Mexico. Trade with the new American settlements in the Missouri Valley was discouraged until Mexico achieved independence from Spain in 1821. The independent Mexican republic, which promptly assumed control of New Mexico, legalized economic contacts with the United States.

As early as 1822, William Becknell took the first wagon loads of merchandise across the plains from Missouri to New Mexico, gaining the title Father of the Santa Fe Trail. This important caravan route, operating from Westport (now part of Kansas City) and Independence, Missouri, grew by leaps and bounds. The spring wagon train in 1824, for example, carried $30,000 in goods to Santa Fe and returned with $180,000 in precious metals and $10,000 in furs. In 1860, the route was used by 3,033 wagons, 9,084 men, 6,147 mules, and 27,920 oxen. However, the laying of the Atchison, Topeka, and Santa Fe Railroad to Santa Fe in 1880 sounded the death knell for the famous trail.

At the outbreak of the Mexican War in 1846, the Army of the West, commanded by Brigadier General Stephen Watts Kearny, crossed into New Mexican territory and occupied Las Vegas on August 15 and Santa Fe three days later. On August 23, the construction of Fort Marcy, the first U.S. military fort in New Mexico, began northeast of Santa Fe. On September 22, Kearny set up a civil government for New Mexico, appointing Charles Bent, a partner in the largest southwestern fur-trading company, as governor. At the end of the Mexican War in 1848, the Treaty of Guadalupe Hidalgo ceded Mexican New Mexico, which encompassed present-day Arizona and other territory, to the United States.

Delegates meeting at Santa Fe on October 10, 1848, petitioned Congress for a civil territorial government and for an end to Texan claims to New Mexican land. In May 1850 a constitutional convention framed a constitution for the state of New Mexico, which was subsequently ratified by the inhabitants and submitted to Congress. However, the bid for statehood failed. Instead, a provision of the Compromise of 1850, namely the Organic Act of the Territory of New Mexico, made New Mexico a territory and granted it a civil territorial government. Texas, by then a state, relinquished all claims to the area. The newly established Territory of New Mexico extended all the way to California. It was enlarged in 1853 by the purchase from Mexico of 45,535 square miles west of the Rio Grande and south of the Gila River, known as the Gadsden Purchase.

New Mexico's present boundaries were fixed in the early 1860s. The creation of the Territory of Colorado on February 28, 1861, took away the northeastern section of New Mexico territory, while the Territory of Arizona was fashioned out of New Mexico's western half on February 24, 1863.

New Mexico was a frontier backwater during the Civil War. In 1861, only 22 slaves lived in the sparsely settled territory, and it was of little strategic importance to either the Union or the Confederacy. For the settlers, however, the withdrawal of Union troops, felt to be more essential elsewhere on the military front, meant that large sections of New Mexico lay open to devastating Apache and Navajo raids. Conflicts with the tribes continued after the war, due in large part to the American policy of confining native peoples to reservations in the poorer lands bypassed by white settlers. A peace commission negotiated a treaty with the Navajos in 1868, permitting them to transfer to reservations set up on their home ground of northwestern New Mexico and northeastern Arizona. New reservations in other sections of the territory were also established for the Mescalero Apache in 1873 and for the Jicarilla Apache in 1880. Nevertheless, Geronimo, one of the last prominent Apache leaders, went on the warpath as late as 1885 before his final capture and deportation from the territory.

Another bid for statehood was blocked in 1906, when the people of Arizona rejected a bill proposing Arizona's joint statehood with New Mexico. New Mexico's half-century struggle to obtain statehood ended on June 20, 1910, when Congress passed the enabling act providing for the admission of New Mexico and Arizona as separate states, once each had adopted a suitable state constitution. On January 6, 1912, New Mexico, having fulfilled the requirement, formally entered the Union.

The "Four Freedoms" Enunciated

World War II was well under way in Europe when President Franklin D. Roosevelt made his memorable "Four Freedoms" speech to the United States Congress on January 6, 1941. Although the United States, still technically neutral, did not enter the war on the side of the Allies until after the Japanese attack on Pearl Harbor on December 7 of that year, the United States was already increasing its supply-and-assistance role as the "arsenal of democracy."

The president's address of January 6, 1941, presented as his annual message to Congress, was widely quoted as summarizing the goals that

Americans stood ready to defend. His listing of the "four essential human freedoms" was subsequently used to epitomize the ideology of the Allied democracies as opposed to that of their Nazi and Fascist opponents. In the portion of his speech most frequently cited, FDR said:

In the future days, which we seek to make secure, we look forward to a world founded upon four essential human freedoms.

The first is freedom of speech and expression, everywhere in the world.

The second is freedom of every person to worship God in his own way, everywhere in the world.

The third is freedom from want, which, translated into world terms, means economic understandings which will secure to every nation a healthy peacetime life for its inhabitants everywhere in the world.

The fourth is freedom from fear, which, translated into world terms, means a worldwide reduction of armaments to such a point and in such a thorough fashion that no nation will be in a position to commit an act of physical aggression against any neighbor, anywhere in the world.

The Four Freedoms address was followed, in March 1941, by congressional enactment of the Lend-Lease Act, permitting the lending, leasing, sale, or transfer of arms, equipment, and supplies to any country whose defense the president deemed vital to that of the United States. The lend-lease legislation, which Roosevelt had recommended in his Four Freedoms speech, contributed significantly to the material superiority of the Allies over the Axis powers and to the ultimate defeat of the latter. The statement of goals contained in the presidential message of January 6, 1941, was later amplified by the declaration known as the Atlantic Charter, issued jointly by President Roosevelt and British prime minister Winston Churchill.

Charles Sumner's Birthday

Senator Charles Sumner, one of America's most outspoken abolitionists, was born on January 6, 1811, in Boston, Massachusetts. He went to Harvard at the age of 15, graduated in 1830, and then went on to Harvard Law School, which he attended until 1833. He went into the private practice of law, but soon became bored, and amused himself by periodically lecturing at Harvard Law School and by traveling to Europe. For many years he drifted, unenthusiastically practicing law, but he did manage to develop an interest in public speak-

ing and became one of Boston's most popular lecturers by the end of the 1840s. His populist views alienated conservative Boston's society class, but the Democrats and members of the Free Soil Party (an influential third party of the time) admired him, and nominated him for the United States Senate.

Sumner won the contest and entered the Senate on December 1, 1851. One of his first actions was to deliver a blistering speech against the Fugitive Slave Act, which as part of the Compromise of 1850 permitted slave owners to pursue their escaped "property" anywhere in the country, North or South. Sumner soon became a leader of the radical abolitionist faction in the Senate, and unsuccessfully sought to reverse the decision to let the Kansas and Nebraska territories decide for themselves whether to permit slavery within their boundaries. This decision, a compromise between Northern "Free" and Southern "Slave" forces, was causing considerable violence in the territories as members of both factions went there to try to influence the outcome by force. Kansas, where most of the conflict occurred, was nicknamed "Bleeding Kansas" at the time.

When the new Republican Party emerged in the mid-1850s, Sumner was influential in its organization. The old Whig Party disappeared, and many northern Democrats joined the Republicans. One of the leading planks of the Republican Party was the abolition of slavery, and Sumner redoubled his efforts to eliminate the South's "peculiar institution." On May 20, 1856, Sumner gave a speech on the Senate floor entitled "The Crime Against Kansas," which in particular criticized the role of Andrew Pickens Butler of South Carolina. Preston Brooks, a representative from South Carolina who was Senator Butler's nephew, went into the Senate chamber on May 22 to exact revenge and proceeded to beat Sumner with a heavy walking stick.

Sumner was seated when the assault began, and was unable to escape from his desk while his more youthful adversary continued to beat him. The injuries were severe, and it was years before Sumner could resume his duties in the Senate. In the meantime, members of Congress began to carry guns and knives for protection. Northerners condemned the assault on Sumner as barbaric, but many Southerners applauded Preston Brooks and sent him new walking sticks. The incident dramatized the deterioration in North-South relations, which were drifting slowly to secession and the Civil War.

After recovering from his injuries, Sumner returned to the Senate in 1860, just in time to see the eruption of the Civil War. He chaired the Senate Foreign Relations Committee from 1861 to 1871, and joined the Radical Republicans after the Civil War who sought unsuccessfully to impeach President Andrew Johnson from office. He died on March 11, 1874, in Washington, D.C.

January 7

Millard Fillmore's Birthday

U.S. Senate Historical Office

Millard Fillmore

Millard Fillmore, the 13th president of the United States, was born at Locke (now Summerhill) in Cayuga County, New York, on January 7, 1800. He was the oldest son and second child of Nathaniel Fillmore, who had moved to Locke from Bennington, Vermont, in 1798. He took his first name from his mother, the former Phoebe Millard. The family name of Fillmore originally had been spelled Phillmore, and was so noted when its first known American member bought an estate at Beverly, Massachusetts, in 1704.

Young Fillmore worked on his father's farm and served as an apprentice in several trades. His formal schooling was meager, but he had tutors, including Abigail Powers, with whom he fell in love and eventually married. Fillmore was able to support himself by teaching while he learned the law, a study that began at the age of 18 by reading law in the office of a local county judge and ended when he was admitted to the bar of Erie County

in 1823. Fillmore moved to Buffalo in 1830, where he developed an interest in politics and was elected to the New York state assembly on the Anti-Masonic ticket in 1828. After serving three terms in the state legislature, he was elected to the House of Representatives in 1832. He did not run in 1834 but returned to Congress in 1836 and was twice reelected.

An anti-Jacksonian, Fillmore was a follower of Henry Clay, even though he refused to go along with Clay's fight for re-establishment of the Bank of the United States. When the Whigs obtained a majority in the House in the election of 1840, Fillmore was made chairman of the powerful Ways and Means Committee and took an active part in framing the protective tariff law of 1842. Two years later, an unsuccessful attempt was made to nominate Fillmore for vice president. He was, however, nominated that year to be the Whig candidate for governor of New York. Running against Silas Wright, the Democratic candidate, he was narrowly defeated. In 1847, Fillmore was elected as comptroller of New York State. The following year, with strong support from Clay and his followers, he received the Whig nomination for vice president.

After running on the winning ticket with Zachary Taylor, Fillmore resigned his state office on February 20, 1849, to take up his duties in Washington. He could hardly have guessed that with the death of President Taylor on July 9, 1850, he would himself become president in little more than a year. His unexpected accession to the office of chief executive came at a time of grave national crisis. Debate over the issue of extension or nonextension of slavery to new territories had been raging for a decade, raising sectional passions as had no issue before it. Things reached a fever pitch after the end of the Mexican-American War, when Congress was confronted with the question of what to do with the territory the United States had acquired from Mexico. In particular, the debate focused on California's proposed admission to the Union and the question of whether it would be a slave or a free state. Partisans of both views hardened their stands, with the antislavery contingent, centered in the North, vowing every effort to prevent the further extension of slavery; and the proponents of slavery, largely in the cotton-growing South, threatening secession if their view was not adopted.

Although Fillmore privately deplored slavery, he considered the threat to national unity an even graver danger and carefully refrained from taking sides. Meanwhile, a historic debate raged for eight months in the Senate over what is known as the Compromise of 1850, the set of measures devised by Henry Clay to ease tensions between the North and the South. Among other things, Clay's formula provided for the admission of California as a free state, the organization of New Mexico as a territory with no restrictions regarding slavery, adjustment of the disputed border between Texas and New Mexico, abolition of the slave trade in the District of Columbia, and the enactment of a more stringent Fugitive Slave Act.

Although President Taylor had opposed the Clay compromise, Fillmore had intimated to his chief a few days before the latter's death that, in the event of a Senate tie, he would vote in favor of the measures. When he became president, Fillmore exerted the full weight of his influence in favor of the compromise at a time when it was on the verge of defeat. As it turned out, his support was decisive in ensuring passage. He thus stood with Clay in postponing for a decade the confrontation that would nearly tear the nation asunder in civil war. In his anxiety to preserve the Union, Fillmore even signed the much-abhorred Fugitive Slave Act, exposing himself to bitter denunciation by Northern abolitionists and helping to terminate his tenure in the presidency.

Fillmore's supporters, chiefly Southern Whigs, sought to bring about his renomination in 1852 but failed. Not even General Winfield Scott, who did receive the nomination, could win. In fact, the election marked the final disintegration of the already hopelessly divided Whig Party, and Fillmore was to be the last Whig president. He was, however, nominated by the American or Know-Nothing Party in 1856, while the new Republican Party nominated John C. Frémont. Fillmore, running a poor third in that election, received 874,534 votes; Frémont received 1,341,264; and James C. Buchanan, the Democratic candidate, ran up a total of 1,838,169. Opposing Lincoln's conduct of the Civil War, Fillmore supported General George McClellan for president in the campaign of 1864, and during the Reconstruction period that followed he joined President Andrew Johnson in opposing the policies of the Republican-dominated Congress.

Obviously, Fillmore was not idle in retirement. He was involved in establishing a number of civic and cultural institutions in Buffalo, among them the Buffalo Historical Society and the Buffalo General Hospital. In 1855, Oxford University offered him the degree of doctor of civil laws, but he declined the honor on the ground that he had no literary or scientific achievements that would justify his accepting it. Five years after the death of his wife in 1853, Fillmore was married again, to the widowed Caroline C. McIntosh. The retired president died on March 8, 1874, in Buffalo. He is buried there, in the Forest Lawn Cemetery.

Panama Canal Traversed

On January 7, 1914, the vessel *Alex. La Valley* made the first passage through the Panama Canal. On August 3 the SS *Ancon* became the first ocean steamer to pass through it, and the canal was officially opened on August 15, 1914.

This opening solved a problem of international commerce that had originally presented itself to the Western world in 1453, when Constantinople fell to the Turks and the great land routes to India and the Orient were closed to Christian Europe. Within half a century, Christopher Columbus set forth in search of a westward water route to the Far East; subsequent explorers soon discovered that the North and South American continents blocked the way. From the 16th century onward, the creation of an interoceanic waterway was considered. Vasco Núñez de Balboa, the discoverer of the Pacific Ocean, having explored the Isthmus of Panama in vain for a legendary strait, proposed that the Atlantic and Pacific be joined by a water route through present-day Panama. Hernando Cortes, the conqueror of Mexico, made a similar suggestion. Charles V, the 16th-century emperor of the Holy Roman Empire and king of Spain (as Charles I), went so far as to have survey routes of the area mapped out in detail in preparation for the construction of a canal.

Explorations and plans continued to multiply. They reached a height in the 19th century, during America's age of expansion from Atlantic coast to Pacific coast. The westward thrust of settlement emphasized the need for such a waterway, and several times during the 1800s, creation of a canal under at least partial American control seemed assured. Then, however, the focus of canal-building efforts centered upon Nicaragua rather than Panama. During the 1840s, the conflicting interests of the United States and Great Britain over control of the proposed waterway caused friction, until the Anglo-American Clayton-Bulwer Treaty of 1850 provided that neither country would seek exclusive control of the isthmus or of any canal across it.

The topography of the Central American isthmus remained unknown or at best vague until the California gold rush of 1848–1849. Would-be prospectors seeking to travel from east to west developed an alternate water route to the long Cape Horn voyage. Instead of traveling around the cape, they sailed from eastern U.S. ports, crossed the isthmus overland, and on the Pacific coast boarded a ship for California. Construction of a canal was delayed once again, however, when the United States was distracted by the Civil War and Reconstruction, so the French undertook to engineer and finance a canal project. In 1876 an association was formed in Paris to draw up surveys, and in 1879 the Panama Canal Company was organized with Vicomte Ferdinand de Lesseps, the engineer of the Suez Canal, as president. Excavations for a sea-level canal from Colon on the Atlantic to Panama on the Pacific started in 1881; however, the project proved impractical from an engineering standpoint. In 1887 the French company changed to a lock canal, but, plagued by heat, disease, costly mistakes, and financial difficulties, including misuse of funds, the company was forced to declare bankruptcy in 1889. Over $260 million had been spent. The firm was reorganized as the New Panama Canal Company in 1894, primarily with the intention of unloading the canal project on some willing buyer.

The Spanish-American War of 1898 served to renew interest in the United States in a canal project. Some groups advocated the purchase of the French Panama Canal Company properties; others backed an American business syndicate that had obtained a concession from Nicaragua. A congressional commission, formed to assess the two routes, recommended the one across Nicaragua, since the French were demanding $109 million for their dubious assets.

However, the eruption of a volcano on Nicaraguan soil, as well as the reduction of the French concession price to $40 million, caused a reversal. After the way was cleared with Great Britain in the Hay-Pauncefote Treaty of 1901, which gave the United States the sole right to operate a canal, Congress passed the Spooner Act on June 28, 1902. It authorized President Theodore Roosevelt to acquire the rights and property of the New Panama Canal Company from the French, provided that Colombia (of which the area of the Isthmus of Panama was at that time a province) agreed to grant perpetual control of the required strip of land. On January 22, 1903, Secretary of State John Hay and Colombian representative Tomas Herran signed the necessary treaty, leasing to the United States a 10-mile-wide zone for 100 years.

However, when the Colombian government procrastinated, failing to ratify the treaty, the inhabitants of what is now Panama, actively encouraged by American supporters of the canal project, revolted. The revolt was carefully timed to coincide with the arrival of the American warship *Nashville* in Panamanian waters to prevent Colombian forces from suppressing the revolt, since Panama and Colombia are not connected by land and any force would have to arrive by sea. Panama then declared its independence from Colombia on November 3, 1903. The new Republic of Panama was recognized by the United States three days

later. On November 18, Panama signed the Hay-Bunau-Varilla Treaty, giving the United States the right to build a canal in return for payment of $10 million, a $250,000 annuity beginning in 1913, and a guarantee of Panama's independence. Even though many of the rights provided were later relinquished, the hastily negotiated treaty earned the lasting ill will of Panamanians by granting the United States in perpetuity all rights to the 10-by-50-mile strip of land that was to serve as the site of the canal.

On May 4, 1904, the United States took formal possession of the Canal Zone, and in 1906 construction began under John F. Stevens on a canal with three intricate sets of high-level locks. It was brought to completion by chief engineer George W. Goethals, an army officer who, with his associates, overcame monumental technical, personnel, and health problems. Lieutenant Colonel William C. Gorgas of the Army Medical Department supervised an extensive sanitation program, thus enabling long-term construction in the tropical environment. The canal was opened to international sea commerce on August 15, 1914.

Then as now, the Panama Canal is one of the engineering marvels of the world. It has proved to be especially valuable as a strategic link in the defense of the Western Hemisphere, having facilitated the movement of war materials and servicemen to fighting fronts during World War II and the Korean War. Today, however, the canal has become somewhat antiquated. The development of oil supertankers and aircraft carriers means that the world's largest ships can't use the canal and have to go around South America. Many people have advocated a new canal, built entirely at sea level so that locks to raise and lower ships would be unnecessary.

By the 1960s, the "gunboat diplomacy" means by which the United States had acquired the Canal Zone and built the canal were becoming an issue in American-Panamanian relations, with the result that a series of treaty renegotiations began. Agreement on a new treaty to establish a more modern and equitable relationship was delayed by several factors, notably the unstable Panamanian political situation and rise to power of a nondemocratic military junta. Many Americans felt that surrendering any aspect of control over the Canal Zone was unpatriotic, not to mention dangerous, given the new Panamanian junta, which would not necessarily be an American ally in the future and could conceivably act to hinder American shipping if disputes arose between the two countries. Nevertheless, the Carter administration finally reached an agreement with Panama over the form of a new canal relationship.

On September 7, 1977, President Jimmy Carter and General Torrijos signed new Panama Canal treaties, calling for the transfer of the Panama Canal and the Canal Zone by 2000. The signing, which took place in the Pan American Building in Washington, D.C., was witnessed by diplomats representing 26 other American nations. U.S. ratification faced strong opposition, but the Senate voted on March 16, 1978, to ratify the pact guaranteeing neutrality of the canal and on April 18 to ratify the treaty governing operations and defense and the eventual transfer of the canal to Panama on December 31, 1999.

Russian Orthodox Christmas

January 7 is observed as Christmas by the Russian Orthodox community in the United States, since the Russian Orthodox Church still uses the Julian calendar introduced by Julius Caesar in the year 46 B.C. The Russian Orthodox community numbers in the hundreds of thousands, and is particularly large in San Francisco and New York.

According to legend, in the year A.D. 863 two brothers, Cyril and Methodius, set out from Constantinople, the capital of the Byzantine Empire, to convert the Slavs of "Rus," or Russia. The Slavs were still mostly pagan, worshipping Perun, the God of Thunder, or Dazhbog, God of the Sun. There was no written Slavic language, so Cyril devised an alphabet still known as "Cyrillic" in order to translate the Bible and other religious works. By 945, a mission had been established in Kiev, then the largest Russian city and capital of the largest Russian principality.

That same year, the ruler of Kiev, Prince Vladimir, sent representatives far and wide to investigate the various monotheistic faiths and help him decide which to adopt for his people. He rejected Catholicism because of the power of the papacy. He rejected Islam, reportedly because Muslims are forbidden alcohol and he doubted that the Russians would ever give up drink. He also rejected Judaism, because he felt that since the Jews had no country they must be in disfavor with God. However, the emissaries to Constantinople had sent back glowing reports about the beauty of the Greek churches, which impressed Vladimir as a sign of divine favor, so he embraced Orthodoxy for his people. Once established in Kiev, over the centuries the Orthodox Church converted the Russians of Moscow and the other Russian principalities.

During the Middle Ages, Russia was largely cut off from Byzantium, due to the Mongols and other invaders. The church became the Russian Orthodox Church, with its own traditions and no longer subject to Constantinople. Unfortunately, the church also became an instrument of state power, preaching obedience to authority and the czar in return for the privileges granted to the clergy. When the Romanov dynasty collapsed in 1917, the Soviets adopted an official state policy of atheism and persecuted Orthodox Christians who refused to abandon their faith, or at least keep their observances sufficiently discreet to avoid notice. Many churches were closed, and leading clerics such as Metropolitan Anthony of Kiev went into exile.

On November 20, 1920, Patriarch Tikhon, the last free primate of the Russian Orthodox Church, issued a decree authorizing the formation of the Russian Orthodox Church outside Russia. In the United States, the church grew as Russians fleeing the Soviet Union arrived, and also with the arrival of other Orthodox believers from Eastern Europe after World War II. Today, Russian Orthodox parishes are spread across the country, and they have maintained the tradition of observing their Christmas on January 7.

First Transatlantic Telephone Service

Transatlantic telephone service was pioneered by the American Telephone and Telegraph company (AT&T). AT&T engineers began experimenting with transatlantic communication as early as 1915, briefly achieving two-way radio communication between Virginia and Paris, France. America's entry into World War I put a hold on further developments. By 1925, AT&T was retreating from world markets, and in that year AT&T president Walter S. Gifford sold most of AT&T's assets outside the United States and Canada to the newly organized International Telephone and Telegraph Company for $33 million. However, interest in transatlantic telephone communication remained high, particularly between New York and London. Of course, speedy written communication was already available by telegraph, but oral communication could be achieved only by telephone service.

By 1926, AT&T engineers were confident that reliable two-way telephone service by radio could be established and maintained. It would be expensive, but AT&T figured that the market would be there. For example, since New York and London were the world's financial capitals, telephone service would make it possible to communicate between Wall Street and The City (London's financial district). On January 7, 1927, commercial telephone service by radio was opened between New York and London. Thirty-one calls were made that day, at the astronomical price of $75 for each five minutes.

Transatlantic telephone service was a success, and AT&T expanded it to other countries in Europe. In 1929 the S.S. *Leviathan* became the first ocean liner to offer telephone service to its passengers. In the 1930s telephone service expanded across the Pacific, reaching Hawaii in 1931 and Tokyo, Japan, in 1934. By 1935 a radio-telephone signal could circle the world, but telephone service based on radio transmissions had its weaknesses, notably vulnerability to bad weather. The transition to telephone service by undersea cable came in 1956, when the first transatlantic cable was laid, and in 1964, when the first transpacific cable was laid.

First Commercial Bank Established in the United States

On January 7, 1782, the Bank of North America in Philadelphia, Pennsylvania, opened its doors, becoming the first commercial bank in the United States.

The American Revolution, which began in 1776, was undergoing a serious crisis by the end of the 1770s. The crisis was not just military, but financial as well. The Continental Congress issued paper currency to help finance the war, but the "Continentals" were rapidly becoming worthless. Congress turned to Pennsylvania financier and businessman Robert Morris, one of the signers of the Declaration of Independence, and appointed him superintendent of finance. Morris was a large importer of arms and supplies for the army, and he had chaired a secret congressional committee organized to obtain foreign aid and assistance.

Morris told Congress that the war effort required a commercial bank to act as the financial arm of the government and stabilize the currency. Thus, in 1781 Congress passed legislation authorizing the creation of the Bank of North America under Morris's stewardship. The Bank of North America was financed largely by government funds and a loan from France, with some additional financing by private investors. It issued two new series of bank notes to help finance the war. One series was backed by the assets of the bank, while the other series, nicknamed "Morris notes," was backed by Robert Morris's considerable personal fortune.

The Bank of North America helped to stabilize the financial situation somewhat. Morris held his post as superintendent of finance until 1784, losing much of his personal fortune in the process, and later came under fire for having allegedly misused his authority while in office. The bank not only inaugurated commercial banking in the United States, but the precedent of an independent and yet government-sponsored central bank helped pave the way for the Bank of the United States in the 19th century, and indirectly for the modern Federal Reserve System.

January 8

Battle of New Orleans

The Battle of New Orleans, during which Andrew Jackson commanded victorious American forces and laid the way for his own political career and eventual rise to the presidency, is remembered as a brilliant victory for American arms and as the last battle of the indecisive War of 1812.

Ironically, the Battle of New Orleans was fought after the treaty of peace had been signed. American representatives, including John Quincy Adams, James A. Bayard, and Henry Clay, had been sent to Europe to negotiate a peace. They met the British representatives at Ghent and after long negotiations signed a treaty ending the war on December 24, 1814. Methods of communication, however, were so slow that news of the signing of the treaty did not reach the British and American forces in North America for several weeks.

The New Orleans campaign was undertaken by Major General Sir Edward Pakenham, commander of the expedition. The goal was to take the city and port of New Orleans, which is at the mouth of the Mississippi River. By controlling this port, the British could block all of the American commerce coming downriver from the Midwest and the newly settled territories of the Louisiana Purchase. At this point in history, commerce depended almost entirely on river routes and access to the Atlantic Ocean via the Mississippi into the Gulf of Mexico.

Pakenham arrived off the coast of Louisiana with a fleet of some 50 ships and 7,500 soldiers on December 10, 1814. On December 23 he reached a point about eight miles from New Orleans with a detachment of troops. He was attacked by General Andrew Jackson but successfully resisted the assault, although his advance was checked. The next morning, Jackson fell back to Chalmette, near New Orleans, and ordered his troops to throw up earthworks. On January 1, 1815, the British tried to break the American lines with artillery fire but were unsuccessful. On January 8 they attempted to take the American position by frontal assault, but they were met by such vigorous resistance that within half an hour some 2,000 of their men were dead or wounded, in contrast to no more than 13 American dead and 58 wounded. General Pakenham himself was killed, along with two other gen-

Battle of New Orleans

erals. The British retreated to their ships ten days later.

The victory made Andrew Jackson a national hero and laid the foundation for the political strength that later made him president. In New Orleans, people joyously danced in the streets. More significantly, the United States had redeemed itself militarily in the War of 1812, which had gone badly for the country and involved the humiliating burning of Washington, D.C., by British forces. The young United States was in no position to carry the war to British soil, much less retaliate against the British capital of London, but the victory of American forces at New Orleans in the face of Britain's overwhelming naval superiority impressed the world.

The victory is marked annually on January 8 in New Orleans. In Jackson Square, a statue by Clark Mills shows the general astride his horse. Several miles outside the city other ceremonies take place at the scene of the battle, now known as Chalmette National Historical Park. One of the most notable early celebrations of the anniversary of the Battle of New Orleans occurred on January 8, 1828, when Jackson went to the city during his campaign for the presidency and was guest of honor at a large Democratic Party gathering.

Eleventh Amendment Declared Ratified

Under the federal system that the Constitution of 1787 established, in the United States certain powers are vested in the national government and the remainder are retained by the individual states. The framers of the Constitution outlined in detail the areas over which the central government was to exercise jurisdiction, but in 1793 a dispute arose over the constitutional clause permitting lawsuits "between a State, or the citizens thereof, and foreign States, citizens or subjects." To curtail the federal government's authority over such judicial matters, Congress in March 1794 sent the 11th Amendment to the states for their approval. The amendment was declared ratified on January 8, 1798.

The demand for the 11th Amendment stemmed from the Supreme Court's 1793 ruling in the case of *Chisholm* v. *Georgia*. In 1793 two South Carolinians representing a British creditor initiated suit in the U.S. Supreme Court against the state of Georgia to gain restitution for goods provided to the state during the American Revolution. Georgia argued that the nation's highest tribunal had no jurisdiction in the matter, since a sovereign state could not be sued without its consent. The Supreme Court ruled otherwise. By a four-to-one decision, the Court accepted the case, ruled against the state of Georgia, and ordered it to pay the debt under consideration.

The court based its decision on Article III of the Constitution, which establishes the judicial power of the United States and vests it in one Supreme Court. Within Article III's grant of jurisdiction to the Supreme Court is Section 2, clause (1), which states that "The judicial power shall extend to all cases, in law and equity, arising under this Constitution, the laws of the United States, and Treaties made, or which shall be made, under their authority . . . between a State, or the citizens thereof, and foreign States, citizens or subjects." When Congress created the federal court system that the Chisolm plaintiffs used to initiate their lawsuit, it had not considered that it was now providing a federal forum for lawsuits against the states. Further, under the principles inherited from English common law, both the states and the federal government were considered to be "sovereigns" immune from lawsuits by "subjects" unless the "sovereign" consented. In fact, this legal principle is still very much alive: A myriad of state and federal statutes waiving sovereign immunity make it possible for modern litigants to sue their governments for damages. In 1793, however, the idea of a federal lawsuit proceeding against a state's will was too radical to be accepted.

Reaction to the Chisholm decision was immediate. The lower house of the Georgia legislature approved a bill making any federal marshal who tried to collect the debt in question a felon. The legislatures of other states protested the Supreme Court's ruling only slightly less vehemently. And, more important, the states instructed their representatives in Congress to take action to prevent a repetition of what they believed to be a violation of their sovereign rights. On March 4, 1794, Congress passed the 11th Amendment by the required two-thirds majority in both the House and the Senate, and sent the amendment to the states for ratification. After the requisite three-fourths of the states had approved the measure, it became effective on February 7, 1795.

As ratified, the 11th Amendment states that "The judicial power of the United States shall not be construed to extend to any suit in law or in equity, commenced or prosecuted against one of the United States by citizens of another State, or by citizens or subjects of any foreign State." It is one of the few constitutional amendments passed specifically to reverse a particular Supreme Court decision.

Elvis Presley's Birthday

Elvis Aaron Presley, later to be known as the King of Rock and Roll, the King of Western Bop, Elvis the Pelvis, the Hillbilly Cat, or simply "The King," was born on January 8, 1935, in East Tupelo, Mississippi. As a child, he sang with his parents at Pentecostal churches in Tupelo and was exposed to gospel music at revival meetings. His parents gave him his first guitar on his 11th birthday.

The Presley family moved to Memphis, Tennessee, in 1948. After graduating from high school in 1953, Elvis had a short-lived career as a truck driver. In June of that year, he was "discovered" when he went to the local Sun Records studio to make a private recording of "My Happiness" for his mother. Sun Records president Sam Phillips was impressed by Elvis's style, despite Elvis's then controversial use of African American rhythms in his music. In 1954 "Blue Moon of Kentucky" was released, and became Elvis's first big hit.

After touring the South and releasing some more country- and-western songs, Elvis left Sun Records and signed up with "Colonel" Tom Parker, who became his personal manager. In 1955 Parker signed Elvis with RCA records, a major national label, and Elvis's release of "Heartbreak Hotel" became a national hit. Elvis's music appealed to pop and rhythm- and-blues fans in addition to country music listeners, and his songs ranked high on survey lists of all three types of music. In 1956 Elvis released a two-sided single, "Don't Be Cruel / Hound Dog," which became a top hit on all three lists. The single earned him an appearance on the popular *Ed Sullivan Show*.

On September 9, 1956, before an estimated television audience of 54 million people, Elvis played his hits. The appearance was a big success, but Elvis was televised only from the waist up. His performances on stage, during which he would swing his hips while singing, were thought to be too suggestive. Another issue was the African American influence in Elvis's music—"Elvis the Pelvis" seemed a little too close to the unwritten divide between blacks and whites for 1950s television producers.

Elvis released more hits in the late 1950s, such as "Love Me Tender" and "All Shook Up." He also starred in a series of B-movie musicals, beginning with *Love Me Tender*. Unlike his music, which in later years gained respect for its innovativeness, Elvis's movies had few redeeming qualities other than their commercial success.

Elvis was drafted by the army on March 24, 1958, but as a celebrity he was treated with kid gloves, and even managed to record some more hits before he was released on March 5, 1960. After leaving the army, Elvis continued to record songs and appear in movies, but he also moved into some new areas. He recorded his first album of gospel music, *His Hand in Mine*, in 1960 and another gospel album, *How Great Thou Art*, which was released in 1967. He also decided to start a family, and married Priscilla Beaulieu on May 1, 1967. His only child, daughter Lisa Marie, was born on February 1, 1968.

Elvis's popularity had begun to fade by the late 1960s. He had been left behind by the British invasion, acid rock, heavy metal, and Woodstock developments of 1960s music that were propelling new performers to the top of the charts. He attempted a comeback in 1968, putting together a television special that was aired on NBC on December 3 of that year. The show, which featured some elaborate production numbers, fared well. Elvis followed up with some new releases, including an attempt at racial and social consciousness with "In the Ghetto." Beginning on July 31, 1969, Elvis also became a regular performer in the Las Vegas hotels and casinos, where he appealed to an aging audience of fans and where his glitzy attire helped disguise his growing weight problem.

Elvis's last major hit album was *Aloha from Hawaii* in 1973. His lifestyle had become increasingly unhealthy. In addition to gaining weight, he had a problem with alcohol and substance abuse. Some of his odder habits included shooting television sets with a pistol when the programs began to irritate him, and indulging in his favorite snack, a whole loaf of Italian bread stuffed with peanut butter and cooked bacon. He was divorced from Priscilla on October 11, 1973. His live performances became increasingly listless, and his last act was in Indianapolis on June 26, 1977. On August 16, 1977, at his lavish Graceland mansion in Memphis, Tennessee, Elvis died of heart failure. Since he was only 42, and had a history of abusing prescription drugs, the assumption is that he died of an overdose of barbiturate depressants.

After his death, "The King" quickly became an American icon. This was in part due to the efforts of Priscilla, who inherited most of Elvis's estate and shrewdly parlayed the copyright, licensing, and royalty rights into a fortune reputedly worth hundreds of millions of dollars. Graceland has become a major tourist attraction since it was opened to the public in 1982, and the Post Office has even issued a special Presley postage stamp. There is even a theory, fanned by the tabloid press, that Elvis is still alive and that he faked his own death. In 1986, Elvis became one of the first inductees into the Rock and Roll Hall of Fame. By some estimates, his total record sales had topped the 1 billion mark by the mid-1990s.

AT&T Agrees to Split Up Its Telephone Monopoly

On January 8, 1982, the American Telephone and Telegraph Company, known as AT&T or "Ma Bell," consented to a historic devolution of its traditional monopoly over American telephone service when it agreed to the spinoff of its 22 local Bell System companies. The divestiture of these local companies, henceforth known as the "Baby Bells," represented the voluntary loss of roughly 80 percent of AT&T's assets.

Alexander Graham Bell, the inventor of the telephone, organized the Bell Telephone company in 1877. In 1899, the name changed to its current form, and the company became the giant of the American telephone business. For many decades, AT&T was considered a "natural monopoly," but in 1949 the first of a series of antitrust actions was brought by the Department of Justice. In that year, the department challenged AT&T's ownership of Western Electric, the Bell System's major phone equipment manufacturer. The action was settled in 1956, when the government agreed to let AT&T keep Western Electric in return for AT&T's consent to keep its business activities within the regulated telephone arena. In 1968, however, the Federal Communications Commission challenged AT&T's telephone equipment monopoly. Finally, in 1974, the Department of Justice challenged AT&T's monopoly over long-distance telephone service, an action that led to lengthy litigation in the federal courts throughout the 1970s.

The 1970s litigation was vigorously supported by such prospective competitors as MCI, then just an upstart in the telecommunications business. By the early 1980s, Congress was seriously considering some new and very restrictive regulations on AT&T's business. As a consequence, AT&T chairman Charles Brown entered into a series of negotiations that led to the January 8, 1982, agreement. Under the agreement's terms, AT&T would be freed from the restrictions of the old 1956 decree and could enter telecommunications and computer markets that had previously been forbidden. The price, however, was divestiture of the local Bell companies. After the spinoff, seven regional "Baby Bell" phone companies emerged, having consolidated the 22 Bell companies into viable competitive entities.

The settlement agreement was modified somewhat by the federal judge in charge, District Judge Harold Greene, but overall it went into effect by the mid-1980s. Although AT&T was bereft of its local subsidiaries, it prospered in the new areas of business now open to it, and by the 1990s had built a telephone, data transmission, computer, and Internet business worth nearly $100 billion. In fact, further spinoffs were inaugurated on AT&T's own initiative, such as the divestiture of Bell Laboratories into the newly formed Lucent Technologies.

January 9

First Successful Balloon Flight in the United States

Through the ages people have dreamed of flying. In legends, the ancients recounted tales of intrepid individuals who dared to ascend into the sky, and throughout the course of history many persons such as Leonardo da Vinci tried to design machines that would allow human beings to defy the force of gravity. Efforts to imitate the birds of the air progressed slowly, but finally, in 1783, the first successful manned balloon flight took place in France. Ten years later, on January 9, 1793, a hydrogen-filled balloon carried a man above the territory of the United States.

A French citizen, Jean Pierre Blanchard, also known as François Blanchard, was the man responsible for the first balloon flight in the United States. The idea of flying had fascinated Blanchard from an early age. He studied birds in flight and even constructed an ingenious, albeit unsuccessful, flying machine before his fellow countrymen Joseph and Jacques Etienne Montgolfier in 1783 produced the first hot-air balloon capable of carrying a man. The Montgolfier invention turned Blanchard's attention to lighter-than-air craft. Between 1783 and 1792 he used Montgolfier balloons to make more than 40 flights that delighted and thrilled audiences in such European cities as Berlin, Warsaw, and Vienna. He also accompanied Dr. John Jeffries of Boston, by balloon, on the first air flight across the English Channel in 1785, an achievement that at the time was hailed as the eighth wonder of the world.

Like the Europeans, Americans were enthusiastic about air travel by balloon. As early as 1784, Peter Carnes tried to duplicate the European achievement. In Baltimore, Maryland, in June 1784, Carnes was able to raise a captive balloon carrying a 13-year-old boy, but when Carnes attempted a second ascension at Philadelphia one month later, his balloon burst into flames. In the years that followed other Americans made efforts to ascend into the sky, but none were successful.

Believing that many Americans were eager to see a balloon ascension and would pay for the privilege, 39-year-old Blanchard set sail from Hamburg on September 30, 1792. He landed in Phila-

delphia on December 9 and immediately made arrangements for his historic flight. Local newspapers carried advertisements inviting interested persons to pay five dollars so they might see the spectacle. A general feeling of excitement swept through Philadelphia as January 9, 1793, the day of the ascent, approached.

Blanchard chose the courtyard of Philadelphia's Walnut Street Prison as the starting point of his flight. The brick walls of the jail yard protected Blanchard's balloon from the curious who might be tempted to tamper with it, and also prevented people who had not paid the necessary five dollars from observing the event. At 9:00 A.M., inflation of the massive balloon started. A band provided musical background as the huge yellow silk balloon was filled with hydrogen.

Promptly at 10:00 A.M., Blanchard came before the throng of spectators, who included President George Washington and the minister plenipotentiary of France. Washington presented Blanchard, who spoke no English, with a letter explaining the Frenchman's mission to any person he might encounter after his descent. This first presidential message to be airborne read:

> The bearer hereof, Mr. Blanchard, a citizen of France, proposing to ascend in a balloon from the city of Philadelphia, at 10 o'clock, A.M. this day, to pass in such direction and to descend in such places as circumstances may render most convenient, these are therefore to recommend to all citizens of the United States, and others, that in his passage, descent, return or journeying elsewhere, they oppose no hindrance or molestation to the said Mr. Blanchard; and, that on the contrary, they receive and aid him with that humanity and good will, which may render honor to their country, and justice to an individual so distinguished by his efforts to establish and advance an art, in order to make it useful to mankind in general.

After Blanchard accepted the "passport" from Washington, the artillery fired one last time. Then Blanchard entered the blue, spangled boat under the massive balloon, tossed out some of the ballast, and slowly the balloon carried him skyward. As Blanchard ascended, he waved a flag, which bore the colors of the United States on one side and those of France on the other, and he doffed his feathered hat to the delighted crowd below. Reflecting on his reactions as he rose above the walls of the jail yard, the Frenchman reported:

> I could not help being surprised and astonished, when, elevated at a certain height over the city, I turned my eyes towards the

immense number of people, which covered the open places, the roofs of the houses, the steeples, the streets and the roads, over which my flight carried me in the free space of air. What a sight! How delicious for me to enjoy it.

Blanchard soared over Philadelphia, until air currents caught his craft and propelled it east toward Delaware. During his journey eastward, Blanchard performed a number of experiments that American scientists had requested. When he reached maximum altitude, he took his pulse, determined that the balloon had risen to a height of 5,812 feet, and discovered that a magnet that could lift five and one half ounces on the ground could raise only four ounces at that altitude. After completing his scientific observations, Blanchard began his descent by alternately letting air escape from the balloon and throwing out ballast. His first two efforts to land were frustrated when he encountered a dense forest and then a swamp, but on his third try he found a suitable area situated in a thick wood. The descent was easily accomplished, and at 10:56 A.M., 46 minutes after leaving the Walnut Street Prison yard, Blanchard set foot on the ground just outside Woodbury in Gloucester County, New Jersey.

As Blanchard began to consult his compass so that he could calculate his exact location, a local townsman approached the balloon. The sight of the Frenchman's strange craft astonished and frightened the man, but Blanchard reassured him by offering him some of his wine. Within minutes a second townsman appeared, and then others. They read Washington's missive, and proceeded to help Blanchard pack up his equipment and load it on a cart for the return journey to Philadelphia. Arriving in Philadelphia at 7:00 P.M., he paid his respects to Washington and presented the president with the flag that he had waved during his balloon ascent that morning.

Blanchard's flight thrilled the city, but unfortunately most people chose to watch the spectacle from outside the Walnut Street Prison walls, so that Blanchard did not raise enough money to meet his expenses. Thus, in the months following, he undertook a number of projects to earn additional funds. He wrote an account of his flight, which was sold at five and a half cents per copy, and he gave a number of aeronautical exhibitions. These ventures were only moderately successful, and Blanchard returned to France at the end of the year.

Connecticut Ratifies the Constitution

On January 9, 1788, Connecticut became the fifth state to ratify the United States Constitution, doing so by an overwhelming 128 to 40 vote in the ratifying convention.

Three eminent statesmen, Oliver Ellsworth, William Samuel Johnson, and Roger Sherman, represented Connecticut at the Constitutional Convention in Philadelphia in 1787. Oliver Ellsworth, 42 years old, was a state superior court judge and an accomplished orator. William Samuel Johnson was one of America's leading intellectuals. The 60-year-old scholar had been a lawyer and a judge, and had recently become the president of Columbia College. Roger Sherman, mayor of New Haven, had been a shoemaker, almanac maker, lawyer, and judge during his 66 years. He had a keen mind and was an extraordinarily shrewd politician. Sherman was one of the signers of the Declaration of Independence and a member of the Continental Congress.

Connecticut was at a disadvantage under the Articles of Confederation. In colonial days, the state had traded livestock, especially to the West Indies, but the British closed the market after the Revolution. Designed for carrying animals, Connecticut's fleet was unsuited for shipping other commodities, and the state's businessmen did not have the money to build new vessels. Unable to compete for transatlantic trade, Connecticut became dependent on New York for its European imports. Money, which Connecticut needed to pay its war debts and to invest in various manufacturing and mercantile enterprises, went instead to Manhattan merchants and to the coffers of the New York state government, which levied heavy import duties.

Deprived of control of its fortunes, Connecticut hoped that a new constitution would spread prosperity more equitably among the states. The Connecticut legislature authorized the state's representatives to the Constitutional Convention at Philadelphia to "discuss upon such Alterations and Provisions agreeable to the general principles of Republican Government as they shall think proper to render the federal Constitution adequate to the exigencies of Government and the preservation of the Union." Oliver Ellsworth, William Samuel Johnson, and Roger Sherman took these directions seriously and worked vigorously to create a document that would foster the interests of both their state and the nation.

Connecticut's goal was the difficult one of strengthening the Union without undermining the sovereignty of the states. Along with the other smaller states, Connecticut opposed the Virginia

Plan, which would have allotted representation in the Congress on the basis of population, and preferred the New Jersey Plan, which would have provided each state with a single vote in the national legislature. Connecticut was not doctrinaire in this matter, however, and its delegates were instrumental in the adoption of a solution acceptable to both large and small states. Historians have sometimes dubbed this "Great Compromise," which authorized representation by population in the lower house and an equal vote for each state in the upper house, the "Connecticut Compromise," in recognition of the efforts of Ellsworth, Johnson, and Sherman.

The Constitutional Convention ended its work on September 17, 1787, and in November of that year the Connecticut legislature issued a call for the election of delegates to a ratifying convention, which was to meet in Hartford. In the weeks before the elections Federalists continued a newspaper campaign, which they had been conducting for several months, in favor of the new Constitution. The elections took place in early December at town meetings throughout the state, but the meaning of the outcome was not immediately clear, because the communities did not instruct their representatives either to ratify or reject the new frame of government.

When the ratifying convention opened at Hartford on January 4, 1788, the Federalists immediately took control of the proceedings. Matthew Griswold of Lyme was president of the gathering and Jedediah Strong of Litchfield its secretary. Oliver Ellsworth began the debates with a speech on behalf of ratification. A strong Union was necessary, Ellsworth argued, for purposes of defense, economy, internal harmony, and Connecticut's survival in the midst of powerful neighboring states. Ellsworth's fellow delegates found his arguments persuasive, and on January 9, 1788, then voted 128 to 40 to accept the Constitution. For purposes of establishing a chronology of the admission of the states into the Union, historians typically use the dates of their ratification of the Constitution, so Connecticut is considered to be the fifth state to join the Union.

Richard M. Nixon's Birthday

Richard Milhous Nixon, the nation's 37th chief executive, experienced extremes of glory and humiliation during his career in public life. When he first ran as the Republican candidate for president in 1960, he suffered a narrow defeat at the hands of Democrat John F. Kennedy. Two years later, he experienced an embarrassing loss to Edmund Brown in the gubernatorial election in his home

Library of Congress

Richard M. Nixon

state of California. In 1968, however, he made one of the most remarkable political comebacks in American history, winning the presidency from the Democrats. Nixon experienced an even more impressive victory on November 7, 1972, when he won reelection by a vote that carried 49 of the 50 states and gave him the second highest percentage of the popular vote in the nation's history. His presidency is marked by a number of noteworthy achievements, including diplomatic negotiations with both the Soviet Union and the People's Republic of China, but is also marked by the Watergate scandal and the national humiliation on August 9, 1974, when Nixon became the first president in American history to resign rather than be impeached from office.

Richard M. Nixon was born in Yorba Linda, California, on January 9, 1913. The second of the five sons of Francis and Hannah Milhous Nixon, he spent his first years on his father's lemon farm and at the age of nine moved with his family to Whittier, California. Young Nixon attended local public schools and in 1930 entered Whittier College. During his college years, he was active in debate and student politics. He served as class president in his freshman year and, as a senior, won election as president of the Whittier student body. Ranking second in his 1934 graduating class, Nixon won a scholarship for further study at the Duke University Law School.

Like many other students during the Great Depression, Nixon had to work hard to remain in school. To supplement his scholarship at Duke, he held a number of jobs, which included working in the law school library and for individual professors. He was elected to the Order of the Coif, the honorary legal fraternity, and graduated third in his class in 1937, receiving his LL.B. degree with honors. That same year, he returned to Whittier. In the fall he was admitted to the California Bar Association and joined the law firm of Wingert and Bewley (later Wingert, Bewley and Nixon).

The young attorney remained with the southern California firm for five years. During that time he worked on corporate and tax cases, and in addition acted as town attorney in La Habra, a small town near Whittier. Shortly after the United States' entry into World War II, Nixon went to Washington, D.C., where he worked for about six months as an attorney in the tire-rationing section of the Office of Price Administration. In June 1942 he accepted appointment as a lieutenant, junior grade, in the Naval Reserve. After training, he served in the South Pacific as officer in charge of the South Pacific Combat Air Transport Command at Guadalcanal and Green Island. He later carried out various stateside assignments for the Navy's Bureau of Aeronautics. By the time of his discharge in early 1946, Nixon had advanced to the rank of lieutenant commander.

Also in 1946, Nixon sought his first elective office. Even before his release from the navy, a group of California Republicans endorsed his candidacy for the United States House of Representatives from the state's 12th Congressional District. Nixon did not disappoint these initial supporters. Early in 1946 he captured his party's nomination for Congress, and in the November elections he unseated the Democratic incumbent H. Jerry Voorhis in a campaign that foreshadowed those of his later political career. Displaying a deep understanding of the temper of his constituents and an adroit sense of politics, he took a strong stand against Communism; indeed, he alleged that his opponent had the backing of a Communist-dominated organization and argued that a vote for Voorhis would be a vote for Communism. In the early postwar years such a campaign had widespread appeal, and Nixon gained a reputation as a fighter against Communism that eventually brought him to national prominence.

Nixon served two terms in the House of Representatives, during which time he worked on some of its most influential committees. As a member of the House Committee on Education and Labor, he aided in drafting the Labor-Management Act of 1947, popularly known as the Taft-Hartley Act.

Nixon was also a member of the Select Committee on Foreign Aid, which was sent to Europe to examine the war-ravaged economies of that continent, and whose recommendations helped cement bipartisan support for the Marshall Plan. However, the activity that most advanced Nixon's career prior to 1950 was his membership in the controversial House Un-American Activities Committee. The young congressman worked on the bill requiring alleged Communist-front organizations in the United States to register with the attorney general, and he also helped with the committee's investigations into alleged Communist infiltration of government, schools, and other organizations. When in 1948 Whittaker Chambers, an editor of *Time* magazine, accused Alger Hiss, the president of the Carnegie Endowment for International Peace and a former member of the State Department, of having belonged to the Communist Party, Nixon played a leading role in the ensuing investigation. It was largely due to Nixon's persistent efforts that Hiss was indicted and ultimately convicted of perjury.

Nixon's conduct of the Hiss case alienated some portions of the populace. Nixon himself later wrote that it "left a residue of hatred and hostility toward me . . . among substantial segments of the press and intellectual community." However, most Americans approved of Nixon's impressive performance in the Hiss investigation. Nixon became an increasingly prominent figure in national politics, and in 1950 ran for the United States Senate. His campaign against the Democratic candidate, Representative Helen Gahagan Douglas, was hard fought, and feelings on both sides were heated. Nixon accused Mrs. Douglas of being soft on Communism; she, in turn, gave him the nickname Tricky Dick, which was to stay with him for life. Nixon nonetheless won the election and entered the Senate in December 1950, shortly after the resignation of incumbent senator Sheridan Downey.

During his years in the Senate, Nixon served on the Labor and Public Welfare Committee and on the Expenditures in Executive Departments Committee. In addition to his official duties in Washington, Nixon, in 1951 and 1952, spoke before numerous Republican groups across the country, and these speaking engagements worked to enhance his reputation among the most influential members of the party. When he addressed a New York State fund-raising dinner in May 1952, Nixon favorably impressed Thomas E. Dewey, the Republican presidential candidate in 1944 and 1948 and a trusted adviser of General Dwight D. Eisenhower. Two months later, when Eisenhower captured the Republican presidential nomination,

Dewey and others suggested Nixon as a possible running mate. Eisenhower agreed to their proposal, and at the age of 39 Richard Nixon became a candidate for the second-highest elective office in the nation.

Senator Karl Mundt identified the three issues on which the Republican campaign focused as K1 C2: Korea, Communism, and Corruption. The bloody war in Korea, the Democrats' alleged softness on Communism, and several scandals involving instances of corruption among some administration officials were obvious targets for Republican politicians seeking to oust Democratic incumbents. The Democrats, however, temporarily turned one element of the Republican attack back against the GOP. Midway through the 1952 campaign, Nixon was accused of accepting contributions from California businessmen to a private fund designed to offset political expenses.

Temporarily unnerved by the scandal, some Republican leaders called for Nixon to withdraw from the race. Determined to stay, Nixon took the novel step of using television to take his case to the public, and on prime-time TV emotionally proclaimed his innocence of any wrongdoing and denied that any part of the fund had ever been devoted to personal use. In an oblique reference to allegations that the wives of some Democratic officials had received improper gifts of furs, Nixon noted that his wife, Pat, wore a "respectable Republican cloth coat." Nixon also mentioned the family cocker spaniel, Checkers, which he claimed was the only personal gift he received in office. Finally, Nixon asked viewers to determine his future by sending their opinions of his candidacy to the Republican National Committee. The audience response to the famous "Checkers speech" was overwhelmingly favorable; Nixon's opponents within the Republican Party were forced to retreat; and he stayed on the ticket.

On November 4, 1952, Eisenhower and Nixon scored an overwhelming victory over their Democratic opponents, former governor Adlai E. Stevenson of Illinois and Senator John J. Sparkman of Alabama. The Republicans received approximately 33,936,000 votes and the Democrats approximately 27,315,000, for an electoral college victory of 442 to 89. Under Eisenhower, Nixon served an important role as liaison with the various Republican factions, and chaired a number of Cabinet meetings when Eisenhower was incapacitated due to his frequent heart trouble. In 1956 the Eisenhower-Nixon ticket was reelected in another big victory over the Democrats. Nixon's second term as vice president was marred by his trip in the spring of 1958 to South America, where unfriendly mobs assaulted the Nixons in Lima, Peru,

and Caracas, Venezuela. Nixon recovered somewhat in 1957, when he visited Moscow, where he opened the American National Exhibition. At a display of kitchen appliances, Soviet premier Nikita S. Khrushchev engaged the American vice president in a heated discussion of issues on which the United States and the Soviet Union differed. Nixon handled the awkward situation well, and his conduct during the so-called "kitchen debate" was widely applauded in the United States.

Despite a lukewarm endorsement from Eisenhower, who found Nixon to be politically useful but was not personally fond of him, Nixon won the Republican presidential nomination in 1960 and chose Henry Cabot Lodge of Massachusetts as his running mate. The Democrats selected Senator John F. Kennedy, also of Massachusetts, and Senate majority leader Lyndon B. Johnson. During the course of the 1960 campaign, Nixon and Kennedy met in a historic series of nationally televised debates. Nixon, looking pale and having refused cosmetic assistance for the camera, gave a bad impression next to the tanned and youthful Kennedy. Interestingly, people who listened to the debate on radio rather than viewing it on TV typically felt that Nixon won the debate on the merits. Reactions to the other television debates were more evenly balanced, but that first debate was an important factor in the outcome of the November election, in which Kennedy defeated Nixon by a narrow margin of approximately 118,000 votes.

After 14 years of national public service, Nixon returned to California in 1961. He joined a Los Angeles law firm, and in 1962 he published his political memoir *Six Crises*. That same year he again sought elective office, this time running for governor of California against the Democratic incumbent, Edmund "Pat" Brown. On election day, Brown defeated Nixon by almost 300,000 votes. Nixon contended that unfair treatment by the press had largely been responsible for both this defeat and his failure to win the 1960 presidential race. The day after the election, Nixon revealed his bitterness when he told a group of newsmen that "you won't have Nixon to kick around any more because, gentlemen, this is my last press conference."

In 1963 Nixon moved to New York City, where he became a partner in one of the city's largest law firms, soon to be renamed Nixon, Mudge, Rose, Guthrie and Alexander. Most observers believed that Nixon's political career had ended, but the former vice president continued to be active in the Republican Party and, unlike many prominent Republicans, he endorsed and worked for the election of Arizona senator Barry Goldwater, the party's presidential nominee in 1964. Although Goldwater was soundly defeated by Democrat Lyndon B. Johnson, Nixon's political career revived, and he increasingly appeared to be a likely presidential candidate in 1968. In July 1968, after strong showings in the state primaries, the Republican National Convention in Miami Beach, Florida, chose Nixon as its nominee for president on the first ballot.

In the November election, divisions within the Democratic Party and the third-party candidacy of George C. Wallace of Alabama helped Nixon and his running mate, Governor Spiro T. Agnew of Maryland, achieve victory over the Democratic candidates Hubert Humphrey and Ed Muskie. The Nixon-Agnew ticket received 31,785,480 votes; the Democrats received 31,275,165 votes; and Wallace received 9,906,473 votes. Wallace, whose support came almost exclusively from Southern Democrats, swung the election in Nixon's favor.

On January 20, 1969, Nixon took the oath of office and became the 37th president of the United States. The most immediate issue for Nixon was what to do about the increasingly unpopular war in Vietnam. As critics of the war grew more strident in their demand that the United States end its involvement on behalf of South Vietnam, Nixon responded by accelerating the plan by which South Vietnamese troops were trained to defend their country, thereby permitting the gradual withdrawal of American servicemen. Vietnamization, as the plan was known, did not satisfy all opponents of the war, but it enabled Nixon to reduce the number of American troops in Vietnam from about 542,500 in February 1969 to 368,000 in late 1970, with the promise of further reductions to come.

In foreign policy, Nixon undertook a historic reversal of American cold war policy by announcing in July 1971 that he would personally visit the People's Republic of China. (See February 21, "President Nixon Goes to China," for further information.) In 1972, Nixon visited the Soviet Union, beginning the period of thaw in cold war relations known as détente. Meanwhile, America's presence in Vietnam continued to decline, and by year's end the American force was down to less than 30,000 and still shrinking. After tortuous negotiations, a dubious peace pact was eventually signed in Paris on January 27, 1973, providing for a cease-fire, the release of all military prisoners of war and foreign civilians, the withdrawal within 60 days of the 23,000-man U.S. force then in South Vietnam, and the creation of an international force to supervise the truce. North Vietnamese troops already in the South were allowed to remain, but

according to the agreement they were not to be replaced, and both the United States and North Vietnam agreed to respect the South Vietnamese people's right to self-determination. Neither side really believed that the pact would create a lasting peace, but now Nixon could claim that he had achieved "peace with honor" and get America out of Vietnam. North Vietnam simply waited until Nixon was out of office and resumed the war during the Ford administration, correctly guessing that America would not want to reenter the conflict despite the breach of treaty, and South Vietnam fell on April 30, 1975.

With 60.8 percent of the popular vote, Nixon was reelected on November 7, 1972, beating the Democratic challenger Senator George McGovern of South Dakota. Despite his apparently overwhelming victory, Nixon faced a new and increasingly serious problem: Watergate. During the 1972 campaign, on June 17, five men, including James W. McCord Jr., security adviser for the Committee for the Reelection of the President, were arrested in the act of burglarizing the Democratic National Committee's headquarters at Washington's Watergate complex. President Nixon disavowed any prior knowledge of the escapade. On August 29 he stated that "no one in the White House staff, no one in this administration, presently employed, was involved. . . ." Most people believed him, and the prediction by Senator McGovern that the Watergate scandal would become a major campaign issue never materialized.

By the end of January 1973, the five burglars and their two accomplices had pleaded guilty to felonies or had been convicted of them. But Federal District Court judge John J. Sirica, who presided at the trials, doubted that the whole truth had been revealed, a suspicion strengthened by a letter he received from McCord, which he made public at the March 23 sentencing hearing. McCord claimed that the defendants had been under pressure to plead guilty and to suppress facts in order to protect higher ranking officials. On March 24, McCord testified before the Senate Select Committee on Presidential Campaign Activities, which had been established on February 7, that White House counsel John Dean and campaign official Jeb Magruder had prior knowledge of the Watergate break-in. After these allegations, Nixon reversed his former noncooperative attitude toward the Senate Select Committee, and in a televised address on April 30 took general responsibility for (while denying knowledge of) any wrongdoing during the 1972 presidential campaign. Nixon also announced the resignations of Dean; H. R. Haldeman, White House chief of staff; John D. Ehrlichman, his chief counselor for domestic affairs; and Attorney General Richard G. Kleindienst. At the same time the president announced his nomination of Elliot Richardson to become the new attorney general, stating that Richardson would have authority to appoint a special prosecutor with full powers to investigate the Watergate affair. The man Richardson chose for that position was Archibald Cox, a Harvard Law School professor and former U.S. solicitor general.

The Senate Select Committee (later known as the Watergate Committee), under chairman Sam J. Ervin Jr. of North Carolina, began televised public hearings on the Watergate scandal on May 17, 1973. Dean testified from June 25 to June 29 that Nixon had encouraged efforts to cover up Watergate and had discussed with him the possibility of executive clemency for the conspirators and the payment of hush money. Dean also reported that the White House had engaged in illegal efforts to suppress political opposition and to harass persons noted on an "enemies list." Several officials implicated by Dean, including Haldeman, Ehrlichman, and former attorney general John Mitchell, who had served as campaign chairman from March 1 to July 1, 1972, denied Dean's allegations in subsequent testimony before the Ervin committee.

Hopes for discovering the truth rose when former White House aide Alexander P. Butterfield told the senators on July 16 that since early 1970 the president had tape-recorded all conversations in his offices at the White House and at the Executive Office Building. Both Senator Ervin and Watergate special prosecutor Cox immediately asked Nixon to hand over the tapes relevant to their investigations. Nixon refused the Senate Watergate Committee's request on the grounds that compliance would violate executive privilege and on the constitutional doctrine of the separation of powers of the three branches of government. Cox was similarly refused access to the tapes. Both Cox and Ervin then subpoenaed the documents, and the matter went to Judge Sirica for decision. The judge stated that he lacked authority to enforce the Senate committee's order. Regarding Cox's subpoena, Sirica informed the president on August 29 that he himself would have to examine the tapes before deciding whether executive privilege had been properly invoked. Rather than comply, the president appealed the judge's ruling.

On October 12 the U.S. Court of Appeals for the District of Columbia affirmed Sirica's decision, asserting that the president was not above the law and that the Constitution does not mention any executive privileges. Rather than take the case to the Supreme Court, as many had assumed he would, Nixon put forward a compromise plan by which he would personally summarize the requested tapes, have the summary's accuracy verified by Senator John C. Stennis of Mississippi after permitting him to hear the tapes, and provide the verified summary to the Watergate investigators. When Cox rejected this compromise, the president ordered him, as an employee of the executive branch, to cease further efforts to acquire the tapes and related materials through the courts.

Refusing to follow this instruction, Cox explained his reasons at a televised news conference on October 20. That evening, at presidential instruction, Attorney General Elliot Richardson was ordered to dismiss Cox. Richardson resigned rather than participate in what came to be known as the Saturday Night Massacre. His second in command, Deputy Attorney General William D. Ruckelshaus, also refused to carry out the president's order and was promptly fired. Solicitor General Robert H. Bork finally executed the discharge order.

However, public reaction to the firing of Cox was so widespread and so hostile that Nixon was finally forced to release the tapes. The announcement that the president would comply was made by a Nixon lawyer in Sirica's court on October 23. Later, however, another member of Nixon's defense team stated that two crucially important conversations had not been recorded. Still later, he reported that an 18.5-minute gap existed in the tape of a conference between Nixon and Haldeman three days after the Watergate break-in. It developed that there were gaps in some other tapes as well. Judge Sirica turned most of the tapes over to Leon Jaworski, the new special prosecutor whom Nixon, under the pressure of public opinion, had named on November 1 to replace Cox.

On March 1, 1974, a federal grand jury handed up to Judge Sirica indictments of Mitchell, Haldeman, Ehrlichman, and four other former White House or presidential campaign aides on charges of conspiracy in the Watergate cover-up. Doubting that an incumbent president would be liable to indictment, the panel did not indict Nixon. Instead, it took the unusual step of giving to Sirica a sealed report, outlining its findings about the chief executive's involvement, that designated him as an unindicted co-conspirator. Other inquiries were going forward at the same time. On February 6, 1974, the House of Representatives voted 410 to 4 to grant to its Judiciary Committee, under chairman Peter Rodino of New Jersey, the power to pursue an inquiry as to whether grounds existed for the impeachment of the president. In March the committee received White House tapes and documents that earlier had been provided to the Watergate grand jury. However, the president refused a request for 42 additional tapes, and the committee issued a subpoena for them on April 11. Seven days later another subpoena, issued by Judge Sirica at the request of special prosecutor Jaworski, demanded that the President provide tape recordings of 64 conversations and related material.

Unwilling to give up the tapes, yet hoping to reverse the tide that was increasingly running against him, Nixon on April 30 instead released more than 1,250 pages of edited transcripts from the tapes. Of the 42 tapes that the Judiciary Committee had subpoenaed, 11 were declared to be nonexistent or missing. Those transcripts that were published only further tarnished the president's reputation. Not only did they reveal a profane and cynical side of the publicly upright Nixon, but they belied his professed concern for reaching the truth about Watergate.

On July 9 the House Judiciary Committee issued its own transcripts of eight tapes that it possessed. Comparison with the White House transcripts showed important discrepancies that were unfavorable to the president. During the remaining days of its investigation, the committee (composed of 21 Democrats and 17 Republicans) closely examined and debated the available evidence. Beginning on July 24, most of its deliberations were nationally televised. On July 27, after exhaustive debate of the issues involved, the committee, by a bipartisan 27 to 11 vote, passed an article of impeachment that it planned to present for vote by the whole House, accusing Nixon of obstruction of justice. On July 29 a second article of impeachment, passed by a vote of 28 to 10, charged him with abuse of power, failing in his constitutional duty to take care that the laws be faithfully executed, and engaging in conduct violating the constitutional rights of citizens. This conduct included the following:

(1) He has, . . . personally and through . . . subordinates and agents, endeavored to obtain from the Internal Revenue Service . . . confidential information contained in income tax returns for purposes not authorized by law, and to cause, in violation of the constitutional rights of citizens, income tax audits or other . . . investigations to be . . . conducted in a discriminatory manner.

(2) He misused the Federal Bureau of Investigation, the Secret Service, and other executive personnel, in violation or disregard of the constitutional rights of citizens, by directing, or authorizing such agencies

or personnel to conduct . . . electronic surveillance or other investigations for purposes unrelated to national security, the enforcement of laws, or any other lawful function of his office. . . .

(3) He has . . . personally and through . . . subordinates and agents . . . authorized . . . a secret investigative unit within the office of the President . . . which unlawfully utilized the resources of the Central Intelligence Agency [and] engaged in covert and unlawful activities.

On July 30, by a vote of 21 to 17, the committee passed a third article of impeachment accusing the president of contempt of Congress for failure to obey the committee's subpoenas for Watergate tapes and related materials. As for the 64 additional tapes ordered by Judge Sirica on behalf of special prosecutor Jaworski, after the White House moved to appeal the order, Jaworski, on May 24, asked the Supreme Court to rule on the matter directly in the interests of speed. The high court's decision, issued on July 24, the same day the Judiciary Committee's televised hearings began, ultimately proved even more disastrous for Nixon than the Judiciary Committee's action. With Associate Justice William Rehnquist, who had served in the Justice Department under Mitchell, withdrawing from the case, the remaining eight members unanimously sustained an order by Judge Sirica that the president must turn over the tapes. They rejected the contention that either executive privilege or the doctrine of the separation of powers was reason to withhold evidence from a criminal prosecution. Faced with this unanimous, unequivocal decision, Nixon had no choice but to comply.

The contents of the subpoenaed tapes were extremely incriminating. Three conversations between Nixon and Haldeman on June 23, 1972, six days after the Watergate break-in, showed clearly that the president had tried to impede the FBI's investigation of the Watergate affair and that he was motivated by political concerns rather than legitimate national security interests. Support for the president had collapsed by now, with even his staunchest defenders on the House Judiciary Committee convinced that the conversations of June 23, 1972, constituted the "smoking pistol" of presidential complicity. On Wednesday, August 7, Republican representative John Rhodes and Republican senators Hugh Scott and Barry Goldwater met with Nixon to tell him that his supporters in Congress had diminished to a handful and that impeachment and conviction were inevitable.

The president appeared on national television at 9:00 P.M. the following evening and announced that he would resign at noon the next day. In a brief and dignified speech, he summed up the achievements of his presidency and stated that he was leaving because his political base in the Congress had eroded. On the morning of August 9, 1974, he bade farewell to members of his administration with an extemporaneous and highly emotional televised address. Escorted by Vice President Gerald Ford, who in a few hours was to be sworn in as the new president, Nixon, his wife Pat, their daughter Tricia, and her husband Edward Cox left the White House by helicopter on the first leg of his return to San Clemente, California.

Scarcely a month later, on September 8, President Ford granted Nixon a pardon for "all offenses against the United States which he . . . has committed or may have committed or taken part in" during his presidency. Nixon accepted the pardon and expressed sorrow for his handling of Watergate, but he did not confess to any criminal wrongdoing. The pardon was controversial, pleasing those who did not wish to see a former president face trial or imprisonment but outraging others who thought it a travesty of the concept of equal justice under law. If Nixon and Ford had an agreement that Nixon's resignation would be followed by Ford's pardon when Ford became president, that secret has been well kept, and there has never been any direct admission or evidence of such.

After a period of isolation, Nixon became restless in retirement. He conducted a series of lengthy television interviews with journalist David Frost and published his autobiography. When the Republicans retook the White House in 1981 after the 1980 electoral victory of Ronald Reagan, Nixon gradually assumed the position of elder statesman within the GOP, especially in matters with respect to Soviet and Chinese relations. Nixon also advised Reagan's successors, the Republican George Bush and then the Democrat Bill Clinton. After the death of his wife Pat, Nixon's health rapidly deteriorated, and he died of a stroke on April 22, 1994. Despite his best efforts, the memories of Watergate were too deep for Nixon to ever entirely redeem himself in the public eye.

Joan Baez's Birthday

1960s folk music legend and social activist Joan Baez was born on January 9, 1941, in Staten Island, New York. In high school, she committed her first act of civil disobedience when she refused to leave school during an air raid drill, and developed an interest in the philosophy of social change through nonviolence. After graduating from high school, Joan briefly attended Boston University's School of Fine and Applied Arts in 1958, but she dropped out in order to play folk music in the avant-garde coffee house scene.

She was an instant success. In 1959 she was invited to the prestigious Newport Folk Festival, where her straightforward singing style and guitar rhythms impressed the audience. The following year, Vanguard released her first album. Having achieved national prominence, Baez used her fame to help promote a variety of social causes. For example, in 1962 her concert tours through the segregated South were booked only at African American colleges, so that discrimination would be impossible. In 1964, as an advocate of nonviolence and one of the earliest opponents of the Vietnam War, she publicly announced that she would begin withholding the percentage of her taxes that went toward defense spending. For the next ten years, Baez held back approximately half of her income taxes. She also marched with Dr. Martin Luther King Jr. in Mississippi.

Her political activities helped rather than hurt her musical career. In 1967 the conservative Daughters of the American Revolution refused to let her use Constitution Hall in Washington, D.C. In response, Baez held a free concert at the Washington Monument that attracted 30,000 fans, far more than the seating capacity of Constitutional Hall. She was arrested for protesting outside a military installation in Oakland, but after her release from prison she was invited to perform at the historic Woodstock Music Festival in the summer of 1969.

In 1971 Baez released her biggest hit, "The Night They Drove Old Dixie Down." During the 1970s she frequently toured with Bob Dylan, another famous folk singer. She also did work for Amnesty International, and she visited Hanoi during the Vietnam War. Her interest in human rights led her to organize the Humanitas International Human Rights Committee in 1979. During the 1980s she gave a concert in front of the Cathedral of Notre Dame that was broadcast worldwide, and she did several benefit performances with Paul Simon for the cause of nuclear disarmament. She also participated in the Live Aid concert of 1985, which was organized to raise funds for famine and poverty relief in Africa. Her music career began to fade in the 1990s, and the release of her album *Play Me Backwards* in 1992 was unsuccessful in reviving interest in her type of music. Nevertheless, Baez still has a strong and loyal following of folk music and 1960s music fans.

Joan Baez has published two autobiographies, *Daybreak* in 1968 and *And a Voice to Sing With: A Memoir* in 1987, the latter of which made the *New York Times* national best-seller list.

Carrie Catt's Birthday

Carrie Lane Chapman Catt was born on January 9, 1859, in Ripon, Wisconsin, to Lucius Lane and Maria Clinton. After the Civil War, the Lanes moved to Charles City, Iowa, and Carrie would live in Iowa for much of her life. At the age of 12, she learned that women were not allowed to vote, and her outrage was so strong that she spent the rest of her life crusading for the right to vote and for women's rights.

In 1877 Carrie enrolled in Iowa State College, where she completed the four-year curriculum in three years and graduated at the top of her class. Since military training was then compulsory for land grant college students, she organized a "G" company of women who trained with broomsticks instead of rifles. After she graduated, Carrie Lane was hired as a high school principal in Mason City, Iowa, and she became the superintendent of all Mason City schools in 1883. It was then that she met Leo Chapman, a newspaper editor, whom she married in 1885. Unfortunately, her husband died the next year. After spending some time as a newspaper reporter in California, she returned to Iowa and went into the women's suffrage movement full time. This decision was made possible by her second marriage, to George W. Catt in 1890, since her husband owned an engineering company and was willing to finance her activities.

Carrie Chapman Catt was president of the National American Woman Suffrage Association from 1900 to 1904 and of the International Woman Suffrage Alliance from 1904 to 1923. Her greatest ambition was realized when the Nineteenth Amendment was ratified in 1920 (see August 26), giving women the right to vote. Foreseeing the adoption of the amendment, in 1919 Carrie had proposed creating a league to organize and inform women voters. On February 14, 1920, the National American Woman Suffrage Association changed its name to the League of Women Voters. Catt summed up the organization's mission as follows:

> What is the League? A group of enfranchised women who want not merely to vote, but to vote for something. The vote is a tool with which to work, and for years they have struggled and sacrificed to secure it. Now, they want to build a better world for their neighbors and their posterity.

The league still exists today, and has played an important role in organizing such activities as presidential debates on television. During the 1920s and 1930s, Catt also worked to promote international peace and disarmament, and she chaired the National Committee on the Cause and Cure of War from 1925 to 1932. In her final years, she retired to New Rochelle, New York, where she died on March 9, 1947. She was buried in Woodlawn Cemetery in New York City.

George Balanchine's Birthday

Originally Georgi Melitonovich Balanchivadze, George Balanchine was born on January 9, 1904, in St. Petersburg, Russia. He attended a ballet school sponsored by the imperial Russian government and survived the Bolshevik Revolution of 1917 to defect in 1924 with a group of dancers while on tour in Europe. Sergei Diaghilev invited Balanchine to join the Diaghilev Company in Paris, where Balanchine served as a choreographer. In 1932 he helped found Les Ballets Russes in Monte Carlo.

In 1933 philanthropist Lincoln Kirstein invited Balanchine to the United States, and Balanchine left Europe for New York in October of that year. With Kirstein, Balanchine established the School of American Ballet, which opened on January 1, 1934, and has survived to the present day. At the school, Balanchine choreographed his first American ballet, "Serenade," which was first performed in March 1935 and was one of Balanchine's favorites for the rest of his life. In 1946 he and Kirstein founded the Ballet Society, which became the New York City Ballet in 1948. Morton Baum, chairman of the New York City Center's finance committee, decided to expand the center's existing sponsorship of the New York City Opera to include facilities and sponsorship for Balanchine's New York City Ballet.

Thanks to Balanchine's leadership, the New York City Ballet became one of the world's great ballets, due to his brilliant choreography and infusion of the "Ballet Russe" classical style into the performances. Balanchine was involved in hundreds of ballets, far too numerous to list here, but some of his most memorable productions were *The Four Temperaments* in 1946, *The Nutcracker* in 1954 and again in 1964, *Stars and Stripes* in 1958, *Don Quixote* in 1965, and *Jewels* in 1967. His productions of *Orpheus* and *Swan Lake* were important as well. Balanchine also did some work as a movie and musical choreographer.

From his arrival in America until his death, Balanchine spent most of his life in New York City. He died there on April 30, 1983.

January 10

League of Nations Established

One of the most far-reaching results of World War I was the establishment of the League of Nations on January 10, 1920. As the war pursued its relentless course, the public in both Europe and the United States, shocked by the appalling losses, pressed for the establishment of an international peace organization that might prevent such destruction and suffering in the future.

Plans for such a league had long been proposed by unofficial organizations in Great Britain, France, and the United States. The concept had won the support of many influential leaders in public and private life, including former president William H. Taft and the British statesmen Sir Edward Grey and Lord Robert Cecil. By the spring of 1915, the name League of Nations was already in use among small interested groups. Both parties in the presidential campaign of 1916 backed U.S. membership in such an organization in their political platforms. The incumbent president, Woodrow Wilson, was an ardent advocate of the league. His famous Fourteen Points, which he proclaimed in January 1918 as essential for the peace settlement, called for the establishment of "a general association of nations . . . affording mutual guarantees of political independence and territorial integrity to great and small States alike."

At the end of World War I, President Wilson urged strongly that provisions for a League of Nations be inserted into the peace treaty. A commission was appointed at the Paris Peace Conference, composed of two delegates each from the United States, France, Great Britain, Italy, and Japan, with representatives of five smaller powers subsequently added, to study the different forms that the League of Nations might take. Several 19th-century developments in international cooperation provided valuable precedents to guide the plan makers. These included the growth of such international agencies and bureaus as the Universal Postal Union, founded in 1874; the creation of the Permanent Court of Arbitration at the Hague Peace Conference of 1907; and the proliferation of international treaties, such as the multilateral International Copyright Convention of 1870.

After several meetings, the commission agreed upon a final draft, entitled the "Covenant of the League of Nations," and inserted it into the Treaty of Versailles. The covenant was submitted for approval on February 14, 1919, and the final amended text was unanimously adopted by the conference on April 28, 1919. The concise document of 26 articles set up the central organs of the League of Nations (assembly, council, and secretariat) as well as a broad network of auxiliary institutions of a primarily legal and political, or economic and social, nature. Geneva, Switzerland, was designated as the organization's headquarters. The league formally came into existence on January 10, 1920, the date of the ratification of the Treaty of Versailles by Germany.

The establishment of the league was a decisive step in the history of international relations. It was the first permanent international body of general purpose to encompass much of the world community. The 32 Allied states that had signed the peace treaties, as well as 13 neutral states, were asked to join. Moreover, other countries could become members provided that two-thirds of the league assembly approved. On its formal inauguration, there were only 23 members, but the total had risen to 42 by November 1920. Egypt became the 63rd and last league member in 1937, although by that time several leading countries had withdrawn from the organization.

The leading cause of the league's eventual collapse was the failure of the United States to become a member. President Wilson vigorously campaigned for Senate ratification, but both the nation and the Senate were leaning toward a return to the traditional policy of isolationism. The issue of joining the league entered the presidential campaign of 1920, with the Democratic candidate, James M. Cox, favoring it and the Republican candidate, Warren G. Harding, taking an equivocal position. The Republicans won by a large majority, and the United States never joined the league, although it cooperated to a limited extent in peace-enforcement activities during the 1930s.

Without the United States as a member, the league drifted, incapable of dealing with either the economic turmoil or the military conflicts of the 1920s and especially the 1930s. When the Japanese army attacked Manchuria in 1931, the league was helpless to protect China. In October 1935, the Italian dictator Benito Mussolini invaded Ethiopia and annexed it despite the economic sanctions that 52 league member states imposed. When confronted with league disapproval, Japan simply withdrew from the league in 1933, and Italy withdrew in 1937. Germany, admitted to the league in 1926, also withdrew in 1933. Adolf Hitler remilitarized the Rhineland in 1934 and denounced the Treaty of Versailles two years later, but the league did nothing. A swift series of crises in the late 1930s, including the Spanish Civil War and the German annexations of Austria and Czechoslovakia, marked the doom of the league as an agency for the preservation of peace. Small states realized that the organization could not protect them against superior enemy forces. When World War II broke out in September 1939 with the German invasion of Poland, no nation seriously suggested that the matter be submitted to the league for effective action. The Finnish appeal for help against the Soviet attack in 1939 was a mere formality.

Thus weakened, the League of Nations reduced its Geneva secretariat to a skeleton staff in 1940. No further meetings were held during World War II. In the last years of the war, the Allies, although rejecting any idea of reviving the league covenant, which was still nominally in force, began to plan for a future international organization. The league was ultimately replaced by the United Nations, and the League of Nations officially dissolved itself in April 1946. Its services and property, most notably the Palace of Nations in Geneva, were turned over to the United Nations.

The league did have some successes, however. It was closely associated with the International Labor Organization, founded in 1919 to improve labor conditions throughout the world, and with the Permanent Court of International Justice formed at The Hague in 1921.

Publication of *Common Sense* by Thomas Paine

See also January 29, Thomas Paine's Birthday.

Thomas Paine published his most famous treatise, *Common Sense*, on January 10, 1776. In a way, the publication of this revolutionary pamphlet began in London, where Thomas Paine met Benjamin Franklin, then a colonial representative to Great Britain. With Franklin's encouragement and some letters of reference, Paine went to Philadelphia in 1774 to become an editor for a new publication titled *Pennsylvania Magazine*. He also published some works anonymously. In 1775, he began to work on *Common Sense*.

Common Sense was published in Philadelphia and Boston, sometimes anonymously, and went on sale for two shillings. It was an instant sensation, and did more to stimulate popular dissent with British rule than any other publication on the eve of the American Revolution. By the end of 1776, over 20 different editions had been published. Sales would eventually reach half a million copies, an impressive figure given that the population of the colonies was no more than three million. Copies were also reprinted in the newspapers.

The basic tenet of *Common Sense* was that the British monarchy was no longer a viable or fair system of government for the colonies, and that since the colonies were being exploited and misruled, it was "common sense" to get a new form of government that truly represented the people. There was also an ideological premise, namely that the Old World was contaminated by oppression and the privileges of the upper classes, and that only in the New World could human freedom truly be achieved. Thus, Paine wrote that "the cause of America is in a great measure the cause of mankind." Further, perhaps foreseeing the waves of immigrants in years to come, Paine stated that a free America could become a haven for people fleeing tyranny:

> O! Ye that love mankind! Ye that dare oppose not only the tyranny but the tyrant, stand forth! Every spot of the Old World is overrun with oppression. Freedom hath been hunted round the globe. Asia and Africa have long expelled her. Europe regards her like a stranger, and England hath given her warning to depart. O! Receive the fugitive, and prepare in time an asylum for mankind.

Thomas Jefferson later stated that Paine's discourse about America and the need to establish a democracy "rendered useless almost everything written before on the structures of government." After the Declaration of Independence was issued and the Revolution began, Paine gave most of his revenues from the publication of *Common Sense* to the struggling colonial cause.

The United States Establishes Diplomatic Relations with the Vatican

On January 10, 1984, the United States reestablished formal diplomatic relations with the Vatican when William A. Wilson became the U.S. ambassador to the Holy See.

This issue over diplomatic relations with the Vatican has been somewhat controversial, since the United States has a tradition, seen in the First Amendment to the Constitution, of keeping government separate from organized religion. Nevertheless, President George Washington appointed the first representative to the Holy See, a consul. In 1848 President James Polk promoted the Vatican consulate to a legation, but instructed the minister to the Vatican to "carefully avoid even the appearance of interfering in ecclesiastical questions, whether these relate to the United States or any other portion of the world."

During the process of Italy's reunification in the 1860s, the new Italian state took the Vatican's territorial possessions around Rome, known as the Papal States. The Vatican was reduced to its present size, consisting of the area immediately surrounding the Vatican buildings in the middle of Rome. Now that the Vatican was bereft of its territorial dominions, and there was a new nation of Italy with its capital in Rome, in 1867 the United States stopped sending envoys.

In 1939 President Franklin D. Roosevelt appointed Myron Taylor the U.S. special envoy to the Vatican, a position that Taylor held until 1950. By appointing a special envoy, the United States could maintain de facto diplomatic relations with the Vatican without having to address the politically uncomfortable fact that the Vatican was not really a nation with territory, but a church or religious institution. President Ronald Reagan, however, decided to end the charade and reestablish formal relations. Whatever its religious status, the reality was that the Vatican was an important player on the international political scene. Reagan appointed William A. Wilson as ambassador, and he was confirmed by the Senate and took his post effective January 10, 1984.

After Wilson's appointment, several organizations initiated lawsuits alleging that diplomatic relations with the Vatican violated the Constitution. The litigants included Baptist and Evangelical church organizations, whose history has involved centuries of dispute with the Catholic Church. There were also some Catholic litigants, concerned that American relations with the Vatican might turn into a vehicle for the government to exercise influence over papal appointments in the American clergy. As of the present date, however, these challenges have been unsuccessful.

January 11

Alexander Hamilton's Birthday

Alexander Hamilton was one of the most brilliant and influential figures of the American Revolutionary era. He occupied a focal point in the struggle for liberty and in the formation of the fledgling country, from the very onset of armed hostilities with Great Britain to the close of President John Adams's term in office more than a quarter of a century later.

Alexander Hamilton was born on January 11 at Charlestown on the island of Nevis in the Leeward group of the British West Indies. He was probably born in the mid-1750s, but the exact year is uncertain. His father was James Hamilton, fourth son of Alexander Hamilton, Laird of Cambuskeith in the parish of Stevenston, Ayrshire, Scotland; his mother was Rachel Faucitt (Fawcett) Lavien, the daughter of a French Huguenot physician and the wife of John Michael Lavien, a planter of either north German or Danish extraction. She left Lavien in 1750, according to the divorce petition he later filed, and went to live with James Hamilton instead. But James Hamilton proved to be nothing but a drifting trader, and as Alexander Hamilton later commented, his father's fortunes soon "went to wreck." Rachel Lavien, eventually abandoned by James Hamilton, supported the Hamilton household by running a small store and seeking aid from her relatives. She died on February 26, 1768.

Little is known about Alexander Hamilton's childhood. At approximately the age of 11 he was earning a living as an apprentice clerk in the trading establishment of Nicholas Cruger and David Beekman, New York businessmen who had settled on the Danish-owned island of St. Croix. The young boy, a virtual orphan thrown upon the charity of relatives, was determined to do well. Although physically frail, he was highly intelligent and his ambition, industry, and superior mental powers soon brought him rapid advancement. When ill health forced Cruger to leave for the North American mainland for a while, he named his capable assistant manager-in-charge.

In early September 1772, Alexander Hamilton wrote about a devastating hurricane that had swept St. Croix the preceding month. His essay was accepted for publication in the *Royal Danish-American Gazette*, the leading English newspaper of the Danish islands, and printed on October 3. It was well-received, and his family and friends encouraged him to pursue an education in America. Hamilton sailed from Nevis for Boston and entered the grammar school of Frances Barber at Elizabethtown, New Jersey, in order to master Latin, Greek, and mathematics. Afterwards, Hamilton entered King's College in New York City. His advanced studies were soon disrupted by the mounting colonial insurrection against Great Britain.

On July 6, 1774, the young college student attended an open-air mass meeting in New York City, called to consider a congress of the colonies. Hamilton spoke on behalf of the growing revolutionary movement, and began to write letters, essays, and pamphlets in favor of independence. Hamilton also began to serve in the New York militia groups that were being organized, and he left college in 1776 when the provincial congress of New York appointed him captain of a militia company.

Captain Hamilton reportedly received his baptism of fire at the battle of Long Island on August 27, 1776. He was also present at the battles of White Plains, Trenton, and Princeton. On March 1, 1777, General George Washington made Hamilton one of his aides-de-camp, with the formal rank of lieutenant colonel and informal status as confidential secretary. The new position was ideal for Hamilton, who was determined to prove himself and attain success on Washington's staff.

Hamilton spent most of his time drafting reports and communications, and also acted as liaison officer to the French forces aiding the Americans because of his fluency in the French language. He distinguished himself in Washington's service, but he became dissatisfied with his administrative duties and resigned in February 1781 to seek a combat position. General Washington gave him the command of a brigade of light infantry, and Hamilton served in the Battle of Yorktown where the Americans finally defeated the British once and for all.

After Yorktown, Hamilton was elected one of New York's delegates to the Continental Congress, where he served in 1782 and 1783. Here he had an opportunity to utilize the knowledge of military and political affairs that he had gained as Washington's aide and secretary, an opportunity that catapulted him into the midst of the political debates of the day. Publicly and privately, Hamilton voiced his alarm over the instability of the Articles of Confederation, and helped organize the Constitutional Convention in Philadelphia that eventually all 13 states agreed to attend.

Hamilton's role as one of three New York delegates to the Constitutional Convention, which began in 1787, was not so significant as his advocacy of the new Constitution formulated at the momentous meeting. He ranks as one of the most renowned Federalists, as the staunch backers of the strong new federal government called themselves. The Federalists, anxious to obtain ratification of the Constitution by all of the states, issued a flurry of newspaper articles and pamphlets. Most brilliant among this literature of persuasion was the series of essays written in New York under the name Publius. The first letter was printed in the New York *Independent Journal* of October 27, 1787. By mid-August 1788, a total of 85 letters had appeared in various New York newspapers.

Although known to be the joint output of Hamilton, Madison, and John Jay, these "Federalist Papers" still pose questions concerning the exact number prepared by each man, especially since some of the essays were collaborations. Hamilton, having composed at least three-fifths or an estimated 51 letters, was the chief author; Madison contributed as many as 26; Hamilton and Madison together wrote at least 3; and Jay wrote 5. The remarkable series, soon published in book form as *The Federalist* and reprinted several times during Hamilton's lifetime, is now regarded as the funda-mental historic treatise on the Constitution of the United States. The fight over ratification in predominantly Antifederalist New York state was extremely difficult but, thanks to Hamilton's efforts, New York eventually ratified the Constitution.

When George Washington became the first president of the United States in 1789, Hamilton rejoined the staff of his former commanding officer as secretary of the treasury. Hamilton's extraordinary business experience as a youth, during which he had achieved financial success by the time he was a teenager, was a motivating factor. Although the new United States teetered on the edge of bankruptcy, Hamilton successfully stabilized the situation by establishing a national mint, attracting foreign capital, and paying the Revolutionary War debt in full. Many of these measures were very unpopular, however. Some states that had paid their particular war debts in full objected when other states, who were still in debt, were bailed out by the federal government at Hamilton's initiative. An excise tax on whiskey that Hamilton had sponsored sparked a grass-roots rebellion in western Pennsylvania that had to be put down by calling out the state militia. Despite these setbacks, the value of Hamilton's financial policies was clearly recognized: George Washington stated that "our public credit stands on that ground which three years ago it would have been considered as a species of madness to have foretold."

One unexpected side effect of Hamilton's financial measures was the creation of the two-party political system that has lasted until the present day. The Federalists supported his initiatives, and a new party led by Thomas Jefferson and James Madison called the Democratic-Republicans opposed them. Of course, there were other differences between the two factions: Hamilton wanted the United States to become an industrial, urban nation with a strong central government, while Jefferson preferred a nation of small towns and self-sufficient farmers with as little central government as possible. Thus, Hamilton's differences with Jefferson and Madison helped spark the split that has evolved through the centuries into the modern American political system. The tension between Hamilton and Jefferson caused Hamilton to resign as secretary of the treasury on January 31, 1795, and return to his private business pursuits in New York City.

Hamilton eventually retired from the public limelight to the pleasures of family life and his country estate, the Grange, overlooking the Hudson River. However, he had by no means completely broken his ties with the Federalists. Though his status was unofficial, his advice was still sought on both domestic and foreign policy, and he drafted many state papers, including a version of Washington's famous farewell address in 1796.

In the presidential election of 1800, Aaron Burr tied with Thomas Jefferson in the Electoral College, and lost the ensuing election contest in the House of Representatives wherein the House (pursuant to the procedures mandated by the Constitution) made Jefferson the president and Burr the vice president. Hamilton agreed with his old adversary Jefferson on one thing: Burr was erratic, unstable, and dangerous. When Jefferson dropped Burr as his vice president in the 1804 campaign, Burr blamed Hamilton for the decision and challenged Hamilton to a duel.

Hamilton was personally opposed to the institution of dueling, but in the early 19th century the social pressure to defend one's honor was too strong for him to resist. The duel was held on July 11, 1804, in Weehawken, New Jersey, near New York City. Burr fired a shot directly into Hamilton's body, whereas Hamilton was uncertain and made no shot at Burr. Burr walked away from the duel unscathed, while Hamilton endured 32 hours of agony until he died the next day. For the public, however, Hamilton was the victor. In death he was eulogized and praised as a patriot; the opposition to his policies was forgotten; and Burr became a political pariah who eventually turned traitor.

Surgeon General Issues First Report on the Dangers of Smoking

Smoking is literally as old as America itself. Tobacco was unknown to the Europeans until the discovery of the New World by Christopher Columbus in 1492, when he found the natives of the Caribbean islands smoking it. Tobacco was introduced to Europe in the course of the 16th century; in 1585 the English explorer Sir Francis Drake brought some to England. Pipe smoking became fashionable; the health risks were largely unknown.

The growing demand for tobacco stimulated the exploration and settlement of the early colonies. The mid-Atlantic regions of Virginia and North Carolina were ideal in terms of climate and soil for the growing of tobacco, and its cultivation goes as far back as the settlement of Jamestown, with the first recorded tobacco crop being planted as early as 1615. Tobacco was often used as a medium of exchange in the currency-short colonies. It became a major American export to England and Europe, and the trade continued to expand after the American Revolution. Until the late 19th century, people smoked tobacco in pipes or in the form of cigars. It was also used in the form of

chewing tobacco or snuff, which is inhaled through the nostrils. In 1881, however, the cigarette-making machine was invented. This invention served to further expand the popularity of smoking. Cigarettes with filters became popular in the 1950s, and by the early 1960s most adult Americans smoked.

It is probably difficult for the generations since the 1950s and 1960s to remember when smoking was considered the norm and nonsmokers were in the minority. Smoking was common in movie theaters, in elevators, and on airplanes and other forms of public transportation. Most offices and public places had ashtrays, and few restaurants were segregated into smoking versus nonsmoking areas. Smoking was commonplace and even glamorized on television, in advertising, and in the motion pictures. Thus, it came as something of a shock when on January 11, 1964, the United States surgeon general, Luther Terry, issued the first official government findings that "smoking may be hazardous to your health."

For several decades, some doctors had been concerned about the potential health risks of smoking. Autopsies had revealed a higher than normal amount of cancer, lung disease, and heart problems in smokers. These ailments also afflict nonsmokers, however, and both the public and the tobacco industry resisted the notion that such an ingrained social custom as smoking might be dangerous. But as the medical evidence mounted, acceptance slowly grew. By the 1970s, Congress had acted to curb cigarette advertising on television and had forced the tobacco industry to print warning labels on cigarette packs. By the 1980s, some private legal actions were being taken against the tobacco industry by ex-smokers or on behalf of deceased smokers for the damages caused by the tobacco industry's failure to disclose what it knew about the risks of smoking. Finally, federal, state, and local legislation was passed against smoking in public accommodations, and measures were taken to educate the public about the risks of smoking.

The tobacco industry strongly resisted all of these encroachments, and bitterly contested every suggestion that smoking was dangerous or that the tobacco industry should be held liable for having encouraged smoking. The industry had enormous assets at its disposal and fought most of the legal actions against it to a standstill. As late as the mid-1990s, tobacco industry executives testifying under oath before Congress were still declaring that smoking was not dangerous and that the tobacco industry had never attempted to conceal evidence to the contrary. Given the now vast amount of medical evidence, and some intriguing leaks by former members of the tobacco industry, popular skepticism was strong.

As of this writing in the late 1990s, the tobacco industry appears to be losing its war to defend smoking. A coalition of state attorneys general forced the industry to agree to a multibillion-dollar settlement to pay for the health costs inflicted by smoking, and also to accept additional curbs on cigarette advertising. Federal measures are also being initiated, and there is discussion in some quarters of a curb on tobacco exports. Finally, in the decades since Luther Terry issued his famous report on the risks of smoking, millions of Americans have quit the habit, and the percentage of smokers in the population continues to decline year after year.

Alice Paul's Birthday

Alice Paul, one of the first feminists and the founder of the National Woman's Party, was born in Moorestown, New Jersey, on January 11, 1885. She went to Swarthmore College and later received her doctorate from the University of Pennsylvania. In 1906, barely in her twenties, she went to England to work in a London settlement house. She was active in the British women's rights movement and was arrested several times for "suffragist agitation."

In 1910 she returned to the United States, where she continued her work in the feminist movement. In 1912 she became the chairperson of the Congressional Committee of the National Woman Suffrage Association. The next year, she helped to establish a more activist organization, named the Congressional Union for Woman's Suffrage, which in 1917 agreed to merge with the Woman's Party to form the National Woman's Party.

During the rest of her long life, Alice Paul worked for the cause of achieving equal rights for women. After the 19th Amendment in 1920 gave women the right to vote, she became a lawyer in order to more effectively pursue her causes. She helped introduce the first proposed Equal Rights Amendment to Congress in 1923, but it failed to pass. In 1942 she was appointed chairperson of the National Woman's Party.

Although Alice Paul lived to see an Equal Rights Amendment pass Congress in 1970, as of this writing no Equal Rights Amendment has been ratified by the required three-fourths majority of the states. She died in Moorestown, New Jersey, on July 9, 1977.

January 12

John Hancock's Birthday

John Hancock, the first person to sign the American Declaration of Independence, was born on January 12, 1737, in North Braintree, Massachusetts. He graduated from Harvard College in 1754 and went into business with his uncle Thomas Hancock in the family's trading firm. In 1760 he went to London to learn more about the business. In 1763 he became a partner in the firm, and when his uncle died in 1764 John Hancock inherited the entire business.

Now a man of substantial means, Hancock entered politics. He was elected to the Massachusetts Colonial Assembly in 1766, having already made a name for himself by opposing the Stamp Act passed by the British Parliament in 1765. His first serious conflict with the British authorities came in 1768, when his ship *Liberty* was seized for smuggling when it unloaded a cargo of wine without paying the new import tax levied by Parliament.

Hancock's strong opposition to British colonial policies quickly made him a popular figure in Massachusetts politics. In 1770, after the infamous Boston Massacre, he served on a colonial committee that worked for the removal of British soldiers from the city of Boston. After the skirmishes between the colonial militia and the British at Lexington and Concord in April 1775, Hancock began to work closely with Samuel Adams, another leading figure of the American Revolution. Hancock's credentials as a leading patriot were confirmed when the British specifically excluded him and Adams from the amnesty offered to the colonial rebels several months later.

Hancock became a delegate to the Second Continental Congress in 1775. For the first two years, he was that body's presiding officer. During this time he had the distinction to become the first delegate to sign the Declaration of Independence in 1776. His famous signature, several inches long, was a deliberate act on his part so that the King of England could read the signature "without having to remove his glasses." This popular legend became the basis for the expression to "put one's John Hancock" on a document. Hancock served in the Second Continental Congress until 1780, when he was elected as the first governor of the State of Massachusetts.

Hancock resigned the governorship in 1785, but was once again elected to the post in 1787. He stayed in office until his death, and presided over the Massachusetts Convention that would eventually ratify the Constitution of the United States, which he and the Massachusetts Federalists supported. He was apparently a popular governor, although there was some criticism of his handling of Shays's Rebellion in the 1780s. His critics denounced him for indecisiveness and his alleged habit of endorsing only popular measures. Nevertheless, Hancock's political career was certainly long and successful. He died on October 8, 1793.

John Winthrop's Birthday

John Winthrop, governor of the Massachusetts Bay Colony and historian of the Puritans, was born at Edwardstone in the English county of Suffolk on January 12, 1588. An earnest Puritan and a natural leader, Winthrop enrolled at Cambridge University's Trinity College at the age of 14 but left without graduating. At 17 he was married, and at 18 he became a justice of the peace. In his own county, where he was lord of the manor of Groton, he became a person of reputation and property. He subsequently studied law and practiced in London with considerable success.

Winthrop was attracted to the growing Puritan faith in England and joined the Puritan leaders who had formed the Massachusetts Bay Company for the settlement of New England. The Puritans chose Winthrop as their leader, and Winthrop commanded the fleet of four ships that landed some 700 to 900 settlers at what is now Salem, Massachusetts, on June 22, 1630. The colony moved several times in the next few months, eventually settling on the Shawmut peninsula, which the colonists named Boston and would become the modern city of the same name.

Thus began the "Bible Commonwealth," the colony intended by its Puritan leaders as an example to others, one that they hoped would bring no dishonor to the name of God. The early history of the colony is inseparable from that of Winthrop, the man of conscience who was elected its governor 12 times. After an unfortunate first winter, in which roughly a fifth of the settlers died of starvation or disease, the colonists found their means of survival in the sea. What was to be a substantial business in fishing, trading, and shipbuilding began with the launching in 1631 of the first Massachusetts-built ship, rapidly followed by others.

The Puritans gradually succeeded in taming the new land and starting farms, which attracted more settlers from the Puritan communities back in England. In little more than a decade, the population of the colony was close to 15,000. The influx was encouraged by Governor Winthrop, who had described the country of New England as "exceeding good and the climate very like our own." More

privately, he had written to his wife, "I thank God, I like so well to be here, as I do not repent my coming, and if I were to come again, I would not have altered my course."

It was consistent with Winthrop's way of thinking that he should regard government as an agent of religion. He opposed unlimited democracy. The colony he led was governed by the learned, the religious, and thus the few. It was a Puritan theocracy in which the authority of the clergy extended far beyond the pulpit, and dissenters like Roger Williams and Anne Hutchinson were banished. Although the government of the Massachusetts Bay Colony was intolerant of dissent internally, Winthrop led some of the first struggles for American independence externally. As governor, he consistently defended the colony against coercion from England. He also advocated, as early as 1637, an alliance of New England colonies, and when the New England Confederation came into being in 1643, he was its first president.

A portrait of Winthrop, presumably done by a contemporary, shows him as a spare, contemplative man with dark hair and beard, tight-lipped, with a long, thin nose and perfectly arched brows echoed by the perfectly arched wrinkles of a lean forehead. He died in office in 1649. He was survived by his son John, who eventually became the governor of Connecticut. Winthrop is also survived by an important historical work, namely his journal of the Massachusetts Bay Colony, which he began while en route from England in 1630. This journal would be published in later years as *The History of New England from 1630 to 1649.*

January 13

Salmon P. Chase's Birthday

Salmon Portland Chase, the sixth chief justice of the United States, was born on January 13, 1808, in Cornish, New Hampshire. He was the eighth of eleven children in a family whose forebears came from England to Newbury, Massachusetts, in 1640. Chase's father, Ithamar Chase, was a farmer and tavern keeper who, as a member of the Federalist Party, held a variety of state and local offices. His mother, the former Janette Ralston, was a descendant of Scottish settlers.

When his father died around 1817, Salmon Chase went to live with his uncle, Philander Chase, the Episcopal bishop of Ohio. He studied at the minister's church school at Worthington, near Columbus, and in 1821 entered Cincinnati College, where his uncle had just accepted the presidency. Young Chase left the institution after

and in 1855 he was a successful Republican gubernatorial candidate in Ohio. Chase sought the Republican presidential nomination in 1856, but lost
it to Colonel John C. Frémont. He won reelection
as Ohio governor in 1857 and remained in that
post until the outbreak of the Civil War.

Governor Chase vied for the Republican presidential nomination in 1860, but the delegates at
the Chicago convention made Abraham Lincoln
their choice. Chase vigorously supported the successful candidacy of Lincoln, and himself won a
second term in the U.S. Senate. The new chief executive rewarded Chase's loyalty by offering him
the post of secretary of the treasury, and Chase resigned from the Senate to join the cabinet in this
capacity.

As secretary of the treasury, Chase directed the
country's finances during the turbulent years of
the Civil War. With the aid of financier Jay Cooke,
he successfully sold the bonds necessary to raise
money for the Union's military machine. Chase
thought that Lincoln was a weak leader in the
struggle with the Confederacy, and tentatively explored the idea of challenging Lincoln for the Republican nomination during the wartime election
of 1864, but prudently backed off. Chase's differences with Lincoln forced Chase to resign from
the treasury, but Lincoln nevertheless picked
Chase to fill the vacancy in the Supreme Court
caused by the death of Chief Justice Roger Brooke
Taney on October 12, 1864.

Chase accepted, and remained as chief justice
until his death in 1873. During his tenure he presided over a variety of cases that evolved from the
aftermath of the Civil War, and reorganized and
reopened the federal courts in the South. He opposed the prosecution of Confederate leader Jefferson Davis for treason and helped delay the trial
until President Andrew Johnson's declaration of
universal amnesty freed Davis. As chief justice,
Chase also presided over the 1868 Senate impeachment trial of President Johnson. The Radical
Republicans, intent on ousting Johnson from office, sought to downgrade Chase's role as presiding judge in the Senate and attempted to bypass
traditional legal procedures concerning evidence
and testimony. However, Chase successfully defended the Senate's function as a court of law and
defeated efforts to deprive him of the right to cast
tie-breaking votes. The chief justice's integrity
helped preserve the decorum of the proceedings
and gave Johnson, who narrowly won acquittal,
some chance for a fair trial.

Chief Justice Chase still longed to be president.
In 1868, unimpressed by Ulysses S. Grant, the Republican candidate, Chase made himself available
for the Democratic nomination. His platform of

By Leon van Loo. Collection of the Supreme Court of the
United States.

Salmon P. Chase

less than a year, and after several months of study
was able to enter Dartmouth College as a junior.
After graduating from college, he went to Washington, D.C., to administer a boys' school. He soon
became a friend of William Wirt, the attorney general of the United States under Presidents James
Monroe and John Quincy Adams. Chase undertook the study of law with Wirt as his mentor, and
on December 14, 1829, was admitted to the bar.

Chase returned to Cincinnati in 1830 to begin
the practice of law. He also undertook a variety of
intellectual, literary, and scholarly activities. He
helped establish the Cincinnati Lyceum and became an author and lecturer. In the years from
1833 to 1835 he published a three-volume compilation entitled *Statutes of Ohio*. Opposition to slavery also became a cornerstone of Chase's philosophy in the 1830s. He served as attorney for a number of runaway black slaves and also defended
James G. Birney, an early abolitionist leader, before the Ohio Supreme Court against charges of
harboring fugitive slaves.

In the 1840s, Chase became active in politics,
working with such antislavery political parties as
the Liberty Party and the Free Soil Party. He
briefly joined the Democrats, who helped him get
elected to the U.S. Senate in 1849, but the Democratic Party was eventually dominated by the proslavery Southern faction of the party. Chase therefore allied himself with the new Republican Party,

universal amnesty for Southerners and universal manhood suffrage to protect the freed blacks disenchanted some delegates, and the convention instead chose Horatio Seymour of New York. In 1872 there were liberal Republicans who sought to nominate Chase as a candidate against Grant, since these Republicans opposed the corruption of the Grant administration, but ill health as well as other factors removed Chase from the running.

Salmon Chase married three times and was the father of six daughters. He wed Katherine Jane Garniss on March 4, 1834, but she died on December 1 of the following year. He was married again on September 26, 1839, to Eliza Ann Smith, who remained his wife until her death on September 29, 1845. Finally, Chase wed Sarah Bella Dunlop Ludlow on November 6, 1846; she died on January 13, 1852. It was more than two decades later when the chief justice himself died, on May 7, 1873, after a stroke.

Horatio Alger's Birthday

The writer Horatio Alger Jr. was born in Revere, Massachusetts, on January 13, 1834. He graduated from Harvard College in 1852. His parents allowed him to travel to Europe, where he spent several years writing for various newspapers. His father, however, eventually began to pressure Alger to enter Harvard Divinity School. Alger acquiesced, and received his degree in 1860.

After several more years in Europe, in 1864 Alger was ordained as a Unitarian minister. Shortly thereafter, he became the chaplain of a lodging house for young men in New York City. Based upon his experiences there, Alger began to write stories about the struggles and achievements of youth. His first work, *Ragged Dick* (1867), established the pattern for most of his writings. His stories concerned young people who, through hard work and perseverance, "pull themselves up by their bootstraps" and go from rags to riches. In a country that was undergoing rapid industrialization and urbanization, Alger's traditional themes of American self-reliance and triumph in the face of adversity resonated with the public. *Ragged Dick* became a best-seller, and was followed by *Luck and Pluck* (1869) and *Tattered Tom* (1871). Over his lifetime, Horatio Alger would write more than 100 works with similar themes. He also wrote several popular biographies, including *From Canal Boy to President* (1881; the story of President James Garfield) and *Abraham Lincoln, The Backwoods Boy* (1883). Both biographies reiterated the familiar story line of how a person could raise himself from poverty and obscurity to attain wealth or fame by moral virtue and perseverance.

Alger was certainly as industrious in his writing as his young male heroes were in their careers, and his works were popular for many decades. Although their literary content is not exceptional, a new generation of hardworking immigrants and factory workers found them inspirational. Horatio Alger died in Natick, Massachusetts, on July 18, 1899, at the age of 65.

Stephen Foster Memorial Day

The anniversary of the death of the great song and ballad writer Stephen Foster on January 13, 1864, is marked annually by proclamation of the president as the national Stephen Foster Memorial Day. Presidential proclamation 2957 of December 13, 1951, designated January 13 as the day for "appropriate ceremonies, pilgrimages to his shrines, and musical programs featuring his compositions."

Stephen Collins Foster was born on July 4, 1826, in what is now Pittsburgh, Pennsylvania. The 10th of 11 children of a prosperous family, he was six when he first gave indications of what his father called his "strange talent" for music. Foster learned how to play the piano and began to play for the various "blackface" minstrel shows of the time, in which white actors wearing makeup imitated and mocked African Americans (who were, of course, still slaves at the time).

Since Foster had no inclination toward formal training in music and his family did not urge him to pursue such study, his technical background was always minimal. He briefly attended Jefferson College and later went to work as a bookkeeper for a brother in Cincinnati. It was in Cincinnati that several of his songs were published locally (in 1848), and one of them, "Oh! Susanna," swept the country shortly thereafter. This sensation prompted him to become a full-time songwriter.

Although some of his compositions were the sentimental ballads of the day, he found his best outlet in minstrel shows, selling many of his numbers to E. P. Christy, who headed a famous troupe. Foster usually wrote both the words and music for his compositions. Despite the phenomenal growth of his popularity between 1850 and 1854, however, he was a poor businessman and never reaped the proportionate financial returns. His songs, which ultimately numbered more than 200, include such famous tunes as "Camptown Races," "Jeanie with the Light Brown Hair" (which he wrote for his wife Jane), and the slow waltz "Beautiful Dreamer."

Poverty forced Foster to sell his compositions for immediate cash at the sacrifice of future royalties. The quality of his work deteriorated under the pressure for quick compensation, complicated by the alcoholism and (according to at least one source) tuberculosis with which he was afflicted after 1860. He spent his last years alone, living in rooming houses in New York City's Bowery slum. There he suffered a fall that proved to be fatal. He died, at the age of 37, in the charity ward of Bellevue Hospital on January 13, 1864. Tragic as his short life was, he was not forgotten, and in 1940 he was the first musician elected to the Hall of Fame for Great Americans.

January 14

Benedict Arnold's Birthday

Benedict Arnold, arguably the country's most dazzling Revolutionary War general as well as its most notorious traitor, was born on January 14, 1741, in Norwich, Connecticut. The Arnolds were an old and respected New England family. When Benedict was in his teens, he became an apprentice to a druggist. He did not enjoy this profession, however, and joined the Connecticut militia. At the age of 16 he was one of the soldiers who marched against Fort William Henry in the French and Indian War of 1754–1763. Eventually he became a captain in the Connecticut militia.

When Arnold's father died in 1761, Benedict moved to New Haven, Connecticut, returning for a time to the druggist trade and also engaging in trade with the West Indies. He became a successful businessman and expanded his enterprises to include trading with Canada. The outbreak of the American Revolution, however, caused him to return to a military career.

Arnold was one of the few military officers in the colonial militia with some experience, and thus he rose quickly and had the opportunity to demonstrate his abilities. After the skirmishes at Lexington and Concord in Massachusetts, Arnold (now a colonel) teamed with Vermont militia leader Ethan Allen and the "Green Mountain Boys" in the capture of Fort Ticonderoga in 1775. He then swept northward through Lake Champlain, reducing a fort and destroying a number of British boats. His next venture, a bold attempt to capture the city of Quebec, was very nearly a disaster. With about 1,000 men, he marched to Canada through the wilderness in the dead of winter to join with Richard Montgomery's forces in an assault on the strategic city, but his men were exhausted, the attack was repulsed, and during the battle Arnold was seriously wounded. He was finally forced to abandon the siege and retreat down Lake Champlain, where he built a small fleet and attacked his pursuers so hotly that they gave up the chase, leav-

ing Fort Ticonderoga safely in American control. For his bravery at Quebec, Arnold had been promoted to brigadier general; now his daring and resourcefulness led many to see him as the Continental Army's shining star. Others saw only arrogance and recklessness, and he was treated shabbily by Congress, which early in 1777 promoted a number of his juniors in service to the level of major general, making them his superiors in rank. George Washington himself protested on Arnold's behalf, but Congress was unmoved. Arnold felt he had been insulted by timid, inferior men, and resented it bitterly. Although he was tardily created major general later in the year, after his role in defending Connecticut, his seniority was still at issue. He handed in his resignation, but was persuaded by Washington to withdraw it when news came of a British plan to divide the colonies by a three-pronged attack through upstate New York. In the Saratoga campaign that followed, Arnold covered himself with glory and contributed much to the decisive American victory. Even his personal enemies were silenced, at least for a time, and his seniority was restored, but a second wound, in the left leg, made him unfit for the kind of arduous campaigning that he loved.

Appointed military commander of the city of Philadephia in 1778, Arnold plunged into the social scene and went deeply into debt. These circumstances led to allegations that he was abusing his office, an investigation by the Executive Council of Pennsylvania, and, at Arnold's own request, a court-martial, which ultimately cleared him of any serious wrongdoing. The reprimand he received, however, deepened his bitterness. Meanwhile, in the spring of 1779 he had married Peggy Shippen, the daughter of a wealthy Philadelphia loyalist; shortly thereafter he began to deal secretly with the British, passing along information and promising to do more when the opportunity arose.

It was not long in coming. In 1780, as soon as he was placed in charge of the garrison at West Point, New York (later the site of the United States Military Academy), Arnold entered into an agreement with the British general Sir Henry Clinton to hand over this key position to the enemy. For his treason, Arnold would receive a substantial amount of money (he demanded a minimum of 10,000 pounds sterling) and a commission in the British army. The plot was uncovered when Arnold's British liaison, Major John André, was captured behind American lines with papers containing the details. Thus incriminated, Arnold fled to the British-held city of New York; André, left in American hands, was hanged as a spy. Although the plot had been foiled, the British rewarded Arnold with the rank of brigadier general and approximately 6,000 pounds; as a British officer, he led two fierce raids against his former compatriots. After the war he was allowed to relocate to London, England.

Despite his services, however, he was never fully accepted into British society. The stigma of being a traitor remained with him even in England, although he was able to establish another West Indies commercial trading enterprise. His final years were largely spent with his wife and children. He died (still in debt) in London on June 14, 1801. A statue of his left boot, considered by Americans the only relic of his honor, can be found in the Saratoga National Historical Park.

Ratification of the Treaty of Paris

For all practical purposes, the American Revolution ended with the surrender of British commander Lord Cornwallis after the Battle of Yorktown, Virginia, in 1781. However, officially there was a state of war until the peace pact known as the Treaty of Paris was agreed upon between Great Britain and its former colonies. After a delay of nearly two years, the Treaty of Paris, by which "His Britannic Majesty acknowledges the . . . United States . . . to be free Sovereign and independent," was finally signed on September 3, 1783. But not until the Continental Congress, meeting in Annapolis, Maryland, had ratified the treaty did the United States legally "assume among the Powers of the earth, the separate and equal station" of which the Declaration of Independence had spoken.

Ratification did not come easily. Indeed, it was uncertain for a time whether one of the key provisions of the Treaty of Paris, namely that it be ratified and returned to England within six months, could be met at all. The six-month period was due to expire in March 1784, and two months had to be allowed for the ocean crossing. As Representative Thomas Jefferson of Virginia repeatedly pointed out, the need for action was urgent. However, the mood of the states was leisurely. It was not until late November 1783 that the first representatives to the Congress arrived at Annapolis.

Finally, after the insistent prodding of Thomas Jefferson, a quorum was assembled. The delegates from Connecticut arrived on January 13, 1784. South Carolina congressman Richard Beresford, until then ill in a Philadelphia hotel, arrived the next day. From then on, not a minute was lost. Meeting in the Maryland State House, which then was serving as the temporary capitol of the nation, the Continental Congress ratified the Treaty of Paris on the very day of Beresford's arrival. Thus, it was on January 14, 1784, that the United States

of America officially took its place as a sovereign, free, and independent nation among nations.

January 15

Edward Teller's Birthday

Edward Teller, the father of the American hydrogen bomb, was born in Budapest, Hungary, on January 15, 1908. At the time, Hungary was part of the Austro-Hungarian Empire. Teller spent his childhood in Hungary, and displayed an exceptional aptitude for mathematics. His parents sent him to private schools, and when he was 18 he left Hungary to pursue advanced studies in Germany.

In Germany, Teller studied chemical engineering and physics. He was admitted to the University of Munich in 1928, but later transferred to the University of Leipzig in order to study under Professor Werner Heisenberg. Heisenberg was at the forefront of quantum physics, the study of the most elemental subatomic particles. Heisenberg would eventually expand upon Albert Einstein's theories of relativity and formulate the famous Heisenberg Uncertainty Principle, which states that the positions of subatomic particles can never be known with certainty. After receiving his doctorate in 1930, Teller became a research associate at the University of Göttingen, where he stayed from 1931 until 1933. When the Nazi Party came to power, Teller left Germany for Denmark, and studied with another famous quantum physicist, Niels Bohr. Teller worked with Bohr in Copenhagen, but then moved to London and eventually the United States, where in 1935 he accepted a position with George Washington University in Washington, D.C. As a professor of physics in the United States, Teller would be safe from the turmoil of World War II which would engulf both Germany and his native Hungary.

Teller became an American citizen in 1941. He formed a close relationship with Russian physicist George Gamow, who had also fled the turmoil of his homeland, and the two worked together to formulate the Gamow-Teller Principles for classifying subatomic particle behavior during the process of radioactive decay. They and other foreign scientists, including Albert Einstein and Leo Szilard, who had also come to America, put the United States at the forefront of nuclear physics. However, the Nazi regime in Germany also had some formidable scientific resources, and there was great concern during World War II that the Germans might discover how to construct a nuclear fission weapon before the United States did. Since the Nazi nuclear effort was headed by Heisenberg,

Teller's former mentor, the danger that the Nazis might develop an atomic bomb first was apparently very real. When President Roosevelt established the Manhattan Project, Teller joined the effort and worked with J. Robert Oppenheimer at the famous Los Alamos, New Mexico, research center and test site. Teller made important contributions to the development of the atomic bomb, although Oppenheimer has traditionally received the credit for being the father of the bomb. It was Teller who theorized that the energy released by an atomic bomb's nuclear fission explosion might create the environment necessary for an even more explosive nuclear fusion reaction. In essence, an atomic bomb explosion could be used as the trigger mechanism for an even bigger hydrogen bomb nuclear fusion explosion.

After World War II, Teller wanted to pursue the development of a hydrogen bomb. The American government was largely unenthusiastic until the Soviet Union developed and detonated its own atomic device in 1949, which prompted President Harry S. Truman to give Teller and his fellow scientists the go-ahead. Some scientists, including Oppenheimer, questioned the need for an H-bomb. Since Russian cities were smaller than American cities, atomic bombs were more than sufficient to devastate the industrial and population centers of the Soviet Union. Hydrogen bombs, with their greater destructive power, were not really necessary according to this viewpoint. But hydrogen bombs would be useful against large American cities, such as New York and Los Angeles, which might not be totally destroyed by conventional atomic bombs, so the development of the H-bomb might actually be counterproductive, in that it might encourage the Russians to develop their own fusion weapons and thus put American cities at greater risk. Despite such arguments, the H-bomb was developed, and in 1952 it was successfully tested at Eniwetok in the Pacific Ocean. Its success confirmed Teller's theories.

After a long and distinguished career, including many publications and books, Teller retired in 1975. As of this writing, he resides in Palo Alto, California. He has continued to be active politically, promoting the development of nuclear energy and such cold war programs as the Strategic Defense Initiative of the Reagan presidency. Teller's strong support of national defense and technological development may well stem from his childhood in war-torn Europe and his flight from Nazi Germany. He also serves as a research fellow at Stanford University's Hoover Institute for the Study of War, Revolution and Peace.

Vermont Declares Independence from the British

Vermont did not exist as a separate entity before 1776. In the colonial period both New Hampshire and New York claimed the Green Mountain region which now comprises Vermont, and speculators from both these provinces invested in Vermont lands. In 1764 the British royal government granted the disputed area to New York, but this action did little to resolve the question. The coming of the American Revolution allowed Vermonters to settle their own fate; the people of the Green Mountains took advantage of the chaos created by the dissolution of the British Empire in America and on January 15, 1777, declared their independence.

Vermont's difficulties in the mid-18th century arose from the problems of settling the area. The first European to explore the region was the Frenchman Samuel de Champlain, who arrived in 1609. As a result of his discovery, France controlled the Green Mountain region for the next 150 years. During that time the French established several forts in present-day Vermont to protect French Canada from invasion by the hostile Iroquois Indians, and Roman Catholic missionaries ventured into the rugged Green Mountains to attempt to Christianize the natives. However, the French were not interested in actually settling the area, and they built only a few small towns along the eastern shore of Lake Champlain.

Although the French had little intention of colonizing Vermont, they soon realized that the geographical position of the Green Mountain area provided them with easy access to the English settlements in northern Massachusetts. Repeatedly during the first half of the 18th century, the French or their Indian allies in Canada passed through Vermont and without warning fell upon the vulnerable English towns along the Massachusetts frontier. These raids terrorized the inhabitants of the remote settlements: During the 1704 attack on Deerfield, Massachusetts, alone, roughly 50 English colonists were killed and more than 100 were taken captive.

To protect the colonists in northern Massachusetts, the British launched a number of retaliatory raids against the French and their Native American allies in the area of present-day Vermont. They also constructed a series of forts just north of the settlements that were in danger of enemy attack. Fort Dummer, begun in 1724 just north of the Massachusetts border near what is now Brattleboro, is significant because it was the first permanent English settlement in the Green Mountain region; but Fort Number Four, built at

Charlestown, New Hampshire, in 1740 afforded the greatest protection to the English settlements in the Connecticut River valley.

The English victory during the French and Indian War of 1754–1763 ended the threat of enemy attack on the remote Massachusetts settlements and assured British control of the Vermont area. However, even before 1763 the royal governors of New Hampshire and New York had involved themselves in the affairs of the Green Mountain region. As early as 1750 Governor Benning Wentworth of New Hampshire realized that great profits could be made by making grants of land in the Vermont area to speculators. Wentworth's authority to dispose of the Green Mountain region was questionable, for New Hampshire's western boundary had never been established. Wentworth merely assumed that New Hampshire's jurisdiction, like that of neighboring Connecticut and Massachusetts, extended to a line 20 miles east of the Hudson River, and proceeded to grant substantial areas in present-day Vermont to New Hampshire investors.

Between 1750 and 1764, Wentworth made grants of land for 138 towns in the Vermont area to New Hampshire speculators. The governors of New York believed that their own colony rightfully controlled the Green Mountain region, and repeatedly protested to the Crown about Wentworth's "New Hampshire Grants."

In 1764 the Crown acknowledged New York's claim to Vermont by declaring the western bank of the Connecticut River "to be the boundary between the said two provinces of New Hampshire and New York." Unfortunately, this proclamation made no reference to jurisdiction over the Vermont area prior to 1764. Therefore, controversy continued: New Hampshirites argued that political authority over Vermont had shifted to New York in 1764 but that the land titles previously given by Wentworth were still valid, while New Yorkers insisted that they had always controlled the Vermont area, and the governor of New York proceeded to make his own land grants to speculators.

For more than a decade the dispute over Vermont raged. The governor of New York was willing to confirm the land titles of those persons who had actually settled in the Vermont areas granted by New Hampshire, but he would not validate the much larger claims held by the colony's absentee speculators. The New Hampshire speculators looked for assistance to John Wentworth, who had succeeded his uncle as governor of New Hampshire. Both as governor and as "Surveyor General of the King's Woods," Wentworth befriended the land investors, but his contribution in the fight against New York authorities could not match that

of the most famous of the speculators, Ethan Allen.

A native of Connecticut, Ethan Allen first emerged as a leader of the New Hampshire grantees in 1770. After an unsuccessful attempt to defend the validity of New Hampshire land titles before a New York court that year, Allen rather ambiguously announced that "the gods of the hills are not the gods of the valleys." Then he returned to Vermont, where he worked to align the actual settlers of the Green Mountain area with the absentee speculators who held New Hampshire grants.

Allen argued that the lands of the settlers would be safe only if all New Hampshire titles were confirmed. He also urged those who lived in what is now Vermont to oppose New York authorities, with force if necessary. The efficacy of this strategy was demonstrated in the fall of 1770 when a group of about 100 Vermonters successfully turned back a New York posse that had come to the Green Mountains to oust a settler. Within a short time, 11 towns in the western part of the Green Mountains had raised military companies, and Allen was appointed to be their "Colonel-Commandant."

In the early years of their existence, the Green Mountain Boys, as the band led by Allen was known, counted among their membership only a small portion of the residents of what is today western Vermont. Nevertheless, the organization was able to block New York's efforts to extend its authority over the Vermont area. The resistance was so successful that in 1774 the New York assembly ordered the leaders of the Green Mountain Boys to be tried *in absentia* and executed if apprehended. This so-called Bloody Act did nothing to curtail the activities of Allen and his followers; indeed, it served to gain them additional popular support.

Deteriorating relations between England and the American colonies in the 1770s added a new dimension to the politics of the struggle of the Green Mountain Boys. Allen and his cohorts quickly reevaluated the situation and made England the primary target of their wrath. The mother country was the authority to which both New York and New Hampshire looked for support in their claims on Vermont. England's departure from the American scene would deprive New York of the Crown's 1764 decision as a cudgel to use against the Green Mountain Boys, and it would also destroy any pretensions that New Hampshire would have to control of Vermont. Allen began to dream of a completely independent Vermont, which (if England lost Canada, too) might even enjoy access to the Atlantic Ocean through the St. Lawrence River.

Shortly after the first skirmishes of the American Revolution at Lexington and Concord in April 1775, Allen proposed a campaign against the British Fort Ticonderoga at the head of Lake Champlain. The plan was well received, and troops from Massachusetts and Connecticut joined Allen and 100 Green Mountain Boys for an attack on Ticonderoga. The British fort fell on May 10, 1775. Two days later, the British contingent at nearby Crown Point likewise surrendered to the Green Mountain Boys under Seth Warner.

After the capture of Ticonderoga, Allen urged pressing the northern campaign, for, as he wrote to the Continental Congress, "advancing an army into Canada will be agreeable to our friends, and it is bad policy to fear the resentment of an army." Congress approved the expedition against the province of Quebec, and Allen served without a commission in the campaign. He was captured outside Montreal, but the Americans, assisted by a regiment of Green Mountain Boys, captured Montreal in November 1775. Their success in Canada was short-lived, however. Near the city of Quebec, British forces repulsed the colonists' subsequent attack of December 31, 1775, and forced them to retreat to the safety of Fort Ticonderoga.

While British forces in Canada prepared to launch a counter-invasion southward, the inhabitants of present-day Vermont struggled with the difficulties of their political status. In January 1776, 49 leading citizens, still angered by what they considered to be New York's "land-jobbing," issued a declaration in which they refused to join with New York "in such a manner as might in the future be detrimental to our private property." Eight months later, after New York and the other 12 colonies had declared their independence from Britain, the same group decided to poll the residents of the New Hampshire Grants, as Vermont was then known, about the feasibility of forming a "separate district." In time, the decisive step of declaring independence from New York was taken. On January 15, 1777, at a meeting at Westminster, the Green Mountain Boys and others disenchanted with both New York and New Hampshire announced the formation of the state of New Connecticut. A district in Pennsylvania had already taken the name New Connecticut, however. Thus, by June 1777 the rebels in the "Grants" decided to call their lands Vermont, from the French words *vert* and *mont*, meaning "green" and "mountain."

By the time a convention met at Windsor in July 1777 to formulate a constitution, British forces had overwhelmed the American defenders at Ticonderoga and threatened to invade. But the American victory over British general Burgoyne's forces at the battle of Bennington late in the summer of 1777 saved the fledgling state. Vermont would face other crises before it ratified the U.S. Constitution in 1791 and became the 14th state, but the Green Mountain Boys had survived their first trials.

January 16

Operation Desert Storm Begins

On January 16, 1991, the United States and allied forces began to move against Iraqi military positions in occupied Kuwait and the surrounding territory of southern Iraq. This was the beginning of Operation Desert Storm, one of the major military confrontations of the 1990s.

The events leading up to Operation Desert Storm go back to the 1980s, when Iraqi dictator Saddam Hussein tried to take advantage of the revolutionary turmoil in neighboring Iran by attacking that country. Hussein thought that the disorganized Iranians would be an easy target for Iraqi territorial expansionism, but he was mistaken. After a long and expensive war, the conflict ended in a stalemate. In order to sustain his military effort, Hussein had imported large amounts of military equipment, driving his country deeply into debt. He had even borrowed money from neighboring Arab states, such as Kuwait on Iraq's southeastern border along the Persian Gulf—states that were themselves afraid that Iranian revolutionary sentiment might spread and lead to the overthrow of their conservative monarchies. Thus, during the Iraq-Iran War, Kuwait was in the ironic position of being on the Iraqi side.

After the war, Hussein struggled to reassert his authority, domestically and abroad. Iraq is an oil-producing and exporting country, but its oil reserves are limited, and thus it was unable to generate the funds necessary to pay off its foreign debts quickly. In 1990 Hussein began to pressure Kuwait for financial assistance, since Kuwait has sizable oil reserves of its own but only a small population and a weak military to defend its wealth. On July 17, 1990, Hussein accused Kuwait of excessive exploitation of the Rumailia oil field, which straddles both Iraqi and Kuwaiti territory. April Glaspie, the American ambassador to Iraq, mistakenly informed Hussein that the United States was not interested in the issue, despite the ominous implications. On August 2, Hussein sent Iraqi forces into Kuwait and quickly occupied the country. He still commanded an impressive military machine, and was in an excellent position to expand into the lightly defended kingdom of Saudi

Arabia and the other Persian Gulf oil-producing states, which would effectively make him the master of a considerable portion of the world's oil resources.

U.S. president George Bush had no significant military presence in the Persian Gulf to counter the Iraqi military threat. He initiated a series of international economic sanctions through the United Nations and began assembling an American expeditionary force that would eventually number in the hundreds of thousands. He also secured military and financial assistance from American allies throughout the world and from Arab states in the region that had now come to consider Iraq (rather than Iran) the principal regional threat.

On November 29, 1990, the United Nations Security Council gave Iraq until January 15, 1991, to withdraw its forces from Kuwait and authorized the use of all necessary force by the United States and its allies to force Iraqi compliance. This measure, Security Council Resolution 678, was followed on January 12, 1991, by a resolution of the United States Congress authorizing the use of American troops against Iraq. The January 12 vote came after several months of fruitless negotiations and Iraqi stonewalling.

On January 16, 1991, the Bush administration announced that "the liberation of Kuwait has begun." American military aircraft began thousands of bombing missions and missile attacks against Iraqi military targets. American military technology, such as infrared night vision and "stealth" radar-invisible planes, made the attacks devastatingly effective. The Iraqis attempted to retaliate with missile attacks of their own, launching SCUD missiles purchased from the Soviet Union many years before. Despite some limited successes, the missile attacks were ineffective in thwarting the overwhelming American onslaught. By February 23, 1991, Iraqi military bases, airfields, and other strategic sites were largely in ruins, and the American-led ground forces took the offensive.

Rather than attack the entrenched Iraqi positions in Kuwait directly, American commander general Norman Schwartzkopf conducted a sweeping end run around the Iraqi flank by going into the desert territory of southern Iraq and coming around the Iraqi forces in Kuwait from the side. Demoralized and disorganized, and frequently abandoned by their own officers who retreated for the safety of the Iraqi interior, Hussein's soldiers surrendered in droves. Some Iraqi units actually surrendered to television cameramen who had followed the ground forces into liberated Kuwait. The American victory was one of the most one-sided in the history of warfare. At every engagement, those Iraqi forces who chose to

fight were crushed with few or no American or allied casualties, and most of Saddam Hussein's war machine was destroyed.

Rather than face the prospect of an American occupation of Iraq, Hussein quickly agreed to the terms of a United Nations cease-fire agreement. As of this writing, however, enforcement of the peace terms has been an ongoing problem and a contentious issue for both the United States and the United Nations. For example, Hussein, who stayed in power after the Gulf War ended, has continued to thwart United Nations efforts to monitor Iraq for illegal development of nuclear, chemical, and biological weapons. Thus, although Operation Desert Storm was successful in its objective of restoring the legitimate government of Kuwait, it remains to be seen whether the collateral objective of defeating the territorial ambitions of Saddam Hussein will be realized.

Eighteenth Amendment Ratified

For more than a century, temperance advocates worked to rid the United States of alcohol abuse. The active supporters of Prohibition were never more than a minority of the nation's population, but as a result of their efforts, the 18th Amendment to the Constitution, which forbade the import and export of intoxicating liquors and outlawed their "manufacture, sale, or transportation . . . within . . . the United States and all territory subject to the jurisdiction thereof for beverage purposes," gained the approval of the requisite three-fourths of the states by January 16, 1919. By its own terms, the 18th Amendment went into effect one year from the date of its ratification, on January 16, 1920.

Over the years, the temperance crusade had drawn support from a number of sources. Early in the 19th century, clergymen and other persons with strong religious affiliations formed the core of the temperance movement, while in the decades that followed, women's organizations (most notably the Women's Christian Temperance Union under Frances E. Willard) became the chief protagonists. In 1872 Prohibitionists even formed their own political party and ran a candidate for president. When this attempt at direct political action failed to attract sufficient voters to their cause, temperance advocates organized the Anti-Saloon League in 1893 to persuade members of the Republican and Democratic parties to support anti-liquor laws.

Temperance workers of the 19th century enjoyed some success. A number of states passed anti-liquor legislation, and hundreds of thousands of people signed pledges promising to abstain from alcohol. However, it was not until the early 1900s that the Prohibition movement gained widespread support. The Anti-Saloon League launched a massive campaign to outlaw liquor, and by 1914 about a quarter of the states had enacted anti-liquor laws. The growing success of the Prohibition movement may also have been a manifestation of the general spirit of Progressive reform that swept the United States at the turn of the century.

The Progressive era, as the first decade or so of the 20th century was known, was a time of major reforms in the United States. Convinced of the possibility of effecting social improvement through law, the Progressives worked for a number of causes, including women's suffrage, government regulation of business, direct election of U.S. senators, and the elimination of child labor. Many Progressives believed that Prohibition would eliminate the many evils of alcohol, such as poverty, illness, violence, crime, broken homes, and wrecked lives.

Prohibitionists failed to win sufficient congressional support for an amendment outlawing alcoholic beverages in 1913, but the movement against liquor continued to gain supporters as the decade progressed. The United States' involvement in World War I somewhat strengthened the momentum. The Lever Act of 1917, passed to ensure adequate food supplies for prosecution of the war, forbade the use of grain for the distillation of alcoholic beverages, and by temporarily eliminating a major portion of the country's liquor supply proved the feasibility of nationwide abstinence. On a less admirable plane, war fever created a widespread distaste for beer among certain sectors of the American populace, simply because that beverage had long been associated with the German nation.

By 1917 the United States was ready for what Herbert Hoover called the "noble experiment." On December 18, 1917, Congress sent to the states the proposed 18th Amendment, which would outlaw the sale, import, and export of alcoholic beverages beginning one year after the amendment's ratification. The amendment also gave both the national and the state legislatures power to enforce Prohibition. On January 16, 1919, the amendment received the approval of the requisite three-fourths of the states, and on January 16, 1920, it went into effect. The one-year delay was designed to give the country time to prepare.

Even before the 18th Amendment became effective, Congress, on October 28, 1919, passed the National Prohibition Enforcement Act, more commonly known as the Volstead Act. This act vested administration of Prohibition in the Bureau of Internal Revenue and created the post of Com-

missioner of Prohibition. But the bureau's force had at its peak only 3,000 agents, a number inadequate for the mammoth task of controlling illegal liquor traffic. Further, there was a substantial portion of the public that disagreed with Prohibition. Thus, throughout the 1920s and the early 1930s, Prohibition legislation was openly flouted. In Rhode Island, a state that refused to ratify the 18th Amendment, alcoholic beverages were openly sold in grocery stores; elsewhere, many persons distilled their own spirits, frequented speakeasies, or patronized bootleggers.

For 13 years the 18th Amendment remained in force. However, the open defiance of Prohibition created as many social problems as the alcohol abuse it sought to curtail, including the growth of organized crime syndicates that arose to satisfy the demand for liquor and produced such notorious gangsters as Al Capone. In February 1933, Congress recommended repeal of the 18th Amendment. Only 10 months later, on December 5, 1933, three-fourths of the states approved the 21st Amendment and Prohibition came to an end in the United States.

January 17

Benjamin Franklin's Birthday

Library of Congress

Benjamin Franklin at the Constitutional Convention.

Benjamin Franklin, born in Boston, Massachusetts, on January 17, 1706, is famous for his contributions to American history as a printer, writer, scientist, inventor, statesman, philanthropist, public servant, and diplomat.

Franklin was the 15th of Josiah Franklin's 17 children, and the tenth son. As a boy, he worked for a year in his father's candle shop, and then was apprenticed at the age of 12 to his brother James, who founded one of the first American newspapers. This was the *New England Courant*, which carried Benjamin Franklin's earliest (although anonymously) published works. Although the terms of Franklin's apprenticeship required him to serve until he was 20 years old, he quarreled with his brother when he was 17 and ran away to New York. Unable to find work there, he went to Philadelphia. Although he arrived almost penniless, he soon found friends and employment.

In 1725, when Franklin was 19, Sir William Keith, governor of the colony of Pennsylvania, encouraged him to go to London. Keith promised letters of credit and introduction so that Franklin could buy equipment for a printing office, return to Philadelphia, and set up a business. When the governor's promises failed to materialize, Franklin found himself alone, friendless, and jobless in London. With his customary resourcefulness, however, he quickly found employment as a printer. He remained in London for a year and a half and then returned to Philadelphia, where he began a successful printing business of his own. His printing career eventually helped Franklin enter politics, since he had a platform for publishing his own views on the need for American independence in the decades leading up to the American Revolution.

Franklin was America's best-known representative abroad in its days as a new nation struggling for independence and recognition. As statesman and diplomat, he helped draft and eventually signed the Declaration of Independence, was instrumental in securing French support for the American cause, laid the groundwork for the treaty that brought a successful conclusion to the American Revolution, and helped negotiate the compromises that led to adoption of the U.S. Constitution. He also served his home city of Philadelphia, Pennsylvania, in many ways and represented the state of Pennsylvania in a variety of official capacities, including as a member of the Pennsylvania assembly and as president of the Pennsylvania executive council.

As a scientist, he experimented tirelessly, identifying lightning with electricity by means of his famous investigation with a kite during a storm. This experiment and others brought him renown in both America and Europe. As an inventor, Franklin conceived such varied items as the fuel-saving Franklin stove, bifocal lenses, and the lightning rod. His practical nature, as well as the wit and wisdom that became his hallmarks, was expressed in essays and in aphorisms that are still famous today. Many of them concerned such virtues as thrift, industry, honesty, and moderation. His unique style brought success to his printing ventures, particularly *Poor Richard's Almanack*, which was published annually from 1732 to 1757.

Franklin's wide-ranging interests involved him in many other activities, associating his name with a list of accomplishments that few biographies can equal for length or significance. Among other things, he was instrumental in founding the country's first hospital, the Pennsylvania Hospital in Philadelphia; the first subscription library, the Library Company of Philadelphia; and one of the first insurance companies, the Philadelphia Contributionship for the Insurance of Houses from Loss by Fire. Having earlier reorganized the postal system of the colonies, he served as the country's first postmaster general. Franklin organized Philadelphia's first fire company, proposed a police force, drew up a plan for paving the streets, and was responsible for better lighting and other civic improvements. He was also instrumental in the establishment of the American Philosophical Society and the University of Pennsylvania. Benjamin Franklin died in Philadelphia on April 17, 1790.

January 18

Daniel Webster's Birthday

Daniel Webster, who won fame as an orator, statesman, and constitutional lawyer, was born in Salisbury (now part of Franklin), New Hampshire, on January 18, 1782. His father was a New England farmer who had served as a soldier in the American Revolution. Daniel received a preliminary education in neighborhood schools. The boy demonstrated precocious intellectual abilities, and in 1796 his father managed to enroll him at Phillips Exeter Academy in Exeter, New Hampshire, and then at prestigious Dartmouth College. Daniel graduated from Dartmouth in 1801 at the age of 19.

He vacillated between a career as a schoolteacher and a career as a lawyer, finally settling on the latter. After serving in Boston as a clerk in the firm of the noted lawyer Christopher Gore, Webster was admitted to the bar in March 1805. He first practiced law in Boscawen, New Hampshire, and in 1807 continued his profession in Portsmouth, New Hampshire. Also drawn into politics, he was elected to the U.S. House of Representatives from the Portsmouth district in 1812, and was reelected two years later.

In 1816 Webster moved to Boston and devoted himself to his law practice. His rapid success in that field has been attributed to his dramatic voice, penetrating gaze, persuasive arguments, and quick grasp of the key issues at stake. He came to national attention in 1818–1819 while successfully defending his alma mater in the famous Dartmouth College case, wherein the Supreme Court made an important legal decision about the limits imposed by the Constitution on the government when it comes to altering the terms of legally valid documents. During the next several years, Webster also took part in other cases of national importance, including *McCulloch* v. *Maryland*, *Gibbons* v. *Ogden*, and *Osborn* v. *The Bank of the United States*.

In the meantime, Webster gained a nationwide reputation as a public orator, speaking, for example, at the Plymouth, Massachusetts, bicentennial in 1820 and at the 50th anniversary of the battle of Bunker Hill in 1825. In 1822, he was once again elected to the House of Representatives, this time from a Boston district, and he was twice reelected by an overwhelming vote. In the election of 1827, he was chosen to represent Massachusetts in the U.S. Senate, where he served without interruption until 1841 and became a leading political figure. As a champion of New England economic interests, he supported the protective tariff of 1828. He denounced the Southern position concerning states' rights and the nullification of federal laws in a famous debate with Robert Hayne of South Carolina. His thunderous defense of the Union included the famous words "Liberty and Union, now and forever, one and inseparable!"

In 1832 and 1833, Webster backed President Andrew Jackson in arguing against nullification with another South Carolinian, John C. Calhoun. On many other issues, however, especially fiscal matters pertaining to the Bank of the United States, Webster was at odds with Jackson. In 1836 Webster received the electoral vote of Massachusetts as the presidential candidate of the New England Whigs although he did not win the election itself, and in 1840 he declined the nomination for vice president. President William Henry Harrison made him secretary of state, a post he retained under President John Tyler after Harrison's sudden death in 1841. When Tyler broke with his Whig cabinet in September 1841, Webster was the only cabinet member who did not hand in his resignation, thereby gaining the enmity of some of his fellow Whigs. After completing the negotiations for the Webster-Ashburton Treaty of 1842, which settled a boundary dispute between Maine and English-held Canada, Webster resigned from office and resumed law practice in Boston.

Webster entered the Senate for a second time in 1845. As senator, he followed the Whig policy of opposing the war with Mexico and the annexation of Texas. He aspired to the nomination for president in 1848, and denounced bitterly the Whig selection of the Mexican War hero General Zachary Taylor. The defeat of Mexico and the subsequent vast acquisition of territory stirred up a great debate over slavery, which threatened to split the Union. Although Webster condemned slavery as evil, he regarded the preservation of the Union as a more desirable goal than the abolition of slavery. Risking his own popularity among New Englanders, especially the abolitionists, he actively supported Henry Clay's Compromise of 1850, which he believed to be the only course to avert civil strife. In his last notable speech in the Senate, known as the Seventh of March [1850] speech, he advocated compromise on the issue of the extension of slavery. He was roundly denounced for it in the North.

From 1850 until his health deteriorated in 1852, Daniel Webster served as secretary of state under President Millard Fillmore. When Webster died at his home in Marshfield, Massachusetts, on October 24, 1852, there was widespread mourning at the passing of one of the most brilliant men the United States had produced. On July 4, 1970, the building at Marshfield that had once served as Webster's study and law office was opened to the public as a historical monument.

Muhammad Ali's Birthday

Muhammad Ali was born Cassius Marcellus Clay Jr. in Louisville, Kentucky, on January 17, 1942. His parents were Cassius Marcellus Clay Sr. and Odessa Grady Clay, blue-collar African Americans. His boxing career began at the age of 12, when he rode a new bicycle to a Louisville children's event. When his bike was stolen, he went to the police and told Officer Joe Martin that he wanted to "kick the butt" of the person who stole his bicycle. Officer Martin, who happened to be the boxing coach at the local gym, encouraged young Cassius to channel his anger into amateur boxing.

Cassius Clay weighed roughly 90 pounds when he began his boxing career. However, during his teenage years, he grew rapidly in both size and expertise. In 1957, at the age of 16, he won his first Golden Gloves competition. Clay would eventually take two national Golden Glove titles, in addition to winning 103 amateur boxing matches while only losing five contests.

Boxing soon began to dominate Cassius Clay's life. In high school, he was a mediocre student, and despite his obsession with pugilism he had a reputation for being rather shy. In 1960, at the age of 18, he turned professional after fighting Tunney Hunsaker. Angelo Dundee became his trainer, and remained with him for many years. The young boxer achieved national recognition in 1964 when he fought heavyweight champion Charles "Sonny" Liston on February 25 for the title. Clay was a seven-to-one underdog. With his youth and superior agility, however, he defeated Liston, becoming one of the youngest heavyweight champions in history. After this victory, he made history by also stating that he would renounce his "slave name" of Cassius Marcellus Clay. Before the media, he announced that he had joined the Nation of Islam, a fundamentalist African American separatist religious organization led by Elijah Muhammad and the controversial Malcolm X. Henceforth, Cassius Clay would be known to the world by his adopted name of Muhammad Ali.

During the remainder of the 1960s, Ali successfully retained his self-proclaimed title of being "The Greatest" in boxing. He fought Liston in a rematch, and also such other noteworthy heavyweight contenders as Floyd Patterson, Cleveland Williams, Ernie Terrell, and Zora Folley. He also earned a reputation for witticism, especially with his off-the-cuff rhymes about himself and his opponents. "Float like a butterfly, sting like a bee" became his slogan.

In 1967 Muhammad Ali entered a controversial period of his career. He was drafted by the United States Army for service in the Vietnam War, but on April 28, 1967, declared that he would refuse to serve on the grounds that he was an Islamic minister and thus a conscientious objector. He also stated that he had "no quarrel with the Viet Cong." He was subsequently deprived of his titles by the boxing authorities and prosecuted as a draft dodger in federal court. In 1970, after a series of appeals, the U.S. Supreme Court overturned Ali's conviction and upheld his right to refuse the draft based on his Islamic principles. Thus vindicated, he was able to reenter the world of boxing.

By the 1970s, however, Ali was approaching his thirties and was thus past his prime for professional boxing. In the "fight of the century" on March 8, 1971, Ali was defeated by "Smokin'" Joe Frazier. Ali reclaimed his prestige in 1974, however, when he beat Frazier in a rematch. Further, on October 30, 1974, in the famous "Rumble in the Jungle" in Zaire, Ali defeated the current heavyweight champion George Foreman and despite three-to-one odds became one of the few men ever to recapture a heavyweight boxing title.

Ali successfully defended his title through the mid-1970s, but during a match with Joe Frazier called the "Thrilla in Manila" (so named because it was located in the Philippines), Ali's age began to show even though he retained his title. In 1978, Ali was defeated by Olympic gold medalist Leon Spinks. He was able to regain his title from Spinks in a rematch several months later, but his career was clearly nearing its end. On June 27, 1979, he decided to retire and surrendered his title. He briefly came out of retirement in 1980, but was defeated by the current heavyweight champion Larry Holmes on October 2. After that experience, Muhammad Ali decided once and for all to make his retirement final. Now afflicted with Parkinson's disease, he made a rare public appearance to light the flame at the opening ceremonies of the 1996 Summer Olympics.

January 19

Robert E. Lee's Birthday

Robert E. Lee's birthday was made a legal holiday in the state of Georgia in 1889. Virginia, where the anniversary is observed as Lee-Jackson Day, followed Georgia's example in 1890. Other states that also note the Confederate general's birthday as a legal holiday, either on January 19 or on the third Monday of the month, are Alabama, Arkansas, Florida, Kentucky, Louisiana, Mississippi, North Carolina, South Carolina, Tennessee, and Texas.

Lee, who is regarded by many military authorities as the ablest strategist of the Civil War, was born at Stratford, his family's estate in Westmoreland County, Virginia, on January 19, 1807. He was the son of Henry Lee, known as Light-Horse Harry Lee, a distinguished soldier of the American Revolution. His mother (his father's second wife) was the former Anne Hill Carter, a daughter of Charles Carter, part of a Virginia family as famous as the Lees.

Henry Lee was forced to leave Stratford in 1811 because of unfortunate investments and complicated ownership rights. Young Robert E. Lee and his family moved to Alexandria, Virginia, located near the nation's capital of Washington, D.C., where they soon occupied a handsome Georgian mansion. Lee's father was seldom at home and had little contact with his family before his death on March 25, 1818. Nonetheless, inspired by his father's military career, young Lee sought admission to the United States Military Academy at West Point, which he entered in 1825. He graduated second in his class and was the first cadet to complete the course without receiving a single demerit.

Entering the army as a second lieutenant of engineers, Lee served as assistant engineer at Fort Monroe, Virginia, from May 1831 to November 1834. While there, he was married on June 30, 1831, to Mary Ann Randolph Custis, the only daughter of George Washington Parke Custis (grandson of Martha Washington), who lived on the estate originally known as Arlington, across the Potomac from Washington and near Lee's former home of Alexandria. Arlington House, where Lee and his bride settled and raised their family, has since become known as the Custis-Lee Mansion. Visited by thousands annually, it stands within what is now Arlington National Cemetery, directly overlooking the grave of President John F. Kennedy and a panoramic view of Washington. The mansion, administered by the National Park Service, was named a permanent memorial by act of Congress in 1955.

After his marriage, young Lee was assigned to various engineering duties until 1846, when war broke out between the United States and Mexico. Lee, then a captain, first reported for service as assistant engineer to Brigadier General John E. Wool, the commander of a secondary force stationed at San Antonio, Texas. Transferred to the expedition that landed at Vera Cruz, Mexico, he won the esteem and admiration of General Winfield Scott, its commander, and performed valuable service in planning for the capture of Mexico City. Lee returned from the Mexican War with his military reputation established at the age of 42 and was promoted to the rank of colonel. He was then put in charge of the construction of Fort Carroll in Baltimore Harbor, Maryland.

After serving there from September 1848 to April 1852, Lee was appointed to fill the post of superintendent at West Point. He remained in this position until March 1855, when Secretary of War Jefferson Davis appointed him lieutenant colonel of the Second Cavalry Regiment. Lee's orders to leave for western Texas to take his first field command came the next month. Later, in 1857, Colonel Lee obtained an extended leave of absence to supervise the running of Arlington. While in Virginia, in December 1859 Lee was called upon to put down the uprising at Harpers Ferry led by antislavery crusader John Brown. Brown was captured and eventually executed after a famous trial for treason against the state of Virginia.

From this duty, Lee returned to the Texas border, only to be summoned to Washington, D.C., in February 1861 to meet the crisis of his life. In December 1860 South Carolina, soon to be followed by other Southern states, had declared its secession over the issues of slavery and state sovereignty. General Scott placed Lee, his favorite officer, on standing order with the intention of promoting him immediately if civil war should erupt.

Although Lee was no politician, he was an intelligent observer and had watched with concern and sadness the mounting strife that would lead to the Civil War. Considering slavery an evil, he, like many of his fellow Virginia landowners, had freed his slaves, but he was equally convinced that any effort to wipe out slavery by force would be a grave mistake. When the secession movement began to gain momentum, Lee hoped that the issue might be settled peacefully. Loyal to the federal government and to the U.S. Army, he was convinced of the advantages of the Union on the one hand, while on the other he adamantly insisted upon the right of each state to secede from that Union at will. It was in keeping with the tradition in which he had been raised that if Virginia seceded he would go with it as a matter of course. Shortly before the crisis, he wrote:

> I can anticipate no greater calamity for the country than the dissolution of the Union. . . . Still, a union that can only be maintained by swords and bayonets, and in which strife and civil war are to take the place of brotherly love and kindness, has no charms for me. If the Union is dissolved and the Government dispersed I shall return to my native State and share the miseries of my people and, save in defense, will draw my sword no more.

Some historians point out that Lee, who has such a reputation for being a man of honor, was nevertheless deserting the U.S. Army and breaking his duty of loyalty to that Union that had consistently recognized and rewarded his service.

Events moved more rapidly and radically than Lee had wished. On April 12, 1861, the firing on Fort Sumter touched off the Civil War. General Scott promptly advised President Lincoln to offer Lee the field command of the U.S. Army. On April 18, Francis P. Blair, a top presidential adviser, informed Lee that the president had authorized such an offer. Lee declined the offer and discussed the situation with General Scott, who advised him that he should either resign from the army or accept whatever duty was assigned to him. On April 19, while at Arlington, Lee learned that a Virginia convention had voted in favor of secession and would submit the issue to the people for ratification. Persuaded that secession would not wait for referendum, he resigned from the army on April 20.

Having already refused the command of what soon would be the Union forces in the Civil War, Robert E. Lee now began his rise to leadership of the forces that would oppose them. On April 23 he assumed command of the military and naval forces of Virginia, reorganizing them thoroughly. He was soon made military adviser, with the rank of general, to Jefferson Davis, who had become president of the Confederacy.

In March 1862, President Davis summoned Lee to Richmond, Virginia, in the capacity of military adviser. Lee devised the successful strategy to divert the massive federal reinforcements intended to bolster the Union advance on Richmond, the capital of the Confederacy. After Confederate general Joseph E. Johnston was wounded during the Peninsular campaign in May 1862, Lee assumed command of the Army of Northern Virginia on June 1. His brilliant leadership of that army during the next three years was to earn him a place among the world's renowned commanders, and his varied campaigns were to lead him from Virginia to Pennsylvania.

Assuming the offensive upon taking command, Lee ended the threat to Richmond in the Seven Days battles in late June and early July 1862. Resoundingly defeating Union general John Pope at the second battle of Bull Run at the end of August, Lee was himself checked in his first invasion of Union territory at Antietam, Maryland, in September. The Southern general skillfully repulsed federal advances under generals A. E. Burnside and Joseph Hooker at the battles of Fredericksburg, Virginia, on December 13, and Chancellorsville, Virginia, in May 1863.

Lee's defeat at Gettysburg in the summer of 1863 came after the death of General "Stonewall" Jackson, his ablest officer, had forced the reorganizing of the command of his army with less experienced men. The Gettysburg campaign forced Lee to reshape his military strategy. Previously, he had hoped that a stunning Southern victory on Northern ground would compel the enemy to sue for peace. Afterwards, aware that increasingly limited manpower and material resources could no longer sustain such a policy, Lee attempted, with dilatory tactics, to wear down the resolve of the North by preventing a conclusive showdown.

Pitted against Lee, however, was the equally persistent and stubborn Ulysses S. Grant, the Union general who had successfully besieged and captured the strategic Confederate city of Vicksburg, Mississippi, on the Mississippi River. President Lincoln appointed Grant commander of the federal armies in March 1864. Grant, acutely assessing the situation, realized that Lee's Army of Northern Virginia was the chief obstacle to Union victory and was determined to force Lee to fight. Lee was able to repulse Grant's direct attacks in the Wilderness campaign during May and June of 1864. Nevertheless, Grant managed to trap Lee in the grueling siege of Petersburg, the crucial support center south of Richmond, which lasted during the winter of 1864 and into spring of 1865. This move confined the Southern general to the immediate defense of the Richmond area, depriving him of the opportunity for rapid maneuvers, which had so far helped to offset the numerically superior Union forces.

Lee's appointment as general-in-chief of all the Confederate armies on February 6, 1865, was an empty gesture, intended primarily to improve morale in the crumbling Confederacy. In the spring of 1865, Grant broke through the Petersburg defenses. Lee abandoned the lines around Richmond and unsuccessfully attempted to unite with General Joseph Johnston's forces in North Carolina. Grant pursued Lee, eventually encircling the remnants of the Confederate army and forcing Lee to surrender on April 9, 1865, at the small town of Appomattox Court House, Virginia. Lee's surrender brought the war to an end for all practical purposes, although some scattered Confederate forces continued to fight for a while.

Lee returned as a paroled prisoner of war to Richmond. He could not return to Arlington. That estate, situated on the line of defenses protecting Washington, was occupied by federal troops and became a Union army camp shortly after the Lees departed for Richmond. The federal government confiscated the Lees' land and turned the property into a military cemetery, now known as the Arlington National Cemetery. Begun as a burial place for Civil War dead, Arlington today contains graves of dead from all wars in which the United States has participated, and is the largest and most famous of the national cemeteries.

After the Civil War, Lee resolutely avoided participation in the many war-kindled controversies that still rankled the nation. Choosing from the positions offered him, in September 1865 he accepted the presidency of Washington College at Lexington, Virginia, and devoted the remaining years of his life to raising its standards of scholarship and increasing the number of its students. He died on October 12, 1870, at Lexington. His wife died three years later.

Shortly after the end of the war, Lee had requested a pardon and restoration of his citizenship from President Andrew Johnson. A required oath of allegiance, which he swore on the same day he assumed the presidency of Washington College, apparently never reached the proper federal authorities. It was discovered 100 years after his death, in 1970, in the National Archives. Five years later, with the overwhelming approval of both houses of Congress, citizenship was belatedly restored to Robert E. Lee.

Perceptive of his enemy's weak points, quick to grasp the potentialities of a military situation, and intuitively anticipating his opponents' moves, Robert E. Lee possessed many assets as a commander. Both as a general and as a person, he commanded the respect and devotion of his men. He was almost universally regarded as the epitome of the Southern gentleman. In his memory, the trustees of Washington College changed its name to Washington and Lee. The university's Lee Chapel, which Lee himself designed, contains his crypt. The chapel was restored as part of the four-year Civil War centennial observed throughout the United States in the early 1960s.

Edgar Allan Poe's Birthday

Edgar Allan Poe was born in Boston on January 19, 1809. Both his father, David Poe Jr., the son of a patriot in the American Revolution, and his mother, the British-born Elizabeth Arnold Poe, were actors, and Poe was carried about the country with them in his infancy. Both parents died in 1811, and the Poe children were distributed among foster parents.

Young Poe was taken into the home of a successful Richmond merchant, John Allan, and his wife. Allan's wife, who was childless, became Poe's foster mother. In 1815, the Allans took the boy with them to Scotland and England, where he studied at several schools, including the Manor House School near London. He received additional schooling after the family's return to Richmond five years later. In 1826 Poe entered Thomas Jefferson's new University of Virginia at Charlottesville, where he read widely in contemporary literature and showed great proficiency in the study of Latin, Greek, French, Spanish, and Italian. Being pressed for funds, however, he meanwhile accumulated a gambling debt in a vain attempt to meet his expenses. He also demonstrated that alcohol, even in small amounts, had a disastrous effect upon him, signaling the beginning of his struggle with a weakness that he was to battle the rest of his life.

Neither circumstance was pleasing to Allan, who refused to pay Poe's debt, took him out of college, and put him to work in his own business. Poe soon ran away to Boston, where his first published work, *Tamerlane and Other Poems*, was brought out in paperback in 1827. In desperate need, he enlisted in the U.S. army in the same year. He served for two years under the assumed name of Edgar A. Perry and was promoted to sergeant major before securing an honorable discharge. His guardian, with whom he was reconciled for a time, then helped with his application for an appointment to the U.S. Military Academy at West Point. Poe was expelled from the academy after only six months, however, due to his poor attitude.

Beginning his attempt to support himself by writing, Poe went to New York, where his next volume of poems was published in 1831. Not long afterwards he moved to Baltimore. It was while he was living there that Poe, whose work had gone largely unnoticed until then, turned from verse to prose fiction. Drawing upon his own peculiar and often macabre genius, he showed himself to be the master of a unique form of short story. His writing—mysterious, full of suspense, rhythmic, at once controlled and passionate—has been often copied but never duplicated.

Poe's earliest real recognition came in 1833, when he won a prize offered by the Baltimore *Saturday Visitor* for his tale "A MS. Found in a Bottle." Publication of the story led indirectly to Poe's becoming a contributor to, and from 1835 to 1837 editor of, the *Southern Literary Messenger* in Richmond, whose circulation increased sevenfold as a result of his editing and brilliant literary criticism. Meanwhile, he married his 13-year-old cousin, Virginia Clemm, and in 1837 moved to New York with her and her mother. Unable to support his family there, the next year he went to Philadelphia, where he worked as a freelance writer and as an editor, first of *Burton's Gentleman's Magazine* and then of *Graham's Magazine*. In the latter magazine, Poe published his pioneering detective story, "The Murders in the Rue Morgue."

Poe's talent increased the circulation of *Graham's* tenfold, making it the leading literary magazine in the United States before he left it in 1842. The next year he won a prize of $100 for his story "The Gold Bug," which was printed in Philadelphia's *Dollar Newspaper* and became the best-known example of the detective story. The publication of this and other tales notwithstanding, it was a time of extreme hardship. Poe, with no resources, was often in need of the necessities of life, and his wife, whom he would later memorialize as his "beautiful Annabel Lee," was ill with tuberculosis. They moved to New York in 1844 and Poe became subeditor of the New York *Evening Mirror*, which published "The Raven," his most famous poem. The next year he became, for some months, editor of the *Broadway Journal*.

In the spring of 1846, Poe rented a small cottage at Fordham, now part of New York City's borough of the Bronx. It was in this house, now a museum (in Poe Park on Grand Concourse at East 193rd Street), that his wife died in January 1847, leaving him overcome with grief. It was also here that he composed some of his best-known lyrics, including his haunting poem "The Bells." His other works included "The Fall of the House of Usher," "The Pit and the Pendulum," and "The Tell-Tale Heart." Poe, who suffered from cardiovascular problems, outlived his wife by less than three years.

In the summer of 1849, Poe returned to Richmond, but he left for New York again in late September. En route to New York, he fell ill in Baltimore and was taken unconscious to a hospital. When he died on October 7, 1849, he was buried in an unmarked grave in the churchyard of Baltimore's Westminster Presbyterian Church. The grave was not marked until 1875, when Baltimore schoolteachers successfully raised enough money to erect a modest headstone.

Poe died at the age of 40, after a short, turbulent, troubled, and often unhappy life. However, history remembers him as one of America's greatest writers and a pioneer in suspense and horror fiction.

Isaiah Thomas's Birthday

Isaiah Thomas, an important but often overlooked figure in the American Revolution, was born in Boston, Massachusetts, on January 19, 1749. He was the youngest of three children in an impoverished Boston family. At the age of six, he became an indentured servant to Boston printer Zachariah Fowle, where as a printer's apprentice he began his future career.

Thomas's indentured servitude ended when he was 16, and after moving several times he came to settle in Worcester, Massachusetts, where he opened his own publishing business. He was active in the growing colonial dissent movement against British rule, and was particularly outspoken in his criticism of the Stamp Act of 1765. Beginning in 1771, he began to secretly meet with leaders of the colonial movement, including such notable figures as John Hancock, James Otis, and Paul Revere. On November 14, 1771, he began to publish an underground periodical titled *The Massachusetts Spy*. When the American Revolution began in 1775, the British occupation of the city of Boston forced Thomas to flee Worcester with his family. During the Revolution, he served in the first skirmishes at Lexington and Concord, and continued to print pro-colonial literature.

After the Revolution Thomas returned to Worcester and resumed his printing enterprise. During his lifetime his shop produced hundreds of titles. He also wrote a two-volume treatise on the printing industry, *The History of Printing in America With a Biography of Printers and an Account of Newspapers*, published in 1810. This work is perhaps the leading authority on the printing industry in America during colonial times and the early post-Revolutionary era. Isaiah Thomas died on April 4, 1831, in Worcester.

January 20

Martin Luther King Day

This is a movable event.

Martin Luther King Jr. had a simple dream, "that one day this nation will live out the true meaning of its creed: 'We hold these truths to be self-evident, that all men are created equal.'" Born on January 15, 1929, King devoted his life to trying to transform this ideal into reality. A personification of hope and justice to some, and an object of scorn and vilification to others, King pursued his dream until an assassin struck him down in Memphis, Tennessee, on April 4, 1968.

The son of Martin Luther King Sr., pastor of the Ebenezer Baptist Church in Atlanta, Georgia, young King attended public schools in that city and then went to Atlanta's Morehouse College. It was during his junior year there that he decided on a career in the ministry. He was ordained in his father's church in 1947.

Following his graduation from Morehouse in 1948, King continued his studies at the racially integrated Crozer Theological Seminary in Chester, Pennsylvania. He was an outstanding student and the first African American in the school's history to be elected class president. He received the B.D. degree and won a fellowship for further graduate study. In 1951 King began his doctoral studies in theology at Boston University. There he met Coretta Scott, a graduate student in music, and in 1953 they were married. King eventually completed his doctoral dissertation and in 1958 was awarded a Ph.D. degree, but in the meantime his work in the civil rights movement had brought him national prominence.

In 1954, King returned to the South to become pastor of the Dexter Avenue Baptist Church in Montgomery, Alabama. For a year, the young minister performed routine duties for his largely black congregation. Then, on December 1, 1955, Rosa Parks, a black seamstress in Montgomery, refused to obey a bus driver's order to give up her seat to a white male passenger. Rosa Parks's defiance of the segregationist practice of forcing blacks to sit in the rear of buses and to surrender their seats to whites resulted in her being fined $14. It also marked the beginning of a citywide bus boycott by Montgomery's 50,000 black residents. Montgomery's established black leaders initiated the boycott, but they chose King, who was a relatively recent arrival in the city and who had not yet identified himself with any local black faction, to lead the campaign. The boycott aroused national attention and gave King an opportunity to dramatize his belief in the efficacy of peaceful civil disobedience.

When in the course of the boycott he was arrested, the 27-year-old minister exhorted his followers, "If we are arrested every day, if we are exploited every day . . . don't ever let anyone pull you so low as to hate them." Even when his home was bombed, King cautioned more militant blacks against seeking violent revenge. And, in the end, his belief in peaceful protest seemed justified. After the Supreme Court ruled on November 13, 1956, that segregation on buses was unconstitutional, city authorities announced compliance. Integrated bus service was begun in Montgomery on December 21, 1956.

The Montgomery bus boycott made King an undisputed leader in the civil rights movement. In 1957 he helped organize the Southern Christian Leadership Conference, composed of black ministers and professionals, which gave him an organizational base upon which he extended his civil rights campaign throughout the South. During 1961, the conference sponsored freedom rides. On these rides, teams composed of black and white volunteers (mostly young people) tested southern compliance with the 1956 Supreme Court decision banning segregation on buses and other transport facilities.

In April 1963 King launched a massive civil rights campaign in Birmingham, Alabama. For five weeks, black citizens participated in protest marches and sit-ins at lunch counters where they traditionally had been refused service, and they picketed stores that condoned segregationist practices. These peaceful activities elicited a violent response from many of Birmingham's white citizens. The police turned dogs and firehoses on the demonstrators, and white supremacists were responsible for the bombing of a black church, which caused the deaths of four young black girls.

King was arrested during the Birmingham campaign and spent five days in jail. During his confinement, he issued a 9,000-word letter in which he recorded his feeling that "the Negro's great stumbling block in the stride toward freedom is not the White Citizens Counciler or the Ku Klux Klanner, but the white moderate who is more devoted to order than to justice."

After Birmingham the cry of "Freedom Now" resounded throughout the United States. Protest marches, picketing, and sit-ins took place in many localities during the summer of 1963, but the culmination of the campaign for civil rights was the march on Washington that took place on August 28 of that year. More than 200,000 blacks and whites gathered in the nation's capital on that day to demand racial equality and, in the shadow of the Lincoln Memorial, this great throng heard Martin Luther King Jr. exclaim:

I am happy to join with you today in what will go down in history as the greatest demonstration for freedom in the history of our nation.

Five score years ago, a great American, in whose symbolic shadow we stand today, signed the Emancipation Proclamation. This momentous decree came as a great beacon light of hope to millions of Negro slaves, who had been seared in the flames of withering injustice. It came as a joyous daybreak to end the long night of their captivity. But one hundred years later, the Negro still is not free. One hundred years later, the life of the Negro is still sadly crippled by the manacles of segregation and the chains of discrimination.

One hundred years later, the Negro lives on a lonely island of poverty in the midst of a vast ocean of material prosperity. One hundred years later, the Negro is still languishing in the corners of American society and finds himself an exile in his own land. So we've come here today to dramatize a shameful condition.

In a sense we have come to our nation's capital to cash a check. When the architects of our republic wrote the magnificent words of the Constitution and the Declaration of Independence, they were signing a promissory note to which every American was to fall heir.

This note was a promise that all men, yes, black men as well as white men, would be guaranteed the inalienable rights of life, liberty and the pursuit of happiness.

It is obvious today that America has defaulted on this promissory note insofar as her citizens of color are concerned. Instead of honoring this sacred obligation, America has given the Negro people a bad check, a check which has come back marked "insufficient funds."

But we refuse to believe that the bank of justice is bankrupt. We refuse to believe that there are insufficient funds in the great vaults of opportunity of this nation. So we have come to cash this check, a check that will give us upon demand the riches of freedom and the security of justice.

We have also come to this hallowed spot to remind America of the fierce urgency of Now. This is no time to engage in the luxury of cooling off or to take the tranquilizing drug of gradualism. Now is the time to make real the promises of democracy. Now is the time to rise from the dark and desolate valley of segregation to the sunlit path of racial justice. Now is the time to lift our nation from the quicksands of racial injustice to the solid rock of brotherhood. Now is the time to make justice a reality for all of God's children.

It would be fatal for the nation to overlook the urgency of the moment. This sweltering summer of the Negro's legitimate discontent will not pass until there is an invigorating autumn of freedom and equality. Nineteen sixty-three is not an end but a beginning. Those who hope that the Negro needed to blow off steam and will now be content will have a rude awakening if the nation returns to business as usual.

There will be neither rest nor tranquility in America until the Negro is granted his citizenship rights. The whirlwinds of revolt will continue to shake the foundations of our nation until the bright day of justice emerges.

But there is something that I must say to my people who stand on the warm threshold which leads into the palace of justice. In the process of gaining our rightful place we must not be guilty of wrongful deeds.

Let us not seek to satisfy our thirst for freedom by drinking from the cup of bitterness and hatred. We must ever conduct our struggle on the high plane of dignity and discipline. We must not allow our creative protest to degenerate into physical violence. Again and again we must rise to the majestic heights of meeting physical force with soul force.

The marvelous new militancy which has engulfed the Negro community must not lead us to a distrust of all white people, for many of our white brothers, as evidenced by their presence here today, have come to realize that their destiny is tied up with our destiny. They have come to realize that their freedom is inextricably bound to our freedom. We cannot walk alone.

And as we walk, we must make the pledge that we shall always march ahead. We cannot turn back. There are those who are asking the devotees of civil rights, "When will you be satisfied?" We can never be satisfied as long as the Negro is the victim of the unspeakable horrors of police brutality.

We can never be satisfied as long as our bodies, heavy with the fatigue of travel, cannot gain lodging in the motels of the highways and the hotels of the cities. We cannot be satisfied as long as a Negro in Mississippi cannot vote and a Negro in New York believes he has nothing for which to vote.

No, no, we are not satisfied and we will not be satisfied until justice rolls down like waters and righteousness like a mighty stream.

I am not unmindful that some of you have come here out of great trials and tribulations. Some of you have come fresh from narrow jail cells. Some of you have come from areas where your quest for freedom left you battered by the storms of persecutions and staggered by the winds of police brutality. You have been the veterans of creative suffering. Continue to work with the faith that unearned suffering is redemptive.

Go back to Mississippi, go back to Alabama, go back to South Carolina, go back to Georgia, go back to Louisiana, go back to the slums and ghettos of our northern cities, knowing that somehow this situation can and will be changed.

Let us not wallow in the valley of despair. I say to you today, my friends, that even though we face the difficulties of today and tomorrow, I still have a dream. It is a dream deeply rooted in the American dream.

I have a dream that one day this nation will rise up and live out the true meaning of its creed—we hold these truths to be self-evident: that all men are created equal.

I have a dream that one day on the red hills of Georgia the sons of former slaves and the sons of former slave owners will be able to sit down together at the table of brotherhood.

I have a dream that one day even the state of Mississippi, a state sweltering with the heat of injustice, sweltering with the heat of oppression, will be transformed into an oasis of freedom and justice.

I have a dream that my four little children will one day live in a nation where they will not be judged by the color of their skin but by the content of their character.

I have a dream today!

I have a dream that one day, down in Alabama, with its vicious racists, with its governor having his lips dripping with the words of interposition and nullification; one day right down in Alabama little black boys and black girls will be able to join hands with little white boys and white girls as sisters and brothers.

I have a dream today!

I have a dream that one day every valley shall be exalted, and every hill and mountain shall be made low, the rough places will be made plain and the crooked places will be made straight and the glory of the Lord shall be revealed and all flesh shall see it together.

This is our hope. This is the faith that I will go back to the South with. With this faith we will be able to hew out of the mountain of despair a stone of hope. With this faith we will be able to transform the jangling discords of our nation into a beautiful symphony of brotherhood. With this faith we will be able to work together, to pray together, to struggle together, to go to jail together, to stand up for freedom together, knowing that we will be free one day. This will be the day, this will be the day when all of God's children will be able to sing with new meaning "My country 'tis of thee, sweet land of liberty, of thee I sing. Land where my fathers died, land of the Pilgrim's pride, from every mountainside, let freedom ring!" And if America is to be a great nation, this must become true.

And so let freedom ring from the prodigious hilltops of New Hampshire.

Let freedom ring from the mighty mountains of New York.

Let freedom ring from the heightening Alleghenies of Pennsylvania.

Let freedom ring from the snow-capped Rockies of Colorado.

Let freedom ring from the curvaceous slopes of California.

But not only that.

Let freedom ring from Stone Mountain of Georgia.

Let freedom ring from Lookout Mountain of Tennessee.

Let freedom ring from every hill and molehill of Mississippi, from every mountainside, let freedom ring!

And when this happens, when we allow freedom to ring, when we let it ring from every tenement and every hamlet, from every state and every city, we will be able to speed up that day when all of God's children, black men and white men, Jews and Gentiles, Protestants and Catholics, will be able to join hands and sing in the words of the old Negro spiritual, "Free at last, free at last. Thank God Almighty, we are free at last."

In 1965, civil rights activists turned their attention to the registration of black voters. In March of that year the Southern Christian Leadership Conference organized, and King led, demonstrations against unfair voting requirements in Selma, Alabama. As had been the case the year before in Birmingham, white racists in Selma reacted violently to the campaign. Police treated the demonstrators harshly, and hundreds of blacks were arrested. King himself was beaten and kicked, but after the drive ended 25,000 persons marched from Selma to Montgomery and there, from the steps of the state capitol, he addressed the assembled crowd.

In 1966, King took his civil rights campaign north. For several months he worked in a rented tenement in Chicago and attempted to initiate efforts to improve the city's slum housing. He led a march on the city hall to demand housing, welfare, education, and job reforms, and he also headed several protest marches into all-white neighborhoods, where he encountered hostility. King had only limited success in Chicago, but city officials and real estate brokers agreed to try to decrease housing segregation.

In the wake of several northern race riots in 1965 and 1966, black militants began to challenge King's moderate, nonviolent methods. King never repudiated those who marched to the rallying cry of "black power," but he remained true to his belief in nonviolence, saying: "The Negro needs the white man to free him from his fears. The white man needs the Negro to free him from his guilt. A doctrine of black supremacy is as evil as a doctrine of white supremacy."

King began to expand the scope of his movement to include other issues besides the fight for basic legal rights such as voting and using public facilities. He was an outspoken critic of American involvement in Vietnam, arguing that the war effort consumed resources that might otherwise have benefited the nation's poor. And he sought to dramatize the plight of the underprivileged with a Poor People's Campaign that was scheduled to begin in Washington, D.C., on April 22, 1968.

As planned, thousands of African Americans encamped in the nation's capital in the summer of 1968 to demonstrate to Congress the need for legislation that would provide better economic opportunities for the nation's poor. But their leader was not with them. On April 3, 1968, King went to Memphis, Tennessee, to help organize a strike of the city's predominantly black sanitation workers. There, on April 4, 1968, James Earl Ray fired a shot that killed King on the balcony of the motel where King had been staying. The shot ended the life of a man commonly acknowledged as one of history's greatest leaders in the continuing struggle to achieve full equality for the nation's black citizens. Violent riots broke out in many cities after King's assassination. There have been periodic allegations that Ray was part of a larger conspiracy against King, but none of these allegations has been proven conclusively as of this date.

During his lifetime, Martin Luther King Jr. was honored by many nations and was a recipient of the Nobel Peace Prize. Today, he is honored by the federal holiday known as Martin Luther King Day, which takes place on the third Monday of every January. Throughout the nation, many highways, schools, parks, housing projects, and other civic works have been dedicated to King.

Inauguration Day

The term of the president of the United States started on March 4 until the adoption of the 20th Amendment to the Constitution in 1933. Presidents elected since then have taken office on January 20. Franklin Delano Roosevelt was the first chief executive to do so at the time of his second inauguration in January 1937. When Inauguration Day falls on a Sunday, the oath of office is administered privately, on or ahead of schedule, but the public ceremonies are generally transferred to the following day. This was the case in 1821, 1849, 1877, and 1917, when the ceremonies took place on March 5, and in 1957 and 1985, when they were conducted on January 21. In future years, Inauguration Day will also have to be postponed a day in 2013 and 2041.

It was more or less by accident that the nation's first president, George Washington, was not inaugurated until April 30, 1789. Part of the cause was delay in assembling a quorum of the legislators who were needed to count the presidential votes. Although they were due in New York City, then the nation's capital, on March 4, it was not until April 6 that a quorum was achieved and the votes counted. Washington was informed of his unanimous election on April 14 and left his home at Mt. Vernon, Virginia, for the capital two days later. After arriving in New York, he took the oath of office on the steps of the old Federal Hall.

At the beginning of his second term in 1793, Washington took the oath in front of Independence Hall in Philadelphia, then serving as the capital. John Adams was also inaugurated in Philadelphia, in 1797, but by the time Thomas Jefferson was elected, the seat of government had been moved to Washington, D.C., and it was there that his inauguration took place in 1801. Escorted by a body of militia and a procession of citizens, Jefferson walked to the Capitol from a nearby boardinghouse and took the oath of office in the Senate chamber. In 1809, James Madison was the first president to take the oath in the hall of the House of Representatives, which was used for the ceremony again in 1813, 1821, 1825, and 1833. In 1817, James Monroe was sworn in at the east portico of the Capitol, and this became the customary location for the presidential oath-taking for over a century and a half. However, some recent presidents, beginning with Ronald Reagan, have preferred to be sworn in at the west front of the Capitol, since that side overlooks scenic lawns and gardens.

Over the years, the inauguration ceremonies have slowly developed into a set pattern. At noon, or shortly thereafter, the chief justice of the United States Supreme Court administers the oath of office to the president, who customarily rests his hand on the Bible as he declares: "I do solemnly swear that I will faithfully execute the office of President of the United States, and will, to the best of my ability, preserve, protect and defend the Constitution of the United States." After taking this oath, which is mandated by the Constitution, the chief executive delivers an inaugural address. In 1841, William Henry Harrison gave the longest address (a one hour and forty-five minute speech of some 8,500 words); George Washington delivered the shortest (approximately 135 words) at his second inauguration in 1793. Harrison also has the unenviable distinction of being the only president to die because of his inaugural address: He gave his speech without a coat or hat despite the cold weather, contracted pneumonia, and died a month later.

Today, Inauguration Day is also the occasion for a variety of parades and events in the nation's capital. The size of the parades has varied greatly, depending upon such factors as world and national conditions, the president's personal inclination, and weather. Washington can experience some very severe winter storms in the month of January, and a fair share of inaugural celebrations have been hampered by blizzard or downpour. Even when weather is not an overriding consideration, inaugural festivities usually are more modest when a president is elected to a second term or when a change in the presidency does not involve a change in political party.

Leon Ames's Birthday

Leon Waycoff, later known as Leon Ames, was born in Portland, Indiana, on January 20, 1903. Although he was never one of the great movie stars, he was an important figure in the movie industry and one of the most long-lived of actors, with a list of film credits that spans over 50 years.

Ames's first movie was the 1932 horror classic *Murders in the Rue Morgue*. He would ultimately appear in more than 100 movies. He was primarily a character actor, and played in westerns, comedies, dramas, and romances. Some of his more famous movies include the classic *Meet Me in St. Louis* (1944), *The Postman Always Rings Twice* (1946), *Little Women* (1949), and *The Absent-Minded Professor* (1961).

In addition to his prolific movie career, Ames was active in the Screen Actors Guild. In 1933 he was one of the 19 actors who met in order to form that organization. The guild has grown to represent tens of thousands of people involved in the movie industry. Ames served as a member of the guild's board of directors for over 30 years, and was chosen as its recording secretary in 1947. He also served as vice president from 1952 to 1956 and as president from 1957 to 1958.

In his later years, Ames ceased to be actively involved in the Screen Actors Guild, but he continued his vigorous movie career. He appeared in films such as *Peggy Sue Got Married* (1986) while in his eighties. Ames died on October 12, 1993, at the age of 90 in Laguna Beach, California.

January 21

Stonewall Jackson's Birthday

Thomas Jonathan Jackson, better known as "Stonewall," was born on January 21, 1824, in Clarksburg, Virginia (now part of West Virginia). The state of Virginia, regarding Jackson as a Virginian who won most of his fame as a Confederate general within its borders, considers him one of its heroes. Virginia observes the anniversary of his birth in conjunction with that of Robert E. Lee (see January 19) and Martin Luther King (see Jan-

uary 20). The third Monday in January is therefore a state holiday known as Lee-Jackson-King Day.

Stonewall Jackson was the son of Jonathan Jackson, a lawyer who died when his son was a small boy, leaving the family almost destitute. Young Jackson later added Jonathan as a middle name in memory of his father. After his widowed mother had remarried, only to die soon afterwards, Thomas Jackson was reared by an uncle, Cummins Jackson. Through hard work and self-discipline, since he had little opportunity for education beyond attendance at a small country school, Jackson obtained in 1842 an appointment to the U.S. Military Academy at West Point, New York. Although handicapped by inadequate preparation, he graduated in the upper third of his class and received a commission as a second lieutenant of artillery in 1846.

The young officer was sent almost immediately to serve in the Mexican War. In Mexico, he distinguished himself at the conflicts in Veracruz, Cerro Gordo, and Chapultepec. He became a major within 18 months of his graduation. From 1848 to 1851, Jackson was stationed at Fort Columbus and Fort Hamilton, both in New York Harbor. In 1851 he received orders transferring him to Florida, but decided instead to take a position at the Virginia Military Institute in Lexington, Virginia, and resigned his commission in February 1852.

Jackson returned from a trip to Europe in 1856 to find that the threat of war, which he considered "the sum of all evils," was growing between the North and the South. He remained at the Virginia Military Institute until the sectional differences erupted in the Civil War in April 1861. He then offered his services to the seceding state of Virginia and was ordered to Richmond with part of the Virginia Military Institute cadet corps. When Jackson received a commission as colonel of infantry and was assigned to command strategic Harpers Ferry, one member of the Virginia Convention, which had to approve the appointment, asked, "Who is this Major Jackson?" Samuel McDowell Moore, the representative for Rockbridge County, in which Lexington was located, replied, "He is one who, if you order him to hold a post, will never leave it alive to be occupied by the enemy."

On June 17, 1861, Jackson was promoted to the rank of brigadier general. He was soon called upon to help defeat the strong Union assault in the first battle of Bull Run on July 21. The impetuosity of the first federal attack caused confusion in the Confederate ranks, with 2,000 men "shouting each some suggestion to his neighbor, their voices mingling with the noise of the shells hurtling through the trees overhead." As the outcome of the battle hung in suspense, there occurred one of the dramatic episodes of the war. Confederate brigadier general Barnard E. Bee, trying desperately to rally his panic-stricken troops, glanced toward nearby Henry Hill, where he saw Jackson and his men standing bold and steadfast. Grasping inspiration from the moment, Bee achieved immortality by shouting: "Look, there is Jackson standing like a stone wall. Rally behind the Virginians!" The Southern forces rallied; the Union assault was repulsed; and the sobriquet "Stonewall" was forever attached to Jackson's name.

Stonewall Jackson's subsequent career as a soldier was brilliant. Promoted to major general on October 7, 1861, he was given command of the Confederate forces in the Shenandoah Valley on November 5. His campaign from March to June 1862 is sometimes considered the most remarkable display of strategy and tactics in American history. It is regarded as a classic example of what a meager force can accomplish when commanded by a leader who realizes the importance of determination, mobility, and secrecy in warfare. With incredible speed, Jackson's army marched and countermarched a total of 630 miles to defeat four Union armies in 39 days. His dashing campaign staved off massive federal attacks on beleaguered Richmond and kept Washington, braced for a Southern invasion, on the brink of nervous prostration for weeks on end. With audacity tempered by skill, Jackson, with fewer than 20,000 men, neutralized the action of over 175,000 enemy troops.

A Confederate soldier tersely summarized Jackson's style of action: "All Old Jackson gave us was a musket, a hundred rounds, and a . . . blanket, and he druv us like hell." Jackson was definitely something of a character. He was often dirty and unkempt in his personal appearance, refused for religious reasons to fight on a Sunday, and was very shy and taciturn in public. However, he was a successful commander, so when Robert E. Lee succeeded to the command of the Army of Northern Virginia on June 1, 1862, he summoned Jackson to take part in the Seven Days battles on the Yorktown peninsula late in that month.

Despite unspectacular actions at places such as White Oak Swamp and Beaver Creek Dam, Jackson showed his mettle in August by executing one of his renowned marches. In its course he destroyed the federal base at Manassas Junction on August 27, and, a few days later, participated in the offensive against General John Pope at the second battle of Bull Run, which permitted Lee to carry the war out of Virginia and into enemy territory. Leading Lee's drive into Maryland, Jackson seized Harpers Ferry on September 15, 1862, and distinguished himself again at Antietam two days later. At the close of 1862, owing to the military genius of Lee and Jackson, Union forces were as far from Richmond as they had been at the beginning of the year.

Jackson, having been promoted to lieutenant general on October 10, 1862, was henceforth recognized as Lee's right-hand man and was given command over one of the two corps into which the Army of Northern Virginia had been divided. After the resumption of the Union offensive in the spring of 1863, Jackson and Lee planned to attack General Joseph Hooker's troops, camped near Chancellorsville, Virginia, in a thick, dismal forest almost 15 miles square, termed the Wilderness. During the night of May 1–2, the two Southern commanders devised one of the most daring strokes in the course of the war. Although Hooker had about 100,000 men and the Confederates had fewer than half that number, Lee and Jackson boldly agreed to split their force. Lee, with fewer than 20,000 men, would hold the ground, while Jackson would lead the remaining men through the dense undergrowth to launch a surprise attack on the enemy flank. In the afternoon of May 2, Jackson's soldiers, having accomplished the move undetected, stormed out, red battle flags waving, in a formation more than a mile wide and three divisions deep. Within minutes the Union flank had crumbled, its broken remnants dispersing in confusion, while Lee pounded in front.

Upon learning the news of the Union defeat, President Abraham Lincoln exclaimed: "My God! My God! What will the country say?" However, Chancellorsville was the costliest victory the South ever won. In addition to suffering some 13,000 casualties, Jackson, out surveying his position after dark, was mistaken by some of his own soldiers for the enemy and attacked. Reeling in the saddle, the general sustained three wounds, with bullets penetrating his right hand and smashing his left arm from elbow to shoulder. After his left arm had been amputated in a field hospital behind the lines, Jackson was moved to safer quarters near Guiney's Station, Virginia.

Hearing about Jackson's injury, General Lee wrote on May 3, 1863: "General: I have just received your note, informing me that you were wounded. I cannot express my regret at the occurrence. Could I have directed events, I should have chosen for the good of the country to be disabled in your stead. I congratulate you upon the victory, which is due to your skill and energy." While Jackson was being treated, Lee wrote, "He has lost his left arm, but I have lost my right," a reference to Lee's dependence on Jackson as his right-hand man. On May 7, Jackson developed pneumonia, and three days later he died at the age of 39, murmuring, "Let us cross over the river and rest under the shade of the trees."

The death of Stonewall Jackson was disastrous for the Confederate cause. Never again would Lee have at his side a fellow commander who could so swiftly grasp his strategy and so brilliantly execute it. Never again would the Southern army carry out those bold thrusts that had enabled it to wrest victory from numerically superior forces. Although his career in high field command lasted only a little over two years, Jackson is regarded as one of the most brilliant military leaders of the Civil War. In accordance with his last wishes, he was buried in Lexington, Virginia.

John Breckinridge's Birthday

John Cabell Breckinridge, the fourteenth vice president of the United States, was born on January 21, 1821, in Lexington, Kentucky. He attended Centre College in Danville, Kentucky, and graduated in 1837. He became a lawyer, but entered the United States Army in order to serve in the Mexican War.

After the war he decided to enter politics and was elected to the Kentucky House of Representatives. He was elected to the U.S. House of Representatives in Washington in 1851 and served there until 1855. Like most southerners, Breckinridge was a Democrat, and he became a leader in the effort to resist the abolition of slavery. In the presidential campaign of 1856, the Democratic candidate was James Buchanan and Breckinridge was the vice-presidential candidate. After Buchanan's election, Breckinridge served as vice president until 1860, when the proslavery faction of the Democratic Party nominated him as their candidate against Republican Abraham Lincoln and two other splinter candidates (Stephen Douglas and John Bell). Breckinridge came in second in the four-man race, receiving 72 electoral votes to Lincoln's 180, while the remaining two candidates combined received a total of only 51.

After Lincoln's election, Breckinridge briefly served as United States senator from Kentucky, but with the outbreak of the Civil War in 1861 he left office in order to serve the Confederacy. He rose to the rank of general, and saw action at Shiloh, Vicksburg, Chickamauga, and New Market. In January 1865 he was appointed the Confederacy's secretary of war. Shortly thereafter, however, he had to leave the Confederate capital of Richmond, Virginia, as the approaching Union forces threatened to occupy the city. He helped negotiate an amnesty for Confederate troops and then left for Florida, from which he traveled to Cuba, then England, and eventually Canada. After receiving a pardon, he returned to the United States in 1869 and spent the rest of his life practicing law

in Lexington, Kentucky. Breckinridge died on May 17, 1875.

Wolfman Jack's Birthday

Robert Smith, better known as Wolfman Jack, the pioneering radio disc jockey, was born in Brooklyn, New York, on January 21, 1938. In the early 1960s, when rock and roll music was still relatively new and somewhat controversial, he achieved fame as a disc jockey for XERF-AM in Mexico. The Mexican border station was widely listened to in the United States, since it broadcast at 25,000 watts, approximately five times the legal limit for American radio stations at the time.

Smith adopted the name Wolfman Jack, since radio disc jockeys were expected to have nicknames and he liked horror movies. From the Mexican radio station, he was free to broadcast a variety of rock and roll, blues, and hillbilly music that was still shunned by many American stations. Further, he was free to develop his on-the-air demeanor, particularly his wolf howls and other eccentricities. As rock and roll music became more popular in the 1960s, Wolfman Jack went from being controversial to being mainstream. During the 1970s he appeared in the 1973 movie classic *American Graffiti*; hosted his own television program, *The Wolfman Jack Show*; and appeared in several advertising campaigns.

During the rest of his life, Wolfman Jack made periodic radio, television, and motion picture appearances. He was displaced in notoriety, however, by such arrivals as Howard Stern and Don Imus. In 1995 he went on tour to promote his new book, *Have Mercy, the Confession of the Original Party Animal*. However, his party animal days caught up with him. Upon returning home to Belvidere, North Carolina, he died of a heart attack on July 1, 1995.

January 22

The Supreme Court Holds That Abortion Is a Constitutional Right

On January 22, 1973, the Supreme Court of the United States decided the case of *Roe* v. *Wade*, setting forth one of the most far-reaching constitutional precedents in stating that a woman has a constitutional right to obtain an abortion as an aspect of her protected rights of privacy. Despite some refinements and subsequent limitations, as of this writing in the late 1990s the *Roe* decision still holds.

The Supreme Court's written decision was a lengthy one, containing many legal complications, but the *Roe* decision can be summarized as follows:

(1) During the first three months of her pregnancy (the "first trimester"), a woman has a largely unfettered right to obtain an abortion, and no law can prohibit her from obtaining one or seeking the advice and assistance of a doctor.

(2) For the second three months of the pregnancy (the "second trimester"), the law may impose reasonable regulations on the abortion process, but these restrictions must be reasonably related to the mother's health and not simply a means of denying access to abortion services.

(3) In the final three months of the pregnancy (the "third trimester"), when the fetus is recognizably human and largely capable of life independent of the mother, the law has considerable authority to regulate and even forbid abortion procedures.

Historically, it had almost always been illegal to obtain an abortion. Under the common law of England, which the American colonies largely inherited after the American Revolution, an abortion was a felony subject to the very severe punishments of the time. Throughout the 19th century and into the 20th century, underground or "back alley" abortions were available, but only at some considerable risk to the health of the mother and at the risk of criminal prosecution of both her and the doctor involved. In many states, it was also illegal to distribute information about birth control. By the 1960s, approximately a dozen states had moderated their abortion restrictions, but for most American women access to an abortion was either impossible, extremely risky, or extremely expensive, available only to those wealthy enough to travel to countries such as Sweden where abortions were legal. Beginning with such cases as *Griswold* v. *Connecticut* (1965), however, the Supreme Court of the United States indicated an increasing willingness to consider extending the various constitutional rights of privacy provided by the United States Constitution to a woman's decision to obtain an abortion.

In 1969, a 21-year-old woman named Norma McCorvey became pregnant and wanted to abort her fetus in her home state of Texas. However, under Texas law abortions were illegal except when necessary to save the mother's life. McCorvey's situation became a test case for civil rights groups looking to challenge antiabortion laws. To protect her privacy, McCorvey was named "Jane Roe" in the lawsuit. After several years of litigation, the case reached the Supreme Court, where it was argued before the nine justices on December 13, 1971, and reargued on October 11, 1972. In a deeply divided decision, riddled with dissents and reservations, the Court set forth its holding that a woman had the right to an abortion according to the three-trimester framework outlined above.

The Supreme Court's decision was a landmark affirmation of the constitutional right to an abortion, but in the following decades it sparked considerable political controversy. For the supporters of a woman's right to an abortion, it was something less than the outright endorsement that they were looking for. For opponents, it was a dangerous exercise of power by the Supreme Court over policy matters that traditionally had been left to the legislature, and an infringement on traditional religious and moral sensibilities.

The debate over abortion turned into a touchy political issue, and overturning the *Roe* decision became a goal of the Republican Party in 1980 with the election of Ronald Reagan to the presidency. Although the decision has been tested in the courts by various groups, including in some instances by the federal government itself, as of this writing *Roe* remains largely intact. Given the difficulty of reconciling the value of saving human life with the right of women to self-determination, many Americans agreed with President Bill Clinton in the 1990s when he stated that abortions should ideally be "safe, legal, and rare."

Frederick Moore Vinson's Birthday

Frederick Moore Vinson, the 13th chief justice of the United States, was born in Louisa, Kentucky, on January 22, 1890. Vinson, who during his long political career served in all three branches of government, came from a family of modest means. James Vinson, the jailkeeper in Louisa, died shortly after the birth of his son Frederick, and responsibility for raising the baby fell upon his widow, Virginia Ferguson Vinson. Determined that her son should receive a good education, she took in boarders to earn money. Frederick himself contributed to the family funds by running errands and working in local stores.

Vinson prepared at Kentucky Normal School to be a teacher, but by the time of his graduation in 1908, he had decided not to pursue a career in education. Instead, he enrolled at Centre College of Kentucky in Danville. There he excelled in his studies, graduated first in his class in 1909, and then remained at Centre to work for a degree in law. During his years in law school, Vinson taught mathematics in a local preparatory school to help support himself. This extracurricular work did not

By Harris and Ewing. Collection of the Supreme Court of the United States.

Frederick Moore Vinson

prevent him from achieving an outstanding academic record. He received his law degree in 1911 and was awarded both the junior and the senior law prizes.

Vinson then returned to Louisa, where he opened his own law office. Two years later he became Louisa's city attorney, a post he held until 1917, when he joined the U.S. Army. He remained in the military throughout World War I, and when the war ended he resumed his law practice and his career in public service. The young veteran became commonwealth attorney for Kentucky's 32nd judicial district in 1921. Three years later, he was a successful Democratic candidate for the U.S. House of Representatives.

With the exception of 1928, when a large number of Democrats lost in the face of a Republican landslide headed by presidential candidate Herbert Hoover, Vinson was returned to Congress in every election from 1926 to 1938. He supported most New Deal legislation and was an especially ardent proponent of measures benefiting labor. In particular, he advocated the Guffey-Snyder Bituminous Coal Stabilization Act of 1935, which sought to regulate the soft coal industry according to the provisions of the National Recovery Act soft coal code. When the Supreme Court found this act unconstitutional in 1936, he cosponsored the Guffey-Vinson Bituminous Coal Act of 1937. This measure promulgated a code of fair competition

in the soft coal industry, provided federal regulation of bituminous coal output, imposed a revenue tax on soft coal, and penalized those producers who did not adhere to the code with a heavy tax.

During his last years in Congress, Vinson served as chairman of the influential tax subcommittee of the House Ways and Means Committee. Shortly after assuming that post in 1936, he worked for and won congressional approval of a tax on undistributed profits. He was also largely responsible for congressional passage of the Revenue Act of 1938, which made several important modifications in the federal tax structure.

In 1938 President Franklin D. Roosevelt appointed Vinson an associate justice of the U.S. Court of Appeals for the District of Columbia, and in 1942 named him the chief judge of the three-member Emergency Court of Appeals, which was set up to handle disputes arising from World War II price controls. Vinson remained on the bench until May 1943; he then moved to the executive branch of the government, where he became the director of the Office of Economic Stabilization. In this post he grappled with the difficult task of curbing inflation in the wartime economy. Although he alienated many people during his two-year tenure, his efforts were fairly successful.

Vinson became the director of the Office of War Mobilization and Reconversion in April 1945 and held that position until President Harry S. Truman appointed him secretary of the treasury three months later, on July 23, 1945. Vinson's knowledge of tax problems and his experience as a member of Congress made him an excellent choice to head the Treasury Department during the difficult transition from a wartime to a peacetime economy. He served in the post for less than one year, but in that short time he was able to recommend and secure congressional approval for a bill that provided for the first reduction in federal tax rates in 14 years and that exempted almost 12 million people from the tax rolls.

In 1946, President Truman nominated Vinson to be chief justice of the United States Supreme Court, and in June of that year the Senate confirmed the appointment. Truman's selection of Vinson to succeed the late chief justice Harlan F. Stone was no doubt prompted as much by Vinson's reputation as a mediator as by his legal expertise. In 1946 the associate justices of the Supreme Court were divided into two factions. The groups, one led by Justice Hugo Black of Alabama and the other by Justice Robert Jackson of New York, differed on personal as well as constitutional issues, and reports of feuds among the Supreme Court members had resulted in a serious loss of prestige to the high tribunal.

Truman's faith in Vinson's abilities as a peace-maker were not unfounded. Within a year of his confirmation as chief justice, overt hostility among the associate justices had come to an end. During Vinson's seven years as chief justice, the Supreme Court ruled on far fewer cases than it had in the years prior to World War II, but the 758 decisions that were handed down during his tenure involved some of the most pressing issues of the postwar era, such as labor relations and civil rights.

In one of the first cases to come before the Court after his confirmation, Chief Justice Vinson concurred in the decision upholding fines against the United Mine Workers and the union's chief, John L. Lewis, for contempt of court in continuing a 1946 coal strike after the federal government had seized the mines. Vinson also wrote the major-ity opinion in the 1950 case of the *American Com-munications Association, CIO, et al. v. Douds*, which found the provision of the controversial Taft-Hartley Act of 1947 requiring labor union of-ficers to sign a non-Communist affidavit to be con-stitutional. However, Vinson was not always on the side of the majority in labor decisions. When the Court, by a six-to-three vote in 1952, invalidated President Truman's seizure of the strikebound steel plants that year, Vinson defended the presi-dent's action, saying in a dissenting opinion that the Founding Fathers "created a government sub-ject to law but not left subject to inertia when vigor and initiative are required."

Between 1948 and 1950, the Supreme Court heard and ruled on a number of important cases dealing with racial segregation in state universi-ties. In the 1948 decision in the case of *Sipuel* v. *Board of Regents*, the Court ruled that Oklahoma could not refuse to admit a qualified black to the state's law school unless it made equivalent legal training available to him within the state. As a re-sult of this opinion, Texas set up a separate law school for the blacks of that state. In the 1950 case of *Sweatt* v. *Painter*, however, the Court ruled that this law school was inferior to that of the Universi-ty of Texas. In reaching this verdict, the Court took into account such qualitative factors as the pres-tige of faculty members and opportunities for con-tact with distinguished lawyers and judges. The *Sweatt* opinion had broad implications. It was eventually interpreted to mean that black gradu-ate schools were by their very nature inferior and unequal, and that for this reason states could not refuse to open all their publicly supported schools of higher learning to blacks.

In the case of *McLaurin* v. *Oklahoma State Re-gents*, the Vinson court took yet another step to-ward ending the "separate but equal" doctrine that had prevailed since the *Plessy* v. *Ferguson* decision

of 1896. The *McLaurin* case involved the rights of black students in state universities. In 1950 the Court ruled in this case that black students who had gained admission to state schools of higher learning could not be segregated within these schools or in any other way be treated in a differ-ent or discriminatory manner.

Vinson, who had been mentioned as a possible Democratic presidential candidate in 1952, died unexpectedly of a heart attack on September 8, 1953. He was survived by his widow, Roberta Dix-on Vinson, and his two sons, Frederick Jr. and James Robert Vinson.

January 23

Twenty-Fourth Amendment Ratified

The 24th Amendment to the Constitution, forbid-ding collection of a poll tax as a requirement for voting in elections, became effective on January 23, 1964, when it was ratified by the South Dakota legislature. As the 38th state to take such action, South Dakota completed the requirement that three-fourths of the nation's states ratify an amendment before it can become law. The mea-sure was formalized in Washington, D.C., on Feb-ruary 4, when Bernard L. Boutin, head of the General Services Administration, after receiving notification of South Dakota's action, issued a doc-ument certifying that the ratification process had been completed. President Lyndon B. Johnson, who signed the document as a witness, declared, "Today, the people of this land have abolished the poll tax as a condition for voting. By this act they have reaffirmed the simple but unbreakable theme of this Republic: Nothing is so valuable as liberty and nothing is so necessary to liberty as the freedom to vote without bans or barriers." Presi-dent Johnson also noted that, with enactment of the 24th Amendment, "there can be no one too poor to vote. . . . The only enemy to voting that we face today is indifference. Too many of our citi-zens treat casually what other people in other lands are ready to die for."

Specifically affected by the new amendment were the poll taxes that had existed until then in the five southern states of Alabama, Arkansas, Mississippi, Texas, and Virginia. Some of these states attempted to continue the poll taxes in state and local elections but national elections were a different matter. With passage of the 24th Amend-ment, the presidential election of November 1964 became the first in which no state exacted a poll tax.

The road to enactment of the 24th Amendment was a long one, beginning some 20 years earlier with congressional attempts to outlaw poll taxes by statute. Three different anti–poll tax bills passed by the House of Representatives were defeated in the Senate by filibusters conducted by southern senators. In 1949 a southerner of a different mind, Spessard L. Holland of Florida, introduced a proposal for abolishing poll taxes by means of a constitutional amendment. Each and every year until 1962, when the Senate finally voted its approval, Senator Holland reintroduced his proposal with a larger and larger number of co-sponsors, until finally there were 67 co-sponsors at the time of passage.

Senate approval of the 24th Amendment resolution on March 27 was followed by House approval by a vote of 295 to 86 on August 27. The measure was submitted to the states on September 14, 1962. Illinois was the first to concur officially (on November 14) in the long process of ratification. The measure officially became a part of the U.S. Constitution on February 4, 1964. As finally approved, the 24th Amendment to the Constitution reads as follows:

SECTION 1. The right of citizens of the United States to vote in any primary or other election for President or Vice President, for electors for President or Vice President, or for Senator or Representative in Congress, shall not be denied or abridged by the United States or any State by reason of failure to pay any poll tax or other tax. SECTION 2. The Congress shall have the power to enforce this article by appropriate legislation.

Elizabeth Blackwell, First Woman in the United States to Receive a Medical Degree

On January 23, 1849, Elizabeth Blackwell made history when the Medical Institution of Geneva, New York, awarded her a medical degree, making her the first woman in the United States to officially become a doctor. Previously, women had been limited to such roles as midwives and nurses.

Elizabeth Blackwell was born in Bristol, England, on February 3, 1821. She was raised in a socially progressive family, and her father was active in the social reform movements of the time. She and her sisters were encouraged to consider careers outside the home, a concept that was almost unheard of in that day and age. In 1832, after her father's business was destroyed by fire, the family immigrated to the United States and settled in New York City.

In 1838, the family relocated to Cincinnati, Ohio, where Elizabeth's father passed away. In order to support themselves, the Blackwells opened a boarding school, and Elizabeth learned how to teach. In 1842 she left Cincinnati to accept a position in Henderson, Kentucky, and in 1844 she moved again to Asheville, North Carolina. There she began to pursue her interest in medicine, and she began to study both privately and with the assistance of some male doctors willing to tutor her. For several years, these means of independent study were all that were available to her, as her efforts to seek admission to a medical school were fruitless. In 1848, however, Geneva College in upstate New York granted her request for admission. Whether Geneva's decision was due to its progressive tendencies is questionable, as several sources indicate that she was admitted simply as a practical joke. Apparently the faculty submitted the matter to the student body (all male, of course), stipulating that the application would have to be unanimously approved if Blackwell was going to be admitted. The student body, finding some humor in the situation, did not cast a single negative vote.

At the time, the required curriculum was only one year long. Apparently, Elizabeth gained some measure of respect from her professors and fellow students. A hospital in Philadelphia allowed her to treat patients in the summer of 1848, although again her peers were reluctant to accept her.

After graduating from Geneva on January 23, 1849, Dr. Blackwell left for Europe to pursue additional studies in medicine. In 1851 she returned to New York City and opened her own practice. She was shunned by her fellow doctors and by the public, but in 1856 her sister and another female friend, both of whom had recently also attended medical school, joined her enterprise. The team eventually founded a hospital, the New York Infirmary for Women and Children. The institution prospered, and established a medical school for women that would graduate hundreds of female doctors before it merged in 1899 with the Medical School of Cornell University.

Dr. Blackwell spent most of her final years in England, where she continued to teach and advocate increased opportunities for women in the medical profession. She died in Hastings, England, on May 31, 1910.

January 24

California Gold Rush

On the morning of January 24, 1848, a carpenter named James W. Marshall made a chance discovery of gold, which touched off the California gold rush. Hired by the wealthy landowner and entrepreneur John A. Sutter, Marshall was overseeing the construction of a mill on the south fork of the American River in the northern California valley called Coloma, or "beautiful vale," by Native Americans. He was inspecting the work when the gleam of metal in the streambed attracted his attention. Reaching down into the water, he brought up golden flakes, placed them in his hat, and dashed into the mill, shouting, "Boys, I believe I've found a gold mine." The carpenter conducted a series of inconclusive tests to discover whether he had really found gold; he then took three ounces of the metal to his employer at Sutter's Fort, some 40 miles downriver.

John A. Sutter realized that the discovery, if highly publicized, might very well destroy his vast enterprises in California. Born of Swiss parents, Johann Augustus Suter, as he had been baptized, had immigrated to America in his early thirties and amassed a fortune. Possessed of an adventurous spirit, he gradually moved westward. He gained experience trading in the northwest Oregon country before settling in Mexican-owned California in 1839. Sutter induced the Mexican authorities to grant him approximately 49,000 acres in the lower Sacramento Valley; in return, he agreed to create a fortified outpost as a deterrent to the ever increasing numbers of American settlers who were encroaching on Mexican territory in the western part of the present United States. The enterprising proprietor constructed not only a fort but also a colony of houses, warehouses, and stores, as well as a distillery, mill, tannery, and blanket factory at the confluence of the Sacramento and American rivers. Sutter rapidly expanded his holdings to 146,000 acres, a little empire that he dubbed New Helvetia. The short, stubby "feudal baron of the Sacramento Valley" later boasted that "I was everything: patriarch, priest, father, and judge."

Sutter's Fort, strategically located where several central and northern overland routes to the West Coast joined after winding through the high Sierra Nevadas, became a mecca for weary immigrants, a busy trading post, a rendezvous for frontiersmen, and a convenient open door to California for American settlers. Sutter's unconcealed sympathy for the Americans, as well as his wealth, power, and independence, made him an object of suspicion in the eyes of the Mexican officials. In 1846, the outbreak of hostilities between the Americans and Mexicans in California merged with the larger question of the war between the United States and Mexico. Sutter at first maintained at least an appearance of loyalty to Mexico; it soon became evident, though, that he was more than willing to condone American dominance.

American control of the region did not become official until early in 1848, when California was ceded to the United States by the Treaty of Guadalupe-Hildago. Marshall had already made his discovery of gold, but the Mexican government was unaware of that event. It was not the first time that gold had been unearthed in California. In the early 1840s, for example, Mexicans had mined scattered deposits in the Placerita Canyon near Los Angeles. The discovery of 1848, however, was soon seen to be a mammoth lode of gold-bearing quartz extending some 150 miles along the western foothills of the Sierra Nevada. Erosion and weathering had freed particles of ore from gold-bearing veins; rapid mountain waters had swept them away and deposited them, when the current slackened, in easily accessible rock crevices and streambeds.

Sutter tried to keep the discovery quiet, but the news spread like wildfire, and by June 1848 much of the population of nearby San Francisco was on its way to Sutter's property. One city newspaper editor commented that the entire area resounded "with the sordid cry of 'Gold, Gold, GOLD!' while the field is left half-planted, the house half-built, and everything neglected but the manufacture of shovels and pick axes." The gold fever spread to other California settlements at Santa Barbara, San Diego, and Monterey.

The first prospectors rushed to the goldfields in the late spring and early summer of 1848, and seemed to stumble upon gold everywhere in the scenic hills. Drought had dried up the mountain streams, revealing gold-bearing gravel. One group took 273 pounds of gold washings from the Feather River in seven weeks, while the first gold seekers to tap the Yuba River resources earned $75,000 in three months. The majority of gold hunters in the initial rush averaged $25 to $30 a day. Life for those prospecting in the long narrow mineral strip was relatively comfortable except for meager food supplies.

The situation changed drastically, however, as reports of the gold strikes spread throughout the Pacific region. Newcomers from Hawaii, Oregon, and northern Mexico poured into California via ships, wagon caravans, and horseback in the summer and fall of 1848. Mining camps, erected haphazardly, mushroomed furiously and fell apart just as rapidly when the gold deposits petered out. Food prices mounted: Eggs sold for as high as $3 apiece and flour at $800 a barrel. By the end of the year, between 5,000 and 10,000 people were working the diggings along the western slopes of the Sierra Nevada.

The news of the discovery at Sutter's Mill and the subsequent lucky strikes took months to reach the eastern part of the United States. California newspaper accounts, carried across the continent by couriers such as Kit Carson, did not arrive in the East until August 1848. The many stories related by prospectors were often discounted as tall tales. Nevertheless, by the close of 1848, easterners were aware that something extraordinary had occurred in California.

The American military governor of California at Monterey, Colonel Richard Mason, had visited the mineral belt in June 1848 to straighten out the confused reports flooding his office. At several of the sites his aide, William T. Sherman, sketched maps which, together with a letter and gold sample, were rushed to Washington, D.C. In his annual message to Congress, on December 5, 1848, President James K. Polk exuberantly reported: "The accounts of the abundance of gold in that territory are of such extraordinary character as would scarcely command belief were they not corroborated by the authentic reports of officers in the public service." As if to back his first official confirmation of the discovery, two days later a courier reached Washington with 230 ounces of California gold. The last doubts vanished, and the invasion of 1849 got under way.

It is impossible to determine accurately the number of persons who participated in the gold rush of 1849. Estimates range from 60,000 to 100,000, more than three-fourths of whom were Americans, with the remainder coming from Western Europe, Australia, South America, and Asia. Within a month of President Polk's message, would-be gold prospectors jammed shipping offices and chartered some 60 vessels regardless of their age or seaworthiness. By February 8, 1849, a total of 136 ships had embarked from Atlantic ports. The *New York Herald* reported: "In every Atlantic seaport, vessels are being filled up, societies are being formed, husbands are preparing to leave their wives, sons are parting with their mothers, and bachelors are abandoning their comforts; all are rushing head over heels toward the El Dorado on the Pacific."

Some 15,000 people sailed from the East Coast in 1849 to California, traveling around South America (since the Panama Canal was not yet built) and making the 18,000-mile trip in six to eight months, with the average being nearly 200 days. Conditions were abominable in the confined quarters, but they were still superior to the alternative of trying to cross the Isthmus of Panama by foot or horseback, since Panama contained dangerous terrain and disease-infested swamps. Other "forty-niners" used the central and southern over-land trails through the continental United States. An estimated 45,000 prospectors followed the central route; they set out from midwestern towns such as Independence or Saint Joseph, Missouri, and climbed the high passes of the Sierra Nevada to the Pacific foothills. About 10,000 people chose the southern route, which was less mountainous and had a more pleasant climate. They usually trekked along the Santa Fe Trail or western Texas trails, and later followed either the Gila River or the Old Spanish Trail into southern California.

Life was far from easy for the prospectors who reached California: There were thousands of newcomers, mostly men, crammed into small settlements. The very names are indicative of living conditions within the camps: Hangtown, Whisky Diggings, Poverty Hill, Poker Flat, Bedbug. As one disillusioned miner commented: "There's nothing to do but hang around the saloons, get drunk and fight, or lie out in the snow and die." Crime flourished among the newcomers, whose ranks included an increasing number of undesirable drifters who found it easier to gain gold by robbery, murder, and claim-jumping than by toiling for it themselves. More than 1,000 murders were committed in San Francisco during the first eight years of the gold rush, and the situation was worse at the diggings. A favorite tune ran:

Oh, what was your name in the States?
Was it Thompson or Johnson or Bates?
Did you murder your wife and fly for your life?
Say, what was your name in the States?

Domestic life was practically nonexistent. In 1850, women composed only 8 percent of California's population, and even this low figure fell to 2 percent in the mining belt. Most forty-niners hardly made ends meet, and rich strikes came to only a few gold seekers. Interestingly enough, the rare fortunes amassed often resulted indirectly from the mining bonanza. Leland Stanford sold the registered claims he had staked out for more than half a million dollars. Mark Hopkins used the money from his one strike to purchase hardware to resell at exorbitant prices in the camps. Charles Crocker and Collis P. Huntington ran prosperous dry goods and hardware businesses. All four invested $15,000 apiece in the Central Pacific Railroad Company in 1861 and were catapulted into the multimillionaire bracket.

John A. Sutter, however, was not among the fortune makers. As he had feared, the discovery of gold was his ruination. Squatters trespassed on his land and his workers deserted him. Silent mills, decaying hides, unharvested fields, and plundered warehouses were all that remained of his once mighty empire. The little capital left to Sutter was depleted when the U.S. Supreme Court ruled that his land title was invalid, and he was forced to reimburse those persons to whom he had granted subtitles. Annually, from 1871 until his death in 1880, the bankrupt ex-magnate unsuccessfully petitioned Congress for reimbursement for his property and services.

In 1849, $10 million came from the California mines. In 1852 they produced a high of $81 million. However, the surface deposits soon dwindled and large companies, financed with Eastern funds, transformed the unsystematic rush into an efficient industry. In 1853 and 1854 extractions were valued at some $68 million; from 1865 through 1885 they were valued at about $15 million to $20 million yearly. Today, only memories and ruins mark the gold rush trail. Coloma, the settlement that sprang up around Sutter's Mill, is the center of a State Historical Park dedicated to the discovery of gold.

Edith Wharton's Birthday

The author and Pulitzer Prize winner Edith Wharton was born on January 24, 1862, in New York City. Her family were members of New York's upper-crust society, tracing their lineage back to the colonial era and to the Dutch settlement of New Amsterdam, which eventually became New York. Thus born into a family of wealth and privilege, as a child she found her life controlled by the rigid social customs of the Victorian era.

As a female, she had few outlets to vent her frustrations, so she turned to writing. She began to write short stories and demonstrated an exceptional literary ability. Her first book was privately printed in 1878 when she was only 16. In 1885 she married a wealthy banker, Edward Wharton, who was also a member of the society class. However, Edith was unhappy in her marriage, again because of the restraints imposed by custom on the lives and freedom of women. After several nervous breakdowns, she obtained a divorce in 1913.

Her work first began to achieve wide public circulation in the 1890s, when she wrote a number of short stories for *Scribner's* magazine. Wharton's first major work came in 1902, when she published the novel *The Valley of Decision*. This was followed by *The House of Mirth* in 1905. Like so much of her writing, the principal theme in the latter work was the narrow life and many restrictions imposed by Victorian social codes. *The House of Mirth* became a best-seller, and with her literary reputation thus established, Wharton moved in 1907 to France, where she spent the rest of her life.

Wharton was a prolific writer. During her lifetime she wrote 11 volumes of short stories, 17 novels, and scores of short stories, novellas, and other works. In 1920 the novel *The Age of Innocence* won her the Pulitzer Prize. Also noteworthy are the novels *Ethan Frome* in 1911, *The Custom of the Country* in 1913, the short stories collected in *Old New York* in 1924, and her autobiography *A Backward Glance* in 1934.

In the 1990s movie versions of *The Age of Innocence* and *Ethan Frome* were produced. Wharton died on August 11, 1937, in France at St. Brice-sous-forêt.

January 25

Robert Burns's Birthday

The poet Robert Burns, revered by the Scots and people of Scottish ancestry, was born on January 25, 1759, in a cottage at Alloway, Scotland. He was the eldest son of William Burns, a farmer of modest means. Robert worked on his father's farm as a plowboy until he was 15. The boy was eager to learn and read the *Spectator*, Locke's *Essays*, and Pope's translation of the *Iliad*. He went to school for a time and learned a little Latin and French. In 1781 he was apprenticed to a flax dresser, but before he began to work, the shop burned down, and he was left without work or money.

Burns was 25 when his father died, and he wrote his father's epitaph, the last line of which declared that "even his failings leaned to virtue's side." Now the head of his family, Robert, with his brother Gilbert, rented the farm of Mossgiel near Mauchline, Scotland. He toiled there for four years, barely earning a living, and in 1786 decided to emigrate. He secured a job as a bookkeeper on an estate in Jamaica, bought his ticket for the West Indies, and arranged for his first small volume of poems to be published. Entitled *Poems, Chiefly in the Scottish Dialect*, it received such an enthusiastic response that he changed his mind and decided not to leave.

The financial return from the book was minimal, but the social returns were much greater. The "plowboy poet" was invited to Edinburgh and welcomed by the city's literary society. Sir Walter Scott, then a boy of 15, saw Burns and described him this way: "His countenance was more massive than it looks in any of his portraits. There was a strong expression of shrewdness in his lineaments; the eye indicated the poetic character and temperament. It was large and of a dark cast, and literally glowed when he spoke with feeling or interest. I never saw such another eye in a human head."

The second edition of the volume of poems, which appeared in 1787, yielded Burns more money. With the proceeds, he took a walking tour throughout the Border towns of England and the eastern Highlands of Scotland, eventually returning to Ayrshire, Scotland, where he bought another farm and married a woman named Jean Armour. In 1789 Burns received an appointment as excise officer of the local district, and two years later he was promoted to a similar post at Dumfries. At about this time he was asked to help find, and to write or rewrite words for, the traditional Scottish song, collected by George Thomson. This and a similar project begun earlier for James Johnson, in addition to his duties as excise officer, kept Burns busy for most of the rest of his life.

The bulk of Burns's songs, building on folk tradition and portraying the life of rural Scotland, were contained in Johnson's multivolume *Scots Musical Museum* and the several volumes of Thomson's *Select Collection of Original Scottish Airs*. Despite his family's financial need, Burns refused payment, except honorariums, for the songs, which constitute his best-known work and which he himself regarded as a service to Scotland. His longer works express a humorous sympathy for human frailty and a dislike of cant, as well as an ardent egalitarianism—rank, wealth, and social propriety were not, in Burns's opinion, adequate measures of human worth.

Burns died on July 21, 1796, at the early age of 37. Before his death, he had done more than any person before or since to recreate the entire body of Scottish song, which he came upon in fragmentary and disorganized form and left as an example of lyric beauty. His fame throughout the world has grown with the years. Scottish American societies often celebrate his birthday with a festive dinner featuring haggis, scotch whiskey, and recitations of the poet's verses.

Feast of St. Paul's Conversion

The Feast of the Conversion of St. Paul, observed by Christian churches on January 25, celebrates the transformation of Saul of Tarsus, scourge of Christians, into St. Paul, apostle, missionary, leader of Christians, and martyr. It is not known with certainty just when this feast was first observed, but it is mentioned in the church calendars and other works of the eighth and ninth centuries, and Pope Innocent III (1198–1216) urged that it be celebrated. Listed as a "solemn" festival in the records of the Council of Oxford in 1222, during the reign of England's King Henry III, the feast continued to be observed by the Anglican Church after its separation from Rome and was brought to the American colonies by English settlers.

Saul of Tarsus was a well-educated and fiercely dedicated Jew, a Pharisee and member of the tribe of Benjamin. He was named after Saul, the first king of Israel, who was also a Benjamite, and became known as Paul after his conversion to Christianity.

Although he had been educated "at the feet of Gamaliel," who was greatly respected for his learning and who himself was a tolerant person (Acts 5:34–40), Saul of Tarsus had a fiery nature and became an anti-Christian extremist. He thought that Christians blasphemed and felt that Christianity was a threat to his religion. Saul scoured Jerusalem for Christians, and when he found them he had them bound and delivered to prison or to death. He was a witness to the stoning of St. Stephen, the first Christian martyr, as the New Testament notes in Acts 8:1: "and Saul was consenting to his death."

After considerable success in rooting out Christians in Jerusalem, Saul, "breathing threats and murder against the disciples of the Lord," decided to journey to Damascus and continue what he felt was his holy work in that city. Securing authority from the chief priest to bind "any belonging to the [Christian] Way" and take them back to Jerusalem, Saul set forth for Damascus. It was on the road there that his dramatic conversion took place, perhaps a few years after Jesus' death.

Many years later, between A.D. 60 and 62, Paul gave to King Agrippa his own account of his conversion, as recorded in the 26th (and also the 9th and 22nd) chapter of Acts. The events leading to Paul's appearance before Agrippa began in Jerusalem when some Jewish pilgrims from Asia, who had seen him in the Temple, erroneously thought that he had violated its sanctity by taking Gentiles into the Temple with him. Seeing him again later (according to the report in Acts 21), they accused him of this and of teaching against their law. In the process, they stirred up members of a Jerusalem mob, who beat Paul and sought to kill him. Roman soldiers arrested him, in effect rescuing him, and placed him in protective custody. While incarcerated, Paul, learning of a plot against his life, demanded his rights as a Roman citizen and asked to be sent to Rome for trial. The procurator (or governor) of Judea, Porcius Festus, agreed. However, the procurator decided to investigate the charges against Paul so that they might be specified before Paul was sent to Rome. Since he himself could find nothing against Paul, Festus discussed the case with the visiting King Agrippa.

Summoned before Agrippa, Paul brought to bear all his education in law and theology to show that, contrary to the charges against him, he had not turned away from Judaism when he embraced

Christianity. Instead, Paul promoted Christianity as the fulfillment of Judaism (Acts 26). At the end of Paul's defense, the account goes, the king and the governor and those listening withdrew and "said to one another, 'This man is doing nothing to deserve death or imprisonment.' And Agrippa said to Festus, 'This man could have been set free if he had not appealed to Caesar.' " As it was, Paul was sent to Rome, where a few years later he was beheaded during Nero's persecution of Christians. Between the time of his conversion and his death, Paul was a leader in spreading the young Christian religion.

Florence Mills's Birthday

Florence Mills, one of the leading African American singers of the Harlem Renaissance in the 1920s, was born on January 25, 1896, in Washington, D.C. As a young woman, Florence developed an interest in the jazz music phenomenon sweeping the African American cultural world.

Jazz music originated in New Orleans, Louisiana, during World War I. It was an active, fast-paced form of music that quickly spread through African American urban communities, the Harlem neighborhood of New York City in particular. Most whites considered jazz scandalous and fit only for "Negroes," but such famous jazz musicians as Louis Armstrong and Duke Ellington managed to eventually attain a certain level of respectability. Mills, however, had two obstacles to overcome: Not only was she black, but she was a woman.

The largely African American community of Harlem provided Mills with a home where she could develop her talents. At the time, Harlem was not associated with the sort of grim urban poverty and crime that it is today, but was the center of African American cultural and artistic life. The 1920s are often referred to as the period of the "Harlem Renaissance." Mills became a popular singer and dancer in the Harlem nightclubs and speakeasies in such places as Lenox Avenue, where the famous Cotton Club was located. Mills appeared on Broadway as well, and was even offered a position in the prestigious Ziegfeld Follies. On June 27, 1924, she became the first African American woman to be featured at the well-known Palace Theater.

Florence Mills died on November 1, 1927, in New York City at the age of 31. The exact circumstances are unclear. Her death was greatly mourned, and over 100,000 people gathered in Harlem to honor her memory. Although the Harlem Renaissance would eventually fade and Florence Mills's fame would be eclipsed by that of more prominent African American musicians, she remains a pioneering figure for African American women.

January 26

Douglas MacArthur's Birthday

General of the Army Douglas MacArthur, supreme commander of the Allied forces in the southwest Pacific during World War II, came from a celebrated army family. Born in Little Rock, Arkansas, on January 26, 1880, he was the son of Mary P. Hardy and Lieutenant General Arthur MacArthur, who served for a time as military governor of the Philippines and eventually became the army's senior ranking officer.

Young Douglas MacArthur attended the U.S. Military Academy at West Point, New York, and graduated in 1903, the first in his class of 93. Commissioned a second lieutenant and assigned to the Corps of Engineers, he was sent by his own choice to the Philippines. He also served in California, in Japan as an aide to his father, and as an aide to President Theodore Roosevelt in Washington, D.C. In 1908, after graduating from the Engineering School of Application, he joined Company K, Third Battalion of Engineers, at Fort Leavenworth, Kansas. During the next four years he also served at San Antonio, Texas, and in the Panama Canal Zone, rising to the rank of captain. He was then ordered back to Washington, D.C., where he was appointed to the General Staff Corps. He served from April to September 1914 in the Vera Cruz expedition against Mexico.

In September 1917, after the United States' entry into World War I, MacArthur was appointed chief of staff of the 42nd Division with the rank of colonel. He conceived the idea of naming this division the Rainbow Division, since it was composed of National Guard units from 27 states and represented the diversity of America. During the war, MacArthur participated in the Champagne-Marne and Aisne-Marne defensives. Given the temporary rank of brigadier general in June 1918, he was placed in command of the 84th Infantry Brigade and led it in the St. Mihiel, Essey, Pannes, Woevre, Meuse-Argonne, and Sedan offensives. He created a sensation by insisting on going into battle with his men. Twice wounded in action, he was decorated 13 times and cited an additional 7 times.

The Armistice of 1918 found MacArthur temporarily commanding the 42nd Division once more before serving with the Army of Occupation in Germany until April of the following year. Returning to the United States, he became supcrintendent of the U.S. Military Academy at West Point in June 1919. In the three years that he held the post he revitalized the academy by modernizing military training, broadening the curriculum, and instituting compulsory intramural athletics. He was formally commissioned a brigadier general in January 1920.

In 1922 MacArthur left again for the Philippines, where he served in several command posts before being promoted to major general in January 1925. After intervals as commander of the Fourth Corps Area in Atlanta and the Third Corps Area in Baltimore, he returned to the Pacific for two years as commanding general of the Philippines. When President Hoover named MacArthur chief of staff of the U.S. Army in November 1930, he was the youngest man ever to hold the position. He was made a four-star general at the same time, the youngest since Ulysses S. Grant. In his new post MacArthur worked to modernize the army, directing its mechanization and motorization. He also urged recognition of the airplane's military potential, and prepared some of the basic manpower and industrial mobilization plans later used during World War II. In the isolationist climate of the 1930s, however, he was unpopular for his belief that Germany and Japan, then arming, posed a military threat.

With Japan embarked on its program of territorial expansion, President Franklin D. Roosevelt appointed MacArthur (who was due to retire as chief of staff) head of the American military mission to the newly created Commonwealth Government of the Philippines in 1935. In that capacity, he directed the organization of the islands' defenses. After President Quezon of the Philippines commissioned him as field marshal of the Philippine army in 1936, MacArthur took a leave of absence from the U.S. Army, but he was recalled to active duty on July 26, 1941, as tensions continued to grow between the United States and Japan. Designated commanding general of army forces in the Far East, he was put in command of United States and Philippine troops. On December 7, 1941, Japan attacked the American naval installation at Pearl Harbor, Hawaii, precipitating the United States' entry into World War II.

Japan attacked Malaya and the Philippines the same day as it did Pearl Harbor. Earlier defensive preparations notwithstanding, the attackers quickly overran most of the Philippines. MacArthur's outnumbered men were forced to withdraw from Manila to the Bataan peninsula and the island of Corregidor, where they put up their now legendary defense before being forced to capitulate in the spring of 1942.

Assigned to the defense of Australia by President Roosevelt, MacArthur left the Philippines in March before the American forces surrendered. His arrival in Australia, after a 3,000-mile dash over Japanese-controlled waters, prompted his subsequently famous declaration: "I came through and I shall return." "I shall return" became synonymous with MacArthur's vow to return to and liberate the Philippines from Japanese control.

In April 1942 MacArthur was made supreme commander of Allied forces in the Southwest Pacific Area. His command complemented that of Admiral Chester W. Nimitz in the North Pacific, Central Pacific, and South Pacific areas. Both men operated under the overall strategic direction of the U.S. Joint Chiefs of Staff.

After the battles of the Coral Sea and Midway had raged in other Pacific areas, and while the Guadalcanal campaign proceeded to the east, MacArthur launched a counterattack to secure Papua, the southeastern section of New Guinea, in September 1942. The end of enemy resistance in this region, which he announced on January 23, 1943, was followed by actions under his command to secure New Britain and neighboring straits. Then, his main New Guinea campaign, a brilliant "leapfrog" operation along the northern coast toward the Philippines, proceeded from January to September 1944.

True to his word, MacArthur returned to the Philippines, wading ashore on the east coast of Leyte on October 20, 1944, and calling on the Filipinos to rise and support him. The land battle for Leyte was accompanied by one of the great naval battles of modern times, from October 23 to 26, 1944, during which the U.S. Navy defeated the Japanese naval forces off Leyte and allowed the Allied forces under MacArthur to continue their advances. On Luzon, which the Allies invaded on January 9, 1945, and in some other parts of the islands, hostilities lasted until July and even later, although Manila and Corregidor were liberated by early March.

Confronted by the Allies' advances on land and sea, and by the dropping of atomic bombs on Hiroshima and Nagasaki, Japan indicated its willingness to surrender on August 14, 1945. World War II came to a close with the official surrender ceremonies held on September 2, 1945, aboard the battleship *Missouri* in Tokyo Bay. MacArthur, who had been made a five-star general late in 1944, was appointed Supreme Allied Commander to accept the surrender and command the American occupation force in Japan. He spent the next five years there, supervising reconstruction and the establishment of a democratic form of government.

January 26

In 1950, after North Korean troops invaded South Korea, MacArthur was appointed commander of the United Nations forces sent to oppose the action. In reality, the UN contingent was dominated by the American troops, as the North Korean invasion was a thinly veiled challenge to American power by the People's Republic of China and the Soviet Union. MacArthur was able to stop the North Korean advance at Pusan in southern South Korea, and to conceive and brilliantly execute a surprise landing far to the North Korean rear at Inchon. As MacArthur's forces around Pusan moved north to meet the Inchon forces, the North Korean army was routed and nearly destroyed. American forces subsequently crossed the 38th parallel, which roughly divided North and South Korea, and proceeded as far as North Korea's Yalu River boundary with Communist China. They were turned back, however, by the sudden invasion of Chinese army troops, who far outnumbered the Americans. The Chinese government claimed that the troops were "volunteers" who had gone to serve with their Communist North Korean brethren, but the truth was that the Chinese were nervous about having an American military presence on their border and gambled that the Americans would not use nuclear weapons or attack China itself to retaliate. Using nuclear weapons and/or attacking China might mean war with the Soviet Union, which at that time was China's ally.

The Chinese gamble succeeded. MacArthur publicly stated that the Communist bases in Manchuria should be bombed and the Chinese coast blockaded to bring an end to hostilities. President Truman, determined not to escalate the conflict, disagreed and was eventually forced to dismiss the unruly MacArthur from his command on April 11, 1951. It was an unpopular move by Truman: MacArthur was a war hero, had many admirers and supporters in the United States, and was correct in pointing out that the United States was now at war with China more than it was with the defeated North Koreans.

MacArthur returned to the United States like a conquering hero, complete with a ticker tape parade up New York's Broadway and a memorable address to a joint session of Congress, in which he made the famous statement that "old soldiers never die, they just fade away" (the text of his speech is at April 19). In retirement he served as chairman of the board of the Remington Rand Corporation. He died in New York City on April 5, 1964, and was buried in Norfolk, Virginia. In 1971 Norfolk was the city of first-day issue for a commemorative stamp bearing MacArthur's likeness and released on his January 26 birthday.

Michigan Admitted to the Union

Michigan, the 26th state, was admitted to the Union on January 26, 1837. The Michigan area was probably first visited by Europeans when the Frenchman Étienne Brulé reached the Sault Ste. Marie narrows, strategically located between Lake Superior and Lake Huron, in 1618. He was followed by other explorers, fur traders, and missionaries, including Jean Nicolet, who reached Sault Ste. Marie in 1634. Sault Ste. Marie was the site of Michigan's first permanent settlement, founded in 1668 by Père Jacques Marquette as a Jesuit mission. Detroit, as strategic in its way as Sault Ste. Marie, since it effectively controls the entrance to Lake Huron and Lake Erie, was founded in 1701 by the French under Antoine de la Mothe Cadillac.

The lands now within the boundaries of the state of Michigan passed to the English in 1760 and 1761 and to the United States in 1783, with the signing of the Treaty of Paris after the conclusion of the American Revolution. It was 1796, though, before the British actually surrendered Detroit and Mackinac. At first part of the Northwest Territory (from 1787), then part of the new Indiana Territory (from 1803), Michigan was organized as a separate territory in 1805. Although the region was again occupied by Great Britain during the War of 1812, it was virtually all recovered within the next year.

Michigan was enlarged by the cession of Indian lands between 1814 and 1836. It set up a state government without federal sanction and applied for statehood in 1835, although its actual admission was delayed until January 26, 1837, by a boundary dispute with Ohio and by debate in Congress over maintaining the balance between free and slave states. With the admission of Arkansas, a slave state, in 1836, Michigan's statehood was assured. Under both the Missouri Compromise of 1820 and the earlier Northwest Ordinance of 1787, slavery was prohibited in the region occupied by Michigan; it could thus enter the Union as a free state, offsetting Arkansas. January 26, the anniversary of Michigan's actual admission in 1837, was formally observed as Michigan Day in earlier years.

The capital of Michigan is Lansing. With a coastline on four of the Great Lakes, Michigan has excellent transportation facilities, which have furthered industrial development. Detroit, is a world leader in the manufacture of automobiles and other motor vehicles, an industry that suffered greatly in the 1970s and 1980s under the twin blows of gasoline price increases and Japanese competition, but which recovered significantly in the

1990s. With the 1959 opening of the St. Lawrence Seaway, which turned the Great Lakes cities into international ports, Michigan has also become an important shipping area.

Angela Davis's Birthday

Angela Davis, the famous African American academic and political activist, was born on January 26, 1944, in Birmingham, Alabama, to B. Frank Davis and Sallye E. Davis. She attended Brandeis University, graduated in 1965, and then went to graduate school at the University of California in San Diego.

Like many young people during the turbulent 1960s, she was attracted to civil rights causes, particularly the more radical and extreme factions. In 1968 she joined the Communist Party and began to advocate physical confrontation as a means of achieving social justice. In 1969 she became a professor of philosophy at the University of California in Los Angeles, but she was shortly removed from her position due to her growing radicalism.

Davis is most remembered for her alleged involvement in the attempted escape of San Quentin inmate James McClain. This incident took place during proceedings against McClain on August 7, 1970, in the Marin County, California, courthouse. Several gunmen stormed the courtroom where McClain was held and attempted to escape with him and several hostages. The attempt was unsuccessful, and several people, including McClain, were killed in the ensuing shootout. Davis was accused of purchasing a shotgun for and otherwise assisting the radical group—Soledad Brothers—that had attempted this rescue. After a controversial trial, she was acquitted.

Davis was released from prison after more than a year of incarceration during the trial process. Despite the opposition of California governor (and future president) Ronald Reagan, she was able to return to academia and become the first African American woman to hold a fully tenured professor's position at the University of California at Santa Cruz. She continued her involvement with activist causes, and published a number of essays concerning racial issues in the United States as well as her autobiography. In 1980, she was the vice-presidential nominee of the Communist Party. In addition to her radical political work, she has been active in prisoners' rights groups and was elected to the board of directors of the National Black Women's Health Project. As of this writing in the late 1990s, Angela Davis continues her activities both in academia and in areas of social reform. She will be remembered as a symbolic figure of the struggles of the 1960s.

Paul Newman's Birthday

Paul Newman, one of America's most famous actors, was born in Cleveland, Ohio, on January 26, 1925. He was educated at Kenyon College and attended the Yale Drama School in 1951 and 1952.

Newman's Broadway debut was in 1953, when he had a part in William Inge's *Picnic*. His acting ability and youthful good looks won him a contract with Warner Brothers, and his first movie role was as the star of *The Silver Chalice* in 1954. Newman went on to appear in a number of famous movies, including *Cat on a Hot Tin Roof* (1958), *The Long Hot Summer* (1958), *Exodus* (1960), *The Hustler* (1961), *Hud* (1963), *Cool Hand Luke* (1967), *Butch Cassidy and the Sundance Kid* (1969), *The Sting* (1973), *Absence of Malice* (1981), *The Color of Money* (1986), and *Nobody's Fool* (1994).

In addition to his successful acting career, Paul Newman is noted for his charitable works. Beginning in the early 1980s, he began to endorse a variety of products such as popcorn, salad dressing, and spaghetti sauce that carry the name "Newman's Own." Profits from these ventures go to a variety of philanthropic organizations, and in 1994 the Academy of Motion Picture Arts and Sciences conferred a humanitarian award upon him. As of this writing, Newman's charitable efforts have raised approximately $100 million. Although he no longer pursues his movie career as actively as before, Newman participates in other ventures, such as the 1994 Ken Burns documentary on the history of baseball. He has received several Academy Awards.

January 27

Samuel Gompers's Birthday

Samuel Gompers, the first president of the American Federation of Labor and the man who guided the course of organized labor in the United States for more than four decades, was born on January 27, 1850, in London, England. After attending school for four years, he was apprenticed in his father's trade of cigar making. When he was 13, his family moved to the United States and settled in New York City.

Within a year, young Gompers had joined the New York Cigarmakers' Union, and he became active in the social clubs and fraternal orders of New York's East Side. Although he attended lectures at Cooper Union, most of his education came from the reading materials that were purchased from common funds for the shops of master cigar makers, where workers took turns reading to one another. He was also exposed to various theories of socialism and to the revolutionary tradition of some of the European immigrants with whom he came in contact. He became a naturalized citizen in 1872.

To better the lot of working people, he looked for inspiration to the British trade unions and their Trade Union Congress. After the panic of 1873, with its attendant hardships, and a long strike in 1877, which nearly wrecked the Cigarmakers' Union, he and Adolph Strasser reorganized the Cigarmakers along British lines. Strasser became the union's international president; Gompers became president of the New York local; and their thinking became known as the "new unionism." Central to it was their belief that labor should concentrate on immediate economic goals and avoid the kind of political radicalism and utopian social experiments on which some earlier reformers had dissipated their energies. They also sought to remedy two previous handicaps to union activity: lack of strike funds and the absence of central control. They raised membership dues, gave national officers jurisdiction over funds, and prepared to establish sickness, accident, and unemployment benefits for workers.

In the process, the Cigarmakers became a model for other unions. But Gompers and Strasser, seeing the need for a national federation of trade unions, which could lobby for favorable legislation and act defensively against employer opposition, regarded their reorganization of the Cigarmakers as merely a first step. In 1881 they were among the main organizers of the Federation of Organized Trades and Labor Unions.

The federation was reorganized as the American Federation of Labor at a convention in Columbus, Ohio, on December 8, 1886. Gompers was elected president of the new AFL and, except for one year (1895), held the position for the rest of his life. He worked for what he considered to be the just goals of labor: higher wages, shorter hours, and greater freedom. He held that the national federation should have authority over local unions, although the authority was to be by moral force, or "organized consent to collective action," rather than by arbitrary rule. The national organization was supposed to exercise only the powers delegated to it by the organization's constitution or by annual conventions of members.

Since the AFL was composed of craft unions, the membership, which increased from under 200,000 in 1886 to over 1,750,000 by 1904, consisted largely of skilled workers. Under Gompers's leadership, the AFL based its efforts to achieve a better living for its members on collective bargaining and on such weapons as the strike, the boycott,

and picketing. There was resistance from the government and big business: Strikes were often crushed by the use of strikebreakers, court injunctions, and state or federal troops. In the face of such pressures, Gompers abandoned his political neutrality in the presidential election of 1908, lending his unofficial support to the Democrat, William Jennings Bryan, who ran without success on a pro-labor platform.

In 1912 the climate for labor improved with the election of Woodrow Wilson as president of the United States. Wilson had received the support of the AFL during his campaign, and after his election he succeeded in getting a progressive program of legislation passed through Congress. Two examples of legislation enacted while he was president were the Adamson Act and the Clayton Antitrust Act, which supplemented the Sherman Antitrust Act. The Adamson Act provided an eight-hour day for workers on interstate railroads, while the Clayton Antitrust Act recognized strikes, boycotts, and peaceful picketing as labor's legal rights; drastically limited the use of court injunctions in labor disputes; and held that labor organizations were not illegal combinations in restraint of trade. Although the Clayton Antitrust Act, at first hailed by Gompers as "labor's *Magna Carta*," was much weakened by judicial interpretation, the act's general provisions are now regarded as basic rights.

One weakness of the AFL, however, was that it was largely the domain of skilled craft workers. Unskilled workers and semiskilled factory floor workers were not actively solicited or targeted for unionization. This void would eventually be filled by the Congress of Industrial Organizations (CIO), which decades later would merge with the AFL to form the modern AFL-CIO labor organization that dominates American unions.

Gompers, who was recognized as an important public figure as the strength of labor grew, served as President Wilson's official and unofficial adviser on labor and organized the War Committee on Labor during World War I. As head of this group and as a member of the Advisory Commission to the Council of National Defense, he led the AFL in active support of the war effort. The war years were a period of substantial gains and vastly increased membership for the labor movement. There was a period of decline in the 1920s, however, prompting the AFL to consider once more its policy of aloofness from politics. In the presidential election of 1924, the organization gave its support, this time officially, to Robert M. LaFollette, who ran unsuccessfully on the third-party Progressive ticket.

Gompers died that same year, in San Antonio, Texas, on December 13. His authoritative account of the rise and growth of American trade unionism, *Seventy Years of Life and Labor*, was published the next year.

Hyman G. Rickover's Birthday

Hyman G. Rickover, the famous United States admiral and father of the nuclear-powered navy, was born in Makow, Russia, on January 27, 1900. His home town later became part of Poland. In 1906, his family left for the United States and settled in Chicago, Illinois.

After graduating from high school, Rickover was able to obtain admission to the United States Naval Academy at Annapolis, Maryland, thanks to the sponsorship of Congressman Adolph Sabath, a family friend. In 1922 Rickover graduated from the academy, having placed in the upper fifth of his class. He was posted to the destroyer *La Vallette*. It was on this vessel that he first impressed his superiors with his engineering ability. He used his tour of duty on the *La Vallette* to take correspondence courses to further his education. His hard work earned him a transfer to the battleship *Nevada*, one of the frontline warships in the navy at the time. As the officer primarily responsible for the electrical engineering aboard the battleship, he developed an interest in this particular specialty, and several years later returned to the Naval Academy to take graduate level classes in electrical engineering. He also took some classes at Columbia University, where he met and married Ruth Masters.

After graduation, Rickover returned to the fleet, this time to the battleship *California*. At the time, the United States was developing and expanding its fleet of submarines. Rickover developed an interest in this new technology, and by 1930 he was admitted to the navy's submarine school. His interest in submarines would remain with him for the rest of his career.

Rickover held a variety of posts throughout the years leading up to World War II, including his one and only command, on the minesweeper *Finch*. Afterwards his positions were purely administrative—appropriately, given his organizational abilities and engineering skills. For example, he reformed several of the navy's procurement and supply divisions, and helped the navy obtain innovative new minesweeping technology. He was promoted several times, and by 1943 he was a senior officer.

After World War II, Rickover was assigned to help supervise operations at Oak Ridge, Tennessee, one of the atomic energy development sites in the famous Manhattan Project. The experience he gained there enabled him to become head of both the Naval Reactors Branch of the U.S. Atomic Energy Commission and the U.S. Navy's Nuclear Power Division. With this authority, and his previous experience both in engineering and with submarines, Rickover was in a position to pursue his conviction that the development of nuclear-powered submarines was vital to American naval supremacy in the cold war with the Soviet Union. His efforts led to the design and construction of the USS *Nautilus*, the world's first nuclear-powered submarine, in the 1950s.

Now an admiral, Rickover's abilities and his blunt personality earned him both respect and resentment within the military establishment. Although his achievement with the *Nautilus* and the development of America's nuclear submarine fleet earned him the title of "Father of the Nuclear Navy," he was also outspoken in his criticism of what President Eisenhower would one day term the "military-industrial complex." For example, Rickover once dryly noted that in order to "increase the efficiency of the Department of Defense, you must first abolish it." His bluntness and criticisms did not, however, stop him from working further to promote the expansion of the navy's nuclear fleet. In addition to nuclear submarines, he helped spur the development of the nuclear surface fleet, exemplified by America's present-day fleet of American nuclear-powered aircraft carriers. Rickover was convinced that, despite numerous safety concerns, only nuclear power could provide the American navy with the travel range and freedom from refueling necessary to carry out missions around the world and counter the Soviet enemy. Although the danger of nuclear mishaps is of course present with a nuclear Navy, it remains a fact that America's submarine and carrier fleet is unsurpassed throughout the world and that during the cold war the Soviets were never able to seriously challenge American dominance of the oceans.

Rickover was in the United States Navy for a total of 63 years, and attained the rank of four-star admiral. In his spare time, such as it was, he wrote several books criticizing the state of the American educational system. He prolonged his retirement until 1982, when in his 80s he was finally forced to leave active service. He died in Arlington, Virginia, on July 8, 1986, and was buried in Arlington National Cemetery.

January 28

Space Shuttle *Challenger* Explodes

On January 28, 1986, one of the worst disasters in the American space program occurred when the space shuttle *Challenger* exploded just over one minute from its launch at the Kennedy Space Center on Cape Canaveral, Florida.

The roots of the *Challenger* disaster go back to the origins of the American space program in the early 1960s, when President John F. Kennedy made it a national priority to put a man on the Moon and achieve superiority in space over America's cold war enemy, the Soviet Union. At the time, the Soviet Union appeared to be winning the "space race," so Congress was willing to finance enormously expensive space programs out of a concern for national security. The fear was that if the Soviets conquered space first, they would be in a position to dominate the world from distances unattainable by the Americans. However unfounded these fears might have been in hindsight, the space program achieved its goal of putting a man on the Moon by the end of the 1960s, and the notion of conquering space generated such popular enthusiasm that the space program continued to maintain wide public support. Further, over the years the various technological spinoffs of the space program, such as the semiconductor chip and advances in the aerospace industry, convinced people of the economic benefits of space exploration.

By the early 1970s, however, there had been several manned missions to the Moon and further ones were increasingly marginal as far as their scientific value was concerned. In addition, NASA's ambitious plan for a Mars mission was prohibitively expensive. Further exploration of the solar system was consigned to satellite probes, and attention began to focus on the utility of a spacecraft that could be used again and again. Thus began the plans for a space shuttle, and the development of the American fleet of space shuttles of which *Challenger* was a member.

By 1986, space shuttle launches had become relatively routine, and NASA was preparing the launch of Mission 51-L, the tenth flight of the shuttle *Challenger*. In order to achieve media publicity for what was becoming a rather ordinary event, NASA had promoted the fact that in this particular launch the shuttle's crew would include, for the first time, an ordinary citizen, namely teacher Christa McAuliffe. The shuttle's commander was Francis Scobee and there were five other crew members, for a total of seven people

aboard. When the spacecraft launched at approximately 11:39 A.M., there were hundreds of millions of television viewers who were unfortunate enough, 74 seconds later, to see the *Challenger* explode before attaining orbit and within sight of the launch pad.

The nation was stunned by the *Challenger* disaster, particularly after the publicity given to the inclusion of Christa McAuliffe. After a lengthy investigation and much criticism of NASA, the government determined that defects in the "O-ring" devices for sealing joints in the rocket boosters used to launch the shuttle were the cause of the explosion. Abnormally cold temperatures at the Florida launch site contributed to the mishap as well. After this investigation and some redevelopment of the space shuttle design, the program eventually resumed. However, the incident helped remind NASA and the public of how dangerous the business of space exploration can be, and how much more needs to be learned before space can truly be conquered.

The United States Withdraws from Cuba

The termination, on January 28, 1909, of the provisional government that had marked the United States' second intervention in Cuban affairs also marked the establishment for the second time of an independent Cuban republic. That republic had come into being after the Spanish-American War of 1898, in which the United States intervened on behalf of Cuban insurgents who opposed Spanish rule of their island. The Treaty of Paris (1898), which concluded the hostilities, saw the virtual dissolution of the Spanish empire. Puerto Rico and Guam were ceded to the United States, as were the Philippine Islands, in return for $20 million. Spain also relinquished all authority over Cuba, which became an independent republic under American protection.

For three and a half years afterwards, Cuban affairs were administered by the U.S. War Department, briefly through General John R. Brooke and then through General Leonard Wood. The goal was to prepare the way for an independent but subservient Cuba. The American authorities held an election of Cuban delegates for a convention which, in February 1901, completed work on a constitution for a Cuban republic. As a condition for the end of military occupation, the convention reluctantly agreed to attach to Cuba's constitution what was known as the Platt Amendment. Designed to preserve Cuba's dependence on the United States, the Platt Amendment provided for American naval bases in Cuba and permitted U.S.

intervention in Cuban affairs. After the amendment was accepted, Cubans were allowed to elect a president and a Congress, which they did on December 31, 1901. With the inauguration of Tomas Estrada Palma, a leading anti-Spanish revolutionary, as the Cuban republic's first president, the United States formally withdrew from Cuba on May 20, 1902.

After new elections, which followed in late 1905 and early 1906, Tomas Estrada Palma became president for the second time, with the support of Cuban conservatives. Although he attempted to lead Cuba to economic prosperity, his administration, plagued by corruption and veterans' pension requests, failed to bring about demanded reforms. Claiming fraud in the elections, supporters of the Cuban Liberal Party under José Miguel Gómez revolted against the Palma administration in August 1906.

President Palma, invoking the Platt Amendment, declared that he was unable to maintain order and asked the United States to intervene. At first reluctant to interfere, the United States sent mediators, headed by Secretary of War (later President) William Howard Taft, who attempted to effect a compromise. When this attempt failed, President Palma and his cabinet resigned, leaving the island without a government.

To restore order the United States proclaimed a provisional government on September 29, 1906, under Taft. He was succeeded as provisional governor by Charles E. Magoon the next month. After order had been restored and new laws drafted by a U.S.–headed advisory committee, a new election was held in November 1908. With the inauguration of José Miguel Gómez, leader of the 1906 rebellion, as president on January 28, 1909, American administration of the island officially ceased for the second time.

January 29

Kansas Admitted to the Union

The admission of Kansas to the Union as the 34th state on January 29, 1861, brought to a close one of the most important chapters of American history. That chapter had begun seven years earlier when Kansas was organized as a territory under the controversial Kansas-Nebraska Act passed by Congress on May 30, 1854.

The repercussions of the Kansas-Nebraska Act, which opened the way for the extension of slavery to the West, were widespread. Debate over the act intensified pro- and antislavery sentiments across the country, making slavery the most inflammatory issue in the land. Passage of the measure inaugurated an era of bloodshed in Kansas that in some ways foreshadowed the Civil War. Politically there were repercussions too, for opposition to the Kansas-Nebraska Act cut across party lines and led to the formation of the new Republican Party by antislavery Whigs and Democrats and members of some other groups, including the Free-Soil Party, which opposed the extension of slavery.

The history of Kansas began when most of what is now Kansas came into American possession through the Louisiana Purchase in 1803. The rest of Kansas came into American possession after the Mexican War, which ended in defeat for Mexico and a massive transfer to the United States of Mexican territory, including much of the Midwest and Southwest. Sections of Kansas were designated as Indian territory by the U.S. government. From 1835 until 1850, part of Kansas was also claimed by Texas, a claim that ended when Texas ceased to be an independent nation and joined the United States as a state. Kansas itself was organized as a state in 1861.

The prelude to statehood began in 1804, when Lewis and Clark passed through Kansas on their famous voyage of exploration and discovery through the Louisiana Purchase. The vast prairies subsequently were crossed and recrossed by such explorers as Zebulon M. Pike, John C. Frémont, and Stephen H. Long, who dismissed the whole area now known as the nation's wheat belt as "uninhabitable by a people depending on agriculture." Beginning in 1821, the Santa Fe Trail stretched across the entire length of Kansas. Westward migration through the region continued in the 1830s, and in the 1840s the Oregon Trail carried thousands of Pacific-bound emigrants across the northeastern corner.

However, these were all people with destinations farther west. Actual settlement in the Kansas area began when a group of Presbyterians founded the first Kansas mission in 1824. This was followed by the establishment of Fort Leavenworth in 1827, Fort Scott in 1842, and Fort Riley in 1853. Large numbers of permanent settlers did not pour in, however, until Kansas was officially designated a territory by the Kansas-Nebraska Act, signed into law by President Franklin Pierce on May 30, 1854.

The Kansas-Nebraska Act provided that the residents of the territory that now constitutes the modern states of Kansas and Nebraska would decide for themselves whether they would become free states without slavery, or slave states. It was a North- versus-South issue in the years leading up to the Civil War: Northern states were free states; Southern states were slave states; and both North and South wanted new states joining the Union to be on their side. Previously, the Missouri Compromise had established an imaginary line running across the country, north of which new states became free states and south of which new states became slave states. The Kansas-Nebraska Act, however, repealed the Missouri Compromise and in effect left it to the settlers to literally fight it out for themselves. Nebraska, which borders Kansas on the north, was far enough north that it was fairly certain to enter the Union as a free state. Kansas, on the other hand, is almost dead center in the United States geographically. Settlers and sympathizers from both sides flooded to Kansas, determined to use any means, peaceful and otherwise, to bring Kansas into the Union on their side.

The conflicts between the two sides often turned violent, earning Kansas the nickname "bleeding Kansas." Antislavery newcomers settled in Lawrence, Topeka, and Osawatomie. Advocates of slavery founded Leavenworth, Atchison, and Lecompton. On March 30, 1855, an election for a territorial legislature was held, and 5,427 proslavery votes were cast out of a total of 6,307, which was rather suspicious since there were only 2,905 legal voters in the territory. The discrepancy was accounted for by proslavery Missourians who had crossed the border to stuff the ballot boxes and intimidate voters. Territorial governor A. H. Reeder set aside the election in six of the districts and ordered a new election that resulted in victory for the antislavery candidates.

Proslavery advocates, however, were able to seize effective control of the first territorial legislature that met at Pawnee, Kansas, on July 2, 1855. This majority expelled the members chosen at the second election ordered by the governor, and passed acts making it a capital offense to assist slaves in escaping either to or from the territory and a felony to circulate antislavery publications or to challenge the right to hold slaves. Not content with this, the legislature also required all voters to swear to support the Fugitive Slave Law, and eventually secured Governor Reeder's removal from office.

Antislavery advocates refused to recognize the legality of the territorial government and in a convention held at Topeka between October 23 and November 11, 1855, they adopted a constitution prohibiting slavery after July 4, 1857, and excluding blacks from Kansas. After their constitution was adopted at a December election, the Free-Soil, or abolitionist, contingent went on to choose state officers and a legislature and set up a rival government in January 1856.

Although the abolitionists wished to avoid armed conflict, violence came when a sheriff of the proslavery government was shot at Lawrence while trying to seize a prisoner. Antislavery leaders were indicted for treason and imprisoned, and on May 21, 1856, a proslavery mob sacked Lawrence. Three days later, the fiery abolitionist John Brown and his sons retaliated by killing five proslavery men at Pottawatomie Creek. Civil war between the two factions began, and continued throughout the month of June until federal troops intervened and restored order.

The Free-Soil legislature met at Topeka on July 4, 1856. Dispersed by federal troops, it made another attempt to meet on January 6, 1857, but its members were arrested. Robert J. Walker, who by then had become governor of the territory (the sixth in a rapidly changing series of governors), succeeded in arranging a compromise with the Free-Soilers, who agreed to take part in another election for a territorial legislature in October 1857.

Although the abolitionists won the election, the pro-slavery party meanwhile had called a convention to meet in Lecompton, where they adopted the proslavery Lecompton Constitution on November 7, 1857. Declaring that the right of slaveholders in Kansas to own slaves was inviolable, this constitution prohibited the legislature from passing any act of emancipation or preventing the importation of slaves. Then, on December 21, 1857, the people of the territory were called upon to decide whether they would have a constitution with slavery (i.e., with the Lecompton provisions) or without.

The proslavery vote was 6,226, more than half of which was polled along the Missouri border, where there were not more than 1,000 qualified voters. Since the great body of antislavery partisans regarded the election as farcical and refrained from voting, the opposition vote was only 569. Following this, the entire Lecompton Constitution was submitted to the voters by the territorial legislature on January 4, 1858, with 10,226 votes cast against the measure and fewer than 200 for it. The issue was then taken to Congress, where the Senate ignored the verdict of territory residents and voted to admit Kansas as a state with the Lecompton Constitution. The House of Representatives rejected this bill, however, instead passing legislation that put the Lecompton Constitution to another referendum by Kansas voters.

In a ringing defeat for the proslavery forces, Kansas voters once again rejected the Lecompton Constitution, finally ending the struggle to establish slavery in Kansas. The antislavery Wyandotte Constitution was subsequently adopted by Kansas voters on October 4, 1859. Kansas was admitted to the Union as a free state on January 29, 1861, just as the Civil War was beginning.

William McKinley's Birthday

Library of Congress

William McKinley

William McKinley, the 25th president of the United States, was born in Niles, Ohio, on January 29, 1843. Of Scots-Irish ancestry, he was the seventh of the nine children of William and Nancy Allison McKinley. His great-grandfather, David McKinley, was a soldier in the American Revolution. His father and grandfather were engaged in the iron industry, and he worked with his father as a boy.

After the family moved to Poland, Ohio, McKinley prepared for college at Poland Academy and subsequently entered Allegheny College at Meadville, Pennsylvania. Unable to complete his work towards a degree due to lack of funds, he returned to Poland and obtained employment as a teacher. He was still teaching when the Civil War broke out, but not long afterwards, on June 11, 1861, he enlisted in the 23rd Regiment of Ohio Volunteer Infantry commanded by Brigadier General William S. Rosecrans. Rutherford B. Hayes, a Republican later elected president, succeeded Rosecrans as commander, and on September 24, 1862, commissioned McKinley a second lieutenant for gallantry in the field. McKinley continued with the regiment throughout the war, reaching the rank of major.

When he was mustered out of the army after the Civil War, McKinley began the study of law in the office of an Ohio judge and completed his preparation at the Albany Law School. He was admitted to the bar in 1867 and opened an office in Canton, Ohio. Immediately becoming active as a Republican, he worked on behalf of Ulysses S. Grant's successful candidacy in the presidential campaign of 1868. McKinley's own political career began the next year, when he was elected prosecuting attorney for Ohio's Stark County, an unusual achievement for a Republican since the county was normally Democratic.

McKinley loyally supported the candidacy of his former commander, Rutherford B. Hayes, for the governorship of Ohio in 1875. Elected to the U.S. House of Representatives in 1876, McKinley served there for seven terms, which were interrupted by only a single defeat (in 1882). In time, he became the Republican leader in the House and rose to the chairmanship of the Ways and Means Committee. A highly protective tariff act drawn up by that committee was known by his name, the McKinley Tariff Act.

McKinley lost the House election of 1890 as a result of a reapportionment of Ohio's congressional districts. Democrats, in control of the state legislature, gerrymandered his district to give their party a majority. However, the defeat represented hardly a pause in his upward career. He was elected governor of Ohio on the Republican ticket in 1891 and was easily reelected in 1893. With this triumph behind him, he was nominated by the Republicans for the presidency in 1896. McKinley defeated William Jennings Bryan, the Democratic-Populist candidate, by an electoral vote of 271 to 176.

The chief event during McKinley's presidency was the Spanish-American War of 1898, which he carried to a successful conclusion. The treaty of peace that concluded the war provided that Spain withdraw from Cuba and cede the islands of Puerto Rico, Guam, and the Philippines to the United States. McKinley was reelected president in 1900, defeating Bryan once again, but his second term was tragically short. On September 6, 1901, he was shot while attending a public reception at the Pan American Exposition in Buffalo, New York, and he died on September 14.

Although rarely celebrated anymore, McKinley's birthday was once honored as Carnation Day. The celebration was proposed by Lewis G. Reynolds of Dayton, Ohio. In a letter to the editor of the *New York Tribune*, published on January 22, 1903, he said:

It is proper that some annual observance be held in memory of William McKinley. The same loyal impulse that prompted the stoppage of almost all the wheels of industry for those few moments on the day of his burial may find annual expression in this tribute suggested by the Carnation League. The plan of the movement is a simple, inexpensive and attractive one and can be taken part in by the old and the young of either sex. A beautiful, fragrant flower worn in the lapel of the coat or at the throat or in the hair in silent memory of a public servant whose life was forfeited because he was our servant is what is contemplated. The fact that the carnation was President McKinley's favorite flower and was always found in his buttonhole is the reason for its choice as a league symbol. On all other days of the year it will be what it is today, the common people's flower, but on September 14 [it was first proposed to observe the day of McKinley's death] it becomes especially the President's flower and will be worn in silent tribute to his memory. . . . If the Carnation League of America serves the purpose of a perennial memorial to a faithful public servant and at the same time fosters a national brotherhood of patriotism it will be worthy of our people.

McKinley's birthday, not the day of his death, became Carnation Day. In the decades to come America would see more great presidents, not to mention more presidential assassinations, and over time the observance of Carnation Day faded into obscurity.

Thomas Paine's Birthday

Thomas Paine, the writer and propagandist whose essays on independence inflamed the colonists by clarifying the issues for which the American Revolution would be fought, was born at Thetford in Norfolk, England, on January 29, 1737. Forced by poverty to leave school at the age of 13, he joined his Quaker father in the trade of corset making. He followed this trade intermittently in various parts of England and also worked at one time or another as a sailor, excise officer, tobacconist, grocer, and schoolteacher, meanwhile educating himself by reading books on politics, social issues, and science.

In England, Paine was oppressed by poverty, the death of his first wife, and an unhappy second marriage. Armed with letters of introduction from Benjamin Franklin, whom he had met in London,

he immigrated to Philadelphia in the fall of 1774. There he became editor of the *Pennsylvania Magazine*, attached himself to the patriot cause, and soon proved to be an exceptional writer. His pamphlet *Common Sense*, arguing that the American colonies owed no allegiance to the British crown and "should forthwith be independent," was published on January 10, 1776 (see January 10). It had a decisive effect in the colonies, where public opinion hovered irresolutely between the alternatives of limited revolt and an attempt to gain independence. Though it did nothing to alter the apathy of some, the pamphlet, in the understated words of George Washington, "worked a powerful change in the minds of many men."

Six months after the publication of *Common Sense*, the Declaration of Independence was adopted by the Second Continental Congress in Philadelphia on July 4, 1776. The clashes later recognized as the beginning of the American Revolution had already taken place in 1775 at Lexington, Concord, and Bunker Hill. After the Declaration of Independence, however, the colonies would soon be in open and total rebellion.

Paine served briefly in George Washington's army in 1776, and on a November night during the New Jersey retreat demonstrated the truth of a comment Franklin had made: that while some could rule and many could fight, "only Paine can write for us." Huddled over a drum, Paine poured his fervor into what became the first of the essays in *The Crisis*, starting with the memorable words "These are the times that try men's souls." Widely read and influential, *The Crisis* was printed and reprinted throughout the Revolution, giving substantial encouragement to the new nation's first patriots.

During the late 1770s, Paine served as secretary of the congressional committee on foreign affairs and then as clerk of the Pennsylvania assembly. In 1781 he went with John Laurens to France, successfully seeking financial aid for the former colonies. At the suggestion of George Washington, Congress voted Paine $800 for his services to the nation. Paine was subsequently presented by the state of New York with a 300-acre farm at New Rochelle and by Congress with an additional $3,000 in 1785.

After the Revolution, Paine spent the years from 1787 until 1802 in England and France. Although his original purpose was to generate interest in a new form of iron bridge that he had invented, he attracted more attention as a propagandist bent on turning both England and France into republics. Paine's *Rights of Man* defended the 1789 French Revolution, which had periodically degenerated into mob violence and disorder. *Rights of*

Man gave a spirited defense of the republican form of government with a written constitution, universal male suffrage, and no artificial distinctions of birth and rank. The sentiments did not win Paine the friendship of the British government, which indicted him for treason and suppressed the pamphlet, fearing that it would lead (as Paine hoped) to revolution in Great Britain.

Before Paine could be brought to trial, however, he escaped to France and rapidly became involved in French revolutionary politics. After becoming a French citizen, he was elected as a delegate to the revolutionary National Convention, which discussed the deposing of King Louis XVI. Paine served for a year in the convention. He was attached to the moderate Girondist Party and counseled exile, rather than execution, for the king, arousing the suspicions of Robespierre and the increasingly radical Jacobin political faction. After the Jacobins had crushed the Girondists and instituted the Reign of Terror, Paine was arrested and imprisoned for about 10 months, beginning on December 28, 1793. Late in 1794, after the fall of Robespierre, he was reinstated in the National Convention.

Paine's controversial *Age of Reason*, which appeared in two parts in 1794 and 1796, was a defense of deism, the doctrine that reason and nature, as seen in the logical design of the universe, are in themselves and without benefit of supernatural revelation sufficient proof of the existence of God. Although *The Age of Reason* attacked a strictly literal interpretation of the Bible, it was, in Paine's words, written "lest in the general wreck of superstition . . . we lost sight of morality . . . humanity, and . . . the theology that is true."

Thomas Jefferson commented favorably on *The Age of Reason*, while Jefferson's American political opponents in the Federalist Party accused Paine of being an atheist, a charge that long persisted. Paine's own tactlessness, and such works as his vitriolic *Letter to Washington* in 1796, did not increase his popularity. When Paine returned to the United States in 1802 he discovered that, although his services to the cause of freedom had not been wholly forgotten, he was almost completely ostracized. He spent the last seven years of his life in poverty and deteriorating health. After his death in New York City on June 8, 1809, he was buried in a corner of his farm at New Rochelle, where a monument was erected to him in 1839. His body, however, was removed to England in 1819. Despite the controversy that marked his seldom placid life, Paine is respected as a patriot and leading figure of the American Revolution.

Clinton Administration Announces New Policy Concerning Gays in the Military

On January 29, 1993, President Bill Clinton's administration announced a new policy concerning the treatment of homosexuals in the United States military establishment, popularly termed "don't ask, don't tell." This policy decision was an attempt to reconcile what had become a difficult issue in the military in particular and in American society in general.

Popular acceptance of homosexuals in American society, who often prefer the term "gay" and/or "lesbian," has developed slowly. Although by the 1990s it was possible to function as an openly gay member of society, popular prejudice and scorn remained high and many gays preferred to remain "in the closet," practicing their personal preferences in private while publicly maintaining an apparently mainstream lifestyle. This was particularly true in the military, where the genders were typically segregated and the idea of sexual activity in all-male or all-female quarters was troubling. Although illicit sexual encounters between members of the same sex in the military are probably as old as warfare itself, the outwardly strict moral regime and appearance of clean-cut traditional values has always been a part of maintaining military pride and morale. Thus, the interests of individual preferences clashed with the perceived need to maintain military discipline.

The traditional approach to gays in the military was simple: homosexuality was outlawed. Regulation AR135-175 (1982) stated that "if a member (of the United States Armed Forces) states that he or she is a homosexual, then that member will be removed from the military." The "don't ask, don't tell" policy, approved by Congress in November 1993, barred homosexuals from military service only if they did or said anything that reflected their sexual orientation. However, the military was no longer allowed to ask recruits about their sexual preference. Essentially, gays were permitted to serve in the military so long as they were circumspect in their activities.

The new policy pleased no one. Civil rights and gay rights groups accused the Clinton administration of forcing gays and lesbians to remain in the closet. Conservative groups accused the administration of hypocrisy in formulating a policy with such a self-contradictory approach. As of this writing, the "don't ask, don't tell" policy has survived several challenges in the federal courts and before the Supreme Court itself.

January 30

Oprah Winfrey's Birthday

Oprah Winfrey, one of the most successful black women in the entertainment industry, was born on January 29, 1954, in Kosciusko, Mississippi. At the age of six, she moved to Milwaukee and lived with her mother, but she ran away from home at the age of 13 in order to escape an abusive environment. She then went to Nashville, Tennessee, to live with her father.

Under her father Vernon Winfrey's strict upbringing, Oprah flourished and became a model student. She won a scholarship to Tennessee State University, where she pursued her interest in journalism and became the first black female to announce the news at the local television station in Nashville. She graduated from Tennessee State University in 1976.

For the next eight years, Oprah held a variety of jobs with regional television stations. In 1984 she became the host of the talk show *AM Chicago*. The next year, this program was renamed *The Oprah Winfrey Show*. It was this program that gave her national recognition, and in 1986 it was carried nationwide. Not only did the program deal with controversial issues in a straightforward and appealing manner, but Oprah's personality won her a wide following. Oprah also found the time to pursue a movie career, starring as Sophia in the award-winning film *The Color Purple* (1985) and also appearing in *Native Son* (1986).

Oprah's success won her considerable wealth in addition to fame. With the profits from her television talk show, movies, and other activities such as her own book club, Oprah Winfrey ranks as one of the wealthiest African Americans (and possibly the wealthiest African American woman) in America as of this writing. She continues to actively pursue her various career interests.

January 30

Franklin D. Roosevelt's Birthday

One of the United States' most influential presidents, Franklin Delano Roosevelt (FDR), the 32nd to hold the office, was born on January 30, 1882, on his family's Hudson Valley estate at Hyde Park, New York. Roosevelt began his presidency during the darkest days of the Great Depression, giving decisive leadership to an apprehensive nation on the brink of despair. He was still at the helm eight years later when the Japanese attack on Pearl Harbor precipitated the United States' entry into World War II, and he guided the country's course almost until the end of that global conflict.

Library of Congress

Franklin D. Roosevelt

In all, he served as president a little more than 12 years, longer than any other person.

Roosevelt was descended on his father's side from Claes Martenszan van Rosenvelt, who arrived in New Amsterdam, the predecessor to modern New York City, in about 1649 from the Netherlands. The New World ancestors of his mother, the former Sara Delano, dated back to Philippe de la Noye, of French-Dutch lineage, who arrived in Plymouth colony in the 1620s. Franklin's father, James Roosevelt, was vicepresident of the Delaware & Hudson Railroad and lived on the estate at Hyde Park that his family had owned for a hundred years. His only child Franklin grew up there, educated by governesses and tutors, and spent summer vacations on Campobello Island, where he developed a lifetime interest in ships and sailing.

At 14, young Franklin Roosevelt was sent to the strict Groton School in Groton, Massachusetts. He attended Harvard University from 1900 to 1904, during which time his father died. After graduation, Roosevelt developed an interest in politics, thanks to the political success of his fifth cousin, Republican president Theodore Roosevelt. Also after graduation, Roosevelt married. During his years at Harvard, Roosevelt had fallen in love with his shy fifth-cousin-once-removed, Anna Eleanor Roosevelt, self-described as the "ugly duckling" of her socially prominent family. Eleanor Roosevelt, who was to win such admiration in the course of her lifetime that she would ultimately be referred to as the First Lady of the World, was the niece of Theodore Roosevelt, who gave her away when she married Franklin Roosevelt on March 17, 1905.

Meanwhile, FDR had entered Columbia Law School in the fall of 1904. Following a delayed honeymoon in Europe, the young couple lived in a house on East 36th Street in New York City. The first of their six children was born in 1906. After Roosevelt passed the New York State bar examination in 1907, he began to practice law in New York City with the firm of Carter, Ledyard and Milburn, an association that lasted about three years. One of his fellow law clerks later recalled his having explained during this period that he wanted, at the first chance, to run for public office and that he would, in fact, like to be president.

While practicing law, in which he had only limited interest, Roosevelt also spent a good deal of time at Hyde Park, managing the family property and participating in community affairs. The opportunity to run for office was not long in coming. As the son of a leading local family, he was offered his district's Democratic nomination for the state Senate in 1910. He was elected after an energetic campaign, even though the district usually voted Republican, and was reelected in 1912. In Albany, he attracted notice as the leader of a group of Democrats who rebelled against the dominance of the Tammany Hall political organization in New York City Democratic politics. In 1911 and 1912 he was prominent in the effort to secure the Democratic presidential nomination for Woodrow Wilson, organizing independent Democrats for Wilson and leading an unofficial delegation to the Democratic convention in Baltimore. After Wilson won the presidency in the 1912 election, FDR served as assistant secretary of the navy from 1913 to 1920.

Roosevelt unsuccessfully ran for the U.S. Senate in 1914. He also unsuccessfully sought the Democratic nomination for vicepresident in the 1920 election, although the Democrats lost that election anyway to Republican Warren G. Harding. Then came a crippling attack of polio in August 1921, which imperiled both Roosevelt's political career and his very life. FDR survived polio, but his legs were largely paralyzed. In the course of time he learned how to walk with crutches, and then with a cane while his legs were supported by iron braces. He also acquired his famous estate at Warm Springs, Georgia, where he found relief from the pain in his legs by bathing in the warm springs there.

By 1924, FDR's health had returned and he resumed work. He left his law firm, Emmet, Marvin and Roosevelt, and returned to politics. He supported Governor Alfred E. Smith of New York's unsuccessful bid for the Democratic Party presidential nomination in 1924. In 1928 Roosevelt again supported Smith, who this time successfully obtained the Democratic nomination for president but was defeated in the election by Republican Herbert Hoover. Also in 1928, Smith persuaded Roosevelt to run as the Democratic candidate for governor of New York State. After a vigorous campaign, and in the face of a Republican sweep of most of the nation, Roosevelt was successful in his bid for the governorship. He was reelected governor in 1930.

Meanwhile, the Great Depression had begun, following the stock market crash of 1929. It was against this background that the Democrats met in Chicago in 1932 to choose a candidate for president. On the fourth ballot the delegates chose Roosevelt. In his acceptance speech, Roosevelt pledged "a New Deal for the American people." With his vice-presidential running mate, John Nance Garner, Roosevelt won overwhelmingly in November over the ticket headed by President Hoover, receiving over 22 million popular votes to Hoover's 15 million and 472 electoral college votes to Hoover's 59. The Democrats also won overwhelming majorities in the Senate and the House of Representatives.

The nation's economic crisis deepened in the period between election day and Roosevelt's inauguration on March 4, 1933. By the time he took office, the nation's unemployed numbered between 12 and 15 million; one-seventh of the population was subsisting on public or private relief; industrial production was down to about half that of 1929; hundreds of factories had closed; and over 5,000 banks had failed. A mood bordering on panic pervaded the country. Roosevelt, however, was prepared for action. In the interim between election and inauguration, he gathered around him a group of advisers later referred to as the Brain Trust. They and other experts set their minds to devising programs to meet the crisis.

On Inauguration Day, a Saturday, the new president set the tone for what was to come. Confident and optimistic, he declared in his inaugural address that "the only thing we have to fear is fear itself." On Sunday, March 5, he issued two proclamations. One called the 73rd Congress to meet in special session on Thursday, March 9. The other declared a four-day bank holiday beginning on Monday, March 6, which closed all the nation's banks. Most banks, once their fiscal soundness was determined, were permitted to reopen very quickly thereafter under new and stricter controls.

Roosevelt's New Deal began with the famous first "Hundred Days" in office, as Congress acted with breathtaking speed to pass an impressive body of New Deal legislation in less than a hundred days. Laws were passed to stabilize the banking system, create jobs, give financial assistance to the needy, ensure better farm income, protect home owners, begin a vast program of public works, and reform the securities markets. The titles of some of these measures are indicative of their scope: the Emergency Banking Act, the Emergency Farm Mortgage Act, the National Employment System Act, the Home Owners Refinancing Act, the Glass-Steagall Banking Act (which created the Federal Deposit Insurance Corporation), the Farm Credit Act, etc.

Further, a number of important government agencies were established. Among them were the Civilian Conservation Corps, which provided work for up to a quarter of a million young men; the Agricultural Adjustment Administration, which undertook to raise agricultural purchasing power by subsidizing farmers; and the Tennessee Valley Authority, which brought dams and electric power to some of the nation's poorest areas. Also born in the hundred-day period were the National Recovery Administration, created under the National Industrial Recovery Act, and the Public Works Administration.

There were other important measures after the Hundred Days period. An act was passed creating the Securities and Exchange Commission, with the power to regulate the securities markets. The National Labor Relations Act was passed in 1935, strengthening labor's power to bargain collectively, providing guarantees against coercion by employers, and establishing the National Labor Relations Board with the power to supervise labor elections. The Social Security Act was also passed in 1935. Finally, during Roosevelt's first term in office the United States went off the gold standard, meaning that except for some international transactions, the dollar was no longer backed by government gold reserves.

Roosevelt was renominated at the Democratic National Convention in Philadelphia in June 1936 for the November 1936 presidential ticket. He won reelection by a precedent-shattering margin of more than 11 million in the popular vote and all but eight of the electoral votes. He carried every state except Maine and Vermont against the Republican ticket headed by Governor Alfred M. Landon of Kansas. In early 1937 Roosevelt became the first president inaugurated under the terms of the 20th Amendment to the U.S. Constitution, which set January 20 as the date on which presidential terms begin.

More New Deal legislation was passed in FDR's second term. Among them were the Bituminous Coal Act, the Farm Tenancy Act, the Wagner-Steagall Housing Act, the second Agricultural Adjustment Act, and the Fair Labor Standards Act, establishing the first hourly minimum wage and providing for the 40-hour work week. For a time it looked like the Depression was about to end, but the economic recovery collapsed in 1937. Also during Roosevelt's second term, he proposed the controversial Supreme Court "packing plan." The Supreme Court, which is composed of nine justices, had nullified a number of New Deal laws. Frustrated, Roosevelt wanted to expand the Court to 17 justices, which would give him the power to nominate eight new justices loyal only to him and make the Court more compliant. This proposal was extremely unpopular both in Congress and with the public, since it was a blatant effort to subvert the venerable Supreme Court, and Roosevelt shortly abandoned it.

Meanwhile, the rise of dictatorships in Europe threatened the peace that had lasted since the end of World War I. Most Americans wanted to stay out of foreign affairs. As Germany and Japan became increasingly aggressive, however, Roosevelt sought to prepare the country for the seemingly inevitable war. He secured funds for expansion of the U.S. Navy in both the Atlantic and the Pacific oceans, persuaded Congress to let the U.S. sell arms to Britain and France, and increased defense spending overall. Roosevelt also authorized the transfer of 50 navy destroyers to the British in exchange for 99-year leases on eight naval and air bases in the Western Hemisphere. Finally, FDR secured passage of the Selective Training and Service Act, the nation's first peacetime draft law.

As World War II approached, Roosevelt took another unprecedented step: He decided to run for a third term as president in the upcoming 1940 elections. At the time, there was no Constitutional restriction on the number of terms that a president could serve. George Washington, however, had once stated that a president should not serve more than two terms and himself left office as the nation's first president after two terms. Since Washington's time, no president had dared to break with that precedent, but Roosevelt chose to run anyway. He won the election, but by a smaller margin than in previous elections.

In March 1941, FDR secured passage of the Lend-Lease Act, which provided that the president could "loan" arms and supplies to any nation whose defense the president judged to be essential to the security of the United States. Initially intended primarily for Britain, Lend-Lease assistance was later extended to other countries, eventually reaching a total of more than $50 billion. Britain's prime minister Winston Churchill referred to the legislation as the "most unsordid act in the history of any nation." After World War II, repayment of these "loans" was largely forgiven by Congress.

With the passage of the Lend-Lease Act, the United States, still technically neutral, had all but abandoned its claim to that status. In the summer and fall of 1941, relations between the U.S. and the "Axis," the term for the alliance between Germany, Italy, and Japan, became increasingly strained. War finally broke out when Japan attacked the American naval installation at Pearl Harbor, Hawaii, on December 7, 1941, "a date which," Roosevelt declared, "shall live in infamy." The next day, FDR asked Congress to declare that "since [that] unprovoked and dastardly attack . . . a state of war has existed between the United States and the Japanese Empire." Within four hours both houses of Congress had approved the declaration of war with only a single dissenting vote. On December 11, Japan's Axis partners declared war against the United States, and the U.S. reciprocated by declaring war on them the same day.

Although tough years were ahead, America's entry into the war put the Axis on the defensive, and the Allies gradually liberated the territories seized by the Germans, Italians, and Japanese. Roosevelt's role in the war was, of course, immense. He authorized a mammoth effort, known as the Manhattan Project, to develop the atomic bomb. He also periodically met with the other major Allied leaders, including British prime minister Winston Churchill and Soviet dictator Joseph Stalin.

In 1944, with the war still raging, Roosevelt was nominated by the Democrats for an unprecedented fourth term. With his vice-presidential running mate, Harry S. Truman, he defeated Republican Thomas E. Dewey. Soon after his fourth inauguration, a sick and aged FDR left to meet with Churchill and Stalin in the February 1945 conference at Yalta in the Russian Crimea, on the Black Sea. There the leaders discussed the final defeat of the Axis and the details of postwar occupation and boundaries, as well as the establishment of the United Nations. President Roosevelt, however, did not live to see the final Allied victory. On April 12, 1945, he was stricken with a massive cerebral hemorrhage at his estate in Warm Springs, Georgia.

Roosevelt's body was taken from Warm Springs to Washington, D.C. The flag-draped coffin remained briefly in the East Room of the White House, while on the Capitol the flag flew at half-mast. Later, Roosevelt's body was taken to his family estate at Hyde Park and buried in the rose garden, the grave marked as he had requested with a plain white marble tombstone. In the 1990s a modest memorial to FDR was built in Washington, D.C., to honor his memory.

Gene Hackman's Birthday

One of America's favorite actors, Gene Hackman was born on January 30, 1930, in San Bernadino, California. His family moved to Danville, Illinois, where he spent the bulk of his childhood. He was a rebellious teenager, and dropped out of high school at the age of 16 in order to enlist with the United States Marine Corps.

Hackman was a Marine for three years. During his time in the military, he was trained as a radio operator and developed an interest in the media. After leaving the service, he entered the University of Illinois under the G.I. Bill, where he took classes in journalism and the emerging field of television production. After graduating from the University of Illinois, he attended the School of Radio Technique in New York City.

For several years, Hackman held a variety of small-time jobs, until he finally decided to focus his energies on acting. At the age of 30, which many considered to be too old to begin an acting career, he entered the famous Pasadena Playhouse in order to study. His first movie role was in a low-budget gangster production called *Mad Dog Coll* (1961). Although this movie was hardly a box office hit, it caused Hackman to be noticed by the famous actor and director Warren Beatty. Thanks to Beatty, Hackman landed a role in the film classic *Bonnie and Clyde* (1967), which resulted in an Oscar nomination for Hackman and his rise to prominence.

In the decades since Gene Hackman's breakthrough in *Bonnie and Clyde*, he has been in a wide variety of movies, many of which have won critical acclaim and recognition for him at the Oscars. Some of his most famous movies include *I Never Sang for My Father* (1970), *The French Connection* (1971), *The Poseidon Adventure* (1972), *Superman* (1978), *Mississippi Burning* (1988), *Postcards from the Edge* (1990), and *Unforgiven* (1992).

January 31

Jackie Robinson's Birthday

Jack Roosevelt Robinson, later known as Jackie Robinson, one of the ground-breaking figures of professional baseball and American race relations, was born on January 31, 1919, in Cairo, Georgia. His parents were poor sharecroppers, but managed to leave the South and settle in Pasadena, California. Jackie was one of five children.

From an early age, Robinson demonstrated exceptional athletic ability. He attended Pasadena Junior College (later Pasadena City College) for a time, but in 1939 he was awarded an athletic scholarship to the prestigious University of California at Los Angeles (UCLA). At the university, Robinson made varsity history when he became the first person to win letters in four sports: baseball, basketball, football, and track. However, in 1941 Robinson left UCLA and enlisted in the United States Army.

Financial considerations may have prompted Robinson's decision to leave the university before graduating. At any rate, his military career appeared promising when he was admitted to Officer Candidate School and was eventually commissioned as a second lieutenant. However, his military career ended abruptly after an incident at Ft. Hood, Texas, where he protested the discriminatory practices of the still segregated army. Specifically, Robinson refused to sit in the back of a segregated bus. After a court-martial, he was acquitted but was forced to leave the service with an honorable discharge at the rank of first lieutenant. In 1945, the year after he left the army, Robinson began his famous baseball career.

At the time, professional baseball was a segregated sport, and African American teams were known as the "Negro Leagues." Robinson joined one of these teams, the Kansas City Monarchs. His exceptional abilities attracted the attention of Branch Rickey, the head of the Brooklyn Dodgers (later the Los Angeles Dodgers). At the time, the Brooklyn Dodgers were a struggling team, perennially at the bottom of the standings in their league. Thus, Branch Rickey was willing to break the social taboo against mixing blacks and whites, and he offered Robinson a position with the Dodgers.

When Jackie Robinson joined the Brooklyn Dodgers in 1947, he became the first African American player in the major leagues. He helped the Dodgers win their league with a batting average of .297, and was voted Rookie of the Year. In 1949, he was chosen as the Most Valuable Player in his league after batting an astonishing .342. With Robinson at bat, the Brooklyn Dodgers went on to win several more league championships and eventually the World Series in 1955. After being traded to the New York Giants in 1957, Robinson retired from baseball, finishing with a lifetime batting average of .311. In 1962 he became the first

African American to be inducted into the Baseball Hall of Fame.

Although Jackie Robinson's baseball career was enormously successful, he sas often extremely unhappy. As the first African American in major league baseball, he had to endure the verbal and physical abuse directed at him by the crowds, opposing teams, and even his fellow Dodgers.

After retiring from baseball, Robinson moved to New York, where he became the vice-president of the Chock Full O'Nuts company and also got involved with a variety of African American businesses in the predominantly black Harlem district of New York City. In the late 1960s Robinson became a prominent civil rights advocate, and New York governor Nelson Rockefeller appointed him special assistant for civil rights.

Jackie Robinson died on October 24, 1972, in Stamford, Connecticut, still active and having planned to attend a conference on drug abuse that very day. The epitaph on his tombstone summarizes his approach towards life: "A life is not important except in the impact it has on other lives."

Norman Mailer's Birthday

Norman Mailer, one of America's most famous and controversial writers, was born in Long Branch, New Jersey, on January 31, 1923. He grew up in the New York City borough of Brooklyn, and was admitted to Harvard University in 1939. Mailer developed an interest in writing during his college years, but after graduation in 1943 he was drafted into the United States Army to serve in World War II.

Mailer's wartime service became the inspiration for his first novel, the famous work *The Naked and the Dead* (1948). In addition to establishing a national reputation for Mailer, the novel has been described as one of the most significant literary works of the Second World War. In the 1950s Mailer became involved with a variety of antiwar and socially activist causes, helping to establish publications such as the *Village Voice* and *Dissent*. In the 1960s he was active in protests against the Vietnam War, and in 1967 was jailed for helping to lead a massive protest march against the Pentagon.

In addition to pursuing his various social and political causes, Mailer continued to be an active and productive writer. Some of his more famous works after *The Naked and the Dead* include *Barbary Shore* (1951), *The Deer Park* (1955), *Advertisements for Myself* (1959), *The Presidential Papers* (1963), *An American Dream* (1964), *Why Are We in Vietnam?* (1967), *The Armies of the Night* (1968), *A Fire on the Moon* (1970), *The Prisoner* of *Sex* (1971), *Marilyn* (1973), *A Transit to Narcissus* (1978), *The Executioner's Song* (1979), and *Tough Guys Don't Dance* (1983). Some of his later works, however, such as his account of the Kennedy assassination in *Oswald's Tale: An American Mystery* (1995), received very mixed reviews.

Norman Mailer continues to maintain an active literary career. He has had six marriages, and has nine children.

James G. Blaine's Birthday

James G. Blaine, one of the late 19th century's leading politicians, was born in West Brownsville, Pennsylvania, on January 31, 1830. He graduated from Washington (now Washington and Jefferson) College in Washington, Pennsylvania, at the age of 17. After spending the next several years as a teacher and student of law in Kentucky and Pennsylvania, he moved to Augusta, Maine, and became part-owner and editor of the *Kennebec Journal* in 1854.

Attending the first national convention of the newly organized Republican Party in 1856, Blaine played an active role in the formation of that party in Maine. As a journalist he was instrumental in making the name Republican widely known in the East. In 1857 he became editor of the *Advertiser* in Portland, Maine, a position that he held for three years.

Blaine was elected to the state legislature in 1858 and rose to the post of speaker two years later. In the meantime, he had been made chairman of the Republican state committee. He was elected to the national House of Representatives in 1862 and served there until 1876, holding the position of speaker of the House from 1869 until 1875.

Blaine had ambitions for the Republican presidential nomination in 1876, but the publication of what were known as the Mulligan letters, suggesting that he had used his political influence for personal profit, weakened his support, and he lost the nomination. Immediately after that year's election, however, he was appointed by the state of Maine to fill a vacancy in the U.S. Senate. Soon afterwards, he was elected to a full Senate term. Blaine was again a candidate for his party's presidential nomination in 1880, but failed for a second time to receive it.

President James Garfield, elected in 1880, appointed Blaine secretary of state, but after Garfield's assassination in 1881, Blaine resigned. Before he stepped down, he sought modification of the Clayton-Bulwer Treaty of 1850 between the United States and Great Britain. Modification of its terms was not accomplished until after Blaine's death, but when it did take place, with the Hay-Pauncefote Treaty of 1901, the British consented to the construction of an American-controlled seaway across the Isthmus of Panama, laying the groundwork for the Panama Canal.

In 1884 Blain finally won the Republican nomination and ran against Grover Cleveland. With the independent Republicans, or "mugwumps," leaving the party ticket and opposing Blaine's election, Cleveland was successful. His margin of victory was so narrow, however, that some observers laid the blame for Blaine's defeat on a single issue: his failure to promptly denounce the speech of a supporter who called the Democrats the party of "Rum" (meaning drinking), "Romanism" (meaning Catholics), "and Rebellion" (meaning the defeated South, which was mostly Democratic). The offending comment was made by the Reverend Samuel D. Burchard at New York City's Fifth Avenue Hotel on October 29, 1884.

Blaine became secretary of state a second time, under President Benjamin Harrison in 1889. Long the champion of an inter-American system that would provide for arbitration to offset tensions and prevent conflicts, and that would also facilitate planning of cooperative measures for the mutual advantage of the United States and Latin America, Blaine presided over the first Pan-American Conference on October 2, 1889. Also favoring increased trade within the hemisphere, he urged the adoption of trade reciprocity treaties with Latin American nations.

Blaine was the author of *Twenty Years of Congress*, an autobiographical work, and a volume of political addresses. He resigned as secretary of state in June 1892 for health reasons, and died in Washington, D.C., on January 27, 1893.

February

February (from Februarius, derived from the Latin *februa* for "feast of purification"), is the second month in the Gregorian, or New Style, calendar in use today. It usually has 28 days, although in leap years (see February 29) it consists of 29. Like January, February was originally omitted from the early Roman calendar, which contained only 10 months, March through December. To complete the calendar year, the Romans inserted a number of extra days or an occasional intercalary month in the "dead" season of midwinter, between the last month of the year (December) and the first month of the next year (March). According to tradition, Numa Pompilius, the legendary second Roman king (about 715–672 B.C.), created the months of Januarius and Februarius out of this previously unnamed period. He is said to have inaugurated a complicated calendar, operating on a four-year cycle, in which the number of days allotted to February varied from 23 to 29, depending upon the year.

Julius Caesar revised the length of the months in his calendar reform, which was adopted in 45 B.C. (see Appendix A: The Calendar). His calendar, which is now known as the Julian, or Old Style, calendar, made February a month of 28 days, but in every fourth year February contained an extra day between February 23 and 24. The Romans, counting back from March 1 (the Kalends, or first day of the month) called "both" February 24ths the sixth of the Kalends of March, hence the term *bisextile*, literally meaning "sixth twice," for a leap year. Another explanation, although no longer credited, has been given to account for the changes in the lengths of the months. This holds that the Emperor Augustus, after it was proposed that a month be named for him, insisted out of vanity that the month contain 31 days, as many as the longer months. Specifically, he supposedly did not wish his month to have fewer days than July, named after Julius Caesar. Augustus, so the story goes, therefore stole time from February to add to August, which previously had fewer than 31 days.

The name *Februarius* arose from the Roman ceremonies of religious purification and expiation that took place during that month in anticipation of the new year, which originally began on March 1. Among the most important festivals was the Lupercalia, the ancient feast of fruitfulness, or fertility, on February 15. This celebration had originated in early Roman times, when the small settlement on the Palatine Hill earned its livelihood by cultivating the soil and keeping flocks and herds. The rites were under the supervision of a corporation of priests called the Luperci, divided into two colleges called Quinctillani and Fabiani, each headed by a master (*magister*). In 44 B.C. a third college, the Luperci Iulii, was instituted in honor of Julius Caesar, and on February 15 of that year, Mark Antony, as its master, offered to make Caesar king just a month before the latter's assassination. (Shakespeare alludes to this in Mark Antony's famous oration in *Julius Caesar*: "You all did see that on the Lupercal / I thrice presented him a kingly crown, / Which he did thrice refuse.")

It is not known if the ritual honored a particular deity, such as a god Lupercus. Some scholars claim that the Lupercalia honored a pastoral deity, probably Faunus. Whatever the case, the Lupercalian rites began as the priests assembled in the cave of Lupercal on the southwestern part of the Palatine Hill, where Romulus and Remus, the legendary founders of Rome, were supposed to have been nourished by a she-wolf. There the priests sacrificed goats and a young dog, after which the foreheads of two youthful Luperci of high rank were smeared with the blood of the victims. After the blood had been wiped off with wool dipped in milk, ritual required that the two youths laugh. Following a sacrificial feast, they stripped themselves naked to don only a loincloth fashioned from the skins of the slain goats. Holding strips of the hides, they ran around the walls of the old Palatine community, striking all those whom they encountered, but especially women, a ritual that was believed to ensure fertility and safe delivery in childbirth. The feast probably also served as a rustic purification rite to protect animals and crops.

The Lupercalia continued to be observed well into the Christian era. Several scholars contend that Pope Gelasius I introduced the Feast of the Purification of the Virgin Mary, also known as Candlemas, in A.D. 494 to counteract the excesses of the pagan Lupercalia.

The Saxons called the month of February Sprout-kale, from the fact that kale sprouted at that season. They later changed the name to Solmonath, in recognition of the returning strength of the sun. The early medieval Frankish emperor Charlemagne used the designation Hornung, referring to the shedding of horns by stags. The lucky birthstone often associated with February is the amethyst, which symbolizes sincerity.

February 1

John Ford's Birthday

The legendary film director John Ford was born Sean Aloysius Feeney on February 1, 1895, in Cape Elizabeth, Maine. As his name suggests, he was born to Irish immigrants, and later Anglicized his name to John Ford. In 1913 he graduated from high school and left for California with dreams of finding fame and fortune in Hollywood. Unlike most such aspirants, he succeeded.

John Ford began behind the scenes, as the person in charge of sets and props, as in *Lucille Love, Girl of Mystery* (1914), for which he was the property master. By 1917 he had become a director, and his first work was the movie *Bucking Broadway*. He was only in his early twenties, but he showed exceptional ability, and in the emerging film industry of the time a young person could advance quickly. Most of the films that Ford would produce during his career would be westerns.

In 1935, Ford achieved nationwide recognition when he was awarded his first Academy Award for best director in *The Informer*. During the next few years, he directed several of his most famous movies, including *Stagecoach* (1939), *Young Mr. Lincoln* (1939), *The Grapes of Wrath* (1940), and *How Green Was My Valley* (1941). During World War II, he produced several war-related documentaries and short films. The most notable of these was his award-winning documentary on the Battle of Midway (1942).

After the war, Ford produced such classics as *My Darling Clementine* (1946) and *The Searchers* (1956). He also directed *The Quiet Man* (1952), which starred western actor John Wayne but was set in the Irish countryside and displayed an interestingly sentimental side to Ford's personality. *The Quiet Man* was also an Academy Award winner for Ford.

John Ford's Hollywood career spanned over five decades. By the 1960s, interest in conventional westerns was fading, and he was becoming eclipsed by a younger generation of film directors. However, he was responsible for several more great movies, including *How the West Was Won* (1962), *The Man Who Shot Liberty Valance* (1962), and *Seven Women* (1966). In 1973 the American Film Institute awarded Ford its Life Achievement Award, making him the first director to receive this honor. He died shortly thereafter on August 31, 1973, at Palm Desert, California.

Clark Gable's Birthday

Movie star William Clark Gable was born on February 1, 1901, in Cadiz, Ohio, into a working-class family. He was a grade-school dropout, and worked in a variety of blue-collar jobs, temporarily finding employment in such occupations as lumberjack and tire factory worker. By his early twenties, he had developed an interest in acting and joined a traveling theater group.

Gable worked in several theater productions, and performed in the 1928 Broadway production *Machinal*, but did not achieve recognition until his debut in the 1931 movie western *The Painted Desert*. After this performance, MGM Studios signed him on at the initial rate of $350 per week.

Gable quickly became a popular actor, due in large part to his charm and dashing good looks. MGM cast him in a wide variety of romances, and he appeared with such famous leading ladies as Joan Crawford, Greta Garbo, Jean Harlowe, Carole Lombard, and Norma Shearer. He also appeared with Claudette Colbert in his first award-winning movie, *It Happened One Night* (1934). His most famous role, however, was in the David O. Selznick production of *Gone With the Wind* (1939), in which he was cast as Rhett Butler, the swashbuckling suitor of beautiful but headstrong Scarlett O'Hara. Gable's performance in what has become an American film classic is considered to be the great achievement of his career.

February 1

After the tragic death of his wife, actress Carole Lombard, and a tour of duty in the Army Air Corps during World War II, Gable returned to Hollywood in 1945. He was a bona fide war hero, having been awarded several medals and the Distinguished Flying Cross, which further enhanced his popularity. Although he never again starred in a film of such magnitude as *Gone With the Wind*, he did appear in some fairly notable movies, including *The Hucksters* (1947), *Mogambo* (1953), *Run Silent, Run Deep* (1958,) and *Teacher's Pet* (1958).

Clark Gable's last movie was the John Huston production of *The Misfits* (released in 1961). He had a heart attack just days after the final scenes were shot and died on November 16, 1960.

Victor Herbert's Birthday

Famous composer and conductor Victor Herbert was born in Dublin, Ireland, on February 1, 1859. He was the son of Edward Herbert, an attorney, and Fanny Lover Herbert. After the death of his father, young Victor and his mother went to live near London, in the home of his maternal grandfather.

After Victor's grandfather introduced him to music, his mother, an accomplished pianist, began giving him piano lessons. So obvious were Victor's musical gifts that his grandfather urged that he be taken to Germany for further training. Accordingly, in 1867 he went with his mother to a village on Lake Constance. After his mother met and married a German physician, Carl Schmid, the family moved to Stuttgart, where Victor received academic training and studied music at the Stuttgart Conservatory. He specialized in playing the cello, studying under Bernhard Cossmann, one of the virtuoso cellists of the century, in Baden-Baden. Herbert recalled years later, "I had exceptional advantages. . . . My lessons were no 15-minute affairs, and then away at something else. I was under the constant eye of my master, and I could not help making rapid progress."

Launched upon a successful musical career, Herbert spent some four years touring Europe, giving solo performances and playing in both small-town and important symphony orchestras, principally in Germany, Austria, France, and Italy. Some of the orchestras were conducted by world-renowned musicians, Brahms and Liszt among them, and the experience provided rigorous training. In 1882 Herbert became first cellist with the Eduard Strauss orchestra in Vienna. In 1883 he returned to Stuttgart, where he was engaged by the conductor of the Stuttgart Royal Orchestra, the violinist and composer Max Seifritz. Recognizing

young Herbert's abilities in composition, Seifritz gave him lessons and encouraged him to begin composing seriously. Herbert's first two works of consequence, a suite and a concerto, were introduced by the Stuttgart orchestra with himself as soloist.

By this time Herbert was courting Theresa Foerster, prima donna of the Vienna Court Opera. When she was offered a contract with the Metropolitan Opera Company in New York City, she agreed to accept only on the condition that Herbert, by then her fiancé, be employed as cellist with the Metropolitan Opera House orchestra. The young couple was married on August 14, 1886, and sailed for the United States soon afterwards.

Victor Herbert embraced his adopted land, and ultimately influenced its musical heritage. For a number of years, he won fame as a leading cellist with such renowned orchestras as the Theodore Thomas Orchestra and the New York Philharmonic. From the late 1880s on, he also attracted increasing notice as a conductor. He served as associate conductor at the Worcester, Massachusetts, music festival, where his oratorio *The Captive* was performed in 1891. In 1893 he became bandmaster of the famous 22nd Regiment Band of the New York National Guard; in 1898, principal conductor of the Pittsburgh Symphony Orchestra; and after 1904, director of his own concert assemblage, the immensely popular Victor Herbert's New York Orchestra.

Although eminently successful as an instrumentalist and conductor, Victor Herbert is now best known as a composer. In 1893 a Boston light opera company commissioned him to compose what was to be the first in a large repertory of Herbert operettas: *Prince Ananias*, first performed in New York City on November 20, 1894. After *Prince Ananias* followed *The Wizard of the Nile* (1895), *The Serenade* (1897), and *The Fortune Teller* (1898), which launched Herbert on a brilliant career as a Broadway composer. Until the end of the first decade of the 20th century, he poured forth captivating operettas, among them *Babes in Toyland* (1903), *Mlle. Modiste* (1905), *The Red Mill* (1906), and *Naughty Marietta* (1910). His catchy and superbly orchestrated tunes included "March of the Toys," "Toyland," "Gypsy Love Song," "Kiss Me Again," "Every Day Is Ladies' Day with Me," "Sweet Mystery of Life," "I'm Falling in Love with Someone," and "Italian Street Song." Many listeners shared the view of Andrew Carnegie, the American industrialist and philanthropist, who once commented: "My idea of heaven is to be able to sit and listen to the music of Victor Herbert all I want to."

The carefree waltz era, into which Herbert had injected his magnetic music, drew to a close with the outbreak of World War I. Although he continued his musical productivity, and was responsible for some noteworthy songs and productions, for the most part his career went into decline thereafter.

In 1913, while dining at Shanley's, a well-known New York restaurant, Herbert happened to hear the orchestra there perform several of his melodies. Convinced that living composers should receive compensation for the use of their copyrighted music, he initiated a lawsuit against Shanley's, which was waged in the courts for four years. In 1917 the U.S. Supreme Court decided in Herbert's favor, holding that copyright owners should be paid royalties for public performances of their works staged for profit. Herbert was also one of the nine founders of a voluntary, nonprofit organization created to safeguard and further the interests of lyricists, composers, and publishers, a group that evolved over time into the influential American Society of Composers, Authors, and Publishers.

Herbert suffered a fatal heart attack in the office of his doctor in New York on May 26, 1924. At the time of his death, in the era of jazz and ragtime, he considered himself part of a bygone era. However, his passing marked the demise not of a has-been, but of a composer whose works merit a place as classics of the American musical theater. As the music critic Deems Taylor wrote in the *New York World* on June 1, 1924, Herbert "raised light opera music to a degree of harmonic sophistication that it had never before reached."

American Lutheran Church Merger Completed

The merger of the American Lutheran Church, the Evangelical Lutheran Church, and the United Evangelical Lutheran Church took place during a convention in Minneapolis, Minnesota, on April 22–24, 1960. The combined organizations took the name of the American Lutheran Church. The newly combined body became constitutionally operative on January 1, 1961.

Combining the 1,059,195 baptized members of the original American Lutheran Church with the 1,174,494 members of the Evangelical Lutheran Church and the 73,091 members of the United Evangelical Lutheran Church, the new denomination brought together Lutherans of Danish, German, and Norwegian heritage. A fourth group, the 88,396-member Lutheran Free Church, joined on February 1, 1963. The merger of the Lutheran churches was thus completed on that date.

A United Testimony on Faith and Life, adopted by the uniting churches approximately nine years before the initial merger became effective, sets forth the thinking that led to the union. Having "walked and worked together for . . . more than twenty years," the Testimony said, the concerned churches

have learned to know one another both as to doctrine and as to manner of life. . . . Coming out of varying backgrounds . . . they have learned to cherish one another's contributions to the fullness of the Church's life in Christ. Through closer acquaintance and deepening fellowship they have found that the common roots of their faith, in the Holy Scriptures and in the Lutheran Confessions, have given them a common life in communion with the one Lord and Savior.

Their loyalty to the Gospel of Jesus Christ, their Lutheran heritage, and the desperate need of the world seem to call for further exploration of the possibilities of closer fellowship, greater understanding, and closer organizational cooperation or union.

"Battle Hymn of the Republic"

First published in *Atlantic Monthly* on February 1, 1862, Julia Ward Howe's "Battle Hymn of the Republic" is a classic song from the Civil War era. It is set forth below:

Mine eyes have seen the glory of the coming of the Lord
He is trampling out the vintage where the grapes of wrath are stored,
He has loosed the fateful lightning of his terrible swift sword
His truth is marching on.
  Glory! Glory! Hallelujah!
  Glory! Glory! Hallelujah!
  Glory! Glory! Hallelujah!
  His truth is marching on.
I have seen him in the watchfires of a hundred circling camps
They have built him an altar in the evening dews and damps
I can read his righteous sentence by the dim and flaring lamps
His day is marching on.
Chorus
I have read a fiery gospel writ in burnished rows of steel,
'As ye deal with my contemners, so with you my grace shall deal';

Let the hero, born of woman, crush the
   serpent with his heel
Since God is marching on.
Chorus
He has sounded forth the trumpet that
   shall never call retreat
He is sifting out the hearts of men before
   his judgment seat
Oh, be swift, my soul, to answer him, be ju-
   bilant my feet!
Our God is marching on.
Chorus
In the beauty of the lilies Christ was born
   across the sea,
With a glory in his bosom that transfigures
   you and me,
As he died to make men holy, let us die to
   make men free
While God is marching on.
Chorus

Sung to the tune of "John Brown's Body," it became the anthem of the Union and is still a favorite
choral work.

February 2

Groundhog Day

Groundhog Day is celebrated as a time for forecasting the weather for the next six weeks. The
custom of observing the weather on this day to discover what the future weather would be was
brought to America by immigrants from Great
Britain and Germany. The theory is that if the
groundhog, or woodchuck, comes out of his winter
quarters on this day and sees his shadow, there will
be six more weeks of winter, but if the day is
cloudy he will not return to his winter quarters for
a long sleep, as the winter weather will soon give
way to spring.

In Germany, it was the badger that supposedly
broke its hibernation to observe the skies; in the
United States, the belief was transferred to the
groundhog or woodchuck. The English and the
Scots had many rhymes in which the belief was
embodied, although they tied the custom to Candlemas Day (see separate entry below), among
them the following:

If Candlemas Day be dry and fair,
The half o' winter's to come and mair;
If Candlemas Day be wet and foul,
The half o' winter's gone at Yule.
If Candlemas Day be fair and bright,
Winter will have another flight;
But if it be dark with clouds and rain,
Winter is gone, and will not come again.

Nowhere in the United States is as much attention paid to Groundhog Day, or as much fun derived from it, as in Pennsylvania, which was largely
settled by Germans. Punxsutawney, in the western
part of the state, calls itself the "original home of
the great weather prognosticator, His Majesty, the
Punxsutawney Groundhog." Since 1887, members
of the Punxsutawney Groundhog Club have
trekked to nearby Gobblers Knob early on the
morning of February 2 to note the appearance of
the groundhog. There are also a number of observances in the Pennsylvania Dutch region of southeastern Pennsylvania.

Dartmouth College Case Decided

The Supreme Court, as guardian and interpreter
of the Constitution, has exerted a tremendous influence on all aspects of American life. Throughout its history, the high tribunal has stood in judgment on social, political, and economic problems;
its decisions, from which there can be no appeal
short of constitutional amendment, have helped
the nation shape its response to its most pressing
issues.

The first two decades of the 19th century witnessed a period of financial chaos in the United
States. To force Great Britain to act more favorably toward the United States, Presidents Thomas
Jefferson and James Madison instituted a series of
trade embargo acts, which lasted from 1806 to
1811. These trade restrictions and the British
blockade of American seaports during the War of
1812 severely hampered the country's commerce.
As a consequence the national economy, which
had been based on the export of agricultural produce and various other raw materials to foreign
markets, stagnated and then declined.

Deprived of their opportunities to trade,
American entrepreneurs turned to domestic manufacturing. It was during this period that corporations became an increasingly popular means of
conducting business: A corporation can own property and conduct business like an individual, but
the stockholder investors are not personally liable
for its debts and obligations. There was one substantial drawback to this. Corporations operated
under charters granted by their respective state
legislatures, and until the 1819 Supreme Court
decision in *Trustees of Dartmouth College* v.
Woodward, the inviolability of these charter rights
against future legislative tampering had not been
determined.

The controversy that led to the historic 1819
ruling stemmed from the New Hampshire legislature's attempt to alter the 50-year-old charter of
Dartmouth College. In 1754 the Reverend Elea-

zar Wheelock, a Congregational minister, had established Moore's Indian Charity School in the part of Lebanon, Connecticut, that is now Columbia. Although Wheelock's institution failed in 1768, his hopes of bringing both secular and religious education to the wilds of upper New England soon revived. In 1769 King George III granted a charter for the establishment of a college in New Hampshire, and shortly afterward the colony's governor offered a substantial land grant to encourage Wheelock to found the institution authorized by the English monarch.

Wheelock quickly accepted the challenge. Accompanied by about 30 students and some other settlers, he organized a township on the eastern bank of the Connecticut River in 1770. There, in the same year, he opened Dartmouth College, named in honor of the second earl of Dartmouth.

Dartmouth College operated under its original charter and remained under Congregational administration for the next 46 years. Then, in 1816, the school became entangled in a political-religious feud that for several years had pitted New Hampshire's Jeffersonian Republicans, who were predominantly Presbyterian, against the state's largely Congregational Federalists. The Republicans won control of the legislature in 1816 and at once initiated measures designed to undermine the opposition party's influence on the college. They increased the number of trustees from 12 to 21, transferred the privilege of appointment from the trustees to the state legislature, and created a board of overseers to supervise the actions of the trustees. All of these innovations were clear violations of Dartmouth's 1769 charter, a fact the school's original trustees were quick to note. The trustees brought suit against the legislature on the grounds that its actions violated the Constitution, which forbids arbitrary inference with contractual obligations.

When New Hampshire's highest court upheld the legislature, the Dartmouth trustees appealed to the U.S. Supreme Court. When the case came before the Court in 1819, the college's chief advocate was an alumnus, Daniel Webster. Webster served his alma mater well. Indeed, his impassioned conclusion in Dartmouth's defense is one of the best-known arguments in American legal annals:

> Sir, you may destroy this little institution. It is weak. It is in your hands! I know it is one of the lesser lights on the literary horizon of the country. You may put it out. But if you do so, you must carry through your work. You must extinguish, one after another, all those great lights of science, which, for more than a century, have thrown their radiance over our land.

> It is, Sir, as I have said, a small college and yet, there are those who love it. . . .

> Sir, I care not how others feel, but, for myself, when I see my Alma Mater surrounded, like Caesar in the senate house, by those who are reiterating stab on stab, I would not, for this right hand, have her turn to me, and say, *et tu quoque, mi fili* [and you also, my son].

Despite the eloquence of Webster's words, the Court had to rule on two very unemotional issues: Was a corporate charter a contract? And, if so, was the contract protected by the Constitution?

On February 2, 1819, Chief Justice John Marshall handed down the Court's decision. On both issues the ruling favored Dartmouth College. In Marshall's words, the charter was "plainly a contract to which the donors, the trustees, and the crown (to whose rights and obligations New Hampshire succeeds) were the original parties. . . . It is a contract for the security and disposition of property. . . . It is, then, a contract within the letter of the Constitution."

The Dartmouth College decision not only safeguarded the college from legislative encroachments, but it ensured the security of all corporate enterprises operating under the authority of legislative charters. The decision was modified, however, when in *Charles River Bridge* v. *Warren Bridge* (1837) the Supreme Court ruled that "while the rights of private property are sacredly guarded we must not forget that the community also have rights," recognizing the police power of the states over corporations to protect the public interest from private infringement.

A postage stamp commemorating the Dartmouth College case was issued in September 1969, during the college's 200th anniversary celebration.

Candlemas, or The Feast of the Presentation of the Lord

Candlemas, or the Feast of the Presentation of the Lord, sometimes also referred to as the Feast of the Purification of Mary, is observed on February 2 by the Roman Catholic, Episcopalian, Lutheran, and some Eastern Orthodox Churches. The feast celebrates the occasion when Mary, as required by Jewish law, went to the temple in Jerusalem to be purified 40 days after giving birth to a son and to present that son, Jesus, to God. The event is described in the second chapter of Luke.

At the time, Simeon, a holy man living in Jerusalem, had been longing for the appearance of the Messiah and, as the King James version of the Bible relates:

February 2

It was revealed unto him by the Holy Spirit, that he should not see death, before he had seen the Lord's Christ. And he came by the Spirit into the temple: and when the parents brought in the child Jesus, to do for him after the custom of the law, then took he him up in his arms, and blessed God, and said, Lord, now lettest thou thy servant depart in peace according to thy word: For mine eyes have seen thy salvation, which thou hast prepared before the face of all people; a light to lighten the Gentiles, and the glory of thy people Israel. And Joseph and . . . Mary marveled at those things which were spoken of him; And Simeon blessed them.

Candlemas was celebrated in very early times, the 4th century A.D. or earlier, by Christians in the eastern part of the Roman Empire. When December 25 was designated as the anniversary of the Nativity, or Christmas day, Candlemas became fixed at February 2 because it was 40 days after the celebration of the birth of Christ just as Mary had brought the baby Jesus to the temple 40 days after giving birth.

The Feast of the Presentation of the Lord was introduced into the Western church and adopted at Rome in the 7th century A.D. The blessing of candles became commonplace about the 11th century, especially in England, where it was a major ceremony, thus giving the day its name of Candlemas (Candle mass). Authorities differ on how the day came to be connected with lighted candles. The candle-carrying ceremonies seem to have been derived from ancient Roman customs. One plausible theory holds that Candlemas grew out of the Roman Feast of Purification, when Romans paraded about the city of Rome with lighted candles early in February. The Roman feast was for the goddess Ceres, who according to legend sought her daughter Proserpine by candlelight after Pluto, the god of the underworld, had carried her away to the nether realm of darkness. According to this theory, the church fathers simply modified the pagan Roman custom, which they found difficult to root out, so that it honored Christ the Light of the World and Mary, his mother.

For many years, February 2 was regarded as the close of the Christmas season, when Yuletide decorations had to be removed to prevent bad luck. Candlemas was also long regarded as a particularly favorable day for weather prognostications, and the traditions associated with Groundhog Day derive from this fact (see the separate essay on Groundhog Day above).

Wystan Hugh Auden's Birthday

The poet W. H. Auden was born in York, England, on February 2, 1907. His father was a distinguished physician, but Auden had no desire to follow in his father's footsteps, and became a poet when he was still in his teens. In 1925 he entered Christ Church College of the University of Oxford, where he was able to develop his artistic leanings.

At Oxford, Auden formed friendships with other youthful poets and intellectuals, including C. D. Lewis, Stephen Spender, and Louis MacNeice. These friendships, particularly with MacNeice, would last for decades. Auden graduated in 1928, and after a brief stay in Germany he returned to Great Britain and found employment as a schoolteacher. In 1930, his book *Poems* was published, and thus at the age of 23 Auden first achieved widespread recognition.

Like many intellectuals of the post–World War I period in England, Auden had pronounced leftist views, and his poetry of the 1930s criticized capitalism and the social values of English society. He also began to travel, and produced *Letters from Iceland* (1937) followed by *Journey to a War* (1939) after a visit to war-torn China. With the onset of World War II in Europe, Auden moved to the United States and, disillusioned with political remedies, became a Christian, although never a conventionally pious one. In 1946 he became an American citizen. His long allegorical poem "The Age of Anxiety" (1947) won the 1948 Pulitzer Prize for Poetry.

Having achieved fame as an American poet, Auden went on to produce such books as *Nones* (1951), *The Shield of Achilles* (1955), and *Collected Longer Poems* (1969). His later poetry is more introspective and contemplative than his early work. He also wrote literary criticism and, in collaboration with Chester Kallman, the American poet who became his companion, a number of opera libretti, the most notable being *The Rake's Progress*, with music by Igor Stravinsky. Auden lived most of the time in New York's East Village, but in 1972 decided to return to Christ Church at Oxford after receiving an invitation to become a resident writer there. He died shortly thereafter, on September 28, 1973, in Vienna, while on a visit to Austria.

February 3

Illinois Becomes a Territory

On February 3, 1809, President Thomas Jefferson approved the congressional act that organized the western part of the Indiana Territory as the Territory of Illinois. The new entity extended all the way from the Ohio River to the Canadian border and included all of what is now Illinois, most of what is now Wisconsin, and areas in what are today Minnesota and Michigan.

In 1809 Illinois was for the most part an unsettled wilderness. As early as 1673 the French Jesuit Jacques Marquette and his compatriot Louis Joliet explored part of the region. Returning to Canada after an expedition down the Mississippi River, Marquette and Joliet, on the advice of Indians who inhabited the area, set out on the Illinois River. The Frenchmen followed the Illinois on its northwestern course until they reached the Des Plaines River. Then they proceeded up the Des Plaines to a creek that ran east to a low ridge separating the Mississippi basin from the Great Lakes. A portage across the ridge brought the explorers to the south fork of the Chicago River, and from there they continued eastward to Lake Michigan.

Marquette and Joliet were probably the first Europeans to explore Illinois, and several areas in the state commemorate their visit. A portion of the portage that they discovered in 1673 was later preserved as the Chicago Portage National Historic Site. Marquette and Joliet also recorded seeing the Kaskaskia Indian village on their 1673 journey, and Marquette established a mission at the village in 1675. Although Marquette and Joliet were the first Europeans to visit Illinois, credit for establishing the first European settlements in the area belongs to another French explorer, René-Robert Cavelier de La Salle.

In 1679 La Salle set out to discover the mouth of the Mississippi River. In the course of his explorations, he spent considerable time in Illinois, and he came to realize the strategic importance of the Illinois River, which provides a water route from Canada to the Mississippi River. To guarantee French control of this waterway, he built two forts on the river: Fort St. Louis near Ottawa, Illinois, and Fort Crevecoeur near Lake Peoria. The actual settlement of Illinois proceeded very slowly, however. In Illinois, as well as in other places in the New World, the French devoted their efforts to establishing missions and trading posts rather than towns. However, some of the larger missions and posts eventually attracted permanent settlers. For example, the town of Kaskaskia was established

near the mouth of the Kaskaskia River around 1703, and Cahokia was founded a little below the mouth of the Missouri River several years earlier.

Illinois remained under French control for about a century. In 1712, when Antoine Crozat was granted temporary possession of Louisiana, the Illinois River was made its northern boundary; and in 1721 more than half the area of what is now the state of Illinois, as well as other territory, was included in the seventh civil and military district of Louisiana, which was named Illinois. The French, however, concentrated their energies on developing the lower Mississippi valley and never tapped the rich resources of Illinois.

With the Treaty of Paris of 1763, France ceded the territory between the Ohio and Mississippi rivers, including Illinois, to Great Britain. Beginning in 1769, Britain allowed settlers from Virginia and its other seaboard colonies to migrate to the newly acquired lands, and as a result of this policy the population of Illinois slowly grew between 1769 and 1774. Then, in 1774, Parliament passed the Quebec Act. The act, which annexed all the territory north of the Ohio River and east of the Mississippi River to the Province of Quebec, and recognized the validity of French civil law in Quebec, deeply antagonized the English colonists. As a result, migration to Illinois and the other areas of the Northwest came to a halt.

During the American Revolution the predominantly French population of Illinois supported the British; nevertheless, the patriots were able to score a number of notable victories in the area. In January 1778 Governor Patrick Henry of Virginia gave George Rogers Clark command of an army of 175 men. Clark and his army surprised and defeated the British at Kaskaskia and Cahokia in the summer of 1778, and by the fall of that year won control of the entire Illinois country. Clark's victories in Illinois and at Vincennes, Indiana, in 1779 were especially important because they helped establish the American claim to the Northwest in the peace negotiations with the British that concluded the American Revolution in 1783.

As a result of the Treaty of Paris of 1783, Illinois came under the jurisdiction of the new American nation. The status of Illinois and the other areas in the Northwest caused a considerable problem. Several states claimed the Northwest Territory because their colonial charters set their western boundaries at either the Mississippi River or the Pacific Ocean. The dispute over land claims even threatened the ratification of the Articles of Confederation, but in 1781 Virginia agreed to cede its western territories to the national government, and by 1786 the other states with western claims had followed Virginia's lead. The following year

February 3

Congress approved the Northwest Ordinance, which established a territorial government for the area north of the Ohio River.

In 1800 the Indiana Territory was organized, and the Illinois country was included in this new jurisdiction. Illinois remained a part of the Indiana Territory until February 3, 1809, when the Territory of Illinois was established. Gaining territorial status was a watershed in Illinois history: Before 1809 only a few thousand people had settled in the area, but between 1810 and 1820 the population of Illinois multiplied fivefold. With congressional approval, a territorial legislature was chosen in 1812, and a constitution was adopted by the people of the area the same year. In 1818 Illinois was admitted as the 21st state in the Union.

Gertrude Stein's Birthday

Although she was an expatriate for much of her life, Gertrude Stein qualifies as one of America's greatest writers. She was born on February 3, 1874, in Allegheny, Pennsylvania, and spent most of her childhood in Oakland, California. In 1893 she was admitted to prestigious Radcliffe College, where she studied with such noted scholars as William James. She graduated from Radcliffe in 1897 and went on to medical school, but left in 1901 without finishing her degree. Stein began to write, and in 1903 moved to Paris, France, where she resided for the rest of her life despite the interruptions of World War I and World War II.

Stein's first major work was *Three Lives* in 1909, concerning the lives of three working-class women. Her next major work, *The Making of Americans*, was not published until 1925 due to her unconventional and difficult writing style. However, *The Making of Americans* was well-received both in Europe and in the United States, and firmly established Stein as a leader in the avant-garde literary movement.

Even before her writing made her famous, Stein had become a significant figure within the artistic communities of Europe. She and her brother Leo, who were independently wealthy, were patrons of struggling painters such as Henri Matisse and Pablo Picasso who later became famous. Further, she opened her home to the other American writers who came to Paris after World War I in order to enjoy the European literary scene, and her circle of friends included Ernest Hemingway, Ezra Pound, and Thornton Wilder. It was Gertrude Stein who coined the phrase "lost generation" for this group of writers.

In the 1930s, Stein wrote *The Autobiography of Alice B. Toklas* (1933), which proved to be the best-selling work of her career. Some of her later works, such as *Four Saints in Three Acts*, were turned into operas by the composer Virgil Thomson. Although Stein made periodic visits to the United States and was successful on the American lecture circuit, she chose to remain in France when World War II began and survived the Nazi occupation. When American forces finally liberated Paris, she made an effort to meet and talk with the young American soldiers, and recounted some of their experiences in *Brewsie and Willie* (1946).

Stein died on July 27, 1946, in Paris. One of her works, the opera *The Mother of Us All*, concerning the life of feminist Susan B. Anthony, was released posthumously in 1947.

Buddy Holly Killed in Plane Crash

On February 3, 1959, also known as "The Day the Music Died," the famous rock and roll musician Buddy Holly was killed in a plane crash that also claimed the lives of fellow musicians Ritchie Valenz and J. P. "The Big Bopper" Richardson. At the age of 22, Buddy Holly's career thus came to a tragic end.

Charles Hardin Holley was born on September 7, 1936. As a child he was given the nickname Buddy, and when his musical career began his last name Holley was shortened to Holly after it was misspelled in a recording contract. As a youth, Buddy Holly lived in Lubbock, Texas, where he first sang for some local country-and-western clubs. He became attracted to rock-and-roll music, however, largely due to the influence of new singers such as Elvis Presley. With his band, the Crickets, Holly wrote and sang "That'll Be The Day" in 1957. It became an overnight success. Another hit, "Peggy Sue," was released the same year.

By 1959, Buddy Holly had become one of the country's most popular rock-and-roll musicians, although he experienced a breakup with The Crickets. He appeared on such television shows as *The Ed Sullivan Show* and *American Bandstand*. During a tour that included Ritchie Valenz and "The Big Bopper," Holly decided to charter a small four-passenger plane to fly from Clear Lake, Iowa, to the next destination on their itinerary. The plane crashed shortly after takeoff and all three musicians were killed, as was the pilot.

In later years, Buddy Holly's fast-paced, light-hearted style was recognized as one of the pioneering influences in rock and roll music. In 1971 a hit song by Don McLean called "American Pie" idolized Buddy Holly (in addition to other greats of rock and roll) in its lyrics and coined the phrase "The Day the Music Died" for the events of February 3, 1959.

February 4

Betty Friedan's Birthday

Betty Naomi Friedan, the famous author and feminist, was born on February 4, 1921, in Peoria, Illinois. As a child, she was encouraged to develop her talents by her parents, especially her mother, who had once been a journalist. Betty followed in her mother's footsteps, and began to write for her high school newspaper. At the age of 17, she was admitted to Smith College in Massachusetts.

Friedan graduated from Smith in 1942 with a degree in psychology. In 1943 she began graduate study at the University of California at Berkeley, but left after one year to take a position as a reporter in New York City. After several years as a journalist, in 1947 she married Carl Friedan, and by 1949 she had become a full-time housewife, taking care of a household that would eventually include three children.

In the 1950s most women were still expected to be wives and mothers, and although more women than ever were working outside the home, they typically received less compensation than men and were not allowed to advance to senior positions. Friedan became increasingly dissatisfied with her role as a traditional homemaker, and in 1956 sent a questionnaire to her fellow Smith College alumnae to determine whether her peers were experiencing the same degree of dissatisfaction that she was. The informal survey revealed that her fellow graduates had many of the same reservations that she did about domestic life. Open discussion about these sorts of feelings was still socially taboo, however, and Friedan had difficulty finding publishers who would print her articles about women's issues. In 1960, however, she convinced *Good Housekeeping* magazine to print her article entitled "Women Are People Too!"

Although controversial, Friedan's article received a positive response and generated a considerable amount of mail from sympathetic female readers. In 1963, she released her masterpiece, *The Feminine Mystique*. This revolutionary work shortly became a bestseller. The essential theme of the book is that the traditional belief that a woman should be content in her role as the daughter, wife, or mother of a man was stifling the talents and distorting the lives of most American women. This narrow concept of womanhood was what Friedan meant by the phrase "feminine mystique."

Friedan's book and her new fame thrust her into the budding feminist movement of the 1960s. She became a leader in the cause for equal rights, and founded the National Organization for Women (NOW) in 1966. Friedan was also NOW's first president, serving until 1970. In the early 1970s she contributed to the formation of the National Women's Political Caucus, the First Women's Bank, and the International Feminist Congress. Not unexpectedly, however, her new role as a feminist leader strained her marriage, and she was divorced in 1969.

In many ways, Betty Friedan's career peaked in the early 1970s, with the end of what could loosely be termed the "civil rights era." However, as of this writing in the late 1990s, she has continued to be an ardent supporter of women's rights, including the effort to add an Equal Rights Amendment to the United States Constitution. She has also written several more books, including *It Changed My Life* (1976), concerning her career as a political activist; *The Second Stage* (1981), concerning her evolving notions of feminism; and *The Fountain of Age* (1993), concerning creative approaches toward the problems of senior citizens.

Impeachment Trial of Supreme Court Justice Samuel Chase Begins

One of the most important legal proceedings in the history of American constitutional law began on February 4, 1805, when the U.S. Senate opened its impeachment trial of Supreme Court justice Samuel Chase. When Chase was eventually acquitted, it was a victory for the independence of the judicial system, the third branch of the federal government. It was also a serious embarrassment for President Thomas Jefferson.

The Constitution of the United States divides the federal government into three branches that are supposed to be equal. These are the executive, the legislative, and the judicial. The executive consists of the president and the various agencies of the federal government; the legislative consists of Congress and its affiliated bodies; and the judicial consists of the U.S. Supreme Court at the apex of a federal court system that interprets the nation's laws and enforces the Constitution. Congress has the right to impeach, or remove from office, officials of the federal government, including but not limited to the president and the justices of the Supreme Court. In order to be impeached, the accused must be guilty of "high crimes and misdemeanors." The Senate of the United States conducts the impeachment trial. At this trial, a two-thirds majority vote of the senators is necessary to convict and thus remove the person from office. There are practically no restrictions on the trial procedure in the Senate.

February 5

The first two presidents of the United States, George Washington and John Adams, were members of the Federalist Party. In 1800, however, Thomas Jefferson was elected president as the candidate of the Democratic-Republican Party. As Jefferson sought to consolidate his control over the federal government, he ran into the opposition of the justices of the Supreme Court, who had been appointed by the preceding Federalist administrations and were mostly Federalist sympathizers. The Democratic-Republicans sought to tame the Supreme Court, and brought largely trumped-up charges against Justice Samuel Chase. Chase was a hero of the American Revolution, a delegate to the Continental Congress, and one of the signers of the Declaration of Independence. His Federalist views were very strong, perhaps inappropriately so for a person holding judicial office, but there was very little evidence to suggest that his conduct was illegal.

Nevertheless, Chase became the first target of the Democratic-Republican majority in Congress's move against the Federalist judiciary, although many prominent Democratic-Republicans had their reservations (see June 2, concerning John Randolph). At stake was not only Chase's career and reputation, but potentially also those of Supreme Court chief justice John Marshall, who would be the next logical target if Chase were successfully impeached. In what has been, as of this writing, the one and only impeachment trial of a Supreme Court justice, enough Democratic-Republicans in the Senate joined with the minority coalition of Federalist senators to acquit Chase on March 1, 1805. The acquittal helped secure the independence of the Supreme Court, and Chase resumed his activities as a justice until he died on June 19, 1811.

Mark Hopkins's Birthday

Mark Hopkins, one of the most distinguished educators of his generation and president of Williams College in Williamstown, Massachusetts, from 1836 to 1872, was born in Stockbridge, Massachusetts, on February 4, 1802, the son of a farmer. He entered Williams College as a sophomore and graduated in 1824. Thereafter, he began the study of medicine, but returned to Williams in 1825 to tutor for two years. He then entered Berkshire Medical School at Pittsfield, Massachusetts, from which he graduated in 1829. After graduation, he practiced medicine in New York City and then Binghamton, New York, before once again returning to Williams College in 1830 to accept a position as professor of moral philosophy and rhetoric. He eventually rose to become president of the college.

Hopkins was ordained as a Congregational minister in 1836. When he resigned as president of the college in 1872, he retained the professorship of moral philosophy and continued as pastor of the college church. During his tenure at Williams, Hopkins was revered as an educator and for arousing the interest and enthusiasm of his students. President James A. Garfield, a graduate of Williams, is credited with saying at a dinner of Williams alumni in New York that a log in the woods with Mark Hopkins on one end and a student on the other would be as good as a university. Once, when a student in Hopkins's moral philosophy class asked him who would go to heaven, he replied that he did not know, but that he was sure that no one would go there who would not feel at home.

Hopkins died at Williamstown on June 17, 1887. He was elected to the Hall of Fame for Great Americans in 1915.

February 5

Roger Williams Arrives in America

Roger Williams, one of the most famous defenders of religious liberty in America's colonial period, was born in England, probably in London, the son of James and Alice Williams. Although the exact date of his birth is not certain, it was probably between 1603 and 1607.

As a youth, Williams was educated at Pembroke College of Cambridge University, and graduated with a bachelor of arts degree in 1627. Interested in theology, he was ordained in the Church of England and became chaplain to the household of Sir William Masham at Otes, Essex. However, he became increasingly rebellious against what he regarded as the errors of the church and the lack of religious freedom under the autocratic King Charles I. Williams became a Puritan and then a Separatist, one of those who advocated a complete and overt break from the Church of England.

Williams and his family left England to join the Puritan-dominated Massachusetts Bay Colony in America, arriving in Boston on February 5, 1631. He declined an invitation to serve as teacher of the church there because he found its members "an unseparated people," refusing to sever completely their ties with the Church of England even while avoiding what they considered to be the church's intolerance. Instead, he took a position as the teacher to the church at Salem, Massachusetts, where he got into trouble for denying the right of civil magistrates to punish persons for religious offenses. As the theocratic Massachusetts Bay government insisted on this right, Williams left for the Plymouth Colony, dominated by Separatists, where he preached and began his missionary work with the Indians.

In 1633 Williams returned to Massachusetts to serve as pastor of the church at Salem, where he preached that the power of the civil magistrates extended only to the bodies and goods of men and not to their consciences. He also spoke out against the validity of the Massachusetts Bay Colony charter, under which the king, Williams asserted, had violated Indian rights by giving away land that was not his to give. Such convictions, and his stand for the absolute freedom of conscience, led to his banishment from the Massachusetts Bay Colony by the General Court late in 1635.

Plans were made to deport him to England, but Williams, learning of his impending arrest, fled south to Narragansett Bay with a few followers in January 1636. After suffering the deprivations of a harsh New England winter, he crossed to the west bank of the adjacent Seekonk River. There, on land that he bought from the Indians, he founded the city of Providence, the earliest Rhode Island settlement, in June 1636. Establishing a government founded on complete religious toleration, he made the colony a refuge from religious persecution that drew settlers from England and Massachusetts.

In addition to the separation of church and state, which was a basic tenet of the colony he founded at Rhode Island, Williams consistently championed the cause of democratic government. Three more communities—Portsmouth, Newport, and Warwick—had sprung up around Narragansett Bay by 1643, when Williams went to England to secure from Parliament a charter that would give legal sanction to the Rhode Island settlements and protect them from rival land claims by the Massachusetts Bay and Plymouth colonies. The charter was issued in March 1644, and the entire colony was officially designated the Providence Plantations. Although boundary disputes with Massachusetts, and later with Connecticut, continued into the 18th century, the new colony's survival as a separate entity was assured. The principle of religious freedom was reconfirmed by a new charter granted by King Charles II in 1663. In that document, the colony was renamed the Rhode Island and Providence Plantations, which remained its official designation until it gained independence in the American Revolution.

In 1654, Williams was elected the first president of the colony. He held that position for three years. Afterwards he served in a variety of lesser colonial posts until his death in 1683. He also wrote extensively on religious issues and Indian languages.

Adlai Stevenson's Birthday

Adlai Ewing Stevenson, a prominent Democratic politician and twice the nominee of his party for the presidency, was born on February 5, 1900, in Los Angeles, California. He was born into one of the most distinguished families in American politics.

The Stevenson family was from Illinois, and had long been active in the politics of that state. One of Adlai's great-grandfathers, Jesse Fell, had helped establish the Republican Party and get Abraham Lincoln elected to the presidency. The later Stevensons, however, were predominantly Democrats, and Adlai's grandfather was vice-president during the second administration of President Grover Cleveland. Adlai's father, Lewis Stevenson, had also served as the Illinois secretary of state.

With such patrician roots, it was natural that Stevenson followed his family tradition of entering into Democratic politics. After receiving his education at Princeton University and his law degree at Northwestern University, he became a prominent lawyer in Chicago, Illinois. During the 1930s, the administration of President Franklin D. Roosevelt recognized his talents, and Stevenson served in both the Department of the Navy and the Department of State.

Toward the end of World War II, Adlai Stevenson earned a name for himself at the conferences in San Francisco, California, that led to the creation of the United Nations and the drafting of the UN Charter. After the war, he returned to Illinois and decided to run for governor. In 1948 he defeated the incumbent Republican governor by over half a million votes. During his four-year administration, Stevenson enacted many reforms and impressed even the Republicans with his initiatives and his personal integrity. By 1952 he was one of the leading candidates for the Democratic presidential nomination in the upcoming national elections.

At the same time, however, General Dwight D. Eisenhower was also entering national politics. As one of the most famous military leaders of World War II, he was courted by both the major political parties, but eventually decided to run on the Republican platform in 1952. When Stevenson won the Democratic nomination in 1952, and again in 1956, he faced the almost impossible obstacle of overcoming Eisenhower's popularity and war record. In contrast to Eisenhower, Stevenson came across as overly intellectual, weak on the military issues of the cold war, and "soft on Communism." He was popular with college students and helped bring many of them into the Democratic

Party and thus into the more activist Democratic politics of the 1960s, but lost both the 1952 and 1956 presidential campaigns to Eisenhower by substantial margins.

As a reward for Stevenson's loyalty to the Democratic Party, when Democratic president John F. Kennedy took office in 1961, he appointed Stevenson ambassador to the United Nations. Stevenson served in this position until his death on July 14, 1965, in London, England. His oldest son, Adlai E. Stevenson III, continued the Stevenson family tradition of political involvement and served two terms in the United States Senate from 1971 until 1983.

Dwight L. Moody's Birthday

Dwight Lyman Moody, a famous 19th-century preacher, was born in East Northfield, Massachusetts, on February 5, 1837. His earliest memory was the sudden death of his father when he was four years old. His mother was left in impoverished circumstances but managed to keep her family together. Dwight was schooled locally, did chores, and worked for neighboring farmers in the summer. His first public speech, at the age of 16, before a town meeting ended in failure when he forgot what he had intended to say.

Moody went to Boston, Massachusetts, when he was 17 and, after a dismal period of job hunting, went to work for two uncles in their boot and shoe business there. They agreed that he might perform odd jobs in their store on the condition that he board at a place of their selection, refrain from drinking and gambling, and attend Mount Vernon Church and the young men's Sabbath school. In view of Moody's lack of enthusiasm for the last requirement, his decision to become a preacher was surprising.

In 1856 Moody moved to Chicago, Illinois, where he continued in the boot and shoe business. While showing great business ability and prospering, during his nonworking hours he spent all of his spare time as a Sunday-school teacher and superintendent. In 1860 he completely withdrew from business to become an independent city missionary. As an outgrowth of his Sunday-school and slum mission work, he founded what later came to be known as the Moody Memorial Church. From 1861 to 1873, pastor Moody was a member of the Christian commission of the Young Men's Christian Association. He also became president of the Chicago YMCA and encouraged formation of YMCA chapters on college campuses.

In 1870 Moody, then 33, met the organist and singer Ira D. Sankey, who became his associate in the dozens of evangelistic campaigns that he led

in the years that followed. They began their first campaigns in Great Britain in 1873. During the next quarter century, Moody preached to millions throughout Great Britain and America. He also founded the Moody Bible Institute in Chicago in 1889. He died at his home, known as the Homestead, on December 22, 1899.

Charro Days Fiesta

This is a movable event.

A Texan-Mexican border fiesta known as Charro Days, held every year in Brownsville, Texas, and spilling across the border into Matamoros, Mexico, takes place every year in February. It originally took place on the Thursday of the weekend before Lent (hence this essay from the previous edition of this book stays at this day), but now typically takes place on the last Thursday in February. The celebration attracts roughly 150,000 visitors a year.

Brownsville is situated on the Rio Grande River, opposite Matamoros on the Mexican side. Together they constitute a major border crossing point. The proximity of the two cities originally gave rise to the idea of a fiesta recreating the color and romance of the old border area, where Latin Americans and Anglo-Americans met against a background of turbulent history. Initially Charro Days, which originated in Brownsville in 1938, was purely local. However, its fame spread until it drew tourists from all over the United States and from Mexico as well.

Visitors to the Charro Days Fiesta frequently don costumes and participate in the festivities instead of remaining mere spectators. The fiesta has been officially proclaimed in Matamoros, as well as Brownsville, ever since 1961, although it had the cooperation of Mexican authorities for many years before that. Today, fiesta events take place in both cities.

Charro was the name of a costume worn by the Spanish dons who once ruled Mexico. The term later was extended by popular usage to include the Mexican equestrian outfit. During Charro Days, celebrants sometimes wear variations of the charro costume. It consists of tight-fitting riding breeches trimmed with white suede or silver, a heavily embroidered short jacket, a colorful flowing tie, a serape draped over one shoulder, and a large sombrero. Sometimes women wear the traditional *china poblana* attire, which consists of a brightly colored sequined skirt, a silk shawl, and an embroidered blouse.

February 6

Ronald Reagan's Birthday

U.S. Senate Historical Office

Ronald Reagan

Ronald Wilson Reagan, the 40th president of the United States (1981–1989), was born on February 6, 1911, in Tampico, Illinois. His parents, John and Nelle Reagan, were of Irish ancestry. John Reagan was a traveling shoe salesman who had difficulty keeping his family in one place for any extended period of time. The family eventually settled in Dixon, Illinois, where Ronald Reagan spent most of his childhood and received his early education.

Reagan's childhood was difficult, in part because his father was an alcoholic. After he graduated from high school in 1928, he successfully obtained a scholarship to Eureka College, located near Peoria, Illinois. There he majored in economics and excelled in a number of intramural sports. He also developed an interest in politics when he served as president of the student body for one year.

Reagan graduated from college in 1932, during the depths of the Great Depression, and the only employment that he could obtain was as a sports announcer with a small radio station. He developed an interest in the media and acting, and in 1937 went to Hollywood, where Warner Brothers gave him a contract after a successful screen test. Reagan's movie career quickly blossomed, and he starred in a wide variety of films for over 20 years.

Most of these were "B" movies— such as *Bedtime for Bonzo* (1951), concerning the adventures of a playful ape—although there were some respectable features such as *Knute Rockne: All American* (1940) and *King's Row* (1942).

Reagan's movie career helped him secure the presidency of the prestigious Screen Actors Guild from 1947 until 1952. During this period, his first marriage to actress Jane Wyman ended in divorce in 1948. Reagan remarried in 1952, to another actress named Nancy Davis.

Reagan was at first a Democrat, but throughout the 1950s and into the 1960s he was increasingly attracted by the conservative ideals of the Republican Party. His first entry into politics was during the 1960s, when he had already passed his 50th birthday. In 1964 he used his experience as a former television announcer for the General Electric Theater to deliver a brilliant televised speech in favor of Barry Goldwater, the Republican presidential candidate in that year's national elections. Goldwater was eventually defeated, but Reagan attracted the attention of his fellow Republicans, and they convinced him to run for governor of California.

In 1966 Reagan defeated Edmund G. ("Pat") Brown, the incumbent Democratic governor, by nearly one million votes. He served as governor of California until 1975, during which period he frequently spoke out against what he perceived as the excesses of the civil rights movement and the anti–Vietnam War protests of the era. Reagan first sought the Republican presidential nomination in 1968, but lost to Richard Nixon. In 1976 he was defeated by incumbent Gerald Ford in a hotly contested campaign.

When Ford lost to Democrat Jimmy Carter in the 1976 presidential election, Reagan had another chance to campaign for the presidency. During the Carter years, many people became dissatisfied with the stagnant domestic economy, high inflation, and foreign policy failures, particularly the Iran hostage crisis of the late 1970s. During that crisis, a revolutionary government in Iran held 52 Americans for over a year without any successful counteraction by the Carter administration. Reagan's strong, confident message of national rejuvenation and his imposing television demeanor helped sway public opinion, and he not only won the Republican nomination for president in 1980, but defeated Carter by 489 electoral votes to 49.

The Reagan presidency spanned eight years, and involved a major shift in the national priorities of the federal government. First, Reagan endorsed an idea called "supply side economics," which proposed that the national economy could be revitalized by cutting taxes on the theory that the resulting economic stimulation would lead to new growth that would eventually generate more tax revenue than was lost in the initial tax cut itself. Although the 1980s did see some significant economic growth and eventually an end to the inflation of the 1970s, there were enormous budget deficits that did not end until the Democratic administration of Bill Clinton in the 1990s. Further, Reagan approved massive increases in defense spending aimed against America's cold war enemy, the Soviet Union. Although this defense spending was controversial and possibly wasteful in certain respects, many historians are convinced that the Soviets realized that they could never match America's economic resources in the military sphere, and so eventually decided to end the cold war. Finally, the Reagan administration is noted for being the first to appoint a woman to the United States Supreme Court, namely Sandra Day O'Connor.

Reagan was reelected in 1984, by an even more crushing majority of 525 electoral votes as opposed to 13 electoral votes for his Democratic opponent, Walter Mondale. Reagan continued to pursue his domestic and foreign policy agendas, and successfully concluded several important agreements with the new Soviet leader, Mikhail Gorbachev. He also supported the Tax Reform Act of 1986, which was the first major overhaul of the Internal Revenue Code since the 1950s and helped to curb many abuses in addition to simplifying the income tax system. Although there was a dangerous stock market crash in October 1987, the national economy remained strong through the end of the Reagan presidency, and he left office with fairly strong approval ratings.

Reagan was succeeded as president by his vice president, George Bush. Although the Reagan presidency in many ways helped to end the cold war in a manner favorable to the United States, the massive budget deficits that were Reagan's legacy helped to defeat Bush in 1992 and return the Democrats to the White House. The national debt nearly quadrupled in the Reagan-Bush years from 1981 to 1993. As of this writing, former president Reagan has begun to experience some serious health problems, including Alzheimer's disease, now that he is well into his eighties has largely receded from public view. He lives in California with his wife Nancy.

Aaron Burr's Birthday

Aaron Burr, whose popularity and political skill almost made him president of the United States, was born in Newark, New Jersey, on February 6, 1756. His father was the Reverend Aaron Burr,

U.S. Senate Historical Office

Aaron Burr

the second president of the College of New Jersey, which later became Princeton University; and his maternal grandfather was Jonathan Edwards, a New England Calvinist theologian.

Young Aaron, whose parents died when he was an infant, was raised in the home of a relative. He showed exceptional intelligence at an early age, entering the sophomore class at the College of New Jersey when he was 13 and graduating with distinction at 16. He studied theology for a while and toyed with the idea of following his father's profession, but in 1774 he gave this up to begin the study of law. With the outbreak of the American Revolution, he interrupted his studies to enlist in the Continental army.

Burr served as a captain on the staff of Benedict Arnold during Arnold's unsuccessful campaign against the British at Quebec. After assignment to General Washington's staff for a few weeks, Burr was then transferred to the command of General Israel Putnam. Promoted to the rank of lieutenant colonel in 1777, he remained in the army until March 1779, when he resigned because of ill health. The next year, he resumed the study of law. Admitted to the bar in 1782, he opened a law office in Albany, New York. He was married that same year to Theodosia Prevost, ten years his senior and the widow of a British officer. A daughter, Theodosia Burr, was born in 1783.

During that year, Burr moved his family to New York City, where he entered politics. He briefly served in the New York legislature, and was appointed state attorney general by Governor George Clinton in 1789. In 1791 he was elected to the U.S. Senate, defeating Philip Schuyler, the father-in-law of Alexander Hamilton, Burr's longtime rival and secretary of the treasury. Burr, a Jeffersonian Republican who opposed Hamilton's Federalist financial policies, failed to be reelected to the Senate in 1797. However, he was once again elected to the New York state legislature in that year and served there until 1799.

Meanwhile, Burr's star was rising on the national horizon. In the presidential election of 1796 he received 30 electoral votes. In 1800 he ran with Thomas Jefferson as a Jeffersonian Republican against the Federalist candidates, John Adams and Charles C. Pinckney. Jefferson and Burr triumphed over their opponents, but tied with each other at 73 votes each in the Electoral College, due to the flawed system of casting electoral votes in existence at that time. In the case of an electoral tie, the Constitution mandates that it is up to the House of Representatives to decide the outcome of the election. The election of 1800 thus went to the House, which was controlled by the Federalists. For a time they thought of supporting Burr, but after six days of balloting and Hamilton's clear indication that he regarded Jefferson as the lesser of two evils, the House elected Jefferson president on the 36th ballot. As runner-up, Burr automatically became vice president. (The 12th Amendment, ratified in 1804, would provide for the separate election of president and vice president in the future.)

As the Senate's presiding officer, Burr won respect from both friends and opponents. His last act as vice president was to preside over the impeachment trial of Supreme Court justice Samuel Chase. Jefferson wanted Justice Chase removed, and the friends of his administration sought to influence Burr by offering appointments to office for members of the Burr family. Burr, however, presided "with the dignity and impartiality of an angel and with the rigor of a devil," and the justice was acquitted.

Meanwhile, Burr had fallen into disfavor with the Jeffersonian Republicans and was replaced as the vice-presidential candidate by New York governor George Clinton in the election of 1804. It was also in 1804 that Burr, nominated for the governorship of New York, again had his ambitions thwarted by Hamilton, whose opposition contributed to his defeat. After the election Burr challenged Hamilton to a duel, which was still an accepted means of resolving personal disputes. The

duel, one of history's most famous, took place at Weehawken, New Jersey, on July 11, 1804. It brought to an end not only the life of Alexander Hamilton, who received a fatal bullet wound, but also the political career of Aaron Burr.

Burr became a political and social pariah for killing the popular Hamilton. He was charged with murder by authorities in New York and New Jersey, and fled south. After drifting to the newly acquired Louisiana Territory, he entered into a wild scheme to lead the secession of the West from the Union and establish himself as an independent ruler. Betrayed by a co-conspirator, he was arrested and tried for treason in the U.S. Circuit Court at Richmond, Virginia. Found not guilty of an "overt act" of treason, as required by the Constitution, he was acquitted on September 1, 1807. Despite this fact, he always remained guilty in the public mind.

In 1808 Burr went to England, where he sought help for a plan to drive the Spanish from Mexico. When he failed to get assistance, he took his proposal to France but was unsuccessful there as well. He returned, impoverished, to the United States in 1812 and resumed the practice of law in New York. In July 1833, the 77-year-old Burr, whose first wife had died many years before, was married to the wealthy and flamboyant young widow Eliza Brown Jumel. With the spendthrift Burr threatening to squander her fortune, they separated after four months. Following some colorful proceedings, the divorce decree was officially issued on September 14, 1836, which was the same day that Burr died, in a Staten Island hotel in New York City.

Massachusetts Ratifies the Constitution

On February 6, 1788, Massachusetts became the sixth state to ratify the United States Constitution. Of the earlier five, only Pennsylvania was a major state, so the addition of Massachusetts to the list of affirmative votes was an important victory for the supporters of the new form of government. The debate over the Constitution in the Bay State was intense, and the Federalists had to use all of their powers of persuasiveness and sense of political compromise to achieve their goal.

In the years immediately after the American Revolution, Massachusetts found the Articles of Confederation increasingly inadequate. As early as 1785, Governor James Bowdoin in his inaugural address called for a convention to amend the articles. Massachusetts was heavily dependent on trade, and its shipowners were being squeezed by the often discriminatory and excessive trade regulations imposed by other states. Domestic matters, such as the passage of inflationary paper money legislation and an insurrection of poor farmers led by Captain Daniel Shays in the western part of Massachusetts, also produced calls for a stronger government.

When the Continental Congress on February 21, 1787, asked the states to appoint delegates to a Constitutional Convention, Massachusetts dispatched Francis Dana, Elbridge Gerry, Nathaniel Gorham, Rufus King, and Caleb Strong. Dana never attended the gathering, and Strong returned home in August, but Gerry, Gorham, and King remained in Philadelphia until the conclusion of the Constitutional Convention on September 17, 1787. Gerry served as chairman of the Grand Committee of the convention, composed of one delegate from each state, which worked out several important compromises between the large and small states. King was a member of the Committee of Style and Arrangement, which prepared the final draft of the proposed Constitution. Gerry, however, refused to support the final draft of the Constitution, objecting to the extensive powers to be granted to the national congress.

Having completed its task, the Continental Congress submitted the Constitution to the states for ratification. On October 18, 1787, the Massachusetts General Court issued a call for a ratifying convention to meet in January 1788. On the appointed day, 364 delegates from 318 towns met; 46 communities, mostly in the Maine district, which was then part of Massachusetts, sent no representatives. Gorham, King, and Strong won election to the ratification meeting. They eagerly supported the proposed Constitution, as did such other notables as former governor James Bowdoin. The Antifederalist opposition lacked such an elite leadership group.

Supporters of the Constitution worked vigorously to persuade the public. Federalist essays in favor of the Constitution flooded the newspapers and popular periodicals. The Federalists also won over the politically powerful governor, John Hancock, to their side. On January 31, 1788, Hancock announced his support for the Constitution. After some additional debate, on February 6, 1788, the Massachusetts convention voted 187 to 168 to ratify the Constitution. Counties near the coast, including the commercial seats in Suffolk and Essex counties, gave the strongest support to ratification. Agrarian interior areas, such as Worcester, provided the bulk of negative votes.

France Recognizes the United States

On February 6, 1778, a formal treaty of alliance between France and the United States was signed in Paris. It was the result of intricate negotiations that had been conducted secretly since 1775.

Ever since its defeat at the hands of Great Britain in the Seven Years War (1756–1763), the French government had awaited an opportune moment for revenge. Its goal was to recapture its previous dominance in European affairs. The American Revolution presented an ideal opportunity to undermine the British and redress the balance of power in France's favor. The French minister of foreign affairs, Charles Gravier, Comte de Vergennes, fully realized the possibilities offered by the colonial revolt. He wrote in 1778: "Providence has marked this era for the humiliation of a proud and greedy power . . . glory and inestimable advantages will result."

French manufacturers hoped for trade opportunities with the United States, which up until then had been cut off by the restrictive British Acts of Trade. In fact, after the Revolution ended, Vergennes commented to his minister of finance: "always keep in mind that in separating the United States from Great Britain it was above all their commerce which we wanted." There were other reasons that influenced the French to sympathize with the American cause, however. French intellectuals, including Voltaire, tended to idealize the Americans as a simple, unpretentious people with all the virtues of self-made "natural men." To them, America represented a utopia, which would eventually guide the Old World toward an improved way of life.

The American colonists, in turn, realized the logic of seeking aid from Britain's age-old enemy. Soon after the outbreak of the American Revolution in April 1775, they began wooing France. In November 1775, the Continental Congress appointed a committee on foreign relations. Less than half a year later Silas Deane, an American lawyer and merchant, was dispatched to Paris. Although ostensibly a business agent, Deane had in reality been entrusted with the task of securing arms, supplies, and clothing for the American troops. With the knowledge and protection of King Louis XVI and the French government, a bogus company, Roderigue Hortalez et Cie., was set up. It provided vital military assistance to the hard-pressed revolutionaries. In addition to this partisan help, American ships, including privateers preying on British vessels, were welcomed at French seaports.

Once the Declaration of Independence was adopted on July 4, 1776, the Continental Congress decided that other European states, including Spain, Prussia, and Austria, should also be solicited for aid and that the existing ties with France should be tightened. Benjamin Franklin (see his entry at January 17) and Arthur Lee were appointed commissioners to France to assist Silas Deane. In December 1776 the two newcomers arrived in Paris with proposals for a treaty of friendship and commerce. When the American forces came close to defeat during the winter of 1776–1777, Congress, eager to persuade France to become an ally, authorized Franklin to draw up a military alliance. The American agents were able to secure more war supplies, but they were unsuccessful in persuading the absolutist French monarchy to intervene openly on behalf of the anti-monarchical American Revolution.

The French government reversed its decision, however, and abandoned its policy of all aid "short of war" in the late fall of 1777 after the Americans defeated the British at Saratoga. Vergennes was concerned that the British might make a settlement with the Americans, thereby thwarting his ambition to undermine British supremacy. Indeed, upon receiving news of the British defeat at Saratoga, British prime minister Lord North advocated an end to the war. King George III, although ready to concede almost complete autonomy to the colonists, still demanded that they acknowledge his sovereignty. The French government moved quickly to recognize American independence in order to prevent a British-American reconciliation, and initiated preparations for a formal alliance.

Thus, two treaties were signed on February 6, 1778. The Treaty of Amity and Commerce provided that France and the independent United States would grant each other favorable trade terms, while the Treaty of Alliance secured French assistance for the American war effort against Great Britain. Eleven days later, the British Parliament considered a conciliatory bill authorizing a special peace commission to offer the colonists extensive concessions to be guaranteed by treaty, and the bill was passed. Lord North hoped that the new measures would prevent the Continental Congress from ratifying the French alliance. The peace commission, headed by the Earl of Carlisle, did not reach Philadelphia until June 6, 1778. On March 20, meanwhile, King Louis XVI of France had already formally received the American commissioners and shortly thereafter had named Conrad Gerard as the first French minister to the United States. Congress, learning of the Franco-American alliance on May 2, 1778, unanimously ratified the two treaties two days later. On September 11, 1778, it resolved to appoint a minister to France and three days later named Benjamin Franklin to the post.

French military and naval assistance helped the Americans turn the tide against the British. Further, in April 1779 the French government persuaded the Spanish Empire to become a French ally and help the Americans. The Spanish, who hoped to win Gibraltar from Great Britain, allowed American privateers to use New Orleans (then held by the Spanish) as a base and seized some British outposts in West Florida. The French-American alliance of February 6, 1778, thus became the first major step in turning the American Revolution into a war with important implications for Europe.

Twentieth Amendment Ratified

The 20th Amendment to the Constitution of the United States, known as the "lame duck" amendment, provides that the terms of the president and vice president shall begin on January 20 and those of senators and representatives on January 3 instead of the previous date of March 4 established by the Constitution in 1787. Further, the amendment provides that Congress shall convene on January 3 of each year instead of the first Monday in December, which was the date established by the Constitution.

The 20th Amendment, proposed to the state legislatures by the 72nd Congress in March 1932, was proclaimed ratified on February 6, 1933, with 36 of the existing 48 states having ratified it. By October 15, 1933, the amendment had been ratified by all of the 48 states. The amendment also provides rules for the presidential succession in case of the death, or failure to qualify, of a president-elect.

When the Constitution was originally adopted, the date of March 4 was selected for the president's inauguration in order to provide time for election returns to be assembled and for newly elected candidates to reach the capital. By the time the 20th Amendment was proposed, however, improved methods of transportation and communication had made this long delay after the November elections unnecessary. The customary short session of Congress, beginning in December and attended by members who had been defeated the month before, popularly called "lame ducks," was similarly outdated.

Chinese New Year

This is a movable event.

Although the Gregorian calendar was adopted in China in 1912, the Chinese people in China, Taiwan, and abroad continue to regard the date given in the old Chinese lunar calendar as the beginning of the new year. According to that calendar, the year has 354 days and 12 lunar months, about half of them with 30 days and the other half with 29. In order to make the months correspond with the movements of the earth around the sun, a 13th month is inserted every two or three years. The new year begins on the new moon and may occur at any time from January 21 through February 19. The years are named for the animals of the Chinese zodiac: rat, ox, tiger, hare, dragon, snake, horse, sheep, monkey, rooster, dog, and pig, in that order. Each 12-year cycle begins with another year of the rat.

For Americans of Chinese descent, 1976, the American bicentennial year, was the year of the dragon, the most auspicious sign in the Chinese zodiac according to ancient almanacs. The year 2000 was likewise a dragon year. The arrival of the new year is celebrated with festivities, parades, costumes, and fireworks in Chinese communities throughout the United States.

February 7

John Deere's Birthday

John Deere, developer of the steel plow that helped open the Midwest to pioneer farmers, was born in Rutland, Vermont, on February 7, 1804. He grew up in Middlebury, Vermont. In addition to receiving his grade school education there, he served as an apprentice to a blacksmith.

Deere proved to be exceptionally skilled at his chosen profession, earning a reputation for producing high-quality implements. In the 1830s, however, an economic depression swept the United States. Deere relocated to Grand Detour, Illinois, in 1837. Like many people of the time, he sought economic opportunities on the expanding American frontier.

Deere soon established a thriving business, serving the needs of the farmers and settlers who were moving into Illinois and the Midwest in great numbers. However, the farming conditions of the Midwest were quite different from these of Deere's native Vermont. The soil of the great plains was rich and deep, but the thick turf, intertwined with roots, was difficult to plow with the traditional cast-iron plows in use at the time. Deere solved the problem by taking an old steel sawmill blade and bending it into an ingenious shape. His stronger steel plow not only cut into thick soil, but had a shaped upper surface that lifted the plowed soil up and away from the cutting blade.

By the 1840s Deere and his business partner, Major Leonard Andrus, were selling thousands of plows a year. One of Deere's biggest problems was how to obtain high-quality steel from reliable suppliers. At the time, steel was still a relatively rare and expensive commodity, since the large-scale development of the American steel industry was still decades away. For a time, Deere obtained steel from English suppliers, but this was a cumbersome process because the steel had to be shipped across the Atlantic and then by river and wagon to the Illinois frontier. Finally, he found reliable suppliers in Pittsburgh, Pennsylvania, and was thus able to expand his facilities and increase production.

By the 1850s Deere's enterprise was manufacturing tens of thousands of steel plows a year. Before John Deere's steel plow, many pioneers and farmers had considered the Great Plains that cover America's Midwest as simply an obstacle to be crossed in order to get to more desirable locations such as Oregon or California. Now that the technology was available to turn the grassy plains into productive farmland, however, states such as Kansas, Nebraska, and Iowa could be settled by large numbers of newcomers.

In the late 1860s John Deere incorporated his enterprise as Deere & Company, which has continued to thrive through the present day. In 1869 Deere withdrew from the active management of the company, putting his son Charles in charge. John Deere died on May 17, 1886, in Moline, Illinois.

The Beatles Arrive in the United States

On February 7, 1964, the legendary rock group known as the Beatles landed in the United States at the beginning of what would be one of the most successful tours in music history. During their stay in the United States, which included an historic appearance on the popular Ed Sullivan television show, the Beatles paved the way for a variety of British rock-and-roll groups in the future. This influx of British groups, which included the equally legendary Rolling Stones, has been nicknamed "the British invasion" and is one of the cultural hallmarks of that turbulent era known as the 1960s.

When the Beatles arrived in 1964, the four musicians who comprised the group—George Harrison, John Lennon, Paul McCartney, and Ringo Starr—were already famous, and their music was listened to by millions in both the United States and Great Britain. They began, however, as an obscure band in Liverpool, England. In 1956, John Lennon organized "The Quarrymen." His friend Paul McCartney joined the next year. At first, the group survived by imitating more popular performers such as Elvis Presley in order to eke out a living. As the band became increasingly popular, Harrison and Starr joined the group, and they were given the opportunity to perform in Hamburg, West Germany. By this time, they called themselves the Silver Beetles, in order to play on the popularity of Buddy Holly and the Crickets. Increasingly, however, the word Beetles was deliberately misspelled as Beatles in order to play on the "beat" counterculture of the era. Ultimately, the name was shortened to "The Beatles."

It was during their tour of Hamburg that the Beatles made contacts who eventually enabled them to get a contract with EMI Records. In October 1962 the Beatles' first single, "Love Me Do," was released. The fresh style and upbeat tempo made the song a hit. The band followed with a rapid succession of other singles, including "Please, Please Me," which became the number-one song on the American Top Ten. The Beatles had been waiting for a number-one hit to make their first appearance in the United States, so that they would be riding a crest of popularity, and this strategy proved successful. After their American visit, the craze known as "Beatlemania" swept the country, and the group went on to produce many more successful songs and albums and several popular movies. In later years the group broke up over artistic and other differences, and John Lennon was the victim of a tragic assassination. However, the band and its music live on as one of the most significant cultural emblems of the 20th century.

The Baltimore Fire

A massive fire swept some 150 acres of downtown Baltimore on February 7, 1904. It destroyed most of the city's business center, with a loss of roughly $70-150 million, an enormous sum for that time. The Baltimore Fire, which raged for about 30 hours, was the biggest fire since the Chicago Fire of 1871.

When the fire was over, 80 business blocks and some 2,600 buildings had been demolished. During the next three years, however, reconstruction proceeded swiftly. Much of the work was supervised by the Burnt District Commission. Before the activity was over, Baltimore's business district was almost entirely rebuilt, and what had not been rebuilt had been renovated.

Skyscrapers made their first appearance in Baltimore during this period. Other improvements coincided with the new construction. Cesspools gave way to sewers, for example, and cobblestones gave way to smooth pavements. In addition a modern system for purifying the city's water supply was installed. The beginnings of modern Baltimore date from the conflagration of 1904.

February 8

James Dean's Birthday

The legendary film actor and pop culture icon James Dean was born on February 8, 1931, in Fairmont, Indiana. Shortly thereafter, the family moved to California. Dean's mother died of cancer in Los Angeles in 1940, and he went to live with his aunt and uncle back in Indiana. As a teenager, he developed an interest in acting, which was encouraged by Adline Nall, a teacher at the local high school. Dean appeared in several high school productions, and continued to pursue this interest when he enrolled in Santa Monica City College in 1950. A year later, he dropped out of college and went to work as a full-time actor.

After several minor roles, including bit parts on various television shows, Dean landed a role in the Broadway production of *See the Jaguar*. Whether due to his acting ability or his youthful good looks, Dean was a success, and in 1954 he landed another Broadway role in *The Immoralist*. He was spotted by agents for Warner Brothers Studios, who gave him a screen test and signed him to a movie contract. For his first major movie, *East of Eden*, Dean received an advance of only $700.

East of Eden was a major box office hit, and Warner Brothers decided to extend Dean's contract. Now a popular film star, Dean started to earn a more respectable income, part of which he used to indulge his passion for sports cars. It proved to be an unfortunate choice of hobbies: Shortly after he filmed *Rebel Without a Cause* and *Giant*, he crashed his Porsche into another vehicle while on the way to a race car event in Salinas, California. The accident, which occurred on September 30, 1955, proved fatal for the 24-year-old Dean.

His final two movies were released posthumously, and *Rebel Without a Cause* became popular not only for the quality of his performance in the role of the troubled young man, but also because of the parallels between the actor and his movie character. Dean's lifestyle epitomized the "live fast and die young" outlook often admired by young people and idealized by popular culture. The turbulent 1960s, in which a younger generation began to challenge the values of society, helped to further enshrine Dean as one of Hollywood's legends.

Boy Scouts of America Founded

The anniversary of the founding of the Boy Scouts of America, on February 8, 1910, is observed every year by that multimillion-member organization. Boy scouting began around the turn of the 20th century with the publication of a military pamphlet, "Aids to Scouting," by a British cavalry officer named Robert Baden-Powell, who had scouted extensively on the Indian and African frontiers. He came to world renown and national acclaim as the defender of Mafeking during the Boer War in South Africa, and his pamphlet achieved popularity for its emphasis on the need for building a strong character to cope with the rigors of service on the frontiers of the British Empire.

Challenged to lend his prestige and talents as a writer and illustrator to promote scouting as an activity for existing youth groups, Baden-Powell conducted an experimental camp for boys of varied backgrounds. His subsequent book, *Scouting for Boys*, was an immediate success upon its publication in 1908, and Baden-Powell resigned from the British army to devote the rest of his life to the Boy Scouts. For this work he was knighted and later made Lord Baden-Powell of Gilwell. As chief scout of the world, he saw millions of boys pass through the ranks of scouting in many countries before he died in Kenya at the age of 84 in 1941.

In 1909 a newspaper publisher from Chicago named William D. Boyce was lost in a London fog when a boy came up and saluted, saying, "May I be of service to you, sir?" Boyce told him the street address he was seeking, and the boy took him there. The publisher offered the boy a shilling, but the boy refused it, saluting again. "Sir, I am a Scout," he said. "Scouts do not accept tips for courtesies." Startled, Boyce asked for an explanation, and the boy told him of the British Boy Scout Association and offered to take him to its headquarters. At the Scout office, Boyce learned of the work of Sir Robert Baden-Powell and the organization.

Boyce returned to the United States, and early in 1909 started the organization known as the Boy Scouts of America. The organization was eventually chartered by the U.S. Congress in 1916. Since then, tens of millions of boys have received Scout training. The aim of the Boy Scouts of America has always been to develop the character and personal fitness of boys, particularly through outdoor activities. There are standards of achievement for advancing from rank to rank within the several phases of the program, and most of the Scout activities emphasize the skills required for advancement. The organization's charter and bylaws proclaimed the intention to "promote, through organization, and cooperation with other agencies, the ability of boys to do things for themselves and others, to train them in Scoutcraft, and to teach them patriotism, courage, self-reliance, and kindred virtues."

The scouting movement, which is nonsectarian and without military or political connection, also promotes other activities such as nature conservation and forestry.

February 9

William Henry Harrison's Birthday

Library of Congress

William Henry Harrison

William Henry Harrison, the ninth president of the United States, was born at the plantation of Berkeley in Charles County, Virginia, on February 9, 1773. He was the third son of Benjamin Harrison, whose ancestors came to America from England in 1633.

Benjamin Harrison served as governor of Virginia and was one of the signers of the Declaration of Independence. His son William Henry entered Hampden-Sidney College in 1787. In 1790 William went to Richmond, Virginia, to study medicine, and a few months later he went to Philadelphia, Pennsylvania, to continue his medical studies under Benjamin Rush. After his father's death in 1791, William decided to enter the army and was commissioned as an ensign in the First Infantry Regiment. He served in the Northwest Territory, rose to the rank of lieutenant, and was an aide-de-camp to General Anthony Wayne.

After further promotion to the rank of captain, Harrison resigned from the army in 1798 and was appointed secretary of the Northwest Territory. The next year he was elected as its first delegate to Congress. He was influential in obtaining passage of the act that divided the Northwest Territory into the territories of Ohio and Indiana, and in 1800 he was appointed governor of the new Indiana Territory. As governor, he was presented with two utterly irreconcilable assignments: to see that the Native Americans were treated fairly by the settlers, and to secure the cession of as much Native American land as possible for the U.S. government. Harrison succeeded in obtaining grants of millions of acres of land in Indiana and in what became the territory of Illinois in 1809. Not surprisingly, however, the Native Americans resented the influx of white settlers, and the Shawnee chief Tecumseh set about forming a confederation of tribes to prevent the occupation of their lands. In November 1811, Harrison led a force of about 1,000 men against the allied tribes in the battle of Tippecanoe, defeated them, and took possession of their settlements there. The site of the encounter was later designated as the Tippecanoe Battlefield State Memorial, located near Lafayette, Indiana.

After the War of 1812 between the United States and Great Britain began, Harrison was named a brigadier general and given command of the U.S. Army forces in the Northwest Territory. He saw active service in battles against the British forces and their tribal allies. His victory at the battle of the Thames (near Chatham, Ontario), which resulted in the death of Tecumseh on October 5, 1813, virtually ended British activities in the Northwest Territory and was followed by the pacification of most of the tribes of the region.

Harrison was succeeded as governor of Indiana in March 1813 by Thomas Posey and was promoted to the rank of major general. In May 1814 he resigned from the army for the second time and took up residence on his farm at North Bend, Ohio, near Cincinnati. He was elected to the U.S. House of Representatives in 1816 and served there until 1819. He then served as a member of the Ohio State Senate from 1819 until 1821, and was subsequently elected to the U.S. Senate, where he served beginning in 1825 and chaired the Committee on Military Affairs.

After three years in the Senate, through the influence of his mentor Henry Clay, Harrison was appointed as the first U.S. envoy to the newly independent nation of Colombia. Arriving in Bogotá, Colombia, in February 1829, at a time when the enemies of President Simón Bolívar (who had liberated the region from Spain) were in open revolt, Harrison was accused of sympathizing with the revolutionaries. He was recalled the following summer by President Andrew Jackson. Back in the United States, Harrison was an unsuccessful candidate for president in 1836, running as a Whig and receiving only 73 electoral votes against Martin Van Buren's 170. Undiscouraged, Harrison's supporters immediately began to organize a movement to secure his nomination in the 1840 election. The three leading Whig contenders for the nomination were Harrison, Daniel Webster, and Henry Clay. Webster withdrew in December 1839, and his influence, along with that of political leader Thurlow Weed of New York, was strong enough to win the nomination for Harrison. John Tyler joined Harrison's ticket as the candidate for vice president.

The 1840 campaign is remembered for its slogans, like "Tippecanoe and Tyler too!", Tippecanoe of course being a reference to Harrison by way of his famous military victory. Harrison was elected with 234 electoral votes against 60 for the Democrats' Martin Van Buren.

Inaugurated on March 4, 1841, Harrison refused to wear his hat and coat despite the miserably cold weather. After riding a white horse to the Capitol, he delivered a lengthy outdoor inaugural address. Afterwards, he came down with pneumonia and died on April 4, 1841. Some 48 years later, Harrison's grandson, Benjamin Harrison, would be elected president, marking the only grandfather-grandson presidential sequence in American history to this day.

Gasparilla Festival

This is a movable event.

In 1904 the port city of Tampa, Florida, located on Florida's west coast, began to hold a Gasparilla festival based on the exploits of José Gaspar, a famous Spanish pirate of the late 18th century who referred to himself by the diminutive term Gasparilla, or "little Gaspar." In that year a company of business and social leaders organized a club that they called Ye Mystic Krewe of Gasparilla. In the years since, the former pirate festival has evolved into one of Florida's largest celebrations, attracting hundreds of thousands of spectators and participants.

The idea for the Gasparilla festival originated with George W. Hardee, a New Orleans man who in 1904 was working in Tampa for the federal government. Seeking a way to add color to a May festival that was being planned in Tampa, he seized upon the legends about Gasparilla, who had conducted his pirate activities in the neighboring Gulf of Mexico. A few weeks after Hardee presented his idea to several city leaders, Ye Mystic Krewe of Gasparilla was formed. Plans were then made to secure costumes and provide for parades and festivities. The Gasparilla festival was later moved to February, to take place on the Monday following the first Tuesday in the month.

It is said that Spanish-born José Gaspar, the villain-hero of the Gasparilla festival, was the last of the pirates to sail the Spanish Main. Although facts are few and some scholars doubt that there ever was such a person, evidence points to the probability that the bloodthirsty Gaspar existed. Reportedly he was a lieutenant in the Royal Spanish Navy and began his career as a pirate by leading a mutiny aboard a Spanish warship in 1783. From then until his death in 1821, he terrorized Florida's Gulf Coast, reportedly capturing and burning dozens of ships. He met his end when he attacked a U.S. Navy warship, the USS *Enterprise*, which he had mistaken for an unarmed merchant vessel. The *Enterprise* fired on Gaspar's ship, inflicting serious damage. According to legend, Gaspar committed suicide to avoid being captured as sailors from the *Enterprise* boarded his vessel.

February 10

Mardi Gras, or Shrove Tuesday

This is a movable event.

Shrove Tuesday, or Mardi Gras, is the day immediately preceding the beginning of Lent on Ash Wednesday. Like the dates of Lent, a period of fasting and penitence in which Christians prepare for Easter, Shrove Tuesday is a movable observance whose date depends on the date of Easter. Ash Wednesday is 40 days before Easter, not counting Sundays, and thus Shrove Tuesday is 41 days before Easter.

As observed in New Orleans, Mardi Gras is probably the United States' most elaborate celebration. The day is observed as a legal holiday in many parts of Louisiana. Traditionally, Shrove Tuesday was the concluding day of the carnival festivities that preceded the austere period of Lent, especially in the Roman Catholic countries. Although by the Middle Ages the church had put its imprint upon the celebrations, or at least allowed dispensation for what could not be easily suppressed, the idea of carnival probably originated with pre-Christian pagan rites. These rituals, particularly including fertility rites, marked the approach of spring, with its attendant rebirth of nature, and sought to ensure good crops. Not only the ancient Egyptians, but also the Greeks and Romans, celebrated at about this time of year.

Carnival as it survives today spread from Rome, where masked and costumed revelers took part in annual processions and pelted one another with confetti. During the Middle Ages, Florence and Venice became famous for their carnival pageantry, replete with floats, splendid costumes and masks, and, in the case of Venice, flower-decked gondolas. Major Spanish cities staged sumptuous carnivals and lavish balls, and the Portuguese held floral balls and mock battles with confetti. Beginning in the 1400s the French, whose term *mardi gras* translates literally as "fat Tuesday," also had costume balls. Their celebrations came to include long, float-filled parades, flower battles, and, in some places, a Shrove Tuesday procession led by a fat ox. To the Germans, the night before Lent became known as *Fastnacht*, meaning the night before the fast.

In England, Shrove Tuesday was the preferred term. The verb "to shrive" means to hear or make confession and to grant absolution or impose penance. The Anglo-Saxon *Ecclesiastical Institutes* refers to the custom of going to confess one's sins in order to approach Lent with appropriate penitence: "In the week immediately before Lent everyone shall go to his confessor and confess his deeds and the confessor shrive him." Accordingly, the last three days before Lent, namely Shrove Sunday, Shrove Monday, and Shrove Tuesday, were collectively known as Shrovetide.

The idea of pre-Lent carnivals in general and a climactic Shrove Tuesday celebration in particular spread from Europe to the Western Hemisphere. The Puritans disapproved of the practice and did not observe it in New England, but the French who settled Louisiana and New Orleans did, and they brought the French term *mardi gras* with them. New Orleans, Louisiana, is now the site of North America's most flamboyant, and one of the world's most famous, celebrations collectively known as Mardi Gras. Mardi Gras has also been periodically observed in parts of Florida, Mississippi, and Tennessee, and also in parts of northern Maine where there are towns that were settled by people from French Quebec.

The wearing of masks, which is still customary on Mardi Gras, dates back at least as far as the Middle Ages to the Mardi Gras celebrations of France and Italy. The first recorded instance of processions of masked celebrants in New Orleans was in 1838. In 1857 New Orleans also began the custom of celebrating Mardi Gras with float parades. Some of the most elaborate parades and the heaviest partying are in the old French Quarter of New Orleans, where the streets and famous wrought-iron balconies of houses along the line of march are crowded with people.

In the 1980s and 1990s, the annual Mardi Gras celebration in New Orleans began to suffer from some grim developments. The free and easy sexual climate of Mardi Gras was devastated by AIDS, which was particularly damaging to the gay community. Further, the economic decay of the New Orleans area sparked a dramatic increase in crime, to the point where in some areas official signs were posted warning people to not venture outside after dark. Nevertheless, Mardi Gras remains a popular celebration and a major tourist attraction for New Orleans.

Twenty-fifth Amendment Ratified

On February 10, 1967, the 25th Amendment, establishing clear lines of succession in case of presidential disability, became part of the U.S. Constitution after being ratified by the required two-thirds majority of 38 states. In a parliamentary photo finish, the legislatures of North Dakota, Minnesota, and Nevada competed for the honor of being the 38th state to ratify the amendment.

The amendment, which empowers the vice president to act as president when the president is physically or mentally unable to perform the duties of his or her office, also enables the president to nominate a vice president if that post should become vacant. Under previous provisions of the Constitution, it was clear that the vice president would take up the duties of the presidency in case of the president's death, removal, resignation, or inability to discharge his responsibilities. However, the Constitution was silent as to how a presidential disability would be determined.

This ambiguity led to a situation in which the vice president was not clearly empowered to take over either in the case of President James A. Garfield, who was incapacitated for ten weeks prior to his death in 1881, or of President Woodrow Wilson, who was bedridden and unable to transact official business for most of the 18 months before his second term expired in 1921. When Vice President Lyndon B. Johnson was elevated to the presidency after the assassination of President John F. Kennedy in November 1963, the office of vice president was left vacant for almost 14 months, a reminder that the Constitution also did not provide a means for appointing a new vice president.

On July 6, 1965, Congress proposed the 25th Amendment, which was designed to ensure the continuity of presidential power. In slightly abbreviated form, its text is as follows:

Section I

In case of the removal of the President from office or his death or resignation, the Vice President shall become President.

Section II

Whenever there is a vacancy in the office of Vice President, the President shall nominate a Vice President who shall take the office upon confirmation by a majority vote of both houses of Congress.

Section III

Whenever the President transmits to the President pro tempore of the Senate and the Speaker of the House of Representatives his written declaration that he is unable to discharge the powers and duties of his office, and until he transmits to them a written declaration to the contrary, such powers and duties shall be discharged by the Vice President as Acting President.

Section IV

Whenever the Vice President and a majority of either the principal officers of the executive departments or of such other body as Congress may by law provide, transmit to the President pro tempore of the Senate and the Speaker of the House of Representatives their written declaration that the President is unable to discharge the powers and duties of his office, the Vice President shall immediately assume [these] powers and duties . . . as Acting President.

Thereafter, when the President transmits to the President . . . of the Senate and the Speaker of the House . . . his written declaration that no inability exists, he shall resume . . . his office unless the Vice President and a majority of either the principal officers of the executive department or of such other body as Congress may . . . provide, transmit within four days . . . their written declaration that the President is unable to discharge . . . his office. Thereupon Congress shall decide the issue. . . .

If the Congress . . . determines by two-thirds vote of both houses that the President is unable to discharge . . . his office, the Vice President shall continue to discharge the same as Acting President; otherwise, the President shall resume the powers and duties of his office.

Section II of the 25th Amendment was first applied in 1973, following the resignation of Vice President Spiro T. Agnew. President Richard M. Nixon nominated Gerald R. Ford, who was sworn in as vice president on December 6, 1973. A year later the same provision was again exercised. Upon Nixon's resignation from the presidency, the first such resignation in American history, Ford became president on August 9, 1974, and subsequently nominated former New York governor Nelson A. Rockefeller for the vice-presidency. Rockefeller took the oath of office on December 19, 1974.

First Medal of Honor in World War II

On February 10, 1942, President Franklin D. Roosevelt posthumously awarded the Medal of Honor to Second Lieutenant Alexander R. Nininger for giving his life during the Battle of Bataan. Nininger became the first recipient of the Medal of Honor during World War II.

After the Japanese attacked Pearl Harbor on December 7, 1941, American forces were initially on the defensive throughout the Pacific. The United States was still transitioning from peacetime, while the Japanese had a large and battle-hardened military machine. One of Japan's first targets was the Philippines, which had been under American control since the Spanish-American War (see the Treaty of Paris essay below). The small American occupation force fought bravely, but it was no match for the invaders, and reinforcements were not yet available.

Alexander "Sandy" Nininger was born on October 30, 1918, in Atlanta, Georgia. After being commissioned as a second lieutenant in the infantry, he was stationed in the Philippines as his first assignment when America entered World War II. Nininger was serving in Company A, 57th Infantry of the Philippine Scouts, when the Japanese landed and the Americans were forced to establish defensive positions in what would become the famous Battle of Bataan. On January 9, 1942, the main Japanese offensive began.

The Americans sought to turn the tide of battle by committing their reserves, producing eight days of intense combat that ultimately failed to stop the Japanese advance. During this time, Lieu-

tenant Nininger's reconnaissance patrol came under attack. Single-handedly, Nininger charged into the enemy position, armed only with a rifle and some grenades. He reportedly grabbed a Japanese machine gun and killed at least 40 enemy soldiers before he was fatally shot. For his heroism "above and beyond the call of duty," Nininger earned the Medal of Honor.

Treaty of Paris Becomes Effective

At the conclusion of the Spanish-American War in 1898, a commission was appointed to negotiate a treaty of peace. American and Spanish commissioners met in Paris, France, and agreed on treaty terms under which Spain ceded the Philippine Islands, the island of Guam, and the island of Puerto Rico to the United States for $20 million. Spain also agreed to withdraw from Cuba and leave the settlement of affairs on that island to the United States, which subsequently administered Cuban affairs on a temporary basis until May 1902 and again from late 1906 until early 1909.

The treaty was submitted to the U.S. Senate by President William McKinley on January 4, 1899, for ratification. A memorable debate on it was conducted in open session, with opponents of the measure leveling charges of imperialism, particularly in regard to the projected U.S. acquisition of the Philippine Islands. Departing from the position of much of his party, Republican senator George F. Hoar of Massachusetts opposed ratification on the ground that the United States had no constitutional power to hold the Philippine Islands. However, Senator John C. Spooner of Wisconsin, another Republican, said that the islands constituted "the bitter fruits of the war" and insisted that the United States had the right to acquire territory, although he did not think it expedient for the United States to hold "permanent dominion over far distant lands and people."

While the debate was in progress, William Jennings Bryan, who had been the Democratic candidate for president in 1896, went to Washington and advised Democratic senators to vote for ratification of the treaty, even though he opposed permanent U.S. acquisition of the Philippines. His support turned out to be decisive. As the Republicans did not have the two-thirds majority necessary for ratification, Democratic votes were needed if the treaty was to become effective. After several more weeks of debate, the vote was taken on February 6, 1899, and the treaty was ratified with only one vote to spare. Of those voting for the measure, ten were Democrats. Three Republicans voted against ratification.

The treaty was returned to President McKinley, who signed it on February 10, 1899, completing ratification. This act marked the official conclusion of the Spanish-American War.

February 11

Ash Wednesday

This is a movable event.

Ash Wednesday is observed by the Western branch of the Christian Church, both Roman Catholic and Protestant, as the first day of Lent. In the Eastern Byzantine rite, the first day of Lent is marked on the Monday before Ash Wednesday of the Roman rite. The date of Ash Wednesday is movable, occurring between February 4 and March 11, depending upon the date of Easter.

The origin of the Lent season before Easter dates back to early Christian times, perhaps as early as the 4th century. Pope Gregory I the Great (A.D. 590–604) established Ash Wednesday as the beginning day of this period of preparation and penance. Biblical precedent undoubtedly determined the number of days considered appropriate for Christians to prepare for the great feast of the Resurrection: Christ had fasted 40 days in the desert; God's Chosen People had stayed 40 years in the desert; Moses had spent 40 days on Mount Sinai; and the giant Goliath had threatened Israel for 40 days until he was slain by David. Pope Gregory I urged disciplinary practices in a spirit of self-examination and penitence not only on Ash Wednesday but throughout Lent. He wrote, "From this day unto the joys of [Easter] there are six weeks coming . . . that we, who through the past year have lived too much for ourselves, should mortify ourselves to our Creator . . . through abstinence."

The name Ash Wednesday refers to the use of ashes, symbolizing penance, a custom that can be traced to the Bible. In the early church, "sackcloth and ashes" were used as signs of repentance for grave sins. In a public display of penance, offenders such as criminals and adulterers were compelled to walk barefooted and in sackcloth into church to receive holy water and ashes. It is not known when the practice of distributing ashes not only to public penitents but to all members of the congregation became widespread; it was probably sometime in the 9th century. A passage from Aelfric's *Lives of the Saints*, written in England in 996–997, seems to indicate that the custom was already commonly observed:

We read in the books both in the Old Law and the New that the men who repented of their sins bestrewed themselves with ashes and clothed their bodies with sack cloth. Now let us do this little at the beginning of our Lent that we strew ashes upon our heads to signify that we ought to repent of our sins during the Lenten fast.

Some Roman Catholics still observe the custom of receiving ashes on Ash Wednesday, by having blessed ashes marked on their foreheads by a priest. This custom has largely disappeared in Protestant churches.

Thomas Alva Edison's Birthday

On February 11, 1847, Thomas Alva Edison was born in Milan, Ohio. He was of Dutch ancestry on his father's side and Scottish on his mother's. When he was seven the family moved to Port Huron, Michigan, where Edison had his only formal schooling, for three months in 1854. He was, however, an eager reader and developed a strong interest in chemistry by the time he was ten. Two years later Edison became a newsboy for the Grand Trunk Railway. At 15 he began to earn a living as a telegraph operator. He subsequently pursued this occupation in a number of cities, while devoting most of his free time to study and scientific experiments.

Edison's first patent was for an electrical vote recorder in 1868. Over the next decade, he also invented an improved form of stock ticker-tape machine; devised duplex, quadruplex, and automatic telegraph systems; discovered the phenomenon of "etheric force," which became the foundation of wireless telegraphy; and invented the "electric pen." The last item developed into the mimeograph machine, a prototype for the modern photocopier.

Edison accumulated $40,000 from selling various telegraphic appliances. With this money he opened his own laboratory at Menlo Park, New Jersey, in 1876. This was the famous "invention factory" where Edison and his team of scientists achieved their greatest successes. In 1877 and 1878 Edison developed the carbon transmitter, which improved upon Alexander Graham Bell's newly invented telephone and helped make the telephone commercially practical. It also helped lead to the development of the microphone.

Because so many modern inventions have come about as a synthesis of the contributions of many, the task of establishing priority has often been difficult. But when Edison in 1877 applied for a patent on the phonograph, now regarded as one of the outstanding examples of his inventive imagination, the U.S. Patent Office could find no precedent for the invention. Edison's initial model, which cost $18, was a primitive device consisting of a tinfoil-covered cylinder cranked by hand. When he perfected a motor-driven model a decade afterwards, he utilized cylindrical records made of wax. The improved version rapidly came into widespread use. Subsequently he introduced a new form of phonograph, which substituted a flat disk for the cylinder and employed a diamond needle to reproduce music. The invention of the phonograph also led to Edison's invention of the first dictating machine.

On October 21, 1879, Edison succeeded in inventing the first incandescent electric light bulb of practical value, suitable for inexpensive production and wide distribution. It contained a loop of carbonized cotton thread that shone for more than 13 hours before it sputtered out. Edison shortly developed improved, longer-lasting light bulbs. In the meantime, he had incorporated the Edison Electric Light Company. To go with his new light bulb, he developed whole new systems to generate, distribute, regulate, and measure electricity for light, heat, and power. As these systems evolved he produced more inventions, such as electric switches, safety fuses, insulated wire, light sockets, junction boxes, and underground conductors. In the early 1880s his efforts resulted in the construction of the world's first central electric power plants. One of these was in London, England, and the other was the Pearl Street plant in New York City.

In 1886, Edison moved into Glenmont, a mansion in West Orange, New Jersey, that was to be his home for the rest of his life. A year later he also moved his laboratory to West Orange. This laboratory, with its emphasis on team, rather than individual, research, may have been Edison's most important invention of all, since it served as the prototype for the team concept so widespread in industrial and scientific research today. In 1962 the laboratory buildings and the mansion were officially designated the Edison National Historic Site, administered by the National Park Service.

Edison soon developed an interest in motion picture technology. On October 6, 1889, he demonstrated the Kinetoscope, which made the motion picture a reality. The Kinetoscope was a peephole device in which photographs of a moving object, taken in rapid succession, could be viewed on a new type of film recently introduced by George Eastman, the founder of Kodak. Edison's device, which contained no means of projecting the pictures on a screen, was improved to provide for this after he acquired the patent for a projector that Thomas Armat invented in 1895. The resulting combination was known as the Vitascope.

Edison's company produced hundreds of early silent movies, including the historic *Great Train Robbery*, the world's first movie Western. It was directed and shot by Edwin S. Porter, an Edison cameraman, in 1903. By synchronizing the Kinetoscope with his phonograph, Edison in 1913 also introduced the Kinetophone, the first talking movie. Talking pictures, produced by others, transformed the movie industry in the late 1920s.

In all, Edison was granted over 1,000 patents. The firms that made and marketed his inventions were in time consolidated into the Edison General Electric Company, which eventually became the General Electric Company. Nicknamed "The Wizard of Menlo Park," Edison was honored and revered for the rest of his life. He died at West Orange on October 18, 1931.

Melville W. Fuller's Birthday

By J. E. Purdy. Collection of the Supreme Court of the United States.

Melville W. Fuller

Melville Weston Fuller, eighth chief justice of the United States Supreme Court, was born in Augusta, Maine, on February 11, 1833. He was the son of Frederick A. Fuller and Catherine M. Weston, both of whom belonged to prominent New England families. Melville Fuller's ancestors included Edward Fuller (whose name appeared on the Mayflower Compact of 1620), distinguished educators and churchmen, and men eminent in law. His father, both his grandfathers, and six uncles were either judges or lawyers. His maternal grandfather, Nathan Weston, was a justice of the Supreme Court of Maine from 1820 to 1841 and for seven years served as its chief justice.

In September 1849 Melville Fuller, then 16, entered Bowdoin College in Brunswick, Maine. He graduated with honors in the class of 1853. He subsequently began the study of law in the offices of two uncles, Nathan Weston and George Melville Weston, in Bangor, Maine. Starting in the fall of 1854, he attended Harvard Law School for six months, and was admitted to the Maine bar in 1855. He practiced in Bangor for a few months, then in the summer of 1855 went to Augusta, Maine, where he and another uncle, Benjamin A. G. Fuller, became editors of *The Age*, a well-known Maine Democratic newspaper. Melville also served as president of the Common Council of the city and as city solicitor.

Just as his life was becoming established in Augusta, Fuller left for the West, probably out of disappointment over a broken marriage engagement. He moved to Chicago, Illinois, in May 1856. He was admitted to the Illinois bar, and by September of 1856 had become a partner in the law firm of Pearson and Dow. Fuller shortly made a name for himself as an exceptional lawyer, and in November 1861 was elected one of four delegates to represent Chicago at a convention to be held at Springfield, Illinois, the following January to revise the constitution of the state of Illinois.

In 1862 Fuller was elected a member of the Illinois House of Representatives. He took office in January 1863, and by the session's end was all but the leader of the house. As a delegate from Illinois to the Democratic national conventions of 1864, 1872, 1876, and 1880, he acquired a national reputation in Democratic politics. Sound money, free trade, states' rights, governmental economy, and preservation of civil liberties were the pillars of his political thinking. After Grover Cleveland became president of the United States in 1885, he asked Fuller, with whom he was on friendly terms, to assume several government positions. Eight months after his inauguration, Cleveland suggested that Fuller become chairman of the Civil Service Commission; he later asked him to become solicitor general and one of three Pacific Railway commissioners. Fuller refused these offers on the grounds that they would be detrimental to his family life.

Fuller was married twice. On June 28, 1858, he married Calista O. Reynolds, daughter of a leading Chicago meatpacker; she died on November 13, 1864, leaving him with two young daughters. On May 30, 1866, he married Mary Ellen Coolbaugh, daughter of the president of Chicago's largest bank. She and Fuller had six additional children. When the office of chief justice of the U.S. Supreme Court became vacant due to the death of Morrison R. Waite on March 23, 1888, President Cleveland nominated Fuller for the post on April 30, 1888. The opportunity to lead the nation's highest court proved to be too tempting, and this time Fuller took the job offer.

Fuller wrote over 850 opinions during his tenure on the Court. In his 22 years as chief justice, he leaned towards strict construction of the Constitution in deciding issues. He was respected by his colleagues on the Court for his diplomacy and administrative abilities. When he first assumed the chief justiceship, the Court was more than four years behind in its case workload; in a few years' time, Fuller had brought the calendar up to date, and he struggled to keep it so during the remainder of his life. Supreme Court justice Oliver Wendell Holmes aptly summarized Fuller's executive abilities: "He had the business of the Court at his fingers' ends, he was perfectly courageous, prompt, decided. He turned off the matters that daily called for action easily, swiftly, with the least possible friction . . . and with a humor that relieved any tension with a laugh."

On December 11, 1889, a little more than a year after taking his seat on the bench, Chief Justice Fuller was selected to deliver the address commemorating the 100th anniversary of the inauguration of George Washington as first president of the United States, before both houses of Congress. In 1897 he accepted appointment to a commission established to deal with the long-standing boundary dispute between Venezuela and British Guiana; in 1899 he was a member of the arbitration commission that sat in Paris to settle the dispute. From 1900 to 1910 he served as a member of the Permanent Court of Arbitration at The Hague, in the Netherlands. Despite his declining health, particularly after the death of his second wife in the summer of 1904, Chief Justice Fuller served with distinction in all his functions until his own death at Sorrento, Maine, on July 4, 1910.

Nelson Mandela Released After Years of U.S. Pressure

Nelson Rolihlahla Mandela, South Africa's first black president and a leading figure in the struggle against apartheid, was born on July 18, 1918, in Transkei, South Africa, to a royal family of the Tembu, a branch of the Xhosa people. He was educated by missionaries, but was expelled from Fort Hare University in 1940 for participating in a strike. He soon returned to school, however, and graduated from the University of South Africa with a law degree.

Mandela joined Walter Sisulu and Oliver Tambo to establish South Africa's first black law firm. The three were also active in the African National Congress, which worked for decades to liberate the native black majority of South Africa from the rule of its white European minority. The linchpin of the system of white rule was apartheid, a South African form of segregation similar to that which used to exist in the American South, but even more stringent and ruthlessly enforced by the South African police and military.

The authorities arrested Mandela several times, but he was acquitted of treason charges in 1961. However, shortly thereafter he began to openly advocate armed resistance, and sought assistance from sympathetic foreign organizations that often had socialist or communist leanings. He successfully eluded the police for some time, but was finally captured on August 5, 1962. He was convicted of treasonable offenses and jailed. He would spend nearly three decades in some of South Africa's harshest maximum-security prisons.

The South African government was reluctant to execute troublesome political prisoners such as Mandela, because of the potential for bad publicity and international outrage, preferring instead to let them fade away into obscurity while they were incarcerated. Mandela's wife, Winnie Mandela, refused to let this happen, initiating an international campaign for Nelson Mandela's release. Further, by the 1980s the world community in general and the United States in particular were pressuring South Africa to end apartheid and permit majority rule. Most of this pressure was in the form of international trade sanctions and other economic measures.

By the end of the 1980s, apartheid was crumbling. The South African government had deep reservations about freeing Mandela, since he refused to renounce violence as a means to accomplish change, but it eventually acquiesced. On February 11, 1990, Mandela was released. Shortly thereafter he visited the United States, where he was enthusiastically received by the public during his speaking engagements.

Although initially reluctant to endorse nonviolence, Mandela proved to be the most conciliatory figure in South African history. He successfully managed the peaceful transition to power of the black majority and became South Africa's first black president. Black rule was established without a bloody civil war, and Mandela gained the respect of the international community.

February 12

Abraham Lincoln's Birthday

Abraham Lincoln was born in Hardin County, Kentucky, on February 12, 1809. Lincoln is universally regarded as one of the nation's great presidents. For many decades his birthday was observed as an official holiday, but in the late 20th century this observance was combined with President George Washington's birthday in the holiday known as Presidents' Day (see February 17).

Abraham Lincoln was the son of Thomas and Nancy Hanks Lincoln. Samuel Lincoln, his first American ancestor, came from the town of Hingham, near Norwich, England. The son of a disinherited father, Samuel Lincoln immigrated in 1637 to the namesake town of Hingham, Massachusetts, where he settled the next year. Descendants of Samuel Lincoln migrated west and southward to Pennsylvania and Virginia. Lincoln's grandfather went to Jefferson County, Kentucky.

Abraham Lincoln's father, Thomas, an unschooled frontiersman frequently on the move, lived in various places in Kentucky. The family moved to Spencer County, Indiana, in 1816. There Abraham Lincoln's mother, Nancy, died of a fever in 1818 on the farm where he later grew to adulthood. The site, south of Lincoln City, was established in 1963 as the Lincoln Boyhood National Memorial, adjacent to Lincoln State Park.

When Lincoln was 21 his family moved to Illinois. They settled ten miles west of Decatur, at a site later designated as the Lincoln Trail Homestead State Park. Lincoln worked as a farm laborer and then struck out on his own, working at a variety of occupations. Among other things, he served as a store clerk in New Salem. He must have impressed his neighbors with his ability, for in 1832 he was chosen as captain of a company of volunteers for service in the Black Hawk War against enemy Native Americans. When he returned from the campaign he settled in New Salem and became a partner in the general store there. He was also postmaster and a deputy surveyor. In his spare time, such as it was, he studied law and eventually became a lawyer when he passed the bar in 1836.

At 25, Lincoln was elected to the Illinois state legislature. He served there for four terms, 1834–1841. He moved to Springfield, which had just become the state capital, the next year and opened a law office there. Also in 1842, he married Mary Todd. Lincoln was elected a representative to the U.S. Congress in 1846 and began serving the following year, but he chose not to run for reelection when his two-year term expired. Oddly enough, he

President Lincoln's Cabinet

rose to greater prominence in his supposed retirement to private life. Returning to law, he practiced in Springfield and on a wide traveling route or "circuit" throughout much of Illinois. As a lawyer, Lincoln was noted for his oratorical skills, thorough preparation, quick grasp of the issues, and an honesty that became legendary.

The burning issue of the day was whether slavery would be allowed to extend westward as the nation grew. Lincoln opposed such an extension. Like thousands of other former Whigs, he found himself drawn to the new Republican Party, which antislavery Whigs and Democrats, together with Free-Soilers, had begun forming in Michigan in 1854. At the 1856 state convention in Bloomington, Illinois, where the Illinois branch of the Republican Party was formed, Lincoln made a strong antislavery speech. He supported the Republican candidate, John C. Frémont, for president in the 1856 election, but Frémont lost to Democrat James Buchanan.

In 1858 Lincoln was nominated for the U.S. Senate by the Illinois Republicans to run against Stephen Douglas, the Democratic candidate for the same seat. During the campaign Lincoln and Douglas debated the issues in a series of seven public meetings, the famous "Lincoln-Douglas debates," which lifted Lincoln into the national consciousness even though he ultimately did not win the election. He was nominated for the presidency at the Republican convention in Chicago in May 1860, and went on to win the election of November 1860, despite fierce opposition from Democrats and southerners who opposed his antislavery stance. The Southern states had threatened to secede from the Union if Lincoln were elected, and began to do so after the results of the November election were reported. Meanwhile, incumbent president James Buchanan did nothing to stop the slow dissolution of the United States.

By the time Lincoln took office on March 4, 1861, seven Southern states had already seceded from the Union. The Civil War broke out on April 12, 1861, when South Carolina forces fired on Fort Sumter.

The Civil War was fought and won under Lincoln's direction. Although his primary concern was originally to quell hostilities and keep the nation whole, he realized before long that the issue could not be successfully concluded so long as the institution of slavery remained in force. Accordingly, in September 1862, he issued a proclamation declaring his intention of freeing all the slaves in the rebelling states on January 1, 1863 (see January 1, The Emancipation Proclamation). The proclamation was consistent with his address at Gettysburg the next year, which declared in part: "Four score

and seven years ago our fathers brought forth upon this continent a new nation, conceived in liberty and dedicated to the proposition that all men are created equal."

Lincoln was reelected to the presidency in November 1864. There was no time, however, to carry out the promise of his second inaugural address. Made as victory drew near for the Union forces, it urged on the nation a policy of reconciliation toward the secessionist South: "With malice toward none, with charity for all . . . let us strive to finish the work we are in; to bind up the nation's wounds." However, Lincoln was shot in Ford's Theatre in Washington, D.C., by John Wilkes Booth, an actor, on April 14, 1865. The President died the following morning, and his policy of leniency toward the defeated South died with him.

Today, Lincoln's memory is honored by the Lincoln Memorial, a great monument in classic Greek style in Washington's West Potomac Park, enshrining a massive statue of a seated Lincoln. The Lincoln Memorial began when Senator Shelby Moore Cullom of Illinois introduced a bill in Congress in 1910 providing for the erection of a memorial in the national capital. The bill was passed in 1911, creating a commission to take charge of the work. Former president William H. Taft became chairman of the commission, which approved a design for the building by New York architect Henry Bacon and commissioned the sculptor Daniel Chester French to execute the work. Workmen broke ground for the Lincoln Memorial on Lincoln's birthday in 1914, and the cornerstone was laid a year later to the day. The building was dedicated on Memorial Day, May 30, 1922.

Senate Acts to Preserve Political Balance

On February 12, 1791, the United States Senate voted to admit Vermont into the Union as a state and transmitted the appropriate legislation to the House of Representatives, where it was ultimately approved. A few weeks earlier, the Senate had also voted to admit Kentucky as a state. This legislation was also ultimately approved by the House.

The admission of Vermont and Kentucky to the Union is covered in more detail at March 4 and June 1, respectively. Although a variety of considerations were involved, it is historically significant that the Senate chose to coordinate the admission of a Northern state with the admission of a Southern state. The result was that the North-South political balance in the Senate would not be disturbed. Although it was probably not the dominant consideration at the time, it established a precedent that would affect politics for seven decades until the Civil War.

When the United States Constitution was written in 1787, North and South were roughly balanced in terms of economic and political strength. In fact, in certain ways the South was the stronger, since Virginia had the largest population of all the states and the first president, George Washington, was a Virginian. In the House of Representatives, where representation is based on population, Virginia received 19 seats, more than any other state, after the first census was taken. The country's population was fairly evenly distributed among the other Northern and Southern states. For example, both New York and North Carolina received ten seats each in the first House of Representatives. Southern cities were on a par with northern cities: Charleston, South Carolina, ranked with Boston, New York, and Philadelphia as one of America's major urban centers. Thus, as one of the "big" states, Virginia had initially resisted the Constitutional Convention's decision to establish a Senate wherein every state, regardless of population, would receive two senators. Virginia's outlook would change dramatically over the next several decades, however.

In the 19th century, America continued to expand westward, and new states were added in both the North and the South. However, the population growth of the North greatly exceeded that of the South, in part due to the wave of industrialization which largely bypassed the agrarian South. By 1850, the date of the last pre–Civil War apportionment of delegates to the House of Representatives, New York had four times as many seats as North Carolina, and Virginia had become one of the smaller states in the House. Thus, in the years leading up to the Civil War, the South had to maintain its political influence by preserving political parity in the Senate. Since neither the North nor the South wanted to stop the admission of new states to the Union, a compromise was reached: A new Southern state would be admitted for every new Northern state. Both sides would thus receive an equal increase in the number of United States senators. In the Missouri Compromise of 1820, for example, the admission of the Southern state of Missouri and the Northern state of Maine were timed to coincide.

Of course, with the Civil War this political juggling act that found its precedent with the Senate's vote on February 12, 1791, came to an end.

Founding of the Georgia Colony

On February 12, 1733, James Oglethorpe, together with 120 other colonists from England, disembarked at Yamacraw Bluff in what is now Savannah, Georgia, to start a new colony. An unlikely combination of altruistic and imperialistic desires motivated Oglethorpe and the other colonists: They wanted to provide a refuge for England's oppressed and often imprisoned debtor class, and at the same time they realized the importance of creating a colony that would serve as a buffer between Britain's southern colonies and the Spanish who occupied Florida.

In the centuries since Oglethorpe and his followers arrived at Savannah, Georgians have observed February 12 in many ways. The earliest settlers marked the occasion by firing salutes and giving toasts in honor of Oglethorpe and the other colonies. Large-scale celebrations took place in the state on February 12, 1833, the centennial of the landing of the Oglethorpe party, and newspapers on that day suspended publication so that their employees might attend the festivities. In 1908 a river pageant was held in Savannah to commemorate the 175th anniversary of the 1733 landing.

In 1909 John M. Slaton, the president of the Georgia state senate, introduced a bill to make Georgia Day or Oglethorpe Day an official state observance. The bill was approved on August 13, 1909.

February 13

International Slave Trade Outlawed

During the Constitutional Convention of 1787 in Philadelphia, Pennsylvania, the assembled delegates from the 13 colonies that would eventually form the United States of America addressed the question of whether slavery should be permitted in the new nation. Most Northerners, and many Southerners, were opposed to slavery. However, slavery was already a deeply rooted institution, especially in the South, and the time was not yet ripe for emancipation.

If American slaves could not be emancipated, however, then perhaps at the very least measures could be taken to prevent more slaves from being brought into the country. At this point in history, the international slave trade was a thriving business. Trading ships from America, Great Britain, and other countries sailed to the West African coast to purchase or capture Africans for use as slaves. The persons thus forced into bondage were sold to plantation owners in the American South, the Caribbean, and Latin America. It took months for the sailing ships of the time to cross the Atlantic Ocean to the New World, and the people held on board were shackled and chained in cramped quarters and extremely poor conditions. It was not uncommon for a third of the human cargo to die in transit.

Many of the delegates to the Constitutional Convention believed that, if the new United States were truly to become an enlightened nation, it should act to abolish its role in the international slave trade. However, there were vested economic interests at stake in both the North and the South. Northern merchants ran most of the slave trade with West Africa, and Southern plantation owners were unwilling to give up a source of cheap labor. The result was a compromise. The international slave trade would be abolished, but not for 20 years.

The final version of the Constitution contained a clause in Article I, Section 9, which states that "the migration or importation of such persons as any of the states now existing shall think proper to admit, shall not be prohibited by the Congress prior to the year one thousand eight hundred and eight, but a tax or duty may be imposed on such importation, not exceeding ten dollars for each person." The gist of this provision was that Congress could not forbid the international slave trade until 1808, but it could impose a minor tax on the trade, and the individual states themselves were free to close their ports to slave traders. On February 13, 1807, with the foregoing clause about to expire, Congress passed legislation that forever abolished the importation of slaves into the United States after January 1, 1808. This legislation did not emancipate those slaves already present in the country, nor did it prevent people from buying and selling African Americans born within it, but it was a step on the road toward the end of slavery that would not be completed until the Civil War.

Anchorage Fur Rendezvous

This is a movable event.

The Anchorage Fur Rendezvous, a ten-day community-wide celebration that begins on the second Friday of every February in Anchorage, Alaska, grew from obscure beginnings to become one of Alaska's biggest events. The highlight of the Rendezvous, nicknamed the "Rondy," continues to be the annual World's Championship Sled Dog Races, which are run in three heats. Other attractions over the years have included parades, miners and trappers balls, the coronation of a Fur Rendezvous queen, beard-judging contests, selection of a king and queen regent from the ranks of longtime Alaskan residents, Eskimo dances and blanket tosses, and vaudeville performances.

The World's Championship Sled Dog Races draw mushers and their teams of huskies, malamutes, and other dog breeds from Alaska, many parts of Canada, and as far away as New England. (Dr. Roland Lombard of Wayland, Massachusetts, scored upset victories over local mushers to become the world champion sled dog racer in 1963, 1964, 1965, 1967, 1969, 1970, 1971, and 1974.) The Rondy also features other athletic events, which have included the All-Alaska Basketball Classic, the All-Alaska Judo Tournament, the Curling Bonspiel, the Alaska Table Tennis Championships, the World's Championship Cross-Country Snowmobile Race, the State Indoor Rifle Championship, a cross-country ski trek, snowshoe racing, auto racing, hockey, and weight lifting. There have also been less athletic events such as chess tournaments, bridge tournaments, and photography contests.

Often referred to as the Mardi Gras of the North, the Anchorage Fur Rendezvous had its inception in 1936. In 1937 it acquired its present name from the trappers' custom of bringing fur pelts to town for sale. Fur and fur products, much emphasized in the first years of the Rendezvous, receive far less attention today. Variously managed in its early years by civic groups, fraternal and service organizations, special committees, and the Anchorage Chamber of Commerce, the Fur Rendezvous came under the sponsorship of Greater Anchorage, Inc., when the nonprofit organization was founded in 1955. Under the supervision of the GAI, the originally modest Rendezvous expanded from a 3-day event to the present 10-day festival.

First Fugitive Slave Law

On February 13, 1793, the Fugitive Slave Act of 1793 went into effect after it was signed by President George Washington. It was the first in a series of laws that would invoke the power of the federal government to assist slaveowners in recapturing their human property.

The 1793 Fugitive Slave Law contained provisions that required federal and state officials to assist slaveowners looking for runaway slaves. In the decades leading up to the Civil War, more fugitive slave laws would be passed, and although their provisions would become more and more stringent, they would in fact become less and less effective. This was due to the abolition movement that arose in the early 19th century, which motivated northerners to help runaway slaves through such mechanisms as the famous "Underground Railroad" system of hideouts. Many runaway slaves took new identities in the North, settled in the frontier territories, or went to Canada in order to remove themselves from the jurisdiction of the fugitive slave laws. Slaveowners had a victory in the *Dred Scott* decision of 1856, wherein the Supreme Court held that an African American slave remained a slave wherever he or she went in the United States, but the eruption of the Civil War a few years later would eventually end slavery.

At the time of the first fugitive slave law's passage in 1793, many people considered slavery to be a dying institution. When Eli Whitney invented the cotton gin, however, slavery was revitalized in the South. The cotton gin spurred a vast increase in Southern cotton production, which stimulated a demand for slave labor to work the plantations. With a new economic justification for their "peculiar institution," Southerners consistently sought tougher federal enforcement of their right to recapture those slaves who attempted to reach freedom.

First American Magazine

February 13, 1741, marked the appearance of America's first magazine, Andrew Bradford's *American Magazine, or A Monthly View of the Political State of the British Colonies*, published in Philadelphia, Pennsylvania. Like its closest successor, Benjamin Franklin's *General Magazine, and Historical Chronicle, for All the British Plantations in America*, which appeared in print in the same city three days later, it bore the date of January 1741.

Both magazines were short-lived. Bradford's publication met its demise in three months. Franklin's survived it by only three more. Both were forerunners, however, of the approximately 100 magazines that were eventually founded in the American colonies and of the numberless periodical publications that have succeeded them since.

February 14

St. Valentine's Day

The story of what has become the year's most romantic day, February 14, began in a decidedly unromantic way, with the early Christian martyrs. The histories of early Christian martyrs mention at least two saints named Valentine associated with February 14. One of them is described as a priest of Rome and another as a bishop of a city called Interamna. Both men suffered martyrdom in the second half of the 3rd century A.D.

Little is known of either of the most commonly mentioned Valentines. The few known facts of their lives are so interwoven with undocumented

tradition that it is impossible to separate fact from legend. The theories about how the name Valentine came to be connected with the day on which lovers send gifts to one another also are varied. One is based on the belief throughout rural Europe during the Middle Ages that the birds began to mate on February 14. Chaucer, in his "Parliament of Foules," refers to the belief in this way:

> For this was Seynt Valentyne's day.
> When every foul cometh ther to choose his mate.

English literature, following Chaucer, contains frequent references to February 14 as sacred to lovers. Shakespeare, Drayton, and Gay are among those who mention it in this connection, and the diarist Samuel Pepys several times discusses the day and its related customs. *The Paston Letters*, covering the period from 1422 to 1509, contains a letter by Dame Elizabeth Brews to John Paston, with whom she hoped to arrange a match for her daughter, which runs this way: "And cousin mine, upon Monday is St. Valentine's day and every bird chooseth himself a mate, and if it like you to come on Thursday night and make provision that you may abide till then, I trust God that ye shall speak to my husband and I shall pray that we may bring the matter to a conclusion." The affair must have been managed to her satisfaction, for among the letters is one addressed by the young woman herself "unto my right-well beloved Valentine, John Paston, Esquire."

Some scholars who do not think that the old opinion about the mating of the birds on February 14 is sufficient to explain the connection between St. Valentine's Day and lovers suggest that the association grew out of the similarity between the Norman word *galantin*, meaning a lover of women, and the name of the saint. They think that Galantin's Day, with the initial "g" frequently pronounced as "v," led to confusion in the popular mind. Another theory is that the association with lovers is a survival in Christianized form of a practice that occurred on February 14, the day before the ancient Roman feast of the Lupercalia. At that time the names of young women were put in a box from which they were drawn by chance, an arrangement under which a young man became the suitor of a young woman for the next year, or at least became her partner for the festival. Supposedly the early Christian clergy objected to this custom, and tried to substitute the names of saints for the names of young women, with the idea being that each young man would try to emulate the saint whose name was drawn for him during the next 12 months.

The drawing of the names of young women from a box on Valentine's Day continued for centuries. The young men and women who were paired by this method were expected to give presents to each other. Over the centuries, the custom evolved to where in modern times only the male is expected to give a gift or present flowers.

In the United States, the observance of Valentine's Day and the exchanging of valentine cards reached what was probably an all-time high in popularity about the time of the Civil War. An 1863 periodical published in Boston remarked that "with the exception of Christmas there is no festival throughout the year which is invested with half the interest belonging to this cherished anniversary." Commercially printed valentines have been available since roughly 1800 and have almost entirely replaced the handmade valentines of former days, with the exception of those still fabricated by children in kindergartens and the lower primary grades.

The modern observance of Valentine's Day brings gladness not only to millions of people every year, but also to the greeting card, candy, and flower industries. Shortly after New Year, stores are stocked for this next major card-sending occasion. As the day approaches, candy stores are filled with red, heart-shaped boxes of chocolates and candies, and florists begin taking orders for what has become one of their busiest days of the year. Despite the commercialism that has been introduced into Valentine's Day, however, its romantic significance and importance have remained.

Frederick Douglass's Birthday

February 14 is the day on which, according to his own calculations, the abolitionist orator and journalist Frederick Douglass was born in 1817 in Tuckahoe, Maryland. Frederick Augustus Washington Bailey, as Douglass was originally known, was the son of Harriet Bailey, a black slave of part-Indian blood, and an unknown white father. His only recollections of his mother were "a few hasty visits in the night on foot," Douglass said later, adding that he had "hardly become a thinking thing" when he "first learned to hate slavery."

He was eight years old when he left the care of his grandmother to spend a year working on the plantation managed by his master, Captain Aaron Anthony. His next duties, in the service of the family of Hugh Auld in Baltimore, Maryland, marked a turning point in his life. Mrs. Auld helped point him in a new direction by secretly teaching him to read and write, knowledge that he soon employed in writing passes for runaway slaves.

Douglass was 16 when he was returned to the plantation on the death of his master. In due time he was hired out to, and brutally flogged by, a man named Covey, whose scars he bore on his back for the rest of his life. In 1836, during subsequent service to William Freeland of St. Michael's, Maryland, Douglass attempted unsuccessfully to escape. Instead, he was returned to the Aulds in Baltimore. He was 19 by then, and Hugh Auld had him apprenticed to a ship caulker. During this apprenticeship, Douglass's second, and this time successful, escape attempt took place on September 3, 1838. He posed as a sailor and managed to escape by rail, first to New York City, where he married a young, free black woman, and then to the greater safety of New Bedford, Massachusetts. There he protected his identity by assuming the name of Douglass, borrowed from the hero of Sir Walter Scott's *Lady of the Lake*, and found employment as a day laborer for three years.

In the summer of 1841, Douglass attended a meeting of the Massachusetts Anti-Slavery Society on Nantucket Island, and found himself delivering an extemporaneous address. So effective was his passionate oratory that he was made an agent of the society and spent the next four years, at some danger to himself, lecturing throughout New England in favor of abolition. His words were so eloquent that some listeners, persuading themselves that a man of his capabilities could never have been a slave, accused him of being a fraud. To set the record straight, he published an autobiography, *Narrative of the Life of Frederick Douglass*, in 1845.

The possibility of recapture as a fugitive slave was a continuing problem. To avoid the danger, Douglass spent the years 1845–1847 in England and Ireland, where his lectures did much to sway British public opinion in favor of abolition. He did not return to the United States until his freedom had been purchased with the help of some English friends.

Upon his return, Douglass settled in Rochester, New York, where he founded the weekly antislavery newspaper *North Star*. His reputation as an orator continued to grow, especially when he began to speak in favor of giving the right to vote to women. He also worked with Harriet Beecher Stowe in an effort to set up an industrial school for young blacks. At first a follower of the abolitionist editor William Lloyd Garrison, after 1851 Douglass supported the more conservative James G. Birney, who favored abolition by constitutional political methods. Once the bloodletting of the Civil War had become inevitable, Douglass was among the first to urge that the Union army use black troops, and he helped to form two regiments from Massachusetts.

During the post–Civil War period of Reconstruction, Douglass turned to demanding land and ballots for the freed blacks, so that he who had become "in law, free" would not remain "in fact, a slave." After Reconstruction, Douglass served as marshal of the District of Columbia from 1877 to 1881, and then became recorder of deeds for the district. His second marriage, in 1884, to Helen Pitts, a white woman, caused a controversy that he dismissed lightly, remarking that as his first wife had been the color of his mother his second was the color of his father. Douglass subsequently served as the U.S. minister and consul general to Haiti from 1889 to 1891. He continued his active support of civil rights for blacks and other social reforms until the end of his life. On the day of his death, February 20, 1895, he had attended a women's rights convention.

Arizona Admitted to the Union

On February 14, 1912, President William Howard Taft signed the proclamation admitting the Arizona Territory to the Union as a state.

Arizona has a very ancient history. Archaeological finds indicate that human beings have lived in what is now Arizona for at least 10,000 years, perhaps even for 20,000 years or longer. Some of the notable remnants of early Native American cultures that can be seen today are cliff dwellings, fortifications, and ruins from the years between 800 and 1500. Written records of the region's history began about four centuries ago. The first European to go to Arizona was probably Fray Marcos de Niza in 1539. He returned to Spanish Mexico with tall tales, spun by the natives to please him, of the "Seven Cities of Cíbola," where "gold and silver were the only metals" and in common use by the natives. The fabled seven cities, which Marcos de Niza claimed to have sighted but apparently did not visit, were in fact the impoverished villages of the Zuni Indians in what is now northwestern New Mexico, close to the Arizona border.

Unfounded as they were, the reports set in motion the great expedition of 1540–1542 headed by Francisco Vásquez de Coronado, who set forth from Mexico to secure the rumored riches and conquer the region for Spain. Crossing Arizona to Cíbola, he dispatched several subsidiary parties to different areas. García López de Cárdenas thus became the first European to see the Grand Canyon. Pedro de Tovar explored the Hopi Indian villages. An allied group under Hernando de Alarcón meanwhile investigated the mouth of the Colorado River far to the south. Coronado's main force continued east across New Mexico and explored parts of the Great Plains in what are now Texas and Kansas before returning to Mexico.

European settlement was slow. The soil was arid, and no riches were found. The native tribes fiercely defended their land, and there was bloodshed intermittently for nearly 300 years. Those who went to Arizona were mostly missionaries from Spanish Mexico. Missionary efforts by the Jesuits continued until 1767, when they fell out of favor in Spain and were replaced by the Franciscans. Mexican domination replaced Spanish domination after the conclusion of the Mexican Revolution in 1821, but the only important non-native settlements in Arizona were those at Tubac and Tucson. In 1826, however, American fur trappers began coming in by way of the Gila River valley. After 1840, soldiers, adventurers, and a few pioneer settlers filtered into Arizona. So did prospectors, particularly after the beginning of the California gold rush in 1848 and Henry Wickenburg's gold strike northwest of Phoenix in 1863.

Most of Arizona, namely everything north of the Gila River, was ceded to the United States by Mexico at the end of the Mexican War in 1848. It became part of the Territory of New Mexico, created in 1850. That part of Arizona between the Gila and the present Mexican boundary was added to the territory in 1853 by the Gadsden Purchase. Under its terms, certain boundary vaguenesses were clarified and the United States acquired, for an eventual price of $10 million, land that explorations had indicated was desirable for a proposed southern railroad route to the Pacific Ocean.

In 1856 a convention at Tucson petitioned Congress for the right to create a separate Arizona territory, but Congress, divided over the question of slavery in the territories, put the matter aside. Early in the Civil War, the Confederacy recognized Arizona as a separate territory. Texas Confederate troops occupied southern Arizona for a few months in 1862 before Union troops from California reoccupied the area for the federal government. It was not until February 24, 1863, that a separate territory of Arizona was officially established by Congress.

A movement for Arizona statehood began to assume more definite shape in 1891 when residents ratified a state constitution framed by the legislature at the new territorial capital of Phoenix. Congress, however, failed to approve the constitution and also rejected later bills providing for statehood. The people of Arizona in turn rejected proposed congressional legislation that would have admitted Arizona and New Mexico as a single state.

Finally, a new state constitution submitted in 1910 was approved by Congress and President William Howard Taft, on the condition that a clause providing for the recall of judges be eliminated. After that condition was accepted by the territorial electorate, Arizona was formally admitted as the 48th state on February 14, 1912. The last word on judges, however, came from the people of Arizona, who restored the controversial provision to the state constitution before their first year of statehood had ended.

Oregon Admitted to the Union

On February 14, 1859, Oregon joined the Union. Although Oregon's admission to statehood was considerably complicated by the dispute over slavery, this 33rd member managed to overcome these difficulties and gain statehood just months before slavery divided the United States and threw the country into the Civil War.

The first government in Oregon came into existence during the period when both the United States and Great Britain (which still occupied Canada) claimed the area between the 42nd parallel on the south and parallel 54° 40' on the north. The two countries jointly occupied the Oregon Country, which included the present-day state of Washington, under an 1818 agreement. A limited form of local self-government was established in 1841. In 1843 came the first really large group of American settlers to reach the area by means of the Oregon Trail, the vanguard of a tide of travelers that would swell to a flood. By 1844 the expansionist demand "Fifty-four forty or fight!" had become a Democratic campaign slogan, meaning that the United States should seize control of the whole Oregon area up to the northern 54° 40' parallel.

When the inhabitants of Oregon received word in 1846 that the United States and Great Britain had reached a compromise establishing the 49th parallel as the boundary between the United States and Canada in the Oregon region, they expected that the U.S. Congress would quickly provide a territorial government for their region. President James K. Polk recommended territorial status for Oregon, and a bill was introduced in Congress that would have brought such a government into existence. However, southern congressmen feared the creation of a northern territory in which slavery would almost certainly be outlawed. They therefore prevented passage in 1847 of the legislation necessary to bring the Oregon Territory into being.

In November 1847 members of the native Cayuse tribe killed the Protestant missionaries Marcus and Narcissa Whitman and other members of the mission established at Waiilatpu, near the site of present-day Walla Walla, Washington. This incident precipitated clashes between the Cayuse tribe and the Oregon settlers, and the emergency situation forced Congress in 1848 to reconsider territorial government for that portion of the Pacific Northwest lying below the 49th parallel. In 1848 southern congressmen again attempted to block the creation of a territory where slavery would be outlawed, but this time they did not succeed. The bill organizing an Oregon Territory without slavery—containing the area bounded by the 42nd and 49th parallels, the Rocky Mountains, and the Pacific Ocean—passed both houses of Congress on August 14, 1848, and the measure was signed by President Polk.

Polk immediately appointed a governor and other officials for the new territory. They arrived in Oregon City on March 2, 1849, and the following day the territorial government of Oregon was established. In 1853, Congress reduced the size of Oregon by separating the region north of the Columbia River to form the Territory of Washington. Oregon assumed its present dimensions south of the Columbia and the 46th parallel.

For more than a year after Oregon's acquisition of territorial status, Congress took no action to confirm the land titles of settlers in the Pacific Northwest. Then, in September 1850, Congress approved the Donation Land Act. This legislation guaranteed 640 acres to every married couple that settled in the territory before December 1, 1850, and stipulated that half this acreage belonged outright to the wife. The law also provided 160 acres to each husband and an additional 160 to each wife who took up residence in Oregon after December 1, 1850, but before December 1, 1853.

The Donation Land Act and the discovery in 1848 of gold in nearby California spurred the growth of Oregon, which in turn caused troubles. In 1853 Native American uprisings began in southern Oregon, where recently arrived settlers had displaced the tribes from their lands. Hostilities continued for several years, but by 1858 the native tribes had been defeated and confined to several reservations located along Oregon's northern coast and in the relatively barren eastern portion of the territory.

Congress took up the subject of statehood for Oregon in 1856. The House of Representatives passed an enabling bill that authorized the territory to call a convention to draw up a state constitution, but the Senate defeated the measure, again due to resistance from southern politicians. Even antislavery Republicans were wary of admitting Oregon, which had a reputation for favoring the Democratic Party.

Undaunted, the residents of Oregon in 1857 voted overwhelmingly to form a state government. In accordance with the popular will, the territorial legislature summoned a constitutional convention, which opened on August 17, 1857. When Oregon citizens went to the polls on November 9, 1857, to vote on the proposed constitution, its supporters won by a majority of 3,980 votes. An even larger majority of 5,082 voted against slavery. Congress was still bitterly divided on whether to admit the territory to the Union, but on February 14, 1859, it voted, by an extremely narrow margin, for admission.

February 15

Vietnam War: Ho Chi Minh Writes to President Johnson

The Vietnam War of the 1960s and early 1970s (see various articles throughout this book) was one of the most controversial wars in American history. In the beginning, most Americans considered it a necessary war, needed to prevent communist North Vietnam from conquering pro-American South Vietnam. A victory by North Vietnam was considered to be a victory for the communist powers of the Soviet Union and the People's Republic of China, then bitter cold-war enemies of the United States. President Lyndon B. Johnson (served from 1963 until 1969) endorsed this viewpoint, and made massive increases in the American commitment to South Vietnam.

Although the war escalated, Johnson was unable to obtain the victory he so desperately sought. There were various peace initiatives with Ho Chi Minh, the leader of North Vietnam, who had been struggling to achieve a unified and independent Vietnam for decades. Keenly aware of the growing discontent with the war among the American people and Johnson's desire for an exit from the increasingly costly conflict, Ho Chi Minh demanded an unconditional cessation of the American bombing raids against North Vietnam as a precondition for further negotiations. This demand came in a letter on February 15, 1967. In the same letter, Ho also insisted upon an eventual total withdrawal of the American forces.

Although Johnson ordered several temporary halts to the raids against North Vietnam, the resulting negotiations failed. Nevertheless, Ho Chi Minh's letter, reprinted below, provides an excellent statement of the North Vietnamese position concerning the war, set forth with characteristic resolve. In later years, the American public would come to accept elements of this position, although not the representation of North Vietnam as a peace-loving country. Ho Chi Minh did not live to see the victory of his forces; he died in 1969.

To His Excellency Mr. Lyndon B. Johnson, President, United States of America
Your Excellency:

On February 10, 1967, I received your message. This is my reply. Vietnam is thousands of miles away from the United States. The Vietnamese people have never done any harm to the United States. But contrary to the pledges made by its representative at the 1954 Geneva conference, the U.S. has ceaselessly intervened in Vietnam, it has unleashed and intensified the war of aggression in North Vietnam with a view to prolonging the partition of Vietnam and turning South Vietnam into a neo-colony and a military base of the United States. For over two years now, the U.S. government has, with its air and naval forces, carried the war to the Democratic Republic of (North) Vietnam, an independent and sovereign country.

The U.S. government has committed war crimes, crimes against peace and against mankind. In South Vietnam, half a million U.S. and satellite troops have resorted to the most inhuman weapons and most barbarous methods of warfare, such as napalm, toxic chemicals and gases, to massacre our compatriots, destroy crops, and raze villages to the ground. In North Vietnam, thousands of U.S. aircraft have dropped hundreds of thousands of tons of bombs, destroying towns, villages, factories, schools. In your message, you apparently deplore the sufferings and destruction in Vietnam. May I ask you: Who has perpetrated these monstrous crimes? It is the United States and satellite troops. The U.S. government is entirely responsible for the extremely serious situation in Vietnam.

The U.S. war of aggression against the Vietnamese people constitutes a challenge to the countries of the socialist camp, a threat to the national independence movement, and a serious danger to peace in Asia and the world.

The Vietnamese people deeply love independence, freedom and peace. But in the face of U.S. aggression, they have risen up, united as one man, fearless of sacrifices and hardships. They are determined to carry on their resistance until they have won genuine independence and freedom and true peace. Our just cause enjoys strong sympathy and support from the peoples of the whole world, including broad sections of the American people.

The U.S. government has unleashed the war of aggression in Vietnam. It must cease this aggression. This is the only way to restoration of peace. The U.S. government must stop definitely and unconditionally its bombing raids and all other acts of war against the Democratic Republic of Vietnam, withdraw from South Vietnam all U.S. and satellite troops, recognize the South Vietnam National Front for Liberation, and let the Vietnamese people settle themselves their own affairs. Such is the basis of the five-point stand of the government of the Democratic Republic of Vietnam, which embodies the essential principles and provision of the 1954 Geneva Agreements on Vietnam; it is the basis of a correct political solution to the Vietnam problem.

In your message you suggested direct talks between the Democratic Republic of Vietnam and the United States. If the U.S. government really wants these talks, it must first of all stop unconditionally its bombing raids and all other acts of war against the Democratic Republic of Vietnam. It is only after the unconditional cessation of U.S. bombing raids and all other acts of war against the Democratic Republic of Vietnam that the Democratic Republic of Vietnam and the U.S. could enter into talks and discuss questions concerning the two sides.

The Vietnamese people will never submit to force, they will never accept talks under threat of bombs.

Our cause is absolutely just. It is to be hoped that the U.S. government will act in accordance with reason.

Sincerely,

Ho Chi Minh

Susan B. Anthony's Birthday

On February 15, 1820, women's rights leader Susan B. Anthony was born. The information concerning her life and her life's work is contained in entries at June 18 (Susan B. Anthony Fined for Voting) and August 26 (Nineteenth Amendment Proclaimed Ratified, Women's Equality Day).

Battleship *Maine* Memorial Day

The American battleship *Maine*, under the command of Captain Charles D. Sigsbee, was sent to Spanish-ruled Cuba in January 1898 as tensions were growing between Spain and the United States over who should control Cuba. The ship was sent as a show of strength and to protect Americans residing and doing business in Cuba. The Spanish government had been charged with human rights abuses, and lurid stories about Spanish cruelties had turned American public opinion against Spain and in favor of the struggling Cuban revolutionaries of the time, who sought to free Cuba from Spain.

The United States was a growing power, both militarily and economically, and most people favored continued territorial expansion. Spain, on the other hand, was on the decline and had lost virtually all of its once vast empire. Thus, the Spanish possession of Cuba, a short distance off American shores, presented an ideal opportunity for America to flex its muscle while ostensibly acting to protect Cuban freedom fighters. For months, American diplomats in Madrid, Spain, had been pressuring the Spanish government to yield de facto control over Cuba to the United States.

On February 15, 1898, the Spanish warship *Alfonso XII* and the American commercial steamship *City of Washington* were anchored near the *Maine* in Havana harbor. The day had been unusually warm for the season. The evening heat was so oppressive that the officers and men on the two battleships and the passengers on the merchant ship were relaxing, trying to keep cool. At 9:00 p.m., Captain Sigsbee had just finished writing a report to Theodore Roosevelt, then the assistant secretary of the U.S. Navy, on the advisability of continuing the practice of placing torpedo tubes on cruisers and battleships. He was about to begin another letter, this time to his wife. At 9:10 the bugler began to blow taps.

By 9:40 p.m. everything was quiet on the ship and the captain was folding the letter he had just written to his wife. In an instant, as the captain explained afterward, "there came a bursting, rending and crashing sound or roar of immense volume, followed by a succession of heavy, ominous metallic sounds and reverberations." An explosion had occurred under the sleeping quarters of the crew, wrecking the vessel so completely that it sank within a very short time. The *Maine* had a complement of 26 officers and 328 men. Two of the officers and 250 of the men were killed outright, and eight died later in Havana hospitals. Captain Sigsbee was the last man to leave the ship. He took refuge on the *City of Washington* and sent the following dispatch to the Department of the Navy:

Maine blown up in Havana harbor . . . tonight and destroyed. Wounded and others on board Spanish man-of-war and Ward

Line steamer. Send lighthouse tenders from Key West for crew and the few pieces of equipment above water. No one has clothing other than that upon him. Public opinion should be suspended until further report. All officers believed to be saved. Jenkins and Merritt not yet accounted for. Many Spanish officers, including representatives of General Blanco [the island's Spanish captain-general] now with me to express sympathy.

Charles W. Newton, a captain in the National Guard, was in Havana at the time of the explosion. He had gone there with General Arthur L. Goodrich, the owner of the Hartford, Connecticut, newspaper *Courant*, to see if conditions were as bad as reported. He and General Goodrich were seated in a park overlooking the harbor when the explosion occurred. His description of the event and of conditions in Cuba generally was particularly vivid:

Thousands of natives, driven into the city by the Spaniards, were starving. Every morning the authorities would line up men suspected of inciting to revolt and shoot them down. There were street riots all the time. Nevertheless the Spanish officers had a gay time and there were bull fights all the time. That night (February 15) we left the Hotel Inglaterra and went to sit in the park. There was plenty of high feeling and we thought maybe the hotel would be blown up. However, nothing serious had happened and I said to Arthur: "We'll be leaving for home tomorrow and nothing much has happened. I wouldn't mind seeing some excitement, even if we had to swim out to the *Maine* for protection." Just as I said these words there was a great flash out on the water and a few seconds later a big boom. We could barely see the *Maine* in the darkness. It began sinking slowly by the stern. Its powder magazines let go, just like a fireworks blast. It was awful. The ship continued to burn for hours, just that portion that remained out of water. Goodrich and I were afraid that would be a signal for a general fight, so we ran to a warehouse and took shelter until three o'clock in the morning. Then we got aboard the *City of Washington* to which Admiral Sigsbee was taken after every living man had been removed from the *Maine*. Two days later we returned to the States.

The immediate impression in the United States was that the Spanish authorities were responsible for the destruction of the ship. This popular impression, fueled by American expansionist sentiment and the bad press concerning Spanish human rights abuses in Cuba, led to the Spanish-American War in April 1898. The war resulted in the expulsion of Spain from the island and nominal independence for Cuba under American supervision.

As far as the destruction of the *Maine* was concerned, however, a naval court of inquiry that sat in the case found that although the explosion was, in its opinion, caused externally by an underwater mine, it was impossible to "obtain evidence fixing the responsibility . . . upon any person or persons." An independent Spanish investigation had an entirely different conclusion from that of the American board of inquiry, namely that the *Maine* was wrecked by an interior explosion. Some authorities believe that the disaster was accidental, even if the explosion was external. In any event, the exact circumstances surrounding the catastrophe are likely to remain a mystery forever.

The wreck of the *Maine* remained in Havana harbor for 14 years. On February 15, 1909, the Havana Camp of the Spanish War Veterans was organized, and its first act was to adopt a resolution calling on Congress to lift the wreck, recover the bodies of the dead that were still in it, and tow the ruined hull out to sea and sink it. Similar resolutions were adopted by the Spanish War Veterans and by other organizations in the United States, and on May 9, 1910, Congress authorized the work to be done. It was completed on March 16, 1912, and memorial services were held in Havana over the bodies of an estimated 64 sailors taken from the wreck. The recovered bodies were buried in Arlington National Cemetery. A monument to the *Maine* was subsequently erected by the government of Cuba in Havana and dedicated on February 15, 1926. Memorial exercises were held annually at its base for many years thereafter.

Cyrus McCormick's Birthday

Cyrus Hall McCormick, whose reaper is said to have been second only to the railroad in its importance to the development of the United States, was born on February 15, 1809, in Virginia's Rockbridge County. His father, Robert McCormick, was a farmer and inventor who had spent two decades trying, unsuccessfully, to develop a grain-cutting machine when his 22-year-old son took up the task. With careful study and using different principles from his father's, young McCormick managed to construct a horse-operated reaper that received its first public demonstration in a Virginia wheat field late in July 1831. Astonished viewers saw that it could cut as much grain as six men with scythes.

McCormick patented the reaper on June 21, 1834. During the rest of the decade, he kept adding improvements to his machine. However, it was not until after the panic of 1837, which contributed to the demise of the iron-manufacturing business in which he and his father had been engaged, that McCormick devoted all his energies to the reaper. By 1845 it was in use on most of the larger western farms. McCormick, a rarity among inventors in also possessing a good business sense, soon became convinced that he should supervise all the manufacturing himself, in his own factory, and that it should be located near the Midwest's expanding wheat fields.

He opened his factory in Chicago, Illinois, in 1847. Although he was faced with widespread competition after his original patent expired in 1848, he had by then proven the usefulness of his product. By 1850 he had managed to establish a nationwide business. His reaper was the chief attraction of the 1851 London World's Fair, and by 1856 McCormick reapers were selling at the rate of roughly 4,000 a year. McCormick had long since become a millionaire. His machine, which he continued to improve until his death, played an important role in helping the North win the Civil War, by enabling the Union to feed both soldiers and civilians while also securing funds from Europe by means of a lucrative export trade in grain.

As for the longer-range implications of McCormick's reaper, its importance can hardly be overestimated. The reaper revolutionized agriculture, changing the way of life of large segments of the population, vitally affecting the nation's economy, and giving important impetus to the settlement of the frontier. Armed with labor-saving machines that made it possible to farm more land with fewer people, farmers were encouraged to migrate westward, clearing and cultivating new territories as they went. With the advent of the reaper, farming became mass production—agriculture for sale as well as merely for use. The success of the reaper fostered the development of other labor-saving farm machinery, which not only increased farm output but also freed large numbers of farmers to settle in the country's cities and contribute to the growth of the nation's new industries.

McCormick, although he is known primarily as an inventor, also contributed to modern business methods. In some ways foreshadowing Henry Ford, he stressed the invention of machinery that made mass production possible in his factory. Approximately 20 years after his death on May 13, 1884, his McCormick Harvesting Machine Company was consolidated with other firms to become the International Harvester Company, one of the world's largest manufacturers of agricultural equipment.

Russell H. Conwell's Birthday

Russell H. Conwell, a famous 19th-century clergyman and philanthropist, was born in the Berkshire Hills at South Worthington, Massachusetts, on February 15, 1843. The son of a poor abolitionist family, he was born in a two-room farmhouse that served as a way station for the Underground Railroad. He attended the district school four miles away, and before he was 10 years old he had committed to memory the first three books of Milton's *Paradise Lost*. Later he attended Wilbraham Academy, a boys' preparatory school near Springfield, Massachusetts, and during that time taught at a district school. He graduated in 1859 at the age of 16.

In 1860 Conwell entered Yale University, but he did not stay to complete his law studies there. In 1862, responding to President Abraham Lincoln's call for men to serve in the Union forces in the Civil War, he left school and enlisted for military duty. He organized a company of men from his home county, was unanimously elected their captain, and at the age of 19 received his commission from Massachusetts governor John Albion Andrew.

After reaching the rank of lieutenant colonel, Conwell was sent home after being seriously wounded in the Battle of Kenesaw Mountain in northwest Georgia. At the close of the war he entered the law school at Union University in Albany, New York, and upon graduating in 1865 was admitted to the bar. He then went to Minnesota, where he opened a law office in Minneapolis. To add to his income, he became the Minneapolis correspondent of the *St. Paul Press* and shortly thereafter, with the aid of some businessmen, founded the *Minneapolis Daily Chronicle*. Meanwhile, he continued to tend to his growing law practice and taught music and elocution in his spare time.

In 1874 Conwell took up residence in Newton Center, a Boston, Massachusetts, suburb and the seat of the Baptist Newton Theological Seminary. It was there that he decided to become a minister. He closed his law office in 1878 and offered his services to a struggling Baptist church in Lexington, Massachusetts, where he was ordained in 1879. There were only 18 people in his first congregation, but the next Sunday the church was crowded. On the third Sunday the services were held in the town hall, where they continued to be held until a new and larger church was built. Conwell remained in Lexington for 18 months and then was asked to become pastor of a church formed by members of the Tenth Baptist Church in Philadelphia, Pennsylvania. Responding to the call of the small and debt-ridden congregation, Conwell assumed duties as pastor of the Grace Baptist Church on Thanksgiving Day, 1882. As his congregation grew, he saw the need for a new church building. In 1891 he organized the new Baptist Temple, which eventually grew into one of the largest institutional churches in the United States, numbering among its offspring three hospitals and Philadelphia's Temple University.

In 1923, in recognition of his work, Conwell was given the Philadelphia Award, which was presented annually to a deserving citizen of the city. The award consisted of a gold medal and a cash prize of $10,000, drawn from a trust fund established by Edward Bok, the longtime editor of the *Ladies' Home Journal*. Conwell devoted the money to charity. A lecturer in frequent demand, he earned an estimated $10 million on the lecture circuit over the years, most of which also went to charity. He died in Philadelphia on December 6, 1925. After his death, Conwell's birthday was designated by Temple University, of which he was the founder and first president, as Founder's Day.

Elihu Root's Birthday

Elihu Root was born on February 15, 1845, in Clinton, New York. His father was a mathematics professor at Hamilton College, which Elihu eventually attended and from which he graduated first in his class. Root graduated from New York University Law School in 1867, and within a few years became a prominent corporate lawyer. He represented some of the largest banks and railroads of the 19th century.

Predictably, as a corporate lawyer Root favored the Republicans, who among other things stood for the traditional "gold standard" underlying the American dollar and international finance. Beyond local New York politics, however, Root was not a well-known figure until 1899, when President McKinley asked him to become secretary of war. Root served from 1899 until 1904, during which time he successfully reorganized the entire War Department. He also established the military's War College and expanded the U.S. Military Academy at West Point. Finally, Root participated in the drafting of the Platt Amendment, which gave the U.S. government the power to intervene in Cuba in order to preserve Cuban independence after the Spanish-American War, during which the United States had forced Spain to let Cuba leave the Spanish Empire.

In 1905 President Theodore Roosevelt made Elihu Root his secretary of state. Root reorganized the American consular service abroad and negotiated certain important agreements with Japan. He

left the State Department in 1909 and successfully ran for the U.S. Senate. In the Senate, where he served from 1909 to 1915, he was active in fisheries legislation and supported the "New Freedom" initiatives of Democratic president Woodrow Wilson. After he left the Senate, Root served as ambassador extraordinary to Russia during World War I, but failed to keep the Russians in the war against the Germans.

After World War I, Root continued to be active in the field of international arbitration, always a field of special interest to him. He participated in the Washington Naval Conference of 1921–1922, the Five Power Treaty limiting naval armament, the creation of the Central American Court of Justice, and the creation of the Permanent Court of International Justice. He also served as the first president of the Carnegie Endowment for International Peace. Root died on February 7, 1937, in New York City shortly before his 92nd birthday.

February 16

Cushing Eells's Birthday

Cushing Eells, the founder of Whitman College in Walla Walla, Washington, was a Congregationalist missionary to the Native Americans of the Pacific Northwest during that region's early settlement in the 1800s. The college, which was founded in 1859, is Washington's oldest institution of higher learning. It is also a memorial to Dr. Marcus Whitman and his wife Narcissa, friends and fellow missionaries of Eells who were killed at their mission in Washington in 1847.

Eells was born in Massachusetts on February 16, 1810. At the age of 15 he decided to dedicate his life to missionary work. In 1834 he graduated from Williams College in Williamstown, Massachusetts, and in 1837 graduated from the Hartford Theological Seminary in Hartford, Connecticut, known at that time as the East Windsor Theological Institute. Choosing South Africa as his field of work, Eells was commissioned as a missionary to the Zulus by the American Board of Commissioners for Foreign Missions. However, a war among the Zulus prevented him from going to Africa.

Instead, Eells remained in the United States, where he became important in pioneering missionary efforts to the Pacific Northwest. He and his wife were sent to the Oregon Territory in 1838. It took them a year to reach what is now eastern Washington, where in the spring of 1839 they began their work with the Spokane tribe. Eells built a log cabin and lived there for nine years, preaching to the tribes. On November 29, 1847, Dr.

Whitman, his wife, and 12 others were killed in an incident with the natives, forcing Eells and his family to flee south and take refuge in the Willamette Valley. He did not return until the resulting warfare in the region had ended in 1858 and the area was reopened for American settlers. Coming to Waiilatpu in 1859, he found only the ruins of the Whitman mission and the unmarked common grave of the victims. There, Eells vowed to build a school in honor of Whitman.

On December 20, 1859, his vision of a school became a reality when the territorial legislature of Washington granted a charter for the Whitman Seminary. The first building was dedicated in October 1866, and Eells assumed charge of the school soon after it opened. In 1883 an amended charter was granted to Whitman College, and in 1907 the school became nondenominational. Meanwhile, Eells continued to preach and travel about Washington founding new churches. He helped organize churches at Cheney, Chewelah, Colfax, Medical Lake, Skokomish, Spokane, Sprague, and Walla Walla. When he died in 1893, he left $5,000, about all that he possessed, to Whitman College. After his death, clergyman and author Lyman Abbott described Cushing Eells as a "man of quiet and beautiful character, of unsurpassed consecration, and one to whom the republic of the United States owes a far greater debt than to many who have occupied a more conspicuous place in its history."

February 17

Thomas J. Watson Sr.'s Birthday

Thomas J. Watson Sr., the founder of International Business Machines (IBM), was born in Campbell, New York, on February 17, 1874. Although his name is not as widely known as that of other industrialists such as Andrew Carnegie or John D. Rockefeller, Watson certainly deserves equal stature, since IBM would become one of the largest and most successful corporations in the world.

After attending the Elmira School of Commerce, Watson found employment with a small cash register company as a salesman, and in 1895 was hired by the National Cash Register company. National Cash Register, the predecessor to the modern NCR Corporation, was the leader in the field of mechanical cash registers. Watson became the company's general sales manager, but he had a falling out with president John H. Patterson in 1912 due to an antitrust investigation.

In 1914, Watson became president of the Computing-Tabulating-Recording Corporation, which manufactured the first primitive computers. These early machines were mostly mechanical and were based on punch cards. A punch card was a piece of paper, roughly the size of a modern business envelope, which had rows of numbers and was perforated or "punched" in order to carry information. Punch cards first became widespread in the late 19th century, when they were used by the federal government to help record information taken in the national census. In modified forms, they would be used in various applications until the early 1980s. In Watson's time, they represented the cutting edge of high technology.

The company changed its name to International Business Machines in 1924, and has kept that name ever since. Watson was an outstanding salesman, and he had a genius for corporate organization. He paid his sales people well and gave them a variety of job benefits, but in return he expected their loyalty. Through such measures as a strict dress code, he enforced a unique IBM corporate culture. Watson also hired some of the best scientific minds of the time to develop IBM's product lines. The result was a highly disciplined and motivated work force, which by the end of World War II had come to dominate both the domestic and the international computer industry.

Of course, the computer industry at the time was rather small. IBM was heavily dependent on government contracts, such as the computerization of the new Social Security program in the 1930s. The onset of the cold war in the late 1940s increased demand from the American defense establishment, which helped contribute not only to IBM's growth but also to further technological advances.

In 1952 Thomas Watson Jr. inherited IBM's presidency from his father. The elder Watson died several years later, on June 19, 1956, in New York City. The company he built would go on to thrive in the 1960s, and IBM computers helped make the space program possible. Although slow and incredibly bulky by modern standards, IBM's mainframe computers could perform calculations at a speed that had previously seemed impossible. Not only was IBM one of America's blue chip companies, but the name IBM was synonymous with American industrial superiority in the world.

IBM was at its zenith in the 1970s. Despite several antitrust actions, it continued to thrive and to bring out even bigger and better computers, such as the IBM 360. The few corporations that tried to take on IBM directly, such as General Electric, suffered serious financial losses. However, IBM missed several important new developments in the computer industry. Other companies, such as Ross Perot's Electronic Data Systems (EDS), were beginning to specialize in data processing services. IBM, slow to enter the field, let EDS take the lead. When the first desktop personal computers were introduced, IBM chose to rely on its traditional mainframes, and thus in the 1980s other companies such as Microsoft and Apple Computer were dominating what would become a revolutionary segment of the marketplace.

By the late 1980s IBM was struggling to maintain its dominant position. It was forced to pay large dividends to prop up its stock, and for the first time resorted to massive layoffs to cut costs. In the early 1990s the company revamped its management and wrote off billions of dollars in losses. It began to recover, however, thanks to a new and improved product line and more emphasis on the PC market. As of this writing, the company has recovered some of its lost glory, although it is unlikely that it will ever gain the near-monopoly status that it had during the pioneering days of Thomas J. Watson Sr.

Presidents' Day

This is a movable event.

Until the early 1970s, President George Washington's birthday (see February 22) and President Abraham Lincoln's birthday (see February 12) were separate public holidays observed by the federal government and in most states. Public Law 90-363, changing the federal observance of certain holidays to Mondays, was enacted by the United States Congress in 1968 and became effective in 1971. According to the provisions of this Monday Holiday Law, Washington's birthday and Lincoln's birthday would be jointly observed as a legal public holiday on the third Monday in February.

Hawaii, Nebraska, Ohio, and the American possession of the Northern Marianas have enacted parallel legislation to officially observe Presidents' Day. Regardless of these local enactments, Presidents' Day is in fact observed nationwide. One of the results of its creation, however, has been a declining interest in observances related specifically to Washington and Lincoln. Presidents' Day has evolved to become a somewhat general observance in honor of all the American presidents.

February 18

Helen Gurley Brown's Birthday

Helen Gurley Brown, the "Cosmo Girl," was born on February 18, 1922, in Green Forest, Arkansas. She had no formal education beyond high school, and became a secretary at the age of 18. For over 20 years, she would hold a variety of secretarial and clerical positions. However, during her employment as a copywriter for a Los Angeles advertising company, she wrote a book titled *Sex and the Single Girl*. Published in 1962 when Brown was 40 years old, the book was revolutionary for a time in which women were expected to focus on becoming wives and mothers. Brown's book, which contained advice on how a single woman should lead her love life, became a bestseller.

Brown's success attracted the attention of publishing magnate William Randolph Hearst. One of Hearst's publications was *Cosmopolitan* magazine, founded in 1886 and acquired by Hearst in 1905. It was a fairly mainstream publication for midwestern women with a variety of noncontroversial articles and literary pieces. To help boost the magazine's stagnant circulation, in 1965 Hearst hired Brown as *Cosmopolitan*'s editor. Her mission was to transform the magazine into a publication for modern young women, and she succeeded brilliantly.

Brown focused *Cosmopolitan* on issues of sexual relationships and the sexual revolution of the 1960s. During her tenure, circulation would eventually reach 3 million in the mid-1980s, and as of this writing *Cosmopolitan* continues to remain a major women's magazine. Not only were the articles and advice both frank and relevant, but Brown successfully boosted sales with such controversial innovations as male centerfolds. The first such centerfold, intended to be the woman's counterpart of those in publications such as *Playboy*, appeared in 1972 with a layout of the actor and sex symbol Burt Reynolds.

Brown ran *Cosmopolitan* until 1997, when she retired at the age of 74. Her 32 years there saw many changes in the issues confronted by modern women, and Brown ceased to be at the cutting edge of developments. Circulation peaked in the mid-1980s in large part due to *Cosmopolitan*'s hesitancy about discussing matters such as AIDS, as well as Brown's derision for the emerging concept and legal implications of sexual harassment. *Cosmopolitan*'s advice on matters of flirtation and its covers with chesty young models began to seem slightly old-fashioned. When Brown stepped down, she was succeeded by Bonnie Fuller, who was more than three decades younger.

Helen Gurley Brown made important contributions to publishing during her leadership of *Cosmopolitan*. In addition, *Sex and the Single Girl* and Brown's later books were important steps in the evolution of modern feminism.

Jefferson Davis Inaugurated

See also June 3, Jefferson Davis's Birthday.

By the time Jefferson Davis, who had served as United States senator from Mississippi from 1847 to 1851, returned to the Senate in 1857 after a stint as secretary of war, he had become the acknowledged leader of the Southern bloc in the years leading up to the Civil War. A strong champion of states' rights, Davis favored the extension of slavery into the western territories and economic development of the South as a counterbalance to Northern power.

Davis had little to do with the movement for secession until Mississippi, on January 9, 1861, became part of the Confederacy, which would fight the Union through four long years of Civil War (1861–1865). After Mississippi's action, Davis, a reluctant secessionist, stated in a Senate speech that the states had the constitutional right to secede from the Union and that Congress had no right to interfere with the domestic institutions of any state. Withdrawing from the Senate on January 21, 1861, he cast his lot with his home state.

Although Davis would rather have been offered the command of Southern military forces, members of the Confederate congress meeting in Montgomery, Alabama, unanimously chose him as president of the new Confederacy's provisional government on February 9, 1861. He was inaugurated at Montgomery on February 18, 1861, and began to organize the new government. Soon after his inauguration, there was a popular election in the Confederacy, in which he was elected president for a six-year term. Thus, Davis was inaugurated for the second time on February 22, 1862, at Richmond, Virginia, which became the Confederate capital.

February 19

Franklin D. Roosevelt Orders Japanese American Internment

The Japanese American community in the United States began with the first Japanese immigrants in the 1890s. Like other Asian immigrants, such as the Chinese, they faced considerable discrimination and were relegated to low-paying manual labor. Nevertheless, the community thrived, numbering in the tens of thousands when the Japanese Exclusion Act was enacted by Congress in 1924. Because the easiest way to reach the United States from Japan is obviously to cross the Pacific Ocean, most of the Japanese American community was located on the west coast and on Hawaii. Despite the restrictions on further Japanese immigration, the community continued to expand by virtue of children born and raised in the United States. These American descendants, known as the Nisei, were thoroughly Americanized and often spoke English better than Japanese.

During the 1930s, relations between the United States and the Japanese Empire became increasingly tense. The Japanese invasion of China led to Japan's departure from the League of Nations. As the Japanese continued to pursue their policy of Pacific expansionism, the administration of President Franklin D. Roosevelt began to place restrictions on American exports of petroleum and other resources necessary for the Japanese economy. These measures and other factors led to the Japanese surprise attack on Pearl Harbor on December 7, 1941, which FDR labeled "a day that will live in infamy."

It was the sensational and bitterly resented Japanese attack on Pearl Harbor that led to America's entry into World War II. Shortly after declaring war on Japan, the United States declared war on Nazi Germany and Fascist Italy, and in fact that European theater of World War II would consume far more resources than the Pacific operations against Japan. Nevertheless, unlike the German American and Italian American individuals in the United States, the Japanese were easy targets for racial discrimination because they were so obviously different in appearance from the Caucasian majority.

On February 19, 1942, a few months after the bombing of Pearl Harbor, President Roosevelt issued Executive Order No. 9066 directing the internment of Japanese Americans. The Japanese were thought to be potential saboteurs and enemy agents who should be rounded up and placed in prison camps in the interests of national security. FDR ordered the Japanese to report to certain facilities, while persons of German and Italian descent were left free to continue leading normal lives.

Not only were Japanese Americans forced to spend the bulk of World War II as prisoners, but many lost everything they owned. There was no protection for Japanese American businesses, homes, and personal possessions. The process of releasing the internees began on December 17,

1944, with the revocation of Executive Order No. 9066. Congress made a token effort at restitution with the Japanese American Evacuation Claims Act of 1948, but even successful claimants typically received only a fraction of their lost property. It was not until 1988 that President George Bush signed into law a more comprehensive restitution measure, and finally gave the Nisei an official apology on behalf of the nation. Unfortunately, nearly one-half of the World War II internees had already died.

Supreme Court Declares Initiatives and Referendums Valid

Two cornerstones of the reform movement that swept the United States at the beginning of the 20th century were the initiative and the referendum, forms of direct legislation designed to ensure the triumph of popular will over any obstructionism by recalcitrant legislatures.

Under the initiative, a specified percentage or number of a state's voters can initiate legislation by means of a popular petition. If by state law the proposal then goes directly before the people in a popular election, the method is known as the direct initiative. If the proposal must go to the legislature for approval before it can become law, the procedure is known as the indirect initiative. In either case, the effect is to force consideration of a proposal and ensure that it is put to a vote.

The referendum is applied to measures approved by a legislative body. Under the terms of the referendum, a particular number of citizens can force the state legislature to submit a measure that it has passed to a vote of the people before that measure becomes law. In the United States, the kind of referendum most commonly employed is the so-called optional type, instituted by a petition of the people. There is also what is known as the mandatory referendum, by which some state constitutions and local charters require that certain kinds of laws always be submitted to the electorate for approval.

The initiative and referendum were first adopted by South Dakota in 1898, and then by Oregon in 1902. In due course, the validity of these methods of direct legislation was disputed, and a test case was taken to the United States Supreme Court for final decision. The Court decided on February 19, 1912, that the adoption of such political devices as the initiative and referendum lies within the discretion of the people of the states and that when these devices are adopted the courts must accept them.

However, the initiative and referendum as applied to state and local proposals are not applicable to matters concerning the United States Constitution. The state of Ohio discovered this when it attempted to submit a federal constitutional amendment to its voters for ratification. The validity of such ratification was disputed, and the Supreme Court held that a state had no power to change the method of amending the U.S. Constitution as laid down in that document itself. Thus, constitutional amendments must still be submitted to the legislatures of the states or to conventions in the states called for the purpose of considering them. An amendment to the federal Constitution becomes effective only after three-fourths of the state legislatures or specially called conventions have ratified it.

The initiative and referendum were patterned on the forms of direct legislation that came into wide use in Switzerland after 1830. Actually, however, the initiative was recognized in America as early as 1777, when Georgia gave voters the exclusive right to propose amendments to its state constitution. The automatic referendum on state constitutions (as opposed to the federal constitution) and amendments to them, which has been called a purely American invention, was first used in adopting the constitution of Massachusetts in 1780. Connecticut adopted the obligatory referendum, for amendments to the state constitution proposed by the legislature, in 1818.

February 20

John Glenn Orbits the Earth

On February 20, 1962, boosted aloft by an Atlas-D rocket, the *Friendship 7* space capsule, carrying astronaut John H. Glenn Jr., soared into space from a launch pad at Cape Canaveral, Florida. Under the aegis of the National Aeronautics and Space Administration (NASA) and its Project Mercury, Glenn was the first American and the third man to orbit the Earth. The first two men to orbit the Earth were Soviets.

An estimated 135 million people followed television coverage of his flight at some time during the day, while millions more kept pace by radio. The launch took place at 9:47 a.m. Eastern Standard Time. At 9:48, Lieutenant Colonel Glenn was reported experiencing the space-travel phenomenon of weightlessness. At 9:59 it was confirmed that he was in orbit. At 10:09 a tracking station in Nigeria made radio contact with him; 19 minutes later he was over the Indian Ocean; 12 minutes after that, he had seen the lights of Perth, Australia, turned on for him in a special gesture of greeting. In another 29 minutes, he was in radio contact with a tracking station in Mexico. At 11:24, an hour and 37 minutes after liftoff, he had completed his first orbit.

Meanwhile, as NASA's Mercury Control Center at Cape Canaveral broadcast a tape recording, waiting millions heard his ebullient voice, speaking from space: "Flight turning out real fine. . . . Capsule is in good shape. . . . All systems are Go. . . . Zero G [gravity] and I feel fine. . . . Oh! that view is tremendous."

In the next few hours Glenn repeated the process twice, and reports were transmitted back from tracking stations around the globe. The flight's three orbits were completed despite erratic behavior in the automatic system controlling the attitude of his capsule, a problem he solved by manual control, and despite the alarm caused by a malfunctioning signal. Fortunately the signal was wrong in indicating that the heat shield, which was to prevent his capsule from incinerating in the heat of reentering the Earth's atmosphere, had become unlatched.

The heat shield remained intact during the scheduled firing of three retrorockets to slow the capsule and bring it out of orbit. As expected, radio contact was momentarily lost during reentry. Relieved listeners heard Glenn's voice again at 2:35: "Boy, that was a real fireball."

Glenn's capsule splashed into the Atlantic Ocean, off the Bahamas, at 2:43. The pickup was accomplished 18 minutes later by the destroyer *Noa*. Shortly after emerging from his capsule, Glenn received the telephoned congratulations of President John F. Kennedy, who declared in a statement that space "is the new ocean, and I believe the United States must sail on it and be in a position second to none."

Counting technical personnel and the 15,000 people, mostly aboard ships, who stood by for recovery, search, and rescue operations, some 30,000 people played a part, directly or indirectly, in Glenn's feat. During his 4 hours and 56 minutes of flight, the astronaut had orbited the Earth three times and traveled a distance of about 81,000 miles. Traveling at altitudes that varied from 99 to 162 miles, he achieved a speed of 17,545 miles per hour. His history-making trip through space, which succeeded those of the Russians Yuri Gagarin (1 orbit) and Gherman Titov (17 orbits) in 1961, was followed by other efforts, including the flights of Scott Carpenter and Walter Schirra (3 and 6 orbits, respectively, in 1962) and Gordon Cooper (22 orbits in 1963), as well as both countries' efforts to place men on the moon, a goal achieved by the United States on July 20, 1969.

Glenn returned to a hero's welcome and honors too numerous to list. After two days of debriefing on Grand Turk Island, he was flown to Florida for a reunion with his family. His wife and two children were escorted to Florida by President Kennedy, who presented the Distinguished Service Medal to Glenn in a ceremony at Cape Canaveral. Other celebrations followed in quick succession: a February 26, 1962, parade in Washington, D.C., where Glenn addressed a joint session of Congress and testified in support of the administration's space program; a March 1 ticker-tape parade and luncheon in New York, where Glenn and his six fellow Mercury astronauts were honored by Mayor Robert F. Wagner and other dignitaries; and a March 3 welcome by 50,000 people in Glenn's hometown of New Concord, Ohio.

John Glenn, who was born in nearby Cambridge, Ohio, on July 18, 1921, grew up in New Concord. At high school he won letters in football, tennis, and basketball, and was elected president of the junior class. He enrolled at New Concord's Muskingum College (which has since granted him an honorary degree), but left in his third year to train as a naval aviation cadet. He was commissioned a second lieutenant in the U.S. Marine Corps in March 1943 and promoted in the ensuing years.

During World War II, Glenn flew 59 fighter-bomber missions in the Pacific. Afterwards he served in northern China and in Guam, became a flight instructor, and attended amphibious warfare school. After a jet refresher course, he was assigned to duty in the Korean War, in the course of which he flew another 90 missions. He subsequently became a test pilot and served with the Fighter Design Branch of the navy's Bureau of Aeronautics in Washington, D.C. He made headlines on July 16, 1957, when he made the first transcontinental flight at supersonic speed, from Los Angeles to New York. For this feat, and his service in World War II and Korea, he was five times awarded the Distinguished Flying Cross and 19 times the Air Medal.

Glenn became a lieutenant colonel on April 1, 1959. Eight days later, he was among the seven chosen from 110 military test pilots who had volunteered to become the country's first astronauts. The long preparation for space flight that followed included intensive study of such subjects as desert and water survival, geography, meteorology, aviation biology, astronomy, astronautics, and astrophysics. The preparation also included exposure to simulated phenomena of space travel, including weightlessness, high heat, and strong gravitational forces.

Glenn served as backup pilot for astronaut Alan B. Shepard in May 1961 and astronaut Virgil I. Grissom in July 1961, helping to accomplish the first U.S. suborbital flights. He was chosen on November 29, 1961, to make the United States' first manned orbital flight. He once said: "People are afraid of the future, of the unknown. If a man faces up to it and takes the dare of the future, he can have some control over his destiny. That's an exciting idea to me."

After his historic flight, Glenn rose to the rank of full colonel, and retired from the Marine Corps in 1964. After a failed bid in 1970, he successfully went after the Democratic nomination for one of Ohio's seats in the U.S. Senate in 1974. He was victorious in the November election, defeating his Republican opponent by a margin of more than two to one. He expressed some interest in running for president during the 1980s, but abandoned the idea when popular enthusiasm failed to materialize.

In the late 1990s Glenn was chosen to serve as an honorary member of a space shuttle flight, despite his advanced age. He successfully completed the mission, proving that senior citizens could withstand the rigors of space travel.

Joseph Jefferson's Birthday

Joseph Jefferson, one of the most distinguished American actors of the 19th century, was born in Philadelphia, Pennsylvania, on February 20, 1829. The fourth actor in a family of actors and managers, he made his stage debut at the age of three as Cora's child in Kotzebue's *Pizzaro*. At the age of four he appeared in Washington, D.C., in one of Thomas Dartmouth Rice's popular *Jim Crow* minstrel shows. His father, who began to play in western and southern cities in 1838, died of yellow fever in Mobile, Alabama, on November 24, 1842, and was buried in that city's Magnolia Cemetery.

After his father's death, Jefferson spent many years as a strolling player and for a brief time in 1856 studied in Europe. In November of that year, he joined actress Laura Keene's company in New York, and in 1857 he scored a success in the role of Dr. Pangloss in George Colman's *The Heir at Law*. A year later he won fame for his portrayal of Asa Trenchard, opposite the English actor E. A. Sothern, in Tom Taylor's *Our American Cousin*.

While gaining prominence as an actor, Jefferson began to search for a character around whom a play could be written. He finally settled on Rip Van Winkle and wrote a short play about him. His 1859 dramatization of the Washington Irving story was only moderately successful, however. While in England in 1865, he commissioned the Irish American playwright Dion Boucicault to revise the play. The Boucicault version, with Jefferson in the leading role, opened in London at the Adelphi Theatre in 1865. An immediate success, Jefferson's *Rip Van Winkle* was performed before London audiences for 170 successive nights. Returning to the United States in 1866, he re-created the part in performances throughout the country, achieving both financial success and popular acclaim.

During his long career, Jefferson was a friend of many leading figures of the day. He and President Grover Cleveland both had summer homes in Buzzards Bay, Massachusetts, and the two frequently went fishing together. When not working, Jefferson spent his winters at his large plantation in Louisiana. He was also a landscape painter and the author of an autobiography, originally published in *Century Magazine* (1889–1890). He was a member of the American Academy of Arts and Letters, and in 1893 succeeded Edwin Booth as lifetime president of the club, mainly for actors, known as The Players. Jefferson died on Easter Sunday, April 23, 1905, in Palm Beach, Florida, a year after his last stage appearance on May 7, 1904, in Paterson, New Jersey.

February 21

President Nixon Goes to China

See also January 9, Richard M. Nixon's Birthday.

During his political career in the 1950s and 1960s, Richard Nixon was the archetypal "cold warrior." He was a staunch Republican, advocating a strong military posture toward the communist nations of the Soviet Union and the People's Republic of China during the cold war that began in the late 1940s and ended in the early 1990s. The two communist nations were far from united, however. Although the Soviets and the Communist Chinese were allies during the 1950s, they began to drift apart for a variety of reasons, including the Soviet tendency to treat China as the junior partner in the alliance and the historic enmity between the old Russian and Chinese empires.

By the 1960s the Sino-Soviet alliance was largely over. China pursued an independent foreign policy, collaborating with the Soviets only when it served their mutual interests, such as in Vietnam, where both countries desired America's defeat.

When Nixon became president, he realized that there was an opportunity to exploit the rift between the Soviets and the Chinese. Like the Americans, the Chinese were concerned about

Soviet expansionism. With a population of roughly one billion and its own arsenal of nuclear weapons, China could be a powerful ally.

In a dramatic shift from his previous cold war positions, Nixon announced in July 1971 that he would personally visit the People's Republic of China. The United States had not officially recognized China since 1949, when the Communist regime took over the Chinese mainland from the Nationalist Chinese forces of Generalissimo Chiang Kai-shek. Nixon's pronouncement was only one of a series of steps, including an easing of trade and travel restrictions, that were taken during his administration to come, in his words, "urgently to grips with the reality of China."

Nixon's historic trip began on February 21, 1972. He met with Chairman Mao Tse-tung and the other senior Chinese leaders and began the process of normalizing diplomatic relations between the two countries. A temporary agreement was reached on one important matter. The forces of Chiang Kai-shek that left mainland China after the communist takeover had taken refuge on the offshore Chinese island of Taiwan, where they had built a prosperous and independent society that claimed to be the legitimate government of China. Although Taiwan's claim to China was unrealistic, America had supported Taiwan throughout the cold war, but the Communist Chinese insisted that there could only be one Chinese government. Such a situation would naturally mean domination by the mainland Communists over the Taiwanese. In a carefully worded statement, on February 27, 1972, President Nixon and Premier Chou En-Lai jointly issued the Shanghai Communiqué, which stated that "the United States acknowledges that all Chinese on either side of the Taiwan Strait maintain there is but one China and that Taiwan is a part of China."

Although ambiguously worded, the Shanghai Communiqué effectively transferred American diplomatic recognition from Taiwan to mainland China. On January 1, 1979, the United States and the People's Republic of China officially normalized diplomatic relations. American diplomatic relations with Taiwan continued, but through supposedly "unofficial" channels. As of this writing in the late 1990s, there have been negotiations between the Chinese and the Taiwanese concerning the peaceful absorption of Taiwan back into mainland China, which now has a booming capitalist economy under the umbrella of its old communist leadership.

President Nixon's historic visit to China in 1972 made it possible for the United States to develop relations with one of the largest nations on Earth, one that may well be an industrial superpower in the future.

Washington Monument Dedicated

By the time the stark white obelisk called the Washington Monument was finally dedicated in Washington, D.C., on Saturday, February 21, 1885, nearly 100 years had gone into the planning and execution of a fitting memorial to the first president in the nation's capital. The monument was first suggested by Major Pierre Charles L'Enfant, when he submitted the master plan for the new city of Washington, D.C., in 1791.

The Washington Monument sits on a small hill, mirrored in a reflecting pool and ringed by 50 American flags, one for each state. It is the centerpiece of a north-south view that stretches from the White House to the Jefferson Memorial, and of an even more compelling east-west vista extending from the domed Capitol to the Lincoln Memorial. Washington himself had selected the same site for a monument, but he had seen it as a memorial to the "unknown soldier" of the American Revolution, not to himself.

The idea of a monument in honor of the first president was proposed to Congress within a week after Washington's death in 1799. The generally sympathetic legislators looked at designs but took no action for many years. Finally, a speech by Henry Clay helped spur action, and a private organization, the Washington National Monument Society, was established in 1832 with the purpose of raising funds for the project. Over 15 years the society obtained some $87,000 and selected Robert Mills as architect of the proposed monument.

Remembered today as the United States' first native-born professional architect and the creator of such Washington landmarks as the Post Office, Treasury building, and former Patent Office (later the Fine Arts and Portrait Galleries), Mills planned a granite shaft faced with white marble. Although the finished monument was slightly lower than in Mills's original plan (it stands 555 feet, 5 inches instead of 600 feet), its other dimensions (55 feet square at the base and 34 feet square at the top) are close to his original specifications. However, the ornate base proposed by Mills was eliminated, some believe fortunately, from the austerely handsome final result.

Building the Washington Monument took almost as long as planning it. The site admired by L'Enfant and Washington was selected, and the cornerstone was laid on July 4, 1848. Robert C. Winthrop, speaker of the House of Representatives, delivered a dedication speech. During the first stage of construction, the monument rose to just over 150 feet, a so-called "high-water mark" still visible today. Work had to be abandoned in 1854, as the Monument Society's funds had been exhausted and an appeal for more money had met with no response. The Civil War further delayed completion.

Finally, in 1876, Congress appropriated funds and set the Army Corps of Engineers to work to complete the project in marble that did not quite match the original stone in color. Construction was finished on December 6, 1884, when the capstone was put in place. Arrangements were made by Congress for the dedication of the completed obelisk, and on Saturday, February 21, 1885, ceremonies were held at the monument's base and in the House of Representatives. The speaker for the occasion was the same Robert C. Winthrop who had spoken at the laying of the cornerstone 37 years earlier. The total cost of completing the monument was estimated at between $1.2 million and $1.3 million.

February 22

George Washington's Birthday

Library of Congress

George Washington

George Washington was born on February 22, 1732. For many decades his birthday was observed as an official holiday, but in the late 20th century this observance was combined with President Abraham Lincoln's birthday in the holiday known as Presidents' Day (see February 17).

Washington was born at Bridges Creek in Westmoreland County, Virginia. His parents were Augustine Washington and his second wife, Mary Ball Washington. When Augustine Washington died in 1743, George Washington's older half brother Lawrence inherited the main family lands and named them Mount Vernon. The brothers lived together on this property for several years before George Washington moved to a farm near Fredericksburg, Virginia, which was his patrimony.

Washington was a member of an influential family, but in other respects his youth was ordinary. He cut short his education at the age of 15; he had acquired some proficiency in mathematics, but his grasp of other subjects was limited. Stories of Washington's precocious adolescence, like the widely repeated cherry-tree episode, were the fabrications of early biographers such as Parson Mason Weems, who wrote *The Life and Memorable Actions of George Washington*.

Washington benefited from the marriage of his half brother to Anne Fairfax, a member of one of the leading families of Virginia. In 1748 the Fairfaxes allowed Washington to assist James Genn in his survey of their properties in Virginia's Shenandoah Valley. Washington found this experience rewarding and perfected his techniques so well that in 1749 he became public surveyor for Culpeper County. He was very close to his half brother Lawrence, who became almost a second father to him after their own father's death. In 1751 the two journeyed together to Barbados, where it was hoped that Lawrence, suffering from tuberculosis, would recover his health. Unfortunately the trip was unsuccessful. Lawrence died in 1752, following his return to Virginia. George, then scarcely out of his teens, became executor of Lawrence's estate and received title to the family home of Mount Vernon.

In 1753 Governor Robert Dinwiddie of Virginia chose Washington, despite his youthful 21 years, as his emissary to the French forces attempting to fortify territory claimed by Virginia northwest of the colony. Washington had to travel almost as far north as Lake Erie to deliver to the proper commander the ultimatum demanding French withdrawal. Not unexpectedly his adversaries refused, and Washington returned to Virginia with the bad news. The Virginia authorities decided that a more aggressive policy would be necessary to curb the French threat, and in 1754 Washington led two companies north to build a fort at the confluence of the Allegheny and Monongahela Rivers, where the Ohio River is formed (now Pittsburgh, Pennsylvania). Washington discovered that the French had already established a post, Fort Duquesne, on the site. He was able to inflict some damage by defeating a party of French and their native allies at Great Meadows on May 27, 1754. The French counterattacked and captured Washington, together with his men, in a battle on July 3, 1754, at Fort Necessity, the Virginians' aptly named camp. Released by the French, the soldiers returned to Virginia.

British troops under General Edward Braddock arrived in 1755 and undertook an expedition with the Virginia militia against the French. Braddock chose Washington, who knew the terrain to be covered, as his aide-de-camp. The joint effort met defeat on July 9, 1755, at the Battle of Monongahela. Braddock was mortally wounded, and Washington's appointment expired with the general's death. In the autumn of 1755, Governor Dinwiddie commissioned Washington as a colonel in command of the provincial militia. Given the responsibility of defending 350 miles of frontier with 700 irregular troops, Washington learned many military skills that later served him well. In 1758 he cooperated in another Anglo-Virginian venture against the French at Fort Duquesne. The troops, under General John Forbes, managed to force the French to abandon the stronghold.

On January 6, 1759, Washington married Martha Dandridge Custis, the widow of Daniel Parke Custis. By this marriage he added approximately $100,000 worth of property to his estate, becoming one of the wealthiest men in the colonies. The union failed to produce children, but Washington took his wife's offspring as his own and proved to be a devoted stepfather.

In 1758 Washington was elected to the Virginia House of Burgesses and served in that body for most of the years leading up to the American Revolution. As troubles with the British increased, he found himself on the side of the rebels. He denounced the Stamp Act of 1765, commenting to an associate that the Parliament "hath no more right to put their hands in my pocket, without my consent, than I have to put my hands in yours for money." In 1770 he supported a ban on British imports as a means of putting pressure on the London government. He did not approve of the Boston Tea Party of 1773, but he did sympathize with Massachusetts's determination to stand up to the British government. When the governor of Virginia dissolved the House of Burgesses in 1774, Washington participated in the illegal meetings of the ex-legislators in the Raleigh Tavern in Williamsburg, Virginia.

Virginia sent Washington as a representative to the First Continental Congress, which met in Philadelphia, Pennsylvania, in 1774 to petition King George III for the redress of colonial grievances.

He was also a delegate to the Second Continental Congress, which met in Philadelphia in May 1775. Washington served on committees that drafted military regulations and prepared the defense of New York City.

New Englanders, who had already clashed with British soldiers in April 1775 at the towns of Lexington and Concord in Massachusetts, were eager to win southern support for their struggle. At the time, Virginia had the largest population in the colonies, so John Adams, a leader of the Massachusetts contingent, encouraged the Congress to appoint Washington as commander of the American armies. Washington accepted the post and received his commission on June 17, 1775. He refused all monetary compensation except for his expenses, which was actually less noble than it sounds, since he had expensive tastes that were now billed to the Congress.

Washington personally directed the siege that wrested control of Boston from the British during the winter of 1775–1776, and led the unsuccessful defense of New York City in the fall of 1776. His troops defeated the British in daring attacks on Trenton, New Jersey, in 1776 and Princeton, New Jersey, in early 1777, but they were less successful during the following summer, when the Americans lost the city of Philadelphia. Washington led the final Middle Atlantic operations in New Jersey in 1778, and was present at the defeat of Lord Cornwallis at Yorktown in October 1781, which essentially secured the American victory over the British. General Washington's greatest quality was not as a strategist or tactician, but as an inspiring leader of men under the most stressful of conditions. He was able to keep the tattered Continental army together during the harsh winter of 1777–1778 at Valley Forge, Pennsylvania, which probably saved the colonials from defeat.

After the Revolution, Washington retired to Mount Vernon, where he hoped to resume a normal private life. However, the needs of the fledgling United States, weakly allied under the Articles of Confederation, again drew him into public affairs. Delegates from Virginia and Maryland met at his estate to resolve their mutual problems, and the success of these discussions led to the larger convention at Annapolis in 1786, at which five states were represented. The Annapolis participants issued a call for a Constitutional Convention to meet in Philadelphia in May 1787.

Delegates from all 13 states attended the Philadelphia meeting and chose Washington, who represented Virginia, to preside at the conference. Washington let everyone know that he favored the creation of a strong national government equipped to meet the needs of the United States. The popular general was the logical choice to fill the office of chief executive, to which he was elected under the terms of the new Constitution.

After an arduous journey, Washington took the oath of office on April 30, 1789, as the first president of the United States, on the balcony of the Federal Hall in New York City. He spent a good deal of his first months in office choosing people to assist him in running the executive branch. He selected his fellow Virginian Thomas Jefferson to be secretary of state and Alexander Hamilton of New York to be secretary of the treasury. Jefferson and Hamilton had opposing views about the future of the United States, and Washington suffered great strains trying to keep peace between his two most powerful associates. Jefferson favored an alliance with France and maintenance of federal powers at the minimum level, whereas Hamilton was more sympathetic to England and thought a powerful central government essential to the country's growth. In the end the president found himself leaning more toward the position of Hamilton's Federalist faction, and Jefferson, the chief spirit of the emerging Democratic-Republican Party, resigned his post in 1793.

Washington was unanimously reelected president in 1792. He devoted much of his second term to keeping the United States out of the war between England and France. On April 22, 1793, he issued his Neutrality Proclamation, in which he warned Americans not to engage in hostile actions against England or France because the United States was at peace with both of them. Again, in his Farewell Address of September 17, 1796, Washington warned the nation to stay clear of permanent alliances with foreign powers. The Farewell Address was never actually given by Washington in a speech, but was printed in newspapers, first in the pages of the Philadelphia *American Daily Advertiser*.

George Washington retired from public office at the end of his second term as president and returned to Mount Vernon. In December 1799 he contracted a severe throat infection after a long ride in a snowstorm. The 18th-century medical technique of bloodletting only sapped his strength, and he died on December 14, 1799.

There are many other essays relevant to the life of George Washington appearing throughout this book. See the index for further details.

James Russell Lowell's Birthday

James Russell Lowell, a prominent 19th-century American writer and critic, had a rich and varied career as poet, essayist, crusader, editor, professor, and diplomat. Lowell was born in Cambridge,

Massachusetts, on February 22, 1819, in Elmwood, the same house in which he would die in 1891. His father was the Reverend Charles Lowell, minister of the West Church of Boston. His mother was Harriet Brackett Spence of New Hampshire. He was reared in comfort, studied at the classical school of William Wells in Cambridge, and entered Harvard College. When he graduated in 1838, he knew and loved literature and was the class poet. He then entered Harvard Law School, graduating in 1840, but never practiced law.

In 1843 Lowell co-edited *The Pioneer: A Literary and Critical Magazine*. During its short life, Edgar Allan Poe, Nathaniel Hawthorne, John Greenleaf Whittier, and Elizabeth Barrett Browning contributed to the magazine. At the time of his marriage in December 1844, he had also launched himself as a poet and critic in his own treatises as well as in magazines. His wife, Maria Lowell, was a committed abolitionist. Through her and the couple's friends, Lowell enlisted in the antislavery cause. He went to Philadelphia, Pennsylvania, for several months, just after his marriage, to serve as an editorial writer for the *Pennsylvania Freeman*. Later he was a corresponding editor of the *National Anti-Slavery Standard* in New York. In 1845, at the time of the annexation of Texas as a slave state, Lowell composed "The Present Crisis," an often quoted poem:

> Once to every man and nation
> Comes the moment to decide,
> In the strife of truth with falsehood,
> For the good or evil side. . . .

Also in 1848, Lowell published *The Bigelow Papers*, in which he satirized the American war with Mexico. Like many other New Englanders, Lowell opposed the Mexican War on the grounds that it would extend slavery and increase the influence of the southern states in the Union. In the *Papers* he deftly caricatured the ideal of military glory and ridiculed jingoistic journalism. The work gained Lowell a considerable political as well as literary following.

Lowell's first child died at the age of 15 months, early in 1847. This death inspired "She Came and Went," "The Changeling," and "The First Snowfall," some of his best-known short poems. Later that year a second daughter, who would survive Lowell, was born. However, Lowell would lose two more children in infancy, and also his wife, who died on October 27, 1853. The loss of his beloved wife was a tragic blow to Lowell.

In 1855 he gave a series of public lectures at the Lowell Institute in Boston. Soon afterward Harvard appointed him the Smith Professor of French, Spanish, and belles-lettres to succeed

Henry Wadsworth Longfellow upon his resignation. In 1857 Lowell became the first editor of the newly founded *Atlantic Monthly* magazine. Under his skillful editorship the magazine became an important vehicle for liberal thought on politics and religion, gathering a group of the nation's finest writers of that period. Lowell continued as editor and as a regular contributor until 1862. In 1864 he became joint editor of the *North American Review* with Charles Eliot Norton.

Participation in these journals encouraged him to publish his literary studies as professor, as well as his reflections on contemporary letters. He also continued to write poetry, which became more reflective and less lyrical. Literary and political criticism predominated in his later writings, and most of his books after 1863 were collected essays. Placed at the literary center of things, James Russell Lowell developed into one of the most famous critics of the period. The Civil War also rekindled Lowell's earlier passion for freedom and social change, and he composed a second series of *The Bigelow Papers* in support of the Union cause against the Confederacy.

In 1876, at the age of 57, Lowell had a brief role in politics as a delegate to the Republican National Convention, where he helped elect Rutherford B. Hayes as the nominee for president over James G. Blaine. Afterwards Lowell was a member of the Electoral College, where he supported his pledge to Hayes against Samuel J. Tilden, the Democratic candidate, in a contest of unprecedented closeness. For this service to the barely victorious Republican Party, Lowell was asked to become the American envoy to Spain. He served in Madrid from 1877 to 1880, using the time partly to improve his knowledge of Spanish and Spanish literature. On the basis of his diplomatic success, Lowell was made minister to Great Britain in 1880. In England he was admired for his grace in public speaking and his witty, urbane conversation.

In February 1885 his second wife, Frances Lowell, died after a long illness. In June of that year Lowell retired to private life. He died on August 12, 1891, at the age of 73 and was buried in Mount Auburn Cemetery in Cambridge, Massachusetts. In 1905 he was elected to the Hall of Fame for Great Americans.

Adams-Onis Florida Purchase Treaty Signed

The Adams-Onis Treaty, signed in Washington, D.C., on February 22, 1819, by U.S. secretary of state John Quincy Adams and Spanish minister Luis de Onis, is also known as the Florida Purchase Treaty, the Treaty of 1819, and the Trans-

continental Treaty. Under its terms, Spain abandoned its claim to West Florida and ceded East Florida to the United States in return for $5 million, which the United States agreed to pay toward the claims of American citizens against Spain. "West Florida" was basically the panhandle region of modern Florida, except that the panhandle in those days extended across the gulf coast of Alabama and Mississippi into Louisiana. "East Florida" was the rest of Florida's peninsula, considered to be largely uninhabitable due to the vast swamps and hot weather.

Also under the treaty's terms, the United States gave up its claim to Texas, which of course was later rescinded. The treaty did serve, however, to define the southern boundary of the Louisiana Purchase. The western boundary of that huge region had never been a question, since the area was commonly held to extend to the Rocky Mountains. However, the vagueness of the southern boundary had caused endless confusion ever since the United States acquired the vast Louisiana Territory in 1803. Specifically, the Adams-Onis Treaty established the Louisiana Purchase boundary as extending from the mouth of the Sabine River on what is now the Louisiana-Texas border, northward along the Sabine to the 32nd Parallel, thence north to the Red River, west along the Red River to 100 degrees longitude, north to the Arkansas River, west and north along that waterway to its source, thence to the 42nd Parallel, and west along that line to the Pacific Ocean. Thus was established the boundary between Spanish Mexico (which would soon be independent) and the United States. By agreeing to the 42nd Parallel line, which eventually became the northern border of California, Nevada, and Utah, Spain also effectively abandoned its claim to the Oregon Territory northward.

The Adams-Onis Treaty received final ratification by the U.S. Senate on February 19, 1821.

February 23

The Lend-Lease Agreement

The United States entered World War II after the Japanese attacked Pearl Harbor. At the time, Great Britain was on the verge of defeat by German forces and badly in need of American supplies. In order to assist the British, President Franklin D. Roosevelt proposed to "lend" the British various supplies. It was a politically expedient means of sending aid to the British without openly calling it a subsidy. After World War II the United States canceled Britain's Lend-Lease debt.

The Lend-Lease Agreement was entered into on February 23, 1942, although in fact the United States had been sending aid for some time. A copy of the agreement is set forth below:

ARTICLE I

The Government of the United States of America will continue to supply the Government of the United Kingdom with such defense articles, defense services, and defense information as the President shall authorize to be transferred or provided.

ARTICLE II

The Government of the United Kingdom will continue to contribute to the defense of the United States of America and the strengthening thereof and will provide such articles, services, facilities or information as it may be in a position to supply.

ARTICLE III

The Government of the United Kingdom will not without the consent of the President of the United States of America transfer title to, or possession of, any defense article or defense information transferred to it [under the act of Congress authorizing Lend-Lease] or permit the use thereof by anyone not an officer, employee, or agent of the Government of the United Kingdom.

ARTICLE IV

If, as a result of the transfer to the Government of the United Kingdom of any defense article or defense information, it becomes necessary for that Government to take any action or make any payment in order fully to protect any of the rights of a citizen of the United States of America who has patent rights in and to any such defense article or information, the Government of the United Kingdom will take such action or make such payment when requested to do so by the President of the United States of America.

ARTICLE V

The Government of the United Kingdom will return to the United States of America at the end of the present emergency, as determined by the President, such defense articles transferred under this Agreement as shall not have been destroyed, lost or consumed and as shall be determined by the President to be useful in the defense of the United States of America or of the Western Hemisphere or to be otherwise of use to the United States of America.

ARTICLE VI

In the final determination of the benefits to be provided to the United States of America by the Government of the United Kingdom full cognizance shall be taken of all property, services, information, facilities, or other benefits or considerations provided by the Government of the United Kingdom subsequent to March 11, 1941, and accepted or acknowledged by the President on behalf of the United States of America.

ARTICLE VII

In the final determination of the benefits to be provided to the United States of America by the Government of the United Kingdom in return for aid furnished under the Act of Congress of March 11, 1941, the terms and conditions thereof shall be such as not to burden commerce between the two countries, but to promote mutually advantageous economic relations between them and the betterment of worldwide economic relations. To that end, they shall include provision for agreed action by the United States of America and the United Kingdom, open to participation by all other countries of like mind, directed to the expansion, by appropriate international and domestic measures, of production, employment, and the exchange and consumption of goods, which are the material foundations of the liberty and welfare of all peoples; to the elimination of all forms of discriminatory treatment in international commerce, and to the reduction of tariffs and other trade barriers; and, in general, to the attainment of all the economic objectives set forth in the Joint Declaration made on August 14, 1941, by the President of the United States of America and the Prime Minister of the United Kingdom.

At an early convenient date, conversations shall be begun between the two Governments with a view to determining, in the light of governing economic conditions, the best means of attaining the above stated objectives by their own agreed action and of seeking the agreed action of other like-minded Governments.

ARTICLE VIII

This Agreement shall take effect as from this day's date. It shall continue in force until a date to be agreed upon by the two Governments.

Signed and sealed at Washington in duplicate this twenty-third day of February 1942.

February 24

Emma Willard's Birthday

The pioneering efforts made in the 19th century toward the improvement of women's education in the United States owed much of their early success to the work of Emma Hart Willard. Descended from Thomas Hooker and other leaders of the Connecticut colony, Emma was born on February 23, 1787, in Berlin, Connecticut, where she spent her early years and received her schooling. She began teaching at the age of 16, and only four years later (in 1807) became head of the Middlebury (Vermont) Female Academy. She held that post until 1809, when she married a prominent Middlebury physician, Dr. John Willard.

In 1814, motivated by a desire to raise the level of female education in the United States, Emma Willard opened her home in Middlebury as a boarding school for girls. She made innovative additions to the curriculum then usually offered to women by offering such subjects as mathematics and philosophy, previously taught only to men. Although advanced for its time, the school, known as the Middlebury Female Seminary, was successful.

In 1819 Willard addressed the New York State legislature and set forth her "Plan for Improving Female Education," in which she proposed state aid in the founding of girls' schools and equality of educational opportunities for women. The plan was rejected by the legislature but found favor with New York governor DeWitt Clinton, who invited the educator to move her Middlebury school to Waterford, New York. Later in 1819, the New York legislature chartered the school as the Waterford Academy, but still provided no financial assistance. In 1821, on the invitation of local citizens and with the aid of private loans, Willard moved her school to Troy, New York, where it became known as the Troy Female Seminary. It was the first school in the United States to offer college-level education to women. Under her direction, the seminary won fame not only nationally but abroad.

Retiring from the active management of the seminary in 1838, Willard traveled, wrote, and lectured extensively on behalf of public education and women's education. She wrote several widely used textbooks, and published a volume of verse entitled *The Fulfillment of a Promise*, in which the best-known poem is "Rocked in the Cradle of the Deep." She died in Troy, New York, on April 15, 1870. In recognition of the importance of her life's work, Emma Willard was elected to the Hall of Fame for Great Americans in 1905, one of the first three women so honored. In 1892 the Troy Female Seminary was renamed the Emma Willard

School in her honor. As emerging women's colleges gradually replaced female seminaries, it was later reorganized as a secondary-level school.

The Battle of Buena Vista

One of the crucial battles of the Mexican War between Mexico and the United States was fought in February 1847 at Buena Vista, a small settlement south of Saltillo in the Mexican state of Coahuila. The battle marked the successful end of the American military campaign in northern Mexico and secured the reputation of General Zachary Taylor, who shortly afterwards became a national hero and was later elected president.

Commanding a force of about 4,800 men, the advancing Taylor occupied a strong position near Buena Vista on February 21, 1847. There he waited for the expected attack by General Antonio López de Santa Anna, who had arrived from the south with a force of about 20,000 troops. The Mexican attack began with a skirmish on the afternoon of February 22 and ended, after a great deal of seesawing, with what amounted to a victory for the vastly outnumbered Americans. Jefferson Davis, future president of the Confederacy during the Civil War, was then a U.S. Army captain and distinguished himself for gallantry during the bloody battle. After the fighting ended late on February 23, the Americans held a distinct advantage and Mexican morale was low. Santa Anna retreated southward during the night. The American victory weakened the Mexican forces and contributed to the success of General Winfield Scott's campaign to the south, which resulted in the fall of Mexico City in September 1847 and the subsequent conclusion of the Mexican War.

February 24

Supreme Court Decides *Marbury* v. *Madison*, Establishing the Doctrine of Judicial Review

In what was possibly the most important decision in American legal history, on February 24, 1803, the Supreme Court issued its decision in the case of *Marbury* v. *Madison*. The case established the doctrine of judicial review, while establishing the Supreme Court's right to determine the constitutionality or unconstitutionality of laws.

After the American Revolution, American politics was dominated by two political parties, the Federalists and the Democratic-Republicans. In general, the Federalists believed in a strong central government and the development of an industrial economy similar to that of England. The Democratic-Republicans, founded by Thomas Jefferson, believed in limited central government, states' rights, and preserving the traditional American agrarian economy. The first two presidents of the United States, George Washington and John Adams, were Federalists. In the election of 1800, however, Thomas Jefferson narrowly emerged as the victor.

Federalist president John Adams had until March 3, 1801, to serve out his term before Jefferson became president. He used this time to appoint dozens of sympathetic Federalists to the federal judiciary, including 42 justices of the peace for the District of Columbia. Although these commissions were signed and sealed by the end of Adams's term, they had not been delivered by the time Jefferson became president. Jefferson ordered James Madison, the new secretary of state and the individual now holding the commissions, not to deliver them. He took the position that the commissions were invalid and of no effect until such time as they were delivered.

One of the Federalist appointees, William Marbury, decided to challenge the actions of the Jefferson administration. He filed a petition with the Supreme Court on December 16, 1801, which for procedural reasons named James Madison personally as the defendant. The petition requested that the Supreme Court use its power under the Judiciary Act of 1789 to order Madison to deliver the commission that would make Marbury a justice of the peace. The Judiciary Act clearly gave the Supreme Court the power to grant Marbury's petition by issuing a "writ of mandamus."

Granting Marbury's request would have been an easy decision for Supreme Court justice John Marshall, since Marshall was a Federalist who had served as President Adams's secretary of state in the previous administration and had signed and sealed the very commissions that were at issue in this lawsuit. However, Marshall was conscious of the fact that the Supreme Court and the federal judiciary in general were the weakest of the three branches of government. Unlike the executive branch of the presidency, which controls the military and the agencies of government, or the legislative branch of Congress, which controls taxation and spending, the Supreme Court and the judiciary have little more than the respect and prestige given to them by the Constitution and the public to enforce their decisions. At the time, this level of respect was limited, since the Constitution was only a few years old. Therefore, Marshall was cautious about issuing an order against the Jefferson administration that he could not really enforce and

that might prove to be an embarrassment for the Court should Jefferson refuse to obey it. However, Marshall was conscious of the need to take some sort of strong action, and to assert the Court's authority in some respect.

Marshall and the other Supreme Court justices resolved both problems masterfully. The decision in *Marbury* v. *Madison* stated that Marbury's legal rights had indeed been violated by the Jefferson administration, and that Marbury was clearly entitled to the order he requested under the Judiciary Act, but that the Judiciary Act in giving the Supreme Court this power had overstepped the boundaries set forth by the Constitution and was thus invalid. The Supreme Court thus declared that the Judiciary Act was unconstitutional, and held that it was the Supreme Court's right and power to declare whether acts of Congress were constitutionally permissible. In refusing to take on Jefferson directly, Marshall had indirectly asserted a greater and more significant power for the Court, namely the principle of judicial review.

The Supreme Court's decision left William Marbury empty-handed, even though the Court had clearly stated that Jefferson had acted wrongly. Nevertheless, *Marbury* v. *Madison* was a positive development in the evolution of the American judicial system and the separation of powers among the three branches of government. It gave the Supreme Court the power to strike down unconstitutional laws while recognizing the limitations that the Constitution puts on the Court with respect to interference in the other branches of government.

Chester Nimitz's Birthday

Chester William Nimitz, who became commander in chief of the U.S. Pacific Fleet in World War II and led the American naval forces to victory in the Pacific, was born on February 24, 1885, in Fredericksburg, Texas. While still in high school, Nimitiz hoped to become a soldier, and applied for entrance to the United States Military Academy at West Point. Lack of vacancies there, however, led him to take a qualifying examination for entrance into the Naval Academy at Annapolis. He passed the examination and in 1901, at the age of 15, was admitted to the academy. He never actually received his high school diploma until October 1945, a month after he signed the Japanese surrender papers at the end of World War II. On that occasion, the 60-year-old Nimitz, dressed in his fleet admiral's uniform and escorted by cowboys on horseback, rode on a horse-drawn buckboard from his nearby boyhood home to receive his long-awaited diploma at a ceremony at the Tivy High School in Kerrville, Texas.

At Annapolis, Nimitz excelled in mathematics and physical education. In January 1905, he graduated seventh in his class, with the rank of midshipman. He served on the battleship *Ohio* and other ships before being transferred to submarine duty. He was given command of the submarine *Plunger*, and later rose to command the Atlantic Submarine Flotilla in the years leading up to World War I. During this time, he was awarded a Silver Life Saving Medal for bravery in saving one of his crewmen from drowning.

Shortly after his marriage to Catherine Vance Freeman in 1913, Nimitz spent a brief time in Germany and Belgium studying diesel engines. Returning to the United States that same year, he applied his new knowledge to the building of the navy's first diesel engine for the oil tanker *Maumee*, and in 1916, already a lieutenant commander, he served as that vessel's executive officer and chief engineer. During World War I, from August 1917 to February 1918, Nimitz was again assigned to submarines, as aide and later as chief of staff to Rear Admiral Samuel B. Robison, commander of the Atlantic Submarine Fleet.

In the following years, Nimitz held numerous posts on shore and at sea. In 1920 he received the Victory Medal with Escort Clasp for his services as commander of the cruiser *Chicago*. In 1926, now a commander, Nimitz was sent to establish a Naval Reserve Officers' Training Corps unit at the University of California. He subsequently commanded two different submarine divisions and various surface vessels. Then, from 1935 to 1938, he served as assistant chief of the Bureau of Navigation, assuming duty as chief of that bureau in 1939.

By 1938 Nimitz had reached the rank of rear admiral, and in 1940 he was one of the two candidates for the post of commander in chief of the Pacific Fleet. Although the assignment was given to the other candidate, Husband E. Kimmel, the latter's service in that capacity was short-lived. The Japanese surprise attack on Pearl Harbor on December 7, 1941, which precipitated the U.S. entry into World War II, changed the course of events for individuals as well as nations. Pending an investigation of the Pearl Harbor disaster, Admiral Kimmel was relieved of his post, and on December 31, 1941, Rear Admiral Nimitz became the new commander in chief of the Pacific Fleet.

In April 1942, Nimitz assumed the additional title of Commander in Chief, Pacific Ocean Areas. The U.S. Joint Chiefs of Staff, which supervised the war effort, divided the Pacific Ocean into three areas for organizational purposes, and put them under Nimitz's authority. These were the North Pacific Area (above the 42nd parallel); the

Central Pacific Area (including the Hawaiian, Marshall, Mariana, Caroline, Palau, and Ryukyu islands, as well as Midway, Tarawa, and Iwo Jima); and the South Pacific Area (south of the equator). As the war progressed, Nimitz retained direct command of the first two areas while delegating direction of forces in the third area at first to Vice Admiral Robert L. Ghormley and later to Admiral William F. Halsey. The overall command of Nimitz, whose subordinates also included admirals Thomas C. Kinkaid, Marc A. Mitscher, Richmond K. Turner, and Raymond A. Spruance, complemented that of General Douglas MacArthur, supreme commander of the Allied forces in the Southwest Pacific Area.

Nimitz set out to chart the course of victory almost immediately after assuming his new command. While new ships were being built to replace those lost at Pearl Harbor, he strengthened his combat teams and established repair stations and maintenance squadrons to support his new fleet. Under his direction, the Pacific Fleet was rebuilt to a strength of some 2 million men and 1,000 ships. As fast as men, ships, and weapons became available, he switched from defensive to offensive operations, successfully engaging the Japanese in the battle of the Coral Sea and at Midway. A later series of successful battles included action at Tarawa in the Gilbert Islands in late 1943, a great naval victory in the battle of the Philippine Sea (also known as the first battle of the Philippines) in June 1944, and the occupation of the adjacent Mariana Islands, including Saipan, Guam, and Tinian, in June and July of the same year. Occupation of the Palau Islands (Peleliu, Angaur, Ulithi, and others), located southwest of the Marianas, followed. A presidential citation summarized Nimitz's contribution to the final victory:

> Initiating the final phase in the battle for victory in the Pacific, [he] attacked the Marianas, invading Saipan, inflicting a decisive defeat on the Japanese Fleet in the First Battle of the Philippines and capturing Guam and Tinian. In vital continuing operations, his Fleet Forces isolated the enemy-held bastions of the Central and Eastern Carolines and secured in quick succession Peleliu, Angaur and Ulithi.

With the landings in the Palaus in mid-September 1944, forces under Nimitz had advanced more than 4,500 miles across the Pacific from Hawaii since the American entry into the war. After difficult early campaigns in southeastern New Guinea and New Britain, forces under General MacArthur had meanwhile traversed nearly 1,500 miles from the Admiralty Islands by way of northwestern New Guinea to the island of

Morotai. The twin drives under Nimitz and Mac-Arthur brought the Allies to the threshold of the Japanese-held Philippine Islands. The presidential citation quoted above continued with a description of the climactic joint operations to liberate the Philippines:

> With reconnaissance of the main beaches on [the island of] Leyte effected, approach channels cleared and opposition neutralized . . . the challenge by powerful task forces of the Japanese Fleet resulted in a historic victory in the three-phased Battle for Leyte Gulf.

One of the great naval battles of modern times, the Battle of Leyte Gulf in October 1944 dissipated the Japanese naval threat and allowed Allied land forces to continue their advances until Luzon, the chief Philippine island, was finally declared secure in July 1945.

After Leyte came the successful amphibious assaults on Iwo Jima and Okinawa. Marine, army, and naval forces cooperated against bitter Japanese opposition in various stages of these two bloody campaigns. While the battles raged, Japanese suicide planes inflicted heavy damage in an attempt to drive Allied naval power from the western Pacific. The attempt was unsuccessful, however, and the two hard-fought actions took the Allied Pacific forces to the doorstep of Japan. Even when their situation became desperate, the Japanese authorities at first refused to heed the surrender ultimatum issued in late July 1945 during the conference of Allied leaders at Potsdam, Germany. (The Potsdam Conference of U.S. president Truman, British prime minister Churchill, and Soviet premier Stalin followed the surrender of Nazi Germany, Japan's World War II ally, in early May 1945.) The Japanese did not surrender until after the United States used atomic bombs against the Japanese cities of Hiroshima and Nagasaki in early August 1945.

Nimitz rose to the rank of five-star admiral shortly thereafter. On September 2, 1945, aboard the USS *Missouri* in Tokyo Bay, he participated in the signing of the Japanese surrender papers, which formally brought World War II to a close. Before and after the war's end, Admiral Nimitz was the recipient of scores of honors, both in the United States and abroad. They included at least 19 honorary degrees. More than a dozen foreign nations awarded Nimitz their major decorations, while the United States paid tribute to him by designating October 5, 1945, as Nimitz Day in Washington, D.C. The occasion was observed with a ceremony at the White House, during which President Harry S. Truman presented Admiral Nimitz with a medal for his wartime service as commander in chief of the Pacific Fleet and Pacific Ocean Areas.

After World War II, Nimitz remained on continuous active duty in the navy, serving in various capacities. From December 1945 to December 1947 he was chief of naval operations, and in 1948, in San Francisco, he served as special assistant to the secretary of the navy on the Western Sea Frontier. After 1947 he made his home at the Naval Quarters on Yerba Buena Island in San Francisco, where he lived for the rest of his life. Nimitz died on February 20, 1966, four days before his 81st birthday. Learning of his death, Secretary of Defense Robert S. McNamara said: "The world has lost a distinguished citizen whose energies and vision were devoted without stint to a long lifetime of service. In the death of Admiral Nimitz the nation has lost one of our greatest naval leaders."

Arizona Territory Established

Arizona, which earlier had been part of the Territory of New Mexico, was organized as a separate territory by an act of Congress on February 24, 1863 (see also February 14, Arizona Admitted to the Union). The new territorial government was organized at Navajo Springs on December 29, 1863.

The centennial of Arizona's creation as a territory was marked in various parts of the state in 1963 and 1964. In Phoenix, an historical pageant was presented nightly from April 19 to 28, 1963, at the state fairgrounds. Called *The Arizona Story*, the pageant involved a cast of about 1,000 (not to mention cattle, horses, and covered wagons) and traced the region's history from the time of Spanish conquistadores to the present day.

Phoenix has been the capital of Arizona since 1889, when it was made the capital of the Arizona Territory.

February 25

Sixteenth Amendment Ratified

The United States Constitution of 1787 placed certain restrictions on the federal government's power to levy direct taxes on citizens such as the modern federal income tax. The Founding Fathers were sensitive to the concerns of the states, who in 1787 had reservations about submitting themselves to federal authority, so they inserted legal requirements that essentially made it very difficult to impose a federal income tax.

For over a century, the federal government did not really need an income tax. The budget was small, except in times of national crisis such as the Civil War, and import tariffs were more than sufficient to fund federal programs. By the late 19th century, however, the United States was becoming one of the world's great powers. The federal government was building a modern military establishment and had an expanding bureaucracy, and pressure was growing for new social programs. To help raise the necessary revenue, Congress attempted to impose a mild tax on upper-class incomes, but the legislation was struck down by the Supreme Court as unconstitutional.

As with all provisions of the Constitution, the restriction on income taxes could be eliminated through an amendment approved by two-thirds of both the House of Representatives and the Senate and subsequently ratified by three-fourths of the states. The 16th Amendment to the Constitution was sent to the state legislatures for ratification by the 61st Congress in 1909, and was declared ratified in 1913. This amendment provides for a federal income tax, stating in its entirety that "The Congress shall have power to lay and collect taxes on incomes, from whatever sources derived, without apportionment among the several States, and without regard to any census or enumeration." Despite its many flaws, the income tax that was subsequently imposed has enabled the federal government to finance many necessary programs.

National Bank Act

During the Civil War, the Union government found it necessary to borrow large amounts of money to finance the war effort. Unfortunately, there was no national banking system under federal control: Two attempts at creating a permanent federal bank of the United States had failed. Further, there was no real supervision over the banking system in general, and anyone who complied with a number of minimal requirements could organize a bank. The needs of the Union government, coupled with the losses and confusion resulting from uncertain banking conditions in much of the country, prompted plans to create a more satisfactory banking system.

Soon after the start of the Civil War, it was proposed that banks be permitted to organize under a new federal law and issue circulating notes based on government bonds. These bonds, purchased from the government by the banks, were to serve as security for their notes. It was some time, however, before Congress was able to agree on the plan. Finally, in February 1863, the legislation usually referred to as the National Bank Act was

passed. It was signed by President Abraham Lincoln on February 25, 1963. This act, together with amendments adopted later, authorized banks to be incorporated throughout the country under federal law and to operate in a strictly controlled way, thus supplying the nation with a safe, uniform bank-note currency. The act established minimums for cash reserves and provided that part of the reserves could be deposited in certain central reserve banks. In addition, it regulated the capital of the banks according to population.

It was hoped that the act would create a market for government bonds, but at first the plan did not work as well as expected. However, when an act was passed by Congress in March 1865 imposing a prohibitive 10 percent tax on the circulating notes of nonfederal banks, more than 1,000 of them converted themselves into federal banks by taking out federal charters. One of the purposes of the tax was also to force the notes of the state banks out of circulation, since many of these banks had abused their power to issue bank notes.

The power to issue bank notes that circulate as money was retained by the national banks until March 11, 1935. In actual practice, however, the note-issuing function had gradually been taken over by the Federal Reserve Banks since the creation of the Federal Reserve System as the central bank of the United States in 1913. Comprised of 12 regional banks, the Federal Reserve System is coordinated by a central board in Washington, D.C. The National Bank Act was an important stepping stone on the path toward the creation of the modern federal banking system.

February 26

Grand Canyon National Park Established

On February 26, 1919, Congress acted to protect one of America's greatest natural landmarks by establishing the Grand Canyon National Park. This scenic treasure, carved out by the Colorado River over millions of years, cuts through northwest Arizona and covers over a million acres. Millions of tourists visit the site every year.

The first people to see the Grand Canyon were Stone Age hunter-gatherers who had crossed over into North America from Asia and were migrating southward. At the time, the eastern tip of Siberia and the western tip of Alaska were not separated by the Bering Strait, so the ancestors of today's Native Americans had come into the New World. Apparently bands of hunter-gatherers lived in the Grand Canyon vicinity for roughly ten thousand years.

Somewhere between 1000 B.C. and A.D. 1000, a more advanced, agricultural civilization arose, dominated by the Anasazi people. They built well-organized and prosperous communities called pueblos, and traded extensively with neighboring societies. By A.D. 1300, however, most of the Anasazi communities in the Grand Canyon region had been abandoned, for reasons that are unclear but which may relate to the limited water supply and the difficulty of supporting a large agricultural community in an arid terrain.

By the time of the Spanish arrival in the New World, the Navajo were the dominant Native American tribe in the Grand Canyon region, and their people have survived into modern times, now inhabiting a reservation located near the national park itself. In the 16th century, explorers under the leadership of Francisco Vásquez de Coronado became the first European to see the Grand Canyon. The Grand Canyon region became part of the territory of the Spanish empire in the New World, but outside of such settlements as Santa Fe, New Mexico, the Spanish took little interest in developing the region.

When the United States began to expand westward, American frontiersmen opened the Santa Fe Trail between American settlements in Missouri and the Spanish southwest. The land-hungry Americans forced Mexico, which inherited the area from Spain when Mexico gained its independence, to cede the modern-day southwestern region of the United States after the Mexican War of 1848. The Grand Canyon thus became the possession of the United States.

Until the Civil War, the Grand Canyon area was considered largely inhospitable, fit only for outlaws and renegade Native American tribes. In the late 19th century, however, the era of the "robber barons" began. The West was open to mining companies looking to exploit natural resources, and there were no restrictions on the methods used for extracting valuable metals from the land. Many Americans, including President Theodore Roosevelt, became increasingly concerned about the effects of unrestricted development and mining on the natural beauty of the rapidly diminishing frontier. After a visit to the Grand Canyon in 1903, Roosevelt saw to the passage of legislation that increased federal protection for the canyon and gave it the status of a national monument.

It was the act of February 26, 1919, that first made the Grand Canyon a national park. In 1975, federal protection was further expanded by the administration of President Gerald Ford, who acted to roughly double the size of the park. Today, the Grand Canyon National Park is one of the most popular tourist attractions in the country.

Buffalo Bill's Birthday

The famed scout, "Indian fighter," and showman William Frederick Cody, popularly known as Buffalo Bill, was born on a farm near Le Claire in Scott County, Iowa, on February 26, 1846. Cody spent part of his childhood in Kansas after his father, Isaac Cody, moved to Salt Creek Valley, near Fort Leavenworth, in 1854. Left to his own resources after his father's death in 1857, and having received little schooling, Cody began to work at the age of 11 as a mounted messenger for the freighting firm of Russell, Majors and Waddell. In 1860, when the firm initiated the Pony Express, Cody, at the age of 14, was among its first riders.

Cody's scouting career began early in the Civil War. In 1863 he served as a Union scout with the Ninth Kansas Cavalry in its operations against the Kiowa and Comanche native tribes, and in 1864 he enlisted in the regular United States Army and again served as a scout in military campaigns in Tennessee and Missouri.

After the Civil War, from 1867 to 1868, Cody was employed by the firm of Goddard Brothers to provide buffalo meat for the builders of the Kansas Pacific Railroad. His exceptional hunting skills soon earned him the nickname of Buffalo Bill; he estimated that he killed 4,280 buffalo within 17 months. He returned to scouting in 1868, serving as chief scout for the Fifth U.S. Cavalry for four years. In 1872 he was persuaded by Colonel E. Z. C. Judson, who wrote under the name of Ned Buntline, to appear in his play based on Cody's scouting adventures, *Scouts of the Prairies*. Cody played the leading role for four years. Then, in 1876, he rejoined the U.S. Army in a war against the Sioux tribe. That year, during one of the campaigns of the war, Cody killed the Cheyenne chief Yellow Hand in a duel. The story of that feat quickly spread through the popular dime novels of the day, making Buffalo Bill a hero of the wild West.

In 1872 Cody was elected to the Nebraska legislature, but he declined to serve. With a partner, he established a cattle ranch north of North Platte, Nebraska, which later served as rehearsal grounds for his Wild West Show. In 1882 he organized a rodeo at the request of the North Platte citizens as a Fourth of July celebration. On that occasion, Buffalo Bill presented a three-day western show, complete with cowboys and Indians, buffalo and bronco riding. Its success led to the organization in 1883 of the traveling Wild West Show, which played to enthusiastic audiences throughout America and Europe. In 1887 the show played in London for Queen Victoria's Jubilee, and in 1893 it scored a great success at Chicago's World's Fair.

It featured such personalities as sharpshooter Annie Oakley and, for one season, Chief Sitting Bull. In the last Sioux resurgence of 1890–1891, William Cody and the Native Americans who toured with his show were involved in the peace negotiations.

After 1894 Cody made his home on the TE Ranch in Wyoming. He continued to tour with his show, and at the same time devoted much energy to the development of the surrounding country. Fond of the home of his last 20 years, Cody wanted to be buried on Cedar Mountain overlooking the Buffalo Bill Dam and the town of Cody. However, he fell ill en route to his home and died in Denver, Colorado, on January 10, 1917. He was buried atop Colorado's Lookout Mountain, some 16 miles west of Denver, within sight of the Continental Divide and a magnificent panorama of the Rocky Mountains. His burial ground became the site of a museum containing his guns, clothing, and other mementos.

The hero of numerous western tales, Buffalo Bill was himself the author of several books describing his frontier adventures. Among them was an autobiography entitled *The Life of Hon. William F. Cody Known as Buffalo Bill*.

February 27

Henry Wadsworth Longfellow's Birthday

Henry Wadsworth Longfellow, one of the most popular American poets of the 19th century, was born on February 27, 1807, in Portland, Maine. His poems are some of the most widely read works in English, and have been translated into dozens of other languages. During Longfellow's lifetime his popularity in England rivaled that of Alfred Lord Tennyson, the British poet laureate. The Poet's Corner of Westminster Abbey displays a memorial bust of Longfellow, the first American to be so honored.

His father, Stephen Longfellow, was a prosperous lawyer and a trustee of Bowdoin College in Brunswick, Maine. His mother, born Zilpah Wadsworth, was descended from the Mayflower Pilgrims John Alden and Priscilla Mullens Alden. In highly fictionalized form, Longfellow told the story of these two famous forebears in his long narrative poem "The Courtship of Miles Standish."

Longfellow entered Bowdoin College as a sophomore and graduated in 1825 in the same class as Nathaniel Hawthorne and one class behind Franklin Pierce, who later became the 14th president of the United States. Although his father

wanted him to be a lawyer, Longfellow decided to pursue a literary career. Bowdoin provided an acceptable solution to both father and son by offering Longfellow a newly created professorship in modern languages and sending him to Europe for three years of preparation for the new post. By the time he returned to the United States to take up his teaching duties at Bowdoin late in 1829, Longfellow had a knowledge of French, Spanish, German, and Italian. He remained at Bowdoin until 1835, when he resigned. After another year of study in Europe, he became professor of modern languages and belles-lettres at Harvard. During that year of study abroad, Longfellow's first wife, the former Mary Potter, died in childbirth.

Longfellow's long and distinguished career at Harvard and his many contributions to the teaching of modern languages and literature have been overshadowed by his own writings. He was at Harvard for 18 years (1836–1854), during which time he introduced thousands of students to the literary treasures of Europe, some of which he himself had translated. He resigned from his Harvard professorship when he was 47 years old to devote himself to writing.

The year after his resignation he brought out "The Song of Hiawatha," one of his most famous poems, and three years later "The Courtship of Miles Standish." His "Tales of a Wayside Inn" was nearly completed when tragedy shook his life. His second wife Frances was burned to death when she accidentally set her dress on fire in 1861. Longfellow subsequently immersed himself in work, which included translating Dante's *Divine Comedy*. His other works include "The Psalm of Life," "The Wreck of the Hesperus," "The Village Blacksmith," "Excelsior," and "Evangeline."

Longfellow died on March 24, 1882, having achieved fame and wealth. His influence on American poetry and literature was enormous. When the Hall of Fame for Great Americans was opened in New York City in 1900, he was among the first to be elected for inclusion.

Twenty-second Amendment Ratified

When the founding fathers drew up the United States Constitution in 1787, they devoted considerable attention to the office of the president. They specified who would be eligible to hold the office, outlined the manner in which the chief executive was to be elected, detailed his (or her) powers and duties, and provided for the president's removal if convicted of "treason, bribery, or other high crimes and misdemeanors." Yet nowhere in the original frame of government did the founders of the nation set a limit upon the number of four-year terms that an individual could hold as president. Not until 164 years after the adoption of the Constitution, when ratification of the 22nd Amendment was completed on February 27, 1951, was a restriction placed on the number of terms a president could serve.

Even though the federal Constitution had not specifically limited the period that any individual could serve as chief executive, George Washington, the first president, began the tradition of stepping down from office after two terms. From 1796 until 1940, all of the presidents followed Washington's example. President Ulysses S. Grant considered running for a third term, but he abandoned the notion after the House of Representatives passed a nonbinding resolution strongly supporting the tradition of a two-term limit. Then, in 1940, President Franklin D. Roosevelt broke the tradition. Roosevelt, a Democrat, ran for and won a third term as president in 1940, and then, four years later, ran again and was elected for a fourth term.

Roosevelt's long tenure as president dismayed many people. The Republicans felt that his personal popularity and charisma denied a perhaps equally qualified member of their party from being elected president; other individuals, for less partisan reasons, argued that such monopolization of so powerful an office might one day lead to authoritarian rule. During Roosevelt's lifetime, Congress took no official action on the matter of presidential tenure. Two years after his death, however, Congress in March 1947 submitted the 22nd Amendment to the states for approval.

It took nearly four years for the amendment to be approved by the requisite three-fourths of the states. There were only 48 states at the time, so ratification was completed when the 36th state, Minnesota, approved the amendment on February 27, 1951. Administrator of General Services Jess Larson certified on March 1, 1951, that the new addition to the Constitution had been adopted by the required number of states.

The 22nd Amendment establishes two terms as the maximum length of time any one person can hold the nation's highest office. The amendment also sets a limit of one additional term for any person who served more than two years of a term to which another individual had been elected. This means that when a president dies in office, and the vice president becomes president, if the vice president is president for two years or more he or she can run for only one more term. However, this latter provision did "not apply to any person holding the office of President, when this Article was proposed by the Congress." Thus, Vice President Harry S. Truman, who became president upon Roosevelt's death in April 1945, served the three remaining years of his predecessor's term, and then was elected to his own four-year term in 1948, could have sought another term as president in 1952. Truman chose not to run again, however.

State Department Blames Vietnam War on Communist Aggression

On February 27, 1965, the United States Department of State released an official report concerning the Vietnam War. It is a fascinating historical piece from the cold war, viewing the Vietnam conflict entirely through the narrow ideological prism of the time. The legitimate historical, economic, social, and political grievances of the Vietnamese people are brushed aside, and the blame for the war is placed squarely on the communist North Vietnamese. Edited excerpts from this report, entitled "Aggression from the North," are set forth below. The viewpoints expressed therein, such as the statement that "the war in Vietnam is not a spontaneous and local rebellion against the established government," help explain why the American government would stubbornly cling to the Vietnam conflict for another decade.

South Vietnam is fighting for its life against a brutal campaign of terror and armed attack inspired, directed, supplied and controlled by the Communist regime in Hanoi [the capital of North Vietnam]. This flagrant aggression has been going on for years, but recently the pace has quickened and the threat has now become acute.

The war in Vietnam is a new kind of war, a fact as yet poorly understood in most parts of the world. Much of the confusion that prevails in the thinking of many people, and even governments, stems from this basic misunderstanding. In Vietnam a totally new brand of aggression has been loosed against an independent people who want to make their way in peace and freedom.

Above all, the war in Vietnam is not a spontaneous and local rebellion against the established government.

In Vietnam a Communist government has set out deliberately to conquer a sovereign people in a neighboring state. And to achieve its end, it has used every resource of its own government to carry out its carefully planned program of concealed aggression. North Vietnam's commitment to seize control of the South is no less total than was the commitment of the regime in North Korea in 1950. But knowing the consequences of the latter's undisguised attack, the planners in Hanoi have tried desperately to conceal their hand. They have failed and their aggression is as real as that of an invading army.

This report is a summary of the massive evidence of North Vietnamese aggression obtained by the Government of South Vietnam. This evidence has been jointly analyzed by South Vietnamese and American experts. The evidence shows that the hard core of the Communist forces attacking South Vietnam were trained in the North and ordered into the South by Hanoi. It shows that the key leadership of the Vietcong, the officers and much of the cadre, many of the technicians, political organizers, and propagandists have come from the North and operate under Hanoi's direction. It shows that the training of essential military personnel and their infiltration into the South is directed by the Military High Command in Hanoi. In recent months new types of weapons have been introduced in the VC army, for which all ammunition must come from outside sources. Communist China and other Communist states have been the prime suppliers of these weapons and ammunition, and they have been channeled primarily through North Vietnam.

The directing force behind the effort to conqueror South Vietnam is the Communist Party in the North, the Lao Dong (Workers) Party. As in every Communist state, the party is an integral part of the regime itself. North Vietnamese officials have expressed their firm determination to absorb South Vietnam into the Communist world. Through its Central Committee, which controls the Government of the North, the Lao Dong Party directs the total political and military effort of the Vietcong. The Military High Command in the North trains the military men and sends them into South Vietnam. The Central Research Agency, North Vietnam's central intelligence organization, directs the elaborate espionage and subversion effort.

Under Hanoi's overall direction, the Communists have established an extensive machine for carrying on the war within South Vietnam.

The focal point is the Central Office for South Vietnam with its political and military subsections and other specialized agencies. A subordinate part of this Central Office is the Liberation Front for South Vietnam. The front was formed at Hanoi's order in 1960. Its principal function is to influence opinion abroad and to create the false impression that the aggression in South Vietnam is an indigenous rebellion against the established Government.

For more than ten years the people and the Government of South Vietnam, exercising the inherent right of self-defense, have fought back against these efforts to extend Communist power south across the 17th parallel. The United States has responded to the appeals of the Government of the Republic of Vietnam for help in this defense of the freedom and independence of its land and its people.

The record is conclusive. It establishes beyond question that North Vietnam is carrying out a carefully conceived plan of aggression against the South. It shows that North Vietnam has intensified its efforts in the years since it was condemned by the International Control Commission. It proves that Hanoi continues to press its systematic program of armed aggression into South Vietnam. This aggression violates the United Nations Charter. It is directly contrary to the Geneva Accords of 1954 and of 1962 to which North Vietnam is a party. It is a fundamental threat to the freedom and security of South Vietnam.

The people of South Vietnam have chosen to resist this threat. At their request, the United States has taken its place beside them in their defensive struggle.

The United States seeks no territory, no military bases, no favored position. But we have learned the meaning of aggression elsewhere in the post-war world, and we have met it.

If peace can be restored in South Vietnam, the United States will be ready at once to reduce its military involvement. But it will not abandon friends who want to remain free. It will do what must be done to help them. The choice now between peace and continued and increasingly destructive conflict is one for the authorities in Hanoi to make.

February 28

Explosion of the "Peacemaker"

The United States Navy steamship *Princeton* lay in the Potomac River in February 1844 waiting to be shown off. Captain Robert F. Stockton, the commander, had invited President John Tyler; his cabinet; many members of Congress; the president's fiancée, Julia Gardiner; and approximately 300 other distinguished guests to take an excursion aboard the *Princeton* on February 28. They would be able to inspect the first warship to be driven by a screw propeller. The ship had a steam power plant and an iron hull that made it virtually invulnerable to enemy shot and shell.

The *Princeton* was designed by John Ericsson, whose most famous design, the ironclad *Monitor*, was to make history in the Civil War. A naturalized American citizen of Swedish origin, Ericsson was to contribute greatly to the American military through his many marine designs and ordnance inventions.

One of his earliest interests was artillery. Because of the limitations of 19th-century technology, the forging and casting of cannons was a tremendous challenge. By trying a new approach, Ericsson forged a huge cannon named "the Oregon." Perhaps the most enormous cannon in any navy of the time, it had a 12-inch bore, was 13 feet long, weighed 16,000 pounds, and fired 225-pound cannonballs. It was carefully designed with iron reinforcing bands. Ericsson tested his masterpiece hundreds of times at a naval testing ground at Sandy Hook, New Jersey. The cannon's breech developed a crack during the test firing, but after reinforcement it was as strong as ever, and was mounted on the *Princeton*'s foredeck.

Captain Stockton was pleased with the Oregon, but not satisfied. He had also grown inordinately resentful of the talented Ericsson. The captain decided that he should have two great cannons instead of one, and set about the task of providing the second one himself, ignoring Ericsson's cautions about the difficulties and dangers inherent in iron forging and cannon casting. At the Hamersley Foundry in Philadelphia, Pennsylvania, far from Ericsson's interference, Stockton produced what he considered his masterpiece. The Peacemaker, bigger than the Oregon except for the equal bore, was 14 feet long, weighed 25,000 pounds, and was a foot thicker at the breech than the Oregon. But it was without reinforcing bands. And it had not been carefully tested before it was mounted alongside the Oregon.

On the day of the great excursion, the *Princeton* steamed down the Potomac, and the guests gathered around for the firing of the Peacemaker. The Oregon was ignored, as was the absent Ericsson, who was never invited to set foot aboard the ship he had designed. Loaded with 40 pounds of powder for each 225-pound cannonball, the Peacemaker impressed the guests, as was intended. After three or four balls had been shot, Captain Stockton invited the guests to move to the dining room below where they would enjoy drinks, music, and a sumptuous banquet.

During the festivities, a ship's officer informed the captain that a guest was above and requested another firing of the Peacemaker. The captain refused, until he learned that the request came from Secretary of the Navy Thomas W. Gilmer. Stockton went up on deck to do the actual firing himself. A number of guests gathered around the cannon to watch. The Peacemaker was loaded with 25 pounds of powder, a smaller charge than usual. Yet when it was fired, a tremendous explosion shook the ship. The left side of the Peacemaker burst, and several thousand pounds of iron fragments went hurtling into the crowd gathered to the left of the cannon.

Among those killed were Secretary of State Abel P. Upshur; Secretary of the Navy Gilmer; Virgil Maxcy, former charge d'affaires in Belgium; Commodore Beverly Kennon, chief of the navy's Bureau of Construction; David Gardiner, father of the president's fiancée; President Tyler's personal servant of many years; and two members of the cannon crew. Among those stunned by the explosion but not seriously injured were Captain Stockton and nine sailors. Senator Thomas Hart Benton of Missouri suffered a burst eardrum, while Mrs. Gilmer, remarkably, was unhurt.

The *Princeton* set forth for Alexandria, Virginia (which is across the Potomac from Washington, D.C., and was then a port town), at full speed, and anchored around 4:30 p.m. The passengers were taken back to Washington, D.C., by the steamer *I. Johnson*. The next day the bodies of the dead were moved to the White House, where they lay in state in the East Room until the funeral, which took place at the Capitol on Saturday, March 2, 1844. A committee appointed to investigate the tragedy exonerated Captain Stockton.

Linus Pauling's Birthday

Linus Carl Pauling, one of America's greatest scientists, was born on February 28, 1901 in Portland, Oregon. His father, Herman W. Pauling, died when Linus was nine years old. Linus entered Oregon Agricultural College in 1917, and eventually graduated from the California Institute of Technology ("Cal Tech") in 1925 with his Ph.D. in Chemistry.

Pauling became a professor of chemistry at Cal Tech, and began to experiment in the fields of X-ray crystallography, molecular bonds, and quantum mechanics. The result was the landmark treatise *The Nature of the Chemical Bond*, published in 1939. This book alone would have established Pauling as one of America's premier scientists. It explains how molecules are formed and held together and also examines the complex interactions between atoms of carbon, hydrogen, and other elements within organic molecules.

During the 1950s Pauling's work in the area of organic chemistry led him to take an interest in the search for the structure of the DNA molecule. At the time, DNA was known to be the basis of life, but the exact structure of the molecule was unknown. In 1953 Pauling claimed to have solved the riddle of DNA's structure, but his structural hypothesis proved to be wrong and he lost the DNA race to James D. Watson and Francis Crick, who discovered the famous double-helix structure. Pauling continued to be an active researcher, however. For example, his studies helped pinpoint the cause of sickle cell anemia, which afflicts millions of people. During his career, Pauling would receive two Nobel Prizes.

In addition to his scientific work, Pauling was active in the antiwar movement. He strongly criticized the American government for stockpiling nuclear weapons, and advocated disarmament. His book *No More War!* was published in 1958. He also helped circulate a petition against the testing of nuclear weapons that was eventually signed by thousands of his fellow scientists. Pauling's work in the cause of peace earned him the second of his Nobel Prizes, the Nobel Peace Prize in 1962 (the first was in 1954 for chemistry). Unfortunately, he also had to endure accusations of harboring Communist sympathies.

During the 1970s Pauling developed a fascination with the potential health benefits of vitamin C. He claimed that vitamin C could help prevent both the common cold and cancer. These propositions met with decidedly mixed reactions in the scientific community, although as of this writing there is no conclusive data to either confirm or deny Pauling's beliefs. Pauling died of cancer on August 19, 1994, in Big Sur, California.

R. J. Reynolds Abandons "Smokeless" Cigarette Project

On February 28, 1989, the R. J. Reynolds Tobacco Company terminated the brand of cigarettes known as Premiers. Premiers were supposed to give smokers the taste and pleasure of smoking without most of the smoke and other side effects of ordinary cigarettes. It turned out to be one of the most spectacular failures in corporate history.

R. J. Reynolds is one of the oldest and most respected names in the American tobacco industry. By the 1980s, however, the industry was on the defensive due to the health risks of tobacco. RJR responded in part by diversifying, and acquired Nabisco, a major snack food concern whose product lines include Oreo brand cookies. RJR also decided to invest in "healthier" cigarette projects such as Premiers. However, after nearly half a billion dollars in research and development, Premiers proved to be a disaster. The cigarettes used an advanced carbon filter, but if they were lit with an ordinary match, the sulfur in the match flame precipitated a very unpleasant odor.

By early 1989 RJR had decided to abandon the project rather than pump additional funds into improving Premiers. RJR also had other concerns, such as a lengthy and expensive struggle for ownership of the company during the leveraged-buyout mania of the late 1980s.

February 29

Leap Year

See also the essay in this book's appendix on the Calendar, which contains some discussion on calendar reform and how leap years might one day be eliminated.

Leap Year, which occurs every four years, has 366 days instead of 365, the extra day always falling on February 29. The origin of Leap Year can be traced to the calendar reform initiated by the Roman ruler Julius Caesar and adopted in 45 B.C. After consulting his astronomers, Caesar determined that the solar year was 365 days and six hours long. At the end of four years, the extra six hours per year made an additional day. Caesar therefore decreed that following three years of 365 days each, there should be a fourth year of 366 days. He added the extra day to February, which, having only 28 days, was the shortest month of his new Roman calendar. It was inserted between February 23 and 24.

However, not even Julius Caesar's sweeping reform made the calendar perfectly exact. Since the Earth actually takes 365 days, five hours, 48 minutes, and a little over 45 seconds to revolve around the Sun, Caesar's move to fix the mean length of the year at 365 ¼ days caused an ever widening discrepancy between the Julian calendar and the seasons of the year. In March 1582 Pope Gregory XIII therefore abolished the use of the Julian or Old Style calendar and substituted what became known as the Gregorian or New Style calendar. In so doing, he not only canceled 10 days, but also acted to correct the inaccuracy of the Julian system, which amounted to three days every 400 years. After some calculation, he ordered that Leap Year be omitted in all centenary years from then on, except those that are divisible by 400. Thus, the years 1600 and 2000 are Leap Years because they can be divided by 400, but 1700, 1800, and 1900 are not. The Gregorian calendar brought the calendar year in line with the actual time that it takes the Earth to orbit the Sun, except for a discrepancy of 26 seconds a year, which will add up to a full day only after 3,323 years have passed.

The reason that the English term Leap Year is used for Julius Caesar's innovation is unknown, but a number of explanations have been proposed. According to the most widely held hypothesis, the extra day every four years and the day preceding it were once regarded as one in the eyes of the law. The regular day, however, was deemed the "legal" day, while the additional day was judged not to be legally a day. Lacking legal status in the English courts, February 29 was therefore missed or "leaped over" in the records, since whatever happened on February 29 was dated February 28.

There was once an interesting tradition in the British isles that single women could propose to unmarried men on February 29 and throughout Leap Year. According to popular belief, the association of marriage with Leap Year can be traced to an ancient Irish legend concerning St. Patrick and St. Bridget, set in 5th-century Ireland. Bridget complained to Patrick that her charges in the nunnery were unhappy because they were denied the chance to ever propose marriage. Celibacy in religious orders was then based on private vows, not church requirements. Patrick suggested that women be given the privilege of proposing every seven years. Bridget begged that the right be allowed every four years, and Patrick obliged by granting Leap Year, "the longest of the lot." In 1288 the Scottish Parliament enacted the following law:

> It is statut and ordaint that during the rein of hir maist blissit Megeste, for ilk yeare known as lepe yeare, ilk mayden ladye of bothe highe and lowe estait shall hae liberte to bespeke ye man she likes, albeit he refuses to taik hir to be his lawful wyfe, he shall be mulcted in ye sum ane pundis or less, as his estait may be; except and awis gif he can make it appeare that he is bethrothit ane ither woman he then shall be free.

Similar laws giving women the prerogative to propose during Leap Year were soon introduced on the European continent as well. The custom was legalized throughout France and by the 15th century in parts of Italy, such as Genoa and Florence. It eventually spread to the United States, where it is a well-known tradition, but one that is no longer taken seriously.

Ann Lee's Birthday

Ann Lee was the founder of the Shaker sect in America. Born the daughter of a blacksmith on February 29, 1736, in Manchester, England, Ann was sent to work at an early age with her five brothers and two sisters, and she remained illiterate throughout her life. First she worked as a cotton mill laborer, then as a cook in the Manchester Infirmary, and eventually as a cutter of fur for hats.

In 1758 she joined a society called the Shaking Quakers, or Shakers, which had been formed during the Quaker revival of 1747 under Jane and James Wardley. The arrival in England of some exiled radical French Calvinists known as Camisards had set off the revival, and the name "Shaking Quakers" and soon "Shakers" attached itself to those English Quakers who began to follow Camisard worship, meditating, then trembling, shaking, shouting, marching, and singing.

Four years after becoming a Shaker, Lee married Abraham Standerin (Stanley or Standley in Shaker history), who was a blacksmith in Manchester. Her health seriously declined, and the four children she bore died in infancy. She later became obsessed with the idea that sexual relations were sinful and began to preach celibacy. During a jail term in 1770 for "profaning the Sabbath," she had a vision of Jesus, which confirmed her faith. After her release from prison she continued to preach publicly, and the English Shakers soon acknowledged her as the Wardleys' successor and as their leader. Thereafter she was called Ann the Word or Mother Ann, and her position on sex and marriage was incorporated into Shaker belief. Marriage was not prohibited, but it was held to be imperfect as compared to celibacy, which was intended to make followers less self-seeking and to purify them for the expected Second Coming of Jesus.

In 1774, at the age of 38, Ann Lee felt herself directed in a vision to leave England for the American colonies, which were then on the verge of rebellion against Great Britain. Her band of eight followers arrived in New York City on August 6, 1774, and eventually settled near Albany, New York. For several years they lived communally, constructing buildings and conducting religious meetings. After her death in 1784 the Shakers organized themselves into the United Society of Believers in Christ's Second Appearing.

After Lee left England, the Shakers died out there, but in America the movement continued to grow. Her conversions were greatly helped by the Baptist and Congregational revivalism that swept eastern New York and western Massachusetts in the 1780s. The Shakers refused to bear arms or take oaths, in keeping with their Quaker origins, and thus were suspected of British sympathies during the American Revolution. In July 1780 the authorities in Albany arrested Lee and the Shaker elders on the charge of high treason and imprisoned her for several months.

Mother Ann died on September 8, 1784, at the age of 48. Under her successors, the Shaker sect did reasonably well. Shaker preachers were able to establish five new societies, in Ohio, Kentucky, and Indiana. In 1894 a society was founded as far south as Narcoosee, Florida, but it closed in 1910. In all, 18 Shaker societies have existed in the United States. Shakerism reached its greatest numerical strength in the 1830s, when there were perhaps 6,000 members in the various communities. The sect has become practically extinct in modern times.

Shaker communities were organized in families of 30 to 90 men and women. In these a tension was maintained between separation of, and cooperation between, the sexes. Shaker men and women worked, ate, and slept separately, but their lives were joined in the community, governed by a council of elders. Their separate quarters were together in a single building. The Shaker societies cared for thousands of homeless children and orphans over the years, educating them and teaching them trades. At 21 an individual could leave the community or stay to become a Shaker, as he or she preferred. When married couples wished to join, they tested Shaker life for a trial period. If the couple wished to stay, husband and wife thereafter lived apart, entrusting the care of their children to the community.

March

March, named after Mars, the Roman god of war, is the third month of the modern, or Gregorian, calendar and has 31 days. The early Romans, following a precedent attributed to Romulus, the legendary founder of Rome, started their calendar year with March (Martius). They originally designated only ten months, March through December (seen in the derivation of December from the Latin word for ten, *decem*). It was reputedly the second Roman king, Numa Pompilius (roughly 715–672 B.C.), who divided the previously unnamed "dead" season of midwinter into January and February and added these two months to the end of the other ten. Thus March retained its position as the first month and also continued to be the beginning of the yearly cycle of Roman religious festivals.

In 153 B.C. the Roman state designated January 1 as New Year's Day, thereby turning the 11th month, Januarius, into the first month of the year. This order was kept under the calendar reform that Julius Caesar instituted in 46 B.C., creating the Julian, or Old Style, Calendar (see Appendix A: The Calendar). For a long time, however, older traditions prevailed and most Romans still considered March as the first month. Even after the fall of the Roman Empire and throughout the Middle Ages, local diversity prevailed, although March 25 was generally accepted as the beginning of the calendar year in western Europe. Only with the pope's introduction of the Gregorian, or New Style, calendar in 1582 (see Appendix A: The Calendar) did January 1 assume predominance as New Year's Day in Roman Catholic countries. In most Protestant countries, there was a delay before the new calendar, with its January 1 new year, was adopted. Scotland adopted the January 1 new year, but not the new calendar, in 1600. In England and its colonies the change to the new calendar, decreed by act of Parliament in 1751, became effective in 1752. In the early colonial days in the Americas, the year therefore began in March. Thus a transaction that began on February 27, 1720, and ended on April 2, 1721, lasted only a little more than a month, not 13 months, as might have been thought.

According to Roman belief, the god for whom the month of March was named was the father of Romulus. The second-ranking god after Jupiter, Mars was considered from the earliest times to be one of the most important Roman deities.

Ultimately, he became known as the god of war and guardian of the Roman state. In this capacity, he was served by a warrior-priesthood (the Salii, or "leapers") who were responsible for conducting elaborate festivities in his honor. Numbering 24 and divided into two groups located on the Palatine and Collini Hills, the Salii were arrayed in ancient warrior dress: a short military cloak; helmet; breastplate; sword, spear, or staff; and sacred shields (*ancilia*), said to have been the gift of Jupiter. Thus clad in the symbolic armor of the Roman state, the priests marched about Rome on several occasions during the month of March to herald the coming military campaigns in the spring fighting season. In the course of these processions, they danced, displayed their weapons, chanted to the gods, and offered sacrifices of horses, bulls, and rams. Most important of these festivities dedicated wholly or partially to Mars were Feriae Martius, or New Year's Day in the old Roman calendar (March 1); the second Equirria, when horse races were held on the Campus Martius or "Field of Mars" in preparation for the opening of the season of arms (March 14); Quinquatrus, originally the feast of Mars, later changed into a feast of Minerva (March 19); and Tubilustrium, the purification of the war trumpets (March 23).

Although the Tubilustrium marked the end of the March rites, the god of war was also honored in October, when both the sacred shields and the weapons of the army were purified and retired for winter. The worship of Mars then seems to have been at a standstill, until the advent of spring warfare was announced by the Quirinalia on February 17 (Quirinus closely resembled the war god) and the first Equirria on February 27 (when the cavalry horses were ceremonially purified, or lustrated).

Since spring was the season for renewed activity not only in war but also in agriculture, Mars seems to have appropriately served both as god of war and as god of vegetation. From earliest times, he was invoked to avert storms, disease, and famine, and to promote the prosperity of crops, animals, and farms. Certain characteristics of the Mars cult at Rome bear out his dual role. His festival months of March and October are periods of growth, ripening, and harvesting, while the leaping of his priests also could have been intended to encourage fertility of the soil, especially the growth of grain. Moreover, sacred to Mars were not only the spear and shield but also the wolf, woodpecker, and fig tree. It is therefore evident that Mars became prominent as a chief deity of the Italic peoples early in their settlement of the Italian peninsula, and the Mars cult reflected their daily activities of clearing forests and cultivating crops, as well as of waging war.

The old Saxon name for the month the Romans had called Martius was Hlyd-monath, meaning "the boisterous month"; it was also occasionally called Lencten-monath, meaning "lengthening month," as the days are then perceptibly longer. The Dutch called it Lent-maand for the same reason. In North America, the Sioux, counting their year as starting with the vernal equinox in March, referred to March as the "month of bad eyes." According to an old saying in England and Scotland, possibly based on weather conditions, March borrowed from April the last three days in the month, which are termed the borrowed days. The lucky birthstone often associated with March is the aquamarine, which symbolizes courage.

March 1

Nebraska Admitted to the Union

Nebraska was admitted to the Union on March 1, 1867. Popular history reports that Francisco Vásquez de Coronado entered Nebraska in 1541 during his unsuccessful search for the mythical kingdom of Quivira and the Seven Cities of Cíbo-

la. Many scholars doubt that he visited the region, however. In any event, few followed in Coronado's alleged footsteps during the next two centuries. Fur traders occasionally passed through, and in 1714 French explorer Etienne Veniard, Sieur de Bourgmont, first called the land "Nebraska." The word probably comes from the Oto Indian word *Nebrathka* or *Nibthaska*, meaning "flat water," a reference to the shallow Platte River, a tributary of the Missouri.

The United States acquired title to Nebraska in 1803 as part of the Louisiana Purchase. After that time a number of men investigated the territory, including Lewis and Clark, who passed through in the course of their survey expedition. Major Stephen H. Long called the area a "great desert," which succinctly reported the impression of most early observers.

Beginning in the 1820s, the Platte Valley, Nebraska's most important topographic feature, became a significant part of the road to the Far West. Fur traders were the first Europeans to use the thoroughfare, and the pioneers soon followed. In 1841 the first group of settlers heading for the vast Oregon region passed through the Platte Valley along the south bank of the river. Their path became the Oregon Trail. In 1847 Brigham Young led the Mormons to Utah along the opposite bank.

Nebraska's political history began with Illinois senator Stephen A. Douglas's dream of a transcontinental railroad with Chicago, Illinois, as its eastern terminus. Congress would not authorize construction of the line until there was a civil government established in the sprawling Nebraska region through which the line would have to pass. Southerners were hesitant to organize the territory, as it lay north of the Missouri Compromise line of demarcation between slave states and free states, and so was potentially a free state that would add to the North's political and economic strength. Douglas overcame their objections with his Kansas-Nebraska Act, which nullified the Missouri Compromise by dividing the region into two territories, with the inhabitants of each having the right to permit or prohibit slavery. The act resulted in bloody feuds between the proslavery and antislavery factions, particularly in Kansas, but enabled the region to be organized as territories.

During its territorial period, Nebraska grew slowly but steadily. Omaha was the capital, and Brownville, Nebraska City, Plattsmouth, and Florence became important towns. The chief business of the region was overland transportation, including wagons, stagecoaches, and, in 1860–1861, the Pony Express. The Homestead Act of 1862 (awarding 160 acres to each pioneer who settled the frontier) and the development of the railroads greatly encouraged immigration. The former made it economically feasible for farmers to obtain land, while the latter made it possible to settle in the interior, away from the territory's eastern boundary, the Missouri River.

Nebraskans rejected opportunities to join the Union in 1860 and 1864, but in 1866 they finally approved a constitution drafted by the territorial legislature. Nebraska became the 37th state on March 1, 1867. The representatives of the populous South Platte region controlled the first state legislature, and moved the capital from Omaha to the village of Lancaster, which they renamed Lincoln.

Ohio Admitted to the Union

In 1803 Ohio became the 17th state in the Union. It was the first state to be created from the Northwest Territory acquired from Great Britain after the American Revolution. The date of Ohio's admission to the Union was not definitely designated in 1803. However, during the state's sesquicentennial year of 1953, a joint resolution of Congress declared that Ohio had officially joined the Union on March 1, 1803, the date when its state legislature convened for the first time.

An important step toward the eventual creation of the first state in the Northwest region was taken in 1798, when a census showed that the territory had more than the 5,000 adult male residents required for the territory to advance to the second, or representative, stage of government. In December of that year, Northwest Territory governor Arthur St. Clair issued a proclamation ordering the election of a territorial legislature, which was to meet in Cincinnati. The call to select representatives evoked a mixed response. The inhabitants of what is now Ohio were eager to choose delegates to the proposed legislative gathering, but the residents of the more westerly regions of the Northwest Territory were reluctant to assume the financial burden of sending representatives to distant Cincinnati.

The western regions' reluctance to send delegates to underscored the difficulty of governing the large Northwest Territory and revived interest in plans for subdividing the area. St. Clair seized the opportunity to put forth his suggestion to create three separate territories with seats of government at Marietta, Cincinnati, and Vincennes. The Jeffersonian Democratic-Republicans objected to his proposal, since they realized that it would divide the strongly Republican Scioto Valley and thereby indefinitely delay Ohio's admission to statehood. Instead they advocated that the Northwest be split into only two territories and that the

dividing line extend from the mouth of the Kentucky River (west of Cincinnati) to Fort Recovery in what is now eastern Indiana, and from that point directly north to the Canadian border. Under this proposal, the western part of the region, to be known as the Indiana Territory with its capital at Vincennes, would have included most of what are now Indiana, Illinois, and Wisconsin, part of Minnesota, and the western half of Michigan. The diminished remainder of the Northwest Territory, with its seat of government at Chillicothe, was to include all of Ohio and the eastern part of Michigan. The plan of the Jeffersonian Republicans gained the approval of the United States Congress on May 7, 1800.

The advocates of statehood pressed for Ohio's admission into the Union. Congress and President Thomas Jefferson were sympathetic to this desire, and on April 30, 1802, Jefferson signed an enabling act passed by Congress. The act authorized the election of delegates to a convention, which would meet on the first Monday in November 1802 to consider the feasibility of statehood and to draw up a constitution for the proposed new state. It also revised Ohio's western boundary and essentially established the state's present-day borders.

Ohioans enthusiastically responded to news of the enabling act, and the 35 delegates to the November convention reflected the citizenry's desire for statehood. One observer counted 26 Jeffersonian Republicans, 7 Federalists, and 2 persons of unknown political affiliation among the representatives to the convention. The forces favoring statehood were so strong that by the time the delegates met on November 1, 1802, the few emissaries who opposed Ohio's admission to the Union realized that further resistance was futile, and when the vote on statehood was taken only one delegate dissented.

Shortly after the opening of the November meeting, Governor St. Clair (who opposed statehood) received permission to address the gathering in an unofficial capacity. He could not reconcile himself to the inevitability of Ohio's statehood, and he denounced the enabling act as "in truth a nullity," which, he said, had divested the people of the territory "of the rights they were in possession of without a hearing, bartered away like sheep in a market." The speech infuriated the Republicans; President Jefferson removed St. Clair from office, and the former governor, who never again held a public position, retired to Pennsylvania, where he died in 1818.

Ignoring St. Clair's protestations, the convention drew up the constitution for the new state in only 25 days. Reflecting the difficulties its framers had had with St. Clair, the document severely restricted the powers of the governor. The constitution also provided for a supreme court of three (later four) justices, but it vested the greatest authority in the new state in a legislature consisting of two chambers.

The people of Ohio were not called upon to ratify this 1802 constitution. Instead, the convention merely called upon them to elect the new state's legislature and scheduled that body to meet on the first Tuesday in March 1803. In the meantime, Thomas Worthington carried Ohio's acceptance of statehood to Washington, D.C., along with a copy of the new constitution, signed by all the members of the November 1802 convention. Federal laws were extended over Ohio on February 19, 1802. However, Congress did not mark Ohio's admission to the Union with any official ceremonies or statements. Thus, in 1953 the day of the first meeting of the Ohio legislature (March 1, 1803) was selected as the date on which Ohio had become a state.

Chillicothe was Ohio's state capital until 1810, when the seat of government was moved to Zanesville. In 1812 the government returned temporarily to Chillicothe, and then moved to Columbus, which became Ohio's permanent capital in 1816.

St. David's Day

March 1 is the day St. David, patron saint of Wales, is honored. St. David's Day is celebrated not only in Wales but by Welsh groups all over the world, and those of Welsh ancestry in the United States have observed this celebration from early times. There was a large migration of Welsh to Pennsylvania at the end of the 17th century, and they gave Welsh names to many settlements near Philadelphia: Bala Cynwyd, Bryn Mawr, St. David's, and Berwyn. Nearby farming areas settled by Welsh were named Gwynedd Valley, Pennlyn, and North Wales.

According to the Welsh Society of Philadelphia, a group of Welsh purchased a tract of 30,000 acres adjacent to Philadelphia in 1681. It was thereafter known as the Welsh Barony, which was paid for in part by a fee of one shilling for every 100 acres, payable to the proprietor every St. David's Day. By the terms of the purchase, the "barony" was to be a separate realm, wherein all causes, crimes, and disputes were to be heard and determined by Welsh officers and tribunals, using the Welsh language.

These settlers maintained the Welsh language and Welsh customs and evinced a zeal to preserve interest in Welsh history and traditions. To further these aims, they established the St. David's Society, sometimes referred to as the Welsh Society. In

the February 25, 1729, issue of the *Pennsylvania Gazette*, the notice of the settlers' intention to form a society appeared:

> We are informed that several Gentlemen and other Persons of Reputation, of the honorable Stock of Ancient Bretons, design to erect themselves into a Society, to meet annually on the first day of March, or St. David's Day, so-called. In order thereto, on the first of next Month, there will be a Sermon preached in the ancient British language by Dr. Wayman in this City, and a Psalm set to the Organ; from thence the Society are to go and partake of a handsome Collation at the House of Robert Davis, at the Queen's Head, in King Street.

St. David himself left no writings confirming the significant dates and events of his life. However, it is known that he was a monk, an ascetic, and a bishop who founded or restored many monasteries and greatly influenced religious life in Wales. He was probably born around the year A.D. 460 and probably died around A.D. 500 According to tradition, his birthplace was Henfynw in Cardiganshire, Wales. He became the first bishop of Mynyw (now called St. David's) in Pembrokeshire, Wales, where he founded his first monastery and where he later died on March 1. In 1120 the cult of St. David was approved by Pope Calixtus II. Special indulgences were granted to those who made a pilgrimage to St. David's shrine in the cathedral in Pembrokeshire.

In celebrations of St. David's Day, it was the custom for Welshmen to wear on their helmets or hats a leek, the floral emblem of Wales. In some places, including the United States, the daffodil often replaced the leek.

Texas Annexed by the United States

On March 1, 1845, President John Tyler signed into effect the joint congressional resolution providing for the annexation of Texas by the United States. The measure had been passed by the Senate on February 27, 1845, and by the House of Representatives on February 28, 1845.

No one asked the opinion of Mexico, which before the battle of San Jacinto on April 21, 1836, considered itself to be in possession of Texas (see March 2, Texas Independence Day, for a more extensive discussion). The annexation of Texas was one of the principal causes of the war between the United States and Mexico, which began in 1846. Texas became the 28th state of the Union on December 29, 1845.

March 2

Texas Independence Day

March 2, Texas Independence Day, commemorates one of the most important events in Texas history: the Texas declaration of independence from Mexico in 1836.

The first steps toward Texan independence began as early as 1810, when the region was still a Spanish possession. Once Mexico successfully revolted against Spain and gained control over Texas in 1821, American settlements grew rapidly. American settlers like Stephen Austin were, according to a contemporary observer, "spreading out like oil upon a cloth." The number of Americans in Texas, which had exceeded 7,000 early in the 1820s, tripled within the next decade and continued to swell rapidly thereafter. Colonies were established at such places as Brazoria, Washington-on-the-Brazos, San Felipe de Austin, Anahuac, and Gonzales. Mexico, beset by revolution and a rapid succession of administrations, was experiencing a confused period of politics after the birth of the Republic of Mexico in 1824. Its harried government was thus in no position to handle the Texans, who were alienated by linguistic, cultural, and religious differences as well as by their own political aspirations. Mexico, fearing an Anglo-American seizure of Texas, made sporadic attempts to tighten control over the area by restricting foreign immigration, encouraging Mexican colonization, abolishing slavery, levying high duties, and establishing military garrisons.

As tension mounted and grievances remained unredressed, there occurred the first in a series of political moves that would eventually lead to open revolt. Representatives from every important community in Texas except San Antonio gathered at San Felipe de Austin in October 1832. In their attempt to seek greater liberties under Mexican law, they appointed committees to draft memorials asking for repeal of the ban on immigration and for tariff reductions, efficient and just local government, permission to organize their own militia, and reform in the means for the issuance of land titles. Most of all, the Texan colonists desired the separation of Texas from the Mexican state of Coahuila, to which it was joined politically, and the admission of Texas to Mexican statehood on an equal footing with the states of the Mexican nation. The proposals were reconsidered and reaffirmed at a second convention in San Felipe de Austin in April 1833, and a constitution for the proposed new state of Texas was also written. Stephen Austin was sent to Mexico with these proposals, but he was imprisoned for nearly two years, a move that served to aggravate the already strained relations between Texans and the Mexican national government.

As long as the hope of similar resistance in other parts of the Mexican republic existed, the Texans' position was tenable, but in 1834 Antonio López de Santa Anna established himself as the reactionary dictator of Mexico. His forces crushed the opposition in one Mexican state after another, until only the Texans remained. A "consultation" of Texans met at San Felipe de Austin from October 16 to November 14, 1835, and issued a "declaration of the causes of taking up arms." It stated that Texas would continue to be loyal to Mexico as long as that nation was governed by the constitution of 1824, which Santa Anna had virtually overthrown. The Texans were not yet engaged in actual revolt against Mexico, however, and the conference voted down a motion to secede by a large majority.

It soon became increasingly evident that the struggle for a Mexican federal constitution was hopeless, and as Santa Anna's army marched toward the border, the Texans found themselves faced with the dilemma of choosing between total submission to the new regime or adoption of a new framework for the continuation of their struggle. As early as December 20, 1835, the citizens of Goliad issued a declaration of independence from Mexico. By mid-January 1836, the lingering hopes of conservatives were dispelled when Austin, released from prison in Mexico a few months before, encouraged open rebellion and complete separation from Mexico.

The "declaration of the causes of taking up arms" had included a statement in which the Texans reserved the right "to withdraw from the union, to establish an independent government, or to adopt such measures as [may seem] best calculated to protect . . . rights and liberties." In this spirit, delegates from nearly all sections of Texas were elected on February 1, 1836, and were asked to convene in a month's time at Washington-on-the-Brazos.

Washington-on-the-Brazos, the first settlement in Stephen Austin's land grant of 1821, sprawled over the bluff above the muddy waters of the Rio de los Brazos de Dios (River of the Arms of God). The town was still very backward in 1836, judging from the description made on February 13, 1836, by William Fairfax Gray, a lieutenant colonel in the Virginia militia:

> Left Washington at 10 o'clock. Glad to get out of so disgusting a place. It is laid out in the woods; about a dozen wretched cabins or shanties constitute the city; not one decent house in it, and only one well defined

street, which consists of an opening cut out of the woods. The stumps still standing. A rare place to hold a national convention in. They will have to leave it promptly to avoid starvation.

Nevertheless, 58 delegates assembled there on March 2, 1836. Many had come hundreds of miles on horseback and had left their families exposed to danger. The delegates could not have foreseen, when they were elected the previous month, that their meetings would coincide with military disaster on the Texas frontier. Even as they convened, Santa Anna's assault on the Alamo, begun on February 23, was nearing its tragic end (see March 6). The entire border defenses lay exposed, and the Mexican troops were preparing to advance into the heart of Texas. The delegates' first act was to appoint a five-man committee to draft a declaration of independence. The committee, probably headed by George C. Childress, drew up a document enumerating 14 specific grievances against Mexico and declaring Texan independence:

The necessity of self-preservation, therefore, now decrees our eternal political separation.

We therefore, the delegates, with plenary powers, of the people of Texas, in solemn convention assembled, appealing to a candid world for the necessities of our condition, do hereby resolve and declare that our political connection with the Mexican nation has forever ended; and that the people of Texas do now constitute a free, sovereign and independent republic. . . . Conscious of the rectitude of our intentions, we fearlessly and confidently commit the issue to the decision of the Supreme Arbiter of the destinies of nations.

The declaration was unanimously adopted on March 2, 1836, and was signed the following day.

The convention at Washington-on-the-Brazos labored 17 days in an unfinished one-story wooden structure. "In lieu of glass," read one account, "cotton cloth was stretched across the windows, which partially excluded the cold wind." Meeting almost constantly in two, sometimes three, sessions daily, the convention's members worked to prepare for the separation of Texas from Mexico. They drew up and adopted a constitution, provided for military forces to defend the new Texan republic by appointing Sam Houston commander in chief of all land forces of Texas, and formed an interim government with David G. Burnet as provisional president. On March 17, 1836, the new government of the republic, together with most of the inhabitants of Washington- on-the-Brazos, fled before the invading Mexican army.

The new Republic of Texas was eventually victorious, however, and forced Mexico to recognize its independence on April 21, 1836, at the battle of San Jacinto. It remained an independent nation under its Lone Star flag for ten years. The United States recognized Texan independence on March 3, 1837.

Texas was annexed by the United States on March 1, 1845 (see March 1), in an action that was a principal cause of the Mexican War. Texas subsequently became part of the United States when it entered the Union as the 28th state on December 29, 1845.

Sam Houston's Birthday

For Texans, March 2 not only commemorates Texas Independence Day (see above), but also the birthday of Sam Houston. Houston, of Scotch-Irish descent, was born near Lexington, Virginia, on March 2, 1793. After his father died in 1806, his mother resettled in the Tennessee frontier country. Rather than submit to working as a clerk in a trader's store, Houston ran away from home at the age of 15 to live with a Cherokee tribe for nearly three years. He then fought in the Creek campaign under Andrew Jackson in 1814, and was seriously wounded in the Battle of Horseshoe Bend.

Houston went on to study law, was admitted to the bar in 1818, and practiced in Lebanon, Tennessee. He also did well in state and national politics. From 1823 to 1827, he represented the ninth district of Tennessee in the U.S. House of Representatives. In 1827 the Jacksonian Democrats swept him to victory as governor of the state, and his political future seemed bright. Following a disastrous marriage, however, Houston resigned the governorship in 1829 and once more went to live with the Cherokees, who adopted him and gave him the name Co-lon-neh (the raven). In 1830 and 1832 he visited Washington, D.C., where he worked to expose the frauds perpetrated by government agents against Native American tribes. President Jackson commissioned him in December 1832 to work out treaties with the tribes in Texas.

Determined to become a permanent Texas settler himself, Houston settled at Nacogdoches and for a short time practiced law. He was quickly recognized as a natural leader for the aggressive, land-hungry pioneers who opposed Mexican rule. Houston was elected a delegate to a meeting at San Felipe in April 1833 and was a member of the Washington-on-the-Brazos convention that declared Texas's independence. Appointed commander in chief of the revolutionary forces, General Houston was at first severely criticized in the dark days after the loss of the Alamo for his retreat before Santa Anna's superior forces. He redeemed himself at the battle of San Jacinto on April 21, 1836, where the Texans were victorious.

The war hero was elected president of the new Republic of Texas on September 1, 1836, and the new capital was named in his honor. He held office until December 1838, and then again from 1841 to 1844. After Texas was admitted to the United States, he was one of the first U.S. senators sent from Texas to Washington, D.C. A dedicated Union Democrat, he served for 14 years until his inflexible unionism caused his defeat in the years leading up to the Civil War. Elected governor of Texas for the third time in 1859, Houston adamantly opposed secession and refused to join the Confederacy. Because of this, he was deposed from the governorship in March 1861. He died in Huntsville, Texas, two years later.

Pioneer 10 Launched; First Probe to Leave the Solar System

Less than three years after the first person landed on the Moon, another milestone was reached when the first satellite probe was launched with a trajectory designed to take it out of Earth's solar system and into interstellar space.

Pioneer 10 was launched on March 2, 1972. Not only was it the first probe designed to leave the solar system, but it was the first designed to fly by the planet Jupiter and gather scientific data for transmission back to Earth. The idea was to accomplish two objectives. First, Jupiter, which is the largest planet in the solar system, had never been probed by satellites. Second, with a carefully calculated trajectory designed to take *Pioneer* close to Jupiter but not too close, Jupiter's enormous gravity could be used to increase the probe's speed and propel it on its way. The concept is called a "slingshot" trajectory.

Pioneer 10 carried a complement of scientific instruments in order to scan Jupiter. It came within 125,000 miles of the planet on December 3, 1973, and the slingshot trajectory was successful. The spacecraft transmitted close-up photographs back to Earth, in addition to valuable information about Jupiter's atmosphere, magnetic fields, radioactive particles, and so forth. *Pioneer 10* also scanned several of Jupiter's moons.

Unlike the Jupiter mission, *Pioneer*'s travel into interstellar space had no specific mission objective. First, it will be thousands of years before *Pioneer* comes near another star, since even the closest stellar object is trillions of miles away. Second, even with its four on-board nuclear generators, *Pi-*

oneer is too small to continue transmissions to Earth throughout its interstellar journey. If life exists elsewhere in the universe, however, there is the possibility that some intelligent species might find *Pioneer* in space. Therefore, the probe was launched with a special plaque attached to it, containing drawings that show the location of Earth's solar system and nude depictions of both a male and a female in order to give an alien species some idea of the human race.

By December 1, 1997, *Pioneer 10* was over 6 billion miles from Earth and traveling at over 27,000 miles per hour. In the empty vastness of interstellar space, the probe had little to report. Further, many of its instruments had already failed. Therefore, by March 31, 1997, NASA had already ceased to actively monitor the mission.

March 3

Free Speech Is Limited by "Clear and Present Danger"

The First Amendment to the Constitution of the United States guarantees Americans various rights, including freedom of speech. The Founding Fathers did not state, however, whether this was an unlimited right or whether reasonable limitations could be placed on freedom of speech in certain circumstances. In the case of *U.S.* v. *Schenck*, the Supreme Court on March 3, 1919, stated that freedom of speech could be limited only if the speech in question presented a "clear and present danger."

The Schenck case began during World War I, when the Wilson administration secured the passage of several laws aimed at curbing "subversive activity," though the more likely objective was to curb opposition to America's entry into the war. Congress passed the Sedition Act, which made it illegal to speak out against the war or criticize the United States; the Sabotage Act, which made it illegal to "obstruct" the war effort; and the Espionage Act, which criminalized a variety of "treasonous" activities and gave the Post Office the power to censor the mail. It was pursuant to the Espionage Act, passed on May 11, 1917, that Charles T. Schenck was prosecuted.

Schenck was a leader in the American Socialist Party. After the United States entered the war and began to draft hundreds of thousands of young men for military service, Schenck approved the distribution of leaflets against the draft. The leaflets went out through the mail and were detected by the Post Office, and Schenck was arrested. He defended his actions on the grounds that the leaflets were constitutionally permissible under the free speech guarantee of the First Amendment. He was convicted and appealed the verdict, and the case eventually reached the U.S. Supreme Court.

In a decision written by the distinguished Supreme Court justice Oliver Wendell Holmes, the Supreme Court upheld Schenck's conviction. The Court stated that in normal circumstances the antiwar leaflets would probably be protected speech, but that the circumstances were different when the nation was at war. Using the famous analogy of a man shouting "fire" in a crowded opera house, Holmes stated that whether speech was protected by the First Amendment depended on whether the time and circumstances demonstrated that the speech posed a "clear and present danger" to public safety or other important interests such as the war effort. The application of this principle to Schenck's particular situation was questionable, since Schenck and the socialist organization had merely distributed leaflets rather than getting involved in any violent activity. Nevertheless, the case established an important precedent, namely that freedom of speech is not an unlimited right and that society has the power to impose reasonable restraints to protect the other interests of its citizens.

Alexander Graham Bell's Birthday

Alexander Graham Bell, the inventor of the telephone, was born in Edinburgh, Scotland, on March 3, 1847. He was the son of Alexander Melville Bell, a teacher of the deaf who developed a physiological alphabet called Visible Speech, which showed the position of the vocal organs as they formed sounds. The younger Bell, also interested in the problems of the deaf, worked with his father and used the alphabet to teach the deaf to speak.

Bell was educated at the University of Edinburgh and at University College in London. In 1870 the family migrated to Canada, and both father and son began lecturing in Canada and the United States. Beginning in 1871, Bell lectured on speech training in various major cities, including Boston, Massachusetts, where he did pioneering work with the deaf, and in 1872 opened a school to train teachers of the deaf. He was appointed professor of vocal physiology and the mechanics of speech at Boston University the following year.

When first in Boston, Bell was employed by Gardiner Greene Hubbard, an attorney, to teach his deaf daughter, Mabel. Mabel and Bell later married. While teaching in Boston, Bell also conducted experiments with electricity. Hubbard became interested in the work, and in 1873 he and Salem merchant Thomas Sanders (whose deaf son was also a Bell pupil) offered to finance a project. Bell was trying to transmit many signals over one wire. He finally succeeded with an invention called the harmonic telegraph. It was the solving of this problem, plus his acute musical ear and knowledge of the mechanics of human speech and hearing, that enabled Bell to invent the telephone, an instrument that transmits and receives alternating pitches over a wire, duplicating the human voice electrically.

The first words successfully transmitted over the telephone were the famous ones Bell spoke to his assistant, who was waiting in another room: "Mr. Watson, come here, I want you." Bell was issued his first patent for the telephone on March 7, 1876. The most significant demonstration occurred that summer at Philadelphia's Centennial Exhibition, where Bell introduced his invention during the July 4 celebration. Since then, his creation has revolutionized communications all over the world.

The Bell Telephone Company was formed by Bell, Hubbard, and Sanders in July 1877. Bell took little interest in the company after 1881, although he testified frequently in lawsuits to defend his patent. He reaped large profits from his stake in the business. Until the late 20th century, when it was broken up, the Bell System nearly monopolized local and long-distance telephone service in the United States under a parent corporation named the American Telegraph and Telephone Company.

In 1880 the French government awarded Bell the Volta prize for his invention of the telephone. He used this money and the profits from his patent to establish the Volta Laboratory in Washington, D.C. A division of this laboratory, the Volta Bureau for the Deaf, was established by Bell for the advancement and dissemination of knowledge relating to the deaf. It was later renamed the Alexander Graham Bell Association for the Deaf.

Bell became an American citizen in 1882. He lived in Washington, D.C., for most of the rest of his life, devoting himself to research in many fields. It was at the Volta Laboratory that the first successful phonograph record was produced. Bell also invented the photophone, a device that transmits sound by light rays, and the audiometer, an instrument that measures the intensity of sounds. In addition, while serving as president of the National Geographic Society (1896–1904), he worked to promote popular membership in the society and helped develop its technical journal into today's widely known *National Geographic* magazine.

Beginning in 1895, Bell developed an interest in aviation. He invented the tetrahedral kite, which carried a man aloft, and encouraged Samuel Pierpont Langley's experiments with heavier-than-air craft. In 1907, with Glenn H. Curtiss and others, Bell founded the Aerial Experiment Association, which contributed substantially to early aviation. It developed and built flying machines that were demonstrated in three successful public flights in 1908. In contrast to the earlier flights of the Wright brothers, which took place in a remote location and received little attention, these demonstrations aroused widespread interest in aviation progress. Bell and his associates also developed the tricycle landing gear and the aileron, a hinged, movable section of an airplane wing still used to control flight.

Another of Bell's interests was marine engineering; his hydrofoil speedboat, developed with F. W. Baldwin, set a world record of 70.86 mph in 1919. He also tinkered in genetics, breeding a flock of sheep that bore mostly twins. While in his Canadian summer home near Baddeck on Cape Breton Island, Nova Scotia, Bell died on August 2, 1922. He was buried atop a nearby mountain.

Florida Admitted to the Union

Florida was the last of the Atlantic seaboard states to gain admission to the Union. Twenty-four tumultuous years passed from the time the United States acquired possession of the Florida territory from Spain before statehood was granted, on March 3, 1845.

The United States acquired Florida from Spain under the Adams-Onis Treaty (known also as the Florida Purchase Treaty) of February 1821. Formal transfer of the territory to the United States was made on July 17, 1821. Fewer than 5,000 settlers lived in Florida at the time. The only sizable settlements were at Pensacola on the north Florida panhandle and at the towns of St. Augustine and Fernandina on the Atlantic coast. The man chosen to be the first American governor was Andrew Jackson, military hero and later president of the United States. He was no stranger to the area. With his troops, Jackson had twice captured Spanish-held Pensacola, once during the War of 1812, just prior to his victory in the battle of New Orleans, and again in 1818. He was unsuccessful in his new post, however, and after eight months he resigned.

Florida was organized as a territory in 1822. More settlers came to the northern part of the territory, but settlement of south Florida was slow due to the hot and humid climate and swampy terrain. So greedy for land were the newcomers that

they brought great pressure to bear on the U.S. Congress to remove the Seminole tribe from the territory and make the entire area available for settlement. The Seminoles were actually an amalgam of Native American tribes, many of whom had intermarried with runaway slaves from the American states who had fled to Florida for sanctuary under Spanish rule. As the number of settlers increased and pushed steadily southward and into the interior of the peninsula, they came into conflict with the Seminoles.

After a series of costly wars with the Seminoles in the 1830s and 1840s, the federal government finally prevailed. Some of the Seminoles were forced to emigrate to Oklahoma, but many were able to stay in Florida reservations, which still exist today. The famous Seminole leader Osceola fell into federal hands and died in prison in Charleston, South Carolina.

In 1824, Tallahassee, on the north Florida panhandle, was selected as the capital of the new territory. It was an important Native American town at least as early as 1539, when the Spanish explorer Hernando de Soto and his party visited it; its name, of Native American origin, means "old town." The development of Tallahassee and north Florida was spurred by the construction of a road linking Pensacola with St. Augustine. Pensacola, with its excellent harbor, was of major importance during the period of Spanish sovereignty. St. Augustine, the oldest city in the United States, dated its existence as a permanent settlement from 1565, when Pedro Menendez de Avilés claimed the site for Spain. In the area between these two historic cities, many large plantations were founded after American sovereignty was established. New towns came into existence, and a substantial number of northerners settled in those along the eastern coast. Jacksonville, near the mouth of the St. Johns River, about 35 miles north northwest of St. Augustine, was laid out as a town in 1822.

Floridians gained the right to elect their territorial legislative council in 1826. The council was superseded in 1838 by a state house of representatives and a senate. In December 1838 and January 1839 a convention meeting in the town of St. Joseph drafted a proposed state constitution. The citizens of Florida, however, held varying opinions as to the desirability of gaining statehood. Ratification of the proposed constitution was by a slim margin of about 100 votes. The resulting controversy and delay went hand in hand with the congressional desire not to admit another Southern slave state, as Florida would be, without admitting a free state at the same time. Finally, when Iowa was ready for admission as a free state, Florida was admitted to the Union on March 3, 1845, as the 27th state, with its capital at Tallahassee.

Only 16 years later, on January 10, 1861, Florida declared itself seceded from the Union and joined with other Southern states to form the Confederate States of America. During the ensuing Civil War, Union forces captured Florida's chief ports and blockaded its coast, but the area's many inlets provided both refuge and bases of operation for blockade runners. The interior of the state remained in Southern hands, and, apart from a major battle at Olustee in 1864 and another engagement outside Tallahassee in 1865 (both resulting in Confederate victories), there was little actual fighting in Florida. Throughout the war Florida was an important source of supplies, foodstuffs, and manpower for the rest of the Confederacy.

At the close of the Civil War in 1865, a new state government was organized and a new state constitution was framed. However, neither met with federal approval, for Florida's proposed constitution withheld the vote from African Americans and the new legislature in 1866 refused to ratify the 14th Amendment to the U.S. Constitution, which included a provision granting citizenship to former slaves. In accordance with the federal Reconstruction policies in effect in the South, therefore, a quasi-military government was instituted in Florida, which became part of the Third Military District. In early 1868 a revised state constitution was drafted, which proved to be acceptable to the federal government given Florida's acceptance of a stipulation that universal manhood suffrage would never be repealed. The U.S. Congress voted to restore the full rights of statehood, including representation in Congress, to Florida on June 25, 1868.

March 4

Vermont Admitted to the Union

On March 4, 1791, Vermont gained statehood. Vermont was not one of the 13 original states. Indeed, the inhabitants of the Green Mountains in 1777 took advantage of the chaos of the American Revolution to declare themselves independent of their neighboring states as well as of Great Britain. However, in the years that followed Vermont's 1777 declaration of independence (see January 15), Vermont repeatedly tried to become a member of the Union. For more than a decade its status remained controversial, but finally the disputes over the region were resolved, and in 1791 the area won acceptance as the 14th state.

The convention that declared Vermont's independence on January 15, 1777, did not bring a unified Vermont into existence. The southwestern area around Bennington strongly supported an independent status for Vermont, but the remainder of what is now the state was less enthusiastic. Most of the region east of the Green Mountains in the Connecticut Valley considered joining the New Hampshire towns east of the Connecticut River in a separate "Valley state," and the southeastern portion of Vermont, which was heavily populated by settlers from New York, retained strong ties with that state. In addition, British forces occupied most of the northern region, including all the territory along Lake Champlain, so that area had no opportunity to align itself with the new Vermont government.

Despite the lack of unified support for a separate Vermont, a convention met at Windsor in July 1777 to draw up a state constitution. The Vermont frame of government drew heavily from that adopted by Pennsylvania in 1776, but included several additions. Vermont's constitution was the first to specifically prohibit slavery and to provide for universal manhood suffrage. The 1777 document was never submitted to Vermont's inhabitants for ratification; nevertheless, it became and substantially remains their basic frame of government. The framers of the Vermont Constitution hoped that after they had drawn up that document, the Continental Congress would approve their application for statehood. Their aspirations were ill founded, however. The Congress upheld New York's contention that it had jurisdiction over the Green Mountain area and denounced Vermont's claims to independence.

In May 1778, Ethan Allen, who nearly three years earlier had been taken prisoner by the British during the American revolutionaries' unsuccessful campaign against Quebec, was exchanged and returned to Vermont. A land speculator whose financial interests would be best served if Vermont were independent of New York, Allen used his considerable talents in the years that followed to strengthen the state. Since his influence was greatest in the Bennington area, he worked particularly hard to ensure the dominance of that region in the politics of the new state.

At the first meeting of the Vermont legislature in the spring of 1778, the representatives from the Connecticut Valley put forth a plan to include the New Hampshire areas located east of the Connecticut River within the jurisdiction of Vermont. A number of towns on the western frontier of New Hampshire were dissatisfied with what they believed to be inadequate representation in that state's legislature, and were willing to transfer their loyalties to the new state of Vermont. Allen, however, opposed the admission of these towns because they would shift the balance of political control from western Vermont to the Connecticut Valley. He wrote to the governors of Vermont and New Hampshire protesting the former state's admission of the New Hampshire towns, and he traveled to Philadelphia, Pennsylvania, where he promised the New Hampshire delegate to the Continental Congress that the towns on the eastern bank of the Connecticut River would be returned to his state if New Hampshire supported Vermont's application for statehood. When he returned to Vermont, Allen gave the state legislature an extremely negative report on the reaction of Congress to Vermont's taking over the New Hampshire towns. He warned that "the whole power of the United States of America will join to annihilate the State of Vermont, to vindicate the right of New Hampshire. . . ." Allen's dire words had their intended result. In the fall of 1778, the Vermont legislature decided not to recognize the inclusion of the New Hampshire towns in the eastern Vermont counties, and when the representatives reconvened in the western Vermont town of Bennington in February 1779, the western delegates, who this time outnumbered their eastern counterparts 29 to 21, were able to end the New Hampshire towns' association with Vermont.

As a result of the legislature's ejection of the New Hampshire towns, most of the area west of the Connecticut River declined further connection with Vermont. The fledgling Green Mountain State was thus reduced to a small number of western towns and a few isolated eastern towns. Allen worked to intimidate settlers into staying with Vermont. For example, since the inhabitants of Cumberland County refused to acknowledge Vermont's draft law, Allen used this excuse to lead 100 of his Vermont followers into its precincts. There, he arrested 36 persons who sympathized with New York. As a show of force, Allen persuaded a Vermont court to fine these "Yorkers." Vermont's governor, Thomas Chittenden, eventually pardoned the Yorkers, but the incident had considerable impact. The Yorkers wrote to New York governor George Clinton that Allen was "more to be dreaded than death with all its terrors," and Clinton in turn made a protest to the Continental Congress.

Although the Revolutionary War against Britain dominated the attentions of the Continental Congress, in 1779 that body realized that it could no longer ignore the Vermont question. Congress asked the bordering states of New York, New Hampshire, and Massachusetts to allow the national government to establish their respective boundaries. Vermont, however, was not asked to participate in these negotiations. Exclusion from the deliberations greatly antagonized the Vermont

legislature that met in October 1779, and that body reaffirmed its independent status.

The ongoing war delayed the Continental Congress's consideration of the problem. Meanwhile some Vermont leaders, perhaps acting on the belief that the Congress would never recognize an independent Vermont, began to explore the practicality of an alliance with British Canada. Ethan Allen and his brother, Ira Allen, realized that an enlarged Vermont would improve their bargaining power with the British. Thus, with the help of the loyalists who inhabited the Connecticut Valley, Ira Allen persuaded or intimidated a large number of the towns on both sides of that river to rejoin Vermont in April 1781. Then, due to the efforts of Ethan Allen, a number of towns located between the Hudson River and the area claimed by Vermont also voted to join Vermont.

News of Vermont's interest in negotiating with the British, and its absorption of New York and New Hampshire towns, quickly came to the attention of the Continental Congress. Ethan Allen even admitted to the president of the congress that he had corresponded with the British colonel Beverly Robinson. Allen showed no remorse over his activities, stating: "I am as resolutely determined to defend the independence of Vermont as Congress that of the United States. . . ."

For a time it seemed that Vermont might gain admission to the Union in 1781, but Congress could not acquiesce to Vermont's absorption of the New York and New Hampshire towns, and resolved that Vermont would be granted statehood if the towns in question were returned to the respective states. Unwilling to give up the towns, the Allens and some of their political allies continued to explore a possible rapprochement with the British. However, the American victory over the British at Yorktown in the fall of 1781 ended the American Revolution and with it any hope of a feasible Vermont-British agreement.

Vermont agreed to give up the towns in question, but it did not immediately gain admission into the United States. Southern members of Congress were reluctant to increase the number of New England states in the Union, while those who represented states with western claims balked at establishing a state in an area claimed by one of the original states. Congress's failure to accept Vermont as a state disappointed many inhabitants of that region and briefly revived interest in a reunion with the British. However, in the Treaty of Paris of 1783 the British recognized the northern boundary of the United States to be the 45th parallel and thus tacitly acknowledged the jurisdiction of the new American nation over the area of Vermont.

March 4

After the adoption of the United States Constitution in 1787, Alexander Hamilton of New York persuaded Congress to reconsider Vermont's statehood. In 1789, New York, which had previously blocked efforts to create a new state from the area that it claimed, agreed to consider a compromise. Settlement of the decades-old controversy followed in 1790. New York received $30,000 from Vermont in settlement of all land claims, and in turn agreed to Vermont's admission to the Union. On January 6, 1791, Vermont ratified the U.S. Constitution, and on March 4, 1791, Congress voted unanimously for Vermont to become the 14th member of the United States.

Casimir Pulaski's Birthday

The ideals and adventure of the American Revolution inspired a number of noteworthy Europeans to take up arms and help fight for the independence of the 13 American colonies. Men such as the Marquis de Lafayette of France, Baron Friedrich von Steuben of Germany, and Thaddeus Kosciuszko of Poland rendered invaluable assistance to the colonists during the war against Great Britain. Several representatives of foreign nobility lost their lives while attempting to win America's freedom. Count Casimir Pulaski was one of those men.

Born in Warka, Poland, on March 4, 1748, Pulaski was the son of Count Joseph Pulaski, an ardent nationalist and the founder of the Confederation of the Bar, an organization that attempted to prevent foreign domination of Poland in the mid-18th century. In 1767, at the age of 19, Casimir Pulaski joined the fight to preserve the independence of his homeland. He fought bravely for several years, and scored a number of victories. However, the Polish army was no match for its stronger adversaries, and in 1772 Prussia, Russia, and Austria partitioned Poland. Pulaski's estate was confiscated, and the young nobleman was forced to seek refuge in Turkey.

For three years Pulaski tried to persuade Turkey to attack Russia, but his efforts failed, and in 1775 he went to Paris. Mutual acquaintances there brought him together with Benjamin Franklin and Silas Deane. These American envoys were impressed by Pulaski's military background and believed that he might substantially aid the colonial cause. Penniless and in need of employment, Pulaski readily agreed to their suggestion that he fight on behalf of the Americans. With a letter of introduction from Franklin to George Washington, the commander in chief of the Continental army, the Polish count sailed from France in June 1777.

Pulaski arrived in America just as the Continental army was being reorganized. When Washington heard of his considerable experience with the Polish cavalry, he recommended that Pulaski be given command of the new mounted units. On September 15, 1777, the Continental Congress appointed Pulaski to the rank of brigadier general and named him to the post of Commander of the Horse.

After taking part in the battle of Germantown on October 4, 1777, Pulaski spent the winter of 1777 doing outpost duty at Trenton and Flemington, New Jersey. With General Anthony Wayne he also conducted several expeditions designed to obtain provisions for the Continental soldiers, then in their harsh winter quarters at nearby Valley Forge, Pennsylvania. However, his association with the army was not happy. Unable to speak English and unwilling to subordinate himself even to Washington, Pulaski failed to maintain the respect of the troops under his command. In March 1778 he resigned from the army.

With the permission of Congress, Pulaski then raised an independent cavalry corps. Still, things did not go well for him. In September 1778, after he complained that he was "languishing in a state of inactivity," Congress ordered his unit to guard American supplies at Little Egg Harbor, New Jersey. In early October 1775, however, a surprise British attack at Little Egg almost destroyed his volunteer legion. The following month Pulaski was sent to Minisink on the Delaware River to protect the inhabitants of the area from attack by Native American tribes. This new assignment did not please him, and on November 26, 1778, he wrote that he had "nothing but bears to fight." After 1778 the scene of the major military confrontations between the British and the Americans shifted to the south. Under orders from Congress, Pulaski proceeded to South Carolina in February 1779 to assist General Benjamin Lincoln, the American commander of the southern forces. This change in the theater of his operations did not relieve Pulaski's frustrations. In May 1779 the British under the command of General Augustine Prevost badly defeated his cavalry corps, and in August Pulaski again complained to Congress of "ill treatment."

Despite his dissatisfaction, Pulaski continued to fight for the American cause. During the unsuccessful American attempt to wrest Savannah, Georgia, from British control on October 9, 1779, he led a gallant, if perhaps foolhardy, cavalry attack against the enemy defenses. He was mortally wounded during this action and died on October 11, 1779. Despite his problematic career, he was honored as a hero of the American Revolution, and a number of towns and counties in Arkansas, Georgia, Illinois, Indiana, Kentucky, Mississippi, Missouri, New York, Tennessee, and Virginia are named Pulaski to commemorate his service.

First Meeting of the First Congress

On March 4, 1789, the first session of the First Congress began. It was the first convening of the United States Congress pursuant to the Constitution.

Congress has its origins in the Continental Congress of the American Revolution. During the postwar period of the Articles of Confederation (1781–1787), what little national government there was, was vested in the Congress. However, the Articles of Confederation proved to be a weak and ineffective form of government, so at the urging of George Washington and other leaders a Constitutional Convention met in Philadelphia, Pennsylvania, on May 25, 1787, to reform the system. The convention soon went beyond its original mandate to simply revise the Articles of Confederation and crafted an entirely new form of government in the Constitution of the United States.

The Constitution provided for a stronger federal government, consisting of the executive (the presidency), the judicial (the Supreme Court and a federal court system), and the legislative (Congress). Congress consists of two branches, the Senate and the House of representatives. Senators are elected for six-year terms, and Representatives are elected for two-year terms. Thus, every two years there is a congressional election. Since the first congressional election was in November 1788, the Congress that convened afterwards on March 4, 1789, was the First Congress. Two years later the Second Congress met; four years later the Third Congress met; and so forth until 144 years later when the 73rd Congress met on March 4, 1933. During that Congress, the 20th Amendment to the Constitution took effect, which provides that Congress meets on January 3 (see the essay at January 3, Congress Meets) rather than March 4. Then, the 74th Congress met on January 3, 1935; two years later the 75th Congress met; and so forth to the present day.

The Constitution was just the beginning of the process of building a national government. When the First Congress met, most of the senators and representatives were absent, still en route to the temporary national capital of New York City. President George Washington had not even been inaugurated yet. Nevertheless, during its term the First Congress was able to create the building blocks of the federal bureaucracy, establishing such key agencies as the departments of State, Treasury, and War. In addition, the First Congress approved the Bill of Rights and sent it to the states for ratification.

March 5

The Boston Massacre

When British troops were quartered in Boston, Massachusetts, in 1768, the people of the city, especially the radicals favoring independence for the American colonies, resented it. There were frequent but minor clashes between the civilians and the soldiers. One such clash occurred on March 5, 1770, when seven soldiers under the command of Captain Thomas Preston were pelted with stones and snowballs in King Street (later State Street) by a crowd of 50 or 60 people. In the tension of the moment, one of the soldiers fired his weapon, and the others followed him. Three people in the crowd were killed outright, and two others were mortally wounded.

One of the men killed was one of the crowd's leaders, Crispus Attucks, who is often referred to as the first martyr of the American Revolution. Attucks was born in slavery about 1723 in the area of Framingham, Massachusetts, and is believed to have been of mixed African, white, and Native American ancestry. In 1738 his master, Colonel Buckminster, sold him to William Brown. At the age of 27, Attucks took his first step toward liberty by running away from Brown. Brown searched for him but was unsuccessful. By the time that Attucks led members of the crowd from Dock Square to King Street, where they confronted the British soldiers, he had worked as a sailor for 20 years on whaling ships.

Champions of American independence, including Paul Revere, whose engraving of what was later known as the Boston Massacre became a propaganda classic, lost no time in exploiting Attucks's death. Attucks was buried, after an impressive funeral march, in the historic Granary Burying Ground on Tremont Street, where his body was later joined by those of other early patriots of the American cause, including Revere himself and Samuel Adams. On the day following the Boston Massacre, a meeting was held in an overflowing Faneuil Hall, where speeches were made denouncing the massacre and demanding that the British troops be removed from the city at once.

A week after the Boston Massacre, the British troops were transferred to Castle Island in Boston Harbor. In November 1770, the soldiers and their commander were tried for murder and were defended by John Adams and Josiah Quincy. Two were found guilty of manslaughter and received light sentences, and the others were acquitted. Although Adams, as a lawyer, defended the soldiers, as a colonial patriot he wrote in 1816: "Not the Battle of Lexington, not the surrender of Burgoyne or Cornwallis, were more important events in American history than the battle of King Street on March 5, 1770."

The next year the people of Boston, including many distinguished citizens, held a meeting in Old South Meeting House to commemorate the event. This custom of observing the anniversary of the Boston Massacre on March 5 was encouraged by the Sons of Liberty, who staged a procession and various speeches to keep up resentment against the British. The observance was intended to show "the fatal effects of the policy of standing armies, and . . . of quartering regular troops in populous cities in time of peace." As the previous quote from John Adams suggests, the Boston Massacre became a seminal event in the budding American Revolution.

Winston Churchill Makes His "Iron Curtain" Speech in the U.S.

After World War II ended in 1945, the United States shortly found itself in a new form of world conflict. America's wartime ally, the Soviet Union, had fought and defeated the Nazis in eastern Europe. However, the Soviets wanted to become a Communist superpower that could compete with the United States for world domination. Therefore, they did not withdraw their armies from Eastern Europe after the war, but installed subservient Communist puppet regimes and forced the Eastern European nations to join an alliance known as the Warsaw Pact. The United States would counter the Soviet threat by creating the North Atlantic Treaty Organization, which included America's west European allies.

The two superpowers, the two alliances, and ultimately the whole world would then enter that uneasy period of hostility known as the cold war. During this period, although there were many military confrontations, neither side dared to use the nuclear weapons it possessed. The cold war ended when the Soviet Union collapsed in 1991.

Winston Churchill, the prime minister of Great Britain during World War II, foresaw the onset of the cold war when the Soviets began to consolidate their control over eastern Europe. During a famous speech at Westminster College in Fulton, Missouri, where he was the guest of President Harry Truman and received an honorary degree, Churchill coined the phrase "Iron Curtain" in describing how the Soviets were closing off their do-

mains from the rest of the world. The speech helped make the American public more aware of the Soviet threat and galvanized support for cold war measures. Churchill's speech, given on March 5, 1946, was lengthy. The most relevant parts are set forth below.

The United States stands at this time at the pinnacle of world power. It is a solemn moment for the American democracy. For with this primacy in power is also joined an awe-inspiring accountability to the future. As you look around you, you must feel not only the sense of duty done, but also you must feel anxiety lest you fall below the level of achievement. Opportunity is here now, clear and shining, for both our countries. To reject it or ignore it or fritter it away will bring upon us all the long reproaches of the aftertime.

I have a strong admiration and regard for the valiant Russian people and for my wartime comrade, Marshal Stalin. There is deep sympathy and goodwill in Britain, and I doubt not here also, toward the peoples of all the Russias and a resolve to persevere through many differences and rebuffs in establishing lasting friendships. It is my duty, however, to place before you certain facts about the present position in Europe. From Stettin in the Baltic to Trieste in the Adriatic an Iron Curtain has descended across the Continent. Behind that line lie all the capitals of the ancient states of Central and Eastern Europe. Warsaw, Berlin, Prague, Vienna, Budapest, Belgrade, Bucharest and Sofia; all these famous cities and the populations around them lie in what I must call the Soviet sphere, and all are subject, in one form or another, not only to Soviet influence but to a very high and in some cases increasing measure of control from Moscow.

Twice the United States has had to send several millions of its young men across the Atlantic to fight the wars. But now we all can find any nation, wherever it may dwell, between dusk and dawn. Surely we should work with conscious purpose for a grand pacification of Europe within the structure of the United Nations and in accordance with our Charter.

I repulse the idea that a new war is inevitable; still more that it is imminent. It is because I am sure that our fortunes are still in our own hands and that we hold the power to save the future, that I feel the duty to speak out now that I have the occasion and the opportunity to do so. I do not believe that Soviet Russia desires war. What they desire is the fruits of war and the indefinite expansion of their power and doctrines. But what we have to consider here today, while time remains, is the permanent prevention of war and the establishment of conditions of freedom and democracy as rapidly as possible in all countries. Our difficulties and dangers will not be removed by closing our eyes to them. They will not be removed by mere waiting to see what happens, nor will they be removed by a policy of appeasement.

What is needed is a settlement, and the longer this is delayed, the more difficult it will be and the greater our dangers will become. From what I have seen of our Russian friends and allies during the war, I am convinced that there is nothing they admire so much as strength, and there is nothing for which they have less respect than for weakness, especially military weakness. For that reason the old doctrine of a balance of power is unsound. We cannot afford, if we can help it, to work on narrow margins, offering temptations to a trial of strength.

Last time I saw it all coming and I cried aloud to my own fellow countrymen and to the world, but no one paid any attention. Up till the year 1933 or even 1935, Germany might have been saved from the awful fate which has overtaken her and we might all have been spared the miseries Hitler let loose upon mankind. There never was a war in history easier to prevent by timely action than the one which has just desolated such great areas of the globe. It could have been prevented, in my belief, without the firing of a single shot, and Germany might be powerful, prosperous and honored today; but no one would listen and one by one we were all sucked into the awful whirlpool.

We must not let it happen again.

If we adhere faithfully to the Charter of the United Nations and walk forward in sedate and sober strength, seeking no one's land or treasure, seeking to lay no arbitrary control upon the thoughts of men, if all British moral and material forces and convictions are joined with your own in fraternal association, the high roads of the future will be clear, not only for us but for all, not only for our time but for a century to come.

March 6

The Fall of the Alamo

The anniversary of the fall of the Alamo, on March 6, 1836, in San Antonio, Texas, has great significance for Texans. Originally, the Alamo (today a national historic landmark) was known as Mission San Antonio de Valero, in honor of a Spanish viceroy. Its history extends back to the early days of Spanish settlement in Texas.

A Spanish expedition discovered a native village called Yanaguana in 1691 and renamed the spot San Antonio de Padua. In the 1710s construction of a mission was begun by friars and artisans led by the Spanish Franciscan Fray Antonio de San Buenaventura y Olivares. After a severe hurricane destroyed the primitive structure in 1724, the mission was moved to a nearby location, which became its permanent site. The predecessor of four other missions along an eight-mile stretch of the San Antonio River, Mission San Antonio de Valero originally consisted of a chapel, a two-story adobe convent and hospital building, a convent yard, and a plaza some two and a half acres in extent. The first stone of the chapel was laid on May 8, 1744. The finished structure, with its walls of hewn stone 4 feet thick and 22 and a half feet high, was formally dedicated in the 1750s. Surrounding the mission complex was a strong wall, 8 feet high and varying in thickness from 2 and a half to 3 and a half feet.

With the disappearance of the native tribes from the vicinity, Mission San Antonio de Valero ceased to operate as a church institution in 1793. Unoccupied for several years, the abandoned and partially collapsed mission was secularized and fortified. It was used off and on as a barracks by Spanish troops in the early 19th century. A record of an 1803 baptism held in the former mission chapel already referred to the location as the Alamo. According to some historians, the name Alamo is derived from the name of one of the military companies that occupied the mission, the Flying Company of San Carlos de Parras, from the Pueblo de San Jose y Santiago del Alamo in Mexico. Early records of these troops referred to their home in abbreviated fashion as the "pueblo del Alamo." Other scholars claim that the name came from the fact that the grounds around the mission were once covered with a grove of cottonwood trees, or in Spanish *alamos*.

Falling progressively into decay, the Alamo was a forgotten ruin, more than 100 years old and filled with debris, when the historic siege and massacre that took place there in 1836 made its name a rallying cry in Texas's struggle for independence from Mexico. Beginning in the early 1820s, American colonists under leaders like Stephen Austin began arriving in Texas. The Mexican government, which originally had a lenient policy toward American immigration, gradually grew distrustful of the colonists' increasing political ambitions and overwhelming numbers. Fearing an American seizure of Texas, the Mexicans enacted a series of stringent measures aimed at tightening political control over the Texas area and restricting American immigration.

The settlers began to resist Mexican rule (see March 2, Texas Independence Day). The situation reached crisis proportions when General Antonio López de Santa Anna established himself as the reactionary dictator of Mexico, overthrowing the Mexican Republic. In 1835 Santa Anna ordered Mexican troops northward to bring the Texans to heel. The first serious clash occurred at Gonzales on October 2, when a volunteer Texan army, armed with squirrel guns and hunting knives, defeated a Mexican force. Most of the Texan combatants, however, still had ambiguous feelings about what political goals they hoped to achieve from resistance. As one soldier wrote: "I cannot remember that there was any distinct understanding as to the position we were to assume toward Mexico. Some were for independence, some for the Constitution of 1824 [virtually voided by Santa Anna's arbitrary takeover], and some for anything, just so it was a row. But we were all ready to fight."

A week later, a force of about 50 Texans stormed the fort at Goliad to capture $10,000 worth of military supplies. A "consultation" of Texans, meeting at San Felipe de Austin from October 16 to November 14, 1835, issued a "declaration of the causes of taking up arms," but no attempt was made to secede from Mexico. After seizing the Goliad arsenal, the Texans besieged San Antonio, where Santa Anna had sent his brother-in-law, General Martin Perfecto de Cos, to command the northern Mexican forces. On December 5 the Texans inched their way house by house into the town. By the night of December 8, they had forced a Mexican surrender in the partially ruined Alamo. It was humiliating for the Mexicans to relinquish a stronghold that they had held for more than 100 years, especially since it was their last foothold in Texas suitable as a base for military operations.

By the close of 1835, Mexican troops had withdrawn from Texas, and many Texans thought the fighting was over. However, Santa Anna was actually assembling a large army under his personal command. He reportedly boasted: "If the Americans do not beware, I shall march through their own country and plant the Mexican flag in Washington."

During this uncertain period, confusion, apathy, and bickering throughout Texas prevented the orderly supervision of military affairs. Some Texan leaders were convinced, however, that the Alamo in San Antonio should be held to bar Santa Anna's expected march into the interior. Colonel William Barret Travis, a young South Carolina lawyer who had earned a reputation as a firebrand for driving out the Mexican garrison at Anahuac, Texas, in June 1835, lightly garrisoned the Alamo with about 150 volunteers. Among them was James Bowie, an American land speculator and prospector in Texas, as well as a noted frontiersman whose epic-making deeds were already legend and after whom the bowie knife was named. David "Davy" Crockett, another famed hunter and scout, who had reportedly shot 105 bears in one year and who had served in Congress for three terms, was also present. James Butler Bonham, after borrowing funds to journey to Texas to fight, joined his lifelong friend Travis. In addition, some 20 to 30 noncombatants sought refuge within the walls of the mission compound.

Once Santa Anna and about 1,000 Mexican troops had laid siege to the Alamo on February 23, 1836, they hoisted a blood-red flag signifying no quarter. The outnumbered and outgunned Texans responded to the demand for unconditional surrender with a cannon blast. Their position deteriorated steadily during the first days of the siege, when the arrival of reinforcements swelled Mexican forces to an estimated 4,000 to 5,000 men. Travis, fully aware of the perilous situation, sent for aid from other Texan outposts in a message dated February 24, 1836, and addressed "To the People of Texas and all Americans in the World":

> I call on you in the name of Liberty, of patriotism and everything dear to the American character to come to our aid with all dispatch. The enemy is receiving reinforcements daily and will no doubt increase to three or four thousand in four or five days. If this call is neglected, I am determined to sustain myself as long as possible and die like a soldier who never forgets what is due to his honor and that of his country. VICTORY OR DEATH.

The appeal was answered by a mere 32 men, who slipped through the lines at 3:00 a.m. on March 1, 1836. While Santa Anna fired upon the mission walls for many days without making a breach, delegates at Washington-on-the-Brazos were drawing up a declaration of independence for Texas, issued on March 2, 1836 (see March 2, Texas Independence Day). Their action thus fulfilled one of Colonel Travis's last wishes, made in a letter to a friend:

Let the Convention go on and make a Declaration of Independence. . . . Let the Government declare [the Mexicans] public enemies, otherwise she is acting a suicidal part. . . . I shall treat them as such, unless I have superior orders to the contrary. . . . My respects to all friends, and confusion to all enemies. God bless you.

At daybreak on March 6, 1836, the 13th day of the Alamo siege, the Mexicans attacked in force. An eyewitness described the steady fire of cannons and small arms as a "constant thunder." Twice repulsed, the Mexicans breached the walls on the third attempt. Travis fell as they penetrated the mission. "The Texans defended desperately every inch of the fort," reported a Mexican solider, "muzzle to muzzle, hand to hand, musket and rifle, bayonet and bowie knife." Finally, however, the superior Mexican numbers prevailed. The last survivors withdrew to the stone barracks and former chapel, and fought to their death. Jim Bowie, confined to bed with a raging fever, fired from his cot in the chapel building until he was slain. Most authorities agree that Davy Crockett died at his post, although some maintain that he was one of five prisoners killed in cold blood after the battle upon the order of Santa Anna. No male defender survived; some male servants and slaves, however, were among the 15 or more persons who were spared. The Texans' bodies were piled on layers of brush and wood and burned. The estimates of Mexican losses during the battle vary from 600 to 1,600.

The fall of the Alamo mobilized the Texans, and they went into the battle of San Jacinto on April 21, 1836, with the cry "Remember the Alamo." They defeated Santa Anna and the Mexican forces, took him prisoner, and forced him to sign a treaty pledging the use of his influence to bring about a recognition of their independence.

March 7

Salvador Dali Museum Opens in St. Petersburg, Florida

On March 7, 1982, the Salvador Dali Museum opened in St. Petersburg, Florida. It contains the largest collection of works by the famous Spanish artist Salvador Dali in the world.

Dali was born in Spain on May 11, 1904. He attended the San Fernando Academy of Fine Arts in the Spanish capital of Madrid. During the 1920s, he became a leader in the surrealist movement, which used unconventional imagery to express feelings and emotions. He gained international recognition after an exhibit of his paintings in Pittsburgh, Pennsylvania, in 1928. In 1931 Dali produced what is perhaps his most famous piece, the painting *Persistence of Memory*. When World War II began, he left Europe for the United States.

Dali lived in America from 1940 until 1948. During this period, he met Reynolds and Eleanor Morse, a wealthy couple from Cleveland, Ohio. The Morses became Dali's friends and patrons, and their collection of his works would become the basis for the future Salvador Dali Museum.

Dali produced many more works after World War II. Some of the most famous contained religious themes, such as *Christ of St. John of the Cross* and *The Sacrament of the Last Supper*. Many of Dali's works defy classification, however. This is illustrated by the names of such paintings as *Swans Reflecting Elephants*, *The Hallucinogenic Toreador*, *Metamorphosis of Narcissus*, and *Geopolitical Child Witnesses the Birth of a New Man*. Dali died in Spain on January 23, 1989, of cardiovascular problems.

The decades following World War II also saw the growth of the Morse collection of Dali's works. The Morses invested millions in acquiring Dali's paintings, and their gamble paid off. By the 1980s the collection was tentatively estimated to be worth hundreds of millions of dollars. The Morses had established a public gallery in Beechwood, Ohio, but the collection was outgrowing the limited space available on the premises. Therefore, they decided to donate the Dali works to a museum, so that the collection could be properly housed and displayed. Further, once donated the collection could not be split up after their death or sold to pay estate taxes.

Several museums expressed interest in the Morse collection, but an attorney in St. Petersburg, Florida, named James Martin convinced the Morses to donate their collection to a museum that would be established by the local community. The initiative was supported by the state of Florida, and so the many hundreds of Dali paintings, watercolors, sketches, sculptures, and memorabilia came to their new home in downtown St. Petersburg on the waterfront in what has become the center of a thriving artistic community.

Luther Burbank's Birthday

Luther Burbank was born on a farm in Lancaster, Massachusetts, on March 7, 1849. He was educated until he reached the age of 15 in public schools, and then at the Lancaster Academy. He also read extensively in the local library, including the works of Charles Darwin. Burbank began market gardening in a small way as a youth and then, at 21, bought land near Lunenburg, Massachusetts, to begin his life's work of plant breeding. Within three years he had developed a new variety of potato that later became known as the Burbank potato. Shortly after that, in 1875, he migrated to Santa Rosa, California, where he established a nursery and greenhouse.

For the rest of his life he lived and worked there, experimenting with the production of new varieties of flowers, fruits, and vegetables. Their improvement through plant breeding, which utilized the methods of selection and hybridization, as well as grafting, has helped farmers use their land more productively and has contributed greatly to the agricultural economy of California and the nation in general. Burbank produced new strains of tomatoes, corn, squash, beans, peas, artichokes, asparagus, corn, chives, and rhubarb, among other innovations. He also worked extensively with plums, prunes, and berries and developed new varieties of daisies, roses, and lilies. In all, during more than 50 years of work, Burbank developed over 800 new strains and varieties of plants through experimentation with countless numbers of seedlings. Since his purpose was a practical rather than a theoretical one, he did not keep systematic records of his experiments, and many details concerning his work are not available to scientists interested in heredity. His work, however, stimulated worldwide interest in the field of plant breeding.

Burbank's work is described in his writings, which include *New Creations* (1893–1901), a series of catalogs describing new plant varieties; the 12-volume *Luther Burbank: His Methods and Discoveries*; the 8-volume *How Plants Are Trained to Work for Man*; and, with Wilbur Hall, *The Harvest of the Years and Partner of Nature*. Burbank died on April 11, 1926. At the time, he was working on more than 3,000 experiments and was growing thousands of botanical species, many of them native to other countries.

March 8

Simon Cameron's Birthday

Simon Cameron, the first powerful state boss in American politics, was born on March 8, 1799, in Lancaster County, Pennsylvania. Orphaned at the age of nine and receiving little schooling, he was thrown on his own resources early in life. His early years were spent in newspaper publishing, a trade that brought him into contact with the worlds of both business and politics. He became an appren-

tice in a printing office in Harrisburg, Pennsylvania, and worked there until he was 22, when he went to Doylestown, Pennsylvania, to edit a Democratic newspaper. He returned to Harrisburg as a partner in a newspaper enterprise one year later, worked for a short time in Washington, D.C., and then returned again to Harrisburg as the owner of the *Harrisburg Republican* (not affiliated with the future Republican Party).

Thus, by the age of 25, Cameron was well-established in business and was beginning to be influential in the state Democratic Party. Ownership of the newspaper gave him influence in state and national politics, and he became an associate of James Buchanan, later to be elected president. In 1826 Cameron was appointed state printer, a profitable post that provided the means for branching out into the many business interests that, together with shrewd investments, later brought him a great fortune. Once he accumulated enough capital, he pursued his fortune in banking, canal and railroad construction, iron and steel manufacturing, and eventually railroads. He began buying small local railroads and later united them into a network known as the Northern Central line.

Meanwhile, Cameron's political strength and ambitions increased. He promoted the nomination of Andrew Jackson for the presidency in 1828 and the election of James Buchanan to the Senate in 1834. In 1845 Cameron himself was elected to replace Buchanan in the Senate when Buchanan left to enter President James Polk's cabinet. Cameron was by this time well on his way to becoming one of the most powerful political bosses in the country. However, he had maneuvered his election to the Senate through means that brought him the enmity of Buchanan (who had had another candidate in mind) and the regular Democratic Party members. Cameron was supported in that election by a coalition that included members of the opposition Whig Party. His next two attempts at reelection to the Senate were unsuccessful, but he succeeded on his third try, in 1857, as the candidate of the newly formed Republican Party.

In 1860, Cameron was unsuccessful in seeking the Republican nomination for president, and eventually gave his support to Abraham Lincoln in return for a promise made by Lincoln's campaign managers for a cabinet post. Lincoln kept the promise, appointing Cameron as secretary of war, but with considerable reluctance. The president's misgivings proved justified when corruption in the awarding of army contracts and appointments aroused the nation. Cameron had run the war office with the same favoritism that characterized his tactics in Pennsylvania.

Largely to ease him out of the cabinet, Lincoln sent Cameron to Russia as the American representative to the czar's capital at St. Petersburg. While there, Cameron succeeded in getting Russia's support for the Union side during the Civil War. Within a year, though, he resigned and returned to the United States to campaign, unsuccessfully, for a seat in the Senate. Undaunted, he tried again in 1867 and won a seat, which he held until he resigned ten years later so that he could relinquish the seat to his son, James Donald Cameron.

Cameron's son kept the seat in the Senate for many years, and was secretary of war under President Ulysses S. Grant. The son also assumed control of the Republican machine in Pennsylvania, which he ran for two decades. Following the younger Cameron, the state political dynasty was controlled successively by Matthew Stanley Quay, Boies Penrose, William S. Vare, and Joseph R. Grundy, each selected by his predecessor. This Republican machine was so powerful that it dominated Pennsylvania politics until 1936, when President Franklin D. Roosevelt carried the state for the Democrats in that year's elections.

Simon Cameron spent the final years of his life in retirement. He died at the age of 90, on June 26, 1889. Attributed to him is a famous cynical definition of an honest politician as "one who, when he is bought, will stay bought."

Oliver Wendell Holmes Jr.'s Birthday

Photo by Harris and Ewing. Collection of the Supreme Court of the United States.

Oliver Wendell Holmes Jr.

Oliver Wendell Holmes Jr., the celebrated American jurist, was born in Boston, Massachusetts, on March 8, 1841. A member of a very well-known family of clergymen, lawyers, and judges, he inherited their Puritan sense of responsibility along with his father's wit and charm. His father's friends were such men as Ralph Waldo Emerson, James Russell Lowell, and Henry Wadsworth Longfellow. The son, growing up among these Boston notables while his father became famous as a poet and as the author of *The Autocrat of the Breakfast Table*, demonstrated a critical and independent spirit as well as an interest in philosophy and art.

Holmes received the best education available and was admitted to Harvard College. Just after his graduation from Harvard in 1861, he was commissioned in the Massachusetts 20th Volunteers, one of the most decorated units of the Union Army in the Civil War. On the staff of General H. G. Wright, Holmes fought in some of the bloodiest battles of the war (Ball's Bluff, Antietam, and Fredericksburg) and was wounded three times. He was the subject of his father's essay, "The Captain."

Upon returning to Boston as a hero, he shocked those who talked of warfare in glorious terms by calling war an "organized bore." He went on to attend Harvard Law School, graduating in 1866. After being admitted to the bar in 1867, he began practicing in Boston, where his reputation grew rapidly. In addition to working with a Boston law firm, he began lecturing as an instructor on constitutional law at Harvard Law School and contributed as a writer and editor to the *American Law Review*. In 1880 Holmes delivered a series of lectures at Boston's Lowell Institute, which were published the following year in the book that made him famous: *The Common Law*.

As a result of the international acclaim for the book, Holmes was offered the newly created Weld Chair Harvard Law School in 1882. Within another year he was appointed an associate justice of the Supreme Judicial Court of Massachusetts. He was associated with the Massachusetts court for 20 years, contributing to nearly 1,300 legal opinions and serving for the last three years as its chief justice.

In 1902 Justice Holmes was appointed an associate justice of the U.S. Supreme Court by President Theodore Roosevelt. Holmes held the post for 30 years, earning his place in judicial history as one of the Court's greatest members, unsurpassed in the depth of his perception and the originality of his exposition. It is the work of the Supreme Court to interpret the Constitution, and when the decision of the nine members of the Court is not unanimous, both the dissenting and the majority opinions are studied. During his years with the Court, Justice Holmes delivered so many dissenting opinions that he came to be known as the Great Dissenter, but his dissents have been highly influential, serving as precedents for many of today's legal decisions. He was considered the leader of the liberal wing of the Court, since he usually ruled to permit social legislation, although he was not sympathetic to all of the views considered liberal in his day. A strong advocate of judicial restraint, he believed that the will of the electorate, or its elected representatives, should not be lightly thwarted by the courts.

Many of Holmes's legal decisions were of lasting importance. For example, in the case of *Schenck* v. *U.S.* (1919), a case governing the interpretation of the First Amendment's language protecting freedom of speech, he ruled that "the question in every case is whether . . . words are used in such circumstances and are of such a nature as to create a clear and present danger." The "clear and present danger" phrase has since become a staple of First Amendment legal analysis.

Holmes resigned from the Supreme Court in 1932 at the age of 90 and died three years later, on March 6, 1935. In addition to *The Common Law*, his published works include *Speeches* (1891, revised in 1913 and 1938), *Collected Legal Papers* (1920), *Dissenting Opinions of Mr. Justice Holmes* (1929), *Representative Opinions of Mr. Justice Holmes* (1931), *Justice Oliver Wendell Holmes: His Book Notices and Uncollected Letters and Papers* (1936), and two volumes of letters (1941 and 1953).

Battle of Pea Ridge

In the Civil War's Battle of Pea Ridge, also known as the Battle of Elkhorn Tavern, Union forces scored an important victory over the Confederates in the western theater of the war across the Mississippi River. The battle claimed nearly 6,000 casualties: over 1,300 Union soldiers and over 4,500 Confederate soldiers.

The campaign began on March 6, 1862. Major General Samuel R. Curtis commanded the Union forces in the vicinity of Pea Ridge, Arkansas, while Major General Earl Van Dorn commanded forces of the Confederate Army of the West. In the evening of March 6, Van Dorn's Confederates moved to outflank Curtis's position near Pea Ridge, with the goal of dividing the Union forces. Curtis discovered the enemy's maneuver, however, and on March 7 moved to meet Van Dorn. The resulting clash halted the Confederates. Van Dorn attacked again, this time taking the strategic Elkhorn Tav-

ern area. On March 8 Curtis regrouped and deployed both his troops and artillery against the enemy. The Confederates, low on ammunition, were forced to withdraw back across the Mississippi.

After Pea Ridge, the Union held the upper hand in the West.

March 9

Supreme Court Expands Freedom of the Press

On March 9, 1964, the United States Supreme Court issued its decision in the case of *New York Times* v. *Sullivan*. It was a historic decision that limited the ability of public figures to suppress their critics by suing for libel or slander.

In 1960 the Committee to Defend Martin Luther King and the Struggle for Freedom in the South had a full page advertisement published in the *New York Times* newspaper stating that the recent arrest of Reverend Martin Luther King Jr. in Alabama was part of a conspiracy to suppress the civil rights movement. L. B. Sullivan, city commissioner for Montgomery, Alabama, sued the *New York Times* for libel. The lawsuit was brought in an Alabama state court, before a sympathetic southern judge and jury, and under Alabama's libel law Sullivan did not even have to prove that he had suffered damages. The jury returned a verdict in Sullivan's favor and awarded him a $500,000 judgment.

On August 30, 1962, the Alabama Supreme Court upheld the judgment. The case then went to the United States Supreme Court, whose decision on March 9, 1964, reversed the Alabama courts' rulings and invalidated the judgment. The Supreme Court held that public figures such as Sullivan had to prove "actual malice" in order to recover for libel or slander. In other words, unlike ordinary individuals, someone in the public limelight has to prove that a statement was made with knowledge of its falsity or with reckless disregard of whether it was true or false in order to win a lawsuit.

The scope of the *New York Times* v. *Sullivan* decision was initially limited to persons holding office in federal, state, or local governments. However, it became the basis for expanding the "actual malice" standard to anyone who is a public figure. The term "public figure" includes not only public officials but movie stars, business leaders, and others who are widely known. Although it can certainly be argued that the decision to make it harder for public figures to sue for libel and slander has led to abuses by the press and some unwarranted intrusions of privacy, it also acts to prevent the suppression of legitimate criticism and debate that is necessary for a free society. More pragmatically, the *Sullivan* decision prevented southern state officials from using state laws to suppress the civil rights movement during the 1960s.

Edwin Forrest's Birthday

Edwin Forrest was the first American actor to win international acclaim. Born in Philadelphia, Pennsylvania, on March 9, 1806, of Scottish and German parentage, Forrest made his debut in Philadelphia when he was only 14, playing in *Douglas* by John Home. He gained experience by touring the frontier circuit for several years and then playing supporting roles with the English actor Edmund Kean. When Forrest was 20 he scored a brilliant success while making his New York debut in Shakespeare's *Othello*. The performance established him as one of the great tragedians of his century.

Over the next 10 years Forrest established himself as one of America's greatest actors, playing various Shakespearean tragic roles and commissioning tragedies by American playwrights to provide vehicles for his vigorous style of acting. In 1836 he appeared at the Drury Lane Theatre in London, England, in a specially written play, *The Gladiator*, by Robert M. Bird, which provided the actor with one of his most successful roles as Spartacus.

Forrest's success in England and the United States was so great that he amassed a large fortune. He built a castle, which he called Fonthill, on the Hudson River. Later he sold the castle and bought an estate in the northern part of Philadelphia, which he called Spring Brook. Forrest died at Spring Brook on December 12, 1872, of a stroke. He left the greater part of his estate to found the Edwin Forrest Home for Retired Actors in Philadelphia.

March 10

Death of Harriet Tubman

Harriet Tubman, the famous abolitionist and "conductor" in the Underground Railroad, died on March 10, 1913, in Auburn, New York. She was born into slavery around 1820 or 1821 in Dorchester County on the eastern shore of Maryland. Thus, when she died she was probably in her early 90s. Tubman lived a remarkably long time even by modern standards. It is that much more remarkable when it is remembered that very few slaves lived past the age of 50.

At the time of Tubman's birth, Maryland was a slave state. Her childhood was hard, and when she was 13 an overseer struck her with a two-pound weight for disobedience. Tubman's skull was fractured, and she would suffer from blackouts for the rest of her life. In 1849 she learned that she was likely to be sold and decided to escape. She successfully made her way to the free state of Pennsylvania.

Having achieved freedom, Tubman vowed to help rescue other less fortunate blacks, and found support from northern abolitionists. She made the first of her many trips into slave territory when she went to Baltimore, Maryland, and successfully helped several members of her family escape. Over a dozen more trips into the South followed, and Tubman helped hundreds of slaves escape during the 1850s. Despite her lack of formal education or training, she proved to be an excellent leader and organizer. She was given the nickname "Moses" by her admirers, as Moses had led the enslaved Jews from Egypt to a promised land where they were free. Naturally, she was hated by southerners and slaveowners. At one point, there was a $40,000 bounty on her head in Maryland.

After the onset of the Civil War, Tubman joined the Union army. She served in a variety of capacities, including cook, nurse, scout, and spy. She served primarily in the Carolinas, earning several commendations from Union officers. During these military campaigns in southern territory, she also helped many slaves escape from their masters.

When the Civil War ended, Tubman came to settle in Auburn, New York, and was active in fund-raising for new schools to help educate the freed slaves. She also began a home for elderly African Americans, which was where she was living when she died in 1913. Despite her service to the Union during the Civil War, she never received a veteran's pension or other benefits.

Albany Becomes the Capital of New York

Albany, New York, is located at a strategic crossroads of navigable waterways and overland transportation routes. The area was the object of several early colonization efforts. In 1540 the French established a short-lived trading post in the area. The region reverted to wilderness until 1609, when Henry Hudson sailed the ship *Half Moon* 142 miles up the river that today bears his name. He claimed the territory around Albany, and within five years his Dutch employers and sponsors had established a trading post, Fort Nassau. The Dutch abandoned the post in 1619, however. The first actual settlers were 18 families sent by the Dutch West India Company, who arrived in 1624.

Disembarking on the banks of the Hudson 17 years after the English had settled at Jamestown, Virginia, and three years after the Pilgrims had established their colony at Plymouth, Massachusetts, these settlers built Fort Orange. It was the third oldest permanent settlement within the borders of the 13 original American colonies. Eventually the Dutch possessions in New York were conquered by the English, and in 1664 the name of the village was changed to Albany in honor of the Duke of York and Albany, who later became King James II of England.

In 1686 Thomas Dongan, governor of the colony of New York, granted Albany a city charter. This document, the oldest city charter in the United States, gave complete control of all vacant lands within the city limits to the mayor, aldermen, and common people. Pieter Schuyler was the first mayor. Perhaps the most significant event to occur in the city was the famous intercolonial conference of 1754, known as the Albany Congress. At this meeting, delegates from the New England colonies, New York, Pennsylvania, and Maryland considered Benjamin Franklin's plan for a federation of colonies. Many historians consider this to have been the first attempt at intercolonial cooperation prior to the American Revolution.

Albany was the seat of government of New York at various points during New York's colonial history and during the turmoil of the American Revolution, but it was not until March 10, 1797, that Albany was selected as the permanent capital of New York state.

March 11

Worldwide Influenza Epidemic Strikes the United States

It is of course widely known that America was involved in World War I and that there was considerable loss of life in that conflict. Curiously, another event that in fact claimed many more lives than World War I has faded into obscurity. This was the worldwide influenza epidemic, which reached the United States on March 11, 1918, as World War I was drawing to a close. On this date, over 100 servicemen at Fort Riley, Kansas, came down with the illness. In the years following World War I and through the early 1920s, roughly half a million Americans would die from the flu.

In modern times, the flu is considered a minor ailment with symptoms that can be treated with over-the-counter drugs; powerful antibiotics can be used if complications develop. This was not the case in 1918. In addition, the particular strain of influenza that was spreading around the world at that time was much more deadly than any flu virus seen since. It is uncertain where the virus of 1918 originated, although it was nicknamed the "Spanish Influenza."

The limited medical knowledge of the time made it possible for the disease to spread very rapidly. For example, when nurses and other hospital personnel wore surgical masks to protect themselves while treating patients with the flu, they often did not pull the mask up over their nostrils. It was not yet understood that a virus could be inhaled through the nasal cavities just as easily as through the mouth, so the result was that these medical personnel became carriers of the flu themselves.

Worldwide, the loss of life may have been as high as 40 million people, approximately 2 percent of the world's population. The loss of life was even higher in some Pacific Island communities where the natives were more susceptible to outside diseases. As with most deadly epidemics, however, the flu virus began to fade. This is a fairly predictable outcome for most viruses, since a disease that kills its host hinders its own chances for survival.

There were unusually serious flu outbreaks in 1957 and 1968 as well. In any year, there is a regular "flu season" that begins with the onset of colder temperatures in the fall. Approximately 20,000 people die of the flu every year in the United States.

The Blizzard of 1888

The legendary blizzard of 1888, one of the most famous snowstorms in American history, hit the northeastern states on March 11 of that year. High winds, low temperatures, and heavy snowfall continued for 36 hours. The winds whipped the snowfall into impassable drifts, and people lost all sense of direction in the driving, swirling snow. The result was some 400 deaths.

One victim was Roscoe Conkling, the leader of the Republican Party in New York and United States senator from 1867 to 1881. Conkling, at the time in private law practice, walked from his office on Wall Street to his house on 14th Street during the blizzard. He died about a month later from the effects of exposure.

In New York City the 20.9-inch snowfall was blown into 12-foot-high drifts. In some areas, such as Herald Square, the snow drifts were reportedly as high as 30 feet. Transportation was brought to a standstill, except for sleighs, and the stock exchanges closed. Communications were cut off, and telegraph messages from New York City to Boston had to be transmitted by way of England.

New Yorkers were marooned in their homes, threatened by a food panic in addition to their other worries. Because of the snowdrifts, fire-fighting equipment could not reach fires, which caused an estimated property loss of $25 million.

Not long after the storm, an organization called the Blizzard Men of 1888 was formed in New York City. For years, members of the group met each year to mark the anniversary of the storm by recalling their experiences. Although the stories they exchanged seemed like tall tales, there was probably little need for exaggeration. One member, who had been a boy in Philadelphia at the time of the storm, recalled that the snowdrifts reached the second-story windows of his house and that 28 horses were hitched to the snowplow on the streetcar tracks. Another member reported that the wind velocity had reached 84 miles per hour, and a salesman in a shoe store reported that he sold 1,200 pairs of men's rubber boots that week.

There have been heavier snowfalls since, but no storm has equaled the Great Blizzard of 1888 in the unfortunate combination of severe cold, strong winds, heavy snowfall, number of human casualties, and extent of property damage.

March 12

Girl Scouts Founded

March 12 is the anniversary of Juliette Gordon Low's 1912 founding of the Girl Scouts of the United States of America, in Savannah, Georgia. It is observed every year by the organization's members, who number in the millions.

Low was born on October 31, 1860. One of the six children of Eleanor Kinzie Gordon and Captain William Washington Gordon, she was an adventurous child with a penchant for pets, games, drawing, and writing and an early flair for organization, as evidenced in the Helpful Hands club she formed to make clothes for needy children. At age 14 she was sent to boarding school in Virginia, and she later attended a French school in New York City. On November 21, 1886, she married a wealthy Englishman, William Mackay Low, whose family owned a house on Savannah's Lafayette Square. The couple took up residence in London, England, where Juliette became socially prominent. She returned to the United States during the Spanish-American War of 1898, helping her mother organize a hospital for soldiers in Florida, where her father, by then a general, was stationed. At the war's end, she rejoined her husband in England.

After the death of her husband in 1905, Low filled the next six years' uncertainty about the purpose of her life with art studies and travel. In the spring of 1911, her interest in the scouting movement was aroused through a chance meeting with Sir Robert S. S. Baden-Powell, who had founded the Boy Scouts three years earlier (see February 8). The enthusiasm of Baden-Powell and his sister Agnes, who in 1910 had joined him to form the Girl Guides as a sister organization to the Boy Scouts, proved to be contagious. In a short time, Low became a Girl Guide leader, starting her first troop in a lonely valley of Scotland during the summer of 1911. On her return to London in the fall, she founded two more troops.

In 1912 she transported the Girl Guides idea to Savannah, where she organized 18 girls from a friend's school into the first American troop on March 12. The first name in the register that the girls signed was that of a Daisy Gordon, Low's niece, who has since been frequently honored as the first Girl Scout. For a time, Low herself led the troop, teaching fire building, simple outdoor cookery, knot tying, and other skills that were novelties to the girls of 1912. Meanwhile, she also trained new leaders to carry on the work.

In 1913, the year that the name of the American organization was changed from Girl Guides to Girl Scouts, Low opened a national headquarters in Washington, D.C. As a result of her energetic promotional activities, inquiries poured into the new office from all parts of the country, and membership increased rapidly. Low retired from the presidency of the organization in 1920, receiving the title of founder, and devoted her remaining years to the development of international guiding, acting as liaison between the Girl Scouts of the United States and Girl Guide organizations in European countries.

At the time of Low's death, on January 17, 1927, there were more than 140,000 Girl Scouts, with troops in every state of the Union. Membership continued to grow under new leadership after her death. During World War II, a liberty ship was named in her honor, and in 1954 the city of Savannah, where she had been laid to rest in her Girl Scout uniform, named a new school after her. The Girl Scouts were officially chartered by the United States Congress on March 16, 1950.

President Truman Announces the "Truman Doctrine"

See also May 8, Harry S. Truman's Birthday.

After World War II, the United States became embroiled in a new conflict, known as the cold war. Although President Harry S. Truman tried diplomatic initiatives, it quickly became clear that stronger measures were necessary. By 1947 the Soviets had consolidated their control over the nations of Eastern Europe that they had "liberated" from the Nazis. Greece and Turkey were in danger of falling within the Soviet sphere of influence, as well. Although the Soviets had not occupied those two countries, the Greeks and the Turks were dependent on British military and economic assistance, which Great Britain could no longer afford.

On March 12, 1947, President Truman gave a speech in which he proposed aid for Greece and Turkey. Further, Truman stated that he supported aid for any country anywhere in the world that was struggling to stay free, a policy that would become known as the "Truman Doctrine." His speech was successful in getting Congress to approve the requested aid for the Greeks and Turks. The relevant excerpts are set forth below:

The gravity of the situation which confronts the world today necessitates my appearance before a joint session of the Congress. The foreign policy and the national security of this country are involved.

One aspect of the present situation, which I wish to present to you at this time for your consideration and decision, concerns Greece and Turkey. The United States has received from the Greek Government an urgent appeal for financial and economic assistance. Preliminary reports from the American Economic Mission now in Greece and reports from the American Ambassador in Greece corroborate the statement of the Greek Government that assistance is imperative if Greece is to survive as a free nation.

I do not believe that the American people and the Congress wish to turn a deaf ear to the appeal of the Greek Government. Greece is not a rich country. Lack of sufficient natural resources has always forced the Greek people to work hard to make both ends meet. Since 1940, this industrious and peace-loving country has suffered invasion, four years of cruel enemy occupation, and bitter internal strife. When forces of liberation entered Greece they found that the retreating Germans had destroyed virtually all the railways, roads, port facilities, communications and merchant marine. More than a thousand villages had been burned. Eighty-five per cent of the children were tubercular. Livestock, poultry and draft animals had almost

disappeared. Inflation had wiped out practically all savings.

As a result of these tragic conditions, a [communist and pro-Soviet] military minority, exploiting human want and misery, was able to create political chaos which, until now, has made economic recovery impossible. Greece is today without funds to finance the importation of those goods which are essential to bare subsistence. Under these circumstances the people of Greece cannot make progress in solving their problems of reconstruction. Greece is in desperate need of financial and economic assistance to enable it to resume purchases of food, clothing, fuel and seeds. These are indispensable for the subsistence of its people and are obtainable only from abroad. Greece must have help to import the goods necessary to restore internal order and security so essential for economic and political recovery.

The very existence of the Greek state is today threatened by the terrorist activities of several thousand armed men, led by Communists, who defy the Government's authority at a number of points, particularly along the northern boundaries. A commission appointed by the United Nations Security Council is at present investigating disturbed conditions in northern Greece and alleged border violations along the frontier between Greece on the one hand and Albania, Bulgaria and Yugoslavia on the other. Meanwhile, the Greek Government is unable to cope with the situation. The Greek Army is small and poorly equipped. It needs supplies and equipment if it is to restore the authority of the Government throughout Greek territory. Greece must have assistance if it is to become a self-supporting and self-respecting democracy.

The British Government, which has been helping Greece, can give no further financial or economic aid after March. Great Britain finds itself under the necessity of reducing or liquidating its commitments in several parts of the world, including Greece. We have considered how the United Nations might assist in this crisis. But the situation is an urgent one requiring immediate action, and the United Nations and its related organizations are not in a position to extend help of the kind that is required.

Greece's neighbor, Turkey, also deserves our attention. The future of Turkey as an independent and economically sound State is clearly no less important to the freedom-loving peoples of the world than the future of Greece. The circumstances in which Turkey finds itself today are considerably different from those of Greece. Turkey has been spared the disasters that have beset Greece. And during the war, the United States and Great Britain furnished Turkey with material aid. Nevertheless, Turkey now needs our support.

Since the war Turkey has sought financial assistance from Great Britain and the United States for the purpose of effecting that modernization necessary for the maintenance of its national integrity. That integrity is essential to the preservation of order in the Middle East. The British Government has informed us that, owing to its own difficulties, it can no longer extend financial or economic aid to Turkey. As in the case of Greece, if Turkey is to have the assistance it needs, the United States must supply it. We are the only country able to provide that help.

I am fully aware of the broad implications involved if the United States extends assistance to Greece and Turkey, and I shall discuss these implications with you at this time. One of the primary objectives of the foreign policy of the United States is the creation of conditions in which we and other nations will be able to work out a way of life free from coercion. This was a fundamental issue in the war with Germany and Japan. Our victory was won over countries which sought to impose their will, and their way of life, upon other nations.

To ensure the peaceful development of nations, free from coercion, the United States has taken a leading part in establishing the United Nations. The United Nations is designed to make possible lasting freedom and independence for all its members. We shall not realize our objectives, however, unless we are willing to help free people to maintain their free institutions and their national integrity against aggressive movements that seek to impose upon them totalitarian regimes. This is no more than a frank recognition that totalitarian regimes imposed on free peoples, by direct or indirect aggression, undermine the foundations of international peace and hence the security of the United States.

The peoples of a number of countries of the world have recently had totalitarian regimes forced upon them against their will. The Government of the United States has made frequent protests against coercion and intimidation in violation of the Yalta agreement, in Poland, Rumania, and Bulgaria. I must also state that in a number of other countries there have been similar developments.

At the present moment in world history nearly every nation must choose between alternative ways of life. The choice is too often not a free one. One way of life is based upon the will of the majority, and is distinguished by free institutions, representative government, free elections, guaranties of individual liberty, freedom of speech and religion, and freedom from political oppression. The second way of life is based upon the will of a minority forcibly imposed upon the majority. It relies upon terror and oppression, a controlled press and radio, fixed elections, and the suppression of personal freedoms.

I believe that it must be the policy of the United States to support free peoples who are resisting attempted subjugation by armed minorities or by outside pressures. I believe that we must assist free peoples to work out their own destinies in their own way. I believe that our help should be primarily through economic and financial aid which is essential to economic stability and orderly political processes. The world is not static, and the status quo is not sacred. But we cannot allow changes in the status quo in violation of the Charter of the United Nations by such methods as coercion, or by such subterfuges as political infiltration. In helping free and independent nations to maintain their freedom, the United States will be giving effect to the principles of the Charter of the United Nations.

It is necessary only to glance at a map to realize that the survival and integrity of the Greek nation are of grave importance in a much wider situation. If Greece should fall under the control of an armed minority, the effect upon its neighbor, Turkey, would be immediate and serious. Confusion and disorder might well spread throughout the entire Middle East. Moreover, the disappearance of Greece as an independent State would have a profound effect upon those countries in Europe whose peoples are struggling against great difficulties to maintain their freedoms and their independence while they repair the damages of war. It would be an unspeakable tragedy if these countries, which have struggled so long against overwhelming odds, should lose that victory for which they sacrificed so much. Collapse of free institutions and loss of independence would be disastrous not only for them but for the world. Discouragement and possibly failure would quickly be the lot of neighboring peoples striving to maintain their freedom and independence.

Should we fail to aid Greece and Turkey in this fateful hour, the effect will be far-reaching to the West as well as to the East. We must take immediate and resolute action.

This is a serious course upon which we embark. l would not recommend it except that the alternative is much more serious. The United States contributed $341,000,000,000 toward winning World War II. This is an investment in world freedom and world peace. The assistance that I am recommending for Greece and Turkey amounts to little more than one-tenth of 1 per cent of this investment. It is only common sense that we should safeguard this investment and make sure that it was not in vain. The seeds of totalitarian regimes are nurtured by misery and want. They spread and grow in the evil soil of poverty and strife. They reach their full growth when the hope of a people for a better life has died. We must keep that hope alive.

The free peoples of the world look to us for support in maintaining their freedoms. If we falter in our leadership, we may endanger the peace of the world and we shall surely endanger the welfare of our own nation. Great responsibilities have been placed upon us by the swift movement of events. I am confident that the Congress will face these responsibilities squarely.

March 13

L. Ron Hubbard's Birthday

Lafayette Ronald Hubbard, the founder of the Church of Scientology, was born on March 13, 1911, in Tilden, Nebraska. His father was a naval officer, and the family moved frequently. Young Hubbard had an adventurous spirit, and in 1927, at the age of 16, he took a steamship from San Francisco, California, to Asia. He traveled through many of the ports on the Pacific Rim before eventually reuniting with his father in Guam. After several years of travel, Hubbard returned to the United States. In 1930 he entered George Washington University in Washington, D.C.

In college, Hubbard developed an interest in both nuclear physics and the functioning of the human mind. He also began to write fiction, which became his full-time profession after leaving college. Eventually, he wrote hundreds of novels and short stories covering a variety of genres. He is best known for his science fiction stories, which he contributed to such magazines as *Unknown* and *Astounding Science Fiction*.

After serving in the United States Navy during World War II, Hubbard's interest in the workings of the human mind began to dominate his life. He developed a means of psychiatric treatment called Dianetics that attempts to improve mental hygiene by confronting unpleasant memories and experiences buried in the subconscious. Hubbard believed that these "engrams" were at the root of human unhappiness. In 1950 Hubbard's book *Dianetics: The Modern Science of Mental Health* was published. The book was enormously popular, and even as of this writing in the late 1990s, it continues to sell in the millions.

In the following years, Hubbard continued his research into Dianetics and gained many followers. He claimed that there was a relationship between subatomic physics and the operation of the human mind, and further concluded that what he saw as the success of Dianetics was due to the fundamentally spiritual nature of the mind. Having thus entered into the realm of religious philosophy, Hubbard and his followers founded the Church of Scientology in 1954. In the following decades, Scientology would grow to become a worldwide religion that claims to have millions of followers.

In addition to Dianetics, Scientology attempts to apply scientific principles to ethics and morals. The Church of Scientology also believes in reincarnation.

Hubbard's work for the church did not prevent him from continuing to be a prolific writer. In the early 1980s, he produced a massive 10-volume science fiction novel entitled *Mission Earth* that contained over a million words and was a top-10 bestseller. He died on January 24, 1986, in California. Despite some criticism about its financial operations, the Church of Scientology continues to thrive and sponsors a number of programs to help rehabilitate criminals and drug addicts.

Discovery of Pluto Announced

On March 13, 1930, the discovery of the ninth planet in the solar system was officially announced. The announcement was deliberately timed to coincide with the birthday of Percival Lowell, the American astronomer who was born on March 13, 1855, and predicted the existence of what he termed "Planet X." When this Planet X was discovered, it was named Pluto partly to honor Lowell's memory, as explained below.

The solar system consists of the Sun and nine major planets. A space traveler moving outward from the Sun would encounter the nine planets in the following order: Mercury, Venus, Earth, Mars, Jupiter, Saturn, Uranus, Neptune, and Pluto. Mercury is roughly 35 million miles from the Sun, a tiny distance by astronomical standards, while the outer planets are billions of miles away. The existence of Mercury, Venus, Mars, Jupiter, and Saturn has been known since ancient times, as those planets can be observed with the naked eye from Earth. Thus, for centuries it was assumed that there were only six planets, including Earth.

By the 1700s, telescopes were in wide use. In 1781 a British astronomer named William Herschel discovered the seventh planet, Uranus. Uranus cannot be seen with the naked eye, since it is nearly two billion miles from the Sun, almost twice as far away as Saturn, the farthest out of the first six planets. Shortly after its discovery, astronomers noticed that the orbit of this new planet did not follow the path predicted by the laws of physics. In the 1820s, a German mathematician predicted that the reason for this discrepancy must be due to the gravitational influence of an unknown eighth planet even further away from the Sun than Uranus. This eighth planet was discovered in 1846, and was named Neptune.

Neptune's existence accounted for nearly all of the discrepancies in Uranus's orbit, but there were enough remaining gaps to lead American astronomer Percival Lowell to conclude that there must be yet another planet in the solar system. Lowell had made a name for himself as an astronomer with his observations of Mars, and in the 1890s he had founded the prestigious Lowell Observatory in Flagstaff, Arizona. Independently wealthy, he financed the observatory's search for the ninth planet. Unfortunately, Lowell died of a stroke on November 12, 1916, before his dream could be realized.

It was an amateur astronomer named Clyde Tombaugh, working in cooperation with the Lowell Observatory, who eventually made the breakthrough. He spent months taking telescopic photographs of various sections of the night sky. Although Pluto is billions of miles away, it is much closer to Earth than even the closest star, so over time any point of light in the sky that was a planet would eventually appear to move as it orbited the Sun while the stars in the background would appear to stand still. By using a succession of photographic plates taken of the same sections of the night sky but at different times, Tombaugh was able to determine that one particular object was in fact moving. This object turned out to be the elusive ninth planet.

The planet was named Pluto after the Roman god of the underworld, which seemed appropriate for a planet that was so far from the Sun. Further, the first two letters of the word Pluto are P and L, which are the initials of Percival Lowell.

Pluto has one moon, named Charon.

March 14

Albert Einstein's Birthday

Scientific inquiry, said Albert Einstein, one of the greatest physicists the world has known, is prompted by "the cosmic religious experience" and the attempt to experience all existence "as a unity full of significance."

Einstein, whose thinking laid the foundation of the atomic age and paved the road to the exploration of space, was born at Ulm, Germany, on March 14, 1879. After study in mathematics and physics, he graduated from the Federal Institute of Technology in Zurich in 1900. In 1902 he was appointed examiner of patents at the Swiss Patent Office in Berne, a position that gave him modest financial security, as well as time for contemplation and the pursuit of personal projects.

One of these projects was work toward a Ph.D. degree, which he received from the University of Zurich in 1905. The other was the publication that same year of a series of papers of incalculable importance. One of them changed the concept of the basic building blocks of matter and energy by enlarging upon Max Planck's theory that radiant energy is given out not in a steady wave, but in tiny particles or "quanta" that are essentially "packages" of energy. This paper, which among other things explained the photoelectric effect (the basis of electronics), came to have far-reaching practical applications, including television. It also garnered Einstein the 1921 Nobel Prize in physics.

Another one of the 1905 papers explained the movement of small particles suspended in liquids. Two others, dealing with the inertia of energy and the characteristics of electricity in motion, were steps toward Einstein's historic 1905 publication

March 13

"The Special Theory of Relativity." Together with a later work, "The General Theory of Relativity," the Special Theory altered the concept of the universe. For one thing, it obliterated the age-old distinction between matter and energy. As Einstein showed with his now famous equation $E=mc^2$, matter and energy are interchangeable, a truth demonstrated by the explosion of the first atomic bomb at Alamogordo, New Mexico, on July 16, 1945.

Einstein's Special Theory also showed that the supposed absolutes of space, time, and mass, by which people were accustomed to measuring the universe, were not actually absolutes. Space, time, and mass can contract and expand in complex, interrelated ways depending on such factors as the speed of an object in motion. Thus, the mass of a moving body increases with its speed in relation to a stationary observer, and would become infinite if the moving body could reach the speed of light (which, however, is impossible for ordinary matter).

Einstein's theory of relativity, presented at an Austrian scientific congress in 1908, was greeted with acclaim and a deluge of teaching offers. A series of prestigious academic posts followed in Zurich, Prague, and Leiden. In 1913 a position was created for him, the directorship of Berlin's Kaiser Wilhelm Institute. A year later, his election to the Prussian Academy of Sciences brought him a stipend that allowed him to devote himself full-time to research. Einstein's General Theory of Relativity (1916) grew out of this period of freedom. In it he pointed out that, in terms of the universe at large, it is useless to speak of three-dimensional space without taking the fourth dimension of time into account. His theory forever changed the idea of space and time as two separate entities; instead the universe is to be perceived as a four-dimensional "space-time continuum." Einstein's mathematics made it possible to deal with this universe in which time is the fourth dimension.

The General Theory is also remarkable for Einstein's ideas concerning gravity, which is not, he said, a "force" as commonly thought. Stars, planets, and other bodies in space do not exert a force upon each other across space. Instead, their mass is a physical presence that causes a "warping" or "curving" of the space-time continuum around that mass, and this curving influences other nearby bodies (which, in turn, also curve space and influence their neighbors). The situation is somewhat like placing objects on a tightly stretched blanket: A bowling ball placed on such a blanket would create a deeper impression in the blanket than a ping-pong ball placed nearby, and would probably cause the ping-pong ball to roll toward it. However, the bowling ball has exerted no "force" on the ping-pong ball.

Einstein went on to reveal some other unexpected characteristics of gravity: It can affect time, for time intervals vary according to the gravitational field in question, and it can affect light, causing it to pass through a gravitational field in a curve instead of in the expected straight line. In short, Einstein explained that the universe is not at all like a great, precisely conditioned machine, as had been thought since the time of Isaac Newton. Everything in it is in constant motion, the parts interacting to alter one another's behavior and characteristics. It is, however, an orderly universe in its own way, and Einstein sought to define the laws of nature that govern that order. In this attempt, he perceived "the illimitable superior spirit who reveals himself in the slight details we are able to perceive with our frail and feeble minds."

Einstein was married to his cousin, Elsa Einstein, a widow, in 1917, after his first marriage ended in divorce. In the years that followed, he received many of the Western world's important honors, wrote a number of books on scientific and other subjects, and was active in humanitarian causes. In 1933, after the rise of Hitler in Germany, Einstein (an anti-Fascist, pacifist, and Jew) moved to Princeton, New Jersey. He became an American citizen in 1940. In Princeton, Einstein was associated with the Institute for Advanced Study for the rest of his life, continuing to work there even after his official retirement in 1945.

In 1939, concerned about Nazi nuclear research, Einstein wrote President Franklin D. Roosevelt about the possibility of an atomic war. This letter eventually resulted in the Manhattan Project of World War II and the development of the atomic bomb. After World War II, Einstein devoted much of his energy to urging disarmament and some form of world government. In 1952 he was offered the presidency of Israel. He declined, feeling himself unsuited for the post. Instead, he continued his research into the Unified Field Theory, an attempt to harmonize quantum theory (which deals with the smallest of subatomic and other particles) with relativity (which deals with large masses and bodies traveling at enormous speeds). Later work by other scientists went further toward establishing a Unified Field Theory, and suggested that Einstein had come close to his goal of ultimate synthesis. Unfortunately, he did not live to realize the extent of his achievement. On April 18, 1955, he died of a ruptured aorta. He left as his legacy new vistas of scientific knowledge so vast that their eventual implications have as yet only been glimpsed.

Eli Whitney Patents the Cotton Gin

Eli Whitney, a native of Massachusetts, was born in rural Westboro on December 8, 1765. As a boy, he showed little enthusiasm for study, but he excelled in the use of his hands as he learned craftsmanship in his father's metalworking shop. Belatedly deciding (at age 18) that he would like to go on to college, he taught school for several years to earn the funds for this purpose. He went on to attend Yale, and graduated at the age of 26.

After graduation, Whitney went to Savannah, Georgia, to be a tutor. He taught and lived at Mulberry Grove, a plantation belonging to the widow of the Revolutionary War general Nathanael Greene. While he was there, some of Mrs. Greene's planter friends complained about the problems of cotton production and asked Whitney if he could invent a machine for separating the seed from the fiber. Relatively little cotton was then grown in the South because of the tedious process of freeing the seed from the fiber by hand.

Whitney soon conceived of a device that could separate cottonseeds from fibers. In 1793 he produced the first cotton gin, for which he obtained a patent on March 14, 1794. The gin was a cylinder, covered with many metal teeth that revolved against a grate of closely spaced parallel bars holding the cotton full of seeds. The teeth of the cylinder pulled the cotton fibers through the bars, leaving the seeds behind. This process made possible a 50-fold increase in the average daily output of cotton. Modern ginning technology has evolved from Whitney's system.

Following the invention of the cotton gin, the cultivation of cotton in the South expanded rapidly. Unfortunately, slave labor became that much more profitable as plantation owners sought more workers for their cotton fields. The great increase in production benefited mill owners as well as planters, since it led to the wide use of cotton fabrics, which were made even more economical by the later development of the power loom.

South Carolina gave Whitney an award of $50,000 in recognition of the importance of his invention, but since Congress refused to renew his patent in 1812, he received relatively little profit from the machine that revolutionized the economy of the South and had a profound effect throughout the world. Whitney later devoted himself to the more profitable business of munitions manufacture, and he introduced an important innovation with his concept of interchangeable parts. He died in New Haven, Connecticut, on January 8, 1825.

Union Forces take New Berne, North Carolina

On March 14, 1862, during the Civil War, Union forces took the strategic town of New Berne in Craven County, North Carolina. It was an important step in Union general Ambrose Burnside's North Carolina campaign and became the staging point for many later operations.

Burnside's forces were opposed by the Confederates under Brigadier General Lawrence Branch. On March 11 Burnside moved his forces from their coastal landing site at Roanoke Island. Supported by Union gunboats, on March 13 he moved up the Neuse River and landed his forces on the river's south bank near New Berne. The next day he attacked Branch's defenses with several brigades. After several hours of fighting, the Confederates were forced to abandon their positions and the Union took the town. Burnside also captured dozens of heavy artillery pieces.

New Berne was an important Union victory, securing as it did a town with strategic river and rail assets.

March 15

Andrew Jackson's Birthday

Library of Congress

Andrew Jackson

Andrew Jackson, the seventh president of the United States, was born at the Waxhaw settlement on the border line then disputed by North and South Carolina, on March 15, 1767. Both states have since claimed him as their native son, although most sources agree with Jackson, who in later years said that he had been born in South Carolina. Of Scotch-Irish descent, he was born to parents who had emigrated from Ireland to the American frontier.

Perhaps it was the rigor of Jackson's early life that instilled in him the stubbornness that later earned him the nickname Old Hickory. His father died a few days before he was born. His mother, Elizabeth Hutchinson Jackson, died in 1780. His two older brothers also died during the closing years of the American Revolution, leaving him alone in the world at an early age. Meanwhile, Jackson had begun his own military career at the age of 14 by taking part in a local skirmish after the British invasion of the Carolinas. Briefly a prisoner of the British, he declined to polish a captor's boots with the announcement that he was "a prisoner of war, not a servant."

Jackson was 17 and the Revolution was over when he began to study law at Salisbury, North Carolina, in 1784. He was admitted to the bar in 1787. The next year, he was appointed prosecuting attorney for the region of North Carolina that would eventually become the state of Tennessee. Having settled in what was then the stockaded frontier community of Nashville, he developed a thriving law practice, engaged in land speculation, and earned the loyalty of the landowners and creditors who became his political allies for the next three decades. He also became acquainted with Rachel Donelson Robards, daughter of Mrs. John Donelson, in whose home he lodged. In the mistaken belief that she was legally divorced from the absent Captain Lewis Robards, Rachel Robards and Jackson, both 24, were married in August 1791. The divorce was not actually granted until two years later, however, and a second wedding ceremony was performed on January 17, 1794.

In January 1796 Jackson became a delegate to the convention that framed a constitution for the state of Tennessee. Later that year he was elected as the new state's first representative to the House of Representatives in Washington, D.C. He was elected to the U.S. Senate in 1797, but resigned after serving about a year. He returned to Tennessee, where he served as a judge of the state's superior court from 1798 to 1804. He returned to private life in the latter year, living as a planter and engaging in a variety of business and mercantile enterprises. Meanwhile, he had become the commanding general of the Tennessee militia in 1802,

a post that he still held when the War of 1812 against Britain was officially declared by Congress. In mid-1812 Jackson offered his services and those of the militia he commanded to the federal government.

Jackson and his men were sent to fight the Red Sticks faction of the Creek native tribe, who were allied with the British and posed a threat to the southern frontier. A months-long campaign culminated in Jackson's final triumph in March 1814 at the battle of Horseshoe Bend in east central Alabama. The victory secured millions of acres of Creek land in present-day Alabama and Georgia, opening a vast new region to settlement. Jackson next invaded Florida, which was blatantly illegal since Florida was then a Spanish possession and Spain was not at war with America, and took the port city of Pensacola, where some British ships were docked. Jackson also won a significant victory against the British at the Battle of New Orleans on January 8, 1815 (see January 8 for further details). The victory made Jackson a national hero and set him firmly on the road to the White House.

Although offered the post of secretary of war by President James Monroe, Jackson preferred to remain in the army. In 1818 he received orders to conquer the independent Seminole tribe and the runaway slaves who had crossed into Spanish Florida, thus achieving freedom. Jackson once again invaded Spanish Florida and led his troops to Pensacola, where they captured the Spanish fort. On the way he hanged two British subjects, whom he accused of inciting the Seminoles. This foray helped the United States purchase Florida from Spain, since Jackson's feats demonstrated Spain's weakness in the area.

The Adams-Onis Treaty, by which the United States purchased Florida, was signed in 1819 (see February 22) but was not ratified until 1821. In the latter year Jackson was appointed provisional governor of the territory. He immediately antagonized the inhabitants by imprisoning one of the two Spanish governors on charges of failing to abide by the terms of the treaty. His relations with the government in Washington, D.C., were also poor. After only eight months, he resigned.

Jackson decided to run for president in the 1824 election. There were four contenders for the presidency in this election, each of them representing a different part of the disintegrating Democratic-Republican Party. The Electoral College gave the largest number of votes, 99, to Jackson. Secretary of State John Quincy Adams received 84; Secretary of the Treasury William Harris Crawford, 41; and Henry Clay, speaker of the House of Representatives, 37. Thus, no candidate received a majority of the vote. In accordance with the Constitution, the outcome of the election was to be decided by the House of Representatives. At this point Clay gave his support to Adams, which ensured Adams's election to the presidency.

Jackson ran again in 1828. His supporters opposed Adams's policies, which were based on the philosophy of a strong central government, and depicted Jackson as an advocate of states' rights. Even though Jackson was no uneducated backwoodsman, his supporters built up a homespun image of the man that had particular appeal in the western and southern regions then being settled. They pictured Adams as one of an "aristocratic" minority that was controlling the government. The Democratic-Republican Party accordingly split into two factions. Adams was chosen to be the presidential candidate of the faction that called itself the National Republican Party, the forerunner of the modern Republican Party. His only opponent was Jackson, the candidate of the faction that became the modern Democratic Party.

Jackson was victorious. The 1828 popular vote was 647,286 for Jackson and 508,864 for Adams; Jackson received 178 electoral votes to Adams's 83. On the evening of Inauguration Day, Jackson held a reception for the public at the White House. It was a noisy, drunken affair attended by about 20,000 people, who did thousands of dollars' worth of damage to the residence. Upon assuming office, Jackson began rewarding his supporters with government positions, even when doing so involved removing capable officeholders. This was called the "spoils system," a play on the ancient proverb that "to the victor go the spoils," and introduced an element of corruption into government offices that would last until the civil service reform legislation of the late 19th century. Jackson also sought to abolish the second Bank of the United States, which was a forerunner of the modern central banking system, a decision that became an important issue when he stood for reelection in 1832.

Despite these controversies, in the 1832 election Jackson was swept back into office with 56.6 percent of the popular vote and 219 electoral votes, while his opponent Henry Clay garnered only 49 electoral votes. Jackson was now free to move against the second Bank of the United States, and successfully crushed it, a move that resulted in a financial panic and the depression of 1833–1834. The Senate officially censured Jackson for his actions concerning the bank, the first such presidential censure ever, which was not removed for three years.

Another major issue during Jackson's administration was the question of the right of a state to nullify a federal law. The exponents of the doctrine of nullification, including Vice President John C. Calhoun, who resigned in December 1832 to become a senator from South Carolina and a leader of those advocating states' rights, contended that the individual states could nullify any federal law they deemed to be unconstitutional. Jackson contended that the states had no such power. The issue became critical when Calhoun and others declared the protective tariff act of 1832 to be unconstitutional, arguing that it was discriminatory because it aided the industrial North and hurt the agricultural South. When South Carolina threatened to secede from the Union if any federal action was taken to force its citizens to pay the higher import duties, Jackson stood firm and made preparations for possible military action. A compromise was reached, however, involving a new tariff bill that provided for a gradual reduction in duties. Jackson's actions preserved the Union but only postponed the North-South split that led to the Civil War.

Jackson still enjoyed great popularity at the end of his second term, so great that he probably could have been elected for a third term. However, since George Washington had established the precedent that no president should hold more than two terms, Jackson declined to be considered for renomination. But as head of the Democratic Party, he virtually dictated the choice of its next candidate, Martin Van Buren. His endorsement ensured the latter's election to the presidency in 1836.

After leaving office in 1837, Jackson lived quietly at his Tennessee home, the Hermitage. In 1804 he had bought 1,200 acres near Nashville, and for 15 years he and his wife had lived in a log cabin that was standing on the grounds at the time of his purchase. When he returned from the Seminole wars, he decided to build a new house for his wife. The stately colonial brick mansion was completed in 1819. Jackson had it enlarged in 1831 and rebuilt after a disastrous fire in 1834. Upon his death at the Hermitage on June 8, 1845, he was buried beside his wife in the garden. The couple had no children.

Despite the questionable aspects of his presidency and his personal character, in 1910 Andrew Jackson was elected to the Hall of Fame for Great Americans. He has been and continues to be honored in many other ways as well. For example, various places have been named after him. Among them are the cities of Jackson, the capital of Mississippi; Jacksonville, Florida; and Jackson, Tennessee.

See also the essays concerning the Trail of Tears at June 23 and Oklahoma Admitted to the Union at November 16.

March 15

Maine Admitted to the Union

Maine, the largest of the New England states, was admitted to the Union on March 15, 1820, as the 23rd state. Archaeological evidence indicates that humans inhabited the area as early as prehistoric times. The earliest inhabitants are called the Red Paint People because their graves customarily contained various quantities of a bright red pigment, powdered hematite. Later tribes in Newfoundland and New England used this pigment to color their huts, canoes, weapons, and bodies.

European exploration of the area probably began with Leif Ericson, the Viking son of Eric the Red, in the 10th or 11th century. Five hundred years passed without further exploration, until Columbus discovered the New World in 1492. During the years 1497–1499, the explorer John Cabot made several voyages to the North Atlantic coast of the Americas in the service of England's King Henry VII. England later based its territorial claims on Cabot's voyages, although for many years thereafter it more or less ignored the new land.

Giovanni da Verrazano (or Verrazzano), an Italian navigator in the service of France, sighted Maine in 1524, a year before the Spanish explorer Estevan Gómez. In subsequent years many Europeans came but most of them, seeking a route to the Indies, merely sailed past Maine. In the first decade of the 17th century, the kings of England and France each granted charters for the area of the New World that included Maine. There followed over a century of bitter competition, filled with raids, claims, and counterclaims. Under charter from France's King Henry IV in 1604, Pierre du Guast, Sieur de Monts, accompanied by adventurers such as the famous Samuel de Champlain, established the first Maine colony on St. Croix Island at the mouth of the St. Croix River. After a hard winter, the French colonists left St. Croix and moved across the Bay of Fundy to Port Royal (later Annapolis Royal), Nova Scotia. Champlain, however, continued to explore Maine, discovering many of its rivers, providing the first detailed maps of the islands off the mainland, and mapping the jagged coastline with its many natural harbors. The French, including the many missionaries who later followed the Sieur de Monts to the New World, were more successful in establishing friendly relations with the Native Americans than were the English explorers who arrived later.

The first British newcomer, Captain George Weymouth (or Waymouth), landed at Monhegan Island in 1605. He obtained valuable information that helped future English colonists, but also guaranteed those colonists a hostile reception by kidnapping five natives to take back to England. That infamous act, plus subsequent years of continual incursions by white men and constant breaking of treaties, ensured long years of warfare in Maine.

When he returned to England with his five captives, Weymouth's adventures caught the imagination of many of his countrymen, including Sir Ferdinando Gorges, military governor of Plymouth, England. In 1606, when King James I granted a charter to the Plymouth Company, Sir Ferdinando and Sir John Popham underwrote an expedition to the New World to be led by Sir John's nephew, George Popham. Arriving at Allen's Island, one of the present Georges Islands, on Sunday, August 9, 1607, the colonists gathered for prayers of thanksgiving, the first English religious service on New England soil. The Popham colony was established near the mouth of the Kennebec River on the Sagadahoc Peninsula.

The colonists, however, had not brought sufficient supplies, and more than half of them returned to England in December 1607, promising to send supplies as soon as possible. George Popham stayed, but, like several of the other settlers, he did not survive the harsh winter. In the spring, the ship bringing supplies from England arrived with news of the death of Sir John Popham. Rather than face another Maine winter, the disheartened colonists returned home in September 1608 aboard the first ship to be built in the New World, the *Virginia of Sagadahoc*.

The name New England was apparently given to the area by Captain John Smith, who in 1614 put in briefly at Monhegan Island and the abandoned Popham colony site and charted the coast from Rhode Island to Nova Scotia. He returned to England with a rich cargo of furs and fish and reported that the land was suitable for settlement. However, the hardships suffered by the Popham colony were not put aside easily. To prove that Europeans could endure the climate, Captain Richard Vines and his 16-man crew spent the winter of 1616–1617 at a site at the mouth of the Saco River. A few years later, Vines returned and established the first successful settlement at Saco, an achievement that was followed by other coastal settlements west of Penobscot Bay.

In 1635 Sir Ferdinando Gorges, appointed governor-general of New England, sent his nephew William Gorges to act as his deputy in the New World. The latter set about organizing the government, and in 1639 Maine's first legislative and judicial court was held at Saco. In 1639 Sir Ferdinando received the charter for "The Province and Countie of Maine" from Charles I of England. The name Maine was probably taken from the region of Maine in northwest France as a salute to

Charles's queen consort, Henrietta Maria, daughter of King Henry IV of France.

After Sir Ferdinando's death in 1647, Parliament invalidated his grant, but his heirs, disregarding Parliament's action, sent a deputy governor to Maine. With the confusion of grants and leadership, Maine settlers tried to form their own body politic. Their effort met with no great success, and the province of Maine came under the rule of the Massachusetts Bay Colony in 1652, despite the protests of the Maine settlers. King Charles II restored the charter for the province of Maine to Ferdinando Gorges, grandson of the earlier Sir Ferdinando, in 1664. Massachusetts judges were ordered out of Maine, and royal commissioners went in to establish an independent government. There followed a long period of political upheaval, squabbling about rights, and native warfare, which reduced the number of Maine settlements to three or four. In 1677, during this period, Gorges sold all rights to Maine to Massachusetts for 1,250 English pounds.

The British sovereigns William and Mary gave Massachusetts its second charter in 1691, and the province of Maine became the district of Maine, governed by Massachusetts. By 1732 the European population of Maine had been either wiped out or driven out by the long years of native wars. To stimulate resettlement, Massachusetts offered free land in Maine. Within a decade Maine's settler population grew to 12,000, but again the settlers were entangled in warfare with the native tribes.

The people of the District of Maine began to agitate for separation from Massachusetts at the close of the American Revolution. They did not succeed until 1820, when Maine was admitted to the Union as a free state through the Missouri Compromise, in which Missouri was also admitted to the Union but as a slave state in order to preserve the political balance between the free states in the North and the slave states in the South. Maine's population at that time was 298,335. Its capital, first at Portland, was moved to Augusta in 1832.

Ruth Bader Ginsburg's Birthday

Supreme Court justice Ruth Bader Ginsburg was born on March 15, 1933, in Brooklyn, New York, to Nathan and Celia Bader. She was educated at Cornell University, graduating Phi Beta Kappa, and in 1956 went to Harvard Law School. During her last year there she transferred to Columbia Law School, from which she graduated in 1959.

Photograph by Richard Strauss, Smithsonian Institution, Courtesy the Supreme Court of the United States.

Ruth Bader Ginsburg

Despite her impressive academic credentials, as a woman Ginsburg had difficulty securing employment, which may help explain her long-standing interest in sex discrimination issues. She finally obtained a clerkship with Judge Edmund L. Palmieri of the Federal District Court in New York City, where she stayed until 1961. Afterwards, she went into academia, becoming a professor at Rutgers University School of Law from 1963 to 1972 and then at Columbia Law School from 1972 to 1980.

Ginsburg's interest in women's legal issues manifested itself when she helped establish the American Civil Liberties Union's Women's Rights Project in 1972. She also wrote several books and articles on sex discrimination. Her prominence in the field attracted the attention of President Jimmy Carter, who nominated her to the United States Court of Appeals for the District of Columbia Circuit. She was sworn in on June 30, 1980.

The District of Columbia Court of Appeals has traditionally been a stepping-stone for potential Supreme Court nominees. It gives promising judges the chance to learn the political ropes in Washington, D.C., and become experienced in certain types of federal litigation that take place only in the nation's capital. When Carter lost the presidential election in November 1980, however, the liberal Ginsburg was shunned by the Republican administrations of Ronald Reagan and George

Bush, which held the White House for twelve years.

When Democrat Bill Clinton won the presidential election of November 1992, Ginsburg got her chance. After the appropriate opening in the Supreme Court occurred, Clinton nominated her, and she took her oath as associate justice on August 10, 1993. Ginsburg is the second woman to ever serve on the nation's highest court, after Sandra Day O'Conner.

March 16

James Madison's Birthday

Library of Congress

James Madison

James Madison, the fourth president of the United States and a major architect of the Constitution, was born at the home of his maternal grandparents in Port Conway, Virginia, on March 16, 1751. Soon afterwards, his mother returned with her son to her husband's home, Montpelier, a plantation in Orange County, Virginia. It was at Montpelier, just a few miles northeast of the home of Thomas Jefferson, Madison's lifetime associate, that Madison spent his youth and later his retirement years.

A Scottish tutor began his formal schooling when he was 12. Madison studied the classics and the French and Spanish languages. Later, after further tutoring, he entered the College of New Jersey (now Princeton University). While there, he excelled in the study of history and government and was one of the founders of the American Whig Society, a debating club that became famous in the history of the college. Completing a four-year course in three years, he graduated in 1771, but remained at the college for part of another year to study Hebrew, ethics, theology, and law. He continued his studies in law and theology, after his return to Virginia, and it was eventually said of him that "he knew more of theology than most ministers."

The first political issue he concerned himself with was the controversy raging in Virginia over religious toleration. Madison, who felt that the free exercise of religion was a matter of right and not of mere toleration, argued in favor of religious freedom and against the principle of an established church, as in Virginia, where the Church of England held sway. In 1776 he became a delegate to the Virginia constitutional convention. As a member of the committee that drafted the constitution, including that portion of the document known as the Declaration of Rights, he was influential in formulating the article on religious freedom whose adoption eventually had significance far beyond Virginia's borders.

Madison was elected to the Governor's Council in 1778 and served there until late the next year. He was sent as a delegate to the Continental Congress during the later stages of the American Revolution and served there from March 1780 until December 1783, when he returned home because of illness in his father's family. During the next few years away from the congress, Madison resumed his study of the law in order, as he wrote to the Virginina statesman Edmund Randolph, to have a profession in which he could "depend as little as possible on the labour of slaves." He also began studies of confederacies throughout history, which gave him an understanding of the national government as it then existed under the Articles of Confederation. He wrote Jefferson, then in France, asking him to buy books, especially "whatever may throw light on the general constitution and droit public [public law] of the several confederacies which have existed."

Madison was not away from public service for long, for he was elected by his county to the Virginia House of Delegates in 1784. He served there until 1786, playing a major part in securing passage of the article on religious freedom that disestablished the Anglican Church. In so doing, he and Thomas Jefferson defeated a project, supported by Patrick Henry and others, to impose a general tax for the support of religion. During those years, Madison also opposed proposals for the issue of paper money, since the states issuing the money were not supplying the federal treasury with the funds needed to back that money. Madison was also influential in bringing about a series of interstate conferences dealing with commercial problems, which ultimately led to the calling of the Constitutional Convention in Philadelphia, Pennsylvania, in 1787. Having once again been elected to the Continental Congress, in May 1787 he took his seat in the Constitutional Convention as a delegate from Virginia.

In preparation for this important responsibility, Madison in April 1787 prepared a paper based on his studies of confederacies, in which he declared that a confederacy could not survive long if it acted exclusively upon states and failed to act directly on individuals as well. He fashioned an outline for reorganizing the government that strongly influenced the work of the Constitutional Convention. In his recommendations of April 1787, he set forth his views on various provisions that he felt should be embodied in the proposed constitution. He wrote that the large states should have more representatives in the national legislature than the small states, that the national government should have "positive and complete authority in all cases which require uniformity," that the national supremacy should extend to the judiciary departments, that the national legislature should be composed of two houses with differing terms of office, that there should be a national executive, and that the national government should guarantee the tranquility of the states against internal as well as external dangers.

Madison played a prominent part in the deliberations of the Constitutional Convention, attending every session and taking copious notes on the debates. These notes, which were eventually published in 1840 as his *Journal of the Federal Convention*, are the most complete records of the proceedings. He also contributed to a brilliant series of essays written by himself, John Jay, and Alexander Hamilton that were published in New York newspapers under the signature of "Publius." Defending the new Constitution and urging its ratification, these papers, now classics, were published in book form as *The Federalist Papers* in 1788 after the Constitution had been officially adopted by the Constitutional Convention in Philadelphia on September 17, 1787. After it was transmitted to the Continental Congress, the Constitution was sent to the state legislatures for submission in turn to the delegates of the states' specially chosen ratifying conventions.

Madison was active in securing the approval of the Virginia ratifying convention. With allies that included John Marshall, later chief justice of the United States, he opposed the Antifederalist faction led by Patrick Henry, George Mason, and others, winning Virginia's approval for the new Constitution by a majority of 10 votes. However, this effort cost Madison valuable political support in Virginia, and he was not elected to a seat in the first Senate under the new Constitution. Instead, he was elected a member of the House of Representatives and served in this capacity from 1789 to 1797. Madison soon became a leader of the House and was active in framing the legislation necessary for the organization of the new government, including proposals for the establishment of three of the first executive departments: Foreign Affairs (now the State Department), the Treasury, and War (now the Department of Defense). He also proposed nine amendments to the new Constitution that became the basis of the ten now known as the Bill of Rights. Madison retired from Congress at the expiration of his term on March 3, 1797.

During this period of his life, Madison, a bachelor until he was in his 40s, married the vivacious Dorothea "Dolley" Payne Todd, a young Quaker widow from Philadelphia. Dolley Madison, famous as a charming and tactful hostess, was a great asset to the scholarly Madison, first at Montpelier and later at the White House. She was hostess at the White House not only during her eight years as First Lady, but also in the previous eight years, when she was unofficial hostess for the widowed Thomas Jefferson.

Following his service as a member of Congress, Madison remained in retirement less than a year, for in 1798 he began working with Jefferson to oppose the repressive Federalist legislation known as the Alien and Sedition Acts. Madison (now a member of Jefferson's Antifederalist Party, the Democratic-Republicans) drew up the states' rights resolutions adopted by the Virginia legislature, condemning the acts as unconstitutional and declaring,

> In case of deliberate, palpable and dangerous exercise of other powers not granted by the said compact [the Constitution], the states, who are parties thereto, have the right and are duty bound to interpose for arresting the progress of the evil, and for maintaining within their respective limits the authorities, rights and liberties appertaining to them.

Madison later explained that he did not mean that a state could by its own action nullify an act of Congress, but that if the states regarded such an act as unconstitutional they should either work for its repeal or for an amendment to the Constitution that would invalidate it.

Jefferson was elected the third president of the United States in 1800, and he appointed Madison his secretary of state. Madison was Jefferson's chief adviser during his two terms of office. Madison himself was elected to the presidency in 1808 and took office in March 1809.

During Madison's administration, the major problem confronting the United States was dealing with the issues arising out of the Napoleonic wars in Europe. Jefferson, and later Madison, tried to maintain neutrality, but neither France nor England respected this position; it was impossible to resolve the conflicting interests. Ultimately, Britain's impressment of American sailors and seizure of cargoes, together with suspected British instigation of Native American uprisings, brought about popular demand for declaring war. Congress was dominated by the "War Hawks" of the South and West and, although the country was not prepared to fight, Madison agreed to their demands by advising a congressional declaration of war against Great Britain on June 1, 1812. The war, now known as the War of 1812, then was called "Mr. Madison's War" by those who opposed it, principally northeasterners. Meanwhile, Madison was reelected to a second term in the election of 1812.

Congress did not take adequate economic measures to provide for the war, and for this and other reasons, the conflict was initially filled with disasters for the United States. A low point came in August 1814, when the British briefly took Washington, D.C., and set fire to the White House and other landmarks. Thereafter, the United States achieved some notable victories. As the tide turned against the British, Madison regained much of his popularity. The war was concluded with the Treaty of Ghent on December 24, 1814.

After the end of his second term, on March 4, 1817, Madison returned to private life. His last years were spent at Montpelier. He supported Jefferson in founding the University of Virginia in 1819, and became its rector following Jefferson's death in 1826. Madison died at Montpelier at the age of 84, on June 28, 1836. He and his wife, who outlived him by more than a decade, were buried on his estate.

United States Military Academy Founded

March 16 marks the anniversary of the founding of the United States Military Academy at West Point by an act of Congress dated March 16, 1802. The original act authorized the creation of a Corps of Engineers, setting its strength at five officers and ten cadets, and provided that it be stationed at West Point, New York, and constitute a military academy. Today the faculty numbers in the hundreds, and the student body Corps of Cadets numbers in the thousands.

In October 1975 Congress approved and President Gerald R. Ford signed into law legislation directing that women be admitted to West Point and the other U.S. service academies. The admission of women to West Point in July 1976 changed a 174-year-old policy of exclusively male admissions, yet the quality and integrity of the Corps of Cadets was preserved. Every cadet, male or female, is subject to the same rigorous requirements for admission, training, graduation, and commissioning, except for those minimum essential adjustments required because of physiological differences.

West Point, situated on the west bank of the Hudson River about 50 miles north of New York City, was an important military post during the American Revolution and has been occupied continuously by regular army troops since January 20, 1778. The experience of the American Revolution called attention to the need for a national military academy for the training of the country's armed forces. In May 1776 General Henry Knox, the American Revolutionary officer and adviser to General George Washington, urged the establishment of such an academy. With Washington's approval, Congress on October 1 of the same year adopted a resolution appointing a committee to prepare plans for the school. On June 20, 1777, it was ordered that a corps organized as "a military school for young gentlemen previous to their being appointed to marching regiments" be created. In 1781, at the request of General Washington, the resulting corps was marched from Philadelphia to join the garrison at West Point, where an engineering school, a laboratory, and a library had already been opened.

Originally the grounds of what is now the academy consisted of 1,795 acres purchased in 1790 from Stephen Moore; today the site comprises roughly 16,000 acres. The buildings used for the school were destroyed by fire in 1796, and the work of the academy was suspended until 1801.

The academy as it is now known was formally organized on March 16, 1802. Its original purpose was to train technicians for all branches of the military service, as well as to encourage the study of military arts nationwide. The War of 1812 focused attention on the need for trained officers, and President James Madison convinced Congress of the importance of making the academy a scientific as well as a military college. Congress, by an act of April 29, 1812, increased the strength of the Corps of Cadets to 250, enlarged the academic staff, and placed the cadets under the discipline of published regulations. The act of 1812 also required that the cadets be taught "all the duties of a private, a noncommissioned officer, and an officer," a requirement that according to Emory Upton in *The Military Policy of the United States* (1904) was the "key to the character for efficiency and discipline which the graduates have since maintained."

The four-year, college-level course at the United States Military Academy leads to the bachelor of science degree and a commission as a second lieutenant in the United States Army. The academy produces officer-graduates who are trained leaders, with academic and military knowledge enabling them to discharge their duties in a wide range of specialized fields. Training in both the standard academic and advanced studies programs is designed to provide cadets with a foundation in the basic sciences, applied sciences and engineering, language and literature, and national security and public affairs. Elective courses permit cadets to concentrate on areas that are of particular interest to them.

The list of famous West Point graduates is a long one, including such names as President Ulysses S. Grant; General Robert E. Lee; General John J. Pershing, commander in chief of the American Expeditionary Forces in World War I; President Dwight D. Eisenhower; General George S. Patton Jr.; and General of the Army Douglas MacArthur. On the academy's grounds stand a number of monuments memorializing noted graduates, including those who died in combat while upholding the West Point motto, "Duty, Honor, Country."

My Lai Massacre

The massacre at My Lai was one of the most infamous incidents of the Vietnam War. It has come to symbolize the grimmest aspects of American involvement in Vietnam, and is a disturbing reminder that Americans are capable of committing atrocities during wartime.

By the late 1960s the Vietnam War had become a major conflict, and hundreds of thousands of American soldiers were sent to fight. It was a frustrating war for the Americans, since the Viet Cong used innovative guerrilla tactics and hid with ease in the jungles and tropical terrain of Vietnam. American forces began to conduct "search and destroy" missions for the elusive Viet Cong and their bases, and it was during such a mission in the Quang Ngai province of South Vietnam that the My Lai massacre occurred.

The 105 soldiers of Charlie Company, 11th Light Infantry Brigade, had been fighting long and hard. The enemy appeared to be everywhere; mines and booby traps had injured several men; and much of the local population that the Americans were supposedly protecting sympathized with the enemy and helped hide Viet Cong stockpiles of weapons and food. On March 16, 1968, Lieutenant William Calley's First Platoon of Charlie Company entered the village of My Lai. Under orders to "destroy the enemy," Calley had villagers pushed into a ditch and shot. The soldiers went on a rampage and shot men, women, and children indiscriminately, with no real effort to determine who might actually be the enemy. Roughly 500 Vietnamese were killed.

In addition to the obvious immorality of Calley's actions, the My Lai massacre violated the laws of war, which prohibit the killing of civilians without military necessity. An American cameraman happened to be present in My Lai on the day of the massacre, and despite the army's attempt at a cover-up, the photographs and the story were eventually leaked to the public. The resulting outcry forced the administration of President Richard Nixon to order an investigation.

Despite some resistance from the military establishment and the destruction of relevant evidence, charges were finally brought against Calley on September 6, 1969, under the Uniform Code of Military Justice. He was charged with the murder of 109 "Oriental human beings," as the army curiously termed it. The court-martial began on November 17, 1970, and on March 29, 1971, Calley was found guilty of the murder of at least 22 of the villagers. Although this was but a fraction of the actual death toll, the rules of evidence said that each murder had to be proved separately and "beyond a reasonable doubt" under the law. Even as it was, the conviction was sufficient to permit Calley's execution by hanging. Instead, Calley was given a dishonorable discharge and sentenced to life imprisonment. The sentence was reduced to 20 years in August 1971.

Charges were also brought against others involved in the My Lai massacre, but Calley was the only one convicted. Many people felt that Calley was a scapegoat for both the military and the antiwar movement: He was a convenient target in an incident for which many were to blame, from the top of the command structure down to Calley's platoon level. President Nixon was one of those inclined to be lenient toward Calley, and arranged for his release in 1974 after serving only a few years of the sentence.

March 17

St. Patrick's Day

The Feast of St. Patrick, bishop and confessor, is celebrated on March 17. St. Patrick is the patron saint of Ireland, and St. Patrick's Day is observed by millions of Irish Americans. The occasion has also expanded beyond the Irish American community, and St. Patrick's Day festivities are popular throughout America on March 17.

Many of the facts about Patrick have been buried under centuries of Irish legend, and there is a great deal of controversy and speculation about the chronology of events in his life and especially about the date of his death. Patrick was born between A.D. 385 and 389, possibly in Bannavem Taberniae, a village near the mouth of the Severn River in what is now Wales, when the region was part of the Roman Empire; hence he is described as a Romano-Briton. His father, Calpurnius or Calpornius, was a Roman official. Although his parents were Christian and Patrick was baptized, he was a worldly youth who gave little thought to religion. However, when he was about 16, a group of Irish pirates raided the area of Bannavem Taberniae and carried off Patrick and hundreds of other young men and women to be sold as slaves in Ireland. For six years, possibly in Slemish in County Antrim, Patrick worked as a herdsman, and during this time of slavery and frequent solitude he felt an increasing awareness of God. Patrick's *Confession*, which he wrote when he was older, opens with this passage:

> I, Patrick, a sinner, the most rustic and the least of all the faithful, and in the estimation of very many deemed contemptible, had for my father Calpornius, a deacon, the son of Potitus, a presbyter, who belonged to the village of Bannavem Taberniae; for close thereto he had a small villa, where I was made a captive.

> At the time I was barely 16 years of age, I knew not the true God; and I was led to Ireland in captivity with many thousand persons according to our deserts, for we turned away from God and kept not His commandments, and we were not obedient to our priests who used to admonish us about our salvation. And the Lord brought us the indignation of His wrath, and scattered us amongst many nations even to the utmost part of the earth, where now my littleness may be seen amongst strangers.

> And there the Lord opened the understanding of my unbelief so that at length I might recall to mind my sins and be converted with all my heart to the Lord, my God, who hath regarded my humility and taken pity on my youth and my ignorance, and kept watch over me before I knew Him, and before I had discretion, and could distinguish between good and evil; and He protected me and consoled me as a father does his son.

During his sixth year of slavery, Patrick had a dream in which he was told to escape. Following the instructions given him in the dream, he made his way to the harbor and boarded a ship, which carried him out of captivity. He returned to his home, much less worldly than when he had left it. While he was enjoying his reunion with his family and the warmth and comforts of home, however, he heard "the voice of the Irish" calling him to go back to Ireland, and he determined that he must return to the land where he had found his faith to share that faith with the Irish people.

In preparation for this he went to the Continent, traveling to Gaul (modern-day France), Italy, and some of the Mediterranean islands, visiting monasteries and living the life of a religious man. For approximately a dozen years he stayed in Gaul under the tutelage of St. Germanus (or Germain), the bishop of Auxerre. Patrick had from the first made known his desire to return to Ireland but, perhaps because his education had been so long ignored and was considered inadequate, his religious superiors did not grant his request. St. Palladius was chosen over Patrick as the first bishop of Ireland. After a year or two in Ireland, however, Palladius went to Scotland, and Patrick took his place, probably in 431 or 432.

Patrick's arrival in Ireland was greatly opposed by the druid priests, who wielded great political and religious authority. They captured Patrick many times, but he always escaped. He traveled in all parts of Ireland, making converts to Christianity and founding monasteries, schools, and churches, which would in time turn pagan Ireland into the "Isle of Saints."

Not all of the opposition came from the druids. Some clergymen objected to Patrick's mission and methods. There was, for instance, much dispute over such things as the great bonfires that were spring rites. As various people became Christians, the bonfires were often prohibited on the grounds that they constituted a pagan ritual. St. Patrick caused much consternation by "christening" the spring fires, making them a symbol of Christ, the Light of the World. Traditionally, Patrick started his bonfire at Easter on the Hill of Slane (Slaine) in County Meath. Through the centuries, opposition to the Christianized fire rite diminished, and it became part of the Irish Easter rituals.

Patrick, who is referred to as the Father and the Founder of the Church in Ireland, established his headquarters at Armagh. After approximately 30 years of what was one of the most successful missionary lives on record, he retired to Saul in Downpatrick, where he died on March 17 in or about the year 461. He was buried in Downpatrick in County Down, and many pilgrims have visited the stone carved there with a "P," which supposedly marks his grave.

Many of the legends about Patrick are portrayed in pictures and statues of the saint. The most famous emblem associated with him is the shamrock, which he supposedly showed to a king to convey the idea of the Holy Trinity. Others include the cross, harp, and baptismal font (signifying his many converts). Patrick is also associated with images of serpents, as he is said to have driven all the snakes out of Ireland.

British Troops Evacuate Boston

The evacuation of Boston by British troops took place on March 17, 1776. The event became the occasion for annual celebrations for many years afterwards. The 200th anniversary was observed in 1976, during the nationwide celebration of the American Revolution Bicentennial.

At the outbreak of the American Revolution, the peninsula of Boston was highly vulnerable to attack either from Charlestown, located on an arm of land to the north, which the British had secured at a staggering cost in the Battle of Bunker Hill; or from Dorchester Heights, on another arm of land to the south. Because of miscalculation or exhaustion after their Bunker Hill engagement with the colonials, the British failed to immediately follow up their victory with what would have been the logical next step: an assault on Dorchester Heights.

George Washington, who took command of the Continental army two and a half weeks after the Bunker Hill battle, was quick to take advantage of the British oversight. After training and equipping his ill-prepared force, he proceeded with what history has termed the Siege of Boston. As soon as he had amassed sufficient ammunition and weaponry, notably the British cannon hauled from the captured Fort Ticonderoga, he was able to take Dorchester Heights without opposition. On the evening of March 4, 1776, while American forces kept up fire on British lines to obscure what was going on to the rear, the American general John Thomas took possession of the heights with 2,000

handpicked men. Since fortifications were an immediate necessity and the frozen ground made it impossible for the men to dig in, they carried with them prefabricated entrenchments consisting of timber frames. These works were loaded on 350 wagons and carts, which moved with the army in the dark. Having arrived on the heights, the men erected a timber wall, fronted it with an additional fortification made of felled trees, and placed barrels filled with stones before that. It was, in the words of one observer, "a most astonishing night's work." When day broke on the morning of March 5, the British saw two redoubts on the heights, armed with cannons and commanding the city.

General Sir William Howe, the British commander, was astounded, and Vice Admiral Molyneux Shuldham, whose ships were now vulnerable to bombardment, stated that if the Americans could not be driven from their position he could not keep a single vessel in Boston Harbor. Accordingly, a company of 2,400 soldiers under the command of Sir Hugh Percy was dispatched in boats, under cover of darkness, to dislodge the enemy. But the New England weather was on the side of the Americans. A sudden storm drove some of the boats ashore, and it rained so hard in the morning that none of the British troops could move. Even with good weather, the attack would have been launched against almost impossible odds. With bad weather, it was delayed long enough for the Americans to make their position impervious to assault.

General Howe called a council of war, which decided that the city the British had occupied for so long should be evacuated. Howe offered to take his forces from the city if they were allowed to go without molestation. Washington consented, but maintained a close watch, ready to attack if the British made a hostile move. The actual evacuation was delayed until March 17, when the British troops were taken aboard their ships along with some 1,000 Loyalists. After pausing off Nantasket for 10 days, the fleet sailed for Nova Scotia. After the evacuation was completed, the Continental Congress thanked Washington for the delivery of the city from the British and awarded him a gold medal.

Roger Brooke Taney's Birthday

The life of Roger Brooke Taney spanned the historic years from the American Revolution to the Civil War. A member of a wealthy, slave-owning family, he was born on March 17, 1777, in Calvert County, Maryland. By the time of his death in Washington, D.C., on October 12, 1864, he was chief justice of the United States. During his 28

Photo by George P. Healy. Collection of the Supreme Court of the United States.

Roger Brooke Taney

years on the Supreme Court bench, he helped formulate several momentous decisions that affected the course of the nation.

After graduating from Dickinson College in Carlisle, Pennsylvania, in 1795, Taney read law and gained admission to the bar of Calvert County, Maryland, in 1799. He was elected a delegate to the general assembly of the state and in 1801 moved to Frederick, Maryland. Taney served in the state senate from 1816 to 1821. In 1823 he took up residence in Baltimore and from 1827 to 1831 was attorney general of Maryland.

Originally a Federalist, the young Taney broke with the party in 1812. During the following years, the nation experienced a period of one-party politics in which various factions among the Jeffersonian Republicans, later known as the Democratic-Republicans, vied for dominance. By 1824 Taney had allied himself with the group led by Andrew Jackson of Tennessee.

In the 1824 presidential election, Jackson received more popular votes than any of the other three candidates—John Quincy Adams of Massachusetts, Henry Clay of Kentucky, and William H. Crawford of Georgia—but failed to secure the necessary majority of electoral votes. The selection of the president fell to the House of Representatives, which chose Adams. Jackson's supporters felt cheated and began preparations for the next election. In Baltimore, Taney and his associ-

ates staged a Jackson gala in conjunction with ceremonies commemorating the city's successful resistance against the British in the War of 1812. The festivities commenced with the firing of a cannon and a parade of 700 marshals. Orators described the exploits of Old Hickory, as Jackson was called, against the British, and the crowd responded with cheers for their idol. Thanks to Taney and his other supporters, Jackson won the presidency in the 1828 election, and he did not forget those who had helped him. In 1831 the president took Taney into his cabinet as attorney general.

Taney entered his post during a period of crisis, the struggle over the fate of the second Bank of the United States. Incorporated in 1816 for a period of 20 years, the bank had an ambivalent identity as a private enterprise and as a public servant holding the deposits of the United States Treasury. Under the leadership of Nicholas Biddle of Philadelphia, the institution served as a strong central bank that regulated the money supply and thereby kept a check on the expansion of credit. Unfortunately, its very effectiveness gained it enemies. Many state bankers resented the advantage that federal patronage gave their giant competitor. Others felt that the bank's conservative policies unduly hampered their activities, which sometimes far exceeded the bounds of sound financial judgment. In addition, some strict-constructionist Democratic-Republicans like Andrew Jackson believed that the government had exceeded its constitutional powers in establishing the institution.

President Jackson wanted a simple deposit bank associated with the treasury, with no power to make loans or acquire property. Senator Thomas Hart Benton of Missouri, Jackson's close friend, renewed the attack on the bank in 1831, putting particular emphasis on what he regarded as the institution's overbearing role in the national economy. Although the bank's charter was not due to expire until 1836, Biddle, alarmed by the attack, decided to force the issue by requesting early renewal. Congress passed the bill extending the bank's existence, but the president vetoed it on July 10, 1832. Jackson's executive statement was weak in economic theory, but it was strong in democratic philosophy and included a denunciation of all laws granting special privileges to the powerful. Taney played a part in drafting the statement, and was responsible for the section in which Jackson argued that the president was not bound by the interpretation of the Constitution enunciated by the Supreme Court.

Some historians have suggested that Taney's interests in the Union Bank of Maryland, for which he was counsel, influenced his position. Whatever the reason, Taney remained a foe of Biddle. In

1833 Jackson decided to cripple the Bank of the United States by removing all federal money from its vaults. When Secretary of the Treasury William J. Duane opposed this course, the president secured for Taney a temporary appointment to the treasury post, and the compliant Taney carried out Jackson's wishes.

In 1835, Jackson appointed Taney an associate justice of the United States Supreme Court, but the Senate refrained from acting on the appointment. The death of Chief Justice John Marshall on July 6, 1835, gave the president another opportunity to reward his friend, and he nominated Taney to become the nation's new chief justice. This time the Senate gave its consent, and Taney took his seat on the Supreme Court. He was the fifth chief justice in American history and the first Roman Catholic to hold that high honor.

On the bench, Taney acted against some of the trends set by Marshall. He curbed monopolies and weakened his illustrious predecessor's defense of the sanctity of contracts (see February 2, Dartmouth College Case Decided), as can be seen in his decision in the *Charles River Bridge* v. *Warren Bridge* case. This found Taney arguing that Massachusetts, which had authorized the building of a toll bridge by the Charles River Bridge Company in 1785, did not impair its original contract by authorizing the construction of the nearby Warren Bridge in 1828.

Taney's most important decision came in 1857, over the volatile slavery issue. The Dred Scott case involved questions concerning the legal rights of African Americans, the extent of Congress's power over slavery, and the matter of whether the Missouri Compromise was constitutional. The chief justice's conservative, pro-Southern interpretations inflamed Northern opinion and aggravated the feelings of distrust and anger that were then tearing the nation apart. The case, among the most famous in the history of the Supreme Court, provided a key point of dispute in the critical period preceding the Civil War.

In 1832 or 1833 John Emerson of St. Louis had purchased the slave Dred Scott. Emerson became an army surgeon and took Scott with him on assignment to Rock Island, in Illinois, a state that had no slavery. He later moved with Scott to Fort Snelling, located in federal territory (now Minnesota) above the 36° 30′ north latitude. Except in Missouri, the Missouri Compromise, passed by Congress in 1820, had outlawed slavery north of that line in all of the vast, trans-Mississippi area earlier acquired through the Louisiana Purchase. Emerson returned to slave-holding Missouri in 1838, and Dred Scott accompanied him.

Emerson died several years later, and in 1846 Scott attempted to buy his freedom and that of his wife from the doctor's widow. When the latter refused his request, Scott, with the assistance of an army officer and a lawyer, took his case to court in St. Louis. The lower court ruled in his favor, accepting the argument that Scott's earlier residence in a free state and territory had ended his servitude. The Missouri Supreme Court reversed the decision, justifying its stand on the basis of a Missouri law that declared that any slave who voluntarily returned from a free state automatically resumed his bonds.

Mrs. Emerson's remarriage to Calvin C. Chaffee, a Massachusetts politician with antislavery leanings, further complicated matters. Under Missouri law she lost jurisdiction over Emerson's estate, including slaves, which had been left in trust for her daughter. John F. A. Sanford of New York, Mrs. Chaffee's brother, became administrator of the Emerson property. Scott's lawyers immediately renewed the litigation, but this time brought their case before the federal courts because the plaintiff and defendant were no longer residents of the same state.

Before a U.S. circuit court, Sanford argued that Scott, as a slave, was not a citizen of Missouri and had no right to bring suit. Judge R. W. Wells rejected this contention but found that the law supported the Emerson estate's right to retain Scott. At that point, Scott's lawyers decided to appeal to the Supreme Court.

The justices heard the case in 1856 and deliberated on February 15, 1857. Justice Samuel Nelson of New York held that, by Missouri law, Scott remained a slave despite his temporary residence on free soil. Nelson's moderate opinion would have limited the Court's involvement in the slavery controversy, but his fellow judges thought it inadequate. The proslavery majority, particularly James Wayne of Georgia, wanted a strong pronouncement to counteract the long dissenting statements promised by antislavery justices Benjamin Curtis of Massachusetts and John McLean of Ohio.

Each of the nine justices issued an opinion, but the majority agreed that slaves could not be citizens and that the Missouri Compromise was unconstitutional. Chief Justice Taney's statement was particularly inflammatory. He argued that at the time of the signing of the Declaration of Independence and drafting of the Constitution, slaves "were considered as a subordinate and inferior class of beings . . . and whether emancipated or not . . . had no rights or privileges but such as those who held the power and the government might choose to grant them." Thus, Dred Scott could not be a citizen and had no right to sue in the circuit court.

Taney then proceeded to consider the legality of the Missouri Compromise. The chief justice stated that the 1820 agreement was invalid because it violated the constitutional provision (namely the 5th Amendment) that forbids the deprivation of property without due process of law. He held, in effect, that Congress could not enact legislation that limited slaveholders' property rights.

Roger Brooke Taney remained chief justice until his death in 1864. He was buried in Frederick, Maryland, which erected a monument in his honor. Interestingly enough, before he died Taney acted to free his own slaves.

March 18

John C. Calhoun's Birthday

John Caldwell Calhoun, the controversial pre–Civil War champion of Southern interests, was born on March 18, 1782, in the Abbeville District of South Carolina. His father, an Irish immigrant named "Pat" Calhoun, was a farmer and political leader. Young Calhoun was largely self-taught until, at the age of 18, he was schooled by his brother-in-law, the Reverend Moses Waddel, who later became president of the University of Georgia. Thus prepared, Calhoun was able to enter the junior class at Yale College, from which he graduated in 1804. He subsequently studied at the Litchfield, Connecticut, Law School.

In 1807 Calhoun was admitted to the bar in his native South Carolina, and shortly thereafter he was elected a member of the South Carolina legislature. He served in the sessions of 1808 and 1809, during the debate over a state constitutional amendment that adjusted the legislative apportionment of the state's two distinct regions, the wealthy low-country and the poorer up-country. Calhoun, who always considered himself an up-countryman, became associated with low-country interests as well, and he gained entrance into South Carolina plantation society when he married his aristocratic cousin, Floride Bonneau Calhoun of Charleston, in 1811.

Calhoun's nearly four decades on the national political scene began the same year, when he was elected to the United States House of Representatives, just as Henry Clay was becoming speaker of the House. The two men quickly became leaders of the young "War Hawks," who urged President James Madison into the War of 1812 with Britain. Calhoun followed a nationalistic course in other respects as well, voting for the protective tariff of 1816 and, like Clay, promoting what was called the

"American system" to bring improvements and prosperity to all sections of the country.

For a time, Calhoun joined with those who favored the use of federal funds to build new national roads and canals. Named chairman of a committee to consider setting up a permanent fund for this purpose, he urged passage of his so-called bonus bill with arguments that were curious in view of his later philosophy: The very size of the United States, he said, was a threat to its unity, and new roads and canals would help overcome this difficulty. Congress passed the bill, but it was vetoed by President Madison.

Calhoun served in the House of Representatives until 1817, when he became secretary of war, a post he held during President Monroe's two terms of office. During the election of 1824, he was an unsuccessful presidential contender along with Andrew Jackson, William H. Crawford, and Clay. However, he was elected to the vice presidency under the successful candidate, John Quincy Adams. Four years later, Calhoun was reelected vice president under Jackson, whose victory he had helped make possible.

Meanwhile, Calhoun's thinking had changed since the days when he favored protective tariffs and federal funds for highways. For one thing, Calhoun himself had become a farmer, and the cotton- and slave-based Southern economy had begun a drastic decline. For another, he had been impressed, during the debate over the 1820 Missouri Compromise, with the thinking of John Randolph, who had called attention to a fundamental point: If the South admitted the right of the Northern congressional majority to prohibit slavery in the new territories, it would in the process be recognizing simple majority rule. Calhoun's changed views on tariffs were evident in 1827, when he used his vote as vice president to defeat in the Senate a bill that would have increased protection for New England woolen manufacturers and sheep raisers.

Another turning point came during the discussion of the so-called Tariff of Abominations of 1828, which he opposed on the grounds that it was unconstitutional and benefited the North at the expense of the South. He set forth his arguments in his famous South Carolina Exposition, the first systematized presentation of the doctrine of nullification and states' rights. Briefly, he held that the states, which had created the Union, were the final authority as to whether acts of the federal government were constitutional; and that it was the duty and privilege of each state to nullify a law it deemed unconstitutional, so that the law had no force within its boundaries unless three-fourths of the states could agree on a constitutional amendment to uphold it.

The doctrine, which translated what might have been mere opinion into a plan of action, had long-lasting implications. Segregationists were still quoting it well over a century later, during the intensified drive for civil rights that characterized the 1960s. But its first application came much earlier: South Carolina voted to nullify the tariff of 1832 (and 1828). In so doing, it added fuel to a controversy between Calhoun and President Jackson that had been ignited, or at least fanned, by political enemies bent on ruining Calhoun's chances for the presidency. Calhoun contributed his share to the ill feeling by objecting to Jackson's spoils system of political reward. When South Carolina, armed with Calhoun's Exposition, voted for nullification, Jackson viewed the action as close to anarchy and threatened to arrest Calhoun. Calhoun resigned as vice president in 1832 and was succeeded by Martin Van Buren.

Within a year of his resignation, Calhoun returned to Washington in the new role of United States senator from South Carolina, which he filled (except for a brief interlude as President Tyler's secretary of state in 1844–1845) until the end of his life. As senator, he opposed both big business and big government, while seeking to unite the Democratic Party and devote it to states' rights and agricultural interests. He secured the annexation of Texas (as secretary of state) and opposed the war with Mexico in 1846–1848. The nullification crisis, meanwhile, had been averted under the compromise tariff of 1833 sponsored by Henry Clay. However, the questions of slavery and states' rights remained unanswered. In 1833 they were the subjects of a historic debate between Calhoun and Daniel Webster that defined the concepts of government held by the supporters and opponents of slavery.

By the time of the debate over the Compromise of 1850, Calhoun was thinking most specifically of the need for legislation that would safeguard economic interests on a regional basis, restoring the balance between the economically slow South and the rapidly developing North. The debate over the Compromise of 1850, which Calhoun opposed, partly because it provided for the admission of California as a free state, marked the last appearance of the Senate's "great triumvirate" of Clay, Webster, and Calhoun, with Calhoun defending Southern interests and calling for an end to Northern agitation against slavery. His arguments made it evident that he clearly understood the threat to the Southern economy inherent in proposals for abolition.

Unfortunately, by the time he was scheduled to present these views, on March 4, 1850, Calhoun, ill and anxious, was too weak to make a speech, al-though he dragged himself to the Senate to hear his argument read by Senator Mason of Virginia. Calhoun died on March 31. The events of the next decade gave tragic emphasis to the warning he had issued a few weeks before: The South, he had said, "cannot remain, as things now are, consistently with honor and safety, in the Union." In a sense, he had foreseen the upcoming Civil War.

Grover Cleveland's Birthday

Library of Congress

Grover Cleveland

Stephen Grover Cleveland, president of the United States from 1885 to 1889 and again from 1893 to 1897, is known as the 22nd and 24th president because of the interval between his terms. He was born in the Old Manse of the First Presbyterian Church of Caldwell, New Jersey, on March 18, 1837, the fifth of nine children of Anne Neal Cleveland and the Reverend Richard Falley Cleveland, a descendant of an early colonial family. Named for his father's predecessor in the pastorate, young Cleveland dropped the name Stephen in childhood.

When he was very young, the family moved from Caldwell to Fayetteville, New York. He attended school there until family financial troubles forced him to work in a village store. In 1850, when his family moved to Clinton, New York, Cleveland entered the Clinton academy to prepare for Hamilton College. However, his father's death in 1853 caused him to give up his college plans to help support his mother and the younger children.

After spending a year as a bookkeeper and a teacher in the New York Institution for the Blind in New York City, Cleveland moved west in search of better opportunities. In Buffalo, New York, he stopped to work on an uncle's book for stock farmers. Soon he became a law student and clerk in the firm of Rogers, Bowen and Rogers. He was admitted to the bar in 1859 at the age of 22.

At the outbreak of the Civil War, Cleveland chose not to follow two brothers into the Union army. When drafted in 1863, he hired a substitute as provided for in the conscription law of the time. Political opponents later suggested that Cleveland's decision indicated Southern sympathies, but his supporters claimed that it was due to the fact that he was supporting his mother and two sisters.

In Buffalo, Cleveland joined the Democratic Party with his law associates and became very active locally. He first entered public life in 1863 when he was appointed assistant district attorney for Erie County. While participating in politics in the 1860s and 1870s, he was building a flourishing law practice, to which he would return whenever defeated for public office. The first defeat came immediately, in 1865, in an election for county district attorney. In 1870, however, he was elected sheriff of Erie County. A decade later, in 1881, the Democrats nominated the 44-year-old bachelor for mayor of Buffalo and won. Cleveland was so successful in his broad attack on the political corruption in Buffalo that, before he had served a full year, the Democrats in the state nominated him for governor of New York. Because he was not a part of the inner circle of state politicians, Cleveland drew many independent and reform Republican votes in 1882, winning the governorship by a large plurality.

Cleveland's burgeoning reputation prompted the national Democratic Party to nominate him for the presidency before his term as governor had ended, despite objections from the Tammany bosses of the Democratic organization in New York City. In 1884 the Democratic Party had been without national power for 23 years, ever since the Civil War. Party leaders saw their opportunity to defeat a divided and demoralized Republican Party by running Cleveland, a Northern governor, on a reform platform. After a bitter mudslinging campaign, Cleveland defeated James G. Blaine by a narrow popular majority but with a clear victory in the Electoral College.

During his first administration, Cleveland strongly supported the creation of a federal civil service based on competitive examinations to re-

place the spoils system of political patronage that dated back to the presidency of Andrew Jackson. He vetoed many private pension bills designed to reward congressmen's friends and constituents, and he also vetoed a bill that would have compensated veterans for nonmilitary disabilities. In addition, he attacked high American tariffs on imports as inflationary, stating that they unduly rewarded protected industries at the expense of consumers. The election campaign of 1888 opened amid public furor over an administration-favored bill to lower tariffs.

Also during his first administration, on June 2, 1886, Cleveland, then 49, married his former ward, the beautiful 21-year-old Frances Folsom, in the Blue Room of the White House. He was the first president to have his wedding ceremony in the White House.

In 1888 the Democrats renominated Grover Cleveland despite opposition within the party. Although he won the popular vote by a slender plurality, Cleveland lost to Benjamin Harrison, the Republican candidate, by 168 to 233 electoral votes. He returned to law practice in New York City for the next four years. In 1892, however, he was renominated for president by the Democrats in the face of fierce opposition from Tammany Hall. In this election, he defeated Harrison and James B. Weaver, the third-party Populist candidate, by a sound margin in the Electoral College, though with only a small plurality of the popular vote.

The United States was beset by economic strife as Cleveland's second administration opened. A financial panic soon after he took office touched off one of the most severe depressions in American history. The public blamed Cleveland and the Democrats for events whose long-range causes were little understood, and the Democratic Party itself split into factions with conflicting views on monetary policies. Cleveland fought to limit the silver currency in circulation in an attempt to avert inflation. The "pro-silver" congressmen bitterly opposed him. These pro-silver forces spoke for the agrarian sections of the country, which were suffering severe hardship and looked to the free coinage of silver for inflationary economic relief.

President Cleveland achieved the repeal of the Sherman Silver Purchase Act of 1890 with the help of the Republican minority in Congress. This action failed to reverse the depression, however. While business continued to grapple with failures and uncertainty, unemployment rose and wages dropped. Also during Cleveland's second term, the Pullman railroad works in Chicago were the scene of a fierce labor war, which spread into a major rail strike, with riots and bloodshed in a number of places. Over the protests of the governor of Illinois, the president sent federal troops to Chicago to put down the strike, in the name of moving the mail and assuring interstate commerce. The business world applauded the president's action, but organized labor was embittered.

Cleveland was extremely unpopular when he left the presidency. In 1896 antiadministration forces gained control of the Democratic national convention and refused to endorse Cleveland, instead nominating William Jennings Bryan (see March 19) on a free-silver platform. Cleveland then retired to Princeton, New Jersey, where he was soon elected a trustee of Princeton University and named the Stafford Little lecturer on public affairs. In 1905 he agreed to serve on a three-man board of trustees to reorganize the Equitable Life Assurance Society. In retirement his views on business were often sought, and he had the leisure time to write two books and numerous articles.

In the last years of his life, Cleveland's unpopularity with the electorate faded, and he came more and more to be regarded as one of the political sages of the country. At his death on June 24, 1908, expressions of esteem poured forth, no doubt in part to allay earlier bitterness, but also because he had come to symbolize to Americans certain cherished ideals and virtues. President William Howard Taft wrote for the 75th anniversary of Cleveland's birth:

> Grover Cleveland earned the sincere gratitude of his countrymen. . . . He was a great President . . . because he was a patriot with the highest sense of public duty, because he was a statesman of clear perceptions, of the utmost courage of his convictions and of great plainness of speech, because he was a man of high character . . . and because throughout his political life he showed these rugged virtues of the public servant and citizen.

The Supreme Court Expands the Right to Counsel

It has long been recognized that defendants in criminal prosecutions have the right to legal assistance. Not until *Gideon* v. *Wainwright*, however, did the Supreme Court state that this right extended to indigent defendants, who must be provided with an attorney at the government's expense. Prior to the *Gideon* decision on March 18, 1963, criminal defendants were expected to hire their own attorney regardless of whether they had the economic means to do so.

There were some exceptions to this rule, such as in murder cases, but for the most part the Supreme Court had not extended any special privileges to defendants who were too poor to hire their own attorney. The *Gideon* case, which arose during the tenure of Supreme Court justice Earl Warren (see also Earl Warren's Birthday at March 19), caused the Court to reconsider its previous stance and expand the right to counsel.

Clarence Earl Gideon was a middle-aged drifter who worked part-time in a poolroom in Panama City, Florida. When the poolroom was burglarized, the evidence pointed toward Gideon, who was arrested and prosecuted. He was too poor to hire an attorney, and the state successfully secured a conviction. He was sentenced to five years imprisonment after a trial that lasted just one day. While in prison, Gideon became a jailhouse lawyer, writing his own petitions, despite a lack of formal education, in an attempt to fight his conviction. After a lengthy procedural process through the Florida state courts, Gideon's handwritten pleas eventually reached the United States Supreme Court in Washington, D.C.

To Gideon's credit, his petition was sufficiently well- written, and intriguing in its insistence that all felony defendants are entitled to appointed counsel if they cannot afford one, that the Supreme Court decided to hear his case. As his counsel, Gideon was given Abe Fortas, one of the country's most distinguished attorneys. The Court held that Gideon's position was correct, since an impoverished defendant who was forced to mount a defense without an attorney would not receive a fair trial as guaranteed by the Constitution.

Having thus established a landmark precedent, Gideon was given a retrial in Florida. Now defended by an attorney, he was acquitted of the poolroom burglary.

March 19

William Jennings Bryan's Birthday

William Jennings Bryan, who was the most popular leader of the Democratic Party for many years, was born in Salem, Illinois, on March 19, 1860. In 1881, he graduated from Illinois College, where a college oratory prize foreshadowed his later career. He graduated from the Union College of Law in Chicago in 1883 and began law practice in Jacksonville, Illinois. In 1887 he moved to Lincoln, Nebraska, where in 1890 he was elected to the U.S. House of Representatives. He served there for two terms.

In Congress, Bryan made full use of his gift of oratory. The Democrats of the time attributed the Panic of 1893 to the gold standard and felt that bimetallism (a currency based on both gold and silver, silver being in plentiful supply from the silver mines of the American West) was the panacea for the depression that followed the panic. Bryan became the party's leading proponent of the free coinage of silver at the ratio of 16 ounces of silver to one ounce of gold.

While in the House, Bryan unsuccessfully sought election to the Senate. He became editor of the *Omaha World-Herald* in 1894, resigning in 1896 after he was nominated for the presidency by the Democratic National Convention. The nomination was a signal honor for Bryan, then only 36, and a tribute to his persuasiveness as a speaker. As a delegate to the convention, he mounted the platform on the third day and delivered his famous "Cross of Gold" speech in denunciation of the gold standard. It ended with a resounding declaration that is still included in collections of famous quotations: "You shall not press down upon the brow of labor this crown of thorns, you shall not crucify mankind upon a cross of gold." Enthusiastically applauded, Bryan was nominated for president on the fifth roll call the next day. The National Silver Party and the Populists also endorsed him, but he was defeated by William McKinley, the Republican candidate.

Again nominated by his party's convention in 1900, Bryan was once more defeated by McKinley. He then returned to Lincoln, Nebraska, where he established and edited *The Commoner*, a weekly newspaper that kept his name and views before the people for many years. Called the Great Commoner, Bryan dedicated himself to speaking for "the toiling masses," who idolized their champion.

Bryan was nominated for the presidency for the third time in 1908, but was once again defeated, this time by the Republican William Howard Taft. Bryan's influence in his party nonetheless continued, and he helped secured the nomination of Woodrow Wilson in 1912. Wilson, successful in his campaign, took Bryan into his cabinet as secretary of state, an office that Bryan resigned in June 1915 because of his opposition to the president's war policy. As secretary of state, Bryan had negotiated a large number of arbitration treaties that he had hoped would prevent war.

In the course of his career, Bryan was influential on behalf of a number of important measures that eventually were adopted. Women's suffrage, the direct election of senators, Prohibition, the income tax, and legal requirements for the public disclosure of newspaper ownership were among them. Over the years, Bryan also became one of the country's best-known advocates of Fundamentalism. As a Fundamentalist, he believed that the Bible should be interpreted literally in every instance. He accordingly regarded Darwin's theory of evolution as the root of many of the theological errors of the day, and he was instrumental in drafting state legislation forbidding the teaching of evolution in public schools. This measure became law in Oklahoma, Mississippi, and Tennessee.

After Bryan retired from politics, he divided his time between selling real estate in Florida (where he moved in 1921) and promoting Fundamentalism. Thus, in 1925, when John T. Scopes, a biology teacher in the high school at Dayton, Tennessee, was charged with teaching evolution in the public schools in violation of Tennessee's state law, Bryan volunteered to act as an attorney for the prosecution. Scopes, represented by the famous defense attorney Clarence Darrow (see related essays throughout this book), was convicted but never sentenced. Bryan himself never left Dayton. Weakened by his exertions in the heat of a southern summer, he died on July 26, 1925, five days after the trial.

A college named after Bryan was founded in Dayton, Ohio, in 1930. He was further memorialized in Salem, Illinois, his birthplace, where a statue of him by Gutzon Borglum was erected.

Earl Warren's Birthday

Photo by Robert Oakes. Collection of the Supreme Court of the United States.

Earl Warren

Earl Warren, the 14th chief justice of the United States Supreme Court, was born on March 19, 1891, in Los Angeles, California. His father, Methias Warren, who changed the family's surname from Varren, had come in his infancy to the United States from Stavanger, Norway. Warren's mother, Crystal Hernlund Warren, emigrated from Sweden when she was young and spent her formative years in Minnesota.

Methias Warren, an employee of the Southern Pacific Railroad, was an early member of Eugene V. Debs's American Railway Union and in 1895 lost his job when he joined a strike against the line. He later prospered as a master railroad car repairman and as a dabbler in real estate. The elder Warren met a tragic death in 1938, when an unidentified robber murdered him.

Earl Warren worked at a variety of odd jobs after school and during summer vacations: He delivered newspapers, drove an ice wagon, sold books, and acted as a railroad callboy rounding up train crews. He also worked as a cub reporter for a newspaper, the Bakersfield Californian. He prepared for his later career by studying political science for three years at the University of California at Berkeley and then entering that institution's school of law. He received a B.L. degree in 1912 and a J.D. in 1914, and on May 14, 1914, he achieved admission to the state bar. He joined the legal department of the Associated Oil Company in San Francisco but then moved across the bay to become a law clerk in the firm of Robinson and Robinson in Oakland.

When the United States entered World War I in 1917, Warren applied for the Army Officer Training Corps, but minor surgery made it impossible for him to be available before the quotas were filled. Undaunted, he enlisted as an infantryman and took basic training at Camp Lewis, Washington. The young lawyer managed to advance from private to first sergeant in four weeks and became an officer candidate in January 1918. Commissioned a second lieutenant in May of that year, he instructed recruits at Camp Lee, Virginia, and officer trainees at Fort MacArthur, Texas. He left active duty as a first lieutenant on December 11, 1918, but retained a captaincy in the reserves until 1935.

In 1919 assemblyman Leon Gray, a onetime member of Robinson and Robinson, helped Warren secure the post of clerk of the judiciary committee of the lower house of the California legislature. After the legislative session ended, Warren joined Gray's law office in Oakland, but he quickly moved on to become deputy attorney for that city (1919–1920). In May 1920 Ezra Decoto, the district attorney of Alameda County, appointed Warren as one of his assistants, and by 1923 the rising public servant had become chief deputy district attorney. Warren, who also served as legal adviser to the Alameda Board of Supervisors, succeeded Decoto as district attorney when his mentor resigned in 1925, and he persuaded voters to grant him a full term in the 1926 campaign. Reelected in 1930 and 1934, he earned a reputation as a crime fighter and "racket buster."

Warren was a successful public prosecutor for 13 years, but found the role a distressing one. "I never heard a jury bring in a verdict of guilty," he once commented, "but that I felt sick at the pit of my stomach." Much to his credit, as district attorney he never had a conviction reversed by a higher court.

A Republican who served as a national committeeman for the party from 1936 through 1938, Warren nonetheless won the nomination of the Democrats and Progressives as well as of the Republicans when he successfully sought election as attorney general of California in 1938. He immediately made good his pledge of nonpartisanship by urging a jury to convict the secretary of the outgoing Republican governor for selling pardons to prisoners. As attorney general, Warren closed the flourishing but illegal dog-racing tracks in the state and harassed gambling ships operating in the Pacific just beyond the coastal jurisdiction of the state.

At the outbreak of World War II, Warren focused his attention on national security and shaped the Uniform Sabotage Prevention Act, or Warren Act. In the uneasy days after the Japanese attack on the naval installation at Pearl Harbor on December 7, 1941, he actively supported the forced removal of 110,000 Japanese aliens and Nisei (Japanese Americans) from strategic spots along the West Coast to inland detention camps. In later years, he shared with many others strong feelings of guilt about that period of history.

Warren ran for governor of California in 1942, easily defeating the Democratic incumbent, Culbert Olson, by 342,000 votes. Characteristically, he promised a bipartisan administration and vowed: "I am a Republican, but . . . I shall seek the support of people of both parties. I can do this honorably because I am independent, and therefore in a position to serve the people fairly, regardless of their politics or mine." He was reelected in 1946. In 1950 he became California's first three-term chief executive when he decisively defeated James Roosevelt, the son of President Franklin D. Roosevelt.

As governor, Warren appointed both Democrats and Republicans to important political positions and increased the responsiveness and efficiency of several agencies, including the Public Works and Industrial Relations departments. He advocated a variety of programs directed at easing the burdens on the less affluent: He supported a reduction in the sales tax, raised old age pensions, expanded unemployment insurance coverage, and encouraged the appropriation of funds for child-care centers. He won wide recognition for his programs and became an aspirant for national office.

Warren gave the keynote speech at the Republican National Convention in 1944 and led the California delegation into the camp of Thomas E. Dewey, the governor of New York. In November 1947 he announced that he wanted to be the party's candidate for president in the following year, but he lost the contest to Dewey. Although he had declined the vice-presidential nomination in 1944, he accepted it in 1948. To the surprise of almost everyone, the Dewey-Warren combination, heavily favored by the pollsters to win the November election, failed to oust Democrat Harry S. Truman from the White House. Warren again sought the presidential nomination in 1952, but Dwight D. Eisenhower became the Republican standard-bearer instead.

Although Warren had no experience as a member of the judiciary, in 1953 President Eisenhower appointed him to succeed the deceased Fred M. Vinson as chief justice of the United States Supreme Court. Eisenhower noted that Warren's "reputation for integrity, honesty, middle-of-the-road philosophy, experience in government, experience in the law" showed him to be a man who had "no ends to serve except the United States." On October 5, 1953, Associate Justice Hugo L. Black administered the oath of office to Warren as the new leader of the Supreme Court.

In his earliest days on the high bench, Warren seemed to follow the lead of Associate Justice Felix Frankfurter, the Court's most eloquent spokesman for traditional jurisprudence. Frankfurter thought that the Court should thwart the will of the Congress or the state legislatures only in those rare instances when a law clearly contradicted the Constitution. Warren was neither a deep theoretician nor a legal technician. His major desire, he told the editors of *Fortune* magazine, was to be fair. "A legal system," he said, "is simply a mature and sophisticated attempt, never perfected, to institutionalize this sense of justice and to free men from the terror and unpredictability of arbitrary force."

As Warren gained experience on the bench, he aligned himself less frequently with Frankfurter and agreed almost consistently with Black. The latter was an ardent civil libertarian and defender of the Bill of Rights. With Warren and Black in the lead, the Court after 1954 worked vigorously to enforce individual rights when they were denied and to protect them when they were threatened. Warren's earnest desire was that the Supreme Court be a "people's court."

The justices in 1954 reversed a decision, which their predecessors had made in the 1896 case of *Plessy* v. *Ferguson*, that stated that restricting African Americans to separate but equal public facilities did not constitute illegal discrimination. Relying heavily on psychological and sociological arguments, the Court in the historic case of *Brown* v. *Board of Education of Topeka* unanimously stated that racially segregated elementary schools were inherently unequal and that their existence denied equal protection of the law to African Americans. The Court ordered the states to place public schools on a racially nondiscriminatory basis "with all deliberate speed." Some localities complied quickly, but many others resisted the ruling for decades, and school desegregation would not become the norm until the 1970s.

From 1960 to 1966 the Warren Court made it clear that civil authorities could not deprive individuals suspected of crimes of their basic rights as guaranteed under the Constitution. In *Mapp* v. *Ohio* (1961), the justices forbade states from introducing at trials evidence obtained through unreasonable search or seizure. In the landmark case of *Gideon* v. *Wainwright* (1963), the Court affirmed the right of indigent persons to court-appointed counsel at state felony trials. In the cases of *Escobedo* v. *Illinois* (1964) and *Miranda* v. *Arizona* (1966), the Court declared that police at the time of arrest must inform prisoners of their right to see a lawyer and stated that suspects have the right to have counsel present during interrogations.

Many of the Supreme Court decisions during Warren's tenure as chief justice were controversial, and some conservative groups demanded that Congress remove him from the bench. Many citizens were particularly distressed by the Court's ruling in the case of *Engel* v. *Vitale* (1962), that the New York State Board of Regents could not draw up a prayer for use in public school classrooms. In keeping with the doctrine of the separation of church and state, the justices, divided six to one, argued that, even if pupils retained the right not to participate, "it is no part of the business of government to compose official prayers to be recited as a part of a religious program carried on by government." In the case of the *School District of Abington Township* v. *Schempp* (1963), the Court banned Bible reading and recitation of the Lord's Prayer in public schools.

Politically, the Warren Court's most significant decisions may have been those that dealt with apportionment of seats in state legislatures. Traditionally, a disproportionately large number of delegates from rural areas held seats in many state assemblies and senates and in the U.S. House of Representatives, thus wielding the power to prevent legislation designed to alleviate urban distress. In *Baker* v. *Carr* (1962), the Court agreed to hear cases related to the problem, and in *Reynolds* v. *Sims* (1964) it determined that the states must apportion both chambers of their legislatures by population in such a way as to treat all their citizens as equally as possible. In the case of *Westberry* v. *Saunders* (1964), the justices declared that all congressional districts should include approximately the same number of inhabitants.

After the assassination of President John F. Kennedy in 1963 (see November 22), President Lyndon B. Johnson placed on Warren's shoulders the heavy responsibility of conducting the government's inquiry into that tragedy. The chief justice and six other noted Americans worked for almost a year on the case. On September 27, 1964, the Warren Commission issued its 888-page report, which concluded that Lee Harvey Oswald, acting independently, fatally shot Kennedy in Dallas, Texas. The commission's findings have been challenged by many who are convinced that not all the facts have been disclosed.

In mid-June 1968, Warren informed President Johnson that he wished to retire from the Court. He stepped down at the end of the next Court year in June 1969. At a press conference, Warren expressed satisfaction with his 16 years on the bench and listed *Baker* v. *Carr* (reapportionment), *Brown* v. *Board of Education* (desegregation), and *Gideon* v. *Wainwright* (rights of accused persons) as his three most significant decisions. President Richard M. Nixon appointed Warren F. Burger to replace Warren as chief justice.

On October 14, 1925, Warren married Nina Palmquist Meyer, a Swedish-born widow, and adopted her son, James. The Warrens became the parents of five more children: Earl Jr., Robert, Virginia, Dorothy, and Nina. Warren, a Baptist and a Mason, made a habit of starting and concluding each day by reading from the Bible. For recreation, he favored deer and duck hunting and was an avid baseball and football fan. The man who, it has frequently been said, exerted the most profound influence on his country's law and way of life since the time of Chief Justice John Marshall a century and a half earlier died on July 9, 1974, at the age of 83. Following a U.S. Army honor funeral, he was buried in Arlington National Cemetery.

March 20

Burrhus F. Skinner's Birthday

Famed behavorial psychologist Burrhus Frederic Skinner was born on March 20, 1904, in Susquehanna, Pennsylvania. His father was a lawyer, and hoped that the young Skinner would follow in his footsteps. However, Skinner developed an interest in writing, and attended Hamilton College where he graduated with a degree in English in 1926.

After receiving his Ph.D. from Harvard in 1931, Skinner became a professor of psychology at the University of Minnesota. During the 1930s he became a leader in the school of behavioral psychology. According to this philosophy, human psychology is dominated by external stimuli, namely experiences that shape our behavior. According to Skinner, behavior can be conditioned by consistent positive or negative reinforcement (reward or punishment) for certain actions. In 1938 Skinner wrote *The Behavior of Organisms*, which presented his conclusions. Although controversial in some respects, namely the role of free will and individuality in human behavior, *The Behavior of Organisms* established Skinner's reputation as one of America's leading psychologists.

In 1948 Skinner joined the faculty of Harvard University, where he would remain until his retirement in 1974. During his career he developed several new teaching methods based on his psychological theories, in which students were taught to master a certain set of facts before moving onto the next level. This form of "programmed instruction" led to the development of several types of teaching machines. Skinner's book *The Technology of Teaching* was published in 1968. He also developed a mechanism to improve the study of behavioral activity in laboratory animals, namely the "Skinner Box." This device was a small box or cage, typically enclosed in glass, which contained a test subject such as a rat or a mouse. The animal could be observed and subjected to various stimuli with a minimum of external interference, and the box could be connected to devices such as a feeder that would release food pellets when the animal was to be given a reward as positive reinforcement for acting in the desired manner.

Skinner also wrote *Walden 2* (1948) and *Beyond Freedom and Dignity* (1971). In both books, he envisioned a form of utopian or ideal society based on mass conditioning and behavioral modification. Some critics have found Skinner's writings on social issues to be disturbing, given the conflict between mass conditioning and traditional notions of democracy and self-determination.

Nevertheless, Skinner was one of the great contributors to the evolution of modern psychology. He died on August 18, 1990, in Cambridge, Massachusetts.

Neal Dow's Birthday

An early leader in the temperance movement, which assumed prominence in the United States in the 19th and early 20th centuries, Neal Dow became world-famous as the Father of Prohibition in Maine, the first state to prohibit the sale of liquor. Born in Portland, Maine, on March 20, 1804, Dow was trained by his Quaker parents in the principles of peace, industry, thrift, and temperance. Although he espoused these principles throughout his life, he was eventually dismissed from the Society of Friends (the official name of the Quaker organization) because he came to disagree with it on the propriety of using weapons.

Educated at the Friends Academy in New Bedford, Massachusetts, Dow joined his father in the tanning business and accumulated a large fortune. His first temperance speech was made in opposition to serving liquor at a dinner of the Deluge Engine Company of Portland. His plea was successful, and no liquor was served to the firemen.

Dow was a delegate to the first temperance convention in Maine when the State Temperance Society was organized in 1834. Four years later he helped found the Maine Temperance Union, whose members were pledged to total abstinence from liquor. It was not until 1845, however, that he persuaded this organization to support legislation forbidding the sale of intoxicants in the state. The Maine legislature passed the first state prohibitory law the next year, though it was too weak to be fully effective.

Dow, elected mayor of Portland in 1851, was immediately made chairman of a committee to urge more stringent antiliquor legislation. He drafted a bill that was passed by large majorities in both houses of the state legislature and then signed into law by Governor John Hubbard on June 2, 1851, which is generally regarded as the date when Prohibition began in Maine. The statute became widely known as the Maine Law. In the next 10 years it served as the model for Prohibition laws in more than a dozen other states. Dow was reelected mayor of Portland in 1855, in which year the Maine Law was temporarily repealed. It was reenacted in response to popular sentiment in 1858.

Dow was 57 years old when the Civil War erupted. Nearly as intense in his opposition to slavery as to alcohol, he volunteered his services on behalf of the Union and became colonel of the 13th Regiment of Maine volunteers. During the conflict he rose to the rank of brigadier general. Twice wounded, he was taken prisoner while recuperating. He was eventually exchanged for a Confederate major general, Fitzhugh Lee, and returned home. After the war, he continued to speak and write on behalf of Prohibition, traveling extensively in the process. He was the candidate of the Prohibition Party for president in the election of 1880, winning a total of 10,305 votes. Four years later, owing to his efforts, the constitution of Maine was amended to prohibit the sale of intoxicants in the state, as the Maine law already did.

By the time Dow died in Portland on October 2, 1897, the temperance movement, which had waned during the years of the Civil War and the following decade, had seen a resurgence under the leadership of Frances E. Willard of the Woman's Christian Temperance Union and others. Temperance groups triumphed in 1919 with passage of the 18th Amendment, legislating Prohibition on a nationwide scale. Few of those who had worked hardest for the measure lived to see their labors undone with passage of the 21st Amendment, which repealed the 18th Amendment, in 1933 after a stormy period of attempted enforcement and all but universal violation of the law. Since then the question of abstaining from alcohol has generally been regarded as a matter for personal decision, although there are still a number of counties and municipalities in various parts of the country where the availability of alcoholic beverages is determined by local option.

March 21

Spring Begins

In the United States, and the north temperate zones generally, the season of fresh growth and new life known as spring begins about March 21 of every year. The exact moment when the Sun is at the vernal equinox, officially signaling the change of seasons, varies slightly from year to year because of the oscillations and wobbling motions that the Earth manifests both in its rotation on its axis and in its elliptical course around the Sun.

The ecliptic, the plane in which the Earth revolves around the Sun, is divided into four 90-degree sections, each beginning with a definite point: two solstices and two equinoxes. The amount of time taken by the Sun to cover each of these divisions is termed a season. The season of spring begins at the vernal equinox when the Sun, as seen from the Earth, passes through the intersection of the ecliptic and the celestial equator, having then a longitude of exactly 0 degrees. Its rays extend from the North to the South Pole, and day and night are an equal 12 hours throughout the world.

In antiquity the start of the year was often reckoned from the vernal equinox, which was also chosen as the point from which to calculate and observe the 12 constellations of the zodiac, beginning with the sign of Aries. The vernal equinox has since been known as the first point of Aries, and spring is therefore said to begin when the sun enters the zodiac sign of Aries. Hipparchus, the 2nd-century B.C. Greek astronomer whose calculations form the groundwork of the present zodiacal system, correctly estimated that because of the precession of the equinoxes (the retrograde motion of the equinoctial points), the vernal equinox moves slightly west each year. Therefore, the first point of Aries, which during Hipparchus's time was found in the constellation Aries, is now in Pisces, the next constellation to the west.

During the spring season, the Sun leaves the celestial equator and progresses along the ecliptic north of the equator. At the summer solstice (see June 21), the Sun enters the zodiac sign of Cancer, having reached a longitude of 90 degrees and its maximum northerly ascent. The season of spring then ends. In terms of earthly weather, the four seasons do not invariably coincide with the astronomical seasons. In many parts of North America, where spring is popularly considered to comprise the months of March, April, and May, the climate of March may still be that of winter, and May can sometimes seem like summer. In Great Britain, spring is popularly thought to include February, March, and April.

The difference in the seasons, notably the consistent variation in weather, is caused by the tilt of the Earth's axis, as well as by its elliptical course around the Sun. When the North Pole inclines away from the Sun around December 21, the time of the winter solstice and the beginning of winter (see December 21), the sun's rays are slanted, solar heat is less concentrated, and temperatures consequently are low. By the end of spring the North Pole points directly toward the Sun, and the opposite conditions prevail. In the Southern Hemisphere, since the movement of the South Pole is opposite to that of the North Pole, the seasons are reversed. Astronomical spring starts there about September 21 and ends about December 21.

Spring, a transitional period between the extreme temperature cycles of winter and summer, is the chief season of planting and germination, when life, light, and apparent order in the universe once more prevail over what the ancients regarded as the chaos of the dark, barren winter season.

Spring profoundly influenced the ancients and played an important role in mythology, folklore, and art. Ancient painters and sculptors often depicted spring as a female figure carrying flowers. The early Christians regarded the seasons as symbolic of the course of human life, seeing spring as rebirth or resurrection after the death that winter symbolized. The practice of adorning basilicas with symbolic representations of the seasons continued into the Middle Ages, culminating in the 13th century with the beautifully carved depictions of the seasons and the individual months in the French cathedrals of Paris, Chartres, and Reims. These spring scenes reveal the harsh realities of the laborer's everyday tasks in preparing the fields for cultivation and dressing the vineyards. Renaissance artists tended to view spring more lightheartedly: Sandro Botticelli's famous painting *The Primavera* is a prime example of the glorification of the joys of awakening nature.

Pleasure at the annual greening and blossoming of the landscape is still much in evidence today, particularly as reflected in the numerous flower festivals and house-and-garden tours that take place across the nation each year. The season is marked by all kinds of beginnings: seed plantings, graduations, and weddings. Even the season's major religious holidays epitomize the arrival of spring, at least indirectly. The Jewish Passover refers to renaissance, or, more exactly, release from physical and spiritual bondage and from the labors of winter. The Christian Easter (which may have borrowed its name from Eostre, Teutonic goddess of spring and fertility) is also a celebration of resurrection.

Earth Day

As of this writing, there is no universally recognized fixed date for the observance of Earth Day. Many people observe Earth Day on April 22, for the reasons set forth below.

The modern environmental movement first began to gain momentum in the 1960s. At some point in the late 1960s, the concept of celebrating an annual Earth Day to focus attention on environmental issues developed. Several prominent individuals have taken the credit for being the first to propose Earth Day, including former senator Gaylord Nelson (Democrat from Wisconsin) and John McConnell, President of WE, Inc. (later the Earth Society). In the fall of 1969, the San Francisco Board of Supervisors voted to hold a local Earth Day observance on March 21, 1970. March 21, being the first day of spring and thus the rebirth of nature after winter, seemed like a logical date to celebrate the natural beauty of the Earth.

However, there was another environmental observance planned for the spring of 1970, namely the "National Environmental Teach-In." The sponsors of this event were preparing a massive, one-day national event on April 22, 1970, and they decided to change the name to Earth Day.

Thus, although Earth Day was first celebrated on March 21, 1970, the first national Earth Day took place on April 22. Millions of Americans participated in rallies and other events. Earth Day has been observed annually ever since, on one date or the other. Many organizations, including the United Nations, follow the March 21 line of reasoning and schedule their observances for the first day of spring. However, April 22 continues to remain a popular date as well. In certain localities, Earth Day events take place on other dates in the spring, sometimes timed to coincide with a convenient weekend. As of yet, there is no federal observance or holiday to help establish a uniform date for the observance of Earth Day.

Since the first Earth Day in 1970, the environmental movement has successfully pursued its agenda in several areas. Congress has passed clean-air and clean-water legislation to help curb pollution. Cities such as Pittsburgh, Pennsylvania, which used to be synonymous with industrial smog and grime, have been rejuvenated. Anti-littering legislation has cleaned up the nation's highways, which older readers may remember used to be strewn with trash until a $500 penalty for throwing refuse out the window was imposed. Some of the worst toxic waste dumps have been cleaned up, and most communities have some sort of mandatory recycling program for newspapers, plastics, glass, and metal containers. Dozens of other initiatives have been taken at the federal, state, and local. Critics of the environmental movement point to the massive costs involved and the burden of government regulation, while environmental activists believe that still more needs to be done in the face of new threats such as global warming (the increase in Earth's temperature due to atmospheric pollution) and the industrialization of populous countries such as China and India.

March 22

The First Native American Treaty

On March 22, 1621, Governor John Carver of the Plymouth colony made a treaty with Massasoit, sachem of the Wampanoags, pledging friendship and alliance between the Wampanoags and the colonists. This was the first treaty between a native tribe and the European settlers made within the 13 colonies. It remained in effect for 54 years, during which time it was respected by both parties.

The territory over which Massasoit ruled embraced nearly all of southeastern Massachusetts. By the time the Plymouth colonists arrived in 1620, however, the Wampanoags, though still powerful, had been reduced in number by a mysterious pestilence, variously described as smallpox, yellow fever, or plague, which had struck them down several years earlier. The epidemic had a devastating effect, killing off perhaps a third of all Indians in southern New England, upsetting the balance of power between the various tribes, and perhaps contributing to the willingness of the Wampanoags to make friends with the colonists. Those involved in the preliminary conversations that led to the treaty included Edward Winslow (who later became governor of Plymouth colony) and two English-speaking natives living in the area. The two natives were Squanto, a Pawtuxet, and Samoset, a Pemaquid.

The treaty of peace and alliance signed by Massasoit and Governor Carver appears in slightly differing forms in William Bradford's *The History of Plymouth Plantation*, in Nathaniel Morton's *New-Englands Memorial*, and in *Mourt's Relation*, named for the author of its preface. *Mourt's Relation*, which appeared in London in 1622, was the earliest account of the Plymouth Pilgrims. As edited by Dwight B. Heath under the title *A Journal of the Pilgrims at Plymouth* (New York, 1963), *Mourt's Relation* contained this version of the treaty:

1. That neither he [Massasoit] nor any of his should injure or do hurt to any of our people.
2. And if any of his did hurt to any of ours, he should send the offender, that we might punish him.
3. That if any of our tools were taken away when our people were at work, he should cause them to be restored, and if ours did any harm to any of his, we would do the like to them.
4. If any did unjustly war against him, we would aid him; if any did war against us, he should aid us.
5. He should send to his neighbor confederates, to certify them of this, that they might not wrong us, but might be likewise comprised in the conditions of peace.
6. That when their men came to us, they should leave their bows and arrows behind them, as we should do our pieces when we came to them.

Lastly, that doing thus, King James would esteem of him as his friend and ally.

The treaty worked well. A contributor to *Mourt's Relation* wrote: "We have found the Indians very faithful in their covenant of peace with us, very loving and ready to pleasure us. So that there is now great peace amongst the Indians . . . and we, for our part, walk as peaceably and safely in the wood as in the highways in England."

Peace between the colonists and natives lasted throughout the life of the Wampanoag chief. After Massasoit's death in 1661, his son Wamsutta (Alexander) succeeded him. In 1662 Wamsutta died (murdered by the English, the Wampanoags suspected), and his brother Metacomet (whom the colonists called King Philip) became chief. Encroachment by the colonists on tribal territory and the settlers' execution in 1675 of three native warriors accused of murdering a pro-settler informer led directly to what is known as King Philip's War. Directed against colonists throughout New England, the war involved not only the Wampanoags but all the tribes with which Metacomet in the previous decade had been making treaties in anticipation of a stand against the growing colonial tide.

In the course of the devastating war, 52 of the region's 90 towns were attacked by natives. Roughly a dozen of them were completely destroyed; others were deserted; and all suffered damage. Perhaps 1,000 colonists, including 600 men of military age, and eventually 3,000 natives lost their lives.

Eleven days after his wife and son were captured on August 1, 1676, Metacomet was himself killed, and his head was cut off to be exhibited on top of a pole at Plymouth for the next quarter century. The war, which resulted in the virtual destruction of the Wampanoags and an end to native resistance throughout southern New England, did not terminate with the death of Metacomet. On frontiers as far north as the Penobscot River in Maine, it dragged on until 1678, involving numerous tribes.

Palm Sunday

This is a movable event.

For Christians the world over, Palm Sunday, commemorating Jesus Christ's triumphal entry into Jerusalem, ushers in one of the most important and solemn weeks of the church year. A movable feast, Palm Sunday is always celebrated a week before Easter, and its date each year depends on the date set for Easter (see March 29). The days between the two Sundays comprise Holy Week, a period especially devoted to the commemoration of the events of the last week of Jesus' life on earth. According to Christian belief, it was during Holy Week (sometimes called Great Week) that Jesus performed the essential work of the Redemption, that is, redeeming human beings from the bondage of sin.

Christian theologians hold that the Redemption is one unified event encompassing Christ's Passion (that is, suffering), death, and Resurrection. From the earliest times, Holy Week was considered the Christian Passover, signaling Jesus' passing over from this life to life with his heavenly father (God). The events and circumstances of the Redemption had been foretold in the Old Testament, and the New Testament records that Jesus alluded several times to his Passion, death, and Resurrection. The drama of the Redemption, the core of Christianity, began to unfold on Palm Sunday with Jesus' entry into Jerusalem.

Knowing full well what awaited him in Jerusalem, Jesus went to that holy city for the Feast of the Passover, according to Jewish custom. He was greeted as a triumphant king by the people, who had heard about or witnessed his miracles and looked to him as the temporal ruler sent in answer to their prayers for a leader who would deliver them from the domination of the Roman Empire. All four Gospels in the New Testament record Jesus' entry into Jerusalem; the specific accounts are found in Matthew 21:1–11, Mark 11:1–10, Luke 19:28–40, and John 12:12–16. Among these biblical reports of the first Palm Sunday, the briefest is the summary found in the Gospel of John:

> The next day a great crowd who had come to the feast [the Passover] heard that Jesus was coming to Jerusalem. So they took branches of palm trees and went out to meet him, crying, "Hosanna! Blessed be he who comes in the name of the Lord, even the King of Israel!" And Jesus found a young ass and sat upon it; as it is written, "Fear not, daughter of Zion; behold thy king is coming, sitting on an ass's colt!"

It is often stated that the animal Jesus chose to ride symbolized humility and was the antithesis of violence, war, or domination by force; and that the image of a horse, by contrast, would have been one of arrogance, as of a temporal ruler returning victorious from battle. In keeping with this, many Christians also hear on Palm Sunday a reading from Philippians (2:5-11):

> Let this mind be in you, which was also in Christ Jesus: Who . . . made himself of no reputation, and took upon him the form of a servant, and was made in the likeness of men: And . . . humbled himself, and became obedient unto death, even the death of the cross.

The Palm Sunday account in the Gospel of John also explains the crowd's exuberant expectations concerning Jesus, and the Pharisees' antagonism, which would lead to his arrest, trial, and death:

> The crowd that had been with him when he called Lazarus out of the tomb and raised him from the dead bore witness. The reason why the crowd went to meet him was that they heard he had done this sign. The Pharisees then said to one another, "You see that you can do nothing; look, the world has gone after him."

Celebration of Palm Sunday by Eastern Orthodox churches sometimes coincides with and sometimes follows the date set in the Western Christian churches. Throughout Holy Week, worship services are scheduled in the Albanian, Bulgarian, Carpatho-Russian, Greek, Russian, Serbian, Syrian, Ukrainian, and other Orthodox churches. Palms are distributed in some of the Eastern churches, but in others, branches of some other tree are used. This custom is particularly prevalent among those whose origins are in northern regions where palms are not available.

After the persecutions of Christians abated in the 4th century A.D., people from many countries made Holy Week pilgrimages to Jerusalem. One such pilgrim, a Spanish woman named Eutheria (Etheria), or Silvia, kept a journal that provides one of the earliest accounts of the Palm Sunday celebration in Jerusalem, dating from about A.D. 390. It describes how the crowds of pilgrims gathered on the Mount of Olives and listened to the account of Jesus's entry into Jerusalem, and then, singing and waving palm and olive branches, marched toward the city.

Purim (Feast of Lots)

This is a movable event.

Purim, the Feast of Lots, is celebrated by Jews on the 14th day of the month of Adar, a date that falls in either February or March. A day of great rejoicing, it commemorates the deliverance of the Jews in Shushan, the capital of Persia, from a plot to destroy them. The story is told in the Book of Esther, one of the five small Megillot, or Scrolls, of the Bible that are read on five different Jewish holidays.

The story begins as King Ahasuerus, commonly identified with Xerxes, decides to depose his queen, Vashti, because she refuses to obey him. During his search for a successor to Vashti, many beautiful maidens are presented to him. Finally the king selects Esther, an orphan (originally named Hadassah) brought up by her cousin Mordecai. The fact that both are Jews is not known by Ahasuerus.

At this time the king's prime minister, Haman, holds a parade through the streets of Shushan. Everyone who sees Haman is required to bow down before him, and all obey except Mordecai, who says that as a Jew he must bow only before God. This enrages Haman, who convinces king Ahasuerus that the Jews are a useless and disloyal people and should be exterminated. Haman draws lots, or purim, to fix the date for the slaughter of the Jews and for the confiscation of Jewish property.

When Mordecai hears of the cruel proclamation, he persuades Queen Esther to undertake the deliverance of her people. She directs a fast of three days by all Jews, including herself, after which she is to go before the king, although the queen is not expected to appear before him unless summoned. Esther's appearance delights the king, who receives her graciously and promises to dine with her and Haman on two successive nights. On the night after the first banquet the king, sleepless, orders the national records read aloud to him. The part that is read tells of the revelation, by Mordecai, of a plot against the king's life, a service for which Mordecai has never been rewarded. Upon hearing this, the king calls his prime minister and asks him, "What shall be done to the man whom the King delighteth to honor?"

Haman, thinking that the king means to honor him, suggests a pageant through the streets of Shushan at which a great noble will attend the honored man. Thereupon the king orders a pageant in honor of Mordecai and commands Haman, who is appalled at this turn of A.D.S, to attend Mordecai. The next night, at the second banquet, Esther reveals to the king that she is a Jew and begs him to rescind the order for the destruction of her and her people. The king, realizing the extent of Haman's plot, revokes his decree and orders that Haman and all his sons be hanged on the gallows that Haman had prepared for Mordecai. In addition, Ahasuerus appoints Mordecai his prime minister and issues an order permitting the Jews to slay their enemies on the day that the Jews themselves were to have been killed. Then, as the Book of Esther records (9:20–28):

> Mordecai . . . sent letters unto all the Jews that were in all the provinces of the King Ahasuerus . . . to enjoin them that they should keep the fourteenth day of the month Adar . . . yearly, [the day] wherein the Jews had rest from their enemies, and the month which was turned unto them from sorrow to gladness, and from mourning into a good day; that they should make them days of feasting and gladness, and of sending portions one to another, and gifts

to the poor. And the Jews took upon them to do as . . . Mordecai had written unto them; because Haman . . . the enemy of all the Jews, had devised against the Jews to destroy them, and had cast Pur, that is, the lot, to . . . destroy them; but when [Esther] came before the king, he commanded by letters that [Haman's] wicked device, which he had devised against the Jews, should return upon his own head; and that he and his sons should be hanged on the gallows. Wherefore they called these days Purim after the name of Pur. . . . The Jews ordained, and took upon them . . . that [this day] should be remembered and kept throughout every generation.

Today, Jews celebrate Purim as prescribed in the Book of Esther. It is a day of feasting and rejoicing. The festival meal, which begins in late afternoon on the 14th of Adar, may extend until late in the evening. Since Purim is only a semiholiday, there is no religious prohibition against working. Unlike most of the other Jewish holidays, Purim has no marked religious features, other than the portrayal of Esther's loyalty to her people and her courage. The Book of Esther itself contains no mention of God. The main content of the services held in synagogues on Purim is the reading of the Megillah or scroll of the Book of Esther, and an expression of hope and confidence that the Jews will survive every future Haman as they have survived those in the past.

Stamp Act Signed

On March 22, 1765, King George III approved the Stamp Act, the first direct tax ever levied upon the American colonies by Parliament, little realizing the vehemence of the protest that the act would provoke. George Grenville, chancellor of the exchequer, estimated that this act, which required tax stamps to be affixed to various colonial legal documents and commercial papers, would yield revenues of 60,000 pounds a year. This sum, together with impost receipts, would have paid approximately a third of the yearly cost of maintaining the 10,000 British troops defending American borders against French invasion, substantially alleviating the burden borne by the sorely pressed English taxpayers.

The American colonists, however, refused to accept the Stamp Act as a justifiable means of contributing to their own defense. Instead, shouts of "No taxation without representation" echoed up and down the American seaboard, and the following year Parliament was forced to repeal the act.

March 23

Wernher Von Braun's Birthday

Wernher von Braun, one of the pioneers in the field of rocket science, was born on March 23, 1912, in Wirsitz, Germany. His parents were Baron Magnus von Braun and Baroness Emmy von Braun. As a child he was fascinated by science fiction, and began to study mathematics and physics in order to understand the principles of rocketry, which was in its infancy at that time.

Von Braun entered the Berlin Institute of Technology in 1930 and graduated in 1932 with a degree in mechanical engineering. He began to work for the German army's missile program while he completed his studies at the University of Berlin from 1932 to 1934. During the 1930s he helped develop the V-2 rocket and jet engine prototypes for military aircraft. Eventually he was relocated to the testing grounds at Peenemunde on Germany's Baltic coastline. Peenemunde is one of the most famous names in the history of rocket science: Many important advances were made there, albeit in the pursuit of Nazi military objectives during World War II. Toward the end of the war, American troops approached Preenemunde from the west while Russian troops approached from the east. Von Braun arranged for the surrender of himself and hundreds of German rocket scientists to the Americans.

In "Operation Paperclip," von Braun and over a hundred other German scientists were eventually brought to the United States. They were sent to Fort Bliss, Texas, to work on the American missile program. Picking up where he had left off in Peenemunde, von Braun helped develop new rockets, such as the Redstone. In 1950 he was transferred to the military facilities in Huntsville, Alabama. He received his American citizenship on April 14, 1955.

Von Braun lived in Huntsville until 1970. He was a leader in the Jupiter and Saturn rocket programs, and helped develop the *Saturn V* that eventually carried astronauts to the Moon. He was also the director of NASA's Marshall Space Flight Center and contributed to the development of *Skylab*, the first space station. Von Braun retired in the early 1970s, going to work for Fairchild Industries in the Washington, D.C., area. He died on June 16, 1977. During his lifetime, von Braun saw rockets go from science fiction to fact and helped the United States become the world's leader in space exploration.

Patrick Henry's Speech for Liberty

When a provincial convention assembled in Virginia in March 1775, Patrick Henry, regarding war as inevitable, introduced a resolution providing for the organization of the militia in order to put the Virginia colony in shape for what would eventually be the American Revolution. The proposal was bitterly opposed by the Loyalists. On March 23, Henry defended his resolution in one of his most famous speeches. It reportedly concluded with the ringing words:

> There is no retreat but in submission to slavery. Our chains are already forged. Their clanking may be heard on the plains of Boston. The next gale that sweeps from the North will bring the clash of resounding arms. Our brethren are already in the field. Why stand we here idle? What is it that the gentlemen wish? What would they have? Is life so dear or peace so sweet as to be purchased at the price of chains and slavery? Forbid it, Almighty God! I know not what course others may take, but as for me, give me liberty, or give me death!

Henry's prophecy of the "clash of arms" from the north was fulfilled within less than a month, for on April 19 the battles of Lexington and Concord were fought. Henry's speech, which fanned the flames of the American Revolution, still stands as a masterpiece of patriotic oratory.

Henry was born on May 29, 1736, in Studley, Hanover County, Virginia. After failing twice as a storekeeper and once as a farmer, he was admitted to the bar in 1760. His courtroom oratory as a trial lawyer soon won him a wide reputation and an impressive practice in Virginia. In 1765, at the age of 29, he was elected to the Virginia legislature, the House of Burgesses. That same year he wrote the Virginia Resolutions, which included not only a denunciation of the Stamp Act (see March 22) but also an assertion of the right of the colonies to legislate for themselves, independently of the British Parliament.

After 1774 and 1775, when he went to Philadelphia, Pennsylvania, as a delegate to the First Continental Congress and part of the Second, most of Henry's public life was divided between serving as governor of Virginia and serving in the Virginia legislature. Chosen the first governor of Virginia in May 1776, he was reelected in 1777 and 1778, serving the maximum continuous time allowable under Virginia's new constitution. Later, however, he was Virginia's governor again (1784–1786), between terms in the Virginia legislature (1780–1784 and 1787–1790).

Frustrated in his own military ambitions, Henry effectively supported George Washington in many ways. In 1778 he sent George Rogers Clark on a military expedition to the Illinois country, which led to the expulsion of the British from the Northwest.

In the last decade or so of his life, Henry was offered but declined some of the most prestigious national offices, including those of secretary of state in Washington's cabinet (1795), chief justice of the Supreme Court (1795), envoy to France (1799), governor of Virginia (1796), and United States senator (1794). He agreed to serve again in the Virginia legislature, to which he was elected in 1799, but died on June 6, 1799, at his home called Red Hill, five miles east of Brookneal, Virginia, before he could take his seat.

March 24

NATO Intervenes in Kosovo

The North Atlantic Treaty Organization (NATO) is an important mutual security alliance formed by the United States, Great Britain, and most of Western Europe after World War II to counter the Soviet-led Warsaw Pact. The Warsaw Pact comprised the Soviet Union and the puppet communist regimes it had installed in most of Eastern Europe when its troops overran the Nazis. During the cold war, which lasted until the 1991 collapse of the Soviet Union, NATO and the Warsaw Pact maintained an uneasy peace.

Yugoslavia was one of the few Eastern European states to have escaped the Soviet grip. Although it was led by a communist strongman, Josip Broz Tito, he had come to power by leading the local resistance movement that ousted the Nazis, and so the Soviets had never "liberated" Yugoslav territory. Tito kept Yugoslavia independent, while also keeping a tight rein on his people. Comprised of the states of Bosnia, Croatia, Macedonia, Montenegro, Serbia, and Slovenia, Tito's Yugoslavia had a diverse ethnic and religious population and a history of bitter internecine conflict, but peace was maintained until the death of the strongman on May 4, 1980.

After Tito's death, Yugoslavia began to slowly dissolve, as old ethnic and religious tensions resurfaced. In Serbia, the largest and most powerful of the six Yugoslav states, a new strongman named Slobodan Milosevic rose to power during the 1980s. He tried to use Serbian power to hold Yugoslavia together, even though he had limited support outside of Serbia and was distrusted by non-Serbian ethnic groups. Throughout the 1980s and most of the 1990s, protracted conflicts ensued as Milosevic struggled to consolidate his power. One by one, however, the non-Serbian states slipped out of Milosevic's grasp until his would-be "Yugoslav" federation consisted only of Serbia and Montenegro. He acquired a modicum of new territory by supporting the Serbian faction in Bosnia, in a brutal campaign that alarmed non-Serbs throughout the region, but finally ethnic independence movements began to surface within Serbia itself. In 1998 Milosevic moved to crush a separatist movement within the Serbian province of Kosovo, primarily Albanian in population and Muslim in religion.

Meanwhile, after the collapse of the Soviet Union and the dissolution of the Warsaw Pact, NATO began to change from a cold war alliance of Western powers to a more inclusive, all-European peacekeeping organization. At first NATO was primarily concerned with the dismantling of the Soviet military machine, the reduction of nuclear stockpiles, and the establishment of peaceful relations with Russia. Over time, however, both NATO and the United States became increasingly concerned about the situation in the former Yugoslavia, as evidence of Serbian war crimes, mass executions, and other atrocities began to mount.

When Milosevic moved against Kosovo in 1998, the United States and NATO decided to take aggressive action. A humanitarian disaster loomed as Serbian troops began to force the mass exodus of the Albanian population of Kosovo, using murder and rape to inspire fear among the refugees. With President Bill Clinton's backing, and after diplomatic initiatives had failed, NATO forces intervened directly by launching Operation Allied Force on March 24, 1999. This campaign, the first attack against a sovereign country by NATO since it was created, marked a historic change in the role of NATO and its potential rise as a comprehensive European peacekeeping organization.

Operation Allied Force consisted primarily of using NATO's overwhelming air superiority against Serbian military targets. There were also bombing raids on strategic sites in the Serbian capital of Belgrade. After nearly three months of relentless attacks, Milosevic capitulated and began to withdraw his forces from Kosovo. On June 11, 1999, NATO ceased its offensive and the Albanian refugees began to return to their homeland. Meanwhile, Milosevic's power continued to erode as even Montenegro began to push for independence from Serbia. Whether Milosevic will remain in power is uncertain as of this writing. What is certain is that NATO has redefined its role in European security considerably from the days of the cold war.

John Wesley Powell's Birthday

John Wesley Powell, born on March 24, 1834, in Mount Morris, New York, was the first American to explore the treacherous canyons of the Green and Colorado rivers by boat. His daring trip began on May 24, 1869, and was completed on August 29 of the same year. The journey took Powell and his group of 11 men through nearly 900 miles of uncharted waterways.

John Wesley Powell was the son of Joseph and Mary (Dean) Powell, who had emigrated from England. His father was a Methodist Episcopal preacher who spent most of his life bringing the gospel to western frontier towns. It was not until young Powell was in his late teens that his father finally settled the family in Wheaton, Illinois. Because of this nomadic early life, Powell's formal schooling was constantly interrupted and most of his education was received at home. He showed an interest in natural history and botany, but after settling in Wheaton he chose to prepare to follow his father's profession and studied at the Illinois Institute (later Wheaton College), Oberlin College, and Illinois College. However, in 1854 he enrolled in the State Natural History Society, and during the following years he became absorbed in trips and collections, traveling alone down the Mississippi, Illinois, and Ohio rivers. His collections brought him some recognition, and in 1858 he was made secretary of the Illinois Society of Natural History.

Powell's career was interrupted by the outbreak of the Civil War, in which he enlisted as a Union soldier. He soon became an officer and a member of General Ulysses S. Grant's staff. In 1862 he was wounded at the battle of Shiloh and lost his right arm at the elbow. Nevertheless, he returned to active duty, and by the time he was honorably discharged on January 14, 1865, he had risen to the rank of brevet lieutenant colonel. While in the army, he had married his cousin Emma Dean.

After Powell's discharge he was appointed professor of geology at Illinois Wesleyan University, and a year later he became lecturer and curator of the museum of Illinois Normal University. In 1868, while still serving as curator, he formulated a plan to lead a boat expedition down the unexplored canyons of the Green and Colorado rivers. The following year he received grants from the federal government and the Smithsonian Institution to help finance an exploration party with four boats. Although this daring trip made Powell something of a national hero, it was not until his second trip, in 1871–1872, that he made substantial geological findings. On this later expedition he was accompanied by such famous geologists as

Grove Karl Gilbert, Clarence E. Dutton, and W. H. Holmes. Together they formulated some of the basic principles of structural, or geotectonic, geology. Powell later described his findings in two publications, *The Exploration of the Colorado River of the West* (1875) and *The Geology of the Eastern Portion of the Uinta Mountains* (1876).

Powell continued his explorations of the area until 1875, when he was named director of the second division of the U.S. Geological and Geographical Survey of the Territories (known after 1877 as the Survey of the Rocky Mountain Region). This post enabled him to gather extensive information on the plateau country and the peoples of Utah, western Colorado, and northern Arizona. He became alarmed by the ruinous consequences of dry land homesteading and unscrupulous land speculation, and in 1879 issued the prophetic *Report of the Lands of the Arid Region of the United States*. In this report, Powell expressed a fear that poor land policies might cause irreparable damage to the soil resources of the West. His recommendations for new land management programs went unheeded until the tragic Dust Bowl years of the 1930s, when the report's guidelines became the foundation of a reformed national land policy.

In 1879, when all western survey divisions were consolidated as the U.S. Geological Survey under Clarence King's directorship, Powell was chosen to oversee the new Bureau of American Ethnology of the Smithsonian Institution, studying Native American tribes. Upon King's resignation in 1880, Powell was named director of the Geological Survey as well. Under his guidance, the survey became the largest and most powerful bureau of its kind in the world, and a model scientific organization. Powell initiated an innovative series of detailed geologic and topographic maps. However, his attempts to improve land management in the West were opposed by speculators and undermined by congressional budget cuts. In 1894 he resigned from the Geological Survey but continued to serve as head of the Bureau of American Ethnology. He also wrote several philosophical treatises, among them *Truth and Error, or the Science of Intellection*, published in 1898. He died on September 23, 1902.

March 25

Gloria Steinem's Birthday

The famous feminist Gloria Steinem was born in Toledo, Ohio, on March 25, 1934, to Leo and Ruth Steinem. Steinem's mother was emotionally un-stable and her parents were separated when she was 10 years old. Despite her troubled childhood, however, she excelled in school and eventually obtained admission to prestigious Smith College.

Steinem graduated magna cum laude from Smith in 1956 with a degree in government. She was also awarded a postgraduate scholarship for two years of study in India. Upon her return to the United States, she became the head of the Independent Research Service in Cambridge, Massachusetts. However, in 1960 she decided to pursue her interest in journalism on a full-time basis. She began to write articles for magazines such as *Help!* and briefly went undercover as a Playboy "bunny" in one of the Playboy clubs in order to write an award-winning exposé. By the mid-1960s she was a regular contributor to such well-known magazines as *Cosmopolitan*, *Esquire*, *Glamour*, *McCall's*, and *Vogue*.

Steinem gained a reputation as one of the leading voices of the feminist movement. She used this reputation and her journalistic experience to start the magazine *Ms.* in January 1972. Although the designation "Ms." for women has become commonplace as of this writing in the late 1990s, in the early 1970s it was a controversial emblem of the feminist movement. Most feminists considered the distinction in titles for women—"Miss" or "Mrs."—to be a sexist relic, and developed the "Ms." designation so that women could have the same anonymity with respect to their marital status that was enjoyed by men. In addition to making a statement with its title, *Ms.* magazine proved to be a very well-written publication and attracted a wide readership.

Gloria Steinem has also been active in the abortion rights movement and the effort to ratify an Equal Rights Amendment to the United States Constitution. She has written several books, including *Outrageous Acts and Everyday Rebellions* (1983), *Marilyn* (1986), *Revolution from Within: A Book of Self-Esteem* (1992), and *Moving Beyond Words* (1994). As of this writing, Steinem continues to be a popular figure on the lecture circuit and is still a consulting editor for *Ms.* magazine.

Greek Independence Day

Greek Independence Day, commemorating March 25, 1821, the day the Greeks began their long struggle for independence from the Ottoman Empire (Turkey), which had ruled Greece for almost 400 years, is a day of celebration for millions of Greek Americans.

Greek freedom from the subjugation of the Ottoman Turks had been dreamed of for many generations before Alexander Ypsilanti (1792–1828) proclaimed Greece independent in 1821, thus beginning the wars that stretched over almost a decade before freedom was at last obtained. Ypsilanti was a Phanariot, that is, a member of an educated class of Greeks who lived in Constantinople in the Greek quarter, which was called the Phanar. Since the Muslim Turks generally would not condescend to learn foreign languages, the sultan customarily chose from among the educated Greeks of Constantinople when he sought a governor for one of the Ottoman Empire's many provinces. In these positions, the Phanariots earned a reputation as greedy and unjust rulers, often more despised by their subjects than the Muslim conquerors.

Control of many of these provinces passed, at times, from Ottoman to other Asian or European powers. Often the same provinces were ruled alternately by Turkey and Russia. Two such provinces were Moldavia and Walachia, now regions in modern Romania, which at that time had sizable Greek populations. The Ypsilanti family had held high official pots in both Moldavia and Walachia for many years. Alexander Ypsilanti's grandfather, who was also named Alexander (circa 1725–1807), had served as governor of each of the two provinces and was ultimately executed by the sultan for alleged conspiracy.

His son, Constantine (1760–1816), served as governor as well, first of Moldavia and then of Walachia. Although the Greeks, many of whom had scattered throughout Europe after the Turkish conquest of Greece in the 15th century, would have preferred independence, lacking that they preferred the rule of Christian Russians to that of Muslim Turks. Because of his suspected pro-Russian inclinations, Constantine, then governor of Walachia, was deposed by the Turkish sultan but was reinstated shortly thereafter when Russia occupied the province during one of its wars with Turkey.

Constantine had supported the Serbian insurrection against the Turks in 1804 and hoped to gather an army to fight for Greek independence. His plans were foiled by the Treaty of Tilsit between Russia and France in 1807, and he instead found himself a political exile, seeking refuge in Russia. His hopes were carried to completion by his two sons, Alexander and Demetrios (1793–1832).

The brothers had gone with their exiled father to Russia and had both served in the Russian army. Alexander, who became a general, had been made leader of the Philike Hetairia, a secret organization formed to work for Greek independence. Ypsilanti was a revered name to Greeks in Moldavia and Walachia. Along with the governor of Moldavia, they rallied to Alexander when, in 1821, with strong Russian support, he staged a revolt at Jassy, Moldavia's capital, and boldly proclaimed Greek independence from Ottoman rule. Unfortunately, the Romanians of the region, who had endured cruel and unjust treatment by the Phanariots for many generations, turned on the Greeks, helping the Turks to victory and winning Romanian rule for themselves.

After his defeat, Alexander fled to Austria, seeking refuge, and was instead imprisoned there. His younger brother, Demetrios, who had been at his side during the revolt, later went to the Peloponnesus, the southern most region of continental Greece, and entered a rebellion there of Greeks against Turks.

The Greeks fought bravely, and their degree of success from 1821 through 1824 surprised and confounded the Ottoman army. To turn the tide of the war, the sultan sought and received the intervention of Egyptian forces. From 1825 to 1827 the Greeks fought what was almost inevitably a losing battle against Egyptian and Turkish armies. Finally Britain, France, and Russia stepped in and, lending support to the Greeks from 1827 to 1829, not only routed the Egyptian and Turkish forces but also demanded and received the sultan's recognition of Greece's independence.

Demetrios Ypsilanti has been honored by the naming of an American city. Ypsilanti, a city situated between Detroit and Ann Arbor in southeastern Michigan, began as a Native American village and French trading post about 1809 and was settled in 1823, while the Greek struggle for independence was capturing worldwide admiration.

First Colonists Arrive in Maryland

On March 25, 1634, the first colonists arrived in Maryland. This was the first proprietary colony on the American mainland, named after Henrietta Maria, the consort of King Charles I of England.

In 1632 Charles appointed George Calvert, Lord Baltimore, the proprietor of 10 million acres of land between 40 degrees north latitude and the south bank of the Potomac River. The king, in return for one-fifth of any gold or silver found there and for the symbolic payment of two arrowheads a year, granted the proprietor almost absolute control over the colony. Lord Baltimore could make laws with the consent of the freeholders, establish courts, levy taxes, control commerce, and grant lands. Maryland was essentially a feudal barony in the wilderness.

Lord Baltimore, who had been a member of the London Company and the Council for New England, was an early leader in the colonization of America. In 1622 he received a grant of part of Newfoundland and established the colony of Avalon there. He visited Newfoundland in 1625 and Virginia in 1629 and, finding the southern climate more to his liking, decided to undertake another settlement in the latter vicinity. As proprietor, Baltimore could garner great profits by renting some lands while retaining the rest until the growth of the colony increased their value. Moreover, religion, as well as economics, interested him in the venture. A convert to Catholicism in 1624, Baltimore envisioned Maryland as a refuge for his fellow Catholics, who suffered much in Anglican England.

Cecilius Calvert, the second Lord Baltimore, received Maryland's charter in June 1632, shortly after his father's death. He spent much of his fortune recruiting some 200 men and women, who set sail for the colony from England on November 22, 1633, on two ships named the *Ark* and the *Dove*. These ships sailed the West Indian route across the Atlantic, stopping at Barbados and arriving at Chesapeake Bay on February 27, 1634. Led by their 28-year-old governor, Leonard Calvert, the brother of the second Lord Baltimore, the colonists on March 25 erected a cross on St. Clements Island (also known as Blakiston Island) and held a thanksgiving service. A few days later they established St. Mary's, a few miles north of the Potomac River, as their capital.

The population had a mixed composition from the beginning. Most of the original immigrants were Anglicans, but two Jesuits and 17 Catholic couples were among the group. The Protestant preponderance increased when disaffected Puritans left Anglican Virginia and established Providence (later Annapolis), Maryland. Increasing danger to the colony's religious peace and its character as a haven for Catholics prompted Lord Baltimore to instruct Governor William Stone, a Protestant, to have the legislature pass an "act concerning Religion." This toleration act, which granted religious liberty to all who affirmed a belief in the divinity of Jesus Christ, marked a limited but significant step forward in 1649.

The Feast of the Annunciation

The Christian Feast of the Annunciation celebrates the announcement made by the angel Gabriel to Mary that she was chosen to become the mother of Jesus. According to the Christian faith, Jesus was miraculously conceived at the instant of her consent. Therefore, the date is set at nine months before Christmas, the feast celebrating Jesus' birth. The feast was instituted in the East in about A.D. 430. Roman Catholic observance dates from the 7th century.

The New Testament account of the Annunciation, as it appears in the King James Version of the Bible in Luke 1:26–38, follows:

> The angel Gabriel was sent from God unto a city of Galilee, named Nazareth, to a virgin espoused to a man whose name was Joseph, of the house of David; and the virgin's name was Mary. And the angel came in unto her, and said, "Hail, thou that art highly favored, the Lord is with thee; blessed art thou among women." And when she saw him, she was troubled at his saying, and cast in her mind what manner of salutation this should be. And the angel said unto her: "Fear not, Mary: for thou hast found favor with God. And, behold, thou shalt conceive in thy womb, and bring forth a son, and shalt call his name Jesus. He shall be great, and shall be called the Son of the Highest; and the Lord God shall give unto him the throne of his father David: And he shall reign over the house of Jacob forever; and of his kingdom there shall be no end." Then said Mary unto the angel, "How shall this be, seeing I know not a man?" And the angel answered and said unto her, "The Holy Ghost shall come upon thee, and the power of the Highest shall overshadow thee: therefore also that holy thing which shall be born of thee shall be called the Son of God. And, behold, thy cousin Elisabeth, she hath also conceived a son in her old age; and this is the sixth month with her, who was called barren. For with God nothing shall be impossible." And Mary said, "Behold the handmaid of the Lord; be it unto me according to thy word." And the angel departed from her.

March 26

Robert Frost's Birthday

Robert Lee Frost, a poet who is closely identified with New England, was born not there but in San Francisco, California, on March 26, 1874. He was the son of William Prescott Frost Jr. and Isabelle Moodie Frost. During his 88 years, Frost became the United States' unofficial poet laureate, one of the few poets of his time whose work was widely read and loved by the public in addition to being acclaimed by critics.

Many years passed before Frost's poetry was recognized and accepted, years when he drifted from one kind of work to another and in and out of school. He spent his first 11 years in the hurly-burly of young San Francisco, where he participated in campaigns with his politically active father, marching in torchlight processions and filling saloons with literature. (A Southern sympathizer during the Civil War, Frost's father named his son for the Confederate general Robert E. Lee.) Upon his father's death, Robert, his mother, and his younger sister returned to his father's native New England for the burial. Short on funds, they stayed in the area, settling in Lawrence, Massachusetts.

To support her family, Robert's mother went to work as a teacher. Although she helped her son, he was a poor student throughout elementary school. However, in high school his interest was fired so strongly that he graduated as co-valedictorian of his class, sharing the honor with a girl named Elinor White, who later became his wife. His enthusiasm for poetry also developed in high school, and poems of his were published in the school paper.

With the financial help of his paternal grandfather, who hoped that he would become a lawyer, Frost enrolled at Dartmouth College in 1892, but he was unhappy there and left after only a few months. He subsequently turned his attentions to teaching, farming, and newspaper reporting, all the while continuing to write poetry. Elinor White was determined to complete her college education before marriage; as soon as she graduated from St. Lawrence University in 1895, she and Frost were wed.

Having decided to qualify himself to teach Latin and Greek, Frost in 1897 entered Harvard College (again with the financial aid of his grandfather). He did well and was granted a scholarship, but after two years he withdrew again from academic life. By then he had two children. Disappointed by Frost's failure to continue his formal education, his grandfather bought a farm in Derry, New Hampshire, and gave him the use of it in 1900. It was a rather poor farm and, as Frost himself admitted, he never worked too hard at farming. He therefore went back to teaching to augment his income and his reputation in that field grew rapidly. He was eventually offered a one-year post to teach psychology at the New Hampshire State Normal School in Plymouth, and he accepted.

At about this time, under the terms of his grandfather's will, the ownership of the Derry farm was transferred to Frost. Although his poem "My Butterfly, an Elegy" had been published in the New York Independent when he was only 20,

Frost had generally been unsuccessful in gaining any real acceptance of his poetry. In hopes that the literary climate in England might be more favorable, he sold the farm and in 1912 sailed for England with his wife and four children. There he became acquainted with various poets, including Ezra Pound, Edward Thomas, Lascelles Abercrombie, and W. W. Gibson. The latter two men were members of a group of English poets known as Georgians, who wrote poems in the traditional meters about nature and rural life.

Frost soon set to work compiling a collection of poems that he had written over the years. It was accepted by the first publisher to whom he submitted it, and came out in 1913 under the title A Boy's Will. The volume won the 39-year-old poet immediate recognition. A second collection, which was published the following year as North of Boston, won not only critical acclaim for Frost but also, for the first time, financial success.

American publishers quickly became interested in Frost. He and his family returned to the United States in 1915 just after the American publication of North of Boston, when his fame was spreading.

Frost returned to New England and bought a farm near Franconia, New Hampshire. Five years later he bought another farm near Shaftsbury, Vermont. He continued writing and was much sought after to lecture and to read his poetry, which he did very effectively. Though he had never earned a college degree, he was associated during the rest of his life as a faculty member with such institutions as Amherst College, the University of Michigan, Harvard University, and Dartmouth College. More than 40 honorary degrees were conferred on him by colleges and universities in the United States and Great Britain. He was also one of the earliest poets-in-residence; he held his first such post at the University of Michigan from 1921 to 1923.

Teaching by the book was not Frost's style. He felt that students could get that sort of learning either on their own or from other teachers. He was concerned with challenging them to discover their own ways of expressing their thoughts and feelings about common situations and experiences. Once, Frost asked his students whether there was anything in the papers they had just handed to him that any of them would like to keep. When there were no affirmative answers, he tossed all the papers into the wastebasket, remarking that he "wasn't going to be a perfunctory corrector of perfunctory writing."

The poet's private life was not serene. His sister became mentally ill, and of his four children who survived childhood, a daughter died following childbirth and his son committed suicide. The death of Frost's wife in 1938 was another blow from which he had great difficulty recovering. His public attitude was one of steadfastness, affirmation, and humor, but he had a complex personality. Those who knew him well found him to be sometimes gloomy, cantankerous, petty, and mean, but never defeated.

Among the best known of Frost's lyric poems are "Mowing," "Revelation," "The Tuft of Flowers" (all contained in the volume titled *A Boy's Will*); "The Road Not Taken," "Birches, A Time to Talk" (all in the volume *Mountain Interval*); "Fire and Ice," "Stopping by Woods on a Snowy Evening" (both in the volume *New Hampshire*); "Acquainted with the Night" (in the volume *West-Running Brook*); "Directive" (in the volume *Steeple Bush*); and "Take Something Like a Star" (in the volume *An Afterword*). His well-known narrative poems and essayistic poetic reflections include "Mending Wall," "The Death of the Hired Man," "Home Burial," "The Wood-Pile" (all in the volume *North of Boston*); "New Hampshire," "Paul's Wife," "Two Witches" (all in the volume *New Hampshire*); and the title poem of *West-Running Brook*.

Frost also wrote two plays in blank verse, *A Masque of Reason* and *A Masque of Mercy*, both dealing with biblical characters. They were less well-received than his other works.

Frost had the unique distinction of being awarded the Pulitzer Prize in poetry four times. He was elected a member of the National Institute of Arts and Letters and of its prestigious inner body, the American Academy of Arts and Letters, and received the institute's gold medal. In 1958 he held the post of consultant in poetry at the Library of Congress, and in 1962 the Congressional Gold Medal was conferred upon him. Frost also traveled abroad three times at the request of the State Department as a goodwill ambassador for the United States. His first such trip was to South America in 1954. In 1961 he went to Israel and Greece. In 1962, the year before his death, he traveled to the Soviet Union, where he realized his hope of having a face-to-face meeting with Premier Nikita Khrushchev and put forth his personal appeal for a rivalry for excellence between the two great powers, rather than a rivalry of ideology.

One of Frost's most gratifying honors was president-elect John F. Kennedy's invitation to read a poem at the president's inaugural ceremonies. Frost and Kennedy greatly admired each other, and the two had become good friends. It was the first time a poet participated in a presidential inauguration.

On his 80th birthday, in musing about what honor he most desired, Frost said he would like to leave behind "a few poems it would be hard to get rid of." In fact, he had the highly unusual experience of seeing his work become classic while he was still living. His poems were published in 22 languages, and American editions set publishing records for poetry.

Frost died on January 29, 1963, in a hospital in Boston, after cancer surgery. He was mourned the world over. Among the many tributes were those of President Kennedy and Premier Khrushchev. A poetic tribute was printed in the Soviet government newspaper *Izvestia*. A few months later an anthology of Frost's poetry was published in the Soviet Union for the first time; although over 10,000 copies were printed, bookstores' supplies were exhausted a few days after publication.

The poet was buried on a hillside in the Old Bennington Cemetery in Old Bennington, Vermont, not far from Shaftsbury, where he had made his home for many years. Frost's grave and those of his wife and four of his children were marked by an elaborately carved seven-foot slab of blue granite. "I had a lover's quarrel with the world" is the epitaph Frost chose for himself; it is a line from his poem "The Lesson for Today."

Sandra Day O'Connor's Birthday

Photograph by Dane Penland, Smithsonian Institution, Courtesy the Supreme Court of the United States.

Sandra Day O'Connor

Sandra Day O'Connor, the first woman to become a justice of the United States Supreme Court, was born on March 26, 1930, in El Paso, Texas. Her parents were prosperous cattle ranchers. She proved to be an exceptional student, and graduated from high school in 1946 at the age of 16. From high school she went to Stanford University, graduating in 1950 with a degree in economics. She then entered Stanford Law School, one of the most prestigious law schools in the nation.

Although law school normally takes three years to complete, O'Connor graduated in two years, finishing near the top of her class. Despite her outstanding academic credentials, she found it nearly impossible to secure employment in the private sector. Most law firms were reluctant to hire a female attorney, so O'Connor had to take a series of government jobs. In 1957 she became a full-time housewife, taking care of her three children.

She resumed her career in 1964 when she served in the presidential campaign of Arizona Republican Barry Goldwater. Although Goldwater lost the election to Democrat Lyndon B. Johnson, he remained an influential figure in Arizona politics and helped secure the position of assistant attorney general for O'Connor. She served in that position until 1969, when she was appointed by Arizona governor Jack Williams to a vacant seat in the Arizona state senate. O'Connor became a leader in the Republican Party, and in 1972 she became the Senate's majority leader. In 1974, however, she decided to leave her career in state politics and enter the judiciary. She became a judge in the Superior Court for Mariposa County.

O'Connor was a superior court judge until 1979. That year, Governor Bruce Babbitt appointed her to the Arizona Court of Appeals, an intermediate appellate court in the Arizona court system.

Although O'Connor certainly had an impressive career resume, a nomination for justice of the United States Supreme Court typically requires service in the federal courts or some other emblem of national prominence. However, during his successful 1980 presidential campaign, Republican Ronald Reagan pledged to be the first president to appoint a woman to the Supreme Court. After a thorough selection process, he decided upon O'Connor, and on July 7, 1981, officially nominated her. She was confirmed by the United States Senate on September 22, 1981.

Although O'Connor has deep Republican roots, she has typically taken a moderate stand on the Supreme Court. In fact, her views in favor of the Equal Rights Amendment have drawn some criticism from conservatives. Further, despite her personal opposition to abortion, she has refrained from siding with those justices who would overturn the landmark decision of *Roe* v. *Wade* (1973), which holds that a woman has a constitutional right to an abortion. Over the course of her career, Justice O'Connor has earned the respect of the legal community and has become one of the country's most outstanding jurists.

Holy or Maundy Thursday

This is a movable event.

On Holy Thursday, the Thursday before Easter (see March 29), Christians commemorate the major events that occurred on this day in the earthly life of Jesus Christ. Three of these events are best known as the Last Supper, the Agony in the Garden, and Judas's betrayal of Jesus with a kiss. After this betrayal, Jesus was seized and led off for questioning by the Pharisees and elders, who then bound him over to guards to be brought the next day before Pontius Pilate, the Roman procurator of Judea, who the high priests insisted should condemn him to death (see March 27, Good Friday).

On Holy Thursday, Christian churches celebrate Christ's institution, during the Last Supper, of the Eucharist (also known as Communion or the Lord's Supper). Note is also taken on this day of Jesus' reminder to his disciples of the commandment of brotherly love, which is central to Christian belief. It is also in remembrance of Jesus's demonstration of humility that the ritual of the washing of feet continues to be carried out on Holy Thursday in some churches today. The minister does the ceremonial washing of the feet, usually of 12 men chosen from the clergy or from the lay congregation. The number 12 represents the number of the apostles whose feet Jesus washed. Centuries ago, kings and other rulers often washed the feet of the poor, choosing as many poor people as the number of years that the ruler had lived.

In most churches the main ritual of Holy Thursday is the Service of the Lord's Supper, commemorating the Passover meal that Jesus shared with his Apostles and his institution of the Eucharist during that event. The Gospel of Matthew (26:26–29) recounts the occasion:

Now as they were eating, Jesus took bread, and blessed, and broke it, and gave it to the disciples and said, "Take, eat; this is my body." And he took a cup, and when he had given thanks he gave it to them, saying, "Drink of it, all of you; for this is my blood of the covenant, which is poured out for many for the forgiveness of sins. I tell you I shall not drink again of this fruit of the vine until that day when I drink it new with you in my Father's kingdom."

Holy Thursday is also called Great Thursday, especially in Slavic countries, because of the important events it marks. Less obvious is the derivation of the name "Maundy Thursday," which comes from the Latin word for commandment, *mandatum*, the first word in a hymn sung during the ritual of the washing of feet. The words of the hymn come from the Gospel of John (13:34–35), which quotes Jesus's statement to his disciples on the first Holy Thursday: "A new commandment I give to you, that you love one another. . . . By this all men will know that you are my disciples, if you have love for one another." The mass on Holy Thursday begins what Roman Catholics refer to as the sacred triduum, the three days before Easter Sunday, which are considered together as the Lord's Passover. During the Gloria Patri of the Holy Thursday mass, the bells or chimes ring out in Roman Catholic churches for the last time until the Easter Mass of the Resurrection. The solemn joy of Holy Thursday then gives way to the somber tone of Good Friday.

Prince Kuhio Day in Hawaii

The Prince Kuhio festival held every year in Hawaii pays tribute to a man who represented the Hawaiian people during their struggle to maintain their old traditions while emerging as a modern republic. A full-blooded Hawaiian, Prince Jonah Kuhio Kalanianaole was born of royal ancestry on March 26, 1871, on the island of Kauai. His mother and father, High Chief David Kahalepouli Piikoi and Princess Kinoiki Kekaulike, died when he and his two older brothers were very young. Their maternal aunt, Kapiolani, consort of King Kalakaua, the last reigning monarch of what was then the Kingdom of Hawaii, adopted the children. The king and queen began their reign in 1874, and the children were made princes by royal proclamation 10 years later.

As a possible successor to the throne, Prince Kuhio was sent to private schools and colleges in Honolulu, California, and England to receive the best education possible. However, in 1893 the course of his future was suddenly altered. The Hawaiian monarchy was overthrown, and the Republic of Hawaii was established. A steadfast royalist, Kuhio joined a group of revolutionaries engaged in acts to overthrow the new republic and restore the monarchy. Their acts quickly led to their arrest, and Prince Kuhio was sentenced to one year in prison. While in prison he was visited frequently by Elizabeth Kahanu Kaauwai, daughter of a chief of Maui, whom he married upon his release and pardon in 1895.

The following years were filled with inner struggle for Prince Kuhio. The abolition of the monarchy, and with it many of the old traditions, was something that the young prince had great difficulty coping with. He traveled abroad for several years and even contemplated taking up permanent residence in a foreign country. However, in 1901 he decided to return to his native land and serve his people within the new framework of government. While the prince had been abroad, Hawaii had become a territory of the United States, and upon his return he found many political parties vying for power. In 1902 he decided to join the Republican Party and was nominated as a candidate for election as the first delegate to represent the Territory of Hawaii in Congress. He was elected to his first term in 1903 and was reelected for the next 10 consecutive terms until his death in 1921.

During his political career he worked tirelessly for the Hawaiian people. His concern for the diminishing numbers of his race prompted him to urge the passage of the Hawaiian Homes Commission Act. This act, which was passed in 1921, provided homesteads for Hawaiians at nominal rents and for government loans to the settlers. Some of his other accomplishments were the development of Pearl Harbor as a strategic military base, the establishment in 1917 of the Hawaiian Civic Club to help preserve Hawaiian culture, and the designation of Kilauea volcano as a national park. Kuhio died on January 7, 1921, and his remains were entombed at the Royal Mausoleum in Nuuanu Valley on the island of Oahu.

March 27

1964 Alaska Earthquake

The most severe earthquake to ever strike North America, and the second strongest ever recorded anywhere in the world at the time, hit Alaska on March 27, 1964. Registering at least 8.4 on the Richter Magnitude Scale, it exceeded even the 8.25 fury of the San Francisco quake of 1906.

The damage was worst in Anchorage, the 49th state's largest city, where the entire downtown business section was leveled, whole streets dropped as much as 20 feet, and cars and shattered buildings piled up on top of one another. The trouble was compounded by quake-caused landslides, made worse by the fact that much of the Anchorage area rested on an unstable layer of wet clay. In the most spectacular of many landslide disasters, 77 suburban Anchorage homes, borne on a slippery carpet of moving earth, tumbled over a bluff into Cook Inlet.

Landslides, rockslides, and snow avalanches occurred elsewhere in southern Alaska, especially in the coastal regions, and tidal waves struck as well. Such Alaskan ports as Kodiak, Kenai, Seward, Cordova, and Valdez suffered major damage. The town of Valdez, where every building was damaged, had to be totally rebuilt on a safer site four miles away from the old one. Giant waves also wrecked coastal regions in Canada, Oregon, and California. Even as far away as Hawaii, Siberia, and Japan, quake-triggered tidal waves wrought havoc, and sections of earth moved up or down nearly five inches in Houston, Texas.

In all, 114 lives were lost on the North American borders of the Pacific Ocean, a toll that would have been higher had the quake not taken place at 5:36 p.m., just after the business areas that suffered heavily had partly emptied. Property damage from the earthquake soared to an estimated $750 million, some $200 million of it in greater Anchorage alone. Less than two years later, however, that determined community had recovered and was bigger than ever, with the debris barely visible to remind one that it could all happen again.

Good Friday

This is a movable event.

Good Friday, the Friday before Easter Sunday, is one of the most significant days of the Christian calendar. On this day Christians commemorate the suffering and death of Jesus Christ on the cross. (See also March 22, Palm Sunday, and March 29, Easter.)

To the early Christians, who regarded Jesus as the son of God and long-hoped-for Messiah, the original Good Friday seemed to mark the end of all that they had hoped and believed in. Their despair deepened when Jesus did not miraculously descend from the cross and triumph over the temporal powers in the manner of an earthly king or conqueror. Not until Easter Sunday, with the Resurrection, did their faith and hope revive.

In view of the grief associated with the crucifixion, many have questioned why the day observed as its anniversary is known in English as Good Friday. One theory is that the term is a corruption of the earlier "God's Friday." Another theory holds that the "Good" refers to the good that came to humankind through the life and death of Jesus. In various periods and places, the day has also been known as Long Friday, Holy Friday, and Great Friday. Christians today still relive the sorrow of the first Good Friday. The observance extends from Good Friday until Holy Saturday evening, which in many churches is marked by an Easter Vigil service beginning after sundown and extending into the beginning of the new day of Easter.

Whatever the exact form of their worship, Christians of all denominations also associate with Good Friday the prophetic words from the 53rd chapter of Isaiah commonly read as part of Good Friday services: "He was despised and rejected by men; a man of sorrows, and acquainted with grief; . . . Surely he has borne our griefs and carried our sorrows; . . . he was wounded for our transgressions, he was bruised for our iniquities; upon him was the chastisement that made us whole. . . . the Lord has laid on him the iniquity of us all."

Like most events of Holy Week, Good Friday has inspired artists for centuries. Michelangelo's *Pietà*, a sculpture of Mary holding the body of her crucified son, is perhaps the best-known example. Richard Wagner's *Parsifal*, the opera based on the search for the Holy Grail, is frequently heard during Holy Week and includes a passage known as the "Good Friday Spell."

March 28

Nuclear Accident at Three Mile Island

On March 28, 1979, the most serious civilian nuclear accident in American history occurred at the Three Mile Island nuclear power facility near Harrisburg, Pennsylvania. A meltdown of the core nearly occurred, which would have contaminated the region for many miles and put thousands of lives at risk.

The Three Mile Island facility was operated by Metropolitan Edison. Reactor Number Two had been in operation only since December 1978 when the incident took place. Around 4:00 a.m., an accidental coolant leak began, which went undetected by the staff. When the temperature of the nuclear core began to rise, a series of human errors aggravated the problem. The temperature increased to over 5,000 degrees Fahrenheit, resulting in a partial meltdown of the core and massive gas emissions.

Two days later, on March 30, 1979, Pennsylvania governor Richard Thornburgh announced that all young children and pregnant women should evacuate the Three Mile Island area. Although the amount of radiation released was actually very low, young children and pregnant women are especially vulnerable. Several days later, President Jimmy Carter personally visited the vicinity, and declared that the situation was under control thanks to the efforts of the authorities and Metropolitan Edison.

A presidential commission eventually concluded that there was no serious adverse health effect on the public from the Three Mile Island accident. However, the cleanup of the site would take over a decade and cost nearly $1 billion. Further, the nuclear power industry was seriously discredited, and the construction of new nuclear power facilities in the United States came to a virtual halt.

Those who oppose nuclear power as too risky cite Three Mile Island as an example of why fossil fuels should remain the primary energy source. Supporters of nuclear power consider Three Mile Island to be a regrettable anomaly in the otherwise excellent safety record of nuclear facilities. Further, supporters point to the health risks of dependence on oil, such as air pollution and oil spills from supertankers.

Holy Saturday

This is a movable event.

The day before Easter is called Holy Saturday or the Vigil of Easter. In the words of the revised Roman Missal, "On Holy Saturday, the Church waits at the Lord's tomb, meditating on His suffering and death." Until recent decades, in most Western Christian churches no services were held on Holy Saturday. It was as if all activity had been suspended, the same state Jesus' followers were in on the day after the crucifixion: Jesus had died but he had not yet risen.

As observed by Roman Catholics, the traditional Easter vigil service begins after nightfall and consists of four parts. It opens with the Service of Light, which takes place in a darkened church or area outside the church. The dark symbolizes the death of Jesus, the Light of the World. The congregation gathers around the priests, ministers, deacons, and acolytes as the celebrant lights a new fire, symbolizing Jesus' passing from death to life. The blessing of the fire is followed by the blessing of the new paschal (Easter) candle, which during the Vigil service will be placed on the main altar of the church, where it will remain until Ascension Day, a period symbolizing the 40 days Jesus remained with his disciples between his resurrection and his ascension into heaven.

The service then continues with part two of the Easter Vigil, the Liturgy of the Word. This consists of a series of readings from the Old Testament, always including the account from Exodus of the Israelites' safe passage through the Red Sea, followed by the New Testament readings of the Epistle and the Gospel. The third part of the Vigil service is the Liturgy of Baptism, which includes the blessing of water and the baptismal font. The final part of the service is the Mass, or Liturgy of the Eucharist, wherein the faithful participate in communion.

March 29

Easter

This is a movable event.

Easter Sunday, commemorating the resurrection of Jesus Christ, is the most important event of the Christian ecclesiastical year, even more important than Christmas. Christians, who believe in the divinity of Jesus, base this divinity in part on the miracles Jesus performed while he was on earth and particularly on the culminating miracle of his resurrection from the dead on the third day after he was crucified. Jesus himself had foretold his resurrection, to which there are many references in the New Testament, as well as in the prophecies of the Old Testament. Christians believe that the resurrection was the fulfillment of those prophecies.

The story of the resurrection is told in each of the four Gospels in the New Testament: Matthew 27:57–28:10; Mark 15:42–16:12; Luke 23:50–24:50; and John 19:38–20:30. According to the Gospel of Matthew, after Jesus died on the cross, Joseph of Arimathea, a wealthy man who was a secret disciple of Jesus, obtained permission to bury him from Pontius Pilate, the Roman procurator of Judea:

> And Joseph took the body, and wrapped it in a clean linen shroud, and laid it in his own new tomb, which he had hewn in the rock; and he rolled a great stone to the door of the tomb, and departed. . . . Now after the sabbath, toward the dawn of [Sunday,] the first day of the week, Mary Magdalene and the other Mary went to see the sepulchre. And behold, there was a great earthquake; for an angel of the Lord descended from heaven and came and rolled back the stone, and sat upon it. His appearance was like lightning, and his raiment white as snow. And for fear of him the guards trembled and became like dead men. But the angel said to the women, "Do not be afraid; for I know that you seek Jesus who was crucified. He is not here; for he has risen, as he said. Come, see the place where he lay. Then go quickly and tell his disciples that he has risen from the dead, and behold, he is going before you to Galilee; there you will see him. . . ." So they departed quickly from the tomb with fear and great joy,

and ran to tell his disciples. And behold Jesus met them and said, "Hail!" And they came up and took hold of his feet and worshiped him. Then Jesus said to them, "Do not be afraid; go and tell my brethren to go to Galilee, and there they will see me."

Easter is the culmination of Holy Week. For Christians throughout the world, the Feast of Easter, celebrating the risen Christ's victory over death, is the foundation of their faith: During the preceding Holy Week, Jesus suffered and died for humankind, thus offering all people hope of redemption. In Jesus' resurrection from the dead on the first Easter Sunday, Christians find reaffirmation of his divinity and hope for their own victory over death. This belief is expressed in the following traditional hymn, often sung in Christian churches during Easter services:

Christ the Lord is ris'n today, Alleluia!
Sons of men and angels say, Alleluia!
Raise your joys and triumphs high, Alleluia!
Sing, ye heav'ns, and earth reply, Alleluia!
Lives again our glorious King: Alleluia!
Where, O death, is now thy sting? Alleluia!
Dying once, he all doth save: Alleluia!
Where thy victory, O grave? Alleluia!

The subject of the timing of Easter has been controversial from the early centuries of the Christian Church. Indeed, setting the date of Easter, and determining when it should fall in each future year, were extremely complicated matters. Since Good Friday and Easter took place during the Jewish feast of Passover, any effort to establish the date of Easter was bound to be influenced to some extent by the Jewish calendar and by the lunar cycles on which the months of the Jewish calendar depend. However, the Julian calendar then in use by most Christians was a solar calendar (like today's Gregorian calendar, which succeeded it). In view of the natural incompatibility of the lunar and solar cycles, both of which were involved in calculating the date of Easter, there was a built-in difficulty in establishing the date to begin with (see Appendix A: The Calendar).

The week-long Passover festival begins after sundown on the 14th day of the month of Nisan. Since the resurrection took place during Passover, some early Christians, known as Quartodecimans, chose to observe Easter on the 14th of Nisan. In the Jewish calendar, this is a fixed date. As translated into terms of the Julian (and later the Gregorian) calendar, however, it appears as a movable feast whose date can vary widely from year to year. Further, in both calendars, the 14th of Nisan (or its Julian equivalent) could fall on any day of the week. Although this did not trouble the Quartodecimans, other early Christians felt strongly that

Easter should always be celebrated on a Sunday, since according to the Bible that was the day of the actual resurrection. Much of what came to be known as the Easter Controversy centered on this difference of opinion, with the Quartodecimans ultimately overruled.

Other considerations also accounted for a lack of uniformity as to the date on which Christians observed Easter in the early centuries of the Church. One complicating factor was that astronomers in different centers of the Mediterranean world possessed differing degrees of astronomical knowledge or used different methods of calculation, and in consequence they achieved different results when attempting to compute the correct date for the observance of Easter.

Finally, the question of the date of Easter was taken up by the Ecumenical Council of Nicaea, presided over by Emperor Constantine, in A.D. 325. Although the exact wording of the Nicene ruling on Easter is uncertain, and some specifics remained to be agreed upon in later centuries, the council apparently did decide important elements of the rule that eventually predominated. The council's synodical letter, together with a letter from Emperor Constantine, indicates two decisions: that all Christians should thenceforth celebrate Easter together, after the fashion of the Roman and Alexandrian churches (whose reckonings were not fully identical at the time, however); and that the celebration of Easter should not coincide with the beginning of the Jewish Passover.

Both Eastern Orthodox and Western Christians have since cited the authority of the Nicene Council for their Easter rule, even though the dates on which they celebrate Easter usually differ, according to their somewhat different interpretations. This rule, as it came to be formulated, was that Easter should be celebrated on the first Sunday after the first full moon on or after the vernal equinox. Some scholars assert that the Easter rule contained the additional stipulation that Easter must be observed after the beginning of Passover, in order to follow the biblical sequence of events. Western Christians, whose Easter can fall on any Sunday from March 22 to April 25, do not adhere to this additional requirement, while Eastern Orthodox churches do. The result is that, while the Eastern Orthodox Easter may coincide with the Western celebration in some years, it more frequently occurs from one to five weeks later than the Western feast.

In either case, Easter is a "movable" feast, whose date changes each year, in both West and East. It should be noted, however, that even though the date of Passover is not a factor in determining the date of Easter among Western Christians, it is generally agreed that there is more than a chronological link between the two feasts. Indeed, Easter is often referred to as "the Christian Passover."

The dates of numerous Christian observances are determined by the date of Easter each year. The events leading up to the resurrection of Jesus are described in connection with Holy Thursday (see March 26), Good Friday (see March 27), and Holy Saturday (see March 28). As for the difference in the Easter date between West and East, for many years there have been renewed attempts by some church leaders to set a date that would be acceptable to all Christians. One result of the Second Vatican Council, held under Roman Catholic auspices between 1962 and 1965, was the "Constitution on the Sacred Liturgy," indicating openness to such an idea.

The name Easter does not appear in the Bible, and the origin of the English word is uncertain. The Venerable Bede, the 8th-century English monk and scholar, suggested that the word may have derived from the Anglo-Saxon name of a Teutonic goddess of spring and fertility, Eostre, or Eastre, whose symbol was the hare. Other possible derivations have been suggested as well. Certainly, people celebrated spring rites long before the time of Jesus, rejoicing that winter was dead and that spring had been reborn.

In the United States, Easter is a celebration with both sacred and secular traditions, whose origins have often been forgotten. The colored Easter eggs, used almost universally, derive from the fact that the egg was an ancient symbol of life and hence was deemed suitable for celebrating the resurrection. Furthermore, in many countries eggs were among the foods not permitted during Lent in the days when Lenten fasts were more rigid than now, and thus they were relished on Easter along with many other special foods. If some children grow up with the strange idea of Easter bunnies laying Easter eggs, it is only because the fertility of the rabbit makes that animal a symbol of life also.

John Tyler's Birthday

John Tyler, the tenth president of the United States, was born on March 29, 1790, at Greenway, his family's home, near Williamsburg in Charles City County, Virginia. His father, John Tyler, had an illustrious career of public service as governor of Virginia, as speaker of the Virginia House of Delegates, and as a federal district judge.

John Tyler graduated from the College of William and Mary in Williamsburg in 1807 and was admitted to the Virginia bar in 1809. At the age of

Library of Congress

John Tyler

21 he was elected to the Virginia House of Delegates as a member of the Jeffersonian Republicans, forerunners of the Democratic-Republicans and the present-day Democratic Party. He served five consecutive terms in the state legislature before being elected in 1816 to the national House of Representatives in Washington, D.C., consistently siding with the states' rights wing of his party.

Prompted by ill health and business considerations, Tyler resigned from Congress in 1821. He returned home and lived there as a private citizen until 1823, when he was again elected to the state legislature. In 1825 he was elected governor of Virginia. During his two years in that post, he gave priority to the development of roads and schools, as his father had done before him.

Tyler resigned from the governorship after his election to the United States Senate in 1827, taking his Senate seat on March 4 of that year. Elected for a second Senate term, Tyler continued to alienate his fellow Democratic-Republicans by opposing President Andrew Jackson, a stance that was sharpened by the president's refusal in 1833 to continue the deposit of federal funds in the Bank of the United States. When Henry Clay introduced a resolution to censure the president for this action, Tyler voted for it. Tyler resigned his Senate seat in February 1836 when the Virginia legislature adopted a resolution requiring the two Virginia senators to vote to expunge the resolution of censure from the record. Rather than vote as instructed, Tyler left the Senate and the Democratic-Republicans. Later in 1836, now a member of the Whig Party which had been formed by Andrew Jackson's adversaries, he was defeated for vice president on a states' rights Whig ticket. He returned once again to the Virginia legislature in 1838.

In 1840 General William Henry Harrison, who had been lauded as the hero of the battle of Tippecanoe, was elected president on the Whig ticket, with Tyler as his vice president. Their campaign slogan, "Tippecanoe and Tyler Too," is one of the most famous in American electoral history. One month after his inauguration, Harrison became the first American president to die in office. With no precedent for guidance, there was much discussion about whether the vice president should succeed as president or should simply serve as acting president until new elections could be held. Tyler, however, was successful in maintaining his claim to both the title and the powers of the presidency.

Almost immediately, his independent stance alienated the Whigs as thoroughly as it had earlier alienated the Democratic-Republicans. For most of his three years and 11 months in office he was, as he has been called by historians, a "president without a party." Notwithstanding the lack of support, Tyler was an effective chief executive. During his administration, a treaty was negotiated with China, permitting increased American trade with that country; the Seminole War was terminated; Dorr's Rebellion in Rhode Island was quelled without the introduction of federal troops; the Monroe Doctrine was enforced and strengthened; and the Webster-Ashburton treaty with Great Britain resolved some lingering questions about the exact northeastern boundaries of the United States (a decades-old discord between Canada and the United States). Perhaps Tyler's most notable achievement was the annexation of Texas. It was just two days before the end of his presidency that he signed the joint congressional resolution for the annexation, on March 1, 1845, marking the first time that a joint resolution was employed in foreign relations instead of a treaty.

Also to Tyler's credit was the reform and reorganization of the navy and the encouragement of its scientific work. For example, he called for the establishment of a depot for nautical charts and instruments, which developed into the United States Naval Observatory. He also signed an act testing the feasibility of setting up a national system of magnetic telegraphs, which had wide-ranging effects, especially in the United States Weather Bureau.

The Whigs, who controlled both houses of Congress, sought the rechartering of the Bank of the United States, an action to which Tyler was now much opposed. Twice the Whigs passed a bill to recharter the bank, and twice President Tyler vetoed it. His cabinet members, all appointed by Harrison, responded by resigning en masse with the single exception of Secretary of State Daniel Webster, who stayed only long enough to complete the negotiation of the Canadian border treaty.

In 1844, the Whigs selected Henry Clay as their presidential candidate. Tyler, who returned to the Democratic-Republican Party that year, threw his support to nominee James K. Polk, who won the election and was inaugurated as president on March 4, 1845. Tyler subsequently retired to Sherwood Forest, a 1,200-acre plantation a few miles from his Greenway birthplace, and lived the life of a Virginia gentleman. With him was his second wife, Julia Gardiner Tyler of Gardiner's Island, New York, whom he had married on June 26, 1844. His first wife, Letitia Christian, had died in 1842.

Although he consistently supported Southern positions during the years of his retirement, even while hoping that the institution of slavery would die a natural death, Tyler initially stood firmly against secession. Shortly before the outbreak of the Civil War, he suggested that the border states meet to discuss compromises that might save the Union. The resulting convention was called by the Virginia Assembly and met in Washington in February 1861, with Tyler acting as chairman. It was only after the peace effort had proved futile that he voted for secession in the Virginia secession convention and served in the Provisional Confederate Congress. He was elected to the Confederate House of Representatives, but died on January 18, 1862, in Richmond, before he could take his seat.

First Colonists In Delaware

On March 29, 1638, Swedish settlers under the command of a Dutchman, Peter Minuit, sailed up the Delaware River and founded the colony of New Sweden, erecting Fort Christina where Wilmington now stands. The Fort Christina Monument later marked their landing place at a point called The Rocks. This landing marked the start of the first permanent settlement in what was later to become the state of Delaware.

The history of the original Swedish colony is short but colorful. Although its population never exceeded 300 or 400 people, they and their ancestors bequeathed a considerable Swedish heritage to the region. The most important of the governors of New Sweden who succeeded Minuit was a severe but well-qualified man of profane tongue and mammoth proportions, the 400-pound Johan Bjornsson Printz. He governed the colony from 1643 to 1653, making Tinicum "Island," at what is now Essington, just southwest of Philadelphia, Pennsylvania, the capital of New Sweden.

Governor Printz was succeeded by another Swede, Johan Rising, who arrived in 1654 and immediately seized Fort Casimir, which the Dutch (who all along had regarded the Swedish settlements as encroachments) had built between Fort Christina and the sea. The Swedish triumph over the Dutch was short-lived, however, for in 1655 the entire colony of New Sweden was taken over by the Dutch under the autocratic Peter Stuyvesant. Stuyvesant was the governor of New Netherland to the north, which had as its principal settlement New Amsterdam, later New York City.

The tenure of the Dutch was also short. In 1664 the entire Delaware country, along with New Netherland, was seized by the English, since the English were at war with the Dutch in Europe. The area thus came under the sway of the duke of York, later James II. Even though his title to the Delaware region did not actually become legal until later, the duke, on August 24, 1682, transferred the area to William Penn, the Quaker colonist, who sought unimpeded water access for his new colony of Pennsylvania. What would later be Delaware thus became the Three Lower Counties of Pennsylvania.

Delaware remained part of Pennsylvania until 1776, when Delaware became a separate state with the adoption of a state constitution on September 21, after struggling for separate political power during most of its 94 years. The same year, Delaware joined the other colonies in signing the Declaration of Independence. Later, on December 7, 1787, it became the first state to adopt the Constitution of the United States.

Twenty-third Amendment Ratified

With the ratification on March 29, 1961, of the 23rd Amendment to the Constitution, the previously disenfranchised residents of the District of Columbia, the seat of national government, were empowered for the first time to vote in elections for the president and vice president of the United States. Although the amendment enabled Washingtonians to vote in presidential elections, they still had no representation in Congress, and their municipal government would remain subject to the supervision of Congress.

In accordance with the provisions of the 23rd Amendment, the District of Columbia was accorded three electoral votes, equivalent to the minimum number that a state can receive under the Constitution. In its essential portions, the amendment read as follows:

> SECTION 1. The District constituting the seat of Government of the United States appoint . . . a number of electors of President and Vice President equal to the . . . number of Senators and Representatives in Congress to which the District would be entitled if it were a State . . . ; they shall be . . . considered, for the purposes of the election of President and Vice President, to be electors appointed by a State. . . .
>
> SECTION 2. The Congress shall have power to enforce this article by appropriate legislation.

Ratification of the 23rd Amendment was completed when Kansas became the 38th state to approve the measure, completing the necessary three-fourths of the states required by the Constitution for ratification. Approval by the Ohio legislature followed 42 minutes after that of Kansas. In the final count, Arkansas was the only state to refuse its approval. The amendment was formally declared a part of the Constitution on April 3, 1961.

March 30

Easter Monday

This is a movable event.

The day after Easter Sunday is called Easter Monday, or Pasch Monday, a word derived through the Greek, Latin, and Old French from the Hebrew word for Passover: *Pesah* or *Pesach*.

Easter Sunday, in addition to being one of the most significant Christian religious observances, also marks the end of Lent. In years past, Lent was truly "the penitential season," and devout Christians practiced great austerities, fasting, abstaining entirely from certain types of food, and avoiding most forms of public entertainment for the six weeks preceding Easter. Therefore, when Easter finally dawned, people celebrated. It was the time for feasting, games, and fun, as well as worship. Folk customs vary somewhat from country to country, but in most European countries the celebrations extended beyond Easter Sunday and continued into, or throughout, the following week.

Before Christianity, ancient European peoples held spring celebrations following the winter. Since the egg has traditionally symbolized life, it often figured prominently in the celebrations of spring. Near and Far Eastern mythologies abound with stories centering on eggs and their symbolism. The various Easter-related games and contests using eggs, still common in many countries, probably had their inception in Egypt and other parts of the ancient world. The custom came with the European settlers to the United States, and developed into such interesting traditions as the annual White House Easter egg roll.

Actually, egg-rolling contests had been a custom in England and other European countries for centuries. In these contests, children would roll hard-boiled eggs down a hill, and the child who rolled the greatest number of eggs without cracking the shells was the winner. At some point in the 19th century, the tradition developed of holding a White House–sponsored Easter egg roll on Capitol Hill for the children of Washington, D.C. A contemporary description of the children gathered on the Capitol's terraced grounds on the occasion of Washington's first Easter Monday egg-rolling contest indicates that the event was a success:

> At first the children sit sedately in long rows; each has brought a basket of gay-colored hard-boiled eggs, and those on the upper terrace send them rolling to the line next below, and those pass on the ribbon-like streams to other hundreds at the foot, who scramble for the hopping eggs and hurry panting to the top to start them down again. And as the sport warms, those on top who have rolled all the eggs they brought finally roll themselves, shrieking with laughter. Now comes a swirl of curls, ribbons and furbelows, somebody's dainty maid indifferent to bumps and grass stains. A set of boys who started in a line of six with joined hands are trying to come down in somersaults without breaking the chain. On all sides the older folks stand by to watch the games of this infant carnival.

From the beginning, adults were not admitted unless accompanied by a child, a stipulation put to profitable use by enterprising young Americans who, for a fee, would escort adults past the gates and then return for others who wished to get a closer look at the chaotic proceedings. Except for an interruption during the Civil War, the Easter Monday egg roll took place on the Capitol grounds from its inauguration until 1877, when the locale was changed during the administration of President Rutherford B. Hayes. After Capitol officials

complained that the grass was being ruined by the thousands of pairs of small feet, the tradition was saved by the president's wife, Lucy Webb Hayes, who invited the children to use the White House lawn. At the time, the First Family numbered five children among its members, two of whom, Fanny (9) and Scott (6), were young enough to enjoy the event themselves. From that time, April 2, 1877, to the present, the Easter Monday egg roll has been held on the most famous lawn in the land, and it is customary for a member of the First Family to make an appearance for the occasion.

The White House egg roll, suspended during World War I, was revived in 1921 by President Warren G. Harding. Discontinued again during World War II, and for some time thereafter, the custom was again revived on April 6, 1953, by President Dwight D. Eisenhower and First Lady Mamie Eisenhower.

Seward's Day in Alaska

This is a movable event.

Seward's Day celebrates the signing, on March 30, 1867, of the treaty purchasing Alaska from Czarist Russia for $7 million. It is an annual observance in Alaska, and since 1971 it has been observed on the last Monday in March of every year. The treaty negotiated by William Henry Seward, then secretary of state under President Andrew Johnson, was not highly regarded in his time, however. Alaska was called "Seward's folly," "Seward's icebox," and "Johnson's polar bear garden" until the discovery of gold in the region changed public opinion.

Seward, an expansionist, had acted quickly and quietly. With the Russian minister Baron Edoard de Stoeckl, he worked out the details in an all-night meeting. The treaty was signed by the two men at 4:00 a.m. on March 30 and on the same day was presented to the United States Senate for ratification. The senators, annoyed with the speed and secrecy of Seward's actions, debated for a week but finally ratified the treaty by a one-vote margin on April 9, 1867.

The Russian flag had flown in Alaska since the middle of the 18th century. Czar Peter the Great had in 1725 commissioned the Danish navigator Vitus Jonassen Bering to determine whether Asia was separated from America or whether it was one continuous land mass. Preparations were necessarily lengthy, and Bering finally sailed in 1728. On that first voyage, he discovered that the two continents were indeed divided by what is now called the Bering Strait. Actually, at one point only about 50 miles of water separate the two continents.

Bering found some islands but, perhaps because of fog, did not see the Alaskan mainland until 1741, during his second voyage. Returning home, he was shipwrecked and died on what is now called Bering Island in the Bering Sea. His men built a new ship out of the wreckage of the old one and finally reached Russian soil with tales of a wealth of furs to be had from the herds of seals that they had seen. For several decades thereafter, Russian adventurers and seal hunters from other nations plundered the seas and shores of Alaska. During this time, Russians set up trading posts and settlements along Alaska's coast.

By the mid-19th century, the seal herds were decimated by wanton slaughter, and Russia was more interested in preventing the British Empire from dominating the Pacific Ocean than in pursuing the exploitation of Alaska. The United States, which was expanding into the Pacific region and frequently had conflicts with Great Britain, could only be an asset in Russia's efforts to thwart British ambitions. Thus, the Russians decided to sell their North American colony to the land-hungry Americans. The negotiations proceeded slowly during the administration of President James Buchanan, and were interrupted by the American Civil War. However, they were resumed with Seward, who had been secretary of state in Abraham Lincoln's cabinet and continued in that post when Andrew Johnson assumed the presidency after Lincoln's assassination. Baron de Stoeckl helped get congressional approval by employing skillful lobbyists and also by allegedly paying substantial sums to at least two influential and supposedly incorruptible members of Congress.

Although the formal transfer ceremonies had taken place in Sitka on October 18, 1867, Congress did not actually pass the appropriations bill to pay Russia for Alaska until July 14, 1868. Seward's price for Alaska no longer seems high. Each year Alaska's natural resources return many times the original investment, particularly in the areas of oil and natural gas. Its other resources include gold, seafood, lumber, silver, copper, lead, platinum, uranium, tungsten, and molybdenum. Seward was 71 when he died on October 10, 1872, in Auburn, New York.

Fifteenth Amendment Ratified

The 15th Amendment to the Constitution, one of three early post–Civil War amendments intended to secure the rights of African Americans as persons and as citizens, was proclaimed ratified on March 30, 1870, thirteen months after it had been proposed in Congress. As ratified by the states, the amendment reads as follows:

SECTION 1. The right of citizens of the United States to vote shall not be denied or abridged by the United States or by any State on account of race, color, or previous condition of servitude.
SECTION 2. The Congress shall have power to enforce this article by appropriate legislation.

Unfortunately, the 15th Amendment was unsuccessful in securing equal rights for African Americans until the 1960s. First, until the 1960s the Supreme Court chose to narrowly construe this amendment, permitting such injustices as segregation. Second, African Americans had very little economic or political power, so they were largely without the means to enforce their constitutional rights. Third, organizations such as the Ku Klux Klan used violence to intimidate those African Americans who spoke out against oppression, particularly in the South.

March 31

Virgin Islands Transfer Day

March 31 commemorates the date on which the Virgin Islands were formerly transferred from Danish to American control in 1917. The Virgin Islands are a group of about 100 small islands, islets, and cays in the Caribbean. Covering a total area of about 200 square miles, they are located about 34 miles east of Puerto Rico and extend for approximately 60 miles. They dominate the Anegada passage between the Atlantic Ocean and the Caribbean Sea. St. Croix, St. Thomas, St. John, and Tortola are among the nine major islands in the group.

Christopher Columbus discovered the Virgin Islands on his second voyage to the New World in 1493. He named them Las Virgines in honor of St. Ursula and her companions. The islands had previously been called Ay Ay by their inhabitants, the Caribs and Arawaks. Since in 1494 King Ferdinand and Queen Isabella of Spain were given a papal grant to all lands west of the 46th meridian of longitude, the Virgin Islands became Spanish territory. Their subsequent history was that of colonial expansion and exploitation by European powers: in the 16th century by Spain and during the 17th century by the English, Dutch, French, and Danes, who contested Spain's supremacy. In the 1650s the French gained possession of St. Croix. In 1666 the British occupied Tortola, which had been controlled by the Dutch since 1648. The Danish West Indian Company settled St. Thomas in the early 1670s, giving the name Taphus to the first community, which later became known as Charlotte Amalie. The company claimed St. John a decade later, and purchased St. Croix from France in 1733. The Danish West Indian Company's control lasted until the Danish ruler King Frederick V purchased the islands in 1754. They remained a royal colony, known as the Danish West Indies, until 1917. Only twice during this long period did a foreign power, namely Great Britain, occupy the islands: once in 1801 and again from 1807 to 1815.

The Danes introduced slave labor to work the profitable sugar plantations. Even after the bottom had dropped out of the sugar market, the Danish West Indies continued throughout the 19th century to enjoy a commercial boom as a free port and as a coaling station in the days of sailing vessels and paddle steamers. However, long-haul steamships and the opening of the Panama Canal robbed the islands, especially St. Thomas with its fine harbor of Charlotte Amalie, of much of their economic value.

After the sugar boom ended, Denmark expressed interest in selling the colony. As early as 1865, the United States reacted favorably, but the Senate opposed the negotiations. Rising support for the Panama Canal project resulted in renewed American interest in the Virgin Islands in 1902, but this time the Danish legislature rejected the treaty of transfer. In the early stages of World War I, when Denmark expected a German invasion at any moment, the American government grew increasingly apprehensive that the Germans would seize the strategic Danish colony, which lay so close to one of the approaches to the Panama Canal. American officials assailed the Danes with a combination of pleas and threats, voiced in diplomatic language and implying that "certain circumstances" involving "another European power" could result in U.S. occupation of the Danish West Indies. Moreover, the argument went, the sale of the islands would remove one of the chief incentives for a German invasion of Denmark. As part of the agreement, the United States would recognize Danish rule over Greenland.

Denmark finally agreed to sell its possessions in the Virgin Islands, namely the three large islands of St. Thomas, St. Croix, and St. John, together with about 50 small islets and cays with a total area of 132 square miles, provided that the United States submit to terms that would "not lead to haggling" and that the islands would retain their free-port status forever. In 1917 the United States government offered $25 million ($295 per acre), then regarded as an exorbitant sum for land that amounted to hardly more than a tenth of the size of Rhode Island, the smallest state.

Once the terms were mutually acceptable, the formal transfer ceremony took place on March 31, 1917. In Washington, D.C., the Danish minister, Constantine Brun, accepted payment. The news was immediately telegraphed to New York, then cabled to San Juan, Puerto Rico, flashed by wireless to the cruiser Hancock in the harbor at Charlotte Amalie, and carried ashore to St. Thomas via rowboat. There, Danish and American honor guards in white uniforms stood in formation on opposite sides of the parade ground before red-walled Fort Christian. Once the message had been delivered, at 4:48 p.m, the Danish honor guard presented arms, the Danish national anthem was played, and a cannon boomed 21 times as the red and white Danish flag was slowly lowered for the final time after 251 years of Danish rule. At 4:53 p.m. the American honor guard presented arms, a band played the "Star-Spangled Banner," and to the roar of the cannon the American flag was raised. As a last gesture, Admiral Henri Konow of Denmark and Admiral Edwin T. Pollock of the United States Navy drew their ceremonial swords.

After 1918, when the German threat subsided with the defeat of Germany in World War I, the Virgin Islands dropped into obscurity. Aside from the fact that the American flag flew over government buildings, the transfer of sovereignty resulted in little change. The islands retained their Danish flavor, and even the currency remained Danish until 1934. Originally under the supervision of the Department of the Navy, the Virgin Islands were transferred to the control of the Department of the Interior in 1931.

The United States had purchased the islands primarily for their strategic importance, and together with Culebra Island and Vieques (or Crab) Island, administered by Puerto Rico, they were considered one of the most vital keys to the defense of the Panama Canal Zone and the Caribbean. A more unexpected result, however, was the transformation of this poverty-stricken territory into a vacationers' paradise. Although Prohibition and the declining sugar trade had left the islands so destitute that Congress had had to appropriate over $400,000 in 1930 for relief work, decades later the Virgin Islands became a major tourist center of the Western Hemisphere. Post–World War II economic prosperity in the United States, expanding airline networks, the islands' free-port status, and their scenic and climatic assets all combined to boost the local economy. Today, millions of tourists visit the islands every year.

April

April is the fourth month of the modern, or Gregorian, calendar and has 30 days. It was formerly the second month in the ancient Roman year, when March began the calendar. The origin of its name has been lost. The most commonly accepted theory is that *Aprilis*, the Roman name for the month, is derived from the Latin verb *aperire*, meaning "to open," in allusion to the opening, or blossoming, of buds of trees and flowers in this season. On the other hand, the Romans sometimes named months for divinities. April was sacred to Venus, the Roman goddess of love, and her festival was held on the first day of the month. Some scholars have therefore conjectured that the month Aprilis had originally been called *Aphrilis*, a Latin name derived from Aphrodite, the Greek goddess of love, whom the Romans equated with Venus.

A number of important Roman festivals took place in April. On April 4, the Megalesia (or Megalensia) honored Cybele, the *Magna Mater* or Great Mother, a goddess whose cult was native to Phrygia in Asia Minor (now central Turkey). The cult had been established at Rome on April 4, 204 B.C. in the Temple of Victory on the Palatine Hill. In 191 B.C. a special temple was erected on the hill in Cybele's honor. Her festival was marked by a procession and banquet, as well as by combined games and scenic performances known as the *ludi megalenses*.

April 15 was the Fordicidia, or Feast of the Cows, when ancient rites were conducted to ensure the prosperity of the crops. A cow in calf (*forda*) was sacrificed, and attendants of the vestal virgins then took the calf from its mother to burn it. Its ashes, gathered up by the vestals, were used a few days later at the Parilia. This was the annual Roman festival of flocks and herds, staged on April 21 in honor of Pales, the pastoral deity (god or goddess) and special protector of cattle. The lus-

tral rite, which was celebrated in early spring to purify the animals, stalls, and herdsmen, consisted of several stages.

After the sheep and shepherds had been sprinkled with water, the cattle stalls were cleansed with laurel-twig brooms and decorated with leaves and wreaths. Sulphur, laurel, and rosemary, together with olive wood, were then burned, their smoke wafting through the barns to purify the flocks and herds. Gifts of milk, meat, cakes, and millet were offered to Pales. The senior vestal virgin handed the celebrants the ashes of the calf that had been slain on April 15 at the Fordicidia. By then, the ashes had been mixed with the blood of the horse that had been sacrificed to Mars, the god of war, in the previous October. Finally (in a ceremony that anticipated the customs and superstitions associated with the later Midsummer's Eve bonfires) the sheep and cattle were forced to leap across bonfires of hay and straw. The herdsmen imitated them, as, facing east, they jumped three times over the flames to conclude the lustration and guarantee prosperity and propagation.

The Parilia, a basically pastoral rite reflecting a rural environment, undoubtedly originated long before the founding of the city of Rome which, according to tradition, occurred in 753 B.C. It is said that Romulus, the founder of Rome, had himself played a significant role in conducting the cleansing and renewal rituals of the Parilia. The rite was therefore accorded a conspicuously important place in the Roman state calendar: April 21 was set aside to commemorate not only Pales but also the founding of Rome. A public holiday known as the *Natalis urbis Romae* (birthday of the city of Rome), the day was marked by music, street dancing, and general revelry.

On April 25 the Robigalia was held, special ceremonies honoring Robigus, the spirit of mildew, who was invoked to ward off any threat of red mildew from the crops. The ceremonies were performed in a sacred grove north of Rome.

Starting on April 28 the Romans celebrated the boisterous Floralia, the festival honoring Flora, the goddess of flowers. Instituted in 238 B.C., the Floralia was originally a movable feast whose dates were determined by the progress of crops and plants. In 173 B.C., after violent storms had severely damaged the crops and vineyards, the Roman senate decreed it an annual festival extending six days from April 28, the anniversary of the founding of Flora's temple, through May 3. The riotous celebrations included licentious dramatic productions and games and were usually accompanied by excessive drinking.

April was called Ostermonath or Eosturmonath by the Anglo-Saxons, after Ostra or Eostre or Eastre, the goddess of spring, from whom the Christian festival of Easter may also derive its name. The gemstone associated with April is the diamond, which symbolizes innocence.

April 1

April Fools' Day

April Fools' Day, or All Fools' Day, takes its name from a centuries-old tradition among the English, Scots, and French of playing practical jokes on April 1. The day has persisted in American culture since colonial times, although it has naturally not received official recognition or encouragement from schools or governments. It has been called "a holiday of the mind, not of the state."

Perhaps one reason for the persistence of April Fools' Day is that children in the United States are often introduced to it within the family, either by having jokes played on them that underscore their gullibility or by one parent's playing a joke on the other, giving a glimpse of the childlike spirit in adults and an occasion for shared laughter at grown-ups. The aim of April fooling has always been to put over some prank or impossible request on an unwary person who has not yet noticed what day it is. When the fooled person grows confused or realizes that he or she has been taken in, the joker calls out "April fool!"

In earlier times the most popular form of April fooling was the "fool's errand," in which an unsuspecting person is sent on an absurd mission; for example, to buy some pigeon's milk or a copy of the *History of Adam's Grandfather*. In France the fool might have been sent for some sweet vinegar

or for a stick with one end. Of course everyone the fooled person approaches for help at once perceives the joke. "Thus by contrivers' inadvertent jest, one fool exposed makes pastime for the rest," runs an old rhyme.

Many different explanations have been offered for the origins of April Fools' Day. Some may be as fanciful as April Fools' jokes themselves. In 1760 the dilemma was set in verse in *Poor Robin's Almanac*:

The first of April, some do say,
Is set apart for All Fools' Day.
But why the people call it so,
Nor I, nor they themselves do know.
But on this day are people sent
On purpose for pure merriment.

One rather unlikely explanation is that the day arose from an ancient farcical representation of the sending of Jesus from Annas to Caiaphas, from Caiaphas to Pilate, from Pilate to Herod, and from Herod back to Pilate at the time of Jesus' trial and crucifixion. Another debatable theory is that April Fools' Day is a relic of the festival of Cerealia, held at the beginning of April in Roman times. This festival recalled the legend in which the goddess Ceres, hearing the echo of the screams of her daughter Proserpina as she is being carried off to the lower world from the Elysian meadows by Pluto, goes in search of Proserpina's voice. However, Ceres' search is a fool's errand, for it is impossible to find the echo. It is also sometimes asserted that April Fools' Day is a remnant of an ancient Celtic custom concerning the beginning of spring.

The impression prevails, however, that the custom of April fooling had something to do with the observance of the spring equinox (usually March 21 in the Gregorian calendar). It is striking that at this time of year, although not precisely on April 1, customs of fooling people have been found in lands as far apart as Sweden, Portugal, and India. The similarity of April fooling to one aspect of the Hindu festival of Holi (or Huli) has especially fascinated folklorists. Originating in an ancient fertility rite at the beginning of spring, Holi is a five-day Hindu festival celebrated with bonfires and outdoor dancing. For centuries unsuspecting persons have been sent on fool's errands on the final day of Holi, March 31, just as they are on April Fools' Day. In modern times, however, Holi seems to be losing its appeal.

Certain scholars have argued that the strong resemblance between April Fools' Day and the last day of Holi indicates a prehistoric common Indo-European origin, attesting to the great antiquity of April Fools' Day. Whatever its global affinities, the tradition of April Fools' Day was brought early to the American colonies by English, Scottish, and

French settlers. However, its beginnings in Great Britain are unclear. The first allusion to All Fools' Day in English literature dates from the end of the 17th century (*Dawks's Newsletter*, April 2, 1698). Literary allusions become more frequent from the time of Addison and Steele's *Spectator* (1711–1712; 1714), but of course April fooling existed before it was mentioned in print. Many historians believe that the custom was prevalent in France earlier than in Britain.

April fooling may have first become customary in France after the adoption of a calendar reform by young Charles IX in 1564, making the calendar year begin on January 1. The influential King Philip II of Spain had recently decreed January 1 New Year's for his realm, and this had also been the practice in ancient Rome for a number of centuries, beginning before the time of Jesus Christ. Through much of France in the Middle Ages, however, New Year's Day had been observed on March 25 at the time of Lady Day, or the Feast of the Annunciation. This plan had been favored by the medieval Church because the bacchanalian flavor of the old pagan celebration of the new year on January 1 was thus avoided. Furthermore, with March 25 as its beginning, the year commenced on the traditional anniversary of the angel's announcement to Mary that she would bear a son, that is, on the anniversary of the conception of Jesus.

Like most medieval festivals, New Year's had been celebrated throughout the week following the festival day. This period of seven days after March 25 was called the octave of New Year's, because with the festival day it lasted eight days. Under the old (Julian) calendar arrangement, most French people had exchanged calls and given gifts on April 1, the final day of the New Year's octave. Charles IX's proclamation of 1564, changing New Year's Day to January 1, took several years to be recognized because of slow communications and popular attachment to tradition. Conservatives especially objected to the change. In time, jokers began to ridicule the conservatives' attachment to the old New Year's by making calls of pretended ceremony and sending them mock gifts on April 1. It is thought that the widespread French tradition of April fooling arose from this. In England and the British colonies, March 25 remained the New Year until 1751–1752, so April fooling may have been imported into Great Britain and then the Americas from the French.

First Speaker of the House Is Chosen

On April 1, 1789, Frederick Augustus Conrad Muhlenberg was elected as the first speaker of the United States House of Representatives. Under the Constitution, which had just taken effect, the speaker of the House is the leader of the House of Representatives, which together with the Senate comprises the Congress of the United States.

Muhlenberg was a member of the "Administration" Party, which would later become the Federalist Party and is one of the remote predecessors of the modern Republican Party. He was a former Lutheran minister from Pennsylvania who had previously served as speaker in the Pennsylvania State House of Representatives and as a member of the Continental Congress that preceded the Congress devised by the Constitution.

April 2

United States Mint Established

As Article I, section 8, of the United States Constitution conferred on Congress the exclusive power to coin money and to regulate its value, it became necessary to make some provision to exercise this power. In January 1791, Alexander Hamilton, the first secretary of the treasury, dealt with the coinage problem in his report to Congress. Hamilton's recommendations, which were strongly influenced by the thinking of Thomas Jefferson and the financier Robert Morris, called for three major provisions: (1) a decimal system of coinage; (2) the dollar as the basic unit of money; and (3) bimetallism, with both silver and gold as legal tender in a ratio of 15 to 1. Under Hamilton's recommendation, the gold dollar would contain 24.75 grains of pure gold and the silver dollar would contain 371.25 grains of pure silver.

On April 2, 1792, Congress ratified this plan and passed an act establishing a mint for the coinage of money. The word "mint" is derived from a Latin term meaning money. The first coins—copper cents and half cents—came from the mint in 1793. Silver dollars were first coined in 1794. Gold eagles ($10) and half eagles ($5) appeared in 1795, and soon afterward half-dollars, quarters, and 10-cent and 5-cent pieces were also produced on a large scale.

Only Massachusetts, which between 1652 and 1683 minted the famous pine-tree shilling, successfully coined money during the colonial period. Instead, the colonies generally relied on English money, the Spanish dollar, ordinary barter, tobacco and other warehouse receipts, emergency issues of paper currency, and other expedients. Such an inadequate supply of money was a major grievance against Great Britain up to the time of the American Revolution. After the colonies united to resist Great Britain, the Second Continental Congress authorized an issue of paper money. Provision was made for its redemption within three years, and each colony was held responsible for its proper proportion of the issue. Because the first issue of $3 million was inadequate, there were many subsequent issues, and all pretense of redemption was abandoned. The currency's value depreciated until in 1782 it took 500 Continental dollars to buy one Spanish silver dollar. George Washington once said that it took a wagonload of money to buy a wagonload of provisions. The depreciation was so great that people got in the habit of saying of a useless thing that it was "not worth a Continental."

Despite attempts to stabilize finances during the Confederation period, currency continued to be one of the major problems plaguing the new nation. Seen in this perspective, Hamilton's plan was viewed by many as a panacea that would place American finances on a sound footing. However, the system, which undervalued gold, proved to be a complete failure, and not until after the Civil War was there a really satisfactory national coinage.

The first mint, provided for in the act of 1792, was opened in Philadelphia, Pennsylvania. Over the succeeding two centuries, mints were also opened in San Francisco, California; New Orleans, Louisiana; Carson City, Nevada; Dahlonega, Georgia; Charlotte, North Carolina; and Denver, Colorado. Most of these other mints were short-lived, however. There have also been many changes in the laws governing coinage and in the denominations of coins in use since the first Philadelphia Mint began coining money in 1793. For example, gold and silver are no longer used in American coins. In addition, certain denominations have been eliminated, such as the half-cent, 2-cent, 3-cent, and 20-cent pieces and the silver half-dime (which was replaced by the nickel).

President Wilson Urges Congress to Approve the U.S. Entry into World War I

By the spring of 1917, the United States was about to enter World War I (see April 6 for background information). President Wilson finally decided to ask Congress to declare war, and called Congress into special session on April 2, 1917. The relevant parts of Wilson's address, announcing that "the

world must be made safe for democracy," are set forth below. Congress complied. The House of Representatives voted for war on April 4, 1917, and the Senate voted for war on April 6, 1917.

I have called the Congress into extraordinary session because there are serious, very serious, choices of policy to be made, and made immediately, which it was neither right nor constitutionally permissible that I should assume the responsibility of making. On the third of February last I officially laid before you the extraordinary announcement of the Imperial German Government that on and after the first day of February it was its purpose to put aside all restraints of law or of humanity and use its submarines to sink every vessel that sought to approach either the ports of Great Britain and Ireland or the western coasts of Europe or any of the ports controlled by the enemies of Germany within the Mediterranean. That had seemed to be the object of the German submarine warfare earlier in the war, but since April of last year the Imperial Government had somewhat restrained the commanders of its undersea craft in conformity with its promise then given to us that passenger boats should not be sunk and that due warning would be given to all other vessels which its submarines might seek to destroy when no resistance was offered or escape attempted, and care taken that their crews were given at least a fair chance to save their lives in their open boats. It is a war against all nations. American ships have been sunk, American lives taken, in ways which it has stirred us very deeply to learn of, but the ships and people of other neutral and friendly nations have been sunk and overwhelmed in the waters in the same way. There has been no discrimination. The challenge is to all mankind. Each nation must decide for itself how it will meet it. The choice we make for ourselves must be made with a moderation of counsel and a temperateness of judgment befitting our character and our motives as a nation. We must put excited feeling away. Our motive will not be revenge or the victorious assertion of the physical might of the nation, but only the vindication of right, of human right, of which we are only a single champion.

When I addressed the Congress on the twenty-sixth of February last I thought that it would suffice to assert our neutral rights with arms, our right to use the seas against unlawful interference, our right to keep our people safe against unlawful violence. But armed neutrality, it now appears, is impracticable.

With a profound sense of the solemn and even tragical character of the step I am taking and of the grave responsibilities which it involves, but in unhesitating obedience to what I deem my constitutional duty, I advise that the Congress declare the recent course of the Imperial German Government to be in fact nothing less than war against the government and people of the United States; that it formally accept the status of belligerent which has thus been thrust upon it, and that it take immediate steps not only to put the country in a more thorough state of defense but also to exert all its power and employ all its resources to bring the Government of the German Empire to terms and end the war.

What this will involve is clear. It will involve the utmost practicable cooperation in counsel and action with the governments now at war with Germany, and, as incident to that, the extension to those governments of the most liberal financial credit, in order that our resources may so far as possible be added to theirs. It will involve the organization and mobilization of all the material resources of the country to supply the materials of war and serve the incidental needs of the Nation in the most abundant and yet the most economical and efficient way possible. It will involve the immediate full equipment of the navy in all respects but particularly in supplying it with the best means of dealing with the enemy's submarines. It will involve the immediate addition to the armed forces of the United States already provided for by law in case of war of at least five hundred thousand men, who should, in my opinion, be chosen upon the principle of universal liability to service, and also the authorization of subsequent additional increments of equal force so soon as they may be needed and can be handled in training. It will involve also, of course, the granting of adequate credits to the Government, sustained, I hope, so far as they can equitably be sustained by the present generation, by well conceived taxation.

While we do these things, these deeply momentous things, let us be very clear, and make very clear to all the world what our motives and our objects are. My own thought has not been driven from its habitual and normal course by the unhappy events of the last two months, and I do not believe that the thought of the Nation has been altered or clouded by them. I have exactly the same things in mind now that I had in mind when I addressed the Senate on the twenty-second of January last, the same that I had in mind when I addressed the Congress on the third of February and on the twenty-sixth of February. Our object now, as then, is to vindicate the principles of peace and justice in the life of the world as against selfish and autocratic power and to set up amongst the really free and self-governed peoples of the world such a concert of purpose and of action as will henceforth insure the observance of those principles. Neutrality is no longer feasible or desirable where the peace of the world is involved and the freedom of its peoples, and the menace to that peace and freedom lies in the existence of autocratic governments backed by organized force which is controlled wholly by their will, not by the will of their people. We have seen the last of neutrality in such circumstances. We are at the beginning of an age in which it will be insisted that the same standards of conduct and of responsibility for wrong done shall be observed among nations and their governments that are observed among the individual citizens of civilized states.

We have no quarrel with the German people. We have no feeling towards them but one of sympathy and friendship. It was not upon their impulse that their government acted in entering this war. It was not with their previous knowledge or approval. It was a war determined upon as wars used to be determined upon in the old, unhappy days when peoples were nowhere consulted by their rulers and wars were provoked and waged in the interest of dynasties or of little groups of ambitious men who were accustomed to use their fellow men as pawns and tools. Self-governed nations do not fill their neighbor states with spies or set the course of intrigue to bring about some critical posture of affairs which will give them an opportunity to strike and make conquest. Such designs can be successfully worked out only under cover and where no one has the right to ask questions.

Cunningly contrived plans of deception or aggression, carried, it may be, from generation to generation, can be worked out and kept from the light only within the privacy of courts or behind the carefully guarded confidences of a narrow and privileged class. They are happily impossible where public opinion commands and insists upon full information concerning all the nation's affairs.

A steadfast concert for peace can never be maintained except by a partnership of democratic nations. No autocratic government could be trusted to keep faith within it or observe its covenants. It must be a league of honor, a partnership of opinion. Intrigue would eat its vitals away; the plottings of inner circles who could plan what they would and render account to no one would be a corruption seated at its very heart. Only free peoples can hold their purpose and their honor steady to a common end and prefer the interests of mankind to any narrow interest of their own.

One of the things that has served to convince us that the Prussian autocracy was not and could never be our friend is that from the very outset of the present war it has filled our unsuspecting communities and even our offices of government with spies and set criminal intrigues everywhere afoot against our national unity of counsel, our peace within and without, our industries and our commerce. Indeed it is now evident that its spies were here even before the war began; and it is unhappily not a matter of conjecture but a fact proved in our courts of justice that the intrigues which have more than once come perilously near to disturbing the peace and dislocating the industries of the country have been carried on at the instigation, with the support, and even under the personal direction of official agents of the Imperial Government accredited to the Government of the United States. Even in checking these things and trying to extirpate them we have sought to put the most generous interpretation possible upon them because we knew that their source lay, not in any hostile feeling or purpose of the German people towards us (who were, no doubt, as ignorant of them as we ourselves were), but only in the selfish designs of a Government that did what it pleased and told its people nothing. But they have played their part in serving to convince us

at last that that Government entertains no real friendship for us and means to act against our peace and security at its convenience. That it means to stir up enemies against us at our very doors, the intercepted [Zimmerman Note] to the German Minister at Mexico City is eloquent evidence.

We are accepting this challenge of hostile purpose because we know that in such a Government, following such methods, we can never have a friend; and that in the presence of its organized power, always lying in wait to accomplish we know not what purpose, there can be no assured security for the democratic Governments of the world. We are now about to accept gauge of battle with this natural foe to liberty and shall, if necessary, spend the whole force of the nation to check and nullify its pretensions and its power. We are glad, now that we see the facts with no veil of false pretense about them, to fight thus for the ultimate peace of the world and for the liberation of its peoples, the German peoples included: for the rights of nations great and small and the privilege of men everywhere to choose their way of life and of obedience. The world must be made safe for democracy. Its peace must be planted upon the tested foundations of political liberty. We have no selfish ends to serve.

We desire no conquest, no dominion. We seek no indemnities for ourselves, no material compensation for the sacrifices we shall freely make. We are but one of the champions of the rights of mankind. We shall be satisfied when those rights have been made as secure as the faith and the freedom of nations can make them. Just because we fight without rancor and without selfish object, seeking nothing for ourselves but what we shall wish to share with all free peoples, we shall, I feel confident, conduct our operations as belligerents without passion and ourselves observe with proud punctilio the principles of right and of fair play we profess to be fighting for.

It will be all the easier for us to conduct ourselves as belligerents in a high spirit of right and fairness because we act without animus, not in enmity towards a people or with the desire to bring any injury or disadvantage upon them, but only in armed opposition to an irresponsible government which has thrown aside all considerations of humanity and of right and is running amuck. We are, let me say again, the sincere friends of the German people, and shall desire nothing so much as the early re-establishment of intimate relations of mutual advantage between us, however hard it may be for them, for the time being, to believe that this is spoken from our hearts. We have borne with their present Government through all these bitter months because of that friendship, exercising a patience and forbearance which would otherwise have been impossible. We shall, happily, still have an opportunity to prove that friendship in our daily attitude and actions towards the millions of men and women of German birth and native sympathy who live amongst us and share our life, and we shall be proud to prove it towards all who are in fact loyal to their neighbors and to the Government in the hour of test. They are, most of them, as true and loyal Americans as if they had never known any other fealty or allegiance. They will be prompt to stand with us in rebuking and restraining the few who may be of a different mind and purpose. If there should be disloyalty, it will be dealt with with a firm hand of stern repression; but, if it lifts its head at all, it will lift it only here and there and without countenance except from a lawless and malignant few.

It is a distressing and oppressive duty, Gentlemen of the Congress, which I have performed in thus addressing you. There are, it may be, many months of fiery trial and sacrifice ahead of us. It is a fearful thing to lead this great peaceful people into war, into the most terrible and disastrous of all wars, civilization itself seeming to be in the balance. But the right is more precious than peace, and we shall fight for the things which we have always carried nearest our hearts, for democracy, for the right of those who submit to authority to have a voice in their own Governments, for the rights and liberties of small nations, for a universal dominion of right by such a concert of free peoples as shall bring peace and safety to all nations and make the world itself at last free. To such a task we can dedicate our lives and our fortunes, everything that we are and everything that we have, with the pride of those who know that the day has come when America is privileged to spend her blood and her might for the principles that gave her birth and happiness and the peace which she has

treasured. God helping her, she can do no other.

April 3

Washington Irving's Birthday

Washington Irving, the first American writer to gain international fame, was born in New York City on April 3, 1783. The youngest of 11 children of a prosperous merchant, he was pampered and indulged, especially by his brothers. His family's warmth molded his warm, generous character and helped make possible his whimsical, polished, sophisticated style as a writer.

Irving was sickly from early boyhood, which turned out be somewhat advantageous, as he was exempt from the rigors of formal education to which all of his brothers had been subjected. Further, to regain his health, he often traveled in the United States, Canada, and Europe. These travels brought him a cosmopolitan attitude and a store of material for future writing.

Starting in his teens, Irving frequently traveled up the Hudson River to stay with married sisters who lived in the country. It was there that he became absorbed in the legends and folklore of the early Dutch settlers that appear in so much of his work. Given more leisure than his older brothers, who were working in the family business or practicing their own professions, he was free to pursue his own interests in theatrical, literary, and social circles. He did not have a college education, but since it was considered necessary for every young gentleman to be trained in a profession, he studied law intermittently in the offices of Josiah Ogden Hoffman. If Irving was lukewarm about the law, he was ardent about Hoffman's daughter Matilda, and the two became engaged.

During this period, Irving wrote a series of whimsical essays, which were published (1802–1803) in the *Morning Chronicle*, his brother Peter's paper, under the pen name of Jonathan Oldstyle, Gent (the first of many pseudonyms that Irving was to use). At 21 he went to Europe for his health and remained for two years. Returning to New York, he finished his study of law and passed the bar examination late in 1806. Meanwhile, with his brother William, J. K. Paulding, and other friends, he was collaborating on a collection of essays entitled *Salmagundi; or, The Whim-Whams and Opinions of Launcelot Langstaff, and Others* (1807–1808).

In 1809 Irving published *Diedrich Knickerbocker's History of New York*, which made him internationally famous. However, tragedy struck when his fiancée Matilda died suddenly. Stunned with sorrow, Irving became aimless and restless and there followed a 10-year moratorium on his writings. His brothers tried vainly to interest him in several projects that they hoped would occupy his mind. Finally, in 1811 he took up residence in Washington, D.C., as a lobbyist for the family's importing firm. It was an essentially social job for which he was eminently suited. He was warmly welcomed into diplomatic and political circles as one of the country's most famous writers. During the War of 1812, after the British burned the capital, Irving served briefly as aide-de-camp to Governor Daniel D. Tompkins, acquiring the rank of staff colonel with the Iron Grays of the New York State militia.

In 1815 the importing enterprise began to falter, and Irving set out for England to attend to the firm's interests in Liverpool. He could do little to save the business, but he made important literary contacts in London, most notably with Sir Walter Scott and Lord Byron, both of whom had admired his work. Scott's encouragement, and perhaps the family's business reverses, formed the turning point in Irving's long-neglected literary career, and he began to write again. *The Sketch Book of Geoffrey Crayon, Gent.* (1819–1820), a collection that included "Rip Van Winkle" and "The Legend of Sleepy Hollow," was a great success in England and the United States.

For the next several years, Irving continued to travel, often in quest of health, and wrote about the places he visited (Germany, Austria, France, Spain, and England) and their histories or legends. Early in 1826 he was invited to the American legation in Spain to translate Martin Fernandez de Navarrete's book on Columbus. He became fascinated with the subject and wrote his own *Life and Voyages of Christopher Columbus* (1828) and *The Companions of Columbus* (1831).

Absorbed in Spain and its Moorish heritage, Irving lived for a while in the Alhambra, the Moorish citadel in Granada, and later wrote *The Conquest of Granada* (1829) and *The Alhambra* (1832). From Spain, he went to London, where he served as secretary of the American legation from 1829 to 1832. By the time he returned to New York in 1832, he had been away from home for 17 years, yet he was tumultuously received. The public had followed his career with interest and pride, and his *Knickerbocker's History* had grown in popularity. The United States had its first literary idol.

These were years of great excitement in America's Wild West. Irving traveled to the western frontier and wrote *A Tour of the Prairies* (1835). *The Adventures of Captain Bonneville* was published in 1837, and *Astoria*, written with a nephew, came out in 1836.

In 1835 Irving moved into Sunnyside, a house located in Tarrytown, New York, on the Hudson River. He lived in the house, which he described as "a little, old-fashioned stone mansion, all made up of gable ends and as full of angles and corners as an old cocked hat," for the rest of his life, except from 1842 to 1846, when he was the American minister to Spain. Although his home was a busy place, with visits from friends, dignitaries, and relatives, Irving continued to write, concentrating mostly on biographies. His last published work was the five-volume biography *George Washington* (1855–1859).

Washington Irving died at Sunnyside on November 28, 1859, and was buried in the churchyard of the Old Dutch Church of Sleepy Hollow in North Tarrytown.

The XYZ Affair

During the administration of President John Adams (1796–1800), the second president of the United States, the country nearly went to war with its former ally France. During the American Revolution, the French had assisted the colonies with money, supplies, and military advisors. After the revolution, however, the French monarchy was overthrown and war broke out between France and Great Britain.

Because of its ties with both countries, the United States was drawn into the conflict. In 1797, the year that Adams was inaugurated as president, three American representatives were present in France: Charles C. Pickney, Elbridge Gerry, and John Marshall. Charles-Maurice de Talleyrand-Périgard, the French foreign minister, sent to the Americans three agents who demanded a loan for the French government and a bribe for certain French officials. Pickney refused, stating that the Americans would pay "not a sixpence." The American representatives reported the affair to President Adams, who then reported it to Congress on April 3, 1798.

The incident became known as the XYZ Affair, since the three agents were named anonymously as "X, Y and Z." It was considered an insult to American honor, no small matter in this era. There was considerable support in Congress and in the public for a war with France. However, the United States was not in a position to enter into another war with one of Europe's great powers so quickly after the American Revolution, and cooler heads prevailed.

April 4

Martin Luther King Jr. Assassinated

Martin Luther King Jr. arrived in Memphis, Tennessee, on April 3, 1968, to organize support for the city's predominantly black sanitation workers, who had been on strike since February 12. Speaking before a gathering of 2,000 people that evening, King spoke of the inevitable dangers faced by those who fought for civil rights. He concluded:

> Like anybody, I would like to live a long life; longevity has its grace, but I'm not concerned about that now. I just want to do God's will. And He's allowed me to go up to the mountain. And I've looked over, and I've seen the promised land. I may not get there with you, but I want you to know tonight that we as a people will get to the promised land. So I'm happy tonight. I'm not worried about anything. I'm not fearing any man. Mine eyes have seen the glory of the coming of the Lord.

King's eloquence was prophetic; the next day, April 4, 1968, an assassin's bullet struck him down.

That day, he and his aides had worked in his room at the Lorraine Motel, which they had chosen because of its black ownership. Toward evening their meeting ended, and the participants prepared to go to dinner. King stepped onto the balcony outside his room and chatted with a member of his staff, the Reverend Jesse Jackson, who was standing below in a parking lot. Jackson introduced the musician Ben Branch, who was scheduled to play at that evening's church rally. The civil rights leader, leaning over the railing, greeted Branch and asked him to play the spiritual "Precious Lord" at the gathering. As King straightened up, he was shot by a .30-06 bullet, which pierced his face and neck. The impact of the bullet lifted him off his feet and dropped him on his back on the concrete balcony floor.

Jesse Jackson, Ralph Abernathy, Andrew Young, and other associates rushed to the fallen leader. They tried, unsuccessfully, to stop the bleeding. A fire department ambulance carried King to St. Joseph's Hospital, but the surgery performed there failed to revive him, and doctors pronounced him dead.

King's assassin had fired the fatal bullet from a dingy boardinghouse across the street from the Lorraine Motel. The suspect, later identified as James Earl Ray, an escaped convict, fled the site, but local, state, and federal law enforcement officers were soon tracking him. The authorities finally captured Ray at a London airport. Back in the United States, a jury convicted him of murder and sentenced him to 99 years in the penitentiary.

Upon hearing of King's assassination, national leaders expressed a sense of horror. Vice President Hubert Humphrey, attending a congressional dinner, stated: "Martin Luther King stands with our other American martyrs in the cause of freedom and justice. . . . The apostle of nonviolence has been the victim of violence. . . . An America of full freedom, full and equal opportunity, is the living memorial he deserves, and it shall be his living memorial."

President Lyndon B. Johnson asked every citizen to reject the blind violence that struck down the nonviolent King, but not all Americans responded to his plea. Nights and days of rioting, looting, and burning plagued many cities, as some African Americans angrily reacted to the news of the murder. Youths rampaged through the streets of ghettos, burning large sections of their own communities and despoiling the stores of African Americans as well as other merchants. Washington, D.C., which had escaped serious urban riots in the earlier 1960s, suffered the worst damage. The plundering began on the Thursday evening when King was shot and continued for several days. Looters struck stores only two blocks from the White House, and arsonists set blazes whose smoke hung over government buildings. On Friday, President Johnson called for 6,500 army and National Guard troops to aid the city's 2,900 police officers, and he soon sent for another 6,000 regulars. By late Saturday, the soldiers and police were able to restore some order.

Chicago, the site of King's unsuccessful campaigns for open housing in 1966, also felt the wrath of rioters. Looters, arsonists, and a few snipers battled the police. Chicago officials finally had to use 12,500 federal soldiers and Illinois guardsmen to restore order. New York City, meanwhile, escaped relatively unscathed. Although window-breakers and looters were active in some African American areas, police restraint, the cooperation of community leaders in Harlem, and the presence there of Mayor John Lindsay on the nights following the assassination helped to calm the anger.

Coretta Scott King, the wife of the slain leader, stepped forward to continue her husband's work. On April 8, the day before King was buried, she led between 20,000 to 40,000 marchers through the streets of Memphis in a demonstration in support of the sanitation workers her husband had wanted to help. Walter P. Reuther, president of the United Automobile Workers; Benjamin Spock, pediatrician and Vietnam War opponent; Charles S. Cogen, president of the American Federation of Teachers; Harry Van Arsdale, president of the New York City Labor Council; John deLury, president of the Uniformed Sanitation Men's Association of New York; actors Ossie Davis and Godfrey Cambridge; singer Harry Belafonte; and representatives John Conyers and William Fitts Ryan were among the dignitaries who marched in the front ranks with Coretta King. At the Memphis city hall, she addressed the crowd, challenging all to carry on her husband's work. She reminded the throng of what King had often said, that an unearned suffering is redemptive.

> If you give your life to a cause in which you believe, and which is right and just, and it is, and if your life comes to an end as a result of this then your life could not have been lived in a more redemptive way.

"I think," she declared, "that this is what my husband has done."

In anticipation of the funeral, many communities held special commemorative services. President Johnson declared April 7 Martin Luther King Memorial Day. In New York City, thousands of people gathered at lunchtime on April 8 in a Manhattan garment center meeting sponsored by District 65 of the Retail, Wholesale, and Department Store Union. At approximately the same time, 500 people who had marched downtown from Harlem held a memorial service at the United Nations Plaza. Mayor Lindsay attended both events. Also on April 8, some 200 diplomats and United Nations staff members attended a memorial service for King at the Church Center for the United Nations. Arthur Goldberg, the United States ambassador to the United Nations, led the American delegation. Philip A. Johnson, associate general secretary of the World Council of Churches in the United States, reminded the worshipers that commemorations were only the beginning and that "the world now awaits the only eloquence that will make any difference, the eloquence of deed."

On April 9 people from all stations in life gathered in Atlanta, Georgia, to attend King's funeral. Among them were members of Congress, many governors, and leading representatives of major religions. Funeral services began at 10:43 a.m. at the Ebenezer Baptist Church, of which King and his father, the Reverend Martin Luther King Sr., had been co-pastors. At the request of Coretta King, the ceremony included a taped excerpt from the last sermon preached by King at the church. In the talk, King described what he hoped would be his eulogy:

> If any of you are around when I have to meet my day, I don't want a long funeral. And if you get somebody to deliver the eulogy, tell him not to talk too long. . . . Tell him not to mention that I have a Nobel Peace Prize, that isn't important.

> Tell him not to mention that I have 300 or 400 other awards; that's not important.
> Tell him not to mention where I went to school.
> I'd like somebody to mention that day that Martin Luther King Jr. tried to give his life serving others.
> I'd like for somebody to say that day that Martin Luther King Jr. tried to love somebody. . . .
> I want you to be able to say that day that I did try to feed the hungry. I want you to be able to say that day that I did try in my life to clothe the naked. I want you to say on that day that I did try in my life to visit those who were in prison. And I want you to say that I tried to love and serve humanity.
> Yes, if you want to, say that I was a drum major. Say that I was a drum major for justice. Say that I was a drum major for peace. I was a drum major for righteousness.
> And all of the other shallow things will not matter.

When the services ended after noon, the pallbearers carried the coffin from the church, and to symbolize King's identification with the poor placed it upon a faded green wooden wagon drawn by two mules. Then, about 50,000 mourners began the three-and-a-half mile march through the streets of Atlanta to Morehouse College, which King had attended. At Morehouse, Benjamin H. Mays, president emeritus of the college, gave a eulogy as part of the 90-minute program:

> I make bold to assert that it took more courage for King to practice nonviolence than it took his assassin to fire the fatal shot. The assassin is a coward: he committed his foul act and fled. When Martin Luther King disobeyed an unjust law, he accepted the consequences of his actions. He never ran away and he never begged for mercy. . . . He was supra-race, supra-nation, supra-denomination, supra-class, and supra-culture. He belonged to the world and to mankind. Now he belongs to posterity.

King's body was carried in a hearse from the college to South View Cemetery, a burial area established by African Americans after the Civil War. There, at approximately 5:30 p.m., he was buried beside his grandparents. The epitaph on his tombstone catches the irony of his life and death: "Free at last, free at last; thank God Almighty I'm free at last."

April 4

Puyallup Valley Daffodil Festival

This is a movable event.

Washington's Puyallup Valley Daffodil Festival takes place early every spring. The 18-mile-long Puyallup Valley is located east of Tacoma, Washington, between Puget Sound and snowcapped Mount Rainier. To draw attention to the tens of millions of daffodils that cover the valley in spring, civic leaders in Tacoma and the valley communities of Puyallup, Sumner, Orting, Fife, and Spanaway sponsor the festival each year. It customarily begins in April, when the blooms are at their best. Besides the magnificent fields of daffodils, dozens of events contribute to the success of the festivities. They have included the coronation of a "daffodil queen," a grand floral parade, an Arabian horse show, a marine regatta, and track, field, and other sports competitions.

The state of Washington has a strong flower industry, thanks to ideal soil, moisture, mild winters, and other growing conditions together with innovations in the use of machinery in the fields. The state produces a significant percentage of the nation's daffodil bulbs. A large portion of the state's acreage in bulb production can be found in the Puyallup Valley, where the bulb industry started as early as 1910 when George Lawler made the first, albeit small-scale, commercial plantings. The United States Department of Agriculture examined the valley in 1923 to seek a substitute crop for the area's hop production, which was hard hit with the advent of Prohibition. Acting upon the department's recommendation that the region would be an excellent place for extensive bulb production, W. H. Paulhams of Sumner summoned a meeting of all persons eager to implement the suggestion.

The year 1925 is generally given as the start of Puyallup Valley's fame as a bulb center. In addition to the sale of bulbs, there was a large market for forcers (bulbs placed in hothouses and forced into early spring bloom) and for cut flowers (used for spring and Easter promotions, especially in department stores). Today, despite some foreign competition, millions of daffodils are shipped every year from the Puyallup Valley.

The first Puyallup Valley Daffodil Festival was held on April 6, 1926, at the estate of Charles Orton, near Sumner, under the auspices of the Sumner Garden Club. Civic leaders from 15 nearby towns attended the garden party, held amid many varieties of blooming daffodils. The following year the Sumner chamber of commerce sponsored a bulb banquet and, with help from the Tacoma and Puyallup chambers of commerce, chose a daffodil queen from one of the valley communities. As visitors from Tacoma and Seattle flocked to visit the blooming fields on weekends in late March and early April, the modest festivities became well-known. Representatives from the participating communities met in 1934, creating a steering committee to form a more ambitious program of events. From these small beginnings the present festival was born in 1934. It remains an active and popular event.

Flag Act of 1818

On June 14, 1777, the Continental Congress approved a flag for the United States consisting of 13 alternate red and white stripes and a union of 13 white stars on a blue field. Congress evidently intended to continue to represent each state with a star and a stripe because, following the admission of Vermont and Kentucky to the Union, it voted on January 13, 1794, to add two stars and two stripes to the national banner. This act became effective on May 1, 1795, and the flag remained unchanged for 23 years.

When Congress met to consider the flag in 1818, however, five more states had joined the Union, and several territories were also petitioning for statehood. No longer was it feasible to continue the old plan for the flag. For this reason, on April 4, 1818, President James Monroe signed a congressional bill providing that the flag be redesigned, that the number of stripes be reduced to the original 13, and that there be 20 stars. The act further ordered that "on the admission of every new state into the Union one star be added to the union of the flag and that such addition shall take effect on the Fourth of July next succeeding such admission."

The flag has been made in accordance with this design since that date. It was last redesigned in 1959, when it underwent two revisions. At the admission of Alaska to the Union on January 3, President Dwight D. Eisenhower ordered that, effective on July 4 of that year, the flag would consist of 49 stars arranged in seven rows of seven stars each, with alternate rows indented. After Hawaii became a state on August 21, 1959, the flag was again altered, and the present 50-star flag with five rows of six stars each and four rows of five stars each became the nation's official banner on July 4, 1960.

April 5

Booker T. Washington's Birthday

Booker Taliaferro Washington was born on April 5, 1856, in the cramped slave quarters of James Burroughs's plantation near Halesford in Franklin County, Virginia. The son of a mixed-race slave mother and a white father, Washington lived the first seven years of his life as a slave. In 1865, after emancipation, his mother moved with her family to Malden, West Virginia, where young Washington soon found work in a salt furnace and then in a coal mine. In spite of the exhausting work in the mines, he also managed to go to public school for a few months.

In 1872, determined to pursue his ambition for learning, Washington set off with only $1.50 in his pocket to walk the 300 miles to the Hampton Institute in Virginia. There he earned the esteem of General Samuel C. Armstrong, the director of the school. Washington studied at the Hampton Institute for three years, working as a janitor at the school to pay his expenses. Upon graduation he returned to Malden, where he taught for two years at a school for African Americans. There he instructed children during the daytime and adults at night. In 1878 he left Malden to attend Wayland Seminary in Washington, D.C., and eight months later he returned to the Hampton Institute to take charge of its night school. While at Hampton he also helped start an educational program for 75 Native Americans.

In 1881 General Armstrong recommended Washington to be principal of the just established Tuskegee Normal and Industrial Institute, later known as Tuskegee Institute, Alabama's first school to train African American teachers. The start was inauspicious. Arriving there to open the school on July 4, Washington found only a miserable house, $2,000 in teaching salaries provided by the state, and a handful of pupils. By the time of his death in 1915, however, he had built Tuskegee into a school with a national reputation, an endowment of some $2 million, and a plant of more than 100 well-equipped buildings, where over 1,500 students studied 38 trades and professions under nearly 200 faculty members.

The physical expansion of the institute testified to Washington's success as an educator, since he had made Tuskegee the proving ground for his theories on industrial education. Washington felt that, for the African American, "the opportunity to earn a dollar in a factory just now is worth infinitely more than the opportunity to spend a dollar in an opera house." While emphasizing the dignity of manual labor and the importance of cleanliness, proper diet, and other good habits, he also stressed the necessity of knowing a trade. At Tuskegee he tried to provide students with a useful education. He felt that the best interests of African Americans were more likely to be served by providing them with education and the opportunity for material advancement than through political agitation for civil and voting rights.

In 1895 Washington spoke at the Cotton States Exposition in Atlanta. In his speech he referred to black-white relations, saying: "In all things that are purely social we can be as separate as the five fingers, yet one as the hand in all things essential to mutual progress." This speech, which some regarded as a tacit acceptance of segregation and others saw as an attempt to conciliate the races, brought Washington instant national recognition. Especially in the white world, he came to be regarded as the leading spokesman for African Americans, and he was increasingly in demand, both in the United States and in Europe, as a public speaker. Those who wished to establish or contribute to African American educational institutions sought his advice before allocating their funds, and African Americans seeking federal appointments sought his endorsement. In 1905 President Theodore Roosevelt, like President William McKinley before him, visited Tuskegee, paying its founder a great honor. Other influential admirers were President William Howard Taft and industrialists Andrew Carnegie and John D. Rockefeller.

The emphasis placed by Washington on the potential rather than the grievances of African Americans, as well as his ability and willingness to compromise, contributed to his acceptance by whites. However, this acceptance led to opposition from other African American leaders, such as W. E. B. DuBois. They feared that Washington's stress on industrial education might keep African Americans in virtual bondage and regarded his attitude toward the white establishment as excessively conciliatory. Those who opposed his views stressed the importance of fighting for political and civil rights, something Washington thought unwise and sought to avoid. Many historians feel that Washington adopted the only approach that could have been effective during the turn-of-the-century era in which he came to prominence, though others contest that assertion.

Washington's lifelong concerns were broad, including not only the Tuskegee Institute and the immediate community around it, but also the well-being of all African Americans in the United States. In 1892 he founded the Tuskegee Conference, which dealt with rural problems encountered by African Americans in Alabama and encouraged self-improvement. The National Negro Business League, which Washington started in 1890, reached African American businessmen all over the country. His ideas also found expression in his public-speaking tours and in the many books he wrote, among them his best-selling autobiography, *Up from Slavery* (1901), which has been widely translated. Among his other books are *The Future of the American Negro* (1899); *Life of Frederick Douglass*, about the influential black abolitionist (1907); and a second autobiography, *My Larger Education* (1911).

Washington's strenuous work hastened his death, and he died on November 14, 1915. He was buried near the chapel at Tuskegee Institute. In 1945 Washington was elected to the Hall of Fame for Great Americans in New York City.

Elihu Yale's Birthday

Elihu Yale, one of the earliest benefactors of what is now Yale University, was born in or near Boston, Massachusetts, on April 5, 1649. His father, David Yale, who had emigrated from Wales in 1638, was one of the early settlers of New Haven, Connecticut, now the home of Yale University. The man for whom the university is named never actually saw New Haven, since his parents moved to Massachusetts before he was born and returned to Great Britain when he was about three years old.

Elihu Yale was educated in London and, when he was about 21, joined the British East India Company. He was sent to Madras, India, and worked his way up in the organization. In 1687 he was made governor of Fort St. George in Madras, a post that he held until 1692. He stayed in India as a private merchant-trader and returned to London a wealthy man in 1699.

In 1701 a group of Connecticut clergymen started the Collegiate School, later to become Yale University. Most of the students lived in the homes of the founding clergymen-teachers, who were scattered in many towns in the colony of Connecticut. In 1716 the founders began to build in New Haven, but soon realized that they needed more money than could be raised locally. Jeremiah Dummer, the colony's agent in England, was interested in the school and asked Yale, who was already known as a philanthropist, for assistance. So, it is said, did Cotton Mather, one of the teachers at the school. One of them evidently suggested that the grateful trustees might name the school after the benefactor they so desperately needed: "If what is forming at New Haven might wear the name of Yale College, it would be better than a name of sons and daughters."

Thus persuaded, Elihu Yale, then close to 70, dispatched nine bales of goods, including books, rich fabrics from India, and a portrait of King George I. Sold on arrival in Boston, the goods brought 562 pounds and 12 shillings, the largest gift that the school would receive for more than 100 years. The trustees of the school heard the good news just before commencement in 1718 and immediately voted to name the new building Yale College.

Elihu Yale died in London on July 8, 1721, and was buried on July 22 in the churchyard of St. Giles in Wrexham, North Wales, near Liverpool, England. Yale College became Yale University in 1887.

First Presidential Veto Cast

On April 5, 1792, President George Washington cast the first veto in American legislative history.

The United States Constitution of 1787 gives the president the power to veto laws enacted by Congress. By the spring of 1792, during the Second Congress (1791–1793), an occasion had arisen for President Washington to exercise this power for the first time. Congress had enacted legislation concerning the apportionment of seats in the House of Representatives, which contained certain provisions that Washington disagreed with. Washington vetoed the bill on April 5 and returned it to Congress. Pursuant to the Constitution, Congress can override a veto, but only if two-thirds of the House of Representatives and two-thirds of the Senate vote to override.

On April 6, 1792, an attempt in the House to override the veto failed by a vote of 28 in favor of an override to 33 against. The Senate did not hold a vote, since it would be pointless after the action in the House, and thus Washington's first use of the chief executive's veto prerogative stood. In the centuries since 1792, many vetoes have been overridden by Congress, but the veto power remains one of the most potent weapons at the president's disposal in his dealings with Congress.

Bette Davis's Birthday

Ruth Elizabeth Davis, later known as Bette Davis, was born on April 5, 1908, in Lowell, Massachusetts. As a child she developed an interest in acting, which her mother encouraged. In the late 1920s she moved to New York and eventually landed a contract with Universal Pictures. One of her first films was *Bad Sister* (1931), in which she was cast with Humphrey Bogart, one of the most popular actors of the time.

Still only in her 20s, Davis won an Oscar for Best Actress after her performance in *Dangerous* (1935). She would go on to act in over 80 movies, earning a total of ten Academy Award nominations. In fact, legend has it that the nickname "Oscar" for the Academy Award comes from Davis, who thought that the trophy statuette given to Academy Award winners had a diminutive rear end that resembled the anatomy of her husband Harmon Oscar Nelson Jr.

Some of Davis's most famous movies include *Jezebel* (1938), *The Little Foxes* (1941), *Now, Voyager* (1942), *The Corn Is Green* (1945), *All About Eve* (1950), *John Paul Jones* (1959), *Whatever Happened to Baby Jane* (1962), and *Dead Ringer* (1964). Her last significant appearance was in *Wicked Stepmother* (1989). She died on October 6, 1989, in Neuilly-sur-Seine, France. During her lifetime, she was honored with the American Film Institute's Life Achievement Award, the first actress to receive one.

April 6

The United States Enters World War I

In the summer of 1914, the major European powers went to war. When the fighting ended more than four years later, 28 nations on five continents had become involved in the conflict. Alliance commitments and immediate threats to their national and economic security forced many countries to lose no time in placing their armies on the battlefield. Others, including the United States, attempted to maintain a neutral position and waited several years before making the momentous decision to declare war.

At the outset of hostilities in Europe, President Woodrow Wilson appealed to the people of the United States to be "impartial in thought as well as action." For many of the country's 32 million foreign-born people or children of immigrant parents, such disinterest in the outcome of the war was difficult. However, even among those who openly sympathized with one side or the other, there were few in 1914 who wanted the nation to intervene in the war. For almost three years, the United States clung to its neutral status despite numerous provocations both by the Allies (chiefly Britain, France, and Russia) and by the Central Powers (chiefly Germany, Austria-Hungary, and the Ottoman Empire of Turkey). As a neutral, the United States had the theoretical right to trade with any belligerent. In practice, the British blockade of the North Atlantic severely limited American commerce with Germany and Austria. The British even forbade commerce in such basics as foodstuffs, and forced neutral merchant vessels to put in at Allied ports, where they were searched for contraband goods. In addition, the British established import quotas for neutral nations located near Germany and blacklisted a number of American firms suspected of dealing with the enemy. The Wilson administration protested all of these measures, but to no avail.

The Germans were also a problem. The German navy planned to break the Allied blockade with its submarine fleet. A relatively new weapon, which could easily be destroyed when on the water's surface, the submarine or U-boat (from the German *Unterseeboot*), as it was also called, relied on surprise attack. It could not, as the ordinary rules of war required, search an enemy merchant ship for contraband and make provision for the safety of passengers and crew before sinking a vessel. In February 1915 the Germans announced their intention to launch submarine torpedoes without warning against all enemy merchant ships encountered in the waters surrounding the British Isles. Realizing the danger inherent in this policy for Americans traveling aboard non- American vessels, Wilson notified the Germans that he would hold them to "strict accountability" if any American citizens lost their lives or property because of Germany's submarine operations. On May 7, 1915, a German torpedo struck the British Cunard liner *Lusitania*, and 128 Americans died as the ship sank. Wilson strongly protested this action, and the German government finally assured him that it would modify its submarine activities.

Despite this promise, U-boat operations continued. On March 24, 1916, several Americans were injured when the French ship *Sussex* was torpedoed. Wilson threatened to break diplomatic relations with Germany unless that government immediately abandoned its "present methods of submarine warfare against passenger and freight-carrying vessels." The Germans did not want to risk American intervention in the war. For that reason, on May 4, 1916, they promised to discontinue sinking merchant ships without warning on the condition that the United States compel Britain to also account for its violations of neutral rights.

The *Sussex* pledge, as it was called, allowed the United States to remain neutral for a while longer, but in Europe the fighting continued. In December 1916 Wilson attempted to mediate a settlement of the war. This effort, like similar ones in January 1915 and January 1916, proved unsuccessful. Neither the Allies nor the Central Powers were interested in beginning negotiations to end hostilities, and Wilson's plea for a "peace without victory" went unheeded.

Until 1917 the United States was able to maintain its uneasy neutral position. Then, on January 31 of that year, the German government announced that it was about to renew total submarine warfare against merchant shipping in the waters off the British Isles and in the Mediterranean. The Germans realized that this action might bring the United States into the war on the side of the Allies, but they believed that they would be able to subdue England before American forces could be mobilized. Their strategy was very nearly successful.

On February 3, 1917, Wilson severed diplomatic relations with Germany, but the United States was still reluctant to enter the war. Congress even denied the President power to arm the nation's merchant vessels. However, Wilson was able to override what he considered to be the decision of "a little group of willful men representing no opinion but their own." His advisers uncovered a 1797 statute authorizing the president to arm the merchant fleet, and Wilson relied on this law.

By March 1917 it was becoming increasingly apparent that American interests were being jeopardized by the European war and that the United States would eventually be forced to intervene in the conflict. On March 1 Wilson made public the Zimmermann Note. This message from German foreign secretary Arthur Zimmermann to the German ambassador in Mexico had been intercepted by British intelligence. It proposed that the ambassador induce the Mexican government to ally itself with Germany if the United States went to war against the Central Powers; in return, Germany would help Mexico regain its "lost territory in New Mexico, Texas, and Arizona." The message also suggested that Mexico press Japan to ally itself with Germany.

The Zimmermann Note helped turn public opinion against Germany. Wilson called Congress into special session on April 2, 1917, and, announcing that "the world must be made safe for democracy," asked Congress to declare war (see also April 2, where the text of Wilson's war message is set forth).

It was a curious call to arms, since the Allies Wilson sought to join were far from committed to democracy. The Russians were in the midst of a revolution against their autocratic czar, and the British and French controlled vast colonial empires in Asia and Africa where the inhabitants had no say in their government. Nevertheless, on April 4 the House of Representatives approved the war resolution, and two days later the Senate also agreed. The United States had entered World War I.

Mormon Church Formally Organized

The Church of Jesus Christ of Latter-Day Saints, unofficially known as the Mormon Church, was formally organized on April 6, 1830.

The religious body had its inception in visions reportedly experienced by the prophet Joseph Smith Jr. in 1820 and 1823. By Smith's account, the first of these took place when he acted on the biblical promise of James 1:5, namely that "if any of you lack wisdom, let him ask of God, that giveth to all men liberally . . . and it shall be given him," and inquired which of the many contending Christian sects was right. He reportedly was informed that he must join none of them, for they were all in error.

It was in 1823, according to Smith, that he learned from the angel Moroni of the existence of secret records, written upon gold plates, that told of the ancient inhabitants of North America and set forth "the fullness of the everlasting Gospel" as Christ had delivered it to them after his Resurrection. Later, Smith would deduce from the mysterious, pictographic script on the plates that these ancient inhabitants were descended from Israelites via the tribe of Joseph, whose members had reached North America by migration.

In the visions of 1823, Smith recounted, he learned of the plates' location: hidden in a hill named Cumorah in ancient times. The hill was located between Palmyra and Manchester, New York. However, he related, although he visited the place annually as instructed, nearly four years passed before Moroni granted him permission to remove the plates and begin their translation with the aid of marvelous stones provided with them. Moroni, in Mormon belief, was the son of Mormon, a fourth-century prophet. According to Latter-Day Saints tradition, it was primarily Mormon's abridgment of earlier records that was preserved on the gold plates revealed to Smith.

The translation of the plates, which would appear as *The Book of Mormon* (published in 1830), was performed by Smith with the aid of the schoolteacher Oliver Cowdery and others, who transcribed the records from his dictation. It was in the course of the deciphering, according to Smith, that John the Baptist appeared to Cowdery and him on May 15, 1829, and ordained them into the Priesthood of Aaron. The priestly order, one of two recognized by Mormons, bears the name of the brother of Moses, generally regarded as the first high priest of Israel. Less than a year later, according to the testimony of Smith, the Apostles Peter, James, and John also appeared to the two men and bestowed upon them the Melchizedek

Priesthood, named for the biblical "priest of the most high God."

It was while *The Book of Mormon* was in the hands of the printer that Joseph Smith Jr., Oliver Cowdery, Hyrum Smith, Samuel H. Smith, Peter Whitmer Jr., and David Whitmer gathered at Fayette, New York, and organized the Church of Jesus Christ of Latter-Day Saints under New York state laws. The Mormons, with their hotly contested views and sometimes controversial customs, were hounded by prejudice, hostility, and the repeated threat of mob violence throughout their early years. It was the antagonism or suspicion of their non-Mormon neighbors ("Gentiles," as the Mormons called them) that lay at the root of each of their increasingly arduous migrations.

The first move (in 1831) was to Kirtland, Ohio, where the Latter-Day Saints built a temple. Subsequent removals found the Mormons successively establishing residence in western Missouri; in the place they named Nauvoo, Illinois; and ultimately in the Great Salt Lake Valley in Utah, where they founded Salt Lake City in 1847. Their arrival there, under the leadership of Brigham Young, signaled the end of a heroic trek. It included a disastrous encampment near the site of Omaha, Nebraska, where 600 died during the winter of 1846–1847. The journey also included passage over the difficult terrain of the Rocky Mountains. Indeed, the story of Mormon migration is one of the epics of the settlement of the West.

From the beginning, no difficulty deterred the Latter-Day Saints from those objectives they perceived as the will of God, particularly the restoration of what they believed to be the true church and Gospel of Christ in keeping with their founder's original calling. Within a month of the formal organization of the church on April 6, 1830, the Mormons sent out missionaries to the surrounding states. Missionaries were sent to Canada in 1833 and to Great Britain in 1837. Five years later, eight ships were chartered to carry Mormon converts from Britain to the United States. These steps were the beginning of the Mormon missionary work that in modern times encompasses hundreds of missions in dozens of countries.

North Pole Discovered

The discovery of the North Pole by men of three races on April 6, 1909, was the culmination of nearly a quarter century of effort. Those who reached the pole on that date were Robert E. Peary, a white man who originated and led the effort; Matthew A. Henson, an African American man who had served as ship's cook, carpenter, and blacksmith and then as Peary's servant before be-

coming his co-explorer and most valuable assistant; and four Eskimo guides (Coqueeh, Ootah, Eginwah, and Seegloo).

Peary, who was born at Cresson, Pennsylvania, on May 6, 1856, graduated from Bowdoin College in 1877. After graduation he served as a cartographic draftsman in the U.S. Coast and Geodetic Survey for two years before becoming an engineer in the navy in 1881. As part of the navy's corps of civil engineers, to which he remained attached until his retirement (with leaves for his explorations), he served as assistant engineer in chief of the Nicaragua Canal survey.

Having meanwhile become interested in Arctic exploration, Peary made his first trip to the far north in 1886. His association with Henson, whom he had met when the latter was a clerk in a Washington clothing store, dates from this first expedition, in which Henson, then about 19, served as a member of the crew. In Greenland, Peary and a Danish friend journeyed inland from Disko Bay and over the Greenland ice sheet for a distance of 100 miles, reaching a height of 7,500 feet above sea level.

Seven companions accompanied Peary on his second exploration of Greenland in 1891. They included his wife and Henson, who was to accompany him on all of his Arctic explorations and twice save his life, as Peary would once save his. On this tour, Peary made several contributions to scientific knowledge, the most important of which was the verification of Greenland's island formation. He also proved that the polar ice cap extended beyond 82 degrees north latitude and discovered the Melville meteorite on Melville Bay. Peary also encountered the "Arctic highlanders," an isolated Eskimo tribe. He befriended them, and they assisted with his later surveys. Henson, meanwhile, was learning the Eskimo language and becoming a master sled dog driver and an expert in the numerous other skills necessary for arctic survival.

Peary continued his work with further expeditions in 1893–1895 and voyages during the summers of 1896 and 1897. In 1898 he announced his intention to travel to the North Pole. During the next four years, he sought possible routes from camps at Etah on the northwest coast of Greenland and Fort Conger on neighboring Ellesmere Island. Despite all his efforts, he fell short of reaching the pole on several attempts, including those of 1902, when he reached 84 degrees 17 minutes north latitude, and 1905, when he reached 87 degrees 6 minutes.

Undaunted by these failures, Peary and his party set sail on July 17, 1908, on the ship *Roosevelt* on still another expedition to the pole. They spent the winter in a base camp on Ellesmere Island and on March 1, 1909, began the final trek north from Cape Columbia. On April 6, Peary and his party reached the top of the world. This was after days of exhausting effort during which they had traveled 18 to 20 hours a day, menaced by the cold and dwindling food supplies. Henson reached the pole first with two of the Eskimos. Peary, exhausted and barely able to walk, arrived 45 minutes later and took a reading, which confirmed Henson's calculation of their location. Henson then proudly planted the American flag at the North Pole, 90 degrees north.

The men built an igloo and camped for more than 30 hours at the pole, making astronomical observations. At 4:00 p.m. on April 7 they headed south and, with favorable conditions, made the return trip to Cape Columbia in 16 days. The effort cost the life of one Eskimo, who drowned during the return trip.

When Peary and his party reached Newfoundland, Canada, they found that they were not the only ones claiming to have reached the North Pole. Dr. Frederick A. Cook, who had served as the surgeon on Peary's 1891 expedition, said that he was the first to perform the feat, but his report failed to withstand scrutiny. The National Geographic Society accepted the discovery of the Peary expedition as the authentic one, and Congress voted its thanks and promoted Peary to rear admiral. This was in 1911, the year of Peary's retirement from the navy. He received numerous other awards as well, including the rank of grand officer of the French Legion of Honor, before his death on February 20, 1920. He was buried at Arlington National Cemetery in Arlington, Virginia, just outside Washington, D.C.

Henson received some of his recognition rather belatedly. In 1945 Congress awarded him a medal for "outstanding service to the Government of the United States in the field of science," and near the end of his life President Dwight D. Eisenhower honored him at the White House. Henson, born on August 8, 1866, in Charles County, Maryland, died at the age of 88 in New York City on March 9, 1955. He died two months before the death of Ootah, the last survivor of the trip to the Pole, who died near Thule, Greenland, at the age of 80 in May 1955.

April 7

National Cherry Blossom Festival

This is a movable event.

The National Cherry Blossom Festival, held annually in Washington, D.C., in April or late March depending on the weather and the state of the cherry blooms, had its origin in a friendly gesture by the city of Tokyo, Japan. In 1912 Tokyo mayor Yukio Ozaki gave 3,000 cherry trees to Washington as a symbol of Japan's wish for good relations with the United States. The first of the trees, which today surround Washington's graceful Tidal Basin, were planted on March 27, 1912, by First Lady Helen Herron Taft, wife of President William Howard Taft. She was accompanied by Viscountess Chinda, wife of Yasuya Uchida, the Japanese ambassador to the United States.

The first ceremony connected with the trees took place in April 1927, when some Washington schoolchildren reenacted the original planting. This pageant was repeated annually until 1934, when the District of Columbia government put on a more ambitious, three-day program including the crowning of the first Cherry Blossom Festival queen. The festival was discontinued during World War II, and several patriotic groups sought to have the trees destroyed since the country was at war with Japan. Fortunately, they were unsuccessful. Beginning in 1949, Cherry Blossom princesses were chosen from every state to participate in the festival.

The Washington Convention and Visitors Bureau became the sole sponsor of the postwar festival in 1948 and expanded the program to a week. In 1974 the National Conference of State Societies took over as sponsor, with the Downtown Jaycees sponsoring a related parade. As of this writing in the late 1990s, the National Cherry Blossom Festival is sponsored by National Cherry Blossom Festival, Inc., a coalition of public and private organizations. In 1994 the festival was expanded again to two weeks.

The festival is timed to coincide with the blossoming of the cherry trees, which usually takes place between March 20 and April 15. According to records maintained by the National Park Service, the earliest known blooming of the cherry trees on any given year was on March 15, 1990, and the latest was on April 18, 1958.

The *Alabama* Claims

On April 7, 1865, the United States and Great Britain began correspondence on the matter of damages arising from the Civil War. The Americans were the more aggrieved party, seeking compensation for the multimillion-dollar losses inflicted on their commerce by English-built Confederate warships. Captain Raphael Semmes's *Alabama*, the most notorious of these raiders, captured 62 merchant vessels in two years before the Union cruiser *Kearsarge* sent it to the bottom of Cherbourg harbor in June 1864. The *Alabama's* career was so remarkable that the whole controversy over war reparations was dubbed the *Alabama* Claims Dispute.

The United States charged that the British government had contravened its own foreign enlistment law of 1819, which prohibited British subjects from outfitting ships to engage in wars in which their country was neutral. The British only belatedly responded to the complaints of the American minister, Charles Francis Adams, thus allowing the *Alabama* to escape unmolested from its Liverpool shipyard. The Americans also charged that the British had not exercised adequate care to prevent other ships from operating out of their West Indian ports.

In their defense, the British pointed to their seizures in 1863 of the raider *Alexandra* and of two ironclad "Laird rams," all of which had been intended for Confederate use. The British government was willing to negotiate, however, and eventually the new American minister, Reverdy Johnson, and Prime Minister Gladstone's foreign secretary, Lord Clarendon, agreed to submit the question to an arbitrator. They concurred that the arbitrator was to be selected by four commissioners, with two each to be chosen by the United States and Great Britain.

Unfortunately, the road to compromise was not to be that smooth. Prodded by the bellicose Charles Sumner, who thought that the cession of Canada to the United States would provide a more proper solution, the Senate rejected the Johnson-Clarendon Convention by a vote of 54 to 1. Only when Senator Sumner lost his position as chairman of the Senate Foreign Relations Committee was President Grant's secretary of state, Hamilton Fish, able to obtain a settlement. In the resulting Treaty of Washington of 1871, the British government expressed regret and agreed to make reparations, the amount of which a tribunal of arbitration would determine. The president of the United States, the queen of England, the king of Italy, the president of the Swiss Confederation, and the emperor of Brazil each appointed one member to this board, which met at Geneva, Switzerland, from December 1871 to September 1872. The tribunal awarded the United States $15.5 million in gold for losses caused by the raiders, but rejected an American request for additional money to compensate for such "indirect" damages as the transfer of a number of ships to foreign registry.

This event marked one of the first times that two major nations used an international arbitration commission to settle a dispute amicably. On June 23, 1874, Congress created a court of claims to which American business interests could submit proof of their losses and collect their proper share of the British compensation. However, many years passed before all the cases were settled.

April 8

Ponce de León Claims Florida for Spain

Although the peninsula of Florida was sighted by earlier navigators (it was shown on the 1502 Cantino map of the New World), its first known European visitor was the Spanish adventurer and explorer Juan Ponce de León. On April 8, 1513, scarcely more than 20 years after Christopher Columbus's discovery of America, Ponce de León claimed Florida for Spain.

Juan Ponce de León was born in San Servos, León, Spain, about 1460. After fighting against the Moors of Granada, he accompanied Columbus on the latter's second voyage to America in 1493. From 1502 to 1504 he assisted in the conquest of Higuey, the eastern region of Hispaniola, and was appointed *adelantado* or governor of that province. On August 12, 1508, he found an excellent port on the island of San Juan Bautista, later to be renamed Puerto Rico, which had been discovered by Columbus in November 1493. Ponce de León explored the island in 1508, and became its temporary governor the following year. He and his companions established a colony at Caparra near what is now San Juan. Having apparently amassed a fortune in gold, land, and slaves, the explorer was ready for new adventures.

Ponce de León lived in an age in which adventurers were drawn to the Gulf of Mexico region in the hope of finding a passage to the Pacific or in quest of mythical riches and wonders. One prevalent myth was that related by the inhabitants of the Caribbean area about the Fountain of Youth, a spring whose health-restoring waters granted the mental and physical powers of youth to the aged. Peter Martyr, Ponce de León's contemporary and author of *The Decades of the New World or West*

India, addressed to Pope Leo X, wrote one of the few contemporary literary accounts of it:

> Among the islands on the North side of Hispaniola there is one about 325 leagues distant, as they say which have searched the same, in which there is a continual spring of running water, of such marvelous virtue, that the water thereof being drunk, perhaps with some diet, maketh older men young again. And I here must make protestation to your holiness not to think this to be said lightly or rashly, for they have so spread this rumor for a truth throughout all the court, that not only all the people, but also many of them whom wisdom or fortune hath divided from the common sort, think it to be true. But if you should ask my opinion herein, I will answer that I will not attribute so great power to nature, but God hath no less reserved this prerogative to himself. . . .

Ponce de León, having lived for some time in the West Indies, undoubtedly knew of this myth, although it is not known what his opinion of it may have been. In any event, the fabled spring did not figure prominently among the inducements that attracted him toward new adventure. A patent authorizing him to search for and conquer the unknown Bimini Islands north of Cuba, the supposed location of this spring, was granted by the Spanish king Ferdinand V on February 23, 1512. This patent dealt with more prosaic matters: the crown's share in any gold deposits and the subjugation of the natives as slaves in the mines. Although many scholars have now completely dismissed the tale about a fabulous fountain as motivation for Ponce de León's voyage, it is nevertheless possible that the Spanish adventurer (then aged 53) was not averse to including this quest among other tantalizing goals.

In any case, he sailed from Puerto Rico with three vessels on March 3, 1513, on a northwestern course. After landing briefly at San Salvador in the Bahamas, he threaded his way through uncharted islands. On March 27 he probably sighted one of the Abaco Islands (the most northerly of the Bahamas) and soon afterwards an extensive unknown coastline. Having no grounds for suspecting that the landmass was anything more than just another island, Ponce de León followed the coast northward. He probably sailed from near Palm Beach, Florida, to a spot somewhere between what are now St. Augustine and the mouth of the St. Johns River. There, near the 30th parallel, his expedition landed early in April and remained for a short time. On April 8, 1513, in the name of the Spanish king, Ponce de León took possession of the "is-land," which he named La Florida. The great Spanish historian Antonio de Herrera (1559–1625), who is thought to have had access to Ponce de León's original notes or logbook (now lost), wrote an account of the voyage. According to this, the area was named La Florida "because it had a very pretty view of many cool woodlands, and it was level and uniform: and because, moreover, they discovered it in the time of the Feast of Flowers (the season of Easter)."

Ponce de León continued northward briefly, but then reversed his course and returned southward along the Atlantic east coast of Florida, went around the Florida peninsula through the Florida Keys, and advanced up the west coast of Florida in the Gulf of Mexico. The native inhabitants of La Florida, then consisting of four tribes—the Calusa, Tegesta, Timucua, and Apalachee—resisted conquest. Further, there was no sign of gold, or of the rejuvenating waters of the Fountain of Youth.

After seven weeks of sailing, Ponce de León still had not circumnavigated the "island." Disillusioned, he turned back on May 23, 1513, and arrived in Puerto Rico, empty-handed, on September 21. In tracing much of the coastline of Florida, however, he had contributed a noteworthy geographical service.

After helping to quell a revolt that had flared up in Puerto Rico during his absence, Ponce de León returned to Spain in 1514. He seems to have given a highly favorable account of his exploits, since, on September 27, he obtained a royal grant to colonize "the island of Bimini and the island of Florida," of which he was appointed civil and military governor.

Other adventures, such as an expedition against the Caribs who inhabited the Lesser Antilles, as well as lack of finances, prevented Ponce de León from immediately embarking for Florida. Only in 1521 did he decide to take possession of the area under the authority of his patent. Gathering together two vessels and 200 men,

> as a good colonist, he took mares and heifers and swine and sheep and goats, and all kinds of domestic animals useful in the service of mankind: and also for the cultivation and tillage of the field he was supplied with all [kinds of] seed, as if the business of colonization consisted of nothing more than to arrive, and cultivate the land and pasture his livestock.

Sailing from Puerto Rico on February 20, 1521, Ponce de León and his companions probably landed near Charlotte Harbor on the west coast of Florida. Native American resistance and the outbreak of disease demoralized the Spaniards and hindered the growth of their colony, which persisted for five months. After its leader himself was severely wounded in a skirmish, the entire Spanish expedition abandoned the venture and sailed for Havana, Cuba. Juan Ponce de León died soon afterwards, in June 1521.

Expeditions by subsequent Spanish explorers, especially Pánfilo de Narváez and Hernando de Soto, established the fact that Florida was not an island and bolstered Spain's claim to an immense area covering much of the present southeastern United States. Alarmed at the encroachments of French adventurers in the early 1560s, King Philip II of Spain commissioned Pedro Menéndez de Avilés to drive out the French and firmly implant Spanish colonies in Florida. The founding of St. Augustine, the oldest city in the United States, in 1565, was therefore the first permanent result of the claim that Juan Ponce de León had made more than a half century before.

John Randolph and Henry Clay Fight a Duel

On April 8, 1826, Senator John Randolph of Virginia and Secretary of State Henry Clay, formerly the speaker of the United States House of Representatives for many years, fought a duel. It is noteworthy because it involved two such prominent individuals.

Biographies of John Randolph and Henry Clay are set forth at June 2 and April 12, respectively. Both men were distinguished figures in American politics during the early 19th century. Randolph was a supporter of Andrew Jackson. During the presidential election of 1824, Jackson was one of four candidates for the nation's highest office. The other candidates were John Quincy Adams, Secretary of State William H. Crawford, and Henry Clay. Jackson won the highest number of popular votes but did not secure the necessary majority in the electoral college, and so pursuant to the Constitution the election went to the House of Representatives to decide who would become the next president. Clay threw his supporters and his influence as former speaker of the House behind Adams, who was chosen as president. Like many of Jackson's supporters, Randolph was furious.

Randolph, who was a skilled speaker, launched scathing denunciations of both President Adams and Clay, who became Adams's secretary of state. Clay finally grew angry at the insults and challenged Randolph to a duel. The two men met on a dueling field on April 8, 1826, to settle their differences. They took careful aim at each other with their pistols, but both missed. (Given the inaccurate firearms of the period, this was not an uncommon occurrence.) In the second exchange of gun-

fire, Clay fired first and missed again. Randolph then deliberately fired his weapon into the air in order to miss Clay. Impressed by this gesture, Clay announced that his honor was satisfied, and the duel ended without injury to either man.

This episode was not the first instance in which political differences were resolved through the primitive institution of dueling. However, other political adversaries were not so lucky in avoiding injury. During the famous duel between Alexander Hamilton and Aaron Burr at Weehawken, New Jersey, on July 11, 1804, Hamilton was killed.

For centuries, dueling had been a form of private justice not only in the American colonies, but in England and most of Europe, especially where matters of personal honor were concerned. Duels were fought with swords or other weapons until firearms became widespread. The early dueling pistols were only accurate at short ranges and were prone to misfire or not fire at all. However, they presented a test of courage for the duelers, who would typically attempt to stand without showing fear while they exchanged shots with their opponent.

By the early 19th century, many states were acting to outlaw dueling, which was increasingly regarded as a barbaric custom. By the end of the century, the custom had virtually disappeared.

Death of Kurt Cobain

The body of "Generation X" icon Kurt Cobain was discovered on April 8, 1994. He had committed suicide in his home several days earlier, but his corpse was not discovered until an electrician came to his residence. Cobain was the lead singer and guitarist for Nirvana, a leading "alternative" or "grunge" rock and roll group of the late 1980s and early 1990s. It was this movement that made Seattle, Washington, one of the centers of the modern music industry.

Cobain was born on February 20, 1967, in Aberdeen, Washington. When he was eight years old, his parents separated. It was a traumatic event for Cobain, one that helped propel him into the rebellious world of garage bands and grunge rock. In the late 1980s he formed Nirvana with bass guitarist Krist Novoselic. Their debut album, *Bleach*, was recorded for less than $1,000, but it succeeded in gaining recognition for the group. In 1991, Nirvana released the album *Nevermind*, which sold millions of copies within months. This was followed by worldwide tours, and Cobain became both wealthy and famous.

Despite Nirvana's success, Cobain's personal life was far from happy. He suffered from gastrointestinal problems and a serious heroin addiction.

April 9

He underwent medical treatment for both problems, with no success. His marriage to entertainer and actress Courtney Love appeared to be a successful one, resulting in the birth of daughter Frances, but still Cobain could not find peace. Around April 6, 1994, he went into the garage of his Seattle home and killed himself with a shotgun. He left a rambling suicide note, which expressed his love for his wife and daughter.

Some detractors have accused Cobain of trying to become a martyr through suicide. Admirers compare him to Jim Morrison and other music pioneers, who happened to have unfortunate and ultimately tragic personal lives. As of this writing in the late 1990s, the true legacy of Kurt Cobain remains undetermined.

April 9

Lee Surrenders at Appomattox

On April 9, 1865, in the quiet town of Appomattox Court House, Virginia, General Ulysses S. Grant of the Union army accepted the surrender of General Robert E. Lee of the Confederacy. Lee's surrender effectively ended the American Civil War after four blood-stained years and the loss of more than 600,000 lives.

Time had run out for the Confederate States of America in the spring of 1865. General Grant was in Virginia, close to Richmond, the Confederate capital, and laying siege to the nearby city of Petersburg which supplied Richmond. On March 25, 1865, Lee unsuccessfully tried to smash through the besieging Union forces at Petersburg's Fort Stedman. After his defeat convinced him that the capital could not be held much longer, Lee made contingency plans, in case of a forced withdrawal, to extricate his men and go south to North Carolina. There, he hoped, they could join forces with General Joseph E. Johnston's troops.

The Union army had 115,000 men and the Confederate army 54,000. Grant used his numerical superiority to envelop the enemy. From March 30 to April 1 at Five Forks, detachments from the two armies fought for possession of the Southside Railroad, Lee's best hope for escape should Richmond and Petersburg fall. Union general Philip H. Sheridan's horsemen defeated Southern troops under General George E. Pickett and captured 5,200 of them.

Back at Petersburg, General Grant probed relentlessly at the Confederate lines. When Lee had to dispatch three brigades to cover the defeated Pickett's reorganization, the Union's VI Corps made a decisive breakthrough opposite Fort Fish-

er on April 2. The Confederates under General James Longstreet held Petersburg until nightfall, when the Southern troops evacuated that town and Richmond. General Godfrey Weitzel of the Union army entered the Confederate capital on April 3 and accepted its surrender.

From the Petersburg and Richmond area, the men of Lee's army headed for Amelia Court House, where they hoped to get desperately needed rations and take the Richmond and Danville Railroad south to join Johnston. Sheridan pursued the Confederates south of the Appomattox River, where one of General George A. Custer's Union cavalry brigades defeated an element of General Fitzhugh Lee's horse troops at Namozine Church on April 3. The rest of Robert E. Lee's men retreated north of the James River.

When the Confederates converged at Amelia Court House, they found no food and learned that Sheridan had reached Jetersville, thus cutting off the Richmond and Danville Railroad escape route. Lee had no choice but to lead his men to the west. On April 5 Sheridan sent General Henry E. Davies's cavalry brigade northwest from Jetersville to search for the enemy. At nearby Paineville, the First Pennsylvania Cavalry fell upon the Southerners' wagon train and burned 200 vehicles. The next day the Union forces destroyed the rear guard of General Richard S. Ewell's U.S. troops at Sayler's Creek. On April 6 the Southerners sustained between 7,000 and 8,000 casualties.

The remnants of the Confederate army reached Farmville, Virginia, on April 7. They received rations at last and were able to repulse Union attacks. Lee renewed the withdrawal that night. On the morning of April 8, Custer found another Confederate supply train at Appomattox Station and captured it along with 30 artillery pieces. He then proceeded a few miles northeast and discovered the Southern line of defense drawn up southwest of Appomattox Court House.

Hungry and exhausted, Lee's men could run no farther. The Southern commander knew that April 9 would be decisive. At 5:00 a.m. he sent Fitzhugh Lee's cavalry against hastily constructed earthworks along the Bent Creek Road. The Confederates were momentarily successful, but the Union infantry soon enveloped their position. When the II and VI Corps attacked Longstreet's rear guard, Lee knew the end had come. His opponent had written to him on April 7, inviting him to surrender, and now the Virginian said to his aides: "There is nothing left for me to do but to go and see General Grant, and I would rather die a thousand deaths."

General Lee put on a fresh dress uniform and rode to the farmhouse of Wilbur McLean in Appomattox Court House. At 1:30 p.m., General Grant arrived in his mud-spattered fatigues. The two men tried to ease the tension by conversing about the Mexican War, during which they had briefly met as comrades. They then quickly came to terms that were quite conciliatory. The Confederate officers and men were released upon giving their pledge to not take up arms against the United States again. The officers were permitted to keep their sidearms and horses. When Lee pointed out that some of his enlisted men also had their own horses and mules, Grant allowed those to be retained as well.

Joseph E. Johnston's army was still in the field, but he surrendered to General William T. Sherman at Durham Station, North Carolina, on April 18, 1865. President Andrew Johnson, who succeeded the assassinated Abraham Lincoln, rejected the originally proffered terms, which included concessions of a political nature, so Sherman obtained a simple military surrender on April 26.

La Salle Reaches the Mouth of the Mississippi River

Many explorers during the 16th and 17th centuries directed their efforts toward finding a water route leading west across the continent of North America to the Orient. These quests for a passage to the treasures of the East were futile. However, the early adventurers in the interior regions of what is now the United States did come upon a mighty north-south waterway. Early in 1682, René-Robert Cavelier, Sieur de La Salle, led the first party of Europeans to navigate the Mississippi from its juncture with the Illinois River to the Gulf of Mexico. On April 9, 1682, the expedition reached the river's mouth, and on that day La Salle claimed the vast territory lying on either side of the "Father of Waters," as well as on the borders of all its tributaries, for France.

La Salle was born in 1643 in Rouen, France. The son of a wealthy burgher, he received an excellent education. He attended the Jesuit college in his native city and then at the urging of his father entered the Society of Jesus to become a Jesuit. The regimented life of the Jesuits held little appeal for La Salle, and shortly after his father's death in 1665 he left the order. The following year, at the age of 23, he went to Montreal, where Jean Cavelier, his elder brother and a member of the Sulpician order, had settled. The Sulpicians, who held the seigneury of Montreal, assisted La Salle by granting him land along the St. Lawrence River.

For two years La Salle worked to develop his lands. However, stories of the West so attracted him that in 1669 he abandoned his agricultural efforts. In July of that year he set out from Montreal with a group of Sulpicians who intended to start missions in the West. Traveling up the St. Lawrence River to Lake Ontario, the party made its way west along the lake's southern shore. At a village on the far side of the lake, the expedition encountered the great French explorer Louis Joliet, who persuaded the missionaries to push on to the Northwest. La Salle, however, decided to continue on his own to explore the region south of Lakes Erie and Ontario.

The exact location of La Salle's adventures between 1669 and 1673 is unknown. He later claimed to have discovered the Ohio River and to have descended that waterway as far as the site of Louisville, Kentucky, during this period.

La Salle's explorations made him a favorite of the Comte de Frontenac, the governor of the French territories in North America known as New France, who shared his interest in the interior of the American continent. Shortly after becoming governor in 1672, Frontenac subdued the Iroquois and built a fortification on the northern shore of Lake Ontario (today the site of Kingston, Ontario), which he named after himself. Frontenac wanted official sanction for the fort, which he had erected on his own initiative, and a monopoly of the fur trade in the region. To accomplish these ends, he sent La Salle to France in 1674 to plead his case before the court. La Salle's mission was successful, and the explorer gained Fort Frontenac as a seigneury and exclusive rights to trade in the area.

After his return to America in 1674, La Salle used Fort Frontenac as a base of operations for his fur-trading ventures and probably for expeditions through the region of the upper Great Lakes. He returned to France in 1677 to seek additional favors from the king, and again he succeeded. He gained a title of nobility and permission to explore the West and trade in all furs except beaver.

The Jesuit priest Jacques Marquette and the explorer Louis Joliet came upon the Mississippi River and navigated its waters as far south as its junction with the Arkansas River in 1673. They had little interest in the waterway, since it flowed in a north-south direction, rather than westward across the continent. La Salle, however, realized the importance of the river and decided to claim the bordering lands for France. In 1679 he embarked on his first attempt to go down the Mississippi. Traveling by canoe, he and his companions went along the west shore of Lake Michigan from Green Bay to the mouth of the St. Joseph River in Michigan.

There the party joined with La Salle's chief lieutenant, Henri de Tonti, and the men under his command. The 34-member expedition then went up the St. Joseph, crossed overland to the Kankakee, and descended that river to the Illinois. Continuing their journey westward, they went down the Illinois and in January 1680 reached Lake Peoria, where they built Fort Crèvecoeur.

Late in February 1680, La Salle sent friar Louis Hennepin, together with Michel Accault (or Accou) and Antoine Auguella, to investigate the area of the upper Mississippi. Captured by the Sioux in April 1680, the three men were taken as prisoners to the region of Minnesota. The Sioux allowed their captives considerable freedom. Hennepin and his companions acquired knowledge of Minnesota and discovered the Falls of St. Anthony, at the site of Minneapolis, before another renowned French explorer, Daniel Greysolon, Sieur Duluth, effected their rescue in the summer of 1680.

Meanwhile, La Salle and four others returned to Fort Frontenac to settle outstanding debts and to obtain additional supplies. Starting early in the spring, they took 65 days to reach their destination. Business affairs detained La Salle at Frontenac for several months, and not until late autumn did he and his companions return to Fort Crèvecoeur.

While he was away, La Salle put Tonti in charge of Fort Crèvecoeur, and he had such confidence in his lieutenant that he expected upon his return to be able to continue his expedition to the Mississippi. This was not to be, however. During his absence, La Salle sent a messenger instructing Tonti to occupy a natural fortification, now known as Starved Rock, which he had noticed en route up the Illinois River. Tonti went north to this site, but later was forced to vacate it in the face of an imminent Iroquois attack. With Tonti occupied by this errand and La Salle at Frontenac, very few of the adventurers with the expedition were left to defend Fort Crèvecoeur. Faced with an impending attack by the Iroquois, the missionaries and defenders fled the fort.

As La Salle was making his way back to Crèvecoeur, he received word that the fort had been abandoned. Deeply concerned about the safety of Tonti, he journeyed as far as the Mississippi to search for him. La Salle finally returned east to Frontenac without finding any trace of his lieutenant. Tonti, who had been captured, managed to gain his freedom, and in June 1681 he and La Salle were reunited at Mackinac.

Undaunted by the failure of his first venture to the Mississippi, La Salle set out again early in 1682, accompanied by Tonti and more than 50 men. Traveling by way of the portage at Chicago

that had been discovered by Marquette and Joliet in 1673, the party reached the Mississippi on February 6, 1682. La Salle's expedition proceeded down the mighty river without difficulty, passing the site of New Orleans on April 6, 1682, and three days later arriving at the Gulf of Mexico. There La Salle unfurled the white Bourbon banner and claimed the lands watered by the Mississippi and all its tributaries "in the name of the most high, mighty, invincible and victorious Louis the Great, by Grace of God King of France."

To hold the area he had claimed, La Salle planned to establish forts and colonies in the Illinois region and at the mouth of the Mississippi. In December 1682 he started work on Fort St. Louis along the Illinois River. He sent two men to the site of Chicago to build another outpost at the important portage there, which provided a connecting link between the Great Lakes and the Mississippi. However, just as La Salle seemed about to cement his vast empire, Joseph Antoine Lefebvres, Sieur de La Barre, replaced Frontenac as governor of New France. Unlike his predecessor, La Barre did not favor La Salle, and took drastic measures against him, ordering the explorer to surrender command of his fort on the Illinois River and recalling him to Quebec to question him regarding alleged misdemeanors.

La Salle decided to take his case to the French monarch. Louis XIV had originally believed the explorer's expedition along the Mississippi to be "wholly useless." However, by the time La Salle arrived in France, that nation was at war with Spain and the king recognized the strategic value of holding the Mississippi against an enemy that was also interested in the area. After naming La Salle governor of Louisiana and restoring to him all of his former commands and privileges, Louis equipped the explorer with four ships so that he might establish a colony at the mouth of the Mississippi. The expedition left France in July 1684, but the mission was ill fated. The Spanish captured the main supply vessel, and La Salle became ill in the West Indies, where the expedition began to unravel during his long recuperation. After he continued on his way with less than half of his original contingent, his ships overshot the mouth of the Mississippi, landing instead at Matagorda Bay in Texas, where La Salle was disappointed in his initial hope that the bay would turn out to be the great river's western outlet.

The party built a fort near the Garcitas River and subsisted on the buffalo that inhabited the region. Their situation became desperate. Repeated attempts to find a land route to the Mississippi failed. Meanwhile, two of their remaining three ships had been wrecked and the third had returned to France. Finally, in 1686 La Salle and some others in the party made an effort to find their way to Canada to seek help. They again set off in search of the Mississippi, which they knew could lead them there. Their search was once again unsuccessful.

In January 1687, La Salle and about half of the 45 remaining members of the expedition once again went forth to try to obtain assistance. La Salle was not to survive. After traveling overland for several months, his men mutinied on March 18, 1687, near what is now Navasota, Texas. They killed La Salle and left the body of the man who had gained such a vast territory for France to be devoured by animals.

Hugh Hefner's Birthday

Hugh Marston Hefner, the famous and controversial founder of *Playboy* magazine, was born on April 9, 1926, in Chicago, Illinois. He had a strict Methodist upbringing, and his parents forbade cursing, drinking, smoking, and sexual activity. He attended the University of Illinois and graduated in 1949.

Hefner's upbringing must have contributed to his future career path. After college, he went to work for *Esquire* magazine, which at the time had a reputation for approaching the boundaries of sexual propriety. By modern standards, the articles and photographs in *Esquire* were somewhat tame, but for Hefner they were the inspiration to begin his own magazine and explore sexual issues that were considered taboo. After raising several thousand dollars from his friends, he began to publish *Playboy* in 1953.

Playboy, with its page-length pictures of nude and seminude women, was scandalous in the 1950s. Despite widespread criticism and some legal complications, however, the magazine thrived and by the 1960s was selling millions of copies a year. Hefner expanded his business into the Playboy Clubs, where women dressed in bunny outfits, served drinks, and provided entertainment for a largely male audience.

Hefner flaunted his fame and fortune, hosting elaborate parties at his Playboy Mansion and keeping dozens of female guests in his household. But he was in many ways still the product of his conservative midwestern upbringing. He preferred soft drinks to alcoholic beverages and refused to compete with more hardcore competition such as Larry Flynt's *Hustler*. Although not as hardcore as *Hustler*, Bob Guccione's *Penthouse* magazine also presented serious competition. *Playboy* began to lose market share, and the Playboy Clubs lost their popularity. Furthermore, public pressure and a

revitalized conservative Christian fundamentalist movement caused several chain stores, such as Seven-Eleven, to stop carrying *Playboy*.

In 1982 Hefner went into semiretirement, appointing his daughter Christie as president of his business. It proved to be an excellent choice, as Christie Hefner managed to revitalize the operation by focusing on a more upscale audience. As of this writing, Hugh Hefner enjoys a quiet life out of the public limelight. Whether he should be admired as a pioneer in the open discussion of sexual issues or reviled as a pornographer is a question for the reader and for history to decide, but it is certainly true that he was a groundbreaker in the field of magazine publishing and one of the most famous figures in the sexual revolution of the 1960s.

April 10

Salvation Army Founder's Day

When the Salvation Army celebrates Founder's Day, it marks the birthday of William Booth, the remarkable Englishman who began the organization.

William Booth was born on April 10, 1829, in Nottingham, England. His father, not very successful in his own trade as a builder, wanted a secure future for his son and therefore apprenticed him to a pawnbroker to learn what was a lucrative profession in 19th-century England. Behind the pawnbroker's counter, young Booth was barraged by situations of human misery and economic suffering; it was an experience that influenced his whole life's work. Another factor, equally important, helped mold the man and his career. When he was about 15, Booth experienced religious conversion in a Wesleyan Methodist chapel. He felt particularly drawn to preaching, and while he was a pawnbroker's apprentice he served locally as a Methodist lay preacher.

At age 19, his apprenticeship over, he sought work in the pawnshops of Nottingham. Failing to find a position, in 1849 he finally moved to London, where he found employment with a pawnbroker in Walworth. There, too, he dedicated his hours after work to preaching. However, he wanted to be involved in more evangelical work than was possible in his duties as an official lay preacher, so he began holding open-air meetings, a move that did not sit well with his local minister. Booth subsequently joined the Methodist New Connexion, the first group to secede from the Wesleyan Methodist Church, and after completing his studies he was ordained as a minister in 1858.

April 10

Catherine Mumford (1829–1890) was one of the group that left the original Methodism, and she and Booth were married in 1855. Catherine Mumford Booth was as remarkable as her husband. Brought up by religious parents, she was schooled in the theology of the day. Because of poor health in adolescence, she received most of her education at home. The invalid youngster grew into a strong-minded woman, an untiring social worker who spent her time and energies for and among the poor and championed social causes such as women's rights. Her belief that women had the right to preach the Gospel was outlined in the cogent pamphlet "Female Ministry" (1859), and she set an example by beginning to preach in her husband's church at Gateshead, in the north of England, in 1860. Her talent for oratory, combined with her religious convictions and her dedication to social causes, later made her a well-known speaker at meeting halls in London's West End. It was because of her urging and support that William Booth gave up his secure life as a Methodist minister to embark in 1861 on a career of itinerant evangelism, which he felt was his true vocation.

After four years of traveling and preaching throughout England, Booth severed all connections with formal religion, largely because his plan for taking the Gospel message to city slum dwellers was too radical for his church to accept. He became an independent evangelist and settled with his family in London in 1865. Invited to speak at open-air and tent meetings in London's East End, a slum district notorious for its crime rate, human degradation, and misery, Booth made his first appearance there on July 2, 1865. The Salvation Army consequently regards that day as its founding date.

Before long, Booth was regularly leading outdoor meetings in the East End and getting a tremendous response. His religious zeal and genius for organization instilled in the people he reached the desire to reach out and help others in turn. His movement, first called the East London Revival Society, soon became known as the Christian Mission. In 1878 it was renamed the Salvation Army and carefully organized with military ranks, uniforms, flags, bands, and books of orders and regulations, with Booth as its first commander.

It was Booth's initial intention simply to bring the Gospel to the millions of people who had never attended any church. Most of all, he wanted to reach those people who, he thought, might not be welcomed by "respectable" church congregations. Soon, however, he realized that his preaching could not be optimally effective while people lacked the basic essentials of food, shelter, and warm clothing. Therefore, the work was expanded from street preaching to the organization of social reforms and the establishment of food and shelter depots, children's homes, and agencies for helping discharged criminals. Soon people began to refer to members of Booth's army as the purveyors of "soup, soap, and salvation."

Booth really did reach for "lost souls." Before he was scheduled to speak at a rally, he would send out word to the far reaches of the slum areas, "Come, drunk or sober." Salvation Army members would go to street corners, as they still do, and there play drums, cornets, and tambourines to attract audiences. As crowds gathered, the group would preach the Gospel and offer hope to the people in the audiences.

For many years the Salvation Army was greeted with a great deal of hostility, which came from the more conventional forms of organized religion and also from established society and government. Some of the opposition even came from the poor whom Booth was trying to help. The army's street preachers were kicked, beaten, and showered with eggs, and the very people who bore the brunt of these attacks were sometimes placed in jail for disturbing the peace. Despite all obstacles, however, the organization finally prevailed. Its numbers grew vastly, as did the variety of work in which members engaged, endeavoring to meet human need in any form.

Soon the Salvation Army was carried to many nations. In 1880 George Scott Railton and seven women were sent from England to organize the Salvation Army in the United States. Their efforts were received by Americans very much as the efforts of William Booth had first been received in London. However, in the course of time the value of their work was appreciated, and Railton and his successors received valuable support from people interested in helping the unfortunate and destitute. In addition, the Salvation Army established outposts in 18 other countries around the world during the 1880s.

In 1890 Booth, in collaboration with W. T. Stead, published his most influential book, *In Darkest England and the Way Out*. In this work he explained his efforts and gave concrete proposals for relieving poverty and loneliness, dealing with vice and moral danger, and salvaging wasted lives. Slowly Booth was given recognition: by the city of London, which made him a freeman; by Oxford University, which conferred an honorary doctorate upon him; and by the British government, which invited him to the coronation of King Edward VII in 1902. That same year, Booth accepted an invitation to open a session of the United States Senate with a prayer.

Catherine Mumford Booth lived to see only some of the honors and recognition conferred upon her husband and the organization that she had so effectively helped to build. She was "promoted to glory," in the Salvation Army's phrase, in 1890 in Clacton, England. The Booths' eight children had also played roles in building the Salvation Army. After their mother's death, however, two sons and a daughter left the organization because of disagreements and dissension. One of these was Ballington Booth, who later formed the Volunteers of America, an organization in some respects similar to the one he had left.

In spite of increasing loss of sight and ultimately blindness, Booth continued his evangelical and humanitarian works until he was past 80. He made his last public appearance in London's Royal Albert Hall on his 83rd birthday. Four months later, on August 20, 1912, he died in London.

Although he lived in the Victorian age, when such issues were avoided, William Booth did not shrink from discussions of poverty, prostitution, illegitimacy, homelessness, hunger, alcoholism, drug addiction, and crime. He dealt with them by providing homes, training schools, soup kitchens, hospitals, and other needed services. Counseling, help in adjustment for released prisoners, work rehabilitation programs, a missing persons bureau, camps, residences, family service agencies, rehabilitation programs for alcoholics and drug addicts, and daycare centers are some of the services that the Salvation Army now provides. The group also works in times of disaster—such as wars, earthquakes, floods, and fires—when it provides food, shelter, clothing, and comfort to victims.

April 11

Charles Evans Hughes's Birthday

Charles Evans Hughes, the 11th chief justice of the United States Supreme Court, was born in Glens Falls, New York, on April 11, 1862. The only son of Mary Catherine Connelly Hughes and the Reverend David Charles Hughes, a Baptist preacher who had emigrated from Wales in 1855, he was a precocious youth. He completed high school at the age of 13, and after a year of independent study he enrolled at Madison (now Colgate) University. Hughes remained at the school for two years, but when his father accepted the pastorate of a Baptist church in Providence, Rhode Island, in 1878, he transferred to Brown University so that he might continue to live near his parents. His academic record at Brown was outstanding; he was elected to Phi Beta Kappa and graduated third in his class in 1881.

Photo by Harris and Ewing, Collection of the Supreme Court of the United States.

Charles Evans Hughes

After teaching for a year in Delhi, New York, Hughes entered Columbia University Law School. Again he excelled in his studies; at his graduation in 1884 he received his LL.B. degree with highest honors and was presented with a three-year fellowship. That same year he was also admitted to the bar and began practicing law with the distinguished New York City firm of Chamberlain, Carter and Hornblower.

By 1891 Hughes's relentless attention to his work had severely impaired his health. To regain his strength, he temporarily gave up private practice and accepted a teaching position at the Cornell University Law School in Ithaca, New York. In 1893 he returned to New York City, where be became associated with the firm of Carter, Hughes, and Dwight and at the same time served as a special lecturer at both the Cornell University Law School and the New York Law School.

Hughes's public career began in 1905. He first served as counsel to a New York state legislative commission investigating gas costs, and then directed a probe into the practices of the state's insurance companies. His efforts in both investigations met with great success. His disclosures drastically curtailed the corrupt practices of the state's utility companies, and he won nationwide recognition for changing New York's insurance business "from a public swindle into a public trust."

Running on the Republican ticket in 1906, Hughes defeated his Democratic rival, the publisher William Randolph Hearst, to win election as governor of New York. He was reelected in 1908, and his two terms in office were notable for several major reforms. New York became one of the first states in the nation to establish a Public Service Commission to regulate utility rates, and the governor also secured legislative approval for labor and welfare bills, changes in the operation of the state government, and laws designed to reduce illegal racetrack gambling.

In 1910 President William Howard Taft named Hughes associate justice of the United States Supreme Court. Hughes's appointment occurred just as the Court began to hear cases testing the constitutionality of new Progressive legislation. It was a critical period in the history of American reform: If the Court upheld the Progressives' laws, it would open the way to more extensive federal and state involvement in matters such as regulation of industry and railroads, limitation of working hours, and prohibition of child labor. If the Court found this legislation unconstitutional, the reform movement would be severely set back. Hughes understood the significance of these cases, and the majority of his opinions during his six-year tenure reflected his support for most of the Progressive reform efforts.

In 1916 Hughes resigned from the Court to accept the Republican nomination for president. During the months before the election he toured the country in an effort to defeat his Democratic rival, the incumbent president Woodrow Wilson. Wilson, however, had widespread support because of his domestic policies and efforts to maintain American neutrality in World War I. He won the election, and Hughes left public life to resume his private law practice.

He returned to government service in 1921, when Republican president Warren G. Harding selected him to be secretary of state. As the head of the State Department, Hughes negotiated a separate peace with Germany after the Senate rejected the Treaty of Versailles. Even more important, he did his utmost to ensure American participation in world affairs despite the country's policy of isolationism after World War I. Hughes won worldwide acceptance for his scheme of naval arms limitations; he was largely responsible for the adoption of several treaties designed to stabilize the politics of the Far East; he assisted several Latin American countries in settling their boundary disputes; and he gained approval for the Dawes Plan to reduce German reparations payments and thereby restore the European economy. However, despite his repeated efforts, the Senate refused to approve U.S. membership in the League of Nations.

In 1925 Hughes resigned as secretary of state and once again devoted himself to private legal practice. The firm of Hughes, Rounds, Schurman and Dwight represented some of the largest corporations in the country. Hughes was also active in the field of international cooperation. Between 1926 and 1930 he served at various times as a member of the Permanent Court of Arbitration at the Hague, as chairman of the U.S. delegation to the Pan American Conference, and as a judge of the Permanent Court of International Justice.

The nomination of Hughes for chief justice of the United States Supreme Court in 1930 by President Herbert Hoover elicited an adverse reaction from liberals in the Senate. During the 1920s the conservative members of the Supreme Court had declared unconstitutional many laws designed to effect social and economic change. Hughes's activities as a corporation lawyer made him a perfect symbol of all that the liberals found objectionable in the Court. They agreed with Senator George Norris of Nebraska when he said of Hughes, "No man in public life so exemplified the influence of powerful combinations in the financial and political world," and they worked hard to block his nomination. The Senate's heated debate over Hughes lasted four days, but on February 14, 1930, he was confirmed as chief justice by a vote of 52 to 26.

During the 1930s, cases testing the constitutionality of the highly controversial and innovative New Deal measures came before the Court. Since the four conservative justices (George Sutherland, Willis Van Devanter, James McReynolds, and Pierce Butler) consistently rejected this legislation and the liberal coalition of Louis Brandeis, Benjamin Cardozo, and Harlan Stone as frequently upheld it, the votes of the unaligned Hughes and his colleague Owen Roberts were critical in determining the fate of many New Deal laws. Hughes agreed with the majority of the Court when it struck down the National Recovery Administration and the Agricultural Adjustment Act in 1935 and 1936, while his votes helped sustain such other important legislation as the Tennessee Valley Authority, the Wagner Act, and Social Security laws.

Hughes served as chief justice until 1941, when he wrote to President Franklin D. Roosevelt that "considerations of age and health make it necessary that I be relieved of the duties which I have been discharging with increasing difficulty." He died in Osterville, on Cape Cod, Massachusetts, at the age of 86 on August 27, 1948.

Congress Proclaims Cessation of American Revolution Hostilities

Although the Treaty of Paris, which officially established peaceful relations between Great Britain and the new United States, would not be signed until September 3, 1783, and ratified by Congress until January 14, 1784, the American Revolution had effectively ended with the British surrender at Yorktown on October 19, 1781. Thus, in response to the progress made during the peace treaty negotiations, on April 11, 1783, Congress issued a proclamation declaring a cessation of hostilities. This proclamation, edited in some minor respects, is set forth below:

By the United States of America in Congress Assembled. A Proclamation, Declaring the Cessation of Arms, as well by Sea as by Land, agreed upon between the United States of America and His Britannic Majesty; and enjoining the Observance thereof.

Whereas Provisional Articles were signed at Paris on the Thirtieth Day of November last, between the Ministers Plenipotentiary of the United States of America for treating of Peace, and the Minister Plenipotentiary of His Britannic Majesty to be inserted in and to constitute the Treaty of Peace proposed to be concluded between the United States of America and his Britannic Majesty, when Terms of Peace should be agreed upon between their Most Christian and Britannic Majesties:

And Whereas Preliminaries for restoring Peace between their Most Christian and Britannic Majesties were signed at Versailles, on the Twentieth Day of January last, by the Ministers of their Most Christian and Britannic Majesties:

And Whereas Preliminaries for restoring Peace between the said King of Great Britain and the King of Spain were also signed at Versailles, on the same Twentieth Day of January last.

By which said Preliminary Articles it hath been agreed, That as soon as the same were ratified, Hostilities between the said Kings, their Kingdoms, States and Subjects, should Cease in all Parts of the World; and it was farther agreed, That all Vessels and Effects that might be taken in the Channel and in the North Seas, after the Space of Twelve Days from the Ratification of the said Preliminary Articles, should be restored; that the Term should be One Month from the channel and

North Seas as far as the Canary Islands inclusively, whether in the Ocean or the Mediterranean, Two Months from the said Canary Islands as far as the Equinoctial Line or Equator; and lastly, Five Months in all other Parts of the World, without any Exception or more particular description of time or Place:

And Whereas it was Declared by the Minister Plenipotentiary of the King of Great Britain, in the Name and by the express Order of the King his Master, on the said Twentieth day of January last, that the said United States of America, their Subjects and their Possessions shall be comprised in the above mentioned Suspension of Arms, at the same Epochs, and in the same manner, as the three Crowns above mentioned, their Subjects and Possessions respectively; upon Condition that on the Part, and in the Name of the United States of America, a similar Declaration shall be Delivered, expressly Declaring their Assent to the said Suspension of Arms, and containing an Assurance of the most perfect Reciprocity on their Part:

And Whereas the Ministers Plenipotentiary of these United States, did, on the same Twentieth Day of January, in the Name and by the Authority of the said United States, accept the said Declaration, and declare that the said States should cause all Hostilities to Cease against His Britannic Majesty, his Subjects and his Possessions, at the Terms and Epochs agreed upon between His said Majesty the King of Great-Britain, His Majesty the King of France, and His Majesty the King of Spain, so, and in the same Manner, as had been agreed upon between those Three Crowns, and to produce the same Effects:

And Whereas the Ratifications of the said Preliminary Articles between their Most Christian and Britannic Majesties were exchanged by their Ministers on the Third Day of February last, and between His Britannic Majesty and the King of Spain on the Ninth Day of February last:

And Whereas it is Our Will and Pleasure that the Cessation of Hostilities between the United States of America and his Britannic Majesty, should be conformable to the Epochs fixed between their Most Christian and Britannic Majesties;

We have thought fit to make known the same to the Citizens of these States and we hereby strictly Charge and Command all our Officers, both by Sea and Land, and others, Subjects of these United States, to Forbear all Acts of Hostility, either by Sea or by Land, against His Britannic Majesty or his Subjects, from and after the respective Times agreed upon between their Most Christian and Britannic Majesties as aforesaid.

And We do further require all Governors and others, the Executive Powers of these United States respectively, to cause this our Proclamation to be made Public, to the end that the same be duly observed within their several Jurisdictions.

Done in Congress, at Philadelphia, this Eleventh Day of April, in the Year of our Lord One Thousand Seven Hundred and Eighty-Three, and of our Sovereignty and Independence the Seventh.

Civil Rights Act of 1968

On April 11, 1968, President Lyndon B. Johnson signed the Civil Rights Act of 1968 into law. The legislation made it a federal crime to engage in such activities as harming civil rights workers, crossing state borders to incite riot, and manufacturing, selling, or demonstrating firearms and certain kinds of explosives for use in riots. In addition, it extended broad rights to Native Americans in their dealings with the courts, with their tribal governments, and with authorities on the local, state, and federal levels. Perhaps the most important part of the act banned racial discrimination in the sale and rental of approximately 80 percent of the homes and apartments in the United States.

Before 1968, a number of states had passed "open housing laws," barring racial discrimination in the selling and renting of real estate. Many observers believed that these statutes were important steps toward eventually ending the racial polarization of American society and urged Congress to adopt similar federal legislation against segregated housing. As early as 1966, President Johnson proposed an open housing bill to Congress, but despite strong support from some members, the majority were reluctant to approve such a measure.

In both 1966 and 1967, Congress refused to pass an open housing bill, and opponents of the legislation were hopeful of again defeating a fair housing statute in 1968. Then, early in April 1968, the civil rights leader Martin Luther King Jr. was killed by an assassin's bullet (see April 4). King's murder outraged the nation and precipitated riots in the urban ghettos of cities across the country.

A few weeks before King's death, the National Advisory Commission on Civil Disorders, which President Johnson had established after the Detroit and Newark riots of 1967, had made public its findings. In its report, the commission warned of the prevalence of white racism and noted that "our nation is moving toward two societies, one black, one white; separate and unequal." The wave of violence that swept the nation in April 1968 dramatized the commission's grimly prophetic findings. The combined circumstances of King's death, the riots that followed, and the commission's call for "common opportunities for all within a single society" helped spur Congress to act affirmatively on the Civil Rights Act of 1968.

By April 10, 1968, both the Senate and the House of Representatives had approved the bill, and on April 11, 1968 (exactly one week after the assassination of King), President Johnson signed it into law. Recalling the long and arduous battle to gain enactment of the bill, Johnson said:

We did not get it in 1966. We pleaded for it again in 1967, but the Congress took no action that year. We asked for it again this year, and now at long last this afternoon its day has come.

I do not exaggerate when I say that the proudest moments of my Presidency have been times such as this when I have signed into law the promises of a century.

As President Johnson stated after signing the new legislation, "In the Civil Rights Act of 1968 America does move forward and the bell of freedom rings out a little louder."

April 12

The Civil War Begins

The sectional conflict that led to the firing on Fort Sumter on April 12, 1861, had a long history. The institution of slavery had plagued the United States from the nation's earliest existence. At the time of the American Revolution, critics of the patriots' opposition to Great Britain asked how the colonists could decry tyranny while holding half a million people in bondage. Some Southerners withheld support of the Declaration of Independence until Thomas Jefferson agreed to delete from it his denunciation of slavery. At the Constitutional Convention in 1787, the founding fathers spent days arguing about slavery, the slave trade, and the effect of the presence of a host of unfree blacks in the South on proposals concerning taxation and representation.

In the first half of the 19th century, the North grew rapidly. It began to industrialize, and millions of immigrants came to the region to work in the factories. The South, however, stayed mostly agricultural and fell behind in population and economic power. This caused a shift in political power, as the House of Representatives, which is based on population, was increasingly dominated by the North. To prevent Congress from being dominated by the North, the South began to focus on the other chamber, the Senate, where every state is guaranteed two seats regardless of size. Accordingly, the South advocated the expansion of slavery into the western territories that would one day become states. Major political battles ensued as Northerners became increasingly angered by the expansionist appetite of the "slavocracy" and Southerners developed an intense fear of the national government as a threat to their slave society.

Only grudging accommodations prevented even greater troubles. The Compromise of 1820 admitted Missouri to the Union as a slave state in return for the entrance of Maine as a free state, thus preserving the South's equal voice in the Senate. The Missouri Compromise also forbade the extension of slavery into the Louisiana Territory above a specific northern latitude.

Many Americans condemned the War with Mexico from 1846 to 1848 as an attempt by supporters of the South to extend the area available for slavery. Twice during the conflict, David Wilmot, a Pennsylvania Democrat, won strong Northern support by proposing a ban on the introduction of slavery into any territory taken from Mexico, but Congress rejected this Wilmot Proviso. The Compromise of 1850 partially calmed the North by establishing California as a free state and by ending the slave trade in the nation's capital of Washington, D.C.; on the other hand, the South received a strong law requiring the return of fugitive slaves.

After 1850, hopes of compromise faded as slavery became a moral issue beyond political solution. Harriet Beecher Stowe's *Uncle Tom's Cabin*, which appeared in book form in 1852, filled many Northerners with repulsion for the treatment of human beings as mere chattels. The decision of the Supreme Court in the Dred Scott case of 1857—that the Missouri Compromise represented an unconstitutional limitation on the property rights of slave owners—alienated even more residents of the free states.

Southerners also found the situation intolerable. Denounced as immoral, they countered with a description of slavery as a benefit that "civilized" the slave. Angered by the cries of abolitionists, slaveholders saw little reason why they should not have the opportunity to extend the institution to the western territories. Political parties, the vehicles of compromise, found themselves unable to overcome the new spirit of discord. Reflecting the inflexibility of their constituents, the Democratic Party broke into factions, and the Whigs totally disbanded. Gradually, dissidents from all camps formed the Republican Party, which was based on opposition to the extension of slavery. Both Republicans and Democrats recognized that the 1860 presidential election would be crucial.

Senator Stephen A. Douglas of Illinois, the leading contender for the Democratic nomination, advocated that the residents of the territories, prior to admission to the Union, have the power to accept or outlaw slavery within their own areas. Antislavery Northerners distrusted Douglas because he had formulated the Kansas-Nebraska Act of 1854 (see January 29), which applied this policy of "popular sovereignty" to the Kansas and Nebraska territories. Southerners disliked Douglas because he argued that people could keep slave owners out of their territories by simply not passing the police regulations necessary to maintain the system.

Douglas remained the strongest candidate when the Democratic convention opened in Charleston, South Carolina, on April 23, 1860, but he did not have enough strength to control the gathering. When a majority of the delegates accepted popular sovereignty as part of the platform, the representatives of eight Southern states walked out, making it impossible for Douglas to garner the two-thirds vote necessary for nomination. The Democrats adjourned and reconvened in Baltimore, Maryland, on June 8, but the Southerners again bolted rather than accept Douglas. The remaining delegates thereupon nominated him.

Dissident Southern Democrats held their own convention in Baltimore on June 28, 1860, and drew up a platform demanding an equal opportunity to take part in the settlement of the territories. They then nominated John C. Breckenridge of Kentucky for president. In May the newly formed Constitutional Union party, a coalition of conservatives from several defunct political organizations, had also met in Baltimore and chosen John Bell of Tennessee to run on a platform denouncing sectionalism and encouraging support of the Constitution.

The Republicans had convened in Chicago, Illinois, on May 16, jubilant over the chaotic state of the Democrats. They nominated Abraham Lincoln of Illinois, Douglas's unsuccessful opponent in the 1858 senatorial election and a foe of the extension of slavery into the territories. Lincoln received 1,866,452 votes in the November 6, 1860, election, only a plurality of those cast, but he won the necessary majority in the electoral college with 180 votes, not one of which came from a slave state. Douglas obtained 1,375,157 votes, but his strength was so dispersed that he garnered only 12 electoral ballots. Breckenridge won 847,953 votes and 72 electoral votes, all from slave states. Bell won 590,631 votes and 39 electoral votes from slave-owning border states.

Many Southerners were unable to reconcile themselves to Lincoln's election. Although he claimed not to be an abolitionist, he was the candidate of the North's antislavery party. Furthermore, Lincoln's victory confirmed the increasing political and economic dominance of the Northeast and West. Unable to maintain their relative strength, Southerners looked away from the Union toward a country of their own. On December 20, 1860, South Carolina, the most defiant of the Southern states, repealed its ratification of the United States Constitution and announced its secession from the United States. Mississippi, Florida, and Alabama followed suit in 1861, on January 9, 10, and 11, respectively. The similar actions of Georgia on January 19, Louisiana on January 26, and Texas on February 1 brought to seven the number of rebellious states. On February 4 the first six met in Montgomery, Alabama, to form the Confederate States of America, and Texas soon joined the new confederation as well.

Not all Southerners were in accord with the secessionists. Some, known as cooperationists, wanted to give Lincoln time to show his intentions: If he proved to be an abolitionist, then the slave states could leave with a demonstration of unity rather than in a piecemeal manner. Georgia cooperationists conducted a vigorous but futile campaign against secession. In Texas, Governor Sam Houston, an ardent Unionist, held out until the secessionists forced him to call a special convention. That gathering decided that Texas should withdraw from the Union, and it won the approval of a plebiscite for its decision.

James Buchanan remained in the White House during the opening months of the secession crisis. A lame-duck president with Southern sympathies, he was politically and psychologically unable to act effectively against the rebellious states. Other leaders took up the slack and attempted to engineer a compromise satisfactory to the contending sections. Senator John J. Crittenden of Kentucky put forward the most important proposal, which offered federal protection for slavery in the states where it already existed and permission for the institution to expand into the Southwest.

Lincoln had no authority to act prior to his inauguration, but he exerted a powerful behind-the-scenes influence. Through his friends, the president-elect made it clear that he would not accept any proposal that authorized the extension of slavery into the territories and thus doomed the hopes of Crittenden and others who wished to conciliate the South. The nation could only wait for the March 4 ceremony at which the new president would take office and announce his plans.

In his first inaugural address, Lincoln outlined his obligations and intentions, but he avoided a call to action. He declared the constitutional separation of the states to be as impossible as a physical one, and he affirmed that he had an "oath in Heaven . . . to preserve, protect, and defend" the United States. Yet Lincoln offered to support a constitutional amendment that would guarantee the domestic institutions of the states, including slavery, and promised that the federal government would not resort to violence unless attacked. The new president ended his speech with the hope that "the mystic chords of memory, stretching from every battlefield and patriot grave to every living heart and hearthstone all over this broad land, will yet swell the chorus of the Union when again touched, as surely they will be, by the better angels of our nature."

Once in office, Lincoln had to deal with the gravest threat to the national government, the demand of the Confederate States of America for the surrender of the four remaining federal forts in the South. Forts Jefferson and Taylor in Florida appeared secure, but to assure the safety of Fort Pickens, Florida, Lincoln ordered troops waiting in Pensacola harbor to join the forces already at that outpost. In January 1861, however, the *Star of the West*, a merchant steamer bearing reinforcements and provisions for Fort Sumter, had been driven away from Charleston harbor by South Carolina forces. By the time of Lincoln's inauguration, Major Robert Anderson's garrison at Fort Sumter had supplies for only six additional weeks.

On March 5, 1861, the day after Lincoln assumed office, Secretary of State William H. Seward brought the president letters from Anderson, reporting that his situation was virtually hopeless. In light of the commander's pessimism, Seward and the aged General Winfield Scott advised the president to surrender Fort Sumter. During the following weeks, Seward and Scott continued to bring Lincoln messages from Southern Unionists and Northern conservatives, urging him not to provoke South Carolina lest the remaining slave states also declare secession. On March 15 the cabinet advised the president to withdraw Union forces from the fort.

Many Americans strenuously opposed any concession on Sumter, however. Some Republicans advised the president that surrender to the Confederates on this point would destroy both the party and the government. Postmaster General Montgomery Blair and his father, Francis P. Blair, formerly a trusted adviser of Andrew Jackson, warned Lincoln that to evacuate the fort would be an ignominious "surrender of the Union." Blair's brother-in-law, Gustavus Vasa Fox, a retired naval officer, presented a plan to relieve Sumter with troops and supplies.

The president kept his silence for several weeks. While sending Fox to inspect Fort Sumter, Lincoln also dispatched his friend Stephen A. Hurlbut, who had relatives in Charleston, to visit the South Carolina capital. On March 27 Hurlbut reported that even the moderates in the state would fire on any ship that attempted to bring provisions, let alone troops, to Sumter. After a state dinner on March 28, Lincoln informed his cabinet that Scott now advocated abandoning both Pickens and Sumter as a means of guaranteeing the support of the remaining slave states for the Union. The proposal did not sit well with the cabinet. The next day the cabinet reversed its former position, and all the members save Seward argued that Lincoln should hold both Pickens and Sumter. The President then issued orders for expeditions to both outposts.

On April 1, Secretary Seward, dismayed by the failure of his policy to win acceptance, offered a desperate alternative solution. He advocated that the president conciliate the South by yielding Sumter while holding Pickens and unify the nation through the creation and exploitation of a crisis with a foreign nation. Lincoln rejected the proposal and stated that his policy would be to maintain all federal positions.

On April 4, Lincoln told Fox to carry out his plans for an expedition including a chartered steamboat with 200 soldiers and one year's provisions, a gunboat, three tugs, and three warships, one of which was later diverted to the Pickens convoy. The president advised Major Anderson of the mission and, on April 6, dispatched a message to the governor of South Carolina to inform him of the shipment of provisions to Fort Sumter. The South Carolina authorities dared not allow the reinforcement of Sumter, lest the fort indefinitely threaten the activity of one of the Confederacy's leading ports. The governor ordered General Pierre G. T. Beauregard on April 11 to demand Anderson's surrender. The Union major asked for permission to delay evacuation until his supplies ran out, but the Confederates, aware that the relief ships were approaching, refused his request.

The Confederates gave Anderson until 4:00 a.m. on April 12, 1861, to surrender Fort Sumter. When the major held firm past the deadline, Beauregard ordered the Charleston shore batteries to fire on the fort. It is often alleged that it was Edmund B. Ruffin, the South Carolina radical, who pulled the lanyard that set off the first shot. At 2:30 p.m. on April 13, after 34 hours of intense but bloodless bombardment, the Union troops, their ammunition expended, surrendered their burnt-out post. In the interim, Fox's ships arrived and, with the permission of the Southerners, took the defenders off their island fort. Jefferson Davis, the president of the Confederate States, condemned Lincoln's Sumter policy as a maneuver designed to make the South appear to be the aggressor.

In the attempt to provision Sumter, Lincoln followed a strategy of calculated risk to preserve the Union. The president believed that the government would gain nothing by the surrender of Sumter, but he also recognized that any expedition to provision the fort would be fraught with risks. The North might suffer a psychological defeat if the mission failed; worse, the federal government might well seem the aggressor if in the course of the operation the Confederates managed to draw the first fire from the fort.

The firing on Fort Sumter began the Civil War. On April 15, 1861, Lincoln issued a proclamation asking the states to provide 75,000 militiamen to put down the insurrection in the South. On April 19 he ordered the navy to blockade the ports of the Confederacy.

The state of Virginia, previously divided on the question, declared its secession from the Union on April 17. A number of Virginians who were leaders in the U.S. Army, most notably Robert E. Lee, followed their state into secession. Arkansas, Tennessee, and North Carolina also joined the Confederacy, on May 6, 7, and 20, respectively. The slave states of Delaware, Maryland, Kentucky, and Missouri remained loyal to the Union. The Delaware legislature raised troops in response to Lincoln's call, and pro-Northern elements in Maryland, with the aid of the federal government, arrested officials with Confederate sympathies. Kentucky at first announced its neutrality, but it called for federal troops when it was invaded by the Southern army. Missouri underwent an internal conflict to determine its allegiance, with the pro-Union forces gaining victory by March 1862.

Confederate armies enjoyed early successes, especially on July 21, 1861, at the first battle of Bull Run in Virginia, near Washington, D.C. There General Joseph E. Johnston repulsed an attack by Union forces under Brigadier General Irvin Mc-

Dowell and, with the aid of reinforcements under General Thomas J. ("Stonewall") Jackson, drove them in a disorderly retreat toward Washington. Northerners were shocked by the Confederate victory, and Lincoln replaced McDowell with Major General George B. McClellan.

Northern armies were more successful in 1862, although the Confederates scored a repeat victory near Bull Run on August 29 and 30, 1862. Earlier in the year, Union forces under General Ulysses S. Grant had defeated the Confederates in Tennessee at Fort Henry on February 6 and at Fort Donelson on February 16. Grant's men turned what was almost a defeat into a victory at Shiloh in Tennessee on April 6 and 7. On September 17, McClellan won a technical victory in one of the bloodiest battles of the war, defeating the Southerners in a near standoff at Antietam, Maryland. The killed and wounded totaled close to 24,000, more or less evenly divided between the two sides. McClellan's victory gave President Lincoln enough political leverage to issue on New Year's Day, 1863, the Emancipation Proclamation, ordering the freeing of slaves in areas controlled by the rebels (see January 1).

The turning point of the Civil War came in 1863 with the Union victory at Gettysburg, Pennsylvania, which ended the South's attempt to invade the North and end the war. On July 4, Grant accepted the surrender of Vicksburg, Mississippi, thus assuring Northern control of the Mississippi River and dividing the South in half. These twin successes ended all Southern hopes of obtaining aid from friendly foreign nations such as Great Britain.

Union forces continued the attack in 1864. General William T. Sherman set out from Chattanooga, Tennessee, on May 7 on his famous march through Georgia and captured Atlanta on September 2. On November 14, Sherman began his March to the Sea, during which his men cut a wide path of destruction between Atlanta and the port city of Savannah, which fell on December 22. In the spring of 1864, Grant began a siege of nearly 10 months outside Petersburg, Virginia, near the Confederate capital of Richmond. The costly operation eventually brought final victory.

By the spring of 1865, the Southerners were no longer able to hold off their opponents. On April 2, the Confederate commander, General Robert E. Lee, evacuated both Petersburg and Richmond. Grant requested Lee's surrender on April 7, and two days later he received it at Appomattox Court House, Virginia. Lee's surrender virtually ended the war (see April 9). Northerners rejoiced at the restoration of the Union, but the assassination of President Lincoln by John Wilkes Booth on April 14 brought a time of mourning rather than celebration.

The Civil War was the costliest war in American history. Between 33 and 40 percent of the Union and Confederate soldiers involved became casualties. The North suffered 359,528 dead and 275,175 wounded, while the South suffered 258,000 dead and at least 100,000 wounded. The social, economic, and psychological devastation cannot be calculated.

Henry Clay's Birthday

Henry Clay, the Great Compromiser and legislative leader of the pre–Civil War period, and three times candidate for the presidency, was born in Virginia's Hanover County on April 12, 1777. He was the seventh of nine children of prosperous parents, John Clay and Elizabeth Hudson Clay. High-spirited, impulsive, intelligent, and above all ambitious, he was far from handicapped by his lack of formal schooling. As a young man he studied under two of Virginia's most noted lawyers, after being named secretary to one of them, and was admitted to the bar at the age of 20.

Preceded by his mother, Clay soon moved to a land of opportunity for young lawyers, namely Kentucky, then the scene of frequent land-claim litigation. In 1797 he settled in Lexington, then the cultural center of the frontier, and two years later he married Lucretia Hart, the daughter of a wealthy local businessman. Shrewd, skillful in debate, and with a flair for oratory, he became one of Kentucky's leading lawyers by the time he was 23.

He entered politics as a Jeffersonian Republican. He served from 1803 to 1806 as a member, and from 1807 to 1809 as speaker, of the Kentucky legislature. In 1806 and again in 1809, the state of Kentucky sent him to Washington to fill unexpired terms in the United States Senate. After that, Clay was seldom absent from the national capital. Elected to the U.S. House of Representatives, he served there, usually as speaker, from 1811 until 1825 (except for a period devoted to personal affairs from 1821 to 1823). An ardent nationalist who favored American expansion and championed the economic interests of western pioneers, he joined them in their demands that the British (long suspected of instigating Native American attacks) be forced out of Canada and compelled to recognize American rights on the high seas. With John C. Calhoun (see March 18), he headed the young congressional War Hawks who pushed President James Madison into the War of 1812 with Britain. Two years later, Clay was one of the commissioners who negotiated the Treaty of Ghent which established peace.

Back in Congress, Clay popularized, although he did not invent, the "American system" associated with his name, namely a program designed to bring prosperity to the United States. The program called for the development and interdependence of the country's three major regions and their products: the East (manufactures), the South (cotton), and the West (food). Clay accordingly advocated passage of the tariff acts of 1816 and 1824 to protect manufacturers, and he backed legislation for internal improvements at government expense, including new roads and canals. Reversing his earlier position on another big issue of the day, he also favored creation of the second Bank of the United States as a guarantor of a stable currency and proposed that revenues from the sale of public lands be distributed to state governments. He became the great champion of recognition for the new Latin American republics and futilely nurtured hopes of being named secretary of state by President James Monroe. In 1819 he incurred the enmity of Andrew Jackson by urging that Jackson be censured for his invasion of Florida (see March 15).

Outspoken though he was, Clay was also congenial and could be conciliatory. He performed what may have been his greatest service as a compromiser. In 1820 he became known as the "Great Pacificator" for his tact in dealing with the controversy over Missouri's admission to the Union as a slave state. To ease the furor, he helped frame the famous Missouri Compromise, which was designed to preserve the balance between free and slave states and, it was hoped, to settle similar questions in the future. Under its provisions, Missouri was admitted as a slave state and Maine as a free state, and slavery was prohibited in the Louisiana Territory north of a specified northern latitude running east to west across the country.

It was during James Monroe's second term as president that the Jeffersonian Republican organization broke into factions, one of which later became the Democratic Party, headed by supporters of Jackson. The presidential election of 1824 saw four major candidates: Jackson, John Quincy Adams, William H. Crawford, and Clay. Clay, as speaker of the House, was the most powerful man in Congress. He was also in the position of kingmaker, since the election ended with no clear victor, and pursuant to the Constitution the House would have to elect the next president. Clay controlled enough votes to decide the election, and to the everlasting resentment of Jackson, he swung his support to Adams. Jackson had received more popular votes, but Adams became president and named Clay secretary of state, a position he held from 1825 to 1829.

When Jackson defeated Adams for the presidency in the election of 1828, Clay retired temporarily to the 600 stately acres of Ashland, his estate in Lexington, from which he fired off criticisms of Jackson's administration and maintained contact with national political leaders. In 1831 Clay was elected to the Senate. Later the same year, he became a presidential nominee on the National Republican ticket. He was soundly defeated by Jackson in the ensuing election, largely because of Clay's support of the national bank.

Clay served in the Senate from 1831 to 1842 and from 1849 to 1852. He helped to conciliate South Carolina, eliminating the threat of secession during the so-called nullification crisis, by sponsoring the compromise tariff of 1833. The next year, the Senate adopted Clay's resolution censuring President Jackson for having removed government deposits from the national bank. The resolution was expunged in 1837. Jackson's successor, Martin Van Buren, skirted the troublesome bank issue by establishing an independent federal treasury system over Clay's opposition.

In 1840 the ever aspiring Clay was denied the Whig nomination for president. William Henry Harrison, a man less prominently identified with the bank issue, ran successfully against Van Buren, but died after a month in office. The fact that Harrison's successor, Vice President John Tyler, was a supposed Clay supporter did not save Clay from a period of frustration during which most of his legislative proposals were defeated or vetoed by the president.

Clay resigned from the Senate in 1842. When Tyler's unsuitability for the Whig leadership became apparent, the party, in search of a candidate for 1844, turned to Clay. He ran against the ardent expansionist James K. Polk, a Democrat, and went down bitterly to his third defeat in a presidential election. He hoped in vain for renomination in 1848. By then, however, he had reached the age of 71, and the Whigs passed him by in favor of a military hero, General Zachary Taylor, who became the nation's 12th president.

When Clay returned to the Senate in 1849, it was just in time to serve his nation once more as the Great Compromiser. His Compromise of 1850 was designed to quell the growing controversy between North and South over the extension of slavery into new territories. The compromise provided, among other things, that California would be admitted as a free state and that the large territory acquired as a result of the Mexican War would be organized without regard to slavery. With its passage, sectional tensions eased and the Civil War was postponed for a decade.

Clay, whose health had already begun to fail in the year of his last great triumph, declined steadily thereafter. On June 29, 1852, he died of tuberculosis in Washington's National Hotel. Four of his 11 children survived him. Clay was buried in the heart of Kentucky's bluegrass country at Lexington Cemetery.

Halifax Independence Day

April 12 commemorates the date in 1776 when the provincial congress of North Carolina authorized the colony's delegates to the Second Continental Congress to join with representatives from the other colonies in a Declaration of Independence. Several factors precipitated this first official sanction of separation from Great Britain, including the increasing realization that the mother country would never agree to American demands and the growing belief in the possibility of a colonial military victory.

On the eve of the American Revolution, political sentiment in North Carolina was fairly evenly divided. The Lowland Scots and Scotch-Irish, who had come to the colony early in the 18th century and controlled North Carolina's government, provided the impetus for the patriot movement. The Highland Scots, who had recently settled in the Piedmont region and resented exclusion from public office by the earlier arrivals, formed the core of Loyalist support. In August 1775 the royal governor, Josiah Martin, had been forced to flee to the safety of a British ship anchored in the Cape Fear River, but, recognizing the strength of the Loyalists, he represented to the home government that if they were supported by a body of British troops the colony might be kept under control.

In the winter of 1775–1776, a British force under Sir Henry Clinton was sent to North Carolina. Commissions were issued to influential men in the colony. These men, under the direction of Governor Martin, enlisted about 1,500 Loyalists. The patriots, aware of what was going on, called out the militia and took the field under Colonel James Moore. When Sir Henry Clinton was expected at Cape Fear, 80-year-old General Donald McDonald, in command of the Loyalist force, moved to join him. Colonel Moore ordered parties of militia to post themselves at Moore's Creek Bridge, over which McDonald would have to pass. The patriots fought a decisive battle at this bridge on February 27, 1776, defeating the Loyalists, taking 850 prisoners, and capturing a large store of military supplies. Inspired by this victory, on April 12 delegates elected to a provincial congress that met at Halifax, North Carolina, unanimously adopted a resolution allowing their representatives to the

Second Continental Congress "to concur with the delegates of the other Colonies in declaring Independency."

April 13

Thomas Jefferson's Birthday

Library of Congress

Thomas Jefferson

Unique in the wide range of his interests and talents, Thomas Jefferson, the third president of the United States, was undoubtedly one of the most gifted of Americans. A leader in the American Revolution, he was also a statesman, diplomat, scholar, linguist, writer, philosopher, political theorist, architect, engineer, scientist, and farmer. He was honored at home and in Europe as the foremost American thinker of his time.

Thomas Jefferson was born at Shadwell, his family's farm in Goochland County, Virginia, on April 13, 1743. His father, Peter Jefferson, had married Jane Randolph, a member of one of the most prominent families in Virginia, and become a successful planter, surveyor, and member of the House of Burgesses. Young Thomas enjoyed the advantages of a scion of a leading Virginia family. He received his early training in small private schools and then went to the College of William and Mary in Williamsburg, from which he graduated in 1762. He completed his education by reading law with Judge George Wythe, the outstanding legal teacher of the era, and was admitted to the bar in 1767.

At the age of 14, Jefferson, who was the eldest son, inherited the 2,500-acre Shadwell estate and its 30 slaves from his father. During the decade preceding the American Revolution, he supplemented the income from Shadwell with that of his thriving law practice. He entered the colony's House of Burgesses in 1769, and at the age of 27 he became a county lieutenant. On January 1, 1772, he married Martha Wayles Skelton, a widow and the daughter of John Wayles, a prominent lawyer. They lived at Shadwell, where Jefferson was in the process of building Monticello, the home he had personally designed. The couple would have five children, two surviving to adulthood.

Jefferson was one of a number of young men, including Patrick Henry and Richard Henry Lee, who took the lead in opposing England's colonial policy in the 1770s. In 1773 these three were among the 11 men appointed by the House of Burgesses to an intercolonial committee of correspondence to voice grievances. In 1774 Jefferson wrote "A Summary View of the Rights of British America," his most important contribution to pre-Revolutionary thought. Grounding his position on a philosophy of natural rights, he argued that Parliament had authority over neither internal nor external colonial affairs. He then went on to claim that only through the king were the provinces bound to England.

On June 21, 1775, two months after the beginning of the Revolution, Virginia sent Jefferson to the Continental Congress. His first major act was the writing, with John Dickinson, of the "Declaration of the Causes and Necessities of Taking Up Arms." This document, adopted on July 6 by Congress, stated that colonists would die before they were enslaved by Britain and implied that America might possibly accept a foreign ally. Jefferson soon thereafter drafted a letter to the British prime minister, Lord North, rejecting North's proposal that the American colonies tax themselves for their own defense rather than be taxed by Britain.

By the spring of 1776, American sentiment was strongly in favor of independence from Britain. In June, Congress appointed a committee consisting of Jefferson, Benjamin Franklin, John Adams, Robert Livingston, and Roger Sherman to draw up a Declaration of Independence. The committee decided that Jefferson should draft the document, and accepted it with few changes. Perhaps his most enduring work, the Declaration of Independence eloquently expresses his belief in a political theory based upon natural rights and reflects the influence of the English philosopher John Locke and of French theorists. It is also evidence of the increasing radicalism of Jefferson and many of his contemporaries: In 1774 he had accepted the king as the tie to Britain, but in 1776 he rejected even this connection, supporting the revolutionary position with a listing of "abuses and usurpations" on the part of King George III.

Jefferson returned to Virginia during the Revolution. In September 1776 he left the Continental Congress and again took a seat in the House of Burgesses. There he worked hard to implement the theories underlying the Declaration of Independence in Virginia, most of which was then controlled by a small number of rich slave owners. He was instrumental in obtaining the abolition of the feudal vestiges of primogeniture and entail, and he drafted an ordinance (later used as a model for the First Amendment) for religious freedom, which, when passed, disestablished the Anglican Church. He also initiated a public school system. All these measures worked to undermine social stratification based on artificial privileges. However, his efforts to curtail the major abuse of Virginia society met with failure, for he was not able to win acceptance for his proposals to end the slave trade and to gradually emancipate the slaves.

Jefferson became governor of Virginia in 1779. The British invaded the state during his administration from 1779 to 1781. Some critics claimed that Jefferson's handling of Virginia's defenses was inept, but a legislative investigation later cleared his name. He remained out of office for two years afterward and used the respite from the controversy to write *Notes on the State of Virginia*, which was published in Paris in 1785. The death of his wife on September 6, 1782, left Jefferson disconsolate; in 1783 he was elected to Congress and decided to accept the office to help overcome his depression.

During his one-year stay in Congress, Jefferson devised and was responsible for the adoption of the nation's decimal system of currency. He also drew up the Ordinance of 1784, which never went into effect but which served as the basis of the Northwest Ordinance three years later. In addition, he worked on the Land Ordinance of 1785, the provisions of which are still used today in determining township boundaries. Jefferson left Congress in 1784 to go to France to negotiate a commercial treaty. There he succeeded Benjamin Franklin as minister to France and served in that post until 1789. Meanwhile, in his private life, he seems to have begun an intimate relationship with the slave woman Sally Hemings, continuing over several decades. DNA evidence suggests that he fathered one of her children.

The Constitutional Convention took place in 1787 while Jefferson was absent from the United States, and at first he worried about the instrument of government that the convention had produced. He was sent a draft of the Constitution by James Madison and approved it, but was disturbed by the omission of a bill of rights to preserve individual freedom. His qualms were removed, however, when a bill of rights was promised, and he accepted the position of secretary of state in the new United States government under President George Washington.

In his new office, Jefferson found himself frequently at odds with Alexander Hamilton, the secretary of the treasury. Domestically, he opposed Hamilton's attempt to strengthen the national government at the expense of the states. In foreign affairs, Jefferson sympathized with the French revolution against despotism, and wished to support France in its struggle against external enemies such as Britain. Hamilton, on the other hand, wanted the United States to be allied with Britain. Despite Jefferson's efforts, Hamilton's policies gained favor with President Washington, and on December 31, 1793, Jefferson resigned in protest.

Jefferson returned to private life for three years, but even in his absence those who were disenchanted with the administration looked to him as their leader. These dissidents had formed an Antifederalist faction strong enough to attempt to win control of the government in the national election. The Antifederalists, then called Republicans, came to be known as Jeffersonian Republicans or Democratic-Republicans. By the 1830s they were officially known as the Democrats.

In 1796 Jefferson became vice president under the Federalist president John Adams. He opposed a number of Federalist measures, such as the Alien and Sedition Acts, which restricted individual liberties, including freedom of speech and of the press. He drafted resolutions passed by the legislature of Kentucky, which declared that the states had the right to judge when the national government overstepped its constitutional limitations.

When Adams and Jefferson met in the presidential election of 1800, the latter was victorious. In the electoral college, both he and Aaron Burr, also a Democratic-Republican, received 73 votes, but the House of Representatives declared Jefferson president and Burr his vice president. Ironically, Hamilton, his former archrival, was one of his stronger supporters, since Hamilton distrusted Burr even more than he disapproved of Jefferson. Jefferson's greatest achievement as president was probably the 1803 purchase from France of the 828,000-square-mile Louisiana Territory for $15 million, virtually doubling the nation's size,

and his dispatching of Meriwether Lewis and William Clark to explore the newly acquired land.

In 1804 Jefferson was reelected president. One of his major concerns during his second administration was preventing American involvement in the Napoleonic wars between Great Britain and France, while safeguarding the rights of Americans as citizens of a neutral nation. Repeated futile efforts, including the passage of the Non-Importation Act of 1806 and diplomatic negotiations, were made to halt the increasing British seizures of American vessels and the impressment of their seamen. In June 1807 the British frigate *Leopard* fired upon the American frigate *Chesapeake* when the *Chesapeake*'s captain refused to let the vessel be searched for British deserters. In an attempt to salvage American neutrality, Jefferson signed the Embargo Act, which virtually forbade all trade with foreign nations. This measure was so unpopular and economically injurious that in 1809, just before he left office, Jefferson was obliged to sign the Non-Intercourse Act, which replaced the Embargo Act and permitted trade with all nations except England and France.

After 60 years of government service, Jefferson retired to Virginia, where he remained for the rest of his life. There he assumed the task of founding the University of Virginia at Charlottesville. He led the legislative campaign for establishment of the university, and was also the architect of the buildings and the curriculum; procured the faculty, books, and scientific equipment in England and on the Continent; and served as chairman of the governing board. The university opened in 1825 with an enrollment of 40 students.

At Monticello, Jefferson spent time renovating his home, experimenting with farming methods, and designing mechanical devices. He served as adviser to Presidents James Madison and James Monroe and renewed his friendship with John Adams, with whom he carried on an extensive correspondence. Jefferson died on July 4, 1826, the 50th anniversary of the Declaration of Independence. John Adams also died that same day.

A number of impressive monuments honor Jefferson. A 60-foot-high head of Jefferson, along with the heads of George Washington, Abraham Lincoln, and Theodore Roosevelt, was designed and carved by Gutzon Borglum on the cliff of Mount Rushmore National Park, 25 miles south of Rapid City in the Black Hills of South Dakota (see also the following essay).

Jefferson Memorial Dedicated

Washington, D.C., is the site of the Jefferson Memorial, which was dedicated on April 13, 1943.

Rudolph Evans's 19-foot-tall statue of the third president of the United States stands on a black granite pedestal in the center of the domed, white marble memorial beside the cherry-tree-rimmed Tidal Basin. Jefferson's own words adorn the memorial's inner walls, one of which bears what must be his most famous utterance, from the Declaration of Independence:

> We hold these truths to be self-evident, that all men are created equal, that they are endowed by their Creator with certain unalienable Rights, that among these are Life, Liberty, and the pursuit of Happiness. That to secure these rights, Governments are instituted among Men. . . . We . . . solemnly Publish and Declare, That these . . . Colonies are, and of Right ought to be Free and Independent States. . . . And for the support of this Declaration, with a firm reliance on the Protection of Divine Providence, we mutually pledge . . . our Lives, our Fortunes and our sacred Honor.

Jefferson's pledge, "I have sworn upon the altar of God eternal hostility against every form of tyranny over the mind of man," is inscribed around the base of the dome that covers his monument.

April 14

Abraham Lincoln Assassinated

It was on April 14, 1865, at about 10:30 p.m., that President Abraham Lincoln was fatally shot in the back of the head as he sat in a box seat at Ford's Theatre in Washington, D.C., while viewing a performance of *Our American Cousin*, by Tom Taylor. The assassin, John Wilkes Booth, felt his action would somehow help the devastated South, which had just recently surrendered to the Union. Booth was apprehended 12 days later at a farm near Bowling Green, Virginia, where he too was fatally shot (either by himself or by a pursuing soldier, Boston Corbett). President Lincoln, who never regained consciousness, was taken across the street to a boarding house owned by William Petersen, a tailor, and died there at 7:21 on the morning of April 15.

In life, Lincoln had had his political foes. In death he had almost none. The nation now embarked on a demonstration of grief that was as remarkable for its depth as for its unanimity. The poet and biographer Carl Sandburg described the country's shock at the death of Lincoln:

Thousands on thousands would remember as long as they lived the exact place where they had been standing or seated or lying down when the news came to them, recalling precisely in details and particulars where they were and what they were doing when the dread news arrived.

Lincoln, who had dreamed of the event beforehand, was the first U.S. president to be assassinated. He was also the first president to lie in state in the rotunda of the Capitol, where his body was on view on April 19 and 20, after lying in state at the White House. The next day his bier was conveyed to the railroad station, where it commenced a long journey back to Springfield, Illinois, his home for 24 years before he became president. The funeral procession, which reversed the route Lincoln had followed to his first inauguration, took 12 days. The train, draped in dark bunting, made stops en route while people in Baltimore, Harrisburg, Philadelphia, New York, Albany, Utica, Syracuse, Cleveland, Columbus, Indianapolis, and Chicago paid their respects.

It was Lincoln himself who had unknowingly pointed to the appropriateness of Springfield as his place of burial. Departing from there on February 11, 1861, to assume the presidency, he had expressed himself, characteristically, with a candor all could comprehend:

> My friends, no one, not in my situation, can appreciate my feelings of sadness at this parting. To this place, and the kindness of these people, I owe everything. Here I have lived for a quarter of a century, and have passed from a young man to an old man. Here my children have been born, and one is buried. I now leave, not knowing when or whether ever I may return, and with a task before me greater than that which rested upon Washington. Without the assistance of that Divine Being who ever attended him, I cannot succeed. With that assistance, I cannot fail.

His funeral in Springfield was held on May 4, 1865. Secretary of War Edwin M. Stanton spoke the most memorable words as he looked on the lifeless face of Lincoln: "Now he belongs to the ages." The two most famous memorials to Lincoln are the Lincoln Memorial by Daniel Chester French in Washington's Potomac Park, facing the Washington Monument and the Capitol across a long vista, and the 60-foot-high head of Lincoln at Mount Rushmore. The sculpture of Lincoln's head, along with those of Presidents George Washington, Thomas Jefferson, and Theodore Roosevelt, were designed and carved by Gutzon Borglum on the towering cliff of Mount Rushmore

National Memorial, 25 miles south of Rapid City in the Black Hills of South Dakota.

Pan American Day

April 14 is Pan American Day, a time for emphasis on the culture, contributions, and harmonious interrelation of Latin and North American nations. The first official celebration took place in 1931, but its origins go back much further to what is frequently called the first Pan American Conference. This gathering, called and presided over by President Benjamin Harrison's secretary of state, James G. Blaine, opened in Washington, D.C., on October 2, 1889, and remained in session until April 21, 1890. Officially, it was titled the First International Conference of American States.

On April 14, the date still celebrated, the conference adopted a resolution forming what has since grown in scope to become the Organization of American States (OAS), the world's oldest international organization and a powerful force for preserving hemispheric peace and cooperation. Initially, however, the organization was more immediately concerned with the collection and distribution of commercial information, and its name was the International Union of American Republics. Composed of nations in North, Central, and South America, the union operated from a permanent office in Washington, D.C. Subsequently designated the Pan American Union, the Washington office continued to serve as the OAS's permanent general secretariat.

It was on May 7, 1930, that the governing board of the International Union of American Republics adopted a resolution setting forth the desirability of observing a day to be known as Pan American Day in all the American republics. The proposal went on to suggest April 14, the date of the resolution that had created the Union of American Republics, as an appropriate date. According to the recommendation, each government represented in the union was to designate that day as Pan American Day and provide for the display within its borders of the flags of the various American nations.

The governments acted on the recommendation, each in its own way. In the United States, President Herbert Hoover issued a proclamation on March 7, 1931, ordering that the flag be displayed on all government buildings on April 14 and inviting schools, civic associations, and the people of the United States to observe the day with appropriate ceremonies, "thereby giving expression to the spirit of continental solidarity and to the sentiments of cordiality and friendly feeling which the government and people of the United States entertain toward the peoples and governments of the other republics of the American continent." Pan American Day was thus observed for the first time in 1931. The ceremonies in Washington were held in the Pan American Building, attended by the president and the members of his cabinet and by the diplomatic representatives of the other American republics.

In 1948 the representatives of 21 American republics, meeting in Bogotá, Colombia, at the Ninth International Conference of American States, chartered the new Organization of American States. In so doing, they replaced the International Union of American Republics and gave the inter-American system its first comprehensive constitution. The purposes of the OAS were the consideration of mutual concerns in economic, technical, cultural, political, and legal matters; the preservation of hemispheric peace; and the maintenance of collective security. The Treaty of Reciprocal Assistance, signed by member states at Rio de Janeiro in 1947, stated that an attack upon one American state should be considered as an attack upon all. It was in light of hemispheric provisions for mutual defense that the OAS voted approval of the action of President John F. Kennedy, who on October 22, 1962, announced an embargo on Soviet shipping of offensive weapons to Communist Cuba, where launching sites for Soviet missiles had been discovered.

April 15

Federal Income Tax Deadline

Every year tens of millions of Americans work to meet the deadline for filing their federal income tax returns. (The deadline is typically extended to the next business day when April 15 occurs on a Saturday or Sunday.) Even though the federal income tax has become a fact of American life, it has not always been so. Prior to the Civil War, there was no income tax, and the federal government was able to finance its operations largely through the revenues generated by import tariffs. The federal government was also much smaller in those days; there were no federal social programs and the military budget was very limited.

The first income tax was instituted during the Civil War. Faced with the extraordinary costs of the conflict, both the North and the South decided to tax personal incomes as a means of raising much needed revenues. These first levies were only emergency measures, however, and the end of the war brought immediate repeal of the tax legislation. The federal government returned to its traditional reliance on import tariffs for revenue, supplemented by property taxes.

In the late 19th century, populist and agrarian groups began to call for a federal income tax. The theory was that such a tax would be paid primarily by the rich. The money generated thereby could replace the import tariffs, which raised the cost of goods for farmers, workers, and other ordinary people, and could also replace the property taxes paid by farmers and other landowners who were frequently short on cash. In 1892 the platform of the Populists, a new third party with widespread appeal in the agrarian South and West, called for a graduated income tax. James B. Weaver, the party's candidate in the ensuing presidential contest, garnered over a million votes, and his success indicated to the Democrats and Republicans that they could no longer ignore the issue. Within two years Congress passed the Wilson-Gorman Tariff, which slightly reduced import duties and imposed a 2 percent tax on annual incomes exceeding $4,000 (which at the time was a rather impressive income).

Opponents of the new income tax took the law to court. The test case, *Pollock* v. *Farmers' Loan and Trust Company*, came before the Supreme Court in 1895. The Court heard the legal arguments for two days and then handed down its decision. By a five-to-four vote it found the income tax provision of the Wilson-Gorman Tariff to be a direct tax and therefore a violation of Article 1 of the Constitution, which stipulates that such taxes must be apportioned among the states on the basis of population.

This historic decision made a new constitutional amendment the absolute prerequisite for any further income tax legislation. Several years elapsed before the proponents of the tax could acquire sufficient support for such an amendment, but the rise of the Progressive reform movement of the early 20th century ensured their ultimate success. Finally, on July 12, 1909, Congress agreed to the 16th Amendment and submitted it to the states for ratification. Just over three-and-a-half years later, on February 25, 1913, the amendment, which allows Congress to tax incomes "without apportionment among the several States, and without regard to any census or enumeration," gained the approval of the necessary three-fourths of the states and became part of the Constitution.

Income tax rates have increased considerably since 1913, when the Underwood-Simmons Tariff Act provided for the first constitutional levy, namely 1 percent on incomes over $4,000. During the First and Second World Wars, the income tax was greatly increased and provided much needed revenue to finance the war effort. During World War II, Congress passed legislation creating the modern system of income tax withholding, whereby taxes are withheld from paychecks as a credit against the final yearly tax obligation calculated by the taxpayer on or before April 15 of the next year.

Thomas H. Gallaudet Starts the First School for the Deaf

The first school for the deaf was founded on April 15, 1817, in Hartford, Connecticut. It was named the Connecticut Asylum for the Education and Instruction of Deaf and Dumb Persons. Later renamed the American School for the Deaf, it has survived to the present day.

The founder of the school was Thomas H. Gallaudet, the pioneer teacher of the deaf in the United States. He was born on December 10, 1787, in Philadelphia, Pennsylvania, of Huguenot ancestors who had fled to America from France at the time of the revocation of the Edict of Nantes. When he was 13 years old, his family moved to Hartford.

Gallaudet graduated from Yale in 1805. During the next seven years he divided his time between studying law, teaching, working in a business office, and traveling for his health. He then decided to study for the ministry and graduated from Andover Theological Seminary in 1814. Becoming acquainted with a deaf child named Alice Cogswell at about the time of his graduation, he urged her father to hire a special teacher for her. The father, joining with others, responded by sending Gallaudet to Europe to learn the methods in use there for teaching the deaf. Gallaudet accordingly spent several months studying under Abbé Sicard at the Royal Institute for Deaf Mutes (Institut Royal des Sourds-Muets) in Paris. He also visited England, where he studied the teaching methods of Thomas Braidwood and of the latter's successor, Joseph Watson.

Gallaudet returned to America in 1816 with the brilliant educator Laurent Clerc, who was himself deaf and who had studied and taught at the Royal Institute for Deaf Mutes. With the aid of Clerc, Gallaudet raised the money to open his school for the deaf in Hartford. Made principal of the school, Gallaudet held the post for 13 years. Apart from his pioneering work with individual pupils, he made important contributions in training others who founded similar schools.

Other members of Gallaudet's family shared his interests. His oldest son, also named Thomas, became a minister to the deaf and his youngest son, Edward Miner Gallaudet, opened a school for deaf mutes in Washington, D.C. The upper branch of this school developed into Gallaudet

College. The institution was named for the senior Gallaudet, who died in Hartford on September 10, 1851.

April 16

Washington Departs for His Inauguration

On April 16, 1789, George Washington set out from his estate at Mount Vernon in Virginia. His destination was New York City, where he was to be inaugurated as the first president of the United States.

Washington's inauguration was the culmination of more than seven years of debate about the form of government best suited for the fledgling nation. The Treaty of Paris of 1783, which ended the Revolutionary War, ushered in a period of political turmoil. With the Articles of Confederation, under which the original 13 states were joined, the national government was almost totally dependent upon the good will of the individual states and had very little power of its own. Washington, pessimistic about the country's future, wrote on May 18, 1786, that "something must be done, or the fabric must fall, for it is certainly tottering." At first he advocated amending the Articles of Confederation, but later, following the outbreak of Shays's Rebellion and virtual civil war in Massachusetts in 1786, he urged more radical reforms toward the formation of "an indissoluble union."

The practical needs of the young nation inevitably drew Washington back into public affairs, although he had hoped to enjoy a private life at Mount Vernon after leading the Revolutionary forces to victory. As early as the spring of 1785 he opened his estate to delegates from Virginia and Maryland, whose discussions there resolved common problems concerning the navigation of the Potomac River. The meetings led to the larger Annapolis Convention in 1786, attended by delegates from five states. The report of these participants included a call for a convention "to render the Constitution of the Federal Government adequate to the exigencies of the Union."

George Washington was chosen as one of Virginia's five delegates to the Constitutional Convention, which met in Philadelphia, Pennsylvania, in May 1787. After a quorum had been obtained, he was unanimously elected the convention's pres-

Library of Congress

Washington is sworn in as president.

ident by the delegates from the 12 states represented (Rhode Island did not participate). In the four months during which he presided, Washington remained silent in the debate, but on the side he made it known that he desired the formation of a strong national government. Although he again expressed his wish to retire quietly from the public eye, he was the most capable leader to serve as the nation's chief executive under the new constitution, which was ratified by the states in 1788. Members of the electoral college, meeting on February 4, 1789, were unanimous in voting him as president. The election, however, was not yet official. The Constitution required that Congress convene and that the president of the Senate open the ballots in the presence of both the Senate and the House.

The Continental Congress had intended that the newly established government should convene on "the first Wednesday in March next," namely March 4, 1789, at Federal Hall in New York City, which was the national capital at the time. By March 5, a mere handful of the legislators needed to count the presidential vote had assembled. A quorum still had not been reached by March 30.

Washington, awaiting the official decision, was in the meantime making careful preparations for his departure from Mount Vernon. Although he was one of the largest landowners in Virginia at the time, he was short on funds, and needed to borrow money to pay off his debts in Virginia and finance his relocation to New York. Forced to appeal to personal acquaintances since his credit was not judged good enough, Washington contacted "the most monied man I was acquainted with," namely Charles Carroll of Carrollton, Maryland, who declined the request because of his own financial difficulties. At last Richard Conway, a wealthy resident of Alexandria, Virginia, responded favorably to the following letter sent by Washington on March 4, 1789:

> Never till within these two years have I experienced the want of money. Short crops, and other causes not entirely within my control, make me feel it now very sensibly. To collect money without the invention of Suits seems impractical . . . and Land, which I have offered for sale, will not command cash at an undervalue, if at all. Under this statement, I am inclined to . . . borrow Money on Interest.

Conway at first lent Washington 500 English pounds at 6 percent interest, then extended a further loan of 100 pounds to cover his expenses on his trip to New York City.

On April 6, 1789, the necessary quorum was obtained and the electoral votes tallied. Charles Thomson, who had served as secretary of the Continental Congress, informed Washington of his unanimous election about noon on April 14, made a brief speech, and extended a letter from the president pro tempore of the Senate, which said in part: "Suffer me, Sir, to indulge the hope, that so auspicious a mark of public confidence will meet your approbation." Washington accepted the appointment, stating "I shall therefore be in readiness to set out the day after tomorrow." However, his personal sentiments about his decision were better reflected in the letter that he had written to Henry Knox shortly beforehand:

> My movements to the chair of Government will be accompanied by feelings not unlike those of a culprit who is going to the place of his execution: so unwilling am I, in the evening of a life nearly consumed in public cares, to quit a peaceful abode for an Ocean of difficulties, without that competency of political skill, abilities and inclination which is necessary to manage the helm. . . . Integrity and firmness is all I can promise.

On April 16, 1789, Washington left his home. His progress from Virginia to New York was a triumphal procession far different from the "quiet entry devoid of ceremony" he had requested. Speeches, toasts, cannon shots, militia parades, banners, and archways decorated with laurel marked each step of the long and somewhat taxing journey. At Trenton, New Jersey, there were lengthy speeches and 13 young girls in white, flowered attire to represent the 13 states of the Union. This celebration made an especially vivid impact, offering as it did such a marked contrast with the icy crossing of the Delaware River that Washington's ragged troops had made at that very spot in 1776 during the darkest days of the Revolution.

On April 23, Washington embarked from Elizabeth Town, New Jersey, for New York City on an elaborate barge rowed by 13 pilots dressed in white smocks and black-fringed hats. It had been constructed for the event with funds donated by 46 prominent citizens. The 15-mile boat trip took the president-elect past Staten Island, through the Upper Bay and inner harbor to Murray's Wharf at the foot of Wall Street in Lower Manhattan. Washington later commented in his diary:

> The display of boats which attended and joined us on this occasion, some with vocal and some with instrumental music on board; the decorations of the ships; the roar of cannon and the loud acclamations of the people, which rent the skies as I

passed along the wharves, filled my mind with sensations as painful (considering the reverse of this scene, which may be the case after all my labors to do good) as they were pleasing.

At the landing, richly carpeted steps and crimson upholstered railings added to the effect. One spectator observed that "the General was obliged to wipe his eyes several times." Once Washington had reached his new quarters at Cherry Street, dignitaries and former officers pressed forward to greet him. Later that evening, Governor George Clinton of New York gave a banquet in his honor.

The inauguration itself did not take place for another week. During the following days, members of Congress heatedly argued issues of etiquette and nomenclature. Finally the Senate, which had favored designating the chief executive as "His Highness the President of the United States of America and Protector of the Rights of the Same," agreed to follow the House's simpler title of "The President of the United States." In the meantime Washington reworked and polished his inaugural address, discarding a prepared 64-page speech and substituting instead a short text that, when read, lasted less than 20 minutes.

On the morning of April 30, inauguration day, Washington awoke at dawn to the thunder of 13 cannon shots and the ringing of church bells. At noon he donned a suit of brown broadcloth with silver buttons decorated with spread eagles, put on silver-buttoned shoes, and strapped on his dress sword. Washington proceeded to Federal Hall at Wall and Nassau Streets. A crimson canopy, a dais with an armchair, a small table, and a large Bible on a red pillow had been placed on the balcony of the Senate Chamber there. Robert R. Livingston, the chancellor of the state of New York, administered the presidential oath and then exclaimed: "Long live George Washington, President of the United States!" President Washington retired inside the Senate Chamber to read to Congress his inaugural address in a voice described as "deep, a little tremulous." After the ceremony, he attended a service at St. Paul's Chapel on Broadway and was then escorted to his place of residence to rest before the evening receptions and fireworks.

The president resided at Cherry Street until February 23, 1790. The government changed the location of the capital to Philadelphia in 1790, and Washington took the oath of office for his second term in that city on March 4, 1793.

April 17

J. P. Morgan's Birthday

John Pierpont Morgan, one of America's most famous bankers and financiers, was born on April 17, 1837, in Hartford, Connecticut. His father was a banker, who in 1854 became a partner in a major London banking house. After receiving his education in Switzerland and Germany, young Morgan decided to follow in his father's footsteps. In 1857 Morgan went to work for a firm on Wall Street, and in 1860 he became the New York agent for his father's banking firm.

During the Civil War, Morgan was involved in a variety of business ventures and was accused of being a war profiteer. Although no such charge was ever conclusively proven, it is certain that after the Civil War he emerged as one of Wall Street's leading financiers at the head of his own firm. Morgan then developed an interest in the area of railroad finance. The post–Civil War resumption of America's westward expansion meant a corresponding expansion of the nation's railroad system in order to transport people and goods to and from the frontier, and the potential profits were enormous in a day and age when the railroad business was largely unregulated.

Although the railroad business was potentially lucrative, many railroads were in deep financial trouble because of bad management, dishonest financial practices, speculation, over-expansion, and cutthroat competition. Morgan acted as banker and financial manager for many American railroads, overseeing their reorganization and reaping enormous profits for his services while putting the industry on a sounder footing in the process. His experience in the field of corporate reorganizations, mergers, and finance made him America's leading investment banker.

In the 1890s Morgan began to move beyond the field of railroad finance as he led the effort to put together such well-known corporate giants as American Telephone & Telegraph, General Electric, International Harvester, and United States Steel. U.S. Steel is particularly noteworthy since it was the first billion dollar corporation in American history.

Morgan was also a prominent political figure. Since he was effectively the leader of the nation's banking industry, the federal government turned to him for assistance in 1895 when there was a financial crisis and a run on gold reserves. At the time, the nation's currency was based on gold, but the Federal Reserve System did not yet exist and the federal government still had very limited resources. Morgan stepped in as the nation's banker, and helped President Grover Cleveland raise enough capital to get through the crisis. In 1907 Morgan helped resolve another crisis, namely a stock market collapse on Wall Street.

When J. P. Morgan died on March 31, 1913, in Rome, Italy, his son J. P. Morgan Jr. inherited the Morgan banking empire. The younger Morgan was an important figure in his own right, and helped raise money for America's allies during World War I. When the elder Morgan died in 1913, he left behind a substantial art collection, which is now housed in the Morgan Wing of New York's Metropolitan Museum of Art; rare books and prints are housed in the Morgan Library, some fifty blocks south.

The Bay of Pigs Invasion

On April 17, 1961, over a thousand Cuban exiles armed and trained by the United States landed at the *Bahia de Cochinos* or Bay of Pigs on Cuba's southern coastline. Their unsuccessful attempt to overthrow the communist regime of Cuban dictator Fidel Castro would become a major embarrassment for the administration of President John F. Kennedy and was a serious setback in America's conduct of the cold war.

Fidel Castro was an educated man, and his admiration for American freedom and democracy was one of the factors that helped inspire him to lead a revolt against the corrupt Cuban government of Fulgencio Batista. After several years of guerrilla warfare, Castro finally deposed Batista in 1959. From the beginning, the American government was suspicious of Castro. For decades, Cuba had been a peaceful Caribbean backwater nation, where the local government was willing to let American business interests develop lucrative casinos and sugar interests in return for some discreet bribes and payoffs. Cuba became a tourist haven, and the American government was content to ignore the corrupt practices of both big business and organized crime. Castro's takeover shattered this paternalistic relationship.

Unfortunately, at the time of Castro's rise to power the cold war between the United States and the Soviet Union was in its heyday. Both countries viewed revolutionary developments in countries such as Cuba through the prism of cold war competition, and thus the United States sought to reassert its control over a country which had historically been a part of the American sphere of influence and which would be a valuable Soviet asset, given its location just off American shores.

Observing America's hostile reaction, the senior Soviet leadership predicted that Cuba would come to the Soviet Union "like iron filings to a magnet." They were correct. The revolutionary fervor of Castro and his people was transferred to the cause of communism. Before he left office, President Eisenhower approved plans for the training of a small army of Cuban exiles to lead an invasion of their homeland and overthrow Castro. There was no shortage of willing Cuban exiles in the United States, since thousands of people had fled Cuba in the wake of the turmoil that followed Castro's seizure of power, and many of them were anxious to return to their homes, businesses, and property. For the United States, an invasion by Cuban exiles would be a convenient ruse because the American government could claim that it was a purely Cuban matter that did not involve the United States. In fact, the entire operation would be supervised from start to finish by the Central Intelligence Agency (CIA).

When he took office, President Kennedy approved the Bay of Pigs operation. Just months after Kennedy's inauguration in January 1961, the Cuban force landed at the Bay of Pigs on April 17. The result was a disaster. Instead of receiving sympathy and support from the local population, the force was decimated by Castro's army. Those not killed were taken prisoner. Although American military forces were nearby, the Kennedy administration chose not to intervene on the exiles' behalf when it became clear that defeat was imminent. Such an intervention would have been a clear signal that it was an American-sponsored operation. The result was a victory for Castro and the new Cuban-Soviet alliance, and President Kennedy was severely criticized for his conduct of the affair. Many historians believe that the incident led indirectly to more serious cold war confrontations in the years to follow, such as the Cuban missile crisis when the Soviets attempted to deploy nuclear weapons on Cuban soil, because the Soviets perceived Kennedy to be a vulnerable president and a weak leader.

April 18

Clarence Darrow's Birthday

Clarence Seward Darrow, one of the most famous criminal lawyers in the history of the United States, pursued a lifelong campaign against hatred, ignorance, prejudice, and bigotry. Darrow repeatedly represented the underdog, attempting to secure for his clients equal rights, equal protection, and a fair trial. For example, during the 1903 anthracite coal strike he reminded the arbitration commission selected by President Theodore Roosevelt that the coal mine operators, not the workers, possessed every asset in the hearings: "Their social advantages are better, their religious privileges are better, they speak the English language better. . . . They can hire . . . expert accountants, and they have got the advantage of us in almost every particular, and we will admit all that" at which point, the chairman interjected, "All except the lawyers."

Born near Kinsman, Ohio, on April 18, 1857, Clarence Darrow completed only one year of law school when he was admitted to the bar of Ohio in 1878. After practicing law in Ashtabula, Ohio, he settled in 1887 in Chicago, Illinois, where he soon made an impression as a public speaker and lawyer. He won the respect and friendship of a powerful supporter, John Peter Altgeld, an established attorney and political leader who was to be elected governor of Illinois in 1892. Through Altgeld's influence, Darrow was appointed assistant corporation counsel, and then acting corporation counsel of Chicago. Darrow and Altgeld shared a deep concern for the so-called Haymarket anarchists, a common bond which helped to draw them even closer together.

Not long before Darrow went to Chicago, the city had been violently disrupted by the Haymarket Square riot. During a mass rally condemning police brutality in the McCormick Works strike, a bomb had been hurled, killing seven policemen and wounding 67 other persons. Eight anarchists were arrested as perpetrators. Although conclusive evidence was lacking, all were found guilty. Four of the men were executed, one committed suicide on the eve of his execution, one received a 15-year prison sentence, and the remaining two were condemned to life imprisonment. Convinced that their trial had been a travesty, Darrow became involved in the amnesty movement for the three jailed anarchists, and in 1893 he was instrumental in persuading Governor Altgeld not only to pardon the imprisoned men, but also to exonerate their fellow anarchists who had been executed.

After serving a few years as Chicago's legal adviser, Darrow accepted the position of general attorney for the Chicago & North Western Railway. In 1894 the American Railway Union, under the presidency of Eugene Victor Debs, boycotted the servicing of pullman cars in support of the striking workers of the Pullman Car Company of Pullman, Illinois, whose wages had been cut. Darrow found himself siding with the strikers and hard pressed to reconcile his own sympathies with the position he had to uphold as representative of the railroad corporation. When the railroads were granted an injunction against the strikers and Debs was indicted for conspiracy and imprisoned, the highly regarded corporation lawyer gave up his lucrative career. He became the champion of labor before the union was recognized as a lawful organization entitled to wield the weapons of the strike and boycott to improve wages and working conditions. Darrow's celebrated defense of Eugene Debs brought him nationwide recognition in labor and criminal affairs. From then on until he retired, Darrow exerted his courtroom skill in a series of notable trials embracing a variety of controversial causes.

The William D. Haywood, Charles H. Moyer, George Pettibone, and Steve Adams cases revolved around the bombing murder of Frank Steunenberg, former governor of Idaho, on December 20, 1905. The 1920 communist labor case, involving the 1919 Illinois Sedition Act, centered upon 20 communists who had been accused of advocating a forceful overthrow of the government. In the Scopes trial of 1925, Darrow served as defense counsel for a Tennessee schoolteacher who had violated a state law that prohibited the teaching in public schools of Darwin's theory of evolution (see July 10, Scopes "Monkey Trial" Begins, for further information). In this trial, one of Darrow's targets was the fundamentalist political leader and orator William Jennings Bryan, a member of the prosecution staff.

One of the most famous of Darrow's defenses was in the 1924 Chicago "thrill" murder trial of two youths, Nathan Leopold and Richard Loeb, both sons of prominent, respected, and wealthy Chicago businessmen. Wanting to commit the perfect crime "for the sake of a thrill," the two kidnapped and murdered 14-year-old Bobby Franks. Darrow, having been begged to defend the youths despite their confessions, accepted the difficult assignment not, as was rumored at the time, because of the fee expected from the millionaire parents, but because of the opportunity that the case offered for expressing his ideas against capital punishment. The 67-year-old veteran attorney delivered a moving, 12-hour-long plea, by which he saved his clients from execution on the grounds of temporary insanity. A contemporary newspaper reporter commented that the lines in Darrow's face were "deeper, the eyes haggard. But there was no sign of physical weariness in the speech, only a spiritual weariness with the cruelties of the world." Nathan Leopold, whose parole in 1958 and later death triggered a revival of public interest in Clarence Darrow, once remarked that Darrow was "the kindest man I have ever known. To me, at least, Mr. Darrow's fundamental characteristic was his deep-seated all-embracing kindness. . . . He hated superficiality and refused to conform for conformity's sake."

Indeed, Darrow remained steadfast in his convictions to the end of his life. In 1934 he was asked by President Franklin D. Roosevelt to serve as chairman of a board reviewing charges that the National Recovery Administration (NRA) was siding with big business. The Darrow review board investigated some 3,000 complaints and 34 NRA industrial codes during 47 public hearings spread over a four-month period. Although admitting that the NRA had accomplished much in eradicating child labor and shortening working hours, Darrow was still convinced that "not in many years have monopolistic tendencies in industry been so forwarded and strengthened as they have been through the perversion of an act excellently intended to restore prosperity and promote general welfare." As *Newsweek* magazine noted: "Clarence Darrow is on one of his peculiarly cool and deadly rampages again. As a foreman of a kind of governmental grand jury to tell the administration how the NRA is working, he has brought in a report saying it's doing perfectly terrible." In the following year, the Supreme Court declared the compulsory code system of the NRA unconstitutional.

The public image of Darrow, whom Lincoln Steffens called "the attorney for the damned," was that of an uncommonly learned and moving orator, whose speeches were filled with historical examples, quotations, and analogies drawn from wide reading. The true magnetism of the often disheveled figure who paced back and forth in court with his hands in his pockets, shoulders hunched, and head bowed was his keen intuition about human nature. Sometimes angry, scathing, and pitiless, sometimes witty and jovial, sometimes tearful, he used emotions as well as logistics and rhetoric to achieve his goals. He died on March 13, 1938. As the eulogy delivered at his funeral stressed:

> In his heart was infinite pity and mercy for the poor, the oppressed, the weak and erring; all races, all colors, all creeds, and all human kind. Clarence Darrow made the way easier for man. He preached not doctrine but love and pity, the only virtues that can make this world any better.

The San Francisco Earthquake and Fire

At 5:12 a.m. on April 18, 1906, the ground began to quake under San Francisco, California, to the sound of jangling church bells. The tremor signaled the displacement of land surfaces along the San Andreas fault from Upper Mattole in Humboldt County to San Juan in Benito County, a distance of 270 miles. The earthquake was the worst to that date in the United States: The tremor lasted 60 to 75 seconds and reached 8.25 points on the Richter scale. Shock waves traveled to Los Angeles in the south and to Coos Bay, Oregon, 750 miles to the north. Residents of Winnemuca, Nevada, 300 miles to the east, also felt the ground tremble. Displacement was mostly horizontal, reaching an apex of 21 feet at Tomales Bay. There was little vertical shifting.

The earthquake was felt most intensely in San Francisco, where the effect reminded one writer of "a terrier shaking a rat." It took many lives throughout the city, with the greatest number of the dead concentrated in the produce district and the area south of Market Street. The tremor subsided within minutes, but it set off more than fifty fires, which quickly became the main danger. The worst, which razed the Hayes Valley section, began when a woman attempted to cook on a stove that the quake had damaged. It immediately became known as the Ham and Eggs Fire. Within 20 hours flames consumed most of the business district and all of the area south of Market Street, Chinatown, and Hayes Valley. Public transportation and the telegraph were inoperative, and 100,000 people were homeless. The fire continued to burn for two and a half days before it was brought under control.

Since San Francisco's water pipes broke early in the disaster, the fire fighters were forced to draw water from the nearby San Francisco Bay to save most of the wharves and a number of buildings. Experts used dynamite to raze structures and create a firebreak to control the westward advance of the flames along Van Ness Avenue. However, less capable use of explosives in other areas served only to start more blazes. Finally, after the water mains were repaired, San Franciscans were able to put out the fires.

The conflagration was the worst in American history. It consumed an area six times as large as that destroyed in the great London fire of 1666. The earthquake and its aftermath leveled 490 city blocks containing 2,831 acres, and did an estimated $500 million worth of damage. The business district and three-fifths of the city's homes and lodgings were in ruins. Worst of all, 450 people died in the disaster. Bleak as the disaster was, San Francisco had brighter days ahead. Rebuilding in earthquake-proof and fire-resistant materials began almost immediately. San Franciscans completed the task quickly, and in 1915 their beautiful new city was the host of the Panama Pacific International Exposition.

April 19

World War II: "Jimmy" Doolittle's Bombing Raid on Japan

After the Japanese raid on Pearl Harbor on December 7, 1941, the United States entered World War II. During the first few months of 1942, the Japanese pursued their offensive in the Pacific, while the American military struggled to rebuild and make the transition from peace to war. In an effort to regain the initiative and improve public morale, plans were made to take the war to the enemy in the form of a bombing raid on Japan. Japan was an ideal target for bombers, since not only did it have concentrated urban and industrial centers, but many structures were made in the traditional manner with wood and paper that caught fire easily.

Lieutenant Colonel James "Jimmy" Doolittle was chosen to carry out a raid with a squadron of B-25 bombers. The B-25 was a medium bomber with limited range, but could be launched from an aircraft carrier, which was an advantage since at the time America had no airfields within reasonable striking distance of Japan. It was a risky plan. Launching bombers rather than fighters from an aircraft carrier involves heavier aircraft and other problems, notably the difficulty of landing again. In fact, the B-25s would not be able to return, and would have to fly on from Japan to friendly airfields in eastern China held by Chinese forces at war with Japan. From China, the planes could go on to Burma and join the Allied forces there.

The USS *Hornet* was chosen to be the carrier. Twenty-four B-25s were assigned, and the hand-picked aviators were not told the specifics of the mission. On February 3, 1942, there was a successful B-25 test launch from the *Hornet*. The military came to realize, however, that the planes would have to be stripped of some weaponry in order to reduce weight, and that extra fuel storage was needed. In effect, the planes would be vunerable flying gas cans traveling at low altitudes to avoid detection. Finally, the size of the mission was reduced to 16 planes, given the space limitations of the *Hornet*. Each plane would carry four 500-pound bombs. The *Hornet* with Doolittle's B-25s aboard departed on April 2, 1942.

On April 18, 1942, Doolittle's 16 planes successfully launched off the *Hornet* and set their course for Japan. They were forced, however, to leave ahead of schedule and further from Japan than originally planned because a Japanese naval vessel had been sighted and it was feared that the *Hornet* would be intercepted. The bombers reached Japan, and struck targets in Kobe, Nagoya, Yokohama, and most importantly the capital of Tokyo, with none of the B-25s being shot down. After the raids, however, problems occurred.

The weather turned bad. Poor visibility made it impossible to find the Chinese airfields, and 15 of the bombers became lost. Most of the crews, however, were able to parachute to safety before their planes crashed. Only one plane landed intact, having found an airfield near the Soviet city of Vladivostock on the North Pacific coast. In total, ten men were killed or injured, and eight were captured by the Japanese. Doolittle himself successfully made it back to the United States.

Although he lost his entire squadron, Doolittle was given a hero's welcome and promoted to Brigadier General. Further, he was awarded the prestigious Medal of Honor. His primary achievement was not military in nature, but was in having delivered the first blow to the enemy homeland and given American morale a badly needed boost.

April 19

Battles of Lexington and Concord ("Patriots' Day")

The American Revolution began on April 19, 1775, with the battles of Lexington and Concord in Massachusetts. The anniversary of the "shot heard round the world" was historically observed as Patriots' Day, although this observance declined significantly in the late 20th century.

Massachusetts was tense in the spring of 1775. Since the previous year the province had languished under the so-called Intolerable Acts, which were imposed by the British Parliament in retribution for the Boston Tea Party of December 16, 1773. England ordered the port of Boston closed until the colonists paid for the shipment of tea, which had been destroyed to protest taxation by Parliament. The governor's powers were increased to the detriment of local autonomy, and royal officials were put beyond the jurisdiction of provincial courts in capital cases.

The royal government's actions provoked a hostile response in the Massachusetts Colony. In October 1774 Massachusetts set up a provincial congress, an extralegal legislative body with revolutionary tendencies. Committees of Correspondence communicated the incendiary message of Massachusetts' experience to the other American colonies. Militia units drilled with special intensity, and the colonials seized British military stores in Boston and Charlestown and accumulated their own supplies in Concord and Worcester.

General Thomas Gage, the British commander in chief in America, who had taken over the governorship of the unruly province in 1774, received authorization on April 14, 1775, to take decisive action to regain control of events. Determined to seize the colonists' supplies in Concord, he kept the mission a secret, waiting until the last minute to inform Lieutenant Colonel Francis Smith, the commander of the expedition, of his objective. Despite all of Gage's precautions, the watchful and suspicious Americans became aware of the plans. Brigadier General Hugh Percy learned that the colonists were expecting trouble and told the governor, but Gage thought it too late to turn back.

At about 10:00 p.m. on April 18, the colonial leader Joseph Warren dispatched William Dawes to warn their comrades at Concord. As Dawes was going by way of Boston Neck, Warren shortly afterwards sent Paul Revere by another route across Charlestown Neck. The two riders reached Lexington and then set out for Concord. Between 1:00 and 2:00 a.m. they ran into a British patrol assigned by Gage to intercept messengers. Dawes escaped, but the soldiers seized Revere, whom they released shortly thereafter. The poet Henry Wadsworth Longfellow made Revere and his ride known to the world; Dawes is remembered only by historians.

Lieutenant Colonel Smith and his second-in-command, Marine Major John Pitcairn, had an elite British force of approximately 700 men, making up eight infantry and eight grenadier companies, at their disposal for the mission. At dusk on April 18 they assembled their men on Boston Common, and in the darkness they made their way to a spot near what is now Park Square, where the men boarded boats. The oars were muffled as they silently rowed to Phips Farm, now East Cambridge. Wet and uncomfortable, the redcoats landed before midnight and spent two hours awaiting extra provisions. The column then began its march, crossing a waist-deep ford to avoid using a noisy wooden bridge.

Pitcairn led the advance guard of six light companies. His men encountered the patrol that had captured Revere. These men passed on the false report, which Revere had invented for their benefit, that 500 militiamen were waiting at Lexington. Pitcairn proceeded slowly, allowing Smith's men to catch up in case he needed reinforcements, and reached Lexington at about 5:00 a.m.

At sunrise on April 19, Captain John Parker and a small force of about 70 armed men were assembled on Lexington green, while other minutemen were retrieving gunpowder from the meeting-house where they had hidden it. Pitcairn formed his numerically superior force in a battle line and ordered the colonists to lay down their arms. Tradition relates that Captain Parker had instructed his men: "Don't fire unless fired upon! But if they

want a war, let it begin here." Actually, the captain was more prudent. Recognizing that resistance would be futile, Parker ordered his men to disperse. Suddenly, however, gunfire crackled and a quick fight ensued, leaving eight Americans dead and ten wounded; only one British soldier was injured.

Who really fired "the shot heard round the world"? Nineteenth-century American historians, such as George Bancroft, blamed the British; John Fiske went so far as to claim that Major Pitcairn personally fired the first shot. Twentieth-century scholars are less certain, because it seems that the militiamen on the green did not fire and that Pitcairn did not give the order to shoot. Most likely the culprit was an American spectator or an impetuous or nervous British soldier.

Smith and Pitcairn proceeded from Lexington to Concord, six miles away. The British searched the town and Barrett's Farm for provisions, but they found little, since the colonials had removed most of the supplies. The delay, however, permitted about 400 militiamen under Major John Buttrick to close in on the British companies stationed at Concord's North Bridge. A battle between the Americans and British ensued. Each side suffered several casualties as the colonists drove the British regulars back in disorder.

Smith regrouped his men and left Concord about noon. The retreat was bloody as Americans hidden behind fences, bushes, and buildings sniped at and ambushed the British column. The unorthodox tactics exacted a high number of British casualties. Some 1,400 reinforcements under General Percy joined the disheartened column at Lexington, and both contingents set out for Boston. The return was just as bloody as the colonials continued their sniping, and the British, in retaliation, looted and burned houses along the road and killed all of the male inhabitants. By dusk the British had reached Charlestown Neck and the protection of their naval guns. Overall, 19 officers and 250 enlisted men had been killed or wounded that day.

The battle aroused the people of the colonies. Those in New England resolved to confine the British army to Boston. New Hampshire voted to raise 2,000 men; Connecticut, 6,000; Rhode Island, 1,500; and Massachusetts, 13,600. The city was soon encircled by colonial troops. The news spread from colony to colony. Arms and ammunition were seized, provincial congresses were formed, and before the end of the summer the power of the royal governors had been completely destroyed.

April 19

Attack on the Branch Davidian Compound in Waco, Texas

After a 51-day confrontation between the U.S. government and members of the Branch Davidian cult, on the morning of April 19, 1993, agents from the Bureau of Alcohol, Tobacco and Firearms (ATF) assaulted the sect's compound in Waco, Texas. Using armored vehicles, they injected tear gas into the building, and six hours later, a fire ensued that burned unchecked for 30 minutes, consuming the building and those inside. The group's leader David Koresh and more than 80 of his followers perished, although autopsies of recovered bodies later revealed that seven—including Koresh—had died before the blaze of gunshot wounds to the head that were either self-inflicted or a result of execution. Attorney General Janet Reno, who had approved the raid, admitted that evening that the government had made a terrible mistake. An investigation ensued, and two reports—one by the Treasury Department and the other by the Justice Department—blamed the ATF for bungling the original plans to seize Koresh and for covering up mistakes that compromised the safety of government agents and those in the compound.

The Branch Davidians are a splinter sect of the Seventh-Day Adventist Church, and like the Adventists (who have repudiated them) believe in a literal interpretation of the Bible and immanent apocalypse. The sect is financed primarily through its members' savings. The 33-year-old Koresh, born Vernon Howell, began recruiting for the group in the 1970s and became its leader in 1987 after a violent struggle with another member, George Roden, that resulted in the latter's death. Koresh was charged with the murder but his trial ended in a hung jury. Koresh was a charismatic leader who believed and taught that he was the Messiah and frequently spoke of an apocalyptic confrontation with law enforcement officers that would presage the end of the world. His followers remained faithful to him until the end, despite reports that he sexually abused many of the women and children inside the compound.

Those allegations were among several that prompted the ATF to lay siege to the compound in Waco on February 28, 1993. The agents also acted on reports that the sect was stockpiling illegal weapons and chemicals that could be used to make explosives. Four federal agents and six cult members were killed in a shootout when ATF officials arrived to serve Karesh with search and arrest warrants. That began the 51-day confrontation, in which agents tried to force the members out of the compound in a variety of ways, such as by overwhelming them with unpleasant music and grisly sound effects. While several people did leave the compound before the April 19 attack, most remained with Koresh, including 17 children.

Just before 6:00 a.m. on April 19, the ATF called Koresh to notify him that they were about to use tear gas to eject the Davidians from the compound. Shortly thereafter they began ramming holes into the main building with a long boom attached to the front of an armored vehicle, through which the tear gas CS was injected into compound. The agency claimed to have opted for this quick strike because they feared Branch members would commit mass suicide, although the nine survivors of the attack later denied any plans for such an act. The fire broke out shortly after noon and spread rapidly, due to 30-mile-an-hour winds and the building's wooden construction. The compound was still smoldering when speculation began that the agency had either inadvertently or deliberately caused the fire, perhaps by its use of CS. But while CS has been known to be lethal to individuals with preexisting health conditions, it is not deemed a significant fire hazard. Investigations conducted the day after the fire determined it had been set from within the compound, and 11 eavesdropping devices planted by the FBI in the building revealed discussions by Branch members about dousing the hallways and rooms with fuel to be set afire when agents entered. It is still not certain that they actually followed through with these plans. Firefighters were also kept from the scene for over 20 minutes, apparently for their own safety.

After the first report on the Waco disaster was issued in early October 1993, Treasury Secretary Lloyd Bentsen dismissed the head of the ATF Stephen E. Higgins and suspended five other officials. By October 4 two more top officials from the bureau had resigned over their disagreement with the report. The Justice Department's findings, issued the day after the Treasury Department's, offered similar conclusions, but while severely critical of the ATF, the report largely exonerated Janet Reno, who would maintain her post as attorney general through both of President Bill Clinton's administrations.

Eleven Branch Davidians were tried on murder and conspiracy charges in connection with the deaths of the four ATF agents during the original raid on the compound on Februrary 28. All were acquitted of these more serious charges, but seven were found guilty of illegal weapons possession. Five of them received 40 years in prison for their roles that day—10 years for voluntary manslaughter and 30 years for weapons violations. The others received sentences ranging from three to 20 years in prison, and all were fined in amounts that varied from $2,000 to $50,000.

Bombing of the Alfred P. Murrah Federal Building in Oklahoma City

In what has been called the worst terrorist attack on American soil, at 9:00 a.m. on April 19, 1995, a bomb destroyed the Alfred P. Murrah Federal Building in Oklahoma City, Oklahoma. The blast, occurring two years to the day after the attack on the Branch Davidian compound in Waco, Texas (see article above), injured 850 people and killed 168, most of them government employees and 15 of them children at a day care center on the second floor. Two former U.S. Army veterans, Timothy McVeigh and Terry Nichols, were convicted of the bombing—McVeigh for conspiracy and murder and Nichols on lesser charges.

The building housed a number of federal agencies, including the Bureau of Alcohol, Tobacco and Firearms; the Secret Service; and the Drug Enforcement Administration. These were concluded to be the terrorists' primary targets in retaliation for the Waco incident and a prior one at Ruby Ridge, Idaho, in which the wife and teenaged son of Randy Weaver, a white supremacist, were mistakenly shot by marshals from the Federal Bureau of Investigation during a 1990 attempt to arrest Weaver on illegal weapons charges. After the Oklahoma City bombing, several people signed affidavits stating that the 26-year-old McVeigh, a veteran of the Persian Gulf War, had extreme right-wing views and was sympathetic to the Branch Davidians. He had apparently expressed outrage over the Waco attack, and he was also photographed by government agents in the crowd that gathered outside of the Davidian compound before that confrontation ended.

On the Monday before the 1995 bombing, McVeigh is said to have rented a Ryder truck in Junction City, Kansas, using a forged South Dakota driver's license with 4-19-93 (the date of the Waco raid) printed as the date of issue. He allegedly packed the truck with 4,800 pounds of explosives made of ammonium nitrate fertilizer and diesel fuel and parked it across the street from the Murrah Building on the morning of April 19. The explosion, which took place at one of the busiest times of day, as employees were arriving for work, ripped a huge crater in the front of the building and destroyed other nearby facilities, including a Y.M.C.A. and the main office of the newspaper *The Journal Record*. McVeigh was arrested later in Perry, Oklahoma, 60 miles north of Oklahoma City, for driving without a license plate and was connected to the bombing after Perry authorities

recognized him from a picture circulated by the FBI. Shortly after that, Nichols surrendered to police in Herington, Kansas, after hearing that he was wanted for questioning in the case. McVeigh and Nichols were indicted in August, while a third man, Michael J. Fortier, who served with them at Fort Riley, Kansas, pleaded guilty to knowing of plans for the attack ahead of time and decided to cooperate with federal prosecutors.

Separate trials for McVeigh and Nichols took place in Denver, Colorado, in 1997. McVeigh, who was tried first, was convicted on June 3 and was given the death penalty on June 14. Terry Nichols was convicted on December 24 of conspiracy and involuntary manslaughter but was acquitted of murder. He was sentenced to life in prison without the possibility of parole.

In October 1998, Vice President Al Gore broke ground for a memorial to the victims of the bombing alongside the former site of the Murrah Building. This memorial was scheduled to open in phases beginning in late 1999 and when completed will include an empty chair for each person who died in the blast, a reflecting pool, and the headquarters of a National Memorial Institute for the Prevention of Terrorism and Violence. Other features of the memorial will be the chain-link fence that was erected around the site shortly after the bombing, to which mourners attached cards, flowers, and other expressions of condolence, and an elm tree that survived the blast and is now known as the Survivor Tree. In addition, in December 1999 unidentifiable fragmentary remains of some of the victims were placed in a single coffin and buried in a memorial grove at the Oklahoma state capitol. A new $40 million facility to be called the Federal Campus is scheduled to open in 2002 as a replacement for the Murrah Building one block from the former site.

General Douglas MacArthur's "Old Soldiers Never Die" Address

See also January 26, Douglas MacArthur's Birthday.

General Douglas MacArthur, the legendary military leader and hero of World War II, was relieved of command by President Harry S. Truman on April 11, 1951. MacArthur's dismissal came after a series of policy differences and personality clashes between MacArthur and Truman that eventually became irreconcilable. Upon returning to the United States, on April 19, 1951, MacArthur gave his famous "Old Soldiers Never Die" farewell speech to a joint session of Congress. Afterwards he retired to private life, staying fairly active but never again returning to the national limelight with the same prominence.

The relevant portions of the speech are set forth below:

I stand on this rostrum with a sense of deep humility and great pride; humility in the wake of those great architects of our history who have stood here before me, pride in the reflection that this home of legislative debate represents human liberty in the purest form yet devised. Here are centered the hopes and aspirations and faith of the entire human race.

I do not stand here as advocate for any partisan cause, for the issues are fundamental and reach quite beyond the realm of partisan considerations. They must be resolved on the highest plane of national interest if our course is to prove sound and our future protected. I trust, therefore, that you will do me the justice of receiving that which I have to say as solely expressing the considered viewpoint of a fellow American.

I address you with neither rancor nor bitterness in the fading twilight of life, with but one purpose in mind: to serve my country. The issues are global, and so interlocked that to consider the problems of one sector oblivious to those of another is to court disaster for the whole. While Asia is commonly referred to as the gateway to Europe, it is no less true that Europe is the gateway to Asia, and the broad influence of the one cannot fail to have its impact upon the other. There are those who claim our strength is inadequate to protect on both fronts, that we cannot divide our effort. I can think of no greater expression of defeatism. If a potential enemy can divide his strength on two fronts, it is for us to counter his efforts. The Communist threat is a global one. Its successful advance in one sector threatens the destruction of every other sector. You cannot appease or otherwise surrender to communism in Asia without simultaneously undermining our efforts to halt its advance in Europe.

While I was not consulted prior to the President's decision to intervene in support of the republic of Korea, that decision, from a military standpoint, proved a sound one. As I say, it proved a sound one, as we hurled back the invader and decimated his forces. Our victory was complete, and our objectives within reach, when Red China intervened with numerically superior ground forces. This created a new war and an entirely new situation, a situation not contemplated when our forces were committed against the North Korean invaders; a situation which called for new decisions in the diplomatic sphere to permit the realistic adjustment of military strategy. Such decisions have not been forthcoming.

While no man in his right mind would advocate sending our ground forces into continental China, and such was never given a thought, the new situation did urgently demand a drastic revision of strategic planning if our political aim was to defeat this new enemy as we had defeated the old. Apart from the military need, as I saw it, to neutralize the sanctuary protection given the enemy north of the [Chinese border at the Yalu River], I felt that military necessity in the conduct of the war made necessary:

(1) The intensification of our economic blockade against China,

(2) The imposition of a naval blockade against the China coast,

(3) Removal of restrictions on air reconnaissance of China's coastal area, and of Manchuria,

(4) Removal of restrictions on the forces of the republic of China on Formosa, with logistical support to contribute to their effective operations against the Chinese mainland.

For entertaining these views, all professionally designed to support our forces committed to Korea and to bring hostilities to an end with the least possible delay and at a saving of countless American and Allied lives, I have been severely criticized in lay circles, principally abroad, despite my understanding that from a military standpoint the above views have been fully shared in the past by practically every military leader concerned with the Korean campaign, including our own Joint Chiefs of Staff. I called for reinforcements, but was informed that reinforcements were not available. I made clear that if not permitted to destroy the enemy built-up bases north of the Yalu, if not permitted to utilize the friendly Chinese force of some 600,000 men on Formosa [Taiwan], if not permitted to blockade the China coast to prevent the Chinese Reds from getting succor from without, and if there were to be no hope of major reinforcements, the position of the command from the military standpoint forbade victory. We could hold in Korea by constant maneuver and at an approximate area where our supply-line advantages were in balance with the supply-line disadvantages of the enemy, but we could hope at best for only an indecisive campaign with its terrible and constant attrition upon our forces if the enemy utilized his full military potential.

I have constantly called for the new political decisions essential to a solution. Efforts have been made to distort my position. It has been said in effect that I was a warmonger. Nothing could be further from the truth. I know war as few other men now living know it, and nothing to me is more revolting. I have long advocated its complete abolition, as its very destructiveness on both friend and foe has rendered it useless as a means of settling international disputes. Indeed, on the second day of September 1945, just following the surrender of the Japanese nation on the battleship Missouri, I formally cautioned as follows:

"Men since the beginning of time have sought peace. Various methods through the ages have been attempted to devise an international process to prevent or settle disputes between nations. From the very start workable methods were found in so far as individual citizens were concerned, but the mechanics of an instrumentality of larger international scope have never been successful. Military alliances, balances of power, leagues of nations, all in turn failed, leaving the only path to be by way of the crucible of war. The utter destructiveness of war now blocks out this alternative. We have had our last chance. If we will not devise some greater and more equitable system, our Armageddon will be at our door. The problem basically is theological and involves a spiritual recrudescence, an improvement of human character that will synchronize with our almost matchless advances in science, art, literature, and all material and cultural developments of the past two thousand years. It must be of the spirit if we are to save the flesh."

But once war is forced upon us, there is no other alternative than to apply every available means to bring it to a swift end. War's very object is victory, not prolonged indecision. In war there is no substitute for victory.

There are some who for varying reasons would appease Red China. They are blind to history's clear lesson, for history teaches with unmistakable emphasis that appeasement but begets new and bloodier war. It points to no single instance where this end has justified that means, where appeasement has led to more than a sham peace. Like blackmail, it lays the basis for new and successively greater demands until, as in blackmail, violence becomes the only other alternative. Why, my soldiers asked of me, surrender military advantages to an enemy in the field? I could not answer. Some may say to avoid spread of the conflict into an all-out war with China. Others, to avoid Soviet intervention. Neither explanation seems valid, for China is already engaging with the maximum power it can commit, and the Soviet Union will not necessarily mesh its actions with our moves. Like a cobra, any new enemy will more likely strike whenever it feels that the relativity in military or other potential is in its favor on a worldwide basis.

The tragedy of Korea is further heightened by the fact that its military action is confined to its territorial limits. It condemns that nation, which it is our purpose to save, to suffer the devastating impact of full naval and air bombardment while the enemy's sanctuaries are fully protected from such attack and devastation. Of the nations of the world, Korea alone, up to now, is the sole one which has risked its all against communism. The magnificence of the courage and fortitude of the Korean people defies description. They have chosen to risk death rather than slavery. Their last words to me were: "Don't scuttle the Pacific."

I have just left your fighting sons in Korea. They have met all tests there, and I can report to you without reservation that they are splendid in every way. It was my constant effort to preserve them and end this savage conflict honorably and with the least loss of time and a minimum sacrifice of life. Its growing bloodshed has caused me the deepest anguish and anxiety. Those gallant men will remain often in my thoughts and in my prayers always.

I am closing my 52 years of military service. When I joined the army, even before the turn of the century, it was the fulfillment of all of my boyish hopes and dreams. The world has turned over many times since I took the oath on the plain at West Point, and the hopes and dreams have long since vanished, but I still remember the refrain of one of the most popular barracks ballads of that day which proclaimed most proudly that old soldiers never die; they just fade away. And like the old soldier of that ballad, I now close my military career and just fade away, an old soldier who tried to do his duty as God gave him the light to see that duty. Good-bye.

April 20

Death of Pontiac, Ottawa Chieftain

One of the first great Native American leaders, Pontiac, died on April 20, 1769. His exact date of birth is unknown, although it was probably sometime in the year 1720. He was a warrior chief of the powerful Ottawa tribe in the Great Lakes area.

French explorers and traders were the first to make contact with the Ottawa as the French began to chart the Great Lakes region in the 1600s. The Ottawas were part of the Algonquin-speaking family of tribes, and were active traders with both the European newcomers and the other tribes. By the time that Pontiac was born, the Ottawas had become French allies, and were dependent on French guns, gunpowder, and trade goods. They fought with the French in the frontier wars between Great Britain and France that erupted intermittently from the late 1600s until the 1760s when Britain finally prevailed.

The details of Pontiac's early life are sketchy at best. He gained a reputation as a powerful warrior and was loyal to the French. Unlike the British, the French were primarily traders and brought few settlers with them, thus posing a limited threat to the Ottawa people. During the French and Indian War (1756–1763), the last of the British-French frontier wars, the British gained the upper hand. French forts, including the important site of Fort Detroit (now Detroit, Michigan), were taken by Great Britain. By 1760, the British had displaced the French from the Great Lakes region.

Unlike the French, the British refused to provide the Ottawas and other tribes with guns, food, and tobacco in return for their acquiescence to European rule. The aggrieved tribes thus turned to Pontiac for leadership, and in 1763 he forged a Native American confederacy against the British. Pontiac hoped to retake Fort Detroit and bring the French back to the Great Lakes, but the British discovered his plans and successfully held the fort when Pontiac attacked.

Frustrated, Pontiac attacked the other British positions in the Great Lakes and Ohio Valley region, taking all of the British forts between Fort Detroit and what is now Pittsburgh, Pennsylvania. He also added more tribes to his alliance. When it became clear that the British were defeating the French in Europe and the other theaters of the war (also known as the Seven Years War), however, many tribes began to leave Pontiac's cause. The British successfully reinforced Fort Detroit, and began to reassert their authority. Pontiac's warriors were largely free to come and go as they pleased and the confederacy of tribes was at best loosely organized, whereas the British soldiers were highly disciplined and armed with modern weapons. Finally, the French never sent the assistance that Pontiac expected.

The result was Pontiac's defeat by the end of 1763. He continued to fight the British and attempted to revive his confederacy, but in 1765 he accepted the inevitable and swore allegiance to the British. While traveling in Illinois, Pontiac was murdered on April 20, 1769, by a warrior of the Peoria tribe, who may have been paid by the British.

The Hague Peace Palace

During the last quarter of the 19th century all of the European powers except Great Britain introduced the principle of compulsory military training for every able-bodied male citizen. The growth of vast national armies resulting from this policy convinced many that the specter of world war was at hand. However, there were some who would not passively accept the possibility of such a disaster. Innumerable peace societies sprang up in Europe and the United States, and their members argued that if the major national governments would agree to limit armaments and arbitrate international disputes war might be avoided.

Hopes for world peace were encouraged when Czar Nicholas II of Russia suggested that an international conference meet at The Hague in 1899 to consider a general disarmament. Although the participating nations could not agree to a limitation on arms, the meeting did result in the establishment of the first permanent court of international arbitration. The court had one glaring defect, namely that there was no mechanism by which nations could be forced to submit their claims to arbitration, but in the euphoric months immediately following the first Hague Peace Conference this aspect was overlooked. Attention centered instead on providing a suitable peace palace at The Hague.

Shortly after the conference had adjourned, Lyudvig von Martins, the Russian minister in Berlin, approached Andrew White, the American ambassador at The Hague, with the suggestion that one of the latter's compatriots might be able to contribute the funds needed for the construction of the peace palace. White immediately thought of American industrialist Andrew Carnegie. In the years following the Civil War, Carnegie had ruthlessly built his fortune in the steel industry, but by 1899 he had embarked upon an extraordinary philanthropic career. White wrote to Carnegie concerning the palace, and after several months of desultory correspondence received an invitation to Carnegie's castle in Scotland. Carnegie said nothing of the peace palace until the final day of White's visit, when he agreed to supply the necessary funds if such an agreement proved acceptable to the government of the Netherlands.

An accord with the Dutch was reached, and on April 20, 1903, Carnegie donated $1.5 million for the peace palace. Construction of the building on land contributed by the Dutch government was begun in 1907 and completed in 1913. Since then it has served as the seat of the Permanent Court of Arbitration. The Permanent Court of International Justice, established in 1922, and its successor the International Court of Justice, created in 1946 as an organ of the United Nations, have also been housed in The Hague Peace Palace.

April 21

Passover (*Pesach*)

This is a movable event.

Passover (in Hebrew, *Pesach*), or the Feast of Unleavened Bread, is one of the most important and elaborate celebrations of the Jewish year. As it began more than 3,000 years ago and continues to the present day, it is also one of the oldest festivals known to history. Beginning at sundown on the 14th day of the month of Nisan (March–April), the Passover is observed by Orthodox and Conservative Jews for the next eight days, and by Reform Jews for the next seven. Its high point is the *seder*, a ceremonial meal served in all Jewish homes on the first night; and by Conservative, Orthodox, and some Reform Jews on the second night as well. Many Reform synagogues observe a home seder one night and on the other have a community seder in the synagogue for members and their guests. The seder is also served in hotels or central meeting halls for those away from home.

Passover is a celebration of the Exodus, the deliverance of the Jews under Moses after their many generations of captivity in Egypt. Thus it is a festival of freedom from bondage, marking the real beginning of the Jewish nation. The entire story of the Jews' deliverance, including their safe passage across the Red Sea, is recounted in the Old Testament in the Book of Exodus. According to this account the Jews, obeying the commands of Moses, remained in their homes on the fateful night before their exodus from Egypt. They were dressed and ready for their journey, and ate unleavened bread and the sacrificial (or paschal) lamb. Fulfilling Moses' prediction, the firstborn of the Egyptians were slain by the hand of God, both humans and animals, so that no Egyptian household remained without its dead.

The term *Passover* refers to the way in which God, when he smote the firstborn of the Egyptians, passed over the homes of the Jews in Egypt, since their lintels and doorposts had been marked with the blood of sacrificial lambs in accordance with God's instructions to Moses. Fulfillment of the prediction caused the Pharaoh to summon Moses in the night and urge him to depart in haste from the land with his people. Later, reconsidering the loss of their servants, the Jews, the Egyptians pursued them and were drowned by the waters of the Red Sea. According to the biblical account, the Red Sea parted to allow the Jews to pass on dry land, but closed upon and drowned the pursuing Egyptians.

After the Jews reached the Promised Land in Israel some 40 years later, they continued Passover as Moses had originally instructed them. Except for the now discontinued offering of sacrificial lambs on the eve of Passover, an annual ritual from the Jews' entry into Israel until the destruction of the Second Temple in Jerusalem, the Passover rites of biblical times have been observed to this day. Essentially the observance is a reliving, on an individual basis, of the original Passover experience and an expression of gratitude for it. It also serves to preserve the history of the people and to instruct the young. Passover customs are deliberately arranged for the enjoyment of children and for their participation.

In preparation for the Passover celebration, Jewish houses are cleaned, traditional foods are prepared, and special dishes and cooking utensils, unused during the rest of the year, are placed in readiness. During the seven or eight days of the actual Passover observance only unleavened bread, the traditional matzos or bread of affliction, commemorating the Jews' hasty departure from Egypt before the leaven or yeast in their bread had time to rise, is eaten. On the night before Passover eve, Orthodox Jews make certain that there is no yeast or leavened bread in their homes.

The seder finds the head of the family in the place of honor, provided (like other males) with cushions in memory of the ancient manner of freemen who reclined at the table, and with his family, guests, and servants all seated with him in recognition of the equality of all before God. In the center of the table are the symbolic Passover foods, including unleavened bread; bitter herbs in remembrance of the hardships of slavery; a roasted egg, as a free will or voluntary offering; salt water, signifying tears; *haroset*, a mixture of apples, nuts, cinnamon, and wine, representing the bricks and mortar used in Egypt; and a roasted shank bone of lamb, symbolizing the sacrificial lamb of tradition. There is wine on the table, and four cups or glasses are drunk by each participant, each cup at a fixed point in the ceremonial meal, with a fifth cup placed on the table for the prophet Elijah who, it is believed, will pave the way for the coming of the Messiah.

The focal point of the seder is the reading aloud of the story of the Exodus. The account, as related in the Haggadah, is in response to four questions, asked by the youngest child of the family, as to the meaning of the evening and its customs, beginning with the traditional "Why is this night different from other nights?" Commencing his answers, the head of the household responds: "We were slaves in Egypt, but the Lord our God brought us out with a mighty hand and an outstretched arm." In addition to the Exodus account, the seder includes benedictions, psalms, and prayers of thanksgiving.

Texas Wins Independence From Mexico

One of the most important days of the year for Texans is April 21, the anniversary of the Battle of San Jacinto in 1836, after which Mexico was forced to recognize the independence of Texas.

Mexico itself had been independent from Spain for only 15 years at the time of the battle, and, like Spain before, Mexico considered the area of Texas to be within its boundaries. The United States had asserted a claim to the region based on the Louisiana Purchase from France in 1803, but the claim was rather tenuous, especially given the Adams-Onis Treaty of 1819, by which the United States acquired Florida from Spain while renouncing its claim to Texas. Nevertheless, American settlers began to arrive in Texas, attracted by the vast available lands and the lenient attitude of the Mexican authorities towards Americans in Texas.

The first direct step towards Texas's independence came in 1810, at the beginning of the revolution by which Mexico eventually expelled the Spanish who had ruled Mexico for so long. The Texans chose that moment to set up a government of their own, with Nacogdoches as their capital. Texas's independence at that time was brief, however, since the forces of Spain—which would hold on to power until 1821—quickly broke up the new Texas government.

In 1820 Moses Austin petitioned the Spanish governor of Texas for a grant of land big enough to provide farms for 300 families of American settlers. He learned in 1821 that his request had been granted, but he died before he could carry out his plan for settlement. Instead, the idea was implemented by his son, Stephen Austin, who secured confirmation of his father's grant from the new Mexican government and learned that he could have as much land as he wished, at no cost, and at a location of his own choice. Mexico continued to offer large gifts of land, either to individual settlers or to the *empresarios* who, like Austin, contracted to bring settlers in. The result of the official generosity was a flood of American settlers. The number exceeded 7,000 early in the 1820s, tripled within the next decade, and continued to swell thereafter.

In 1826 the American settlers, desiring independence, proclaimed the eastern part of Texas an independent republic. As such it survived for only a short time. It was after this act of insurrection that the Mexican authorities in 1827 ordered a stop to further American immigration, although they did not enforce the order until about 1830. Then, the Mexicans dispatched troops to carry out their decrees, ejecting recent arrivals. Two years later there was another revolt, followed by the calling of a convention, which elected Stephen Austin as president. The authority of Mexico over Texas nonetheless continued, and Austin was sent to Mexico to demand reforms. Instead of getting a hearing, he was imprisoned.

After his release in July 1835, Austin became involved in the Texas Revolution. The first battle of that revolution was fought on October 2, 1835, at Gonzales. After this victory, the Texans captured San Antonio, where they fortified themselves in the Alamo. Santa Anna, the Mexican general and dictator, began his long siege of that bastion on February 23, 1836. During this siege, another conference of Texans, meeting on March 2, formally declared Texas to be independent of Mexico (see March 2). It was just four days later, on March 6, 1836, that the outnumbered defenders of the Alamo were overcome by Santa Anna's men (see March 6). The provisional government of Texas, meeting on the day of the defeat, appointed Sam Houston "commander in chief of all land forces of the Texian Army, regulars, volunteers and militia," supplementing his earlier appointment as commander only of regulars. Directly after the new appointment, Houston went to Gonzales and there learned of the Alamo disaster. Gathering an army as he went, Houston retreated east toward the Brazos River, followed closely by Santa Anna. Arriving at the point where Buffalo Bayou joins the San Jacinto River, Houston made camp and waited for Santa Anna's troops.

On the afternoon of April 21, 1836, Santa Anna's men failed to post lookouts. Nearly 1,600 strong, they were taken by surprise by Houston's force of some 900 Texans, who had crossed a mile of prairie to reach them, screened only by sparse trees and rising ground and inspired by the slogan "Remember the Alamo." The battle was short, and cost the Mexicans 630 killed and 730 taken prisoner, compared to only nine Texan casualties. Santa Anna was taken prisoner the next day, and forced to sign a treaty by which he pledged to do what he could to secure the recognition of Texas as an independent republic, with boundaries extending as far south as the Rio Grande. The battle of San Jacinto, one of the most decisive in American history, confirmed the independence of Texas and also paved the way for its annexation by the United States on March 1, 1845.

Spanish-American War Begins

Replying to a declaration of war by Spain on April 24, 1898, the United States declared that a state of war had been in effect between the two countries since April 21, the day when the main squadron of the U.S. Atlantic fleet had been ordered to Cuban waters.

The conflict had its origins in Spain's attempt to maintain its position as a power in the New World. The pride and remembered glory of a once vast empire played an important role in Spanish determination to retain control of Cuba. Spanish voyages of exploration and settlement during the 15th and 16th centuries had created an empire that included large areas within what is now the United States, Mexico, Central America, all of South America except Brazil, small areas in Africa and the Far East, and various islands around the globe. Spain remained a great imperial power until the time of the Napoleonic Wars. Then in 1808 the French emperor Napoléon I put his brother Joseph on the throne of French-occupied Spain. The result was a series of upheavals in Spain and in the Spanish colonies. By 1819 all but Cuba, the Philippine Islands, and some holdings in the Caribbean, Africa, and the Far East had gained their independence.

After a Cuban revolt in 1895, Spain introduced the *reconcentrado* system, under which peasant families were relocated in fortified cities while the countryside was ravaged to destroy the insurgents' sources of supply. This policy, like the earlier unsuccessful Ten Years' War for independence (1868–1878), brought great suffering to Cuba's rural population and increased sympathy in the United States. Proinsurgent feelings were also inflamed by sensational coverage of Cuban events in the so-called "yellow press," notably William Randolph Hearst's *New York Journal* and Joseph Pulitzer's *New York World*. The rivalry between the two newspapers appeared to have reached its apex with inflammatory accounts of the sinking of the American battleship USS *Maine*, with a loss of 260 lives, in Havana harbor on February 15, 1898 (see February 15).

The *Maine* had been sent to Havana for the protection of American citizens and property in Cuba. American involvement had grown significantly, and Americans had a huge stake in the island's economy, with substantial sugar and mining investments in addition to trading and shipping interests. Another factor was the American hope of building an Atlantic-to-Pacific canal across the Central American isthmus; Cuba's location was strategic in any such project. Although many Americans, including President William McKinley, had hoped for a peaceful settlement of the Cuban situation, war sentiment was fed by the exaggerated Hearst and Pulitzer reports and by the proexpansionist sentiments of the time.

On April 11, 1898, President McKinley asked Congress for the authority to intervene in Cuba. Congress responded with resolutions that demanded Spain's withdrawal from Cuba and defined terms for American intervention. On April 22, Congress passed an act authorizing the enlistment of volunteer troops. The Spanish declaration of war, which came two days later, was followed by the United States's retroactive declaration, placing the beginning of hostilities on April 21.

The war itself was a brief and one-sided contest, with some of the major engagements fought halfway around the world, such as in the Philippine Islands at the Battle of Manila Bay. Action in Cuba included encounters at Santiago, where most of the Spanish fleet was destroyed; at Las Guasimas and El Caney; and at San Juan Hill, where the volunteer Rough Riders of Theodore Roosevelt and Leonard Wood won fame.

An armistice supposedly stopping the fighting (though an attack on Manila took place the following day) was signed on August 12, 1898. Details of

The Rough Riders after their victory at San Juan Hill.

the peace (see January 28, The United States Withdraws from Cuba) were set forth in the Treaty of Paris of 1898, signed on December 10. The treaty was ratified by the Senate on February 6, 1899, and signed by the president four days later. Spain emerged from the conflict with all but the last remnants of its colonial empire gone and its long influence in the New World at an end. Cuba became an independent republic under American protection. Thus, by the end of the war, the United States had become a world power, with new interests in the Pacific and an increased stake in the affairs of the Caribbean.

John Muir's Birthday

John Muir, naturalist and founder of the Sierra Club, was born on April 21, 1838, in Dunbar, Scotland. The Muir family came to America in 1849, when he was 11, and they settled in Wisconsin. Life was hard on the frontier farm, but he came to love nature and the American wilderness. Despite the lack of educational opportunities, Muir learned to read, and studied by himself whenever he could find the time. He successfully gained admission to the University of Wisconsin in Madison.

Muir studied natural science, and left the university in 1863. He began to explore the American countryside on foot, wandering across the country and taking various odd jobs to support himself. His travels took him through the American South,

where he came down with malaria in Florida, and then cross-country to California in 1868. After a brief stay in San Francisco, he left the city for the Californian wilderness, settling in the scenic Yosemite Valley. He frequently corresponded with Ralph Waldo Emerson, describing the beauty of the valley and the surrounding mountains.

In 1880 Muir married and moved to Martinez, California, although he continued to visit Yosemite. During his trips he became increasingly concerned about the pace of development, the rapidly increasing population of California, and the resulting threat posed to the pristine wilderness. He corresponded with a friend who was the editor of *Century* magazine, writing, among other things, "let us do something to make the mountains glad." Muir's concerns eventually led to the foundation of the Sierra Club, which has grown to become one of the leading environmental preservation organizations in the United States today.

Muir also worked with President Theodore Roosevelt to preserve national treasures such as the Yosemite Valley, which today remains an unspoiled wilderness protected by the federal government. Muir succumbed to pneumonia on December 24, 1914, in Los Angeles, California.

April 22

President George Washington Issues Neutrality Proclamation

In April 1793, Great Britain went to war with the new Republic of France, established after the overthrow of King Louis XVI. The United States was caught in the middle, unwilling to take sides against either the powerful British Empire or the French, who had aided the Americans during the American Revolution. Further, there were substantial trade interests with both countries. On April 22, 1793, President George Washington declared that the United States would be neutral, and issued a famous proclamation to that effect. (See also February 22, George Washington's Birthday.)

The proclamation is set forth below:

Whereas it appears that a state of war exists between Austria, Prussia, Sardinia, Great Britain, and the United Netherlands, of the one part, and France on the other; and the duty and interest of the United States require, that they should with sincerity and good faith adopt and pursue a conduct friendly and impartial toward the belligerent Powers,

I have therefore thought fit by these present to declare the disposition of the United States to observe the conduct aforesaid towards those Powers respectfully; and to exhort and warn the citizens of the United States carefully to avoid all acts and proceedings whatsoever, which may in any manner tend to contravene such disposition.

And I do hereby also make known, that whatsoever of the citizens of the United States shall render himself liable to punishment or forfeiture under the law of nations, by committing, aiding, or abetting hostilities against any of the said Powers, or by carrying to any of them those articles which are deemed contraband by the modern usage of nations, will not receive the protection of the United States, against such punishment or forfeiture; and further, that I have given instructions to those officers, to whom it belongs, to cause prosecutions to be instituted against all persons, who shall, within the cognizance of the courts of the United States, violate the law of nations, with respect to the Powers at war, or any of them.

In testimony whereof, I have caused the seal of the United States of America to be affixed to these present, and signed the same with my hand. Done at the city of Philadelphia, the twenty-second day of April, one thousand seven hundred and ninety-three, and of the Independence of the United States of America the seventeenth.

Arbor Day

"Other holidays repose upon the past; Arbor Day proposes for the future." The words of the originator of Arbor Day, Julius Sterling Morton, pinpoint the significance of this day, which focuses on the value of trees. Today conservation of the natural environment is universally acknowledged to be of major importance; however, Morton was one of the earliest conservationists at a time when even the term was unknown. In honor of Morton, a Nebraska City newspaper editor in 1872 proposed the first Arbor Day as an occasion for tree planting, and Nebraska began to celebrate Arbor Day as an annual event on April 22. The observance has subsequently spread throughout the country.

One of the first Americans to concern himself seriously with the need for tree conservation was the pioneering John Chapman, who became known as Johnny Appleseed. A few years after the American Revolution, Chapman set out from his native Massachusetts with a pouch of apple seeds and little else. Fruit trees were scarce in the developing western areas, so he wandered through present-day Pennsylvania, Ohio, Illinois, and Indiana, planting apple trees. Several decades later Julius Sterling Morton, who became known as the Father of Arbor Day, also went west, when he was only a child. At the age of two Morton, who had been born in Adams, New York, on April 22, 1832, moved with his family to Michigan, where he received his elementary education at the Methodist Episcopal Academy in Albion. Entering the University of Michigan, he transferred to Union College in Schenectady, New York, from which he graduated in 1854 with a B.A. degree. Morton married in October 1854, and the following year he and his wife settled on the treeless plains of Nebraska, where he edited the Nebraska City News and also became active in politics. In the course of his career he served as a member of the Nebraska territorial legislature, as secretary of the territory, and for a time as acting territorial governor. After Nebraska gained statehood in 1867, he ran unsuccessfully as a Democratic candidate for the governorship, and also ran unsuccessfully for a seat in the United States Senate.

Morton worked to improve agricultural methods through his newspaper writings and in other ways. He was a member of the state board of agriculture and was appointed secretary of agriculture by President Grover Cleveland, serving in that capacity from 1893 to 1897. At the same time (1893–1896) he was president of the American Forestry Association. He died in 1902.

Believing that the Nebraska prairie area in which he homesteaded would benefit from trees, which could serve as windbreaks, hold moisture in the soil, and provide lumber needed for shelter, Morton began planting trees and urging his neighbors to do the same. He felt, however, that his idea was not catching on rapidly enough, and when he joined the state board of agriculture he seized the opportunity to propose that a specific day be set aside for the planting of trees. His resolution included a provision for prizes to be awarded to the county agricultural society and to the individual who properly planted the largest number of trees on the first Arbor Day, and he proposed April 10, 1872, for that designation. The idea proved unexpectedly popular: A million trees were planted in Nebraska on that one day alone.

So successful was the day that it was made an annual event in 1884, and in 1885 the state legislature passed an act specifying April 22, the anniversary of Morton's birth, as the date on which Arbor Day would thenceforth be celebrated as a legal holiday. About 350 million trees were planted in Nebraska within 16 years after that first Arbor Day in 1872. Interest in tree planting continued, and today the state has a national forest planted by Nebraskans that covers more than 200,000 acres and from which seedlings are provided to other countries that have seriously depleted forests.

Agricultural organizations and town authorities promoted the observance of Arbor Day, and three years after its inception in Nebraska two other states, Kansas and Tennessee, also observed an Arbor Day, as did Minnesota the following year. Much greater stimulus was provided, however, by Ohio's first observance in April 1882. It was timed to coincide with the meeting in Cincinnati of the American Forestry Association and the American Forestry Congress. The success and popularity of the Ohio event helped encourage other states to adopt their own Arbor Day observances. Today, in many localities, Arbor Day has been subsumed by Earth Day, a celebration with many of the same goals. See the article on Earth Day, March 21.

Oklahoma Land Rush Begins

On April 22, 1889, a frantic land "run" opened up the first section of what is now Oklahoma to American settlement. Known as the Unassigned Lands, the area consisted of approximately two million acres in the center of the vast region then called the Indian Territory. The 1889 run was instrumental in paving the way for the organization of the Oklahoma Territory in 1890 and eventual statehood in 1907.

The land rush of April 22, 1889, was a major development in the history of the hitherto entirely Native American–populated area. Apart from the plains tribes who had roamed there earlier, most Native Americans had arrived in the region as a result of the federal government's policy by which tribes in the southeast Atlantic seaboard region were transplanted from their ancestral homes to locations west of the Mississippi River in the 1820s, 1830s, and 1840s. The removal effort reached massive proportions after Andrew Jackson became president in 1829. On May 28, 1830, Congress passed the Indian Removal Act, empowering the president to "negotiate" with tribes to give up their eastern holdings in exchange for land beyond the Mississippi, which was to be theirs "as long as the grass grows, or water runs," in the words of Jackson. When the tribes resisted removal, the American military supervised a vast, involuntary, and tragedy-filled exodus to the West. The infamous Trail of Tears occurred during this period.

The large, vaguely defined trans-Mississippi region that became popularly known as the Indian Territory gained a more official status in 1834, when Congress set aside an area including all of what is now Oklahoma, except the panhandle, as the Indian Territory. The unsettled region, regarded as a barren wilderness fit only for savages, was divided among what were called the Five Civilized Tribes (the Chickasaw, Creek, Seminole, Choctaw, and Cherokee) who had been driven from the Southeast. After these tribes had, for the most part, sided with the Confederacy during the Civil War, the federal government in 1866 split the Indian Territory from north to south and forced the five tribes to relinquish the western part of their lands. From 1866 to 1883 the government made numerous small grants from this vast new territory at its disposal to other tribes, among them the Cheyenne, Apache, Arapahoe, Comanche, Kiowa, and Pottawatomie. By the mid-1880s, the only major land block that had not yet been assigned was the central region known as the Unassigned Lands, and later as Old Oklahoma, or the Oklahoma District.

When the settlement of the West picked up again after the hiatus of the Civil War, the Indian Territory, once thought to be of little value, grew more and more attractive to American pioneers.

Cattle drovers, traveling from northern Texas across the Indian Territory to the railroad depots in Kansas, quickly discovered that the herds grew fat on the lush grasslands. The region's most famous longhorn trail was reputedly named after Jesse Chisholm, a mixed-blood Cherokee who used the route after the Civil War to get supplies to his trading post at Anadarko. Passing through the sites of several modern-day Oklahoma towns, such as Waurika, Duncan, Marlow, El Reno, and Enid, the trail reached the busy stockyards of Abilene, Kansas. In 1871 some 700,000 cattle were driven over the Chisholm Trail, while in the peak period of 1867 to 1871, an estimated 40,000 boxcars carted 1.5 million longhorns to slaughterhouses in Chicago and Kansas City. The rapidly developing range cattle industry so enhanced the worth of the Indian Territory that Americans vied to rent pastures on Indian land and ran prosperous ranches nominally under Indian ownership.

Soon not only cattlemen but land-hungry homesteaders coveted the Indian Territory. Even before the railroad had reached the area of Oklahoma in the early 1870s, white settlers had illegally squatted on Indian Territory land, ignoring all treaties. In the late 1870s newspaper articles urged settlement of what was referred to erroneously as "public land" open to homestead entry. Spurred on by these accounts, several groups of homesteaders drew up elaborate colonization schemes and to a limited extent implemented them until ejected by federal soldiers. President Rutherford B. Hayes was finally forced to reiterate officially the ban on settlement in 1879 and again the following year. Nevertheless, pressure to open the Indian Territory, especially the central Unassigned Lands, increased steadily until the "boomers," persons "booming" or pushing for settlement of the region, succeeded in transferring the issue to Washington, D.C.

Agitation by railroad companies, land speculators, and impatient frontier farmers eventually caused Congress to modify its policy and open at least part of the Indian Territory to settlement. In 1885 Congress empowered the president to conduct negotiations with the Creek and Seminole to extinguish all possible tribal claims to the central Unassigned Lands. By 1889 the government had managed to obtain, through coercion and other methods, a clear title to the unoccupied land. Soon afterwards President Benjamin Harrison announced that the Oklahoma District, previously called the Unassigned Lands, would be opened to entry under the Homestead Act of 1862 precisely at high noon on April 22, 1889. Each successful homesteader would be permitted to claim one 160-acre plot free of charge.

The actual land run was a scene of confusion, making a fascinating page in American history. Estimates of the number of persons who milled along the border on the morning of the historic event range all the way from 20,000 to 100,000. The United States Army did its utmost to keep the excited settlers restrained behind the starting line. However, some wily opportunists, known as "sooners" (thus accounting for Oklahoma's nickname, the Sooner State), managed to evade the guards and sneak into the district before the official opening. The few sooners who were later caught lost their claims, but many succeeded in carrying off the gamble.

At noon on April 22, the federally appointed timekeepers at the border signaled a cavalry trumpeter stationed on high ground. He in turn sounded "dinner-call" on his bugle, thus setting in motion one of the wildest and most extensive land runs in history. The whooping settlers, mainly midwesterners and southerners, tore across the line by various means of transportation: horses, wagons, and even bicycles. The prospect of free land had been so alluring that by nightfall nearly all of the almost two million acres were occupied, some claims having as many as six contenders. What at dawn had been a barren prairie was by dusk staked-out homesteads and bustling tent-and-shack communities boasting populations as high as 15,000. Among the towns that sprang into existence were Oklahoma City, Guthrie, Kingfisher, Edmond, and Norman.

The land rush of 1889 triggered a series of additional runs in 1891, 1892, and 1893, as the federal government attempted to regulate migration by allowing homesteaders to settle only one new section at a time. Especially prominent was the opening of the Cherokee Outlet on September 16, 1893. The homesteading procedure was completed by lottery and allotment in the opening years of the 20th century.

In 1890 the Oklahoma Territory was created around a nucleus consisting primarily of the panhandle and the now booming Oklahoma District. Other western sections of Oklahoma were gradually added to the Oklahoma Territory. The eastern area still owned by the Five Civilized Tribes became known as Indian Territory (not to be confused with the original Indian Territory set aside by Congress in 1834). The two territories combined to enter the Union as the state of Oklahoma on November 16, 1907.

April 23

James Buchanan's Birthday

Library of Congress

James Buchanan

James Buchanan, 15th president of the United States just before the outbreak of the Civil War, was born near Mercersburg, Pennsylvania, on April 23, 1791, to James and Elizabeth Speer Buchanan. His father was a Scotch-Irish Presbyterian who had gone in 1783 to south-central Pennsylvania, where he became a successful storekeeper. Young James Buchanan attended a school in Mercersburg and graduated in 1809 from Dickinson College in Carlisle. He read law for three years in Lancaster, and at the age of 21 was admitted to the bar.

Buchanan proved to be an exceptionally able lawyer. Within three years his earnings were more than $11,000, a very large income at that time. The legal learning and oratorical skill that made him a fine lawyer also recommended him for politics. He entered the Pennsylvania House of Representatives in 1814 as a Federalist and served two terms. Buchanan then expected to retire from politics, but personal calamity intervened. His fiancée died suddenly, before he was able to heal a quarrel that had caused her to break their engagement. Buchanan put aside thoughts of marriage and turned completely to politics. He never married. Later, his orphaned niece, Harriet Lane, acted as his hostess, surrounding him with the most charming society of the time.

Buchanan was elected to Congress in 1820 and served for a decade in the House of Representatives, eventually becoming chairman of the judiciary committee. The disbanding of the Federalist Party in the 1820s forced him, as a moderate, to choose between the Whig Party and the Democratic-Republican Party (soon after to be called the Democratic Party). He chose the Democrats, unlike many Federalists, and soon established cordial relations with Andrew Jackson, whom he actively supported for president in 1828.

In 1830, after again attempting to retire from politics, Buchanan accepted the ambassadorship to Russia. His stay in St. Petersburg was marked by successes that won him popularity at home, such as negotiating an important commercial treaty between Russia and the United States. On his return to the United States in 1833, Buchanan was elected from Pennsylvania to fill an unfinished term in the United States Senate and was twice reelected. He became an important "party man," supporting the programs of Presidents Jackson and Martin Van Buren.

In the decades leading up to the Civil War, slavery divided the country. As senator, Buchanan shared the common opinion of Pennsylvanians that slavery was morally evil, and he upheld the constitutional right to petition for abolition. At the same time he emphasized that, under the Constitution, Congress had no control over slavery in the states and held that the national government had a duty to protect slavery where it existed. Buchanan also publicly sympathized with Southern whites' fears that abolitionism would set off slave revolts, endangering white homes. He criticized abolitionist "fanaticism," while his positions avoided the question of the extension of slavery into the territories.

The Democrats nominated James K. Polk in the election of 1844, passing over the favorite-son candidacy of Buchanan. When Buchanan delivered Pennsylvania's uncertain electoral votes to Polk, he gained a claim to high office. Polk named him his secretary of state. Though the initiative in foreign affairs was as often the president's as his own, Buchanan served in the post with distinction from 1845 to 1849 and greatly enhanced his public popularity. An expansionist, Buchanan employed his diplomatic skill in resolving the dispute with Britain over Oregon and in the question of the annexation of Texas. In settling the Mexican War, he was subordinate to Polk. However, Buchanan was largely responsible for the president's reiterations of the Monroe Doctrine to deter further British involvement in the Western Hemisphere. As secretary of state, Buchanan was strongly interested in Central America, and he personally opened the dormant question of Cuba with an unsuccessful attempt to purchase the island from Spain.

When the Whigs won the presidency in 1848 with Zachary Taylor, Buchanan retired to Wheatland, a country estate near Lancaster. In 1852 friends made a great effort to win the Democratic nomination for Buchanan, but the party's convention eventually chose the unknown Franklin Pierce of New Hampshire. Buchanan campaigned vigorously for Pierce and must have been severely disappointed to be offered the ministry to Great Britain, rather than an influential position at home, after Pierce's victory.

Buchanan's two years in Great Britain shielded him from the controversies over the extension of slavery under Pierce. His popularity with white Southerners and many Democrats was heightened by the Ostend Manifesto, which he secretly drew up at Ostend, Belgium, with the American ministers to Spain and France in October 1854. The manifesto contained a historical discussion of the Cuban question followed by the recommendation that the United States purchase Cuba from Spain, or, if Spain refused to sell, that Cuba be seized. The authors were anxious to prevent European interference, especially the possible emancipation of slaves in Cuba, or a slave revolution. The manifesto read in part: "We should . . . be recreant to our duty . . . should we permit Cuba to be Africanized and become a second St. Domingo, with all its attendant horrors to the white race, and suffer the flames to extend to our neighboring shores, seriously to endanger or actually to consume the fair fabric of our Union."

The document also argued that "self-preservation is the first law of nature, with States as with individuals." In the event that Cuba became necessary to American safety, then "by every law, human and divine, we shall be justified in wresting it from Spain if we possess the power." The United States government repudiated the manifesto, but Buchanan's popularity persisted with the proslavery Southerners.

In 1856 Buchanan became the Democratic nominee for president, on a platform stating that the Compromise of 1850 (including the Fugitive Slave Act) was final and reiterating that Congress should not interfere with slavery in the territories. When he spoke during the campaign, which was not often, he denounced the abolitionists. He was elected by popular plurality over John C. Frémont, the first nominee of the newly organized Republican Party, and Millard Fillmore, the candidate of the Whig and American ("Know-Nothing") parties.

James Buchanan hoped to heal the increasingly bitter sectionalism of the country. The warnings given by the realignment of political parties, namely the destruction of the Whigs and the growth of the Republican Party as a force hostile to the South and slavery, seem not to have alarmed him. The new president genuinely relied on "strict construction" of the Constitution and judicial decision to fashion a compromise between proslavery and antislavery forces and to avert internal warfare. Thus, in his inaugural address, Buchanan referred to slavery in the territories as "happily a matter of but little practical importance" because the Supreme Court would shortly settle the question "speedily and finally." Buchanan's allusion was to the Dred Scott decision, which would soon infuriate the North. By dividing his cabinet equally between Northerners and Southerners, Buchanan sought to maintain a delicately balanced peace. He was a man divided in roles and interests, close in politics and friendship to many wealthy white Southerners and clearly a white supremacist, but deeply opposed to secession and morally opposed to slavery. Under the circumstances, he lashed out most at the group pushing the conflict to total crisis, namely the abolitionists.

Buchanan's hoped-for successes in foreign policy were wholly overshadowed by the financial panic of 1857 and the struggle over slavery in Kansas. In 1858 Buchanan favored granting Kansas statehood under the proslavery Lecompton Constitution. This decision identified the administration with the Southern Democrats and precipitated revolt among the supporters of Stephen A. Douglas, opening the way to Abraham Lincoln's election in November 1860.

Buchanan has been charged with fostering secession by his argument that although the states had no right to secede, the federal government had no power to prevent them, since it could employ force in a state only at the demand of the lawful authorities. Further, his reluctance to act after South Carolina announced its secession on December 20, 1860, threw the entire burden of reversing secession on Lincoln.

Early in 1861 Buchanan moved slowly to oppose South Carolina. He refused to remove federal troops from Charleston harbor and tried to reinforce the garrison there, he also announced his intention to protect federal property if it was attacked. Not finding constitutional authority to act beyond this, he simply held on until Lincoln's inauguration in March 1861 and then retired to Wheatland. During the Civil War, he backed the federal government as a Union Democrat and wrote a careful defense of his administration. He died on June 1, 1868, at the age of 77.

April 23

St. George's Day

The feast of St. George, patron saint of England since the Middle Ages, is celebrated by Roman Catholics and many Protestants on April 23. However, long before the Middle Ages, St. George was greatly venerated in the East and so his day is celebrated by many Eastern Orthodox churches (often on a different date, however, since Orthodox churches sometimes still use the Old Style or Julian calendar).

Although there are many traditions about St. George, little is known about him except that he was martyred in the year 303 in Diospolis (now Lydda, or Lod), in Palestine. A decree attributed to Pope Gelasius I at the end of the 5th century includes St. George among those saints "whose names are reverenced among men, but whose actions are known only to God."

According to one tradition, George was born in Asia Minor, then a province of the Roman Empire. He joined the Roman army and rose to the rank of captain. When the Roman emperor Diocletian began to persecute Christians, George rebuked the emperor. He was immediately imprisoned and subjected to such cruel torture that the Eastern churches call him the Great Martyr. The most popular legend, namely the slaying of the dragon, did not appear until the 12th century. According to the story (possibly based on ancient Greek myth), an enormous dragon satisfied its hunger with human victims. The terrorized populace drew lots to determine who should be offered to the dragon, and one day the lot fell to the king's young daughter. The princess, dressed as a bride, was sent off to the marshy lair of the dragon. George happened to be riding by and asked her where she was going. When he heard her story, he insisted on fighting the dragon. After a fierce struggle he transfixed the monster with his spear. Then he asked the princess for the sash around her waist, of which he made a leash that he tied about the neck of the dragon. The princess led the monster like a lamb back to the city, and George told the people not to be afraid, but only to be baptized and accept Christianity. The people were all converted and George then cut off the dragon's head. To this day the emblem of St. George is a dragon.

St. George was the patron of soldiers and a great hero in the East for many centuries before his name spread to England in the eighth century. English churches were dedicated to St. George before the Norman Conquest in 1066. By the time of the Middle Ages, when knighthood flourished, George was given all the attributes of a knight and became more and more identified with England. Observance of Saint George's Day came with the English settlers to the American colonies, and the first St. George Society in America was organized in Philadelphia, Pennsylvania, on April 23, 1729.

For many years thereafter, members held an annual dinner to celebrate St. George's Day. This society was succeeded in 1772 by an organization that described itself as the "Society of the Sons of St. George established at Philadelphia for the advice and assistance of Englishmen in distress." Among its early members were William Penn, founder of Pennsylvania; the merchant Robert Morris, a signer of the Declaration of Independence, who has been called the "financier of the American Revolution"; and Benjamin Franklin. Organizations like the Society of the Sons of St. George continue to exist across the country and celebrate St. George's Day.

William Shakespeare's Birthday

The accepted date of the birth of William Shakespeare is April 23, 1564. The only available records show that he was baptized on April 26, and since it was the custom to have the baptism three days after birth, the date may be correct. Although the poet and dramatist was regarded with affection and respect by his contemporaries, and although he himself had predicted that "not marble, nor the gilded monument of princes shall outlive this powerful rhyme," he could have hardly envisaged the pinnacle of fame on which he stands today. As Ben Jonson, his fellow playwright and friend, wrote a few years after his death, Shakespeare "was not of an age but for all time."

William Shakespeare was the third of eight children and the eldest son born to John and Mary Shakespeare at Stratford-upon-Avon. His father was prominent in municipal affairs, rising to become high bailiff and justice of the peace in the town. His mother was a member of the prosperous, landed Arden family. Young Shakespeare undoubtedly received a fairly sound education. At 18 he married Anne Hathaway; they had three children before he set out for London sometime between 1584 and 1590. There Shakespeare probably served first as a stage apprentice, performing minor parts and menial tasks; but by 1592 he had become an established actor and a rising dramatist.

In 1594 or 1595 Shakespeare joined the dramatic company known as the Lord Chamberlain's Men (later the King's Men), where he enjoyed the dual function of playwright and performer. Hardworking and with an eye for business, he became part-owner of the new Globe Playhouse in London in 1599 and, in 1609, of the Blackfriars Theatre. Having amassed a moderate fortune, he retired to his family and property in Stratford around 1610. There he died on his 53rd birthday, April 23, 1616. During his lifetime he produced an incomparable body of work: a sequence of 154 sonnets, several long poems, and 37 plays.

Appreciation for Shakespeare came with the English settlers to the American colonies and has persisted into modern times. For example, the Folger Shakespeare Memorial Library, located two blocks from the Capitol in Washington, D.C., is a world-famous research library and museum devoted to Shakespearean works and memorabilia. It derives its name from its benefactor, Henry Clay Folger, the first president of the Standard Oil Company of New York, who amassed one of the most extensive Shakespeare collections in the world. To house the material Folger commissioned the construction of the library. It was dedicated by President Herbert Hoover on April 23, 1932, the 368th anniversary of Shakespeare's birth.

United Methodist Church Formed

On April 23, 1968, the 10,289,214-member Methodist Church and the 746,099-member Evangelical United Brethren Church merged to form the United Methodist Church. The uniting conference, which settled the administrative and legal technicalities arising from such a merger, was attended by 400 accredited Evangelical United Brethren delegates and 800 Methodist representatives. They officially inaugurated the United Methodist Church by participating in a joint service and procession in the Dallas Memorial Auditorium.

In uniting, the two churches followed a well-established ecumenical tradition, for each one had resulted from a previous merger. The Methodist Church, which traces its origins back to the beliefs and preaching of the Anglican clergyman John Wesley in the early 18th century, was the product of the merger of the Methodist Episcopal Church, the Methodist Episcopal Church South, and the Methodist Protestant Church, on May 10, 1939. The Evangelical United Brethren Church, with its membership mostly in Pennsylvania and Ohio, was formed in 1946 when two denominations, the Evangelical Church and the Church of the United Brethren in Christ, agreed to unite; they both originated among the German-speaking population in Pennsylvania as part of the evangelistic movements of the late 18th and early 19th centuries. Jacob Albright (1759–1808), a Lutheran who converted to Methodism, founded what became the Evangelical Church, and Philip William Otterbein (1726–1813), a minister of the German Reformed Church, was a founder of the Church of the United Brethren in Christ.

The two merging Protestant churches, whose general conferences adopted the plan of union in November 1966, shared a common religious and historical background. They held the same basic doctrines of faith with emphasis upon a life devoted to Christ and prayer, and even their ecclesiastical organizations, both episcopal with bishops as heads, were similar. In fact, had it not been for the fact that the Methodist Church was initially directed to English-speaking persons and the Evangelical Church and the Church of the United Brethren in Christ to German-speaking persons, the separate bodies might have formed one church from the very beginning.

Opposition to the Vietnam War Intensifies

Determining when public opinion about the Vietnam War began to turn from supportive to hostile is difficult. Most scholars believe this occurred in the late 1960s or early 1970s, as American involvement in the war escalated. Hundreds of thousands of armed forces personnel had become involved and casualties were increasing. Given the American policy of short troop rotations, in which the standard tour of duty in Vietnam was one year, more and more veterans of the war were returning home with tales to relate to their friends and families. Many of these veterans shared the growing antiwar sentiment, and some of them formed an organization called Vietnam Veterans Against the War. Their personal accounts of the conduct of the war were powerful and disturbing, and the organization became an important factor in turning public opinion.

On April 23, 1971, a veteran named John Kerry (later a United States senator and an occasional contender for the Democratic Party's presidential nomination) testified on behalf of the VVAW before the Senate Foreign Relations Committee. In an impassioned plea to save American lives and American honor, he called into question the rationale for the war itself ("there is nothing in South Vietnam . . . which realistically threatens the United States"), the good faith of America's South Vietnamese allies, and the validity of the U.S. military's much publicized gains against the enemy. He pointed out that the majority of the South Vietnamese people, caught between two opposing camps, simply wanted the war to be over, and he reported that American troops were becoming profoundly demoralized. (At a meeting in Detroit a few months previously, he said, a number of veterans had confessed to what can only be described as atrocities, committed with the full knowledge and consent of their commanding officers.) Kerry asked whether any of this was truly in the nation's interest; if it was not, then continuation of the war was in fact a face-saving exercise, conducted with a brutal disregard of the human cost. Testimony such as this, from veterans who had served honorably in the field, had a decisive impact on people who were uncertain about the Vietnam War, while those who were already opposed to it took heart at the unexpected support. The full text of Kerry's statement is reproduced below.

I would like to talk on behalf of all those veterans and say that several months ago in Detroit we had an investigation at which over 150 honorably discharged, and many very highly decorated, veterans testified to war crimes committed in Southeast Asia. These were not isolated incidents but crimes committed on a day-to-day basis with the full awareness of officers at all levels of command. It is impossible to describe to you exactly what did happen in Detroit—the emotions in the room and the feelings of the men who were reliving their experiences in Vietnam. They relived the absolute horror of what this country, in a sense, made them do.

They told stories that at times they had personally raped, cut off ears, cut off heads, taped wires from portable telephones to human genitals and turned up the power, cut off limbs, blown up bodies, randomly shot at civilians, razed villages in fashion reminiscent of Genghis Khan, shot cattle and dogs for fun, poisoned food stocks, and generally ravaged the countryside of South Vietnam in addition to the normal ravage of war and the normal and very particular ravaging which is done by the applied bombing power of this country.

We call this investigation the Winter Soldier Investigation. The term "Winter Soldier" is a play on words of Thomas Paine's in 1776 when he spoke of the Sunshine Patriots and summertime soldiers who deserted at Valley Forge because the going was rough.

We who have come here to Washington have come here because we feel we have to be winter soldiers now. We could come back to this country, we could be quiet, we could hold our silence, we could not tell what went on in Vietnam, but we feel because of what threatens this country, not the reds, but the crimes which we are committing that threaten it, that we have to speak out.

In our opinion and from our experience, there is nothing in South Vietnam which could happen that realistically threatens the United States of America. And to attempt to justify the loss of one American life in Vietnam, Cambodia, or Laos by linking such loss to the preservation of freedom, which those misfits supposedly abuse, is to us the height of criminal hypocrisy, and it is that kind of hypocrisy which we feel has torn this country.

We found that not only was it a civil war, an effort by a people who had for years been seeking their liberation from any colonial influence whatsoever, but also we found that the Vietnamese whom we had enthusiastically molded after our own image were hard put to take up the fight against the threat we were supposedly saving them from.

We found most people didn't even know the difference between communism and democracy. They only wanted to work in rice paddies without helicopters strafing them and bombs with napalm burning their villages and tearing their country apart. They wanted everything to do with the war, particularly with this foreign presence of the United States of America, to leave them alone in peace, and they practiced the art of survival by siding with whichever military force was present at a particular time, be it Viet Cong, North Vietnamese, or American.

We found also that all too often American men were dying in those rice paddies for want of support from their allies. We saw first hand how monies from American taxes were used for a corrupt dictatorial regime. We saw that many people in this country had a one-sided idea of who was kept free by the flag, and blacks provided the highest percentage of casualties. We saw Vietnam ravaged equally by American bombs and search-and-destroy missions, as well as by Viet Cong terrorism, and yet we listened while this country tried to blame all of the havoc on the Viet Cong.

We rationalized destroying villages in order to save them. We saw America lose her sense of morality as she accepted very coolly a My Lai and refused to give up the image of American soldiers who hand out chocolate bars and chewing gum.

We learned the meaning of free fire zones, shooting anything that moves, and we watched while America placed a cheapness on the lives of Orientals.

We watched the United States falsification of body counts, in fact the glorification of body counts. We listened while month after month we were told the back of the enemy was about to break. We fought using weapons against "Oriental human beings." We fought using weapons against those people which I do not believe this country would dream of using were we fighting in the European theater. We watched while men charged up hills because a general said that hill has to be taken, and after losing one platoon or two platoons they marched away to leave the hill for reoccupation by the North Vietnamese. We watched pride allow the most unimportant battles to be blown into extravaganzas, because we couldn't lose, and we couldn't retreat, and because it didn't matter how many American bodies were lost to prove that point, and so there were Hamburger Hills and Khe Sanhs and Hill 81s and Fire Base 6s, and so many others.

Now we are told that the men who fought there must watch quietly while American lives are lost so that we can exercise the incredible arrogance of Vietnamizing the Vietnamese.

Each day to facilitate the process by which the United States washes her hands of Vietnam someone has to give up his life so that the United States doesn't have to admit something that the entire world already knows, so that we can't say that we have made a mistake. Someone has to die so that President Nixon won't be, and these are his words, "the first President to lose a war."

We are asking Americans to think about that, because how do you ask a man to be the last man to die in Vietnam? How do you ask a man to be the last man to die for a mistake? We are here in Washington to say that the problem of this war is not just a question of war and diplomacy. It is part and parcel of everything that we are trying as human beings to communicate to people in this country, the question of racism which is rampant in the military, and so many other questions such as the use of weapons; the hypocrisy in our taking umbrage at the Geneva Conventions and using that as justification for a continuation of this war when we are more guilty than any other body of violations of those Geneva Conventions; in the use of free fire zones, harassment interdiction fire, search and destroy missions, the bombings, the torture of prisoners, all accepted policy by many units in South Vietnam. That is what we are trying to say. It is part and parcel of everything.

An American Indian friend of mine who lives in the Indian Nation of Alcatraz put it to me very succinctly. He told me how as a boy on an Indian reservation he had watched television and he used to cheer the cowboys when they came in and shot the Indians, and then suddenly one day he stopped in Vietnam and he said, "My God, I am doing to these people the very same thing that was done to my people," and he stopped. And that is what we are trying to say, that we think this thing has to end.

We are here to ask, and we are here to ask vehemently, where are the leaders of our country? Where is the leadership? We're here to ask where are McNamara, Rostow, Bundy, Kilpatrick, and so many

Where are they now that we, the men they sent off to war, have returned? These are the commanders who have deserted their troops. And there is no more serious crime in the laws of war. The Army says they never leave their wounded. The Marines say they never even leave their dead. These men have left all the casualties and retreated behind a pious shield of public rectitude. They've left the real stuff of their reputations bleaching behind them in the sun in this country.

We wish that a merciful God could wipe away our own memories of that service as easily as this administration has wiped away their memories of us. But all that they have done and all that they can do by this denial is to make more clear than ever our own determination to undertake one last mission: to search out and destroy the last vestige of this barbaric war, to pacify our own hearts, to conquer the hate and fear that have driven this country these last ten years and more. And more. And so when thirty years from now our brothers go down the street without a leg, without an arm, or a face, and small boys ask why, we will be able to say "Vietnam" and not mean a desert, not a filthy obscene memory, but mean instead where America finally turned and where soldiers like us helped it in the turning.

April 24

Library of Congress Created

On April 24, 1800, the Congress of the United States created the Library of Congress by approving an act providing "for the purchase of such books as may be necessary for the use of Congress at the said city of Washington, and for fitting up a suitable apartment for containing them." Although originally intended specifically as a parliamentary collection to aid the legislative branch of the government, the Library of Congress in its approximately two centuries of existence has expanded its services until, despite its name, it has become the national library of the United States. Besides serving members of Congress and other government officials, the reference library meets the needs of the general public, scholars, and libraries both in this country and abroad.

Ranking as one of the largest libraries in the world, the Library of Congress possesses outstanding collections of manuscripts, prints, maps, motion pictures, records, and books, as well as tapes, microfiche, and microfilm. It also offers such added benefits as an extensive computer system and a detailed Web site on the Internet. The library is maintained chiefly by congressional appropriations, but also derives funds from private donations. The hundreds of millions of dollars in the library's annual budget today are a far cry from the $5,000 Congress set aside for book purchases at the institution's founding in 1800.

The original nucleus of 3,000 volumes, amassed from 1800 to 1814 and housed in the Capitol, was burned on August 24, 1814, in the British attack on Washington, D.C., during the War of 1812. The loss was mitigated by the purchase in January 1815 of former President Thomas Jefferson's private library, comprising more than 6,000 volumes. This splendid collection, considered remarkable in its day, formed the basis around which the library built up its holdings in diverse fields. However, it too suffered a Capitol blaze, namely an unexpected fire on December 24, 1851, and was reduced by half.

Despite setbacks, the Library of Congress continued to augment its collection substantially during the course of the 19th century through annual congressional appropriations; special purchases, such as the Peter Force collection of primary materials relating to American history (1867) and the Rochambeau collection pertaining to the American Revolution (1883); bequests; foreign exchanges; and items transferred from other government agencies, including the Smithsonian collec-

tion of almost 40,000 volumes (1866). Moreover, in 1870 a congressional act made the Library of Congress the official depository of copyrighted and official publications. In 1897 a copyright department was set up on the library premises. The library also approved the purchase of the presidential papers of George Washington, James Monroe, Thomas Jefferson, and James Madison, a project that has since grown to encompass millions of items in several dozen presidential collections. The personal papers of other famous men and women have been gradually acquired as well.

By the end of the 19th century, the Library of Congress housed an extensive national reference collection comprising some 740,000 volumes, 250,000 prints, 40,000 maps, 200,000 pieces of music, and 18,000 bound newspaper volumes. The cramped Capitol "apartment" stipulated by the congressional act of 1800 had long been inadequate, and in 1897 the library transferred its holdings to a new $7 million Italian Renaissance–style main building on Capitol Hill near the Congress. As the institution added personnel, services, and more material during the 20th century, the library began to add annex buildings in the Capitol Hill area, including the massive Madison building annex across from the main building which contains the extensive law library holdings.

Hubble Space Telescope Deployed

The Hubble Space Telescope was deployed in orbit around the Earth on April 24, 1990. It began a new era of space exploration through long-distance observation, and has helped astronomers and scientists learn more about the solar system and the universe.

Telescopes have been in existence for centuries. In some of the modern observatories, it is now possible to see objects that are billions of light years away. However, there is one fundamental limitation on Earth-bound telescopes, namely the Earth's atmosphere itself. Cloud cover and bad weather make precise observations impossible. Even with the clearest skies, the atmosphere will blur and distort observations to some degree. The expression "twinkle, twinkle, little star" itself comes from the visible atmospheric distortions of starlight, since stars themselves obviously do not twinkle. Finally, the rotation of the Earth means that observatories cannot avoid the interference of daylight on their activities, nor can they observe particular areas of the night sky for more than a few hours.

A telescope in outer space, however, is free from atmospheric interference and most of the other Earth-bound disadvantages that traditional observatories labor under. As early as World War II, astronomers began to conceive of a "Large Space Telescope," but it remained nothing more than a fantasy until the first satellites were launched into orbit in the late 1950s. Unfortunately for the astronomers, most of the funds in the American space program during the 1960s and early 1970s were directed towards the Moon missions and various military projects. By the late 1970s, however, Congress was looking for projects with practical applications. One such project was the space shuttle, and interest also developed in the idea of an orbital telescope. The first significant funds for an orbital telescope were allocated in 1977, and the project was named after astronomer Edwin Hubble in 1984.

By the time it was deployed, the Hubble cost nearly two billion dollars. It went through a series of design changes, and the original plan to have the Hubble returned to Earth every few years for servicing was scrapped as impractical. Since the Hubble was to be deployed in Earth orbit by a space shuttle rather than launched on its own, the project was delayed for several years after the space shuttle *Challenger* explosion of January 28, 1986, slowed the shuttle program. Finally, however, the Hubble was placed in orbit on April 24, 1990, from the space shuttle *Discovery* several hundred miles above the surface of the Earth.

A serious problem developed almost immediately after deployment. There was a flaw in the Hubble's primary mirror, used to reflect and focus light for observations, which had apparently occurred during the mirror's construction but was not detected prior to deployment. The flaw was not entirely correctable, since the mirror could not be removed or replaced, but a servicing mission in 1993 by another shuttle was able to overcome most of the observational difficulties. Even with the flaw, however, the pictures and data transmitted by the Hubble proved far superior than anything previously obtained from Earth-bound observatories. The Hubble was a success.

The Hubble is solar-powered and runs 24 hours a day. It has been used to observe the birth of stars, the formation of distant galaxies, and to confirm the existence of planets in orbit around stars other than the Sun. The Hubble also took pictures of a storm that covered the entire surface of Saturn, which is 95 times more massive than Earth, and of the violent explosions generated when the Shoemaker-Levy comet fragmented and collided with Jupiter. Finally, the Hubble has a variety of other scientific instruments aboard, such as the Faint Object Camera and the Faint Object Spectograph to assist in long-range readings.

April 25

Edward R. Murrow's Birthday

Edward Roscoe Murrow, one of America's greatest journalists, was born on April 25, 1908, in Polecat Creek, North Carolina, to Ethel Lamb and Roscoe Murrow. His first name was originally Egbert, but he changed it to Edward when he was in his teens. During high school, a teacher named Ruth Lawson encouraged Murrow's interest in public speaking, which he pursued when he entered Washington State College (later renamed Washington State University) in 1926.

While at Washington State, Murrow appeared in several student theatrical productions, and was elected president of the student body. He graduated in 1930. That same year, he was also chosen to be president of the prestigious National Student Federation of America (NSFA). Murrow spent most of the next two years traveling, but in 1932 he resigned from the NSFA and took a position with the Institute of International Education, which helped resettle a number of intellectuals fleeing the Hitler regime in Nazi Germany.

In 1935 Murrow went to work for the Columbia Broadcasting System (CBS) as its director of educational programming. He became the head of CBS's European Bureau in 1937 and moved to London, England. Beginning with the German occupation of Austria in 1938, Murrow covered the breaking events of World War II, leading his broadcasts with the famous phrase "This is London. . . ." In 1940 he covered the Blitz, namely the German attempt to force England's surrender through repeated bombing raids on London. Murrow stayed in London during this period, despite the risk to himself and his staff, and his broadcasts were widely followed in the United States.

During the war, Murrow also covered events in North Africa and Europe as the Allied armies advanced. He accompanied a highly dangerous bombing raid against the German capital of Berlin, and covered the Allied liberation of the notorious concentration camp at Buchenwald. After the war, he returned to the United States and became a CBS vice president. Murrow missed being a broadcaster, however, and returned to the airwaves in 1947. He worked on several radio programs, including the popular *Hear It Now* show, which became *See It Now* in 1951 after it was adapted for television.

See It Now, a weekly documentary series, covered politics, the Korean War, and the anticommunist witch hunts of Senator Joseph McCarthy (Republican from Wisconsin). Murrow broke with the journalistic tradition of avoiding controversial topics, and his 1954 program concerning McCarthy is credited with helping to expose the senator's excesses. Shortly thereafter, McCarthy was officially censured by the Senate. Murrow also worked on the interview program *Person to Person*, which began in 1953. Poor sponsor support, however, led to *See It Now*'s cancellation in 1958. Murrow's hard-hitting journalism was simply not good business for CBS's corporate sponsors, who preferred noncontroversial light entertainment shows.

Murrow started another television show, called *Small World*. He also worked for *CBS Reports*, which replaced *See It Now*, and produced the award-winning documentary *Harvest of Shame* on the plight of migrant farm workers. *Harvest of Shame* aired on November 25, 1960. Shortly after his inauguration in January 1961, President John F. Kennedy offered the directorship of the United States Information Agency (USIA) to Murrow. Murrow accepted, partly because of his declining health and partly because of continued problems with CBS's corporate sponsors.

Poor health continued to plague Murrow, who was a heavy smoker and eventually lost a lung to cancer. He resigned from the USIA late in 1963 and died on April 27, 1965, in Pawling, New York.

Feast of St. Mark

The Feast of St. Mark, one of the four Evangelists, is observed on April 25 by the Roman Catholic, Greek Orthodox, and some Protestant churches. Mark, whose full name was John Mark, was not one of the 12 Apostles but was one of the larger number of disciples, the band of men who were closely associated with the apostles.

Sometime between A.D. 64 and 70, Mark wrote his Gospel, one of the four Gospels on the life of Jesus in the New Testament. According to tradition, Mark became the first bishop of Alexandria and was martyred there about 74 or 75. His followers reportedly obtained possession of his body and put it in a sepulcher, which became a shrine visited by the faithful. Early in the 9th century Venetian merchants trading in Alexandria are said to have acquired the relics and carried them to Venice, where a church was built over them. This original church was destroyed by fire in 967. The present Basilica of St. Mark in Venice, graced with delicate masonry and studded with mosaics, is one of the most famous churches in the world. Its main structure, designed by Byzantine architects, was completed in 1071. In following centuries, embellishments were added, so that the basilica today is a mixture of Byzantine and Gothic architecture,

richly adorned with sculpture and rare forms of marble. What are said to be the remains of St. Mark, the patron saint of Venice since the ninth century, lie under the main altar.

An English superstition holds that on the eve of St. Mark apparitions of those who will die within the ensuing year can be seen in the churchyard. In Maxwell Anderson's 1942 play *The Eve of St. Mark*, a young American solider, who will not return from the war, appears in spirit to his mother and his sweetheart.

April 26

John James Audubon's Birthday

John James Audubon, the artist and naturalist whose drawings of the birds of North America broke new ground in the field of ornithology, was born on April 26, 1785, the son of a Creole woman who died several years later. The place of his birth is said to be Les Cayes, Haiti. Regarded by most authorities as the son of Captain Jean Audubon, a trader, planter, and officer in the French navy, and his Creole mistress, young Audubon was taken to France in 1789, where he was formally adopted several years later by Captain Audubon and his wife. Educated in France, although he had little enthusiasm for formal studies, Audubon lived there in relative luxury.

It is uncertain how Audubon first came to draw birds. There is no doubt, however, that the interest that began as an apparently spontaneous pastime never waned. Sent to study drawing in Paris under the French painter Jacques Louis David, Audubon found himself impatient with the dull plaster casts that he was expected to draw, and he felt too restricted with only black chalk on white paper. On his own he experimented in watercolors with the bright hues that would later characterize his work. Even working independently, however, he found that neither carefully constructed wooden birds nor ordinary stuffed birds could serve as adequate models for the impression of life he hoped to capture on paper.

His chance for concentrated study of birds in their natural surroundings came in 1803 when he was sent to America, supposedly to enter business, and settled at Mill Grove, an estate northwest of Philadelphia that was owned by his father. There, on Perkiomen Creek and in the surrounding countryside, young Audubon began in earnest to paint the birds of North America. It was while Audubon was living at Mill Grove that he met Lucy Blakewell, whom he married in 1808 and whose love and admiration sustained him when others thought his work impractical. It was during their courtship that Audubon, painting a portrait of her, accidentally discovered the technique of softening his watercolor tones with an overlay of pastel crayons, a process that was to give a special quality to his later bird drawings.

Important as it was, Audubon's time at Mill Grove was actually rather brief and interrupted by a year-long stay in France during which he saw his father and stepmother for the last time. Audubon returned to the United States in 1806 and opened a general store in Louisville, Kentucky. In 1810 the store, never a success and neglected by Audubon in favor of his other interests, was moved to a more westerly Ohio River location in Henderson, Kentucky. The site was chosen by him because it was on the route of a great American bird migration. When Audubon lived in Henderson, however, it seemed unlikely that he would ever be famous. Plagued by a series of unsuccessful business ventures, he was bankrupt by 1819. Forced to sell all he owned, he moved his family for a brief time to Shippingport (near Louisville, Kentucky), where he sought unsuccessfully to gain a living by turning out portraits and giving drawing lessons. He also played his flute or violin at local balls and taught young people the dance steps he had learned long before in France. The family also lived briefly in Cincinnati, Ohio, where Audubon was employed to stuff and mount birds and fishes for the city's new Western Museum.

Wherever Audubon went during these difficult early years, he followed the same pattern, employing every talent he possessed to eke out a precarious living by means that would still permit him to move towards his main goal of discovering, studying, and painting the birds of North America. If these were years of slow accomplishment, they were also years of exasperating frustration, discovery mixed with the hardships of poverty, and long separations from his family. His wife supplemented the family income as a teacher and governess.

In 1820, encouraged by his wife, Audubon determined to complete his studies of North American birds and embarked by flatboat on a painting and drawing excursion that was to take him all the way down the Mississippi and allow him to explore its banks, always tirelessly in search of new varieties of birds to paint. Coming to rest in New Orleans, Louisiana, an ideal setting from which to embark on bird searching excursions, he earned a meager livelihood by painting portraits and giving drawing lessons, although clients were scarce. Often penniless, he was engaged at last for a summer of tutoring at Oakley plantation, four miles east of St. Francisville, in Louisiana's West Feliciana Parish. Audubon came to love the area,

which he had time to explore thoroughly, producing 32 of his most famous bird paintings in the process.

Audubon's summer at Oakley brought him sufficient funds to send for his wife, who joined him in New Orleans. When her position as a governess there ended abruptly, she was engaged as a governess at Weyanoke, the home of a family named Percy, at Little Bayou Sara. Audubon was also hired by the Percy family, to give music, drawing, and dancing lessons to local children, again with the understanding that he also would have time for his own work. By October 1822 he had accumulated over 200 bird paintings that pleased him and set off for Philadelphia, Pennsylvania, in search of a publisher. After a winter-long pause in Shippingport, where he earned money for the trip by turning out popular paintings of American scenery, he arrived in the spring of 1823 in Philadelphia, where he found encouragement but no publisher. In New York, which he visited in the summer, he found neither, though in both places he was advised that his best chance of publication lay in Europe.

First, however, Audubon returned to see his family at Bayou Sara, after a long trip with work stops whenever he ran out of money. In the spring of 1826, having accumulated sufficient funds and over 400 bird portraits, he sailed from New Orleans to Liverpool, England. In Europe his work began to receive attention. Exhibitions of his paintings in Liverpool, Manchester, and Edinburgh attracted wide interest and brought a flurry of invitations, introductions to influential persons, recognition in art and scientific circles, and demands for the shy Audubon to appear at dinners and meetings of learned societies. As always, money was a pressing problem, and he worked furiously, occupied not only with the paintings that paid his expenses, but also with socializing and public appearances, which were important in his effort to get his bird paintings published.

In London, Audubon became acquainted with a skillful engraver, Robert Havell Jr., beginning what was to be a long association. Audubon's best-known work, the generously proportioned *Birds of America*, with engravings by Havell, was published in elephant folio size, allowing for the life-size portrayal of birds on which Audubon had always insisted. It appeared in parts between 1827 and 1838.

After a return trip to America in 1829, Audubon returned to Britain with his wife, who relinquished the security of her teaching position in order to accompany her husband and assist in his ambitions. Audubon decided to supplement *Birds of America*, which would ultimately boast 435 hand-colored plates, with a text. This *Ornithological Biography*, describing the birds and containing numerous vignettes of life on the American frontier, eventually ran to five volumes, published from 1831 to 1839, and was supplemented by a systematic index and catalog, *A Synopsis of the Birds of North America* (1839). In these works Audubon had the assistance and collaboration of a young Scottish naturalist, William MacGillivray, who was responsible for much of the scientific information.

From 1826 until 1839, when the vast undertaking on which he had labored for so many years with alternating delight and despair was finally completed, Audubon divided his time between Europe and America. He traveled to the Florida Keys, Labrador, and Texas in search of new birds. His sons, Victor and John, assisted in his work, as they were to continue to do after Audubon's final return to the United States in 1839. Settling, typically, where he could overlook one of the nation's great waterways, he purchased a small estate above the Hudson River. There, aided by his sons, Audubon undertook an ambitious new work named *Viviparous Quadrupeds of North America*. Two volumes of plates for the new enterprise came out in parts in 1845 and 1846, and the three-volume text was issued between 1846 and 1854. Before the text was completed, however, Audubon died on January 27, 1851.

Lucy Audubon, who survived her husband by many years, returned to teaching to support herself. One of her pupils, George Bird Grinnell, became editor of *Forest and Stream* and in 1886 organized a society for the study and protection of birds, which he named the Audubon Society. Many branches were soon formed, and in 1905 the National Association of Audubon Societies was organized. Today, this organization, its name now simplified to the National Audubon Society, is one of the largest groups devoted to the conservation of wildlife, scenic beauty, and other natural resources.

Confederate Memorial Day

Confederate Memorial Day, widely observed in southern states, is celebrated on a variety of dates depending on the state. Florida and Georgia observe it on April 26. On this date in 1865, two notable events took place. One was the final surrender of Confederate General Joseph E. Johnston to the Union army's General William T. Sherman near Durham, North Carolina. That historic encounter took place 17 days after the surrender of General Robert E. Lee, commander in chief of Confederate forces, to General Ulysses S. Grant at Appomattox Court House, Virginia (see April 9). On the same day that Johnston and Sherman were meeting near Durham, some women in Vicksburg, Mississippi, were performing a gesture of private grief and salutation by decorating the graves of soldiers who had fallen in the course of the conflict. In so doing, Sue Landon Vaughan and her companions paid tribute to those killed before the end of the 47-day siege of strategically located Vicksburg on July 4, two years earlier.

As early as 1866, honoring the graves of Confederate war dead had become an annual custom in communities throughout the South. In Columbus, Mississippi, a group of women decorating the graves of Confederate soldiers—mostly casualties of the battle of Shiloh—extended their efforts to the graves of some Union prisoners of war who were buried nearby. This spontaneous act of kindness was widely reported and widely appreciated, especially by bereaved Northerners; many saw, in shared grief, a way of reuniting the nation. Francis Miles Finch, a young attorney in Ithaca, New York, honored the incident with a poem called *The Blue and the Gray*. Reprinted in newspapers, memorized by students, and widely discussed throughout the nation, it appeared originally in the September 1867 issue of the *Atlantic Monthly* and read in part as follows:

> By the flow of the inland river,
> Whence the fleets of iron have fled,
> Where the blades of the grave grass quiver,
> Asleep are the ranks of the dead;
> Under the sod and the dew,
> Waiting the judgment day;
> Under the one, the Blue;
> Under the other, the Gray. . . .
> From the silence of sorrowful hours
> The desolate mourners go,
> Lovingly laden with flowers
> Alike for the friend and the foe;
> Under the sod and the dew,
> Waiting the judgment day;
> Under the roses, the Blue;
> Under the lilies, the Gray. . . .
> Sadly, but not with upbraiding,
> The generous deed was done;
> In the storm of the years that are fading
> No braver battle was won;
> Under the sod and the dew,
> Waiting the judgment day;
> Under the blossoms, the Blue;
> Under the garlands, the Gray.

In addition to the state observances, some individual communities have established their own date for honoring Confederate Memorial Day. The choice of date is often tied to an event of local historical importance. Winchester, Virginia, for example, began observing it on the anniversary of the death of General Turner Ashby, and Petersburg, Virginia, began observing it on the anniversary of its defense against a massive Union siege.

Frederick Law Olmsted's Birthday

Frederick Law Olmsted, the father of American urban landscape architecture, was born in Hartford, Connecticut, on April 26, 1822. A man of varied accomplishments, he devoted his talents primarily to the improvement of life in cities throughout the United States through the development of public parks. Olmsted's imagination and expertise created Manhattan's Central and Riverside parks, Brooklyn's Prospect Park, Boston's Franklin Park, Philadelphia's Fairmount Park, and St. Louis's Forest Park, among others.

Olmsted was the son of John Olmsted, a successful merchant whose forebears arrived in Boston from England in 1632, and Charlotte Law Hull Olmsted. The boy's mother died when he was four years old, and his father then married Mary Ann Bull, a deeply religious woman. Olmsted's father and stepmother shared a love for nature, which they communicated to Frederick and his younger brother John.

Aware of the shortcomings of his own education, Olmsted's father decided not to take responsibility for his son's instruction and instead delegated it to a series of country parsons. Ironically, these clergymen were apparently fundamentalist and anti-intellectual, the antithesis of what the elder Olmsted intended. Frederick Olmsted reacted negatively to the narrow ways of these teachers, and his experiences left him hostile to organized religion.

In 1837 Olmsted planned to attend Yale College, but sumac poisoning so weakened his eyesight that he could not continue his education. Instead he became an apprentice to Frederick A. Barton, a civil engineer in Andover, Massachusetts, and subsequently Collinsville, Connecticut. During his two and a half years with Barton, Olmsted acquired many of the skills that he would later put to use.

In August 1840 Olmsted began to pursue a career in commerce, as a clerk with Benkard and Hutton, a French dry-goods importer in New York. He left this employment in March 1842 and spent the next year attending lectures at Yale. In April 1843 he signed on as an apprentice seaman on the *Ronaldson*. Olmsted spent a year on the *Ronaldson*, and during that time he sailed to China, but he gave up the sea upon the completion of the voyage.

Upon returning to the United States, Olmsted decided to devote himself to scientific farming. He received his first training at the farm of David Brooks, his uncle, in Cheshire, Connecticut. He also attended lectures at Yale on geology and scientific farming given by professors Benjamin Silliman and John T. Norton. He then spent from April to October 1846 at the prize-winning farm of George Geddes near Owego, New York. In 1847, John Olmsted bought his son a small farm at Sachem Head, Connecticut. This venture did not prosper, and in January 1848 the elder Olmsted purchased another farm for him on Staten Island, New York. Frederick Olmsted turned his new holding into a beautiful homestead as well as a model of scientific agricultural management, but again the undertaking was not a financial success.

In 1850 Olmsted sailed for Europe with his brother and a friend, Charles Loring Brace. They spent four weeks on the Continent and then made a walking tour of rural Britain. In 1852 Olmsted published the product of his journey, *Walks and Talks of an American Farmer in England*. Critics acclaimed Olmsted's first book, and Henry J. Raymond, who only a short time before had founded the *New York Times*, was favorably impressed by the author. Raymond noted that Olmsted shared his view that the radical abolitionists were presenting a distorted image of the United States abroad. Raymond accordingly commissioned Olmsted, who like him was a Free-Soil Whig, to travel through the South and make reports on life and manners there.

In 1856 Olmsted published his reports as *A Journey in the Seaboard Slave States*. Shortly thereafter he traveled to Texas with his brother and then returned to the North alone via New Orleans and Richmond. After this second visit, Olmsted published *A Journey Through Texas* in 1857 and *A Journey in the Back Country* in 1860. The three books, condensed into two volumes that appeared as *The Cotton Kingdom* (1861), contained powerful descriptions of the antebellum South. Olmsted's appraisal was harsh. He concluded that the South had rejected democracy in favor of protecting the interests of a small, self-styled aristocracy and was appalled by the brutalities of slavery.

Olmsted's travels convinced him of the superiority of the North's urban-commercial complexity, which held the promise of a better life for vast numbers of people. He was not blind to the deficiencies of municipalities like New York, Boston, and Philadelphia, but he blamed the overwhelming pursuit of profit rather than urban life for these flaws. The erstwhile farmer envisioned the city as the ultimate hope as well as the apparent destiny of 19th-century America, but recognized that improving the quality of urban life was imperative.

Two tendencies in city life particularly disturbed Olmsted. He believed that the density of population of the great centers was hazardous to health and created an atmosphere in which the inhabitants, unable to develop stable relationships with their neighbors, became apprehensive, hard, and selfish. Olmsted noted with dismay that such conditions led businessmen and merchants, the leaders of urban America, to make their residences away from the cities that had produced their wealth. Reacting positively to the challenge, Olmsted decided to devote the rest of his life to an attempt to rehabilitate American cities. His principal goal was the creation of environments that would entice the social elite to remain in the urban areas and that would offer public recreation areas. Eventually, Olmsted came to see the ideal city as a unit with a core devoted to business and administrative activities, and with contiguous suburban areas, thus combining the best features of the countryside with the amenities of urban life.

In 1857 influential New Yorkers urged Olmsted, who had been a friend of the early landscaper Andrew Jackson Downing, to apply for the superintendency of Central Park, which the city (then consisting only of Manhattan Island) was to construct according to the plan of Captain Egbert L. Viele. Olmsted, who received endorsements from such notables as Peter Cooper and Washington Irving, received the post on September 11, 1857. He associated himself with the English architect Calvert Vaux, and the two men submitted a plan called Greensward, which in 1858 won a competition for a new design for the park.

Olmsted became architect-in-chief of Central Park on May 17, 1858. He and Vaux struggled against politicians who sought to make the enterprise a reservoir of patronage. Years passed before the project was completed, but by 1860 Olmsted and Vaux had achieved some successes, and the park became popular with residents. Olmsted had transformed an area of rocks, swamps, and pastures into an artful arrangement of wooded hills, artificial lakes, and gentle fields.

The Civil War interrupted Olmsted's new career. He took a leave of absence to serve as general secretary of the United States Sanitary Commission, the privately supported, volunteer organization whose functions were later taken over by the American Red Cross. Olmsted's duties included the establishment of field hospitals and supervision of the care of the wounded and dying. In 1863 Olmsted resigned from the commission, physically and emotionally exhausted, but he found the time to help establish the Union League, which was created in part to aid in soldier relief.

Political pressures prompted Olmsted and Vaux to resign from their Central Park assignment. In August 1863 Olmsted, in the hope of restoring his health, accepted the position of superintendent of the Freemont Mariposa mining estates in California. During two years in the West, Olmsted helped set up the Yosemite Park state reservation, now Yosemite National Park, and served as the area's first commissioner. He also designed Golden Gate Park in San Francisco, the Oakland Cemetery, and the grounds and residential village of the University of California at Berkeley.

Olmsted returned to New York in 1865 and made the city his center of operations for the next 13 years. In the summer of 1865, Olmsted and Vaux were reappointed as landscape architects of Central Park. Olmsted continued his efforts until 1878, when political complications finally ended his association with the project. In the intervening years between 1865 and 1878, Olmsted and Vaux, who in 1860 had been named "landscape architects and designers to the Commissioners north of 155th Street," had also laid out Riverside Park and the upper reaches of Manhattan Island. In addition, they drew up comprehensive plans for the development of Brooklyn, which was an independent city until 1898, and created Brooklyn's Prospect Park. Olmsted also made plans for improvements on Staten Island, New York, and for land subdivisions in Irvington and Tarrytown in Westchester County.

Other communities also gained the benefits of Olmsted's talents between 1865 and 1878. He designed several municipal parks, including South Park in Chicago, Illinois, and the Mount Royal Park in Montreal, Canada, and he created the beautiful residential suburb of Riverside, near Chicago. In 1874, in recognition of his achievements, Olmsted received the assignment of landscaping the grounds of the Capitol in Washington, D.C.

In 1878 Olmsted moved to Boston. He devoted his efforts to the design of the park system of Boston, including Franklin Park in the West Roxbury section. In cooperation with Professors Asa Gray and Charles Sprague Sargent, he planned the notable Arnold Arboretum, also in the West Roxbury area. In addition, Olmsted was engaged in a number of projects outside the Boston region. He collaborated with Leopold Eidlitz and H. H. Richardson in the design of the state capitol at Albany, New York; took part in the site selection and development of plans for Stanford University in Palo Alto, California; and was occupied with devising a program for the protection of Niagara Falls. Olmsted continued to create and make suggestions for urban parks, including Belle Isle Park in Detroit,

Michigan, and Morningside Park in New York City.

Two projects drew most of Olmsted's attention during his final years. He took special interest in the creation of Biltmore, George W. Vanderbilt's estate in Asheville, North Carolina, and designed other retreats for Vanderbilt and for Rockefeller. Fittingly, it was Olmsted who laid out the grounds for the great White City of the World's Columbian Exposition in Chicago in 1893. This remarkable collaboration of architects and artists was intended to give inspiration for the design of future urban communities, and it gave rise to the American "City Beautiful" movement. The grounds for the exposition later became Chicago's Jackson Park. Frederick Law Olmsted retired in 1895, and died on August 28, 1903.

Cape Henry Day

The establishment of Jamestown, Virginia, the first capital of the Virginia colony and the earliest English permanent settlement in the region, was on May 13, 1607. It preceded by more than a decade the better known landing of the Pilgrims at Plymouth Rock in 1620. The founders of Jamestown, namely Captain Christopher Newport and his band of adventurers, landed at Cape Henry, Virginia, on April 26, 1607. The event is remembered as Cape Henry Day.

Located on the south side of Chesapeake Bay, ten miles east of present-day Norfolk, Virginia, the Cape Henry promontory must have been a welcome sight to the weary English voyagers. Its appearance on the horizon signaled the conclusion of an arduous four-month journey across the Atlantic Ocean. Captain Newport, Edward Wingfield, Bartholomew Gosnold, and 30 others disembarked on April 26. They were impressed by the beauty of the country and, after a skirmish with some natives, returned to their vessels for the night. The expedition of 110 men and four boys had made the voyage in three vessels, of which the largest, the *Susan Constant*, measured 75 feet. A group of men went ashore on the second day and spent some time in exploration. On April 29 the men set up a wooden cross and named the area Cape Henry in honor of the Prince of Wales, the eldest son of James I. They then renewed their trek inland to the site that became Jamestown.

In 1896 the Association for the Preservation of Virginia Antiquities commemorated the landing by placing a plaque on the nearby Old Cape Henry Lighthouse, the first lighthouse erected by the federal government. The Cape Henry Memorial, consisting of a quarter acre of ground and a cross erected in 1935 by the Daughters of the American Colonists, later marked the location of the landing.

April 27

Ulysses S. Grant's Birthday

Library of Congress

Ulysses S. Grant

Ulysses Simpson Grant, the 18th president of the United States, was born April 27, 1822, in Point Pleasant, Ohio. He was baptized Hiram Ulysses Grant by his parents, Hannah Simpson Grant and Jesse Root Grant. Jesse Grant, a tanner by trade, moved with his family to Georgetown, Ohio, in 1823. Though without formal education himself, he insisted that his children be educated, and young Ulysses S. Grant was sent to school. Further, Jesse Grant obtained for his son an appointment to the United States Military Academy at West Point in 1839. Although not enthusiastic about the prospect of a military career, young Grant set off for the East. The congressman who recommended Grant to West Point had erroneously presented his name as Ulysses Simpson Grant, and Grant accepted the change.

His career at the academy was generally undistinguished. Although he was the best horseman there, he was only an average student, except in mathematics, in which he excelled. He was quiet, courted no one's favor, and counted the days until he could escape from military life. His graduation in 1843, 21st in a class of 39 cadets, entailed a period of service as an army officer. Grant hoped to serve in the cavalry, but instead he was commissioned a brevet second lieutenant in the infantry.

April 27

In 1845 Grant joined the army of General Zachary Taylor in Texas. Though he opposed the Mexican War on principle, Grant fought with great personal bravery throughout the conflict. He distinguished himself at Monterrey by a daring ride through enemy lines in search of ammunition. After the war, Grant married Julia Dent on August 22, 1848. He was stationed at Sackett's Harbor, New York, until 1852, when he and his regiment were ordered to the Pacific Coast via Panama. Because of the danger of the assignment, Julia Grant did not follow.

The trip was extremely challenging. Cholera struck, and Grant buried most of his men en route. He spent the next two years in the wilds of the Pacific Northwest, lonely for his wife and child, Frederick. His promotion to the rank of captain in 1853 was small consolation. Grant took to drink and resigned from the army after being censured for intoxication. Dispirited and without money, he rejoined his family in St. Louis in August 1854. After he unsuccessfully tried to earn a living as a farmer, real estate agent, and customhouse clerk, he went to work in a leather goods store owned by his father and run by two of his brothers in Galena, Illinois. However, their condescending attitude made his stay uncomfortable.

In April 1861 the federal installation at Fort Sumter was bombarded by Confederate guns, and President Abraham Lincoln called for volunteers. Responding to the call, Grant volunteered for military service. Once back in the army, however, he was shuttled from one menial job to another. He was drillmaster, then military clerk, then mustering officer. He asked to lead a regiment, but his letter making the request was never answered. After six weeks of uncertainty, he was appointed colonel of the 21st Illinois Volunteers Infantry Regiment. He had drilled his men scarcely a month when they were ordered to Missouri.

Grant, to his own surprise, was promoted to brigadier general. Within two months, he was commanding 20,000 green troops. In January 1862, Grant was ordered to move up the Tennessee River in a plan to drive out the Confederates holding West Tennessee by attacking their weak center at Fort Henry on the Tennessee River and nearby Fort Donelson on the Cumberland River. Fort Henry quickly succumbed on February 6 to cannon fire from gunboats. Fort Donelson's batteries, however, repulsed the federal gunboats, and on February 15 the garrison attempted to fight its way free of the Union forces. Grant came upon the scene of battle late in the day to see his center and right flank about to collapse. In a cool maneuver, he attacked with his left and carried the day. The following morning he won unconditional surrender. This victory gave his initials, U.S.G., a new meaning—"Unconditional Surrender Grant"—and provided the discouraged North, which had not won a battle since the war had begun, with renewed spirit.

Grant wished to pursue the fleeing enemy further up the Tennessee River, but was hampered by a lack of will to pursue that proved habitual on the part of many of the Union's senior officers. Instead of allowing Grant to follow up his advantage, General Henry W. Halleck diverted some of Grant's troops for another operation and slowed his main force, allowing Confederate troops to regroup 40,000 strong at Corinth, near Tennessee's southern border.

Grant's army lay at Pittsburgh Landing, waiting for reinforcements before engaging the enemy. However, the Confederates did not wait, but attacked Grant frontally in a surprise attack on April 6, 1862. The ensuing battle of Shiloh was extremely bloody and poorly led on both sides. Having made little preparation for defense or security on April 6, the Union forces were driven back in confusion, until their backs were at the Tennessee River. Grant had badly injured his foot, but chose to spend the night with his men on muddy ground under torrential rains. The next morning, the arrival of fresh troops gave Grant the confidence to counterattack. His attack, when he was expected to retreat across the river, finally turned the battle into a victory of sorts.

The Confederate troops were driven off. Out of 63,000 Union troops, 13,000 were wounded, killed, or missing in the encounter, as were nearly 11,000 of 40,000 Confederates.

Grant was widely criticized for his leadership and tactics at Shiloh. Not expecting an attack, he had chosen to drill his new recruits rather than dig them into trenches. Grant responded to his critics with silence. Lincoln, however, announced, "I can't spare this man; he fights."

The eastern theater of the Civil War gave Lincoln most cause for concern. There the Union's formidable Army of the Potomac was so timidly and unimaginatively led that even Confederate mistakes did not result in Union gains. Even so, the battles of Antietam in September 1862 and Gettysburg in July 1863 finally blunted the offensive capability of the South. In the West, the Confederates still held one stronghold: Vicksburg, Mississippi, on the Mississippi River. Grant spent the latter part of 1862 trying fruitlessly to cut through the muddy woods north of Vicksburg. Meanwhile, the national press was vituperative, calling him an inept drunkard, and the Confederates expected him to retreat to Memphis in disgrace. Grant persisted, however, and in January

1863 sent his army of 36,000 down the Mississippi by steamer to a point opposite Vicksburg. Twenty-five miles south of that point, he crossed the river, then cut loose from his supply line and marched 35 miles northeast until he was directly east of Vicksburg. Meanwhile, General John C. Pemberton, commanding the Confederates at Vicksburg, was completely fooled by a raucous diversionary attack known as Grierson's Raid.

The Union forces in the area then joined together. Skirmishing as they went, Grant's 36,000 troops won the day through brilliant maneuvering across terrain that was heavily wooded and cut by deep ravines. Initially outnumbered (though they were later reinforced), the Union troops were caught between Confederate troops to their east and the strong force defending Vicksburg to the west. Grant drove off the eastern forces, made an about-face, and proceeded to outflank and outfight the Confederates outside Vicksburg. A siege was established, and the city surrendered on July 4, the day after the Confederates had been stopped at Gettysburg. After Port Hudson, Louisiana, surrendered four days later, the Mississippi was in Union hands, and the Confederacy was cut in two.

Lincoln promoted Grant to major general in the regular army after the fall of Vicksburg. His direction of the bloody Chattanooga campaign in the fall opened the way for a Union drive toward Atlanta. Then, on March 9, 1864, Grant (now with the rank of lieutenant general) was given command of all the federal armies and went to Virginia to direct the Union's most important military force, General Meade's Army of the Potomac.

Grant was the first of Lincoln's generals to agree wholly with Lincoln's war plan: to press in simultaneously upon the South from three directions. By maintaining this simultaneous offensive, the Union armies would nullify the South's advantage of interior defense lines and the South's smaller armies would be denied mobility; the Confederacy would be cut into pieces. This was Grant's strategy. It proved costly, but it worked.

In May 1864 Grant marched the Army of the Potomac south and met Lee's army in the wilderness near Chancellorsville, Virginia. The fighting through the dense underbrush resulted in many casualties, but was indecisive. Then, in a series of bloody battles that included Spotsylvania, North Anna River, and Cold Harbor, the indomitable Grant drove the brilliant Lee slowly southward, past Richmond. At Petersburg came a new stage in warfare, forecasting the grimness of World War I. Both armies settled into opposing lines of trenches, occasionally making costly forays over open ground.

President Lincoln narrowly weathered the election of 1864, emerging as the victor. Shortly afterwards, in mid-November 1864, General Sherman left the Atlanta area and began his march to the sea. While Sherman's army moved across the South, Grant's strength continued to grow. On April 2, 1865, Lee finally broke contact with Grant's forces in front of Petersburg after the long siege and set out towards the west, with Grant in pursuit. Union cavalry raced ahead, and Lee's army surrendered at the little town of Appomattox Court House, Virginia, where Lee surrendered to Grant on April 9, 1865, effectively ending the Civil War.

Grant, the war hero, was nominated for president on the Republican ticket in 1868. He won the election by a large electoral vote, although he had only a slight edge in the popular tally. For a time, he enjoyed life in the White House. He tried to run the administrative branch of government like an army staff, but had some difficulties on that account. In the conduct of foreign affairs, he gave his very competent secretary of state, Hamilton Fish, a free hand. Fish's skill contributed to the amicable settlement by international arbitration of the Alabama Claims dispute over damage done by British-built Confederate warships during the Civil War.

Questions of finance were central to Grant's domestic policy. During the war, paper money "greenbacks" had been issued to raise money for the government. Many greenbacks had been purchased by speculators. With the rise in value of this paper currency, a dispute arose over whether it should be redeemed at original rates or at current value. Generally speaking, eastern business interests wanted a deflationary policy, while debtors and speculators hoped for an inflationary policy. With inside information on administration policy, two stock speculators, Jay Gould and James Fisk, organized a corner on gold, thus precipitating a disastrous day on Wall Street known as Black Friday on September 24, 1869. By dumping gold onto the open market, the treasury foiled the scheme. The machinations of Gould and Fisk were the beginning of a whole series of scandals that were to besmirch both the first and second administrations of Grant.

Grant was an uncomplicated, patriotic man who expected others to attend to the business of government in the same spirit. Some others, however, did not hold this attitude but went into government to get rich. Although Grant himself introduced some reforms, he suspected no one and refused to listen to cries for the kind of thoroughgoing civil service reform that was obviously needed. Thus, a split arose within Republican ranks. Members of one section of the party dubbed themselves Reform, or Liberal, Republicans. Their interest was to rid the Republican Party of the spoils system, political corruption, and vindictiveness toward the former Confederate states. In May 1872 this Liberal Republican faction met and nominated the brilliant but erratic Horace Greeley for president. His nomination was also endorsed by the Democrats. The regular, or Radical, Republicans were still interested in preserving the voting rights of African Americans, whereas this concern had faded from the minds of Liberal Republicans. Nominated on a Radical Republican platform, Grant was reelected by a wide margin, carrying all but six states.

Grant's second term was marked by a wave of corruption at all levels of government. The effort to build a railroad to the Pacific became infested with speculators and unprincipled legislators scheming to line their pockets. In St. Louis and elsewhere, a Whiskey Ring defrauded the government of several million dollars in taxes with the aid of treasury officials and Grant's private secretary. The war, interior, and postal departments were all scenes of scandals. Grant himself was never proven to be corrupt or dishonest in his governmental activities, and in fact he left the White House with rather poor finances.

With a few thousand dollars saved from his presidential salary, Grant set out in May 1877 to see Europe. He traveled for two years, returning home in the autumn of 1879. Grant retired to an apartment on New York City's upper East Side in 1881. He lived on the income from gifts of admirers totaling $250,000, which he invested. These investments eventually went bad, however, and in 1884 Grant entered an unsuccessful business partnership in which he was badly exploited. Meanwhile, perhaps as a result of his lifelong addiction to cigars, Grant contracted throat cancer. Knowing that he had not long to live, he agreed to write a book of personal memoirs to provide his family with an income. For the quiet to do this work, Grant was moved to what would later be known as the Grant Cottage, at Mount McGregor, New York. In severe pain, he worked stoically. He completed the manuscript on July 19, 1885, and died four days later. The memoirs, remarkable for their straightforwardness and eloquence, were published by Mark Twain. They sold well and eventually brought Grant's family almost $500,000.

The Grant Memorial Association was soon formed to erect a suitable monument over his grave. John Duncan designed a massive structure whose interior is reminiscent of Napoléon's Tomb. Over 90,000 people contributed to build the memorial, which is at Riverside Drive and West 122nd Street in New York City. It was opened to the public in 1897, and since that time has been visited by millions. Inside are mural maps of battles and busts of other Civil War heroes. The site was declared General Grant National Memorial on May 1, 1959.

"Fast Day" in New Hampshire

This is a movable event.

New Hampshire is the only state in which there is still a legal holiday known as Fast Day. Although it was for years marked on the last Thursday of April, the state legislature in 1949 shifted the observance to the fourth Monday in April. In so doing, it anticipated the trend toward Monday holidays of more recent years. Although the date of Fast Day is set by statute, it is customary for the governor to issue a proclamation officially designating the day each year.

So far as the general public is concerned, the original purpose of the day as an occasion of spiritual significance marked by prayer and fasting is now largely overlooked. The prayer services and special exercises that were once customary have much diminished in number. As one resident summarized it, Fast Day today is much more commonly used as "an opportunity for recreation, opening up summer camps, the performance of spring chores, and out-of-town shopping." Governor H. Styles Bridges took note of this fact as early as 1935, in explaining New Hampshire's custom of observing Fast Day:

> The fact that the season of outdoor sport is then opening in this latitude tends to secure a general observance of the day so far as ceasing from labor is concerned. . . . I do not know personally of any instance of its observance by fasting. Some church services are held and the official proclamation usually recalls the original reason for establishing Fast Day, and the existing need for a continuance of the thought that inspired the first observance.

In colonial times, days of "public humiliation, fasting and prayer" were commonly proclaimed by the royal governors in New England, usually about the middle of April. For generations, prayers for a bountiful harvest characterized New England's spring Fast Days. The earliest official record of a Fast Day proclamation issued in New Hampshire appeared in the provincial papers of 1679. That proclamation designated February 26 for the commemoration. Later acts of the New Hampshire legislature confirmed the Fast Day observance in 1861 and 1899, with the last Thursday of April traditionally set aside for the purpose, until the 1949 change.

Long before that, however, there had been changes elsewhere. In most places, the custom of observing Fast Day had faded out, both in statute and in practice, after the American Revolution. Massachusetts formally abolished its Fast Day in 1895 and substituted Patriots' Day on the grounds that the former occasion no longer retained the austere religious character it had once had. A few years later, Maine repealed the law establishing its Fast Day for similar reasons. In New Hampshire there were also thoughts of dropping the observance. The earliest known effort to abolish Fast Day occurred in 1897, when Governor Ramsdell, in a message to the legislature, urged it to follow the example of Massachusetts. His recommendation was not adopted. Similar later proposals were also defeated, and a concerted anti–Fast Day effort in 1917 came to naught. To this day, New Hampshire retains its now unique observance.

April 28

James Monroe's Birthday

Library of Congress

James Monroe

James Monroe, the fifth president of the United States and promulgator of the Monroe Doctrine, was born in Westmoreland County, Virginia, on April 28, 1758. Of Scottish and Welsh ancestry, he

was the eldest of five children of Spence Monroe, a farmer and circuit judge, and Elizabeth Jones Monroe.

Monroe was tutored at home until he was 12 and then attended a parson's school. A member of the gentry, he entered the College of William and Mary at 16, but after only two years left to join the Continental army. Rising from the rank of lieutenant to lieutenant-colonel in four years, he fought in many of the most famous battles of the American Revolution, including those at Harlem Heights, White Plains, Trenton, Brandywine, Germantown, and Monmouth.

By 1780 Monroe's military career was at an end, and he returned to his native state, where he studied law with Thomas Jefferson. In 1782 Monroe was elected to the Virginia legislature, and the next year he was sent to the Continental Congress, where he remained for three years. In 1786 he was admitted to the bar and began to practice law in Fredericksburg. That same year he returned to politics by being elected to the Virginia Assembly. As a member of the Virginia ratifying convention of 1788, Monroe worked with such Antifederalists as Patrick Henry to defeat the proposed Constitution. Their efforts, however, were doomed to failure, and Monroe came to accept the new frame of government.

A member of the United States Senate from 1790 to 1794, Monroe was active in the party of the Jeffersonian Republicans (later known as Democratic-Republicans and ultimately as the Democrats), which opposed many policies of the Washington administration. President Washington appointed Monroe as minister to France in 1794, but Monroe's failure to assuage the French hostility aroused by the Jay Treaty between the United States and England led to his recall two years later.

Monroe later served as governor of Virginia from 1799 to 1802. Meanwhile, the election of the Democratic-Republican candidate, Thomas Jefferson, to the presidency in 1800 assured Monroe of a place of importance in the national government. In 1802 and 1803 he and Robert R. Livingston, with instructions only to purchase New Orleans and West Florida from France, exceeded their authority and doubled the area of the United States by acquiring the entire Louisiana Territory. After completing these spectacularly successful negotiations, Monroe served as minister to England in 1804 and then went to Madrid, where he failed to settle a boundary dispute between the United States and Spain. Nevertheless, Jefferson dispatched him in 1806 to England to negotiate a treaty along with William Pinkney. The mission, whose purpose was to effect a cessation of British interference with American commerce and to receive indemnity for seizure of vessels, resulted in the Monroe-Pinkney Treaty. Its terms were so weak, however, that Jefferson did not even submit it to the Senate.

Monroe was elected governor of Virginia a second time in 1810, but he resigned after several months to become secretary of state in the cabinet of President James Madison in April 1811. In 1814 he was appointed secretary of war to replace John Armstrong, who resigned under public pressure after the British burning of Washington, D.C., during the War of 1812. He also continued serving as secretary of state until the conclusion of the war.

In 1816 Monroe was elected president, receiving almost 85 percent of the electoral votes. By the time Monroe ran for reelection in 1820, the Federalist Party, which had supported such unpopular causes as the War of 1812 and had not won the presidency in 20 years, had virtually disintegrated. For this reason, Monroe captured all but one electoral vote, and the absence of party bickering and dispute during his administration has led historians to characterize his time in office as the "era of good feeling."

Monroe's best known action as president was the issuance, on December 2, 1823, of the doctrine that bears his name. The Monroe Doctrine, a declaration that was directed against European attempts to restore the power of Spain in Latin America and against Russian encroachments in the northern Pacific coast region of North America, clearly rejected any further European interference in the Americas and established the United States as the protector of the Western Hemisphere. The pertinent part of the message follows:

> We owe it, therefore, to candor and to the amicable relations existing between the United States and [the European] Powers to declare that we should consider any attempt on their part to extend their system to any portion of this hemisphere as dangerous to our peace and safety.

> With the existing colonies and dependencies of any European Power we have not interfered and we shall not interfere. But with the Governments who have declared their independence, and maintained it, and whose independence we have, on great consideration, and just principles, acknowledged, we could not view any interposition for the purpose of oppressing them, or controlling, in any manner, their destiny, by any European Power in any other light than as the manifestation of an unfriendly disposition towards the United States.

His presidency completed, Monroe retired in 1825 to his handsome Oak Hill estate in Loudon County, Virginia. He remained active, becoming a regent of the University of Virginia in 1826 and serving in the 1829 Virginia Constitutional Convention, which amended the state constitution. Congress awarded him $30,000 in 1826 to ease the monetary problems caused by expenditures in public service, but in 1830 he was forced to move to New York City, with his daughter, because of financial difficulties.

Monroe's death, like that of John Adams and Thomas Jefferson, who died within a few hours of each other in 1826, came on the anniversary of the nation's independence. While in New York, Monroe died on July 4, 1831. His remains were reinterred in 1858, the centennial year of his birth, with great ceremony at Hollywood Cemetery in Richmond, Virginia.

Maryland Ratifies the Constitution

Maryland, on April 28, 1788, officially became the seventh state to ratify the proposed United States Constitution. In actuality, the delegates performed the act of ratification on Saturday, April 26. After the signing, the document was taken to a print shop. The shop was closed until Monday, however, and the paper was redated April 28.

As in Delaware, New Jersey, Georgia, and Connecticut, supporters of the new government faced little opposition in Maryland. Thus, ratification was accomplished quickly and without much bitter argument or political maneuvering. Maryland was among the earlier proponents of strengthening the Articles of Confederation. In March 1785, four commissioners from Maryland met with four counterparts from Virginia at George Washington's Mount Vernon residence to discuss problems relating to the navigation of Chesapeake Bay and the Potomac River. The negotiators quickly reached agreement on jurisdiction over the Potomac and on the apportionment of the expenses for marking the Chesapeake channel. In their report the representatives suggested that their respective legislatures adopt uniform currency, commercial regulations, and customs duties. The Maryland legislature approved the plan and suggested that Delaware and Pennsylvania be included in future discussions of matters of mutual interest.

After Congress called on February 21, 1787, for the assembling of the Constitutional Convention, Maryland agreed to send a five-man delegation. The legislature initially appointed Charles Carroll of Carrollton, Gabriel Duvall, Robert Hanson Harrison, Thomas Sim Lee, and Thomas Stone, but all of them declined to serve. Apparently, domestic political considerations, including opposition to plans to issue large amounts of paper money, seemed more important than the Constitutional Convention to these noted leaders. Two weeks after the date set for the opening of the Philadelphia, Pennsylvania, gathering, the Maryland legislature named another, much less distinguished, five-man contingent.

Luther Martin, then in his early 40s, was the most capable member of the delegation. A lawyer and former schoolteacher, Martin had been a member of the Confederation Congress and state attorney general. At the convention he became a prominent foe of plans to strengthen the federal government.

James McHenry, an Irish-born surgeon, served as secretary to George Washington during the American Revolution and became his trusted friend. Only 33, he had served in the Maryland senate and in the Confederation Congress. He made little impression at the convention.

Daniel Jenifer of St. Thomas, 64, was the senior member of the Maryland contingent. A man of means, respected in his home state, he had served in Congress and was one of Maryland's commissioners at the Mount Vernon conference. Amiable, but aware of his shortcomings as a politician, Jenifer was not outspoken in Philadelphia.

Daniel Carroll and John Francis Mercer both had experience in the Confederation Congress. Affluent and well-connected, these two men were rising Maryland politicians in 1787. Carroll was 56, and Mercer, at 28, was the youngest member of the delegation.

Maryland's contribution to the Constitutional Convention was not noteworthy. Predictably, this small state supported resolutions granting each state an equal vote in the Senate, but the delegation was not able to reach a decision on the preferred system of voting in the House of Representatives. Eventually, however, Maryland gave its assent to the Great Compromise, which provided for equal representation of states in the Senate and proportional representation by population in the House.

Contentious Luther Martin spoke out vociferously against granting excessive power to the central government. On June 27 and June 28, 1787, Martin made a two-day speech to the weary delegates, arguing against congressional representation proportional to population. Although Martin's position that the national government should be formed for the states rather than for individuals was plausible, his rambling harangue only antagonized his fellow convention members.

In September, the Constitutional Convention concluded its business in Philadelphia. Maryland's delegates joined those of the other states in signing the proposed federal Constitution, which they sent to Congress for referral to the states for approval. The framers then returned to their home states to prepare to take part in the process of ratification. After the October 1787 state elections, the Maryland legislature began its consideration of the new Constitution. The delegates to the convention gave their accounts of the Philadelphia proceedings, and their impressions varied. Luther Martin presented an indictment of the new frame of government, which later appeared in print as *The Genuine Information*, while James McHenry ably refuted Martin's contentions and spoke in favor of the proposed Constitution.

Maryland's state Senate called for a ratifying convention, and proposed that the election of convention delegates take place in January 1788 and that the convention assemble early in March. In the Maryland House, Samuel Chase and other Antifederalist leaders persuaded the members to postpone the election and convention until April, remove the property qualifications for candidates, and omit the statements in favor of ratification from the call for the convention. The Senate, for the sake of quick ratification, agreed to the House's terms. Voters appeared at the polls in unusually large numbers on election day. Approximately 10,000 Marylanders cast ballots, and a large majority of them chose candidates favoring the Constitution; the Federalists elected 65 delegates and the Antifederalists 12. When the convention met, the Federalists simply allowed opposition speakers such as Chase and Martin to express their views and then called for an immediate vote on ratification. Late on Saturday, April 26, 1788, the Maryland convention approved the new Constitution by a vote of 63 to 11.

Various factors led Maryland to strongly favor the new Constitution. A small state, Maryland looked forward to the protection that a powerful national government could provide. Baltimore merchants and manufacturers also found advantages in certain provisions of the new Constitution. Finally, the Maryland Federalists drew much support from the tobacco-planting aristocracy, which hoped that the new government would be able to curb democratic programs, suggested by such men as Samuel Chase, that would undermine their political and economic dominance.

Maryland and the 12 other colonies that separated from England became states at the time of the Declaration of Independence. For purposes of establishing a chronological order of the entry of these 13 states into the Union, however, historians have used the dates of their ratification of the Constitution. Thus Maryland is listed as the seventh state.

Washington State Apple Blossom Festival

This is a movable event.

The Washington State Apple Blossom Festival is held annually in the central apple-growing region of Washington state. Beginning in 1970, the festival, which is timed to include the first weekend in May, was extended to a full six days from Tuesday through Sunday. In 1972 the celebration was expanded to nine days. By 1997 it was eleven days long, lasting from April 24 through May 4, although the exact dates may change from year to year. It is at this time of year that the apple orchards are in full bloom.

The Washington State Apple Blossom Festival has the distinction of being the oldest blossom festival in the United States, as well as the state's oldest major civic event. Its origins go back to 1920, when Mrs. E. Wagner, a native of New Zealand, recalled the blossom festival in her former homeland and suggested to the Ladies' Musical Club that a similar celebration be held in Wenatchee, Washington. The first of the Blossom Days, as the festival was initially entitled, was conceived as a modest musical tribute to the chief industry of the developing community. A simple program held in Memorial Park consisted of speeches and songs. In 1921 the first festival queen was chosen from the student body of the local high school to "rule over" the Wenatchee Valley, and a parade was staged. By 1923 the one-day event had grown to include not only a queen but a King Apple and four lesser queens. Only the selection of the Apple Blossom Queen survived as an annual feature, but during the first 10 years a pageant, show, fireworks display, and other events were added, and neighboring communities were invited to participate.

Community effort grew more extensive, and Blossom Days became known as the Wenatchee Apple Blossom Festival, or the North-Central Wenatchee Apple Blossom Festival. It was held annually with the exception of 1932 and the years during World War II. By 1946 the first day of a then two-day celebration included a schoolchildren's costume parade, a royal banquet, and a queen's ball attended by the governor and other dignitaries. The second day featured the festival parade with floats, followed by the coronation of the Apple Blossom Festival Queen and a pageant presented by high school students. Evening entertainment consisted of a baseball game and a fireworks display.

Although financed and produced by Wenatchee, the festival was designated the Washington State Apple Blossom Festival in 1947. The change of title was made in view of the festival's importance as one of the nation's largest civic celebrations and in recognition of the widespread participation of people throughout the state and the Pacific Northwest. In 1967 the festival formed a sister relationship with the Aomori Apple Blossom Festival of Japan, and the Washington State Apple Blossom Queen traveled to Japan as guest of the Aomori Broadcasting Company, which sponsored the Japanese event.

April 29

Oliver Ellsworth's Birthday

Photo by William Wheeler after Ralph Carl, Collection of the Supreme Court of the United States.

Oliver Ellsworth

Oliver Ellsworth was the third chief justice of the United States Supreme Court, serving from 1796 to 1800, following John Jay and John Rutledge. Though the chief justiceship crowned his career, Ellsworth made his deepest contributions to American government in his earlier political roles, most strikingly in the United States Senate. He was also a framer of the Constitution.

Ellsworth was born on April 29, 1745, in Windsor, Connecticut, the second son of Captain David Ellsworth and Jemima Leavitt Ellsworth. His father wanted him to become a clergyman, and so he was educated by the Reverend Joseph Bellamy of Bethlehem, Connecticut, and then sent to Yale College in 1762. He remained at Yale for two years, then transferred to the College of New Jersey (now Princeton University). He graduated from college in 1766 and returned home to study theology with the Reverend John Smalley of New Britain, Connecticut. Within less than a year Ellsworth decided to abandon theology and study law. He worked at it for four years, teaching part of the time.

In 1771 he was admitted to the bar. He tried to practice law at Windsor but had so few clients that he had to support himself by farming and chopping wood. The next year he married Abigail Wolcott of East Windsor. Not possessing a horse, he had to walk to Hartford when court was in session, a round trip of 20 miles. In 1775 Ellsworth moved to Hartford, where his practice improved rapidly. Four years later Noah Webster, who began the study of law in his office, said that Ellsworth had from 1,000 to 1,500 cases on his lists and that there was hardly a suit tried in the city in which Ellsworth did not appear on one side or the other. By shrewd management he built his income into a fortune.

Ellsworth entered politics as a representative of Hartford in the Connecticut general assembly. In 1777, at the age of 32, he was appointed state's attorney for Hartford County. In 1780 he became a member of the Governor's Council, serving until 1785, when he was made a judge of the state superior court. He served in that capacity for four years until he became a United States Senator from Connecticut.

From 1777 to 1783, during the American Revolution, Ellsworth divided his energies between service to Connecticut and to the struggling central government of the 13 former colonies. While state's attorney, he also became one of Connecticut's delegates to the Continental Congress. There he was active on important committees and was reelected five times, until in 1783 he declined to serve further. He had served simultaneously on Connecticut's Council of Safety and as one of five on its Committee of the Pay Table.

After the Revolution, the Articles of Confederation proved to be an ineffective system of government, and the Constitutional Convention was called at Philadelphia, Pennsylvania, in 1787 to draft a new federal constitution. Ellsworth, along with Roger Sherman and William Samuel Johnson, represented Connecticut. He became a member of the important committee on detail that wrote the first and decisive draft of the Constitution. With Sherman he proposed the crucial "Connecticut compromise," providing for a federal legislature of two houses: in the upper house each state was to be equally represented; in the lower house representation was to be on the basis of population. This arrangement ended the quarrel between the large and small states at the convention, and it continues to be an essential feature of the federal system in the United States. Ellsworth is also credited with the insertion of the term "United States" in the Constitution, although this phrase had been adopted 11 years earlier by the Continental Congress to replace the name "United Colonies" and therefore was probably not Ellsworth's own invention. Among his other positions at the convention, Ellsworth backed the continuance of the international slave trade, arguing that moral responsibility should remain with the people of those states that legally sanctioned it.

It is said that Ellsworth did not wait for the convention to conclude but rushed home to work for Connecticut's ratification of the Constitution. During the ratification debates his "Letters to a Landholder," appearing in the *Connecticut Courant* and the *American Mercury* (1787–1788), were widely circulated and had an influence somewhat like that of the *Federalist* papers by Alexander Hamilton, James Madison, and John Jay in New York.

At the age of 44, tall, dignified, and commanding, Ellsworth was chosen as one of the first two senators from Connecticut to the newly formed United States Senate. He seems to have been especially suited to the work necessitated by the newness of the government, and his great familiarity with organizational and administrative matters gave him a predominant place among his Senate colleagues during the next seven years. The first rules of the Senate were reported by Ellsworth, and he put forward a plan for printing its official journal. Ellsworth also shaped the report on the first 12 proposed amendments to the Constitution, ten of which were ratified and became the Bill of Rights. During his term, Ellsworth also wrote the measure that admitted North Carolina to the Union and designed the act that forced Rhode Island to join. He helped draw up the government of the territory south of the Ohio, framed the first bill regulating the consular service, and energetically supported Hamilton's scheme for funding the national debt and for incorporating the Bank of the United States. Ellsworth's most weighty single contribution was the organization of the federal judiciary. He was the chief author of the Federal Judiciary Act of 1789, which remains the foundation of the federal court system.

April 30

In 1796 Ellsworth resigned from the Senate to accept appointment by President Washington as chief justice of the United States Supreme Court, after John Rutledge failed to receive Senate confirmation and William Cushing, the senior associate justice, had declined. (Technically Rutledge may be considered the second chief justice, and therefore Ellsworth the third, even though Rutledge's appointment was never confirmed. In fact, Rutledge was acting chief justice from his presidential appointment on July 1, 1795, until his rejection by the Senate on December 15, 1795. Ellsworth was named by Washington on March 4, 1796.) Historians have found Ellsworth to be an unremarkable chief justice whose opinions reveal common sense but no outstanding knowledge of the law. The position of justice gave little scope for the forensic talents that had given Ellsworth his skill at the bar, in the Constitutional Convention, and in the Senate.

In 1799 Ellsworth very reluctantly accepted President John Adams's call to go to France with William Vans Murray and William R. Davie in a commission to negotiate a settlement of grievances, particularly the restrictions placed on American vessels. Adams was anxious to avert a war, which many in his own Federalist Party wanted, and Ellsworth agreed that negotiation was the lesser evil. The disappointing terms offered by Napoléon I did not fulfill the commissioners' instructions or hopes, but a compromise was arranged providing for freedom of commerce between France and the United States. The Treaty of Morfontaine (September 30, 1800), commonly known as the Convention of 1800, was ratified by the Senate when Napoléon agreed that it should supersede and abrogate the treaties of 1778, thus formally releasing the United States from its defensive alliance with France.

The hardships of the winter journey to France, which took four months because of storms, ruined Ellsworth's health. He resigned the chief justiceship while still in France and did not return with the other commissioners, but remained in England for a time in an effort to recover his health. He returned to America in the spring of 1801, still ill, and took up his residence in his native Windsor. He was appointed chief justice of the Connecticut Supreme Court, but was unable to serve. For the next six years, after he had "begun to die," as he wrote a friend, he occupied himself with agriculture, reading theology, and writing a weekly column on agricultural topics for the *Connecticut Courant*. He died on November 26, 1807, at the age of 62 in the stately frame house in which he lived in Windsor.

April 30

Fall of Saigon

By the early 1970s, with the mounting casualties, economic burden, and domestic unpopularity of the Vietnam War, President Richard Nixon's administration was attempting to extricate the United States from the conflict. (See various related essays throughout this book.) Determined to not be the first American president to "lose a war," however, Nixon wanted "peace with honor." He instituted a campaign of heavy bombing raids on North Vietnam, including the capital of Hanoi, on the theory that this would force the North Vietnamese to resume the protracted negotiations which had gone on for years but had yet to produce any agreement.

It worked. On January 8, 1973, American representative Henry Kissinger and North Vietnamese representative Le Duc Tho resumed talks in Paris. Thirteen days later Nixon announced "progress" in the peace negotiations, and suspended bombing in all of North Vietnam, as well as mining, shelling, and other offensive actions. Kissinger and Tho held one additional session. Then, on January 23, President Nixon reported that the representatives had initiated an agreement "to end the war and bring peace with honor in Vietnam and Southeast Asia."

On January 27 representatives of the United States, Hanoi, the Viet Cong, and Saigon signed the Vietnam peace pact in Paris. The agreement specified, among other things, that all military prisoners of war and foreign civilians would be released, that the 23,700-man American force in South Vietnam would be withdrawn within 60 days, and that an international force composed of Canadians, Hungarians, Indonesians, and Poles would supervise the truce. North Vietnamese troops already in the South were allowed to remain, but they could not be replaced. Both the United States and North Vietnam agreed to respect "the South Vietnamese people's right to self-determination." The cease-fire went into effect at 7:00 p.m. Eastern Standard Time and brought the United States' longest and most controversial involvement in a war to its conclusion.

The extrication of the United States from the hostilities, however, did not mean that the fighting stopped. During the spring of 1973, violations of the truce were so frequent and flagrant that representatives of the United States, North Vietnam, South Vietnam, and the Viet Cong signed a second peace agreement in South Vietnam on June 13, 1973. Called an "amplification and consolidation" of the earlier Paris accord, the new document stipulated that all military actions in South Vietnam end at noon Greenwich Mean Time on June 15, 1973, and that commanders of the opposing forces meet within 24 hours of that time to ensure compliance with the truce and to guarantee medical attention for all combatants. It also specified that the United States would no longer fly reconnaissance missions over North Vietnam, would resume mine-sweeping operations in North Vietnamese waters, and would resume talks regarding aid to North Vietnam.

Even after the second cease-fire, fighting in Vietnam continued. Although neither the South nor the North conducted a major offensive during 1973, the Saigon government estimated that nearly 16,000 South Vietnamese and some 45,000 North Vietnamese and Viet Cong died in guerrilla operations and skirmishes between January 27, 1973, and January 27, 1974.

Through 1974 the bloody war continued in stalemate. North Vietnamese and Viet Cong troops conducted limited offensives against areas controlled by the Saigon government. Meanwhile, the United States continued to aid its ally. About 5,000 Americans remained in South Vietnam as civilian advisers, and Congress appropriated hundreds of millions of dollars in military aid. At home the United States endured the long-festering political scandal that in August of 1974 brought about the resignation of Nixon and the succession of Gerald R. Ford to the presidency.

The major Communist offensive that many observers had expected came in March of 1975. Early in the month, North Vietnamese and Viet Cong troops struck the Central Highlands provinces of Kontum, Pleiku, and Darlac. In the two weeks of fighting that followed, the Communists severed the two main highways leading from the highlands, took a number of key outposts, captured the provincial capital of Ban Me Thuot, and caused about 100,000 persons to flee to the coast of the South China Sea. The forces of the Saigon government were unable to stem the Communist advance, and on March 18, 1975, President Nguyen Van Thieu ordered a retreat from the strategic Central Highlands area.

Communist control of the Central Highlands effectively isolated the northern provinces of South Vietnam from the remainder of the nation, and within days of their success in the Highlands the Communists gained command of two-thirds of the northern area of the country. By sacrificing this region, the Saigon government hoped that it would be capable of defending the rich and populous southern part of the nation and the narrow strip running northward from Saigon along the coast of the South China Sea to Hue.

Through the last days of March 1975 and into the beginning of April, the Communist forces continued their victories. By April 10 the North Vietnamese and Viet Cong controlled Hue and Da Nang in the north and turned their attention toward isolating Saigon. The situation in South Vietnam was so critical that on April 11 President Ford appealed to Congress for nearly $1 billion in military and humanitarian aid so that the Southeast Asian nation might save itself. Reaction was favorable to Ford's request for $250 million to be used for humanitarian purposes and for authority to call upon American troops to ensure the evacuation of American citizens from Vietnam. However, the fact that the South Vietnamese army had already abandoned a billion dollars worth of arms and supplies to the enemy made Congress unwilling to approve the expenditure of $722 million for further military assistance.

During mid-April 1975, South Vietnam's remaining defenses rapidly crumbled, and with 10 divisions of the North Vietnamese army surrounding Saigon, President Thieu resigned on April 21. When the Communists refused to negotiate a peace with Thieu's former vice president and successor, Tran Van Huong, he too left office, and on April 28 General Duong Van Minh was sworn in as the new president. Both the North Vietnamese and Viet Cong were favorable to Minh, but they would not deal with him until all 1,000 Americans remaining in Vietnam had left. On April 29 American helicopters carried out this emergency evacuation. The following day, April 30, 1975, President Minh announced the unconditional surrender of South Vietnam. After more than a decade of fighting, the loss of 180,000 South Vietnamese troops, 58,000 Americans, an unknown number of Northern and Viet Cong forces, and hundreds of thousands of civilians, the Vietnam War had finally ended.

Louisiana Admitted to the Union

On April 30, 1812, Louisiana became the 18th state in the United States of America. It was the first state to be carved out of the vast area of the Louisiana Purchase, which stretched across a vast portion of the continental United States and would in later years be divided into many other states. Thus, it was quite appropriate that Louisiana formally gained statehood on the ninth anniversary of the official date of cession of the Louisiana Territory.

The nine-year period from the beginning of American jurisdiction over Louisiana in 1803 to statehood in 1812 was a time of considerable difficulty and frustration for the inhabitants of that region. The vast area of Louisiana came under the control of France in 1682, when René-Robert Cavelier, Sieur de La Salle, reached the mouth of the Mississippi River and claimed the lands bordering the river and its tributaries for King Louis XIV. The first French settlers came to what is now Louisiana in 1699, and they, and those who followed, firmly established the customs, government, and language of their homeland in the area at the mouth of the river.

For more than 70 years following La Salle's explorations, the Mississippi valley, including what is now Louisiana, remained under French control. Then, in 1762, France ceded its claim to the area west of the Mississippi to Spain. Spanish rule over the vast territory lasted until 1800 when Spain returned the area to France. However, even during the time of Spanish jurisdiction, the settlers clung to their French language and traditions. The American purchase from France of the vast, ill-defined area west of the Mississippi in 1803 disrupted the lives of the inhabitants of New Orleans and the surrounding countryside to a much greater extent than had the previous period of Spanish rule.

On March 26, 1804, the United States Congress passed an act dividing the Louisiana Purchase into two parts: the Territory of Orleans, comprising that "portion south of the Mississippi Territory and on an east and west line, to commence on the Mississippi River at the thirty-third degree of north latitude and extend west to the western boundary of the cession"; and the District of Louisiana, composed of the remainder of the area purchased. The act provided that the District of Louisiana, or upper Louisiana, as it was also known, be placed under the jurisdiction of the government of the Indiana Territory, but it established a separate government for the Territory of Orleans.

The government that Congress set up for the Territory of Orleans was unlike any other then existing in the United States or its territories. It consisted of a governor vested with full executive powers, to be appointed by the president; a 13-member legislative council, to be named by the president; a superior court of three judges, also to be presidential appointees; "and such inferior courts and justices of the peace as the Legislature of the Territory might establish." English was made the official language of the territory, and "the importation of slaves from foreign countries was forbidden, and that of those from the United States was allowed only to citizens, bona fide owners, removing to the Territory."

The congressional debate preceding the passage of the 1804 act was heated. One Massachusetts representative claimed that the inhabitants of the new territory were not ready for full citizenship and should be treated "as if they were a conquered country." Others disagreed. Indeed, some members of Congress felt that the government established for the Territory of Orleans was too harsh and even contrary to the treaty of cession, which guaranteed that "the inhabitants of the ceded territory [the Louisiana Purchase] shall be incorporated in the union of the United States and admitted as soon as possible according to the principles of the federal Constitution to the enjoyment of all the rights, advantages and immunities of citizens of the United States."

The government that Congress established for the Territory of Orleans greatly dissatisfied the residents of what is now Louisiana. They had expected immediate admission to statehood and resented the territorial status that Congress imposed. Furthermore, they disliked the introduction of jury trials, a phenomenon that previously had no place in their legal system, and they were unhappy that English was now the territory's official language since few could read or speak it. To protest the Act of 1804, the mayor of New Orleans resigned, and on June 1, 1804, a group of planters and merchants met in New Orleans to initiate more practical measures. They drew up petitions asking Congress to repeal the legislation relating to the division of the Louisiana Purchase and to the prohibitions against the importation of slaves. They also decided to request immediate statehood for Louisiana. In the following weeks, they circulated these memorials among the populace, and late in the summer they sent a committee of three to Washington, D.C., to place their demands before Congress.

In November 1804 President Thomas Jefferson suggested to Congress that improvements be made in the government of the Louisiana Purchase territory, and in December 1804 Pierre Darbigny, Pierre Sauvé, and Jean Noel Destréhan presented to the House of Representatives the petition that had been circulated through the Orleans territory during the previous summer. In 1805 Congress acted quickly to correct the harsher aspects of the government it had established the previous year. On March 2 it passed an act setting up a separate territorial government for upper Louisiana and created a government for the Orleans territory that was similar to that established for the Northwest Territory in 1787. The New Orleans government consisted of a house of representatives to be elected by the inhabitants of the territory; a legislative council whose five members were to be chosen by the president from among ten nominees presented by the elected house; and a governor, secretary, and judges of the superior court, who would be named by the president with the consent of the Senate. The 1805 act also provided that the territory be admitted to statehood as soon as its free population numbered 60,000.

The new government did not entirely please the inhabitants of the Orleans territory, and one official remarked that "the people of Louisiana complained that in this form, as in the preceding, their lives and property were in some degree at the disposal of a single individual." In addition, the territory was plagued by external difficulties. In 1806 Spanish troops attempted to establish a post near Natchitoches in an area claimed by the United States. About the same time Aaron Burr, the former vice president of the United States, became involved in a plot that included a plan to detach an area of the Louisiana Purchase from the United States. Fortunately, neither the Spanish raids nor the alleged Burr conspiracy developed into a major threat to the Orleans territory. Instead, the area continued to prosper, and by 1809 the territorial legislature petitioned Congress for statehood. William C. C. Claiborne, the territorial governor, forwarded the petition to Washington with a letter listing a number of reasons for denying the legislature's request. Nevertheless, the Senate approved the petition in March 1810. The House of Representatives, however, sent it to a committee, and Congress adjourned before the House had voted on the question.

In December 1810 Louisiana's request for admission to the Union again came before Congress. Opponents of the statehood bill cited the difficulties posed by the ill-defined boundaries between the territory and the possessions claimed by Spain in the Southwest, and the French culture of almost all the inhabitants. However, Congress had promised that the Territory of Orleans would be admitted to the Union when its population reached 60,000 free inhabitants, and the 1810 federal census showed the area to have 76,550 free residents. On February 11, 1811, Congress authorized the Orleans territory to draw up a state constitution. A convention meeting from November 1811 to January 1812 formulated the necessary frame of government for Louisiana and on April 8, 1812, Congress gave its approval to this work.

The new state of Louisiana was originally to have encompassed the area of the present state west of the Mississippi and the Isle of Orleans. However, only four days after Congress had approved Louisiana's constitution, it passed an act that added the area of West Florida between the Mississippi and Pearl Rivers (the so-called Florida Parishes) to the new state. Thus it was a substantially enlarged area that ended its territorial status and officially became the state of Louisiana on April 30, 1812.

Like other Southern states, Louisiana declared its secession from the Union shortly before the beginning of the Civil War. Its full rights of statehood were restored in July 1868, after the drafting of a new constitution that enfranchised African American citizens. The constitution of 1868 was succeeded by the far more restrictive one of 1898, and that in turn was succeeded by a number of others.

Congress Establishes the United States Navy

The first American navy was established by the Continental Congress during the American Revolution. After the Revolution, however, the nation had political and economic problems that caused it to lose interest in maintaining a significant naval force. Although Great Britain had a formidable navy, hostilities had ceased, and it was easier to simply let the old Continental navy fade away. By 1785 the last Continental vessel had been sold to raise funds for the financially strapped government.

The United States Constitution of 1787 gave the country a stronger government, and renewed the desire to have an American navy. Further, the country was by then on the verge of war with both Great Britain and France over interference with American shipping in the Atlantic. Pirates from northern Africa, coming from a region then known as the Barbary Coast, also harassed American merchants. On January 2, 1794, the House of Representatives passed a resolution recommending the creation of a national naval force, and a committee established to study the matter recommended that six ships be commissioned. The Senate approved, and on March 27, 1794, those first six ships were approved.

Although the first ships had been authorized, that did not mean that the United States had a navy. Those first ships, named the *Chesapeake*, *Congress*, *Constellation*, *Constitution*, *President*, and *United States*, were built in civilian ports under the nominal supervision of government personnel. Further, a peace treaty with the Barbary pirates caused Congress to slow the pace of construction. Renewed tensions with France, however, finally convinced Congress that an American navy was necessary and inevitable. On April 30, 1798, Congress established the Department of the Navy, in effect creating the United States Navy. Benjamin Stoddert became the first secretary of the navy. In the twentieth century, the Department of the Navy would be absorbed by the modern-day Department of Defense.

April 30

Shenandoah Apple Blossom Festival

This is a movable event.

Every year, beginning on the Thursday closest to May 1, Winchester, the seat of Frederick County in Virginia's historic Shenandoah Valley, is the site of the Shenandoah Apple Blossom Festival. Winchester, which is Virginia's apple center, hosts this fete to provide a jubilant welcome to spring against a colorful backdrop of extensive apple orchards in full bloom. Frederick County and adjoining Clarke County produce millions of bushels of apples every year.

The festival has been celebrated annually, with the exception of the World War II years, since 1924. Early in that year Frank L. Sublett was elected the first president of Shenandoah Valley, Inc., a regional chamber of commerce for the 140-mile-long valley between the Blue Ridge and Allegheny mountains. He proposed that the city of Winchester stage an Apple Blossom Festival as its contribution toward the organization's campaign "to publicize the historic, scenic, and industrial assets of this already far-famed section of Virginia and West Virginia." The undertaking was approved at a large meeting held in Winchester on April 22. A phrase from the benediction pronounced at the close of the meeting was adopted as a motto: "The bounties of nature are the gift of God."

On May 3, 1924, some 30,000 persons jammed the streets of Winchester to view the first festival parade, which included several bands, fire fighting equipment, and makeshift floats. The U.S. assistant secretary of war J. W. Weeks crowned Elizabeth Steck as Apple Blossom Queen at an official coronation on the steps of Winchester's Handley High School. The purpose of the Apple Blossom Festival is still "to welcome spring, celebrate the blossoming of the apple trees, and call attention to the apple industry of the area," but from its modest beginnings the event has grown significantly and visitors now number in the hundreds of thousands.

Walpurgis Night or Spring Festival

The spring festival known as Walpurgis Night takes place on April 30, the eve of one of the feast days of St. Walpurgis. It is observed by many Scandinavian American organizations, especially in areas that have a large population of Scandinavian descent.

Walpurgis Night, often simply called "spring festival," takes its name from St. Walpurgis (or Walpurga, Walburga, or Valborg), an English missionary and abbess in Germany who died about 780. It is not known why the festival, which has come down through Nordic and Teutonic tradition, was named for her, but the observance took the place of a pagan festival that had earlier marked the beginning of summer. The occasion is popularly celebrated in some Scandinavian countries today. In Sweden, for example, people build fires, sing traditional spring songs, and make speeches welcoming the spring.

In the long history of superstitions connected with Walpurgis Night, the customary fires have had the purpose of frightening away witches who, according to popular lore, ride broomsticks, he-goats, and other conveyances to an appointed rendezvous on this date. The meeting is said to take place on a high mountain. Traditionally the site preferred is the Brocken, the tallest peak of Germany's Harz Mountains, and scene of the witches' sabbath in Goethe's *Faust*.

May

May, originally the third month, Maius, of the ancient Roman calendar, is the fifth month of the Gregorian or New Style calendar used today. It has 31 days. The origin of the name is uncertain. Some scholars derive the word from the Latin *maiores*, meaning "elders," contending that the month was intended to honor the senior members of the population just as the following month, Junius from *iuniores*, meaning "juniors," commemorated the younger generation. A more widely accepted theory holds that May is derived from Maia, a name bestowed on two different goddesses in ancient mythology. The more important of the two goddesses was the Greek Maia, the eldest of the Pleiades, who were the seven daughters of Atlas, the god who bore the world on his shoulders, and the Oceanid nymph Pleione. In a cave on Cyllene (a mountain in northeastern Arcadia, Greece), Maia gave birth to Hermes. Hermes, who corresponds to the Roman god Mercury, was known as the swift messenger of the gods and as the god of commerce and trade.

The Romans tended to identify the Greek Maia with a more obscure Roman goddess of spring known as Maia Maiesta, to whom the priests of Vulcan, the god of fire, offered sacrifices on the first day of May. To add to the confusion, Maia Maiesta was in turn sometimes identified with Bona Dea, the "good goddess" of fertility in both the earth and in women. This probably occurred because Bona Dea's festival also fell on May 1, the dedication date of her temple on the Aventine Hill. Bona Dea was variously described as the sister, daughter, or wife of Faunus, the ancient rustic Roman god worshiped as the bestower of fertility in men. Accordingly she was occasionally called Fauna. As befitted a prophetic goddess who revealed her oracles only to females, Bona Dea's temple was taken care of and her rites attended

solely by women, all males being strictly excluded. Even her name was never uttered in front of a man. At the festival of Bona Dea on May 1, a vestal virgin performed the required rituals at night in the house of the current consul or praetor.

On May 1, May Day, which fell in the midst of the Floralia (see April), the Romans customarily went in procession to the grove of the Camenae on the outskirts of Rome. Located there was the grotto of Egeria, the spirit of the local stream who, legend claimed, had been the spouse and adviser of the ancient Roman king Numa Pompilius. The grief and tears Egeria displayed at her husband's death supposedly caused her to be changed into a stream.

The Romans regarded May as unlucky for marriages since the festival of the unhappy dead, the Lemuria, took place that month. Held on May 9, 11, and 13, the Lemuria was a private domestic ritual to honor the *lemures*, or *larvae*, the ghosts of dead persons. In its original form the Lemuria had probably been a sort of expulsion ritual to frighten away evil spirits in spring, when demons were traditionally very active. Especially bothersome were those spirits who either lacked kinsmen or wandered about unappeased, threatening to revenge various oversights, such as the failure to provide fitting burial rites for them. In the course of time, the ceremony was transformed into a private appeasement of family ghosts, conducted in individual households. To quiet these spirits and prevent them from returning to scare the living, the head of the family arose at midnight. Having washed his hands, he went through the house barefooted, tossing black beans over his shoulder without glancing back and exclaiming: "With these beans, I redeem myself and my family." He carried out this procedure nine times. It was believed that the ghosts followed in his footsteps and gathered up the beans. The family head then repeated the hand-washing and banged brass vessels together loudly. In the final stage of the ritual, he commanded nine times: "Ghosts of my fathers, depart." Then, he was at last permitted to look behind himself. The Roman belief that May was an inauspicious month for marriages supposedly helps to account for the popularity of June as the month for weddings.

The Anglo-Saxons called May Thrimilce because the cows could then be milked three times daily. The birthstone associated with May is the emerald, which symbolizes love and success, a rather ironic tradition given the foregoing discussion.

May 1

May Day

May Day ranks as one of the oldest holidays in the world. Since antiquity the first of May has been celebrated with a variety of festivities. Many pre-Christian civilizations voiced their thankfulness to the gods for the arrival of spring and the rebirth of nature. The Romans, especially, held a feast in honor of the flower goddess Flora and the coming of May. With variations, the ancient Roman celebration became embedded in the western European tradition, especially in the British Isles, where a significant Celtic religious festival had been held on May 1 and its eve. In Elizabethan England, May Day with its maypole and general merriment was one of the most significant holidays of the year. To a limited extent the May Day observances were carried to the New World.

In the past, May Day was a common observance, and young children would go "a-maying" and dance on greens and school lawns. May queens were occasionally chosen to reign over college campuses. In Hawaii, May Day became known as Lei Day (see the separate entry below), a festive occasion for donning colorful garlands of flowers as a sign of friendship and goodwill. In the 20th century, however, May Day observances began to fade. The reason was that labor-related observances began to supersede the holiday. In the United States, although the official Labor Day (in September) is far removed from May Day, socialists, communists, and other leftists have traditionally held rallies and demonstrations on May 1. In communist nations, such as the old Soviet Union, May Day was transformed into an occasion for exhibiting military might and glorifying the state. In reaction to these May Day displays and the cold war between the United States and the Soviet

Union, popular May Day observances fell off and alternative events such as Loyalty Day (see the separate entry below) were introduced, with limited success.

Some scholars claim that the May Day festivities can be traced to the spring festivals of India and Egypt, when the renewal of the fertility of nature was celebrated. In ancient Greece, the revelers expressed gratitude to Demeter, the goddess of agriculture and vegetation, who had once again rejuvenated nature and instilled new fruitfulness in the world. Of all the ancient festivities, the Roman Floralia bears the greatest similarity to the later May Day celebrations of western Europe. It was held in honor of Flora, the goddess of flowers and springtime. Although tradition gives credit for originating the festival to Romulus, the legendary founder of Rome in 753 B.C., the festival is actually believed to have been instituted in Rome in 238 B.C. The Floralia was first a movable feast whose annual date depended upon the progress of crops and flowers. In 173 B.C., however, when unseasonable weather had seriously delayed the blossoming of flowers, the Roman senate made definite arrangements for its celebration and made it an annual festival extending from April 28 to May 3.

The festivities, which sometimes involved dramatic productions and games, were most important at the Temple of Flora in Rome. Traditionally, the first person to lay a wreath or garland on the statue of Flora was guaranteed good fortune in the coming months. Chains formed of entwined blossoms were wound around the temple columns, while white-robed women and girls, adorned with flowers, scattered petals along the streets nearby. Children fashioned small statues of Flora, which they decorated with blossoms. With the advent of Christianity, these "May-dolls" became crude images of the Virgin Mary.

The beginning of May, in particular May 1 and its eve, was also a sacred time elsewhere in Europe. The priestly druids, in the Celtic communities of pre-Christian northern and western Europe, celebrated the feast of Beltane on May 1. Although originally common to all Celtic peoples, the rites were observed especially in Ireland and Scotland. The most noteworthy ceremony was the kindling of sacred bonfires termed "beltane fires." The origin of the word *beltane* is unknown, although it appears to be the name of the god Bel, combined with the Celtic word for fire, *teome*, thus "Bel's fires." Bel may have been connected with the Celtic god Belenos, whose cult was well known in Gaul. Although it is uncertain whether Bel was a solar deity, the timing of the festivities around May 1 suggests that they were intended to honor and stimulate the sun as a life-giving force at the beginning of the warm weather.

Cormac, the early 10th-century archbishop of Cashel, Ireland, provided the first recorded reference to the age-old Celtic custom of lighting bonfires on the hills on May Day Eve. Various ancient rites were performed about them. The participants leapt over the flames to ensure diverse blessings: to win husbands, to guarantee fertility and safe childbirth, to ward off illness. Even cattle were driven between two fires to protect them from disease. The embers were scattered on the fields to assure a good growing season and harvest. The fire rites were also considered a precaution against evil spirits and other sinister powers, which supposedly roamed the earth on May Eve.

The ancient Celtic custom of lighting bonfires on hilltops continued throughout the Middle Ages in the British Isles and lingered on as a vestige of the druidical Beltane rite until the late 18th century. However, May Day celebrations, as practiced in England especially, owed far more to Roman than Celtic influences. Undoubtedly the Romans who occupied Britain from the 1st century A.D. to the early 5th century introduced there the revels connected with the festival of Flora. In medieval and Tudor England, May Day was a universally celebrated public holiday, a festival of nature following the winter months. All classes of people, even royalty and nobility, rose at dawn to go "a-maying." Women rose before sunrise to wash their faces with the dew, a custom believed to beautify the skin. The 17th-century English diarist Samuel Pepys alludes to such an excursion in his famous diary, stating that his wife got up about 3:00 a.m. to "go with her coach abroad, to gather May-dew. . . ." As late as 1791, a London newspaper reported that "yesterday, being the first of May, a number of persons went to the fields and bathed their faces with the dew on the grass with the idea that it would render them beautiful." There was also the custom of dancing around the maypole, although that custom fell off after the Puritan movement of the 17th century disapproved of such "frivolity."

Although May Day seems to be a part of England's tradition more than of any other country's, it was observed in various ways throughout western Europe. In France, for example, some people rose early May Day morning to find the first lilies of the valley in the woods. They pressed the flowers to send as tokens of love and affection to friends. In some cantons of Switzerland, village bachelors chopped down small pines (*maitannli*) on May Day Eve and decorated them with blossoms and streamers. They then planted the trees before the houses of their sweethearts. May Day Eve was also a popular holiday full of folk traditions in Scandinavia.

In the United States, May Day never enjoyed quite the same kind of tradition and ceremony that it enjoyed in England and Europe. The Puritans, objecting to all secular celebrations, carried with them to America their dislike of May Day. For example, the inhabitants of the Plymouth colony in New England were scandalized when, on May 1, 1627, an Anglican named Thomas Morton dared to erect an 80-foot pine maypole, decorated with flowers, ribbons, and antlers, at his nearby plantation of Merry Mount. Moreover, it was rumored that Morton and his cohorts had even danced with Native American women. The stern Puritan leader John Endecott had the pole chopped down and all festivities halted. He renamed Merry Mount, calling it "Mount Dagon" after the Philistine idol that fell before the ark. Morton, charged with having traded arms with the natives, was deported to England.

Labor Observances

For many workers around the world, May Day is not a time for reviving old customs and merrymaking, but is a day dedicated to the interests of the laborer. It is observed in practically every advanced industrial country except the United States, and is a public holiday in several countries of western Europe. In 1833 Robert Owen, the British social reformer, was the first to tentatively suggest honoring labor on May 1.

Oddly enough, although the United States observes Labor Day officially in early September, the first strong link between May 1 and labor was formed in this country. In 1884 a number of American trade unions chose May 1 as the day "from which eight hours shall constitute a day's labor." The decision to launch an intensive campaign for an eight-hour work day resulted in widespread strikes, including one set for May 1, 1886. During a demonstration that ensued on May 4, 1886, at Chicago's Haymarket Square, a bomb exploded, killing 11 people and wounding over 100 others. In the late 1880s several states named May 1 as Labor Day, although the American Knights of Labor had instituted Labor Day on the first Monday in September as far back as 1882. In 1889 the first Paris congress of the Second International, acting on the suggestion of a German socialist, resolved:

> There shall be organized a great international demonstration at a fixed date, so that on the agreed day, in every country, and in every town, the workers shall call upon the state for legal reduction of the working day to eight hours. . . . In view of the fact that a similar demonstration has been decided

upon by the American Federation of Labor for the First of May 1890 . . . this date is adopted for the international demonstration.

On May 1, 1890, there were large militant demonstrations in European capitals and industrial cities, as well as numerous May Day meetings in the United States. In 1894 the United States Congress made the official date of Labor Day the first Monday in September, a designation that remains in force today. The International Labor Day, however, remained May 1. Labor's struggle, against opposition, to enforce its right to an annual May Day holiday abroad led to frequent and bloody battles. Police were often called in as bombs were hurled and buildings burned in many European cities. In the end, the workers gained their way. May 1 soon became an occasion not only for demonstrations on behalf of the cause of labor, but also for rallies by radicals, communists, and socialists to show opposition to the government. At the third congress of the Second International at Zurich in 1893, speakers urged that May Day also

serve as a demonstration of the determined will of the working class to destroy class distinctions through social change and thus enter on the road, the only road, leading to peace for all peoples, to international peace.

The communist and socialist overtones of the event, in addition to the cold war between the United States and the Soviet Union, have prevented May Day from being officially recognized as a labor holiday in the United States or from gaining popular acceptance in that regard. As early as the 1920s and 1930s, the communist May Day had become a time for massive military reviews in Moscow's Red Square. As Communist rule expanded, similar demonstrations of armed power were staged in satellite countries. These demonstrations were significantly reduced, however, when the Soviet Union collapsed in 1991.

Spanish-American War: Battle of Manila Bay

When the Spanish-American War broke out on April 21, 1898 (see April 21), Commodore George Dewey was in Hong Kong with four cruisers, namely his flagship *Olympia*, the *Baltimore*, the *Boston*, and the *Raleigh*, as well as two gunboats, the *Concord* and the *Petrel*. He received orders on April 24 from Secretary of the Navy John Davis Long "to proceed to the Philippine Islands; commence operations at once against the Spanish fleet; capture vessels or destroy."

Dewey's Asian Squadron sailed immediately, and arrived at the entrance to Manila Bay on the evening of April 30. The Spanish fleet, under the command of Admiral Patricio Montojo and consisting of four cruisers, three gunboats, and three other vessels in poor repair, lay off Cavite naval point. At 5:40 a.m. on May 1, when the American ships were about 5,000 yards from the Spanish fleet, Dewey quietly ordered Captain C. V. Gridley, the commander of his flagship: "You may fire when you are ready, Gridley."

The American fleet then raked the Spanish line, swinging in an oval pattern past the Spanish ships at a range of between 5,000 and 2,000 yards. Upon receiving an erroneous report that there was a shortage of ammunition, Dewey ordered a temporary ceasefire at 7:35 a.m., but at 11:16 he renewed action. An hour and a quarter later, the battle was over.

The Spanish fleet, with not one-third of the American firing power, had been completely disabled or destroyed. Spanish losses were 381 men killed and wounded. None of the American ships were damaged; eight men were wounded. Within 10 days of the battle, Dewey had been promoted to the rank of rear admiral. Congress authorized bronze medals to be struck and awarded to the officers and men who had taken part in the battle, and on March 3, 1899, Dewey was named admiral of the navy. The title was especially created for him by Congress the previous day.

Since Dewey did not have enough men to occupy Manila, he blockaded the bay. Finally, on August 13, the day after an armistice was signed between the United States and Spain, American troops under Major General Wesley Merritt, supported by Dewey's fleet, occupied the city. On February 10, 1899, the Treaty of Paris, formally ending the Spanish-American War, was signed by President William McKinley. Under its terms the United States took possession of the Philippine Islands in return for the payment of $20 million.

For many years, the anniversary of the Battle of Manila Bay was celebrated annually by the Dewey Congressional Medal Men's Association, composed of the officers and men who took part in the battle. Other organizations of war veterans usually participated in the celebration. The exercises were held for a number of years in the Philadelphia Navy Yard, where the *Olympia* was docked after it was put out of commission in 1922. It was customary to hold a parade of war veterans in one of the streets leading to the navy yard in advance of the formal exercises on board the *Olympia*. At the celebration in 1934, Admiral Dewey's flag, which was shot down during the battle of May 1, was restored to the ship and hoisted to its proper place.

Today, there are no longer any major celebrations of the Battle of Manila Bay.

Loyalty Day

In 1947 the United States Veterans of Foreign Wars designated May Day as Loyalty Day, a day to reaffirm loyalty to the United States. It was intended to be a "direct positive weapon" against communism, especially the American Communist Party, which observed the communist tradition of holding May Day rallies. The American communist movement was never more than a fringe element, but the "red scare" of the times led to enthusiastic support of the Loyalty Day innovation by civic organizations, schools, churches, and the armed forces. A joint resolution of the United States Congress officially designated May 1 of each year as Loyalty Day, and all persons were urged to "fly the U.S. flag and observe Loyalty Day in schools and other suitable places with appropriate ceremonies."

Recognition of Loyalty Day spread rapidly as governors and mayors throughout the country endorsed the observance. School programs, flag presentations, sermons on loyalty, patriotic exercises, and parades marked the occasion. By the late 1960s, however, the political ramifications of the unpopular Vietnam War had seriously affected the popularity of Loyalty Day. Loyalty Day had never been much more than a countermeasure to the perceived threat of communist May Day, and as such its celebration never recovered significantly after the Vietnam War ended. Some scattered local observances can still be found today.

Law Day

Another way of observing May Day was inaugurated through the efforts of the American Bar Association. In 1958, upon its urging, President Dwight D. Eisenhower instituted Law Day on May 1. It was not a coincidence that Law Day also fell on May Day. Like Loyalty Day, it was conceived as another attempt to emphasize the fact that the United States is a nation dedicated to the principle of democratic government under law, essentially an anticommunist cold war initiative. Its avowed educational and patriotic purposes were: "to foster respect for law; to increase public understanding of the place of law in American life; to point up the contrast between freedom under law in the United States and governmental tyranny under Communism." It became an official nationwide observance in 1961, when a joint resolution of Congress designated May 1 as Law Day, and in his procla-

mation President John F. Kennedy asked all Americans to display the flag and observe the occasion "with suitable ceremonies." Law Day was also proclaimed annually by governors and mayors across the nation. In the years since the 1960s, however, Law Day observances have fallen to a handful of minor events.

Lei Day in Hawaii

Quite apart from political connotations, May Day, a day associated with flowers since antiquity, has added significance in Hawaii. It is dedicated to the lei, the handsome garland of flowers which is Hawaii's traditional sign of friendship. The wearing of the lei is still observed, largely because of the tourist trade, and the millions of annual visitors to the islands are frequently welcomed with necklaces of carnations, jasmines, or orchids. Although leis are thus presented and worn many times during the year, a special effort has historically been made on May 1 to have everyone wear a lei and honor Hawaiian traditions.

It was in 1928 that the poet Don Blanding voiced the idea of having a special day on which to honor the lei, proposing that the custom be carried out each year. In response, a writer suggested that the day be May Day, not only a time traditionally connected with flowers, but also one when blossoms were especially aesthetic in Hawaii. The slogan, "Lei Day is May Day," caught the popular imagination. The annual Lei Day festivities, which began on May 1, 1928, have traditionally involved such activities as large popular celebrations in the city of Honolulu, parades, schoolchildren in homemade costumes, and Polynesian cultural performances.

May 2

North Korea–South Korea Joint Communiqué

Although a 1953 armistice ended three years of fighting in Korea (see essays on the Korean War throughout this book), North Korea and South Korea never executed a formal peace treaty. Their governments remained bitter enemies. The United States, which had supported South Korea during the conflict, had to establish a permanent military presence along the border between the two countries to preserve the peace and protect South Korea. The problem was exacerbated by the cold-war conflict between the United States and two supporters of communist North Korea, namely the

Soviet Union and the People's Republic of China. It took decades for negotiations concerning a formal peace treaty and the possibility of eventual reunification of the two Koreas to make any progress.

Beginning on May 2, 1972, representatives of North Korea and South Korea met to discuss these issues. The result was the Joint Communiqué, formally issued on July 4, 1972. It was a general statement of principles committing the two sides to peaceful progress toward reunification, which both agreed was a desirable goal, though not one to be dictated by any third party. In the Joint Communiqué, the two Koreas announced that they would continue negotiations, eschew aggression and provocative rhetoric, and carry out certain exchanges. Perhaps most importantly, they agreed to install a direct telephone line between their rival capitals (Seoul and Pyongyang) to lessen the risk of a military incident or a misunderstanding that might endanger the peace. The Joint Communiqé helped lead to a more concrete pact in 1991 (see December 13).

Kentucky Derby

This is a movable event.

The Kentucky Derby, first run in 1875, is held every year on the first Saturday of May at Churchill Downs in Louisville, Kentucky. It derives its name from another well-known horse race, instituted in 1780 by the 12th earl of Derby and held annually at Epsom Downs near London. The Kentucky Derby ranks as one of the top sporting events in the United States. With the Belmont Stakes (run at the Belmont Park, near New York City) and the Preakness (run at the Pimlico Race Course, near Baltimore, Maryland), the Kentucky Derby is one of horse racing's Triple Crown races. Only a horse that has won all three races in one year, like Secretariat in 1973, can qualify as a Triple Crown winner.

Kentuckians have long been interested in horse racing and breeding. The first horse races in Lexington were staged in 1787, and the first jockey club was organized 10 years later. Over two centuries of tradition and experience, as well as ideal natural conditions, have made the Lexington and Louisville area of Kentucky one of the leading centers for the raising of thoroughbred horses. In this area, bluegrass combines with the unusually rich vegetation to produce lush bluegreen meadows. Graceful thoroughbreds on the hundreds of horse farms in the heart of the bluegrass country have become the very symbol of the Blue Grass State.

The inspiration behind the Kentucky Derby came from Colonel Meriwether Lewis Clark Jr., who developed most of the rules governing the sport of horse racing in the United States. In 1875 Colonel Clark organized Churchill Downs as the Louisville Jockey Club, and he served as president of the track from 1875 to 1894. As part of the Churchill Downs program, he offered the Kentucky Derby. The race was to be for three-year-old horses, which is when horses are in their prime, carrying weight not in excess of 126 pounds.

The first Derby race, on May 17, 1875, was a deliberate attempt by the Louisville aristocracy to transplant the social ambiance of the English Derby. The day after the race, the local press dwelt upon the stylish crowd and 10,000 carriages present at the 80-acre track and lawn of Churchill Downs before mentioning that a horse named Aristides had won the race. The first running was a memorable one. Aristides, owned by H. Price McGrath, a Kentucky horse breeder and gambler, had been entered as a pacemaker for Chesapeake, also owned by McGrath. Aristides ran so well, however, that when the time came for Chesapeake to pass him, Chesapeake was too far behind to overtake his pacemaker. Seeing what had happened, McGrath signaled Aristides' jockey to go for the finish line. Aristides reached the wire a winner in a little over two-and-a-half minutes, then the fastest on record for a three- year-old-at the mile and one-half distance (in 1896 the course was shortened to a mile and one-quarter).

Over the next few years, the Kentucky Derby continued to gain in popularity. A visitor to Derby Day in 1877 described the setting and influx of spectators as follows: "Green fields and woodlands lay on the left, a cottage dotted here and there over the plain. Behind, the Nashville railroad winding its way like a snake through the woodlands. In front there was a vast cloud of dust that indicated the road over which the vast throng was approaching."

In 1878 the Short Line Railroad added a special 19-car train to accommodate Derby fans. For the 1882 running, the seating capacity at Churchill Downs was doubled. Following the death of Colonel Clark in 1899, however, interest in racing at Churchill Downs declined for several seasons. In an attempt to recapture its lost prestige, Colonel Matt J. Winn agreed to become general manager of the track in 1902. He scheduled the race for Saturday rather than a weekday, and he turned the Kentucky Derby from an inbred Louisville social occasion into a nationwide attraction. With his knack for showmanship and promotion, Colonel Winn set the race well on the way to ranking as one of the best-known sporting events in the world.

May 3

First Medical School in the United States

On May 3, 1765, John Morgan presented, at a special meeting of the board of trustees of the College of Philadelphia (now the University of Pennsylvania), a proposal for the establishment of a "professorship . . . of Physick and Surgery, as well as the several occupations attending upon these necessary and useful arts." On the same day, he was chosen to be the college's "professor of the Theory and Practice of Physick." At commencement exercises, on May 30 and 31 of that year, Morgan outlined his philosophy of medical education and the manner in which it would be taught. William Shippen Jr. was appointed professor of anatomy and surgery at a subsequent meeting of the trustees in September 1765. In establishing a medical department with the appointment of Morgan and Shippen, the College of Philadelphia founded the country's first medical school. The first classes began in November of the same year. The University of Pennsylvania's School of Medicine, into which the new school evolved, observed the bicentennial of medical education in the United States in 1965.

Morgan, a graduate of the College of Philadelphia, had studied medicine with a Philadelphia physician and served for three years as surgeon in the French and Indian War. He then went abroad and continued his studies in Paris, London, and Edinburgh. He graduated from the University of Edinburgh with a medical degree in 1763. While abroad he conceived the idea of establishing a medical school in the United States. It was on his return that he suggested the plan to the trustees of the College of Philadelphia. Later, from 1775 to 1777, he was director-general of hospitals and physician in chief of the Continental army. He subsequently undertook what became a substantial medical practice, corresponded with learned persons, and was the author of several publications. He died in Philadelphia on October 15, 1789.

Shippen, who had been lecturing on anatomy and operating the nation's first maternity hospital since 1762, was a pioneer in making obstetrics a recognized branch of medicine. From the appointment of Morgan and Shippen as its first professors, the College of Philadelphia developed one of the great medical colleges of the country—the first of the professional schools now maintained by the University of Pennsylvania, and the first school for postgraduate professional training established in the United States. Shippen, who served from 1777 to 1781 as chief of the Continental army's medical department, became a founder and president, from 1805 to 1808, of the College of Physicians of Philadelphia. He died in 1808.

Rural Life Sunday (also known as Soil Stewardship Sunday)

This is a movable event.

In an era of increasing concern about the abuse of the environment, the emphasis of Rural Life Sunday is on the concept that the Earth belongs to God, who has merely granted humanity the use of it, along with the responsibility of caring for it wisely. The day is observed in the United States in both rural and urban areas on the fifth Sunday after Easter. Known also as Rogation Sunday, a term deriving from the Latin *rogare*, "to ask," it had its origin in France in the second half of the 5th century when Mamertus, bishop of Vienne, designated Rogation Sunday and the following Monday, Tuesday, and Wednesday (Rogation Days) as a time of penitence and of praying for God's beneficence and protection from evil. As was natural in view of the spring season, the prayers said on these days came to stress agricultural concerns, with entreaties for God's blessing upon the soil, the seed, and the cultivators of the earth. These days immediately precede Ascension Day, which falls on Thursday of the same week.

The day was first observed as Rural Life Sunday in 1929, at the suggestion of the International Association of Agricultural Missions (IAAM), and according to plans adopted by the Home Missions Council of North America (HMCNA) and the Federal Council of Churches (FCC). All Christian churches were invited to observe the day with a special service prescribed by the FCC, which included prayers and hymns.

In 1950 the IAAM, the HMCNA, and the FCC combined with eight other independent religious bodies to form the National Council of the Churches of Christ in the United States of America (NCCCUSA), a cooperative federation that came to represent dozens of Protestant and Eastern Orthodox denominations. Rural Life Sunday has historically been sponsored in the NCCCUSA and the National Catholic Rural Life Conference.

Rural Life Sunday has been observed annually by churches of many Christian denominations throughout the United States ever since its inception in 1929. The forms of the observance are left largely to the discretion of the individual churches. The seeds and soil are still blessed in many localities, but there is also considerable stress on the unity of all of life and the interdependence of all segments of society. The week beginning with Rural Life Sunday is now often observed as Soil Stewardship Week, and the Sunday itself is alternatively termed Soil Stewardship Sunday. As a result of the broadening of emphasis in recent decades, observances now include a call for individual action on problems connected with air, water, and noise pollution, in addition to the preservation of natural resources.

May 4

Horace Mann's Birthday

The life of Horace Mann, coinciding as it did with the great reform movements of the first half of the 19th century, prompts the familiar question as to whether the times created the man, the man the times, or both. On May 4, 1796, Mann—who was to become known as the Father of American Public Education—was born into a poverty-stricken family in Franklin, Massachusetts. His early formal education was sporadic, totaling eight to ten weeks a year at the hands of poor teachers. However, he received a continuous informal education, self-administered in the Franklin town library. With the help of an itinerant schoolmaster's occasional tutoring, Mann managed to enter Brown University as a sophomore at the age of 20. He graduated with high honors in 1819. His valedictory address, which has been described as a model of humanitarian optimism, gave promise of things to come.

Mann returned to Brown briefly to tutor (1819–1821) in Latin and Greek. Meanwhile, however, he read law with an attorney from Wrentham, Massachusetts, and it was not long before he turned his full attention to that field. He attended the Litchfield Law School in Connecticut and was admitted to the Massachusetts bar in 1823. Mann practiced law at Dedham (where he first settled) and Boston (where he moved later) until 1837. In the meantime, he spoke out in favor of a number of humanitarian and reform causes, and demonstrated his legal training and skill in public speaking. In 1827 he was elected to the Massachusetts house of representatives. He served there until 1833, when he became, for four years, a member of the state senate. As a representative, he had been instrumental in establishing in Worcester a state hospital for the mentally ill. As senator, more specifically as president of the senate during his last two years in the state legislature, he signed the bill that made history in 1837 by establishing a state board of education.

Ignoring the advice of friends, Mann, to whom the cause of education had long been important, put aside law and politics and became secretary of the new state board of education. Thanks to his moral leadership and driving energy, the board's influence extended far beyond what its limited powers would have led anyone to expect. He worked to arouse public opinion in favor of increased appropriations for schools and better facilities and teacher training. He helped secure a new state law that required children under 12 to spend at least six months of the year in school. During his 12 years in office, Massachusetts's appropriations for public education were more than doubled. Fifty new public high schools were opened. Under his leadership, many of the ills of Massachusetts's decentralized educational system, which had placed control of schools with economy-bent local districts, were overcome by the reassertion of a centralized state influence. Teaching methods and curricula were revised and teachers' salaries raised. During his tenure Mann also found time to establish and edit the biweekly *Common School Journal*.

Mann also lectured extensively and issued 12 annual reports to the board of education. These reports, covering a wide range of topics and illuminating many problems, substantially influenced the course of education in the United States. The reports, which declared that a republic cannot for long be both ignorant and free, set forth the argument for the public school, championing universal education. They called for nonsectarian schools, open to children from all social, ethnic, and religious backgrounds, to be financed and controlled by a concerned citizenry. In 1843 Mann made a five-month tour of Europe. He devoted his annual report that year to a survey of European educational conditions and methods. Among other things, he recommended the abandonment of corporal punishment.

The suggestion aroused the opposition of those who feared that it would undermine classroom discipline, just as the idea of nonsectarian schools had brought opposition from the clergy, and the establishment of a state board of education had prompted charges that local authority was being violated. With public opinion marshaled behind them, however, most of Mann's views ultimately triumphed. Their effect upon the American educational system was revolutionary.

In 1848 Mann resigned from the school board to fill the seat made vacant in the United States House of Representatives by the death of representative and former President John Quincy Adams. As was the case with a number of other reformers, Mann's humanitarian zeal extended to more than one cause. During his five years in Congress, he made no secret of his strong abolitionist sentiments. In 1852 he was defeated as the Free-Soil Party's candidate for governor of Massachusetts.

However, although his remaining years were few, his strong idealism, ability to contribute, and willingness to serve were still substantial. In 1858, when he was in his 50s, he became the first president of Antioch College in Yellow Springs, Ohio, a new nonsectarian college founded a year earlier. Antioch, which was committed to equal opportunities for blacks and women, became a pioneer institution in both education and a now widely known cooperative work-study program.

In June 1859 Mann counseled one of Antioch's graduating classes with words that might have served as his own epitaph: "Be ashamed to die until you have won some victory for humanity." When he himself died on August 2 of the same year, he had no cause for shame. He was survived by his wife, the former Mary Peabody. She was one of Massachusetts's famous Peabody sisters; the others were Elizabeth, the noted educator and transcendentalist, and Sophia, the wife of Nathaniel Hawthorne.

Rhode Island Independence Day

Every year Rhode Island celebrates two Independence Days: July 4 and May 4. The latter is the anniversary of Rhode Island's own renunciation of allegiance to Britain, two months before the national Declaration of Independence.

Britain's post-1765 imperial policy had devastated the economy of the tiny Rhode Island colony. The inhabitants were traders, and the basis of their commerce was the sugar and molasses that for decades had been obtained from the French and Spanish West Indies. The Sugar Act of 1764, however, prohibited such exchange. The American colonists were forced to trade with only the British island possessions in the Caribbean, where sugar and molasses were more expensive and less abundant.

To enforce the new mercantile regulations, British revenue ships plied the coastal waters in search of smugglers. One of the most efficient, and therefore despised, of these vessels was the *Gaspee*, which patrolled Narragansett Bay off Rhode Island. On June 9, 1772, the *Gaspee* went aground on a sandspit near Providence, and the colonists seized the opportunity to end its career. That night a party of men boarded the *Gaspee*, terrorized the crew, and then set the vessel aflame.

This action was a serious offense. The British government sent a special commission to Rhode Island to investigate the incident, and empowered its members to transfer the scene of the suspects' trial to England. The commission never made any arrests, but the provincial press widely publicized Britain's theoretical violation of an accused individual's right to trial by a jury composed of members of his community.

The *Gaspee* experience made Rhode Islanders particularly sensitive to every British infraction of colonial rights thereafter. Following the Boston Tea Party, Rhode Island joined the outcry against the harsh retaliatory measures imposed by the British. The general assembly enthusiastically sent delegates to the First Continental Congress and authorized charters for several new military companies. Throughout the colony, arms manufacturers and ammunition stores steadily increased. The fighting at Lexington and Concord on April 19, 1775, likewise roused Rhode Island, and within a month a 1,500-man army was sent to Boston to act "for the safety and preservation of any of the colonies."

Relations between Great Britain and its American colonies worsened during the remainder of 1775, and by the time the general assembly met in May 1776 the desire for independence was strong in Rhode Island. Traditionally, each elected officer in the colony had sworn allegiance to the king before assuming his duties. This practice ended on May 4, 1776, when both houses of the general assembly approved an act repealing the old "Act for the more effectually securing to His Majesty, the allegiance of his subjects, in this his Colony and Dominion of Rhode Island and Providence Plantations."

The preamble to the new act related that protection and allegiance were reciprocal and asserted that the king, in violation of the compact, had introduced fleets and armies into the colony to force upon the people a detestable tyranny. It further asserted that under such circumstances it became the right and duty of a people to make use of the means at hand for their preservation, and that therefore the former act of allegiance was repealed. The new act directed that in all writs and processes of law, wherever the name and authority of the king had been employed, there should be substituted "the Governor and Company of the English Colony of Rhode Island and Providence Plantations." It was also declared that the courts were no longer to be the king's courts and that written instruments should no longer bear the year of the king's reign.

The bold deed of Rhode Island was an important step toward independence, and rebellion spread quickly after May 4. On May 15 a Virginia convention instructed its delegates to the Second Continental Congress to "declare the United Colonies free and independent states." Less than a month later, on June 11, the Congress appointed a committee consisting of Thomas Jefferson, John Adams, Benjamin Franklin, Roger Sherman, and Robert R. Livingston. The product of their work was the Declaration of Independence of July 1776.

World War II: Last Major German Contingents Surrender

On May 4, 1945, the last major German contingents in the western front surrendered. These forces, in northwest Germany, Holland, and other scattered locations, were the remnants of the once-mighty Nazi war machine that had nearly conquered the world a few years earlier. A copy of the surrender document is set forth below. Several days later, the general surrender of Germany took place (see May 8, Victory in Europe Day).

Instrument of Surrender of all German armed forces in Holland, in northwest Germany including all islands, and in Denmark.

1. The German Command agrees to the surrender of all armed forces in Holland, in northwest Germany, including the Frisian Islands and Heligoland and all islands, in Schleswig-Holstein, and in Denmark to the Commander-in-Chief 21 Army Group.

This to include all naval ships in these areas.

These forces to lay down their arms and to surrender unconditionally.

2. All hostilities on land, on sea, or in the air by German forces in the above areas to cease at 0800 hours British Double Summer Time on Saturday 5 May 1945.

3. The German command to carry out at once, and without argument or comment, all further orders that will be issued by the Allied Powers on any subject.

4. Disobedience of orders, or failure to comply with them, will be regarded as a breach of these surrender terms and will be dealt with by the Allied Powers in accordance with the laws and usages of war.

5. This instrument of surrender is independent of, without prejudice to, and will be superseded by any general instrument of surrender imposed by or on behalf of the Allied Powers and applicable to Germany and the German armed forces as a whole.

6. This instrument of surrender is written in English and in German. The English version is the authentic text.

7. The decision of the Allied Powers will be final if any doubt or dispute arise as to the meaning or interpretation of the surrender terms.

May 5

Battle of the Wilderness

On May 5, 1864, the Battle of the Wilderness began near Fredericksburg, Virginia. Although the Union forces were badly bloodied, this time they did not retreat, and the final phase of the Civil War began. Henceforth, Confederate forces were constantly on the retreat, and it was only a matter of time before the Union's victory.

During the previous year, Confederate forces were still strong enough to carry the war to the North. General Robert E. Lee invaded Pennsylvania during the summer of 1863, but was defeated in early July at the Battle of Gettysburg. Although Gettysburg was a major Union victory and a turning point in the war, President Abraham Lincoln was dissatisfied with Commanding General George Meade's reluctance to pursue Lee's retreating army. Lee's Army of Northern Virginia was the strongest of the Confederate armies and had won a number of important victories over Union forces. Since Lee's military genius had made him a legend in the North as well as the South, his less talented Union counterparts were reluctant to take him on, even though Union generals typically had superior forces at their disposal. It was a problem that had plagued the Union and President Lincoln throughout the war: The Union had more people, more soldiers, more industrial facilities, and a larger economy than the Confederacy, but inferior military leadership.

There was one general, however, who would not retreat from Lee. This was Ulysses S. Grant, who became the commander of all the Union armies in the spring of 1864. If not as skilled as Lee, Grant was willing to use the Union's superior troop strength to press the attack regardless of the losses. Although it was a ruthless strategy, it was in fact true that the Union could absorb significant troop losses on the battlefield, while the Confederacy could not.

Grant began to move southward towards the Confederate capital of Richmond, Virginia. Readers in the mid-Atlantic region know that today

Richmond is a mere 90-minute drive from Washington, D.C., on the interstate highway system. However, during the Civil War that short distance was the most hotly contested stretch of land in the nation. Union offensive had always ended in defeat and retreat. In May 1864, however, the war entered a new phase when Grant brought an army of 118,000 men against 62,000 Confederates troops. The two forces met in the vicinity of Fredericksburg, Virginia, roughly halfway between Washington, D.C., and Richmond.

The engagement began on May 5, 1864. Lee outmaneuvered Grant's advancing forces, luring them into a dense forest region known as the Wilderness. The battle lasted until May 7, and when it was over Grant had sustained 18,400 casualties to Lee's 11,400. Lee was still outmanned and outgunned, however. Unlike his predecessors, Grant continued the Union offensive, pushing past Lee's flank and on towards Richmond, thereby forcing Lee to fall back. There were more bloody battles ahead, but the Union would eventually take Richmond and crush both Lee and the Confederacy with its superior numbers.

Cinco de Mayo

One of the great days in Mexican history is known as the Cinco de Mayo, or the Fifth of May. It is the anniversary of the 1862 battle of Puebla, in which Mexican forces against overwhelming odds defeated French invaders. The battle itself was not of great military importance, since the victory represented only a temporary setback for the French troops, but it nevertheless appealed to the imagination of the Mexicans and gave them the confidence they needed to achieve victory in the long run. May 5, a national holiday in Mexico, is therefore celebrated with festivities by Mexicans both at home and in foreign countries. In the United States, the anniversary is observed by Mexican Americans everywhere, especially in the states that border Mexico—Texas, Arizona, New Mexico, and California.

The following events led to the much celebrated battle. Mexico had defaulted on payments due in bonds sold to France, Spain, and England. An arrangement was made by the three European countries at a conference held in London on October 30, 1861, to make a joint naval demonstration against Mexico in order to compel payment to the bondholders. Fleets of the three powers sailed for Veracruz, arriving there near the end of the year. It was announced that there was no intention of conquering Mexico and that nothing was desired but a settlement of just claims. A conference was arranged with Mexican representatives, and a pre-

liminary agreement was reached. Thereupon the British and Spanish fleets sailed for home in April 1862. However, French emperor Napoléon III, Charles-Louis-Napoléon, who was eager to establish a centralized monarchy under French control in Mexico as a means of achieving hegemony in Spanish America, started a war of conquest.

On May 4, 1862, the commander of the French forces communicated this message to France's minister of war:

We have over the Mexicans such superiority of race, of discipline, and organization that I beg Your Excellency inform the Emperor that tomorrow, at the head of 6,000 of my choice troops, I will attack, and I consider that Mexico is mine.

When he attacked the forts of Loreto and Guadalupe on May 5, however, 2,000 Mexican soldiers under General Ignacio Zaragoza drove the invaders back with serious losses and finally won the day. The French ultimately conquered the country, and put Archduke Maximilian of Austria, the brother of Emperor Francis Joseph, on the throne on June 12, 1864, only to have him deposed and shot by the Mexicans on June 19, 1867, after a troubled reign. The city of Puebla, Mexico, which had been known as Puebla de los Angeles, changed its name to Puebla de Zaragoza as a tribute to the general who had defended it from the French. The body of the general was placed in the Panteon de San Fernando in the capital, Mexico City. This hero of the 1862 battle had been born on March 24, 1829, in Goliad, Texas, when Texas was still part of Mexico and the town was called Bahia del Espiritu Santo. His birthplace site was designated a Texas state park in 1960 and dedicated on May 5, 1967.

May 6

The *Hindenburg* Disaster at Lakehurst, New Jersey

One of the most famous disasters in aviation history occurred on May 6, 1937, when the German dirigible *Hindenburg* burst into flames just as it was supposed to moor at Lakehurst, New Jersey.

At the time, lighter-than-air vessels were still a viable alternative to airplanes as a means of transatlantic transportation. The airplanes of the time were limited in range and required constant refueling. Dirigibles, on the other hand, used a relatively simple technology in the form of a torpedo-shaped balloon. Further, dirigibles actually had a rather impressive safety record, in many ways superior to that of contemporary aircraft.

May 5

The *Hindenburg* still holds the record for being the largest flying vessel ever built by man. It was 882 feet long, only 78 feet shorter than the famous ocean liner *Titanic*, and far larger than today's Boeing 747 jumbo jet. The *Hindenburg* was built by Germany's Zeppelin Company and was the pride of the Nazi regime in the 1930s.

As with all airships, during the construction of the *Hindenburg* the Zeppelin Company had to decide which particular lighter-than-air gas to use in order to fill the balloon. The traditional choices were hydrogen, which is the lightest of all gases, or helium, which is the next lightest. Although hydrogen has the advantage of giving extra lifting power, hydrogen is flammable, whereas helium is not. Helium was difficult to get in Nazi Germany, however. The only known natural deposits of helium were located in the United States, which was increasingly suspicious of the Germans. Thus, the decision was made to use hydrogen. When it was launched, the *Hindenburg* appeared to be a success. The vessel flew 18 transatlantic trips between Germany and the United States before meeting its unfortunate end.

The *Hindenburg* was primarily a passenger ship, transporting people to and from Germany and the town of Lakehurst, New Jersey. Lakehurst was chosen because it was an elegant resort town at the time, and had an airfield specially built for dirigibles by the United States Navy for the navy's airship program and available for civilian use. As the *Hindenburg* approached the Lakehurst airfield on the evening of May 6, 1937, there were no outward signs of any problem. For reasons that are still unknown, the ship suddenly burst into flames and began to crash land. Because of the flammable gas, the flames spread quickly. Luckily, however, the airship had already made most of its descent towards the ground. Of the 97 persons aboard the Hindenburg, only 36 died.

What made the *Hindenburg* disaster so famous was the presence of photographers and newspeople at the airfield on that evening. Many people heard the stirring words of radio announcer Herb Morrison, describing the event live and on-the-air while it occurred: "It's burning, bursting into flames, and it's falling on the mooring mast and all the folks. This is one of the worst catastrophes in the world . . . oh, the humanity and all the passengers!" The phrase "oh, the humanity" and the photographs of the massive burning *Hindenburg* forever tarnished the reputation of dirigibles.

Today, some dirigibles remain in use, primarily for special events, but they are constructed so that they can be lifted by helium alone. The *Goodyear* blimp, which is used to televise sporting events, is an example.

Congress Passes First Legislation

The modern-day Congress, established by the Constitution of the United States, first met in 1789. On May 6, 1789, Congress passed its first piece of legislation. It was largely an administrative measure, entitled "An Act to Regulate the Time and Manner of Administering Certain Oaths." This legislation was necessary in order to have a legally binding means of taking those pledges required by the Constitution of certain key state and federal officials. For example, all members of Congress and the various state legislative bodies are required to pledge their support and loyalty to the Constitution when they take office.

Legislation concerning the administration of oaths and the penalties for breaking them has existed ever since this first enactment by the First Congress. After the Civil War, it was a matter of some controversy with respect to officers in the Confederate army and officials in the Confederate government. Prior to the Civil War, many of these people had held positions in the government or military that required them to take an oath to the United States Constitution, which they then broke when they chose to serve the states that seceded from the Union. Ultimately, however, most of these persons were treated with leniency.

Civil Rights Act of 1960

The Civil Rights Act of 1960 became law on May 6, 1960. It had passed by a vote of 311 to 109 in the House of Representatives on March 24, 1960, and by a vote of 71 to 18 in the Senate on April 8, 1960.

In the 1960 Civil Rights Act, Congress increased the legal protections for people exercising their right to vote, meaning primarily African Americans in the South where legal restrictions and illegal intimidation had effectively deprived nonwhites of the right to vote. The act also increased the penalties for bombings, lynchings, and other tactics used by such groups as the Ku Klux Klan to prevent African Americans from voting and from registering to vote. The act expanded upon the previous Civil Rights Act of 1957, and was an important step in the civil rights movement, which would gain momentum as the 1960s progressed. It did not, however, succeed in its objective of protecting the civil rights of African Americans, and thus tougher civil rights laws were passed in the middle and late 1960s that finally achieved this aim.

May 7

Twenty-seventh Amendment Ratified

The Bill of Rights, namely the first 10 amendments to the Constitution, was actually a package of 12 amendments sent by the First Congress to the states in 1789 for ratification. The states ratified ten of the amendments, such as the First Amendment, which protects freedom of speech, and those ten became the Bill of Rights. Two amendments, however, were not ratified by the states. One was a lengthy provision concerning the apportionment of the House of Representatives. The other was a provision stating that "No law varying the compensation for the services of the Senators and Representatives shall take effect, unless an election of Representatives shall have intervened," which after two centuries of obscurity was ratified on May 7, 1992.

The purpose behind what would become the 27th Amendment was to make sure that Congress would have to go through at least one election before a pay raise, or even in theory a pay cut, could take effect. Congress would thus be able to change the pay for future Congresses, but not for itself, and so there would be a safety-catch on the ability of legislators to manipulate their own compensation. Most attention is given to congressional pay raises, but in theory pay cuts could be just as dangerous: Independently wealthy members of Congress could pass a pay cut, survive on their own resources, and be in a position to dominate their less fortunate impoverished colleagues.

In 1982 a Texas state legislative aide named Gregory D. Watson learned about this unratified amendment. Watson began a one-man campaign to revive the amendment, and successfully convinced state legislatures around the country to ratify it. The unpopularity of recent congressional pay raises helped stimulate interest. On May 7, 1992, Michigan became the 38th state to ratify the amendment, thus achieving ratification by the required three-fourths of the states. There was some debate over whether an amendment could be ratified after two centuries in limbo, but on May 13, 1992, the National Archives announced that it would exercise its power to officially certify the 27th Amendment as ratified. Although technically not necessary, on May 20, 1992, Congress also issued its formal approval.

Sinking of the *Lusitania*

On May 7, 1915, the British Cunard liner *Lusitania* was torpedoed without warning by a German submarine. The liner was en route from New York to Liverpool, England, and was off the coast of Ireland when it was struck. Though hit by only one torpedo, the ship quickly sank, with the loss of 1,198 passengers, of whom 128 were American. Among those drowned were Charles Frohman, a well-known theatrical manager; Elbert Hubbard, the popular author and lecturer; and Alfred G. Vanderbilt, a son of the railroad magnate Cornelius Vanderbilt.

At the time of the *Lusitania* sinking, World War I, which had begun in August 1914, had bogged down in prolonged and bloody trench warfare. Thus, both Germany and the major Allies (Britain, France, and Russia) looked for other means to break the deadlock. With submarine warfare, Germany tried to wrest control of the high seas from Great Britain and in February 1915 announced that merchant vessels in British waters would be sunk without warning. The reason for the no-warning policy was that submarines had to surface in order to give warning, and when surfaced they were vulnerable to the artillery pieces and other weapons that the British had begun to mount on civilian vessels for just this sort of opportunity.

The United States, while officially neutral, had become a major source of supplies and munitions for the British. There was some trade with Germany and its allies, namely Austria-Hungary and Turkey, but much less than with the Allies (who had in any case blockaded German ports). Thus, when Britain protested the German position on unarmed ships, the American government supported the British view. Germany, meanwhile, asserted that passengers on transatlantic ships were serving merely as a screen for military shipping, and in fact the *Lusitania* was carrying troops and munitions as well as passengers. Just before the *Lusitania* sailed, the German embassy in Washington, D.C., posted a newspaper notice to prospective passengers on British ships, warning that they might be sunk. Since no one believed that Germany would dare attack the *Lusitania*, or any ship carrying Americans, the warning was ignored. The timing of the advertisement, however, does support the viewpoint that Germany had in fact modified its no-warning policy by announcing its intent to sink the *Lusitania*.

In the United States, popular shock and outrage followed the sinking, which was seen as a cold-blooded attack on civilians. But public opinion was divided on the advisability of entering a European conflict. Most Americans thought the United States should stay out of it; those who were willing to consider military action were divided between supporters of Britain (the "mother country") and supporters of Germany (the "fatherland" for German Americans as well as the "enemy-of-my-enemy" for the majority of Irish Americans). Southerners were also anti-British, because of German purchases of American cotton. President Woodrow Wilson reacted cautiously, through diplomatic channels. Nevertheless, his stern protest to the German government prompted the resignation of his own secretary of state, William Jennings Bryan, who felt that Wilson was coming dangerously close to taking sides. The German government promised to sink no more ocean liners unless warnings had been delivered and arrangements made to protect the lives of noncombatants, and all was quiet for a time. But a slow drift toward war had begun: In the months to come, the United States would find it increasingly difficult to remain neutral, and would finally be drawn into the conflict on the Allied side. The sinking of the *Lusitania* was a significant step in this direction.

Ascension Day

This is a movable event.

The Feast of the Ascension celebrates Jesus Christ's departure from the midst of his apostles and his ascension into heaven, as described in the New Testament, 40 days after his Resurrection (see March 29, Easter Sunday). During those 40 days, Jesus was reported to have met with the apostles on many occasions, telling them what he expected of them: "You shall be my witnesses . . . to the ends of the earth." Then, on the first Ascension Day, when the apostles were gathered together, Jesus led them out to the Mount of Olives. There he departed from them and, as they watched, ascended into heaven.

In the church calendar, the Feast of the Ascension marks the close of Eastertide, climaxing the events of the death and resurrection of Jesus Christ. Services are held on Ascension Day in many churches, including the Episcopalian, Lutheran, Eastern Orthodox, and Roman Catholic denominations. The date of the Eastern Orthodox observance of Ascension Day, though it falls on the traditional 40th day after Easter, customarily differs from that in Western churches because the rules by which the Eastern Orthodox churches calculate the date of Easter differ from those followed by the churches of the West.

In most churches, Ascension Day services include readings chosen from those portions of the New Testament that describe the last acts of Jesus during his time on earth. The Gospel of St. Luke, for example, closes with a brief account of the events of that original Ascension Day:

And he led them out as far as to Bethany and he lifted up his hands, and blessed them. And it came to pass, while he blessed them, he was parted from them, and carried up to heaven. And they worshipped him, and returned to Jerusalem with great joy: And were continually in the temple, praising and blessing God. Amen.

In his prelude to the Acts of the Apostles, St. Luke gives a more thorough account:

The former treatise have I made, O Theophilus, of all that Jesus began both to do and teach, until the day on which he was taken up, after that he through the Holy Ghost had given commandments unto the apostles whom he had chosen: to whom also he showed himself alive after his passion by many infallible proofs, being seen of them forty days, and speaking of the things pertaining to the kingdom of God: and, being assembled together with them, commanded them that they should not depart from Jerusalem, but wait for the promise of the Father, which, saith he, ye have heard of me. For John truly baptized with water; but ye shall be baptized with the Holy Ghost not many days hence. When they therefore were come together, they asked of him, saying, Lord, wilt thou at this time restore again the kingdom to Israel? And he said unto them, It is not for you to know the times or the seasons, which the Father hath put in his own power. But ye shall receive power, after that the Holy Ghost is come upon you: and ye shall be witnesses unto me both in Jerusalem and in all Judea, and in Samaria, and unto the uttermost part of the earth. And when he had spoken these things, while they beheld, he was taken up; and a cloud received him out of their sight. And while they looked steadfastly toward heaven as he went up, behold, two men stood by them in white apparel; which also said, Ye men of Galilee, why stand ye gazing up into heaven? This same Jesus, which is taken up from you into heaven, shall so come in like manner as ye have seen him go into heaven. Then returned they unto Jerusalem from the mount called Olivet, which is from Jerusalem a sabbath day's journey.

Other works also express the theological significance of the Ascension. Part of the preface of the mass celebrated in the Roman Catholic Church on Ascension Day reads: "Christ was lifted up to Heaven to make us sharers in His divinity." St. John Chrysostom, writing in the 4th century, said:

"Through the mystery of the Ascension we, who seemed unworthy of God's earth, are taken up into heaven."

According to tradition, the Feast of the Ascension is one of the earliest festivals of the Christian Church, dating from A.D. 68. No written record of its celebration as a liturgical feast, however, occurs before the 4th century. Over the centuries, many customs grew up around the celebration of the feast. For example, during the Middle Ages it was traditional for people to dine on pheasant, partridge, or some other bird on Ascension Day in commemoration of the fact that Jesus had "flown" to heaven. During church services from about the 13th to the 17th centuries, it was quite common for celebrants to reenact the Ascension by raising a crucifix or a statue of the resurrected Jesus, suspended from a rope, until it disappeared through an opening in the church roof.

May 8

Victory in Europe (V-E) Day

World War II ended in Europe, although it continued in Asia, on May 7, 1945, when Germany surrendered unconditionally to the western Allies and the Soviet Union at Reims, France. It was 2:41 a.m. (8:41 p.m. of the previous day on the east coast of the United States) when the act of military surrender was signed in a large schoolhouse, the advance headquarters of General Dwight D. Eisenhower, supreme commander of the Allied Expeditionary Forces. However, the surrender did not become effective until approximately midnight of May 8, the date officially celebrated in the United States as Victory in Europe (V-E) Day. From Washington, D.C., President Harry S. Truman announced on radio the end of World War II in Europe and issued a proclamation:

The Allied Armies, through sacrifice and devotion and with God's help, have won from Germany a final and unconditional surrender. The Western World has been freed of the evil forces which for five years and longer have imprisoned the bodies and broken the lives of millions upon millions of free-born men. They have violated their churches, destroyed their homes, corrupted their children and murdered their loved ones. Our armies of liberation have restored freedom to these suffering peoples, whose spirit and will the oppressors could never enslave.

Much remains to be done. The victory in the West must now be won in the East. The whole world must be cleansed of the evil from which half the world has been freed. United, the peace-loving nations have demonstrated in the West that their arms are stronger by far than the might of dictators or the tyranny of military cliques that once called us soft and weak. The power of our peoples to defend themselves against all enemies will be proved in the Pacific as it has been proved in Europe.

For the triumph of spirit and of arms we have won, and for its promise to peoples everywhere who join us in love of freedom, it is fitting that we, as a nation, give thanks to Almighty God, who has strengthened us and given us this victory.

Now, therefore, I, Harry S. Truman, President of the United States of America, do hereby appoint Sunday, May 13, 1945, to be a day of prayer. I call upon the people of the United States, whatever their faith, to unite in offering joyful thanks to God for the victory we have won and to pray that He will support us to the end of our present struggle and guide us into the way of peace. I also call upon my countrymen to dedicate this day of prayer to the memory of those who have given their lives to make possible our victory.

There was rejoicing throughout the United States on V-E Day, but awareness of the war in the Pacific still to be won tempered the general relief, as did the national grief over the death of President Franklin D. Roosevelt. Public demonstrations were moderate compared to the triumphant victory mood that was to sweep the nation on V-J Day (Victory over Japan) several months later in August.

In New York and other large cities, crowds resembling those of New Year's Eve gathered to express their jubilation by tooting horns and staging impromptu celebrations. On the other hand, business as usual was the rule in most offices, factories, and defense plants, where employees reported for their shifts and went quietly about their work. Perhaps the most significant indication of a prevailing spirit of intense but sober interest in the event was the fact, revealed by a radio poll, that 64 percent of all adult listeners, then the largest radio audience in history, tuned in President Truman's address officially confirming the surrender.

Today, although V-E Day is not widely celebrated, it remains a day of historic interest with vivid personal memories for many Americans.

Harry S. Truman's Birthday

Library of Congress

Harry S. Truman

The man who was thrust unexpectedly, while World War II still raged, into the presidency of the United States and leadership of the free world was born in Lamar, Missouri, on May 8, 1884. Just under 61 years later, he was catapulted into office by the sudden death of President Franklin D. Roosevelt on April 12, 1945.

Harry S. Truman was the first of three children born to John Anderson Truman and his wife, the former Martha Ellen Young. His grandparents, of English and Scottish descent, had come to Missouri from Kentucky four decades earlier. By giving him a middle initial only, his parents avoided the choice of naming him for grandfather Anderson Shippe Truman or grandfather Solomon Young. The initial S was frequently used without a period, often by Truman himself in signing his name with a continuous stroke. In his autobiographical books, however, he used S. and indicated that he had no preference between the two forms.

During Truman's earliest years, the family moved several times, living for five years on Missouri farms. In 1890 they settled in Independence, a suburb of Kansas City, in Missouri's Jackson County. As a boy, Truman was a shy youth who wore glasses and avoided sports, becoming a voracious reader. His grandfather Young's tales of leading wagon trains and driving cattle across the unsettled West to California and Utah helped stimulate in him a tremendous appetite for historical information. Another source of later pleasure, though it inspired other boys' taunts at the time, was playing the piano.

After a family financial setback ruled out college, and poor eyesight kept him out of the United States Military Academy at West Point, Truman held several jobs. He also joined the National Guard, and served until 1911. When his unit was called up in 1917, during World War I, he reenlisted. After attending the Fort Still, Oklahoma Artillery School, Truman was shipped to France where as a captain he commanded Battery D of the 129th Field Artillery, 35th Division, American Expeditionary Force. He saw action at St. Mihiel, in the Meuse-Argonne offensive, and at Verdun. A skillful leader, he revealed an ability to win the respect and affection of even the most hard-bitten men. After the war he remained in the Army Reserve and was promoted through the ranks to colonel.

When he returned to Independence, Missouri, in 1919, he married Elizabeth (Bess) Wallace, whom he claimed to have loved since the day they met at a Sunday school picnic when she was five and he was six. In 1924 their only child, Mary Margaret, was born. After his marriage, Truman opened a men's clothing store in Kansas City with an army companion. The venture, successful at first, failed in the economic recession of 1921. Although his partner went through bankruptcy proceedings, Truman refused to do so, and over the next 15 years he paid his creditors in full, a total of about $28,000.

John Truman had long been active in Democratic politics, and his son Harry became involved as a matter of course. The self-confidence Harry Truman gained from his wartime leadership increased his readiness for political office, and in 1922 he announced his candidacy for the post of judge of the Jackson County Court (an administrative board of supervisors, despite its name). After several months of impressive campaigning he won the support of Thomas J. Pendergast, the boss of the Democratic machine that controlled politics in Kansas City and later in much of Missouri. Truman had been introduced to Pendergast by the political leader's nephew, whom he had known in the army. Thus began a long political association, one for which Truman would later be criticized when allegations of the machine's corruption were made. While Truman, a person of strong party and personal allegiance, maintained his loyalty to the Pendergasts through the years, he disclaimed any subservience to them and avoided any involvement in graft or corruption. Through his personal integrity and his own vote-getting ability, he managed to maintain a relatively independent position in relation to the organization.

Truman's attractiveness as a candidate was enhanced by his excellent war record and his extensive contacts through active membership in the American Legion, the Army Reserve, the Baptist Church, and the Masons. These factors combined to give him wide support and he won the election for judge of the Jackson County Court. The post was administrative, not judicial, but Truman felt that some knowledge of the law would be helpful to his career and so he began two years of evening study at the Kansas City School of Law. Although he was defeated for reelection in 1924, when he had strong opposition from the Ku Klux Klan as well as from a rival Democratic faction, he was a successful candidate in 1926 and again in 1930 for presiding judge of the county court (which included Kansas City in its jurisdiction). His years of service in these county court posts, which involved the supervision of all county roads and public buildings, demonstrated his flair for efficiency and his honesty in handling a large budget.

Having developed a solid political base by 1934, Truman asked Pendergast for his support for a higher position, and Pendergast proposed Truman for nomination to the United States Senate. After a hard fight in the Democratic primary, Truman easily won the election, despite predictions that he would be a puppet of the machine. In his campaign, he endorsed the New Deal policies of President Franklin Delano Roosevelt.

During his first term as senator, Truman worked quietly and hard. He became knowledgeable in the field of transportation and was instrumental in the drafting of the Civil Aeronautics Act of 1938 and the Transportation Act of 1940. Burton K. Wheeler, chairman of the Senate's Interstate Commerce Committee, of which Truman was a member, taught him how to conduct an investigation. When the names of Missouri politicians surfaced during the probe into railroad financing that preceded formulation of the transportation act, Pendergast was among those who put pressure upon subcommittee chairman Truman. Truman responded by instructing committee investigators to treat the investigation like all others. However, he fought strenuously but unsuccessfully in the Senate to prevent reappointment of a federal district attorney for western Missouri who had won election fraud convictions against 35 ward leaders of the Pendergast organization.

As Truman's Senate term neared its end in 1940, Pendergast was in jail, his machine had collapsed, and some 47,000 names fraudulently included on Missouri voting lists had been removed.

Truman was criticized for his association with the machine; and he had not attracted favorable notice from President Roosevelt, whose New Deal programs Truman had staunchly supported. These handicaps notwithstanding, Truman characteristically decided to make every effort to win renomination. When two anti-Pendergast candidates joined the race, they succeeded in canceling each other out and Truman again walked off with the Democratic nomination. He won election again, but by a considerably slimmer margin than in 1934.

After personally investigating reports that graft and waste were rampant in the growing national defense program, including allegations of favoritism in the awarding of defense contracts in his home state, an outraged Truman began his second Senate term by introducing a bill to establish a Senate watchdog committee. The Special Committee to Investigate Contracts under the national defense program was created in March 1941 with Truman as chairman. The wide-ranging Truman Committee, noted for its courage and impartiality, exposed many forms and areas of corruption and waste, propelling its chairman into national prominence. It was credited with saving the government hundreds of millions of dollars during World War II.

When President Roosevelt decided to run for a fourth term in 1944, his vice president, Henry A. Wallace, had lost considerable support from Democrats who thought him too liberal. Roosevelt, anxious to replace him with a candidate who was backed by all factions of the party, turned to the well-respected Truman. In addition to chairing his committee, Truman was also serving on six others, including the important Appropriations, Military Affairs, and Interstate Commerce committees.

Roosevelt won the 1944 election, and Truman became vice president in January 1945. Roosevelt did not confide in Truman, however, or prepare him in any way for the presidency. Less than three months later, both Truman and the nation were stunned by Roosevelt's sudden death from a cerebral hemorrhage on April 12, 1945. Truman thus became the 33rd president of the United States and the first to ever succeed to the office in wartime. His sense of awe of the presidency, and his feeling of unpreparedness, found expression when he said to a group of reporters, "Boys, if you ever pray, pray for me now."

Truman retained Roosevelt's cabinet for the time being. He also maintained Roosevelt's war policies, and so the conclusion of World War II was carried out in accordance with the plans put into effect before Roosevelt's death. On May 8,

1945, Germany surrendered to the Allies, effectively ending the war in Europe. In the Far East, however, the war continued and Truman was called upon to make a decision of surpassing importance. On April 25 he learned for the first time, from Secretary of War Henry L. Stimson, that the United States was developing the atomic bomb, a weapon judged capable of causing unprecedented devastation. The question was whether this weapon should be used against Japan. Truman made the critical decision that it should, believing that its use would shorten the war and ultimately save more lives than it would cost by ending the bloody conflict as soon as possible.

Truman met at Potsdam, Germany, with British prime minister Winston Churchill and Soviet premier Joseph Stalin during the last half of July 1945. Most of the agreements at the Potsdam Conference concerned Europe, the postwar occupation, and control of Germany. Machinery was set up for the formulation of peace treaties, and Japan was given an unconditional surrender ultimatum.

The first atomic bomb was dropped on August 6, 1945, on the Japanese city of Hiroshima, and three days later, on August 9, Nagasaki was bombed as well. The death toll from the two strikes was more than 100,000; damage was catastrophic, and casualties from radiation poisoning continued for years afterward. On August 8, meanwhile, the Soviet Union joined the war against the badly shaken Japanese. On August 14 Japan surrendered.

After World War II, the next international crisis was the growing cold war between the United States and the Soviet Union. The Soviet Union, no longer America's ally, was challenging the United States for the dominant position in world affairs. At first, Truman's response to Soviet aggression seemed confined to ineffective verbal weapons. However, upon learning in early 1947 that Great Britain could no longer afford to provide economic and military aid to Greece and Turkey, both struggling to remain free of communist domination, Truman seized the opportunity to offer American aid to those two countries. He also offered American assistance in general "to support free peoples who are resisting attempted subjugation by armed minorities or by outside pressures." This new policy, designed to contain Soviet expansion and halt the spread of communism, became known as the Truman Doctrine.

The highly successful Marshall Plan, suggested by Secretary of State George C. Marshall in June 1947, was an outgrowth of the Truman Doctrine. Officially known as the European Recovery Program, the Marshall Plan dispensed some $12.5 billion during its nearly four years of existence (1948–1951), contributing importantly towards rebuilding war-shattered economies in Western Europe, where it also was credited with preventing communist takeovers. Participation in the plan was also offered to, but rejected by, the Soviet Union and its Eastern European satellites.

The cold war had many fronts: diplomatic, political, and military. In Germany the lack of agreement among the former Allies prevented progress toward a peace settlement. The Western occupying powers (the United States, Great Britain, and France) therefore began making plans, with German approval, to unite the sectors under their control. In hopes of thwarting their plans, the Soviet Union in June 1948 blockaded all land routes to West Berlin, which was also under the control of the three Western powers but completely surrounded by the Soviet occupation zone of Germany. President Truman, who long before had concluded that the Russians respected only force, would not consider abandoning the city to them. He immediately instituted an airlift that, with British participation, brought in needed provisions for almost a year until the Soviets relented and withdrew the blockade.

Trying to steer the country on a course that would avoid both inflation and recession as the booming wartime economy underwent reconversion to peacetime activities was one of Truman's major concerns. In this connection he urged continuation of price controls, a higher minimum wage, increased unemployment benefits, expanded social security coverage, national health insurance, large-scale federal subsidies for housing, and a full-employment plan. He also advocated civil rights guarantees and job rights for African Americans, a federal antilynching law, abolition of the poll tax, and universal military training. Most of these initiatives failed to pass Congress. However, Truman was successful in achieving unification of the three branches of the armed forces into one Department of Defense, and in bringing about the desegregation of the military.

By the 1948 election, many segments of the public were unhappy either with the postwar inflation or with one or another of Truman's domestic policies. Convinced that the president could not be reelected, Democratic Party leaders tried to persuade General Dwight D. Eisenhower to let his name be placed in nomination for the candidacy. When Eisenhower refused, the party felt it had no other choice but Truman. During the campaign that followed, almost every politician and pollster, Republican and Democrat, believed Truman to be a sure loser. The strong civil rights plank in the party platform alienated the traditionally Democratic South, and Governor J. Strom Thurmond of South Carolina drew considerable support there as presidential nominee of the new States' Rights ("Dixiecrat") Party. Democratic strength was also lost in the large northern and western cities to Henry A. Wallace on the ticket of the Progressive Party, which had been newly formed by discontented liberals.

Almost alone, Truman believed he could get through to the people with his message. He campaigned by riding trains nearly 32,000 miles across the nation, addressing friendly crowds from back platforms at whistle stops. In his extemporaneous, hard-hitting talks, which became known as his "give 'em hell" speeches, he presented himself as the defender of Roosevelt's New Deal policies and disclaimed responsibility for the legislative failures of what he called the "do-nothing" Republican-controlled 80th Congress. In contrast with Truman, whose efforts were unsparing and vigorous, the Republican candidate, New York's governor Thomas E. Dewey, appeared overconfident and unwilling to discuss the issues. Election night was unforgettable. Accepting Dewey's victory as a foregone conclusion, an early edition of the next day's *Chicago Tribune* proclaimed in a banner headline, "Dewey Defeats Truman." Truman relished that headline for years to come, for morning showed him to be unquestionably the winner with more than 24.1 million votes to roughly 22 million for Dewey. The electoral college vote was 303 to 189. Thurmond and Wallace had received roughly a million votes apiece.

Truman immediately renewed his efforts to secure adoption of his Fair Deal programs. In this he was no more successful than he had been during his first term. Although returned to Democratic control, Congress was in reality again dominated by an unsympathetic coalition of Republicans and southern Democrats. In 1950, involvement in the Korean War brought about financial strains and economic controls that were to be additional obstacles in the path of Truman's domestic goals.

One major accomplishment during Truman's second term was the signing in 1949 of the North Atlantic Treaty and the creation of the North Atlantic Treaty Organization (NATO) to carry out the treaty's objectives of cooperation and collective self-defense among the United States, Canada, and Western European signatories. Continuing to support Truman's foreign policy, Congress passed the Mutual Defense Assistance Act of 1949 to provide large amounts of military aid to NATO members and other friendly nations.

When Communist North Korean forces equipped by the Soviet Union invaded South Korea on June 25, 1950, Truman promptly called for a special session of the United Nations Security Council. The Soviet Union was a member of the Security Council, but was boycotting the body at the time. Thus, without Soviet interference, the Security Council branded the North Korean action as unprovoked aggression and requested that United Nations members aid South Korea. Truman ordered American forces into action under General Douglas MacArthur, a decision that he later called the most difficult of his presidency. One reason for his decision was his fear that the fledgling United Nations, whose strongest free-world member was the United States, would be severely weakened if it was unable to repel this flagrant aggression. Another consideration was the belief that the communists were testing, in Korea, the willingness of the United States to fulfill the promises it had made through the Truman Doctrine and various collective security treaties. Failure to act, the president believed, would encourage future communist encroachment in the Middle East and Western Europe, and weaken the confidence of free-world nations that the United States could be relied upon to honor its commitments to them.

After being pushed to the southern tip of the Korean peninsula, American forces made a daring landing at Inchon, in the northernmost part of South Korea, near the capital city of Seoul, in September 1950. Maintaining their powerful offensive, by late 1950 they had driven the invaders far back into North Korea, advancing almost to the Chinese border despite Chinese warnings. On November 26, 1950, the Chinese Communists entered the battle in strength and, joining the North Koreans, pushed the American and UN forces back, driving into South Korea and recapturing Seoul. The Chinese government stated that its forces were "volunteers" who had joined the North Korean cause on their own initiative, and despite this transparent falsehood the United States never declared war on China for entering the conflict, since broadening the war to include Communist China risked a nuclear confrontation with the Soviet Union.

Although General MacArthur was aware of Truman's desire to avoid escalating the conflict, he began to publicly urge that American forces bomb air bases in China. Because of his insubordination, and in order to ensure that American policy be clearly understood, Truman took the controversial step of removing the venerated MacArthur from his command in April 1951 and replacing him with General Matthew B. Ridgway.

Meanwhile, the American and UN forces had battled their way back to retake Seoul and by late spring of 1951 the battlefront had stabilized in the area around the 38th Parallel. In an atmosphere of stalemate, truce negotiations began in July 1951, but were not completed until two years later, after Truman's term of office had ended.

The 22nd Amendment to the Constitution, ratified in 1951 (see February 27), limited a president to two terms in office (each term being four years), but exempted Truman since he was still in office. Nevertheless, Truman announced in March 1952 his decision not to seek another term. Never having had "the complex of being a big shot," as he put it, Truman found the transition from major world figure to private citizen of Independence, Missouri, relatively easy. With his zest for living, his consuming interest in politics, and his fund of historical knowledge, he followed domestic and world affairs closely. Even former critics of some of his policies held him in high regard, and there was wide interest in his views on current events.

Truman was quoted as saying that he expected to live to be 90, and he almost did. Death came to the spirited former president in a Kansas City hospital on December 26, 1972, at the age of 88. By then the political differences of the past had dimmed with time. He was remembered for his integrity, courage, decisiveness, and willingness to accept responsibility without trying to shift blame to others, as reflected in the famous sign on his White House desk: "The buck stops here." Often extremely unpopular during his presidency, Truman is now considered one of America's greatest presidents.

May 9

John Brown's Birthday

John Brown, a radical advocate of the abolition of slavery in the United States, was born in Torrington, Connecticut, on May 9, 1800. His father, Owen Brown, was an abolitionist and helped slaves escape to freedom in the North or in Canada by means of the Underground Railroad. John Brown's mother, Ruth Mills Brown, died when he was eight years old.

Brown spent his boyhood in Hudson, Ohio. He had little formal education, and later in life he said that to him school meant confinement and restraint. He liked to read, but he loved roaming in the wilderness even more. When he was 20, Brown married Dianthe Lusk, and they had seven children. In 1825 the family settled in Richmond, Pennsylvania, setting up a tannery and an Underground Railroad station. During his travels, Brown engaged in many different kinds of businesses, working in tanneries, land speculating, sheep raising, and farming, but he was unsuccessful in all of

them. In 1831 his wife died, and shortly afterwards Brown remarried. His second wife, the former Mary Anne Day, bore him 13 more children. Brown's continued economic failures, coupled with the problems of supporting an enormous family, led him in 1849 to go to North Elba, near what is now Lake Placid, New York. There, on land donated by a wealthy New York abolitionist, a free black farming community had been established. Brown stayed for two years, trying to help the community.

In 1855 five of Brown's sons went to Kansas to establish a homestead and to help win the territory for freedom. A few months after his sons' arrival in Kansas, Brown responded to their plea for help in fighting the proslavery forces from neighboring Missouri, and joined them at the Osawatomie colony. He soon became the leader of the antislavery men, as well as the captain of the local militia. The sack of the town of Lawrence on May 24, 1856, by proslavery men helped turn the cause of "free soil" into a crusade and stimulated Brown, who believed he was following the will of God, to retaliate. Three days later he led a small group of men on a raid to Pottawatomie, where they brutally killed five proslavery men. In revenge, a large group of proslavery men from Missouri sacked and burned Osawatomie on August 30. The border warfare continued until it was finally suppressed by federal troops in mid-September.

The epithet "Old Osawatomie" Brown acquired in Kansas made him a terror to all proslavery men and a hero to many abolitionists. Ralph Waldo Emerson called him "a pure idealist of artless goodness." When Brown returned east from Kansas in 1856, he met the abolitionists of the Massachusetts State Kansas Committee who had been supplying him and other Free-Soilers with arms, supplies, and money. Brown by this time had become obsessed with the cause of abolition and the need to free the slaves. In 1858 he returned to Kansas and made a daring raid on a Missouri plantation, liberating 11 slaves. Eluding his pursuers, he guided the slaves safely to Canada.

That year, with the financial and moral encouragement of many abolitionists, including Frederick Douglass, Brown held a convention in Canada (Chatham, Ontario) and disclosed his plan to liberate the slaves by setting up a free state in the mountains of Virginia to which the slaves could flee. The convention adopted a provisional constitution for the state and named Brown commander in chief.

Brown proceeded to put his plan into effect by renting a farm across the river from Harpers Ferry, Virginia (now West Virginia). There he gathered a small group of men, black and white, and on the night of October 16, 1859, crossed the river and seized the federal armory and rifle-works. A small group of his men went to nearby Charlestown, Virginia (now Charles Town, West Virginia), to seize hostages and recruit slaves. Then Brown and his followers retreated into the brick fire engine house in the armory compound. By morning the news of the raid had spread and 17 militia companies were blocking the roads to any escape.

Brown and his men managed to fight off the militia. However, when soldiers under the command of Robert E. Lee (then a federal officer, although he would become a famous Confederate general in future years) attacked the engine house, the abolitionists were overcome. Brown was captured fighting next to the bodies of his two dead sons. He was tried in a Virginia court at Charlestown and convicted of "treason and of conspiring and advising with slaves and others to rebel, and of murder in the first degree." Despite 17 affidavits attesting that Brown was insane (as his mother had been), Governor Henry A. Wise decided not to have Brown examined, and the question of Brown's sanity remains a matter of historical debate. He was sentenced to death and hanged at Charlestown on December 2, 1859.

Although the expected slave uprising never occurred after the signal at Harpers Ferry, Brown's behavior during his trial enhanced his stature among abolitionists. He consistently maintained that he was an instrument in God's hands and he refused to be held accountable to anyone but God for his mission to free the slaves. Brown accepted his death sentence with a confident declaration: "I cannot now better serve the cause I love . . . than to die for it."

The passions aroused by Brown's raid and his death even more sharply divided antislavery and proslavery factions in the United States. The former glorified him as a martyr to the cause of human freedom, while the latter vilified him as a common assassin. When the Civil War broke out, the memory of John Brown was kept alive by Union troops who marched into battle singing: "John Brown's body lies a-mouldering in the grave but his soul goes marching on."

In 1906, almost 50 years after the well-remembered raid, the spirit of "Old John Brown" was evoked by 100 men and women who gathered at Harpers Ferry at the birth of the civil rights movement. Led by W. E. B. Du Bois, the African American scholar and writer, the movement had begun a year before at a secret meeting at Niagara Falls. Abandoning secrecy, the group met at Harpers Ferry and, in an "Address to the Nation," written by Du Bois, clearly enunciated its demands. The address was both a declaration of independence from Booker T. Washington and his policies of compromise and a program for the future: "We claim for ourselves every single right that belongs to a freeborn American . . . and until we get these rights we will never cease to protest and assail the ears of America." Three years later the Niagara militants joined with a larger group of men and women to found the National Association for the Advancement of Colored People, which has worked vigorously since its inception on behalf of equality.

May 10

Mother's Day

This is a movable event.

Every year Americans set aside the second Sunday in May to pay tribute to their mothers. Across the land, children of all ages use the occasion to honor their mothers with tokens of appreciation such as flowers and candy, or with more personal expressions of affection, such as cards, telephone calls, and visits. The day, which provides an excellent opportunity for remembering mothers and expressing gratitude to them, is one of the most widely celebrated holidays of the year.

Americans are not alone in honoring their mothers on a special day; nor did they originate the idea. Both the ancient Greeks and Romans held festivals to pay tribute to mothers, and Christians during the Middle Ages honored Mary, the mother of Jesus, with appropriate observances every year. In England the fourth Sunday in Lent was celebrated as Mothering Sunday, and in Yugoslavia a similar event was traditionally held shortly before Christmas season; on their respective holidays Britons and Slavs visited their mothers and brought them small gifts.

In comparison with these early European observances, the establishment of a similar holiday in the United States is of relatively recent origin. During the Civil War, Julia Ward Howe, the author of "The Battle Hymn of the Republic," suggested that July 4 be renamed Mother's Day and urged that the occasion be used for promoting peace. Howe's idea was never put into effect, but shortly after the end of the Civil War, Anna Reeves Jarvis of Grafton, West Virginia, began to work for a similar holiday. In 1868, Jarvis organized a committee in her home town to sponsor a Mother's Friendship Day. The object of this observance was to reunite families that had been divided during the Civil War. Mother's Friendship Day allegedly brought together a number of brothers who had formerly fought against one another, but Jarvis's dream of an annual "memorial mother's day, commemorating [each mother] for the service she renders to humanity in every field" did not gain widespread acceptance during her lifetime.

Others also showed an early interest in establishing Mother's Day. In 1887 Mary Towles Sasseen, a teacher in Henderson, Kentucky, organized a special musical affair to honor her pupils' mothers. This tribute became an annual event in her classes, but she did not content herself with the success of this celebration. Until her death in 1916, Sasseen worked unceasingly to popularize such recognition of mothers. In 1893 she published a pamphlet describing her classroom ceremonies and for years she traveled across the nation urging other educators to adopt similar observances in their schools.

While Sasseen was promoting her plan, Frank E. Herring of South Bend, Indiana, also took up the cause of establishing Mother's Day. In an address to his fellow members of the Fraternal Order of Eagles in 1904, Herring suggested that mothers be honored throughout the nation on a special day every year.

Although the previously mentioned people have justly been given credit for their contributions to the establishment of Mother's Day, Anna M. Jarvis, daughter of Anna Reeves Jarvis, was most directly responsible for organizing the observance in the United States. On May 9, 1907, the second anniversary of her mother's death, she invited friends to her home in Philadelphia, Pennsylvania. At this gathering, she outlined her plan for making her mother's dream of a nationwide day in honor of mothers, living and deceased, a reality. The following year she carried out her hope. On May 10, 1908, the second Sunday of the month, church services in which mothers were honored were held in both Grafton, West Virginia, and in Philadelphia.

The 1908 observance was only the beginning of Jarvis's efforts. For years, she worked diligently to popularize her idea. She wrote hundreds of letters to church and business leaders, newspaper editors, and members of Congress, and she even brought the need for a Mother's Day observance to the attention of the president of the United States. Jarvis's single-minded labors were rewarded. In 1910 the governor of West Virginia issued the first Mother's Day proclamation, and by 1911 Mother's Day services were held in all the states of the Union. In 1914 President Woodrow Wilson, responding to a joint resolution of Congress, issued a proclamation setting aside the second Sunday in May "for displaying the American Flag, and

as a public expression of our love and reverence for the mothers of our country."

Mother's Day quickly won popular acceptance both at home and abroad. In the United States and in many foreign nations, church services patterned after those held in 1908, as well as personal expressions of appreciation to mothers, became customary on the second Sunday in May. Many persons also observed the custom of wearing carnations on the occasion, a custom which has fallen into disuse in recent decades. In 1934 the post office further commemorated Mother's Day by issuing a three-cent stamp depicting the famed portrait of James McNeill Whistler's mother.

Meanwhile, Jarvis continued her efforts to make Mother's Day truly an occasion on which children would show their appreciation to their mothers. In return for her work, she won numerous honors. She was a delegate to the World Sunday School Convention in Zurich, Switzerland, in 1913; she spoke before many noteworthy groups; and Japan acclaimed her Mother's Day idea "a great American gift." However, as commercialization began to encroach upon the observance of the day, she became embittered. She initiated lawsuits against those seeking profits from Mother's Day, and when these failed she turned away from the world. Within a short time she lost her property, and her blind sister Elsinore, to whom she had devoted her life, died. In the face of such misfortune, her own health failed, and in November 1944 she was forced to ask for public assistance. Realizing her desperate plight, some friends came to her aid and provided funds so that she might spend her final years in a private sanatorium in West Chester, Pennsylvania. Deaf, nearly blind, and childless, the woman whose efforts had brought happiness to countless mothers died in 1948.

Today, Mother's Day is celebrated throughout the world. In the United States the president and the governors of many states issue proclamations declaring the second Sunday in May to be Mother's Day. Observances of the day of course center around the family. Many churches hold special services on Mother's Day, and sermons are generally based on themes indicating the unique bond between mother and child.

The First Transcontinental Railroad

The vision of connecting the east and west coasts of the North American continent with railroad tracks originated among those interested in trade with Asia, and even before the Mexican War the New York merchant Asa Whitney had advocated this enterprise. American acquisition of California and the discovery of gold in that state provided the final impetus that prompted Congress in March 1853 to authorize a survey of the possible routes westward from the Mississippi River.

Bitter sectional rivalries, however, prevented the selection of an eastern terminus and route, and the depression following the Panic of 1857 ended hopes that the proposal would quickly become a reality. Only when the Civil War brought an end to support for a southern route were the Republicans able to fulfill their 1860 platform pledge to rescue the transcontinental railroad from its planning-board limbo. On July 1, 1862, President Abraham Lincoln signed the first Pacific Railroad Act, which authorized the Central Pacific and the new Union Pacific to construct the transcontinental line. The former railroad was to build eastward from California and the latter westward from the Missouri River. The government gave the companies alternate sections of public lands in a checkerboard pattern contiguous to both sides of the right of way. A 30-year loan in government bonds provided a per-mile-of-track subsidy of $16,000 over the plains, $32,000 on the plateau between the Rocky Mountains and Sierra Nevada, and $48,000 across the mountains.

The Central Pacific Railroad, directed by Collis P. Huntington and Leland Stanford, broke ground on January 8, 1863, at Sacramento, California. The Union Pacific began its construction at Omaha, Nebraska, on December 2, 1862, with a ceremony highlighted by a speech by George F. Train, the appropriately named merchant and author. Progress was slow, however. In 1864 a more generous second Pacific Railroad Act doubled the land grants and gave the government a second instead of a first mortgage on railroad property. Labor shortages were more persistent, but General Grenville M. Dodge, the chief engineer of the Union Pacific, managed well with crews of ex-soldiers and Irish immigrants brought from New York City. Charles Crocker, Dodge's Central Pacific counterpart, found his work force by importing more than 6,000 Chinese laborers. The United States Army protected the Union's employees from raids by the Sioux, and the Central Pacific placated the less warlike western tribes by giving the chiefs free rides.

The railroaders drove relentlessly through summers and winters in a race for government mileage subsidies. This quest for speed proved to be quite expensive. Experts have estimated that working through the winter snows of the high Sierras, and other daring exploits, increased construction costs by 70 percent. Both companies reached Utah early in 1869 and their forward crews passed each other with parallel lines. The Congress named Promontory, Utah, as a compromise nexus for the railroads. At final tally, the Union Pacific had built 1,086 miles of track and the Central Pacific 689 miles, but the latter had had to deal with mountains.

Officials from both companies met at Promontory on May 10, 1869, for ceremonies joining the two lines. President Leland Stanford of the Central Pacific and Vice President Thomas C. Durant of the Union Pacific used a hammer of Nevada silver to drive the final spike, a golden one, into a tie of polished California laurel. Each took turns delivering the blows until Stanford completed the job. Telegraph operators reported each strike of the mallet and the completion of the project set off wild celebrations throughout the nation. The federal government later established the Golden Spike National Historic Site to mark the spot where the two railroad companies met.

The Methodist Church Merger Becomes Effective

The merger of the Methodist Episcopal Church, the Methodist Episcopal Church (South), and the Methodist Protestant Church to form the Methodist Church took place on May 10, 1939, during a uniting conference at Kansas City, Missouri, held from April 26 through May 10. Nine hundred delegates and 50 bishops attended. On the final evening 14,000 persons, mostly Methodists, from all parts of the country packed the auditorium to witness the closing events. After a solemn procession of delegates, bishops, and the three chairmen of the joint commission for church union (Bishops John M. Moore, Edwin H. Hughes, and James H. Straughn), the "Declaration of Union" was read. It was then adopted without dissent by the assembled bishops.

As the episcopal address, read by Bishop John M. Moore on the first day of the conference, had stressed, the movement toward union was a logical one. The merging church organizations, having split in the past over issues of church government, had never diverged in doctrine:

On the larger matters we are already in agreement. Since we have never separated in faith, we will have no theological discussions. . . . This Methodism is no fabrication of ambitious, selfish ecclesiastics. It is rather the flowing together of great streams going out to the same seas.

The merger, Bishop Straughn later commented, therefore gave all members the supreme satisfaction that "we are together again in one family, one home, witnessing to earnest yearning for an obedience to that ancient prayer for the unity of Christ's people." His thought was similar in spirit to the congratulatory message that President Franklin Delano Roosevelt sent the conference from his Warm Springs, Georgia, retreat:

> To a world distracted by malice, envy, and ill will, the Kansas City assembly is a harbinger of better things. . . . The Methodists have pointed the way to union. May God prosper the work and hasten the day when Christians of all confessions shall present a united front to combat the forces of strife that threaten our heritage of religion.

The Methodist movement started in the early 18th century with the evangelistic preaching of John Wesley (1703–1791), an Anglican clergyman and a fellow of Lincoln College, Oxford, who was assisted by his brother Charles and George Whitefield. Small numbers of Oxford students who gathered about these men to share their personal Christian experiences were soon dubbed Methodists, in reference to the methodical manner in which they strictly observed what they saw to be their religious duties. Members of the Holy Club, as the group was called, were punctilious in their daily worship and study, set themselves a schedule for visiting the sick and those in prison, and conducted schools among the poor.

The emphasis of Methodism was on personal salvation through faith, fellowship in Christian service, and love for others. The stress of the movement was on religion as an inner experience, on conversion, and on testimony, and it was characterized by the strong social conscience of its adherents. It was brought to the American colonies in the mid-18th century. Without Wesley's knowledge, local preachers, especially Irish immigrants, began to spread his beliefs in Maryland about 1764 and in New York two years later. By 1768 groups of Methodists in Maryland, Pennsylvania, New York, and New Jersey had modeled themselves upon Wesley's English "societies." American independence from England following the Revolution necessitated the establishment of an independent Methodist ecclesiastical body in the United States. The Methodist Episcopal Church, which adopted the order of worship and religious precepts set down by Wesley, came into being at the Christmas Conference held in Baltimore, Maryland, on December 24, 1784. The first General Conference, the supreme policy-making body of the church, met in 1792.

Several schisms occurred in the church, although none was caused by doctrinal differences. The first serious split was in 1830. The dispute centered about the issue of lay representation in the church governing body, and reflected the general desire of the reformers to establish a broader base in church administration by limiting episcopal power. The controversy resulted in the formation of the Methodist Protestant Church in Baltimore, a non-episcopal church with equal lay and clerical representation in its conferences that spread rapidly in Maryland, Pennsylvania, and neighboring states. Four years after its founding, it had a membership of 26,587.

The separation of the Methodist Episcopal Church, South, took place in May 1845 at a meeting in Louisville, Kentucky, called by southern church leaders. The division materialized in general over the increasingly bitter issue of slavery and specifically over the suspension of a slaveholding bishop who was not acceptable to northern Methodists. Despite its organization as an independent body, the 460,000-member Methodist Episcopal Church, South, retained the same doctrines and discipline as the parent Methodist Episcopal Church; however, at its first general conference following the Civil War, it adopted the position of the Methodist Protestant Church in allowing both lay and clerical representation at its general and annual conferences.

Since the two major schisms had not been caused by doctrinal divergences, the reconciliation of the three Methodist churches was broached as early as the 1870s. In fact, in 1868 the Methodist Episcopal Church had already moved towards clerical and lay representation at its conferences, a trend that eventually resolved the chief issue that had caused the formation of the Methodist Protestant Church in 1830. In 1870 the way was paved for healing the Methodist division between north and south when the General Conference of southern delegates welcomed northern representatives. In 1905 the two Methodist Episcopal bodies agreed on a joint hymnal and order of worship.

The movement for unification of the three major Methodist churches gained momentum in the 20th century. The first plan for union between the northern and southern Methodist Episcopal Churches, voted upon in the mid-1920s, was adopted by the Methodist Episcopal Church but rejected by the Methodist Episcopal Church, South. In the 1930s a new plan of union, this time including the Methodist Protestant Church as well, won the support necessary for adoption. The reunion of May 10, 1939, brought together the largest number of Protestants (approximately 8 million) that had as yet been merged. On April 23, 1968, the Methodist Church also absorbed the Evangelical United Brethren Church to form the United Methodist Church (see April 23).

Fort Ticonderoga Falls

Emerging from the 4:00 a.m. darkness on May 10, 1775, Ethan Allen and his Green Mountain Boys caught the British by surprise and captured Fort Ticonderoga, at the junction of Lakes Champlain and George, in the first offensive action of the American Revolution. Benedict Arnold, later best known as a traitor to the American cause, helped conceive the action and was among those who crossed with Allen from the Vermont to the New York side of Lake Champlain to participate in the daring exploit. This first American victory in the war not only yielded control of vital waterways leading to Canada and to New York City, it also provided the colonists with badly needed cannons, which were dragged the following winter all the way to Boston. There they were crucial in the action of Dorchester Heights that resulted in expulsion of the British (see March 17, British Troops Evacuate Boston).

May 11

Minnesota Admitted to the Union

On May 11, 1858, Minnesota became the 32nd state to join the Union. Before admission to statehood, the region had a rich history as the home of several Native American tribes, the scene of European explorers' and fur trappers' adventures, and an area that had attracted thousands of hopeful pioneers. As a state located in the heart of America's "breadbasket," Minnesota continued to make important contributions to the history and strength of the nation.

Apart from the 14th-century Norsemen who, some have alleged, may have reached the area, Frenchmen, seeking fur pelts and a western passage through the North American continent, were the first Europeans to go to what is now called Minnesota. Pierre Ésprit Radisson and Médart Chouart, Sieur des Groseilliers, may have visited the region, possibly even as early as 1654 or 1655. Daniel Greysolon, Sieur Duluth (Dulhut), led a party to Minnesota in 1679 for the purpose of improving relations between the Chippewa and Sioux tribes who inhabited the region. On the western shore of Lake Superior, near the site of the city that today bears his name, Duluth held a council with the Sioux. Then, Duluth and his men continued inland to the Mille Lacs Sioux village, where he recorded that "on the second of July, 1679, I had the honor to set up the arms of His Majesty in the great village of Nadouecioux called Izatys, where no Frenchman had ever been, nor to the Songakitons and Quetbatons, distant 26 leagues from the first, where I also set up the arms of His Majesty in the same year 1679." Duluth sent members of his expedition to probe the wilderness west of Mille Lacs, and they reported seeing a "great lake whose water is not good to drink." However, the exact area they explored is unknown; perhaps they reached the Pacific Ocean or came upon the Great Salt Lake.

In 1680 Louis Hennepin, a Flemish priest sent by René-Robert Cavelier de La Salle to explore the area of the upper Mississippi, discovered the Falls of St. Anthony. The adventures surrounding Hennepin's coming upon this great power source, which centuries later helped make Minneapolis the milling center of the United States, were recounted in the *Description de la Louisiane*, which was published in Paris in 1683. Whether Hennepin himself actually wrote this book is questionable, but there is no doubt that its tales about the Minnesota wilderness aroused great interest in Europe.

Meanwhile, French explorers and trappers continued to venture into the region of Minnesota. In 1700 Pierre Charles Le Sueur led a party up the Minnesota River to the Blue Earth River. There he built Fort L'Huillier, a small post that for two years was a lucrative fur-trading center.

Between 1701 and 1714 the War of the Spanish Succession occupied the energies of the French in both the Old and New Worlds. On the North American continent, the hostilities with England put a temporary end to explorations in the Northwest, and not until 1727 did the French again sponsor an expedition to that region. In that year, however, René Boucher de La Perrière led a party into the area of the upper Mississippi. In September the expedition landed at the upper end of Minnesota's Lake Pepin, where Fort Beauharnois was built. The fortification, which included a number of buildings and a small chapel, might have served as a base for French explorations farther west. But La Perrière returned to Montreal in 1728, and shortly after his departure the soldiers at Beauharnois became involved in attacks and counterattacks against the Fox and Sioux tribes.

In 1731 Pierre Gaultier de Varennes de la Vérendrye led an expedition into Minnesota. The men in the Vérendrye party established Fort St. Pierre at the western end of Rainy Lake in 1731, and built the larger Fort St. Charles at Lake of the Woods in 1732. The latter fortification served as a base of operations for extensive French explorations in the Midwest during the decades that followed. Between 1756 and 1763, French and English forces again clashed, and the English victory in the French and Indian War cost France its empire in the New World. By a secret treaty, France in 1762 ceded the area west of the Mississippi to Spain, and by the Treaty of Paris of 1763 it surrendered Canada and its claims east of the Mississippi to England. These treaties technically divided control of Minnesota between Spain and England, but in practice the latter nation controlled the entire Minnesota region for the next 50 years, even though by the Treaty of Paris of 1783 England officially turned over its claim to eastern Minnesota to the new American nation, which made it part of the newly created Northwest Territory four years later.

During England's half-century of dominance of Minnesota, a thriving fur trade developed in the area. Independent traders were active in the Minnesota wilds at this time, but the North West Company, an organization of Montreal businessmen, conducted by far the most extensive operations in the area. Every year during the last decades of the 18th century, pelts worth tens of thousands of dollars were collected at Grand Portage and from there sent to Montreal, where they were reshipped to Europe. As the center of the British fur trade, Grand Portage, located on the western shore of Lake Superior in northeastern Minnesota, has a place of great importance in the state's history. Accordingly, Grand Portage was declared a national monument in 1958.

Although the United States formally gained control of eastern Minnesota by the Treaty of Paris of 1783, and of western Minnesota by the Louisiana Purchase of 1803, the nation did not make any substantial efforts to exert its authority in the area until after the War of 1812. Then, realizing that American claims to the Midwest would be recognized only if the nation actually occupied the area, the United States built a series of frontier forts that would serve as defenses against foreign enemies. In 1819 a United States Army expedition, which was taken over by Colonel Josiah Snelling the following year, set out to build the first American fortification in Minnesota. Located at the juncture of the Minnesota and Mississippi Rivers on land that explorer Zebulon M. Pike had purchased in 1805 from the Sioux, the fort was virtually completed by 1822. Originally known as Fort St. Anthony, it was renamed Fort Snelling in 1825. As an "isle of safety" in the wilderness and as a center from which expeditions could explore, survey, and eventually settle the surrounding region, Fort Snelling played a critical role in the growth of Minnesota.

Although the United States effectively removed the British presence from the upper Mississippi region in the years following the War of 1812, Minnesota did not attract American settlers for several decades. Instead, as had been the case during the periods of French and British dominance, most Europeans who visited Minnesota in the early 19th century were either explorers or fur trappers. Like their predecessors, these adventurers played an important part in Minnesota's history. The explorers conducted numerous expeditions into the Minnesota wilderness and eventually discovered Lake Itasca, the source of the Mississippi River, while the traders, most of whom were associated with John Jacob Astor's American Fur Company, reaped great profits from the pelts of the region.

Changes in fashion, which curtailed the demand for furs in the 1830s and 1840s, brought an end to the dominance of the trappers and explorers in Minnesota. In 1837, meanwhile, the American government negotiated treaties with the Sioux and Chippewa that extinguished the tribes' title to the triangle of land between the Mississippi and lower St. Croix Rivers. This opened the first wedge to permanent settlement, and within a few years the influx of migrants (which neighboring areas had already experienced) began to reach Minnesota. Lumberers followed the fur traders into the region. Minnesota became not only a major lumbering area, but also an important transportation center, first as the northern terminus of the growing traffic on the Mississippi River, and later as the western terminus of the inland waterway extending through the Great Lakes to points east. Ultimately, after the opening of the St. Lawrence Seaway in the 20th century, the inland water route would stretch all the way to the Atlantic Ocean, paralleling the path of the early fur traders.

With new interest in the region, the population of what would soon be the state of Minnesota mounted. By 1849 about 4,000 American settlers inhabited the area, and the towns of St. Paul and Stillwater counted 910 and 609 residents, respectively. During the 19th century, much of the area of present Minnesota was successively included in the jurisdictions of the Indiana, Illinois, Michigan, Wisconsin, and Iowa Territories. Michigan gained statehood in 1837, and Iowa in 1846. When Wisconsin was admitted to the Union in 1846, Minnesota's legal status was temporarily ambiguous. Faced with this situation, a convention that met at Stillwater on August 26, 1848, decided to send Henry Hastings Sibley as a delegate to the national Congress. Sibley asked Congress to form a new territory of Minnesota to serve the needs of the area's residents, and Congress complied on March 3, 1849.

In 1851, 1854, and 1855 the United States government concluded treaties with the Sioux and Chippewa that opened to settlement most of the area in Minnesota west of the Mississippi and about half the northern region of the territory. The opening of these rich lands resulted in a population boom of almost unprecedented dimensions. Between 1850 and 1857 Minnesota's population grew from 6,077 to 150,037, and countless farms and towns appeared across the expanse of the territory. The expansion of the railroads after the Civil War would account for further large gains.

Minnesota did not remain a territory for long. Its rapid growth quickly made it eligible for statehood, and on February 26, 1857, Congress approved an enabling act that empowered Minnesota officials to call a constitutional convention. The convention met on July 13, 1857, and by August 28, 1857, it had drawn up a state constitution. This document was approved in a popular referendum on October 13, 1857, and was submitted to President James Buchanan on January 6, 1858. In the nation's capital, Minnesota's application for admission to the Union became entangled with the more controversial issue of Kansas's statehood (see January 29), so that several months passed before Congress finally approved the application on May 11, 1858, and Minnesota was admitted to the Union as the 32nd state.

Colonies of New Haven and Connecticut Unite

The first general court of Connecticut to include representatives from the towns that had comprised the New Haven Colony met on May 11, 1665. This was more than three years after John Winthrop Jr. had obtained a royal charter granting Connecticut jurisdiction over the area previously controlled by New Haven.

Prior to 1662, neither Connecticut nor New Haven had a royal charter. Colonization of both areas took place without the legal sanction of the king. It was the natural migration of Massachusetts inhabitants that accounted for the settlement of Connecticut. In 1635 the attraction of the colony's rich farmlands caused an exodus from Dorchester and Watertown to the area around Hartford. The following year, the Reverend Thomas Hooker arrived, and under his guidance a compact of government was drawn up. The Fundamental Orders of Connecticut closely followed the system of government then operative in Massachusetts. The only major deviation from the Massachusetts model was the provision for citizenship. In Massachusetts, membership in the Puritan Congregational Church was a prerequisite for admission to political privileges, but in Connecticut the only requirement was acceptance by the majority of householders in the township. Since the original

settlers were staunch Puritans, however, only those with similar religious beliefs proved "acceptable," and in practice Congregational Church members also controlled Connecticut. The Fundamental Orders remained the sole basis of the colony's government for more than 20 years. Not until 1660 was any effort made to obtain royal recognition.

The colony at New Haven was likewise established without a royal charter. Under the leadership of the Reverend John Davenport and Theophilus Eaton, a merchant, Puritans fleeing religious persecution in England arrived in New England in 1637. They stopped briefly at Boston, but the religious controversies then raging in that town made them unwilling to stay. Instead, the followers of Davenport and Eaton decided to found a new settlement. In the spring of 1638, without royal knowledge of their activity, they established New Haven on the shore of Long Island Sound. Other towns quickly sprang up around the original settlement, and in 1643 the common need for protection caused Stamford, Guilford, and Milford to join with New Haven. The new colony limited citizenship to church members. Many of New Haven's leading citizens were merchants, and under their influence the colony quickly expanded. By 1662 it controlled a number of new settlements on the sound, several towns on Long Island, and a struggling colony in Delaware.

The English civil war afforded the Connecticut and New Haven colonies protection for two decades. The parliamentary government executed King Charles I in 1649, and Oliver Cromwell and his Puritans held the reins of power until 1660. Royal authority was reestablished with the restoration of Charles II to the throne in that year, and any colonial government that ignored the crown thenceforth risked its own existence.

Connecticut was quick to curry favor with the king. In 1662 the colony sent John Winthrop Jr. to England to negotiate for a charter. New Haven failed to take similar action. It could not afford the luxury of sending an emissary to the king, and its reputation as a refuge for Charles I's regicides made it unlikely that Charles II would have turned a favorable ear even if such a delegate had appeared at court. The charter that Winthrop received in 1662 incorporated New Haven into the Connecticut Colony. New Haven, however, refused to accept this action and for nearly two years struggled to maintain its independent existence. It petitioned the colonial organization known as the New England Confederation to redress its grievances against Connecticut, and at first that body upheld New Haven. However, the English conquest of New Netherland in 1664 ended any hope of continued independence. The Roman Catholic duke of York controlled New Netherland, and his charter could be interpreted so as to include the New Haven area within his jurisdiction. Fearing Catholic domain, the confederation quickly reversed itself, and in September 1664 agreed to Connecticut's control of the New Haven region. In November 1664 royal commissioners, disregarding the Duke of York's claim, established Long Island Sound as Connecticut's southern boundary.

New Haven reluctantly agreed to these terms on December 15, 1664. A formal act of submission was passed on January 5, 1665, and on May 11 the first general court of the combined colonies was held.

May 12

Florence Nightingale's Birthday

May 12, 1820, marks the birth of Florence Nightingale, whose pioneer endeavors in nursing inspired progress in the hospital systems of both England and the United States. She was born in Florence, Italy, the second daughter of well-to-do and cultured British parents. Vivacious and intelligent, she was an intensely emotional child, who at a young age developed an extraordinary capacity for self-criticism and introspection. In 1837 she felt that she heard the voice of God summoning her to service, and by 1844 her uncertainties about the form that this service should take had been resolved and nursing became her profession. At that time hospitals were popularly regarded as little better than poorhouses; patients were neglected, and nursing was considered a disreputable calling. Indeed, most nurses themselves considered their occupation as meaningless or, at most, menial. Almost all were untrained and many were also alcoholics or prostitutes.

Although her socially ambitious mother was determined to arrange a marriage for her, Nightingale refused. After years of misery and frustration caused by family opposition to her chosen career, she was finally allowed to gain her first nursing experience with the Protestant deaconesses at Kaiserswerth, Germany, in 1851. She also trained briefly with the Sisters of St. Vincent de Paul in Paris. Firmly committed to the goal of lifting nursing into an honorable occupation for women, in 1853 she became the superintendent of a small hospital, the Institution for the Care of Sick Gentlewomen in Distressed Circumstances, on Harley Street, London.

Through study and tireless attention to detail, Nightingale made herself an expert in hospital administration. Her reorganization at Harley Street soon became widely admired. Meanwhile, in March 1854 the Crimean War erupted between Britain and France on one side and Russia on the other over Russian encroachments on Turkey. By October of that year England reverberated with reports about the appalling neglect of British soldiers wounded in the conflict. The work that Florence Nightingale had conducted at Harley Street with such success prompted a request by British war secretary Sidney Herbert that she take charge of an official plan for introducing female nurses into British army hospitals in the Crimean Peninsula. He made clear to her that if the nursing project succeeded, "an enormous amount of good will have been done now . . . a prejudice [against women in military nursing] will have been broken through and a precedent established which will multiply the good to all time."

It was a challenge that the woman who would become known as the founder of modern nursing could not refuse. She went to the front with 38 nurses and established a new type of war hospital at Scutari and Balaklava. Nightingale triumphed over bureaucratic jealousy, resentment, and intrigue, and managed to secure necessary supplies, enforce discipline, and introduce sanitary reforms into hospital buildings that were neglected, filthy, and lacking in adequate utilities. She frequently worked 20 hours at a time, making nightly inspections of the wards with a lamp in her hand. Within months of her arrival, the mortality rate among patients had been slashed. Her efforts to ease the sufferings of wounded soldiers stirred the imagination of people in all parts of the world, including poet Henry Wadsworth Longfellow, who was inspired to write "Santa Filomena" (1857), with its famous verse:

> A Lady with a Lamp shall stand
> In the great history of the land,
> A noble type of good,
> Heroic womanhood.

Upon her return to England, Nightingale deliberately sought to escape the fame that surrounded her. She intended to devote the rest of her life to the British army and studied food, housing, and sanitary conditions in military establishments at home and in India. Over time, however, she also turned to civil as well as military nursing. In July 1860, with a testimonial fund of 45,000 British pounds raised for her benefit after the war, she opened the Nightingale School and Home for training nurses at St. Thomas's Hospital, London. Professional nursing as it is known today is said to date from this time.

Nightingale was highly critical of the low repute in which nursing was held by contemporary opinion. She wrote, scathingly: "No man, not even a doctor, ever gives any other definition of what a nurse should be than this: 'devoted and obedient.' This definition would do just as well for a porter. It might even do for a horse." She also said: "It seems a commonly received idea among men, and even among women themselves, that it requires nothing but a disappointment in love, or incapacity in other things, to turn a woman into a good nurse." She insisted that the training and education of a nurse consist of two aspects of equal weight: acquisition of formal knowledge, involving a rigorous routine, and character development. So as not to perpetuate the criticism to which their calling was already subjected, her nurses were required to be beyond reproach in their personal lives as well as in their profession.

Although her health was poor after years of deprivation and overwork, Nightingale's advice was constantly sought on matters of sanitation and nursing throughout her long life. In 1907 she became the first woman to receive the British Order of Merit. By 1910—the 50th anniversary of the founding of the Nightingale training school, and the year of her death at the age of 90—over 1,000 training schools for nurses had opened in the United States alone.

May 13

Jamestown Colony Founded

On May 13, 1607, a colonizing expedition sponsored by the London Company disembarked 50 miles from the mouth of the James River and established the first permanent English settlement in America. Jamestown was not an immediate success, however. Expectations of a lucrative trade with the natives and dreams of vast gold and silver discoveries had prompted the 105 colonists (mostly disbanded soldiers and fortune hunters) to come to the New World. They were ill-prepared to cope with the malarial swamps of the region and had little interest in farming, despite the rich soil of the region.

Seventy-three settlers fell victim to famine and disease during the first seven months of Jamestown's existence. Despite this dismal beginning, the London Company (sometimes called the Virginia Company) continued to send men and supplies to the colony and these, combined with Captain John Smith's compulsory work program, saved Jamestown. The "starving time" ended in 1610. However, the introduction of tobacco by John Rolfe in 1612 was the most significant factor in improving the colony's fortunes. By 1614 the colonists were exporting their tobacco to England and the profits gained from this single product allowed Virginia to become economically self-sufficient.

To attract more settlers to Virginia, the London Company in 1619 repealed the harsh code of martial law that had been instituted in 1612. In its place the company instructed the colony's governor to call a general assembly. Twenty-two burgesses (each town, plantation, or 100 people selected two representatives) gathered in Jamestown from August 9 to 14, 1619. This first colonial legislature marked the beginning of representative government in America. Although ravaged by fire during Bacon's Rebellion in 1676, Jamestown continued to be the meeting place of the House of Burgesses and thus the capital of the Virginia until 1700, when the seat of government was moved to Williamsburg.

Mexican War Begins

The congressional declaration of war against Mexico on May 12, 1846, was the culmination of a long series of events. Primarily, the powerful and expanding American nation was eager to acquire and settle Mexico's vast but thinly populated possessions in the Southwest, which included Texas (see March 2, Texas Independence Day; and April 21, San Jacinto Day). Further, Mexico was weak militarily, had practically no industrial base, and was not under the protection of any major European power, which made it an easy target for American expansion. Finally, President James K. Polk had promised to expand American territory as much as possible, a politically popular theme at the time, and war with Mexico was an ideal opportunity.

The 1845 annexation of Texas and controversy over what constituted its southern border was what set off the war more directly. Texas, according to Texans, extended all the way south to the Rio Grande. Mexico claimed, however, that Texas extended only as far as the Nueces River.

Even in the United States, the measure for annexation was controversial. Unable to secure the two-thirds vote necessary for Senate ratification of the measure, proponents presented it as a joint congressional resolution instead. Providing for Texas to be admitted directly to statehood, the measure passed both chambers of Congress by a simple majority and was signed by President John Tyler on March 1, 1845 (see March 1), just before he left office and Polk came in. Texas became a state on December 29, 1845.

Accordingly, President Polk dispatched John Slidell on a diplomatic mission to Mexico in November 1845. Slidell's assignment was to secure Mexico's agreement on the Rio Grande as the southern boundary of Texas. If feasible, he also was to arrange the purchase of California and New Mexico, for which the United States was prepared to offer $30 million to $40 million and assumption of certain civilian legal claims against Mexico. Slidell's stay in Mexico dragged on for months while the Mexican government, under the pressure of local politics, declined to receive him. The final refusal came on March 12, 1846.

Four days earlier an American army under the command of General Zachary Taylor had begun advancing from the Nueces River, where he had been since the previous summer, to the mouth of the Rio Grande, where he arrived on March 24, 1846. Elements of Taylor's force followed the river inland to a point opposite Matamoros, where the Mexicans had assembled between 5,000 and 6,000 men. In the weeks that followed, both armies devoted themselves to building fortifications. The spark was not long in coming. On April 24 the Mexican commander sent word that, in his view, hostilities were already under way. That very day, 1,600 Mexicans crossed the Rio Grande, killed or wounded 16 members of an American reconnaissance party, and captured most of the rest. Advised of the news, President Polk delivered, with the approval of his cabinet, a war message in which he asserted that "Mexico has . . . shed American blood upon . . . American soil." Although some Americans questioned whether hostilities had begun on American or on Mexican soil, a declaration of war was passed by the House of Representatives the same day, May 11, and by the Senate the following day. Thus, the war with Mexico officially began on May 13, 1846.

Even before war had been declared officially, "Old Rough and Ready" Taylor, who became a national hero during the hostilities, had driven the Mexicans back across the Rio Grande. Taylor won victories at Palo Alto and Resaca de la Palma, in the vicinity of Matamoros. He occupied Matamoros itself on May 18 and took Monterrey on September 24. The conflict in northern Mexico ended before the winter was over with Taylor's defeat of the victor of the Alamo, General Antonio López de Santa Anna, in the battle of Buena Vista on February 22 and 23, 1847.

In the meantime, two other aspects of the war went forward. These were the United States's blockade of Mexico's east and west coast ports and the occupation of New Mexico, a vast region embracing most of what is now the American southwest, by Colonel Stephen Kearny. From New Mexico, Kearny's instructions took him with part of his force to California. On the way he learned of the "bear flag revolt" of a handful of American settlers in the Sacramento Valley. The settlers had declared California independent in June 1845 and prepared to challenge Mexico as the Texas settlers had done earlier. The adventurer Kit Carson and Captain John C. Frémont of the U.S. Army, who was in California at the time, joined forces with the rebels. On the California coast, the navy took possession of Monterey, San Francisco, and Los Angeles. In the north of California other points were occupied with little resistance. When Kearny arrived in San Diego in December 1846, he was able to proceed with setting up a provisional California government.

Back on the Mexican front, General Winfield Scott meanwhile proposed, and Polk approved, an expedition to Veracruz. When that city fell to Scott on March 29, 1847, the way was opened to victories at Cerro Gordo, Contreras, Churubusco, Molino del Rey, and the hill of Chapultepec, which dominated the capital, Mexico City. When Chapultepec was won, the American forces entered Mexico City on September 13 and 14, 1847. For all intents and purposes, the war ended several days later. Technically, however, it was concluded on February 2, 1848, with the signing of the Treaty of Guadalupe Hidalgo (see February 2). In accordance with the terms of this agreement, Mexico gave up all claim to Texas and recognized the Rio Grande as its own northern boundary. Mexico also ceded both California and New Mexico to the United States. In return the United States paid Mexico $15 million and assumed the claims of its nationals against the Mexican government.

Tulip Time Festival

This is a movable event.

The nation's fifth largest annual festival, namely the annual Tulip Time Festival, takes place in early to mid May in Holland, Michigan. By the late 1990s the festival comprised over a week's worth of activities. The city, founded by Dutch immigrants in 1846, is one of the nation's largest centers of Dutch culture.

The idea that tulips should be planted as a civic undertaking to beautify the city of Holland originated as the suggestion of Lida Rogers, a local high school biology teacher, in 1927. A hundred thousand bulbs were planted the next fall to such public acclaim that more were planted for the next year. The phrase "Tulip Time in Holland," coined for news releases describing the project, encouraged an already mounting public interest. Before long, residents found themselves searching for added festival atmosphere to go with the tulips.

The first official Tulip Time Festival followed in 1929. It has been an annual event ever since, attracting visitors by the hundreds of thousands. There are participants in authentic Dutch costumes, parades, bands, floats, traditional Dutch "Klompen" dancers with wooden shoes, baton twirling contests, and musical events.

May 14

United States Recognizes Israel

Of particular importance to American Jews is the close relationship between the United States and the nation of Israel, which began on May 14, 1948, when President Harry S. Truman officially recognized the newly created state.

The region roughly comprised by modern-day Israel (and to an extent Lebanon and Jordan) is of immense historical and religious importance. It is the "Promised Land" of the Old Testament, where Moses brought the Jews from Egypt, out of captivity. For millennia Jews of the world have regarded this region, and such important sites as the city of Jerusalem, as the center of their religion. The Middle East, however, has a history of turbulence, which shows no signs of abating. The Promised Land was conquered by a succession of invaders, including the Assyrians, Babylonians, Persians, Romans, Byzantines, Arabs, Mongols, and Turks. Later religions, namely Christianity and Islam, also developed important ties to the region. Thus, the claim of the Jews that Israel was "their" homeland has long been the subject of divisive, and often violent, controversy.

The Ottoman Empire of the Turks controlled Israel and most of the Middle East from the time of the Renaissance until the early 20th century. As Ottoman rule weakened, British influence in the region grew stronger. During World War I, the Ottomans sided with the Central Powers of Germany and Austria-Hungary, who lost to the Allies, led by Britain, France, and the United States. As a consequence, the Ottoman Empire was dismantled, and new nation-states were carved out of formerly Ottoman territory. One of these was Palestine, which in 1922 the League of Nations formally gave to the British to govern.

During World War I, Jewish leaders had lobbied the British government to establish a homeland for the Jews of the world in Palestine once the war ended. Britain was sympathetic, in part because of the influence of wealthy and powerful British Jews. An official statement in 1917, known as the Balfour Declaration, endorsed the concept of a Jewish homeland in Palestine on behalf of the British Empire (see September 21, Congress Endorses the Balfour Declaration). Jews flocked to Palestine, particularly from Germany after the Nazis rose to power in the 1930s. The Arab inhabitants of the region, fearful that the influx of Jewish settlers would displace them, began to resist. By the late 1930s there were sporadic guerrilla clashes between the Jews and the native Palestinians. Beginning in 1939, in an effort to maintain peace and order, Britain began to restrict Jewish immigration into Palestine.

Nazi persecution convinced many Jews that the creation of a homeland for the Jewish people was vital. Jews had lived in Germany for centuries, making immense contributions to German culture and economic prosperity and serving loyally in the Kaiser's armies during World War I. Even so, they had not been safe from hatred and bigotry. Many Jews felt that only a strong and independent Jewish state could protect them, and they turned their eyes toward the United States in hope of assistance, since Britain had distanced itself from their cause.

President Harry S. Truman supported the idea. He believed in the principle of national self-determination, which had been a cornerstone of President Woodrow Wilson's foreign policy during World War I. Despite resistance from some advisors, who were concerned about alienating the Arabs and creating opportunities for the Soviet Union to exploit, Truman backed the establishment of a Jewish state.

World War II had taxed the resources of the British nation heavily, so that it was no longer capable of sustaining its worldwide empire. Unable to prevent or effectively control the violent clashes that had resumed between the Jews and the Arabs in Palestine, Britain turned to the United Nations. In 1947 the United Nations General Assembly set up the Special Committee on Palestine, which recommended that British rule over Palestine be terminated and the region divided into two states. One would be Arab and the other Jewish. This attempt at compromise pleased neither the Arabs nor the Jews. Nevertheless, on November 29, 1947, the General Assembly approved the plan. The result was United Nations Resolution 181, creating a Jewish state, an Arab state, and an international "free zone" around the city of Jerusalem.

On May 14, 1948, the provisional government of the newly established Jewish state announced the new nation of Israel. That same day, President Truman recognized Israel on behalf of the United States.

The new nation was immediately plunged into war when neighboring Arab states, opposed to partition, invaded en masse to crush the fledgling Jewish homeland. Nevertheless Israel survived and even won additional territory, thanks in large part to American economic and military assistance. The United States was a loyal ally in the decades that followed as well, during which Israel endured several more wars. In return, Israel became a bastion of pro-American support in the Middle East during the difficult days of the cold war. (See related articles throughout this book.)

Antioch College Chartered

On May 14, 1852, Antioch College, located in Yellow Springs, 18 miles east of Dayton in southwestern Ohio, was chartered. It was the earliest American educational institution of first-class standing that was both nonsectarian and fully coeducational.

The idea for such a college had been broached as early as 1837 by members of the Christian Connexion, a religious body that had arisen in various eastern states at the beginning of the century. The movement to establish an innovative college began to gather momentum in 1849 under the impetus of Alpheus Marshall Merrifield, a building contractor in Worcester, Massachusetts. On May 8 and 9, 1850, an informally chosen committee on education gathered in New York to draw up plans for a college to be submitted to delegates from widely scattered Christian Connexion congregations in the United States and Canada at a national convention in October 1850 in Marion, New York. There it was resolved that "our responsibility to the community, and the advancement of our interests . . . demand of us the establishment of a College" and that "this College shall afford equal privileges to both sexes."

In recognition of the financial support of Ohio members, who contributed six times as much money as members in all the other states combined, it was decided to locate the college in that state. Yellow Springs was selected as the site, and construction of campus buildings began early in 1852. Upon its completion, Antioch Hall, designed to accommodate 1,000 students, was one of the largest buildings in Ohio. By January 26, 1852, the decision had been made to close the proposed curriculum to theological study, a step that was significant for the institution's pioneering role in nonsectarian education on the college level.

The Committee on Faculty then approached Horace Mann (see May 4) to ask whether he would accept the presidency of the new college which would admit students without regard to sex,

color, or religious affiliation. The 56-year-old Mann, who for 12 years had been secretary of the Massachusetts Board of Education, was a well-known educator and social reformer noted for furthering common school education and teacher training. He was attracted by the idea of having a free hand in developing Antioch College and commented: "It involves considerations of vast importance; not to myself merely, these I could easily dispose of; but considerations of vast importance to the rising generations of the country in whom I feel so deep an interest."

Mann was elected president of Antioch on September 17, 1852. Dedication and inauguration ceremonies took place on October 5, 1853, and a permanent board of trustees was elected on September 4 of the following year. The new college was the object of much attention. When it opened its doors in the fall of 1853, it had attracted over 1,000 applicants, most of whom were unprepared. Of the 150 students who took the required written entrance examinations, only 8 passed; others were enrolled in a related preparatory school. During Mann's six-year presidency, 40 students (nine women and 31 men) graduated from the college, while 325 other college students and over 1,500 preparatory students were directly influenced by his educational methods.

Mann was imbued with an "enthusiasm for humanity." He aimed at the individual's highest possible development and stressed that a combination of scholarship and character development would result in intellectual and spiritual freedom. To attain this end, Mann planned a curriculum modeled on the highest academic standards of the period, as practiced in the top eastern colleges. Courses in science, history, composition, literature, and modern languages were supplemented by electives in drawing, design, and music. As the president stated with pride: "In all this Great West, ours is the only institution, of a first-class character, which is not, directly or indirectly, under the influence of the old-school theology." Great stress was also placed upon hygiene, general conduct, and moral habits.

Elected president of Antioch College three times, Mann devoted the last years before his death on August 2, 1859, to fulfilling these goals and experienced perhaps greater satisfaction in his achievements than in his previous accomplishments as a lawyer, politician, and state official. As his wife, Mary Peabody Mann, wrote in a letter to her sister Sophia Peabody Hawthorne (the wife of Nathaniel Hawthorne) in 1858: "What Mr. Mann has done in these five years for five hundred or more young people is worth all the toils and labors of his life." One of his students later summarized

Mann's achievements: He established high literary and moral standards; he raised educational requirements on all levels; he demonstrated the practicality of coeducation; and he imparted the mastery of knowledge while promoting both self-reliance and improved health among students.

After the first few decades of its existence, Antioch College experienced a decline that was not arrested until the 1920s. Then, Arthur E. Morgan, an educator and noted civil engineer, was selected president of Antioch. In 1921 he began to revitalize the college by revamping the curriculum around the goal of "learning what life means and how to make the most of it." The school still has a reputation for widely divergent learning environments, cultural pluralism, individualized attention, openness to educational experimentation, and extensive training outside the classroom. In line with Horace Mann's last words to his students, "be ashamed to die until you have won some victory for humanity," the college stresses the application of knowledge to civic action.

Congress Attempts to Protect Native American Territories

The conflict between America's westward expansion and the rights of Native American tribes in the path of this expansion was always crucial. Ultimately, Native American societies were simply swept aside by the superior numbers, economic power, and military capabilities of the American settlers. During the colonial period and for some decades after the American Revolution, however, various Native American tribes were able to deal with the United States from a certain position of strength. For example, Cherokee communities thrived until the presidency of Andrew Jackson, and the Seminole in Florida defeated the United States Army on several occasions.

During the colonial era, the British sought to prevent American settlers from going beyond the Allegheny Mountains that served as a natural boundary between the 13 colonies and the interior of the North American continent. The British did not have the means to enforce this policy, however, particularly in the face of America's rapidly growing population and the influx of European immigrants. British attempts to limit trans-Allegheny settlement were in fact one of the colonial grievances that led to the American Revolution. After the Revolution, however, the independent United States inherited many of the political considerations that had led to the British policy in the first place. Native American tribes served as a buffer between the British possessions in Canada to the north and other European powers such as

France and Spain to the west and south. Further, if American settlers were to encroach on Native American lands there was the risk of frontier warfare, something that the fledgling United States wanted to avoid, for the Native American tribes were still capable of mounting significant military campaigns.

The United States was not willing to stop the settlement of the Northwest Territory won from Britain, which roughly comprises the region of modern-day states of Ohio, Illinois, and Indiana, but on May 14, 1796, the federal government decided to implement a "hands-off" policy with respect to other tribal lands along the frontier. On that date, Congress passed "an Act to regulate trade and intercourse with the Indian tribes," which made it illegal for American settlers to hunt, fish, or trap on the lands of certain tribes deemed important enough for protection. Congress, however, was just as ineffective as the British in attempting to slow down the steamroller of westward settlement and expansion. There was no effective means of policing the frontier, and the temptation to grab available land was too strong for settlers to resist.

George Lucas's Birthday

George Lucas, one of America's most famous movie directors and producers, was born on May 14, 1944, in Modesto, California. He attended Modesto Junior College and then the University of Southern California, graduating in 1966. While at USC, he produced a student film called *THX-1138*. It was a success, and became the basis for the feature-length movie *THX-1138* released in 1971.

THX-1138 was a science fiction movie, concerning life in a futuristic underground community that depersonalized human existence. When an individual seeks to escape and reach the surface of the Earth and freedom, law enforcement androids begin a deadly pursuit. The movie attracted the attention of such film industry moguls as Francis Ford Coppola, who encouraged Lucas to produce *American Graffiti* in 1973. *American Graffiti*, concerning the experiences of teenagers in the early 1960s, was a box office hit. However, Lucas's next film was an even greater hit. In 1977, 20th Century Fox released *Star Wars*, which is one of the most popular and profitable movies in history.

Star Wars also led the movie industry into the next generation of special effects. Many of these special effects were developed by Lucas's own company, Industrial Light & Magic. *Star Wars* helped initiate a wave of big-budget science fiction movies in the 1980s and 1990s, transforming the movie industry. Lucas, who has described *Star Wars* as the fourth episode in what is to be a nine-part space epic, has gone on to produce parts 5 and 6—*The Empire Strikes Back* (1980) and *Return of the Jedi* (1983)—as well as part 1, *The Phantom Menace* (1999), which he directed himself. He has also produced three films of old-time adventure: *Raiders of the Lost Ark* (1981), *Indiana Jones and the Temple of Doom* (1984), and *Indiana Jones and the Last Crusade* (1989), all directed with tongue-in-cheek panache by his friend Steven Spielberg, and all featuring Harrison Ford as a dashing archeologist.

Lewis and Clark Depart on Their Expedition

The Treaty of Paris of 1783, which established the independence of the United States, gave the fledgling nation title to all lands east of the Mississippi River. In the colonial period, settlement had extended inland only to the Allegheny Mountains, and observers thought that generations would pass before American cities and farms would border the Mississippi. Still, the citizens of the adventurous young nation not only sought to reach the river, but also dreamed of laying claim to the vast expanse between it and the Pacific Ocean. Early in 1803, President Thomas Jefferson persuaded Congress to appropriate $2,500 for an exploration of the uncharted trans-Mississippi region, and with the Louisiana Purchase of 1803 he bought from France the vast territory between the Mississippi and the Rocky Mountains.

Jefferson named Meriwether Lewis and William Clark, military men who had spent considerable time in wilderness areas, to lead an exploring party that would probe the newly acquired territory and the region beyond the Rocky Mountains. Lewis and Clark and the more than 40 soldiers and civilians with them spent the winter of 1803–1804 near what is now St. Louis, Missouri, preparing for their mission. Then, on May 14, 1804, the expedition set out on the adventure, which lasted two years and took the explorers through areas of the Northwest that hitherto had not been visited by Americans. Their historic overland journey ended in 1806 with their triumphant return to St. Louis and a world that had thought them lost forever (see the index for the related essays contained throughout this book).

May 15

Continental Congress Resolves to Put Colonies in State of Defense

On May 10, 1775, the Second Continental Congress met in Philadelphia, Pennsylvania, to coordinate the actions of the American colonies in the continuing crisis with Great Britain. News from Massachusetts of the battles of April 19 at Lexington and Concord, and allegations of atrocities committed by British troops retreating from those engagements to Boston, angered moderate delegates and drove even conservatives like John Dickinson of Pennsylvania to despair of the possibilities of reconciliation. Five days later, on May 15, the congress took an important step toward a total military rebellion against Great Britain, resolving that "these colonies be immediately put in a state of defence."

Congress advised the colonies to prepare their militia units, in which all able-bodied men between the ages of 16 and 50 were supposed to serve. The Philadelphia delegates offered a general plan for the most efficient organization of militia companies, the combination of these smaller groups into battalions and regiments, and the proper allocation of officers throughout the structure. The congressional directive granted company-size elements the power to select their own leaders, and authorized proindependence groups to appoint regimental officers on the provincial level.

In a decision of even greater importance, the Philadelphia assembly took steps to establish an intercolonial Continental army. John Adams of Massachusetts offered the forces besieging the British troops in Boston as the nucleus of the Continental army, and the congress on June 14, 1775, resolved to raise six additional companies in Pennsylvania, Maryland, and Virginia to assist in the New England operations. The delegates requested the colonies to raise specified numbers of troops and authorized them to appoint officers up to the rank of colonel.

Congress reserved for itself the power to choose generals in the Continental army and decided immediately to name a commander in chief. George Washington was the leading candidate for the post. Forty-three years of age, the Virginian had gained military experience in the French and Indian War, serving for a time as an American aide-de-camp to the ill-fated General Edward Braddock. The fact that Washington was one of the wealthiest men in America made him attractive to conservatives. In politics he was a moderate, acceptable to both radicals and conservatives. On June 15, 1775, Thomas Johnson of Maryland nominated Washington as commander in chief. John Adams, New England's radical spokesman, seconded the selection in the hope of enlisting southern support for beleaguered Massachusetts, and the delegates gave their unanimous consent.

Washington, who attended the session in his Virginia militia uniform, accepted the post. He made a modest speech to the congress and offered to serve without salary. The new commander then prepared to depart for Massachusetts to join the colonial soldiers encircling Boston, where the British troops had taken refuge. On June 17, 1775, the congress named a number of other generals, including Artemas Ward, Charles Lee, Philip Schuyler, and Israel Putnam as major generals. The delegates also designated Horatio Gates as adjutant general, James Warren of Massachusetts as paymaster general of the main army, and Jonathan Trumbull Jr. as paymaster of the forces in New York. The congress then deferred to Washington for the selection of officers for the posts of quartermaster general and commissary of artillery.

Aware of the vulnerability of the provincial legislatures to the powers of the royal governors, the congress on July 18, 1775, advised the colonies to appoint extralegal committees of safety to supervise matters relating to defense during the recesses of the colonial assemblies. The provinces quickly responded, and the committees of safety became strong bodies, which sometimes operated in arbitrary ways to obtain the cooperation of the reluctant. At the same time, the Continental Congress reminded the colonies to ensure the safety of their harbors and seacoasts.

Congress next faced the problem of raising money for the defenses. Gouverneur Morris of New York was most active in developing a plan to issue paper money, which the delegates adopted on June 22, 1775. According to the proposal, the congress was to issue not more than $2 million in bills of credit backed by Spanish milled dollars. The confederated colonies then pledged to redeem them within seven years, with each colony paying a share of the debt proportionate to the size of its population.

As subsidiary measures to secure the American military position, the congress took action to improve relations with the colonies' Canadian and Native American neighbors, to establish a post office, and to set up a military hospital. The congress on May 29, 1775, requested the "oppressed inhabitants of Canada" to extend cooperation to American efforts to preserve liberty. On July 13 the delegates appointed commissioners to secure treaties of neutrality with the tribes in the north-

ern and middle colonies, and on July 19 designated other negotiators to deal with the tribes in the south. On July 26 the congress named Benjamin Franklin postmaster general and authorized the erection of a string of stations from New England to Georgia that would offer the ways and means "for the speedy and secure conveyance of Intelligence from one end of the Continent to the other." Finally, on July 27 the assembly made provisions for a hospital establishment, including a director general and chief physician, four surgeons, one apothecary, two storekeepers, one nurse to every 10 sick, 20 surgeons' mates, and occasional laborers. Benjamin Church of Boston, who later proved to be an informer for the British, became the director-general and chief physician.

Before adjourning on August 2, 1775, the delegates issued two important declarations. Much to the distress of the radicals, the congress on July 5 adopted the Olive Branch Petition, designed by John Dickinson of Pennsylvania as a final plea for reconciliation between England and its colonies. The petition, which King George III eventually refused to receive, restated the Americans' grievances, professed the colonists' attachment to the crown, and begged that the monarch prevent further hostile action until a peaceable solution could be achieved. On July 6 the assemblage endorsed a "Declaration of the Causes and Necessity of Taking Up Arms," a statement drafted by John Dickinson and Thomas Jefferson, which rejected independence as a goal but presented the colonial point of view in the most forceful manner:

> We are reduced to the alternative of chusing an unconditional submission to the tyranny of irritated ministers, or resistance by force. The latter is our choice. We have counted the cost of this contest, and find nothing so dreadful as voluntary slavery. . . . Our cause is just. Our union is perfect. Our internal resources are great, and, if necessary, foreign assistance is undoubtedly attainable. . . . With hearts fortified with these animating reflections, we most solemnly, before God and the world, declare, that, exerting the utmost energy of those powers which our beneficent Creator hath graciously bestowed upon us, the arms we have been compelled by our enemies to assume, we will, in defiance of every hazard, with unabating firmness and perseverance, employ for the preservation of our liberties; being with one mind resolved to die freemen rather than to live slaves.

The words of this declaration were to be more prophetic than those of the Olive Branch Petition. Lexington and Concord became not isolated incidents but the first battles of the American Revolution, a protracted war between the united colonies and Great Britain. Fortunately for the Americans, the actions taken by the Second Continental Congress proved a solid foundation on which they were able to construct a lasting triumph and a new nation.

May 16

Official Apology Issued for Tuskegee Experiments

On May 16, 1997, President Bill Clinton issued a national apology for the infamous federally funded experiments at the Tuskegee Institute in Alabama. In these experiments, African American men suffering from syphilis were offered free medical care under a special government program. The unstated purpose of the program, however, was to observe and analyze the progress of the disease, in the interests of medical science; no real treatment was ever intended and none was provided. Indeed, treatment was deliberately withheld, even after an antibiotic cure had been discovered. The men were also denied basic information about their condition, which may have put their families at risk. The study, which began in 1932, continued for forty years; it was terminated after it became public knowledge in 1972. By that time most of the men were dead. Outrage over the Tuskegee experiments, which were among the most flagrant instances of racial bias and unethical behavior in American science, was an important factor in the movement to create strict guidelines for research in the future, and to make informed consent a legal necessity. Speaking for the nation on May 16, 1997, the president apologized to the men and their families, to the county and institute where the experiments had been conducted, and to the African American community as a whole. He also announced new guidelines for medical research, to be published within a year; a grant to Tuskegee University for the development of a center for the study of bioethics; and fellowships for graduate work in that field.

Armed Forces Day

This is a movable event.

To increase military efficiency and encourage interservice cooperation, Congress on July 26, 1947, approved the National Security Act. This legislation coordinated the army, navy, and air force into a single national military establishment, created the new cabinet post of secretary of defense, and consolidated the executive Departments of War and of the Navy into a single Department of Defense. In keeping with this emphasis on the unity and common purposes of the various branches of the United States military, a new day of observance, Armed Forces Day, came into existence in 1949. Armed Services Day is observed annually on the third Saturday in May.

Prior to 1949, the three branches of the armed services held elaborate observances on three separate days of the year. The army held its observance on April 6, the anniversary of American entry into World War I; the navy held its on the October 27 birth date of Theodore Roosevelt, its champion; and the air force held its on the second Saturday in September, close to the date when it was first established as a separate service on September 18, 1947. President Harry S. Truman's proclamation of 1949, initiating the third Saturday in May as Armed Forces Day, did not totally eliminate these individual celebrations. However, it did more or less reduce them to intraservice or private commemorations designed to promote the particular traditions and achievements of each of the branches of the armed forces.

Commemorations of each service unit's days of importance are generally confined to military installations, but celebrations of Armed Forces Day reach a much wider audience. Every year the president of the United States and the governors of several states issue official proclamations declaring the third Saturday in May as Armed Forces Day. Throughout the country both civilians and the military participate in the day's events. Citizens express their gratitude to the nation's millions of service members with parades, special church services, military balls, and other events. The armed forces, for their part, take the opportunity to acquaint the public with the latest military advances. Many army posts hold open houses featuring tactical and weapons displays, the navy often permits civilians to tour vessels in port, and some air force bases present demonstrations of precision flying. Often the president and highly placed members of the defense establishment are witnesses to special exhibitions of the nation's defense readiness.

May 17

Supreme Court Orders School Desegregation

History was made on May 17, 1954, when the United States Supreme Court ruled unanimously in the case of *Brown* v. *Board of Education* that racial segregation in public schools was unconstitutional. Specifically, it held that school segregation violated both the equal protection clause of the 14th Amendment and the due process clause of the Fifth Amendment. No matter how "equal" separate schools for black and white students might be, the decision held, the very quality of being separate was "inherently unequal." The new ruling overturned the Court's 1896 decision in *Plessy* v. *Ferguson* that segregated facilities, if equal, did not constitute discrimination. *Plessy* had established the famous "separate but equal" doctrine that for the next 58 years was used to justify the segregation of schools and many other facilities.

With the Court's 1954 decision, any such basis for the prolonging of segregation ceased to exist. The implications of the decision, as later spelled out through directions to lower courts and in a second *Brown* case, extended considerably beyond public schools to include public housing developments, public parks, and tax-supported colleges and universities. As attempts to flout the ruling touched off what was to become a mammoth drive for civil rights in other areas as well, the decision's indirect effects extended still further.

Opposition to the school desegregation order was initially most pronounced in the South, where it was first put into effect. Until the *Brown* case, legal segregation had prevailed throughout the South. Public places were segregated by state and local law, and the idea of desegregated public facilities of any kind ran counter to decades of custom. Moderate opinion notwithstanding, most deep South and border states devised foot-dragging tactics to thwart desegregation. In some places violence was perpetrated by segregationist extremists who also sought, by intimidation, to deprive African Americans of their right to vote. Later, however, when implementation of the school desegregation ruling began in other parts of the country, it was realized that antidesegregation sentiment was not merely a regional matter. Vocal opposition to the Supreme Court decision was also encountered in the north, midwest and west. There, school segregation, where it existed, was not a matter of law but *de facto*, resulting from widespread segregated housing patterns. Contro-versy over establishing racial balance in schools, especially if this meant busing students out of their own neighborhoods or across suburban boundary lines, was often as vociferous above the Mason-Dixon Line as below it.

The Supreme Court followed its 1954 decision with several others. One, on May 31, 1955, emphasized that the desegregation of schools must proceed "with all deliberate speed." A second, on May 27, 1963, pointedly stressed that the concept of "deliberate speed" did not countenance "indefinite delay in elimination of racial barriers in schools," and called for the prompt vindication of "plain and present constitutional rights."

Meanwhile, in September 1957, Congress had enacted the first Civil Rights Act since 1875. Important as the new act was, it seemed to intensify resistance to school desegregation. The inevitable confrontation between federal and state authority on this issue came that same month at Little Rock, Arkansas, when Governor Orval Faubus called out the state national guard to prevent nine black children from entering the previously all-white Central High School, to avert, as he declared, public disorder. When the governor defied a federal district court order to admit the children, President Dwight D. Eisenhower dispatched federal troops to ensure their enrollment.

Against this background of resistance to legally required desegregation, African Americans, who had waited a century for the equality promised them after the Civil War, were losing their patience. There began a new, widespread, and determined drive to achieve what a century of waiting had failed to provide. Although it was set in motion as an indirect result of the Supreme Court's school desegregation ruling, the goals of this broad civil rights drive extended far beyond schools to include demands for an end to discrimination in many other areas as well, among them voting, employment, and housing. Part of the effort centered around a long series of court battles, waged initially by the National Association for the Advancement of Colored People (NAACP) and subsequently also by the United States Department of Justice and others. More spectacular, however, was the wave of carefully planned nonviolent demonstrations that swept the country in the late 1950s and throughout the 1960s. They included such tactics as picketing, boycotts, mass meetings, sit-ins at segregated lunch counters and restaurants, marches, prayer meetings, voter registration drives, and the Freedom Rides in which interracial groups of travelers eventually forced the desegregation of interstate buses, trains, and waiting rooms.

One of the movement's leaders and chief spokesman was the young southern African American minister Martin Luther King Jr. (see January 20), who based his concept of love on the teachings of Jesus and his practical strategy on the tactics of nonviolent protest enunciated by Henry David Thoreau and perfected by India's Mahatma Gandhi. Support for the rights movement was interracial. It came from students, religious leaders, individuals of varied backgrounds, and civil rights organizations. The latter included the NAACP, the Urban League, King's own Southern Christian Leadership Conference, and organizations such as the Congress of Racial Equality (CORE) and the Student Nonviolent Coordinating Committee (SNCC) that later moved away from the civil rights moderates to take a more activist position.

As the rights drive progressed, laying bare the issues and bringing attention to them, the various forms of protest shifted their focus, with the name of one community after another taking its place in news headlines across the nation. Among the hundreds of demonstrations that took place, there were scores of key engagements. A few of the most crucial were the following:

(1) The successful, year-long boycott, beginning in December 1955, to desegregate the buses of Montgomery, Alabama. It was this boycott that first brought King and the civil rights movement to worldwide attention.

(2) The confrontations between state and federal power at Little Rock, Arkansas, in 1957 and at Oxford, Mississippi, in 1962, where James Meredith became the first black student to enter the University of Mississippi.

(3) The massive demonstrations at Birmingham, Alabama, in the summer of 1963. Greeted with harsh police measures, the Birmingham protests set off a nationwide chain reaction of demonstrations, including the famous March on Washington of 1963 (see January 1, Emancipation Proclamation), and did much to ensure the passage of the Civil Rights Act of 1964.

(4) The Mississippi Freedom Summer in 1964, a large-scale voter registration drive gruesomely punctuated by the murder of three young civil rights workers.

(5) The demonstrations against restrictive voter registration requirements in Alabama, begun in February 1965 at Selma, where the brutal police beatings of the demonstrators sparked nationwide indignation and ensured congressional passage of the Voting Rights Act of 1965. The upheaval at Selma was followed by a triumphant, five-day civil rights march from Selma to the state capital at Montgomery.

As for the fate of school desegregation, the original issue that had sparked the larger civil rights drive, it was in the 17 southern and border states that had required segregation by law (and another four that allowed it) that the Supreme Court's *Brown* v. *Board of Education* decision of 1954 first had effect. The Court waited until May 1955 before spelling out the principles it recommended for compliance with its historic ruling. After it did so, the District of Columbia promptly desegregated its schools, and some of the border states moved without delay to set up programs for desegregation in the gradual manner that the Court initially envisioned. Elsewhere in the region, the first reaction to the desegregation ruling was one of fierce noncompliance. After that, progress toward integration began at a snail-like pace. It was not, however, totally absent. In the 11 southern states, the percentage of black children attending school with whites crept slowly upwards from no more than 2.5 percent at the beginning of the 1964–1965 school year to approximately 7.7 percent by February 1966 and to 16 percent in 1967. Such increase as there was came with the encouragement of the Civil Rights Act of 1964 and the prodding of the federal government.

Just before the start of the school year in 1969, federal officials were forecasting that the proportion of blacks going to desegregated schools in the 11 southern states would be close to 40 percent, or double that of the previous year. Still, the pace of integration during the 15 years following *Brown* had been sluggish, and in October 1969 the Supreme Court once again underscored the ruling by handing down its emphatic "desegregate now" decision. This ruling stressed that "'all deliberate speed' for desegregation is no longer constitutionally permissible. . . . The obligation of every school district is to terminate dual school systems at once and to operate now and hereafter only unitary schools." The Court showed the following January that it meant what it said when it refused a request by certain southern school districts to temporarily postpone their scheduled desegregation.

Desegregation continued in the 1970s, accompanied by further court actions, more protests, and many unfortunate incidents of violence. Contributing to the change, and to the turmoil, was a Supreme Court ruling in April 1971 that municipalities could be required to bus pupils to schools outside the pupils' own neighborhoods, if necessary, to overcome segregation. Busing was enormously controversial, and there were many antibusing riots and protests during the 1970s. By the 1980s, however, desegregated schools had become a fact of American life. Due to the economic disparity between blacks and whites, however, most poor urban schools remain largely black and most prosperous suburban schools remain largely white. Whether this lingering *de facto* segregation will continue in the 21st century remains to be seen.

Pentecost

This is a movable event.

Pentecost (or Whitsunday, as it is commonly called in Britain) is a movable feast, celebrated on the seventh Sunday or 50th day after Easter, counting Easter as the first day. Since antiquity Pentecost has ranked among the principal feasts of the Christian Church. Its name, meaning "50th" (day), derives from the Greek language. Pentecost has a threefold significance: It commemorates the descent of the Holy Spirit upon the apostles, the assembling of the first Christian community, and the official birthday of the Christian Church. Initially, Pentecost was so intimately linked with Easter, commemorating the Resurrection of Jesus (see March 29), that the 50 days separating the two celebrations were considered one continuous season of rejoicing. The seventh Sunday after Easter was regarded as the apex of this paschal season and officially closed Eastertide. Its crucial position in the church year is evident from the fact that the pre-Reformation Christian churches generally number the Sundays following Pentecost as the first Sunday after Pentecost, the second Sunday after Pentecost, and so forth.

The story of the first Pentecost is related in detail by Luke in the second chapter of the Acts of the Apostles. Obedient to the command of Jesus, after his ascension (see May 7) which took place 40 days after the first Easter, the apostles gathered with Mary and the other disciples in Jerusalem to await the coming of the Holy Spirit. On one occasion at the close of his earthly life, Jesus had promised that he would pray to God that the "Comforter" might come to abide with them (John 14:16–17). On another occasion, he had declared: "And, behold, I send the promise of my Father upon you: but tarry ye in the city of Jerusalem, until ye be imbued with power from on high" (Luke 24:49). Uncertain of what to expect, the apostles followed their instructions, keeping a prayerful vigil in an upper room.

The 10th day of their vigil was the important Jewish feast of Shavuot. It was also known as the Feast of the First Fruits, since it was a celebration of thanksgiving for the first fruits of the wheat and barley harvest after the spring planting. Another designation it had received was the Feast of

Weeks, occurring as it did at the close of a "week of weeks" or after the seven-week harvest period, which had started on the second day of Passover (see April 21). Since the Feast of Shavout fell on the sixth day of the month of Sivan, the 50th day after the first day of Passover, the feast had gained yet another name, Pentecost. Finally, according to ancient Jewish tradition, the Feast of Shavuot was also the anniversary of Moses' receiving of the Ten Commandments, centuries before.

As the apostles were praying in one room on this highly significant Feast of Shavuot, or Pentecost, the Holy Spirit appeared to them:

> When the day of Pentecost had come, they [the followers of Jesus] were all together in one place. And suddenly a sound came from heaven like the rush of a mighty wind, and it filled all the house where they were sitting. And there appeared to them tongues as of fire, distributed and resting on each one of them. And they were all filled with the Holy Spirit and began to speak in other tongues, as the Spirit gave them utterance.

In line with Jesus' promise, "But ye shall receive power, after the Holy Spirit is come upon you: and ye shall be witnesses unto me, both in Jerusalem, and in all Judea, and in Samaria, and unto the uttermost part of the earth" (Acts 1:8), the apostles underwent a transformation. The once huddled band of frightened men became a dynamic company that bore witness to the teachings of Jesus and began to spread the Christian faith. Supposedly they received the "gift of tongues" in this missionary connection, namely the ability to speak in diverse languages. Luke recorded (Acts 2:7–8; 12–18) that the pilgrims who had come to Jerusalem for Shavuot were astonished:

> [They] marveled, saying one to another, Behold, are not all these which speak Galileans? And how hear we every man in our own tongue, wherein we were born? . . . And they were all amazed, and were in doubt, saying one to another, What meaneth this? Others mocking said, These men are full of new wine. But Peter, standing up with the eleven, lifted up his voice, and said unto them, Ye men of Judea, and all ye that dwell at Jerusalem, be this known unto you, and hearken to my words: for these are not drunken, as ye suppose, seeing it is but the third hour of the day. But this is that which was spoken by the prophet Joel; And it shall come to pass in the last days, saith God, I will pour out of my Spirit upon all flesh: and your sons and your daughters shall prophesy, and your young men shall

see visions, and your old men shall dream dreams.

Pentecost, although replete with Jewish significance, thus gained a Christian meaning independent of and yet connected with the Jewish festival. Just as the Feast of Shavuot thanked God for the first fruits of the earth, the Christian Pentecost was a feast of thanks to God for the first fruits of the Holy Spirit, procured through Jesus' death on the cross. Just as Shavuot was considered the anniversary of the bestowal of the Ten Commandments, so Pentecost became the birthday of the Christian Church. It is uncertain when Pentecost began to be observed annually by Christians, but it may have been as early as the first century A.D. As far as the term *Pentecost* is concerned, the early fathers of the church frequently referred to the whole 50-day period from Easter to Pentecost as "Pentecost." It soon became a noteworthy occasion for Christian celebration, marked with special sermons, readings, prayers, and hymns expressing the mood of thanksgiving and praise. In fact, the Council of Nicaea in A.D. 325 specifically banned any form of kneeling during the Pentecost season as evidence of too penitential an attitude and for the same reason outlawed fasting.

Norwegian Constitution Day

Norwegians, and many Americans of Norwegian descent, observe May 17 as Norwegian Constitution Day.

The Norwegian Constitution was one of the many results of the political upheaval caused by the Napoleonic Wars in the 19th century. Prior to and during the wars, Norway was joined with Denmark in the Twin Kingdoms of Denmark and Norway. The ruler of the Twin Kingdoms, Frederick VI, resided in Denmark and considered himself primarily a Danish king. His policies reflected a disregard for Norway. During the wars, Frederick allied himself with Napoléon Bonaparte against Great Britain and Sweden. This alliance caused great hardships for Norway: Its shipping was curtailed because of the British blockade of its coast, and Norway's long border with Sweden left it exposed to the constant possibility of invasion. More importantly, however, Frederick's involvement with Napoléon threatened the very existence of the Twin Kingdoms because the British, Russians, and Prussians agreed to allow Sweden to annex Norway after the French emperor's final defeat.

In October 1813 Napoléon was crushed at the battle of Leipzig, and within a few weeks the Swedes marched against Denmark to force the cession of Norway. The Swedes defeated the Danes in the region of Holstein, and on January 14, 1814, Frederick agreed to a peace. In accordance with the resulting Treaty of Kiel, Denmark ceded Norway to Sweden.

News of the Treaty of Kiel reached the Norwegian capital of Christiania (now Oslo) on January 24, 1814. The citizenry was outraged by the idea of Norway's union with its longtime enemy Sweden, and Crown Prince Frederick Christian Augustus, a cousin of King Frederick who served as his commander in chief in Norway, was reluctant to abandon his hereditary claim to the Norwegian throne. Thus, the Norwegians and the crown prince joined forces to make Norway an independent nation. Although the crown prince initially planned to proclaim himself king of an independent Norway by virtue of his hereditary claim to the Norwegian throne, he met strong resistance to such an action. Many Norwegian leaders argued that after Frederick VI renounced his rule, sovereignty returned to the people of Norway. The crown prince accepted this reasoning, and called an assembly to write a constitution for the nation. That body came together at Eidsvoll, near the capital, on April 10, 1814.

On May 17, 1814, the assembly completed its work, and on that same day the constitution was signed and Frederick Christian Augustus was chosen king. The new frame of government established a limited and hereditary monarchy and, like the United States Constitution of 1787, it provided for a division of power among the executive, legislative, and judicial branches of government. The king, together with a council of state or cabinet, was to exercise executive authority. Legislative power would rest with the National Assembly, or *Storting*. Judicial authority was to be the prerogative of the nation's courts of law. The 1814 constitution reflected liberal political thought; not only did it outline the form of the new national government, but it included guarantees of basic human and civil rights.

In theory, the Norwegian constitution established a "free, independent, indivisible and inalienable kingdom." In practice, however, the nation did not have the strength to guarantee the existence of such a government. Sweden, on the other hand, did have a powerful army, and in July 1814 its troops invaded Norway to enforce the provisions of the Treaty of Kiel. The Swedes easily defeated their weaker neighbors, and after only a few weeks of fighting the Norwegians agreed to an armistice. After months of negotiations, Norway and Sweden agreed to the Act of Union in August 1815, in which Norway "voluntarily" entered into a union with Sweden. However, the act of 1815 recognized Norway's sovereignty over its internal affairs and did not impair the guarantees of the 1814 constitution.

The union of Norway and Sweden under one king lasted until a separation was effected in 1905. Although altered numerous times during the past two centuries, the constitution of 1814 is still Norway's basic frame of government and is revered as such by her citizens. For many years, Norwegians have set aside May 17 to commemorate its adoption. In the United States, Norwegian American communities often celebrate the event as well, such as the town of Stoughton, Wisconsin, which calls itself the Norse Capital of the United States (with some justification, since 80 percent of its population is of Norwegian descent).

May 18

The Supreme Court Approves Segregation

On May 18, 1896, the United States Supreme Court handed down one of the most infamous legal decisions in American history. In *Plessy* v. *Ferguson*, the Court sanctioned segregation in the South, inaugurating an era in which African Americans would in fact be second-class citizens.

The Civil War ended slavery. After the war, the 13th, 14th, and 15th Amendments to the United States Constitution were ratified in order to guarantee the civil liberties of the newly freed slaves. The legacy of slavery, however, was not so easily eradicated. Most African Americans were poor, had never been educated, and lived as tenant farmers on land owned by whites. When Southern states were readmitted to the Union during Reconstruction, Southern whites began to reassert their power over the economically and politically vulnerable blacks. For example, in order to prevent blacks from voting, poll taxes were imposed. The tax was usually nominal, and thus affordable for whites, but sufficiently onerous for poor blacks that it effectively disenfranchised them. Other examples include literacy tests, which prevented the illiterate from voting and again impacted blacks more than whites.

By the late 19th century, southern states had also passed the first segregation laws, establishing separate schools and other public facilities for blacks and whites. The federal government made some attempts to preserve the civil rights of African Americans, but political support outside of the black community was weak. Further, there were many southerners on the Supreme Court, who in such cases as *U.S.* v. *Cruikshank* (1875) began to hobble the civil rights powers of the federal government with narrow interpretations of the Constitution and the post–Civil War amendments.

One particular southern segregation law was an 1890 Louisiana statute "that all railway companies carrying passengers in their coaches in this state shall provide equal but separate accommodations for the white and colored races. . . ." On June 7, 1892, a 30-year-old shoemaker named Homer Plessy bought a ticket for travel on the East Louisiana Railroad from New Orleans to Covington, Louisiana. Although he was seven-eighths white in ancestry, under Louisiana law Plessy was still required to sit in the "black" railroad car, and was arrested when he refused to leave the car for whites only. He was tried and convicted for violating the law.

Although the penalty was $25 or 20 days in jail, Plessy pursued his case all the way to the United States Supreme Court. In a nearly unanimous decision, the Court upheld Plessy's conviction, stating that if segregated facilities were "separate but equal" there was no constitutional violation. The Court ignored the fact that in reality separate facilities would be inherently unequal, because of the implication of racial inferiority and the lack of any practical mechanism for enforcing the "equal" portion of the equation. Only Justice John M. Harlan dissented from the Court's decision, stating that "our Constitution is color-blind, and neither knows nor tolerates classes among citizens."

After *Plessy*, segregation was constitutionally permissible for decades. Beginning in the late 1940s, however, cracks in the institution began to develop. For example, the Supreme Court held that segregated law schools were inherently unequal, since as lawyers the justices knew that the social contacts made in law school could be just as important as the quality of education in a lawyer's career. This precedent led indirectly to the landmark case of *Brown* v. *Board of Education* (1954; see the essay on May 17), which held that segregated public schools were unconstitutional. In its holding, the Court effectively overturned *Plessy* v. *Ferguson*. *Brown* was followed by other Court decisions striking down other aspects of segregation, and unlike the Reconstruction era these decisions were backed by strong federal civil rights laws. By the 1970s segregation was all but over, and *Plessy* became no more than an unfortunate historic relic.

Rhode Island Colony Acts to Prohibit Perpetual Slavery

Before January 1, 1808, when the Slave Trade Act forbidding the importation of slaves into the United States took effect, aversion to slavery was based primarily on moral and religious grounds. The Puritans and Quakers especially opposed slavery, but neither of these colonial groups developed an effective plan for abolishing it. Starting on May 18, 1652, however, the General Court of Election held at Warwick, Rhode Island, with Samuel Gorton, the founder of Warwick, as moderator, enacted during its three-day session one of the first colonial laws limiting slavery.

One of several "Acts and Orders" (which were devoted principally to a revision of practice and procedure in trial courts), the statute carefully stipulated the period in which any person, black or white, could be kept in slavery in the colony:

> Whereas, there is a common course practised amongst Englishmen to buy negers [sic], to that end that they may have them for service or slaves forever; for the preventinge of such practices among us, let it be ordered, that no blacke mankind or white [may be] forced by covenant bond, or otherwise, to serve any man or his assignes longer than ten years, or until they come to be 24 years of age, if they be taken in under 14, from the time of their coming within the Liberties of the Collonie, and at the end or terme of ten years . . . [are to be set] free, as is the manner with the English servants. And that man that will not let them goe free, or shall sell them away elsewhere, to that end that they may be enslaved to others for a long time, he or they shall forfeit to the Collonie forty pounds.

This law against perpetual slavery is judged to be, with one exception, the first legislative enactment for the suppression of involuntary servitude in the history of the United States. Previously the Massachusetts "Body of Liberties" of 1641, drawn up chiefly by Nathaniel Ward, the lawyer, clergyman, and author, had included a provision that there should "never be any bond slaverie, villinage or captivitie amongst us unles it be lawful captives taken in just warres, and such strangers as willingly selle themselves or are sold to us." In 1646 the Massachusetts general court enforced this provision by ordering that certain blacks, who had been unlawfully transported from Africa, be returned to their native land together with a letter expressing the disapproval of the court.

Although the 1652 Rhode Island statute was enforced for some time, it had either been repealed or had fallen into disuse by the beginning of the 18th century. A Rhode Island act in February 1708 recognized perpetual slavery, placing a duty of three English pounds on all blacks imported. From 1700 onwards, Rhode Island citizens engaged to a greater and greater extent in the flourishing slave-carrying trade. Although they did not import many slaves for their own use, the Rhode Islanders became the greatest slave traders in the American colonies, operating a sort of clearinghouse for other areas. Only in 1779 did Rhode Island pass an act preventing the sale of slaves out of the state. In 1784, eight years after the Declaration of Independence, Rhode Island's legislature approved a law to gradually abolish slavery in the state. Three years later an act prohibiting participation in the slave trade finally set a fine of 1,000 pounds on every vessel caught in such a venture and 100 pounds on each slave transported.

May 19

Malcolm X's Birthday

Malcolm X was born as Malcolm Little in Omaha, Nebraska, on May 19, 1925. His father, the Reverend Earl Little, was a Baptist minister who was active in Marcus Garvey's Universal Negro Improvement Association. As an outspoken civil rights activist, Little became a target for white racism, and was murdered after receiving death threats from the Ku Klux Klan.

At the time of his father's murder in 1931, young Malcolm Little was only six years old. After his mother suffered a nervous breakdown, Malcolm lived in a foster home, a reform school, and with a variety of relatives. He dropped out of school at the age of 15, and began a life of crime. He made money in drugs and prostitution, and was eventually arrested and prosecuted for burglary. In 1946 he was sent to prison in Charlestown, Massachusetts.

During his six years in prison, Malcolm became acquainted with the black Muslim movement known as the Nation of Islam. He learned about the teachings of the Honorable Elijah Muhammad from another inmate and became a convert in 1947. Malcolm began to educate himself and corresponded with Muhammad himself, who took an interest in Malcolm's situation. After his release from prison in 1952, Malcolm Little became Malcolm X and went to Detroit, Michigan, in order to work at Muhammad's side.

Malcolm X became the foremost spokesman for the Nation of Islam. He was intelligent and articulate. The sincerity of his conversion was evident from the passion of his speeches. In a day and age when segregation was still accepted as normal, Malcolm insisted on nothing less than complete freedom for African Americans and heaped derision on those who pointed to the first tentative gains in the civil rights movement as evidence of progress. Malcolm was also successful in bringing more converts to the Nation of Islam. Most of the

William Bradford's Death

converts were from northern urban communities, however, and the majority of the African American community preferred to remain Christian no matter how much they sympathized with Malcolm X's stance on civil rights.

In 1958 Malcolm married Sister Betty X. She was also a member of the Nation of Islam. The couple would eventually have six children.

A rift developed between Malcolm X and the Nation of Islam in 1963. Now one of the organization's most prominent spokesmen, Malcolm X was severely criticized for certain comments that he made after President John F. Kennedy was assassinated. Specifically, Malcolm stated that the assassination was the white man's "chickens coming home to roost." This comment caused Muhammad to suspend Malcolm from the Nation of Islam on December 4, 1963. Malcolm also claimed to have found evidence of various sexual improprieties committed by Muhammad, and by March 1964 the split between the two men was so great that Malcolm decided to start his own Muslim organization.

Malcolm X created the Muslim Mosque, his own personal ministry. On April 22, 1964, he went on a pilgrimage to Mecca in Saudi Arabia. Such a visit to Islam's holiest city is called a *hajj*, and is required by the Qur'an (Islam's foremost holy book) for all true Muslims at least once in their lifetime. During that pilgrimage, Malcolm X became acquainted with a variety of other Muslims, many of whom were white. After having seen how Islam had cut across racial barriers, Malcolm X returned to the United States and began to speak out in favor of racial conciliation. He also took a new name El-Hajj Malik al-Shabazz. Most people, then and now, nevertheless continue to refer to him as Malcolm X. On June 28, 1964, Malcolm formed the Organization of Afro-American Unity.

Malcolm X was assassinated by three gunmen on February 21, 1965, while making a speech in the Audubon Ballroom in New York City. Many people believed that the Nation of Islam was involved in the assassination, but this suspicion has never been conclusively proven. Together with Martin Luther King Jr., Malcolm X is regarded as one of the foremost African American civil rights leaders of the 1960s. Although Malcolm X preferred a more militant approach to achieving equality, before he died he came to appreciate King's philosophy of nonviolence and became less critical of other mainstream (and Christian) African American civil rights leaders.

William Bradford, the governor of Plymouth colony and historian of the Pilgrims, was probably born in March 1590, at Austerfield in the English county of Yorkshire. He was only a year old when his father died, leaving the boy's rearing, as a farmer, to his uncles and grandfather. When he was 12, Bradford first read the Scriptures. At Scrooby in Nottinghamshire, he ignored the counsel of friends in order to attend meetings of a dissident religious sect, the Separatists, in the home of Elder William Brewster. The group, which favored separation from the "pudle of corruption"—the established Church of England—was the target of local persecution and also felt the wrath of King James I, who warned the Separatists to conform or be harried out of the land. Under the leadership of Elder Brewster and pastor John Robinson, members of the Scrooby congregation fled to a tolerant Holland in 1608. Bradford, who was not more than 19 at the time, went with them, first to Amsterdam and a year later to Leyden, where he was apprenticed to a silk manufacturer. Despite his relative youthfulness, he became a leader of the group.

Although the congregation's membership tripled in exile, life was economically hard for its members, their children were increasingly "Dutchified," and the group lacked the kind of autonomy best suited to the unhampered carrying out of its religious ideals. By 1617, with the prodding of Bradford and others, a number of members had determined to move to the New World. Lengthy negotiations brought forth the offer of financial backing by London merchants, a charter from the Virginia Company of London, and a proposal that the Separatists form a joint-stock company to set up a trading post in America. Bradford and Brewster were among the 35 who accepted the offer. With 67 Londoners (most of them probably not Separatists), they boarded the *Mayflower* at Plymouth, England, and set sail on September 16, 1620. Contrary to their plans, they dropped anchor outside Virginia Company jurisdiction, and consequently outside the legal provisions of their patent, in the harbor of what is now Provincetown, Massachusetts, on November 21, 1620. Before landing, they drew up the Mayflower Compact, which became one of the written landmarks of democracy. It was designed, according to Bradford's account, to prevent the defection of certain restless souls who threatened to strike out on their own when they found themselves in a legal no-man's-land.

Bradford, who was among the 41 adult males who had signed the compact, was also among those who set out by small boat to find a spot that might prove more "fitt for situation" than Provincetown's barren sand dunes. The die was cast when they sighted Plymouth, across Cape Cod Bay, on December 21, 1620, and returned to Provincetown for the rest of the voyagers, who have been referred to as Pilgrims ever since their permanent settlement at Plymouth.

The discovery of what was variously known as Plymouth, New Plymouth, and Plimoth Plantation as a suitable place for habitation was preceded by tragedy. While Bradford helped choose a permanent site, his wife Dorothy May drowned in Cape Cod Bay on December 17. It was the beginning of the tragedies that filled the Pilgrims' first winter. Their "victuals being much spente" in the course of their ocean voyage, their struggle to build houses and find food at Plymouth was made more difficult by exposure, pneumonia, tuberculosis, and scurvy. Over half the group died during the first few years. Bradford himself was seriously ill but recovered, fortunately for the surviving colonists, who unanimously elected him governor after the death of Governor John Carver in 1621.

Although he pressed for rotation of the office, Bradford, who exercised wide governmental and religious authority in the settlement's early years, was reelected governor for all but five of the next 35 years. Under his prudent guidance, fortified by the judicious advice of Elder Brewster, the colony became politically and economically sound. One of the governor's early acts was the signing of a treaty with neighboring native tribes, who instructed the colonists in cultivation and partook with them of the first American Thanksgiving feast in the fall of 1621. The colony was put on a sounder legal footing the same year, when it obtained a charter from the New England Council. In 1623 Bradford put an end to the communal land system first employed and granted each male colonist an acre as his own. A plentiful harvest followed and the settlers subsequently also found some small profit in the fur trade. By 1627 Bradford and the other Pilgrim fathers were able to buy out the London merchants who had financed their expedition, thus severing their financial connection with England. Although it was his purpose to maintain Plymouth as a separate and independent colony, Bradford cooperated with other colonies in such enterprises as the war against the Pequot tribe and was four times a delegate to, and twice president of, the New England Confederation (a military alliance of Plymouth with the colonies of Massachusetts Bay, Connecticut, and New Haven).

A self-taught man, Bradford was skilled in several languages and possessed a simple and direct prose style. The most notable of his several writings, *History of Plymouth Plantation, 1620–1647*, is among the major literary accomplishments of his day. Although the manuscript was completed in 1651, six years before Bradford's death at Plymouth on May 19, 1657, it was not published in full until 1856, after its discovery in London following a long disappearance.

Although the Plymouth colony, which sent out offshoots in the form of neighboring towns, grew to include a sizable area, it was eventually overshadowed by the Massachusetts Bay Colony, by which it was absorbed in 1691. Plymouth nevertheless retains historical significance as the second permanent English settlement in America; and Bradford as its historian and leading statesman.

Formation of the New England Confederation

On May 19, 1643, delegates from Massachusetts Bay, Plymouth, New Haven, and Connecticut met at Boston and adopted the 12 articles of the New England Confederation "for mutual safety and welfare." In so doing they reacted to the precariousness of life in the frontier settlements. From 1636 to 1637, for instance, war with the Pequot tribe of Connecticut had brought tremendous suffering and bloodshed to the colonists. The tribes on whose lands they encroached were not the only problem of the colonists, who were equally threatened by the expansion of the Dutch and French into territory claimed by the English.

The individual colonies could not safely stand alone against such obstacles. Thus, the common danger posed by the Dutch, French, and Native Americans drove them to form the first intercolonial union. Under their written agreement, each colony through its general court annually chose two church members to be delegates to the New England Confederation. The confederation had no control over the internal affairs of any colony, but the consent of six of the eight commissioners was sufficient to determine matters of intercolonial concern. Their jurisdiction included declarations of both offensive and defensive wars, apportionment of defense expenses, supervision of relations with the tribes, and approval of foreign treaties.

Despite its seemingly great powers, the confederation could not prevent the New Haven colony from being absorbed by Connecticut when King Charles II of Britain granted the latter colony its charter in 1662. This failure cost the confederation much prestige, but its fortunes revived during

King Philip's War from 1675 to 1676. In that time of grave danger, the confederation successfully coordinated the colonists' efforts against the hostile Wampanoag tribe. However, Massachusetts' attempts to dominate the organization after the Native American crisis caused bitter feelings, and the confederation was dissolved in 1684. This was shortly after England had revoked the charter of the Massachusetts Bay Colony, whose theocratic government had always been reluctant to recognize its dependency on the mother country and had often resorted to foot-dragging and evasion to avoid compliance with British policy. The necessity for replacing the charter with some other form of royal control prompted Britain to try out in New England a long-contemplated plan for improving colonial administration by consolidating the colonies into a few large provinces. With others, the same colonies that had participated in the New England Confederation were thus again united, but in a less voluntary way under the Dominion of New England established in 1686.

The dominion, at first set up on a temporary basis under a New Englander named Joseph Dudley, became a more formal unit with the arrival of Sir Edmund Andros in December of 1686. Commissioned by King James II as governor of the Dominion of New England, Andros ruled an extensive area that ultimately included the colonies or regions of Massachusetts Bay, Plymouth, Maine, New Hampshire, Rhode Island, and Connecticut, to which were added New York and New Jersey. A tactless man, strict in enforcement of unwelcome edicts, and overzealous (the colonists thought) in his royalist administration, Andros was arrested and sent back to England by Boston Puritans when they learned in April 1689 that James II had been deposed. Under these circumstances, the Dominion of New England came to an abrupt end, and no further plans were put forward for consolidating the colonies.

May 20

Dolley Madison's Birthday

Dolley (commonly but incorrectly called "Dolly") Madison, wife of James Madison, the fourth president of the United States, has become legendary as the outstanding hostess of the early American presidencies and as one of the best loved American first ladies. She was born Dorothea Dandridge Payne on May 20, 1768, in what is now Guilford County, North Carolina, where her Virginian parents were spending a year with an uncle. She was the eldest daughter of John Payne and Mary Coles Payne, a cousin of Patrick Henry.

Dolley Madison

The family returned to Virginia while she was still an infant and lived at Scotchtown in Hanover County until she was 15. Probably one of the oldest plantation houses in Virginia, built around 1719, Scotchtown had belonged to Patrick Henry from 1771 to 1778. Coming conscientiously to abhor slavery, John Payne, a Quaker, freed his slaves in 1783. He moved to Philadelphia, Pennsylvania, where he engaged unsuccessfully in business. After his death in 1792, his widow supported herself by keeping a boardinghouse for men in Philadelphia.

On January 7, 1790, at the age of 21, Dolley Payne married John Todd Jr., a lawyer of the city and a member of the Quaker Society of Friends, to which her own family also belonged. In 1791 the Todds purchased a house on the corner of Fourth and Walnut Streets near Independence Hall in Philadelphia. Dolley Todd and her husband had two sons, but only John Payne Todd, born on February 29, 1792, lived to maturity. His father and brother were less fortunate. The elder John Todd died on October 24, 1793, during a yellow fever epidemic that killed between 4,000 to 5,000 people, roughly one-tenth the population of Philadelphia. Their second infant son died a few hours afterwards. After her husband's death, young Dolley Todd and her surviving son lived with her mother in Philadelphia.

Dolley Todd was introduced to James Madison by Aaron Burr, then a senator. Madison was in Philadelphia as a representative to Congress from Virginia. On September 15, 1794, the 43-year-old bachelor, famous for his work in drafting the United States Constitution and in arguing for its adoption, married Dolley Todd at the home of her sister, Mrs. George Steptoe Washington, at Harewood in Jefferson County, Virginia (now part of West Virginia). By a twist of fate years later, this sister, the then-widowed Lucy Payne Washington, was to remarry in the Madisons' home at the White House. It would be the first White House wedding, held on March 29, 1812, and Dolley Madison was hostess.

It has been said that Dolley Todd accepted Madison's marriage proposal even though he was 17 years older and an inch shorter, and had been rejected by at least one other woman. Blue-eyed, black-haired Dolley Madison complemented her frail, scholarly husband well, and they were apparently very happy together during their 41 years of marriage. Her warmth, charm, and great gifts as a hostess assisted him in politics. In the following decades she became the toast of Washington, D.C., through her natural friendliness, her keen memory of persons and their interests, and her unfailing tact.

When President Thomas Jefferson appointed James Madison secretary of state in 1801, Dolley Madison moved into the center of the social life of the capital, and there she continued for the next 16 years. As Jefferson was a widower, he often invited the gracious, capable Dolley Madison to act as his official hostess at the White House. She helped create the Jeffersonian style of hospitality, cutting back the earlier pomp of entertainment under George Washington and John Adams but generously drawing together the most interesting people in the capital for conversation with the president. By her own presence and style, Dolley Madison helped to lend social grace to Jefferson's administration.

In 1809, when her husband became president, Dolley Madison followed Jefferson's taste in furnishing the White House and entertaining in a manner more Continental than English. However, presidential entertaining became more elaborate under the Madisons. She was, for example, hostess at the first inaugural ball, which was held in Long's Hotel on Capitol Hill on January 20. All personal additions that the Madisons made to the White House, however, were destroyed when the British burned the mansion on August 24, 1814. Instructed by her husband to flee the advancing army, Dolley Madison waited stubbornly until the very last minute to leave. She is famous for having saved a carriage-full of state papers and for insisting that Gilbert Stuart's portrait of George Washington be removed from its frame and rescued. This painting now hangs in the East Room of the White House and is the one object saved from President Adams's time. The Madisons lived out their second term in private residences while the mansion was being reconstructed.

When Madison's term expired in 1817, Dolley Madison went with him to Montpelier, his estate in Orange County, Virginia, and presided gracefully over his house and his plantation until his death in 1836. Earlier she had helped him enlarge Montpelier following Jefferson's suggestions for a stately portico.

Immediately after her husband's death, Dolley Madison devoted herself to preparing his manuscript of the debates in the Constitutional Convention (1787) for publication. This was bought by the United States government under President Andrew Jackson. In 1837, nearly 70, she returned to Washington with her adopted niece Anna Payne, and again became a noted and respected social figure, though privately her last years were troubled by financial difficulties and the waywardness of her son. In 1844 Dolley Madison's appearance in the visitor's gallery of the House of Representatives evoked a motion, which passed unanimously, to grant her an honorary seat in the House. Her last public appearance was at a reception in the White House in February 1849, when she passed through the rooms on the arm of President James K. Polk. She died on July 12, 1849, at the age of 81.

Some years later, her grandniece Lucia B. Cutts published a selection of Dolley Madison's private letters, with biographical introductions, as *Memoirs and Letters of Dolly Madison, Wife of James Madison, President of the United States*. The volume has been mistakenly referred to as Dolley Madison's "diary," in the same genre as *A White House Diary* (1970) by Lady Bird Johnson, wife of President Lyndon B. Johnson. Actually, Dolley Madison's letters were written, as her editor says, "without the most remote idea of publication" over a period of 50 years.

Mecklenburg Independence Day

May 20 in North Carolina commemorates the alleged adoption of the Mecklenburg Declaration of Independence on this date in 1775. A popular tradition holds that Colonel Thomas Polk, commander of the Mecklenburg County militia, after consulting community leaders, ordered each company of citizen soldiers to select two delegates to attend a convention in Charlotte. They reportedly met on

May 19, 1775, with the intention of setting up a local government, as the British government had declared the colonies to be in a state of rebellion.
During the debates, the story continues, a messenger arrived with news that the colonials had fought
battles against the British at Lexington and Concord in Massachusetts the previous month.
Aroused by this news, many delegates reportedly
brought far-reaching resolutions before the convention. At 2:00 a.m. on May 20, 1775, according
to the legend, the delegates adopted the Mecklenburg Declaration of Independence.

Many historians doubt this account, however,
and there is strong evidence to support the belief
that the declaration is, in the words of Thomas Jefferson, a "spurious document." The actual course
of events in North Carolina in May 1775 seems to
have been as follows:

On May 31 a convention met in Mecklenburg
County and passed a series of resolutions that "an-
nulled and vacated all civil and military commissions granted by the Crown." The delegates further pledged that "until Parliament should resign
its arbitrary pretensions" the provincial congress
would exercise all legislative and executive powers
within the colony. These bold resolves were then
sent to the North Carolina delegation at the Second Continental Congress then meeting in Philadelphia, but they were never presented to the
Philadelphia gathering.

Much to the Mecklenburg colonials' chagrin,
the first accounts of the American revolution
passed over the proceedings of May 31, 1775, in
silence. Those who had participated in the convention would not be so easily ignored, however,
and in the following decades they used every
means to make certain that they were accorded an
honored place. After a fire in 1800 destroyed the
records of the Mecklenburg Convention, North
Carolina's one-time revolutionaries, who became
further and further removed from the facts as time
went on, had to rely on their recollections to prove
their case. On April 30, 1819, the *Raleigh Register*
published what Joseph Graham, one of the delegates, remembered to have been the Mecklenburg
Declaration of Independence of May 20, 1775.
Events that had taken place over a period of many
months, 44 years earlier, blended into a single experience in Graham's fading memory and he em-
bellished the substance of the convention's resolves with the immortal phrases of Thomas Jefferson's Declaration of Independence.

The genuineness of the so-called Mecklenburg
Declaration of Independence was widely accepted
until the discovery in 1847 of a Charleston newspaper of June 16, 1775, containing the proceedings of the Mecklenburg Convention. The old

newspaper challenged the authenticity of the
Mecklenburg Declaration of Independence for
two serious reasons: It proved that the delegates
had met on May 31 rather than May 20; and in setting forth the full text of the resolutions it showed
that they contained no mention of "independence."

Even though the North Carolina colonialists
may not have been the first to call for independence, the action of Mecklenburg County marked
an important step on the road to the American
Revolution. The resolves of May 1775, bearing as
they do the unmistakable stamp of rebellion, still
merit the attention of historians of the period.

May 21

Lindbergh Lands in Paris

Setting out on May 20, 1927, Charles Augustus
Lindbergh flew nonstop from New York to Paris
to win a $25,000 prize offered for the first success-
ful flight of this kind across the Atlantic. Taking off
from Roosevelt Field on Long Island, New York,
he covered 3,610 miles in 33 and one half hours,
landing the next day at Le Bourget airfield just
outside Paris.

Lindbergh, only 25 years old, caught the imagination of millions of people around the world. At
Le Bourget, he escaped being mobbed by wildly
cheering crowds when they mistakenly carried off
someone else. The French government made him
a Chevalier of the Legion of Honor. He was also
welcomed in Brussels and London before his triumphant return to the United States.

Lindbergh's interest in flying had developed
early in life. Born in Detroit on February 4, 1902,
he grew up in Little Falls, Minnesota, and in
Washington, D.C., where his father represented
Minnesota's sixth district in Congress. Young
Lindbergh attended the University of Wisconsin
at Madison, but gave up his studies after less than
two years there in order to study flying. He soloed
in 1923, and enlisted in the United States Air Service Reserve in 1924. In 1926 he became an air-
mail pilot. When the prize for a nonstop flight to
Paris was offered by a French American philanthropist named Raymond Orteig, Lindbergh went
to San Diego, California, to supervise the construction of a custom- designed monoplane with
the financial backing of several St. Louis businessmen. The plane was appropriately named *Spirit of
St. Louis*. On May 10, 1927, Lindbergh flew the
aircraft from San Diego, via St. Louis, Missouri, to
New York in a record-breaking 21 hours and 20
minutes.

Although it is often remembered as such, Lindbergh's solo trip to Paris was not the first nonstop transatlantic flight. That record is held by the British aviators Captain John Alcock and Lieutenant Arthur Whitten Brown, who flew from Newfoundland to Ireland in June 1919. However, Lindbergh's was the first transatlantic solo flight, and it is he who was best remembered. Lindbergh's honors upon returning home began with a Broadway parade and the award of both a Congressional Medal of Honor and the first Distinguished Flying Cross. In 1928 he received the Woodrow Wilson Award for Distinguished Service.

Lindbergh actively contributed to the progress of early aviation. Apart from flying the goodwill tours to many countries, which served to intensify interest in the future of flying, he served as a technical adviser to the aeronautics branch of the United States Department of Commerce and also to private airlines, personally pioneering many of their routes in the early days of commercial flying. His career also influenced the development of military aviation. Among other things, Lindbergh helped the visionary work of the little-known rocket pioneer Robert H. Goddard, obtaining financial backing for the man who was mercilessly taunted for his talk of sending men to the Moon in giant rockets. In the 1930s Lindbergh also worked with the surgeon and biologist Alexis Carrel on the construction of a perfusion pump, or mechanical heart, used experimentally to keep organs alive outside the body.

Lindbergh's personal life was always marked by his modesty and desire for privacy, particularly after he and his wife, Anne Morrow Lindbergh, endured the harrowing press exposure that surrounded the kidnapping and murder of their young son and the ensuing sensational murder trial in the early 1930s. To escape publicity they lived for a time in Europe before returning to the United States in 1939.

Despite a flurry of unpopularity occasioned by his strong support of an isolationist foreign policy during the early days of World War II, Lindbergh quietly threw himself into the Allied effort once the United States entered the war, contributing significantly to the aviation advances of the time. He served as a consultant to aircraft manufacturers and in this capacity also flew combat missions in the Pacific. He also acted as a civilian consultant to the military. In the early postwar period, he went to Europe with a navy technical mission to look into Germany's wartime aviation advances. Until 1941, and beginning again in 1954, he held reserve commissions in the Army Air Corps and its successor, the air force. His writings include *We*, published in 1929, and *The Spirit of St. Louis*,

which won him a Pulitzer Prize after its publication in 1953. Some of Anne Lindbergh's books, such as *North to the Orient* (1935) and *Listen! The Wind* (1938), describe their flights together. Charles Lindbergh died on August 26, 1974.

May 22

National Maritime Day

National Maritime Day, observed annually on May 22, commemorates the contribution of commercial shipping to the prosperity of the United States. Seafaring people discovered and settled the nation, and their descendants have maintained a continuing interest in transoceanic trade. From the clipper ships of the 19th century to modern times, Americans have helped lead the way in the faster and safer transportation of vital and valuable cargoes.

Appropriately, the celebration of National Maritime Day occurs on May 22, the anniversary of the 1819 sailing of the *Savannah*, the first steam-propelled vessel to attempt a transatlantic crossing. Owned by a Georgia steamboat company, the *Savannah* was constructed at the Corlears Hook shipyard in New York. Nothing was left to chance; the vessel was fitted out with both a steam engine and sails. It left New York on March 8, 1819, and after eight and a half days at sea arrived in its home port of Savannah, Georgia.

In actuality, the *Savannah* had been built for use in the coastal trade between New York and Georgia, but the Panic of 1819 so depressed the nation's commerce that its owners were forced to abandon their original plan. They decided instead to sell their ship abroad and scheduled it to sail on May 20, 1819. The accidental drowning of one of the crewmen delayed the *Savannah*'s departure until May 22, when it left port laden with only the 1,500 bushels of coal and the 25 cords of wood necessary to power the engine across the Atlantic. Advertisements in a local newspaper announcing the voyage had attracted neither passengers nor cargo.

The *Savannah* crossed the Atlantic with ease, but the first use of steam on a transatlantic voyage resulted in one amusing incident. Authorities at the naval station at Cape Clear in Ireland sighted large amounts of smoke billowing from the *Savannah* and, not knowing of its steam engine, they concluded it was on fire. They dispatched a royal cutter, the *Kite*, to her assistance and the English sail craft chased the American ship for almost an entire day before it was realized that a steam engine and not an uncontrolled fire was responsible for the smoke clouds.

After 29 days at sea, the *Savannah* arrived in Liverpool, England, on June 20. Sailing vessels had crossed the Atlantic in less time, and according to her log the *Savannah* had used the steam engine for only about 90 hours of the voyage. However, the novelty of using steam during a transoceanic passage attracted great attention in Liverpool. People crowded at the waterfront to greet the American craft, and during the 25 days that it remained in the English port many people went aboard the *Savannah*. At least part of their excitement and curiosity, however, was caused by unfounded rumors that the ship might attempt to win the large reward offered by Jerome Bonaparte for rescuing his brother, Napoléon Bonaparte, from St. Helena.

From England, the *Savannah* went to Stockholm, Sweden. Despite the eagerness of the Swedish king to purchase the ship, a satisfactory financial agreement could not be reached in Stockholm, and so the *Savannah* set out for St. Petersburg, Russia, on September 5, 1819. The Russian government had previously expressed interest in acquiring a steam vessel, but even though the czar himself may have gone on a short excursion aboard the American ship, no sale was made.

On October 10, 1819, the *Savannah* began its trip back to the United States. Since the high cost of coal in Europe made the use of its engine too expensive, it relied entirely upon the sails during the return passage, and not until it reached the mouth of the Savannah River was the engine fired. The arrival home on November 30 attracted little attention. After sustaining large fire losses in January 1820, the owners of the *Savannah* were forced to sell their ship at auction. Its engine was removed, and the ship was put in service as a coastal sailing packet. It was wrecked during a storm off Long Island in November 1821.

Short as its existence was, the *Savannah* has a just claim to fame as the first vessel to use steam to cross the Atlantic. Recognition of the importance of the 1819 voyage in the history of the merchant marine was accorded in 1962 when the world's first nuclear-powered merchant ship, built as a joint project of the United States Maritime Commission and the Atomic Energy Commission, was named the NS *Savannah*. The greatest acknowledgment of the *Savannah*'s accomplishment, however, was the choice of May 22, the date of the beginning of her transoceanic passage, for the observance of National Maritime Day. In accordance with a joint resolution of Congress, President Franklin D. Roosevelt issued the first proclamation designating May 22 as National Maritime Day in 1933. In honor of the contributions of the merchant marine to America, the president called

upon the citizens of the United States to fly the flag on their homes and ordered government officials to display the national banner on all federal buildings. The president of the United States still issues a proclamation designating the observance every year.

President Lyndon Johnson Promotes the "Great Society"

See also August 27, Lyndon B. Johnson's Birthday.

During his administration in the 1960s, President Lyndon Johnson pushed a variety of social programs and civic initiatives through Congress. He gave the label "Great Society" to his package of legislation, just as Franklin D. Roosevelt had his "New Deal." On May 22, 1964, President Johnson gave a speech that announced his Great Society ideas, and set forth the proposals that his administration planned to pursue through the 1960s. Relevant excerpts from the famous "Great Society" speech are set forth below.

The purpose of protecting the life of our Nation and preserving the liberty of our citizens is to pursue the happiness of our people. Our success in that pursuit is the test of our success as a Nation. For a century we labored to settle and to subdue a continent. For half a century we called upon unbounded invention and untiring industry to create an order of plenty for all of our people. The challenge of the next half century is whether we have the wisdom to use that wealth to enrich and elevate our national life, and to advance the quality of our American civilization.

Your imagination, your initiative, and your indignation will determine whether we build a society where progress is the servant of our needs, or a society where old values and new visions are buried under unbridled growth. For in your time we have the opportunity to move not only toward the rich society and the powerful society, but upward to the Great Society.

The Great Society rests on abundance and liberty for all. It demands an end to poverty and racial injustice, to which we are totally committed in our time. But that is just the beginning. The Great Society is a place where every child can find knowledge to enrich his mind and to enlarge his talents. It is a place where leisure is a welcome chance to build and reflect, not a feared cause of boredom and restlessness. It is a place where the city of man serves not only the needs of the body and the demands of commerce but the desire for beauty and the hunger for community.

It is a place where man can renew contact with nature. It is a place which honors creation for its own sake and for what it adds to the understanding of the race. It is a place where men are more concerned with the quality of their goals than the quantity of their goods. But most of all, the Great Society is not a safe harbor, a resting place, a final objective, a finished work. It is a challenge constantly renewed, beckoning us toward a destiny where the meaning of our lives matches the marvelous products of our labor.

So I want to talk to you today about three places where we begin to build the Great Society; in our cities, in our countryside, and in our classrooms. Many of you will live to see the day, perhaps 50 years from now, when there will be 400 million Americans, four-fifths of them in urban areas. In the remainder of this century urban population will double, city land will double, and we will have to build homes, highways and facilities equal to all those built since this country was first settled. So in the next 40 years we must rebuild the entire urban United States.

Aristotle said: "Men come together in cities in order to live, but they remain together in order to live the good life." It is harder and harder to live the good life in American cities today. The catalog of ills is long: There is the decay of the centers and the despoiling of the suburbs. There is not enough housing for our people or transportation for our traffic. Open land is vanishing and old landmarks are violated. Worst of all, expansion is eroding the precious and time honored values of community with neighbors and communion with nature. The loss of these values breeds loneliness and boredom and indifference.

Our society will never be great until our cities are great. Today the frontier of imagination and innovation is inside those cities and not beyond their borders. New experiments are already going on. It will be the task of your generation to make the American city a place where future generations will come, not only to live but to live the good life.

A second place where we begin to build the Great Society is in our countryside. We have always prided ourselves on being not only America the strong and America the free, but America the beautiful. Today that beauty is in danger. The water we drink, the food we eat, the very air that we breathe, are threatened with pollution. Our parks are overcrowded, our seashores overburdened. Green fields and dense forests are disappearing. A few years ago we were greatly concerned about the "Ugly American." Today we must act to prevent an ugly America. For once the battle is lost, once our natural splendor is destroyed, it can never be recaptured. And once man can no longer walk with beauty or wonder at nature his spirit will wither and his sustenance be wasted.

A third place to build the Great Society is in the classrooms of America. There your children's lives will be shaped. Our society will not be great until every young mind is set free to scan the farthest reaches of thought and imagination. We are still far from that goal. Today, eight million adult Americans, more than the entire population of Michigan, have not finished five years of school. Nearly twenty million have not finished eight years of school. Nearly 54 million, nearly more than one-quarter of all America, have not even finished high school. Each year more than 100,000 high school graduates, with proved ability, do not enter college because they cannot afford it. And if we cannot educate today's youth, what will we do in 1970 when elementary school enrollment will be 5 million greater than 1960?

In many places, classrooms are overcrowded and curricula are outdated. Most of our qualified teachers are underpaid, and many of our paid teachers are unqualified. So we must give every child a place to sit and a teacher to learn from. Poverty must not be a bar to learning, and learning must offer an escape from poverty. But more classrooms and more teachers are not enough. We must seek an educational system which grows in excellence as it grows in size. This means better training for our teachers. It means preparing youth to enjoy their hours of leisure as well as their hours of labor. It means exploring new techniques of teaching, to find new ways to stimulate the love of learning and the capacity for creation.

These are three of the central issues of the Great Society. While our Government has many programs directed at those issues, I do not pretend that we have the full answer to those problems. But I do promise this: We are going to assemble the best thought and the broadest knowledge from all over the world to find those answers for America. I intend to establish working groups to prepare a series of White House conferences and meetings on the cities, on natural beauty, on the quality of education, and on other emerging challenges. And from these meetings and from this inspiration and from these studies we will begin to set our course toward the Great Society.

The solution to these problems does not rest on a massive program in Washington, nor can it rely solely on the strained resources of local authority. They require us to create new concepts of cooperation, a creative federalism, between the National Capital and the leaders of local communities.

There are those timid souls who say this battle cannot be won; that we are condemned to a soulless wealth. I do not agree. We have the power to shape the civilization that we want. But we need your will, your labor, your hearts, if we are to build that kind of society. Those who came to this land sought to build more than just a new country. They sought a new world.

So let us from this moment begin our work so that in the future men will look back and say: It was then, after a long and weary way, that man turned the exploits of his genius to the full enrichment of his life.

May 23

South Carolina Ratifies the Constitution

On May 23, 1788, South Carolina became the eighth state to ratify the federal Constitution. Historians accordingly list South Carolina eighth in the chronology of the admission of the 50 states to the Union. Of course, South Carolina and the other 12 colonies had assumed statehood more than a decade before the meeting of the 1787 Constitutional Convention, when they promulgated the Declaration of Independence in July 1776.

Four delegates represented South Carolina at the Constitutional Convention held in Philadelphia, Pennsylvania, in 1787. Pierce Butler, an English noble by birth, came to America as an officer in the British army. He eventually sold his commission and settled in the New World. Butler, 43

years old in 1787, had served in the South Carolina legislature and had recently won election to the federal Congress. Charles Pinckney, brilliant but annoyingly aggressive, was only 29 years old and one of the convention's youngest members. Charles Cotesworth Pinckney, only in his early 40s in 1787, had risen to the rank of brigadier general during the American Revolution. A cousin of Charles Pinckney, he had received his education at Oxford University in England and was a prominent lawyer. John Rutledge, then in his late 40s, was the leader of the South Carolina contingent. Rutledge, who served South Carolina as congressman, governor, and chancellor, was a renowned orator and was influential in the drafting of the Constitution.

Charles Pinckney was one of the more active members of the convention. After Edmund Randolph presented Virginia's proposals for an ideal Constitution on May 29, 1787, the brash young South Carolinian submitted his own plan of union. The Pinckney plan did not have the breadth of the Randolph resolutions, but it did prove useful on a number of minor points to the Committee of Detail, which made the first full draft of the Constitution.

John Rutledge of South Carolina was the chairman of the Committee of Detail, on which Edmund Randolph of Virginia, Nathaniel Gorham of Massachusetts, Oliver Ellsworth of Connecticut, and James Wilson of Pennsylvania also served. Rutledge and Randolph were influential in the committee's decision to recommend that the Constitution not interfere with the slave trade, allow no tax on exports, and require a two-thirds vote of both houses to impose levies on imports. In later debate the convention accepted the provision concerning taxes on exports but, on the advice of a compromise committee composed of one delegate from each state, forbade interference with the slave trade only until 1808 and authorized the Congress to place duties on imports by a simple majority vote.

The Philadelphia convention completed its work on September 17, 1787, and official copies of the proposed Constitution first appeared in South Carolina on October 4 of that year. Propaganda pieces from Pennsylvania in support of the new government and from New York in opposition to it soon followed in the newspapers. By December groups of South Carolinians formed on each side and issued their own arguments.

South Carolina's vulnerability to attacks from the sea by foreign enemies or on the frontier from Native American tribes fostered a general approval of the proposed Constitution. The state had suffered greatly during the American Revolution, and looked for protection by creating a strong national government. Low-country planters, a number of whom were experiencing financial difficulties, were the chief opponents of the new frame of government. These planters tended to be parochial in their political outlook, and also disliked the provisions of the Constitution that discouraged legislation favorable to debtors.

Convening in January 1788, the South Carolina legislature (despite the objections of former governor Rawling Loundes, who opposed the Constitution) ordered the election of delegates for a ratifying convention and established April 11 and April 12 as the dates for the election. The Federalists achieved success in the contests for delegates and were ready to assume control of the ratification caucus when it convened on May 6. With the conclusion foregone, the delegates spent two weeks in desultory debate and issued a resolution declaring that all powers not expressly delegated by the Constitution to the central government were reserved to the states. Then, the South Carolina representatives, by a margin of 149 to 73 votes, ratified the Constitution of the United States on May 23, 1788.

Captain Kidd Hanged

Captain William Kidd, perhaps the most famous of all pirates, belied the stereotype of a buccaneer. Historians know little of his early life, except that he was born about 1645 in Greenock, Scotland, the son of John Kidd, a Calvinist minister. Neither a hardened criminal nor a social outcast, Kidd first appears in the records around 1690 as a respectable New York City shipowner and a staunch supporter of the English government.

Shortly before then, England's Glorious Revolution of 1688 had brought Protestant William III and his wife Mary to the throne in place of the Roman Catholic James II. War with France ensued when that country gave shelter to the deposed monarch and took up his cause. The French government, employing a common wartime tactic, commissioned privateers to prey on English shipping. Kidd, in turn, put his ship to the service of William and Mary and did his best to protect England's commerce in the area of the West Indies.

Financially, Kidd was secure. In 1691 he married Sarah Oort, the widow of John Oort, a sea captain, and of William Cox, a wealthy merchant. On the tax assessment list of 1695 Kidd held a place among the wealthiest 10 percent of the New York City population. Kidd's house, located in Manhattan's East Ward, stood on Queen Street, fronting the strand of the East River. In the fall of 1695, Kidd met in London with Robert Livingston, a fellow Scot who was one of the leading men in the New York colony. Together with Richard Coote, the earl of Bellomont, they planned an expedition to enrich themselves and to rid the seas of the pirates that plagued the trade of England's East India Company. On October 10, 1695, Kidd signed an agreement to command the expedition and to divide one-fifth of the profits with Livingston, who was to help finance the venture. The earl of Bellomont, who became governor of New York, New Hampshire, and Massachusetts in 1697, promised to provide four-fifths of the necessary capital in return for a corresponding amount of the gain. The earl managed to raise his share by accepting as partners some of the most powerful men of the realm, including the lord chancellor, the first lord of the Admiralty, the earl of Oxford, the earl of Romney, and the duke of Shrewsbury.

On April 23, 1696, Captain Kidd left Plymouth, England, in the *Adventure Galley*, a 287-ton vessel that carried 34 guns. He sailed to New York City, where he added more men to his crew. While in his home port, Kidd lent his runner and tackle to help in the erection of the original Trinity Church, the principal Anglican church in the colony. The *Adventure Galley* hoisted anchor again on September 6, rounded the Cape of Good Hope in December, and proceeded to Madagascar, a pirate haven.

Conditions aboard the *Adventure Galley* were harsh. The ship leaked and one-third of the crew died on the voyage to Madagascar. The men were to receive no pay unless they took prizes, and their early lack of success increased their dissatisfaction. The crew became mutinous and, at some point, the strain proved too much for the captain. Kidd cast off his role as protector for that of predator and the pirate hunter turned to piracy. On January 30, 1698, he took his most valuable prize, the Armenian ship *Quedagh Merchant*, a 400- to 500-ton vessel worth perhaps as much as 70,000 English pounds.

Many knowledgeable persons had suspected that Kidd's mission might be perverted. Benjamin Fletcher, a leading figure in the New York colony, was unimpressed by Kidd's crew. In 1697 Fletcher wrote to the Lords of Trade in England:

> Many flockt to him from all parts men of desperate fortunes and necessitous in expectation of getting vast treasure. He sailed from hence with 150 men as I am informed great part of them are of this province. It is generally believed here, they will have money "per fas aut nefas," that if he misse of the design intended for which he has commission, 'twill not be in Kidd's power to govern such a hord of men under no pay.

Having scuttled the *Adventure Galley* and transferred his crew to the *Quedagh Merchant*, Kidd left Madagascar in September 1698. By April 1699 he had arrived at Anguilla in the West Indies, where he learned that the government had declared him and his crew to be pirates. He then set sail for the mainland in a fresh vessel, the *Antonio*. When he reached Oyster Bay on Long Island, New York, he met with his friend James Emmot, the most important attorney in New York City. Emmot served as a negotiator between Kidd and Governor Bellomont, and arranged for the captain to surrender himself.

Kidd landed in Boston on July 2, 1699, expecting that the governor would pardon him. The captain attempted to excuse his activities as involuntary deeds forced upon him by a mutinous crew. Bellomont, who had drawn Kidd ashore with the lure of possible pardon, was not satisfied with the explanation and imprisoned him.

Bellomont sent Kidd to England as a prisoner. On April 14, 1700, the Board of Admiralty questioned the captain and committed him to the jail at Newgate. The House of Commons, hoping to be able to implicate some of the peers who had financed Kidd's expedition, ordered him to appear before it prior to standing trial. The captain therefore languished in Newgate until the next session of Parliament, in March 1701. Unable to involve the financiers, the commissioners then sent Kidd to stand trial.

William Kidd went to the "Old Bailey" criminal court on May 8, 1701. The prosecution charged him with the killing of William Moore, a gunner on the *Adventure Galley*. The captain admitted that he struck the sailor with a bucket, but claimed he did it in the course of subduing a mutiny. The judge held that it was intentional murder, and the court convicted Kidd. The government also charged him with piracy against five ships. Kidd defended himself by saying that the vessels carried French passes, but the court again found him guilty.

Most historians agree that the trial of Captain Kidd was conducted questionably. The prisoner had no qualified counsel and the only witnesses against him were two hardly disinterested men from the *Adventure Galley*. The charge of murder in the Moore case seems unduly harsh inasmuch as Kidd could hardly have premeditated it. The captain had taken French passes from two vessels, but the prosecution suppressed this evidence.

On May 9, 1701, the judge sentenced Captain William Kidd to be hanged. The prisoner responded, "My Lord, it is a very hard sentence. For my part I am innocentest of them all, only I have been sworn against by perjured persons." On May 23,

1701, Kidd was hanged, protesting his innocence to the end. Years after his death, Captain Kidd became a center of legend and controversy. Stories of his buried treasure drove many to fruitless searches for hidden riches. The questionable proceedings at his trial won sympathizers for Kidd who doubted his guilt. The full story will probably never be known.

May 24

Bob Dylan's Birthday

Rock-and-roll legend Bob Dylan was born as Robert Allen Zimmerman on May 24, 1941, in Duluth, Minnesota. His family moved to the mining town of Hibbing, Minnesota, in 1947, where young Zimmerman would spend his youth. As a teenager he developed a fascination with the pioneering rock stars of the 1950s, such as Elvis Presley and Little Richard. He even formed some groups of his own, such as the Golden Chords, although these would not be lasting affiliations.

After graduating from Hibbing High School in 1959, Zimmerman entered the University of Minnesota. He was more interested in his music, however, and dropped out of college after his freshman year. It was at that time that he took the name Bob Dylan, possibly to honor his favorite poet, Dylan Thomas. He went to New York City's trendy Greenwich Village district to enter the booming folk music movement, which was a more intellectual and serious offshoot of rock and roll.

Dylan developed his own distinctive, somewhat nasal style, and became a hit in Greenwich Village's coffee house scene. He also befriended folk legend Woody Guthrie and other artists. John Hammond of Columbia Records signed Dylan to a contract, and the debut album *Bob Dylan* was released in 1962. It was followed by *The Freewheelin' Bob Dylan* in 1963, which contained such classic Dylan pieces as "Blowin' in the Wind" and "A Hard Rain's Gonna Fall."

More Dylan hits followed in 1964 with *The Times They Are A-Changin*. The album contained a song with the same title that epitomized the restless spirit of the turbulent 1960s with its many protest movements. More albums followed through the mid-1960s, such as *Another Side of Bob Dylan*, *Bringing It All Back Home*, *Blonde on Blonde*, and *Highway 61 Revisited*. Some of his most popular songs were "It Ain't Me Babe," "Mr. Tambourine Man," "It's All Over Now, Baby Blue," and "Like a Rolling Stone." During this period, Dylan began to play the electric guitar in his songs and transformed the traditional acoustical sound of folk music.

Dylan had reached his peak at the age of 25. On July 29, 1966, he nearly died from injuries received in a motorcycle accident. Further, he had undergone a bitter breakup with longtime girlfriend Suze Rotolo. After the accident, Dylan retreated from public life with his new companion, Sara Lowndes. He continued to write songs, gravitating toward country music, and did the musical score for the movie *Pat Garrett and Billy the Kid*. However, he never regained his previous stature in the rock-and-roll movement, although his songs continued to be popular and his albums sold in the millions.

Most of Dylan's new releases in the 1970s were considered mediocre and received poor reviews. However, he managed to make a comeback in the 1980s, and was also applauded for his participation in the "We Are The World" and "Farm Aid" benefit performances. Noteworthy new albums included *Oh Mercy* in 1989 and the award-winning *World Gone Wrong* in 1993.

Samuel F. B. Morse Opens the First U.S. Telegraph Line

It was on May 24, 1844, that the United States's first telegraph line was formally opened, with the initial message clicked out by the man who had produced the first practical telegraph instrument, Samuel Finley Breese Morse. The historic line stretched from Washington, D.C., to Baltimore, Maryland, and carried as Morse's first officially telegraphed words the sentence "What hath God wrought." Actually, however, earlier messages had been sent during the line's construction. One of them, on May 1 of the same year, had brought to Washington the news that the Whigs, meeting in Baltimore, had nominated Henry Clay as their candidate for the presidency. The telegraphed news, which arrived in Washington an hour before a train carrying the same information, heralded a new era of rapid communications.

Morse's invention followed a century in which Europeans, and some Americans, had experimented with the idea of communicating by electrically transmitted signals. His was not, as he thought for some years, the first electric telegraph to be proposed. There was, for instance, the detailed description of an electromagnetic telegraph published by Joseph Henry in 1831, several years before Morse completed construction of his first working telegraph on or about 1835. At that time, Morse was known mainly as a portrait painter and as the chief founder and first president of the National Academy of Design.

Born in Charlestown, Massachusetts, on April 27, 1791, Morse was the son of the noted clergyman and geographer Jedidiah Morse and graduated from Yale in 1810 before studying painting at London's Royal Academy under Washington Allston. In the process of becoming one of the most respected American artists of his time, Morse had put in years of artistic effort, some of them impoverished, in such cities as Boston, Charleston, New York, and Washington. He had been studying art in Europe and was on his way back to New York, where the institution now known as New York University would soon appoint him professor of painting and sculpture, when his life was altered by a thought-provoking conversation on shipboard. The year was 1832 and the conversation, about the newly developed electromagnet, prompted Morse to wonder "why intelligence may not be transmitted instantaneously by electricity."

Morse immediately set down his original idea of an electromagnetic telegraph. Subsequently, he developed an apparatus involving a sender and a receiver, which was improved after much experimentation by the addition of Joseph Henry's magnet. Morse's most important contribution to the telegraph was a system of electromagnetic renewers or relays that made it possible to send long-distance messages by way of many stations and branch lines.

Politically, Morse was active in the anti-Catholic nativist movement and was its candidate for mayor of New York City in 1836 and again in 1841. In 1837 he gave up painting to work full-time on the telegraph, filing a caveat at the patent office in Washington, D.C., and also beginning a vain attempt to secure European patents. Leonard Gale, a scientific colleague at the university, and Alfred Vail, who gave financial and other assistance, became partners in Morse's enterprise that same year. A third partner, Representative F. O. J. Smith, was acquired in 1838 while Morse was trying to persuade Congress to construct an experimental telegraph line. By that year, Morse had also worked out the Morse code, an alphabet of dots and dashes for use with his machine.

In 1843 Congress appropriated $30,000 for construction of the experimental line from Washington to Baltimore, and Vail, who was more persevering than the other early partners, received Morse's first official message at the Baltimore end of the line on May 24, 1844. The same year, the Patent Office granted Morse his patent. Although Congress in 1847 decided not to continue the government's ownership of the 44-mile experimental line, enthusiasm for Morse's telegraph spread like wildfire. Numerous private companies were organized under his patent privileges. As new instruments were patented in the 1840s and 1850s, Morse, who had his own characteristic flair for controversy, found himself immersed in litigation. By 1854 matters had progressed as far as the Supreme Court, which upheld his patent rights.

By the time of the Civil War, the telegraph was playing an important communications role, particularly in the more industrialized North. Like the railroad and the McCormick reaper, the telegraph was important in the economic and social development of the United States. In contrast to Morse's lean early days, his last years were filled with honors and financial rewards. He died in New York City on April 2, 1872. Until the telephone came into use, Morse's telegraph provided the public with its only means of rapid communication.

May 25

Ralph Waldo Emerson's Birthday

Ralph Waldo Emerson was born on May 25, 1803, in Boston, Massachusetts, to the Reverend William and Ruth (Haskins) Emerson. Ancestry and education would have placed him in the upper class of Boston, but the family was not wealthy. When Emerson was eight years old, his father, the cosmopolitan and literary minister of Boston's oldest church, died and left the education of the children to his wife. The young Emerson attended the Boston Latin School, and with the help of various jobs and his mother's economies was able to attend Harvard College, from which he graduated at the age of 18 and earned the title of class poet.

For several years afterwards, Emerson taught at a girls' school run by his brother. After some hesitation he decided to prepare for the ministry, following seven direct ancestors in this field. In 1825 Emerson entered Harvard Divinity School, where he was "approbated" to preach the next year and earned money by giving sermons while he continued his studies. Slowed by poor health, Emerson wintered in St. Augustine, Florida.

At divinity school, Emerson discovered his oratorical skills and found that his strength lay in the exercise of "moral imagination" more than in the systematic defense of doctrine. Though already disturbed about certain church teachings, he was pushed ahead by ambition, and in 1829 was called to the pulpit of the Second Unitarian Church of Boston and ordained. Soon afterwards he married Ellen Tucker of New Hampshire. Meanwhile, his fame as a preacher in Unitarian circles grew; but underneath the fame, he was restless.

Emerson was open to the "new voices" of the times, including those of Thomas Carlyle, Samuel Taylor Coleridge, and the Swedenborgians. Also at this time, his older brother returned from Germany with word of Johann Wolfgang von Goethe and of the new biblical criticism with its systematic doubt about the historicity of miracles. Emerson's sermons took on a characteristic idealism, stressing personal "uses of the spirit" rather than traditional Christianity. After his wife died of tuberculosis in 1831, however, Emerson found it increasingly difficult to continue as a minister. He desired a freer and more vital vocational framework in which to express his intellectual and spiritual ideas. In the summer of 1832, at the age of 29, he refused as a matter of conscience to administer the symbolic Lord's Supper to his congregation, no longer regarding it as necessary. In this way Emerson provoked the termination of his ministry.

Released from previous restrictions, but in bad health and without a clear alternative for his life, Emerson sailed for the Mediterranean. He traveled in Italy, England, and Scotland, seeking out such distinguished persons as Carlyle, Coleridge, and William Wordsworth in hopes that the example of these great men would illuminate and fortify him in his search for his own experience of God. Returning to America in 1833, Emerson began to write his epic work *Nature*. He also continued the journal he had begun as a Harvard undergraduate, which became a mine of ideas for later essays. Above all he launched himself as a lecturer, offering courses in natural history and biography. If a little unusual for a former minister, these subjects derived naturally from Emerson's emerging philosophy. For him the picture of natural history developing in Europe and America through the study and classification of animal and plant species confirmed the spiritual connection between man and nature. Biography enabled him to explore models of human greatness and moral self-reliance.

Emerson's literary career was aided by the spread of "lyceums" at this time. The first lyceum had been founded at Millbury, Massachusetts, in 1826 by Josiah Holbrook, a collaborator of the educator Horace Mann. It offered a paid-in-advance series of lectures to satisfy the public's craving for knowledge on a variety of subjects. As the lyceum movement expanded westward in the 1830s, offering townspeople a new form of education, entertainment, and a social occasion other than weekly prayer meetings, Emerson became a favorite speaker. Much of his livelihood would come from such lecturing, and often it was money hard earned, for travel from town to town at the time involved many inconveniences, delays, and discomforts.

As early as 1834 Emerson made his home in Concord, Massachusetts. The following year he married Lydia Jackson of Plymouth, Massachusetts, bringing her to live first in the Old Manse, which his grandfather had built around 1765. In 1836 the Emersons moved to what became known as the Emerson House. In this square frame house, he lived and worked until his death. For two years after 1841, young Henry David Thoreau joined the Emerson household and wrote there under Emerson's tutelage, in exchange for performing certain household and editorial duties. Emerson encouraged the young individualist, editing his poems, and supporting his writings on nature. His encouragement of Thoreau is just one example of the leadership that Emerson gave to his intellectual contemporaries. However, his peaceful married life in Concord, with its daily schedule of writing, walking, and conversation with friends, is deceptive, for it was from this calm haven that Emerson launched a philosophic attack upon old religious and scientific beliefs that shook traditional New England.

Emerson rejected the contemporary mechanistic, deterministic, and materialist philosophy of man and nature in favor of a philosophy that was new in its bases. He laid down its essentials in the essay entitled *Nature*, which stated that men were not merely passive recipients of sensations from the external world, bound by material causes and effects over which they had no control. In such a world there was no place for passionate spirit and real piety; and men became strangers to themselves. The truth was rather that all nature was a great living organic reality, immanent with spirit, still unfolding, and embracing man, the most active of her creatures, in an intimate bond. Man shared with nature the indwelling of the Over-Soul, which Emerson defined as "that Unity, that Over-Soul, within which every man's particular being is contained and made one with all other." Thanks to his powers of perception, man was capable of understanding nature's laws. Through his ideas he could participate fully in the yet-to-be formed future and fashion from nature a world suited to human needs.

In 1837, in the Phi Beta Kappa address at Harvard College, Emerson applied his insights directly to the attitudes behind the educational process of his day. Entitled *The American Scholar*, his talk was an impassioned plea for Americans to do their own thinking and no longer lean on the cultures of Europe and the ancient world. The address made him famous, and the next year Emerson was asked to deliver an address at the Harvard Divinity School. Once again he spoke with a directness and courage born of a philosophy not adopted from others but won for himself. He attacked the Christian church as dead and the ministry as antiquated, and called on the scholar to free himself from the church and seek "a new revelation commensurate to the present age."

The response to this speech was extremely negative. Emerson was not welcomed at Harvard for a generation, and for a time he was virtually *persona non grata* on the lecture circuit as well. The experience drove home to him the fact that ideas do not themselves bring reform, at least in any immediate sense. Nevertheless, his ideas made him the spokesman for a group of like-minded New England thinkers, known as the Transcendentalists, who included in their number certain persons very interested in reform. Among this group were Thoreau; author-philosopher Orestes Brownson; clergyman-abolitionist Theodore Parker; educator and mystic Bronson Alcott; the influential Unitarian minister William Ellery Channing; Unitarian clergyman and reformer James Freeman Clarke; and author, critic, and feminist Margaret Fuller, who was the first editor of the Transcendentalists' magazine, *The Dial*.

Emerson himself took over the editorship of that publication in 1842. As editor, he stressed poetry and metaphysics rather than questions of practical reform, which did not arouse his sympathy any more than did the experiments of some of his friends in utopian communal living. The only reform that seemed to Emerson of lasting value was individual moral regeneration, and he wrote and spoke eloquently on its behalf.

The Emerson work entitled *Essays, First Series* appeared in 1841. The collection included one of his finest pieces, "Self-Reliance." "To believe your own thought," Emerson wrote, "to believe that what is true for you in your private heart is true for all men, that is genius. . . . In every work of genius we recognize our own rejected thoughts; they come back to us with a certain alienated majesty. Great works of art . . . teach us to abide by our spontaneous impression with good-humored inflexibility. . . ." He also wrote, more pungently:

> Society everywhere is in conspiracy against the manhood of every one of its members. . . . The virtue most in request is conformity. . . . The objection to conforming to usages that have become dead to you is that it scatters your force. It loses your time and blurs the impression of your character. . . . It is easy to see that a greater self-reliance must work a revolution in all the offices and relations of men. . . .

Essays, Second Series (1844) took up similar themes but gave greater weight to Emerson's experience of limitations in pursuing his high goal of self-activation. In *Representative Men* (1849), he increasingly balanced the test of action with the test of perception in his judgment of men.

Emerson's interests shifted as tensions in the nation grew during the 1850s. The great and bitter issues of this period in American politics fill the work entitled *Journal*. Always sympathetic to the abolitionist cause, he became outspoken in his criticism of slavery. On the eve of the Civil War he established the Saturday Club, a group of distinguished New Englanders who met for monthly discussions. The group included Nathaniel Hawthorne, Henry Wadsworth Longfellow, Louis Agassiz, Oliver Wendell Holmes, and John Lothrop Motley. Along the way Emerson in 1855 became one of the first critics to appreciate the gifts of Walt Whitman.

Emerson began to decline intellectually during the 1860s, although a second volume of his poems, *May Day and Other Pieces*, appeared in 1867. In the 1870s Emerson grew amiably senile. He died on April 27, 1882, at Concord, and was buried there on Author's Ridge in Sleepy Hollow Cemetery. In 1900 he was elected to the Hall of Fame for Great Americans.

Indianapolis 500

This is a movable event.

Every year, on the Sunday of Memorial Day weekend, the world's most famous race car event takes place in Indianapolis, Indiana. The Indianapolis 500, held at the Indianapolis Motor Speedway, consists of 200 laps around a two-and-a-half-mile track for a total of 500 miles. Hence the name "Indianapolis 500." The racecars are sleek, aerodynamically enhanced vehicles, subject to uniform size and design regulations that nevertheless permit engineering innovations by individual race teams.

The first Indianapolis 500 race was held in 1911. Today, the event hosts hundreds of thousands of spectators, and millions more watch on television. Set forth below is a list of the Indy 500 champions.

Year	Champion	Avg. Speed (mph)
1911	Ray Harroun	74
1912	Joe Dawson	78
1913	Jules Goux	75
1914	Rene Thomas	82
1915	Ralph DePalma	89
1916	Dario Resta	84
1917-1918:	No races	
1919	Howard Wilcox	88
1920	Gaston Chevrolet	88
1921	Tommy Milton	89
1922	Jimmy Murphy	94
1923	Tommy Milton	90
1924	L. L. Corum	98
1925	Peter DePaolo	101
1926	Frank Lockhart	95
1927	George Souders	97
1928	Louis Meyer	99
1929	Ray Keech	97
1930	Billy Arnold	100
1931	Louis Schneider	96
1932	Fred Frame	104
1933	Louis Meyer	104
1934	William Cummings	104
1935	Kelly Petillo	106
1936	Louis Meyer	109
1937	Wilbur Shaw	113
1938	Floyd Roberts	117
1939	Wilbur Shaw	115
1940	Wilbur Shaw	114
1941	Floyd Davis	115
1942-1945:	No races	
1946	George Robson	114
1947	Mauri Rose	116
1948	Mauri Rose	119
1949	Bill Holland	121
1950	Johnnie Parsons	124
1951	Lee Wallard	126
1952	Troy Ruttman	129
1953	Bill Vukovich	129
1954	Bill Vukovich	131
1955	Bob Sweikert	128
1956	Pat Flaherty	128
1957	Sam Hanks	136
1958	Jim Bryan	134
1959	Roger Ward	136
1960	Jim Rathman	139
1961	A. J. Foyt	139
1962	Roger Ward	140
1963	Parnelli Jones	143
1964	A. J. Foyt	147
1965	Jimmy Clark	150
1966	Graham Hill	144
1967	A. J. Foyt	151
1968	Bobby Unser	153
1969	Mario Andretti	157
1970	Al Unser Sr.	156
1971	Al Unser Sr.	158
1972	Mark Donohue	163
1973	Gordon Johncock	159
1974	Johnny Rutherford	159
1975	Bobby Unser	149
1976	Johnny Rutherford	149
1977	A. J. Foyt	161

1978	Al Unser Sr.	161
1979	Rick Mears	159
1980	Johnny Rutherford	143
1981	Bobby Unser	139
1982	Gordon Johncock	162
1983	Tom Sneva	162
1984	Rick Mears	164
1985	Danny Sullivan	153
1986	Bobby Rahal	171
1987	Al Unser Sr.	162
1988	Rick Mears	145
1989	Emerson Fittipaldi	168
1990	Arie Luyendyk	186
1991	Rick Mears	176
1992	Al Unser Jr.	134
1993	Emerson Fittipaldi	157
1994	Al Unser Jr.	161
1995	Jacques Villenueve	154
1996	Buddy Lazier	148
1997	Arie Luyendyk	146
1998	Eddie Cheever	145
1999	Kenny Brack	153

Constitutional Convention Opens

The American Revolution made the United States independent, but it did not give the new country national unity. In 1777 the common desire for freedom from Great Britain had bound the 13 original states into a government based on the Articles of Confederation. However, in the years following the Peace of Paris of 1783, a number of incidents repeatedly illustrated the inadequacy of the confederation government, and by 1787 many shared the sentiment of George Washington that "something must be done or the fabric will fall." To revise and strengthen the Articles of Confederation, a convention of representatives of the various states opened in Philadelphia, Pennsylvania, on May 25, 1787. In the months that followed, the delegates to the Philadelphia meeting drew up the United States Constitution, which has served as the nation's frame of government ever since.

May 26

Montana Becomes a Territory

During the dark days of the Civil War, while federal troops were fighting to preserve the integrity of the Union, the United States Congress was faced with the necessity of establishing a viable government in the area of what is now Montana. In the spring of 1864 Congress passed an enabling act creating the Territory of Montana. On May 26, 1864, President Abraham Lincoln signed this measure into law.

An area rich with natural resources and rugged beauty, Montana yielded slowly to the intrusion of settlers. In 1742 or 1743 the French fur traders François La Vérendrye and Louis Joseph La Vérendrye, his brother, probably visited eastern Montana. The snowcapped peaks of the American West captivated François, and he reportedly exclaimed: "this is truly the Land of the Shining Mountains." However, the Vérendryes returned to Canada without exploring western Montana, and for the remainder of the 18th century only an occasional fur trader disturbed the tranquil wilderness.

Shortly after he purchased the Louisiana Territory from Napoléon Bonaparte in 1803, President Thomas Jefferson authorized the American explorers Meriwether Lewis and William Clark to undertake an extensive expedition through the newly acquired lands. With the assistance of their Native American guide, Sacagawea, Lewis and Clark proceeded west across Montana on their trek to the Pacific in 1805. Then, on their return east in 1806, they undertook the first major explorations of the Montana region by Americans. Lewis and several members of the party ventured into northern Montana in the area of the Marias River while, farther south, Clark and his companions surveyed the valley of the Yellowstone River.

Lewis and Clark found many streams rich with beaver in Montana, and their reports of excellent trapping opportunities quickly attracted fur traders to the region. In 1807 Manuel Lisa of New Orleans, Louisiana, outfitted 42 men and led them to the mouth of the Bighorn River. There they constructed Montana's first trading post.

Lisa was only the first of many fur traders to tap Montana's beaver resources. During the next 70 years, trappers, working on their own or for British or American companies, took thousands of pelts out of the Montana wilds. Vast fortunes were amassed from this beaver trade, the most notable of which was that made by John Jacob Astor and his American Fur Company.

Although most of the newcomers were only interested in fur profits, others wanted to bring Christianity to the native tribes that inhabited Montana. In 1841 the Belgian-born Jesuit priest Pierre-Jean De Smet founded St. Mary's Mission in the Bitterroot Valley. Three years later another Jesuit, Italian-born Anthony Ravalli, joined the western Montana mission. Father Ravalli was a man of many talents: In addition to evangelizing he built a sawmill and a gristmill, and dispensed herbal medicines to the Native Americans. After the Jesuits were forced to leave the Bitterroot Valley in 1850, Father Ravalli established the St. Ignatius Mission and a boarding school for Native

Americans in the Mission Valley of northwestern Montana.

Only trappers seeking beaver skins and missionaries seeking converts thus braved the Montana wilderness prior to 1860. In the next decade, however, the discovery of gold brought thousands of prospectors to the region. As early as 1852 François Finlay may have found the first evidence of gold deposits, and in 1858 James and Granville Stuart definitely made gold strikes. The Stuarts staked their claim in the spring of 1862, but it was not these initial discoveries that brought the population boom to Montana.

The strike that lured so many prospectors occurred in July 1862 when John White and his party discovered gold along Grasshopper Creek. By the fall of 1862, it was apparent that this discovery was a major find, and news of the new goldfield spread quickly. The town of Bannack was immediately laid out near the site of the strike, and by the spring of 1863 the area had almost 1,000 inhabitants.

On May 26, 1863, six prospectors found an even more lucrative gold deposit along a small creek in the foothills of Montana's Tobacco Root range. The prospectors named the gold-rich area Alder Gulch because of the large number of alder trees on the banks of the creek, and for a time they tried to keep their discovery secret. Their efforts to conceal the location failed, however, and within six months of the strike approximately 10,000 gold seekers had flocked to Alder Gulch (which was soon known as Virginia City), and by mid-1864 the population of the area had swelled to some 35,000.

In July 1864 gold was also discovered at Last Chance Gulch north of Virginia City. Again, thousands of prospectors swarmed to the new mining fields, and Last Chance Gulch soon became the site of Helena, which was Montana's third boom town and eventually became its capital.

The gold rush necessitated the establishment of a viable and easily accessible government for Montana. The Montana area east of the Rocky Mountains, which came under United States jurisdiction as a result of the Louisiana Purchase, had since 1803 been (in succession) a part of the Louisiana Territory and then the Missouri Territory, the Nebraska Territory, and the Dakota Territory. The mountainous western region of Montana remained under the control of Great Britain until the Oregon Treaty of 1846, under which Britain recognized American authority in the area. In 1848 northwestern Montana was included in the Oregon Territory, and later it was incorporated into the Washington Territory. In March 1863, when Congress created the Idaho Territory from the area of what is now Montana, Idaho, and virtu-

ally all of Wyoming, the entire eastern and western sections of Montana came under a single government for the first time.

The Montana mining camps and boom towns were breeding grounds of lawlessness and violence, and it soon became apparent that the territorial capital (now Lewiston, Idaho) was too distant and inaccessible to deal effectively with the problems of the gold fields of present-day Montana. In the spring of 1864 Congress responded to the need for a new territory. Thus, on May 26, 1864, President Abraham Lincoln signed the enabling act creating the Montana Territory.

For 25 years thereafter Montana existed as a territory. During that time the territorial capital was moved several times: from Bannack, the original capital, to Virginia City in 1865, and to Helena in 1875. Montana prospered during the latter half of the 19th century, and mining continued to be the major source of income, although prospectors gradually turned their attention from gold to silver and finally to copper.

The Montana Territory was also the scene of Custer's Last Stand. In June 1876 Sioux and Cheyenne warriors annihilated the United States Army troops commanded by General George Custer. The incident was, of course, the most famous Native American military victory. However, the triumph was short-lived, and eventually the tribes of Montana were forced onto small reservations.

May 27

Cornelius Vanderbilt's Birthday

Cornelius Vanderbilt, the American capitalist and industrialist who ranks as one of the great promoters of American steamship and railroad lines, was born in Staten Island, New York, on May 27, 1794. His paternal Dutch ancestors, who settled on Long Island in the late 1600s, wrote their name "Van der bilt." His parents were Cornelius Vander Bilt and Phebe Hand Vander Bilt. The industrialist himself preferred the form "Van Derbilt." This preference notwithstanding, however, other family members consolidated the name to "Vanderbilt" within his lifetime, and he is customarily referred to in that way.

The elder Cornelius Vander Bilt was a farmer of modest circumstances. As a member of a large family with little means, young Cornelius Vanderbilt had to help his father at an early age and consequently received little formal schooling. At 16, the enterprising youth borrowed enough money from his parents to purchase a modest sailing ship with which to transport passengers and farm produce between Staten Island and Manhattan. Within the next few years he built up his business by provisioning forts in the New York City harbor during the War of 1812, buying sturdy schooners for an eastern seaboard trade between New England and the South, and engaging in shipping up and down the Hudson River.

In 1818 Vanderbilt abandoned his private ventures to serve as captain on Thomas Gibbons's ferry line between New York City and New Brunswick, New Jersey, which was a vital link for passenger and freight transport between New York and Philadelphia. It was during his 11 years as captain that Cornelius Vanderbilt first displayed the ruthless side of his character in contesting, on Gibbons's behalf, a steam navigation monopoly in New York waters that the state legislature had previously granted to the rival Robert Fulton. The tenacious Captain Vanderbilt held out against fierce odds until 1824, when the Supreme Court in the famous case of *Gibbons* v. *Ogden* invalidated such monopolies as unconstitutional.

In 1829 the ambitious businessman invested his savings to establish his own steamboat enterprise on the Hudson River. By cutting rates and engaging in similar cutthroat practices to eliminate or intimidate competitors, he was soon able to extend his network to the Long Island Sound region and even to Providence, Rhode Island, and Boston, Massachusetts. By the age of 40 Vanderbilt had amassed roughly half a million dollars. In 1840 he had an elaborate mansion built on Staten Island for himself, his wife (the former Sophia Johnson, whom he had married in 1813), and their numerous children. A few years later the social-climbing head of the household transferred his family to a townhouse on Washington Place in Manhattan.

The 1850s made Vanderbilt, already a millionaire and nicknamed "Commodore" Vanderbilt, into a business colossus. The discovery of gold in California and the subsequent gold rush offered him a chance to open up his own transportation network to the West Coast, not across the Isthmus of Panama or around South America like other routes, but across the Isthmus of Nicaragua. The investment involved in creating the land-and-sea route (docks, a 12-mile-long asphalt road through practically impassable terrain, and the construction of eight steamers to ply between the United States and Nicaragua) was substantial. However, the Accessory Transit Company, as the precarious venture had been chartered, was eminently successful. By drastically reducing the New York–San Francisco fare and offering a shorter route, the skillful manipulator gained much of the land-sea passenger trade and reportedly netted some $10 million.

Between 1855 and 1861 Vanderbilt operated a transatlantic freight and passenger service between New York City and Le Havre, France. He hoped to reap considerable profits while the Crimean War, which had broken out in 1854, occupied his British competitors. With the outbreak of the American Civil War, however, he abandoned this disappointing venture, and indeed all shipping enterprises, to turn his attention to railroads.

In the early 1860s Vanderbilt purchased stock in the New York and Harlem Railroad at a low price. Somewhat later, he bought stock in the Harlem line's main competitor, the Hudson River Railroad. By 1867 the financier and manager had gained control of the New York Central Railroad, which ran between Albany and Buffalo. In each of these takeovers, the Commodore showed himself to be even more domineering and ruthless than his unscrupulous rivals, who did their best to ruin him. Only in the case of the Erie Railway, the stock of which Vanderbilt tried to control in 1868, was he outwitted by opponents, who flooded the market with fraudulent shares. Although the railroad magnate lost a small fortune in this abortive effort, he quickly recouped his losses by vastly expanding his railroad network.

Vanderbilt first united the New York Central and Hudson River lines in 1869; three years later he leased the Harlem Railroad to it, thereby fashioning an efficiently run and highly lucrative system from three formerly unimpressive enterprises. Then, starting in 1873, he acquired the Lake Shore & Michigan Southern, Michigan Central, and Canada Southern railways, which enabled him to extend his transportation network from New York City to Chicago, Illinois. As part of this extensive through-service, he built Grand Central Terminal in New York City.

The entrepreneur died in New York on January 4, 1877. He bequeathed the bulk of his wealth, estimated at over $100 million, to his son William Henry and left most of the remainder to his second wife (since his first wife Sophia Vanderbilt had died in 1868) and his daughters. Tight-fisted with his money, Vanderbilt refused to bestow philanthropic gifts until the last years of his life. In 1873 he made his most memorable contribution, to the small Central University of the Methodist Episcopal Church in Nashville, which had been chartered the previous year and which opened in 1875. The Commodore eventually endowed this educational institution, which was renamed Vanderbilt University in his honor, with a million dollars.

Rachel Carson's Birthday

Rachel Louise Carson, sometimes referred to as the mother of the environmental movement, was born on May 27, 1907, in Springdale, Pennsylvania. She attended the Pennsylvania College for Women, later known as Chatham College, and graduated in 1929 with honors. Her outstanding academic record earned her a scholarship to Johns Hopkins University in Baltimore, Maryland, from which she graduated in 1932 with a master's degree in zoology.

Rachel Carson began her career as a writer for the United States Bureau of Fisheries, scripting a radio show called *Romance under the Waters*. In 1936 she joined the Bureau of Fisheries as a full-time biologist, but continued her writing activities. Eventually, she would oversee all of the U.S. Fish and Wildlife Service's publications.

Carson also began to publish her own works, beginning with some newspaper and magazine articles. In 1941 she published her first book, *Under the Sea Wind*. This was followed by *Food from the Sea: Fish and Shellfish of New England* (1943) and *Food from the Sea: Fish and Shellfish of the South Atlantic* (1944). In 1951 she published the work that first made her famous, *The Sea Around Us*. Having thus achieved a national reputation, Carson left the government in 1952 in order to pursue a full-time literary career.

Throughout the 1950s Carson continued to write books and articles concerning the ocean environment. Beginning in 1957, however, she developed an interest in the hazards posed to the environment by the indiscriminate use of chemical pesticides. It was a new area for Carson, since her specialty was marine biology, but she spent years researching the problem and meticulously gathered an impressive body of scientific evidence. The result was her most famous book, *Silent Spring*, published in 1962.

Silent Spring, which was a bestseller, drew national attention to environmental issues and helped bring about a ban on DDT. It also stimulated public support for such later initiatives as the creation of the Environmental Protection Agency. Carson, however, would not live to see the growth of the environmental movement that she had helped to create. She died of cancer on April 14, 1964, in Silver Spring, Maryland.

Hubert Humphrey's Birthday

Hubert Horatio Humphrey, the 38th vice president of the United States and one of the most prominent politicians in the mid-20th century, was born on May 27, 1911, in Wallace, South Dakota.

U.S. Senate Historical Office

Hubert Humphrey

He was raised in Doland, South Dakota, and worked in his father's drug store. He entered the University of Minnesota in order to study pharmacy, but was forced to interrupt his studies when the Great Depression began. Although he ultimately received a degree in 1933 from the Denver College of Pharmacy, his interests turned toward politics. Humphrey returned to the University of Minnesota in order to study political science, and graduated with honors in 1939. He received his master's degree in 1940 from Louisiana State University.

Humphrey's political career began in 1943 when he ran for mayor of Minneapolis, Minnesota. He lost the campaign, but nevertheless became a leader in the Minnesota Democratic Party, and helped the Democrats absorb the Farmer-Labor Party, which was a significant third-party influence in Minnesota politics. In 1945 Humphrey once again ran for mayor of Minneapolis, and this time he won.

Humphrey was reelected mayor in 1947. In 1948 he entered national politics when he was elected to the United States Senate. He was reelected to the Senate in 1954 and again in 1960. Humphrey was a leader of the liberal wing of the Democratic Party, and became the Senate majority whip in 1961 (meaning he occupied the number two position in the party that controlled the Senate, which at the time was the Democrats). Humphrey was active in such initiatives as the creation of the Peace Corps, civil rights legislation, Medicare, and the ratification of the Limited Nuclear Test Ban Treaty. In 1964 Humphrey became the Democrats' vice-presidential nominee in the presidential campaign of Lyndon B. Johnson.

As vice president, Humphrey reversed his earlier opposition to the Vietnam War, a position that was in line with the Johnson administration's official platform. However, this change of heart alienated many of Humphrey's liberal supporters. Many felt that Humphrey had knuckled under to Johnson, who was committed to victory in Vietnam.

A series of unlikely events propelled Humphrey to the status of presidential contender in 1968. First, President Johnson announced that he would not run in the 1968 presidential election. Second, during the 1968 Democratic primaries, the popular Senator Robert F. Kennedy was assassinated. Humphrey thus remained as one of the few viable candidates, and despite some opposition eventually secured the nomination of his party.

The presidential election of 1968 was a close one, marked by the third-party candidacy of George Wallace, the former governor of Alabama. Wallace, a former Democrat, had strong support in the South, where white opposition to the civil rights agenda of northern Democrats such as Humphrey was strong. Perhaps because of Wallace's candidacy, Humphrey lost the election to Republican candidate Richard M. Nixon by a narrow margin.

After his 1968 presidential defeat, Humphrey was once again elected to the Senate in 1970. He ran in the Democratic presidential primaries of 1972, but lost to George McGovern, and afterwards decided to abandon his ambitions for the presidency. Despite the onset of cancer, Humphrey began another term in the Senate in 1976. He died on January 13, 1978, in Waverly, Minnesota.

May 28

Louis Agassiz's Birthday

Jean Louis Rodolphe Agassiz, the charismatic apostle of natural history and one of America's most outstanding teachers of science, was born at Môtier-en-Vully in the French-speaking canton of Fribourg, Switzerland, on May 28, 1807, the son of a Protestant pastor. At the age of 10 he was sent to the preparatory school in Bienne, where he struggled with "the rudiments of many desperate studies." At 15 he went to the academy at Lausanne, and two years later he began medical studies at the University of Zurich.

Itinerant, like most students in German universities, Agassiz enrolled at Heidelberg in 1826. In 1827 he transferred to the larger University of Munich, and became an ardent student of Ignaz von Döllinger, the pioneer embryologist. In Munich, Agassiz labored over a rich collection of Brazilian fishes, brought back in 1821 by two outstanding German naturalists. Agassiz's work *Fishes of Brazil* was published in 1829 with many colored plates and was hailed as a most important scientific record of local fish fauna. Just 22 years old, Agassiz received his doctorate at Erlangen in 1829 on the basis of this first book. The next year, Agassiz went on to take the degree of doctor of medicine at Munich. Simultaneously, he launched investigations of fish fossils that would result in superb works over the next 15 years, particularly his five-volume *Recherches sur les poissons fossiles* (1833–1844). This became a foundation work for research into all forms of extinct life.

Upon leaving Munich late in 1830, however, Agassiz could only wonder whether he would have to devote himself to the practice of medicine in order to earn a living. Financing his scientific schemes was to be a constant difficulty. Late in 1831 he left for Paris, then the center of zoological and medical research. There he spent part of each day studying the fossil fishes in the Museum of Natural History of the Jardin des Plantes. Soon Georges Cuvier, the renowned comparative anatomist, became interested in Agassiz and assigned to him the entire subject of fossil fishes, giving him his own notes and collections.

Despite poverty as a student in the Latin Quarter of Paris, Cuvier's protégé was becoming famous. Alexander von Humboldt, the celebrated Prussian naturalist and explorer, sought Agassiz out. Humboldt helped Agassiz continue his investigations by advancing him money and assisted Agassiz more permanently in 1832 by arranging a special professorship in natural history at Neuchâtel, sponsored by the king of Prussia. This position gave Agassiz an essential base, but little income and insecure tenure. Undaunted, he plunged into teaching and turned the town of Neuchâtel into a center of scientific activity.

In 1833 Agassiz married Cécile Braun, the sister of his friend Alexander Braun. A highly gifted artist, she was responsible for some of the finest plates in her husband's works on fossil and freshwater fishes. In 1835 their son Alexander was born, and later two daughters, Ida and Pauline. Agassiz also took a number of close friends and colleagues into his household. Simultaneously, he set up a lithographic press to publish his works. In 1838 his position as professor was made more secure and financially rewarding by a sizable grant of funds for public education in the canton of Neuchâtel, once again provided by the king of Prussia. The improvement was to be a mixed blessing, however, because Agassiz expanded his work far beyond his means.

Through his drive and enthusiasm, Agassiz was able to both carry old projects forward and initiate new ones before he had irretrievably overextended his resources. Between 1839 and 1845, numerous volumes on ichthyology and mollusks appeared. *Nomenclator Zoologicus*, his painstaking work on classification, came out between 1842 and 1846. These publications elicited interest in several countries, including Great Britain and the United States. In addition, in the summer of 1836 Agassiz had entered a new line of research on the action of glaciers in shaping the earth's surface. Accepting the glacial theory of other investigators in the Rhône valley, Agassiz perceived that glaciers must have acted on a far larger area of Europe. He began to look for evidence in Switzerland of the hypothesized period of extreme cold. In 1837, in a famous address at Neuchâtel, Agassiz argued that there had been glacial action from the North Pole as far south as the Mediterranean and Caspian Seas. Late in 1840 his two-volume work *Études sur les Glaciers* appeared, followed by two other works on glaciers. Before Agassiz's death the main lines of his theory were widely accepted.

In 1845 his establishment at Neuchâtel succumbed to economic and personal strains. The press was closed down. Several close friends departed. Cécile Agassiz, frail and careworn, asked to return with the children to her old home in Carlsruhe. Members of Agassiz's family saved him from financial disaster, but his debts were to burden him for years. Although he had earlier declined positions in several larger European cities, when Agassiz set out in 1846 on a long planned trip to the United States, everyone sensed that the move would probably be permanent. Acclaimed in Paris and England, he embarked for the New World on the great adventure of the second half of his life.

Despite his depression over family and financial problems, Agassiz threw himself into his new work, traveling the eastern seaboard of the United States to meet scientists and government officials. Agassiz later spoke of his new country as "a land where Nature was rich, but tools and workmen few and traditions none." Amidst this dearth, he soon became the leading figure in American natural history. Joined by old coworkers from Neuchâtel, Agassiz established himself in Cambridge, Massachusetts. Early in 1848 he accepted the chair of natural history at the new Lawrence Scientific School of Harvard University.

That same year, before they could be reunited, Cécile Agassiz died in Europe of tuberculosis. From this time on, Agassiz's ties to America grew stronger, and he became a naturalized citizen in 1861. In 1850 he married Elizabeth Cabot Cary of Boston, who assisted him in his later work. Soon thereafter he brought his children to the United States. To help finance her husband's work, Elizabeth Agassiz opened a school for girls. The profits from the school also went to pay off the debts Agassiz had contracted before coming to America. In addition to teaching, writing, and collecting, Agassiz traveled extensively throughout the United States, lecturing to large and interested audiences on scientific subjects. Probably the most significant of his American works were the four volumes of his *Contributions to the Natural History of the United States*.

In 1859, after strenuous efforts to raise funds and make zoological collections for the project, he presided over the opening of Harvard's Museum of Comparative Zoology. In the summer of 1873 he opened the Anderson School of Natural History on Penikese Island in Buzzards Bay, Massachusetts, giving actuality to his novel idea of a summer school where he could train teachers of science. In an old barn on the island, he lectured daily on a great range of subjects to the 20 women and 30 men he had selected from the hundreds of applicants.

Agassiz made journeys to Brazil (1865), to the Rocky Mountains (1868), and to Cuban waters (1869); and in late 1871 he set out with his wife on a sea voyage around South America to California. The trip, though exhausting, enabled him to see evidence of glaciation in Chile. Louis Agassiz died in Cambridge on December 14, 1873, and was greatly mourned by his students. "He had been a student all his life long, and when he died he was younger than any of them," one wrote. Agassiz was buried in the Mount Auburn Cemetery in Cambridge, with a large boulder from the Aar Glacier in Switzerland placed over his grave as a monument. He was elected to the Hall of Fame for Great Americans in 1915, the first year foreign-born citizens were admitted.

United Presbyterian Church Formed

The way was paved for the creation of the new United Presbyterian Church in the United States when two previously separate bodies, namely the Presbyterian Church in the United States and the United Presbyterian Church of North America (UPCNA), agreed after years of discussion to unite. In doing so, they followed a venerable tradition, for each church had behind it a long history of other mergers. The former Presbyterian Church in the United States can point to important unions in its history in 1758, 1801, and 1870, and to the 1906 union with the Cumberland Presbyterians and the 1920 union with the Welsh Calvinistic Methodist Church. In the case of the former UPCNA, the history of mergers goes back to 1782, when the Reformed Presbyterians and the Associate Presbyterians joined in one of the earliest church unions in America. The resulting body went into the UPCNA union in 1858.

The merger of the Presbyterian Church in the United States with the UPCNA came about after Concurrent Declarations were distributed throughout both churches as part of a plan of union. The declarations "convenanted and agreed" that each of the uniting bodies would elect, according to its own form of government, "a General Assembly to meet on the twenty-sixth or twenty-seventh day of May, 1958, at Pittsburgh." After each of the general assemblies met separately, commissioners of the two groups were to meet together on May 28, 1958, to "be constituted as one body." A description of this joint meeting, which served as the opening session of the general assembly of the new united church, appeared in *The General Assembly News* published the next day. "USA Presbyterians and United Presbyterians have joined hands," said the account, and "a new chapter in church history has been written. With the . . . symbolic clasp of hands [of moderators Harold R. Martin of the USA Presbyterians and Robert N. Montgomery of the United Presbyterians] a new Church yesterday came into being."

May 29

John F. Kennedy's Birthday

For many Americans the election of John Fitzgerald Kennedy as the 35th president of the United States in 1960 marked the beginning of a new era in this country's political history. Kennedy was the first Roman Catholic and the youngest man ever to be elected as chief executive. He was also the first person born in the 20th century to hold the nation's highest office.

Born in Brookline, Massachusetts, on May 29, 1917, Kennedy was descended from two politically conscious Irish American families that had emigrated from Ireland to Boston shortly after potato blight and economic upheavals had struck their homeland in the 1840s. Kennedy's grandfathers, Patrick J. Kennedy and John F. ("Honey Fitz") Fitzgerald, became closely associated with the local Democratic Party: Patrick Kennedy served in

Library of Congress

John F. Kennedy

the Massachusetts legislature, and Fitzgerald won election as mayor of Boston. In 1914 the marriage of Joseph P. Kennedy and Rose Fitzgerald united the two families. John Fitzgerald Kennedy was the second eldest of Joseph and Rose Kennedy's four sons and five daughters.

Joseph P. Kennedy was an extraordinarily successful businessman. Despite the relatively modest means of his family, he attended Harvard College, and upon graduation in 1912 began a career in banking. During the 1920s he amassed a substantial fortune from his investments in motion pictures, real estate, and other enterprises, and unlike many magnates of his era he escaped unscathed from the stock market crash of 1929. There have also been allegations, none clearly proven, that he was involved in bootlegging during Prohibition. Joseph Kennedy himself was never a candidate for elective office, but he was deeply interested in the Democratic Party. He made large contributions to the presidential campaign of Franklin D. Roosevelt in 1932; in return, Roosevelt appointed him chairman of the newly established Securities and Exchange Commission, where his business expertise proved especially helpful in drafting legislation designed to regulate the stock market. Joseph Kennedy also served as American ambassador to Great Britain. His business empire continued to grow, and by the 1950s his fortune was rumored to be in the hundreds of millions.

John F. Kennedy, like his brothers and sisters, grew up in comfortable homes and attended some of the nation's most prestigious preparatory schools and colleges. He was enrolled at the age of 13 at Canterbury, a Catholic preparatory school staffed by laymen, but transferred after a year to the nonsectarian Choate School, where he completed his secondary education before entering Princeton University. Illness forced him to leave the college before the end of his freshman year, but the following autumn he resumed his studies at Harvard.

Kennedy's college years coincided with a time of world crisis. The future president had unusual opportunities to combine knowledge gained in the classroom with his own firsthand observations. As a government major at Harvard, he benefited from the teachings of some of the nation's most prominent political scientists and historians, men who in the late 1930s were acutely aware of the growing Nazi menace. Moreover, in 1938 Kennedy spent six months in London assisting his father, who was then serving as ambassador. This stay in England gave the young student an excellent opportunity to witness for himself the British response to the Nazi aggression of the 1930s, and he used the insights gained from the experience in writing his senior thesis. This thesis, in which Kennedy attempted to explain England's hesitant reaction to German rearmament, was extremely perceptive and in 1940 it was published in expanded form in the United States and Great Britain with the title *Why England Slept*.

After graduating cum laude from Harvard in 1940, Kennedy briefly attended the Stanford University Graduate School of Business, and then spent several months traveling through South America. Late in 1941, when the United States's entry into World War II seemed imminent, Kennedy joined the navy. As an officer he served in the South Pacific theater, where he commanded one of the small PT torpedo boats that patrolled off the Solomon Islands.

On April 25, 1943, Kennedy assumed command of *PT-109*, the vessel on which, only a little more than four months later, his courage and strength were put to their first serious test. On the night of August 2, 1943, the Japanese destroyer *Amagiri* rammed *PT-109*. The force of the destroyer sliced the American craft in half and plunged its 11-man crew into the waters of Ferguson Passage. Burning gasoline spewed forth from the wrecked torpedo boat, setting the waters of the passage aflame. Lieutenant Kennedy remained calm, directed the rescue of his crew, and personally saved the lives of three of the men. Kennedy and the other survivors found refuge on a small unoccupied island,

and during the days that followed he swam long distances to obtain food and aid for his men. Finally, on the sixth day of the ordeal the crew was rescued.

Kennedy's bravery did not go unnoticed. For his deeds in August 1943 he subsequently received the Purple Heart and the Navy and Marine Corps Medal. Injuries sustained during his courageous exploits and an attack of malaria ended Kennedy's active military service, however. Later in 1943 he returned to the United States, and in 1945 he was honorably discharged from the navy.

After leaving the navy, Kennedy, like many other young men who had served their country during World War II, had to make a decision about his future career. He did not originally plan to seek public office. Members of the Kennedy family had expected that the eldest son, navy pilot Joseph P. Kennedy Jr., would enter politics, but this hope was cut short when he was killed in a plane crash during the war. Deeply affected by his older brother's death, John Kennedy in 1945 compiled a memorial volume, *As We Remember Joe*, which was privately printed. Shortly afterwards he decided to pursue the career that had been the choice of his late brother.

Appropriately, Kennedy sought his first elective office in East Boston, the low-income area with a large immigrant population that several decades before had been the scene of both his grandfathers' political activities. Announcing his candidacy for the Democratic nomination for the United States House of Representatives in the 11th Congressional District of Massachusetts early in 1946, Kennedy, with the assistance of his family and friends, campaigned long and hard against several of the party's veterans and won the primary. Since the district was overwhelmingly Democratic, Kennedy's victory in the primary virtually guaranteed his election in the November contest. As expected, on November 5, 1946, he easily defeated his Republican rival and at the age of 29 began his political career as a member of the House of Representatives.

East Boston voters returned Kennedy to Congress in 1948 and 1950, and for the six years he represented the 11th district he continuously worked to expand federal programs, such as public housing, social security, and minimum-wage laws, that benefited his constituents. However, in 1952 the young politician decided not to run for another term in the House. Instead he sought the Senate seat held by the Republican Henry Cabot Lodge.

The incumbent Lodge was well-known and popular throughout Massachusetts; in contrast, Kennedy had almost no following outside of Boston. However, Kennedy was backed by his father's vast fortune. Assisted by family, friends, and thousands of volunteers, he conducted a massive and intense grass-roots campaign. This hard work brought results: On November 4, 1952, when the landslide presidential victory of Dwight D. Eisenhower carried hundreds of other Republican candidates into local, state, and federal offices throughout the nation, the Democratic Kennedy defeated Lodge by a narrow margin to become the junior senator from Massachusetts.

On September 12, 1953, Kennedy married the beautiful and socially prominent Jacqueline Lee Bouvier, who was 12 years his junior. Shortly after their marriage, Kennedy became increasingly disabled by an old spinal injury, and in October 1954 and again in February 1955 he underwent major surgery. A product of the months of convalescence that followed was his book *Profiles in Courage*, a study of American statesmen who had risked their political careers for what they believed to be the needs of their nation. Published in 1956, *Profiles in Courage* immediately became a bestseller, and in May 1957 it won the Pulitzer Prize for biography.

During his years in the House and for the first half of his Senate term, Kennedy concerned himself primarily with the issues that particularly interested or affected his Massachusetts constituents. However, when he resumed his congressional duties after his prolonged convalescence, national rather than local or state affairs attracted his attention. His determination to run for higher office became evident at the Democratic National Convention in 1956. Adlai Stevenson, the party's presidential nominee, declined to name a running mate, and instead left the choice of a vice-presidential candidate to a vote of the delegates. Seizing this opportunity, Kennedy mounted a strong, if last-minute, campaign for the nomination in which he was narrowly defeated by Senator Estes Kefauver of Tennessee. Kennedy's efforts were not entirely unrewarded, however. He proved himself to be a formidable contender and, perhaps more importantly, came to the attention of the millions of television viewers across the nation who watched the convention proceedings. Kennedy was reelected to the Senate in 1958.

Shortly after the defeat of Stevenson in 1956, Kennedy launched a nationwide campaign to gain the 1960 Democratic presidential nomination. During the four intervening years, the Massachusetts senator had developed the organization that would help him win his goal. Through his personal appearances and writings, he also made himself known to the voters of the United States. Kennedy's tactics were successful. He won all the state primaries he entered in 1960, including a critical contest in West Virginia, where an overwhelmingly Protestant electorate dispelled the notion that a Catholic candidate could not be victorious.

The Democratic National Convention of 1960 selected Kennedy as its presidential candidate on the first ballot. Then, to the surprise of many, Kennedy asked Senator Lyndon B. Johnson (the Senate majority leader), who had himself aspired to the nomination, to be his running mate. Johnson agreed, and the Democratic slate was complete. For its ticket, the Republican National Convention in 1960 chose Vice President Richard Milhous Nixon and Kennedy's earlier political rival, Henry Cabot Lodge.

Throughout the fall of 1960 Kennedy and Nixon waged tireless campaigns to win popular support. Kennedy drew strength from his father's millions and the loyal Democratic Party organization. Nixon's strength stemmed from his close association with the popular President Eisenhower and from his own experience as vice president, which suggested an ability to hold his own with the hostile Soviet Union in foreign affairs. The turning point of the 1960 presidential race, however, may have been the series of four televised debates between the candidates, which gave voters an opportunity to assess their positions on important issues, and unintentionally also tested each man's television presence. The young, handsome Kennedy projected a better image on television than Nixon, and this factor may well have won Kennedy the election.

On November 8, 1960, the voters of the United States cast a record 68.8 million ballots, and elected Kennedy over Nixon by a narrow margin of fewer than 120,000 votes in the closest popular vote in the nation's history. In the electoral college the tally was 303 votes to 219.

John Fitzgerald Kennedy took the oath of office as the 35th president of the United States on January 20, 1961. A number of notable Americans participated in the ceremonies: Richard Cardinal Cushing of Boston offered the invocation, Marian Anderson sang the national anthem, and Robert Frost read one of his poems. Kennedy's inaugural address, urging Americans to "ask not what your country can do for you, ask what you can do for your country," was memorable. The new chief executive also asserted, "Now the trumpet summons us again . . . to bear the burden of a long twilight struggle . . . against the common enemies of man: tyranny, poverty, disease, and war itself."

Both challenges were in keeping with what observers would later mark as Kennedy's greatest contribution: a quality of leadership that extracted from others their best efforts toward specific goals. Many felt themselves influenced by his later reminder to a group of young people visiting the White House that "the Greeks defined happiness as the full use of your powers along the lines of excellence."

As he had promised in his inaugural address, Kennedy successfully sought the enactment of programs designed to assist the "people in the huts and villages of half the world." The Alliance for Progress, an ambitious but ultimately less-than-successful program for the economic growth and social improvement of Latin America, was launched in August 1961 at an Inter-American Conference at Punta del Este, Uruguay. The Peace Corps, which offered Americans a unique opportunity to spend approximately two years living and working with peoples in underdeveloped countries, was a more successful attempt to aid emerging nations throughout the world.

In the realm of foreign affairs, Kennedy's record was a mixture of notable triumphs and dangerous setbacks. He allowed the Central Intelligence Agency to carry out plans laid before his administration for an invasion of Cuba by anti-Communist refugees from that island. Between 1,400 and 1,500 exiles landed on April 17, 1961, at the Bay of Pigs, but suffered defeat when an anticipated mass insurrection by the Cuban people failed to materialize. Severely embarrassed, the administration nevertheless successfully encouraged the creation of a private committee, which ransomed 1,178 invasion prisoners for $62 million.

Cuban premier Fidel Castro, after repelling the Bay of Pigs invasion, turned to the Soviet Union for military support and allowed the Soviets to install secret missile sites in Cuba. From these locations, 90 miles from American soil, the Soviets could launch missiles capable of striking deep into the American heartland. Reconnaissance by American observation planes uncovered the Soviet activities. Taking a decisive stand, on October 22, 1962, President Kennedy announced that the United States would prevent the delivery of offensive weapons to Cuba. Kennedy demanded that the Soviets abandon the bases and stated that the United States would "regard any nuclear missile launched from Cuba against any nation in the Western Hemisphere as an attack by the Soviet Union on the United States, requiring a full retaliatory response upon the Soviet Union." After a week of intense negotiations, Soviet premier Nikita S. Khrushchev agreed to dismantle all the installations in return for an American pledge not to invade Cuba.

Meanwhile, the divided city of Berlin, Germany, had proved to be another Soviet-American sore point. After World War II, the victorious allies had carved Germany into four occupation zones and the capital city of Berlin into four occupation zones as well. The American, British, and French occupation zones of Germany became the nation of West Germany. The Soviet zone became the Soviet puppet state of East Germany. Berlin was located in the heart of East Germany, but the Americans, British, and French held on to their occupation zones of Berlin and thus the city was split into West Berlin and East Berlin.

In June 1961 the Soviet Union, still technically in a state of war with a divided Germany, announced that it planned to sign a separate peace treaty with East Germany by the end of the year. The Soviet Union also demanded that West Berlin become a demilitarized "free city" at the same time, asserting that this step would mean an end to Allied access and other Allied rights. Vehemently asserting the legality of the Allied presence, President Kennedy responded in July by doubling the American draft call and recalling certain reserve and National Guard units to active duty in order to add 200,000 men to the armed forces of the United States. On August 13 the East Germans erected the fortified Berlin Wall, which physically sealed off the eastern sector of Berlin and cut off the substantial flow of East German refugees into West Berlin. After a period of pronounced tension, however, the crisis passed without further conflict and eventually the Russians and East Germans eased their harassment of West Berlin. Two years later, in June 1963, the residents of that beleaguered outpost gave Kennedy a hero's welcome when he visited the city. He won even greater affection from them by proclaiming "Ich bin ein Berliner," meaning "I am a Berliner," in solidarity against Soviet domination (in German *ein berliner* usually refers to a jelly doughnut, but Kennedy's audience understood his intention).

President Kennedy gave wholehearted support to American efforts in space exploration. During his administration the nation increased its expenditures in that area fivefold, and the president promised that an American would land on the moon before the end of the 1960s. On July 20, 1969, two American astronauts fulfilled the president's pledge by becoming the first human beings to set foot on the lunar surface.

During his presidential campaign, Kennedy had stressed the necessity of improving the American economy, which was then suffering from a recession. As president he managed to stimulate the sluggish economy by accelerating federal purchasing and construction programs, by the early release of more than $1 billion in state highway funds, and by putting $1 billion in credit into the home construction industry. During his administration, however, increasing hostility developed between the White House and the business community. Anxious to prevent inflation, the president gave special attention to the steel industry, whose wage and price structure affected so many other aspects of the economy. After steel manufacturers insisted on raising their prices in April 1962, Kennedy, by applying strong economic pressure, forced the producers to return to the earlier lower price levels. His victory earned him the enmity of many business people

As a northern liberal, Kennedy sympathized with the aspirations of African Americans, but he included no comprehensive civil rights legislation in his presidential agenda for fear of alienating the conservative southern Democrats who otherwise supported him. In 1962, however, his hand was forced when he had to use army troops and federalized National Guard units to secure the admission of an African American student, James Meredith, to the University of Mississippi. In 1963 Kennedy used federal National Guardsmen to watch over the integration of the University of Alabama.

John F. Kennedy was president for roughly 1,000 days. During that time American involvement in Vietnam and other areas of Southeast Asia increased moderately, but the beginnings of a thaw in the cold war were also noticeable, and in 1963 the Soviet Union and the United States signed the Nuclear Test Ban Treaty. Kennedy's presidency was also notable for a new, vital style. John and Jacqueline Kennedy and their two children Caroline and John Jr. quickly captured the imagination of the nation, and their activities were widely reported by the media. Certainly the Kennedys exuded a youthful vibrance, and their interests seemed unending. Jacqueline Kennedy was responsible for redecorating the public rooms of the White House and inviting a glittering array of cultural and intellectual leaders to the executive mansion.

An assassin's bullet abruptly ended the life of John Fitzgerald Kennedy on November 22, 1963, as he rode in a motorcade through the streets of Dallas, Texas (see November 22). The entire nation mourned the tragic death of the chief executive. Many millions watched on television as the 35th president was buried at Arlington National Cemetery on November 25.

Both of President Kennedy's younger brothers, Robert F. and Edward M. Kennedy, served in the Senate. Many of the former president's compatriots hoped to see his goals and promise carried forward when Robert Kennedy, who had served as his attorney general and closest adviser, announced early in 1968 that he would seek the Democratic nomination for president. In another tragedy that shook the nation to its roots, Robert Kennedy was shot down by an assassin just after claiming victory in the California presidential primary. He died in Los Angeles just over 25 hours later, on June 6, 1968.

Wisconsin Admitted to the Union

Wisconsin, the 30th state, entered the Union on May 29, 1848. It was the last state to be formed in its entirety from the old Northwest Territory, which the United States had acquired after the American Revolution. Including the whole area north of the Ohio River and east of the Mississippi River, the territory held within its boundaries the present-day states of Illinois, Indiana, Michigan, Ohio, parts of Minnesota, and Wisconsin.

Jean Nicolet, a Frenchman, was the first known European to visit Wisconsin. Nicolet's sojourn at Green Bay in 1634 began a highly profitable fur trade between his countrymen and the native tribes of the region. In 1654 and 1655 Mért Chouart des Groseilliers and Pierre Esprit Radisson explored the Green Bay region of present Wisconsin. From 1659 to 1660 they investigated the Lake Superior section of Wisconsin. In 1660 seven French traders went to Chequamegon Bay on Lake Superior, and between 1679 and 1689 Daniel Greysolon Duluth investigated the lands west of Lake Superior and some tributaries of the Mississippi River. Nicolas Perrot in the same era built posts, extended French influence among the native tribes, and officially claimed the whole upper Mississippi for the king of France in 1689.

Roman Catholic priests were among the earliest Europeans in Wisconsin. The Jesuit Réne Ménard, who accompanied the Chequamegon Bay exploration in 1660, was the first of many missionaries who worked in what is now Wisconsin among such tribes as the Winnebago, Chippewa, Menominee, Fox, Sauk, and Potawatomie. Father Claude Allouez founded a mission at Chequamegon Bay in 1665, and later established a successful mission at De Pere. Father Jacques Marquette (see June 1), forced to abandon the Chequamegon mission in 1671, went on to found the mission of St. Ignace on the north shore of the Straits of Mackinac. There he was joined by Louis Joliet in December 1672. The next spring the two embarked on an expedition of the upper Mississippi territory.

Early in the 18th century, England emerged as France's primary adversary in the Wisconsin area. Native allies of the French killed a band of the Fox near Detroit in 1712, and a series of wars lasting until 1740 between the French and the area tribes ensued. In the French and Indian War from 1754 to 1763, England ultimately defeated the French and drove them from North America. The English then solidified their control of the region by putting down the native insurgency led by Chief Pontiac in 1765 and by taking over operation of the fur trade.

Wisconsin's traders remained loyal to England during the American Revolution. One of them, the mixed-blood Charles Michel de Langlade, who had fought against the English in the French and Indian War, led raids against American settlements west of the Allegheny Mountains in the later conflict. The efforts of the pro-British traders were to no avail, however, and Wisconsin became part of the United States by the Treaty of Paris, which concluded the American Revolution in 1783. British traders from Montreal nevertheless continued to exploit the fur trade in the area until the conclusion of the War of 1812.

United States Army garrisons erected at Fort Howard (Green Bay) and Fort Crawford (Prairie du Chien) in 1816 gave evidence of increased American activity in Wisconsin. The area was part of the Indiana Territory from 1800 until 1809 and part of the Illinois Territory from 1809 to 1818. In 1818 Wisconsin became part of the Michigan Territory until 1836, sending representatives to the legislature's sessions in Detroit after 1824. Between 1829 and 1848, 11 treaties extinguished Native American titles to Wisconsin land and increased the acreage available to American settlers.

Americans began to go to Wisconsin in significant numbers after the War of 1812. Members of the American Fur Company capitalized on an 1816 law excluding foreigners from the pelt trade. After 1822 miners poured into the southwestern sector of Wisconsin to search for lead deposits; their numbers reached 2,500 by 1830. Many of the miners returned south every autumn to avoid the harsh winters, and they earned the nickname "suckers" after a Mississippi River fish with similar habits. The more hardy adventurers, who passed the winters in hillside caves in Wisconsin, gained the sobriquet "badgers," and this tenacious creature became a nickname for the state and its people.

Pioneers continued to enter Wisconsin, especially after the Black Hawk War of 1832 broke the remaining power of the Native Americans. The government opened public land offices at Mineral Point in 1834 and at Green Bay in 1835. By the end of 1836 settlers, many of whom came from eastern states, had purchased 878,014 acres. These newcomers gravitated towards the southeast region of Wisconsin and founded Milwaukee and other cities along the Lake Michigan shore.

Wisconsin gained territorial status in 1836, with its territory extending all the way west to the Missouri River. Henry Dodge, a hero in the Black Hawk War, became governor. The first legislature, which met at Old Belmont in Lafayette County, selected Madison as the permanent capital. Although it shrank in size when the Iowa Territory, extending west from the Mississippi to the Missouri, was carved out of it in 1838, the Wisconsin Territory continued to grow in population. On August 10, 1846, Congress authorized the convocation of a constitutional convention, a key step on the road to statehood. The electorate rejected the first proposed constitution, which had controversial provisions concerning women's rights and an elective judicial system. A second convention drew up a frame of government more acceptable to the voters, and Wisconsin entered the Union on May 29, 1848.

Rhode Island Ratifies the Constitution

Rhode Island, on May 29, 1790, became the last of the 13 original states to ratify the United States Constitution. In the time intervening since the end of the Constitutional Convention at Philadelphia, Pennsylvania, in September 1787, the Rhode Island legislature seven times refused to call a ratifying convention, and the Antifederalist forces defeated the Constitution once in a plebiscite. Only after the national government had been in operation for more than a year, with George Washington as president, did Rhode Island call a convention. The convention delegates acquiesced in the new arrangement by the narrow vote of 34 to 32.

Rhode Island did not respond to a congressional summons in 1787 to send delegates to the Constitutional Convention at Philadelphia. The smallest state was faring well under the Articles of Confederation, which gave each state one vote in the Congress regardless of the size of its population and required unanimous approval for any changes in the frame of government. Economically, Rhode Island prospered in the years after the American Revolution, and its success was due in part to congressional impotence to regulate foreign trade. In 1782 Rhode Island's rejection doomed a proposed amendment that would have given the Confederation Congress the power to levy a 5 percent duty on imports. Rhode Island earned its livelihood in commerce, and feared that it would lose control of its destiny under such a provision. Of equal importance, the little state did not want to lose the revenues that accrued from its own schedule of import duties, and were used by the state to retire the Revolutionary War debts that it owed to its citizens.

Perhaps as many as three-fourths of the Rhode Island electorate owned state securities, which the government had pledged to honor in full. Returns from commercial duties serviced most of the debt in the early postwar period, but the state had to resort to sizable direct taxation on property in ensuing years as the burden of interest increased severalfold. Rhode Islanders were in the awkward position of paying heavy taxes to pay interest on money owed to themselves, and in 1786 they resorted to issuing large amounts of paper money in the hope of being able to liquidate the debt in two to seven years.

The state's residents initially found little that seemed attractive in either the Philadelphia Convention of 1787 or the Constitution that its delegates produced. To begin with, these New Englanders were the heirs of a strong democratic tradition, and they instinctively distrusted the powerful central government called for by the Constitution. In addition, they were in the midst of their paper money plan, which went into operation in September 1787. At such a time Rhode Islanders could have little enthusiasm for the new frame of government and its conservative monetary policies, which would not countenance their state's experiment in debt retirement.

In its October 1787 session, one month after the conclusion of the Philadelphia convention, Rhode Island's legislature met and began its evaluation of the Constitution. To the chagrin of the Federalists, who favored the new scheme of government, the Antifederalists dawdled and put off consideration of proposals to call a ratification convention until the February session. The Rhode Island legislature also ordered the printing and distribution of 1,000 copies of the Constitution so that "the freemen may have an opportunity of forming their sentiments" of the new government and communicate these feelings to the assembly.

At the February session in 1788, William Bradford of Bristol, Henry Marchant and George Champlin of Newport, and Benjamin Arnold and Jabez Bowen of Providence spoke in favor of the convocation of a ratifying convention. The Antifederalists, led by Jonathan J. Hazard of Charlestown and Job Comstock of East Greenwich, countered their arguments and defeated their proposal by a large majority. The opponents of the Constitution adopted a substitute proposal by a vote of 43 to 15 to submit the Constitution directly to the freemen of Rhode Island in their town meetings.

Meeting on March 24, 1788, the Rhode Island freemen defeated the Constitution proposal by a vote of 2,708 to 237. Federalists generally refused to participate in these proceedings and their abstention accounts for part of the lopsided margin of victory. Rather than cast their ballots, supporters of the Constitution, especially in the cities of Providence and Newport, issued resolutions calling for a ratification convention like those held in the other states. Also in March, Federalists in the state legislature repeated their proposal for the convocation of a ratifying convention, again in vain, as the opposition won by a 27-vote margin. Despite this defeat, the supporters of the new government remained undaunted and took heart when New Hampshire on June 21, 1788, ratified the Constitution. Victory in New Hampshire provided the Federalists with the minimum of nine states necessary to put the new Constitution into effect on a national level.

Five more times between 1788 and 1789, Antifederalists in the Rhode Island legislature defeated Federalist proposals for the calling of a ratifying convention. The opponents of the Constitution won by a vote of 40 to 14 in October 1788, by 44 to 12 in December 1788, and by similarly lopsided margins in March, June, and late fall 1789. Despite these victories, every day of successful operation of the United States under the new Constitution brought increased pressure on Rhode Island to join the Union.

In the summer of 1789, the United States Congress decreed that after January 15, 1790, all goods entering the United States through members of the old confederation that had refused to ratify the Constitution (namely North Carolina and Rhode Island) should be taxed as items entering from foreign countries, unless they had actually been made within the two states' own boundaries. On a more positive note, Congress in October 1789 sent to the governors of the various states 12 proposed constitutional amendments designed to placate critics who feared that the central government would limit civil liberties. Reacting to these proposals, North Carolina reversed itself, and on November 21, 1789, accepted the new federal government. North Carolina's capitulation left Rhode Island isolated in an untenable position as the year 1790 approached.

Reconvening on January 11, 1790, the Rhode Island legislature once again took up the issue of the Constitution. After much debate the Federalist proposal to call a ratifying convention in the state assembly on January 15 won by a vote of 34 to 29. The next day, a Saturday, the state senate received the measure from the assembly, but rejected it. Unhappy with this outcome, the assembly met in special session on Sunday and repeated its call for a convention. With one Antifederalist—who was a preacher—absent because he objected to the conduct of governmental affairs on Sunday, the senate then reconsidered the bill. Governor

John Collins, although nominally an Antifederalist, cast the deciding ballot in favor of the convocation of a convention.

Winning approval for a ratifying convention was but the beginning of the contest for Rhode Island Federalists. On election day, February 9, 1790, the opponents of the Constitution elected a majority of the delegates chosen for the ratifying convention, which met on March 1 at the old state house in South Kingstown. The Antifederalists elected Lieutenant Governor Owen as chairman of the convention. Owen and Jonathan J. Hazard provided the Antifederalists with leadership, and Jabez Bowen and Henry Marchant led the Federalists.

The Antifederalist leaders were not confident of victory. Indeed, there were some grounds for their fears that less determined delegates would be swayed by the Federalists, who suggested that the convention ratify the Constitution in the expectation that beneficial amendments, including a Bill of Rights, would soon be added to the Constitution. Hoping that an Antifederalist victory in the spring legislative elections would impress the weak of spirit, the opponents of the Constitution voted to adjourn the convention until May 24, 1790.

As expected, the Antifederalists scored a sweeping victory in the April 21 elections, but other political developments diminished the significance of their victory. By the time the delegates to the ratifying convention had reassembled, they had learned that the Congress was considering punitive legislation against Rhode Island. Many federal legislators wanted to end commercial relations between the Union and the state and to demand from recalcitrant Rhode Island quick repayment of its Revolutionary War debt. Upset by these possibilities, the leaders of Providence made it known that the city was ready, if the convention rejected the Constitution, to secede from Rhode Island and seek accommodation with the United States.

The second Rhode Island ratifying convention lasted less than one week. Confronted by threats from both Congress and the city of Providence, the delegates could not listen only to the popular voice expressed in the spring elections. Late in the afternoon of May 29, 1790, the delegates voted 34 to 32 to accept the Constitution, and the governor immediately informed President Washington of the news. A special session of the state legislature quickly chose Rhode Island's first two United States Senators, and in August the people elected delegates to the House of Representatives in Washington, D.C.

Rhode Island and the 12 other American colonies became states in 1776 when they declared their independence from England. However, for purposes of establishing the chronological order in which these states entered the Union, historians customarily use the dates on which they ratified the Constitution. According to this computation, Rhode Island is the 13th member of the United States.

Patrick Henry's Birthday

On May 29, 1765, nine days after he became a member of Virginia's House of Burgesses, the fiery young orator Patrick Henry introduced in that legislative body what history recalls as the Virginia Resolutions. Seven in number, Henry's militant resolutions were written in opposition to the much loathed Stamp Act. They asserted the colonies' right to legislate for themselves and upheld the principle of no taxation without representation.

Even though they were softened somewhat by subsequent actions of the legislature, the resolutions were published by colonial newspapers in their entire original form. Quoted throughout the colonies, they caused turmoil from Boston, Massachusetts, to Charleston, South Carolina, and encouraged the movement that became the American Revolution.

Young Henry had turned 29 the day he presented his resolutions. The well-remembered speech with which he introduced them called to the attention of King George III the disastrous fate of some earlier rulers. It concluded with the lines: "Caesar had his Brutus, Charles the First his Cromwell, and George the Third [at this point, Henry's impassioned speech is said to have been punctuated with cries of "Treason!"] may profit by their example! If this be treason, make the most of it."

The words today are only slightly less familiar than the "give me liberty or give me death" with which Henry concluded his most celebrated speech of all. However, that was not until 10 years later, on March 23, 1775 (see March 23).

May 30

Memorial Day

This is a movable event.

Honoring the dead has been a practice of many civilizations. The ancient Druids, Greeks, and Romans decorated the graves of their loved ones with garlands of flowers. Among the Chinese, the centuries-old Festival of Tombs, an ancestral remembrance day known as *Ch'ing Ming*, has long been a special occasion for visiting cemeteries and for performing rituals in memory of the dead. So has Japan's ancient Feast of Lanterns, or *Bon*, when Japanese welcome the visiting souls of the departed and light their way back to the hereafter with lanterns sent across the waters in miniature boats. In Christian countries, there is All Souls' Day. It is a day for decorating graves with wreaths, flowers, or candles.

In the United States, the dead veterans of the nation's various wars have been honored on a secular holiday now known as Memorial Day since the time of the Civil War. The location and date of the first ceremony paying tribute to the dead is disputed, but even before the fighting in the Civil War had ended, women in many communities of the South had begun the practice of placing flowers on the graves of fallen Confederate soldiers.

Spontaneous gestures of remembrance also took place in the North, as in the village of Waterloo, New York, which honored its war dead on May 5, 1866, by closing its businesses for the day, flying the flag at half-mast, decorating the graves of fallen soldiers, and holding other ceremonies at the three cemeteries in the area. In 1967 a proclamation of President Lyndon B. Johnson and a joint congressional resolution officially recognized Waterloo as "the birthplace of Memorial Day." The community responded on May 30 of that year by dedicating the Waterloo Memorial Day Museum, which contained relics of the 1866 event and Civil War memorabilia.

"Firsts" are difficult to establish, however, particularly for an observance like Memorial Day, which had its origins in numerous, widely separated, individual acts of commemoration. It is not surprising, therefore, that Waterloo's claim to priority is disputed by a number of other communities. One such is Boalsburg in central Pennsylvania, which some years ago erected a sign proclaiming itself "Boalsburg, an American village, birthplace of Memorial Day." The claim dates to a Sunday in October 1864 when Emma Hunter, placing flowers on the grave of her father (Colonel James Hunter, who had commanded the 49th Pennsylvania Regiment in the battle of Gettysburg the previous year), encountered a Mrs. Meyer paying similar tribute at the grave of her son. The two women agreed to meet the following year to again decorate the burial places, and their idea, gradually adopted by others, was an established custom in Boalsburg by May 30, 1869. Other early observances took place in Vicksburg, Mississippi; Petersburg, Virginia; Charleston, South Carolina; Columbus, Mississippi; Lynchburg, Virginia; and on Belle Isle at Richmond, Virginia.

In the years immediately following the end of the Civil War, an increasing number of memorial observances, similar to those held earlier, took place throughout the nation. Delegations of women from the North also visited cemeteries in the South where Union soldiers were buried and decorated their graves with flowers. Adjutant General Norton P. Chipman of the Grand Army of the Republic (G.A.R.), the organization of Union veterans, realized that the nation was eager to honor those who had died in the fighting, and he suggested to General John A. Logan, the commander in chief of the G.A.R., that arrangements be made for the organization to decorate the graves of Union soldiers on a uniform date throughout the country. General Logan approved the plan and issued an order to all G.A.R. posts:

The thirtieth day of May, 1868, is designated for the purpose of strewing with flowers or otherwise decorating the graves of comrades who died in defense of their country during the late rebellion, and whose bodies now lie in almost every city, village and hamlet churchyard in the land. In this observance no form of ceremony is prescribed, but posts and comrades will in their own way arrange such fitting services and testimonials of respect as circumstances may permit.

It is the purpose of the commander-in-chief to inaugurate this observance with the hope that it will be kept up from year to year while a survivor of the war remains to honor the memory of his departed comrades. He earnestly desires the public press to call attention to this order and lend its friendly aid in bringing it to the notice of comrades in all parts of the country in time for simultaneous compliance therewith.

Department commanders will use every effort to make this order effective.

The first national Memorial Day on May 30, 1868, was the occasion of more than 100 exercises honoring those who had died in the Civil War. The most noteworthy ceremonies of the day were held at Arlington National Cemetery in Arlington, Virginia, just outside Washington, D.C. General Ulysses S. Grant was present at the services, and General James A. Garfield was the main speaker. Garfield noted, in part:

I am oppressed with a sense of the impropriety of uttering words on this occasion. If silence is ever golden, it must be here beside the graves of fifteen thousand men whose lives were more significant than speech and whose death was a poem the music of which can never be sung. With words we make promises, plight faith, praise virtue. Promises may not be kept; plighted faith may be broken; and vaunted virtue be only the cunning mask of vice. We do not know one promise these men made, one pledge they gave, one word they spoke; but we do know they summed up and perfected, by one supreme act, the highest virtues of men and citizens. For love of country they accepted death, and thus resolved all doubts, and made immortal their patriotism and virtue.

Observances of Memorial Day quickly multiplied in the years following 1868. In 1869 more than 300 exercises marked the day, and in 1873 New York became the first state to designate May 30 a legal holiday. Rhode Island followed New York's lead in 1874, Vermont in 1876, New Hampshire in 1877, Wisconsin in 1879, and Massachusetts and Ohio in 1881. Memorial Day gained such rapid acceptance that by 1890 it was a legal holiday in all the northern states. Today, Memorial Day is a federal holiday and a legal holiday throughout the nation. The passage of time has brought about a number of changes in the observance, however. Most notable is the fact that Memorial Day is no longer purely a Civil War event; it is an occasion for honoring all those men and women who have died in the service of the United States.

Moreover, the date of Memorial Day is no longer fixed on the traditional May 30. On June 28, 1968, President Lyndon B. Johnson signed legislation shifting the dates of certain holidays to provide Americans with an increased number of three-day weekends. One provision of the new statute was that Memorial Day be observed on the last Monday of May every year. By 1971 most of the states had followed the federal precedent and set their particular state observances of Memorial Day for the last Monday of May as well.

The large national cemeteries, where thousands of war dead are buried, are the scenes of the most extensive ceremonies on Memorial Day. Arlington National Cemetery continues to be the site of one of the nation's most elaborate observances. On Memorial Day in 1958 the bodies of unknown servicemen who had died in World War II and the Korean War were interred next to the Unknown Soldier of World War I, and every year on Memorial Day the president or a representative places a wreath at the Tomb of the Unknown Soldier. Near the austerely simple tomb, on a terrace commanding a dramatic view of the nation's Capitol across the Potomac in Washington, is the Greek-style Arlington Memorial Amphitheater. It is within this oval, open-air structure of white marble that a high-ranking government official addresses the several thousand onlookers who generally attend the Memorial Day services, which follow the wreath laying.

Memorial Day observances are by no means limited to the big national cemeteries. In towns and cities across the land, veterans' groups, civic organizations, family groups, and individuals decorate graves with flowers or with small American flags on and in advance of Memorial Day. On the day itself, flags fly at half-mast, and relatives and friends visit the final resting places of their loved ones. In many communities, large and small, there are parades, usually leading from the business center to the local cemetery. Alternatively, the parade destination may be a park or square where a monument or other special memorial stands. Parade participants include veterans, armed forces personnel, and members of various civic organizations.

May 31

Seventeenth Amendment Proclaimed Ratified

The men who assembled in Philadelphia in 1787 to draw up the United States Constitution both respected and feared the citizenry of the new nation. The experience of the American Revolution had taught them that a government cannot remain unresponsive to the will of its constituents. A democratic system had no precedent in modern history, however, and many argued that the masses could not be trusted to govern themselves responsibly. Under these circumstances, the Constitutional Convention labored to establish a frame of government that would both ensure the voice of the people and curb the feared "excess of democracy." The process that the Constitution specified for the selection of the national legislature clearly reflected this dual objective. The document gave the people at large the right to elect their delegates to the House of Representatives, but reserved to the supposedly more learned and experienced state legislatures the power to elect the members of the Senate.

This system proved adequate until the end of the 19th century. As the era of the robber barons advanced, corporate control and corruption of state legislatures steadily increased. More and more of these bodies sent senators to Washington, D.C., who failed to represent the best interests of their constituencies and instead worked unscrupulously for legislation favorable to the great financial powers within their respective states. During the first decade of the 20th century the reputation of the Senate reached its nadir. Federal courts indicted three of its members for accepting bribes, and more than 12 others faced charges of similar corrupt practices.

Americans have always prided themselves, however naively, on the pristine qualities of their political institutions and found such abuses disturbing. The response was to make the political process more responsive to popular control. Convinced that the citizenry was capable of selecting the best people to fill the Senate, reformers argued that direct popular election of Senators would ensure the integrity of that body. Such a change in electoral procedure required a constitutional amendment. Both the House and the Senate must approve proposed constitutional amendments by a two-thirds majority, so the Senate was able to block its own reform for many years by refusing to give the necessary approval. Reform was temporarily halted on the national level, but this did not deter the reformers. Instead, they channeled their efforts toward altering election practices within the individual states.

The chief weapon in the campaign to restore good government was the primary election, the method by which candidates for public office are directly chosen by the people. In the first decade of the 20th century, the primary won wide acceptance throughout the nation, and by 1909 the electorate in 29 states were effectively selecting their own senatorial nominees. The state legislatures subsequently elected these candidates, but it became increasingly evident that this action was a mere formality.

The voice of the people in determining their representation in the Senate could not be denied. A scandal involving the election of William Lorimer, an Illinois political boss, in 1909 forced the Senate to end its resistance to a constitutional amendment. By May 16, 1912, both houses of Congress had given their approval to the 17th Amendment and sent it to the states for ratification. Just over a year later, on May 31, 1913, a proclamation by the secretary of state declared the amendment to have been ratified by the necessary three-fourths of the states, and it became part of the Constitution.

Walt Whitman's Birthday

Walt Whitman, one of the most original American poets of the 19th century, whose work was the precursor of free verse, shattered traditional patterns of poetry. His poetry, which was revolutionary both in form and content, met with a mixed reception from the contemporary public. Some readers were offended by its sensuality and its rugged, un-

conventional phrases. Others praised its freedom, inventiveness, and extraordinary vitality.

Life, death ("lovely . . . soothing . . . delicate death") and rebirth were among Whitman's greatest themes. So too was the symbolic "I," often interpreted as egotism, by which he identified himself and all humanity as one with the universe and one another. *Leaves of Grass*, one of his most famous works, opens with what may be the archetypal Whitman poem, eventually called "Song of Myself," although it was at first untitled. Among its nearly 2,000 lines of quintessential Whitman are these:

> I celebrate myself, and sing myself,
> And what I assume you shall assume,
> For every atom belonging to me as good
> belongs to you. . . .
> And I know that the spirit of God is the
> brother of my own. . . .
> I am the mate and companion of people,
> all just as immortal and fathomless
> as myself,
> (They do not know how immortal, but I
> know.) . . .
> And I know the amplitude of time.
> I am the poet of the Body and I am the
> poet of the Soul. . . .
> I am the poet of the woman the same as the
> man. . . .
> I hear all sounds running together, com-
> bined, fused or following,
> Sounds of the city and sounds out of the
> city, sounds of the day and night. . . .
> I believe a leaf of grass is no less than the
> journey-work of the stars. . . .
> I have said that the soul is not more than
> the body,
> And I have said that the body is not more
> than the soul,
> And nothing, not God, is greater to one
> than one's self is,
> And whoever walks a furlong without sym-
> pathy walks to his own funeral drest
> in his shroud. . . .

Whitman's words have perhaps even more import today than in his own century. One example of his modern flavor comes from his essay *Democratic Vistas*, written in 1871:

> I say we had best look our times and lands
> searchingly in the face, like a physician di-
> agnosing some deep disease. Never was
> there, perhaps, more hollowness at heart
> than at present, and here in the United
> States. Genuine belief seems to have left
> us. The underlying principles of the States
> are not honestly believ'd in, (for all this
> hectic glow, and these melo-dramatic

screamings,) nor is humanity itself believ'd in. What penetrating eye does not everywhere see through the mask? The spectacle is appaling. We live in an atmosphere of hypocrisy throughout. . . . It is as if we were somehow being endow'd with a vast and more and more thoroughly-appointed body, and then left with little or no soul.

Whitman was born on May 31, 1819, in Huntington (on Long Island), New York, in a house built by his father. He was the second of eight children. The family moved from Long Island, where Whitman's father tried to make a living as a farmer, to Brooklyn and then back to another town on Long Island. Whitman attended school in Brooklyn until he was 11, and then went to work as an errand boy in a law office. The lawyers encouraged him to continue his education, providing him with books, study space, and time to read comfortably between chores. He went on educating himself at newspaper and printing offices, where he worked as a printer's devil and then as an apprentice printer.

When serious fires and economic disasters swept New York City and made printing jobs scarce, Whitman returned to Long Island and, at age 17, took the first of a series of teaching posts. Conveniently for Whitman, who had much else to occupy him, school terms were only three months long at the time. He taught in seven different schools between 1835 and 1841. On June 16, 1838, the 19-year-old Whitman started his own newspaper, *The Long Islander*, which he ran for a year.

Whitman's newspaper career overlapped his teaching career. He held many newspaper jobs between 1838 and 1849, becoming the editor of the Brooklyn *Eagle* when he was 27. Whitman quit the newspaper business in 1849 and went to work for his father, building houses in Brooklyn. Thereafter, at various times, he was carpenter, printer, journalist, poet, and proprietor of a bookstore in Brooklyn. He finally gathered a selection of 12 of his poems, which he published in 1855 as *Leaves of Grass*. Whitman had probably begun work on the poems as early as 1847. He was to revise and add to the original *Leaves of Grass* until the last year of his life, bringing out a total of nine editions. Of these the last (1892) version, containing several hundred poems, was by Whitman's own deathbed statement the one definitive edition. It contained, one commentator said, all of Whitman's poems "that are worth reading."

In 1862, during the Civil War, Whitman went to Washington, D.C., to care for his younger brother George, who had been wounded while serving as a lieutenant with the 159th New York Regiment in Virginia. Though his brother's injury was less severe than had been feared, the conditions of other wounded men and the lack of care so appalled Whitman that he stayed on for three years as a volunteer nurse, treating both Northern and Southern soldiers, writing journalistic accounts of what he saw, and gathering notes for poems. A book of his war poems, *Drum-Taps*, was published in 1865. Whitman's two famous Lincoln poems, "O Captain! My Captain!" and "When Lilacs Last in the Dooryard Bloom'd," were among those to come out of this period.

To support himself during this time, he worked as a clerk in a government office. He lost that job in 1865 because his superior disapproved of *Leaves of Grass*, which he found indecent. Whitman's friends rallied to his cause, and that same year Whitman obtained a clerkship in the Treasury Department. Out of that fracas came the nickname "Good Gray Poet" for Whitman, which was the title of a pamphlet written by a friend during the campaign to reinstate Whitman in government employment.

In 1873 Whitman suffered a paralytic stroke, which left him a semi-invalid for the rest of his life. He moved to Camden, New Jersey, where he lived with one of his brothers until his death on March 26, 1892. Whitman was buried in a tomb of rough-cut stone, which he designed, in Camden's Harleigh Cemetery. The Walt Whitman Home at 330 Mickle Street in Camden became a state museum in 1923.

Hillary Rodham Clinton's Graduation Address from Wellesley College

Hillary Diane Rodham, future wife of President William Jefferson Clinton (elected in 1992 and 1996) and first lady, was born on October 26, 1946, in Chicago, Illinois. Her interest in social issues began at an early age, and intensified in 1965 when she entered Wellesley College in Massachusetts. In 1969 she was asked to give the commencement address for her graduating class. Her speech, given on May 31, 1969, was quite different from the traditional mild commencement address normally heard at college graduations. In her typically assertive and freethinking manner, traits that would distinguish her as a future first lady, Hillary Rodham exhorted her graduating class to help make the world a better place. She also criticized one of the previous speakers, Senator Edward Brooke, for being out of touch with modern issues.

Her speech gained national attention, and several commentators accurately stated that Hillary Rodham appeared to be a woman with a bright and promising future. Relevant excerpts are set forth below:

I find myself reacting just briefly to some of the things that Senator Brooke said. This has to be brief because I do have a little speech to give. Part of the problem with empathy with professed goals is that empathy doesn't do us anything. We've had lots of empathy; we've had lots of sympathy, but we feel that for too long our leaders have used politics as the art of the possible. And the challenge now is to practice politics as the art of making what appears to be impossible, possible.

What does it mean to hear that 13.3 percent of the people in this country are below the poverty line? That's a percentage. We're not interested in social reconstruction; it's human reconstruction. How can we talk about percentages and trends? The complexities are not lost in our analyses, but perhaps they're just put into what we consider a more human and eventually a more progressive perspective. The question about possible and impossible was one that we brought with us to Wellesley four years ago. We arrived not yet knowing what was not possible. Consequently, we expected a lot. Our attitudes are easily understood, having grown up, having come to consciousness in the first five years of this decade; years dominated by men with dreams, men in the civil rights movement, the Peace Corps, the space program; so we arrived at Wellesley and we found, all of us have found, that there was a gap between expectation and realities. But it wasn't a discouraging gap and it didn't turn us into cynical, bitter old women at the age of 18. It just inspired us to do something about that gap.

Many of the issues that I've mentioned—those of sharing power and responsibility, those of assuming power and responsibility—have been general concerns on campuses throughout the world. But underlying those concerns there is a theme, a theme which is so trite and so old because the words are so familiar. It talks about integrity and trust and respect. Words have a funny way of trapping our minds on the way to our tongues but there are necessary means even in this multimedia age for attempting to come to grasps with some of the inarticulate maybe even inarticulate things that we're feeling. We are, all of us, exploring a world that none

of us understands and attempting to create within that uncertainty. But there are some things we feel: feelings that our prevailing, acquisitive, and competitive corporate life, including tragically the universities, is not the way of life for us. We're searching for more immediate, ecstatic and penetrating modes of living. And so our questions, our questions about our institutions, about our colleges, about our churches, about our government continue. The questions about those institutions are familiar to all of us.

Every protest, every dissent, whether it's an individual academic paper, Founder's parking lot demonstration, is unabashedly an attempt to forge an identity in this particular age. That attempt at forging for many of us over the past four years has meant coming to terms with our humanness. Within the context of a society that we perceive, now we can talk about reality, and I would like to talk about reality sometime, authentic reality, inauthentic reality, and what we have to accept of what we see; but our perception of it is that it hovers often between the possibility of disaster and the potentiality for imaginatively responding to men's needs. There's a very strange conservative strain that goes through a lot of New Left, collegiate protests that I find very intriguing because it harkens back to a lot of the old virtues, to the fulfillment of original ideas. And it's also a very unique American experience. It's such a great adventure. If the experiment in human living doesn't work in this country, in this age, it's not going to work anywhere. But we also know that to be educated, the goal of it must be human liberation. A liberation enabling each of us to fulfill our capacity so as to be free to create within and around ourselves. To be educated to freedom must be evidenced in action, and here again is where we ask ourselves, as we have asked our parents and our teachers, questions about integrity, trust, and respect. Those three words mean different things to all of us. Some of the things they can mean, for instance:

Integrity, the courage to be whole, to try to mold an entire person in this particular context, living in relation to one another in the full poetry of existence. If the only tool we have ultimately to use is our lives, so we use it in the way we can by choosing a way to live that will demonstrate the way we feel and the way we know. Integrity, a man like Paul Santmire [a Christian theologian writing on social and ethical issues].

Trust. This is one word that when I asked the class at our rehearsal what it was they wanted me to say for them, everyone came up to me and said, "Talk about trust, talk about the lack of trust both for us and the way we feel about others. Talk about the trust bust." What can you say about it? What can you say about a feeling that permeates a generation and that perhaps is not even understood by those who are distrusted? All they can do is keep trying again and again and again. There's that wonderful line in *East Coker* by Eliot about there's only the trying, again and again and again; to win again what we've lost before.

And then Respect. There's that mutuality of respect between people where you don't see people as percentage points. Where you don't manipulate people. Where you're not interested in social engineering for people. The struggle for an integrated life existing in an atmosphere of communal trust and respect is one with desperately important political and social consequences. And the word "consequence" of course catapults us into the future. One of the most tragic things that happened yesterday, a beautiful day, was that I was talking to a woman who said that she wouldn't want to be me for anything in the world. She wouldn't want to live today and look ahead to what it is she sees because she is afraid. Fear is always with us but we just don't have time for it. Not now.

There are two people I would like to thank before concluding. That's Ellie Acheson, who is the spearhead for this, and also Nancy Scheibner who wrote this poem which is the last thing I would like to read.

My entrance into the world of
   so-called "social problems"
Must be with quiet laughter, or
   not at all.
The hollow men of anger and
   bitterness
The bountiful ladies of righteous
   degradation
All must be left to a bygone age.
And the purpose of history is to
   provide a receptacle
For all those myths and oddments
Which oddly we have acquired
And for which we would become
   unburdened
To create a newer world

To translate the future into the
   present
We have no need of false
   revolutions
In a world where categories tend
   to tyrannize our minds
And hang our lives up on narrow
   pegs.
It is well at every given moment to
   seek the limits in our lives.
And once those limits are
   understood
To understand that limitations no
   longer exist.
Earth could be fair. And you and I
   must be free
Not to save the world in a glorious
   crusade
Not to kill ourselves with a
   nameless gnawing pain
But to practice with all the skill of
   our being
The art of making possible.

June

June, the Latin form of which is Junius, was formerly the fourth month in the old Roman calendar. It is the sixth month in the Gregorian, or New Style, calendar in use today and has 30 days. There are many theories about the origin of the name. In the *Fasti* (a poetical description of the Roman festivals from January through June, commingling superstitions, folklore, history, and descriptions of religious observances), the Roman poet Ovid states that the name is derived from *juniores*, "youths." Thus, June is a month dedicated to the young, just as May, with a name that derives from *maiores*, "elders," is a month dedicated to the old. In another passage, however, Ovid has Juno, the sister and wife of Jupiter, the chief of the gods, claim that June had been named in her honor.

The Romans regarded Juno primarily as the guardian of all women and protector of their lives in all crucial moments. Her special relationship with women is easily seen in the diverse forms under which she was worshiped. As Juno Unxia and Pronuba, she played a leading role in furthering and protecting marriages. As Juno Caprotina, she was invoked for aid by female slaves. As Juno Lucina, she was turned to as a source of strength in time of childbirth. As Juno Sospita, she was called upon as a rescuer in perilous situations. Finally, as Juno Regina, the queen of the gods, she was worshiped in conjunction with Jupiter on the Capitoline Hill in Rome.

Not only did Ovid himself put forth conflicting theories on the derivation of the name, but other authorities both ancient and modern have suggested additional hypotheses as well. One is that June comes from the Roman clan name Junius. Another connects June with an individual member of the Junius clan, namely Lucius Junius Brutus, a distinguished Roman leader who liberated the Romans from their oppressive Etruscan overlords on or

about 510 B.C. According to tradition, the father and older brother of Lucius Junius Brutus had been killed by the Tarquins, the ruling dynasty of Etruscan kings. He himself had avoided death at the hands of King Tarquin the Proud by pretending to be an idiot. Later, he was instrumental in inciting a widespread revolt against the Etruscans and expelling their dynasty. An early fifth-century A.D. Roman writer, Ambrosius Theodosius Macrobius, explained that June had therefore been named after Lucius Junius Brutus since "in this month, that is, on the Kalends of June [the first day of the month], after Tarquin had been driven out, he, bound by his vow, erected a shrine to . . . Carna [the goddess of the internal organs of the body] on the Caelian mount [one of the seven hills of ancient Rome]."

The Roman hero was subsequently elected one of the first praetors, since the office of consul did not yet exist, of the newly established Roman republic. When Lucius Junius Brutus's two sons plotted to restore the Etruscan monarchy, he ordered them executed for conspiracy. He was slain in combat with the son of his mortal enemy (Tarquin the Proud), who was attempting to reestablish the Etruscan dynasty.

The tale recounting the naming of June in honor of Lucius Junius Brutus was probably invented many years after the death of that Roman hero, perhaps as late as the first century A.D. It may have been disseminated by Julius Caesar (102 B.C.–44 B.C.) or Augustus Caesar (63 B.C.–A.D. 14), either of whom would have had good reason to find such a precedent useful in justifying and sanctioning his own policy of calling a month after himself.

One of the most important June festivals in Rome was that of Vesta, the goddess of the hearth, which took place from June 7 to 15. It was considered such a sacred occasion that all secular activities were kept to a minimum: Even marriages could not be celebrated. During the festival, a number of rituals were performed. On the central day of the Vestalia, June 9, three senior vestal virgins prepared a sacred cake of mola (meal), mixing it with salt. This *mola salsa*, or salt meal, was offered to Vesta in her temple, the oldest in Rome, alleged to have been constructed on the Palatine Hill by the legendary King Numa Pompilius in 716 ᴮᶜ The festival of Vesta concluded with the cleansing of the temple storehouse in anticipation of the approaching harvest. The storehouse was considered to be of great significance, since not only Vesta, as goddess of the hearth, but also the Penates, the deities of the household, dwelled there to protect the food supplies of the city.

Apart from the period of the Vestalia, Roman women believed that June was the most favorable month for marrying. It is probable that this view arose in part from the belief that May marriages were unlucky and in part from Ovid's theory that June was named for Juno, the protector of women and guardian of marriages. However this may be, the popularity of June as a marriage month has survived through the centuries.

The Anglo-Saxons variously called June "the dry month," "midsummer month," "the earlier mild month" (before July, "the mild month"), and "joy time." June is the month of the summer solstice, the time when the sun has apparently moved to the point farthest north from the equator and seems to stand still before moving south again, hence the word *solstice* (of Latin origin, meaning a "standing still of the sun"). The lucky birthstones frequently associated with June are the pearl, symbolizing health and longevity, and the moonstone.

June 1

Kentucky Admitted to the Union

Kentucky, originally a part of Virginia, was admitted to the Union as the 15th state on June 1, 1792, by an act of Congress that had been approved on February 4 of the same year. Following the passage of the act, a constitutional convention met in Danville, Kentucky, on April 2 and completed its work on April 19. The constitution drafted by the convention went into effect on June 1 without being first submitted to the people for ratification.

The area of what is now called Kentucky attracted the attention of both the French and the English in the 17th and 18th centuries. The first Europeans who touched upon its borders were adventurers looking for an all-water passage west to the Pacific Ocean. In the second half of the 17th century, the great French explorer René-Robert Cavelier de La Salle may have followed the course of the Ohio River to the falls near which the city of Louisville is now situated. In 1682 he claimed the vast region drained by the Mississippi River and its tributaries, including Kentucky, for King Louis XIV and called it Louisiana.

For more than 100 years after La Salle's explorations, only isolated bands of fur traders and hunters penetrated the region and brought back tales of a beautiful but almost deserted land beyond the Appalachian Mountains. However, as one Native American chief predicted, the area was to be a "dark and bloody ground." None of the tribes that roamed the territory—Cherokee, Shawnee, Seneca, or Iroquois—had been successful in securing the rich hunting grounds, which were full of bears, deer, and buffalo, as its own domain. Thus there were internecine struggles for possession; and further troubles occurred when white settlers arrived in the area.

The first exploration of practical importance was undertaken in 1750, when British interest in the region, stimulated by rivalry with the French for supremacy not only in the Ohio River valley but also in all of North America, mushroomed. In that year Thomas Walker (1714–1794), a Virginian physician and land agent for the Loyal Land Company of Charlottesville, Virginia, crossed a natural passage (near the point where Virginia, Kentucky, and Tennessee now meet) from Virginia into what is now eastern Kentucky. He named it the Cumberland Gap after William Augustus, duke of Cumberland, the third son of King George II of England. Scouting for a suitable spot for a settlement, he explored the Big Sandy region of Kentucky.

Within a few months of Walker's expedition, the Ohio Land Company dispatched the frontiersman Christopher Gist on a similar surveying mission. Tracing an old Native American trail, Gist reached the falls of the Ohio and returned east via Walker's Cumberland Gap route. Although both Walker and Gist penned vivid accounts of their travels, their ventures into the "dark and bloody ground" were not immediately fruitful in encouraging settlement, because of the fierce frontier warfare between the French and the British. Only after the British victory in the French and Indian Wars, confirmed in the Treaty of Paris of 1763, did settlers from the eastern seaboard area start to trickle into Kentucky. In so doing, they blatantly defied the royal proclamation of 1763, which guaranteed the local tribes their hunting grounds west of the Appalachians and prohibited white penetration of the vast western expanse.

June 1

The first major movement of white settlers into Kentucky was instigated by Colonel Richard Henderson, a North Carolinian attorney and land speculator who, with others, founded the Transylvania Company with the express design of throwing open most of Kentucky. In 1769 the renowned backwoodsman Daniel Boone, who soon began to act as an agent for the Transylvania Company, started the arduous task of exploring the Kentucky wilderness and pinpointing suitable spots for settlement (see June 7, Daniel Boone Reaches Kentucky).

Numerous hunters and surveyors followed in Boone's footsteps. One of the most important was James Harrod, who in 1774 founded Harrodstown (now Harrodsburg), the first permanent settlement within the borders of the present state, eight miles south of the Kentucky River in eastern Kentucky. In March 1775 Richard Henderson and several of his Transylvania Company partners, imbued with somewhat grandiose plans for a 14th colony of Transylvania in the region, met with more than 1,000 Cherokee at Sycamore Shoals on the Watauga River near what is now Elizabethton, Tennessee. For several thousand English pounds, they purchased a piece of land, reputedly Cherokee-owned, covering most of Kentucky and part of Tennessee. Earlier the same month, even before the treaty was signed, the Transylvania Company had dispatched Daniel Boone and a party of 30 to perform one of Boone's outstanding accomplishments. This accomplishment was the clearing of the trail that would become famous as the Wilderness Road, extending some 250 miles from the Long Island of the Holston River in northeastern Tennessee west and north through the Cumberland Gap to the Kentucky River, deep in Kentucky.

In this venture the Transylvania Company was acting illegally, as it had no right to purchase the immense region which, far from lying exclusively in Cherokee hands, fell partly within the chartered boundaries of Virginia and partly within those of North Carolina. The area was in fact disputed between the two colonies. On December 6, 1776, Virginia affirmed its authority over the region by creating Kentucky County, practically covering the entire extent of today's state, out of this western land.

The prosperous Virginia plantation owners, who controlled the colony's government, soon found themselves very much occupied with Revolutionary War campaigns on their own soil and failed to provide adequate protection for distant Kentucky County. The self-reliant frontiersmen had to fend for themselves against British-instigated tribal raids. However, between 1775 and 1795 thousands of pioneers from Virginia, Maryland, Pennsylvania, and especially the Carolinas continued to pour through the Cumberland Gap over the Wilderness Road or float down the Ohio River on barges to Kentucky. As early as 1780, Kentucky County was split into three sections: Fayette, Jefferson, and Lincoln counties, and the 1790 census showed a population of 73,667.

Many Kentuckians, convinced that Virginia could not provide sufficient protection and governmental supervision, came to advocate independent statehood. Others favored the creation of a separate nation. A few even contemplated alliance with Louisiana, then under Spanish rule. A number of conventions, held at Danville starting in 1784, prepared the groundwork for statehood. Virginia responded favorably to the idea of ceding the title to its western land, provided that Congress admit Kentucky as a state. Congress passed the preliminary act in February 1791; a state constitution was drafted in April of the following year; and on June 1, 1792, Kentucky became the 15th state of the Union and the first one west of the Appalachian Mountains. The state constitution granted full manhood suffrage, making Kentucky the first state in the nation to extend such a right.

By the start of the 19th century, even Kentucky's Native American difficulties had been alleviated with General Anthony Wayne's decisive victory over the British-supported tribes at the Battle of Fallen Timbers near Toledo, Ohio, in August 1794. The question of free navigation down the Mississippi River to the Spanish-held port of New Orleans, a factor indispensable to the state's economic prosperity, was temporarily solved in 1795 by the so-called Pinckney's Treaty with Spain and permanently guaranteed by the Louisiana Purchase in 1803. Between 1800 and 1850 Kentucky grew quickly, strategically located as it was, with developing trade and shipping on the Ohio and Mississippi Rivers.

Like the other border states, Kentucky was split by divisive cultural, economic, and geographical interests. Its slaveholding farmers of the central Blue Grass country and poor whites of the mountain regions were torn by the same political and social rivalry that characterized the relationship between the tidewater gentlemen farmers and mountain frontiersmen of Virginia. Their reliance on slavery and their aristocratic social ties, on the one hand, caused many Kentuckians to sympathize with the South just before the outbreak of the Civil War, while Northern business connections and pro-Union political traditions inclined others to side with the North. Both the vocal antislavery element and the equally outspoken proslavery faction lost to the conciliatory group, which aimed at compromise and a united nation above all (in the tradition of Kentucky's statesman Henry Clay, the Great Compromiser).

With passions running high for both North and South in Kentucky, the birthplace of the Union's Abraham Lincoln and the Confederacy's Jefferson Davis, the inhabitants preferred to remain technically neutral. During the course of the Civil War, however, Kentucky's strategic location was to make it a buffer zone and battlefield for invading forces, and its citizens would join the armies of both sides.

Despite Kentucky's official declaration of neutrality, war came to the area with the invasion of southern Kentucky by Confederate troops early in September 1861. With its neutrality thus ended, the state officially announced its allegiance to the Union, even though the divisions among the populace remained. Union forces under the then little-known Ulysses S. Grant reacted to the Confederate incursion by taking Paducah, Kentucky, which controlled the entrance to both the Tennessee and Cumberland Rivers, and by seizing Fort Henry and Fort Donelson, Confederate posts that were respectively located on the two rivers just over the border in Tennessee.

Both Confederate and Union troops entered Kentucky again before the war was over. The Confederate invasion of central Kentucky in late summer and fall of 1862 brought Union forces in hot pursuit. The eventual collision of the two armies, near Perryville on October 8, ended somewhat inconclusively but with the Confederate forces departing from the state. Thereafter Kentucky was devoid of armed Confederates, except for guerrilla activity, which persisted until the end of the war. The strategically situated Ohio River community of Louisville had been secured by Union forces early in the war, on September 21, 1861. Established as a Union military headquarters, it remained a major supply depot throughout the North-South hostilities and largely escaped the ravages of war.

Kentucky's particularly deep divisions among friends and kin were reflective of its status as a border state. Typical of the divided households, ironically, was that of Mary Todd Lincoln, the wife of President Abraham Lincoln. Her brother, three half brothers, and three half sisters' husbands went South to serve the Confederacy. Appropriately, in view of the deep divisions, Kentucky was represented by a star on both the Union and Confederate flags.

After the Civil War, Kentucky saw the growth of industrialization as well as the development of the state's tourist attractions. Horse breeding and horse racing, epitomized by the famous Kentucky Derby, became practically synonymous with the Bluegrass State.

Tennessee Admitted to the Union

In 1929 the Tennessee legislature passed an act designating June 1, the anniversary of the admission of Tennessee to the Union, as Statehood Day. Tennessee's admission in 1796 as the 16th state was the climax of a long and complicated struggle for an independent status separate from the previously settled areas of Virginia and North Carolina.

The Spanish, French, and English, in turn, touched upon, explored, and laid claim to the region that is now Tennessee, setting off a rivalry for its possession that was not settled in favor of the English until the Treaty of Paris in 1763. The Spanish explorer Hernando de Soto was probably the first European to set foot within the boundaries of the present state. He may have crossed the southeastern section as early as 1540 on his march from Florida. In about 1541 he and his men, having reached the Mississippi River, stopped hastily to gather supplies and construct crude rafts on a lofty bluff, presumed to be the site of Memphis in southwestern Tennessee. There was, however, no attempt at colonization.

Over 130 years passed before other Europeans visited the area. Starting in the late 17th century, French adventurers, including the intrepid missionary Jacques Marquette and his companion Louis Joliet, explored the Mississippi River and its tributaries and undoubtedly visited the western portion of Tennessee. The explorer René-Robert Cavelier de La Salle considered this western region part of the vast area of French Louisiana and constructed Fort Prud'homme near what is now Memphis in about 1682. Subsequent French explorers erected Fort Assumption at the same strategic location.

The Spanish and French explorations of Tennessee were minimal in comparison with the inroads made by English fur traders and hunters in the 18th century. Although Virginians are known to have traded with the local tribes there as early as the 1670s, the 1750 expedition led by the Virginia physician and land agent Thomas Walker, who also penetrated the area of Kentucky, is regarded as the decisive beginning of the steady English probing of the region.

In 1756, during the French and Indian Wars, British soldiers established Fort Loudoun (named after John Campbell, the fourth earl of Loudoun, then commander in chief of the British military establishment in North America) on the Little Tennessee River some 30 miles south of what is now

June 1

Knoxville. Four years later Cherokee warriors attacked the outpost's garrison and the scattered frontiersmen it defended. After the British victory in the protracted struggle for supremacy in North America had been achieved in 1763, Native Americans, especially the Cherokee, were partially appeased by a royal proclamation guaranteeing them their hunting grounds west of the Appalachian Mountains and forbidding colonists along the eastern seaboard from settling on these lands.

Lured by tales spun by hunters and speculators, land-hungry Virginians and North Carolinians nevertheless ventured west across the mountains. In 1769 border settlers, primarily from Pittsylvania County, Virginia, built a few log cabins along the Holston and Watauga Rivers in what they presumed to be Virginian soil, but which was in reality the northeastern corner of Tennessee. When the western boundary between Virginia and North Carolina was subsequently surveyed, the settlements were discovered to be in what then was North Carolina.

The hardy, self-sufficient residents of the first Watauga River valley settlements met in 1772 to form a "homespun government" for the "preservation of their ideals of liberty." This "government" became known as the Watauga Association. For the first time frontiersmen west of the Alleghenies had joined together in drawing up a written agreement for civil government. The general committee of 13, empowered to act as a legislature, elected five of its members to wield executive and judicial powers. A clerk, an attorney, and a sheriff were also elected. The laws of the Royal Colony of Virginia served as models "so near as the situation of affairs would admit," and provisions for recording deeds and wills were stipulated. The Watauga Association survived for several years, and it soon gained additional support from the Brown Settlement, which had been made on the Nolichucky River in the early 1770s.

Any thought the Wataugans may have had of eventually founding a separate royal colony became obsolete with the outbreak of the Revolutionary War in 1775. Instead they organized their area into the Washington District. In 1777 the district, at the request of its residents, was formally annexed to North Carolina and gave its name (changed to Washington County) to North Carolina's entire territorial claim west of the Alleghenies to the Mississippi River. The frontiersmen, including such fighters as John "Nolichucky Jack" Sevier, participated in several Revolutionary War campaigns, helping to defeat the British in the important battle of Kings Mountain in October 1780 in South Carolina. Meanwhile, exploration and settlement over the mountains continued apace. The

war years saw the creation of Nashborough (later Nashville), founded by the ubiquitous explorer James Robertson, sometimes dubbed the Father of Tennessee.

After the Revolution, North Carolina, wishing to avoid the financial burden of defending its westernmost territory, ceded it to the federal government in 1784 on condition that the cession be accepted within two years. The Watauga River valley settlers in eastern Tennessee were upset by this action, taken without their approval, and were disturbed at the prospect of finding themselves without any government protection whatsoever. They met in convention at Jonesboro on August 23, 1784, and declared their intention of forming a new state of Franklin (at first dubbed "Frankland," or "land of the free"). They deemed the move essential to ensure protection against Native American attacks, validity of land titles, and a stable government. Delegates were chosen for a later convention, which would organize the new governmental apparatus.

North Carolina reversed its decision, repealed the act of cession, and tried to reclaim the territory. The precarious civil government of Franklin was beset with financial problems, Native American difficulties, and a struggle to wrest recognition from North Carolina and the United States Congress. It tottered on for four years under the leadership of the war hero John Sevier, now governor, whose annual salary had to be paid in animal skins. The Franklinites and the Cumberland settlers eventually found it necessary to gain support by intriguing with Spanish Louisiana, whose control of the mouth of the Mississippi River vitally affected the area's economic development.

By the late 1780s, the situation in Franklin was confused. North Carolina put an abrupt halt to the possibility of having the territory fall under the control of Spanish Louisiana by reenacting the cession of its western claim. Sevier was arrested on charges of treason. Congress accepted the cession, and on May 26, 1790, created the "Territory of the United States South of the River Ohio" with William Blount as governor. Blount had served as a member of the Continental Congress and delegate to the federal Constitutional Convention. Finally, arrangements were made for its admission to the Union as a state. A constitutional convention met in January 1796 at Knoxville, the first capital, and drafted the constitution, which Thomas Jefferson described as "the least imperfect and most republican" of any state. It went into effect without submission to a popular vote, and on June 1, 1796, Tennessee, with substantially its present borders, became the 16th state of the Union. John Sevier, having been pardoned and restored to favor, became the first governor of the state and served several terms.

Settlers flocked into Tennessee by land and water, especially through the Cumberland Gap over the famous Wilderness Road hacked out by Daniel Boone. The state's population numbered over 100,000 by 1800, and prosperous centers such as Memphis, soon a leading town of the cotton-growing delta, sprang into existence during the next half century. The state nurtured many famous fighters, including Andrew Jackson, Sam Houston, and Davy Crockett. It gained its nickname "the Volunteer State" from the high number of volunteers who answered the call to service when the Mexican War broke out in 1846.

After the election of Abraham Lincoln as president of the United States in 1860, and the subsequent formation of the Confederacy, the people of Tennessee, in February 1861, voted down a proposal to summon a convention to consider the question of secession. Public opinion shifted rapidly, however, with the firing on Fort Sumter in the spring of 1861, the beginning of the Civil War. A second popular referendum, held on June 8, 1861, saw the victory of the pro-Confederate faction as secession was approved by two-thirds of the voters, those against the move being east Tennesseans who owned few slaves and were loyal Unionists. On June 24 the governor of Tennessee issued a proclamation declaring the state's independence of the federal government, thus making Tennessee the last of the 11 Southern states to leave the Union.

In the meantime, a pro-Union convention of delegates representing all the eastern and some of the middle counties had been held on June 17 and had petitioned the United States Congress for admission of their area to the Union as an independent state. The request was denied.

Home to an extensive river network that provided ideal invasion routes during the conflict, Tennessee was, after Virginia, the second bloodiest battlefied of the Civil War. According to one historian, over 450 minor skirmishes and major encounters took place within Tennessee's boundaries.

In February 1865 an amendment to the Tennessee state constitution of 1834 liberated the slaves. In 1866 Tennessee became the first of the former Confederate states to have its statehood privileges restored, thereby escaping the congressional Reconstruction. However, radical Republicans in power enforced Reconstruction-like measures in Tennessee, and the postwar era was marked by bitter feelings.

Starting in the late 19th century, Tennessee developed its mining, manufacturing, and other industrial assets. A landmark in American economic history was the creation of the Tennessee Valley Authority (TVA), an independent government corporate agency, by Congress in 1933. The TVA contributed to the development of the entire Tennessee River basin and stimulated the state's industrial and tourist potentialities in a variety of ways: furnishing cheap hydroelectric power, improving river navigation, preventing floods, and planning forest and soil conservation projects.

Jacques Marquette's Birthday

Jacques Marquette, the gentle young French Jesuit who journeyed to the New World in 1666 as a quiet missionary, is celebrated in history as the co-discoverer, with Louis Joliet, of the Mississippi River.

The eldest son of a prominent and fairly prosperous family in Laon, France, Jacques Marquette was born on June 1, 1637. When he was nine he was sent to Reims (Rheims) to be educated by Jesuits. After receiving his college degree at the age of 17, he entered the Society of Jesus at Nancy, France, on October 7, 1654. During his school days and throughout his Jesuit training period, he heard reports of French Jesuits' adventures in the New World. From the time he was nine years old, he had wanted to become a foreign missionary, and this ambition never deserted him. Five years after he joined the Jesuit religious community, he volunteered to go as a missionary to whatever land his superiors elected, but he was encouraged instead to continue his training.

In 1665, with a master's degree completed and nearing the end of his long Jesuit training, Marquette again volunteered. The time was ripe for sending more missionaries to the New World; more specifically, Jesuits were sought to work with the native tribes of New France, as French Canada was then called. First, however, Marquette was ordained in the cathedral at Toul, France, on March 7, 1666. On September 20 he arrived in Quebec.

Shortly thereafter, he set out for Trois Riviéres (Three Rivers), about 70 miles from Quebec on the St. Lawrence River. There, under the direction of Father Gabriel Druillettes, Marquette, like other uninitiated Jesuit missionaries, spent two years in training. This training included learning native tribal languages and customs, in addition to wilderness survival. Marquette had a facility for learning languages, and he became familiar with at least six native tongues. More important, he grew to know and respect the natives.

June 1

In 1668 Marquette was assigned to work with the Chippewa at Sault Sainte Marie, which had been founded two years earlier by Father Claude Allouez as the first permanent mission in Michigan. The next year Marquette was sent to work with the Huron and Ottawa at La Pointe de St. Esprit on Chequamegon Bay in Wisconsin, another mission founded by Father Allouez.

While at La Pointe, Marquette heard many tales of the Great River. He became interested mainly because if such a river did exist it would provide a route for missionaries to reach many more tribes living in the hinterland and thought, until then, to be geographically inaccessible. In 1671 intertribal hostility broke out, and the Sioux drove the Huron and other tribes that Marquette had befriended out of La Pointe. With his native friends Marquette went east and founded a mission at the site of St. Ignace on the Straits of Mackinac, in the Upper Peninsula of Michigan.

Toward the end of 1672, Louis Joliet appeared at St. Ignace. Joliet, Canadian born and educated, had been sent to France for a year to be trained in hydrography, the study of bodies of water. He traveled the Great Lakes area for many years as a trapper and trader. Joliet also knew the native tribes and the geography of that part of Canada, Wisconsin, and Michigan as well as any other explorer. He too had heard stories about the Great River and in 1672 had been commissioned by the French government to locate the river and chart its course. The French, like the Spanish, speculated that the Mississippi might flow to the Pacific Ocean, opening new worlds and providing access to Asia.

Marquette was appointed to accompany Joliet for several reasons. First, it was the custom of French expeditions to take a priest along as chaplain for the explorers. The second reason had to do with the Jesuits' wish to learn more about that uncharted area in order to establish a mission among the Illinois tribe. Marquette, who knew the Illinois dialect and customs, thus was a particularly appropriate choice to accompany Joliet and his five woodsmen-adventurers.

Their preparations having been made during the winter, the seven men set out in two birch canoes on May 17, 1673. Marquette was then 36 years old and Joliet was 28. The explorers went through the Straits of Mackinac, across Lake Michigan to Green Bay, and into the Fox River. They stopped to seek advice and aid from members of the Mascouten tribe at the Jesuit Mission of St. Francis Xavier, near what is now De Pere, Wisconsin. This mission was, as Marquette wrote in his journal, "the terminus of previous French explorations. They have gone no further than this place." There were limits beyond which even the natives would not go, as the voyagers learned when they asked for guides.

Father Marquette's journal reads:

The following day which was June 10 [1673], two Miami who were assigned to us as guides embarked with us in the presence of a throng of Indians who stood dumbfounded by the spectacle of seven Frenchmen in two canoes undertaking what seemed to them such an extraordinarily hazardous expedition. We were led to believe that about nine miles up the river we could cross to a stream which emptied into the Mississippi. Furthermore, we were pretty sure that we had to travel west southwest, but the route was so cluttered with swamps and small lakes that it is easy to go astray, especially since the river is so full of wild rice that it is difficult to determine the channel. That is why we needed the two guides. They served us well, and led us to the portage [now Portage, Wisconsin] which is only two-and-a-half miles long. After the Indians helped us to carry the canoes over to the river, they left us to the care of Providence, alone in this unexplored land.

A later entry in the journal takes up the narrative: "A hundred-twenty miles of paddling brought us to the mouth of our river at 42½ degrees north latitude. On the 17th day of June, with a joy that I cannot express, we floated out upon the Mississippi River."

Eight days later, following a footpath from the river to a village, the explorers came upon friendly Illinois tribespeople who warned them that if they continued they would face many dangers from the river itself and from hostile tribes. The explorers decided to go on nonetheless, and the Illinois presented Marquette with a symbolic feathered peace pipe, widely respected by various tribes. As they continued down the river, the explorers did indeed have arrows shot at them, but Marquette raised the peace pipe high, and the two canoes were given safe passage.

When they approached the mouth of the Arkansas River, they met Akansea tribespeople who warned them that if they went farther they would meet not only hostile tribes with firearms but also hostile white men. The Akansea told them that the mouth of the great river was only five days away. By this time the French explorers knew that the Mississippi emptied into the Gulf of Mexico and not the Pacific. They realized that the white men the Akansea warned about were the Spanish, who had known about the lower Mississippi for over

100 years. Since France and Spain were traditional enemies in the Old World, and rivals in the New, Marquette and Joliet thought it the better part of valor to turn around rather than risk capture and have their information about the river lost to France. Less than ten years later, in 1682, the French explorer René-Robert Cavelier de La Salle reached the mouth of the Mississippi and claimed the river, its tributaries, and the land adjacent for France, naming it Louisiana in honor of King Louis XIV.

On July 17, 1673, Marquette, Joliet, and their men reversed their course. Having traveled down the west bank of the Mississippi, they made the difficult return upstream along the east bank. They paddled upriver (up several rivers, in fact, namely the Mississippi, the Illinois, and the Des Plaines) before they discovered the famous Chicago Portage, which henceforth would link the waters of the Mississippi with those of the Great Lakes for explorers, traders, and settlers. Beyond the portage, Marquette and Joliet continued on the Chicago River, which led them to Lake Michigan. They became the first Europeans to land on the site of Chicago, where those two bodies of water meet. Four months and 2,000 miles after they had embarked on their historic journey, the explorers arrived back at the Mission of St. Francis Xavier (De Pere, Wisconsin) in September 1673.

The trip had taken its toll on Marquette's health, and he stayed at the mission while Joliet, anxious to get his maps and information back to New France's Governor Frontenac, hastened to depart for Canada. Unfortunately, within sight of Montreal, his canoe overturned in the Lachine Rapids, and Joliet's notes and maps were lost, although he himself survived. Because of this mishap, Marquette's journal became the official account of the expedition.

Marquette, feeling somewhat stronger by the autumn of 1674, left De Pere to return to the Illinois tribe and establish a mission. He got as far as Chicago, where a severe winter and his recurring ill health forced him to stay until spring. In April he completed his journey to the Illinois, preaching to the tribe on Holy Thursday and Easter Sunday. By this time he was aware that his health would not be restored, and he explained to the Illinois that he wished to return to his home at the mission in St. Ignace, 300 miles away.

Marquette was so weak by this time that he had to be carried and cared for. Several Illinois tribespeople accompanied him on his return trip to St. Ignace, which he had left in company with Joliet just two years before. As the Illinois paddled the canoe up Lake Michigan, Marquette grew weaker. Finally, he asked them to stop and take him ashore

to die. They took him to a high hill near the mouth of what is now Marquette River. There, within a few hours, Marquette died peacefully on May 18, 1675.

June 2

John Randolph's Birthday

John Randolph was born on June 2, 1773, in Cawsons, Virginia, later part of the city of Hopewell. His background was distinguished; the Randolphs were one of the leading families in Virginia, and his maternal relations, the Blands, were equally prominent. Young Randolph was both brilliant and restless. In 1787 he enrolled in the College of New Jersey, now Princeton University. He remained there one year and then studied briefly at Columbia College. In 1791 he returned to his native state and completed the last two years of his formal education at the College of William and Mary.

In 1799 Randolph was elected to the House of Representatives. The new congressman's political career began during a time of sharp party divisions. The Federalists advocated a strong central government, while the Democratic-Republicans favored state's rights. Randolph was an ardent Democratic-Republican, and the election of Thomas Jefferson, his party's leader, to the presidency in 1880 ensured Randolph's rapid political advance. At 28 he not only became the chairman of the powerful Ways and Means Committee, but also was his party's spokesman in the House of Representatives.

Randolph's break with the Democratic-Republican leadership began in 1804. In that year Jefferson decided to move against the Federalist-dominated judiciary branch and, in particular, against Associate Justice of the Supreme Court Samuel Chase. Chase had enjoyed a distinguished career. He was a signer of the Declaration of Independence and a member of the Continental Congress; in 1796 President George Washington had appointed him to the Supreme Court. Chase, however, was also a staunch Federalist, and some of his rulings had been prejudiced by his strong partisan feelings. His continued presence on the bench was intolerable to the Democratic-Republicans, but according to the Constitution he could be removed from office only if found guilty of "high crimes and misdemeanors."

Randolph was given the responsibility for securing such a conviction. The evidence against Chase was speculative. The Democratic-Republican leadership, however, ignored this fact and, when the justice was acquitted, blamed Randolph for mismanaging the impeachment proceedings. Following the Chase trial, growing philosophical differences widened the gap between him and the leaders of his party. After 1804 Democratic-Republicans such as Jefferson, James Madison, and James Monroe began to espouse nationalist policies similar to those advocated by the Federalists. Randolph viewed such actions as contrary to the original principles of the party. He soon emerged as the leader of the former Democratic-Republicans who contended that the party's leaders were betraying its fundamental states' rights doctrine.

Jefferson's faction remained in power until the election of Andrew Jackson in 1828, and throughout most of this period Randolph, as a member of the House of Representatives, opposed the bulk of the party's important actions. It was his belief that Jefferson's Embargo Act in 1806, the presidential candidacy of James Madison in 1808, the War of 1812, the chartering of the second Bank of the United States in 1816, and the Missouri Compromise in 1820 were all violations of the party's states' rights doctrine. Randolph was especially harsh in his treatment of Henry Clay. A brilliant orator, Randolph used his talents in his numerous attacks upon the nationalist President John Quincy Adams and Clay, who was Adams's secretary of state.

Randolph's branding of Adams and Clay as "a combination of a Puritan and a blackleg" led to a duel between himself and Clay in which neither was wounded.

In 1831 Randolph was appointed minister to Russia. However, after he had served for only one month, illness forced him to resign. Throughout his life, Randolph had been troubled by several chronic illnesses. After 1831 his health failed rapidly. He died in Philadelphia on May 24, 1833. He was buried in Roanoke, the site of his father's homestead. According to tradition, he left instructions that his face be turned to the west so that he might keep his eye on the Kentuckian Henry Clay. In 1879 Randolph's remains were moved to Richmond.

June 3

Jefferson Davis's Birthday

The tenth child of Samuel Davis, a Revolutionary War veteran, Jefferson Davis (named for Thomas Jefferson) was born in a farm cabin in Christian County, Kentucky, on June 3, 1808. His father had lived near Atlanta, Georgia, for a time after the American Revolution, and then moved with his family to Christian County in central Kentucky, where he made a living by raising cattle and growing tobacco. Ironically, his youngest son, the future president of the Confederacy, was born scarcely a hundred miles from the Kentucky birthplace of Abraham Lincoln, his Civil War adversary. The Lincoln family moved north from Kentucky, eventually settling in Illinois; the Davis family moved south, to Wilkinson County, Mississippi, shortly after the birth of Jefferson.

When Jefferson was only seven, he rode on ponyback hundreds of miles northward to become a student in the Roman Catholic Seminary in Washington County, Kentucky, which his Baptist parents had permitted him to enter. After two years he returned home to study in the local schools, subsequently entering Transylvania University at Lexington, Kentucky, in 1821 at the age of 13. When he was 16, he received an appointment to the United States Military Academy at West Point. Upon his graduation in 1828, he was commissioned a second lieutenant in the United States Army (Robert E. Lee was in the class a year behind him). Davis spent seven years in army posts in Wisconsin and Illinois, and served in the Black Hawk War, in which Abraham Lincoln also served. While stationed at Fort Crawford, Wisconsin, commanded by Colonel Zachary Taylor, Davis met Sarah Knox Taylor, Taylor's daughter, and married her in 1835 against her father's will. Three months after their marriage she died of malaria.

Davis resigned from the army before the marriage and returned to his home in Mississippi. With a small inheritance from his father and a larger sum from his eldest brother Joseph, who was wealthy, he settled a plantation called Brierfield on rough land overlooking the Mississippi River. This land adjoined several of his brother's plantations, and the area, a large peninsula in the Mississippi, was known as Davis Bend.

Davis spent the next ten years overseeing the plantation. He worked his land alongside his slaves and is reputed to have treated them well. One unusual aspect of his plantation was his institution of a black jury system to try slave offenses. He was one of the "enlightened" planters who saw slavery as a necessary evil. In 1845 Davis entered the local aristocracy when he married Varina Howell. Elected as a Democrat to the 29th Congress, he served in the House of Representatives until June 1846, when he resigned to serve in the Mexican War, organizing a volunteer regiment known as the Mississippi Rifles. Under his former father-in-law, General Taylor, Davis and his regiment fought valiantly. Davis won widespread praise for his bravery at the battle of Buena Vista, and from then on thought of himself as a surpassing military commander.

Withdrawing from the army in 1847, Davis was elected to the United States Senate from Mississippi. He was an avid supporter of President James K. Polk and his expansionist policies. Davis's vision was essentially one in which the South would expand into the "empty" areas of the West, thus gaining in national political power. He opposed California's entrance into the Union as a free state in 1850. This California question, and the whole inflammatory issue of free versus slave states and territories, contributed to a wave of secessionist sentiment throughout the South.

In 1851 Davis resigned from the Senate to run for governor of Mississippi. The election was a conflict among extreme states' rightists, Southern nationalists, and "cooperationists." Davis's campaign appears to have been designed to allow the Mississippi Democratic Party a face-saving retreat from the brink of secession. Losing the election, he returned to his plantation, but in 1853 he was appointed secretary of war by President Franklin Pierce.

Davis's years as secretary of war were among his happiest. His health was robust, and he enjoyed the endless rounds of social events that were a part of Washington governmental life. He was responsible for the acquisition from Mexico of the strip of territory in the Southwest known as the Gadsden Purchase, which he wanted in American hands so that a railroad to the Pacific might be built through the South to the West.

At the close of his service as secretary of war, Davis was again sent to the Senate by Mississippi. Until his state declared secession, he hoped for some plan short of an actual break with the Union, although he never doubted the right of the South to secede. On January 21, 1861, he announced the secession of his state (which had actually taken place 12 days earlier) and withdrew from the Senate himself.

Mississippi immediately appointed Davis to command its state troops, although he himself had hoped to be commander of all the South's armies. Eventually, he was chosen as a compromise president by a convention of seceding states, in an effort to attract uncommitted Southern states to the Confederacy. Although he was not the first choice for many Southerners, Davis was widely respected as a moderate Southern nationalist. He was inaugurated provisional president at Montgomery, Alabama, on February 18, 1861 (see February 18). Then, with the choice confirmed by an election in October 1861, he was again inaugurated, formally, at Richmond, Virginia (which by then had become the capital of the Confederacy), on February 22,

1862. Meanwhile, the Civil War, which was to wrack the nation for four years, had begun with the firing on Fort Sumter on April 12, 1861.

Austere, now in frail health, and often irritable, Davis was plagued by a lack of cooperation among the Confederate states. When he tried to tax the states and institute a draft, he was bitterly opposed by extreme states' rightists, who called him a dictator. As the conflict dragged on, the South's manpower reserves were drastically depleted. Increasingly, there were calls for the enlistment of slaves into the army. Robert E. Lee finally lent his support to this plan, even to the extent of offering freedom to those slaves who would fight for the Confederacy. Finally, on March 13, 1865, in the most desperate hours for the South, Davis signed the Negro Soldier Law, authorizing the enlistment of blacks but leaving their emancipation to their masters and to the states. A few regiments were raised, but the war was soon over.

When Richmond fell, Davis fled toward Mexico. Captured at Irwinville, Georgia, on May 10, 1865, he was imprisoned at Fort Monroe for two years but was never brought to trial, partly because the political status of the Confederate states during the war was never definitively settled. Two former enemies of the South Horace Greeley and Gerritt Smith came forward, and Davis was released on their bond on May 13, 1867. The war had impoverished him, and he lived at Beauvoir, an estate near Biloxi, Mississippi, on the Gulf Coast. The estate was owned, and later bequeathed to him, by Sarah Dorsey, a friend of his wife's.

Since Davis refused to ask the federal government for a pardon, he never retrieved any of his former privileges or properties. He spent three years writing *The Rise and Fall of the Confederate Government*. He died at the age of 82 in New Orleans, Louisiana, on December 6, 1889. His birthday is still honored as a holiday in several southern states.

June 4

Jack Jouett's Ride

This is a movable event.

Jack Jouett Day, which commemorates an act of heroism during the American Revolution, is celebrated on the first Saturday in June in Charlottesville, Virginia. The event had more than just local significance, however. Through the night of June 3 and into the dawn of June 4, 1781, young John Jouett Jr., always known as Jack, galloped at great peril for some 45 miles along an abandoned road to warn Governor Thomas Jefferson and the Virginian legislature that British forces were closing in on them.

Born on December 7, 1754, in Albemarle County, Virginia, Jouett became a captain in the Virginia militia. He was the second son of the former Mourning Harris and John Jouett Sr., owner of the Swan Tavern at the county seat of Charlottesville and a member of the American branch of the De Jouhet family, prominent French Huguenots who had fled to England after the revocation of the Edict of Nantes in France. Before the outbreak of the American Revolution, young Jack Jouett, with 202 other citizens, had signed the Albemarle Declaration renouncing allegiance to King George III of England. Later he had urged the acceptance of the Declaration of Independence in Virginia.

Jouett's father, who helped provision American troops during the Revolution, owned a farm six miles east of Louisa, Virginia. Thus, Jack Jouett Jr. was somewhere in the vicinity of Cuckoo Tavern, Louisa County, at the critical moment. To his amazement the captain saw British lieutenant colonel Banastre Tarleton (known as the Hunting Leopard) sweep by at the head of 180 dragoons and 70 mounted infantry. Jouett at once guessed that Tarleton's goal was the capture of Thomas Jefferson, then at his home of Monticello, near Charlottesville, and of the general assembly of Virginia. As the Revolution progressed, the latter body had moved west, first from Williamsburg to Richmond and then from Richmond to Charlottesville. Tarleton's raiders, sent by Lieutenant General Lord Charles Cornwallis, had as of yet gone undetected even though Cuckoo Tavern was only a 24-hour ride from Charlottesville in normal circumstances.

Jouett's alertness and courage, his guerrilla-like knowledge of the countryside, and the swiftness of his thoroughbred mare enabled him to accomplish his self-assigned mission. In the tensest of races, he covered the distance from Cuckoo Tavern to Charlottesville between roughly 10 o'clock at night and 4:30 the next morning. Since the British were on the main road, he used a track nearly impassable in places, and the lashing branches overhead are said to have permanently scarred his face. He narrowly escaped capture several times by the troops he was paralleling, and if it had not been just a day before the full moon, the ride would probably have been impossible.

Jouett arrived before dawn at Jefferson's mountaintop home, after crossing the Rivanna River at the Milton Ford and warning the colonists guarding it. He immediately roused Jefferson and his guests, giving them time to make plans coolly and to secure important papers. Nevertheless Jefferson barely escaped; he relied on his telescope to tell him when the enemy reached Charlottesville, and by that time a detachment was nearly upon him.

After a glass of wine, Jouett had meanwhile remounted and dashed across the few miles from Monticello to Charlottesville to awaken the other Virginia legislators. They hastily convened and agreed to meet three days later at Staunton, in Virginia's Shenandoah Valley. Seven laggards, among them the renowned pioneer Daniel Boone, were captured by Tarleton's men but the main group escaped.

By his warning, Jouett saved not only Jefferson, but three others who had also signed the Declaration of Independence: Richard Henry Lee, Thomas Nelson Jr., and Benjamin Harrison, ancestor of two future presidents. Also saved were the famous orator Patrick Henry and John Tyler Sr., father of the future president of that name. Had Jouett not steeled himself for his ride, these prominent rebels, who had given crucial leadership to the Revolution, almost certainly would have been taken into captivity and run the strong risk of trial for treason in Great Britain. At the time of Jouett's ride it was impossible for the colonists to guess that the British surrender at Yorktown was only months away. As of June 1781 fortune seemed to have turned against the colonists, and the capture of the Virginia leaders would have been a severe blow to American morale.

Safely in Staunton on June 15, 1781, Virginia's general assembly passed a resolution commending Jouett for his "activity and enterprise" and ordering that he be presented with "an elegant sword and a pair of pistols as a memorial" of their high esteem for his service. The pistols were delivered in 1783, but the sword, ordered by Governor James Monroe from Paris, did not follow until 1804.

Two years after his tumultuous ride Jouett moved across the mountains to the wilderness part of Virginia, which would soon become the state of Kentucky. He settled first in Mercer County, near Harrodsburg. There he married Sallie Robards, sister of Lewis Robards, the husband of Rachel Donelson Robards, who later married Andrew Jackson. Since he sat in the Virginian general assembly as a representative of Mercer County, Jouett became involved in Lewis Robards's embittered efforts to divorce his wife by an act of the legislature. Jouett was later a warm friend of Andrew Jackson and visited often at the Hermitage, Jackson's home outside Nashville, Tennessee. Jouett was also on close terms with Kentucky's great congressman Henry Clay. After supporting Kentucky's separation from Virginia as an independent state, Jouett sat for several terms in the Kentucky legislature, first from Mercer County and then from Woodford County after he moved there. He foresaw the importance of the bluegrass country in stock breeding, and was a pioneer in importing horses and cattle from England.

Jouett died in 1822 at the age of 67 in Bath County, Kentucky. His burial place has been located in the family graveyard at Peeled Oak, Bath County. It has been said that "fame hung back from Jack Jouett." Until a resurgence of interest in Revolutionary War history in Charlottesville, the gripping ride of June 3–4, 1781, was largely forgotten. In 1922 the Jack Jouett Chapter of the Daughters of the American Revolution was organized in Charlottesville. Its members worked to commemorate Jouett's exploit and to further his recognition.

June 5

Gold Clause Repealed

On June 5, 1933, Congress, by joint resolution, revoked the clause in federal and private obligations that stipulated that payment was to be made in gold. Henceforth legal tender currency would be the accepted medium for fulfilling such contracts. This action, which came close to the end of Franklin Delano Roosevelt's famous first "Hundred Days" as president, was an attempt to make the government's then-recent abandonment of the gold standard more effective.

Under a gold standard monetary system the basic unit is a fixed weight of gold or is kept at the value of such a fixed weight. The Currency Act of March 14, 1900, had made the gold dollar, which weighed 25.8 grains, nine-tenths fine, the basic unit of value. The system was fiscally conservative in that it did not allow the money supply to keep pace with the world economy's increasing need for currency and because the provision that the holder of any type of American legal tender could exchange it for gold on demand discouraged any moves toward inflation.

Roosevelt, believing that the gold standard only reinforced the deflationary trend present in the Great Depression, which had plagued the nation since 1929, sought to secure greater control over the value of the dollar for the government. The president had plans to achieve recovery through monetary manipulation; he thought that a controlled devaluation of the dollar would encourage exports, raise domestic prices, and lead to an increase in production. A presidential proclamation on March 5, 1933, invalidated the redemption in gold provision of the Currency Act of 1900 and forbade the exportation of the metal without United States treasury approval. The Emergency Banking Relief Act of March 9 authorized the secretary of the treasury to call in all gold and gold certificates, and provided a maximum penalty of ten years' imprisonment and a fine of $10,000 for those who hoarded the metal. On April 19 Roosevelt announced that the United States was no longer on the gold standard.

The abandonment of the gold standard did boost prices temporarily as the exchange value of the dollar declined, but when winter approached the economy faltered. Following the theories of Professors George Warren and Frank Pearson of Cornell University, the government again resorted to currency inflation and began to buy gold until its per-ounce value rose in December 1933 to $34.06 from the October level of $29.01. This action was ineffective in improving the economy, however, and Roosevelt finally decided to stabilize the dollar. In accordance with the Gold Reserve Act of January 30, 1934, he set the price of gold at $35 an ounce, thereby reducing the dollar to 59.06 percent of its pre-1933 value. Further, Roosevelt lowered the amount of gold reserves that the Treasury was required to maintain to only 25 percent of the value of paper money in circulation. Thus, from 1934 to 1970 the nation was on a modified gold standard, sometimes called a gold bullion standard. In 1970, however, the dollar was cut free from virtually any gold standard when the Treasury was no longer required to maintain even a 25 percent gold backing of its notes, and as of December 31, 1974, the United States government once again permitted the private ownership of gold for the first time since 1933.

Portland Rose Festival

This is a movable event.

Portland is renowned as the City of Roses and is the home of the famous Portland Rose Festival. Located on both banks of the Willamette River, near its confluence with the Columbia River, the city is Oregon's largest and is noted for attractive residential sections, parks, and flower gardens.

Portland's association with the rose extends back into the history of Oregon. Probably in the early 19th century, traders of the Hudson's Bay Company, carrying with them seeds of the wild rose from England, introduced the earliest roses into the Pacific Northwest. Finding a congenial home in the rich Oregon soil, the wild rose became known as the Oregon Sweet Briar and still flourishes in the Portland region. From the 1840s on, pioneers arriving by way of the Oregon Trail (the beaten path from Independence, Missouri, to Willamette Valley, Oregon) brought rose plants with them. Hastily erected log cabins and crude houses throughout the area were soon bedecked with roses. One variety in particular, which came to be known as the Mission Rose, grew from slips cut from a prolific parent bush located at the Jason Lee Methodist Mission near Salem.

Every June since 1907, with the exception of 1918 and 1926, Portland has staged an elaborate rose festival. Growing from a notable city event to one of America's outstanding civic pageants, the festival is the biggest event in Portland, as well as the world's largest celebration of the rose. It comprises events of a Mardi Gras–like diversity, including a rose show, carnivals, sports events, stage entertainment, and a ski tournament on the slopes of Mt. Hood, east of the city. The grand floral parade attracts bands, floats, and marching units from all over the country.

The rose festival's origins go back to 1888, when H. L. Pittock held a rose show in a tent in her front yard at Tenth and Washington Streets, later called the Pittock Block, and invited her friends and neighbors to exhibit roses. On May 21, 1889, the Trinity Church Guild sponsored a rose show. During the next few years a rose show was part of either the flower festival held by the local women's club or the floral show held by the state horticultural society.

In 1902 the Portland Rose Society was organized. J. C. Card was elected president and F. V. Holman vice president. On June 10, 1904, the society, to supplement its annual exhibition, staged the Portland Rose Society Fiesta, highlighted by a floral parade with decorated carriages, bicycles, and automobiles. The fiesta was judged a success and was repeated in the two succeeding years.

As part of its Lewis and Clark Centennial Exposition, Portland presented on June 3, 1905, the greatest amateur rose show that had ever been held in the United States. It was remembered for the introduction of a new red rose named J. B. Clarke and for a speech by Mayor Harry Lane suggesting a Portland "festival of roses." In 1906 Holman, who by then had risen to the presidency of the Portland Rose Society, carried forward the mayor's enthusiasm by proposing to some of the leading citizens that a festival be held in conjunction with the annual rose show. A plan was agreed upon, and on June 20 and June 21, twenty illuminated floats on flatcars, driven on the rail of Portland's electric trolley network, were the chief attractions of the first Rose Festival pageant. The

festival also included an exhibition of 10,000 roses and other flowers in the Forestry Building and a parade of automobiles and horse-drawn carriages decorated with flowers. It was so successful that within the month enthusiastic citizens, mostly businessmen, incorporated the Rose Festival Association with a capital stock of $10,000 and the declared purpose of holding an annual floral event which, it was thought, would call favorable attention to both the state of Oregon and the city of Portland.

By 1910, when the first moving pictures of the festival were taken, the automobile had so increased in popularity and efficiency that that year's festival had a five-mile-long procession of decorated cars and trucks. A train of six trolley cars was loaded with roses, and on one of the days during the week-long festival, the roses were thrown from the cars to the spectators lining the sidewalks. Another highlight was an aerial exhibition demonstrating a dirigible. In 1915 the rapidly growing festival was widely advertised by the slogan "The Whole World Knows the Portland Rose." In subsequent years other promotional events advertised the city as a rose center. The Union Pacific named a special train the Portland Rose. Members of the city's Women's Advertising Club would meet arriving trains and hand each passenger a rose; they gave an honorary membership in the Mystic Order of the Rose to distinguished visitors, including Franklin Delano Roosevelt, Herbert Hoover, and Amelia Earhart, who were initiated with the pledge that they speak or write of Portland as the "city of roses." Rose cuttings were made available for free distribution; in 1946 a supply of 30,000 was exhausted in less than two hours.

By 1922 the Portland Rose Festival had become so popular that floats were entered in the parade not only from Portland but also from other communities in Oregon and from California, Washington, and British Columbia. As the festival increased in size, so did the number of events. By the late 1990s there were approximately 80 events covering some 25 days and drawing an estimated 2 million people. The date of the festival can vary from year to year, but it typically covers the period from late May to late June.

June 6

World War II: D Day

In the early hours of June 6, 1944, forces of the World War II Allies (American, British, Canadian, and French) embarked from England to launch an invasion of continental Europe. Across the cold waters of the English Channel, the greatest armada ever assembled made its way toward the beaches of Normandy in France. This D day assault, the product of three years of planning, broke the Nazi stranglehold on the Continent and led to the eventual surrender of Germany and its Axis partners.

British strategists had begun planning for an invasion of Europe after Germany's conquest of France in 1940 had driven the Allies from the Continent. At the Atlantic Conference of August 1941 the British outlined their strategy to the Americans. They envisioned the operation as a coup de grâce to be administered to the Nazis only after blockade, air bombardment, and internal subversive action had severely weakened Germany. Britain deeply wished to avoid repetition of the bloody infantry contests of World War I.

The attack by Japan, Germany's Far Eastern ally, on the American naval base at Pearl Harbor on December 7, 1941, brought the United States into the war against the Axis powers and introduced a new trend into the military planning. American strategists stressed the need to defeat Germany's ground forces in order to break the will to fight and did not want to delay the invasion of Europe until the Nazis were moribund. Garman successes on the eastern front against the Soviet Union, which had been brought into the war on the Allied side in the summer of 1941, increased the necessity of striking early.

General Dwight D. Eisenhower, appointed on March 9, 1942, by United States chief of staff general George C. Marshall to be head of the Operations Division of the War Department, strongly advocated an early cross-Channel invasion of Europe from England. For reasons of communications and logistics, England was best located to serve as the base of operations and it already had airfields from which to bombard Germany. Eisenhower considered the cross-Channel assault so vital he argued that the United States should shift its focus of operations from the Atlantic to the Pacific theater if the Allies did not agree to the plan.

President Franklin D. Roosevelt approved the plans of the War Department and sent Marshall and presidential assistant Harry Hopkins to England to present arguments in favor of the cross-Channel invasion. The American envoys also impressed upon the British chiefs of staff the importance of allowing the American forces time to gain combat experience. The mission was a success: On April 14, 1942, the British endorsed the American plan for an invasion, and the Allies agreed to 1943 as the target date.

Meanwhile, British strategists suggested campaigns in North Africa or the Middle East to divert the Germans' attention from the hard-pressed Russians. Although American military men feared that such Mediterranean adventures might upset the scheduling of the main invasion, they reluctantly accepted the plan for a North African landing. However, execution of the North African operation, the initiation of the Italian campaign, and the increased activity in the Southwest Pacific delayed preparations for the European invasion. Planners soon realized that the assault could not come until 1944.

In January 1943 at the Casablanca Conference, the British and American combined chiefs of staff created an office to prepare for the invasion of northern Europe. Lieutenant General Sir Frederick Morgan of Britain became the chief of staff to the supreme allied commander, who had not yet been named. COSSAC, as Morgan's office became known, immediately began planning and chose the beaches of Normandy as the landing site for the invasion. The Quadrant Conference of August 1943 approved Morgan's work, and the Teheran Conference in November gave the final approval to a May 1944 cross-Channel assault.

Most observers expected General Marshall to command the European invasion, but in December 1943 General Dwight D. Eisenhower, then the head of the European Theater of Operations for the United States Army (ETOUSA), received the appointment. Eisenhower had been battle-tested in the Mediterranean campaigns and had the personality necessary to keep the Anglo-American military alliance operating smoothly. Marshall continued as chief of staff, a post in which his strategic and organizational abilities were most valuable.

On January 17, 1944, Eisenhower took command of the Supreme Headquarters Allied Expeditionary Forces (SHAEF), which replaced COSSAC. Air Chief Marshal Sir Arthur William Tedder of Britain became deputy supreme commander and General Walter Bedell Smith of the United States became chief of staff. Admiral Sir Bertram Ramsay and Air Chief Marshal Sir Trafford Leigh-Mallory commanded the naval and air elements of the expeditionary forces.

SHAEF devised plans for a Normandy landing to be followed by an advance across a wide front. After driving the Germans back across the Rhine River, the Allies would then envelop the industrialized Ruhr region. The final assault would thrust deep into Germany to destroy the Nazis in their homeland.

June 6

May 1944 was the month originally set for the invasion, but Eisenhower rescheduled it for June to increase the strike force from three to five divisions. Allied air forces made use of the delay and the good flying weather to attack Axis transportation centers and coastal defenses throughout the month of May. During the final month the Allied forces practiced their beach landing techniques.

SHAEF established three landing zones for the Allied armies. The British Second Army, composed of English and Canadian troops and commanded by Lieutenant General M. C. Dempsey, was to strike between Bayeux and Caen at beaches designated Sword, Juno, and Gold. Lieutenant General Omar Bradley's United States First Army had two landing sites to the right (or west) of the British: The V Corps under Major General Leonard T. Gerow was to invade at Omaha Beach and the VII Corps under Major General J. Lawton Collins had Utah Beach on the right flank as its objective.

German defenses in Normandy were strong, but several factors favored the Allies. Adolph Hitler and Field Marshal Gerd von Rundstedt, the German commander in chief for the west, expected that the Allied invasion would strike at Pas de Calais, near Belgium, where the Channel was narrowest and not in Normandy. Von Rundstedt also thought that the enemy should be allowed to land and then be destroyed by well-placed mechanized reserves. Fortunately for the Allies, the Nazis followed the alternative philosophy of General Field Marshal Erwin Rommel, commander of German Army Group B in the Netherlands-Loire district, that the Germans must stop the invaders at the coast. Consequently, the Germans spread their defenses along the coast and failed to keep a sufficient reserve force to counter penetration of their front lines. Allied air superiority further limited the Nazis' defensive capabilities.

Eisenhower's burden increased as D day approached. Plans called for the 82nd and 101st Airborne Divisions of the U.S. Army to drop behind German lines, but Leigh-Mallory continued to argue that the jumps would bring excessive casualties. Omar Bradley argued that the airborne phase was absolutely necessary to prevent disaster at Utah Beach, and Eisenhower decided to follow his advice.

Factors of the moon, tide, and time of sunrise limited D day to June 5, 6, or 7. Early on the morning of June 4, Group Captain J. M. Stagg, chief Allied meteorologist, informed General Eisenhower that the weather on June 5 would be unfavorable because of 45-mile-per-hour winds expected to hit the Normandy beaches. Although June 4 was a beautiful day, with no visible hint of what the next

day held, Eisenhower took Stagg's advice and postponed the invasion for 24 hours. As Stagg had predicted, June 5 was stormy. However, on the morning of the fifth the group captain was able to forecast acceptable weather for June 6. Eisenhower again accepted his word and set the assault for the following morning.

Late on the night of June 5, more than 900 planes and 100 gliders of the U.S. Ninth Air Force took off from British fields with the parachute jumpers of the 82nd and 101st Divisions. Fog and heavy antiaircraft fire awaited them at the coast of France and caused the soldiers to land in groups scattered over a much larger area than planned. Nevertheless, Leigh-Mallory's fears proved unfounded, and the paratroopers, fighting in small groups, managed to secure bridges and access roads to Utah Beach. Their efforts contributed greatly to the battle's outcome.

In the early hours of June 6, the huge armada began to move across the Channel: 1,796 and 931 vessels carried the three British divisions and the two American divisions, respectively. About halfway across the Channel, the faster combat vessels moved ahead to their predesignated positions while the transport vessels bearing the troops and equipment moved behind them.

An hour and a half before sunrise, the preliminary naval bombardment began. Ten minutes later, 480 B-24s dropped 1,285 tons of bombs on the mainland. Unfortunately for the Allies, the projectiles landed behind, rather than on, the beach defenses. As the naval and air attack began, the transports, standing 11 miles offshore out of range of the German batteries, unloaded troops and equipment into smaller Landing Craft Transports (LCTs). The LCTs then undertook the hazardous run to the beaches.

Tanks comprised the first assault wave heading for Omaha Beach. The commander of the LCTs in the western sector of the beach recognized that the seas were too rough for normal procedures and brought even the amphibious tanks to the shoreline. An army captain in the eastern sector was not so prudent and lost 27 of his 32 amphibious tanks when he launched the tracked vehicles 5,000 yards from the beach.

Eight waves of infantrymen and one artillery unit followed the tanks onto Omaha Beach. German defenses were even stronger than expected because Allied intelligence had missed the presence of the 352nd Infantry Division in the area. American casualties ran as high as 66 percent in some sectors of the beach, but the troops gradually pushed inland. Utah Beach, unprotected by cliffs like those overlooking Omaha, posed fewer problems for the attacking Americans. The reservists and foreign volunteers comprising the Nazis' defending 709th Regiment lacked the fighting spirit of the units encountered elsewhere. Moreover, poor communications made the Germans' situation worse; General Friedrich Dollman of the Seventh Army did not even learn of the attack until hours after it began.

In the other D day landings, British, Canadian, and French soldiers successfully stormed Gold, Juno, and Sword Beaches. Their experiences paralleled those of the Americans at Utah, rather than Omaha, Beach. By the end of the first day the Allies had established bases at each of the five invasion points.

The Normandy struggle continued until July. The American V Corps took Isigny, and on June 12 the VII Corps took the key city of Carentan. Then General Joseph ("Lightning Joe") Lawton Collins began a drive across the Cotentin Peninsula to capture the port city of Cherbourg. Obeying Hitler's orders to fight until the end, the Germans withstood a terrific pounding, but the battle came to a close on June 26 with the capture of the city and a large number of its defenders, including General Karl Wilhelm von Schlieben.

Approximately 130,000 men landed at Normandy during D day; 72,215 were British and Canadian, 57,300 were American. The British dropped 7,900 paratroopers and the Americans 15,000. British and Canadian forces suffered more than 4,000 casualties, and about 6,000 Americans were killed or wounded. In June 1994 President Bill Clinton personally visited Normandy to honor the 50th anniversary of the D day invasion and the American lives lost during the battle.

Confederate Memorial Day in Winchester, Virginia

The Civil War divided the nation into two armed camps, but the North and South shared a common grief in the staggering loss of life that both sides suffered during the conflict. No war in the history of the United States ever produced more casualties in proportion to the number of combatants involved; the Confederate army counted approximately 258,000 soldiers killed, while the Union dead numbered more than 359,000. Sorrow was so intense in the last days of the war and in the years that followed that a number of places in both the North and the South held special ceremonies to honor those who had fallen in battle. These services gradually became traditional. Today there is the national Memorial Day, and many southern states take note of special Confederate memorial days. A number of these observances take place on the anniversary of events of special significance to

particular localities. Of these, one notable example takes place in Winchester, Virginia, where June 6 has been commemorated since 1866.

During the Civil War the Shenandoah Valley, in which Winchester is located, was important to the Confederacy both as a source of provisions and as a possible route for an invasion of the North. Six major battles were fought in the vicinity of Winchester; the town changed hands more than 70 times as Confederate and Union forces alternately exercised control of the region. The extensive fighting that took place in the valley resulted in a large number of casualties. Estimates of the number of Northern and Southern soldiers who died in the area of Winchester are generally placed at about 7,500.

Because of the exigencies of war, many of the battle dead were buried in hastily dug graves, and soon after the fighting ended the inappropriateness of these final resting places became apparent. As early as the spring of 1865, only weeks after Robert E. Lee's surrender at Appomattox, farmers preparing to plant their fields in the area unearthed the bodies of several Confederate soldiers. The likelihood that such desecration would recur greatly disturbed one citizen of Winchester, Mrs. Philip Williams, who had headed the town's women's relief corps during the war. She decided to secure a proper resting place for the Southern war dead.

Together with her sister-in-law, Mrs. A. H. H. Boyd, Mrs. Williams organized the women who had nursed and otherwise assisted the soldiers who fought in the vicinity of Winchester into the Ladies Confederate Memorial Association. The avowed purposes of the association were to reinter in one graveyard all those who had died for the Confederate cause within a 12- to 15-mile radius of Winchester, and to encourage people of the region to come to the proposed cemetery every year to decorate the grave sites with flowers and evergreens. To finance the purchase of land for the cemetery, the association and a committee of town representatives appealed to the citizens of the South. The economic plight of the former Confederate states after the war was desperate, but the Winchester appeal received an overwhelmingly favorable response. By the spring of 1866, sufficient funds were accumulated so that the association could buy land for the cemetery and begin the arduous task of reinterment.

The work of removing the bodies of the 2,494 Confederate dead who were buried in graves scattered in the Winchester area proceeded rapidly. By the fall of 1866 their reinterment was completed, and on October 25 of that year Stonewall Cemetery was officially dedicated. Thousands of people were present for the October 25 services. Former Virginian governor Henry A. Wise addressed the assembly, and the remains of General Turner Ashby, a wealthy and influential Shenandoah Valley planter and politician who had died on June 6, 1862, during a rearguard action at Harrisonburg, Virginia, were brought from the University of Virginia to their final resting place at Stonewall Cemetery. In the years to follow, June 6, the anniversary of the death of General Ashby, became the traditional date for the Winchester memorial observances.

YMCA Founded

Although it consisted of only 12 members at its birth in London on June 6, 1844, the Young Men's Christian Association (YMCA) was destined to become a significant international organization. Within seven years, a YMCA was founded in Boston, Massachusetts. Today, the YMCA has millions of members throughout the United States and the world. Its sister organization, the Young Women's Christian Association (YWCA), had its beginnings in England 11 years after the YMCA. The YWCA also has millions of members in the United States and throughout the world.

George Williams was the founder of the YMCA. He was born on October 11, 1821. At the age of 15 he left his farm home in Dulverton, Somerset, to work in London. With the advent of the Industrial Revolution, many young men migrated from rural areas to newly developing urban areas, which were ill prepared to cope with the influx. Such communities offered little in the way of constructive diversions or intellectual stimulation, and large numbers of those who were separated from their families were drawn to gambling halls, pubs, and brothels. Deeply disturbed by what he felt to be a general lack of religion, Williams began to organize prayer meetings for his London co-workers and in some nearby villages. As enthusiasm grew, a Bible class was started, and missionary and literary societies were formed. The owner of the drygoods firm (George Hitchcock and Company) for which Williams was a clerk became a supporter and made larger quarters in the shop available for meetings. Meanwhile, prayer groups had developed among workers in other companies.

On June 6, 1844, Williams proposed to a meeting of members of his and another business house that they form a "Society for Improving the Spiritual Condition of Young Men engaged in the drapery and other trades." The proposal was unanimously approved, and the name Young Men's Christian Association was given to the society thus created. A reading room was established to serve

as the center for its activities, which consisted primarily of discussions, lectures, personal counseling, Bible study, and prayer meetings. The society grew rapidly, and branches were formed in various cities. By 1851 there were 24 YMCAs, with a total of 2,700 members, functioning in Great Britain.

The founders' enthusiasm propelled the movement across the English Channel to Europe. There it was so widely accepted that 30,360 young men were active in 397 YMCAs in seven European countries by 1854. The international body later known as the World Alliance of Young Men's Christian Associations was formed the following year in Paris, during the first world conference of YMCAs. Williams, who remained active in the association, was knighted for his work by Queen Victoria in 1894, 11 years before his death.

Among the first YMCAs to be formed outside Great Britain was the one founded in Boston, Massachusetts, in 1851. Upon reading an article about the London YMCA, Thomas V. Sullivan, a retired sea captain who had involved himself with religious work and was making news as a "missionary-at-large" on the Boston waterfront, knew he had come to the end of his search for an instrument through which to broaden his work. He brought together more than 30 young men to discuss his idea, and on December 29, 1851, in the chapel of the historic Old South Meeting House, the Boston YMCA was founded on the same principles as those of the London society.

Within three years 48 other YMCAs had developed across the country, and they continued to multiply. In 1854 the YMCAs of Canada (where a YMCA had been formed in Montreal a month before the one in Boston) and those of the United States joined in a cooperative international committee. Not until 1924 did the American associations organize their own separate national council (though the international committee also continued to function).

The purposes of American YMCAs broadened considerably beginning in the late 1850s, when classes in language, music, and gymnastics were first offered. Branches were organized to serve special groups, such as railroad workers, members of the armed forces, college students, and increasingly large numbers of rural young men who were moving to the cities. The maintenance of youth hostels and residences became an important service. Around 1900, YMCA night schools and classes in industrial education were instituted. Physical and social recreation were stressed. Physical fitness became a byword, and the YMCA assumed a position of leadership in offering swimming and water safety instruction. These various activities have continued to the present day, and in modern times have been expanded to included such things as substance abuse counseling.

The founding of the YWCA had an impetus similar to that of the founding of the YMCA. In 1855 two organizations dedicated to improving the situation of women were formed by women in England. The General Female Training Institute was founded by Mary Jane Kinnaird (Lady Kinnaird) primarily to house nurses returning from the Crimean War. Concern for the spiritual needs of all women prompted Emma Robarts to form the Prayer Union. In 1859 the two merged as the YWCA.

The plight of young women drawn to the cities as a result of the Industrial Revolution was just as bad as that of the men. In the United States their need for guidance, housing, and opportunities for recreation soon brought about the founding of the first American YWCA. Its genesis was in the Prayer Union Circle, almost immediately renamed the Ladies' Christian Association, formed by Caroline D. Roberts in 1858 in New York City.

Eight years later a YWCA was established in Boston, and thereafter the movement spread rapidly, as the YMCA had for a number of years. Help in securing jobs was another need that was soon met, through placement services and vocational training. Classes were offered in penmanship, bookkeeping, stenography, sewing-machine operation, practical nursing, and, when it was decided that females were strong enough, typing (or "typewriting" as it was called). Other activities included group singing and classes in astronomy, physiology, and calisthenics. Swimming became a major activity in the 1890s and remains an important part of the extensive health, physical education, and recreation program.

Establishment of the first YWCA summer camp, Sea Rest, at Asbury Park, New Jersey, in 1874, made inexpensive vacations possible for working women. Today, the YWCA also maintains many day camps and child-care centers. It was, in fact, a pioneer in the field of day nurseries.

As circumstances and needs have changed, the concerns and activities of the YWCA have changed in emphasis, though not in purpose. In its attempt to improve conditions for working women, the YWCA was a leader in advocating an eight-hour working day, prohibition of night work, and the right of labor to organize. It was also an early advocate of unemployment insurance, and later it supported the Equal Rights Amendment. Many independent organizations had their birth in the YWCA, among them the National Federation of Business and Professional Women's Clubs.

June 7

Daniel Boone Reaches Kentucky

On June 7, 1769, Daniel Boone, America's most famous frontiersman, reportedly first glimpsed "Kentucke," the virgin woodland that would eventually become the 15th state of the Union in 1792. The June 7 date is taken from the writings of John Filson, a Kentucky pioneer born in Pennsylvania, who went to Kentucky in 1783 and taught school. Filson wrote *The Discovery, Settlement and Present State of Kentucky*, published in 1784 with an appendix titled *The Adventures of Col. Daniel Boon*. The information in the appendix, written in the first person, supposedly came from Boone, although Filson was the actual author. The schoolmaster's style apparently pleased the unlettered Boone, who declared that every word of Filson's account was true. Historians, however, do not consider the work completely reliable.

Whatever the historical inaccuracies in Filson's book, it served to spread the name of Daniel Boone to people of many countries who were excited by the American adventure and the heroes of the New World. Boone became the prototype of the rugged individualist—courageous, self-sufficient, and highly intelligent. A number of editions of Filson's book were published, including several in London and Paris, and the Boone "autobiography" no doubt inspired the seven stanzas Lord Byron devoted to Boone in the eighth canto of *Don Juan*, published in 1823.

Boone was not the first non–Native American to see Kentucky. Several others had preceded him. However, more than any other man, Boone opened Kentucky and the West to American settlers, literally leading them on foot by way of what is now called the Wilderness Road through the Cumberland Gap.

Daniel Boone is believed to have been born on November 2, 1734, about 11 miles from Reading, Pennsylvania, of Quaker parents. His grandfather George Boone, a weaver and small farmer, had left his home near Exeter, England, and came to America in 1717, arriving in Philadelphia on October 10 of that year. His son Squire (a name, not a title) followed his father's vocations and also raised stock and became a blacksmith. Squire Boone's son Daniel, who had little or no regular schooling, helped with his father's work from early youth. By the time he was 12, he was an expert hunter. Even before his father had given him his first rifle, he had proved his marksmanship and hunting prowess with a spear.

As the spring thaw came to Pennsylvania in 1750, the family started for North Carolina. En route they stopped for about a year in the Shenandoah Valley, arriving at their destination (Buffalo Lick on the north fork of the Yadkin River) in 1751. Four years later, when a contingent of North Carolina militia joined a British military expedition against the French stronghold of Fort Duquesne (now Pittsburgh), Daniel Boone went along as a wagoner and may even have met the British commander's aide-de-camp, the 23-year-old Colonel George Washington.

General Edward Braddock, commander of British forces in North America and leader of the expedition, had been in America for only five months. He and his British regulars were unfamiliar with Native American fighting methods and, scornful of the colonials, ignored their warnings and suggestions. On July 9, 1755, while crossing the Monongahela River, Braddock and his men were attacked by a French and native force of about half their number, and the battle turned into a bloody rout. Two-thirds of Braddock's troops were killed or wounded. Braddock himself was mortally wounded and died four days later.

Boone escaped on one of his horses, as did John Finley, a Virginian hunter and trader who like Boone had joined Braddock as a wagoner. The acquaintance of the two men was to prove significant. Finley had already been to Kentucky and with great excitement described the wilderness to Boone.

Boone returned home to North Carolina where, on August 14, 1756, he married 17-year-old Rebeccah Bryan, a neighbor. She was to bear him ten children, and she may have inspired Boone's famous (albeit sexist) saying that all a man needed was a good gun, a good horse, and a good wife. In 1759 he moved his young family to Virginia, away from the threat of local Cherokee, who bitterly resented settlements in what had historically been their domain.

Over the next few years Boone probably took part in other battles of the French and Indian War, which continued until its official conclusion with the Treaty of Paris of 1763, thereby expelling the French from Canada and the Ohio River valley. The British followed up their victory over the French by moving to eliminate several sources of friction in the New World. One such British move, based on the belief that encroachment by settlers lay at the root of Native American unrest, was issuing the Proclamation of 1763. This document, which forbade settlement west of the Appalachian Mountains, was widely ignored by frontiersmen and land speculators. In the end it was simply one more on the list of colonial grievances against the British crown before the American Revolution.

Boone, always restless and eager for new areas to explore, was fascinated by stories about Florida, which the British took from Spain in 1763. After a visit to Florida, Boone returned home in 1765 and declared that he would like to settle in Pensacola. His wife, however, objected and Boone abandoned the project. Some time later, when John Finley visited Boone, the two men decided to head for Kentucky. Setting out on May 1, 1769, Finley, Boone, and Boone's brother-in-law John Stuart took along three other men to act as skinners and camp aides. The party evidently passed through the Cumberland Gap on June 7, and made camp in what is now Estill County in Kentucky.

In the next four or five months the party accumulated many pelts and hides, but Boone and Stuart were captured by Shawnee. By the time the two were released and returned to their party, the other men, even Finley, had had their fill of Kentucky and were ready to head back to their settlements. About the time that Finley and the skinners left, Boone's brother Squire appeared, accompanied by a man named Neeley. Some time later Stuart set out alone to hunt or explore and never returned to camp. The Boones and Neeley waited anxiously at their winter camp site for Stuart to return. After a while Neeley, who could stand the wilderness no longer, also departed. It was not until five years later that Boone, while clearing the Wilderness Road, came upon what might have been a clue to John Stuart's fate: a powder horn initialed J. S., not far from a human skeleton.

When Squire Boone had to go back to civilization in May 1770 to sell the brothers' accumulated pelts and get more ammunition, Daniel was left alone for what turned out to be three months of exploring this virgin land of beautiful hills and trees. At some time during this period another group of hunters, supposing themselves alone in the wilderness, were frightened by what seemed to them the sound of weird howling, unlike anything they had ever heard before. Investigation showed, however, that it was "only [Boone] . . . lying on a deerskin, alone in the wilderness, singing to the sunset out of his joyous heart."

Squire Boone returned to the base camp on July 27, and the Boones continued their long hunt until March 1771, when they gathered up their valuable pelts and at last started home. On the way they were attacked by Native Americans and robbed of their furs. They escaped with their lives and returned to the colonial settlements to tell of their adventures. In September 1773, with about 40 others including his own family, Boone set out for the Kentucky region with packhorses, livestock, other supplies, and plans to settle. However, his group was driven back by the local tribes, who killed some of their number, including Boone's oldest son, 16-year-old James.

After the Powell Valley Massacre, as the settlers were to call it, most of the group returned to North Carolina. Boone and his family, however, spent the winter on the neighboring Clinch River, where they found an abandoned cabin. In May 1774 Boone set off alone to stand once more at the side of his son's grave in Powell Valley. He was later to describe the visit as the most melancholy moment of his life.

One of the men interested in land speculation west of the Appalachians was the Scottish peer Lord Dunmore, then British colonial governor of Virginia. He had sent out several parties of surveyors to Kentucky, and some of them were still there when the war between Virginians and the native tribes, which came to be known as Lord Dunmore's War, broke out. Lord Dunmore assigned Boone to track down the surveyors and warn them of their danger. This Boone did, but before he returned he stopped to visit the new settlement of Harrodsburg, Kentucky, founded in 1774 and which was to become Kentucky's first permanent settlement. A competent surveyor himself, he took the time to lay off some lots and claim land. Then he headed back home to the Clinch, covering an 800-mile stretch of wilderness in two months.

Lord Dunmore's War was still raging, and Boone, a lieutenant of the Virginia militia, joined the forces of Andrew Lewis and may have been one of the 1,100 frontiersmen who fought the Shawnee warriors led by Chief Cornstalk on October 10, 1774. As a result of that battle, which took place at Point Pleasant in what is now West Virginia, Native American power was diminished in the Ohio River valley and the way west was opened for additional American settlers.

Meanwhile, revolutionary sentiments were running high on the eastern seaboard. With official British attention concentrating on stifling the spark of revolt, speculators began to eye the rich land of Kentucky. Among them was Colonel Richard Henderson, a North Carolinian attorney and a judge in the king's court. Like others he ignored the British prohibition against the westward movement of settlers across the Appalachians. Henderson and a group of men founded the Transylvania Company with the intention of opening most of present-day Kentucky to settlers, under the name Transylvania, which he hoped would be recognized as the 14th colony. Boone thus became an agent for Henderson's Transylvania Company and took on the assignment of exploring the territory, negotiating with the resident Cherokee and

other tribes, and leading settlers through the wilderness to their new land of Transylvania.

On March 17, 1775, about 1,000 Cherokee gathered at Sycamore Shoals on the Watauga River, near what is now Elizabethton, Tennessee, close to the North Carolina border. There, in exchange for several thousand British pounds worth of trinkets and goods, Cherokee chiefs signed a treaty relinquishing Kentucky and deeding the land bounded by the Ohio and Kentucky Rivers, and extending to the south watershed of the Cumberland River to Richard Henderson and his Transylvania Company.

Boone could not wait through the socializing and oratory that preceded the treaty; he was a week into his journey by the day of the actual signing. With the first contingent of settlers, Boone set out to mark and clear the 250 miles from the Long Island of the Holston River in northeastern Tennessee to the Kentucky River deep in Kentucky. Boone marked the pioneer trail that would be known as the Wilderness Road following the trace, or path, made by buffalo and Native Americans, clearing brush, chopping branches, blazing trees, and using stone markers along the miles of mountain ridges, through almost impassable valleys and across rushing streams. The men in Boone's trailblazing party knew they were on a great adventure, and some of them kept diaries. One man wrote about a "turrible mountain that tried us all almost to death to git over it and we lodge this night . . . under a grait mountain & Roast a fine fat turkey for our supper." Although Boone and his men had clearly marked the trail, the literal wilderness of the Wilderness Road was still to be reckoned with. It would be 20 years before wagons could be used on the trail, but in those 20 years 100,000 people took themselves and their possessions over the mountainous passes and into Kentucky.

On April 1, 1775, Boone and his men arrived at their destination and began building a fort. Their settlement, which was to become Boonesboro (or Boonesborough), was southeast of what is now Lexington, Kentucky. Henderson was not far behind. Once arrived, most of the men would not be kept within the protective walls of the fort, but set about claiming their own parcels of land and building houses to which they could bring their wives and families. Under the aegis of Richard Henderson, Daniel and Squire Boone and delegates from other Kentucky settlements gathered on May 23, 1775, to decide the rules by which they would be governed.

During the next two years, while the 13 colonies were becoming increasingly involved in the Revolutionary War against Britain, Boone was fully occupied by hunting, trapping, surveying, and defending the new Kentucky settlements against Native American raids and attacks—many of which were encouraged by the British. When Kentucky became a county of Virginia in late 1776, Boone was made a captain of the Virginia militia. He was later promoted to major and then to lieutenant colonel.

In February 1778 Boone and a group of 30 Boonesboro men went to the Blue Licks on the Licking River to obtain salt for the settlement. Leaving the salt camp one day to check his beaver traps, Boone was captured by a war party. Taken back to the Shawnee camp, he learned from Chief Blackfish that the Shawnee were on their way to take Boonesboro. Boone, famous for his speed in running, was also a fast thinker. He convinced Blackfish that the winter was no time to take the women and children of Boonesboro through the deep woods and up to the British commander in Detroit, who would buy the captives from the Shawnee. Instead, Boone suggested, he would talk the men at Blue Licks into surrendering if Blackfish promised that they would not be tortured or humiliated by having to run the gauntlet. Blackfish agreed, the men surrendered, and the Shawnee made their way with their captives to Detroit where the prisoners were delivered into British hands, except for Boone, whose popularity with the Shawnee was so high that they refused to sell him to the British commander. Instead they adopted him into their tribe as the son of Chief Blackfish and gave him the name Sheltowee, which means "big turtle." For months Boone lived with Shawnee as a captive.

When Boone learned that the Shawnee were again planning a full-scale attack on Boonesboro and that he, as the adopted son of the chief, was to go along and persuade the settlers to surrender, he escaped. He traveled so fast that the Shawnee were unable to catch him; he covered 160 miles in four days (three days on foot). He was a strange but welcome sight when he returned to Boonesboro, his head shorn free of his usually long hair except for the Shawnee-style scalp lock. Having warned the settlers of the imminent attack, Boone led a group of scouts and fighters north into Ohio to strike at the oncoming Shawnee and then raced back to help in the defense of Boonesboro. He got back to the fort on September 6, just a day before the arrival of Blackfish and 450 Shawnee warriors. Although there were only 50 rifles within Boonesboro's fortified walls, many of them fired by boys, the Shawnee were driven off.

After spending some time in the east, Boone returned to Kentucky with his family and more settlers in October 1779. In 1780 he established Boone's Station near what is now Athens, Kentucky. It was also in 1780 that the county of Kentucky was divided into three parts, and Boone was elected to the Virginia legislature.

The Commonwealth of Kentucky was admitted to the Union as the 15th state on June 1, 1792. Boone, in spite of his enormous service to Kentucky as a pioneer, founder, soldier, and legislator, now found himself bankrupt and in debt. He had laid claim to 100,000 acres of land, but had been careless about filing claims. That, plus the fact that Virginia had never recognized the Transylvania Company's original land claims, and the general confusion and incompetence of early land courts, left him with no defense to protect his property. One by one a series of ejectment suits wiped out Boone's ownership of his many tracts of land. Disgusted, Boone put Kentucky behind him forever. In 1799 he set out for what is now Missouri, then part of the vast Spanish province of Louisiana. Boone, in his mid 60s, had unusually high physical stamina. He prepared for the trip out of Kentucky by felling a huge tree, which he made into a dugout to transport his wife, children, and household possessions down the Big Sandy River while he and some companions went on foot herding the livestock all the way.

Once in Missouri, it seemed for a while that Boone had finally received the recognition he deserved. The Spanish officials of the area welcomed him warmly and granted him a large tract of land at the mouth of the Femme Osage Creek near the Missouri River. On July 11, 1800, he was appointed chief magistrate for the Spanish crown of the Femme Osage District. Once again, however, land ownership became an uncertain thing. First, Spain ceded Louisiana to France in 1800. Then, only three years later, the vast province was sold to the United States in the Louisiana Purchase. Boone's land title, guaranteed by the Spanish governor, was voided by American land commissioners on technicalities. Finally, after many government delays and many petitions by Boone, his large land holdings in Missouri were restored to him in part by the direct intercession of Congress in 1814. Boone sold the land and traveled back to Kentucky to pay his debts, which according to popular legend "left him with a great sense of satisfaction and 50 cents."

Boone's wife, Rebeccah, died in 1813 after 56 years of marriage. Boone went to live with his son Nathan in what was probably Missouri's first stone residence. He continued to hunt and trap and enjoy life until, nearly 86 years old, he died on September 26, 1820. Missouri's territorial legislature went into mourning for Boone, the prototype of the American frontiersman. Just three years after his death, James Fenimore Cooper published the first of his Leatherstocking Tales, which were frontier adventure novels based at least in part on Boone's exploits. Although Boone and his wife both died in Missouri, their remains were returned to Frankfort, Kentucky, in 1845, where they were reinterred and a monument erected in their memory.

Liberty Bell Hung in Independence Hall

The Liberty Bell, America's famous symbol of independence and freedom, dates back to before the American Revolution. It was hung in Philadelphia's Independence Hall, then known as the State House, on June 7, 1753.

William Penn, for whom the Commonwealth of Pennsylvania was named, received a royal charter from the British monarchy in 1701. This charter gave the colony certain privileges and liberties, and gave expression to Penn's far-reaching ideas concerning human freedom and citizen involvement in government. In 1751 the Pennsylvania assembly decided to honor the 50th anniversary of Penn's charter, and authorized the purchase of a massive commemorative bell to be hung in Philadelphia. It was to contain the biblical quotation "Proclaim Liberty throughout all the land unto all the inhabitants thereof " (Leviticus 25:10). Not only was this quotation an appropriate sentiment given Penn's political beliefs, but it was an excerpt from a biblical passage that speaks of "honoring the fiftieth year."

The bell was ordered from Whitechapel Foundry in London, England. It arrived in Philadelphia on September 1, 1752, and was hung on March 10, 1753. However, on its first ring a massive crack appeared. The bell was apparently too brittle, and so it was taken to a Philadelphia foundry, where it was melted down and recast with copper added in order to make the new bell less brittle. The new bell was hung on March 29, 1753, but many people were dissatisfied with the sound. Once again, the bell was taken down and recast. The third and final bell, weighing over a ton, was hung on June 7, 1753. There was still some dissatisfaction over the sound quality, but this version of the Liberty Bell became permanent.

During the remainder of the colonial era, the Liberty Bell was used to summon the Pennsylvania assembly, call public meetings, and celebrate special events. However, in the 1760s the colonies became increasingly restive under British rule, and thus the uses of the Liberty Bell also changed, and it was rung to call public meetings about unpopular British laws like the Stamp Act. During the American Revolution, it was used to announce the battles at Lexington and Concord in 1775. However, the bell's most famous ringing was on July 8, 1776, when it announced the signing of the Declaration of Independence several days earlier and summoned the people to hear its first public reading.

In late 1777 the Liberty Bell was removed from Philadelphia in order to protect it from the advancing British forces. The British, upon taking Philadelphia, would have melted the bell and used the metal to forge cannon balls and other forms of ammunition. The bell was hidden in a church in Allentown, Pennsylvania, until it could be returned to Philadelphia. After the Revolution the bell was once again used for public announcements, but in 1835 a large crack appeared. Legend has it that the occasion was the tolling of the death of Supreme Court justice John Marshall. By 1846 the crack had become so large that the bell was effectively unusable.

The Liberty Bell, which was placed in a special Liberty Bell Pavilion near Independence Hall in 1976, the year of America's bicentennial, has become a national symbol. The cracked bell was also the favorite symbol of the abolitionists before the Civil War, representing how American freedom was flawed with the evil of slavery.

June 8

Frank Lloyd Wright's Birthday

One of the most inventive of modern architects and, in the judgment of many, the greatest, was Frank Lloyd Wright. Cantankerous, opinionated, an iconoclast, and a genius, he exerted an enormous influence on contemporary architecture in the United States and Europe.

The man who was to design more than 600 completed buildings and foment a revolution in design with his concepts of "organic architecture," namely architecture in which buildings harmonize with their users and surroundings, was born on June 8, 1869, in Richland Center, Wisconsin. His interest in architecture already declared, he entered the University of Wisconsin at the age of 15, even though it had no courses in his subject. For this reason his formal training was in civil engineering, rather than in architecture, a fact that had a profound effect on his work. Engineering was the tool around which he could wrap his originality and his willingness to innovate.

Wright left the university in 1887 before graduating. He went to Chicago, took a job as a draftsman, and in 1888 designed his first executed work.

It was a house for his aunts at Spring Green, Wisconsin. The same year, he went to work in the Chicago office of Louis Sullivan, who shared his aversion to classic form, taught him the basics of architecture, and instilled in him ideas for radical design. Sullivan, sometimes called the Father of Modern Architecture, was the only architect to whom Wright ever admitted a debt (though he later deplored the skyscraper construction in which Sullivan had pioneered). Wright, who at 19 became chief designer under Sullivan and his partner Dankmar Adler, was given a five-year contract. This enabled Wright to begin building his own house in suburban Oak Park in 1889 and to marry Catherine Lee Clark Tobin in 1890. They had six children.

It fell to Wright to handle most of the firm's residential commissions, while Sullivan and Adler concentrated on commercial buildings. Wright took on outside assignments also, a practice that led to a break with his employers. He set up his own business in 1893 and turned out designs in keeping with his precepts of organic architecture. Wright believed, for instance, that the style of a building should be subordinate to human needs and that it should seem to grow out of its surroundings and harmonize with them in the color and texture of its materials. Further, he held that interior space should be open, free, and with a minimum of confining walls. There should be, in effect, a blending of indoor and outdoor space. Rebelling against the conventional box, he built a series of long, low, ground-hugging houses with sweeping horizontal lines and overhanging eaves. This new form was known as "prairie style." Two examples of this style are the Coonley house (1908) in Riverside, Illinois, and the Robie house (1909), which was later designated a national historical landmark by the Department of the Interior.

Wright had already erected two nonresidential buildings, which became famous. One of these, the Larkin Company's administration building (1904) in Buffalo, New York, was the first office building to have air conditioning, doors of plate glass, and double-glass windows. The other building, the Unity Temple (1906) in Oak Park, Illinois, marked a turning point in the use of poured concrete for a monumental public building.

Wright went to Europe in 1909 in connection with the Berlin publication of a portfolio of his work, which had wide influence in Europe. After he returned home he began work in Spring Green, Wisconsin, on Taliesin East, whose Welsh name means "shining brow." Designed to be a studio, farm, and school, as well as "a home where icicles by invitation might beautify the eaves," it was twice destroyed by fire (in 1914 and 1925) and twice rebuilt. Wright's most notable work of the period, however, was his revolutionary design for the Imperial Hotel in earthquake-prone Tokyo. Completed in 1922, it was placed on a cushion of soft mud and employed a unique arrangement of concrete supports and cantilevered floors. With an elastic edifice whose walls and floors had a sliding quality never before achieved, it was the only large structure in Tokyo to survive the disastrous earthquake of 1923. Wright also developed a new method of construction, which utilized precast concrete blocks threaded with steel reinforcing rods. Sometimes, as with the Millard house (1923) in Pasadena, California, the blocks would be pierced and patterned, giving the appearance of a kind of woven house.

Also during the 1920s, Wright was married for a second time in 1922 and a third time in 1928. In 1932 he set up the Taliesin Fellowship. Ultimately, between 40 and 65 young architects studied with him every year, spending the April-November term at Taliesin East and the December-March term in Taliesin West, which Wright began constructing near Phoenix, New Mexico, in 1938. Wright wrote many books and frequently took to the lecture circuit, as often as not to denounce the "international style" of modern architecture. In his later years he continued to turn out a series of remarkable buildings. Perhaps the most outstanding was Fallingwater (1936), the E. J. Kaufmann house, spectacularly cantilevered over a waterfall in Bear Run, Pennsylvania. Along with a $500,000 endowment for its maintenance, the structure was presented in 1963 to the Western Pennsylvania Conservancy for use as a recreation center. Wright's accomplishments also include the S. C. Johnson and Son administration building (1939) and research tower (1950) in Racine, Wisconsin; "Usonian" houses (among them the Friedman house near Pleasantville, New York) which he envisioned as ideal democratic American architecture; the V. C. Morris gift shop (1949) in San Francisco; and the Price Tower (1956) in Bartlesville, Oklahoma. One of his largest commissions was his design of 16 buildings planned for construction on the campus of Florida Southern College at Lakeland between 1936 and 1960.

Controversial to the last, Wright died at the age of 89 on April 9, 1959, in Phoenix, Arizona. He died just a few months before his circular Guggenheim Museum, shaped in the form of a spiral ramp, opened in New York City amid a storm of comment, pro and con. Among the projects of Wright's that have been completed since 1959 by his associates are two other circular buildings, the Greek Orthodox Church (1963) in Milwaukee,

Wisconsin, and the Grady Gammage Auditorium of Arizona State University at Tempe (1964).

June 9

Siege of Petersburg, Virginia

In the city of Petersburg, Virginia, June 9 is the traditional date of observance for Confederate Memorial Day. The day commemorates the heroic defense of the city on that day in 1864 during the Civil War. A crucial rail and supply center, Petersburg commanded the southern approach to the Confederate capital of Richmond, 22 miles to the north. Union general Ulysses S. Grant, leading General George G. Meade's Army of the Potomac, had tried to reach Richmond from the north, but had been kept at bay by the Army of Northern Virginia under General Robert E. Lee at the bloody battles of The Wilderness and Spotsylvania Court House in May 1864. Although neither of these operations was a federal victory, since together they cost the Union 33,000 men, Grant resumed his advance southward and Lee was compelled to retreat.

Drawing nearly opposite Richmond at nearby Cold Harbor on June 3, Grant then attempted a major assault on the Confederate forces. He had, however, underestimated the staying power of Lee's army. Grant's force was defeated. Losing 12,000 men on that one day alone, the Union commander abandoned the idea of a direct onslaught on Richmond and sidestepped skillfully, withdrawing to the east. His plan was now to bypass Richmond and focus his attention on Petersburg, the life-sustaining funnel through which food and supplies had to pass to Richmond. If Petersburg could be taken, he reasoned, Richmond and perhaps the Confederacy itself would fall. To achieve the objective, Grant planned not merely to withdraw eastward from his own trenches, as his initial moves seemed to indicate, but to turn his withdrawal into a wide- swinging, reverse-flanking maneuver that would take his men south across the James River and then abruptly westward toward Petersburg.

As Grant had suspected, Petersburg was weakly held, although it was strongly fortified. It was defended at the time by a 2,400-man brigade under Brigadier General Henry Alexander Wise, which had been hastily reinforced to some extent by a contingent from the command of General P. G. T. Beauregard. Beauregard's main force, which would soon move up to Petersburg's defense, was then located at Bermuda Hundred, a short distance northeast, keeping an eye on the principal Union force of Major General Benjamin F. Butler, commanding officer of the Army of the James. The Confederates had largely bottled up Butler's forces behind his own defense lines, on Bermuda Hundred neck at the junction of the James and Appomattox Rivers. Acting on Grant's orders, Butler nonetheless was able to send General Quincy A. Gillmore over the Appomattox River on June 9 at the head of what was to prove an abortive expedition against Petersburg. Had the federals realized how lightly the city was held, and had General Gillmore not been hampered by the habitual caution he shared with Butler and other high-ranking officers in the Army of the James, Petersburg might have been taken at that time.

The federal force, which numbered perhaps 4,500 men, approached the city by two routes. Encountering formidable earthworks on the City Point Road and suffering a repulse on the Jerusalem Plank Road, Gillmore concluded that the city was too strongly fortified to take. Thus thwarted, he turned back and was abruptly relieved of his command by Butler. June 9, the day of this victory, is remembered by Petersburg as one of its hours of glory.

On the night of June 12, however, Grant began the delicate operation of moving his 100,000-man army east from Cold Harbor, completely misleading Lee, who still thought that Grant meant to attack Richmond. Grant then made his sharp turn to the south, and on the night of June 14 began the carefully planned crossing of the James. It would take two days to complete. Meanwhile, Grant ordered Butler to reinforce Brigadier General William Farrar "Baldy" Smith's force and send it across the Appomattox River on the morning of June 15 to strike at Petersburg, this time with real muscle. The June 15 onslaught was the beginning of four days of repeated attacks and bloodshed. They were marked by valor on the part of soldiers on both sides. For the Confederates, these were days of extraordinary skill and leadership by General Beauregard, who now held the city but could muster no more than 9,000 infantry for his defense. However, for the federal generals, who had at their disposal some 35,000 hard-fighting men, these were days of blunder, confusion, poor staff work, tangled communications, and missed opportunity.

Now apprised of Grant's intentions, Lee began moving south from Richmond. Lee's forces began pouring into Petersburg during the afternoon of July 18. By night the city's lines were strongly held by Lee's men. Even General Beauregard later declared that Petersburg had earlier been "clearly at the mercy of the federal commander, who had all but captured it" on June 15, but failed to grasp the prize he could have had. Now, however, it was too late. The city was so firmly held that the chances for a successful frontal assault by the federals had diminished to the vanishing point.

Grant reluctantly settled down for a siege, which was to last almost ten months. Much of the action during that seemingly endless period centered upon the attempts of both sides to control the railroad supply lines that were so vital to the Confederacy. The most dramatic incident of the siege, however, was the result of a suggestion by members of the 48th Pennsylvania Regiment, many of them former coal miners. Receiving approval for their plan, the men dug a tunnel 511 feet long, extending from the Union lines to a point under a key Confederate fort. The tunnel ended with lateral branches extending 40 feet in either direction. Filled with four tons of powder, these were exploded on the morning of July 30, 1864. Although the resulting blast created an opening through which Union soldiers were supposed to rush beyond the Confederate lines, their movement was slowed by a combination of orders that were not carried out, instructions that were never given, and a total lack of leadership on the part of subordinate officers. The Union move had been perfectly planned, but it was totally wrecked in the execution.

Word of exactly what they were supposed to do had never reached the men involved. Lacking this information, they piled into the enormous crater created by the explosion, together with large numbers of half-entombed Confederate wounded, rather than going around the crater and seizing positions beyond as intended. Mistaking the crater for some sort of sheltered position, like an outsized rifle pit, and with no leadership to the contrary (not one commander of the four divisions involved was in front leading his men), they simply stayed there. A whole precious hour, an opportunity to charge forward unopposed, elapsed before Confederates from other sectors of the Petersburg defense were able to make a substantial response. By the end of that hour, however, Confederate guns had been placed in a position to shell the crater, reinforcements had been rushed into place, and artillery activated. The unfortunate, ill-led invaders were mowed down with deadly fire, and the already stalled Union advance ground to a halt. Grant afterward referred to the event as a "disaster," the "saddest affair I have witnessed in this war." Confederate general William Mahone, who was instrumental in the repulse, concurred in a scathing postwar comment on the ineptitude involved.

After the debacle at the crater, the federals' siege of Petersburg went on for month after wearying month, punctuated by abortive Union thrusts in the direction of Richmond and the dispatch of expeditions to sever crucial rail lines. Thrust and expedition alike were met by Confederate countermoves, but Grant finally took over a portion of the Weldon Railroad and was extending his line around to the left in an effort to surround and isolate Petersburg. At last a decisive moment came on April 1, 1865, when forces under General Philip Sheridan scored a crushing defeat over Confederate troops at Five Forks, southwest of Petersburg.

The victory was pivotal. Grant, who in the evening learned of the success, ordered an immediate general assault on Petersburg. The town bombardment continued throughout April 2. That night the Confederates began crossing to the one possible escape route, on the north side of the Appomattox River. When Petersburg fell, Richmond did too. Its evacuation also began after dark on April 2. The next day Major General Godfrey Weitzel entered Richmond, and Grant rode into Petersburg. It was the beginning of the Confederate retreat, which ended with the surrender of Lee to Grant at Appomattox Court House (see April 9).

In 1865 the local women of Petersburg marked the first anniversary of the city's transient triumph by decorating the graves of the city's defenders in the graveyard south of historic Old Blandford Church. In so doing, they initiated what was to be an annual custom of long duration. Some 30,000 Confederate soldiers were eventually buried in Blandford Cemetery.

June 10

Founding of Alcoholics Anonymous

Alcoholics Anonymous (AA), the international organization dedicated to helping alcoholics cope with their addiction, was founded on June 10, 1935, in Akron, Ohio. The founders were Robert Smith, known as "Doctor Bob," and a stockbroker named William G. Wilson. In keeping with AA's tradition of maintaining the anonymity of its members, these founders are known as Dr. Bob S. and Bill W. in AA history.

Both men were alcoholics wanting to recover from their addiction. However, in an age when alcoholism was considered to be a moral defect and alcoholics were subject to scorn and ridicule, help was hard to find. Thus, they decided to establish Alcoholics Anonymous, an organization that would help alcoholics recover but would respect their privacy and their desire to avoid public disclosure. By the late 1930s there were AA groups in the cities of Akron and Cleveland, Ohio, and New York. In 1939 the organization published its manifesto, explaining AA's philosophy of recovery. This philosophy contains a mixture of psychological and spiritual principles. At its core is the 12-step program, which is not mandatory but strongly recommended, for alcoholics to pass through:

(1) Admit we are powerless over alcohol, that our lives have become unmanageable.

(2) Come to believe that a power greater than ourselves can restore us to sanity.

(3) Make a decision to turn our will and our lives over to the care of God as we understand Him.

(4) Make a searching and fearless moral inventory of ourselves.

(5) Admit to God, to ourselves and to another human being the exact nature of our wrongs.

(6) Become entirely ready to have God remove all these defects of character.

(7) Humbly ask Him to remove our shortcomings.

(8) Make a list of all persons we have harmed and become willing to make amends to them all.

(9) Make direct amends to such people wherever possible, except when to do so would injure them or others.

(10) Continue to take personal inventory and when we are wrong promptly admit it.

(11) Seek through prayer and meditation to improve our conscious contact with God as we understand Him, praying only for knowledge of His will for us and the power to carry that out.

(12) Have a spiritual awakening as the result of these steps, and try to carry this message to alcoholics and to practice these principles in all our affairs.

Currently, AA has over 2 million recovering members in the United States and throughout the world. Approximately one-third are women. No dues are required; anyone can become a member who wants to stop drinking; and AA is nondenominational, although religion is a strong part of its program. Robert Smith died on November 16, 1950, and William Wilson, on January 24, 1971.

Shavuot (Jewish Feast of Weeks)

This is a movable event.

The Feast of Weeks is one of the three great Jewish pilgrimage festivals, the others being Passover and Sukkot (Deuteronomy 16:16). One of the "joyous" holidays, Shavuot begins on the sixth of the Hebrew month of Sivan (May or June), 50 days

after the first day of Passover (and thus is sometimes called the Jewish Pentecost, from the Greek word meaning "fiftieth"). A day of grateful rejoicing, Shavuot celebrates the gifts of the harvest and, more importantly, commemorates the event in Jewish history which was God's gift of the Ten Commandments to Moses on Mt. Sinai. In the Bible (Exodus 34:22) Shavuot is also referred to as *Hag HaKatzir*, that is, Feast of the Harvest and as *Yom HaBikhurim*, literally the Day of the First Fruits.

Shavuot is observed at the end of the wheat and barley harvest season. The counting of the weeks begins on the second day of Passover with the offering of an *omer*, or sheaf, of barley (Leviticus 23:10, 15–16; Deuteronomy 16:9–10); the word *sabbath* used in Leviticus ("And ye shall count unto you from the morrow after the sabbath . . .") has been interpreted as meaning in this context the first day of the feast of Passover. When the Temple in Jerusalem was standing, all adult male Jews were expected to bring their first omer of barley to the temple as a thanksgiving offering. In addition, they were directed to offer their first fruits of the harvest, which were often two loaves of bread baked from the new wheat. After the temple was destroyed in A.D. 70, however, Jews simply recited the prayers associated with the offering of the omer and the first fruits.

The 49 days or seven weeks between the offering of the omer and the first day of Shavuot are marked by the custom of "the counting of the omer." Traditionally, Orthodox Jews say a prayer every evening in the synagogues. On the first evening of Shavuot, they stay in the synagogues late into the night reading a compilation of prayers and passages from the Bible. On the following night the Book of Psalms is read. Meanwhile, however, they have passed through the sad, six-week period that extends from the last day of Passover until Shavuot. These are called the Sefirah days, a time for Orthodox and Conservative Jews of partial mourning when no weddings or celebrations are allowed.

Shavuot, like almost all of the other Jewish holidays, has a historical significance as well as an agricultural one. After the destruction of the Second Temple this aspect—the celebration of the giving of the Torah on Mt. Sinai, and the confirmation of a covenant between God and the Jews—was emphasized. Thus, Shavuot is also called *zeman matan toratenu*, "the season of the giving of our law." While Passover celebrates the Exodus from Egypt, the time when the Jews received physical freedom, Shavuot marks the time when the Jews received spiritual freedom.

June 11

President Kennedy Addresses the Nation on Civil Rights

See also May 29, John F. Kennedy's Birthday.

By the early 1960s the civil rights movement was beginning to sweep the country, and much of the segregated South was thrown into turmoil. Segregation, a way of life that had existed for a century, was challenged by a new generation of African Americans who were no longer willing to accept second-class status. One of the most notable clashes occurred in Alabama, where the Kennedy administration was forced to use the National Guard in order to enforce court-ordered desegregation of the University of Alabama. Without the federal troops, the African- American students seeking admittance would have been beaten or even killed with the tacit approval of Alabama state authorities.

President Kennedy had at first been reluctant to embrace civil rights causes, since he was a Democrat and the South had been largely Democratic ever since the Civil War. Endorsing civil rights did, in fact, begin a process that would make the South largely Republican by the 1990s. However, the injustice of segregation could no longer be ignored, and on June 11, 1963, Kennedy addressed the nation. Kennedy firmly stated that the federal government would support the students in particular and African American rights in general. It was a sweeping commitment on behalf of the entire nation, and relevant excerpts are set forth below:

> Good evening, my fellow citizens. This afternoon, following a series of threats and defiant statements, the presence of Alabama National Guardsmen was required on the University of Alabama to carry out the final and unequivocal order of the United States District Court of the Northern District of Alabama. That order called for the admission of two clearly qualified young Alabama residents who happened to have been born Negro.
>
> I hope that every American, regardless of where he lives, will stop and examine his conscience about this and other related incidents. This nation was founded by men of many nations and backgrounds. It was founded on the principle that all men are created equal, and that the rights of every man are diminished when the rights of one man are threatened. Today we are committed to a worldwide struggle to promote and protect the rights of all who wish to be free. And when Americans are sent to Vietnam or West Berlin, we do not ask for whites only. It ought to be possible, therefore, for American students of any color to attend any public institution they select without having to be backed up by troops.
>
> It ought to be possible for American consumers of any color to receive equal service in places of public accommodation, such as hotels and restaurants and theaters and retail stores, without being forced to resort to demonstrations in the street, and it ought to be possible for American citizens of any color to register and to vote in a free election without interference or fear of reprisal.
>
> It ought to be possible, in short, for every American to enjoy the privileges of being American without regard to his race or his color. In short, every American ought to have the right to be treated as he would wish to be treated, as one would wish his children to be treated. But this is not the case. The Negro baby born in America today, regardless of the section of the nation in which he is born, has about one-half as much chance of completing a high school as a white baby born in the same place on the same day, one-third as much chance of completing college, one-third as much chance of becoming a professional man, twice as much chance of becoming unemployed, about one-seventh as much chance of earning $10,000 a year, a life expectancy which is seven years shorter, and the prospects of earning only half as much.
>
> This is not a sectional issue. Difficulties over segregation and discrimination exist in every city, in every state of the Union, producing in many cities a rising tide of discontent that threatens the public safety. Nor is this a partisan issue. In a time of domestic crisis men of good will and generosity should be able to unite regardless of party or politics. This is not even a legal or legislative issue alone. It is better to settle these matters in the courts than on the streets, and new laws are needed at every level, but law alone cannot make men see right.
>
> We are confronted primarily with a moral issue. It is as old as the scriptures and is as clear as the American Constitution. The heart of the question is whether all Americans are to be afforded equal rights and equal opportunities, whether we

are going to treat our fellow Americans as we want to be treated. If an American, because his skin is dark, cannot eat lunch in a restaurant open to the public, if he cannot send his children to the best public school available, if he cannot vote for the public officials who represent him, if, in short, he cannot enjoy the full and free life which all of us want, then who among us would be content to have the color of his skin changed and stand in his place?

Who among us would then be content with the counsels of patience and delay? One hundred years of delay have passed since President Lincoln freed the slaves, yet their heirs, their grandsons, are not fully free. They are not yet freed from the bonds of injustice. They are not yet freed from social and economic oppression. And this nation, for all its hopes and all its boasts, will not be fully free until all its citizens are free.

We preach freedom around the world, and we mean it, and we cherish our freedom here at home, but are we to say to the world, and much more importantly, to each other that this is a land of the free except for the Negroes; that we have no second-class citizens except Negroes; that we have no class or caste system, no ghettos, no master race except with respect to Negroes?

Now the time has come for this nation to fulfill its promise. The events in Birmingham and elsewhere have so increased the cries for equality that no city or state or legislative body can prudently choose to ignore them. The fires of frustration and discord are burning in every city, North and South, where legal remedies are not at hand. Redress is sought in the streets, in demonstrations, parades, and protests which create tensions and threaten violence and threaten lives.

We face, therefore, a moral crisis as a country and as a people. It cannot be met by repressive police action. It cannot be left to increased demonstrations in the streets. It cannot be quieted by token moves or talk. It is a time to act in the Congress, in your state and local legislative body and, above all, in all of our daily lives. It is not enough to pin the blame on others, to say this is a problem of one section of the country or another, or deplore the fact that we face. A great change is at hand, and our task, our obligation, is to make that revolu-

tion, that change, peaceful and constructive for all. Those who do nothing are inviting shame as well as violence. Those who act boldly are recognizing right as well as reality.

Next week I shall ask the Congress of the United States to act, to make a commitment it has not fully made in this century to the proposition that race has no place in American life or law. The federal judiciary has upheld that proposition in a series of forthright cases. The executive branch has adopted that proposition in the conduct of its affairs, including the employment of federal personnel, the use of federal facilities, and the sale of federally financed housing. But there are other necessary measures which only the Congress can provide, and they must be provided at this session. The old code of equity law under which we live commands for every wrong a remedy, but in too many communities, in too many parts of the country, wrongs are inflicted on Negro citizens and there are no remedies at law. Unless the Congress acts, their only remedy is in the street. I am, therefore, asking the Congress to enact legislation giving all Americans the right to be served in facilities which are open to the public hotels, restaurants, theaters, retail stores, and similar establishments.

This seems to me to be an elementary right. Its denial is an arbitrary indignity that no American in 1963 should have to endure, but many do.

I am also asking Congress to authorize the federal Government to participate more fully in lawsuits designed to end segregation in public education. We have succeeded in persuading many districts to desegregate voluntarily. Dozens have admitted Negroes without violence. Today a Negro is attending a state supported institution in every one of our 50 States, but the pace is very slow.

Too many Negro children entering segregated grade schools at the time of the Supreme Court's decision nine years ago will enter segregated high schools this fall, having suffered a loss which can never be restored. The lack of an adequate education denies the Negro a chance to get a decent job. The orderly implementation of the Supreme Court decision, therefore, cannot be left solely to those who may not have the economic resources to carry the legal action or who may be subject to harassment.

Other features will be also requested, including greater protection for the right to vote. But legislation, I repeat, cannot solve this problem alone. It must be solved in the homes of every American in every community across our country. In this respect, I want to pay tribute to those citizens North and South who have been working in their communities to make life better for all. They are acting not out of a sense of legal duty but out of a sense of human decency. Like our soldiers and sailors in all parts of the world they are meeting freedom's challenge on the firing line, and I salute them for their honor and their courage. My fellow Americans, this is a problem which faces us all, in every city of the North as well as the South. Today there are Negroes unemployed, two or three times as many compared to whites, inadequate in education, moving into the large cities, unable to find work, young people particularly out of work, without hope, denied equal rights, denied the opportunity to eat at a restaurant or lunch counter or go to a movie theater, denied the right to a decent education, denied almost today the right to attend a state university even though qualified. It seems to me that these are matters which concern us all, not merely presidents or congressmen or governors, but every citizen of the United States.

This is one country. It has become one country because all of us and all the people who came here had an equal chance to develop their talents. We cannot say to 10 percent of the population that you can't have that right; that your children can't have the chance to develop whatever talents they have; that the only way that they are going to get their rights is to go into the streets and demonstrate. I think we owe them and we owe ourselves a better country than that. Therefore, I am asking for your help in making it easier for us to move ahead and to provide the kind of equality of treatment which we would want ourselves; to give a chance for every child to be educated to the limit of his talents.

We have a right to expect that the Negro community will be responsible, will uphold the law, but they have a right to expect that the law will be fair, that the Constitution will be color blind, as Justice Harlan said at the turn of the century. This is what we are talking about and this is a matter which concerns this country and what it stands for, and in meeting it I ask the support of all our citizens.

King Kamehameha Day in Hawaii

In Hawaii the citizens have set aside June 11 as an annual state holiday on which to celebrate the memory of King Kamehameha, who united the Polynesian Islands into a single kingdom.

For centuries the Hawaiian archipelago with its native Polynesian inhabitants remained isolated from the rest of the world. Then, in 1778 the English explorer Captain James Cook commanded the first European ships to visit the islands. Cook named his discovery the Sandwich Islands in honor of the first lord of the Admiralty, the earl of Sandwich, and lost his life in a scuffle with the natives. In the years that followed Cook's visit, an ever-increasing number of American and European vessels plied the Pacific, and many visited the Sandwich Islands. For the most part the Hawaiians received the foreigners hospitably. They replenished the ships' supplies of food and water, and in return received metal tools, armaments, and other trade goods.

Kamehameha I, who was to bring the islands under a unified government, was a powerful warrior and the nephew of Kalaniopuu, the king of the island of Hawaii itself. Shortly after the death of his uncle in 1782, Kamehameha (whose date of birth is uncertain) became the leader of the chiefs of the western part of the island, and with their assistance he defeated his cousin King Kiwalao at the battle of Mokuohai. The victory gave Kamehameha and his allies undisputed control of the northwestern part of the island of Hawaii.

In 1782 and again around 1785 Kamehameha tried to conquer the remainder of Hawaii, and in 1786 he launched an attack against the neighboring island of Maui. These efforts were not successful. Kamehameha returned to western Hawaii and during the next four years accumulated a sizable supply of European arms. Then, in 1790 Kamehameha resumed battle. This time he subdued Maui, Lanai, and Molokai, but before he could complete his campaign, his cousin Keoua, the brother of Kiwalao, attacked his territory on the island of Hawaii, thereby forcing Kamehameha to return to Hawaii to protect his lands.

By the summer of 1791, Kamehameha had defeated Keoua and gained control of the entire island of Hawaii. However, while Kamehameha was fighting to secure and expand his holdings on Hawaii, the chiefs of the leeward islands rebelled. Kahekili and Kaeo, the kings of Molokai and Maui, respectively, even attempted to invade Kamehameha's territory on Hawaii, but were defeated and forced to return to Maui.

Peace reigned in the islands for several years. Then in 1794 King Kahekili, who controlled Maui, Lanai, Molokai, and Oahu, and who indirectly ruled Kauai, died. Within a short time after Kahekili's death, his brother Kaeo and his son Kalanikuple were at war. When Kaeo threatened to attack Kalanikuple, the latter king appealed to the commanders of the three British and American ships then at Honolulu for assistance. The commanders gave Kalanikuple ammunition and advice, and with this aid he defeated Kaeo.

Emboldened by his successful victory over Kaeo, Kalanikuple decided to attack Kamehameha on Hawaii. To aid in this venture, Kalanikuple seized the two British ships that had previously assisted him, and on January 12, 1795, the vessels, with the king and his chiefs on board, put to sea. However, Kalanikuple's plot was foiled. Soon after the ships left the harbor, two British mates retook the vessels, put Kalanikuple and his queen adrift in a canoe, and then steered a course for Hawaii. Kamehameha seized the opportunity afforded by the failure of Kalanikuple's operation. Quickly gaining possession of Maui and Molokai, he pushed northward to Oahu. Kalanikuple's warriors on that island valiantly resisted Kamehameha's forces, but by the summer of 1795 Kamehameha had won control of the island.

After 1795 only the island of Kauai and its dependency Niihau remained outside Kamehameha's jurisdiction. The aggressive king attempted an invasion in 1796, but had to postpone it when he lost most of his canoes in the tempestuous seas between Oahu and Kauai. Later in the year Kamehameha returned to Hawaii to put down a rebellion, and so Kauai was again spared.

Kamehameha remained on Hawaii until 1802, building a fleet of special double canoes and acquiring a stockpile of military equipment to ensure his victory in the next attack on Kauai. Then, Kamehameha took his army and fleet to Maui, and late in 1803 or early in 1804 he moved to Oahu to launch the invasion. However, an epidemic decimated his forces before he could assault Kauai.

Kamehameha finally acquired Kauai by peaceful means. As early as 1805 he appealed to King Kaumualii to recognize his sovereignty and to pay him an annual tribute. The Kauaian leader was willing to accept these terms, but, fearing for his life, he refused Kamehameha's demand that he make his submission in person at Oahu. In 1810, through the mediation efforts of an American trader, Captain Nathan Winship, Kaumualii finally agreed to go to Oahu. There he recognized Kamehameha as his overlord.

Having unified the islands under his rule, Kamehameha returned to his native island of Hawaii in 1812. During the last years of his life he lived mainly at Kailua, in the Kona district of the island. The Hawaiian archipelago remained peaceful and stable, and Kamehameha devoted his time to encouraging trade and agriculture, to rebuilding the *heiaus* (temples to the gods), and to pursuing his favorite avocation, fishing.

The kingdom founded by Kamehameha the Great, as he came to be known, lasted almost 100 years. After his death in 1819 his son Kamehameha II succeeded him as ruler of Hawaii. Kamehameha II outlawed the traditional taboo system and welcomed the American traders and missionaries. Upon the death of Kamehameha II, his brother Kamehameha III became king. The liberal Kamehameha III ruled the island for 30 years, and during that time he organized a constitutional government and undertook a program whereby land was more equitably distributed amongst the archipelago's inhabitants. The last direct descendants of Kamehameha I to rule the Hawaiian Islands were his grandsons: Kamehameha IV, whose reign lasted from 1854 to 1863, and Kamehameha V, who ruled from 1863 to 1872. Control of the archipelago then passed to Lunalilo, who ruled for only one year and was succeeded by Kalakaua. He died without an heir in 1891, thus allowing his sister Liliuokalani to assume the throne. Ousted by a coup in 1893, she was Hawaii's last royal ruler.

Today, Hawaiians recall the creation and early history of the Hawaiian kingdom and Kamehameha I's importance as the unifier of the islands. It was in 1872 that Kamehameha V proclaimed June 11 a day to honor his grandfather. The day is still celebrated every year as Kamehameha Day, a legal holiday in Hawaii and an occasion of great festivity.

June 12

George Bush's Birthday

George Herbert Walker Bush, the 41st president of the United States was born on June 12, 1924, in Milton, Massachusetts, to Dorothy and Prescott Bush. His father was a successful businessman and served in the United States Senate from 1952 to 1962.

Bush received his grade school education at the prestigious Phillips Academy in Andover, Massachusetts. He graduated on his 18th birthday, June 12, 1942. At the time the United States was engaged in World War II, and so like many young men of this era, Bush postponed his college educa-

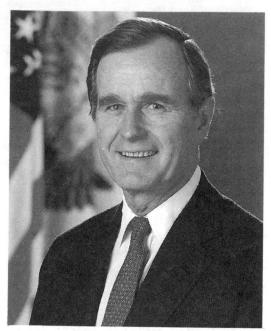

U.S. Senate Historical Office

George Bush

Republican National Committee, and director of the Central Intelligence Agency. While chairman of the Republican National Committee, he coordinated the party's defensive public relations strategy for President Richard Nixon during the Watergate episode. In 1980 Bush decided to enter the Republican primaries for the party's nomination in the upcoming November presidential elections.

Bush lost in the primaries to Ronald Reagan, but had enough supporters to secure the nomination for vice president. Reagan and Bush won the 1980 election and were reelected in 1984. Bush was implicated in the Iran-Contra scandal, in which weapons were illegally sold to Iran to finance pro-American rebels in Nicaragua, but he denied involvement and no determinative evidence of his complicity was ever uncovered. In 1988 Bush ran for president, and with Reagan's endorsement won the Republican nomination and then the election.

George Bush took his oath of office on January 20, 1989. During his presidency the Soviet Union collapsed, thus ending the cold war, which had begun in the late 1940s. Bush's skillful diplomacy helped make it possible for the Soviet leadership to surrender power without losing face and to let the nations within the communist empire establish free and democratic governments. It was one of the rare occasions in human history when a totalitarian regime backed by a formidable military machine voluntarily, and with relatively little bloodshed, accepted the breakup of its power. Further, when Iraqi president Saddam Hussein invaded neighboring Kuwait in the summer of 1990, Bush organized the military campaign known as Operation Desert Storm that forcibly removed the Iraqis from Kuwait early in 1991 (see other entries in this book). Bush was able to forge an unlikely Middle East alliance of Arab states to back the American forces against Hussein, due in large part to the personal contacts that he had made with Arab leaders as director of the CIA.

At home, however, Bush was less successful. Despite record public approval ratings, he was unable to mount a serious economic recovery program when the country entered a severe recession in the fall of 1990. He also reneged on his famous 1988 presidential campaign pledge to not raise taxes, during which he said "read my lips" in making his promise. This quip came back to haunt Bush when his detractors accused him of lying. Bush also opposed such popular measures as extending the period for collecting unemployment benefits, even though a growing number of people were unable to find jobs because of the recession. Finally, Bush supported the controversial savings and loan bailout, in which the government

tion and enlisted in the military. He entered the U.S. Navy as a seaman second class, and was commissioned as a navy pilot in June 1943. Bush was the youngest pilot in navy history.

During the war, Bush flew torpedo bombers in the Pacific against the Japanese. On September 2, 1944, his aircraft was hit by enemy fire and he was forced to bail out over the ocean after completing his mission. He was rescued by a submarine and eventually awarded the Distinguished Flying Cross. Bush left the navy in 1945, which was also the year that he married Barbara Pierce.

After the war Bush attended Yale University, graduating with an economics degree in 1948. He moved to Texas and became a successful businessman, making millions in the petroleum industry. In 1964 he decided to follow in his father's footsteps by entering politics, but his campaign for the United States Senate failed. He ran again in 1966, this time for the Texas Seventh District's seat in the United States House of Representatives, and won. During his freshman term Bush was chosen to serve on the powerful Ways and Means Committee, which writes tax legislation, an honor usually reserved for senior representatives. He left the House in 1970 to run for the Senate again, but lost once more.

During the 1970s Bush served in a number of important government positions. He was an ambassador to the United Nations, an envoy to the People's Republic of China, the chairman of the pumped hundreds of billions of dollars to rescue the savings and loan industry after years of lax government supervision and corrupt financial practices. Many of the financiers and other individuals responsible for the collapse escaped unscathed, while thousands of ordinary savers received no government assistance.

The result was plummeting approval ratings, especially since the public blamed Bush for the poor economy. During the fall of 1992, Bush ran for re-election, but was defeated by Democrat William Jefferson Clinton. The popular vote was 43 percent for Clinton, 38 percent for Bush, and 19 percent for the independent candidate, H. Ross Perot. Many Republicans bitterly accused Perot of causing Bush's defeat, although polls conducted shortly after the election indicated that even without Perot the Bush campaign would have lost. Bush, like many vice presidents who become president after a popular predecessor, thus served only one term. He left office on January 20, 1993.

George Bush now lives in Houston, Texas. He is the father of six children, one of whom died of leukemia, and has over a dozen grandchildren. Two sons, George and Jeb, have also entered politics. George Bush Sr.'s advice and counsel are still frequently sought by Republicans and Democrats alike, especially in the area of foreign policy.

Philippine Independence Day

The Philippine Islands were for several centuries under foreign domination before the establishment of independence in 1946. The story of how June 12 came to be observed as Philippine Independence Day dates from the beginning of that domination.

Spain, on the basis of the discoveries made by Ferdinand Magellan, was the first European nation to claim possession of the Philippines. Magellan, Portuguese by birth, reached the islands in 1521 during his circumnavigation of the world. The Filipinos received the Europeans with hostility and killed Magellan. In 1564 another Spanish explorer, Miguel López de Legazpi, sailed from Mexico to the Philippines and conquered the islands.

Other European nations envied Spain's control of the strategic Philippine archipelago along the Pacific trade routes. On October 6, 1762, during the Seven Years' War, British soldiers captured Manila, the principal city of the islands, but the Treaty of Paris of February 10, 1763, which ended the conflict, restored the islands to the Spanish. In the 19th century the strength of Spain ebbed, however, and the merchant ships of Great Britain and the United States came to dominate the commerce of the area.

The Filipinos, never fully reconciled to Spanish control, began a series of rebellions in 1843. Native priests, especially Father Peláez and Father Opolinario de la Cruz, spearheaded the movements. Although abortive, these uprisings fostered the development of strong nationalistic feelings in the islands, which, with the opening of the Suez Canal in 1869, became even more important in the world economy.

Revolution in Spain ousted Queen Isabella II in 1868 and led to the establishment of a new regime. The new government sent a number of creative administrators to the Philippines, and they allowed the islands greater autonomy, permitted the publication of liberal journals, and tolerated freer political discussions. The collapse of the Spanish regime in 1871, however, ended the experiment and a reactionary governor-general took office in Manila. Responding to a small mutiny of Filipino soldiers at Cavite in January 1871, the restored government executed three priests, sent a number of leaders to penal colonies, and exiled various intellectuals.

Despite the Spanish abuses, many Filipino leaders were willing to remain within the Spanish empire. The Propaganda Movement, a publicity campaign started in Madrid by Filipino exiles, sought reform rather than revolution. Jos Rizal, the author of *Noli Me Tangere* (Touch Me Not), which described the hardships endured by the islanders, became the leader of the group. Rizal returned to Manila in 1892 and founded the Liga Filipino to encourage the political and social advancement of his people. However, within a short time Spanish officials exiled him to the island of Mindanao, and both the Propaganda Movement and the Liga Filipino became moribund.

More militant Filipinos abandoned the conciliatory approach of the Propaganda Movement. In Manila in July 1892 Andrés Bonifacio founded a secret society, the Katipunan (Sons of the People), whose avowed goal was to win independence by force. In 1896 Spanish officials sought to arrest the leaders of the Katipunan, but instead set off a wave of violent uprisings throughout the Philippines. The Spanish retaliated with repressive tactics, including the execution of José Rizal on charges of sedition, even though he had actually advised the rebels to be more moderate.

In 1897 Emilio Aguinaldo emerged as the foremost rebel leader, and a revolutionary assembly proclaimed a provisional republic and named him president. Aguinaldo proved unable to defeat the Spanish in battle, however, and in December 1897 agreed to the Pact of Biac-na-bato by which the insurgent leaders voluntarily exiled themselves to Hong Kong. In return the Spanish agreed to pay the rebels for the surrender of their weapons and to assist families that had been harmed by the war. Unfortunately, neither side lived up to the agreement.

In 1898, as a consequence of the Spanish-American War, the United States became involved in the struggles of the Filipinos. On the evening of April 30, Commodore George Dewey's Asiatic Squadron sailed into Manila Bay in search of the Spanish fleet, which it easily overwhelmed in a brief, one-sided operation early the following morning (see May 1, Spanish-American War: Battle of Manila Bay). Lacking the necessary manpower to undertake land operations against Manila, Dewey simply blockaded the port. Meanwhile, Emilio Aguinaldo was called back from exile by the Americans to lead a native insurrection against the Spanish. On June 12, the day that would ultimately be recalled as Philippine Independence Day, Aguinaldo declared the islands independent and established a provisional government. By the end of July, reinforcements arrived from the United States. On August 13 General Wesley Merritt, supported by Aguinaldo, attacked Manila and on the following day received the Spanish capitulation.

Negotiations necessarily involved the fate of the Philippines. Resolved to have a ship-coaling station in the Far Pacific, unwilling to allow the Spanish to reassert their colonial control, and fearful that another world power would attempt to seize the area, President William McKinley decided that the United States would take over the islands. A number of Americans, some for altruistic, anti-imperialist reasons and others on account of racist biases, opposed the acquisition of the area. However, the Senate on February 6, 1899, ratified the Treaty of Paris, which ended the Spanish-American War and in the process America acquired the Philippines for $20 million.

Aguinaldo and other Filipino leaders, who expected the United States to grant immediate self-government, were disappointed by the American acquisition. Even before the United States approved the Treaty of Paris, the rebel leader on January 5, 1899, had called for the Philippine people to declare their independence. On February 4 the populace rose in revolt against the latest foreign occupiers. Guerrilla warfare between the United States Army and the Filipino rebels continued for several years, but the Filipinos were eventually defeated. In March 1901 Aguinaldo himself was captured.

On January 20, 1899, President McKinley appointed President Jacob Schurman of Cornell University to lead a fact-finding commission to determine the future of the Philippines. The investi-

gators concluded that the Filipinos desired and deserved independence, but required training and experience before they would be able to assume the responsibilities of autonomy. Schurman advocated an extensive educational program and opportunities in local self-government to equip the islanders for the future. Federal Circuit Judge William Howard Taft led the second Philippine Commission, established by President McKinley on April 7, 1900, to establish civil government on the islands. American military rule of the archipelago ended on June 12, 1901, and Taft's five-man commission took office on July 4, 1901. Taft proclaimed equal rights for all Filipinos, separated church and state, instituted freedom of assembly and of the press, and began to put Schurman's proposals into effect. The commission later added three Filipino members.

The United States Congress, by the passage of the Pacific Organic Act on July 1, 1902, increased the strength of democratic government in the islands. The bill created a popular assembly as the lower house of a bicameral legislature in which the Taft commission became the senior body. A governor-general appointed by the United States exercised executive powers. At the inauguration of the assembly chosen in the first general elections in 1909, the United States renewed its promise of eventual independence for the islands.

Passage of the Jones Act on August 29, 1916, marked another step toward Philippine independence. The bill reaffirmed American commitment to independence for the islanders and gave them effective control of their domestic affairs. The act provided for male suffrage and a bill of rights, established an elective senate in place of the Philippine Commission, and vested judicial power in the Supreme Court of the Philippines. In 1934 Congress passed the Tydings-McDuffie Act, which called for the creation on July 4, 1936, of a Philippine Commonwealth under a native chief executive. Manuel Luis Quezon y Molina became the first president and Sergio Osmeña the first vice president of the commonwealth. The United States retained control of foreign relations and kept troops in the islands, but promised that in ten years the Philippines would become an independent republic.

World War II unavoidably delayed the planned transfer of sovereignty. Japan invaded and occupied the Philippines in 1942, and set up a puppet republic the following year. Filipino resistance fighters opposed the Japanese and shared in the final Allied victory. The United States honored its promise and granted full independence to the Philippines on July 4, 1946. Manila celebrated on that day with speeches, flag raisings, planes circling overhead, a 21-gun salute, and a parade led by crack troops of the Philippine army, which the United States had returned to Philippine command on June 30. Paul McNutt, the retiring U.S. commissioner, whom President Harry S. Truman had appointed as the first American ambassador to the Philippines, read the formal proclamation that transformed the commonwealth into a republic. Manuel Roxas y Acuña, the republic's first president, delivered a public address, as did General Douglas MacArthur, who had liberated the islands from the Japanese.

Conscious of their historic ties with the United States, for many years the Filipinos chose July 4 as their Independence Day in order to parallel the American Independence Day celebration. However, in 1962 President Diosdada Macapagal changed the date of the observance to June 12, the anniversary of the declaration of Philippine independence from Spain made by Emilio Aguinaldo in 1898.

June 13

Supreme Court Expands Right Against Self-Incrimination in *Miranda* v. *Arizona*

The United States Constitution guarantees American citizens a wide variety of rights. One of these is contained in the Fifth Amendment, which states in part that no one "shall be compelled in any criminal case to be a witness against himself." On June 13, 1966, the Supreme Court issued its decision in the historic case of *Miranda* v. *Arizona* that clarified and expanded this fundamental constitutional protection for people who are arrested and accused of committing a crime.

Like most constitutional protections, the right to not incriminate oneself originates in English legal history. Before the 1600s English prosecutors could use torture to force confessions from criminal suspects, and suspects could also be legally compelled to give incriminating testimony at their trials. When the United States achieved independence, most of the Founding Fathers who wrote the Constitution were lawyers and were well aware of the abuses in the English system. Thus, the right against self-incrimination was included in the Fifth Amendment. There was, however, no requirement that suspects be told of this right. Although the use of torture to obtain confessions has been fairly rare in American history, the police have certainly used many other forms of physical and psychological coercion to obtain confessions.

In March 1963 Ernesto Miranda, who already had a criminal record, was arrested and charged with the rape of an 18-year-old woman. In a police lineup with several other Mexicans, the victim tentatively identified him as her attacker, although she was not certain. The police then interrogated Miranda, telling him that he had been positively identified, and he signed a confession. The written confession, prepared by the police, stated that he understood his rights even though the police had not told him that he did not have to incriminate himself.

Fortunately for Miranda, he received a competent court-appointed attorney, who challenged the confession and pursued the case all the way to the Supreme Court of the United States. The Supreme Court, under the leadership of Chief Justice Earl Warren, had already been leaning toward a more liberal interpretation of constitutional rights. The Court's decision, issued by the chief justice himself, stated that "prior to any questioning, the person must be warned that he has a right to remain silent, that any statement he does make may be used as evidence against him, and that he has a right to the presence of an attorney. . . ." Although there was some initial resistance, these warnings have now become a routine part of every criminal arrest, and are popularly known as the Miranda warnings. If a suspect is not properly "Mirandized," the case may well be thrown out of court.

The *Miranda* decision has become an important part of the constitutional protections that the American legal system affords criminal suspects, and helps enforce the right against self-incrimination. Miranda himself, however, left a less admirable legacy. He was retried without the confession, but nevertheless found guilty and convicted. After serving his sentence, he was killed in a barroom brawl.

Feast of St. Anthony of Padua

The Feast of St. Anthony of Padua is celebrated by Roman Catholics on June 13. Statues and pictures of St. Anthony usually show him carrying the child Jesus in his arms and holding the lily.

Anthony was born in Lisbon, Portugal, around August 15, 1195. After 1211 his father, a knight, served the Portuguese king Alfonso II. When he was 15, Ferdinand, as he had been christened, entered the Canons Regular of St. Augustine, a religious order in Lisbon, and took the name Anthony. Two years later, he was transferred to the Augustinian monastery at Coimbra.

At Coimbra, the Augustinians had an excellent school of biblical studies, and for eight years Anthony immersed himself in the history, language, and interpretation of scripture. He was made guest-master of the house at Coimbra, caring for the needs of travelers and guests. His life was changed abruptly by one group of these guests. They were five Franciscan friars who were en route to Morocco as missionaries. Shortly after they arrived in Morocco, the five Franciscans were murdered and their remains were returned to Coimbra for burial. Although he had known them only briefly, Anthony was deeply shocked by their deaths and could not keep his mind on his studies. He decided that he too would join the Franciscans and go to Morocco, knowing that he risked a martyr's death.

Although Anthony was successful in getting to Morocco as a Franciscan, poor health struck him shortly after he landed there and his superiors ordered him home. The ship that was supposed to carry him back to Portugal, however, was blown off course by a storm and Anthony landed at Messina in Sicily in about 1220 to 1221. He probably accepted this as God's will inasmuch as Italy was the home of St. Francis of Assisi, who had founded the Franciscan order. Anthony reported to his Franciscan superiors in Italy and was sent to a hospice in Forli, where he did menial chores. His superiors there were not aware of his great learning or his ability as a preacher and, but for an accident, they might never have known.

The discovery took place when a large group of important clergy and laymen were gathered for an ordination ceremony at Forli and the invited speaker did not appear. None of the Franciscans volunteered to step in, and the superior abruptly called on Anthony to preach. The sophisticated and learned audience was stunned by this unknown friar's mastery of scripture, his charm, and his preaching talents. From that time on, Anthony was assigned as preacher to all of Italy. With his Franciscan companions he traveled from town to town and drew crowds so large that town squares could not hold them.

Anthony gave his last sermon during Lent in Padua, which was literally invaded for the occasion. Neither food nor accommodations for the crowd could be found, but the people kept coming. After this, the weary and sick Anthony was invited to rest at the estate of a friend outside the city. While they were walking on the grounds there, his companions saw a large tree whose branches could be formed into a roof, and they made a rustic shelter there for Anthony, appropriate for the Franciscan way of life. On June 13, 1231, as he rested under this tree, Anthony had a premonition of his own death. Not wishing to inconvenience his host, he asked his companions to take him back to the monastery at Padua. They put him in an ox cart and began the hot, dusty journey toward the city. Before they reached there, however, Anthony's condition worsened and they stopped instead at a convent in Arcella, where they propped him up in a sitting position to ease his discomfort. Although he was having great trouble breathing, he began to sing a hymn and with the words still on his lips, he died. He was not quite 36 years old.

Anthony was canonized within a year after his death, on May 30, 1232, by Pope Gregory IX. The pope also declared him a teacher of the church. Anthony also received the title of confessor, accorded to saints who have lived lives of outstanding sanctity and heroic virtue but who have not been martyred. On January 16, 1946, Pope Pius XII declared Anthony a doctor of the church with the title Doctor Evangelicus in honor of his great preaching ability. Many churches in the United States are named for St. Anthony of Padua, especially in Italian American communities; a shrine church is located in New York's Little Italy. Statues of St. Anthony usually show him holding the Christ Child, in reference to a vision he once experienced.

June 14

Flag Day

See also January 1, First National Flag.

The creation of an American nation from the 13 colonies that rebelled against Great Britain in 1776 was not easily accomplished. Prior to their decision to end their connection with the mother country, the colonies had enjoyed separate existences and had established few intercolonial ties. However, their common struggle against British rule brought the colonies more than independence. Gradually, they acquired a sense of national identity. As a symbol of this new unity the former British colonies adopted a national flag on June 14, 1777.

During the initial battles of the American Revolution, the rebels fought under the banners of the individual colonies or even those of local militia companies. For example, colonials from Massachusetts marched under banners depicting a pine tree emblem, while some units of minutemen in Pennsylvania and Virginia gave their allegiance to a flag bearing a coiled rattlesnake and the warning "Don't Tread on Me." Other early revolutionary flags included the banner adopted by the associators of Hanover, Pennsylvania, showing a rifleman and carrying the words "Liberty or Death"; the flag of two militia units at Charleston, South Carolina, proclaiming "Liberty" in white letters on a blue field; and the so-called Bunker Hill Flag, a British-blue flag that the colonists modified by the addition of a pine tree to the St. George's Cross.

Such a great diversity of flags reflected a similar lack of unity in the rebels' efforts against Great Britain. The first "national" flag was the Continental Colors, also known as the Grand Union Flag, and became so on a purely unofficial basis. Commander in Chief George Washington designated it to be flown to celebrate the formation of the Continental army, which was announced on New Year's Day in 1776 (see January 1, First National Flag). The flag, with 13 alternating red and white stripes and a field bearing the crosses of St. George and St. Andrew, may have been in use elsewhere as early as the fall of 1775. The Grand Union Flag, as it became known, was an appropriate selection. The colonists had not yet declared independence, and the presence of the British Union design in the field symbolized many Americans' hope of eventual reconciliation with Britain. However, at the same time the pattern of 13 stripes, one for each colony, was tacit recognition of the rebels' increasing unity of purpose.

The Grand Union Flag was first raised on January 1, 1776, on Prospect Hill in Somerville, near Washington's headquarters at Cambridge, Massachusetts. In the months that followed, the banner, which bore no symbol associated with a particular colony or locality and which was thus a truly national design, won wide acceptance. The flag flew from colonial masts along the entire Atlantic seaboard. However, the Continental Congress's declaration of independence in July made the banner, incorporating the British Union Flag in its design, obsolete. Thus, the congress never officially accepted the flag. Nevertheless, the Grand Union Flag's significance as this country's first national flag should not be underestimated. In recognition of its importance, a granite memorial tower and observatory was dedicated on Prospect Hill in 1903. Inscribed on its side were the words:

> From this eminence on January 1, 1776, the flag of the United Colonies, bearing thirteen stripes and the crosses of St. George and St. Andrew first waved defiance to a foe.

Concerned with the business of conducting the war against Great Britain, the Continental Congress did not give its attention to the matter of an official national banner until almost a year after the adoption of the Declaration of Independence. Then, on June 14, 1777, Congress resolved:

> That the flag of the thirteen United States be thirteen stripes, alternate red and white; that the union [field] be thirteen stars, white in a blue field, representing a new constellation.

The 1777 legislation provided only the barest specifications for the new flag. It did not limit the number of points in the design of the stars, it did not set forth a particular arrangement for the stars and stripes, nor did it designate a designer for the national banner. Numerous contradictory and unsubstantiated legends attribute the creation of the first Stars and Stripes flag to such various personages as John Hulbert of Long Island, New York; John Paul Jones, the American naval hero; and Francis Hopkinson, a signer of the Declaration of Independence. However, tradition generally credits Betsy Ross with making the original Stars and Stripes banner. The story of the Philadelphia upholsterer dates from 1870, when her grandson, William J. Canby, read a paper before the Historical Society of Pennsylvania.

Canby based his report on conversations with Ross that had taken place shortly before her death in 1836. At the time of these talks, she was 84 and her grandson was 11. In 1857 Canby wrote down his grandmother's recollections, and in 1870 he published her story, 94 years after the fact. The appealing vignette of General Washington visiting the needlewoman quickly caught the popular imagination, and Ross's name became linked with the banner of 13 alternate red and white stripes and a blue field bearing a circle of 13 five-pointed stars. Historians, however, have not been able to corroborate Canby's report. The only provable facts known about Ross are that she was a patriot upholsterer living in Philadelphia during the American Revolution, and that some time before May 1777 she made several Pennsylvania naval flags of unknown design.

Just as the identity of the designer and maker of the original Stars and Stripes flag is shrouded in mystery, the exact date of its first raising is also unknown. Authorities do agree that the flag gained increasing acceptance during the summer of 1777, and most believe that rebel forces first fought under the flag at the battle of Bennington, Vermont, in August 1777. The Bennington flag is recognized as the oldest Stars and Stripes banner. Its design reflects the latitude the Continental Congress allowed flagmakers in its specifications. The blue field is nine stripes in width; 11 of its 13 seven-pointed stars are arranged in an arch over the numerals "76" on the field, while the remaining two occupy the upper corners. Interesting as well is the fact that the highest and lowest of the flag's 13 stripes are white rather than red.

Historians do not know if the Continental army regularly fought under the Stars and Stripes following its introduction on the battlefield at Bennington, but there is no doubt that the American navy consistently flew the flag from the masts of its ships. Indeed, Navy Commander John Paul Jones once wrote:

> The Flag and I are twins. . . . So long as we can float, we shall float together. If we must sink, we shall go down as one.

Jones was true to the flag. When the commander sailed his sloop, the *Ranger*, from Portsmouth, New Hampshire, on November 1, 1777, the national banner went to sea for the first time. When French men-of-war saluted the ship as it left Quiberon Bay in France on February 14, 1778, foreign vessels acknowledged the Stars and Stripes for the first time.

Although many flag "firsts" are associated with exploits of the American Revolution, it was the winning of independence in 1783 that made the Stars and Stripes the legally recognized banner of the United States. With nationhood, however, some changes were effected in the flag; for as the young republic matured and expanded, its flag reflected its growth. In January 1794, shortly after the admission of Vermont and Kentucky to the Union, Congress made the first of several alterations in the flag legislation of 1777. Yet, like similar enactments that have followed during the course of American history, the 1794 law (which added two stars and two stripes to the banner to represent the two new states) did not change the flag's basic design of stars and stripes.

The 15-star and 15-stripe flag approved in 1794 served as this country's banner from 1795 to 1818, and is perhaps best remembered as Francis Scott Key's inspiration for the national anthem. The circumstances surrounding Scott's writing were quite dramatic. Harsh fighting took place between British and American forces during the War of 1812, and a particularly bitter battle occurred from September 12 to September 14, 1814, when the British attacked Baltimore, Maryland. Key was aboard a warship in the city's harbor throughout the conflict, and at the break of dawn on September 14 he sought some assurance that the enemy had not penetrated the American defenses. The sight of the national flag flying over Fort McHenry quickly quieted his fears, and his elation upon seeing the flag prompted him to write the famous verses of "The Star-Spangled Banner." In 1931 Congress officially adopted Key's song as the national anthem.

Upon the admission of Vermont and Kentucky to the Union, two new stars and two new stripes had been added to the flag. However, in 1818 so many new states carved from the Old Northwest Territory were either applying for statehood or about to do so that Congress realized it would no longer be practical to increase the number of stripes in the flag. For this reason, Congress passed a third law affecting the national banner. The measure, which went into operation on July 4, 1818, fixed the number of stripes in the flag at 13 and provided for the automatic addition of a new star for each state entering the Union thereafter.

Following the adoption of the 1818 legislation, Congress approved no significant flag law for almost 100 years. During the remainder of the 19th century and in the early 20th century, flags were made according to the prescribed stars and stripes design, but there were still no official specifications regarding the placement and proportions of the stars and stripes. Then in 1912 President William Howard Taft issued two executive orders that ended the latitude previously allowed flagmakers. Taft's orders established the proportions of the height and width of the flag and its field, and the proportionate width of each stripe and diameter of each star. Also beginning in 1912, the government began to standardize the arrangement of the stars on the flag's field.

As the visible symbol of the nation, the Stars and Stripes rapidly won the respect of American citizens. Slower to gain popular acceptance was the establishment of formal ceremonies centering around the banner. In fact, the first Flag Day observance did not take place until June 14, 1861, almost a century after the official adoption of the flag. It occurred then only because the people of Hartford, Connecticut, wished to express their support for the Union during the opening days of the Civil War. In 1877 Congress ordered that the flag be flown over public buildings every June 14.

During the final years of the 19th century, observances of Flag Day on June 14 won only gradual recognition. In 1889 George Bolch, the principal of a free kindergarten for the poor in New York City, decided to hold patriotic exercises on June 14. The ceremonies at Bolch's school attracted considerable attention, and within a short time the New York State legislature passed a law providing that:

> It shall be the duty of the State Superintendent of Public Schools to prepare a program making special provision for observance in the public schools of . . . Flag Day.

In accordance with this act the superintendent ordered that the flag be displayed on every public school building beginning at nine o'clock in the morning, and that appropriate patriotic exercises also be held.

Citizens in other areas of the nation also worked to promote Flag Day. William T. Kerr, who resided first in Pittsburgh, Pennsylvania, and later in Philadelphia, is recognized by many as the Father of Flag Day. As a schoolboy, Kerr began to urge the observance of the day, and his enthusiasm never waned. Interest was also shown by Bernard J. Cigrand of Chicago, a navy officer and flag historian. Cigrand had a leading role in persuading the American Flag Day Association, which was founded in his home city in 1894, to schedule its observances on June 14 rather than on the third Saturday in June as had been its original intention. Still another person closely associated with establishing Flag Day was Joseph H. Hart, a businessman of Allentown, Pennsylvania. Hart led a campaign to urge that a special flag day be set aside, and as a result of his efforts the Allentown Flag Day Association was formed in 1907.

Because of the work of Kerr and the others, the desire to celebrate Flag Day came to the attention of the American public. As early as 1893 the mayor of Philadelphia ordered that the flag be displayed on all city buildings on June 14. Four years later, the governor of New York similarly commanded that the flag be flown over all public structures on that day. In 1916 President Woodrow Wilson issued a proclamation asking the nation to observe June 14 as Flag Day, and President Calvin Coolidge acted similarly in 1927. It was not until August 3, 1949, however, that Congress finally agreed to a joint resolution, and President Harry S. Truman officially designated June 14 as Flag Day. Programs on the day traditionally center around the "Pledge of Allegiance to the Flag," which was written by James B. Upham and Francis Bellamy in 1892.

Harriet Beecher Stowe's Birthday

Harriet Elizabeth Beecher Stowe, author of the inflammatory book *Uncle Tom's Cabin* (probably the most effective piece of antislavery literature ever published), was born in Litchfield, Connecticut, on June 14, 1811, daughter of the noted Calvinist clergyman Lyman Beecher. The role of her mother, who died when she was four, was more or less taken over by her oldest sister Catharine.

Harriet Beecher grew up in a stern Puritan household full of ideas and devotion to causes. Of her father's 13 children by three marriages, she and her brother Henry Ward Beecher earned lasting reputations, and at least five other brothers and sisters (including Catharine) were prominent in their own lifetimes for their work in education, the ministry, abolition, and women's rights. Harriet was at first a student in the school that her sister

had set up in Hartford, Connecticut, and subsequently taught there. She was about 21 when her father gave up the pulpit of Boston's Park Street Church to become president of Cincinnati's new Lane Theological Seminary, which apart from training ministers came to be an abolitionist center. In Cincinnati Catharine promptly set up a pioneering, if short-lived, college for women named the Western Female Institute. Harriet served as an assistant in this enterprise, and did some writing for local journals. Meanwhile, her brother Henry studied at the seminary, where his professors included Calvin Ellis Stowe, a scholar versed in Greek, Arabic, and Hebrew. On January 6, 1836, Calvin Stowe and Harriet Beecher were married.

In spite of the want and worry occasioned by her husband's uncertain health, Harriet Beecher Stowe labored constantly over her writing in the years that followed. She wrote stories and essays, and her first book was *The Mayflower, or Sketches of Scenes and Characters among the Descendants of the Pilgrims* (1843). Her 18 years in Cincinnati also gave her the opportunity to observe the institution of slavery as practiced in the nearby slave state of Kentucky, just across the Ohio River, and as movingly reported by fugitive slaves passing through Cincinnati.

When her husband was appointed professor of religion at his alma mater, Bowdoin College, the family moved to Brunswick, Maine, in 1850. Meanwhile, the North reverberated with abolitionist sentiment and agitation against the new Fugitive Slave Law. In Brunswick she received a deluge of letters describing the tragic effects of the law. Burning with inspiration, she wrote *Uncle Tom's Cabin* for an antislavery newspaper in Washington, D.C. Her hero became the best-known black character in fiction: Uncle Tom, a pious, elderly slave of sterling character, subjected (after the death of a kind master) to the fatal cruelties imposed by Simon Legree. Eliza, Topsy, and Little Eva were other memorable characters.

As a newspaper serial (June 5, 1851–April 1, 1852), the supposedly true-to-life story caused little stir. However, when it was published in book form in 1852, a storm of controversy broke loose both in the United States and around the world. The first American novel to sell more than a million copies, it was translated into at least 23 languages. In Europe its appearance was a literary event, with Thomas Macaulay, Heinrich Heine, George Sand, and Leo Tolstoy among its admirers. Surprisingly, considering Stowe's views, the book did not attempt to place all of the blame on the slaveholding South, but left it to the Yankee-born Simon Legree to epitomize the worst evils of slavery. *Uncle Tom's Cabin* was enormously influential in spreading the abolitionist cause. A legend arose that when she met President Abraham Lincoln during the Civil War, he greeted her with "So you're the little woman who wrote the book that made this great war!"

Stowe's second antislavery novel, *Dred: A Tale of the Great Dismal Swamp*, came out in 1856. She subsequently contributed to the new magazine *Atlantic Monthly* and also to publications such as the *Independent* and the *Christian Union*. She also turned from sociological novels to fiction depicting New England life, as in *The Minister's Wooing* (1859), a romance that challenged the strict Calvinism long espoused by her family, and *The Pearl of Orr's Island* (1862), set in a Maine fishing village.

In 1852 Stowe's husband had become a professor at the Theological Seminary in Andover, Massachusetts, where the family lived until his retirement in 1863, after which they moved to Hartford. She remained in Hartford in seclusion after her husband's death in 1886, and died on July 1, 1896, at the age of 85. Stowe was buried with her husband at Andover.

The Continental Congress Establishes the Continental Army

More than a year before the signing of the Declaration of Independence, the Second Continental Congress established the Continental, or American, army. The colonials who fought in the earliest battles of the American Revolution, at Lexington, Concord, and Fort Ticonderoga, had been members of New England militia companies. These local units were able to endure the first clashes with the British, but they could not provide sufficient men or arms for extensive campaigns against the enemy. Successful long-term resistance to the British required intercolonial cooperation.

Less than a month after the battles of Lexington and Concord, the Massachusetts provincial congress requested the Second Continental Congress, then meeting in Philadelphia, to consider such "matters as may be necessary to the defense of this colony and particularly the state of the army therein." Massachusetts needed weapons and supplies from the other colonies. In return it offered to allow the Continental Congress to assume the "regulation and general direction" of the 15,000 New England troops then besieging British-held Boston "for the general defense of the rights of America." The congress agreed to this arrangement. It sent flour and gunpowder to Massachusetts, and then took steps to unify the military forces of the various colonies.

The most important actions toward the creation of an intercolonial army took place in June 1775. On June 14, the congress ordered the formulation of a "draft of rules and regulations for the government of the army" and recruited ten rifle companies from Pennsylvania, Maryland, and Virginia for service in Massachusetts. The following day the Philadelphia gathering appointed George Washington of Virginia to be "General and Commander in Chief of the Army of the United Colonies" and began to name generals for Continental commissions. Although the Continental Congress all but disbanded the army in June 1784, the modern United States Army effectively dates from June 14, 1775, the date of the establishment of the Continental army.

June 15

Arkansas Admitted to the Union

On June 15, 1836, Arkansas became the 25th state to be admitted to the Union. Arkansas was the third state to be created from the vast area of the Louisiana Purchase. Thus, like its neighboring south-central states, it was visited and ruled by the Spanish and French before coming under the jurisdiction of the United States.

The first European to visit the region that is today Arkansas was the Spanish explorer Hernando de Soto. The exact path of de Soto's 1541 explorations is unknown, but it is probable that his party crossed the Mississippi near present-day Helena, Arkansas, proceeded northward to the mouth of the St. Francis River, and then went southwest to the Arkansas River. De Soto's search for gold next took him farther west to Hot Springs and Caddo Gap. After he and his companions failed to find the precious metal, they journeyed down the Ouachita River, and after wintering at either Camden or Calion they continued on into the area that is now the state of Louisiana.

De Soto's party did not establish any permanent settlements in Arkansas, and no other Europeans ventured into the Arkansas region for more than 130 years. Then, in 1673 the French explorers Jacques Marquette and Louis Joliet sailed down the Mississippi as far as the mouth of the Arkansas River. Marquette and Joliet remained at the Native American village of Mitchigamea, close to the junction of the Mississippi and Arkansas, for about one month. Having learned that the Mississippi emptied into the Gulf of Mexico, and having been warned of both hostile native tribes and hostile Spanish to the south, the French decided to return north to Canada.

Like de Soto before them, Marquette and Joliet left no permanent reminder of their sojourn in Arkansas. This, however, was not the case with the next Europeans to visit the region. Early in 1682 a party of Frenchmen led by René-Robert Cavelier de La Salle journeyed down the Mississippi and on April 9 reached its mouth. La Salle claimed all the territory bordering the Mississippi and its tributaries for King Louis XIV of France and planned to fortify the region from the Great Lakes to the Gulf of Mexico. However, he died in 1687 while attempting to establish the first settlement in the vast area he had claimed for France. Meanwhile, in June 1686 his lieutenant, Henri de Tonti, who had set out on an unsuccessful expedition to find his leader, built a small fort in Arkansas.

This first permanent European settlement in Arkansas was modest. Tonti left only six Frenchmen in 1686 at what became known as Arkansas Post, and within one year four of these men had abandoned the fort. Tonti, who is known as the Father of Arkansas, continued to assist at the settlement. He granted the Catholic Church a large tract of land near the post and arranged for a priest to minister to the residents of the settlement and to preach to the neighboring native tribes.

Tonti's faith in the Arkansas Post was not unfounded. Located about 15 miles west of the Mississippi, near the junction of the White and Arkansas Rivers, the post served early settlers, trappers, and hunters. Its significance as a trading center was drastically diminished when New Orleans was established at the mouth of the Mississippi in 1718, but throughout the period of French rule over Louisiana the post served as an important link between French settlements along the Gulf of Mexico and those in the upper Mississippi Valley.

Even after the establishment of the Arkansas Post, however, settlement of the surrounding area proceeded very slowly. In 1718 the Scottish financier John Law was given a tract of 80,000 acres on the Arkansas River about seven miles from the post. Law planned to colonize this land with about 1,500 settlers from Germany and France. The first contingent, of about 800 (mostly from the Alsace region of modern-day France), arrived in Arkansas in 1720. They built cabins on Law's land and with the assistance of friendly natives managed to survive their first winter in America. Within the year, however, Law went bankrupt and without his financial backing the settlement collapsed. The colonists abandoned the Arkansas settlement and many resettled a few miles outside New Orleans.

Law's unsuccessful venture was the only major attempt to colonize Arkansas during the period of French rule. Some French trappers and priests entered the area during the first half of the 18th century, and the many rivers, prairies, bayous, and mountains that bear French names are a reminder of these early adventurers. However, the number of Europeans who came to Arkansas during the French period was extremely small, and thus in 1762 when France ceded its lands west of the Mississippi to Spain only 88 people inhabited the Arkansas Post.

Under Spanish rule the population of Arkansas continued to grow slowly. A number of new settlements were made, including those at Montgomery's Landing, Hopefield, Portia, and Dardanelle. A census in 1785 revealed that the European residents totaled only 196 persons. In 1800 Spain transferred the entire trans-Mississippi region back to France, and three years later, when the area came under the jurisdiction of the United States as a result of the Louisiana Purchase, Arkansas could still count only about 600 non–Native American inhabitants.

For administrative reasons, the United States Congress divided the Louisiana Purchase region into two separate territories in 1804 and included Arkansas in the District of Louisiana, or Upper Louisiana as it was also known. In 1805 Congress gave Upper Louisiana separate territorial status and designated the lower part of present Missouri and all of present Arkansas as the District of New Madrid within the new territory. The following year the District of New Madrid was further subdivided when its southern region was recognized as the District of Arkansas.

During the first years of American control, fairly extensive explorations were undertaken in Arkansas. The entire length of the Arkansas River was mapped and the course of the Ouachita River was plotted as far west as Hot Springs. Still, during this period Arkansas attracted few new permanent residents, and by 1810 the number of non-native inhabitants had risen to only 1,062. After Louisiana gained statehood in 1812, Congress changed the name of the territory of Upper Louisiana, which included Arkansas, to the Missouri Territory. Until 1819 Arkansas remained a part of the Missouri Territory, and during that time Arkansas attracted a number of settlers from the section of the territory that today comprises southeastern Missouri. These new residents were victims of the New Madrid earthquake of 1811–1812, which was felt over an enormous area and rocked a section of the Mississippi Valley extending southward 300 miles from the mouth of the Ohio. The disaster so devastated parts of southeastern Missouri that in 1815 the federal government authorized persons who had inhabited that hapless region to select other unorganized lands located elsewhere in the territory.

June 15

In 1819 Congress separated the area of Arkansas and most of what is today Oklahoma from the Missouri Territory and created from these regions the new Arkansas Territory. The territorial capital, first at Arkansas Post, was moved to Little Rock in 1821. When Congress considered territorial status for Arkansas, antislavery forces attempted to amend its territorial act so that no more slaves could be brought into the territory and those already there would be freed when they reached 25 years of age. The opponents of slavery won Senate approval for their measures, but the House of Representatives rejected the ban against slavery and thereby allowed it to continue in the region.

When Arkansas became a territory in 1819, the total number of non–Native American residents was about 14,000. In the years that followed, the population grew steadily. The victims of the New Madrid earthquake and veterans of the War of 1812, who had been promised land bounties at the time of their enlistments, helped account for the increase in Arkansas inhabitants during the two decades after 1819. Even more important was the fact that after the Missouri Compromise of 1820, banning slavery north of a latitude that bisected the country into a free North and slave South, Arkansas was the only southern area where slavery could expand westward.

In the 1820s and 1830s cotton was by far the most profitable commodity produced in the United States. However, cotton quickly exhausted the soil of the southeastern states where it was first intensively cultivated, and planters were forced to seek new lands farther west. Arkansas's climate proved to be ideally suited to the growing of cotton, and since there was no restriction against slaves in the territory, many planters chose to establish themselves in the underpopulated territory.

By 1833 the population of Arkansas had increased to 40,026, and many residents began to think of statehood. This number was almost 20,000 short of the 60,000 inhabitants required for admission to the Union. Nevertheless, in December 1833 Arkansas's congressional delegate asked the Committee on Territories to report "as to the expediency of admitting the Territory into the Union as a state." At the same time that Congress was considering Arkansas's statehood, it received a similar request from Michigan. Since Michigan was to be a free state, its admission to the Union would upset the sectional balance of free and slave states, which had been established by the Missouri Compromise of 1820 unless proslave Arkansas also gained statehood.

Southerners regarded the situation as urgent. In 1835 Arkansas's delegate to Congress wrote: "Let Michigan get into the union without us, and we are then completely at the mercy of both houses of Congress." To prevent this from happening, Arkansas lawmakers took an unprecedented step. When a census in 1835 showed that Arkansas had more than the 60,000 residents necessary for statehood, the governor sent a message to the territorial legislature expressing his feeling that "there can be no doubt but that, upon the application of the representatives of the people, Congress will freely grant to the people of Arkansas the requisite powers." However, the Arkansas legislature did not wait for the federal Congress to initiate action regarding Arkansas statehood. Instead, the legislature, which met in October 1835, passed a bill calling for the election of delegates to a convention that would meet in January 1836 to draw up a state constitution.

By the end of January 1836 Arkansas's constitution was completed and a copy was sent to Congress. The admission bill easily passed the Senate, but in the House there were extended debates on the propriety of Arkansas's having formed a state constitution before receiving federal authorization to do so and also on the presence in the constitution of clauses permitting slavery in the new state. Even so, the forces opposing Arkansas statehood were not sufficiently strong enough to permanently block the area's admission to the Union. On June 6 Arkansas's congressional delegate persuaded the House to adopt a resolution that it would "consider until disposed of" the Arkansas and Michigan statehood bills. Seven days later the House passed the Michigan bill, and after 25 hours of further debate also approved Arkansas's statehood application. On June 15, 1836, President Andrew Jackson signed the bill making Arkansas the 25th member of the United States.

After the outbreak of the Civil War, Arkansas declared its secession on May 6, 1861. Full privileges of statehood were not restored until June 1868, after a new constitution enfranchising blacks had been drawn up under Reconstruction auspices and provision had been made for ratification of the 14th Amendment, a prerequisite for restoration to the Union.

Oregon Treaty Ratified

Asserting the "clear and unquestionable" title of the United States to all of the Oregon country, a vast region occupied jointly by the United States and Great Britain, the Democratic platform of 1844 pressed for what it called the "reoccupation" of Oregon. It thus placed the party squarely in favor of what an 1845 magazine article was to call the nation's "manifest destiny to overspread the continent allotted by Providence for the free development of our yearly multiplying millions." The phrase "manifest destiny," written in connection with the annexation of Texas, was applied to the Oregon dispute in an influential newspaper editorial and in the halls of Congress. It soon swept the entire nation.

The Oregon country, which stretched from the Rocky Mountains to the Pacific Ocean and from the 42nd Parallel on the south to the 54th Parallel and 40 minutes on the north, included what are now the states of Washington, Oregon, Idaho, and parts of Wyoming and Montana, as well as Vancouver Island and much more of what became the Canadian province of British Columbia. The United States and Great Britain found themselves in joint possession of this huge tract after Spain and Russia abandoned their own conflicting claims to the area. Spain, which had once claimed the whole Pacific coast, in effect surrendered all rights north of California to the United States in the Florida Purchase Treaty of 1819. Russia, which once claimed the coast as far south as San Francisco, abandoned all rights below the parallel 54° 40' in a treaty concluded with the United States in 1824.

Both of the remaining contenders had substantial claims to the region. Britain based its claim on an agreement with Spain in 1790 and on the explorations of Captains James Cook and George Vancouver, and Sir Alexander McKenzie. Also supporting the British claims were the early fur trading enterprises of the Hudson Bay Company and the establishment of Fort McLeod as the first settlement in the Oregon interior in 1805. The United States rested its claims to the Oregon country on the Spanish and Russian treaties previously mentioned, on Captain Robert Gray's discovery of the Columbia River in 1792, on Meriwether Lewis and William Clark's extensive expedition of 1804–1806, on the fur-trading post with which John Jacob Astor founded Astoria, Oregon, in 1811, and on the presence of thousands of American settlers who streamed over the Oregon Trail beginning in the 1840s.

As joint occupants of the huge area, Britain and the United States found themselves unable to agree on how to divide it. They sidestepped the issue in 1818 with a treaty providing for ten years' joint occupation. In 1827 they renewed the understanding indefinitely, but agreed that either party could terminate the agreement on one year's notice. In the meantime, negotiations went on. Beginning in 1826 the United States repeatedly offered to agree to a boundary along the 49th parallel, which already marked the country's border

from what is now northern Minnesota to the Rockies. The British preferred the Columbia River, largely below the 49th Parallel, as a boundary. They also wanted access to Puget Sound and the Strait of Juan de Fuca between Vancouver Island and what later became the state of Washington.

An event that had a marked effect on the Oregon question took place late in 1841, when Senator Lewis F. Linn of Missouri brought before the Congress a bill that had it been enacted would have provided military protection for the Oregon Trail and a grant of free land to every adult male immigrant who found his way to Oregon. Though the bill failed to pass in the final showdown two years later, the discussion surrounding it did much to encourage American settlement of the Oregon country. While the matter hung in the air, many a land-hungry settler set out for Oregon in anticipation of the bill's passage. As the Oregon Trail began to swarm with immigrants, British apprehensions rose. So did Americans' interest in the new land. When Oregon became an issue in the presidential campaign of 1844, expansionists welcomed the uncompromising stand of the successful Democratic candidate, James K. Polk, and the campaign slogan of "Fifty-four Forty or Fight."

With friction between the two countries intensified by the campaign and the British stand stiffened, Polk asked Congress's permission to give the required one year's notice to end the agreement for joint occupation. Between Polk's request (in his first annual message to Congress, on December 2, 1845) and the introduction of the appropriate resolution in the House of Representatives on January 5, 1846, Britain asked the United States to renew its earlier offer to settle along the 49th parallel. Polk refused, but he did allow his secretary of state, in late February, to advise the American envoy in London that negotiations would be reopened if Great Britain initiated the step.

While Britain waited for a politically feasible moment to conciliate on this point, debate dragged on in Congress. Finally, on April 23, 1846, the resolution for ending the joint occupation of Oregon was passed by both chambers and transmitted to President Polk. He delivered the required one year's notice on May 21. The notice was followed shortly by action from the British, in the form of a draft treaty, which reached Washington on June 6. It suggested that the contested boundary be along the 49th parallel to the Pacific, with Vancouver Island going to Britain. It also sought to guarantee free navigation of waters neighboring the island for both parties and of the Columbia River below the 49th parallel for Britain. Polk felt that the treaty was reasonable, but in view of his own strong stand on the whole Oregon question, he took the unusual step of asking the advice of the Senate before formally submitting the treaty for that body's ratification. Senate reaction was favorable and formal submission of the treaty followed. It was ratified on June 15, 1846.

June 16

Franklin D. Roosevelt's Hundred Days

When Franklin D. Roosevelt took office as the 32nd president of the United States on March 4, 1933, a massive economic depression was gripping the nation. Between 12 million to 15 million Americans were unemployed, almost all the country's banks were either closed or operating under state-imposed restrictions, and the majority of the public was convinced that nothing could be done to stem the course of the great financial crisis. The new chief executive realized that the most pressing task before him was to dispel the general feeling of helplessness that had fallen on the nation. On March 5 Roosevelt proclaimed a four-day national bank holiday beginning on Monday, March 6, and he summoned the 73rd Congress to convene its first session on Thursday, March 9. The period from March 9 to June 16, 1933, has become famous as Roosevelt's Hundred Days. During that time the president electrified the country by taking a number of vigorous actions designed to alleviate the most pressing problems of the Great Depression. By so doing, he restored to the nation the self-confidence needed for economic recovery.

The banking crisis, which paralyzed the nation's financial operations, was Roosevelt's first concern. The financial emergency of 1933 might even have prompted so drastic a step as nationalization of the banking industry, but Roosevelt chose a more conservative approach. The Emergency Banking Act, which he sent to Congress on March 9, gave the president broad discretionary powers over transactions in gold, provided severe penalties for hoarding, authorized an issue of new federal reserve notes, and permitted the reopening of sound banks and the reorganization of insolvent ones. Shortly after Congress convened, both the House and the Senate approved the president's banking bill. Three days later, on Sunday evening, March 12, Roosevelt broadcast his first "fireside chat" over the radio. He assured the American people of the safety of their banks, and when the banks began to reopen on Monday, March 13, citizens showed their confidence in the new president by depositing more funds than they withdrew.

Only hours after the banking bill was approved, and days before he knew of its effect, on March 10 Roosevelt sent a second message to Congress. This time he asked for power to cut $400 million from veterans' payments and another $100 million from federal employees' salaries. A number of members of Congress opposed Roosevelt's Economy Act, but despite their disapproval the bill passed the House on March 11 and the Senate four days later. Next, Roosevelt turned his attention to a more serious matter. The 1932 Democratic platform had pledged an end to Prohibition, and in February 1933 the 72nd Congress had voted to repeal the 18th (Prohibition) Amendment. However, before the 21st (Repeal) Amendment could gain the approval of the requisite three-fourths of states, the new chief executive announced at dinner on March 12 that "I think this would be a good time for beer." The following day he sent a bill to Congress that modified the Volstead Act in order to legalize beer and light wines, thereby supplying additional revenue. That week Congress approved the measure, and on March 22 Roosevelt signed the Beer-Wine Revenue Act into law.

Encouraged by his initial successes with Congress, Roosevelt decided to use the first session to try to gain approval of additional legislation. On March 16 he sent his farm bill to Capitol Hill. Roosevelt's proposals for raising the incomes of farmers included a domestic allotment plan that sought to reduce crop surpluses by restricting the acreage under cultivation and cash subsidies for farmers who agreed to limit their production. This Agricultural Adjustment Act easily passed the House, but met some opposition in the Senate. The act and a related measure, namely the Emergency Farm Mortgage Act, which provided for the refinancing of farm mortgages, gained approval on May 12 shortly after the Farmer's Holiday Association had threatened to begin a nationwide agricultural strike.

During his first weeks in office, Roosevelt also won passage of legislation designed to alleviate the suffering caused by the massive unemployment resulting from the depression. On March 21 he sent his unemployment relief message to Congress. Roosevelt urged the national legislature to create a Civilian Conservation Corps and to appropriate federal funds for the relief projects being carried out by state and municipal governments. Congress responded by approving the Civilian Conservation Corps Reforestation Relief Act on March 31 and the Federal Emergency Relief Act on May 12. The former measure established the Civilian Conservation Corps, which provided work in the nation's forests and on public projects for men between the ages of 18 and 25. The latter authorized outright grants totaling $500 million for city and state relief.

The unemployed also benefited from other legislation passed during the Hundred Days. When Roosevelt took office, banks were foreclosing on home mortgages at the rate of more than 1,000 per day. To deal with this situation, Congress approved the Home Owners Refinancing Act. The act, which went into effect on June 13, 1933, created the Home Owners Loan Corporation. During its three-year existence, the corporation helped more than 20 percent of the nation's homeowners retain their dwellings.

While much of the legislation in the spring of 1933 provided short-term assistance to millions of Americans, Roosevelt and the Congress realized that a much broader program was necessary to revive the economy. In mid-May he sent the National Industrial Recovery Act (NIRA) to Congress. Despite considerable opposition in the Senate, the bill won congressional approval and was signed into law on June 16. The NIRA called for self-regulation of the nation's industries under government supervision. Under the act, industrial and trade organizations were permitted to draw up fair competition codes and the president was authorized to prescribe similar codes for industries that failed to enter into voluntary agreements. The codes, which permitted price agreements and established production quotas, were exempt from antitrust laws. The National Recovery Administration, a governmental agency set up under the NIRA, was empowered to ensure compliance with and prevent abuses of the codes. NIRA also gave a measure of protection to workers: It provided for a minimum wage and guaranteed the right of workers "to organize and bargain collectively through representatives of their own choosing." Another part of the NIRA was the Public Works Administration, set up under Title II of the act with a $3.3 billion appropriation for the construction of roads, buildings, and other facilities whose undertaking would increase employment.

Roosevelt and Congress also began to make some progress toward curbing the abuses in the securities and banking industries that had contributed to the economic crisis of the depression. The Securities Act of 1933, which became law on May 27, required the disclosure of complete information to investors about new issues of securities that were being offered publicly or sold through the mails and other means of interstate commerce. It also required most new issues to be registered with the Federal Trade Commission, later with the Securities and Exchange Commission. The Glass-Steagall Banking Act of 1933, which went into effect on June 16, created the Federal Deposit Insurance Corporation. The corporation guaranteed individual bank deposits up to $5,000, and other provisions of the act enabled the Federal Reserve Board to curb excessive speculation on credit, separated commercial banking from investment banking, and permitted savings and industrial banks to join the Federal Reserve System.

In addition to approving legislation designed to relieve the misery of the depression and to curtail abuses that helped bring about the economic collapse, the 73rd Congress also established the Tennessee Valley Authority (TVA). Throughout the 1920s a number of members of Congress had urged that the hydroelectric and munitions plants built during World War I at Muscle Shoals, Alabama, be used to manufacture fertilizer and to provide power for Tennessee Valley residents. Twice Congress had approved federal operations at Muscle Shoals, but Presidents Herbert Hoover and Calvin Coolidge both vetoed the bills. Roosevelt, however, envisioned the TVA as more than a power-generating facility. He saw it as an opportunity to experiment in regional development planning, and wanted the TVA to engage in such wide-ranging activities as flood control, soil conservation, and the diversification of the area's industries. On April 10 Roosevelt brought the Tennessee Valley Act to the attention of Congress. The legislature quickly approved the bill, and on May 18 the TVA became a reality.

The Hundred Days, for all its activity, was just the beginning of the New Deal. It did not solve the problems of the Great Depression, and when Congress left Washington, D.C., on June 16, 1933, after the conclusion of the first session, the economy was still in the doldrums. However, the national attitude had undergone a radical transformation. The public responded positively to the actions of their energetic president, and gone was much of the feeling of hopelessness that had frustrated Americans to the point of despair in March when Roosevelt took office.

June 17

Newt Gingrich's Birthday

Newton Leroy Gingrich, future Speaker of the House of Representatives, was born on June 17, 1943, in Harrisburg, Pennsylvania, to Kathleen Daugherty, who was separated from Newt's biological father, Newton C. McPherson. She remarried in 1946 to Robert Gingrich, who became Newt's stepfather.

Gingrich was a precocious child and a voracious reader. He was also an animal lover, and at the age of ten successfully lobbied the local authorities to open a zoo. Since his stepfather was in the military, however, his family was constantly on the move. They eventually settled in Columbus, Georgia, where he attended Baker High School. He struck up a romance with his geometry teacher, Jacqueline Battley. Gingrich graduated in 1961, and the two were married in 1962 (they divorced in 1981, and he remarried that same year to Marianne Ginther).

After graduating from Emory University in Atlanta, Georgia, in 1965 with a degree in history, he went to Tulane University in New Orleans, Louisiana, to pursue graduate studies. After receiving his doctorate in history in 1971, Gingrich found employment as a professor on the faculty of West Georgia College, where he would teach until 1978. Meanwhile, he decided to pursue his interest in politics, and ran for the House of Representatives in 1974. He lost that year, and again in 1976, but in 1978 he won and took the House seat for Georgia's Sixth District.

Gingrich was a Republican activist looking to revitalize the party with new ideas and to lead a new generation of Republicans back into the majority. The Democrats had been the majority party in the House since the 1950s, but Gingrich was convinced that they were vulnerable, particularly on ethical issues. Many of his detractors labeled him a "bomb-thrower" for his extremely vocal and public accusations, but his charges were effective. After decades in power, many Democrats had become accustomed to using the "perks" of power in ways that were questionable. One such Democrat was the Speaker of the House Jim Wright, who used his position for personal financial gain by, for instance, promoting his autobiography on the lecture circuit. Gingrich initiated an investigation that eventually led to Wright's resignation on May 31, 1989.

That same year, Gingrich's fellow Republicans elected him to the position of Republican party whip in the House. Since the Republicans were still the minority party, he thus became the House minority whip. As a whip, he was responsible for getting out the vote and ensuring party loyalty in key legislative battles. It was the second most powerful position in the House Republican organization, behind the position of minority leader, then held by Republican Robert Michel.

In the November 1992 elections, Republican president George Bush lost to Democrat Bill Clinton, while the Democrats continued to be the majority party in both the House and the Senate. Even though the Democrats controlled both the executive and legislative branches of the federal government, Gingrich was nevertheless optimistic. He organized a Republican initiative known as the Contract with America during the 1994 midterm elections, a package of reform proposals that included a balanced budget amendment to the Constitution and term limits for senators and representatives. Further, Gingrich's leadership inspired many young Republicans running for Congress that year, and their enthusiasm won over many voters.

The result was a historic upset. In the 1994 elections, the Republicans gained 54 seats in the House, making them the new majority party with 230 of the 435 seats. The Republicans also became the majority party in the Senate, and so now they would control Congress instead of the Democrats. Since Michel chose to leave the House rather than run for reelection in 1994, Gingrich advanced from the number two Republican party position in the House to the number one position formerly held by Michel. Now that the Republicans were in control of the House, he became the Speaker of the House in January 1995 when the 104th Congress began.

When Gingrich first took office, he immediately pursued the aggressive agenda of the Contract with America. There were many legislative successes, but also many failures. Clinton was still president, and his fellow Democrats had enough seats left in Congress to prevent presidential vetoes from being overturned by the required two-thirds majority. After a legislative stalemate among the Republicans and Clinton's 1995 shutdown of the federal government, Gingrich decided to pursue a more conciliatory agenda. Many of the more hard-line party members resented his move toward the moderate mainstream of American politics, and they slammed Gingrich for the disappointing results of the 1998 midterm elections in which the Republicans lost several seats. The result was Gingrich's ouster from the speakership and his resignation from the House.

Battle of Bunker Hill

Buoyed by the victories that marked the beginning of the American Revolution at Lexington and Concord (see April 19) in 1775, the Massachusetts rebels moved on the city of Boston, where the British soldiers had taken refuge. On April 23 the New England colonies agreed to raise an army of 30,000 men. Connecticut, New Hampshire, and Rhode Island were unable to send their full quotas, but by June 1775 some 15,000 colonials had gathered in the towns outside Boston.

General Artemas Ward, the commander in chief of the Massachusetts contingent, held the rebel center with 9,000 men at Cambridge. Major General John Thomas commanded the army's right wing, comprising 5,000 men stationed at Dorchester, Jamaica Plains, and Roxbury. The remaining forces, including Colonel John Stark's New Hampshire regiment, covered the colonists' left flank at Charlestown Neck, Chelsea, and Medford. Thomas Gage, the governor of Massachusetts and the commander in chief of the British forces in America, had 6,500 soldiers in the Boston garrison. King George III had ordered him to proclaim martial law in Massachusetts, but the rebels' numerical superiority suggested that he rely on tact. General Gage had Major General John Burgoyne issue a proclamation offering amnesty to all colonists who laid down their arms, with the exception of the rebel leaders Samuel Adams and John Hancock. Burgoyne's proclamation was largely ignored by the colonists.

Military preparations then replaced political maneuvering. General Gage planned to take Dorchester Heights, an unoccupied strategic high ground lying on the periphery of Boston. Learning of the British plans on June 13, the rebels decided to move first and fortify another dominant position, Bunker Hill on Charlestown Neck. On the evening of June 16, Colonel William Prescott collected a force of about 1,200 men on Cambridge common and began the march to Charlestown Neck. Brigadier General Israel Putnam of Connecticut met them there with entrenching equipment. The troops moved beyond Bunker Hill to what later became known as Breed's Hill. There Prescott revealed to his fellow officers the nature of their mission and requested their advice as to the best location for the fortifications. His council of officers decided to put the main effort into the defense of Breed's Hill; Bunker Hill, adjacent to the north, would be a secondary location.

Work began at midnight under the direction of Colonel Richard Gridley, who had gained engineering experience during the French and Indian War. At 4:00 a.m. dawn revealed the colonial entrenchments to the men aboard the British sloop *Lively*. They turned their guns on the Americans, but their fire was ineffective against the rebel stronghold. At a council of war, General Gage and his staff decided that they must oust the Americans from their new position as quickly as possible. Unable to see how far the rebel defenses extended, the British commanders chose to land troops at Moulton's Point on Charlestown Neck, a safe spot out of range of the rebel redoubt. According to the plan devised by Major General William Howe, the British soldiers would then launch a two-pronged attack on the Americans, namely an assault on the front and an enveloping movement around the rebels' left flank.

The necessity of waiting for the high tide and other preparations delayed the start of the operation for about six hours. The Americans used the interval to strengthen their position. Colonels John Stark and James Read arrived with their regiments from Medford. Stark placed most of his men along the undefended beach between the Mystic River and the eastern end of the rebel line. He detached the remainder to assist Captain Thomas Knowlton, whose soldiers were stationed behind a railed fence barricade to his right.

Fifteen hundred British landed around 1:00 p.m., but Howe decided to wait for reinforcements to assist in the assault on the improved American line. Soon, the 47th Regiment, the First Marine Battalion, and six additional companies joined the British troops on the beachhead. Brigadier General Robert Pigot advanced with the 38th and 43rd regiments against the redoubt, but their effort was stopped by the colonial marksmen's musket fire. Simultaneously with Pigot's movement, Howe led the drive on the American left. Grenadiers and elements of the 5th and 52nd British regiments hit the rail fence head-on, while 11 light infantry companies attempted to turn the left flank of the American line. The rebels beat back both groups with heavy fire. Stark arranged his men in three ranks, one of which was always firing as the other two reloaded. The British light infantry alone left 96 of its men dead on the field.

Howe quickly regrouped his forces and attempted a second assault. This time the British light infantry executed a secondary attack on the American left, while Howe and Pigot went after the redoubt. The Americans waited until their opponents were within 100 feet before driving them back with their fire.

Sir Henry Clinton joined Howe and Pigot on the beachhead after this second failure. The three British generals then prepared for a third assault on the colonial redoubt. This time they ordered their troops to drop the 100 to 125 pounds of equipment that each had carried on the previous attempts. Reinforced with fresh troops 400 strong, the British again moved forward against the redoubt. Preparing for a bayonet charge, the British advanced in column until they were within ten yards of the defenders. The Americans, critically short of ammunition, fought gallantly, even engaging in hand-to-hand combat with stones against the British bayonets. Finally, the attackers, after suffering heavy casualties, took the position and the rebels fell back. The British, however, were so exhausted that they pursued the Americans only as far as neighboring Bunker Hill.

One hundred forty Americans, including Joseph Warren, the president of Massachusetts's provincial congress, died in the battle of Bunker Hill, and another 300 were wounded. British losses were much higher. Of the 2,500 British soldiers involved in the encounter, 40 percent were casualties—19 officers and 207 men died, while 70 officers and 758 men fell wounded.

The battle of Bunker Hill encouraged the colonists and discouraged any thoughts of reconciliation with the mother country. The Americans had proved to themselves that they could stand up to the British. Further, the battle showed the British that the rebels were not to be underestimated, and they postponed indefinitely any thoughts of occupying Dorchester Heights. George Washington, who arrived on July 2, 1775, to take command of the forces surrounding Boston, was able to wait until he had sufficient guns and ammunition. In March 1776 he took the Heights without opposition. Rapidly fortifying the position, he thereby rendered the British position in Boston untenable. On March 17, 1776, Howe and his forces departed from the city by ship (see March 17).

The Supreme Court Expands Fair Housing Rights

On April 11, 1968, the Civil Rights Act of 1968, signed by President Lyndon B. Johnson, became effective. It included fair housing provisions, although concern was voiced that they fell short of entirely condemning racial discrimination in housing. A little more than two months later, on June 17, 1968, the United States Supreme Court went beyond the 1968 statute. In a 7 to 2 decision, the Court upheld the validity of a sweeping 102-year-old law that specifically forbade racial discrimination in selling or renting any kind of property.

The almost forgotten law, dating from 1866 and invoked once in 1903 in the *United States* v. *Morris*, had been promulgated to strengthen the effectiveness of the 13th Amendment (1865), which states that "neither slavery nor involuntary servitude shall exist within the United States, or any place subject to their jurisdiction." The Civil Rights Act of 1866 had explicitly provided "that all . . . citizens of the United States . . . of every race and color, without regard to any previous condition of slavery . . . shall have the same right, in every State and Territory in the United States . . . to inherit, purchase, lease, sell, hold, and convey real and personal property . . . as is enjoyed by white citizens. . . ."

Most of the handful of lawyers aware of the existence of the Reconstruction-era law generally assumed that it had aimed merely at assuring the rights of former slaves to possess property. In 1966, however, lawyers for the National Committee Against Discrimination in Housing attempted, by resurrecting the 1866 statute, to get around the long-standing failure of the United States Congress to enact fair housing provisions. In the case of *Jones* v. *Mayer*, they represented Joseph Lee Jones, an African American bail bondsman in St. Louis and his white wife, Barbara Jo, who had not been allowed to purchase a home in a St. Louis development because he was black. The case, which the interracial couple had initiated on September 2, 1965, was dismissed by the federal trial court and then by the Court of Appeals for the Eighth Circuit, both of which ruled that neither the 1866 statute nor for that matter the Constitution forbids racial discrimination in property transactions by private owners.

The Supreme Court's 1968 ruling on the side of the Joneses reached beyond the less sweeping fair housing provisions (intended by January 1, 1970, to cover about 80 percent of all housing sold or rented in the country) that had been enacted by Congress in the Civil Rights Act of 1968. That legislation immediately banned discrimination in the sale or rental of 900,000 federally insured housing units; then by January 1, 1969, in 19.8 million multifamily housing units; and thirdly, by January 1, 1970, in 31.3 million single-family houses where sale or rental was handled by a broker.

According to the 1866 law, racial discrimination is prohibited even in real estate transactions involving single-family homes sold or rented privately by their owners without a broker and also in multifamily units. Justice Potter Stewart summed up the majority opinion as follows:

> At the very least, the freedom that Congress is empowered to secure under the Thirteenth Amendment includes the freedom to buy whatever a white man can buy, the right to live wherever a white man can live. If Congress cannot say that being a free man means at least this much, then the Thirteenth Amendment made a promise the Nation cannot keep.

June 18

Susan B. Anthony Fined for Voting

In order to test the constitutional rights of women with respect to citizenship and voting, feminist leader Susan B. Anthony led a group of women in an attempt to register and vote in a Rochester, New York, election in 1872. Their action set off a celebrated legal case. Anthony was arrested, tried, and on June 18, 1872, sentenced to pay a fine. Adamant in her refusal to do so, she was allowed to go free by a judge who wished to avoid further publicity and controversy.

Susan Brownell Anthony was born in Adams, Massachusetts, on February 15, 1820. As Quakers, her parents belonged to a group that had always recognized the equal rights of women, an attitude that their daughter inherited. A person of remarkable intellect and strong personality, she was educated at her father's school and subsequently served as a teacher herself for 15 years.

Her first reform activities were in the field of temperance. When she was prevented from addressing a temperance meeting because of her sex, she joined with others in 1852 to form the Woman's State Temperance Society of New York. She also lectured widely, urging the abolition of slavery. However, she came to realize that women could work effectively for social reform only if they obtained the same rights and privileges as men, and she eventually turned her principal efforts toward that end.

Prior to the Civil War, the causes of abolition and women's rights were usually linked. In 1848, however, a separate women's rights convention was held at Seneca Falls, New York, by Elizabeth Cady Stanton and other early feminist leaders. It was followed by other women's meetings, including one at Worcester, Massachusetts, in 1850, headed by Lucy Stone. After the Civil War, when women found themselves excluded from the equal rights granted to the former slaves, a separate women's rights movement began in earnest.

Anthony, who has been described as the dynamic force that galvanized the new women's movement into effective action, first met the pioneering Stanton at a temperance meeting in 1851. Thus began a friendship that lasted 50 years. With Stanton, Anthony worked to reform New York's state laws concerning women's rights over their children and control of their own earnings and property. Together the two women brought out the militant women's rights newspaper *The Revolution* from 1868 to 1870, with Anthony as publisher and Stanton as an editor.

In 1869 they organized the National Woman Suffrage Association (NWSA). Stanton was elected president of the new organization and Anthony became head of its executive committee. The stated purpose of the organization, which held an annual national convention for the next 50 years, was to secure women's voting rights by means of a constitutional amendment. The Anthony Woman Suffrage Amendment was introduced before a congressional hearing in 1868, the first of a half-century of unsuccessful annual presentations.

Across the nation and in Europe, Anthony lectured eloquently on behalf of suffrage and contributed to leading magazines. With Stanton and Matilda Joslyn Gage, she compiled the first three volumes of the *History of Woman Suffrage*, which ultimately embraced the years from 1881 to 1922.

While the NWSA began its effort on the national level, the American Woman Suffrage Association, founded in 1869 under the leadership of Stone and others, was specifically geared for work in the states. In 1890 the two organizations merged as the National American Woman Suffrage Association. Anthony served from 1892 to 1900 as president of the new group, which pressed its campaign on both the state and national levels. In 1888 she organized the International Council of Women and in 1904 the International Woman Suffrage Alliance.

Anthony died in Rochester, New York, on March 13, 1906. Her advocacy had influenced the granting of women's voting rights by several states. Further, her work paved the way for the passage of the 19th Amendment, which in 1920 finally gave American women the right to vote. In 1950 she was elected to the Hall of Fame for Great Americans in New York City.

War of 1812 Begins

The War of 1812 began with a declaration of war on Great Britain by the United States on June 18, 1812. The declaration of war, which came after heated debate between congressional "hawks" such as Henry Clay and John C. Calhoun, and "doves" such as John Randolph, was a result of such matters as Britain's violation of American rights on the high seas. These violations included searching American vessels and impressing American seamen into the British navy. All this was within the context of Britain's long-standing war with France. That, in turn, was part of the Napoleonic Wars, which had been going on for years and involved most of Europe at one time or another.

France tried to exclude British goods, or goods cleared through Britain, from countries under French control on the European continent. Britain forbade international trade with France or French dependencies without first touching at English ports. Further, both countries sought to restrict the rights of neutrals. In view of British naval superiority, the French measures had less effect on American shipping than the British ban, which extended to trade in American ships between Europe and the West Indies—a lucrative trade that American shippers were anxious to engage in.

Americans, especially in the West, chafed at the suspected British incitement of Native American warfare on the frontier. Such hostilities served as a barrier to westward expansion by the new United States, and gave Native American settlements the potential of becoming (as the British hoped they would) a permanent buffer state between the United States and British possessions in Canada.

Although these were the obvious causes of conflict, certain less manifest reasons, such as the desire of western and southern Americans to acquire Canada and Florida, helped create a climate for war. It was not until after Congress passed the declaration of war, however, that President James Madison realized how ill-equipped for such a contest his young nation was or how baseless were the hopes of hawks who dreamed of taking Canada in one sudden swoop.

Had Britain not been preoccupied with war in Europe, it is entirely possible that the United States would have lost the War of 1812. To begin with, three American expeditions aimed at Montreal in the summer of 1812 came to naught. So did early American successes at sea, like the triumph of the naval vessels *Constitution* over the *Guerriere* and the *United States* over the *Macedonian*. The principal American achievements of the war were on the Great Lakes. They included such accomplishments as Oliver H. Perry's Lake Erie victory over Britain's Great Lakes fleet in September 1813. It was also in 1813 that William Henry Harrison defeated British and native forces in the Battle of the Thames, in which the tribal chief Tecumseh was killed. However, after a number of other engagements which saw successes on both sides, the war in the north was a draw late in the summer of 1814.

Meanwhile, Britain used its superior naval strength in the Atlantic to capture American shipping and blockade the eastern seaboard, which had a devastating effect both on American commerce and on government revenues. The British also embarked on a series of hit-and-run attacks along the coast, and landed at Bladensburg, Maryland, in August 1814. Continuing on to Washington, D.C., they burned the White House and other public buildings. Not very long afterward, however, British forces were turned back before they reached Baltimore, notwithstanding the ferocity of their September 13–14 naval bombardment of Fort McHenry. It was that assault that inspired Francis Scott Key, who witnessed the event, to write "The Star-Spangled Banner."

The British had every reason to be confident about the war, since the Americans were primarily on the defensive and the war was being fought on American rather than British territory. Neverthe-less, they entered into peace negotiations, and in the end both sides found it expedient to back down from their strongly stated original demands and to sign the Treaty of Ghent on December 24, 1814, in Ghent, Belgium. The treaty dealt with none of the issues over which the war had ostensibly been fought, but it ended a serious military and financial drain on both governments.

In the meantime, the British fleet that had been turned back at Baltimore retreated to Jamaica. From there they launched an attack on New Orleans, Louisiana, which controlled the mouth of the Mississippi River. The Battle of New Orleans (see January 8) was actually fought some two weeks after the peace treaty had been signed, but the news had not yet reached the combatants. Although that battle obviously had no effect on the already concluded terms of peace, it was important in restoring the confidence of the young American nation, which then embarked on a period of renewed continental expansion.

June 19

French and Indian War: The Albany Congress Convenes

Several times during the 17th and 18th centuries, the British colonies in North America, while retaining their separate identities and governments, joined together for reasons of mutual defense and assistance. For example, in as early as 1643, Massachusetts Bay, Plymouth, Connecticut, and New Haven formed the New England Confederation, an association empowered to declare war, settle intercolonial problems, and deal with Native American affairs. Other ventures in intercolonial cooperation took place against the backdrop of the worldwide struggle for empire between England and France. In North America, conflicts related to this rivalry extended, off and on, for three-quarters of a century from 1689 until the Treaty of Paris of 1763.

During King William's War of 1689 to 1697, New York coordinated its defense (in 1690) with that of its neighbors Connecticut and Massachusetts. Governor Benjamin Fletcher of New York suggested that provinces as far away as Virginia provide troops to protect his colony's frontiers. At the time of Queen Anne's War of 1702 to 1713, plans for concerted colonial action were put forth, and during King George's War of 1744 to 1748, a combined force of men from the New England colonies directed a campaign against the French stronghold of Louisbourg on Nova Scotia's Cape Breton Island. Perhaps the most notable attempt of the colonies to work together before the difficult years of the American Revolution was the Albany congress that convened on June 19, 1754, on the eve of the French and Indian War. It was this conflict that would end in 1763 with the ousting of the French from virtually all of North America.

In the early 1750s the possibility of an alliance between the Iroquois and the French posed a great threat to the British colonies in America. Realizing this danger, in the autumn of 1753 the British Board of Trade sought to strengthen the wavering Iroquois loyalty by asking the representatives of Virginia, Maryland, Pennsylvania, New Jersey, New York, New Hampshire, and Massachusetts to meet together to settle any difficulties that they might have with the native tribes. When the intercolonial conference convened in Albany, Virginia was preoccupied with its own dealings with the Ohio River valley tribes and thus did not send a representative to the meeting. However, most of the other colonies complied with the British request.

The representatives to the Albany congress included some of the most outstanding leaders of the colonies. Among others, Massachusetts sent Thomas Hutchinson, who had served as speaker of the general court and who was a member of the provincial council. Rhode Island's delegation included its chief justice, Stephen Hopkins, who in 1755 became the colony's governor and later signed the Declaration of Independence. New York was represented by its lieutenant governor, James De Lancey. From Pennsylvania came undoubtedly the most important member, Benjamin Franklin.

A total of 25 colonial delegates met with the 150 Iroquois who attended the Albany congress, and the Iroquois Nation cited serious grievances against the British. In particular, they resented the colonists' (and especially the New Yorkers') abuses of the fur trade and their encroachment on Iroquoian lands. In addition, Chief Hendrick of the Mohawks (one of the tribes in the Iroquois Nation) remarked that from 1751 to 1754 the colonists had neglected the tribes, whereas "the French are a subtle and vigilant people, ever using their utmost endeavors to seduce and bring our people over to them." Hendrick then went on to deny the colonists' accusations that the Iroquois were permitting the French to occupy their lands. He took the colonies to task for failing to provide adequate defenses for their own borders. Finally, he concluded by charging that certain Albany merchants were involved in trading munitions with the French in Canada.

The Albany delegates responded to each of the Iroquois grievances. Their explanations of the colonists' past behavior and their promises of improved conduct in the future at least superficially satisfied the Iroquois, and in the days following July 5, 1754, they seemed willing to renew their friendship with the British. The Iroquois asked for a prohibition on the sale of rum in their territory, requested that a church be erected at Canojoharie in the Mohawk Valley "to make us Religious and lead better lives," and warned the British of the dangers of leaving their frontier regions unprotected. Then, on July 9, 1754, the parties concluded their official negotiations, and a few days later the Iroquois returned to their homes with 30 wagonloads of gifts.

Although called for the specific purpose of cementing closer relations with the Iroquois, the Albany congress also considered a much broader issue. On June 24 the question "whether a Union of all the Colonies is not at present absolutely necessary for their security and defense" came before the assembly. A number of the Albany delegates had no authorization from their respective colonies to discuss the possibility of establishing an intercolonial union, but this did not impede their consideration of the matter. The representatives unanimously agreed that a colonial union could best handle the emergency situation created by the threatened alliance between the French and the native tribes, and they then proceeded to examine various plans for setting up the proposed union.

Even before the opening of the Albany congress, Benjamin Franklin had recognized the urgent need for a union of the British colonies. The French had taken possession of the forks of the Ohio River in May 1754. Writing in his *Pennsylvania Gazette* that month, Franklin noted:

> The confidence of the French in this undertaking seems well grounded in the present disunited state of the British colonies, and the extreme difficulty of bringing so many different governments and assemblies to agree to any speedy and effectual measures for our common defence and security, while our enemies have the great advantage of being under one direction, with one council, and one purse.

As early as 1751 Franklin had devised a preliminary plan of union, and he incorporated many of his earlier ideas in the "Short Hints toward a Scheme for Uniting the Northern Colonies," which he presented to the Albany congress. Franklin's "Short Hints" provided for a supracolonial government to be established by an act of Parliament and to consist of a grand council and a president-general. According to the plan, the assembly of each colony would select at least one member of the council, and the larger colonies would have additional representation in that body proportioned according to the "sums they pay yearly to the General Treasury." The president-general would be an appointee of the Crown and have the power to veto all of the acts of the grand council. The authority of the grand council and the president-general would be extensive; they would attend to Native American treaties, control the course of British settlement, erect forts, provide soldiers, and in short do "everything . . . necessary for the defense and support of the Colonies in General, and increasing and extending their settlements, etc."

The Albany congress also considered plans of union advanced by Richard Peters of Pennsylvania, Thomas Hutchinson of Massachusetts, and Thomas Pownall, the sympathetic freelance observer of colonial defense problems who held important posts in several colonies before his eventual return to England. After their deliberation, the delegates chose Franklin's outline as the basis for the colonial union they deemed necessary. On July 10 the congress prepared the final draft of the "Plan of a Proposed Union." It called for an act of Parliament to form a union of all British colonies in North America, excepting Nova Scotia and Georgia, in which "each Colony may retain its present constitution." It also provided for a president-general, appointed by the Crown and having final veto power, and a grand council, whose members would be elected by the colonial assemblies. Finally, it vested in the president-general and grand council the responsibility for Native American affairs and other matters related to the defense of the colonies.

Despite the strong arguments favoring the creation of a colonial union, the plan of a "general Government" of the colonies in America was emphatically rejected by both the colonial assemblies and the British government. In 1754 the Americans believed that a centralized union threatened the individual autonomy of each colony and the British thought that a general government encroached upon the royal prerogative. However, the "Albany Plan of Union," which provided for a central government whose member colonies would retain their separate identities, foreshadowed other governments in America. Less than three decades later, the Articles of Confederation of 1781 embodied the plan's federal ideas, and in 1787 Federalist thinking provided the basis for the United States Constitution.

June 20

West Virginia Admitted to the Union

On December 31, 1862, Congress passed an act providing for the admission of West Virginia to the Union as an independent state on condition that certain changes be made in its proposed constitution. Those changes were made, and on April 20, 1863, President Abraham Lincoln issued a proclamation that admission should take effect 60 days later. Thus, West Virginia entered the Union as the 35th state on June 20, 1863.

West Virginia's admission to the Union was unusual since it was born out of the Civil War. The movement for independence from Virginia, which the state was originally part of, originated long before June 20, 1863, extending back into the early history of this country.

Artifacts, skeletons, and numerous conical-shaped mounds found in West Virginia, especially along the Ohio and Kanawha Rivers, indicate that the area was settled by the prehistoric Mound Builders. By the late 17th century, when European settlers began to appear in the region, less sedentary tribes regarded this mountainous territory (traversed by three major native trails) primarily as a convenient hunting ground. Permanent European colonization came fairly late and was the result of pressure exerted by the English-French rivalry over possession of the Ohio River valley. The English struggle for control of the region began in 1671, when Major General Abraham Wood, a seasoned frontiersman, sent an exploratory party from what is now Petersburg, Virginia, to study "the ebbing and flowing of the waters on the other side of the mountains." Captain Thomas Batts crossed the Allegheny Mountains and may have traced the course of the New River as far as the falls of the Great Kanawha. About the same time, René-Robert Cavelier de La Salle and other French explorers traversed the Mississippi River and its tributaries, planting colonies near the mouth of the Ohio River.

Both powers were determined to manipulate the nomadic native tribes for purposes of trade and strategy. Scores of traders and trappers passed through sections of what is now West Virginia in the late 17th and early 18th centuries. In 1716 Governor Alexander Spotswood of Virginia and 30 cavaliers crossed the Blue Ridge Mountains and may have reached what is now the West Virginia county of Pendleton. According to tradition, the first permanent non-native settlement in West Virginia was made in 1731 by a Welshman, Morgan Morgan, on Mill Creek in Berkeley County.

Within a few years, ambitious and resourceful Welsh, Scotch-Irish, and German pioneers, trekking from Pennsylvania and Maryland, had occupied the area along the rivers emptying into the Potomac River from the south. Much of this land, some of which was surveyed by George Washington when he was a young man working as a surveyor, technically belonged to Lord Thomas Fairfax as proprietor of the Northern Neck of Virginia.

The English eventually triumphed over the French, and the native tribes (who had mostly sided with the French) were forced to sell an immense area of land that included West Virginia to the British. The large-scale trans-Allegheny migration that followed triggered both vigorous tribal resistance and a royal proclamation barring colonists from settlement west of the Alleghenies. Nevertheless, an estimated 25,000 to 30,000 immigrants spilled over the mountains to settle the upper Ohio River valley before the American Revolution. The first United States census, taken in 1790, showed a population of 55,873 for the region of West Virginia.

As early as 1776 the separatist tendencies of the western Virginians gave rise to thoughts about breaking off from eastern Virginia and establishing a new colony to be called Vandalia. Neither this plan nor subsequent schemes to found a state of Westsylvania in 1783 materialized. The history of western Virginia from the end of the Revolutionary War to the outbreak of the Civil War revolved around the increasingly bitter division between the eastern and western sections of the region. The two areas differed in many respects. Rolling hills and vast plantations characterized the Tidewater and Piedmont parts of Virginia in the east, offering a striking contrast with the mountainous Allegheny and trans-Allegheny sections, where small-scale, diversified farming prevailed. The Anglican and Episcopalian slave-owning gentlemen farmers of primarily English origin who inhabited eastern Virginia tended to look down upon the German, Scotch-Irish, and Welsh frontiersmen of western Virginia who owned few slaves and belonged to dissenting religious sects. The two groups differed radically on matters such as taxation, public improvements, and the basis for political representation.

West Virginia's dissent was not alleviated by the changes made in the Virginia constitution in 1830 and 1851. Bitterness and friction mounted steadily, and the intensified regional controversy over slavery (with eastern Virginians for and western Virginians against the institution) sparked the final crisis. In response to the firing on Fort Sumter in April 1861, the Virginia convention, meeting at the capital of Richmond, threw in its lot with the Confederacy and passed an ordinance of secession from the Union. There was much dissatisfaction in the west, with two-thirds of western Virginia's representatives voting against the measure. Meetings of protest were held, and on May 13, 1861, delegates from 26 western counties and what is now Frederick County, Virginia, met at Wheeling and called a convention to meet on June 11. At this second Wheeling convention, representatives from 34 counties branded the Virginia secession null and void, and declared the state government offices at Richmond vacant—in effect announcing their independence. Following the passage of a resolution that called for the organization of the "Restored Government of Virginia" on the basis of loyalty to the Union, they elected Francis H. Pierpont as provisional governor. Waitman T. Willey and John S. Carlile were named as Virginia's two United States senators and were admitted to the Senate in Washington, D.C., replacing Virginia's former United States senators, who had followed their state into the Confederacy.

On August 20, 1861, the second Wheeling convention voted 48 to 27 to create the new state of Kanawha, as it was first called, containing 39 western counties. The decision was overwhelmingly approved in a popular referendum on October 24. In late November 1861, another convention met at Wheeling to draft a state constitution. One of the convention's acts was to discard the name Kanawha in favor of West Virginia. It also decided the boundaries of the new state. Since it was of great economic and military value to control that area of northern Virginia crossed by the main line of the Baltimore and Ohio Railroad on its route west, it was deemed advisable to add to the western counties an additional parcel of eastern counties, thus accounting for the irregularly shaped "eastern panhandle" of present West Virginia. Other additions subsequently enlarged the state to its present dimensions.

In fulfillment of the federal Constitution's requirement that "no new States shall be formed or erected within the Jurisdiction of any other State . . . without the consent of the Legislatures of the States concerned as well as of the Congress," the legislature of Virginia's "restored government" (namely the government at Wheeling, which was loyal to the Union, as distinct from Virginia's Confederate regime at Richmond) gave formal assent to the separation of West Virginia from Virginia. Once Congress voted to admit the new state of West Virginia, the fate of the new political entity rested with President Abraham Lincoln. After careful debate the president justified the action as a war measure and remarked, "It is said that the admission of West Virginia is secession. Well, if we call it by that name, there is still difference enough between secession against the Constitution and secession in favor of the Constitution."

West Virginia's constitution was overwhelmingly ratified by the people of the region on March 26, 1863. Lincoln issued his proclamation of the new entity's impending statehood on April 20, and on June 20, 1863, after new state and county officers had been elected, West Virginia officially entered the Union. The so-called restored government of Virginia left West Virginia and relocated to Alexandria, Virginia, a suburb of the federal capital of Washington, D.C., and occupied by Union troops. Arthur I. Boreman was inaugurated as West Virginia's first governor and established his government at Wheeling. During the Civil War, West Virginia was the scene of countless raids and sharp political splits within families. For example, Thomas J. "Stonewall" Jackson, a native of what is now West Virginia, remained loyal to Virginia and played a leading role as a top-ranking Confederate general, while his sister remained a confirmed Unionist.

First Thanksgiving Day Proclamation

See also November 26, Thanksgiving Day.

During colonial times, there was no set Thanksgiving Day. Although Thanksgiving was observed by the Pilgrims on various dates throughout the 1600s, the first official proclamation establishing a set Thanksgiving Day did not appear until June 20, 1676. On that day the town council of Charlestown, Massachusetts, met and decided to proclaim June 29 as a day of thanksgiving. Obviously, this date did not survive into modern times, but it was a historic first. The Charlestown proclamation is set forth below:

> The Holy God having by a long and Continual Series of his Afflictive dispensations in and by the present War with the Heathen Natives of this land, written and brought to pass bitter things against his own Covenant people in this wilderness, yet so that we evidently discern that in the midst of his judgments he hath remembered mercy, having remembered his footstool in the day of his sore displeasure against us for our sins, with many singular Intimations of his Fatherly Compassion, and regard; reserving many of our Towns from Desolation Threatened, and attempted by the Enemy, and giving us especially of late with many of our Confederates many signal Advantages against them, without such Disadvantage to ourselves as formerly we have been sensible of, if it be

the Lord's mercy that we are not consumed, it certainly bespeaks our positive Thankfulness, when our Enemies are in any measure disappointed or destroyed; and fearing the Lord should take notice under so many Intimations of his returning mercy, we should be found an Insensible people, as not standing before Him with Thanksgiving, as well as lading him with our Complaints in the time of pressing Afflictions:

> The Council has thought mete to appoint and set apart the 29th day of this instant June, as a day of Solemn Thanksgiving and praise to God for such his Goodness and Favour, many Particulars of which mercy might be Instanced, but we doubt not those who are sensible of God's Afflictions, have been as diligent to espy him returning to us; and that the Lord may behold us as a People offering Praise and thereby glorifying Him; the Council doth commend it to the Respective Ministers, Elders and people of this Jurisdiction; Solemnly and seriously to keep the same Beseeching that being persuaded by the mercies of God we may all, even this whole people offer up our bodies and souls as a living and acceptable Service unto God by Jesus Christ.

June 21

Summer Begins

In the United States and the north temperate zones generally, summer begins on approximately June 21 of every year. Actually, the precise moment at which the Sun reaches the summer solstice, officially marking the change of season, differs slightly from one year to the next because of the multitude of oscillations and wobbling motions that the Earth manifests during its daily rotation on its axis and in its annual elliptical orbit about the Sun.

Each of the four seasons has a precise astronomical beginning. The ecliptic, the plane in which the Sun appears to revolve around the earth and in which the earth actually revolves around the Sun, is divided into four 90-degree sections. Each section starts with a definite point: two equinoxes and two solstices. Summer begins at the summer solstice (from the Latin *solstitium*, derived from *sol* meaning "sun" and *sistere* meaning "to stand still") located halfway between the vernal equinox, which marks the start of spring (see

March 21), and the autumnal equinox, which marks the start of fall (see September 21). The time span needed by the Sun to cover the 90-degree section from the summer solstice to the autumnal equinox is termed the season of summer.

Summer is also said, somewhat anachronistically, to begin when the Sun enters the zodiac sign of Cancer, the crab. The second-century Greek astronomer Hipparchus, whose calculations form the basis of the zodiacal system, estimated correctly that in his time the summer solstice began when the Sun entered this sign. He also noted that owing to precession, namely the retrograde motion of the equinoctial points, there is a gradual displacement of the constellations in regard to them. After a slow-motion cycle lasting 25,800 years, the constellations will again be in the same zodiacal positions as in Hipparchus's time, when the summer solstice was found in the constellation of Cancer. Currently, it is actually in the sign of Gemini.

Around June 21 the Sun reaches its greatest northern declination, a term used by astronomers to correspond with terrestrial latitude. At this point in time the period of daylight in the Northern Hemisphere is at its longest and the period of nighttime is at its shortest. During the course of summer the Sun's northern declination constantly decreases, and the days gradually shorten while the nights gradually lengthen. As observed from the terrestrial equator, the Sun crosses closer and closer to the meridian until the autumnal equinox, when it reaches a celestial longitude of 180 degrees and a declination of 0 degrees and is said to enter the sign of Libra. The season of summer then terminates.

At the summer solstice, when the North Pole reaches its greatest degree of tilt toward the Sun, the amount of solar radiation absorbed by the Northern Hemisphere is at its highest and so summer is the hottest season of the year. In the Southern Hemisphere the seasons are reversed, since when the North Pole of the Earth is tilted toward the Sun, the South Pole of the Earth is pointed away from the Sun. Astronomical summer in the Southern Hemisphere starts around December 21 and ends around March 21.

Because of the extended days of sunshine and the resulting period of high temperatures, summer is the prime growing season for plant life. Like the other seasons, it influenced the development of mythology and folklore. For example, Midsummer Day (June 24) with its elaborate solar rites was an especially important festival in ancient and medieval times. There are still many other festivals and events also associated with summer, taking their impetus in whole or in part from the characteristic climate of the season. In ancient and medieval art, summer was frequently personified as a woman carrying sheaves of grain and a sickle.

The Constitution Ratified

In 1776 most of the colonies that broke away from England had existed for over a century. Diverse in economy and social organization, they were bound together by a common danger rather than a common identity. To an extent, the rebel states were as reluctant to surrender their independence from each other as they were eager to win it from Great Britain. The Articles of Confederation, under which they were loosely united in 1777 to prosecute the war, reflected this desire for autonomy.

In reality, the Articles of Confederation established the apparatus of an alliance rather than of a government. There was no provision for a national executive, as the states vested power in a Congress where each of them held one vote. Congress's authority was limited to certain specified areas, and even in these areas it took the approval of nine states to enact legislation. The agreement of all 13 members was necessary to institute any changes in the frame of government.

Postwar difficulties amply illustrated the shortcomings of the confederation. The government's inability to make the states comply with the terms of the Treaty of Paris, requiring the payment of debts owed to British subjects, gave England an excuse not to evacuate its garrisons in the northwest region of the United States. The American economy suffered as the states failed to give Congress the power to levy duties on imports, a measure that would have enabled the government to extract commercial concessions from foreign countries. By 1787 George Washington warned that "something must be done or the fabric will fall; it is certainly tottering."

In 1785 Virginia and Maryland took the first steps leading to the revamping of the government. Delegates from these states arranged to confer with Washington at Mount Vernon on the problem of navigation rights in the Potomac River and Chesapeake Bay. Representatives from Pennsylvania and Delaware were present to negotiate related questions. Encouraged by this effort at cooperation, James Madison suggested to the Virginia legislature that it invite all of the states to a meeting in Annapolis, Maryland, to discuss commercial matters. Only five states sent emissaries to the Annapolis convention of September 1786, and so the delegates called for a new gathering to meet in Philadelphia in May 1787 "to render the Constitution of the Federal Government adequate to the exigencies of the Union." On February 21, 1787,

Architect of the Capitol

Depiction of the signing of the Constitution.

Congress approved the planned convention, provided it work "for the sole and express purpose of revising the Articles of Confederation."

May 14 was supposed to be the opening day, but the convention did not attain the necessary quorum of seven states until May 25. In all, however, 55 delegates from 12 states attended the gathering (Rhode Island refused to participate). Some of the most notable leaders of the Revolutionary era were present, including George Washington and the elder statesman of the new nation, Benjamin Franklin, then 81. However, most of the members were young, having an average age of 42 years. Only eight had signed the Declaration of Independence. The majority were college graduates and almost all were professional men, chiefly lawyers.

The convention unanimously chose George Washington to be its president. He took no part in the discussions, but he put his prestige on the side of those forces advocating a strong central government. Each state had one vote and, provided there was a quorum, the majority vote of the states present would decide issues. The members met from 10:00 A.M. to 3:00 P.M. every day from May 29 to September 17, except for Sundays, a two-day Fourth of July recess, and the ten days between July 26 and August 6.

The delegates realized that they could not heed Congress's admonition to restrict themselves to a mere revision of the Articles of Confederation.

Even if there had been no other problems, the stipulation requiring unanimous consent to change made it unfeasible to work within the framework of the articles. So, on May 30 the convention members resolved that their task was the establishment of a national government. The convention's goal was to create a central government strong enough to unify and direct the nation, yet not so strong as to endanger the rights of the citizenry and of the individual states. The new government would necessarily be a federation of the states and, as James Madison later pointed out in the *Federalist* essays, the diversity inherent in this type of structure greatly limited its capacity for power. To further protect against the central authority's power to encroach on liberty, the delegates, following the concepts of the French political theorist Charles-Louis de Secondat, Baron de La Bréde et de Montesquieu, divided the proposed national government into three balanced branches (executive, legislative, and judicial), each of which could check the power of the other two.

The composition of the new Congress constituted a major problem for the convention. Frustrated by the one-state, one-vote principle of the Articles of Confederation, the larger states wanted greater influence in the national legislature. On May 29 Edmund Randolph of Virginia suggested a system of government favorable to the larger states. The Virginia plan provided for a bicameral Congress in which each state's membership would be proportioned to its free population. On June 15 William Paterson of New Jersey offered a counterproposal more to the liking of the smaller states. The New Jersey plan, as it became known, gave each state equal representation in a unicameral national legislature with significantly increased powers.

The solution to the conflict between the large and small states, and proportional versus equal representation, was eventually based on a suggestion that had been introduced by Roger Sherman of Connecticut. The Great Compromise, as it was later called, provided for a bicameral legislature in which each state would have an equal voice in the upper house of Congress, but would be represented in proportion to its population in the lower house. In the ensuing discussions the delegates agreed that representatives to the lower house would be elected directly by the citizens, whereas the members of the upper house would be selected by the individual state legislatures (this of course refers to the Senate: The 17th Amendment, ratified in 1913, eventually provided for the direct election of senators).

The Great Compromise removed the largest obstacle to the success of the convention. Further compromises dissolved the remaining difficulties. The delegates decided that taxation, like representation in the lower house of Congress, would be proportioned among the states according to population and that for both purposes five black slaves would count as three free persons. The southern states, whose economy centered around the sale in the world market of tobacco and other staples produced by slave labor, won an agreement that there would be no taxation of exports and no ban on the importation of slaves for the next 20 years.

The manner of electing the president was the final important issue. A committee composed of one delegate from each state devised the electoral college system. According to this system, each state would choose, in a manner prescribed by its legislature, a number of electors equal to its total representation in both houses of Congress. The electors of each state would meet and vote for two persons, at least one of whom was not a resident of their state. The person who attained the majority of the electoral votes was to become president and the person who received the next highest number of votes was to become vice president. If no candidate gained the necessary majority, then the House of Representatives, with each state having one vote, would choose the president.

Oliver Ellsworth of Connecticut, Nathaniel Gorham of Massachusetts, Edmund Randolph of Virginia, John Rutledge of South Carolina, and James Wilson of Pennsylvania comprised the Committee of Detail, which drew up the first draft of the Constitution. On September 8 the convention appointed Alexander Hamilton of New York, William S. Johnson of Connecticut, Rufus King of Massachusetts, James Madison of Virginia, and Gouverneur Morris of Pennsylvania as a Committee of Style and Arrangement to prepare the final report. The convention delegates met for the final time on Monday, September 17. They were urged to vote favorably on the fruit of their collective labors in a speech written by the ailing Benjamin Franklin and read to them that day by James Wilson. Franklin's persuasive words have often been quoted since:

I confess that there are several parts of this Constitution which I do not at present approve, but I am not sure I shall never approve them. . . .

I doubt too whether any other convention . . . may be able to make a better Constitution. For when you assemble a number of men to have the advantage of their joint wisdom, you inevitably assemble with those men all their prejudices, . . . passions, . . . errors of opinion, . . . local interests, and . . . selfish views. . . . It therefore astonishes me . . . to find this system approaching so near to perfection as it does. . . .

Thus, I consent . . . to this Constitution because I expect no better, and because I am not sure that it is not the best. . . . On the whole, . . . I cannot help expressing a wish that every member of the convention who may still have objections to it would, with me, . . . doubt a little of his own infallibility and, to make manifest our unanimity put his name to this instrument.

Thus encouraged, the delegates approved the Constitution and sent it to the Congress with a recommendation that it be referred to the states for ratification by special conventions. Thirty-nine of the 42 delegates who had stayed to the end of the proceedings signed the document. As they stepped forward to affix their signatures, the ever-observant Franklin reflected on the half-Sun depicted on the back of the chair that Washington had occupied throughout the months of deliberations. James Madison recorded Franklin's words in his journal:

I have often and often in the course of the session, and the vicissitudes of my hopes and fears as to its issue, looked at that [sun] behind the President without being able to tell whether it was rising or setting. But now at length I have the happiness to know that it is a rising and not a setting sun.

Contrary to the requirement of the Articles of Confederation, the Philadelphia convention determined that ratification by nine states would put the new Constitution into effect. Not everyone, however, approved of the new document. The opponents of the new Constitution, known as Antifederalists, worried about the absence of specific protections for individual liberties and feared that the new central authority would seriously undermine the powers of local governments. Promises of future amendments, which would constitute a Bill of Rights, won a number of undecided voters to the cause of ratification as did arguments such as those put forth by Alexander Hamilton, John Jay, and James Madison in *The Federalist*.

The people in each of the 13 states elected representatives for special conventions to discuss ratification. Delaware, Pennsylvania (after some controversy), New Jersey, Georgia, and Connecticut ratified quickly. Federalists then won a narrow victory in Massachusetts and easier ones in Maryland and South Carolina. New Hampshire, on June 21, 1788, became the ninth state to support the new frame of government, thus putting it into operation. Virginia and New York soon followed. North Carolina and Rhode Island were dissatisfied with the proposed Constitution and did not immediately join the Union. However, North Carolina finally accepted the new system in November 1789 and Rhode Island in May 1790.

New Hampshire Ratifies the Constitution

Although the statehood of the 13 original states dates from their declaration of independence from Great Britain in 1776, historians customarily place the first 13 states in chronological order according to the date on which they ratified the federal Constitution of 1787. Since New Hampshire on June 21, 1788, became the ninth state to ratify the Constitution, it is generally considered the ninth state in the Union.

New Hampshire was one of the smaller and less populous of the 13 original states, and its approval of the new frame of government was therefore probably not so essential to the success of the federal experiment as that of some of the larger states. In another respect, however, New Hampshire's approval was pivotal. Article VII of the Constitution specified that the agreement of nine states would be necessary to bring the new government into existence. It was thus the affirmation of New Hampshire, the ninth state, that made the Constitution of 1787 legally operative.

To gain New Hampshire's approval of the Constitution, the Federalists, as those who favored the new frame of government were known, had to overcome considerable apathy. The state had for the most part fared well under the Articles of Confederation, and many New Hampshirites failed to recognize the urgent need to reform the government. In fact, the state legislature did not even respond to the appeal of the 1786 Annapolis convention that the states send delegates to a convention the following May to consider revisions of the Articles of Confederation. New Hampshire was therefore not represented when the Constitutional Convention convened in Philadelphia on May 25, 1787.

Since the New Hampshire legislature claimed that the state could not afford to send delegates to the Constitutional Convention, John Langdon, a wealthy citizen, offered to pay the expenses of such representatives. With the financial obstacle removed, the legislature late in June 1787 named four deputies: Langdon, Nicholas Gilman, John Pickering, and Benjamin West. They were sent to the Philadelphia convention "to discuss and decide upon the most effectual means to remedy the defects of our federal Union." Pickering and West never attended the constitutional meetings, but Langdon and Gilman arrived in Philadelphia at the end of July 1787.

By the time that Langdon (who had served as Speaker of the New Hampshire House of Representatives, president of the state, and delegate to Congress) and Gilman (who had also been a member of Congress) appeared at the convention, most of the major issues before that body had been resolved. The New Hampshire delegates therefore did not engage in public debate on such problems as representation in the national Congress, but their private correspondence indicates that they agreed with the compromises worked out by the other members of the convention. Langdon and Gilman remained in Philadelphia until September 1787, and during the final weeks of the meetings on the Constitution they helped decide such important questions as the length of terms for the president, senators, and representatives, and the power of Congress to regulate foreign and interstate commerce.

The Constitutional Convention concluded its work on September 17, 1787, and then submitted the new frame of government to the states. Supporters of the Constitution in New Hampshire immediately launched a campaign to win their state's approval of the document, and the state president, John Sullivan, called the legislature into special session in December to select a ratifying convention. Since many towns refused to bear the added expense of sending a representative to the special session, there was no quorum in attendance at the December meeting. However, despite the absence of more than two-thirds of the legislators, the December session was able to set the time and place for the ratifying convention. Realizing that the voters were hesitant to accept any additional burdens, they scheduled the ratifying convention to run concurrently with the regular session of the legislature, which was to take place at Exeter in mid-February 1788.

Many of the towns that had refused to finance delegates to the special legislative session took advantage of the opportunity to send representatives to the regular legislative session and the ratifying convention. In mid-February 1788, when the first session of the convention met, the vast majority of New Hampshire's towns were represented, and that gathering considered the merits of the Constitution without further delay. For ten days the convention debated the frame of government, and during that time the Federalists came to realize that a majority of the delegates opposed the document. Fearing that ratification would be defeated if a vote were immediately taken on the Constitution, they requested and won a four-month adjournment.

Federalist support was concentrated around Portsmouth, situated at the mouth of the Piscataqua River, since the fishing and shipbuilding industries of that area would greatly profit from the national regulation of commerce proposed by the new Constitution. However, the Piscataqua region alone could not bring about ratification, and to gain additional votes the supporters of the Constitution waged a spirited campaign during the four-month adjournment. The Federalists aimed their efforts at New Hampshire's northern towns and those situated along the Connecticut River, because their representatives seemed most likely to change their negative votes. This tactic was successful. On June 17, 1788, the delegates reconvened. They debated the question of ratification for four days. Then, on June 21, 1788, by a vote of 57 to 47, New Hampshire became the ninth state to ratify the Constitution.

Father's Day

This is a movable event.

The third Sunday of June is generally observed as Father's Day throughout the United States. Although an isolated church service in Fairmont, West Virginia, honored fathers in July 1908 at the suggestion of Jessica Clinton Clayton, it is Sonora Louise Smart Dodd of Spokane, Washington, who is most frequently credited with originating the idea for a Father's Day observance in 1909 that spread far beyond the confines of her own church.

Her inspiration was her own father, William Smart, a Civil War veteran who had been widowed when his daughter and five sons were very young. Realization of the difficulties he must have had raising his young, motherless family on a farm in eastern Washington and appreciation for his constant devotion to his family sparked Dodd's desire to honor all fathers.

Because her idea for the observance of Father's Day centered around special church services, Dodd discussed the idea with her minister. Through him she put the idea to the Spokane Ministerial Association and the Spokane Ministers Alliance. Members of the clergy approved of the project. With the city's Young Men's Christian Association also joining in sponsorship, the first Father's Day was celebrated in Spokane on the third Sunday of June in 1910, with local ministers calling the attention of their congregations to the appreciation fathers deserved. June 19 was the actual date of that initial observance. The first Father's Day proclamations were released by the mayor of Spokane and the governor of Washington, M. E. Hay, who followed the lead of Spokane in setting the third Sunday in June as the date for the observance. The orator and political leader William Jennings Bryan also endorsed the idea, stating that "too much emphasis cannot be placed upon the relation between parent and child."

President Woodrow Wilson officially approved the idea for a national Father's Day in 1916. While Wilson was still president, a Father's Day of a different kind was observed on November 24, 1918, when at the suggestion of *Stars and Stripes*, the official newspaper of the World War I American Expeditionary Force in France, the fathers at home wrote to their sons in the field and the sons in the field wrote home. Arrangements were made for the delivery of the letters without delay and, since the war had ended with the armistice celebrated 13 days earlier, delivery was possible without risk.

Father's Day is also celebrated in many foreign countries, although not necessarily on the same day as in the United States.

June 22

HMS *Leopard* Fires on the USS *Chesapeake*

On June 22, 1807, the British frigate HMS *Leopard* engaged the American frigate USS *Chesapeake* in the waters off Norfolk, Virginia. Three

Americans lost their lives during the encounter, and 18 more were wounded. The incident was one of the most serious in a number of events that gradually led the United States and Great Britain into the War of 1812.

After the American Revolution, Great Britain was drawn into conflict with the revolutionary government of France on the European continent and on the high seas. Eventually, Napoléon Bonaparte emerged as the dictator of France and led the French in a long series of wars against the British. Economics inevitably drew the Americans into the ongoing British-French struggles. The United States was a commercial nation involved in carrying goods across the Atlantic. When war broke out, both England and France turned to the United States to supplement their merchant marines. The plight of the European powers offered the Americans great profits, but risks accompanied the new opportunities.

Britain's naval dominance in the Atlantic made the French especially dependent on the American maritime fleet. In times of peace, France did not allow American vessels to carry goods between its Caribbean colonies and Europe, but during its struggles against Great Britain, France opened the West Indies to American traders. The British naturally protested, invoking their "Rule of 1756," which declared that trade prohibited in peace had to remain illegal in war and they threatened to seize American vessels carrying French products.

American merchants used a tactic known as the "broken voyage" to circumvent British objections to their trade with France. American traders picked up their cargoes in the French West Indies and first brought them to American ports, where the goods were theoretically unloaded and taxed, thereby "breaking" the voyage. Then merchants reshipped the original items to French ports as American rather than West Indian products.

Britain temporarily accepted this ruse. In a court case involving the *Polly*, an American ship seized by the British navy, the British in 1800 accepted the defense's contention of a "broken voyage." However, as the war with France became more intense, and the Americans began to only "touch base" in United States ports without actually unloading or paying levies, the British attitude hardened. In the *Essex* case of 1805, the British prize courts, reversing an earlier court decision, outlawed the re-export trade.

The *Essex* decision was only the first of a series of actions that adversely affected American shipping interests. In May 1806 the English instituted a "paper blockade," namely one not supported by ships stationed off the affected ports, of Europe from the Elbe River to Brest. In November 1806

Napoléon issued the equally unenforceable Berlin Decree, which forbade all commerce with Britain and authorized the seizure of vessels trading with the British. Finally, in January 1807 the British retaliated with an order barring ships from the coasts of France and its allies.

England controlled the seas and was in a better position than France to enforce its decrees. The Americans thus directed most of their wrath against the British, and by 1807 the relationship between the United States and England had badly deteriorated. The *Leopard-Chesapeake* affair took place during this tense period. The timing only aggravated the consequences of the incident, which was a serious matter in its own right. The confrontation, which concerned the impressment issue, another dimension of the question of neutral rights, brought Britain and the United States to the brink of war.

Impressment, in the Anglo-American context, was the British practice of stopping and searching American vessels, and of removing sailors born in the British Isles so they might serve in the Royal Navy. The British, desperately in need of sailors to battle the French, justified their actions on the principle of "once an Englishman always an Englishman." Some of the impressed men had been legally naturalized as United States citizens, others had obtained naturalization papers illegally, and a number were actually deserters from the British navy. All had found the high wages of the American peacetime fleet more attractive than either the poor pay of England's commercial vessels or the prospects of battle faced by the British navy. Whatever the actual background of these pirated mariners, the high-handed manner in which the British seized them was a continuing source of friction between the United States and England.

Although impressment had long provoked American ill-feeling toward Great Britain, not until 1807 did the issue become so important that the United States considered war. On March 7, 1807, a number of the crew of the British 16-gun sloop *Halifax*, which was cruising in American waters, seized a lifeboat and used it to escape to Norfolk, Virginia. The commander of the *Halifax* complained to the British consul and to American naval authorities in Norfolk in an effort to regain his sailors, but received no satisfaction. Instead, when the officer met the deserters on the streets of Norfolk, one of them, Jenkin Ratford, began to swear at him and declared that in the land of liberty he could do what he pleased.

Angered by their inability to retrieve deserters, some of whom had allegedly signed on the American frigate *Chesapeake*, the commander of the *Halifax* and a number of other officers complained to their commander, Admiral George Cranfield Berkeley in Nova Scotia, Canada. Without waiting for advice from London, Berkeley issued a fateful order. He directed that all captains and commanders of British vessels, should they meet the *Chesapeake* outside the territorial waters of the United States, stop the frigate and search it for deserters from the British warships *Bellona, Belleisle, Triumph, Chichester, Halifax,* and *Zenobia*.

Captain S. P. Humphreys, commander of the *Leopard,* carried Berkeley's order, dated June 1, 1807, to Chesapeake Bay. Humphreys arrived at nearby Lynnhaven Bay on June 21, and at 6:00 a.m. the next day anchored a short distance to the east, about three miles north of Cape Henry. At 7:15 a.m. on June 22, the *Chesapeake* weighed anchor from Norfolk and set sail for the Mediterranean Sea. As the *Chesapeake* passed Lynnhaven Bay at 9:00 a.m., the British battleship *Bellona* sighted it and signaled to the *Leopard* to lift anchor and reconnoiter.

Hours passed before the *Leopard* and *Chesapeake* made contact. At 3:30 p.m. the British vessel hailed the American about eight to ten miles southeast by east from Cape Henry. The British announced that they had dispatches for Commodore James Barron, the American commander. Barron, who thought that the English merely wanted him to carry mail to Europe, as a traditional naval courtesy, invited them to send an officer on board the *Chesapeake.* Lieutenant Meade from the *Leopard* met Commodore Barron shortly before 4:00 P.M. He presented a note from Captain Humphreys explaining Admiral Berkeley's directive and demanding the right to carry it out. Expecting that Humphreys would respect his word, Barron wrote a reply stating that he was not aware of the presence among his crew of any deserters from the ships mentioned in Berkeley's list and that he could not allow his ship to be searched.

Meade returned to the *Leopard* with Barron's message. Humphreys, however, did not believe that Berkeley's orders allowed him to accept the American answer. The English captain brought his vessel nearer to the American and called, "Commodore Barron, you must be aware of the necessity I am under of complying with the order of my commander in chief." Barron, knowing that the crew of the *Chesapeake* would require at least half an hour to prepare the frigate for combat, sought to delay. Twice Barron called through his trumpet, "I do not hear what you say." After the second exchange the *Leopard* fired a single shot across the bow of the *Chesapeake,* and a minute later another. At 4:30 p.m. the British ship opened up with all its weaponry against the helpless American frigate. The *Leopard* fired three full broadsides pointblank into the *Chesapeake* at a distance of not more than 200 feet. The Americans managed to fire only a single shot.

Twenty-two shots ripped the *Chesapeake's* hull, and ten tore the sails. The firing mutilated the three masts and cut much of the rigging. Three American sailors died, eight suffered severe wounds, and ten less serious injuries. Barron had no choice but to strike his colors and surrender. When the firing ceased, several British officers boarded the *Chesapeake.* They seized three men who they claimed had deserted from the *Melampus.* Berkeley's order had not mentioned that vessel, and the men, two whites and one black, were actually American citizens who had been illegally impressed into service on the *Melampus.* The British also found Jenkin Ratford who, unknown to Barron, had joined the *Chesapeake* under the name Wilson.

Barron, in accord with his situation as a defeated commander, offered to turn the *Chesapeake* over to British control. Humphreys's instructions, however, did not call for capturing the frigate and so he declined to take the vessel. The Americans, degraded and outraged, then turned their battered vessel and headed back to Norfolk.

The American public was angered by Britain's cavalier treatment of the *Chesapeake,* and many favored military retaliation. President Thomas Jefferson, however, sought to avoid war and relied instead on economic measures and other steps. After ordering British warships out of American waters, he called a special session of Congress for October 1807, and secured from the legislators an appropriation of $850,000 with which to strengthen the United States Navy. In December Congress, on Jefferson's recommendation, passed an embargo act. According to its provisions, which Jefferson saw as a form of "peaceful coercion," all American vessels were forbidden to sail for foreign ports and foreign ships were barred from carrying goods out of American ports. All exports were prohibited. Unfortunately, Jefferson's embargo backfired. It harmed the American economy more than the economies of Britain and France, and was repealed several years later.

The question of reparations for damage inflicted on the *Chesapeake* was not laid to rest until November 1811, when the United States accepted a British offer of settlement. Even with reparations paid and with two of the impressed seamen returned (the other two were dead, one having been hanged as a deserter), the question of British impressment of American seamen remained an important issue when differences between the United States and Great Britain finally culminated in the War of 1812.

June 23

Midsummer, or St. John's Eve

Long before the Christian Era, Midsummer Eve and Midsummer Day (see June 24) were celebrated throughout Europe near the time of the summer solstice, when the days are longest and the Sun appears to be at its highest point in the sky. (See June 21, Summer Begins.) The practice probably began with early Sun worshipers who built fires to symbolize the Sun and expressed in their celebration their year-round dependence on the Sun's life-giving light and warmth and their joy at the arrival of summer weather. Numerous customs, notably dancing around the fires and leaping over the flames or embers to ensure a variety of blessings, grew up around the belief that the fires had a mystical power to cure people of diseases and protect them from various dangers such as the fire-fearing witches or evil spirits who were supposedly at large on Midsummer Eve.

All-night festivities became the rule, and as Sun worship faded, leaving behind a legacy of bonfires and associated customs, the emphasis on Midsummer Eve turned to young lovers and romance. Some of the hopes nurtured by the celebration are summed up by Puck in Shakespeare's *A Midsummer-Night's Dream*: "Jack shall have Jill; Naught shall go ill; The man shall have his mare again, and all shall be well." In keeping with the belief that Midsummer Eve was a night when supernatural beings roamed the earth, customs developed in some places similar to the "trick-or-treat" of Halloween, with people going from door to door begging for sweets or other gifts.

When the Feast of the Nativity of St. John the Baptist was instituted on June 24, early in the history of the Christian Church, many of the established forms of celebrating Midsummer's Day and Midsummer's Eve were transferred to St. John's Eve and feast day. This was somewhat contradictory, since the pagans had celebrated midsummer as an excuse for unbridled license, while the austere John had exhorted people to "repent, for the kingdom of heaven is at hand." The custom of lighting bonfires was largely retained, however. Religious authorities could justify this by citing Jesus' description of John the Baptist, related in the Fourth Gospel (John 5:35): "He was a burning and a shining light: and ye were willing for a season to rejoice in his light." Some Midsummer Eve customs were brought to the United States by the European settlers, particularly those from Scandinavia, but aside from some local celebrations the event has largely faded into obscurity.

Unto These Hills Cherokee Historical Drama

This is a movable event.

Something of the heartache, suffering, and heroism of the Cherokee people is captured in a historical drama presented every summer in the town of Cherokee, North Carolina, capital of the Eastern Band of Cherokee who live on the Cherokee reservation at the edge of Great Smoky Mountains National Park. The drama, Kermit Hunter's *Unto These Hills*, records the history of the Cherokee's tragic relations with Europeans and Americans from the time of Hernando de Soto's explorations in 1540 to the Cherokee's forced removal in 1838–1839 from their native Smoky Mountains to the so-called Indian Territory (now Oklahoma) by way of the grave-strewn Trail of Tears. The title is taken from Psalm 121:1–2: "I will lift up mine eyes unto the hills . . . ."

Although the Indian Territory was land that the United States government had set aside as a home for the Five Civilized Tribes of the Southeast (the Cherokee, Chickasaw, Choctaw, Creek, and Seminole), who were largely removed to it between 1820 and 1845, it was soon divided with western tribes. Later it was swallowed up entirely by Oklahoma when it became a state in 1907. Apparently forgotten was President Andrew Jackson's promise to the tribes that their land grants would last "as long as the grass grows, or water runs."

The Cherokee who take part in North Carolina's annual drama-spectacle are descendants of the handful of Cherokee who escaped removal to the Indian Territory by hiding in remote regions of the Smoky Mountains. They and their descendants became known as the Eastern Band of Cherokee as distinguished from the larger group of Cherokee, who became unwilling residents of the Indian Territory under conditions of great hardship.

During the tide of westward expansion that settled the United States, while pushing the Native Americans farther and farther from their original lands, American settlers exhibited a lust for land no matter how acquired. Frontier fever was high in 1828, when Andrew Jackson, the champion of the frontier, was elected president. By then the so-called spirit of the frontier (which was far from unopposed in Congress and elsewhere) could be loosely translated as "move the Indians out by any means."

One of the early steps of Jackson's administration was the enactment in 1830 of the Indian Removal Act, authorizing the president to initiate exchanges of real estate by which native tribes would be given land beyond the Mississippi in exchange for their eastern holdings. Although the act made no provision for the forcible removal of the tribes, it might as well have. State laws, particularly in Georgia (where many of the Cherokee lived), Mississippi, and Alabama, discriminated against the native tribes and blocked their access to legal recourse. The federal government, on the one hand, tried to induce the tribal nations to sign treaties giving up their eastern lands. On the other hand, it declared itself unable to protect the tribes against the abuses and repeated treaty violations made possible under state laws.

Under these pressures, the Choctaw, Chickasaw, and Creek more or less agreed to or were forced into removal between 1830 and 1836. In Florida, some of the Seminole successfully resisted relocation, and the ensuing Seminole Wars proved costly for the American government. The Cherokee, who next to the Seminole resisted longest, probably suffered the most. After a treaty bitterly opposed by most Cherokee was signed by a minority group, United States Army troops under General Winfield Scott were ordered to remove the entire tribe. Cherokee in Georgia, North Carolina, and neighboring regions were hunted down and herded into detention camps. Divided into 1,000-member contingents, they were moved to the Indian Territory during the harsh winter months of 1838–1839. Some 17,000 Cherokee made the 1,000-mile trip to Oklahoma, most of them on foot since there were only enough wagons for children and the elderly or disabled. The arduousness of the journey and the Cherokee's grief at leaving their homes and farmlands was compounded by the army's lack of experience in moving large numbers of people and by unscrupulous suppliers who reneged on their contracts to supply the travelers' needs. Nearly one out of every four Cherokee died en route from the cold, of exposure, or of resulting diseases. As one contemporary source reported in the *New York Observer*, "They buried 14 or 15 at every stopping place . . ." and went "ten miles per day only on the average."

The drama *Unto These Hills*, which has been staged annually at Cherokee since 1950, concerns those Cherokee who hid in the Smoky Mountains to escape deportation and the heroism of the Cherokee Tsali, who sacrificed his own life to keep General Scott from hunting his people down to the very last. The performance involves over 130 actors, and is staged almost daily from mid- to late-June until August, although the exact dates can vary from year to year. By the late 1990s, the drama and its related festivities had an annual attendance of nearly 100,000 people.

June 24

Henry Ward Beecher's Birthday

One of the most famous pulpit orators in American history, Henry Ward Beecher was born on June 24, 1813, in Litchfield, Connecticut. The eighth child of a noted Calvinist preacher, Lyman Beecher, he was the brother of novelist Harriet Beecher Stowe (see June 14).

Henry Beecher was educated at Mount Pleasant Collegiate Institute in Amherst, Massachusetts, and at Amherst College, which he graduated from in 1834. He was never a great student, but he achieved popularity as a leader and became an excellent public speaker. Beecher followed his college training with three postgraduate years at Cincinnati's Lane Theological Seminary, of which his father had become president in 1832, and began his preaching as an independent Presbyterian in Cincinnati.

In 1837 he married Eunice White Bullard, and also accepted his first pastorate. The pastorate was a Presbyterian church in Lawrenceburg, Indiana, with a membership of 20. Two years later he became minister of a Presbyterian church in Indianapolis, where he remained for close to eight years. As a minister he emphasized the love of God and stressed the joy and glory of Christian life. Believing that God "loves a man in his sins for the sake of helping him out of them," Beecher was convinced that the test of preaching was its effectiveness in bringing about a moral change in the listener. His mounting reputation, as a pulpit and lecture-platform orator, was widened with the publication of his *Seven Lectures to Young Men* (1844), on coping with the perils and vice of frontier settlements.

In 1847 Beecher accepted a call to the pulpit that he was to occupy for the rest of his life, in the newly established Plymouth Congregational Church in Brooklyn, New York. His preaching there drew huge crowds, averaging some 2,500 a week by the early 1850s. His sermons, printed in pamphlet form, were circulated widely and his church came to claim the largest membership of any in the country. Throughout the nation and beyond, Beecher's statements and personal life became the subject of interest and he became a newsworthy, and at times controversial, figure.

Eventually, he became one of the leading champions of the abolition of slavery, favoring civil disobedience of the Fugitive Slave Law while opposing the armed coercion of the slave states. As a popular speaker, Beecher frequently employed strong rhetoric, particularly on behalf of moral causes like abolition. Once, as the national debate arose over whether the Kansas Territory would enter the Union as a free state or a slave state, he went so far as to assert that rifles were greater moral agencies than the Bible. This utterance gave rise to the term "Beecher's Bibles," which pro-Northern settlers in Kansas applied to their Sharps repeating rifles, used in their conflicts with pro-Southern settlers.

Uncle Tom's Cabin (1852), written by Beecher's sister Harriet, was already inflaming tempers on the subject of slavery. During the Civil War, he traveled to England in 1863 and defended the Union position to audiences that were at first hostile to the Northern viewpoint, but warmed to the cause under Beecher's influence. Like many other abolitionists, Beecher was a champion of women's suffrage as well. He also advocated civil service reform. After the Civil War he supported a moderate Reconstruction policy. A modernist in religion, he supported such controversial theories as the doctrine of evolution and accepted scientific biblical criticism, while holding firmly to his belief in miracles. In addition to his addresses and sermons, Beecher expressed his outspoken and often courageous views in the *Independent*, a Congregational publication that he edited for several years beginning in 1861, and in the nondenominational *Christian Union* (later the *Outlook*), which he edited from 1870 to 1881.

His later years were to some extent blighted by a scandal involving him, at least by reputation, with the wife of Theodore Tilton, who had been Beecher's friend and protégé. Even Beecher eventually realized that he had been indiscreet, but whether only indiscretion had been involved was never entirely clarified, either by the adultery suit brought by Tilton in 1874 or by the two ecclesiastical tribunals that exonerated Beecher without entirely managing to restore his reputation.

Through all the scandal, Beecher's Brooklyn congregation was staunch in its loyalty, and he remained active for another decade, continuing to exert an influence on public issues, among them the successful candidacy of Grover Cleveland for the presidency in 1884. Over the years Beecher was the author of a number of published works in addition to his sermons. They included *Star Papers* (1855), *New Star Papers* (1859), *American Rebellion: Report of Speeches Delivered in England* (1864), and *Norwood: A Tale of Village Life in New England* (1867). Two of his most important works were *Evolution and Religion* (1885) and the four-volume *Life of Jesus the Christ* (1871–1891).

One of the most widely known ministers that the country has ever seen, Beecher died suddenly of apoplexy on March 8, 1887. He was survived by his wife and four of their ten children. As pastor of Plymouth Church, he was succeeded by a former editorial associate, Lyman Abbott.

Berlin Airlift of 1948 Begins

See also June 26, President Kennedy Speaks in West Berlin, and May 8, Harry S. Truman's Birthday.

In 1948, the cold war had just begun. One flash point was the divided city of Berlin. After World War II, the victorious Allies divided Nazi Germany into four zones: American, British, French, and Soviet. The first three zones would become West Germany, and the Soviet zone in the east would become East Germany. Unfortunately, the former capital of Berlin was located entirely in the Soviet zone. It too was divided into American, British, French and Soviet zones, and again the first three zones became West Berlin and the Soviet zone became East Berlin.

Isolated West Berlin was an easy target for Soviet pressure, such as cutting off supply routes. On June 24, 1948, the Soviet Union chose to do exactly that. The Soviets closed the East German roads to Western traffic, preventing supply trucks from reaching West Berlin. However, the Soviets could not prevent aircraft from flying in and out of West Berlin unless they were willing to shoot them down, a step that would almost certainly mean war with the United States.

With President Truman's approval, air force general Curtis LeMay began to resupply West Berlin by air. The task was a formidable one: Over two million people would need food, clothing, medicine, coal, and other supplies. Since there were only three adequate airfields in West Berlin, more would have to be built. Further, the air force would have to constantly refuel and reload its cargo aircraft, diverting crucial resources from the already tense military situation with the Soviets. In the meantime, negotiations with the Soviets proceeded at a snail's pace.

On July 14, 1948, the Soviets refused to lift their blockade. They claimed that West Berlin was properly part of the Soviet zone of East Germany. After consulting with its allies, the United States told the Soviets that it would continue to hold West Berlin. Further, the air force beefed up its fighter and bomber forces just in case war broke out. When this was accomplished, extra cargo planes were brought in to intensify the West Berlin supply missions. The Soviets made many threats, but never seriously attempted to interfere with the airlift.

The supply missions lasted for nearly a year. Finally, the Soviets relented and permitted the resumption of normal ground transportation. During the period of the airlift, over one and a half million tons of supplies were brought in, an astonishing achievement for the aircraft of the time.

Feast of the Nativity of St. John the Baptist

In the words of Jesus, as reported in Matthew 11:11, "Truly, I say to you, among those born of women there has risen no one greater than John the Baptist." Mentioned by all four of the Gospels, John was the cousin and precursor of Jesus.

John was indeed unique. His coming was foretold by the prophets Isaiah and Jeremiah. He was born during the reign of Herod, when his parents were advanced in years. When he began to preach, his popularity was so great that civil and religious authorities thought him a potential source of danger and rebellion. Despite his austerity and outspokenness, people flocked to hear him and to be baptized by him.

In those Christian churches that commemorate the lives of saints, St. John the Baptist ranks high in liturgical importance. While most other saints' feasts are celebrated on the day of their death, St. John's feast is celebrated on the day of his birth. In fact, the Feast of the Nativity of St. John the Baptist is one of the oldest introduced into the liturgies of the Eastern and Western churches. For many centuries the feast was celebrated, like the Nativity of Jesus, with three masses, one said at midnight, the second at dawn, and the third on the morning of the feast. This unusual honor resulted from the tradition, upheld by the Church fathers, that John was sanctified, that is freed from the stain of original sin, in his mother's womb. According to tradition this happened when the Virgin Mary visited Elizabeth, John's mother, three months before his birth.

After John grew to manhood, he became a hermit, living in the wilderness until the time came for his public ministry. Then, according to Luke 3:1:

> Now in the fifteenth year of the reign of Tiberius Caesar, Pontius Pilate being governor of Judea, and Herod being tetrarch of Galilee, . . . the word of God came to John . . . in the wilderness; and he went into all the region about the Jordan, preaching a baptism of repentance for the forgiveness of sins.

The Gospel of Matthew takes up the report in chapter 3:

> In those days came John the Baptist, preaching in the wilderness of Judea, "Repent, for the kingdom of heaven is at hand." For this is he who was spoken of by the prophet Isaiah when he said, "The voice of one crying in the wilderness: Prepare the way of the Lord, make his paths straight." Now John wore a garment of camel's hair, and a leather girdle around his waist; and his food was locusts and wild honey. Then went out to him Jerusalem and all Judea and all the region about the Jordan, and they were baptized by him in the river Jordan, confessing their sins.

The Jewish priests and people had been awaiting the Messiah, whose coming had been foretold by the Old Testament prophets, and many of them thought that John was he. John, however, denied this. He stated that his mission was to prepare the way for the Messiah. Asked why he was baptizing if he was not the Christ, John replied, "I baptize . . . with water for repentance, but he who is coming after me is mightier than I, whose sandals I am not worthy to carry; he will baptize you with the Holy Spirit and with fire."

This took place in Bethany, according to the Gospel of John, which goes on to relate that the next day John the Baptist, who had never met Jesus, saw him approaching and declared him to be "the Lamb of God, who takes away the sin of the world." As related in the sixth chapter of Mark, John continued his ministry of preaching repentance for sins, baptizing the people, and preparing them to receive the Messiah until his great popularity with the people and his outspokenness caused King Herod Antipas to imprison and execute him.

Although the time span of his public ministry was short, John's influence was great. Because he had pointed out Jesus Christ as the Lamb of God, some of his own disciples, among them the Apostles Andrew and John, went on to follow Jesus. John's influence was still evident 30 years later when the Apostle Paul on his journeys met and baptized people who had not known Jesus but who had been baptized by John.

The Feast of the Nativity of St. John the Baptist on June 24 occurs near the summer solstice, when the days begin to grow shorter. The Christian observance thus conveniently coincided with, and eventually superseded, the older pagan revelries that for centuries had taken place on or about June 24 near the time of the summer solstice. Apparently, however, the selection of June 24 as the Feast of the Nativity of St. John the Baptist was based merely on the fact that, according to Scripture, John was six months older than Jesus. Following the Roman custom of calculating dates by counting backward from the Kalends, or first day of the following month, Church authorities retrospectively fixed the birth of Christ at eight days before the Kalends of January, namely on December 25. John's nativity, then, was put at eight days before the Kalends of July, and since June has only 30 days, the feast was assigned to June 24.

Midsummer Day

The celebration of Midsummer has existed throughout Europe from pre-Christian times. Christian and pagan customs long ago became curiously mingled. The traditional bonfires and revelry of Midsummer Night are remnants of ancient Sun worship (see June 23, Midsummer's Eve). The Feast of the Nativity of St. John the Baptist, whom Jesus called "a burning and a shining light," came to be celebrated on Midsummer Day.

The term *midsummer* is actually a misnomer, since Midsummer Day does not occur in the middle of summer. Rather, it is near the time of the summer solstice, which marks the beginning of summer (see June 21) in the Northern Hemisphere. It is at this time of year that the days are longest, and people are reminded of their year-round dependence on the Sun's life-giving light and warmth. European settlers, particularly those from Scandinavia (sun-starved much of the year), brought their Midsummer traditions with them to the United States. In modern times, however, the occasion has fallen into obscurity.

June 25

Custer's Last Stand

George Armstrong Custer was born on December 5, 1839, the son of Emanuel and Maria Ward Fitzpatrick Custer of New Rumley in Harrison County, Ohio. He spent most of his youth in Monroe, Michigan, where he lived with Lydia Reed, his half sister. In 1857 he left the Midwest for the United States Military Academy at West Point, New York.

At West Point Custer displayed few talents. He was constantly in trouble, earned numerous demerits, and graduated near the bottom of the class of 1861. The new second lieutenant then rushed off to join his unit, the Second U.S. Cavalry, and arrived in time to participate in the first battle of Bull Run, an early defeat for the Union forces in the Civil War.

Custer rose through the ranks with amazing speed. At the age of 23 he became the youngest brigadier general in the annals of the United States Army, and two years later he won a temporary promotion to the rank of major general. The recipient of many awards, Custer had the honor of accepting the flag of truce of the Confederate Army of Northern Virginia at Appomattox Courthouse at the end of the Civil War.

Peace brought a reduction in the size of the army, and most officers surrendered their wartime commissions. Custer reverted to a lieutenant colonel, and took command of the Seventh Cavalry. He and his wife, the former Elizabeth Bacon, made their home on the remote posts of the western frontier. In 1874 Custer's Seventh Cavalry left Fort Abraham Lincoln in the Dakota Territory to explore the Black Hills. The region was part of the Great Sioux Reservation, set aside by an 1868 treaty signed at Fort Laramie, Wyoming, for the Sioux and Cheyenne tribes. However, prospectors with Custer's 1874 expedition confirmed the existence of gold deposits in the Black Hills, and miners soon invaded the reservation lands.

The army sought to keep the fortune hunters away, but lacked the necessary manpower. The tribes therefore assumed the task of defending their lands, which they considered to be religiously sacred. Bands of Sioux and Cheyenne roamed the Black Hills and killed a number of American intruders. Some of the bands joined forces with Crazy Horse and Sitting Bull, determined leaders who had taken no part in the 1868 treaty. They rejected a government ultimatum to return to their reservation settlements by January 31, 1876.

In 1876 the army designed a campaign to encircle and capture the militant Sioux and Cheyenne who were in southeastern Montana. General George Crook marched north from Fort Fetterman in Wyoming, Colonel John Gibbon came east from Fort Ellis in Montana, and General Alfred Terry moved west from Fort Abraham Lincoln in the Dakotas. The three were to join forces near the Yellowstone River and conduct their operation.

Terry and Gibbon met in June and camped at the mouth of the Rosebud Creek in Montana. On June 22 Custer's Seventh Cavalry, the largest element in Terry's command, proceeded south down the creek to reconnoiter. By the morning of June 25 the Seventh had reached the crest of the divide separating the Rosebud from the Little Bighorn River, and the scouts spotted smoke in the valley, indicating that the warriors might be there. Suspecting that the Sioux had discovered his whereabouts, Custer decided to attack immediately rather than wait until June 26 as Terry had planned. Custer divided the Seventh into three battalions, the largest of which he led himself. He proceeded west with five companies along the north bank of a stream leading toward the Little Bighorn Valley. Major Marcus A. Reno led three companies in a course parallel to Custer's, but on the other side of the water. Captain Frederick A. Benteen proceeded in the same direction with three companies, but farther to the south.

Major Reno crossed the Little Bighorn River at about 2:30 p.m. and encountered a surprisingly large band of natives. The troopers dismounted and managed to hold off their opponents for half an hour, but finally had to retreat back across the Little Bighorn. They took up defensive positions and were not a factor in the rest of the battle.

Custer had evidently planned to attack the Sioux and Cheyenne on the right flank and the rear. Unfortunately for Custer's battalion of Seventh cavalrymen, Reno had to fall back before his commander was able to cross the Little Bighorn. The Sioux and Cheyenne were therefore able to turn their full attention to Custer's men. Perhaps as many as 5,000 set out after the approximately 225 troopers. The overwhelmingly outnumbered cavalrymen shot their own horses and used their bodies as shelter from the enemy's bullets and arrows. This gruesome tactic was of no avail: The native warriors killed every one of the cavalrymen.

Major Reno, joined by Captain Benteen, maintained his position through the night. The Sioux and Cheyenne attacked again at dawn on June 26 and continued their harassment until late afternoon, when they withdrew. The cavalrymen feared that the native warriors might return, however, and continued to act cautiously. General Terry and Colonel Gibbon left the mouth of Rosebud Creek on June 21 and traveled west along the Yellowstone River. They then turned south and proceeded up the Bighorn River. On June 27 an advance party led by Lieutenant Bradley came upon the Custer battlefield and met the troopers of Reno and Benteen. The following day those remnants of the Seventh Cavalry began burying their dead.

The war continued for years, and the army eventually began to gain the upper hand. In 1877 Chief Crazy Horse, who had led the enemy at the battle of Little Bighorn, attempted to negotiate with the soldiers at Fort Robinson. He was betrayed and killed with a bayonet. Other die-hard warriors fled across the border into Canada. From this vantage they attempted to continue their fight, but the cause was hopeless. Finally, in July 1881 Sitting Bull and his followers returned to the United States and surrendered. Nine years later, on December 29, 1890, the Sioux met their final defeat when the army ambushed a group of Sioux (many of them unarmed) at Wounded Knee, South Dakota. Wounded Knee was once again the site of violence in 1973, when militant Native Americans occupying the historic site clashed with federal officers.

Korean War Begins

The years following World War II brought not peace but a new kind of conflict. The Western powers, led by the United States, and the Communist bloc, led by the Soviet Union, vied with each other in a tense struggle for global domination termed the cold war. Both sides managed to avoid direct military confrontation, since a "hot" war would inevitably involve nuclear weapons and thus the destruction of the world, but they tested each other's resolve in third-party arenas. One such arena was the Korean peninsula in Asia.

After World War II, control of Korea had passed from Japan to the Soviet Union and the United States. In 1945 these two powers temporarily divided the country at the 38th Parallel, with the Soviet Union responsible for the northern half and the United States for the southern. In theory a single, independent Korean republic was to be established within a short time, but postwar hostility interfered with this plan. Instead, by 1948 two separate governments existed in Korea: the Democratic People's Republic in the north, recognized by the Soviet Union; and the Republic of Korea in the south, backed by the United States.

Soviet and American troops withdrew from Korea in 1948 and 1949, respectively. The Soviets left behind a well-trained and well-equipped native army in North Korea, while the Americans handed over the defense of South Korea to a weak and ineffective military. North Korea did not delay for long in taking advantage of the situation.

On June 25, 1950, North Korean armored divisions crossed the 38th Parallel and within three days captured the South Korean capital of Seoul. This aggressive action immediately spurred the free world to take measures to prevent the complete Communist takeover of South Korea. After its June 25 call for a cease-fire went unheeded, the United Nations Security Council on June 27 appealed to its members to "furnish such assistance to the Republic of Korea as may be necessary to repel the armed attack and restore international peace and security." The United States responded quickly. That same day President Harry S. Truman ordered United States naval and air forces to proceed to Korea, and on June 30 he ordered American ground troops into the combat zone.

Although 16 nations had military personnel in Korea by the beginning of July 1950, American troops constituted more than 80 percent of the entire United Nations (UN) forces. In the first months of combat the UN troops and their South Korean allies continuously lost ground to the North Koreans, and at the end of August the fighting centered around Pusan in southeastern Korea. The tide of battle turned in early September. Under the direction of their commander, General Douglas MacArthur, the UN forces not only held their position at Pusan but began a successful counteroffensive. Seoul was recaptured on September 26, and by October 1 the troops of the Communist North had been driven above the 38th Parallel.

Buoyed by the September victories, the UN General Assembly on October 7 authorized MacArthur to take the necessary steps to ensure "a unified, independent, and democratic Korea." United Nations troops crossed the 38th Parallel on October 9, and by the end of the month they had pushed the Communists back to the Manchurian border between North Korea and its fellow Communist nation, the People's Republic of China. The UN and American forces did not hold this position for long. Chinese foreign minister Chou Enlai had warned that the people of his country would not "supinely tolerate seeing their neighbors being savagely invaded by imperialists." On November 26 the Chinese launched a massive counterattack.

The Chinese pushed the UN and American troops south below the 38th Parallel, reoccupying the cities of Pyongyang and Seoul. Officially, the Chinese government claimed that its troops were independent "volunteers," who had joined their fellow North Korean Communists in the struggle. Although this story was transparently false, the United States never officially declared war on China for the attack, since China was allied with the Soviet Union and an all-out war might lead to a United States–Soviet nuclear confrontation.

By the end of January 1951, the UN forces had rallied. They battled their way back to the 38th Parallel and even won some territory in the eastern sector north of that dividing line. Yet they could not score a major victory against the Communists. In the spring of 1951 a front stabilized, along which fighting continued for the next two years. Truce negotiations began in July 1951. For almost two years they dragged on, and at times it seemed as though agreement would never be reached. Then finally, on July 27, 1953, an armistice was signed ending the Korean War. In accordance with the terms of the armistice, South Korea acquired approximately 1,500 square miles of

territory above the 38th Parallel, which had previously been the border between the north and south. It was a costly gain, since the combined number of American, UN, and South Korean casualties was 498,255 and the forces of North Korea were reported to have suffered approximately 1.6 million killed and wounded.

Virginia Ratifies the Constitution

On June 25, 1788, Virginia became the tenth state to ratify the United States Constitution. Although the new frame of government officially became the law of the land after adoption by nine of the 13 states, approval by Virginia, the largest and most influential of the states, was critical to its success. Moreover, Virginia's decision gave the Federalists in New York enough leverage to bring that prosperous and centrally located state into the new Union.

During the years following the American Revolution, Virginians ranked among the foremost critics of the Articles of Confederation. In 1785 George Washington served as host at Mount Vernon to delegates from Virginia and Maryland who sought to resolve the difficulties involved in navigation of the Potomac River and Chesapeake Bay. In 1786, at Virginia's invitation, representatives from five states met in Annapolis, Maryland, for a convention on commercial affairs. The delegates proposed that the Congress convene a Continental convention "to render the constitution of the Federal Government adequate to the exigencies of the Union." When the Congress made provision for such a gathering, Virginia was the first state to appoint representatives to the Philadelphia convention.

Seven delegates represented Virginia at the Constitutional Convention held in Philadelphia from May through September 1787. George Washington, the commander in chief of American forces during the Revolution, served as president of the gathering. At 55 years of age, the general was perhaps the most popular man in the new nation. James Madison, 36 years old, was essentially a scholar in politics, whose thorough knowledge of public affairs convinced many of his greatness. George Wythe, 61 years of age, was a signer of the Declaration of Independence, a judge of Virginia's high court of chancery, and a professor of law at the famous College of William and Mary. George Mason, 62 years of age, was the author of the Virginia Declaration of Rights and supported the wide distribution of governmental power among the states. Edmund Randolph, governor of Virginia, John Blair, a member of the state's judiciary, and James McClurg, once professor of medicine at William and Mary, completed the delegation. Patrick Henry, a localist who "smelt a rat," declined to serve. Richard Henry Lee and Thomas Nelson, who also won election to the convention, followed Henry's example.

On May 29, Edmund Randolph, on behalf of the Virginia delegation, suggested a program of action to the convention. Presented in the form of 15 resolutions, the Virginia plan was essentially a new frame of government designed to replace rather than to revise the Articles of Confederation. The Randolph resolutions, which appeared to actually be the handiwork of James Madison, provided for the separate branches of government: the executive, the judiciary, and a bicameral legislature.

Under the Virginia plan, the lower house would be elected directly by the people. These delegates in turn would choose the members of the upper house from nominations made by the state legislatures. Each state was to receive representation in both chambers in proportion to its population or to the amount of its contribution to the national treasury. The national legislature was to have all the authority of the Confederation Congress, additional powers to meet situations beyond the competence of the separate states, and the right to annual state laws that violated the Articles of Union. Further, under the Virginia plan the legislature was to select an executive, eligible for only one term, and a national judiciary, including supreme and inferior courts. The judiciary was to have jurisdiction over maritime questions, cases involving foreigners, and matters affecting the "national peace and harmony." The executive and a "convenient number of the national judiciary" were to constitute a council of revision, which could veto acts of the national legislature.

The Constitutional Convention on May 30 formed itself into a committee of the whole and debated the Virginia plan until June 13, when the delegates received a report embodying Randolph's program in 19 resolutions. Many at the Philadelphia gathering, especially members from the smaller states, were hostile to the Virginia vision of the United States. On June 15, William Paterson of New Jersey presented a set of revisions of the Articles of Confederation more in accord with their philosophy. On June 19, after three days of debate, the delegates voted to pursue the formation of a new government following the Virginia guidelines.

Virginia's Plan of Union, altered by some significant compromises, became the basis of the Constitution, which the convention formulated during July and August. The delegates made representation in the lower house proportional to population,

but assigned an equal number of seats in the upper house to each state. Among other important changes the state legislatures received the right to select the members of the upper house, and the president became eligible for reelection. On September 17 the convention gave its final approval to the proposed Constitution and referred it, via the Congress, to the states for ratification.

Convening in October 1787, the Virginia legislature immediately considered the convocation of a ratification convention. The House wanted to schedule the special election of delegates for March 1788 and the convention for May, but acquiesced in the Senate's request to delay these events until April and June respectively. Both supporters and opponents of the proposed Constitution thus had months to try to convince the populace of the correctness of their positions.

Antifederalist propagandists managed to produce much more newsprint than did the supporters of the Constitution. Statements against the new frame of government by the revolutionary firebrand Richard Henry Lee, and by two Virginia delegates to the Philadelphia convention, namely George Mason and Edmund Randolph who both refused to sign the completed Constitution, circulated through the state. Federalist writers were not so prolific, and not even the *Federalist* papers were so influential as the statements by the Virginia dissidents.

However, the Federalists proved more adept than their opponents in the focusing of campaigns on specific contests and in the selection of candidates. The advocates of the new Constitution paid special attention to the area west of the Blue Ridge Mountains, which would elect 46 delegates and where almost no printed matter had circulated. They also put forward as candidates many military heroes, in the hope that the voters might associate them with the revered George Washington, the Federalists' best asset.

April's election of delegates to the Virginia ratifying convention justified the Federalists' tactics. They won 85 seats or fully one-half of 170 contests. The Antifederalists could count 66 of the victors in their ranks and perhaps three others categorized as "doubtful." Little is known about 16 of the delegates, 12 of whom came from what is now Kentucky and 4 from the trans-Allegheny region.

Patrick Henry led the Antifederalist forces in the ratifying convention. George Mason, who refused to sign the new Constitution because it allowed the continuation of the slave trade and permitted the imposition of duties on commerce by a simple majority rather than by a two-thirds vote, assisted him. Henry managed to convert three of the supposed Federalists by his vivid descriptions of the loss of liberty that he claimed ratification would produce, and won over ten of the Kentuckians with arguments that the federal authorities would bargain away the rights of navigation of the Mississippi River.

Having no single delegate capable of matching Patrick Henry in prestige and oratorical powers, the Federalists made maximum use of the number of highly capable individuals in their ranks. Edmund Pendleton and George Wythe lent their prestige to the Federalist cause, and James Madison and John Marshall provided two keen intellects to counter Henry's arguments. Madison's success in persuading Edmund Randolph to change his mind and support ratification not only embarrassed the Antifederalists, but added a shrewd political strategist to the Federalist side. By their combined efforts the Federalists managed to persuade the four trans-Alleghenians, two of the Kentuckians, and one of the "doubtful" delegates to affirm the new Constitution. When the final tally was taken on June 25, 1788, the Federalists had won by 89 to 79 votes.

A variety of factors produced a Federalist victory in Virginia. Especially important was the harsh wartime experience of Virginia, which convinced many of the necessity for a strong Union. There was also the influence of most of Virginia's greatest statesmen, including the incomparable George Washington. Virginia's ratification of the Constitution on June 25, 1788, has led historians to rank the state 10th in the chronological list of the admission of states to the Union.

United Church of Christ Formed

The first union in the United States of churches with differing forms of church government and divergent historical backgrounds took place on June 25, 1957, when the General Council of the Congregational Christian Churches and the Evangelical and Reformed Church came together to form the United Church of Christ. The purpose of the union, in the words of a church representative, was "to express more fully the oneness in Christ of the churches composing it, to make more effective their common witness in Him, and to serve His kingdom in the world."

Each of the uniting bodies was itself the result of earlier mergers. One of the uniting denominations, the Evangelical and Reformed Church, had come into being with the union in 1934 of the Evangelical Synod of North America and the Reformed Church in the United States. Brought to this country by immigrants from Germany and Switzerland, both groups had their roots in the Reformation movement in Europe, tracing their lineage to John Calvin, Martin Luther, Philipp Melanchthon, and Huldrych Zwingli. In America the Evangelical Synod had its origins in Missouri in 1840, whereas the Reformed Church had begun in Pennsylvania in 1725.

The other uniting denomination, the General Council of the Congregational Christian Churches, was formed in 1931 when the Congregational and Christian Churches, each resulting from several previous unions and each tracing its ancestry largely to Reformation movements in England, came together. Congregationalism had been brought to the New World by the Pilgrims who founded the colony at Plymouth and by the Puritans who settled in the Massachusetts Bay Colony. In this country the Congregationalists were joined by the Congregational Methodists in 1892, by the Evangelical Protestants in 1923, and by the German Congregationalists in 1925. The Christian Church had brought together Methodists from North Carolina, Baptists from Vermont, and Presbyterians from Kentucky in 1820.

June 26

President Kennedy Speaks in West Berlin

See also May 29, John F. Kennedy's Birthday.

During the turbulent period of the cold war, relations between the United States and the Soviet Union were usually tense and sometimes came dangerously close to open "hot" warfare. One flash point was the divided city of Berlin. After World War II, the victorious Allies divided Nazi Germany into four zones: American, British, French, and Soviet. The first three zones became West Germany, and the Soviet zone in the east became East Germany. Unfortunately, the former capital of Berlin was located entirely in the Soviet zone. It too was divided into American, British, French and Soviet zones, and again the first three zones became West Berlin and the Soviet zone became East Berlin. Isolated West Berlin, with its vulnerable supply routes, was an easy target for Soviet pressure (see June 24).

A series of crises in the early 1960s, including the construction by the Communists of a fortified barrier between the eastern and western zones, caused President John F. Kennedy to make a personal visit to West Berlin, where he made a famous speech reaffirming America's commitment. It was during this address that Kennedy used the phrase "Ich bin ein Berliner," "I am a Berliner," to express the depth of his commitment. Excerpts from the speech, given on June 26, 1963, are set forth below:

I am proud to come to this city as the guest of your distinguished mayor, who has symbolized throughout the world the fighting spirit of West Berlin. And I am proud to visit the Federal Republic with your distinguished chancellor, who for so many years has committed [West] Germany to democracy and freedom and progress, and to come here in the company of my fellow American General Clay, who has been in this city during its great moments of crisis and will come again if ever needed.

Two thousand years ago the proudest boast was *Civis Romanus sum*. Today, in the world of freedom, the proudest boast is *Ich bin ein Berliner*. I appreciate my interpreter translating my German!

There are many people in the world who really don't understand, or say they don't, what is the great issue between free world and the Communist world. Let them come to Berlin. There are some who say that communism is the wave of the future. Let them come to Berlin. And there are some who say in Europe and elsewhere we can work with the Communists. Let them come to Berlin. And there are even a few who say that it is true that communism is an evil system, but it permits us to make economic progress. *Lass sie nach Berlin kommen*. Let them come to Berlin.

Freedom has many difficulties and democracy is not perfect, but we have never had to put a wall up to keep our people in, to prevent them from leaving us. I want to say, on behalf of my countrymen, who live many miles away on the other side of the Atlantic, who are far distant from you, that they take the greatest pride that they have been able to share with you, even from a distance, the story of the last 18 years. I know of no town, no city, that has been besieged for 18 years that still lives with the vitality and the force, and the hope and the determination of the city of West Berlin. While the wall is the most obvious and vivid demonstration of the failures of the Communist system, for all the world to see, we take no satisfaction in it, for it is, as your mayor has said, an offense not only against history but an offense against humanity, separating families, dividing husbands and wives and brothers and sisters, and dividing a people who wish to be joined together.

What is true of this city is true of Germany; real, lasting peace in Europe can never be assured as long as one German

out of four is denied the elementary right of free men, and that is to make a free choice. In 18 years of peace and good faith, this generation of Germans has earned the right to be free, including the right to unite their families and their nation in lasting peace, with good will to all people. You live in a defended island of freedom, but your life is part of the main. So let me ask you, as I close, to lift your eyes beyond the dangers of today, to the hopes of tomorrow, beyond the freedom merely of this city of Berlin, or your country of Germany, to the advance of freedom everywhere, beyond the wall to the day of peace with justice, beyond yourselves and ourselves to all mankind.

Freedom is indivisible, and when one man is enslaved, all are not free. When all are free, then we can look forward to that day when this city will be joined as one and this country and this great continent of Europe in a peaceful and hopeful globe. When that day finally comes, as it will, the people of West Berlin can take sober satisfaction in the fact that they were in the front lines for almost two decades.

All free men, wherever they may live, are citizens of Berlin, and, therefore, as a free man, I take pride in the words *Ich bin ein Berliner*.

World War I: American Troops Land in France

The United States Congress declared war on Germany on April 6, 1917 (see April 6, United States Enters World War I). Less than three months later, on June 26, 1917, several units of the United States First Infantry Division disembarked in France. Several more months elapsed before the country mobilized sufficient military strength to influence the outcome of the war.

The United States Army numbered only 200,000 enlisted men and officers in April 1917. However, the nation acted quickly to meet the urgent need for additional troops. On May 18, 1917, Congress approved the Selective Service Act, and in less than a month more than nine million American men between the ages of 21 and 30 had registered for the draft. To train the new recruits and inductees, 32 camps and other facilities were built. By the end of the war these installations had prepared nearly four million men, only about half of whom were draftees, for service in the army.

General John J. Pershing, who landed in France on June 14, 1917, commanded the American Expeditionary Force (AEF). "Lafayette, we are here," the statement often attributed to Pershing, was actually made on July 4 at the tomb of Lafayette by Colonel Charles E. Stanton, chief disbursing officer of the AEF. According to Pershing's orders, American troops were to remain "a distinct and separate component of the combined [Allied] force." The exigencies of war at times necessitated abandoning this plan. However, for the most part the army did maintain an independent role, subject after April 1918 to the supreme Allied commander, Marshal Ferdinand Foch of France.

By the time that the fighting ended on November 11, 1918, more than two million American soldiers had landed in France. Of these, approximately 1.4 million saw combat. Their presence decisively influenced the outcome of the war. They gave the Allies numerical superiority on the western front and contributed to such significant victories as Belleau Wood, Saint-Mihiel, and Meuse-Argonne.

June 27

H. Ross Perot's Birthday

H. Ross Perot, businessman, philanthropist, and independent presidential candidate, was born on June 27, 1930, in Texarkana, Texas. Texarkana was a small town, struggling to cope with the Great Depression. Young Perot's personality was shaped by the experience: He learned the importance of hard work, frugality, and personal initiative. As a child, he made extra money by working a paper route through the toughest and most dangerous section of Texarkana, riding his horse at a gallop while he threw the newspapers. He went on to attend Texarkana Junior College, and then successfully obtained admission to the United States Naval Academy.

While at the academy, Perot met and married Margot Birmingham. He was a leader at the academy, and had a reputation for being exceptionally circumspect in his personal habits, abstaining from drinking, smoking, and the other habits of young men. He graduated in 1953, but resigned his commission in 1957. Although Perot always admired servicemen and has supported many veterans' causes, he was dissatisfied with navy life and looked forward to leaving.

Perot went to work as a salesman for International Business Machines (IBM), then the undisputed leader of the American computer industry. IBM's success was due to its dedicated scientists and work force, who lived in a highly disciplined corporate environment. The "IBM man" observed strict rules of conduct, came to work in conservative clothing, and was rewarded for his loyalty with high pay and a policy of no-layoffs. Perot prospered at IBM, and exceeded his sales quotas in record time. However, he was frustrated by his inability to rise as far and fast as he desired, and was unable to generate interest within IBM for his idea of expanding into data processing services. Perot left IBM, and on his 32nd birthday in 1962 formed Electronic Data Systems (EDS) with $1,000 borrowed from his wife.

By the late 1960s, that $1,000 investment was worth nearly a billion. Perot had correctly identified an unfilled niche in the area of data processing, and with the help of several important Medicare and Medicaid contracts, EDS became a thriving business. When the company went public, Perot's stock made him one of America's richest men. He used some of his money to launch a one-man relief expedition to the American prisoners of war (POWs) in North Vietnam during the Vietnam War. His effort to fly in humanitarian supplies was only partially successful, due to resistance by the North Vietnamese authorities, but the publicity generated by the effort forced the Vietnamese to improve POW conditions. It also stimulated the budding POW-relief movement within the United States.

EDS continued to grow throughout the 1970s, especially in its overseas operations. One profit center was the Middle East nation of Iran, which was seeking to modernize under the ambitious but repressive Shah. When the country underwent a revolution, sparked in large part by Muslim fundamentalism, several EDS employees were caught in the capital of Teheran and held hostage by agents of the new government. Scores of other Americans were also caught in what became the Iran Hostage Crisis. The administration of President Jimmy Carter (1977–1981) was unable or unwilling to act quickly enough to satisfy Perot, who has always cultivated a relationship of fierce loyalty with his employees.

Perot personally led a daring rescue operation directly into Iran at the head of a team of EDS volunteers trained by a friend of Perot's, retired colonel Arthur "Bull" Simmons. Despite some close calls, the mission was successful and the EDS captives were brought out of Iran. Ken Follett wrote a book about the mission, *On the Wings of Eagles*, which also became a movie. The title was based on Perot's comment about human nature and how challenging it was to find quality individuals such as those EDS volunteers who went into Iran: "Eagles don't flock together, you have to find them one at a time."

In 1984 Perot sold EDS to General Motors (GM) for over two billion dollars. He also became a member of GM's board of directors, and promptly began to criticize GM's management and the company's operations. Perot was forced to leave GM, in exchange for a $700-million settlement, and the carmaker would go on to experience record losses and drops in market share before finally adopting many of the reforms Perot had suggested. Meanwhile, Perot established another data processing business, Perot Systems.

Perot now had roughly three billion dollars to finance his other ambitions. One of these ambitions was politics. During the 1980s, Perot accepted a challenge to reform the Texas state public school system, and pursued stricter academic standards that would force high school athletes to maintain an acceptable grade point average under a "no pass, no play" policy. In early 1992, during an interview with talk show host Larry King, Perot stated that he might be willing to run for president in the upcoming November 1992 presidential elections. His statement generated a massive, unexpected response.

Perhaps because of public dissatisfaction with the two-party system or the state of American politics, a "draft Perot" movement sprang into life. Volunteers in all 50 states began to work for Perot's inclusion on the ballot. Perot was evasive about declaring his candidacy, but he obviously enjoyed the limelight. His straightforward no-nonsense attitude and focus on substantive issues, such as reducing the budget deficit that had risen to over $300 billion a year under President George Bush, made him popular. In the spring of 1992, Perot ranked higher in the polls than both incumbent President George Bush and Democratic front-runner Bill Clinton. However, Perot decided to drop out of the race, citing a bizarre Republican plot to discredit him and disrupt a daughter's upcoming wedding. The incident seriously discredited Perot, but he decided to reenter the race in October 1992, and had a remarkable comeback. He was invited to the nationally televised presidential debates, where he proved to be exceptionally well-spoken, and in the November election took 19 percent of the vote to Clinton's 43 percent and Bush's 38 percent. He came in third place, but it was the best performance by an independent since Theodore Roosevelt in 1912. Perot drew voters almost equally from both the Republican and Democratic Parties.

After the 1992 election, Perot went on to form the Reform Party. He tried and failed to sway public opinion against the North American Free Trade Agreement (NAFTA), partly because of a dismal performance debating NAFTA with Vice President Al Gore on the Larry King show. Perot ran for president again in 1996, this time as the Reform Party's candidate, capturing roughly 8 percent of the vote. The Republicans, who blamed George Bush's 1992 loss on Perot's independent candidacy, engineered Perot's exclusion from the 1996 television debates and so contributed to his diminished standing. Further, Perot blocked former Colorado governor Dick Lamm's attempt to enter the Reform Party's primaries, and by thus refusing to loosen his personal control over his pet party, Perot discredited its claim as a legitimate third choice in American politics.

Helen Keller's Birthday

Helen Adams Keller, the heroic blind and deaf American who by her courage, spirit, and remarkable achievements made valuable contributions to the education of other blind and deaf persons, was born a normal child in Tuscumbia, Alabama, on June 27, 1880. Her family on her father's side was connected with the Lees and Spotswoods of Virginia and on her mother's side with the Adamses and Everetts of Massachusetts.

When Helen Keller was about 19 months old, a short but devastating illness, perhaps scarlet fever, robbed her of her sight, hearing, and consequently of her articulate speech. Locked in darkness and silence, she became a wild, unruly child, full of rage and rarely smiling. Worried about her education, not knowing if indeed she could be taught or whether they could find a teacher, her parents consulted a Baltimore eye specialist who felt that their child was educable. The specialist suggested that the Kellers consult Alexander Graham Bell, inventor of the telephone, who was also deeply involved in educating the deaf to speak.

Bell directed the Kellers to his son-in-law, Michael Anagnos, who was then director of the Perkins Institution in South Boston (later the Perkins School for the Blind in Watertown, Massachusetts). Helen's mother had already read about the Perkins Institution in Charles Dickens's *American Notes*, in which he wrote of Laura Bridgman, the first blind and deaf person to successfully be educated and who was trained at Perkins.

The teacher selected for Helen was Anne Mansfield Sullivan, who at the age of 10 had been put into Tewksbury Almshouse and was later sent to Perkins because of her own partial blindness. At Perkins, Annie Sullivan, as she came to be known, learned the hand alphabet used to communicate with the blind deaf. Her own vision was improved by treatment, and she graduated from Perkins the year before the Kellers began their search for someone to teach their daughter. She was 20 years old when she arrived at the Keller house in Tuscumbia.

Helen later wrote, "The most important day I remember in all my life is the one on which my teacher came to me. It was the third of March, 1887, three months before I was seven years old." That first meeting was stormy. Brought forward to greet her new teacher, Helen grabbed Sullivan's purse and groped about in it for candy. Finding none, she flew into a rage that lasted for days. These events were dramatized in William Gibson's play *The Miracle Worker*, which opened on Broadway in October 1959 and was based on Nella Braddy's book *Anne Sullivan Macy: The Story behind Helen Keller* (1933). *The Miracle Worker*, a powerful drama that won many awards first as a play and later as a film, was seen by millions of people all over the world.

When Sullivan finally gained Helen's attention, she began to spell words into the child's hand. This method, so useful with the deaf, had its drawbacks with someone who had been blind from infancy. The various patterns traced on her palm by her teacher signified nothing to the child. One day as the two were walking outdoors, they passed a pump in the yard near the house. As Keller later told it:

> We walked down the path to the well-house, attracted by the fragrance of the honeysuckle with which it was covered. Someone was drawing water and my teacher placed my hand under the spout. As the cool stream gushed over one hand, she spelled into the other the word "water," first slowly, then rapidly. I stood still, my whole attention fixed upon the motions of her fingers. Suddenly I felt a misty consciousness as of something forgotten, a thrill of returning thought, and somehow the mystery of language was revealed to me. I knew then that "w-a-t-e-r" meant the wonderful cool something that was flowing over my hand. That living word awakened my soul, gave it light, hope, joy, set it free. There were barriers still, it is true, but barriers that in time could be swept away.

For the next 50 years Sullivan, whom Keller always called Teacher, was there to help sweep away barriers for her student. Soon the eager child knew many words besides "water" and, with a zeal for knowledge, learned whole sentences and then whole stories within just three months after Sullivan's arrival. It was at this time that the young teacher wrote to Michael Anagnos at the Perkins Institution: "Something tells me that I am going to succeed beyond all my dreams."

In May 1888 Keller, not quite eight years old, was taken to the Perkins Institution. There she learned to read braille, and for the first time she met and played with other afflicted children. Eager to learn how to speak, she was taken to the Horace Mann School for the Deaf, in Boston, in the spring of 1890. There she met her first speech teacher, Sarah Fuller, who taught her to "hear" or lip-read by placing her fingers on the lips and throat of the person speaking. Despite instruction, Keller's speech was never completely clear and, though she was understandable if she used short words and spoke slowly, it was usually necessary for her companion to repeat her words for others at social gatherings or when she was lecturing before audiences.

Keller's formal schooling began when she was 14, at the Wright-Humason School for the Deaf, in New York City, and was continued in Massachusetts at the Cambridge School for Young Ladies, where she prepared to enter Radcliffe College. She passed the Radcliffe entrance examination, which was the same given to nonhandicapped applicants, and entered Radcliffe in 1900.

Her years at Radcliffe were marked by endurance, perseverance, and sheer obstinacy on the part of Keller and of Sullivan, who had to spell into her pupil's hand every word of the textbooks and lectures. Keller could write and also use a typewriter with skill by this time. Her assignments for an English composition course, conducted by Harvard's famous Professor Charles Townsend Copeland, became chapters in her most widely read book, *The Story of My Life*, which was serialized in the *Ladies' Home Journal* and first published as a book in 1902. It has since been published in dozens of languages. She was to continue her writing career for most of her life. In 1904 Keller graduated cum laude from Radcliffe, receiving her Bachelor of Arts degree with honors in German and English. The next year Annie Sullivan married John Macy, a social critic, and Keller lived with them. Influenced by Macy's political thought and by her own braille reading of H. G. Wells and Karl Marx and Friedrich Engels, Keller joined the Socialist Party in 1909 and was for many years an active member.

After World War I, popular tastes did not run to her inspirational type of writing and, needing an income, she ventured into vaudeville with Sullivan at her side. With a 20-minute act, they toured the country between 1920 and 1924. The curtain went up on a drawing room setting, and to the background music of Felix Mendelssohn's *Spring Song*, Sullivan made her entrance and told the audience something about Keller's life. Then, her pupil came on stage and said a few words for herself. A *New York Times* review of the debut at the Palace Theater in New York City said "Helen Keller has conquered again, and the Monday afternoon audience at the Palace, one of the most critical and cynical in the world, was hers." For her part, Keller loved the excitement of her new career. She developed a lifelong interest in the theater and formed friendships with such diverse artists as Jascha Heifetz, Harpo Marx, Sophie Tucker, and Charlie Chaplin.

Keller felt that her real life's work, however, was to help in the education and rehabilitation of handicapped children and adults, especially those with afflictions similar to hers. She had been active to some degree in this type of work since 1915, when the Permanent Blind Relief War Fund (later called the American Braille Press) was founded and she was named a member of its first board of directors.

From 1924 until her death, she was a staff member of the American Foundation for the Blind and traveled extensively in the United States, lecturing and promoting for increased help for the blind. In the 1920s, Keller, the Macys, and Polly Thomson, who had joined the household in 1914, all moved from Wrentham, Massachusetts, to Forest Hills in Queens, New York. After the death of John Macy in 1932 and of her beloved Annie Sullivan in 1936, Keller moved with Polly Thomson to Westport, Connecticut, which was within commuting distance of New York City.

When the American Braille Press became the American Foundation for Overseas Blind, working jointly with the American Foundation for the Blind, Keller was appointed its counselor on international relations. In this capacity she traveled tirelessly, circling the globe on behalf of the blind. Her achievements and warm personality impressed audiences, and her work for the blind was monumentally successful. Between 1946 and 1957 she visited 35 countries on five continents, working to improve the education, vocational training, and living conditions for the blind of all nations. She had amazing stamina even at the age of 75, when she made a 40,000-mile, five-month tour through Asia.

Keller died in her home in Westport, Connecticut, on June 1, 1968, less than a month before her 88th birthday. After a private cremation, a funeral service was held in Washington Cathedral, Washington, D.C. Her ashes were buried in the cathedral's St. Joseph's Chapel, next to her companions in life, Anne Sullivan Macy and Polly Thomson (the latter had died in 1960). Keller's writings, articles, and books spanned a period of 55 years, in addition to her still widely read autobiography. Shortly before her death she remarked that "I believe that all through these dark and silent years God has been using my life for a purpose I do not know. But one day I shall understand and then I will be satisfied."

United Nations Authorizes Allied Intervention in Korean War

The Korean War began on June 25, 1950, when the forces of Soviet-supported North Korea invaded American-supported South Korea (see June 25, Korean War Begins). It was part of the cold war struggle between the two superpowers, which began after World War II and did not end until the collapse of the Soviet Union in 1991. If North Korea conquered South Korea, the Soviets would then control the entire Korean peninsula and be in a position to threaten Japan. South Korea was hopelessly outmatched by the superior North Korean forces, but the United States was unwilling to intervene on South Korea's behalf without some sort of international endorsement. This came in the form of a resolution by the United Nations Security Council approving a multinational Allied force to repel the North Koreans, a force that would in reality be spearheaded by the United States. The Soviets, who were members of the Security Council, could have vetoed the resolution; they had absented themselves from the Council, however, and so the Americans were able to get the resolution passed.

The text of the resolution passed on June 27, 1950, is set forth below.

The Security Council,

HAVING DETERMINED that the armed attack upon the Republic of Korea by forces from North Korea constitutes a breach of the peace,

HAVING CALLED FOR an immediate cessation of hostilities, and

HAVING CALLED UPON the authorities of North Korea to withdraw forthwith their armed forces to the 38th parallel, and

HAVING NOTED from the report of the United Nations Commission for Korea that the authorities in North Korea have neither ceased hostilities nor withdrawn their armed forces to the 38th parallel and that urgent military measures are required to restore international peace and security, and

HAVING NOTED the appeal from the Republic of Korea to the United Nations for immediate and effective steps to secure peace and security,

RECOMMENDS that the Members of the United Nations furnish such assistance to the Republic of Korea as may be necessary to repel the armed attack and to restore international peace and security in the area.

Pennsylvania Dutch Folk Festival

This is a movable event.

One of the country's most written about festivals is the Pennsylvania Dutch Folk Festival held annually in Kutztown, Pennsylvania. The dates can vary, but traditionally, the festival begins in late June, ends in early July, and includes July 4. The celebration centers on the arts, crafts, farming methods, food, and folkways of the so-called Pennsylvania Dutch.

The Pennsylvania Dutch, who today inhabit the farm regions of southeastern Pennsylvania, are descendants of the Germans (*Deutsch*, which sounded like "Dutch" to English-speaking Americans) of various religious sects who flocked to Pennsylvania in the early and mid-1700s. War-weary and persecuted, they were attracted by the promise of religious freedom in the colony, which the idealistic Quaker William Penn had established in 1681. Today's Amish are descendants of these early settlers, and due to their religious beliefs they avoid using electricity, telephones, and automobiles; drive about in horse-drawn carriages; refuse to take oaths or perform military service; and dress somberly in the garb of their ancestors. Men wear black coats, broad-brimmed flat hats, and beards if they are married. Women wear long skirts, aprons, high-button boots, and bonnets. The Amish do not usually participate in the Kutztown festival, however, since they consider it too worldly for their beliefs.

The Pennsylvania Dutch Folk Festival first took form in 1950, two years after the nonprofit Pennsylvania Folklife Society, which sponsored it, was founded by Professors Alfred L. Shoemaker, Don Yoder, and J. William Frey. Attendance has fluctuated over the decades, and was approximately 75,000 a year in the late 1990s.

June 28

World War I: Archduke Francis Ferdinand Assassinated

On the evening of August 4, 1914, Sir Edward Grey, England's foreign secretary, looked out from his office window into the London twilight.

"The lamps are going out all over Europe," he said. "We shall not see them lit again in our lifetime." His country and the Continental powers were entering a night of war; before dawn ten million people would die.

The incident that precipitated World War I had occurred only a few weeks before Grey made his prophetic statement. The Balkans had been the scene of several crises involving the independent kingdom of Serbia and the Austro-Hungarian empire. Serbia envisioned itself as the center of a future pan-Slavic state, but Austria-Hungary frustrated these ambitions by its annexation of Bosnia-Herzegovina in 1908 and its continuing efforts to acquire still more territory in the area. Relations between the two countries deteriorated to such an extent that in 1911 the Serbs formed a secret terrorist organization called Union or Death, popularly known as The Black Hand, that was against Austria-Hungary.

On June 28, 1914, the heir to the Austro-Hungarian throne, Archduke Francis Ferdinand, and his wife, Archduchess Sofia, planned to inspect the army at Sarajevo, the capital of Bosnia-Herzegovina. Since June 28 was the date of the Turkish conquest of the old Serbian kingdom in 1389, and also the anniversary of the Serbian victory over Turkey in the Second Balkan War in 1913, Serbian nationalists considered the timing of the archduke's visit to be an intolerable insult to their country. In revenge, The Black Hand decided to assassinate him. As Francis Ferdinand toured Sarajevo, he escaped injury from a hand grenade. However, his assassinator Gavrilo Princip waited for him as his motorcade slowed at a river crossing. Princip fired two shots with an automatic pistol. The first shot killed the archduchess. The second shot struck the archduke, who uttered the single word "Sofia" and then died.

The assassination of Francis Ferdinand shocked the world. More importantly, it provided a focus for the tensions that had been growing in Europe. For 40 years conflicting national interests, economies, and ambitions had driven the Continental powers to prepare for such a crisis. France, Germany, Italy, Austria, and Russia each possessed huge standing armies, and strategic alliances further ensured each country's military might. Thus, Europe was ready for war by 1914, and throughout the summer of that year the Triple Alliance of Germany, Austria-Hungary, and Italy edged toward combat with the Triple Entente of England, France, and Russia, later to be known as the Allies.

Only a week after the archduke's assassination, Germany signed a diplomatic "blank check." With this guarantee of German support for any action it might take, on July 23 Austria-Hungary issued an ultimatum to Serbia, which Austria-Hungary blamed for the assassination. Although the Serbian government agreed to many of the ultimatum's demands, it refused to allow the Austrian police or military to participate in its investigation of the Black Hand plot. Austria-Hungary, however, would accept nothing less than total compliance with the ultimatum, and on July 28 declared war on Serbia.

Austria-Hungary's declaration initiated a chain reaction as the other European powers in turn honored their alliance commitments. On July 29 Russia, responding to its agreement to aid Serbia, started the full mobilization of its armies. Although German efforts to effect an Austrian-Russian settlement temporarily decreased these activities, Russia renewed its total mobilization on August 1.

Events proceeded rapidly after this decision: On August 1 Germany declared war on Russia, while France readied its troops in support of the czar. The following day Germany announced its intention to violate Belgian neutrality; two days later Great Britain responded to this action by joining forces with France and Russia. When Austria-Hungary went to war against Russia on August 6, only a little more than a week had passed since the Austro-Hungarian declaration against Serbia. Yet, in that short time all the members of the Triple Alliance and the Triple Entente (with the exception of Italy, which remained neutral until 1915 and then switched sides by joining the Allies) had brought their troops to the battlefield.

World War I: Treaty of Versailles Signed

World War I began in Europe, but before the fighting ended at 11:00 a.m. on November 11, 1918, 28 nations on five continents had become involved. Airplanes, tanks, modern submarines, and poison gas had seen their first wartime use, and these new weapons had contributed to unprecedented war losses. Ten million people had died; 20 million had been wounded; and direct war costs had reached an estimated $180.5 billion.

Peace negotiations began shortly after the November armistice, and on June 28, 1919, the fifth anniversary of Archduke Francis Ferdinand's assassination, the Treaty of Versailles, chief among the five treaties that terminated World War I, was signed by a vanquished Germany and the victorious Allies. Other treaties dealt respectively with Austria and Hungary, by then separated, and the other enemy states of Bulgaria and Turkey. According to the Treaty of Versailles, Germany accepted full responsibility for the war, made sub-

stantial territorial cessions, and agreed to a drastic limitation of its army and navy. The treaty also required Germany to pay for the civilian damage caused by the war and to bear the costs of the occupation armies.

However, reparations were not the sole concern of the delegates at Versailles. The peacemakers of 1919 were interested in preventing another world conflict. Toward this end, the Versailles treaty provided for the establishment of the League of Nations (see January 10), an organization designed to arbitrate future international disputes.

The Versailles treaty was ratified by the governments of most of the combatants. However, the Senate of the United States refused to accept the Versailles arrangement, and the United States never became a member of the League of Nations.

Lutheran Church in America Organized

One important example of the trend toward church unity that has characterized the 20th century took place when the Lutheran Church in America (LCA) was organized at Detroit in 1962. On June 28 of that year the LCA came into being by consolidation of the American Evangelical Lutheran Church (of Danish background, founded in 1874), the Augustana Evangelical Lutheran Church (of Swedish background, founded in 1860), the Finnish Evangelical Lutheran Church (founded in 1890), and the United Lutheran Church in America (of German background, founded in 1918). The merger took place after six and a half years of negotiation by representatives of the four denominations concerned, and the new LCA began functioning formally on January 1, 1963.

June 29

Atlantis-Mir Docking

A milestone in the history of space flight occurred on June 29, 1995, when the American space shuttle *Atlantis* joined the orbiting Russian space station *Mir* for the first Russian-American space shuttle–space station docking ever. The *Atlantis's* mission was also the 100th manned space flight sponsored by the United States.

The crew of the space shuttle consisted of Commander Robert L. Gibson, Pilot Charles J. Precourt, Payload Commander Ellen S. Baker, and Mission Specialists Gregory J. Harbaugh and Bonnie J. Dunbar. Accompanying them were two Russian cosmonauts: Commander Anatoly Y. Solovyev and Flight Engineer Nikolai M. Budarin. The launch took place from Cape Canaveral, Florida, on June 27, 1995. It had originally been scheduled for May 1995, but *Mir* had to be reconfigured for docking operations with the American spacecraft; this and other delays pushed the launch date into June.

Atlantis launched without incident and docked with *Mir* on June 29, roughly 200 miles above Russia's Lake Baikal. *Atlantis*'s crew then entered the space station, where they were welcomed by Commander Vladimir N. Dezhurov and Flight Engineer Gennady M. Strekalov, Russian cosmonauts, and Mission Specialist Norman E. Thagard, an American astronaut who had been part of *Mir*'s crew for the entire three-month tour of duty. After the official ceremonies, the Americans and Russians carried out joint operations for five days. Supplies and equipment were exchanged, with *Atlantis* replenishing *Mir*'s vital stores of air and water, while Solovyev and Budarin prepared to take over *Mir*'s operation from their predecessors.

Atlantis detached from *Mir* on July 4, 1995, following a formal farewell ceremony. The old *Mir* crew joined the *Atlantis* crew for the voyage back to Earth (this was the first time a crew that had been transported to the station by rocket returned home by space shuttle). *Atlantis* landed at Cape Canaveral on July 7, 1995.

Official Report on the Hiroshima and Nagasaki Atomic Bombings Issued

The United States dropped two atomic bombs on Japan toward the end of World War II, one on the city of Hiroshima on August 6, 1945, and one on the city of Nagasaki on August 9, 1945. During the American occupation of Japan, the Manhattan Engineer District (relating to the Manhattan Project that developed the atomic bomb) under the command of General Leslie Groves undertook a thorough investigation. The goal was to get a better idea of the potential of this new weapon and the consequences of its use. On June 29, 1946, their report was issued.

One particularly interesting section is the portion that describes the power of an atomic explosion. This sobering passage is set forth below in virtually its entirety, and it should be kept in mind that the weapons used at Hiroshima and Nagasaki were mild by modern standards. Both of the atomic bombs had an explosive yield of roughly 20 kilotons (20,000 tons of TNT), and today many countries including the United States have weapons with explosive yields in the megatons (millions of tons of TNT).

The most striking difference between the explosion of an atomic bomb and that of an ordinary TNT bomb is of course in magnitude; as the President announced after the Hiroshima attack, the explosive energy of each of the atomic bombs was equivalent to about 20,000 tons of TNT. But in addition to its vastly greater power, an atomic explosion has several other very special characteristics. Ordinary explosion is a chemical reaction in which energy is released by the rearrangement of the atoms of the explosive material. In an atomic explosion the identity of the atoms, not simply their arrangement, is changed. A considerable fraction of the mass of the explosive charge, which may be Uranium 235 or Plutonium, is transformed into energy. Einstein's equation, $E=mc^2$, shows that matter that is transformed into energy may yield a total energy equivalent to the mass multiplied by the square of the velocity of light. The significance of the equation is easily seen when one recalls that the velocity of light is 186,000 miles per second. The energy released when a pound of TNT explodes would, if converted entirely into heat, raise the temperature of 36 lbs. of water from freezing temperature (32 deg F) to boiling temperature (212 deg F). The nuclear fission of a pound of uranium would produce an equal temperature rise in over 200 million pounds of water.

The explosive effect of an ordinary material such as TNT is derived from the rapid conversion of solid TNT to gas, which occupies initially the same volume as the solid; it exerts intense pressures on the surrounding air and expands rapidly to a volume many times larger than the initial volume. A wave of high pressure thus rapidly moves outward from the center of the explosion and is the major cause of damage from ordinary high explosives. An atomic bomb also generates a wave of high pressure which is in fact of much higher pressure than that from ordinary explosions; and this wave is again the major cause of damage to buildings and other structures. It differs from the pressure wave of a blockbuster in the size of the area over which high pressures are generated. It also differs in the duration of the pressure pulse at any given point: the pressure from a blockbuster lasts for a few milliseconds (a millisecond is one thousandth of a second) only, that from the atomic bomb for nearly a second, and was felt by observers both in Japan and in New Mexico [during the test detonation] as a very strong wind going by.

The next greatest difference between the atomic bomb and the TNT explosion is the fact that the atomic bomb gives off greater amounts of radiation. Most of this radiation is "light" of some wavelength ranging from the so-called heat radiations of very long wavelength to the so-called gamma rays which have wavelengths even shorter than the X-rays used in medicine. All of these radiations travel at the same speed; this, the speed of light, is 186,000 miles per second. The radiations are intense enough to kill people within an appreciable distance from the explosion, and are in fact the major cause of deaths and injuries apart from mechanical injuries. The greatest number of radiation injuries was probably due to the ultraviolet rays which have a wavelength slightly shorter than visible light and which caused flash burn comparable to severe sunburn. After these, the gamma rays of ultra short wavelength are most important; these cause injuries similar to those from overdoses of X-rays.

The origin of the gamma rays is different from that of the bulk of the radiation: the latter is caused by the extremely high temperatures in the bomb, in the same way as light is emitted from the hot surface of the sun or from the wires in an incandescent lamp. The gamma rays on the other hand are emitted by the atomic nuclei themselves when they are transformed in the fission process. The gamma rays are therefore specific to the atomic bomb and are completely absent in TNT explosions. The light of longer wavelength (visible and ultraviolet) is also emitted by a TNT explosion, but with much smaller intensity than by an atomic bomb, which makes it insignificant as far as damage is concerned.

A large fraction of the gamma rays is emitted in the first few microseconds (millionths of a second) of the atomic explosion, together with neutrons which are also produced in the nuclear fission. The neutrons have much less damage effect than the gamma rays because they have a smaller intensity and also because they are strongly absorbed in air and therefore can penetrate only to relatively small distances from the explosion: at a thousand yards the neutron intensity is negligible. After the nuclear emission, strong gamma radiation continues to come from the exploded bomb. This generates from the fission products and continues for about one minute until all of the explosion products have risen to such a height that the intensity received on the ground is negligible. A large number of beta rays are also emitted during this time, but they are unimportant because their range is not very great, only a few feet. The range of alpha particles from the unused active material and fissionable material of the bomb is even smaller.

Apart from the gamma radiation ordinary light is emitted, some of which is visible and some of which is the ultraviolet rays mainly responsible for flash burns. The emission of light starts a few milliseconds after the nuclear explosion when the energy from the explosion reaches the air surrounding the bomb. The observer sees then a ball of fire which rapidly grows in size. During most of the early time, the ball of fire extends as far as the wave of high pressure. As the ball of fire grows, its temperature and brightness decrease. Several milliseconds after the initiation of the explosion, the brightness of the ball of fire goes through a minimum, then it gets somewhat brighter and remains at the order of a few times the brightness of the sun for a period of 10 to 15 seconds for an observer at six miles distance. Most of the radiation is given off after this point of maximum brightness. Also after this maximum, the pressure waves run ahead of the ball of fire.

The ball of fire rapidly expands from the size of the bomb to a radius of several hundred feet at one second after the explosion. After this the most striking feature is the rise of the ball of fire at the rate of about 30 yards per second. Meanwhile it also continues to expand by mixing with the cooler air surrounding it. At the end of the first minute the ball has expanded to a radius of several hundred yards and risen to a height of about one mile. The shock wave has by now reached a radius of 15 miles and its pressure dropped to less than 1/10 of a pound per square inch. The ball now loses its brilliance and appears as a great cloud of smoke: the pulverized material of the bomb. This cloud continues to rise vertically and finally mushrooms out at an altitude of about 25,000 feet depending upon meteorological conditions. The cloud reaches a maximum height of between

50,000 and 70,000 feet in a time of over 30 minutes.

To summarize, radiation comes in two bursts: an extremely intense one lasting only about 3 milliseconds and a less intense one of much longer duration lasting several seconds. The second burst contains by far the larger fraction of the total light energy, more than 90 percent. But the first flash is especially large in ultraviolet radiation which is biologically more effective. Moreover, because the heat in this flash comes in such a short time, there is no time for any cooling to take place, and the temperature of a person's skin can be raised 50 degrees centigrade by the flash of visible and ultraviolet rays in the first millisecond at a distance of 4,000 yards. People may be injured by flash burns at even larger distances. Gamma radiation danger does not extend nearly so far and neutron radiation danger is still more limited. The high skin temperatures result from the first flash of high intensity radiation and are probably as significant for injuries as the total dosages which come mainly from the second more sustained burst of radiation. The combination of skin temperature increase plus large ultraviolet flux inside 4,000 yards is injurious in all cases to exposed personnel. Beyond this point there may be cases of injury, depending upon the individual sensitivity. The infrared dosage is probably less important because of its smaller intensity.

Feast of Saints Peter and Paul

The Feast of Saints Peter and Paul has been celebrated by Christians on June 29 since the early centuries of the Christian Era. The oldest extant church calendar, one found in a Roman work in A.D. 354, bears witness to this fact, listing the joint celebration of the two important Apostles on June 29.

Around the year 319 the Emperor Constantine had basilicas built in Rome over the supposed tombs of the two saints. According to tradition, St. Peter was crucified head down on Vatican Hill. An oratory was built over his burial place by Anacletus, who was pope from A.D. 76 to 88. The great Basilica of St. Peter, Rome's largest church, stands on the same site. St. Paul was reportedly beheaded and buried on the Ostian Way, where his basilica, called St. Paul's Outside the Walls, now stands. (The walls referred to in the name of Rome's second largest church are the city fortifications built by Emperor Aurelian in the third century A.D.)

By the end of the fourth century, great crowds of the faithful flocked to Rome annually for the June 29 feast day, making a pilgrimage from St. Peter's Basilica to St. Paul's, which was located on the other side of the city. The pope would first celebrate a mass at St. Peter's and then proceed to St. Paul's to celebrate a second mass on the same morning. Eastern Orthodox churches, which honor the two saints by observing a special Lenten season named for them, also celebrate the feast of Saints Peter and Paul on June 29. So do many Protestant churches.

The Apostles Peter and Paul were very different in origin and background, and yet they became the two strongest pillars of the early church. Each traveled, Paul more than Peter, preaching the message of Jesus to thousands of people and building the foundations of the church in many countries and against terrible odds. Both died in Rome, as noted earlier, almost certainly as martyrs during Nero's persecution of Christians between A.D. 64 and 67.

Peter, the Prince of Apostles, known as Simon bar-Jona (son of Jona), was a simple Galilean fisherman living in Bethsaida when Jesus called him and his brother with the words recorded in Matthew 4:19: "Follow me and I will make you fishers of men." Peter was present at most of the important events of Jesus' earthly ministry and was the first apostle to whom he appeared after the Resurrection. He was the acknowledged leader of the apostles from the beginning, and Roman Catholics consider him the first pope.

In contrast to the uneducated Peter, who had been with Jesus from the beginning of his public ministry and who effortlessly accepted him as the Son of God, the well-educated Paul had never met Jesus. In fact, he was very likely the foremost anti-Christian of the day. Paul, known as Saul before his conversion, was born probably a year after Jesus at Tarsus in Cilicia, a region of southeastern Asia Minor. He was a prominent Jew and a Roman citizen, becoming active in the movement to persecute Christians. So consuming was his desire to root out Christianity that he obtained authority from the high Jewish priest in Jerusalem to go to Damascus to continue his search for Christians. One of the most famous stories from the New Testament concerns Saul's dramatic conversion on the road to Damascus by a blinding light from heaven and the voice of Jesus saying, "Saul, Saul, why do you persecute me?" Saul became a Christian—changing his name to Paul—and one of the most important Christian missionaries the world has ever seen.

St. Peter is the patron saint of fishermen and sailors in some areas, as well as of keymakers since according to Matthew 16:19 he was to carry the keys of Christ's kingdom. Since the 10th century he has been referred to in popular tradition as the heavenly gatekeeper, who guards the celestial premises and admits or turns away applicants according to their merits. Local observances in St. Peter's honor can still be found in scattered American fishing communities and in those areas with large Roman Catholic populations.

June 30

The "Pentagon Papers" Case Is Decided

By the early 1970s, the ongoing Vietnam War had generated serious domestic opposition within the United States. Some of this opposition manifested itself in the form of protest rallies, the public burning of draft cards, and picketing outside military recruitment and induction centers. Dissent also developed within the military establishment itself.

One such dissenter was Daniel Ellsberg, who had worked for both the Department of Defense and the Rand Corporation, a prestigious research organization and think-tank. Ellsberg and a friend stole a top-secret dossier entitled "History of United States Decision-Making Process on Vietnam Policy" that contained thousands of pages of documents. They also stole a study of the famous Gulf of Tonkin incident, in which a clash between American and North Vietnamese naval vessels led to congressional approval for greater American involvement in the Vietnam conflict. Ellsberg and his friend passed the documents on to both the *New York Times* and the *Washington Post* newspapers.

On June 13, 1971, the *New York Times* began publishing excerpts from these so-called "Pentagon Papers," with more excerpts following in the its daily editions. On June 15 the administration of President Richard Nixon began proceedings in federal court for a restraining order against the *Times*. When the *Post* began publishing its own excerpts from the Pentagon Papers, the government began parallel proceedings against the *Post*, but they were secondary to the legal action against the *Times*.

The proceedings moved with lightning speed through the federal court system, since the government claimed that national security was being compromised, while the *Times* invoked the important First Amendment protection of freedom of the press. Hearings, decisions, and appeals that would normally take years were handled in a matter of days. On June 18, 1971, a federal district court in New York City held a hearing, and on the 19th it issued its decision. Although the district court denied the government an injunction, it restrained the *Times* from further publication while the government filed its appeal. This appeal was heard by a court of appeals on the 22nd, and was denied on the 23rd. The case then went to the United States Supreme Court on June 24, the parties argued their case before the Court in Washington, D.C., on the 26th, and the Court issued its decision on June 30, 1971.

The Supreme Court upheld the right of the *New York Times*, and other newspapers such as the *Post*, to publish the Pentagon Papers. Although the Court did not give the press an unlimited right to publish whatever it wished regardless of national security, it did hold that the government always has a heavy burden of proof in seeking an injunction against the press, which had not been met in this case. In fact, although they were sensationalized by these proceedings, the Pentagon Papers were actually rather unremarkable except to historians. The Pentagon Papers case is one of the strongest reaffirmations of freedom of the press in modern times.

Ellsberg was eventually prosecuted for the initial crime of having stolen the Pentagon Papers in the first place, which was not protected by the Constitution. The case was dismissed, however, when it was revealed that the Nixon administration had illegally wiretapped Ellsberg's personal conversations.

Twenty-sixth Amendment Ratified

Eighteen-year-olds gained the right to vote in all elections, federal, state, and local, with the ratification of the 26th Amendment to the United States Constitution on June 30, 1971. The amendment was approved by Congress and submitted to the states for ratification on March 23, 1971. It was ratified in only three months and seven days, far more rapidly than was the previous record holder, the 12th Amendment, which took six months and six days.

The text of the 26th Amendment is as follows:
Section 1. The right of citizens of the United States, who are eighteen years of age or older, to vote shall not be denied or abridged by the United States or any state on account of age.
Section 2. The Congress shall have the power to enforce this article by appropriate legislation.

When Congress approved an extension of the Voting Rights Act of 1965 in June 1970, it attached to the measure an amendment that would have lowered the voting age to 18 in all elections, effective January 1, 1971. As of the time of Congress's extension of the act, only four states had given the vote to persons under 21 years of age. Georgia and Kentucky allowed 18-year-olds to vote, Alaska 19-year-olds, and Hawaii 20-year-olds. Although President Richard M. Nixon declared himself in favor of a lowered voting age, he and many constitutional experts believed that such a change could not be applied to local and state elections by congressional legislation. The president therefore pressed for a constitutional amendment to guarantee the vote to 18-year-olds, while at the same time asking for an immediate court test of the constitutionality of the new legislation.

By a narrow five to four majority, the justices of the U.S. Supreme Court ruled on December 21, 1970, that the provision of the law empowering 18-year-olds to vote in presidential, vice-presidential, and congressional elections was constitutional. However, it ruled invalid that part of the law that lowered the voting age in state and local elections, stating that Congress does not have authority to legislate in that area.

On the day that the court handed down its decision, Senator Edward M. Kennedy, a Democrat from Massachusetts, introduced into the Senate a draft of a constitutional amendment to give 18-year-olds the vote in all elections. As soon as Congress had given final (and overwhelming) approval, the amendment was ratified by the states of Minnesota, Connecticut, Delaware, Tennessee, and Washington (March 23, 1971). Other states acted swiftly as well, and the necessary approval of three-fourths of all the states was obtained on June 30, 1971, when Ohio became the 38th state to ratify the amendment. As of that date, therefore, the United States acquired an additional 11 million eligible voters, aged 18 to 21.

Granting 18- to 21-year-old citizens the right to vote corrected a great injustice. Although young people have often been called upon to fight in this country's wars, they have frequently been too young to vote for or against the people who send them off to war. This question of being "old enough to take a bullet but too young for the ballot box" reached its climax during the Vietnam War with its massive student protests. The perceived unfairness was the impetus behind the 26th Amendment. Unfortunately, after the Vietnam War the 18- to 21-year-old segment of the population proved to be largely uninterested in politics, and voter turnout in that group is one of the lowest in American society. Even "young people" issues such as the gradual rise in the states' drinking ages from 18 to 21 in the 1980s failed to significantly increase participation in the electoral process.

July

July, originally the fifth month of the Roman year, was accordingly known as Quintilis, derived from the Latin word for five, *quinque*. When the ancient calendar was revised, January and February being added to the beginning of the calendar year, July became the seventh month but still retained its original name. It was renamed July in 44 B.C. in honor of Gaius Julius Caesar (102 B.C.–44 B.C.), the Roman statesman, military leader, and writer. Ambrosius Theodosius Macrobius, a Roman writer of the early fifth century A.D., explained the circumstances behind the change of name: "The month was called Julius in honor of the dictator Julius Caesar in accordance with a law proposed by the consul Marcus Antonius, the son of Marcus. It was so called because Julius had been born in this month on the fourth day before the Ides of Quintilis [the 15th day of July]."

Mark Antony (83 B.C.–30 B.C.), a kinsman of Caesar's, had unsuccessfully tried to persuade the Romans to make Caesar emperor. The best that he could do was to induce the Roman senate to vote to Julius Caesar the tribute of having his birth month called after him. The number of days allotted July, previously only 30, was also raised to 31. Mark Antony played a prominent role in subsequent Roman history as well, although he is perhaps most widely remembered for his fatal affair with the Egyptian queen Cleopatra.

The naming of July after Julius Caesar was the first historical example of applying to the Roman calendar the custom, practiced especially in the eastern part of the Mediterranean world, of calling a month after a living ruler. The honorific month seems to be of Athenian origin, the first person known to have received the privilege in the Greek calendar being the ancient king of Macedon and conqueror of Athens, Demetrius Poliocretes, in 307 B.C. The custom then spread throughout the East and eventually to Rome.

The honor was a tribute to Julius Caesar, who after the long years of civil strife had undertaken numerous administrative reforms in Rome, including the revision of the inaccurate ancient calendar. The resulting calendar, adopted in 45 B.C. (see Appendix A: The Calendar), remained in popular usage until Pope Gregory XIII revised it in the 16th century.

July 7 was the festival of Juno Caprotina, in honor of Juno in her role as the protector of female slaves. On July 8 the important festival of Castor and Pollux, the twins called the Dioscuri, took place. Castor and Pollux were identified with the zodiacal constellation Gemini. The cult of the twins, identified with athletic and military prowess, was a popular one in Rome and a temple was erected in their honor in the Forum.

The Anglo-Saxons called the month of July Litha-se-oefterra, meaning "lithe" or "mild"; Heg-monath, meaning "hay month"; and Maed-monath, because the meadows were in bloom and the cattle were then turned out to feed. Until the end of the 18th century, the name of the month was pronounced with the accent on the first syllable (as noted in Samuel Johnson's dictionary), thus recalling its derivation from *Julius*. For example, the English poets Sir John Suckling and William Wordsworth rhymed it with "newly" and "truly" respectively. The lucky birthstone often associated with July is the ruby, which symbolizes contentment.

July 1

Civil War: Battle of Gettysburg Begins

Victory and conquest are only occasionally synonymous. During the Civil War, the goal of the South was not to conquer the North, but to gain from it a recognition of the Confederacy's self-proclaimed independence from the Union. To win meant not to lose, and, in that perspective, the Southern invasion of Northern territory during the summer of 1863 was a tactic of offense in a strategy of defense. The Confederate leaders hoped that a thrust deep into hitherto secure Union states would undermine the enemy's morale and significantly increase the already sizable number of Northerners willing to accommodate the Confederacy's demands. Such an attack would also shift the theater of conflict into Union territory and might force the recall of Union forces in Southern territory.

Confederate general Robert E. Lee spent the month of June 1863 maneuvering the three corps of his 89,000-man Army of Northern Virginia north from Fredericksburg, Virginia, toward Pennsylvania. Union general Joseph Hooker followed Lee's path, and kept his 120,000-man Army of the Potomac interposed between the enemy and the Union capital at Washington, D.C. Hooker, angered by interference from the Union general-in-chief Henry W. Halleck, asked to be relieved of command, and President Abraham Lincoln ordered General George G. Meade to take the assignment in Hooker's stead. Meade's objective was to catch and defeat Lee before he could cross the Susquehanna River and attack the Pennsylvania state capital of Harrisburg.

By the end of June the opposing armies had crossed the Pennsylvania state line and were concentrated near Gettysburg, approximately 36 miles southwest of Harrisburg. On the morning of July 1, elements of the two forces accidentally met, touching off the most memorable battle of the Civil War: the battle of Gettysburg. Major General John Buford's federal cavalry, scouting ahead of the main units, encountered General James J. Pettigrew's brigade of Lieutenant General Ambrose P. Hill's Confederate III Corps as it moved toward Gettysburg to capture a supply of shoes reported to be there. Buford recognized the importance of the town as a communications center and undertook a valiant effort to defend it. Although badly outnumbered, his cavalrymen repulsed assaults by Confederate units commanded by Major Generals Henry Heth and William D. Pender. The Union

I and XI Corps, under Major Generals John F. Reynolds and Oliver O. Howard, respectively, soon came to Buford's aid.

The fighting, which began at roughly 10:00 a.m., slackened around noon. The Confederates had taken McPherson's Ridge west of Gettysburg and were threatening to overrun Seminary Ridge, their next objective. During the afternoon, the battle resumed as the Confederate II Corps under Lieutenant General Richard S. Ewell arrived in the battle area. The Confederates drove the Union I and XI Corps from Seminary Ridge back to Cemetery Hill. Although the first day of the battle of Gettysburg thus ended as a Southern victory, Meade decided that this was the proper time for a showdown with Lee.

During the night of July 1–2, Meade aligned the main body of Union troops along Cemetery Ridge, which ran in a north-south direction. Expecting that Lee would attack his northern flank in an attempt to cut his lines of communication along the nearby Baltimore Pike, Meade placed additional troops in the area of Cemetery and Culp's Hills to the northeast of the ridge. He gave little coverage to Round Top and Little Round Top on his southern flank.

Lee dispersed his army along the Union front with Ewell's corps on the north, Hill's in the center, and Lieutenant General James Longstreet's I Corps on the south. The Confederate commander had considered attacking the enemy's northern flank, but Ewell's report that he would not be able to take Cemetery and Culp's Hills dissuaded him. Lee's attention then focused on the Union southern flank, which he planned to attack with two of Longstreet's divisions. He ordered Ewell and Hill to make secondary attacks in their sectors to prevent Meade from sending assistance to the exposed flank.

After numerous delays, the second day's fighting began around 4:00 p.m. as Major General John Bell Hood's division of Longstreet's I Corps drove forward. Severe fighting ensued in what historians refer to as the Wheat Field, the Apple Orchard, and the Peach Orchard on the southern flank, and Hood suffered a wound that permanently deprived him of the use of his left arm. Hill and Ewell failed to attack with sufficient vigor in their sectors, however, and Meade was able to shift his troops and stop the rebel advance.

Both sides held councils of war after the July 2 engagement. The progress of the battle had discouraged Meade, but with some hesitation he decided to continue his stand in Gettysburg. Lee, on the other hand, was confident that the next day would bring victory. Morale was high, the Confederates were gaining ground, and Major General

George E. Pickett had just arrived with a fresh division. Lee planned to assault the center of the Union line with ten brigades supported by 159 artillery pieces. Only Longstreet disagreed: He thought that the Confederates should first let the Union take the offense, and then repulse them with heavy losses as they had done at Bull Run, Antietam, and Fredericksburg.

General Longstreet commanded the Confederate force that made the assault on July 3. Historians have called the action Pickett's Charge, but that Virginian general led only four of the ten Confederate brigades that engaged the Union forces. The Confederate infantry began its attack around 1:45 P.m. They advanced steadily with Brigadier General James Pettigrew's four brigades on the left and Pickett's men on the right. Major General Isaac R. Trimble's two brigades followed Pettigrew's troops.

Meade guessed that Lee would strike his center, because Lee had previously attacked both flanks. The Union forces accordingly worked through the night perfecting their defenses and were ready for the Confederate assault. As the Confederates drew close, heavy fire opened into the two brigades on Pettigrew's left flank. Trimble's men were not in a good position to give assistance, and so the Confederate line began to collapse. The battle ended as Longstreet withdrew and reorganized his forces.

Rain on July 4 prevented the expected Union attack, and Lee took advantage of the weather to begin his retreat to southern territory. The Confederate military effort had reached its peak: Although few recognized it at the time, the turning point of the Civil War had been reached.

Approximately 88,000 Union troops and 75,000 Confederate troops participated in the battle of Gettysburg. There is considerable disagreement about the accuracy of the casualty reports, but approximately 3,155 Union soldiers and 3,903 Confederate soldiers lost their lives. The total number of wounded, missing, and dead reached approximately 23,049 for the Union and 28,063 for the Confederacy. The battlefield became a national park on February 11, 1895, and is today a popular historical landmark that attracts thousands of tourists every year. Over a thousand monuments and markers can be seen.

World War II: The Bretton Woods Conference Begins

On July 1, 1944, the United Nations Monetary and Financial Conference began at Bretton Woods, a popular vacation resort in New Hampshire. Over time, this important conference has become popularly referred to as the Bretton Woods Conference. It was the culmination of proposals concerning the necessity of an international currency fund that dated back to the mid-1930s. As World War II entered its final stages, these ideas saw fruition in the broader context of American support for international organizations such as the United Nations to help guarantee postwar political, economic, and military stability.

The conference ended on July 22, 1944, when the 45 participating nations adopted the Articles of Agreement. These articles led to the establishment of the International Monetary Fund (IMF) and the International Bank for Reconstruction and Development. The conference endorsed the principles of free market economics and international trade, and adopted the United States's dollar as the world's international currency. In taking the latter position, the conference was in fact recognizing that the United States was now the world's predominant economic power and would inevitably be shouldering the burden of worldwide reconstruction since it had the only major economy not ravaged by war.

Of the institutions established by the Bretton Woods Conference, the IMF has particular importance in international finance. It began operating in 1947, and currently has roughly 200 participating member nations. It is charged with promoting the expansion of international trade, maintaining orderly currency rates, assisting member nations with balance of trade surpluses and deficits, and encouraging the free flow of capital across national borders. Membership is open to all sovereign and independent countries.

Naturally, the United States plays a leading role in the activities of the IMF. As with all nations, America is assigned a certain quota in IMF special drawing rights (SDRs), which are fiscal units that represent a country's relative share of world economic output. Despite the rapid industrialization of the third world over the past several decades, and the rise of Japan as a major economic power, the United States still wields considerable influence in IMF determinations. The IMF has on occasion been important in assisting American allies, such as certain important third-world nations in the 1970s who experienced financial difficulties and received assistance from the IMF as a lender of last resort. The IMF has also been important in assisting the formerly Communist nations of the Soviet Union and Eastern Europe in their transition to market-based economies after the end of the cold war.

The IMF is headquartered in Washington, D.C. Its executive authority consists of a board of governors composed of officials from the member nations. There is also a 22-member executive board that supervises day-to-day functions.

July 2

Thurgood Marshall's Birthday

Photo by Harris and Ewing, Collection of the Supreme Court of the United States.

Thurgood Marshall

Thurgood Marshall, the first African American justice of the United States Supreme Court, was born in Baltimore, Maryland, on July 2, 1908. His father was William Canfield Marshall, a railroad porter. His mother was Norma Arica Marshall, a graduate of New York City's Columbia Teacher's College. Marshall grew up in Baltimore and attended a segregated high school, from which he graduated at the age of 16. He entered Lincoln University in Chester, Pennsylvania, and graduated in 1930. Marshall then entered Howard University Law School in Washington, D.C., and graduated in 1933 at the top of his class.

After law school, Marshall returned to Baltimore where he entered private practice. In 1936, however, he joined the national legal staff of the National Association for the Advancement of Colored People (NAACP). The NAACP is one of the nation's leading African American civil rights organizations, and the legal staff was charged with both protecting and expanding civil rights guarantees. In 1938 Marshall became the chief legal officer.

Marshall soon demonstrated his excellent legal skills. He litigated a wide variety of cases in both state and federal courts, and represented the NAACP in legal arguments before the United States Supreme Court. In 1940 the NAACP established a Legal Defense and Education Fund with Marshall as its head. It was Marshall's task to use the courts as a means of overturning the wide variety of racial segregation laws then in force throughout the country, most notably in the South. Marshall went on to argue a total of 32 cases before the United States Supreme Court and won 29 of them. His strategy was to begin with attacking segregated schools, in particular, segregated graduate schools and law schools, for which he felt that the Supreme Court justices—as law school graduates themselves—would have a particular affinity.

In 1950, in the case of *Sweatt* v. *Painter*, Marshall successfully persuaded the Supreme Court to order the integration of the law schools at the University of Texas and the University of Oklahoma. This victory was the opening wedge in his campaign against segregated schools, which culminated in the landmark Supreme Court decision of *Brown* v. *Board of Education* in 1954. Although it took roughly two decades to implement, this historic decision declared that racial discrimination in all public schools from the elementary level on up was unconstitutional.

This victory cemented Marshall's reputation in the national legal community. As the civil rights movement gained momentum, and further legal victories ended segregation in other areas, Marshall was increasingly considered for a position in the federal judiciary. In 1961 President John F. Kennedy appointed him as a judge for the United States Court of Appeals for the Second Circuit. Despite strong opposition from southerners in the United States Senate, which tied up the proceedings for several months, Marshall was ultimately confirmed. During his four-year tenure on the second circuit, Marshall wrote over 100 opinions, none of which were overturned by the Supreme Court. In 1965 President Lyndon B. Johnson appointed Marshall the solicitor general of the United States, which is charged with the responsibility of representing the United States government before the Supreme Court.

On June 13, 1967, President Johnson nominated Marshall to succeed Supreme Court justice Thomas C. Clark. Marshall, the first African American Supreme Court justice, was confirmed by the United States Senate on August 30, 1967.

During the nearly 24 years that Marshall served on the Court, he took consistently liberal positions on the issues presented before it. Naturally, he supported the constitutionality and vigorous enforcement of federal civil rights laws that had been enacted during the Johnson administration and were used with increasing aggressiveness by the federal authorities to eradicate segregation and curb racism. Under the leadership of Chief Justice Earl Warren, Marshall was typically in the majority when the Court issued its opinions. In the 1970s, however, both the nation in general and the Supreme Court in particular became increasingly conservative. This trend was more pronounced after the election of Ronald Reagan to the presidency in 1980. Over this passage of time, Marshall increasingly found himself in the minority, writing dissenting opinions on such topics as the constitutionality of the death penalty. Marshall strongly believed that not only was the death penalty unconstitutional under the Eighth Amendment, which forbids cruel and unusual punishment, but that it was a punishment disproportionately directed at members of minority communities. Although the available evidence does suggest that the percentage of African Americans out of the total number of persons executed for capital crimes is much higher than the total percentage of African Americans present in the general population, Marshall was unsuccessful in convincing the Court to strike down death penalty laws as inherently unconstitutional.

Nevertheless, Marshall's career on the Court was successful and he was a highly respected justice. On June 27, 1991, suffering from poor health and now 82 years old, Marshall retired from the Supreme Court. He died in Washington, D.C., on January 24, 1993, of heart failure.

President James A. Garfield Assassinated

At the conclusion of a cabinet meeting on June 30, 1881, President James A. Garfield (see November 19) asked Robert Lincoln, the secretary of war and the son of Abraham Lincoln, about a nightmare that President Lincoln had shortly before his assassination. The secretary told of the dream in which his father had seen a corpse on display in the East Room of the White House. In the dream, President Lincoln asks, "Who is dead in the White House?" and the sentry guarding the body replies, "The president." Garfield and the other officials listened intently as Robert Lincoln recounted the incident, but they were only momentarily impressed by its prophetic quality. No one present would have believed that only two days later, on July 2, 1881, an assassin's bullet would strike Garfield.

The day of the tragedy was to have been the beginning of a holiday for the 20th president of the United States. To escape the hot Washington summer, Garfield planned to go to the New Jersey seaside resort of Elberon and then on to Williamstown, Massachusetts, where he was to attend his 25th class reunion at Williams College. A special railroad car had been reserved for the president and his accompanying cabinet members, which was attached to the train that was scheduled to leave Washington's Baltimore and Potomac Railway depot at 9:30 a.m. on July 2, 1881.

Garfield and his secretary of state, James G. Blaine, arrived at the railroad station at Sixth and B Streets at about 9:20 a.m. on the fateful day. After remaining in Blaine's carriage for roughly ten minutes, the two men made their way to the train. The waiting room of the depot was almost deserted, but as the president and secretary of state passed the empty benches, two gunshots rang out. The bullets found their intended target; Garfield gasped, "My God, what is this?" and sank to the floor.

Garfield's assailant, Charles J. Guiteau, fled from the scene immediately after firing the shots even though he realized that he would not be able to escape and was ready to accept imprisonment. He feared, however, that the inflamed emotions of the moment might result in his being lynched on the spot. When patrolman Patrick Kearney caught and arrested Guiteau, Guiteau said, "Keep quiet, my friend. I wish to go to jail."

Guiteau's life had always been as erratic and yet calculating as his actions and words at the Baltimore and Potomac depot. His father, Luther Guiteau, was the superintendent of schools for Freeport, Illinois, and a friend of John H. Noyes, the founder of the polygamous utopian community at Oneida, New York. Young Charles Guiteau joined the Oneida group in his late teens, but found farm life uninteresting. He left for New York City, where he tried to promote his religious views in a short-lived newspaper called the *New York Theocrat*. Moving to Chicago, he married there and found a position as a clerk in a law firm. For over ten years, Guiteau made his living by swindling and cheating gullible merchants, pawnbrokers, and boardinghouse owners.

Beginning in 1873, Guiteau fell on hard times. His wife grew tired of his questionable activities and divorced him. The newspapers exposed his improper behavior as a collections lawyer. Guiteau became increasingly unbalanced, and began to entertain the delusion that he would eventually become president of the United States.

The shooting of President Garfield.

James Garfield's candidacy for president in 1880 sparked Guiteau's hopes. He offered his services as a public speaker to the Republican Party and passed out copies of his prepared speech, "Garfield and Hancock," to all who would accept them. Guiteau even sent a copy to Garfield himself with the suggestion that Guiteau should receive an appointment as United States Consul to Vienna, Austria, as a reward. After Garfield's inauguration, Guiteau managed to see the president at the White House, where he begged Garfield for an appointment as consul in Paris, France. When the president ignored him, Guiteau sought the assistance of Secretary of State Blaine, who also ignored him. Frustrated beyond his limited endurance, Guiteau (in a letter that Garfield probably never saw) warned the president to remove Blaine or "you and the Republican Party will come to grief."

Blaming Garfield personally for his plight, Guiteau came to believe that he was part of a divine plan to kill the president. On June 6, 1881, with money borrowed from a cousin, Guiteau bought a .44-caliber British Bulldog pistol, a box of cartridges, and a penknife from O'Meara's Gun Shop. He selected a pistol with a white bone handle because, as he later testified at his trial, he believed that it would look better in a museum.

For the next four weeks Guiteau divided his time between target practice at an isolated place along the Potomac and following Garfield through the streets of the capital. Guiteau let several opportunities to shoot the president pass. However, when he heard that Garfield would be leaving Washington on July 2, he decided that that day would give him the ideal opportunity to carry out his plan.

Early on July 2, Guiteau wrote a letter explaining his intended actions. He asserted that he held no ill will toward Garfield, but that the "President's tragic death was a sad necessity, [and] . . . it will unite the Republican Party and save the Republic." Then, Guiteau left for the depot.

One of Guiteau's two shots merely grazed Garfield's left arm. The other bullet, however, lodged in Garfield's back and proved to be a mortal wound. In a state of deep shock and only partially conscious, the president was moved to the second floor of the depot. Members of the cabinet quickly gathered at his side. The sight of the stricken president was particularly upsetting to Robert Lincoln, and he remarked in dismay: "How many hours of sorrow I have passed in this town."

The first doctors to examine Garfield believed that the president would not live out the day. They did, however, permit him to be moved. In a bed hastily mounted on a wagon, he was brought back to the White House only a few hours after he had started out for his intended summer holiday.

For two days Garfield was close to death. On July 5, however, his condition stabilized and for the first time since the shooting he was able to eat and retain food. The many doctors attending the president concluded that the bullet had entered his back, been deflected downward through his peritoneal cavity, and was embedded in the front wall of his abdomen. However, since they were unsure of its exact location, they hesitated to probe for the bullet. Instead, their treatment of the president amounted to little more than intensive nursing care, and blood poisoning posed the greatest threat to Garfield's life in the days that followed.

Room number 18, situated on the south side of the second floor of the White House and commanding a view of the Potomac River, became Garfield's sickroom. The doctors attending the president allowed his wife, Lucretia, and his children to visit frequently. Several trusted advisers and the wives of cabinet members were also permitted to see him; the latter often helped fan Garfield during the hot Washington summer.

Since he had survived the initial crisis, many observers believed that Garfield would recover. However, on July 23 he took a turn for the worse, and his condition steadily deteriorated. The track taken by the bullet through Garfield's body had become infected, but at that time there were no antibiotics for treatment. In short, the doctors were helpless. They did, however, enlist the help of inventor Alexander Graham Bell in their effort to find the bullet. By the end of July, Bell had devised an electrical instrument with which he hoped to pinpoint the bullet's location. On August 1, Bell used his invention on Garfield. The findings were inconclusive, however, and it is questionable whether the president would have survived the necessary surgery to remove the bullet anyway.

Throughout his long ordeal, Garfield displayed courage and fortitude. By the end of August, however, his physical condition was "absolutely critical" according to a friend. The heat of the Washington summer compounded the president's suffering, and he desperately wanted to leave the nation's capital. At first his doctors were reluctant to move him, but they finally agreed that a stay at the seashore might prove beneficial. Charles Franklyn offered Garfield the use of his 25-room house in Elberon, New Jersey, and plans to transport the stricken president to that resort were quickly put in motion.

Garfield withstood the railroad trip to Elberon on September 6, 1881, so well that hopes for his eventual recovery resurged. Several days later, however, the weakened president developed pneumonia. On September 19, 1881, he complained of severe chest pains, and in the evening he lost consciousness. He died at 10:35 p.m. that evening.

Garfield's death plunged the nation into mourning. On September 21 his body was returned to Washington, and for the next two days the president's casket lay in state in the rotunda of the Capitol Building. During that time more than 100,000 persons filed past the bier. On September 23 a special service honoring President Garfield took place in the rotunda, and then his remains were placed aboard a funeral train and carried to their final resting place in Cleveland, Ohio.

As the train passed through the major cities, towns, and villages along its route, bells tolled to express the nation's grief. Thousands of citizens stood along the railroad tracks and paid their final respects to the president. In downtown Cleveland a public funeral was held for Garfield, and then his remains were entombed at Lakeview Cemetery several miles away. Public observances honoring Garfield did not conclude until February 27, 1882, when President Chester A. Arthur eulogized his predecessor before a joint session of Congress.

On November 14, 1881, the trial of Garfield's assassin began. Guiteau based his defense on a plea of insanity, but on January 5, 1882, he was found guilty as charged. He was hanged on June 30, 1882, before a crowd of over 200 spectators.

Garfield's death produced one positive result. The bizarre motivation of his assassin emphasized the abuses of the spoils system, whereby governmental jobs were distributed as rewards for support during election campaigns. In the months following Garfield's death, an outraged public demanded an end to this system, resulting in the passage of the Pendleton Act, which reformed the federal bureaucracy and established the modern Civil Service.

Civil Rights Act of 1964

On July 2, 1964, the most sweeping civil rights legislation since the Reconstruction era was signed into law in a nationally televised ceremony by President Lyndon B. Johnson, who had personally overseen the legislative effort in Congress.

The initiatives contained within the Civil Rights Act of 1964 were originally proposed by President John F. Kennedy. The widespread grief following his assassination in 1963 helped mobilize popular support for civil rights causes. Johnson, who had once served as Senate majority leader and was an astute politician, took advantage of this support and used it to push the act through Congress despite some stiff resistance by Southern Democrats.

As passed by substantial majorities (290 to 130 in the House of Representatives and 73 to 27 in the Senate), the Civil Rights Act of 1964 prohibited discrimination on the basis of race in public accommodations, in publicly owned or operated facilities, in employment and union membership, and in the registration of voters. Although generally requiring remedies to be attempted first on a local or state basis, the law authorized the United States attorney general to initiate legal actions to end discrimination in jobs, public accommodations, and public facilities. The attorney general was also authorized to assist in private civil rights suits of general public importance.

One important feature of the act was that it authorized the attorney general to bring school desegregation suits in cases where private citizens were unable to sue effectively. It was hoped that these actions would hasten school desegregation, which had gone on at a foot-dragging pace since the Supreme Court's historic 1954 ruling in *Brown* v. *Board of Education*. Another important provision was Title VI, which prohibited discrimination in all federally aided projects and programs throughout the country, and provided for the cutoff of federal funds where discrimination persisted. Since the amount of federal aid to state and local programs is considerable, Title VI provided yet another incentive to state and local authorities to comply with the federal policy of desegregation.

The act also

(1) made a sixth-grade education a (rebuttable) qualification for voting;

(2) authorized technical and financial help in the desegregation of school districts;

(3) established a federal Equal Employment Opportunity Commission to investigate and fight alleged discrimination in employment;

(4) created a Community Relations Service, as part of the Department of Commerce, to help localities reconcile racial disputes;

(5) increased access to the federal courts for state criminal defendants alleging civil rights violations; and

(6) ordered the Census Bureau to assemble statistics, by race, on registration and voting in certain areas designated by the Commission on Civil Rights.

Hussey's Reaper First Exhibited

Obed Hussey of Maryland exhibited a reaper in public for the first time on July 2, 1833, on the grounds of the Hamilton County Agricultural Society in New York state. Late in December of that same year, he obtained a patent on the reaper.

There had been reaping machines long before Hussey's. The Roman historian Pliny, writing in A.D. 23, mentions one used in the lowlands of Gaul (modern-day France). It consisted of a cart carrying a box. On the front edge of the box were sharp projecting teeth. Pushed through the grain by an ox, it caught the heads of the grain, and a man sitting in the box raked them in. Reapers did not become widespread until the 19th century, however, since the technology used was so primitive.

Hussey's machine contained pointed knives, which vibrated through a bar and cut the grain. The grain fell on a platform, and was raked by a man riding on the machine. Although Hussey was the first to secure a patent for a practical reaper, he had a competitor in Cyrus H. McCormick (see February 15), who first demonstrated his reaper in 1831. McCormick's machine, patented in 1834, was similar to Hussey's in many respects but generally regarded as superior. Although Hussey manufactured his machine in competition with McCormick from 1834 to 1858, he was eventually overshadowed by his rival. Hussey died in 1860.

July 3

Idaho Admitted to the Union

On July 3, 1890, Idaho entered the Union as the 43rd state. The name of the new state was first used during the 1850s to designate a region in what is now Colorado that was later known as Idaho Springs. The word *Idaho* is derived from the Shoshone *Ee-Da-How*, referring possibly to the ubiquitous purple flowers of the area, but also translated as "gem of the mountains" or "behold the sun coming down the mountain."

Idaho was originally part of the vast northwest Oregon, or Columbia River, country claimed by Spain, Russia, Great Britain, and the United States. In 1818 a treaty provided for joint rule of the area by the United States and Great Britain. At first limited to ten years, joint rule was later extended. In 1846 the United States gained sole possession of the Oregon country below the 49th parallel. The American claim to this northwestern area stemmed primarily from the explorations by Meriwether Lewis and William Clark, who were probably the first non-native people to pass through Idaho, in 1805. En route to the Pacific, they crossed the Continental Divide at Lemhi Pass, traversed the Bitterroot Mountains, and followed the Clearwater, Snake, and Columbia Rivers. They passed through the same part of Idaho again the next year on their return.

Reports of the numerous fur-bearing animals in the area attracted trappers, the majority of whom were acting on behalf of large fur companies. In 1809 David Thompson, a noted explorer for the British North West Company, penetrated Idaho from the north and erected the trading post of Kully-spell House on the eastern banks of Lake Pend Oreille. In the spring of 1810 alone, the region's pelt yield totaled almost fifty 90-pound packs. Also in 1810 Andrew Henry of the Missouri Fur Company made an unsuccessful attempt to establish a trading post near what is now Rexburg, Idaho. In 1811 Wilson Price Hunt, representing John Jacob Astor's Pacific Fur Company, explored the Snake River country. Captain B. L. E. Bonneville's expedition entered the region in 1832, and two years later Fort Hall was built by Nathaniel Wyeth of Boston, Massachusetts, on the east bank of the upper Snake River.

The Reverend Henry H. Spaulding helped establish a settlement at Lapwai, near what is now Lewiston, Idaho, in 1836. Several years later Jesuit priests led by Father P. J. De Smet founded a missionary settlement on the Coeur d'Alene River. Mormon missionaries, extending their horizons northward from their settlement in Salt Lake City, Utah, set up a mission and colony in the valley of the Lemhi River in 1855. They left three years later, however, due to early frosts, plagues of grasshoppers, and poor relations with the local Bannock and Shoshone tribes.

None of these early settlements were truly permanent. On June 15, 1860, however, another pioneering band of Mormons established a settlement in Franklin, in the southeastern part of Idaho. June 15, the anniversary of their arrival, was proclaimed Idaho Pioneer Day in 1911.

Although many settlers passed through the Oregon Trail beginning in the 1840s, going through southern Idaho en route to further destinations, they passed Idaho by. Thus the Idaho region, which had been transferred from the Oregon Territory to the newly formed Washington Territory in 1853, continued to rank among the "unsettled" portions of the West. It was only the backwash of the westward movement that finally resulted in any significant settlement. In 1860 Captain E. D. Pierce's discovery of gold at Orofino Creek, a tributary of the Clearwater River, lured hordes of prospectors from Oregon, Washington, California, and Nevada to Idaho. Mining towns mushroomed as the gold strike was followed by others on the Salmon River in 1861, on the Boise River basin in 1862, and on the Owyhee River in 1863.

The competing gold rushes stimulated the growth of rival mining centers, one in the north around Lewiston, the other in the south around Boise and Idaho City (first named Bannock). Numerous and vocal enough to demand a new government separate from that of the Washington Territory, the miners were also willing to join forces in order to achieve independent territorial status. The bill setting up the Territory of Idaho was signed by President Abraham Lincoln on March 3, 1863, during the Civil War.

The new territory, comprising the eastern portions of the Washington Territory and the western portions of the Dakota Territory, was one of the largest ever created in the United States. It included all of what are now the states of Idaho, Montana, and Wyoming, as well as small portions of North Dakota, South Dakota, and Nebraska. On March 17, 1863, William H. Wallace was appointed as the first territorial governor by President Lincoln. In July of that year, Governor Wallace proclaimed Lewiston the territorial capital, and it was there that the first and second sessions of the territorial legislature were held in December 1863 and November 1864, respectively. Soon afterward the capital was transferred to Boise, where it has remained ever since.

The Idaho Territory of 1863 was short-lived. The territorial act itself provided that nothing in it should be so construed as to prevent the government of the United States "from attaching any portion of said territory to any other state or territory." A little over a year later, Montana gold prospectors persuaded Congress to create the Montana Territory out of a large northern section of the Idaho Territory. In 1868 Wyoming was also taken away, leaving Idaho roughly as it is now.

As the Idaho Territory progressed agriculturally and industrially, a movement for statehood gained momentum. A state constitution was adopted in 1889, and Idaho entered the Union the following year. Mormon polygamy was an important issue in Idaho during these early days. Ever since the 1860s, large numbers of Mormon settlers had come into southern Idaho. In 1883 Idaho's territorial legislature began passing laws that denied polygamists the right to vote and that restricted the Mormons in other ways. Polygamy was violation of federal law as well. After the constitutionality of antipolygamy legislation was upheld by the United States Supreme Court in 1890, the leaders of the Mormon Church ruled that polygamy was not an essential article of faith, and Idaho removed its anti-Mormon restrictions.

Death of Jim Morrison

James Douglas Morrison was born in Melbourne, Florida, on December 8, 1943. His parents were George Stephen Morrison and Clara Clarke Morrison. Stephen Morrison was a naval officer, and his career kept the family constantly on the move. While the family was stationed in Albuquerque, New Mexico, in 1947, young Jim Morrison witnessed an event that he later said changed his life.

July 4

While the family was driving through the New Mexico desert, they came across a traffic accident in which a truck filled with Native American workers had been smashed. There were dead men strewn about the highway, and young Jim was profoundly disturbed by the sight. It may well be that this experience, perhaps compounded with his later drug use, explains some of the moodiness of Morrison's music.

After high school, Jim returned to Florida. In February 1964 he transferred from Florida State University to the Theatre Arts Department of the University of California at Los Angeles (UCLA), which was where he met John Densmore, Robby Krieger, and Ray Manzarek. The four formed a rock and roll group named The Doors, and after Jim's graduation from UCLA in 1965, the group began to pursue their musical ambitions on a full-time basis.

They earned a strong reputation by opening for such popular contemporary groups as The Animals, Buffalo Springfield, and The Byrds. After a disappointing round of negotiations with Columbia Records, the group was eventually signed by Elektra Records, and their first album *The Doors* was released in 1967. This album, which became a number-one hit, included the rock classics "Light My Fire" and "The End." Despite a variety of legal problems surrounding the frequently raucous and occasionally violent nature of their public performances, the group enjoyed strong popularity over the next several years and released such additional hit albums as *Waiting for the Sun* in 1968 and *L.A. Woman* in 1970. Unfortunately, during the height of his success, Morrison was experiencing severe personal problems, including heavy drug use. In 1971 Morrison took a vacation to France, where he died on July 3, 1971, of an overdose.

Like the actor James Dean, Morrison's short, turbulent, but creatively inspired life helped to make him a cultural icon. During his career, he released a total of seven albums, published four books, and wrote a wide variety of poetry and essays. The Doors, with their particular brand of psychedelic and often hypnotic music, have become recognized as one of the classics of rock and roll. In 1991 the movie *The Doors*, produced by Oliver Stone, was released. Interest in the music of The Doors in general and the life of Jim Morrison in particular continues to remain strong.

John Singleton Copley's Birthday

America's foremost colonial portrait artist, John Singleton Copley was born on July 3, 1738, in Boston, Massachusetts. When he was ten, his wid-

owed mother married Peter Pelham, a painter and engraver. Young John Copley learned a great deal about art from his stepfather and the artists who regularly held workshops in Pelham's studio.

By the age of 18, Copley was a professional portrait artist. His clarity of style and remarkable characterization made him popular. Soon he had commissions to paint the portraits of many of the most important people in New England. Shortly after his painting *Boy with a Squirrel* was exhibited in London in 1766, Copley was elected a fellow of the Society of Artists of Great Britain. In 1769 Copley married Suzannah Clarke, the daughter of a wealthy Boston merchant. The couple lived on Beacon Hill where their son, also named John Singleton Copley, was born in 1772.

In June 1774, just before the American Revolution, Copley left Boston with his family. He studied art in Europe for a while before finally settling in London. He was enormously successful in Great Britain, and received commissions to paint the portraits of members of the royal family, in addition to other notables. His studies in Italy had broadened his style, and in addition to portraits he began to paint historical subjects. His early American portraits, however, have usually won higher praise than his later work.

Toward the end of his life, Copley suffered from illness and financial problems. His son, who had become a successful British lawyer, helped support him. Copley died in London on September 3, 1815. His son went on to become a baron in 1827. Under the title Lord Lyndhurst, he served as lord chancellor of England three times, and led the Tories in Parliament's House of Lords.

July 4

Independence Day

Declaring independence from Great Britain was something of a last resort for the Americans. Thomas Jefferson, the author of the Declaration of Independence, wrote in June 1775 that "I am sincerely one of those . . . who would rather be in dependence on Great Britain, properly limited, than on any other nation on earth, or than on no nation."

After the French and Indian War ended in 1763, relations between the American colonies and Great Britain soured. The British government, in severe financial distress as a result of wartime military expenditures, sought to streamline its colonial administration and increase tax revenue from the colonies. In particular, King George III and his ministers wanted the colonists to pay

Thomas Jefferson, future president of the United States, presenting the Declaration of Independence.

for some part of their own defense. Many Americans, however, objected to the new British taxes. Measures such as the Stamp Act of 1765 drew especially strong opposition. The Stamp Act was repealed in 1766, but the Townshend Acts of 1767 levied new taxes. Merchants retaliated by boycotting British imports, and by 1770 all of the Townshend duties had been repealed except for the tax on tea.

Great Britain sent troops to maintain order in the colonies, but clashes between the colonists and British soldiers erupted. In 1770 the Boston Massacre took place when British soldiers fired into an angry mob. Attempts at reconciliation were made, but colonial discontent continued to grow. In 1773 opposition to the tea tax and to the tea monopoly of the British East India Company led a group of colonials to stage the famous Boston Tea Party (see December 16). In order to punish the rebellious colonists, Parliament passed the Coercive or "Intolerable" Acts of 1774, which authorized the closing of Boston harbor and prohibited town meetings without the governor's consent.

On September 5, 1774, the First Continental Congress convened in Philadelphia, Pennsylvania. The congress condemned the Coercive Acts, denounced Britain's imposition of taxes, and adopted a declaration of rights, which included the rights

of "life, liberty and property." The bloodshed at Lexington, Concord, and Bunker Hill in Massachusetts during 1775, together with the king's proclamation of August 23, 1775, stating that the Americans were in rebellion, further weakened the bonds between Great Britain and the colonies. By 1776 many of the colonists were ready to accept the inflammatory rhetoric of Thomas Paine's *Common Sense* (see January 29), with its description of King George as the "royal brute" and its call for an end to his reign in the New World.

In the spring of 1776, the movement for independence continued to advance. On April 12, 1776, the North Carolina convention instructed its delegates to the Second Continental Congress, then meeting in Philadelphia, to vote for independence. In turn, the Virginia convention, which met in Williamsburg, Virginia, on May 15, directed its delegates to ask the congress to "declare the United Colonies free and independent states, absolved from all allegiance to, or dependence on the Crown or Parliament of Great Britain." On the same day the Continental Congress, at the suggestion of John Adams, recommended that the various colonies assume all the powers of government.

Richard Henry Lee, a delegate from Virginia, brought the question of independence before the Second Continental Congress on June 7, 1776. With John Adams's support, Lee made the following motion: "Resolved, that these United Colonies are, and of right ought to be, free and independent States, that they are absolved from all allegiance to the British Crown, and that all political connection between them and the State of Great Britain is, and ought to be, totally dissolved." In subsequent debate moderate representatives persuaded their colleagues to delay a final vote for three weeks. In the meantime, however, "that no time be lost, in case the Congress agree thereto," John Adams, Benjamin Franklin, Thomas Jefferson, Robert R. Livingston, and Roger Sherman were appointed to draft a declaration of independence.

On July 1, 1776, the congress resumed debate on the Lee resolution and approved it the following day. On July 2, 1776, congress formally voted for independence. That same day, Jefferson brought his committee's proposed declaration of independence before the delegates, who debated its merits for two days and made certain revisions. The final version was ratified on July 4, 1776. John Hancock, the president of the congress, and Charles Thomson, its secretary, signed the document that same day. On July 9, 1776, the provincial congress of New York ordered its delegates to the Second Continental Congress, who had abstained from voting on July 4, to endorse the document. Thus, on July 19, 1776, the congress resolved to have the "unanimous declaration" written on parchment.

Written primarily by Thomas Jefferson, one of the most eloquent as well as one of the youngest of the revolutionary leaders, the Declaration of Independence begins with a preamble, which is an assertion of philosophical principles concerning natural rights. "The Unanimous Declaration of the Thirteen United States of America," as the document was titled, began with these ringing assertions:

> When in the Course of human events, it becomes necessary for one people to dissolve the political bands which have connected them with another, and to assume among the Powers of the earth, the separate and equal station to which the Laws of Nature and of Nature's God entitle them, a decent Respect to the Opinions of Mankind requires that they should declare the causes which impel them to the Separation.
>
> We hold these Truths to be self-evident, that all men are created equal, that they are endowed by their Creator with certain unalienable Rights, that among these are Life, Liberty, and the pursuit of Happiness. That to secure these rights, Governments are instituted among Men, deriving their just powers from the consent of the governed, that whenever any Form of Government becomes destructive of these Ends, it is the Right of the People to alter or to abolish it, and to institute a new Government . . . .

There is a complete copy of the Declaration of Independence in the appendices to this book.

Many years later, on May 8, 1825, Thomas Jefferson wrote to Richard Henry Lee that his task in drafting the Declaration of Independence had been

> not to find out new principles, or new arguments, never before thought of, not merely to say things which had never been said before; but to place before mankind the common sense of the subject, [in] terms so plain and firm as to command their assent, and to justify ourselves in the independent stand we [were] impelled to take. Neither aiming at originality of principle or sentiment, nor yet copied from any particular and previous writing, it was intended to be an expression of the American mind. . . . All its authority rests then on the harmonizing sentiments of the day, whether expressed in conversation, in letters, printed essays, or the elementary books of public

right, as Aristotle, Cicero, Locke, Sidney, etc.

Specific colonial grievances are set forth in the second section of the Declaration of Independence. Significantly, the authors did not mention Parliament, whose authority over the colonies they challenged, but instead blamed King George III for all of the wrongs. By declaring the monarch the villain and terminating their allegiance to him, the rebels severed what they alleged to be their sole link with the British Empire.

The third and final part of the Declaration of Independence was a reiteration of the Lee resolution, asserting that the colonies were now independent from Great Britain. The document ended with the delegates' statement that "for the support of this Declaration, . . . we mutually pledge to each other our Lives, our Fortunes, and our Sacred Honor."

The people of Philadelphia were the first to hear the Declaration of Independence. John Nixon, a member of Philadelphia's Committee of Public Safety, read it aloud to them on July 8, 1776, in the yard of the Pennsylvania State House (now known as Independence Hall). There was great popular exultation and church bells rang long into the night. The militia even used up some of their precious gunpowder to fire volleys in salutes to independence. News of the Declaration of Independence spread throughout the colonies in the weeks and months that followed.

On July 2, 1777, it occurred to an individual (whose name has been lost) in Philadelphia that the first anniversary of independence should be celebrated. Although rather hastily prepared, by all accounts the celebration that day was a success. Thus, for a time it appeared that independence would be celebrated annually on July 2. John Adams, like most of his contemporaries, certainly thought so. "It ought to be commemorated," Adams wrote, "as the day of deliverance, by solemn acts of devotion to God Almighty. It ought to be solemnized with pomp and parade, with shows, games, sports, guns, bells, bonfires, and illuminations, from one end of this continent to the other, from this time forward, forevermore." Over time, however, July 4 (the anniversary of the approval of the Declaration of Independence) became the more popular day for holding Independence Day celebrations. Today July 4 is a federal holiday, and festivities are held throughout the country in virtually every major city.

Calvin Coolidge's Birthday

Calvin Coolidge, the 30th president of the United States, was born in the tiny community of Plym-

Library of Congress

Calvin Coolidge

outh Notch in the Green Mountains of Vermont on July 4, 1872. He was named John Calvin for his father, but later dropped the first name. Coolidge's ancestors had immigrated to the American colonies from England in the 1630s. John Coolidge Sr. was a farmer and operated a country store. He was also a politician and served two terms in the Vermont legislature. Calvin Coolidge's mother died when young Calvin was only 12 years old.

Young Coolidge attended the Plymouth district school until 1885, when he entered the academy at Ludlow, ten miles from his home. He completed his preparation for college at St. Johnsbury Academy, entering Amherst College in 1891. He graduated with honors in 1895. His essay, "The Causes of the American Revolution," was awarded a gold medal by the American Historical Society as the best college senior essay on history.

In the autumn of 1895, Coolidge began to study law in the offices of Hammond and Field in Northampton, Massachusetts, and was admitted to the bar two years later. Shortly thereafter, he began his climb up the ladder of Republican politics. He served on the city council of Northampton in 1899, was city solicitor for the next two years, and then clerk of the courts for one year. Elected to the lower house of the Massachusetts legislature, Coolidge served there from 1907 to 1908. He was then elected mayor of Northampton from 1910 to 1911. A member of the state senate for the following three years, he served as president of

that body from 1914 to 1915. In his address on taking the chair position, he stated his conception of the nature of law:

> Men do not make laws. They do but discover them. Laws must be justified by something more than the will of the majority. They must rest on the eternal foundation of righteousness. That state is the most fortunate which has the aptest instruments for the discovery of laws.

Beginning in 1916, Coolidge served three consecutive one-year terms as lieutenant governor of Massachusetts. He was elected governor in 1918 and held that office for two terms (1919–1920). As governor, Coolidge captured the national spotlight in 1919 with his deployment of the state militia to keep order after Boston's police went on strike for higher wages and better working conditions. The entire police force was dismissed and replaced. Coolidge, replying to the objections of Samuel Gompers, president of the American Federation of Labor, stated that "there is no right to strike against the public safety by anybody, anywhere, any time." His response to the public concern for law and order was greeted with nationwide approval, and Coolidge rode the wave of popularity into another term as governor.

After this episode, prominent Republicans began to consider Coolidge as a possible nominee for national office. During the 1920 Republican National Convention, Warren G. Harding was nominated as the party's presidential candidate, and Coolidge as the vice-presidential candidate. The Republicans won the election, and Coolidge was sworn in on March 4, 1921.

On August 2, 1923, Coolidge assumed the presidency when President Harding died suddenly while returning from a trip to Alaska. The news of Harding's death reached Coolidge while he was visiting his father in Plymouth, Vermont. At 2:47 a.m. on August 3, he took the oath of office by the light of a kerosene lamp in the sitting room of the house. It was administered by his father, who was now a justice of the peace. He then left for Washington, D.C., to serve out Harding's term of office. Coolidge ran for president in the 1924 elections and won.

Coolidge's presidency was not an activist one. He had a hands-off attitude toward big business, and undertook no major social initiatives. He believed in high protectionist import tariffs, low taxes, reduced immigration quotas, economy in government, and noninvolvement in international affairs. Coolidge did not run for reelection in 1928.

Coolidge retired to Northampton, Massachusetts, where he bought a large house. He had planned to practice law, but his health failed, and he died on January 5, 1933. He was buried in a rural cemetery at Plymouth Notch, Vermont, near the little white house where he was born.

Nathaniel Hawthorne's Birthday

Nathaniel Hawthorne, one of America's greatest fiction writers, was born on July 4, 1804, in Salem, Massachusetts. His ancestors were Puritans, one of whom was William Hathorne (as the name was originally spelled), a settler of the Massachusetts Bay Colony under Governor John Winthrop and later a magistrate in Salem. Both William Hathorne, who ordered a Quaker woman whipped in public, and his son John, who was a judge at the infamous Salem witch trials, seem to have exemplified the stern and intolerant aspect of Puritanism that influenced Hawthorne's life.

Nathaniel Hawthorne's own father, a sea captain, died in a distant port when his son Nathaniel was only four years old. Although young Hawthorne had three sisters, he grew up with books as his chief companions. He learned about Puritan history, and speculated as to whether his family's declining fortunes could be some sort of divine punishment for the injustices that his ancestors had committed. After his graduation in 1825 from Bowdoin College in Brunswick, Maine, Hawthorne returned to his mother's home in Salem, where he lived for over ten years in almost complete solitude.

His first important work was a collection of what he called *Twice-Told Tales*, published earlier in various magazines, which appeared in 1837 and in an enlarged edition in 1842. The collection contains many of the tales now regarded as classics, among them moral allegories such as the story called "The Ambitious Guest," in which the narrator relates (in a mountain inn just below the avalanche that is about to destroy him) his hopes for earthly immortality. There is also the poignant story "The Minister's Black Veil," and historical sketches such as "Endicott and the Red Cross" and "The Maypole of Merry Mount."

In 1839 financial problems led Hawthorne to take a post in the Boston Custom House. By 1841, however, he was back at his literary endeavors, producing several children's books: *Grandfather's Chair, Famous Old People, Liberty Tree*, and *Biographical Stories for Children*. He also spent some time at the Transcendentalist community at Brook Farm in West Roxbury, Massachusetts.

During this time, Hawthorne fell in love with Sophia Peabody, a prominent figure in Boston society. They married in 1842 and moved to the Old Manse in Concord, Massachusetts. These were happy times for Hawthorne, as reported in his *Passages from the American Notebooks* and *The Old Manse*. They also provided the title for a second collection of tales, *Mosses from an Old Manse* (1846) which, like its predecessor, was more of an artistic than a financial success. Unable to pay the rent, Hawthorne and his family moved to his mother's home in Salem late in 1845. By 1846 he had used certain political contacts to secure a position in the Custom House at Salem, which he held until a Whig victory over the Democrats resulted in his dismissal three years later.

Unemployed, Hawthorne used his time to write his masterpiece, *The Scarlet Letter* (1850). One of the greatest American novels, the book exemplifies Hawthorne's deftness in dissecting human character, his mastery of symbolism, and his skill in creating a pervasive and almost hypnotic mood. As in other Hawthorne works, the message is an essentially Christian one: that as inevitable as sin is in human nature, divine redemption is possible.

The book made Hawthorne famous. He moved to the vicinity of Lenox, Massachusetts, where he became acquainted with Herman Melville. Hawthorne then wrote the somber *House of the Seven Gables* (1851), in which the sins of a father are visited upon successive generations. The novel was followed by *The Blithedale Romance* (1852), which drew upon Brook Farm as its setting; by a collection of tales in *The Snow Image and Other Twice-Told Tales* (1852); and by two more children's books: *A Wonder-Book for Girls and Boys* (1852) and *Tanglewood Tales* (1853).

In the spring of 1852, Hawthorne purchased a large house known as The Wayside. It was at The Wayside that Hawthorne produced a campaign biography of Franklin Pierce, who was elected president in 1852. In 1853 Hawthorne was rewarded with a lucrative appointment as the United States consul in Liverpool, England. He resigned in 1857, but remained abroad, traveling with his family for the next two years in Italy, which served as the setting for *The Marble Faun* (1860), a novel that once again examined the problem of evil, exploring the possible contribution of sin and remorse to spiritual maturity. In 1860 Hawthorne returned to the United States, and shortly thereafter his health began to fail.

Our Old Home (1863), which contains some of the material from his English journals, was the last of his books to be published during his lifetime. He died in his sleep on May 19, 1864, in Plymouth, New Hampshire, during a trip.

July 5

Admiral David G. Farragut's Birthday

David Glasgow Farragut, probably the most famous Union naval officer of the Civil War, was born on July 5, 1801, in Campbell's Station, Tennessee, a few miles southwest of Knoxville. His father, George, was the son of Spanish parents and had served with distinction during the American Revolution. After the Revolution, George Farragut settled in Tennessee and married Elizabeth Shine, a young woman of Scottish descent.

In 1807 President Thomas Jefferson appointed George Farragut sailing master of the United States Navy, and the family moved to New Orleans, Louisiana. David's mother died there when he was seven, and after the age of nine he never saw his father again. Fortunately, Commander David Porter, in charge of the New Orleans naval station, adopted the youngster in gratitude for the care that the Farragut family had previously given to his father during a terminal illness.

At Porter's request, on December 17, 1810, the secretary of the navy appointed nine-year-old Farragut a midshipman. In 1811 Farragut went on his first naval voyage, which was aboard Porter's frigate, the *Essex*. During the War of 1812, the *Essex* cruised in the Pacific Ocean and successfully captured several enemy vessels. The young Farragut performed his shipboard duties well. When Porter decided to take the captured enemy vessels to the Chilean port of Valparaiso, he made his 12-year-old protégé the master of one of the prizes, the *Alexander Barclay*. This trip marked the end of Farragut's service in the War of 1812, however. The British ships *Phoebe* and *Cherub* trapped and sank the *Essex* in Valparaiso harbor on March 28, 1814. Farragut was captured and remained a prisoner until November 1814.

From 1815 until 1820 Farragut sailed the Mediterranean aboard several vessels, namely the *Independence*, the *Washington*, and the *Franklin*. He served as an aide to Commodore William Bainbridge, then to Commodore Charles Chauncey, and finally to Captain Gallagher. The young Farragut then accompanied his naval schoolmaster, Charles Folsom, to the North African port city of Tunis. Farragut spent nine months there, studying French, Italian, English, and mathematics.

In 1821 Farragut briefly returned to the United States, but he decided to resume serving with Porter. Porter commanded a fleet that was engaged in antipiracy operations, and Farragut served with him for two years. During this tour, Porter gave the young man command of his first ship, the *Ferret*.

Farragut married Susan C. Marchant of Norfolk, Virginia, on September 24, 1823. He was devoted to his wife, but she was ill for many years and died in 1840. On December 26, 1843, Farragut married Virginia Loyall, the daughter of a prominent Norfolk citizen. As both his spouses came from the same city, Farragut felt strong ties with Norfolk and made it his home until 1861.

Meanwhile, Farragut was promoted to lieutenant in 1825 and set sail on the *Brandywine*, which returned the Marquis de Lafayette to France after his famous American tour. During the next 15 years, a slack period for the United States Navy, he gained additional experience sailing in the waters off Mexico and Brazil. In September 1841 he was promoted to commander and took command of the sloop *Decatur*.

The Mexican War (1846–1848) gave valuable experience to many American military leaders, but Farragut found it a period of great frustration. Not until February 1847 did the navy respond to his request for duty in the Gulf of Mexico and grant him command of the sloop *Saratoga*. Even this assignment failed to satisfy him, however, for he received only insignificant blockading assignments in the gulf waters.

Commander Farragut held a variety of posts during the 1850s. He served as assistant inspector of ordnance and in 1854 published the results of his research in this field in *Experiments to Ascertain the Strength and Endurance of Navy Guns*. In August 1854 he left for the western frontier to establish a navy yard at Mare Island, California, where he was also promoted to captain in 1855. He returned to the east just before the Civil War broke out, and spent the winter of 1860–1861 in Norfolk while Southern states seceded from the Union and formed the Confederate States of America.

On April 17, 1861, the Virginia Secession Convention passed the ordinance that took Virginia out of the Union. Farragut was unable to accept this decision, and on the following day he moved his family north, to the village of Hastings-on-the-Hudson in New York. He remained there until September 1861, when he was made a member of the naval board that had convened at New York City. Farragut's decision to leave his Virginia home in order to remain loyal to the federal government had impressed his superiors, and on January 9, 1862, he was appointed commander of the Gulf of Mexico Blockading Squadron. On January 20, 1862, Farragut was ordered to destroy the defenses guarding New Orleans and capture the city. Farragut set sail on February 2, 1862, from Hampton Roads in the new steamer sloop *Hartford*, which served as his flagship on the mission.

By mid-April 1862 the Union task force was ready to begin its operation against a formidable enemy. Fort Jackson on the west side of the Mississippi, Fort St. Philip on the east side, and a Confederate flotilla guarded New Orleans. On April 18, 1862, Union navy commander David D. Porter (the son of Farragut's foster father) opened the battle by bombarding Fort Jackson. His efforts continued for several days without any significant effect.

Farragut finally broke the stalemate with the daring decision to run his ships past the forts without completing their destruction. At dawn on April 24, 1862, he sailed his 17 vessels past the fortifications. Despite heavy enemy fire, all but three survived. Next, the Union forces engaged and destroyed the Confederate flotilla. This action stripped New Orleans of its defenses, and on April 25, 1862, the city surrendered to Farragut. President Lincoln and the Congress were properly grateful to the audacious Farragut, and on July 30, 1862, Farragut received a promotion to rear admiral. He was the first man to ever hold that rank in the United States Navy.

Blockade duties, necessary but uneventful, occupied most of Farragut's time for the next year and a half. In January 1864, however, he set sail from New York City for the Gulf of Mexico to command an assault on Alabama's Mobile Bay at the mouth of the Mobile River. Fort Morgan on the east side and Fort Gaines on the west side protected the entrance to the bay, which was blocked by mines or "torpedoes," except for a narrow passage lane. On August 5, 1864, Farragut attempted to breach the defenses.

The ironclad vessel *Tecumseh* struck a mine and sank, losing all aboard. Immediately the warning "Torpedoes ahead!" was sounded, and the advance slowed. Farragut was undeterred, however, and uttered the famous phrase "Damn the torpedoes! Full speed ahead!" His ship, the *Hartford*, took the lead. The Union armada soon passed the forts, dispersed the defending Confederate flotilla, and Mobile Bay, the last important Confederate port on the Gulf coast, fell to Farragut. Fort Gaines surrendered two days later on August 7, 1864, and Fort Morgan on August 23, 1864.

In December 1864 President Lincoln appointed Farragut to the newly created rank of vice admiral. In July 1866 Farragut received another unprecedented promotion, to full admiral. Like the vice admiralcy, the rank was created especially for him. Sixty-five years of life and long service in enemy waters had taken their toll on Farragut by this time, and the government granted him a leave of absence to recuperate. He went to New York City and, with a gift of $50,000 from the city's leading citizens, bought a residence there.

Farragut was given command of the navy's European Squadron in April 1867 and he set sail on the *Franklin*. His voyage turned into a goodwill tour that lasted until his return to New York City on November 10, 1869. Farragut died on August 14, 1870, while traveling. He was interred at New York City's Woodlawn Cemetery.

P. T. Barnum's Birthday

Phineas Taylor Barnum was born in Bethel, near Danbury, Connecticut, on July 5, 1810. Until he went to New York City at the age of 24, he pursued a variety of unremarkable occupations and edited an antislavery newspaper in Danbury.

The expression "there's a sucker born every minute" has been attributed to Barnum. Whether he actually made this statement is uncertain, but it certainly summed up his approach to business. His career as a showman began in 1835, when he purchased and then exhibited a black woman named Joice Heth, who was roughly 80 years old. He claimed that she was 161, and said that she had been the nurse of George Washington. Barnum followed this first test of public credulity by purchasing both Scudder's American Museum and Peale's Museum in 1841. He used their combined collections for his new American Museum, which he operated in New York City from 1842 until 1865. The museum, which was really a circus, included such attractions as a woolly horse, the "original" Siamese twins (Chang and Eng), and the Fiji mermaid (constructed from the top half of a monkey and the bottom half of a fish). There was also the celebrated midget General Tom Thumb, who was eventually seen by some 20 million people.

One of Barnum's greatest coups took place in 1850, when he hired the Swedish singer Jenny Lind for a 95-concert tour of the eastern United States. As a result of his skillful promotion, the tickets sold for as much as $650, an enormous sum for the time. The tour netted $176,675 for Lind and $500,000 for Barnum.

Barnum retired in 1855 and lived in Iranistan, one of several homes that he owned in Bridgeport, Connecticut. He subsequently became mayor of the city and served in the Connecticut legislature. Eventually, he was forced out of retirement due to some bad business ventures that resulted in his bankruptcy. Barnum reopened his American Museum in New York City and embarked on his last great venture, "The Greatest Show on Earth," a massive circus and menagerie that premiered in

1871. It was a huge success, and ten years later Barnum merged with a competitor to form the Barnum & Bailey Circus.

One of the greatest attractions was Jumbo, a six-and-a-half ton elephant purchased by Barnum from London's Royal Zoological Society. "The only mastodon left on earth," as Barnum called Jumbo, was later preserved at the Barnum Museum of Natural History at Tufts University in honor of Barnum (a university trustee). Barnum's other contributions to circus history included the addition of a second, and later a third, ring to the circus. The innovation, which delighted spectators, is of course known as the "three-ring circus."

Barnum also wrote several books, including his autobiography. He died on April 7, 1891, in Philadelphia, Pennsylvania. The circus was sold to the Ringling brothers in 1907, and became part of the famous Ringling Brothers and Barnum & Bailey Circus. Barnum's slogan, "The Greatest Show on Earth," was adopted by the Ringlings.

July 6

John Paul Jones's Birthday

John Paul Jones, the distinguished American naval commander, was born John Paul in the parish of Kirkbean in Kirkcudbrightshire, Scotland, on July 6, 1747. His father, also named John Paul, was the gardener for William Craik, a member of Parliament. The younger John Paul attended the parish school until the age of 12, when he began his naval career as an apprentice aboard the *Friendship*. His training as a member of the ship's crew was brief, however. During his first voyage, which was to the Virginia colony, the *Friendship*'s owner suffered financial problems that forced him to terminate John Paul's apprenticeship.

Fortunately, John Paul had relatives in America. His elder brother, William, worked in Fredericksburg, Virginia, as a tailor. John Paul stayed with him for a while, but returned to sea when he was 19. For several years he served on slave trading vessels in the Atlantic. In 1769 he took command of his first ship, a merchant vessel engaged in West Indies trade. On his second voyage he had the ship's carpenter flogged for neglect of duty, not an unusual disciplinary measure for the times, but the man died at sea several weeks later. The carpenter's father charged John Paul with murder, but he was cleared of this charge. Shortly thereafter, John Paul became captain of the *Betsey*, from London. In 1773 the crew of this vessel mutinied, and during the ensuing struggle John Paul killed the leader of the mutineers. He insisted that it was

an accident, but decided to avoid resolving the matter with the authorities by returning to Fredericksburg incognito and assuming the new name of John Paul Jones.

The American Revolution ended Jones's self-imposed exile from the sea. He offered his services to the Continental Congress and on December 7, 1775, was commissioned as a lieutenant. He was first assigned to the *Alfred*, and in 1776 moved on to command the *Providence*. Jones quickly proved to be of value to the American cause: On one cruise alone his vessel captured 16 ships. On June 14, 1777, he received command of the sloop *Ranger* and sailed for France. After refitting his ship in Brest, France, he set out for the Irish Sea on April 10, 1778. Thirteen days later he entered the English harbor of Whitehaven, where he spiked the guns in the forts and made an unsuccessful attempt to burn the ships there. Then he went to St. Mary's Island in Solway Firth, intending to seize the earl of Selkirk as a hostage. Finding that the earl was not on the island, Jones crossed the sea to the Irish coast and captured the British sloop *Drake* after an hour's battle. Twenty-eight days after its departure, the *Ranger* returned to Brest with many prisoners and seven captured ships.

The French, who were about to go to war against Great Britain, were impressed by Jones's raids and in January 1779 gave him the command of the *Duc de Duras*, an old vessel with 40 cannons. Refitted and renamed the *Bonhomme Richard* in honor of Benjamin Franklin, the author of *Poor Richard's Almanac*, Jones sailed from L'Orient with a complement of several other ships on August 14, 1779. En route to the British coast, this small squadron took 17 ships. Then, on September 23, 1779, Jones sighted a fleet of 39 British merchant ships, convoyed by the 44-gun vessel *Serapis* and the 22-gun *Countess of Scarborough*.

Only three of Jones's ships took part in the ensuing battle. He attacked the *Serapis* with the *Bonhomme Richard* and skillfully maneuvered the two ships together. The British had the advantage at first, but when the commander of the *Serapis* called upon Jones to surrender, he replied, "I have not yet begun to fight." An American grenade set off a powder explosion on the deck of the *Serapis*, and after the British ship's main mast collapsed, its commander surrendered. Jones transferred his crew from the burning *Bonhomme Richard* to the *Serapis* and took his prize to Texel, Holland.

The *Bonhomme Richard–Serapis* engagement assured Jones's fame as a naval leader. Among other honors, Jones received the French cross of the Institution of Military Merit. Upon his return to the United States in February 1781, Congress thanked him formally and on June 26, 1781, gave him command of the *America*, which was then being built in Portsmouth, New Hampshire. It was to be the largest ship in the Continental navy. Jones spent a year supervising its construction, but after its completion the vessel was given to France.

In 1783 the Continental navy was disbanded. Jones had captured some valuable ships during his raids, and he returned to Europe to collect the proceeds from their disposal and remit the funds to the American government. The mission was successful, and he came back to the United States for the last time in 1787. On October 17 of that year, Congress awarded Jones a gold medal for his services to the country. He was the only officer of the Continental navy to receive such an honor.

In 1788 Jones accepted an offer from Empress Catherine the Great to serve in the Imperial Russian Navy and fight against the Turks. Commissioned as rear admiral, Jones took command of a Russian squadron in the Black Sea on May 26, 1788, but because of the jealousy of the Russian officers he was unable to function effectively. Catherine, however, conferred on him the cross of the Order of St. Anne. He went to Paris, France, in June 1790, where he spent the rest of his life, and died on July 18, 1792. Jones was buried in the old St. Louis Cemetery for Foreign Protestants. In 1905 his remains were returned to the United States and reinterred at the United States Naval Academy in Annapolis, Maryland.

Republican Party Founded

The Republican Party arose during a period of widespread popular dissatisfaction with existing political parties. Although there is some controversy surrounding the exact time and place of its beginnings, a July 6, 1854, meeting at Jackson, Michigan, which selected the party's first statewide slate of candidates, is considered by many to be the occasion of the party's founding.

Slavery was one of the major issues leading to the formation of the party. The Missouri Compromise of 1820 had temporarily eased the conflict. In that year Henry Clay of Kentucky engineered an agreement that allowed Missouri to enter the Union as a slave state, while banning slavery in the rest of the Louisiana Purchase north of a specified latitude running across the continental United States. It was only a temporary expedient, however, since it would maintain sectional peace only as long as there were equal numbers of slave states and free states. Other legislative compromises, such as the Compromise of 1850, were equally unsatisfactory in resolving the schism.

Northern dissatisfaction over the political stalemate led to the creation of the new party. On February 28, 1854, an important meeting was held in Ripon, Wisconsin. The 50 dissident members of the existing Whig, Democratic, and Free-Soil Parties who met there were determined to organize a more assertive antislavery political alternative. Allen Bovay, one of the organizers of this gathering, persuaded Horace Greeley, the editor of the influential *New York Tribune*, to urge dissident factions throughout the North to adopt the name Republican.

The new party grew rapidly. Republican candidates ran for state and congressional offices in 1854. On February 22, 1856, an informal meeting in Pittsburgh, Pennsylvania, called for a national convention in Philadelphia, Pennsylvania, on June 17, 1856, to select candidates for president and vice president. All of the northern states were represented, as well as the southern states of Maryland, Virginia, and Kentucky. There were also representatives from the territories of Minnesota, Nebraska, and Kansas as well as from the District of Columbia. Robert Emmet of New York, formerly a Democrat, was the temporary chairman, and Colonel Henry S. Lane of Indiana was the permanent presiding officer.

The famous explorer Colonel John C. Frémont, who had also served as a senator from California, won the new party's presidential nomination. William L. Dayton of New Jersey was the choice for vice president. The party platform supported Congress's right and obligation to bar slavery from the western territories. James Buchanan of Pennsylvania, the Democratic candidate, won the 1856 election with 174 electoral votes, but Frémont made an impressive showing with 114 electoral votes. He took 11 of the 16 free states. Millard Fillmore, the candidate of the nativist American (Know-Nothing) Party, won only Maryland's eight electoral votes.

In 1858, however, the Republicans won control of the United States House of Representatives. The prospects looked good for the presidential election in 1860. That year the national convention met on May 16 at the Chicago Wigwam and selected Abraham Lincoln as its presidential nominee on the third ballot. Hannibal Hamlin of Maine was the nominee for vice president.

The 1860 Republican platform emphasized the nonextension of slavery, but there were other planks as well. The party supported protectionist import tariffs, homestead legislation, and the construction of a transcontinental railroad. Most of the new party's members were from the Whig Party, but there were many northern Democrats as well.

Lincoln received less than 40 percent of the popular vote, but won the election. He received 180 electoral votes in contrast to 72 for the southern Democrat John C. Breckinridge of Kentucky and 39 for Constitutional Unionist John Bell of Tennessee. Stephen A. Douglas, the Democratic candidate, finished second in the popular vote but received only 12 votes in the electoral college. The Southern states began to secede from the Union after Lincoln's victory, and the Civil War followed shortly thereafter. The Republican Party has survived and prospered to the present day, however, and together with the Democratic Party is a cornerstone of the American two-party political system.

July 7

California Proclaimed Part of the United States

Large numbers of Americans did not arrive in California, a province of Mexico, until the colonization of the San Joaquin Valley began in 1843. Even by 1846, only about 500 Americans had settled among the 8,000 to 12,000 Mexicans of Spanish descent and 24,000 Native Americans in the area. Nevertheless, American interest in this large and fertile Mexican province was great. Shortly after the Mexican War erupted, an American naval officer claimed California for the United States on July 7, 1846.

Throughout the 1840s, Americans were eager to add California to the Union. In 1842 Commodore Thomas Catesby Jones, incorrectly believing that the United States and Mexico were at war and that a British fleet was ready to seize California, set sail from the coast of Peru. Jones landed at Monterey and raised the American flag there on October 20, 1842, before the United States consul in Monterey, Thomas O. Larkin, advised him that the two nations were still at peace. Commodore Jones promptly lowered the flag, President John Tyler apologized to Mexico, and the United States made reparations.

James K. Polk, who succeeded Tyler as president, was much more aggressive in pursuing the expansion of the United States to the Pacific Ocean in fulfillment of its "manifest destiny." In October 1845 Polk appointed Thomas Larkin as confidential agent with the assignment of encouraging Californians to join the Union or at least to declare independence under the protection of the United States. Polk's hopes for California soon came to fruition, thanks to the efforts of John C. Frémont and to the outbreak of war with Mexico.

Undertaking his third important government exploring expedition, Frémont, then a young brevet captain in the United States Topographical Corps, reached the California frontier in December 1845 and camped near Sutter's Fort. From Sutter's Fort, Frémont traveled with a single companion to Monterey, more than 100 miles to the south. Monterey was the headquarters of General José Castro, the military commandant of California. Meeting with Castro, Frémont received what seemed to be the commandant's tacit approval for his expedition to remain in California, reprovision themselves, and explore further. In February 1846, Frémont's expedition camped some 13 miles southeast of San José, roughly midway between San Francisco and Monterey. All was quiet until late February, when the expedition moved on toward the main settlements of the province, including Monterey. Keeping east and inland of that center, Frémont camped some 25 miles from Monterey, near Salinas. The movements of his well-armed band alarmed the Mexican authorities, and Castro ordered the Frémont party out of the area. Angered, Frémont refused, raising the American flag and standing his ground for three days on nearby Hawk's Peak in the Gabilan Mountains. When Castro prepared to attack with his superior forces, Frémont decided to withdraw.

Frémont was at Klamath Lake on the Oregon frontier by May 9, 1846, when Marine Lieutenant Archibald H. Gillespie reached him with what may have been secret orders. In any case, Frémont and his expedition returned to California immediately, where they camped on the Sacramento River, not far from Sutter's Fort.

As Frémont approached, the Mexican leaders in California, who had long been feuding, were at odds over the issue of allegiance with Mexico. Castro announced his support for General Mariano Paredes, who had deposed José Herrera as president of Mexico. However, the civil governor of Mexican California, Pío Pico, responded by calling for a general council in Santa Barbara. It was widely thought that the purpose of this council would be to proclaim California's independence and place it under the protection of a foreign government such as Great Britain or France. In response to this internal challenge, Castro diverted his attention from the Americans and dispatched forces against Pico's headquarters at Los Angeles. Castro also ranged up and down northern California in a troop-raising effort designed to meet threats from any quarter, foreign or domestic.

With Frémont's encouragement, American settlers in the Sacramento Valley took advantage of Castro's preoccupation, seizing the opportunity to attack a Castro force on June 10, 1846. On June

14, 1846, another American party captured Sonoma, north of San Francisco. With their unanimous consent, one of the settlers, William B. Ide, drew up a proclamation declaring the independence of the American settlements. The insurgents claimed that the Mexicans had promised them lands and a republican form of government, but had instead imposed a dictatorship and forbidden them to buy or rent land.

William L. Todd, a nephew of Mary Todd Lincoln, designed a flag for the newly proclaimed Republic of California. The flag had a white field with the name of the republic, a picture of a grizzly bear, and a star. Not surprisingly, historians came to call the uprising the Bear Flag Revolt. Frémont himself reached Sonoma on June 25, 1846, and shortly thereafter became the leader of the Bear Flag republic.

The life of the fledgling California republic was short, however, for the Mexican War quickly brought American military intervention to the area. Commodore John D. Sloat, the commander of the United States Navy's Pacific Squadron, was anchored off Mazatlán on Mexico's west coast. He had learned by late May 1846 that war had broken out in Texas between the United States and Mexico. Acting on standing orders for such a development, Sloat set sail for California on June 8, 1846. Sloat's flagship, the *Savannah*, arrived at Monterey on July 2, 1846.

On July 7, 1846, Commodore Sloat sent Captain William Mervine with 250 marines and seamen ashore to claim California for the United States. Sloat raised the American flag and issued a proclamation that was read to the populace in both Spanish and in English. He guaranteed the civil and religious rights of persons who accepted American authority, and allowed those who chose to refuse it to either remain neutral or to leave. Those who decided to depart would receive time to sell their property. Sloat promised to not interfere with existing real estate titles or the property of the clergy, and announced that the military would take no private property without giving just compensation. Several months of conflict followed throughout California, and there was tension between the leaders of the different American forces involved, but eventually the Americans defeated the Mexicans. The Treaty of Cahuenga of January 13, 1847, provided for the withdrawal of Mexican forces from California.

July 8

John D. Rockefeller Sr.'s Birthday

John Davison Rockefeller, the famous American industrialist and philanthropist, was born on July 8, 1839, to William and Eliza Rockefeller in the small town of Richford, New York. His father was a trader and also owned a farm. When John was 12 years old, his family moved to Cleveland, Ohio, where he attended high school for two years. That was the extent of his formal education. At the age of 16 he became a clerk in a Cleveland produce business. Despite his low wages, he saved a little every week. Thus, at the age of 20, he was able to open his own produce business, with M. B. Clark as his partner.

During the Civil War, Rockefeller prospered as a wholesaler in grain, hay, and meat, accumulating a small fortune of $50,000 by 1865. He became a leading member of Cleveland's Erie Street Baptist Church, and began the practice of donating one-tenth of his income to charity. In 1864 he married Laura Celestia Spelman. The couple would eventually have four children: Bessie, Alta, Edith, and John D. Rockefeller Jr.

From such modest beginnings, Rockefeller went on to become one of the wealthiest and most powerful men in American history. It was in the petroleum industry that he made his fortune. Whale oil, used for lamps, was becoming increasingly scarce and expensive. In western Pennsylvania, however, naturally occurring deposits of underground petroleum were discovered. E. L. Drake, drilling for oil near Titusville, Pennsylvania, released a gusher on August 27, 1859, and the rush was on to enter the oil business.

Four years later, Rockefeller and Clark entered oil refining as a sideline after seeing the business opportunities afforded by a recent railroad link between Cleveland and the oil lands of Pennsylvania. They bought one small Cleveland refinery and hired some experienced personnel. By the end of the Civil War, Rockefeller had decided to expand his operations and leave the produce business. He bought out Clark and reorganized the partnership into Rockefeller and Andrews. To build a second, larger refinery in Cleveland called the Standard Works, Rockefeller brought his brother William (1841–1922) into a firm called William Rockefeller and Co. Not long afterward, an eastern affiliate was established in New York. By drawing talented men to his enterprises, Rockefeller magnified his own keen abilities many times. For example, in 1867 Henry M. Flagler, later an important industrialist in his own right, joined the Rockefeller enterprise.

Rockefeller saw that any field so lucrative and so easily entered as oil would eventually be crowded with competitors. To enhance his profits, he learned how to thin out the ranks by taking over or intimidating competitors. By 1870 he dominated the refining industry in Cleveland. Then he formed the Standard Oil Company of Ohio, with himself as president. This joint-stock corporation, which attracted a number of investors, absorbed his earlier enterprises and employed more than 1,000 workers.

Until this time Rockefeller had concentrated on refining. However, since crude oil was worthless to the consumer, refining put him at the strategic center of the entire petroleum business. As Rockefeller clearly saw, any refiner who could monopolize this essential process would be able to dictate terms to producers and set prices for wholesalers and consumers. He ruthlessly pursued his competitors, but also introduced important technological advances to the business and a variety of innovative cost-cutting measures,. A highly accurate cost-accounting system was one product of his fine sense for detail. Soon his firms were making their own barrels and erecting their own warehouses. To bring the refineries into more direct touch with wholesalers, he invested in fleets of barges and tankers. He also bought up as much of the pipelines from the oil fields to the railroads as he could, to lessen dependence on outsiders and to gain another point of control.

In order to realize his dream of establishing a petroleum monopoly, Rockefeller also needed favorable rates from the railroads for his oil shipments. Since railroad rates were not standardized at the time and the business was highly competitive, a customer as large as Standard Oil could demand lower rates than smaller customers offering less business. Rockefeller saw that discriminatory rates (more flatteringly referred to as "preferential") would keep competitors' prices higher than his and contribute to their failure. Under-the-counter rebates from railroad companies to the strongest shippers were a common form of such discriminatory pricing. Though not strictly illegal at the time, Rockefeller and Flagler's tactics were coercive and grasping in the extreme.

In 1882 Rockefeller and his associates created a new business organization, the Standard Oil Trust, capitalized at $70 million and centralizing roughly 40 companies. In this trust, the stockholders placed their shares in the hands of nine trustees, among them Rockefeller, in exchange for trust certificates of ownership. The combined Rockefeller enterprises controlled approximately 90 percent of petroleum refining in the United States, and dominated the world market for petroleum products. Through efficient marketing systems, price wars against rivals, and other measures Standard Oil went on to capture the wholesale trade as well as the retail trade of the entire United States in petroleum products. Once in control, however, Standard Oil raised prices to recoup its losses, and thereafter could maintain prices at a level of its choosing.

The result was that popular opinion turned against Rockefeller, while his organization earned enormous profits and paid lucrative dividends to its stockholders. Crusading journalists, later derided by their targets as "muckrakers," led the attack against Rockefeller and other wealthy monopolists such as Andrew Carnegie. It took several decades, but eventually federal antitrust legislation and a series of important court decisions forced Rockefeller to dissolve his trust. Some important spin-off companies included Standard Oil of New Jersey (later known as Exxon), Standard Oil of Ohio (later known as Sohio), and Standard Oil of Indiana.

After the Standard Oil breakup, which occurred in 1911, John D. Rockefeller decided to retire and devote the rest of his life to his long-standing interest in philanthropy. He had already helped to establish the University of Chicago in 1891 and the Rockefeller Institute for Medical Research in 1901 (later the Rockefeller University). In 1913 he founded the Rockefeller Foundation, dedicated to promoting "the well-being of mankind throughout the world." In 1918 Rockefeller established the Laura Spelman Rockefeller Memorial Foundation in memory of his wife, to further the social sciences and child welfare (later consolidated with the Rockefeller Foundation). Rockefeller also made significant contributions to the Baptist Church, the Young Men's Christian Association, and the Anti-Saloon League (a pro-Prohibition organization).

Rockefeller died at his home in Ormond Beach, Florida, on May 23, 1937, at the age of 97.

American Revolution: Olive Branch Petition

As the American Revolution began to unfold in the spring and early summer of 1775, moderates in the Continental Congress pressed for a diplomatic alternative to an open break with Great Britain. Thus, on July 8, 1775, representatives of nearly all the colonies signed a petition to King George III expressing their discontent with British rule and setting forth their desire for peaceful reconciliation. It is referred to as the Olive Branch Petition, in reference to the ancient use of olive branches as a symbol of peace. Inevitably, it was rejected by the British, and war became increasingly unavoidable.

July 8

A copy of the Olive Branch Petition is set forth below:

To the King's Most Excellent Majesty. Most Gracious Sovereign:

We your Majesty's faithful subjects of the colonies of New-Hampshire, Massachussetts-Bay, Rhode Island and Providence Plantations, Connecticut, New York, New Jersey, Pennsylvania, the counties of New Castle, Kent and Sussex on Delaware, Maryland, Virginia, North Carolina and South Carolina, in behalf of ourselves and the inhabitants of these colonies, who have deputed us to represent them in general Congress, entreat your Majesty's gracious attention to this our humble petition.

The union between our Mother Country and these colonies, and the energy of mild and just government, produced benefits so remarkably important, and afforded such an assurance of their permanency and increase, that the wonder and envy of other Nations were excited, while they beheld Great Britain rising to a power the most extraordinary the world had ever known. Her rivals observing, that there was no probability of this happy connection being broken by civil dissentions, and apprehending its future effects, if left any longer undisturbed, resolved to prevent her receiving such continual and formidable accessions of wealth and strength, by checking the growth of these settlements from which they were to be derived.

In the prosecution of this attempt events so unfavourable to the design took place, that every friend to the interests of Great Britain and these colonies entertained pleasing and reasonable expectations of seeing an additional force and extension immediately given to the operations of the union hitherto experienced, by an enlargement of the dominions of the Crown, and the removal of ancient and warlike enemies to a greater distance.

At the conclusion therefore of the late war, the most glorious and advantageous that ever had been carried on by British arms, your loyal colonists having contributed to its success, by such repeated and strenuous exertions, as frequently procured them the distinguished approbation of your Majesty, of the late king, and of Parliament, doubted not but that they should be permitted with the rest of the empire, to share in the blessings of peace and the emoluments of victory and con-

quest. While these recent and honorable acknowledgments of their merits remained on record in the journals and acts of the august legislature the Parliament, undefaced by the imputation or even the suspicion of any offence, they were alarmed by a new system of Statutes and regulations adopted for the administration of the colonies, that filled their minds with the most painful fears and jealousies; and to their inexpressible astonishment perceived the dangers of a foreign quarrel quickly succeeded by domestic dangers, in their judgment of a more dreadful kind.

Nor were their anxieties alleviated by any tendency in this system to promote the welfare of the Mother Country. For although its effects were more immediately felt by them, yet its influence appeared to be injurious to the commerce and prosperity of Great Britain.

We shall decline the ungrateful task of describing the irksome variety of artifices practised by many of your Majestys ministers, the delusive pretences, fruitless terrors, and unavailing severities, that have from time to time been dealt out by them, in their attempts to execute this impolitic plan, or of tracing through a series of years past the progress of the unhappy differences between Great Britain and these colonies which have flowed from this fatal source.

Your Majestys ministers persevering in their measures and proceeding to open hostilities for enforcing them, have compelled us to arm in our own defence, and have engaged us in a controversy so peculiarly abhorrent to the affection of your still faithful colonists, that when we consider whom we must oppose in this contest, and if it continues, what may be the consequences, our own particular misfortunes are accounted by us, only as parts of our distress.

Knowing, to what violent resentments and incurable animosities, civil discords are apt to exasperate and inflame the contending parties, we think ourselves required by indispensable obligations to Almighty God, to your Majesty, to our fellow subjects, and to ourselves, immediately to use all the means in our power not incompatible with our safety, for stopping the further effusion of blood, and for averting the impending calamities that threaten the British Empire.

Thus called upon to address your Majesty on affairs of such moment to America, and probably to all your dominions, we are earnestly desirous of performing this office with the utmost deference for your Majesty; and we therefore pray, that your royal magnanimity and benevolence may make the most favourable construction of our expressions on so uncommon an occasion. Could we represent in their full force the sentiments that agitate the minds of us your dutiful subjects, we are persuaded, your Majesty would ascribe any seeming deviation from reverence, and our language, and even in our conduct, not to any reprehensible intention but to the impossibility or reconciling the usual appearances of respect with a just attention to our own preservation against those artful and cruel enemies, who abuse your royal confidence and authority for the purpose of effecting our destruction.

Attached to your Majestys person, family and government with all the devotion that principle and affection can inspire, connected with Great Britain by the strongest ties that can unite societies, and deploring every event that tends in any degree to weaken them, we solemnly assure your Majesty, that we not only most ardently desire the former harmony between her and these colonies may be restored but that a concord may be established between them upon so firm a basis, as to perpetuate its blessings uninterrupted by any future dissentions to succeeding generations in both countries, and to transmit your Majestys name to posterity adorned with that signal and lasting glory that has attended the memory of those illustrious personages, whose virtues and abilities have extricated states from dangerous convulsions, and by securing happiness to others, have erected the most noble and durable monuments to their own fame.

We beg leave further to assure your Majesty that notwithstanding the sufferings of your loyal colonists during the course of the present controversy, our breasts retain too tender a regard for the kingdom from which we derive our origin to request such a reconciliation as might in any manner be inconsistent with her dignity or her welfare. These, related as we are to her, honor and duty, as well as inclination induce us to support and advance; and the apprehensions that now oppress our hearts with unspeakable grief, being once removed, your Majesty will find your faithful subjects on this continent ready and willing at all times, as they ever have been with their lives and fortunes to assert and maintain the rights and interests of your Majesty and of our Mother Country.

We therefore beseech your Majesty, that your royal authority and influence may be graciously interposed to procure us relief from our afflicting fears and jealousies occasioned by the system before mentioned, and to settle peace through every part of your dominions, with all humility submitting to your Majesty's wise consideration, whether it may not be expedient for facilitating those important purposes, that your Majesty be pleased to direct some mode by which the united applications of your faithful colonists to the throne, in pursuance of their common councils, may be improved into a happy and permanent reconciliation; and that in the meantime measures be taken for preventing the further destruction of the lives of your Majesty's subjects; and that such statutes as more immediately distress any of your Majestys colonies be repealed. For by such arrangements as your Majestys wisdom can form for collecting the united sense of your American people, we are convinced, your Majesty would receive such satisfactory proofs of the disposition of the colonists towards their sovereign and the parent state, that the wished-for opportunity would soon be restored to them, of evincing the sincerity of their professions by every testimony of devotion becoming the most dutiful subjects and the most affectionate colonists.

That your Majesty may enjoy a long and prosperous reign, and that your descendants may govern your dominions with honor to themselves and happiness to their subjects is our sincere and fervent prayer.

July 9

French and Indian War: The Battle of the Monongahela

Great Britain and France were enemies in the New World as well as in the Old World, and by the mid-18th century their ambitions in the former were as irreconcilable as in the latter. The Ohio River valley, the gateway to the American West, became the focus of the conflict in the 1750s. The British expected their colonies to expand into the region, and the colony of Virginia, whose charter gave it a claim to the region, granted over one million acres of land to groups of speculators and promoters such as the Ohio Company and the Loyal Land Company. The French, on the other hand, viewed the trans-Allegheny area as the natural connection between their settlements in Canada and those in Louisiana. Canada's governor, the Comte de La Galissonière, promoted France's claim by sending out an expedition of soldiers that planted lead plates in the ground at important locations which proclaimed France's right to the territory.

Both countries elaborately justified their respective claims to the Ohio River valley. In several cases, British colonial charters granted all land from the Atlantic to the Pacific, and in the Treaty of Lancaster of 1744, Britain purchased the Ohio River valley region from the Iroquois tribe who claimed title by right of conquest. French claims were based on the exploration of the area in 1679 by René-Robert Cavelier de La Salle. Galissonière's plaques announced "the renewal of possession which we have taken of the said river Ohio, and of all those which fall into it, and of all the territories on both sides as far as the source of the said rivers, as the preceding kings of France have enjoyed or ought to have enjoyed it, and which they have maintained by arms and by treaties, particularly by those of Ryswick, Utrecht, and Aix-la-Chapelle."

Neither Great Britain nor France followed up their claims with significant settlements until the Marquis Duquesne, who assumed the Canadian governorship in 1752 and built French forts in 1753 at Presque Isle and Fort Le Boeuf (later Erie and Waterford in modern-day Pennsylvania, respectively). These wooden forts presented a greater threat than mere lead plaques, and Lieutenant Governor Robert Dinwiddie of Virginia answered the challenge by sending a young militia major, the 21-year-old George Washington, with a letter warning the French to leave the area. On December 11, 1753, Washington delivered the message to Captain Jacques Legardeur de St. Pierre at Fort Le Boeuf. The French commandant rejected the request and the young Virginian returned home.

Backwoods diplomacy degenerated into a wilderness war within a few months. On April 17, 1754, a detachment of over 1,000 French soldiers surprised, captured, and then released a band of 41 Virginians under Ensign Edward Ward as they were erecting a fort at the forks of the Ohio (the confluence of the Allegheny and Monongahela Rivers, later the site of Pittsburgh, Pennsylvania).

The French razed the structure and replaced it with Fort Duquesne (which the British would one day rebuild as Fort Pitt). As Ward retreated he encountered Washington, arriving with 120 soldiers belatedly sent to protect the fort builders. Determined to recapture the site, on May 28, 1754, Washington attacked and defeated a French advance party at Jumonville Glen, approximately five miles east of what is now Uniontown, Pennsylvania. Washington then relocated to Great Meadows, where he built the modest and appropriately named Fort Necessity. Reinforcements joined him at the encampment, and he received word of his promotion to colonel, but neither additional numbers nor increased rank enabled him to hold off the enemy. The French captured Fort Necessity on July 3, 1754, and sent Washington and his men back to Virginia. George Washington's only surrender became the opening battle of the French and Indian War.

The Ohio River valley dispute was only one part of a greater Anglo-French conflict in America, and the arrival of Major General Edward Braddock in February 1755 as commander in chief of British forces indicated that a general frontier war was imminent. British campaign plans included attacks on Fort Niagara by the Massachusetts governor, Major General William Shirley, and on Fort St. Frederic at Crown Point, New York, by William Johnson, the colony's Indian agent. Braddock himself intended to drive the French from Fort Duquesne.

Two regular Irish regiments formed the core of the force that Major General Braddock had assembled across the Allegheny Mountains at Fort Cumberland, Maryland. The addition of three independent companies and eleven companies of Virginia, North Carolina, and Maryland militia brought the complement to 2,500 men. The expedition left Fort Cumberland on June 7, 1755, but difficult terrain and inadequate transportation reduced its speed to two miles a day. At the suggestion of George Washington, who accompanied Braddock as a civilian aide-de-camp, the British commander reduced the size of the force to a lightly supplied contingent of 1,450 men capable of completing the 110-mile journey with speed. The streamlined column renewed the trek on June 20, 1755, traversing the Alleghenies.

By July 9, 1755, the Anglo-American expedition was near Fort Duquesne, crossing the Monongahela where the town of Braddock was later located. As the vanguard, under Lieutenant Colonel Thomas Gage, advanced toward the location selected for the final encampment, it encountered a party of approximately 290 French regulars and militia supported by more than 600 natives. Gage, later famous as the British commander in chief in the colonies at the beginning of the American Revolution, quickly lined up his men and fired on the French. Colonel Gage probably could have broken through the enemy line, but not knowing its strength, he retreated instead.

Upon hearing the commotion, Braddock ordered the main body of his force forward. Tremendous confusion ensued as it ran into Gage's retreating troops. Captain Jean Dumas, who had assumed command of the French force when Captain Daniel de Beaujeu was killed, took advantage of the situation by deploying his men on both sides of the road along which the British and Americans were proceeding. The French brought intense fire to bear on the Anglo-American column. Braddock personally had five horses shot from under him and then fell himself, mortally wounded. In the three-hour battle, Braddock's expedition lost 63 of its 83 officers and almost 1,000 soldiers killed or wounded. The French lost fewer than 60 men.

The survivors of the battle of the Monongahela, as the engagement came to be known, escaped to their campsite east of Uniontown, where Braddock died on July 13, 1755. The British had lost the first major battle of the French and Indian War, which they also referred to as the Seven Years' War. Trained British soldiers had proved to be inadequate in frontier fighting: As Washington commented, they had been "most scandalously beaten by a trifling body of men." However, better days would come for the British, who would ultimately achieve victory over the French and end the war in 1763.

July 10

Scopes "Monkey Trial" Begins

See the related article concerning Clarence Darrow's Birthday at April 18.

Until the 19th century, most people in the Christian world believed that all life on earth was created by God in six days, as related by the Book of Genesis in the Bible. According to traditional theology, God created animals and plants in addition to human beings, all of which remained unchanged throughout time. The creation of the world was also supposed to have been relatively recent, having taken place some six or seven thousand years ago depending upon the interpretation of particular events and the life spans of certain individuals described in the Old Testament. By the 19th century, however, science had developed to the point where some glaring errors in this traditional theological outlook had become apparent. For example, there was fossil evidence of extinct species, such as woolly mammoths and dinosaurs, that went back thousands and even millions of years before the events referred to in the Bible. Charles Darwin published his famous works concerning the evolution of species, suggesting that human beings might well have developed from apes over the course of time. The principles of adaptation and development that Darwin set forth are generally referred to as the theory of evolution.

Naturally, there was some resistance to these new ideas, since they challenged centuries of tradition and some fundamental religious beliefs. In the American south religious fundamentalists influenced several state legislatures to pass bills against the teaching of the theory of evolution in public schools. One state that passed such legislation was Tennessee, which in February 1925 made it illegal to discuss any theory other than traditional biblical creationism in state classrooms.

The American Civil Liberties Union, a leading civil rights organization, decided to find a "test case" with which to challenge the Tennessee law in the courts. The forum for the historic encounter between the supporters of evolution and the supporters of traditional biblical creationism was the town of Dayton, Tennessee. The town was small, economically depressed and declining in population, so the local officials decided that having a prominent court case take place within their community could only help bring in much-needed business and tourist dollars. Therefore, they enlisted a young schoolteacher named John T. Scopes for help in their cause. Scopes, who believed in evolution, officially broke the law on April 24, 1925, by teaching it to his Rhea County High School science class. He was indicted by the Tennessee authorities shortly thereafter, and the case went to trial on July 10, 1925.

As predicted, the case attracted nationwide media attention. It was nicknamed the "Monkey Trial" in a sarcastic reference to the proposition that human beings were descended from the apes. Due to a special arrangement, the prosecution was headed by William Jennings Bryan, the famous although unsuccessful Democratic candidate for president in previous years and one of the most notable populists in American history (see related articles throughout this book). Bryan was a deeply religious man, and the same faith that made him give the famous "cross of gold" speech at the 1896 Democratic Convention, using biblical analogies in favor of more liberal monetary policies, now led him to join the fundamentalists' crusade against the teaching of evolution. The defense was headed by the famous trial lawyer Clarence Darrow.

What followed was a battle between two great orators, Bryan and Darrow. At first, Bryan appeared to have the upper hand, since the prosecution successfully convinced the judge to exclude the bulk of the scientific evidence that supported the theory of evolution. The judge held that this evidence was "irrelevant" to the charge of breaking Tennessee law. Bryan spoke eloquently on behalf of the traditional biblical notions concerning the divine creation of mankind. However, as the trial appeared to be nearing a close, Darrow took the unusual step of calling Bryan to the witness stand as an expert on the Bible. Bryan agreed, unwittingly subjecting himself to ruthless cross-examination by Darrow. Darrow successfully exposed various contradictions in the Book of Genesis, embarrassing Bryan in the process, who left the stand a shaken man.

The case ended on July 21, 1925, with a verdict of guilty and a nominal $100 fine assessed against Scopes. Although technically a victory for the supporters of creationism, in fact it has gone down in history as one of the landmark events in the progress of modern scientific thought. Although antievolution statutes remained on the books in Tennessee and several other states for many years, they were almost entirely discredited by the Scopes trial. Despite their competition during the trial, Darrow and Bryan always maintained a certain respect for each other, and Darrow was one of the first to express regrets when Bryan died several days after the conclusion of the trial in Dayton.

World War II: Allied Troops Land in Sicily

In January 1943 President Franklin D. Roosevelt and Prime Minister Winston Churchill of Great Britain met at Casablanca, Morocco, to discuss offensives. American military strategists wanted to concentrate on gathering men and material in Great Britain in preparation for a cross-Channel invasion of mainland Europe. The British argued that such an assault would not be possible for another year, and convinced the Americans of the necessity of maintaining pressure on the Mediterranean area. As a result of the conference, Roosevelt and Churchill ordered General Dwight D. Eisenhower to set in motion Operation Husky, an invasion of the island of Sicily.

Allied strategists wanted Sicily in order to secure the Mediterranean lines of communication. Control of the island, in addition to North Africa, would allow the Americans and British to dominate the Mediterranean Sea at one of its most narrow and critical points. The planners also hoped to divert some German attention from the Soviet Union, to make possible Turkey's entrance into the war as an active ally, and to put pressure on Italy. However, they did not initially envisage the island as the stepping stone to the Italian mainland that it subsequently became. Attacks on Sardinia and Corsica would have been more logical starting points for a European invasion, because occupation of those islands would have forced a broader dispersal of Axis troops along the western Italian coast. Only at the Trident conference in Washington, D.C., in May 1943 did Churchill obtain Roosevelt's consent for Eisenhower to exploit Operation Husky with the objective of eliminating Italy from the war.

Eisenhower's final plan placed General Harold R. L. G. Alexander in command of the Allied ground forces, which received the designation "Fifteenth Army Group." General George Patton's Seventh Army made up the American element. General Bernard L. Montgomery's Eighth Army, which had distinguished itself in North Africa, was the British component. Patton's and Montgomery's forces were to strike simultaneously at the southeastern corner of Sicily on July 10, 1943.

Patton's Seventh Army, which had responsibility for the western sector of the landing beach, divided into three groups for the invasion. Major General Lucian Truscott's Joss Force was to land in the Licata area, secure the port and airfield, protect the attackers' western flank, and make contact on the eastern flank with the Second Corps. Lieutenant General Omar Bradley's Shark Force was to land in the Gela-Scoglitti area, capture the airfields at Ponte Olivo and Comiso, and make contact with the American Third Division on the left and the British on the right. Major General Hugh J. Gaffey's Kool Force was to act as the reserve.

Montgomery's Eighth Army, which had responsibility for the eastern area of the invasion zone, was to attack at the same hour as the Americans. The British were to establish beachheads between Syracuse on the east and Pozzallo on the west, and coordinate with Bradley's Second Corps in the vicinity of Ragusa. The Eighth Army was also supposed to capture the airfields in the region and continue its attack north toward the major port of Catania.

During June and into early July 1943, Allied fliers weakened the Axis defenses in the invasion area with severe bombardments. The attacks enabled the Allies to capture the islands of Lampedusa, Linosa, and Pantelleria, located between Tunisia and Sicily, thereby depriving the enemy of advanced air bases. The bombers repeatedly struck bases in Sicily, Sardinia, and Italy, putting many ground installations out of operation and reducing the number of planes available to the defenders to 1,400. These missions culminated in a major raid on the night of July 9, 1943, just hours before the troops landed on the beaches.

General Patton assembled and trained his men at North African ports from Bizerte all the way west to Algiers, and Montgomery similarly used the island of Malta and towns as far east as Port Said and Alexandria. On the morning of July 9, 1943, ships bearing both armies approached Malta and proceeded toward the objective. At 2:30 A.m. on July 10, 1943, the troops made their landings against little opposition, a sign that they had achieved tactical surprise.

Initially, the American and British elements were successful. On the right flank of Bradley's Second Corps, Major General Troy H. Middleton's 45th Infantry Division secured Scoglitti and Vittoria, while on the left flank Major General Terry de la Mesa Allen's First Infantry Division landed near Gela. Men from Joss Force captured Licata by 11:30 A.m. Montgomery's troops took a major highway bridge over the Anapo River near Syracuse, seized Avola and Noto, and advanced toward Pachino.

On July 11 and July 12, the Germans and Italians counterattacked several times in the vicinity of the Gela beachhead. The Americans repulsed the attackers on all occasions, and the invaders continued their operations. The American 45th Division captured airfields at Comiso and Biscari on July 11 and July 14, respectively, and the First Division took the air base at Ponte Olivo on July 12. The British proceeded north from their landing sites, seizing Palazzolo and Vizzini by July 14.

Air reconnaissance revealed that the German and Italian defenders were withdrawing to the northeast, fighting only delaying actions and making local counterattacks. General Alexander modified his strategy accordingly and ordered the Seventh Army to attack toward the northwest instead of concentrating on protecting the left flank of the Eighth Army. Montgomery was to continue his advance up the eastern coastline around both sides of Mt. Etna and to make the port of Messina his final objective. Alexander hoped to split the enemy forces, isolate the western portion of the island, and cut off the main route of escape to the Italian mainland.

Patton established a Provisional Corps under Major General Geoffrey Keyes, deputy commander of the Seventh Army, to assist the Second Corps in the American operations in the northwest. Composed basically of the Third Infantry Division, the Second Armored Division, and the 82nd Airborne Division, the Provisional Corps had the city of Palermo as its major objective. Between July 15 and July 23, the Seventh Army made important advances, and on the evening of July 22 the Provisional Corps seized Palermo. On the next day Patton entered the city in triumph with the Second Armored Division. News of Palermo's fall had immediate repercussions in Italy, where on July 24 and July 25, 1943, a coup toppled the Mussolini government.

Montgomery's drive toward Catania encountered heavy resistance from German and Italian forces. Recognizing Montgomery's hesitance to continue a frontal attack along the coast, General Alexander modified his battle plan, and ordered Patton to strike eastward from Palermo toward Messina to cut off the enemy's route of retreat. Montgomery decided to refrain from offensive operations south of Catania until Patton had reached a position from which they could launch a coordinated final attack. Unfortunately, a week of delays allowed the enemy to develop a system of strong defenses.

General Patton pushed east from Palermo along the only two possible routes in these mountainous regions of Sicily, sending the 45th Division along the coast and the 1st Division along the Gangi-Nicosia-Randazzo road. On August 2, the Seventh Army reached the San Fratello-Troina area and Montgomery's Eighth Army pushed north to the Simeto River. The Germans and Italians had by that time realized that the loss of Sicily was inevitable. On July 31, General Alfredo Guzzoni decided to evacuate the Italian troops. Shortly thereafter Field Marshal Albert Kesselring, supreme commander of German forces in Italy, authorized the withdrawal of the German troops.

American and British forces continued to attack the retreating enemy, but were unable to prevent their successful evacuation to the Italian mainland. Patton attempted three amphibious landings behind the German lines, but even these daring maneuvers failed to disrupt the enemy's skillful retreat. The Allies entered Messina on August 17, 1943, but by then the Germans had escaped from Sicily, taking with them 100,000 troops, 9,800 vehicles, and 47 tanks.

James Abbott McNeill Whistler's Birthday

One of the most famous paintings in the world, popularly called *Whistler's Mother*, went begging for a buyer for 20 years. The portrait was formally titled *Mrs. George Washington Whistler* and was later referred to by the artist as *Arrangement in Grey and Black No. 1.* The Royal Academy in London refused to show it in 1872. When the portrait was exhibited in the United States, it could not find a purchaser even at a ridiculously low price. Finally, in 1891 the French government bought it for $600. Not until 1926 was it finally given its present place of honor in the Louvre.

James Abbott McNeill Whistler, who lived abroad most of his life, was born in Lowell, Massachusetts, on July 10, 1834. Whistler's grandfather, John Whistler, was Irish by birth and served in the British army under General John Burgoyne during the American Revolution. After his discharge he returned to America, became an officer in the American army, and was the commandant of Fort Wayne when his son George Washington Whistler was born.

George Washington Whistler also enlisted in the army and distinguished himself as a draftsman while a student at the United States Military Academy at West Point. Graduating in 1819 as a second lieutenant, he had several surveying and teaching assignments before he and another West Pointer, William Gibbs McNeill, were assigned to working on railroads. Whistler helped to plan the location and supervised the construction of the Baltimore and Ohio and the Baltimore and Susquehanna railroads.

In 1833 George Washington Whistler resigned from the army to become an engineer in Lowell, Massachusetts, where his son James Abbott McNeill Whistler was born. The elder Whistler continued to supervise railroad construction and also became consulting engineer for the Western Railroad of Massachusetts and chief engineer for that line in 1840. His engineering skills received much notice and acclaim, and he was eventually invited to work for the Russian government. His family joined him in St. Petersburg, Russia, in 1843 when James Whistler was nine years old.

While in Russia, the boy studied at the Academy of Fine Arts. After the elder Whistler's death in 1849, the family returned to America and settled in Pomfret, Connecticut, where young Whistler was sent to school to prepare for entrance to West Point. He entered the military academy in 1851, but dropped out after three years. However, he was immensely proud of his West Point days for the rest of his life. "Had silicon been a gas, I would have been a major general," he once declared (he had failed chemistry). For about a year afterward, Whistler worked as a draftsman and map engraver for the Coast Survey in Washington, D.C., learning the techniques of etching.

In 1855, with an annual allowance of $350, he sailed for Paris, France, to study with the classicist Swiss painter Charles Gleyre. As it turned out, Whistler never returned to the United States but spent the rest of his life in Europe, chiefly in Paris and London. Largely self-trained, he was influenced by the naturalism of Jean Désiré Gustave Courbet and the English Pre-Raphaelites, the strong tonalities of Velásquez, and the serenity of Japanese art. However, he did not belong to one school of art—strongly individualistic in all things, Whistler imitated no one. Although his early landscapes (mostly nocturnal urban subjects) were realistic, he later rejected realism, saying "if the man who paints only the tree or flower or other surface he sees before him were an artist, the king of artists would be the photographer."

If Whistler can be said to have settled anywhere, it was in the Chelsea district of London, long favored by artists and writers. Appreciation of Whistler's paintings was slow in coming. However, Whistler did earn a considerable reputation as an etcher, publishing his first group of etchings in Paris in 1858. Four hundred plates reveal that he was a prodigious worker in etchings as well as in lithographs, watercolors, pastels, and oils.

A lengthy libel action against a well-known English art critic hurt Whistler financially, and he was forced into bankruptcy. In September 1879 he went to Venice and produced some new etchings, which were well-received when he returned to London. His fortunes began to recover, and in 1886 he became president of the Royal Society of British Artists. During his two-year tenure, he accomplished much to bridge the gap between French and British art and to improve the manner in which paintings were displayed.

Whistler's life achieved a measure of stability when on August 11, 1888, he married Beatrix Godwin, the widow of his architect friend Edward William Godwin. Her death on May 10, 1896, was a shattering blow to Whistler. In 1897, when the International Society of Sculptors, Painters, and Engravers was established and asked him to be president, he accepted and immersed himself in the work.

By the turn of the 20th century, Whistler's health was failing and voyages to Africa, Corsica, and other places brought no improvement. He returned to London in 1901 and died there on July 17, 1903. He was buried in Chiswick Cemetery on July 22, 1903.

Although he received little recognition as an artist before the age of 50, Whistler died a man of many honors. He was an officer of the French Legion of Honor and a member of German, French, Italian, and English societies of artists. A stela honoring Whistler and designed by Augustus Saint-Gaudens was erected at West Point. Soon after Whistler's death a memorial exhibition of his works was shown in London, New York City, and

Boston. In 1930 Whistler was also elected to the Hall of Fame for Great Americans.

Wyoming Admitted to the Union

On July 10, 1890, Wyoming became the 44th state to join the Union.

The first non-native to enter Wyoming was probably the explorer John Colter in 1806. He had been a member of the Lewis and Clark expedition. However, when that party began its return journey east in 1806, Colter decided to remain in the Pacific Northwest. Throughout 1806 he trapped in the area south and east of what is now Yellowstone National Park, and in 1807 his search for pelts took him into the park area itself.

During the early decades of the 19th century, the Pacific Northwest attracted many fur trappers, and these woodsmen explored much of Wyoming. In 1811 a party of 50 trappers sponsored by John Jacob Astor's Pacific Fur Company and led by Wilson Price Hunt crossed Wyoming on its way from St. Louis to the mouth of the Columbia River, where they built Fort Astoria. This expedition proved the feasibility of a central overland route to the Pacific Ocean. The following year, members of the 1811 group returning to St. Louis under the leadership of Robert Stuart again traveled through Wyoming, using a more southerly route than on their outward journey.

Even after the expeditions of Hunt and Stuart, fur trappers confined their activities to eastern Wyoming until 1824, when a party led by Thomas Fitzpatrick crossed the Continental Divide at South Pass. Fitzpatrick (or Broken Hand, chief of the Mountain Men, as he was known to the native tribes) is often credited with the discovery of this important pass. However, even if he was not actually the first non-native to come upon the crossing point, it was because of his efforts that the South Pass was publicized.

The Wyoming wilderness remained the domain of native tribes and fur trappers during the 1820s and 1830s. Every year trappers and natives met with representatives of eastern fur companies at the annual "fur trade rendezvous" and exchanged their pelts for supplies and trade goods. The first permanent trading post in Wyoming was established near the junction of the Laramie and North Platte rivers in 1834. Initially known as Fort William, then as Fort John, and finally as Fort Laramie, this settlement quickly became the center of the Wyoming fur trade. In 1849 the federal government purchased the fort, and until 1890 it served as a garrison for army troops.

In 1841 settlers started to flock to Oregon, and a new era in the history of Wyoming began. One of the most popular routes to the Pacific was the 2,000-mile Oregon Trail, which extended from Independence, Missouri, to Fort Vancouver in the Oregon country. Much of the trail adhered closely to the route that the trappers Robert Stuart and Thomas Fitzpatrick had blazed decades earlier. It proceeded from Independence to the Platte River and followed that waterway's north branch from the western part of what is now Nebraska. After continuing to Fort Laramie in southeastern Wyoming, the trail continued west across the southern part of Wyoming and through the famous South Pass in the Rocky Mountains. After reaching Fort Bridger in the southwestern section of Wyoming, the trail continued northwest to the Snake River valley, which it followed to Fort Boise. From there the route continued via the Grande Ronde Valley and across the Blue Mountains to the Columbia River, and along that river until it eventually ended at Fort Vancouver.

Between 1841 and 1869 more than 300,000 people went west along the Oregon Trail, and in so doing passed through Wyoming. Some went to the Oregon country. Others, after the discovery of gold in California in 1849, branched southwest in what is now Idaho and found their fortune in the California gold fields. Only a handful of this vast number decided to remain in Wyoming. However, the westward migration had a lasting effect on the area, for Wyoming became a vital link between the Pacific Northwest and the central and eastern United States. Early in the 1850s, stagecoaches provided monthly service across Wyoming. By 1860 the Pony Express served the area, and in 1861 a telegraph system was established, with stations at such places as Fort Laramie, South Pass, and Fort Bridger.

In 1861 the Civil War began. The war effort necessitated the removal of large numbers of federal troops from garrison duty in the Pacific Northwest, and as the soldiers left Wyoming, clashes between settlers and the native tribes increased. There were many skirmishes from 1862 to 1864. In 1865 the hostilities became so serious that the year was known as the Bloody Year on the Plains. At the end of the Civil War several United States Army expeditions were sent out to quell the troubles, and they established a precarious peace with the Sioux in 1868. However, the skirmishes did not end until 1876, when the army decisively defeated the native tribes.

In 1867 a major gold discovery was made in South Pass, and within a short time 15 mining camps had opened in the area. At about the same time the Union Pacific Railroad started to push across southern Wyoming. The town of Cheyenne was established in southeastern Wyoming in 1867, and a number of smaller settlements along the route of the railroad followed in quick succession.

As early as 1865, a proposal had been made to establish a separate government for Wyoming, and the area's substantial population increase following the gold strike of 1867 and the advance of the railroad spurred action on this proposition. On July 25, 1868, the Wyoming Organic Act, which created the Territory of Wyoming out of parts of the territories of Utah, Dakota, and Idaho, was approved. Cheyenne was selected to be the territorial capital. Wyoming's first legislature convened there on October 12, 1869, and it was during this session that the women of the territory were given the right to vote. It was a historic first for women's rights (see related essays throughout this book).

Wyoming prospered as a territory. Shortly after the Civil War, Texas cattlemen began to move their stock north to graze on Wyoming's great open ranges, and by 1884 approximately 800,000 head of cattle had journeyed along the Long Trail from Texas to Wyoming. In the 1880s settlers also began to establish homesteads in the territory. In only two years, more than three million acres that had previously been owned by the government or the railroads passed into private hands. In only ten years, the territory's population increased by roughly 300 percent.

On July 10, 1890, Wyoming was admitted into the Union. When news of its statehood reached Wyoming, there was great rejoicing. In Cheyenne most buildings were draped with red, white, and blue bunting, and on July 23, 1890, a parade took place. After the parade official ceremonies took place at the capitol building. Theresa A. Jenkins was the principal speaker at these exercises, and Esther Morris, who had largely been responsible for gaining the passage of the woman's suffrage bill in 1869, presented a flag to the state government. Morris said:

> On behalf of the women of Wyoming, and in grateful recognition of the high privilege of citizenship that has been conferred upon us, I have the honor to present to the State of Wyoming this beautiful flag. May it always remain the emblem of our liberties, and the flag of the Union forever.

July 11

John Quincy Adams's Birthday

John Quincy Adams, the eldest son of John and Abigail Smith Adams, was born on July 11, 1767,

Library of Congress

John Quincy Adams

in the section of Braintree, Massachusetts, that later became part of the city of Quincy. His father (see October 30), who was already criticizing British colonial policy in articles for the *Boston Gazette*, was soon to emerge as a leader in the struggle for independence and would eventually become the second president of the United States. The younger Adams followed in his father's footsteps and eventually became the sixth president of the United States.

In 1778, at the age of 10, John Quincy Adams accompanied his father on a mission to France. Placed in a school at Passy, he studied French and Latin. In 1780, while his father was on a diplomatic mission in Amsterdam, he attended the Latin School in that city. The next year Francis Dana, the American envoy to Russia, took the youth to St. Petersburg as his secretary. John Quincy Adams performed similar services for his father in 1782 and 1783 before returning to the United States. The young Adams graduated from Harvard in 1787, and after gaining admission to the bar in 1790, he began to practice law in Boston, Massachusetts.

After the elections of 1788, John Adams became vice president under President George Washington. Washington soon found use for Adams's son. He named the young Adams, still in his twenties, minister to Holland in 1794. Adams held that post for two years. After the elections of 1796, the elder Adams succeeded Washington as president, and John Quincy Adams became minister to Prussia for the term of his father's presidency.

Both John Adams and John Quincy Adams were Federalists. After the elections of 1800, however, Thomas Jefferson became president. Jefferson was the founder of the rival Democratic-Republican Party. Thus, John Quincy Adams was forced to find a new career. He won a seat in the Massachusetts state senate in April 1802, but failed to achieve election to the United States House of Representatives in November of that same year. In 1803, however, he did succeed in become a United States senator. Ironically, he supported some of President Jefferson's more controversial policies, and as a result was forced to resign.

Adams went on to become a professor of rhetoric and oratory at Harvard College, a position that he held from 1806 to 1809. Afterwards President James Madison appointed him as minister to Russia, where Adams served until 1814. It was also in 1814 that Adams served with James Bayard, Henry Clay, Albert Gallatin, and Jonathan Russell on the peace commission that negotiated the Treaty of Ghent, ending the War of 1812 with Great Britain. Adams then became minister to Great Britain.

President James Monroe appointed Adams the secretary of state in 1817, an office that he filled with ability and distinction. He helped obtain the cession of Florida from Spain in 1819 and contributed greatly to the proclamation of the Monroe Doctrine. It was on his advice that President Monroe made the latter declaration unilaterally, instead of in tandem with Great Britain as the British foreign secretary George Canning had suggested. Adams thought "it would be more candid, as well as more dignified, to avow our principles explicitly to Russia and France, than to come in as a cock-boat in the wake of the British man-of-war."

Adams was ready to make his bid for the White House in 1824. Andrew Jackson defeated him in the popular vote, but none of the four candidates (Jackson with 99 electoral college votes, Adams with 84, William Crawford with 41, and Henry Clay with 37) received the necessary electoral majority. On February 8, 1825, the United States House of Representatives, with each state voting as a bloc, chose Adams to be the next president over Jackson by a vote of 13 to 7, with Crawford receiving the remaining four votes. In this crucial contest Clay gave his support to Adams, and later became Adams's secretary of state. Followers of Jackson, however, saw this as evidence of a "corrupt bargain."

As president, Adams was unremarkable. Further, his support for a program of internal improvements and a national university alienated large numbers of his sectionally divided constituents. When he ran for reelection in 1828, he was soundly defeated by Jackson.

Adams returned home in defeat, but a year after his retirement he was elected to the House of Representatives by a district in Massachusetts and was reelected every two years for the remainder of his life. Becoming prominently identified with the cause of abolition in these later years, he opposed the annexation of Texas in 1836 and the extension of slavery to new territories in the West. He also fought the House's "gag rule," which forbade the discussion of slavery on the House floor.

At the age of 80, Adams suffered a stroke while present in the House of Representatives on February 21, 1848. He was carried to the Speaker of the House's office, where he died two days later. Adams was buried beside his father in Quincy, Massachusetts.

The Chester Gillette Murder

What has often been described as the murder of the century took place on July 11, 1906, when Chester Ellsworth Gillette murdered Grace "Billie" Brown in Herkimer County, New York.

Gillette was born in Montana in 1884. He was raised according to strict Christian values, and even did some work for the Salvation Army as a child. Gillette went on to attend Oberlin College, which was well known for its school of theology and its missionary work in China. After graduation, he went to work for a wealthy uncle in Cortland, New York, who owned a dress factory. Gillette did well in business and became a prominent figure in local social circles. However, an affair with young Grace Brown stood to ruin his chances of rising higher by marrying into local gentry.

Brown, a lowly clerk in the dress factory, became involved with Gillette and eventually became pregnant. In that day and age, marriage was the only respectable way of resolving an out-of-wedlock pregnancy. Gillette, however, did not want to surrender his ambitions, so he turned to crime instead. On July 9, 1906, Gillette took Brown on a trip through upstate New York that ended at Big Moose Lake in Herkimer County.

On July 11 Gillette rented a rowboat and took Brown out on the lake. When out of sight of the shore, Gillette clubbed her to death with a tennis racquet. After throwing her corpse into the lake, he returned to shore, buried the tennis racquet, and checked in at a local hotel. While there, he made a fateful blunder by asking the hotel clerk whether a drowning on the lake had been reported. This raised suspicions when the local police discovered Brown's body, and Gillette was arrested.

Without any sign of grief, Gillette claimed that Brown had committed suicide by jumping into the lake after they had argued about her pregnancy. Gillette's lack of emotion made the police even more suspicious, and when the tennis racquet was discovered (broken in several places from the heavy blows on Brown),he was charged with murder. He took his imprisonment stoically, encouraging the press to treat his case as a major society scandal and even selling photographs of himself so he could pay for catered meals in his jail cell.

Gillette's trial began on November 12, 1906. He continued to claim that Brown had jumped in the lake and that the boat had capsized in the process, making it impossible for him to rescue her. Further, he claimed that as Brown jumped and the boat capsized she banged her head on the boat, thus explaining the evidence of blows to her skull. His attorneys also argued that his calm demeanor afterward, and lack of an attempt to flee, showed his innocence. The jury did not accept these defenses, however, and on December 4, 1906, they returned a verdict of guilty. The judge sentenced Gillette to die by electrocution.

After a series of appeals, Gillette finally went to the electric chair on March 30, 1908. His case became more than just another society scandal and sordid romance when Theodore Dreiser wrote *An American Tragedy* (1925), based in part on the Gillette case.

July 12

George Washington Carver's Birthday

George Washington Carver, the agricultural chemist whose gift for practical experimentation was to improve the quality of life for millions of farmers, especially in the South, was born on July 12, 1861, on the Moses Carver plantation near Diamond Grove, Missouri. He was born a slave.

Near the end of the Civil War, Carver and his mother were kidnapped by a band of marauders. Tiny, suffering from exposure, and ill with whooping cough, he alone was retrieved by a posse sent out by his master, Moses Carver, with a $300 racehorse as ransom. Young Carver was raised by Moses Carver and his wife, who encouraged him to study and read the Bible. Even as a child, he showed a talent for growing things, which caused him to be called a "plant doctor." When he was ten

years old he struck out on his own, working at odd jobs to support himself while he went to school for two years in nearby Neosho, Missouri. He went on to Fort Scott, Kansas, and eventually to Minneapolis, Kansas, where he put himself through high school and began to earn money for college by doing various odd jobs.

In 1890 Carver was accepted by Simpson College in Indianola, Iowa, after being refused by another college. He subsisted during his first week there on the ten cents he had left after paying his tuition: Five cents purchased cornmeal and five cents suet, his diet for the week. Subsequently, he supported himself by laundering the clothes of fellow students while he lived in a woodshed.

At first Carver studied voice and piano, but his instructor encouraged him to abandon the idea of an art career in favor of scientific agriculture. When the idea took hold, Carver's instructor helped him enter the Iowa State College of Agriculture and Mechanic Arts (later Iowa State University). He arrived with no material possessions, and lived in a college office that he paid for by working as a janitor. Carver worked at various other odd jobs, but still managed a full schedule of academic and extracurricular activities. After he received his B.S. degree in 1894, he was made head of the college greenhouse and placed in charge of bacteriological laboratory work in systematic botany while he earned his master's degree in agriculture, which he received in 1896.

Soon afterward, Booker T. Washington invited Carver to become the first director of the Tuskegee Institute's Department of Agricultural Research. It was there that Carver embarked on the projects that won him international renown. Traveling through the countryside, he urged farmers to diversify their crops by planting peanuts and sweet potatoes, which would enrich the soil, instead of concentrating exclusively on cotton, which exhausted it. He then set out to find uses for these new crops.

The results of his work were astonishing. From peanuts he developed over 300 products, including milk, cheese, coffee, flour, soap, lard, cooking oils, dyes, stains, paper, plastic, insulating board, and linoleum. From sweet potatoes he developed more than 100 products, among them starch, tapioca, molasses, breakfast foods, vinegar, ink, synthetic rubber, shoe blacking, library paste, and mucilage for use on postage stamps. He derived scores of useful products from pecan nuts and many others from soybeans. Carver constantly demonstrated to poor farmers how they could use the things around them, such as local clays to whitewash their cabins, garden vegetables for more nutritious diets, and compost to nourish the soil.

Carver remained at Tuskegee for the rest of his life. In 1940 he donated his life savings of $33,000 to establish at Tuskegee the George Washington Carver Foundation to continue and expand his research and experiments. He became a well-known lecturer and one of the nation's most influential agronomists. Carver received a variety of honors: election as a fellow of the Royal Society of Arts in London, England; honorary degrees from Simpson College, the University of Rochester, and Selma University; the Thomas A. Edison Foundation Award; the Roosevelt medal for distinguished service in the field of science; and the Spingarn medal from the National Association for the Advancement of Colored People. He died at the Tuskegee Institute on January 5, 1943.

Henry David Thoreau's Birthday

Henry David Thoreau, the writer, poet, and naturalist who believed in shaping one's life by inner principle, was born on July 12, 1817, in Concord, Massachusetts. His father manufactured graphite pencils and his mother ran a boardinghouse. As a boy he enjoyed outdoor activities such as hunting and fishing. He studied at the Concord Academy and entered Harvard College in 1833.

Quiet by nature, he held himself apart from college life and exhibited some of the independent spirit that was to rule his later life. He attended chapel in a green coat "because the rules required black" and studied well but had little regard for the rank system. During these years he came into contact with believers in Transcendentalism, who stressed the relationship between the in-dwelling spirit in nature and the in-dwelling spirit of human beings, took intuition to be the highest form of knowledge, and glorified individualism.

Their thinking struck a responsive chord in Thoreau, who in 1837 demonstrated his own individuality with a nonconformist commencement piece scorning "the commercial spirit." It was during the same commencement week that America's leading Transcendentalist, Ralph Waldo Emerson, presented at Harvard his stirring declaration of intellectual independence from Europe in "The American Scholar." Among other things the address advised the seeker of truth (in words Thoreau later would live out) that "the ancient precept 'Know thyself' and the modern precept 'Study nature' [had] become at last one maxim."

Thoreau and Emerson became close friends in the following years. Emerson helped turn Thoreau to nature writing, edited his poems, introduced him to leading literary figures, and in 1843 sent him to New York City. Thoreau failed to find a market for his works, however, and returned home

disappointed and in debt. He summarized the next year with a brief entry in his journal: "Made pencils in 1844."

The great spiritual adventure of his life and the period of his most ecstatic communication with nature began on July 4, 1845, when he commenced a two-year stay in a simple cabin that he built in the woods on the shore of Concord's Walden Pond. In the resulting masterpiece *Walden: or Life in the Woods*, he later explained that he went there "because I wished to live deliberately, to front only the essential facts of life, and see if I could not learn what it had to teach, and not, when I came to die, discover that I had not lived." His experience in choosing this self-reliant and independent course led him to counsel others: "If a man does not keep pace with his companions, perhaps it is because he hears a different drummer. Let him step to the music which he hears, however measured or far away." Perhaps it was this philosophy that led him to protest the Mexican War by not paying his state poll taxes, for which he was briefly jailed.

In September 1847 Thoreau returned to civilization and spent almost all of the rest of his life in his father's house. He helped in the family business, worked as a surveyor, participated in social activities, and took daily walks around Concord. *Walden* was published in 1854, and is now recognized as a classic in American literature. Thoreau was also active in the movement to abolish slavery. He died on May 6, 1862.

July 13

Northwest Ordinance Enacted

Even during the fighting of the American Revolution, the Continental Congress was laying plans for the future expansion of the United States. Legislators with a vision of a large united nation sought to obtain control of the lands that now comprise the modern Midwest, located west of the thirteen colonies on the Atlantic and east of the Mississippi River. New York, Connecticut, Virginia, and Massachusetts had various claims to these lands by virtue of their colonial charters and titles. In 1780, however, the Continental Congress promised to use any western lands surrendered to the "firm league of friendship" of the states under the Articles of Confederation for the good of the whole country and eventually create out of the domain several new and equal states. Virginia responded to the pledge by renouncing its claim in 1781, and New York (1781), Massachusetts (1785), and Connecticut (1786) followed suit.

The Continental Congress quickly established a committee under Thomas Jefferson of Virginia to devise a plan of government for the "Northwest" territory (meaning it occupied the northwest portion of the American frontier in those days), which included 265,878 square miles of land and water. On March 1, 1784, the day that congress accepted Virginia's cession of its western claims, Jefferson presented his program. He proposed that the government eventually carve no more than ten new states from the territory. Believing that democracy fared best in small jurisdictions, Jefferson, who seriously underestimated the size of the area, urged that none of the ten new states be larger than 150 square miles. His scheme also advocated the abolition of slavery and universal male suffrage, and promised a great deal of self-government for the inhabitants. Settlers, upon their petition or by direction from the congress, could set up a government modeled on the constitution and laws of any one of the 13 original states. When the population reached 20,000 or more, they could devise a republican constitution of their own choosing. Finally, when the inhabitants of the territory became as numerous as the population of the least populous state, they could apply for admission to the Union. The Continental Congress rejected Jefferson's suggestion banning slavery, but accepted the rest of his proposal on April 23, 1784.

Administrative obstacles delayed the implementation of Jefferson's territorial ordinance, and conservatives in the congress strove to undo his work. Led by Rufus King of Massachusetts, the conservatives persuaded the congress to empower the appointed territorial governor with an absolute veto, and to limit the right to vote and to hold office to property owners. Under the influence of King and his supporters, the continental congress also raised the number of inhabitants required for the organization of a territorial legislature from 500 to 5,000 and set the population needed for admission to the Union at a figure equal to one-thirteenth of the population of the original states.

In 1786 the congress decided to revamp its territorial enactments. A committee, led by Nathan Dane, modified Jefferson's program. On July 13, 1787, the Continental Congress passed what was possibly the most significant piece of legislation enacted during the period of the Articles of Confederation. This legislation, the Northwest Ordinance, became model legislation for the admission of new states to the Union. It placed a congressionally appointed governor, secretary, and three judges in charge of the territory initially, and promised the establishment of a bicameral legislature when the free adult white male population

reached 5,000 or more. The ordinance provided for the eventual creation of three to five fully equal states, each of which would have a population of at least 60,000 as a prerequisite for statehood. Congress guaranteed freedom of worship, trial by jury, and publicly supported education. Further, in accordance with Jefferson's original proposal, the congress banned slavery in the Northwest Territory.

Arthur St. Clair became the first governor of what was officially known as the Territory Northwest of the River Ohio. In May 1800 Congress divided the Northwest Territory into two new territories, separated by a boundary line from the mouth of the Kentucky River north to Canada. The diminished Territory Northwest of the River Ohio, with its capital at Chillicothe, Ohio, lay east of the line. The Indiana Territory, with its capital at Vincennes, lay to the west. William Henry Harrison, who became the first governor of the Indiana Territory, was later elected president of the United States.

Ohio, admitted to the Union as the 17th state in 1803, was the first state formed from the Northwest Territory. The United States Congress created the Michigan and Illinois Territories from the Indiana Territory in 1805 and 1809, respectively. Illinois gained statehood in 1818 (see December 3) and Michigan gained statehood in 1837 (see January 26). The remainder of the Indiana Territory became the state of Indiana in 1816. A portion of the Michigan Territory was reorganized as the Wisconsin Territory in 1836, and gained admission to the Union as the state of Wisconsin in 1848. Eventually a small portion of what had been the Northwest Territory became a part of the Territory of Minnesota, which gained statehood in 1858.

July 14

Gerald R. Ford's Birthday

Gerald R. Ford, the 38th president of the United States, was born Leslie Lynch King Jr. on July 14, 1913, in Omaha, Nebraska. He was the only child of Dorothy Gardner King and Leslie King, a wool trader. His parents were divorced in 1915, and his mother returned with her two-year-old son to her family in Grand Rapids, Michigan. There she married Gerald R. Ford, a paint salesman, who adopted her son and gave him his own name.

Young Gerald Ford made a name for himself in high school football. In his junior and senior years he was chosen All-State center, and his team won the state championship in the latter year. His football prowess helped him gain a scholarship to the

University of Michigan. Ford was named the most valuable player in his senior year, and his skill on the field again opened a door for him.

Offered a position as assistant football coach and coach of the boxing team at Yale University, Ford felt that it might give him the chance to realize his ambition to attend law school. Not until his fourth year at Yale, however, was he able to persuade the law school faculty to let him take courses. In 1941 he graduated in the top third of a class in which almost 80 percent were members of Phi Beta Kappa.

Returning to Grand Rapids with his law degree, Ford was admitted to the Michigan Bar and put organized sports behind him. With the intention of specializing in labor law, he opened an office with Philip Buchen, a friend from the University of Michigan. However, his plans were changed less than six months later by the United States's entry into World War II. Ford enlisted in the navy in 1942 and, with his background in sports, was assigned to a physical training unit. For a year he worked unhappily with aviation cadets at the University of North Carolina at Chapel Hill, until his superiors finally agreed to his requests for transfer to active duty.

The USS *Monterey*, a new light aircraft carrier on which Ford subsequently served as both director of physical training and as an assistant navigation officer, saw significant action in the Pacific as part of the United States Third Fleet. Ford said it was a lucky ship. Though it was repeatedly under attack, its worst enemy turned out to be the great Pacific typhoon of December 1944, a severe storm that took 800 lives and capsized three destroyers. Ford was almost one of the 800. Losing his footing, he slid across the flight deck and over the edge, fortunately dropping to a catwalk beneath the deck rather than into the raging sea.

In 47 months of active duty, Ford accumulated ten battle stars and an excellent service record. Upon his release from active duty, he became a lieutenant commander in the naval reserve. In late 1945 he returned to live with his parents in Grand Rapids, and joined a highly respected law firm. As he became involved in the struggles of young veterans and their families to find housing, he learned that their difficulties stemmed from the banking, zoning, and real estate interests controlled by the local Republican political boss. Ford helped form the Independent Veterans Association, which lobbied vigorously against these abuses, and its considerable degree of success elated Ford and turned his thoughts toward political office.

In 1948 Ford was elected to the United States House of Representatives. During the campaign, he began to court Elizabeth (Betty) Bloomer War-

ren, and the two were married on October 15, 1948. Gerald and Betty Ford would eventually have four children: Michael Gerald, John Gardner, Steven Meigs, and Susan Elizabeth.

Ford became a member of the House Appropriations Committee during his second term, and this position provided a number of opportunities, particularly after he gained a reputation as the House member most knowledgeable about defense spending budgets. In early 1952 Ford was one of a group of Republican congressmen urging Dwight D. Eisenhower to seek the Republican presidential nomination that year. Eisenhower was nominated and elected, with Richard M. Nixon as his vice president. Nixon had also served in the House, and was one of Ford's friends. Ford would support Nixon on a number of occasions, such as in 1956 when a segment of the party favored another vice-presidential nominee for Eisenhower's second term.

Ford was a loyal party man, and he represented a conservative district. As a legislator he usually followed the views of his party. He indicated deep reservations about civil rights laws, but finally voted for those that seemed sure to pass. His positions on social welfare legislation and defense policy were strongly conservative. After President John F. Kennedy was killed in 1963, President Lyndon B. Johnson named Ford the Republican House member to serve on the Warren Commission to investigate the circumstances of the assassination.

Nixon was elected president in 1968 and reelected in 1972, and when Vice President Spiro Agnew resigned in October 1973, Nixon quickly nominated Ford to fill the vacancy, pursuant to the recently ratified 25th Amendment to the Constitution (see related articles on this topic throughout this book). Ford, though politically ambitious, nevertheless had to do some hard thinking. He had promised his wife that he would retire from politics, probably to law practice in Grand Rapids, after his next term. However, he ultimately decided to accept the nomination. On December 6, 1973, in the chamber of the House of Representatives, Ford was sworn in as the 40th vice president of the United States.

By the end of July 1974, disclosures resulting from the Watergate investigation led the House Judiciary Committee to adopt Articles of Impeachment charging President Nixon with obstruction of justice and other abuses of power. By early August an almost complete defection from the president had occurred among members of the House, who were about to vote on whether to accept the impeachment articles. Advised of the probability of his impeachment, on August 8,

1974, Nixon announced his decision to resign. At noon on August 9, 1974, Gerald R. Ford was sworn in as president.

The new president pledged to work closely with Congress, and to refrain from what the legislature considered to be the usurpation of its powers by several of his predecessors. He moved slowly in making cabinet and staff changes. On August 20, 1974, he nominated Nelson Rockefeller, the former governor of New York, to be his vice president. After lengthy congressional hearings, Rockefeller was finally confirmed in December 1974.

On Sunday, September 8, 1974, Ford made the most controversial decision of his administration. He announced that he was granting an unconditional pardon to former president Nixon for any crimes he "may have committed or taken part in" during his tenure as chief executive. The move was taken with almost no consultation and drew enormous criticism on the grounds that a pardon could not be granted when there had been no confession of guilt and that justice was not served by this action. Rather than putting the Watergate affair to rest, as Ford had hoped, his action kept this divisive national issue alive. On October 17, 1974, Ford personally testified before a subcommittee of the House Judiciary Committee that there had been no "deal" with Nixon concerning the pardon. However, public opinion was skeptical. The resulting political backlash cost the Republicans a considerable number of seats in the midterm congressional elections of November 1974.

Ford decided to run in the 1976 presidential election, and secured the nomination of his party despite fierce opposition from supporters of future president Ronald Reagan. However, he lost to the Democratic candidate, Jimmy Carter. The popular vote was 40.8 million for Carter and 39.1 million for Ford. The electoral vote was 297 for Carter, 240 for Ford, and 1 for Reagan. In January 1977 Carter was inaugurated as the 39th president and Ford left the White House.

July 15

Mother Frances Cabrini's Birthday

Francesca Xaviera Cabrini, known as Mother Cabrini, was the first American citizen to be proclaimed a saint of the Roman Catholic Church. She was born on July 15, 1850, in the village of Sant'Angelo Lodigiano in the Lombard region of northern Italy. Although she was the 13th child of her parents, Francesca Maria (as she was christened) was only the fourth to survive. She looked so fragile at birth that immediate baptism was advised. Her frail health was to be a lifelong burden.

Early in life, Francesca Cabrini decided that she wanted to go to China as a missionary nun when she grew up. At her confirmation, when she was seven, she took her name from the Jesuit missionary St. Francis Xavier. When she was old enough, Cabrini sought admission to several convents, but was refused because of her poor health. She was subsequently offered a temporary teaching job in the nearby village of Vivardo, where she remained for two years. When the Vivardo pastor was transferred to the town of Codogno and found himself with a problem concerning an orphanage for girls, he sent for Cabrini. The dismal orphanage, unclean and located in the midst of tenements, factories, and open sewers, was being mismanaged. Young Cabrini was to spend six of the worst years of her life in this place. She worked to clean the run-down building and took loving care of the orphans, some not much younger than she was.

After three years she again asked permission to take religious vows, as did seven of her charges. On September 14, 1877, the eight took the vows of poverty, chastity, and obedience. She herself was appointed superior of the orphanage and became known as Mother Cabrini. In 1880 she founded the Missionary Sisters of the Sacred Heart, and moved with her sisters to an abandoned monastery in the Codogno countryside. Within a year the building had to be enlarged to accommodate more orphans and more young women who wanted to join Mother Cabrini's missionary institute.

Cabrini's school and orphanage in the Codogno motherhouse soon became known for its efficiency, high quality of teaching, and spiritual character. Requests came from other towns and cities for Mother Cabrini to found schools, orphanages, and branches of the motherhouse. By 1887 she had founded seven houses. In that same year, she decided to establish a missionary institute in Rome, and seek papal consent to establish foreign missions. Her longtime adviser, Monsignor Antonio Serrati, discouraged her several times but could not deter her. On September 24, 1887, she and another sister boarded a train for Rome. There they were again discouraged, this time by the cardinal-vicar, and advised to return home. Instead, Mother Cabrini simply remained in Rome and pressed her case with the cardinal-vicar whenever she could. Finally, on October 22, 1887, he asked her to start not one but two houses (a free school in Rome and a nursery in a suburb). On March 12, 1888, Mother Cabrini received papal recognition and approval of her institute and the missionary work she had so long dreamed of doing.

One of the people who assumed an unexpected importance in Mother Cabrini's life was Giovanni Scalabrini, bishop of Piacenza, whom she had met when she opened a college in that city. He had taken as his special concern the cause of the impoverished Italians who were then emigrating en masse. After a visit to the United States, where he saw the conditions under which they were living, he returned to Italy and founded a religious order to help Italian emigrants. Some of his priests had just opened a small church in the Italian section of New York City, and Bishop Scalabrini asked Mother Cabrini to help.

Although reluctant at first, Mother Cabrini eventually accepted the assignment. On March 23, 1889, she and six of her missionary sisters sailed from the French port of Le Havre on a ship carrying 1,300 passengers. Of the 900 emigrants in steerage, 700 were Italian. During the voyage Mother Cabrini talked to many of them, and by the time the ship reached New York on March 31, 1889, she had some practical understanding of their hopes and problems.

When Mother Cabrini and her nuns landed, there was no one to meet them. Although they knew little English, they found their way to the rectory, where they were received cordially but with obvious surprise. The orphanage that supposedly awaited Mother Cabrini in New York had never materialized, and a letter from Archbishop Corrigan instructing her to defer her trip had not arrived in Italy before her departure. Nevertheless, Cabrini began her work. A newspaper report of May 1889 described her efforts:

> . . . young ladies with radiant faces dressed in plain black religious hoods and robes . . . [are] seen coursing the overcrowded streets of Little Italy. . . . These young nuns hardly speak English. The Directoress of their congregation is "Madre Francesca Cabrini," a diminutive, youthful lady with great eyes and an attractive smiling face. She does not know the English language, but she knows the universal language of the human spirit.

Although Mother Cabrini eventually did learn English, she never lost either her Italian accent or her fluency in the "language of the . . . spirit." She went on to establish orphanages, schools, and hospitals in many cities in the United States and in other countries around the world as well. Her motto was "I can do all things through him who strengthens me" (Philippians 4:13). For the last five years of her life, however, she confined her extensive travels to the United States for health reasons. She was in Chicago, Illinois, when she died on December 22, 1917. In the 67 years of her life, she had established 67 houses in many parts of the world. She was canonized by Pope Pius XII on July 7, 1946.

First United States–Soviet Joint Space Mission

On July 15, 1975, the United States and the Soviet empire, bitter enemies in the cold war that lasted from the end of World War II until the collapse of the Soviet Union in 1991, commenced a historic space linkup known as the Apollo-Soyuz Test Project. Both countries had invested heavily in their respective space programs over the years for a variety of political and military reasons, and had competed in space just as heatedly as they competed on Earth. The Soviets achieved the first successful satellite launch and other milestones, but the United States was the first to land a man on the Moon. In the early 1970s, a movement toward the easing of tensions, known as détente, caused both countries to make symbolic gestures of reconciliation. One of these was the decision to hold a linkup between an American *Apollo* spacecraft and a Soviet *Soyuz* spacecraft in order to effect the first joint space mission.

The *Soyuz 19* spacecraft was launched first that day, from the Soviet facility known as the Baikonur Cosmodrome in Kazakhstan, then a part of the Soviet Union but now an independent nation. It carried Commander Aleksei A. Leonov and flight engineer Valeri N. Kubasov. Just over seven hours later, the *Apollo 18* spacecraft was launched from the Kennedy Space Center at Cape Canaveral, Florida. It carried Commander Thomas P. Stafford, docking module pilot Deke Slayton, and module pilot Vance D. Brand.

The two spacecraft successfully linked up, forming what was in effect a five-person space station. The crews performed a variety of scientific tests, including growing ultrafine crystals that could only be produced in space due to the weightlessness present in orbiting vehicles. Docking systems and the compatibility of Soviet and American equipment were also tested. Ground control stations in the United States and the Soviet Union cooperated in the monitoring of the mission, exchanging information such as tracking data. Meanwhile, the mission members shared their respective vehicles, ate meals together, and got to know each other both professionally and personally.

Apollo and *Soyuz* were linked for just under two days. The *Soyuz* detached first, returning to the Soviet Union and landing on July 21, 1975. The *Apollo* remained in orbit for a few days longer, returning to Earth with a splashdown in the Pacific

Ocean on July 24, 1975. In addition to marking a thaw in U.S.-Soviet relations, the mission set a precedent for future nonpolitical cooperative ventures. Since the 1991 breakup of the Soviet Union, the Russian space authorities who took over the Soviet space programs and facilities have maintained a fairly close relationship with their American counterparts, thanks in part to such precedents.

July 16

Mary Baker Eddy's Birthday

Seemingly a failure by the time she was middle-aged, Mary Baker Eddy later became one of the most remarkable women of the 19th century. Her influence extended to all parts of the United States and to many other countries through the religion that she founded, namely the Church of Christ, Scientist. Its members are more familiarly known as Christian Scientists, who believe in the practice of spiritual healing based on the teaching that cause and effect are mental and that sin, sickness, and death will be destroyed by a full understanding of Jesus' teaching and ministry.

Mary Baker was born in Bow, New Hampshire, on July 16, 1821. She was the youngest of six children of Mark and Abigail Baker, both descendants of old New England families. Too frail to attend school regularly, she received instruction at home from her family, mostly from her college-educated brother Albert. When Mary was 14, the family moved to Sanbornton Bridge (later Tilton), New Hampshire. When her health permitted, Mary attended Sanbornton Academy and also Holmes Academy in Plymouth, several miles away. According to parish records, she joined the Congregational Church in Sanbornton when she was 17.

In December 1843 Mary Baker married George W. Glover, whose sister had married her oldest brother, Samuel, some ten years earlier. After their wedding the couple went to Charleston, South Carolina, where Glover had a building and contracting business. The following July, Glover died. Mary returned to her family in New Hampshire, where on September 11, 1844, she gave birth to her only child, George Glover.

After her mother's death in 1849 and her father's later remarriage, Mary left home and began what must have been the most difficult period of her life. For many bleak years she moved between New Hampshire, Maine, and Massachusetts, living with family and friends, and in rented rooms. She was destitute and ill, with no home of her own. She had a number of suitors, however, and finally married Daniel Patterson. Patterson was an itinerant dentist with an interest in homeopathic medicine that the sickly Mary Baker shared. He was a poor husband, however, and they were often separated (she ultimately secured a divorce in 1873).

Meanwhile, homeopathic remedies had not helped her. She had, however, heard the stories that had spread throughout New England of remarkable cures effected by a faith healer, Phineas Parkhurst Quimby. Her hopes for a cure awakened, she traveled to Portland, Maine, for her first meeting with Quimby, which took place on October 10, 1862. Her health was temporarily improved by his treatment, and for a while she became his disciple, even helping to treat some of his patients. Her lifelong concern about her own poor health and her great devotion to the Bible made it easy for her to accept Quimby's assertion that he had discovered Jesus' secrets of healing. Quimby further believed that the Bible provided the key to solving all the problems of the world.

In January 1866, Quimby died. Mary wrote a poem "On the Death of P. P. Quimby Who Healed with the Truth That Christ Taught" that was published in a local newspaper. On February 1, 1866, just a few weeks after Quimby's death, Mary slipped on some ice and injured her chronically troublesome back. Three days later, still confined to her bed, she read the New Testament passage in Matthew 9:2–8 that tells of Jesus' healing a paralytic:

> And, behold, they brought to him a man sick of the palsy, lying on a bed: and Jesus seeing their faith said unto the sick of the palsy; Son, be of good cheer; thy sins be forgiven thee. And, behold, certain of the scribes said within themselves, This man blasphemeth. And Jesus knowing their thoughts said, Wherefore think ye evil in your hearts? For whether is easier, to say, Thy sins be forgiven thee; or to say, Arise, and walk? But that ye may know that the Son of man hath power on earth to forgive sins, (then saith he to the sick of the palsy) Arise, take up thy bed, and go unto thine house. And he arose, and departed to his house. But when the multitudes saw it, they marvelled, and glorified God, which had given such power unto men.

In her book *Miscellaneous Writings* (1896), Mary recalled the importance of the occasion: "As I read, the healing Truth dawned upon my sense; and the result was that I rose, dressed myself, and ever after was in better health than I had before enjoyed." Thus was the beginning of Christian Science, established in February 1866, a date officially accepted as the beginning of the church that now has thousands of branches around the world.

During the years that followed her recovery, Mary began to delve more into the healing ministry of religion. She also devoted herself to what she regarded as the even more important task of formulating her thoughts on how healing should be practiced and teaching others her philosophy of healing. Mary let people read her works, and soon small groups gathered around her to learn and discuss her thoughts about healing. Many of these people became her pupils and were later established as healers in their own right. Her fortunes improved by 1875, and that same year she brought out the first version of *Science and Health*, which became the Christian Science textbook. All told, 382 editions of the work were published during her lifetime.

On January 1, 1877, Mary Baker Glover, then 55, married one of her disciples, Asa Gilbert Eddy. From that time forward she was known as Mary Baker Eddy. Her husband, a sewing machine salesman, became the first of her students to use the title Christian Science practitioner. Their marriage was short-lived, since he died of heart disease on June 3, 1882.

Mary Baker Eddy not only drew up the tenets of her new church, but chose the directors, the 12 charter members, and the 20 additional persons known as first members of the First Church of Christ, Scientist. She also laid down the administrative bylaws in the *Church Manual*, a publication that she had personally revised through 89 editions by the time of her death. In 1879 the Church of Christ, Scientist, with its headquarters in Boston, was chartered under Massachusetts law. Mother Eddy, as her disciples called her, became pastor and was ordained by her followers in a special ceremony. Her students fanned out across the country. In 1908 she oversaw the first publication of *The Christian Science Monitor*, which soon became a well respected national newspaper.

Mary Baker Eddy died on December 3, 1910. Her church has prospered in the decades since then. It has occasionally drawn criticism, however, for its reliance on faith over and above secular science and modern medicine.

The Starting Date of the Islamic Calendar

The Islamic calendar, which many Americans of the Islamic faith follow, has as its beginning date July 16, 622, of the more common Christian Era calendar. It was on that date that the prophet Mohammed left Mecca for Medina, then called Yathrib, in what is known as the *Hegira* or "flight."

Caliph Umar I, the first to systematize the Islamic calendar, decided to use the Hegira as an epochal date of reference, since it was that event which led to the establishment of Islam in Medina and its later spread through Arabia. Thus, in the Islamic calendar, July 16, 622, is known as the first day of the first month of the year of the Hegira. Umar finalized his calendar in 639.

The Islamic calendar is based on lunar months, not on the solar year like the Christian Era calendar (see Appendix A: The Calendar). Months begin when the first lunar crescent after the New Moon is sighted in the sky after sunset. Islamic months last 29 to 30 days. There are 12 months in the year, for a total of 354 to 355 days, 11 or 12 days less than in the solar year. Because of the shorter year, Islamic months are not pinned to a particular season but retrogress, over time, from spring to winter to fall to summer and then back to spring again. Holidays dated by the Islamic calendar have no fixed parallel point of reference in the Christian Era calendar, but appear as movable events. (The same, of course, is true when Christian Era dates are expressed on the Islamic calendar.)

The twelve months of the Islamic calendar are:
(1) Muharram
(2) Safar
(3) Rabi' al-Awwal
(4) Rabi' al-Thaani
(5) Jumada al-Ooola
(6) Jumada al-Ukhra
(7) Rajab
(8) Sha'ban
(9) Ramadan
(10) Shawwal
(11) Dhu al-Qa'dah
(12) Dhu al-Hijjah.

Years in the Islamic calendar are typically abbreviated A.H., after the Latin words *Anno Hegirae*.

July 17

John Jacob Astor's Birthday

John Jacob Astor was born in the village of Waldorf near Heidelberg, Germany, on July 17, 1763, the third son of a butcher. He decided to leave home at the age of 16 after his brother George had already established a musical instrument store in London. In 1780 John Astor set out on foot for the Rhine. He worked his way down the river on a timber raft, earning enough for passage to England. Astor worked for his brother in London, learning English and all that he could about America. In

November 1783, after the Treaty of Paris was signed following the conclusion of the American Revolution, he embarked for the United States. His vessel was frozen in the Chesapeake Bay for two months en route to Baltimore, and this delay gave him time for conversations with a passenger who was engaged in the fur trade. Astor then decided to enter that business.

By 1786 Astor had established himself in the fur trade and was making purchasing trips as far west as Mackinaw, in what is now northern Michigan. As a result of tireless effort and sharp business practices, by 1800 Astor had built up a fortune of $250,000 and became the country's leading fur trader. He also began to purchase New York real estate in large amounts. Shortly before his death a half century later, Astor asserted that "could I begin life again knowing what I now know, I would buy every foot of land on the island of Manhattan." By that time the growth of American cities had become rapid, and Astor saw how enormous the profits in real estate would continue to be.

In the early years of the 19th century, however, Astor was preoccupied with the fur trade. His men were already dominating the fur trade of the Great Lakes region when President Thomas Jefferson's acquisition of the huge Louisiana Purchase in 1803 sparked Astor's imagination and opened broader trading vistas. Astor followed the reports of Meriwether Lewis and William Clark's expedition of 1804–1806 with keen interest. In 1808 he consolidated his holdings into the American Fur Company, chartered in New York state, and also established the Pacific Fur Company and the South West Company as subsidiaries.

By this time Astor was fully engaged in a twin commercial struggle to monopolize the American fur trade and to compete with the great Canadian fur interests, particularly the Hudson's Bay Company and the Northwest Company. Astor devised a daring scheme to further both these ends, and but for larger international circumstances his plan might have succeeded. Wishing to circumvent the St. Louis merchants' hold over the western fur trade, he decided to establish a base at the mouth of the Columbia River, the farthest point reached by Lewis and Clark. Such a depot, as yet undreamed of by anyone else, would enable his companies to ship precious furs directly to eager Chinese markets across the Pacific. Middlemen would be avoided, and his furs would bring even larger profits in exchange for Chinese tea. According to his plan, tea would be carried straight from China to Europe to be exchanged once again at high profits for goods to be imported to the United States at still further profit. To complete the global circuit, a ship with goods for trappers would be dispatched from the Atlantic coast to go around South America to the Oregon Territory.

In 1810–1811, Astor sent out a land party to lay commercial claim to the area explored five years earlier by Lewis and Clark and to interest native tribes in trapping for the Pacific Fur Company. At the same time Astor equipped a sea party for the long trip around Cape Horn, with orders to establish and provision Fort Astoria at the mouth of the Columbia River and to await the overland party.

By land, harsh competition with the Northwest Company hindered the venture from an early point, as did native tribal hostility. Despite many difficulties, however, Fort Astoria was established in 1811 on the south bank of the Columbia some 12 miles from the open sea. If the War of 1812 with Great Britain had not broken out, the settlement might have become permanent. However, after a calamitous expedition by the settlers to trade with a native tribe, Astor's supply ships were cut off by the British navy in 1813. Following these reverses, Astor's field partners sold Fort Astoria's trading goods and abandoned the company's posts to its rivals.

If the War of 1812 undercut his western vision, John Jacob Astor made millions from it by lending money at exorbitant rates to a desperate United States government in 1814. In spite of his retreat from the far western fur trade, he shortly achieved a virtual monopoly of the trade within American territory. By 1817 his men controlled the Mississippi Valley, often riding roughshod over government officials. After 1822 they controlled the upper Missouri Valley as well. This monopoly continued after his retirement from the fur trade in 1834.

Astor was then 70 years old, and his withdrawal from the fur trade was doubtless prompted in part by weariness. Moreover, despite his vigorous campaign against the Rocky Mountain Fur Company, an American competitor, Astor was disappointed in the profits from furs. By 1834 the great days of the fur trade were behind, as Astor had astutely calculated. After 1838 the market rapidly declined as other products replaced fur in fashionable men's hats. However, in all that the fur trade had wrought on the North American continent, John Jacob Astor had had a large role. The trade's "mountain men" had done much to mark out wilderness paths and the most advantageous sites for settlement.

John Jacob Astor devoted his later years to managing his fortune. He died in his New York home on March 29, 1848, at the age of 84. His estate was conservatively estimated at $20 million, an enormous fortune in those days.

Florida Ceded to the United States

Florida was claimed for Spain on Easter Day in 1513 by Juan Ponce de León. During the next half century, the peninsula was explored by other Spaniards, such as Pánfilo de Narváez, who perished by shipwreck in the Gulf of Mexico after he fled from natives in northwest Florida. There was also Hernando de Soto, who landed on Florida's west coast and explored 4,000 miles to the north and west before he too perished. Tristán de Luna founded Pensacola on Florida's Gulf Coast panhandle, and Pedro Menéndez de Avilés founded the city of St. Augustine on Florida's east coast.

Two centuries passed before the rivalries of European powers for North American lands reached their peak. However, a foreshadowing of what was to come took place after a group of French Huguenots established a fort at the mouth of the St. Johns River, above St. Augustine in 1564. In two bloody battles, the Spanish under Menéndez drove the French out the following year. With the threat of foreign competition thus removed, Spanish control of Florida remained uninterrupted until 1763.

The year 1763 marked the conclusion of the Seven Years' War in Europe, of which the French and Indian War was the American aspect. Peace became official with the 1763 Treaty of Paris between victorious Great Britain on the one hand, and France and Spain on the other. One of the provisions of that document was that Havana, Cuba, which the British had conquered, would be returned to Spain in exchange for Florida. Great Britain also received from France additional land that extended the area of Florida from that state's present border at the Perdido River all the way to the Mississippi, though it did not include strategically located New Orleans.

The treaty marked the start of two decades of British rule in Florida. It was a period of prosperity, during which the British separated the region into East and West Florida with the Apalachicola River as the dividing line. East Florida was similar to, but somewhat smaller than, the present state of Florida.

It was during Britain's 20-year control of the Floridas that the 13 American colonies revolted. The Floridas remained loyal to Britain during the American Revolution and were a haven for Loyalists, who flocked there from the rebelling colonies. When the American Revolution formally ended with the 1783 Treaty of Paris between Great Britain and the new United States, relations between European powers again influenced the fate of the Florida region. Related treaties that Britain signed respectively with France (an ally of the United States) and Spain (an ally of France) became effective simultaneously with the Treaty of Paris. In accordance with the Anglo-Spanish agreement, the Floridas were retroceded to Spain in return for the abandonment of Spanish hopes for gaining British-occupied Gibraltar.

Spain was to have control of the Floridas until 1821. This time, however, its grasp was not so firm and it was to weaken even more as time went on. For years after the United States acquired the vast Louisiana Purchase territory from France in 1803, debate raged as to whether West Florida (or at least that portion between the Perdido and Mississippi Rivers) had been included in the transaction as the United States claimed. The Louisiana Purchase, meanwhile, served as an impetus for the ever-continuing westward thrust that would eventually carry American settlers all the way to the Pacific Ocean. They were already moving into West Florida and neighboring areas.

In 1810 President James Madison declared West Florida to be under the jurisdiction of the United States. Two years later, portions of West Florida were lopped off by the United States Congress, which annexed the area west of the Pearl River to the new state of Louisiana and incorporated the land between the Pearl and Perdido Rivers into the Mississippi Territory. The latter strip of Gulf Coast was subsequently divided between Mississippi, which became a state in 1817, and Alabama, which became a state in 1819.

Control of West Florida by the Spanish, who still claimed the disputed region, became even more tenuous after the outbreak of the War of 1812 between the United States and Great Britain. Part of the area, including the Spanish fort at Mobile and the land between Mobile and the Perdido, was occupied by American general James Wilkinson's forces in 1813. Late in 1814, Andrew Jackson captured Spanish Pensacola en route to his triumph in the battle of New Orleans. Jackson, again without authorization, took Pensacola for a second time in 1818.

Negotiations that the United States hoped would end the Florida controversy were going on between the United States and Spain, but were interrupted by what the Spanish regarded as the warlike nature of Jackson's incursion. Nevertheless the Spanish, preoccupied by difficulties at home and revolutions in South America, were willing to settle. The result was the Adams-Onis Treaty, by which Spain abandoned its claim to West Florida and ceded East Florida to the United States in return for $5 million that the United States agreed to credit toward claims of its citizens against Spain (see related essays throughout this book).

Columbia University Opens

King's College, later known as Columbia University, opened on July 17, 1754, in New York City after several years of controversy. The New York colonial legislature in 1746 made provisions to raise money for the school through public lotteries. The colony amassed 17,000 British pounds within five years and gave it to the trustees, but disagreements threatened the future of the project. Dissenting Protestants felt uneasy about the role of the Church of England in the administration of the institution: Two-thirds of the trustees were Anglicans and some were even vestrymen of Trinity Church. William Livingston, a lawyer, Presbyterian, and member of the leading family in the colony, argued for a liberal nonsectarian college in a series of articles in the newspaper known as the *Independent Reflector*. In reality, Livingston merely wanted to prevent the establishment of an Anglican college, but he argued in libertarian terms. He stated that a sectarian institution would intensify animosities in the religiously heterogeneous province and perhaps enable the faction that controlled higher education to dominate the colony. Livingston envisioned a college established by the colonial assembly as the most desirable solution since it would make it possible for all factions to have a voice in educational matters.

The charter of King's College was a conciliatory document designed to resolve the dispute and unify all factions in the support of the school. The result was to make the college almost nonsectarian. Indeed, of all the institutions of higher learning established in the colonies prior to the American Revolution, only King's College never had a theology faculty associated with it.

Although the college officially dates its existence from October 31, 1754, namely the day on which its charter from King George II was granted, by that time it had already been in operation for a few months. The Reverend Samuel Johnson of Stratford, Connecticut, assumed the office of president on July 17, 1754, and greeted the first class of eight students.

The capture of New York City by the British in 1776 closed the college for the duration of the American Revolution and its buildings served as a military hospital. The institution reopened after the New York state legislature granted it another charter and a new name, namely Columbia College, on May 1, 1784. This revised document ended the former requirement that the institution's president be an Episcopalian and that selections from the liturgy of the Church of England be used at the school's religious services. In 1787 title to Columbia was transferred from the state to the trustees.

Columbia officially became a university in 1896, the change in terminology reflecting almost a century and a half of growth. The law school opened in 1858, a school of engineering in 1864, and a school of architecture in 1896.

July 18

John Rutledge's Death

Photo by Robert Hinkley, Collection of the Supreme Court of the United States.

John Rutledge

John Rutledge was born in Charleston (then Charlestown), South Carolina, or possibly in nearby Christ Church Parish, in September 1739 on an unknown day. His father, John Rutledge, had emigrated from England in 1735 and settled in Charleston, marrying Sarah Hext. John, the eldest of their seven children, was born soon after his mother turned 15. By birth he belonged to the cultivated planter class of coastal South Carolina, whose wealth from rice and indigo assured their social and political dominance of the colony in the 18th century.

John Rutledge Sr. supervised his son's education until his death in 1750, when John was 11. The boy was also taught by the minister of Christ Church and by a classics tutor. He was then sent to London to study law in the Middle Temple. In 1760 Rutledge was admitted to the bar, and in 1761 he returned to Charleston to practice. Two years later he married Elizabeth Grimké; the couple would eventually have ten children.

John Rutledge entered politics in 1762, when he was elected from Christ Church Parish to the Carolina Commons House. He was to hold this seat for 14 years, until he became the leader of the rebellious colony in 1776. His rise was rapid. At the age of 25 he became attorney general of South Carolina (1764–1765), and in 1765 he was sent as a delegate to the colonial congress called to protest the Stamp Act. There he chaired the committee that wrote the petition against the act to the House of Lords.

In 1774 Rutledge reappeared in intercolonial politics as a representative to the First Continental Congress in Philadelphia, Pennsylvania. He had gained the confidence of the Carolina merchants as well as of the more bellicose planters in the hot discussions of the previous months. In Philadelphia, Rutledge first argued for colonial self-government within the British Empire. This position, together with his successful battle to exempt rice from the boycott list against Britain, put Rutledge in a very strong political position within South Carolina. The next year he was reelected as delegate to the Second Continental Congress. He urged that regular governments be set up in the colonies, replacing those directed by royal governors. On November 4, 1775, the congress advised South Carolina to proceed accordingly if necessary.

Armed with this directive and prepared to break with Great Britain, Rutledge returned to South Carolina. His election to the Council of Safety and service on the committee that wrote the South Carolina constitution of 1776 fulfilled his ambition to play a major role in the reorganization of the colony. In March 1776, when the South Carolina congress adopted the new constitution, it also chose the 37-year-old Rutledge as its president.

As chief executive of the first independent government in the American colonies, John Rutledge led South Carolina reasonably well. He successfully defended Charleston against British attacks on June 28, 1776, at Fort Moultrie. This victory freed the southern colonies from invasion for nearly three years. In addition, the colony prospered economically.

In 1778 Rutledge vetoed a more liberal constitution for South Carolina and resigned the presidency. However, when invasion was again imminent in February 1779, he was recalled and elected governor. He took the field, desperately combating the British with inadequate forces. In May 1780, after a siege of two months, Charleston surrendered. The legislature vested Rutledge with plenary powers before adjourning. He then went to the North Carolina border towns, implored George Washington and congress for aid, and encouraged local militia officers such as "Swamp Fox" Francis Marion to undertake what amounted to guerrilla warfare. As the fighting continued in 1781, Rutledge took steps to restore civil government. He issued terms of pardon and called for an election of members to an assembly to meet in January 1782. Soon thereafter, he stepped down as governor.

Once peace was restored, in 1782 Rutledge was elected to both the state assembly and the Continental Congress. In 1784 his election to the chancery court of South Carolina launched his judicial career, and from 1784 to 1790 he sat in the South Carolina House of Representatives. However, in 1787 his efforts were required on the national level. With Charles Cotesworth Pinckney, Charles Pinckney, and Pierce Butler, he represented South Carolina at the Constitutional Convention in Philadelphia, where he served as chairman of the Committee on Detail. During the convention he worked on behalf of the interests of the planters of the lower south in general and of South Carolina in particular. Rutledge vigorously opposed restrictions on the slave trade and was influential in the compromise that extended the trade to 1808. He argued that society should be divided into classes for representation and that office holding should be restricted to men of property. Rutledge also championed legislative supremacy rather than an independent executive and urged the assumption of states' debts by the national government.

After an active role in the South Carolina ratifying convention, in 1789 Rutledge was appointed senior associate justice of the United States Supreme Court by President George Washington. In 1791, however, he resigned to become chief justice of the South Carolina state supreme court. In 1795, after John Jay's retirement, he indicated his interest in the chief justiceship of the United States Supreme Court to President Washington. The president appointed Rutledge in July 1795 during a recess of Congress, and Rutledge presided at the August sitting of the court. However, on December 15, 1795, the Senate refused to confirm his appointment. Whether it was because of his bitter public attack on the Jay Treaty earlier in the year or because of his increasing mental instability is not wholly clear. Since the death of his wife in 1792, John Rutledge had suffered intermittent attacks of insanity, and after his rejection by the Senate his mind failed completely. He died on July 18, 1800, and was buried in the churchyard of St. Michael's at Charleston.

The Presidential Succession Act of 1947

The United States Constitution provides for both a president and a vice president. In Article II, Section 1, clause 6, it also states,

In Case of the Removal of the President from Office, or of his Death, Resignation, or Inability to discharge the Powers and Duties of the said Office, the Same shall devolve on the Vice President, and the Congress may by Law provide for the Case of Removal, Death, Resignation or Inability, both of the President and Vice President, declaring what Officer shall then act as President, and such Officer shall act accordingly, until the Disability be removed, or a President shall be elected.

In other words, the vice president succeeds the president, but after that it is up to Congress to establish the order of succession. On July 18, 1947, Congress passed the Presidential Succession Act, which sets forth the modern order of succession. It states that, after the vice president, the order of succession to the presidency is: (1) the Speaker of the House of Representatives and then (2) the president pro tempore of the Senate. After those two persons, the line of succession goes to the secretaries of the various cabinet departments in the order in which they were created. Thus, since the State Department is the oldest cabinet department, the secretary of state would be next in line after the president pro tempore of the Senate. Here is the list of succession for cabinet officers:

(1) secretary of state
(2) secretary of the treasury
(3) secretary of defense
(4) attorney general
(5) secretary of the interior
(6) secretary of agriculture
(7) secretary of commerce
(8) secretary of labor
(9) secretary of health and human services
(10) secretary of housing and urban development
(11) secretary of transportation
(12) secretary of energy
(13) secretary of education, and
(14) secretary of veterans affairs

Of course, all of the people in the line of succession must satisfy the constitutional requirements for becoming president. Each must be: (1) a natural born citizen of the United States; (2) at least 35 years old; and (3) a resident of the United States for at least 14 years. If someone does not meet these qualifications, the succession goes to the next person in line.

July 19

First Women's Rights Convention: Seneca Falls, New York

The American movement for women's rights had its formal start on July 19, 1848, when the first convention to discuss the rights of women was held at Seneca Falls, New York. It was attended largely by residents of western New York state.

This was the beginning of the organized women's movement, even though a few voices had been raised since colonial days. In 1647 Margaret Brent appeared before the Maryland assembly to demand the right to vote in an unprecedented and ultimately unsuccessful appeal. Thomas Paine, the writer best known for his advocacy of the American Revolution, was also a consistent champion of the vote for women. Other early proponents of equality for women included the Quakers, who historically favored granting women the right to vote.

Some delegates to the Continental Congress also favored enfranchising women, and the matter was debated while the United States Constitution was being drafted. So intense were the feelings for and against, however, that the congress was forced to sidestep the issue by leaving it to the individual states to formulate voting laws that might also give the franchise to women. Also sidestepped was the subject of slavery, on which the delegates were similarly unable to agree. In order to achieve ratification of the Constitution, it was considered necessary to keep the status of women and slaves unresolved.

Books such as *A Vindication of the Rights of Women* (1792), by the British writer Mary Wollstonecraft, had an influence in intellectual circles on both sides of the Atlantic. So too did later works such as *The Equality of the Sexes* (1838), by the southern abolitionist Sarah Grimké, and *Woman in the 19th Century* (1845), by the literary critic and reformer Margaret Fuller. These were isolated works, however. In mid-19th-century America, the traditional belief that women were inferior and that their only proper roles were childbearing and housekeeping still held sway. Rare were those who accepted women as adult human beings with fully developed individual attributes and innate rights equal to those of men.

The fact that women were regarded as second- or third-class beings became unmistakably clear to two American women active in the cause of abolition when they journeyed to London, England, in 1840 to attend the World Anti-Slavery Convention. One of them was Lucretia Coffin Mott of

Philadelphia, Pennsylvania. A devoted reformer, she was, like her husband, James Mott, an ardent Quaker. She had traveled extensively as a lecturer, speaking at Quaker meetings in various parts of the United States. The other woman was a youthful resident of Seneca Falls, namely Elizabeth Cady Stanton (see related essays throughout this book) who had traveled with her husband, Henry Brewster Stanton, to attend the London meeting. Because they were women, however, Mott and Stanton were denied official accreditation and could not be seated in the convention. Their attempt to participate touched off a lengthy debate in which noted clergymen put forward the claim that equal status for women was contrary to God's will. Finally (unlike six less fortunate women who had also been excluded), Mott and Stanton were granted the privilege of being seated where they could hear the proceedings, but they were hidden from view by a curtain and denied the right to speak.

The rebuff was to have historic consequences, for it convinced Mott that an emphasis should now be placed on women's rights. The subject occupied much of her attention for the rest of her life. Stanton, who was to become a dynamic advocate of equality, was strongly influenced by Mott. The discussions that they held in London led directly to the Women's Rights Convention in 1848 at Seneca Falls.

The gathering, held in the chapel of the Wesleyan Methodist Church, approved Stanton's celebrated bill of rights for women. This was the famous Declaration of Sentiments, patterned after the Declaration of Independence, asserting that women are the equals of men and are entitled to all the rights and privileges of citizenship. These rights included the right to hold property, to control their own wages, and to have a voice in the management of their children in addition to the right to vote. The Declaration of Sentiments also demanded wider educational and professional opportunities for women.

A similar convention was held in 1850 in Salem, Ohio, a Quaker center and an important link in the Underground Railroad. It was followed by the first national women's rights convention, which took place in Worcester, Massachusetts, in the autumn of 1850 under the leadership of Lucy Stone. Some 250 delegates were present at the Worcester gathering, representing nine states.

The organized effort to achieve equal rights for women begun at Seneca Falls led to some small early victories. For example, in 1852 Kentucky passed a law permitting widows with children of school age to vote for school district trustees. Other states enacted legislation permitting married

women to own property in their own names. It would be many decades, however, before more significant progress was made (see the related articles throughout this book).

George McGovern's Birthday

George Stanley McGovern was born in Avon, South Dakota, on July 19, 1922. The McGovern family eventually moved to Mitchell, South Dakota, where his father secured a position as a Methodist minister. Young George McGovern was active in his high school debate team, and developed an interest in politics.

In 1940 McGovern won a scholarship to Dakota Wesleyan University. The United States entered World War II in 1941, and McGovern was drafted into the U.S. Army Air Force in 1943. He served in the European theater as the pilot of a B-24 bomber. McGovern flew 35 missions and was eventually awarded the Distinguished Flying Cross. After the war he returned to academia and began graduate studies in history at Northwestern University. McGovern earned his doctorate, and in 1952 returned to South Dakota Wesleyan to teach. However, in 1953 he quit his job in order to become the executive secretary of the South Dakota Democratic Party organization.

McGovern first entered national politics in 1956 when he was elected to the United States House of Representatives. He was reelected to the House, but lost his first bid for the United States Senate in 1960. He was eventually rewarded for his loyalty to the Democratic Party with positions as special assistant to President John F. Kennedy and as the director of the Food for Peace Program. In 1962 McGovern again ran for the Senate, and this time he won.

During the 1960s Senator McGovern began to distance himself from official Democratic support for the Vietnam War, and became a prominent critic of the prowar policies of President Lyndon B. Johnson. He participated in antiwar activities, and became a leading spokesman for the more liberal wing of the Democratic Party and American politics in general. McGovern did support the Johnson administration, however, when it came to increased funding for such government activities as antihunger programs. He also reluctantly endorsed the nomination of Hubert Humphrey, Johnson's vice president, for president at the 1968 Democratic Convention despite Humphrey's support for the Vietnam War.

In 1969 McGovern became the chairman of a committee established to reform the Democratic Party. He worked to make the party more open for women and minorities. McGovern's position made him a leading figure in the Democratic organization, and in 1972 he decided to run for the party's nomination as its presidential candidate. Despite the opposition of many more conservative Democrats, he won the party primaries and secured the nomination. However, his campaign against Republican candidate Richard M. Nixon went badly. McGovern was forced to abandon his running mate for vice president, Senator Thomas F. Eagleton, due to Eagleton's mental health problems and replace him with Sargent Shriver. Further, McGovern's liberal policy positions alienated most mainstream Americans, resulting in an electoral landslide for Nixon.

Nixon won with 520 electoral votes to McGovern's 17, in which he carried only Massachusetts and the District of Columbia. Despite this stinging defeat, he was reelected to the Senate in 1974. In 1980 he lost to Republican James Abdnor in another Republican landslide election, this time led by Ronald Reagan who took the presidency that year from Democrat Jimmy Carter. The nation had become increasingly conservative, making liberals like McGovern seem somewhat antiquated, and the end of the Vietnam War in the mid-1970s made his popularity with respect to that issue moot. He attempted to reenter Democratic Party politics in 1984 by entering the primaries for that year's presidential nomination, but he terminated his campaign after finishing third in the Massachusetts primary. He continues to write and lecture on politics and foreign policy; a 1996 book describing his daughter's tragic struggle with alcoholism was well received by reviewers.

July 20

First Manned Landing on the Moon

On July 20, 1969, at 4:17 p.m. eastern daylight time a spacecraft launched by the United States glided in and came to rest in the Sea of Tranquility on the Moon. At 10:51 p.m. the door of the lunar module *Eagle* opened. Astronaut Neil A. Armstrong slowly descended the steps of his craft and five minutes later stepped onto the Moon. That step, and his historic words "That's one small step for a man, one giant leap for mankind," were seen and heard by an estimated 600 million people on Earth.

Armstrong, a 38-year-old civilian and commander of the Apollo 11 mission, was joined on the Moon 18 minutes later by air force colonel Edwin E. "Buzz" Aldrin Jr. Aldrin was 39 years old and pilot of the lunar module. Armstrong's first act after stepping outside the module was to pause on the second rung of the nine-step ladder and pull a lanyard, releasing a television camera that transmitted to the world the sight of his very first steps on the Moon. After Aldrin joined him they showed television viewers a plaque, which would remain on the Moon, with the words: "Here men from the planet Earth first set foot upon the Moon July 1969 A.D. We came in peace for all mankind." The men then planted an American flag made of metal on the lunar surface, stepped back, and saluted.

The mission was the first attempt ever at a manned Moon landing. The flight had been launched from Cape Kennedy, Florida, on July 16 at 9:32 a.m. eastern daylight time atop a 363-foot Saturn 5 launch rocket. Aboard with Armstrong and Aldrin was 38-year-old air force lieutenant colonel Michael Collins, pilot of the command module *Columbia*, which would circle the Moon during the mission and then take the astronauts back to Earth.

Columbia and *Eagle*, together with the Saturn rocket launcher, constituted Apollo 11. After separation from one another, the Apollo 11 components were referred to by their individual names. In describing early phases of the space trip, however, commentators used the collective name "Apollo."

Less than 12 minutes after launch, after two of the Saturn's three stages had fired in succession, Apollo 11 went into a two-and-a-half-hour orbit around the Earth. The orbiting was to assure that the astronauts had a vehicle that functioned properly and was fully capable of continuing the mission. Then a firing of the Saturn's third-stage engine boosted Apollo 11 out of its 115-mile-high orbit and into a trajectory toward the Moon. The astronauts separated the *Columbia* command ship in which they were situated from the Saturn's third stage, turned the *Columbia* around, and locked its nose into a connecting device on the *Eagle* lunar landing craft that was still connected to the third stage of the Saturn launch vehicle. The linked command ship and lunar module now pulled free of the Saturn's third stage.

After a three-day flight, the joined command ship *Columbia* and the lunar module *Eagle* swept into an orbit around the Moon. Aldrin and Armstrong then dressed in white pressurized space suits and, leaving Collins behind in the command craft, crawled through a tunnel into the lunar module. Once inside it, they activated the electrical power and checked all the instrument settings on the cockpit panel. The *Eagle's* four legs with yard-wide footpads were extended from the ship, ready to land it on the Moon's surface. Then the *Eagle* and the *Columbia* were separated. When all of the latches were loosened, Armstrong radioed ground control: "The *Eagle* has wings."

The *Columbia* remained in orbit around the Moon while the *Eagle* began its historic descent. After the descent rocket was fired, the *Eagle* coasted toward the target area on the Moon under its automatic guidance system. When they were about 400 feet from the surface, the astronauts saw that their ship's navigation and guidance system was taking them into a rocky crater surrounded by huge boulders. Further, it was some distance beyond the intended landing site. In addition, they received an alarm signal indicating that the onboard computer was being overworked. Taking manual control of the ship, Armstrong quickly accelerated its speed and took it four additional miles to a safe landing spot. The craft touched down with only a few seconds of fuel remaining. Then Armstrong radioed: "Houston, Tranquility Base here. The *Eagle* has landed." Houston responded: "Roger, Tranquility, we copy you on the ground. You got a bunch of guys about to turn blue. We're breathing again. Thanks a lot."

The first duty after landing was to check the spacecraft's systems, its supplies of oxygen and fuel, and its ascent engine to be sure that the men would be able to leave the surface of the Moon. Suiting up for the moonwalk took more than three hours. Once on the Moon, the astronauts checked and photographed the *Eagle* from all angles to be certain that no flight or landing damage had occurred. They studied the depressions, roughly one or two inches deep, that the *Eagle's* footpads had made in the Moon's surface dust. Then they tested the best way to run and walk on the Moon, which has only one-sixth of Earth's gravity. Their efforts made it seem as if they were frolicking with childlike excitement, trying two-legged kangaroo jumps and then hopping in slow motion with six- to eight-foot strides.

The astronauts' scientific work included gathering 48 pounds of rocks and soil samples to take back to Earth. They also took a sample of subsurface soil. In the process, Aldrin found that he could force a core tube only about five inches downward into the lunar soil, and yet that same lunar soil was surprisingly easy to move sideways. The astronauts set up a solar wind composition detector, a seismic detector, and a laser reflector. The men also took dozens of photographs during their two-hour-and-21-minute walk on the Moon.

On July 21, 1969, at 1:54 p.m. eastern daylight time, after spending more than 21 hours on the Moon, Armstrong fired the rocket that returned the *Eagle* to lunar orbit. At 5:35 p.m. approximately 69 miles from the Moon, the craft redocked with the command module and the two astronauts reentered the *Columbia*. They then jettisoned the lunar module. After an emergency-free return

trip, the *Columbia* made a perfect splashdown in the Pacific Ocean at 12:50 p.m. eastern daylight time on July 24. Helicopters took the astronauts and their capsule to the aircraft carrier USS *Hornet*, where the men were put in quarantine. On August 10 they were released and treated as heroes by an excited nation and world.

The Moon landing was the result of years of scientific preparation and the expenditure of billions of dollars. Although both the United States and the Soviet Union had been engaged in extensive space research, on April 12, 1961, the Soviets were the first to place a man (cosmonaut Yuri Gagarin) in orbit around Earth. On May 25, 1961, President John F. Kennedy addressed Congress on the challenges of a successful space program for the United States. He said: "I believe we should go to the Moon . . . before this decade is out." Support for the space program solidified after his assassination, and the United States became the first country to reach the Moon. Despite their early victories, the Soviets had neither the technology nor the economic resources to surpass the United States in the "space race."

About the crew of Apollo 11:

Neil A. Armstrong was born in Wapakoneta, Ohio, on August 5, 1930. He took flying lessons as a teenager and received his pilot's license on his 16th birthday. He was an aviator in the United States Navy from 1949 until 1952, and flew 78 combat missions during the Korean War. After his naval service he completed his studies at Purdue University and in 1955 received a bachelor of science degree in aeronautical engineering. He then became a test pilot at Edwards Air Force Base in California, flying the F-100, F-101, and F-50 as well as the X-1 and X-15 rocket planes, setting records for speed and altitude. After he was named the first civilian astronaut in September 1962, his first assignment was to be backup command pilot to L. Gordon Cooper on the *Gemini 5* mission. Armstrong served as command pilot on the *Gemini 8* flight in March 1966. In this capacity he performed the first docking of two spacecraft in orbit. Training for the Apollo missions in 1968, he was almost killed when his lunar landing trainer lost power and crashed. He was named commander of the Apollo 11 in January 1969.

Edwin E. Aldrin was born in Montclair, New Jersey, on January 20, 1930. He graduated third in his class of 475 from the United States Military Academy at West Point in 1951. Following his father, who had been an officer in the United States Army Air Corps (piloting biplanes and setting several cross-country speed records), Aldrin transferred to the air force and earned his wings within a year. Like Armstrong, Aldrin also served in the

Korean War. A pilot of F-86 fighters, he completed 66 combat missions, and also received the Distinguished Flying Cross. He was awarded a doctorate in aeronautics by the Massachusetts Institute of Technology in 1963, and in October of that same year he became the first holder of a doctoral degree chosen to become an American astronaut. In November 1966, as pilot of the last flight in the Gemini series, he spent slightly over five and a half hours outside his craft in a spacewalk performing a number of engineering and scientific assignments.

Michael Collins, the pilot of the command module *Columbia*, was born on October 31, 1930, in Rome, Italy, where his father was serving as military attaché to the United States Embassy. Collins, a graduate of the United States Military Academy at West Point, subsequently transferred to the air force and was sent to California. There he became an experimental flight test officer at Edwards Air Force Base. One of the 14 astronauts appointed in October 1963 by the National Aeronautics and Space Administration, Collins finished his basic training at the Manned Spacecraft Center in Houston, Texas, and was named backup pilot to James Lovell Jr. on the *Gemini 7* flight. His initial space flight mission was in July 1966, when he served as pilot of *Gemini 10*. He was named to the crew of Apollo 8, but back surgery ultimately prevented his participation. The Apollo 11 flight was Collins's last mission as an astronaut.

The American Space Program Since the First Moon Landing

The American space program has evolved considerably since the Moon landing of July 20, 1969. Several important events are discussed elsewhere in this book; consult the Index for further information. In summary, after several more Apollo Moon landings, government funding was gradually moved into areas that were considered more cost-effective or productive. First, the space shuttle program was inaugurated. Second, a series of research satellites and deep space exploratory probes were launched. Third, there were new initiatives such as the Hubble Space Telescope. Beginning in the late 1990s, there was some discussion of a new manned space initiative, perhaps a voyage to Mars in cooperation with Russian space authorities (who have continued many of their space programs despite the collapse of the Soviet Union in 1991).

A timeline of some of the major events in the American space program since the first Moon landing is set forth below:

November 14, 1969: Apollo 12, the second successful lunar landing mission, is launched.

April 11, 1970: Apollo 13 is launched, but suffers an explosion in its oxygen tanks. Its Moon landing is aborted, but the crew returns safely.

January 31, 1971: Apollo 14, the third successful lunar landing mission, is launched.

May 30, 1971: *Mariner 9* is launched, which becomes the first satellite to survey Mars from orbit.

July 26, 1971: Apollo 15, the fourth successful lunar landing mission, is launched.

July 30, 1971: Apollo 15 astronauts David Scott and James Irwin drive the first Moon rover.

March 2, 1972: *Pioneer 10* is launched toward Jupiter, and returns the first close-up images in 1973. After passing by Jupiter, itstrajectory took it out beyond the Solar System. Should it ever come into contact with intelligent life, it carries information about Earth, its location, its people, its languages, and its sounds.

April 16, 1972: Apollo 16, the fifth successful lunar landing mission, is launched.

December 7, 1972: Apollo 17, the sixth and last successful lunar landing mission, is launched.

April 5, 1973: *Pioneer 11* is launched and travels past Jupiter in 1974 and Saturn in 1979.

May 14, 1973: The *Skylab* is launched.

November 3, 1973: *Mariner 10* is launched toward Venus and Mercury.

July 1975: American Apollo 18 and Soviet Soyuz 19 are launched and successfully dock, achieving the first United States–Soviet joint space rendezvous.

July 20, 1976: *Viking 1* takes pictures of the surface of Mars.

September 3, 1976: *Viking 2* lands on Mars on the Plain of Utopia.

August–September 1977: *Voyager 1* and *Voyager 2* are launched toward Jupiter and Saturn, respectively.

December 1978: Two *Pioneer* spacecraft survey and map Venus.

September 1, 1979: *Pioneer 11* reaches Saturn.

April 12, 1981: The space shuttle *Columbia* is launched.

April 4, 1983: The space shuttle *Challenger* is launched.

June 19, 1983: Sally Ride, aboard the space shuttle *Challenger*, becomes the first American woman in space.

August 30, 1984: The space shuttle *Discovery* is launched.

October 3, 1985: The space shuttle *Atlantis* is launched.

January 28, 1986: The space shuttle *Challenger* explodes shortly after launch, killing all of its crew.

May 4, 1989: The space shuttle *Atlantis* successfully deploys the *Magellan* satellite.

October 18, 1989: The *Galileo* satellite is launched from the space shuttle *Atlantis* and begins its trek toward Jupiter.

April 24, 1990: The space shuttle *Discovery* deploys the Edwin P. Hubble Space Telescope astronomical observatory.

May 2, 1992: The space shuttle *Endeavor* is launched.

January 25, 1994: The *Clementine*, an advanced military satellite, is launched but ultimately malfunctions.

February 6, 1995: The space shuttle *Discovery* begins docking procedures with the Russian space station *Mir*, the first shuttle–*Mir* rendezvous.

February 17, 1996: The first of the Discovery series of satellites is launched, namely the *Near Earth Asteroid Rendezvous* (NEAR) spacecraft.

July 21

Ernest Hemingway's Birthday

Ernest Miller Hemingway, one of the greatest writers of the 20th century, was born in Oak Park, Illinois, on July 21, 1899. He was the second of Clarence and Grace Hall Hemingway's six children, with four sisters and one brother. The Hemingways lived in an upper-middle-class suburb of Chicago that Hemingway later referred to as a place of "wide lawns and narrow minds." He was alienated by its conservative isolationist nature, and as a youth took to solitary activities such as hunting and fishing that would be hobbies of his for life and inspire much of the naturalism in his work.

Hemingway attended the Oak Park public schools as a child, graduating from high school in the spring of 1917. He worked briefly for the *Kansas City Star* newspaper as a reporter, but when he turned 18 he decided to enlist in the military in order to serve in World War I. Even though he was rejected due to poor vision, he was able to join the Red Cross as an ambulance driver, and left for Europe in May 1918. He first went to Paris, France, and then to Milan, Italy.

Almost immediately after he arrived in Milan, there was a disastrous munitions factory explosion. Hemingway helped clean up the scattered corpses and wreckage, which affected him deeply. A few weeks later, he was injured near the front lines by shrapnel from an exploding mortar shell. Nevertheless, he was still able to take a wounded Italian soldier to a first aid station for medical treatment. For his heroism, Hemingway was awarded the Italian Silver Medal for Valor.

After the war, Hemingway returned to Oak Park in January 1919. Bored, he eventually took a position with the *Toronto Star* weekly newspaper. With his new wife, Hadley Richardson, he left for Europe in 1921 as the *Star*'s correspondent. They set up house in Paris, France, where Hemingway met such literary giants as Ezra Pound and Gertrude Stein, who labeled these postwar expatriates a "lost generation." Hemingway covered an international conference in Geneva in April 1922, events in the Ruhr valley in 1923, and other matters for the *Star*. However, his real interest was in developing his skills as a novelist with help from his literary friends. Some of his early stories included "Indian Camp" and "Cross-Country Snow."

Hemingway went on to write a short-story collection, *In Our Time* (1925), the successful novel *The Sun Also Rises* (1926), and another short-story collection, *Men Without Women* (1927). In 1929 came his groundbreaking work, *A Farewell to Arms*. Based on his war experiences, this novel was widely praised and established him as one of the greatest writers of the age.

Hemingway's personal life, however, was rather tumultuous despite his professional success. He divorced his wife in 1927, remarried to Pauline Pfeiffer, and in 1928 relocated to Key West, Florida. It would not be his last divorce and remarriage. Hemingway avidly pursued his interest in fishing in Key West, but also found the time to attend such exotic events as the bullfights at Pamplona, Spain. In 1932 he published a book about bullfighting entitled *Death in the Afternoon*, and in 1935 *Green Hills of Africa*, about big-game hunting on safari. Works of fiction included *Winner Take Nothing* (1933), *To Have and Have Not* (1937), and *The First Forty-nine Hours and Other Stories* (1938), which contained two of his most famous pieces: "The Snows of Kilimanjaro" and "The Short Happy Life of Francis Macomber."

In 1937 Hemingway went to Spain as a war correspondent covering the Spanish civil war in which Francisco Franco, the head of the rebel Nationalist government, ultimately triumphed. He wrote several works about the war, including a play, *The Fifth Column* (1938), and the best-selling novel *For Whom the Bell Tolls* (1940). Hemingway also served as a correspondent covering the D day landing in June 1944. After the war he published *The Old Man and the Sea* (1952), another classic of American literature.

Despite his literary success, and his receipt of the Nobel Prize for Literature in 1954, Hemingway continued to experience turmoil and deep depression in his personal life. He experimented with shock therapy, but ultimately resorted to suicide on July 2, 1961, when he killed himself with a shotgun, just as his father had. Hemingway was buried in Sun Valley, Idaho. His memoir of 1920s Paris, *A Moveable Feast*, was published posthumously in 1964.

July 22

Robert Dole's Birthday

Robert Joseph Dole, a prominent United States senator and Republican political leader, was born in Russell, Kansas, on July 22, 1923. He entered the University of Kansas in 1941, but joined the military in 1943 in order to serve in World War II.

Dole had a distinguished record of service in the war, serving as a combat infantry officer. During the Allies' Italian campaign he was badly wounded, and eventually was discharged and sent home to Kansas in a body cast to recuperate. It was a painful and humiliating episode in Dole's life. During a train journey, his fellow soldiers even used his body cast to put out their cigarettes. Nevertheless, Dole's recovery was largely successful, although he would never regain the full use of his right arm. He went back to academia, completing both college and law school. In 1950 Dole entered politics, successfully winning election to the Kansas state legislature on the Republican ticket.

After serving for two years as a state representative, in 1952 Dole ran for and won the position of prosecuting attorney of Russell County, Kansas. He held that position for eight years. In 1960 he entered national politics when he was elected to the United States House of Representatives in Washington, D.C., where he would serve from 1961 to 1969. He supported most of the Republican Party's positions, including its opposition to the increased social spending of President Johnson's Great Society programs, but he did come out in favor of legislation to assist the handicapped due to his personal experience in that area.

In 1968 Dole ran for the United States Senate and won. He was a strong supporter of Richard Nixon, who ran for president that year and also won. As a loyal party member with strong leadership skills, Dole began to rise within the party organization. He became the chairman of the Republican National Committee in 1971. In 1973, however, he resigned from that position after a series of disagreements with the Nixon administration over such matters as Dole's support for civil rights legislation.

Dole emerged relatively unscathed from the Watergate scandal that forced Nixon to resign the presidency on August 9, 1974. Gerald R. Ford, who succeeded Nixon as president, chose Dole as his candidate for vice president on the Republican ticket in the 1976 presidential election. Ford lost by a narrow margin, due in no small measure to the stigma surrounding his pardon of former president Nixon for Watergate crimes. Dole's performance in the campaign was unremarkable: His dry midwestern humor often came across as terse or bitter, and he was not a popular figure.

Despite his loss in the election, Dole continued to serve in the Senate and he would go on to serve for nearly 30 years. He was reelected in 1974, 1980, 1986, and 1992. He ran for the 1980 Republican presidential nomination but lost to Ronald Reagan. Within the Senate, he became the leader of the Senate Republicans beginning with the 99th Congress in 1985, and would serve in that position until his resignation from office in 1996. Dole tried again for the Republican presidential nomination in 1988, but this time was defeated by Reagan's vice president, George Bush.

Although he was over 70, the landslide Republican victory in the 1994 midterm congressional elections that gave the party a majority in both the House and the Senate for the first time since the 1950s encouraged Dole to try for the presidency yet again. This time he was successful in gaining the Republican nomination, despite several stumbles in the primaries. Dole resigned from the Senate in June 1996 to pursue his campaign on a full-time basis free of his duties as Republican leader.

Dole lost the presidential election in a three-way race between the incumbent, Democrat President Bill Clinton, and independent candidate H. Ross Perot. Although neither opponent openly made an issue of it, it was clear that Dole's advanced age was a factor in his defeat. Further, Dole endorsed a massive tax proposal that most analysts criticized as both fiscally unsound and as a transparent attempt to lure voters away from the popular President Clinton.

After the elections, Dole went into retirement but occasionally spoke out on selected public policy issues. In 1999 his wife of over 20 years, Elizabeth Hanford Dole, decided to enter Republican presidential politics herself. She is an accomplished public servant in her own right, having served in such positions as the head of the American Red Cross and the secretary of transportation, and was a popular figure during Dole's 1996 presidential campaign. As of this writing, however, her presidential aspirations remain unfulfilled.

July 23

James Cardinal Gibbons's Birthday

James Gibbons, the Roman Catholic cardinal whom Theodore Roosevelt praised in 1917 as the most venerated, respected, and useful citizen of the United States, was born in Baltimore, Maryland, on July 23, 1834. The son of Irish immigrants, he spent his childhood in both the United States and Ireland. In 1837 the family returned to Ireland, staying there for ten years before returning to America. After a few years in New Orleans, Louisiana, the family moved back to Baltimore.

Drawn to the priesthood, Gibbons prepared for his vocation by attending St. Charles College in Ellicott City, Maryland, near Baltimore. After graduating in 1859, he studied theology at Baltimore's St. Mary's Seminary. He was ordained a Roman Catholic priest on June 30, 1861. Later that year, he was named pastor of St. Bridget's Church in the Baltimore suburb of Canton. During the Civil War, Gibbons served as a volunteer chaplain at nearby Fort McHenry.

While a local pastor, Gibbons demonstrated exceptional administrative skills, and in 1865 he was appointed secretary to Archbishop Martin J. Spalding of Baltimore. The following year, Gibbons greatly impressed the participants at the Second Plenary Council of Baltimore, which had been assembled to improve the governance of the Catholic Church in the United States. The council established important guidelines in matters pertaining to education, clerical conduct, ecclesiastical property, parochial duties, and the organization of dioceses.

In 1868 Gibbons was given the difficult task of organizing and heading the newly established vicarate apostolic of North Carolina. He became the youngest consecrated bishop in the entire Catholic Church, and he participated in the Vatican Council of 1869–1870 in Rome. In 1872 he left North Carolina to become the bishop of Richmond, Virginia.

During his nine years in the South, Gibbons conceived of an easily understandable brief summary of the doctrines of the Roman Catholic faith. His famous exposition of Catholic doctrine, *The Faith of Our Fathers*, was the result. This work became one of the most widely read statements of Catholic beliefs ever written. Throughout his career, despite his busy schedule, Gibbons frequently wrote articles on topics of national concern for leading periodicals. He also wrote several other books, including *Our Christian Heritage*, *The Ambassador of Christ*, and the autobiography *A Retrospect of Fifty Years*.

In 1877 Gibbons was appointed coadjutor to and designated successor of the archbishop of Baltimore, James R. Bayley. Five months later, Bayley died, and Gibbons became the new archbishop of the oldest archdiocese in the United States. He became the first native of the city to serve in this position.

In 1883 Pope Leo XIII appointed Archbishop Gibbons "apostolic delegate" with the authority to preside over the Third Plenary Council of Baltimore. The council was attended by 14 archbishops and 60 bishops of the United States. This council, which convened in 1884, introduced new catechisms and decided to establish a Catholic University of America in Washington, D.C. A dedicated supporter of Catholic higher education, Gibbons served as the first chancellor of the university when it opened in 1889 and as president of the board of trustees until his death in 1921.

On June 30, 1886, Pope Leo XIII named Archbishop Gibbons the second American cardinal (Pope Pius IX had named Archbishop John McCloskey of New York City the first American cardinal in 1875). He was officially installed as cardinal on March 25, 1887.

As cardinal, Gibbons was active in a wide number of civic, humanitarian, and religious causes. He sided with organized labor when he opposed a Quebec prelate's condemnation of the Canadian branch of the Knights of Labor as a secret society incompatible with the Roman Catholic faith. Although the condemnation was at first upheld by Rome, Gibbons came to labor's defense and convinced the pope that the organization could not be considered in this light. Owing to his efforts, the ban was lifted.

Coming from an immigrant family, Cardinal Gibbons was also acutely aware of the problems involved in integrating the Catholic Church into American society, where a suspicion of Catholicism as "un-American" was deeply rooted. Popular concern that Roman Catholics would hand the nation over to the pope and his "foreign priestcraft" mounted in the late 19th century, when as many as half a million Catholic immigrants came to the United States in a single year. Gibbons strongly favored the early assimilation of these newcomers into the general American population. He therefore reacted vehemently against the so-called Cahensly movement, which advocated the nomination of Catholic bishops in the United States according to the representation of national immigrant groups within a particular diocese (a German bishop for German-speaking Catholics, for example). The cardinal opposed this idea, on the grounds that such "foreign enclaves" in the United States would ultimately work to the detriment of the Catholic Church in America, causing it to be regarded as a threatening foreign institution.

Many Americans, Catholics and non-Catholics, respected Cardinal Gibbons and admired his support for progressive social reform. In 1911 many of the nation's leading citizens, led by President William H. Taft, assembled in Washington, D.C., to pay a special tribute to Cardinal Gibbons. He died ten years later, on March 24, 1921.

July 24

Mormon Pioneer Day in Utah

The history of Utah as a political community dates from the arrival of Brigham Young and his fellow members of the Church of Jesus Christ of Latter-Day Saints, unofficially known as the Mormons, in the Great Salt Lake Valley on July 24, 1847. This anniversary, which has been celebrated every year since 1849, was made a legal holiday by the Utah territorial legislature on March 9, 1882, and is still observed in the state.

In 1820 Joseph Smith (see related essays throughout this book), the Mormon founder and prophet, first aroused enmity by telling his neighbors in the area around Palmyra, New York, that he had received visions from God. Smith published the *Book of Mormon*, formally organized his church on April 6, 1830, and rapidly gained converts. As early as 1831, the sect, hounded by persecution and prejudice, was forced to begin its long exodus. Over the next decade the Mormons moved from New York to Kirtland, Ohio; then to several localities in Missouri, including Independence and Far West; and finally to Illinois. Members of the church settled in Commerce, Illinois, which Joseph Smith renamed Nauvoo (meaning "the beautiful plantation"). Smith reigned supreme as mayor of Nauvoo, commander of its militia, and head of his religion. There too, however, nonbelievers (termed "Gentiles" by the Mormons) envied the Mormons' prosperity and political influence. Rumors about the practice of polygamy caused a stir. When Smith ordered the destruction of a newspaper that was critical of his policies, the result was mob violence and his imprisonment. He was murdered in jail at Carthage, Illinois, on June 27, 1844.

Although disputes about the succession to leadership in the church followed, with some splintering into factions, the majority of Mormons chose to follow Brigham Young. Young was a 43-year-old churchman and a strong leader. The continued hostility in the surrounding Illinois communities after Smith's death convinced Young that the only

place where the Mormons could find refuge would be in an isolated and desolate terrain, far beyond the frontier to the west. Determined that this should be the Mormon's last exile, the resolute leader meant to go so far that the "new Zion" would have time to grow to independent strength before animosity could again menace it. Familiar with the accounts of expeditions under Captain John C. Frémont and other western explorers, Young and his colleagues were drawn to an area known as the Great Salt Lake.

The autumn and winter of 1845 were devoted to preparations for the 1,000-mile trek. Instead of one mass exodus, Young organized the faithful into parties, then into companies, hundreds, fifties, and tens. Skilled craftsmen, hunters, and even brass bands were assigned to each party. Scouts were sent ahead to locate suitable way stations, plant crops, build bridges and cabins, dig wells, and establish ferries. Early in 1846, after promising his followers that "the angels of God will go with you, even as they went with the children of Israel when Moses led them from the land of Egypt," Young led the vanguard of 2,000 followers from Nauvoo across the frozen Mississippi River to Iowa. There they established the Camp of Israel.

As soon as additional companies could be assembled on the Iowa side of the river, they too started on the trail for the West. Dragging their heavily loaded wagons across Iowa, they halted only long enough to set up temporary settlements for those who followed. These settlements included Garden Grove, 150 miles from Nauvoo; Mount Pisgah, 100 miles beyond; Council Bluffs on the Missouri River; and finally Winter Quarters near Omaha, Nebraska, where more than 600 sod houses and log cabins were constructed and food was stored. Riding from Council Bluffs, Iowa, to the Mississippi River, a witness declared that 12,000 Mormons were drifting across Iowa in July 1846. Entering Nauvoo in the fall, an anti-Mormon mob found a deserted city.

The following spring, in April 1847, Young and his advance party organized to continue the migration. For three and a half months they journeyed across the prairie and over the mountains. Meanwhile, Young became ill with what was called "mountain fever." For a time it looked as if he, like Moses, would see the promised land but never enter it. In order to reach the Salt Lake Valley without delay, his party was divided into two groups. One, commanded by Orson Pratt, pushed forward and reached the destination on July 22, 1847. On July 23 Young, riding in a wagon, was driven from the trail to an elevation from which he could gaze over the surrounding country. The Great Basin, in which the Great Salt Lake lies, was spread out before him. He said, "Enough, this is the place. Drive on." A monument was later built on that site.

At first Young's followers were not so sure about the new location. As they broke through the Wasatch Range, they viewed "a broad and barren plain hemmed in by mountains, blistering in the burning rays of the midsummer sun," "the paradise of the lizard, the cricket, and the rattlesnake." However, the pioneers were dedicated to the task of transforming their settlement into a place where they could "become a mighty people in the midst of the Rocky Mountains." On July 24, after Young had arrived in the valley, the embryonic city was laid out with solemn ceremonies and consecrated. The land on which the faithful settled was officially Mexican territory, not to be formally ceded to the United States until 1848 in the Treaty of Guadalupe Hildago that ended the Mexican War. However, the only inhabitants for hundreds of miles were scattered bands of seminomadic native tribes.

By the end of autumn 1847, about 2,000 Mormons had reached the Salt Lake Valley. The immigrants suffered great hardships for the first year or so, especially when their fields were invaded by hordes of grasshoppers. The settlers were saved by white gulls that devoured the insects, known as Mormon crickets.

The westward movement of gold seekers to California from 1849 onward soon made the Mormons prosperous. Their new city was on one of the routes to the West Coast, and thousands passed through the valley. Although Young thundered that "gold is for the paving of streets [and] the business of a Saint is to stay home and make his fields green," he did not forbid his followers from making a profit by selling horses and supplies to the travelers.

New Mormon converts from the East, and also from England and Scandinavia, poured into the Salt Lake Valley. It is estimated that between 1847 and 1869, when the Union Pacific railroad to the West Coast was completed, some 80,000 followed the Mormon Trail. Most of them traveled in covered wagons, but some actually pushed their belongings all the way in handcarts. Under the guidance of the older pioneers, these settlers spread out along the western slopes of the Wasatch Mountains, then along fertile valleys with adequate water supplies. Within a few years, more than 400 communities had been established. On March 10, 1849, the Mormons organized the provisional state of Deseret, a word taken from the *Book of Mormon* meaning "honeybee." On September 9, 1850, the Territory of Utah was set up,

thus slowly linking the Mormons' destiny to the mainstream of American life (see related essays throughout this book).

After the poor harvests of 1847 and 1848, the crops of 1849 were so good that a great celebration was planned for the anniversary of the founding of the city. It was the first of many July 24 celebrations to come.

Pioneer Day in Other Western States

Pioneer Day is celebrated not only in Utah but also in the surrounding states, some of which have a large Mormon population. As emigrants from the eastern United States and abroad (especially from England and Scandinavia) swelled the Mormon ranks in and around Salt Lake City, Brigham Young organized his aggressive theocracy into the provisional state of Deseret. Deseret means "honeybee" and is a word taken from the *Book of Mormon*. Young's projected empire embraced what is now Utah, Nevada, and parts of Arizona, California, Colorado, Idaho, New Mexico, Oregon, and Wyoming. Young's ambitious plans for Deseret were doomed to failure, however, for Congress set up the much smaller Territory of Utah in 1850. Nevertheless, Mormon colonists spread out into the areas once claimed as part of Deseret.

The first Mormon attempt to expand northward beyond Utah was made in May 1855. Brigham Young dispatched 27 men under the command of Thomas Smith to set up a mission and colony in the Lemhi River Valley of Idaho, then a 22-day trip from Salt Lake City. After three years of hardships, the settlers gave up and returned home. In June 1860 a second, more successful band of Mormon settlers established a permanent agricultural settlement at Franklin in the southeastern section of the present state of Idaho. These Mormons who left Utah took with them the custom of celebrating July 24 as Pioneer Day. To mark the anniversary, they held morning religious services and a program of speeches, songs, and recitations, followed by a round of family or community banquets, races, and games. Pioneer Day is still observed by Mormons in Idaho. There are sporadic observances in Arizona, Nevada, and Wyoming as well, where the Mormons also settled.

July 25

Puerto Rican Constitution Day

One of Puerto Rico's most important holidays takes place annually on July 25, the anniversary of its founding as a commonwealth and of the adoption of its new constitution on July 25, 1952. By the terms of this constitution, Puerto Rico became a self-governing commonwealth voluntarily associated with the United States. Puerto Ricans retained their United States citizenship (granted by the Jones Act in 1917) but were exempted from federal taxes and could not take part in presidential elections.

Under the 1952 constitution Puerto Ricans were empowered to elect a governor and a legislature, composed of a senate and a house of representatives, by direct vote for four-year terms. Until 1948, when the journalist and reformer Luis Muñoz Marín won the first popular election for governor, executive officials had been appointed by the president of the United States, to which Puerto Rico had been ceded by Spain after the Spanish-American War in 1898. Amendment of the Jones Act in 1947 gave Puerto Ricans the right to elect their own governor. Muñoz, who was instrumental in securing commonwealth status for Puerto Rico, voluntarily stepped down from the governorship on January 3, 1965, after four terms in office. During his administration the success of Operation Bootstrap economic programs in raising Puerto Rico's standard of living made the commonwealth a model for underdeveloped nations around the world.

Under the 1952 constitution, which provides for the division of power between executive, legislative, and judicial branches of the Puerto Rican government, islanders also elect a resident commissioner who is sent with a voice but no vote to the United States Congress in Washington, D.C.

Perhaps the most interesting feature of Puerto Rico's commonwealth relationship with the United States is that, while the arrangement is permanent as long as it is agreeable to both parties, it can be changed by mutual consent. The relationship came about after Puerto Rico's election of 1948 failed to produce a majority in favor either of statehood or of complete independence. The search for a third alternative led the resident commissioner in Washington, D.C., to introduce a bill giving Puerto Ricans a chance to vote on whether they wanted to prepare their own constitution under a compact with the United States. Congressional passage of the bill was followed by a 1951 referendum in which Puerto Ricans indicated their approval of the idea by a large majority.

Early the next year, Puerto Rican representatives of varying political views met in a convention to draft a constitution. On March 3, 1952, the island's electorate approved the document by a vote of more than four to one. On July 3 it was ratified by the United States Congress. Finally, on July 25, 1952, the Commonwealth of Puerto Rico and the constitution that established it were proclaimed. On July 23, 1967, just two days before the 15th anniversary of Puerto Rico's Constitution, island residents in a referendum confirmed their preference for remaining a commonwealth. The vote was 425,081 in favor of commonwealth status; 273,315 in favor of statehood; and 4,205 for complete independence.

Thomas Eakins's Birthday

Thomas Cowperthwait Eakins, one of the most important American realist painters of the 19th century, was born in Philadelphia, Pennsylvania, on July 25, 1844. He entered the Pennsylvania Academy of the Fine Arts in 1861 and studied there until 1866. Afterward, Eakins went to Europe, spending several years in Paris, France, where he attended the École des Beaux-Arts. He was particularly attracted to the work of such greats as the famous Dutch master Rembrandt Harmensz van Rijn and the Spanish artists José Ribera and Diego Rodríguez Velásquez.

Eakins returned to Philadelphia in 1870 and spent most of the rest of his life there. He rejoined the Pennsylvania Academy of the Fine Arts in 1873 as an instructor, and became the institution's director in 1876. Eakins revamped the course of studies, introducing classes on scientific topics such as anatomy and dissection in order to help aspiring artists depict the human form more realistically. He also worked with, and painted at, the local Jefferson Medical College. Eakins's support of having nude models, however, was too revolutionary for the times and he was forced to resign in 1886.

Some of Eakins's greatest paintings include: *Max Schmitt in a Single Scull* (1871), *The Biglen Brothers Racing* (1873), *The Gross Clinic* (1875), *The Pathetic Song* (1881), *Miss Van Buren* (circa 1886–1890), *The Agnew Clinic* (1889), *Portrait of Mrs. Samuel Murray* (1897), and *Mary Adeline Williams* (1899).

Eakins's work was uncompromisingly realistic, and his graphic portrayals of surgery in *The Gross Clinic* and *The Agnew Clinic* works were highly unconventional at the time. His family was prosperous, however, and so he was able to continue his work despite being shunned by many art patrons and critics. Eakins also painted personal portraits, native Philadelphia scenes, and some works concerning his family and friends. He died in Philadelphia on June 25, 1916. Even though he was unpopular during most of his painting career, like many other groundbreaking artists, in later years his work came to be appreciated and admired.

Eakin is now generally recognized as one of the most important influences on American naturalism.

July 26

New York Ratifies the Constitution

New York emerged from the American Revolution in a most favored position. Its strategic location, which made the state a critical objective in the war, promised to bring commercial advantages. New York City was the best natural ocean port in the United States, and the Hudson and Mohawk Rivers offered the easiest route to the vast interior of the new nation. Governor George Clinton was especially eager to exploit New York's potential without interference. He saw no reason for New York to support national programs that would inevitably draw money from his state's coffers to help improve the less well-situated states.

George Clinton thus regarded the Articles of Confederation, which bestowed only minimal powers on the central government, as a desirable arrangement. Despite assurances to General George Washington that he would support "every measure which has a tendency to cement the Union, and to give to the national councils that energy which may be necessary for the general welfare," Clinton consistently stymied attempts to increase the powers of the central authorities. In particular, the governor was hostile to legislative proposals that offered the Continental Congress greater control over the customs revenues generated in the port of New York. Clinton agreed that the congress should receive the duties, but demanded that the state alone have the power to levy and collect those taxes.

Alexander Hamilton was the leading opponent of Clinton's parochial view of New York's role in the Union. Hamilton believed that New York's real greatness lay in becoming the cornerstone of a powerful nation rather than in remaining the most prosperous member of a collection of autonomous states.

In the years immediately following the American Revolution, the deficiencies of the Articles of Confederation became apparent. The central government lacked the authority necessary to resolve elementary interstate problems; even worse, the national leaders were virtually impotent in international matters.

In 1786 the Continental Congress called for delegates from the states to meet in Annapolis, Maryland, to discuss methods of strengthening the national government. Hamilton represented New York at the gathering, which emissaries from New Jersey, Pennsylvania, Delaware, and Virginia also attended, and proposed that the states bestow greater powers on the national government. Hamilton's exhortation stirred the Continental Congress to ask all the states to send delegates to Philadelphia, Pennsylvania, to discuss revision of the Articles of Confederation.

New York's legislature responded to the congress's request and dispatched Alexander Hamilton, Robert Yates, and John Lansing Jr. to Philadelphia. Clinton hoped that Yates and Lansing, who shared the governor's view of the Union, would be able to frustrate Hamilton's dream of a stronger federation. At the convention each state would have one vote, and if Yates and Lansing cooperated they could deprive the nationalists of New York's critical support.

At the Constitutional Convention, Hamilton supported a more powerful central government that could appoint state governors and veto state legislation. He even proposed that presidents and senators hold office for life. Unable to win support for his extreme program, Hamilton accepted the more modest proposals of James Madison of Virginia, who also desired an entirely new frame of government with greatly increased federal powers. Yates and Lansing rejected Madison's suggestions as going beyond the "revision" of the Articles of Confederation for which the New York legislature had commissioned them to participate. Both men withdrew from the convention and returned home with the apparent approval of Governor Clinton. Hamilton had no authority to cast New York's ballot independently, but he remained in Philadelphia and affixed his signature to the constitutional proposal finally adopted by the convention.

On September 28, 1787, the Continental Congress transmitted a draft of the Constitution, which required the assent of nine of the 13 states for adoption, to the state legislatures. In New York the proposed Constitution divided both the political leadership and the populace. Clinton led the opponents of ratification, and sought to prevent the calling of a ratifying convention. Alexander Hamilton worked vigorously on behalf of the new Constitution and, together with Madison and his fellow New Yorker John Jay, produced the *Federalist* papers, which were a series of essays eloquently advocating the nationalist cause.

In January 1788 Egbert Benson proposed in the New York legislature that the state hold a convention to consider the proposed Constitution. The legislature accepted his suggestion, and 61 delegates gathered at the courthouse in Poughkeepsie on June 17, 1788. Advocates of ratification were initially disappointed because two-thirds of the body opposed adoption of the new frame of government. Nevertheless, Federalists like Hamilton, Jay, Robert Livingston, Robert Morris, and James Duane undertook the difficult task of changing their adversaries' minds.

Hamilton argued that the new Constitution would add strength and vigor to the government without weakening the liberties protected under the Articles of Confederation. Melancton Smith forcefully presented the Antifederalists' arguments. Smith particularly warned that a far-off national government that had the support of an army and navy and maintained contacts with the nations of Europe would pose a grave threat to popular liberty.

Clinton's supporters apparently had the convention under their control, but Hamilton slowly undercut their position. Besides using eloquent arguments, he established contacts with delegates meeting in constitutional conventions in Virginia and New Hampshire. When New Hampshire and Virginia respectively became the ninth and tenth states to ratify the Constitution, Hamilton announced to the Poughkeepsie gathering that the new Constitution would soon go into effect and warned that New York was in danger of being omitted from the Union.

The defeat of the Virginian Antifederalists, led by Patrick Henry, was a severe blow to Clinton. Support for the opponents of the Constitution quickly waned, and even Melancton Smith became a convert to Federalism. Finally, on July 26, 1788, by a vote of 30 to 27, the Poughkeepsie convention ratified the Constitution. Although in a sense the original 13 colonies became states at the time that they declared their independence from Great Britain in 1776, they are generally ranked according to the order in which they ratified the Constitution. New York was the 11th to ratify the Constitution and is thus considered to be the 11th state.

July 27

First Permanent Transatlantic Cable Completed

Telegraphic communications between the United States and Great Britain have been uninterrupted ever since July 27, 1866, when the spanning of the Atlantic Ocean by underwater telegraphic cable was permanently achieved. There was a briefly successful cable some eight years earlier by means of which British queen Victoria and American president James Buchanan exchanged greetings on August 16, 1858. Queen Victoria cabled:

The Queen is convinced that the President will join with her in fervently hoping that the electric cable, which now connects Great Britain with the United States, will prove an additional link between the nations, whose friendship is founded on their common interest and reciprocal esteem.

In reply, President Buchanan echoed the queen's sentiments in wishing that

the Atlantic Telegraph might, under the blessing of Heaven, prove to be a bond of perpetual peace and friendship between the kindred nations, and an instrument destined by Divine Providence to diffuse religion, civilization, liberty and law throughout the world.

The general public greeted the news of the first transatlantic cable with wild acclaim. The feat had been accomplished through the cooperation of both governments, with financing and technical support from the public and private sectors of both countries and with the active participation of both countries' navies. However, the driving force for the cable was an individual named Cyrus West Field, an American merchant and entrepreneur.

Field was born on November 30, 1819, in Stockbridge, Massachusetts, to the Reverend David Dudley Field and Submit Dickinson Field. Two of his brothers became prominent lawyers, namely David Dudley Field in New York City and Stephen Johnson Field, who served on the U.S. Supreme Court. Cyrus West Field, however, struck out early into the business world and left home at the age of 15 for several years' work in New York City. He then spent a short time in Lee, Massachusetts, where he assisted his brother Matthew, a paper manufacturer. In 1840 young Field briefly went into the paper business for himself in Westfield, Massachusetts. Not long afterward, however, he accepted a partnership in the firm of E. Root & Company, wholesale paper dealers in New York City. When the Root establishment failed in 1841, he formed his own firm, Cyrus W. Field & Company. It was so successful that by the time he was 33, Field felt that he had worked hard enough and had accumulated enough money (more than a quarter million dollars) to retire. His intention was to enjoy life and to see the world. He visited Europe with his wife, Mary Bryan Stone Field, in 1849 and in 1853 he took a trip through South America.

At the family's Thanksgiving dinner in 1853, Field's brother Matthew asked whether he would be interested in a project that intrigued Matthew and a friend, Canadian engineer Frederick Newton Gisborne. The project, no doubt inspired by the cable connecting England and France in 1845 and another connecting Scotland and Ireland in 1853, had as its goal the laying of an underwater telegraph line across the Gulf of St. Lawrence to connect Newfoundland and the North American mainland. Not only did Cyrus Field become interested in the Gulf of St. Lawrence project, but he decided to take on the decidedly more ambitious project of laying a cable all the way across the Atlantic Ocean.

Knowing that the enormous undertaking would require scientific, financial, and governmental support, he immediately set about communicating with and organizing the various sectors. He talked to the people involved with the cables already laid between Britain and France and between Scotland and Ireland, such as John W. Brett of the British-French venture, who became his associate. Field also sought advice from others, including Samuel F. B. Morse, the father of the telegraph, and Matthew Fontaine Maury, the naval officer and oceanographer who was head of the United States Naval Observatory and Hydrographical Office for many years. For financial backing, Field approached influential friends and neighbors such as Peter Cooper, Moses Taylor, Marshall Owen Roberts, and Chandler White. With them, Field formed the New York, Newfoundland, and London Telegraph Company, chartered on May 6, 1854, with its headquarters in New York.

In the summer of 1856 Field took his family to reside in England, where he had much work to do. He met with Charles Tilston Bright, the young British engineer who worked on the underwater cable connecting Scotland and Ireland. In December 1856 they gathered British financiers and organized the Atlantic Telegraph Company with its headquarters in London. Bright, initially the company's engineer in chief and consulting engineer later in the cable laying project, was knighted for his work in 1858. Field, the director of both the London and New York companies from the beginning, had successfully generated scientific and financial support on both sides of the Atlantic.

The work of establishing land lines in the rugged territory of Newfoundland had already begun. The first underwater cable across the Gulf of St. Lawrence, started in August 1855, failed but another cable was successfully laid the following year. Land lines connected Newfoundland with the underwater cable across the gulf and with land lines from the southern shore of the gulf to New York City and other eastern points in the United States.

In order to proceed with the transatlantic cable from Newfoundland to Great Britain, Field went to Washington, D.C., to gain official approval for the project. After long delays and much debate on Capitol Hill, the cable bill was finally passed and signed on March 3, 1857, by President Franklin Pierce.

The United States and Great Britain assigned naval personnel and ships to cooperate in the venture. For that first attempt in 1857, the plan was for the American steamship *Niagara*, starting from Valentia, Ireland, to lay out the first half of the cable. Sailing with the *Niagara* was the British ship *Agamemnon*, carrying the second half of the cable. At approximately midpoint in the Atlantic, the two halves were to be spliced and the *Agamemnon* was to continue the laying of the cable to Newfoundland. However, the *Niagara*'s line snapped after only about 350 miles of cable had been laid. The first attempt thus ended unsuccessfully. Meanwhile, in the economic depression of 1857, Field's personal fortune was depleted. Though not bankrupt, he was no longer wealthy. Still, he continued to work on the transatlantic cable project without pay. In spite of his financial problems, he was able not only to raise capital for the venture, but also to supervise changes in the ships and equipment that included methods and materials to improve cable insulation. For the second cable laying attempt, the ships were to first splice the cable at midpoint in the Atlantic and then take off for their respective shores. The midocean meeting took place on June 25, 1858, but the attempt was given up on June 28.

On the third attempt, almost everyone involved with the cable venture, including the directors of both the British and American financing companies, was disheartened. There was no send-off celebration when the cable fleet departed. It was later reported that "Mr. Field was the only man on board [the *Niagara*] who kept up his courage through it all."

On July 29, 1858, the splice was made in midocean and the ships sailed off as planned, going through heavy weather and high winds. Cable engineers, mechanics, and naval personnel, fearful that passing merchant ships might inadvertently damage the cable as it was let out, scrambled to correct mechanical snags and to make navigational maneuvers to compensate for compasses gone awry. On August 14, 1858, when the *Niagara* sailed into Trinity Bay, Newfoundland, the *Agamemnon* was already harbored in Valentia Bay. The first transatlantic cable had been laid. The first shore-to-shore message was sent from the British directors to the American directors: "Glory to God in the highest and on earth Peace, goodwill toward men." Field was in Newfoundland when this message came via cable. However, he and a team of men had to go into the Newfoundland woods to repair the land lines before the message could be relayed to New York and other East Coast points. The first through message, received by transatlantic cable at Newfoundland and transmitted via land lines and the Gulf of St. Lawrence cable to the eastern seaboard of the United States, was that from Queen Victoria to President Buchanan on August 16, 1858.

The accomplishment was hailed on both sides of the Atlantic. One account described the enthusiastic reaction in New York City:

> Flags went up everywhere, the cannon roared and the church bells rang clamorously while the name of Cyrus Field was greeted with boisterous cheers as the hero of the hour, fit to be named with that of Benjamin Franklin and Columbus. There seemed no limit to the tumultuous rejoicing. New York City was illuminated by a great torchlight parade and a grand public reception was given in honor of [Field] and the other members of the company with the officers of the ships included.

As Field was getting into his carriage to go to the New York reception, he was handed a message cabled from the directors of the London company. When he read it at the reception, the "cheering was half-frantic." No one knew at the time that it would be the last message to be transmitted via that cable. Poor insulation against the seawater was given as the reason for the cable's malfunction on September 1, 1858, after approximately three weeks of operation. People on both sides of the Atlantic were now skeptical and even suspicious. Field and his companies were accused of fraud.

For several years, further attempts to lay a transatlantic cable were stymied by negative public feeling, lack of financing, and the outbreak of the Civil War. Field himself, however, continued his efforts to restore interest in and gain financial backing for the undertaking. In later years, he described these times: "Great was our discouragement and severe also were our struggles to raise money for what seemed to many people an insane venture."

It was not until 1865 that the fourth attempt to span the Atlantic Ocean by electric cable was undertaken. The world's largest steamship, the *Great Eastern*, was hired by Field and specially fitted for the task of laying cable. The ship departed from Ireland on July 23, 1865. Some 1,200 miles of cable had been laid when, only two or three days from Newfoundland, the cable snapped. Finally, a year later, the fifth attempt was successful. The *Great Eastern* departed from Ireland on July 13, 1866, and on July 27, 1866, Field stepped ashore at Newfoundland. Thus, the first permanent transatlantic cable was officially completed on that date.

Cyrus Field was once again greeted as a hero with parades, luncheons, receptions, and medals of recognition from many governments. He had shown that great bodies of water could be spanned by underwater cables. Field pursued a variety of business ventures for the rest of his life, and died on July 12, 1892, at the age of 72.

July 28

Fourteenth Amendment Proclaimed Ratified

The 14th Amendment to the Constitution of the United States of America, the second of three (namely the 13th, 14th, and 15th Amendments) that are commonly called the Reconstruction or post–Civil War amendments to the Constitution, received the necessary two-thirds majority of both chambers of Congress on June 8, 1866. It was then submitted to the states for ratification, which requires a three-fourths majority. Ratification was completed by July 9, 1868. The states of the former Confederate States of America were required to ratify it in order to rejoin the Union.

The 13th Amendment had abolished slavery, while the 14th Amendment defined national citizenship, using terms that included African Americans. It also guaranteed the personal rights and property rights of such citizens, granting to all persons born or naturalized in the United States equal protection and due process under the law.

Although the 14th Amendment's primary purpose was to guarantee African Americans the same rights that were enjoyed by other Americans, and to ensure the constitutionality of legislation enacted to secure these rights, its terms are general in scope. The guarantees of due process and equal protection have been invoked in a wide variety of civil rights cases, although it was not until the 1950s that the Supreme Court was willing to expand its interpretation of these rights to strike down major pieces of state legislation. Furthermore, for a long time (beginning in the late 19th century and ending roughly in the 1950s and 1960s), the Supreme Court used a narrow definition of what constituted actions by the "states" rather than by individuals. The former are covered by the 14th Amendment but the latter are not.

In its entirety, the first section of the 14th Amendment reads as follows:

> All persons born or naturalized in the United States, and subject to the jurisdiction thereof, are citizens of the United States and of the State wherein they reside. No State shall make or enforce any law which

shall abridge the privileges or immunities of citizens of the United States, nor shall any State deprive any person of life, liberty, or property without due process of law; nor deny to any person within its jurisdiction the equal protection of the laws.

The second section provides for a proportionate reduction of representation in Congress when a state denies or abridges the right of any citizens to vote in federal or state elections. This section was largely forgotten until the civil rights turmoil of the 1960s, when it was used to help force southern compliance to federal voting rights initiatives.

Section three excluded from Congress, and from federal and state office, any person "who, having previously taken an oath" in any such capacity "to support the Constitution of the United States, shall have engaged in insurrection or rebellion against the same." What this meant was that all the federal and state legislators, together with certain others, who had sided with the Confederacy during the Civil War were ineligible for office. Upon taking office, before the Civil War, they would have been required by Article VI of the Constitution to take the aforementioned oath to support the Constitution and thus they broke their oath in siding with the Confederacy. However, Congress was given the power to grant exceptions, and it did so rather liberally.

Section four pledged the payment of Union debts, but forbade the payment of Confederate debts or, as it was phrased, of "any debt or obligation incurred in aid of insurrection or rebellion against the United States. . . ."

The fifth and final section empowered Congress to enforce the amendment's provisions by appropriate legislation.

"Bonus Army" Evicted From Washington, D.C.

On July 28, 1932, one of the more sordid incidents of the Great Depression occurred when the federal government used force to drive the impoverished, protesting veterans known as the "Bonus Army" from Washington, D.C.

The incident had its roots in the years immediately following World War I, when hundreds of thousands of American servicemen were demobilized after the fighting ended. In the Soldiers Bonus Bill, passed on April 21, 1924, Congress authorized a bonus for war veterans based on their length of service. The bonus was to be in the form of a 20-year annuity policy. As with most Americans, however, the onset of the Great Depression after the stock market crash of 1929 hit veterans hard. Millions of people lost their jobs and their

savings, and those who were able to stay employed saw their wages fall by an average of 60 percent from 1929 to 1932.

Beginning on May 29, 1932, veterans' groups began to gather in Washington, D.C., to petition the federal government for early payments on their service benefits under the Soldiers Bonus Bill. They hoped this would alleviate their current economic problems. The mass of veterans, nicknamed the "Bonus Expeditionary Force" or the "Bonus Army," camped out at Anacostia Flats, where they constructed a temporary settlement derisively called a "Hooverville," after President Herbert Hoover, who was widely blamed for the nation's economic misfortunes. The veterans' numbers increased to roughly 20,000 during the summer of 1932.

On June 15, 1932, the House of Representatives approved Bonus Bill legislation in favor of the veterans' demands by a vote of 211 to 176. However, on June 17 the Senate rejected the Bonus Bill by a vote of 62 to 18, and so the legislation died. The veterans responded by marching in protest along Pennsylvania Avenue past the White House in what was nicknamed the "Death March." The federal authorities became concerned about the possibility of riots and civil unrest, especially after several incidents between the marchers and the police took place in the stifling summer heat. Although many of the veterans had already accepted their defeat and begun to leave the city, the government decided to take more forceful action to bring the matter to a close.

Roughly 10,000 veterans were still in Washington, D.C., on July 28, 1932. President Hoover ordered the secretary of war to command General Douglas MacArthur, then the army chief of staff, to remove the remnants of the Bonus Army. MacArthur led federal troops from the nearby military bases at Fort Myer and Fort Washington against the Bonus Army. One unit was commanded by Major George S. Patton, who like MacArthur had fought in World War I, possibly commanding some of the men he now attacked, and would go on to become one of the leading military figures of World War II. Backed by cavalry and even some tanks, the troops marched with fixed bayonets and cleared downtown Washington, D.C., of the protesting veterans. Then they proceeded to the settlement at Anacostia Flats, forcing the veterans and their families to evacuate and leveling their tents and shanties.

The Bonus Army movement ended in failure, but in crushing the veterans President Hoover further diminished his already low standing in the public eye. Several months later, Democrat Franklin D. Roosevelt would defeat him in the 1932 presidential elections.

Veterans' Bonus March

July 29

Pony Penning on Chincoteague Island

This is a movable event.

Every year in late July the inhabitants of Chincoteague, Virginia, and thousands of visitors participate in the annual pony penning. Chincoteague is a quiet fishing town on Chincoteague Island, roughly 90 miles from Virginia Beach and 135 miles from Williamsburg via the Chesapeake Bay Bridge–Tunnel. Since 1924, with the exception of the World War II years, the annual festivities there have included as its highlight the wild pony penning and sale.

The origin of the wild "ponies," which are actually stunted horses, is a matter of some debate. They are known to have roamed the small islands off what is now the Virginia and Maryland coast since the 17th century, and various theories account for their presence. Two popular explanations trace their history back to the early Spanish explorers. One theory holds that the small, wiry horses are the descendants of the survivors of a 16th-century shipwreck. Its adherents claim that a Spanish galleon carrying a cargo of Spanish mustangs was wrecked off Assateague, the 37-mile-long barrier island parallel to the coast of Maryland and Virginia, whose name (given by the native Gingoteague tribe) means "a running stream between." Early settlers in the area supposedly came across the skeleton of the ship. Another widely held theory maintains that early adventurers, perhaps pirates, deposited the ponies on Assateague Island for grazing purposes and for unknown reasons never reclaimed them.

The horses, distinguished by thick curly manes and long flowing tails, roamed the remote sandy island with its low dunes and extensive salt marshes. The scanty diet of salt-marsh grass apparently stunted their growth. Becoming increasingly wild and adventuresome, the rapidly multiplying herd frequently sought refuge from the lashing Atlantic storms by crossing over to nearby Chincoteague Island. Then, only a narrow waterway separated Chincoteague from Assateague, but the waterway later widened into what became the Assateague Channel.

Unlike barren Assateague Island, the wooded seven-mile-long, mile-and-a-half-wide Chincoteague Island (whose name means "beautiful land across the waters") had been settled since 1671. Jumping the inhabitants' split log fences, the wild ponies foraged for food in vegetable gardens and corn fields. In an effort to prevent these destructive pony raids, sometime in the late 17th or early 18th century the islanders inaugurated the first annual pony roundup and penning. The owner of a section of marshland was generally permitted to claim any wild horses found grazing on the property and offer them for sale.

In subsequent years, numerous mainland colonists, having been informed of the pony penning date (usually around August 10), went to Chincoteague Island to appraise and buy the penned ponies that had been rounded up from Chincoteague and Assateague Islands. Races, free liquor, and food were additional inducements for visitors. Only men were allowed to attend the annual event, which was originally held on the southern end of Chincoteague Island.

The waterway dividing Chincoteague and Assateague Islands gradually became too wide for even the intrepid ponies to cross with ease. Assateague, especially, became overrun with multiplying livestock. The increasingly popular pony penning and sale was then routinely supplemented by a "pony swim," during which the horses were forced to cross the Assateague Channel from Assateague to Chincoteague Island.

In 1924, 14 men formed the Chincoteague Volunteer Fire Company. Since their original capital consisted of only $4.16, the volunteers decided to stage an annual carnival in July to raise funds for fire fighting equipment. To ensure continued interest in the island's traditional festivity, the pony penning celebration became the focal point of a two-week carnival program. Concerned that the wild pony herd might eventually become depleted, the firemen established their own breeding herd by buying 80 ponies.

Both the pony penning festival and the horses themselves gained widespread fame when Marguerite Henry, a well-known author of children's books, became an admirer of the Chincoteague islanders and their ponies and wrote several stories about them. *Misty of Chincoteague*, published in 1947 and made into a movie in 1960, brought the Chincoteague horses national prominence. In 1943 the Chincoteague National Wildlife Refuge was established on Assateague Island, containing 9,030 acres in Virginia and 417 acres of salt marsh in Maryland. In 1965 the Chincoteague National Wildlife Refuge was incorporated into the 39,500-acre Assateague Island National Seashore. Today the herd, consisting of several hundred horses, shares its ancestral home with snow geese, waterfowl, peregrine falcons, and other wildlife.

Alexis de Tocqueville's Birthday

Alexis-Charles-Henri Clérel de Tocqueville, a French aristocrat who wrote *Democracy in America* (1835–1840), one of the leading studies of the American people and American political institutions, was born on July 29, 1805, in Verneuil, France. His parents were Hervé-Bonaventure Clérel de Tocqueville and Louise Le Péletier de Rosanbo, both of aristocratic ancestry. Tocqueville was educated in Metz, France, and then studied law in Paris. In 1827 he became a judge at the French court of law in Versailles.

In 1831 Tocqueville and a companion were given an 18-month leave of study to write a report on the penal system in the United States for the benefit of the French government. They left on April 2, 1831, and arrived at Newport, Rhode Island, on May 9. Their travels took them through New York, west to Lake Michigan, and south to New Orleans, Louisiana. On February 20, 1832, they embarked on their return voyage to France. Once home, they wrote their work: *Du systéme pénitentiaire aux États-Unis et de son application en France* (or *The Penitentiary System in the United States and its Application in France*). It was well-received, and inspired Tocqueville to begin writing *De la démocratie en Amérique* (or *Democracy in America*).

It took Tocqueville until 1840 to finish the entire work. It dealt with his impressions of the influence of religion, wealth, journalism, class structure, racism, the government, and the judiciary on American democracy. Overall, it was a positive as well as insightful analysis of American democracy as seen through the eyes of a neutral observer. He did have some criticisms, however, notably concerning the potential for tyranny in a system where there were limited restraints on majority rule. Nevertheless, *Democracy in America* has since become one of the standard reference works for historians, almost on a par with the famous *Federalist* papers.

Tocqueville went on to become a successful politician and a member of the French Chamber of Deputies. He served in that body until the French revolution of 1848, and supported such American ideals as an independent judicial system. After the 1848 unrest, which resulted in the abdication of French ruler Louis-Philippe, Tocqueville was elected to the new National Assembly and even served briefly as minister of foreign affairs. In 1851, however, Charles-Louis-Napoléon Bonaparte (a descendant of the famous Napoléon Bonaparte) staged a coup d'etat and became the new French autocrat. Tocqueville opposed the coup, and decided to retire from public service.

During his retirement, Tocqueville published in 1856 *L'Ancien Régime et la Révolution* (or *The Old Regime and the Revolution*), which discusses the collapse of the Bourbon dynasty and the French Revolution of 1789. Tocqueville died on April 16, 1859, in Cannes, France.

July 30

Henry Ford's Birthday

Perhaps more than any other, the name of automobile manufacturer Henry Ford has come to be synonymous with mass production. His innovation was the efficient use of that cornerstone of production: the assembly line. A pioneer in the development of the automobile, Ford "put the nation on wheels" with his Model T. With his principles of increased efficiency, increased volume, lower prices, and higher wages, he brought the automobile, once the toy of the rich, within the reach of the many.

Ford was born on a farm near Dearborn, Michigan, on July 30, 1863. He attended school until he was 15, then became an apprentice machinist in Detroit, where he repaired watches in his spare time. Ford eventually attended business college, and at the age of 24 married Clara Bryant on April 11, 1888.

Ford became a mechanical engineer, and later chief engineer, for the Edison Illuminating Company. In his free time he tinkered in his backyard shop with a two-cylinder internal combustion engine, powered by gasoline, which he had personally designed. The motor was successfully tested in 1893. Three years later, Ford made history by harnessing his engine to a homemade frame mounted on bicycle wheels and driving it to Dearborn. Although his was not the first gas-powered automobile, it was destined to change the face of America as had no other device before it.

Ford left the Edison Illuminating Company in 1899. After brief associations with two groups of investors, and an attempt at developing racing cars, he found new financial backing and organized the Ford Motor Company with himself as president in 1903. The young company was hard-pressed financially until the introduction in 1905 of its Model N, bearing a $500 price tag, which astonished the manufacturers of more expensive cars.

However, even more revolutionary was Ford's introduction of the Model T in 1908, commonly known as the "flivver" or the "Tin Lizzie." The vehicle swept the country. The subject of verse, cartoons, and jokes, it was later immortalized in an essay by E. B. White. Whole new industries grew up around it. The company's capital stock was increased to $2 million. By 1911 Ford had more than 4,000 employees and a new plant in Highland Park, Michigan. Before the demise of the Model T in 1927, 15 million had been sold worldwide.

Ford accomplished this remarkable production feat by his introduction, in 1913, of standardized, interchangeable car parts. He also introduced assembly-line techniques whereby moving conveyor belts transported the parts, on which each laborer quickly performed one simple task, from worker to worker. The manufacturing process thus became a constantly moving, integrated, and timed operation. As Ford's principles of mass production were applied in industries across the land, American industry expanded and the American standard of living rose.

At Ford plants, production soared, along with worker discontent over monotony and increases in production quotas. Ford stabilized his labor force by instituting the highest wages in the industry and introducing the eight-hour workday. In the process he doubled the company's profits from $30 million in 1914 to $60 million in 1916, while lowering automobile prices almost annually. His policies resulted in handsome profits, which he largely plowed back into plant expansion. He also found time in 1918 to campaign, unsuccessfully, for the United States Senate on the Democratic ticket.

Ford held the company presidency until 1919, the year a new plant was constructed at River Rouge, Michigan. He then handed his title to his son, Edsel. Meanwhile though, the senior Ford had purchased enough stock to control the company and operate it in his own autocratic, suspicious, and sometimes reactionary way for many more years.

While competitors were introducing yearly style changes, color variety, and mechanical improvements, Ford defied his management, clinging to the outmoded features of the Model T. It was available in black only. By 1927, however, even Ford realized that it had seen its day. The Model A was introduced in 1928, the V-8 in 1932, and a yearly changeover thereafter. These reforms were too late, however, to prevent Ford's loss of first place in the industry to General Motors.

Ford's relations with his labor force did not go smoothly either. Despite his pioneering wage policies, profit-sharing plan, and paternalistic concern, workers complained about Depression-wrought wage cuts and layoffs. There were also grievances about the speed and tension under which they worked, about the company's "sociological department" which investigated their private lives, and about its repressive campaign against union organizing. Ford's running battle with labor erupted in violence in 1932 and 1937. It culminated in hearings before the National Labor Relations Board (NLRB), which found the company guilty of repeated labor violations. There was a bitter strike in 1941. After an NLRB-ordered election in which 70 percent of the workers designated the United Automobile Workers as their bargaining agent, Ford finally agreed to a union contract. He was the last major automobile manufacturer to do so.

When the Japanese attack on Pearl Harbor brought the United States into World War II in December 1941, Ford put aside his pacifist convictions to construct the huge Willow Run plant and manufacture airplanes, tanks, armored cars, jeeps, and engines for the government. The company was employing well over 100,000 persons, and war production was at its height, when Ford was shaken by an event from which he never fully recovered: the death of his only child, Edsel, in 1943. Now 80, Ford resumed the presidency until his grandson Henry Ford II (later chairman of the board) succeeded him in 1945.

Ford himself died of a cerebral hemorrhage on April 7, 1947. He left an empire estimated in the billions. Like his son, he bequeathed the largest share of his company holdings to the nonprofit Ford Foundation, which the two had established in 1936 for the "advancing [of] human welfare." The Ford Foundation is now one of the largest private philanthropic institutions in the world.

July 31

Milton Friedman's Birthday

Milton Friedman, one of America's greatest economists and economic theoreticians, was born on July 31, 1912, in Brooklyn, New York. His parents were Jeno and Sarah Friedman, immigrants from the Carpatho-Ruthenian province of Austria-Hungary. Shortly after his birth, the family moved to Rahway, New Jersey, where his father eked out a meager living, barely supporting his wife and children.

In 1928, only 15 years old, Milton Friedman graduated from Rahway High School. Although his father had died, leaving the family even more destitute than before, Milton was able to attend college thanks to a scholarship from Rutgers University. While majoring in mathematics and economics, he supplemented this assistance with various odd jobs, and graduated in 1932. That same year, he entered the University of Chicago's Economics Department for graduate studies, receiving his M.A. degree in 1933.

After further study at Columbia and Chicago, Friedman found employment with the federal government in Washington, D.C., as a New Deal economist for President Franklin D. Roosevelt's administration. He worked in a variety of positions until 1946, when he received his Ph.D. from Columbia and accepted an offer from the University of Chicago to teach economic theory. Friedman was to remain there, working on the theories that made him famous, for most of the rest of his professional career. As summarized in his 1976 Nobel Prize for Economics, Friedman is noted "for his achievements in the field of consumption analysis, monetary history and theory and for his demonstration of the complexity of stabilization policy."

In 1957 Friedman wrote what is perhaps his most important work, A Theory of the Consumption Function. He pointed out various flaws in accepted economic theory about the regularity and predictability of personal consumption, arguing that people adjust their consumption on the basis of their long-range expectations, not their current income. This work influenced the empirical standards used in economic analysis and introduced the concept of "permanent income."

In the 1960s Friedman became one of the leaders of the conservative "monetarist" free market school of economic theory, which holds that careful regulation of the money supply rather than government spending is the best way to protect and encourage economic growth. He served as an economics adviser to Republican Senator Barry Goldwater in his 1964 campaign for the presidency and also worked for the 1968 campaign of Republican candidate Richard Nixon. However, Friedman turned down a variety of offers to serve in high-level government positions, preferring instead to remain in academia. He wrote a number of books, including Capitalism and Freedom (1962), A Monetary History of the United States, 1867–1960 (1963), Dollars and Deficits (1968), A Theoretical Framework for Monetary Analysis (1971), and Free to Choose (1980).

Friedman retired from the University of Chicago in 1977. He still does some occasional work for the school, however, and also serves as a Senior Research Fellow at the Hoover Institution of Stanford University.

August

August is the eighth month of the Gregorian, or New Style, calendar now in use and has 31 days. In the ancient Roman calendar, which began in March, August was the sixth month and was therefore called Sextilis, a name derived from the Latin word for six, *sex*. Even after the old calendar was revised, January and February being added to the start of the year, August continued to be called by its old name, despite the fact that it was now the eighth month. In 44 B.C. Mark Antony, as consul, had the name of the month preceding August changed by decree of the Roman senate from Quintilis to Julius in honor of Gaius Julius Caesar, then dictator of the Roman state. In the same fashion, Sextilis was renamed Augustus in 27 B.C. as a tribute to the first Roman emperor, Augustus Caesar

Augustus was born in 63 B.C. and originally named Gaius Octavius, or more popularly Octavian. He was the grandson of Julius Caesar's sister. When Octavian was a youth, he showed such promise that Julius Caesar not only took personal interest in his education, but also designated him as his heir without the boy's knowledge. The young Octavian was abroad pursuing his studies when in 44 B.C. he learned of Julius Caesar's assassination. Octavian immediately set out for Italy, where he was formally adopted into the Julian clan and received the name Gaius Julius Caesar Octavianus.

Determined to make the most of his inheritance, Octavian was soon accepted as one of the emerging leaders during a very confused political situation. Overcoming considerable opposition, he gained a foothold in the capital city of Rome, secured the consulship in 43 B.C., and then skillfully allied himself with his chief contender for power, Mark Antony. Together with Lepidus, the two leaders formed a triumvirate, or three-man dicta-

torship. Then Octavian and Mark Antony fulfilled a vow of vengeance against Julius Caesar's assassins, defeating the forces of the conspirators, Marcus Junius Brutus and Gaius Cassius Longinus, at Philippi in Macedonia in 42 B.C. Eleven years later Octavian triumphed over Mark Antony in the naval battle of Actium. He thus cleared the road of all important rivals and without further opposition carried through a final seizure of power. In 29 B.C. Octavian was made emperor.

Octavian preferred to regard himself, in public at any rate, as the first citizen, or *princeps*, of the Roman state. He gradually assumed, however, the honors and powers commensurate with his unchallenged political position. On January 17, 27 B.C., for example, the Roman senate granted him the title of honor *Augustus*, meaning "venerable" or "reverend." This designation was adopted by all succeeding Roman emperors.

Since July had been named for Julius Caesar, Augustus thought that a month should bear his own name as well. The emperor chose the month following July and decreed that it should be called after himself. The early fifth-century Roman writer Ambrosius Theodosius Macrobius explained the emperor's reasons for this choice:

> [After July] August comes next, which formerly was called Sextilis, until it was devoted to the honor of Augustus by a *senatus consultum*, whose text I have given below: "Since the imperator Caesar Augustus in the month Sextilis entered upon his first consulship [in 43 B.C.] and led three triumphs into the city [the triple triumph for Illyria, Actium, and Egypt on August 13, 14, and 15 in 29 B.C.] and the legions were led down from the Janiculum [one of the seven hills of Rome] and followed his auspices and trust, and since in this month also

Egypt was brought under the sway of the Roman people [in 30 B.C.] and since in this month an end was made of the civil wars, and since for these reasons this month is and has been most fortunate for this empire, it pleases the senate that this month be called Augustus."

In addition to conferring his name on Sextilis, the emperor Augustus supposedly took one day (from February, in one version of the story; from September, in another) to add to August, making it 31 days long, just like July. Reportedly he did not want "his" month to be outdone by Julius Caesar's, even by a day.

In the third week of August, after the harvesting and planting, the Romans celebrated the Consualia, the festival of Consus, the Roman god of the harvest. Consus, who was probably also the deity of the storage bin and guardian of secrets, was the cult partner of the goddess of sowing and reaping known as Consiva, or Ops. According to yet another hypothesis about his undoubtedly varied functions, Consus was the god of good counsel. He is said to have advised the founder of Rome, Romulus, to stage a notorious event known as the rape of the Sabine women. The Sabines were a people who lived in the Sabine Hills of central Italy northeast of Rome, and when they came to Rome to participate in the first Consualia, the Romans ambushed them and forced their women into servitude as wives for Roman men.

Another noteworthy Roman festival, the Vulcanalia, took place on August 23 in honor of Vulcan, the god of fire and flame. In an effort to improve fire prevention, Emperor Augustus had the city of Rome divided into small districts set up to facilitate fire fighting. He was therefore also honored as Volcanus Quietus Augustus, since Vulcan was called upon to prevent fires.

The Anglo-Saxon name for August was Weodmonath, or the month when the weeds flourished. The lucky birthstone associated with August is the peridot, which symbolizes married happiness.

August 1

Colorado Admitted to the Union

On August 1, 1876, President Ulysses S. Grant signed the proclamation admitting Colorado to the Union as the 38th state. Events celebrating "Colorado Day" are frequently held in Central City, a historic mining town that is considered by many to be the "birthplace of Colorado." It was near there that John Gregory discovered the celebrated gold deposits on May 6, 1859, in the steep gulch

that later bore his name. The area became known as "the richest square mile on earth" until the title was forfeited to another of the state's mining regions, Cripple Creek, 30 years later. The more than $75 million worth of minerals and metals from Central City was of vital importance in keeping the smaller plains settlements alive.

Four centuries before the discovery of America by Europeans, sedentary, agricultural cliff dwellers constructed their multistoried "apartment houses" in the canyons of the southernmost region of what is now Colorado. The first Europeans to enter the area were the Spanish, who traveled from Mexico to christianize the natives and seek riches. In the 1540s Francisco Vásquez de Coronado probably touched upon Colorado during his quest for the fabled Seven Cities of Cíbola, where the streets were supposedly paved with gold. Throughout the 17th century, small Spanish expeditions continued to explore the area and as early as 1700 French explorers reached the Rocky Mountains. The profitable fur trade also enticed the first American, James Purcell, into the Colorado region in 1803.

The largely uncharted wilderness still remained practically virgin territory for Europeans when the United States gained the vast, vaguely defined region between the Mississippi River and the Rocky Mountains in the Louisiana Purchase of 1803. Several expeditionary parties, including Zebulon M. Pike's (1806), Stephen H. Long's (1820), and John C. Frémont's (1842–1843 and 1845), were commissioned by the federal government. Overland trails were mapped out and several private forts were constructed, but settlement did not really start in earnest until the United States acquired the rest of Colorado by cession from Mexico in 1848 following the Mexican War. Texas yielded some additional territory in 1850.

Settlers from Georgia and Kansas entered Colorado as gold seekers in 1858. Green Russell, a Georgia prospector, found gold in the Little Dry Creek near the south edge of Denver that very year. When the first great gold discoveries were made in the winter and spring of 1859 in Idaho Springs, near Central City, and in other places, prospectors flocked to Colorado. The free-for-all days of the mining camps had begun. Horace Greeley, the editor of the *New York Tribune*, was among the first easterners to arrive at the strike near Central City. He vividly described its 4,000 new residents who slept, cooked, and ate outdoors.

The political development during the next two decades was chaotic. In 1858 "Arapahoe county," in which all of Colorado was included, was considered part of the Kansas Territory. A delegate was nevertheless dispatched to Washington, D.C., to secure the admission of an independent territory called Jefferson. After a movement for statehood was inaugurated, a constitution drawn up, submitted to the people and rejected, the illegal territory of Jefferson was formed. Its provisional legislature managed to operate until Congress passed the bill for territorial status on February 28, 1861. William Gilpin, the first governor, bestowed the name *Colorado* from the Spanish word for "red" or "colored." By that time the population had risen to 20,798 males, 4,484 females, and 89 free blacks. In the 1860s other unsuccessful attempts were made to organize a state government. In 1867 President Andrew Johnson vetoed an enabling act prepared by the Republican Party.

Finally an enabling act of Congress, passed on March 3, 1875, provided for the admission of the territory as a state. It contained some unusual provisions. It directed as a condition of admission that the constitution should provide by ordinance, irrevocable without the consent of the United States and the people of the state, the following provisions: that perfect religious toleration should be secured; that the people should disclaim all right to the unappropriated public lands; that the lands should remain at the sole disposition of the United States; that the land in Colorado belonging to citizens of the United States living outside the state should not be taxed at a higher rate than the lands belonging to residents; and that no tax should be levied on lands or property of the United States.

The constitution was framed at a convention held at Denver from December 20, 1875, to March 14, 1876, and the people of the territory adopted it on July 1, 1876. The final admission proclamation of President Grant was dated August 1, 1876.

Herman Melville's Birthday

Herman Melville, the novelist and poet, was born on August 1, 1819, in New York, New York. His large family, which included his seven brothers and sisters, moved to Albany, New York, in 1830 after suffering financial reverses. Two years later his father, a once-prosperous importer, died in bankruptcy.

Melville's scant formal education at the Albany Academy ended when he was 15. Then and in later life, however, he read voraciously, beginning with the works in his father's library. He found conventional employment (as a bank and store clerk, as a farmhand, and as a schoolteacher), uninteresting and in 1837 he chose the sea as the best way to combine adventure with self-support.

His first voyage was in 1839 as a cabin boy on a trader going from New York to Liverpool, England. On January 3, 1841, he shipped out on the whaler *Acushnet*, which was to provide the background for his masterpiece, *Moby Dick*. The vessel was bound for the South Seas from what was then the whaling capital of the world—New Bedford, Massachusetts.

After a year and a half of hardships under the *Acushnet*'s tyrannical captain, Melville jumped ship with a companion at the Marquesas Islands. He escaped on an Australian whaler to Tahiti, where he participated in a minor mutiny and was imprisoned briefly. Melville wandered through the South Pacific to various other islands, and eventually found his way to Honolulu, Hawaii, where he enlisted as a seaman on the U.S. Navy frigate *United States*. It took him to Boston, where he was discharged in the year from which, he later said, "I date my life" (1844). It marked the beginning of the writing career on which he now embarked.

Melville's first book, *Typee* (1846), based on his experiences in the Marquesas, was an immediate success. Its sequel, *Omoo* (1847), was a fictionalized version of his adventures in Tahiti and combined humor with serious social commentary.

After Melville's marriage in August 1847 to Elizabeth Shaw, the daughter of the chief justice of Massachusetts, he moved to New York City where he wrote *Mardi* (1849). It was a political and moral allegory in which imaginary South Seas islands represented various countries. The book was hard to understand and poorly received.

Under financial pressure, Melville hastily reverted to what the public had liked before, turning out *Redburn* (based on his voyage to Liverpool) in 1849, and *White-Jacket* (drawing on his experiences aboard the *United States*) in 1850. That year, after attending to publishing business in England and visiting France briefly, he decided to reduce living expenses by moving his family to Arrowhead, a farm near Pittsfield, Massachusetts.

It was at Pittsfield that Melville began his friendship with novelist Nathaniel Hawthorne, then living in nearby Lenox, who shared Melville's interest in combining symbolism with romance. The two men spent long hours together, and Melville, encouraged by Hawthorne's example, embarked on the serious book he was determined to write: *Moby Dick* (1851). It is one of the world's great epics, a tale of whales and whaling, God, man, and nature. Behind it lay Melville's love of ideal virtues and his deep disillusionment at the apparent heartlessness of nature, the savagery of humanity, and the seeming indifference of a God who permits the noble and the unworthy to suffer alike. Richly allegorical and with many levels of meaning, the novel tells of the mutilated Captain Ahab's maniacal search for revenge against the great white whale that has severed his leg and seems to him to represent "all evil . . . visibly personified, and made practically assailable." The book failed to achieve popularity for its deeper level or as a suspenseful, action-filled tale of adventure.

If the writing of his supreme work had drained Melville of energy, its reception left him disappointed, bitter, in debt to his publishers, and ill. His following works were equally unsuccessful: *Pierre: or the Ambiguities* (1852), *Israel Potter* (1855), and *The Confidence-Man* (1857). Seeking solace in religion, Melville traveled to Europe and the Middle East in 1856–1857. Upon his return he supplemented his meager income by lecturing. Finally, he sold his farm to a brother in 1863 and moved back to New York City, where he was appointed as a customs inspector in 1866. He held the post for 19 years, until a bequest placed him in comfortable circumstances. Melville's only works in this period were his Civil War poems *Battle-Pieces* (1866), the long religious poem "Clarel" (1876), and some other poetry.

When Melville died on September 28, 1891, he had lived so long in voluntary seclusion that the event was marked by only a few lines in the press. He left two notable travel diaries and a short novel that he had just completed—*Billy Budd*. Eloquent and subtly symbolic, this celebrated work was another tale of the sea and dealt with what Melville saw as the tendency of the forces of evil to triumph over the qualities of innocence and beauty. It was not published until 1924, following the 1919 centennial of Melville's birth and a sudden revival of interest in the South Seas. Melville's reputation continued to grow, and he is now recognized as one of America's greatest novelists.

Francis Scott Key's Birthday

Francis Scott Key wrote the words (not the music) of what is now known as "The Star-Spangled Banner," the national anthem of the United States. The occasion for the poem was the British bombardment of Baltimore's Fort McHenry during the War of 1812. Key, on board a British ship in the harbor where he had been negotiating the release of a friend held prisoner by the British, was an accidental witness to the assault. His anxious watch to see if the fort would remain in American hands at the conclusion of the bombardment on the morning of September 14, 1814, and his joyous relief "that our flag was still there" prompted him to write his work (see September 12, War of 1812: Battle of North Point, Maryland).

Key was born on August 1, 1779, on his family's estate, Terra Rubra, in Frederick (later Carroll) County, Maryland. His parents were John Ross Key, a prosperous farmer, and Ann Phoebe Charlton Key. His great-grandfather Philip Key came to Maryland from England around 1720. Key attended St. John's College in Annapolis, Maryland, from 1789 to 1796 and after graduation read law in the Annapolis office of Judge Jeremiah Townley Chase of the Maryland general court. One of his colleagues was Roger B. Taney, who, after their studies, accompanied Key on his return to Frederick to set up practice. Taney subsequently married Key's sister, Anne, and would later become the fifth chief justice of the United States Supreme Court.

On January 19, 1802, Key married Mary Tayloe Lloyd. They had six sons and five daughters. Key moved with his family to the Georgetown region of Washington, D.C., in 1805 and became a law partner of his uncle Philip Barton Key. Key had a quick logical mind that made him an effective speaker and helped in his extensive practice in the federal courts. A deeply religious person, he gave serious thought in 1814 to entering the clergy. He was a delegate to the general conventions of the Episcopal Church from 1814 to 1826 and for many years served as lay reader of St. John's Church in Georgetown.

Key moved from the Georgetown area to downtown Washington, D.C., around 1830 and was the United States attorney for the District of Columbia from 1833 to 1841. In October 1833 President Andrew Jackson sent him to Alabama to negotiate a settlement between the state and federal government over the Creek tribe's lands. On January 11, 1843, while visiting a daughter in Baltimore, Key died of pleurisy at the age of 63.

John Alden Day

This is a movable event.

Plymouth was a small, poor, and relatively short-lived colony. Yet its inhabitants earned a place of special prominence in American history, and few of the Pilgrims are better known than John Alden, the hero of Henry Wadsworth Longfellow's poem "The Courtship of Miles Standish." Longfellow's narrative poem is without historical foundation, since there is no evidence that Alden ever competed with Standish, who was perhaps 15 years his senior, for the affection of Priscilla Mullens. However, John Alden did indeed marry Priscilla Mullens shortly after the *Mayflower*'s arrival on the Massachusetts coast in 1620, and Longfellow was one of their descendants.

August 2

Alden was born in eastern England around 1599. Aside from this vague information, nothing is known about his early life. The first definite statement regarding Alden is contained in the history *Of Plymoth Plantation*, written by William Bradford. According to Bradford, the Pilgrims hired the 21-year-old Alden as a cooper, or barrel-maker, shortly before their departure from Southampton, England. The young man's presence on the *Mayflower* satisfied an act of Parliament that required every seagoing vessel carrying beer to employ a cooper. On the voyage across the Atlantic, Alden kept the beer casks in good repair. He decided to remain with the settlers after their arrival in the New World.

Before disembarking on the Massachusetts coast, Alden and the 40 other adult male passengers signed the Mayflower Compact, a preliminary plan of government. The youngest to agree to this famed document, he devoted his entire life to the service of the "civil body politic" that the compact advocated. In 1627 Alden was one of the eight "undertakers" who assumed the responsibility for the colony's debts. In addition, he held many of the most important positions in the colony. Alden was a member of the colony's council of war in all times of impending crisis, served as treasurer of the colony from 1656 to 1658, was governor's assistant for 44 years, and served as deputy governor in 1664, 1665, and 1677.

Alden settled first in Plymouth. There he probably built a house similar to those erected by the other Pilgrims: a small, one-room, clapboard structure with a thatched roof. (Contrary to popular belief the first settlers of eastern Massachusetts never constructed log cabins. This type of building did not appear in North America until Swedish settlers arrived in Delaware in the 1640s.) Alden remained in Plymouth until 1627 when he and a number of colonists, including Myles (or Miles) Standish, decided to set up another town at Duxbury about ten miles from the original settlement. The Plymouth general court approved this plan and in that same year granted Alden 169 acres upon which to establish his farm.

John and Priscilla Alden lived for many years in Duxbury, where most of their 11 children were born. Alden also received a substantial land grant in nearby Bridgewater. John Alden, the last surviving signer of the Mayflower Compact, died in 1687 at the age of 89. John Alden Day, a local observance celebrated on the first Saturday in August, honors his life.

August 2

James Baldwin's Birthday

James Arthur Baldwin, an important African American novelist, was born on August 2, 1924, in Harlem, New York. His stepfather was a poor Pentecostal preacher. Young Baldwin was an outstanding student, and served as a junior minister at the local Pentecostal church. He graduated from high school in 1942, and went to work in order to help support his family. After his stepfather died in 1943, Baldwin moved to Greenwich Village, New York, in order to become a writer.

Baldwin's early work won him a fellowship, and he moved to Paris, France, where he would live for most of the rest of his life. He wrote his first novel there, entitled *Go Tell It on the Mountain* (1953). It concerned the condition of African Americans in the United States, and established him as one of the best writers on the subject. Baldwin, who was gay, then wrote *Giovanni's Room* (1956) concerning a homosexual relationship. *Another Country* followed in 1962, which was panned by the critics for its graphic sexual portrayals. Nevertheless, during the 1960s Baldwin achieved his greatest popularity as he critiqued the racial and sexual inequities in American society and become one of the most influential spokesmen for the civil rights movement.

Some of Baldwin's most significant works include *The Fire Next Time* (1963), *Tell Me How Long the Train's Been Gone* (1968), and *No Name in the Street* (1972), again concerning the injustices inflicted on African Americans and their struggle for identity. During his career, Baldwin also wrote several notable and reasonably successful Broadway plays, such as *The Amen Corner* (1955) and *Blues for Mister Charlie* (1964).

As the 1970s progressed the civil rights movement began to lose steam and Baldwin began to lose some of the popularity he had as a younger man. Nevertheless, he still produced some great works, such as *If Beale Street Could Talk* (1974), concerning the injustice of the American judicial system, and *Just Above My Head* (1979), concerning a homosexual gospel singer. A compilation of his nonfiction works, containing many pieces on the protest movement, was published in *The Price of the Ticket* (1985).

Baldwin died of cancer in St. Paul de Vence, France, on December 1, 1987.

August 3

The USS *Nautilus* Cruises under the North Pole

Columbus Departs for the New World

Christopher Columbus and the approximately 90 sailors who set forth on August 3, 1492, in three small ships to sail the Atlantic rank among the world's greatest pioneers and adventurers. Lured by the rich East Indies trade, mariners had sought an ocean route to the Orient for many years before Columbus's voyage. With the encouragement of Prince Henry the Navigator, the Portuguese made significant advances in navigation during the first half of the 15th century and conducted extensive explorations along the western coast of Africa. In 1488 Bartolomeu Dias of Portugal rounded the Cape of Good Hope at the southern tip of Africa, but a mutiny prevented him from continuing on to the Orient. His fellow mariner Vasco da Gama was the first to sail to India via the African route in 1497.

While the Portuguese concentrated on finding an eastern ocean passage to the Orient, Christopher Columbus, a Genoese sailor, made plans for a western voyage. By this time many educated people in Europe had come to realize that the world was round, not flat. Columbus reasoned that by sailing west along a northern latitude he could eventually reach Japan. In theory he was correct, but Columbus underestimated the distance between Europe and Japan by roughly 8,000 miles. Of course, he also never suspected the existence of the New World continents.

It was not easy for Columbus to find financial backing. He was turned down by King John II of Portugal; the city of Genoa; and King Henry VII of England, before King Ferdinand and Queen Isabella of Spain agreed to underwrite his expedition in 1486. It was not until January 1492, however, when the Spanish war against the Moors had ended with the fall of Granada that the monarchs were finally able to finance Columbus's voyage. In April 1492 arrangements for the expedition were concluded, and under the terms of the agreement Spain was to acquire "certain islands and mainland in the Western Ocean" and Columbus as "admiral of all the ocean seas" was appointed governor general with control over the trade of any territory he might discover. The Spanish monarchs provided Columbus with three small sailing ships, namely the flagship *Santa María*; the *Niña*, captained by Vincente Yáñez Pinzón; and the *Pinta*, under Martín Alonso Pinzón. On August 3, 1492, they set sail from Palos in southern Spain (see related essays throughout this book).

The first voyage beneath the North Pole, which is essentially one massive icecap floating on the Arctic Ocean and which unlike the South Pole does not rest on any land mass underneath, was made by the nuclear submarine USS *Nautilus* in August 1958. The *Nautilus* submerged off the northern coast of Alaska near Point Barrow on August 1, 1958. On August 3, at 11:15 p.m., the ship passed beneath the pole. It was the first time that a ship had reached the North Pole, and the vessel resurfaced on August 5 in the Arctic Ocean between Greenland and Spitsbergen. For 96 hours the *Nautilus* had cruised under the polar ice cap, covering a distance of 1,830 miles at a depth of approximately 400 feet beneath the ice cap. At times the ice above was 80 feet thick, with the thinnest layer being ten feet thick.

The *Nautilus* was the first submarine in the world to be propelled by nuclear power. Launched at Groton, Connecticut, in 1954, and commissioned in January 1955, the ship was capable of cruising underwater indefinitely at a speed of more than 20 knots. It was "refueled" with a new reactor core for the first time in March 1957 after cruising over 60,000 miles. In September 1957, on one of three secret trial runs in preparation for the major feat that lay ahead of it, the ship spent five and a half days cruising 1,383 miles under the Arctic ice. By the end of October 1957, it had logged a total of more than 100,000 miles.

A transpolar crossing was first attempted by the *Nautilus* in June 1958, but at that time the ice in an area north of the Bering Strait had not yet melted sufficiently to allow passage beneath it. The vessel returned to Pearl Harbor, Hawaii. On July 23, 1958, it left Pearl Harbor for its subsequent successful crossing under the North Pole. Codenamed Operation Northwest Passage, the mission was shrouded in secrecy by the United States Navy. The public knew nothing of the history-making voyage until August 8, 1958, when the success of the operation was disclosed by the Dwight D. Eisenhower administration.

During the *Nautilus*'s cruises beneath the ice, various scientific tests and measurements were made. The salinity and temperature of the water were measured, and ocean depths to 13,410 feet were determined by more than 11,000 soundings. In addition, a number of underwater mountain ranges were discovered.

The captain of the *Nautilus* was Commander William R. Anderson. The success of his pioneering mission enhanced the international prestige of the United States at a time when it had been challenged by the Soviet Union's successful launching in October 1957 of *Sputnik I*, the first artificial satellite sent into orbit around Earth. President Eisenhower awarded Anderson the Legion of Merit in a ceremony at the White House. In addition, the Presidential Unit Citation, an award never before given in peacetime, was awarded to the ship's officers and men. Anderson later wrote a book entitled *Nautilus 90° North* about the polar voyage.

August 4

John Peter Zenger Acquitted

Freedom of the press, regarded throughout the world as a cornerstone of liberty, is a constitutional principle of recent origin. Some historians argue that the theory gained acceptance in the Western Hemisphere no earlier than the late 18th century. Until then, most political thinkers retained the ancient suspicion that free expression would undermine the state.

In England, freedom of speech, the antecedent of freedom of the press, originated as a protection for legislators against the monarchy rather than as a civil right. During the 17th century, Parliament twice overthrew Stuart kings to establish this principle. Having guaranteed their freedom of expression by the Glorious Revolution of 1688, the House of Commons and the House of Lords showed no interest in extending this right to the citizenry.

The English boasted that they enjoyed freedom of expression, but construed the term very narrowly. Sir William Blackstone, the 18th-century author of *Commentaries on the Laws of England* (1765–1769), stated that freedom of the press "consists in laying no previous restraints upon publications, and not in freedom from censure for criminal matter when published." Blackstone further argued that his position did not inhibit free thought, but simply prevented the dissemination of destructive sentiments.

The government's primary weapon in its war on criticism was the law of seditious libel. Inherently vague, the concept outlawed any comment, true or false, that might lower the popular opinion of the authorities or disturb the peace. Indeed, England's Star Chamber ruled in 1606 that an accurate statement against the government was a worse libel than a deceitful one, for the former created scandal whereas the latter merely breached the peace.

Eighteenth-century political and intellectual developments slowly erased age-old theories of free expression and replaced them with a more libertarian attitude. In the American colonies, colonial leaders actively supported the movement insofar as it helped them curb the power of the governors appointed by the British to rule over them. As did so many of the colonial struggles for increased liberty, the controversy over freedom of the press produced a number of heroes, of whom John Peter Zenger is the most famous.

In 1710 at the age of 13, John Peter Zenger emigrated to America from the German Palatinate, a refugee from the War of the Spanish Succession. His mother later apprenticed him to William Bradford, the first printer in the New York colony. Zenger left Bradford's employ after Bradford in 1725 established the *Gazette*, the colony's first newspaper and a publication subservient to the government.

Zenger's independent efforts at printing fared poorly, but his iconoclastic ways pleased the leaders of the party opposed to the government. In 1733 they offered him the financial support necessary to bring out an antiadministration newspaper. Zenger established the *Weekly Journal* and chose William Cosby, the new governor of New York, as the object of its scorn.

An avaricious man, William Cosby insisted that the New York colonial assembly grant him a gift of money beyond his salary and appointed his son secretary of East and West Jersey. In an extraordinarily bold move, Cosby then demanded half of his salary for the time between his appointment in Great Britain and his arrival in New York. When Rip Van Dam—who as acting governor had legally earned the money—refused to bow to his wishes, Cosby brought the matter to the courts. Knowing that he would have no chance before a jury, the governor took the case before the Supreme Court of Judicature, which sat without a jury.

Cosby's attempt to enrich himself by manipulating the legal system so angered Lewis Morris, the chief justice, that he stepped down from the bench and announced that he would sit on no more cases. The governor removed Morris from his post and installed the more pliable James De Lancey. Morris counterattacked by running for the assembly seat from the town of Eastchester. A veteran of New York and New Jersey politics, he easily defeated Cosby's candidate.

Undaunted, Cosby continued his assault upon New York's leaders by calling into question the validity of the patents giving them title to vast sections of the colony's land. The governor touched on a sensitive issue, since the validity of most New York patents was open to question, and to challenge them had long been considered an unpopular and unfair political tactic. The opposition responded by savagely satirizing the administration in Zenger's newspaper.

James Alexander, a respected lawyer and landholder, provided most of the copy that the *Weekly Journal* devoted to the governor and his cronies. Items described the recorder of New York City as a five-foot five-inch spaniel and the sheriff as a four-foot monkey. Zenger's press worked overtime printing ballads denouncing Cosby as a "knave" and rejoicing in the victory of his enemies in the annual elections for the common council.

Governor Cosby ultimately decided to punish Zenger directly. On November 17, 1734, the council had the printer arrested and held incommunicado for three days. James Alexander and another noted lawyer, William Smith, secured a writ of *habeas corpus* and had Zenger brought before the court. Chief Justice De Lancey set the bail at a prohibitively high figure and sent Zenger back into jail.

Zenger spent the next ten months in confinement, yet every issue of the *Weekly Journal*, save one, made its scheduled appearance. He carried on his business by communicating with his wife and servants through the door of his cell, and fulfilled his promise to "entertain" his readers "as formerly."

Meeting in January 1735, a grand jury failed to indict Zenger for any crime. Richard Bradley, the attorney general of New York, then filed an "information," an unpopular means of avoiding the indictment procedure by having a government officer directly accuse the prisoner of a crime. Bradley charged that Zenger was guilty of seditious libel for declaring that the colony's liberties were in danger.

James Alexander and William Smith acted as Zenger's counsel at his arraignment before the court in April 1735. They immediately questioned De Lancey's right to sit as chief justice, since he held his commission at Governor Cosby's pleasure and not on the less political basis of good behavior tenure. Enraged, De Lancey disbarred both Alexander and Smith for contempt and appointed John Chambers as Zenger's attorney. Chambers did a competent job in a delicate situation, and managed to secure for the prisoner a jury sympathetic to his cause.

Attorney General Bradley opened the trial by reading the "information," which included inflammatory statements from the *Weekly Journal*. Chambers, employing the defensive strategy traditional in libel cases, responded that Zenger had not committed a crime because he had not clearly identified the objects of his accusations. A man

stepped forward, however, and announced that he spoke on behalf of the defendant. The distinguished addition to the trial was Andrew Hamilton, Philadelphia's leading lawyer.

Taking over the trial, Hamilton began by admitting that Zenger printed the two allegedly seditious copies of the *Weekly Journal*. Bradley, referring to a number of old Star Chamber cases in which the court ruled that the truth of printed accusations was irrelevant, stated that Zenger was obviously guilty of libel. Seeing his opportunity, Hamilton rhetorically asked whether the attorney general desired to resurrect the arbitrary Star Chamber, long dismantled in England, and establish it in New York. The defense attorney then stated that the truth or falsity of Zenger's words was of paramount importance.

Chief Justice De Lancey recognized that Hamilton had effectively put Cosby on trial, and quickly tried to undo Hamilton's work: "It is far from being a justification of a libel that the contents thereof are true, or that the person upon whom it is made had a bad reputation," said the judge, "since the greater appearance there is of truth in any malicious invective, so much the more provoking it is."

Thwarted by the judge, Hamilton turned to the jury, and argued his case to them. Remarking that the suppression of evidence itself provided the strongest evidence, Hamilton argued that Zenger's accusations were obviously accurate. He then denounced oppressors who would silence those who opposed them, and called on the jury to strike a blow for liberty against arbitrary authority.

In his instructions to the jury, De Lancey ordered the jurors to disregard Hamilton and determine only the facts. Namely, had Zenger published the material in question? The court would then determine the law, namely was the material libelous? Ignoring De Lancey, the jurors quickly returned a verdict of not guilty. Cheering erupted in the hall, and that night, August 4, 1735, celebrations took place in New York City. It was a victory for the principle of freedom of the press.

August 5

John Eliot Baptized

John Eliot, later known as the "apostle to the Indians," was baptized according to the rites of the Anglican Church at Hertfordshire, England, on August 5, 1604. Eliot is presumed to have been born a few days before, but the exact date of his birth is unknown. At the age of 15 he entered Jesus College at Cambridge University. There he excelled in his studies of the classics, and at the same time became increasingly convinced of the rectitude of Puritan theological teachings. After receiving his bachelor of arts degree in 1622, he accepted a position at the grammar school in Little Badden. His superior at the school was the Reverend Thomas Hooker, the Puritan who later founded the colony of Connecticut. Contact with Hooker helped strengthen Eliot's commitment to the Puritan way of life, and before long he decided to become a minister and to emigrate to New England.

Arriving in Boston on November 3, 1631, Eliot substituted as the town's spiritual leader during the temporary absence of its regular minister, John Wilson. Upon Wilson's return, the congregation invited Eliot to remain as its teacher, but instead he accepted a similar offer from the newly formed church in nearby Roxbury. For over 60 years Eliot served the congregation faithfully and during that time became one of New England's most respected ministers.

His duties in Roxbury brought Eliot into close contact with the Native Americans in the area, and he decided in the early 1640s to attempt to convert them to Christianity. Before this undertaking could begin, however, Eliot had to master the Algonquian language. In the absence of phonetic guides and printed vocabularies, this was no easy task. Undeterred, he studied the language diligently for several years under the tutelage of Cochenoe, a Long Island native whom the Puritans had taken captive during the Pequot War of 1637. By 1646 Eliot became sufficiently fluent to begin proselytizing.

Eliot preached to the native tribes for the first time at Nonantum (later Newton), Massachusetts, on October 28, 1646. Although he began with a prayer in English, he conducted the major portion of the three-hour service in his listeners' own language. This initial effort was a great success, and within a short time Eliot had converted a number of natives. In addition to preaching and attracting missionaries and funds for future proselytizing efforts, Eliot sought to convert more natives by making Christianity available to them in printed form. In 1654 he published a catechism that served both to summarize Christian religious beliefs and to familiarize the native peoples with his written version of their language. In 1650 he began a translation of the Bible into an Algonquian language. Published in 1663, Eliot's Indian Bible was the first Bible printed in North America.

Until his death on May 21, 1690, Eliot's efforts to convert the native peoples never ceased. His success was definitely limited, and much of his work was undone by the bitter fighting during King Philip's War beginning in 1675. Regardless,

Eliot's work as a linguist and translator during the early colonial period was significant.

Limited Nuclear Test Ban Treaty Signed

In a milestone of the cold war, on August 5, 1963, the United States signed a limited nuclear test ban treaty with the Soviet Union and the United Kingdom. The three countries pledged "not to carry out any nuclear weapon test explosion, or any other nuclear explosion" in the atmosphere, under water, or in outer space. The treaty also prohibited tests that would cause radioactive fallout to occur outside of the territory of the country conducting the test.

The treaty was the result of years of test ban discussion that began in the early 1950s. On June 10, 1963, President John F. Kennedy announced that the three countries, who were the world's dominant nuclear powers, would hold meetings in Moscow, Russia. Soviet premier Nikita Khrushchev called for an agreement outlawing nuclear tests in the atmosphere, under water, and in outer space on July 2, 1963. The Moscow meetings began on July 15, 1963.

The discussions proceeded swiftly, a rather unusual occurrence in the normally testy United States–Soviet relationship. In less than two weeks the terms of the treaty were agreed upon, and it was initialed on July 25, 1963. The formal signing took place in Moscow on August 5, 1963, with Secretary of State Dean Rusk representing the United States, Foreign Minister Andrei Gromyko representing the Soviet Union, and Foreign Minister Lord Home representing the United Kingdom.

On September 24, 1963, the United States Senate ratified the treaty by a vote of 80 to 19. It was signed by President Kennedy on October 7, 1963, and entered into force on October 10, 1963. The treaty was of unlimited duration, but permitted amendments. In later years the treaty was occasionally criticized as too limited, but at the time it was an important first step in the process of imposing nuclear arms limitations.

Set forth below is a copy of the treaty, whose formal title is actually *Treaty Banning Nuclear Weapon Tests in the Atmosphere, in Outer Space and Under Water*.

> The Governments of the United States of America, the United Kingdom of Great Britain and Northern Ireland, and the Union of Soviet Socialist Republics, hereinafter referred to as the "Original Parties,"
>
> Proclaiming as their principal aim the speediest possible achievement of an agreement on general and complete disar-

mament under strict international control in accordance with the objectives of the United Nations which would put an end to the armaments race and eliminate the incentive to the production and testing of all kinds of weapons, including nuclear weapons.

Seeking to achieve the discontinuance of all test explosions of nuclear weapons for all time, determined to continue negotiations to this end, and desiring to put an end to the contamination of man's environment by radioactive substances,

Have agreed as follows:

Article I.

1. Each of the Parties to this Treaty undertakes to prohibit, to prevent, and not to carry out any nuclear weapon test explosion, or any other nuclear explosion, at any place under its jurisdiction or control:

(a) in the atmosphere; beyond its limits, including outer space; or under water, including territorial waters or high seas; or

(b) in any other environment if such explosion causes radioactive debris to be present outside the territorial limits of the State under whose jurisdiction or control such explosion is conducted. It is understood in this connection that the provisions of this subparagraph are without prejudice to the conclusion of a Treaty resulting in the permanent banning of all nuclear test explosions, including all such explosions underground, the conclusion of which, as the Parties have stated in the Preamble to this Treaty, they seek to achieve.

2. Each of the Parties to this Treaty undertakes furthermore to refrain from causing, encouraging, or in any way participating in, the carrying out of any nuclear weapon test explosion, or any other nuclear explosion, anywhere which would take place in any of the environments described, or have the effect referred to, in paragraph 1 of this Article.

Article II.

1. Any Party may propose amendments to this Treaty. The text of any proposed amendment shall be submitted to the Depository Governments which shall circulate it to all Parties to this Treaty. Thereafter, if requested to do so by one-third or more of the Parties, the Depository Governments shall convene a conference, to which they shall invite all the Parties, to consider such amendment.

2. Any amendment to this Treaty must be approved by a majority of the votes of all the Parties to this Treaty, including the votes of all of the Original Parties. The amendment shall enter into force for all Parties upon the deposit of instruments of ratification by a majority of all the Parties, including the instruments of ratification of all of the Original Parties.

Article III.

1. This Treaty shall be open to all States for signature. Any State which does not sign this Treaty before its entry into force in accordance with paragraph 3 of this Article may accede to it at any time.

2. This Treaty shall be subject to ratification by signatory States. Instruments of ratification and instruments of accession shall be deposited with the Governments of the Original Parties—the United States of America, the United Kingdom of Great Britain and Northern Ireland, and the Union of Soviet Socialist Republics— which are hereby designated the Depository Governments.

3. This Treaty shall enter into force after its ratification by all the Original Parties and the deposit of their instruments of ratification.

4. For States whose instruments of ratification or accession are deposited subsequent to the entry into force of this Treaty, it shall enter into force on the date of the deposit of their instruments of ratification or accession.

5. The Depository Governments shall promptly inform all signatory and acceding States of the date of each signature, the date of deposit of each instrument of ratification of and accession to this Treaty, the date of its entry into force, and the date of receipt of any requests for conferences or other notices.

6. This Treaty shall be registered by the Depository Governments pursuant to Article 102 of the Charter of the United Nations.

Article IV.

This Treaty shall be of unlimited duration.

Each Party shall in exercising its national sovereignty have the right to withdraw from the Treaty if it decides that extraordinary events, related to the subject matter of this Treaty, have jeopardized the supreme interests of its country. It shall give notice of such withdrawal to all other

Parties to the Treaty three months in advance.

Article V.

This Treaty, of which the English and Russian texts are equally authentic, shall be deposited in the archives of the Depository Governments. Duly certified copies of this Treaty shall be transmitted by the Depository Governments to the Governments of the signatory and acceding States.

IN WITNESS WHEREOF the undersigned, duly authorized, have signed this Treaty.

DONE in triplicate at the city of Moscow the fifth day of August, one thousand nine hundred and sixty-three.

August 6

World War II: United States Uses the First Atomic Bomb Against Japan

The first atomic bomb used in warfare was dropped on Hiroshima, Japan, at 7:15 p.m. on August 5, 1945, Washington, D.C., time. It was 8:15 a.m. on August 6, Tokyo time. The bomb was dropped from an American B-29 Superfortress bomber called *Enola Gay* and piloted by Colonel Paul W. Tibbets Jr.

Hiroshima, the seaport capital of Hiroshima prefecture on the island of Honshu in southwest Japan, was the country's eighth largest city and consisted of five islands interconnected by bridges. It was a center of Japanese arts as well as of heavy industry. When the lone Superfortress appeared over the city, there was no alert or rush for shelter and the inhabitants went about their morning tasks. The *Enola Gay* released its lethal cargo, a bomb with an explosive force of approximately 20,000 tons of TNT that descended five miles by parachute and then burst over the target. A flash of blinding intensity and an earthshaking shock followed. Colonel Tibbets reported: "It was like looking over a tar barrel boiling. There was lots of black smoke and dust and rubble. . . . We couldn't see the city at all through the thick layer of dust nor could we see the fires beneath."

It is estimated that out of a population of over 343,000, between 70,000 to 80,000 people died immediately from the blast and fire, and at least 37,000 were injured. The figure rises to a staggering total of almost 200,000 if one counts all those who later suffered from the delayed effects of acute radiation poisoning. Of Hiroshima's total 6.9 square miles, some 60 percent of the city center disappeared; approximately 4.1 square miles were instantly and completely incinerated.

On August 6 (Washington, D.C., time) President Harry S. Truman was having lunch with the crew on board the cruiser USS *Augusta* on the fourth day of his trip home from the Potsdam Conference in Europe when he was given a terse but urgent message. It said: "Big bomb dropped on Hiroshima. . . . First reports indicate complete success which was even more conspicuous than earlier test." He then announced the startling news of the atomic bomb. Until that date the existence of the weapon had been a closely guarded secret. In fact only a handful of the thousands of scientists and technicians who developed the first bombs actually knew the ultimate nature of their work.

The research known as the Manhattan Project was initiated by President Franklin D. Roosevelt in response to a warning from leading atomic scientists who arrived in the United States as refugees from tyranny in their own countries. In 1939 Hungarian-born Leo Szilard was working on the problem of uranium fission at Columbia University with the Italian Nobel Prize winner Enrico Fermi. Frustrated by the slow rate of nuclear research in the United States, Szilard, like other nuclear scientists, was aware that German scientists had already succeeded in splitting the atom, and he was fearful for the free nations of the world if Germany should be the first to develop an atomic bomb. He urged Princeton physics professor Eugene P. Wigner, a fellow Hungarian, to join him in seeking the help of the German-born physicist Albert Einstein in urging the American government to explore the adaptation of atomic fission for military purposes.

At their suggestion, Einstein composed a historic letter to Roosevelt on August 2, 1939. World War II had broken out in Europe on September 1, before the letter with supporting technical documents was delivered in person to Roosevelt on October 11, 1939. It was delivered by the Russian-born economist Alexander Sachs, an acquaintance of Szilard and a friend of Roosevelt who served as intermediary. Einstein's letter said in part,

. . . it may become possible to set up a nuclear chain reaction in a large mass of uranium, by which vast amounts of power and large quantities of new radium-like elements would be generated. . . .

This new phenomenon would also lead to the construction of bombs. . . . A single bomb of this type, carried by boat and exploded in a port, might very well destroy the whole port, together with some of the surrounding territory.

Spurred on by Einstein's letter and associated warnings that the Germans were already working on atomic fission, the president initiated a daring enterprise that eventually cost some $2 billion. On December 2, 1942, Fermi and other scientists of the Manhattan Project (which had been placed under the general direction of General Leslie R. Groves) brought about, in a former squash court under the University of Chicago's Stagg Field Stadium, the first self-sustaining nuclear chain reaction. Two immense plants were constructed for the task of producing the bomb. One was at Oak Ridge, Tennessee, to separate a uranium derivative known as U-235. The other was at the Hanford Engineer Works in Richland, Washington, to make plutonium. At Los Alamos, New Mexico, a special laboratory under the direction of J. Robert Oppenheimer was set up to work out the technical problems of fashioning a bomb shell for a weapon that so far existed only in the minds of scientists. The first atomic device was detonated on July 16, 1945, near Alamogordo Air Base, New Mexico.

So secret was the entire process of research and manufacturing that Vice President Harry Truman did not learn of the bomb's development until after he became president following Roosevelt's death in April 1945. His decision to use the bomb against Japan is the subject of continuing historical debate. Truman wrote that he made the decision on the basis of evidence that Japan's military leaders would not surrender short of a costly invasion involving the loss of an estimated half million American lives. He was given sharply divided advice about using the bomb. Some scientists and political advisers urged that a "demonstration" of the bomb before representatives of the United Nations on some desert island should be afforded the Japanese before the incineration of one of their cities. However, many others argued that American bombers were already pounding Japanese cities, and that the difference between a conventional rain of death and atomic destruction was of no consequence to those killed. Moreover, direct military use of the weapon without specific warning of its nature would provide the United States with a means of saving face if the experiment proved to be a fiasco.

On July 26, 1945, the leaders of the American and British governments, with the concurrence of Nationalist China, issued the so-called Potsdam Declaration or Proclamation. It called for Japan to proclaim the "unconditional surrender of all Japanese armed forces, and to provide proper and adequate assurances of their good faith in such action." When the bombing of Hiroshima did not produce the unconditional surrender that the Allies had demanded, a second atomic bomb was dropped around 11:00 a.m. on August 9 (Tokyo time) on Nagasaki. Nagasaki was a railroad terminal and port for Japanese naval and military operations in the Pacific, located on the west coast of Kyushu Island. The bomb fell four miles from the city center in an outlying industrial district. Out of Nagasaki's 250,000 inhabitants, it is estimated that more than 35,000 were killed and 60,000 were injured. The following morning the Japanese government made known its willingness to offer an unconditional surrender on the basis of the Allies' Potsdam Declaration, with the one proviso that Hirohito remain emperor. The *New York Times* reported in enormous captions the jubilant response of American forces in the Pacific: "GI's in Pacific Go Wild With Joy; 'Let 'Em Keep Emperor,' They Say." The Allies raised no serious objection to the request, provided that the emperor be subject to the supreme commander of the Allied powers. With this decision, the war was all but over. The formal surrender ceremonies took place aboard the battleship *Missouri* in Tokyo Bay on September 2, Tokyo time.

When he first announced the dropping of the atomic bomb on Hiroshima, President Truman informed the world of how the American government planned to deal with the new technology: "I shall give further consideration . . . as to how atomic power can become a powerful and forceful influence toward the maintenance of world peace." Following the war he placed before the newly organized United Nations a proposal that all humanity be made the guardian of atomic power. The Soviet Union vetoed this bold proposal in 1947, since it was working feverishly to develop an atomic bomb of its own and did not want international inspectors on Soviet soil. They succeeded in 1949. Another, more powerful bomb was also to come. In 1950 President Truman approved the development of a hydrogen bomb, which was first detonated in 1952. One year later the Soviets also tested an H-bomb.

The anniversary of the dropping of the first atomic bomb is marked with the annual Peace Festival by residents and visitors in the largely rebuilt city of Hiroshima. The commemoration of prayer and remembrance, held every year since 1947 at Peace Memorial Park, is the city's most important yearly event.

Voting Rights Act of 1965

After a symbolic ceremony in the rotunda of the Capitol Building in Washington, D.C., on August 6, 1965, President Lyndon B. Johnson signed the Voting Rights Act of 1965 into law. The law was designed to carry out the provisions of a measure that had been taken 95 years earlier. This was the 15th Amendment to the United States Constitution providing that "the right of citizens . . . to vote shall not be denied or abridged by the United States or by any State on account of race, color, or previous condition of servitude."

Genuine as the intent of the amendment was, in 1965 there were still parts of the country where blacks and other minorities were prevented from voting on the grounds (among others) that they had failed to pass literacy tests, failed to interpret sections of the Constitution adequately, failed to locate registrars, or failed to call during the registrars' often nebulous office hours. Although rarely admitted openly, obviously the denial of voting rights to blacks was deliberate. Different criteria were applied to white and black would-be voters and the spirit of the 15th Amendment was being deliberately violated.

The Voting Rights Act of 1965 had as its goal the removal of bars to voting everywhere in the United States, not just in the South where they were particularly prevalent. Reinforcing the Civil Rights Act of 1964, the new act sought to guarantee the right of every citizen to vote. It specified federal action to prevent local practices that had the effect, whatever the given reason, of denying the right to vote on account of race. In concrete terms, the act called for the suspension of all such devices as literacy tests, constitutional interpretations, registration forms, or required recommendations by registered voters. This provision was applied to states and counties where less than 50 percent of adult residents had voted in 1964. The act also empowered the United States attorney general to dispatch federal examiners to register black voters in those areas if he felt that local registrars were failing to do their job.

As thus spelled out, the law applied principally to Alabama, Alaska, Georgia, Louisiana, Mississippi, South Carolina, Virginia, and parts of North Carolina. It also applied to scattered counties in Arizona, Idaho, and Hawaii. The new act further directed the attorney general to bring court tests to challenge the constitutionality of poll taxes as a requirement for voting in state and local elections. This provision was directed at the four states of Alabama, Mississippi, Texas, and Virginia that still had such taxes. Poll taxes as a requirement for voting in federal elections had already been banned with the ratification of the 24th Amendment to the Constitution in January 1964.

The passage of the Voting Rights Act of 1965 was followed by a dramatic upturn in the number of blacks registered to vote. Nearly 250,000 were newly registered by the end of 1965, a third of them by federal registrars. Much remained to be done, however. Attorney General Nicholas Katzenbach was criticized by some for being too fast and by others for being too slow in sending federal registrars to areas of low black registration. It was not until the 1970s that the voter registration abuses were largely eradicated. In 1975 the act was broadened to protect the voting rights of non-English-speaking minorities, including Native Americans, Mexican Americans, and Asian Americans.

First Evidence of Extraterrestrial Life Announced

On August 6, 1996, Daniel S. Goldin, the head of the National Aeronautics and Space Administration (NASA), issued a historic press release:

NASA has made a startling discovery that points to the possibility that a primitive form of microscopic life may have existed on Mars more than three billion years ago. The research is based on a sophisticated examination of an ancient Martian meteorite that landed on Earth some 13,000 years ago. The evidence is exciting, even compelling, but not conclusive. It is a discovery that demands further scientific investigation. NASA is ready to assist the process of rigorous scientific investigation and lively scientific debate that will follow this discovery.

I want everyone to understand that we are not talking about "little green men." These are extremely small, single-cell structures that somewhat resemble bacteria on Earth. There is no evidence or suggestion that any higher life form ever existed on Mars.

Despite the caveats contained within Goldin's statement, its importance was nonetheless clear: For the first time, there was demonstrable scientific evidence of the existence of life on a planet other than Earth.

The discovery was due to a program, dating back to the late 1960s, involving the collection of meteorites from Antarctica. For reasons that are not entirely understood, certain regions of Antarctica have high concentrations of meteorites that originated from the Moon and Mars. These meteorites are the result of asteroid collisions with the Moon or Mars that blasted chunks of rock into space, which eventually landed on Earth millions of years later. Space probe landings on Mars in the 1970s, which sampled and tested the Martian surface, enabled scientists to identify which meteorites came from Mars.

The next day, August 7, 1996, NASA scientists gave a nationally broadcast press briefing setting forth the details and background of their discovery. Their official statement is set forth below:

A NASA research team of scientists at the Johnson Space Center and at Stanford University has found evidence that strongly suggests primitive life may have existed on Mars more than 3.6 billion years ago.

The NASA-funded team found the first organic molecules thought to be of Martian origin; several mineral features characteristic of biological activity; and possible microscopic fossils of primitive, bacteria-like organisms inside of an ancient Martian rock that fell to Earth as a meteorite. . . .

The igneous rock in the 4.2-pound, potato-sized meteorite has been age-dated to about 4.5 billion years, the period when the planet Mars formed. The rock is believed to have originated underneath the Martian surface and to have been extensively fractured by impacts as meteorites bombarded the planets in the early inner solar system. Between 3.6 billion and 4 billion years ago, a time when it is generally thought that the planet was warmer and wetter, water is believed to have penetrated fractures in the subsurface rock, possibly forming an underground water system.

Because the water was saturated with carbon dioxide from the Martian atmosphere, carbonate minerals were deposited in the fractures. The team's findings indicate living organisms may also have assisted in the formation of the carbonate, and some remains of the microscopic organisms may have become fossilized, in a fashion similar to the formation of fossils in limestone on Earth. Then, 15 million years ago, a huge comet or asteroid struck Mars, ejecting a piece of the rock from its subsurface location with enough force to escape the planet. For millions of years, the chunk of rock floated through space. It encountered Earth's atmosphere 13,000 years ago and fell in Antarctica as a meteorite.

It is in the tiny globs of carbonate that the researchers found a number of features that can be interpreted as suggesting past life. Stanford found easily detectable amounts of organic molecules called polycyclic aromatic hydrocarbons (PAHs) concentrated in the vicinity of the carbonate.

Researchers at JSC found mineral compounds commonly associated with microscopic organisms and the possible microscopic fossil structures.

The largest of the possible fossils are less than 1/100th the diameter of a human hair, and most are about 1/1000th the diameter of a human hair—small enough that it would take about a thousand laid end-to-end to span the dot at the end of this sentence. Some are egg-shaped while others are tubular.

In appearance and size, the structures are strikingly similar to microscopic fossils of the tiniest bacteria found on Earth.

The meteorite, called ALH84001, was found in 1984 in Allan Hills ice field, Antarctica, by an annual expedition of the National Science Foundation's Antarctic Meteorite Program. It was preserved for study in JSC's Meteorite Processing Laboratory and its possible Martian origin was not recognized until 1993. It is one of only 12 meteorites identified so far that match the unique Martian chemistry measured by the Viking spacecraft that landed on Mars in 1976. ALH84001 is by far the oldest of the 12 Martian meteorites, more than three times as old as any other.

Many of the team's findings were made possible only because of very recent technological advances in high-resolution scanning electron microscopy and laser mass spectrometry. Only a few years ago, many of the features that they report were undetectable. Although past studies of this meteorite and others of Martian origin failed to detect evidence of past life, they were generally performed using lower levels of magnification, without the benefit of the technology used in this research. The recent discovery of extremely small bacteria on Earth, called nanobacteria, prompted the team to perform this work at a much finer scale than past efforts. . . .

The team of researchers includes a wide variety of expertise, including microbiology, mineralogy, analytical techniques, geochemistry, and organic chemistry, and the analysis crossed all of these disciplines. . . .

The team found unusual compounds—iron sulfides and magnetite—that are commonly produced by anaerobic bacteria and other microscopic organisms on Earth. The compounds were found in locations directly associated with the fossil-like structures and carbonate globules in the meteorite. Extreme conditions—conditions very unlikely to have been encountered by the meteorite—would have been required to produce these compounds in close proximity to one another if life were not involved. The carbonate also contained tiny grains of magnetite that are almost identical to magnetic fossil remnants often left by certain bacteria found on Earth.

Other minerals commonly associated with biological activity on Earth were found in the carbonate as well.

The formation of the carbonate or fossils by living organisms while the meteorite was in the Antarctic was deemed unlikely for several reasons. The carbonate was age-dated using a parent-daughter isotope method and found to be 3.6 billion years old, and the organic molecules were first detected well within the ancient carbonate. In addition, the team analyzed representative samples of other meteorites from Antarctica and found no evidence of fossil-like structures, organic molecules or possible biologically produced compounds and minerals similar to those in the ALH84001 meteorite. The composition and location of PAHs organic molecules found in the meteorite also appeared to confirm that the possible evidence of life was extraterrestrial.

Since the August 1996 announcement, the Martian fossil samples have undergone additional exhaustive tests, and no evidence contradicting the NASA findings that life did indeed develop independently on Mars has been found. Although microscopic bacteria may be unexciting to science fiction fans, it is nevertheless proof that "we are not alone."

August 7

Gulf of Tonkin Resolution Approved

In the years following the end of World War II, the "domino theory," as set forth by President Dwight D. Eisenhower on April 7, 1954, guided American leaders in formulating policy in Southeast Asia. Presidents John F. Kennedy and Lyndon B. Johnson, who succeeded Dwight D. Eisenhower, agreed that if the Communists were victorious in South Vietnam all of Southeast Asia would fall to the enemy. Both presidents therefore decided to safeguard South Vietnam from Communist encroachment. Kennedy's years as president witnessed increased American involvement in the small nation, and after Congress approved the Gulf of Tonkin Resolution on August 7, 1964,

the Johnson administration escalated military participation dramatically.

The United States became entangled in Vietnam during the last years of French colonial domination of Southeast Asia. At the end of World War II, Vietnamese nationalists, many of whom had become identified with Ho Chi Minh's Communist-dominated Vietminh (or League for the Independence of Vietnam), desired independence for their homeland. France, however, had no intention of surrendering control of Vietnam or any other part of its Indochinese empire. Realizing that neither the United States nor the powers of Western Europe would support a war to stifle a movement for Vietnamese independence, French leaders decided to transform the image of their military efforts into a fight against communism. As part of this undertaking, the French in 1949 set up a quasi-independent government in Vietnam headed by former emperor Bao Dai. The new regime lacked true autonomy and failed to satisfy Vietnamese nationalists, but it accomplished its purpose. American leaders believed the new French-supported Vietnamese government was a bulwark against communism and the anti-American Communist regimes in China and the Soviet Union. On February 7, 1950, the United States recognized the Bao Dai government and during the next four years provided some $2.6 billion to assist France in Vietnam.

Despite such enormous economic aid, France was unable to put down what the Vietminh and those allied with them saw as a struggle for self-determination. In the spring of 1954 France committed its best troops to the protection of the fortress of Dienbienphu in Vietnam's northern province of Tonkin. The French military command believed this tactic would lure the Vietminh into an engagement that would result in a decisive defeat of the insurgents, but their reasoning proved wrong. Supplied with artillery by China, the Vietminh besieged Dienbienphu and captured the fortress on May 7, 1954.

The fall of Dienbienphu marked the end of French military efforts in Vietnam. The Geneva armistice and agreements of July 20 and 21, 1954, provided for a cease-fire in Vietnam and partitioned the war-ravaged nation at the 17th Parallel. Ho Chi Minh was given control of the North, and the government of Bao Dai was recognized in the South. The division was to be temporary: The Geneva agreements also called for a free election to be held under international supervision in July 1956 to decide the question of Vietnamese unification.

Unwilling to participate in negotiations with the Communists, the United States did not sign or endorse the Geneva agreements. An official statement was issued, however, warning that the United States "would view any renewal of the aggression in violation of the . . . agreements with grave concern."

In the months following the 1954 armistice, American involvement in South Vietnam deepened. With American approval, Bao Dai selected Ngo Dinh Diem, the nationalist leader of Vietnam's powerful Roman Catholic minority, to be prime minister. American leaders believed Diem would be able to build South Vietnam into a stronghold against communism, and on October 23, 1954, President Eisenhower notified Diem that the United States would assist Vietnam to become "a strong, viable state, capable of resisting attempted subversion or aggression through military means." In the same message, however, Eisenhower also warned that "the Government of the United States expects that this aid will be met by performance on the part of the Government of Vietnam in undertaking needed reforms."

In October 1955 Diem, after a one-sided government-controlled referendum ousted Bao Dai, proclaimed himself president of the Republic of Vietnam. The United States immediately recognized the new regime, while continuing its liberal financial assistance to South Vietnam.

The Geneva accords called for a general election to be held in Vietnam in July 1956, but in July of the previous year, Diem announced that his government had not signed the Geneva agreements and therefore was not bound by them. Thus, he stated that no referendum would take place in Vietnam until the conditions for a free election were present in the North. Ho Chi Minh and the Vietminh, who most observers believed would have easily won the election, were eager for the referendum. They repeatedly called upon Diem's Saigon government to enter into discussions so that arrangements might be made for the elections, but the South Vietnamese, with the support of the United States, refused.

Conditions in Vietnam steadily deteriorated. After 1956 Communist guerrillas, popularly known as the Vietcong, began to make raids in the South. The Diem government proved itself unable to stem the terrorists. Between 1956 and 1960 the United States sent several hundred military advisers to South Vietnam and financial aid estimated by some to have averaged as much as $300 million a year. Despite this massive assistance to the Saigon government, the Vietcong gained strength and in December 1960 joined with non-Communist anti-Diem insurgents to form the National Liberation Front (NLF) of South Vietnam.

By the autumn of 1961 the NLF had perhaps as much as 80 percent of the South Vietnamese countryside under its influence and so threatened the Diem government that on October 18, 1961, Diem declared "a state of emergency." The United States acted quickly to provide assistance. On December 11, 1961, two army helicopter companies, the first American military units to become directly involved in combat support, arrived in Saigon. On December 14 President Kennedy reaffirmed American support of South Vietnam and authorized the addition of 1,500 military advisers to the more than 600 already in South Vietnam.

Throughout 1962 American involvement in Vietnam steadily increased. By February the number of military personnel in South Vietnam climbed to 4,000, and in early March Pentagon officials admitted that American pilots were flying some combat missions there. The United States did not become directly involved in ground fighting during 1962, but by the end of the year, 11,300 American troops were stationed in South Vietnam.

Despite American aid, the Diem regime made no progress against the enemy. The Army of the Republic of Vietnam (ARVN) repeatedly proved itself incapable of holding its own against the Vietcong. On one occasion, during January 1963 in the Mekong Delta, 200 Vietcong were able to repulse the advance of 2,000 government troops supported by armor and air units. Moreover, such failings by his military force were not the only problems facing Diem in 1963.

For some time prior to 1963 the Buddhists who formed the majority of Vietnam's population had resented the favoritism Diem showed toward the Catholic minority and had chafed under the oppressive measures carried out by Diem's brother, Ngo Dinh Nhu, who headed the secret police. Then, on May 8, 1963, the police in Hue fired into a crowd demonstrating against an order prohibiting the flying of Buddhist flags during a religious festival. The incident precipitated a major crisis. On June 11 a Buddhist monk immolated himself in Saigon to protest the Hue shooting, and during the summer of 1963 several others followed his example. By August South Vietnam was in such turmoil that Diem declared martial law so that order could be restored.

On September 16, 1963, only 11 days after martial law was lifted, Diem permitted national elections to take place in South Vietnam. By allowing only candidates who had won prior governmental approval to seek election, Diem totally ignored the months of protest and unrest that had preceded the September 27 canvass. In any event, the days of his corrupt and authoritarian regime were numbered. On November 1, 1963, a group of officers in the South Vietnamese armed forces, with the tacit approval of the United States, overthrew the Diem government. The following day they murdered Diem and his brother Nhu and set up a military junta to rule South Vietnam.

After the downfall of Diem, South Vietnam's internal political situation was chaotic. Worried that the cause of anticommunism might fail, the United States continued to support the Saigon government. On January 1, 1964, Lyndon B. Johnson, who had succeeded to the presidency following the assassination of President Kennedy, assured South Vietnamese leaders that "we shall maintain in Vietnam American personnel and materiel as needed to assist you in achieving victory." By March and April high administration advisers were considering what they would come to see as the necessity for a major increase in the American role in Vietnam.

In the spring of 1964 the Joint Chiefs of Staff prepared a list of possible bombing targets in North Vietnam. During the first half of the year, American advisers provided the South Vietnamese with training and equipment for guerrilla operations, reconnaissance missions, and raids against coastal installations in North Vietnam. It was all part of a program, code-named Operation 34A, of covert military pressures against the North. In addition, United States Navy destroyers secretly patrolled the Gulf of Tonkin, directly east of North Vietnam, conducting reconnaissance, monitoring Communist radio broadcasts, and collecting information about North Vietnamese radar installations. By summer, with the military situation of anti-Communist South Vietnam particularly precarious, the Johnson administration was maneuvering to gain approval for a congressional resolution that would in effect authorize undeclared war should that seem necessary.

The first of two incidents that led to just such a resolution took place on August 2, 1964, when North Vietnamese PT boats allegedly fired on the American destroyer *Maddox* cruising in the Gulf of Tonkin. President Johnson ordered a second destroyer, the *C. Turner Joy*, added to the navy patrol and protested the "unprovoked attack" to Hanoi. A second North Vietnamese attack on the *Maddox* and the *C. Turner Joy* allegedly took place in the same area on August 4, although there were no visual sightings in the pitch-dark night. President Johnson retaliated by ordering planes to bomb strategic targets in North Vietnam, the first overt military action undertaken by the United States in the area.

On August 5, 1964, President Johnson asked Congress to promise full support for American forces in South Vietnam in order "to promote the maintenance of international peace and security in Southeast Asia." The response was quick and predictable. At the time, Congress and the American public had no knowledge of Operation 34A, nor of any possible confusion surrounding the Gulf of Tonkin incidents. These appeared as clear examples of unprovoked North Vietnamese aggression, and the Gulf of Tonkin Resolution, which Congress quickly passed on August 7, 1964, appeared to be a clearly warranted response.

The resolution, which passed 416 to 0 in the House of Representatives and 88 to 2 in the Senate, gave the president the power "to take all necessary measures to repel any armed attack against the forces of the United States and to prevent further aggression." The resolution also stated that "the United States is . . . prepared, as the President determines, to take all necessary steps, including the use of armed force, to assist any member or protocol State of the Southeast Asia Collective Defense Treaty requesting assistance in defense of its freedom."

Although the Gulf of Tonkin Resolution did not authorize a full-scale war in so many words, it was, in effect, a blank check, and American participation in the fighting in South Vietnam dramatically increased in the years following its approval.

George Washington Issues Whiskey Rebellion Proclamation

In the years following the adoption of the United States Constitution of 1787, the federal government of the young United States struggled to assert its authority. The population was widespread and rapidly expanding into the frontier. In order to raise revenue and exercise some control over the frontier population, in 1791 Congress enacted an excise tax on whiskey. The tax was extremely unpopular in western Pennsylvania, which produced much of the nation's whiskey, and riots broke out that led to organized resistance to federal authority. To restore order, on August 7, 1794, President George Washington called out the militias of four states in order to crush the rebellion. It took several months, but the operation was eventually successful, and it was important historically as a test of federal power. A copy of Washington's proclamation is set forth below:

> Whereas, combinations to defeat the execution of the laws laying duties upon spirits distilled within the United States and upon stills have from the time of the commencement of those laws existed in some of the western parts of Pennsylvania;

And whereas, the said combinations, proceeding in a manner subversive equally of the just authority of government and of the rights of individuals, have hitherto effected their dangerous and criminal purpose by the influence of certain irregular meetings whose proceedings have tended to encourage and uphold the spirit of opposition by misrepresentations of the laws calculated to render them odious; by endeavors to deter those who might be so disposed from accepting offices under them through fear of public resentment and of injury to person and property, and to compel those who had accepted such offices by actual violence to surrender or forbear the execution of them; by circulation vindictive menaces against all those who should otherwise, directly or indirectly, aid in the execution of the said laws, or who, yielding to the dictates of conscience and to a sense of obligation, should themselves comply therewith; by actually injuring and destroying the property of persons who were understood to have so complied; by inflicting cruel and humiliating punishments upon private citizens for no other cause than that of appearing to be the friends of the laws; by intercepting the public officers on the highways, abusing, assaulting, and otherwise ill treating them; by going into their houses in the night, gaining admittance by force, taking away their papers, and committing other outrages, employing for these unwarrantable purposes the agency of armed banditti disguised in such manner as for the most part to escape discovery;

And whereas, the endeavors of the legislature to obviate objections to the said laws by lowering the duties and by other alterations conducive to the convenience of those whom they immediately affect (though they have given satisfaction in other quarters), and the endeavors of the executive officers to conciliate a compliance with the laws by explanations, by forbearance, and even by particular accommodations founded on the suggestion of local considerations, have been disappointed of their effect by the machinations of persons whose industry to excite resistance has increased with every appearance of a disposition among the people to relax in their opposition and to acquiesce in the laws, insomuch that many persons in the said western parts of Pennsylvania have at length been hardy enough to perpetrate acts,

which I am advised amount to treason, being overt acts of levying war against the United States, the said persons having on the 16th and 17th of July last past proceeded in arms (on the second day amounting to several hundreds) to the house of John Neville, inspector of the revenue for the fourth survey of the district of Pennsylvania; having repeatedly attacked the said house with the persons therein, wounding some of them; having seized David Lenox, marshal of the district of Pennsylvania, who previous thereto had been fired upon while in the execution of his duty by a party of armed men, detaining him for some time prisoner, till, for the preservation of his life and the obtaining of his liberty, he found it necessary to enter into stipulations to forbear the execution of certain official duties touching processes issuing out of a court of the United States; and having finally obliged the said inspector of the revenue and the said marshal from considerations of personal safety to fly from that part of the country, in order, by a circuitous route, to proceed to the seat of government, avowing as the motives of these outrageous proceedings an intention to prevent by force of arms the execution of the said laws, to oblige the said inspector of the revenue to renounce his said office, to withstand by open violence the lawful authority of the government of the United States, and to compel thereby an alteration in the measures of the legislature and a repeal of the laws aforesaid;

And whereas, by a law of the United States entitled "An act to provide for calling forth the militia to execute the laws of the Union, suppress insurrections, and repel invasions," it is enacted that whenever the laws of the United States shall be opposed or the execution thereof obstructed in any state by combinations too powerful to be suppressed by the ordinary course of judicial proceedings or by the powers vested in the marshals by that act, the same being notified by an associate justice or the district judge, it shall be lawful for the President of the United States to call forth the militia of such state to suppress such combinations and to cause the laws to be duly executed. And if the militia of a state, when such combinations may happen, shall refuse or be insufficient to suppress the same, it shall be lawful for the President, if the legislature of the United States shall not be in session, to call forth and employ such numbers of the militia of any other state or states most convenient thereto as may be necessary; and the use of the militia so to be called forth may be continued, if necessary, until the expiration of thirty days after the commencement of the ensuing session; Provided always, that, whenever it may be necessary in the judgment of the President to use the military force hereby directed to be called forth, the President shall forthwith, and previous thereto, by proclamation, command such insurgents to disperse and retire peaceably to their respective abodes within a limited time;

And whereas, James Wilson, an associate justice, on the 4th instant, by writing under his hand, did from evidence which had been laid before him notify to me that "in the counties of Washington and Allegany, in Pennsylvania, laws of the United States are opposed and the execution thereof obstructed by combinations too powerful to be suppressed by the ordinary course of judicial proceedings or by the powers vested in the marshal of that district";

And whereas, it is in my judgment necessary under the circumstances of the case to take measures for calling forth the militia in order to suppress the combinations aforesaid, and to cause the laws to be duly executed; and I have accordingly determined so to do, feeling the deepest regret for the occasion, but withal the most solemn conviction that the essential interests of the Union demand it, that the very existence of government and the fundamental principles of social order are materially involved in the issue, and that the patriotism and firmness of all good citizens are seriously called upon, as occasions may require, to aid in the effectual suppression of so fatal a spirit;

Therefore, and in pursuance of the proviso above recited, I, George Washington, President of the United States, do hereby command all persons, being insurgents, as aforesaid, and all others whom it may concern, on or before the 1st day of September next to disperse and retire peaceably to their respective abodes. And I do moreover warn all persons whomsoever against aiding, abetting, or comforting the perpetrators of the aforesaid treasonable acts; and do require all officers and other citizens, according to their respective duties and the laws of the land, to exert their utmost endeavors to prevent and suppress such dangerous proceedings.

In testimony whereof I have caused the seal of the United States of America to be affixed to these presents, and signed the same with my hand. Done at the city of Philadelphia the seventh day of August, one thousand seven hundred and ninety-four, and of the independence of the United States of America the nineteenth.

August 8

Charles A. Dana's Birthday

Charles Anderson Dana, one of the most influential newspaper editors in the decades before and after the Civil War, was born in Hinsdale, New Hampshire, on August 8, 1819. When he was nine years old, following his mother's death, he was sent to live with an uncle in Buffalo, New York. He worked from the time he was 12, first on a farm and then as a clerk in his uncle's store, educating himself in his free moments.

Dana's self-education was evidently of high caliber, since Harvard accepted him as a student in 1839. Although Dana ranked high in his class during his first term, his eyesight became impaired by the long hours of study, and he left Harvard in 1841. However, 20 years later Harvard gave him an honorary Bachelor of Arts degree as of the class of 1843, the year he would have graduated.

Probably while he was at Harvard, Dana became acquainted with George Ripley, a Unitarian minister and Harvard graduate who preached in Boston from 1826 to 1841. Ripley left Boston in 1841 to start Brook Farm, one of the most famous of the numerous experiments in communal living that sprang into existence in the early and middle 19th century. The concept of Brook Farm was to strive for intellectual freedom and a society of educated, cultivated, and liberal-minded persons in a simple setting away from the competition and distractions of the outside world. It appealed greatly to the idealistic Dana, who went to Brook Farm in 1841 and stayed for five years. Dana and Nathaniel Hawthorne were among the original shareholders of Brook Farm, which comprised 160 acres in West Roxbury, Massachusetts, nine miles from Boston. Dana and Hawthorne served together as the institution's first directors of agriculture, but Hawthorne, unable to write in the idyllic setting, left after six months.

During his years at Brook Farm, Dana wrote for *The Harbinger*, the Brook Farm publication edited by Ripley. He also wrote for *The Dial*, the literary magazine put out by New England Transcendentalists. After he left Brook Farm in 1846, which was soon to fail, Dana wrote for the Boston *Chronotype*.

Joining the *New York Tribune* in 1847 with a starting pay of $10 weekly, Dana soon rose to be managing editor, second in importance only to the paper's editor and publisher, Horace Greeley. The creation of the post of managing editor was one of Greeley's many contributions to American journalism. Both men had strong personalities, and increasingly they clashed on many points, especially about the Civil War. The friction between the militant Dana and the pacifist Greeley became intolerable and, after 15 years, Dana left the *Tribune* on March 28, 1862.

Secretary of War Edwin Stanton, who had often received Dana's editorial support, immediately appointed Dana as a special investigating agent for the War Department. In that capacity Dana, who was present at the campaigns of Vicksburg, Chickamauga, and Chattanooga, sent Stanton reports from the front. He gave valuable aid to Generals Ulysses S. Grant and William Tecumseh Sherman, and urged Stanton to name Grant supreme commander of all the armies in the field. Dana served as second assistant secretary of war from 1864 until July 7, 1865, when he resigned from the War Department.

After the war Dana edited the *Chicago Republican*. When it folded, he returned to New York in 1868 as editor and part-owner of the *New York Sun*, which he ran until his death. Under his leadership, the *Sun* became known as "the newspaperman's newspaper." However, Dana's erratic editorials showed that the Brook Farm idealist had become skeptical and cynical. While he could endear himself to newspaper colleagues, he had the reputation of never forgiving a grudge or supposed slight, or of dropping a point. An example was the hotly disputed presidential election of 1876, in which the *Sun* had supported the unsuccessful Democratic candidate Samuel Jones Tilden. After the inauguration of Republican Rutherford B. Hayes, the paper persisted in using such references as "His Fraudulency the President."

On October 17, 1897, Dana died at his home on Dosoris Island in Glen Cove, New York. In addition to his newspaper activities, during his lifetime he edited one of the most successful anthologies of American verse, *The Household Book of Poetry* (1857). With Ripley he edited the *New American Cyclopaedia* (1858–1863). He also wrote *The Art of Newspaper Making* (1895); *Recollections of the*

Civil War, considered by some to be his greatest book; and *Eastern Journeys*. The last two were published posthumously in 1898.

The Wilmot Proviso of 1846

In the decades preceding the Mexican War, which began on May 12, 1846 (see related essays throughout this book), Americans began to settle in the vast expanse of Mexican territory that is now Texas, California, and the American Southwest. At first the settlers came at the invitation of the Mexican authorities, who were looking to populate the largely empty region, but over time the Mexicans became concerned about the often-rebellious American pioneers and began to clamp down both on immigration and on political dissent. Several incidents between the United States and Mexico, plus the expansionist policies of President James K. Polk, led to the outbreak of war.

The United States achieved victory in the summer of 1847 when it took the Mexican capital of Mexico City, although the formal cessation of hostilities did not take place until February 2, 1848, with the signing of the Treaty of Guadalupe-Hidalgo. Long beforehand, however, there was concern over whether slavery would be permitted in the territory that might (and probably would) be seized from Mexico. In these pre–Civil War years, there was a precarious political balance between the slave states of the South and the free states of the North. The North, with its larger population, controlled the House of Representatives in which representation is determined by the number of people in a state. The South, however, was able to check this power in the Senate where every state has two senators regardless of population.

On August 8, 1846, the House approved a proposal by Representative David Wilmot, from Pennsylvania, known as the Wilmot Proviso. It would have prevented the expansion of slavery into any territory taken from Mexico. The proviso came in the form of an amendment to an appropriations bill, which was not voted on by the Senate that year before the Senate adjourned. Determined to keep the initiative alive, however, the House passed the proviso again on February 1, 1847. The Senate voted it down, and ultimately the issue of slavery was addressed in the package of legislation known as the Compromise of 1850. Essentially, slavery would be permitted in certain parts of the territory taken from Mexico if the residents wished it.

The dispute over the Wilmot Proviso inflamed passions on both sides over slavery and made many northerners concerned over the future of the United States with such a divided sectional political system. These concerns helped lead in part to the creation of the Republican Party with its strong antislavery platform.

August 9

Free-Soil Party Organized

The two-party political system in the United States is based on the belief that the problems that the government must deal with may be solved by political compromise. For most of the history of the American republic this premise has held true. However, in the mid-19th century the national government grappled with the difficult issue of slavery, which could not be resolved through the usual method of partisan give-and-take. Political compromise ultimately proved to be impossible. Before the very existence of the federal Union was challenged, however, the course of debate over slavery led to the formation of a significant third party in the form of the Free-Soil Party. It first convened on August 9, 1848.

Although abolitionists had denounced slavery prior to the 1840s, the annexation of Texas in 1845 and additional areas obtained in 1848 as a result of the American victory in the Mexican War brought a new intensity to their arguments. Opponents of slavery viewed the new territories as regions into which the institution they so detested might be extended. Accordingly, in 1846 Representative David Wilmot of Pennsylvania proposed a prohibition against slavery in any territory that might be taken from Mexico. This Wilmot Proviso failed to win congressional approval, but the expansion of slavery became an increasingly important issue in the years that followed.

The debate over the Wilmot Proviso raised a major constitutional question: Did Congress have the power to prevent the extension of slavery to the new territories? Many northerners argued that the national legislature had the authority to prevent such expansion. In a sense, with the Ordinance of 1787, which banned slavery in the old Northwest Territory, it had already done so. Southerners, on the other hand, denied that Congress possessed such power. They claimed that such interference with slaveholding was a direct violation of property rights guaranteed by the Constitution. Finally, there was yet another viewpoint. A large number of influential westerners supported the doctrine of "popular sovereignty." According to this theory, the actual settlers of the new territories should be allowed to decide the question of slavery for themselves.

Although the expansion of slavery and the question of Congress's power to prevent its introduction into the territories were the most important issues in the election of 1848, both major political parties tried to avoid taking an absolute stand on these problems. The Democrats chose Senator Lewis Cass, former governor of the Michigan Territory and an advocate of popular sovereignty, as their presidential candidate. The Whigs selected General Zachary Taylor, the Mexican War "Hero of Buena Vista" to be their standard-bearer. Neither nominee pleased the "Barnburner" Democrats, so called because they were allegedly willing to "burn down the Democratic barn" to eliminate the proslavery Democrats. The party nominees displeased the "Conscience Whigs" as well, who were also strongly opposed to slavery.

Unable to accept either of the candidates offered by the two major parties, the Barnburner Democrats, Conscience Whigs, and other dissidents decided to form a third party. On August 9, 1848, some 465 representatives from 18 states met in Buffalo, New York, to organize the Free-Soil Party. The delegates came from varied backgrounds, but for one reason or another all of them opposed the extension of slavery into the territories that the United States had acquired from Mexico.

The Free-Soil Party chose Martin Van Buren, former president of the United States and a Barnburner Democrat, as its presidential nominee, and Charles Francis Adams, the son of President John Quincy Adams and a conscience Whig, as its vice-presidential candidate. In their platform, the Buffalo delegates attacked the expansion of slavery into the newly acquired territories, favored the habitation of these areas by bona fide white settlers, and approved certain river and harbor improvements. They summed up the goals of their new party with their slogan Free Soil, Free Speech, Free Labor, and Free Men.

In the November 1848 election, Van Buren and Adams polled only 291,263 popular votes and failed to carry a single state. However, the young party had an important effect on the outcome of the presidential contest. The Free-Soilers drew away so many ballots from the regular Democrats in New York that Lewis Cass, the Democratic presidential candidate, failed to carry that key state. The lack of unity among Democrats lost him the election.

More significant than the impact of the Free-Soilers on the 1848 election was the lasting effect that the party exerted on national politics. Though the party never again garnered as many votes as it did in 1848, when its presidential ticket won slightly over ten percent of the ballots and elected nine representatives to Congress, the very existence of the Free-Soil Party forcefully demonstrated the strength and intensity of the slavery issue. In the years between 1848 and 1854 it served as an important channel for antislavery sentiment.

The Free-Soil Party lasted only six years. In 1852 its presidential and vice-presidential nominees, John P. Hale of New Hampshire and George W. Julian of Indiana, won only roughly five percent of the popular vote. The party never participated in another national contest, for in 1854 its membership found another political home in the newly created Republican Party.

Webster-Ashburton Treaty Signed

For more than half a century, the location of the northeastern border between the United States and Canada was disputed. The Treaty of Paris of 1783 specified that the boundary separating the new American nation from its British neighbor to the north extended

> from the north-west angle of Nova Scotia, viz—that angle which is formed by a line drawn due north from the source of the St. Croix river to the highlands, along the said highlands which divide those rivers that empty themselves into the St. Lawrence, from those which fall into the Atlantic ocean to the north westernmost head of the Connecticut river—thence down along the middle of that river to the 45th degree of north latitude; from thence in a line due west on that latitude until it strikes the river Iroquois or Cataraqui.

Unfortunately, the wording of the 1783 settlement was open to several interpretations, and not until the signing of the Webster-Ashburton Treaty on August 9, 1842, was the issue finally resolved.

Prior to the 1842 treaty, Great Britain and the United States made several unsuccessful attempts to settle the border controversy. In 1798 a commission composed of representatives from both nations was able to reach agreement concerning which of several rivers in the disputed area was actually the St. Croix River specified in the 1783 treaty. However, efforts in 1803 and 1807 failed to produce a settlement concerning where the line from the St. Croix reached the highlands. Between 1816 and 1822 the United States and Britain again tried to resolve this difficulty, but without success. In 1827 the king of the Netherlands agreed to arbitrate the matter. Four years later the king found the 1783 treaty to be "inexplicable and impracticable" and suggested a completely arbitrary division of the disputed territory. The United States refused to accept this compromise.

In the winter of 1838–1839 the boundary dispute threatened to become the cause of armed conflict. Beginning in 1820 the legislatures of Maine and Massachusetts had made extensive grants of land in the Aroostook Valley to American citizens. The British, however, also claimed the rich area and in 1838 Canadian lumberjacks started cutting timber there. To protect the interests of American settlers, in January 1839 the Maine legislature named Rufus McIntire a land agent and instructed him to expel the Canadian loggers from the valley. On February 12, 1839, the Canadians arrested McIntire. This action and the Canadians' determination to remain in the area resulted in the calling up of militias in both Maine and New Brunswick. The Nova Scotia legislature and the United States Congress voted for substantial war appropriations. As preparations for the so-called Aroostook War continued, President Martin Van Buren sent General Winfield Scott to Maine. In March 1839 Scott was able to persuade the governor of Maine and the lieutenant governor of New Brunswick to agree to a truce. The Aroostook War thus ended without bloodshed, but the boundary issue remained unresolved.

Although the need to establish the northeastern boundary between Canada and the United States became increasingly urgent during the 1830s, several incidents not directly related to the disputed area complicated negotiations between Great Britain and the United States. After the failure of an insurrection in Canada in 1837, rebel leader William Lyon Mackenzie and some of his followers took refuge on Navy Island, which is located on the Canadian side of the Niagara River. The assistance of New Yorkers hostile to the British enabled the Mackenzie group to launch a number of attacks against the Canadian frontier in the fall of 1837. To prevent further depredations a party of Canadian militia on December 29, 1837, crossed to the American side of the river. They destroyed the steamboat *Caroline*, which had been used to carry supplies and arms to the rebels, and killed Amos Durfee, an American citizen.

Tensions between the United States and Britain over the *Caroline* and several minor incidents began to abate in 1839, but hostilities soon flared up again. In November 1840 Alexander McLeod, a Canadian deputy sheriff, boasted in a New York tavern that he had participated in the *Caroline* affair and had personally killed Durfee. New York authorities promptly charged McLeod with murder. On December 13, 1840, the British, claiming that McLeod had acted under military orders, protested his arrest. This admission that the *Caroline* action had received official sanction served only to further antagonize the already excited residents of northern New York. Federal authorities, claiming to have no jurisdiction in the McLeod case, announced that they could not comply with Britain's demand for his release. McLeod accordingly was brought to trial. Many observers believed that conviction of the Canadian would have precipitated a serious international crisis. This ominous possibility was averted when a jury found McLeod innocent of Durfee's murder on October 12, 1841. Despite the outcome of the trial, the McLeod case placed a great strain on Anglo-American ties.

Relations between Britain and the United States further deteriorated late in 1841. Britain had outlawed its slave trade in 1807 and abolished slavery throughout the empire in 1834, but British efforts to end slaving were seriously hampered, since the American ban on the trade was loosely enforced. For decades both nations had harbored ill-feelings regarding slave trade activities in particular and naval rights in general. The *Creole* incident intensified these antagonisms.

On October 27, 1841, the American brig *Creole* set sail with a cargo of slaves from Hampton Roads, Virginia, on a voyage to New Orleans. The slaves revolted, gained control of the vessel, and ordered it to put in at the British port of Nassau in the Bahamas. The British authorities charged several of the slaves with mutiny and murder, but then freed most of them. American secretary of state Daniel Webster immediately protested the latter action. He asked for the return of the "mutineers and murderers and the recognized property" of citizens of the United States, but the British did not comply.

Against this background of mutual provocations and minor incidents, Anglo-American relations suddenly took a sharp turn for the better in 1842. In September 1841 Sir Robert Peel had replaced Lord Melbourne as Britain's prime minister, and the new government named Lord Aberdeen to head the Foreign Office. Aberdeen strongly desired to settle the long-standing grievances between Britain and the United States, most notably the matter of the northeastern boundary. In the spring of 1842 he sent a special minister, Alexander Baring, the first Baron Ashburton, to Washington, D.C.

Lord Ashburton, the head of the House of Baring, London's great banking institution, entered into negotiations with Daniel Webster on June 13, 1842. Like the king of the Netherlands before them, Ashburton and Webster concluded that the 1783 Treaty of Paris was too vague to permit a boundary settlement. They put aside that document and worked out an arbitrary division of the disputed lands. The treaty, which Ashburton and Webster signed on August 9, 1842, and which sub-

sequently received the approval of their respective governments, ended the decades-long controversy over the northeastern boundary and settled a number of other issues. In a supplementary exchange of notes Ashburton unofficially apologized for the *Caroline* and McLeod cases, thereby disposing of these matters.

According to the Webster-Ashburton Treaty, the British received 5,000 square miles lying north of the Aroostook Valley in what is now New Brunswick, the region needed for the military road connecting Halifax and Quebec. In return the United States gained about 7,000 square miles of the 12,000 in question. Maine retained the Aroostook Valley, and both Maine and Massachusetts were indemnified in the amount of $150,000 by the United States for abandoning their claims to the area that had been awarded to New Brunswick. In addition, the northern boundary of Vermont and eastern New York State was set at about a half mile north of the 45th Parallel. This gave the United States control of a military outpost accidentally built on Canadian soil near the head of Lake Champlain in what is now New York State. The United States–Canadian border then followed a previously agreed-upon course through the Great Lakes and their connecting waterways to Lake Superior. A compromise between Webster and Ashburton fixed the border west from there to Lake of the Woods at the present boundary line. This gave the United States the 6,500 square miles of northeastern Minnesota that was later found to be the site of the rich Mesabi iron ore deposits. The treaty also established mutual extradition procedures for seven nonpolitical crimes, authorized joint squadrons to suppress slaving along the African coast, and gave the United States the right to navigate the St. John River, which empties into the Bay of Fundy at St. John, New Brunswick.

August 10

Herbert Hoover's Birthday

Herbert Clark Hoover, a great humanitarian and the 31st president of the United States, was born on August 10, 1874, in West Branch, Iowa. West Branch had been founded as a Quaker settlement by his ancestors in 1853. His father, Jesse Clark Hoover, a blacksmith and farm equipment dealer, was descended from Quakers who had settled in Pennsylvania in 1738. The forebears of Hoover's mother, Huldah Randall Minthorn Hoover, were also Quakers. They migrated to New England in 1630.

Herbert Hoover

Herbert Hoover was only six when his father died of typhoid fever. His mother supported three children by sewing. In 1884 she died of pneumonia, and the children were cared for by relatives. Young Hoover went to live in Oregon with an uncle. After attending a small Quaker academy in Newberg, Oregon, at 17 Hoover decided to become an engineer. In 1891 he was accepted into the first class at Stanford University. During the summers, he worked for the Arkansas and United States geological surveys. Specializing in mining engineering and geology, he graduated in 1895.

At the time, the country was suffering from an economic depression, and Hoover found that his degree was worth little in the job market. He managed to find work as a miner until the mine went bankrupt a year later. Then, in 1896 he sought work from the mining engineer and entrepreneur Louis Janin. Janin hired Hoover as an office boy but soon sent him to assist in an extensive northern Californian mining project. The next year Hoover received a job, on Janin's recommendation, as a consulting engineer to develop newly discovered Australian gold deposits for the British mining firm of Bewick, Moreing, and Company.

From that time onward Hoover's fortunes improved. At 24 he was earning the substantial sum of $7,500 per year. Hoover remained in Australia for two years until he accepted the challenge of organizing mining and transportation facilities for the Chinese government's Imperial Bureau of Mines. On his way to China, Hoover detoured to California, where he married his Stanford sweetheart, Lou Henry, on February 10, 1899.

The Boxer Rebellion, an effort to expel colonial powers from China, flared up in 1900 just as the Hoovers arrived. Many lives were lost during the upheaval, and the rebellion was subdued only by the arrival of an international army representing countries with interests in China. Foreshadowing the kind of initiative that was to make him famous, Hoover took charge of the safety of Westerners trapped by the uprising and managed to obtain food for them.

After the rebellion, China closed its Bureau of Mines and in 1901 Hoover returned to private industry as a partner in Bewick, Moreing, and Company. In 1908 Hoover left Bewick, Moreing to establish his own firm, and in 1909 published the book *Principles of Mining*.

The outbreak of World War I found the Hoovers in England. It also found 120,000 Americans stranded abroad, with their credit cut off. Hoover quickly built an organization to help these unfortunate travelers get home. In the course of the venture, Hoover's group loaned $1.5 million, of which they lost only $300. For his relief efforts Hoover received public acclaim and was appointed head of the Commission for Relief, in Belgium. During four war-torn years this commission moved five million tons of food through Allied and German blockades to feed starving millions in Belgium and northern France.

In April 1917 the United States entered the war, and President Woodrow Wilson called Hoover back to the United States to head the United States Food Administration. He was given broad powers to regulate food production, foreign food purchases, and food distribution, which he managed without recourse to rationing. Hoover's persuasive powers, abetted by price incentives, resulted in the tripling of American farm production. In order to feed the fighting men, Americans were urged to "hooverize," namely to consume less food.

Hostilities ceased on November 11, 1918. With the armistice in effect, Hoover was called upon by the Allied governments of Britain, France, the United States, and Italy to direct relief efforts throughout 30 European countries. Hoover directed the distribution of approximately $3.5 billion to feed and clothe Europeans left without resources by the war. Under this effort, more than 23 million tons of food, clothing, and medicine were made available.

Peace treaties signed by the separate countries during 1919 brought both the war and Hoover's official work to an end. However, with American support he continued his relief efforts, establishing the American Relief Administration (ARA) and persuading Congress to appropriate $100 million for the relief of children, while privately raising another $200 million himself. He first concentrated his efforts in Poland and Rumania, where typhus raged. Then in 1921 famine struck Russia, threatening the lives of 20 million people, mostly children. The strains between the United States and the new revolutionary government in Russia notwithstanding, Hoover managed to raise $75 million in relief money. This effort continued from 1921 to 1923 and was conducted under the authority of the ARA.

Popular because of his humanitarian efforts, Hoover was mentioned by both American political parties as a potential presidential candidate. He declared that he was a Republican, but announced that he would not be a candidate. Party bosses picked a dark horse candidate, Warren G. Harding. When elected, Harding appointed Hoover secretary of commerce. He remained at his post throughout the administrations of Harding and Calvin Coolidge. As secretary of commerce, Hoover established housing and highway safety programs, began government regulation of the infant radio and aviation industries, and persuaded manufacturers to establish standardization codes for appliance parts. He also offered a program to reorganize the federal government. Harding submitted the proposal to the Congress, but it was turned down. In 1927 Hoover oversaw massive relief efforts for the Mississippi basin area, which had been devastated by floods.

When Coolidge declined to run for the presidency in 1928, Hoover was the obvious choice. He was nominated and entered the campaign against Al Smith, the Democratic nominee. With prosperity apparently available to all Americans after eight years of Republican administration, it is doubtful that any Democrat could have won—Hoover was elected by a landslide.

The presidency, however, soon turned into a nightmare for Hoover. Only seven months after he entered the White House, the stock market crashed (see October 29). With the prices of watered or worthless stocks swollen far beyond their real worth by rampant speculation, the confidence upon which speculation had been built suddenly vanished. With no customers for stocks, prices tumbled and panic gripped the financial community. Hoover himself had been worried about the runaway economy and had protested the policy of easy money to the Federal Reserve.

Now, although somewhat alarmed himself, Hoover tried to restore confidence among investors. When the expected upswing in the market never came, however, his optimism rang hollow. An international monetary crisis followed, and banks began to call in loans to repay their foreign debts. Americans, meanwhile, commenced withdrawing their savings. Fear spread across the country, and businesses finally refused to honor their pledges to Hoover on holding wage levels. Wages tumbled, consumers stopped buying, factories closed, and unemployment soared.

Hoover responded by establishing the Emergency Relief Organization and a huge federal loan agency, the Reconstruction Finance Corporation. The latter agency secured loans for businesses, banks, farmers, and even states. However, Hoover insisted that direct relief was not a proper function of the national government. In this, he was relying on the American tradition of voluntarism. So convinced was he of the superiority of community self-help that he refused to believe advisers who reported widespread hunger throughout the country. Voluntarism failed: Community and state treasuries were quickly exhausted, businessmen looked after themselves and cut wages, banks called in loans. Further, most people began to blame Hoover, who to the end of his term doggedly vetoed all Democratic social legislation. When 17,000 unemployed veterans on a Bonus March camped on the Capitol grounds to dramatize their plight, Hoover ordered them evicted. Under the direction of Douglas MacArthur, the veterans were driven out with sabers, fixed bayonets, and tanks. (See July 28, Bonus Army Evicted From Washington, D.C.)

Renominated at the Republican National Convention in 1932, Hoover defended his policies during the campaign. His Democratic opponent, Franklin D. Roosevelt, pledged to enact experimental social legislation. Roosevelt also promised to repeal Prohibition, which was increasingly unpopular and unenforceable. Hoover was soundly defeated in the November 1932 election.

Hoover remained active during his retirement. Under President Harry S. Truman and again under President Dwight D. Eisenhower, he was called upon to head the Commission on Organization of the Executive Branch of the Government. It was called the Hoover Commission and was charged with finding ways of making the federal government more efficient. Hoover wrote more than 30 books, including his three-volume memoirs. At his alma mater, Stanford University, Hoover founded the prestigious Hoover Institution on War, Revolution, and Peace. He died on October 20, 1964.

Missouri Admitted to the Union

On August 10, 1821, President James Monroe proclaimed the admission of Missouri to the Union. Monroe's action brought an end to the controversy that erupted shortly after Congress first considered Missouri's application for statehood in 1818. By the so-called Missouri Compromise, Missouri gained statehood with a constitution containing no restrictions against slavery. Maine entered the Union as a free state, and slavery was prohibited in the area of the Louisiana Purchase north of latitude 36 degrees and 30 minutes. However, the compromise was only a temporary solution to the serious problems that stemmed from the existence of slavery in the United States. Former presidents Thomas Jefferson and John Adams respectively referred to the Missouri controversy as "a fire bell in the night" and "a title-page to a great tragic volume." Their fears were justified, for the same issues that divided the United States in 1820 plunged the nation into the Civil War in 1860.

Missouri, the second state to be created from the vast area of the Louisiana Purchase (see related essays throughout this book), had passed from French to Spanish control and back again to the French before coming under the jurisdiction of the United States in 1803. During their periods of rule, both the French and Spanish had permitted slavery throughout the Louisiana Purchase region, and thus well before 1803 the practice was firmly implanted in Missouri. When the United States purchased Louisiana, it promised by the treaty of cession to protect the liberty, property, and religion of the inhabitants of the trans-Mississippi Louisiana Purchase area. Most observers assumed that slaves were included in this guarantee of property, but Congress's failure to specifically provide for slavery in its first act pertaining to Louisiana displeased Missourians. Some feared that such silence might "create the presumption of a disposition in Congress to abolish at a future day slavery altogether in the district."

When lower Louisiana, which had been known as the Territory of Orleans, was admitted to the Union in 1812 as a slave state named Louisiana, the huge upper Louisiana region was renamed the Missouri Territory. At that time, Representative Abner Lacock of Pennsylvania moved to prohibit the admission of slaves into the Missouri Territory. The United States, however, was on the brink of war with Great Britain in 1812, and congressional fears that a restriction on slavery in Missouri might create great dissension throughout the South at a time of crisis caused Lacock's motion to be overwhelmingly defeated. However, an elective legislature for the Missouri Territory was authorized in

1812 and again in 1816 after the population in the area began to swell with new settlers.

In 1817 residents of Missouri began to petition Congress for permission to frame a constitution as a preliminary move to statehood. Congress considered the request in 1818 but failed to act upon the enabling legislation reported by a House committee. The inhabitants of Missouri continued to press the issue. In November 1818 they again petitioned Congress for permission to form a state government, and in December 1818 Speaker of the House Henry Clay presented their request to the House of Representatives.

A large number of slaveholding settlers from Virginia, North Carolina, Kentucky, and Tennessee had migrated to the Missouri region after 1803, and there was no doubt that the majority of its residents favored the continuation of slavery. However, Missouri's admission as a slave state was not to be easily accomplished. When the House took up the question of Missouri statehood on February 13, 1819, Representative James Tallmadge Jr. of New York proposed the following amendment to the admission bill:

> That the further introduction of slavery or involuntary servitude be prohibited, except for the punishment of crimes, whereof the party shall be duly convicted; and that all children of slaves, born within the said state, after the admission thereof into the Union, shall be free, but may be held to service until the age of twenty-five years.

For several days, the representatives debated the Tallmadge amendment. The antislavery forces argued that any decision made on Missouri would affect not only that state but the entire region west of the Mississippi. Denouncing slavery, they claimed that Congress had the power to require an amendment against slavery in the constitution of any new state admitted to the Union. On the other side, the proponents of slavery, including Henry Clay, countered that "the cause of humanity" necessitated allowing slavery in the frontier. They argued that such expansion would provide more adequate food supplies and better living conditions for slaves than were to be had in the South. They also denied that Congress had the right to require prohibitions against slavery in the constitutions of any new states, and they argued that the 1803 cession treaty between the United States and France specifically prevented congressional interference with slavery in any state created from the Louisiana Purchase.

Voting on the Tallmadge amendment, the House approved the measure by February 17, 1819, and then sent it to the Senate, where it faced stronger opposition. In the spring of 1819, 10 slave states and 11 free states were represented in the Senate. However, many residents of Illinois, which was counted on the side of the predominantly antislavery North, strongly sympathized with the South and both Illinois senators were slaveholders. They opposed the Tallmadge amendment, and their votes helped the South defeat the antislavery measure in the Senate. On March 2, 1819, the Senate passed the Missouri statehood bill without the defeated Tallmadge amendment. The following day, the House refused to admit Missouri as a slave state, and the 15th Congress adjourned on March 3, 1819, leaving the future status of Missouri unresolved.

By the fall of 1819 the admission of Missouri had become a national issue. The debate, no longer confined to Congress or the disputed area, stirred popular interest, and mass protest meetings were held in many northern communities. The question was further complicated because Massachusetts had agreed, in June 1819, to allow its northern section to become the independent state of Maine. Maine applied for statehood shortly after Congress convened in December 1819, and since Maine was to be an additional free state, the North greeted its request with enthusiasm. Moreover, the North, with its larger population, controlled the House of Representatives so that the Maine statehood bill passed by a substantial margin on January 3, 1820.

However, Maine's application for admission to the Union faced strong opposition in the Senate. On December 14, 1819, Alabama had gained statehood, thereby making the number of slave states in the Union equal to the number of free states. Since each state sent two representatives to the Senate, and the Illinois senators consistently voted with the South, southerners could count on a clear Senate majority in 1820. Further, the South had no intention of giving up its control of the Senate by allowing the admission of another free state to disrupt the sectional balance. As early as December 30, 1819, Henry Clay presented an ultimatum to the free states: "If you refuse to admit Missouri also free of condition, we see no reason why you shall take to yourselves privileges which you deny to her, and until you grant them also to her, we will not admit [Maine]."

Maine's application for admission to the Union was thus inextricably tied to the fate of Missouri. On January 3, 1820, the House approved the aforementioned bill admitting only Maine to statehood. The following month, when the Senate considered the Maine statehood bill, it added an amendment also allowing Missouri to prepare for statehood by forming a state constitution that would have no restrictions against slavery. In addi-

tion, the Senate also attached to the bill an amendment suggested by Senator Jesse B. Thomas of Illinois:

That, in all that territory ceded by France to the United States, under the name of Louisiana, which lies north of thirty-six degrees and thirty minutes north latitude, excepting only such part thereof as is included within the limits of the State contemplated by this act, slavery and involuntary servitude, otherwise than in the punishment of crimes whereof the party shall have been duly convicted, shall be and is hereby forever prohibited: Provided, always, That any person escaping into the same, from whom labor or service is lawfully claimed in any State or Territory of the United States, such fugitive may be lawfully reclaimed and conveyed to the person claiming his or her labor or service as aforesaid.

In short, the Senate version of the Maine bill was a plan to resolve the 1820 controversy by permitting Missouri to form a constitution with no restriction against slavery, admitting Maine as a free state, allowing slavery to exist in the unsettled regions that today are part of Arkansas and Oklahoma, and outlawing slavery in the remainder of the Louisiana Purchase north of latitude 36 degrees 30 minutes. That latitude constituted the southern boundary of Missouri.

The southern majority in the Senate passed the bill joining Missouri and Maine statehood and including the Thomas amendment. However, the North was not satisfied with the compromise and used its majority in the House to defeat the Senate compromise plan late in February 1820. The House rejection of the Senate compromise bill and its subsequent passage on March 1, 1820, of a Missouri statehood bill with an amendment restricting slavery created a stalemate. The Senate would not consider any alternative to its compromise plan, and the House refused to approve the admission of Missouri as a slave state. In an attempt to break this deadlock, the Senate requested that a conference committee be set up with the House. The report of the joint committee was made public on March 2, 1820. It recommended: (1) withdrawal of the Senate's amendments to the Maine statehood bill that allowed Missouri to form a state government with slavery and that restricted slavery in the Louisiana Purchase; (2) removal of the clause restricting slavery in the Missouri statehood bill passed by the House on March 1, 1820; and (3) the addition to the Missouri admission bill of a provision prohibiting slavery in all areas of the Louisiana Purchase north of latitude 36 degrees 30 minutes except in the new state of Missouri.

Since northern representatives opposed the admission of Missouri as a slave state and many southern representatives were against a restriction on the expansion of slavery, the House would have defeated the compromise resolutions of the joint congressional committee if they had been voted on as a single bill. For this reason, Henry Clay used his influence to see that each of the committee proposals was voted on separately. Thus, Clay was able to gain slim majority votes in the House for each of the recommendations. The Senate also went along with the committee proposals, and on March 3, 1820, a bill was passed admitting Maine to the Union as a free state. On March 6 Missouri gained the right to form a constitution and form a state government with no restrictions on slavery, and on the same day a bill was passed banning slavery from the remainder of the Louisiana Purchase north of latitude 36 degrees 30 minutes.

The Missouri Compromise of 1820, as the measures are collectively known, ended the crisis that erupted over the expansion of slavery into new states to be created from the Louisiana Purchase territory. It did not, however, immediately bring Missouri into the Union as a state. Its constitution had to first gain the approval of both the House and Senate. Missourians framed a constitution not only permitting slavery but also forbidding free blacks and mulattoes from entering the state and making it illegal for the legislature to free slaves without their owners' consent. These two latter portions of the Missouri constitution served as the basis for the dispute over Missouri that continued into 1821.

On December 12, 1820, the Senate approved a Missouri statehood bill saying nothing specific against the two controversial clauses of its constitution but including the ambiguous proviso that "nothing herein contained shall be so construed as to give the assent of Congress to any provision in the constitution of Missouri, if any such there be, which contravenes that clause in the Constitution of the United States which declares that the citizens of each State shall be entitled to all privileges and immunities of citizens in the several States."

This so-called Pontius Pilate proviso did not satisfy those who opposed Missouri's gaining statehood with no restrictions against slavery and who were particularly determined to fight against the clauses in the Missouri constitution barring free blacks from the state and impeding the liberation of slaves. Their strength, of course, lay in the House of Representatives where the North enjoyed a clear majority. On December 13, 1820, the question of Missouri statehood came to a House vote and on that day it was defeated by 93 to 79.

Throughout January and February 1821 the Missouri controversy, or the "misery debate" as it was also known, dragged on. During this time a number of compromise plans were put forth, but both sides adamantly refused to yield any ground. The situation was potentially explosive. Southerners felt the North had betrayed the spirit of compromise of 1820 by refusing to admit Missouri to statehood, and in the early months of 1821, some threatened to secede from the Union. On February 22, 1821, Henry Clay proposed that a joint congressional committee meet to attempt to resolve the Missouri dispute before the 16th Congress adjourned. When the joint committee, composed of 23 representatives of the House and seven members of the Senate, convened Clay proposed.

> that Missouri shall be admitted into this union on an equal footing with the original States in all respects whatever, upon the fundamental condition, that the fourth clause of the twenty-sixth section of the third article of the constitution submitted on the part of said State to Congress shall never be construed to authorize the passage of any law . . . by which any citizen of . . . the States in this Union shall be excluded from the enjoyment of any of the privileges and immunities to which such citizen is entitled under the Constitution of the United States: Provided, That the Legislature of the said State, by a solemn public act, shall declare the assent of the said State to the said fundamental condition and shall transmit to the President of the United States, on or before the fourth Monday in November next, an authentic copy of the said act; upon the receipt whereof the President, by proclamation, shall announce the fact: whereupon, and without any further proceeding on the part of Congress the admission of the said State into this Union shall be considered as complete.

As he had anticipated, Clay was able to influence most of the committee members and he successfully gained approval of his resolution. On February 26, 1821, he reported his compromise plan to the House, which passed the resolution on that same day. The Senate rapidly followed suit, and the agreement became official on March 2, 1821.

Clay's so-called Second Missouri Compromise did not automatically guarantee Missouri statehood. His resolution made the admission of Missouri conditional upon its legislature's promising never to pass laws that would discriminate against citizens (technically, including free blacks and mu-lattoes) of another state. Even after Clay's bill gained the approval of Congress, some northerners hoped that the Missouri legislature would not make such a pledge. They were disappointed in their hopes, however. In June 1821 the Missouri lawmakers made the necessary promise, albeit phrased in defiant and sarcastic language, and on August 10, 1821, President Monroe proclaimed the admission of Missouri as the 24th state of the Union.

August 11

Alex Haley's Birthday

Alex Murray Palmer Haley, one of the most prominent African American authors of the 20th century, was born on August 11, 1921, in Ithaca, New York. His parents were Simon and Bertha Palmer Haley, and he grew up in Henning, Tennessee. As a youngster, he heard many stories about the family's past, including tales of one Kunta Kinte in Africa who was captured and sold into slavery in America during the late 18th century.

Haley enlisted in the United States Coast Guard in 1939. During his service at sea he began to write in his spare time and became a journalist. After 20 years with the Coast Guard, Haley retired in 1959 and began to write pieces for such magazines as *Playboy* and *Reader's Digest*. He achieved national prominence in 1965 with the publication of his first book, *The Autobiography of Malcolm X*, written in cooperation with Malcolm X (formerly known as Malcolm Little), the leader of the controversial Nation of Islam movement. The book was widely praised and sold millions of copies.

Shortly after finishing the book on Malcolm X, Haley began to research his family's ancestry with an eye toward producing both a good novel and a serious work on the subject of African American heritage in the United States. It took him over a decade to research the life of Kunta Kinte and other Haley ancestors; the result was the best-selling book *Roots: The Saga of an American Family* (1976). Further, the television miniseries of *Roots*, aired from January 23 to January 30, 1977, became one of the most popular programs in history. Over 100 million people watched it, a record for the time. A second television miniseries, *Roots: The Next Generations*, aired in 1979 and covered Haley's family history after the Civil War.

Roots won special citations from both the National Book Award and the Pulitzer Prize committees in 1977. Haley, however, was later accused of falsifying certain accounts, particularly with respect to his research in West Africa and consultations with a local *griote*, or bard, concerning an oral history that supposedly referred to Kunta Kinte. Some litigation and out-of-court settlements followed, but *Roots* still remained popular and spawned such book and television sequels as *Queen*, in 1993.

Haley died of a heart attack on February 10, 1992, in Seattle, Washington, and was buried at the Alex Haley Museum in Henning, Tennessee. His works gave a new perspective to the civil rights movement, from the coverage of important leaders such as Malcolm X to inspiring a new appreciation for African American heritage in the *Roots* books.

Tishah B'Av

This is a movable event.

Tishah B'Av, the ninth day of the Hebrew month of Av (July or August), is a day of remembrance for the destruction of the first and second Temples in Jerusalem. The First Temple, built by King Solomon, was destroyed in 586 B.C. by the Babylonians under Nebuchadnezzar. It was rebuilt after the Jews returned from their exile in Babylonia. However, the Second Temple was in turn destroyed by Titus, the Roman emperor in A.D. 70.

According to rabbinic tradition, these two catastrophes for the Jewish people occurred on the same day: the ninth day of Av. Furthermore, the complete destruction of Jerusalem by the Romans a year after the suppression of the revolt of Bar Kochba (or Bar Cochba) in A.D. 135 is also supposed to have taken place on Tishah B'Av. Thus, Tishah B'Av became a day of mourning associated with a number of events in Jewish history.

During the Middle Ages, the significance of the day increased, especially after the expulsion of the Jews from Spain in 1492 on Tishah B'Av. Many Jews also use the day to commemorate the murder of six million European Jews by the Nazis during World War II.

Orthodox Jews traditionally fast on Tishah B'Av. Their synagogues are draped in black. The curtain covering the ark, where the scrolls of the Bible are kept, is removed and the ark is either left bare or covered with black cloth. The scrolls too may be dressed in black. The Book of Lamentations is read. Special prayers, dirges, and laments called *kinot* are also chanted. For Jews living in Israel, this is a special day to pray at the Western Wall (the so-called Wailing Wall) of the Second Temple, which is the only remnant of the temple still standing.

Some Jews, however, do not observe Tishah B'Av because they believe that the Jews are not in exile today, now that the nation of Israel has been established.

August 12

Hawaii Annexed to the United States

Hawaii, which was formally annexed to the United States on August 12, 1898, attracted American attention as early as the first quarter of the 19th century. Merchants, missionaries, and whalers all found the islands important and made Honolulu a major port before California entered the Union. The American government recognized the usefulness of the islands, and on December 20, 1842, President John Tyler informed Congress that foreign interference in the area would "create dissatisfaction on the part of the United States."

Thoughts of the United States annexing Hawaii existed before the Civil War. In 1854 David L. Gregg, a commissioner sent to the isles by President Franklin Pierce, drew up a draft treaty making Hawaii a state. However, the administration was reluctant to send it to the Congress. William H. Seward, who served as secretary of state to Presidents Abraham Lincoln and Andrew Johnson and who was responsible for the purchase of Alaska, entertained a similar vision but also abandoned it for fear of domestic opposition.

The United States and Hawaii developed close commercial ties. By a reciprocity agreement of January 30, 1875, the two nations agreed to admit without duties a variety of items, including unrefined sugar. This agreement was a boon to the sugar planters of the islands, who gained an advantage over the planters of other nations in dealing with the United States. In 1887 the governments of Hawaii and the United States agreed to renew this commercial arrangement.

Within a short time, however, unrelated events in the United States and in Hawaii darkened the prospects of the islands' sugar planters, many of whom were of American descent. The McKinley tariff of 1890 deprived them of their trade advantage by authorizing duty-free importation of sugar to the United States from all the nations of the world. In Hawaii, the strong-willed Queen Liliuokalani succeeded her brother King Kalakaua in 1891.

In January 1893 American-led opponents of Liliuokalani staged a relatively bloodless coup aimed at establishing a republican government that would seek annexation to the United States. John L. Stevens, the American minister in Hawaii, actively assisted the uprising by calling for sailors and marines from the cruiser USS *Boston* to land in Honolulu. Stevens also raised the American flag in the capital and declared the islands to be a protectorate of the United States. Secretary of State John W. Foster acted with equal haste to recognize the new republic and signed an annexation treaty on February 14, 1893.

Grover Cleveland, a Democrat, replaced the Republican Benjamin Harrison as president in March 1893 before the Senate concluded debate on the annexation treaty. Doubtful that the revolutionary government represented the will of the native Hawaiian majority, Cleveland withdrew the treaty from the Senate on March 9, 1893. Two days later he appointed Representative James H. Blount, onetime chairman of the House Foreign Relations Committee, as his emissary to investigate the whole matter. Upon arriving in Hawaii, Blount declared the protectorate ended, and he reported to the president that the Hawaiians did not wish annexation.

Cleveland considered restoring Liliuokalani to her throne, but the queen's express intention to behead her opponents and the stability of the republican government in Hawaii combined to thwart his ambitions. He passed the problem to the Congress, which coupled a statement renouncing intervention in the islands' affairs with a warning to other powers to follow an equally benign course. In the summer of 1894 Cleveland extended official recognition to an undemocratic government established by the island's white minority, and the Wilson-Gorman Tariff of that year restored the islands' sugar planters to their former position.

Expansionist sentiment grew stronger in the United States during the late 1890s. In 1898 the nation went to war with Spain over the fate of Cuba, where a popular revolutionary movement was being suppressed by the ruling Spanish imperial authorities. Expansionist Americans, including those who wished to annex Hawaii, found the wartime period an auspicious one to promote their cause.

William McKinley, a Republican who became president in March 1897, favored the annexation of Hawaii. He had promised to raise tariffs, but did not want to undo the reciprocity agreement with the islands. Annexation would eliminate any question of conflict. Moreover, Japan, angered by immigration limits leveled against its citizens by the Hawaiians, had threateningly dispatched a cruiser to Honolulu. This show of force from the increasingly powerful Japanese disturbed many Americans.

In May 1897 President McKinley decided to proceed with the annexation of Hawaii, and on June 16, 1897, Secretary of State John Sherman signed an annexation treaty with the Hawaiian government. Japan immediately protested the act, but withdrew its complaint in December 1897 when the United States promised to protect the rights of Japanese nationals in Hawaii.

Domestic sugar growers and anti-imperialists opposed the incorporation of Hawaii into the United States, and enough United States senators agreed with them to make it impossible for the annexationists to gain the two-thirds vote necessary for approval of the treaty. Undaunted, the expansionists turned to another tactic: annexation by a joint resolution of Congress, which required only the support of a simple majority of the legislators. On July 7, 1898, Congress passed, and President McKinley signed, the Newlands resolution, and on August 12, 1898, Hawaii officially became part of the United States. Congress on April 30, 1900, granted the islands territorial status, which they maintained until 1959 when they gained admission to the Union as the 50th state.

Cecil B. DeMille's Birthday

Cecil Blount DeMille, the great movie director and producer known for his spectacular biblical epics, was born in Ashfield, Massachusetts, on August 12, 1881. He attended Pennsylvania Military College and the American Academy of Dramatic Arts. DeMille's family was in the theater business, and he worked with his brother William on a variety of projects that included learning management skills. After over a decade of working with William, in 1913 he teamed up with film industry pioneers Samuel Goldwyn and Jesse Lasky.

DeMille became the director-general of the Jesse L. Lasky Feature Play Company. In 1914 he directed his first silent movie, *The Squaw Man*, which also happened to be the first movie produced in Hollywood, California. Nearly 80 more movies would follow during his long career. In 1921, DeMille established his own production group, Cecil B. DeMille Productions. Although he produced several well-received westerns, it was in 1923 that he produced his first silent classic, *The Ten Commandments*. Thereafter, he became a recognized master in the art of directing lavish historical productions, particularly on biblical themes, such as *The King of Kings* (1927).

Cecil B. DeMille Productions worked primarily with the Lasky organization, which later became Paramount Pictures, until 1928. In that year DeMille went to Metro-Goldwyn-Mayer (MGM), where he made three "talkie" movies using the new sound technology. However, these films were not successful, so he returned to Paramount in 1931. He made his comeback with such hits as *The Sign of the Cross* (1932), *Cleopatra* (1934), and *The Crusades* (1935). DeMille also made several successful western and frontier movies, including *The Plainsman* (1936), *Union Pacific* (1939), *Northwest Mounted Police* (1940), and *Reap the Wild Wind* (1942).

DeMille entered the greatest phase of his career in 1949 when he produced *Samson and Delilah*. This was followed by *The Greatest Show on Earth* in 1952 and the famous award-winning remake of *The Ten Commandments* in 1956 starring Charlton Heston and Yul Brynner. He died on January 21, 1959, in Hollywood after experiencing heart problems.

August 13

Lucy Stone's Birthday

Lucy Stone, a leading women's rights activist and abolitionist of the 19th century, was born on August 13, 1818, near West Brookfield, Massachusetts. She was still a child when she became indignant at the second-class treatment accorded women, and she decided to study Greek and Hebrew so that she could decide whether biblical pronouncements on the subjection of women had been translated accurately. In time, she enrolled at the first coeducational college in the country, Oberlin College. She graduated from Oberlin in 1847, and gave her first lecture on women's rights that same year.

An ardent abolitionist, Stone was engaged as a regular lecturer by the Anti-Slavery Society in 1848. Although her duties demanded that Saturday evenings and Sundays be devoted to the cause of emancipation of slaves, she also lectured widely on the emancipation of women. Pictured by biographers as approachable, good-natured, and dynamic, she became popular as a lecturer.

When Stone and the abolitionist Henry Brown Blackwell were married in 1855, they agreed that she, as his equal, would retain her original surname. Her husband joined her in protesting the inequalities of the marriage laws of the time and afterward worked with her for women's rights. At the time of their marriage, they drew up a joint statement that said in part:

> While acknowledging our mutual affection by publicly assuming the relationship of husband and wife, yet, in justice to ourselves and a great principle, we deem it our duty to declare that this act on our part im-

plies no sanction of nor promise of voluntary obedience to such of the present laws of marriage as refuse to recognize the wife as an independent, rational being, while they confer upon the husband an injurious and unnatural superiority, investing him with legal powers which no honorable man would exercise, and which no man should possess. . . .

We believe that personal independence and equal human rights can never be forfeited except for crime; that marriage should be an equal and permanent partnership, and so recognized by law; that, until it is so recognized, married partners should provide against the radical injustice of present laws by every means in their power. . . .

Thus, reverencing law, we enter our protest against rules and customs which are unworthy of the name, since they violate justice, the essence of law.

In 1869 Stone, as she was called, took a leading part in founding the American Woman Suffrage Association (AWSA), which sought women's voting rights by organizing to exert pressure on the various state legislatures. In contrast, the National Woman Suffrage Association (NWSA), organized that same year by Susan B. Anthony and Elizabeth Cady Stanton, began its suffrage work with appeals on the national level.

In 1870 Stone founded the *Woman's Journal* in Boston, Massachusetts. With her husband she edited the publication beginning in 1872. Later they had the assistance of Alice Stone Blackwell, their daughter, who succeeded them. After 1890, when the AWSA combined with the NWSA, the *Woman's Journal* became the official organ of the resulting merger that was known as the National American Woman Suffrage Association. Stone continued her editorial duties until her death on October 18, 1893.

Annie Oakley's Birthday

Phoebe Anne Oakley Mozee, later known as Annie Oakley, was born on August 13, 1860, in Patterson, Ohio. Her father died when she was a small child. When she was only eight years old, Oakley first demonstrated her uncanny skill with a rifle. Taking aim at a squirrel with an old muzzle-loader that her father had once owned, she shot the animal through the throat for a clean kill. Tales of her skill began to spread quickly: It was said that she could shoot through a playing card with the thin edge turned toward her and hit dimes thrown into the air. Many of these tales appear to be valid because she was certainly an extraordinary marksperson.

As a hunter, Oakley shot wild game for her impoverished family's dinner table and also for sale to restaurants in nearby Cincinnati. She was prized for her ability to kill animals with clean shots, like the squirrel of her youth, so that no bullets or buckshot would be left in the carcass to damage the teeth of consumers. Oakley began to appear in local shooting tournaments, and in one match she defeated a famous competitor named Frank Butler. The two began to court and were later married. As a husband and wife team, they began to tour the country as performers, and joined the famous Buffalo Bill's Wild West Show in 1885. For her stage name, Oakley took the name Annie Oakley, which she considered suitably "fancy" for promotional reasons.

Oakley toured with the Buffalo Bill troupe until 1901, when she was injured in a train accident. Although she was partially paralyzed for the rest of her life, Oakley nevertheless remained active. She participated in shooting tournaments, instructed hundreds of women in the proper use of firearms at no charge, and helped raise money for a wide variety of charities. Oakley died on November 3, 1926, in Greenville, Ohio. In 1946 she became the central figure of the hit Broadway musical *Annie Get Your Gun*, by Irving Berlin.

August 14

World War II: Victory over Japan (V-J) Day

Since the actual and official conclusions of wars are seldom identical, it is not surprising that there is some confusion as to the exact end of World War II in the Pacific arena. The formal act of surrender by Japan took place aboard the battleship USS *Missouri* in Tokyo Bay on September 2, 1945 (Tokyo time; it was September 1 in Washington, D.C.). President Harry S. Truman proclaimed the following day, namely September 2 (Washington, D.C., time) as Victory over Japan (V-J) Day. However, Japan's capitulation had already been announced on August 14, and it is this date that is generally remembered as V-J Day.

As the war in Europe was drawing to a close in April 1945, the Pacific Allied forces were reorganized in expectation of a major push against the chief remaining enemy—the Japanese. General Douglas MacArthur was made commander of all United States Army forces in the Pacific. Admiral Chester W. Nimitz had command of all United States Navy units. The Eighth Air Force under Lieutenant General James H. Doolittle and the 20th Air Force under Lieutenant General Nathan

F. Twining were joined to form the United States Strategic Air Forces under General Carl Spaatz. Lieutenant General George C. Kenney commanded the United States Far Eastern Air Force.

During the spring and summer of 1945, the Japanese home islands were subjected to intensive air attacks, among them the massive firebombing raid on Tokyo on March 9 and 10, 1945, in which it is estimated that over 80,000 people were killed. B-29 Superfortresses and other bombers based on islands or on navy aircraft carriers carried out systematic bombing attacks on an intensifying scale. They included both high-altitude precision bombing and low-altitude incendiary bombing on Japanese urban centers such as Osaka, Nagoya, and Kobe, and on individual industrial targets. The Japanese home islands were also subjected to naval bombardment by American and British units, and American submarines took a mounting toll of Japanese merchant vessels and warships. On May 25, 1945, the Joint Chiefs of Staff laid plans for an invasion of Kyushu, one of the main islands of Japan, on November 1, 1945. The Tokyo plains area of Honshu was scheduled for invasion on March 1, 1946.

In mid-July 1945, while attending the Potsdam Conference in Europe with the leaders of Great Britain and the Soviet Union, President Truman learned of the successful detonation of the world's first atomic device during a test conducted on July 16 near the Alamogordo air base in New Mexico. On July 26 the heads of state of the United States and Britain, with the concurrence of Nationalist China, issued the so-called Potsdam Declaration, or Proclamation, calling upon Japan to proclaim the "unconditional surrender of all Japanese armed forces, and to provide proper and adequate assurances of their good faith in such action."

Earlier, on May 8, 1945, Truman had already announced that unconditional surrender involved the end of military rule in Japan. However, he stressed that it did not signify the "extermination or enslavement" of the Japanese. Although by the summer of 1945 Japanese leaders, with the exception of a few militant diehards, were seeking means of ending the war, they were not yet prepared to accept unconditional surrender. Further, neither Truman's May statement nor the Potsdam Declaration made it clear what the future status of the Japanese emperor or empire would be. Thus, on July 28 the Japanese rejected the Allies' ultimatum. In the meantime the leaders of Japan continued to search for an honorable way to surrender.

The United States proceeded to use atomic bombs against the Japanese cities of Hiroshima and Nagasaki on August 6 and August 9, 1945, respectively. The Japanese were unable to cope immediately with the meaning of the new weapon. Faced with utter ruin, they could hardly believe their helpless position. Moreover, on August 8 the Soviet Union declared war against Japan, a step agreed upon earlier by the Allies and reaffirmed at the Potsdam conference.

On August 9 the divided members of the Japanese Supreme Council for the Direction of War convened and became deadlocked on the course of action, an impasse which even the news of the Nagasaki bombing failed to break. They prevailed upon Emperor Hirohito to summon an imperial conference. This was an unprecedented step since the emperor, albeit the titular ruler of the Japanese empire, normally played a passive role in government and only received word of policy decisions that had already been made. Shortly before midnight on August 9, Japan's chief political and military leaders gathered in an underground air raid shelter adjoining the Imperial Library. There, Hirohito, when asked for an opinion, approved the proposal for seeking peace. He stated, "I cannot bear to see my innocent people suffer any longer." His prestige carried enough weight to settle the deadlock.

On August 10 the Japanese government made known its willingness to accept an unconditional surrender based on the Allies' Potsdam Declaration, provided that the emperor was retained. The Allies raised no serious objection to this request, with the one proviso that "from the moment of surrender the authority of the Emperor and the Japanese Government to rule the state shall be subject to the Supreme Commander for the Allied powers who will take such steps as he deems proper to effectuate the surrender terms." After intense debate, the Japanese accepted the Allied proviso on August 14. General Douglas MacArthur was then appointed Supreme Commander for the Allied Powers to oversee the occupation of Japan.

At 7:00 p.m. Eastern War Time, August 14, 1945, the moving electric sign on the Times Tower in New York City flashed the words "Official—Truman announces Japanese surrender." It set off an unparalleled demonstration. The terrific roar that greeted the announcement on the Times Tower lasted for 20 minutes and practically deafened the participants. People began pouring into Times Square from the subways and buses and on foot, and in a short time they were packed so solidly that individual movement was impossible. By 10:00 p.m. the Manhattan police estimated that two million people were in the Times Square area, setting an all-time record.

World War II: The Atlantic Charter

The entry of the United States into World War II was slow and hesitant. Japan's bombing of Pearl Harbor on December 7, 1941, finally propelled the country into war against the Axis powers of Germany, Italy, and Japan. However, earlier events in 1941 had clearly indicated the direction of American sympathies in favor of the Allies. On March 11, 1941, the Lend-Lease Act went into effect. This act empowered President Franklin D. Roosevelt to sell, lend, lease, transfer, or exchange war materials with any country whose defense he considered vital to American security. Passage of Lend-Lease occurred at a critical stage in the Allied struggle: The strains of the war, which had begun in Europe on September 1, 1939, had depleted the financial resources of Great Britain. At the time, Britain was the only major Ally that had not been overrun by Nazi Germany. Without American armaments it would have lacked the equipment needed to continue its fight.

As the Lend-Lease Act provided the material aid necessary for the Allied war effort, the Atlantic Charter supplied the equally essential moral support. This joint declaration, issued on August 14, 1941, was the outcome of a secret meeting from August 9 to August 12, 1941, between President Roosevelt and Prime Minister Winston Churchill of Britain aboard the American cruiser USS *Augusta* and the British battleship HMS *Prince of Wales* in Argentia Bay off Newfoundland, Canada. Basically, the principles embodied in the charter were those urged by President Woodrow Wilson during the peace conference at Versailles following World War I. The Atlantic Charter denounced territorial aggression and supported the right of people to live under a government of their own choosing. It also supported unrestricted trade and access to raw materials, freedom from want and fear, freedom of the seas, and the disarmament of belligerent nations. The charter did not formally ally or legally bind the two nations, but it demonstrated that the United States and Great Britain shared identical postwar aims. By September 1941 the document had been endorsed by 15 nations.

A copy of the Atlantic Charter is set forth below:

> The President of the United States of America and the Prime Minister, Mr. Churchill, representing His Majesty's Government in the United Kingdom, being met together, deem it right to make known certain common principles in the national policies of their respective countries on which they base their hopes for a better future for the world.

> First, their countries seek no aggrandizement, territorial or other;

> Second, they desire to see no territorial changes that do not accord with the freely expressed wishes of the peoples concerned;

> Third, they respect the right of all peoples to choose the form of government under which they will live; and they wish to see sovereign rights and self government restored to those who have been forcibly deprived of them;

> Fourth, they will endeavor, with due respect for their existing obligations, to further the enjoyment by all States, great or small, victor or vanquished, of access, on equal terms, to the trade and to the raw materials of the world which are needed for their economic prosperity;

> Fifth, they desire to bring about the fullest collaboration between all nations in the economic field with the object of securing, for all, improved labor standards, economic advancement and social security;

> Sixth, after the final destruction of the Nazi tyranny, they hope to see established a peace which will afford to all nations the means of dwelling in safety within their own boundaries, and which will afford assurance that all the men in all lands may live out their lives in freedom from fear and want;

> Seventh, such a peace should enable all men to traverse the high seas and oceans without hindrance;

> Eighth, they believe that all of the nations of the world, for realistic as well as spiritual reasons must come to the abandonment of the use of force. Since no future peace can be maintained if land, sea or air armaments continue to be employed by nations which threaten, or may threaten, aggression outside of their frontiers, they believe, pending the establishment of a wider and permanent system of general security, that the disarmament of such nations is essential. They will likewise aid and encourage all other practicable measure which will lighten for peace-loving peoples the crushing burden of armaments.

August 15

Woodstock Begins

The Woodstock Music and Art Fair, one of the greatest musical events in history as well as one of the most important symbols of the 1960s counterculture movement, began on August 15, 1969, and lasted for just over three days. Nearly half a million people attended the event in rural New York State and the traffic was so heavy that it shut down the New York State Thruway and brought in a bevy of state and local authorities to help preserve order. It was certainly more raucous than the "Three Days of Peace and Music" that it was promoted as, and yet many participants and members of the general public alive at the time remember it fondly.

Woodstock was the brainchild of four men, Artie Kornfeld, Michael Lang, John Roberts, and Joel Rosenman. It was primarily financed by Roberts, who came from a wealthy family and had inherited millions. Kornfeld was a vice president at Capitol Records who had worked on a variety of hit records. Lang had production and management experience: In 1968 he produced one of the biggest concerts of the decade, the Miami Pop Festival. Rosenman was a graduate of Yale Law School who had taken to playing guitar for lounge music groups in various hotels.

Originally, the four had planned to open a recording studio in the town of Woodstock, New York. It was about a hundred miles from New York City, and at the time it was a "hip" artists community frequented by such popular performers as The Band, Bob Dylan, Tim Hardin, Jimi Hendrix, Janis Joplin, and Van Morrison. To further their plan, the four settled on the idea of holding a concert. They formed Woodstock Ventures, and each held 25 percent interest in the corporation. Ideally, the concert would both promote and provide funds for the contemplated recording studio. Even though they originally envisioned only some 50,000 participants, the promoters had trouble finding a suitable site, since the rural authorities balked at the "large" number of attendees. Finally, the promoters arranged to lease a large field from a dairy farmer named Max Yasgur in the vicinity of Bethel, a town about 50 miles from Woodstock. Thus, Woodstock never actually took place in Woodstock, although the name stuck.

Despite their problems with finding a suitable location, the promoters were nevertheless able to cleverly and effectively promote the event. They carefully cultivated a very trendy image, advertising in fashionable underground publications like the *Village Voice* and *Rolling Stone* magazine. They then began to run ads in such major newspapers as the *New York Times*. Arnold Skolnick designed the eye-catching Woodstock logo of a dove perched on the handle of a guitar (although the "dove" was really a catbird).

Since it was such a speculative venture, Woodstock had to pay premium prices to line up popular performers, but it succeeded in scheduling some of the greatest legends of rock and roll. They included:

Joan Baez
The Band
Blood, Sweat & Tears
Paul Butterfield
Canned Heat
Joe Cocker
Country Joe and the Fish
Credence Clearwater Revival
Crosby, Stills and Nash
The Grateful Dead
Arlo Guthrie
Tim Hardin
Richie Havens
Jimi Hendrix
Jefferson Airplane
Janis Joplin
Santana
John Sebastian
Sha-Na-Na
Ravi Shankar
Sly & The Family Stone
Ten Years After
The Who
Johnny Winter
Neil Young

Further, the promoters got Michael Wadleigh to film the event, which eventually resulted in the award-winning documentary *Woodstock*.

By all historical criteria, the event was a success: It drew record crowds, some of the greatest music of the age was played, and it was all captured on tape and on film for posterity. It was laden, however, with administrative blunders and logistical nightmares, such as massive traffic jams, limited space for all the attendees to camp out, inadequate sanitary and medical facilities, not enough food and water, and widespread use of illegal narcotics.

In many ways, Woodstock also represented the end of an era. In the 1970s the counterculture movement began to fade and interest in 1960s-style music declined. Nevertheless, interest in Woodstock as a historical and cultural event remained high, and even inspired a 25th anniversary celebration in 1994 called Woodstock II. It was held in Saugerties, New York, just a few miles from the original site.

August 16

American Revolution: Battle of Bennington

During the summer of 1777, British forces in America undertook a campaign to suppress the rebellion of the colonies against Great Britain. Major General John Burgoyne devised a strategy that included a three-pronged attack on New York's upper Hudson River valley. Burgoyne himself led the main column of more than 7,000 men south from Canada. On July 5, 1777, his men took possession of Fort Ticonderoga, which the Americans had abandoned as the enemy drew near. He then resumed the advance toward Albany, New York.

By the time Burgoyne reached Fort George at the end of July, he realized that his supply line, stretching 185 miles back to Canada, was inadequate for the expedition. His forces badly needed provisions as well as horses to pull wagons and serve as mounts for the 250 German dragoons that the Duke of Brunswick had contributed to the British cause. Upon the advice of his German subordinate General Baron Friedrich Adolphus von Riedesel, Burgoyne decided to send a detachment into western New England to arouse popular support for the royal government and to obtain cattle, horses, and carriages.

Burgoyne designated Lieutenant Colonel Friedrich Baum, the commander of the Brunswick dragoons, to go to Manchester, in what is now Vermont. However, a last-minute intelligence report indicated that the party could more easily capture the stores in Bennington where only 300 to 400 militiamen guarded an American supply depot. On August 11 Baum started his force of 374 Germans, 50 British marksmen, and 300 Tories, Canadians, and native tribesmen toward Bennington.

On July 24 George Washington, commander in chief of the Continental army, had placed Major General Benjamin Lincoln of Massachusetts in charge of the militia units forming east of the Hudson River to oppose Burgoyne. Lincoln performed well, but was unable to win the submission of John Stark, the commander of New Hampshire's 1,500-man contingent. Stark had resigned from the Continental army in March 1777, when Congress failed to promote him from colonel, and accepted New Hampshire's commission as a brigadier general. Lincoln prudently treated Stark as an ally rather than as a subordinate, approving his plan to operate independently and to harass Burgoyne's rear forces.

General Stark's wanderings took his brigade to Bennington before Baum reached there. On August 13 the militia leader dispatched 200 men to investigate native hostilities around neighboring Cambridge in what is now New York State, and the patrol discovered that the natives were only part of a larger operation. Stark decided to intercept the enemy force, now that he was aware of its existence, and sent word to Lieutenant Colonel Seth Warner to bring his Green Mountain Boys from Manchester to assist in the campaign.

On the morning of August 15 an American forward party made the first contact with Baum's troops at Van Schaick's Mill. The colonists fired one volley and then retreated. The skirmish and the necessity of repairing the burned St. Luke's Bridge across Little White Creek delayed the enemy, but they soon resumed their advance. Baum soon found himself 25 miles from his parent unit and facing a force twice his size. Logic called for retreat. Instead, Baum sent a message to Burgoyne requesting a small number of reinforcements, and proceeded to ineptly deploy his inadequate forces. The German commander placed 150 men on the far, or enemy, side of the Walloomsac River in hastily constructed earthworks called the Tory Redoubt. He kept his largest contingent of 200 men in the Dragoon Redoubt on the near side of the river and scattered the rest of his troops in smaller detachments.

Rain prevented a battle on August 15, but Stark attacked on the afternoon of August 16. He sent 300 rangers and Bennington militiamen to approach the Dragoon Redoubt from the left and attack the enemy's rear guard. Colonel Moses Nichols simultaneously led 200 New Hampshire men to assault the redoubt from the right. Stark sent another 200 men under Colonels David Hobart and Thomas Stickney to engage the defenders of the Tory Redoubt. Hobart approached from the left and Stickney from the right. Stark then led his main column of almost 1,300 men down the Bennington Road.

The Tory Redoubt and the scattered enemy positions quickly fell, but Baum's dragoons held their ground. Having expended most of their ammunition by 5:00 p.m., the Germans attempted to cut their way out with their swords. They made some progress, but surrendered when Baum was mortally wounded.

Both Baum and Stark had called for reinforcements, and the arrival of the new troops precipitated the second phase of the battle. Lieutenant Colonel Francis Breymann's force of 650 Germans came in time to halt Stark's pursuit of retreating soldiers from Baum's expedition. However, Seth Warner's 350 Green Mountain Boys then made

contact with Breymann near what was later Walloomsac, New York. The Germans held their
ground until they ran low on ammunition, and
then they attempted to retreat. The Americans
managed to capture a number of them, but two-
thirds of the force slipped away after dark.

Stark reported 14 Americans killed and 42
wounded. Enemy losses totaled 207 dead and 700
captured. Only nine of the Brunswick dragoons
managed to get back to Burgoyne. The British
commander had lost a tenth of his men and gained
nothing.

Madonna's Birthday

Madonna Louise Veronica Ciccone, otherwise
known as Madonna—one of America's most popular female singers—was born on August 16, 1958,
in Bay City, Michigan. As a child she showed a talent for the performing arts, and in particular she
excelled in the dancing classes offered by the
Catholic school where she received her education.
As a sensual teenager, however, she struggled with
the authoritarian and puritanical atmosphere of
the school and of her home. She was admitted to
the University of Michigan on a dance scholarship,
but dropped out after two years.

Moving to New York City, Madonna wanted to
enter show business. Unlike the vast majority of
such aspirants, she succeeded. It was not an easy
road, though. For years she lived in a cheap boardinghouse and worked in a variety of menial jobs.
Finally, she and several friends formed a band,
which gave her the opportunity to develop her
singing and songwriting skills in the New York
nightclub circuit. Madonna signed some small
record deals with Gotham Records and Sire Records that got her noticed. In 1983 her first album,
Madonna, was released and became a hit.

Madonna generated three top-ten singles, and
was followed by the hugely successful *Like a Virgin* album in 1984. The rise of televised music vid-
eos, broadcast by such entities as Music Television
(MTV), also helped Madonna because it gave her
a chance to use her dancing skills. She became a
superstar, and in 1985 appeared in her first motion
picture, *Desperately Seeking Susan*. It was a popular movie, and helped cement Madonna's credentials as an actress in addition to a singer. *Like a
Virgin* was followed by *True Blue* (1986), *Like a
Prayer* (1989), *Blonde Ambition* (1990), and *Bedtime Stories* (1994). More movies followed as well:
Shanghai Surprise (1986), *Who's That Girl?*
(1987), *Dick Tracy* (1990), *Truth or Dare* (1991),
Shadows and Fog (1992), *A League of Their Own*
(1992), *Body of Evidence* (1993), and the musical
Evita (1996). Madonna has also published a best-
selling book entitled *Sex* (1992).

August 17

Davy Crockett's Birthday

David Crockett, better known as Davy, was born
on August 17, 1786, near what was later Greeneville in Hawkins County, Tennessee. His paternal grandparents were from Ireland, and his father John Crockett was born either there or on the
voyage to the New World. John Crockett, who
took part in the American victory at the battle of
King's Mountain on October 7, 1780, during the
Revolution, married Rebecca Hawkins from
Maryland. Around 1783 they moved from North
Carolina to Tennessee, where Crockett became a
tavern keeper.

Davy Crockett ran away from home when he
was 13 to avoid a beating. He wandered for three
years and made his way to Baltimore before he returned home. Crockett spent his first year back in
Tennessee working to pay off debts incurred by
his father. While still a teenager Crockett married
Polly Findlay, and, with $15 borrowed from a
friend, rented a homestead. His career as a farmer
was a failure, and they moved near the Alabama
border. Polly Crockett died around 1815, leaving
her husband with three children. He later married
Elizabeth Patton, and they had two more children.

Adventure and politics interested Crockett. In
1813 and 1814 he served as a scout under General
Andrew Jackson in the war against the Creek tribe.
Crockett performed his duties well, but left the
service early and hired a substitute to complete his
enlistment service. As a frontiersman, Crockett
was continuously on the move. With his family he
went farther west, and became a justice of the
peace when Tennessee's Giles County absorbed
his new home. His fortunes continued to improve:
He became a colonel of the district's militia and
won election to the state legislature in 1821. When
the Crocketts migrated to the western border of
Tennessee, near the junction of the Obion and
Mississippi Rivers, he was again elected to the legislature.

In 1826 Crockett was elected to the United
States Congress. If a famous tall tale has any accuracy, he undoubtedly made an impression. "I'm
David Crockett," he is said to have announced,
"fresh from the backwoods, half horse, half alliga-
tor, a little touched with snapping turtle. I can
wade the Mississippi, leap the Ohio, ride a streak
of lightning, slip without a scratch down a honey
locust, whip my weight in wildcats, hug a bear too
close for comfort, and eat any man opposed to
Jackson."

In reality, however, Crockett's relationship with Andrew Jackson was far from smooth. As a state legislator, Crockett had opposed his former commander's selection as senator from Tennessee, but in 1828 he gave his backing to Jackson's successful campaign for the White House. During their tenures in Washington, D.C., Crockett and Jackson frequently clashed. To his credit, Crockett opposed the president's support of Alabama, Georgia, and Mississippi in their violation of the treaty rights of the Cherokee, Chickasaw, Choctaw, and Creek tribes.

Crockett's temerity cost him the 1830 congressional election, but he managed to regain his seat two years later despite Jackson's landslide victory in the presidential contest of 1832. Crockett's success against such odds and his opposition to Jackson's veto of the renewal of the charter for the second Bank of the United States made him the hero of the antiadministration forces. The Whig Party adopted the backwoodsman and in 1834 sent him on a tour of the Northeast.

Life and industry in Philadelphia, New York, and Boston pleased Crockett. He was particularly impressed by the system of factories that his Whig mentors had developed in New England. He thought that the mill workers of Lowell, Massachusetts, were especially blessed: "There is every enjoyment of life realized by these people and there can be but a few who are not happy."

In 1834 Crockett lost his congressional seat again. He remained active in politics for a little while longer, and in 1835 authored a scurrilous biography of Vice President Martin Van Buren, whom Jackson had selected to succeed him in office. However, troubles in Texas diverted Crockett's attention from politics. Texas was Mexican territory, but the many Americans who had settled there were anxious to be independent or become part of the United States. The Americans revolted in 1835, and Crockett went off to join their fight.

The Texans under Sam Houston's leadership cleared the province of Mexican garrisons in 1835, but the enemy soon returned. On February 23, 1836, General Antonio López de Santa Anna appeared with more than 6,000 men before the Texan outpost, the Alamo mission at San Antonio. Inside the Alamo were 145 men, including Davy Crockett, which Lieutenant Colonel William Travis and James Bowie jointly commanded. Soon 32 additional men came to their aid.

Santa Anna demanded that the fort surrender, but the defenders refused to lay down their arms. "I have sustained a continual Bombardment and cannonade for 24 hours and have not lost a man," Travis answered. "Our flag still proudly waves from the wall. I shall never surrender or re-treat. . . . Victory or death." A siege ensued for 13 days, and on the morning of March 6, 1836, Santa Anna launched his assault. After failing twice the Mexicans breached the walls on the third try. The Texans had not suffered many casualties, but were almost out of ammunition and were physically exhausted. The fighting continued inside the fortress, but gradually the Mexicans killed all the defenders, including Davy Crockett and 12 other Tennessee volunteers.

Fulton's Steamboat Sails

Robert Fulton did many remarkable things during his 50 years of life, but he did not invent the steamship as Americans often credit him with doing. He did, however, successfully develop the first steamboat that was commercially practical.

Harnessing steam power had been considered since the time of the ancient Greeks. It was certainly contemplated by Hero of Alexandria, a Greek mathematician and inventor (circa third century A.D.). Again contrary to public opinion, the first steam engine was not invented by James Watt. Watt, a Scottish instrument maker working at the University of Glasgow, discovered some interesting things when he was repairing a steam engine that had been patented in 1705 by Thomas Newcomen and Thomas Savery. In 1769, when Watt patented his improvements on the steam engine, he gave the world the most practical source of steam power that had been seen up to that time.

Many engineers began to experiment with powering ships by steam. Among these were the Americans John Fitch and James Rumsey, whose steam-powered ships successfully sailed less than two decades after Watt patented his piston steam engine. However, it remained for Fulton to make the application of steam power to ships practical enough to be used commercially.

Born on November 14, 1765, on a farm in Little Britain, Pennsylvania, about 22 miles south of Lancaster, Fulton showed great mechanical talent and inventiveness early in his life. When he was 14 he enjoyed fishing with a group of boys, but he balked at the exertion required to pole the boat out to the fishing spot, so he designed a paddlewheel vessel. While still in his teens he built a skyrocket to celebrate Independence Day. He liked talking with craftsmen and watching them work, and he learned much this way, becoming an expert gunsmith while the American Revolution was being fought.

After the war Fulton was apprenticed to a jeweler in Philadelphia. Two or three years later, still in Philadelphia, he became self-employed as a painter of landscapes and portraits. He also did miniatures, which were very much in vogue. His success enabled him to buy a small farm for his mother. In 1786 he went to London, England, and studied under another Pennsylvania-born painter, Benjamin West. Fulton's paintings had a fairly good reception in England and France, but his interests turned more and more to canal engineering and mechanical invention. Abandoning art in 1793, he wrote his *Treatise on the Improvement of Canal Investigation*, which appeared in 1796 but failed to interest anyone in his canal proposals.

In the spring of 1797 Fulton moved to France, where he drew plans for a submarine. Despite rejection from the French government, in 1800 Fulton successfully launched his submersible, the *Nautilus*. He stayed in the submerged vessel for six hours, receiving air from an above-water tube. He later improved the *Nautilus* by devising an onboard supply of compressed air, a horizontal rudder, and other refinements. Nevertheless, the French still rejected the *Nautilus*, and Fulton turned to experimenting with steamboats.

Fulton then went into partnership with Robert R. Livingston, who was appointed as American minister to France in 1801 by President Thomas Jefferson and helped negotiate the Louisiana Purchase in 1803. Livingston had been experimenting with steamboats and held a monopoly on steamboating in New York waters. He financed Fulton's experiments, and together they launched Fulton's first steamboat on France's Seine River in 1802.

Having spent 20 years abroad, Fulton returned to the United States in 1806, still working on improvements for what he called "The Steamboat" and others called "Fulton's Folly." On August 17, 1807, a few days after a trial run, Fulton's vessel made its historic trip up the Hudson (or North) River from New York City to Albany. The trip of 150 miles took 32 hours, and the return trip an additional 30 hours. Fulton thus proved that it could be done, and regular commercial schedules, beginning in the fall, were advertised for his "North River Steamboat."

Substantially rebuilt, and lengthened from 140 to 149 feet, the ship was registered in 1808 as *The North River Steamboat of Clermont*, which the press shortened to *Clermont*. Clermont was the name of the house in which Fulton married Harriet Livingston, the cousin of his partner. Over the next few years more steamboats were built to ply the Hudson River route. Fulton set up an engine works in New Jersey and continued to design steamboats of all sorts, including ferries used on the Hudson and East Rivers, which border Manhattan. He designed the *New Orleans*, which sailed on the Mississippi River in 1811. During the War of 1812 Fulton built the ship *Demologos*,

which he conceived of as a floating fort to defend New York harbor. It was launched shortly before the war ended in December 1814.

Having spent his comparatively short life making great practical contributions by improving upon the inventions of others, Fulton died in New York City on February 24, 1815.

Marcus Garvey's Birthday

Marcus Mosiah Garvey, the prominent black nationalist, was born in St. Ann's Bay, Jamaica, on August 17, 1887, to Marcus and Sarah Garvey. He was the youngest of 11 children and grew up under conditions of extreme prejudice in British-ruled Jamaica. Garvey had to leave school at the age of 14 and take employment as a printer's apprentice, but was able to educate himself by reading voraciously.

Garvey traveled through Central America for a few years, and then in 1912 he went to London, England. He met several African nationalists, did some writing for radical black publications, and eventually decided to become a crusader for black rights. In 1914 he returned to Jamaica and established the Universal Negro Improvement and Conservation Association and African Community League, more popularly known as the Universal Negro Improvement Association (UNIA). The objective was to improve the condition of blacks throughout the world.

In 1916 Garvey went to the United States to raise funds and settled in the Harlem district of New York City. He became a leading political figure in the largely African American community of Harlem, and made it the headquarters for the UNIA in 1918. Shortly thereafter, he began to publish *Negro World*, a nationalist newspaper. It was a success, and became one of the most prominent black publications in the United States. The paper also helped bring new members into the UNIA, and affiliate chapters of the organization were opened in a number of major cities.

Garvey believed that blacks should return to Africa and build their own nation-states, free of white domination. In order to further this goal and provide the necessary transportation he founded a steamship company called the Black Star Line in 1919. He also established an organization to promote black economic independence, called the Negro Factories Corporation. Although these enterprises were largely unsuccessful, the publicity did help to bring more members into the UNIA, and at one point Garvey claimed that the organization had two million members. He also held a worldwide convention of UNIA members that issued a "Declaration of the Rights of the Negro

Peoples of the World" in 1920 in addition to adopting a black, red, and green flag as their standard.

Garvey's questionable fundraising activities and financial dealings with respect to his enterprises, however, drew the attention of the American authorities. It may well be that this attention was inspired by racial prejudice. Regardless, on January 12, 1921, the United States government charged Garvey with mail fraud relating to his use of the mails to sell stock. Garvey represented himself at his trial, but was convicted despite the eloquence of his speeches and sent to prison in 1925. In 1927, however, President Calvin Coolidge commuted Garvey's sentence. He was deported back to Jamaica, where he attempted to revive the UNIA movement but failed. Eventually, Garvey made his way to London, where he died on July 10, 1940.

Despite the tragic nature of his downfall, Marcus Garvey remains an important figure in the struggle for civil rights. His powerful advocacy of self-determination has influenced many African American leaders, and in his native Jamaica he is recognized as a national hero.

August 18

First United States Government Maritime Expedition Sets Sail

Exploration has played an important role in American history. The earliest Europeans to visit America conducted extensive expeditions into the continent, and only decades after the United States achieved independence, the young nation sponsored several western explorations. These included the expeditions of Meriwether Lewis and William Clark (1804–1806) and Zebulon Pike (1806–1807). As increasing numbers of merchant vessels entered the trade between China and the Pacific Northwest, and whaling vessels made their dangerous voyages to the South Seas, Americans also sought knowledge about the oceans. On August 18, 1838, the first marine expedition sponsored by the federal government set sail from Hampton Roads, Virginia, to survey maritime routes in the Pacific Ocean and South Seas.

Lieutenant Charles Wilkes commanded the expedition. The 40-year-old Wilkes, who since 1833 had headed the Depot of Charts and Instruments in Washington, D.C. (from which later developed the Naval Observatory and the Hydrographic Office), was well qualified for the task before him. He had personally selected many of the astronomical and other scientific instruments that equipped

his squadron of four naval vessels: the *Vincennes*, *Peacock*, *Porpoise*, and *Relief*. There were also two pilot boats, the *Sea Gull* and *Flying Fish*. The success of the expedition did not depend on Wilkes's talents alone, however. Noted civilian specialists, including geologist and mineralogist James D. Dana, botanist W. R. Rich, artist Alfred T. Agate, zoologist Charles Pickering, and artist and naturalist Titian Ramsay Peale were also among the 440 men who embarked on the 1838 expedition.

The expedition reached Rio de Janeiro, Brazil, on November 24, 1838. After a stay of more than three weeks in that city, the squadron returned to sea on December 17. Continuing south, it sailed the entire length of South America and rounded Cape Horn, though the *Relief* turned out to be so slow that it had to be left behind in Tierra del Fuego. Below Cape Horn, the explorers sighted the northernmost of the South Shetland Islands and continued south for their first incursion into the Antarctic. The expedition split into two sections for this initial investigation. Under Wilkes's second in command, Lieutenant William L. Hudson, the *Peacock* and *Flying Fish* explored the Bellingshausen Sea west of Palmer Peninsula, which points from Antarctica toward the southern tip of South America.

The *Porpoise* and *Sea Gull*, under Wilkes, investigated the region east of the Palmer Peninsula in the ice-filled Weddell Sea where they experienced the piercing Antarctic cold. They also encountered great beauty: "I have rarely seen a finer sight," wrote Wilkes. "The sea was literally studded with . . . beautiful [ice] masses . . . of pure white . . . all . . . shades of opal, . . . emerald green, and occasionally . . . some of deep black, forming a strong contrast to the pure white."

The long Antarctic winter was now at hand, however, and both sections of the expedition retreated northward. Wilkes, with three vessels, headed for Valparaiso, Chile. He arrived on April 13, 1839. He dispatched the *Flying Fish* and the *Sea Gull* to Tierra del Fuego to pick up the *Relief* and escort it around Cape Horn. When the latter ship proved too feeble to be useful and had to be sent home, the two smaller vessels proceeded around the treacherous Horn alone, en route to join the others in Valparaiso. They were separated, however, on April 26, 1839, during a severe storm, and the *Sea Gull* was never seen again.

On May 1 the remainder of the expedition (rejoined by the *Vincennes*, which had also remained in Tierra del Fuego during the journey into the Antarctic) left Valparaiso. Twelve days later they arrived at Callao, the seaport of Lima, Peru. The explorers remained in the Peruvian capital for more than two months before they departed on

July 13 with their four remaining vessels—the *Vincennes*, *Peacock*, *Porpoise*, and *Flying Fish*—taking a westerly course that would permit extensive scientific observations in the South Pacific and the collection of many valuable specimens. The scientists carefully noted the exact location of each of the many small islands they encountered. They also went ashore many times, examined the terrain of the islands, and made contact with the inhabitants.

On September 12 the expedition reached Tahiti. The scientists made extensive surveys of the island, and Lieutenant Wilkes negotiated a commercial treaty with the principal tribal chiefs. On October 10 the Americans left Tahiti and, continuing westward, arrived at Pago-Pago, Samoa, on October 18. After staying for only one day in Pago-Pago, they pushed on to the neighboring island of Upota. There they purchased provisions, explored the interior of the island, and made detailed observations of the tides. On November 10 they sailed southward and encountered many small islands before entering the harbor of Sydney, Australia, on November 27.

The expedition remained in Sydney for almost a month. On December 26 they began an exploring cruise in the Antarctic Ocean. Dense fog and driving rain hampered the vessels as they made their way south. However, on January 10, 1840, the weather cleared and the explorers caught their first glimpses of icebergs. The following day they came upon even more spectacular ice formations, some of which they estimated to be five miles long and 300 feet high.

On January 19 the explorers sighted land, and during the weeks that followed they confirmed the existence of a theretofore undiscovered continent. On several occasions their boats sailed fairly close to the Antarctic land mass, thereby enabling the scientists to observe and gather specimens of the rock and sand of the continent. The discovery that Antarctica was, in fact, a continent was undoubtedly the most spectacular achievement of the expedition. In honor of its commander, a large region of the southernmost continent later bore the name Wilkes Land.

On February 21 the Americans began their return north. On March 11 they arrived back in Sydney. The squadron set sail again on March 19 and 11 days later reached New Zealand. Departing from New Zealand on April 6, the expedition made its way northeast and on April 24 put in at Tonga. The Americans continued their journey on May 4 and within two days landed at Levuka in the Fiji Islands.

Deciding to conduct detailed surveys, the expedition remained in the Fiji Islands for several months. When they had completed their scientific observations, the party left the Fiji Islands on August 11. After sailing in a northeasterly direction for more than six weeks, they arrived at the Hawaiian Islands on September 30, 1840. The explorers remained there for six months, during which time they collected much valuable data. They descended into the crater of the great volcano of Mount Kilauea and obtained specimens of volcanic rock and lava. They also explored Maui and some of the smaller islands.

From Hawaii the Americans took a northeast course, and on April 28, 1841, they reached the northwest coast of North America. During the months that followed, they conducted extensive surveys of Washington and Oregon, and the data provided by these investigations proved extremely useful during the dispute between the United States and Great Britain over the Oregon Territory in the mid-1840s. The area to the south also interested the explorers, and early in September, 39 members began an overland journey to San Francisco. This party made detailed reports on the animals and vegetation they encountered as they proceeded south.

The overland party rejoined the maritime expedition in San Francisco on October 9, 1841, and at the end of October the entire American squadron returned to sea. Proceeding west they secured provisions in Honolulu, Hawaii, on November 19 and reached Singapore on January 22, 1842. They again set sail on February 25 and arrived 13 days later at St. Helena off the west coast of Africa. From St. Helena the expedition continued its circumnavigation of the globe. The American ships crossed the Atlantic, touching at Rio de Janeiro, and finally reached New York City on June 10, 1842.

The report of the 47-month expedition was published in 19 volumes. Wilkes contributed the *Narrative of the United States Exploring Expedition* (five volumes plus atlas). He also edited the scientific reports and was the author of the hydrography and meteorology volumes.

Marshall Field's Birthday

Marshall Field, the great retailing magnate, was born near Conway, Massachusetts, on August 18, 1834, to John and Fidelia Field. As a youth he worked on the family farm and was educated in the local public schools. At the age of 17 Field took a clerical job with a dry-goods store in Pittsfield, Massachusetts. In 1856 he went to Chicago, Illinois, and took a job with the retailing firm of Cooley, Wadsworth and Company. Field became a partner in 1860.

He was both a retailing pioneer and a shrewd opportunist. Field emphasized customer service, instituted a "one price for all" policy, extended consumer credit liberally, and accepted returned merchandise without question. At the time, these were controversial innovations, but Field helped to make them the industry standards that they are today. In 1865 Field and another partner, Levi Zeigler Leiter, joined with Chicago retailer and real estate developer Potter Palmer. Field became the senior partner in 1867 when Palmer retired, and the firm was renamed Field, Leiter and Company. It relocated to premises on State Street, one of Chicago's major thoroughfares, in 1868. The Great Fire of 1871 destroyed the store, but Field took advantage of the disaster to erect an even larger emporium. This massive and ornate building, designed by D.H. Burnham with Charles Atwood, became Chicago's leading department store, and further expansions followed. As the flagship store of Field's firm, renamed Marshall Field and Company in 1881, it came to occupy an entire city block. Branch stores were opened in New York City and major cities abroad. Field was also noted for his pioneering advances in window displays and retail advertising.

Field, who was also a successful real estate investor and a noted philanthropist, died on January 16, 1906, in New York City. His estate, worth over a hundred million dollars, made him one of the wealthiest men in America. During his lifetime, Field gave generously to the University of Chicago and his own Field Museum of Natural History, which became one of the finest museums in the world. His descendants also went on to become important and influential men in their own right. Marshall Field III (1893–1956), Field's grandson, founded the *Chicago Sun-Times* newspaper. He was also the publisher of the popular *World Book Encyclopedia* and came to own such major publishing houses as Simon & Schuster and Pocket Books. Marshall Field IV (1916–1965) was a publisher as well, and expanded into radio and television broadcasting. The Field family also maintained an active involvement with charitable organizations.

August 19

William Jefferson Clinton's Birthday

Bill Clinton, the 42nd president of the United States, was born William Jefferson Blythe III on August 19, 1946, in Hope, Arkansas. His father,

The White House

Bill Clinton

William Jefferson Blythe Jr. was killed in an automobile accident just a few months before Clinton was born. Clinton's mother, Virginia Cassidy Blythe, moved to New Orleans, Louisiana, to study nursing while he stayed in Hope with his grandparents Eldridge and Edith Cassidy. They owned a small grocery store, and despite the official policies of segregation that pervaded the South at that time, they treated their black customers equally with white customers. Young Clinton grew up in an atmosphere of racial tolerance unique for most southern white males of his generation, and it influenced his later political outlook by encouraging him to endorse progressive social agendas.

In 1950 Clinton's mother remarried, this time to a car salesman named Roger Clinton. Shortly thereafter the family moved to Hot Springs, Arkansas, where Clinton received his grade school education. He was popular and a natural leader. In high school, during the presidency of John F. Kennedy (1961–1963), Clinton went to Washington, D.C., as part of the Boys' Nation youth leadership conference. He met Kennedy in the White House and shook his hand in the Rose Garden, an experience that Clinton later described as one of the most memorable in his life and one that eventually caused him to enter politics.

In addition to being an exceptional student, Clinton was active in church and charity activities. He also found time to become proficient on the saxophone, and during his later political career he

would occasionally entertain audiences with impromptu performances. After high school Clinton
entered Georgetown University in Washington,
D.C., in 1964. In addition to his studies, he in-
terned in the offices of Senator J. William Fulbright of Arkansas. He admired Fulbright, who
became his mentor and taught him about politics.
Clinton graduated from Georgetown in 1968 with
a degree in International Affairs and a Rhodes
Scholarship for further study at Oxford University
in Great Britain. Clinton would become the first
president to have earned the coveted title of
Rhodes Scholar.

Clinton studied at Oxford until 1970, when he
was accepted to Yale University Law School. During that time he met his future wife, fellow student
Hillary Diane Rodham. After Clinton graduated in
1973, he returned to Arkansas to teach at the University of Arkansas Law School. In 1974 he began
his first political campaign by running for the
United States House of Representatives against
Republican incumbent John Paul Hammersch-
midt in the Third District of Arkansas. Clinton lost
the race.

After marrying Hillary on October 11, 1975,
Clinton reentered politics in 1976 by working for
the successful presidential campaign of Democratic candidate Jimmy Carter. That same year, he
was elected attorney general of Arkansas. In 1978
he successfully campaigned for and won the Arkansas governorship, becoming one of the youngest governors in history. Clinton pursued a progressive Democratic agenda, increasing funding
for education and highways. His daughter Chelsea
was born on February 27, 1980.

Clinton lost his bid for reelection in November
1980 due to several unpopular policies, such as
higher car taxes to fund his programs. He returned
to office in 1982, however, and went back to his
progressive agenda (albeit with more political as-
tuteness). Clinton's successes, such as improving
the Arkansas educational system, gained national
attention and helped him rise in prominence within the Democratic Party. In 1986 Clinton became
the chairman of the National Governors' Association, and in 1990 he became the head of the Democratic Leadership Council. He also continued to
be reelected as governor of Arkansas.

In the fall of 1991, Clinton decided to enter the
Democratic primaries for nomination as the presidential candidate in the upcoming elections of
1992. It was a grueling campaign. The Republican
incumbent, President George Bush, was enormously popular after the American victory against
Iraq in Operation Desert Storm. There were also
a number of strong Democratic challengers for
the nomination. Further, an alleged sex scandal

with Gennifer Flowers nearly destroyed Clinton's
campaign. However, the entry of independent
candidate H. Ross Perot into the presidential contest in the spring of 1992 added more interesting
twists. Perot criticized many of Bush's policies,
and during the resulting Perot-Bush feud Clinton
was able to reach the public with his campaign
themes. Running on a platform of better health
care, increased funding for education, and fiscal
stimulus to bolster the lagging economy, Clinton
was able to win not only the Democratic nomination but also the November 1992 election. He received 43 percent of the popular vote (370 votes
in the electoral college), Bush received 38 percent
(168 electoral votes), and Perot received 19 percent (no electoral votes). Clinton's vice president
was Albert A. Gore Jr., formerly a senator from
Tennessee.

President Clinton was reelected together with
Gore in November 1996. He defeated Republican
candidate Robert Dole and Reform Party candidate H. Ross Perot (the Reform Party was formed
after Perot's run as an independent in 1992) with
49 percent of the popular vote (379 votes in the
electoral college) to Dole's 41 percent (159 electoral votes) and Perot's 10 percent (no electoral
votes). Unfortunately, as of the late 1990s, it is difficult to make an objective assessment of the Clinton presidency. The reader is referred to *Facts
about the Presidents* and *Facts about the Congress*, two other works issued by the H. W. Wilson
Company, for the statistical information. It is certainly safe to say, however, that Clinton's achievements have included:

(1) Eliminating the persistent federal budget deficit and achieving the first budget
surplus since the 1950s.

(2) Getting the North American Free
Trade Agreement and the General Agreement on Tariffs and Trade, two major international trade deregulation compacts,
passed by Congress.

(3) Achieving a peaceful transition of power in Haiti from the military dictatorship of
Raoul Cedras to a civilian government.

(4) Promoting pro-growth, moderate economic policies that led to one of the greatest economic expansions in American history and record declines in unemployment
and interest rates.

Some of his more noteworthy failures have
been:

(1) Inability to persuade Congress to adopt
his program for health care reform. (The
promise of such a program had been part
of his 1992 campaign.)

(2) Neglecting his role as leader of the Democratic Party in 1994, when the Republicans were able to take control of both houses of Congress in the midterm congressional elections.

Certain questionable financial dealings with respect to a real estate development known as Whitewater in Arkansas before he became president led to a serious scandal during Clinton's first administration and the appointment of an independent counsel to investigate the matter. This investigation gradually expanded to other matters, such as Clinton's conduct while governor of Arkansas with respect to a female state employee named Paula Jones. Allegedly, Clinton exposed himself to her in a hotel room. Not only did she bring a lawsuit, but the incident became the subject of a massive investigation by the independent counsel into whether or not Clinton had engaged in unlawful conduct in trying to cover up evidence regarding his sexual behavior. The independent counsel's investigation became the basis for the impeachment of Clinton by the House of Representatives and his subsequent trial and acquittal by the Senate. A summary timeline follows:

August 1994: Former judge Kenneth Starr was appointed the independent counsel.

June 1995: Monica Lewinsky became a White House intern.

November 1995: A sexual relationship began between Clinton and Lewinsky.

January 1998: A friend of Lewinsky's named Linda Tripp tape-recorded telephone conversations between herself and Lewinsky concerning the relationship with Clinton and turned the tapes over to Starr's staff. The material was considered relevant to the Paula Jones matter because Clinton had denied a pattern of behavior showing a tendency toward sexual promiscuity.

August 17, 1998: Clinton confesses to his extramarital affair with Lewinsky in a nationally televised speech. His confession contradicts his previous denials.

September 10, 1998: Starr's report was delivered to the United States House of Representatives, as required by statute, for consideration with respect to impeachable offenses under the Constitution.

December 12, 1998: The House Judiciary Committee approved four Articles of Impeachment for consideration by the full House.

December 19, 1998: The House voted to impeach President Clinton, approving two of the four Articles of Impeachment.

January 7, 1999: As mandated by the Constitution, an impeachment trial began in the Senate.

February 12, 1999: The Senate impeachment trial ended. On one of the two Articles of Impeachment, concerning perjury, the vote was 55-45 in favor and thus short of the required two-thirds majority required to remove a president from office. On the other article, concerning obstruction of justice, the vote was 50-50 and also short of the necessary two-thirds majority. Clinton was therefore acquitted.

Clinton was only the second president in United States history to have been impeached. The first was Andrew Johnson, in 1868; he was also acquitted, though by a very narrow margin. President Richard M. Nixon was threatened with impeachment over Watergate in 1974, but resigned from office before the full House could consider the charges.

War of 1812: The USS *Constitution* Engages the British

The War of 1812 pitted the young American nation against Great Britain, the mightiest sea power of the era. When hostilities between the two nations began in June 1812, 11 British ships of the line, together with 34 frigates and 52 smaller warships, patrolled American waters. In comparison, American naval resources consisted of only four frigates and about 12 other warships capable of fighting on the open sea. The addition of several hundred armed American merchant vessels, which harassed British commerce throughout the war, considerably aided the American effort. However, from the beginning it was clear that the American navy was no match for the British.

English newspapers reflected the contempt that the British felt for their adversaries. One paper described the USS *Constitution*, one of the four American frigates, as "a bundle of pine boards sailing under a bit of striped bunting" and claimed that "a few broadsides from England's wooden walls would drive the paltry striped bunting from the ocean."

A few days later the *Constitution*'s performance necessitated a reconsideration of these words. Under the command of Captain Isaac Hull, the *Constitution* sailed from Chesapeake Bay on July 12, 1812, to join forces with an American squadron then sailing off the waters of New York. En route a number of British vessels, including the frigate *Guerrière*, sighted the lone American ship and pursued it for three days and two nights. Hull was able to outmaneuver his adversaries, however, and the American frigate escaped to the safety of Boston harbor.

On August 12, 1812, the *Constitution* left Boston, and seven days later, while cruising 200 miles off the Maine coast, again met the *Guerrière*. This time a confrontation between the two vessels was unavoidable. The 30-minute battle that ensued on August 19, 1812, resulted in 79 British casualties and the destruction of the *Guerrière*. The Americans, however, suffered only 14 casualties and minor damage to their ship. In fact, the *Constitution's* ability to withstand British attack was so great that one of its gunners allegedly exclaimed, "Her sides must be made of iron!" Although tradition holds that this is the source of the nickname Old Ironsides, some claim that the incident merely confirmed an already widespread usage. According to these sources, the name originated at the time of the ship's construction because the oak planking was bent into place without first undergoing the customary steaming and softening process.

A hero's welcome awaited Hull when he returned to Boston. On the other side of the Atlantic, the stunned *London Times* reported, "Never before in the history of the world did an English frigate strike to an American." The *Constitution's* victory was a great boost to American morale, and an equally great blow to British pride. Aside from this, however, the battle itself had little long-range significance. The regular American navy was too weak to withstand the superior British fleet, and during most of the remainder of the war British ships kept the *Constitution* and the other frigates confined to their homeports.

The contribution of Old Ironsides to American history is not limited to the defeat of the *Guerrière*. The 44-gun frigate was one of the first six warships Congress ordered built when it reactivated the United States Navy in 1794. Launched on October 21, 1797, the ship served in the Tripolitan War of 1801 to 1805. Several times during the War of 1812 it escaped British surveillance to put a number of enemy vessels out of commission. In 1830 the navy declared it unseaworthy, and it would have been scuttled for parts had not Oliver Wendell Holmes's stirring poem "Old Ironsides" gained the ship a last-minute reprieve.

After extensive renovation, the *Constitution* returned to service in 1833. For another 22 years it saw active duty, but in 1855 deterioration again reached such an extent that it was retired to the Portsmouth Navy Yard. Partially restored in 1877, it made a final transatlantic crossing in that same year. The *Constitution* sailed only intermittently thereafter, and in 1897 returned to the Boston Naval Shipyard where it was used as a barracks ship

until 1927. After its restoration in 1931, it became a popular tourist attraction.

National Aviation Day

National Aviation Day, observed annually on August 19, celebrates the progress of aviation since the 120-foot hop of Wilbur and Orville Wright at Kitty Hawk, North Carolina, in 1903. Over the years the airplane has become an increasingly important factor in commerce and warfare, and America's success in the skies has been vital to its economic strength and national security.

On May 11, 1939, the United States Congress adopted a resolution to set aside a special day each year to commemorate the contributions of the aircraft industry and to stimulate interest in aviation. In accordance with this legislation, on July 25, 1939, President Franklin D. Roosevelt proclaimed August 19, the anniversary of Orville Wright's birth, as National Aviation Day and encouraged all American citizens to observe it.

August 20

Benjamin Harrison's Birthday

Benjamin Harrison, the 23rd president of the United States, was born on August 20, 1833, in North Bend, Ohio. He came from a wealthy family of the planter class, heavily involved in politics. Harrison's great-grandfather Benjamin Harrison was a governor of Virginia and one of the signers of the Declaration of Independence. The governor's son William Henry Harrison (who settled in Ohio) became the ninth president of the United States in 1841. It was a memorable event in the life of his seven-year-old grandchild, Benjamin Harrison. Young Benjamin's father, John Scott Harrison (the eldest son of William Henry), lived on a farm adjacent to the estate of the new president. John Harrison was himself twice elected to the United States House of Representatives as a Whig. His second wife, Elizabeth Irwin Harrison, was Benjamin Harrison's mother.

Harrison received private tutoring before entering Farmers' College in Walnut Hills, Ohio. He studied for three years at Farmers' College before transferring to Miami University at Oxford, Ohio, from which he graduated in 1852. Harrison was a good student, especially drawn to political science and history. Following college, Harrison studied law for two years before being admitted to the bar. On October 20, 1853, Harrison married Caroline Lavinia Scott.

In 1854 Harrison established his own law practice in Indianapolis, Indiana. His practice flourished in the burgeoning state capital. Talented as a public speaker, Harrison became involved with the infant Republican Party, making addresses on behalf of Republican candidates and policies. He was elected city attorney of Indianapolis in 1857. In 1860, and again in 1864, he was elected reporter of the Indiana state supreme court.

After the outbreak of the Civil War, in 1862 Harrison helped raise the volunteer 70th Indiana Infantry Regiment, and was appointed its colonel. At first his men guarded railroads and took part in minor encounters in Kentucky and Tennessee. In 1864, however, his regiment was attached to the command of General William T. Sherman and engaged in the difficult campaign that culminated with the capture of Atlanta, Georgia. Harrison's skill in commanding his men won him promotion to the brevet rank of brigadier general. Harrison was diverted from further direct military action by the request of Governor Oliver P. Morton that he return to Indiana to help campaign in the 1864 elections against the "Copperhead" Democrats who sympathized with the Confederacy.

After the war Harrison resumed the practice of law and was soon recognized as one of the leading lawyers of the state. He was noted for his excellent memory, eloquent presentation, and analytical mind. He tried for the Republican gubernatorial nomination in 1872 but was not selected. Four years later he was nominated, but not elected. In 1880 Harrison was chairman of the Indiana delegation at the Republican National Convention, and supported the swing of delegates that gave the nomination to James A. Garfield of Ohio. When elected, Garfield offered him a cabinet post, but Harrison declined it since he had just been elected by the Indiana legislature to serve in the United States Senate.

As a senator, Harrison supported further expansion into the territories and the admission of new states to the Union. He also supported the establishment of a national park system. As a Republican, he backed the party's position in favor of continued high tariffs on imports. He was also instrumental in the passage of the Interstate Commerce Act of 1887 before the expiration of his term. He had lost the support of the Indiana legislature the previous fall and had not been reelected (at the time, senators were chosen by the individual state legislatures, not directly elected by the people). However, at the Republican National Convention of 1888 he was nominated to run for president. In the election Harrison won over incumbent Grover Cleveland by 233 to 168 electoral votes, even though Cleveland received a larger popular vote.

As president, Harrison pushed ahead with plans to increase the number of states. In April 1889 Oklahoma was opened to new settlers after the Creek and Seminole tribes were paid to move out. During Harrison's administration, North Dakota, South Dakota, Montana, Washington, Idaho, and Wyoming became states.

During the winter of 1889–1890, representatives of various Latin American countries met in Washington, D.C., in the first Pan American Congress, with the goal of establishing closer ties. However, the Latin American image of the United States did not improve during Harrison's term. One particularly unpleasant incident was a dispute involving American sailors in Chile, which resulted in a forced apology from the Chilean government.

Harrison's administration saw the passage of some important legislation. Measures were enacted to strengthen the army and the navy. Public clamor for some restraints on the activities of giant "trusts" was placated with the Sherman Antitrust Act. The Sherman Silver Purchase Act satisfied western Republicans, while the McKinley Tariff Act slightly raised tariff schedules for eastern, business-oriented Republicans. In addition, a new veterans' pension bill vastly increased payments to Civil War veterans.

A number of factors led to Harrison's defeat in 1892. Although the United States was rapidly being transformed from an agrarian to an urban and industrial country, neither Harrison and the Republicans, nor their political opponents, took into serious consideration the nation's increasing labor problems. Labor unrest, populist farmer movements, and problems in the economy led to a call for a change in leadership. In the presidential election of 1892, Grover Cleveland was again the Democratic nominee. After the balloting was over, Cleveland had received 277 electoral votes and Harrison had received 145 electoral votes. Populist candidate James B. Weaver received 22 electoral votes.

Another factor in Harrison's defeat may have been his rather cold personality. Acting Attorney General William Howard Taft noted this problem in 1890:

> The President is not popular with the members of either house. His manner of treating them is not at all fortunate, and when they have an interview with him they generally come away mad. . . . I think this is exceedingly unfortunate, because I am sure we have never had a man in the White House who was more conscientiously seeking to do his duty.

Harrison returned to his law practice in Indianapolis, handling many important court cases in the ensuing years. He also accepted numerous invitations to make public addresses, and he wrote articles for various magazines. A series of pieces that appeared in the *Ladies' Home Journal* on the nature of the federal government was later revised and issued as the book *This Country of Ours*. For many years it was a standard reference work for schools and colleges. Harrison also published *Views of an Ex-President*, a volume of essays originally presented as speeches. He was active on behalf of Republican candidates in the elections of 1894 and 1896. In addition, he was chosen to be senior counsel for Venezuela in its boundary dispute with British Guiana. After nearly two years of preparation, he presented the Venezuelan case before an arbitration tribunal in Paris in 1899. Before his impressive closing argument was half finished, the British counsel recognized that defeat was imminent and indicated as much in a message home.

Harrison's first wife had died in the White House in 1892, after suffering a long illness. In 1896 he remarried to Mary Scott Lord Dimmick, a relative of his first wife. The couple became parents of a daughter named Elizabeth. During his first marriage, Harrison had fathered two children, Russell and Mary. Throughout his postpresidential years, Harrison retained the interest he had always had in the activities of the Presbyterian Church. He was an elder of the church, taught a men's Bible class, was superintendent of a Sunday school, and was several times a delegate to the general assembly of the Presbyterian Church.

He died of pneumonia on March 13, 1901. His burial place was Crown Hill Cemetery in Indianapolis.

First Probe Is Launched Toward Mars

The Viking mission to Mars, which became the first to achieve a successful landing on the surface of that planet, was launched by the National Aeronautics and Space Administration (NASA) in the summer of 1975. The mission consisted of two spacecraft, *Viking 1* and *Viking 2*. Each of these spacecraft consisted of an orbiter and a lander. Years of developing the Viking project culminated on August 20, 1975, with the launch of *Viking 1*, the first part of the mission.

The purpose of the Viking project was to scan the Martian surface, take air and soil samples, and search for any evidence of life. *Viking 1* reached Mars on June 19, 1976, and went into orbit around the planet to map the surface for suitable landing

sites. Then, on July 20 the *Viking 1* lander module detached from the orbiter vehicle. It descended to the surface and landed at a site known as Chryse Planitia. The lander took photographic scans of the Martian surface and transmitted them back to Earth. These images revealed surface features that could only have been caused by water erosion, indicating that there was once surface water on Mars. It transmitted images for years, finally ceasing operation on November 13, 1982. The Viking lander also took a wide variety of atmospheric measurements and determined that the soil at the landing site consisted of iron-rich clay. It did not, however, find evidence of life presently existing on Mars (as opposed to evidence of life existing on Mars in the past, which was discovered in the 1990s—see August 6, First Evidence of Extraterrestrial Life Announced).

The second part of the mission, *Viking 2*, was launched September 9, 1975. It reached Mars on August 7, 1976, and the *Viking 2* lander descended to the region known as Utopia Planitia on September 3, 1976.

August 21

Hawaii Admitted to the Union

Hawaii became the 50th state of the United States on August 21, 1959.

Captain James Cook of the British navy was the first European to visit Hawaii, reaching the Pacific archipelago in 1778. Many other Westerners followed, including a large number of American merchants, missionaries, and whalers who migrated to the islands in the 19th century. The United States eventually gained control of Hawaii's economy and government, and annexed the islands in 1898.

Consisting of over 100 islands formed by volcanic eruptions, Hawaii is located approximately 2,400 miles west of San Francisco, California. Hawaii, Oahu, Maui, Kahoolawe, Lanai, Molokai, Kauai, and Niihau are the major islands. Honolulu, the capital city, is on the island of Oahu and is by far the state's biggest population center.

Seafaring Polynesians, probably from Tahiti, first settled the islands. The arrival of Westerners, however, devastated the native Hawaiian population, which has been reduced to a fraction of its former size. Today, Hawaii is a polyglot mixture of cultures with mainland, native Hawaiian, Chinese, Filipino, Japanese, and other ancestries.

The United States Congress granted Hawaii territorial status in 1900. In 1919 Congress considered a bill that would grant the islands statehood. This proposal failed, however, and 40 more years passed before the advocates of statehood achieved success. On March 12, 1959, the United States House of Representatives completed congressional action by passing the Hawaiian Statehood Bill, and President Dwight D. Eisenhower signed the bill on March 18, 1959. The citizens of Hawaii ratified the act by a margin of nearly 17 to 1 at the June 27, 1959, plebiscite, and on July 28 they elected their first state governor, senators, and representatives. President Eisenhower brought the long process to its culmination by signing the Hawaiian Statehood Proclamation, which officially admitted the new state to the Union on August 21, 1959. The American flag was accordingly redesigned to contain its present field of 50 stars. The third Friday in every August is now a Hawaiian state holiday to commemorate the event.

American Bar Association Formed

The American Bar Association (ABA), the leading organization for attorneys in the United States, was founded on August 21, 1878, in Saratoga Springs, New York. It was created in response to a multistate initiative for a national code of legal ethics and a national body in which to debate legal issues facing American attorneys. Lawyers representing 21 states were present at the organizing convention.

According to its charter, which has remained largely intact to the present day, the primary purpose of the ABA is "to be the national representative of the legal profession, serving the public and the profession by promoting justice, professional excellence and respect for the law." As such, the ABA is a voluntary association. Membership is not mandatory, since attorneys are licensed and regulated by the bar associations of the 50 states, the District of Columbia, and the various American territories and possessions. Even though the ABA cannot effectively regulate or discipline its members, it has achieved prominence as the leading organization for national legal issues, and so roughly half of all American attorneys and a considerable number of judges belong to it even though they are not required to do so.

ABA membership is open to any attorney admitted to practice and in good standing with the bar association of any state, territory, or other jurisdiction within the United States. Certain nonlawyers, like court personnel and law librarians, are also eligible to join as associates.

The ABA has nearly half a million members. It works to promote uniform legal codes among the states, establish standardized codes of ethics and rules of practice, and reform inadequacies in the legal system. It also functions as a lobbying and support organization for lawyers. For example, a wide variety of specialized ABA branches serve attorneys that practice in such diverse fields as antitrust and taxation.

August 22

First America's Cup Race

On August 22, 1851, the schooner *America* triumphed in the first of a long series of hotly contested races, the most prestigious in international yacht racing today. That first competition had its origin in 1850 with an invitation to a New York businessman from a Londoner. He suggested that the Americans send one of their fastest yachts to England to race in a regatta, sponsored by the British Royal Yacht Squadron, that was to be held in conjunction with the Great Exposition opening at the Crystal Palace in London the following year.

Designed by George Steers, the *America* was 101 feet 9 inches long, with a waterline length of 90 feet 3 inches. It was built by a six-person syndicate of the New York Yacht Club, headed by John C. Stevens, the club's commodore. To hide its speed, the *America* was first sailed to France and then refitted with racing sails. As it sailed for the Isle of Wight where the regatta was to be held, a British cutter enticed it into a race, which the *America* won and thus prematurely revealed its speed.

The English realized that they could not win in an open competition, and there was talk of dropping the challenge to the *America*. Because of pressure from the press and public, however, the *America* was included in the regatta with 14 of England's fastest schooners and cutters. The race took place as scheduled on August 22, 1851, in the coastal waters around the Isle of Wight. When the starting gun was fired, the *America* fouled its anchor and had to haul down and reset its sails. However, even with that delay it quickly caught up and won the race.

The victorious *America* took 10 hours and 37 minutes to sail the course's 58 miles. The victory was not without protest, however, for several British yachtsmen claimed that the *America* had not won. The British interpreted the specified racecourse "outside the Nab" to mean outside Nab Light. The Americans, not realizing the difference between Nab Light and Nab promontory, had sailed outside the tip of land but inside the light. Nevertheless, the Royal Yacht Squadron awarded its Hundred Guinea Cup to the *America* and it was henceforth known as the America's Cup. Commodore Stevens gave it to the New York Yacht Club in 1857.

The *America* was sold to an English buyer a few months after the race. He raced it for a while but then sold it for junk. The schooner was subsequently reconditioned, however, and during the Civil War was used as a blockade runner to and from Confederate ports. Found scuttled near Jacksonville, Florida, it was raised by the Union navy and then used as a blockade ship. After the war it was used as a training ship at the United States Naval Academy at Annapolis, Maryland. The *America* was last seen under sail in 1901. It spent the next 20 years in a Boston shipyard, and in 1921 was towed to Annapolis. In 1940 it was hauled ashore and blocked up. A protective shed was built for it, but four years later the shed collapsed when two feet of ice and snow landed on its roof, and the schooner was shattered in the crash.

The competition for the America's Cup has made that international sailing event an exciting forum for innovative yacht designs and development. The rules of the competition have evolved over the years, with a recurring trend toward boats of greater sail-carrying power, larger rigs, more complicated design, and greater cost. In the late 20th century, innovative hull and keel designs made the Australians leaders in the competition, upsetting America's traditional dominance of the event.

Mormon Tabernacle Choir Gives First Performance

The Mormon Tabernacle Choir gave its first performance on August 22, 1847, in Salt Lake City, Utah. From this performance, given at an outdoor meeting of the Mormon settlers in Utah, the choir has grown to become a famous and highly respected musical ensemble.

Mormon pioneers on the way to Salt Lake used to sing in order to break the tedium of the long trek. Singing around the nightly campfire or at other social occasions was one of the few opportunities for musical entertainment. Given the religious inspiration of their quest to settle Utah, the Mormons naturally had a certain liking for hymns and other forms of spiritual music. The choir was formed barely a month after the Mormons first entered the Salt Lake Valley.

The choir produced its first record in 1910. More than 100 have followed, five of which have been gold records and one of which has been a platinum record. Further, the choir has given a large number of broadcast performances. These performances include weekly appearances on *Music and the Spoken Word*, which has been running continuously since 1929, making it the longest-running radio program in history. Today, the choir consists of over 300 unpaid male and female volunteers. Many of the performers come from families that have sung in the choir for generations. The choir has given live performances at four presidential inaugurations and has performed with such well-known orchestras as the New York Philharmonic Orchestra and the Royal Philharmonic Orchestra of London.

The choir's headquarters has always been, and remains, in Salt Lake City. The heart of the city and of the Mormon Church is Temple Square. The temple itself, the most important center of religious worship in the Mormon faith, was begun by the early pioneers in the 1850s and took 40 years to complete. Adjacent to the temple is the tabernacle, built for the choir, which took 12 years to complete. It has one of the finest acoustical designs in the world and features the Tabernacle Organ, which has some 11,000 pipes. The choir still gives free public performances several times a week.

August 23

Oliver Hazard Perry's Birthday

Oliver Hazard Perry, the great naval hero of the War of 1812, died on August 23, 1819. According to a number of authoritative sources, he was also born on August 23, in 1785. Other scholars claim he was born on August 20. Most, however, agree on the year of his birth and on the place of his birth, namely South Kingstown, Rhode Island. His father, Christopher Raymond Perry, had enjoyed a long seafaring career both in the service of his country and on merchant vessels. In 1798 he was commissioned as a captain in the United States Navy. Perry followed in his father's footsteps, and at the age of 14 he entered the navy as a midshipman. He completed his first tour of duty aboard his father's ship, the *General Greene*, during the brief naval conflict with France in 1799. He then served in the Mediterranean from 1802 to 1803 and again from 1804 to 1805, during the war against the Barbary pirates of North Africa. Commissioned as a lieutenant in 1807, Perry spent his next five years carrying out routine peacetime assignments.

Perry's experience and skill qualified him to serve when hostilities between the United States and Great Britain began in 1812. Given command of American naval forces on Lake Erie early in 1813, he worked at his headquarters in Erie, Pennsylvania, throughout the spring and summer of that year. He prepared his small, ten-vessel fleet for combat. By the end of July 1813 he was ready to begin operations. Not until mid-August, however, were his ships able to elude the British blockade under the command of Robert H. Barclay and sail across the shallow Erie bar into the open waters of the lake. On August 12, 1813, Perry sailed his fleet to Put-in-Bay. The bay, located 20 miles north of Sandusky, Ohio, gave him an excellent base from which to monitor enemy ship positions. He remained there almost a month, awaiting the next British move.

The confrontation between American and British forces for control of Lake Erie came on September 10, 1813. At sunrise the Americans sighted the approaching six-vessel squadron commanded by Barclay and immediately began preparations to meet the challenge. When the British attack began at 11:45 a.m., Perry's ten ships were ready. The actual fighting proceeded according to the American commander's strategy. His flagship, the *Lawrence*, engaged Barclay's strongest ship, the *Detroit*. The *Niagara* fought the *Queen Charlotte*, and the remaining smaller vessels sought out their enemy counterparts.

During the ensuing three-hour encounter, the *Lawrence* sustained such extensive damage that Perry had to abandon his flagship for the safety of the *Niagara*. After intense fighting, the British casualties were 41 dead and 94 wounded, while the American casualties were 27 dead and 96 wounded. In the end, the American force was victorious.

Soon after the British surrender, Perry sent the famous message "We have met the enemy and they are ours" to General William Henry Harrison, the American commander in chief of the western army. In light of Perry's accomplishment, his description of the event was modest. Perry's victory at the battle of Lake Erie gave the United States lasting control of the lake and enabled Harrison to move his forces freely.

Perry became a national hero. When news of his victory reached Washington, D.C., President James Madison promoted him to the rank of captain. Shortly thereafter, the United States Congress passed a resolution expressing its gratitude. In addition, state and local governments also praised his victory. The legislatures of Pennsylvania and Georgia voted Perry their thanks, and the cities of Boston and Newport expressed their admiration with a gift of silver plate.

Perry saw action in several other important engagements during the War of 1812. In October 1813 he assisted in Harrison's capture of Detroit and the successful operation against the British and their native allies at the battle of the Thames, in Ontario. Then he turned his fleet over to Jesse Duncan Elliott, his second in command, and re-

turned to the east. In July 1814 the navy placed the 44-gun vessel *Java* under Perry's command. However, the British blockade prevented this ship from leaving Baltimore harbor.

After the war Perry commanded the *Java* during its two-year tour in the Mediterranean. Upon his return, the navy placed him in charge of a small fleet being sent on a diplomatic mission to Venezuela and Buenos Aires, Argentina. This assignment was to be Perry's last. While sailing down the Orinoco River in Venezuela, he contracted yellow fever. He died several days later on August 23, 1819. Perry's crewmen buried him at Port of Spain in Trinidad, but in 1826 his body was returned to the United States.

Great Britain Issues the Proclamation of Rebellion

On August 23, 1775, faced with the growing rebellion in the American colonies that would soon unfold as the American Revolution, King George III of Great Britain issued the Proclamation of Rebellion. The full text of the document is set forth below:

Whereas many of our subjects in divers parts of our Colonies and Plantations in North America, misled by dangerous and ill-designing men, and forgetting the allegiance which they owe to the power that has protected and supported them; after various disorderly acts committed in disturbance of the publick peace, to the obstruction of lawful commerce, and to the oppression of our loyal subjects carrying on the same; have at length proceeded to open and avowed rebellion, by arraying themselves in a hostile manner, to withstand the execution of the law, and traitorously preparing, ordering and levying war against us:

And whereas, there is reason to apprehend that such rebellion hath been much promoted and encouraged by the traitorous correspondence, counsels and comfort of divers wicked and desperate persons within this realm:

To the end therefore, that none of our subjects may neglect or violate their duty through ignorance thereof, or through any doubt of the protection which the law will afford to their loyalty and zeal, we have thought fit, by and with the advice of our Privy Council, to issue our Royal Proclamation, hereby declaring, that not only all our Officers, civil and military, are obliged to exert their utmost endeavours to suppress such rebellion, and to bring the traitors to justice, but that all our subjects of this Realm, and the dominions thereunto belonging, are bound by law to be aiding and assisting in the suppression of such rebellion, and to disclose and make known all traitorous conspiracies and attempts against us our crown and dignity; and we do accordingly strictly charge and command all our Officers, as well civil as military, and all others our obedient and loyal subjects, to use their utmost endeavours to withstand and suppress such rebellion, and to disclose and make known all treasons and traitorous conspiracies which they shall know to be against us, our crown and dignity; and for that purpose, that they transmit to one of our principal Secretaries of State, or other proper officer, due and full information of all persons who shall be found carrying on correspondence with, or in any manner or degree aiding or abetting the persons now in open arms and rebellion against our Government, within any of our Colonies and Plantations in North America, in order to bring to condign punishment the authors, perpetrators, and abetters of such traitorous designs.

Given at our Court at St. James's the twenty-third day of August, one thousand seven hundred and seventy-five, in the fifteenth year of our reign.

GOD save the KING.

August 24

War of 1812: The British Burn Washington, D.C.

In one of the low points of the War of 1812 for the Americans, British forces were able to temporarily seize the national capital of Washington, D.C., on August 24, 1814, and torch such national monuments as the White House in addition to the government buildings on Capitol Hill (see related articles concerning the War of 1812 throughout this book). First Lady Dolley Madison, wife of President James Madison who was out of the city, recorded the impending British sack of the city in a contemporary letter to her sister Anna. She describes how she was forced to abandon the White House, but took the time to save Gilbert Stuart's famous portrait of George Washington, an act of patriotism that has become famous.

My husband left me yesterday morning to join General Winder. He inquired anxiously whether I had courage or firmness to remain in the President's house until his return on the morrow, or succeeding day, and on my assurance that I had no fear but for him, and the success of our army, he left, beseeching me to take care of myself, and of the Cabinet papers, public and private. I have since received two dispatches from him, written with a pencil. The last is alarming, because he desires I should be ready at a moment's warning to enter my carriage, and leave the city; that the enemy seemed stronger than had at first been reported, and it might happen that they would reach the city with the intention of destroying it. I am accordingly ready; I have pressed as many Cabinet papers into trunks as to fill one carriage; our private property must be sacrificed, as it is impossible to procure wagons for its transportation. I am determined not to go myself until I see Mr. Madison safe, so that he can accompany me, as I hear of much hostility towards him. Disaffection stalks around us. My friends and acquaintances are all gone, even Colonel C. with his hundred, who were stationed as a guard in this enclosure. French John (a faithful servant), with his usual activity and resolution, offers to spike the cannon at the gate, and lay a train of powder, which would blow up the British, should they enter the house. To the last proposition I positively object, without being able to make him understand why all advantages in war may not be taken.

Wednesday Morning, twelve o'clock— Since sunrise I have been turning my spyglass in every direction, and watching with unwearied anxiety, hoping to discover the approach of my dear husband and his friends; but, alas! I can descry only groups of military, wandering in all directions, as if there was a lack of arms, or of spirit to fight for their own fireside.

Three o'clock—Will you believe it, my sister? we have had a battle, or skirmish, near Bladensburg, and here I am still, within sound of the cannon! Mr. Madison comes not. May God protect us! Two messengers, covered with dust, come to bid me fly; but here I mean to wait for him . . . At this late hour a wagon has been procured, and I have had it filled with plate and the most valuable portable articles, belonging to the house. Whether it will reach its des-

The Capitol after it was burnt by the British.

tination, the "Bank of Maryland," or fall into the hands of British soldiery, events must determine. Our kind friend, Mr. Carroll, has come to hasten my departure, and in a very bad humor with me, because I insist on waiting until the large picture of General Washington is secured, and it requires to be unscrewed from the wall. This process was found too tedious for these perilous moments; I have ordered the frame to be broken, and the canvas taken out. It is done! and the precious portrait placed in the hands of two gentlemen of New York, for safe keeping. And now, dear sister, I must leave this house, or the retreating army will make me a prisoner in it by filling up the road I am directed to take. When I shall again write to you, or where I shall be tomorrow, I cannot tell!

Another contemporary account, by a British soldier, describes the actual taking of the White House and the city:

Toward morning a violent storm of rain, accompanied with thunder and lightning, came on, which disturbed the rest of all those who were exposed to it. Yet, in spite of the disagreeableness of getting wet, I can not say that I felt disposed to grumble at the interruption, for it appeared that what I had before considered as superlatively sublime still wanted this to render it complete. The flashes of lightning seemed to vie in brilliancy with the flames which burst from the roofs of burning houses, while the thunder drowned the noise of crumbling walls, and was only interrupted by the occasional roar of cannon, and of large depots of gunpowder, as they one by one exploded. . . .

The consternation of the inhabitants was complete, and to them this was a night of terror. So confident had they been of the success of their troops, that few of them had dreamed of quitting their houses, or abandoning the city; nor was it till the fugitives from the battle began to rush it, filling every place as they came with dismay, that the President himself thought of providing for his safety. That gentleman, as I was credibly informed, had gone forth in the morning with the army, and had continued among his troops till the British forces began to make their appearance. Whether the sight of his enemies cooled his courage or not I can not say, but, according to my informer, no sooner was the glittering of our arms discernible than he began to discover that his presence was more wanted in the Senate than with the army; and having ridden through the ranks, and exhorted every man to do his duty, he hurried back to his own house, that he might prepare a feast for the entertainment of his officers, when they should return victorious. For the truth of these details I will not be answerable; but this much I know, that the feast was actually prepared, though, instead of being devoured by American officers, it went to satisfy the less delicate appetites of a party of English soldiers. When the detachment, sent out to destroy Mr. Madison's house, entered his dining parlor, they found a dinner-table spread, and covers laid for forty guests . . .

They sat down to it, therefore, not indeed in the more orderly manner, but with countenances which would not have disgraced a party of aldermen at a civic feast; and having satisfied their appetites with fewer complaints than would have probably escaped their rival gourmands, and partaken pretty freely of the wines, they finished by setting fire to the house which had so liberally entertained them.

But, as I have just observed, this was a night of dismay to the inhabitants of Washington. They were taken completely by surprise; nor could the arrival of the flood be more unexpected to the natives of the antediluvian world, than the arrival of the British army to them. The first impulse of course tempted them to fly, and the streets were in consequence crowded with soldiers and senators, men, women, and children, horses, carriages, and carts loaded with household furniture, all hastening toward a wooden bridge which crosses the Potomac. The confusion thus occasioned was terrible, and the crowd upon the bridge was such as to endanger its giving way. But Mr. Madison, having escaped among the first, was no sooner safe on the opposite bank of the river than he gave orders that the bridge should be broken down; which being obeyed, the rest were obliged to return, and to trust to the clemency of the victors.

In this manner was the night passed by both parties; and at daybreak next morning the light brigade moved into the city, while the reserve fell back to a height about half a mile in the rear. Little, however, now remained to be done, because everything marked out for destruction was already consumed. Of the senate-house, the President's palace, the barracks, the dockyard, etc., nothing could be seen, except heaps of smoking ruins; and even the bridge, a noble structure upward of a mile in length,

was almost wholly demolished. There was, therefore, no further occasion to scatter the troops, and they were accordingly kept together as much as possible on the capitol hill.

Feast of St. Bartholomew

St. Bartholomew, one of the 12 apostles of Jesus Christ, is identified by many scholars with Nathanael (or Nathaniel) in the scriptures. In listing the apostles, the four Gospels all include Bartholomew, whose name is a form of *bar-Tolmai*, meaning "son of Tolmai," or "Ptolemy."

According to St. John's gospel, Nathanael was resting under a fig tree when he first met Jesus. He was so moved by Jesus that he converted on the spot. According to tradition, Bartholomew spent his apostolic life preaching in Ethiopia, Persia, and other parts of the Middle East. His missionary work ultimately took him to Armenia, where he was martyred by being flayed alive and then beheaded.

The saint's name became linked to an infamous event of the 16th century. This was the St. Bartholomew's Day Massacre, which began on August 24, 1572, initiating the fourth in a series of at least seven civil wars fought in France from 1562 to 1598 and often referred to as the Wars of Religion. The troubles began when the Calvinist Protestant Huguenots held their first French national synod in 1559 and organized a church. Some of the French aristocrats became Huguenots, while others adhered to the traditional Roman Catholic faith. Religious and political strife ensued.

When the Huguenot Henry of Navarre (later Henry IV of France) married the Catholic Margaret of Valois, sister of King Charles IX, many important nobles and other persons traveled to Paris for the wedding on August 18, 1572. Catherine de Medici, King Charles's mother and regent, seized this opportunity to strike at the most powerful Huguenots. She ordered the assassination of Admiral Gaspard de Coligny, a preeminent Huguenot leader. When the attempt failed, on August 22, plans were laid for a full-scale massacre of Protestants two days later, at the Feast of St. Bartholomew. In the bloodbath that followed, Coligny and about 3,000 others were slain in Paris, many more in the provinces, for the conflict spread rapidly. Henry of Navarre eluded death by temporarily changing his religion but was a virtual prisoner of the royal court for the next four years, until he could escape. Not surprisingly, the St. Bartholomew's Day massacre led to a resumption of the civil wars, which continued off and on until 1598, when Henry of Navarre (now once more a Catholic, and now on the throne as Henry IV) instituted a policy of religious toleration with the Edict of Nantes. The revocation of this edict by Louis XIV in 1685 caused many Huguenots to emigrate to America, especially those who were not tied to lands in France. The influx of artisans, professionals, and businessmen would benefit the colonies greatly.

August 25

George C. Wallace's Birthday

George Corley Wallace was born on August 25, 1919, in Clio, a rural town in southeastern Alabama. His father was a farmer and his mother was a county health worker. Wallace attended the University of Alabama and received his law degree in 1942. He also married young Lurleen Burns that same year and then joined the United States Army Air Corps in order to serve in World War II. When he was discharged in 1945, Wallace secured employment as an assistant Alabama state attorney general.

In 1946 Wallace successfully ran for a seat in the Alabama House of Representatives. He went on to become a circuit court judge for his home in Barbour County. Wallace was a charismatic figure, a man of short stature but with a feisty temperament that earned him many followers. He was also a firm believer in the traditional southern politics of racial segregation and states' rights. Wallace made his first bid for the governorship of Alabama in 1958 but lost to John Patterson, because Patterson took an even harder stance in favor of segregation than Wallace.

Wallace won the governorship in the 1962 elections. He took office just as the federal courts were beginning to strike down segregation on constitutional grounds and as the federal government was becoming increasingly active in civil rights enforcement. Wallace strongly resisted the federal authorities' actions in forcing the all-white University of Alabama to desegregate, and achieved notoriety by personally blocking the door when two blacks came to enroll. As "the man in the schoolhouse door" who loudly preached "segregation forever," Wallace became a national figure and one of the most popular politicians among whites in the South.

In the 1964 Democratic primaries for the November presidential election, Wallace ran against incumbent President Lyndon B. Johnson for the party's nomination as its candidate and lost. Johnson, a fellow southerner, embraced civil rights and aggressively pursued desegregation throughout the country in general and the South in particular. Wallace, however, managed to hold on to the governorship. When the Alabama legislature refused to enact legislation that would permit him to serve another term, Wallace had his wife Lurleen run in 1966 and she won the office in his stead. Of course, for all intents and purposes he was the real governor. Lurleen died of cancer in 1968, and was succeeded in office by Lieutenant Governor Albert Brewer.

Also in 1968 Wallace decided to run for the presidency as the third-party candidate of the American Independent Party. He received roughly nine percent of the popular vote, a respectable showing for an independent, and actually won five southern states for a total of 46 electoral votes in the final tally. Wallace's candidacy may well have cost Democratic candidate Hubert Humphrey the election by drawing away traditional southern Democrats. Although his campaign was ostensibly a crusade to preserve states' rights, Wallace was, in fact, a magnet for people who opposed increased federal involvement in civil rights matters.

Wallace remarried to Cornelia Snively, a niece of former governor "Big Jim" Folsom, in 1971. In 1972 he ran for the presidency again, returning to the Democratic Party and embarking on a successful campaign in the party primaries. Wallace was the leading candidate when on May 15, 1972, Arthur H. Bremer, a white laborer from Milwaukee, shot him five times during a visit to a shopping center in Laurel, Maryland, to meet voters in that state's primaries. Wallace survived, but was partially paralyzed because one of the bullets grazed his spine. He spent the rest of his life in a wheelchair. Despite several victories in the state primaries, he lost the 1972 campaign. He ran again in the Democratic primaries in 1976, but lost to Jimmy Carter in the early contests and dropped out. Carter went on to win the nomination.

In 1978 Wallace divorced Cornelia, and in 1979 he retired from politics. In 1981 he remarried to singer Lisa Taylor. Rejuvenated by the marriage (although it ended in divorce), he reentered politics and he was able to revive his career. Wallace renounced segregation, successfully courted African American voters, and defeated Lieutenant Governor George McMillan in the 1982 gubernatorial primaries to take the Democratic nomination and eventually win the governorship. He appointed several African Americans to high-level positions in his administration, and managed to partially rehabilitate his image. However, poor health forced Wallace to return to retirement in 1986. He died on September 13, 1998, in Montgomery, Alabama, of a heart attack at the age of 79.

August 26

Nineteenth Amendment Proclaimed Ratified

On August 26, 1920, Secretary of State Bainbridge Colby proclaimed the 19th Amendment to the United States Constitution in effect after its adoption by three-fourths (36) of the 48 states. Supporters of women's rights rejoiced in this victory after 72 years of organized effort. The wording of the amendment is simple and direct: "The right of citizens of the United States to vote shall not be denied or abridged by the United States or by any State on account of sex." Thus, in November 1920—for the first time in the history of the United States—women throughout the country were able to vote in a presidential election.

The cause of women's suffrage had been pressed by isolated reformers since colonial days. A short-lived "first" came about when the state constitution adopted by New Jersey on July 2, 1776, granted (or seemed to grant) women the right to vote. What the document actually said was that "all Inhabitants" of the colony who had reached the age of majority and fulfilled certain monetary and residency requirements were entitled to vote. The legislature did away with this convenient and perhaps intentional vagueness by providing in the Act of 1807 that "no person shall vote in any state or county election for officers in the government of the United States or of this state unless such person be a free, white male citizen."

The organized campaign for women's suffrage in the United States commenced with Elizabeth Cady Stanton and Lucretia Mott (see related articles throughout this book), who with certain other leaders called the Woman's Rights Convention at Seneca Falls, New York, in 1848. Securing the right to vote became a pressing issue after the Civil War, when women renewed their drive. Rights organizations were formed, such as the National Woman Suffrage Association led by Susan B. Anthony and Elizabeth Cady Stanton, and the American Woman Suffrage Association led by Lucy Stone, Henry Ward Beecher, and others. Annual conventions became a fixed part of their program.

It was in the Wyoming Territory that women first won the right to vote in 1869, largely as a result of Esther Morris's efforts. The women of Utah

Library of Congress

A suffrage march in Washington, D.C.

also received the right to vote in 1869, although Congress temporarily rescinded that right in 1887. When Utah entered the Union in 1896, however, it was with women's suffrage. Women were given the right to vote in Colorado in 1893 and in Idaho in 1896. Later, referendums extended voting rights to women in Washington State (1910) and California (1911). Kansas, Oregon, and Arizona followed suit in 1912, as did Nevada and Montana in 1914. East of the Mississippi, only Illinois gave women the right to vote (in 1913), but only in presidential elections. Finally, New York, which had voted down a suffrage referendum in 1915, passed the measure in 1917.

Work was also going on toward a federal amendment to guarantee the right to vote for all women in the nation. After 1913 the National American Woman Suffrage Association, long active in this endeavor, was joined in the effort by the National Woman's Party (originally known as the Congressional Union), which under the leadership of Alice Paul played a significant role in achieving passage of the amendment.

Their victory, however, did not come easily. The Anthony Woman Suffrage Amendment, as it was known, was first introduced in Congress in its final form in 1878. It was reintroduced in every succeeding Congress, except for the 46th Congress, until 1919, and supporting presentations were patiently repeated before the congressional hearings that were held annually on the measure. The important contributions of women in industry and war during World War I helped create a climate favorable to their enfranchisement on a national level. Ultimately, the support of President Woodrow Wilson was added to the congressional lobbying, state referendum campaigns, picketing, hunger strikes, and other forms of political pressure that marked the drive for a federal amendment. Congress finally passed the amendment and sent it to the states on June 4, 1919.

Then began the 14-month-long campaign that was necessary before the amendment received ratification by three-fourths of the states. That achievement was another closely won contest, with Tennessee as the 36th state granting approval by the narrow margin of one vote in the state legislature. Tennessee's approval, on August 18, 1920, was shortly followed by Secretary Colby's proclamation of the 19th Amendment on August 26, 1920.

France Adopts the Declaration of the Rights of Man

France provided invaluable financial and military assistance to the Americans during the American Revolution. The French were also strongly influenced by the ideals of the American Revolution as expressed in the Declaration of Independence (1776) and the Constitution of the United States (1787). When the French Revolution erupted and King Louis XVI was forced to surrender his autocratic powers, the National Assembly of France adopted the historic Declaration of the Rights of Man on August 26, 1789. It was modeled after the Constitution, and includes such familiar American liberties as freedom of speech and equal protection under the law. Thus, it represents the beginning of the spread of American democratic ideals around the world in the centuries to follow.

Women's Equality Day

August 26, the anniversary of the ratification of the 19th Amendment in 1920, is also celebrated as Women's Equality Day. It was first officially designated as such in 1973 by President Richard M. Nixon. Women's Equality Day also honors the progress in women's rights made over the course of American history. When the present Constitutional system of government first came into being, women were distinctly second-class citizens. For example, Rebekah S. Greathouse, a former assistant United States attorney for the District of Columbia, once summed up the situation of married women in 1789 (when George Washington became the first president of the United States) as follows:

A married woman could not contract for the spending of her own money, even though it had been given to her by her parents or earned by her own labor. She owned no personal property, not even the clothes she wore, nor the jewels her husband gave her. She could not sue in the courts for injury to her person. She could not make a will. Her husband could chastise her or restrain her of her liberty. In short, she was her husband's slave, dependent upon his whims, without appeal to any court, and penniless. . . . She had no right to the control or even the society of her own children, as her husband could transfer the guardianship of them to a third person by deed or will. No woman could vote or hold office, and the disabilities of women when married were advanced as reasons for keeping all women out of various professions.

Library of Congress

Women's Rights rally on the steps of the Capitol.

August 27

Lyndon B. Johnson's Birthday

U.S. Senate Historical Office

Lyndon B. Johnson

Lyndon Baines Johnson, the 36th president of the United States, was the oldest of the five children of Samuel Ealy Johnson Jr. and Rebekah Baines Johnson. He was born on August 27, 1908, at his parents' farm near Stonewall, Texas. When he was five years old, his family moved to Johnson City, a town founded in the 1850s by his paternal grandfather, Samuel Ealy Johnson Sr. There the future president attended public schools. In 1924 he was one of seven members of the graduating class of the Johnson City High School.

Initially uninterested in further study, Johnson spent the next few years wandering and working at various jobs. His travels took him as far west as California, but his love for Texas eventually brought him home. In February 1927 he enrolled in Southwest Texas State Teachers College in San Marcos, Texas.

To earn his tuition, Johnson worked as a janitor, as secretary to the president of the college, and as an elementary school teacher. An energetic young man, he also participated in several extracurricular activities. He was a debater, the editor of the school newspaper, and the founder of a political group on the San Marcos campus. However, neither his outside jobs nor his extracurricular interests distracted Johnson from his studies of history and political science, and in August 1930 he received his B.S. degree.

Following graduation, Johnson accepted a post as a debate teacher in a Houston high school, but politics soon drew his attention away from academia. In 1931 he campaigned on behalf of Richard M. Kleberg, a candidate for the United States House of Representatives, and when Kleberg won the election, he rewarded Johnson by selecting him to be his secretary. Johnson adjusted quickly to life in Washington, D.C. Renewing his acquaintance with Texas representative Sam Rayburn, a friend of his father's (who later served as speaker of the House), he learned much about politics in the nation's capital. In 1933 he was elected speaker of the organization of congressional secretaries known as Little Congress.

In 1935 President Franklin D. Roosevelt appointed Johnson the Texas director of the National Youth Administration. Johnson's position in this New Deal agency gave him an opportunity to help approximately 30,000 young Texans to remain in school or to find jobs. Many of them became loyal supporters. In 1937 Johnson competed against nine other candidates for the seat in Texas's 10th Congressional District, which had been vacated by the death of its incumbent. Running on a New Deal platform that included support for Roosevelt's controversial plan for reorganizing the Supreme Court, Johnson won the April election. On the recommendation of President Roosevelt himself, the freshman member of the House of Representatives was appointed to the House Committee on Naval Affairs.

Johnson was reelected to the House in every election between 1938 and 1948. However, on December 9, 1941, two days after the Japanese attack on Pearl Harbor, he temporarily abandoned his congressional duties and became the first member of Congress to enter active service in the nation's armed forces. Commissioned a lieutenant commander in the United States Navy, he was stationed in the South Pacific and was awarded the Silver Star for bravery before July 1942, when President Roosevelt ordered all members of Congress to return to their posts in the nation's capital.

Although Johnson enjoyed considerable influence in the House and sat on such important committees as the House Armed Services Committee and the Joint Atomic Energy Committee, he aspired to be in the Senate. In 1948 he won election to the Senate, where his power and influence increased rapidly. In 1951 and 1952 he served as the majority whip, or deputy leader, of the Democratic Party in the Senate. In 1953, at the age of 44, he was elected majority leader. As the Democratic leader in the Senate, he also automatically assumed chairmanship of the Senate Democratic Conference, the Democratic Policy Committee,

and the Democratic Steering Committee. These positions gave him considerable control over such vital matters as legislative schedules and committee assignments.

Between 1955 and 1961 Johnson served as the Senate majority leader. The youngest man in history to hold this post, the 46-year-old Texan was one of the most powerful men in the federal government. By means of political maneuvering, he helped win congressional approval of measures that included the 1957 and 1960 civil rights bills, the National Defense Education Act, extension of social security coverage, and liberal appropriations for defense, foreign aid, and the national space program. However, his stands on issues did not always please all the factions of the Democratic Party. Many liberals, for example, considered him too moderate on civil rights and too favorable to the interests of the South. Johnson nevertheless managed to weather such criticism, and until he left the Senate in January 1961 he continued to exercise extraordinary influence in that body.

In 1960 Johnson sought the Democratic presidential nomination, but the party's convention selected John F. Kennedy instead. The day after receiving the nomination, Kennedy asked Johnson to be his running mate, and much to the surprise of many political observers Johnson accepted. Johnson campaigned energetically throughout the fall of 1960. His presence on the ticket undoubtedly won many southern votes for the Democrats, and indeed may have been the decisive factor in the Democrats' victory over the Republican candidates, Richard M. Nixon and Henry Cabot Lodge, in November of 1960.

As vice president, Johnson probably exercised considerably less power than he had as Senate majority leader, and many pundits were quick to remark on his loss of influence. Then, on November 22, 1963, an assassin's bullet killed President Kennedy in Dallas, Texas. Within a half hour of Kennedy's death, Johnson stood before his wife, Mrs. Kennedy, and about 25 other people on the presidential jet Air Force One at Love Field in Dallas and took the oath of office as president of the United States.

During the days immediately following the assassination of Kennedy, the stunned nation mourned its loss. Then, five days after the tragedy in Dallas, the new president addressed a joint session of Congress. His speech was eloquent:

> All I have I would have given gladly not to be standing here today. . . .
>
> This nation has experienced a profound shock and in this critical moment it is our duty, yours and mine, as the Government of the United States to do away with uncer-

tainty and doubt and delays and to show that we are capable of decisive action; that from the brutal loss of our leader we will derive not weakness but strength; that we can and will act, and act now. . . .

This is our challenge: not to hesitate, not to pause, not to turn about and linger over this evil moment, but to continue on our course so that we may fulfill the destiny that history has set for us.

Then Johnson called on Congress to enact the extensive legislative program, including the civil rights bill and the tax reduction bill, that Kennedy had advocated. The first months of the Johnson administration were a time of exceptional legislative activity. Bills that had been stalled in Congress during the Kennedy years were pushed forward by the new president. Before the 88th Congress adjourned in October 1964, it approved an $11.5 billion tax cut and a civil rights bill that protected voting rights and outlawed discrimination in employment and public accommodations. However, not all 1964 legislation stemmed from purely Kennedy-era initiatives. In 1964 Johnson also called upon the nation to begin a "war on poverty," and in August of that year Congress responded by appropriating $947.5 million for the establishment of a federal Office of Economic Opportunity and an extensive antipoverty program.

In August 1964 the Democratic National Convention unanimously nominated Johnson as its presidential candidate and chose Senator Hubert H. Humphrey as his running mate. The Republicans selected two conservative members of their party, Senator Barry Goldwater and Representative William E. Miller, as their candidates. The November 1964 election was a landslide victory for the Democrats, and Johnson defeated his Republican rival by an unprecedented 16 million votes.

In his State of the Union Message on January 4, 1965, Johnson outlined his plan for a "Great Society." His program emphasized the need for adequate health care for the aged, the preservation of natural resources, the elimination of poverty, increased aid to education, and the establishment of a cabinet-level Department of Housing and Urban Development. In the months that followed, the large Democratic majorities that controlled both houses of Congress gave Johnson enough votes to put a number of Great Society measures into effect. Most notably, Congress passed the Medicare bill, which financed medical insurance through social security for those over 65, and the Voting Rights Act, which authorized the attorney general to send federal registrars to enroll black voters in states violating their civil rights.

Johnson's conduct of foreign policy, however, did not prove to be as successful as his handling of domestic affairs. His sending of American troops into the Dominican Republic in 1965, in an effort to prevent a communist takeover of that nation, aroused opposition in many quarters. Even more important, his increasing support of the government of South Vietnam against the opposition of communist North Vietnam and its guerrilla allies became a major source of concern to many American citizens. This was especially true after February 1965, when he authorized bombing attacks against North Vietnam, and after the sharp increase in the number of American troops in Vietnam that began the same year. These steps followed congressional approval of the Gulf of Tonkin Resolution on August 7, 1964, which some commentators have characterized as a blank check for escalation.

Despite Johnson's continued efforts to build a Great Society, after 1965 the vast expenditures necessary to support the war effort in Vietnam sapped the nation's resources. Appropriations for domestic programs suffered, while the American people became increasingly divided over Vietnam. A sizable portion of the citizenry opposed the man who had so deeply involved the nation in a conflict that seemed morally dubious and incapable of solution by a clear-cut victory. Large-scale demonstrations against the war took place in many cities and on college campuses. Public opinion polls showed that the president was steadily losing the confidence of the people.

On March 31, 1968, President Johnson addressed the nation over television and radio. To end the fighting in Vietnam, he announced a new peace initiative. He ordered an end to the American bombing of most of North Vietnam and invited the Hanoi government to join in a "series of mutual moves toward peace." Then Johnson made a dramatic statement:

What we won when all of our people united . . . must not now be lost in suspicion and distrust. . . . I have concluded that I should not permit the Presidency to become involved in the partisan divisions that are developing in this political year.

Accordingly, I shall not seek, and I will not accept, the nomination of my party for another term as your President.

The 1968 Democratic convention nominated Hubert H. Humphrey for president and Senator Edmund S. Muskie as his running mate. The Republicans nominated former vice president Richard M. Nixon and Maryland governor Spiro T. Agnew. Nixon, with only 43 percent of the popular vote, garnered 302 electoral votes as compared with the 191 electoral votes for Humphrey and the 45 of third-party candidate George C. Wallace.

After more than five years as president, Johnson left office in January 1969. Following the inauguration of President Nixon, Johnson and his wife, "Lady Bird" Johnson, returned to their 600-acre ranch near Johnson City, Texas. He died at the ranch on January 22, 1973, of a coronary thrombosis.

Kellogg-Briand Pact "To Outlaw War" Signed

The Kellogg-Briand Pact of 1928, named after United States secretary of state Frank B. Kellogg and French foreign minister Aristide Briand, was signed on August 27, 1928, by 15 nations including the United States in Paris, France. Its formal title was the Treaty for the Renunciation of War, and as the title suggests its purpose was to abolish war as a means of implementing national policy among the major powers in favor of peaceful negotiation or arbitration. The treaty was ratified by the United States Senate on January 16, 1929. It was of course completely unsuccessful in abolishing war, since there was no mechanism for enforcing its provisions.

One view of the historical significance of the Kellogg-Briand Pact is that it shows how paralyzed the major powers were by pacifism after World War I, making them vulnerable to totalitarian aggression. Another view is that, even if unsuccessful in preventing the outbreak of World War II, the pact helped establish the principle of international law that war was no longer an ordinary and acceptable means of resolving disputes.

A copy of the pact is set forth below [prefatory material deleted]:

ARTICLE I. The High Contracting Parties solemnly declare in the names of their respective peoples that they condemn recourse to war for the solution of international controversies, and renounce it, as an instrument of national policy in their relations with one another.

ARTICLE II. The High Contracting Parties agree that the settlement or solution of all disputes or conflicts of whatever nature or of whatever origin they may be, which may arise among them, shall never be sought except by pacific means.

ARTICLE III. The present Treaty shall be ratified by the High Contracting Parties named in the Preamble in accordance with their respective constitutional requirements, and shall take effect as between them as soon as all their several instru-ments of ratification shall have been deposited at Washington.

This Treaty shall, when it has come into effect as prescribed in the preceding paragraph, remain open as long as may be necessary for adherence by all the other Powers of the world. Every instrument evidencing the adherence of a Power shall be deposited at Washington and the Treaty shall immediately upon such deposit become effective as between the Power thus adhering and the other Powers [which are] parties hereto.

It shall be the duty of the Government of the United States to furnish each Government named in the Preamble and every Government subsequently adhering to this Treaty with a certified copy of the Treaty and of every instrument of ratification or adherence. It shall also be the duty of the Government of the United States telegraphically to notify such Governments immediately upon the deposit with it of each instrument of ratification or adherence.

IN FAITH WHEREOF the respective Plenipotentiaries have signed this Treaty in the French and English languages both texts having equal force, and hereunto affix their seals.

August 28

Commercial Radio Broadcasting Begins

The first commercial radio broadcast in history took place in New York City on August 28, 1922, when station WEAF ran an advertisement by the Queensboro Realty Corporation promoting a new apartment complex in the Queens area of New York City.

The roots of radio go back to the 19th century when German scientist Heinrich Hertz and Italian scientist Guglielmo Marconi did the pioneering research with electromagnetic waves that made wireless radio communications possible. In 1920 Frank Conrad, an engineer with the Westinghouse Electrical and Manufacturing Company, started the first radio station: KDKA in Pittsburgh, Pennsylvania. With the introduction of advertising, radio became a profitable commercial venture, and the number of stations across the country soared. By the 1930s, the number of radio stations was large enough so that Orson Wells's famous *War of the Worlds* October 30, 1938, broadcast caused national panic. Radio was also used for more positive purposes, like President Franklin D. Roosevelt's famous "fireside chats" to reassure the nation during the depths of the Great Depression.

In the 1950s the introduction of television began to have a competitive impact on radio broadcasting. By the 1960 presidential elections, television was widespread enough that a televised debate helped Democrat John F. Kennedy defeat Republican Richard M. Nixon. People who listened to the debate on radio generally considered Nixon to be the victor, but television viewers were influenced by the visual impact of the youthful, poised Kennedy and generally considered him the winner. Without the sizable television viewing audience, it is possible that Kennedy could have lost the election.

Despite television, however, commercial radio broadcasting has been able to thrive by adapting to the times. It is not practical to view television in an automobile, but most vehicles have radios; as a result, many radio stations have prospered by catering to the music, news, and other preferences of the driving public. Other radio stations have certain discussion formats, known as talk radio, generally involving popular disc jockeys who both play music and entertain the listener with humorous commentary. By the late 1990s a new phenomenon known as "shock jocks" became increasingly widespread, as radio personalities, such as Howard Stern and Don Imus, increased their ratings by discussing controversial topics on the air, including scandalous sexual matters and extremist politics. Audience participation by telephone added to the popularity of these shows.

Feast of St. Augustine

Saint Augustine of Hippo, one of the greatest figures of the Christian Church, was born on November 13, 354, at Tagaste in Numidia, later Souk-Ahras in Algeria. His father Patricius was an official of the city and a non-Christian. His mother Monica (later canonized) was a devout Christian.

After Augustine finished his literary studies in Tagaste and in Madaura, a nearby town, his father wanted him to continue his education in the great city of Carthage, an ambition that even wealthier fathers of the time rarely held for their sons. As a teenager, Augustine lived in idleness at home while his father accumulated enough money to send him away to study. It was during this period that Augustine began the dissolute life that he was to continue for many years and that he was to condemn so heartily in his *Confessions*, one of the most famous of his writings.

While studying and later teaching rhetoric in Carthage, Augustine put aside all his mother had taught him about Christianity. He sampled many pagan philosophies and finally became a strong advocate of Manichaeanism, a dualistic religion founded by a Persian a century before Augustine's birth. The persuasive Augustine, who had fulfilled his teachers' wishes for him to "excel in the tongue science," made many converts to Manichaeanism before he himself began to have strong doubts about it.

Augustine returned to Tagaste and continued teaching there until he was about 29. He then went to Rome and on to Milan, where he arrived in 384 and began to teach rhetoric. There he became very impressed with the ideas of an eminent Christian intellectual: Ambrose, the bishop of Milan. A Roman born to senatorial aristocracy, Ambrose (who was later canonized) had been a provincial governor with Milan as his headquarters before becoming bishop of that city. During most of his episcopate, Milan was also the capital of the Western Roman Empire.

After the death of Patricius, Monica traveled to Italy to be with her son, always praying for his conversion. After several years of intellectual and emotional conflict within himself and with his educated friends, Augustine decided to become a Christian. He was baptized by Ambrose on Easter Eve in 387. Determined to devote his life to God, Augustine, with his mother and his friend Alypius, returned to North Africa. Monica died during the voyage home.

When Augustine returned to Africa, Valerius, bishop of Hippo (later Bone in Algeria), persuaded him to become a priest. Augustine was ordained in 391, was consecrated bishop in 395, and became bishop of Hippo in 396 after the death of Valerius. As bishop, Augustine made many enduring contributions to the church during the next 35 years. He lived a monastic life with his clergy and strongly encouraged the formation of religious communities. His letters and sermons outlined the basis of the religious and monastic life, emphasizing charity as the foundation for perfection. From his writings evolved the Augustinian rule, now followed by many groups of friars, monks, and nuns.

When Rome was invaded by the Vandals in 410, Christianity was blamed for the fall of the Western Roman Empire. Because of the Christians, their enemies claimed, the gods had been neglected and as a consequence had deserted the Roman Empire. In defense of the church, Augustine wrote *The City of God*, where he asserted that calamity in this world is not due to the neglect of gods. He examined the history and institutions of pagan Rome, distinguished between the City of

God and the worldly city, and discussed their respective origins and goals.

The Vandals, spreading out from Rome, were at the gates of Hippo when Augustine died on August 28, 430. Augustine left a priceless legacy of Christian thought in 113 books and treatises, and more than 200 letters and 500 sermons. St. Augustine, Florida, the oldest city in the United States, was named in honor of this saint.

August 29

Oliver Wendell Holmes's Birthday

Oliver Wendell Holmes, the father of the Supreme Court justice of the same name, was born in Cambridge, Massachusetts, on August 29, 1809. It was the same year that his father, the minister Abiel Holmes, published a historical work entitled *The Annals of America*. Oliver's mother, Sarah Wendell Holmes, was the daughter of the prosperous Oliver Wendell. She was the second wife of Abiel Holmes, who was a childless widower before his remarriage.

As a youngster, Oliver Wendell Holmes received his education at local schools and then for a year at the Phillips Academy in Andover, Massachusetts. He subsequently entered Harvard in 1825, where his classmates elected him class poet. Just a month before Holmes graduated from Harvard, a two-year battle between Calvinists and Unitarians came to a head and his father was ousted from his Cambridge pulpit. Holmes blamed the Calvinists for this bitter blow to his father's pride and career, and for the rest of his life he rarely missed an opportunity to attack Calvinist clergy and doctrines.

After receiving his undergraduate degree, Holmes went on to study law at Harvard. Finding the studies dull (he continued in law for only one year), he turned more and more to writing verse, an avocation that he followed for the rest of his life. In 1830 he switched to the study of medicine, and in that same year published what is perhaps his most famous poem: "Old Ironsides," a tribute to the American frigate USS *Constitution*, which won an important victory in its encounter with the British frigate HMS *Guerrière* during the War of 1812. Holmes's poem stirred the nation to protest this sending of the famous ship to the scrap heap.

Although he was working hard at his medical studies, in 1831 Holmes was still able to publish "The Last Leaf," another poem that gained great popularity. He decided to pursue his medical studies in Paris for an additional two years, but found no time for poetry there. Holmes became

influenced by a group of French clinicians who were skeptical about the effectiveness of drugs then widely prescribed. He was to become a lifelong crusader against the use of unscientific remedies.

Returning from France in December 1835, Holmes received his degree from Harvard. Although he was thus qualified to practice medicine, his real preference was for teaching, and for ten years he combined the two. In 1838 Holmes and other physicians founded the Tremont Medical School, where he taught even while carrying on his private practice and serving for two years (1838–1840) as professor of anatomy at Dartmouth College in Hanover, New Hampshire.

In 1840 Holmes married Amelia Lee Jackson, whose father, Charles Jackson, was a justice of the Supreme Judicial Court of Massachusetts. They had three children. Their first-born, Oliver Wendell Holmes Jr., became known as the Great Dissenter while serving as an associate justice of the United States Supreme Court. His birth in 1841 was followed by that of a sister, Amelia, in 1843, and a brother, Edward, in 1846.

The senior Holmes was offered the teaching post he really wanted in 1847, and for the next 35 years until his retirement in 1882, he was the Parkman professor of anatomy and physiology at Harvard. He encouraged his students to practice medicine on the basis of scientifically proven treatments. Among other things, he introduced the use of the microscope in his classroom. While no original medical discoveries are attributed to Holmes, he lent his prestige and talents to the support of many worthwhile causes and encouraged original research and good methods of practice among American doctors.

He was awarded the Boylston prize in 1836 for his first medical essay "Direct Exploration," which was a convincing argument for the more extensive and frequent use of the stethoscope, an instrument that was then largely ignored in American medicine. His most controversial medical essay, "The Contagiousness of Puerperal Fever" in 1843, indicated that the "childbed fever," which caused the deaths of many women, was transmitted from patient to patient by obstetricians. Four years later similar conclusions were published by a young Hungarian physician named Ignaz Semmelweis, who is credited by medical historians with this important discovery. However, Semmelweis— ridiculed for publishing his theory and for attempting to have doctors wash their hands before attending women in labor—fled Vienna and committed suicide before his theory was accepted. Holmes, meanwhile, was able to withstand the criticism and in 1855 he reprinted his original essay with an eloquent appeal to American doctors to acknowledge the facts. Holmes's other medical writings include the books *Homeopathy and Its Kindred Delusions* (1842) and *Currents and Counter Currents in Medical Science* (1860).

Holmes's reputation as a man of letters soon outstripped his reputation as a man of science. His first volume of verses, *Poems*, was published in 1836. Ralph Waldo Emerson noted that Holmes "could always write or speak to order; partly from the abundance of the stream, which can indifferently fill any provided channel." During the 1840s Holmes became a popular lecturer, regaling the public with his witty observations on almost any subject. The British author William Makepeace Thackeray, after a visit to the United States, declared Holmes to be the best thing he had seen in America.

Holmes's popularity was such that in 1857, when James Russell Lowell was asked to become the editor of a new magazine founded by literary Bostonians, he accepted on the condition that Holmes would be a regular contributor. Holmes not only contributed to the magazine, but gave it its name: the *Atlantic Monthly*, which is still in publication. Holmes died in Boston, at the age of 85, on October 7, 1894. He was elected to the Hall of Fame for Great Americans in 1910.

The Articles of Confederation of the United Colonies of New England

On August 29, 1643, the Articles of Confederation of the United Colonies of New England were finalized "between the Plantations under the Government of the Massachusetts, the Plantations under the Government of New Plymouth, the Plantations under the Government of Connecticut, and the Government of New Haven with the Plantations in Combination therewith." This so-called New England Confederation was a loose union of the British colonies in order to deal with common issues, such as boundary disputes, defense, and relations with the Native American tribes at the time when the mother country seemed preoccupied with European affairs. This regional confederation lasted for over 40 years, and was the first comprehensive attempt at self-government by the American colonies. It came to an end in 1686 when Great Britain established the Dominion of New England, a more centralized form of colonial government with less autonomy for the colonists. Nevertheless, the New England Articles of Confederation set an important precedent in colonial self-government and constituted a step on the path toward independence.

August 30

Huey P. Long's Birthday

Huey Pierce Long was born on August 30, 1893, near Winnfield in Winn Parish, Louisiana. Despite his family's financial difficulties, Long was able to get an education, and he eventually entered Tulane University Law School in 1914. He finished law school in only seven months, and in 1915 was admitted to the bar after a special bar examination. Long first set up his law practice in Winnfield, and shortly thereafter relocated to Shreveport, Louisiana.

In 1918 Long won appointment as the state railroad commissioner, the only state office from which he was not excluded by a minimum age requirement. In this capacity, and later in 1921 as public service commissioner (when the Railroad Commission became the Public Service Commission), he began his long crusade against privately owned public utilities. He succeeded in preventing streetcar fare increases in Shreveport, in reducing telephone rates, and in forcing pipelines to act as common carriers. Long also successfully defended these measures in court when they were challenged.

In 1924, during his service as chairman of the Public Service Commission, Long ran for governor. Although he won much support from the rural parts of the state, Long lost New Orleans and was defeated. Four years later, however, he was elected governor by a large plurality. There were allegations about Long's alleged misconduct and misappropriation of state funds, and some legislators unsuccessfully attempted to impeach him. While in office, one of his major goals was to bring the powerful and undertaxed petroleum industry in the state under control.

Running for the United States Senate in 1930, Long took his case to the people. He blamed the impeachment attack on the Standard Oil Company, one of his favorite targets. Long was elected by a majority of 38,000. With this victory, Long also entrenched himself in Louisiana by establishing a strong political machine. Unwilling to give up the governorship to the politically hostile lieutenant governor, Paul Cyr, Long refused to relinquish his seat. Not until January 1932, when a candidate that he approved of was elected, did Long take his seat in the United States Senate.

As governor, Long made numerous public improvements by passing a free schoolbook law, expanding the facilities of Louisiana State University, and providing a $30 million highway fund to build new roads. He also funded the construction of a new capitol building at Baton Rouge, the state capital. Thirty-four stories high, it stood 450 feet tall and contained 30 varieties of marble.

As senator, Long (nicknamed by himself the Kingfish) seemed to many Americans a clown. His stand on the redistribution of wealth was considered extreme, and though as a Democrat he supported Franklin Delano Roosevelt for president in 1932, by August 1933 Long was in open rebellion against the administration. Faced with domestic political opposition in Louisiana, Long responded by having the Louisiana legislature during 1934–1935 reorganize the state government, creating a virtual dictatorship. By the end of 1935 Long had ended local government in Louisiana and obtained direct control over the appointment of the militia, the judiciary, the police, firemen, schoolteachers, election officials, and tax assessors. He exercised this control over the state while simultaneously continuing to serve in the Senate.

Long's strength in his own state, plus the support generated by his Share-Our-Wealth Society (organized in 1934), which promised a minimum income for every American family, made him a power to be reckoned with as a potential presidential candidate in 1936. Meanwhile, he found the time to write two books, *Every Man a King* (1933) and (optimistically) *My First Days in the White House* (1935).

However, on September 8, 1935, as Long was leaving the state capitol where the Louisiana legislature was in special session, he was shot by Carl A. Weiss, the son-in-law of a political enemy. Weiss was killed on the spot by Long's bodyguards, and Long died two days later on September 10. Whatever his shortcomings, Long was revered by the rural people of Louisiana, and his political career marked the beginning of a Long family dynasty in Louisiana politics. Among his successors in politics were his son Russell B. Long, also a United States senator; a brother Earl who was elected governor three times; and two cousins who were elected to Congress.

Gabriel Prosser's Slave Revolt

On August 30, 1800, an African American slave named Gabriel Prosser led an unsuccessful slave revolt in Richmond, Virginia. Ruthlessly crushed, it became a symbol of the struggle for freedom in the decades to follow before the dream of emancipation would be realized during the Civil War in the 1860s.

Prosser was born sometime in 1776, though the exact date is not certain, on a plantation owned by Thomas Henry Prosser's family in Henrico County, Virginia, not far from Richmond. He received some education in his youth, a rare occurrence for a slave, and was also trained as a blacksmith. This valuable skill gave him the opportunity to travel beyond the Prosser plantation, since like many other such slaves he was hired out by his master for various jobs. He and his fellow skilled slaves suffered under many unfair restrictions and were permitted to retain only a small portion of the payment for their labors, but nevertheless got the chance to see the world beyond their own plantations and to meet each other. Prosser and some other such "privileged" slaves began to plot a rebellion, inspired in part by the example of Haiti where African slaves successfully overthrew their white masters and established their own independent nation.

In 1800 Prosser and his cohorts decided to seize a military arsenal in Richmond. They enlisted other slaves in their cause, planning to kill all the whites after an assault on the city on August 30. Prosser also hoped to capture Governor James Monroe of Virginia, later president of the United States. However, news of the plot was leaked to the authorities, and the state militia was mustered. When roughly 1,000 slaves gathered on August 30 as planned, they also had to contend with massive unexpected rainstorms that washed away a bridge on their route to Richmond. Upon arriving, the slaves were dispersed by the militia, which captured and executed several dozen ringleaders.

Prosser, however, was able to elude the authorities for a while. He traveled down the Chickahominy River looking for a means of escape. Governor Monroe offered a $300 reward, a substantial amount for the times, and on September 24, 1800, Prosser was eventually found and captured on a ship in the port of Norfolk. On October 10, 1800, he was executed by hanging in the center of Richmond.

August 31

James Coburn's Birthday

The famous actor James Coburn Jr. was born on August 31, 1928, in Laurel, Nebraska. His father James Coburn Sr. owned an automobile repair shop that went out of business during the Great Depression. Despite the family's financial problems, however, Coburn was able to study acting at Los Angeles City College and drama at the University of Southern California. He made his acting debut in New York City in a stage performance of *Billy Budd*.

Coburn entered the film industry in 1959, first appearing in a variety of minor supporting roles as a gunfighter in westerns. Then, he was cast in such popular movies as *The Magnificent Seven* (1960), *Hell Is for Heroes* (1962), *The Great Escape* (1963), and *Major Dundee* (1965). It was the 1966 release of the spy movie *Our Man Flint*, however, that helped to make him a superstar. Even though it was clearly an attempt to play off the popularity of the James Bond movies and other secret agent thrillers of the time, *Our Man Flint* was a box-office hit. A sequel, *In Like Flint*, followed in 1967.

Coburn has enjoyed a successful acting career ever since. Some of his most noteworthy movies include *Pat Garrett and Billy the Kid* (1973), *Midway* (1976), *Cross of Iron* (1977), *Sins of the Father* (1985), *Maverick* (1994), *The Avenging Angel* (1995), and *Eraser* (1996). His supporting role in the film *Affliction* (1998) earned Coburn his first Academy Award. He has also established several production companies and has done some directing.

The Charleston Earthquake

One of the most disastrous earthquakes ever experienced east of the Mississippi River occurred late on August 31, 1886. The epicenter was 15 miles northwest of Charleston, South Carolina, where at least three-fourths of the buildings were wrecked or badly damaged. Roughly 100 people were killed in the entire affected area, including over 40 in Charleston itself. The shock was felt as far away as Bermuda, Cuba, and Toronto, Canada.

In the Charleston area, the quake opened deep cracks in the ground, which emitted clouds of sulfurous gas. Falling buildings were the principal cause of death. Many of the victims were people who, after the first tremors, rushed out into the city streets expecting to see the end of the world. They were then exposed to a rain of debris as subsequent shocks brought down walls and roofs.

On December 2, 1977, residents of the Charleston area heard booming sounds, which were believed to be similar to the sounds that had preceded the 1886 quake. The two explosion-like sounds were strong enough to rattle windows. On December 15 two mild quakes in Charleston were preceded by five more booms. On December 20 there were yet two more booms. Records of similar mysterious booms go back for centuries, but the exact cause is as of yet unknown.

September

September is the ninth month of the Gregorian, or New Style, calendar used today and numbers 30 days. As can be seen from its name, derived from the Latin word *septem,* "seven," September was the seventh month in the ancient Roman calendar which began in March. Even after the Roman calendar was revised with the addition of two new months and a New Year beginning in January, September retained its name, although it was thenceforth the ninth month. The chief events in September were the games in honor of Juno, Minerva, and Jupiter, which were called the Ludi Magni or Ludi Romani and began on September 4.

During the time of the Roman Empire, there were numerous attempts to rename September. The months of Quintilis and Sextilis had been renamed July and August, after Julius Caesar and Augustus, in the first century B.C. Once July and August had taken their places in the Roman calendar, it was not surprising that the Roman senate tried to bestow upon succeeding rulers a similar sign of prestige. It was the custom to vote to each new emperor the honors and prerogatives that his predecessors had held, including the "divine honor" of the honorific month. September was especially open to change since it immediately followed July and August.

Shortly after the emperor Augustus's death in A.D. 14 and early in the reign of his successor, Tiberius (A.D. 14–37), the senate proposed to rename September Tiberius. The emperor's refusal seems to have modified but not halted the schemes of his flatterers in the senate. They soon attempted to name his birth month of November after him, but this time Tiberius supposedly stopped all such adulation with the cutting remark "and what will you do if there be 13 Caesars?"

According to the second-century Roman biographer Suetonius, in A.D. 37 at the start of his reign the emperor Caligula (A.D. 37–41) had the Roman senate name September Germanicus in memory of his father, Germanicus Caesar (15 B.C.–A.D. 19), a famous Roman general. The change did not survive Caligula's reign.

The emperor Domitian (A.D. 81–96) also tried to rename September Germanicus, since he himself had adopted this title to commemorate his victories in Germany. Domitian selected September because the *dies imperii,* marking his accession as emperor, fell within that month. Again, however, the change did not survive the tyrannical emperor's death. The early fifth-century writer Ambrosius Theodosius Macrobius commented: "The month September retains its own original name; this month Domitian had usurped with the appellation Germanicus and October with his own name Domitianus. But when it was decreed that the unpropitious word [Domitianus] be erased from every bronze or stone, the months too were freed from the usurpation of a tyrannical appellation."

In yet another move, the Roman senate, probably in A.D. 138, suggested that the inappropriately named September be called Antoninus in honor of Emperor Antoninus Pius (A.D. 138–161), who had been born on the 19th day of the month. The emperor refused.

Conspicuously less modest was the emperor Commodus (A.D. 180–192), who around A.D. 191 had the Roman senate approve the renaming of all 12 months in his honor. Each was to be called after an honorary name that he sometimes assumed, September being designated Augustus for "venerable," or "reverend." The month of August, previously named for the first Roman emperor Augustus, was renamed Commodus so as not to cause conflict. However, Commodus's innovations in the naming of months did not survive his reign.

The last Roman emperor to have his name given to September was Marcus Claudius Tacitus, who ruled for a brief period in A.D. 275–276. According to an account in his unreliable contemporary biography, "he ordered the month September to be called Tacitus because in this month he was born and also made emperor." The name Tacitus, like all others previously bestowed on September, did not survive.

The rapid growth of Christianity by the fourth century A.D., combined with the conversion of the emperor Constantine (A.D. 311–337), struck a severe blow at the Roman state religion with its worship of the emperor as a god. It spelled doom for the "divine honor" of the honorific month. It therefore also marked the end of attempts to rename September in line with the precedent set by July and August.

In early medieval Frankish emperor Charlemagne's calendar, September was known as the harvest month. The Anglo-Saxon name for it was Gerst-monath, or "barley month," since barley was harvested then. After the introduction of Christianity it was sometimes called Halig-monath, or "holy month," in reference to the birth of Mary, the mother of Jesus, on September 8. September is usually the month of the harvest moon, the full moon nearest the time of the autumnal equinox. The harvest moon appears above the horizon around sunset for several days, giving light enough for farmers to continue their harvesting. The lucky birthstone associated with September is the sapphire, which symbolizes clear thinking.

September 1

World War II Begins

World War II, one of the most cataclysmic events of the 20th century, began in Europe when the forces of Adolf Hitler's Nazi Germany invaded Poland on September 1, 1939. The war stemmed from the territorial ambitions of the totalitarian regimes that had emerged against the backdrop of the Great Depression in the 1930s and the conditions created by the peace terms after World War I (see related entries throughout this book). The weak League of Nations, which the United States had never joined, was unable to check aggression and prevent war. The United States, however, would eventually be pulled into the new conflict.

The German invasion of Poland was preceded by aggression elsewhere. Under Hitler, Germany illegally remilitarized the Rhineland in 1936, an-

nexed Austria in 1938, and swallowed up Czechoslovakia in 1939. Germany's ally, in what was initially known as the Rome-Berlin Axis, was Italy. Under the leadership of fascist dictator Benito Mussolini, Italy had conquered Ethiopia in 1936 and Albania in 1939. Another totalitarian regime dominated Japan, which would become the third leading member of the Axis alliance during World War II. Japan had pursued a policy of territorial aggression in Asia throughout most of the 1930s, most notably with its occupation of Manchuria in 1931 and the war against China that followed. Known as the Second Sino-Japanese War, it ultimately would merge into World War II.

Abandoning their unsuccessful policy of appeasement, Great Britain and France declared war against Germany two days after the invasion of Poland. Strong domestic support for a policy of isolationism kept the United States out of the conflict at first, although the United States did send supplies and other assistance to the British and French. The United States did not enter the war until after Japan's attack on the naval installation at Pearl Harbor, Hawaii, on December 7, 1941. That action precipitated an American declaration of war against Japan on the following day. Germany and Italy reacted by declaring war against the United States on December 11, 1941. That same day, the United States Congress (with only one dissenting vote) responded in kind, issuing a declaration of war against Germany and Italy.

After untold suffering and bloodshed, World War II ended in 1945 with victory for the Allies. In Europe the German surrender was signed at 2:41 a.m., local time, on May 7, 1945. After simultaneous announcements by the Allied heads of state, May 8 was officially celebrated by the Americans as Victory in Europe (V-E) Day (see May 8). In the Pacific, Allied victory came several months later, after American forces dropped two atomic bombs on Japan (see August 6 and August 9). The Japanese decision to surrender was announced in Washington, D.C., on August 14, 1945, a day later observed as Victory over Japan (V-J) Day. Formal ratification of the Japanese surrender followed on September 2, 1945 (see September 2).

Walter Reuther's Birthday

Walter Philip Reuther, one of America's leading union organizers, was born on September 1, 1907, in Wheeling, West Virginia. As a youth he worked in the local steel mills. He eventually made his way to Detroit, Michigan, and worked in automobile plants. Despite his blue-collar background, he was able to obtain an education and attended what later became Wayne State University. Reuther became active in the labor movement, which at the time was struggling to organize workers and faced severe opposition from both big business and the government.

In 1932 Reuther was fired by Ford for his pro-union activities, something employers then had the power to do. In order to study labor conditions abroad, he went to the Soviet Union and even worked in a Soviet automobile plant for a while. Reuther returned to the United States in 1935 and resumed his efforts on behalf of American automobile workers, particularly those in the "car capital" of Detroit. In May of that same year, the United Automobile Workers (UAW) union was organized.

The first years of the UAW were turbulent ones. Despite New Deal legislation that favored the unions and permitted them to organize under federal auspices, the automobile companies were able to fight back, often with strong-arm tactics such as hiring thugs to terrorize the workers. Nevertheless, the UAW responded with "sit down" strikes where workers occupied plants and refused to move until their demands were met, despite the risk of physical violence. Reuther himself was involved in one such incident. On March 27, 1937, he and several other prominent UAW organizers, namely Richard Frankensteen, Bob Kanter, and J. J. Kennedy, were handing out leaflets on an overpass leading to a Ford plant when Ford thugs savagely attacked them.

One by one, however, the major automobile manufacturers were forced to accept the inevitable unionization of their workforce under the auspices of the UAW. Reuther became vice president of the UAW in 1942, and supported the official "no strike" policy during World War II in order to ensure that wartime production would not be interrupted by labor strife. After the war, in 1946, he was elected president of the UAW.

Reuther aggressively continued the policy of expanding union membership and secured the benefits of collective bargaining under federal labor legislation passed by Congress during the New Deal. He resisted the weakening of these guarantees in the Taft-Hartley Act of 1947, which sought to restrain some perceived abuses. Under Reuther's leadership the UAW secured cost-of-living adjustments for its members, paid holidays, guaranteed pensions, hospital care, sick leave benefits, and even some limited profit sharing arrangements. He was still president of the UAW and actively pursuing its interests when he and his wife were killed in a plane crash on May 9, 1970, near Black Lake, Michigan.

September 2

Andrew Grove's Birthday

Andrew S. Grove, the pioneering scientist and semiconductor industry magnate, was born as Andras Grof on September 2, 1936, in Budapest, Hungary. His father was a dairy worker and the family was Jewish. During World War II they successfully hid from both the Nazi and the Hungarian Jew-hunters, only to fall under the Soviet Union cold war occupation of Eastern Europe. In 1956, when the Soviet military ruthlessly crushed an abortive Hungarian independence movement, Grof was able to escape to neighboring Austria. From there he made his way to the United States, changing his name to Andrew Grove.

Grove was admitted to the City College of New York and graduated in 1960 with a degree in chemical engineering. He went on to attend the University of California at Berkeley and received his doctorate in 1963. Grove went to work in Silicon Valley, the famous computer and electronics hub in California, for Fairchild Semiconductor's Research and Development Laboratory, and was promoted to assistant director of research and development in 1967. In 1968 he left Fairchild to join Gordon Moore and Robert Noyce in establishing a new semiconductor company called Intel Corporation based in Santa Clara, California.

The first important Intel product was the dynamic random access memory circuit (DRAM) in 1970 for use in mainframe computers. It was followed by the world's first microprocessor, the 4004 chip, in 1971. The 4004 was the first central processing unit (CPU) on a single chip. It was roughly five inches by seven inches in size, incredibly large by modern standards, but it was revolutionary for the times and had as much processing power as the first electronic digital computer (ENIAC) which took up an entire room.

The eight-bit chip followed in 1974 and was used to run the first personal computer, the Altair 8800. In 1979 Grove became the president of Intel, and through strategic marketing initiatives and an aggressive emphasis on producing affordable microchips, Intel chips became the industry standard for the burgeoning personal computer industry. The company became the world leader in the semiconductor industry even though it had to struggle in the mid-1980s with price-cutting by Japanese competitors and sluggish economic conditions. Nevertheless, Intel maintained its dominance in the field, introducing a succession of ever more powerful and efficient chips. Its 286 and 386 processors were widely used in the personal computer clones, which refers to affordable IBM-compatible equipment, that proliferated in the late 1980s. The 486 chip was introduced in 1989, the Pentium chip in 1993, the Pentium Pro chip in 1995, and the Pentium II chip in 1997. By the late 1990s, more than 80 percent of all personal computers used Intel microprocessors.

Grove began to move toward retirement in 1998 when he resigned from his position as chief executive officer of Intel. He has taught some graduate-level courses and has written several books, including *High Output Management* (1983), *One-on-One with Andy Grove* (1987), and *Only the Paranoid Survive* (1996). Grove also contributes to several newspapers and magazines. In 1997 he was named by *Time* magazine as its Man of the Year.

World War II: Japan Surrenders

Following the capitulation of Japan in 1945 (see related essays throughout this book), preparations were begun for the formal ceremonies of surrender. Since there was some unease about the safety of holding such important formalities on the Japanese home islands with the hostilities so recently ended, the ceremonies were held in Tokyo Bay on the battleship USS *Missouri*, surrounded by a large fleet of Allied warships. President Harry S. Truman chose the *Missouri* because it was a new and impressive battleship, it was named after his home state, and it had been christened by his daughter Margaret.

The ceremony was held on September 2, 1945. Foreign Minister Mamoru Shigemitsu and General Yoshijiro Umezu signed the surrender papers for Japan. Those signing for the Allies included General Douglas MacArthur and Admiral Chester W. Nimitz of the United States. There were also representatives from Great Britain, China, the Soviet Union, France, Australia, New Zealand, Canada, and the Netherlands. After the signing was completed, hundreds of aircraft roared over the ships in a massive show of Allied air power. The display was followed by an address broadcast to the United States by General MacArthur, who had been named supreme allied commander to receive the surrender and now had the responsibility for supervising the postwar occupation of Japan.

September 3

Henry Hudson Enters New York Harbor

Henry Hudson, who on September 3, 1609, sailed his vessel, the *Half Moon*, into New York Harbor, was the first European to explore the river that now bears his name. Even though 16th-century mariners, notably the Italian Giovanni da Verrazano, as well as Portuguese, French, and possibly English voyagers, had entered or crossed the river, Hudson was the first to give a full account and to recognize its potential value.

Despite his achievement Hudson remains a mysterious character about whom little information is available. Historians do not know the exact date of his birth and can give only the approximate time of his death. He is believed to have been an Englishman, to have married a woman named Katherine, and to have fathered three sons. His second son, John, accompanied him on the voyages of discovery and perished with him as well.

All that is known with certainty about Hudson's career concerns the four journeys of exploration that he undertook between 1607 and 1611. In each instance a leading company of merchants in either England or the Netherlands commissioned him to find shorter water routes than those then known to the highly prized areas of trade in Asia. Their trust in Hudson suggests that he was already a capable, experienced, and respected mariner.

In 1607 the English Muscovy Company hired Hudson to search for a northeast passage to China, Japan, and the East Indies across the top of Scandinavia and Asia. On May 1 Hudson, his son John, and ten mariners, aboard the 80-ton vessel *Hopewell*, set sail from Gravesend (near London) and about a month later they reached the Shetland Islands. After spending some time on the east coast of Greenland, Hudson sailed east to Spitsbergen. The voyage produced no discoveries, and the *Hopewell* returned to London in September 1607.

In 1608 Hudson set sail on a second voyage, again financed by the Muscovy Company. Its mission was to search for a northeast passage to Asia between Spitsbergen and the Novaya Zemlya Islands in the Arctic Ocean north of Russia, or alternatively to find a strait leading to the Kara Sea. Hudson gathered a crew of 14, including his son John, and in the spring of 1608 set sail from London in the *Hopewell* from London's St. Katherine's Docks on the Thames.

Hudson and his men reached the Lofoten Islands on the west coast of Norway a month later. The explorers continued their journey, rounding the North Cape in June. The arduous passage began to wear down the mariners, and Hudson noted at one point in his log that two of his men claimed to have sighted a mermaid. Soon afterward the *Hopewell* encountered an ice pack, which forced the vessel onto a southeasterly course toward Novaya Zemlya, where they landed. Unable to find a suitable eastward passage through the ice flow, Hudson finally gave up and sailed back to England.

After this second voyage, Hudson went to Holland to discuss the possibility of further explorations with the Dutch East India Company, a commercial group representing merchants from six neighboring areas. The representatives of Amsterdam favored making a deal with Hudson, but the delegates from Zeeland persuaded the organization to delay such an undertaking for at least another year. At that point, the Amsterdam Chamber of the Dutch East India Company, well aware of the French government's desire to obtain Hudson's services, independently made an agreement with the mariner.

Under the terms of a contract signed by Hudson on January 8, 1609, the explorer was to seek a northeast passage to Asia by way of Novaya Zemlya. The Amsterdam Chamber of the East India Company promised to provide Hudson with a well-equipped ship and a crew and paid him 800 guilders. If he returned within a year, the merchants pledged to give him additional compensation, and if he failed to come back, agreed to pay his wife an extra 200 guilders.

Hudson set sail from Amsterdam on April 4, 1609, with a crew of 18 English and Dutch sailors on the *Halve Maen* (*Half Moon*). Ice and cold again awaited Hudson in the northern waters and cut short his quest for a northeastern passage. Frustrated once more in his attempts to reach Asia by way of an Arctic route, he decided to abandon his instructions and try to find a northwest seaway. Equipped with information about the Atlantic coast of America, which Captain John Smith had sent him from Virginia, Hudson reversed his course and sailed for the New World.

The *Half Moon* arrived on the coast of Maine in July 1609. The crew stopped to repair the vessel's torn sails and to cut a new foremast from the abundant timber in the area. For two more weeks the adventurers sailed south, finally reaching a point south of Chesapeake Bay. Then Hudson moved north again and explored Delaware Bay. Still in search of the northwest passage, the captain continued farther north and on September 2, 1609, approached New York's lower bay. Beginning on September 3, he explored and took soundings in the waters at the mouth of what would be known as the Hudson River. On September 12 the vessel passed through the narrows, and the mariners dropped anchor at the southern tip of Manhattan Island.

On September 13 the *Half Moon* began its voyage up the Hudson. By the next day the vessel was as far north as Stony Point and sailed past the Catskill Mountains two days later. On September 19 Hudson reached the approximate location of what is now Albany. From there he proceeded north in a small boat to continue his search for a northwest passage, but he soon realized that the steadily narrowing river could not be a channel to the Pacific. The *Half Moon* weighed anchor and began the journey back down the river on September 23. Rain slowed the descent, and the vessel finally reached the future site of Hoboken, New Jersey, on October 2.

On October 4 the *Half Moon* sailed out of the New York Hharbor into the Atlantic for its homeward voyage, arriving at Dartmouth, England, a month later. In 1610 Hudson set out on his fourth voyage. Sailing this time on behalf of a group of English merchant-adventurers, he again went in search of a northwest passage to Asia. On April 27, with a crew of 23 men on the vessel *Discovery*, he set sail from London. He was never to return.

Sighting the coast of Greenland on June 4, 1610, Hudson continued west and by August 2 passed through the Canadian strait later named for him. On August 3 the *Discovery* entered what would be known as Hudson Bay, which the crew explored for many weeks. Winter soon set in, and in early November Hudson hauled his vessel onto the shore of a southern cove of the bay, which soon became frozen. Scurvy and starvation threatened the crew, who sustained themselves by eating frogs and moss until the weather warmed sufficiently to permit hunting parties to search for food.

In the spring of 1611 Hudson explored to the southwest with a few members of his crew. During his absence Robert Juet, who had had a falling-out with the captain, plotted a mutiny. Upon his return to base, Hudson disregarded the hostility of the men and on June 12, 1611, set sail again in search of the elusive northwest passage. On June 23 Juet and others seized Henry and John Hudson and set them, with seven of their supporters, adrift in a small boat. The mutineers then sailed away. Nothing further was ever heard of Hudson and his companions; they undoubtedly perished shortly thereafter.

Misfortune followed the *Discovery* on its homeward journey. Natives killed several of the mariners, and sickness and starvation took a number of the others, including Robert Juet. Only seven men and a boy were alive when the *Discovery* reached Ireland on September 6, 1611. On July 24, 1618, four of the men were arraigned in London, but they pleaded not guilty and won acquittal from a jury.

World War II: Britain and France Declare War on Germany

On September 3, 1939, Great Britain and France—in the struggle against tyranny that became World War II—declared war on Germany. What was to escalate into the most devastating conflict known had begun two days earlier, when Nazi Germany invaded Poland. Before its end in 1945 in Europe and Asia, the war would become global in nature, involving nations from every continent except Antarctica. The contesting countries were headed by the Axis powers (Germany, Italy, and Japan) and by the Allies (Britain, France, the Soviet Union after it was invaded by Germany in June 1941, and the United States after the attack on Pearl Harbor on December 7, 1941).

America's entry into the conflict was followed by a monumental effort, devoting the human and industrial resources of the nation to the cause of Allied victory. For the United States, as for every nation that participated, this costly war changed history.

September 4

Founding of Los Angeles

Los Angeles, California, was officially founded on September 4, 1781. The moving spirit behind the foundation was Don Felipe de Neve, the Spanish governor of California, who acted in conformity with the Spanish colonial policy that active colonization should start once a local mission center and military forts were established. He recommended to the viceroy of Mexico that a pueblo be built on the spot where, in 1769, a group of explorers and missionaries under Captain Gaspar de Portolá had discovered a native village. They named the fertile valley Portiuncula after a chapel in Italy favored by Saint Francis of Assisi. The establishment of the future city was subsequently ordered by royal decree of King Charles III of Spain.

Every detail was worked out well in advance of settlement. An area of four square leagues out of the 17,500-acre tract was set aside and divided into a small plaza surrounded by seven-acre fields for agriculture, pastures, and royal lands to be leased to citizens. On August 18, 1781, the settlers,

recruits from Mexico, reached the San Gabriel Mission. Lying nine miles to the northeast of the planned site, the mission served as a base where the settlers rested and received instruction about where to live, what to build, what crops to grow, and how much time to give to community undertakings. On September 4 the expedition set out for the newly designated pueblo. It included the 44 settlers (11 men, 11 women, and 22 children), Don Felipe de Neve, and a detachment of soldiers and priests from the San Gabriel Mission. At the site the native villagers gathered to look on as a procession formed and the marchers slowly circled the plaza, invoking God's blessing. The governor gave a formal address, followed by prayers and benediction. Thus the new settlement was established, officially named El Pueblo de Nuestra Señora La Reina de Los Angeles de Portiuncula (The Pueblo of Our Lady Queen of Angels).

The little pueblo first consisted of dwellings with rawhide doors and paneless windows. Three years later the settlers erected a simple adobe church on the plaza. The narrow streets became pools of mud in winter and clouds of dust in summer. By 1800 the population of Los Angeles numbered only 315, living in 30 adobe dwellings with a town hall, guardhouse, army barracks, and grain storehouses.

After Mexico gained independence from Spain in 1821, the settlement experienced frequent political disturbances. In 1835 it was made a city by the Mexican congress, and from 1845 to 1847 it was the capital of California. When the Mexican War broke out between the United States and Mexico, the defenders of Los Angeles fled before advancing American troops under Commodore Robert F. Stockton and Captain John C. Frémont. The American flag was unfurled over Los Angeles on August 13, 1846.

After California was granted admission as the 31st state in the Union on September 9, 1850, the population of Los Angeles rapidly increased, augmented by the California gold rush and later by the completion of the transcontinental railroad, the discovery of oil, and the development of the aircraft and motion picture industries. Between 1890 and 1940, the population grew from 50,395 to 1,504,277, a gain of almost 3,000 percent. Los Angeles is now one of the largest cities in the United States.

The Santa Fe Fiesta

This is a movable event.

The anniversary of the reconquest of New Mexico from the Pueblo tribe in 1692, which was first formally celebrated in September 1712, was renewed by the city of Santa Fe in 1919 and is known as the Santa Fe Fiesta.

The historical background of the celebration dates from 1528, when the battered and hungry survivors of Pánfilo de Narváez's expedition to Florida, fleeing across the Gulf of Mexico from hostile tribes, were shipwrecked off the coast of Texas. Only four men escaped from the ordeal and managed to reach land, probably Galveston Island. They included Álvar Núñez Cabeza de Vaca, who had served as Narváez's treasurer, and a black Moor known as Esteban or Estevanico who had served as guide.

In the nearly eight years that followed, the four labored for native captors, escaped, and wandered thousands of miles through the rugged terrain of the American Southwest. They probably crossed through New Mexico and Arizona, possibly reaching the Gulf of California. Far south of the Rio Grande, they finally encountered other Spanish people near Culiacán. In Mexico they spread tales they had heard about the Pueblo natives and rich northern cities, thus giving rise to the myth about the fabled Seven Cities of Cíbola.

Spurred by these accounts, Antonio de Mendoza, the viceroy of New Spain, dispatched an exploring party under the leadership of the Franciscan missionary Fray Marcos de Niza in 1539. Estevanico, who had become an experienced ambassador to the natives in the previous years of wandering, went with him as guide and scout. The party, accompanied also by native guides, explored southeastern Arizona. Sent ahead as the leader of an advance expedition, Estevanico was the first non-native to see the region of northwestern New Mexico. He discovered the Zuñi tribe. At Hawikuh, their westernmost pueblo, the Zuñis killed him and some of the native guides who had accompanied him.

The three guides who managed to escape hastened back to Fray Marcos with news of the tragedy. Though he promptly turned back for Mexico, the friar's imagination and credulity were undiminished by the disaster. His unsubstantiated report about a land "rich in gold, silver and other wealth" where people were "very rich, the women even wearing belts of gold" aroused such enthusiasm that a year later Captain-General Francisco Vásquez de Coronado, with Fray Marcos as a guide, set out at the head of a military expedition of 1,500 men. After crossing the deserts, mountains, and forests of southeastern Arizona, they arrived five months later at Hawikuh. When the Zuñis refused to submit to Coronado, he subdued them by force.

As it turned out, however, Hawikuh was not one of the golden cities of Cíbola but a "few hovels of clay and stone built upon a high rock" surrounded by barren land. Coronado, spurred on by yet another fabulous tale of the wealthy kingdom of Quivira, continued his explorations, probably as far east as the southern part of what is now Kansas. Bitter and disappointed, he returned to Mexico City in 1542, having found no gold in his 3,000-mile march but having claimed extensive lands for Spain.

Although the legends of riches and glory lingered, a royal ordinance suspended further Spanish exploration of the recently discovered New Mexican area, at least as far as government-sponsored expeditions were concerned. Five decades were to pass before serious colonization of New Mexico would be attempted. Then, in 1598 Don Juan de Oñate, acting on reports about profitable grazing and mining opportunities there, offered to finance a private expedition. Born into a prosperous mining family, he was able to equip the company of colonists—130 families and 270 single men—and supply 7,000 cattle. He established the first permanent European settlement in New Mexico in 1598 at a native pueblo that he renamed San Juan de los Caballeros. It was situated at the confluence of the Chama River and Rio Grande, 30 miles north of what is now Santa Fe.

This provisional Spanish capital of New Mexico was later transferred to the west bank of the Rio Grande and named San Gabriel del Yunque. The colony remained there for several years until the viceroy of New Spain ordered Don Pedro de Peralta, the third governor of "the Kingdom and Provinces of New Mexico," to move it farther south. In the winter of 1609–1610, Peralta built a new capital at a spot known to the natives as Kuapoga, the "place of the shell beads near the water." This modest mud and stone settlement, located at the base of the Sangre de Cristo Mountains, was proclaimed La Villa Real de la Santa Fe de San Francisco de Assisi—the Royal City of the Holy Faith of St. Francis of Assisi, or Santa Fe as the name was abbreviated. Work immediately began on construction of a colonial headquarters at Santa Fe. The result, called the Royal Palace, was a long adobe structure with walls several feet thick. Later known as the Palace of the Governors, it was successively occupied by Spanish captains-general (until 1821, when Mexico won independence from Spain), by Mexican governors (until 1846), and by American territorial governors (until 1907).

By 1617 Spanish villages had spread all along the Rio Grande and the Franciscan friars who accompanied the Spanish soldier-settlers had erected 11 churches and supposedly had converted

14,000 natives. The Spanish and the native tribes lived in relative harmony for 70 years, but dissatisfaction and resentment mounted as some of the natives were enslaved and compelled to work in the mines and others were slain by religious zealots because they rejected conversion. In August 1680 the Pueblo people under the leadership of Popé of Taos, and with the help of the Apache, rose in revolt. They killed 21 Franciscans and all the other Spanish they could find. Governor Antonio Otermín, at the head of a small military force, led the remaining colonists in a hasty retreat from the city. The nearly 1,000 survivors crossed southern New Mexico and reached the safety of El Paso del Norte, where the cities of El Paso, Texas, and Juárez, Mexico, now face each other across the Rio Grande. In the meantime, the natives at Santa Fe "washed away" their baptisms with mud and sacked the churches and the Royal Palace.

After 12 years in exile, awaiting the appearance of a conquistador to win back Santa Fe, the Spanish settlers finally found Captain-General Don Diego de Vargas Zapata y Luján Ponce de León, who had been appointed governor of New Mexico in 1691. Before marching to regain New Mexico for Spain in 1692, de Vargas solemnly vowed that in return for a bloodless victory he would have an annual novena to Our Lady offered in thanksgiving. He successfully negotiated a peace agreement with the natives, and under the royal banner of New Mexico his troops triumphantly entered Santa Fe on September 14, 1692.

With elaborate fanfare, de Vargas took over the Royal Palace. Soon afterward he and his men marched south and rounded up the settlers to escort them back to Santa Fe. They also carried back the statue of Our Lady as patroness and queen of New Mexico and Santa Fe, known as *La Conquistadora*, which had been saved from damage in the 1680 uprising. Renewed native opposition in 1693, however, soon forced the Spanish to fight to keep control of the city.

In the years immediately following the reconquest, the inhabitants of Santa Fe continued to hold their traditional fiesta of La Conquistadora on the first Sunday in October, as had been customary before the revolt. At the same time, they commemorated the 1693 battle for the city, when they had prayed before the statue for victory. In 1712 the city council agreed to inaugurate a special fiesta in memory of the 1692 reconquest as well. The lieutenant governor of New Mexico, Juan Paéz Hurtado (acting in place of the governor, the Marquás de la Peñuela), with the governing body of the city, issued a proclamation on September 16. It required "that in the future the said 14th day [of September] be celebrated with Vespers, Mass, Sermon and Public Procession through the Main Plaza. . . . It is our will that it be [henceforth] celebrated for all time to come . . . and . . . we swear [this] in due form of law."

It is not known how long this order was obeyed, since documentary evidence is lacking. It may have been only in 1712 or may have continued for many years afterward; but in the course of time the fiesta was abandoned. In the 20th century, however, there was renewed interest in having a fiesta. For several years prior to 1911, the Women's Board of Trade of Santa Fe had been holding an annual festival on the town plaza to raise money for the library. Early in that year, the Reverend James Mythen suggested a commemoration of the important events in the history of the city. On July 4, 1911, the women arranged a pageant representing the entry of de Vargas into the city. It was repeated two or three times in succeeding years, but abandoned during World War I. It was not until 1919, therefore, that people began to seriously arrange for an annual celebration. The original date of the fiesta, set in 1712 for September 14, was changed to the Labor Day weekend when the festivities attracted larger numbers of people and spread over a number of days. In the late 1990s, however, it was moved back to the second weekend in September. Roughly 50,000 people typically attend the parades, shows, and food fairs that surround the event.

September 5

The First Continental Congress Convenes

The British regarded the Boston Tea Party of December 16, 1773, as a malicious destruction of property and an affront to the British Empire. Despite some opposition, most Britons thought it necessary to chastise the upstart colonials. Thus, Britain's response to Massachusetts was the Coercive or "Intolerable" Acts, a collection of measures designed both as a punishment and as a preventative.

The Boston Port Bill of March 31, 1774, closed Boston Harbor until Massachusetts made reparations to the East India Company for the lost tea. The Administration of Justice Act of May 20, which authorized the governor and council of Massachusetts to transfer to England certain trials for capital offenses involving British officials, protected government functionaries from harassment by the colonials. The Massachusetts Government Act, also of May 20, 1774, abolished a number of charter rights and severely limited the holding of town meetings. The Quartering Act of June 2 legalized the forced housing of troops in occupied private dwellings in all the American colonies. Although Britain did not intend the Quebec Act of May 20 as a punitive measure, the Americans regarded it as one of the Coercive Acts. They resented the legislation, which granted civil and religious liberties to Canada's predominantly Roman Catholic population and extended Canada's borders far to the south, and perceived it as a threat not only to Protestantism but also to American colonial hopes for westward expansion.

Ships from Britain brought news of the passage of the Port Act to Boston on May 10, 1774. Boston town meetings on May 13 called for all American colonies to suspend trade with Britain and the West Indies. On June 17 Boston refused to pay the demanded reparation to the East India Company. Joseph Warren of the Massachusetts Committee of Correspondence gathered signatures for a Solemn League and Covenant, which pledged subscribers to boycott anyone who continued commerce with Great Britain. Royal Governor Thomas Gage's denunciation of the document as a "traitorous combination" only encouraged more people to sign it.

Colonists elsewhere, uninvolved in the Boston Tea Party issue and exempt from the provisions of most of the Intolerable Acts, were not so anxious to resort to extreme measures. Philadelphians met publicly on May 20, 1774, and rejected Massachusetts's request for suspension of commerce with Britain. Instead, they suggested that every colony send delegates to a congress specially convened to respond to this latest crisis. In New York City on May 23, 1774, the rebel committee of 51 men, under the leadership of Isaac Low, also declined to terminate trade immediately and echoed the call for a Continental Congress. Eighty-nine members of the Virginia House of Burgesses, meeting informally on May 27 in the Long Room of the Raleigh Tavern, reached the same decision as their northern counterparts.

Massachusetts accepted the more moderate position of the other colonies. Its general court on June 17, 1774, appointed five delegates to the congress meeting in Philadelphia in September. Connecticut and Rhode Island also selected representatives during June 1774, and nine more colonies followed suit during July and August. Only in Georgia was the royalist government able to prevent the naming of a contingent.

Fifty-six men from 12 colonies convened in what history would recall as the First Continental Congress. It opened in Philadelphia on September 5, 1774. Joseph Galloway, the speaker of the Pennsylvania colonial assembly, suggested the colony's State House as a meeting place. However, the delegates instead accepted the offer by the city carpenters of their own building. The leaders believed that the choice of Carpenters' Hall would be "highly agreeable to the mechanics and citizens in general." The representatives elected Peyton Randolph of Virginia to be the president of the congress and selected a nondelegate, the radical Charles Thomson of Pennsylvania, as secretary. They also decided that each colony would have one vote in determining questions and pledged to keep the proceedings secret.

The British Parliament's authority to enact legislation affecting the Americas was the center of debate, until Samuel Adams of Massachusetts introduced a set of resolutions that had been drafted by Joseph Warren and adopted on September 9, 1774, by Suffolk, the county in which Boston is located. On September 17 the First Continental Congress also endorsed these declarations in a clear victory for its more radical members. The Suffolk Resolves, as they were called, stated that the Coercive Acts were null and void and thus not to be obeyed. They also advised Massachusetts residents to form an extralegal government that would collect taxes but withhold them from the British until Parliament repealed the Intolerable Acts. Even more foreboding were provisions urging the people to arm themselves as militias and calling for stringent economic sanctions against Britain.

Conservative delegates to the Continental Congress tried to recoup their losses by advocating Joseph Galloway's Plan of a Proposed Union Between Great Britain and the Colonies. The Pennsylvanian called for a grand council composed of delegates selected for three-year terms by each of the colonial assemblies. Together with a president-general appointed by the king and equipped with veto power, the provincial congress would form a separate and subordinate branch of the British legislature. Parliament and the council would each enjoy the right to originate legislation concerning America, but both would have to approve each proposal before it could become law. Radicals found this measure insufficient, and on September 28, 1774, the Continental Congress rejected Galloway's plan by a six to five vote. On October 22, 1774, the congress expunged all reference to it from the minutes.

On October 14, 1774, the Continental Congress issued its Declaration and Resolves, which made the radical claim that, subject only to the king's veto, the provincial legislatures had the sole right to levy taxes on the colonies and to enact measures affecting their internal polity. Parliament's sphere of action was to be restricted to Great Britain and to imperial affairs. The congress denounced 13 acts of Parliament passed since 1763 as violations of American rights and promised to invoke economic sanctions until their repeal.

The Continental Association, a series of agreements adopted by the delegates to the Congress on October 18, 1774, pledged that their colonies would cease all imports from Britain by December 1, 1774, and also terminate the lucrative West Indian slave trade by the same date. In addition, the association called for the boycott of British goods and certain foreign luxury items beginning on March 1, 1775, and set September 1, 1775, as the date for ending American exports to Great Britain, Ireland, and the West Indies. Adding teeth to its resolutions, the Continental Congress provided for the establishment of extralegal machinery to force compliance on local citizens through threats of unfavorable publicity and boycotts.

The First Continental Congress adjourned on October 26, 1774, but made plans to reconvene on May 10, 1775, if Great Britain did not act to resolve the crisis. In less than two months the rebel leaders had taken a giant step toward intercolonial unity. Even more important, the congress's demand that Parliament surrender its voice in American affairs marked a greater development in the growing movement for independence.

September 6

President William McKinley Assassinated

One chapter in a tragic history of assassinations, which would deprive the United States of four of its presidents by 1963, was written on September 6, 1901. The victim was 58-year-old President William McKinley, then six months into his second term. Like other presidents, McKinley was vulnerable to one nearly inescapable requirement of American politics, namely that he be to some degree accessible to the citizenry. In an effort to maintain personal contact with the electorate, McKinley ignored the warnings of his closest adviser by scheduling a reception that would be open to the public during his September 1901 visit to the Pan-American Exposition in Buffalo, New York. McKinley was struck down by an assassin's bullet only minutes after the reception began on September 6.

McKinley had looked forward to his two-day visit to Buffalo. September 5 had been designated President's Day at the Pan-American Exposition and a record-breaking crowd of 116,000 people was present at the fairgrounds to catch a glimpse of the president. By noon more than 50,000 tourists overflowed the vast expanse of the esplanade, and they enthusiastically greeted the president when he entered the fairgrounds amid much pageantry and ceremony. Proceeding along the Triumphal Causeway, McKinley made his way to the flag-draped platform, where he spoke to the crowd about the impossibility of the United States's isolating itself from the rest of the world and the necessity for entering into reciprocal trade treaties. After his speech, McKinley reviewed several military units and then made a brief tour of the fair.

McKinley wanted September 6 to be "the restful day" of his Buffalo visit. On that morning he and his party traveled to nearby Niagara Falls for sight-seeing. In midafternoon they returned to Buffalo so that McKinley might attend the public reception that had been scheduled for 4:00 p.m. in the exposition's Temple of Music. Hours before the reception was to begin, hundreds of people had queued up outside the Temple of Music to await the arrival of the president. Among them was Leon Czolgosz, who carried a .32 caliber Iver-Johnson revolver.

Czolgosz's family had experienced many difficulties. The senior Czolgosz, father of eight, was a Polish immigrant laborer who moved from town to town in Michigan, eventually went to Pittsburgh, and finally settled in Ohio. He never had much money, but by drawing on the earnings of his six sons he was able to buy a farm near Cleveland during the depression of the 1890s.

Leon Czolgosz grew up embittered. The inequities of the American social order appalled him, and he became increasingly interested in socialism. A devotee of Emma Goldman and other anarchists, he looked to violence for redress of the grievances of the American worker and as an outlet for his hostilities. Czolgosz was also a loner, and became a virtual recluse after suffering a nervous breakdown in 1898. He left his job at a Cleveland wire mill and returned to the family farm, where he ate his meals alone, slept an inordinate amount of time, and dissipated his few waking hours in restless idleness. Newspapers fascinated him, and he pored over the account of the assassination of King Humbert of Italy for countless hours.

In July 1901 Czolgosz left his family's home and, after some wanderings, arrived in Buffalo in time for the Pan-American Exposition. Apparently, he did not go there with the intention of killing McKinley, but newspaper stories of the splendid reception planned for the president stirred his resentment. "I didn't believe one man should have so much service," he later said, "and another man should have none."

President McKinley being shot.

He decided to shoot the president and, having no concern for his own safety, determined to do it at close range. Czolgosz realized that the reception would provide the best opportunity for such an act, so early on September 6 he joined the crowd waiting to greet McKinley and calmly stood outside until 4:00 p.m., when the doors opened to allow the holiday throng to file past McKinley. As he approached the president, Czolgosz carefully swathed the gun in his hand with a handkerchief. He reached McKinley's place on the receiving line at 4:07 p.m., and without uttering a word to his target fired two shots. Czolgosz then tried to escape, but shocked onlookers immediately seized him and might have killed him had not the wounded president gasped: "Don't let them hurt him."

One of Czolgosz's bullets ricocheted off the president's ribs, and minutes after the shooting when McKinley was examined at the exposition's emergency hospital, it fell from his clothing. The second bullet created a more serious problem, entering the president's abdomen and causing such extensive damage that the first doctors to examine McKinley decided to operate immediately. Working by the light of the setting sun, the surgeons repaired the lacerations in the walls of the president's stomach, one of several affected organs, but they could not locate the bullet itself. An X-ray machine was being exhibited at the fairgrounds, but the doctors made no use of this six-year-old invention. Instead, they merely cleansed McKinley's

peritoneal cavity and closed the incision, leaving the bullet embedded in his abdomen.

McKinley was shot on a Friday, and during the weekend that followed, Vice President Theodore Roosevelt, most members of the cabinet, and relatives and close friends of the president went to Buffalo to keep their anxious vigil. McKinley's condition was serious, but medical bulletins released on Monday indicated that he was recovering, and those made public on Tuesday led most observers to believe that he was no longer in danger. In fact, McKinley's condition seemed so improved that his relatives returned to their homes in Ohio, governmental officials went back to Washington, D.C., and Vice President Roosevelt joined his family at a retreat that was 12 miles away from the nearest telephone or telegraph.

However, though the president's strong constitution enabled him to rally from the initial trauma of the attack on his life and the surgery that followed, his doctor's optimism for his ultimate recovery was largely unfounded. The possibility of infection along the track taken by the bullet that had lodged in McKinley's body posed a constant threat to his life in this era before antibiotics. The doctors attending him ignored the danger.

For several days McKinley struggled against the gangrene that was spreading through his abdomen. By Thursday, September 12, his resources were taxed beyond their limits and his condition deteriorated. Despite the best efforts of his physicians, McKinley continued to weaken. Late in the afternoon of Friday, September 13, he realized that he was dying and said to his doctors: "It is useless, gentlemen. I think we ought to have a prayer." McKinley's wife was brought to his side. The president whispered: "Good-bye, good-bye, all. It is God's way. His will, not ours, be done." Then he began to whisper the words of his favorite hymn, "Nearer My God to Thee." McKinley died around 2:00 a.m. on September 14, 1901.

News of McKinley's death plunged the nation into mourning. A special train carried the president's body back to Washington, D.C. There McKinley's remains lay first in the East Room of the White House, then in the Capitol, where thousands of citizens went to pay their final respects. When official services concluded in Washington, a funeral procession escorted McKinley's body to the train that would carry him to Canton, Ohio, for burial.

The nation's grief for McKinley had not yet subsided when on September 23, 1901, the trial of his assassin began. After a hearing that lasted only two days, the jury deliberated for less than one hour before finding Czolgosz guilty. He was electrocuted on October 29, 1901, at Auburn State Prison in Auburn, New York.

Lafayette's Birthday

Marie-Joseph-Paul-Yves-Roch-Gilbert du Motier de Lafayette, the French hero of the American Revolution, was born on September 6, 1757. The site of his birth was the 17th-century château of Chavaniac in the province of Auvergne.

Lafayette was only two when his father was killed at the battle of Minden during the Seven Years' War, and 13 when he became an orphan with the death of his mother in 1770. The inheritor of a large fortune, Lafayette was married just three years later to Marie Adrienne Françoise de Noailles, a member of a wealthy and powerful family of the nobility. Bashful and clumsy, young Lafayette was nevertheless anxious to tread in his father's military footsteps. He joined the King's Musketeers in 1771 and was a dragoon captain when the American colonies revolted against Great Britain in 1775. While attending a banquet in honor of the duke of Gloucester in August of that year, the young officer listened enthusiastically to the duke's sympathetic remarks about the American rebels.

Lafayette later wrote in his memoirs, "At the first news of this quarrel, my heart was enrolled in it." He resigned from active service in June 1776 and through Silas Deane, an American agent in Paris, made an agreement to serve in the colonies

without pay but with the rank of major general. The young Frenchman fitted out a ship at his own expense. Despite the obstacles laid in his path by the officially neutral French government (which forbade his departure, issued orders to seize his ship, and even arrested him), Lafayette managed to sail from a Spanish port on April 20, 1777.

With a dozen or so companions, he arrived at Georgetown, South Carolina, on June 13, 1777. He was amazed at the contrast between America and its people and conditions in France. From Charleston, South Carolina, he wrote his impressions to his wife:

What most charms me is, that all the citizens are brethren.

In America, there are no poor, nor even what we call peasantry. Each individual has his own honest property, and the same rights as the most wealthy land proprietor.

Lafayette traveled to Philadelphia, where on July 31, 1777, the Continental Congress accepted his services and resolved that, in view of his "zeal, illustrious family and connections," he should have the rank of major general. Not long afterward he gained the close friendship of General George Washington, to whose staff he was appointed. On September 11 the 20-year-old major general took part in the battle of Brandywine in Pennsylvania. There, Washington suffered defeat in an attempt to prevent the British general Sir William Howe from advancing on the strategic city of Philadelphia. Lafayette received his baptism of fire and showed his mettle by rallying the scattered American troops, although he himself was wounded in the left leg.

Spending the winter at Valley Forge, early in 1778 Lafayette was put in command of a planned invasion of Canada. The expedition was, however, abandoned for lack of supplies. The impatient youth then fought under General Charles Lee at the battle of Monmouth in New Jersey on June 28, 1778. In August he served as a key liaison officer between the American forces and the French fleet under Count Charles d'Estaing, during and after the unsuccessful attack on British-occupied Newport, Rhode Island.

When war broke out between France and Great Britain, Lafayette returned to France, sailing in January 1779 with an elegant sword presented by Congress and a letter of appreciation to King Louis XVI. Acclaimed in Paris and at the Versailles court and created a colonel in the French cavalry, he persuaded the French king to send a land and naval expedition to help the Americans. In April 1780 Lafayette returned to the United States to prepare for the expedition's arrival. He accompanied General Washington to West Point, where the young French officer was a member of the court-martial that gave the death sentence to Major John André, a captured British officer who had plotted with the American general Benedict Arnold to surrender West Point to the British.

Early in 1781 Lafayette was ordered to Virginia with 1,200 troops, drawn from the New England and New Jersey Continental regiments. He arrived at Richmond on April 29, just in time to prevent its capture. Even after he received reinforcements, he had only about 3,000 men to oppose the more than 7,000 troops under the command of the British general Lord Charles Cornwallis. Lafayette avoided any decisive engagement, and explained in a letter to Washington:

> Were I to fight a battle, I should be cut to pieces, the militia dispersed, and the arms lost. Were I to decline fighting, the country would think itself given up. I am therefore determined to skirmish, but not to engage too far, and particularly to take care against their immense and excellent body of horse, whom the militia fear as they would so many wild beasts. . . . Were I anyways equal to the enemy, I should be extremely happy in my present command. But I am not strong enough even to get beaten.

Later in 1781, however, Lafayette received his chance. With the additional forces of the French navy under the French admiral François-Joseph-Paul de Grasse, Marquis de Grasse-Tilly, and a greatly strengthened French-American army (including forces under General Jean-Baptiste-Donatien de Vimeur, Comte de Rochambeau), Washington concentrated 16,000 men around Yorktown. Neatly bottled up, Cornwallis surrendered his army of 7,500 (see October 19). Lafayette was praised for his role in what proved to be the closing military campaign of the Revolutionary War. In December 1781 the hero sailed for home from Boston, and his direct connection with American affairs ended. He died on May 20, 1834, in France.

Jane Addams's Birthday

Jane Addams, the pioneering social worker, was born on September 6, 1860, in Cedarville, Illinois. Shortly after graduating from Rockford College in 1881, she embarked on studies at the Woman's Medical College of Philadelphia but had to give them up because of bad health.

After a two-year convalescence, she traveled in Europe, which affected much of her later life. Her already awakened social conscience, appalled at an auction of rotten vegetables in London, found hope in another London establishment: Toynbee Hall. Probably the first settlement house (or community center, as it might be called today), this enterprise was established in 1884, when the Anglican clergyman Samuel Barnett invited a group of university students to join him and his wife in "settling" in London's deprived Whitechapel area.

Toynbee Hall kindled Addams's interest in settlement-house work. Returning to Chicago, she founded a settlement house dedicated to improving community and civic life. Hull House (formerly the Hull mansion, on Chicago's West Side, which she and Ellen Gates Starr purchased in 1889) was a pioneering institution. Initially, its main purposes were to give welfare assistance to needy families and combat juvenile delinquency by setting up recreation facilities for slum children. It became a beehive of nurseries and sewing clubs, helped large numbers of the neighborhood's foreign-born to learn English and to become citizens, and opened its doors to union meetings.

As resident head of the settlement until her death, Addams was noted for her ability to recruit outstanding workers and hold their loyalty as well as for her knack for disarming would-be critics. Her books and articles brought public support, and the work of Hull House influenced the settlement movement throughout the country.

With her associates, Addams also influenced the course of American politics, championing woman's suffrage and seeking reforms to bring justice to laborers, immigrants, African Americans, and children. With other groups, she campaigned against sweatshops and pressed for many of the early welfare laws. For example, she supported legislation concerning tenement house regulation, factory inspection, workmen's compensation, an eight-hour workday, and the establishment of juvenile court systems.

An affectionate and tactful person who was skilled at dealing with people, Addams was also a prominent pacifist. She devoted a great deal of effort to crusading for peace during the last two decades of her life. In 1915 she presided over the International Congress of Women meeting at The Hague in Holland and became president (1915–1935) of the Women's International League for Peace and Freedom created shortly thereafter.

As Addams became the recognized leader of social settlement work in the United States, Hull House became one of the largest institutions of its kind in the country. Its facilities for recreation and education (which included a day nursery, gymnasium, meeting and recreation rooms, a social-service center, and classrooms for adult education) were supplemented by a music and art school, theater, and summer camp for children. Addams was also instrumental in organizing the first White House Conference on Children in 1909, was named the first woman president of the National Conference on Social Welfare in 1910, took an active part in Theodore Roosevelt's campaign for the presidency on the Progressive Party ticket in 1912, and was named chair of the Woman's Peace Party in 1915. In 1931 she became the first American woman to receive the Nobel Peace Prize, which she shared with Nicholas Murray Butler. She died of cancer on May 21, 1935.

September 7

Labor Day

This is a movable event.

Industrial workers have played a major role in the emergence of the United States as a world power. Labor has contributed to the general prosperity and has buttressed the nation in times of hardship as well as prosperity. Labor Day, an annual celebration that takes place on the first Monday in September, is a national federal holiday. It is also observed in the Virgin Islands and other American territories and possessions, including the Commonwealth of Puerto Rico.

Unfortunately, employers and the government did not always acknowledge the great contributions of workers, nor did they always even recognize the difficulties they faced. In the wake of the Industrial Revolution, most workers toiled long hours for low pay and under difficult conditions. They lacked any real strength with respect to their employers, and were almost totally without the organizational structures that could improve their bargaining position. Efforts to organize the nation's vast work force began to be more meaningful in the decades following the Civil War.

Many of the nation's workers joined the spreading labor union movement. Their struggle for higher wages, better working conditions, and shorter hours was long and arduous. Utilizing such weapons as spontaneous work stoppages, strikes, picketing, and boycotts, they called attention to the harsh conditions under which they lived and worked. Although the unions grew in number and strength, they had only limited success in redressing the grievances of their members.

According to a long-accepted version of events, it was at a meeting of an early labor organization in 1882 that Peter J. McGuire, the founder and general secretary of the new Brotherhood of Carpenters and Joiners, first proposed the idea of setting aside a day to honor labor. McGuire, with other labor leaders, had been influential the previous year in establishing the Federation of Organized Trades and Labor Unions (which was to be reorganized in 1886 as the American Federation of Labor, now part of the American Federation of Labor and Congress of Industrial Organizations [AFL-CIO]). The son of Irish immigrants, McGuire had himself known the extreme poverty that oppressed many laborers in the years following the Civil War. Forced to leave school and go to work at the age of 11, he had held an assortment of low-paying jobs and, according to his later recollection, "was everything but a sword swallower. And sometimes I was so hungry, a sword (with mustard, of course) would have tasted fine."

McGuire's youthful experiences gave him a deep respect for workers and made him determined to improve their condition. He believed that a day should be set aside to honor laborers and to bring their plight to public attention. At a meeting of the New York Central Labor Union on May 8, 1882, he made his idea known. McGuire suggested that the labor holiday be celebrated on the first Monday in September because, in his words, "it would come at the most pleasant season of the year, nearly midway between the Fourth of July and Thanksgiving, and would fill a wide gap in the chronology of legal holidays."

The union enthusiastically approved McGuire's idea, and on September 5, 1882, the first Labor Day observance took place in New York City. The celebration was on a Tuesday, but the change to Monday was made within two years. Although the 1882 observance was confined to New York City, the idea of setting aside a day to honor laborers quickly gained popularity. In 1884, when the Federation of Organized Trades and Labor Unions gave its endorsement to the idea of an annual Labor Day, the occasion was scheduled for the first Monday in September. On that day, parades of workers took place in cities throughout the northeast. Enthusiasm for the new holiday spread rapidly, and the idea was also endorsed by the Knights of Labor organization. By 1895 Labor Day events were taking place in localities across the nation.

On February 21, 1887, Oregon became the first state to recognize Labor Day as a legal holiday. The Oregon statute set the first Saturday in June for the labor observance, and this law remained in force until 1893, when the state's lawmakers moved the date of Labor Day to the first Monday in September. In the meantime other state legislatures also approved statutes establishing the first Monday in September as Labor Day: Colorado, Massachusetts, New Jersey, and New York did so in 1887, and by 1893 the lawmakers of more than 20 other states had legalized the holiday.

In 1893 a bill establishing Labor Day as a federal holiday was introduced in the United States Congress. Both houses gave it their unanimous approval in 1894. On June 28 of that year President Grover Cleveland signed an act making the first Monday in September a legal holiday for federal employees and in the District of Columbia. All of the remaining states and Puerto Rico eventually legalized the day.

Having won legal recognition of Labor Day, workers in the 1890s and early 20th century used the holiday to dramatize their grievances. The large Labor Day parades, which took place in many cities across the nation, proved to be particularly effective. In 1898 Samuel Gompers, the pioneer who served for more than a quarter century as president of the American Federation of Labor, said of the holiday:

> It is regarded as the day for which the toilers in past centuries looked forward, when their rights and their wrongs might be discussed, placed upon a higher plane of thought and feeling; that the workers of our day may not only lay down their tools of labor for a holiday, but upon which they may touch shoulders in marching phalanx and feel the stronger for it; meet at their parks, groves and grounds, and by appropriate speech, counsel with, and pledge to, each other that the coming year shall witness greater effort than the preceding in the grand struggle to make mankind free, true and noble.

The emphasis on Labor Day as an opportunity for bringing workers' problems to public attention has diminished over time, along with the militant tone of some of the earlier observances. Labor organizations still take special note of the holiday, however, and labor leaders usually issue special Labor Day statements.

Many other nations have also set aside days to honor working men and women. However, in most countries it is the traditional May Day (May 1) that is marked as labor's holiday.

The Miss America Pageant

This is a movable event.

The Miss America Pageant, praised by some as an American institution and criticized by others as a sexist relic of times gone by, takes place annually in early September. Regardless of argument, millions of viewers watch the crowning of the now Miss America on network television each year.

Across the country, thousands of persons get involved in the multitude of state and local pageants that precede the Miss America event. Winners at the local level move up to the state pageants, which are often just as elaborate as the national one. The 50 winners on the state level represent their states in the final, suspense-filled week of judging. Contestants receive a variety of scholarships and other prizes. The winner is chosen on the basis of evening gown and swimsuit appearances, personal talents, poise, personality, articulateness, and ability to carry the responsibilities of the title. The highest point is reached with the coronation of the new Miss America, who is typically serenaded by the host with the traditional "There She Is: Miss America" song as she begins her year-long reign by walking regally down the runway.

The Miss America Pageant was held for the first time in 1921, when bathing beauties from eight cities and states lined up on the beach at Atlantic City, New Jersey, for judging. It was held yearly through 1927 and again in 1933. Since 1935, when it resumed in the Marine Ballroom of Atlantic City's Steel Pier, it has been an annual event. By 1940, when the pageant moved to the Convention Hall, there were 46 aspirants from 30 states and the District of Columbia. Every state in the Union was represented for the first time in 1959.

The following is a list of the Miss Americas:

1921: Margaret Gorman of Washington, D.C.
1922: Mary Campbell of Columbus, Ohio
1923: Mary Campbell of Columbus, Ohio
1924: Ruth Malcomson of Philadelphia, Pennsylvania
1925: Fay Lanphier of Oakland, California
1926: Norma Smallwood of Tulsa, Oklahoma
1927: Lois Delander of Joliet, Illinois
1933: Marian Bergeron of West Haven, Connecticut
1935: Henrietta Leaver of Pittsburgh, Pennsylvania
1936: Rose Coyle of Philadelphia, Pennsylvania
1937: Bette Cooper of Bertrand Island, New Jersey
1938: Marilyn Meseke of Marion, Ohio
1939: Patricia Donnelly of Detroit, Michigan
1940: Frances Burke of Philadelphia, Pennsylvania
1941: Rosemary LaPlanche of Los Angeles, California
1942: Jo-Carroll Dennison of Tyler, Texas
1943: Jean Bartel of Los Angeles, California
1944: Venus Ramey of Washington, D.C.

1945: Bess Myerson of New York City, New York

1946: Marilyn Buferd of Los Angeles, California

1947: Barbara Walker of Memphis, Tennessee

1948: BeBe Shopp of Hopkins, Minnesota

1949: Jacque Mercer of Litchfield, Arizona

Prior to 1950, the Miss America winner was designated according to the year in which she won the pageant. Since 1950, however, the winner has been designated according to the following year. Thus, Miss America 1951 was crowned in 1950 and there was no Miss America 1950.

1951: Yolande Betbeze of Mobile, Alabama

1952: Colleen Hutchins of Salt Lake City, Utah

1953: Neva Langley of Macon, Georgia

1954: Evelyn Ay of Ephrata, Pennsylvania

1955: Lee Meriwether of San Francisco, California

1956: Sharon Ritchie of Denver, Colorado

1957: Marian McKnight of Manning, South Carolina

1958: Marilyn Van Derbur of Denver, Colorado

1959: Mary Ann Mobley of Brandon, Mississippi

1960: Lynda Mead of Natchez, Mississippi

1961: Nancy Fleming of Montague, Michigan

1962: Maria Fletcher of Asheville, North Carolina

1963: Jacquelyn Mayer of Sandusky, Ohio

1964: Donna Axum of El Dorado, Arkansas

1965: Vonda Van Dyke of Phoenix, Arizona

1966: Deborah Bryant of Overland Park, Kansas

1967: Jane Jayroe of Laverne, Oklahoma

1968: Debra Barnes of Pittsburgh, Kansas

1969: Judith Ford of Belvidere, Illinois

1970: Pam Eldred of Bloomfield, Michigan

1971: Phyllis George of Denton, Texas

1972: Laurel Schaefer of Bexley, Ohio

1973: Terry Meeuwsen of DePere, Wisconsin

1974: Rebecca King of Denver, Colorado

1975: Shirley Cothran of Denton, Texas

1976: Tawny Godin of Saratoga Springs, New York

1977: Dorothy Benham of Edina, Minnesota

1978: Susan Perkins of Columbus, Ohio

1979: Kylene Barker of Roanoke, Virginia

1980: Cheryl Prewitt of Ackerman, Mississippi

1981: Susan Powell of Elk City, Oklahoma

1982: Elizabeth Ward of Russellville, Arkansas

1983: Debra Maffett of Anaheim, California

1984: Vanessa Williams of Syracuse, New York; succeeded by Suzette Charles of Mays Landing, New Jersey, after Williams resigned due to a scandal over nude photographs.

1985: Sharlene Wells of Salt Lake City, Utah

1986: Susan Akin of Meridian, Mississippi

1987: Kellye Cash of Memphis, Tennessee

1988: Kaye Lani Rae Rafko of Monroe, Michigan

1989: Gretchen Carlson of Anoka, Minnesota

1990: Debbye Turner of Columbia, Missouri

1991: Marjorie Vincent of Oakpark, Illinois

1992: Carolyn Sapp of Honolulu, Hawaii

1993: Leanza Cornett of Jacksonville, Florida

1994: Kimberly Aiken of Columbia, South Carolina

1995: Heather Whitestone of Birmingham, Alabama

1996: Shawntel Smith of Muldrow, Oklahoma

1997: Tara Dawn Holland of Overland Park, Kansas

1998: Kate Shindle of Evanston, Illinois

1999: Nicole Johnson of Roanoke, Virginia

September 8

The Galveston Hurricane of 1900

Beginning on September 8, 1900, a savage hurricane battered the southern coast of Texas for 18 hours without letup, leaving such destruction that it continues to be ranked among the most devastating North Atlantic hurricanes of the 20th century. Although extensive damage was done to farms and villages for several miles east and west, the storm wreaked its greatest havoc on the island city of Galveston, a key southern port that at the time had a population of 38,000 people.

The city of Galveston lies 48 miles southeast of Houston, on Galveston Island. Galveston Island is a sea island some 32 miles long and two miles wide, lying in the Gulf of Mexico about two miles off the Texas coast across the entrance to Galveston Bay. Beautiful beaches line Galveston's gulf front, and a major harbor extends on the bay side for six miles.

The island was known to Spanish explorers from early times. Álvar Núñez Cabeza de Vaca is believed to have been shipwrecked in 1528 off either Galveston or the nearby island of San Luis, and from there he supposedly began traveling through what are now Texas, New Mexico, and Mexico. These travels inspired other expeditions on the North American mainland. The island and bay were named in 1785 by José de Evía, a pilot sent out to survey the Gulf coast by Bernardo de Gálvez, then Spanish governor of Louisiana and later viceroy of Mexico. Americans later gave the settlement an anglicized form of the name "Galveztown," namely Galveston.

The Spaniards settled the island in 1816 under Luis Aury. However, they soon lost control of it to the pirate chieftain Jean Lafitte and his cohorts, who used it as a base from which to prey on the Spanish galleon traffic. The Spanish were unable to curtail Lafitte's plundering, and Galveston remained a nest of pirates and outlaws until 1821 when the United States Navy ordered Lafitte to leave. He departed, burning Galveston behind him in its first great disaster.

The first English-speaking settlement was established on Galveston Island in 1837, and in 1839 the city of Galveston was incorporated under the independent Republic of Texas. The town grew, despite yellow fever epidemics and recurrent hurricanes, and during the American Civil War it was the largest Confederate port on the Gulf coast.

During the Galveston hurricane of 1900, Galveston was lashed by winds of up to 120 miles an hour. Since the weather instruments in Galveston broke at that point, the maximum velocity remains unknown. The barometer fell to 28.48, the lowest on record for the United States up to that time. As the sky turned black and the wind howled, Galvestonians were trapped on their island. The storm hurled gulf waters through the sea-level streets with tidal-wave force. For both life and property, the hurricane was catastrophic.

News reports of the time still capture Galveston's terror. On September 9, 1900, the *Richmond Times-Dispatch* alerted its readers to a special bulletin from Dallas:

> All Texas is in a keen state of doubt and uncertainty tonight concerning the fate of Galveston Island and city, which are shut off from communication. In everybody's mind is the suspicion that a calamity rests behind the lack of information from the Gulf coast. . . . It is said that the bridges leading from the mainland to the island have been swept away by the terrible fury of the wind and the rolling up of the water in the bay, and if this is so it is not seen how the town could have escaped.

When boats were finally able to make the crossing, the spectacle of flattened and desolated Galveston was worse than anything anyone had imagined. The death toll was continually revised upward during succeeding days, until Galveston's dead were estimated at between 5,000 and 8,000. The need to avoid disease by disposing of the bodies at once was so great that those killed could not be very carefully counted. Many persons who were never found were simply presumed to have been swept out to sea. Somewhere between one-seventh and one-fifth of Galveston's population perished.

In addition, almost all of the buildings were struck, and many disappeared entirely. Property damage was estimated at between $20 million to $25 million. Because the best of the cotton crop was then being shipped out through Galveston, the New York Stock Exchange dipped sharply when rumors of the disaster at Galveston first came in.

Founding of St. Augustine, Florida, the Nation's Oldest City

The founding of St. Augustine, Florida, on September 8, 1565, is a tribute to the nation's Spanish heritage. Many Americans, whose history books have placed more stress on the 13 original English colonies, find it something of a shock to be reminded that St. Augustine's founding took place 55 years before the Pilgrims ever set foot on Plymouth Rock and 42 years before the historic settlement at Jamestown, Virginia.

Spain's claim to Florida, a huge region that covered most of the southeast, dated from 1513 when Juan Ponce de León first explored the area. In 1564 a group of French Huguenots established Fort Caroline at the mouth of Florida's St. Johns River, ten miles northeast of what was later Jacksonville. The location had the potential of being used to prey upon Spanish treasure ships, a possibility that was not lost upon King Philip II of Spain. Therefore, he commissioned his leading admiral, Don Pedro Menéndez de Avilés, to drive the French Protestants out and named him proprietor of any colony he managed to establish in Florida.

Menéndez de Avilés first entered the bay of St. Augustine on August 28, 1565, the feast day of the saint for whom he named the bay. He then sailed north to reconnoiter the French position. Menéndez de Avilés returned to St. Augustine, disembarked his colonists on September 6 and 7, and ordered hasty fortification against an anticipated French attack. It was not until the next day, September 8, that the Spanish officially dedicated St.

Augustine "with many banners spread, to the sound of trumpets and salutes of artillery." Mass was said, and Menéndez de Avilés claimed the land in the name of Spain.

When the French appeared as expected several days later, what Menéndez de Avilés's chronicler called a miracle took place. Before they could enter the harbor, much less attack, their ships were driven off by a hurricane and wrecked. During their absence, Menéndez de Avilés attacked their half-empty Fort Caroline, killing 132 Huguenots within an hour. Later he found the shipwreck survivors and had them massacred, "not as Frenchmen but as Lutherans."

The Spanish victories marked the beginning of two and a half centuries of Spanish rule, interrupted only by a short interval of British control (1763–1783) and not terminated until July 17, 1821, when Florida formally passed from Spain to the United States under the terms of the Adams-Onis Treaty (see related essays throughout this book).

First Broadcast of *Star Trek*

The famous television program *Star Trek*, created by Gene Roddenberry, made its broadcast premiere on September 8, 1966. It was aired by the National Broadcasting Corporation (NBC), one of the three major networks existing at the time. *Star Trek* was the story of a spaceship of adventurers, sent on a mission of discovery and exploration throughout the galaxy aboard the starship *Enterprise*. A total of 79 episodes were shown over three seasons before the program was retired.

Star Trek never enjoyed high ratings and was constantly on the verge of cancellation. However, it won a loyal fan base for several reasons. First, the excitement and idealism of the American space program translated into a certain fascination with the idea of interstellar adventure and contacting alien cultures. Second, in many ways the show was revolutionary. Men and women, and blacks and whites were shown interacting in an atmosphere of equality. A black woman (Lieutenant Uhura) was given a position of prominence in the regular cast, and participated in the first interracial kiss ever shown on network television in an episode involving herself and Captain Kirk. Third, the plots were noted for their adult content and treatment of controversial issues in an era when science fiction programs were considered fit mostly for children.

When *Star Trek* went into reruns, a process known as syndication, it gradually became one of the most popular programs ever shown. Throughout the 1970s the number of followers grew, and they began to hold large conventions and other gatherings. A wide variety of science fiction novels with *Star Trek* themes were published, thereby helping to make science fiction a popular and respectable genre of adult fiction.

In 1979 *Star Trek: The Motion Picture* was released. Several more *Star Trek* movies, all featuring members of the original cast, were produced in the 1980s. Then, from 1987 to 1994, *Star Trek: The Next Generation*, the television sequel to *Star Trek*, aired. The sequel earned not only high ratings but also critical acclaim for the quality of its plots, acting, and special effects. Evidence of science fiction's newfound prestige was seen in the large budgets authorized to produce episodes of *Next Generation*. Several *Next Generation* movies followed, and so did two more *Star Trek* spin-offs: *Star Trek Voyager* and *Deep Space Nine*. *Deep Space Nine* departed somewhat from the original *Star Trek* premise of exploration and encounter with the unknown, but *Voyager* is generally regarded as staying fairly true to the original *Star Trek* theme.

September 9

California Admitted to the Union

On September 9, 1850, President Millard Fillmore signed into law a bill that made California the 31st state of the Union. The act of admitting California to the Union was the culmination of a confused political period extending back into the previous 30 years of Californian history.

California, once a Spanish possession, became a Mexican province in the early 1820s after Mexico's successful revolt against Spain. The Californios, including several hundred Americans who had settled in the area, grew increasingly dissatisfied with Mexican rule. They briefly asserted their independence in 1836 and drove out the last Mexican governor in 1845. Under the influence of the American explorer Captain John C. Frémont, a somewhat ragged band of American "revolutionaries" conducted a surprise attack on the Mexican presidio in the pueblo of Sonoma on June 14, 1846. They surrounded the house of the commandant, General Mariano G. Vallejo, and seized the garrison in a practically bloodless battle. The frontiersmen's army then hauled down the Mexican flag, raised its own Bear flag over the Sonoma plaza, and proclaimed the independence of California. A motto read: "A bear stands his ground always, and as long as the stars shine we stand for our cause."

Talk of making California an independent republic came to an abrupt halt three weeks later when the issue merged with a larger question, namely the American declaration of war on Mexico on May 13, 1846. When the news of the war finally reached California, Commodore John D. Sloat of the United States Navy captured the Californian capital of Monterey on July 7. He raised the American flag and claimed California as a military possession of the United States. Two days later the Bear flag was hauled down from the Sonoma plaza.

The Treaty of Guadalupe Hidalgo of February 2, 1848, which ended the Mexican War arranged for the cession of California to the United States. The federal government was therefore obligated to provide a civil government for the region. Settlement of California's political status soon became even more pressing, as news spread that James W. Marshall, while establishing a sawmill for John A. Sutter on the south fork of the American River at Coloma, had discovered gold on January 24, 1848. The discovery touched off the California gold rush.

As thousands of Americans migrated to California, the congressional debate about what should be done with this area of great national importance grew bitter and was deadlocked over the question of slavery. The United States had 15 free states and 15 slave states, so the admission of California to statehood would upset this delicate balance. After a confused period in which Spanish law, American law, and military law were simultaneously administered in California, military governor Brigadier General Benet Riley issued a proclamation on June 3, 1849, "recommending the formation of a State constitution, or a plan for a Territorial government." Forty-eight delegates met in a constitutional convention in Colton Hall in Monterey on September 1, 1849. On October 10 they adopted a state constitution, which was ratified overwhelmingly by the people of California on November 13, 1849, and put into effect a month later. On December 15 the state legislature convened at San Jose and on December 20 Peter H. Burnett was inaugurated as the first governor.

On that same day, Brigadier General Riley issued a proclamation: "A new executive having been elected and installed into office in accordance with the provisions of the constitution of the State, the undersigned hereby resigns his powers as Governor of California." The highest American official in California had recognized California as a state, although legally it had no right to declare itself such without congressional action.

This development precipitated a debate that lasted for eight months in Congress. Since the founders of California had explicitly included in the constitution adopted at Monterey a clause forbidding slavery, the issue was prolonged by pro-slavery members of Congress who desperately fought to prevent the admission of a new free state. From January to September 1850 threats of dissolution of the Union, if California was admitted, were frequently made.

California was finally admitted as a free state in the momentous Compromise of 1850, worked out by Henry Clay. Thus California, cut off from direct contact with the 30 states in the east, entered the Union less than three years after gold had been discovered within its borders. Sharing a distinction possessed by the original 13 states and Texas, it did not pass through customary territorial status.

Civil Rights Act of 1957

In the 1954 case of *Brown* v. *Board of Education*, the United States Supreme Court ordered the desegregation of public schools (see related articles throughout this book), which led to widespread opposition, particularly in the South. Economic pressure, intimidation, and violence were used to delay desegregation and discourage blacks from exercising their right to vote. Finally the United States Congress took action, and the Civil Rights Act of 1957 (the first such measure since the Reconstruction following the Civil War) became law on September 9, 1957.

The Civil Rights Act of 1957 gave the United States attorney general the power to seek federal court injunctions against any violation, or threatened violation, of individual voting rights. It provided for the creation of a special civil rights division within the United States Department of Justice, which subsequently initiated hundreds of legal actions against the infringement or attempted infringement of African American rights. The act established a six-member, bipartisan United States Commission on Civil Rights. This commission was armed with subpoena powers to investigate the alleged deprivation of voting rights, examine federal laws and policies with respect to the equal protection of the laws, and look into any legal developments constituting a denial of such equal protection.

The act was an important step in the budding civil rights movement, although it was later succeeded by more comprehensive and effective legislation.

September 10

John Smith Assumes Jamestown Council Presidency

John Smith, one of the first English colonists in America, was born in Willoughby in Lincolnshire, England, in 1580. He left England around 1596 and became a military adventurer abroad, fighting in wars against the Turks, probably until 1604. Upon his return to England he developed an interest in the London Company (sometimes called the Virginia Company) and became a member of the company-financed expedition that in 1607 established the first permanent English settlement in America at Jamestown, Virginia.

Smith, whom historians have alternately criticized for boastfulness and exaggeration and praised for bravery and resourcefulness, had his ups and downs with the other settlers. When they set sail for Virginia in 1606, he was named in the secret sailing orders as a member of the council for the new community. During the voyage, however, he was charged with sedition and imprisoned. When the ship landed and the secret instructions containing his name were opened, it was decided that he had forfeited his right to sit on the council.

During the colony's bleak first year, the settlers were underfed and wracked by disease. Their leaders, unprepared for frontier hardships, were also unaccustomed to farming. Smith went out on various foraging expeditions, explored, and mapped the countryside surrounding Jamestown, and warded off starvation by trading goods with the native tribes for food.

Smith also found the time to write a personal narrative in 1608, *A True Relation of Such Occurrences and Accidents of Noate As Hath Hapned in Virginia since the First Planting of that Collony*. It was the first book ever published about America and is the most respected of his writings. So successful were Smith's undertakings that he was permitted to take his seat in the council in 1607 and was elected its president in July 1608. A friend, Scrivener, acted in Smith's place until his return from an exploratory trip on September 7, 1608. Smith assumed his presidential duties three days later, on September 10, 1608.

Although he has been described as "in all but name" the leader of the settlement, his council presidency was short-lived. A new charter was granted for the Jamestown colony in 1609, and Smith was left out in the reorganization of the government. He returned to England the same year and henceforth devoted himself to exploration and to writing reminiscences, which encouraged inter-

est in the New World and grew more colorful as the years went by. His *Map of Virginia*, containing a remarkable map and a vivid account of the new land and its native inhabitants, appeared in 1612.

Two years later Smith led an expedition that explored and mapped the American coast from the Penobscot River to Cape Cod. He was responsible for the name New England, bestowed on that region at his request by the Prince of Wales. It is said that such works as his *Description of New England* (1616) proved useful to the Pilgrims on their historic *Mayflower* voyage. Smith also wrote *New Englands Trials*, a tract on fisheries, in 1620. In 1622 he added a report on the colony at Plymouth to it.

The legend that in 1608 during his stay at Jamestown, Pocahontas (daughter of the native chieftain Powhatan) prevailed upon her father to spare Smith's life is not included in the personal narrative that Smith wrote at the time. That story, which appeared in Smith's much later work, *Generall Historie of Virginia, New-England, and the Summer Isles* in 1624, curiously parallels his accounts of generous women who saved him from earlier, similar disasters in other lands. It is often considered as perhaps, though not necessarily, an exaggeration of what really happened.

Also fanciful in its own way was the name Pocahontas, given to the young Matoaka by her tribe in the belief that knowledge of her real name would enable the English settlers to cast evil magic on her. Unfortunately for her, she was taken prisoner by the English in 1612. After her conversion to Christianity her name was changed again, this time to Rebecca. A further change of name took place in April 1614, when she married the colonist John Rolfe, a union that brought peace between the natives and the English in Virginia for several years. Two years after their marriage, Pocahontas went with Rolfe to England. A letter attributed to John Smith and dated 1616 called the sterling qualities of Pocahontas (including the disputed story) to the attention of Anne—consort of England's King James I—who received Pocahontas with royal honors.

Pocahontas became ill and died as she was preparing to return to America in 1617. If she was born in 1595, as historians hesitantly surmise, she was about 22 years of age at the time. Her husband, John Rolfe (whose discovery of a method for curing tobacco laid the foundation for Virginia's later prosperity), died in Virginia in 1622. Smith, who remained in England, survived both John Rolfe and Pocahontas. His literary output included one work against which serious charges of fabrication have been leveled, though not proven: *The True Travels, Adventures, and Observations of Captaine John Smith* (1630). He died in 1631, the year of publication of his last tract, *Advertisements for the Unexperienced Planters of New-England.*

Beginning of the Organization of Petroleum Exporting Countries (OPEC)

The Organization of Petroleum Exporting Countries (OPEC), an international cartel of oil-producing nations involved in the "energy crisis" and other economic disruptions that plagued the American economy in the 1970s, was established during the Baghdad Conference held in Baghdad, Iraq, beginning on September 10, 1960. The founding nations were Iran, Iraq, Kuwait, Saudi Arabia, and Venezuela. They were later joined by Qatar in 1961, Libya and Indonesia in 1962, the United Arab Emirates in 1967, Algeria in 1969, Nigeria in 1971, Ecuador in 1973, and Gabon in 1975. The organization's headquarters have been located in Vienna, Austria, since 1965.

The roots of OPEC go back to the 1950s when western oil companies, backed by the governments of the United States and Great Britain, dominated and operated the vast oil fields of the Middle East and elsewhere in the third world. These oil fields produced millions of barrels of crude oil a day, which then went by tanker or pipeline to refineries and distribution centers in America, Europe, and Japan. The oil companies kept the price of crude oil low in order to minimize their payments to the governments of the nations that actually owned the oil fields. A low price for crude oil benefited both the oil companies, who made a larger profit when they refined the oil into products such as gasoline, and the consumers of western nations, who saved money when buying the products. OPEC was established by the oil-producing nations, the biggest of which were in the Middle East, to form a coordinated response.

The economic growth enjoyed by the industrialized world in the 1960s, plus various wasteful habits such as the popularity of large "gas guzzling" automobiles among consumers, made western nations increasingly dependent on oil imports. By the early 1970s OPEC was able to make its move. The oil-producing nations successfully seized control over their oil fields by "nationalizing" them. They then instituted a series of steep price hikes, backed by production quotas among OPEC members in order to prevent oversupply. The result was economic turmoil in the United States, and high inflation as the price hikes filtered through the economy due to the increased cost of energy (hence the "energy crisis"). The severity of the crisis was underlined when OPEC initiated a week-long embargo on any oil shipments to the United States, in response to America's support of Israel during the Arab-Israeli war of 1973.

Although there was some discussion of a military intervention to break OPEC's hold on oil prices, the United States ultimately let the free market system resolve the situation. After a severe economic recession, the American economy began to rebound in 1975. Furthermore, new oil fields were discovered in Alaska, Mexico, the North Sea, and elsewhere around the world, and smaller, more fuel-efficient automobiles were introduced. Some nations, like France, invested heavily in alternative energy sources such as nuclear power. By the 1980s, these competitive pressures were having an effect. While OPEC lost its ability to effectively dictate the price of crude oil, individual member nations strapped for cash routinely exceeded their assigned production quotas, thereby decreasing OPEC's political and economic significance.

September 11

American Revolution: Battle of Brandywine

In the summer of 1777 the British forces in America conducted two vigorous campaigns to end the movement for colonial independence. In New York State, General John Burgoyne and Lieutenant Colonel Barry St. Leger undertook an unsuccessful joint operation against the American rebels, leading to the British surrender at Saratoga on October 17, 1777. In Pennsylvania, General William Howe, the British commander in chief in North America, was able to capture the rebel capital of Philadelphia after defeating George Washington's troops at Brandywine on September 11, 1777.

After leaving his winter quarters at Morristown, New Jersey, in May 1777 Washington camped at Middlebrook, New Jersey, where he could thwart any attempt by the British to move directly against Philadelphia from their positions in New Brunswick. In June, General Howe, unable to draw the Americans into battle, removed his troops to New York City. From there he planned to advance on Philadelphia by sea. On July 23 some 15,000 of his soldiers set sail from New York in more than 260 ships. Howe's armada reached Delaware Bay on July 29 but found the river approach to Philadelphia heavily defended. The British general accordingly sailed instead to the head of Chesapeake Bay, where his troops disembarked on August 25.

Worn down by the journey and the late summer heat, the British troops then started on an overland trek to Philadelphia.

Howe's movements confused General Washington. However, despite misgivings that his adversary intended to sail up the Hudson River to join Burgoyne and St. Leger, the American commander decided to prepare to defend Philadelphia. When the British army reached Kennett Square on September 10, 1777, they found 11,000 colonials on the north side of Brandywine Creek blocking their advance. The Pennsylvania militia under General John Armstrong defended the Americans left at Pyle's Ford, Generals Nathanael Greene and Anthony Wayne defended the center at Chadds Ford, and General John Sullivan was stationed at the right.

Howe decided to envelop the American flank, employing the same tactic that had previously given him victory on Long Island. He sent Baron Wilhelm von Knyphausen's division in a feint toward Chadds Ford and commanded General Charles Cornwallis's division to encircle Sullivan. When Knyphausen did not seriously attempt to advance, Washington decided that Howe had divided his forces and planned a counterattack across Chadds Ford. However, he abandoned the idea when he received intelligence reports that incorrectly stated that Howe was not trying to outflank him.

Cornwallis crossed the Brandywine at Jeffries Ford, above the end of the American right flank, and fell upon Sullivan's men. The colonials fought bravely, encouraged by the presence of Washington and the young French nobleman Marie-Joseph-Paul-Yves-Roch-Gilbert du Motier de Lafayette, who received a leg wound in the battle. When General Greene committed the American reserves to Sullivan's aid, Knyphausen was able to cross Chadds Ford with little resistance. The Americans managed to hold their ground until sunset, when they withdrew in confusion.

The British suffered over 500 casualties but the Americans suffered more than 1,000. Perhaps Howe could have destroyed Washington's army had he pursued it, but his men were too exhausted for such a chase. The colonials escaped.

The Navajo Nation Fair

This is a movable event.

The giant Navajo fair held annually at Window Rock, Arizona, the capital of the Navajo Nation (the largest of the tribal nations in the United States), is one of the largest Native American fairs in the United States. Not only Navajos but Native Americans representing many other tribes partici-

pate. There are colorful traditional dances and exhibits of a wide variety of clothing, arts and crafts, and other facets of cultures that predate written history. The fair also represents the contribution of Native Americans to American history and is a practical example of cross-cultural influences between the Navajo people and the modern world.

The first Navajo Tribal Fair took place in 1908, in Shiprock, New Mexico, the headquarters of the Northern Navajo Agency. It was the inspiration of the first superintendent of the agency, William T. Shelton. For many years Shelton had helped and guided the Navajo people, and he was eager to exhibit their products and crafts. The main attractions of the fair, in addition to races and rodeos, were the vegetables, canned and preserved foods, improved breeds of animals, arts, crafts, and needlework of the Navajos.

The first Shiprock fair was such a success that it was decided that it would be held on an annual basis. In 1937 the first Window Rock fair was held, capitalizing on the success of the Shiprock event. The Window Rock fair was discontinued during World War II, but it resumed in 1951. It has been held every year since then in early September, with the most recent fair covering five days from September 9 to September 13, 1998. Over 100,000 people attended.

Although the Window Rock fair is a highlight of the Navajo country, there are many other places of interest. Occupying a four-corner area of the Southwest where Arizona, New Mexico, Colorado, and Utah join, the Navajo Nation reservation is some 200 miles wide and 135 miles north to south and offers some of the most scenic vistas in the Southwest. A high tableland, it is crisscrossed by spectacular canyons and sprinkled with eroded buttes and other natural formations, one of the most famous being Window Rock itself. The rock has been important for many centuries in the rites and legends of the Water Way Ceremony, and Navajo people call the formation Tse-ghahodzani, "perforated rock." Traditionally, it was one of only four places where tribal medicine men went to get water for rain ceremonies.

September 12

War of 1812: Battle of North Point, Maryland

September 12, still honored as Maryland Defenders' Day, marks the anniversary of the battle of North Point in the War of 1812. The battle was fought near Baltimore, Maryland, on September 12, 1814—the day before the unsuccessful British bombardment of Baltimore's Fort McHenry, which inspired Francis Scott Key to write "The Star-Spangled Banner."

The War of 1812 began when the United States declared war on Great Britain on June 18, 1812. Despite scattered American successes in the first two years of conflict, the United States lacked the resources to match the naval superiority and other advantages of Great Britain. By the late summer of 1814, prospects for the young American nation were gloomy. The British had instituted a devastating blockade on the Atlantic seaboard and, under Admiral Sir Alexander Cochrane's supervision, were diverting attention from the Canadian border–Great Lakes campaigns with attacks on the east coast. In August the British had attacked Washington, D.C., and set fire to the White House and other public buildings. Rear Admiral Sir George Cockburn, in command of British naval forces in the area, had threatened to burn Baltimore as well.

On September 11 British vessels sailed up Chesapeake Bay and entered the Patapsco River. Early the next morning they landed 6,000 troops at North Point, near Baltimore, and then continued up the Patapsco in preparation for their attack on Fort McHenry, which was fortified with 1,000 troops under Major George Armistead. General Samuel Smith, a United States senator from Maryland, also stood ready in command of some 13,000 regulars and militiamen who had been assembled to defend the city.

When news of the British landing at North Point reached Smith, he sent Brigadier General John Stricker with a force of about 3,200 to watch the movements of the British and act as conditions required. Stricker accordingly sent roughly 150 men ahead, accompanied by sharpshooters, to reconnoiter. The British General Robert Ross, advancing up North Point in command of his troops, had ridden to the head of the column when the sharpshooters, firing from concealed positions, killed him.

The British force continued forward under the second in command, and met the first line of General Stricker's army. The Americans fought hard for two hours before falling back half a mile and waiting for a follow-up attack, which never came. Toward sunset, they withdrew to the defenses on the perimeter of Baltimore. There, joined by reinforcements and still waiting, they spent the rainy night.

Instead of attacking in that direction, however, the British troops halted and camped on the field, while their ships sailed up the Patapsco River toward Fort McHenry. At six the next morning, September 13, the ships began their bombardment of the fort from a distance of two miles, a range that best suited their guns. Back on the North Point side of the city, the British troops watched the shells decimate the fort's occupants while preparing themselves to join in an amphibious assault on the fort once its walls had been breached. The bombardment, however, was unsuccessful.

A few days earlier, a young American lawyer named Francis Scott Key and an American intermediary named John Skinner had boarded one of the British ships to negotiate the release of William Beanes, a friend of Key's whom the British held prisoner. The negotiations were successful, but at a price: Key and Skinner were held by the British until after the attack on Baltimore, and so became unwilling witnesses to the shelling of Fort McHenry.

The 25-hour bombardment ceased shortly after daybreak on September 14, 1814. From their viewpoint, Key and Skinner did not know whether the fort had surrendered. Anxiously, they waited for the day to grow brighter and a breeze to unfurl the limp banner above the fort before they could see that it was the American flag. Relieved and inspired, Key exuberantly wrote on the back of a letter a rough draft of the words that were to become the national anthem of the United States:

O say can you see, by the dawn's early light,
What so proudly we hailed at the twilight's
    last gleaming,
Whose broad stripes and bright stars
    through the perilous fight
O'er the ramparts we watched, were so gal-
    lantly streaming?
And the rockets' red glare, the bombs
    bursting in air,
Gave proof through the night that our flag
    was still there:
O say does that star-spangled banner yet
    wave
O'er the land of the free and the home of
    the brave?

That night, in a Baltimore hotel, Key wrote the words out in full. The next morning he read them to Judge Joseph H. Nicholson, his brother-in-law, who had been one of the defenders of the fort. The judge liked them so well that he took them to the press and had them printed in handbill form under the title of "The Defence of Fort McHenry." The song subsequently appeared in the *Baltimore Patriot* on September 20 and the *Baltimore American* on September 21. Tradition has it that the anthem was first sung in public by the actor Ferdinand Durang.

The popularity of "The Star-Spangled Banner," which was evident in Baltimore, grew more slowly in the rest of the nation. Though it was often sung by Union soldiers during the Civil War, it competed for attention with such other favorites as "America" and "Hail Columbia." In the decades following the Civil War, however, "The Star-Spangled Banner" gained currency, especially in the armed forces. In 1904 the secretary of the navy directed that it be played at morning and evening colors throughout the navy. The army and navy, in response to an executive order by President Woodrow Wilson, have regarded "The Star-Spangled Banner" as the national anthem since 1916. Congress confirmed that order in an act signed by President Herbert Hoover on March 3, 1931.

Jesse Owens's Birthday

Jesse Owens, one of the most famous African American athletes in history, was born James Cleveland Owens on September 12, 1913, in Oakville, Alabama. When he was nine years old, the family moved to Cleveland, Ohio, where he acquired the nickname "Jesse"—a mistaken contraction of his first two initials, J.C. Attending Cleveland's East Technical High School, he exhibited exceptional prowess in track and field competitions. He set world records for high school students in such events as the high jump, the broad jump, and the 100-yard dash.

Courted by a number of colleges and universities, Owens decided to attend Ohio State University. There he set new world records of 26' 8" for the running broad jump and 10.2 seconds for the 100-meter dash. Although he did not graduate from Ohio State until 1937, Owens was invited to participate in the 1936 Olympic Games held in Berlin, Germany, as a member of the track and field team for the United States.

In Germany, Adolf Hitler and the Nazi Party had recently risen to power. Hitler was anxious to enhance the international prestige of his new Third Reich, and was proud of the fact that the capital city of Berlin had been chosen to host the prestigious Olympic events. Furthermore, Hitler and the Nazis believed in the racial superiority of Germans and Germanic peoples over all other ethnic groups, including all people of color. Expecting German athletes to prevail in the events, Hitler was stunned when Owens proceeded to win four gold medals and set several new world records. It was a symbolic victory for African Americans and a rebuke to racists around the world.

After the Olympics and his graduation from college, Owens went on to work in a number of youth-oriented sports education programs. He also participated in several public relations programs sponsored by the government and private

industry, eventually establishing his own public relations firm. Owens's autobiography, *The Jesse Owens Story*, was published in 1970. He also received a number of awards, including the Presidential Medal of Freedom in 1976 and the Living Legend Award in 1979. He died on March 31, 1980, in Tucson, Arizona.

September 13

Death of John Barry

John Barry, a naval hero of the American Revolution, was born at Tacumshane in County Wexford, Ireland, in 1745. The exact date of his birth is unknown. While he was still quite young, his father apprenticed him to a ship's captain. At 14 Barry came to America, where he found employment on a trading ship based out of Philadelphia, Pennsylvania. Hardworking and ambitious, he had become the master of a schooner by his 21st birthday, and in the decade leading up to the revolution he commanded several trading vessels.

When hostilities between the American colonies and Great Britain erupted in 1776, Barry placed his naval skills at the disposal of the Continental Congress. Congress quickly accepted his aid and ordered him to outfit the first fleet sailing from Philadelphia. The Pennsylvania Council of Safety likewise enlisted Barry's assistance and authorized him to build a ship for the colony.

As commander of the brig *Lexington*, Barry was responsible for the first capture in battle of a British warship by a regularly commissioned Continental vessel. The *Lexington*'s seizure of the British ship *Edward* occurred on April 17, 1776. In October of that year, the Continental Congress placed Barry as seventh on its seniority listing of naval captains, and put him in command of the *Effingham*, still under construction. However, the frigate, which was scheduled to put to sea in September 1778, was burned on orders from General George Washington shortly before the British occupied Philadelphia, to keep it from falling into enemy hands.

During the winter of 1777–1778, Barry harassed British supply vessels in the lower Delaware River. He then took command of the 32-gun warship *Raleigh*. Shortly after the *Raleigh* put to sea in September 1778, it encountered a 64-gun British warship with an accompanying frigate. A 48-hour chase ensued, and after a hard-fought battle the *Raleigh* was finally captured near the mouth of the Penobscot River in what is now Maine.

In the fall of 1780 Barry was put in command of the *Alliance* and ordered to take Colonel Henry Laurens to France on a diplomatic mission. On his return voyage he encountered two British warships, the *Atalanta* and the *Trepassy*. In the battle that followed, he was severely wounded, but he continued to fight and eventually forced the enemy to surrender. The captain of one of the ships had been killed, but the captain of the other, when taken aboard the *Alliance*, surrendered his sword. Barry took it and then returned it, saying: "You have merited it, sir. Your king ought to give you a better ship."

As commander of the *Alliance*, Barry continued to inflict considerable damage on the British fleet until the end of the war. The January 1783 encounter between the *Alliance* and the British frigate *Sybil* is generally regarded as the last significant naval battle of the American Revolution.

Barry continued in naval service after the end of the war, and made many suggestions for the improvement of the navy. On June 4, 1794, President George Washington appointed him senior captain of the American naval forces. Although the rank of commodore had not yet been created, the officer in command of more than one ship was popularly known by that title. Barry qualified for this honor since he had twice been in charge of all the United States ships in the West Indies. Barry died on September 13, 1803.

John J. Pershing's Birthday

John Joseph Pershing, commander of the American Expeditionary Force in World War I, was born in Linn County, Missouri, on September 13, 1860. He attended Kirksville's Missouri Normal School and graduated with a teaching degree in 1880. Pershing taught for a while, but eventually entered the United States Military Academy at West Point, New York. He graduated in 1886 and entered active service as a second lieutenant in the United States Army.

Pershing was assigned to the Sixth Cavalry in New Mexico and fought against the Apache tribe. He also participated in the campaign against the Sioux tribe in South Dakota during the winter of 1890–1891, a campaign that included the infamous Wounded Knee massacre. During the mid-1890s, Pershing was assigned to the Tenth Cavalry, which consisted of African American "Buffalo Soldiers." During this service he received the nickname "Black Jack," and his unit fought in the famous Battle of San Juan Hill during the Spanish-American War of 1898.

After the war, which resulted in the American takeover of the Philippines (formerly held by Spain but ceded to the United States), Pershing served from 1899 until 1903 in northern Mindanao fighting native resistance to the occupation. Afterward, he was appointed military attaché to Japan during the Russo-Japanese War of 1905. Pershing was promoted to brigadier general in September 1906, and was the military commander of the Moro Province in the Philippines from 1909 until 1914.

In 1914 Pershing was sent back to the United States to command the 8th Infantry Brigade at the Presidio base in San Francisco, California. While stationed there, he lost his wife and three daughters to a fire. In 1916 Pershing was assigned to the American expedition against Mexican bandit Pancho Villa after Villa's raid on the border town of Columbus, New Mexico, which had caused nearly 20 deaths. Pershing was promoted to major general in September 1916 and full general in October 1917. That same year he was given the command of the American Expeditionary Force sent to France in World War I. He was an effective leader and administrator, although his campaign strategies showed little originality.

Pershing was promoted to general of the armies of the United States in September 1919. He became the army chief of staff in 1921, and helped to reorganize the army during the period of demobilization that followed the war. He retired in September 1924, and wrote his memoirs, which were published under the title *My Experience in the World War One* in 1931. He died on July 15, 1948, in Washington, D.C., and was buried in Arlington National Cemetery.

September 14

Mexican War: American Forces Capture Mexico City

On September 14, 1847, American forces under the command of General Winfield Scott gained control of Mexico City. Scott's capture of the "halls of Montezuma" was the decisive campaign during the Mexican War. The victory led to General Antonio López de Santa Anna's surrender and to Mexico's acceptance in 1848 of the Treaty of Guadalupe Hidalgo. According to that treaty, Mexico recognized the Rio Grande as its northern boundary and ceded California and New Mexico (then comprising much of the present-day American Southwest) to the United States in exchange for $15 million.

Scott's 1847 campaign against Mexico City followed the route taken by Hernando Cortez during his conquest of Mexico more than three centuries earlier. On March 9 the American commander landed his force of more than 10,000 men along the beaches southeast of Veracruz. The soldiers then set about establishing their positions in a wide arc to the rear of the city, thereby cutting the port off from the rest of Mexico. On March 22 this undertaking was completed, and Scott demanded the immediate surrender of Veracruz. When the Mexicans refused, the Americans began a land and naval bombardment of the city. After four days of continuous shelling, negotiations for surrender started on March 26. Three days later American forces occupied the port.

Having gained control of Veracruz, Scott began the overland trek to Mexico City. With fewer than 9,000 troops the American general set out for the inland capital on April 8. His immediate objective was Jalapa, a town whose location 75 miles northwest of Veracruz and 4,250 feet above sea level made it free from the yellow fever that plagued the coastal lowlands. Proceeding along the national highway, Scott's forces advanced with little difficulty until they were about 20 miles from Jalapa. Then, on April 13 they encountered outlying enemy defenses at Plan del Río just below the important mountain pass at Cerro Gordo.

Less than two months after his crushing defeat at Buena Vista in northern Mexico, General Santa Anna had reorganized his army and readied his troops to defend the route leading from Veracruz to Mexico City. Choosing to engage Scott's army at Cerro Gordo, the Mexican general used the natural terrain of the area and his 13,000-man force to advantage. He established defenses extending two miles from the high bluff and river (the Río del Plan) on his right, across the national highway to El Telégrafo (or Telegraph Hill, as the Cerro Gordo eminence was sometimes called) and another rise called La Atalaya on his left.

Although the Mexican troops were well positioned, adroit reconnoitering by Scott's engineers disclosed a path leading to the enemy's left flank. Scott exploited this passage. After the troops cleared away rocks and underbrush, he moved his artillery along the route. Aided by this firepower, American forces were able to capture La Atalaya on April 17. The following morning the troops commanded by General Gideon J. Pillow undertook a diversionary attack against the Mexican right flank. Meanwhile, the main body of American soldiers assaulted Santa Anna's strongest fortification at El Telégrafo. The struggle was brief. By 10:00 a.m. on April 18 the Mexican army had retreated, leaving Scott and his men with more than 3,000 prisoners, a large number of arms, and control of the Cerro Gordo pass.

On April 19 Scott's troops marched into Jalapa. Three days later an expedition under the command of General William Jenkins Worth took control of the city of Perote. However, as his army moved westward, Scott faced a difficult problem. Many of his soldiers were 12-month volunteers, and their enlistments were due to expire in the middle of June. Scott pleaded his case and offered bounties to these volunteers to persuade them to extend their time with the army; but when his efforts failed he reluctantly decided to release them at once. Thus, during the first week in May 1847, about one-third of his force returned to the coast, leaving Scott deep within enemy territory with an army of less than 7,000.

Early in May the forces under Worth continued to advance westward, and on May 15 they captured Puebla. By the end of May, Scott moved his headquarters to that important Mexican city. Awaiting additional troops, Scott's army had to remain in Puebla throughout the months of June and July. During that time the morale of the soldiers sagged badly, but reinforcements gradually came to their assistance. By early August American troops in Puebla numbered nearly 14,000, including 3,000 who were ill.

Setting forth again on August 7, Scott's army (minus the hundreds of sick who were left behind) reached the Valley of Mexico on August 11. With the arduous journey from the coast behind them, the American forces still faced the task of actually conquering the Mexican capital. Following his defeat at Cerro Gordo, Santa Anna had returned to Mexico City. There, having re-established his political power, he strengthened the capital's defenses and organized the 25,000 troops under his command. By the time Scott's army reached the Valley of Mexico, the Mexican general was prepared to meet the American assault.

Santa Anna's strategy was to supplement Mexico City's natural defenses since vast marshlands surrounding the capital made access possible only through a few stone causeways. Santa Anna fortified the most likely of these approaches—at the suburb of Guadalupe Hidalgo to the north and at Mexicalcingo to the south—with infantry and artillery. Between these two sites he erected his strongest defense atop El Peñón, a hill that commanded the main road from the east.

Scott learned of Santa Anna's disposition of his forces through reconnaissance operations. Initially, he thought that Mexicalcingo would be the most vulnerable point at which to attack, but last-minute intelligence gathered by General Worth's men prompted a change of plan. Scott decided to circle around Xochimilco and Chalco Lakes, which lay east of Mexicalcingo, and attack San Augustín, a town far below Santa Anna's southernmost fortifications.

Taking San Augustín, Scott had the option of attacking north toward San Antonio where Santa Anna had quickly established defenses, or west across the Pedregal lava field to Contreras, which was defended by General Gabriel Valencia. The American commander chose the latter course, and on August 19 Pillow's men moved slowly toward Contreras, building a road across the lava field as they advanced. By evening the main element of Pillow's force was in position before Contreras, and a smaller portion had occupied the village of San Gerónimo to the west and discovered a ravine leading behind Valencia's position.

Pillow and Scott decided to attack Valencia from the rear. At 3:00 a.m. on August 20 the Americans began to advance along the ravine leading from San Gerónimo to Contreras. The Mexicans, who were concentrating on Pillow's diversionary force in front of them, were taken by surprise when the American forces struck from behind. The Mexicans suffered heavy casualties before surrendering.

With the fall of Contreras, San Antonio was outflanked and Santa Anna withdrew his forces to Churubusco. The Americans could have advanced directly from Contreras toward Mexico City, but Scott would have had to leave his right flank exposed to Santa Anna. The American commander refused to take the risk and decided to conquer Churubusco before attacking the capital. The Mexicans tenaciously defended their position against the American force, which was weary after the morning's action at Contreras, but by late afternoon Churubusco fell. The Americans found themselves within three miles of Mexico City.

His troops defeated twice in a single day, Santa Anna was anxious to delay further battle. The Mexican commander, rejecting a demand by Scott for immediate surrender, indicated interest in an armistice to permit negotiations. Scott, who also desired to give his weary troops rest, agreed. The negotiators talked until September 6, but failed to reach an agreement. On September 7, Scott moved north to Tacubaya, from which his forces could attack Mexico City's southwestern defenses. Two objectives lay ahead. First, there was the palace of Chapultepec. Second, at the western end of the park surrounding Chapultepec was a group of buildings known as Molino del Rey, where the enemy was supposedly manufacturing guns. On September 8 the Americans attacked Molino del Rey and took it at the cost of more than 700 men.

On September 12 the Americans began to bombard Chapultepec, and on the following morning they assaulted the palace. As a division under Brigadier General John A. Quitman advanced from the south, Pillow led his men from the southwest and Worth's forces came from the west. By 9:30 a.m. Chapultepec had fallen. The attackers pressed on toward Mexico City. Quitman drove for the Belén Gate and Worth for the San Cosmé Gate. Both objectives were taken by nightfall.

Santa Anna decided to save his demoralized troops for another battle, and on the night of September 13 he withdrew his forces to Guadalupe Hidalgo rather than engage the Americans in the streets of the capital. On the morning of September 14 the Mexico City authorities, after an unsuccessful bid for negotiated terms, surrendered to the Americans. Quitman occupied the Grand Plaza and raised the American flag over the palace.

For all intents and purposes, the capture of Mexico City on September 14, 1847, marked the end of the Mexican War. The war's formal conclusion, however, had to await the signing of the Treaty of Guadalupe Hidalgo in February 1848.

Margaret Sanger's Birthday

Margaret Sanger, the founder of the American birth control movement, was born Margaret Louise Higgins on September 14, 1879, in Corning, New York. Her parents were Michael Hennessey Higgins, an Irish stonemason, and Anne Purcell Higgins. Margaret was the sixth of 11 children. Her mother died young, worn out by poverty and frequent pregnancies, but Margaret was able to obtain an education with the help of her sisters. She trained as a nurse at White Plains Hospital.

Shortly before graduating from the nursing program, in 1902 Margaret married William Sanger. They moved to the suburbs of New York City and had three children. Married life did not suit Margaret, and she eventually separated from her husband, although she kept his last name. In the meantime, she became active in liberal and progressive political causes, and began to practice nursing among the city's poor. She developed an interest in women's health issues, especially sex education and birth control, which were not only controversial topics but subject to legislation such as the Comstock Law, pursuant to which Congress had forbidden the dissemination of contraceptives or information about contraception. There were also legal prohibitions at the state level.

In 1912 Margaret Sanger began writing articles for local New York City periodicals. She argued that birth control was a means by which working-class families in general and poor women in particular could free themselves from the economic burden of large families and unwanted pregnancies. Sanger spoke out against the legal restraints on the public discussion of contraception, and in 1914 she began to publish the magazine *The Woman Rebel*, which supported feminism and birth control. The authorities censored her publication, and prosecuted her for violating the law. Sanger went abroad rather than face imprisonment while her influential friends worked to have the charges against her dismissed. They were successful, and by 1916 she had returned to the United States to begin the task of establishing the country's first birth control clinic.

The clinic opened in Brooklyn, New York, in October 1916. It was subjected to police raids, and Sanger herself was briefly imprisoned. However, the publicity surrounding the clinic gained her a number of wealthy patrons who supported the growing birth control movement. With their assistance she prevailed in the courts, achieving an exception to the anticontraceptive information law for medical professionals, and was able to operate her clinic legally with a staff of female doctors. Sanger's Birth Control Clinical Research Bureau became a model for other birth control clinics across the country.

Sanger also resumed her public advocacy activities. In 1917 she started a periodical called *The Birth Control Review*. Then in 1921 she organized the American Birth Control League, serving as its first president until 1928. This organization has survived to the present day, combining with like-minded groups, and is currently called the Planned Parenthood Federation of America. Sanger also helped organize the World Population Conference in 1927, the National Committee on Federal Legislation for Birth Control in 1929 to lobby for birth control legislation, and published her book *My Fight for Birth Control* in 1931. Another book, *Sanger Sanger: An Autobiography*, followed in 1938.

Margaret Sanger was considered too radical by most people of her time, even feminists. She also received severe criticism from the Catholic Church. By the 1940s she had entered semiretirement, moving to Arizona. Nevertheless, she was still able to participate in the formation of the International Planned Parenthood Federation in 1953. She also supported research into more effective and less costly means of contraception, including diaphragms, spermicides, and of course the birth control pill, which was developed during the 1950s.

Margaret Sanger died on September 6, 1966, in Tuscon, Arizona. Shortly before her death, the United States Supreme Court, in 1965, struck down a Connecticut law which made the use or distribution of contraceptives a criminal offense. Declaring that every citizen has a constitutional right to privacy, the Court proceeded to define that right, in a decision with far-reaching implications (*Griswold* v. *Connecticut*, 1965).

September 15

James Fenimore Cooper's Birthday

James Fenimore Cooper, one of America's first major novelists, was born on September 15, 1789, in Burlington, New Jersey. He grew up in Cooperstown, New York, on the shore of Otsego Lake where his father, Judge William Cooper, had a large estate. At Cooperstown, which Judge Cooper founded, the family first lived in a log house and later moved into a mansion known as Otsego Hall. It was built to the specifications of the judge, a Federalist active in New York State politics and one of the largest property owners of the region.

Otsego Hall was on the edge of frontier wilderness, and young Cooper, born to wealth and position, became interested in the native tribes of the region and the life of the frontiersmen. From this background came his best-known works, namely the series of novels called The Leatherstocking Tales. In Cooper's day, Cooperstown villagers used leather to make leggings, aprons, and even petticoats. Leather leggings were referred to as "leatherstockings."

After receiving his preparatory education in the household of an Episcopal rector in Albany, Cooper entered Yale at 13, the youngest in his class. His age notwithstanding, he proved to be the class's best Latin student but showed a lack of discipline. He was expelled in his third year at Yale, reportedly for exploding a charge of gunpowder that he had carefully placed in the lock of a tutor's door.

In an effort to teach his son discipline, Judge Cooper obtained a berth for Cooper as an apprentice seaman. Cooper enjoyed the sailor's life, and received a commission as a midshipman in the United States Navy. He served in the Atlantic Ocean as well as on Lakes Ontario and Champlain. This phase of his life gave him the foundation for the sea stories he would later write.

On January 1, 1811, Cooper married Susan A. DeLancey, the daughter of a wealthy Tory who lived in Mamaroneck in Westchester County, New York. Resigned from the navy, Cooper took up the life of a gentleman farmer, and might have lived happily in that role had his wife not challenged him to write a book. Taking up the challenge, he set about writing *Precaution* (1820), a novel of English life—a fashionable subject far from his own concerns. The book was a failure, but it stirred the creative spirit in Cooper. He later commented, "Ashamed to have fallen into the track of imitation, I endeavoured to repay the wrong done to my own views, by producing a work that should be purely American, and of which love of country should be the theme."

The first fruit of this new approach was *The Spy* (1821), a story of the American Revolution with its scene laid in Westchester County. The book was a huge and immediate success, both in America and abroad, and became the most popular American novel in print. In 1823 and 1824 he produced two significant and well-received novels: *The Pioneers* and *The Pilot*, the first American sea story. *The Pioneers* laid the foundation for the Leatherstocking Tales, five stories that show the American forests and plains, first in their primeval splendor, then entered by woodsmen who are in turn followed by pioneers and settlers, and then vastly changed by the imposition of European culture.

Cooper's hero, Natty Bumppo, is also called Leatherstocking, Hawkeye, the Deerslayer, the Pathfinder, and La Longue Carabine. Whatever he is called, the character remains the simple, self-sufficient, natural man of integrity, courage, and loyalty. By the time Cooper wrote *The Last of the Mohicans* (1826), his popularity at home and abroad was immense. That same year, he decided to take his family and travel abroad. The Coopers were to stay in Europe for seven years, and he obtained the nominal position of United States consul in Lyons, France. His new position did not interfere with his writing output, which included *The Prairie* (1827), the third novel in the Leatherstocking series. Cooper also found the time to write *The Red Rover* (1827), *The Wept of Wishton-Wish* (1829), and *The Water-Witch* (1830). He also wrote a trilogy that, while dealing with social relations in Europe during the Middle Ages, incurred some European displeasure by persistently ranking democracy above aristocracy.

During his stay in Europe, Cooper found himself constantly explaining or defending the United States and all things American. His *Notions of the Americans* (1828) gave much information about Americans and their views, but succeeded only in irritating both his American and European readers. Proud as he was of the young republic, he was not as tactful as he might have been when he pointed out in conversation, novels, and expository writings the superiority of the American way of life over that of Europe's aristocracy.

Cooper returned home to Cooperstown with his family in 1833. A Federalist, he became a critic of the administration of President Andrew Jackson, a Democrat. Cooper's writings turned more and more to social criticism and the defense of American principles that he felt were being sorely abused. His books of social criticism included *A Letter to His Countrymen* (1834); *The Monikins* (1835); *Homeward Bound*, a fictionalized account of the American scene as viewed by Americans just returning from a stay abroad, and its sequel, *Home As Found* (both published in 1838); and *The American Democrat* (1838).

During this same period, Cooper also wrote five books about his travels abroad, which succeeded in raising hackles on both sides of the Atlantic. He gave at least some of his attention again to the pioneers and Native Americans in such novels as *Wyandotte* (1843) and *The Oak-Openings* (1848). In the trilogy called *The Littlepage Manuscripts*, he followed a New York family through three generations: *Satanstoe* (1845), *The Chainbearer* (1846), and *The Redskins* (1846).

If Cooper had a talent for inventive storytelling, he also had a genius for annoying people. From the time he returned to the United States and began criticizing political trends and social changes, he sowed seeds of enmity. As one commentator put it, Cooper became "the most popular author and the most unpopular man in American literature." Newspapers fought back, calling him everything from a snob to antidemocratic and worse. Cooper spent years suing for libel and usually won, neither of which helped his popularity.

Cooper frequently turned to his first love, the sea, during these troubled years and wrote many solid nonfictional works such as *The History of the Navy of the United States of America* (1839), *Lives of Distinguished American Naval Officers* (1842–1845), and *Ned Myers* (1843), the story of a sailor Cooper had met on his first voyage as an apprentice seaman. Some of his novels of this period, also set at sea, were *Mercedes of Castile* (1840); *The Two Admirals* (1842); *The Wing-and-Wing* (1842); *Afloat and Ashore* and its sequel, *Miles Wallingford* (both in 1844); *Jack Tier* (1846–1848); *The Crater* (1847); and *The Sea Lions* (1849). In all, Cooper produced some 50 works during his 30-year literary career.

Although Cooper never failed to be warmly affectionate to his family, he remained sour toward the public to the end of his days and forbade family and friends to authorize any biography of him. He died on September 14, 1851, the day before his 62nd birthday, and was buried in the Episcopal churchyard in Cooperstown.

William Howard Taft's Birthday

Library of Congress

William Howard Taft

William Howard Taft is the only man in the history of the United States who has held both the office of president and the office of chief justice of the United States Supreme Court. His record is also remarkable in that he held public office almost continuously from his early adulthoood until a few weeks before his death. A huge, affable man, Taft was afflicted with a lifelong tendency to procrastinate. He enjoyed the quiet, orderly, and conservative life of the legal profession, particularly in the judicial aspect, and actively disliked the rough-and-tumble of politics.

Taft was born in Cincinnati, Ohio, on September 15, 1857, the son of Alphonso Taft. The elder Taft was attorney general in the cabinet of President Ulysses S. Grant during the last nine months of Grant's second term. Graduating from Yale College in 1878, the second in his class, young William Taft then entered the Law School of Cincinnati College, graduating in 1880. Although he was promptly admitted to the bar, he spent the next year as a law reporter on a Cincinnati newspaper.

In 1881, as a Republican Party prize for his campaign services, Taft was appointed assistant prosecuting attorney for Hamilton County, of which Cincinnati was the county seat. The next year he left that position when he was appointed collector of Internal Revenue for the first district of Ohio. After serving in that post for about a year, he resigned. Taft returned to political office in 1885 with his appointment as assistant solicitor for Hamilton County. In 1886 he married Helen Heron, a cultured and ambitious woman.

The following year Taft was made judge of the Superior Court of Ohio to fill a vacancy, and in 1888 he was elected to complete the term. Aside from the presidency, this was the only elective office he was to hold. Taft himself said that he proceeded in politics by having his "plate the right side up when offices were falling." He resigned his judgeship in 1890 to accept the office of solicitor general of the United States under President Benjamin Harrison. Two years later, the president appointed him circuit judge for the United States Sixth Circuit. Taft accepted the post over the opposition of his wife, who considered the post a poor job with no political future. While still on the bench, Taft also served as dean and professor in the law department of the University of Cincinnati from 1896 to 1900.

During a time of great labor unrest, Taft was to make a number of judicial decisions relating to strikes and injunctions that earned him the enmity of organized labor. Though he agreed that huge industrial trusts needed to be restrained, this did not ally him with labor. As a man trained to the law, Taft mistrusted organizations of workers, who he believed were an uneducated rabble bent on overturning the social order.

President William McKinley took Taft from the bench in 1900 and made him president of the Philippine Commission. When civil government was established in the Philippine Islands, he became governor-general *ex officio*. The status of church lands in the islands was uncertain, and in 1902 during a personal interview with Pope Leo XII, Taft arranged a satisfactory settlement under which $7,239,000 was paid for the lands.

Taft was recalled to the United States by President Theodore Roosevelt in January 1904 to serve as secretary of war. In that capacity, Taft supervised the construction of the Panama Canal. Taft became Roosevelt's trusted aide and was granted powers more than commensurate with his official position. Roosevelt, holding to his promise to not run again, used his influence in 1908 to bring about the nomination of Taft as his successor. Taft was elected by a majority of 159 electoral votes over William Jennings Bryan, the Democratic candidate.

As president, Taft recommended the adoption of an amendment to the Constitution that would permit the levying of income taxes. He urged upon Congress the importance of arranging for a national budget apportioning expenditures within the anticipated national revenues. He negotiated treaties with Great Britain and France providing for the arbitration of disputes that could not be settled by ordinary diplomatic means, but when the Senate began to modify them he withdrew the treaties. During his term there was a controversy over the conservation of natural resources, which resulted in the removal of chief forester Gifford Pinchot and the resignation of Secretary Richard A. Ballinger from the Department of the Interior. There was also much dispute over the enactment of the Payne-Aldrich Tariff, which in its final form hardly affected rates at all, but which offended nearly all of the concerned political factions. Taft's leadership on the tariff issue was, at best, inconsistent, since he had declared himself for higher tariff rates only to reverse himself within a matter of months.

Taft ran for reelection, but a section of his party—known as the Progressives—opposed him on the grounds that he was too conservative and reactionary. When the Republican National Convention met in 1912 and gave him the nomination, the Progressives held an independent gathering known as the Bull Moose convention and nominated Theodore Roosevelt, who had broken with Taft early in Taft's term. Because of the divided opposition the Democrats won the election and Woodrow Wilson became president.

After his retirement from the presidency, Taft became Kent professor of law at Yale University. As his professional duties did not occupy all of his time, he lectured frequently and for a year or more wrote editorial articles for the Philadelphia *Public Ledger*. He was elected president of the American Bar Association in 1913 and 1914, and became the first president of the American Institute of Jurisprudence, an organization formed to improve the administration of the law. He favored the ratification of the Versailles Treaty in 1919, regarding the Covenant of the League of Nations as its most important part.

When Chief Justice Edward Douglass White died in 1921, President Warren G. Harding appointed Taft to succeed White on the Supreme Court. In making his appointment Harding fulfilled a lifelong dream of Taft's, even though Taft had previously turned down a seat on the Supreme Court offered to him by President Theodore Roosevelt. When the second chance came, however, Taft was glad to accept appointment to the Court.

Taft enjoyed his work as chief justice. In this capacity he was guided in his thinking by moderate-to conservative principles. He viewed the more liberal justices, led by Louis D. Brandeis, simply as habitual dissenters. Taft was an excellent legal

administrator and revised the rules of the Court to end long delays in litigation. He resigned from the bench on January 3, 1930, because of ill health and died on March 8 of the same year. Taft was buried in the Arlington National Cemetery at Arlington, Virginia. His son, Robert A. Taft, later became a United States senator, carrying on the political heritage.

September 16

Cherokee Land Rush in Oklahoma, 1893

On September 16, 1893, a famous land "run" opened the section of Oklahoma for settlement that was officially called the Cherokee Outlet, but known more popularly as the Cherokee Strip. September 16, Cherokee Strip Day, is still observed in Oklahoma as an optional holiday.

The Cherokee, one of what were known as the Five Civilized Tribes, have a deep-rooted connection extending back into the first half of the 19th century with several parts of Oklahoma and not just the Outlet. As early as 1809 some of the Cherokee who lived in North and South Carolina, Georgia, Alabama, and Tennessee informed President Thomas Jefferson that they wanted to migrate to new hunting grounds beyond the Mississippi River. At first they were given permission to move into the area of Arkansas. Only limited numbers had made the transfer before mounting white pressure, spurred by the discovery of gold on Cherokee land, forced the removal of the entire tribe from the eastern United States. In 1838, with the approval of President Andrew Jackson, some 16,000 Cherokee—4,000 of whom died en route—were forced along what became known as the Trail of Tears (see related essays throughout this book). A new home awaited them, as it did for the other Civilized Tribes—Chickasaw, Choctaw, Creek, and Seminole—in the vast western region that had been set aside by Congress in 1834 and designated Indian Territory.

In addition to some seven million acres of land in what is now northeastern Oklahoma, the Cherokee received extensive territory to the west, intended not as a homesite but as a "perpetual outlet" to hunting grounds in what are now New Mexico and Colorado. The Outlet encompassed more than six million acres of land, extending from Keystone, Oklahoma, to the 100th meridian, then the western border of the United States. North to south, it stretched from the border of what was to become the state of Kansas to a point three miles north of Hennessey, Oklahoma.

September 17

After the Civil War the federal government forced the Five Civilized Tribes to relinquish the western half of the Indian Territory. From 1866 to 1883 the government used this land to resettle several more tribes, especially the nomadic Plains tribes. The Cherokee were required to give up the eastern end of the Outlet, which was then assigned to the Osage. The Ponca, Oto, and Tonkawa tribes, among others, were settled on reservations in smaller sections of the Outlet. However, a great expanse still remained under Cherokee control.

The open-range cattle industry greatly expanded in the 1870s and 1880s. Cowhands, driving longhorns northward from Texas to Kansas across the Indian Territory, soon discovered that the animals thrived on the grassy plain of the Cherokee Outlet. In 1883 the Cherokee Strip Livestock Association, a group of white ranchers, persuaded the Cherokee Nation to lease its unoccupied Strip for $100,000 a year for five years. The agreement was renewed after its expiration in 1888.

By the late 1870s, both cattlemen and homesteaders, realizing the value of the millions of acres of tribal land, began to demand the opening of the Indian Territory to white settlement. Especially desirable were the two "unoccupied" sections. One was the Unassigned Lands, a two million-acre tract in the center of the Indian Territory later known as Old Oklahoma or the Oklahoma District. The other was the Cherokee Outlet, which, although assigned to the Cherokee, had never been settled. The Unassigned Lands were opened to white migration under the 1862 Homestead Act in a run on April 22, 1889. Other sections of western Indian Territory were gradually occupied by white homesteaders in the subsequent runs of 1891 and 1892.

In the meantime, the federal government was conducting negotiations to obtain a clear title to the Outlet. It terminated the Cherokee Strip Livestock Association's second lease before its expiration, abolished the tribal land allotments that had been granted to several tribes in favor of individual allotments, and purchased the six million acres of the Outlet for $8,595,736.

In the summer of 1893 President Grover Cleveland signed the proclamation opening the region to settlement by means of a land run set for September 16, 1893. Prior to the run, the Outlet was carefully surveyed by government engineers and divided into counties of equal size. County seats, townsites, and 160-acre claims were minutely determined. All that was needed to obtain a claim was to be the first to plant a flag stake at a given spot. Thus speed was essential in securing the best plots.

The lure of free land and the thrill of the race attracted an estimated 100,000 prospective settlers. They swarmed along the borders of the rectangular Cherokee Strip in anticipation of the noon opening on September 16. The majority concentrated in the border towns of Arkansas City and Caldwell in Kansas, on the northern side of the Outlet, and Orlando and Hennessey in Oklahoma on the southern side. Housing, food, water, sanitary facilities, and supplies were inadequate or nonexistent. Eight cavalry troops and four infantry companies guarded the 400-mile border in an effort to protect the area from illegal invasion. Nonetheless, some (called Sooners) managed to slip into the territory, just as they had infiltrated the Oklahoma District before the land rush of 1889.

The multitude of impatient land seekers lined up in the neutral zones starting at dawn on September 16. As the morning sun climbed higher and higher, the tension became almost unbearable. Tempers flared as men, with their animals and vehicles, jockeyed for position. Precisely at noon rifles cracked, and before the reverberations faded away, the frantic race had begun. The crowd charged forward, and the eager homesteaders swept over the prairie. By sunset, 40,000 homesteads of 160 acres each had been claimed throughout the tract, except on the sites allocated for towns.

The land rush of 1893 was the largest and last of the runs that opened the western tribal lands to white settlement. Land lotteries and auctions replaced the often violent runs, completing the homesteading process in the early 20th century. The Cherokee Outlet became part of the Oklahoma Territory, which roughly encompassed the westernmost part of the Indian Territory set aside by Congress in 1834. The eastern half of the congressionally designated Indian Territory still retained that name. Subsequently, the two territories combined to form the state of Oklahoma in 1907.

September 17

Warren E. Burger's Birthday

On May 21, 1969, President Richard M. Nixon selected Warren Earl Burger to succeed the retiring Earl Warren as chief justice of the United States Supreme Court. His appointment as chief justice, following the many landmark decisions that had sprung from the Warren court, signified the end of one era and the beginning of another. The Senate confirmed the president's selection on June 9,

Photo by Robert Oakes, Collection of the Supreme Court of the United States.

Warren E. Burger

and on June 24 Burger was sworn in by Warren as the 15th chief justice in American history.

Burger was born in St. Paul, Minnesota, on September 17, 1907. He was the fourth of the seven children of Charles Joseph Burger, who worked variously as a railroad cargo inspector, traveling salesman, and small farmer, and Katherine Schnittger Burger. At the age of nine he began to deliver newspapers. Later, when he attended John A. Johnson High School in St. Paul, he played the cornet and bugle and was active in track, swimming, football, hockey, and tennis. He served not only as student council president and editor of the school newspaper but also as head of the student court. During his summer vacations he worked on a farm in Red Wing, Minnesota, and also held positions at a Young Men's Christian Association camp where he served as counselor, truck driver, lifeguard, and track coach.

Princeton University, impressed by Burger's many activities, decided to overlook his undistinguished academic record and offer him a partial scholarship. Burger, whose family's financial resources were quite modest, could not afford to accept the offer. Instead he took extension courses at the University of Minnesota from 1925 to 1927 and then entered night classes at St. Paul College of Law (later Mitchell College of Law). Despite having to work while he was studying, Burger managed to earn his law degree, magna cum

laude, in 1931, and to rank third in his graduating class.

Burger was an associate until 1935 with the St. Paul law firm of Boyesen, Otis, and Faricy, and he was a partner until 1953 with its successor, Faricy, Burger, Moore, and Costello. From 1931 until 1953 he taught at St. Paul College of Law and eventually became professor of contract law. He also served as president of the St. Paul Junior Chamber of Commerce in 1935.

A chronic back ailment prevented Burger from joining the military during World War II, so he became a member of the Minnesota Emergency War Labor Board from 1942 to 1947. In 1948 he gained appointment to the Governor's Interracial Commission and remained on it until 1953. He also became the first president of the St. Paul Council on Human Relations, which was designed to promote understanding between the city police and the African American and Mexican American minorities.

Burger, a lifelong Republican, played an important role in the successful gubernatorial campaign of liberal Republican Harold Stassen in 1938. Ten years later, Burger was floor manager for Stassen's unsuccessful run for the presidential nomination at the Republican National Convention in Philadelphia. Burger served again as Stassen's manager in 1952, but when the Minnesotan's bid appeared doomed, he switched his support to Dwight D. Eisenhower and helped assure Eisenhower's first-ballot nomination in a contest with Robert A. Taft of Ohio.

Upon taking office, President Eisenhower appointed Burger as the assistant attorney general in charge of the civil division of the Department of Justice. Burger and his staff of 180 lawyers had the responsibility of representing the government in all civil cases except those involving land or antitrust matters. While attached to the Department of Justice, in 1954 he became a member and legal adviser to the United States delegation to the International Labor Organization in Geneva. In 1955 he represented the government in cases involving Norwegian claims against the United States.

In June 1955 Eisenhower nominated Burger to a seat on the United States Court of Appeals for the District of Columbia Circuit, which has appellate jurisdiction over many federal agencies and departments in Washington, D.C. The Senate confirmed Burger's appointment, and he took office on April 13, 1956. While serving on the court for 13 years, he established a reputation as a conservative jurist and was openly critical of several Supreme Court rulings designed to protect the rights of accused persons. He attacked the *Dur-*

ham rule of 1954, which broadened the definition of criminal insanity, and the *Miranda* decision of 1966, which forbade the police to interrogate a suspect without informing him or her of the right to remain silent and of the right to legal counsel. President Nixon was impressed by Burger, and chose him for the chief justice's position when it opened in 1969.

Burger served as chief justice during a turbulent time. In the early 1970s the Court issued several very important decisions, concerning such matters as abortion rights (*Roe* v. *Wade*) and President Nixon's claim to executive privilege during the Watergate scandal (*United States* v. *Nixon*). As one of the more conservative members of the Court, Burger was often in the minority in these decisions. In the 1980s, however, the increasingly conservative nature of the country and the Supreme Court put him more in the mainstream. President Ronald Reagan, elected to office during the 1980 presidential election, successfully placed more conservatives in the federal judiciary and their presence had a decided impact on the Supreme Court's rulings.

On September 26, 1986, Warren Burger resigned as chief justice after 17 years in office. He served in a variety of positions during his retirement, including chairman of the Commission on the Bicentennial of the United States Constitution and as chancellor of the Smithsonian Institution's Board of Regents. Burger died on June 25, 1995, and was buried at Arlington National Cemetery.

Baron von Steuben's Birthday

Under George Washington, 10,000 poorly supplied soldiers of the Continental army suffered through the winter of 1777–1778 in their Valley Forge, Pennsylvania, encampment trying to keep themselves and their new nation alive. Despite the important American victory at Saratoga in October 1777 (see October 17), the British still held the major cities of New York and Philadelphia and menaced the rebel Congress meeting at York, Pennsylvania. American successes against British and Hessian regulars demonstrated that the colonists were not bumbling rustics, but their inconsistent performance reflected a lack of military finesse and discipline. Baron Friedrich Wilhelm Ludolf Gerhard Augustin von Steuben remedied this deficiency after his arrival at the Valley Forge winter quarters on February 23, 1778.

Steuben was born on September 17, 1730, in the fortress at Magdeburg, Prussia, where his father, an engineer, served as a lieutenant in the army of King Frederick William I. Entering the Prussian officer corps at the age of 17, the younger Steuben served during the Seven Years' War of 1756 to 1763 as a member of the general staff and aide-de-camp to Frederick the Great. The general staff was a sophisticated institution unique to the Prussian military establishment, and Steuben's association with it equipped him with an expertise that would prove invaluable to the rebel cause during the American Revolution.

Discharged from the army with the rank of captain at the conclusion of the Seven Years' War, Steuben became the chamberlain of the prince of Hohenzollern-Hechingen and earned the title of baron. He accompanied the prince to France when financial problems forced the closing of the court in 1771, but by 1776 the burden of his own debts led Steuben to seek other employment. A friend of his in Baden sent Steuben with a letter of introduction to Benjamin Franklin, the American representative in Paris.

Both Franklin and the Comte de Saint-Germain, who was the French minister of war, recognized the Prussian's talents and arranged for him to go to America. Hotalez et Cie., a commercial corporation that covertly supplied French aid to the American colonial rebels, paid for Steuben's passage. The wily Franklin, without the power to offer the baron a commission, ensured his welcome to the colonies by promoting him in a letter to George Washington as "Lieutenant General in the King of Prussia's Service."

Steuben arrived in Portsmouth, New Hampshire, on December 1, 1777, and proceeded overland to York, Pennsylvania. The baron impressed the Continental Congress by offering to serve as a volunteer in the Continental army with no rank or pay, save compensation for his expenses. If the American cause was successful he would expect a suitable reward, but if it met with failure he would make no claim. Congress quickly agreed and dispatched him to join Washington at Valley Forge.

The baron's first task was to introduce the Continental army to the intricacies of military drill, a form of training requiring concentration and cooperation and intended to promote unified action. Steuben's inability to speak English impaired communication with the troops, but he overcame the obstacle by teaching, praising, and swearing at the soldiers through interpreters. He personally instructed a select company of 100 men, which he then employed as a model for the other units. The rapid progress made by the colonials under their Prussian tutor impressed Washington, and at his request Congress on May 5, 1778, appointed Steuben inspector general with the rank of major general. On June 28 the value of Steuben's training was demonstrated in the rout of the British at the battle of Monmouth.

Steuben spent the next winter preparing his "Regulations for the Order and Discipline of the Troops of the United States," a task that language differences made especially difficult. The baron wrote the manual in simple French, and an aide then put it into literary French. A third officer rendered it word for word into English, and another transformed this stilted product into a smoother English translation. The final version became the "blue book" of American military instruction.

Administrative ability was another one of Steuben's assets. During the winter of 1779–1780 he served as Washington's representative to Congress on matters involving the reorganization of the army. More important, the baron developed a system of property accountability that curtailed the egregious waste plaguing the American military.

General Nathanael Greene, who replaced Horatio Gates as American commander in the south in the autumn of 1780 after the disastrous defeat at Camden, New Jersey, gave Steuben the responsibility for defending Virginia. Then, after Lafayette took charge of Virginia in April 1781, Steuben exercised his first field command in America by leading one of Washington's divisions at the climactic battle of Yorktown. His knowledge of siege warfare greatly contributed to the victory, which virtually concluded the colonies' successful revolution against British rule.

In 1783 Steuben helped Washington plan for the future defense of the young United States and demobilize the Continental army. Washington's last official act as commander in chief of the American forces was to write to the baron, expressing the depth of his respect for his Prussian aide:

> Altho' I have taken frequent Opportunities both in public and private, of Acknowledging your great Zeal, Attention and Abilities in performing the duties of your Office; yet, I wish, to make use of this last Moment of my public life, to Signify in the strongest terms, my intire [sic] Approbation of your Conduct, and to express my Sense of the Obligations the public is under to you for your faithful and Meritorious Services.

Steuben received an honorable discharge on March 24, 1784. He remained in the United States after the Revolution, and the legislatures of Pennsylvania and New York both granted him American citizenship. In 1786 New York State granted Steuben 16,000 acres of Mohawk Valley land north of the city of Utica, and in 1790 Congress granted him a yearly pension of $2,500. In expectation of the government's offering him a large sum of money rather than an annuity, Steuben had allowed himself to assume heavy debts, but Secretary of the Treasury Alexander Hamilton and other friends extricated him through a liberal mortgage of his lands. The New York State legislature designated the baron's lands as the Town of Steuben on April 10, 1792. Steuben thereafter spent his winters in New York City and his summers in a log cabin retreat in the township that bore his name. He died there on November 28, 1794.

Citizenship Day

September 17 is the anniversary of the signing of the United States Constitution in 1787. Citizenship Day is the outgrowth of two patriotic celebrations: Constitution Day and "I Am an American" Day. The former observance first took place in Philadelphia, Pennsylvania, on September 17, 1861, shortly after the outbreak of the Civil War. Little is known about the 1861 exercises, aside from the fact that Philadelphians used the anniversary of the signing of the Constitution to reaffirm their devotion to the Union at a time when the secession of many Southern states threatened its very existence.

No other observance of September 17 seems to have occurred until 1887, when Philadelphians marked the centennial of the signing of the Constitution with a mammoth three-day celebration. Buildings throughout the city were draped in red, white, and blue bunting, and an estimated 500,000 visitors, including cabinet members, Supreme Court justices, and the governors of several states, joined Philadelphia residents to witness the many events.

The celebration of September 17 became more widespread during the first decades of the 20th century. Organizations such as the National Security League, the American Bar Association, and the National Society of the Sons of the American Revolution devoted time and effort to popularizing the observance. As early as 1919 at least 22 states and 100 cities sponsored special exercises on September 17 or took note of the anniversary in some other way.

A 1940 act of Congress set aside the third Sunday in May as "I Am an American" Day, and during the next 12 years festivities were held on that day to honor those who, by coming of age or by naturalization, had attained citizenship status. As independent celebrations, both Constitution Day and "I Am an American" Day enjoyed some minor popularity. Because of the close relationship between the Constitution and the duties and privileges of American citizenship, however, there was some opinion in favor of uniting the two observances. In response to this sentiment, Congress in 1952 united the two holidays. The new observance, known as Citizenship Day, has been observed ever since although it is not widely celebrated and is not a federal holiday.

September 18

Cornerstone of the Capitol Laid

Two years after Congress selected the District of Columbia as the site for the national capital in 1790, the district commissioners invited both professional and amateur architects to submit sketches for the city's two most important structures: The presidential residence and the building in which Congress would be housed. The committee charged with choosing the winning entries quickly recognized that James Hoban's design for the executive mansion was the best plan, and the cornerstone for the building was laid on October 13, 1792. Selection of an appropriate design for the Capitol was more difficult.

The French architect Pierre Charles L'Enfant had already laid out the new federal city, and according to his plans the congressional building would occupy a hill that stood "as a pedestal waiting for a monument." The problem was that none of the designs originally entered in the contest reflected this majestic spirit. Some were outlandish, most were mundane. Then, three months after the competition deadline, William Thornton (a physician, painter, and inventor) submitted drawings that were well received. Secretary of State Thomas Jefferson remarked that it "captivated the eyes and judgment of all." The committee agreed and, despite the lateness of his entry, named Thornton the winner of the competition.

During the months that followed, work on the Capitol progressed so rapidly that plans were made to lay the building's cornerstone on September 18, 1793. On that day, the festivities began with a parade. Uniformed members of the Alexandria (Virginia) Volunteer Artillery and the Masonic lodges of Maryland, Virginia, and the District of Columbia escorted President George Washington from Virginia across the Potomac River into Maryland and then on to the President's Square in the federal district. According to one contemporary account, "the procession marched two abreast in the greatest solemn dignity, with music playing, drums beating, colours flying and spectators rejoicing." However, participants in the parade had to contend with the primitive condition of the city before reaching their destination at the top of Capitol Hill. The marchers had to skirt the "great

Serbonian Bog," where Pennsylvania Avenue is now, and cross the Tiber Creek by either stepping from stone to stone or balancing along a single log.

Washington laid the cornerstone himself using a silver trowel and a marble-headed gavel to put the stone in place. Then he attached a silver plate to it that recorded the date of the ceremony as the 13th year after American independence, the first year of his second term, and the year 5793 of Masonry. The official program concluded with a 15-gun volley by the artillery company.

The 1793 cornerstone was only the first of several such markers laid at the Capitol. On August 24, 1818, the cornerstone for a center section that would connect the north and south wings was laid. Completion of this part of the building six years later made Thornton's original plan for a domed center area, flanked by two wings, a reality.

On July 4, 1851, a third cornerstone marked the beginning of work on the much needed additions to the Capitol. Since the North and the South had narrowly averted conflict over the perennial problem of slavery only one year before, it is not surprising that the 1851 ceremony combined the theme of national unity with the traditional Masonic rituals. The actual cornerstone laying recalled the 1793 festivities. Using the same trowel and gavel Washington had used 58 years before, President Millard Fillmore and B. B. French (the grand master of the Masonic fraternity) set the new stone.

For almost a century (from 1863, when the work begun in 1851 was completed) until 1959, no major alterations were made on the Capitol. However, by the mid-20th century the expanding business of the federal government made it necessary to add another part to the building. Greater architectural balance and space for 75 additional Capitol offices were achieved when the center section's East Front was moved forward 32 ½ feet. Still another cornerstone was laid in the course of this construction. President Dwight D. Eisenhower put the Capitol's fourth cornerstone in place on July 4, 1959. The new addition was completed in 1961, with marble replacing the sandstone of the old East Front but following the design of the original sandstone.

The Air Force Becomes an Equal Branch of the Military

The Department of the Air Force, a division of the Department of Defense on an equal footing with the army and the navy, was established on September 18, 1947, pursuant to the National Security Act of 1947. As a result, the old U.S. Army Air Force was transferred from the Department of the

Army to the Department of the Air Force and became known as the United States Air Force.

Military aviation has it roots in the late 18th century, when the French used balloons for reconnaissance at the battle of Fleurus in 1794. During the Civil War (1861–1865), the Union army used balloons on several occasion under the supervision of the U.S. signal corps. In 1892 the signal corps established a permanent balloon unit, which served in the Spanish-American War. The signal corps also lent some support to inventors who claimed to be able to build the first aircraft, without success. These disappointments initially led the military to regard the Wright brothers with some skepticism after their history-making flight of December 17, 1903 (see December 17). Nevertheless, after the Wrights obtained their patents, the army finally gave them a contract for military aircraft in 1909.

Military aviation began to receive regular annual funding from Congress in 1911. Aircraft design and development was spurred by the outbreak of World War I in 1914, in which all of the major combatants sought to exploit the advantages of the new technology, mostly for purposes of reconnaissance. When the United States entered the war in 1917, the army's budding aviation program was transferred from the signal corps to the new U.S. Army Air Service. John D. Ryan, second assistant secretary of war, oversaw its organization. The navy also had an aviation program, although that and its successors were not absorbed into what has become the air force.

During the 1920s, visionaries such as General William "Billy" Mitchell wanted to increase the commitment to and exploitation of military aircraft, with limited success. Unlike the British and the Germans, the American military leadership foresaw primarily ground-support uses for its aircraft and the air service (renamed the U.S. Army Air Corps in 1926). In the 1930s, however, the air corps began to make progress. It developed a fleet of long-range fighters and bombers capable of precision attacks. Although it was a small fleet, outnumbered by the air forces of several other countries, it was an important nucleus when the United States entered World War II in 1941.

After America entered the war, air corps commander Major General Henry H. "Hap" Arnold was given the new title commanding general of the U.S. Army Air Forces (AAF). The AAF was placed directly under the authority of the chief of staff of the army, General George C. Marshall, but enjoyed a certain degree of independence during the war. Arnold also joined the Joint Chiefs of Staff, the central planning body of the American military. He oversaw the expansion of the AAF into an organization with tens of thousands of planes and hundreds of thousands of personnel.

American air power had a vital role in the war effort, both in the European and Pacific theaters. By the end of the war, the strategic and tactical importance of aircraft was clear to all, leading to the establishment of the U.S. Air Force in the National Security Act of 1947. It is commanded by the secretary of the air force.

September 19

George Washington's Farewell Address

George Washington, the first president of the United States, issued his famous Farewell Address on September 19, 1796, as the end of his second term as president approached. Washington cautioned against excessive involvement in the affairs of other nations and involvement in foreign wars. Furthermore, he took a strong position against political factionalism and spoke in favor of national unity. Finally, by announcing his retirement he set a historic precedent that presidents should serve no more than two terms in office (see related articles throughout this book).

A copy of Washington's address is set forth below:

> Friends and Fellow-citizens: The period for a new election of a citizen to administer the executive government of the United States being not far distant, and the time actually arrived when our thoughts must be employed in designating the person who is to be clothed with that important trust, it appears to me proper, especially as it may conduce to a more distinct expression of the public voice, that I should now apprise you of the resolution I have formed to decline being considered among the number of those out of whom a choice is to be made.
>
> I beg you at the same time to do me the justice to be assured that this resolution has not been taken without regard to all the considerations appertaining to the relation which binds a dutiful citizen to his country; and that, in withdrawing the tender of service which silence in my situation might imply, I am influenced by no diminution of zeal for your future interest, no deficiency of grateful respect for your past kindness, but am supported by a full conviction that the step is compatible with both.

The acceptance of and the continuance hitherto in the office to which your suffrages have twice called me have been a uniform sacrifice of inclination to the opinion of duty and to a deference for what appeared to be your desire. I constantly hoped that it would have been much earlier in my power, consistently with motives which I was not at liberty to disregard, to return to that retirement from which I had been reluctantly drawn. The strength of my inclination to do this, previous to the last election, had even led to the preparation of an address to declare it to you; but mature reflection on the then perplexed and critical posture of our affairs with foreign nations, and the unanimous advice of persons entitled to my confidence, impelled me to abandon the idea.

I rejoice that the state of our concerns, external as well as internal, no longer renders the pursuit of inclination incompatible with the sentiment of duty or propriety, and am persuaded, whatever partiality may be retained for my services, that in the present circumstances of our country you will not disapprove of my determination to retire.

The impressions with which I first undertook the arduous trust were explained on the proper occasion. In the discharge of this trust I will only say that I have with good intentions contributed towards the organization and administration of the government the best exertions of which a very fallible judgment was capable. Not unconscious in the outset of the inferiority of my qualifications, experience—in my own eyes, perhaps still more in the eyes of others—has strengthened the motives to diffidence of myself; and every day the increasing weight of years admonishes me more and more that the shade of retirement is as necessary to me as it will be welcome. Satisfied that if any circumstances have given peculiar value to my services they were temporary, I have the consolation to believe that, while choice and prudence invite me to quit the political scene, patriotism does not forbid it. In looking forward to the moment which is intended to terminate the career of my public life, my feelings do not permit me to suspend the deep acknowledgment of that debt of gratitude which I owe to my beloved country for the many honors it has conferred upon me; still more for the steadfast confidence with which it has supported me, and for the opportunities I have thence enjoyed of manifesting my inviolable attachment by services, faithful and persevering, though in usefulness unequal to my zeal. If benefits have resulted to our country from these services, let it always be remembered to your praise, and as an instructive example in our annals, that under circumstances in which the passions, agitated in every direction, were liable to mislead; amidst appearances sometimes dubious, vicissitudes of fortune often discouraging; in situations in which not unfrequently want of success has countenanced the spirit of criticism, the constancy of your support was the essential prop of the efforts and a guarantee of the plans by which they were effected. Profoundly penetrated with this idea, I shall carry it with me to my grave, as a strong incitement to unceasing wishes that Heaven may continue to you the choicest tokens of its beneficence; that your union and brotherly affection may be perpetual; that the free Constitution which is the work of your hands may be sacredly maintained; that its administration in every department may be stamped with wisdom and virtue; that, in fine, the happiness of the people of these States, under the auspices of liberty, may be made complete by so careful a preservation and so prudent a use of this blessing as will acquire to them the glory of recommending it to the applause, the affection, and adoption of every nation which is yet a stranger to it.

Here, perhaps, I ought to stop. But a solicitude for your welfare, which cannot end but with my life, and the apprehension of danger, natural to that solicitude, urge me, on an occasion like the present, to offer to your solemn contemplation, and to recommend to your frequent review, some sentiments which are the result of much reflection, of no inconsiderable observation, and which appear to me all important to the permanency of your felicity as a people. These will be offered to you with the more freedom, as you can only see in them the disinterested warnings of a parting friend, who can possibly have no personal motives to bias his counsel. Nor can I forget, as an encouragement to it, your indulgent reception of my sentiments on a former and not dissimilar occasion.

Interwoven as is the love of liberty with every ligament of your hearts, no recommendation of mine is necessary to fortify or confirm the attachment.

The unity of government which constitutes you one people is also now dear to you. It is justly so; for it is a main pillar in the edifice of your real independence, the support of your tranquillity at home, your peace abroad, of your safety, of your prosperity, of that very liberty which you so highly prize. But as it is easy to foresee that from different causes and from different quarters much pains will be taken, many artifices employed, to weaken in your minds the conviction of this truth; as this is the point of your political fortress against which the batteries of internal and external enemies will be most constantly and actively, though often covertly and insidiously, directed, it is of infinite moment that you should properly estimate the immense value of your national union to your collective and individual happiness; that you should cherish a cordial, habitual, and immovable attachment to it; accustoming yourselves to think and speak of it as of the palladium of your political safety and prosperity, watching for its preservation with jealous anxiety; discountenancing whatever may suggest even a suspicion that it can in any event be abandoned; and indignantly frowning upon the first dawning of every attempt to alienate any portion of our country from the rest, or to enfeeble the sacred ties which now link together the various parts.

For this you have every inducement of sympathy and interest. Citizens, by birth or choice, of a common country, that country has a right to concentrate your affections. The name of American, which belongs to you in your national capacity, must always exalt the just pride of patriotism more than any appellation derived from local discriminations. With slight shades of difference, you have the same religion, manners, habits, and political principles. You have, in a common cause, fought and triumphed together; the independence and liberty you possess are the work of joint councils and joint efforts, of common dangers, sufferings, and successes.

But these considerations, however powerfully they address themselves to your sensibility, are greatly outweighed by those which apply more immediately to your interest. Here every portion of your country finds the most commanding motives for carefully guarding and preserving the union of the whole.

The North, in an unrestrained intercourse with the South, protected by the equal laws of a common government, finds in the productions of the latter great additional resources of maritime and commercial enterprise and precious materials of manufacturing industry. The South, in the same intercourse, benefiting by the agency of the North, sees its agriculture grow and its commerce expand. Turning partly into its own channels the seamen of the North, it finds its particular navigation invigorated; and while it contributes in different ways to nourish and increase the general mass of the national navigation, it looks forward to the protection of a maritime strength, to which itself is unequally adapted. The East, in like intercourse with the West, already finds, and in the progressive improvement of interior communications, by land and water, will more and more find, a valuable vent for the commodities which it brings from abroad or manufactures at home. The West derives from the East supplies requisite to its growth and comfort, and, what is perhaps of still greater consequence, it must of necessity owe the secure enjoyment of indispensable outlets for its own productions to the weight, influence, and the future maritime strength of the Atlantic side of the Union, directed by an indissoluble community of interest as one nation. Any other tenure by which the West can hold this essential advantage, whether derived from its own separate strength, or from an apostate and unnatural connection with any foreign power, must be intrinsically precarious.

While, then, every part of our country thus feels an immediate and particular interest in union, all the parts combined cannot fail to find, in the united mass of means and efforts, greater strength, greater resource, proportionately greater security from external danger, a less frequent interruption of their peace by foreign nations; and, what is of inestimable value, they must derive from union an exemption from those broils and wars between themselves which so frequently afflict neighboring countries not tied together by the same government, which their own rivalships alone would be sufficient to produce, but which opposite foreign alliances, attachments, and intrigues would stimulate and embitter. Hence, likewise, they will avoid the necessity of those overgrown military establishments which, under any form of government, are inauspicious to liberty, and which are to be regarded as particularly hostile to republican liberty. In this sense it is that your union ought to be considered as a main prop of your liberty, and that the love of the one ought to endear to you the preservation of the other.

These considerations speak a persuasive language to every reflecting and virtuous mind, and exhibit the continuance of the Union as a primary object of patriotic desire. Is there a doubt whether a common government can embrace so large a sphere? Let experience solve it. To listen to mere speculation in such a case would be criminal. We are authorized to hope that a proper organization of the whole, with the auxiliary agency of governments for the respective subdivisions, will afford a happy issue to the experiment. It is well worth a fair and full experiment. With such powerful and obvious motives to union, affecting all parts of our country, while experience shall not have demonstrated its impracticability, there will always be reason to distrust the patriotism of those who, in any quarter, may endeavor to weaken its bands.

In contemplating the causes which may disturb our Union, it occurs as a matter of serious concern, that any ground should have been furnished for characterizing parties by geographical discriminations, Northern and Southern, Atlantic and Western, whence designing men may endeavor to excite a belief that there is a real difference of local interests and views. One of the expedients of party to acquire influence within particular districts is to misrepresent the opinions and aims of other districts. You cannot shield yourself too much against the jealousies and heartburnings which spring from these misrepresentations; they tend to render alien to each other those who ought to be bound together by fraternal affection. The inhabitants of our western country have lately had a useful lesson on this head. They have seen in the negotiation by the Executive and in the unanimous ratification by the Senate of the treaty with Spain, and in the universal satisfaction of that event throughout the United States, a decisive proof how unfounded were the suspicions propagated among them of a policy in the general Government and in the Atlantic States unfriendly to their interests in regard to the Mississippi; they have been witnesses to the formation of two treaties, that with Great Britain and that with Spain, which secure to them everything they could desire, in respect to our foreign relations, towards confirming their prosperity. Will it not be their wisdom to rely for the preservation of these advantages on the Union by which they were procured? Will they not henceforth be deaf to those advisers, if such there are, who would sever them from their brethren and connect them with aliens?

To the efficacy and permanency of your Union, a government for the whole is indispensable. No alliances, however strict, between the parts can be an adequate substitute; they must inevitably experience the infractions and interruptions which alliances in all times have experienced. Sensible of this momentous truth, you have improved upon your first essay by the adoption of a Constitution of Government better calculated than your former for an intimate union and for the efficacious management of your common concerns.

This government, the offspring of our own choice, uninfluenced and unawed, adopted upon full investigation and mature deliberation, completely free in its principles, in the distribution of its powers, uniting security with energy, and containing within itself a provision for its own amendment, has a just claim to your confidence and your support. Respect for its authority, compliance with its laws, acquiescence in its measures, are duties enjoined by the fundamental maxims of true liberty. The basis of our political system is the right of the people to make and to alter the Constitution of Government. But the Constitution which at any time exists, until changed by an explicit and authentic act of the whole people, is sacred and obligatory upon all. The very idea of the power and the right of the people to establish government presupposes the duty of every individual to obey the established government.

All obstructions to the execution of the laws, all combinations and associations, under whatever plausible character, with the real design to direct, control, counteract, or awe the regular deliberation and action of the constituted authorities, are destructive of this fundamental principle and of fatal tendency. They serve to organize faction, to give it an artificial and extraordinary force, to put in the place of the delegated will of the nation the will of a party, often a small but artful and enterprising minority of the community; and, according to the alternate triumphs of different parties, to make the public administration the mirror of the ill-concerted and incongruous projects of faction, rather than the organ of consistent and wholesome plans, digested by common councils and modified by mutual interests.

However combinations or associations of the above description may now and then answer popular ends, they are likely, in the course of time and things, to become potent engines by which cunning, ambitious, and unprincipled men will be enabled to subvert the power of the people and to usurp for themselves the reins of government; destroying afterward the very engines which have lifted them to unjust dominion.

Toward the preservation of your government and the permanency of your present happy state it is requisite, not only that you speedily discountenance irregular opposition to its acknowledged authority, but also that you resist with care the spirit of innovation upon its principles, however specious the pretexts. One method of assault may be to effect in the forms of the Constitution alterations which will impair the energy of the system, and thus to undermine what cannot be directly overthrown. In all the changes to which you may be invited, remember that time and habit are at least as necessary to fix the true character of governments as of other human institutions; that experience is the surest standard by which to test the real tendency of the existing Constitution of a country; that facility in changes, upon the credit of mere hypothesis and opinion, exposes to perpetual change, from the endless variety of hypothesis and opinion. And remember especially that for the efficient management of your common interests, in a country so extensive as ours, a government of as much vigor as is consistent with the perfect security of liberty is indispensable. Liberty itself will find in such a government, with powers properly distributed and adjusted, its surest guardian. It is, indeed, little else than a name where the government is too feeble to withstand the enterprises of faction, to confine each member of society within the limits prescribed by the laws, and to maintain all in the secure and tranquil enjoyment of the rights of person and property.

I have already intimated to you the danger of parties in the States, with particular reference to the founding of them on geographical discrimination. Let me now take a more comprehensive view, and warn you, in the most solemn manner, against the baneful effects of the spirit of party generally. This spirit, unfortunately, is inseparable from our nature, having its root in the strongest passions of the human mind. It exists under different shapes in all governments, more or less stifled, controlled, or repressed. But in those of the popular form it is seen in its greatest rankness, and is truly their worst enemy.

The alternate domination of one faction over another, sharpened by the spirit of revenge, natural to party dissensions, which, in different ages and countries, has perpetrated the most horrid enormities, is itself a frightful despotism. But this leads at length to a more formal and permanent despotism. The disorders and miseries which result gradually incline the minds of men to seek security and repose in the absolute power of an individual; and, sooner or later, the chief of some prevailing faction, more able or more fortunate than his competitors, turns this disposition to the purposes of his own elevation on the ruins of public liberty.

Without looking forward to an extremity of this kind, which, nevertheless, ought not to be entirely out of sight, the common and continual mischiefs of the spirit of party are sufficient to make it the interest and duty of a wise people to discourage and restrain it. It serves always to distract the public councils and enfeeble the public administration. It agitates the community with ill-founded jealousies and false alarms; kindles the animosity of one part against another; foments occasionally riot and insurrection. It opens the door to foreign influence and corruption, which finds a facilitated access to the government itself through the channel of party passion. Thus the policy and the will of one country are subjected to the policy and will of another.

There is an opinion that parties, in free countries, are useful checks upon the administration of the government, and serve to keep alive the spirit of liberty. This, within certain limits, is probably true; and, in governments of a monarchical cast, patriotism may look with indulgence, if not with favor, upon the spirit of party. But in those of popular character, in governments purely elective, it is a spirit not to be encouraged. From their natural tendency, it is certain there will always be enough of that spirit for every salutary purpose. And, there being constant danger of excess, the effort ought to be, by force of public opinion, to mitigate and assuage it. A fire not to be quenched, it demands a uniform vigilance to prevent its bursting into a flame, lest, instead of warming, it should consume.

It is important, likewise, that the habits of thinking in a free country should inspire caution in those intrusted with its administration to confine themselves within their respective constitutional spheres, avoiding, in the exercise of the powers of one department, to encroach upon another. The spirit of encroachment tends to consolidate the powers of all the departments in one, and thus to create, whatever the form of government, a real despotism. A just estimate of that love of power, and proneness to abuse it, which predominates in the human heart is sufficient to satisfy us of the truth of this position. The necessity of reciprocal checks in the exercise of political power, by dividing and distributing it into different depositories and constituting each the guardian of the public weal against invasion by the other, has been evinced by experiments ancient and modern: some of them in our country and under our own eyes. To preserve them must be as necessary as to institute them. If, in the opinion of the people, the distribution or modification of the constitutional powers be, in any particular, wrong, let it be corrected by an amendment in the way which the Constitution designates. But let there be no change by usurpation; for though this in one instance may be the instrument of good, it is the customary weapon by which free governments are destroyed. The precedent must always greatly overbalance in permanent evil any partial or transient benefit which the use can at any time yield.

Of all the dispositions and habits which lead to political prosperity, religion and morality are indispensable supports. In vain would that man claim the tribute of patriotism who should labor to subvert these great pillars of human happiness, these firmest props of the destinies of men and citizens. The mere politician, equally with the pious man, ought to respect and cherish them. A volume could not trace all their connection with private and public felicity. Let it simply be asked, where is the security for property, for reputation, for life, if the sense of religious obligation desert the oaths which are the instruments of investigation in courts of justice? And let us with caution indulge the supposition that morality can be maintained without religion. Whatever may be conceded to the influence of refined education on minds of peculiar structure, reason and experience both forbid us to expect that natural morality can prevail in exclusion of religious principles.

It is substantially true that virtue or morality is a necessary spring of popular government. The rule, indeed, extends with more or less force to every species of free government. Who that is a sincere friend to it can look with indifference upon attempts to shake the foundation of the fabric?

Promote, then, as an object of primary importance, institutions for the general diffusion of knowledge. In proportion as the structure of a government gives force to public opinion, it is essential that public opinion should be enlightened. As a very important source of strength and security, cherish public credit. One method of preserving it is to use it as sparingly as possible; avoiding occasions of expense by cultivating peace, but remembering also that timely disbursements to prepare for danger frequently prevent much greater disbursements to repel it; avoiding likewise the accumulation of debt, not only by shunning occasions of expense, but by vigorous exertions in time of peace to discharge the debts which unavoidable wars may have occasioned, not ungenerously throwing upon posterity the burden which we ourselves ought to bear. The execution of these maxims belongs to your representatives; but it is necessary that public opinion should cooperate. To facilitate to them the performance of their duty, it is essential that you should practically bear in mind that towards the payment of debts there must be revenue; that to have revenue there must be taxes; that no taxes can be devised which are not more or less inconvenient and unpleasant; that the intrinsic embarrassment inseparable from the selection of the proper objects, which is always the choice of difficulties, ought to be a decisive motive for a candid construction of the conduct of the Government in making it, and for a spirit of acquiescence in the measures for obtaining revenue which the public exigencies may at any time dictate.

Observe good faith and justice towards all nations; cultivate peace and harmony with all: religion and morality enjoin this conduct; and can it be that good policy does not equally enjoin it? It will be worthy of a free, enlightened, and, at no distant period, a great nation to give to mankind the magnanimous and too novel example of a people always guided by an exalted justice and benevolence. Who can doubt, in the course of time and things, that fruits of such a plan would richly repay any temporary advantages that might be lost by a steady adherence to it? Can it be that Providence has not connected the permanent felicity of a nation with its virtue? The experiment, at least, is recommended by every sentiment which ennobles nature. Alas! is it rendered impossible by its vices?

In the execution of such a plan, nothing is more essential than that permanent, inveterate antipathies against particular nations, and passionate attachments for others, should be excluded; and that, in place of them, just and amicable feelings towards all should be cultivated. The nation which indulges towards another an habitual hatred, or an habitual fondness, is in some degree a slave. It is a slave to its animosity or to its affection, either of which is sufficient to lead it astray from its duty and its interest. Antipathy in one nation against another disposes each more readily to offer insult and injury, to lay hold of slight causes of umbrage, and to be haughty and intractable when accidental or trifling occasions of dispute occur.

Hence frequent collisions, obstinate, envenomed, and bloody contests. The nation, prompted by ill-will and resentment, sometimes impels to war the Government, contrary to the best calculations of policy. The Government sometimes participates in the national propensity, and adopts through passion what reason would reject; at other times, it makes animosity of the nation subservient to projects of hostility instigated by pride, ambition, and other sinister and pernicious motives. The peace often, and sometimes, perhaps, the liberty of nations, has been the victim.

So, likewise, a passionate attachment of one nation for another produces a variety of evils. Sympathy for the favorite nation, facilitating the illusion of an imaginary common interest in cases where no real common interest exists and infusing into one the enmities of the other, betrays the former into a participation in the quarrels and wars of the latter, without adequate inducement or justification. It leads also to concessions to the favorite nation of privileges denied to others, which is apt doubly to injure the nation making the concessions: by unnecessarily parting with what ought to have been retained, and by exciting jealousy, ill-will, and a disposition to retaliate, in the parties from whom equal privileges are withheld; and it gives to ambitious, corrupted, or deluded citizens who devote themselves to the favorite nation facility to betray or sacrifice the interests of their own country without odium, sometimes even with popularity; gilding with the appearances of a virtuous sense of obligation, a commendable deference for public opinion, or laudable zeal for public good, the base or foolish compliances of ambition, corruption, or infatuation.

As avenues to foreign influence, in innumerable ways, such attachments are particularly alarming to the truly enlightened and independent patriot. How many opportunities do they afford to tamper with domestic factions; to practice the arts of seduction; to mislead public opinion; to influence or awe the public councils! Such an attachment of a small or weak nation toward a great and powerful one dooms the former to be the satellite of the latter.

Against the insidious wiles of foreign influence, I conjure you to believe me, fellow-citizens, the jealousy of a free people ought to be constantly awake, since history and experience prove that foreign influence is one of the most baneful foes of republican government. But that jealousy, to be useful, must be impartial; else it becomes the instrument of the very influence to be avoided, instead of a defence against it. Excessive partiality for one foreign nation, and excessive dislike of another, cause those whom they actuate to see danger only on one side, and serve to veil and even second the arts of influence on the other.

Real patriots, who may resist the intrigues of the favorite, are liable to become suspected and odious; while its tools and dupes usurp the applause and confidence of the people to surrender their interests. The great rule of conduct for us in regard to foreign nations is, in extending our commercial relations, to have with them as little political connection as possible. So far as we have already formed engagements, let them be fulfilled with perfect good faith. Here let us stop.

Europe has a set of primary interests, which to us have none or a very remote relation. Hence she must be engaged in frequent controversies, the causes of which are essentially foreign to our concerns. Hence, therefore, it must be unwise in us to implicate ourselves by artificial ties in the ordinary vicissitudes of her politics, or the ordinary combinations and collisions of her friendships and enmities.

Our detached and distant situation invites and enables us to pursue a different course. If we remain one people, under an efficient government, the period is not far off when we may defy material injury and external annoyance; when we may take such an attitude as will cause the neutrality we may at any time resolve upon to be scrupulously respected; when belligerent nations, under the impossibility of making acquisitions upon us, will not lightly hazard the giving us provocation; when we may choose peace or war, as our interest, guided by justice, shall counsel.

Why forego the advantages of so peculiar a situation? Why quit our own, to stand upon foreign ground? Why, by interweaving our destiny with that of any part of Europe, entangle our peace and prosperity in the toils of European ambition, rivalship, interest, humor, or caprice?

'Tis our true policy to steer clear of permanent alliances with any portion of the foreign world; so far, I mean, as we are now at liberty to do it; for let me not be understood as capable of patronizing infidelity to existing engagements. I hold the maxim no less applicable to public than to private affairs, that honesty is always the best policy. I repeat it, therefore, let those engage-

ments be observed in their genuine sense. But, in my opinion, it is unnecessary, and would be unwise, to extend them. Taking care always to keep ourselves, by suitable establishments, in a respectable defensive posture, we may safely trust to temporary alliances for extraordinary emergencies.

Harmony and a liberal intercourse with all nations are recommended by policy, humanity, and interest. But even our commercial policy should hold an equal and impartial hand; neither seeking nor granting exclusive favors or preferences; consulting the natural course of things; diffusing and diversifying, by gentle means, the streams of commerce, but forcing nothing; establishing, with powers so disposed, in order to give trade a stable course, to define the rights of our merchants, and to enable the government to support them, conventional rules of intercourse, the best that present circumstances and mutual opinion will permit, but temporary, and liable to be, from time to time, abandoned or varied, as experience and circumstances shall dictate; constantly keeping in view that it is folly in one nation to look for disinterested favors from another; that it must pay with a portion of its independence for whatever it may accept under that character; that, by such acceptance, it may place itself in the condition of having given equivalents for nominal favors, and yet of being reproached with ingratitude for not giving more. There can be no greater error than to expect or calculate upon real favors from nation to nation. It is an illusion which experience must cure, which a just pride ought to discard.

In offering to you, my countrymen, these counsels of an old and affectionate friend, I dare not hope they will make the strong and lasting impression I could wish, that they will control the usual current of the passions, or prevent our nation from running the course which has hitherto marked the destiny of nations. But if I may even flatter myself that they may be productive of some partial benefit, some occasional good, that they may now and then recur to moderate the fury of party spirit; to warn against the mischief of foreign intrigues; to guard against the impostures of pretended patriotism, this hope will be a full recompense for the solicitude for your welfare by which they have been dictated.

How far, in the discharge of my official duties, I have been guided by the principles which have been delineated, the public records and other evidences of my conduct must witness to you and to the world. To myself, the assurance of my own conscience is that I have at least believed myself to be guided by them.

In relation to the still subsisting war in Europe, my proclamation of the 22d of April, 1793, is the index to my plan. Sanctioned by your approving voice, and by that of your representatives in both Houses of Congress, the spirit of that measure has continually governed me, uninfluenced by any attempts to deter or divert me from it. After deliberate examination, with the aid of the best lights I could obtain, I was well satisfied that our country, under all the circumstances of the case, had a right to take, and was bound in duty and interest to take, a neutral position. Having taken it, I determined, as far as should depend upon me, to maintain it with moderation, perseverance, and firmness.

The considerations which respect the right to hold this conduct it is not necessary on this occasion to detail. I will only observe that, according to my understanding of the matter, that right, so far from being denied by any of the belligerent powers, has been virtually admitted by all.

The duty of holding a neutral conduct may be inferred, without anything more, from the obligation which justice and humanity impose on every nation, in cases in which it is free to act, to maintain inviolate the relations of peace and amity towards other nations. The inducements of interest for observing that conduct will best be referred to your own reflection and experience. With me, a predominant motive has been to endeavor to gain time to our country to settle and mature its yet recent institutions, and to progress without interruption to that degree of strength and consistency which is necessary to give it, humanly speaking, the command of its own fortunes.

Though, in reviewing the incidents of my administration, I am unconscious of intentional error, I am, nevertheless, too sensible of my defects not to think it probable that I may have committed many errors. Whatever they may be, I fervently beseech the Almighty to avert or mitigate the evils to which they may tend. I shall also carry with me the hope that my country will never cease to view them with indulgence, and that, after forty-five years of my life dedicated to its services with an upright zeal, the faults of incompetent abilities will be consigned to oblivion, as myself must soon be to the mansions of rest.

Relying on its kindness in this, as in other things, and actuated by that fervent love toward it, which is so natural to a man who views in it the native soil of himself and his progenitors for several generations, I anticipate with pleasing expectations that retreat in which I promised myself to realize, without alloy, the sweet enjoyment of partaking, in the midst of my fellow-citizens, the benign influence of good laws under a free government, that ever favorite object of my heart, and the happy reward, as I trust, of our mutual cares, labors, and dangers.

American Revolution: First Battle of Saratoga

On September 19, 1777, the first of the two battles of Saratoga took place just south of the town of Saratoga (later renamed Schuylerville) in New York State. Although this first battle was technically a victory for the British, it stopped their advancing forces and denied them their objective, namely Albany, New York.

The second battle of Saratoga, which took place on October 7, 1777, began with a British reconnaissance force directed toward the Continental army positions at nearby Bemis Heights. The Americans defeated the British, whose forces then retreated and eventually surrendered at Saratoga (see October 17). It was this victory that helped convince the French to support the cause of American independence, since the inexperienced colonials had proven that they could defeat the powerful British army. Saratoga was a turning point in the American Revolution.

September 20

Panic of 1873

In associating economic collapse with the stock market crash of 1929 and the subsequent depression, Americans often overlook their earlier economic history, including five crises in the 19th century. The "panics" of 1819, 1837, 1857, 1873, and 1893 were not so severe as the Great Depression of the 20th century, but they caused considerable hardship. Indeed, the panic of 1873 precipitated one of the longest periods of economic contraction in American history, lasting until 1879.

The collapse marked the end of a period of economic expansion that followed the Civil War. By 1869 a transcontinental railroad linked the Atlantic and Pacific coasts of the United States, and numerous new subsidiary routes supplemented the older networks of the eastern half of the nation. In addition to this railroad boom, the influx of immigrants and the overall expansion of the population stimulated the growth of the housing industry.

By 1873 the tight money market had deprived the railroads of investors. The unnecessary expansion of some lines complicated the problems caused by the scarcity of backers, and during the first eight months of the year, 25 railroads found themselves unable to pay the interest on their bonds. Jay Cooke, the chief financier of the Union war effort during the Civil War, fell victim to the railroads' difficulties. With the expectation that European financiers would purchase $100 million worth of bonds from him, Cooke put money obtained from short-term depositors into the Northern Pacific Railroad, which was far from completion. When no foreign backers appeared and the depositors called for their money, Cooke was unable to meet his commitments. The failure of the prestigious Jay Cooke and Company on September 18, 1873, precipitated the collapse of many other firms in similar circumstances and touched off a banking panic that forced the New York Stock Exchange to close on September 20.

Level-headed action by New York bankers quickly terminated the financial panic. On September 24 a five-man committee of the New York Clearing House Association took control of the cash reserves of the organization's member banks and used them freely to restore confidence. By September 27 the monetary crisis was over, and in October bankers' cash reserves began to increase.

Although short-lived, the banking panic did serious damage to the economy. Businesses reduced or canceled orders and were unable to meet their payrolls, while unpaid employees purchased fewer goods. This temporary interruption of the nation's commerce was enough to cause a full-scale economic depression. More than 18,000 businesses, including the majority of the nation's railroads, went bankrupt during the depth of the depression in 1876 and 1877. Half a million workers lost their jobs as a result of the collapse, and countless others had their wages lowered.

Labor problems increased significantly during this depression. On July 17, 1877, workers on the Baltimore and Ohio Railroad went on strike to protest wage cuts, and the stoppage quickly spread to other rail lines across the country. Riots occurred in Baltimore, Maryland; Chicago, Illinois; and St. Louis, Missouri. On July 21, 1877, 26 people died when a Pittsburgh, Pennsylvania, mob battled the militia and then burned almost $10 million worth of railroad property before federal troops, dispatched by President Rutherford B. Hayes, restored order. Prosperity finally returned in 1879 when the government's readoption of the gold standard increased business confidence, and crop shortages in Europe provided a strong demand for American exports.

Upton Sinclair's Birthday

Upton Beall Sinclair, author and crusader for social reform, was born on September 20, 1878, in Baltimore, Maryland. He attended the College of the City of New York, graduating in 1897, and briefly studied at Columbia University. During these years he earned some money by writing pieces for local magazines. In 1900 he moved to Quebec, where he wrote his first novel, *Springtime and Harvest* (1901) (also published as *King Midas*).

Sinclair became involved in liberal politics when he joined the Socialist Party in 1902. He moved back to the United States in 1903, and worked with Jack London, another noted writer, in establishing the Intercollegiate Socialist Society in 1905. He unsuccessfully ran for Congress on the Socialist ticket in 1906, but in that same year published his most famous novel, *The Jungle*. The book was the result of Sinclair's months of research in Chicago, Illinois, concerning the deplorable sanitary conditions in the meat packing industry and the desperate lives of the immigrant workers. This enormously successful book made him a national figure, and President Theodore Roosevelt used the popular sympathy for the reform it generated to achieve congressional passage of the Pure Food and Drug Act in 1906 and to impose tighter federal meat inspection controls. As a political tract, however, *The Jungle* was less successful in generating support for the Socialists or alleviating the conditions in immigrant communities.

During the 1920s Sinclair helped to establish the American Civil Liberties Union, one of the most prominent civil rights organizations in existence today, and made several more unsuccessful bids for Congress. Sinclair also wrote other social and political works, supported Prohibition and the abolition of alcoholic beverages, and attempted to expose abuses in the newspaper business. In 1934 his most famous political bid came when he won the Democratic nomination as the party's candidate for governor of California by running on populist themes that generated wide support during the economic crisis of the Great Depression. Sinclair won 37 percent of the vote, losing to the Republican candidate who took 48 percent of the vote (an independent candidate took most of the remaining votes).

During World War II Sinclair wrote *Dragon's Teeth* (1942), concerning Adolf Hitler's rise to power and the establishment of Nazi Germany. For that work he won the 1943 Pulitzer Prize in fiction. He also wrote *The Autobiography of Upton Sinclair* (1962). He died on November 25, 1968, in Bound Brook, New Jersey, the author of some 90 books.

September 21

Autumn Begins

In the United States and the north temperate zones generally, autumn begins on approximately September 21 of every year. Astronomically, the start of the third season of the year, which comes between summer and winter, can be pinpointed precisely. The ecliptic, the plane in which the Sun appears to revolve about the Earth and in which the Earth actually revolves about the Sun, is divided into four 90-degree sections. Each of these sections commences with a specific point: two equinoxes and two solstices. Autumn starts at the autumnal equinox (Latin *aequinoctium*, from *aequus* meaning "equal" and *nox* meaning "night") situated halfway between the summer solstice, the start of summer (see June 21), and the winter solstice, the start of winter (see December 21). The period from the autumnal equinox to the winter solstice has been designated the season of autumn.

Autumn is also said to begin when the Sun appears to reach the zodiac sign of Libra, the scales (see Appendix D: The Zodiac). That statement is somewhat misleading today since precession, that is the backward movement of the equinoctial points, has caused a retrograde motion of 30 degrees over the past 2,000 years. Thus the autumnal equinox, which used to be found in Libra, is presently in the sign of Virgo the virgin. Only at the completion of a 25,800-year cycle will the autumnal equinox once more be located in Libra.

It is thought that Libra received its designation as "the scales" from the "balancing" or equality of day and night that occurs at the equinoxes, vernal (see March 21) as well as autumnal. Around September 21, the Sun appears to reach the intersection of the celestial equator and the ecliptic, having then a celestial longitude of 180 degrees and

a declination of 0 degrees. Its rays extend from the North to the South Pole.

During the season of autumn, the Sun, having crossed the celestial equator from north to south, progresses along the ecliptic south of it. The Sun's south declination constantly increases. At the winter solstice, when the Sun is said to enter the zodiac sign of Capricorn, it reaches a longitude of 270 degrees and its maximum south declination of minus 23 degrees 27 minutes. Autumn then ends.

Seasonal differences, especially the regular fluctuations in weather, are the result of the tilt of the Earth's axis (23 ½ degrees) as well as of the elliptical nature of its revolution around the Sun. When the North Pole points directly toward the Sun at the summer solstice, the amount of solar radiation absorbed daily by the surface and atmosphere of the northern hemisphere is high. So, consequently, are the temperatures there. By the winter solstice, when the North Pole inclines away from the Sun, opposite conditions prevail. Like spring, autumn is therefore a transitional period between the extremes of summer and winter. In the Southern Hemisphere the seasons are reversed, since the South Pole moves in the opposite direction from the North Pole. There, astronomical autumn begins around March 21 and ends around June 21.

Autumn has always played an important role in the life of the farmer. As the period of harvest, vintage, and fruit gathering, it has left an imprint not only on day-to-day living but also on the development of folklore, mythology, and art. The intimate intertwining of art and nature can be seen in the detailed depictions of the autumn months in the French cathedrals. At Reims, for example, in one of the carved stone scenes portraying the calendar year, fermenting wine is being transferred from vats to casks. The season itself was often personified as a female figure bearing grapes.

Congress Endorses the Balfour Declaration

For thousands of years, the creation of an independent homeland in the Middle East was only a dream for Jews scattered across the world. But in the aftermath of World War I, that dream became a real possibility as control of Palestine, a historic region in the old Ottoman Empire, passed to the victorious British. Palestine included the present-day lands of Israel and Jordan, parts of modern Lebanon, and above all the city of Jerusalem.

Influential British Jews began to petition the British government to allow a Jewish homeland in Palestine. On November 2, 1917, they achieved official endorsement of their cause in the form of a letter from Arthur James Balfour, the British Foreign Secretary, to Baron Lionel Walter Rothschild, a former member of Parliament and a supporter of Zionism. This letter is known as the Balfour Declaration:

Dear Lord Rothschild,

I have much pleasure in conveying to you, on behalf of His Majesty's Government, the following declaration of sympathy with Jewish Zionist aspirations which has been submitted to, and approved by, the Cabinet.

His Majesty's Government view with favour the establishment in Palestine of a national home for the Jewish people, and will use their best endeavours to facilitate the achievement of this object, it being clearly understood that nothing shall be done which may prejudice the civil and religious rights of existing non-Jewish communities in Palestine, or the rights and political status enjoyed by Jews in any other country.

I should be grateful if you would bring this declaration to the knowledge of the Zionist Federation.

Yours sincerely,

Arthur James Balfour

On July 24, 1922, the League of Nations formally recognized British rule over Palestine and the door was opened for Jewish immigration. The British Empire, however, was on the wane. Although the United States was dominated by isolationist sentiment at the time and did not even belong to the League of Nations, it would come to be the world's leading superpower after World War II, and would also become the guarantor of modern Israel's security. Therefore, an important step toward the formation of a Jewish homeland and the modern American-Israeli relationship was taken on September 21, 1922, when Congress endorsed the Balfour Declaration:

Resolved by the Senate and House of Representatives of the United States of America in Congress Assembled:

That the United States of America favors the establishment in Palestine of a national home for the Jewish people, it being clearly understood that nothing shall be done which will prejudice the civil and religious rights of Christian and all other non-Jewish communities in Palestine, and that the holy places and religious buildings and sites in Palestine shall be adequately protected.

The way was open for the later creation of the nation of Israel, under American sponsorship, on May 14, 1948 (see May 14, United States Recognizes Israel).

Delaware Organized as a State

During the American colonial period, Sweden, the Netherlands, and Great Britain successively ruled the area which is now Delaware. England gained control of Delaware in 1664, and in 1682 the duke of York gave William Penn (proprietor of the new colony of Pennsylvania) title to the counties of Kent, New Castle, and Sussex, which today comprise the state of Delaware. The settlers in Delaware at the time were not pleased with their inclusion in Penn's colony, and in 1704 Penn allowed them to hold a separate assembly. However, the governor of Pennsylvania continued to administer the so-called Three Lower Counties.

The American Revolution gave Delaware residents the opportunity to determine their own destiny. Although still technically under the jurisdiction of the governor of Pennsylvania, Delaware sent its own delegates to the Second Continental Congress, which declared the independence of the United States in 1776. In the following August a constitutional convention met to form a government for Kent, New Castle, and Sussex counties. On September 21, 1776, the convention completed organizing the government for the new and autonomous state of Delaware. Later, in 1787 Delaware had the honor of being the first state to ratify the United States Constitution and consequently won for itself the honor of being the first state of the Union.

September 22

American Revolution: Nathan Hale Hanged

Nathan Hale, the son of a prosperous farmer named Richard Hale and his wife, Elizabeth, was born in Coventry, Connecticut, on June 6, 1755. He entered Yale College at the age of 14 and graduated in 1773 with high honors. A friend once described Hale as slightly above average height, blue-eyed, athletic, and as having a "rather sharp or piercing" voice. Shortly after leaving Yale he took a teaching position in East Haddam, Connecticut. He remained there for several months and then moved to New London, Connecticut, where he taught for less than a year.

The first skirmishes of the American Revolution ended Hale's academic career in 1775. Five of his brothers battled the redcoats at Lexington and Concord, and Hale joined the fight on July 6 when he was commissioned as a lieutenant in the Seventh Connecticut militia. He was only 20 at the time of his enlistment, but despite his youth Hale advanced quickly. By the following summer he had earned the rank of captain and commanded a company in New York.

Shortly before the battle of Harlem Heights, General George Washington requested a volunteer for an intelligence mission behind enemy lines. Hale agreed to perform the task. Explaining his reasons for accepting the mission to one of his friends, he stated: "I wish to be useful, and every kind of service, necessary to the public good, becomes honorable by being necessary."

Disguised as a Dutch schoolteacher, Hale left the rebel camp at Harlem Heights around September 12, 1776. For the next nine days he gathered information on the position of the British troops, and was returning to the American side when he was captured by the enemy. The British sentries took Hale to Beekman Mansion, the headquarters of their commander in chief, General William Howe. It was at the mansion that he was allegedly betrayed by his cousin Samuel Hale, who was serving as Howe's deputy commissioner of prisoners. However, even without his cousin's testimony, there was little doubt that Hale was a spy. When captured he was not in uniform, and he had incriminating papers in his possession. Howe did not hesitate to sentence his prisoner. Without allowing him the benefit of a trial, Howe ordered that Hale be hanged the following day.

As he approached death on Sunday, September 22, 1776, the young schoolmaster did not forget his academic training. Inspired by words of the English writer Joseph Addison, "What pity is it that we can die but once to save our country," Hale concluded his speech at the gallows with his own ringing statement: "I only regret that I have but one life to lose for my country."

Peace Corps Created

On September 22, 1961, the United States Congress passed legislation formally establishing the Peace Corps, authorizing it to promote "world peace and friendship" and giving it three objectives: (1) to help the people of interested countries in meeting their needs for trained workers, (2) to help promote a better understanding of Americans on the part of the peoples served, and (3) to help promote a better understanding of other peoples by Americans.

The inspiration for the Peace Corps was based on a speech given on October 14, 1960, by Democratic presidential candidate John F. Kennedy at the University of Michigan. He challenged the assembled students to give two years of their lives to help people in less developed countries. They responded enthusiastically, and formed the Americans Committed to World Responsibility committee to oversee a petition drive asking for the establishment of just such a program. Kennedy went on to win the election, and during his inaugural address on January 20, 1961, he followed up on the idea: "To those peoples in the huts and villages of half the globe struggling to break the bonds of mass misery, we pledge our best efforts to help them help themselves . . . ."

On March 1 Kennedy signed an executive order establishing the Peace Corps and appointed Sargent Shriver as its first director. The first group of volunteers was assembled on August 28, roughly a month before Congress gave its official authorization. They and other Peace Corps volunteers during the idealistic 1960s were inspired by other words of Kennedy's:

And so, my fellow Americans: ask not what your country can do for you, ask what you can do for your country. My fellow citizens of the world: ask not what America will do for you, but what together we can do for the freedom of man.

By June 1966 more than 15,000 Peace Corps volunteers were abroad—the height of the corps' membership. However, many of them had more enthusiasm than expertise, with few skills and little or no relevant useful knowledge with respect to third world problems. Soon, disillusioned by the realities of everyday life in a third world country, among people who were often suspicious or resentful of Americans, many would drop out of the corps. As a result, the administration of the Peace Corps became more professional and pragmatic. Volunteers were screened on the basis of skills and experience, and educational programs for prospective volunteers were established throughout the country.

After some hard times, the corps began to recover. In July 1989 Peace Corps volunteers were chosen by President George Bush to go to Hungary and help assist in the transition of formerly communist Eastern Europe to a free market economy. More volunteers followed in the years afterward on missions to Russia, Poland, and the newly independent Baltic republics of Estonia, Latvia, and Lithuania. By the late 1990s, President William J. Clinton sought to increase funding for the Peace Corps so it could expand its worldwide activities and its membership.

September 23

Lewis and Clark Expedition Completed

The explorers Meriwether Lewis and William Clark arrived in St. Louis, Missouri, on September 23, 1806, to the astonishment of a world that had thought them dead. Their return from the first recorded overland crossing of the continent was celebrated with excitement in St. Louis, where they were "met by all the village." As the news spread, the entire nation celebrated their return.

To anyone familiar with the inquiring mind of President Thomas Jefferson, who had been trying for two decades to further exploration west of the Mississippi, his commissioning of the Lewis and Clark expedition in 1803 should have come as no surprise. When Jefferson named Lewis, a fellow Virginian whom he had known as a boy, as his private secretary in 1801, it was probably with this in mind. Captain Lewis, born on August 18, 1774, near Charlottesville, Virginia, had spent several years in the Northwest Territory while serving in the army. He subsequently added to his qualifications for wilderness survival by traveling to Philadelphia, Pennsylvania, to study botany, zoology, and celestial navigation.

Lewis persuaded Jefferson to let him name his friend Lieutenant William Clark as co-leader of the expedition. With a party of some 40 men, they spent the winter of 1803–1804 at Wood River near St. Louis getting supplies. Before they set out on May 14, 1804, with two dugouts and a 55-foot keelboat, Jefferson had completed the famous Louisiana Purchase whereby the United States acquired a vast territory stretching from the Mississippi to the Rocky Mountains.

The explorers followed the Missouri River, whose treacherous current they fought every mile of the way, along what are now the borders between Kansas and Missouri, and Nebraska and Iowa. By November 2 the explorers had traveled 1,600 miles up river to the Mandan Sioux villages 60 miles above what is now Bismarck, North Dakota. There they built Fort Mandan and spent their second winter among friendly natives who lived in earthen lodges.

In April 1805 the party continued up the Missouri. With them were two guides, Toussaint Charbonneau and his Shoshone wife, Sacagawea, who was purchased by Charbonneau from slave traders. A native of what is now southwestern Montana, the resourceful Sacagawea traveled with her infant on her back while she served as interpreter and principal guide of the expedition.

It took the party nearly a month to make portage around the falls near Great Falls, Montana. As they approached the Rocky Mountains, the Missouri took them through a canyon that they named Gates of the Mountains because of its towering rock walls, which gave the illusion of opening before them and closing behind them like monstrous gates. The explorers also passed the site of Three Forks, at the juncture of three forks of the Missouri River.

Passing landmarks that Sacagawea recognized from her childhood, the explorers then followed the fork of the Missouri that they named the Jefferson to its source in southwestern Montana. Unable to negotiate the Salmon River in nearby Idaho, Lewis and Clark bartered for horses with a Shoshone chief who turned out to be the brother of Sacagawea. Detouring 110 miles north through the Bitterroot Range of the Rockies, they were able to turn west through the Lolo Pass. Ill, nearly starved, and plagued by early snow, they were reduced to eating bear oil and candles before they reached the headwaters of the Clearwater River, where they paused to build canoes.

The Clearwater led into the Snake, and the Snake into the Columbia River, which carried the explorers westward along what is now the boundary between Oregon and Washington. On November 15, 1805, they finally reached the mouth of the Columbia. Clark recorded the event with understandable elation: "Ocian in view! O! the joy."

On March 23, 1806, Lewis and Clark began their comparatively rapid trip back to St. Louis. Just east of the Continental Divide they separated, Lewis going north with one party to explore (and name) the Marias River, Clark going south to explore Yellowstone. Reuniting just below the junction of the Missouri and Yellowstone Rivers, they reached St. Louis on September 23, 1806. They bore with them their remarkable diaries and Clark's detailed maps and drawings.

In providing the first descriptions of the largely unknown territory through which they had traveled, Lewis and Clark helped open the West and gave the United States a valid claim to the Oregon Territory. Lewis and Clark were rewarded with double their promised pay and 1,600 acres apiece of public land. Lewis, who was appointed governor of the Louisiana Territory, died on October 11, 1809. Clark was named superintendent of Indian affairs at St. Louis and became governor of the Missouri Territory, in which capacity he concluded treaties with the native tribes after the War of 1812. He died on September 1, 1838.

Victoria C. Woodhull's Birthday

Victoria Claflin Woodhull, a prominent feminist and the first woman to run as an independent candidate for the presidency, was born on September 23, 1838, in Homer, Ohio. Her parents ran a traveling medicine show, and together with her sister (Tennessee Claflin) Victoria practiced faith healing and spiritualism. At the age of 15, she married Canning Woodhull, but their relationship soured and they soon became estranged. Thus she continued to spend most of her time with Tennessee, touring the Midwest and finally settling in New York City in 1868.

Woodhull became friends with the rich and powerful railroad magnate and entrepreneur Cornelius Vanderbilt. With his assistance, in 1870 she and Tennessee established their own Wall Street brokerage firm. That same year, they also started the newspaper *Woodhull & Claflin's Weekly*, which was a political tract that promoted a number of controversial positions on sexual freedom in addition to women's rights. For example, it endorsed short skirts for women, a notion then considered scandalous. Colonel James H. Blood, Woodhull's male companion, and reform activist Stephen Andrews worked on the paper as well. She also became active in Socialist Party politics.

In 1871 Woodhull became the head of Karl Marx's International Workingmen's Association. She also continued to speak out in favor of women's suffrage, even appearing before the judiciary committee of the United States House of Representatives to give testimony in support of suffrage measures, but her radical politics and indiscreet personal lifestyle alienated many of her fellow feminists and most politicians. Undaunted, in May 1872 she sought and obtained the Equal Rights Party's nomination as its candidate for president in the upcoming November presidential elections. It was a small third-party organization, affiliated with Susan B. Anthony's National American Woman Suffrage Association.

Like most minor third-party candidates in presidential elections, Woodhull received only a token portion of the vote. However, she nevertheless earned the distinction of being the first woman to run for the presidency. Also in 1872 Woodhull and her sister were tried for sending obscene matter through the mails after they published accounts of adultery concerning the prominent clergyman Henry Ward Beecher. The sisters were ultimately acquitted, but their political and journalistic careers were over, and the paper folded in 1876. In 1877 they moved to Great Britain, where both of them married prosperous businessmen. Victoria died on June 10, 1927, in Worcestershire, England.

September 24

John Marshall's Birthday

John Marshall, the fourth chief justice of the United States Supreme Court, was born in Germantown, Virginia, on September 24, 1755. He enlisted in the Continental army in 1776, and fought in several of the important early battles of the American Revolution, namely Brandywine, Germantown, and Monmouth, and spent the harsh winter of 1777–1778 at Valley Forge. In 1780 he resigned his army commission and returned to Virginia, where he attended law lectures at the College of William and Mary in Williamsburg.

Following his admission to the bar in 1781, the fledgling lawyer established his first practice in his native Fauquier County. In 1783 he moved to Richmond, the state capital, where he quickly advanced his legal reputation, and married Mary Willis Ambler, the daughter of Virginia's treasurer. Marshall also served in the Virginia state legislature almost continuously from 1782 to 1797. He was a representative to the state convention that ratified the Constitution of the United States. President George Washington offered him the cabinet post of attorney general in 1795 and the position of American minister to France in 1796, but Marshall declined both offices.

Despite this initial reluctance to enter national politics, in 1797 Marshall consented to go to Paris, France, with C. C. Pinckney and Elbridge Gerry to persuade the French to remove restrictions on American commerce. Although this mission failed, it so increased Marshall's reputation that in 1799 he won election to the United States House of Representatives.

By the end of the 1790s, two distinct political parties had developed in the United States. There were the Federalists, who advocated a strong national government, and the Democratic-Republicans, who favored a more decentralized system. Marshall, an ardent Federalist, served briefly as secretary of state during the administration of President John Adams, a fellow Federalist. Ironically, however, he would exert his greatest influence when the opposing party occupied the White House. In 1800 Thomas Jefferson, the Democratic-Republican candidate, won the presidency. However, just before Adams left office in March 1801 he appointed Marshall as chief justice of the United States Supreme Court. This move ensured the Federalist dominance of the judiciary.

Marshall's accomplishments as chief justice securely established the prestige of the Supreme Court. In the 1803 case of *Marbury* v. *Madison*, he insisted that the Supreme Court had the function to interpret the Constitution and to decide whether the acts of Congress and of the state legislatures exceeded the powers delegated to them. In addition, he himself wrote many of the most important opinions handed down during his 34 years on the bench, and these decisions reflected his belief in a strong national government.

Marshall's most famous defense of such a system of government is contained in his 1819 opinion in the case of *McCulloch* v. *Maryland*: "Let the end be legitimate, let it be within the scope of the Constitution, and all means which are not prohibited, but consist with the letter and spirit of the Constitution, are constitutional." His service to his country ended in 1835. Following a stagecoach accident, he was taken to a Philadelphia hospital and died there on July 6. The Liberty Bell in the tower of Independence Hall was tolled to announce his death.

F. Scott Fitzgerald's Birthday

The writer F. Scott Fitzgerald—a distant relative of Francis Scott Key, the author of the national anthem—was born on September 24, 1896, in Saint Paul, Minnesota. Fitzgerald's parents were Edward and Mary McQuillan Fitzgerald. He was educated at private Catholic schools and was admitted to Princeton University in 1913. There he was an indifferent student, although he honed his writing skills and met a number of other aspiring writers.

Shortly before his scheduled graduation in 1917, which may well have been in doubt because of his poor academic performance, Fitzgerald joined the United States Army. He was commissioned as an officer, and found the time during his training courses to finish his first novel, *This Side of Paradise* (1920). It concerned the life and loves of Amory Blaine, a protagonist who somewhat resembled Fitzgerald himself during his Princeton years. Fitzgerald's evocation of the Jazz Age was influenced by his courtship of Zelda Sayre, a young woman who epitomized the fast-living "flapper" of the 1920s.

Fitzgerald never served in World War I, as the conflict ended shortly before he was scheduled to be shipped overseas. He was discharged in 1919. When his book came out the next year, it was both a financial and a literary success, making Fitzgerald a fairly wealthy man. He married Zelda and became a sought-after writer of short stories for such well know publications as *The Saturday Evening Post*.

In 1922 Fitzgerald produced his second novel, *The Beautiful and the Damned*. It concerned the dissolute life of a young couple and was not as enthusiastically received as his first work. His frustrations increased when his play *The Vegetable* failed miserably in the fall of 1923. Perhaps because of these disappointments, and his stormy relationship with Zelda, Fitzgerald began to drink heavily and gained a reputation as an alcoholic. Nevertheless, he continued to produce popular short stories, which were later issued in book form in a series of compilations.

Fitzgerald moved to Europe in 1924, where he wrote his third and most famous novel, *The Great Gatsby* (1925), which concerns a self-made man's devotion to a vacuous socialite. The work, not widely appreciated at the time, sold poorly. Although he continued to write for magazines and other periodicals, Fitzgerald's personal life deteriorated, and Zelda began to experience mental problems. His fourth novel, *Tender Is the Night* (1934), his thinly veiled account of the relationship with Zelda, had structural problems and lackluster sales.

Having returned to the United States in 1931 and survived both Zelda's breakdown and his own, in 1937 Fitzgerald began to do movie screenwriting in Hollywood, California, on a regular basis. He also wrote *The Last Tycoon* (1941), a novel about Hollywood, but died on December 21, 1940, before it was published. In the decades following his death, the book would gain critical acclaim as a great work, as would *The Great Gatsby*. Fitzgerald has come to be regarded as one of the greatest American authors of the 20th century and of the 1920s in particular.

September 25

Balboa Discovers the Pacific Ocean

Vasco Núñez de Balboa, the Spanish discoverer who led the first band of Europeans to the Pacific, was born at Jeréz de los Caballeros in western Spain about 1475. By birth he was a *hidalgo*, or gentleman, descended from Galician nobles who had become impoverished. Little is known of his life in Spain. Perhaps to repair the family fortunes, he joined a great mercantile expedition to the New World undertaken by Rodrigo de Bastidas in 1501.

The Bastidas group explored the coast of Colombia and the northern coast of the Isthmus of Panama. While linking continents to the north and south, the Isthmus of Panama itself lies in a west-to-east curve. Thus the Caribbean Sea, already familiar to the Spanish by 1500, lies off its northern shore. However, off its southern coast lies the Pacific Ocean, unknown to Europe until Balboa and his men discovered it.

Balboa settled on Hispaniola, the island that Haiti and the Dominican Republic occupy today, and tried farming in the vicinity of Salvatierra. However, his plantation was not financially successful. In 1510, to escape his creditors, Balboa had himself smuggled aboard the caravel that was being sent to provision Alonso de Ojeda's new settlement of San Sebastían that bordered the Gulf of Urabá on the north coast of Colombia. It is said that Balboa hid in a cask of "victuals for the voyage" sent from his farm to the ship.

In this bizarre fashion, he joined his second expedition to the South American continent. This time Balboa sailed under Martín Fernández de Enciso, an adventurous lawyer from Hispaniola who had been engaged by Ojeda. On reaching the coast, however, the provisioning party found that Ojeda had vanished. Only 41 survivors remained in the ruined settlement, led by Francisco Pizarro (who later conquered Peru). While Enciso hesitated, the seasoned Balboa urged that the colony sail west to the other side of the Gulf of Urabá. This would put them on the easternmost part of the Isthmus of Panama in the region called Darién, where Balboa had landed earlier with Bastidas. Balboa's proposal was accepted, and the first permanent European settlement in South America, Santa María de la Antigua del Darién, was established by Enciso's group and the remnant of Ojeda's expedition.

There was a struggle for leadership between Enciso and Balboa, whose initiative had saved the colony. In the end Enciso was deposed, imprisoned, and shipped back to Spain under the watch of one of Balboa's allies. He would stir up trouble for Balboa at the Spanish court, but in the meantime the latter was freed for an important role in the second stage of Spanish exploration. The first stage had been capped by the settlement of Hispaniola, which thereafter declined in vigor and importance.

As leader of the Darién colony, Balboa brought the surrounding area under Spanish control. On an excursion into the interior, Balboa first heard from a native *cacique*, or chief of the great sea across the mountains of Darién and of the gold of Peru. Balboa wrote King Ferdinand V of his conviction that the "Other Sea" and its fabled realms lay near, and he included the natives' estimate that 1,000 soldiers would be needed for its discovery. At this news, King Ferdinand was inspired to authorize a large crown colony (Castilla del Oro), for which 2,000 new colonists were gathered.

Informed that the king was also sending a new governor, Pedro Arias Dávila (often called Pedrarias Dávila), with these reinforcements, Balboa resolved to find the "South Sea" before his replacement could arrive. On September 1, 1513, he set out at the head of 190 Spaniards (one-half his colony) and 800 native allies to cross the Isthmus of Panama. Reaching the summit of the range, Balboa and his men sighted the Pacific on September 25. After falling on his knees to give thanks for the new ocean, Balboa sent Pizarro and two other scouts ahead to find the shore. On September 29 Balboa himself arrived at the Gulf of San Miguel. With banner raised and sword drawn, he strode into the waters, claiming the new ocean and all the lands bordering on it for the crown of Spain. Exploring the region for several months, he returned to Darién on January 18, 1514, and sent messengers to Spain with gifts and the news of his discoveries.

For his success King Ferdinand named Balboa admiral of the South Sea and governor of Panama and Coiba, an island off the southwest coast of Panama, but Arias Dávila remained the governor of Darién. Balboa revisited the Pacific a number of times and began to plan the conquest of Peru and the exploration of the new ocean. However, Arias Dávila, cheated of the great discovery, hounded Balboa and prevented his putting to sea for Peru. The marriage by proxy of one of Arias Dávila's daughters to Balboa exacerbated the feud, and late in 1518 Arias Dávila lured his rival to Acla, imprisoned him, and had him condemned on a trumped-up charge of treason with his right of appeal denied. Balboa was beheaded in January 1519.

Thus, at the age of 44, one of the great conquistadors was executed and his explorations brought to an end. Balboa's comrade Pizarro went on to conquer Peru. Ferdinand Magellan, spurred by the discovery of the new ocean, sailed south and west around what he presumed to be a great peninsula but which was in fact South America. It was Magellan who, seven years after Balboa's original sighting, first called the South Sea the Pacific.

Twelfth Amendment Proclaimed Ratified

Complications in the national election of 1800 inspired the 12th Amendment, which changed the process of selection for the offices of president and vice president. Congress proposed the 12th Amendment in December 1803 and it was ratified on September 25, 1804.

Article II, Section 1 of the United States Constitution entitled each state to appoint a slate of presidential electors every four years equal in number to its total membership in both houses of Congress. These electors, empowered to choose a president and a vice president, could each cast votes for two persons. The individual who received the greatest number of these electoral votes became president, provided that their total exceeded one-half the number of appointed electors. If no one gained such a majority, or if two candidates managed to do so and obtained an equal number of votes, the House of Representatives had the right to make the final decision. In either case, whether the electors or the House chose the president, the person with the second greatest number of votes became vice president.

In the 1790s, because of disputes over domestic and foreign policies, two relatively stable political parties emerged. The founding fathers, who looked upon parties as unhealthy manifestations of division and selfishness, had not envisioned such a development. The appearance of these disciplined voting organizations played havoc with the electoral system created by the Constitution and in 1800 demonstrated that the original process was already obsolete.

Federalists, as one group became known, favored strong central government and a diplomatic stance friendly to Great Britain. Their opponents, the Democratic-Republicans, wanted greater reliance upon local government as a means of preserving civil and individual liberties and generally sympathized with the goals of the French Revolution. President George Washington warned of the dangers of factionalism, but he increasingly sided with the Federalists during his two terms. John Adams, his vice president, openly aligned himself with the Federalists. Thomas Jefferson, Washington's secretary of state until 1793, became the leader of the Democratic-Republicans.

Washington, elected president in 1788 and 1792 without opposition, announced that he would retire after his second term in office. In 1796 candidates from two parties vied for the White House for the first time. Many Federalists favored John Adams for president and Charles Cotesworth Pinckney for vice president, while almost all of the Democratic-Republicans supported Jefferson for president. The party system had not yet attained maturity, and the division of the electoral vote among 13 candidates demonstrated that voting discipline was weak. Adams managed to win the presidency, but not all of his supporters cast their second ballots for Pinckney. As a result, Thomas Jefferson, the choice of Democratic-Republicans and independent-minded

electors, won second place and the office of vice president. He accepted the position and bided his time until 1800 for a second attempt at the White House.

Adams was again the Federalist candidate in 1800, but his even-tempered resolution of America's diplomatic and maritime conflict with France undermined his position with more aggressive Federalists. For example, Alexander Hamilton worked almost openly to defeat Adams and put Pinckney, the Federalist vice-presidential selection, in the White House. Jefferson once more carried the Democratic-Republican banner, and Aaron Burr was his running mate.

Party discipline was rigorous in 1800, and the electors divided their ballots among only five men. John Adams received 65 votes and Pinckney 64. Rhode Island cast one of its Federalist ballots for John Jay rather than for Pinckney to prevent a tied vote, which would have sent the election to the House of Representatives in the event of a Federalist victory. However, the Democratic-Republicans won the contest, and their electors, lacking this foresight, allowed both Jefferson and Burr to gain 73 votes.

Some Federalists saw the Jefferson-Burr tie as their salvation. Still strong in the House of Representatives, where each state would have one vote, they hoped to be able to give the presidency to Burr as the more conservative of the two. Others, like Alexander Hamilton, thought Burr untrustworthy and admitted that, in comparison to Burr, Jefferson had some "pretensions to character."

When balloting began on February 10, 1801, eight states aligned with Jefferson, six with Burr, and two were divided. To be victorious, a candidate needed the votes of a majority, or 9 of the 16 states. The stalemate continued for 35 ballots until February 16, 1801. On that day, Federalist James A. Bayard, the sole representative from Delaware, broke the impasse. Bayard preferred Burr, but thought his cause hopeless. Assured by a friend of Jefferson's, Senator Samuel Smith, that Jefferson did not intend to revoke the major pieces of legislation enacted by the Washington and Adams administrations, Bayard agreed to acquiesce in his election. After Bayard declared his intentions, politicians from both parties worked out an arrangement whereby ten states gave their votes and the election went to Jefferson without a single Federalist having cast a ballot in his favor.

Both victors and vanquished learned from the election of 1800 the weaknesses of the Constitution's original system for selecting the president and vice president. Aside from the obvious disadvantages of ending up with a president and vice president from competing parties (as in 1796), no party wanted to risk losing the fruits of a successful campaign by having a tie force an election into the House of Representatives, where their opponents could block the way to victory. In December 1803 Congress proposed the 12th Amendment, which provided for distinct ballots distinguishing presidential and vice presidential candidates. The states found the amendment acceptable, and it was declared ratified on September 25, 1804.

September 26

John "Johnny Appleseed" Chapman's Birthday

Even during his own lifetime, John Chapman, one of America's true folk heroes, was better known as Johnny Appleseed. An early conservationist and a pioneer in establishing midwestern orchards, he has been called the "patron saint" of American orchards and floriculture. Born September 26, 1774, in Leominster, Massachusetts, Chapman spent most of his life roaming the Midwest, planting orchards with apple seeds or teaching others how to plant and care for apple orchards.

Chapman had nurseries scattered throughout the Midwest, mostly in Ohio, Michigan, and Indiana. He traveled frequently, usually on foot, visiting his nurseries and later his orchards to prune and tend them. He gave or sold apple seeds or saplings to pioneers heading west, sometimes charging a "fippenny bit" (a coin worth about six cents), but more frequently exchanging the saplings for old clothes or promissory notes that were never collected. He was more interested in knowing that the saplings would be properly planted and tended, even in areas he would never see. Chapman himself had gone west of the Alleghenies in advance of the pioneer settlements. With two lashed-together canoes bearing apples from the cider presses of western Pennsylvania, he was seen drifting past Steubenville on the Ohio River in 1800 or 1801, his first recorded appearance in the Midwest. By the latter year, he already had a chain of seedling nurseries flourishing throughout Kentucky and Ohio.

One story has it that as Chapman planted seeds, he often remarked, "Maybe sometime someone will come along here and be hungry. Then they will have apples to eat and apples are God's food." According to that story, "the settlers who followed him called him blessed." Another account notes that "towns had an uncanny way of springing up wherever he selected an orchard site."

Nature was Chapman's first love. As a boy in New England, he often wandered off on long trips searching for flowers and birds. Early in life, he became a disciple of Emanuel Swedenborg, the 18th-century Swedish scientist and religious mystic. Chapman was reportedly a Swedenborgian missionary in Virginia for a time. It may have been in Virginia, even then an important apple-growing region, that John Chapman took the first steps toward becoming Johnny Appleseed. It happened, according to one report, after a horse kicked him in the head, whereupon Chapman envisioned heaven as filled with apple trees in bloom. From that time on, he took as his mission the planting of nurseries and distributing of apple seeds and saplings to all who would grow them. One thing is certain: Chapman became as zealous in planting and caring for apple trees as he was, to the end of his days, in preaching Christianity.

With these two objectives, it is estimated that he covered over 100,000 square miles, meeting and becoming familiar with many groups of settlers. He was easily identifiable and unforgettable because of his eccentricities of dress and manner. For all his walking, Chapman was barefoot most of the time, even in the deep of winter. He wore the roughest of clothes; over short ragged trousers, his tunic was usually a coffee sack with holes cut out for his head and arms. On his head he wore a tin mush pan or iron cooking pot, which he used both as protection from the elements and to prepare the meager fare on which he subsisted.

While frontier settlers variously regarded Johnny Appleseed as a religious fanatic, a borderline saint, or a dedicated horticulturist, Native Americans regarded him as a great medicine man. During his travels Chapman scattered the seeds of many herbs that were thought to have curative powers, such as catnip, rattlesnake weed, horehound, and pennyroyal, and the noxious weed dog fennel, which he mistakenly thought was effective against malaria.

Chapman's home base for more than a quarter century, beginning about 1810, was Ashland County, Ohio. During some of that time he lived with his half sister in a cabin near Mansfield. For the last ten years of his life, however, he made his home in northern Indiana where he continued his dedication to missionary and horticultural work. Returning home from a long, cold trek to care for a damaged orchard, Chapman was stricken with pneumonia. He sought refuge in William Worth's cabin in Allen County, Indiana, where he died in March 1845. Other sources list the date as March 11, 1847. Many of the orchards he planted have survived and prospered to the present day.

George Gershwin's Birthday

George Gershwin was born Jacob Gershvin in Brooklyn, New York, on September 26, 1898. Regardless of the name his Russian-immigrant parents gave him, his family always called him George. When he entered the music field professionally, George changed the spelling of his last name to Gershwin and the family followed suit.

Far from being pushed by his parents, young Gershwin—whose seriousness and enthusiasm were unusually intense, and whose creativity was apparent very early on—came to an awareness of his talent and sensitivity entirely on his own. He studied piano with Charles Hambitzer, who exerted a major influence in Gershwin's musical development. He also studied harmony, theory, and orchestration with Edward Kilenyi. Although he studied at different times with others, these two men were his most important teachers.

Eager to move into the professional world, Gershwin left school at the age of 15 when he was offered a job as pianist and song plugger for a New York music publisher. He was more interested in composing than in playing, and he received the opportunity less than four years later when another music publishing firm put him on the payroll with no other duties than to write songs and show them to the firm for consideration. One of his songs had already been included in a Broadway production by 1916.

The first musical comedy for which Gershwin wrote the entire score, *La, La, Lucille*, was produced in 1919 when he was just 20 years old. A few months later Gershwin's "Swanee" caught the interest of Al Jolson. The popular singer's rendition was such a hit that fans bought more than two million records and a million copies of sheet music in a year's time.

As Gershwin's fame increased, he moved into high gear as a composer for musical comedies. Among those comedies for which he wrote all the music were the *George White's Scandals* (1920–1924), *Lady, Be Good!* (1924), *Tip-Toes* (1925), *Oh, Kay!* (1926), *Funny Face* (1927), *Strike Up the Band* (1927, second version 1930), *Girl Crazy* (1930), and *Of Thee I Sing* (1931). An original and sophisticated style marked Gershwin's popular music. For the most part the lyrics of his songs were written by his older brother, Ira.

Jazz held a powerful fascination for Gershwin from the time of his earliest exposure to music. Convinced of its importance as a native American art form, he was determined that it not be confined to the realm of popular music, but also incorporated into serious music. Accordingly, he tried to make the transition. His first attempt was a one-

act, jazz-idiom opera, *Blue Monday*. Paul Whiteman, the "king of jazz," was so excited by the potential he saw in *Blue Monday* that he suggested Gershwin write a new piece for orchestra for a special jazz concert he was planning. Thus was born *Rhapsody in Blue* for piano and orchestra. It was first performed at Aeolian Hall in New York City on February 12, 1924, with Gershwin at the piano. Music critics were divided in their reactions, but the enthusiasm of the audience was unquestioned.

Gershwin's most ambitious and mature work was the folk opera *Porgy and Bess* (1935), with a libretto by DuBose Heyward, based on the novel *Porgy*. Audiences were at first puzzled by its new form, actually somewhere between musical comedy and opera, but as they became familiar with it, the popularity of the opera, written for an all-black cast, grew, while several of its songs gained wide acceptance as solo pieces. Though Gershwin did not live to see it, within a decade the opera had been performed not only throughout the United States but also in Western Europe and the Soviet Union.

A brilliant pianist, Gershwin frequently performed as a soloist at the premieres or other performances of his works. He also conducted his own music, both symphonic works and musical comedies, at various times. During the mid-1930s he was the host of a radio program on which he often generously showcased the music of unknown composers in addition to playing, conducting, and talking about his own works. He also wrote the musical scores for a number of movies.

Gershwin died suddenly in Hollywood, California, on July 11, 1937, of a brain tumor. He was 38 years old. Despite his untimely death, he left more than 1,000 musical works, which abundantly illustrate the unique Gershwin blend of musical verve, vitality, and brashness with original, sophisticated melodies and ingenious, intricate rhythms.

September 27

Warren Commission Report Released

President John F. Kennedy was assassinated on November 22, 1963 (see November 22 concerning this specific event, as well as related articles throughout this book). Although Lee Harvey Oswald, Kennedy's assassin, was quickly arrested for the crime, he was himself assassinated by Jack Ruby just a few days after the Kennedy killing. The public outcry over the Kennedy assassination and the rapid spread of conspiracy theories made

Kennedy's successor, Lyndon B. Johnson, appoint an investigating committee. Since it was headed by the chief justice of the United States Supreme Court, Earl Warren, it became known as the Warren Commission. In preparing its report, the commission took testimony from 552 persons and also reviewed all the information gathered by government agencies such as the Federal Bureau of Investigation and the Central Intelligence Agency. On September 27, 1964, the Warren Commission issued its report. After detailing the exhaustive investigation, it concluded that Oswald had acted alone and was solely responsible for the assassination.

Samuel Adams's Birthday

The New England patriot and politician Samuel Adams, one of the most persistent and zealous of the agitators for American independence, was born in Boston, Massachusetts, on September 27, 1722. The second cousin of John Adams, he graduated from Harvard College in 1740, briefly studied law, and failed in several business undertakings. He served as a tax collector in Boston from 1756 until 1764. Adams also joined Boston's influential Caucus Club and had become powerful in local politics by 1764. However, it was with the enactment that year of the Sugar Act duties, by which the British Parliament sought to raise money for King George III, that Adams's political career began to take shape.

Adams scathingly denounced measures regarded by the colonists as oppressive, such as the Stamp Act, the Townshend Acts, the Coercive or "Intolerable" Acts, and the provisions for quartering British troops in private homes. In a dozen or more years of pre-Revolutionary activity, he pressed for independence. Adams also worked to set up the Sons of Liberty, took part in the agitation that brought about the Boston Massacre, became a leader in the Boston town meetings, organized the Boston Tea Party, and was instrumental in other retaliatory efforts such as the colonial embargo of British goods.

Adams, a member (1765–1774) and recording clerk (from 1766) of the lower house of the Massachusetts General Court (the legislature), was a master of political organization. His reputation as an opponent of taxation without representation, and as the author of revolutionary newspaper articles and similar incendiary writings—including the Massachusetts Circular Letter and *The Rights of the Colonists as Men, as Christians, and as Subjects*—spread throughout the colonies. He convened Boston's Committee of Correspondence, a widely copied body that the towns and colonies employed to inform one another of their various anti-British actions and to enlist mutual cooperation. A consistent foe of compromise, he stirred the fires of controversy during a period of relative calm in the early 1770s. As a delegate to the Continental Congress (1774–1781), he pressed for immediate independence and was one of the signers of the Declaration of Independence.

The opening incidents of the American Revolution took place at Lexington (where Adams and John Hancock were staying at the time) and, with considerably more bloodshed, at Concord on April 19, 1775. The British governor, General Thomas Gage, offered pardons to any colonists who returned to British allegiance in an effort to stem hostilities. Only Adams and Hancock were excepted from the offer. However, as far as practical effects were concerned, the overture might as well not have been made. Adams continued to play an important role throughout the Revolution. He was a delegate to the convention that framed the Massachusetts constitution in 1779–1780. After hostilities ended with independence for the new United States of America, in 1788 he was also a delegate to the state convention that ratified the new federal Constitution. Ratification was achieved only after Adams's strong Antifederalist stance had been overcome with the promise of Federalist support for various Constitutional amendments, among them a bill of rights and an assurance that all powers not specifically delegated to the central government would be entrusted to the states. He subsequently served as lieutenant governor (1789–1793) and then as governor (1794–1797) of Massachusetts.

On October 2, 1803, six years after his departure from public office, Adams died in Boston. He was interred in the Granary Burying Ground in Boston.

September 28

Frances E. Willard's Birthday

Frances Elizabeth Willard, a reformer in several fields but best known for her successful promotion of the Woman's Christian Temperance Union (WCTU), was born on September 28, 1839, in Churchville, New York. She graduated from the Northwestern Female College at Evanston, Illinois, in 1859. For the next 12 years she held a variety of positions in academia, and also traveled and studied in Europe.

In 1871, after her return to the United States, Willard was named president of the newly formed Evanston College for Ladies. In this capacity, she is said to have been the first female college president to confer degrees upon women. In 1873 Evanston College for Ladies merged with Northwestern University, where Frances Willard promptly became professor of aesthetics and dean of women. She resigned from this position in 1874 after her election as corresponding secretary of the new national WCTU.

This reform-minded society had been organized that year at a meeting in Cleveland, Ohio, assembled in response to a call issued from Chautauqua, New York, and signed by Martha McClellan Brown, Jennie Fowler Willing, and others. Attended by women from 16 states, the gathering at Cleveland was the first of a continuing series of conventions held annually by the WCTU. Like some earlier and less successful temperance efforts, the WCTU sprang into being as a reaction to the increased liquor trade and the political influence of liquor interests that developed in the United States during and after the Civil War. With the more or less concurrent campaign for woman's suffrage, the temperance movement was a harbinger of the national wave of social, political, and economic reform that was to crest in the first two decades of the 20th century.

Annie Wittenmyer, the WCTU's first president, was succeeded in 1879 by Frances Willard, who served as its president until her death. It was she who wrote the declaration of principles adopted by the WCTU upon its founding in 1874. Besides containing a pledge of total abstinence from all intoxicating beverages, the declaration stated:

> We believe in the golden rule and that each man's habits of life should be an example safe and beneficent for every other man to follow; we believe that God created man and woman in His own image, and therefore we believe in one standard of purity for both men and women, and in the equal right of all to hold opinions and to express the same with equal freedom; we believe in a living wage, in an eight hour day, in courts of conciliation and arbitration, in justice as opposed to greed of gain, and in "Peace on earth and good will to men."

In 1883 Willard completed a 30,000-mile organizing tour to every state in the Union and set up a local organization in each of them. With her on the trip, which included visits to every community of more than 10,000 people, was her lifelong friend Anna Gordon, later a president of the WCTU herself. Not surprisingly, the year 1883 marked the WCTU's greatest expansion in the United States. Willard also carried the WCTU program abroad, founding the World Woman's Christian Temperance Union in 1883 and becoming its president in 1891. Further, in 1888 Willard joined the suffragists May Wright Sewall and Susan B. Anthony in founding the National Council of Women. Willard, whose powers of leadership Anthony recognized in describing her as "a bunch of magnetism," became the organization's first president.

During the course of her life, Willard became one of the most famous women of her time. She was especially influential in the temperance movement, but was also important in the effort to achieve woman's suffrage. In many respects, as her declaration for the WCTU indicates, her thinking was ahead of her time. It was she who introduced the now widespread honor system in student government. Willard died on February 17, 1898, and was elected to the Hall of Fame for Great Americans in 1910.

Cabrillo Day in California

In California, September 28 is observed in honor of Juan Rodríguez Cabrillo, the Portuguese explorer who discovered California on this day in 1542. His date of birth is unknown, as is his birthplace, which may have been one of several places in Portugal named Cabril. Cabrillo's last name was apparently a nickname, either assumed by Cabrillo himself or added by contemporaries as a means of differentiating the navigator from others named Juan Rodríguez.

A professional soldier and mariner who served Spain, Cabrillo arrived in Mexico with the expedition of the Spanish conquistador Pánfilo de Narváez in 1520. Participating in the earliest Spanish conquests of Mesoamerica, the adventurer accompanied another conquistador, Hernando Cortez, in the capture of the Aztec capital at what is now Mexico City. He later joined an exploratory party into Oaxaca in southern Mexico. Having proved his mettle, Cabrillo was enlisted by Pedro de Alvarado, the governor of Guatemala, to help subdue the natives. When Alvarado decided to leave Guatemala and explore the as yet unknown area to the northwest of Mexico, he recruited Cabrillo for the expedition.

Interest in the lands northwest of Spanish Mexico was stimulated not only by pure adventurism and curiosity, but also by widespread rumors about the legendary Seven Cities of Cíbola in the fabulous "Isle of California." Moreover, the prospect of establishing profitable trade connections with Asia and of discovering the western mouth of the elusive Northwest Passage (the interoceanic strait that supposedly joined the Atlantic and Pacific Oceans) provided additional allure. In the 50 years following Christopher Columbus's discovery of the New World in 1492, slow but steady progress had been made in penetrating the unexplored regions on both the Atlantic and Pacific sides of the North American continent. In 1513 Vasco Núñez de Balboa discovered the Pacific Ocean. After the western shores of Central America had been explored, tentative steps were made northward along the Pacific coast. By 1539 it was clear that Lower California was a peninsula. In the following year Hernando de Alarcón became the first European to set foot in Upper California when he sailed up the Colorado River from the Gulf of California as far as the Gila River. The stage was therefore set for Cabrillo, who was to be the first European to touch upon the Pacific coastline of what is now the United States.

Cabrillo apparently assisted Alvarado in building the fleet designed for the unexplored northwestern lands, and may have been present when Alvarado was killed while quelling a native revolt on the western coast of Mexico in 1541. The viceroy of New Spain, Antonio de Mendoza, who took responsibility for the fate of the fleet, assigned two ships to Cabrillo. The new commander set sail from Navidad, a small port on the western coast of Mexico, on June 27, 1542. The two vessels crossed the Gulf of California and continued along the western shores of Lower California until, on August 20, they reached Cape Deceit (Cabo del Engaño). At that time it was the northernmost point touched by previous Pacific mariners. Cabrillo's expedition then cautiously skirted the untested coastline. Some 90 days away from their home port, the sailors approached the islands off northern Mexico that are opposite what is now known as San Diego Bay. In the dark they glimpsed native campfires. The following day they sailed into one of the outstanding naturally landlocked harbors of the world, which Cabrillo described as a "closed and very good port." He named it San Miguel (the name San Diego was later given to the bay in November of 1602 by Sebastián Vizcaíno, a Spanish explorer and merchant).

There, on September 28, 1542, the fleet anchored. A handful of its crew disembarked, probably at Ballast Point, a small stretch of land jutting out into the bay. The landing party, although attacked by natives and suffering three casualties, briefly explored the area. Cabrillo laid claim to the "Isle of California" in the name of the king of Spain and Holy Roman Emperor, Charles V, by planting the imperial flag.

On October 3, 1542, the expedition put out to sea once more to further explore the coast of Upper California. Four days later it reached the islands of Catalina and San Clemente. Passing Santa Monica Bay, as well as the Channel Islands, Cabrillo sailed through the Santa Barbara Channel past Point Conception and then far northward beyond Point Reyes north of San Francisco Bay (which he failed to discover).

Driven off course by a severe storm, Cabrillo returned south to winter at what he called Isla de la Posesión, later known as San Miguel Island, the farthest north of the eight Channel Islands off the Santa Barbara coast. He anchored his two ships there on November 23, 1542. On January 3, 1543, Cabrillo died on this island, probably as the result of an infection that developed after he broke a limb sometime earlier on the voyage. He was buried on San Miguel.

After Cabrillo's death, his chief pilot, Bartolomé Ferrelo (or Ferrer), assumed command in fulfillment of the dead leader's last request that the work of the expedition still continue. They accordingly sailed northward along the Pacific coast until March 1, 1543, when they attained their northernmost point, probably the region of the Rogue River in what is now southern Oregon. The expedition returned triumphantly to its home port of Navidad, Mexico, on April 14, 1543.

September 29

Tokyo Rose Is Convicted of Treason

The Tokyo Rose trial, one of only seven American treason trials following World War II, ended on September 29, 1949, with a verdict of guilty.

Iva Ikuko Toguri, the woman who was better known as Tokyo Rose, was born on July 4, 1916, in Los Angeles, California. Her parents had migrated from Japan to California, and Toguri grew up as an American. In July 1941, at the age of 25, Toguri went to Japan for the first time to visit a sick aunt. She stayed with relatives for several months, attending to her sick aunt, and she was left stranded in Japan when war broke out on December 7, 1941, with the bombing of Pearl Harbor.

Toguri was hard-pressed to earn a living in wartime Japan, where food and shelter were both expensive and scarce, and her only skill was her proficiency in English. She worked as a typist for several news agencies and foreign legations before getting a job with Radio Tokyo. In November 1943 Toguri was forced to become one of the several female radio announcers for Radio Tokyo. Although Radio Tokyo broadcasts were made from many different locations throughout the Japanese Empire, which at its height covered much of eastern Asia, the female broadcasters were collectively termed *Tokyo Rose* by American servicemen.

Toguri never used the name Tokyo Rose, and her broadcasts were limited to playing popular American music with a smattering of pro-Japanese propaganda written for her by her supervisors.

Toguri was only one of an estimated 10,000 Japanese Americans trapped in Japan during World War II and forced to cope with the circumstances of the war. She, however, was one of the few singled out for punishment by the American authorities afterward. Toguri was arrested in American-occupied Japan on October 17, 1945, released on October 25, 1946, when the Justice Department expressed doubts on the charges of treason against her, but rearrested on August 28, 1948, in Tokyo. She was brought back to the United States to stand trial in San Francisco, California. Toguri's trial began on July 5, 1949.

Toguri pleaded innocent to the eight treason charges against her. Despite the prevailing public sentiment against Toguri, the trial lasted for nearly three months and the jury was deadlocked. When the jury reported that it was unable to reach a verdict, the judge ordered them to continue deliberating until they had made a decision. Nine of the 12 jurors were willing to vote for a guilty verdict, and after some time the three holdouts were cajoled to capitulate to the majority.

On September 29, 1949, the jury returned with a guilty verdict. Toguri was sentenced to ten years in prison and a $10,000 fine. After serving just over six years in a federal women's prison in West Virginia, she was paroled for good behavior. On January 18, 1977, and after decades of debate over the fairness of her trial, President Gerald Ford pardoned Toguri. She was thus officially exonerated, and her American citizenship was finally restored.

September 30

Feast of St. Jerome

The Feast of St. Jerome, one of the greatest scholars of the early Christian Church, has been celebrated in Rome since the seventh century. Jerome is honored by most branches of Christianity, and his feast day is observed regularly in the Roman Catholic Church.

Jerome (his Latin name was Eusebius Hieronymus, and his literary name was Sophronius) was born in A.D. 347 at Stridon, a town near Aquileia in the extreme northeast part of Italy in the border area near the outlying Roman provinces of Dalmatia and Pannonia. Stridon was destroyed by the Goths in the late fourth century, and its precise location is not known. Jerome's parents were prosperous Christians.

Jerome received an excellent literary and rhetorical education of the type generally given to upper-class boys in Roman times. He studied first at Stridon and later at Rome. The young man learned grammar from Aelius Donatus, the renowned grammarian of the day, and then mastered the art of rhetoric. Jerome frequented the law courts and schools of philosophy. According to his own writings, he often spent his Sundays deciphering inscriptions on the graves of Christian martyrs.

Although raised as a Christian and apparently a practicing believer since childhood, Jerome was not baptized until he was 19, probably by Pope Liberius on Easter Saturday in 366. (Late baptisms, however, were not out of the ordinary in the early days of Christianity.) After completing his studies, he visited Trier, the Roman city in the Moselle River valley in what is now western Germany. There, after closely observing the ascetic way of life, he apparently realized his true vocation. Around 370 the young scholar became a member of a loosely organized community of priests and laymen at Aquileia.

When the group split in 374, Jerome and a few friends journeyed east to the lands where Christianity had first taken root. They passed through Thrace, Athens, Bithynia, Galatia, Pontus, Cappadocia, and Cilicia to Syria, which to Jerome seemed "like a peaceful harbor open to the shipwrecked sailor." At Antioch, however, Jerome became dangerously ill. While lying bedridden in the spring of 375, he experienced a dream that affected his entire life. In it, he was dragged before God, heard a voice saying accusingly, "Thou art a Ciceronian, not a Christian," and was severely beaten.

Jerome, who took the admonition of his dream as a rebuke for his interest in the classics of pagan Rome, underwent a spiritual transformation. He decided to devote the rest of his life to the study of the scriptures. He went into the desert of Chalcis, some 50 miles southeast from Antioch. There, with "no other company but scorpions and wild beasts" he lived the life of a hermit. In order to keep busy, he copied manuscripts and later began to study Hebrew with a Jewish convert to Christianity. Jerome thus started on his lifelong work as a scriptural scholar.

When numerous and sometimes undesirable hermits gathered in the desert around him, Jerome decided to return to Antioch, where he was ordained as a priest. In 379 he traveled to Constantinople to study the scriptures under the famous Greek theologian Gregory Nazianzen. Three years later, Pope Damasus I invited Jerome and Gregory to Rome to resolve some doctrinal disputes. Jerome stayed on as papal secretary. Damasus I soon realized that the scholar's knowledge might be usefully employed for the good of the church. The pope at first suggested revision of biblical texts. However, Jerome soon became aware that an entirely new translation into Latin from the oldest and most reliable Greek and Hebrew manuscripts of the Bible was needed. He plunged into the task, publishing the gospels and the remainder of the New Testament as well as a new version of the Psalms.

Jerome, a supporter of the ascetic way of life, developed an enthusiastic following among the noble Christian women of Rome. Among those to whom he acted as spiritual adviser and tutor were Paula and her daughter Eustochium, both of whom later became saints. Jerome's close friendship with these aristocratic women and his merciless criticism of important Romans, including members of the clergy, aroused much resentment. After the death of Damasus I in 384, who was his protector, Jerome had to return to the east for his own safety.

At Antioch, Jerome was reunited with Paula, Eustochium, and a group of Roman women who wished to devote themselves to an ordered, peaceful, and celibate religious life. After traveling to Palestine and Egypt, where they visited the centers of monasticism, the small band eventually settled down near the Church of the Nativity at Bethlehem. Paula's wealth was used to construct four monasteries—three were for nuns, which Paula supervised until her death in 404, when Eustochium became her successor, and the other was for monks, which Jerome supervised. Jerome eventually translated almost the entire text of the Old Testament. His version gradually superseded all others, and eventually it became known as the Vulgate, or the "popular," edition of the Bible. In 1546 the Council of Trent decreed it the authorized version to be adopted by the Catholic Church as its official text (this did not necessarily imply, however, that other versions were to be rejected).

While in Bethlehem, Jerome also wrote commentaries on many books of the Old Testament and a church history consisting of biographies of 130 Christian authors. After a lingering illness, Jerome died on September 30, 419 or 420. St. Jerome is the patron saint of scholars and librarians.

Truman Capote's Birthday

Truman Capote was born Truman Streckfus Persons on September 30, 1924, in New Orleans, Louisiana. His father had trouble maintaining steady employment to support the family, which led to his parents' divorce when he was a small child. When his mother remarried and took a new last name, Truman became Truman Capote. He attended schools in New York City and Connecticut, but terminated his education at the age of 17 in order to become a writer.

Capote's first novel was *Other Voices, Other Rooms* (1948). It concerned an alienated southern boy's search for his true identity and was controversial because of its bizarre and effeminate characters and dreamlike atmosphere. *A Tree of Night and Other Stories*, a collection of short pieces, followed in 1949 and a second novel, *The Grass Harp*, three years later. Capote began to develop a subsidiary career as a scriptwriter, adapting both *The Grass Harp* and a later story, *House of Flowers*, for the stage and collaborating with John Huston on the screenplay for *Beat the Devil* (1954) and with William Archibald on *The Innocents* (1961). In 1955–56, in the midst of the cold war, he accompanied an American troupe to Russia for some goodwill performances of *Porgy and Bess* and wrote an entertaining report, *The Muses Are Heard* (1956), his first work of journalism; he then returned to fiction with *Breakfast at Tiffany's* (1958), the bittersweet tale of a naive party girl, which (with suitable alterations) became a very successful film. But it was *In Cold Blood* (1966) that made Capote famous. To write this "nonfiction novel" about the brutal murder of a Kansas farm family, Capote immersed himself in the details of the crime, the detective work that broke the case, and the life histories of the stunted young drifters who did it. The book was on the bestseller list for weeks, was made into a movie, and inspired other novelists to experiment with nonfiction as well.

In Cold Blood proved to be the pinnacle of Capote's career. He wrote some noteworthy pieces afterward, but nothing that received such wide acclaim. Late in his life he developed problems with drugs and alcohol and had some well-publicized fights with rival authors and society friends. He died on August 25, 1984.

✄✄✄ ✄
October
✄ ✄ ✄

October is the tenth month of the Gregorian, or New Style, calendar used today and has 31 days. It was the eighth month in the ancient Roman calendar, which started in March. The word *October* is derived from the Latin word for eight, *octo*. Even after the Roman calendar was revised and two new months were added, October retained its outmoded name, although it had become the tenth month of the year.

Several efforts were made to rename October in honor of Roman emperors or their wives. The months of Quintilis and Sextilis had been renamed Julius for Julius Caesar and Augustus for the emperor Augustus in the first century B.C., creating the modern months of July and August. Following this precedent, there was an attempt on the part of the Roman senate shortly after the death of Augustus in A.D. 14 to rename October Livius in honor of Livia, Augustus's wife and the politically influential mother of the new emperor, Tiberius (14–37), by a previous marriage. It was a change that Tiberius refused to sanction, however. Emperor Domitian (81–96) renamed October, his birth month, Domitianus after himself but the change was short-lived. About 138, the Roman senate proposed that September be changed to Antoninus as a tribute to the Emperor Antoninus Pius (138–161). As an accompanying gesture, the senate suggested that the following month, October, be known as Faustinus in honor of Faustina (c. 104–141), Antoninus's wife. The emperor rejected both proposals. A fourth name change was proposed around 191, when it was suggested that October be called Hercules to honor the emperor Commodus (180–192), who sometimes called himself the Roman Hercules. This attempted renaming was also unsuccessful.

On October 13, the Romans celebrated the Fontalia, the festival of the fountains, by scattering flowers over springs. From October 15 to October 19 they honored the war god Mars in a feast known as the Armilustrum. Held as a counterpart to the festival of Mars celebrated in March which marked the beginning of the season for military campaigns, it was the occasion for sacrificing a horse to the god of war and for purifying the sacred war shields and arms of the Roman army before retiring all weapons for winter.

The Anglo-Saxons had three names for October: Win-monath, or "wine month," the time for making wine; Teo-monath, or "tenth month"; and Winterfylleth, from the belief that winter would begin with the full moon of October. The lucky birthstone associated with October is the opal, which symbolizes hope.

October 1

Jimmy Carter's Birthday

Jimmy Carter (James Earl Carter Jr.), the 39th president of the United States, was born on October 1, 1924, in Plains, Georgia, a small town in the state's southwestern peanut and pine tree growing region. James Earl Carter Sr., his father, was a farmer and grocery store manager who launched a business reselling peanuts for processing and later served as a representative in the state legislature. Lillian Gordy Carter, his mother, worked as a nurse at the Plains hospital and served in the Peace Corps as a birth control information specialist in the late 1960s.

Library of Congress

Jimmy Carter

The oldest of four children, Jimmy Carter grew up three miles from Plains in a wooden clapboard house in the unincorporated community of Archery. As a boy he worked in the fields under his father's strict supervision. In his free time he enjoyed hunting and fishing with the children who lived nearby, almost all of whom were black. After his graduation from Plains High School in 1941, Carter became the first member of his family to attend college. He studied at Georgia Southwestern College in Americus for a year, then transferred to the Georgia Institute of Technology in Atlanta in order to fulfill the mathematics requirements for admission to the United States Naval Academy at Annapolis, Maryland. There he began an accelerated wartime program in 1943 and graduated 59th in his class of 820 three years later. Shortly afterward, on July 7, 1946, he married Rosalynn Smith, also of Plains.

Carter proved to be a naval officer of exceptional ability during his two years of service on battleships and five years of service on submarines. His first submarine commander, Captain John B. Williams of the USS *Pomfret*, characterized him as a natural leader "who no matter what he does ends up being the boss." Taking postgraduate evening courses in nuclear physics at Union College in Schenectady, New York, in 1951 the young officer joined the nuclear submarine development program sponsored by the Atomic Energy Commission. He became a senior officer on the *Sea Wolf*, one of the first nuclear powered submarines.

When his father was diagnosed with cancer, Jimmy Carter was forced to take over the family peanut business, then encompassing some 2,500 acres of farmland. He resigned his commission in 1953 and moved his family back to Plains. Through the application of his engineering skills and some bold investments, he eventually built up the enterprise until by the early 1970s it was grossing nearly a million dollars a year. Carter also became active in local civic affairs.

Carter served as chairman of the Sumter County Board of Education from 1955 to 1962, when, angered by the rejection of a school-consolidation plan he had advanced, he became a candidate for the Georgia senate. Although the original ballot count showed that he had lost narrowly, he contested the results on the grounds of voting irregularities. A subsequent suit revealed that he had been beaten by voters "who were dead, jailed, or never at the polls on Election Day," and the outcome was reversed. Elected to a second term in 1964, Carter gained a reputation as a hardworking, moderate liberal.

In September 1966 the still relatively unknown politician passed up an almost certain seat in the United States House of Representatives to run as a liberal in the Democratic gubernatorial primary. His third-place showing behind segregationist Lester G. Maddox and the liberal former governor Ellis Arnall was a bitter disappointment. During the next four years, Carter prepared for the 1970 gubernatorial campaign, building up an effective political network. Skillfully exploiting the weakness of his chief opponent, former governor Carl Sanders, he played up his populist appeal as a simple farmer. Supported by Georgia's rural white and urban blue-collar voters, he won a plurality in the September 8, 1970, Democratic primary and two weeks later secured the runoff election against Sanders. In the November 3 general election he easily defeated television newscaster Hal Suit, his Republican opponent.

Carter served as governor for four years. His massive reorganization of the unwieldy and inefficient state bureaucracy streamlined 300 agencies into 22 "super departments." Carter introduced zero-base budgeting, requiring state officials to justify every program every year. He improved prison and mental health systems and backed consumer and environmental protection programs.

During his term as governor, Carter became involved with national politics. At the July 1972 Democratic convention in Miami, he unsuccessfully nominated Senator Henry M. Jackson as a centrist alternative to liberal Senator George McGovern. That same year, Carter decided to plan his own 1976 presidential bid with a handful of close advisers. He used his honorary chairmanship of the 1974 National Democratic Congressional Campaign to further his political future, monitoring all gubernatorial and congressional campaigns, developing contacts, and starting Carter for President committees.

On December 12, 1974, one month before the expiration of his term as governor, he formally announced his candidacy for the presidency. Using the same populist tactics that had won him the 1970 gubernatorial race, he began to campaign across the nation in January 1975. Overcoming long odds and the opposition of many party regulars, on July 14, 1976, Carter overwhelmingly won the Democratic nomination on the first ballot at the party's national convention at Madison Square Garden in New York City. The following day he named Senator Walter F. ("Fritz") Mondale as his running mate. In the November 1976 elections, Carter won 51 percent of the popular vote against Ford's 48 percent and 297 electoral votes against Ford's 241. Carter was the first president from the deep south since Zachary Taylor of Louisiana was elected in 1848.

Carter's presidency was an embattled one. Shortly after his inauguration on January 20, 1977, he announced his decision to pardon most Vietnam War draft-dodgers, which alienated many conservatives and veterans. Further, he agreed to treaties with Panama that would transition much of the control of the Panama Canal from American to Panamanian authorities. In addition, in 1979 the Soviet Union occupied the central Asian nation of Afghanistan, despite Carter's protests. That same year Iranian revolutionaries toppled the pro-American regime of Shah Mohammed Reza Pahlavi and held dozens of American hostages after they seized the American embassy. Despite lengthy negotiations and an abortive military rescue effort, Carter was unsuccessful in securing their release (they were eventually freed shortly after he left office in 1981). The overall result was a public feeling of American weakness, perceived both at home and abroad.

Carter did succeed in negotiating a peace between Egypt and Israel that resulted in a lasting cessation of hostilities between these two historic enemies. The treaties, known as the Camp David accords because they were negotiated at the presidential retreat of the same name, were signed on March 26, 1979, in Washington, D.C. Nevertheless, this achievement was not enough to rescue Carter's presidency. Compounding his problems were the sluggish national economy and a high inflation rate. The result was a resurgent Republican Party in the presidential elections of 1980, whose candidate Ronald Reagan swept to victory by a margin of 52 percent to Carter's 42 percent. Independent candidate John Anderson received roughly 6 percent of the vote. In the electoral college the vote count was 489 for Reagan and 49 for Carter with none for Anderson.

Many historians consider Carter's presidency a failure. However, as an ex-president he has become a respected and popular figure, successful in his endeavors. He has participated in peacekeeping initiatives with North Korea and Haiti, and has helped monitor elections in war-torn Central America. At home he has helped to promote Habitat for Humanity, a nonprofit organization that helps provide affordable housing for the needy.

William Rehnquist's Birthday

Photograph by Dane Penland, Smithsonian Institution, Courtesy of the Supreme Court of the United States.

William Rehnquist

William Hubbs Rehnquist was born on October 1, 1924, in Milwaukee, Wisconsin. During World War II he served in the United States Army Air Corps, and was honorably discharged with the rank of sergeant. After the war he entered Stanford University, graduating in 1948 with both an undergraduate degree and a master's degree. He was awarded a second master's degree from Harvard University in 1950, and then went on to enter Stanford University Law School.

After graduating from Stanford in 1952, Rehnquist won a coveted law clerkship with Supreme Court justice Robert H. Jackson for the February 1952 to June 1953 term. Upon completion of the clerkship, Rehnquist settled in Phoenix, Arizona, taking up private practice with an emphasis on civil litigation. He was in private practice until 1969, when President Richard M. Nixon offered him the position of assistant attorney general for the Office of Legal Counsel in the Department of Justice. Rehnquist accepted and entered his career with the federal judicial system.

On October 22, 1971, Nixon nominated Rehnquist as an associate justice of the United States Supreme Court. The Senate confirmed the appointment on December 10, 1971, by a vote of 68 to 26. On the bench, Rehnquist was the only abstention in the case of *United States* v. *Nixon*, in which the Court held that executive privilege does not protect American presidents like Nixon from judicial subpoenas of materials such as the Watergate tapes. Through the 1970s and into the 1980s, Rehnquist earned a reputation as one of the more conservative justices with a strong "law-and-order" legal philosophy.

President Ronald Reagan nominated Rehnquist for chief justice of the Supreme Court on June 17, 1986. The Senate confirmed the appointment on September 17, 1986, by a vote of 65 to 33. As chief justice, he led the Supreme Court in a predictably conservative direction. He wrote the majority opinions in such cases as *Lockhart* v. *McCree* (1986), which held that opponents of the death penalty may be excluded from juries in capital cases, and *United States* v. *Armstrong* (1996), which held that racial disparities in convictions for crack-cocaine possession do not prove that drug enforcement laws are racially discriminatory.

In early 1999, pursuant to the constitutional requirements for impeachments, he presided over the trial and acquittal of President William Clinton in the United States Senate.

Rosh Hashanah

This is a movable event.

The Jewish New Year, Rosh Hashanah, falls on the first day of the Hebrew month of Tishri (in the course of September or October), which in 1970 corresponded to October 1. As in the 1978 third edition of this book, October 1 is used as a convenient reference point.

Rosh Hashanah is the first of the ten Penitential Days, which end with Yom Kippur, the Day of Atonement. The Hebrew calendar, which is luni-solar, is divided into 12 lunar months of 29 to 30 days each. A 12-month lunar year contains 353 to 355 days. Since a solar year is about 11 days longer than 12 lunar months, seven times in a 19-year cycle a 13th month is added to the Hebrew calendar.

The beginning of the new year falls between September 5 and October 5. All other Jewish festivals also fall on different dates of the solar secular calendar from year to year.

Rosh Hashanah is also called the Day of Judgment and the Day of Remembrance because, according to Jewish tradition, on this day God remembers all his creatures and judges humanity. According to the traditional Jewish imagery, on Rosh Hashanah God opens three books in which the deeds of every individual are recorded. One book is for the completely wicked, a second is for the perfectly righteous, and a third for those in between. The righteous are at once inscribed and sealed for life, and the wicked for death. Judgment of the middle group is suspended until Yom Kippur, the Day of Atonement. Thus the customary salutation of Jews on Rosh Hashanah eve is "Leshanah tovah tikatevu vetichatemu" or "May you be inscribed and sealed for a good year." In a somewhat different form, this message appears on New Year's greeting cards sent at this time.

Rosh Hashanah, like every day in the Hebrew calendar, starts at sundown on the previous day. In the synagogue the *shofar*, or ram's horn, is blown to mark the beginning of the New Year. The sounds of the shofar summon all Jews to meditation, self-examination, and repentance. Reform Jews typically celebrate Rosh Hashanah at special holiday synagogue services for one day from sundown to sundown, as specified in the Bible, while Orthodox and Conservative Jews often observe the holiday for two days according to later tradition. In the afternoon on the first day of the New Year, Orthodox Jews also take part in the ceremony known as *Tashlikh*, going to a nearby body of water where they recite special prayers and symbolically cast away their sins by shaking out their hems and pockets. The name *Tashlikh* derives from the recitation of the first words of Micah 7:19, "you will cast your sins into the sea."

Although Rosh Hashanah and Yom Kippur are Days of Awe, the High Holy Days of the Jewish year, celebration of the New Year is marked by festivity as well as by prayer. In the evening of the holiday, candles are lighted and a holiday meal is served.

Treaty of San Ildefonso

By the Treaty of Fontainebleau of 1762 and the Treaty of Paris of 1763, France gave up all of its colonial possessions in North America after losing the Seven Years' War (also known as the French and Indian War) with Great Britain. Preoccupied with domestic affairs, the French government for several decades showed no inclination to regain its empire. However, at the beginning of the 19th century Napoléon Bonaparte decided to revive his nation's colonial interests in North America. To carry out his plan, the French government forced Spain to accept the Treaty of San Ildefonso of October 1, 1800, by which Spain returned the vast territory of Louisiana that it had received from France 38 years earlier.

The treaty was a secret agreement, and news of the retrocession did not reach the United States until more than a year later. Nevertheless, the transfer of jurisdiction over the area west of the Mississippi River had an important effect on the historical development of the United States.

News that France had regained possession of the Louisiana Territory disturbed President Thomas Jefferson. He feared that French occupation of the area might jeopardize the security of the United States and restrict American use of the Mississippi River. Thus, as early as 1802 Jefferson instructed Robert R. Livingston, the American minister to France, to begin negotiations for a tract of land on the lower Mississippi that could be used as a port. Alternatively, Livingston was to seek an irrevocable agreement that American citizens would be able to navigate the Mississippi freely and ship their goods through New Orleans. In January 1803 President Jefferson named James Monroe minister plenipotentiary to France to assist Livingston in negotiating these matters. Their task was accomplished with ease, for even before Monroe had reached France in April 1803, Napoléon—having given up on the idea of reviving the French colonial empire in North America—was willing to sell the entire province of Louisiana. Discussions over the terms of sale lasted only a few weeks, and on May 2, 1803, the treaty of cession (antedated to April 30) was signed. According to this document, the United States agreed to pay France $15 million for the vast area between the Mississippi River and the Rocky Mountains. The United States Senate approved the treaty on October 20, 1803, and the nation took formal possession of Louisiana later that same year (see related articles throughout this book).

October 2

American Revolution: Major John André Hanged as a Spy

During the American Revolution, General Benedict Arnold betrayed the colonial cause and plotted with the British to give them control of the vital Hudson River fortification at West Point, New York. The plot failed, and Arnold himself escaped

punishment by fleeing to safety behind British lines. Major John André, the British officer who had plotted with Arnold, was not so fortunate. By order of General George Washington, the commander in chief of the Continental army, André was hanged as a spy on October 2, 1780.

A brilliant young soldier, André first came to the American colonies as a lieutenant in the British army in 1774. Captured the next year at St. John's (north of Lake Champlain) during the abortive American campaign against Canada, André spent a year on parole in Pennsylvania before being exchanged and returning to service with the British army occupying New York City. André's superior officers quickly recognized the young man's abilities. By 1779 he had advanced to the rank of major, and Sir Henry Clinton, the commander in chief of British forces in America, had selected him to be his aide-de-camp and adjutant general.

As Clinton's aide, André was in charge of the British general's correspondence with secret agents and informants, the most notable of whom was Benedict Arnold. Beginning in May 1779 Arnold provided the British with important information regarding American defenses, but not until the summer of 1780 did he gain command of West Point and develop the plan to betray that strategic fortification. Using the pseudonyms Gustavus and John Anderson, Arnold and André exchanged considerable correspondence about the plot against the American garrison. Finally, in August 1780 Clinton agreed to pay Arnold 20,000 British pounds for his assistance in bringing West Point under British control.

On September 20 André ventured up the Hudson River on the British sloop *Vulture*, wearing his British uniform so that he could not be charged as a spy if he was captured behind enemy lines. On September 22, while it was still dark, André was able to go ashore as planned. He and Arnold met in a wooded area across the Hudson from West Point and worked out the specific details for the British takeover of the garrison. They finished at about 4:00 a.m.

Fearing detection if he attempted to return to the *Vulture* now, when dawn was approaching, André decided to wait at the home of a British sympathizer, Joshua Hett Smith, until the next night. This delay proved disastrous for him. As day broke, Colonel James Livingston, a Continental officer who had no knowledge of the plot between Arnold and André, ordered his men to fire on the *Vulture*. The British sloop managed to escape down the Hudson, but its retreat left André stranded within rebel territory.

The departure of the *Vulture* forced André to return to the British forces in New York City by an overland route through perilous countryside. Before beginning the trip André decided to remove his scarlet uniform. By doing so he discarded his chief advantage as well as his worst handicap, for although his military garb made him conspicuous it also guaranteed him protection as a soldier from the reprisals and punishments accorded a captured spy. For his hazardous journey he donned civilian clothes, including a round beaver hat and a long flowing blue cloak, and hid the papers detailing the secrets of West Point's defenses in his boots.

Arnold wrote out special passes so that André would be allowed through the American lines. Then, with Smith as his guide, André set out at nightfall on Friday, September 22, for New York City. Smith accompanied André as far south as the Croton River. There he considered André to be beyond all danger, and shortly after dawn the next day he left the British major to complete the remaining 15 miles of his journey alone.

André's trip continued without mishap until about 9:00 a.m., when he encountered three volunteer militiamen. John Paulding, Issac Van Wart, and David Williams were, probably, adventurers acting under a New York law that permitted them to claim any property they might find on a captured enemy. However, when they stopped André, he mistook them for British sympathizers and in the confusion of the moment revealed his true identity. The militiamen searched their captive, and when they discovered the incriminating papers relating to West Point in his boots, they immediately turned him over to Lieutenant Colonel John Jameson, the commander of the American outposts in the region.

During the two days that followed, American leaders slowly unraveled the complicated plot involving Arnold and André. On September 25 Arnold heard of André's capture and managed to flee to safety with the British just hours before General George Washington arrived in the vicinity of West Point and learned of his subordinate's treachery. André, however, had no hope of escaping punishment. On September 29 a military board consisting of such respected officers as Nathanael Greene, the Marquis de Lafayette, Baron von Steuben, and Henry Knox met to interrogate him. During the hearing, which lasted only one day, the evidence that was presented conclusively indicated that André was guilty of spying.

When Washington heard the board's report, he ordered that André be hanged on October 1. The execution was postponed a day, following General Sir Henry Clinton's request for a delay so that Washington might learn "a true state of facts." However, the British general's efforts on behalf of his aide were futile, and Washington could not agree to André's request to be shot as a soldier rather than hanged as a spy. On October 2 the original orders were carried out and he met his death on the gallows.

André, who had been liked and respected by his fellow soldiers, was mourned by the British army. A monument to the soldier who had plotted with Arnold to advance the cause of Great Britain was erected in Westminster Abbey, where his remains (transferred there in 1826) subsequently found their final resting place.

First Pan American Conference Convenes

On October 2, 1889, the First International Conference of American States convened in Washington, D.C. At this first Pan American Conference, as the 1889 gathering is more commonly known, representatives from all of the nations of the Western Hemisphere except Canada and the Dominican Republic came together for the first time. The meeting thus marked the beginning of an effort toward true international cooperation in the Americas.

The hope that the nations of the Western Hemisphere would come together to discuss matters of common interest originated as early as 1826, when Simon Bolívar, the liberator of South America, invited all the nations of North America and South America to the Congress of Panama. Bolívar's dream of establishing diplomatic unity among the nations of the Americas was premature as the congress adjourned before the American delegation arrived. However, Bolívar's plan was not forgotten.

Representatives of Latin American countries met several times in the mid and late 19th century to discuss possible alliances in the event of foreign attack and to deliberate on some aspects of international law. The United States did not take part in these conferences. In 1881, however, during the brief administration of President James A. Garfield, Secretary of State James G. Blaine invited delegates from the nations in the Western Hemisphere to a meeting to consider ways of "preventing war between the nations of America." International difficulties in Latin America and domestic problems in the United States prevented the conference that was scheduled for 1882 from taking place, but interest in the hemispheric meeting soon revived.

October 3

In 1888 President Grover Cleveland instructed Secretary of State Thomas Bayard to invite the nations to a Pan American conference. Ironically, when the gathering convened on October 2, 1889, Blaine was again secretary of state, appointed by the new president, Benjamin Harrison.

The delegates to the first conference met for more than six months, undertook a railroad tour of the United States, and listened to countless speeches. Since most of the countries of Latin America had strong economic ties with Europe, the representatives rejected the plan for a customs union with the United States that Blaine proposed. However, on April 14, 1890, they created the International Union of American Republics, an information clearinghouse based in Washington, D.C., which later became the Pan American Union. The delegates to the conference also approved a number of recommendations involving sanitary regulations, patents and trademarks, and other matters. Most significantly they established the precedent for later hemispheric cooperation that resulted in the holding of seven other Pan American conferences between 1901 and 1938 and that culminated in the formation of the Organization of American States (OAS) in 1948. The charter of the OAS was the product of the ninth Pan American Conference (officially the Ninth International Conference of American States), which met at Bogotá, Colombia, from March 30 to May 2, 1948.

October 3

George Bancroft's Birthday

George Bancroft, who has been called the Father of American History, was born in Worcester, Massachusetts, on October 3, 1800. The eighth of the 13 children of Aaron and Lucretia Chandler Bancroft, he was descended from old New England families. His forebears included Captain Benjamin Church, the historian of the 1675 war between the Wampanoag tribe and the settlers of New England also known as King Philip's War, and "Tory John" Chandler, who served as a judge in Worcester County before fleeing to England during the American Revolution. Aaron Bancroft, George's father, also had a notable career: He took a leading role in the Unitarian schism from the Congregational Church, serving as the first president of the American Unitarian Association, and also wrote a biography of George Washington that had considerable popularity.

George Bancroft attended local Worcester schools before enrolling at Phillips Exeter Academy in Exeter, New Hampshire, at the age of 11. After a two-year stay at that school, he entered Harvard College. He graduated before his 17th birthday and remained as a divinity student during the following year.

During his years at Harvard, Bancroft so impressed President J. T. Kirkland and a number of professors that in 1818 they arranged for him to continue his studies in Europe, which lasted for four years. In 1820 he received his doctorate from the University of Göttingen. He also studied for a time in Berlin, and then traveled throughout Europe.

In 1822 he returned to the United States and accepted a position as a tutor in Greek at Harvard. Hoping to institute sweeping academic reforms at Harvard, he eventually discovered that the institution was not interested in his recommendations for changing its methods of instruction. Instead Bancroft, with his newly acquired European mannerisms and educational beliefs, became increasingly alienated from his fellow faculty members. By the end of his first year of teaching, he commented, "I have found College a sickening and wearisome place."

In association with Joseph G. Cogswell, who had also studied at Göttingen, in 1823 Bancroft founded the Round Hill School at Northampton, Massachusetts. Modeling the school after the German *gymnasium*, Bancroft and Cogswell tried to put into practice the educational innovations they had seen in operation at Göttingen and other European universities. Round Hill was a bold experiment in educational reform, but it ultimately failed. In 1830 Bancroft sold his interest in the school, and several years later he recorded his dissatisfaction with teaching, noting that it "was a kind of occupation to which I was not peculiarly adapted, and in which many of inferior abilities and attainments could have succeeded as well."

As his interest in teaching waned, Bancroft became increasingly involved in politics. On July 4, 1826, he delivered an address at Springfield, Massachusetts. In this speech on the occasion of the 50th anniversary of American independence, he emphasized the value of the democratic principles advanced by Thomas Jefferson. This address was the beginning of his efforts to propound his democratic beliefs. In the years that followed, he eloquently defended the actions of President Andrew Jackson and other Democrats in numerous articles that appeared in the *North American Review* and other periodicals.

Through his political writings and his activities in public office, Bancroft made substantial contributions to the American political scene, but it is for his historical works that he is best remembered. In 1828 he began writing *A History of the United States from the Discovery of the American Continent to the Present Time*, and by 1834 he completed the first volume. This volume, which treated the development of European colonization of America up to 1660, received an enthusiastic reception. With its basic theme that "the spirit of the colonies demanded freedom from the beginning," Bancroft's history, as the historian J. F. Jameson noted, "caught, and with sincere and enthusiastic conviction repeated to the American people the things which they were saying . . . concerning themselves."

During the next 40 years Bancroft completed ten volumes of his history. The task of writing a history "to the present time" proved impossible, and he carried his unbroken narrative only through the period of the American Revolution. Nevertheless, his work enjoyed great success as it went through at least 20 editions, making him a wealthy man.

Historians in the 20th century, however, have noted some important flaws in the work. The underlying thesis of the *History*, that the American Revolution was the inevitable result of the colonists' continuing search for freedom, often caused Bancroft to distort his account of the development of the American colonies. Moreover, he ignored the social growth of the American colonies and often oversimplified complex issues. Despite these shortcomings his work remains a classic as much respected for its accurate reflection of the spirit of the United States in the 19th century as for its detailing of the history of the nation during the colonial and Revolutionary periods.

Bancroft's overtly political writings and his *History*, which seemed "to vote for Jackson," helped him advance in the Democratic Party. In 1834 he was an unsuccessful candidate for election as representative to the Massachusetts General Court from Northampton. Three years later, President Martin Van Buren appointed the historian to be the collector of the Port of Boston. In 1844, as a delegate to the Democratic National Convention, he played an important role in gaining the presidential nomination for James K. Polk. Bancroft lost his race for governor of Massachusetts in 1844, but as a reward for his political services President Polk selected him to be secretary of the navy. Bancroft held this post for only 18 months, but in that short time he answered a long-felt need by establishing the United States Naval Academy at Annapolis, Maryland.

In 1846 Polk appointed Bancroft to be the American minister to Great Britain. This three-year service in England strengthened his great affection for America, and he commented that "my residence in Europe has but quickened and confirmed my love for the rule of the people." It also gave him access to important documents in London and Paris relating to the American colonies and the Revolution. His extensive research in these materials contributed much to the broad international scope of his *History*.

Returning to the United States in 1849, Bancroft took up residence in New York City. For the next 18 years he devoted himself almost exclusively to his *History*, and during this time he completed volumes IV through IX. During this period Bancroft held no public office, but despite his strong association with the Democratic Party he became a friend and supporter of President Abraham Lincoln, a Republican. Indeed, Bancroft's relationship with the 16th president was such that he was chosen to deliver the February 12, 1866, memorial address on the life and character of Lincoln before the House of Representatives.

Bancroft also enjoyed a close association with Lincoln's successor, Andrew Johnson. In 1867 Johnson appointed the historian to be the American minister to Berlin. Serving in this capacity for seven years, Bancroft helped resolve questions concerning naturalization and trademarks and assisted in arbitrating the boundary between British Columbia and the state of Washington. He also found time during this stay in Europe to gather material for volume X of his *History*, which was published in 1874.

At the age of 74 Bancroft returned to the United States. In 1874 he settled in Washington, D.C., and for the remainder of his life he resided alternately in the nation's capital and Newport, Rhode Island. Bancroft continued his historical writing, and in 1876 he published a "thoroughly revised edition" of his *History*. Six years later his two-volume *History of the Formation of the Constitution of the United States* was published. He again revised his multivolume *History*, producing the "author's last revision" of the work between 1883 and 1885. Bancroft completed one other noteworthy volume *Martin Van Buren to the End of His Public Career* (1889), after his 80th birthday.

He died in Washington, D.C., on January 17, 1891. As a symbol of the nation's grief, President Benjamin Harrison ordered the executive departments in the capital to fly their flags at half-mast.

October 4

Rutherford B. Hayes's Birthday

Library of Congress

Rutherford B. Hayes

Rutherford Birchard Hayes, the 19th president of the United States, was born in Delaware, Ohio, on October 4, 1822. He was the son of Rutherford Hayes and Sophia Birchard Hayes. The senior Rutherford Hayes, who died before his namesake was born, was originally from Vermont. Hard times after the War of 1812 compelled him to join the westward migration, and he and his wife settled in Ohio where he became a farmer and whiskey distiller.

After attending the Methodist Academy in Norwalk, Ohio, Hayes studied at Isaac Webb's private school in Middletown, Connecticut. He then continued his studies at Kenyon College in Gambier, Ohio, from which he graduated in 1842. Deciding to become a lawyer and statesman, he read law in the offices of Sparrow and Matthews in Columbus, Ohio, and then studied for a year and a half at Harvard Law School, and graduated in 1845.

Returning to Ohio, he was admitted to the bar in March 1845 and established a small practice in Lower Sandusky (later Fremont), where his uncle maintained a home and where Hayes himself would later live. Early in 1850 Hayes moved his law practice to Cincinnati, Ohio, where his career soon flourished. In 1851 he declared himself a Whig, and in 1852 he campaigned for the Whig

presidential nominee, Winfield Scott. On December 30, 1852, Hayes married Lucy Ware Webb, whom he had courted since youth. They eventually had seven sons, of whom only four survived infancy, and one daughter.

In 1854 Hayes left the regular Whig Party and, like other radical or "conscience" Whigs, joined the new Republican Party. He served as volunteer counsel for the Underground Railroad, which aided escaped slaves in their flight to Canada. During the height of the Kansas-Nebraska conflict in 1855 Hayes supported the Free-Soilers against the proslavery faction. In 1856 he attended a convention of Ohio State Republicans, which gave its support to John C. Frémont. At the subsequent Republican National Convention in Philadelphia, Pennsylvania, Frémont became the new party's first presidential candidate. As a Republican, Hayes opposed the extension of slavery, but not the existence of the institution itself.

Hayes actively entered politics on his own behalf in 1858, when he ran successfully for the post of city solicitor of Cincinnati. He held this post until the outbreak of the Civil War in 1861, when he joined the Union army as a major. During the war he distinguished himself for bravery and was wounded five times. By 1864 he had advanced in rank to brigadier and the next year was breveted major general. While he was still in the army, he was elected to the United States House of Representatives. Resigning his army position, he served two terms, and then ran for the governor of Ohio in 1867. He won the election and held office from 1868 until 1872 as a reform governor.

After two terms, Hayes retired to an estate at Fremont, Ohio, which had been bequeathed to him by his uncle. However, because the Democrats had carried the state in 1873, the Republicans persuaded Hayes to run for governor again in 1875. He campaigned on a platform pledged to "sound money," opposing Democratic calls for the increased issuance of greenbacks or paper money, and won by a large majority.

Hayes's decisive victory thrust him into the national limelight, and when the Republican National Convention met in Cincinnati the next year it nominated Hayes. Both Democrats and Republicans ran on reform tickets, pledging to clean up the corruption associated with the administration of Republican President Ulysses S. Grant. Hayes had been an effective reform governor in Ohio, while his Democratic opponent Samuel J. Tilden was known as the reformer who had smashed the notorious Tweed Ring before becoming governor of New York.

The election brought no clear-cut decision. The Democrats proclaimed themselves the winners, but the Republicans claimed a narrow victory on the basis of disputed returns from South Carolina, Florida, Louisiana, and Oregon. Without the disputed states, Tilden had 184 electoral votes, one vote short of victory. Only if Hayes received all of the disputed states could he claim the necessary 185 electoral votes and the presidency. The popular vote, however, favored Tilden by 250,000 votes even with the disputed states counted as Republican.

In January 1877 Congress passed a bill establishing an electoral commission of 15 members to settle the matter. The commission idea was supported by the Democrats, who felt it was their best chance to reverse some of the returns in which Republicans claimed victory. The bipartisan commission was to have five senators (three Republicans and two Democrats), five representatives (two Republicans and three Democrats), and five members of the Supreme Court. In the last category, two Republicans and two Democrats were chosen. They, in turn, chose the last member and settled upon Justice David Davis, a liberal Republican who was seen as a potential arbiter between opposing parties of the commission. Davis resigned, however, upsetting the commission's expected makeup. The much more partisan Justice Joseph P. Bradley, chosen to replace him, was a Republican who joined other commission members in what was from then on a purely political approach to voting. It was eight Republicans to seven Democrats on all questions, and Hayes was eventually declared president on March 2, 1877.

As president, he adopted a conciliatory approach to the Democrats and the South by permitting much of the dismantling of Reconstruction. He also proceeded with civil service reforms, but met stiff opposition from members of the "Stalwart" wing of his own party who had entrenched themselves in positions of power during and after the Civil War. Economic reform was another important issue during his administration. Although the country continued to suffer from a depression, Hayes refused to allow government intervention in economic matters.

Early in 1878 Congress passed the Bland-Allison Act over Hayes's veto. This legislation made silver legal tender along with gold and provided for the government's mandatory purchase of $2 million to $4 million worth of silver bullion every month and its coinage into silver dollars. The inflationary impact of the bill was lessened by the conservative administration of the act by the secretary of the treasury.

Keeping his promise to serve only one term, Hayes left the White House in 1881 for his estate at Fremont. He expanded his house and collected an impressive library. When not reading, he busied himself with various philanthropic pursuits. He was president of the American Prison Association from 1883 until his death, and served as president of the board of trustees of the John F. Slater fund to aid the industrial education of southern blacks. As a member of the board of the Peabody Education Fund, he promoted the improvement of southern education. Hayes died on January 17, 1893, at Fremont.

Soviets Launch *Sputnik I*

On October 4, 1957, the Soviet Union—America's principal antagonist during the cold war, which lasted from the late 1940s until the Soviet Union collapsed in 1991—launched the first artificial Earth-orbiting satellite in history. Known as *Sputnik I*, it was about the size of a basketball and weighed roughly 183 pounds. *Sputnik*—meaning "companion," a synonym for "satellite" in Russian—was a political coup for the Soviet Union, and caused the United States to invest heavily in what has become the modern American space program.

The origins of *Sputnik* go back to 1952, when the International Council of Scientific Unions (ICSU) declared July 1, 1957, to December 31, 1958, as the International Geophysical Year because of the predicted cycle of intense solar activity during that period. Although none had ever been built, in October 1954 the ICSU issued a resolution stating the desirability of launching satellites during the International Geophysical Year to map the Earth's surface. In July 1955 the United States approved plans to launch an American satellite, but it was a low-priority item. The Soviets, anxious to demonstrate their technological prowess, invested heavily in rocket technology in conjunction with their nuclear weapons program in order to catch up with the American ballistic missile program. Although in most substantive fields they were still way behind the United States, the Soviet launch of *Sputnik* was an impressive achievement that caught the Americans by surprise.

Sputnik was launched from the Baikonur Cosmodrome in the Central Asian country of Kazakhstan, then part of the Soviet Union. For the next three weeks until its batteries failed, it took measurements concerning such matters as the density of the upper atmosphere and the nature of the ionosphere. On January 4, 1958, after 92 days and some 1,400 rotations around Earth, the satellite's decaying orbit brought it into the atmosphere, where it was burned up by the friction.

The *Sputnik* launch caused a certain amount of panic in the United States due to the prevailing cold war concerns, which often bordered on paranoia, about the Soviet Union. The American government immediately embarked on a crash course to finally build and launch its own satellite. On January 31, 1958, the United States successfully launched the *Explorer I* satellite, carrying instruments that helped discover the rings of magnetic radiation around Earth now known as the Van Allen belts after the scientist James Van Allen.

Furthermore, Congress approved several funding programs for increased science education in the nation's schools and established the National Aeronautics and Space Administration (NASA). NASA became operational effective October 1, 1958, and has coordinated the American space program ever since. Eventually, the Soviets fell behind in the "space race" of the 1960s, and despite their impressive program never matched such American achievements as the Moon landing of 1969. After the collapse of the Soviet Union, its space program was taken over by a Russian agency.

October 5

Chester A. Arthur's Birthday

Library of Congress

Chester A. Arthur

Chester A. Arthur, the 21st president of the United States, was born on October 5, 1829, probably in Fairfield, Vermont. His father, the Reverend William Arthur, was an immigrant from northern Ireland and a Baptist preacher. His mother, Malvina Stone Arthur, was a native of Vermont. Little is known of Chester Arthur's youth. The family changed residences five times before he was nine years old. Arthur graduated with honors from Union College in Schenectady, New York, in 1848, having entered with advanced placement as a sophomore and having worked his way through school by teaching school.

Arthur then took a position as a schoolteacher in North Pownal, Vermont, while studying law in his spare time. In 1853, a year before he was admitted to the bar, he took an apprentice position with a New York City law office. Arthur's family background, which was strongly Whig and abolitionist, led the young lawyer into a number of notable cases. On October 25, 1859, Arthur married Ellen Lewis Herndon, who bore three children before she died of pneumonia in 1880.

Drawn to politics, Arthur was an active member of the Republican Party from the time of its founding in 1854. He served as a delegate to the convention at Saratoga, New York, that organized the state Republican Party and became increasingly involved in the party's local affairs. When the Civil War broke out in 1861, he was serving in the state militia as engineer in chief on the staff of the governor of New York, Edwin D. Morgan. He was charged with the immense task of recruiting, training, equipping, and dispatching soldiers from New York City to the front to serve in the Union army. In January 1863 he retired to his private law practice.

In 1871 President Ulysses S. Grant appointed Arthur collector of customs for the Port of New York, a post that was considered one of the most desirable patronage appointments available. He served as an efficient and, within the bounds of the then-prevalent spoils system, honest official. However, in 1877 the new Republican administration of President Rutherford B. Hayes set out to institute certain civil service reforms. Hayes directed that civil service employees abstain from political involvement. Arthur, together with his political boss, New York's United States senator Roscoe Conkling, decided to fight Hayes on the patronage issue. The Tenure of Office Act of 1867 prevented Hayes from removing Conkling's supporters outright. However, during the congressional recess in 1878, Hayes suspended Arthur among others and made interim appointments. The next session of the Senate refused to overturn Hayes's decision. Although Hayes thus won his battle to have Arthur and other Conkling men removed from office, Conkling himself and the New York Republican machine became even more powerful in politics.

In 1880 Arthur attended the Republican National Convention in Chicago, Illinois, as a delegate-at-large. The New York delegates were mostly "Stalwarts" who wished to renominate Grant for a third term, since Hayes declined to run for reelection. However, James A. Garfield was nominated. In an effort to retain the support of the disenchanted Stalwarts, Arthur was chosen as Garfield's running mate. Despite this effort at reconciliation, the Conkling Republicans gave only grudging support to the ticket. In fact, Conkling had advised Arthur to reject the offer "as you would a red-hot shoe from the forge." However, Arthur, convinced that "the office of Vice President is a greater honor than I ever dreamed of attaining," stood firm. Misgivings were voiced throughout the nation over the selection of such a reputed "spoilsman" as Arthur, while some commentators like E. L. Godkin, editor of the *Nation*, argued, "There is no place in which his powers of mischief will be so small as in the Vice Presidency. . . . It is true General Garfield . . . may die during his term of office, but this is too unlikely a contingency to be worth making extraordinary provision for."

The Republicans won the election by a narrow margin. Garfield's policy of office appointments did not meet with Conkling's approval, and a power struggle ensued. Arthur was not strictly loyal to the president during the contest. After Senator Conkling resigned in protest over an appointment to the collectorship of the Port of New York, Arthur even went to Albany in an unsuccessful attempt to use his influence in behalf of Conkling's reelection.

Garfield had scarcely won his battle against Conkling when on July 2, 1881, he was shot by a mentally unstable office-seeker named Charles J. Guiteau. When Garfield died on September 19, 1881, Arthur took the oath of office as president in his own house in New York City and again three days later in Washington, D.C., before the chief justice of the United States Supreme Court. Arthur thus became president under a good deal of public apprehension, since he was known as a political maneuverer through his longtime association with Conkling. Furthermore, Garfield's assassin claimed to be a Stalwart who wanted Arthur to become president.

Despite such an inauspicious beginning, Arthur tried his best to not be a partisan president. In 1882 he vetoed a bill to restrict Chinese immigration, asserting that it violated existing treaties with China. He also refused to sign a river and harbor development bill on the grounds that it would squander over $18.7 million of public funds by improperly using some of the allocated money for insignificant local projects. A major political issue of this time was the large surplus of funds flowing into the Treasury, a surplus that was largely the result of high tariffs since the Civil War. Some of the funds were used for increased public works projects and for rebuilding and enlarging the United States Navy. Democrats pushed to have the tariffs lowered. Despite recommendations for a downward revision from a special commission, supported by Arthur, another high protective tariff was passed in 1883.

Wherever they turned, the Republicans seemed to be setting up the conditions for Democratic victories at the polls. In 1882 Arthur himself committed what has since been regarded as the greatest political mistake of his administration. He insisted upon the nomination of his secretary of the treasury, Judge Charles J. Folger, for the governorship of New York. The Democrats nominated Grover Cleveland, the reform Democratic mayor of Buffalo, and denounced federal interference in state elections. Cleveland won the election, partly on the strength of public annoyance with Arthur's role in the contest. However, although Arthur continued to support political "bossism" to a certain extent, he also strongly backed the proreform Civil Service Act of 1883.

At the Republican National Convention of 1884, Arthur's name was presented for renomination, but he lost to James G. Blaine, who in turn lost the election to the Democratic reform candidate Grover Cleveland. Arthur returned to New York City, where he died less than two years later, on November 18, 1886. He was buried in Albany, New York.

Tecumseh's Death

Tecumseh, the Shawnee chief and statesman whose federation of Native Americans was almost successful in halting the United States's intrusion into their lands, was probably born in 1768 in a Shawnee village near what was later Springfield, Ohio. His exact date of birth is uncertain.

As a youth, Tecumseh roamed far and wide in hunting expeditions through what would later be called the Northwest Territory. This region included what are now Ohio, Indiana, Illinois, Michigan, and Wisconsin. It was a period in which various native tribes, backed by the British in Canada, sought to check the territorial expansion of the new United States. The aim was to contain frontier settlements south of the Ohio River. Tecumseh himself participated in attacks on Americans traveling down the river. A skilled warrior, he became noted for his role in the Northwest border wars. He also became noted for his humanitarianism, exhibiting clemency toward captives and persuading the Shawnee to abandon their practice of torturing prisoners.

As pioneer settlements spread north of the Ohio River, native opposition stiffened, and was met by various expeditions sent by the American government. One of these, headed by General Anthony Wayne in 1794, defeated the natives at Fallen Timbers, Ohio, and paved the way for the Treaty of Greenville in 1795. However, although the treaty opened much of Ohio and other scattered tracts to settlement and supposedly clarified the boundary between native and non-native lands in the process, all did not go smoothly. In the ensuing conferences between the tribes and settlers, Tecumseh became a leading figure by 1800.

He foresaw the trend of history more clearly than the leaders of many other tribes, realizing that if the tribes were to remain strong they could not afford to retreat any farther. Backed by long tradition, he argued that since all tribes held their grounds in common, no one tribe or chief had the authority to sell or cede land without the agreement of all. He felt one might with as much logic attempt to sell the air or clouds, also natural gifts. Therefore, he held, no sale or cession of native lands could be valid without a consensus of the tribes.

When the United States government ignored this position, Tecumseh and his brother Tenskwatawa, who was an influential shaman, set about organizing a vast confederation of tribes, which they hoped would stem the American advance. The program began with the organization of certain groups of Shawnee into what was called "the Prophet's town," initially located near Greenville, Ohio, and later transferred to a spot near the juncture of the Tippecanoe and Wabash Rivers a few miles above the site of Lafayette, Indiana.

Tecumseh traveled from Wisconsin to Florida urging other tribes to join his confederation. The growth of his coalition was disquieting to Northwest settlers, although Tecumseh pledged to keep the peace. This pledge depended upon the abandonment of certain cessions of native territory, particularly an 1809 agreement that took certain hunting grounds, and on the acceptance of Tecumseh's principle concerning the common ownership of land. William Henry Harrison, the governor of the large Indiana Territory, refused to accept these conditions.

On November 6, 1811, Harrison camped with 1,000 men about a mile away from "the Prophet's town." Apprehensive in Tecumseh's absence,

Tenskwatawa decided against leaving matters to chance. He attacked the encampment at dawn on November 7, thus beginning the famous battle of Tippecanoe. By the end of the next day, Harrison had surmounted heavy losses while forcing the natives back and razing their village. Nearly three decades later the battle furnished a slogan, "Tippecanoe and Tyler Too," on which Harrison and his running mate successfully campaigned for the presidency and vice presidency of the United States. The battle caused the loss of Tenskwatawa's personal influence and largely destroyed the confederacy built by Tecumseh. At a native council in May of the next year, Tecumseh sadly defied any "living creature to say we ever advised anyone . . . to make war on our white brothers." Governor Harrison, he pointed out, "made war on my people in my absence."

During the War of 1812, Tecumseh sided with the British, a position from which he hoped to obtain some advantage for his people. He received the rank of brigadier general in the British army and commanded 2,000 native allies. When British fortunes took a turn for the worse after Oliver Hazard Perry's victory in the battle of Lake Erie, Tecumseh reluctantly covered the retreat of Colonel Henry Proctor, whom he mistrusted and regarded as a coward. "You always told us, that you would never draw your foot off British ground," said Tecumseh to Proctor, "but now . . . we see you are drawing back. . . . Our lives are in the hands of the Great Spirit. We are determined to defend our lands, and if it be his will, we wish to leave our bones upon them."

Tecumseh's words forced Proctor to take a stand against the Americans near Chatham, Ontario. In the ensuing engagement, known as the battle of the Thames on October 5, 1813, the Americans under Harrison were victorious. Tecumseh lost his life in the battle. Rather ironically, he had prepared for the engagement by shedding his British uniform in favor of his native buckskins. His death marked the end of the last desperate stand of the tribes of the northeastern United States against the steady westward advance of American pioneers.

Robert Goddard's Birthday

Robert Hutchings Goddard, a pioneer in the development of modern rocket science, was born on October 5, 1882, in Worcester, Massachusetts. As a youth he fantasized about space travel, going through a deeply introspective personal experience on October 19, 1898, when he climbed into an old tree and began daydreaming about building vehicles that could travel to Mars. On that day he vowed to make space travel his life's pursuit, a vision that was often scorned and ridiculed during his lifetime.

Goddard was educated at Worcester Polytechnic Institute and Clark University, going on to teach physics and experimenting with rockets in his spare time. At that time, the science of rocketry was largely limited to small, primitive short-range military rockets. They were not much better than the first rockets invented by the Chinese roughly a 1,000 years earlier after the development of gunpowder, refined somewhat by the British and others but largely neglected in favor of artillery. Goddard experimented with liquid fuel, using twin-feed designs wherein liquid fuel and liquid oxygen were run through separate tubes into a combustion chamber. On March 16, 1926, at Auburn, Massachusetts, he flight-tested his first liquid fuel rocket, a small device that traveled only a short distance. However, it was a historic event in that it demonstrated the feasibility of liquid fuel rockets. Goddard went on to incorporate innovations concerning such matters as flight stability and reliable fuel flow into his designs that greatly helped advance future rocket development.

He received a grant from the Guggenheim Foundation enabling him to build larger and more sophisticated rockets through the 1930s at a test facility in Roswell, New Mexico. He developed rockets that could travel over a mile with a reasonable degree of accuracy and was awarded hundreds of patents in the process. Goddard's work was used by German scientists during World War II to design the V-2 rocket, the first truly modern ballistic missile. He died on August 10, 1945, before he could see the vindication of his dreams about rockets and space travel with the dawn of the Space Age.

October 6

American Revolution: The British Capture Forts Clinton and Montgomery

British strategists in 1777 devised a three-pronged attack to defeat the American armies in the state of New York and crush the colonists' efforts to gain independence. General John Burgoyne was to lead the main column south from Canada down the Lake Champlain Valley to the upper Hudson River. Colonel Barry St. Leger was to head an auxiliary force east from Oswego through the Mohawk Valley. General William Howe was to bring an army from New York City up the Hudson.

The British executed their plan poorly. General Nicholas Herkimer and his fellow officers led the colonists to victory over St. Leger at Oriskany and Fort Stanwix, New York, in August 1777, and General Thomas Gates produced another American victory by October 17, 1777, over Burgoyne at Saratoga. General Howe, who captured Philadelphia from the American colonists in late September 1777, failed to return to New York in time to take part in the operation. Only General Henry Clinton, commander of the British garrison in New York City, who captured Forts Montgomery and Clinton on October 6, 1777, pursued the mission with any success.

When Howe sailed for Philadelphia on July 23, 1777, Clinton remained in New York City with 4,000 regular and 3,000 American Tory troops to defend the vital urban center. Envious of Burgoyne and Howe, Clinton resented his inactive role of conducting a "damned starved defensive" and feared that the rebels under General George Washington could take his position. Clinton stayed in New York City during July and August awaiting an American assault and avoiding offensive operations.

By September 1777 Burgoyne was encountering stiff resistance, and he asked General Clinton for assistance. The latter, who expected reinforcements to arrive from Britain shortly, promised on September 12 to move against the Hudson Highlands within ten days. Burgoyne, receiving this assurance on September 21 two days after the first battle of Saratoga, decided to delay an operation that might have opened the road to Albany and instead asked Clinton to act as soon as possible.

Clinton's objectives were Forts Montgomery and Clinton, located astride Popolopen Creek in the Hudson Highlands. Only 45 miles north of New York City, the Highlands, to the west of the river, were the highest ground in the area, and formed a natural barrier of easily defensible terrain. Fort Montgomery, located north of Popolopen Creek, was a good position from which to harass shipping going up the Hudson. Its breastworks were strong facing the river but weak on the western side. Fort Clinton lay north of Bear Mountain and on the south side of the deep Popolopen gorge. Fort Clinton was smaller but stronger than Fort Montgomery and was essential to the latter's protection. The land defenses to the two redoubts followed rugged, defensible defiles. A system of riverine obstructions, including a log boom and a great iron chain, stretched across the Hudson River from Fort Montgomery to a point called Anthony's Nose on the eastern shore. A small flotilla supplemented the river defenses.

The reinforcements for General Clinton arrived around September 24, placing his total strength in regulars at 2,700 British and 4,200 Hessian troops. On October 3, somewhat later than promised, Clinton moved north with 3,000 men from New York City up the Hudson River. The force landed at Verplanck's Point on the evening of October 5, across the river and southeast from the two forts.

Major General Israel Putnam, the American commander in the Highlands, had approximately 1,000 Continental soldiers and 400 militiamen on the east side of the river. Clinton immediately engaged a small contingent of the Americans and routed them from their outpost. Putnam quickly drew his men back several miles and called for reinforcements from the west side of the river. The American response, which reduced the number of defenders of the forts, perfectly suited the British plans.

Leaving 1,000 troops on the east side of the Hudson in order to keep Putnam distracted, General Clinton took the major portion of his force across the river to Stony Point under the cover of the dawn fog on October 6. Following a Tory guide named Brom Springster, the British and Hessian soldiers moved quickly through an 850-foot-high pass called the Timp to a trail junction at Doodletown within two and a half miles of Fort Clinton. There, after driving off a small American patrol, Clinton divided his forces. He sent 900 men west around Bear Mountain to cross Popolopen Creek and attack Fort Montgomery from the rear. The remainder moved to a position from which they could attack Fort Clinton from the south, and there they waited for the encircling column to complete its seven-mile trek.

Scouts reported the British landing at Stony Point to Governor George Clinton, the American commander of the two forts (and no relation to the attacking Sir Henry Clinton). The governor had hurried south from Esopus (later Kingston) to direct the defense as soon as he received word of the enemy's approach from Putnam. He dispatched two delaying forces to the Doodletown area, but the British repulsed both of them. The American commander then sent Captain John Fenno with 100 men and an artillery piece to engage the attackers about a mile from the fort. The British and Hessians forced the patrol from its primary position and captured Fenno. American pickets retreated to a secondary line and finally fell back to Fort Montgomery.

By 4:30 p.m. on October 6, the attacking columns had reached their positions before the Forts Montgomery and Clinton. Lieutenant Colonel Campbell commanded the British units at Fort Montgomery. From north to south were the 52nd

Regiment, a group of New York Volunteers, Colonel Beverley Robinson's 400 loyal Americans, Emmerich's Hessian Jagers, and the 57th Regiment. Campbell suffered fatal wounds in the attack, and his soldiers refused to show mercy as they routed the Americans. The attackers spared some of the garrison, however, and Governor George Clinton, the commander of Fort Montgomery, managed to escape.

Sir Henry Clinton directed the successful but costly assault on Fort Clinton, which was under the command of General James Clinton, the brother of Governor Clinton. Lacking room to maneuver, the British general committed the bulk of his forces to a successful frontal attack on the strongly defended southern face of the fort.

Losses were heavy on both sides during the assaults on the two forts. The British may have suffered as many as 300 casualties, including at least 18 officers and 169 enlisted men killed. Approximately 250 of the more than 600 Americans in the forts were killed, wounded, or missing, and the British captured 67 guns and many supplies. The Americans also lost their river flotilla, which was unable to escape north against the wind and was burned after dark.

On October 7 Clinton seized Fort Constitution north of Forts Clinton and Montgomery and across the river from West Point. Then, in response to pleas from Burgoyne, Clinton sent General John Vaughan with 1,700 men and Sir James Wallace with a flotilla north to assist him. Vaughan and Wallace burned Esopus on October 16 and proceeded to Livingston Manor 45 miles south of Albany. Putnam fell back before the advance of Vaughan and Wallace and placed his forces across their route to Burgoyne. Vaughan and Wallace reported the situation to Clinton, who had in the meantime received orders to abandon the Highlands and send reinforcements to Howe in Philadelphia. He instructed them to return toward New York City. So ended the unsuccessful 1777 British campaign in New York.

October 7

James Whitcomb Riley's Birthday

James Whitcomb Riley, the Hoosier Poet, is one of the few American poets to have become wealthy and famous during his lifetime. His popularity was such that he received without delay a letter that Mark Twain had sent from Vienna, addressed to the "Practicing Poet, and a dern capable one, too, Indianapolis, Indiana."

The title *Hoosier Poet* was bestowed on Riley not only because he was born and lived most of his life in Indiana, but also because he so colorfully portrayed the inhabitants of the region. His poems truly depicted their behavior in everyday situations and their feelings about basic issues. For his down-to-earth quality and his interest in "ordinary folk," Riley was sometimes called "the poet of the common people" or "the people's laureate." Many, though not all, of his poems and prose pieces were written in a Hoosier dialect and it is probably for these that he is best remembered. Although he was a regional poet, his fame spread throughout the United States, and his Hoosier-flavored pieces were as well received in large cities as they were in the small towns of Indiana. He wrote over 1,000 poems, which were published in a number of collections in the 1880s and 1890s.

The third of six children, Riley was born on October 7, 1849, in Greenfield, Indiana, about 20 miles from Indianapolis, where he later took up permanent residence. His father was a lawyer, but the legal profession did not appeal to the younger Riley, whose ambition was to be an actor. Never very good at academic subjects, he dropped out of school at 16 and joined an itinerant group of young sign painters who called themselves the Graphics and according to Riley "covered all the barns and fences in the state with advertisements." Later he was a traveling musician and jack-of-all-trades with patent medicine shows, an important source of entertainment for country people of the time.

Riley got his first taste of professional acting by taking part in these skits, whose purpose was to attract crowds. After the free entertainment for which they had gathered, the townspeople would be offered the various medicines and other articles being sold. Not only did Riley act, fiddle, sing, and recite in these entertainments, he also composed many of the skits used. The traveling also brought him into close contact with the Hoosier dialect, which was more pronounced in the rural areas.

After approximately ten years of traveling, Riley took a job with the *Democrat*, a newspaper published in Anderson, Indiana. He began to write verse but was frustrated in his attempts to get published. Having great confidence in his work, he believed it was being rejected not because of its quality but because its author was not well known.

To prove his point, Riley thought out and executed an elaborate prank, which came to be known as the "Leonainie hoax." Using the style of Edgar Allan Poe, he wrote a poem called "To Leonainie." A newspaper editor in Kokomo, Indiana (working for another paper), apparently privy to the hoax, printed a story about the "discovery" of the poem. The poem was handwritten on the flyleaf of a book

known to have been published during Poe's lifetime, and the story suggested that the poem was possibly an unpublished work of Poe's.

The account caused a greater stir than Riley had hoped for. Scholars and literary people all over the country became interested, and many of them were ready to authenticate the poem as Poe's. When the truth was told, however, their fury was unleashed. Riley was called unethical and a fraud. Dismissed from his newspaper job, he felt that he would never be able to hold his head up in public again.

To make a living, Riley went back to sign painting and life as a minstrel with medicine shows, but his exuberance for being on the road was gone. In the midst of his gloom, however, a letter arrived from the editor of the *Indianapolis Journal* offering to publish his poetry. The letter changed Riley's life. He moved to Indianapolis, and from 1877 to 1885 wrote poems that were published in the *Journal*, at first under the pen name of Benjamin F. Johnson of Boone. In 1883 the first collection of his poems was privately published under the title *The Old Swimmin'-Hole and 'Leven More Poems*. One of the poems in this collection, "When the Frost Is on the Punkin," became one of his best known.

The book helped to broaden Riley's fame, and in 1887 he was invited to participate in readings (which were very popular at the time) with such famous writers as Mark Twain, William Dean Howells, George W. Cable, Frank R. Stockton, and Edward Eggleston. Riley's first appearance was in New York City's Chickering Hall, where James Russell Lowell heard Riley read his own poetry. In introducing him the next day, Lowell admitted that, though he previously had been unacquainted with Riley's work, he was so impressed by the recitation that he had spent the night reading Riley's poetry. "Today," Lowell declared, "in presenting him, I can say to you of my own knowledge that you are to have the pleasure of listening to the voice of a true poet."

With this warm praise from the highly respected Lowell added to the deafening applause of appreciative audiences, Riley's fame grew and he received more invitations to appear on the lecture circuit. Soon he teamed up with Edgar Wilson Nye, the American humorist and journalist better known as Bill Nye, and they became some of the most popular lecturers of the time. The two men also collaborated on the book *Nye and Riley's Railway Guide* (1888).

In 1893 Riley, who had lived in hotels and boardinghouses since he left home, moved to a house at 528 Lockerbie Street in Indianapolis where he spent the rest of his life. He never married, but he apparently had an active social life. He received many public honors in his lifetime, including a number of honorary degrees, election to the American Academy of Arts and Letters, and the gold medal for poetry of the National Institute of Arts and Letters. Riley died in Indianapolis on July 22, 1916, and was buried in Crown Hill Cemetery beneath an imposing marble monument supported by Grecian columns on the highest point of land overlooking Indianapolis.

Elijah Muhammad's Birthday

The African American religious leader known as Elijah Muhammad was born as Elijah Poole on October 7, 1897, in Sandersville, Georgia. His father, a former slave, was a Baptist preacher. Poole was forced to leave school at the age of nine in order to work. In 1923 he moved to Detroit with his wife and children, where he met Farad Muhammad (also known as Wallace D. Fard), the founder and leader of a small local group known as the Nation of Islam. Poole was converted to Islam and quickly rose to a senior position within the organization, and in 1932 he established the Nation of Islam's Temple Number Two in Chicago.

After Farad disappeared under mysterious circumstances in 1934, Poole became the leader of the Nation and changed his name to Elijah Muhammad. Given the designation Allah's Messenger, Muhammad galvanized the organization, which became popularly known as the Black Muslims. During World War II, when the United States was at war with the Axis powers, he was imprisoned for sedition after supporting the Japanese on the grounds that they were non-Caucasian. Muhammad had also urged blacks to resist the draft. While in prison he took an interest in converting black inmates to Islam, something that the Nation continues to promote.

After his release from prison in 1946, he returned to his leadership of the Nation, overseeing its continued growth. Its focus was on urban black neighborhoods, promoting separatist Islamic communities and lifestyles. The movement continued to grow, despite the widely publicized split between Muhammad and his former protégé Malcolm X, which ended when Malcolm was assassinated in 1965 (see May 19, Malcolm X).

By the 1970s the Nation of Islam had become large enough to own a variety of prosperous businesses and to have a recognized voice in the civil rights movement. Muhammad began to moderate some of the more radical ideology he had previously espoused, such as the contention that whites are "devils," in order to encourage acceptance of the Nation as a mainstream organization. This process, which continues today under new leadership, was underway when he died on February 25, 1975.

American Revolution: Second Battle of Saratoga

The second battle of Saratoga, which resulted in a resounding British defeat at the hands of the colonials and marked a turning point for the American Revolution, took place on October 7, 1777, in the vicinity of Bemis Heights about three miles north of what is now Stillwater, New York.

Both battles took their name from the town of Saratoga, a few miles farther to the north. Established in 1689, it was burned by native tribes in 1745 and supplanted by Schuylerville in 1831. However, the place was still known as Saratoga when it served as the site for General John Burgoyne's historic surrender to General Horatio Gates on October 17, 1777 (see October 17).

October 8

John Clarke's Birthday

John Clarke, a founder of the colony of Rhode Island and a pioneer of religious liberty in America, was born in Westhorpe in Suffolk, England, on October 8, 1609. One of eight children, Clarke was the son of Thomas Clarke and Rose Kerrich Clarke.

Probably equipped with a university education, Clarke arrived in Boston, Massachusetts, in November 1637. His arrival was just after the general court of the Massachusetts Bay Colony had taken actions to purge the colony of "anti-nomianism," a belief that human salvation depends on faith in the Gospel's message of redemption rather than on rules of behavior. Clarke allied himself with Anne Hutchinson, William Coddington, and other condemned antinomians who, banished from the colony, fled to Exeter, New Hampshire. In the spring of 1638 a party of them, including Clarke, journeyed to Roger Williams's newly established settlement of Providence in the Narragansett Bay area. After conferring with Williams, they decided to buy Aquidneck (later Rhode) Island in Narragansett Bay from the native tribes and settle on it. During the year they founded Pocasset (later Portsmouth) in the northern part of the island, and in the spring of 1639 Clarke, Coddington, and others moved south and established Newport, where Clarke practiced medicine and served as pastor of the church that he helped organize (later referred to as the First Baptist Church). Warwick, the fourth Narragansett Bay settlement and on the mainland like Providence, was founded by Samuel Gorton and settled in 1643.

Among the leaders of the Narragansett Bay settlements, Clarke aligned himself against Coddington and on the side of Roger Williams in support of a political union of the settlements. He also favored religious liberty and, along with Williams, is given credit for the democratic character of the code of laws adopted by the Providence Plantations, which was the name given in 1647 to the union of the Narragansett Bay settlements under a patent that Williams obtained from the English parliament in 1644.

In 1651, after Coddington gained English permission to annul the patent and withdraw Aquidneck and another island from the Providence Plantations colony, Clarke went to England with Williams to get the charter reinstated. They succeeded, and Williams returned to America in 1654. Clarke, however, remained in England for ten or more years to represent the interests of the colony and in 1663 was largely responsible for securing from King Charles II a new charter that reconfirmed the corporate existence of the colony (designated in the new charter as Rhode Island and Providence Plantations) and proclaimed religious liberty within its jurisdiction in words that were later inscribed in part on the south front of the State House in Providence: "to hold forth a lively experiment that a most flourishing civil state may stand and best be maintained . . . with full liberty in religious concernments."

The provisions of this charter were incorporated in the constitution of the state of Rhode Island after the American Revolution and were in effect until 1842 when a new state constitution was adopted.

After Clarke's return to Rhode Island, he served in the general assembly from 1664 to 1669 and was deputy governor for three terms. He died on April 28, 1676.

Jesse Jackson's Birthday

Jesse Jackson, the famous African American civil rights leader, was born Jesse Louis Burns on October 8, 1941, in Greenville, South Carolina. His father left the family, and in 1956 Jesse took his stepfather's name, becoming Jesse Louis Jackson. Graduating from Sterling High School in Greenville in 1959, he entered the University of Illinois in the fall of that same year. He dropped out, but decided to resume his education in 1961 by transferring to North Carolina Agricultural and Technical College. He married Jacqueline Lavinia Brown

in 1962, and the couple would eventually have five children, one of whom went on to serve in the United States Congress.

Jackson entered the civil rights movement in June 1963 when he was arrested in Greensboro, North Carolina, for "inciting to riot and disturbing the peace and dignity of the state" by leading a demonstration. After graduating from school in 1964, he entered the Chicago Theological Seminary, eventually becoming a Baptist minister. The next year, after watching television broadcasts of southern police brutality toward civil rights marchers, Jackson joined Martin Luther King's famous march on Selma, Alabama.

In 1966 Jackson became the head of the Chicago chapter of the Southern Christian Leadership Conference's (SCLC) Operation Breadbasket. The SCLC was at the forefront of the civil rights movement, organizing economic boycotts and other initiatives. Jackson became one of the leaders in King's marches for open housing in Chicago, and in 1967 he became the national director of Operation Breadbasket. In December 1971, however, he left the SCLC in order to organize Operation PUSH (People United to Save Humanity). He became one of the most respected leaders of the African American community, despite a controversial trip to the Middle East in 1979 where he met with leaders who supported certain causes hostile to American interests.

In 1984 Jackson unsuccessfully sought the Democratic Party's nomination as its candidate for president in the upcoming election. He was the first African American to make more than a symbolic bid for such a nomination. That same year he established another civil rights organization, the National Rainbow Coalition. He tried for the Democratic nomination again in 1988, but lost to Michael Dukakis.

Jackson remains active in politics and civil rights causes, fighting such injustices as the disparities in state and federal sentencing laws that send a disproportionately high number of African American men to prison for drug offenses. He has also been important in international peacekeeping initiatives concerning such hot-spots as Yugoslavia.

October 9

The Chicago Fire

Sunday, October 8, 1871, was an unusually warm day in Chicago, Illinois, like too many others in the summer and fall of 1871. City officials were worried because buildings were predominantly wooden, and less than one-quarter of the normal amount of rain had fallen in the preceding months. The fact that many woodworking industries made the city their home only amplified the tinderbox effect. Furthermore, a spectacular fire that claimed four blocks on the night of October 7 added to the uneasiness.

On the evening of October 8, Daniel "Pegleg" Sullivan spent a few minutes visiting his friends Patrick and Catherine O'Leary at their home at 137 DeKoven Street. Then he went across the street and sat down in front of his own house to enjoy the evening breeze. The sight of flames inside the O'Learys' barn ended his relaxation. Sullivan rushed to the building and managed to rescue a calf, but not much else could be done.

The local firewatcher spotted the blaze from his tower, but misjudged its location by a mile. He soon recognized his error, but more valuable time was lost when the alarm operator, for some inexplicable reason, temporarily refused to revise the telegraph message. The flames, aided by a high veering wind, spread quickly. The fire traveled two and a quarter miles in six and a half hours, and continued through the next day. The use of explosives to raze buildings and create a firebreak brought the conflagration under control on the city's south side on October 9. On the north side, where the waterworks were destroyed by the disaster, the flames made their way almost out to the prairie before a rainstorm finally quenched them.

In the space of 27 hours the Chicago fire burned 2,000 acres, destroying 18,000 buildings and causing $196 million in property damage. At least 300 Chicagoans lost their lives, and 90,000 out of a population of approximately 300,000 found themselves homeless.

Speculation about the origin of the fire began while Chicago was still ablaze. Some said that Catherine O'Leary was milking her cow when the animal kicked over a lamp and set the straw in the barn on fire. Others noted that a party had been in progress next door at the McLaughlins' to welcome the brother of McLaughlin's wife, who had recently arrived from Ireland. Perhaps some of the guests had been in the O'Learys' barn and disturbed the cow. A few malicious people accused O'Leary of intentionally starting the blaze in revenge for being taken off the relief rolls, though in reality she had never received public assistance. Daniel Sullivan, the only eyewitness, did not see anyone in the vicinity, and so all that historians can say with certainty is that the fire began in the O'Learys' barn. Curiously, the O'Leary house survived the disaster with only slight damage.

Chicagoans quickly rebuilt their metropolis. They restored the business district within a year; and by 1893 the city was ready to become the site of a great World's Fair.

Leif Erikson Day

In the ninth century A.D. the Vikings emerged from the isolation of their native Norway and began a series of invasions that radically altered the course of world history. For 200 years the Norsemen plundered and pillaged the towns and coastlines of France, Portugal, Spain, Italy, and the British Isles. They established settlements in some of these areas, and eventually gained dominance in one of the northern regions of France, now known after them as Normandy. William the Conqueror, the most famous of the French Normans, invaded Britain in 1066 and quickly brought the English kingdom under his control.

Their thirst for adventure and ability to sail the seas made the Norsemen powerful. They not only raided communities in Europe but dared to venture across uncharted seas to seek out new lands. Proceeding west from Norway, the intrepid Vikings established settlements in the Shetland, Faroe, and Orkney Islands during the eighth century and set up a colony in Iceland in 874. Eric the Red, an exile from Iceland, discovered Greenland in the early 980s. After exploring its lengthy coast for several years, he went back to Iceland and, returning to Greenland with colonists, established two settlements in the western part of the island. These communities lasted for several centuries, but ultimately died out.

The Viking ships also reached the North American coast during the same period. According to Icelandic sagas, Leif the Lucky, the son of Eric the Red and thus also known as Leif Ericson (or Erikson), sailed west from Greenland in the 11th century and discovered a land rich with wild grapes and wheat, which he named Vinland. Evidence of Viking settlements has indeed been found in Newfoundland, and there may have been other as-yet undiscovered settlements on the coast of New England.

For many years Norwegian Americans worked through such organizations as the Leif Erikson Association to establish October 9 as Leif Erikson Day. Their efforts were rewarded in 1964 when President Lyndon B. Johnson proclaimed October 9 as Leif Erikson Day. Since 1964, a presidential proclamation has been issued annually on October 9, and in 1968 the United States Postal Service issued a Leif Erikson commemorative stamp. The governors of several states also issue proclamations on October 9, and states with a large Norwegian American population such as Minnesota and Wisconsin often hold observances on the day. The Sons of Norway, a social organization for both men and women of Scandinavian descent in general and Norwegian Americans in particular, regularly commemorates Leif Erikson Day.

October 10

Yom Kippur

This is a movable event.

Yom Kippur, the Day of Atonement, is the last of the ten Penitential Days that mark the beginning of the Jewish New Year (see October 1, Rosh Hashanah). Yom Kippur is observed on the tenth day of the lunar month of Tishri (in the course of September or October), which fell on October 10 in 1970. Jews traditionally consider Yom Kippur the Sabbath of Sabbaths, the holiest day in the Jewish year. It is a day of prayer and fasting to obtain forgiveness of sins and reconciliation with God through sincere repentance, and is devoted to the regeneration and renewal of moral and religious life.

Before the destruction of the second Temple in Jerusalem in A.D. 70, an elaborate ceremony was practiced, including the offering of sacrifices. The ceremony is described in chapter 16 of Leviticus, the portion of the Bible read during the Yom Kippur synagogue services.

Today, the ancient sacrificial ceremony is recalled by the repetition in the synagogue of a special service, the *Avodah*, or "sacrificial service." The Avodah service describes in poetry and prayer the ritual of confession and sacrifice that the High Priest performed when the Temple was standing. The High Priest recited three confessions of sins, namely one for himself and his household, one for the whole community of priests, and one for the entire Jewish people. The third confession was accompanied by the ritual of the scapegoat, during which the High Priest confessed the sins of Israel while resting his hands on the head of a goat. The priest then sent the scapegoat to die in Azazel, the wilderness.

Since the destruction of the Temple, the importance of individual repentance has been stressed. One of the readings from the Bible on Yom Kippur is Isaiah 57:14–58:14, which teaches that external signs of repentance are not acceptable to God; only a change of heart that affects one's relations with others is true repentance.

The Day of Atonement is observed in modern times by synagogue services that begin in the evening of the preceding day with the chanting of the *Kol Nidre*. This prayer asks for the remission of unfulfilled vows to God, specifically including those made under duress, and indicates the petitioner's desire for a new beginning. It is a tenet of Jewish belief that the remission does not apply to unfulfilled obligations between people. For these or other wrongs, it is incumbent upon the individual to seek the pardon of those wronged. By custom, the day before Yom Kippur is therefore given over to the mutual asking of forgiveness. Some Reform Jews do not chant the Kol Nidre but begin the evening service by reciting Psalm 130, as was done in biblical times.

Traditionally, the scrolls in the ark are clothed in white, and white garments are worn by the rabbi and the cantor during the Yom Kippur synagogue services. These services continue for the whole day. The souls of the dead are included in the community of those remembered on this day. Many Jews visit cemeteries and make special charitable gifts during the days before Yom Kippur. On the day itself, traditional Jews customarily light two candles, one in memory of the dead and the other for the living. The synagogue services include a special *Yizkor*, literally "He will remember," service in memory of the dead. The last section of the synagogue services is the emotion-filled *neilah*, or closing service of the day, which takes place just before sunset. This service is interpreted to mean the closing of the heavenly gates, at the sealing of the divine judgment.

The Day of Atonement services end with the confession of faith and the blowing of the *shofar*, or ram's horn. For some, the break-the-fast dinner that follows may be hearty and include traditional foods: the braided bread known as *challah*, chicken soup, wine, honey or sponge cake, and *taglach* pastry.

Oklahoma Historical Day

Oklahoma Historical Day was inaugurated in 1939 by the state legislature, which passed a resolution directing the governor to proclaim October 10 of each year as a day for commemorating the anniversary of the 1758 birth of Major Jean Pierre Chouteau, the Father of Oklahoma. In 1796 he established at Salina the first permanent non-native settlement within the boundaries of what is now the state of Oklahoma. As early as 1740, French traders and trappers had made settlements in other sections of the state, but these small outposts had all been abandoned by the beginning of the 19th century, making Chouteau's outpost the first of any consequence.

Much of the early history of Oklahoma is connected with the French family named Chouteau. In 1794 Major Chouteau took command of the newly constructed Fort Carondelet on the south bank of the Osage River in what is now Missouri. The fort was intended to protect settlers in the region west of St. Louis from the native attacks caused by intertribal hostility between the Osage people and various other tribes that resented Osage dominance. Major Chouteau and his half brother René Auguste took over a virtual monopoly of the fur trade with the natives of the area, especially the Osage. Spain, which then owned the vast central region known as Spanish Louisiana, at first left them undisturbed. Later, however, the Spanish granted extensive fur trading rights in the area to a young New Orleans-born Spaniard named Manuel Lisa (or Liza) and his French associates. This action threatened to close down the Chouteau trade.

Not easily thwarted in his plans, Major Chouteau began to scout around for another base of operations for his profitable business. In late March 1796 he formed a party of French hunters and traders, and headed southwest from Fort Carondelet into what was then unknown country. Some 400 miles from the fort, he came upon a sizable river, which the natives called Neosho. Chouteau ordered his men to follow *cette grande rivière* and thus unwittingly gave that part of the Neosho River the name it bears today: Grand River. Following this river south, the major found a site for his new trading post. Located near a freshwater spring and a ford across the Grand River, it also had convenient access to an extensive water network via the Grand, Arkansas, and Mississippi Rivers to the New Orleans markets.

One part of the Chouteau party erected a cabin at the site of Salina to serve as a headquarters and trading post, while another group set out to explore the surrounding vicinity. Despite the ideal location of the post, Chouteau was dismayed to learn that within hundreds of miles there were no native villages with which he could trade.

Forced to leave their campsite near the Grand River at least temporarily, Chouteau and his men returned to Fort Carondelet. The major still planned to salvage the family's lucrative trading business, and he skillfully used his power, wealth, and position to create dissension among the Osage people. He persuaded one faction of the tribe to move its villages southwest into the country around the Grand, Arkansas, and Verdigris Rivers and agreed to establish trade with them at the little campsite (Salina) that he had already selected. As soon as the Osage started to move into the area in 1802, the major personally oversaw the reestablishment of the remote outpost. Several thousand Osage were soon shooting and trapping in their new hunting grounds, providing Chouteau's trading post with an abundant supply of pelts. The furs, as Major Chouteau had anticipated, were then piled onto rafts or flatboats and floated down the river network to New Orleans.

Meanwhile, in 1800 France had acquired the territory known as Louisiana by the secret Treaty of San Ildefonso. In 1803 the United States, through the Louisiana Purchase, bought the huge tract which included Oklahoma. Chouteau frequently visited his "American" trading post from 1802 to 1817, when he passed its supervision over to his oldest son, Auguste Pierre. The major retired from the fur trade around 1820, but for several generations his descendants continued to be active not only in expanding the fur trade, but also in settling other places such as Vinita and Chouteau within what is now Oklahoma.

October 11

Eleanor Roosevelt's Birthday

Anna Eleanor Roosevelt, who in the words of President Harry S. Truman became the "First Lady of the World," was born on October 11, 1884, in New York City. The niece of President Theodore Roosevelt and the activist wife of President Franklin Delano Roosevelt, Eleanor Roosevelt became a prominent figure in her own right. By the time of her death at the age of 78 on November 7, 1962, she had traveled to all corners of the earth to speak and act on behalf of social justice, peace, and friendship among nations and peoples.

Eleanor Roosevelt's parents, Elliott and Anna Livingston Hall Roosevelt, were descendants of wealthy old New York families. Claes Van Rosenvelt had arrived in America from the Netherlands in the 1630s, when Manhattan Island was the Dutch colonial city of New Amsterdam. Robert Livingston had come to New York from Scotland in the late 1600s. Both immigrants became the founders of impressive families, and the Livingstons contributed several leaders of the American movement for independence.

Anna Livingston Hall Roosevelt was a beautiful socialite unable to hide her disappointment in the plain appearance of her daughter, whom she called "Granny." In a family noted for its attractive women, Eleanor Roosevelt was an exception. The "ugly duckling," as she was called, Eleanor Roosevelt became self-conscious and withdrawn. Both of her parents died when she was young, and she went to live with her maternal grandmother, Mrs. Valentine Gill Hall. They resided in a brownstone on West 37th Street in New York City most of the time.

Eleanor's grandmother had a narrow conception of the education appropriate for a young lady, centering her granddaughter's early training on such social and homemaking skills as playing the piano and darning socks. Fortunately, when Eleanor was 15, her grandmother agreed to send her to the Allenswood School in London. The school was run by Marie Souvestre, a staunch political liberal who emphasized the rights of the individual. Eleanor Roosevelt spent three years under her tutelage and toured the Continent with her. Returning to the United States at the age of 18, Eleanor made her debut into New York society. She found the role of debutante unsatisfying, and took a position teaching at the Rivington Street Settlement House in Lower Manhattan.

Franklin D. Roosevelt entered Eleanor's life seriously during these years. A student at Harvard, he found in his fifth cousin once removed those qualities that later endeared her to the world. In 1903 the couple announced their engagement, but out of respect for the wishes of Franklin Roosevelt's strong-willed mother, they prolonged their engagement until March 17, 1905. They were married at the home of relatives on Manhattan's upper East Side. Theodore Roosevelt, fresh from his presidential inauguration, gave the bride away. The Roosevelts would have six children, born within 11 years: Anna Eleanor; James; Franklin Jr., who died in infancy; Elliott; a second Franklin Jr.; and John.

Franklin Roosevelt entered politics six years after their marriage and won election to the New York State Senate. In 1913, when President Woodrow Wilson named him to be assistant secretary of the navy, Eleanor Roosevelt accompanied him to Washington, D.C. There she began to emerge as a public figure with the onset of World War I. Horrified by the poor medical treatment that the government gave sailors and marines at St. Elizabeth's, the federal psychiatric hospital, she insisted that the secretary of the interior obtain a larger appropriation for the hospital from Congress.

After the war, the year 1921 brought personal tragedy to the Roosevelts when Franklin Roosevelt contracted polio while vacationing at their summer home on Campobello Island in New Brunswick, Canada. Although his mother expected Franklin to retire as an invalid to Hyde Park, Eleanor was determined that he remain in public life. To renew his interest in politics, she became active in the field herself. She joined the board of the League of Women Voters, participated in the work of the Women's Trade Union League, and assumed an active role in the state committee of the Democratic Party.

Regaining his political enthusiasm, in 1924 Franklin Roosevelt managed Alfred E. Smith's unsuccessful bid for the Democratic presidential nomination. In 1928 he successfully put Smith's name in nomination, and Eleanor Roosevelt directed the women's campaign committee. Smith lost the election to Herbert Hoover, but Franklin Roosevelt won the gubernatorial race in New York.

In 1932, with the nation in economic collapse, Franklin Roosevelt won the presidency of the United States and began preparing his New Deal programs to combat the Great Depression. In Washington, D.C., Eleanor Roosevelt attained national prominence and held unprecedented weekly news conferences. She toured the nation inspecting projects for her disabled husband. During her first eight years in the White House, she averaged 40,000 miles of travel annually. Criticized for her sympathy with left-wing groups, she dissociated herself from any connection with several organizations that proved to be controlled by Communists, while continuing to defend the right of individuals to maintain their political convictions. Her championship of the rights of blacks also raised the hackles of some, but she remained adamant in her pursuit of racial justice and even resigned from the Daughters of the American Revolution when that organization refused the use of Washington's Constitution Hall for a concert by the African-American contralto Marian Anderson.

World War II changed the focus of her activity. In 1942 Eleanor went to England to visit American training bases, becoming the first wife of an American president to go abroad alone and the first to fly across the Atlantic. During the remainder of the war, she also served as assistant director of the Office of Civilian Defense and traveled to remote areas of the world to see troops in the war zones and comfort the wounded.

Eleanor Roosevelt's days in the White House ended with the death of her husband on April 12, 1945. However, she remained in the public eye. In 1945 President Harry S. Truman appointed her as a delegate to the first General Assembly of the United Nations. The next year she chaired the Commission on Human Rights of the United Nations Economic and Social Council, serving until April 1951. She played an important role as one of the chief authors of the Universal Declaration of Human Rights, designed to define fundamental rights and freedoms for peoples throughout the world. President Dwight D. Eisenhower selected a new delegate, but John F. Kennedy returned her to the international body.

Eleanor Roosevelt also remained active in Democratic politics after her husband's death. She supported the unsuccessful bids of Adlai E. Stevenson for the presidency in 1952 and 1956, and endorsed the victorious candidacy of Kennedy in

1960. In New York State, she cast her lot with the liberal reform wing of the party.

On September 26, 1962, Eleanor entered Columbia Presbyterian Medical Center, where it was determined that she suffered from a reactivated case of tuberculosis. Although she was returned to her home, she proved unable to overcome her illness and died on November 7, 1962, four weeks after her 78th birthday. Upon learning of her death, President Kennedy said:

> One of the great ladies in the history of this country has passed from the scene. . . . Our condolences go to all the members of her family, whose grief at the death of this extraordinary woman can be tempered by the knowledge that her memory and spirit will long endure among those who labor for great causes around the world.

Eleanor Roosevelt was buried on November 10, 1962, next to Franklin at Hyde Park. Besides the Roosevelt family, President Kennedy, Vice President Lyndon B. Johnson, and former presidents Harry S. Truman and Dwight D. Eisenhower attended the services. Leading figures from the days of the New Deal and representatives of the United Nations also were present.

Harlan Fiske Stone's Birthday

Photo by Harris and Ewing, Collection of the Supreme Court of the United States.

Harlan Fiske Stone

Harlan Fiske Stone, the 12th chief justice of the United States Supreme Court, was born in Chesterfield, New Hampshire, on October 11, 1872. His father, Frederick Lauson Stone, was a farmer who encouraged his sons to make agriculture their occupation. In 1874 Frederick Stone moved his family to Amherst, Massachusetts, so that his eldest son might attend the state agricultural college (later the University of Massachusetts). His younger son, Harlan, grew up on the family farm.

Originally, Harlan Stone also planned to become a farmer. His admission to Amherst College in 1890, however, was the turning point in his life. During his four years there, he achieved an outstanding record. Among other distinctions, he served as class president, was a member of the football team, and won election to Phi Beta Kappa. After graduating in 1894, Stone taught in a neighboring community for a year and then entered Columbia Law School. Admitted to the bar in 1898, he began his legal practice with the New York law firm of Sullivan and Cromwell and joined the Columbia faculty as a lecturer in that same year.

Both as a practicing attorney and as an academic, Stone enjoyed great success. In 1905 he became a senior partner in the firm of Satterlie, Canfield, and Stone. During the next 18 years he remained an active member of this firm, although for much of the period this practice was not his only concern. In 1907 and from 1910 to 1923, Stone also served as dean of the Columbia Law School. In 1923 Stone resigned both positions and rejoined Sullivan and Cromwell, planning to devote himself to the large corporate practice for which the firm was renowned.

However, it was to be public rather than private service that would give Stone the opportunity to utilize his legal talents fully. In 1924 President Calvin Coolidge appointed Stone attorney general of the United States. Although he held this office for only one year, he initiated reforms that salvaged the reputation of the Department of Justice from the depths into which it had fallen as a result of the scandals of the Harding administration. The following year Coolidge named Stone associate justice of the Supreme Court.

During Stone's 21 years on the bench, three areas of law preoccupied the Supreme Court. In the 1920s the main issue before the tribunal was the extent of power an individual state had to alter its economic system by regulation, prohibition, and taxation. In the 1930s the constitutionality of New Deal legislation that sought to change the nation's economic and legal order was the burning issue. In the 1940s the most noteworthy cases before the Court concerned the validity of wartime measures such as martial law and military courts. Stone wrote more than 600 opinions and dissents dealing with these matters, and an examination of his record shows how closely he aligned himself with the liberal members of the Court.

From the time of his appointment to the Court in 1925 until 1937, Stone and some fellow justices (Oliver Wendell Holmes Jr., Louis Brandeis, and, after Holmes's retirement in 1932, Benjamin Cardozo) rendered opinions that earned them the nickname of "the three great dissenters." In 1937 several of the more conservative justices retired from the Supreme Court, and President Franklin D. Roosevelt selected liberals to fill the vacated positions. This change in the Court's membership resulted in a corresponding change in its rulings. Post-1937 decisions reversed previous opinions, and the majority of the Court after that date accepted many of the positions that Holmes, Brandeis, Stone, and Cardozo had taken in their earlier dissents.

When Chief Justice Charles Evans Hughes retired in 1941, President Roosevelt named Stone as his successor. Stone served five years in this office. He was delivering a dissenting opinion in the case of *Girouard* v. *United States* when he became fatally ill. Stone died on April 22, 1946, in Washington, D.C.

October 12

Columbus Day

This is a movable event.

The identity of the first Europeans to visit the shores of North America is uncertain. The Irish may have reached what is now Canada in the ninth or tenth century. The Vikings reached Vinland, an area of wild grapes and wheat located west of Greenland, around the 11th century. It was only with the voyage of Christopher Columbus in 1492, however, that systematic European exploration and colonization of the New World commenced.

Little is known about the commander of the momentous 1492 expedition. Most historians believe Christopher Columbus, or Christoforo Colombo, was born in Genoa in 1451. His father, Domenico Colombo, was a weaver, and the future navigator may have followed his father's trade during his youth. He is believed to have gone to the sea sometime around 1472.

Columbus arrived in Portugal in 1476 after narrowly escaping death during a naval battle. The young seaman made a number of voyages under the Portuguese flag during the following years and visited England, the African Gold Coast, the Madeira Islands, and the Azores. In 1479 or 1480 he married Felipa de Perestrello, the daughter of the captain of Porto Santo, one of the Madeiras.

Portugal, however, failed to offer Columbus support for his most daring venture. Like many mariners of his time, Columbus dreamed of gaining fame and wealth by finding a water route to the Orient. In 1484 he asked King Joao II of Portugal to provide financial backing for his plan to reach the East Indies by sailing west. The king refused.

Most educated European persons of the 15th century believed the earth to be round and accepted Columbus's plan as theoretically possible. Nevertheless, the best geographers correctly calculated that 10,000 miles lay between Europe and the East Indies, and few were convinced that ships could successfully complete so arduous a voyage. Columbus disagreed, claiming that only 2,400 miles separated the continents, a gross underestimation that was the source of much of his self-confidence and courage.

For years Columbus was unable to obtain financial support for his adventurous undertaking. Then, in 1492 King Ferdinand II and Queen Isabella of Spain agreed to sponsor his voyage. The Spanish monarchs met all of Columbus's requests by providing him with three ships, naming him Admiral of the Ocean Sea, and appointing him viceroy of any territory he might discover. On August 3, 1492, Columbus and his 90-member crew sailed from Palos, Spain, aboard the *Niña*, the *Pinta*, and the *Santa María*. They carried with them a letter from Ferdinand and Isabella addressed to the Grand Khan of China.

Columbus's transatlantic crossing was relatively easy. From Spain his three ships sailed to the Canary Islands, off the coast of Africa. There they took on additional provisions and on September 6 began their voyage west. At first the northeast trade winds took the ships briskly along, but then unfavorable breezes and calms slowed their progress. For more than a month the vessels sailed, almost 2,700 miles, without sighting land. The sailors became mutinous, and in early October they tried to persuade Columbus to turn back. The commander remained steadfast, stating that he would continue the voyage until he found the Indies.

The expedition maintained its westward course, and within a few days Columbus believed he had accomplished his purpose. At 2:00 a.m. on October 12 one of the lookouts on the *Pinta* spotted land. Later that same morning, Columbus and his captains went ashore on an island, named it San Salvador, and planted a cross there.

After exploring what was actually the Bahamas for several weeks, the expedition arrived in Cuba on October 27. On that island, the crew members were amazed to see "many people with a firebrand in the hand . . . to drink the smoke thereof," but were disappointed in their hopes of finding gold and the other reported treasures of the Orient. Columbus and his men left Cuba on December 5, and on the following day they reached the island of Hispaniola or Santo Domingo, which today comprises Haiti and the Dominican Republic. They remained there for more than a month, and after the wreck of the *Santa María* on a reef off the island on December 25, they established a trading colony and named it Navidad.

Leaving a contingent behind at Navidad, the *Niña* and the *Pinta* began the return voyage to Spain on January 16, 1493. Two severe storms battered the vessels on the long trip, but after stops at the Azores and Lisbon the ships finally arrived at their home port of Palos on March 15, 1493. Columbus, having dispatched from Lisbon a letter telling Ferdinand and Isabella of his discovery of what he thought were the Indies, was invited to proceed without delay to the Spanish court at Barcelona, where he was enthusiastically received.

Columbus made three more voyages to the New World. He visited Trinidad, Puerto Rico, Martinique, and Panama. However, his failure to find gold or silver in any of these places caused the Spanish monarchs to lose interest in his expeditions. He spent the last years of his life in relative obscurity. He died in Valladolid, Spain, on May 21, 1506, still believing he had discovered a new route to the Orient.

The first observance of October 12 to take place in the United States occurred in New York City in 1792. That year the Society of St. Tammany (also known as the Columbian Order) sponsored a dinner and organized elaborate ceremonies for the 300th anniversary of Columbus's voyage. As part of the decorations for the event, the society erected a monument in its headquarters. It was only a temporary structure, but it is generally believed to have been the first memorial raised to Columbus in this country.

The 1792 observance attracted only limited interest, and little if any notice of October 12 was taken in the United States during the century that followed. However, in 1892 the nation prepared a massive celebration to honor Columbus on the 400th anniversary of his landing at San Salvador. President Benjamin Harrison issued a proclamation calling upon citizens to participate in commemorative services and requested schools to organize programs. The American people responded enthusiastically, and many localities sponsored special festivities. Preparations for the Columbian Exposition, however, were not completed by 1892, and it was not until the summer of 1893 that the gates of the great fair opened in Chicago. The celebration held at the exposition on October 12 of that year was the most elaborate arranged up to that time.

During the first decade of the 20th century, the Knights of Columbus (a Roman Catholic society for men founded in 1882) repeatedly urged state legislatures to declare October 12 a legal holiday. In 1905 the governor of Colorado issued a proclamation calling on the people of the state to commemorate the day. The next year the mayor of Chicago made a similar request of the residents of that city. However, it was not until 1909 that New York became the first state to pass legislation declaring Columbus Day a holiday. Within a few years other states followed New York's lead.

For many years American presidents proclaimed October 12 as Columbus Day, but in 1968 President Lyndon B. Johnson signed a law designating the day as a federal holiday and setting the day of its observance as the second Monday in October in accordance with the new federal policy of scheduling three-day weekends. This legislation became effective in 1971 and thus Columbus Day has been a "movable event" ever since.

First Use of the Pledge of Allegiance

The Pledge of Allegiance to the Flag of the United States, the oath of loyalty to the United States as represented by its flag, was first written by a Baptist minister named Francis Bellamy in a piece for a popular magazine called *The Youth's Companion*, in September 1892. The pledge was first officially used on October 12, 1892, by order of President Benjamin Harrison during Columbus Day observances. This first pledge read as follows:

I pledge allegiance to my flag and to the republic for which it stands: one nation, indivisible, with liberty and justice for all.

In the 1920s, several patriotic organizations such as the American Legion achieved a modification of the pledge when Congress substituted the words "the flag of the United States of America" for the phrase "my flag" effective on Flag Day, June 14, 1924. In 1954 Congress further amended the pledge by adding the words "under God." The Pledge of Allegiance now reads:

I pledge allegiance to the flag of the United States of America and to the republic for which it stands: one nation under God, indivisible, with liberty and justice for all.

October 13

White House Cornerstone Laid

In 1790, the United States Congress rejected the established urban centers of New York City, New York, and Philadelphia, Pennsylvania, as possible locations for the permanent seat of government. Instead, it chose to express the youth of the nation by placing the federal capital in a new city. Although the site chosen for this massive undertaking was a rather bleak and unpromising stretch of land along the Potomac River between Maryland and Virginia, Congress decided to transform the area into a metropolis. To ensure the success of this project, nothing was left to chance. Congress selected the respected French engineer Pierre Charles L'Enfant to superintend the overall design of the city, and it announced an open competition in which other architects were invited to submit plans for the Capitol building and the president's home.

The design of the president's house captured the imagination of many, and even Secretary of State Thomas Jefferson submitted a plan. From numerous entries, Congress selected that of James Hoban, an Irish architect living in Charleston, South Carolina. Hoban envisioned the presidential mansion as a Georgian country seat. His winning design featured a hipped roof, a balustrade, and alternating window arches—characteristics typical of the Palladian architectural style then enjoying widespread popularity in Europe.

The cornerstone of the presidential residence was laid on October 13, 1792, thereby making it the first federal structure in the national capital. Initial plans called for its completion within eight years, so that it would be ready when the government relocated to Washington, D.C., in 1800. This deadline was not met, however, and the building was still unfinished when it received its first occupant, namely President John Adams on November 1, 1800. The primitive condition of his new living quarters does not seem to have unduly dismayed Adams. Only one day after he moved in, he wrote to his wife, Abigail, the inspiring words that President Franklin Delano Roosevelt later ordered carved on the mantel of the State Dining Room:

I pray Heaven to bestow the best of Blessings on this House and all that shall hereafter inhabit it. May none but honest and wise Men ever rule under this roof.

Every president of the United States since Adams has occupied the residence at 1600 Pennsylvania Avenue. Since then, the building itself has undergone considerable transformation. Only a few years after its completion, the entire interior of the house was destroyed when the British burned Washington on August 24, 1814, during the War of 1812. Reconstruction of the White House began almost immediately under the supervision of its designer, Hoban, and the building was again ready for occupancy in 1816. The South Portico was added in 1824 and the North Portico in 1829. Throughout the remainder of the 19th century, various presidents altered the house to suit their personal preferences and the changing styles of the times.

The presidential mansion assumed its modern appearance during the administration of Theodore Roosevelt. Commissioned by him in 1902, the famed architectural firm of McKim, Mead, and White rid the building of the Victorian trappings so favored by the late-19th-century presidents and renovated the house in the French classical style. They relieved its overcrowded condition with the addition of the West Wing, which housed various executive offices that had previously occupied space in the original structure. The administration's influence on the building was not only architectural: In 1902 Roosevelt also made its popular name, the White House, the official designation of the president's home.

Structural weaknesses necessitated a total renovation of the White House in 1948. In the course of this four-year project, the entire interior of the building was removed and a new basement and foundation were constructed under its original walls. The interior was then reinstalled with only one major deviation from the 1902 design, in that the main stairway was redirected from the Main Hall into the Entrance Hall. In 1961 Jacqueline Kennedy, wife of President John F. Kennedy, created two committees to select appropriate furnishings and paintings to grace the historic building. The work of these committees beautified the house immeasurably. They acquired numerous antiques to supplement the pieces that were originally purchased for the White House, and in particular they sought items dating from the early 19th century, since very few things associated with the presidential mansion during that era had survived. Substantial additions have now also been made to the White House Art Collection so that it includes works representative of every genre of American painting. The most prized possession is probably the Gilbert Stuart portrait of George Washington, saved from the advancing British by Dolley Madison in 1814.

October 14

War of 1812: Battle of Queenston Heights

American forces suffered an important defeat during the War of 1812 in the battle of Queenston Heights on October 13, 1812.

At the time, Canada was still a British possession, and Canadian settlements, ports, and forts were important staging areas for British forces in their war with the United States, while its defenses were limited due to its small population. Therefore, an invasion was planned into the Canadian province of Ontario across the Niagara River from northern New York State. On the night of October 12, 1812, roughly 1,600 troops from the United States Army and the local state militia departed from Lewiston, New York, toward Queenston, Ontario. However, a local Canadian woman named Laura Secord had overheard conversations concerning the invasion.

Secord went to the British forces and reported her discovery to their commander, Major General Sir Isaac Brock. He summoned a combined British, Canadian, and native tribal force of over 2,000 men. On October 13 Brock's forces engaged the Americans at Beaver Dams, stopping their advance, and then attacked the American positions established at Queenston during the night. Nearly 100 Americans were killed and nearly 1,000 were captured. The British incurred few casualties, although Brock himself was killed during the battle. American forces suffered a permanent setback in their designs on Canada.

October 14

Dwight David Eisenhower's Birthday

Dwight David Eisenhower, the 34th president of the United States, was born on October 14, 1890, in Denison, Texas. He was descended from a family that traced its lineage back to the colonial period. The victims of religious persecution in their native Catholic Bavaria, Eisenhower's forebears emigrated to America in the early 1730s. They settled on the Susquehanna River near Harrisburg, Pennsylvania, in 1732 and there helped organize the branch of the pietist Mennonite sect that became known as the River Brethren. A plain, hardworking people, the Eisenhowers remained among the Brethren in the Pennsylvania Dutch region for almost a century and a half.

The lure of the frontier, however, proved to be an irresistible attraction for the Reverend Jacob Eisenhower and his family. In 1878, together with other members of the River Brethren, they moved

Dwight David Eisenhower

to Kansas. The Eisenhowers settled on a 160-acre farm in Abilene, and shortly after their arrival their son David met Ida Elizabeth Stover. In 1885 the couple were married in the United Brethren Church in Lecompton, Kansas.

After several business failures, David Eisenhower took Ida and their two young sons to Denison, Texas. He was working for a local railroad company when his son Dwight was born. In 1892 the Eisenhowers moved back to Abilene, where David eventually began working for a creamery while Ida raised three more sons, making a total of six.

Although Dwight D. Eisenhower, or Ike as he came to be called, did well in high school, he graduated with no definite plans regarding his future. For a year he held various odd jobs, including a brief stint as a semiprofessional baseball player. He finally decided to attend the United States Military Academy at West Point, which he entered on July 1, 1911. His academic record was undistinguished, and at graduation Eisenhower placed 61st in a class of 164. However, his Class of 1915 was not composed of mediocre students: 59 of its members became generals, earning a total of 111 stars, and it is remembered as "the class the stars fell on."

Commissioned a second lieutenant in June 1915, Eisenhower began his active military career with the 19th Infantry Regiment at Fort Sam Houston in San Antonio, Texas. During his first tour of duty in Texas, he met Mamie Geneva Doud. After a brief courtship, they were married on July 1, 1916, at her parents' home in Denver, Colorado.

Eisenhower did not participate in the actual fighting in World War I. During the first year after the United States entered the conflict in April 1917, he held several minor posts at army installations in the United States. His real contribution to the war effort came in 1918, when the 28-year-old captain took command of the Camp Colt tank training center at Gettysburg, Pennsylvania. His assignment was to instruct the soldiers in the methods of tank warfare. This was not an easy task, since the tank had only been in use for a short time after the outbreak of World War I. However, Eisenhower received the Distinguished Service Medal for his "unusual zeal, foresight, and marked administrative ability in the organization, training, and preparation for overseas service of technical troops of the Tank Corps."

In 1920 Eisenhower, who had advanced to the temporary rank of lieutenant colonel during the war, received the permanent commission of major. During the next five years he performed routine peacetime assignments in the United States and in the Panama Canal Zone, but not until 1925 did he really begin to distinguish himself. In August of that year the army selected 275 officers, including Eisenhower, for training at its Command and General Staff School at Fort Leavenworth, Kansas. Eisenhower excelled at the school, and in the following June he graduated at the top of the class.

Although there was no doubt about Eisenhower's superior ability for military organization after 1926, there was little demand for such talents during the isolationist 1920s. Eisenhower's next major assignment was service with the American Battle Monuments Commission, preparing a guide to American battlefields in France. Afterward, Eisenhower served as assistant executive officer to the assistant secretary of war from 1929 to 1933. During that time he helped establish the Army Industrial College and drafted a plan for industrial mobilization in time of war. The latter work came to the attention of General Douglas MacArthur, the chief of staff of the army, and so impressed him that in February 1933 he appointed Eisenhower the senior aide on his personal staff. Moreover, two years later when MacArthur went to the Philippines as military adviser to the new commonwealth, Eisenhower accompanied him as senior military assistant.

Returning to the United States in 1939, Eisenhower, who had been commissioned a lieutenant colonel in 1936, rapidly advanced as the country mobilized for possible entry into what would be World War II. In March 1941 he won the rank of temporary colonel, and three months later was named chief of staff for the Third Army. The Third Army engaged in the extensive war games that took place in Louisiana during the early fall of 1941, and Eisenhower's leadership impressed General George C. Marshall, the chief of staff. On September 29, 1941, Eisenhower was promoted to the temporary rank of brigadier general.

Eisenhower's career changed abruptly when Japanese forces bombed the American naval base at Pearl Harbor, Hawaii, on December 7, 1941, precipitating the entry of the United States into World War II. A week later Marshall ordered Eisenhower to Washington, D.C. Throughout the spring of 1942, he held several key organizational positions. Although Eisenhower had never led troops in combat, he so impressed his superiors with his abilities and tact in carrying out assignments that on June 25, 1942, Marshall named him commanding general of American forces in the European Theater of Operations with the temporary rank of lieutenant general.

Eisenhower arrived at his headquarters in London in July 1942 and almost immediately began preparations for the Allied invasion of North Africa. One of his major tasks during the months of planning and combat that followed was to conciliate the various Allied officers participating in the project. He eventually managed to promote harmony among British, French, and American military leaders.

Named Allied commander in chief, North Africa, on August 14, 1942, Eisenhower moved his headquarters to Algiers. There he directed operations against the German general Erwin Rommel and his Afrika Korps. The Allies suffered several critical reverses during the initial months of fighting, and not until February 1943 did the tide turn. From that point on, however, the Allies gradually gained control. By May 13 the remaining German and Italian troops in North Africa had surrendered. Eisenhower had won his first military campaign.

He next turned his attention to the other side of the Mediterranean by directing the amphibious attack on Sicily in July 1943, which led to its conquest the following month. He also prepared for and directed the early stages of the invasion of Italy. Due to German intervention and difficult terrain, the liberation of Italy was a long, painful process that lasted throughout 1944 and into the spring of 1945.

October 14

On Christmas Eve 1943 President Franklin D. Roosevelt made public Eisenhower's new assignment: He had been selected as supreme commander of the Allied Expeditionary Forces then preparing to invade Nazi Germany's Fortress Europe. D day on June 6, 1944 (see related essays throughout this book), proved to be one of the most important days of Eisenhower's life. Although weather conditions were far from perfect, Eisenhower decided to proceed with the invasion—a judgment that proved correct. This amphibious landing, combined with a heavy air attack, caught the Germans off guard and after days of bitter fighting the Allies established several crucial beachheads on the Normandy coast of German-occupied France.

Securing these footholds in France allowed the Allied campaign against the Axis to accelerate. By the end of August 1944, Paris had been liberated. The Allied cause suffered a setback when Nazi troops briefly rallied at the battle of the Bulge in December 1944, but this was to be Hitler's last major counterattack. By February 1945 the Allied forces had resumed their offensive. In March they entered Germany, and at 2:41 a..m. on May 7, 1945, General Alfred Jodl of the German army unconditionally surrendered at Eisenhower's headquarters in a schoolhouse at Reims, France. The next day, May 8, when the surrender became effective, was celebrated as Victory in Europe (V-E) Day (see May 8).

In the late summer of 1945, Eisenhower became the commander of the American occupation forces and military governor of the zone occupied by the United States. His stay was brief. On November 20, 1945, President Harry S. Truman ordered his recall and named him to succeed General Marshall as the army's chief of staff. Eisenhower held this position until his resignation on February 7, 1948. Three months later, the five-star general of the army (he had attained this highest rank on April 11, 1946) retired from the armed services. As the 1948 presidential election approached, he was sought out as a presidential nominee by both the Democratic and the Republican parties. He chose to decline, and became the president of Columbia University on June 7, 1948. It was a short-lived position, however, and at President Truman's invitation Eisenhower rejoined the military to serve as the temporary chairman of the Joint Chiefs of Staff. In 1950 he assumed command of the military forces of the newly created North Atlantic Treaty Organization (NATO).

From 1950 to 1952 Eisenhower worked to strengthen the military defenses of Western Europe against the possibility of future Soviet aggression. Meanwhile, Republican leaders in the Unit-

ed States, convinced that the general's candidacy would give their party its best chance for success in the 1952 presidential election, waged a campaign to persuade him to accept the nomination. Finally, on January 7, 1952, Eisenhower agreed.

Eisenhower's chief rival for the Republican nomination was the widely respected Senator Robert A. Taft, popularly identified as Mr. Republican. Known for his conservative policies, Taft had strong support when the Republican delegates convened in July 1952. Under the leadership of New York's Governor Thomas E. Dewey, however, Eisenhower's supporters managed to swing several key delegations to Eisenhower. With these crucial votes the general won the nomination after only one ballot. As the party's vice-presidential candidate, the convention then approved Eisenhower's choice of Richard Milhous Nixon, then a California senator.

The November 1952 elections resulted in an overwhelming victory for Eisenhower over his Democratic opponent, Adlai Stevenson. The former general won almost 34 million popular votes and 442 votes in the electoral college. His opponent received 27.3 million popular votes and 89 electoral votes. On January 20, 1953, Eisenhower became the 34th president of the United States.

Eisenhower's first term in office witnessed a general relaxation of tension in both domestic and foreign affairs. Although the conclusion of the war in Korea was the outstanding achievement of his first administration, other policies and actions were also noteworthy, among them his designation of Earl Warren as the nation's 14th chief justice of the United States Supreme Court. This appointment was to have far-reaching consequences, since the Supreme Court under Warren would issue some of the most important civil rights decisions in American history.

Although Eisenhower suffered a heart attack in September 1955 and underwent major intestinal surgery the following June, his doctors declared him physically fit to seek reelection in 1956. The Democrats again nominated Stevenson for president, but his campaign was no more successful than it had been in 1952. Eisenhower received 35.5 million popular votes and 457 electoral votes. Stevenson received 26 million popular votes and 73 electoral votes.

Eisenhower's second term was fraught with crises. The South resisted the Supreme Court's 1954 order to integrate its schools, the national economy entered a three-year recession, the Soviet Union launched *Sputnik I*, the first artificial earth satellite (see October 4), and they also captured an American U-2 reconnaissance plane in the act of violating Soviet airspace. Confronted with these problems, in 1957 Eisenhower sent federal troops to Little Rock, Arkansas, to force compliance with the Supreme Court's desegregation order and signed the first Civil Rights Act since Reconstruction. In February 1958 he announced the launching of *Explorer I*, a small American satellite, which was launched a few days prior on January 31. Shortly after the U-2 incident in 1960, he promised to end American espionage flights.

Before leaving office, Eisenhower issued a famous warning that was all the more remarkable for being voiced by a military man. In the warning he spoke of something "new in the American experience" namely a "conjunction of an immense military establishment and a large arms industry." He further stated:

> We recognize the imperative need for this development. Yet we must not fail to comprehend its grave implication. . . . In the councils of government, we must guard against the acquisition of unwarranted influence, whether sought or unsought, by the military-industrial complex. The potential for the disastrous rise of misplaced power exists and will persist.

The phrase "military-industrial complex" has since become common usage.

After John F. Kennedy was inaugurated as president in January 1961, Eisenhower retired to his 230-acre farm in Gettysburg, Pennsylvania. He wrote his two-volume memoirs, *The White House Years*, compiled a series of personal anecdotes entitled *At Ease: Stories I Tell My Friends*, and advised both Presidents Kennedy and Lyndon B. Johnson. He also found time for his two favorite hobbies—golf and painting. Eisenhower died on March 28, 1969.

William Penn's Birthday

Pennsylvania's history begins with the man whose name it bears. William Penn, the son of the wealthy and influential Admiral Sir William Penn, was born in London on October 24, 1644. His father was a creditor and close friend of both King Charles II and his brother the duke of York, who later became King James II.

Such connections would have guaranteed young Penn's worldly success, but he forsook these advantages for the sake of conscience. He associated himself with George Fox's Society of Friends, commonly called by the then derogatory nickname Quakers, and came to know the oppression reserved for that radical religious group. Christ Church in Oxford expelled the 18-year-old Penn when he interfered with the college's religious services in protest against the established Anglican religion.

Dismayed by the perceived excesses of Restoration England, the Quakers like so many 17th-century dissidents longed to establish a religious refuge in the New World. Penn had the means by which the dream of a Quaker colony could become a reality. His father's death in 1670 left him with a large fortune, including a claim of several thousand pounds against the crown. Travels through northern Europe in 1676 convinced Penn that there was a sufficient number of Quakers and other religious dissidents to populate a new colony. In 1680, probably in lieu of requesting the unpaid royal debt, he petitioned King Charles II for a grant of land in America.

The king's response was favorable, and despite the opposition of Parliament in March 1681 Penn received title to the territory between 43 degrees and 40 degrees north latitude extending west of the Delaware River through five degrees longitude. The following year the duke of York added the three Delaware counties of Newcastle, Sussex, and Kent to Penn's jurisdiction in return for an annual rent of five shillings and a "rose to be paid on the Feast of St. Michael the Archangel."

Penn received his grant at a time when England was becoming interested in exerting more control over its American colonies. For this reason, Penn's charter contained several restrictions not included in earlier grants. Laws could be enacted only with assembly approval, and none could be passed that were contrary to those of England. Decisions of provincial courts could be appealed to the crown, strict obedience to the Navigation Acts was to be maintained, and Parliament's right to tax the colony was affirmed in a rather ambiguous clause. However, Penn was free to establish any form of government that would not violate the charter restrictions.

Penn's first frame of government, which he devised in 1682 while still in England, provided for a governor (Penn himself or his appointee) and a bicameral legislature elected by the freemen of the colony. The upper house or council of 72 members had the power to initiate all bills, and an assembly of 200 to 500 representatives could either approve or reject the proposed legislation. The franchise was open to all men who held a small amount of land or paid taxes. In 1683 a second frame of government reduced the council and assembly to 18 and 32 members, respectively, after the legislature became increasingly aware that their original size prevented efficient operation.

Penn's foresight and planning ensured the success of his colony. To attract settlers to the area, in 1682 he published the pamphlet *Some Account of the Province of Pennsylvania*. The tract, which was translated into German, French, and Dutch, and distributed throughout Europe, guaranteed complete religious freedom to all believers in God and offered liberal terms for obtaining land. Penn himself visited his colony in 1682. During his two-year stay he supervised the planning of the city of Philadelphia. Even more important, his insistence that the colonists treat the native tribes with respect inaugurated what was to be a 70-year period of good relations between the colonists and the Native Americans.

Penn returned to England in 1684 in an attempt to settle his dispute with George Calvert, first baron of Baltimore, over the boundary between Pennsylvania and Maryland. Despite his absence the colony flourished. Settled by immigrants from the British Isles, Holland, the Rhineland, and France, Pennsylvania's population grew from about 1,000 in 1682 to 12,000 in 1689. The economy of the colony also thrived as its exports of wheat, beef, and pork found ready markets in the West Indies.

In 1699 Penn returned to his colony and on November 8, 1701, he issued the Charter of Privileges, the constitution by which Pennsylvania was governed until the American Revolution. This plan provided for a unicameral legislature elected by the freemen and a governor appointed by the proprietor. All laws needed the approval of both the assembly and the chief executive to become effective. The charter also explicitly guaranteed religious freedom to all believers in the "One Almighty God."

The controversy over his colony's southern boundary again called Penn back to England in 1701, but he was unable to reach a satisfactory settlement. The matter was not officially settled until 1764, when the surveyors Charles Mason and Jeremiah Dixon established what is now known as the Mason-Dixon line. During his later years, the agents Penn had entrusted with his fortune cheated him, and he fell deeply into debt. His financial condition deteriorated to the point that he was forced to spend a number of months in debtors' prison. In 1708 his insolvency forced him to mortgage Pennsylvania to trustees. Three years later Penn suffered his first stroke, and the following year two additional attacks left him an invalid. He was virtually helpless until his death in 1718.

October 15

Sukkot

This is a movable event.

In the Jewish calendar, the first full day of Sukkot (the Feast of the Tabernacles or Booths) is the 15th day of the lunar month of Tishri (in the course of September or October). Sukkot, like all other Jewish holidays, begins at sundown on the preceding evening (in 1970 the 15th day of Tishri coincided with October 15).

The holiday lasts for eight days, although only the first two days and last two days are considered full holidays by Orthodox and Conservative Jews. Reform Jews celebrate only the first and last days as full holidays. The last day of Sukkot is called *Shemini Atzeret*, "the Eighth Day of Solemn Assembly." During the Middle Ages a ninth day had the name *Simhat Torah*, "the Rejoicing in the Law." Today Orthodox and Conservative Jews continue to celebrate Simhat Torah as a separate holiday. In Israel Simhat Torah is observed together with Shemini Atzeret on the eighth day of Sukkot. Reform Jews similarly observe Simhat Torah and Shemini Atzeret on the same day.

Although the precise origins are uncertain, it is generally believed that the observance of Sukkot began after the Jews ended their 40 years of wandering in the wilderness and entered the promised land of Canaan. Sukkot is one of the three great pilgrimage festivals, the others being Pesach (Passover) and Shavuot (the Feast of Weeks), during which all male Jews were supposed to go to the Temple in Jerusalem. Since Sukkot occurs at the end of the fruit and wine harvest, it was also one of the three important harvest festivals in ancient times. In the Bible it is referred to as *Hehag*, literally "the Festival."

Sukkot is also referred to in the Bible as *Hag HaAsif*, "the Feast of the Ingathering," and as *Hag HaSukkot*, "the Feast of the Booths." These two names reflect the dual quality of the holiday. Although originally it was only a harvest festival, the *zeman simhatenu*, or "time of our rejoicing," later it acquired a historical significance. The custom of dwelling in booths during Sukkot, although originally probably connected with the harvest, came to commemorate Israel's dwelling in tents during the 40-year wandering in the wilderness. The commandment is given in Leviticus 23:42–43: "Ye shall dwell in booths seven days. . . . That your generations may know that I made the children of Israel to dwell in booths, when I brought them out of the land of Egypt." With the destruction of the second Temple in Jerusalem by the Romans in A.D. 70, many of the ancient customs of Sukkot, especially those having to do with the Temple's sacrificial rituals, were abandoned.

According to Jewish tradition the *sukkah*, or "booth" used during Sukkot, must be specially built for the festival and specially thatched to shut out the hottest rays of the sun by day and yet allow the stars to shine through at night. Thus, one can see the heavens and direct one's heart to God. In ancient times the booth served as a dwelling place for the entire seven days, and every male was supposed to live in a booth unless prevented by illness or another valid cause. For seven days the booth was his actual home, as well as a representation of his religious identity and being. The booth's fragility symbolized the brevity and insecurity of all human life and especially the transitory character of Jewish life throughout most of history. The allusions to wandering in the wilderness were meant to remind Jews at this time of thanksgiving of how dependent upon God they were. Even for those who had better harvests than their neighbors, which in modern times might translate as greater wealth, the command that during Sukkot all Jews should live in booths (which had to conform to certain dimensions) emphasized the equality of all people before God as in the days in the wilderness.

The seventh day of Sukkot is called *Hoshana Rabbah*, literally "the Great Hosanna." Hoshana Rabbah became an important holiday in its own right during the Middle Ages, when it acquired the characteristics of a second Day of Atonement (see October 10, Yom Kippur).

John Kenneth Galbraith's Birthday

John Kenneth Galbraith, the famous economist, was born in Iona Station in Ontario, Canada, on October 15, 1908. He attended the University of Toronto, graduating in 1931 with a degree in economics, and went on to the University of California for graduate studies. Galbraith earned his master's degree in 1933 and his doctorate in 1934. Afterward he took a position as an economics instructor with Harvard University, and eventually became a professor with Princeton University in 1939.

During World War II, Galbraith served with the National Defense Advisory Committee and as the deputy administrator of the Office of Price Administration. He also served as the director of the Office of Economic Security Policy in 1946, which dealt with the postwar challenges posed by the devastated economies of Germany and Japan. In 1949 Galbraith returned to Harvard University as a professor of economics, coming to embrace lib-

eral economic theories. The result was two works that made him a national figure: *American Capitalism* (1951), concerning curbing the economic power of big business, and *The Affluent Society* (1958), in which he argued for a diversion of economic resources into social programs. *The Affluent Society* helped influence many of the policy decisions behind President Lyndon B. Johnson's Great Society initiatives in the mid to late 1960s.

During a leave of absence from Harvard, Galbraith served as an ambassador to India from 1961 to 1963. Through the 1960s and 1970s he continued to be popular in liberal circles for his social spending advocacy, but was dismayed by the shift to the right in American politics. Galbraith unsuccessfully argued against the conservative "supply-side" economic theories implemented by President Ronald Reagan after the 1980 election, and blundered badly by asserting that the centralized command economy of the Soviet Union resulted in a better allocation of resources than in free market societies.

Retired in the 1990s, Galbraith continues to enjoy an active lifestyle. Some of his other writings include *The Great Crash: 1929* (1955), *The Liberal Hour* (1960), *Made to Last* (1964), *The New Industrial State* (1967), and *Ambassador's Journal: A Personal Account of the Kennedy Years* (1969). Galbraith has also written several novels.

October 16

Noah Webster's Birthday

Born in West Hartford, Connecticut, on October 16, 1758, Noah Webster was a descendant of distinguished New England families. His mother Mercy Steele Webster was the great-great-granddaughter of William Bradford, the second governor of the Plymouth colony. His father Noah Webster was descended from John Webster, a founder of the Connecticut colony, who became governor in 1656.

Even as a small child, the young Noah Webster showed an interest in books. He received his early education from the Reverend Nathan Perkins and later from a local Hartford teacher before he entered Yale in 1774. The Revolutionary War broke out two years later, and although he served as a volunteer, Webster managed to complete his studies within four years and graduated in 1778. After his graduation, he decided on a legal career, and earned his living by teaching while studying law in his spare time. In 1781 he passed his bar examinations at Hartford. He continued to teach, however, and did not actively practice law until 1789.

During this period, he taught school in Goshen, New York, and came to realize the critical need for quality American textbooks. Between 1782 and 1785 he wrote his first textbook, *A Grammatical Institute of the English Language*. Intended for use by schoolchildren, it consisted of three parts: a grammar, a reader, and (most famous and widely used) *The American Spelling Book*, also known as *Webster's Spelling Book* or the "Blue-Backed Speller." The great success of the spelling book was largely due to Webster's innovative use of American spellings and pronunciations, as well as to its patriotic theme. Although the speller was the most successful, selling as many as 60 million copies by 1890, the reader also had a number of editions. To the 1787 edition of the reader Webster added "some American pieces under the discovery, history, wars, geography, economy, commerce, government, of this country . . . in order to call the minds of our youth from ancient fables & modern foreign events, and fix them upon objects immediately interesting in this country."

Because he was unable to copyright his works in 13 states, Webster became aware of the need for a uniform national copyright law. In 1782 he began to work for legislation to that end, and he spent the next six years traveling throughout the country lobbying, lecturing, and corresponding with many state legislators. To help defray the expenses he incurred during this fight for a copyright law, Webster taught, gave singing lessons, and wrote several pamphlets. His efforts drew him into politics, and he soon earned a reputation for being an avid Federalist. In 1785 he wrote *Sketches of American Policy*, a pamphlet advocating strong central government that brought him to the attention of George Washington and James Madison. Webster's lobbying efforts were not in vain, and in 1790 Congress enacted a national copyright law.

While agitating for copyright legislation, Webster lectured in Philadelphia, Pennsylvania, and had the opportunity to meet Benjamin Franklin. Their mutual interest in simplified spelling led to prolonged correspondence as well as periodic visits by Webster to Philadelphia. During one of these visits he was introduced to Rebecca Greenleaf, the daughter of a Boston merchant. They were married in Boston, Massachusetts, on October 26, 1789, and subsequently had two sons and six daughters.

Webster practiced law in Hartford from 1789 through 1793. His primary interests, however, were journalism and lexicography. Giving up his legal career in Hartford, he founded two Federalist newspapers in New York, the *Minerva* (later the *Commercial Advertiser*) and the semiweekly *Herald* (later the *Spectator*). In 1798 he moved to New Haven, Connecticut, his interest in the newspapers by then having waned. Eventually, the financial success of his early schoolbooks enabled him to retire, and in 1803 he gave up journalism and turned all of his attention to lexicography.

For the next three years he worked on *A Compendious Dictionary of the English Language*, issued in 1806. This was to be the forerunner of *An American Dictionary of the English Language*, which proved to be one of the most popular publications of the time. Webster labored for 20 years in the compilation of his dictionary, spending a year (1824–1825) in England and France doing research. Published in two volumes in 1828, it contained 70,000 entries with 5,000 new words and nearly 40,000 definitions that had never appeared in any other dictionary. It included many nonliterary words, technical terms, and "Americanisms," and it favored American rather than British spelling. Despite the weakness of its etymologies, Webster's dictionary was a landmark work and a great scholarly achievement. The dictionary, however, was less successful financially than his earlier works (after his death the rights were purchased from his estate by George and Charles Merriam).

In 1812, while compiling his dictionary, Webster moved from New Haven to Amherst, Massachusetts. In 1822 he returned to New Haven, where he lived for the rest of his life. By the time he died in 1843 at the age of 84, Webster had added to his lexicographical works several more dictionaries with abridgments and revisions. His broad range of interests is evidenced in other publications, including *A Brief History of Epidemic and Pestilential Diseases* (1799), *Historical Notices of the Origin and State of Banking Institutions and Insurance Offices* (1802), *Origin, History, and the Connection of the Languages of Western Asia and of Europe* (1807), *A Philosophical and Practical Grammar of the English Language* (1807), *Experiments Respecting Dew* (1809), *History of the United States* (1832), a revision of the *Authorized Version of the Bible* (1833), and numerous political pamphlets and informal essays.

Million Man March

An important African American event, known as the Million Man March, was held on October 16, 1995, in Washington, D.C. It was the brainchild of the controversial Nation of Islam leader Louis Farrakhan. On December 14, 1994, Farrakhan issued a call for black men to hold a "holy day of atonement and reconciliation" in the capital in order to unite behind a greater commitment toward their families and communities across the nation. He asked for one million men from across the country to attend.

There was some criticism of the male-only nature of Farrakhan's call, with accusations of sexism from various women's groups and other organizations within and outside of the African American community. Furthermore, there was some reluctance about holding such a major event under the auspices of the Nation of Islam and Farrakhan. Both have been connected with widely publicized controversies concerning the use of violence in order to achieve racial equality and the relationship of the African American community toward the Jews. Nevertheless, many African American men responded in a positive manner to Farrakhan's call, and thousands began to converge on Washington, D.C., for the October 16 event.

At the march, a number of prominent African American figures addressed the crowd, including the Reverend Jesse Jackson and Maya Angelou. All spoke in favor of increased personal responsibility and increased commitment to the community, and all deplored the self-destructive behavior typified by black-on-black violence and dependence on welfare. The event ended with a stirring and yet relatively nonpartisan speech by Farrakhan. He concluded by having the participants take the following pledge en masse:

I (say your name) pledge that from this day forward I will strive to love my brother, as I love myself.

I pledge that from this day forward I will strive to improve myself spiritually, morally, mentally, socially, politically, and economically for the benefit of my self, my family, and my people.

I pledge that I will strive to build businesses, build houses, build hospitals, build factories, and enter into international trade for the good of myself, my family, and my people.

I pledge that from this day forward I will never raise my hand with a knife or a gun to beat, cut, or shoot any member of my family, or any human being except in self-defense.

I pledge from this day forward I will never abuse my wife by striking her, or disrespecting her, for she is the mother of my children, and the producer of my future.

I pledge that from this day forward I will never engage in the abuse of children, little boys, or little girls for sexual gratification, but I will let them grow in peace to be strong men and women for the future of our people.

I pledge that I will never again use the "B" word to describe any female but particularly my own black sister.

I pledge that from this day forward that I will not poison my body with drugs or that which is destructive to my health or to my well-being.

I pledge from this day forward I will support black newspapers, black radio, and black television. I will support black artists who clean up their act, show respect for themselves, and respect for their people and respect for the ears of the human family.

I pledge that I will do all of this, so help me God.

Estimates of the actual size of the march vary. The National Park Service initially estimated that "only" some 400,000 participants were there, certainly an impressive figure but rather short of Farrakhan's goal. An independent research group, however, used aerial photography to arrive at a figure of over 800,000 attendees. Farrakhan stated his belief that in reality there were over a million participants. Although the actual figure may never be known, certainly the Million Man March will go down in history as an important event in the struggle for civil rights and self-determination in the African American community.

October 17

American Revolution: British Surrender at Saratoga

British general John Burgoyne, nicknamed "Gentleman Johnny" for his love of high living, won the assignment of leading the 1777 summer expedition in the American colonies. British strategy for the campaign grew out of Burgoyne's "Thoughts for Conducting the War on the Side of Canada" submitted on February 28, 1777, to the king and Lord George Germain, the secretary of state for the colonies. Burgoyne was to lead the main body of British troops south from Canada by way of Lake Champlain, capture Fort Ticonderoga in New York (which Ethan Allen and his Green Mountain Boys had wrested from the British just two years earlier), and proceed to Albany. Lieutenant Colonel Barry St. Leger, meanwhile, was to conduct a diversionary operation in the Mohawk valley which he would approach from the west via Lake Ontario. St. Leger would then join Burgoyne at Albany. General William Howe, the commander of the third prong of the offensive, was to bring a large number of men up the Hudson valley from New York City to meet the other two British columns. The objective was to wipe out the rebel forces in centrally located New York, thus splitting the newly formed nation into isolated halves.

October 17

On June 17, 1777, Burgoyne left St. John's, Canada, with a force of 7,700 British, Germans, Canadians, Loyalist Americans, and native warriors. His column reached Ticonderoga by June 30 and forced the American defenders under Major General Arthur St. Clair to evacuate the fort on July 5. Burgoyne resumed his trek southward, but the expedition soon ran short of supplies. To obtain the necessary provisions, Burgoyne sent a party of German dragoons under Lieutenant Colonel Friedrich Baum to raid an American storehouse at Bennington, in what is now Vermont. Colonials under General John Stark defeated the Hessians in the battle of Bennington (see August 16), leaving Burgoyne without the additional supplies he needed and bereft of one-tenth of his original strength.

Considering the fate of the other two British columns, General Burgoyne would have been wise to not press on to Albany. St. Leger left Oswego, New York, on July 26 with a British force of 1,800 Loyalists and native warriors. On August 3 he reached and besieged Fort Stanwix on the Mohawk River. At nearby Oriskany on August 6 a detachment under Mohawk chief Joseph Brant defeated General Nicholas Herkimer's American relief force, but Major General Benedict Arnold managed to bring 1,000 volunteers to the aid of the beleaguered colonial garrison. St. Leger had no choice but to terminate the siege and withdraw. Meanwhile, General Howe left New York City with 15,000 troops on July 23. Rather than march up the Hudson valley as originally expected, however, he sailed for an attack on Philadelphia, Pennsylvania. Howe did not occupy Philadelphia until September 26, much too late to be able to return to the New York campaign.

Despite these difficulties, Burgoyne decided to continue on his mission. On September 13 he crossed the Hudson to its west bank near Saratoga (later Schuylerville), New York, 32 miles north of Albany. The British column, reduced to 6,000 by the Bennington defeat and native desertions, continued a short distance south to the vicinity of Bemis Heights where the Americans were encamped.

Major General Philip Schuyler had supervised the American defense of the upper Hudson region until August 4 when Congress replaced him with General Horatio Gates. The new commander arrived on August 19, and on September 12 moved the army north to well-entrenched positions on Bemis Heights. There, he and his 7,000-man force lay in wait for the British attack. General Burgoyne decided to attempt a reconnaissance in force to test the colonists' strength. On September 19, in the first battle of Saratoga, Burgoyne sent

2,200 men under General Simon Fraser out on the right flank to sweep the Freeman's Farm area. Major General Baron Friedrich Adolphus Riedesel was to move south with 1,100 men along the Hudson River road on the left flank. Burgoyne accompanied the center column of 1,100 troops, whose mission was to move south and then westward to make contact with Fraser.

Gates made no counter-move until Major General Benedict Arnold persuaded him to send Colonel Daniel Morgan's Virginia riflemen and Major Henry Dearborn's light infantry out from his left flank to make contact. Morgan's marksmen ambushed the British center column's advance guard and picked off all of its officers as they stood near the cabin of Freeman's Farm. Burgoyne quickly brought up the rest of the center force and dispersed it along the northern edge of the farm. Seven more American regiments joined Morgan and Dearborn, and the colonists took their positions on the southern side of the farm. The opposing forces fought inconclusively for almost four hours.

Burgoyne wanted to attack the Americans again on September 20, but Fraser asked for a day's respite for his tired troopers. The next day Burgoyne received a letter from Lieutenant General Henry Clinton, whom Howe had left in New York City. Clinton offered to make a diversionary attack against the Hudson Highlands. The British commander thereupon canceled his plans in order to await the outcome of Clinton's venture, which resulted in the British capture of Forts Clinton and Montgomery and the burning of Kingston, but did not materially help Burgoyne.

American strength rose after the first battle of Saratoga, reaching 11,000 by October 7. The colonists continuously harassed Burgoyne's position, and his numbers fell to 5,000 regulars as desertions increased. Finally Burgoyne decided to undertake another reconnaissance in force. If he found the enemy to be vulnerable, he would attack in force on the following day. If not, the British would retreat to stronger position.

Divided into three columns, about 2,100 British troops left their entrenchments to begin the second battle of Saratoga on the morning of October 7, 1777. After a short march, the main body of 1,500 men formed a 1,000-yard line on high ground near Mill Creek. The earl of Balcarres held the right with light infantry, while Major John Acland's British grenadiers were on the left. Riedesel's men formed the center of the British line. General Fraser commanded 600 auxiliaries in a wooded area protecting the right flank.

The British dispositions would have been excellent had the enemy been a European opponent used to frontal attack. The Americans, however, chose to approach through the woods which covered both flanks. In mid-afternoon General Enoch Poor's 800 men struck Acland's flank, routed the grenadiers, and captured the wounded major. Daniel Morgan's riflemen attacked the right flank, drove off Fraser's auxiliaries, and with the aid of Dearborn pushed back Balcarres's forces.

Riedesel's Germans held their ground, unaware that Sir Francis Clerke had been mortally wounded and captured while trying to bring them Burgoyne's order to retreat. As other American units put pressure on the German flanks, Brigadier General Ebenezer Learned's brigade approached them from the front. At that moment, General Benedict Arnold took over control of Learned's brigade. The Germans managed to withstand the colonists' first assault, but then fell back to the Balcarres Redoubt. Arnold's aggressiveness brought the Americans victory. When an attack on the Balcarres Redoubt failed, Arnold led Learned's men in an attack that overran the fortified cabins located between the Balcarres Redoubt and the position of Lieutenant Colonel Heinrich von Breymann, German ally of the British. Then Arnold rushed to the other flank of Breymann's Redoubt and led four regiments in an assault that routed the defenders.

British losses were roughly 600 while the Americans' totaled approximately 150. Arnold's efforts made Burgoyne's position untenable and forced him to fall back. On the night of October 8 the British forces slipped away from the camp and past the sleeping 1,300 Massachusetts militiamen under Brigadier General John Fellows whom Gates had dispatched to prevent Burgoyne's escape to the north. By the night of October 9 the British reached Saratoga, where Burgoyne decided to rest his tired soldiers.

Gates took up the chase on October 10 and quickly caught up with his enemy. Instead of pushing his way back to Canada, Burgoyne clung to his strong defensive position at Saratoga and established his troops there. By October 12 the Americans had enveloped his forces everywhere but to the north. The arrival of Brigadier General John Stark of New Hampshire closed the northern route before the British could withdraw. Burgoyne had no choice but to surrender.

Negotiations over the conditions of surrender consumed several days. Tired of the British commander's delaying tactics, on October 16 Gates demanded that he surrender or fight. Still thinking that Clinton might be coming to save him, Burgoyne reluctantly submitted. On October 17 Burgoyne surrendered his sword to Gates, and the American graciously returned it. The British soldiers laid down their arms, signifying the end of Burgoyne's campaign.

Historians have described the two battles of Saratoga as a turning point in the American Revolution. In the course of the conflict, the colonials defeated a great British army and saved themselves from disaster. Moreover, the victory gave the United States a psychological lift and led France to ally with the young nation against Great Britain, its traditional rival.

The *Federalist* Papers Are First Published

After the Constitutional Convention of 1787 in Philadelphia, Pennsylvania, the proposed Constitution of the United States went to the 13 states for ratification. In order to increase public support for ratification, prominent members of the Federalist Party wrote a series of articles called the *Federalist* papers setting forth the arguments in favor of ratification. Some 85 papers were written by Alexander Hamilton, James Madison, and John Jay under the pseudonym Publius beginning on October 17, 1787, and ending on April 12, 1788. In summary, the *Federalist* papers eloquently argued that a federal form of government under the Constitution would curb the rampant and destructive regionalism and factionalism prevalent under the Articles of Confederation that the former colonies had organized themselves under after the victory over the British in the American Revolution. Despite vehement opposition from the Antifederalists, whose cause was supported by several prominent statesmen, the Federalists prevailed and the Constitution was eventually ratified by all 13 states (see related articles throughout this book, especially the articles concerning state ratification).

The subjects of the *Federalist* papers were:
Federalist 1–14: The importance of the proposed Federal union
No. 1: General Introduction
No. 2–5: Concerning Dangers from Foreign Force and Influence
No. 6–7: Concerning Dangers from Dissensions Between the States
No. 8: The Consequences of Hostilities Between the States
No. 9–10: The Union as a Safeguard Against Domestic Faction and Insurrection
No. 11: The Utility of the Union in Respect to Commercial Relations and a Navy
No. 12: The Utility of the Union in Respect to Revenue
No. 13: Advantage of the Union in Respect to Economy in Government

October 17

October 18

Anniversary of the Transfer of Alaska from Russia to the United States

Alaska Day, an officially recognized observance in the 49th and geographically largest state, commemorates the formal transfer of Alaska from Russia to the United States. That event was the culmination of several months of diplomatic maneuvering (see related articles throughout this book). The transfer took place at Sitka, Alaska, on October 18, 1867. Sitka was the last capital of czarist Russia in Russian America, as Alaska was then called. Alexander Baranof, the first Russian governor of Alaska, had established Sitka as the capital in 1799 (under American control, Juneau has been the capital since 1906).

The last Russian governor, Prince Dmitri Maksoutsoff, was bitterly opposed to the sale of Alaska (as were most of the Russian settlers); he refused to give the 250 American troops sent for the transfer ceremonies permission to land. Eager to get ashore after a rough three-week voyage from San Francisco, California, the troops had to spend an additional ten days confined to their ship off Sitka until the arrival of the Russian and American commissioners authorized to carry out the formalities.

At the appointed hour, the commissioners, Russian and American military personnel, local dignitaries, native tribal chiefs, and ordinary citizens gathered at Castle Hill near the official residence of the Russian governor. The ceremony was to be simple. During alternate salutes by Russian and American guns, the czarist flag was to be lowered, the Stars and Stripes raised and the formal words of transfer and acceptance spoken by the commissioners. The commissioners were Captain Alexei Pestchouroff from St. Petersburg, Russia, and General Lovall H. Rousseau from Washington, D.C. Princess Maksoutsoff, the wife of the governor, waited to receive the Russian ceremonial flag.

In an effort to ease the emotionally charged transfer and as a courtesy to the Russian colonists who were losing their adopted home, the tactful General Rousseau asked that no cheers be given. Nevertheless, the ceremony went badly for the Russians. The wind-whipped Russian imperial double-eagle flag wrapped itself around the flagstaff and became caught in the halyards, as if refusing to be displaced. After much tugging and manipulation of the ropes and equally futile attempts by seamen to climb the 90-foot flagpole, a cradle was hastily made out of rope and a seaman hoisted to the banner.

When the seaman finally retrieved the wind-torn flag, he either fumbled or misunderstood the shouted orders to bring it down. Instead the flag was dropped and a strong gust swept it onto Russian bayonets. The tattered double-eagle was subsequently presented to a weeping Princess Maksoutsoff.

Alaska's road to statehood after this transfer was a long one. After control passed from Russia to the United States, it was governed first by the American army and then by the navy. In 1884 Congress designated the region a "district" under civil authority, and so it remained until August 24, 1912, when it was organized as a territory. The territorial status remained in effect until 1959, when Alaska was admitted to the Union as the 49th state.

Thomas B. Reed's Birthday

Thomas Brackett Reed, Speaker of the United States House of Representatives, was born on October 18, 1839, in Portland, Maine. He attended the public schools and eventually entered Bowdoin College in Brunswick, Maine. After graduating in 1860, Reed studied law, while serving as an assistant paymaster with the United States Navy from April 1864 to November 1865. That same year, he was admitted to the Maine bar and began his own practice in Portland.

Reed was elected to the Maine state house of representatives in 1868 as a Republican. He also served in the Maine state senate, as the attorney general of Maine, and as solicitor of the city of Portland. Reed's career in national politics began in 1876, however, when he was elected to the national House of Representatives in Washington, D.C. During his 22-year tenure, Reed served as chairman of the Committee on the Judiciary, chairman of the Committee on Rules, and Speaker of the House. He became a powerful speaker by imposing the Republican majority's will on the Democratic minority and implementing procedural changes known as the Reed Rules.

In 1896 Reed was a candidate for the Republican Party's nomination for president, but lost to Ohio governor William McKinley, who went on to win the election. Due to a dispute with the McKinley administration over the Spanish-American War, Reed resigned from Congress in 1899. He died in Washington, D.C., on December 7, 1902, and was buried in Portland, Maine.

Feast of St. Luke

The Feast of St. Luke the Evangelist is observed on October 18 by Roman Catholics and other Christian denominations. St. Luke is traditionally regarded as the author of the third Gospel and of the Acts of the Apostles.

Little is known about Luke. He was probably a Greek-speaking gentile who was at some time associated with the city of Antioch, since he seems to have been familiar with the early Christian Church there. According to the church historian Eusebius, whose life bridged the third and fourth centuries A.D., Luke was a Syrian born in Antioch.

Like Paul, with whom he was closely associated, Luke never actually met Jesus. Instead, he was one of the early converts to Christianity after the crucifixion. The fact that Luke's writings are generally considered the most literary of the Gospels is an indication that he was well educated. In writing the Acts of the Apostles, he sometimes employed the first person plural, and from this it is assumed that he accompanied Paul on parts of his second and third missionary journeys. There is some evidence that Luke was also a physician.

Luke probably joined Paul on his second missionary journey around A.D. 50, but remained at Philippi when Paul continued the journey. Luke again joined Paul around 57 and from then on was a fairly constant companion to Paul in his travels throughout Asia Minor, finally accompanying him on his trip to Rome for trial. While Paul was in prison, Luke apparently continued his research for the Gospel, speaking with people who remembered Jesus and could give firsthand accounts of events in his life and describe the early church. Luke escaped Nero's persecutions, which presumably made martyrs of Peter and Paul, and tradition has it that he lived his remaining years in Greece. According to a second-century writer, it was there that Luke died at the age of 84, in Boeotia.

Luke may well have actually interviewed Mary herself, Jesus' mother. In any event, Luke made a number of unique contributions to the New Testament. He is the only gospel writer to provide certain information about the conception, infancy, and childhood of Jesus. The events that Luke alone describes include the annunciation (the announcement by the archangel Gabriel that Mary had been chosen to be the mother of Christ). The words of Luke's account of this event are the basis for two Roman Catholic prayers, the Hail Mary, or Ave Maria, and the less widely known Angelus.

It is not certain when Luke first decided to write the records that would eventually be known as the Gospel of Luke and the Acts of the Apostles. He apparently spent a long time on this task, perhaps two to three decades gathering information. The actual writing is now thought to have taken place at some time between A.D. 70 and 90. The book of Acts traces the early spread of Christianity, moving from Jerusalem to Rome. This supplement to the Gospels covers a period of about 35 years, ranging from the time of Jesus' ascension to heaven to the second year of Paul's imprisonment in Rome.

Luke is the patron saint of physicians and artists.

October 19

The North American Martyrs

The Feast of St. Isaac Jogues and Companions, observed by Roman Catholics, commemorates eight French Jesuit missionaries and martyrs who became the first canonized saints of the North American continent. The eight, all killed between 1642 and 1649, are known collectively as the North American Martyrs. Three of them, Isaac Jogues, René Goupil, and Jean Lalande, were killed in what is now New York State. The other five, Jean de Brébeuf, Antoine Daniel, Gabriel Lalemant, Charles Garnier, and Noël Chabanel, were killed in New France (now Canada). With two exceptions, they were all priests. Goupil and Lalande had joined the missionaries as lay helpers, but at some time between his arrival in the New World in 1640 and his death two years later, Goupil also took the vows of a Jesuit brother.

The story of the North American Martyrs must be seen in the light of the times. In the 17th century and much of the 18th century, France and England were continuously battling over the possession of Canada. In this conflict the Iroquois people of the region were usually allied with the British, more out of hatred for the French and their native allies than any affection for the British.

The French missionaries, making their headquarters in New France in what is now the province of Ontario, wanted to bring the gospel of Christ to the native peoples of the New World. The Iroquois were a confederation of five tribes that stretched across territory including what is now New York State, with the Mohawk on the east and the Seneca on the west. The Oneida, Onondaga, and Cayuga tribes were in the center.

The expansionist Iroquois were at war with the more peaceful Huron, who at that time were settled between Lake Simcoe (north of the eastern part of Lake Ontario) and Georgian Bay to the west. During the years that the French missionaries were working (mostly among the Hurons), the Iroquois repeatedly sent war parties into Huron territory until the Huron were decimated or had fled to new settlements. In 1694, the same year that the last four of the martyrs were killed, the Iroquois succeeded in permanently disrupting the Huron people.

The Jesuits (or Blackrobes, as the natives called them) made their missionary center at Fort Sainte Marie. Father Isaac Jogues had participated in the building of the old fort, which was destroyed in the Iroquois invasion of 1649. It was from Fort Sainte Marie that the Jesuits set out for their Huron missions scattered throughout the countryside.

The year 1642 was a particularly bad one in the land of the Huron. The harvest had been poor, illness was rampant, and clothing was scarce. Even though the Iroquois posed a threat, an expedition had to be sent to Quebec for supplies. The 600 miles of land and water from Fort Sainte Marie to Quebec were in rugged territory made more dangerous by the Iroquois presence in the area. Father Jogues led the expedition, which left in June 1642 and arrived in Quebec in mid-July.

On August 1 he and about 40 others (including Goupil and some high-ranking Huron converts) headed back for the mission with their canoes heavily laden with supplies. The next day they heard the dreaded Iroquois war cry and were immediately ambushed by 70 Mohawk warriors in 12 canoes. Fighting ensued, but the mission convoy was outnumbered. The Mohawk warriors took their captives and booty back to their village of Ossernenon (later Auriesville), New York. During the 12-day trip from the banks of the St. Lawrence to the banks of the Mohawk River, the Mohawk warriors tortured their prisoners, especially the hated French and most especially Father Jogues.

When they arrived in Mohawk territory, the captives were dragged from village to village with the inhabitants of each community inflicting additional brutalities. The captives who did not die were given away as slaves. For a while Jogues and Goupil were kept in a kind of public slavery. It was six weeks before their wounds were even partially healed. Gradually the two men were given some degree of freedom in and around the stockaded village. Sometimes they were permitted to go a short distance up a hill, where they prayed together.

In the village itself there was one rather quiet cabin, where Goupil sometimes went to pray. One day while he was there, a small child came in, and Goupil playfully put his hat on the child's head and made the sign of the cross over him. Just at that moment the child's grandfather happened to look in. He thought the "dog of a Frenchman" was bewitching the child. Enraged, he drove Goupil out of the cabin and plotted to have him killed outside the palisades.

A few days later Goupil and Jogues went to their "hill of prayer" outside the stockade. Evidently sensing their new danger, they offered themselves to God as martyrs. As they came down the hill, reciting the rosary, two warriors approached and ordered them back to the stockade at once. The two continued saying the rosary as they walked downhill with the warriors close behind. Then one of the warriors drew a hatchet from beneath his garments and struck at Goupil's head. Goupil fell to the ground and was attacked a second time. Jogues, seeing the hatchet, knelt down to pray, sure that he would be treated in like manner. Instead he was told to stand. He rushed to his dying companion, and while he was administering absolution he was thrust aside as the warriors cleft Goupil's skull. Thus died the first North American Martyr, on September 29, 1642. Father Jogues later wrote a biography of Goupil, the only North American Martyr whose life was recorded by another of the martyrs.

For more than a year, Jogues remained a slave of the Mohawk people. Some of the natives began to respect him, however, for his bravery and endurance. Although the Dutch at Fort Orange (later Albany) offered to ransom Jogues for the then substantial sum of $200, the natives refused. Once in a while Jogues was able to minister to other Christian captives, comforting them and hearing their confessions.

Finally, in August 1643 he escaped. He made his way to the Dutch settlements, and on November 5 found passage aboard a ship for France by way of England. He reached France in time to attend Mass in a Breton church on Christmas morning. After a 10-day trip on horseback, he arrived at the Jesuit college at Rennes, where his fellow Jesuits (who had long given him up for dead) did not recognize him at first. Jogues was received with acclaim wherever he went. The French queen, Anne of Austria, kissed his mutilated hands, while Pope Urban VIII granted Jogues the one gift he had longed for: permission to say the mass despite the handicap presented by his deformed fingers. In a few months he was back in New France, anxious to continue his work.

Tiring of the perpetual war, the Mohawk people notified the governor of New France that they wished to make peace with the French. In May 1646 Jogues, wearing civilian clothes, was sent down to the Mohawk country as the French ambassador of peace. En route he discovered Lake George on May 30, 1646. Since it was the eve of the Feast of Corpus Christi, he named it Lac du Saint Sacrement, or Lake of the Blessed Sacrament. The name was retained until 1755, when Sir William Johnson, a British colonial leader, renamed it Lake George in honor of England's King George II.

The peace council in the chief Mohawk village ended successfully. Jogues, who hoped to establish a permanent mission among the Mohawk people, stopped at Ossernenon on the way back. Then he returned to Quebec to report to the governor of New France on the successful negotiations. Although Jogues himself felt certain that God wanted him to labor and die among the Mohawks, his Jesuit superiors in New France were understandably hesitant to send him back to Ossernenon. However, the Huron council decided to send a peace mission of its own to the Mohawk people and requested that Father Jogues accompany their representatives. Jogues, determining to go chiefly as a missionary and only secondarily as a peace legate, replied, "I shall go, but I shall not return." He asked for a mission assistant. The young layman who accepted the challenge was Jean Lalande, who had recently come from Dieppe, France, to dedicate his life to helping the Jesuits in New France.

On September 24, 1646, three canoes left Three Rivers on the St. Lawrence River between Quebec and Montreal. One carried Huron representatives on the peace mission, one transported returning Mohawk representatives, and the third carried Jogues, Lalande, and the Huron spokesman. By the time they reached Lake Champlain, however, the Mohawk and Huron had abandoned the party in fear.

As Jogues and Lalande approached Ossernenon, they were received with sullen expressions by a small group of Mohawk who then vanished. Suddenly, a great number of Mohawk appeared, attacked Jogues and Lalande, ripped their clothing, and dragged them to the village. The two missionaries were rescued by the friendly Wolf clan of the Mohawk and learned that some of the warriors, especially those in the Bear clan, blamed the Jesuits and their "sorcery" for the blight and pestilence that the Mohawk had recently suffered. The Wolf clan and the Turtle (or Tortoise) clan spoke on behalf of the Frenchmen, and the next day Jogues was allowed to defend his position and refute the charges before the council of chiefs.

The chiefs then went to the capital village, six miles away, where they deliberated the fate of the missionaries and ultimately declared them innocent. However, it was too late. While the chiefs were deliberating, a warrior entered Jogues's cabin and invited him to a feast. Since refusal of such an invitation would give offense, Jogues decided to follow the warrior to a lodge. As he stooped to enter the door of the lodge, he was killed with a tomahawk. The date was October 18, 1646. The next morning Lalande met the same fate.

Jogues had often expressed the desire to suffer martyrdom. Therefore, when in the spring of 1647 his Jesuit companions in New France heard of his death, they celebrated the Mass of Thanksgiving instead of the usual Requiem Mass. For five of these Jesuits in New France, their own martyrdom was not far off.

On July 4, 1648, Father Antoine Daniel had just celebrated Mass at the Huron village of Teanaustaye, near what was later Hillsdale, Ontario. All the Huron warriors were away from the village when the Iroquois attacked. Daniel hurriedly baptized the women, children, and old men who came to him and urged them to escape through an opening in the palisade. The invaders set fire to the village and killed those who had not escaped in time. Daniel, still wearing his Mass vestments, came out of the chapel to meet the Iroquois. For a moment, stopped by the sight of the priest as he calmly approached them, the Iroquois merely stared. Then they sent a shower of arrows at him and a gunshot killed him.

Father Jean de Brébeuf, at 56 the oldest French missionary in Canada, was one of the first Jesuits sent from France (in 1625) to work among the natives. On March 16, 1649, he and Father Gabriel Lalemant were captured during an Iroquois raid into Huron territory and martyred in the village of St. Ignace, not far from Fort Sainte Marie. Brébeuf died under torture that day and Father Lalemant the following morning.

Father Charles Garnier met martyrdom on December 7, 1649, in another Iroquois raid. Alone among his Huron converts and friends in the village of St. Jean, he blessed and baptized them and urged them to flee from the oncoming Iroquois. As he ran from house to house, an Iroquois shot him three times, tore off his cassock and his black robe, and rushed off in pursuit of the fleeing Huron. The priest recovered sufficiently to try to drag himself toward a mortally wounded Huron to give him absolution, but before he could reach his convert, he was killed.

Garnier's companion, Father Noël Chabanel, was away at the time and never returned. Later a Huron confessed that out of hatred for the faith, which he blamed for all his misfortunes, he had killed Chabanel as he was returning to the mission on December 8, 1649, and had thrown the body into the Nottawasaga River in Ontario.

Remains of three of the eight North American Martyrs (Jean de Brébeuf, Gabriel Lalemant, and Charles Garnier) were partially recovered and enshrined in reliquaries at the National Shrine of the North American Martyrs in Auriesville, New York, and in its Canadian counterpart, the Martyr's Shrine in Midland, Ontario.

The *Peggy Stewart* Incident

The Boston Tea Party, the most famous demonstration against the British Tea Act of 1773 (see related articles throughout this book), inspired violent resistance to the hated legislation in several other American localities as well. In April 1774 the Sons of Liberty dumped tea into New York harbor, and in June and September of the same year mobs forced a Portsmouth, New Hampshire, merchant to reship his cargoes of tea to Nova Scotia. The following December rebels in Greenwich, New Jersey, set fire to a tea shipment. Similar public outrage met efforts to land the duties tea leaves at Annapolis, Maryland, and it was there that one of the most serious incidents of 1774 took place.

On May 14, 1774, the *Peggy Stewart* left London carrying more than a ton of tea that Thomas C. Williams had consigned to his brothers and business partners, James and Joseph, in Annapolis. Williams's action was ill advised. Even before the brig had reached its destination, J. J. Johnson, the London agent for another Annapolis firm, wrote home: "I would not be surprised to hear that you made a Bon Fire of the *Peggy Stewart* as I have a hint that a certain T[homas] W[illiams] has ship'd Tea on Board of her." Johnson accurately prophesied the fate of the vessel and its cargo.

When the *Peggy Stewart* arrived in Annapolis on October 14, its owner, Anthony Stewart, first tried to enter the ship and all the cargo except the tea at the customhouse. The customs official, however, ruled that the entire cargo had to be entered. Stewart yielded to his demand and paid the duty on the tea. News of this action enraged the local rebels, and the Annapolis Committee of Observation immediately called a meeting to deal with the

emergency. Some of those present at this gathering wanted to land and burn the tea without further discussion, but others objected. They argued that no action should be taken on a matter of such importance without consulting all of the inhabitants of Anne Arundel County, in which Annapolis was located. This opinion prevailed, and on October 14 a town meeting was called for October 19.

Both the local committee and Stewart used the next five days to persuade the public of the correctness of their respective positions. The rebels circulated handbills throughout the county, advising the populace that Stewart's actions had jeopardized their liberties. Stewart replied to this charge with a detailed explanation. In defense of his behavior, he disclaimed ever having any interest in the cargo of the *Peggy Stewart*. He argued that the presence of more than 50 passengers aboard his leaky ship had bound him "both in humanity and prudence to enter the vessel and leave the destination of the tea to the Committee."

Stewart's claims had little effect on the citizens who gathered in Annapolis on October 19. Before that date they had judged Stewart and the Williams brothers guilty of offensive behavior. The meeting concerned itself only with obtaining the offenders' signatures on a prepared apology and determining an appropriate punishment. The first matter presented no problem: Stewart and the Williams brothers readily agreed "to acknowledge that we have committed a most daring insult and act of the most pernicious tendency to the liberties of America." Less easily determined was the matter of punishment.

Although the populace unanimously voted to burn the tea, this did not satisfy "the gentlemen from Elk Ridge and Baltimore Town" who called for total destruction of the *Peggy Stewart*. Seven-eighths of the assembly rejected this demand, but the extremists would not be denied. Throughout the day of October 19, they repeatedly threatened Stewart's home and family. Finally, to prevent further violence, the shipowner agreed to burn his vessel. Accompanied by the Williams brothers and some of the radicals, Stewart boarded his ship and sailed to Windmill Point, where he ran it aground. There, Stewart personally set his brig and the entire cargo aflame.

The rebels' harassment of Stewart temporarily ceased after the destruction of his vessel. However, prior to the incident Stewart had been considered a Tory, and after his experience he again took up his opposition to "the enemies of Government." The rebels in turn resumed their tactics. They hanged and burned Stewart in effigy throughout the county, and they eventually forced him to leave his wife, family, and property for the safety of England.

The *"Peggy Stewart* Tea Party," unlike its counterpart in Boston, provoked no response from the British government. England was then attempting to strengthen Loyalist feeling in the southern colonies, and retaliatory measures might have alienated many potential supporters. In addition, there was a basic difference between the tea parties at Boston and Annapolis. In the former harbor, the rebels had destroyed tea belonging to the British East India Company. In the latter, the actual owners of the brig and its cargo of tea had set their goods aflame.

American Revolution: The British Surrender at Yorktown

At 2:00 p.m. on October 19, 1781, Lieutenant General Lord Charles Cornwallis's more than 7,000 British and Hessian troops unhappily tramped down the Hampton Road outside Yorktown, Virginia, to surrender themselves to their American and French adversaries, commanded by General George Washington. There is a tradition that the British band played "The World Turned Upside Down." Indeed the world had altered, since the colonial victory at Yorktown marked the death knell for British control of the 13 American colonies. The peace treaty recognizing American independence would not be signed until September 3, 1783, nor ratified until January 14, 1784, but the sporadic fighting that occurred in the intervening two years was largely insignificant.

The battle of Yorktown took place partially because of disunity within the British high command. General Sir Henry Clinton, the head of the royal forces in America, captured Charleston, South Carolina, in 1780. He returned to New York City and put Lord Cornwallis in charge of the southern district, with strict orders to protect South Carolina. Clinton believed that the British should remain on the defensive, holding key cities like New York, Charleston, and Savannah until the acquisition of 10,000 reinforcements would make more aggressive action possible. The younger, more adventurous Cornwallis wanted to invade North Carolina. His defeat of the colonists under General Horatio Gates at Camden, South Carolina, on August 16, 1780, won the support of Lord George Germain, the secretary of state for the colonies; but defeats in South Carolina at Kings Mountain (October 7, 1780) and Cowpens (January 17, 1781), and a Pyrrhic victory in North Carolina at Guilford Court House (March 15, 1781) thwarted Cornwallis's plans for that region. Therefore, he took his army to Virginia, where he established a base on the York River at Yorktown.

The rebel victory there resulted in large measure from well-coordinated American and French operations. Forces under Washington and Jean-Baptiste-Donatien de Vimeur, Comte de Rochambeau, spent the early summer of 1781 unsuccessfully probing Clinton's defenses near New York City. Then word arrived on August 14 that Admiral François-Joseph-Paul de Grasse would bring his French fleet and more than 3,000 troops to the Chesapeake area and remain there for joint operations until the middle of October. Washington seized the opportunity to trap Cornwallis. He advised the Marquis de Lafayette, who was in Virginia with a large number of troops of the Continental army, to keep the English bottled up on the Yorktown Peninsula. The American commander then prepared to move south. On August 21 some 7,000 allied troops, including Rochambeau's 5,000 French, left their New York encampments and slipped past Clinton for Virginia. On September 5 Admiral de Grasse defeated the British fleet under Sir Thomas Graves off the Chesapeake Capes, and on September 9 Admiral Paul-François-Jean-Nicolas de Barras arrived safely from Rhode Island with siege artillery and provisions. Cornwallis was doomed. The French and American forces slowly enveloped the British positions and by October 6 were ready to begin siege operations. In a night attack on October 15 they captured several strategic positions, and on October 17 Cornwallis asked for terms. As demanded, all of his men surrendered two days later.

Washington's aide-de-camp, Lieutenant Colonel Tench Tilghman, officially informed the Continental Congress in Philadelphia of the good news. Congress voted special honors to the French commanders Rochambeau and de Grasse, and of course to George Washington.

October 20

World War II: General Douglas MacArthur Returns to the Philippines

In the three weeks after the Japanese attack on Pearl Harbor, the Philippine Islands were the scene of desperate defenses led by General Douglas MacArthur and Major General Jonathan M. Wainwright. When Manila and Cavite fell to the Japanese on January 2, 1942, the American and Filipino forces withdrew to the Bataan Peninsula, where they resisted a siege for three months. Bataan fell on April 19 and the defenders retreated to Corregidor Island in Manila Bay. Finally, on May 6 Wainwright surrendered Corregidor and its garrison of 11,500 (see related essays throughout this book).

During the battle for the Philippines, President Franklin D. Roosevelt directed General MacArthur to leave the islands for Australia, where he was to become supreme commander of the Allied forces in the Southwest Pacific Area. MacArthur left Corregidor by boat on March 11 and reached Australia on March 17. Arriving in Australia, MacArthur told reporters of his determination to avenge Allied losses: "The President of the United States ordered me to break through the Japanese lines and proceed from Corregidor to Australia for the purpose, as I understand it, of organizing the American offensive against Japan, a primary object of which is the relief of the Philippines. I came through and I shall return."

MacArthur fulfilled his promise two and a half years later, on October 20, 1944, when he waded ashore at Leyte Island on the first day of the American invasion of the Philippines.

American strategy, developed in the early days of World War II, called for two lines of advance against the Japanese. Admiral Chester W. Nimitz, commander in chief of Pacific Ocean Areas, was to attack westward from the Hawaiian islands. General MacArthur was to proceed northward from Australia. Early in 1944 forces within MacArthur's Southwest Pacific command fought to secure Papua (the southeastern section of New Guinea), seized the Admiralty Islands, and began a series of amphibious assaults along the northern coast of New Guinea. In the Central Pacific Area, forces under Nimitz's command took the Gilbert Islands late in 1943 and invaded the Marshall Islands early in 1944. Meanwhile, additional encounters, including the struggle for the bitterly contested western Solomon Islands, were taking place in other areas of the Pacific. By March 1944 the Joint Chiefs of Staff in Washington, D.C., agreed that the Allies should return to the Philippines, and they proposed November 1944 as the date for an invasion of Mindanao, the southernmost and largest of the Philippine Islands.

During the spring and summer of 1944, MacArthur continued his offensive across the northern coast of New Guinea, leapfrogging his forces in a series of amphibious operations supported by air cover from Nimitz's carriers. By the end of July, MacArthur was at New Guinea's northwest tip. Meanwhile, Nimitz moved farther westward across the Central Pacific. His carrier forces defeated the bulk of the Japanese fleet on June 19 and 20 in the battle of the Philippine Sea. His army and marine divisions took the island of Saipan in July and then stormed Guam. By mid-September 1944, with the invasions of Morotai and the Palau Islands, the stage was set for the retaking of the Philippines.

Flying in support of the Morotai and Palau landings, Admiral William Halsey's carrier planes bombed the central Philippines on September 12 and 14, 1944. The Japanese offered little resistance, and Halsey recommended that MacArthur and Nimitz change the next major objective from Mindanao in the southern Philippines to Leyte. More centrally located, Leyte offered the Allies potential air and logistical bases from which to carry out further operations. The target lay beyond the reach of land-based planes, but Nimitz offered to make aircraft carrier support available. MacArthur immediately agreed to the proposal and set October 20, 1944, as the new date for his return to the Philippines.

Coordinated army and navy operations underlay the Leyte plans. Lieutenant General Walter Krueger's Sixth Army, with over 200,000 men, was responsible for the actual invasion of the island. On October 17 an Army Ranger battalion landed on Dinagat and Suluan, two of several small islands that guard the entrance to Leyte Gulf. However, poor weather conditions forced the postponement of further landings until October 18. Minesweepers began operations to clear the waters for the troop carriers, and on October 20 the full invasion began. At 9:30 a.m. the 21st Regimental Combat Team captured the Panaon Strait. Four divisions then began to land in Leyte Gulf.

Behind the third assault wave of American troops, MacArthur waded ashore on Leyte with Philippine president Sergio Osmeìa. Standing in pouring rain on the island, MacArthur spoke by radio: "People of the Philippines: I have returned. By the grace of Almighty God, our forces stand again on Philippine soil; soil consecrated by the blood of our two peoples." Reporting that President Osmeña was with him, MacArthur urged the Filipinos to rally to him:

> Let the indomitable spirit of Bataan and Corregidor lead on . . . In the name of your sacred dead, strike! Let no heart be faint. Let every arm be steeled. The guidance of Divine God points the way. Follow in His Name to the Holy Grail of righteous victory.

By the end of the year, the Americans secured the rest of Leyte in hard fought campaigns that cost them 15,584 casualties and the Japanese well over 70,000. On January 31, 1945, the 11th Airborne Division made an amphibious landing at Nasugbu, southwest of Manila, and began a drive toward the capital. By February 3 two vanguard columns from the First Cavalry reached the outskirts of the city and seized Malacañan Palace, the official residence of the president of the Philippines. The last Japanese resistance in Manila was overcome by March 4.

Even as the fighting raged, MacArthur reestablished the Philippine government. On February 27, 1945, MacArthur announced the restoration of the constitutional government of President Osmeña in a ceremony at the Malacañan Palace. On July 5, having defeated the remaining Japanese forces in the islands, MacArthur announced that "All the Philippines are now liberated."

Convention of 1818 Signed

On October 20, 1818, representatives of the United States and Great Britain signed a convention in London. The terms of this agreement established the northernmost limits of the Louisiana Purchase by setting the boundary between the United States and Canada at the 49th parallel from the Lake of the Woods west to the crest of the Rocky Mountains. In addition, the 1818 document provided that Oregon country, which lay west of the Rockies, would remain open to settlement by both American and British citizens for ten years without either nation's forfeiting its territorial claim in the Pacific Northwest.

The convention of 1818 also dealt with matters not directly related to territorial disputes. One article granted American citizens fishing rights in the coastal waters of Labrador and Newfoundland. Another renewed the commercial agreement of 1815 that permitted the United States to trade in the East Indies and ended discriminatory duties on imported goods.

October 21

Electric Light Bulb Perfected

On October 21, 1879, Thomas Edison and his associates in Menlo Park, New Jersey, tested an incandescent light bulb that burned for a recorded 13 ½ hours. Their experiment demonstrated the feasibility of electric lighting and thus marked the beginning of a new era.

Edison was not the first to try to devise an electric light bulb. During the half century preceding his achievement, scientists throughout the world had attempted to develop a practical technique for electric lighting. Experiments in Great Britain, Russia, and the United States led to devices that utilized platinum or carbon conductors enclosed in glass globes or tubes. However, the results were disappointing, since these early incandescent light bulbs burned for only a few moments.

Edison briefly experimented with electric lighting in 1876 and again in 1877, but both times he abandoned the project without making any significant advances. In 1878, however, his interest in electric lighting revived. He felt frustrated with the work on the phonograph that had been occupying his attention, and he later recalled, "Just at that time I wanted to take up something new." With the encouragement of Grosvenor P. Lowrey, the general counsel for Western Union, and Professor George F. Barker of the University of Pennsylvania, Edison launched the research project that ultimately produced one of the world's greatest inventions.

Before beginning his own experiments, Edison carefully studied the work of others. He also traveled to Ansonia, Connecticut, in September 1878 to see a display of electric arc lights. The exhibit greatly impressed Edison, but it did not convince him of the utility of the arc light, and he commented to his host William Wallace, "I believe I can beat you making the electric light. I do not think you are working in the right direction."

Late in the autumn of 1878, Edison gave a press interview during which he made public his intention to devise an electrical system capable of lighting New York City. At the time that Edison made his announcement, electric arc lights had been installed in several areas, including the Avenue de l'Opéra in Paris and John Wanamaker's department store in Philadelphia. These lights burned in open globes, emitted a blinding glare and noxious odors, and were wired to a dynamo in series so that they could not be individually operated. Edison was convinced that further work with arc lights would not produce a practical means of household lighting. Instead, he proposed to create an entirely different electric lighting system, one that would be modeled closely on the gas lighting systems that then illuminated many American cities.

Edison's plan seemed visionary. The gas lighting systems then in existence permitted a central gashouse to supply energy via gas mains and smaller branch pipes to thousands of individual jets that could be individually turned on or off. To develop a similar electrical lighting system, Edison not only had to produce a workable light bulb, but had to deal with much more perplexing problems involving electrical resistance, distribution of power, and pressure fluctuation in electrical conductors.

Confident that he could overcome these problems, Edison began work on the project. By choosing to create an entire lighting system rather than a single device, he gained a perspective that eventually allowed him to resolve the difficulties that had stymied other inventors and scientists. He was forced to consider the problems of power distribution and consumption that his predecessors had basically ignored. They had wired their devices to the power source in a series and had constructed low-resistance lights that consumed large quantities of current. Edison realized that such apparatuses were impractical for the lighting network he envisioned, and he decided to investigate other possibilities. He turned his attention to parallel wiring, which would permit each unit to operate independently of the others in a circuit, and he began work on a high-resistance incandescent light bulb that would use little current.

To finance his search for a practical means of electric lighting, Edison's friend and adviser Grosvenor Lowrey persuaded some of the wealthiest people in the United States to invest in the project. In the autumn of 1878 the Edison Electric Light Company was formed to "own, manufacture, operate and license the use of various apparatus used in producing light, heat and power by electricity." In return for agreeing to assign to the corporation any invention or improvement he might make in electric lighting during the following five years, Edison received 2,500 shares of company stock. For their part, such important financial figures as William Henry Vanderbilt, Western Union president Norvin Green, and J. P. Morgan's partner Eggisto Fabbri agreed to pay $50,000 for Edison Electric's remaining 500 shares of stock.

To create a high-resistance incandescent light bulb, Edison first had to find a material that could sustain high temperatures without fusing, melting, or burning out. Although he had a substantial knowledge of the uses of carbon from his work with the phonograph, he was unsuccessful in his initial experiments using strips of carbonized paper for the "burner" or "partial conductor" in the glass globe. Similarly fruitless were his efforts, also in the autumn of 1878, to make a burner out of platinum wire. However, these attempts made Edison aware of the need to produce a greater vacuum in his glass container and to calculate the exact resistance of potential burner materials.

Although Edison originally boasted that his lighting system would be completed within six weeks, the project proved to be much more complicated than he had expected. By the end of the winter of 1878–1879, he and his associates at Menlo Park had experimented with a wide variety of materials in their search for a suitable burner. With the new Sprengel pump, they had raised the vacuum in their glass globes to within one or two millimeters of a total vacuum, and in addition they completed extensive mathematical calculations for electrical conductors, lamp resistance, and dynamo capacities. Their efforts yielded a considerable

amount of valuable data, but even more work remained ahead.

Throughout the spring and summer of 1879, Edison's team concentrated on three major problems: (1) the development of a dynamo that could power their new lighting system, which would require a constant-voltage current in a multiple circuit; (2) the production of a higher vacuum in the glass globe of their incandescent light bulb; and (3) the search for a perfect incandescent material. By the autumn of 1879 they had completed work on a dynamo that converted steam power into electrical energy with 90 percent efficiency and they succeeded in excluding all but a one-millionth part of an atmosphere from their light globes. However, they were still struggling to find the right incandescent material.

After experimenting with more than 1,500 materials for the burner in his light bulb, by the summer of 1879 Edison had resumed his work with carbon. His earlier work with carbon had been unsuccessful because carbon in its natural state is porous and tends to absorb gases. However, during his year of experimentation Edison had learned that it was possible to expel occluded gases by sending a current through the burner material and heating it at the same time that air was being pumped out of the glass globe of the light bulb. This procedure gave the burner substance a greater resistance to high temperature, and permitted Edison to perfect the light bulb with a carbon illuminant, the precursor of today's modern light bulb.

For months Edison and his associates experimented with threadlike carbon filaments. By October 1879, feeling that success was near, they worked around the clock. After hundreds of tests, their labors were rewarded on October 21, 1879. Using a filament of ordinary cotton thread that had been packed with powdered carbon in an earthenware crucible and then heated to a high temperature, Edison began the ninth of a series of experiments. At 1:30 a.m. he attached the filament to a power source. Thirteen and a half hours later, at 3:00 p.m. the following afternoon, the still-burning light demonstrated the feasibility of electric lighting.

On December 21, 1879, the *New York Herald* publicized Edison's successful experiment of October 21. The announcement was greeted with amazement, and the Wizard of Menlo Park (as Edison was nicknamed) was praised both in the United States and abroad.

October 22

Cuban Missile Crisis

In a televised address on October 22, 1962, President John F. Kennedy declared that the United States would take whatever steps were necessary to force the removal from neighboring Cuba of offensive weapons and installations (namely missiles, launching sites, and jet bombers) that had been placed there by the Soviet Union. Pending compliance with this demand, Kennedy announced the imposition of a naval "quarantine" to prevent the further importation of offensive weapons into Cuba.

Failing compliance, the president added, the quarantine (in effect a limited blockade) would merely be an initial step toward more serious military action. Furthermore, he declared that it would be American policy to regard "any nuclear missile launched from Cuba against any nation in the Western Hemisphere as an attack by the Soviet Union on the United States requiring a full retaliatory response on the Soviet Union."

Despite the danger of nuclear confrontation with the Soviet Union, the American naval quarantine went into effect on October 24. For five long days, during which several Cuba-bound Soviet vessels altered their course, the world held its breath. Finally, on October 28 Soviet premier Nikita Sergeyevich Khrushchev informed the United States that the offensive weapons would be removed as quickly as possible.

The Soviet decision was apparently news to Cuban leader Fidel Castro, who regarded it as a betrayal of his alliance with the Soviet Union. Castro's denunciations notwithstanding, the offensive missiles were removed and the missile bases were dismantled by November 20, and the bombers were withdrawn by early December 1962. These developments were preceded by the visits to Cuba of United Nations secretary general U. Thant, who played a key role in the negotiations, and Soviet first deputy premier Anastas Ivanovich Mikoyan.

Krushchev was ousted from power in October 1964 for various reasons that included failures in his agricultural policies. One of his errors, however, was reported to have been the Cuban missile episode (see the related essays throughout this book).

Timothy Leary's Birthday

Timothy Francis Leary, one of the most famous figures of the counterculture movement in the 1960s, was born on October 22, 1920, in Springfield, Massachusetts. A psychologist by training, during the 1940s and 1950s he worked on several projects concerning human interaction and new ideas such as group therapy, and eventually became a professor at Harvard University.

Leary began experimenting with hallucinogenic drugs in the 1960s. He was terminated from his professorship after distributing psilocybin, contained in hallucinogenic mushrooms, to hundreds of students as part of a "study." Leary argued that he was studying the emotional, physical, and social effects on graduate-level volunteers with the goal of finding a cure for mental illness and for violent criminals. When a new drug called Lysergic acid diethylamide (or LSD) appeared, Leary began to experiment with that as well, coming to believe that the substance had positive spiritual, mental, and emotional effects. He did the bulk of his research in Millbrook, New York, surrounded by devotees of the budding "hippie" and antiestablishment movement who were increasingly involved in drug experimentation, often in the hope of achieving greater awareness.

Leary publicly advocated what he considered to be the beneficial aspects of LSD and acquired popular notoriety as a "drug guru" of the 1960s. There were a number of encounters with the authorities, including several police raids on his residence. Nevertheless, Leary continued to advocate the "safe" use of LSD and even published several "instruction manuals" for users. Leary's most famous comment is probably his recommendation to the youngsters of the counterculture movement to "turn on, tune in, drop out." This was essentially a recommendation to experiment with drugs, embrace the music and lifestyle of the 1960s, and reject traditional societal values.

Leary's troubles with the law included an unsuccessful flight to Switzerland for asylum, followed by his extradition and imprisonment. By the time he was released in 1976, the counter-culture movement had largely died. Leary moved to California and became a computer enthusiast, writing programs and authoring a number of books, in addition to appearing on the lecture circuit. Even though Leary was diagnosed with cancer in the early 1990s he remained active, taking a particular interest in the Internet and the World Wide Web. He died on May 31, 1996, in Beverly Hills, California.

October 23

World War II: The Battle of Leyte Gulf

From October 23 to October 26, a decisive naval battle was fought in the Pacific between American and Japanese forces off the Philippine island of Leyte. The battle was precipitated by the American landings on Leyte (see October 20, General Douglas MacArthur Returns to the Philippines), which convinced the Japanese High Command that an all-out effort should be made to stop the campaign of island-hopping that was bringing the Americans closer and closer to Japan itself. If MacArthur's forces, which had landed on Leyte's beaches and were struggling under fire to advance into the mountainous interior, could be attacked from the water as well as the land, they might be crushed, and the reconquest of the Philippines would be halted.

However, for *Sho-Go* ("Operation Victory") to succeed, some of the American ships and planes that were supporting the landing would have to be lured away from the area, so that the Japanese navy could strike. Therefore the Japanese divided their own forces into three parts. One part, coming from Japan, was ordered to stand out to sea and serve as a decoy, in the hope of drawing American ships and planes of the Third Fleet away from Leyte itself. This force included several aircraft carriers and many of Japan's dreaded *kamikaze* (suicide pilots). Two other forces, coming from Singapore and armed with heavy guns, would go around Leyte from the south and from the north, to converge on the Americans in the gulf, who (it was hoped) would be caught by surprise with little support. (The assault was timed to come on a day when many of the American ships would be engaged in refueling operations, so that it would be hard for them to move around.) After the invaders were destroyed, the plan went, the combined Japanese fleet would attack the American Third Fleet from the rear and finish it off. Sho-Go was a good plan from the tactical point of view, but a desperate gamble given Japan's diminishing resources.

The first contact was made on October 23, by two American submarines who were prowling the South China Sea when they unexpectedly encountered a large, fast-moving enemy fleet. They immediately radioed the information back to headquarters and then sank two Japanese cruisers. One of the submarines was subsequently lost when it scraped bottom on a coral reef, but its crew were saved by native partisans; the other acquired a

companion and continued to shadow the enemy fleet, reporting on its location, speed, and direction.

As the Battle of Leyte Gulf was a very large battle, it was also very confusing to the participants. Great numbers of ships and aircraft were in motion over a very wide area. On October 24, American search planes spotted the two fleets from Singapore and an air war began. Waves of Japanese planes attacked American ships and destroyed the aircraft carrier *Princeton*; on the other side, an American bomber hit the battleship *Musashi*. For much of the 24th, however, the opposing forces maneuvered for position while their commanders tried to figure out exactly where the enemy were and what their intentions might be. The heaviest fighting erupted on October 25, in the small hours of the morning. At that time the Japanese force commanded by Vice Admiral Teiji Nishimura coming around the southern side of Leyte was ambushed in the Surigao Strait by the American Seventh Fleet, under the command of Rear Admiral Jesse Olendorf, and virtually annihilated. The Japanese fleet coming around the north side of the island, however, passed through the San Bernadino Strait almost unopposed and approached Leyte Gulf, where it inflicted terrible damage on the more lightly armed American vessels that were guarding the landing area. At one point the Japanese commander, Admiral Takeo Kurita, was in a position to attack the landing itself, but he drew back, realizing that something had happened to the ships that were supposed to meet him there and fearing an American trap. In fact, the Americans had fallen into the Japanese trap. Admiral William "Bull" Halsey had spotted the decoy and gone after it with the better part of the U.S. Third Fleet. This was just what the Japanese had hoped would happen, but Halsey's forces were more aggressive than anticipated: They overtook the decoy fleet and sank most of it before hastening back to Leyte Gulf.

By the 26th, the Japanese were in full retreat, harried by American planes. The Americans had lost six large warships, but the Japanese had lost 24. Casualties were heavy on both sides, and included, significantly, most of Japan's experienced pilots. After the Battle of Leyte Gulf, the Japanese navy was no longer a serious threat to Allied plans.

Francis Hopkinson Smith's Birthday

Francis Hopkinson Smith, one of the most versatile Americans of his generation, was born in Baltimore, Maryland, on October 23, 1838. A maternal great-grandfather, Francis Hopkinson, was a poet and a signer of the Declaration of Independence.

His father, Francis Smith, distinguished himself as a musician, philosopher, and mathematician. The younger Smith continued his family's tradition of wide interests and gained fame as an engineer, artist, and writer.

Financial necessity forced Smith to begin his career as a shipping clerk in his brother's iron foundry, but neither Baltimore nor his brother's business held a lasting attraction for him. Shortly after the Civil War, he moved to New York City, where he set himself up as an engineer. His enterprise flourished and he won important government contracts, including those for the Block Island breakwater, the foundation of the Statue of Liberty, and the Race Rock Lighthouse. Smith considered the latter structure his greatest engineering achievement, and the lighthouse, situated in the rough waters six miles off the coast of New London, Connecticut, demanded the utmost use of its designer's innovative and technical abilities.

Engineering was Smith's occupation, art his passion. A proponent of "art for its own sake and not as a mere means of making money," he believed that a clear-cut distinction between art and earning a livelihood would keep the former "high and noble, [a person's] worthiest and best expression." For 30 years Smith lived by this dictum, devoting his work week to engineering and his spare time to art. His European vacations provided him with his best opportunities to indulge his artistic interests. During one stay in the Mediterranean region he completed 53 pictures in an equal number of days. However, despite the relatively brief periods he allowed for painting, Smith's works are not without artistic merit. He is best known for his watercolors of Venice and charcoal sketchings.

At the age of 53 Smith published his first fictional work, *Colonel Carter of Cartersville*. This collection of tales about an impoverished aristocrat in the post–Civil War South proved so successful that its author gave up his engineering business and turned to writing as a full-time career. Smith wrote many novels, short stories, and travel accounts during the next two decades, some of which were semiautobiographical. He died in New York City on April 7, 1915.

October 24

The United Nations Formally Comes into Existence

During World War II approximately 25 million to 30 million military personnel and civilians were killed, and the property damage was so great that it was impossible to estimate. No war in history had ever produced such appalling statistics. Even before the fighting ended, the Allied leaders recognized their obligation to attempt to prevent a repetition of this tragedy. Toward this end, they began preparations for the creation of a new international organization designed to help maintain world peace.

As early as October 1943 the foreign ministers of Great Britain, the Soviet Union, and the United States met in Moscow and agreed to establish a new peacekeeping organization. During the following year a number of conferences of the so-called United Nations, namely those countries that had agreed to cooperate in the fight against the Axis powers according to the principles laid down in the Atlantic Charter, dealt with specific problems arising from the war. To aid countries that had fallen under Axis control, the United Nations Relief and Rehabilitation Administration was set up on November 9, 1943. To restore and expand educational opportunities, the United Nations Organization for Educational and Cultural Reconstruction was proposed in April 1944. To stabilize international finances the United Nations Monetary and Financial Conference, otherwise known as the Bretton Woods Conference, was held from July 1 to July 22, 1944.

The first discussions concerning the actual establishment of the proposed international peacekeeping organization took place at the Dumbarton Oaks estate in Washington, D.C. Meeting between August 21 and September 27, 1944, representatives of the United States, Great Britain, the Soviet Union, and Nationalist China considered various problems pertaining to the structure of the new agency. The results of these talks, which were released in October 1944, became the basis for the United Nations Charter.

Only one major question, namely voting procedures in the United Nations Security Council, remained unresolved after October 1944. At Dumbarton Oaks the Soviet delegates had insisted that the permanent members of the council should have the right to bar discussion of disputes in which they were involved. The United States would not accept this plan.

On February 3 and 4, 1945, President Franklin D. Roosevelt, British prime minister Winston Churchill, and Soviet premier Joseph Stalin met at Yalta in the Soviet Union to consider among other matters the organization of the United Nations and the critical voting procedure problem in the Security Council. Their talks produced important results. The Soviet Union was allowed three votes in the General Assembly, since the Ukraine and Byelorussia (White Russia) were to be considered independent nations for voting purposes.

The Soviets abandoned their former demands and agreed to a voting formula that allowed each permanent member of the Security Council veto power over the final decisions rather than over the discussions of that body.

With the Big Three powers in agreement on all major issues concerning the structure and organization of the United Nations, representatives of 46 nations gathered at the Opera House in San Francisco, California, on April 25, 1945, to draft the organization's charter. The document, which they unanimously approved on June 26, 1945, provided for the six chief organs of the United Nations: (1) the General Assembly, or policy-making body; (2) the Security Council, which in theory functions in continuous session to resolve international military and political problems; (3) the Economic and Social Council, which is entrusted with the preservation of fundamental human rights and freedoms; (4) the International Court of Justice, which mediates legal disputes between countries; (5) the Trusteeship Council, which was to administer former colonies or "trust territories"; and (6) the Secretariat or administrative agency.

Ratification of the United Nations Charter by the signatory nations was swift. Even the United States Senate, which had rejected the League of Nations three decades earlier, acted quickly and on July 28, 1945, approved American membership. By October 24 the requisite 29 nations, including the five permanent members of the Security Council (Great Britain, France, the United States, the Soviet Union, and China), had ratified the charter and it was on that day that the United Nations came into formal existence. The headquarters of the United Nations is located in New York City, New York.

War Powers Resolution

A historic showdown between the executive branch and the legislative branch of the United States government occurred on October 24, 1973, when President Richard M. Nixon vetoed a bill restricting the president's power to engage American armed in military situations. This bill is popularly known as the War Powers Resolution.

Article I, section 8 of the Constitution grants Congress the exclusive power to declare war. Article II, section 2 vests the president with the powers of commander in chief over the American military. However, it is not clear from the Constitution when the president must obtain a formal declaration of war from Congress before sending American forces into a foreign conflict. The Vietnam War caused this constitutional issue to arise in a way that it never had before.

The Gulf of Tonkin Resolution, passed by Congress on August 7, 1964, provided Congressional approval for military action in Vietnam but fell short of a formal declaration of war. Nevertheless, a war was waged and, with no end in sight, became increasingly unpopular at home. As protests mounted, President Lyndon B. Johnson, who had pursued the war vigorously, decided not to seek reelection. Nixon, the Republican who became president after the November 1968 elections, took office in the face of a growing antiwar movement and a Democrat-controlled Congress. Unable to gain broad support for increased military action but determined not to be the man who "lost" Vietnam, Nixon resorted to a number of covert operations. One of these was the secret bombing of enemy bases located in Cambodia, a neutral country beset with its own internal problems and too weak to prevent infiltration across its borders by either the North Vietnamese looking for a safe retreat or the Americans looking to retaliate. The United States began bombing these enemy bases, which were located in the dense Cambodian jungle far from major cities, in 1969 and continued to do so until 1973, when news of the action leaked out. There was also evidence that the Nixon administration had withheld information and misrepresented facts to Congress.

In an attempt to regain some control, Congress passed the War Powers Resolution in 1973. This limited the president's power to use the military abroad, established reporting requirements, and gave the president only 60 days to use forces in foreign conflicts before having to obtain congressional approval. When Nixon vetoed the resolution, he claimed it was "both unconstitutional and dangerous." However, Congress overrode his veto on November 7, 1973, and the measure went into effect. The War Powers Resolution has remained controversial and has never been tested in court. It is, however, the law, and during the 1990s it had considerable influence on the conduct of military actions in Somalia and Kosovo.

October 25

Richard E. Byrd's Birthday

Admiral Richard Evelyn Byrd, the pioneer aviator and explorer of the Antarctic, was born on October 25, 1888, in Winchester, Virginia. He began exploring early when he was 12 by traveling alone around the world. After attending the Shenandoah Valley Military Academy, Virginia Military Institute, and the University of Virginia, he entered the United States Naval Academy at Annapolis, Maryland. Elected president of his class while a plebe, he was also a member of the football squad and gymnastics team, pursuits that resulted in fractures of his right foot and ankle. They caused him to miss his semiannual examinations and led to a months-long bout with the ankle injury and a race to catch up with his studies. Years after his graduation in 1912, he recalled that "this terrific struggle . . . to graduate taught me a great lesson: that it is by struggle that we progress."

Byrd was assigned to active navy duty, but his injured leg proved too weak for standing long watches, which caused pain throughout his body. He was retired for physical disability in March 1916 but recalled two months later. In his new assignment he worked to organize the navy's Commission on Training Camps, and worried that he would not see combat duty in World War I. The resulting strain on his health was severe. He lost 25 pounds and was ordered by a medical board to take a leave of absence.

He had, however, won the board's permission to learn how to fly aircraft when he fully recuperated. The prospect, which excited him, was better than any medicine. He was pronounced in perfect health two months later, reported to the Naval Aeronautic Station at Pensacola, Florida, and was a full-fledged naval aviator by the spring of 1918. "From that moment . . . ," he later wrote, "my ambition was to make a career out of aviation. Not merely in the sense of routine flying, but rather in the pioneering sense."

During World War I, Byrd commanded the American air patrol operating from Canada. In administrative positions, he subsequently devised several instruments for aerial navigation and played an important role in the development of naval aviation reserves and in the enactment of navy-oriented legislation, such as the establishment of the navy's Bureau of Aeronautics.

His career in polar exploration began in 1925, when he was named commander of the naval aviation unit accompanying Donald B. MacMillan's expedition to the North Polar regions, sponsored by the National Geographic Society. The next year, Byrd and Floyd Bennett returned to the area and on May 9, 1926, became the first persons to fly over the North Pole. At least, that is what Byrd reported; many historians think he fell short of the goal by about 150 miles, and some think he may even have known it. These doubts did not arise at the time, however. Byrd received the Congressional Medal of Honor, the Distinguished Service Medal, and the society's Hubbard Medal. He was praised for his courage by President Calvin Coolidge in an address to National Geographic Society members, and he was promoted to the rank of

commander. He recorded his experiences in *Skyward* (1928). A year later Byrd and three companions were saluted by New Yorkers with a ticker-tape parade up Broadway after making the first nonstop flight to Europe by a multiengined aircraft.

Byrd won additional support from the National Geographic Society for his first expedition to Antarctica (1928–1930). His party set out from New York on August 25, 1928, and in December established a base, Little America, from which Byrd and three others made the first flight over the South Pole on November 29, 1929. The expedition also mapped some 150,000 square miles of Antarctica. Promoted to the rank of rear admiral, Byrd received the society's special medal of honor from President Herbert Hoover and released the report *Little America* in 1930.

His second Antarctic expedition (1933–1935), also with the backing of the National Geographic Society, resulted in the exploration of more than 450,000 square miles of territory. Byrd, who journeyed 123 miles south of the expedition's main Antarctic base to spend a solitary five months making weather observations in a shack beneath the ice, almost lost his life through carbon monoxide poisoning from a defective stove. Knowing his men would risk their lives if they came to rescue him, he refused to send for help, sometimes crawling on his hands and knees to make regular radio reports. He was finally rescued after his faltering signals inadvertently warned of trouble. Welcomed by President Franklin D. Roosevelt on his return, Byrd subsequently published *Discovery* (1935), telling of the expedition, and *Alone* (1938).

From 1939 to 1940 Admiral Byrd returned to Antarctica as the commander of a government sponsored expedition that was set up in conjunction with the United States Antarctic Service, established by President Roosevelt. Expedition achievements included aerial surveys of some 100,000 square miles and the discovery of five mountain ranges, an important peninsula, and five islands.

Byrd was assigned secret duties during World War II, including strategic planning for the chief of naval operations, inspection of advance bases before the marine invasion of Guadalcanal, and the study of American forces in Europe. After the war, in 1946 and 1947, he headed 4,200 men in what was then the largest expedition ever sent to the Antarctic and which discovered more territory than any had previously (1.7 million square miles). Sponsored by the navy, the expedition also tested equipment and made weather and geological observations. Byrd himself again flew over the South Pole and reported that he had photographed from the air "all major gaps in our maps" of Antarctica's coast.

In 1955 Byrd was placed in command of all American activities in the Antarctic, and from 1955 to 1956 he returned to Antarctica as the head of the first phase of the Operation Deepfreeze expedition dispatched in connection with the observation of International Geophysical Year (1957–1958). While there he made his third flight over the South Pole. When he returned home for the last time, in March 1956, huge reaches of Antarctica had been explored and charted. Largely because of his work, the American effort in Antarctica was to continue.

The Admiral of the Ends of the Earth, as Byrd was dubbed, died in Boston, Massachusetts, on March 11, 1957.

October 26

Erie Canal Opens

New York State's Erie Canal, which linked the Great Lakes with the Hudson River and thus with the Atlantic Ocean, opened on October 26, 1825. It helped make New York City the major commercial center to which goods were sent for distribution elsewhere in the northeastern half of the United States.

Geographically, the state of New York was the 19th-century key to the inland empire of America. The Hudson River, passable north from New York City almost 150 miles to Troy, was the only navigable waterway through the Appalachians. Westward from there, the Mohawk Valley pointed the way to the Great Lakes along a chain of natural waterways. As early as 1768, colonial New Yorkers had considered plans to develop their waterways, but the coming of the American Revolution resulted in postponement. Interest rose again after independence was won, and in 1792 the New York legislature, under the prodding of Governor George Clinton, chartered the Western Company and the Northern Inland Lock Navigation Company to connect the Hudson River with Lake Ontario and Lake Champlain, respectively. Northern Inland did little, and Western built a series of short canals at portages rather than a continuous waterway, which somewhat improved communications.

Spurred by a suggestion of President Thomas Jefferson in 1805 that surplus federal revenues might be applied to improving canals and roads, New Yorkers began thinking of a greater canal. In January 1809 James Geddes reported that the best path for an artificial waterway in New York lay along a channel that cut directly across the center of the state from the northern end of the Hudson River to Lake Erie. Joshua Forman, the Onondaga assemblyman who had introduced the legislation commissioning Geddes's study, brought the document to Jefferson's attention. However, the retiring president rejected the idea of building a canal through 350 miles of wilderness as economically unfeasible.

Despite the lack of federal cooperation, New York continued to contemplate building the gigantic waterway. In 1810 Jonas Platt, the minority leader in the New York State senate, and Thomas Eddy, treasurer of Western Inland, persuaded De Witt Clinton, a nephew of George Clinton and a spokesman for the state senate majority, to introduce legislation establishing a commission to lay plans for a canal that would connect the Hudson River with Lakes Erie and Ontario. Distinguished New Yorkers, including Clinton, Eddy, Stephen Van Rensselaer, Simeon De Witt, William North, Peter B. Porter, Robert R. Livingston, and Robert Fulton, made up the commission. In March 1812, in spite of the unavailability of federal funds, the commission reported in favor of the prompt construction of the canal system.

However, the War of 1812 with Great Britain delayed further consideration of the canal scheme until 1815. In December of that year Jonas Platt and Thomas Eddy prompted De Witt Clinton, then serving as mayor of New York City, to write the *New York Memorial*. Purportedly the work of a committee, the document rekindled popular enthusiasm for the project and encouraged other communities to issue similar manifestoes. More than 100,000 residents of the state signed petitions encouraging the legislature to undertake construction.

In 1816 the state assembly approved the project, but the state senate, influenced by members from New York City who saw the venture as beneficial only to upstaters, prevented the commencement of work. Supporters of the canal spent the remainder of the year making additional studies and surveys. Early in 1817 the commissioners reported that the canal to Lake Erie would be 353 miles long and would have 77 locks to compensate for an aggregate rise and fall of 661 feet. The canal would cost $4,881,738, and an additional but shorter waterway to Lake Champlain would require $871,000.

Finally winning legislative approval, the builders broke ground on July 4, 1817. They then began construction on a portion of the central section of the canal between Rome and Utica. When work in this area neared completion in 1819, the legislature authorized extension of the waterway west to Lake Erie and east to the Hudson River.

The work was in the hands of Benjamin Wright, master of the Erie project, and James Geddes, whose responsibilities included supervision of the Champlain sector. They had little engineering experience, but used their expertise as surveyors and knowledge garnered from personal inspections of thousands of miles of canals in England to perform the construction miracle of the era. Geddes, who was over 60 years old at the completion of the work, subsequently also surveyed a route for the Chesapeake and Ohio Canal. Wright, in his 50s at the completion of the Erie waterway, was later chief engineer of the Chesapeake and Ohio project. He and the two men's younger associates came to be regarded as the leading engineers in the United States.

On March 3, 1817, President James Madison, as his last official act, vetoed the Bonus Bill which would have turned over federal money to the states for internal improvements. Stymied in Washington, D.C., it was decided to finance the project by selling stock. Eventually, a sufficient number of investors became interested, and the money was raised to continue the work. On October 22, 1819, the vessel *Chief Engineer* (named in honor of Benjamin Wright) became the first ship to sail on the canal. It traveled the short distance eastward from Rome to Utica and made the return voyage on the following day. Navigation on the completed central section of 96 miles began in May 1820, and on July 4, 1820, Syracuse was the scene of an official celebration of the event. More elaborate festivities took place in the fall of 1823, when New Yorkers marked the completion of the Champlain Canal and the remaining portions of the Erie between the Genesee and Hudson Rivers. Construction proceeded apace, and the Erie Canal was formally opened on October 26, 1825, during elaborate inaugural festivities.

The Erie Canal was an immediate success. By 1830 annual revenues exceeded one million dollars. Land values soared along the route, and cities like Buffalo (the western terminus of the canal) and Rochester (located at the junction of the canal and the Genesee River) grew at an astounding rate. The later emergence of the railroad industry reduced the importance of the Erie Canal somewhat, but it was nevertheless an important 19th-century transportation link to the Midwest and the frontier.

Hillary Rodham Clinton's Birthday

Hillary Diane Rodham, who would become a controversial political figure and a symbol of the changing role of women in American society, was born on October 26, 1947, in Chicago, Illinois, to Hugh and Dorothy Rodham. She entered prestigious Wellesley College in 1965, graduating with high honors in 1969. Rodham gave the commencement address at her class's graduation, the first Wellesley student to ever be given such an honor. Her speech, given on May 31, 1969, was quite different from the traditional mild commencement address normally heard at college graduations. In her typically assertive and free-thinking manner, traits that would distinguish her as a future first lady, Rodham exhorted her graduating class to help make the world a better place. She also criticized one of the previous speakers, Senator Edward Brooke, for being out of touch with modern issues (see May 31).

After college, she entered Yale Law School, where she excelled academically and met her future husband, the future president, William Jefferson Clinton. After graduation, she went to work for the Children's Defense Fund for a year, then on to the United States House of Representatives in 1974, where she worked on the Watergate investigation and preliminary impeachment proceedings against President Richard M. Nixon. Afterward, she moved to Arkansas to begin teaching law at the University of Arkansas and to marry Clinton. The two would eventually have one daughter, Chelsea.

In 1977 she joined the Rose Law Firm, one of Arkansas's leading law firms, where she engaged in the private practice of law until 1992 when William Clinton was elected to the presidency (see the various articles relating to William Clinton and his presidency throughout this book). Twice she was listed as one of the 100 most influential lawyers in the country by the *National Law Journal*. Meanwhile, she became involved in several financial dealings, notably the Whitewater real estate development project, that would be heavily scrutinized during her husband's presidency and draw much criticism from his opponents.

Unwilling to be a traditional first lady and adopt an exclusively social role, as White House hostess, Hillary Clinton took charge of a special commission on health care reform organized early in her husband's first term (1992–1996) as president. Her commission took much longer than expected to formulate its proposals, and the resulting plan was widely criticized for being excessively complicated and expensive. The resulting negative publicity doomed health care reform, a major defeat for the Clinton administration, which had pledged to get legislation enacted. Afterward, the first lady began to take on less public tasks, in particular becoming involved with child welfare issues and publishing *It Takes a Village and Other Lessons Children Teach Us* (1996) on the subject. She gained national attention and much praise for her work in this area.

By the late 1990s she became somewhat estranged from her husband in the wake of the allegations concerning sexual misconduct that plagued his administration and contributed to the impeachment proceedings against him. She is still active in politics, however, and plans to run for senator in the state of New York in the year 2000.

October 27

Theodore Roosevelt's Birthday

Theodore Roosevelt, the 26th president of the United States, was born on October 27, 1858, in New York City, New York. His father's family were identified with the city from its earliest days. Claes Martenszen Van Rosenvelt left the Netherlands for Dutch New Amsterdam in the 1640s. His son Nicholas was a flour bolter and became a municipal alderman in what by then was British New York. The family remained prominent, and the future president's father, also named Theodore, was a man of considerable wealth and importance in civic affairs. Martha Bulloch Roosevelt, the younger Theodore Roosevelt's mother, was the daughter of James Stephen Bulloch of Roswell, Georgia. A descendant of Archibald Bulloch, the first president of the Georgia Provincial Congress, she was of Scotch-Irish and Huguenot lineage.

Handicapped in childhood by asthma and poor eyesight, young Theodore Roosevelt became conscious of his physical shortcomings and undertook strenuous body-building activities. He taught himself riding, shooting, and boxing, and maintained a devotion to these sports throughout his life. His efforts to compensate for his early maladies affected all facets of his character and contributed to his aggressive philosophical outlook and political behavior.

Anxious about their son's delicate health, Roosevelt's parents employed tutors for his education and afforded him opportunities to travel. He graduated from Harvard in 1880 and was a member of Phi Beta Kappa. Roosevelt developed an interest in literature and history, and published in 1882 the first of his 30 books, *The Naval War of 1812*.

In addition to his literary efforts, Roosevelt participated in New York City's Republican Reform Club. His credentials attracted the attention of the party's leadership, and in 1881 he was elected assemblyman from New York's 21st district. During his tenure in this post, Roosevelt gained extensive newspaper coverage for his support of workers' re-

lief and good government legislation. On February 14, 1884, however, his wife Alice Hathaway (whom he had married on October 27, 1880) died just 12 hours after the death of his mother. Despondency over these personal losses, as well as his failure to prevent the presidential nomination of James G. Blaine at the Republican National Convention, led Roosevelt to withdraw temporarily from politics.

With his baby daughter, Alice, Theodore Roosevelt retreated to his ranch lands in the Dakota Territory. He found solace in the cattleman's life and had time to continue his historical writing. His *Hunting Trips of a Ranchman* appeared in 1885 and a biography, *Thomas Hart Benton*, in 1886. In the latter year the campaign trail lured Roosevelt away from the West for candidacy in the New York mayoral election. Abram S. Hewitt, a liberal Democrat, won the contest; Henry George, who advocated a single tax on land, ran second; and Roosevelt an unimpressive third. In the same year, on December 2, 1886, Roosevelt married Edith Kermit Carow, whom he had known since childhood.

Benjamin Harrison's victory in the 1888 presidential election brought the Republicans and Roosevelt to Washington, D.C. The new president recognized the New Yorker's contribution to his campaign by naming him to the Civil Service Commission. In this capacity Roosevelt worked hard to curb the number of unqualified political appointees and to protect competent government employees. During his six-year stay in the capital he greatly increased his knowledge of politics and politicians.

William L. Strong, a Republican reform mayor, called Roosevelt back to New York in 1895 to become president of the Board of Police Commissioners. Roosevelt's fervor and his forceful personality drew attention to the crime, graft, and poverty that plagued the city. His two years in office alienated many politicians, however, who were unaccustomed to such zealous leadership.

In 1897 Senator Henry Cabot Lodge persuaded the new president, William McKinley, to appoint Roosevelt assistant secretary of the navy. An advocate of sea power, Roosevelt (as acting secretary in the absence of John D. Long) on February 27, 1898, anticipated the war with Spain by ordering Admiral George Dewey to prepare his squadron for possible offensive operations in the Philippines. After the Spanish-American War commenced (see related articles throughout this book), Roosevelt resigned his post on May 6, 1898, to take an active part in the fighting.

Cuba, San Juan Hill, and Theodore Roosevelt are inseparable in history. He advocated a strong American military and agreed with Admiral Alfred Thayer Mahan's contention that a powerful navy and overseas bases in places such as the Philippines and Cuba were necessary. Roosevelt also believed that the United States must act in support of justice, and would exhort his men at the base of San Juan Hill: "Gentlemen, the Almighty God and the Just Cause are with you. Gentlemen, Charge!"

Roosevelt's charging troops were the First United States Volunteer Cavalry, a unit raised by Colonel Leonard Wood and Roosevelt himself. Originally ranked as a lieutenant colonel, Roosevelt became colonel and commander of this regiment, nicknamed the Rough Riders, when Wood was promoted. Roosevelt's military exploits and his complaints about the unsanitary and unhealthful conditions that the soldiers had to live in made him an overnight celebrity. He subsequently furthered his growing fame through an account of his experiences in the largely autobiographical *Rough Riders* in 1899.

Meanwhile, Thomas Collier Platt, the leader of New York's Republican Party, saw in the returning hero an answer to his prayer. He knew that only Roosevelt could keep the governor's mansion in the control of the party, which had been discredited by scandals in the administration of the state's canals and its civil service system. Platt persuaded the party's reluctant regulars to support Roosevelt as the Republican candidate for governor in the election of 1898, and Roosevelt accepted the nomination, narrowly winning the election by 18,000 votes.

Governor Roosevelt became a proponent of progressivism, the political reform movement of the time. He supported legislation to improve the civil service system, ameliorate working conditions in factories and other places of employment, and protect inhabitants of tenement houses. The new governor managed to overcome the opposition of Platt and the Republican Party to achieve the enactment of a measure levying taxes on public service corporations.

Roosevelt never totally broke with Platt, but his independence unnerved the party boss. By 1900 Platt, wanting to remove the headstrong Roosevelt from his bailiwick, persuaded a hesitant President William McKinley to take him as his second-term running mate in the upcoming presidential election. Roosevelt's active campaign offset that of William Jennings Bryan, the highly articulate Democratic presidential candidate, and secured a Republican victory in the November election.

On September 6, 1901, Leon Czolgosz shot President McKinley at a public reception during the Pan American Exposition in Buffalo, New York. Eight days later McKinley died and Theodore Roosevelt, at the age of 42, became the youngest president in the history of the United States. Roosevelt's accession brought progressivism to the White House and important changes to the nation.

An accidental president dealing with a conservative Congress, Roosevelt prudently chose not to seek the immediate enactment of a program of progessive legislation. Instead he achieved constructive results and greatly increased the powers of his office through executive action based on existing legislation. Roosevelt became the first of the strong presidents of the 20th century.

President Roosevelt's first years in office coincided with the high point of a period of consolidation in American industry. Many progressives, fearful of the threat to free enterprise, wanted to arrest this trend. Roosevelt, however, considered the process as inevitable. Rather than destroy the new economic monoliths, he preferred to regulate their activities for the public welfare. He avoided asking congressional conservatives for additional legislation and instead vigorously exercised existing federal powers against improper corporate behavior. This policy became known as the Square Deal.

In 1902 the president ordered the Department of Justice to seek the dissolution of the Northern Securities Company, which monopolized the railroads of the Pacific coast. The conglomerate, which united the interests of magnates John Pierpont Morgan, James Jerome Hill, and Edward Henry Harriman, proved to be a popular and easy target. In 1904 the Supreme Court upheld the government's case under the Sherman Antitrust Act of 1890 and established precedents for future government action against the American Tobacco Company, meat packers, and Standard Oil.

Even though he earned a reputation as a "trust buster," Roosevelt often preferred less dramatic approaches to business. He sought arrangements like his 1905 "gentlemen's agreement" with Judge Elbert H. Gary, chairman of the board of United States Steel, whereby the corporation promised to open its records for government inspection and to correct abuses in return for immunity from prosecution. Such accords greatly increased Roosevelt's presidential stature.

Roosevelt's response to labor unrest likewise bypassed Congress, increased the powers of his office, and aided workers. Seeking higher wages, an eight-hour day, and recognition of their union, John Mitchell's United Mine Workers in June

1902 struck the anthracite coal industry. The miners acted with restraint and offered to submit to arbitration, but the operators, who were allied with railroad and Wall Street interests, refused to negotiate. George F. Baer of the Reading Railroad claimed that God supported the employers, and the strike dragged on through the summer.

As winter approached, Roosevelt decided to intervene to ensure an adequate fuel supply for the nation. Early in October 1902 the president summoned both the miners and the operators to the White House. Roosevelt's warning that he might use the United States Army to seize the mines from the operators was effective, and management soon reopened the pits. The settlement, determined by a government commission in 1903, granted the workers a 10 percent raise and a nine-hour day.

Progressive but prudent, Roosevelt did not alienate the conservative leaders in the Republican Party with his first-term liberalism. He faced no serious opposition for the party's 1904 presidential nomination, and in November he defeated Judge Alton B. Parker, the conservative Democratic candidate, by more than 2.5 million votes. As one commentator observed, "Parker ran for the presidency against Theodore Roosevelt and was defeated by acclamation."

Fortified by the electoral vindication of his Square Deal policies, Roosevelt in his second term prodded Congress to enact a comprehensive program of progressive legislation. The lawmakers rejected many of his proposals, especially those that would have benefited labor, but they grudgingly went along on others. The Hepburn Act of 1906 authorized the Interstate Commerce Commission to examine railroad records and set carrier rates, and the Pure Food and Drug Act outlawed the production and sale of adulterated merchandise.

Roosevelt was characteristically aggressive in the field of foreign relations and continued the trend toward greater American involvement in world affairs. In 1905 he played a leading part in the Portsmouth (New Hampshire) Peace Conference, which brought an end to the Russo-Japanese War. As a result of his efforts, American interests in Asia were protected and he became the first American recipient of the Nobel Peace Prize. In 1906 he actively supported the Algeciras Conference, which guaranteed Moroccan independence and averted a Franco-German clash over North Africa.

With respect to Latin America, Roosevelt conducted himself in accord with his own advice: "Speak softly and carry a big stick." When the government of Colombia rejected as inadequate an American offer of ten million dollars to build a ca-

nal across its isthmian territory of Panama, Roosevelt tacitly supported a 1903 revolution by Panamanian nationalists willing to accept the offer. By the Hay-Bunau-Varilla Treaty of 1903, the United States guaranteed Panama's independence from Colombia in return for control of a ten-mile-wide zone across the isthmus.

Roosevelt picked Secretary of War William Howard Taft to succeed him as the Republican leader. Taft received the party's presidential nomination in 1908 and defeated his Democratic opponent William Jennings Bryan by more than a million votes. With the White House secure in the hands of a trusted associate, Roosevelt set off for an African safari vacation.

During his first years in office, Taft turned for support to the Republican old guard conservatives rather than to the Roosevelt liberals. The new president supported the high Payne-Aldrich tariff, retreated on conservation issues, and severely chastised progressives who tried to oust the notorious Speaker of the House, Joseph Cannon. When Roosevelt returned in March 1910 he found himself in the middle of the party controversy. He placed himself firmly on the side of the progressives.

Unable to settle their differences, Taft and Roosevelt fought each other for the 1912 Republican presidential nomination. As the incumbent, Taft was able to secure the nomination through shrewd usage of the party machinery. Roosevelt and his supporters formed a new coalition, the Progressive or "Bull Moose" Party. The Democratic candidate, Woodrow Wilson, received 435 electoral votes and defeated the divided Republicans in the November contest. Roosevelt ran second with 88 votes and Taft a poor third with only eight. Wilson's New Freedom philosophy closely resembled Roosevelt's, except that the victor emphasized preserving competition in business and arresting rather than just controlling the growth of giant corporations.

In Roosevelt's opinion, Wilson was as poor a president as Taft, especially in the realm of foreign affairs. During his first term Wilson cautiously maintained a policy of American neutrality during World War I, which erupted in 1914. Roosevelt disdained the president's unwillingness to arm the United States and increasingly favored open American aid to the Allied powers. In 1916 he strongly supported the unsuccessful bid of Republican candidate Charles Evans Hughes to unseat the incumbent Wilson.

The United States finally entered the war in 1917, and Roosevelt's four sons served in Europe. Quentin Roosevelt lost his life in 1918 while flying over France. Roosevelt offered to raise a division and lead one of its brigades, but Wilson, following the military's advice to leave the fighting to the professionals, rejected the offer. Soon after the war, on January 6, 1919, Roosevelt died in his sleep.

Roosevelt's efforts as secretary of the navy greatly strengthened that branch of the armed forces, and his birthday coincides with the date upon which the Continental Congress in 1775 received the "bill providing for the creation and establishment of a Fleet." It is therefore appropriate that the Navy League of the United States, a civilian organization founded to promote the role of sea power in the nation's defense, has selected October 27 for its observance of Navy Day every year since 1922.

October 28

Statue of Liberty Dedicated

Since its dedication on October 28, 1886, the Statue of Liberty, which stands in New York Harbor, has welcomed millions of immigrants, foreign visitors, and citizens returning to the United States from abroad. The idea for such a statue originated in France during the early 1870s. Having just adopted a republican form of government, the French people wanted to pay a special tribute to the United States, the first modern republic, on the occasion of its 100th anniversary in 1876. The gift chosen to symbolize the lasting friendship between the two countries was Frédéric Auguste Bartholdi's statue *Liberty Enlightening the World*.

In 1875 the newly organized Franco-American Union began to solicit contributions to finance the statue's construction, and by the time of its completion in 1884, the French people had donated the entire cost of $250,000. Bartholdi himself selected the 12-acre Bedloe's Island (renamed Liberty Island in 1960) as the permanent site for his statue, and the United States Congress agreed to its being used for this purpose. To provide a suitable base for the 225-ton figure, American citizens donated $350,000. This money financed the building of a concrete and granite pedestal, and in 1886 the Statue of Liberty was placed upon this structure to begin its symbolic vigil in New York Harbor. Since then hundreds of thousands of tourists visit Liberty Island every year.

A bronze plaque was affixed to the pedestal of the statue in 1903. On this tablet is engraved the famous excerpt from "The New Colossus" by Emma Lazarus:

> . . . Give me your tired, your poor,
> Your huddled masses yearning to breathe free,

> The wretched refuse of your teeming shore,
> Send these, the homeless, tempest-tossed, to me:
> I lift my lamp beside the golden door.

In 1937 the statue, which with its pedestal is 305 feet high, was declared a national monument.

Bill Gates's Birthday

William Henry Gates III, one of the wealthiest men in the world and the driving force behind the enormous success of the Microsoft Corporation, was born on October 28, 1955, in Seattle, Washington. While growing up, Gates developed a fascination with computers and formed a club in high school that wrote programs for local businesses. In 1973 he was admitted to Harvard University.

While at Harvard in 1975, Gates worked with a friend named Paul Allen to develop a version of the computer program known as BASIC for one of the first personal computers made available on the retail market. The two formed Microsoft in order to pursue this interest commercially, and Gates dropped out of Harvard in 1977 in order to give his full attention to the young company. They established their corporate headquarters just outside of Seattle, and by 1980 they had successfully landed a deal with International Business Machines (IBM) to develop computer languages and programs for IBM's start-up line of personal computers. When Allen left the company, Gates became the chairman and chief executive officer of Microsoft, pushing the company into a variety of software fields and operating systems. One of these was the development of MS-DOS in the early 1980s, which became the operating system for IBM personal computers.

Given that at the time IBM was the giant of the computer business, Gates was able to successfully persuade other computer companies to adopt MS-DOS, employing a variety of innovative alliances that eventually made MS-DOS the standard for the computer industry. According to some statistics, by the late 1990s MS-DOS in all its various versions was the operating system for three-quarters of the world's computers. Capitalizing on the advantages of software compatibility, Microsoft introduced such popular products as Windows, which contained a variety of applications that made MS-DOS easy to use and increased its productivity. Windows gained the lion's share of the consumer market due to Microsoft's now-entrenched marketing power in the booming personal computer market.

In the 1990s Gates began to expand Microsoft into the booming Internet, where the World Wide Web promised virtually unlimited commercial opportunities. He also teamed with Craig McCaw, the cellular telecommunications magnate, to organize Teledesic Corporation for the purpose of launching several hundred low-orbit satellites in order to establish a global telecommunications network. However, an antitrust suit brought by the U.S. government threatened to limit Microsoft's expansion. Currently, Gates's net worth is in the tens of billions of dollars. He is married to Melinda French, with whom he has had one daughter.

October 29

Stock Market Crash of 1929

One of the greatest stock market crashes took place on Black Tuesday, October 29, 1929. Trading on that day was the culmination of an almost week-long period of falling prices on the New York Stock Exchange. The Wall Street collapse was the most significant indicator of the depth of the economic depression that the United States and the rest of the world were then entering.

The American economy had done reasonably well during most of the 1920s, and popular faith in the ability of industrial capitalism to ensure prosperity was strong. Rising prices on the stock market reflected this optimism. In the latter half of 1924, a boom period began, which continued through 1925. After a setback in 1926, the boom gained speed in 1927, but the character of the expansion changed. During 1928 the upward spiral no longer reflected solid economic gains, but rather an inordinate amount of speculation.

Less than one million of the 120 million people then living in the United States had ever engaged in stock market speculation, but most of the populace participated in the mania vicariously if not directly. Normally countervailing forces failed to oppose the unhealthy trends. Even the banking community, typically a bastion of financial responsibility, contributed to the boom through newly organized securities outlets. The statement by Yale economics professor Irving Fisher that "stock prices have reached what looks like a permanently high plateau" reflected the optimism prevalent in academic circles.

The stock market began to falter after Roger W. Babson, at his Annual National Business Conference on September 5, 1929, predicted a crash. For the next few weeks Wall Street prices were uneven, but the bull market was definitely finished. The volume of transactions increased, and by October 21 the New York Stock Exchange ticker was unable to keep pace with the flow of business. In the last hour of trading on October 23, some 2.6 million shares changed hands as prices fell sharply.

Wall Street was showing signs of trouble, and the crisis grew to a panic frenzy in the morning hours of Black Thursday, October 24. By 11:00 a.m. so many stockholders were trying to sell that they could not find buyers. To stem the decline, Thomas Lamont of the John Pierpont Morgan banking house and other financial leaders pooled their institutional resources. Their actions restored confidence, and by the close of the trading day the market had regained some strength. Stock prices held their own on Friday and during the short session of Saturday, but they tumbled again on Monday, October 28. This time even the bankers could not counteract the urge to sell.

Commentators have dubbed October 29, 1929, Black Tuesday. That day, 16,410,030 shares were traded on the New York Stock Exchange and the Dow Jones Industrial Average dropped by nearly 13 percent. The crash helped precipitate the Great Depression, and the stock market would not recover its losses for over 20 years. The record one-day percentage losses of Black Tuesday have only been exceeded by the crash of October 19, 1987, on which day the Dow Jones Industrial Average lost over 22 percent of its value. In 1987 the market quickly rebounded, however, and no depression followed.

The Stock Market in American History: Bull and Bear Market Cycles

The previous essay is a classic illustration of the cyclic nature of the stock market. Although over many decades the trend of the market is inevitably upward, given the ever-expanding economy and population of the United States, it is subject to dramatic short-term price swings of which the Crash of 1929 is one of the more famous. When the market is rising, it is called a bull market, and when it is falling, it is called a bear market.

Following the Crash of 1929, the stock market dropped from a high of 381 on the widely-followed stock market index known as the Dow Jones Industrial Average to a low of 41 in 1932, a decline of nearly 90 percent. The public demanded reform, and Congress passed various laws to curb fraud in the sale of securities and the operation of the stock exchanges. Furthermore, the Securities and Exchange Commission, a federal regulatory agency, was established. These measures, plus state legislation known as blue sky laws, have also helped to curb excess speculation in the markets.

It took some 20 years for investor confidence to be restored in the stock market, so that by the 1950s the Dow returned to its late 1920s high and began to exceed it. In the late 1960s the market hit 800 and made little progress for the next 15 years. A series of economic problems, such as high inflation, low growth, rising oil prices, and increasing foreign competition, beset the nation. Particularly devastating was the "Energy Crisis" of the mid-1970s, when the oil cartel known as the Organization of Petroleum Exporting Countries (OPEC) instituted steep increases in the price of petroleum (see related articles throughout this book), thereby hurting corporate profits and stagnating the stock market. It fluctuated from highs of around 1,000 to lows of around 600, and by the early 1980s was at approximately the same 800 level it had reached in the late 1960s.

As the economic problems began to recede, however, the stock market resumed its upward course with confidence. Surging economic growth and corporate profits, plus new investment opportunities such as computer technology and the Internet, helped propel the market to a new high of 10,000 by 1998 and 11,000 by 1999. There were temporary setbacks in 1987 and 1998 (see the previous essay), but they had no lasting importance beyond generating new restrictions, such as limits on stock trading by means of automatic computer programs. The cyclical nature of the economy, however, suggests that the current bull market will eventually give way to something else.

October 30

John Adams's Birthday

John Adams, the son of John and Sarah Boylston Adams, was born on October 30, 1735, in the part of Braintree, Massachusetts, that was later incorporated into the city of Quincy. The Adams family, descended from Henry Adams, who came to America in 1640, had remained obscure farmers and village officials until John's father married into the prominent Boylston clan. John Adams, the first member of the family to attend college, graduated from Harvard in 1755.

Originally, he wanted to become a minister, but doubts about certain Calvinistic tenets caused him to put aside this career. Instead, in 1758 he gained admission to the Massachusetts bar. Six years later, he wed Abigail Smith, the daughter of the Reverend William and Elizabeth Quincy Smith. In the years that followed, Abigail Adams was a constant support to her husband, and her association with the leading families of the colony undoubtedly also helped his career.

The aspiring lawyer and politician took an interest in local affairs, but it was not until the Stamp Act crisis that Adams assumed a leading role in the rebel cause. He attacked the taxation measure in a series of articles published in the *Boston Gazette* in 1765, and wrote the resolutions by which Braintree instructed its representatives in the colonial assembly. He gained prominence as other towns adopted his directives. John Hancock chose Adams to defend him against smuggling charges, and Adams was elected to the Massachusetts General Court in 1769.

Adams rarely allowed his partisan sentiments to interfere with his sense of justice and responsibility. While many of his associates sought to extract all possible propaganda value from the Boston Massacre of March 5, 1770, Adams and Josiah Quincy acted as defense attorneys for Captain Thomas Preston and the six other British soldiers accused of murder. Preston and four of the men won acquittals, and the other two, convicted of manslaughter, received only token punishment.

The British saw the value of a man like Adams and offered him the position of advocate general of the admiralty court. Adams, interpreting this gesture as an attempt to dissociate him from the rebel movement, declined the post.

Pen and paper were his early weapons in the struggle against Great Britain. In 1774, as "Novanglus," he engaged in debate in Boston newspaper columns with Daniel "Massachusettensis" Leonard, a Tory adversary. Elected to the First Continental Congress, Adams helped write the address to King George III and the Declaration of Rights. As a member of the Second Continental Congress he put his pen aside, and on June 7, 1776, he seconded Richard Henry Lee's resolution in favor of severing American ties with the British Empire. He was a member of the committee that drafted the Declaration of Independence, and it was on his motion that George Washington was appointed general of the American army.

Adams became chairman of the Board of War and Ordnance and served in Congress until late in 1777. On November 28 of that year the government nominated him to replace Silas Deane as a commissioner to France. On February 13, 1778, Adams and his son, the ten-year-old John Quincy Adams, set sail across the Atlantic. Adams's experiences in France soon convinced him that a sole envoy could represent American interests better than a commission. In mid-1779, with congressional approval, he returned home and left the task to Benjamin Franklin.

Adams remained in America only long enough to draw up a state constitution for Massachusetts. In November 1779 he set off again for Europe as minister plenipotentiary to negotiate treaties of peace and of amity and commerce with Great Britain. The times were not auspicious for such gestures, however, and Adams made no overtures to the British. In December 1780 Congress made him minister to Holland, and in 1782 he won that country's recognition of and financial support for the United States. With Benjamin Franklin and John Jay, Adams negotiated the Paris Peace Treaty of 1783, which guaranteed American independence and officially ended the American Revolution. From 1785 to 1788 he served as the fledgling nation's first envoy to Britain.

In April 1789 George Washington took office as the first president of the United States under the new Constitution, and John Adams became his vice president. Adams thought his post was "the most insignificant office that ever the invention of man contrived or his imagination conceived," but in his vice-presidential role as president of the Senate he cast 20 deciding votes. Adams retained the vice-presidency in the 1792 election, and in 1796 was the logical choice of the Federalist Party to succeed the retiring President Washington. Alexander Hamilton, knowing he would have little influence in an Adams administration, tried unsuccessfully to turn the election to Charles Cotesworth Pinckney, the Federalists' original choice for the vice presidency. However, Adams won the contest, and Thomas Jefferson, a Democratic-Republican, became his vice president.

The presidency of Adams covered four bitter years. The powerful Hamilton never accepted him, and other Federalists were alienated by his efforts to establish amicable relations with France. He was also blamed for the controversial Alien and Sedition Acts. Adams became extremely unpopular, thereby allowing the Democratic-Republican candidates, Thomas Jefferson and Aaron Burr, to sweep to an easy victory in the election of 1800. The dejected Adams left Washington, D.C., without attending his successor's inauguration. He took no further part in public affairs beyond writing letters and articles. The enmity that had arisen between him and Jefferson because of political differences was removed in the course of time, and the two men engaged in correspondence for years, exchanging reminiscences and expressing their views on current affairs.

Adams's death, on July 4, 1826, occurred only a few hours after the death of Jefferson in Virginia. The nation's second president was buried in the crypt of the First Parish Church in Quincy, Massachusetts. His son John Quincy Adams would become the sixth president of the United States.

World War II: The Moscow Conference

In the fall of 1943 representatives of the United States, the Soviet Union, Great Britain, and China met in Moscow, Russia. They issued the Moscow Declaration on October 30, 1943, which demonstrated their agreement on the restoration of free and independent governments in Austria and Italy, Germany's two largest European allies, after the war. They also agreed to vigorously prosecute German war criminals, given the extent of Nazi atrocities that were being uncovered by the advancing Allied armies.

A copy of the declaration is set forth below.
Joint Four-Nation Declaration

The governments of the United States of America, United Kingdom, the Soviet Union, and China;

United in their determination, in accordance with the declaration by the United Nations of January, 1942, and subsequent declarations, to continue hostilities against those Axis powers with which they respectively are at war until such powers have laid down their arms on the basis of unconditional surrender;

Conscious of their responsibility to secure the liberation of themselves and the peoples allied with them from the menace of aggression;

Recognizing the necessity of insuring a rapid and orderly transition from war to peace and of establishing and maintaining international peace and security with the least diversion of the world's human and economic resources for armaments;
Jointly declare:

1. That their united action, pledged for the prosecution of the war against their respective enemies, will be continued for the organization and maintenance of peace and security.

2. That those of them at war with a common enemy will act together in all matters relating to the surrender and disarmament of that enemy.

3. That they will take all measures deemed by them to be necessary to provide against any violation of the terms imposed upon the enemy.

4. That they recognize the necessity of establishing at the earliest practicable date a general international organization, based on the principle of the sovereign equality of all peace-loving states, and open to membership by all such states, large and

small, for the maintenance of international peace and security.

5. That for the purpose of maintaining international peace and security pending the re-establishment of law and order and the inauguration of a system of general security they will consult with one another and as occasion requires with other members of the United Nations, with a view to joint action on behalf of the community of nations.

6. That after the termination of hostilities they will not employ their military forces within the territories of other states except for the purposes envisaged in this declaration and after joint consultation.

7. That they will confer and cooperate with one another and with other members of the United Nations to bring about a practicable general agreement with respect to the regulation of armaments in the postwar period.

Declaration Regarding Italy

The Foreign Secretaries of the United States, the United Kingdom and the Soviet Union have established that their three governments are in complete agreement that Allied policy toward Italy must be based upon the fundamental principle that Fascism and all its evil influence and configuration shall be completely destroyed and that the Italian people shall be given every opportunity to establish governmental and other institutions based on democratic principles.

The Foreign Secretaries of the United States and the United Kingdom declare that the action of their governments from the inception of the invasion of Italian territory, in so far as paramount military requirements have permitted, has been based upon this policy.

In furtherance of this policy in the future the Foreign Secretaries of the three governments are agreed that the following measures are important and should be put into effect:

1. It is essential that the Italian Government should be made more democratic by inclusion of representatives of those sections of the Italian people who have always opposed Fascism.

2. Freedom of speech, of religious worship, of political belief, of press and of public meeting, shall be restored in full measure to the Italian people, who shall be entitled to form anti-Fascist political groups.

3. All institutions and organizations created by the Fascist regime shall be suppressed.

4. All Fascist or pro-Fascist elements shall be removed from the administration and from institutions and organizations of a public character.

5. All political prisoners of the Fascist regime shall be released and accorded full amnesty.

6. Democratic organs of local government shall be created.

7. Fascist chiefs and army generals known or suspected to be war criminals shall be arrested and handed over to justice.

In making this declaration the three Foreign Secretaries recognize that so long as active military operations continue in Italy the time at which it is possible to give full effect to the principles stated above will be determined by the Commander-in-Chief on the basis of instructions received through the combined chiefs of staff.

The three governments, parties to this declaration, will, at the request of any one of them, consult on this matter. It is further understood that nothing in this resolution is to operate against the right of the Italian people ultimately to choose their own form of government.

Declaration on Austria

The governments of the United Kingdom, the Soviet Union and the United States of America are agreed that Austria, the first free country to fall a victim to Hitlerite aggression, shall be liberated from German domination.

They regard the annexation imposed on Austria by Germany on March 15, 1938, as null and void. They consider themselves as in no way bound by any changes effected in Austria since that date. They declare that they wish to see re-established a free and independent Austria and thereby to open the way for the Austrian people themselves, as well as those neighboring States which will be faced with similar problems, to find that political and economic security which is the only basis for lasting peace. Austria is reminded, however, that she has a responsibility, which she cannot evade, for participation in the war at the side of Hitlerite Germany, and that in the final settlement account will inevitably be taken of her own contribution to her liberation.

Statement on Atrocities

Signed by President Roosevelt, Prime Minister Churchill and Premier Stalin.

The United Kingdom, the United States and the Soviet Union have received from many quarters evidence of atrocities, massacres and cold-blooded mass executions which are being perpetrated by Hitlerite forces in many of the countries they have overrun and from which they are now being steadily expelled. The brutalities of Nazi domination are no new thing, and all peoples or territories in their grip have suffered from the worst form of government by terror. What is new is that many of the territories are now being redeemed by the advancing armies of the liberating powers, and that in their desperation the recoiling Hitlerites and Huns are redoubling their ruthless cruelties. This is now evidenced with particular clearness by monstrous crimes on the territory of the Soviet Union which is being liberated from Hitlerites, and on French and Italian territory.

Accordingly, the aforesaid three Allied powers, speaking in the interest of the thirty-two United Nations, hereby solemnly declare and give full warning of their declaration as follows:

At the time of granting of any armistice to any government which may be set up in Germany, those German officers and men and members of the Nazi Party who have been responsible for or have taken a consenting part in the above atrocities, massacres and executions will be sent back to the countries in which their abominable deeds were done in order that they may be judged and punished according to the laws of these liberated countries and of free governments which will be erected therein. Lists will be compiled in all possible detail from all these countries having regard especially to invaded parts of the Soviet Union, to Poland and Czechoslovakia, to Yugoslavia and Greece including Crete and other islands, to Norway, Denmark, Netherlands, Belgium, Luxembourg, France and Italy.

Thus, Germans who take part in wholesale shooting of Polish officers or in the execution of French, Dutch, Belgian or Norwegian hostages of Cretan peasants, or who have shared in slaughters inflicted on the people of Poland or in territories of the Soviet Union which are now being swept clear of the enemy, will know they will be brought back to the scene of their crimes and judged on the spot by the peoples whom they have outraged.

Let those who have hitherto not imbued their hands with innocent blood beware lest they join the ranks of the guilty, for most assuredly the three Allied powers will pursue them to the uttermost ends of the earth and will deliver them to their accusers in order that justice may be done.

The above declaration is without prejudice to the case of German criminals whose offenses have no particular geographical localization and who will be punished by joint decision of the government of the Allies.

October 31

Halloween

Few holidays have a stranger or more paradoxical history than Halloween. Technically, it is the vigil of All Saints' Day, observed by Roman Catholics and other Christians on November 1. However, some of the customs traditional to Halloween hark back to matters that Christianity for centuries has adamantly opposed: black magic, fortune-telling, ghosts, witches, goblins, fairies, and so on. In many countries, All Hallows' Eve is observed only as an austere religious occasion with extra masses and prayers at the graves of deceased relatives and friends. In the United States, however, Halloween is primarily regarded as a night of festivities and partying. To understand this curious mixture of the religious and the secular, and to realize how the varied customs of Europe have affected the American celebration of Halloween, it is necessary to trace the remote origins of the holiday.

It is generally accepted that Halloween in its more popular or folk aspects represents a combination of druidic practices and classical Roman religious beliefs. Halloween has clear connections with the rites of the druidic priests in the pre-Roman, pre-Christian Celtic communities of northern and western Europe, especially in Ireland and Scotland. The Celtic order of druids performed mystical ceremonies in honor of the great Sun god at various sites. The Celtic year ended on October 31, the eve of *Samhain*, or "summer's end," and on this occasion the white-robed priests celebrated a joint festival for the Sun god and the lord of the dead.

In the agrarian sense, the last day of October was the festival of the waning year. After the ripened grain had been gathered and the cattle had been brought back from the meadows to their stalls, the Sun was thanked for the harvest and given moral support for his coming battle with cold and darkness. The Samhain rites were intended to offset the blight of winter with its perils and anxieties for people and beasts alike. It was also an occasion for feasting, when the food supplies amassed in summer were plentiful.

On this night, Celtic households extinguished the fire in their hearth and gathered at a designated circle, where the priests solemnly quenched the sacred altar fire. Having rubbed together pieces of the sacred oak to kindle a new fire on the altar, the priests passed on the sparks to light great bonfires on the hilltops to honor the Sun god and frighten away any lurking evil spirits. The head female of each family received live embers to kindle a new fire on her hearth, which was to last until the next autumn festival. Blessed fire was thought to protect the home from danger throughout the year.

The Celts also believed that on October 31 the lord of the dead assembled the souls of all those persons who had died in the previous year, and those persons were required to pay for their sins by dwelling in the bodies of animals. Moreover, the spirits of the dead were believed to be allowed a brief visit to their relatives in search of warmth and comfort as winter approached. Since it was believed that the departed souls roaming abroad sometimes played tricks on October 31, the druids sought to appease them and simultaneously honor the Sun god by sacrificing horses and occasionally human beings. Despite Roman efforts to suppress these practices, the ancient Celtic rites survived for centuries. Horses continued to be sacrificed on Samhain as late as A.D. 400. Even after Christianity spread across Europe and the British Isles, oxen were often sacrificed on October 31 "in honor of the saints and sacred relics." In medieval Europe, black cats, chosen as victims in the belief that they were witches in disguise, were burned on that day.

The modern observance of Halloween also reflects influences from the Roman festival honoring Pomona, the goddess of fruits. A grove near Ostia, Italy, was dedicated to the goddess in ancient times, and a harvest festival was held there around November 1 of every year. Scholars believe that offerings of the winter stores of nuts and apples were made to her, and that the deities of fire and water were asked to ensure fertility.

The process of incorporating October 31 into the Christian calendar as All Hallows' Eve took several centuries. The idea of honoring martyrs and saints on a common day grew out of the fact that there were fewer days in the calendar year than there were saints to venerate. In keeping with this idea, during the fourth through the seventh centuries, various localities observed a day for venerating all martyrs at one time (usually in the

spring of the year). It was not until the eighth century that Pope Gregory III moved the feast to November to offset the residual paganism of the old Samhain rites. It was a century later, however, before Pope Gregory IV placed All Saints' Day in the church calendar, decreeing that the day and the vigil of All Hallows' Eve be observed. Even after that, however, the Christianizing of the observance took time.

Halloween folk customs of pagan origin continued to flourish in Ireland, Scotland, Wales, and parts of England well into the 18th century. Rural people, especially those in isolated locations, practiced the ancient rites of dispersing the "spirits" who were out on Halloween stealing milk, harming cattle, and destroying crops. In 1786 the Scottish poet Robert Burns described in "Halloween" a party in which many ancient customs were followed by the young people, although with a touch of skepticism not characteristic of the earlier days.

The widespread observance of Halloween came relatively late to the United States. Most of the early settlers, the majority of whom were Protestant, did not observe All Saints' Day or Halloween. October 31 had little significance in colonial days, although records show that some of the English kept up the secular side of the evening with various festivities. However, Halloween did not become widely observed until the great Irish immigration in the 1840s, following the Irish potato famine. The Irish brought with them not only the religious observances of All Saints' Day and its eve, but also the folklore remnants of the eve of Samhain (even into the 20th century, October 31 is referred to as *Oidhche Shamhna* in Ireland) and the traditional legends of the fairy folk, or "little people." In fact, jack-o'-lanterns, one of the most popular and enduring features of Halloween, are primarily an Irish tradition (although in Ireland people used oversized rutabagas, turnips, and potatoes instead of pumpkins, which was an American adaptation).

By the late 1800s Halloween had become a widespread event in the United States, characterized especially by the custom of children going trick-or-treating in masks and costumes. There are several theories about the origins of trick-or-treating. One claims that the practice stems from the custom of souling, or soul-caking, when the English went around on All Saints' Day and All Souls' Day to ask for soul cakes (square buns with currants) in remembrance of the dead. However, the contemporary custom of trick-or-treating also resembles an ancient Irish practice on Halloween, when groups of peasants went from house to house asking for money in order to buy luxuries for a feast and demanding that fatted calves and black sheep be prepared for the occasion. These contributions were often requested in the name of Muck Olla, a druid deity, or Saint Columba (a monk who in the sixth century converted the Picts and founded a monastery on Iona off the Scottish coast). Threats were made against those who were stingy. Another possibility is that trick-or-treating, as well as masquerading, is derived from the "penny for the Guy" practice in England on November 5, when Guy Fawkes Day festivities (commemorating the foiling of the 1605 Gunpowder Plot to blow up King James I and Parliament) included begging and dressing up in costumes. Finally, some scholars suggest that the custom of wearing Halloween costumes comes from the medieval practice of celebrating All Hallows' Eve with a procession around the local church, with the local populace dressed variously as angels, patron saints, and devils.

Admission of Nevada to the Union

The territory of Nevada was admitted to the Union as the 36th state on October 31, 1864, by proclamation of President Abraham Lincoln, issued in accordance with the provisions of an act passed on March 31 of that year.

The history of Nevada before it entered the Union reflects the interaction of geographical, physical, and human factors. Formed as a result of turbulent geological upheavals, Nevada is a land of many contrasts: vast, arid stretches of sagebrush and creosote bush; lofty mountains extending north to south; and relatively few rivers. Its early inhabitants, the "Basketmakers" and later the Paiute, Shoshone, and Washoe tribes, were preoccupied with struggling to survive. Their sparse population existed on a diet of wild animals, insects, and plants.

The first Europeans to enter the region of Nevada are said to have been Franciscan missionaries en route from Mexico to California in the 1770s. Friar Francisco Garcés probably passed through what is now the extreme southwestern part of the state. Friar Silvestre Vélez de Escalante may have crossed the eastern edge in search of a new route to the coast. Their reports about the forbidding wilderness of mountains and semidesert were sufficient to discourage further exploration for almost 50 years.

Only in the 1820s and 1830s did American and Canadian fur traders and trappers penetrate the unknown region for beaver pelts. Peter Ogden and other members of the Hudson's Bay Company, trading out of the Oregon country, crossed into what is now Nevada from the north and discovered the Humboldt River valley. Jedediah Smith,

an American Fur Company trader from St. Louis, traversed the area of the present state while journeying from the Mississippi to the Pacific. Another adventurer, Joseph Walker, scaled the precipitous Sierra Nevadas into California. In an 1843–1845 expedition, Captain John C. Frémont, guided by the renowned frontier scout Kit Carson (after whom the capital city of Nevada is named), conducted the first systematic exploration of the region. Writing in 1846, the trapper James Clyman still characterized the area as one of the "most sterile barren countrys I have ever traversed . . . [having the] most thirsty appearance of any place I ever witnessed."

In the 1840s wagon trains and gold seekers hurried across the inhospitable territory on the way to California. At the end of the Mexican War, the territory from which Nevada was formed came into the possession of the United States by the Treaty of Guadalupe Hidalgo on February 2, 1848 (see the related essays throughout this book). Since it was adjacent to the Mormon commonwealth that was just being formed in the Salt Lake City area, Nevada was included in the vast Mormon "state" of Deseret proclaimed by the Mormon leader Brigham Young in March 1849. The Mormons soon established a trading post and base for exploration in the Carson River valley. Known as Mormon Station and later as Genoa, it was the first permanent American settlement in Nevada.

When the United States government rejected the Mormon claim to Deseret, most of the area of Nevada was included in the newly organized territory of Utah in 1850. Salt Lake City, seat of the Utah territorial government, proved to be too far distant to provide adequate political control and military protection for the area's westernmost inhabitants. As early as 1851, therefore, these settlers tried to form a more satisfactory and hopefully more independent form of government. In 1854 the Utah legislature quashed all such attempts by including the settlements of the western Utah Territory in a newly created Carson County. In 1859 the people of Carson County made an abortive attempt to form a state government of their own.

In general, life in the area remained quiet until 1859, when Nevada's huge mineral wealth was discovered. The famous Comstock Lode, one of the richest silver deposits ever tapped, yielded silver worth hundreds of millions of dollars. Near its site, the little settlement of Virginia City mushroomed overnight as news of the strike spread like wildfire. In its heyday, Virginia City boasted a population of 30,000 people and 106 saloons. Mark Twain, who was a Virginia City inhabitant from 1862 until 1864, vividly depicted the wild Nevada Days in

Roughing It (1872). He also left little doubt that although the mining boom had unearthed riches underground, the area's physical attractiveness had not improved:

> I overheard a gentleman say the other day, that it was "the d——dest country under the sun" and that comprehensive conception I fully subscribe to. It never rains here, and the dew never falls. No flowers grow here, and no green thing gladdens the eye. The birds that fly over the land carry their provisions with them. Only the crow and the raven tarry with us.

The influx of people seeking quick riches and the lack of effective federal control made lawlessness rampant in the raucous mining towns. In a move partly designed to impose law and order, Congress divided the territory of Utah on March 2, 1861, and out of its western portion created the territory of Nevada. The name, originally designating the snowcapped Sierra Nevada, means "snow-clad" in Spanish. An effort to achieve statehood in 1863 failed. By the following year, however, it had become obvious that two more Republican senatorial votes were needed in Congress in order to push certain antislavery measures through as the Union's victory in the Civil War neared.

Thus, in a political maneuver supported by Republican President Abraham Lincoln, Nevada attained statehood on October 31, 1864, a mere three years after gaining territorial status. Even then, the "battle-born" state formed during the Civil War was considerably short of the 60,000 population theoretically necessary for entry into the Union, a shortcoming that was conveniently overlooked.

In 1866 Nevada reached its present boundaries by acquiring its southern tip from New Mexico and certain eastern lands from Utah.

November

November is the 11th month of the Gregorian, or New Style, calendar in use today and numbers 30 days. As its name indicates, derived from the Latin word *novem*, for "nine," November was the ninth month in the old Roman calendar that began in March. Even after the ancient Roman calendar was revised and two more months were added, November retained its traditional but outmoded name despite having become the 11th month.

The Roman senate, however, sought to rename November in the early first century A.D. In the first century B.C. Quintilis and Sextilis had been renamed Julius and Augustus, respectively, after Julius Caesar and the first Roman emperor, Augustus. These are the modern months of July and August. Based on these precedents, the Roman senate attempted to flatter succeeding rulers by naming months in their honor as well. The senate therefore proposed naming November Tiberius in honor of the second Roman emperor, Tiberius, who ruled from A.D. 14 to A.D. 37. Tiberius rejected the proposal, just as he had rejected a previous proposal to rename September Tiberius. He is said to have once remarked sarcastically, "What will you do if there be 13 Caesars?"

In a much less modest fashion, in roughly 191 A.D. the emperor Commodus (A.D. 180–192) forced the Roman senate to consent to the renaming of all 12 months after himself. Each was to be designated with one of his honorary titles. November was to be called Romanus, or "the Roman," according to one contemporary historian. According to another account, it was to be called Exsuperatorius, signifying that Commodus surpassed all men. However, the new calendar names did not outlive the rule of Commodus.

The Anglo-Saxons called November Windmonath, or "wind month," since the winds blew furiously during this season. The month was also designated Blod-monath, or "bloody month," since it was the time for slaughtering animals for winter food. The lucky birthstone associated with November is the topaz, which symbolizes fidelity.

November 1

All Saints Day

November 1, All Saints' Day, is a feast observed by Roman Catholics, as well as by Episcopalians, Lutherans, and some other Protestant denominations of the Christian religion, in honor of all the saints in heaven known or unknown. The day also used to be called All Hallows' Day or Hallowmass from the Old English word *hallow* meaning "sanctify." In the Roman Catholic Church, All Saints' Day is considered one of the most important observances of the church year, and is preceded by a vigil of preparation on the evening of October 31.

Strangely enough, it is this vigil, All Hallows' Eve, or more familiarly Halloween, that has become the most widely known feature of the observance. All Hallows' Eve was originally intended to be celebrated entirely as a religious occasion with prayers and extra masses, as on the eve of any great feast, and is still commemorated in this fashion in many European and Latin American countries. However, throughout the Middle Ages, especially in the British Isles, the old Celtic religious and folk ways connected with the pagan celebration of Samhain lingered on alongside the ecclesiastical celebration. Today in Great Britain, Ireland, and the United States, October 31 has lost its serious religious tone and is primarily regarded as a night of merrymaking, games, and parties featuring macabre and superstitious themes (see October 31).

November 2

The origin of All Saints' Day is probably to be found in the common veneration of all who either suffered Christian martyrdom in groups or whose names were unknown. As early as the fourth century, following the persecutions under the Roman emperor Diocletian (284–305) and his predecessors, it was suggested that there be a special day to commemorate all the martyrs (the first saints publicly venerated by the early church) since the year was not long enough to assign an individual day for the veneration of each martyr. The Eastern Orthodox church has observed such a day (on various dates) since the fourth century. St. John Chrysostom (345–407), the Greek Father of the Church and later bishop of Constantinople, preached a sermon every year to commemorate all the saints.

In 609 Pope Boniface IV consecrated the Pantheon in Rome, formerly the Roman temple of all the gods, to the Virgin Mary and all martyrs. He also designated the first observance of the feast for May 610. In conjunction with the church's attempt to displace or suppress preexisting pagan cults, Pope Gregory III (731–741) changed the feast from May to November and enlarged it to embrace all saints as well as martyrs. He consecrated a chapel in St. Peter's Basilica at Rome to all the saints. Although the change of date was presumably to combat the lingering Samhain rites, some scholars hold that November was selected so that the multitude of pilgrims flocking to Rome for the feast of the saints could be fed from the fall harvest. In the 830s, Pope Gregory IV (827–844) established the feast in the church calendar as All Saints' Day and required its observance (and the observance of its vigil, All Hallows' Eve) by all churches.

After the Reformation in the 16th century, the feast was generally retained by Protestants in varying degrees of observance, although among some denominations it was either not adopted or soon ceased to be celebrated.

In the United States, All Saints' Day is regularly observed in areas with a significant Roman Catholic population. For example, in New Orleans, Louisiana, a city rooted in French and Spanish customs that go back to the early 1700s, people often visit the cemeteries on this occasion to put flowers on the graves. There are similar observances in Puerto Rico.

November 2

Warren G. Harding's Birthday

Warren Gamaliel Harding, the 29th president of the United States, was born on November 2, 1865, in Blooming Grove, Ohio. He was the oldest of the eight children of Phoebe Elizabeth Dickerson Harding and George Tryon Harding, a farmer and later a physician. The young Harding studied at Ohio Central College for three years, leaving in 1882 and moving with his family to Marion, Ohio. He taught school and studied law for a year.

Having learned the printer's trade by working at the Caledonia *Advertiser*, Harding was hired by the *Democratic Mirror* in Marion in 1884. Irritated by the Democratic bias of the newspaper, however, he quit. With a partner, he purchased the bankrupt *Marion Star* for $300. Harding soon bought out his partner's share and set out to make the enterprise a commercial success. Florence Kling De Wolfe, a widow who became Harding's wife on July 8, 1891, assisted him with the *Star*.

Harding developed an interest in Republican Party politics. Winning a seat in the Ohio state senate in 1898, he served two terms. In 1903 he was successful in his electoral bid for lieutenant governor of Ohio. When his term ended two years later, Harding went back to his newspaper. He ran for governor in 1910, but was defeated by the Democratic candidate. Having earned a reputation as a forceful speaker and loyal Republican, he was chosen by President William Howard Taft to make the Republican National Convention nominating speech in 1912.

Elected to the United States Senate in 1914, Harding began to draw some notice, especially among his fellow politicians. He thus earned the temporary chairmanship of the Republican National Convention of 1916, at which he gave the keynote speech.

As a United States senator, Harding was unexceptional. In foreign affairs he attacked President Woodrow Wilson's policy of restraint when American business interests in Mexico were threatened during the upheavals caused by the Huerta-Carranza conflict and related events in that country. He approved of the American declaration of war against Germany in 1917 and also favored various supporting measures, including provisions for a military draft and the repressive Espionage Act of 1917. After the war he followed the isolationist views of Senator Henry Cabot Lodge on foreign policy, refusing to approve the Treaty of Versailles because it incorporated Wilson's proposal for a League of Nations.

In domestic policy Harding was a defender of big business. He supported protective tariffs and voted against high taxes on excess war profits. He voted in favor of the 18th Amendment that authorized prohibition, but never felt constrained to stop his own heavy drinking.

Harding's loyalty to the Ohio Republican machine won him a dark-horse nomination for the presidency at the 1920 convention. As his political mentor Harry M. Daugherty had predicted, Harding was chosen in a "smoke-filled room" by a handful of party bosses after being asked to swear that there was nothing in his past to keep him from accepting the nomination. During the election, he straddled and tried to ignore the controversial League of Nations issue, while his Democratic opponents James Cox and Franklin D. Roosevelt crusaded for the League. Harding campaigned for high tariffs, curbs on immigration, and a deflationary economy. Having supported the 19th Amendment that gave women the right to vote, Harding reaped much of the new female electorate. Thus, he won the election by large electoral and popular majorities.

Harding was, by all accounts, an ordinary man who people thought would bring "normalcy" back to a country disillusioned with the idealisms of World War I. Instead, he brought incompetence to the highest levels of government. His cabinet was a mixture of excellence, corruption, and mediocrity. Three of his top appointments—Charles Evans Hughes as secretary of state, Andrew W. Mellon as secretary of the treasury, and Herbert Hoover as secretary of commerce—were well-respected. Other appointments, however, were based on personal friendships or political debts rather than on qualifications for office. The predatory cronies and others who surrounded Harding came to be known as the Ohio Gang, and they were quick to take advantage of their positions for personal gain.

Most notorious was Secretary of the Interior Albert B. Fall, who with the passive cooperation of Navy Secretary Edwin M. Denby illegally transferred naval oil reserve lands (including the Teapot Dome reserve in Wyoming) to Interior Department control and then leased them to private oil companies with substantial kickbacks for himself. In time, this Teapot Dome Scandal brought prison sentences for both Fall and oil magnate Harry Sinclair.

Harding's attorney general, Harry Daugherty (a longtime political backer) was also involved in scandals. A Senate committee later found him guilty of misconduct, including the illegal sale of liquor permits and pardons to violators of prohibition statutes. He narrowly escaped incarceration when a jury could not reach a verdict. Daugherty's crony Jesse Smith, who eventually committed suicide, had a desk but no official duties in the Department of Justice. He has been variously described as a dispenser of graft and as the prime "fixer" of the administration. Gaston B. Means, who also held an office in Daugherty's Department of Justice, eventually served time in prison for selling liquor permits. Means afterward reported that he had collected and passed on to Jesse Smith some $7 million in bribes from bootleggers. Harding's choice to administer the Veteran's Bureau, an acquaintance known as "Colonel" Charles R. Forbes, went to Leavenworth after bilking the government of at least half the bureau's congressionally appropriated funds and amassing huge sums from kickbacks and other graft.

The growing scandals of Harding's administration were not offset by any notable record of legislative or executive action. Probably the most outstanding accomplishment of his presidency was the 1921 Washington Conference called at the behest of Secretary of State Hughes to discuss limiting the size of the great powers' navies. The meeting resulted in the signing of nine treaties concerning armaments and territory. Another achievement was the establishment of a federal Bureau of the Budget to coordinate the piecemeal procedure whereby each federal department applied independently to Congress for funds. Harding is also remembered for his presidential pardon of several persons, including the Socialist Eugene V. Debs. They were among the many who had been imprisoned under the provisions of the stringent Espionage Act and the Sedition Act during World War I.

Word of his administration's rampant corruption apparently reached Harding early in 1923. Aware that the scandals would surely become public, Harding left Washington, D.C., on an official visit to Alaska in June 1923 with his wife and a few friends. During his return trip he was stricken by what was diagnosed as ptomaine poisoning. He stopped in San Francisco to rest, but developed bronchial pneumonia, and died on August 2, 1923, of an embolism. Vice President Calvin Coolidge became president and served out the remainder of Harding's term. Not long after Harding's death, the Teapot Dome scandal and the news of other Harding administration corruption became public. At the time of his death, however, most of the corruption had yet to be revealed and thus Harding was mourned throughout the nation. He was buried in Marion, Ohio, on August 10, 1923.

November 2

James K. Polk's Birthday

James Knox Polk, the 11th president of the United States, was the eldest son of Samuel and Jane Knox Polk. Samuel Polk was a farmer and surveyor. His Scotch-Irish ancestors were named Pollock, which was later shortened to Polk.

James Polk was born on November 2, 1795, in Mecklenburg County, North Carolina. Frail from early youth, he channeled his energies into study. In 1806 the family moved to the valley of the Duck River in Tennessee's Maury County. Polk entered the University of North Carolina in 1815 and graduated in 1818 with honors in mathematics and the classics.

He returned to Tennessee and began to study law in Nashville at the offices of Felix Grundy, who was also a prominent politician. Young Polk worked hard and was admitted to the bar in 1820. Returning home to Maury County, he established a law practice in the town of Columbia. His intelligence and diligence quickly brought him success. After three years of law practice, in 1823 he entered the state legislature. Polk was a Democrat, and quickly established a reputation as a well-informed, persuasive speaker. His political principles were modeled after those of Thomas Jefferson, but he soon became a follower of fellow Tennessee politician Andrew Jackson. They grew to be friends and maintained a close political relationship until Jackson's death.

On January 1, 1824, Polk married Sarah Childress of Murfreesboro, Tennessee. In 1825 Polk entered the United States House of Representatives. By 1833 he was one of the leaders of the Democratic Party in Congress. As chairman of the House Ways and Means Committee, he supported President Andrew Jackson's effort to destroy the Bank of the United States. In 1835 Polk became Speaker of the House, and served in that position until 1839 when he decided to seek the governorship of Tennessee. He won the election, serving from 1839 to 1841, but lost subsequent campaigns for reelection in 1841 and 1843.

During the election of 1844, the elderly Andrew Jackson still ran the Democratic Party, and he decided to reward Polk's devotion to Democratic Party policies by supporting him for president. In particular, both Polk and Jackson firmly believed that the United States should continue to expand its territory. At the Democratic National Convention in 1844, despite stiff opposition by former president Martin Van Buren, Polk won the nomination. He became the nation's first dark-horse presidential candidate. His Whig opponents were a divided party, and thus Polk was able to win the election.

Polk's administration had one overriding goal: to increase the territory of the United States as much as possible. The Mexican War that erupted in 1846 eventually helped secure Texas, California, and the Southwest for the United States (see related essays throughout this book). Furthermore, Polk obtained an agreement with Great Britain concerning the disputed Oregon Territory, then jointly ruled by both Britain and the United States. In June 1846 a treaty established a compromise boundary at the 49th Parallel, and secured exclusive American jurisdiction south of that line.

Also during his administration Polk pushed through the enactment of lower tariff schedules known as the Walker Tariff of 1846. That same year he also pushed through Congress the Independent Treasury Bill, which established a national financial system that was not supplanted until the creation of the Federal Reserve System in 1913.

The systematic Polk had thus achieved all of his presidential objectives. In the process, however, he literally worked himself to death. He did not run for a second term in the elections of 1848, and was succeeded in the presidency by Zachary Taylor. Polk left office in bad health, and died shortly thereafter on June 15, 1849, at the age of 54. He was buried at his Nashville, Tennessee, home. In 1893 he was reburied, with his wife, on the grounds of the Tennessee state capitol.

North Dakota Admitted to the Union

As a result of political feuding between the northern and southern parts of the Dakota Territory, North Dakota and South Dakota were admitted to the Union as separate states on November 2, 1889. The two areas had been unable to agree on a capital city, and the argument had grown increasingly heated during the 1870s and 1880s. Thus North Dakota, with its capital at Bismarck, became the 39th state of the United States, and South Dakota, with its capital at Pierre, became the 40th.

At the time of the first recorded visit by a European to the region now constituting North Dakota, that of French-Canadian explorer Pierre Gaultier de Varennes de La Vérendrye in 1738, approximately ten native tribes inhabited the area. Some, such as the Mandan, Arikara, and Hidatsa, lived in villages and were farmers. Other tribes, including the Assiniboin, Crow, and Dakota, were nomadic. They hunted buffalo, whose meat provided food and whose skins they used for clothing and tepees. The Cheyenne and Cree tribes, also in the region, were seminomadic.

The central and southwestern area of what is now North Dakota formed part of the territory of Louisiana, which passed from French to Spanish control by the secret Treaty of Fontainebleau in 1762. Great Britain controlled the rest of the area. The North West Fur Company, a privately owned British fur-trading company, built the first trading post in 1797 at the confluence of the Pembina River and the Red River of the North in the extreme northeastern corner of North Dakota. Numerous fur-trading posts were subsequently established in the British region by various companies, including the Hudson's Bay and North West Fur companies. British fur traders operated not only in the British-dominated valley of the Red River, but also along the Missouri River where Spain permitted them to do a certain amount of trading with the native tribes. Spanish fur traders were also active.

Even after the secret Treaty of San Ildefonso, which returned the vast Louisiana region to France in 1800, Louisiana temporarily remained under Spanish administration. When the United States acquired the huge Louisiana Territory through the Louisiana Purchase in 1803, what had been the Spanish-held part of North Dakota was transferred to the American government. Meriwether Lewis and William Clark were dispatched by President Thomas Jefferson to explore the newly acquired territory, which had roughly doubled the size of the United States. By the fall of 1804 they had reached the point on the eastern bank of the Missouri River (about 14 miles west of what is now Washburn, North Dakota) where they built Fort Mandan.

During the winter that Lewis and Clark spent at the fort, the friendly Hidatsa and Mandan tribes provided supplies for the continuation of their journey to the Pacific coast. Also of great value was the information that the natives provided, as well as the presence of Sacagawea, a Shoshone woman who had been captured by the Hidatsa. The Hidatsa sold her to Toussaint Charbonneau, a Canadian trapper, who then married her. Both Charbonneau and Sacagawea acted as interpreters for Lewis and Clark, but Sacagawea's greatest contribution to the success of the expedition was her ability to guide the party through her home area and procure needed horses from her fellow Shoshone.

Scottish immigrants led by a member of the Hudson's Bay Company, Thomas Douglas (the Earl of Selkirk), came by way of Canada in 1812 to establish at Pembina the first permanent settlement in the region. So bitter was the rivalry between the various fur-trading companies, however, that the settlers were twice driven from their homes by members of the North West Fur Company before Pembina could be established as a permanent settlement.

Meanwhile, Great Britain had refused to recognize American sovereignty in the area, claiming the territory for itself. After the War of 1812, however, Britain formally gave up its claim to the region in 1818 when an agreement between the two countries fixed the 49th Parallel as the boundary between the United States and British North America. This line runs from the Lake of the Woods west to the Rocky Mountains, establishing in the process what serves today as the northern boundary of North Dakota.

From the time of the Lewis and Clark expedition, the Missouri River had been a main avenue of transportation for the fur traders. For almost three decades, small boats plied its waters. Then, in 1832 the *Yellowstone* became the first steamboat to navigate within the area of North Dakota. The steamboat traveled as far as Fort Union, which had been built in 1828 by the American Fur Company of financier John Jacob Astor, the same trading company that owned the *Yellowstone*.

Fort Union was located close to the western border of North Dakota, at the confluence of the Yellowstone and Missouri Rivers. For four decades it was the largest and most important trading post in the upper Missouri region, and it also served as the gathering place for native tribes, artists, scientists, and missionaries. The region attracted such noted persons as John James Audubon, the ornithologist and painter of birds, and George Catlin, the American artist and author who painted hundreds of native portraits and nature scenes. Their various works, including personal journals, provide valuable historical material on the North Dakota area.

Settlement of the region was slow, and the fur traders had it virtually to themselves for a long time. Several native tribes also forcibly resisted the incursions by settlers on their lands. Eventually, a number of American military posts were established. The first was Fort Abercrombie, built in 1857 on the Red River at the eastern border of the state. Despite Sitting Bull's famous victory at Little Big Horn in 1876, American forces successfully overcame the native tribes by the end of the 19th century.

As the number of military posts grew and the native tribes were either subdued or pushed farther west, the flow of settlers into the Dakota region increased. The homestead laws passed by Congress beginning in 1862, which permitted settlers to claim up to 160 acres of free land, also encouraged settlement. Furthermore, the completion of the Northern Pacific Railway as far west as the North Dakota–Montana border in 1881 brought even more settlers. Among these early settlers was Theodore Roosevelt, who eventually purchased two ranches and lived in the region for several years.

The prelude to statehood began in 1868 when the Dakota Territory, which originally included Montana and Wyoming, was reduced in size to contain what is now North Dakota and South Dakota. Due to a conflict between the two regions over where the capital should be located, they were simply admitted as separate states, each with its own capital. The admission of North Dakota, with its capital at Bismarck, was proclaimed by President Benjamin Harrison on November 2, 1889.

South Dakota Admitted to the Union

Along with North Dakota, South Dakota joined the Union on November 2, 1889. The proclamation issued by President Benjamin Harrison made South Dakota the 40th state (North Dakota was officially the 39th state). The region comprising the two states had been united as the Dakota Territory, and had it not been for the protracted and bitter wrangling over the choice of a capital city, it might well have been admitted to the Union as a single state.

Native peoples are known to have lived in South Dakota, at least in the part that lies east of the Missouri River, prior to 1200. These people are known as Mound Builders, from their custom of building mounds of earth in which to bury their dead. The Arikara people were living in villages and farming near the Missouri River when the first Europeans of whom there is record, Louis Joseph and François de Varennes de La Várendrye, passed through South Dakota in 1742 and 1743. Starting out from Manitoba, Canada, these two sons of the French-Canadian explorer Pierre Gaultier de Varennes de La Várendrye were searching—unsuccessfully— for a route to the Pacific Ocean. In 1913 children found a lead plate buried in 1743 on a hill over-looking the Missouri River, opposite what is now the city of Pierre, by the brothers to establish a French claim to the region.

After 1750 the Dakota (or Santee Sioux) tribe, for whom the state is named, became numerous in South Dakota as the increasing number of settlers in Minnesota forced them westward. The movement of settlers into the South Dakota area was slow, however. Fur trappers began to filter in during the latter part of the century, when the region was under Spanish rule. In 1803 the United States acquired title to the land as part of the Louisiana Purchase. For the first time in more than half a century, explorers penetrated the region. At President Thomas Jefferson's behest, Meriwether Lewis and William Clark led an expedition that explored the vast unknown territory acquired in the Louisiana Purchase. During the westward journey from St. Louis to the Pacific coast of Oregon, the Lewis and Clark expedition crossed South Dakota in 1804, and again in 1806 on its return trip.

The success of the expedition prompted more trappers to seek their fortunes in new territory. Trading posts sprang up all over South Dakota, particularly on the banks of the Missouri River. One of the leading posts, Fort Pierre, was established in 1817. It was rebuilt by a subsidiary of the American Fur Company in 1832, a year after that same company had inaugurated steamboat travel on this section of the Missouri River. The fur trade boomed during the next two decades, but no significant permanent settlements were established. In 1856 an attempt was made by land speculators to create a settlement in southeastern South Dakota, at the falls of the Big Sioux River. A Sioux uprising in neighboring Minnesota in 1862, however, forced the settlers to flee.

Access to South Dakota was improved tremendously by the construction of a railroad line from Sioux City, Iowa, which reached Yankton, South Dakota, in 1872. The railroad was extended northward through the eastern part of the state, and reached Watertown in 1878. Many immigrants from northern Europe and Scandinavia made their way across the country to settle in the area of South Dakota east of the Missouri River. In addition, reports of gold lured many to the Black Hills of western South Dakota.

Members of an expedition led by General George A. Custer discovered the precious metal there in July 1874, and thereby set in motion a gold rush. Because the Black Hills were within the Sioux Reservation established by treaty between the United States government and the Sioux in 1868, the government tried to prevent people from entering the area while it attempted to persuade the Sioux to cede the territory. When the Sioux refused and a geological expedition in 1875 reported that the gold deposits were valuable, the government ceased its attempts to keep miners from the Black Hills. Even more valuable gold deposits were found in the vicinity of Deadwood and Lead, where in 1876 the Homestake Lode was discovered. The following two years saw the peak of the rush.

This invasion of their lands was deeply resented by the Sioux, and hostilities flared. Custer himself was killed, as were all of the men in his command, at Little Big Horn. In other battles, however, the Sioux were defeated and in 1877 they were forced to cede the Black Hills region to the government.

Gradually, the native tribes, forced to relinquish title to various parts of their lands, were relocated onto government reservations. One of the most famous tribal leaders who resisted was the powerful Sioux chief Sitting Bull, victor of the 1876 engagement at Little Big Horn. However, in 1881 he decided that he could no longer hold out, and surrendered to the United States authorities. By the end of the 19th century, there was no longer any significant native resistance.

The prelude to statehood began in 1868, when the Dakota Territory, which originally included Montana and Wyoming, was reduced in size to contain what is now North Dakota and South Dakota. Due to a conflict between the two regions over where the capital should be located, they were admitted as separate states, each with their own capital. The admission of South Dakota, with its capital at Pierre, was proclaimed by President Benjamin Harrison on November 2, 1889.

November 3

Edward Douglass White's Birthday

Edward Douglass White, the ninth chief justice of the United States Supreme Court, was the son of Edward D. White and Catherine Ringgold White. He was born in Lafourche Parish, Louisiana, on November 3, 1845, the great-grandson of an Irish immigrant. The White family became increasingly successful in its adopted land, and Edward White's father was prominent in Louisiana politics.

A Catholic, White attended Mount St. Mary's College in Emmitsburg, Maryland, and Georgetown College in Washington, D.C. He left Washington at the beginning of the Civil War to return home and enlist in the Confederate army. Union troops captured him after the fall of Port Hudson in 1863, but soon freed him on parole after he promised not to take up arms again.

White studied law after the Civil War and gained admission to the Louisiana bar in 1868. Entering politics, he won election to the state senate in 1874 and served as a judge on the state supreme court from January 1879 to April 1880. The state legislature selected White as a United States senator and he assumed that post on March 4, 1891.

A bitter feud between President Grover Cleveland and Senator David B. Hill made possible White's elevation to the United States Supreme Court. When Justice Samuel Blatchford of New York died in 1893, Hill thwarted Cleveland's attempt to name one of his loyalists from New York to replace Blatchford. Invoking senatorial courte-

sy, the custom by which the Senate granted its members what were essentially vetoes over appointments of residents from their home states to important federal posts, Hill prevented the confirmation of both William B. Hornblower and Wheeler H. Peckham. Knowing that Hill could not employ the same machinations against a fellow senator, Cleveland then nominated White, who took his seat on the bench on March 12, 1894.

In 1910 President William Howard Taft bypassed his own appointee to the bench, Charles Evans Hughes, to select White as chief justice of the United States. Historians tend to explain the nomination of the Louisiana Democrat as an attempt by the Republican president to make political inroads in the solidly Democratic South. White served as chief justice until his death in Washington, D.C., on May 21, 1921.

During his tenure as associate justice and later chief justice, White passed judgment in many vital cases, particularly in the fields of labor relations and commercial regulation. He opposed attempts by workers to gain better conditions through organization but made some allowance for governmental programs to improve their lot. In cases affecting big business, White consistently found unconstitutional the attempts of the Progressives to stem the growth of giant corporations.

In 1894 Eugene V. Debs, the president of the American Railway Union, defied a federal court injunction and led a strike against the Pullman Company. White concurred in the decision *In re Debs* (1895), which sustained the power of the government to issue injunctions in labor disputes and upheld Debs's citation for contempt. The Court based its opinion on the railroads' importance in interstate commerce and the transportation of the mails.

The Court in *Adair* v. *United States* (1908) declared unconstitutional the provision of the Erdman Act of 1898, which protected the rights of employees of interstate railroads to join unions. White concurred in this decision and in the finding of *Loewe* v. *Lawler* (1908) that a boycott by workers to force unionization constituted a conspiracy in restraint of trade. The latter suit, popularly known as the Danbury Hatters case, marked the first application of the Sherman Antitrust Act of 1890 to labor organizations. White displayed a somewhat more favorable attitude toward legislation that protected individual workers. In *Lochner* v. *New York* (1905) he unsuccessfully supported the constitutionality of a state law regulating the hours of bakery employees, although in *Bunting* v. *Oregon* (1917) he concurred in a decision that voided a similar law.

White saw little necessity to use the Sherman Antitrust Act against its intended targets, namely the large corporations that developed at the end of the 19th century. He concurred in the case of *United States* v. *E. C. Knight Company* (1895), which limited the law's jurisdiction over manufacturing in a highly artificial and strained distinction of that term with respect to commerce. In the *Northern Securities Company* case (1904) he dissented from the majority opinion, which rejuvenated the Sherman Antitrust Act by dissolving a major railroad holding company. White also issued important decisions in *United States* v. *American Tobacco Company* (1911) and *Standard Oil Company of New Jersey et al.* v. *United States* (1911).

General Election Day

This is a movable event.

Voting is both a right and, many feel, an obligation of United States citizenship. The power of the people to choose those who guide their public affairs is one of the principal advantages and ultimate safeguards of democracy.

The date reserved for elections varied from state to state during the early years of the nation. In 1845 the United States Congress took an important step toward establishing uniformity in federal elections by decreeing the first Tuesday after the first Monday in November to be the legal day every four years for the selection of presidential and vice-presidential electors. An 1872 federal statute set the same day for the biennial election of members of the United States House of Representatives. Since the ratification of the 17th Amendment in 1913, United States senators have also been elected by the people on that day.

The United States Constitution gives each state the right to establish voting qualifications for federal electors, and at various times the states have enfranchised only those persons who could meet property ownership, age, gender, residence, or other requirements. However, the adoption of several amendments to the Constitution in and since 1870 has considerably limited the restrictions that the states may set. The 15th Amendment enfranchised those who had previously been denied voting rights because of "race, color, or previous condition of servitude." The 19th Amendment enfranchised women. The 24th Amendment prohibited the imposition of a poll tax as a requirement for voting in national elections. In addition, the Voting Rights Act of 1965 outlawed the use of literacy tests and similar devices to deny the ballot to qualified voters and enabled the United States attorney general to send federal registrars into states and counties in which less than one-half of the voting-age population was registered. In 1971 the 26th Amendment set the voting age at 18 for all elections.

Many Americans, however, do not exercise their right to vote. Even in national elections the voter turnout rate is often barely half of the eligible voters. Organizations such as the League of Women Voters conduct massive campaigns every election year to educate Americans on the necessity of registering and the importance of voting. Most public schools hold special programs designed to acquaint future voters with their rights and responsibilities.

November 4

Will Rogers's Birthday

Will Rogers was born on November 4, 1879, in the Indian Territory halfway between the towns of Claremore and Oologah in what is now Oklahoma. "I usually say I was born in Claremore for convenience, because nobody but an Indian can pronounce Oologah" he once quipped. He was of Cherokee extraction on both sides of his family, and his father, Clem Vann Rogers, was prominent in the affairs of the Cherokee Nation. As Will Rogers told his audiences, "My ancestors didn't come over on the *Mayflower*, they met the boat."

After completing his formal education, including a brief period at the Kemper Military School in Boonville, Missouri, Rogers worked as a cowboy, rope artist, and rough rider. He traveled as far as Argentina, South Africa, and Australia, appearing in steer roping contests and Wild West shows.

Twirling a lariat, he made his first New York City vaudeville appearance in 1905 at Madison Square Garden. It was the beginning of a notable career in show business. He accidentally discovered that talking informally to the audience was a good accompaniment to his rope tricks. The image he projected was of a warm, homespun, gum-chewing, and, as he put it, "natchell" man. In his comments and jokes about current events the humorist delighted listeners by exposing smugness, bias, and hypocrisy wherever he saw them. By 1915 Rogers had achieved stardom on the stage, and beginning in 1916 he appeared in a number of Ziegfeld Follies presentations. His popularity continued to grow when he subsequently starred in motion pictures, wrote syndicated newspaper articles, lectured, performed over the radio, and wrote several books in which shrewd observations on life and politics were clothed in his dry wit.

The warm-hearted Rogers, who became famous as the "cowboy-philosopher" and as the author of the famous phrase "I never met a man I didn't like," was also an ardent fan of aviation. He died on August 15, 1935, with a fellow Oklahoman, the noted aviator Wiley Post, in an airplane crash near Point Barrow, Alaska. The Will Rogers and Wiley Post Monument was later erected at the site, and the Will Rogers Institute for medical care and research was later established in his honor.

Robert Mapplethorpe's Birthday

Robert Mapplethorpe, the controversial artist and photographer, was born on November 4, 1946, in Queens, New York. He was educated at the Pratt Institute of Art, where he studied painting and sculpture but eventually settled on a career in photography. He would become one of the most famous photographers in recent history, honored and reviled in almost equal measure.

Mapplethorpe's portfolio had a heavy emphasis on still lifes, portraits, and studies of the nude, sometimes with sadistic or masochistic themes. Public exhibitions of his work began in 1976, and the pictures displaying homosexuals engaged in sex and sadomasochism against classical backdrops drew both critical acclaim and public notoriety. The sensational nature of this type of work often overshadowed his more conventional but equally noteworthy photographs of celebrities and floral still lifes.

Mapplethorpe held exhibitions at such prestigious museums as the Corcoran Gallery in Washington, D.C. (1978), the Musée National d'Art Moderne in Paris, France (1983), and the Whitney Museum in New York (1988). Some led to such outrage that the museums involved had to either cancel the shows or deal with obscenity charges brought by local authorities. Nevertheless, collections of Mapplethorpe's work have been acquired by the Art Institute of Chicago (located in Chicago, Illinois), the Metropolitan Museum and the Museum of Modern Art (located in New York, New York), the Pompidou Center (located in Paris, France) and the Victoria and Albert Museum (located in London, England). Mapplethorpe died on March 9, 1989, in Boston, Massachusetts.

November 5

John Dickinson Writes the First of the "Farmer's Letters"

On November 5, 1767, John Dickinson wrote the first of the series of his famed "Letters from a Farmer in Pennsylvania to the Inhabitants of the British Colonies." According to the 19th-century literary historian Moses Coit Tyler, publication of the "Farmer's Letters" was "the most brilliant event in the literary history of the [American] Revolution." Aside from their literary merit, the essays are also important because they set forth strong arguments for the colonists' opposition to the hated Townshend Acts of 1767.

In the years following the Treaty of Paris of 1763, the British government tried repeatedly to force the American colonies to bear some of the cost of their own defense. In 1764 Parliament passed the Sugar Act, which increased the duties on foreign refined sugar and other non-British goods. The next year Parliament passed the Stamp Act, levying the first direct tax on the American colonies by requiring tax stamps to be affixed to various articles, including newspapers, pamphlets, almanacs, legal documents, and playing cards.

The colonies protested the Sugar Act by pledging not to import the goods subject to the additional duties specified by that legislation, and their resistance to the Stamp Act was even stronger. Secret organizations, most notably the Sons of Liberty, forced the resignation of all stamp agents in America. The Stamp Act Congress, meeting in October 1765, prepared resolutions demanding the repeal of the act. Colonial merchants refused to import European goods until the stamp tax was ended. The last measure was the most effective: British merchants whose businesses suffered because of the nonimportation agreements appealed to Parliament to repeal the Stamp Act. In March 1766 Parliament agreed to their demands.

Just over a year after the repeal of the Stamp Act, the British government again tried to raise revenue from the American colonies. Persuaded by Chancellor of the Exchequer Charles Townshend that the Americans might accept taxation if it was an "external" levy on trade, in June 1767 Parliament approved import duties on glass, lead paints, paper, and tea. To enforce the collection of these duties, the so-called Townshend Acts set up an American Board of Commissioners of Customs in Boston and established vice-admiralty courts whose judges were to be paid from the fines and judgments collected from the colonials violating the new legislation. These acts also suspended the

New York Assembly until that body agreed to comply with the Quartering Act of 1765, which required colonial governments to provide barracks and other necessities for the British troops garrisoned in America.

In the autumn of 1767, after the American colonists refused to accept the Townshend Acts, the major Atlantic seaports implemented nonimportation procedures in order to force Parliament to rescind the new duties. As the major colonial cities agreed to ban foreign goods, John Dickinson took up his pen on November 5, 1767, to warn his fellow colonists of the dangers of the Townshend Acts.

Dickinson, who was born on November 8, 1732, was fairly typical of the conservative businessmen and other people who led the opposition to the Townshend Acts. The son of a gentleman farmer, he studied law in Philadelphia and London, served in the Assembly of the Lower Counties (the lower legislative house of Delaware), and then won election to the Pennsylvania legislature.

Reflecting the substantial position and conservative nature of their author, the "Farmer's Letters" firmly opposed the Townshend Acts but did not advocate any radical or violent measures to force their repeal. Dickinson recognized force as the ultimate avenue of redress, but he stated eloquently that "the course of Liberty is a cause of too much dignity to be sullied by turbulence and tumult." Instead he urged the colonists to "behave like dutiful children, who have received unmerited blows from a beloved parent. Let us complain to our parent; but let our complaints speak at the same time the language of affliction and veneration."

Although Dickinson counseled his fellow Americans to use moderate means to oppose the Townshend Acts, his "Farmer's Letters" were an important step in the colonists' efforts to set forth the exact nature of their relationship with Great Britain. Dickinson agreed that Parliament had the authority to impose import duties on the colonies for the purpose of regulating the trade of the British Empire, but he argued that Parliament had no right to pass legislation such as the Townshend Acts that were intended primarily to raise revenue. Dickinson also took Parliament to task for suspending the New York Assembly, and he warned the Americans that this action was a threat to the liberties of all the colonies.

Printed anonymously in the *Pennsylvania Chronicle* from the end of November 1767 through January 1768, the "Farmer's Letters" were quickly recognized to be the work of Dickinson. Moreover, the cogent arguments against the Townshend Acts presented in the essays made them extremely popular. They were published in all but four of the 25 newspapers then printed in the colonies, and as a pamphlet that went through at least eight editions. The "Farmer's Letters" were also published and circulated throughout Europe.

So popular were the "Farmer's Letters" that colonial town meetings, grand juries, and other groups voted Dickinson public thanks. The College of New Jersey (later Princeton University) granted him the degree of doctor of laws. The "Farmer's Letters" made Dickinson one of the most respected political theorists in the 1760s and 1770s. He was a member of the First and Second Continental Congresses. In 1776 Dickinson, believing conciliation with Great Britain might still be possible, refused to sign the Declaration of Independence. However, once the colonies decided to separate from Britain, he joined in the fight for independence. He served in Congress during the American Revolution, was elected president of the Supreme Executive Council of Delaware in 1781, held a similar post (equivalent to governor) in Pennsylvania from 1782 to 1785, and represented Delaware at the Constitutional Convention in 1787. Dickinson was also influential in securing the adoption of the new federal Constitution in his two home states: Delaware and Pennsylvania, respectively, were the first two states to ratify the new form of government.

He published two volumes of his writings in 1801, the *The Political Writings of John Dickinson, Esq., Late President of the State of Delaware and of the Commonwealth of Pennsylvania*. Dickinson College in Carlisle, Pennsylvania, chartered in 1783, was named in his honor. He died in Wilmington, Delaware, on February 14, 1808.

Eugene Debs's Birthday

Eugene Victor Debs, the union organizer and five-time Socialist Party candidate for president of the United States, was born on November 5, 1855, in Terre Haute, Indiana. His parents were immigrants from the Alsace region of France. In his early teens Debs began working for the local railroad in addition to holding other jobs, but soon developed an interest in politics and union organizing. In 1875 he took charge of the local Brotherhood of Locomotive Firemen, and became secretary-treasurer of the national Brotherhood from 1880 to 1893. He also served as the clerk of the city of Terre Haute for a time.

In 1885 he was elected to the Indiana state legislature, where he served until 1887. He left the secretary-treasurer of the Brotherhood position in 1893, to become the president of the newly formed American Railway Union. Debs led the union into a major confrontation with the western railroads and the federal government in 1894 when he ordered a strike on behalf of the Pullman railroad car workers. With the assistance of the federal courts, President Grover Cleveland broke the strike and had Debs arrested for violating an injunction against continuing the strike.

During his brief term of imprisonment, Debs met Socialist Party leaders such as Victor Berger. Inspired, he left the American Railway Union in 1897 and in 1900 became the Socialist candidate for president of the United States. Debs received 87,814 votes, a token percentage of the electorate. Nevertheless, he continued working and speaking on behalf of the Socialist movement. He was the Socialist candidate for president again in 1904 (with 402,283 votes), 1908 (420,793 votes), 1912 (900,672 votes), and 1920 (919,799 votes). During World War I he was imprisoned for his antiwar activities, but his sentence was commuted in 1921. Debs's 1920 presidential campaign was, in fact, run while he was behind bars.

During the 1920s he wrote articles for the Socialist Party's weekly publication, *Appeal to Reason*. He also wrote the book *Walls and Bars*, published posthumously in 1927. Debs died on October 20, 1926, in Elmhurst, Illinois.

November 6

John Carroll Appointed First Roman Catholic Bishop in the United States

On November 6, 1789, the see (or diocese) of Baltimore, Maryland, was established when John Carroll received his official appointment as bishop of Baltimore, thus becoming the first Roman Catholic bishop in the United States.

The Carrolls were a wealthy and distinguished family. John Carroll's brother Daniel was one of the signers of the Constitution of the United States, and his cousin Charles Carroll of Carrollton (as he styled himself) was one of the signers of the Declaration of Independence. John Carroll himself was born in Upper Marlborough, Maryland, on January 8, 1738. He received some of his early education at Bohemia Manor, a Jesuit elementary school in northern Maryland. Subsequently, since there were no Catholic high schools and few secondary schools that would take Catholics in that era of religious intolerance, when he was 13 years old he was sent abroad with his cousin Charles to St. Omer's, a well-known school run by English Jesuits in French Flanders. Charles completed his education and returned to America in

1765, while John entered the Jesuit order in Belgium in 1753 and was ordained (probably in 1769) after the traditionally lengthy Jesuit training.

After traveling extensively in Europe (1771–1773) as tutor to the son of a British nobleman named Lord Stourton, Carroll was back at the Jesuit house in Bruges, Belgium, in the summer of 1773 when news arrived that the Jesuit order had been dissolved by papal action on July 21, 1773 (it was restored many years later). Carroll remained at the house until the following October, when government officials invaded it and Carroll was arrested. Lord Arundell of Wardour intervened, and Carroll went to England to serve as family chaplain.

In 1774 Carroll returned to America where he lived with his aged mother at Rock Creek, Maryland, performing priestly duties and ministering to the spiritual needs of people in the area. From the time that he returned to America, he dedicated himself to two goals, both of which he saw achieved in his lifetime. First, as an American, he was a staunch advocate of American independence. Second, as a priest, he hoped to organize the Roman Catholic clergy in America for a more effective ministry.

At the request of the Continental Congress, in 1776 John Carroll accompanied his cousin Charles Carroll, Samuel Chase, and Benjamin Franklin to Canada to ask Canada to either join with the colonies in their fight for independence or to at least remain neutral. The mission failed, and the discouraged Americans made the long journey home. Carroll returned to Philadelphia, Pennsylvania, with the ailing 70-year-old Franklin, who thanked him for his "friendly assistance and tender care."

In 1784, when the pope moved to appoint a vicar general for the Roman Catholic clergy in the United States, it was on Franklin's recommendation that Carroll was named "head of the missions in the provinces . . . of the United States." After receiving his episcopal appointment in 1789, Carroll went to Great Britain to be consecrated by Bishop Charles Walmesley on August 15, 1790, in Lulworth Castle Chapel in Dorset. Carroll returned to America as a consecrated bishop with a diocese—then the only see in the United States—that stretched from the Atlantic Ocean to the Mississippi River and from Canada to Florida.

Even before he had received any official authority, Carroll set about his life's work of building schools, establishing seminaries, and encouraging the formation of religious orders of men and women. In 1789 he founded an "academy" at "George Town on the Patowmack River, Maryland," the first Catholic college in the United States. Carroll lived to see Georgetown raised from college to university rank in 1815, and today Georgetown University is one of the most prestigious institutions of higher learning in the United States.

In 1791 Carroll founded St. Mary's Seminary in Baltimore, the first Catholic seminary (which was closed in 1969) in the United States. Carroll was recognized not only as a founder of Catholic schools, but also as a patron of all educational institutions. He served on the boards of several secular schools and colleges. He was also the president of the Baltimore Library Company from its inception until his death. In 1785 George Washington and John Carroll both received honorary degrees at the second annual commencement of Washington College in Chestertown, Maryland.

The first American bishop visited the first American president in retirement at Mount Vernon, and after Washington's death Carroll preached a eulogy for him at St. Peter's Church in Baltimore on February 22, 1800. In recognition of his patriotism, Carroll was invited to speak at the 1815 laying of the cornerstone of the first Washington Monument to be built (at Charles and Monument streets in Baltimore), but poor health forced him to decline the offer. Carroll, who had been made an archbishop on April 8, 1808, died on December 3, 1815, and was buried in the chapel of St. Mary's Seminary in Baltimore. In 1824 his body was removed to the cathedral. A number of educational centers have been named for him, the oldest and most notable being Cleveland's John Carroll University, founded by Jesuits in 1886.

First College Football Game

The first intercollegiate football game was held on November 6, 1869, between Rutgers University and Princeton University. Columbia, Cornell, and other eastern schools also began to form teams for intercollegiate football competitions, which for a time were primarily the domain of the elite schools. Harvard was reluctant to join the competitions at first, since it wished to retain its own game rules, but beginning in 1874 began to waive its objections. In 1875 representatives from Columbia, Harvard, Princeton, and Yale met at Springfield, Massachusetts, to draft a set of common football rules and to form the Intercollegiate Football Association, which was dissolved in 1894 and succeeded by a rules committee.

In 1905 the National Collegiate Athletic Association (NCAA) was formed to help curb some of the more violent plays and tactics then common in the game. President Theodore Roosevelt sponsored two White House conferences of college athletic officials to encourage such reforms. In December 1905 Chancellor Henry M. MacCrack-

en of New York University held a conference of 13 schools to further discuss modifying the rules of intercollegiate football, and on December 28 the Intercollegiate Athletic Association of the United States (IAAUS) was founded in New York, New York, with 62 initial members. The IAAUS was renamed the NCAA in 1910 and is still the principle authority governing college football in addition to a number of other intercollegiate athletic activities.

Professional football teams began to spring up as well, subject to the rules of various for-profit leagues rather than the NCAA, but for many decades college football was decidedly more popular. This began to change in the 1950s, however, with the spread of television. As a fast-moving action-oriented sport, football was ideal for television, and the professional teams could take their pick of the most talented college players when they graduated. Eventually, professional football began to eclipse college football.

One exception to this rule, however, is the series of post season intercollegiate football contests known as the bowl games (see January 1). Essentially, the best college football teams of the season as determined by national polls of sportswriters and coaches get invited to widely televised bowl games, such as the Rose Bowl, Sugar Bowl, Orange Bowl, and Cotton Bowl. There are many lesser bowl games as well.

November 7

Harvard Established

On November 7, 1636 (or October 28, according to the Julian or Old Style calendar then in use), the General Court of Massachusetts (which was basically the government of the colony) ordered the establishment of a "schoale or colledge" and appropriated 400 English pounds for it. This was an impressive amount for the Massachusetts Bay Colony, whose founding had taken place less than ten years earlier and whose population of under 10,000 had scarcely secured the necessities of life. In fact, the appropriation represented more than half the entire colony's tax levy for 1635 and almost one quarter for 1636.

Since educated clergymen were essential in the theocratic Puritan colony, the establishment of an institution of higher learning was necessary. As *New Englands First Fruits* (1643) stated:

> After God had carried us safe to New England, and wee had builded our houses, provided necessaries for our liveli-hood, rear'd convenient places for Gods worship, and

setled the Civill Government: One of the next things we longed for, and looked after was to advance Learning and perpetuate it to Posterity; dreading to leave an illiterate Ministery to the Churches, when our present Ministers shall lie in the Dust.

The first step in this direction was the general court's order of 1636. The November 7 order did not determine the type of institution to be established, as in whether it would be a boys' boarding school, a college of university standing, or something in between. However, it stipulated that "the next Court [is] to appoint wheare and what building." The following session, which met at Boston on December 17, 1636, had more pressing business at hand. Thus, it was not until the meeting of the general court on November 25, 1637, that the college was "ordered to bee at Newetowne" as Cambridge, Massachusetts, was then known. The founders had probably been influenced in their conception of a university site by the grounds of Cambridge University, where many of the leading men of the colony had been educated. Wishing to find a place level enough for building and protected from the winds and sea, they decided upon Newtown. This fortified capital of the colony, a "spacious plain more like a bowling green than a Wilderness," was nestled between the salt marshes and low hills of the placid Charles River between Charlestown and Watertown.

On December 1, 1637, the session appointed the first board of overseers, consisting of Governor John Winthrop, Deputy-Governor Thomas Dudley, four other magistrates, and six ministers. Presented with the tremendous task of setting up a college that existed only on paper, without property, officers, or students, the board hired the 27-year-old "professor" Nathaniel Eaton. On May 12, 1638, the general court ordered "that Newetowne shall henceforth be called Cambridge" after the English university. Sometime before June 19, 1638, the board housed Eaton and his family in the Peyntree House, which had been described as "one House with a backside and garden about halfe a rood, one Cowhouse with a backside aboute one acker in Cowyarde Rowe." Thus the doors of the first college and what was to become one of the best American educational institutions opened in 1638, probably in July or August and certainly by early September.

On September 17 a letter from Edmund Browne addressed to Sir Simonds D'Ewes proudly stated that "wee have a Cambridge heere, a College erecting, youth lectured, a library, and I suppose there will be a presse this winter." One week later, on September 24, a young Puritan immigrant named John Harvard died in Charlestown.

The *New Englands First Fruits* reported that it had "pleased God to stir up the heart of . . . Mr. Harvard . . . to give the one halfe of his Estate (it being in all about 1,700 pounds) towards the erecting of a Colledge, and all his Library." Although John Harvard did not initiate the institution, secure its charter, or provide money to set the college in operation, he was its first benefactor. On March 23, 1639, the general court, meeting at Boston, "ordered, that the college agreed upon formerly to bee built at Cambrige shal bee called Harvard Colledge."

The dozen or so students of Harvard College studied and lived in the single frame Peyntree House in College Yard. The harsh punishments and scanty diet, which characterized Master Nathaniel Eaton's regime, were exposed in 1639 at a public trial in which Eaton's wife confessed:

And for the bad fish, that they had it brought to table, I am sorry there was that cause of offence given them. I acknowledge my sin in it. And for their mackerel, brought to them with their guts in them, and goat's dung in their hasty pudding, it's utterly unknown to me, but I am much ashamed it should be in the family, and not prevented by myself or servants, and I humbly acknowledge my negligence in it.

In 1640 the almost defunct college received new life with the selection of Henry Dunster, a Cambridge graduate who was soon to prove himself a remarkable teacher and administrator, as the new president. The first commencement took place in 1642, and by the time Harvard celebrated its ten-year anniversary some 1,248 men had received degrees.

Although the primary stated purpose of Harvard College was to provide clergymen for the colonies, graduates actually entered all walks of colonial life. The charter of 1650 dedicated the institution to "the advancement of all good literature, arts, and sciences" and to "the education of the English and Indian youth . . . in knowledge and godlynes." Liberal arts courses were modeled upon those at Oxford and Cambridge, and before long the college had built up a solid curriculum in mathematics and the physical sciences. Harvard also received generous contributions from abroad for the special purpose of educating the "savages." Although a good number of Native Americans were students, only one, Caleb Cheeshahteaumuck, was awarded a bachelor's degree, in 1665.

By the turn of the century, the college's growing liberalism alarmed conservatives, such as the Reverend Solomon Stoddard of Northampton, who wrote that "Places of Learning should not be Places of Riot and Pride; tis not worth the while for persons to be sent to the Colledge to learn to Complement men and Court Women."

Since the board of overseers had proved too unwieldy to run an educational institution, the Massachusetts General Court at President Dunster's request granted Harvard a corporate charter in 1650. The document created a self-perpetuating corporation, the first in North America, composed of Harvard's president, treasurer, and five fellows. They were empowered to function as the executive of the college, subject to veto by the board of overseers in matters of special importance. Known as The President and Fellows of Harvard College, it controlled funds, held property and investments, retained copyrights, made contracts, appointed all officers, and awarded degrees. Many of these administrative features remain in existence today.

At first the board of overseers jointly represented the state and the church. During its early history, the college was closely allied with the Congregational Church (later with the Unitarian), although the state of Masachusetts, as founder and patron, long considered it a state institution. By 1851, however, representation of the clergy on the board of overseers had ceased to be obligatory. Financial help and dependence upon state agencies gradually died out until, in 1865, all connections were formally severed. Starting with John Harvard, Harvard College was increasingly supported by private contributions.

During the second half of the 19th century, Harvard experienced a period of unprecedented development under the presidency of the noted educator Charles W. Eliot. Although the college continued to be the hub of intellectual activity, after 1869 Harvard became a university in the highest sense. Schools that had previously been established—medicine in 1782, divinity in 1816, law in 1817, and dental medicine in 1867—were raised to graduate level. Others were founded: arts and sciences in 1872, business administration in 1908, education in 1920, public health in 1922, design in 1936, and public administration (later the John Fitzgerald Kennedy School of Government) in 1937. Radcliffe College, established in 1879 as an institution of higher learning for women, is officially connected with Harvard. It received its present name in 1894 in honor of Ann Radcliffe, who gave Harvard College its first scholarship in 1643.

Harvard University, an enormous educational complex with a huge endowment, has over the years acquired unique prestige and influence. It is the alma mater of notable Americans in politics, law, science, literature, the arts, business and finance, education, and religion. Among its distin-guished graduates are John Adams, Franklin D. Roosevelt, John F. Kennedy, Ralph Waldo Emerson, Henry James, and Oliver Wendell Holmes. Many foreign students, including future government leaders, are sent to Harvard.

Battle of Tippecanoe

In the tragic and ultimately irreconcilable struggle between Native Americans and westward advancing American settlers, the battle of Tippecanoe on November 7, 1811, is one of the most historic episodes.

Even before the American Revolution, the colonists had looked longingly toward the fertile trans-Appalachian lands. However, the British with their Proclamation of 1763 restricted colonial settlements to the seaboard area east of the mountains. The achievement of American independence in 1783, however, ended the British prohibition against westward expansion. By the Treaty of Paris of 1783, Great Britain ceded the entire area east of the Mississippi to the United States, and the new American nation immediately began preparations to occupy the trans-Appalachian region. As early as 1784 plans were made for organizing the Northwest Territory, namely the area that is now composed of Ohio, Indiana, Illinois, Michigan, and Wisconsin. By 1787 the Northwest Ordinance establishing a government for the territory had gained congressional approval.

The region between the Appalachians and the Mississippi River was already occupied by dozens of native tribes, but the American government argued that the natives had forfeited their claim to the land by fighting on the side of the British during the American Revolution. Consequently, between 1784 and 1786 the Americans forced many tribes in the Northwest Territory to sign treaties giving over their lands to the United States government as war reparations.

By 1786 the native tribes had begun to resist the American encroachment on their lands. The American government, in turn, realized that it could not afford either the vast military expenditures necessary to coerce the natives into relinquishing their lands nor the unfavorable foreign reaction that would accompany such a policy. Thus, after 1786 the United States adopted a new approach to westward expansion. Returning to the British and colonial practice of acknowledging the tribes' right of soil, the government decided to purchase native lands and to set the boundaries of such territorial acquisitions by means of formal treaties.

The government's new policy tacitly assumed that the tribes would willingly agree to sell their lands and accept the settlers' way of life. Indeed, part of the rationale used to justify the acquisition of native territory was that the introduction of such European concepts as individual ownership of property and European methods of intensive agriculture, animal husbandry, and domestic manufacture would ultimately benefit the tribes. This assumption was unrealistic.

The tribes did not want to abandon either their lands or their ways of life, but the relentless influx of American settlers into the Northwest Territory seemed to offer few alternatives. The military victory of General Anthony Wayne at Fallen Timbers in 1794 forced them in 1795 to agree to the Treaty of Greenville, which gave the United States control of sections of eastern and southern Ohio, a strip of land in Indiana, and other, scattered tracts. Even this major cession did not satisfy the lust for land, however. The young nation was determined to expand westward, and from 1801 to 1810 a number of tribes were tricked or coerced into agreeing to a series of treaties that ceded a total of 110 million acres in the Ohio Valley to the United States.

During the first decade of the 19th century, pioneer settlements in the Northwest Territory increased, and incidents of violence likewise became more frequent. Against this background two Shawnee leaders, Tecumseh and his brother Tenskwatawa, who was known as the Prophet, attempted to unite the various tribes against their common enemy. Tecumseh argued that the vast unsettled trans-Appalachian regions belonged to all the tribes in common and that no individual chief or tribe could sell or cede land. Tenskwatawa urged the tribes to cast off all American influence and goods (particularly alcohol) and return to their own ways.

To resist the American advance, Tecumseh tried to organize all the Northwest Territory tribes into one confederation. As he worked to unite the tribes, William Henry Harrison, the governor of the Indiana Territory, continued his relentless effort to bring more native lands under federal control. When in 1809 Harrison persuaded the Delaware, Potawatomie, Miami, and Eel River tribes to accept the Treaty of Fort Wayne, which ceded large areas in Indiana to the United States government, Tecumseh's followers became enraged. By 1810 tribal relations in the territory had deteriorated to such an extent that on several occasions Harrison reported that war seemed imminent. In his reports to the federal government, Harrison tended to blame the activities of British agents for the hostility of the natives, although in reality the cessions of 1809 seem to have caused the climate of tension.

In July 1811 Tecumseh tried to intimidate Harrison by warning him of his intention to enlist aid from the southern tribes. Tecumseh's warning convinced Harrison of the necessity of taking military action against the tribes. He selected Prophetstown, a village where some of Tecumseh's followers lived, near the junction of the Tippecanoe and Wabash Rivers as his target. Harrison waited until Tecumseh had left the village for a southern trip. Then, on November 6, 1811, he and 1,000 soldiers advanced to within a mile of Prophetstown. Thus menaced, the apprehensive natives attacked Harrison's encampment at dawn on November 7. Recoiling from the initial blow, Harrison's men were able to turn the natives back and to raze their village. However, neither side scored a decisive victory. The two contesting forces suffered roughly equal casualties.

The battle of Tippecanoe had both short- and long-range consequences. Most immediately, the encounter served to convince the American settlers that the British were responsible for backing Tecumseh's followers. This feeling resulted in renewed cries for the conquest of Canada as the best means of safeguarding the frontier. The tribes, for their part, saw the battle as additional evidence that the United States would be satisfied with nothing less than complete control of the Northwest Territory. This realization prompted many tribes of the region to ally themselves with the British when the War of 1812 broke out in June. The one-day skirmish at Tippecanoe also produced a hero in the form of William Henry Harrison. His so-called victory brought him to national prominence, and in 1840 under the slogan "Tippecanoe and Tyler Too" he won election as president of the United States.

November 8

Founding of Mount Holyoke College, the First American College for Women

Mount Holyoke College, founded on November 8, 1837, by Mary Lyon, became the first institution for the higher education of women in the United States. Although not the first institution of its kind to be granted a college charter, it was the forerunner in offering young women an education conforming to college standards.

Mary Lyon, a pioneer in the higher education of women, was born on a farm near Buckland, Massachusetts, on February 28, 1797. Her father,

Aaron Lyon, died before she was six years old, leaving seven children to the care of his wife. In 1817, with savings earned from spinning and weaving, Mary Lyon attended the Sanderson Academy in Ashfield, Massachusetts, and later studied in Amherst, Massachusetts.

In 1821 Lyon entered a seminary supervised by the Reverend Joseph Emerson in Byfield, Massachusetts. She remained there for two terms and then became associate principal of an academy in Ashfield. In 1824 she accepted a position as a teacher at the Adams Female Academy in Londonderry, New Hampshire. When the 19th-century custom of making girls remain at home in winter provided a respite from teaching at Londonderry, Lyon taught at her own winter school in Buckland. She terminated this venture in the late 1820s, however, when Zilpah P. Grant (a fellow student at Byfield) opened a seminary in Ipswich, Massachusetts, and asked Lyon to be her assistant. Lyon also made the most of her few opportunities to participate, at least informally, in men's education. She attended natural history lectures at Amherst College and studied chemistry at what was later the Rensselaer Polytechnic Institute.

During these 13 years of teaching at financially insecure seminaries at which girls acquired a smattering of knowledge, Lyon became convinced that there should be an institution for young women that was not dependent for its existence upon the life of the person who opened it. A school, with a board of disinterested trustees, that would "outlive the teachers and the principal," "a permanent institution consecrated to the training of young women for usefulness [and] designed to furnish every advantage which the state of education in this country will allow." She herself had experienced the hurdles then facing any woman who desired an education that was at once sounder in content and more serious in its aim than the curriculum of "ornamental" subjects offered in the typical women's academies of the period. Lyon also wanted an institution that was not limited to the daughters of rich families.

Reinforcing her enthusiasm with common sense, she set about the task of securing the necessary financial aid for her plan. On September 6, 1834, a group of men interested in the project met with her at Ipswich to consider ways of establishing the institution she envisioned. For the next two years she ran a fund-raising campaign as donations ranging from six cents to $1,000 trickled in. Having overcome indifference and antagonism in persuading a reluctant public that women should have educational opportunities comparable to those offered to men at Harvard and Yale, she was able to write on October 9, 1836: "I have lived to see the

time, when a body of gentlemen have ventured to lay the cornerstone of an edifice which will cost about $15,000, and for an institution for females." She predicted that "this will be an era in female education. The work will not stop with this institution."

After nearly four years of preparation and fund-raising, the Mount Holyoke Female Seminary was opened on November 8, 1837, nearly two years after the original charter had passed the Massachusetts legislature on February 11, 1836. Admission requirements were strict, and the entrance age was set at 17. The original course of study, modeled largely on the systematic curriculum offered at Amherst College, included mathematics, English, science, philosophy, and Latin, while music and modern languages were added later. There was no course in domestic science because Lyon did not think that subject had a proper place in a literary institution. To reduce the cost of operating the seminary, she had the students do the housework. A diploma was given after three years of study at the new institution, but Lyon anticipated its evolution into a four-year curriculum, which eventually came in 1861. The teachers were women, with visiting male faculty members from Williams and Amherst Colleges supplementing the instruction of the resident faculty.

Lyon had no doubts about the lasting success of her endeavors and always spoke of Mount Holyoke's original building, which was swept by fire in 1896, as "the first building." Indeed the seminary was immediately popular: At the beginning of its second year, 400 young women seeking admission had to be turned away for lack of room.

Serving as president of Mount Holyoke for nearly 12 years on an annual salary of only $200, Lyon enlarged and expanded the facilities until the institution earned a national reputation for its high standards. She died on March 5, 1849, and was buried on the grounds of the institution.

The Mount Holyoke Female Seminary set the pattern for future independent women's colleges. Other institutions, modeled on Mount Holyoke and upon the educational principles expressed in Lyon's *Tendencies of the Principles Embraced and the System Adopted in the Mount Holyoke Seminary* (1840), sprang up in the United States and abroad.

World War II: U.S. Troops Land in North Africa

On November 8, 1942, American forces under General Dwight D. Eisenhower staged their first major operation in the European theater when they landed in North Africa. Although it was a sideshow to the titanic struggle on the Russian front between Nazi and Soviet armies, North Africa was nevertheless the scene of important engagements between the Germans under General Erwin Rommel and the British (based in Egypt) under General Bernard L. Montgomery. Neither side had yet secured effective control over the region.

The entry of the United States into World War II in December 1941 gave the hard-pressed opponents of Nazism new hope of ultimate victory. Both the British and their Soviet allies wanted the Americans to enter combat as soon as possible, in order to relieve their own weary soldiers of part of the burden. One proposal, favored by American military planners and by the Soviets, was for an early cross-Channel invasion of continental Europe. However, President Franklin D. Roosevelt of the United States and Prime Minister Winston Churchill of Great Britain vetoed this plan as too rash. Instead, in July 1942 they chose North Africa as a more vulnerable invasion target and planned the undertaking for the fall.

On August 14, 1942, Eisenhower received the title of commander in chief of the Allied Expeditionary Force, and assumed responsibility for the North African operation. Major General Mark Clark of the United States was Eisenhower's acting deputy commander in chief, and Admiral Sir Andrew B. Cunningham of Great Britain served as overall naval commander. Brigadier General James H. Doolittle directed American air units, and Air Marshal Sir William L. Welch led the British units.

Casablanca, Oran, and Algiers, politically important cities in western North Africa, became invasion targets. A separate task force received the mission of taking each of these hubs in the rail, highway, and communications systems of the region. French troops, subject to German control, garrisoned the area since, as part of France's colonial empire, that region had fallen to the Nazis. The Western Task Force, composed of American troops, was to leave the United States and sail directly to Casablanca. The Center Task Force, also American but with naval and air components that were largely British, was to embark from Britain and proceed to Oran. The Eastern Task Force, including British as well as American troops, was to depart from Britain and attack Algiers. Having secured their objectives, the Western and Center groups were to be ready to invade Spanish Morocco if it became necessary to repel a possible German invasion launched from Spain. The Eastern Task Force would become the British First Army under Lieutenant General Kenneth A. N. Anderson and would move east to Tunisia.

D day for Operation Torch, the code name for the invasion, was November 8, 1942. By November 7 the Western Task Force was in position, and the ships of the Center and Eastern groups moved past Oran and Algiers (as if to approach Malta or the Suez Canal) and then swung sharply south toward their real objectives under the cover of darkness. As the night of November 7 passed, the men aboard the transports made their final preparations for battle. At each of the three landing sites, the tactics would be similar, as the commanders planned to place units on the coastal flanks of the targets and then take them by envelopment.

Elements of Major General George S. Patton's Western Task Force hit the beach at Casablanca between 4:00 a.m. and 6:00 a.m. on November 8. Hopes that pro-American French officers in Morocco would not oppose the invaders proved unfounded, and the French troops resisted the Americans. Major General Ernest Harmon's men seized Safi, below Casablanca, by 10:15 a.m. on November 8. They took Marrakesh the following day and Mazagan on November 11. On the opposite flank, to the north of Casablanca, the Third Division took Fedala by the afternoon of November 8 and overran the Port of Lyautey airfield on November 10. Patton requested the surrender of Casablanca, and the French commander gave up the struggle on November 11 at 7:00 a.m. pursuant to orders from his superiors in Algiers.

At Oran, Major General Lloyd Fredendall landed his Center Task Force at approximately 1:30 a.m. on November 8, 1942. A direct assault on the city's harbor was a costly failure, but in general the Americans made excellent progress. Fredendall's men enveloped Oran, and on November 10 at 12:30 p.m. the city surrendered. British and American troops of the Eastern Task Force met only light resistance at Algiers, because pro-American French soldiers managed to seize power in the city at the critical moment. By the nightfall of November 8, the Allies were in control.

Hitler saw the danger to Rommel's troops that the Allied invasion posed and immediately sent supplemental forces to Tunisia. General Walther Nehring arrived in Tunis on November 16, 1942, to assume command of the German and Italian units and held control until General Jürgen von Arnim replaced him on December 9. From this stronghold, the Germans hoped to expand their area of control and stop the Allied pincer movement. After several months of heavy fighting, however, they were unsuccessful and the Allies took hundreds of thousands of prisoners. When it was over, North Africa and the Suez Canal were safe from the Axis menace, the Mediterranean was open to Allied shipping, and the Americans and

British began their preparations for the invasion of Sicily.

Montana Admitted to the Union

On February 22, 1889, President Grover Cleveland signed the Omnibus Statehood Bill, which authorized the admission of Montana, North Dakota, South Dakota, Washington, Idaho, and Wyoming into the United States. The Montana territorial government immediately completed the legal steps required by the United States Constitution, and Montana was officially proclaimed the 41st state on November 8, 1889.

The residents of the Montana Territory had desired admission to the Union for some time, but earlier efforts in the direction of statehood had been less successful. Although a constitutional convention had been held in Helena in 1884, it was ignored by the United States Congress, and came to nothing. With the enactment of the enabling legislation of February 22, 1889, however, a new constitutional convention met in Montana on July 4. By the middle of August it had completed a frame of government for approval by the citizenry. On October 1 the people ratified the document by a wide margin and then chose their first state officials. Joseph K. Toole, who had served as the territory's delegate to Congress, became the first governor.

Democrats and Republicans sitting in the first legislature were unable to agree on the choice of United States senators for the new state. Both parties attempted to appoint two of their own members. The Republicans named Wilbur F. Sanders and T. C. Power, and the Democrats selected W. A. Clark and Martin Maginnis. In Washington, D.C., the Senate declared Sanders and Power the winners. This was not the end of the story, however, for the question of who should represent Montana in the Senate would continue to arouse controversy for well over a decade.

Also controversial was the choice of a state capital, with Helena emerging as the victor after several years of contention. The town became the seat of the territorial government in 1875, but in the intervening years several other communities had developed as worthy challengers to its preeminent position. Unable to agree on a site for the capital, the delegates to the constitutional convention put the issue before the voters in 1892. No town won a majority that year, but the people finally resolved the problem in 1894 by selecting Helena over its rival, Anaconda. The mining magnate W. A. Clark reportedly spent at least $500,000 in support of Helena's bid, and Marcus Daly of what later became the Anaconda Copper Mining Company spent over $2.5 million on behalf of Anaconda.

In 1895 the Montana legislature appointed a commission to select a site for the statehouse. A year later, construction began at an unpopulated location approximately one mile east of the famous Last Chance Gulch, where prospectors made a rich gold strike in 1864. The workers completed the central portion of the capitol in January 1902, and Clark was one of the orators at the dedication of the building on July 4, 1902.

November 9

The Great Northeast Power Failure

Tuesday, November 9, 1965, was an average autumn workday in the northeastern United States. As evening approached, however, chaos replaced the usual patterns of activity in the region. Many elevators carrying workers to the ground from the heights of Manhattan's office towers suddenly suspended their hapless riders between floors. In homes across the Northeast, lights dimmed to darkness. November 9 was no longer a typical day: Darkness and quiet settled on the northeastern United States and southeastern Canada. The great power blackout had begun.

The electrical difficulties that produced the largest power blackout that history had ever known started at the Sir Adam Beck II generating plant in Queenston, Ontario. Shortly after 5:00 p.m., its system of circuit breakers and primary and secondary relays protecting the plant's five high-tension lines sensed that one of the lines was overloaded. To safeguard this line, the system cut off power along this artery and diverted the electrical energy to the four remaining lines. This shift had disastrous consequences. The other four lines were already carrying close to full-capacity loads and could not accept the additional surge of power. Within seconds, the protective system closed off the four remaining lines.

The shutdown of the Queenston plant resulted in 1.7 million kilowatts of electricity being diverted back along the interconnected grid of power networks that serviced southeastern Canada and the northeastern United States. The high-tension lines of this grid, which were already carrying heavy loads to meet the great evening demand for electricity, could not absorb this additional power. Their protective systems were activated too, and power was cut off along the major cables serving the Northeast.

The effect of the shutdown was immediate: Rochester, New York, lost its electric service at 5:17; Boston fell into darkness at 5:18; and New York City's lights went out between 5:24 and 5:28.

Eight states—New York, Massachusetts, Connecticut, Rhode Island and parts of New Hampshire, Vermont, Pennsylvania, and New Jersey—and the province of Ontario, Canada, were left without electric power.

Ordinary citizens of the affected area did not at first know that a breakdown in the vast electric system was responsible for the sudden darkness. Many believed that the United States had been sabotaged. So prevalent was this idea that a Cuban official at the United Nations felt obliged to declare to one of the American delegates: "You can't blame me. I was right here all the time."

However, the need to deal with the emergency kept most people from dwelling on the power failure's origins. None of the numerous electrical devices that people had come to rely on in the 20th century could operate on the evening of November 9, 1965. Without lights to control the flow of traffic, automobiles jammed intersections and driving became extremely hazardous. Seeing a chance to make a quick profit, a few opportunists gathered flashlights and candles and then sold them on street corners at many times their normal values. The cloak of darkness and the failure of electric alarm systems that accompanied it also presented problems for law enforcement officials. To prevent looting and other crimes, most off-duty police were recalled to patrol the streets. On the whole, however, a mood of cheerful excitement and improvisation prevailed, once the initial panic had subsided.

The blackout, which disrupted the lives of millions of people, lasted only a few hours. Forty minutes after the power failure began, electric service was restored to Buffalo, New York, and within four hours the lights were on again in Rochester, New York; Toronto, Ontario; and Providence, Rhode Island. New York City, however, remained in darkness for a longer period of time. Not until 5:28 a.m.—12 hours after the blackout had begun—did the city again have electric power.

The day following the power failure, reminders of the blackout surrounded the inhabitants of the Northeast. The New York and American stock exchanges opened 65 minutes late. Approximately one-third of the affected area's labor force failed to report for work, and major retail stores noted a similar percentage drop in their business. Post offices faced mountains of unsorted mail, and banks coped with hundreds of thousands of uncanceled checks. The abrupt stoppage of power had ruined goods in numerous manufacturing plants and food processing facilities.

The United States Federal Power Commission immediately began an investigation of the vast power failure. Within weeks it pinpointed the source of the blackout as the difficulties at the Queenston, Ontario, plant. Investigating authorities also warned electric companies involved of the danger of inadequate power-generating facilities and recommended that more efficient safeguards be used to protect the vast electrical grid system in the future. Despite these precautions, another, smaller blackout occurred in 1979, this one accompanied by considerable looting.

November 10

American Revolution: First Marine Corps Units Formed

The marines have constituted an important element of American military strength since their inception in the 18th century. In engagements at close quarters they defended the vessels on which they sailed by firing their muskets from positions in the ships' rigging, and they formed the landing parties that attempted to board the enemy's crafts. Specialists in amphibious assault landings, the marines also acted as shock troops. They have maintained this latter role, and it is their primary function in modern American warfare.

There were marines long before the United States Marine Corps was founded. Americans served as British marines in the later colonial wars. During the War of Jenkins' Ear from 1739 to 1742 the 43rd Regiment of Foot, more popularly known as Gooch's Marines in honor of its colonel, fought against the French in the West Indies. Colonial Americans also served as marines aboard privateers during the French and Indian War from 1754 to 1763.

Several colonies raised units of marines at the onset of the American Revolution in 1775. A detachment from Connecticut, known in United States Marine folklore as the Original Eight, took part in the capture of Fort Ticonderoga, New York, on May 10, 1775. On November 10, 1775, the Continental Congress resolved to raise its own marine force. According to the act of this date, two battalions composed of men who were "good seamen or so acquainted with maritime affairs as to be able to serve to advantage by sea when required" were authorized. John Hancock, the president of the Continental Congress, appointed Captain Samuel Nichols as the first commandant of this "marine corps."

Captain Nichols set up his headquarters at the Tun Tavern at Water Street and Wilcox Alley in east Philadelphia, Pennsylvania, and began to recruit marines. The tavern's proprietor, Robert Mullan, received a commission as captain and carried on the task of recruiting throughout the Revolution.

Actually, the first marine detachment to serve under the auspices of the Continental Congress preceded the November 1775 resolution. On June 10, 1775, the Congress took control of all American military forces on Lake Champlain, and it also assumed responsibility for a group of 17 Massachusetts colonial marines under Lieutenant James Watson who were part of the ship's complement of the *Enterprise*. These troops also fought in the battle of Valcour Island in October 1776.

Continental marines rendered important service to the revolutionary cause. In March 1776 some 200 marines spearheaded a raid on a British ammunition and supply depot at Nassau in the Bahamas, and from December 1776 into January 1777, marines from the *Hancock* participated in the battles of Trenton and Princeton in New Jersey. The following autumn they assisted in the unsuccessful defense of Philadelphia, Pennsylvania. Marines fought on American soil in many other encounters during the Revolution, and some served with John Paul Jones in his attack on Whitehaven, England, in April 1778.

In 1785, after the Revolution, Congress disbanded the Continental navy and the marines. In 1794, however, the government reversed its decision in response to the continuing harassment of American shipping by the Barbary pirates of North Africa. Finally, on July 11, 1798, Congress established the United States Marine Corps as a specialized service under the secretary of the navy.

The marines have participated in every war in which the United States has been involved and have accomplished more than 300 landings on foreign shores. They fought in the Tripolitan War against the Barbary pirates from 1801 to 1805, in the War of 1812 against Great Britain, in the Mexican War from 1846 to 1848, and in the Civil War. With the expansion of American interests abroad in the 19th and 20th centuries, the marines have played an important role in quelling local disturbances and conflicts. The familiar "Marine's Hymn" lines "From the halls of Montezuma/ To the shores of Tripoli" allude to the wide range of conflicts in which they have been involved.

During both of the world wars in the 20th Century, the marines were engaged in major combat operations. In World War I they fought in France at Belleau Wood, Blanc Mont, the Meuse-Argonne, St. Mihiel, and Soissons. In World War II they spearheaded the landings at Guadalcanal in the Pacific and saw action in such other famous battles as Tarawa, Peleliu, Iwo Jima, and Okinawa. By 1945 the marines had six divisions, four air wings, and a variety of supporting forces.

After World War II the marines remained an important element in the American defense establishment. They fought in the Korean War of 1950 to 1953, participating in the Inchon landing under General Douglas MacArthur, and pioneered the techniques of helicopter assault. In the Vietnam War, Operation Desert Storm, and a variety of other conflicts, the marines have played a critical role in American land, sea, and air operations.

Since 1921 the U.S. Marine Corps has officially celebrated November 10 as its birthday. The location and circumstances of particular marine units influence observances of the event. In Washington, D.C., the battle of Iwo Jima, which was spearheaded by the marines, is commemorated by the Iwo Jima Memorial not far from Arlington National Cemetery. The bronze statue—crafted by Felix de Weldon from a celebrated photograph by Joe Rosenthal, which depicts the raising of the American flag on Mt. Suribachi on Iwo Jima by a group of marines—was dedicated on November 10, 1954.

Kentucky and Virginia Resolutions

In the late 1790s Congress passed a series of legislation known as the Alien and Sedition Acts. These measures sought to suppress political criticism of the government during a time of tense international relations with both Great Britain and France. Many prominent Americans thought that the acts were unconstitutional and an unwarranted extension of federal power over the states. In protest, the legislatures of Kentucky and Virginia asserted their right to nullify unconstitutional federal legislation within their respective state borders. Although the doctrine of state nullification has long since been discredited, these resolutions were important steps in the eventual repeal of the acts and were precedents for the Southern secessionists in the Civil War. Kentucky passed its resolutions, drafted by Thomas Jefferson, on November 10, 1798. Virginia passed its resolutions, drafted by James Madison, on December 24, 1798.

November 11

Veterans Day

At 11:00 a.m. on November 11, 1918, an armistice between the Allies and Central Powers ended the fighting in World War I. As the guns of the victors and the vanquished fell silent, the "war to end all wars" became history.

News of the cease-fire produced mammoth celebrations. Parisians thronged the broad boulevards of their city to demonstrate their jubilation, while in London thousands flocked to the royal palace and to the residence of the prime minister to sing and cheer. In the United States, observances were equally enthusiastic. In New York City, more than one million people jammed Broadway, crowds paraded and danced through other thoroughfares, and tons of ticker tape showered out of windows in the Wall Street area.

The November 11 armistice was a cease-fire, leaving vast problems unresolved. Over 10 million people were dead, huge areas of Europe lay in ruins, and a satisfactory peace settlement was yet to be negotiated. The proclamation issued on November 11, 1919, by President Woodrow Wilson reflected the pride that this nation took in aiding the Allied military victory:

> We were able to bring the vast resources, material and moral, of a great and free people to the assistance of our associates in Europe who had suffered and sacrificed without limit in the cause for which they fought. Out of this victory there arose new possibilities of political freedom and economic concert. The war showed us the strength of great nations acting together for high purposes, and the victory of arms foretells the enduring conquests which can be made in peace when nations act justly and in furtherance of the common interests of men.

> To us in America the reflections of Armistice Day will be filled with solemn pride in the heroism of those who died in the country's service and with gratitude for the victory, both because of the thing from which it has freed us and because of the opportunity it has given America to show her sympathy with peace and justice in the councils of the nations.

Yet the difficulties encountered in attempting to cope with the aftermath of the war produced a somber atmosphere throughout the world in the year that followed the end of the fighting. Many nations noted the first anniversary of the World War armistice on November 11, 1919, with veterans' parades, secular and religious programs, and two minutes of silence in honor of the war dead.

Two years after the 1918 armistice, France and England observed the anniversary by paying tribute to their soldiers who had died in the war. During the dark days of fighting, many soldiers were buried in unmarked graves. In 1920 the French selected one such unidentified French soldier, interred him in a sarcophagus beneath the Arc de Triomphe in Paris, and lit a perpetual flame over his tomb. That same year Great Britain also chose an unknown British soldier and buried him near the tombs of English royalty in Westminster Abbey.

On November 11, 1921, the United States, following the example of France and England, honored its war dead. Months before, the remains of an American soldier had been disinterred in France, taken to the city hall at Châlons-sur-Marne, and placed in a casket inscribed "An unknown American soldier who gave his life in the great war."

After a transatlantic voyage aboard the cruiser *Olympia*, the body of the American unknown soldier arrived in the United States early in November 1921. The remains lay in state in the rotunda of the Capitol in Washington, D.C., for three days. Then, on November 11 the body of the unknown soldier was taken to its final resting place at Arlington National Cemetery in Virginia. Floral tributes and wreaths from all parts of the world decorated the gravesite. Foreign diplomats, members of all branches of the American armed services, and dignitaries including President Warren G. Harding were present for the interment. At 11:00 a.m., the time that the armistice had gone into effect three years earlier, the casket was lowered into the tomb. Above it was placed a block of white marble, bearing the inscription "Here rests in honored glory an American soldier known but to God."

During the 1920s annual observances of the armistice became traditional on both sides of the Atlantic. In England and Canada the commemoration came to be known as Remembrance Day. In the United States it was called Armistice Day or, less commonly, Victory Day. The anniversary did not become a federal holiday until 1938, but as early as 1926 Congress adopted a resolution directing the president to issue an annual proclamation calling on citizens to observe the day.

From the beginning, commemorations of the November 11 armistice paid special tribute to the soldiers who died during World War I. Their graves were decorated and small red artificial poppies were worn to honor them. Poppies were chosen because they grew wild in the fields of Europe; the famous war poem "In Flanders Fields" alludes to the profusion of poppy blossoms. After World War II and the Korean War, however, celebrations of the 1918 cease-fire received less and less attention. In response to this change in attitude, many organizations, particularly veterans' groups, urged that the November 11 holiday be set aside as a day to pay tribute to all those who had served in this nation's armed services. In 1954 Congress passed, and President Dwight D. Eisenhower signed, a bill specifying that Armistice Day would thereafter be known and commemorated as Veterans Day.

Still another change was made in the November 11 observance in June 1968, when President Lyndon B. Johnson signed a law making Veterans Day one of the federal holidays to be observed on a predetermined Monday in order to provide Americans with an additional three-day holiday weekend. The law, which went into effect in 1971, transferred the observance of Veterans Day from November 11 to the fourth Monday of October. However, veterans' organizations did not approve of the movable date, and much confusion resulted. In 1975 Congress passed legislation that made Veterans Day revert to November 11, effective 1978.

Admission of Washington State to the Union

The Oregon Treaty, ratified by the United States Senate on June 15, 1846, amicably terminated a long dispute with Great Britain over the location of the Canadian-American border west of the Rocky Mountains. The Americans, who claimed Pacific territory as far north as 54 degrees 40 minutes north latitude, and the British, who wanted to restrict the expanding young United States to a much more southerly 42 degrees, compromised on a dividing line set at the 49th Parallel. On August 13, 1848, Congress organized the Oregon country below that line into a territory. A sizable region, the new Oregon Territory included what were to be the states of Idaho, Oregon, and Washington, as well as parts of Montana and Wyoming.

In 1844 Michael T. Simmons and John R. Jackson led a group of settlers to Oregon that included George W. Bush, who was of mixed-race descent. When the party discovered that an enactment of the Oregon Provisional Government banned persons of black ancestry from residence in the region, they crossed the Columbia River and in 1845 established the first American communities in the area of Washington. The land, although still part of the Oregon country, was beyond the effective control of the provisional government. Simmons settled at New Market or Tumwater (later Olympia, the state capital). Jackson established his home on the Cowlitz River, and Bush selected what became known as Bush's Prairie for himself.

Few immigrants ventured across the Columbia River in the first years of settlement. The ratification of the Oregon Treaty encouraged the pioneers, but the slaying of the Whitman missionary family by Cayuse warriors at Waillatpu in 1847 frightened away many would-be settlers. The dis-

covery of gold in California diverted still more people from the Puget Sound region, and by 1849 a census by Governor Joseph Lane of the Oregon Territory located only 304 pioneers above the Columbia.

American troops established a fort at Steilacoom in 1849, and their presence ensured security for prospective settlers. Economic opportunity proved to be an even greater inducement to the pioneers, who found in growing California a market for the food, fish, and timber that were so plentiful north of the Columbia River. The region developed quickly in response to these stimuli, attaining a population of 1,049 by the 1850 census.

Settlers pushed north along Puget Sound in 1851 to what was later Alki Point, but found the location inadequate as a port. The following spring they established a town along the inside shoreline of Elliott Bay and named it in honor of Chief Sealth of the Duwamish tribe, though they corrupted his name in the process. Seattle, as they called it, enjoyed an excellent harbor that guaranteed its prosperity.

The residents north of the Columbia River soon became dissatisfied under the jurisdiction of the Oregon government. In order to take care of legal and other matters, they had to travel across many arduous miles of the Pacific Northwest to the territorial capital located south of the river. Furthermore, the legislature neglected to build roads or perform other essential services in the Puget Sound area. Finally, the larger southern population found the attention-demanding northerners to be a nuisance. Both groups decided that the answer to the problem was a separate government for the upper region.

Northerners held a convention at Cowlitz Landing in August 1852 to petition Congress for territorial status. On November 25, 1852, a second convention met at Monticello and the 44-elected delegates repeated the call for the organization of a Territory of Columbia. In Congress Joseph Lane, the Oregon representative and former governor, also advanced the cause of northern independence.

On February 8, 1853, Congress began to discuss a bill to create the Territory of Columbia. Representative Richard Henry Stanton suggested that the area's name be changed to Washington to honor the nation's first president. The legislators passed the amended measure on February 10, and President James K. Polk signed it on March 2, 1853. The new Washington Territory included the land from the Pacific Ocean to the crest of the Rocky Mountains between the 49th and 46th parallels of north latitude, except where the Columbia River formed the southern boundary.

In 1863 Congress created the Territory of Idaho in response to appeals for their own government made by settlers living in Oregon and Washington east of the Cascade Mountains. Inspired by the Idahoans' success, the residents of the Walla Walla region, also east of the Cascades, agitated for separation from Washington and its distant capital at Olympia. In 1876 Congress rejected a bill to annex Walla Walla to Oregon. The discussions surrounding the proposal, however, prompted western Washingtonians (who were anxious to keep their boundaries intact) to work vigorously for statehood. In response to their efforts, the Washington territorial legislature called for the election of delegates to a constitutional convention to meet in Walla Walla.

The convention assembled at Walla Walla on June 11, 1878, and by July 27 it had drafted a constitution. After ratification Thomas Brents, the territorial representative, asked Congress to admit Washington to the Union with the Walla Walla document as the state's basic law. Congress rejected this appeal for two reasons: (1) there was no direct railroad connection with the territory, and (2) it was feared that the region's small population of 75,000 might prove unable to support its own government.

Along with several other territories, Washington frequently requested statehood during the 1880s. Congress, fearful that multiple admissions might upset the equilibrium that was established between the Democratic and Republican parties, turned aside all these motions. In 1889, however, a lame-duck Democratic Congress agreed to admit Montana, North Dakota, South Dakota, and Washington to the Union.

The enabling act, appropriately enacted on George Washington's birthday (February 22, 1889), required the territory to call a constitutional convention. The voters ratified the frame of government devised by the gathering and submitted it to President Benjamin Harrison. He approved the document, and on November 11, 1889, he proclaimed Washington a member of the United States.

November 12

Elizabeth Cady Stanton's Birthday

Elizabeth Cady, later Elizabeth Cady Stanton and one of the leading activists in the field of women's rights, was born on November 12, 1815, in Johnstown, New York. The daughter of a judge, Elizabeth Cady learned in her father's law office of the discriminatory laws affecting women. She was educated at one of the first institutions to provide higher education for women, the Troy Female Academy, later known as the Emma Willard School.

In 1840, at a ceremony that deliberately omitted the customary word "obey" from her vows, Elizabeth Cady was married to the journalist and abolitionist Henry Brewster Stanton. That same year they attended the World International Antislavery convention in London, England. Also in attendance was the Quaker social reformer Lucretia Coffin Mott. Their indignation when female delegates were excluded from the floor of the convention prompted the two women to cooperate and work together for equal rights.

With the assistance of other like-minded activists, Stanton and Mott sent out the call that resulted in the first women's rights convention, held at Seneca Falls, New York, in 1848 (see related essays throughout this book). For this famous Seneca Falls convention, Stanton drew up her bill of rights for women, demanding redress of wrongs and inequities. She insisted (although without Mott's approval) that the declaration include what became the first organized demand for "woman's suffrage" or the right to vote in the United States.

It was in 1851 that Stanton, by now a respected orator and journalist, first met the dynamic Susan B. Anthony (see related essays throughout this book). Their meeting marked the beginning of a half-century's working partnership: Stanton served as writer and editor, Anthony as business manager, and both of them as lecturers. Together with Parker Pillsbury they issued *The Revolution*, a women's rights publication, from 1868 to 1870. In 1869 they organized the National Woman Suffrage Association. Stanton served as president of the association from its founding until 1890, planning suffrage campaigns, appearing before legislative committees, and speaking in favor of liberal divorce laws and complete equality for women. When the association merged with Lucy Stone's American Woman Suffrage Association in 1890, Stanton served for two years as president of that resulting coalition, which was named the National American Woman Suffrage Association.

Stanton was still active and at the forefront of the movement for equal rights when she died on October 26, 1902, in New York City.

The Washington Conference Begins

The International Conference on Naval Limitation, comprised of delegates from the countries of Belgium, China, France, Great Britain, Italy, Japan, the Netherlands, Portugal, and the United States, met in Washington, D.C., from November

12, 1921, to February 6, 1922. Known as the Washington Conference, it imposed restraints on the size of the navies maintained by the major powers in the East Asian portion of the Pacific Ocean.

The Washington Conference resulted in three major treaties:

(1) The Four Power Treaty. Entered into by France, Great Britain, Japan, and the United States, it pledged that those nations would respect each other's possessions in the Pacific.

(2) The Five Power Treaty. Entered into by France, Great Britain, Italy, Japan, and the United States, it imposed a formula for the number of large warships (defined as those over 10,000 tons displacement) that could be maintained by these countries. The formula was a ratio of five ships/five ships/three ships/1.7 ships/1.7 ships for the United States, Great Britain, Japan, France, and Italy in that order. It was the most important of the three treaties.

(3) The Nine Power Treaty. Entered into by all of the nine participating countries at the Washington Conference, it pledged respect for Chinese territorial integrity and the Open Door Policy of free international trade with China. The Chinese were also able to reassert some control over governmental functions that had been seized over the years by the Western powers and Japan.

These three treaties succeeded in maintaining the peace until the 1930s. However, in 1931 an increasingly militaristic Japan invaded China, and in 1934 it renounced the Five Power Treaty. Diplomatic protests notwithstanding, the United States and the other countries that had participated in the Washington Conference took no effective measures to punish Japan for its actions. The Japanese continued on a course of naval buildup and militaristic expansion that would eventually lead to the December 7, 1941, attack on Pearl Harbor and America's entry into World War II.

November 13

Edwin Booth's Birthday

Edwin Thomas Booth, the famous 19th-century Shakespearean tragedian and one of the most distinguished American actors of all time, was born on a farm near Bel Air, Maryland, some 23 miles from Baltimore on November 13, 1833. He was the son of Junius Brutus Booth, an English actor who had settled in the United States in 1821, and Mary Ann Holmes. Edwin Booth was named for Edwin Forrest, an American tragedian, and for Thomas Flynn, an English comedian. In later years he dropped the second name.

While he was still a young boy, Booth traveled around the country on theatrical tours with his father. On September 10, 1849, when he was not yet 16 years old, young Booth made his stage debut at the Boston Museum playing the minor role of Tressel to his father's Richard III in William Shakespeare's *Richard III*. He then performed occasional juvenile parts with his father. The aspiring actor himself appeared as Richard III in April 1851 at the National Theater in New York City, after his father (often drunk and eccentric in behavior) had refused to perform. The next year Booth went with his father to California and acted with mixed success in various plays.

It was not until after the elder Booth's death on November 30, 1852, that Edwin Booth gained recognition in his own right. In 1854 he ventured to Australia with Laura Keene, an English actress who had recently come to the United States. The troupe was unsuccessful, and Booth returned via Hawaii to California, where in 1856 he captured the public's imagination as the leading man of a stock company in Sacramento. He played in the West until September 1856.

Booth was now an experienced actor who not only exhibited the talents of his father, but had also improved upon the latter's acting techniques by adopting a more subdued and natural manner. Feeling himself ready to return to the East, he first toured the southern states. Then in Boston on April 20, 1857, he scored a brilliant success as Sir Giles Overreach in Philip Massinger's *A New Way to Pay Old Debts*. It was praised by the critics. According to one writer: "Young Booth's success was decided. . . . It brought back the most vivid recollections of the fire, the vigor, the strong intellectuality which characterized the acting of his lamented father."

This and other triumphs in various eastern cities, such as his appearance as Richard III in New York City on May 4, 1857, lifted Booth to the top of his profession.

On July 7, 1860, Booth married Mary Devlin, a young actress whom he had first met in November 1856 while rehearsing Romeo to her Juliet. The couple soon sailed to England, where Booth filled engagements in London, Liverpool, and Manchester, where their first daughter Edwina was born in September 1861. The English engagement, although receiving mixed reviews, added to Booth's prestige at home. Upon returning to the United States in August 1862, the actor played to packed audiences at New York City's Winter Garden Theater until the death of his 22-year-old wife in February 1863 caused his brief retirement from the stage.

In 1863 Booth became co-manager of the Winter Garden and presented a number of lavish Shakespearean productions. His *Julius Caesar* of November 25, 1864, starred Booth and his two brothers, Junius Brutus Booth Jr. and John Wilkes Booth, as Brutus, Cassius, and Mark Antony, respectively. From November 26, 1864, to March 22, 1865, Edwin Booth portrayed Hamlet in an impressive run of 100 consecutive nights. This dramatic feat, however, was soon followed by personal tragedy. On April 14, 1865, Edwin's brother John Wilkes Booth, a Southern sympathizer, assassinated President Abraham Lincoln in Ford's Theatre in Washington, D.C. Booth would one day say to fellow actor Joseph Jefferson that the news "was just as if I was struck on the forehead with a hammer." At first he vowed never to act again and retired from the stage for nearly a year. When his return appearance at the Winter Garden was announced for January 3, 1866, the *New York Herald* asked: "Will Booth appear as the assassin of Caesar? That would be, perhaps, the most suitable character." In fact, Booth played the role of Hamlet, and received a standing ovation.

As manager of the Winter Garden, Booth continued to stage sumptuous productions until a disastrous fire struck the theater in March 1867. He recouped his losses and started to build his own theater at 23rd Street and Sixth Avenue in New York City, which opened as Booth's Theater on February 3, 1869. It was also during 1869 that Booth remarried, this time to actress Mary McVicker. Despite excellent box office receipts, the theater went under during the financial crisis of 1873–1874 and declared bankruptcy on January 26, 1874. Booth repaid his debts, however, and went on tour throughout the United States until 1879.

Between 1880 and 1882, Booth appeared in England. He won praise for his interpretation of the role of King Lear, and also co-starred with the renowned English actor Sir Henry Irving. After the death of his second wife, in 1883 Booth toured Germany and Austria. In 1886 he entered into a business and acting contract with the American actor Lawrence Barrett. Booth appeared in repertory performances in New York City from 1887 until Barrett's death in 1891, but the decline in his abilities became increasingly evident. Booth's last stage appearance was at the Brooklyn Academy of Music performance of *Hamlet* on April 4, 1891. He died on June 7, 1893.

Louis Brandeis's Birthday

Louis Dembitz Brandeis, one of the most famous jurists in American history and the first Jewish justice of the United States Supreme Court, was born on November 13, 1856, in Louisville, Kentucky. The son of a wealthy grain merchant, Brandeis received his education in Louisville until 1872, when the family moved to Dresden, Germany, where he attended the Annen Realschule. Upon returning to the United States in 1875, he entered Harvard Law School and graduated in 1877. After a brief period of postgraduate study at Harvard and private practice in St. Louis, Missouri, he relocated to Boston, Massachusetts.

He practiced law in Boston from 1879 to 1897 with the firm Warren & Brandeis. On March 23, 1891, Brandeis married Alice Goldmark. In 1897 he became the senior partner of the newly established firm Brandeis, Dunbar & Nutter, with whom he practiced until 1916. In addition to his successful private practice, Brandeis established a national reputation as an advocate of liberal reforms and actively supported the Progressive wing of the Republican Party. However, in 1912 he endorsed Democrat Woodrow Wilson for president in that year's elections. After Wilson's election, Brandeis became one of his most trusted advisers, and was rewarded on January 28, 1916, with a nomination to the Supreme Court.

Brandeis, whose nomination was confirmed by the Senate on June 1, 1916, was the first person of the Jewish faith in American history to serve on the Court. During his tenure on the bench, he typically sided with the liberal justices, and frequently wrote their dissenting opinion when they were outvoted by the more conservative justices. The liberal justices were in the minority until the late 1930s, when the Court took a dramatically more conciliatory position toward the constitutionality of federal legislation such as President Franklin D. Roosevelt's New Deal package.

Brandeis resigned from the Supreme Court on February 13, 1939. He began working for the Zionist cause, which sought to establish an international Jewish homeland in the Middle East, and continued with this until his death on October 5, 1941, in Washington, D.C. Besides his service on the Supreme Court, Brandeis is also remembered for developing the "Brandeis brief" format in 1908, when he argued and won *Muller* v. *Oregon* before the Court, using a novel type of legal brief incorporating economic, statistical, sociological, and other types of nonlegal information.

November 14

Samuel Seabury Appointed First Protestant Bishop in the United States

A year after the signing of the Treaty of Paris, which ended the American Revolution, Samuel Seabury was consecrated by Episcopalian bishops in Scotland on November 14, 1784, as the first American bishop. Most of the congregations in the former American colonies that had been a part of the Church of England were by then calling themselves Protestant Episcopal, and in the following year they held an organizing convention for the newly forming Protestant Episcopal Church.

Seabury was born in North Groton, Connecticut, on November 30, 1729. His New World roots went back almost a century. One of his ancestors, John Seabury, was among the earliest American colonists when he arrived in Boston from England in 1639. Samuel Seabury spent most of his childhood in Connecticut, but in 1742 he and his family moved to Hempstead in Long Island, New York. The son of a minister, Seabury wanted to devote his life to the same work.

When Seabury graduated from Yale College in 1748 with a bachelor of arts degree, he was too young to be ordained. Therefore, he studied theology and medicine under his father, who was also a physician, and served as a catechist in Huntington, Long Island. He completed his medical education between 1752 to 1753 at the University of Edinburgh in Scotland, and was ordained a priest of the Church of England in London in December 1753.

The Society for the Propagation of the Gospel named Seabury a missionary to the Christ Church parish in New Brunswick, New Jersey, a post that he assumed upon his return to America in 1754. He married Mary Hicks of Staten Island, New York, in 1756. During the next 20 years he also, successively, served Grace Church in Jamaica, Long Island, and St. Peter's Church in Westchester County, New York (later part of the Bronx). Besides putting his medical training to good use, in Westchester he assumed the additional role of schoolmaster. In the early 1760s he was awarded master's degrees by King's College (now Columbia University) and Yale.

Soon after returning to the colonies, Seabury—who as a priest of the Church of England was a faithful servant of the king—began to involve himself in the evolving controversies between Great Britain and the American colonists. He firmly believed that the colonies would benefit by remaining attached to Britain while using peaceful, legal means to seek resolution of their differences.

He wrote newspaper articles and pamphlets, clearly and emphatically putting forth his views. An able defender of the monarch, he increased his activities on behalf of the king as the rift between Britain and the colonies deepened. Four pamphlets he wrote during this later period bear the pseudonym A. W[estchester]. Farmer and are appropriately written in the language of an educated farmer rather than that of a clergyman. One of them aroused so much indignation that, in Connecticut, copies were either tarred, feathered, and nailed to whipping posts or burned publicly. Rebuttals to Seabury's pamphlets were written by Alexander Hamilton, then an undergraduate at King's College and later one of the principal figures in the founding of the new republic.

When the first shots of the Revolution were fired at Lexington and Concord in April 1775, Seabury and other Loyalists went into hiding. He soon emerged, despite that fact that he had publicly identified himself as a Tory leader. In November he was seized and imprisoned in New Haven, Connecticut, for about a month. Freed, he returned to Westchester, but after eight months he decided to seek safety on British-held Long Island.

His familiarity with Long Island and Westchester qualified Seabury to serve as a British army guide for those areas. He also served as chaplain to both the Provincial Hospital in New York and the King's American Regiment, and was a physician for the New York City Almshouse. As a result of the influence of Loyalist friends, at this time Seabury was granted the degree of doctor of divinity by Oxford University in England. He and his family lived in New York City during most of the conflict, even after the Society for the Propagation of the Gospel appointed him missionary to Staten Island (not then a part of New York City) in 1777.

Despite the strength of his loyalty to Britain before and during the Revolution, after the conclusion of the war Seabury gave his full allegiance to the new country. Because church and state were bound together in England, the churches established in the 13 colonies now needed to organize themselves on a new, independent basis. While a part of the Church of England, they had been within the jurisdiction of the bishop of London.

On March 25, 1783, the Episcopal clergy of Connecticut, while meeting in Woodbury, elected Seabury their first bishop. In early June he sailed for England to request consecration by the English bishops. However, his allegiance to the United States and other points concerning church and state relationships proved to be large obstacles.

He waited in England for a year, hoping that action permitting his consecration would be taken. Finally he appealed for consecration to the Scottish Episcopalian bishops, who themselves took no oath of allegiance to the monarch. They consented, and on November 14, 1784, Seabury was consecrated bishop in Aberdeen. A "free and valid episcopate," in Seabury's words, had been secured for the Episcopal Church in America.

In the summer of 1785 he returned to the United States, and from that time until his death he served as bishop of Connecticut, and, beginning in 1790, of Rhode Island as well. He was also the rector of his father's old church, St. James's in New London, Connecticut.

Dispute over the recognition of Seabury as a bishop arose, mainly because of the method of his consecration but partly because of his former Loyalist sympathies. However, at the general convention of 1789, during which the organization of the Protestant Episcopal Church was completed, he was formally recognized as a bishop. By that time an act of Parliament had made it possible for English bishops to consecrate (in 1787) two additional bishops for the United States. The English and Scottish branches of the Anglican Church were thus united with the American Church.

A simple man with strong faith, Seabury worked throughout his life with great determination to expand the influence of the church. During his episcopate his efforts met with considerable success. Upon his death in New London, Connecticut, on February 25, 1796, one of his six children, Charles, succeeded him as rector of St. James's Church. Seabury was buried in the public burying ground in New London, but his remains were later transferred to lie beneath the altar of St. James's Church.

The Apollo 12 Mission to the Moon Is Launched

The Apollo 12 spacecraft, launched by the National Aeronautics and Space Administration (NASA) on November 14, 1969, was the second manned lunar mission. Its objective was lunar exploration and scientific research, and it was crewed by Charles "Pete" Conrad Jr., the commander; Alan L. Bean, the lunar module pilot; and Richard F. Gordon, the command module pilot. The launch took place at the Kennedy Space Center in Cape Canaveral, Florida.

The spacecraft consisted of three parts: a lunar module (LM), a command module (CM), and a service module. The latter two were linked to form the command service module (CSM). The lunar module landed Conrad and Bean on the surface of the Moon in the *Oceanus Procellarum*, or "Sea of Storms," while the command module remained in orbit around the Moon. Primarily using automatic guidance systems, the landing went smoothly. Television cameras mounted on the spacecraft covered the astronauts as they left the vehicle.

Conrad and Bean planted the American flag on the surface of the Moon and then began their tasks. They collected core samples from the lunar surface, took solar wind measurements, and traveled roughly a mile of terrain in the process. The astronauts also examined the remains of the unmanned *Surveyor III* probe, which had landed nearby in April 1967, and retrieved some equipment. Having accomplished their mission, Conrad and Bean returned to the command module, which left the Moon's orbit on November 22 and reached Earth two days later.

The crew of Apollo 12 reentered Earth's atmosphere, splashed down in the Pacific Ocean on November 24, 1969, near American Samoa, and were recovered by the USS *Hornet* of the U.S. Navy. Apollo 12's command module, known as the *Yankee Clipper*, was later placed on display at NASA's Langley Research Center in Hampton, Virginia.

November 15

Articles of Confederation Adopted

Even prior to the Declaration of Independence, the Founding Fathers realized that some form of national government would be necessary for the 13 colonies seeking their independence from Great Britain. Thus, when Virginia's Richard Henry Lee first introduced his resolution for independence on June 7, 1776, he also suggested that "a plan of confederation be prepared and transmitted to the respective colonies for their consideration and approbation." The Second Continental Congress, meeting at Philadelphia, Pennsylvania, responded quickly to this proposal and on June 12, 1776, appointed a committee under John Dickinson's leadership to accomplish this task.

Formulating a system of government acceptable to the various colonies presented a variety of difficulties. The colonies, diverse in their origins and circumstances, were reluctant to establish any form of government that would compromise their individual social traditions and economic interests. Furthermore, every colony jealously guarded its political autonomy. Several attempts to centralize colonial administration had failed in the past: The short-lived Dominion of New England had ended with Great Britain's "Glorious Revolution" in

1688, and in 1754 the colonies had rejected the Albany Plan of Union devised by Benjamin Franklin to ensure their security during the French and Indian War.

The "Articles of Confederation and Perpetual Union," which Dickinson's committee presented to the congress on July 12, 1776, reflected the colonies' distrust of a strong central government. The plan vested power in a congress in which every state would be represented according to population, restricted congress's authority concerning certain vital matters, and made no provision for a viable national executive. No legislation could be enacted without the agreement of nine states, and the consent of all 13 was required to amend the articles.

The wartime concerns of the American Revolution dominated the Continental Congress's attention during the months that followed, and only intermittently did that body consider the proposed plan of confederation. These occasional debates did, however, produce one major change in the articles. On October 7, 1777, the congress provided that each state would have one vote in the congress under the articles. The small states, which had objected to the original recommendation to apportion each state's representation according to its population, now found the proposed articles acceptable. On November 15, 1777, the Continental Congress formally adopted this frame of government, and two days later sent the articles to the individual states for ratification.

The Articles of Confederation could not become operative without the unanimous approval of all 13 colonies, and by February 1779 all but one had given their consent. Maryland, the lone holdout, refused to ratify until the seven states whose colonial charters gave them claims to western lands agreed to transfer jurisdiction over those lands to the national government. As the spokesperson for the six "landless" states, Maryland contended that the states' common war effort justified its demand that the unsettled territories be "considered as common property, subject to be parceled by Congress into free, convenient, and independent governments." Two years passed without compromise, but finally on January 2, 1781, the legislature of Virginia, "preferring the good of the country to every object of smaller importance," agreed to cede its western lands to the federal government. Within a month, New York and Connecticut followed Virginia's example. Although the other states did not surrender their western claims until later, these demonstrations of good faith persuaded Maryland to ratify the articles on February 27, 1781.

The formal ratification of the Articles of Confederation took place on March 1, 1781, as Philadelphia church bells tolled and the *Ariel*, a warship under the command of John Paul Jones, fired a 21-gun salute. Although the Articles of Confederation ultimately proved to be inadequate for the needs of the new nation, necessitating the drafting of the present United States Constitution (see related essays throughout this book), the country's "first constitution" was an important first step toward nationhood.

Georgia O'Keeffe's Birthday

Georgia O'Keeffe, the famous painter, was born on November 15, 1887, in Sun Prairie, Wisconsin. She studied at the Art Institute of Chicago in 1905 and the Art Students League of New York from 1907 to 1908. Afterward, O'Keeffe worked as a commercial artist in Chicago, Illinois, before moving to Texas in 1912 to teach art. She rose to become the head of the art department at West Texas State Normal College from 1916 to 1918. During this period she held her first major exhibitions, sponsored by the New York modernist photographer Alfred Stieglitz, whom she married in 1924.

Stieglitz held exhibitions of O'Keeffe's work, which consisted primarily of highly stylized and modernist landscapes and still lifes, until he died in 1946. Other galleries developed an interest in her work as well, helping her achieve prominence. Much of her most famous work was done on visits to New Mexico, where she painted desert scenery and used single objects, such as a cow's skull in the 1936 painting *Cow's Skull with Red*, presented in close-up views for dramatic effect. After her husband's death, she permanently relocated to New Mexico.

Her work was critically acclaimed, throughout her long life, for its bold colors and patterns, starkly linear subject matter representation, and austerely sensual design. During the 1960s she developed an interest in aerial motifs, painting skyscapes and clouds as they might be seen from the air. One such work was the 24-foot mural *Sky above Clouds*, in 1965. In the 1970s she returned to her earlier style. She died on March 6, 1986, in Santa Fe, New Mexico, at the age of 98.

After her death an autobiographical series of essays entitled *Georgia O'Keeffe* was published in 1987, and the Georgia O'Keeffe Museum, dedicated to her works, was opened in 1997.

November 16

Oklahoma Admitted to the Union

On November 16, 1907, President Theodore Roosevelt signed a proclamation admitting Oklahoma into the Union as the 46th state.

The history of Oklahoma from the early days of its discovery to 20th-century statehood is inextricably woven with the fate of the Native Americans who inhabited its territory. Oklahoma, fittingly enough, derives its name from the Choctaw words *okla*, "people," and *homma*, "red." Native tribes are known to have inhabited the area of the state long before recorded history. About A.D. 1200 a pre-Columbian civilization, which closely resembled the highly developed Mayan culture of Mexico, flourished there. Apparently, this region, a section of which has been described as a "cradle of civilization in North America," witnessed the rise and disintegration of several advanced cultures before the first Europeans arrived in the area.

In the early 1540s, Captain-General Francisco Vásquez de Coronado, at the head of a military expedition of 1,500 men, probably crossed what is now Oklahoma in his quest for the supposed riches of the mythical kingdom of Quivira. He found no gold, but before returning to Mexico City in 1542 he claimed the vast region he had traversed, including Oklahoma, for Spain. Shortly before his death that year, another Spanish explorer, Hernando de Soto, may have journeyed up the Arkansas River into Oklahoma. At the beginning of the next century, Juan de Oñate, having established the first settlement in the area of New Mexico, went off in search of Quivira and led a party across Oklahoma into Kansas.

Although other Spanish explorers and traders visited the area in the early 17th century, permanent settlement was not attempted. In fact, Spain lost its claim to the French who, as a result of expeditions by Louis Joliet and René-Robert Cavelier de La Salle, claimed all of the vast region called Louisiana in 1682. By the secret Treaty of Fontainebleau in 1762, the French ceded to Spain that part of Louisiana west of the Mississippi River. Within a half century, the Spanish returned this huge area to France in the secret treaty of San Ildefonso of 1800. On December 20, 1803, the United States gained possession of the region, including all of Oklahoma except the northwestern panhandle, in the Louisiana Purchase.

Oklahoma had been explored by various French traders and trappers, especially by the Chouteau family of St. Louis, Missouri. In 1796 Major Jean Pierre Chouteau selected the site of Salina as a suitable location for his thriving trade with the Osage tribe, thus establishing the first permanent European settlement in the state. However, colonization was slow, and the land continued to belong to the scattered Plains tribes. In addition to the Osage there were the Kiowa, Comanche, Apache, and Wichita. During the early 19th century, the wild unsettled region was unknown to most people save for a few travelers, traders, and official explorers such as Stephen H. Long. In 1824 Colonel Matthew Arbuckle constructed Forts Towson and Gibson, the first military outposts in Oklahoma.

The Indian Territory was established by Congress in 1834 as the home for the Five Civilized Tribes: Choctaw, Chickasaw, Creek, Seminole, and Cherokee, all victims of American expansion and settlement in the eastern United States. The territory originally comprised all of Oklahoma, with the exception of the panhandle. In the 1830s and 1840s, some 5,000 Choctaw of Mississippi and Louisiana and 4,000 Chickasaw of Mississippi were removed to that eastern section of the Indian Territory that lay south of the Canadian and Arkansas Rivers. Some 16,000 Cherokee from North and South Carolina, Georgia, Alabama, and Tennessee (about 4,000 of whom died of hardship on the march) were forced along what was later called the Trail of Tears to their new home in the Indian Territory. They settled the broad northern strip, except for a small block of land in the northeastern corner that had been set aside for the Quapaw Agency. Finally, some 20,000 Creek of Georgia and Alabama and 3,000 Seminole of Florida were forced into the Indian Territory. They occupied the remaining middle section between the Cherokee on one side and the Choctaw and Chickasaw on the other.

Those tribes who settled the rolling wooded hills and prairies of the eastern part of the Indian Territory adapted well to the new conditions. Making great advances in agriculture, livestock breeding, and flour milling, the prosperous tribes were soon skillfully managing their own affairs. They each formed a separate "Indian republic," developing sophisticated political organizations. Only the Seminole failed to draw up a written constitution and establish laws.

Although the Five Civilized Tribes fought briefly with the Plains tribes, especially the Osage, they settled down peacefully to raise corn and cotton. However, the Civil War greatly affected the tribes, even though no large-scale conflict was waged on Indian Territory soil. The issue of slavery sharply divided the Five Tribes. Most of their members, as slaveholders of Southern background, sided with the Confederacy, while the remainder clung to the Union. Minor but violent internal civil wars tore the Indian Territory asunder. Confederate General Stand Watie, a Cherokee, did not surrender to the federals stationed at Fort Towson until June 23, 1865, thus gaining fame as the last Rebel commander to put down arms.

Following the Civil War, the United States government acted promptly to negotiate new treaties with the Five Civilized Tribes. Partly as punishment for Southern supporters and partly on the grounds that the extensive tribal holdings should be shared with freed slaves and other tribes, the original Indian Territory was divided. The Cherokee reluctantly granted the United States permission to assign what had been approximately the western half of their territory to new tribes. The Seminole, Creek, Choctaw, and Chickasaw concluded similar agreements.

From 1866 to 1883 the federal government made a number of small grants from the vast new land. Displaced tribes, such as the Delaware and Shawnee, and nomadic Plains tribes, such as the Osage, Kansas, Wichita, Iowa, and Kickapoo were resettled onto these grants. Moreover, the United States Army rounded up other Plains tribes—Comanche, Kiowa, Cheyenne, and Arapaho—and gave them land in the southwestern quarter of Oklahoma. Of the portion of Indian Territory that had been ceded to the United States, there soon remained only one major unassigned land block. It was a choice area of approximately two million acres situated near the center of the Indian Territory. The unoccupied region came to be known as the Unassigned Lands, Oklahoma District, or Old Oklahoma.

As the great tide of westward expansion gained momentum after the Civil War, the Indian Territory, once thought worthless and best "given to the Indians," became attractive to settlers (see related articles throughout this book). The homesteading process, involving approximately 17 million acres, was completed at the beginning of the 20th century. The chaotic influx of settlers, besides pushing the tribes into ever-diminishing reservations, also caused serious disruptions in the traditional tribal ways of life.

In 1890 the Oklahoma Territory was created out of that part of the Indian Territory situated south of the Cherokee Outlet and west of the eastern area still occupied by the Five Civilized Tribes. It also included the panhandle, the 34-mile-wide and 167-mile-long strip taken from Texas in 1850, which since then had remained outside the boundaries of any legally constituted state or territory. Much to Congress's embarrassment, it had simply been overlooked. Known as No Man's Land or Public Land Strip on maps, it had attract-

ed some squatters and many outlaws. Its residents had even attempted to seek independent statehood for the area, which was larger than Connecticut, under the name Cimarron Territory.

At first, the Five Civilized Tribes were allowed to maintain their own governments independently of the Oklahoma Territory, provided that they retained their tribal structure. However, the many American settlers who had penetrated the area demanded the abolition of both the tribal governmental structure and the tribal landholding system. In 1893 the United States Congress appointed the Dawes Commission to persuade the tribes to accept the dissolution of their tribal government in favor of government from Washington, D.C., and to implement the policy of breaking up the tribal lands into individual tracts. It was a disaster for the tribes; of the 30 million acres that had originally been granted to them in 1834, less than two million were in native hands on the eve of statehood.

A bid for statehood began as early as 1891 in the Oklahoma Territory, with frequent conventions being held in successive years in Oklahoma City, El Reno, Purcell, Kingfisher, Shawnee, and finally Guthrie. In the Indian Territory, agitation for statehood started on a large scale only in 1905. After the tribal land divisions had been implemented and native "assimilation" hastened, Congress empowered the "twin territories" to apply for admission to the Union as a single state. Two Osage and 55 other delegates from each of the two territories formulated the state constitution at a convention that met at Guthrie on November 20, 1906. The document was completed on April 22, 1907, and its approval was voted by the people of the region on September 17. On November 16, 1907, Oklahoma, with a population of 1.5 million, became the 46th state.

November 17

Congress Finds a Permanent Home

Before its first session at the Capitol in Washington, D.C., on November 17, 1800, Congress (like its predecessors during the American Revolution) met in a number of locations.

In 1774 America was comprised of 13 mainland colonies and approximately 2.5 million people. Only five percent of the population lived in communities of more than 2,000 residents, but these urban areas greatly influenced politics, commerce, and intellectual life. Philadelphia, Pennsylvania, with 28,000 residents, was America's foremost city. The other leading cities were New York City,

New York; Boston, Massachusetts; and Charleston, South Carolina.

Politics and practicality made Philadelphia the first capital of the united colonies. Britain's imposition of what came to be known as the Intolerable Acts on Massachusetts as a punishment for the Boston Tea Party of December 16, 1773, prompted Massachusetts Bay Colony legislators to seek stringent economic sanctions against Britain. More moderate patriot leaders instead sought to contain the radicals and called a Continental Congress to develop an appropriate American response. They chose Philadelphia to be the site of their gathering, as it was both geographically and politically located in the center. Furthermore, unlike New York and Boston, the city of Philadelphia was free from garrisons of British troops.

Twelve colonies sent 56 representatives to the First Continental Congress—with only Georgia abstaining. Joseph Galloway, the conservative speaker of the Pennsylvania assembly, suggested that the colony's statehouse be the meeting chamber. However, the convention members decided instead to accept the local carpenters' offer of their own building. They foresaw this decision as "highly agreeable to the mechanics and citizens in general." The First Continental Congress thus met at Carpenters' Hall from September 5 to October 26, 1774, having resolved to reconvene on May 10, 1775, if British harassment continued.

Meanwhile, what was to develop into the American Revolution had commenced. It began with bloody encounters between American militiamen and British regulars at Lexington and Concord in Massachusetts on April 19, 1775. In the face of the precarious situation, the colonies held fast to their intention to meet again. The Second Continental Congress convened on May 10, 1775, as planned. This time it held its sessions in the Pennsylvania State House, now known as Independence Hall. Over one year later in the same hall, on July 4, 1776, the delegates voted to accept a revised version of Thomas Jefferson's Declaration of Independence, which officially renounced America's allegiance to Great Britain.

Britain's military superiority threatened the colonial cause. General Sir William Howe's troops occupied New York City on September 15, 1776, and by November George Washington's men were in flight to New Jersey. On December 11, 1776, the British chased the rebels into Pennsylvania, and on December 12 Congress decided to abandon its hazardous position in Philadelphia. During the following months Henry Fite's three-story brick house in Baltimore, Maryland, served as the new location for the Continental Congress.

However, American forces soon scored surprise victories in New Jersey—at Trenton on December 26, 1776, and at Princeton on January 3, 1777—which secured New Jersey for the colonials and bolstered morale in neighboring Pennsylvania. Congress soon left its Baltimore refuge and returned to Philadelphia on March 4, 1777. In the summer of 1777, however, General Howe sailed with 15,000 men against Philadelphia. On September 19, the Continental Congress once again fled the city. The representatives met on September 27 in Lancaster, Pennsylvania, and the next day moved on to York, Pennsylvania, where they convened on September 30. Meanwhile, Howe captured Philadelphia on September 26. The rebel legislators endured their exile until the British evacuated the city in June 1778, after which they returned to Philadelphia.

The Continental Congress remained at Philadelphia for the remainder of the Revolution. Later, a demonstration by 300 American soldiers seeking redress of various grievances prompted the body to remove to Princeton, New Jersey, on June 24, 1783. While there, the Continental Congress met in the faculty room of Princeton College in Nassau Hall. Under a plan requiring alternate sessions in Annapolis and Trenton, the legislature adjourned on November 3, 1783, to go to Maryland. The delegates met in Annapolis from November 26, 1783, to June 3, 1784, and at Trenton from November 1 to December 2, 1784. New York City was the final seat of the Congress meeting under the Articles of Confederation, with sessions held there from January 11, 1785, to March 2, 1789.

The Constitutional Convention, held in Philadelphia during the summer of 1787, devised a new frame of government under which elections were held late in 1788. On March 4, 1789, the new Congress convened in New York City, but it did not obtain a quorum until April. Both the Senate and House of Representatives met at Federal Hall at the intersection of Wall and Broad Streets in lower Manhattan. The building had long served as the New York city hall, but the French architect Pierre Charles L'Enfant refurbished it at a cost of $50,000 to suit the needs of its new tenants.

Political exigencies soon had Congress on the move again. On January 14, 1790, Secretary of the Treasury Alexander Hamilton delivered his "First Report on the Public Credit" in which he advocated that the federal government take the responsibility for $21.5 million worth of debts incurred by the states during the Revolution. Hamilton believed the assumption of debts would increase world confidence in the United States and would also strengthen the central government by connecting its well-being with that of the businessmen who held most of the public debt.

Southerners, fearful of national encroachment on state powers, effectively blocked the assumption plan which Hamilton saw as vital to the American economy. He finally won the support of Secretary of State Thomas Jefferson, Representative James Madison, and the Virginians who led the opposition, by agreeing to have the national capital relocated to a more southern area. On July 10, 1790, the House of Representatives authorized the president to pick a ten-mile square district, within a 105-mile stretch on the Potomac River's banks, to be the site. Philadelphia would serve as the interim capital until 1800.

On December 6 Congress began a decade's tenure in Philadelphia, meeting at the county courthouse at Sixth and Chestnut Streets just west of the Pennsylvania State House. The representatives met on the first floor of the building and the senators on the second. The structure, donated by the state for the use of the legislature, became known as Congress Hall. Pennsylvania also built a President's House on Ninth Street between Elm and Chestnut Streets, in which the president resided. The commonwealth hoped, in vain, that its generosity would persuade the federal government to remain in Philadelphia.

President George Washington spent two weeks in October 1790 inspecting possible locations for the nation's capital along the Potomac River. He finally chose a spot on the east bank, as far south as the congressional mandate allowed. The site included land in both Maryland and Virginia, but the city was to be autonomous. The government then bought the property from its owners for $66.50 an acre, which was five times the market value.

Three commissioners, including Associate Supreme Court Justice Thomas Johnson of Maryland, supervised the development of the capital. They made it known in 1791 that it would bear the name of Washington. Major Pierre Charles L'Enfant designed the city by imposing a series of avenues radiating from circles on a grid of numbered and lettered streets. Thomas Jefferson selected the locations for the Capitol (the seat of the Congress) and for the White House.

Congress met in Washington, D.C., for the first time on November 17, 1800. In the same year, President John Adams moved into the White House. The capital had an appropriate frontier quality: Adams swam in the Potomac before breakfast, and his wife, Abigail, dried the family laundry in the East Room. On March 1, 1801, Thomas Jefferson became the first president to be inaugurated in the new city.

The Capitol is an impressive example of early American governmental architecture. The 432-room structure, which covers three and a half acres, is 751 feet long, 350 feet wide, and 287 feet high. Thomas Crawford's bronze statue *Freedom*, erected to the accompaniment of a 35-gun salute on December 3, 1863, stands atop the Capitol dome.

After a 1792 competition, William Thornton was selected by President Washington to design the Capitol, notwithstanding the fact that his entry arrived months after the competition had closed. Thornton shares the credit with French architect Étienne Sulpice Hallet for the basic conception of a central dome flanked by north and south wings. Retained to supervise the execution and revision of Thornton's plans, Hallet sought to introduce changes and was dismissed in 1794. President Washington himself had meanwhile laid the cornerstone in 1793, and construction proceeded under various hands for years. The architect Benjamin H. Latrobe, working from 1803 to 1817, modified the original plans. Charles Bulfinch, who succeeded Latrobe in 1817, completed the structure in 1830. Thornton died in 1828, before the Capitol was completed.

The north wing, the first one finished, originally served as quarters for the House of Representatives, the Senate, and the Supreme Court. In 1807 the House moved to the new south wing, leaving the north section to the Senate. A wooden walkway joined the two wings. British soldiers burned the Capitol, the White House, and other public buildings on August 24, 1814, during the War of 1812. Following the war, the Capitol was reconstructed, and by December 1819 it was once again ready for occupancy and its north and south wings were restored. The central portion of the Capitol, which Bulfinch had begun in 1818, included the east and west fronts and the central rotunda. Topped with a copper-covered wooden dome, the rotunda was virtually completed by 1824.

In 1849 Congress authorized plans for vastly extending the north and south wings and for adding a massive new dome to match the building's new proportions. The new legislative chambers were essentially completed by 1859. Construction on the 4,500-ton cast- and wrought-iron dome began in 1855 and continued until its completion in 1863. The Capitol then remained undisturbed until 1959, when the east front was moved forward 32 feet to provide greater architectural balance.

Anne Hutchinson Banished From Colonial Massachusetts

The founders of the Massachusetts Bay Colony were convinced of the necessity of establishing a model society (or, in John Winthrop's words, "A City upon the Hill") that would serve as a symbol of righteousness to a decadent world. Theological ideals would not remain vague abstractions in the colony envisioned by the Puritan leadership, but would be the very basis of the social order. In 1630 the Massachusetts Bay colonists arrived in New England, determined to make their dream a reality. Within seven years two later arrivals, namely Roger Williams and Anne Marbury Hutchinson, had jeopardized the very existence of the "community of saints."

Dissent was not tolerated in a colony convinced of its own moral rectitude and struggling to make its religious beliefs the foundation of its governmental system. In 1636 Roger Williams so disrupted Massachusetts Bay with his unorthodox teachings that the Puritan leadership banished him to Rhode Island. The following year Anne Hutchinson, the wife of merchant William Hutchinson and the mother of 14 children, posed another perceived threat.

A great admirer of John Cotton, Hutchinson and her family followed that famous Puritan preacher to New England in 1634. Born in Alford (Lincolnshire), England, in 1591, Anne Hutchinson was a woman of keen intellect. Shortly after her arrival she began to hold weekly meetings in her home during which she discussed and explained Cotton's sermons of the previous Sunday. Before long these sessions also gave her an opportunity to air her own theological opinions. Her most serious deviations from Puritan orthodoxy were her insistence that "works," or outward behavior, were not an indication of personal salvation and her claim that every convert came to know the will of God through direct personal revelation. The leaders of the Puritan colony felt that such tenets, taken to their logical conclusions, jeopardized their "errand into the wilderness" by justifying activities detrimental to the social order and by deemphasizing the role of the ministry. They immediately acted to eliminate the threat to their rule.

The first efforts against Hutchinson were circumspect, for her followers included several very influential people. On August 30, 1637, however, a synod of 25 ministers stated that Hutchinson's teachings were heretical. On November 12 the general court ordered her to stand trial on charges of sedition and contempt.

In the early stages of her trial it seemed that Hutchinson would be able to outwit her adversaries, but in the final days of the proceedings her insistence that she had direct personal revelations from God clinched the government's case against her. On November 17 the general court ordered her banished.

Because of the harsh New England winter, Hutchinson was allowed to remain in the colony until spring. In March 1638, however, she was excommunicated in an ecclesiastical trial after she refused to recant. Soon afterward, she departed from Massachusetts. The Hutchinson family and many of her followers sought refuge in Roger Williams's settlement in Rhode Island and on March 7, 1638, founded Pocasset (later Portsmouth). After her husband's death in 1642, Hutchinson moved to New York, first to Long Island and later to the area of what was later New Rochelle. Sometime in either August or September 1643, she and her family, except one daughter, were killed by Native Americans.

November 18

Asa Gray's Birthday

Asa Gray, the pioneering American botanist, was born on November 18, 1810, at Sauquoit in Oneida County, New York. His parents were Moses Gray, a tanner and prosperous farmer, and Roxana Howard Gray. He was the oldest of eight children and attended school in Clinton, nine miles away.

Gray's first training in science came from James Hadley, a professor of chemistry, between 1825 to 1826. Two years afterward, he was intrigued by an article on botany in Brewster's *Edinburgh Encyclopaedia* and bought a botany handbook of his own, which he studied through the winter. That spring, at the age of 17, he first began collecting and identifying plants. In 1831 Gray graduated from the Fairfield (New York) Medical School as a doctor, but he never practiced medicine. Beyond this point, he was taught by senior colleagues and by himself in the field of science. He delivered lectures on botany at the medical school the summer after graduating and from 1832 to 1835 taught science at Bartlett's High School in Utica, New York.

By correspondence he came to know John Torrey, a New York City physician who was a distinguished botanist and mineralogist then engaged in pioneer work discovering, studying, and systematizing the plants of North America. In particular, Torrey was classifying and publishing reports on plant specimens forwarded by a series of western exploratory expeditions sponsored by the United

States government. During summers and on leave from his post in 1835, Gray served as Torrey's companion on several botanical field trips and as his assistant in New York City.

In 1836 Torrey secured for Gray the position of curator of the New York Lyceum of Natural History, later known as the New York Academy of Sciences. Between 1838 and 1843, Torrey and Gray collaborated on *Flora of North America*, a work in which Gray helped revise the procedure for classifying plants. In 1836 Gray published his *Elements of Botany*, the first of a distinguished series of botany textbooks that helped to popularize the study of botany in the United States. His *Botanical Text-Book for Colleges, Schools and Private Students* followed in 1842, and was renamed *Structural Botany* during the sixth edition (1879) after much development and revision. Gray's other publications included *First Lessons in Botany and Vegetable Physiology* (1857), *How Plants Grow* (1858), *Field, Forest and Garden Botany* (1869), *How Plants Behave* (1872), and a second *Elements of Botany* (1887).

Gray accepted the professorship of botany at the newly founded University of Michigan in 1838 and went to Europe to purchase books for the new school. While there he also pursued his botanical studies, visiting Switzerland, Austria, Bavaria, Italy, France, and England and forming lifelong friendships with European botanists. He never actually took up his duties at Michigan, because he was appointed Fisher Professor of Natural History at Harvard in 1842, a chair he held for 46 years. Gray rapidly made Harvard the nation's center of botanical science, creating the department of botany and training many who were to become outstanding botanists. Through wide exchanges he established an herbarium that developed into the largest and most valuable in the country, later named the Gray Herbarium in his honor. He also founded a botany library.

In 1848 Gray married Jane Lathrop Loring. The Grays' home in the Harvard Botanical Garden became a meeting place for botanists from all over the United States and Europe who sought advice about classifying plants. Gray's efforts toward systematizing the flora of North America had put him at the forefront of American botany and in the company of the world's most eminent naturalists. Gray's most important work, *Manual of the Botany of the Northern United States* (1848), was published during this time.

Gray was also an early and constant supporter of Charles Robert Darwin's theory of the evolution of species by natural selection. Darwin first outlined his theory to Gray in a celebrated letter of September 5, 1857, and sent him one of the three advance copies of *On the Origin of Species by Means of Natural Selection* (1859). Gray openly announced his belief that existing species, including humans, derived from previous species rather than being special creations of God. Even though he defended Darwin's theory against those who insisted that it was contrary to the teachings of the Bible, he did not follow certain contemporaries in making Darwinism a substitute religion. He remained a critic as well as an advocate of the theory of natural selection and formed conclusions about plant variations that pointed toward Gregor Mendel's and Hugo De Vries's later discoveries in plant genetics.

Gray was active in the scientific organizations of his day, some of which are still highly influential. He helped found the National Academy of Sciences in 1863 "to investigate, examine, experiment and report upon any subject of science or art desired by any department of [the United States] Government." He was president of the American Academy of Arts and Sciences from 1863 to 1873, and in 1872 he was also president of the American Association for the Advancement of Science. From 1874 until his death in 1888, he was one of the 14 regents of the Smithsonian Institution in Washington, D.C. He was also a member of the Royal Society of London and received honorary degrees from Oxford, Cambridge, and Aberdeen Universities.

Gray died at the age of 77 in Cambridge, Massachusetts, on January 30, 1888, and was buried in Mount Auburn Cemetery. Twelve years later he was elected to the Hall of Fame for Great Americans.

November 19

Civil War: President Abraham Lincoln's Gettysburg Address

During the Civil War, the Union victory at the battle of Gettysburg in July 1863 (see July 1) contributed significantly to the preservation of the United States. During the battle more than 3,000 federal troops died on the Pennsylvania field, falling beside almost 4,000 Confederates.

To commemorate the victory, the Union decided to establish a military graveyard for its soldiers at the site of the Gettysburg victory. The commission in charge of the project planned appropriate services to accompany the consecration of the cemetery on November 19, 1863. They invited a number of dignitaries to attend the ceremonies, and asked Edward Everett, a famous orator and former senator, to deliver the principal address.

To the surprise of the commission, President Abraham Lincoln accepted their courtesy invitation to attend the ceremonies. The chairman, David Wills of Gettysburg, accordingly on November 2, 1863, asked him to deliver "a few appropriate remarks" on the occasion. Lincoln once again agreed, although he had little time to prepare his speech. Secretary of State William H. Seward, Secretary of the Interior John P. Usher, and Postmaster General Francis P. Blair accompanied Lincoln when he left Washington, D.C., on November 18 for the journey to Gettysburg. The train ride consumed the entire day, but contrary to popular belief Lincoln apparently did not work on his speech during the trip to Pennsylvania.

Chairman Wills greeted the presidential party at the Gettysburg station and escorted it to his home. Serenaders and bands gathered outside the Wills house on the town square and called for Lincoln to make an appearance. The president stepped outside, spoke for a few minutes, and then returned to dinner. Around 9:00 p.m. Lincoln went upstairs to his room. Owing to the pressures of war and politics, Lincoln had only written part of his address before he left Washington, D.C. He did some more work on it during the evening of November 18 before going to bed around midnight. Lincoln spent another hour on the morning of November 19, 1863, completing the speech. He then rolled up the two-page speech, tucked it into his tall hat, and left the Wills house to join the procession to the cemetery.

The prayers that began the ceremonies at the burying ground reflected the solemnity of the event and set the tone for Edward Everett's address. The 69-year-old statesman drew on his lifetime of varied experiences as a minister, professor of Greek, and president of Harvard University. He spoke for two hours, ranging in subject matter from the heroes of ancient Greece to a detailed account of the battle of Gettysburg.

The singing of an ode followed Senator Everett's address, and then the president approached the rostrum. Lincoln delivered his message of less than 300 words within two minutes and resumed his seat. Most of the crowd missed his words entirely. Expecting Lincoln to speak for a longer period, they had allowed themselves to be diverted by the activities of a photographer trying to take a picture of the president. Few among the audience recognized the greatness of Lincoln's speech. Secretary Seward kindly said "his speech was not equal to him." Most major newspapers concentrated on Everett's address and ignored the president's words. The *Chicago Times* was critical: "The cheek of every American must tingle with shame as he reads the silly, flat, and dishwatery utterances of the man who has to be pointed out to intelligent foreigners as the President of the United States." The *London Times* thought that a speech "more dull and commonplace it would not be easy to produce."

However, simple words best explain important events, and Lincoln's phrases had captured the meaning of Gettysburg and the Civil War. Lincoln spoke of the sacrifices of the men who had died that a nation might live:

> Fourscore and seven years ago our fathers brought forth on this continent a new nation, conceived in liberty, and dedicated to the proposition that all men are created equal.
>
> Now we are engaged in a great civil war, testing whether that nation, or any nation so conceived and so dedicated, can long endure. We are met on a great battlefield of that war. We have come to dedicate a portion of that field as a final resting place for those who here gave their lives that the nation might live. It is altogether fitting and proper that we should do this.
>
> But, in a larger sense, we cannot dedicate, we cannot consecrate, we cannot hallow, this ground. The brave men, living and dead, who struggled here, have consecrated it far above our poor power to add or detract. The world will little note nor long remember what we say here, but it can never forget what they did here. It is for us, the living, rather, to be dedicated here to the unfinished work which they who fought here have thus far so nobly advanced. It is rather for us to be here dedicated to the great task remaining before us, that from these honored dead we take increased devotion to that cause for which they gave the last full measure of devotion, that we here highly resolve that these dead shall not have died in vain, that this nation, under God, shall have a new birth of freedom, and that government of the people, by the people, for the people, shall not perish from the earth.

Later critics obviously thought more favorably of the Gettysburg Address. Some 50 years later Lord George Nathaniel Curzon, the chancellor of Oxford University in England, expressed the general modern evaluation:

> The Gettysburg Address is far more than a pleasing piece of occasional oratory. It is a pure well of English undefiled. It sets one to inquiring with nothing short of wonder "How knoweth this man letters, having never learned?" The more closely the ad-

dress is analysed the more one must confess astonishment at its choice of words, the precision of its thought, its simplicity, directness, and effectiveness.

James A. Garfield's Birthday

James Abram Garfield, the 20th president of the United States, was born on November 19, 1831, in the tiny frontier community of Orange, Ohio. The youngest of five children, he was the son of a farmer, Abram Garfield. Garfield's father died in 1833, leaving his family in poverty. Eliza Ballou Garfield, the future president's mother, managed through great perseverance to rear and educate her children.

Garfield worked his way through college. He held a number of jobs, including teacher, carpenter, and farmer, and attended the Western Reserve Eclectic Institute in Hiram, Ohio. He later entered Williams College in Williamstown, Massachusetts, from which he graduated in 1856. After graduation he returned to the institute, where he taught ancient languages and literature, and within a year had risen to become president of the institute. In 1858 he married a childhood friend and former fellow student, Lucretia Rudolph.

Entering politics during this same period, Garfield supported the Free-Soil movement and was drawn to the new Republican Party. Having shown himself to be an effective speaker against slavery in 1857 and 1858, he successfully ran for a seat in the Ohio state senate in 1859 on the Republican ticket. He had also learned enough law to be admitted to the bar. When the Civil War began in 1861, Garfield recruited the 42nd Ohio Volunteer Infantry, becoming first its lieutenant colonel and then its colonel. Although without formal military training himself, he trained the regiment, and then led it against Confederate forces at Middle Creek in Kentucky. As a result of his victory, he was raised to the rank of brigadier general of volunteers, one of the youngest Union officers to achieve such a rank.

In Tennessee Garfield took part in the fighting at Shiloh in April 1862, and in September 1863 he served at Chickamauga as chief of staff under General William S. Rosecrans in the Army of the Cumberland. Although rewarded with a promotion to major general of volunteers, Garfield resigned his commission to serve in the United States House of Representatives, to which he had been elected in 1862. He took his seat in Congress in December 1863.

Garfield won reelection eight times in succession, serving in the House of Representatives for a total of 18 years. His rise within Congress was

steady. At first serving on the House Committee on Military Affairs because of his battlefield experience, Garfield later became an expert on fiscal matters and was a member of both the Committee on Appropriations and the Committee on Ways and Means. Although usually a supporter of Republican policies, his backing of a major protective tariff was at best lukewarm, too lukewarm to suit some of his manufacturer constituents in the industrially burgeoning state of Ohio.

Garfield's most difficult campaign for reelection to Congress came in 1874, when attempts were made to link him with two possible conflict of interest situations. One of these was the Credit Mobilier scandal, in which some potentially influential members of Congress received "gifts" of stocks. However, the charges against Garfield were vague and never proven. His career resumed its upward course after his reelection. By this time he had become one of the leading Republicans in the House of Representatives, and in 1876 became the official leader of the House Republicans.

Garfield played an important role during the disputed presidential election of 1876. He served as a "visiting statesman" to oversee the vote count in Louisiana, one of four crucial states that had sent in two conflicting sets of election returns. Garfield was also instrumental in working out the compromise legislation passed by Congress on January 29, 1877, establishing a bipartisan electoral commission to review disputed state returns. Until then, the choice of the new president had hovered inconclusively—depending on which way the disputed electoral votes were counted— between the two principal contenders, Republican Rutherford B. Hayes and Democrat Samuel J. Tilden. Garfield served on the commission as one of the two House Republicans and voted with the majority in favor of Hayes, who was named president.

In 1880 the Ohio state legislature elected Garfield to the United States Senate, but he was destined to never serve in that post. At the Republican National Convention that year, delegates became deadlocked between the presidential choices of two factions of the party. The contestants were the powerful James G. Blaine, leader of the so-called Half Breeds, and former president Ulysses S. Grant, favored by the Stalwarts. On the 36th ballot the convention swung behind Garfield, who was the manager for the candidacy of Ohio's John Sherman (brother of Union general William Tecumseh Sherman). To placate the party's Stalwart faction, Chester A. Arthur was chosen as the vice-presidential candidate. The popular vote was extremely close with Garfield being elected by a plurality of less than 10,000 votes over his Democratic rival, Winfield Scott Hancock. In the electoral college Garfield received 214 votes and Hancock 155 votes.

After his inauguration on March 4, 1881, Garfield began to make appointments designed to conciliate every section of the Republican Party. Senator Roscoe Conkling of New York, the leader of the Stalwart forces, was still unhappy, but after Garfield won his fight for independence in presidential appointments, Conkling resigned his Senate seat.

Before Garfield was able to devote his full attention to affairs of state, he was struck down by an assassin. En route to his 25th class reunion at Williams College on July 2, 1881, he was on his way to his train at the old Baltimore and Potomac Railway Depot in Washington, D.C., when he was shot by Charles J. Guiteau (see July 2). Guiteau was a disappointed office seeker and Stalwart supporter, who said that he shot Garfield in order to make Arthur president. After he was shot, Garfield was unable to transact even the most trivial functions of his office. With Congress not in session and the cabinet deliberating on the status of Vice President Arthur and whether he should be named temporary or even permanent president, a constitutional crisis loomed. As the weeks rolled by, hopes persisted that Garfield might recover. In an attempt to aid his recovery by removing him from the Washington, D.C., summer heat, the president was taken to the seaside resort of Elberon, New Jersey. These efforts and others to save Garfield failed, and he died at Elberon on September 19, 1881.

Garfield's assassination made him a political martyr, and the stricken nation mourned deeply. One funeral was held in Elberon, followed by a state funeral in Washington, D.C., and a third funeral and interment in Cleveland, Ohio. The assassin was hanged on June 30, 1882.

November 20

Robert F. Kennedy's Birthday

Robert Francis Kennedy, one of the most significant and tragic political figures of the 1960s and brother to President John F. Kennedy, was born on November 20, 1925, in Brookline, Massachusetts. He was one of the nine children born to Joseph and Rose Kennedy. Kennedy received his education at Harvard University, graduating in 1948, and his law degree from the University of Virginia Law School, graduating in 1951. He also served in the United States Navy during World War II.

During law school Kennedy married Ethel Skakel. After law school he joined the Department of Justice as a staff attorney, but left in 1952 to manage his brother John's successful campaign for the United States Senate. In the process the two developed a close political working relationship. Robert Kennedy then returned to the public sector, and served as counsel to several Senate committees, most notably with the Senate Permanent Investigations Subcommittee from 1955 to 1957. He helped with the investigation into corrupt practices by Jimmy Hoffa, the notorious head of the Teamsters' Union.

In 1960 Kennedy once again served as campaign manager for his brother John, this time for president of the United States. After winning the election, President John F. Kennedy appointed Robert attorney general, in addition to retaining him as his personal political adviser. As head of the Justice Department, which includes the Federal Bureau of Investigation (FBI), Attorney General Kennedy actively pursued an aggressive civil rights enforcement program despite considerable resistance from his nominal subordinate, FBI head J. Edgar Hoover. Although President Kennedy was occasionally hesitant on civil rights matters, for fear of alienating the large number of his fellow Democrats who were from the South, he generally supported his brother.

After President Kennedy was assassinated on November 22, 1963 (see November 22), Robert Kennedy's power and influence were greatly reduced. He did not get along well with the new president, Lyndon B. Johnson, and thus in 1964 he decided to resign from office. Kennedy then went to New York and campaigned for the United States Senate, winning in the November 1964 elections. He resumed an activist civil rights agenda, this time working vigorously on behalf of antipoverty initiatives. Although Kennedy generally supported the Johnson administration's Great Society program, he disagreed with the president's commitment to maintaining the war in Vietnam, a dispute that influenced Kennedy's decision to run for the Democratic nomination for president in the 1968 primaries. Johnson himself decided to not seek reelection (see related articles throughout this book).

With his fellow Democrat Johnson out of the way, Kennedy became one of the leading contenders for the nomination. However, his presidential campaign, officially announced on March 16, 1968, lasted less than 90 days. On June 5, 1968, while celebrating his victory in the important California primary, Kennedy was shot in Los Angeles by a Jordanian named Sirhan Bishara Sirhan. He died the next day and was buried in Arlington National Cemetery near the tomb of his brother John.

November 21

North Carolina Ratifies the Constitution

On November 21, 1789, North Carolina became the 12th state to ratify the United States Constitution, leaving only Rhode Island still outside the continental union. More than a year earlier, North Carolina had been the first state to refuse to accept the new frame of government.

Early in January 1787 in the final days of the North Carolina legislative session, Governor Richard Caswell presented a letter from the governor of Virginia urging North Carolina's "zealous attention to the present American crisis." Prodded by men like Caswell, William R. Davie, Richard Dobbs Spaight, William Hooper, John Gray Blount, and Archibald Maclaine, the legislators decided to send a delegation to the Constitutional Convention that was to open in Philadelphia, Pennsylvania, in May 1787. They selected two leaders of the conservative faction, William R. Davie and Richard Dobbs Spaight; two political moderates, Richard Caswell and Alexander Martin; and the acknowledged radical spokesman, Willie Jones. Governor Caswell, unable to participate because of ill health, appointed William Blount in his stead and replaced Willie Jones with Hugh Williamson, the former having refused to serve without giving a reason.

According to contemporary accounts, North Carolina's representatives were among the less prominent members of the convention. Davie, an attorney and planter, was in his early thirties and was popular but not prominent. Spaight, a wealthy planter, was less than 30 years old. Blount, a merchant and planter, was regarded as "plain, honest and sincere." Martin, a lawyer, planter, and former governor, had been dismissed from the army for cowardice at the battle of Germantown. Williamson had been a preacher and professor of mathematics at the College of Philadelphia before he became a medical doctor; he was fond of debate but was not a good speaker. All five had served in the American Revolution; all except Alexander Martin had sat in the Congress of the Confederation. Davie, Martin, and Williamson were also college graduates.

Blount and Martin were silent and inactive at the convention, and neither made a speech or served on a committee. Davie was a member of the committee that devised the Great Compro-

mise authorizing each state to send a number of representatives proportional to its population to the lower house of the new Congress and to have equal representation (later defined as two senators per state) in the upper house. Spaight opposed the Great Compromise but suggested the election of senators by the state legislatures. Williamson, who made 73 speeches, proposed the six-year term for senators and acted as spokesman for the North Carolina contingent.

North Carolina was the fourth most populous state in 1787, but on the critical question of the distribution of seats in the Congress it voted with the smaller states in favor of equal representation in the Senate. Members of the delegation, all of whom owned slaves except for Williamson, supported the three-fifths compromise under which five slaves counted as three freemen for purposes of apportioning representation and taxation. They also agreed with the decision to permit the continuation of the international slave trade for 20 years and to forbid the taxation of exports. At the conclusion of the convention, Blount, Spaight, and Williamson signed the Constitution on behalf of their state.

Governor Caswell presented the proposed Constitution to the state legislature on November 21, 1787, the second day of its new session. On December 5, the day set aside for discussion of the document, the lawmakers debated. On December 6 both houses requested all taxpayers to select, at the March 1788 elections, delegates for a ratifying convention that met on July 21, 1788, at Hillsboro.

Federalists and Antifederalists waged spirited and occasionally vicious campaigns in the months before the March elections. Supporters of the Constitution from Pennsylvania sent masses of literature into North Carolina, but North Carolinian James Iredell, who later served for nine years as an associate justice of the United States Supreme Court, provided the most cogent arguments for ratification. He described the "disordered and distracted" state of the country under the Articles of Confederation and suggested that only a "united, vigorous government" could solve the country's problems.

Antifederalists claimed that the establishment of a strong national government would lead to the disintegration of the states, that the spirit of the Constitution favored industry and commerce rather than agriculture, and that the absence of a bill of rights could have grave consequences for the individual. Timothy Bloodworth insisted that the new government would be an "autocratic tyranny, or monarchial monarchy," and the Baptist preacher Lemuel Burkitt of Hertford County predicted that the national capital would be a walled city housing a standing army of at least 50,000 men who would be at liberty to plunder and pillage.

Opponents of the Constitution won a massive victory in the March 1788 election. Although 11 states had already ratified the proposed frame of government, the Antifederalists were sure of success in North Carolina. When the ratification convention met on July 21, 1788, Willie Jones suggested that the meeting vote and adjourn on the first day, because to delay the inevitable outcome was to waste public money. The Federalists managed to prolong the convention for 11 days, but then by a vote of 184 to 84, delegates declared that North Carolina would not ratify the Continental Constitution until a bill of rights had been presented to the Congress and to a second Constitutional Convention. On August 4, 1788, the North Carolina ratification convention adjourned without setting a date to meet again.

North Carolina Federalists were undaunted by the defeat and immediately began circulating petitions for a second ratifying convention. The state senate in November 1788 called for another convention and, although the lower house concurred, the Antifederalists in that body managed to postpone the date of the proposed gathering for a year. The legislators chose to convene in Fayetteville in November 1789.

While North Carolina remained aloof, the new federal government began functioning in the spring of 1789. George Washington, who enjoyed great popularity in North Carolina, became the first president that April and the national authorities engaged in none of the tyrannical practices predicted by the vehement Antifederalists. The United States Congress even proposed 12 amendments to the Constitution, designed to safeguard individual liberties. Ten of those amendments eventually formed the Bill of Rights.

Supporters of the Constitution in North Carolina used the months before the August 1789 elections to educate the public about the advantages of the new government. They succeeded and defeated the Antifederalists in the August canvass, which selected representatives to the November 1789 ratifying convention. Of the 102 delegates chosen in 1789 who had also served at the Hillsboro convention of 1788, 39 were reelected as Federalists and 20 converted to the support of the Constitution in the interim, while the Antifederalists reelected 43 men. Of the 169 new delegates, 135 were Federalists.

North Carolina's second convention opened on November 16, 1789. The caucus lasted only five days, and on November 21, 1789, North Carolina became the 12th state to ratify the Constitution. The final vote was by the decisive margin of 194

to 77. No doubt the election of George Washington, the proposal of the Bill of Rights, and the state's sense of isolation from the rest of the country strongly influenced the final decision.

North Carolina and the other 12 colonies that formed the original Union under the Articles of Confederation became states when they declared their independence from Great Britain in July 1776. However, historians typically determine the chronology of the entrance of these states by the order in which they ratified the Constitution. Thus North Carolina is said to be the 12th state to join the United States of America.

November 22

President John F. Kennedy Assassinated

On Friday, November 22, 1963, John Fitzgerald Kennedy, the 35th president of the United States, was shot as he rode through the streets of Dallas, Texas. Kennedy had gone to Texas to help mend a dispute between factions of the state Democratic Party, whose unified strength he would need in his anticipated bid for reelection in 1964. The president also hoped to address and win over the people of Texas, many of whom were conservatives opposed to him because of his support of liberal causes such as civil rights.

President Kennedy landed at Love Field in Dallas on the morning of November 22 and mingled with the throng of people that came to meet him. With his wife, Jacqueline Bouvier Kennedy, he entered an open limousine with Texas governor John Connally and his wife, and a Secret Service agent from the motorcade. Large crowds cheered the president on his journey, and his apparent rapport with the Texans greatly pleased him. Connally's wife even turned to her guests and stated that the people lining the roadway exemplified the true affection that Texans felt for Kennedy.

Official investigators later reconstructed events as follows: As the cars turned left at Houston Street onto Elm Street, Lee Harvey Oswald peered down at the motorcade from a sixth-floor window in the Texas School Book Depository. Placing a high-powered Italian rifle with a telescopic sight to his shoulder, Oswald fired three shots at the vehicle bearing the Kennedys and the Connallys. Two shots struck the president, one in his head and the other in his neck. One of the bullets, probably the one that struck Kennedy in the neck, also wounded Governor Connally.

November 21

The motorcade sped to Parkland Memorial Hospital. Doctors at the hospital worked desperately, but to no avail, to save the president. Father Oscar L. Huber administered the last rites of the Roman Catholic Church to the dying president, and William K. Clark pronounced him dead as of 1:00 p.m. central standard time.

Lee Harvey Oswald, who allegedly fired the shots that killed the president, had led an unhappy life. He did not fare well as a student or with his classmates, who remembered him as a bookish loner. As a high school dropout, he joined the U.S. Marine Corps, where he was again an outsider and unpopular with fellow servicemen. After his mother suffered an injury, he obtained a hardship discharge to support her but remained at home for only a few days before he went to New Orleans, Louisianna, and obtained work on a freighter, which went to the Soviet Union in October 1959. Oswald, who had been attracted to communism for several years, declared that he was renouncing his American citizenship and obtained a work permit. Distrusted by many Russians, he again became an outsider. With his Russian wife, Marina Nikolaevna Prusakova Oswald, he returned in June 1962 to the United States, where he lived briefly in Fort Worth, Dallas, and New Orleans before returning to Dallas in 1963. He began work at the Texas School Book Depository on October 16, 1963.

According to official reports, Oswald fled the depository after the assassination and made his way to his rooming house by bus, taxicab, and foot. He quickly left the rooming house and was next seen about a mile away at 10th Street and Patton Avenue, where police officer J. D. Tippit stopped the suspicious-looking young man. Oswald spoke briefly to Tippit and then shot the officer four times with a revolver. Having killed Tippit, Oswald fled to the Texas Theater, where the police apprehended him after a brief struggle.

Dallas officials arraigned Oswald for the murders of Kennedy and Tippit, but he denied participation in the deeds. The public may never know much more about Oswald because the 24-year-old suspect soon met his own violent end. On November 24, as police officers were escorting Oswald through the basement of the police headquarters to a vehicle waiting to take him to the county jail, he was assassinated by Jack Ruby, a Dallas nightclub owner. Ruby, convicted of murder, later died of cancer in prison.

Rumors that there was a conspiracy to kill President Kennedy spread quickly after the assassination, particularly in the wake of Oswald's death. Lyndon B. Johnson, who succeeded Kennedy as president, appointed a commission headed by

Chief Justice of the U.S. Supreme Court Earl Warren, to investigate the event. After months of study, the Warren Commission concluded that Oswald had been the sole assassin. Many people remain unconvinced to this day, believing that not all the facts have been revealed.

News of Kennedy's death spread quickly and shocked people throughout the world. Not only Americans, but people in nations everywhere expressed their sorrow and sense of loss. More than a thousand Londoners made their way to the American embassy at Grosvenor Square. Ten thousand Poles signed the condolence book at the American embassy in Warsaw. In Russia, Premier Nikita Sergeyevich Khrushchev and his wife signed the condolence book at Spaso House, the residence of the American ambassador in Moscow. In Rome, Pope Paul VI decried the human "capacity for hate and evil."

American television networks suspended all commercials and devoted their complete attention to covering the tragedy and the events leading to President Kennedy's funeral, which was held on Monday, November 25, 1963. Approximately 175 million viewers in the United States watched the events of the weekend on their television sets. Countless more persons in 23 other countries followed the proceedings by means of American communications satellites.

The events of the long weekend began with the return of the president's body to Washington, D.C. The Secret Service escorted Jacqueline Kennedy and the casket to the presidential plane at Love Field. On board, Judge Sarah Hughes administered the presidential oath of office to Vice President Lyndon B. Johnson, who had accompanied Kennedy to Texas. After the ceremony, Johnson ordered the pilot to return the plane immediately to the capital.

Air Force One, the presidential plane, touched down at Andrews Air Force Base near Washington, D.C., shortly after 6:00 p.m. A hydraulic lift lowered the casket to the ground, where a waiting ambulance carried the body to Bethesda Naval Hospital for burial preparations. At 4:25 a.m. the ambulance returned the president's body to the White House.

On Saturday, November 23, President Kennedy's body lay in repose in the East Room of the White House. Numerous dignitaries paid their last respects. Meanwhile, under the supervision of Jacqueline Kennedy, scores of persons worked to complete the plans for the funeral ceremonies. On Sunday, November 24, tens of thousands of people lined the streets leading from the White House to the Capitol, where Kennedy's body would lie in state until the following day. At 1:10 p.m. the cortege accompanying the president's body left the White House.

Six gray horses pulled the caisson carrying Kennedy's body, which was flanked by an honor guard of 24 military representatives. The pallbearers, with a sailor carrying the presidential flag, followed. Last in line was a riderless black gelding. A black-handled sword in a silver scabbard hung from the saddle, and polished black boots were thrust reversed in the stirrups in an age-old representation of a fallen leader.

When the cortege reached the Capitol, the navy band played "Ruffles and Flourishes," "Hail to the Chief," and the navy hymn as the pallbearers carried the casket up the East Front steps. Inside the Capitol Rotunda, they placed the casket on a bier built almost 100 years earlier to hold the body of President Abraham Lincoln after his assassination. Senate Majority Leader Mike Mansfield, Speaker of the House John W. McCormack, and Chief Justice Earl Warren offered eulogies. After it was opened to the public, almost a quarter of a million people passed by the Kennedy bier during the 21 hours that the Capitol doors remained open.

November 23

Federalist Number Ten is Published

After the Constitutional Convention of 1787 in Philadelphia, Pennsylvania, the proposed Constitution of the United States went to the 13 states for ratification. In order to increase public support for ratification, prominent members of the Federalist Party wrote a series of articles called the *Federalist* papers setting forth the arguments in favor of ratification. Some 85 papers were written by Alexander Hamilton, James Madison, and John Jay under the pseudonym Publius. Perhaps the most famous is *Federalist* Number Ten, published on November 23, 1787. In summary, it argues that a federal form of government under the Constitution would curb factionalism, promote commerce, and prevent local passions from getting too far out of control. Despite vehement opposition from the Antifederalists, whose cause was supported by several prominent statesmen, the Federalists prevailed and the Constitution was eventually ratified by all 13 states (see related articles throughout this book).

A copy of *Federalist* Number Ten is set forth below.

AMONG the numerous advantages promised by a well constructed Union, none deserves to be more accurately developed than its tendency to break and control the violence of faction. The friend of popular governments never finds himself so much alarmed for their character and fate, as when he contemplates their propensity to this dangerous vice. He will not fail, therefore, to set a due value on any plan which, without violating the principles to which he is attached, provides a proper cure for it. The instability, injustice, and confusion introduced into the public councils have, in truth, been the mortal diseases under which popular governments have everywhere perished; as they continue to be the favorite and fruitful topics from which the adversaries to liberty derive their most specious declamations. The valuable improvements made by the American constitutions on the popular models, both ancient and modern, cannot certainly be too much admired; but it would be an unwarrantable partiality, to contend that they have as effectually obviated the danger on this side, as was wished and expected.

Complaints are everywhere heard from our most considerate and virtuous citizens, equally the friends of public and private faith, and of public and personal liberty, that our governments are too unstable, that the public good is disregarded in the conflicts of rival parties, and that measures are too often decided, not according to the rules of justice and the rights of the minor party, but by the superior force of an interested and overbearing majority. However anxiously we may wish that these complaints had no foundation, the evidence, of known facts will not permit us to deny that they are in some degree true. It will be found, indeed, on a candid review of our situation, that some of the distresses under which we labor have been erroneously charged on the operation of our governments; but it will be found, at the same time, that other causes will not alone account for many of our heaviest misfortunes; and, particularly, for that prevailing and increasing distrust of public engagements, and alarm for private rights, which are echoed from one end of the continent to the other.

These must be chiefly, if not wholly, effects of the unsteadiness and injustice with which a factious spirit has tainted our public administrations. By a faction, I understand a number of citizens, whether amounting to a majority or a minority of the whole, who are united and actuated by some common impulse of passion, or of interest, adversed to the rights of other citizens, or to the permanent and aggregate interests of the community.

There are two methods of curing the mischiefs of faction: the one, by removing its causes; the other, by controlling its effects. There are again two methods of removing the causes of faction: the one, by destroying the liberty which is essential to its existence; the other, by giving to every citizen the same opinions, the same passions, and the same interests.

It could never be more truly said than of the first remedy, that it was worse than the disease. Liberty is to faction what air is to fire, an aliment without which it instantly expires. But it could not be less folly to abolish liberty, which is essential to political life, because it nourishes faction, than it would be to wish the annihilation of air, which is essential to animal life, because it imparts to fire its destructive agency.

The second expedient is as impracticable as the first would be unwise. As long as the reason of man continues fallible, and he is at liberty to exercise it, different opinions will be formed. As long as the connection subsists between his reason and his self-love, his opinions and his passions will have a reciprocal influence on each other; and the former will be objects to which the latter will attach themselves.

The diversity in the faculties of men, from which the rights of property originate, is not less an insuperable obstacle to a uniformity of interests. The protection of these faculties is the first object of government. From the protection of different and unequal faculties of acquiring property, the possession of different degrees and kinds of property immediately results; and from the influence of these on the sentiments and views of the respective proprietors, ensues a division of the society into different interests and parties.

The latent causes of faction are thus sown in the nature of man; and we see them everywhere brought into different degrees of activity, according to the different circumstances of civil society. A zeal for different opinions concerning religion, concerning government, and many other points, as well of speculation as of practice; an attachment to different leaders ambitiously contending for pre-eminence and power; or to persons of other descriptions whose fortunes have been interesting to the human passions, have, in turn, divided mankind into parties, inflamed them with mutual animosity, and rendered them much more disposed to vex and oppress each other than to co-operate for their common good. So strong is this propensity of mankind to fall into mutual animosities, that where no substantial occasion presents itself, the most frivolous and fanciful distinctions have been sufficient to kindle their unfriendly passions and excite their most violent conflicts. But the most common and durable source of factions has been the various and unequal distribution of property. Those who hold and those who are without property have ever formed distinct interests in society. Those who are creditors, and those who are debtors, fall under a like discrimination. A landed interest, a manufacturing interest, a mercantile interest, a moneyed interest, with many lesser interests, grow up of necessity in civilized nations, and divide them into different classes, actuated by different sentiments and views.

The regulation of these various and interfering interests forms the principal task of modern legislation, and involves the spirit of party and faction in the necessary and ordinary operations of the government.

No man is allowed to be a judge in his own cause, because his interest would certainly bias his judgment, and, not improbably, corrupt his integrity. With equal, nay with greater reason, a body of men are unfit to be both judges and parties at the same time; yet what are many of the most important acts of legislation, but so many judicial determinations, not indeed concerning the rights of single persons, but concerning the rights of large bodies of citizens? And what are the different classes of legislators but advocates and parties to the causes which they determine? Is a law proposed concerning private debts? It is a question to which the creditors are parties on one side and the debtors on the other. Justice ought to hold the balance between them. Yet the parties are, and must be, themselves the judges; and the most numerous party, or, in other words, the most powerful faction must be expected to prevail. Shall domestic manufactures be encouraged, and in what degree, by restrictions on foreign manufactures? are questions which would be differently decided by the landed and the manufacturing classes, and probably by neither with a sole regard to justice and the public good. The apportionment of taxes on the various descriptions of property is an act which seems to require the most exact impartiality; yet there is, perhaps, no legislative act in which greater opportunity and temptation are given to a predominant party to trample on the rules of justice. Every shilling with which they overburden the inferior number, is a shilling saved to their own pockets.

It is in vain to say that enlightened statesmen will be able to adjust these clashing interests, and render them all subservient to the public good. Enlightened statesmen will not always be at the helm. Nor, in many cases, can such an adjustment be made at all without taking into view indirect and remote considerations, which will rarely prevail over the immediate interest which one party may find in disregarding the rights of another or the good of the whole.

The inference to which we are brought is, that the CAUSES of faction cannot be removed, and that relief is only to be sought in the means of controlling its EFFECTS.

If a faction consists of less than a majority, relief is supplied by the republican principle, which enables the majority to defeat its sinister views by regular vote. It may clog the administration, it may convulse the society; but it will be unable to execute and mask its violence under the forms of the Constitution. When a majority is included in a faction, the form of popular government, on the other hand, enables it to sacrifice to its ruling passion or interest both the public good and the rights of other citizens. To secure the public good and private rights against the danger of such a faction, and at the same time to preserve the spirit and the form of popular government, is then the great object to which our inquiries are directed. Let me add that it is the great desideratum by which this form of government can be rescued from the opprobrium under which it has so long labored, and be recommended to the esteem and adoption of mankind.

By what means is this object attainable? Evidently by one of two only. Either the existence of the same passion or interest in a majority at the same time must be prevented, or the majority, having such coexistent passion or interest, must be rendered, by their number and local situation, unable to concert and carry into effect schemes of oppression. If the impulse and the opportunity be suffered to coincide, we well know that neither moral nor religious motives can be relied on as an adequate control. They are not found to be such on the injustice and violence of individuals, and lose their efficacy in proportion to the number combined together, that is, in proportion as their efficacy becomes needful.

From this view of the subject it may be concluded that a pure democracy, by which I mean a society consisting of a small number of citizens, who assemble and administer the government in person, can admit of no cure for the mischiefs of faction. A common passion or interest will, in almost every case, be felt by a majority of the whole; a communication and concert result from the form of government itself; and there is nothing to check the inducements to sacrifice the weaker party or an obnoxious individual.

Hence it is that such democracies have ever been spectacles of turbulence and contention; have ever been found incompatible with personal security or the rights of property; and have in general been as short in their lives as they have been violent in their deaths. Theoretic politicians, who have patronized this species of government, have erroneously supposed that by reducing mankind to a perfect equality in their political rights, they would, at the same time, be perfectly equalized and assimilated in their possessions, their opinions, and their passions.

A republic, by which I mean a government in which the scheme of representation takes place, opens a different prospect, and promises the cure for which we are seeking. Let us examine the points in which it varies from pure democracy, and we shall comprehend both the nature of the cure and the efficacy which it must derive from the Union.

The two great points of difference between a democracy and a republic are: first, the delegation of the government, in the latter, to a small number of citizens elected by the rest; secondly, the greater number of citizens, and greater sphere of country, over which the latter may be extended.

The effect of the first difference is, on the one hand, to refine and enlarge the public views, by passing them through the medium of a chosen body of citizens, whose wisdom may best discern the true interest of their country, and whose patriotism and love of justice will be least likely to sacrifice it to temporary or partial considerations. Under such a regulation, it may well happen that the public voice, pronounced by the representatives of the people, will be more consonant to the public good than if pronounced by the people themselves, convened for the purpose. On the other hand, the effect may be inverted. Men of factious tempers, of local prejudices, or of sinister designs, may, by intrigue, by corruption, or by other means, first obtain the suffrages, and then betray the interests, of the people. The question resulting is, whether small or extensive republics are more favorable to the election of proper guardians of the public weal; and it is clearly decided in favor of the latter by two obvious considerations:

In the first place, it is to be remarked that, however small the republic may be, the representatives must be raised to a certain number, in order to guard against the cabals of a few; and that, however large it may be, they must be limited to a certain number, in order to guard against the confusion of a multitude. Hence, the number of representatives in the two cases not being in proportion to that of the two constituents, and being proportionally greater in the small republic, it follows that, if the proportion of fit characters be not less in the large than in the small republic, the former will present a greater option, and consequently a greater probability of a fit choice.

In the next place, as each representative will be chosen by a greater number of citizens in the large than in the small republic, it will be more difficult for unworthy candidates to practice with success the vicious arts by which elections are too often carried; and the suffrages of the people being more free, will be more likely to centre in men who possess the most attractive merit and the most diffusive and established characters.

It must be confessed that in this, as in most other cases, there is a mean, on both sides of which inconveniences will be found to lie. By enlarging too much the number of electors, you render the representatives too little acquainted with all their local circumstances and lesser interests; as by reducing it too much, you render him unduly attached to these, and too little fit to comprehend and pursue great and national objects. The federal Constitution forms a happy combination in this respect; the great and aggregate interests being referred to the national, the local and particular to the State legislatures.

The other point of difference is, the greater number of citizens and extent of territory which may be brought within the compass of republican than of democratic government; and it is this circumstance principally which renders factious combinations less to be dreaded in the former than in the latter. The smaller the society, the fewer probably will be the distinct parties and interests composing it; the fewer the distinct parties and interests, the more frequently will a majority be found of the same party; and the smaller the number of individuals composing a majority, and the smaller the compass within which they are placed, the more easily will they concert and execute their plans of oppression. Extend the sphere, and you take in a greater variety of parties and interests; you make it less probable that a majority of the whole will have a common motive to invade the rights of other citizens; or if such a common motive exists, it will be more difficult for all who feel it to discover their own strength, and to act in unison with each other. Besides other impediments, it may be remarked that, where there is a consciousness of unjust or dishonorable purposes, communication is always checked by distrust in proportion to the number whose concurrence is necessary.

Hence, it clearly appears, that the same advantage which a republic has over a democracy, in controlling the effects of faction, is enjoyed by a large over a small republic, is enjoyed by the Union over the States composing it. Does the advantage consist in the substitution of representatives whose enlightened views and virtuous sentiments render them superior to local prejudices and schemes of injustice? It will not be denied that the representation of the Union will be most likely to possess these requisite endowments. Does it consist in the greater security afforded by a greater variety of parties, against the event of any one party being able to outnumber and oppress the rest? In an equal degree does the increased variety of parties comprised within the Union, increase this security. Does it, in fine, consist in the greater obstacles opposed to the concert and accomplishment of the secret wishes of an unjust and interested majority? Here, again, the extent of the Union gives it the most palpable advantage.

The influence of factious leaders may kindle a flame within their particular States, but will be unable to spread a general conflagration through the other States. A religious sect may degenerate into a political faction in a part of the Confederacy; but the variety of sects dispersed over the entire face of it must secure the national councils against any danger from that source. A rage for paper money, for an abolition of debts, for an equal division of property, or for any other improper or wicked project, will be less apt to pervade the whole body of the Union than a particular member of it; in the same proportion as such a malady is more likely to taint a particular county or district, than an entire State.

In the extent and proper structure of the Union, therefore, we behold a republican remedy for the diseases most incident to republican government. And according to the degree of pleasure and pride we feel in being republicans, ought to be our zeal in cherishing the spirit and supporting the character of Federalists.
PUBLIUS.

Franklin Pierce's Birthday

Franklin Pierce, the 14th president of the United States, was born on November 23, 1804, in Hillsboro, New Hampshire. His mother, Anna Kendrick Pierce, and his father, Benjamin Pierce, were of English ancestry. Benjamin Pierce, who had served in the colonial forces during the American Revolution, was a successful Democratic politician. In 1824 Franklin Pierce graduated from Bowdoin College in Brunswick, Maine. By 1827, after studying law under Levi Woodbury (the New Hampshire governor and legislator who later served as an associate justice of the Supreme Court), he was admitted to the bar.

Beginning in 1829 he served in the New Hampshire legislature. The 25-year-old Pierce came to office in the same election that saw his father elected governor of the state for a second term.

Within two years he was the speaker of the legislature. He continued his steady political ascent when, in 1833, he became a member of the United States Congress. His two terms in the House of Representatives were followed by five years in the Senate.

During his congressional years, Pierce was a faithful Jacksonian Democrat, even though he opposed federally financed internal improvements sponsored by Jacksonian politicians. Though he was from a state in which antislavery feelings were strong, Pierce himself had no ideological misgivings about the institution. On the contrary, he felt that the abolitionists were fanatics bent on destroying the Union.

In 1834 Pierce married Jane Means Appleton, the daughter of a former president of Bowdoin. A chronic invalid who suffered from tuberculosis, Jane Pierce disliked politics and her husband's involvement in the political life of Washington, D.C. Due to her prodding, Pierce resigned from the Senate in 1842, returned to Concord, New Hampshire, and built a flourishing legal practice.

For five years after leaving the Senate, Pierce was the leader of New Hampshire's Democratic Party. As a reward for his party loyalty, Pierce became the federal district attorney in Concord. He declined President James K. Polk's subsequent offers of posts such as United States attorney general. In 1847 Pierce entered the army as a private to fight in the Mexican War. Before long he became a colonel and, shortly thereafter, was appointed a brigadier general of volunteers. He marched his men from Veracruz to join in General Winfield Scott's attack on Mexico City, but never actually saw battle himself.

Returning to New Hampshire, Pierce continued to control the Democratic state machine. When he withdrew party support from John Atwood, the Democratic nominee for governor, on grounds that Atwood did not approve of the Democrats' Fugitive Slave Act, Southern Democrats took note of Pierce's support of slaveholders' interests.

Levi Woodbury, who died in 1851, had been regarded by New Hampshire Democrats as a frontrunning candidate for president. After Woodbury's death state party leaders began to discuss Pierce as a possible candidate. During the Democratic National Convention in June 1852, the active candidates—James Buchanan, Stephen Douglas, William Marcy, and Lewis Cass—split the vote and a deadlock developed. Pierce was put forth as a dark horse compromise candidate, and on the 49th ballot the convention finally nominated him. Pierce ultimately received 254 electoral votes in the presidential election of 1852 to 42 for General Winfield Scott, the Whig candidate.

As president, Pierce advocated expansionism in foreign affairs to the point of being provocative at times. Southern slaveholders pressed for the acquisition of Cuba, which had long been eyed by expansionists, regarding it as a potentially rich slave territory. In response to these pressures, Spain began to search suspicious American ships. An incident occurred in 1854 and southerners pressed for war. However, Spain apologized, thus undercutting any grounds for hostilities. With Pierce's knowledge, his ministers to Spain, Great Britain, and France drew up a statement urging the United States to buy Cuba or to take it by force if Spain refused to sell. The news of this supposedly confidential Ostend Manifesto, as it came to be called, was leaked to the press and caused a scandal. Pierce proceeded anyway with his plans to try to buy Cuba from Spain, but was rebuffed by an indignant Spanish government.

Pierce demonstrated little initiative in dealing with the volatile problem of sectionalism. The issue of slavery expansion was moving ominously into the spotlight of domestic politics, but the phlegmatic Pierce all but ignored the dangers. However, some initiatives were taken by Stephen Douglas, the famous Democratic senator from Illinois. Even though in 1853 Pierce had secured the Gadsden Purchase of land from Mexico to facilitate a southern transcontinental railroad, Douglas wanted to reroute the proposed rail line to a central continental route that would run through his state of Illinois.

To accomplish this, and generally to stimulate the growth of the Northwest, Douglas proposed that Congress organize the Great Plains area. To this end, he introduced the Kansas-Nebraska Bill in January 1854. To lure southern support, he proposed to repeal the Missouri Compromise that Henry Clay had framed in 1820, prohibiting slavery in any part of the Louisiana Purchase north of a certain latitude except for Missouri. This call for the repeal of the Missouri Compromise stimulated antagonisms that had simmered since (and before) passage of the series of resolutions known as the Compromise of 1850. Douglas planned to make the repeal of the Missouri Compromise palatable to all by allowing the actual settlers of the new territories to decide for themselves whether they would or would not allow slavery within their borders.

Pierce lined up enough Democrats behind Douglas's Kansas-Nebraska Bill to secure its passage by May 1854. So bitter was the debate it provoked between pro-slavery and antislavery forces that the proposed transcontinental railroad was all but forgotten. Also forgotten was the fact that part of the Kansas-Nebraska Territory did not even be-

long to the United States—it had been signed over to Native Americans "forever," though they were pushed aside soon after the agreement.

Most of the new trouble centered on Kansas, which like Nebraska was organized in 1854. When the new territory was opened to settlement, Missourians streamed across the border, as did immigrants from the southern states and from New England. Each group was determined by sheer numbers to make its view on slavery prevail. What ensued was a period of violence and intimidation known as the era of "bleeding Kansas," which in effect was a rehearsal for the Civil War that would wrack the entire nation before a decade had passed.

Although Pierce hoped for renomination in 1856, his administration was so deeply identified with the politically divisive issue of Kansas that the Democrats decided instead upon James Buchanan, who had not been involved on either side in the Kansas conflict. Although deeply disappointed, Pierce remained a faithful party servant and worked to defeat the newly organized Republican Party.

After relinquishing the presidency on March 4, 1857, Pierce toured Europe for three years before settling down in Concord, New Hampshire. After the 1860 election, he opposed both Southern secession and Republican efforts to prevent secession. He attacked President Abraham Lincoln, a Republican, for enlarging the power of the presidency, even in light of the crisis that befell the nation with the outbreak of the Civil War in 1861. With offended Republicans added to the Northern Democrats who had been alienated earlier by his pro-southern policies in Kansas, Pierce became increasingly unpopular. Public opinion was influenced by his lack of imagination and his phlegmatic attitude toward decision making. He died on October 8, 1869.

November 24

Zachary Taylor's Birthday

When Zachary Taylor was still an infant, the family moved to Louisville, Kentucky, where they lived a rugged frontier life. Richard Taylor decided that Zachary was to be a farmer, while his second son was given the privilege of embarking on an army career. All this changed, however, in 1808 with the sudden death of the elder brother. The tragedy liberated Zachary Taylor from the farm. Two years later he was commissioned as a first lieutenant in the 7th United States Infantry.

While on leave in June 1810 he married Margaret Mackall Smith of Calvert County, Maryland, a marriage that brought them six children. Of their five daughters, only three survived infancy. Their only son, Richard Taylor, became a general in the Confederacy during the Civil War.

In 1810 Zachary Taylor was promoted to captain, and the following year he was given command of Fort Knox in the Indiana Territory under the territorial governor William Henry Harrison. During the War of 1812 against Great Britain, Taylor continued to serve on the northwest frontier. As captain in charge of Fort Harrison, also in Indiana, he was involved in a desperate battle on September 4, 1812, when his 50 troops fought off 400 native tribal warriors. For his leadership in this battle, Taylor was breveted a major.

During 1813 Taylor assisted in defending the frontier from Indiana to Missouri. In the summer of 1814 he was given the assignment of destroying the settlements of hostile tribes at the juncture of the Rock River and the Mississippi River. Defeated by the natives and their British allies, Taylor retreated down the Mississippi to the mouth of the Des Moines River, where he directed the construction of Fort Johnson before returning to the command of Fort Knox in Indiana. After the war's end late in 1814 and the disbanding of forces the following June, Taylor's rank was reduced back to captain. Declining further service in the army at that time, he resigned and returned to his family's farm in Louisville.

Only a year later, President James Madison restored Taylor to the rank of major; Taylor accepted the commission and joined the 3rd Infantry in Green Bay, Wisconsin. Thus began 15 years of garrison duty. During this time, Taylor was transferred from place to place over much of the United States. In 1819 he went to New Orleans for garrison duty as lieutenant colonel of the 4th Infantry. This assignment was followed by four transfers in four years. He subsequently served briefly in Louisville in 1824 and then went to Washington, D.C., as a member of a military board. His next orders took him to Baton Rouge, Louisiana, for two years. Then, in 1829 he was appointed Indian superintendent at Fort Snelling in Minnesota.

Taylor received a promotion to full colonel in charge of the 1st Regiment at Fort Crawford (later Prairie du Chien, Wisconsin) in 1832. Having acquired some experience in frontier warfare with native tribes, in 1837 Taylor was sent to Florida to track down the Seminole in the conflict known as the Second Seminole War. Taylor successfully managed to force the Seminole into a pitched battle. This was at Lake Okeechobee in December 1837. For his victory there, he won promotion to

brigadier general and the applause of an adoring public, which dubbed him Old Rough and Ready. However, another two years of pursuing Seminole convinced Taylor that the Florida Everglades represented a dead end for him professionally. In April 1840 he asked to be relieved.

Assigned to the command of the military department of the Southwest, he was transferred to its headquarters at Baton Rouge, Louisiana. Within a year, Taylor was ordered to duty in Arkansas, where he remained for three years. Then in May 1844 Taylor was assigned to Fort Jesup in nearby western Louisiana. His subsequent assignments in the Southwest were to involve him in the Mexican War. Taylor's role in that conflict would once again bring him public adulation, and would also set him firmly on the road to the presidency.

American settlers in Texas had declared their independence from Mexico in 1836. Mexico was unable to challenge the existence of the Republic of Texas, and annexation by the United States was sought by many. Late in 1845 Texas accepted a congressional resolution providing for annexation. In May 1845, some two months after the passage of the resolution, President James K. Polk had ordered Taylor to prepare to expel "invaders" (meaning Mexicans) from Texas. The next month, Taylor was ordered to organize a site from which to move upon the Rio Grande in a step designed to establish it as the southern boundary of Texas.

As a preliminary move, Taylor advanced into Texas with an army of 4,000 in late July 1845, setting up a base near Corpus Christi. This base was at the mouth of the Nueces River, which Mexico claimed as its northern boundary. Then, in January 1846 Taylor was ordered to move farther south into the disputed territory. He moved to Point Isabel, located on the Gulf of Mexico near the mouth of the Rio Grande. There he established a supply depot known as Fort Polk. Forces under Taylor's command also established Fort Texas, soon known as Fort Brown, on the site of what is now Brownsville, Texas. This fort was a few miles inland on the Rio Grande, at a point opposite Matamoros, Mexico.

On April 24 a unit of Mexican cavalry moved north across the river from Matamoros. Later that same day Taylor sent out a reconnoitering party of dragoons, who were surrounded the next morning and surrendered after suffering several casualties. Taylor sent word of this engagement to Washington, D.C. The news arrived on May 9, after President Polk had already decided to declare war, but still in time to provide an excellent justification. Polk called for war with Mexico and Congress assented on May 13.

In the meantime, Taylor was already pressing on with the fighting. In early May he marched part of his troops from Fort Brown to Point Isabel on the seacoast, where they worked to strengthen Fort Polk and picked up supplies and ammunition. On their return they were intercepted at Palo Alto by a Mexican force three times their size. On May 8 Taylor attacked the Mexicans and drove them back with heavy Mexican and light American casualties. The Mexicans retreated to more secure defensive positions nearby, closely pursued by the Americans, who occupied a neighboring ravine known as the Resaca de la Palma. There the armies battled again on May 9. In confused hand-to-hand fighting the Mexicans were routed, fleeing across the Rio Grande to Matamoros and suffering appalling casualties en route. On May 18 the American army moved upon Matamoros and discovered that the Mexicans had fled.

When news of these victories reached President Polk, he breveted Taylor major general, while Congress awarded him with two gold medals. Taylor was again a hero in the United States, and people began to mention his name in connection with the presidency.

This popularity escaped neither Taylor's nor Polk's attention. As a Democratic president, Polk had a number of political problems to contend with. Since the war had broken out during his administration, it was politically imperative that it be brought to a successful end before the next presidential election, lest it provide fuel for a Whig campaign. However, the only generals capable of conducting the war, Winfield Scott and Zachary Taylor, were both Whigs.

As Polk anticipated, both generals were soon looked upon as potential presidential candidates by the Whig Party. Polk exhibited little confidence in Taylor's military judgment, and as the president and his secretary of war commenced the supervision of every detail of the war from Washington, D.C., Taylor began to voice his suspicion of a conspiracy to keep him from success.

During the summer of 1846 Taylor kept his army stationary while building up his troop strength, complaining all the while about the low quality of his new recruits. Then, on September 20 Taylor led his army in an unauthorized attack on Monterrey, Mexico. He breached the city walls after four days of costly fighting. Considering the cost of total victory too high, Taylor agreed to an eight-week armistice rather than an unconditional surrender. Polk, more than ever convinced of Taylor's incompetence, was furious about the armistice and ordered the pact abrogated.

Early in 1847 Polk sent Taylor a severe reprimand and ordered him not to advance beyond Monterrey. Deliberately disobeying this order, Taylor advanced to Saltillo with close to 5,000 men. They met 15,000 or more Mexicans at nearby Buena Vista on February 22. The Mexicans held the advantage until, badly mauled by artillery and sharpshooting, they withdrew under the cover of darkness during the night of February 23. In the hands of Whig newspapers north of the border, the Americans' defensive stand at Buena Vista became a major triumph for Taylor and was the last major battle in the north of Mexico. Taylor was now a national idol. A grateful Congress awarded him another gold medal, even though Polk refused to praise his victory. General Scott was given command of the planned attack on Mexico City, and was empowered to draw upon Taylor's army for additional personnel.

Taylor, convinced that he was being victimized for political purposes, took a leave of absence. He returned home in November 1847, and after his initial reluctance had subsided, became available for the Whig presidential nomination. At the Whig national convention in June 1848 Taylor was nominated on the fourth ballot over such leaders as Henry Clay, Daniel Webster, and General Scott. Taylor's advantages as a presidential nominee were enormous, for he was uncommitted on every important issue. The South remembered that he was a slaveholder, and the entire country respected him as a military hero. Taylor won the November 1848 election over Democrat Lewis Cass by approximately 140,000 votes.

After entering the White House in March 1849, Taylor lived for only 16 months. His brief presidency was unexceptional but competent. Notable was his judicious handling of the slavery issue at a time when the whole country was preoccupied with the question of the extension of slavery into new territories and states being carved out of the West. While assuring southerners that there would be no attack on the institution of slavery where it already existed, Taylor favored the admission of California as a free state and dampened threats of secession by indicating his determination to preserve the Union at all costs and with force if necessary. However, he did not live to see the passage of Henry Clay's Compromise of 1850, which for the time assuaged sectional tensions.

On July 4, 1850, Taylor succumbed to the heat at a groundbreaking ceremony for the Washington Monument. That night he had a fever, and on July 9 died of what has been variously called cholera morbus and acute gastroenteritis. He was buried in the family plot on Brownsboro Road, seven miles east of Louisville, Kentucky.

November 25

Andrew Carnegie's Birthday

Andrew Carnegie was born in Dunfermline, Scotland, on November 25, 1835. His father, William Carnegie, worked as a hand loomer. At a time when power-driven machinery was rapidly replacing skilled workers in the textile industry, the senior Carnegie's talents were not in demand. To increase the family income, Andrew's mother, Margaret Carnegie, bound shoes and ran a candy shop.

Margaret Carnegie decided that the family should emigrate to the United States in search of greater opportunities. Despite her husband's reluctance to leave their native land, she sold all their household goods and borrowed money for the passage across the Atlantic. On May 19, 1848, the Carnegies set sail from Glasgow, Scotland. After traveling for two months, the family settled in Allegheny, Pennsylvania. Andrew Carnegie, working as a bobbin boy and engine tender in a local textile factory, earned only $1.20 a week in his first job, but his fortunes gradually improved.

At the age of 14, Carnegie became a messenger for the Pittsburgh telegraph office. This job paid more than twice as much as the one he had held previously, and it gave him an opportunity to learn how to send and receive messages. Carnegie proved to be an apt pupil. In fact, he was one of the first telegraphers in this country to be able to read Morse Code. Within a short time, Carnegie was promoted to the position of telegraph operator. Thomas C. Scott, the superintendent of the Pennsylvania Railroad, was quick to recognize his ability. In 1853 Scott hired the 17-year-old Carnegie to be his private secretary and personal telegrapher.

From 1853 to 1865, Carnegie's connection with the Pennsylvania Railroad and his close association with Scott rapidly advanced his career. In 1860 Scott became a vice president of the railroad, and his young protégé was named superintendent of the Pittsburgh division. The following year the Civil War began. So essential to the success of the Northern effort was the transportation of troops and supplies by rail that Scott was appointed assistant secretary of war, while Carnegie was selected to be the superintendent of the eastern military and telegraph lines.

Throughout the war, Carnegie rendered valuable service to the Union cause, but at the same time he also devoted himself to his private business interests. His successful introduction of sleeping cars on the Pennsylvania Railroad brought him his first fortune, since he owned one-eighth of the stock in the company that held the Pullman patents. He also invested in the recently discovered oil fields in Pennsylvania, and in 1862 he reorganized the Keystone Bridge Works so that within a short time the company was profitably constructing iron bridges that greatly improved railroad safety.

In 1865 Carnegie resigned his $200-a-month job with the Pennsylvania Railroad in order to give his full attention to his oil, iron, and other business activities. By 1868 his yearly income averaged $50,000, but his interests were still diversified. He established the Union Iron Mills in 1868, sold railroad securities on commission to European buyers, and retained his oil and bridge construction holdings. In 1873, however, Carnegie decided to concentrate all his resources in steel and established the J. Edgar Thomson Steel Mills.

Carnegie's gamble made him a millionaire. During the last three decades of the 19th century, the United States became the world's chief producer of steel. Foresight and a genius for organization yielded Carnegie enormous profits from this rapid expansion. By 1900 the Carnegie Steel Company virtually controlled the American steel industry, and Carnegie's share of the profits amounted to $25 million.

The employees of Carnegie's steel mills did not always share his success. While Carnegie was in Europe in 1892, the president of his Homestead plant violated its contract with the Amalgamated Association of Iron and Steel Workers and announced a wage cut. When the union members refused to accept this, the factory was shut down and 300 Pinkerton detectives were hired to protect it. Outraged, the workers attacked the Pinkerton men; order was not restored until the state militia intervened. The unsuccessful five-month strike that ensued had far-reaching consequences that retarded the unionization of steel workers for 40 years.

In 1901 the newly formed United States Steel Corporation bought Carnegie's company. Carnegie retired and received $250 million in 5 percent, 50-year bonds for his share in the business. For the remainder of his life, the great steel tycoon devoted himself to philanthropy. In his book *Gospel of Wealth*, Carnegie articulated his belief that a man with excess riches was "the mere trustee and agent for his poorer brethren." He lived according to this dictate, and before his death in 1919 gave away $311 million.

Carnegie is best known for his beneficence to public libraries. He was convinced that libraries "are entitled to a first place for the elevation of the masses of the people," but he also believed that "unless a community is willing to maintain libraries at the public cost, very little good can be obtained from them." For this reason Carnegie only built libraries, requiring local governments to provide them with books and operating funds. Many localities agreed to these stipulations, and Carnegie contributed millions to the construction of libraries. He also helped establish what later became the Carnegie-Mellon University in Pittsburgh, Pennsylvania.

Carnegie lived in quiet luxury after his retirement, and spent six months each year at his castle, Skibo, in Scotland. He also owned a magnificent mansion on Fifth Avenue in New York City. He died on August 11, 1919, at the age of 84, at Shadowbrook, his summer home in Lenox, Massachusetts. Carnegie was survived by his wife, Louise Whitfield Carnegie, and one daughter, Margaret Carnegie Miller.

Evacuation of the British Troops from New York

By the time that the United States and Great Britain signed the Treaty of Paris of 1783, which ended the American Revolution, British forces occupied only two points along the Atlantic coast of the new American nation. One was a lumber area at the mouth of the Penobscot River in what is now Maine, and the other was New York City. The British had captured New York in September 1776 and made it their headquarters and base of operations. They then controlled Manhattan Island, Staten Island, Long Island, and points along the New Jersey side of the Hudson River.

Most of New York's population fled in 1776 when battles raged in the vicinity, but after the British wrested the port from the colonial rebels, many Loyalists and others returned to their homes in the city. Whatever their political preference, everyone lived under harsh conditions aggravated by sickness, lack of supplies, and by fires in 1776 and 1778, which destroyed nearly 600 buildings.

Soon after the announcement of peace in April 1783, colonial supporters began to return to the city in large numbers. Under strict regulations they secured their former houses and lands. Loyalists who feared reprisals or were unwilling to accommodate themselves to the new order left the city in large numbers. Brook Watson, the British commissary general, reported that between January and November 1783 a total of 29,244 men, women, and children abandoned New York on British vessels bound for Canada or Europe.

Sir Guy Carleton, who became the British commander in chief in the concluding stage of the war, had the delicate assignment of suspending hostilities and protecting Loyalists while withdrawing the remaining British forces. When news of the peace arrived, Carleton began the evacuation of New York City by disbanding the Loyalist units and dispatching a number of regulars to the West Indies, Nova Scotia, and England. By November only slightly more than 6,000 troops remained in the port.

General George Washington met Sir Guy Carleton in May 1783 on board the *Greyhound*, anchored off the Hudson River town of Dobbs Ferry, to discuss the evacuation of New York. Carleton assured Washington that the British would leave as soon as Rear Admiral Robert Digby's fleet completed the removal of those Loyalists who wished to leave the United States. Eventually, the two men agreed on November 22 as the final day for the withdrawal operation, but rain caused a postponement until November 25.

Washington, who had disbanded nearly all of the colonial army at Newburgh and West Point, New York, was ready to occupy New York City with a small force as soon as the British departed. On November 19 Washington arrived at Day's Tavern in the company of New York governor George Clinton and several other army officers and state officials.

On Evacuation Day, November 25, two processions took place. The military paraded into the city to officially occupy it and to relieve the British garrison of control. Then Washington and state officers entered the city to take legal possession of it by virtue of their political authority. Governor Clinton established himself in the DeLancey mansion on Queen Street and began to conduct the affairs of government. On December 2 a public fireworks display took place at the Bowling Green. Two days later, George Washington bade farewell to his troops at Fraunces Tavern. Finally, on December 11 the ceremonies concluded with a national day of public thanksgiving observed with a number of religious programs.

November 26

Thanksgiving Day

This is a movable event.

Every year on the fourth Thursday of November the people of the United States pause to express their gratitude for the bounty and good fortune that they enjoy both as individuals and as a nation. Thanksgiving Day is a legal holiday, observed everywhere throughout the United States and in United States territories, as well as in the Commonwealth of Puerto Rico. Customarily, the president of the United States issues a proclamation of Thanksgiving Day, and the governors of many of the 50 states often add their own messages as well.

Although Thanksgiving is one of the most popular holidays in the United States, the idea of setting aside a day to express gratitude for good fortune did not originate in this country. In ancient times many peoples held special festivals in the autumn to give thanks for bountiful harvests. The Greeks honored Demeter, their goddess of agriculture, with a nine-day celebration. In a similar fashion, the Romans paid tribute to Ceres, identified with Demeter. After the crops were gathered, the Anglo-Saxons rejoiced at a *harvest home* that featured a large feast. In Scotland the harvest celebration was known as a *kirn* and included special church services and a substantial dinner. Since biblical days, Jews have given thanks for abundant harvests with the eight-day Feast of Tabernacles, an observance that has continued to modern times.

Thus, since most of the settlers who came to America probably had known some form of thanksgiving day in their homelands, it is not surprising that they transplanted this custom to the New World. The first thanksgiving day service in what was to become the United States was the one held on August 9, 1607, by colonists en route to found the short-lived Popham Colony at what was later Phippsburg, Maine. After their two ships reached one of the Georges Islands off the Maine coast, the Reverend Richard Seymour led the group in "gyvinge God thanks for our happy meting & saffe aryval into the country."

The first permanent English settlement in America was founded at Jamestown, on the James River in Virginia, also in 1607. After the tobacco introduced there in 1612 proved to be a successful crop, plantation settlements, or "hundreds" (an early English designation for areas smaller than counties), sprang up elsewhere along the banks of the James. As early as December 4, 1619, the settlers at one of them (Berkeley Hundred) set aside a day to give thanks for the survival of their small company. The settlers at Berkeley, between what is now Richmond and Charles City, observed December 4 every year with special religious services until 1622, when a conflict with the native tribes almost devastated the colony.

Although the Berkeley thanksgiving was probably the first full celebration of its kind by colonists in the New World, it was another thanksgiving that took place in the Plymouth Colony in 1621 that set the pattern for present-day observances. After landing on the bleak New England coast in 1620, the Pilgrims endured tremendous hardships (see related essays throughout this book). During the winter of 1620 about half of the 101 passengers of the *Mayflower* died. However, those who survived persevered. In the spring and summer of 1621 they constructed a number of wooden houses, and with the aid of Squanto of the Pawtuxet tribe they planted and cultivated fields of corn and barley. In the fall the Pilgrims gathered a rich harvest, and Governor William Bradford proclaimed a day of thanksgiving.

The first Pilgrim thanksgiving probably occurred some time in the middle of October 1621. Governor Bradford "sent four men fowling, so they might in a special manner rejoice together after they had gathered the fruit of their labor." According to Bradford's historical treatise *History of Plimoth Plantation* (published in full in 1856), the hunters brought back a "great store of wild Turkies" and to this were added lobsters, clams, bass, corn, green vegetables, and dried fruits.

The Pilgrims invited Massasoit, the chief of the Wampanoag tribe, to share their feast. Massasoit agreed to attend the celebration, but when he unexpectedly brought along 90 companions the Pilgrim settlers feared that the natives would consume their entire winter larder. Massasoit, recognizing their difficult position, sent his hunters into the forest, who returned with five deer.

For three days the Pilgrims and the Wampanoag shared the bountiful feast. The militia under the leadership of Captain Miles Standish drilled and fired their muskets and cannon to entertain their guests, and in turn the Wampanoag thrilled their hosts with demonstrations of their traditional dances. The group also competed in foot races and other athletic contests.

The Pilgrims did not celebrate a thanksgiving in 1622. Toward the end of July 1623, however, after a rainstorm ended a summer drought and saved the settlers' crops the Plymouth populace again observed a day of thanks. In November, after the crops were gathered, Governor Bradford ordered that "all the Pilgrims with your wives and little ones, do gather at the meetinghouse, on the hill, . . . there to listen to the pastor, and render thanksgiving to the Almighty God for all His blessings."

The Pilgrims never set a regular Thanksgiving day, although they held such observances at various times. A law of November 15, 1636, permitted the governor "to command solemn days of humiliation by fasting, etc., and also for thanksgiving as occasion shall be offered." In the decades that followed, harvest festivals were held sporadically in the area around Boston and in the Massachusetts Bay Colony to the north. In 1665 Connecticut observed a solemn day of thanksgiving on the last Wednesday of October. Beginning in 1644 the

Dutch residents of New Amsterdam set aside special Thank Days, and this custom continued even after the British captured the city and renamed it New York in 1664. Typically, however, the early thanksgiving celebrations were to be found in New England. Colonists in other areas may also have marked thanksgiving occasions of one kind or another, but these were usually local, isolated events.

Appropriately, the American Revolution caused the first Thanksgiving Day to be observed simultaneously throughout all the colonies. The occasion for the celebration was the American victory over the British at Saratoga in October 1777. So important to the rebel cause was this battle that Samuel Adams called upon the Continental Congress to declare a national day of thanks. On November 1, 1777, Congress approved Adams's proclamation, setting December 18 as a day of "Thanksgiving and praise."

During the course of the American Revolution, the Continental Congress called for a number of days of thanksgiving, although none was observed by all of the colonies. A number of local thanksgiving celebrations took place, the most notable of which was at the headquarters of the Continental army at Valley Forge, Pennsylvania, after General George Washington received news that France had allied with the colonies. To celebrate the alliance, Washington ordered his troops to assemble on May 7, 1778. Ceremonies began with the army chaplains offering prayers of gratitude. Then Washington reviewed the troops, 13 cannons fired a salute, and the soldiers shouted, "Long live the king of France and the American states!"

The end of the American Revolution in 1783 secured the independence of the 13 American colonies, and the adoption of the Constitution established a viable government that began to function in 1789. President George Washington proclaimed Thursday, November 26, 1789, to be a day of national thanksgiving. At the request of the president, citizens assembled in churches that day and thanked God.

In 1795 President Washington proclaimed another day of thanksgiving, but after that the national celebration of the holiday lapsed. New Englanders, however, continued the custom of holding harvest feasts every autumn. In other parts of the country, days of thanksgiving were also observed.

The establishment of a national Thanksgiving Day on a permanent annual basis was largely the result of the work of Sarah Josepha Hale. Beginning in 1827, when she was the editor of the *Ladies' Magazine* in Boston, she began to urge the observance of a uniform day throughout the country to express thanks for the blessings of the year.

She continued her work until the *Ladies' Magazine* was consolidated with *Godey's Lady's Book*. As the editor of *Godey's*, a magazine with a circulation of 150,000 and the largest periodical of its kind in the country, she wrote editorial after editorial in support of an annual Thanksgiving Day. She also wrote personal letters to the successive presidents and to the governors of all the states, persuading many of the latter to fix the last Thursday in November as a day of thanksgiving. Her last editorial on the subject appeared in September 1863 and said in part:

> Would it not be a great advantage, socially, nationally, religiously, to have the day of our American Thanksgiving positively settled? Putting aside the sectional feelings and local incidents that might be urged by any single State or isolated territory that desired to choose its own time would it not be more noble, more truly American, to become national in unity when we offer to God our tribute of joy and gratitude for the blessings of the year?

Hale's editorial appeared at a significant moment: The Civil War divided the nation into two armed camps in 1863. For more than two years the Union and Confederate forces had clashed, and only weeks before her editorial appeared thousands of Union and Confederate soldiers had died at the battle of Gettysburg in Pennsylvania (see July 1). Despite the staggering loss of human life, the battle of Gettysburg was an important victory for the Union, which caused great rejoicing throughout the North. This general feeling of elation together with the clamor produced by Hale's editorials helped spur President Abraham Lincoln to issue the proclamation on October 3, 1863, setting the last Thursday in November 1863 as a national Thanksgiving Day.

Lincoln's proclamation, expressing both his gratitude for God's blessings and his hope that the terrible war would come to a speedy end, asked Americans to not forget that prosperity and freedom were God's gifts:

> It has seemed to me fit and proper that they should be solemnly, reverently and gratefully acknowledged as with one heart and one voice by the whole American people. I do, therefor, invite my fellow citizens in every part of the United States, and also those who are at sea and those who are sojourning in foreign lands, to set apart and observe the last Thursday of November next as a day of thanksgiving and praise to our beneficent Father who dwelleth in the heavens.

Ever since 1863 Thanksgiving has been observed annually. In December 1941, Congress formalized this observance with a joint resolution that permanently placed the holiday on the fourth Thursday in November.

Death of Sojourner Truth

Sojourner Truth, the African American abolitionist and an early advocate of women's rights, was born as Isabella on an unknown date in 1797 in Ulster County, New York, on the Hardenbergh plantation. She was born a slave, and was bought and sold by several masters during her youth. When she was about 20 years old, her life was dramatically changed—on July 4, 1827, the New York legislature emancipated slaves within the state's boundaries. After thus obtaining her freedom, in 1829 she moved to New York City and became a street preacher after receiving what she believed to be messages from God.

In 1843 she took the name Sojourner Truth and began traveling across the country, speaking out on behalf of the abolition of slavery despite the openly hostile reactions of many of her audiences. Gaining national attention, Sojourner's appearances would ultimately include speaking before Congress and meeting with two presidents of the United States. She also joined the budding feminist movement in 1850, lending her reputation and powerful oratorical skills to their cause. When the Civil War broke out in 1861, she worked to raise support and funds for military units formed by free black volunteers.

Toward the end of the war Sojourner Truth relocated to Washington, D.C., where she fought segregation laws and worked at the local Freedman's Hospital, which treated former slaves. She continued to make public appearances on behalf of various progressive causes, including temperance and the abolition of capital punishment, but in the mid-1870s she had to limit her schedule due to health problems. Sojourner Truth died on November 26, 1883, in Battle Creek, Michigan.

November 27

Robert R. Livingston's Birthday

Robert R. Livingston—a distinguished jurist, statesman, and political leader during and after the American Revolution, and the man who administered the oath of office to President George Washington—was born in New York City on November 27, 1746. He was the eldest son of Judge Robert R. Livingston and Margaret Beekman Livingston. Born into a family that had attained prominence soon after establishing its roots in the American colonies during the latter part of the 17th century, the younger Robert Livingston became the most important of the numerous members of the family who were public figures in his day.

After completing his education at King's College (now Columbia University) in 1765, he studied law privately. In 1770, the year in which he was admitted to the bar, he married Mary Stevens, the sister of the inventor John Stevens. The couple had two daughters. Livingston was later associated with Stevens in experiments relating to the development of steam navigation. Livingston and John Jay, who subsequently served as the first chief justice of the United States Supreme Court, were law partners for a time. In 1773 Livingston was appointed by the British authorities to the judicial post of recorder of New York City, but because of his sympathy with the goal of independence, he was removed from that office in 1775.

Also in 1775 Livingston was elected as a delegate to the Continental Congress. Perhaps in hopes of exerting pressure on the New York Provincial Congress, which had not yet authorized its delegation to vote in favor of independence, the Continental Congress named Livingston as one of the five delegates appointed to draft the Declaration of Independence. Most of this task was performed by Thomas Jefferson. Because the New York delegation was still not authorized to vote "yea," it abstained from voting when the Lee resolution for independence was adopted by the Continental Congress on July 2, 1776, and when the final version of the Declaration of Independence was adopted two days later (see July 4) by an otherwise unanimous vote.

On July 9 a newly elected New York Provincial Congress finally endorsed the Declaration of Independence. Livingston was in New York as a member of that body on August 2 when the Declaration was signed by most of the delegates to the Continental Congress. His signature was never added, despite his membership on the committee to draft the document.

During this period Livingston served in the Continental Congress on military and finance committees, on the committee charged with working out a plan of confederation for the colonies, and on many others. He played an important role in the drafting of the first New York constitution in 1777, and then served on the commission that governed after the constitution was adopted but before it took effect. One provision of the constitution, proposed by Livingston, was the creation of a council of revision having veto power. The council consisted of the governor, the chancellor, and the justices of the state supreme court. Livingston was appointed to the judicial post of chancellor, which he held until 1801. According to Jefferson, he was "one of the ablest of American lawyers." While on the council of revision, Livingston opposed the confiscation and alienation laws directed against the Loyalists and certain laws conferring special powers on the magistracy. Livingston also served in the Continental Congress again from 1779 to 1781, and participated in various committees concerning military affairs, foreign affairs, finance, and legal organization.

Congress created a department of foreign affairs in 1781, and on August 10, 1781, Livingston was elected its secretary. His organization and operation of the department were efficient, in contrast to the methods previously used by the Continental Congress. During the peace negotiations with Great Britain, initiated in 1782 in Paris, Livingston sent the American negotiators many recommendations and considerable material for discussion. Among his concerns were boundaries, fishing rights, and Caribbean trade. He also took a stand against the repatriation of Loyalists. Livingston's suggestions for minor changes in the provisional draft of the treaty were also included in the final version. In December 1782 he resigned, offering the reason that his expenses as foreign secretary were $3,000 greater that his yearly salary. Dissatisfaction with the congress may also have prompted his resignation, which after some delay became effective in May 1783. Shortly thereafter, Livingston returned to the Continental Congress once again as a member, serving from 1784 to 1785.

Because of its fear that the proposed federal government would interfere with commerce, the New York delegation to the Constitutional Convention of 1787 opposed the newly drafted federal constitution. Livingston's efforts were probably second only to Alexander Hamilton's in gaining ratification of the constitution by New York at a special convention the following year. In his capacity as chancellor of New York, Livingston administered the presidential oath of office to George Washington on April 30, 1789. After the formation of the federal government, Livingston, unhappy at having received no patronage and differing on financial policy with Hamilton (who had become secretary of the treasury), led his influential family in joining the Antifederalist faction. In a contest for the governorship of New York in 1795, he was defeated by Chief Justice John Jay, even though the latter was in Great Britain at the time, negotiating what came to be known as Jay's Treaty.

Livingston had declined the post of minister to France when it was offered to him in 1794 by President Washington, but he accepted it when President Thomas Jefferson offered it again in 1801. Livingston acted firmly, even boldly, as a negotiator. With the help of James Monroe, who had previously served as minister to France, in 1803 he concluded the purchase of the vast territory of Louisiana (see December 20).

After his resignation in 1804, Livingston retired to Clermont, his estate in New York. He was an influential experimenter in scientific agriculture, and in 1791 had with other landowners founded the Society for the Promotion of Agriculture, Arts, and Manufactures (later known as the Society for the Promotion of Useful Arts) to urge and adopt improved methods. His interest in the possibilities of steam navigation led him to aid various inventors, including Robert Fulton, whose *Clermont* was named for Livingston's home and in 1807 became the first successful steam-propelled vessel. For some years Livingston and Fulton held a joint monopoly on steam navigation in New York State, a monopoly that was unpopular and bitterly contested. The resulting legal conflicts were not resolved until after Livingston's death at Clermont, on February 26, 1813.

November 28

World War II: The Teheran Conference

The Allied decision to carry out Operation Overlord, thus opening a second front in western Europe during World War II, was made at the Teheran Conference from November 28 to December 1, 1943. At this historic conference, the Big Three heads of state—President Franklin D. Roosevelt, Prime Minister Winston Churchill of Britain, and Premier Joseph Stalin of the Soviet Union—met at Teheran, the capital of Iran.

During previous conferences, Roosevelt and Churchill had discussed the idea of launching an invasion from Great Britain across the English Channel into northern France. Such a move, long urged by Stalin, was expected to put considerable additional pressure on Nazi Germany, which was already fighting along an extended eastern front ever since the Nazi invasion of the Soviet Union in June 1941. The American and British plan would necessitate the diversion of German troops not only from that sector, but probably also from Italy where Allied forces were trying to advance northward after their invasion of Sicily.

When Roosevelt and Churchill met in mid-January 1943 at Casablanca, Morocco, they agreed that they would not be militarily prepared to open a second front that year. By the time of their next meeting in Washington, D.C., in May 1943, Roosevelt and his American advisers were eager to formulate plans for a cross-Channel invasion of France the following spring. Agreement was reached on a target date of May 1, 1944. Plans for Operation Overlord, which had been prepared by a joint Anglo-American staff, were considered by the Roosevelt and Churchill staffs at a conference in Quebec, Canada, in August 1943. Despite differences of opinion, the importance of the cross-Channel invasion and the target date were reaffirmed.

At a meeting in Cairo, Egypt, in November 1943 that immediately preceded the Teheran Conference, Churchill had proposed delaying Overlord until about July 1, 1944, in order to concentrate more forces in Italy and the Mediterranean. The proposition made the Americans dubious about the expansion of Mediterranean involvements.

Stalin was joined in Teheran by Roosevelt and Churchill on November 28, 1943, and his insistence that the principal emphasis of the European war in 1944 should be a second front strongly influenced the final decision. A new target date of late May or early June 1944 was set. For some time the sorely pressed Russians had been insistent, contending that because of the lack of another major front their troops were virtually the only ones engaging the German military in Europe. During the Teheran Conference, Stalin also endorsed a plan for an invasion of southern France, to which the other leaders agreed. Churchill was particularly eager to reopen the Mediterranean Sea routes to the Soviet Union through the Dardanelles straits, which were controlled by neutral Turkey. He obtained from Stalin a promise to support Turkey if the latter could be induced to enter the war on the side of the Allies.

On June 6, 1944, the second front was opened as Allied forces crossed the English Channel to land on the beaches of Normandy in northern France (see related essays throughout this book). The proposed assault on southern France was postponed, however, in order to not take men and equipment from the offensive then under way in Italy. The southern invasion was actually begun on August 15, 1944, by a combined American and French army. As for British hopes concerning Turkey, they were dashed by what were considered outrageously large Turkish demands for military aid in return for the abandonment of neutrality.

The conferees at Teheran also discussed postwar plans. Formal assurances were given to their host country, Iran, of their respect for its "independence, sovereignty, and territorial integrity," even though Great Britain and the Soviet Union had been vying for spheres of influence in the area. The two countries had occupied Iran in August 1941 to prevent its possible takeover by Germany and to provide a route for the shipment of supplies from the Allies to the Soviet Union. In 1943 Iran protested that the Soviets had isolated the area that they were occupying, preventing contact between it and the rest of the country. The Teheran agreement ostensibly rectified the situation, but in reality it did not. After the end of World War II, in 1945 an allegedly Soviet-influenced rebellion broke out in the region. Not until a number of international protests had been lodged did the Soviet Union withdraw its troops from Iran in 1946.

November 29

Morrison Remick Waite's Birthday

Morrison Remick Waite, the seventh chief justice of the United States Supreme Court, was born in Lyme, Connecticut, on November 29, 1816. His father, Henry Waite, was the descendant of a 17th-century Massachusetts family and a chief justice of the Connecticut Supreme Court. His mother, Maria Selden Waite, was a granddaughter of Colonel Samuel Selden, who earned distinction in the American Revolution.

Waite graduated from Yale College in 1837 and in the following year moved to Maumee City, Ohio, where he studied law in the office of Samuel M. Young. He gained admission to the state bar in 1839, joined Young's firm, and over the next ten years became a specialist in real estate matters, which were often of concern to railroad companies. In 1850 Young moved the office to Toledo, Ohio. Shortly afterward, when Young retired, Morrison Waite and his younger brother Richard took over the practice.

Politics intermittently attracted Morrison Waite's attention. In 1840 he supported the successful Whig presidential candidate, William Henry Harrison, while losing his own bid for a congressional seat later in the decade. In 1849, however, Waite won election to the state legislature, where he served one term. During the Civil War he supported the Union cause and in 1862 unsuccessfully ran for Congress as a Republican.

Great Britain's construction of cruisers for the Confederate navy prompted the United States to seek reparations after the war. In 1871 President Ulysses S. Grant appointed Caleb Cushing, Waite, and William M. Evarts, a Yale classmate of Waite's, to present the American case in Geneva, Switzerland, before an arbitration commission established to settle the issue. Waite and his colleagues deftly handled these "Alabama Claims" negotiations, and the United States eventually received $15.5 million in damages.

Upon his return from Geneva, Waite won election to the Ohio constitutional convention of 1873 and served as its president. On January 19, 1874, President Grant nominated him for chief justice of the United States Supreme Court. Despite his lack of judicial experience, the Senate unanimously confirmed his selection. Waite led the Supreme Court for 14 years and personally delivered its opinion in more than 1,000 cases, a number of which concerned such diverse areas as states rights, civil and personal liberties, and business regulation.

During Waite's tenure as chief justice, the Court severely limited the scope of legislation seeking to protect African Americans. In *United States* v. *Reese* (1876) the Court invalidated several sections of the Ku Klux Klan Act of 1870. In *United States* v. *Cruikshank* (1876) the Court ruled that the 14th Amendment did not authorize Congress to enact progressive legislation to secure civil rights. In *Hall* v. *DeCuir* (1878) the Court nullified a Louisiana Reconstruction act that forbade racial discrimination by common carriers. In 1883 the Court's finding that the Civil Rights Act of 1875 was unconstitutional virtually halted the federal government's efforts to end discrimination against African Americans for decades.

One of Waite's most famous decisions came in *Munn* v. *Illinois*, one of the six *Granger* cases decided in 1877. He found that Illinois could establish rates for grain elevators and railroads in interstate commerce as a legitimate use of the "police power." Borrowing from an argument of Sir Matthew Hale, a 17th-century lord chief justice of England, Waite asserted that the states had the right to regulate private utilities associated with a public interest.

In 1878 Waite became involved with the difficult case of *Reynolds* v. *United States*, which concerned the Mormon practice of polygamy. Did a congressional law that prohibited the custom in the territories violate the religious freedom of the Latter-Day Saints as guaranteed by the First Amendment to the Constitution? Waite argued that the law was valid because the Bill of Rights protected only the freedom to believe in polygamy as a principle, and not to practice it in contravention of existing statutes.

The Waite court also decided several important cases in international law. In the *Wildenhus* case, the Court upheld the right of New Jersey to exercise jurisdiction in the instance of a murder committed aboard a Belgian merchant vessel docked in New Jersey waters. The Court thus guaranteed that local authorities could control matters that would disturb their peace. Referring in another instance to the "necessary and proper" clause of the Constitution, Waite stated in *United States* v. *Arjona* that Congress could punish the counterfeiting of foreign securities.

Republican leaders suggested Waite as a possible presidential candidate, but he declined it, refusing to use his office as a stepping stone to the White House. During his chief justice tenure, he participated actively in civil affairs as a trustee of the Peabody Educational Fund and served as a member of the Yale Corporation. He attended the Protestant Episcopal Church in Washington, D.C., and served as one of its vestrymen.

Waite married his second cousin, Amelia C. Warner of Lyme, Connecticut, on September 21, 1840. They had five children, one of whom died in infancy. Waite himself died in Washington, D.C., on March 23, 1888, of pneumonia.

Marcus Whitman's Death

November 29 marks the anniversary of the death of Marcus Whitman, one of the early missionaries to the Native Americans of the Pacific Northwest, who was killed in 1847 by Cayuse warriors. A physician, Whitman began his missionary work under the auspices of the American Board of Commissioners for Foreign Missions in 1836 when he established a mission among the Cayuse at Waiilatpu in what is now southeastern Washington. On November 29, 1847, over a decade of hard work and uncertainty finally came to an end when the Cayuse attacked the Whitman mission, killing Whitman, his wife, and 12 other people. Later on, vengeful settlers all but annihilated the Cayuse tribe.

Marcus Whitman was born at Federal Hollow (later Rushville), New York, on September 4, 1802. He studied medicine and graduated from the medical school in Fairfield, New York, in 1832. After three years in medical practice, Whitman decided to devote himself to missionary work at a time when the churches in the east were beginning their efforts to convert the Native Americans of the Pacific Northwest. As early as 1834, a young minister named Jason Lee had already established a Methodist mission in the Willamette Valley in

Oregon. Whitman offered his services to the American Board of Commissioners for Foreign Missions, and in 1835 (together with a Presbyterian minister named Samuel Parker) was sent by the board to explore the Oregon country for possible mission sites. The two men traveled with a fur caravan as far west as Idaho, found the prospects for mission work favorable, and parted. Parker continued west and eventually returned to the east on a ship of the Hudson's Bay Company. Whitman returned directly to the east for equipment and missionary workers.

Encouraged by his report, the board commissioned Whitman and a new recruit, Henry H. Spalding, to establish a mission in the Pacific Northwest. Newly married, Whitman, his wife, Spalding, and a group of missionaries departed on the long journey into the distant and still unknown West on February 19, 1836. In July 1836 the group reached the Rocky Mountains. Once over the Rockies they followed the course of the westward-flowing rivers and reached Fort Vancouver on September 12, 1836. While the women remained at the fort, Whitman and Spalding left to find suitable sites for their missions. Whitman established his mission among the Cayuse at Waiilatpu on the Walla Walla River, while Spalding settled some 110 miles east among the Nez Perce at Lapwai near Lewiston, Idaho.

In December 1836 the Whitmans established their first quarters in Waiilatpu in a small, poorly equipped log lean-to. Soon they were teaching the Cayuse their methods of farming and cattle raising, but the tribe was reluctant to learn. Missionary efforts were also met with indifference. However, the mission continued to grow and by the end of 1841 it had built a large mission house, a mill, and a blacksmith shop. Three years after Whitman had established his Waiilatpu station, three other missions were opened by the board in what is now eastern Washington and central Idaho.

As the number of settlers grew, so did dissension and unrest in the Oregon country. By 1847 the provisional government set up by the settlers after the 1846 boundary settlement with Great Britain was troubled by factional disputes. Moreover, the tension between the Protestant and Catholic missions further alienated the Northwest tribes, who were already watching the incoming settlers with growing alarm. The Cayuse grew more antagonistic as more settlers arrived on their lands, while disputes erupted over land, pasture, and game. Finally, the Cayuse fell prey to disease; with the settlers of 1847 came the measles, to which the Cayuse had no resistance. In a short time the disease spread, killing half the tribe.

Blaming the missionaries for their misfortune, a group of Cayuse attacked the Waiilatpu mission and killed 14 people, including Whitman and his wife.

United Nations Approves International Coalition for Operation Desert Storm

As discussed elsewhere in this book, on August 2, 1990, Iraq invaded the neighboring oil-rich country of Kuwait. Unwilling to see Iraq in a position to dominate the strategically and economically important Persian Gulf, where a significant percentage of the world's petroleum reserves are located, the United States decided to intervene. While American forces were assembled, diplomatic initiatives and economic pressures were brought to bear; but despite the overwhelming censure of the international community and several United Nations resolutions calling for an immediate end to the occupation of Kuwait, Iraq's president, Saddam Hussein, refused to withdraw his forces. Therefore, on November 29, 1990, in Resolution 678, the United Nations Security Council authorized an international military coalition led by the United States to intervene and free Kuwait.

The Security Council,

Recalling and reaffirming its resolutions 660 (1990) of 2 August 1990, 661 (1990) of 6 August 1990, 662 (1990) of 9 August 1990, 664 (1990) of 18 August 1990, 665 (1990) of 25 August 1990, 666 (1990) of 13 September 1990, 667 (1990) of 16 September 1990, 669 (1990) of 24 September 1990, 670 (1990) of 25 September 1990, 674 (1990) of 29 October 1990 and 677 (1990) of 28 November 1990,

Noting that, despite all efforts by the United Nations, Iraq refuses to comply with its obligation to implement resolution 660 (1990) and the above-mentioned subsequent resolutions, in flagrant contempt of the Security Council,

Mindful of its duties and responsibilities under the Charter of the United Nations for the maintenance and preservation of international peace and security,

Determined to secure full compliance with its decisions, Acting under the Chapter VII of the Charter,

1. Demands that Iraq comply fully with resolution 660 (1990) and all subsequent relevant resolutions, and decides, while maintaining all its decisions, to allow Iraq one final opportunity, as a pause of goodwill, to do so;

2. Authorizes Member States cooperating with the Government of Kuwait, unless Iraq on or before 15 January 1991 fully implements, as set forth in paragraph 1 above, the foregoing resolutions, to use all necessary means to uphold and implement resolution 660 (1990) and all subsequent relevant resolutions and to restore international peace and security in the area;

3. Requests all States to provide appropriate support for the actions undertaken in pursuance of paragraph 2 of the present resolution;

4. Requests the States concerned to keep the Security Council regularly informed on the progress of actions undertaken pursuant to paragraphs 2 and 3 of the present resolution;

5. Decides to remain seized of the matter.

The resolution was adopted by a vote of 12 to 2 (Cuba and Yemen voting No, and China abstaining). The military campaign that followed became known as Operation Desert Storm.

Advent Begins

This is a movable event.

The season of Advent, observed in most Christian churches, is a four-week preparation for the feast of Christmas that celebrates the birth of Jesus Christ on December 25. It begins on the Sunday nearest St. Andrew's Day, November 30, and includes the four Sundays before Christmas.

The word *advent* is taken from the Latin *adventus*, meaning "coming" or "arrival." Christian churches first observed Advent as an ascetic period of preparation for the feast of the Epiphany, which in commemorating the manifestations of Christ's divinity originally celebrated both his birth and his baptism. In the fourth century, however, the Western churches under Rome decided upon December 25 for a separate commemoration of Christ's nativity. Later in the same century the Eastern churches followed suit, introducing the separate observance of the Nativity on December 25.

The observance of the Advent season eventually underwent a corresponding shift in time. Thus, when Advent was first adopted by Rome, probably some time in the sixth century, it was as a season in preparation for Christmas. In the Middle Ages the faithful fasted during Advent, which was called "the Christmas Lent." Fasting is no longer required.

Advent is regarded as a season in which the faithful should prepare themselves for the three Comings of Jesus Christ: (1) on December 25, (2) at the Last Judgment, and (3) in their daily life. Therefore, it is a remembrance of the past (the historical event of the first Christmas), an anticipation of the future (the Second Coming at the end of time), and an awareness of the continual coming of Christ in each person's life.

November 30

Mark Twain's Birthday

Mark Twain was born Samuel Langhorne Clemens in Florida, Missouri, on November 30, 1835. His father, John Marshall Clemens, was a lawyer and merchant and proud of his Virginian ancestry. His mother, Jane Lampton Clemens, was also of Virginian ancestry. Samuel was their third son and fifth child. When he was four years old, the family moved to Hannibal, Missouri, on the Mississippi River. In Hannibal Judge Marshall, as his father came to be known, was one of the most respected members of the community.

After his father's death in 1847 Samuel Clemens went to work in the village newspaper shop to learn the printer's trade. At 17 he traveled about the country, working as a journeyman printer in St. Louis, Missouri; New York City, New York; Philadelphia, Pennsylvania; and Keokuk, Iowa, where his older brother Orion had a newspaper. Clemens left Keokuk in 1856 and headed for Brazil, determined to make his fortune. Getting as far as the Mississippi River, he spent the winter in St. Louis and Cincinnati, Ohio, before boarding a riverboat and heading down the Ohio River to New Orleans.

The trip reawakened Clemens's boyhood desire to be a riverboat pilot on the Mississippi, and he persuaded the pilot, Horace Bixby, to take him on as an apprentice. The agreement marked the beginning of Clemens's four years on the Mississippi, the last two and a half of them as a licensed pilot. When the Civil War interrupted river traffic, cutting short his new career, Clemens returned to Hannibal where he temporarily drifted into a company of Confederate volunteers. However, his sympathies were with the Union and he left the volunteers after two weeks.

After his brother Orion was appointed secretary of the new Nevada Territory, Clemens became his assistant. The two set off from Missouri on July 25, 1861, on a 20-day stagecoach journey to Carson City, Nevada's capital. By December of that year, Clemens had succumbed to the prospecting fever then rampant in Nevada and set off in hope of finding silver or gold. His mining camp days added greatly to the riverboat education that was to influence his later writing to a marked degree. Financially, however, they added nothing, so he went on to Virginia City, Nevada, in 1862 and became a reporter for the Virginia City *Territorial Enterprise*. It was with that paper, on February 3, 1863, that the first use of the pen name Mark Twain was recorded. The term *mark twain* had become familiar to him during his days on the Mississippi River, when the riverboat leadsmen would call it out to indicate that the depth of water was two fathoms, or 12 feet, and therefore safe.

In 1864 Clemens (henceforth referred to as Twain) went to California to work as a reporter on the *San Francisco Morning Call* and while there he wrote the first of his famous short stories: "The Celebrated Jumping Frog of Calaveras County," which was based on an old tale he heard while visiting the mining town of Angel Camp, California. Twain's frog tale was first printed in New York in *The Saturday Press*, on November 18, 1865, and then was reprinted all over the country.

Commissioned by the *Sacramento Union*, Twain sailed to Hawaii and sent back stories of the islands' history, people, and geographical wonders. As the special traveling correspondent for the newspaper *Alta California*, Twain next set off for Europe. He joined a party of travelers who took the widely publicized first pleasure cruise from America to visit Europe and the Paris Exposition, and then the Holy Land. During his trip, he sent back almost a quarter of a million words, including 53 letters to the *Alta California*, six to the *New York Tribune*, and three to the *New York Herald*. The trip also resulted in his tremendously popular book *Innocents Abroad* (1869), which, drawn from the letters, established him as a national figure. It was followed by *Roughing It* (1872), which described his experiences and the people he met in the West and in Hawaii; a satirical novel called *The Gilded Age* (1873), written in collaboration with Charles Dudley Warner; and *Mark Twain's Sketches, New and Old* (1875). Twain's boyhood adventures in Hannibal and on the Mississippi River inspired his two most famous novels, *The Adventures of Tom Sawyer* (1876) and *The Adventures of Huckleberry Finn* (1884), as well as the autobiographical *Life on the Mississippi* (1883). Among his other popular works are *A Tramp Abroad* (1880) and *A Connecticut Yankee in King Arthur's Court* (1889).

Twain, a wit and raconteur, liked to point out that he had come into this world in the same year that Halley's comet had made one of its rare appearances. In 1909 Twain looked ahead to the expected reappearance of the comet the next year and remarked that it would be the greatest disappointment of his life if he did not go out with it. Halley's comet did indeed reappear on April 20, 1910, and the 76-year-old Twain died the next day at Stormfield, his home in Redding, Connecticut.

Shirley Chisholm's Birthday

Shirley Chisholm, the first African American woman elected to the United States Congress, was born Shirley Anita St. Hill on November 30, 1924, in Brooklyn, New York. Her parents, who immigrated from the Caribbean, were Charles and Ruby St. Hill. She was educated in the Brooklyn public schools and then admitted to Brooklyn College, graduating in 1946. In 1949 she married Conrad Chisholm, and in 1952 she received her master's degree from Columbia University.

Chisholm first went to work as a nursery school teacher and daycare center director. In 1953 she joined the New York City Bureau of Child Welfare, serving as an educational policy consultant from 1959 to 1964. In 1964 she decided to enter politics, running for the 17th Assembly District of New York. Chisholm won, and served in the New York State Assembly from 1964 to 1968. In 1968 she successfully ran for the United States House of Representatives in Washington, D.C., and became the first African American woman to serve in Congress. For seven terms, from 1969 until her retirement in 1983, she represented her Brooklyn constituents in the House.

During her tenure in the House, Chisholm was an outspoken advocate of women's rights and child care issues. She opposed the American involvement in Vietnam, and strongly criticized the seniority system in Congress that for a time threatened to place her in the House Committee on Agriculture despite the fact that she represented an urban district. Chisholm also made a symbolic but unsuccessful bid for the Democratic Party's nomination as its presidential candidate in the 1972 elections.

By the 1980s her liberal politics had fallen out of favor, particularly after the election of President Ronald Reagan, a Republican, in 1980. When Chisholm's second husband, Arthur Hardwick, became ill, she decided to not seek an eighth term in the 1982 congressional elections. After leaving Congress in January 1983, she became a professor at Mount Holyoke College in Massachusetts.

December

December is the 12th and last month of the Gregorian, or New Style, calendar in use today and has 31 days. In the ancient Roman calendar, the year began in March and was divided into ten months, of which December was the last. The name December is derived from the Latin word *decem*, for ten. Even after the Roman calendar was revised and two new months were added, December retained its outmoded name, although it had become the 12th month of the year.

In roughly A.D. 191 there was a short-lived attempt by Emperor Commodus (A.D. 180–192) to rename all the months in his honor. According to one ancient source, the emperor had the Roman senate change December to *Transcendent* after one of his titles. According to another soure, he ordered that the month should be known as *Amazonius* out of devotion for his mistress, Marcia, who dressed like an Amazon female warrior.

The Saturnalia was the most prominent Roman festival held in December. Originally celebrated on December 17, it was gradually extended for seven additional days to December 24, thus encompassing the time of the winter solstice. As its name indicates, the Saturnalia honored the Roman god Saturnus, or Saturn. According to the most widely accepted theory, Saturnus was the god of planting or sowing, since the name is derived from the Latin word *satus*, or sowing. There was also a mythical king Saturnus of Latium in southern Italy who was said to have introduced agriculture into the area. In earliest times, Saturnus apparently became identified with the Greek god Kronos (Cronus in Latin), and his cult took on Greek features.

In Greek legend Kronos was the youngest of the giant Titans, who were the children of Uranus (Heaven) and Gaea (Earth). He led the Titans in revolt against Uranus and ruled the world in the Golden Age of peace and prosperity. Having fathered the mighty Olympian gods, such as Zeus, Poseidon, Demeter, and Hera, Kronos discovered that he was destined to be overthrown by one of his offspring. He therefore ate all but one of the infants, having been duped into swallowing a stone in place of Zeus. Zeus, as predicted, defeated Kronos in battle and gained control of the world. Kronos reputedly made his way to Rome, where he was well received by Janus, the Roman god of doorways, and where his rites were duly celebrated.

The Saturnalia, which evidently either became confused with or drew heavily upon the rites in honor of Kronos, strongly resembled Kronos's agricultural festival in Greece, known as the Kronia. The lively Roman festivities for Saturnus had the usual revelries associated with harvest celebrations, and included feasting, drinking, and gambling. All commercial transactions, public and private, were in abeyance. Law courts and schools were closed. The Roman senate did not meet, and on the first day of the Saturnalia, after a young pig had been sacrificed in the Temple of Saturn in the Roman Forum, the senators put aside their togas to wear a light upper garment known as the *synthesis* that was more in line with the rustic peasant origins of the occasion. Executions, military campaigns, and even daily household chores were suspended. Social distinctions disappeared as all persons greeted one another with a cheerful *Io Saturnalia*, or "Hail Saturnalia." The Romans also exchanged such presents as wax candles and little terra cotta dolls.

The most striking note of the Saturnalia was the unusual reversal of the established ranks of society. Slaves were temporarily freed and even waited upon by their masters, in memory of the mythical Golden Age, when all people were equal. In the eastern provinces of the Roman Empire, a mock king was chosen by lot to rule as Saturnus and preside over the festival. He issued farcical commands and in general was expected to behave ludicrously.

Observance of the Saturnalia continued into the Christian Era. As late as A.D. 303, a Christian soldier named Dasius was executed in Ancona, Italy, for refusing to portray Saturnus at the Saturnalia. The ruins of the Temple of Saturn are still preserved in the Roman Forum. Although there are some fragments remaining from the earliest temple of 497 B.C. and from another erected in 42 B.C., the most extensive remains date from a hastily constructed fourth-century temple in his honor. The inscription on this final building does not even refer to the god himself.

The Anglo-Saxons called December Wintermonath, or winter month. The lucky birthstone associated with December is turquoise, which symbolizes prosperity.

December 1

Presidential Elections of 1824 Deadlocked

On December 1, 1824, the deadlocked 1824 presidential election involving four candidates—John Quincy Adams, Henry Clay, William Harris Crawford, and Andrew Jackson—was turned over for settlement to the United States House of Representatives pursuant to the Constitution. It was the result of the seemingly clear but actually ambiguous method of electing the president of the United States also stipulated in the Constitution.

In 1787, following lengthy debate, the framers of the Constitution agreed on a certain method: "Each State shall appoint, in such a manner as the Legislature thereof may direct, a number of electors, equal to the whole number of Senators and Representatives to which the State may be entitled." It was expected that the electors would, since there was no constitutional provision for a national slate of announced candidates, cast their ballots for individual choices. It was also assumed that only rarely would any one candidate obtain a majority of all the electoral votes cast. The House of Representatives, voting by states with one vote per state, was therefore empowered to elect the president from among the five candidates who had amassed the greatest number of electoral votes. "After the choice of the President," the constitutional provision continued, "the person having the greatest number of votes of the electors shall be the Vice President."

During the course of the early political history of the United States, the electoral system was increasingly subjected to stresses and strains. At first electing the president was very simple, since in 1788 and 1792 George Washington was the only candidate seriously considered. However, as political parties began to emerge starting in the mid-1790s, congressional party caucuses began to decide upon a candidate and recommend him to the electors. There was generally an undisputed electoral majority.

In 1800, for the first time, the election procedures stipulated in the Constitution were put to a test and the vote went to the House of Representatives. The Constitution provided that the "electors shall . . . vote by ballot for two persons" without providing that they stipulate whether the votes they cast were for the president or vice president. Seventy-three electoral votes had been cast for Thomas Jefferson, around whom the new Democratic-Republican Party was formed, and seventy-three votes had gone to Aaron Burr, Jefferson's fellow party member. A prolonged and exhausting House deadlock was broken only on the 36th ballot, on February 17, 1801, and Jefferson was declared president.

The 12th Amendment, which was ratified in 1804, required the electors to vote separately for president and vice president and also reduced to three the number of candidates from among whom the House decision was to be made.

The election of 1824 reflected several new trends in American politics: increased opposition to the congressional caucus as a means of selecting the presidential candidate, dissolution of former party distinctions and the gradual transition to new party groupings, and mounting sectionalism as seen in the candidates themselves and in voter alignment. John C. Calhoun, President James Monroe's secretary of war, declared his candidacy as early as 1821. In July of the following year, the Tennessee legislature nominated Andrew Jackson, a popular military personality who represented the interests of the West and the "common man" everywhere. After doing so, the legislature charged in a formal complaint that the congressional caucus procedure was invalid because the Constitution had not empowered Congress to endorse a candidate for electoral approval. Other states imitated Tennessee's action. The Kentucky legislature nominated a native son, longtime Speaker of the House Henry Clay, in November 1822. New Englander John Quincy Adams, son of the second president and Monroe's secretary of state, was subsequently nominated in Boston, Massachusetts.

When the congressional caucus finally assembled in early 1823, only 66 representatives attended. This rump assembly nominated Georgia politician William Harris Crawford, Monroe's secretary of the treasury. The Crawford selection did not meet with the approval of the state legislatures. Support for Crawford was further weakened when he suffered a stroke several months later and became physically unfit for the presidency.

The candidates, who were outspoken on the issues of cheap public land, tariffs, and internal improvement, waged a lively campaign. Since a uniform election day in all of the states had not yet been set by federal law, the election extended from October 29 to November 22. Andrew Jackson received the highest number not only of popular votes but also of electoral votes (99), Adams second with 84, and Crawford and Clay trailing with 41 and 37, respectively. John Calhoun, who had decided to run as vice president on both the Adams and Jackson tickets, amassed a clear majority of 182 electoral votes out of the 260 cast (with one elector failing to vote). However, Jackson had received only a plurality, not the required majority of electoral votes.

On December 1, 1824, the presidential election went to the House of Representatives for the second time in the nation's history. Henry Clay, who was automatically eliminated from the race as the holder of fourth place, nevertheless wielded enough power to decide the election outcome by swinging his congressional support in favor of one of the remaining three contenders. Although Clay was ardently wooed by all of the candidates, he favored Adams. Crawford's bad health and Jackson's popularity in the west, which competed with Clay's own popularity, weighed against them in his eyes. Moreover, Adams's nationalist politics most closely conformed to Clay's political ideals.

Early in January 1825, Clay advised his supporters to cast their ballots for Adams. On February 9, 1825, the House of Representatives, with a vote of 13 for Adams, seven for Jackson, and four for Crawford, chose Adams as the sixth president of the United States.

The controversial 1824 election had several important side effects. The Jeffersonian Democratic-Republican Party split into two factions, with the Adams-Clay group becoming the National Republicans, and the supporters of Jackson retaining the old name as Democratic-Republicans. Jackson, particularly chagrined at having been deprived of the presidency after initially winning the largest number of electoral and popular votes, began to lay plans for the 1828 presidential election. Adams's appointment of Clay, whose support had won him the presidency, as secretary of state gave currency to the allegations made earlier that Clay and Adams had made a "corrupt bargain." Although the charges were never substantiated, the accusation cast a shadow on Clay's public image during the rest of his career.

Montgomery Bus Boycott Begun

Under the leadership of the Reverend Martin Luther King Jr. (see related essays throughout this book), African American citizens of Montgomery, Alabama, began in 1955 what was to be a 381-day boycott aimed at achieving the desegregation of Montgomery's public buses. The boycott began on December 1, 1955, when a black woman named Rosa Parks refused to give up her bus seat to a white male. The peaceful boycott resulted in the bus company's loss of 65 percent of its usual income. In response to a November 13, 1956, Supreme Court decision prohibiting bus segregation, desegregated service was finally begun in Montgomery on December 21, 1956. The boycott, which helped make King a national figure, was an important early victory in the struggle for civil rights.

December 2

The Monroe Doctrine Promulgated

On December 2, 1823, in a message to Congress, President James Monroe announced the opposition of the United States to European interference in the affairs of the Western Hemisphere. This policy became known as the Monroe Doctrine.

Various actions by the European powers precipitated Monroe's action. In 1821 the Russians, who had been fishing and trading furs in the Pacific Northwest area since the 1741 explorations of Vitus Jonassen Bering, claimed all the territory north of the 51st Parallel and forbade foreign ships from entering the coastal waters. The following year the members of the Quadruple Alliance—Austria, Prussia, France, and Russia—met and considered sending French troops to the newly liberated South American republics in an effort to restore Spain's "legitimate rule" there.

Given these circumstances, the United States did not want to remain silent. The only question was whether it should act unilaterally or in concert with Great Britain. During the South American wars of independence, Britain had established a profitable trading relationship with the former Spanish possessions. Since it would lose these newly won markets if the area returned to Spanish control, Britain opposed the restoration of Spanish rule. In 1823 the British foreign minister, George Canning, attempted to win American support for a joint statement opposing French intervention in South America and guaranteeing that neither signatory power would ever annex any part of the former Spanish empire.

The British suggestion generated a mixed reaction in the United States. Former presidents Thomas Jefferson and James Madison, Monroe's unofficial advisers, welcomed the plan. However, Secretary of State John Quincy Adams argued that it would better serve the United States to act independently. Adams's logic was persuasive; unlike Great Britain, the United States had already recognized six of the South American republics. Further, the United States received no benefits from Great Britain's South American trade, and there was the possibility that the United States might one day add Cuba to its domain.

President Monroe ultimately sided with Adams. His message of December 2, 1823, was a unilateral declaration of the intention of the United States to safeguard the territorial integrity of the Americas. To the Russians he directed the warning that "the American continents . . . are henceforth not to be considered as subjects for future colonization by any European powers." Then, referring to the proposed action to assist Spain in recovering control over its former possessions, he said:

> With the governments who have declared their independence and maintained it . . . we could not view any interposition for the purpose of oppressing them or controlling in any other manner their destiny by any European power in any other light than as the manifestation of an unfriendly disposition toward the United States.

At the time of its promulgation, the Monroe Doctrine attracted little attention. The United States had not even been able to safeguard its own capital from invasion during the War of 1812. How would it be able to protect the entire Western Hemisphere only a decade later? It was not until the United States became a world power that the Monroe Doctrine became truly significant. It was then used to justify such actions as President John F. Kennedy's famous stand in 1962 against the establishment of Soviet missile bases in Cuba during the Cuban missile crisis of the cold war (see October 22).

World War II: First Nuclear Chain Reaction Achieved

On December 2, 1942, the first sustained nuclear chain reaction was achieved at the University of Chicago in Chicago, Illinois, by a team of scientists led by Italian physicist Enrico Fermi. It was a milestone in the history of science, and helped further the development of not only the atomic bomb, but also peaceful pursuits such as nuclear power (see related essays throughout this book).

In the 1930s German scientists Otto Hahn and Fritz Strassman first observed the fission of uranium atoms by neutron bombardment. This led Leo Szilard to theorize that a chain reaction emitting tremendous amounts of energy might possibly be created under artificial conditions. Albert Einstein, whose mathematical theorems on the relationship between mass and energy had helped spur interest in nuclear fission in the first place, wrote a letter to President Franklin D. Roosevelt in 1939 requesting funds for further research. Einstein's request was largely ignored until the United States entered World War II. When Roosevelt learned that the Germans were potentially capable of developing their own nuclear device, he approved the Manhattan Project with the goal of producing an atomic bomb.

The top-secret Manhattan Project was supervised by General Leslie Grove. Since most of the leading nuclear physicists in the United States were Europeans whose countries had fallen under Axis control, and many were also Jews who as a race were targeted by the Nazis for extermination, they readily agreed to join the venture. Fermi, who developed the first artificial radioactive isotopes, worked with Szilard at the University of Chicago to create the first self-sustained chain reaction. Their reactor, or "nuclear pile," was called Chicago Pile Number One (CP-1) and used Uranium-235 embedded in graphite to achieve a controlled reaction based on a steady flow of neutrons to split the U-235 atoms. Each atom thus split generates additional neutrons which split even more atoms, hence the term "chain reaction."

Fermi's nuclear pile produced less than one watt of power when its chain reaction was underway. Nevertheless, it proved the feasibility of nuclear power and the awesome potential of nuclear weapons, ultimately realized in the atomic bombs used to destroy Hiroshima and Nagasaki in 1945 to bring World War II to an end.

December 3

Gilbert Stuart's Birthday

Gilbert Stuart, best known for his life portraits of George Washington, was born near Narragansett, Rhode Island, on December 3, 1755. The family moved to Newport, Rhode Island, where Stuart grew up. He taught himself to draw during these years, and according to a classmate, by the time Stuart was 13 he was copying pictures and drawing portraits.

Cosmo Alexander, a mediocre Scottish artist, arrived in Newport around 1769 and became Stuart's art teacher. Stuart accompanied his teacher to Edinburgh, where Alexander died on August 25, 1772. After unsuccessful attempts to support himself, Stuart worked his way back to America on a coal ship bound for Nova Scotia sometime in 1773 or 1774.

Back in America, Stuart painted and studied music, for which he also showed a definite talent. He decided to cross the Atlantic again, and went to London in November 1775. When he arrived, he tried to support himself by working as a church organist, probably at St. Vedast's Church in Foster Lane. After a period of poverty, he wrote a letter in which he described himself as "just arrived at the age of 21 . . . without the necessarys of life," his "hopes from home Blasted and incapable of returning thither." The letter was a plea for help addressed to Benjamin West, the American painter in London who had advised and befriended many young artists.

The plea brought an immediate response from West. Stuart became his pupil and eventually moved into West's house, where he remained for five years as a student and member of the West household. The Pennsylvania-born West had tremendous influence in London and in the world of art. He was a founder of the Royal Academy of Arts and had the patronage of King George III, who had appointed him historical painter to the king. West's studio was regularly filled with artists and patrons from many countries.

Stuart contributed one portrait to the Royal Academy in 1777, three in 1779, two in 1781, and four in 1782. By 1781 he had already received favorable notice from the critics, and the next year he received public acclaim for his full-length *Portrait of a Gentleman Skating*, for which his friend William Grant of Congalton had posed. Shortly after this success, Stuart moved into rooms of his own at No. 7 Newman Street.

In 1783 Stuart sent nine portraits to the Exhibition of the Incorporated Society of Artists. He was clearly on the road to professional glory, if not financial stability. His list of patrons over the next five years was impressive. In an era in which British painters had brought portraiture to its peak, Stuart at the age of 32 ranked with the greatest of his time, such as Thomas Gainsborough, Sir Joshua Reynolds, George Romney, and Allan Ramsay. Stuart was also commanding huge fees on a par with the acknowledged British masters. However, since Stuart ignored business matters and never

kept books, he sometimes did not know whether he had been paid for the portraits he painted. This lack of attention to business was to have serious consequences.

In 1785 Stuart exhibited at the Royal Academy for the last time. Already known for his lavishness, he rented an expensive house in New Burlington Street, employed a French chef, and entertained on a grand scale. He married Charlotte Coates, the daughter of a physician, on May 10, 1786; they would eventually have 12 children. Although Stuart was successful, charming, and well mannered, the Coates family did not approve of the match.

Stuart, still in his early 30s, had risen to the top of his profession. However, his extravagant spending outran his substantial fees, and to avoid debtors' prison he fled to Ireland sometime in the summer of 1787. He was an immediate success in Dublin, but within five or six years his overspending and neglect of business again put him in a difficult financial situation.

In late 1792 or early 1793 Stuart sailed for New York, arranging to paint the portrait of the ship's owner in exchange for passage. While on the ship, Stuart reportedly explained that he hoped to make his fortune (and enough to pay his creditors in England and Ireland) by painting portraits of George Washington and selling reproductions of them. After working in New York for about a year, he went to Philadelphia in November 1794, which was then the cultural and political center of the United States. It was in Philadelphia that Washington posed for Stuart's first two life portraits of him. The first, known as the Vaughan Type, showing the right side of Washington's face, was painted in the winter of 1795. The second portrait, known as the Lansdowne Type, a life-size standing figure of Washington showing the left side of the face and the right hand outstretched, was begun in April 1796.

Stuart's Philadelphia studio became so crowded with visitors and patrons that the beleaguered artist could not work. He moved to Germantown (later part of Philadelphia) in mid-1796. That fall, at the request of Martha Washington, he painted a third life portrait of the president. Called the Athenaeum Head, it depicts Washington's face and eyes, but the details of his clothing are not complete. Although Stuart could skillfully draw such difficult details as lace as well as any artist, and on occasion did so with a few flicks of his wrist to prove it, he often left a portrait unfinished if he was pleased with it. Sometimes Stuart liked a commissioned portrait so much that he kept the original for himself. In fact, Martha Washington had to settle for a replica of the Athenaeum Head, while Stuart kept the original until his death.

Stuart moved to Washington, D.C., the new national capital, in 1803. In his studio at F and 7th Streets he painted the portraits of many of this country's leaders, including Thomas Jefferson, James Madison, and James Monroe. Stuart was, as one contemporary put it, "worked to death" in Washington. He moved to Boston in the summer of 1805 and spent the rest of his life painting, even though he was in failing health for the last few years and was especially depressed by signs of paralysis in his left arm. He had an attack of gout in the spring of 1828. On July 9, 1828, he died at the age of 72, still in debt, in his home on Essex Street. Survived by his wife and four daughters, Stuart was buried in the Central Burying Grounds on Boston Common. He was one of the original members elected to the Hall of Fame for Great Americans in 1900.

Illinois Admitted to the Union

Throughout the 19th century the people of the United States pushed the borders of their nation relentlessly westward. The old Northwest Territory attracted settlers early in the century, and between 1810 and 1820 tens of thousands of settlers flocked to what is now the Midwest. The population of Illinois alone multiplied so quickly that on December 3, 1818 (only nine years after gaining territorial status), Illinois was admitted to the Union as the 21st state.

One major obstacle blocked the admission of Illinois as a state in 1818. As a part of the old Northwest Territory, Illinois had to adhere to the regulations of the Northwest Ordinance governing the creation of states from the territory. The 1787 ordinance stipulated that a population of 60,000 free inhabitants was required before an area could be admitted as a state. However, in 1818 Illinois had little more than 40,000.

Nevertheless, Daniel Cook, a young lawyer and the publisher of a small newspaper in Kaskaskia, worked to make Illinois a state. On November 20, 1817, he wrote the first of a series of editorials in his paper, *The Western Intelligencer*, urging that Illinois gain statehood before slaveholding Missouri. Cook discovered that it was possible under certain circumstances for a territory to become a state with a population of only 35,000, and since Illinois had over 40,000 residents, he urged the territorial legislature to apply for statehood. Cook's arguments impressed the territorial legislators, and they even incorporated quotations from his editorials in the official request for statehood that they sent to Congress.

Congress approved the application, and on December 3, 1818, President James Monroe signed the act of administration that made Illinois the 21st state. Kaskaskia served as the first capital of the state, but in 1820 the seat of government was moved to Vandalia. Seventeen years later the capital was permanently moved to Springfield.

Daniel Cook had an important role in the state's early history. He served as the state's first attorney general and was elected to several terms in the United States House of Representatives before he died in 1827 at the age of 33. In gratitude for his efforts on behalf of his home state, in 1831 the Illinois legislature named a new county that it had just created in his honor. Cook County has proved to be a substantial memorial to Daniel Cook, for today it is the location of the metropolis of Chicago.

December 4

George Washington Takes Leave of His Officers

George Washington served as the commander in chief of the Continental army throughout the course of the American Revolution. After the 13 colonies achieved independence, however, he had no desire to retain his powerful post. Washington believed that his usefulness to the nation ended on December 4, 1783, when the last British troops set sail from New York City harbor. On that day, he prepared to take leave of the army and return to his Mount Vernon estate in northern Virginia.

Before leaving New York City, Washington had one last meeting with his officers. At noon on December 4 most of the army officers in the city and its environs gathered at Fraunces Tavern in lower Manhattan. The general's farewell was brief:

> With a heart full of gratitude, I now take leave of you. I most devoutly wish that your later days may be as prosperous and happy as your former ones have been glorious and honorable.

Washington then went on to say: "I cannot come to each of you, but shall feel obliged if each of you will come and take me by the hand." General Henry Knox, his successor as commander in chief, approached first. Emotion so gripped Washington that he broke into tears. He embraced Knox and, in turn, each of the other officers. Many years later, a participant described the farewell:

> Such a scene of sorrow and weeping I had never before witnessed. . . . The simple thought that we were then about to part from the man who had conducted us

through a long and bloody war, and under whose conduct the glory and independence of our country had been achieved, and that we should see his face no more in this world seemed to me utterly insupportable.

After embracing the last officer, Washington went to the door of the tavern, raised his arm in a silent farewell, and then stepped outside. An honor guard lined the route to Whitehall, where a barge awaited him, and crowds had assembled along the path to pay him tribute. Washington was too moved to speak. He walked quickly to the wharf and boarded the barge. As the vessel departed he stretched out his arms to bid good-bye to all of the assembled people.

From New York, Washington went by barge to Paulus Hook (later in Jersey City). There a small cavalcade waited to accompany him to Philadelphia, Pennsylvania, and then to Annapolis, Maryland, where Congress was meeting. Both Philadelphia and Annapolis marked his arrival with special festivities and celebrations. However, the glory of a military hero that was accorded Washington was overshadowed by his wish to return to civilian life. On December 23, 1783, he surrendered his commission to the Congress.

The American Anti-Slavery Society Is Organized

On December 4, 1833, the American Anti-Slavery Society held its organizing convention in Philadelphia, Pennsylvania. The society would become an important part of the abolitionist movement that sought to abolish slavery. It issued a constitution that was in many ways a declaration of principles for the abolitionist movement:

Whereas the Most High God "hath made of one blood all nations of men to dwell on all the face of the earth," and hath commanded them to love their neighbors as themselves; and whereas, our National Existence is based upon this principle, as recognized in the Declaration of Independence, "that all mankind are created equal, and that they are endowed by their Creator with certain inalienable rights, among which are life, liberty, and the pursuit of happiness"; and whereas, after the lapse of nearly sixty years since the faith and honor of the American people were pledged to this avowal before Almighty God and the World, nearly one-sixth part of the nation are held in bondage by their fellow-citizens; and whereas, Slavery is contrary to the principles of natural justice, of our re-

publican form of government, and of the Christian religion, and is destructive of the prosperity of the country, while it is endangering the peace, union, and liberties of the States; and whereas, we believe it the duty and interest of the masters immediately to emancipate their slaves, and that no scheme of expatriation, either voluntary or by compulsion, can remove this great and increasing evil; and whereas, we believe that it is practicable, by appeals to the consciences, hearts, and interests of the people, to awaken a public sentiment throughout the nation that will be opposed to the continuance of Slavery in any part of the Republic, and by effecting the speedy abolition of Slavery, prevent a general convulsion; and whereas, we believe we owe it to the oppressed, to our fellow-citizens who hold slaves, to our whole country, to posterity, and to God, to do all that is lawfully in our power to bring about the extinction of Slavery, we do hereby agree, with a prayerful reliance on the Divine aid, to form ourselves into a society. . . .

This Society shall be called the American Anti-Slavery Society . . .

The objects of this Society are the entire abolition of Slavery in the United States. While it admits that each State, in which Slavery exists, has, by the Constitution of the United States, the exclusive right to legislate in regard to its abolition in said State, it shall aim to convince all our fellow-citizens, by arguments addressed to their understandings and consciences, that Slaveholding is a heinous crime in the sight of God, and that the duty, safety, and best interests of all concerned, require its immediate abandonment, without expatriation. The Society will also endeavor, in a constitutional way, to influence Congress to put an end to the domestic Slave trade, and to abolish Slavery in all those portions of our common country which come under its control . . . and likewise to prevent the extension of it to any State that may be hereafter admitted to the Union . . . .

This Society shall aim to elevate the character and condition of the people of color, by encouraging their intellectual, moral, and religious improvement, and by removing public prejudice, that thus they may, according to their intellectual and moral worth, share an equality with the whites, of civil and religious privileges; but this Society will never, in any way, countenance the oppressed in vindicating their rights by resorting to physical force.

December 5

Twenty-first Amendment Proclaimed Ratified

Prohibition represented one of the most ambitious efforts ever undertaken in the United States to legislate personal morality. The "noble experiment," as President Herbert Hoover characterized the outlawing of liquor, began in 1920 a year after the 18th Amendment, which prohibited the sale, import, and export of alcoholic beverages, was declared ratified. It ended on December 5, 1933, when the requisite three-fourths of the states approved the 21st Amendment, which repealed the 18th Amendment.

The 18th Amendment was in effect for 13 years. To put the amendment into operation, Congress had passed the National Prohibition Enforcement Act, also known as the Volstead Act, in October 1919. This act outlawed any beverage containing alcohol in excess of half a percent and created the Prohibition Bureau under the administration of the Bureau of Internal Revenue to ensure compliance with the law.

Efforts to enforce the 18th Amendment and the Volstead Act proved to be time-consuming, expensive, and ineffective. Lacking sufficient staff—numbering only 3,000 agents at its maximum strength—and failing to get wholehearted public cooperation, the Prohibition Bureau could do little to curb the massive illegal traffic in alcoholic beverages that flourished in the United States during the 1920s and early 1930s.

Both individual citizens and organized crime violated the Prohibition laws. Many people made liquor for their personal consumption and concocted "bathtub gin" from grain alcohol diluted with water and flavored with juniper and other oils. During the 1920s such operations occurred in countless homes and only rarely aroused the attention of federal agents. More serious and of greater concern to law enforcement authorities was the large-scale traffic in liquor that was run by organized crime.

Despite Prohibition, large segments of the populace continued to demand their drinks, and crime syndicates were quick to realize the profitability of catering to the thirst for alcoholic beverages. The sale of smuggled foreign liquors or illegally distilled domestic spirits soon became a massive enterprise. So lucrative were its receipts that gang leaders claimed monopolies over liquor traffic in certain areas and conducted limited, but bloody, battles with other mobsters who dared to challenge their "turf." Across the nation criminal elements openly flouted the laws, but nowhere was their defiance as blatant as in Chicago, Illinois. There, under the leadership of the notorious Alphonse "Scarface" Capone, an underworld empire made a mockery of the law by bribing city officials, bombing the warehouses and hijacking the delivery trucks of competitors, and even gunning down opponents in public places.

As incidents of criminal violence became more frequent and disregard for Prohibition more flagrant, many who had supported antiliquor legislation reconsidered their position. In 1928 Prohibition became one of the major issues of the presidential campaign when the Democrats selected a "wet" candidate, Alfred E. Smith of New York, and the Republicans chose a "dry" candidate, Herbert Hoover of Iowa. Several factors influenced the outcome of the election. Hoover represented the agrarian, midwestern, and Protestant tradition. Smith was an Irish Catholic and the product of Manhattan's Lower East Side. To some degree, however, Hoover's overwhelming victory against Smith indicated that the nation was not yet ready in 1928 to abandon Prohibition.

Realizing the difficulty of enforcing Prohibition, in 1929 Hoover appointed an 11-man Law Observance and Enforcement Commission headed by a former attorney general, George W. Wickersham, to explore the problem. Nearly two years later, in January 1931, the investigative body issued its report. The commission detailed the extensive breakdown of law enforcement resulting from Prohibition and noted that the great profits of the illegal liquor traffic and the public hostility to the law made effective compliance with the 18th Amendment almost impossible. The commission, however, recommended that the ban on alcoholic beverages be continued.

Prohibition continued through Hoover's administration, but the election of Franklin Delano Roosevelt in 1932 doomed the 18th Amendment. Even before the procedures necessary to end Prohibition could be completed, Roosevelt recommended and Congress approved the Beer-Wine Revenue Act on March 22, 1933. This legislation amended the Volstead Act and legalized the manufacture and sale of beer and wine containing no more than 3.2 percent alcohol by weight or 4 percent by volume.

On February 20, 1933, Congress approved the 21st Amendment and sent it to the states for ratification. Less than nine months later, the necessary three-fourths of the states had ratified the amendment, and on December 5, 1933, it was declared ratified. The 21st Amendment returned the control of liquor to the states, and all but seven decided to end the total ban on alcoholic beverages.

Martin Van Buren's Birthday

Martin Van Buren, the eighth president of the United States, was born on December 5, 1782, at Kinderhook in upstate New York. His great-grandfather Maes Van Buren had established the family in the region in 1631, having emigrated from Holland to settle as a leaseholder on the Van Rensselaer Manor. Abraham Van Buren, the father of the future president, earned a comfortable living as a small farmer and tavern keeper. Keenly interested in politics, he also fought in the American Revolution and held such minor local offices as town clerk.

Martin Van Buren attended the local schools until, at the age of 14, he became a clerk in the law office of Francis Silvester, who was a staunch Federalist. Even at this early age, Van Buren did not share his employer's political sympathies, and he spent his free moments eagerly reading the literature of the opposition Democratic-Republican Party. In 1800 he worked diligently for the election of his party's candidate, Thomas Jefferson, and the following year he went to New York City where he completed his legal studies with a fellow Democratic-Republican named William Peter Van Ness.

After his admission to the bar in 1803, Van Buren returned to Kinderhook to practice law with his half brother, James I. Van Alen. His political activities on behalf of the Democratic-Republican Party gained Van Buren appointment as the surrogate of New York's Columbia County in 1808. The young lawyer won election as state senator in 1812, and he used the following nine years in that office to build a coalition opposed to the policies of De Witt Clinton, governor of New York. So successful was this undertaking that Van Buren's friends in the legislature, or the Albany Regency as they were better known, became strong enough to elect him to the United States Senate in 1821. His enemies, however, attributed his rapid rise to deviousness rather than political acumen and branded the small-statured legislator the Red Fox of Kinderhook and the Little Magician.

Van Buren arrived at the center of national politics at a time when the Democratic-Republican Party was splitting into several factions. In the presidential contest of 1824, he supported William Crawford, the choice of the traditional party caucus, over the other candidates—Andrew Jackson, John Quincy Adams, and Henry Clay. Adams won the disputed election, and in his inaugural address

called for a broad program of federally sponsored internal improvements along the lines of the "American system" advocated by Clay. Van Buren, whose home state had built the Erie Canal with its own resources, philosophically opposed such federally financed projects. During Adams's years in office, Van Buren increasingly found himself drawn to Andrew Jackson.

Van Buren ran for governor of New York following the death of De Witt Clinton in 1828. He won the election, but after serving only three months resigned to become the secretary of state for the new president, Andrew Jackson. As a member of the cabinet, Van Buren was the president's most trusted adviser. Indeed, he gained favor with Jackson at the same time that the issue of nullification drove Jackson and his vice president, John C. Calhoun, far apart. In 1831 Van Buren resigned as secretary of state and was named minister to Great Britain. This and other signs of favor clearly showed that Jackson had chosen Van Buren to succeed him in the presidency.

Shortly after his arrival in Great Britain, the nomination of Van Buren for the post of ambassador went before the Senate for confirmation. Since that body deadlocked on the issue, it was left to Calhoun to cast the deciding ballot. As expected, Calhoun voted against it, and the nomination was rejected. Van Buren returned to the United States in May 1832, several days after the Democratic Party (whose name had been shortened from Democratic-Republican) nominated him for vice president on the 1832 ticket headed by Jackson. The two men easily won the election and during the next four years amply demonstrated their political compatibility. Van Buren strongly supported Jackson's stand against nullification and against federally financed programs of internal improvements. He also helped eliminate the second Bank of the United States, an institution that Jackson thought was monopolistic in nature.

With Jackson's second term almost completed, Van Buren became the Democratic candidate for president in 1836. The new Whig Party, lacking a leader with national popularity in 1836, ran several candidates with strong sectional appeal in order to prevent Van Buren's getting a majority of the electoral votes. Their strategy was based on the fact that, if no candidate won the needed majority of electoral votes, the House of Representatives (in which anti-Jacksonians were strong) would have to choose the president. This maneuver, however, failed to overcome Jackson's strong support of his vice president and Van Buren won the election with a narrow margin of popular votes and 170 of the 294 electoral votes.

Two months after Van Buren took office as president, the panic of 1837 swept the country. Precipitated by overspeculation, the panic caused many bankruptcies and much human suffering. The new president responded to the economic catastrophe with the Independent Treasury system, which he first outlined to Congress on September 5, 1837. In this message, Van Buren proposed to transfer all government specie (meaning gold and silver) from state banks and private businesses to federal depositories throughout the country. The attempt to completely divorce public finance from the vagaries of the private sector of the economy won the approval of the Senate in October 1837, but it was not approved by the House until June 1840. Even this victory was short-lived, since the Independent Treasury Bill was repealed the following year.

As 1840 approached, Van Buren's chances of winning another four-year term were slim. The 1837 panic and the resulting economic depression were the most significant factors behind his loss of popularity. In addition, the administration's refusal to annex independent Texas and the bloody war to remove the Seminole from Florida alienated large sectors of the electorate. The Whig candidate, William Henry Harrison, labored under none of these disadvantages. As the hero of the battle of Tippecanoe, Harrison, who had little political experience, merely capitalized on his popular appeal and won 234 electoral votes to Van Buren's 60.

Although Van Buren returned to Kinderhook in 1840 after the election and devoted himself to the renovation of Lindenwald, his Gothic-style home, he did not retire from public life. His accurate prediction that the annexation of Texas would involve the United States in a war with Mexico lost him the 1844 Democratic presidential nomination. Four years later the Free-Soilers, a new party organized to prevent the extension of slavery into the territory acquired from Mexico as a result of the war, chose Van Buren to head their ticket. He failed to carry a single state, but his presence in the race drew essential support away from the Democratic candidate Lewis Cass and contributed to the victory of the Whig nominee and Mexican War hero, Zachary Taylor.

Although Van Buren's active participation in political life ended with the 1848 election, his interest in the affairs of government never wavered. Becoming increasingly disenchanted with the Free-Soilers, he rejoined the Democratic Party in 1852. Ardently opposing secession, he was deeply troubled by the Civil War. He died at Kinderhook on July 24, 1862, failing to see the restoration of the Union that he had served for so long.

December 6

The Everglades Become a National Park

Just outside the reaches of Miami at the southern tip of the Florida peninsula is the Everglades National Park, a wilderness preserve containing the largest expanse of subtropical terrain remaining in the United States and one of the world's most unique ecosystems. It covers roughly one and a half million acres of swamps, jungle, and grasslands. The Everglades became a National Park on December 6, 1947.

Human beings first arrived in the Everglades about 11,000 years ago. One group, known as the Tequesta, settled on the southeastern coast. Another group, known as the Calusa, settled in the south and west. They both built settlements at the mouths of rivers, on offshore islands, and other convenient locations. These early inhabitants, sometimes referred to as the "people of the Glades," used primarily shells, bones, and clay to make their tools and implements, given the scarcity of metal or stone in the region. They also built huge mounds, mostly of shells.

By the time that the first Europeans arrived in the area, namely the Spanish in the early 16th century, there were perhaps several thousand people in the thinly populated Everglades. The famous Juan Ponce de León, exploring Florida for gold, stopped briefly at the Everglades. He encountered hostile Calusa, who had heard rumors about the Spanish and their lust for conquest. In 1567 the Spanish returned in force to establish a mission garrisoned by several dozen soldiers under Captain-General Pedro Menendez de Avilés. As more settlers followed over the years, the "people of the Glades," decimated by slave raids and epidemics of new European diseases, almost ceased to exist.

In their absence came other peoples. Members of the Creek tribe arrived after the Creek War of 1813–1814, fleeing from the American settlers and soldiers who had ousted them from Alabama, the Carolinas, and Georgia. As other tribes and runaway black slaves joined them, they became known as the Seminole. When the Americans began to push into north Florida, the south Florida region containing the Everglades and vast Lake Okeechobee became an important haven for the Seminole. They refused to leave Florida when the federal government ordered their relocation to the West across the Mississippi River, and the Seminole Wars followed. The conflicts of 1835 to 1842 and 1855 to 1859 in particular inflicted heavy losses on both sides, with the American forces suffering from the heat and humidity of the region. The United States Army essentially decided to declare victory unilaterally, and the Seminole were permitted to remain in Florida on reservations that included parts of the Everglades.

By the late 19th century, local cities like Miami had grown to significant size. The region was also becoming a popular winter vacation spot for the upper classes, while several prominent philanthropists became interested in the flora and fauna of the Everglades region. Due in part to the efforts of patrons of the National Geographic Society, a small area of Paradise Key was given official protection in 1916, when Royal Palm State Park was established. In the early 1930s conservationist Ernest F. Coe helped introduce legislation into Congress for federal protection of a larger area of the region. The initiative was stalled for many years, but finally it passed and on December 6, 1947, President Harry S. Truman formally announced the creation of the Everglades National Park.

Nevertheless, more work remained for the conservationists in order to ensure effective protection for the park. Marjory Stoneman Douglas wrote the book *The Everglades: River of Grass* (1947), which concerned the uniqueness of the region's ecosystem. She worked with Coe and other like-minded individuals to prevent excessive real estate development in the region, and Congress responded in both 1968 and 1980 by expanding the size of the protected region. Furthermore, in 1996 Congress reversed swamp drainage legislation that had inadvertently caused some severe damage to the ecosystem by interfering with the natural waterways.

The Everglades National Park receives roughly one million visitors a year. Beside being an important preserve for a variety of wildlife, it also offers a protective haven for alligators, which were once an endangered species but are now making a strong comeback.

Feast of St. Nicholas

The feast of St. Nicholas, one of the most popular saints of Christendom, is observed by Protestant, Eastern Orthodox, and Roman Catholic Churches on December 6. Little is known about the saint except that he was bishop of Myra in Lycia, Asia Minor, in the area that is now southern Turkey. Scholars believe that he was born at Patara in Lycia. He died in Myra in the fourth century and was buried in that city's cathedral, which soon became a place of pilgrimage.

In the 11th century Muslim invaders took control of the region, and Christian holy places and shrines were threatened. Christians from the seaport of Bari, in southern Italy, crept into the cathedral of Myra and stole the sacred remains of St. Nicholas. They took the remains to their own city, where they built a basilica in his honor. Thereafter, devotion to St. Nicholas, which had been strong in the East, quickly spread through the West. The saint's body was reinterred in the newly built Romanesque basilica, and Bari became a popular shrine for pilgrims from all over Europe and Asia (particularly from Russia, where the veneration of St. Nicholas was stronger than in any other country). St. Nicholas became the patron saint of Russia and of Greece.

There are many legends about St. Nicholas, who is sometimes called St. Nicholas of Myra, St. Nicholas of Bari, or St. Nicholas the Wonderworker. One legend is that he inherited great wealth and devoted it to charity. An instance of his benevolence is related in a legend concerning a nobleman of his city who had become so poor that he contemplated allowing his three daughters to become prostitutes. When Nicholas heard of this, he secretly went to the nobleman's home three successive nights and threw a bag of gold into the daughters' room on each visit, thus providing a dowry for each of the girls and saving them from disgrace. This incident is supposed to explain why St. Nicholas is connected with the giving of gifts.

It used to be the custom in various parts of Europe for parents to put gifts of sweetmeats and toys in their children's shoes or stockings on St. Nicholas's Eve (December 5). In convent boarding schools, the young women students would leave their stockings at the door of their respective abbesses' rooms, with notes recommending themselves to the generosity of St. Nicholas—the forerunners of letters to Santa Claus. The next morning the abbesses would summon their charges and show them their stockings—supposedly filled by St. Nicholas—stuffed with goodies. Even today, the Netherlands, Switzerland, Germany, and some other European countries maintain the annual tradition of gift-giving on December 5 or December 6.

Still another legend is that three children, butchered by an innkeeper and put into a brine tub, were miraculously restored to life by the intervention of Nicholas. He is also said to have saved sailors in distress at sea and people unjustly condemned to death. In many pictures, Nicholas is represented as bearing three purses to symbolize his generosity—the round bags of gold that he provided as the triple dowry. Those three round bags later evolved into the three balls used as a symbol by pawnbrokers. Indeed, St. Nicholas also became the patron saint of pawnbrokers, as well as of brides, children, sailors, jurists, brewers, coopers, and travelers. Many churches in the United States and Europe are named after him.

St. Nicholas was especially popular among the Dutch immigrants who settled in New York. Over the years, non-Dutch Americans adopted the Dutch name *Sinter Klaas* for St. Nicholas, who became Santa Claus in the American vernacular and who was portrayed in popular art as a cross between the original St. Nicholas and the British Father Christmas. During the 1800s Thomas Nast, the political cartoonist, created a merry-looking Santa Claus dressed in winter furs. Santa Claus as represented today is thus largely an American contribution to the world.

December 7

Delaware Ratifies the Constitution

Delaware, whose 2,057 square miles make it the second smallest state in the Union, was one of the original 13 colonies. Henry Hudson, an Englishman sailing in the employ of the Dutch East India Company, explored the coastline of Delaware in 1609. In the following year a storm blew Samuel Argall's ship into its bay. The Virginian captain called the body of water Delaware Bay in honor of his colony's governor, Thomas West, Lord De La Warr.

Thirty Dutch citizens, who sailed in 1631 from the town of Hoorn under Captain Peter Heyes on *De Walvis*, became the first Europeans to settle in Delaware. This initial colonization effort ended in disaster. For reasons that are unclear, in 1632 members of the native Lenni-Lenape tribe killed the Dutch band and destroyed their Zwaanendael settlement, near what is now Lewes.

Six years after the Dutch failure, the Swedes attempted to establish a colony in Delaware. Around March 29, 1638, Captain Peter Minuit, former governor of the Dutch colony of New Netherland (later New York), led members of a two-vessel expedition ashore near what is now Wilmington. The settlement, which they named Fort Christina in honor of their queen, flourished. During the next 17 years, 12 more expeditions took Swedes to the area.

At the command of Peter Stuyvesant, the governor of New Netherland, the Dutch wrested control of New Sweden from the Swedes in 1655. The Dutch reorganized Fort Casimir, their own former trading post, as New Amstel (later New Castle). Even more important, they introduced town and village government to the colony and set up judicial districts and counties.

Within a decade, England ended the Netherlands' control of the settlement. In 1664, during the Second Anglo-Dutch War, the duke of York (who later became King James II of England) dispatched expeditions to capture enemy settlements in the New World, a task that proved to be easy. New Netherland itself surrendered to Colonel Richard Nichols without any bloodshed, and New Amstel capitulated to Sir Robert Carr after only one brief skirmish.

On August 24, 1682, the duke granted title to the three counties west of the Delaware River and Bay—Kent, New Castle, and Sussex counties—to William Penn, the proprietor of the newly founded Quaker colony of Pennsylvania. In his Frame of Government of 1683, the Quaker leader incorporated the Three Lower Counties into his commonwealth. This action embroiled Penn in a decades-long dispute with Charles Calvert, Baron of Baltimore and the proprietor of the neighboring colony of Maryland, who also claimed jurisdiction over the area. In 1760 the descendants of the original antagonists finally agreed to arbitrate this quarrel, and the English surveyors Charles Mason and Jeremiah Dixon worked from 1763 to 1767 to establish the famous Mason-Dixon Line setting the Pennsylvania-Maryland boundary.

Pennsylvania was a poor guardian of Delaware. The Quaker legislators' indifferent reaction when French and Spanish pirates attacked the little colony during King William's War of 1689–1697 prompted Delawareans to petition for their own government. In 1704 they won the right to hold their own assembly at New Castle, and six years later they gained their own executive council. Penn, however, retained the right to name a single governor to administer both Pennsylvania and Delaware, an arrangement that lasted until the American Revolution. When the Three Lower Counties declared their independence from Great Britain in 1776, they also threw off this last vestige of Pennsylvanian control and became an entirely separate state.

After the Revolution, Delaware became one of the first states to advocate revision of the Articles of Confederation. John Dickinson of Delaware, formerly a Pennsylvanian, presided at the Annapolis (Maryland) Convention of September 1786 at which Delaware, New Jersey, New York, Pennsylvania, and Virginia called for a meeting of all the states to revise the articles. In response to this request, the Constitutional Convention gathered at Philadelphia, Pennsylvania, in May 1787.

Richard Bassett, Gunning Bedford Jr., Jacob Broom, Dickinson, and George Read represented Delaware at the Philadelphia convention during the summer of 1787. Bedford, Dickinson, and Read worked vigorously to preserve the rights and powers of the less populous states with respect to their stronger neighbors. Their efforts were rewarded when the delegates at last agreed to a bicameral national legislature in which each state would have two votes in the Senate and a number of votes proportional to its population in the House of Representatives. With the problem of representation resolved, the delegates quickly compromised their other difficulties. They signed the Constitution on September 17, 1787, and sent it to the states for ratification 11 days later.

On October 24 the Delaware legislature called for a ratifying convention to meet in Dover on December 4. In accordance with the legislature's plan, each of Delaware's three counties held special elections on November 26 and selected ten representatives to the December gathering. The convention met on December 4 at the old State House, and the delegates chose James Latimer to preside. Delaware's leaders were strong nationalists; many were originally from Federalist Philadelphia and all were aware of the benefits that their small state could gain from participation in a strong country. On December 7, 1787, with 30 delegates unanimously agreed, Delaware became the first state to ratify the Constitution and thus to enter the Union.

World War II: The Japanese Attack Pearl Harbor

The background of the Japanese attack on Pearl Harbor on December 7, 1941, which precipitated the United States's entry into World War II, goes back to the period after World War I. In the years following that conflict, Japan sought to become the dominant nation in Asia. As an industrialized, heavily populated nation controlled by military leaders, it had ambitions with respect to China, its gigantic but weak neighbor. In 1931 the Japanese seized the Chinese province of Manchuria, which had valuable ports and natural resources. The invasion, which was condemned by the League of Nations, was only the first of a series of aggressive acts against China. In 1937 they culminated in open warfare, which eventually merged into World War II.

China was only the first objective in the establishment of what the Japanese envisioned as the Greater East Asia Co-Prosperity Sphere. Japan hoped to ultimately include English, French, Dutch, and Portuguese possessions in the Far

East and the Pacific. Events in Europe provided the perfect opportunity when World War II erupted in 1939. The Japanese decided to move against the vulnerable and resource-rich European colonies.

Japan's imperialistic designs soon brought it into a confrontation with the United States. American interest in the Far East had developed in the 19th century, particularly after its acquisition of the Philippine Islands in the Spanish-American War. The United States government was eager to maintain strong economic connections with Asia and urged all nations to agree to an Open Door Policy of free trade with China. Japan's aggression against China threatened American principles and interests, and Japan's aspirations to capitalize on the outbreak of a European war only exacerbated the situation.

Not all Japanese leaders, however, desired war with the United States. Early in 1941 the premier, Prince Fuminaro Konoye, dispatched Admiral Kichisaburo Nomura to Washington, D.C., to discuss a détente with Secretary of State Cordell Hull. Nomura was an inexperienced diplomat unfamiliar with the English language, but he was a spokesman for the Japanese navy, which was more inclined than the army to seek accommodation with the United States. Both Nomura and Hull sought a peaceful resolution of the nations' differences, but misunderstandings and conflicts of interest doomed their efforts.

In the summer of 1941 the Japanese began to finalize their plans for military assaults on the Asian colonies of the Western powers. Although Japan hoped to avoid conflict with the United States, the American government was resolute in its demand for Japanese withdrawal from China, and froze all Japanese assets in the United States when Japan occupied French Indochina. With some mixed feelings, the Japanese leaders decided that their country would have to engage the United States in combat.

By mid-August 1941 Japanese strategists had drafted their plans of operation. The army and navy would simultaneously attack the Philippines and Malaysia and then proceed against the Dutch East Indies. The maneuvers would require precise timing and coordination, but they offered the best flank security for the attackers and promised to provide the maximum element of surprise. During September the Japanese military worked to complete the details of the program and decided to include an attack on the American naval base at Pearl Harbor, Hawaii.

Admiral Isoroku Yamamoto, commander of the Combined Fleet, was the originator of the idea of an attack on Pearl Harbor. Yamamoto argued that the destruction of the American fleet was essential to guarantee the success of the invasion and occupation of Malaysia and the East Indies. Japan had little hope of winning a protracted war with the United States, but its leaders felt that the incapacitation of the United States Pacific Fleet might lead the Americans to a quick settlement favorable to Japanese aspirations in Asia. Although some Japanese naval strategists thought Yamamoto's idea too risky, opposition collapsed when the admiral threatened to resign. In mid-October 1941 the Japanese government formally adopted the plan for an attack on Pearl Harbor.

Premier Konoye still hoped to achieve an agreement with the United States, but he was working under serious limitations. Japanese oil reserves were dwindling, and the approach of winter demanded the completion of tactical operations as soon as possible. Delay might force postponement until spring, when the Russians could use the favorable weather to attack the Japanese in Manchuria. Under pressure from the military, the Konoye government resigned on October 18 and General Hideki Tojo became prime minister.

Tojo decided that if Japan and the United States did not reach an agreement by November 29, 1941, he would set the war plans in motion. The date passed without a settlement. On December 2 Admiral Yamamoto's flagship, which on November 25 had set sail from the Kurile Islands with the rest of the Pearl Harbor Striking Task Force, sent out the message *Niitaka Yama Nabore* ("climb Mount Niitaka"), the prearranged signal to proceed with the attack on Hawaii.

By late November 1941 President Franklin D. Roosevelt and his advisers had recognized the signs of crisis and accepted the possibility of war with Japan. Both political and military leaders anticipated that the Japanese might launch an attack within a few weeks, but they believed that any such operations would take place in the Far East. On November 24 and November 27 the War and Navy Departments dispatched messages to Pacific commanders, warning them of the possibility of an imminent "surprise aggressive movement in any direction," including an attack on the Philippines or Guam. Although the directives stressed the hazards of the situation, they implied that sabotage attempts were the primary danger to the Hawaiian command.

Lieutenant General Walter C. Short, the army commander in the Hawaiian area, took action to ensure the islands' internal security. General Short issued Alert Number 1, a standard directive that increased the number of men on guard against sabotage and subversion. He also ordered the army's new radar equipment into operation between 4:00 and 7:00 a..m., the most likely hours for a carrier-based air raid. However, Short did not consider such an assault probable and decided not to promulgate Alert Number 2, which pertained to procedures against air and surface bombardment. He also did not invoke Number 3, which concerned invasion defenses.

Rear Admiral Husband E. Kimmel, the naval commander in Hawaii, reacted in the same manner as his army counterpart. The fleet remained conscious of the danger of sabotage and instituted a careful antisubmarine patrol, but it dismissed the possibility of an outright Japanese attack. Kimmel refused to send 50 available patrol planes on long-range reconnaissance missions from the island of Oahu. These aircraft might have provided an early warning of the approaching Japanese Task Force.

In the first week of December 1941, Japan's Striking Task Force, composed of six aircraft carriers with more than 360 airplanes, two battleships, two heavy cruisers, six destroyers, and three submarines, continued across the Pacific Ocean. By December 6 the force was 500 miles north of Oahu. From this area it turned south toward the planned launching point, some 200 miles from the intended target. In the meantime, 25 Japanese submarines gathered in the waters south of Pearl Harbor.

At 6:00 a.m. on December 7 the first Japanese attack plane took off from a carrier deck for the two-hour flight to Pearl Harbor. At 7:30 a.m. Hawaii time (1:00 p.m. in Washington, D.C.) the Japanese emissaries to the United States were to announce their nation's decision to go to war and thus prevent accusations of a sneak attack. The stratagem failed, however, when Japanese officials in Washington were slow in decoding the final message from Tokyo. By the time that diplomats Kichisaburo Nomura and Saburo Kurusu arrived at the State Department to announce the severance of relations, it was 2:05 p.m. and bombs were already falling on Hawaii.

American leaders in Washington, D.C., were not surprised by the declaration of the Japanese envoys. Through a decoding innovation known as MAGIC, the United States government had broken the Japanese code system and could routinely decipher even the most highly classified messages. On the morning of December 7, 1941, the Americans intercepted the final section of a 14-part communication from Tokyo which advised the Japanese embassy in Washington of the decision for war. Chief of Staff General George C. Marshall ordered the army to pass the information to the Hawaiian command, but owing to communication problems, the warning did not reach Hawaii until the attack on Pearl Harbor was under way.

Deprived of this last-minute intelligence, the military authorities in Hawaii compounded their misfortune by failing to recognize the telltale signs of an imminent attack. The commander of an American destroyer and an airplane pilot each spotted and engaged one of the two-man midget submarines dispatched by the Japanese to penetrate Pearl Harbor and advise the approaching Japanese planes. The navy began to investigate the reports of these engagements but did not inform the army of its encounters. In two separate instances, American radar operators picked up large flights on their screens, but junior officers on duty assumed the planes to be from American carriers cruising in the vicinity and did not inform headquarters.

At 7:55 a..m. the first wave of Japanese aircraft, including 49 high-level bombers, 51 dive-bombers, 43 fighters, and 40 torpedo planes, struck Pearl Harbor. A second wave, consisting of 54 high-level bombers, 80 dive bombers, and 36 fighters, appeared just before 9:00 a..m. and continued its attack until 9:45 a..m. American naval vessels had been moored side by side in order to limit the possibility of sabotage, and the airplanes were lined nose to nose on the ground for the same purpose. Thus, they were easy targets for the Japanese pilots. Eight battleships, three light cruisers, and eight other naval vessels were destroyed or damaged. The Americans lost almost every plane at the Kaneohe Seaplane Base, the Ewa Marine Air Station, and the Ford Island Naval Air Station. The Japanese destroyed roughly half the bombers at the army's Hickam Field, but failed to inflict significant damage on the repair shops and gasoline storage tanks.

A total of 2,403 American sailors, soldiers, marines, and civilians died in the attack on Pearl Harbor. An additional 1,178 suffered wounds. The destruction of the battleship USS *Arizona* by the explosion of a 16-inch shell bomb in the forward magazine accounted for almost half of the fatalities—men were entombed in the sunken ship. The Japanese announced the loss of 55 of their fliers and nine of the ten men aboard their midget submarines. The sole surviving Japanese seaman became America's first prisoner of war in World War II.

The day following the Pearl Harbor attack, President Roosevelt appeared before a joint session of Congress (see December 8). Declaring that December 7 was "a date which will live in infamy," Roosevelt reported the Japanese attack on Hawaii—and on Malaysia, Hong Kong, Guam, Wake Island, Midway, and the Philippine Islands the same day—and asked Congress for a declaration of war. The congressional resolution was vir-

tually unanimous, and the United States entered the second global war of the 20th century.

December 8

Feast of the Immaculate Conception of Mary

The Feast of the Immaculate Conception celebrates the preservation of the Virgin Mary from the stain of original sin from the moment of her conception in her mother's womb. It is considered by Roman Catholics to be one of the most important feasts honoring the mother of Jesus.

The meaning of the feast is perhaps best summed up in a prayer from the Roman Catholic liturgy for December 8:

O God, by foreseen merits of the death of Christ, you shielded Mary from all stain of sin and preserved the Virgin Mother immaculate at her conception so that she might be a fitting dwelling place for your son.

According to the tenets of the Roman Catholic Church, only Christ and his mother were so preserved from original sin. Some other Christian churches celebrate the conception of the Virgin Mary, but only Roman Catholics have proclaimed the dogma of the Immaculate Conception.

United States Enters World War II

On December 8, 1941, the day after Japan's surprise attack on the United States naval installation at Pearl Harbor, Hawaii (see December 7), President Franklin D. Roosevelt went before a joint session of Congress at 12:30 p.m. to report the events of the attack and request a declaration of war against Japan. The nation held its breath as citizens everywhere listened to the president's words over the radio. Retiring to their separate chambers, the two houses of Congress acted with unprecedented speed. The Senate adopted the war resolution at 1:00 p.m. and the House of Representatives approved it only ten minutes later. The document was signed by the president at 4:10 p.m.

Germany and Italy, the European members of the Axis pact that Japan had formally joined the previous year, responded by declaring war on the United States on December 11. On that same day, the United States reciprocated by declaring war on them in turn. In so doing, the United States joined the British, French, Soviets, and other Allied nations in the monumental struggle of World War II (see related essays throughout this book).

December 9

American Revolution: Battle of Great Bridge, Virginia

In the years leading up to the American Revolution, Virginia, the most important of the southern colonies, generally avoided the confrontations with British authorities that were so common in other colonies like Massachusetts. However, Virginia's politics gradually became radicalized, thanks to firebrands such as Patrick Henry, intellectuals like Thomas Jefferson, and political leaders like Edmund Randolph.

Parliament's enactment of the so-called Intolerable Acts in 1774 to punish Massachusetts for the Boston Tea Party accelerated Virginia's estrangement from Britain. The general assembly of Virginia protested the legislation and ordered that June 1, 1774, be a day of fasting and prayer. In response to this boldness, Governor John Murray, earl of Dunmore, dissolved the assembly, including the representative House of Burgesses. However, the burgesses continued to meet illegally at the Apollo Room of the Raleigh Tavern in Williamsburg and called for a colonial convention to assemble on August 7.

The first Virginia Convention extended the commercial nonintercourse policy to include the nonpayment of debts to Britain and chose delegates to the First Continental Congress. Among the representatives chosen were Richard Bland, Benjamin Harrison, Patrick Henry, Richard Henry Lee, Edmund Pendleton, Peyton Randolph, and George Washington. The convention also published Thomas Jefferson's *A Summary View of the Rights of British America*, which renounced Parliament's authority to legislate on internal or external matters affecting the colonies and suggested that only through the king were the colonies bound to Britain.

Angered by the failure of words to persuade the authorities in Great Britain and outraged by the hardships that Massachusetts was forced to endure under the Intolerable Acts, Virginia held a second convention at St. John's Church in Richmond in March 1775. The delegates were more militant, and Patrick Henry set the tone with his speech concluding, "I know not what course others may take, but as for me, give me liberty, or give me death." The convention adopted Henry's resolution for "embodying, arming and disciplining" the Virginia militia.

Dunmore felt that he had to take action to quell the sedition, so on March 28, 1775, he ordered civil officials to prevent the appointment of delegates to the Second Continental Congress, scheduled for May. Unfortunately for the governor, the local leaders were so united behind the work of the colonial conventions that they would not comply with his directives. On May 12, Dunmore called for a session of Virginia's general assembly to consider the proposals of Britain's prime minister, Lord North, for reconciling Britain and the colonies. The delegates met on June 1 but received the suggestions with hostility. Upset by the rebelliousness of the Virginians and by news of armed clashes in the northern colonies, Dunmore promptly dispatched his wife and children to the safety of the warship *Fowey*. Soon afterward, deciding to leave Williamsburg himself, he joined them and declared the ship to be the new seat of government. With Dunmore away from the city, the burgesses rejected North's plan on June 12 and on June 20 adjourned for the last time. In July the third extralegal Virginia Convention assembled and took over the direction of the colony's affairs.

Dunmore made his way to Norfolk, Virginia's commercial center, where he gathered a flotilla and a small army of Loyalists. Safely ensconced in the port, he was able to strike at Virginians who challenged the royal authority. On October 24 and 25 he sent a naval force to destroy the town of Hampton in retaliation for the burning and looting of a British ship by the residents. On November 7 he declared martial law, and eventually offered to free the slaves and the indentured servants of American rebels. The governor even raised a force composed of several hundred slaves enlisted by him and called Dunmore's Ethiopians.

Colonial leaders recognized that they had to oust Dunmore from Norfolk, lest all southeastern Virginia become a haven for Loyalists. The Virginia Committee of Safety ordered Colonel William Woodford to march on the town with his 3rd Regiment. This decision quickly led to the battle of Great Bridge on December 9, the first encounter of British and American soldiers since Bunker Hill and the first engagement of the Revolution fought in Virginia.

Governor Dunmore chose to meet the advancing Americans at Great Bridge, about nine miles from Norfolk. He established a virtually impregnable position by fortifying one end of a long causeway that covered a defile and was surrounded by tidal swamps. When Colonel Woodford arrived in the area he built a redoubt at the other end of the causeway and placed Lieutenant Travis with 90 men to defend it. The colonel and the rest of his force, which included John Marshall, the future chief justice of the United States Supreme Court, remained on a hill about 400 yards away.

For some unknown reason, perhaps a loss of patience, Dunmore decided to attack the Americans first. By choosing to assume the offense, Dunmore surrendered the advantages natural to the defense in such terrain. To lead the frontal attack down the long, narrow causeway, the governor dispatched Captain Fordyce with 60 grenadiers and approximately 140 regulars. Colonel Samuel (or, in some accounts, William) Leslie with a contingent of some 230 slaves and Virginia Loyalists formed the reserve.

Failing in his first advance, Fordyce regrouped his men and brought up two cannons for support. Again he moved down the causeway toward the American redoubt. Lieutenant Travis held his fire so long that Fordyce became convinced that the rebels had deserted their position. Led by Fordyce, the British charged the American fortifications, only to be met by a last-minute barrage that killed Fordyce and a large number of his men; the rest retreated and returned to Norfolk.

British losses at the battle of Great Bridge reached a total of 62. The only American casualty was a soldier wounded in the hand. Woodford continued his march to Norfolk, which he entered on December 13. Colonel Robert Howe, who had meanwhile arrived with his 2nd North Carolina Regiment, took command of the town on December 14.

Before the Americans reached Norfolk, Lord Dunmore took refuge with a large number of Loyalists on board a ship. The rebels refused his demands for provisions, and he threatened to retaliate by bombarding the town. On January 1, 1776, Dunmore made good his promise by turning his naval cannons on Norfolk and by sending marines ashore to burn the warehouses. In return, the rebels burned the homes of leading Loyalists. Soon fires roared out of control in much of the port. What remained of Norfolk was virtually destroyed the following month to prevent the British from using it again.

In May 1776 Major General Charles Lee arrived in Norfolk and drove Dunmore's flotilla away after a ship-to-shore skirmish. The governor took his collection of British troops, Loyalists, and slaves to Gwynn's Island off Virginia's Mathews County. He then went to Maryland, and finally out to sea, leaving America forever.

Lord Dunmore was the last royal governor of Virginia. The battle of Great Bridge marked not only the end of Dunmore's tenure in Virginia, but also the beginning of the American Revolution in the southern colonies. At the time, Virginia had the largest population of all the colonies, and its economic and military resources would be vital to the colonial cause.

Tip O'Neill's Birthday

Thomas Philip O'Neill Jr., Speaker of the United States House of Representatives from 1977 to 1987, was born on December 9, 1912, in Cambridge, Massachusetts. O'Neill picked up the nickname "Tip" during his childhood after the baseball player James "Tip" O'Neill. He attended the local parochial schools and graduated from St. John's High School in 1931. O'Neill was admitted to Boston College and graduated in 1936. That same year, he was elected to the Massachusetts state House of Representatives on the Democratic Party ticket.

Many of O'Neill's fellow Democratic legislators came from Irish working-class backgrounds similar to his. He became a popular figure, and also proved to be a skillful political strategist. In 1947 he became the Democratic Party leader in the state house and in 1949 he became Speaker of the state house, serving in the position until 1952. It was in that year that O'Neill ran for and was elected to the United States House of Representatives in Washington, D.C. As a former state Speaker he rose quickly through the party ranks, serving on powerful House committees. He did not always toe the Democratic Party line, however, and in the late 1960s he strongly criticized President Lyndon B. Johnson's policy of pursuing the Vietnam War.

Nevertheless, O'Neill became the Democratic majority whip in 1971 and the Democratic majority leader in 1973. When the then speaker of the House, Carl Bert Albert, chose to not run for Congress again in the 1976 elections, O'Neill rose to the speakership when the 95th Congress met in January 1977. He was an effective speaker during the administration of fellow Democrat Jimmy Carter (1976–1980), but found himself out of step with the nation's increasingly conservative leanings when Republican Ronald Reagan defeated Carter in the 1980 presidential elections.

Reagan and the House Republicans were able to force a variety of tax cut measures and defense spending increases through Congress. Many of O'Neill's fellow Democrats, particularly those from the South, voted with the Republicans. Furthermore, the Republicans were successful at publicly attacking the aging, overweight, and visibly slowing O'Neill as part of the Democratic old guard that was the "problem" with Congress. After several years of fighting the Reagan administration's policies, O'Neill decided to retire, and he left Congress in 1987. He died on January 5, 1994, in Boston, Massachusetts.

December 10

Emily Dickinson's Birthday

Emily Dickinson, who was virtually unknown in her own quiet and reclusive lifetime, was born on December 10, 1830, in Amherst, Massachusetts. Her father, Edward Dickinson, was a lawyer, active in politics, and the treasurer of Amherst College. According to one of her letters, he was "too busy with his briefs to notice what we do." Her mother was Emily Norcross Dickinson. Although she grew up with her brother, William, and sister, Lavinia, Emily Dickinson's more frequent companions came to be the "hills, . . . the sundown" and her own soul. Her family was nonetheless close-knit, with no member ever straying far. When William married, he moved next door. Emily and Lavinia, neither of whom ever married, lived all their life in the home they were born in.

Emily Dickinson attended Amherst Academy intermittently until she was 16, when she left home for the first time for Mount Holyoke Female Seminary in nearby South Hadley, where she completed a year's study before abruptly returning home in 1848. Only rarely again in her lifetime did she travel. In 1855 she went to visit her father, then serving in Congress in Washington, D.C. In the summers of 1864 and 1865 she left home for treatment of an eye ailment in Boston and Cambridge.

After her withdrawal from Mount Holyoke, her parents' home and gardens became essentially her world. With the noted exceptions, she lived and died without leaving the green hills of Amherst. As she wrote later, "I never saw a moor, / I never saw the sea; / Yet know I how the heather looks, / And what a wave must be." She found, as she put it, "ecstasy in living" and in nature. Her first few poems were written with the encouragement of Benjamin Newton, a law student in her father's office. However, Dickinson was about 30 when she began writing poetry in earnest.

In April 1862 Dickinson responded to an article in the *Atlantic Monthly* magazine by the critic and clergyman Thomas Wentworth Higginson. She sent him four carefully selected poems with a question that initiated their lifelong correspondence: "Are you too deeply occupied to say if my verse is alive?" Though intrigued by her ingenuity and the originality of her thought, Higginson, like others, was too confused by her unconventionality of expression to consider her ready for publication. His replies, encouragement, and continuing interest were nonetheless of importance to her.

By 1866 the flow of her poetry had almost stopped. Although she wrote occasional verses for the rest of her life, she devoted far more energy to correspondence, which became her only contact with the outside world. After 1870 her seclusion was virtually complete. Years went by in which she did not cross her doorstep. She continued to dress entirely in white, as had been her practice for some years.

Dickinson's father died in 1874, and her mother became an invalid the next year. During a brief respite from personal tragedy, from 1877 until 1884 she developed a friendship with Judge Otis B. Lord of Salem, Massachusetts. He was a widowed friend of her father's who visited often and corresponded regularly. Meanwhile, the other correspondents whose friendship by mail she had cherished for years had died. Her mother also died in 1882, after seven years of invalidism. With the death of her friend Judge Lord in 1884, Dickinson was overtaken by "nervous exhaustion." She died on May 15, 1886, leaving hundreds of unpublished poems.

Even her sister, Lavinia, was astonished by their number. She found a publisher, and *Poems by Emily Dickinson* appeared in 1890, to the accompaniment of critical confusion and public delight. It was followed by *Poems: Second Series* (1891), two volumes of letters (1894), *Poems: Third Series* (1896), *The Single Hound* (1914), *Further Poems* (1929), *Unpublished Poems* (1935), and *Bolts of Melody* (1945).

Human Rights Day and Week

December 10 is observed as Human Rights Day by most member countries of the United Nations. The celebrations mark the anniversary of the unanimous adoption of the Universal Declaration of Human Rights by the United Nations General Assembly on December 10, 1948. In the United States, the observance is often known as Human Rights Week and extends from December 10 through December 16 in order to include another important rights anniversary, December 15, the date that the Bill of Rights became part of the United States Constitution in 1791 (see related essays throughout this book).

The story of how the United Nations' Universal Declaration of Human Rights came into being is not widely known. When the charter for the establishment of the United Nations was drawn up in 1945 in San Francisco, California, it contained repeated references to the "human rights and fundamental freedoms" that it sought to support. It called upon member nations to promote and encourage these rights in cooperation with the world body. However, since the document nowhere spelled out exactly what these rights and freedoms were, it became necessary to frame such a definition before nations could be expected to promote and encourage them in any specific way.

The United Nations Commission on Human Rights was therefore called upon to prepare a statement of principles that could serve as a universal standard. As set forth in 30 articles, the enunciated principles became known as the Universal Declaration of Human Rights. Two of the document's chief authors were Charles Malik, Lebanon's representative to the United Nations, and Eleanor Roosevelt, the American delegate who was also the first to chair the Commission on Human Rights. Only Saudi Arabia, the Union of South Africa, and six Soviet bloc nations abstained from the vote that resulted in the adoption of the Universal Declaration of Human Rights by the General Assembly of the United Nations on December 10, 1948.

The basic principles of the Universal Declaration are embodied in the following sections:

Article 1. All human beings are born free and equal in dignity and rights. They . . . should act towards one another in a spirit of brotherhood.

Article 2. Everyone is entitled to all the rights and freedoms set forth in this Declaration, without distinction of any kind, such as race, colour, sex, language, religion, . . . opinion, national . . . origin, property, birth. . . .

Article 3. Everyone has the right to life, liberty and security of person.

Article 4. No one shall be held in slavery or servitude. . . .

Article 5. No one shall be subjected to torture or to cruel, inhuman or degrading treatment or punishment.

Article 7. All are equal before the law and . . . entitled . . . to equal protection of the law. . . .

Article 10. Everyone is entitled . . . to a fair and public hearing by an independent and impartial tribunal, in the determination of . . . any criminal charge against him.

Article 11. Everyone . . . has the right to be presumed innocent until proved guilty according to law in a public trial [with] all the guarantees necessary for his defence. . . .

Article 12. No one shall be subjected to arbitrary interference with his privacy, family, home or correspondence, nor to attacks upon his honour and reputation. . . .

Article 13. Everyone has the right to leave any country, including his own, and to return to his country. . . .

Article 14. Everyone has the right to seek and enjoy in other countries asylum from persecution. . . .

Article 18. Everyone has the right to freedom of thought, conscience and religion. . . .

Article 19. Everyone has the right to freedom of opinion and expression; this right includes freedom to hold opinions without interference. . . .

Article 20. Everyone has the right to freedom of peaceful assembly and association.

Article 21. Everyone has the right to take part in the government of his country, directly or through freely chosen representatives. . . . The will of the people shall be the basis of the authority of government; this will shall be expressed in periodic and genuine elections which shall be by universal and equal suffrage and shall be held by secret vote. . . .

Article 23. Everyone has the right to work, to free choice of employment, to just and favourable conditions of work. . . . Everyone, without any discrimination, has the right to equal pay for equal work.

Despite the limited success of certain implementing treaties, known as the Covenants on Human Rights, the Universal Declaration of Human Rights remains a towering achievement as a statement of ideals and declaration of purpose. As such, it is one of the landmark documents of human dignity and of the worth, equality, and rights of individuals.

Mississippi Admitted to the Union

The Mississippi Territory, organized in 1798, produced two states. They were Mississippi, the 20th state, and Alabama, the 22nd state. Alabama became a territory in its own right on March 3, 1817, and nine months later on December 10, 1817, the parent territory of Mississippi was admitted to the Union as a state.

Mississippi was once the homeland of the people known as Mound Builders, whose archaeological remains and earthworks excited wonder and admiration when Europeans first encountered them. Scattered about the state are ancient, artificially built hillocks, some rising as high as 60 feet and some covering several acres of ground. The mounds were used as burial sites and perhaps also as sites for temples, fortifications, and places of refuge when the Mississippi River and its tributaries flooded the valleys. The Mound Builders also left many artifacts, including agricultural implements, pottery, stone and wood carvings, and jewelry. Their culture along the lower Mississippi River flourished between 900 and 1500, and appears to have been in decline by the time Europeans arrived in the region.

At the time of European exploration, the region was inhabited by an estimated 30,000 Native Americans. Of these, the most important tribes were the Chickasaw in the north, the Choctaw in the central and southern parts of the region, and the Natchez along the Mississippi River. The first Europeans known for certain to have set foot in what is now Mississippi were a company of Spanish gold seekers led by Hernando de Soto, who arrived in 1540. Battered and exhausted by intermittent warfare with the natives as they journeyed inland from the Atlantic coast, de Soto's company entered Mississippi a few miles north of what is now Columbus. Continuing westward, on May 8, 1541, they came upon the Mississippi River somewhere near what was is now the northwestern boundary of the state. After exploring the region west of the Mississippi, de Soto's company returned to the river. There de Soto died on May 21, 1542, and his body was committed to the waters of the river near Natchez. Since no gold was discovered, Spain had little interest in the region de Soto explored, and it was left undisturbed by Europeans for more than a century.

In 1673 Father Jacques Marquette and Louis Joliet, a trader from New France in Canada, descended the Mississippi River as far south as the mouth of the Arkansas River. Their accounts of the journey inspired further exploration by René-Robert Cavelier de La Salle, who in 1682 claimed the entire Mississippi watershed for France and gave it the name Louisiana in honor of King Louis XIV of France. Other French explorations followed, and in 1699 Pierre Le Moyne, Sieur d'Iberville, founded the first permanent colony in the lower Mississippi valley. The settlement that grew up near the fort, which acquired the name of Biloxi from a local native tribe, alternated with Fort Louis de La Mobile—a settlement soon removed to the site of what is now Mobile, Alabama—as the seat of government for French Louisiana until 1723, when New Orleans in what is now Louisiana became the capital of the French colony.

Territorial disputes arose between the French and the native tribes and between the French and the English, who claimed a part of the Mississippi region as lying within the so-called Carolina grant made in 1629–1630 to Sir Robert Heath by King Charles I of England. Because of these difficulties and bad administration as well, the colony was unprofitable for France. At the end of the French and Indian War in 1763, all of the French Louisiana territory east of the Mississippi River except for New Orleans came under British rule. The southern third of what is now Mississippi and Alabama was incorporated in the new British province of West Florida, which was occupied by Spain during the American Revolution. Mississippi took almost no part in that conflict. Under the Treaty of Paris of 1783, which officially ended the Revolutionary War, Great Britain recognized American claims to land south to the 31st Parallel that included much of what had been part of West Florida.

On April 7, 1798, the Mississippi Territory, comprising the southern portions of modern-day Mississippi and Alabama, was created by an act of Congress. The territory was enlarged in 1804 and 1812 so that it came to encompass all of what are now the states of Mississippi and Alabama. Natchez was the territorial capital until February 1, 1802, when the seat of government was moved to the nearby town of Washington. The territorial period was made stormy by conflicts with the native tribes, internal civil war, border warfare with the Spanish, and the War of 1812.

In March 1817 the Mississippi Territory was reduced when its eastern part was organized as the Alabama Territory. The western part adopted a state constitution on August 15, and on December 10 Congress voted the new state of Mississippi into the Union. The first state governor was David Holmes, the former territorial governor, who served until 1820. The state government held its legislative sessions at Natchez and Washington during the early years of statehood. In 1821 a legislative commission appointed to locate a permanent state capital chose as its site Le Fleur's Bluff on the Pearl River, which was renamed Jackson in honor of Andrew Jackson. The legislature convened at Jackson for the first time in January 1822.

When the issue of secession became critical after the election of Abraham Lincoln as president in 1860, on January 9, 1861, Mississippi voted to secede from the Union, and became the second state of the Confederacy. One of Mississippi's former United States senators, Jefferson Davis, became the first and only president of the Confederate States of America.

A number of Civil War battles were fought in Mississippi, including the Union campaigns against Vicksburg, which were climaxed by a 47-day siege that forced the surrender of the city on July 4, 1863. After the fall of Vicksburg, most of the Confederate troops within the state were moved elsewhere, and Union forces met with little resistance when they occupied Mississippi. The last Confederate forces in Mississippi surrendered on May 4, 1865. Due to the war, the state was in ruins and its manpower was critically depleted. Of the approximately 80,000 men who went to war, only about 28,000 returned and many of the survivors were disabled. Ranking fifth in per capita wealth before the war, Mississippi dropped to last place in the postwar period.

During the first months after the fall of the Confederacy, President Andrew Johnson attempted to follow the policy of reconciliation begun by Lincoln. Mississippi, like the other Southern states, was provisionally administered by a presidentially appointed governor who called a constitutional convention that passed an amendment abolishing slavery and arranged for a general election in the latter part of 1865. However, the officials elected in Mississippi and elsewhere in the South showed little inclination to promote political, economical, or social equality for blacks. While they continued to deny voting rights to blacks, they demanded increased representation in Congress on the grounds that the recognition of citizenship for blacks had enlarged their constituencies. Angered by the unrepentant Southern attitude and also fearful that the Democratic Party would regain political dominance with the support of a revived and predominantly Democratic South, the Republicans in control of Congress moved to disqualify the Southern leadership under the newly enacted 14th Amendment. The 14th Amendment defined citizenship to include both blacks and whites, sought to guarantee the civil rights of blacks against unfavorable legislation by the states, and required equal protection under the law regardless of race. On March 2, 1867, the first Reconstruction Act was passed, challenging the constitutionality of all the Southern governments except Tennessee and dividing the South into five districts under military commanders who were to remain in charge of the various states until each state had fulfilled certain conditions. These conditions included the election, with black participation, of delegates to a convention that would frame a new constitution and establish a new state government providing for black male suffrage. Another requirement was the ratification of the 14th Amendment by the new state legislatures. When these conditions had been met, the state was eligible for restoration to the full privileges of statehood. Mississippi, which was placed in the Fourth Military District, was one of the last three states to comply. Finally, in November 1869 a new state constitution, which abolished slavery and extended the franchise to black citizens, was ratified. On February 23, 1870, Mississippi was restored to its former status within the Union.

Wyoming Passes the First Law Giving Women the Right to Vote

On December 10, 1869, John Campbell, the governor of the Wyoming Territory, approved an act granting the women of the territory the right to vote. As the first law in the history of the United States explicitly to grant suffrage to women, this landmark legislation is a source of great pride to the people of Wyoming.

Esther Hobart Morris was, in large part, responsible for Wyoming's 1869 suffrage law. A native of New York State, she was orphaned at the age of 11 and worked for a number of years as a ladies' hat maker. When she was 28 she married Artemus Slack, a civil engineer. A few years later Slack died, leaving his wife a tract of land in Illinois. She went west to claim her inheritance, but Illinois property laws, which resembled those of many other states, discriminated against women and thus prevented her from obtaining a satisfactory settlement of the estate.

Her experience with Illinois property laws made her an ardent advocate of equal rights for women. She avidly followed the teachings of such feminists as Susan B. Anthony, Elizabeth Cady Stanton, and Lucretia Mott. Her interest in women's rights did not wane after her second marriage, to John Morris, in 1845.

News of a rich gold discovery in South Pass lured John Morris and his three sons to Wyoming around 1867, and Esther (henceforth referred to as Morris) joined them there in either 1868 or 1869. At about the same time that she arrived in her new home, Wyoming gained territorial status. The first election to choose a representative to the new territorial legislature was scheduled to take place in South Pass on September 2, 1869. Morris recognized that this election was an opportunity to advance the cause of equal rights for women.

A few days before the election was to take place, she invited the Democratic candidate, Colonel William Bright, his Republican opponent, Captain H. G. Nickerson, and about 40 other residents of South Pass to her home. After serving tea, Morris asked each candidate to pledge that if elected he would introduce and support a bill giving women of the Wyoming Territory the right to vote. Both Bright and Nickerson agreed to the proposal.

The Democrats swept the 1869 Wyoming election. Bright was elected and at the territorial capital of Cheyenne he kept his promise. On November 28, 1869, he introduced into the council, or upper house of the legislature, a bill granting voting rights to women, which was treated by the legislators as a farce. The members of both the council and the house raucously debated its merits, and then, perhaps believing that the bill would prove embarrassing to Republican governor Campbell, they unexpectedly approved it.

The Democratic legislators expected Governor Campbell to veto the bill, but on December 10, 1869, he signed the act into law, an action that displeased some of the male residents of Wyoming. One lawmaker toasted the new women voters: "To the lovely ladies, once our superiors, now our equals!" In South Pass another dissatisfied man, Justice of the Peace R. S. Barr, announced his resignation effective "whenever some lady shall have been duly appointed to fill the vacancy." To Barr's surprise, his resignation was immediately accepted, and Morris was appointed as his replacement. She thus became the first woman to serve as a justice of the peace.

The women of Wyoming began to exercise their newly won political rights. In fact, even before an election occurred in which the women might cast their ballots, in March 1870 Judge H. J. H. Howe impaneled five women for the grand jury and six for the petit jury in the second district court in Laramie. These first female jurors attracted worldwide attention. Newspaper correspondents came to Laramie to report the proceedings, and the king of Prussia cabled President Ulysses S. Grant to congratulate him on the "progress, enlightenment and civil liberty in America."

After being admitted to the Union in 1890, Wyoming continued to lead the nation in opening full political participation to women. In 1911 Susan Wissler of Dayton, Wyoming, became one of the first women in the United States to serve as mayor. In 1924 Nellie Tayloe Ross was elected governor of Wyoming, becoming the first woman in American history ever to hold a governorship.

December 11

Indiana Admitted to the Union

Indiana began as part of the Northwest Territory, located north and west of the Ohio River and east of the Mississippi River. Originally settled by prehistoric Mound Builders and then by the Miami tribe, the area became a British possession in 1763 by the terms of the Treaty of Paris which ended the French and Indian War. On February 25, 1779, during the American Revolution, colonial militiamen under Lieutenant Colonel George Rogers Clark captured Vincennes, the region's most important town. The United States took title

to the area by the Treaty of Paris of 1783, which concluded the Revolution.

On July 13, 1787, the Continental Congress (still functioning under the Articles of Confederation that predated the Constitution) passed the Northwest Ordinance, placing the territory under a federally appointed governor, secretary, and supreme judiciary of three judges. Congress provided that when 5,000 free male adults had taken up residence in the region, the people could establish an elected bicameral legislature. Eventually, as planned in the ordinance, three to five states would be carved from the Northwest Territory. As history played itself out, five states were created: Indiana, Illinois, Michigan, Ohio, and Wisconsin, while a remaining portion was allotted to Minnesota.

General Anthony Wayne's victory over the native Miamis under their leader, Little Turtle, on August 20, 1794, at Fallen Timbers, near what is now Toledo, removed an obstacle to the settlement of the Northwest Territory. Immigrants quickly moved into the secured land, and on October 28, 1798, Arthur St. Clair, the first governor of the Northwest Territory, authorized the election of a legislature. Both houses of the new body met for the first time on September 24, 1799, and on October 3 they chose William Henry Harrison as the territory's delegate to Congress.

Harrison brought to Congress's attention the inability of the three federal judges to provide adequate court service for the sprawling Northwest Territory. At his suggestion, on May 7, 1800, Congress subdivided the region. The part including modern-day Ohio and part of lower Michigan retained the title of Northwest Territory, and the remainder of the vast area became the Indiana Territory, with its capital at Vincennes. President John Adams appointed Harrison, the descendant of two well-known Virginia families, to be the first governor.

Slavery became a major issue in Indiana politics during the first decade of the 19th century. With the support of Governor Harrison, a convention met at Vincennes in December 1802 and petitioned Congress to repeal the clause of the Northwest Ordinance that outlawed slavery in the territory. When Congress rejected the appeal, the territorial government evaded the ordinance by enacting a system of black and mulatto indentured servitude based on assignable contracts between masters and servants.

Indiana's population grew steadily, and in accord with a proclamation by Governor Harrison the people of the territory elected their own assembly on January 3, 1805. Antislavery forces were strong in the legislature, and in October 1808 the second territorial assembly refused to petition Congress for a modification of the ban on the institution. Harrison, who continued to associate himself with the proslavery faction, found himself increasingly at odds with a number of the delegates.

On January 11, 1805, Congress had detached the Michigan Territory from Indiana. Settlers in the western part of the Indiana Territory likewise sought their independence. Eastern Indianans, who opposed the proslavery attitude of the territory's western residents, also favored separation. Indiana's representative in Congress, Jesse B. Thomas, obtained a solution agreeable to all. Thus, on February 3, 1809, Congress again divided Indiana, creating the Illinois Territory from its western portion.

The fifth Indiana General Assembly, which met from August 15 to September 10, 1814, petitioned Congress to grant statehood to the territory. On April 19, 1816, President James Madison approved an enabling act authorizing Indiana to devise a state constitution and promising admission to the Union. In quick response to Madison's action, 43 Indianans on June 10, 1816, began a constitutional convention at Corydon, which had become the territorial capital in 1811.

The Indiana constitution clearly banned slavery from the proposed state. To placate the proslavery forces and ensure their support for the document, however, the framers validated existing indenture agreements. As was common in that period, many whites felt an aversion to blacks that was equal to their distaste for slavery, and blacks were forbidden to vote or serve in the militia.

Indiana's constitutional convention completed its work on June 29, 1816. On December 11, 1816, President Madison approved a congressional resolution admitting Indiana to the Union. Shortly thereafter, Jonathan Jennings became the state's first governor. Indianapolis became the capital of Indiana in 1824, replacing the less conveniently located Corydon.

December 12

John Jay's Birthday

John Jay, the first chief justice of the United States Supreme Court, was born in New York City, New York, on December 12, 1745. One of the eight surviving children of Peter and Mary Van Cortlandt Jay, the future jurist was descended from two of the most important families in the colony of New York. His Dutch Van Cortlandt forebears had been among the original settlers of New Amsterdam and had gained wealth and power through

their landholding and trading activities. The Jays traced their lineage to Augustus Jay, a Huguenot exile who sought refuge in New York around 1686 and became an influential merchant. John Jay's father was also a well-established businessman, and he provided his son with an excellent education. Young Jay studied first with private tutors and then entered King's College (later Columbia University), graduating in 1764.

After studying in Benjamin Kissam's law office, Jay gained admission to the bar in 1768. Five years later he served as secretary to the royal commission charged with settling a boundary dispute between New York and New Jersey. In 1774 the young lawyer married Sarah Van Brugh Livingston, daughter of William Livingston, who later became the Revolutionary governor of New Jersey.

The crises that eventually culminated in the American Revolution stimulated Jay's political talents. A man of wealth, he favored continuation of the colonies' ties with Britain. As a member of New York's Committee of Fifty-one and as a delegate to the First and Second Continental Congresses, he espoused conservative solutions to colonial problems. Jay was attending a provincial congress in New York when the Declaration of Independence was adopted and therefore did not vote for the resolution. However, he accepted Congress's action, and decided to support the cause of independence.

During the years immediately following the colonies' break with Great Britain, Jay directed his efforts toward strengthening support for the revolution in New York. He worked to gain the state's ratification of the Declaration of Independence in 1776 and was the chairman of the committee that formulated New York's new state constitution in 1777. He served as chief justice of New York until 1779.

In December 1778 Jay returned to the Continental Congress. He was elected president of that body on December 10 and held the post until September 1779 when he was selected to be minister plenipotentiary to Spain. In Madrid from 1780 to 1782, he was not able to gain Spanish recognition of the independence of the United States and succeeded only in obtaining a loan of $170,000.

In the spring of 1782 Benjamin Franklin called Jay to Paris. There, with Franklin and John Adams, he served as a joint commissioner entrusted with the task of negotiating a peace treaty with Great Britain. In this post Jay was instrumental in persuading Franklin to agree to a preliminary peace settlement without first obtaining concurrence from the French government.

When the final peace treaty was concluded in 1783, Jay was offered the appointment of minister to either Great Britain or France. He declined both positions and returned to the United States, intending to resume his private law practice. However, upon his arrival on July 24, 1784, he learned that Congress had named him as secretary of foreign affairs.

Jay supervised the foreign relations of the United States for the next six years. This experience convinced him of the inadequacy of the Articles of Confederation and made him an enthusiastic supporter of a stronger central government. From 1787 to 1788 Jay, together with James Madison and Alexander Hamilton, published the *Federalist* papers, which were the most forceful argument for the ratification of the Constitution and perhaps the most brilliant exposition of American constitutional theory ever written.

In 1790 George Washington appointed Thomas Jefferson secretary of state, and Jay became the first chief justice of the United States Supreme Court. In 1793 he handed down the most famous opinion of his five years on the bench, namely the case of *Chisholm* v. *Georgia*. In this case Jay and the majority of the Court ruled that two citizens of South Carolina could try to recover damages from the state of Georgia by suing in the federal courts. This decision created an immense furor, since many state legislatures interpreted it as an infringement on their sovereignty. As a result of the states' protests, the 11th Amendment to the Constitution, which prohibits a citizen of one state from suing another state in the federal courts (as opposed to the state courts), was proposed by Congress and ratified in 1795.

In 1794 war with Great Britain seemed imminent because of numerous American grievances. The British refused to vacate the Northwest military posts, thus impeding American settlement in the frontier and maintaining control of the fur trade. The British also impressed, or forced, American seamen into the British navy after seizing their vessels. President George Washington named Jay special envoy to negotiate these problems, and on November 1 he succeeded in negotiating a treaty with Great Britain.

The Jay Treaty was a compromise measure. Together with a number of other concessions, it provided for the British withdrawal from the Northwest forts by June 1796. However, it ignored other problems such as impressment, British agitation of the native tribes, and the return of slaves taken during the Revolution. The treaty met with strong resistance at home and only after a long debate did the Senate finally ratify it on June 24, 1795.

By using questionable electioneering practices, George Clinton defeated Jay in the New York gubernatorial election of 1792. Three years later, however, the Federalists succeeded in winning this post for Jay and he served as the governor of New York until 1801. Refusing to become a candidate for a third term, he retired at the age of 56 to his 800-acre estate at Katonah, New York, in the township of Bedford. There, Jay indulged his interests in horticulture and theology. He died on May 17, 1829.

Pennsylvania Ratifies the Constitution

On December 12, 1787, Pennsylvania became the second state to ratify the United States Constitution of 1787. The state's quick acceptance was an important step in the adoption of the new frame of government.

On September 17, 1787, the members of the Constitutional Convention meeting in Philadelphia, Pennsylvania, concluded their labors and remitted their work to the Continental Congress, which was then functioning under the Articles of Confederation and meeting in New York City, the nation's first capital. On September 28 the congress gave its assent and sent the proposed Constitution to each of the 13 states, formerly the colonies of Great Britain. In each state the legislature was asked to call a special convention to examine the proposal and to vote on ratification.

In Pennsylvania, pro-Constitution forces were ready to act immediately. The Federalists, or supporters of the new frame of government, controlled the state legislature in 1787 and were anxious to pass the resolution required to set up a ratifying convention before the end of the session on September 29. If the Federalists had failed to make the enactment, the opponents of the Constitution would have gained invaluable time to organize their forces and even been able to gain control of the legislature. Such a development could have thwarted ratification in Pennsylvania and doomed the adoption of the new Constitution.

As soon as Congress decided to send the Constitution to the states, an express rider was dispatched from New York to Philadelphia with the news. Even before the horseman reached the city with official notification, however, on September 28 one George Clymer proposed in the Pennsylvania legislature that a state convention of deputies (chosen by the voters on the same day and in the same manner as members of the next general assembly) be called to meet at Philadelphia. Robert Whithill protested that no word had yet arrived from the Continental Congress and noted that

Clymer's proposal violated the traditional procedure of notifying the assembly beforehand of the intention of submitting an important measure, of making the matter the order of the day, and of reading the bill three times.

Despite Whitehill's objections, the Federalists won approval by a vote of 43 to 19 for a convention to meet at Philadelphia. Satisfied with their efforts, the deputies then decided to take a recess until 4:00 P.M. before considering the manner of selecting the delegates and the date for their election. Antifederalist leaders used the hours before the afternoon session to plan their strategy. They concluded that their best hope lay in obstructing the conduct of the legislature until the final adjournment scheduled for the following day. These opponents of the Constitution could count only 19 supporters in their ranks, but if all of them stayed away from the meetings of the assembly, the 69-person body (from which several were already absent) would not be able to obtain the quorum of 46 members necessary to carry on its business.

Only 44 deputies appeared at the afternoon session. The speaker ordered the sergeant-at-arms to summon the absentees, but the Antifederalists would not heed the messenger. Lacking a quorum, the speaker had no choice but to adjourn the assembly until the following morning, September 29, the final day of the session. By the opening of the morning session, the messenger from New York had delivered the congressional resolution, but still the Antifederalist delegates stayed away. The speaker again dispatched the sergeant-at-arms and the assistant clerk to gather them. The officers first went to the house of Major Alexander Boyd, where the opposition made their headquarters, and found James M'Calmont and Jacob Miley there. When M'Calmont and Miley refused to return to the State House with the sergeant and the clerk, a mob of citizens who favored the Constitution broke into the representatives' lodgings and dragged them through the streets to the assembly chamber. With the two unwilling and disheveled Antifederalists present, the legislature finally had a quorum and set the election of delegates to the state constitutional convention for the first Tuesday in November 1787.

Opponents of the Constitution feared the extensive powers it would give the central government. They argued that the new frame of government was not a confederation but an undesirable government over individuals that threatened to destroy the sovereignty of the states that was so well protected by the Articles of Confederation. Of equal importance, the Congress would have direct powers over the lives, liberties, and properties of all citizens, and yet the Constitution offered no bill of rights to prevent governmental abuses.

Supporters of the Constitution argued that Congress, rather than being an omnipotent body, would enjoy only those powers expressly granted to it in the Constitution. Further, the new government posed no threat to the states. In fact, the legislatures of each state were to choose each state's United States senators and determine the mode of selection for electors in the electoral college. The Federalists won the debate, and they were swept to victory in the elections for the Pennsylvania assembly and council, which preceded the selection of delegates to the ratifying convention. Their success proved to be prophetic of the outcome of the later elections, which took place on November 6, 1787, and resulted in a crushing Federalist victory.

Pennsylvania's ratifying convention opened on November 21 at the State House in Philadelphia with 60 of the 69 elected delegates in attendance. The opposing sides spent a week arguing about procedures and then devoted two more weeks to a detailed discussion of the proposed Constitution. Finally, on December 12 the members of the convention cast their ballots—46 were in favor of the new government and 23 were against it. The following day the convention, joined by the president and vice-president of Pennsylvania and all the state dignitaries, both civil and military, went in procession to the State House and read the ratification ordinance to a gathering of the citizenry. On December 15 the convention adjourned.

Among the 13 former British colonies, the order of statehood is usually calculated on the basis of the date of ratification of the Constitution. Thus Pennsylvania, which ratified the Constitution only five days after Delaware, is listed as the second state.

December 13

Korean War: North Korea and South Korea Finally Execute a Peace Treaty

On December 13, 1991, Chung Won-shik, the prime minister of the Republic of Korea (South Korea), and Yon Hyong-muk, the premier of the administration council of the Democratic People's Republic of Korea (North Korea), executed a treaty—the Agreement on Reconciliation, Nonaggression, and Exchanges and Cooperation—between their two countries. It was not a full peace treaty, but it was an important step towards reconciliation between North and South Korea after decades of mutual antagonism following the 1953 armistice that effectually ended the Korean War.

As discussed in several articles throughout this book, the Korean War was a major cold-war confrontation between the United States and the Soviet Union, which at the time was allied with the People's Republic of China. With Soviet approval, communist North Korea invaded pro-American South Korea, necessitating American military involvement under the umbrella of a United Nations–sponsored coalition to prevent a North Korean victory. After several years of seesaw military campaigns and tortuous peace negotiations, in addition to Chinese military assistance on North Korea's behalf that nearly led to nuclear war with the United States, an armistice was signed on July 27, 1953.

An uneasy truce followed, in which both sides maintained large armed forces along the border. There were threats to the Demilitarized Zone, a strip of land about 3 miles wide and 150 miles long separating the two nations, but in fact the DMZ remained largely undisturbed (and in time became a refuge for the region's wildlife). Meanwhile, South Korea embraced Western-style capitalism and prospered economically, while rigidly communist North Korea stagnated. Driven in part by the lure of trade and other economic opportunities with South Korea, in addition to the possibility of eventual reunification, the North began to relent on some of its demands for ending the state of war that still officially existed between the two countries. After years of off-and-on talks, the two sides finally executed the reconciliation and nonaggression treaty, formally ending the Korean War and hopefully paving the way for further progress in years to come.

December 14

Alabama Admitted to the Union

On December 14, 1819, Alabama became the 22nd state to enter the Union.

Alabama's existence as a state represents but a brief period in the span of its history. The region has been populated for at least 8,000 years, which is the age of the earliest known relics of human habitation found in rock caves within the state. The people who left the relics seem to have depended on hunting and fishing, and their main food must have been mussels, judging from the piles of shells found at the sites of habitation.

In the period before the Europeans came, Alabama was the home of Mound Builders who left distinctive flat-topped mounds (which were probably the sites of wooden temples) along the Alabama rivers. They grew corn and other crops,

made excellent pottery and fine jewelry, worked copper, carved stone figurines with considerable skill, wove cloth, and generally left evidence of a high state of cultural development.

The largest native tribes encountered by the first European visitors were the Choctaw along the Gulf Coast in southwestern Alabama, the Creek in the southeastern and central parts, and the Cherokee and Chickasaw in the north. So far as is known, the first Europeans to arrive were the Spanish, notably the companies of Alonzo Alvarez de Piñeda in 1519 and of Pánfilo de Narváez in 1528. Both of them sailed along the Gulf Coast and came into contact with the natives there. The first to penetrate inland was Hernando de Soto and his troop of 900-armored soldiers, who entered the northern part of Alabama looking for gold in 1540. Their aggression aroused the resistance of natives they encountered, and in southwestern Alabama they fought the Choctaw, led by Chief Tascalusa.

After Tristán de Luna tried and failed to start a permanent settlement on Mobile Bay in 1559–1561, the region was not troubled by European interference for about a century. Eventually, however, the French penetrated the region. They were lured by the abundance of beaver, whose fur was highly prized in Europe. In 1699 Pierre Le Moyne, Sieur d'Iberville, claimed the region for France and in 1702 his brother, Jean Baptiste Le Moyne, Sieur de Bienville, established Fort Louis de la Mobile, the first permanent European settlement in Alabama. Because of flooding, the settlement was moved downriver in 1710–1711 to the site of what is now Mobile, which was the capital of French Louisiana until 1719 when France went to war with Great Britain and Spain and moved the government to Biloxi, where there was less chance of an attack.

The year 1719 was also notable as the date of the first arrival of slaves, an event that encouraged French settlers to clear land for indigo and rice plantations. Nevertheless, the main economic pursuit of the French continued to be trading in furs. In this activity, they faced competition from the British, who established close trading relations with the Chickasaw. Throughout the mid-1700s, the British and French vied for control of the fur trade. The contest merged into the French and Indian War and finally was settled in favor of the British in 1763, when the French ceded Canada and all of their possessions east of the Mississippi River to Britain under the Treaty of Paris of 1763.

During the American Revolution, a British garrison held the country around Mobile until 1780, when the governor of Spanish Louisiana forced the British to surrender. By the Treaty of Paris of 1783, which ended the American Revolution, and by a related treaty with Spain, Britain ceded northern Alabama to the United States, while southern Alabama, including Mobile, went to Spain. In 1785 a boundary dispute arose between Spain and the United States, and it was not until 1795 that the Treaty of San Lorenzo settled the southern boundary of the American territory at the 31st Parallel, lying about 26 miles above Mobile. By an act of Congress in 1798, land lying above the 31st Parallel between the Chattahoochee River on the east and the Mississippi on the west was organized as the Mississippi Territory, which at first had its northern boundary at 32 degrees 28 minutes north latitude but was extended to the 35th Parallel in 1804. The territory thus came to include most of what are now the states of Mississippi and Alabama.

After negotiating the Louisiana Purchase with France in 1803, the United States claimed, but Spain still controlled, the Mobile region. The United States did not annex the area until 1813. At that time most of the land in what is now Alabama, in practical fact, was still in the possession of the native tribes. Embittered by the Americans' treatment of them, the Creek killed about 500 people at Fort Mims in August 1813. Ultimately Andrew Jackson, with his Tennessee riflemen and his native allies, ended the Creek War (as it was called) by subduing the Creek at the battles of Talladega on November 9, 1813, and Horseshoe Bend on March 27, 1814. The Creek were forced to cede millions of acres of land, and their defeat paved the way for the removal of most of Alabama's Native Americans from the territory.

With the influx of settlers after the removal of the native tribes, the population of the region swelled. On March 3, 1817, Alabama was separated from Mississippi and organized as a territory on its own. Two years later, on March 2, 1819, Congress authorized the Alabama Territory to draft a state constitution, which was done at a constitutional convention meeting from July 5 to August 2. The first Alabama state legislature convened on October 25 of that year, and on November 9, 1819, the territorial governor, William Wyatt Bibb, was chosen as the first state governor. Alabama was admitted to statehood on December 14 by an act of Congress signed by President James Monroe. Until 1820 the seat of government was in Huntsville, then it was moved to Cahaba (the ruins of which are located near Selma) from 1820 to 1826, to Tuscaloosa from 1826 to 1846, and finally to Montgomery from 1846 to the present.

Following the election of President Abraham Lincoln in 1860, a special state convention convened at Montgomery. On January 11, 1861, it passed an ordinance of secession, making Alabama the fourth state to declare its secession from the Union. On February 4 Montgomery became the site of a conference of six southern states—Alabama, Georgia, Florida, Louisiana, Mississippi, and South Carolina—that created the provisional government of the Confederate States of America. The city was the seat of the new Confederate government until June of that year, when Richmond, Virginia, became the Confederate capital. After the Civil War, Alabama was occupied by Union troops. In September 1865 a constitutional convention revoked the ordinance of secession, ratified the 13th Amendment, which abolished slavery, and adopted a new constitution. A new governor and legislature were chosen and were recognized under President Andrew Johnson's liberal conditions for Reconstruction.

In 1866, however, Alabama and most other southern states refused to ratify the 14th Amendment, which under the more stringent congressional plan of Reconstruction by then in force, was a prerequisite for restoration to the Union. (The amendment defined citizenship to include not only whites but blacks, guaranteed equal protection of the laws for all persons, forbade deprivation by any state of any person's "life, liberty, or property," without due process of law," and disqualified for office anyone who had held office under The Confederacy.) Congress responded by refusing to seat Alabama's chosen representatives to Congress. It also passed the Reconstruction Acts of 1867, placing Alabama and other southern states under military rule and calling for new constitutional conventions, which were to provide for state governments guaranteeing the vote to black males and ratifying the 14th Amendment. Delegates were to be elected by universal male suffrage. On June 18, 1868, after a new convention had drawn up a new state constitution and a new legislature had ratified the 14th Amendment, Alabama's rights and privileges of statehood were restored.

George Washington's Death

Like the legendary Roman hero Cincinnatus, George Washington returned to Mount Vernon in Virginia after serving his country in its time of need. From the time of his retirement as president in 1797 until his death two years later, he devoted himself to this property.

On December 12, 1799, Washington set out on horseback. Ignoring the cold rain and snow, he made a five-hour inspection of several areas of his plantation. He returned from his ride with snow clinging to his hair and clothing. The following day he complained of a "trifling" sore throat, although the discomfort did not deter him from his work.

That afternoon, when the storm ended, he went outdoors and marked the trees on the front lawn that he wished cut down. By dinner time his cold was perceptibly worse, and when he attempted to read aloud that evening he was quite hoarse.

By the morning of December 14, his breathing was labored and his speech almost unintelligible. Every effort was made to relieve his condition. Three doctors applied standard remedies and bled him four times, but to no avail. Washington realized this and late that afternoon said: "I feel myself going. I thank you for your attention. You had better not take any more trouble about me; but let me go off quietly; I cannot last long." Several hours later, shortly after 10:00 p.m., he died.

Funeral services took place on December 18. At 3:00 p.m. a solemn procession, which included military personnel, members of the clergy, and representatives from Masonic lodges in addition to friends and relatives, accompanied his casket to the burial vault at Mount Vernon. In the procession was the general's horse, fitted with holsters and pistols. At the vault the Reverend Thomas Davis read the Order of Burial from the Episcopal Prayer Book. There was a brief eulogy, and then Elisha Dick, grand master of the Alexandria Masonic Lodge, conducted full Masonic rites. When these were concluded, cannons mounted on a schooner in the Potomac River began firing and 11 artillery cannons behind the vault retorted. Then there was silence. Washington's funeral ended and everyone departed.

Grief over Washington's death was not limited to those at the burial site, nor did it end with his interment. Across the Atlantic, one London newspaper prophesied: "His fame, bounded by no country, will be confined to no age." In honor of the American president, units of the British fleet blockading the harbor at Brest, France, dropped their ensigns to half-mast. In Paris Napoléon Bonaparte ordered a ten-day requiem.

When the news of Washington's death reached Philadelphia on December 18, Congress recessed. The temporary capital of the nation observed December 26 as a formal day of mourning. At dawn on that day 16 cannons began firing and continued to boom every half hour until 11:00 a.m., when a procession of troops marched to the Lutheran Church. There, Representative Henry Lee of Virginia gave a description of Washington that was to become immortal:

> First in war, first in peace and first in the hearts of his countrymen, he was second to none in the humble and endearing scenes of private life. . . . The purity of his private character gave effulgence to his public virtues.

As a lasting memorial to Washington, Congress voted to build a marble monument in the Capitol Building then being constructed in Washington, D.C. The legislators also wanted the seat of government to be the final resting place of the first president. A crypt was provided beneath the building's dome, and Martha Washington agreed to the transfer of her husband's remains. However, the plan was never carried out. Instead a new vault was constructed at Mount Vernon according to instructions that Washington had personally given before his death. When it was completed in 1831, the bodies of George and Martha Washington (she died in 1802) were moved to this tomb.

December 15

Ratification of the Bill of Rights

Responding to various calls for a bill of rights, by December 15, 1791, nine states had ratified the first ten amendments to the United States Constitution of 1787. With this approval of three-fourths of the 13 states then in the Union, the amendments became part of the Constitution.

Many had criticized the members of the Constitutional Convention for giving the national government too much strength and, conversely, doing little to guarantee individual liberties and protect states' rights. Even the supporters of the Constitution realized the need for such amendments. In 1787 Thomas Jefferson, who as minister to France was a witness to the abuses of that absolute monarchy, wrote to James Madison that "a bill of rights is what the people are entitled to against every government on earth." Jefferson's fellow Virginian, often referred to as the Father of the Constitution, had played a leading role in the framing and adoption of the Constitution. The demand for a series of guarantees of individual and state rights was so strong that the Constitution itself did not receive the necessary approval of three-fourths of the states until assurances were given that the essential amendments would be forthcoming.

The first Congress of the United States, which convened in New York City, New York, on March 4, 1789, considered 145 proposed amendments. On September 25 it submitted 12 of these to the states. The ten that gained approval are known collectively as the Bill of Rights, one of the landmark documents of human freedom. (See the appendix for the full text of the Constitution, including these first ten amendments, and also the other amendments that followed in later years.)

December 16

The 150th anniversary of the adoption of the Bill of Rights in 1941 found the world arming against the totalitarian oppression of the Axis powers. In January 1941 President Franklin D. Roosevelt enlarged upon the guarantees of the Bill of Rights when he proclaimed freedom of speech, freedom of worship, freedom from want, and freedom from fear to be the birthright of all peoples of the world. Later that year he designated December 15, 1941, as Bill of Rights Day and called upon Americans to observe it with suitable patriotic ceremonies. Presidents have issued proclamations designating December 15 as Bill of Rights Day annually since 1962, with the exception of 1967 and 1968, and the governors of a number of states take similar action.

December 16

Boston Tea Party

Tension marked the relationship between Great Britain and its American colonies in the years between the Stamp Act crisis of 1765 and the Boston Massacre in 1770 (see related articles throughout this book). In January 1770 Lord Frederick North took over the leadership of the British government, and on April 12 he obtained King George III's consent to the repeal of the Townshend Act taxes on glass, lead, paints, and paper. Although a three-penny levy on tea remained in force under the act, the colonists' nonimportation campaign petered out after this relaxation. The appointment in August 1772 of North's stepbrother William Legge, the pro-American earl of Dartmouth, as secretary of state for the colonies in place of the earl of Hillsborough further improved relations. Still, differing English and American viewpoints, aspirations, and interests made future conflict almost inevitable.

In 1773 the British government decided to save the British East India Company, which although virtually bankrupt was vital to the preservation of Britain's influence in India. The means chosen was the Tea Act, which authorized the company to sell 600,000 pounds of surplus tea directly to consignees in America without first offering it at auction in England. Furthermore, the Tea Act provided for the remission of all British duties on tea exported to the American colonies, save for the Townshend levy, after May 10, 1773. The act put the East India Company in the enviable position of being able to sell its tea leaves more cheaply than could the colonial merchants who obtained them from middlemen in England. In fact the company could undersell even those Americans who smuggled the commodity from Holland.

Opposition to the plan was vehement in the American colonies. Commentators charged that the East India Company would monopolize the tea trade and then take over all commerce. This argument soon became secondary as colonial leaders learned from informants in England that the true intent of the act was to encourage acceptance of the Townshend tea taxes by making the company's dutied tea cheaper than even the smuggled substitutes. Central to the colonists' opposition was the realization that if they acquiesced to one levy, the British government would then have a precedent to support future financial demands.

Pressure from militant colonial leaders prompted the resignation of the East India Company's consignees in New York and Philadelphia. In Boston the situation was different, however, since Governor Thomas Hutchinson gave full support to the government's plan. His sons, Elisha and Thomas, were tea agents in the city. The younger Thomas was married to the daughter of Richard Clarke, who along with his sons Jonathan and Isaac was another major consignee. Benjamin Faneuil and Edward Winslow, other prominent Bostonians, also represented the company.

On November 2, 1773, the Massachusetts-based Sons of Liberty sent messages to the tea agents to appear at noon on the next day at Boston's Liberty Tree to resign their commissions. When the men failed to appear, the rebels unleashed the town mob, which invaded the lower floor of the building in which the consignees were meeting. Boston's "selectmen" then called a town meeting for Friday, November 5. Chaired by the radical John Hancock, the gathering denounced the Tea Act and called for the resignations of the consignees. Hancock and three other delegates confronted the agents but were unable to influence them. On November 17 Captain James Scott, the commander of Hancock's ship the *Hayley* arrived with news that four shiploads of tea were en route to Boston. That evening a group of Bostonians demonstrated outside the Clarkes' residence and then smashed windows when someone fired a shot at them.

Persistent harassment diminished the consignees' zest for the struggle. On November 18 they rejected another demand by the town meeting for their resignations, but then they asked the colonial government to take responsibility for the tea until conditions allowed it to be disposed of. The prorebel colonials who controlled the Massachusetts Council, one of the few upper houses in the colonies elected by the lower house of the legislature, were unwilling to permit this and refused to consider the request. Governor Hutchinson, meanwhile, dared not take action without the support of his advisers. Finally the consignees agreed to not unload the expected cargoes, at least until new instructions from England allowed them to offer some concessions to the colonials.

Crisis became imminent when the *Dartmouth*, laden with 114 chests of tea, sailed into Boston harbor on Sunday, November 28. The law permitted a 48-hour delay in reporting the arrival of a vessel to the customhouse, and the Boston rebels prevailed upon Francis Rotch, the son of the ship's owner Joseph Rotch, to take full advantage of the respite. In the interim they hoped to persuade Hutchinson to allow the *Dartmouth* to return to England without registering, without unloading the tea, and especially without paying the Townshend duty.

On Monday morning, posted notices called Bostonians to meet at the red brick Faneuil Hall with the words: "Friends! Brethren! Countrymen! The Hour of Destruction or Manly Opposition to the Machinations of Tyranny stares you in the Face." This was not a town meeting duly called by the selectmen but an illegal gathering at which all Bostonians were welcome. When 5,000 appeared at the hall, the meeting adjourned to the more spacious Old South Meeting House not far away. The citizens resolved to send the tea back without paying the duty and again demanded that the consignees resign. Refusing the Bostonians' demands, the agents left the town for their own safety.

The royalist authorities were unimpressed by this demonstration of public disapproval, and on Tuesday, November 30 the ship's captain, James Hall, had to report the *Dartmouth*'s arrival to customhouse officials. Since payment of the Townshend duty was not mandatory until December 17, twenty days after the vessel reached Boston, the authorities decided it was in the best interests of peace to delay the payment as long as possible. At the request of the colonial Committee of Correspondence, Captain Hall meanwhile docked close to the city at Rowe's Wharf and then at Griffin's Wharf, where the government's guns at Castle William could not prevent any forcible attempt to unload the tea.

During the first two weeks of December 1773 two other ships (the *Eleanor* and the *Beaver*, carrying 114 and 112 chests of tea, respectively) arrived at Griffin's Wharf. The fourth expected vessel had run aground before reaching Boston harbor, but its cargo remained intact. Although the presence of additional ships aggravated the situation in Boston, the earliest arrival remained the focal point. Since the *Dartmouth*'s 20-day grace period would expire first, its fate would determine the outcome of the crisis.

The rebels hoped that Rotch would take his vessel and its cargo of tea back to England and in November had exacted a promise to that effect from him. Perhaps having discovered that the authorities could seize his ship if he left the port without receiving their clearance, Rotch in fact made no attempt to set sail. On December 14, three days before the deadline, the colonists accordingly summoned him before another mass meeting at the Old South Meeting House and demanded that he request permission to sail. Rotch obediently appealed for clearance to customs collector Richard Harrison, but the officer refused to grant it. Harrison argued that the ship was registered at the customhouse and could not leave Boston until someone paid the duties on its cargo of tea.

At 10:00 a.m. on December 16 more than 5,000 Massachusetts citizens gathered again at the Old South Meeting House. Rotch reported his failure to gain clearance, and the convention told him to go directly to the governor for an authorization to leave. Governor Hutchinson, adamant throughout the crisis, rejected the shipper's request. The mass meeting reconvened that afternoon and heard Rotch report another rebuff.

Finally, the rebellious firebrand Samuel Adams rose to his feet and declared that he did not know what recourse was left. As if on signal, a group of men disguised as Native Americans appeared at the door at that very moment. Soon the hall filled with cries of "The Mohawks are come!" and "Boston harbor a teapot tonight." It was about 6:00 p.m. when the meeting disbanded and the participants rushed out into the darkness. Led by the "Indians" they made their way to Griffin's Wharf. Between 30 and 60 men, divided into three groups, boarded the *Dartmouth*, the *Eleanor*, and the *Beaver*. While the crowd watched from the shore, the men went to work. They hoisted the tea chests out of the holds and onto the decks, smashed them, and heaved both contents and containers over the sides.

The tea leaves quickly filled the shallow water in which the ships were resting. The rebels completed the Boston Tea Party within only three hours, and managed to destroy more than 90,000 pounds of leaves worth approximately 9,000 British pounds. Outnumbered, the authorities did not intervene.

The colonials soon had to face the consequences of their venture. Although the British East India Company reluctantly accepted the fate of its tea, asking only that the British government compensate its losses, King George III, supported by many Britons, did not view the situation with the same calmness. Boston, long considered a trouble spot, had gone too far in its protests. Tired of being conciliatory, the king determined to coerce the city into obedience.

The earls of Gower and Sandwich, both members of an anti-American faction, dominated the deliberations on the fate of Boston by the seven-member British ministry that handled American colonial affairs. They devised a program to punish the colonists, which the British Parliament enacted on March 25, 1774, as the Boston Port Bill. This piece of legislation, the first of the Coercive, or "Intolerable," Acts, closed the port of Boston until the residents paid for the lost tea. Only ships bearing food, fuel, and military supplies could unload in Boston Harbor, and even these vessels had to first report to Salem, Massachusetts, where the customhouse was moved. The other Intolerable Acts were the Administration of Justice Act of May 20, 1774, enacted to protect British officials from harassment in colonial courts; and the Massachusetts Government Act (enacted on the same day), which seriously curtailed the colony's charter rights and gave the crown- appointed governor additional powers.

These attempts to coerce the colonists were doomed to failure. Angered rather than intimidated, Americans throughout the colonies united behind their fellow citizens in beleaguered Boston and continued on the road to independence.

The New Madrid, Missouri, Earthquake

On December 16, 1811, the residents of New Madrid, Missouri, experienced a devastating earthquake, which was followed by two major shocks on January 23 and February 7, 1812, and nearly 2,000 aftershocks. Only two lives were lost, largely because the region was still relatively unpopulated. Scientifically, however, the event ranks in severity and in size of the area affected with the San Francisco quake of April 18, 1906, and the Alaska quake of March 27, 1964. Although these two resulted in far greater losses of life and property, the earthquake and following shocks centered near New Madrid were felt over a much wider area. The region affected extended all the way from Canada to the Gulf of Mexico.

December 17

Wright Brothers' First Flight

On the chilly morning of December 17, 1903, the Wright brothers managed to get their faltering flying machine off the ground near Kitty Hawk,

North Carolina, thereby becoming the first men to fly and control a powered heavier-than-air machine. Wilbur Wright, born on April 16, 1867, near New Castle, Indiana, was 36. Orville Wright, born in Dayton, Ohio, on August 19, 1871, was 32.

The sons of Milton Wright, a bishop of the United Brethren Church, the brothers were both mechanics. They opened a shop in Dayton in 1892, where they at first sold and repaired bicycles and then also designed and manufactured them. In their spare moments they avidly read accounts of scientific advances. Of particular fascination to them were the experimental glider flights in Germany of the pioneering Otto Lilienthal, whom they always afterwards regarded as their greatest inspiration.

After reading about Lilienthal, the Wrights developed a strong interest in gliding as a sport, and beginning in 1896, they began to investigate the field of flight. Planning to construct a captive glider that would be capable of carrying a man, they first experimented for several years with kites.

The Wright brothers, however, were not the first to conduct aeronautical experiments. Clement Ader of France, Sir Hiram Maxim of England, and Samuel P. Langley of the United States each independently built and tested a flying machine, but failed because they lacked a basic knowledge of the laws of aerodynamics. The same was true of glider experimenters like Otto Lilienthal of Germany and Octave Chanute of the United States, from whom the Wrights also learned much.

Although Lilienthal had balanced his gliding apparatus by shifting the weight of his body, the Wrights doubted that this method could be expanded sufficiently to meet the needs of flight. Instead they surmised that a glider should be constructed so that its right and left wings could be presented to the wind at different angles for lateral balance, which they accomplished by warping or twisting the tips of the wings. Their system, employing a cable arrangement whereby the wing tips could be moved, was patented. It represented an innovative solution to the problem of control in flight, predating the aileron control developed by Alexander Graham Bell and his associates. Together with other theories, the Wrights incorporated their device for lateral control into both the model glider with a five-foot wing span, which they constructed in 1899 and flew like a kite, and the man-supporting glider, which they built in 1900.

Searching for a secluded spot where they could test the man-supporting glider away from spectators, they studied the wind records of the United States Weather Bureau. Their research, and a letter of inquiry to a local postmaster, revealed the area around Kitty Hawk, North Carolina, as a region of steady winds, level sands, and solitude. The location was ideally suited to their purposes.

Arriving in Kitty Hawk in September 1900, they tried out their first glider. A year later they returned with a larger version of the glider. This time, they built a camp just north of Kill Devil Hill near Kitty Hawk. Their experiments were not an instant success, as their gliders mysteriously achieved far less lifting power than existing wind pressure tables had led them to expect. This fact led to their conclusion that calculations based on existing data could not be trusted.

Thus thwarted, the Wrights faced the necessity of starting from scratch to obtain their own information. Returning to Dayton, they constructed a wind tunnel at their bicycle shop. There they investigated the aerodynamic properties of various airfoils, testing more than 200 kinds of miniature wing surfaces in various wing and biplane combinations. The Wrights, who were the first to test miniature wings accurately, sought in this way to determine correct values for lift, drag, and center of pressure. In the process they drew up valuable tables of wind pressure and drift. Indeed, from the figures they compiled, designing an airplane that could fly was possible for the first time. As a result of their experiments, the Wrights also realized that a sharp edge on the front of the airplane wing was inferior to a curved surface. They also learned that employing the cambered type of wing then advocated by others was ineffective.

Armed with their new body of knowledge, they returned to Kill Devil Hill in 1902 with a vastly superior glider, constructed according to their own figures on wind pressure. Incorporating both their control system and their own wing design, it also included a vertical steering rudder and had a wing span of 32 feet. Many of their glides were of more than 600 feet and against a stiffer, 36-mile-per-hour wind than any previous glider had ever challenged. With the 1902 glider, which they flew nearly 1,000 times, the Wrights solved most of the problem of equilibrium.

With the basic problems behind them, they now felt ready to build the historic, machine-powered *Flyer*, a biplane with a wingspan of 40 feet. An adaptation of their successful glider, the new aircraft incorporated a four-cylinder, 12-horsepower engine weighing 170 pounds, which the Wrights had built themselves. It also boasted the first propellers ever constructed for which performance could actually be predicted. Their design was based on the brothers' own calculations. Altogether, counting the weight of its pilot, the new machine weighed 750 pounds. The experiments leading up to it, from 1899 through 1903, cost the Wrights about $1,000.

The Wright brothers returned to their camp at Kill Devil Hill in September 1903, but they did not have their first test flight until December 14, after working through several mechanical problems and waiting for better weather conditions. Winning a coin toss for what he referred to as the "first whack," Wilbur Wright climbed aboard. However, his first trial run ended suddenly after three and a half seconds in the air. Having the craft lift upward too suddenly before it acquired sufficient speed, he stalled the engine, and the craft fell the short distance back to Earth. Two days of repairs were needed after this incident.

On the morning of December 17 the brothers were ready to try again. Though they were temporarily daunted by the wind, which was blowing at between 21 and 27 miles an hour, they decided to proceed when it failed to die down. On level ground at the base of a hill, they laid a 60-foot track that headed straight into the wind. This time Orville Wright lay in the control mechanism on the lower wing beside the engine. "After running the motor a few minutes to heat it up," he subsequently reported, "I released the wire that held the machine to the track, and the machine started forward into the wind." A handful of persons witnessed the historic trial in addition to Wilbur Wright, who first walked and then ran alongside the plane, steadying the wing until the craft rose of its own power and for 12 seconds flew over the sands. As Orville Wright put it: "This flight lasted only 12 seconds, but it was nevertheless the first in . . . history . . . in which a machine carrying a man had raised itself by its own power into the air in full flight, had sailed forward without reduction of speed, and finally landed at a point as high as that from which it started."

During the remainder of the morning, the brothers alternated as pilots for three more successful flights. Each flight longer than the last, the series culminated with Wilbur's flight of 852 feet in 59 seconds, the last *Flyer* would ever make.

The site of the epoch-making flights and the glider experiments that led up to them is now designated as the Wright Brothers National Memorial, a 425-acre area administered by the National Park Service. Its most prominent feature is a 60-foot-high gray granite pylon atop Kill Devil Hill. Not far away, a granite boulder marks the takeoff point for the first flight. Its course, and that of the other three flights of December 17, 1903, are indicated for visitors to see. Nearby are reconstructions of the Wrights' living quarters and hangar. A visitor center, dedicated on December 17, 1960, is also nearby. It houses pertinent exhibits and a fullsized reproduction of the Wrights' famous plane.

December 17

John Greenleaf Whittier's Birthday

John Greenleaf Whittier, the New England poet, politician, journalist, and abolitionist, was born on a farm near Haverhill, Massachusetts, on December 17, 1807. Second of four children in a Quaker household, the largely self-educated Whittier had scant formal schooling. His strongest intellectual influences were his religion and his lifelong love of reading.

Whittier was especially drawn to poetry, and when he was about 14 he was greatly impressed by the works of the Scottish poet Robert Burns, who depicted the 18th-century lifestyle of his fellow rural Scots. Burns's influence on the young American poet was great, and Whittier began writing of his rural New England surroundings and background, thus becoming a pioneer in American regional literature.

In 1826 one of his two sisters sent a copy of his poem "The Exile's Departure" to the *Free Press*, the Newburyport, Massachusetts, newspaper edited by the abolitionist William Lloyd Garrison. Only two years older than Whittier, Garrison encouraged him to continue writing. In 1827, while studying at the newly established Haverhill Academy, Whittier continued his contributions to the *Free Press* and other publications. His father, however, had convinced Whittier that while poetry might be an acceptable hobby it was hardly a practical livelihood.

Whittier accordingly embarked on a journalism career in Boston in 1829, becoming the editor for the *American Manufacturer*, a post which he secured through Garrison. A long-lasting friendship had meanwhile developed between the two young men, who shared strong antislavery convictions. Whittier's editorial post in Boston was followed by a position in Hartford, Connecticut, where he served from 1830 to 1832 as editor of the influential Whig journal *New England Weekly Review*. Throughout this period he continued to write verses, sketches, and tales of New England. His first volume, *Legends of New England*, was published in 1831.

Led by his zeal for social reform, Whittier entered politics in 1832. For several years he followed Garrison's extreme abolitionism. Whittier's antislavery writings, including the widely read militant pamphlet *Justice and Expediency*—which he published at Garrison's urging in June 1833—soon made him one of the best known champions of the abolitionist cause. Like Garrison, who was prominent among the founders of the New England Anti-Slavery Society early in 1832, Whittier was a delegate to the meeting of abolitionists from various states who gathered at Philadelphia in December 1833 to organize the American Anti-Slavery Society.

Devoted to abolition, he traveled to various places to promote the cause and became a familiar lobbyist in Boston and Washington, D.C. He served one term in the Massachusetts legislature during 1835, although he was not healthy enough to continue in the post after being elected for a second time. He spent May to December 1836 as editor of the *Essex Gazette*. Having sold the family farm, he moved with his mother and sister to a new home in Amesbury, Massachusetts, where he lived, except for certain intervals, for the next 40 years. Even after his move to Danvers, Massachusetts, in 1876, Amesbury remained his legal residence.

Two of Whittier's absences from Amesbury were in the spring of 1837, when he spent six months in New York City as a corresponding secretary of the American Anti-Slavery Society; and from March 15, 1838, to February 20, 1840, when he was editor of the *Pennsylvania Freeman* in Philadelphia. On May 17, 1838, Pennsylvania Hall, containing the *Freeman's* offices, was burned to the ground by an antiabolitionist mob.

In 1840 Whittier was forced by ill health to return home to Amesbury, the center of his activities for most of his remaining productive years. Although he continued to be active in the abolitionist movement, he was among those who by 1840 had broken with Garrison. In contrast to his mentor, who abjured politics and relied solely on moral persuasion to make his point, Whittier felt that more could be achieved through politics than polemics. He assisted in founding the short-lived antislavery Liberty Party in 1840, many of whose members helped establish the Free-Soil Party eight years later. Whittier was also among the first to urge the formation of the new Republican Party, in which Free-Soilers and antislavery Whigs and Democrats joined in 1854.

In the years that followed, Whittier continued his abolitionist writings but turned more and more to his own literary career as he found an increasing acceptance in publishing circles. In 1843, along with Nathaniel Hawthorne and Edgar Allan Poe, Whittier was represented in *The Pioneer*, a new but short-lived literary magazine begun by James Russell Lowell. That same year he published *Lays of My Home and Other Poems*. In the following two decades, Whittier published five volumes of prose, including the semifictional *Leaves from Margaret Smith's Journal in the Province of Massachusetts Bay* (1849), and eight volumes of poems. These included *Voices of Freedom* (1846), *Poems* (1849), *Songs of Labor* (1850), *The Chapel of the Hermits* (1853), and *Home Ballads, Poems and Lyrics* (1860).

For 13 years beginning in 1847, Whittier was also corresponding editor of the *National Era*, published in Washington, D.C., in which many of his poems and articles first appeared. (This was the antislavery publication which introduced *Uncle Tom's Cabin* by Harriet Beecher Stowe to the public in 1851–1852.) Whittier also had a long association with the *Atlantic Monthly*, to which he became a frequent contributor after it was established in Boston in 1857. He also wrote for the *Independent*, which was launched in New York in 1848.

Whittier became almost legendary in his popularity. Along with Henry Wadsworth Longfellow, Whittier became a "household poet" in the United States and England. In 1858 he was elected an overseer of Harvard, which honored him with a master's degree in 1860 and a doctorate in 1886. He was a member of the famous Saturday Club of Boston, and his 70th and 80th birthdays were celebrated as literary events. From 1888 to 1889, his complete works were collected in seven volumes. The Quaker Poet, as he was often called, died on September 7, 1892.

December 18

New Jersey Ratifies the Constitution

On December 18, 1787, New Jersey became the third state to ratify the United States Constitution. Only Delaware and Pennsylvania, which had ratified on December 7 and December 12, respectively, had accepted the new government more quickly. New Jerseyans had long been critics of the Articles of Confederation, which preceded the Constitution as the frame of government, and every delegate to the state convention called to vote on the matter voted in favor of the new Constitution.

New Jersey, a prosperous state in the 1780s, was not fortunate in its geographical location. Even though it had a diversified agricultural base which provided a strong foundation for the economy and a number of industrial enterprises, such as eight iron furnaces and hundreds of saw and gristmills, commerce flowed through either New York City to the north or Philadelphia to the south. New Jersey's commercial dependence on New York and Pennsylvania was its principal reason for dissatisfaction with the Articles of Confederation. Under that system the states, rather than the central government, had the right to control commerce. New Jerseyans consequently paid import duties to both New York and Pennsylvania, as well as heavy taxes to support their own state's effort to meet the interest on state and national debts. They hoped that under a new constitution the national government would relieve the state of an enormous burden by collecting all commercial duties and using the receipts to erase both the state and national debts.

In September 1786, delegates from New Jersey, Virginia, Pennsylvania, Delaware, and New York took part in the Annapolis Convention, which sought to improve the Articles of Confederation. The five states empowered their representatives to discuss commercial problems, and New Jersey suggested that they consider other important matters as well. Spurred by New Jersey's willingness to consider broad changes and recognizing that such alterations could be made only through the joint efforts of all 13 states, the Annapolis conferees declined independent action and called for a convention "to render the constitution of the Federal Government adequate to the exigencies of the Union."

New Jersey appointed six delegates to the Constitutional Convention, which opened in Philadelphia in May 1787. David Brearley, 41 years old, was the chief justice of the state. William C. Houston was a lawyer and had been a professor of mathematics at Princeton. William Paterson had been a member of the Continental Congress and attorney general of the state for 11 years. William Livingston was the governor of New Jersey, a post he held until his death in 1790. Captain Jonathan Dayton, who had served with distinction in the American Revolution, was a member of the state legislature and at 26 was one of the youngest delegates. Abraham Clark, the sixth representative, never attended the Philadelphia sessions.

On May 29 Governor Edmund Randolph of Virginia presented a series of resolutions designed to become the basis for any new constitution. This Virginia Plan was strongly nationalist, and its critical provision called for a bicameral legislature with each state represented in both houses in proportion to its contribution of taxes to the national government or to the number of its free inhabitants. The smaller states objected vehemently to the Virginia proposals, and New Jersey offered an alternative solution to the convention.

Speaking on behalf of the New Jersey delegation, on June 15 Paterson laid before the delegates at Philadelphia the New Jersey Plan for a revitalized union. The plan offered Congress additional powers to raise revenue by import duties, stamp taxes, postal charges, and enforceable requisitions upon the states. Congress would also gain the authority to regulate trade and commerce, and its acts and treaties would become the supreme law of the land. The plan also provided for a vetoless executive branch, composed of several individuals and elected by Congress. Congress would be able to appoint a supreme tribunal with original jurisdiction in cases of impeachment and appellate jurisdiction from the states in maritime disputes, cases involving foreigners or treaties, and acts for the regulation of trade or the collection of federal revenue. The nine resolutions contained in New Jersey's proposal embodied important amendments to the Articles of Confederation, but made no provision for changing the unicameral structure of Congress or its equal (as opposed to proportional) representation for each state.

Compromise ultimately produced a solution acceptable to supporters of both the Virginia and New Jersey plans. On June 11 Roger Sherman of Connecticut suggested a two-house national legislature with representation proportional to population in the lower house but with each state having an equal vote in the upper chamber. On July 12 the convention agreed that each state's representation in the lower house should be based on the total of its white population and three-fifths of its black population. On July 16 the delegates also agreed that each state would have an equal vote in the Senate. Having solved the critical question of equal versus proportional representation in the national legislature, the Constitutional Convention was able to conclude its work by September 17.

By a unanimous vote on November 1, the New Jersey legislature called for the election of a state convention to evaluate the Constitution. Late in November those citizens qualified to vote in assembly elections selected 39 men, three from each county, to attend the ratifying caucus. The delegates assembled in Trenton on December 11 and remained in session for one week. After discussing the document section by section, on December 18 the delegates voted to adopt the new frame of government and affixed their signatures to two copies of it, one sent to Congress and the other retained by New Jersey. Among the 13 original colonies, the order of statehood is usually calculated on the basis of the date of ratification of the Constitution. Thus, New Jersey appears as the third state in tabulations that place the 50 states in order.

Lyman Abbott's Birthday

Lyman Abbott, the American clergyman, editor, and author who became one of the best known religious leaders of his time, was born in Roxbury, Massachusetts, on December 18, 1835. He was the son of Jacob Abbott, a teacher and author of 180 books for boys, including 28 volumes in the then well-known Rollo series. The family moved to Maine when Lyman Abbott was about three years old.

After studying law at New York University, Abbott graduated in 1853 and practiced for two or three years. In New York he was greatly influenced by the famous Congregational preacher Henry Ward Beecher, pastor of Brooklyn's Plymouth Church, who was also an author and public speaker.

Shortly after Abbott's marriage to Abby Frances Hamlin in 1855, he decided to abandon law for the ministry and began a course of private study to that end. Ordained in 1860 by a Congregational council in Maine, Abbott became pastor of a church in Terre Haute, Indiana, from 1860 to 1865. In 1865 he returned east to take up the pastorate of a Congregational church in New York City. After the Civil War, Abbott actively participated in reconstruction work through a group of clergymen and lay people interested in providing aid to the freed blacks in the South.

From the beginning of his clerical life, Abbott supplemented his ministerial income with literary and editorial work. In 1876 he joined *The Christian Union*, sharing editorial duties with Henry Ward Beecher, who had been editor of the weekly since 1870. Since Beecher was then involved with many outside interests, Abbott more or less took over the editing of the magazine within a short time. In 1893 he changed its name to *The Outlook*. Under his editorial guidance, the publication became the leading religious weekly in the country during a period when religious publications were among the most influential media in the United States. For Abbott, *The Outlook* was an effective channel for his views on religion, politics, social problems, and scientific progress, and it remained so for the rest of his life.

Beecher died in 1887. Abbott succeeded him in 1888 as pastor of the Brooklyn Plymouth Church, which continued to prosper under his leadership. Abbott, in his sixties, resigned the pastorate in 1899 and spent the remainder of his life directing *The Outlook* and lecturing throughout the country. In addition, he wrote nearly 40 books, which greatly influenced religious thought in the United States. In such works as *The Theology of an Evolutionist* (1897), he assumed the role of mediator between rigid religious views and the current scientific developments that seemed to threaten those views. His other books include *Dictionary of Religious Knowledge* (1902), *Christianity and Social Problems* (1897), *The Rights of Man* (1901), *Industrial Problems* (1905), *The Spirit of Democracy* (1910), *America in the Making* (1911), and *Reminiscences* (1915, revised 1923). Abbott's devotional books include *The Other Room* (1903) and *The*

Great Companion (1904). He also wrote *What Christianity Means to Me* (1921) and a biography of the man who had been his inspiration to enter the ministry and whose career was paralleled by his own in so many ways: *Henry Ward Beecher* (1903).

Abbott was interested in the growing industrialism of his times. He was a leader in the Social Gospel movement and one of the most influential members of the liberal wing of Protestant churches. He died in New York City on October 22, 1922, a few months short of his 87th birthday.

Thirteenth Amendment Proclaimed Ratified

The Emancipation Proclamation, issued by President Abraham Lincoln pursuant to his authority as commander in chief of the Union armed forces on January 1, 1863, proclaimed as free the slaves in those states and parts of states that were then in rebellion in the Civil War. However, slavery still existed in some parts of the Union as the Civil War drew to a close. There was still slavery in some of the border states that had never seceded and in those parts of the South that had been under Union control when Lincoln issued his proclamation.

To extend the abolition of slavery to these areas and secure full congressional sanction for the provisions of his proclamation, Lincoln urged that Congress propose an amendment to the United States Constitution that would end slavery in all parts of the nation. After congressional passage on January 31, 1865, Lincoln put his signature to the measure on February 1 and it was sent to the states for the required three-fourths ratification. This ratification was officially proclaimed by Secretary of State William H. Seward on December 18, 1865.

The text of the 13th Amendment to the Constitution is as follows:

SECTION 1. Neither slavery nor involuntary servitude, except as a punishment for crime whereof the party shall have been duly convicted, shall exist within the United States, or any place subject to their jurisdiction.

SECTION 2. Congress shall have power to enforce this article by appropriate legislation.

December 19

American Revolution: George Washington Camps at Valley Forge

British military plans for 1777 called for a three-pronged advance to converge near Albany, New York, to crush the American rebel army, isolate New England, and quickly terminate the American Revolution. General John Burgoyne was to push down from Canada through Lake Champlain, General Barry St. Leger was to come from Oswego through the Mohawk Valley, and General William Howe was to drive north up the Hudson River from New York City. The colonists thwarted St. Leger's efforts and captured Burgoyne's entire force at the battle of Saratoga (see October 17). Howe never reached the intended rendezvous, as he directed his attention instead to an assault on Philadelphia, Pennsylvania, the seat of the Continental Congress.

The undertaking took longer than Howe had expected. Embarking from New York City with 15,000 troops on July 23, he did not land at Head of Elk (near what is now Elkton, Maryland) until August 25. It was not until September 11 that he defeated General George Washington and his troops, who were blocking the road to Philadelphia at Brandywine Creek. Furthermore, it was not until September 26 that the British captured the city and forced the Continental Congress to flee to York, Pennsylvania. Washington's counterattack at Germantown on October 4 was a failure, and after several more minor engagements he withdrew his forces to their winter quarters at Valley Forge, Pennsylvania.

On December 19 the Americans arrived at their inhospitable campsite, a spot selected by "a speculator, a traitor, or a council of ignoramuses" according to Major General Johann Kalb, a Bavarian volunteer. Militarily, however, the location was desirable since it was close to water and surrounded by a forest which could provide fuel and materials for shelter. Even more important, Valley Forge lay between the Continental Congress at York and the hostile British forces 20 miles away in Philadelphia.

Valley Forge, in American historical lore, has become synonymous with sacrificial suffering. The winter itself was mild, but the men suffered from disease, hunger, and exposure, which together claimed the lives of more than a quarter of Washington's force—3,000 out of 11,000 men.

The common soldiers lived in makeshift quarters until they completed building huts in mid-January 1778. Many could not help in the construction because their lack of clothing made them unfit for winter duty. On December 23 Washington complained to Congress that 2,898 of his troops were "bare foot and otherwise naked." "The want of clothing," Washington stated, "added to the rigor of the season, has occasioned [the men] to suffer such hardships as will not be credited but by those who have been spectators." General Anthony Wayne complained that "the whole army is sick and crawling with vermin." Frostbite naturally preyed upon the ill-clad soldiers, and the Marquis de Lafayette noted that amputations were frequent.

Three times during the winter provisions gave out, and during one week in March 1778 each soldier received only three ounces of meat and three pounds of flour. Over 1,500 horses died of starvation during the crisis. Foraging expeditions by the Americans, as well as by the British in Philadelphia, laid bare the neighboring countryside. Washington was reluctant to alienate the inhabitants by commandeering supplies, but occasionally a farmer was forced to hand over his seed grain at the point of a bayonet.

Greed and bureaucratic inefficiency were at the root of the suffering at Valley Forge. While the soldiers starved, Pennsylvania farmers delivered their grain to Philadelphia, where they could obtain cash payments from the British. Private contractors profited by using government wagons to ship iron and flour out of Pennsylvania, while pork earmarked for Washington's men rotted in New Jersey for lack of transportation.

Congress, alarmed by the situation, revamped the military supply system during the winter. Joseph Wadsworth became commissary general and for the remainder of the war oversaw the procurement of provisions. Nathanael Greene, one of Washington's subordinates, took over the office of quartermaster general from Thomas Mifflin. Greene performed so well that Washington's men fared much better in the next winter quarters at Morristown, New Jersey, even though the weather was more severe than that at Valley Forge.

Despite their hardships, the American soldiers remained steadfast. Occasionally the troops chanted ominously "no pay, no clothes, no provisions, no rum" but desertion did not become a major problem. Indeed, it decreased when the shortages were most grave. History has confirmed the accolade bestowed by John Laurens, Washington's volunteer aide-de-camp, who spoke of "those dear, ragged Continentals whose patience will be the admiration of future ages."

An army stronger in ability as well as in spirit developed at Valley Forge. Major General Friedrich Wilhelm Ludolf Gerhard Augustin von Steuben, a Prussian volunteer, used the long winter hours to train the soldiers in the latest formations and tactics. The soldiers learned the lessons well and repeatedly put them to good use when they resumed their campaigns in the spring of 1778. Today, Valley Forge is a national historic landmark and a major tourist attraction, visited by hundreds of thousands of people every year.

December 20

The Louisiana Purchase

Thomas Jefferson's most far-sighted act as president may well have been the Louisiana Purchase of 1803, which added approximately 828,000 square miles of land between the Mississippi River and the Rocky Mountains to the United States. This acquisition doubled the size of the young nation and guaranteed American control of the Mississippi River and the port of New Orleans. The government ultimately carved all or parts of 13 states from the region: Arkansas, Colorado, Iowa, Kansas, Louisiana, Minnesota, Missouri, Montana, Nebraska, North Dakota, Oklahoma, South Dakota, and Wyoming.

France was the original European owner of Louisiana. In 1682 René-Robert Cavelier de La Salle completed his exploration of the Mississippi River and claimed for France "possession of that river, of all the rivers that enter into it, and all the country watered by them." He then named the region Louisiana in honor of King Louis XIV. The French won general recognition of their title to the area from their chief colonial rivals, the British, by the Treaty of Utrecht of 1713 which ended the War of the Spanish Succession.

La Salle's original claim included lands west of the Mississippi River to the Rocky Mountains and east into what are now Kentucky, Tennessee, and West Virginia. Worn down by the continuing colonial wars of the 18th century, the French government proved unable to retain control of this vast area. By the Treaty of Fontainebleau of November 3, 1762, France compensated Spain for assisting in the unsuccessful French and Indian War (1754–1763) against the British by ceding all of Louisiana west of the Mississippi to Spain as well as the Isle of Orleans east of the river. By the Treaty of Paris of February 10, 1763, which ended the French and Indian War, the British received the remainder of Louisiana east of the river except for the city of New Orleans.

France had not permanently lost interest in the American continent, and under Napoléon Bonaparte it sought to regain some of its former colonies. By the secret Treaty of San Ildefonso in 1800, Spain returned the Louisiana territory west of the Mississippi to France, and the Treaty of Madrid in 1801, confirmed the retrocession. Napoléon probably envisioned the region, which remained temporarily under Spanish administration, as a source of food and supplies for the sugar plantations that he hoped to foster in the West Indies, notably on the French-colonized Caribbean island of Santo Domingo (later Hispaniola, now divided between Haiti and the Dominican Republic).

Rumors of France's resumption of title to Louisiana gravely upset American westerners, whose prosperity depended on free navigation of the Mississippi. Spain was a weak power, and by Pinckney's Treaty of 1795 had permitted United States citizens to sail the river freely and to use New Orleans as a port. France appeared to be a greater threat, and Napoléon aggravated American fears by dispatching 20,000 troops to the Caribbean under General Charles Leclerc to suppress a slave rebellion on Santo Domingo.

President Jefferson recognized that the United States must protect its interests, and in April 1802 he instructed Robert Livingston, the American minister to France, to attempt to buy New Orleans and the Floridas from Napoléon. In October 1802 news that the still-present Spanish intendant had suddenly revoked certain American rights at New Orleans prompted the president to send James Monroe to Paris as minister plenipotentiary with the authority to offer Napoléon $10 million for New Orleans and the Floridas. Monroe's instructions directed him to undertake negotiations to improve Anglo-American relations if the French proved uncooperative.

Circumstances combined to make Monroe's mission extraordinarily successful. In the Caribbean, yellow fever and the insurgents led by Haitian liberator Toussaint L'Ouverture had virtually wiped out Leclerc's expeditionary force. Napoléon, preparing for military action in Europe, could spare no more troops for the New World. In order to raise money and to deprive the British of a valuable but defenseless possession, he decided to offer the whole of Louisiana to the United States for a pittance.

On April 11, 1803, Charles-Maurice de Talleyrand-Périgord, the French foreign minister, presented Napoléon's offer to Livingston. Livingston decided to wait for Monroe, who arrived the following day, before committing his government. Together, they decided that, although their instructions did not cover such an unexpected development, they dared not allow the opportunity to slip away. They quickly entered into negotiations with the French, and on May 2 signed a treaty (antedated April 30) by which the United States was to pay $15 million for the entire Louisiana territory.

Jefferson thought that the government lacked the power under the Constitution to add new territory to the nation, but he feared that the adoption of an enabling amendment would consume too much time and endanger the transaction. Finally he decided that since "the good sense of the country" wanted Louisiana, "the less we say about constitutional difficulties the better."

On October 20 the United States Senate ratified the treaty and on December 20, 1803, the United States took formal possession of Louisiana. Never, as the historian Henry Adams wrote years later, "did the United States government get so much for so little."

The exploration of the land acquired in the Louisiana Purchase began with the Meriwether Lewis and William Clark expedition of 1804–1806. Having received congressional approval early in 1803 for a venture designed to establish friendly relations with the native tribes and to encourage commerce, President Jefferson chose Lewis and Clark to lead the trailblazing scientific party. On August 31 Lewis and Clark began their descent of the Ohio River, and spent the winter in quarters that they set up near St. Louis.

With their more than 40 companions, Lewis and Clark resumed their trek on May 14, 1804, beginning the expedition with their ascent of the Missouri River, which stretched across much of the Louisiana territory. They spent the winter of 1804–1805 in what is now North Dakota. In the spring of 1805 the explorers set out to cross the Rocky Mountains. On November 7, 1805, after seven harrowing months, they came within sight of the Pacific Ocean. The expedition returned to St. Louis on September 23, 1806, having paved the way for the settlement of the west.

American Poet Laureate Established

On December 20, 1985, President Ronald Reagan signed Public Law 99-194, which officially established the position and title of American Poet Laureate. The poet so honored performs light duties for the Library of Congress, such as appearing at designated national ceremonies or giving an occasional reading. The position is an extremely prestigious one, reserved for only the most accomplished poets.

The American laureateship has its roots in the chair of poetry established at the Library of Congress by virtue of an endowment from Archer M. Huntington in 1936. Some of the most prominent American poets in the 20th century have held this chair:

Joseph Auslander (1937–1941)
Allen Tate (1943–1944)
Robert Penn Warren (1944–1945)
Louise Bogan (1945–1946)
Karl Shapiro (1946–1947)
Robert Lowell (1947–1948)
Leonie Adams (1948–1949)
Elizabeth Bishop (1949-1950)
Conrad Aiken (1950–1952)
William Carlos Williams (chosen in 1952
  but did not serve)
Randall Jarrell (1956–1958)
Robert Frost (1958–1959)
Richard Eberhart (1959–1961)
Louis Untermeyer (1961–1963)
Howard Nemerov (1963–1964)
Reed Whittemore (1964–1965)
Stephen Spender (1965–1966)
James Dickey (1966–1968)
William Jay Smith (1968–1970)
William Stafford (1970–1971)
Josephine Jacobsen (1971–1973)
Daniel Hoffman (1973–1974)
Stanley Kunitz (1974–1976)
Robert Hayden (1976–1978)
William Meredith (1978–1980)
Maxine Kumin (1981–1982)
Anthony Hecht (1982–1984)
Robert Fitzgerald (1984–1985, but suf-
  fered from health problems)
Reed Whittemore (1984–1985; Interim
  Consultant in Poetry)
Gwendolyn Brooks (1985–1986)

The first official poet laureate was Robert Penn Warren, who was appointed on February 26, 1986, and served until 1987. Warren's successors were:

Richard Wilbur (1987–1988)
Howard Nemerov (1988–1990)
Mark Strand (1990–1991)
Joseph Brodsky (1991–1992)
Mona Van Duyn (1992–1993)
Rita Dove (1993–1995)
Robert Hass (1995–1997)
Robert Pinsky (1997–1999)

December 21

Winter Begins

In the United States and the north temperate zones generally, winter begins on or about December 21 or 22. The precise moment at which the Sun reaches the winter solstice, formally signaling the change of seasons, varies slightly every year as a result of the many oscillations that the Earth undergoes during its annual elliptical jour-

ney around the Sun and its daily rotation on its axis.

Like the other three seasons, winter has an exact astronomical beginning. The ecliptic, namely the plane in which the Sun seems to revolve around the Earth and in which the Earth actually revolves around the Sun, is divided into four equal 90-degree sections. Each has a specific starting point. While spring and autumn commence at the vernal and autumnal equinoxes respectively, winter and summer begin at their respective solstices. The winter solstice (Latin *solstitium* meaning "solstice," from *sol* meaning "Sun" and *sistere* meaning "to stand still") is situated midway between the autumnal equinox and the vernal equinox. The amount of time the Sun requires to traverse the 90 degree section from the winter solstice to the vernal equinox is known as the season of winter.

Winter is also said to begin when the Sun enters the tenth sign of the zodiac, namely Capricorn or "the Goat" (see Appendix D: The Zodiac). This assertion is actually anachronistic. At the time of Hipparchus, the second century B.C. Greek astronomer who laid the basis of the zodiacal system, the winter solstice began at Capricorn. However, precession, as the retrograde motion of the equinoctial points on the ecliptic is called, has caused each of the 12 constellations of the zodiac to move 30 degrees backwards during the course of the past 2,000 years. The winter solstice is now located in the constellation Sagittarius or "the Archer." Only at the completion of a 25,800-year cycle will it once again be situated in Capricorn.

In the Northern Hemisphere the Sun shines at its weakest during the time of the winter solstice because it then attains its southernmost position in the skies. At its maximum southern declination (a term used by astronomers to correspond with terrestrial latitude), the Sun extends its rays across and beyond the Earth's South Pole as far as minus 23 degrees 27 minutes. Similarly, its rays fall 23 degrees 27 minutes short of the North Pole, striking only the near side of the Arctic Circle. At the same time, the Sun has a longitude of 270 degrees. Thereafter for a few days the Sun seemingly "stands still," so much so that the times of sunrise and sunset differ imperceptibly and the days appear to be of equal length. During the rest of winter, the Sun's southern declination continuously diminishes until the vernal equinox, at which time the Sun reaches both a longitude of 0 degrees and a declination of 0 degrees, thereby completing the yearly cycle of the seasons.

The difference in the seasons, especially the variation in weather, is due to the 23-and-a-half-degree tilt of the Earth's axis and to its elliptical revolution around the Sun. Around December 21 and 22, the North Pole is inclined directly away from the Sun. Since the Sun's rays are slanted, the Earth's atmosphere and surface are exposed to a low amount of daily solar radiation. Consequently, temperatures are cold, even freezing. The most extreme cold wave generally occurs around the beginning of February. In the Southern Hemisphere, as the result of the reverse movement of the South Pole, the seasons are also reversed. Astronomical winter begins around June 21 and ends around September 21.

Winter has a distinct character in the Northern Hemisphere above the Tropic of Cancer. As the season of dormancy, darkness, and cold, it greatly impressed the ancients. They regarded this period of the year as a time of crisis during which the deities of the upper world struggled against the spirits of chaos and evil to assure the return of light, warmth, and fertility. Many pre-Christian seasonal traditions marked the winter solstice, as people of various cultures observed what they deemed to be a significant religious occasion. Huge bonfires were an integral part of elaborate solar rites. As the days slowly lengthened and gave promise of eventual spring, a less solemn and more festive mood ensued. Roman worshippers of the Persian Sun god Mithras celebrated December 25 as the *dies solis invicti nati*, the "birthday of the invincible Sun." The date of Christmas was probably fixed arbitrarily for this same day because it coincided with and offered competition to these alternative festivities (see December 25).

The winter solstice played an important role not only in mythology and religion, but also in art and literature. For example, early basilicas and medieval cathedrals were frequently adorned with symbolic representations of the seasons and of the individual months. Some of the carved stone scenes depicting the calendar year show winter as a season of contrasts between the laborious preparations for the rough weather ahead and the Christmas revelries.

Forefathers' Day

Plymouth Rock has always symbolized America's historic role as a refuge for persecuted peoples, and as such it is a particularly cherished landmark. There, on December 21, 1620, a scouting party sent out from the *Mayflower* went ashore and explored the area of eastern Massachusetts where the second English colony in North America would be established. The Pilgrims who settled Plymouth were seeking freedom, not fortune. Disenchanted with the established Anglican Church of their homeland, they hoped to find a place in the New World in which they could build a model community in accord with their beliefs. Forefathers' Day, observed annually on December 21 in many parts of New England, commemorates their courageous quest.

Pilgrim aptly describes the band that sailed aboard the *Mayflower* seeking a new home, but it does not indicate the group's theological principles. Specifically, they were Separatist Congregationalists. Like the Puritans who settled Massachusetts Bay in 1630, the Pilgrims were Protestants who believed that the authority of the church rested with the people gathered in each parish or congregation, and they were similarly disturbed by the rites and the hierarchical government of the Anglican Church. However, the Puritans and Pilgrims disagreed on the means to bring about church reform. The former thought that the Church of England was a basically good institution from which the vestiges of Roman Catholicism might be purged. The latter group considered it an ungodly organization from which they must separate themselves to ensure their continued moral integrity.

The Pilgrim congregation originally came together at Scrooby Manor in Nottinghamshire, England, shortly before 1606. Most of the 50 or 60 Scrooby worshipers were tenant farmers. They had the advantage of outstanding leaders. William Brewster was bailiff of the manor and had attended Cambridge University. John Robinson, the pastor of the congregation, had earned two degrees from the same institution and was a brilliant preacher.

In 1606 neighbors hostile to the religious radicalism of the Scrooby Church reported its doctrinal and procedural irregularities to the Anglican authorities. The royal officials reacted vehemently to this news, and they arrested and fined some members of the congregation in an effort to force them to conform to the practices of the Church of England. However, this harassment did not lead the group at Scrooby to abandon its beliefs. Instead the congregation decided to leave England and go to Amsterdam, which had already received groups of Separatists. The English ecclesiastical authorities at first resisted the plan, but in 1607 their opposition was overcome and Robinson led the members of his flock to their Dutch refuge.

Although Amsterdam offered the Pilgrims work and religious freedom, the English Separatists were displeased by the multiplicity of sects in that tolerant city. Robinson and the other leaders became particularly disturbed when they realized that some of the earlier Separatist immigrants to Holland had begun to accept the tenets of the Dutch Protestant Church. To keep their fellow believers free from the perceived taint of heresy, they decided that the congregation must move again. In 1609 the Pilgrims set out for Leiden, a city with less religious controversy and diversity.

The entire Pilgrim congregation remained in Leiden for 11 years, but some of its members were discontented. One young leader, William Bradford, cited several reasons for their unhappiness in his later *History of Plimoth Plantation*. They feared becoming involved if war erupted between Holland and Spain, among other reasons. Some members of the congregation were so dissatisfied that by 1617 they were ready to undertake another move. Since America offered the best opportunity for the Separatist band to live according to its beliefs, Deacon John Carver and Robert Cushman returned to England in 1617 to obtain permission and financial support for a settlement in the New World.

In 1620, after three years of negotiations, arrangements for the new colony were completed. However, not all of Robinson's congregation wanted to settle in the New World. The majority decided to remain in Leiden, and the pastor himself agreed to stay with them, while over thirty members were eager to go to America. Under the leadership of Bradford and Brewster they journeyed from Delftshaven to England aboard the vessel *Speedwell* in July 1620.

In England the *Mayflower*, bearing roughly 65 people, most of whom did not share either Puritan or Separatist beliefs, joined the expedition. The *Mayflower* and the *Speedwell* left Southampton for the New World in August 1620, but the *Speedwell* proved to be unseaworthy. It was decided that the *Mayflower* would sail alone, bearing all of the people who still wished to make the trip. The *Mayflower* departed from Plymouth (where the last unsuccessful repairs on the *Speedwell* had been attempted) on September 16, 1620.

On November 19, after 64 days at sea, the Pilgrims reached the coast of Massachusetts. The passengers of the *Mayflower* had originally intended to settle on land controlled by the Virginia Company (sometimes called the London Company), from which they held a charter. However, storms, faulty navigation, sheer joy at the sight of land, and doubt about the legality of their patent caused a change in their plans. Instead of proceeding south to the territory under the jurisdiction of the Virginia Company, they decided to remain in Massachusetts. On November 21 they anchored at what is now Provincetown on the tip of Cape Cod.

Since Massachusetts lay north of the territorial limits of the Pilgrim's charter, their leaders technically had no powers of government in the area. Furthermore, the Pilgrims knew that they would have no chance to establish their envisioned community without at least recognition of their de facto authority by everyone aboard the *Mayflower* (including those who did not share their religious convictions). Consequently, before anyone could disembark, they drew up a document for the self-government of the colony they were about to found. By its terms the signatories constituted themselves as a body politic and promised submission to whatever just and equal laws should thenceforth be enacted by common consent for the good of all. The agreement, signed on November 21 by 41 male passengers, was the famous Mayflower Compact (see Appendix).

The Pilgrim leaders then turned their attention to finding a suitable place for their settlement. For almost a month, parties from the *Mayflower* explored Cape Cod without success. Then, on December 21 some 17 Pilgrim scouts went ashore at Plymouth. Tradition holds that they first stepped on Plymouth Rock. This may be true, since the size, shape, and probable location of the boulder would have facilitated their landing. In any case they were impressed with the harbor and the region adjoining it.

After the scouting party returned to the *Mayflower* and disclosed its favorable findings, three more explorations were undertaken at Plymouth. These expeditions confirmed the original report, and on December 30 the Pilgrims voted to settle there. The *Mayflower*, carrying most of the colonists, then sailed southwest from Provincetown. On January 5, 1621, it arrived in Plymouth Harbor.

Life in Plymouth was not easy. Disease and exposure to the cold claimed the lives of almost half of the settlers during their first winter in Massachusetts. Nevertheless, those who survived remained steadfast in their hope of establishing a colony where they would be free to worship according to their beliefs. By the spring of 1621 the first buildings were completed and the first crops were planted.

Plymouth was never a particularly prosperous colony, and in 1690 it was absorbed by its more powerful neighbor, the Massachusetts Bay Colony which Puritans under John Winthrop had established to the northwest. Yet, the ideals and the devotion of the Pilgrims to their beliefs have inspired many Americans. To honor the memory of the Plymouth settlers, a number of New England jurisdictions observe Forefathers' Day annually on December 21.

December 22

James Oglethorpe's Birthday

The American continents attracted Europeans in the 16th, 17th, and 18th centuries for a variety of reasons. Some sought religious freedom, some wanted adventure, and some were in search of an easy fortune. However, none of these motives brought James Oglethorpe, the founder of Georgia, to the New World. Oglethorpe came to America imbued with the altruistic desire to establish a colony in which the downtrodden and oppressed debtors of England might prosper and become useful and productive citizens.

James Edward Oglethorpe, the son of Sir Theophilus and Lady Eleanor Wall Oglethorpe, was born on December 22, 1696, in London, England. The future philanthropist was educated at Eton and attended Corpus Christi College of Oxford University before abandoning his formal education in 1715 to seek adventure on the European continent. Oglethorpe spent some time in Paris during 1716, served as aide-de-camp to Prince Eugene of Savoy during his campaign against the Turks in 1717, and spent 1718–1719 in Saint-Germain, France, and Urbino, Italy. In 1719 he returned to England, where he took up residence at the family's estate at Godalming, Surrey.

Continuing a tradition of parliamentary service established by his father and two older brothers, Oglethorpe won election to the House of Commons in 1722, serving as a member of Parliament for 32 years. During that time he consistently supported programs that strengthened the British Empire and became increasingly involved with the problem of penal reform, a need for which he first became aware of when a friend was placed in debtors' prison and died there of smallpox amid appalling conditions.

Service as chairman of a parliamentary committee investigating prison conditions in England further convinced Oglethorpe of the deplorable state of that nation's penal system. The large number of persons who were in jail because of their inability to pay small debts particularly bothered him, and the reports of his committee in 1729 and 1730 resulted in limited penal reform and in the release of several thousand debtors from confinement. However, Oglethorpe realized that setting these debtors free was not enough. He believed that the impoverished needed an opportunity to begin a new life. Thus, as a means of bettering the condition of the oppressed, he conceived of the bold plan of establishing a new colony in America as a haven for debtors.

Oglethorpe's proposal coincided with the designs of the British government. During the first decades of the 18th century the Spanish, who controlled Florida, had been a continuing threat to the safety of Britain's southern colonies. To protect these settlements a proposal had been made as early as 1717 to create a new colony that would act as a buffer between South Carolina and Florida. Oglethorpe's desire to establish a new settlement in America gave the government a chance to make this plan a reality.

A parliamentary charter in June 1732 named Oglethorpe and 19 other associates as "Trustees for establishing the colony of Georgia in America." According to the provisions of this document, the trustees were given control of all the area between the Savannah and the Altamaha Rivers extending westward from the sources of these rivers to the Pacific Ocean. Unlike previous British colonial charters, Georgia's charter did not allow the trustees to own land in the new colony or in any other way profit from the venture. Instead they were to hold the colony as a trust for 21 years for the purpose of securing its future and then at the end of that period return control of Georgia to the crown.

An intensive campaign in the summer and fall of 1732 to raise money for the new colony proved so successful that by November 1732 the first settlers were able to embark on what has been called "the greatest social and philanthropic experiment of the age." Oglethorpe himself led the first band of about 35 families across the Atlantic. Landing at Charleston, South Carolina, on January 13, 1733, the Georgia colonists then proceeded southward and on February 12 arrived at the site of Savannah.

Under Oglethorpe's leadership the Georgia colonists maintained friendly relations with the Native Americans. Even before the building of Savannah was completed, Oglethorpe sought out the leaders of the Creek people who inhabited the region. The Englishman and the chiefs came together in Savannah in May 1733 and at this meeting made an agreement by which the Creek sold a portion of their lands to the newcomers and promised to cease dealing with the Spanish. In return, Oglethorpe entered into certain joint trade regulations with the Creek.

Oglethorpe administered the colony for most of its first two years. During that time the population of Georgia grew rapidly, and not merely because of the influx of English debtors. Neither Oglethorpe nor any of the other trustees wished to restrict immigration to the colony. Thus, in the first years of its existence Georgia attracted considerable numbers of non-English dissidents. Among them were Lutherans from Austria and Moravians from Germany, as well as a group of Scottish Highland Presbyterians.

Oglethorpe returned to England late in 1734 to secure additional funds, but he revisited Georgia from 1735 to 1736 and again from 1738 to 1743. In keeping with the colony's function as a buffer against Spanish attack, he built fortifications in 1736 on St. Simons Island at the mouth of the Altamaha River. He also instituted a program of military training. In addition, Oglethorpe made some attempts at city planning, a fact that accounts for the profusion of green parks, open spaces, and carefully laid-out squares in Savannah.

During much of his last stay in Georgia, Oglethorpe was preoccupied with the War of Jenkins' Ear between Great Britain and Spain. Among other things, he led an unsuccessful expedition against Spanish-controlled Florida in 1740. At the battle of Bloody Marsh in 1742 he crushed the Spanish counterattack against Georgia. The latter defeat ended Spanish attempts to control Georgia and ensured the colony's survival.

Georgia successfully served as a buffer between Britain's southern colonies and Spanish Florida, but the colony never fulfilled its trustees' dream that it would become a place in which disadvantaged persons might enjoy useful and productive lives. Much of this failure was caused by the trustees. They limited the amount of land each settler might hold to 50 acres and overlooked the fact that such an area of the Georgia pine barrens was inadequate to support a family. They nobly banned slavery and made Georgia incapable of competing with neighboring slaveholding colonies. They encouraged the production of such items as silk, failing to comprehend that these were unsuited to the Georgia climate. During the 1740s the trustees were forced to make several important modifications in their original plans, but as a trusteeship Georgia never prospered. In 1752, one year before their charter expired, the trustees returned control of the colony to Britain.

In 1743, as the failure of Georgia under the trusteeship was becoming increasingly apparent, Oglethorpe went back to England. Shortly after his return he faced a court martial, but the charges against him were found to be "frivolous . . . and without foundation." He never returned to Georgia.

In 1745 Oglethorpe gained the rank of major general but was court martialed, yet ultimately acquitted, on charges of inept leadership in a campaign to put down a rebellion in the north in that same year. He was made a lieutenant general in 1746 and was breveted a full general in 1756. He lived the remainder of his life in England, surrounded by such notable friends as Samuel John-son, James Boswell, Oliver Goldsmith, Horace Walpole, and Edmund Burke.

Oglethorpe died at the age of 88 on June 30, 1785. He was buried in Cranham Church, Essex.

December 23

Hanukkah

This is a movable event.

Hanukkah, the Jewish festival also known as the Feast of Dedication and the Festival of Lights, begins on the 25th day of the Hebrew month Kislev (November or December), which fell on December 23 in 1970. The actual observance, as with all Jewish holidays, begins at sundown on the preceding day. The holiday continues for eight days, as does Sukkot, on which the original celebration of Hanukkah was modeled. The observance of Hanukkah was instituted in the year 165 B.C. by Judah the Maccabee at the successful conclusion of his three-year war against the Syrians, culminating in the rededication of the Temple in Jerusalem.

The Temple had been desecrated as part of a program of forced Hellenization undertaken by the Syrian-Greek king Antiochus IV Epiphanes. The efforts of Antiochus to suppress the Jewish religion and to institute pagan worship were resisted by a small group of Jewish nationalists originally led by Mattathias of Modin. After his death, it was led by his eldest son, Judah the Maccabee. Using guerrilla tactics, they defeated Antiochus's large army and regained control of the Temple. After the Temple had been cleansed, the rededication of the altar on the 25th of Kislev was celebrated with sacrifices and songs of praise (*hallel*). The Maccabees decreed that a similar celebration was to take place each year, beginning on the anniversary of the rededication.

After the final destruction of the Temple by the Romans in A.D. 70 and the complete loss of Jewish national independence, the spiritual aspect of this holiday was emphasized. According to a rabbinic tradition, the custom of observing Hanukkah for eight days by kindling one light on the first night and one more each successive night arose from the miracle that was supposed to have occurred at the rededication of the Temple. This story states that when Judah went to rekindle the eternal light that was supposed to burn continuously in the Temple he could only find one small container of consecrated oil that had not been desecrated by the Greeks. This small container of oil, only enough to burn for one day, actually lasted eight days until new oil could be prepared and consecrated.

Today, Jews still observe Hanukkah by lighting one candle on the first night, two on the second, three on the third, and so on until on the last night all eight candles are burning. The candles are placed in a menorah or candelabrum, which contains holders for nine candles. The ninth candle is called the *shammash*, "the servant," and is used to light the other candles. The lighted menorah may be placed in a window so that people outside can see it. The menorah stands as a symbol of freedom, of the Jews' love of liberty, and of their willingness to fight for their freedom of conscience in what was one of the first recorded wars for religious freedom. The Hanukkah lights also symbolize the light of faith, which continues to grow even if only a small group of believers remains.

When the candles are lit each night a special blessing is recited:

Blessed art Thou, O Lord our God, King of the Universe, who hast sanctified us by Thy commandments and commanded us to kindle the Hanukkah light.

Blessed art Thou, O Lord our God, King of the Universe, who performed wondrous deeds for our fathers in ancient days at this season.

Because it is forbidden to do any work by the light of the Hanukkah candles, the time during which the candles burn was traditionally spent singing songs and playing games. Most special Hanukkah games involve the *dreidel*, a four-sided top with a brew letter (*nun, gimel, hay,* and *shin*) on each side. The letters stand for the saying: *Nes gadol haya sham,* "A great miracle happened there." In Israel the last word of the saying is often changed to *po*, so that it reads "A great miracle happened here."

Although Hanukkah is technically only a minor Jewish holiday (except for the brief time when the candles are burning there is no prohibition against working) and although, historically speaking, it is a relatively late holiday for Jews, in modern times it has become important because of the establishment of the nation of Israel. The creation of Israel led to a renewed stress on the national aspects of Hanukkah, the liberation that the Jews won, and the fact that it was a victory of the few over the many and of the weak over the strong.

Among some Jews, Hanukkah has also received more emphasis than it once had because it happens to fall at the same time of year as the Christian observance of Christmas. The proximity to Christmas has tended to bring emphasis on the festive part of Hanukkah, especially the exchanging of gifts. Children traditionally receive Hanukkah *gelt*, or money, and other gifts. Parties are held at which the special holiday *latkes* (potato pancakes) are eaten.

Although Hanukkah is celebrated mainly at home among family and friends, special synagogue services are held as well. These services traditionally include reading from the First and Second Books of the Maccabees, in which the story of the revolt is chronicled. The Torah reading of Numbers 7:1 through 8:4, which describe the dedication offering of the princes of Israel, and the singing of *hallel*, emphasize the spiritual victory of the Maccabees and the importance of religious liberty and the survival of Judaism.

Joseph Smith Jr.'s Birthday

Joseph Smith, Jr., the founder of the Church of Jesus Christ of Latter-Day Saints, unofficially known as the Mormon Church, was born in Sharon, Vermont, on December 23, 1805. He was the fourth child of a farmer, Joseph Smith Sr., and Lucy Mack Smith. He was born into an insecure world and never escaped during his short lifetime of 38 years. By the time he was five years old, his impoverished family had moved three times. They settled in Palmyra, New York, on or about 1816. After living there for a short time, they purchased a tract of land a few miles farther south near Manchester. Owing to the family's financial problems, the boy's education was limited to reading, writing, and elementary arithmetic.

In the early 19th century, western New York was the scene of intense religious revivalism. Evangelists from a number of sects competed for the attention and loyalty of a rough and roving frontier population. This period was one of the most fertile in American history for the emergence of prophets, but only one of them was destined for lasting fame. A century after his death, Joseph Smith had a million followers who held his name sacred and his mission divine.

The road that led Joseph Smith to the career of prophet and church founder began in the spring of 1820, when he was 14. Always a dedicated student of the Bible, he was uncertain about which denomination to join. He later wrote:

In the midst of this war of words and tumult of opinions, I often said to myself: "What is to be done? Who of all these parties are right, or are they all wrong together? If any of them be right, which is it, and how shall I know it?"

Smith searched the scriptures and discovered a passage from the book of James (1:5): "If any of you lack wisdom, let him ask of God, that giveth to all men liberally, and upbraideth not; and it shall be given him." He then retreated to a wooded spot near his home and prayed for divine guidance. According to his account, he beheld a pillar of light over his head, from which appeared two figures floating in the air. One of them called him by name and pointed to the other saying, "This is my Beloved Son. Hear Him." Overcoming his fear, the young boy asked which denomination held the truth and was told to not affiliate himself with any because "they draw near to me with their lips but their hearts are far from me."

On September 21, 1823, Smith had a second vision, in which he said an angel named Moroni appeared to him and revealed the hiding place of some golden tablets containing the history of the ancient people of America and the fullness of the gospel of Jesus. The next day, according to Smith's account, the angel guided him to a hill called Cumorah located between Palmyra and Manchester near the Smith home. There he found the plates but was not allowed to take them away with him. On the anniversary of this date, September 22, for the next three years he visited the hill and looked at the plates again. However, on each occasion he was told that it was too soon to reveal them to the world.

On January 18, Smith married Emma Hale, the daughter of Isaac Hale, a Pennsylvania farmer. On September 22 of that year he visited the hill again and was allowed to take the plates away with him. With them came "two stones in silver bows." These stones, fastened to a breastplate, constituted what were called the Urim and Thummim by which he was to translate the mysterious pictographic characters on the plates. Nearly three years were spent in the task, which was performed by Smith with the assistance of schoolteacher Oliver Cowdery, among others.

The record drawn from the plates accounted for some 1,000 years of pre-Columbian American history. It concerned lost tribes from a colony of Israelite origin, whose members were said to have lived in the Western Hemisphere from roughly 600 B.C. to A.D. 421 and to have been the ancestors of Native American. According to this account, the descendants of the Israelite settlers split into two factions. They were the Lamanites, who turned to idolatry and wickedness, and the God-fearing Nephites, who remained true to the teachings of the Lord. In roughly 400, before their civilization was destroyed by the warfare that eventually raged between the two groups, Mormon (the last illustrious Nephite prophet) compiled the history of his people on the golden plates. In part an abridgment of earlier records, Mormon's account also relates scriptural truths revealed to his people by the risen Jesus Christ who visited them in America. It also included the prophecies and genealogies of ancient Israel. It was this record that Mormon is said to have entrusted to his son Moroni, who "hid it up unto the Lord" in Cumorah Hill.

Smith's translation of this work was published in 1830 under the title *The Book of Mormon*. The first edition of 5,000 copies was financed by Martin Harris, a friend of Smith's who with Cowdery and David Whitmer was also one of three witnesses testifying to the plates' authenticity: "We have seen the plates . . . and we also know that they have been translated by the gift and power of God, for His voice hath declared it unto us." Eight additional witnesses also testified to viewing the golden tablets.

While the translation was in progress, according to Smith's account, John the Baptist appeared to him and Cowdery on May 15, 1829, and made them priests after the order of Aaron. Less than a year later, Smith also reported that Peter, James, and John conferred upon them what is known as the Melchizedek priesthood. Thereafter, Smith and Cowdery began to make converts and establish a church, which was organized as a legal entity by Smith and five associates at Fayette in Seneca County, New York, on April 6, 1830, as the Church of Jesus Christ of Latter-Day Saints. Within a month it numbered 40 members.

Attracting its first converts from the rural areas of New England, the church rapidly gained members but was also confronted by prejudice, hostility, and even threats of violence. Convinced that the church would never flourish in such an environment, Smith asked God for advice, which he said came in the form of a revelation: "That ye might escape the powers of the enemy, and be gathered unto me a righteous people, without spot and blameless, I give unto you the commandment that ye should go to Ohio." In 1831 the planned exodus to Kirtland, Ohio, got under way. As a contemporary observer wrote:

> Kirtland presented the appearance of a modern religious Mecca. Like Eastern pilgrims the converts came full of zeal for their new religion. They came in rude vehicles, on horseback, on foot. They came almost any way, filling on their arrival every house, every shop, every barn to the utmost capacity.

There, the first "Stake of Zion" was established, the first Mormon temple erected, and the organization of the church revamped. Groups of Mormons also settled in Jackson County, Missouri, soon designated as the site for their City of Zion, the New Jerusalem. Bitter political, social, and religious differences, however, forced them to seek refuge in the surrounding counties in late 1833. In Ohio, the Kirtland Safety Society, an unchartered church-supported financial organization, survived only long enough to absorb the life savings of its depositors. It collapsed in the national monetary panic of 1837, causing open insurrection in church ranks. The Ohio Mormons went westward to join their brethren in Missouri. Their clashes with the Gentiles, as the Saints called non-Mormons, convinced Governor Lilburn W. Boggs that "the Mormons must be exterminated or driven from the state." In 1838, despite the onset of winter, he summoned the militia to forcibly evict some 12,000 to 15,000 Mormons, who left behind property valued at roughly $200 million. Smith, having surrendered himself as a "hostage," soon escaped from jail to return triumphantly to the faithful, who awaited him in Illinois.

After their midwinter flight from Missouri in 1838–1839, the Mormons took refuge on the banks of the Mississippi River a few miles above Warsaw, Illinois. Smith and his followers settled in the town of Commerce, which they renamed Nauvoo. Amidst swamps and tangled growth, the Mormons quickly built the biggest city in the state. Converts, especially from England, swelled the population to 20,000. With a temple finished, a university planned, and a generous charter from the Illinois legislature, Smith as mayor of Nauvoo might well have been satisfied. However, in 1844 he announced his candidacy for the presidency of the United States. Events that completely obscured all political ambitions soon overtook him with overwhelming rapidity.

On July 12, 1843, Smith had a revelation in favor of the practice of polygamy. A schism developed in the church, and the practice of polygamy, together with other policies, was denounced by the Nauvoo *Expositor*, a newspaper started by the excommunicated schismatics to expose Smith and defend themselves. The paper was suppressed and the printing plant destroyed at the order of Smith and his municipal council.

Since the surrounding countryside had been roused to fury by these arbitrary acts of suppression, Smith, who was lieutenant general of the Nauvoo Legion, instructed his troops to protect the city and was consequently charged with treason. The owner of the suppressed paper obtained an order in Carthage, the county seat, for the removal of Smith to that town on the charge of riot. Having little confidence that he would be granted a fair trial there, Smith submitted his case to another court, which acquitted him. Upon learning that his appearance in Carthage was nevertheless required, he contemplated fleeing to the Rocky Mountains. The combined protests of his wife and church associates, as well as a guarantee of protection by the governor of Illinois, persuaded Smith and his brother Hyrum to go to Carthage. There they were jailed. On June 27, 1844, a mob with their faces smeared with lampblack stormed the jail and murdered the two Smiths.

Although their leader's death was an unspeakable shock to the more than 50,000 Mormons, the Church of Jesus Christ of Latter-Day Saints did not disintegrate as anticipated, even though a serious dispute over succession followed. One faction, having undertaken a partial reorganization in Beloit, Wisconsin, in 1852, eventually chose Joseph Smith III (the son of the founder) as head of what was termed the Reorganized Church of Jesus Christ of Latter-Day Saints. This faction eventually made its headquarters in Independence, Missouri. Another faction, led by an elder of the church named James Jesse Strang, migrated to Beaver Island, Michigan. Strang was subsequently crowned King of Beaver Island by his followers, thereby ruling the only "monarchy" ever created within the boundaries of the United States. However, the majority of Mormons recognized Brigham Young, the senior member of the church's Council of the Twelve Apostles, as the new leader.

As early as 1842, Smith had apparently predicted that "his people could yet be driven to the Rocky Mountains where they would build a city of their own, free from molestation." The persecution and mob violence encountered by the Mormons at Nauvoo made it increasingly clear to Young and other church leaders that such a move was now desirable. Convinced that the Mormons must seek a new refuge in the Far West, Young began to oversee the exodus early in 1846. As rapidly as companies could be organized, the Mormons took the trail for their unknown land of freedom. After enduring innumerable hardships, the first band of pioneers entered the valley of the Great Salt Lake and laid out a new city there on July 24, 1847. Tens of thousands would follow.

Federal Reserve System Established

The Federal Reserve System, the central bank of the United States comprising 12 regional banks coordinated by a central board of governors in Washington, D.C., was established by the Owen-Glass Federal Reserve Act on December 23, 1913. Creation of the Federal Reserve was prompted by flaws in the then-existing National Banking System. Among these were lack of a central bank, inelasticity of both currency and credit, dispersed financial reserves that were sometimes subject to speculative use, and inadequate check-clearing facilities. As originally established and as modified since, particularly by laws enacted during the banking crisis of the early 1930s, the Federal Reserve System is designed to serve as the fiscal agent and depository of the federal government. It also serves to integrate and supervise the nation's banking system (previously composed of thousands of independent banks functioning in widely divergent ways), to provide an elastic currency whose supply expands and contracts with changing business needs, and by controlling the availability of credit to promote sound economic conditions that foster orderly growth and stability.

Establishment of the Federal Reserve System, which was simply superimposed on the old National Banking System, marked the beginning of a new era in the financial history of the United States. National banks were required to entrust a certain percentage of their assets to the Federal Reserve System. For state banks, joining or not joining the Federal Reserve System was a matter of choice. Many did by meeting certain basic conditions, such as meeting minimum capital requirements, maintaining deposits with the regional federal reserve banks, adhering to certain limitations on loans, and submitting to federal examinations.

After enactment of the Owen-Glass Act on December 23, 1913, the Federal Reserve System actually began to operate under supervision of the seven-member board of governors appointed by the president on the following November 14. The 12 federal reserve bank cities and their district numbers are: (1) Boston, (2) New York, (3) Philadelphia, (4) Cleveland, (5) Richmond, (6) Atlanta, (7) Chicago, (8) St. Louis, (9) Minneapolis, (10) Kansas City, (11) Dallas, and (12) San Francisco.

Today, the federal reserve notes that the system is empowered to issue constitute the nation's paper money. They are issued in denominations of $1, $5, $10, $20, $50, $100, $500, $1,000, $5,000, and $10,000, though the $100 note is the highest denomination printed since 1945 in significant quantities since there is little demand for the larger notes. All of the nation's money is manufactured by the United States Treasury Department, either through the Bureau of the Mint, which produces coins, or through the Bureau of Printing and Engraving, which produces paper money.

December 24

Christmas Eve

Like the celebration of Christmas Day (see December 25), the observance of Christmas Eve, or the Vigil of Christmas, on December 24 is a combination of the religious and the secular. December 24, which is primarily a day of preparation for Christmas, is the culmination of the pre-Christmas

Advent season, namely that period of anticipation and preparation that begins approximately four weeks earlier.

The focal point of the Christmas Eve religious celebration is the service of worship held by Christians of all denominations. Some of the services begin at or just before midnight, in correspondence with the assertion by many that Jesus was born at or near this hour. Choral pieces, such as selections from George Frederick Handel's *Messiah*, are often presented and traditional Christmas carols are often sung. Some of the carols whose titles most typify the gladness of the occasion are "Hark, the Herald Angels Sing," "O Little Town of Bethlehem," "Joy to the World," "O Come, All Ye Faithful," and probably the best-known of all, "Silent Night."

In the United States, Christmas Eve is an occasion for family gatherings, for Christmas lights, decorated Christmas trees, and the hanging of stockings from fireplace mantels by small children who hope they will be filled with gifts by Santa Claus before Christmas morning (see December 6). In American families whose children have grown up, Christmas Eve rather than the more customary Christmas Day is sometimes the time for the exchange of Christmas gifts. These gifts stem from the tale of the Three Wise Men who, according to the biblical account, brought gifts to honor the infant Jesus.

In the early 1860s the cartoonist Thomas Nast drew a depiction of Santa Claus for *Harper's Illustrated Weekly* that has essentially set the tone ever since: a round, bearded figure with a red fur-trimmed suit, wide leather belt, and shiny boots. Nast's caricature was so popular that he continued to depict various scenes with Santa Claus every Christmas for nearly 30 years. As children grow older, however, they begin to have doubts about the legend of Santa Claus. In 1897 one child wrote to the *New York Sun*, asking whether there was a Santa Claus. The answer, written by Francis P. Church and printed as an editorial, has become famous as "Yes, Virginia, there is a Santa Claus." It read:

We take pleasure in answering thus prominently the communication below, expressing at the same time our great gratification that its faithful author is numbered among the friends of the *Sun*:
Dear Editor:
I am eight years old. Some of my little friends say there is no Santa Claus. Papa says "If you see it in the *Sun* it's so." Please tell me the truth, is there a Santa Claus?
Virginia O'Hanlon

Virginia, your little friends are wrong. They have been affected by the skepticism of a skeptical age. They do not believe except they see. They think that nothing can be which is not comprehensible by their little minds. All minds, Virginia, whether they be men's or children's, are little. In this great universe of ours man is a mere insect, an ant, in his intellect as compared with the boundless world about him, as measured by the intelligence capable of grasping the whole of truth and knowledge.

Yes, Virginia, there is a Santa Claus. He exists as certainly as love and generosity and devotion exist, and you know that they abound and give to your life its highest beauty and joy. Alas! how dreary would be the world if there were no Santa Claus! It would be as dreary as if there were no Virginias. There would be no childlike faith then, no poetry, no romance to make tolerable this existence. We should have no enjoyment, except in sense and sight. The eternal light with which childhood fills the world would be extinguished.

Not believe in Santa Claus! You might as well not believe in fairies. You might get your papa to hire men to watch in all the chimneys on Christmas eve to catch Santa Claus, but even if you did not see Santa Claus coming down, what would that prove? Nobody sees Santa Claus, but that is no sign that there is no Santa Claus. The most real things in the world are those that neither children nor men can see. Did you ever see fairies dancing on the lawn? Of course not, but that's no proof that they are not there. Nobody can conceive or imagine all the wonders there are unseen and unseeable in the world.

You tear apart the baby's rattle and see what makes the noise inside, but there is a veil covering the unseen world which not the strongest man, nor even the united strength of all the strongest men that ever lived could tear apart. Only faith, poetry, love, romance, can push aside that curtain and view and picture the supernal beauty and glory beyond. Is it all real? Ah, Virginia, in all this world there is nothing else real and abiding.

No Santa Claus! Thank God! he lives and lives forever. A thousand years from now, Virginia, nay, ten times ten thousand years from now, he will continue to make glad the heart of childhood.

War of 1812: Treaty of Ghent Signed

The Treaty of Ghent, concluding the War of 1812 (see various related essays throughout this book) between the United States and Great Britain, was signed by representatives of the two countries in Ghent, Belgium, on Christmas Eve in 1814. Ironically enough, communications of the era were so slow that the war's last engagement—the battle of New Orleans—was not fought until January 8, 1815, after peace had supposedly been restored (see January 8). Officially, however, the Treaty of Ghent brought the conflict to a close.

December 25

Christmas

For Christians, Christmas, which commemorates the birth of Jesus Christ, is one of the most important religious events in the year. It marks the gift from God described in the New Testament: "For God so loved the world, that he gave his only-begotten Son" (John 3:16). In Christian liturgical calendars only the feast of Easter, commemorating the resurrection of Jesus, is of greater significance. Christmas, however, is certainly the most popularly observed occasion of the church year.

Over the centuries, Christmas has become a holiday as well as a holy day. In its social or festive aspect, December 25 is a curious hybrid of the seasonal traditions of numerous peoples: Persian, Roman, Norse, Gothic, and Anglo-Saxon, among others. At first glance, the staggering array of customs seems to have little to do with the birth in a stable at Bethlehem two thousand years ago. Turkey dinners, glittering trees, greeting cards, elaborate store window displays, bell-ringing Santa Clauses on street corners, Yule logs, gifts, and much more make up the special atmosphere of Christmas.

However, not everyone necessarily regards Christmas as an eagerly anticipated time of joyfulness. For example, Ogden Nash once commented that "roses are things which Christmas is not a bed of" and George Bernard Shaw observed that "Christmas is forced on a reluctant . . . nation by . . . shopkeepers and the press." However, regardless of what critics may say about the commercialization and other excesses of Christmas, December 25 is well entrenched both as a respected social institution and as an occasion for religious gratification.

The story of the birth of Jesus is told in the Gospel According to Luke (2:1–2:16) in this way:

And it came to pass in those days, that there went out a decree from Caesar Augustus, that all the world should be taxed. . . . And all went to be taxed, every one into his own city. And Joseph also went up from Galilee, out of the city of Nazareth, into Judea, unto the city of David, which is called Bethlehem (because he was of the house and lineage of David), to be taxed with Mary his espoused wife, being great with child. And so it was, that, while they were there, the days were accomplished that she should be delivered. And she brought forth her firstborn son, and wrapped him in swaddling clothes, and laid him in a manger; because there was no room for them in the inn.

And there were in the same country shepherds abiding in the field, keeping watch over their flock by night. And lo, the angel of the Lord came upon them, and the glory of the Lord shone round about them; and they were sore afraid. And the angel said unto them, "Fear not: for, behold, I bring you good tidings of great joy, which shall be to all the people. For unto you is born this day in the city of David a Saviour, which is Christ the Lord. And this shall be a sign unto you; Ye shall find the babe wrapped in swaddling clothes, lying in a manger."

And suddenly there was with the angel a multitude of the heavenly host praising God, and saying, "Glory to God in the highest, and on earth peace, good will toward men."

And it came to pass, as the angels were gone away from them into heaven, the shepherds said one to another, "Let us now go even unto Bethlehem, and see this thing which is come to pass, which the Lord hath made known unto us."

And they came with haste, and found Mary and Joseph, and the babe lying in a manger.

Although December 25 is observed as the anniversary of the birth of Jesus, the exact date of his birth is unknown. Partly for this reason, Christmas was not one of the earliest feasts of the Christian Church, since there was at first no general consensus about when the anniversary should be observed or even whether it should be observed at all. In fact, many early Christians were convinced that such a divine being could not have had a natural birth. In any event, the observance of birthdays generally was often condemned as a pagan custom repugnant to Christians. It was in this vein that Or-

igen, the North African church father and philosopher, wrote in 245 that it was sinful even to contemplate observing Jesus' birthday "as though He were a King Pharaoh."

Proposals for marking the birthday of Jesus, and attempts to determine when it was, nonetheless persisted. The Gospels furnished few clues, although some scholars have theorized that if, as Luke relates, the shepherds kept watch outdoors in the fields, the birth must have occurred during a warm season since in winter the sheep were usually penned at night in folds. Early Christian theologians in Egypt reportedly fixed the date as May 20, other scholars are said to have chosen late March or April dates, approximating the time of the Jewish Passover, or January 1 coinciding with the Roman new year under the calendar then in use. In fact, dates in almost every month of the year have been suggested by reputable scholars at one time or another. The most frequently put forth, however, were March 25 (which eventually became known as the Feast of the Annunciation or Lady Day), December 25, and January 6.

What seems clear is that early observances connected with the birth of Jesus took place in scattered places on various dates. January 6 emerged as the date most pertinent to the development of the Christmas observance we know today, and at first it was usually a dual celebration noting both the birth and the baptism of Jesus. Known as the Epiphany, meaning appearance or manifestation, the January 6 observance (often referred to since as "Little Christmas") originated in the Eastern churches around the beginning of the third century. The earliest record of any celebration comes from Clement of Alexandria, the Greek theologian, who around 200 mentioned that members of a certain sect in Egypt had commemorated Jesus' baptism on or about January 6.

It was considerably later, in the western part of the Roman Empire, that a separate celebration of Jesus' birth was introduced by the church at Rome. A Christian chronography or almanac issued in 354 showed the existence of such a commemoration and also indicated that the observance had been instituted some two decades earlier.

Even though controversy still surrounds the actual date of Jesus' birth, the December 25 date has long been accepted by most Christian churches. Modern scholars agree, however, that it was selected arbitrarily for practical purposes rather than as a matter of chronological accuracy. The date happened to coincide with the winter solstice, December 25 by the calendar then in use, and thus also coincided with the numerous pagan celebrations connected with the solstice.

The solstitial festivities, which greatly predated Christianity, cut across several cultures. A number of ancient peoples regarded this time of the year as a period of crisis in which the deities of the upper world fought the spirits of disorder and darkness. The Mesopotamians, for example, performed special rites to support their god Marduk in his grim battle against the powers of chaos. The Greeks offered sacrifices in their temples, believing that their chief god Zeus was renewing the struggle against Kronos and the Titans. As victory approached and the lengthening days gave hope of a distant but sure spring, a festive mood ensued. Also during the solstice season, the Romans celebrated the boisterous feast of the Saturnalia in honor of Saturn, the god of agriculture. The followers of the Persian Sun god Mithras, whose cult in Rome vied with Christianity as the most popular religion for a while, observed December 25 as *dies solis invicti nati*, the "birthday of the invincible Sun." Finally, at approximately the same time of the year, the Jews observed (as they still do) the holiday of Hanukkah, which celebrates the rededication of the Temple in Jerusalem.

It was only logical for early Christian leaders to wish to offer some competition to the winter festivals being celebrated at what had long been deemed a vital religious time and to make that period a Christian feast commemorating the birth of Jesus. Acceptance of the December 25 date initiated at Rome for the observance of Christmas spread gradually throughout western Europe, and more slowly in the East. After the Eastern churches adopted the observance of December 25 as Christmas beginning in the latter part of the fourth century, the Western church took up the observance of the Epiphany on January 6. The feast of Christmas continued to spread slowly. Not until 813 did it extend to Germany on a large scale, and it reached Norway only as late as the tenth century.

For several centuries, December 25 was purely a church anniversary, kept with appropriate religious services and later with banquets and perhaps the exchange of simple presents such as candles and clay dolls. As Christianity advanced in northern Europe, however, the local customs connected with the winter solstice rites began to blend with the Christian observance. Several church fathers condemned this assimilation as potentially dangerous and reiterated Augustine of Hippo's fourth-century warning: "We hold this day holy, not like the pagans because of the birth of the sun, but because of him who made it." The majority of the missionaries who penetrated western Europe after the decline of the Roman Empire, however, preferred to follow the tolerant ruling of Pope Gregory I the Great. The pope instructed Augustine of Canterbury, sent to England in 596, to observe old customs and infuse them with Christian significance to propagate the faith "for from obdurate minds it is impossible to cut off everything at once." On this liberal policy hinged the continuation of numerous traditional customs now connected with Christmas.

The pagan traditions adapted "to the praise of God," included the lighting of candles, Yule logs, and huge bonfires to speed the Sun on its way at the time of its yearly "rebirth." These practices easily tied in with the Christian concept of Christ as the Light of the World. During this solstice season of both dread and festivity, the pagans filled their houses with evergreens, mistletoe, holly, and ivy, believing their greenness in midwinter to be evidence of a special power defying winter's ability to kill.

The use of mistletoe at Christmas goes back to the druids, who regarded it with reverence long before the Christian era. In celebration of the winter solstice, they gathered mistletoe, piled it on the altar, and burned it in sacrifice. Sprigs of the yellow-green leaves and waxen white berries were distributed among the people and hung up in their houses. The plant was regarded as a symbol of future hope and peace. Whenever enemies met under the mistletoe they would drop their weapons and embrace. The modern custom of kissing under the mistletoe may have grown out of this ancient practice.

As Christianity spread throughout western Europe in the early Middle Ages, Christmas (the English name dates from the 11th century, when the feast was termed *Cristes Maesse*) grew into an important popular event. Coming at a time during which the common people had some of their rare leisure, between fall harvesting and spring sowing, it quickly developed into a boisterous period of singing, hunting, gambling, and feasting. From early times, the offering of food and drink has been regarded as a sign of hospitality and good will. Accordingly, steaming beverages, especially spiced ale or beer known as *wassail* (derived from the Middle English *waes haeil*, meaning "be thou well" or "to your health") were served during the holiday season. By the 12th century, the giving of gifts (stemming ultimately from the scriptural account of the Three Magi who offered gold, frankincense, and myrrh to the Christ Child) had become common on Christmas.

A number of new Christmas traditions were introduced in the 17th, 18th, and 19th centuries, including the Christmas tree and the greeting card. The Christmas tree, as it is now known, originated in Germany although its history goes back to antiquity. The custom spread slowly throughout other parts of western Europe, being popularized in England only in the 1840s by Prince Albert, Queen Victoria's German consort. The royal family's gigantic tree, bedecked with wax tapers and sweetmeats, set the trend for the rest of Great Britain. Only as late as 1860 did glass baubles replace edible and handmade ornaments. In the early 20th century, brightly colored electric lights replaced burning candles. Soon after the inauguration of England's penny post in 1839, the custom of sending greeting cards arose.

The first clearly recorded Christmas in America was that of 1607 (if one excludes an isolated event in 1604 by the French, who tried unsuccessfully to establish a permanent settlement on St. Croix Island off the coast of Maine). The observance was at Jamestown, Virginia, where about 40 survivors of the original 100 settlers commemorated the day in the crude wooden chapel of their fort. It was not a festive time, but an occasion marked by the uncertainties of survival in the wilderness.

In New England, however, the Puritans tried hard to stamp out the "pagan mockery" of Christmas, penalizing any frivolity. William Bradford's *History of Plimoth Plantation* recounts that the Pilgrims who started their colony on Christmas Day, 1620, worked hard building houses on the occasion and "no man rested all that day" although they were offered to at least "have some Beere." The following year, Governor Bradford found a newly arrived contingent of colonists "at play, openly; some pitching the barr and some at stooleball, and shuch [sic] like sports. So he went to them . . . and tould them that was against his conscience, that they should play and others worke. . . . Since which time nothing hath been attempted that way, at least openly."

In 1659 the general court of Massachusetts enacted a law making any observance of December 25 a penal offense. Massachusetts Bay Colony Puritans were subjected to a five shilling fine for "observing any such day as Christmas." Although the law was repealed in 1681, in deference to the Puritan tradition many years passed before widespread Christmas festivities were held in New England. The solemn note continued until the 19th century, when the influx of German and Irish immigrants undermined the Puritan legacy. In 1856 the poet Henry Wadsworth Longfellow commented: "We are in a transition state about Christmas here in New England. The old Puritan feeling prevents it from being a cheerful hearty holiday; though every year makes it more so." That same year, Massachusetts finally proclaimed Christmas a legal holiday. Historically, however, Arkansas and Louisiana were the first jurisdictions after the formation of the United States to make Christmas a legal holiday (both doing so in 1831).

In 1856 President Franklin Pierce set up the first Christmas tree inside the White House. In 1923 President Calvin Coolidge began the custom of lighting a National Christmas Tree on the White House grounds.

Clara Barton's Birthday

Clarissa Harlowe Barton, founder of the American Red Cross, was born on December 25, 1821, on an Oxford, Massachusetts, farm to Stephen and Sarah Stone Barton. An acutely shy girl, she received most of her education from her older brothers and sisters and began a career in teaching at the age of 15, when her mother acted on advice that the way to cure shyness was to throw responsibility upon her.

After a period of study at the Liberal Institute in Clinton, New York, in 1851, Barton accepted a teaching position in Bordentown, New Jersey, where her fierce energy, and the kind of one-woman campaign for which she was to become noted, led to the abolishing of the fees that pupils had paid to attend school. With the establishment of a free system came an enormous increase in student enrollment, construction of a larger school, opposition to a woman heading it, and the appointment of a male principal, followed shortly by Barton's resignation and attack of nervous exhaustion. In 1854 she moved to Washington, D.C., where she served as a clerk in the United States Patent Office until the outbreak of the Civil War.

Barton's work in providing nursing and supplies for the war wounded began with her aid to the men of the 6th Massachusetts Regiment, who straggled into Washington in April 1861. Later, learning of more war suffering, she ran an advertisement for medical supplies and other necessities in a Worcester, Massachusetts, newspaper and set up her own distribution system to deal with the resulting deluge. With her characteristic flair for the practical, she recognized the need for rushing the provisions to the places where they were most needed and set about securing transportation and permission to pass through the lines. As the war ground on, she labored heroically, acting for a time as superintendent of nurses under the command of General Benjamin Butler. On the whole, however, hers was an unofficial, uncompensated, and nearly single-handed endeavor.

Her work attained a more official status after the war, when she organized the government's Bureau of Records in Washington, D.C., and supervised its search for missing soldiers. In 1869 she was overcome by one of her periods of bad health and went to Europe for a rest, which was cut short by the outbreak of the Franco-Prussian War shortly thereafter. Once again she plunged into wartime service, this time in association with the International Red Cross, which was founded in Geneva, Switzerland, in 1863 and officially sanctioned by the Geneva Convention of 1864. During this war she helped to establish hospitals and distributed supplies in Paris, Belfort, Montpellier, Strasbourg, and Lyons. Meanwhile, Red Cross officials in Geneva asked her why the United States did not join in the Geneva Convention of 1864.

Barton returned to the United States in 1873 with a burning desire to establish an American branch of the Red Cross and bring the United States into the Geneva Convention of 1864. Illness put her ambitions on hold for several years, however. In 1877 she wrote to Switzerland inquiring whether the Red Cross would approve efforts to organize an American branch, adding that if no person was under consideration for the job she would herself be willing to head such an undertaking. The first local chapter was founded in Dansville, New York.

The Red Cross sent Barton instructions on procedure and a letter, addressed to President Rutherford B. Hayes, which invited the United States to join the Geneva Convention and announced the appointment of Clara Barton as the active working head of the Red Cross in America. Thus armed, she embarked on a round of letter-writing, appointments with officials, and pamphleteering to the public and Congress. Her campaign finally achieved its goal with Senate confirmation of the Geneva Convention in 1882. In anticipation of this approval, a National Society of the Red Cross was formed in 1881, with Barton as its first president. She would eventually represent the United States at several international conferences.

One of the most famous women of the 19th century and a leading figure in public life, Barton also supported the campaign for voting rights for women. Barton retired at the age of 82 and spent the last eight years of her life at her home in Glen Echo, Maryland, where she died on April 12, 1912.

Gorbachev Resigns and the Soviet Union Dissolves

This book contains various articles relating to the cold war, that is, the struggle between the United States and the Union of Soviet Socialist Republics that began shortly after World War II when the two superpowers began to compete for political, military, and economic domination of the world

following the defeat of their common enemy. This struggle came to be known as the cold war because both sides were reluctant to engage in a direct, all-out confrontation, given the danger posed by the nuclear weapons they both possessed. They relied instead on covert action, economic attrition, and limited (though costly) engagements, often fought by proxies. Although there were frequent military confrontations, such as the Korean War, the Cuban missile crisis, and the Vietnam War (see related articles throughout this book), these were largely inconclusive. Overall, the cold war was a decades-long stalemate.

By the 1980s, however, the Soviet Union was beginning to disintegrate. Mikhail Gorbachev, elected as president in 1988, began to introduce political and economic reforms into the stagnating totalitarian state, bringing *glasnost,* "openness," and *perestroika,* "reconstruction," into what had been a strict and centralized communist system. The result was a release of pent-up discontent that had been suppressed since 1917, when the Soviet state was created, as well as a resurgence of national feeling in the non-Russian lands of Eastern Europe and Central Asia. Within the Soviet empire, Boris Yeltsin became the head of the Russian Republic, by far the largest of the Soviet states. On June 12, 1991, he became the first democratically elected president of Russia.

Alarmed at the prospect of a breakup of the Soviet Union into its constituent states, on August 19 Soviet military leaders tried to depose Gorbachev. They held him in captivity for several days, but were reluctant to use force to suppress the resulting popular outrage and mass demonstrations in the streets of the Soviet capital of Moscow, fanned in large part by Yeltsin. The coup leaders caved in on August 21, permitting Gorbachev to return, and after that the real power in the Soviet Union lay with Russian President Boris Yeltsin.

Although as head of the Soviet Union Gorbachev was still technically Yeltsin's superior, the Soviet military and bureaucracy began to transfer allegiance to the Russian government under Yeltsin's authority, while outlying nations of the Soviet Union like Lithuania and the Ukraine began to declare independence. The old Soviet states were reorganized by Yeltsin into a loose confederation known as the Commonwealth of Independent States. Yeltsin also began to dismantle the Communist Party apparatus that had existed for over 70 years. On December 25, 1991, Gorbachev announced his resignation and thus officially declared the end of the Soviet Union, which had already been reduced to a shell of its former self. The cold war was over.

December 26

American Revolution: Battle of Trenton

The months following the issuance of the Declaration of Independence on July 4, 1776, were not auspicious ones for the colonial cause. In August and September General William Howe, the British commander in chief, drove General George Washington from Long Island and New York City. Washington retreated north to Westchester County, and after the battle of White Plains on October 28, led his weary troops to Fort Lee, New Jersey. When Lord Charles Cornwallis menaced that outpost with 12 regiments, the colonials surrendered it without a struggle and fled to Newark. From there they went to New Brunswick and then to Trenton, staying one step ahead of their enemies.

Washington knew he could not hold New Jersey. On December 7 he assembled his men and supplies and ferried them across the Delaware River to Pennsylvania. To prevent pursuit, the Americans destroyed as many boats as possible along a 75-mile stretch of the lower Delaware. In the event, General Howe decided to not follow his quarry and ceased operations for the winter. He thought of withdrawing to the Newark area, but ultimately deployed farther forward with positions at Bordentown, Pennington, and Trenton, New Jersey. Such an alignment was less secure militarily, but the British wanted to provide protection for the Loyalists in the region and in any case were contemptuous of American military ability.

The colonials gained strength in Pennsylvania. General John Sullivan brought 2,000 men to Washington's assistance, and General Horatio Gates arrived with 500 more. A thousand "Philadelphia Associators" under Colonel John Cadwalader joined the encampment, as did a regiment of Maryland and Pennsylvania Germans under Colonel Nicholas Haussegger. By December 25 General Washington had about 6,000 men ready for combat.

Several factors prompted Washington to launch an attack almost immediately. For one, he wanted to take advantage of the relative abundance of personnel, because the expiration of enlistments on December 31 would reduce the army to 1,400. He also expected the British to attack across the Delaware as soon as the river was frozen enough to support the weight of troops and supplies, and wanted to disrupt their organization before that time. Finally, the British were vulnerable, especially at the Trenton outpost.

Colonel Johann Rall, a Hessian, commanded the British forces at Trenton. Rall was a professional soldier but thought so little of the rebels that he neglected to take fundamental defensive measures. Contrary to orders, he built no fortifications and sent out no reconnaissance patrols. On the night of December 25, he and his men celebrated Christmas so heartily that the drunken commander had to be carried to bed.

Washington chose the same night to begin a three-pronged attack on Trenton. General James Ewing was to cross at Trenton Ferry with 1,000 men and cut off a line of retreat by occupying the south bank of the Assunpink Creek. Colonel Cadwalader with 2,000 men was to launch a diversionary attack on Bordentown. Neither of these wings was effective: Ewing could not accomplish the crossing, and Cadwalader arrived too late.

The main column was composed of the 2,400 veterans of Generals John Sullivan and Nathanael Greene. Washington planned to lead it across the Delaware at McKonkey's Ferry (later Washington Crossing) and attack Trenton from the north. General John Glover's regiment of Marblehead, Massachusetts, fishermen, who had skillfully evacuated Washington's men from Long Island on August 29 and 30, now carried them across the river in cargo boats. The arduous crossing began at 11:00 p.m., but snow, cold, strong currents, and floating ice delayed its completion until 3:00 a.m. on December 26.

The colonials began their march about 4:00 a.m. At Birmingham they divided into two columns, one taking the Pennington Road to approach Trenton from the north and the other following the river road to attack from the west. Greene commanded, and Washington accompanied, the first column. It included the troops of Generals William Alexander, Hugh Mercer, and Adam Stephens. Sullivan headed the second column, which contained the troops of Generals John Glover, Arthur St. Clair, and Winthrop Sargent.

At 8:00 a.m. the battle commenced. The hours lost in crossing the Delaware deprived the Americans of the advantage of attacking at daybreak, but did not rob them of the element of surprise. Rall and the main body of his troops were still enjoying a morning-after sleep when the firing began. American artillery under Captains Alexander Hamilton and Thomas Forrest quickly silenced the British cannons, while the foot soldiers drove the Hessians in outlying sectors back into Trenton.

Bitter close combat marked the fighting in Trenton. The Hessians withdrew to the east of the town and found themselves encircled. Some 300 to 500 men managed to escape, but 918 surrendered to the Americans. Twenty-two Germans were killed, including Colonel Rall, and 84 were wounded. Historians differ on how many Americans lost their lives, although it is agreed that no more than four fell at Trenton. Captain William Washington and Lieutenant James Monroe (later president of the United States) were among the few wounded.

Washington decided to return to Pennsylvania, as his men were exhausted and the other columns had not been successful in their missions. The withdrawal consumed another day, and it was just as arduous as every other phase of the battle. The British historian George Otto Trevelyan thought the effort worthwhile, noting that "it may be doubted whether so small a number of men ever employed so short a space of time with greater or more lasting results upon the history of the world."

Kwanzaa Begins

Kwanzaa is a word from the Swahili language of Africa that means "first fruits of the harvest." It is the name given to the African American holiday conceived of by Maulana Karenga in 1966. Kwanzaa is a seven-day celebration, beginning on December 26 and ending on January 1 of the new year. It is intended as a supplement to Christmas, not a replacement, although some observants prefer Kwanzaa to the Christmas holiday for reasons that vary from a desire to distance themselves from an American culture dominated by white traditions to a dissatisfaction with Christmas's commercialization. Kwanzaa is not observed in Africa itself.

Each of the seven days of Kwanzaa is dedicated to one of seven guiding principles, as set forth below. The names of the seven principles are also Swahili.

(1) *Umoja*, "unity," stands for unity in the family, community, nation, and race.

(2) *Kujichagulia*, "self-determination," stands for achieving the self-determination of the African American community.

(3) *Ujima*, "collective work and responsibility," stands for working together to solve community problems.

(4) *Ujamaa*, "cooperative economics," stands for supporting stores, businesses, and other economic pillars of the community.

(5) *Nia*, "purpose," stands for helping the African American community achieve greatness.

(6) *Kuumba*, "creativity," stands for working to make the world cleaner, more beautiful, and more rewarding.

(7) *Imani*, "faith," stands for faith in the leaders and the people of the community and in the eventual triumph of the African American struggle.

There are several symbols associated with Kwanzaa. For example, there is the *kinara*, a candle-holder that holds *mshumaa*, "seven candles," which represent the foregoing seven principles. The center candle is black and represents umoja. Three red candles on one side represent nia, kuumba, and imani. Three green candles on the other side represent kujichagulia, ujima, and ujamaa.

On the last night of Kwanzaa, December 31, there is a *karamu* or feast to bring the community together and give thanks to the Creator. Typically it includes food, drinks, and gift-giving.

December 27

The Soviet Union Installs a Puppet Government in Afghanistan

On December 27, 1979, the Soviet Union used its military forces, which had entered the neighboring central Asian nation of Afghanistan just a few days earlier, to install Babrak Karmal as the leader of the Afghan government. The Soviets believed that Karmal, an ally, would be able to effectively control the country and keep it subservient to the Soviet regime. Afghan people surprised the Soviets, however, and the two groups soon became entangled in a military quagmire reminiscent of the American experience in Vietnam.

Afghanistan is a mountainous, land-locked country bordered by the former Soviet Union to the north, Iran to the west, and Pakistan to the south and east. It is poor and economically undeveloped, and the largely rural Islamic population is somewhat isolated from the outside world. Given the country's proximity to the Soviet Union, which during the cold war was always anxious to expand its list of client states through military and economic assistance, world leaders were not surprised when Afghanistan fell into the Soviet sphere of influence. Beginning in the 1950s the Afghan government launched a series of ambitious development plans, but despite efforts to increase trade and expand relations with the United States and other western countries Afghanistan remained dependent on the Soviet Union.

Afghanistan was a monarchy until 1973, when a military coup led by Muhammad Daud ousted the royalist regime. However, like the monarchy before it, the powers of the new central government were checked by local tribal and religious leaders. In 1978 Daud himself was overthrown in another military coup that resulted in the rise to power of Noor Muhammad Taraki. He in turn was ousted in September 1979 by Hafizullah Amin and then murdered. Anxious to secure the position of the communist and pro-Soviet elements in Afghan politics, in December 1979 the Soviets sent their military forces across the border and into the Afghan capital of Kabul. They forced Amin out of power, had him executed, and made Babrak Karmal the titular leader even though the Soviets held the real power.

The United States vigorously protested the Soviet intervention, but was unable and unwilling to take direct action in a country so remote from American shores. However, Karmal's Soviet-supported communist regime was almost immediately opposed by the conservative tribal leaders and Islamic clerics who had traditionally checked the power of the central government in Kabul. Intent on crushing all opposition, Karmal and the Soviets used military force in an effort to enforce their control over the rugged Afghan countryside. A vicious civil war erupted, with the government in control of the major cities and towns, while rebel groups controlled large portions of the countryside.

Seeking to take advantage of the chaotic situation and to thwart the Soviets, under the administration of President Jimmy Carter (1976–1980) the United States decided to give military assistance to the rebels. The weapons were funneled primarily through Pakistan, which was nervous about Soviet ambitions in the region and thus turned a blind eye towards covert American activities along the Pakistan-Afghanistan border. Under the Reagan administration (1980–1988), the assistance to the rebels was greatly increased and even included such advanced weapons as portable Stinger missiles, which could shoot down Soviet jet fighters and combat helicopters.

The Soviets countered by throwing massive military resources into the Afghan war, and endured thousands of casualties. The Afghan people suffered greatly: Roughly one-third of the population was either killed or forced to flee the country. As the Soviet campaign intensified, however, so did assistance to the rebels. More money and weapons came from other Islamic countries, such as Saudi Arabia and neighboring Iran, and the Peoples' Republic of China lent assistance as well. When Mikhail Gorbachev became the leader of the Soviet Union, he decided to disengage from the conflict, which was becoming extremely unpopular with the Soviet public, as part of his broader agenda in seeking better relations with the West and the rest of the world.

In May 1988 Pakistan, the Soviet Union, and the United States signed agreements providing for an end to foreign intervention in Afghanistan. The Soviets withdrew their forces by February 1989, and the communist regime collapsed. While the United States claimed a victory in the cold war, Afghanistan was left to handle its political and social problems by itself. Some of the more extreme fundamentalist groups subsidized by the West have since been implicated in terrorist bombings in other parts of the world.

Feast of St. John

The Feast of St. John, who was an apostle and evangelist, is celebrated by Roman Catholics, Episcopalians, and Lutherans on December 27 and by Eastern Orthodox churches on May 8. St. John is by tradition called the Beloved Disciple in allusion to the anonymous "disciple whom Jesus loved," long identified as John. He is also called St. John the Divine, namely the theologian, because of the theological aspects of the writings ascribed to him, such as the famous opening words of the Gospel of John:

> In the beginning was the Word, and the Word was with God, and the Word was God. He was in the beginning with God; all things were made through him, and without him was not anything made that was made. In him was life, and the life was the light of men. The light shines in the darkness, and the darkness has not overcome it.

St. John is also traditionally reputed to have been the author of three New Testament Epistles and the Book of Revelation or Apocalypse. He is thought to have done his writing in the decade before he died, at a very old age, in about the year 100. However, 20th-century scholarship has cast doubt on whether John was actually the author of these works. The matter is still debated by scholars, and many theories have been put forward as to the authorship of the writings.

John and his older brother James, also later canonized and known as James the Greater, were the sons of Zebedee, a fisherman who lived by the Sea of Galilee. John and James were among the first apostles to be chosen by Jesus, just after Peter and his brother Andrew. The story is told in Matthew 4:18–22:

> As he walked by the Sea of Galilee, he saw two brothers, Simon who is called Peter and Andrew his brother, casting a net into the sea; for they were fishermen. And he said to them, "Follow me, and I will make you fishers of men." Immediately they left their nets and followed him. And going on

from there he saw two other brothers, James the son of Zebedee and John his brother, in the boat . . . mending their nets, and he called them. Immediately they left the boat . . . and followed him.

From that time on, John, James, and Peter, were present at most of the important events of Jesus' life. After the crucifixion, John often preached and traveled with Peter and was arrested at least once with him. After his brother James was martyred, somewhere around 42 or 44, John apparently left Palestine and traveled through Asia Minor (modern day Turkey) teaching Christ's message and establishing the church there. He was considered the head of all Christian communities in Asia Minor. During one period of persecution, he was exiled to the island of Patmos in the Aegean Sea.

Apart from the period of exile on the island, John apparently spent most of his later life in Ephesus, where he died. He was the only apostle to die a natural death, and had lived a long life. According to St. Jerome, when John was very old and too weak to preach, he was still visited by crowds of pilgrims who had traveled far to see the only living apostle and to seek wisdom from him. For them, Jerome states, John compressed to their essence the teachings of Jesus in these words: "Little children, love one another. That is the Lord's command: and if you keep it, that by itself is enough."

December 28

Iowa Admitted to the Union

A scant 13 years after the establishment of its first permanent settlement at Dubuque in 1833, Iowa gained admission to the Union. In fact, having adopted a constitution in 1844, the people of the region had been seeking admission for two years before the proclamation making Iowa the 29th state was signed by President James Polk on December 28, 1846.

Remains of the prehistoric Mound Builder civilization that existed more than 1,000 years ago have been found in the northeastern corner of the state, along the Mississippi River. Some of the mounds built by these early people are in the form of birds and animals. The first Europeans to visit what is now the state of Iowa were the French explorers Father Jacques Marquette and Louis Joliet, who were commissioned by the governor of Canada to explore the Mississippi River. During their voyage down the river, part of which now forms the eastern boundary of the state, their expedition reached Iowa in June 1673. At that time the area was inhabited by various Sioux tribes,

including the Iowa, from whom the state was to take its name. They lived in villages of earthen lodges, doing some farming and hunting bison. Subsequently, these tribes were largely displaced by peoples of Algonquian stock, including the Sauk and Fox, whose economy was similar. Some exploration of the Iowa region was carried out in 1680 by the Flemish missionary Father Louis Hennepin, who led an expedition that was also principally concerned with exploring the Mississippi. Joliet's notes were lost, but both Marquette and Hennepin published accounts of their travels.

France formally claimed the Mississippi valley region, naming it Louisiana (Louisiane) in 1682. In 1762 France ceded the Iowa region and a vast amount of other territory lying west of the Mississippi River to Spain. Not until another 34 years had passed did Spain make the first land grant in the Iowa Territory. In 1796 roughly 189 square miles of land were given to a French Canadian named Julien Dubuque, who, settling in the area in 1788, received permission from the Fox tribe to mine the valuable lead deposits and established a trading post. After Dubuque died in 1810, however, no one remained at his settlement. His land included the site on which the city of Dubuque was later founded.

During the period of Spanish sovereignty, only two additional land grants were made, but neither became the site of a permanent settlement. Then France persuaded Spain to return the Louisiana Territory by the secret Treaty of San Ildefonso in 1800. Despite the treaty provision that France would not subsequently relinquish ownership of Louisiana to any country other than Spain, France negotiated the sale of the entire vast region to the United States in 1803. Known as the Louisiana Purchase, this transaction added more than 800,000 square miles to the area of the United States, the largest single acquisition ever made by this country.

Having acquired this immense tract of land, much of which was known only to the Native Americans who lived on it, President Thomas Jefferson designated Captain Meriwether Lewis and William Clark to organize an exploratory expedition. While the Lewis and Clark expedition was traveling up the Missouri River (which now forms the western boundary of Iowa) in 1804, a member of the expedition named Sergeant Charles Floyd died and was buried on the Iowa side of the river.

Beginning in 1805, what is now Iowa formed part of various administrative territories of the United States. It was first included in the Louisiana Territory from 1805 to 1812, when that huge region was renamed the Missouri Territory. That name held until 1821, when a portion of the area was admitted to the Union as the state of Missouri. For the next 13 years the remainder of the former Missouri Territory, including Iowa, was an unorganized area of the United States. Then, from 1834 to 1836, what is now Iowa was part of the Michigan Territory. Later, from 1836 to 1838, it was included in the Wisconsin Territory. In the latter year, Congress separated Iowa and certain other tracts of land north to Canada and as far west as the Missouri River from the Wisconsin Territory and organized it as the Iowa Territory.

Settlers began to slowly drift into Iowa beginning around 1830. The rate of settlement increased rapidly when opposition to the settlers' incursion by a number of tribes under the leadership of the Sauk chief Black Hawk was terminated by their defeat in 1832. Immediately after this Black Hawk War, the native tribes were forced to cede almost 9,000 square miles of territory on the Iowa side of the Mississippi River. Settlers lost no time in establishing towns along the riverbank. In 1833 Dubuque became the first permanent community to be established, and Burlington and Davenport were among the other early settlements.

Bit by bit, during the twenty years following Black Hawk's defeat, the natives tribes gave up their claims to land in Iowa. A population count in 1836 revealed that 10,531 people had already settled in the region. Within the next four years, 43,112 were making their home in Iowa. Burlington served as the temporary capital of Iowa Territory when it was organized in 1838. In the following year a site on the Iowa River about 30 miles from the Mississippi was selected and laid out as the capital, to be called Iowa City.

Support for statehood developed swiftly. By 1844 a constitution was framed, and an application was made to Congress for admission to the Union. Discussion and debate in Congress concerning the acceptability of the Iowa constitution and the proposed boundaries of the new state consumed two years. A new constitution was adopted in 1846. Finally, on December 28, 1846, the state of Iowa was formally created with Iowa City as its capital. The remainder of the territory was divided some years later among the new states of Minnesota and North and South Dakota.

The area around Des Moines in the south-central part of the state was opened for settlement in 1845, and in 1857 the city of Des Moines replaced Iowa City as the state capital.

Feast of the Holy Innocents (Childermas)

December 28, the Feast of the Holy Innocents, commemorates the innocent male child-martyrs of Bethlehem and its surroundings who were slaughtered by King Herod the Great's soldiers just before the beginning of the first century A.D. The king of Judea, learning of the birth of a prophesied "King of the Jews" and fearful that the unknown child would one day seize his throne, ordered the massacre of all baby boys two years old and under in an effort to kill his supposed rival. In England the traditional name for this anniversary was Childermas.

Christians first began to celebrate the feast towards the end of the fifth century. The date for the observance was arbitrarily set, since no definite information was available about when exactly the incident took place. It must have occurred within two years of Jesus's birth, since males older than the age of two remained unharmed. However, the date of the Nativity was itself highly speculative. Early church leaders therefore decided to hold the commemoration within the Octave or "eight days of Christmas."

The number of infants actually slain has been variously estimated. Some Eastern Orthodox churches, including the Greek and Russian Orthodox, put it at 14,000 boys. The Syrian liturgy refers to the 64,000 Holy Innocents. Medieval authors based their improbable estimate of 144,000 on passages in the Book of Revelation at 14:1–5. Furthermore, medieval artists invariably played up the horror and brutality of the episode by grossly exaggerating the numbers involved. Modern scriptural specialists have reduced the number considerably. Since Bethlehem was a small town at the time of Jesus's birth, the actual number of infants slain is estimated by some authorities to have been as low as 15 to 20.

December 29

Andrew Johnson's Birthday

Andrew Johnson, whose term as the nation's 17th president was among the most troubled in the history of the country, was born in Raleigh, North Carolina, on December 29, 1808. He was the younger son of Mary McDonough Johnson and Jacob Johnson, who died when Andrew was only four years old. Although his mother remarried, the family was not well off, so Johnson was apprenticed to a tailor at 14. His apprenticeship did not permit time for regular schooling, but Johnson managed to study on his own.

In 1826 he moved with his mother and stepfather to Tennessee, where they eventually settled in Greeneville. On May 17, 1827, Johnson married Eliza McCardle, a marriage that brought them five children. His wife helped Johnson study arithmetic and English. He also joined a debating society of students from Greeneville College to improve his public speaking. In 1828 he organized a party of workingmen in opposition to the landed gentry. Elected alderman in Greeneville, Johnson served for two years. In the meantime he bought a tailor shop and established a respectable local business.

Politics began to dominate Johnson's life. In 1830 he was elected mayor and served for three terms. He then successfully ran for the state legislature, starting his term there in 1835. He was defeated for reelection in 1837, but won again in 1839. During his tenure in the Tennessee legislature, Johnson emerged as a Jacksonian Democrat with a special hatred for aristocratic privilege. He moved up to the state senate in 1841 and two years later was elected to the 28th Congress in Washington, D.C., as a representative from Tennessee. He stayed in the House of Representatives for ten years until his district was gerrymandered by Whigs.

During his decade as a representative, Johnson was strongly antiabolitionist. Yet simultaneously he was extremely forward-looking in his views on democratizing government. He supported the direct election of senators, popular election of federal judges, and abolition of the electoral college. He expanded his support base by advocating homestead legislation to provide free land for settlers, a stand designed to appeal to both easterners and westerners.

In 1853 Johnson was elected governor of Tennessee. Running for reelection in 1855, he won as a moderate against the anti-immigrant American (or "Know-Nothing") Party. While governor, he pushed through Tennessee's first state tax in support of public education. He also obtained authorization for a state board of agriculture and a state library. In 1857 the Tennessee legislature sent him to the United States Senate.

In April 1860 Johnson's name was put forward for presidential nomination at the Democratic National Convention in Charleston, South Carolina. When the regular Democratic convention refused to include a pro-slavery platform, the southerners left and refused to support Stephen A. Douglas, who became the party's regular nominee. Though initially indecisive, Johnson finally chose to support the southerners' nominee, John C. Breckinridge.

Immediately after Abraham Lincoln was elected president, a wave of secessionist sentiment swept the South as the Civil War began to erupt. On December 18, 1860, at the time of the South Carolina secession convention, Johnson bravely delivered a speech in the Senate supporting the principle of federal union. The announcement of the secession of South Carolina on December 20 was followed by that of six other southern states. Together they formed the Confederate States of America, later expanded with the admission of four more southern states and commonly referred to as the Confederacy.

Johnson remained conspicuously alone when every other southern senator withdrew from the Senate. Although he was reviled as a traitor by most southerners, northerners praised him as a second Andrew Jackson for his support of the Union above all else. On July 24, 1861, some three months after the Civil War began, Johnson introduced a resolution in a special session of the Senate which declared union and the preservation of the Constitution to be the only war aim of the North. During the winter of 1861–1862 he served on an important joint committee concerning the conduct of the war.

In March 1862 Johnson sacrificed his relatively powerful Senate position to accept President Lincoln's appointment as military governor of Tennessee. Unfortunately for Johnson, however, the Union-oriented eastern portion of Tennessee was overrun by the Confederates and remained in their hands until 1863. Thus he could exercise his official powers only in western Tennessee, an area whose residents were hostile to the Union. Under his guidance, western Tennessee became something of a laboratory for his later moderate views on the reconstruction of the defeated South.

During the summer of 1864, an election year, the Civil War was not going well for the North. Faced with the distinct possibility that northern Democrats might win the presidential election, the Republican Party looked for ways to broaden its popular support, renaming itself the National Union Party to attract prowar Democrats. The sectional image of the party was further modified with Johnson, a prowar Democrat, as the vice-presidential candidate on the ticket with Lincoln. Although the Republicans won the election, Johnson's health was badly sapped by the strenuous campaign. Though still ill (probably with malaria), at the president's request he went to the inauguration, bracing himself with a drink that severely affected him and resulted in a display of intoxication later used as a political bludgeon by his enemies.

Lincoln was shot on April 14, 1865, and when he died the following day Johnson became president. Since the Civil War was virtually concluded five days earlier by Lee's surrender at Appomattox Court House (see related articles throughout this book) after four years of bloody conflict, Johnson found himself facing the unprecedented task of reuniting the divided country.

December 29

The problems of the Reconstruction era were unprecedented, since the Constitution did not anticipate or provide for the possibility of secession. Thus, Reconstruction had to be effected with no guidelines to the solution of important questions. Were the southern states to be regarded as conquered territory, or as states temporarily out of proper order? How should individual Confederate leaders be dealt with: Should they lose not only political power but also economic power as well? What was the status of freed blacks? Did freedom from slavery imply legal, economic, and social equality with whites?

Questions such as these required resolution, and a power struggle developed between the president and Congress over who should make the decisions. Johnson's first statements were approved by northern public opinion. "Treason must be made infamous and traitors must be impoverished," said the new president, a statement that made the Radical Republicans (who did not then control Congress) feel that Johnson would be easier to deal with than Lincoln, who had favored leniency towards the South. The Radicals were, however, to be surprised. Congress left Washington, D.C., for the summer and the Union armies were quickly disbanded. Immediately, Johnson began to formulate a plan for presidential reconstruction of the South. It was his aim to complete the mechanics of restoring the southern states to what Lincoln had called their "proper practical relation with the Union" before Congress reconvened in December 1865. "Readmission" to the Union, a term often used, was not the issue since the federal government had never recognized the right of the Confederate states to secede.

On May 29, 1865, Johnson issued a proclamation embodying an amnesty plan along the lines envisioned by Lincoln. Amnesty was provided for those who would swear allegiance to the Constitution and the Union and to the provisions of the 13th Amendment, which forbade slavery. However, former high officeholders of the Confederacy, those who had mistreated prisoners of war and those whose taxable wealth was over $20,000 were generally barred from pardon. The exclusion of propertied southerners was Johnson's own special provision in the hope of giving power to small farmers. However, many wealthy southerners petitioned Johnson for special pardons, and the president was liberal in granting such requests.

Among Johnson's other early actions as president was his recognition of the new loyal governments set up under Lincoln in the four states of Arkansas, Louisiana, Tennessee, and Virginia. Johnson then went on to organize provisional governments for the seven remaining states of the former Confederacy. In another important action, on December 25, 1865, he issued a general pardon for the offense of treason.

By this time, most of the southern states had satisfied Johnson's liberal criteria for restoration of the privileges of statehood. He also decreed that loyal southerners could determine the qualifications for their own offices. None of these moves endeared Johnson to either the congressional Radicals or to the moderate Republicans, who were increasingly supporting them. Therefore, when Congress returned to Washington, D.C., in December 1865, many of its members were already alarmed over Johnson's apparent *fait accompli*. Under the presidential policy, it was expected that conventions of delegates pledged to support the Union, the Constitution, and the laws concerning emancipation would be called by the provisional governors in the southern states for the purpose of repudiating secession, reframing state constitutions, and preparing for restoration to the Union. These conventions were also expected to accept emancipation and to repudiate Confederate war debts.

Congress's unease was exacerbated when the southern state conventions watered down their resolutions regarding the rejection of slavery and secession. The image of southerners as unrepentant rebels grew as the legislatures of the former Confederate states passed "black codes" that effectively reduced blacks to the level of serfs. Many northerners regarded the new rules as de facto slavery. None of this interested Johnson, who considered Reconstruction to be complete, but was to learn otherwise.

The actions that Johnson had taken during the congressional recess eroded his working relationship with Congress. That body would not yet permit the seating of the newly elected southern congressmen who, under Johnson's Reconstruction program, now stood ready to represent their states in Congress when statehood privileges were restored. In its fear that too many of the South's former leaders were returning to power and that emancipation was not being accepted in good faith, Congress created a joint committee to study all bills pertaining to Reconstruction. In February 1866 Congress also passed a bill to continue the existence of the one-year-old Freedmen's Bureau, a government agency with military authority to protect the civil rights of blacks throughout the South. Johnson promptly vetoed the bill on February 19, 1866, arguing that the federal government had no authority to impose military law during peacetime. He thus held the position that Congress could not override the "black codes" of the southern states.

Three days after delivering his veto of the Freedmen's bill, Johnson spoke to a Washington's birthday gathering. Unwisely, he allowed his audience to prod him into accusing Radical leaders Thaddeus Stevens, Charles Sumner, and Wendell Phillips of something close to treason. These angry statements helped convince Congress that Johnson was worse than merely foolhardy. In the meantime, reports reached Washington, D.C., that political and economic organization attempts by blacks were being met with intimidation in many parts of the South. In response to this, Congress passed a civil rights act. After Johnson's veto, Congress reenacted it on April 9, 1866, over Johnson's veto with the required two-thirds majority in both the House and the Senate. This act defined citizenship to include blacks as well as whites and asserted the right of the federal government to override state governments for the protection of citizens' rights.

Johnson's veto, on the grounds that the Constitution did not warrant such an extension of federal power, had come as something of a surprise, as the bill had been regarded by many as a moderate compromise measure. Overwhelmingly, moderates and cabinet members had urged the president to sign the bill. When he refused, the gulf between himself and Congress became complete. However, many congressmen feared that the bill might indeed be unconstitutional, and so the 14th Amendment (containing many of the same provisions) was approved by Congress and eventually ratified by the states.

Meanwhile, throughout the spring of 1866 violence against southern blacks became more widespread. During May, roving bands of white men burned and shot up the black section of Memphis, Tennessee. By July Congress had passed a new Freedmen's Bill over Johnson's veto. The need for such an agency was immediately evident, for on July 30 white mobs and policemen trapped a political gathering of blacks inside a meeting hall in New Orleans, Louisiana. A merciless hail of bullets through windows and doorways killed 40 people and wounded 136 others.

Incidents such as the New Orleans massacre were used as emotional political material by Radical Republicans during the congressional election campaigns of 1866. In these campaigns, the moderate Republicans might have joined forces with moderate Democrats had Johnson not pushed them into the camp of the Radicals. Thus Johnson's intransigence spelled the end of the wartime Union Party.

A good many other people were also put off by Johnson's "swing around the circle," the disastrous speaking tour he undertook to help the congres-sional campaigns of moderate southern and northern Democrats. He saw them as members of a potentially useful coalition sympathetic to his views. Accompanied by various dignitaries, including General Ulysses S. Grant, Johnson set out on the 19-day tour of key northern cities on August 28, 1866, and made the mistake of repeating one set speech everywhere he went. With national newspapers reporting his past speeches ahead of him, he appeared unimaginative in his defense of his policies. At the same time, many Radical Republicans were denouncing him as an alcoholic and a traitor. Regardless of whether he was either, both charges were calculated to win votes for the Radicals. Their tactics won support in the North, and the voters elected a Congress that was overwhelmingly controlled by Radical Republicans determined to push through a tough Reconstruction program over Johnson's expected vetoes.

In the months that followed, the defeated South (with the exception of Tennessee, whose restoration to the Union had won congressional approval in 1866) was placed under martial law. The first Reconstruction Act, of doubtful constitutionality and passed over a presidential veto on March 2, 1867, declared the other existing southern state governments to be illegal and divided the South into five military districts. Each was under the control of a major-general with an armed force under his command. To achieve restoration, each state was required to hold a constitutional convention whose delegates were to be elected by the universal suffrage of adult males including black males. Excluded from voting were all former Confederate leaders, which in effect meant most of the prior governing class. The states were also required to adopt new constitutions that guaranteed black suffrage and were in harmony with the federal Constitution, to obtain congressional approval of these documents, and to ratify the 14th Amendment.

When the affected states failed to take prompt action along these lines, a second Reconstruction Act was passed on March 23, which authorized military commanders to set up the new state governments beginning with the enrollment of voters. A third Reconstruction Act, passed on July 19 further enlarged the duties and powers of military commanders and totally subjected state civil administrations to their authority. The fourth Reconstruction Act, enacted on March 11, 1868, was designed to keep southern white voter boycotts from nullifying election results since it provided that a majority of those voting (regardless of their number) was sufficient to ratify the new state constitutions. Not by accident, these acts and related measures were designed to thwart control of the military governments in the South by the president, who had exercised this power by virtue of his position as commander in chief.

The prelude to Johnson's impeachment proceedings began when in March 1867 Congress passed the Tenure of Office Act prohibiting the president from dismissing without Senate consent any official appointed by and with Senate approval. This statute was interpreted by many Radicals as extending to a cabinet member like the secretary of war, Edwin M. Stanton, a Radical Republican who had opposed Johnson at every opportunity. On August 12 Johnson dismissed Stanton. The Senate reacted by declaring the removal illegal, and on January 13, 1868, ordered Stanton reinstated. Johnson refused.

Congress opened impeachment proceedings on February 24. Johnson's alleged "high crimes and misdemeanors" were principally related to his violation of the Tenure of Office Act by discharging Stanton. Radical Republican pressure almost succeeded in moving the required two-thirds of the Senate to support impeachment, but the trial ended in May 1868 just one vote short of conviction. Johnson therefore served out his term, but during his remaining year in office he was virtually powerless.

Johnson returned to Tennessee in 1869 and lost his bid for a Senate seat. In 1872 he ran for a seat as representative-at-large, but lost again. Though weakened by an attack of yellow fever in 1873, Johnson won his bid for a position as senator in 1874, thus becoming the first man to return to the Senate after serving as president. He went to Washington, D.C., in March 1875, but while visiting a daughter in Tennessee soon after the Senate's summer adjournment he suffered a paralytic attack and died on July 31, 1875. Johnson was buried in Greeneville, Tennessee.

Woodrow Wilson's Birthday

Thomas Woodrow Wilson, the 28th president of the United States, was born in Staunton, Virginia, on December 29, 1856. His mother, Janet Woodrow Wilson, was of Scottish descent. His father, Joseph R. Wilson, was a Presbyterian minister descended from Scotch-Irish immigrants.

Although Joseph Wilson was reared in Ohio, he moved to Virginia three years before Woodrow was born. The family moved around the South and finally settled in Wilmington, North Carolina, in 1874. Woodrow Wilson attended Davidson College in North Carolina for one year. Another year of home study prepared him for entering the College of New Jersey (renamed Princeton University in 1896), from which he graduated in 1879.

Already aspiring to the life of a statesman, Wilson entered the University of Virginia to study law, as he considered it a prerequisite to high public office. He was subsequently admitted to the bar, but after an unsuccessful year in private practice he reentered academic life. At Johns Hopkins University, where he embarked on graduate studies in history and government, he wrote the doctoral dissertation *Congressional Government*, which, when published, was received with some acclaim.

After leaving Johns Hopkins in 1885, Wilson married Ellen Louise Axson. For the next three years he taught history and political economy at Bryn Mawr College. He also taught for a year at Wesleyan University, and then was appointed professor of jurisprudence and political economy at Princeton. There he earned a high reputation among his colleagues, and in 1902 was elected president of the university. During his eight years in that post he worked to raise academic standards, reorganizing the curriculum, and introducing the preceptorial system, which was designed to bring students and instructors into a closer and more intellectually stimulating relationship with an emphasis on individual guidance by tutors working with small groups of students. He also sought to democratize the student body and to subordinate the social aspects of student life, reducing the influence of the exclusive undergraduate clubs. This aroused bitter opposition, as did some of his building proposals, and Wilson found himself embroiled in controversy.

Meanwhile, his speeches on public affairs were winning favorable attention far beyond Princeton. The New Jersey Democratic organization invited Wilson to run for governor of New Jersey, since the politicians thought he would be naive and malleable in office. Wilson accepted, resigned the presidency of the university in October 1910, and after a vigorous campaign won the election on a reform platform. Confounding the political machine, he followed no advice but his own in office and achieved a record of reform legislation that brought him nationwide admiration.

Wilson began to consider seeking the Democratic nomination for president. Placed in nomination at the 1912 Democratic National Convention, he won the decisive support of William Jennings Bryan on the 14th ballot and became the party's nominee on the 46th ballot. With the Republicans weakened by Theodore Roosevelt's third-party bid for the presidency, Wilson was able to win the election.

During his first term in office, Wilson supported the Underwood Tariff Act, which established the Federal Trade Commission and the Clayton Anti-Trust Act. He also supported the

Federal Reserve Act of 1913, a sweeping piece of banking and currency reform that was to become the cornerstone of the nation's financial structure. Military squabbles with Mexico and the onset of World War I in Europe, however, diverted his attention to foreign affairs.

Wilson tried to be neutral in the war, hoping that he could bring the warring nations to the peace table. Even after a German submarine sank the *Lusitania*, with the loss of over 100 American lives, he declared that despite provocation a nation might be "too proud to fight." A strongly worded note brought assurances from Germany that neutral civilian shipping would not be sunk without warning.

Wilson defended his policy of restraint during the presidential campaign of 1916. His party hailed him as the leader who "kept us out of war." Even so, the election was so close that Wilson went to bed on election night thinking that he had lost and planning to arrange for the immediate transfer of office to his opponent. In the morning, however, he awoke to find that he had won by a slim majority.

After the election Wilson renewed his diplomatic peace efforts, but could not persuade the two sides to negotiate. At this point, Germany decided that the military advantage of unrestricted submarine warfare outweighed the danger of American entry into the war. With the resumption of submarine attacks on American ships, on April 2, 1917, Wilson asked Congress for a declaration of war. Congress complied with his request four days later. A draft bill was passed, and about four million men were mobilized in the ensuing months. Some two million Americans sent to Europe participated in the bloody battles of World War I before the hostilities ended with the armistice of November 11, 1918.

With his wartime addresses stressing a noble conception of the war's purpose as "the ultimate peace of the world"—the war to make the world "safe for democracy"—Wilson did much to strengthen resolve at home and encourage Europe to look to him for salvation. Best known of all his speeches was his address to Congress on January 8, 1918 outlining the Fourteen Points that he felt were necessary for peace. A portion of this historic message is set forth below:

We entered this war because violations of right had occurred which touched us to the quick and made the life of our own people impossible unless they were corrected and the world secure once for all against their recurrence. What we demand in this war, therefore, is nothing peculiar to ourselves. It is that the world be made fit and safe to live in; and particularly that it be made safe for every peace-loving nation which, like our own, wishes to live its own life, determine its own institutions, be assured of justice and fair dealing by the other peoples of the world as against force and selfish aggression. All the peoples of the world are in effect partners in this interest, and for our own part we see very clearly that unless justice be done to others it will not be done to us. The programme of the world's peace, therefore, is our programme; and that programme, the only possible programme, as we see it, is this:

First. Open covenants of peace, openly arrived at, after which there shall be no private international understandings of any kind but diplomacy shall proceed always frankly and in the public view.

Second. Absolute freedom of navigation upon the seas, outside territorial waters, alike in peace and in war, except as the seas may be closed in whole or in part by international action for the enforcement of international covenants.

Third. The removal, so far as possible, of all economic barriers and the establishment of an equality of trade conditions among all the nations consenting to the peace and associating themselves for its maintenance.

Fourth. Adequate guarantees given and taken that national armaments will be reduced to the lowest point consistent with domestic safety.

Fifth. A free, open-minded, and absolutely impartial adjustment of all colonial claims, based upon a strict observance of the principle that in determining all such questions of sovereignty the interests of the populations concerned must have equal weight with the equitable claims of the government whose title is to be determined.

Sixth. The evacuation of all Russian territory and such a settlement of all questions affecting Russia as will secure the best and freest cooperation of the other nations of the world in obtaining for her an unhampered and unembarrassed opportunity for phe independent determination of her own political development and national policy and assure her of a sincere welcome into the society of free nations under institutions of her own choosing; and, more than a welcome, assistance also of every kind that she may need and may herself desire.

The treatment accorded Russia by her sister nations in the months to come will be the acid test of their good will, of their comprehension of her needs as distinguished from their own interests, and of their intelligent and unselfish sympathy.

Seventh. Belgium, the whole world will agree, must be evacuated and restored, without any attempt to limit the sovereignty which she enjoys in common with all other free nations. No other single act will serve as this will serve to restore confidence among the nations in the laws which they have themselves set and determined for the government of their relations with one another. Without this healing act the whole structure and validity of international law is forever impaired.

Eighth. All French territory should be freed and the invaded portions restored, and the wrong done to France by Prussia in 1871 in the matter of Alsace-Lorraine, which has unsettled the peace of the world for nearly fifty years, should be righted, in order that peace may once more be made secure in the interest of all.

Ninth. A readjustment of the frontiers of Italy should be effected along clearly recognizable lines of nationality.

Tenth. The peoples of Austria-Hungary, whose place among the nations we wish to see safeguarded and assured, should be accorded the freest opportunity to autonomous development.

Eleventh. Rumania, Serbia, and Montenegro should be evacuated; occupied territories restored; Serbia accorded free and secure access to the sea; and the relations of the several Balkan states to one another determined by friendly counsel along historically established lines of allegiance and nationality; and international guarantees of the political and economic independence and territorial integrity of the several Balkan states should be entered into.

Twelfth. The Turkish portion of the present Ottoman Empire should be assured a secure sovereignty, but the other nationalities which are now under Turkish rule should be assured an undoubted security of life and an absolutely unmolested opportunity of autonomous development, and the Dardanelles should be permanently opened as a free passage to the ships and commerce of all nations under international guarantees.

Thirteenth. An independent Polish state should be erected which should include the territories inhabited by indisputably Polish populations, which should be assured a free and secure access to the sea, and whose political and economic independence and territorial integrity should be guaranteed by international covenant.

Fourteenth. A general association of nations must be formed under specific covenants for the purpose of affording mutual guarantees of political independence and territorial integrity to great and small states alike.

In regard to these essential rectifications of wrong and assertions of right we feel ourselves to be intimate partners of all the governments and peoples associated together against the Imperialists. We cannot be separated in interest or divided in purpose. We stand together until the end.

For such arrangements and covenants we are willing to fight and to continue to fight until they are achieved; but only because we wish the right to prevail and desire a just and stable peace such as can be secured only by removing the chief provocations to war, which this programme does remove. We have no jealousy of German greatness, and there is nothing in this programme that impairs it. We grudge her no achievement or distinction of learning or of pacific enterprise such as have made her record very bright and very enviable. We do not wish to injure her or to block in any way her legitimate influence or power. We do not wish to fight her either with arms or with hostile arrangements of trade if she is willing to associate herself with us and the other peace- loving nations of the world in covenants of justice and law and fair dealing. We wish her only to accept a place of equality among the peoples of the world, the new world in which we now live, instead of a place of mastery.

When the hostilities ended, Wilson arranged to go to Europe to attend the peace conference. Leaving on December 4, 1918, he was received in London, Rome, and Paris with great enthusiasm. When the conference assembled at Versailles in January 1919, he proposed that the peace treaty contain the covenant of a League of Nations with provisions for averting war in the future. Through diplomatic pressure, Wilson was able to force elements of his peace plan on the unwilling allies, but he also had to make concessions, perhaps more than he realized. To win support for the League of Nations, he assented to the notorious War Guilt Clause in the Treaty of Versailles, by which Germany was made to accept the entire responsibility for the conflict; this was both unfair and unwise, for it convinced most Germans that the treaty was a sham. But the covenant for the League did become part of the final agreement, and Wilson returned from Europe with what he considered a partial victory for principled statesmanship.

He was not welcomed home with any great enthusiasm. Much of the American public viewed the treaty with suspicion, as failing to include sufficient guarantees of American sovereignty, and Wilson's fellow Democrats, who had already suffered losses in the Congressional elections of 1918, were in no mood to support him in an unpopular cause. Wilson refused to compromise; thus, the Senate refused to ratify the treaty, and the United States never joined the League of Nations.

On September 25, 1919, during a strenuous national tour in which he tried to win popular support for the peace treaty, Wilson collapsed and was forced to return to Washington, D.C. A week later he suffered a stroke which largely prevented him from transacting official business and from which he never fully recovered, although he technically remained in office until March 4, 1921. His second wife, Edith Galt Wilson, whom he had married in 1915 after the death of Ellen Wilson, took on some of the duties of the presidency during this period.

Upon Wilson's retirement, he and Edith moved to a red brick Georgian-style house at 2340 S Street, NW, in Washington's Embassy Row section. He lived there until his death on February 3, 1924.

Massacre at Wounded Knee

What has been called the last major military encounter in the United States between government forces and native tribes took place on December 29, 1890, at a spot that is now the site of the town of Wounded Knee on the Pine Ridge Reservation in southwestern South Dakota a few miles above the Nebraska–South Dakota border. A band of 350 hungry and poorly clothed Oglala Sioux, including 230 women and children, had left their reservation in defiance of government orders for a peaceful meeting with another tribe. They were intercepted by a United States Army cavalry unit, to which they surrendered without resistance.

Camp was made for the night at Wounded Knee. The next morning, while soldiers were confiscating the few weapons that the Sioux had, a shot rang out. Immediately thereafter, a melee of shooting erupted. Roughly 250 men, women, and children were killed. Twenty-five or more soldiers died, mainly due to their own crossfire. At Wounded Knee there are now markers and memorials telling of the massacre.

Texas Admitted to the Union

Some eleven years after Texas's declaration of independence from Mexico and six months after the annexation of Texas by the United States, on December 29, 1845, the former republic became the 28th state to enter the Union (see related articles throughout this book).

From 1845 until Alaska's admission to statehood on January 3, 1959, Texas remained the largest of all the states, even though sizable portions of its original land area were siphoned off to New Mexico and Colorado. Smaller portions also became part of Oklahoma, Kansas, and Wyoming in the intervening years.

December 30

The Gadsden Purchase

Although the Treaty of Guadalupe Hidalgo ended the Mexican War in 1848 (see related essays throughout this book) and gave the United States substantial territorial concessions at Mexico's expense, a number of problems arose in the following years that necessitated further negotiations between the two countries. Mexico charged that the United States had failed to deal effectively with continuing Apache raids south of the Rio Grande, a violation of Article XI of the treaty, and demanded reparations of $15 million to $30 million. For its part, the United States wanted control of an area, which today comprises the southern sections of Arizona and New Mexico, to which both countries laid claim.

The issue over this territory began because of an alleged ambiguity in the 1848 treaty. That treaty had definitively fixed the international boundary from El Paso, Texas, east to the Gulf of Mexico. However, west of El Paso the exact location of the line of demarcation was vague because the area was important to both the United States and Mexico. The United States wanted it as a possible route for a transcontinental railroad, while Mexico simply wanted to prevent further losses of territory.

Promoters of the southern transcontinental railroad route had the strong support of Secretary of War Jefferson Davis, who later served as president of the Confederacy during the Civil War. He arranged to send James Gadsden, a railroad president from South Carolina, as the United States minister to Mexico in May 1853. Gadsden's primary objective was to obtain the territory needed for the southern railroad route, but he was also authorized to bargain for any additional land that the Mexican president, General Antonio López de Santa Anna, would agree to sell.

On December 30, 1853, Gadsden completed his successful negotiations with Santa Anna. He had persuaded the Mexicans to agree to the abrogation of Article XI of the 1848 treaty and to give up their claims against the United States. Even more important, he had succeeded in purchasing the Mesilla Valley and 19 million acres south of the Gila River for $15 million.

The United States Senate reduced the payment to $10 million, and the land cession was proportionately lessened to about 29,640 square miles, but this smaller area still included all of the territory needed for the transcontinental railroad. The Senate finally ratified the Gadsen Purchase treaty on April 25, 1854. Ultimately, however, the first transcontinental railroad was not built along this route. In fact, a southern railroad was not completed until several decades after the Civil War.

December 31

New Year's Eve

The approach of the new year has been celebrated on the evening of December 31 since colonial times in the United States. Here, as in many other countries around the world, the custom of greeting the hour of midnight by ringing bells, blowing horns, clashing gongs, tooting whistles, and throwing confetti is widespread. New Year's Eve parties, usually extending into the early hours of New Year's Day on January 1, have become traditional. Friends and relatives gather in homes, hotels, restaurants, and other locations to bid the old year farewell and to welcome in the new. Church services, with quiet meditation and hymn or carol singing, also mark the occasion. So does the traditional making of New Year's resolutions, by which each individual determines to live in an exemplary way, or at least an improved one, in the coming year.

Some of the New Year's Eve traditions rank among the oldest customs known. The raucous din, which is said to have originated in Babylonian and Indian new year's observances, is a relic of the ancient past when the need was felt to frighten away the spirits believed wandering the earth at the year's change. In northern and central Europe, ancient folk beliefs held that prowling devils must be decisively routed on the last night of the year with noise. Men and boys would masquerade in grotesque headdresses and costumes hung with large bells, clowning and dancing about to scare even the most obstinate of demons. Various western European countries buried, burned, or drowned the passing year in effigy. In Scotland, a dummy called the Auld Wife was ignited, while in other parts of the British Isles huge bonfires were lit to "burn out the old year."

Throughout most of continental Europe, December 31 was also known as St. Sylvester's Day, since it was the feast day of Pope Sylvester I (314–335). This holiday had its own peculiar traditions, especially in Belgium, Germany, France, and Switzerland. For example, the boy or girl who rose last on the final day of the year was mockingly called a "Sylvester."

In the United States, feasting, drinking, partying, and noisemaking are traditional ways of "bringing in" the new year. Only during Prohibition, in the 1920s and early 1930s, did New Year's Eve tone down and become a time primarily for small private parties. However, with the repeal of Prohibition in 1933, it again took on the old-time flavor. The explosion of high spirits is especially loud in New York City. Regularly since the early 1900s, masses of revelers have pushed into Times Square and along Broadway to celebrate. Excitement mounts when, just before midnight, a glowing ball with hundreds of lights slowly descends a high pole atop the One Times Square Building to mark the last seconds of the passing year. At midnight it hits bottom and pandemonium breaks loose.

In addition to the secular celebrations, in New York the historic chimes of Old Trinity Church at the head of Wall Street peal forth every year while its congregation kneels in prayer. Many religious denominations hold special services on New Year's Eve from late in the evening until midnight. John Wesley, the English founder of the Methodist Church, established the "watch-night" service as a time for worshippers to review their past, give solemn thought to the future, and rededicate themselves to Christian ways. In England, the first watch-night was conducted about 1742 and became especially popular in the 19th century. St. George's Methodist Episcopal Church in Philadelphia, Pennsylvania, held in 1770 what has been called the first such service in America. The custom was later adopted by a number of Protestant denominations throughout the country. In the Roman Catholic Church, holy hours are held to mark the advent of the new year.

George Marshall's Birthday

George Catlett Marshall, one of the most prominent American soldiers and statesmen of the 20th century, was born on December 31, 1880, in Uniontown, Pennsylvania. He was one of the four children of George Catlett Marshall, a successful entrepreneur in the coal and coke industries, and Laura Bradford Marshall. The younger George Marshall was destined to become the first five-star general in the history of the United States and to hold the vital posts of chief of staff of the army, secretary of state, and secretary of defense.

After graduating from high school, Marshall tried to obtain a congressional appointment to the United States Military Academy at West Point, but the Republicans who dominated his region of Pennsylvania had little use for the petitions of a boy whose father was a Kentucky-born Democrat. In 1897 Marshall instead entered the Virginia Military Institute (VMI), one of the foremost private military colleges, where he developed into an excellent scholar, athlete, and soldier. Academically, he ranked 15th in his class, and he played football well enough to be named a tackle of the All-Southern team. Marshall's fellow students in his final year at VMI selected him for the highest cadet rank, namely senior first captain.

Graduating from college in 1901, Marshall accepted a commission in February 1902 as a second lieutenant in the army. He served in the Philippine Islands with the 30th Infantry Regiment until its return in 1903 to the Oklahoma Territory. After several years of assignments in the west, the young lieutenant attended the Infantry-Cavalry School at Fort Leavenworth, Kansas, from which he graduated with honors in 1907. The army promoted him to first lieutenant in March 1907, and selected him to remain at Fort Leavenworth as a student at the prestigious Army Staff College. He graduated at the head of his class in 1908 and spent the following two years as an instructor at the school, teaching men who were often his senior in age and rank.

By 1913 Marshall had completed tours with the Massachusetts National Guard and with the 4th Infantry. He then returned to the Philippines. World War I began shortly thereafter, and during training exercises designed to improve the army's defensive position in the islands, Marshall demonstrated his abilities as a planner and won acclaim as a master of tactics. He became an aide to General Hunter Liggett, and upon returning to the United States in 1916 he assumed the same role for General James Franklin Bell, a former army chief of staff. Bell thought highly of Marshall, whom he described as "the greatest military genius since Stonewall Jackson."

Marshall, who won promotion to captain in 1916, was a member of the United States Army General Staff at the time of America's entry into World War I in April 1917. In July 1917 he accompanied the 1st Division to France and in the following months served as its operations officer. Marshall laid the plans for actions that took place in the fall of 1917 east of Lunéville, and in the first half of the next year at the Saint-Mihiel, Picardy, and Cantigny battle areas. In the summer of 1918 he moved to the headquarters of the American commander, General John J. Pershing, where he formulated plans for the Saint-Mihiel offensive. Later in the war Marshall became chief of operations for the First Army and chief of staff for the VIII Army Corps.

In September 1919 Marshall returned to the United States as aide-de-camp to General Pershing, a post he held until 1924. Well aware of how the lack of military preparation had hindered American efforts in World War I, the two men proposed the establishment of a trained army of 450,000 men. The National Defense Act of 1920 incorporated the idea, but Congress never appropriated the funds necessary to implement it.

The interwar period of the 1920s and 1930s brought Marshall a variety of assignments. He served three years, beginning in 1924, with the 15th Infantry in Tientsin, China, and returned to the United States to become an instructor at the Army War College in Washington, D.C. During a tour as assistant commandant of the Infantry School at Fort Benning, Georgia, from 1927 until 1932, he introduced and developed new techniques and concepts in the training of officers and enlisted men. He then undertook successive posts as senior instructor to the National Guard and as the commander of the Eighth Infantry and of the Fifth Infantry Brigade.

Marshall rose slowly in rank during the interlude of peace. He had been brevetted as a colonel during World War I but was reverted back to the rank of captain at the end of the conflict. In 1920 he became a major, in 1923 a lieutenant colonel, and in 1933 he achieved the rank of colonel. General Douglas MacArthur, army chief of staff from 1930 to 1935 and one who stressed the importance of combat command experience in the development of a leader, prevented the promotion of staff officer Marshall to general. In October 1936, after MacArthur's brief retirement from the army, Marshall finally gained the coveted single star of a brigadier general.

Marshall quickly became chief military adviser to President Franklin D. Roosevelt in the months prior to the American entry into World War II. In mid-1938 Army Chief of Staff Malin L. Craig and

Assistant Secretary of War Louis Johnson persuaded Roosevelt to make Marshall assistant chief of staff in the army's War Plans Division. Marshall rose to the position of deputy chief of staff in October 1938 and became acting chief of staff the following July. On the advice of General Pershing, Roosevelt in September 1939 passed over 34 more senior general officers and appointed Marshall chief of staff with a four-star rank.

Marshall masterfully directed the American armed forces during World War II. He built a fighting machine of more than ten million men and provided the necessary supplies for its mission. He also chose able leaders for the army, including Dwight David Eisenhower, from the younger and more vigorous members of the officer corps. In recognition of Marshall's efforts, President Roosevelt in December 1944 made him the first American officer ever to wear five stars and to bear the rank of general of the army.

Strategically, Marshall advocated an Allied cross-Channel invasion of Europe as the quickest means to defeat Hitler. He staunchly opposed British prime minister Winston Churchill's proposals for peripheral attacks and thrusts into the southern European underbelly. Ultimately, the Allies implemented Marshall's plan in Operation Overlord, beginning on D day on June 6, 1944. Marshall hoped to command the forces that landed on the Normandy beaches, but Roosevelt, who protested that he would not be able to sleep at night with his chief of staff out of the country, named Eisenhower to the post.

President Roosevelt depended on Marshall as a trusted adviser in diplomatic as well as military affairs. In August 1941 Marshall accompanied the president to his seaborne rendezvous off the coast of Newfoundland with Churchill, a meeting which resulted in the formulation of the Atlantic Charter. Marshall also assisted Roosevelt at wartime conferences with Churchill and other Allied leaders at Casablanca, Quebec, Cairo, Teheran, and Yalta.

Harry S. Truman, who succeeded Roosevelt as president in 1945, continued to employ Marshall as a diplomat. After the conclusion of the European phase of World War II, Truman took Marshall to the Potsdam Conference, at which Truman discussed plans for the postwar period with Prime Minister Anthony Eden of Great Britain and Premier Joseph Stalin of the Soviet Union. In November 1945 Truman dispatched Marshall, who had recently retired as chief of staff, to China to mediate between the Nationalist government of Generalissimo Chiang Kai-shek and its warring communist rivals under Mao Tse-tung. Marshall stayed in China until January 1947, but he was not able to reconcile the differences of the opposing sides.

Marshall served as Truman's secretary of state from 1947 until 1949. In this capacity, he devised what became known as the Marshall Plan. Officially, it was titled the European Recovery Plan, a program that ultimately granted to war-torn nations more than $17 billion to rebuild their economies. Explaining the program in a speech at Harvard University, Marshall stated:

> Our policy is not directed against any country or doctrine but against hunger, poverty, desperation and chaos. . . . We know that . . . the destitute and oppressed of the earth look chiefly to us for sustenance and support until they can face life with self-confidence and assurance.

Both Democratic and Republican members of Congress made the program a major part of the nation's foreign policy. Later the term *Marshall Plan* became slang for other proposals for economic development programs, domestic or foreign, designed to promote or restore self-sufficiency.

General Marshall became the secretary of defense for Truman in 1950 and was responsible for rebuilding American armed forces to meet North Korean aggression against South Korea in concert with other members of the United Nations. In September 1951 Marshall resigned from the cabinet and retired to his estate in Leesburg, Virginia. During the 1950s Senator Joseph McCarthy assailed Marshall as a procommunist, but his baseless slurs did not mar the general's reputation.

Marshall lived out his retirement near Pinehurst, North Carolina, with his second wife, Katherine Tupper Brown Marshall, whom he had married in 1930. His first wife, Elizabeth Carter Coles Marshall, whom he married upon graduation from VMI, had died in 1927. Marshall died at age 78 on October 16, 1959, at Walter Reed Army Hospital in Washington, D.C. During his lifetime, he won decorations from the United States and from 16 foreign nations. In 1953 he became the first professional soldier to ever win the Nobel Peace Prize.

Beginning of Ramadan, the Islamic Month of Fasting

This is a movable event.

Ramadan is the ninth month in the Islamic calendar, and has important religious significance because it is a month of fasting. The Islamic calendar is a lunar calendar, not a solar calendar like the traditional Gregorian calendar, and is 11 days shorter. Thus, for purposes of convenience this book uses December 31, since that is the date on which Ramadan fell in 1997.

Muslims believe that in the month of Ramadan Allah "perfected his blessing upon his people by giving followers the Holy Quran" or Koran, the sacred book of Islam. Devout Muslims are required to perform the *Sawm*, or "Fasting," during this holy month. In fact, this obligation is considered the fourth pillar of the "five pillars" of Islamic faith, and must be observed from dawn until dusk during the whole month. Every adult Muslim, male or female, who is mentally and physically healthy and not a soldier or traveler is required to comply. There are exceptions for women during their period of menstruation and while nursing children.

The fast is a comprehensive ban on all eating, drinking, and intimate sexual contact during the daylight hours. These needs are supposed to be taken care of after dark. Muslims traditionally break their daily Ramadan fast at sunset with a meal called *iftar*, basically meaning "break-fast." The purpose of the fast is to instill devotion and humility through the rigors of hunger, thirst, and abstinence. It is a special devotional observance to help Muslims develop *taqwa*, or "self-restraint, " "the pleasure of Allah." The fast is also supposed to create appreciation for the deprivations suffered by the poor and to encourage charitable works.

When the month of Ramadan comes to an end, there is a special morning prayer and an observance called *eid al-fitr*, or "the feast of the breaking of the fast." Many Muslims hold celebrations such as family reunions at this time. Gift-giving is also common, among family members and to the poor.

APPENDIX A: THE CALENDAR

The word calendar comes from the Latin *calendarium*, or "account book," derived from *calendae*, or "the calends," the first day of the ancient Roman month, on which accounts were due and on which the priests of Rome called the people together to proclaim, or *calare*, that the new moon had been sighted. In English a calendar means, abstractly, a people's settled system of reckoning the passage of time in days. Thus, it is by the calendar that the beginning and length of the years, and their subdivision into parts, such as months and weeks, are established for the community over the long term. See also Appendix B: The Era, Appendix C: The Days of the Week, and the articles on each of the 12 months in the main text.

More substantively, a calendar is a table constructed for handy reference, showing the division of the days of a given year into months and weeks and the date of each day. Calendars laden with detailed notes concerning the weather, holidays, and other social matters are usually called almanacs.

Calendars are primarily based on some combination of celestial observation and observance of the pattern of human activities and rituals. More than once, improved astronomical data have initially conflicted with deep conservatism about the perceived sanctity of the calendar, based on its foundation in ancient religious beliefs and social customs. In fact, the astronomical computations necessary to construct calendars have presented stargazers with problems at every stage. To amass accurate long-term readings of the positions of the heavenly bodies and of the sun's shadow is a delicate task extending over many generations. In addition, three major natural phenomena challenge the ingenuity of calendar makers.

The first challenge is the fact that the moon's cycle of waxing and waning, so striking in its regularity that it provided early peoples with their first effective subdivision of time beyond the alternations of night and day, is not expressible in whole days. On the contrary, the lunar cycle has an average length of slightly more than 29 ½ days, with a possible variation of up to half a day from this average because of the moon's elliptical orbit. These variations are not readily predictable without extensive astronomical records. Thus, these irregularities have always posed serious difficulties for persons attempting to calculate the length of future lunar months. Often the problem was solved by alternating months of 29 and 30 days and ignoring the fact that the appearance of the new moon often did not coincide with its designated date in the calendar. This is the basic rule in the Chinese, Jewish, and Islamic calendars.

The second and third challenges became apparent only as people gradually came to need a longer unit of time than the moon's cycle (one lunar month) to regulate group life. The cycle of the seasons, important to all even in very simple economies, naturally attracted attention. The seasons are governed by the sun rather than the moon, so that observers were gradually led to estimate the exact length of the sun's cycle. This was a very difficult feat and one not accomplished in an entirely satisfactory way before the 16th century A.D. But even methods that were only fairly sophisticated revealed that the solar, or tropical, year was not expressible in whole days, any more than the moon's cycle had been. In fact, one solar cycle requires 365 days, five hours, 48 minutes, and about 46 seconds, or roughly 365 ¼ days.

Long before the observations of the sun were so precise, scholars formed an approximate idea of the length of the solar cycle and faced the problem of how to combine it with their existing moon-based calendars. Once again there was a natural incompatibility: lunar and solar cycles are not readily expressible in terms of each other. In terms of complete lunar months, the closest approximation to the sun's cycle of 365 ¼ days is 12 moon cycles (lunations) or a little more than 354 days, about 11 days too few. As a result, in a purely lunar calendar, such as that required by the prophet Mohammed in the Koran, the months cannot be held in fixed relation to the solstices and equinoxes, the mileposts of the solar, or tropical, year. Instead, the months will arrive progressively earlier in each solar cycle, until eventually their names will have circled through all the seasons. To avoid this instability certain important moon-based calendars, such as the Chinese, were converted to "lunisolar" calendars, in which the lunar months are periodically returned to a stable place in the seasonal cycle by the insertion of an additional lunar month in the calendar every few years. This procedure is known as intercalation. The resulting calendar has months of nearly equal length, closely approximating the actual lunations, but its "years" are of varying length and do not reproduce the solar cycle exactly except over a period of several calendar "years." In certain civilizations, however, observers became particularly attentive to the sun's cycle and devised a truly solar calendar.

At least as early as the third millennium B.C., Egyptian scholars had calculated the solar cycle precisely enough to devise a yearly calendar of 365 days (12 months of 30 days each plus 5 extra days added as festival days at the end of the year). In the third century B.C., later Egyptian experts attempted to introduce a sixth extra day into every fourth year to reflect new computations that placed the solar year more accurately as 365 ¼ days. The Egyptian people, however, resisted, and the proposed "leap year" did not gain wide acceptance.

The earliest Roman calendar was a crude arrangement of ten lunar months, beginning with March (Martius), plus an indeterminably long, unnamed period during the winter when agriculture was moribund and the Roman armies were not at war. In time, two new months, named Januarius and Februarius, were created out of this unnamed period and added at the end of the year. (See the essays concerning January and February in the main text.) March continued as the first month of the year until 153 B.C., when the Roman state decreed that the new year thenceforth would begin on January 1. The result, although slow to gain popular acceptance, was the calendar from which the names and order of our present months descend.

The intercalation of days was necessary from time to time, however, to realign this Roman calendar with the solar cycle and the equinoxes. Unfortunately those who held this duty had so abused their office, often adding or subtracting days merely for political reasons, that by the time of Julius Caesar's rule, the Roman calendar was thoroughly scrambled, with January falling in autumn and the lengths of years being highly unpredictable. A gifted administrator, holding among other titles that of high priest, Caesar decided to reform the calendar so that it would be as nearly self-correcting as possible. In 46 B.C., on the advice of the astronomer Sosigenes, a Greek from Alexandria, Caesar reshaped the Roman calendar and based it upon the Egyptian solar year. He kept the old Roman month names but assigned the months an unequal number of days.

In setting aside the lunar basis of the calendar, Caesar made it necessary for Sosigenes to annex to the new calendar a separate system for calculating the moon's cycles to guide the dating of festivals dependent on the moon's changes. Sosigenes apparently chose the 19-year Metonic lunar cycle from Greece, and he gave his lunar calculations the starting point of March 1 in the solar year.

Caesar's calendar, known as the Julian, or Old Style, calendar, went into effect in 45 B.C. It ordained that three successive "common years" of 365 days should be followed by a fourth year with an extra day intercalated in the month of February to make a total of 366 days (see February 29, Leap Year). In this way the real solar year, estimated by Sosigenes at 365 ¼ days, was systematically expressed in calendar years of whole days. By intercalating 90 days in the year 46–45 B.C., Caesar also made spring begin once more in March.

The Julian reform also reaffirmed January 1 as the start of the Roman calendar year. It should be noted, however, that neither this new year's date nor the Latin month names were adopted in the Eastern portion of the Roman Empire. Furthermore, after Christianity became the official religion of the Roman Empire and imperial rule declined in the West, the use of the Julian calendar did not always involve keeping January 1 as the beginning of the new year in the West. During the Middle Ages, in fact, various dates were used to start the calendar year in different localities.

In the 16th century A.D., support grew for a reform of the now-ancient Julian calendar. One of the problems was the effect of cumulative error on the Church's Easter calendar. The correct calculation of successive Easters was a vast challenge, since it involved adjustments in computing both the solar and the lunar cycles used under the Julian calendar. The chief difficulty stemmed from an error in Sosigenes's original reckoning of the length of the solar year. In fact, the Earth actually takes 11 minutes, 14 seconds less than 365 ¼ days to orbit the sun. As a result the vernal equinox, which marks the beginning of spring, did not hold stable in the Julian calendar but had slipped backward over the centuries from March 25 in Caesar's time to March 11 by the 16th century. This lag, while annoying in an agrarian society used to associating the seasonal changes with certain months, would not have been regarded so seriously had it not been that in the early centuries of Christianity the reckoning of Easter had come to depend upon the date of the spring equinox.

It is frequently asserted that the rule for the computation of the date of Easter was solemnly set down at the great Ecumenical, or General, Council of Nicaea in A.D. 325. While this statement involves considerable telescoping of history, since the council passed no canon on the subject and its synodical letter was not explicit on many points, important elements of the rule that later came to predominate appear to have been agreed upon at the council. In any case, in later centuries both the Western churches and the Eastern Orthodox churches invoked the authority of the Nicene Council for their Easter rule, which came to be formulated as follows: Easter is to be celebrated on the first Sunday after the first full moon on or after the vernal equinox (taken as March 21). In contrast to the churches of the West, Eastern Orthodox churches also insisted that the rule requires that Easter must always occur after the Jewish Passover. To this day, there is no uniform observance of Easter between the Western and Eastern churches in Christianity.

Thus, calendrical projections of the future dates of Easter were highly complex, since they combined solar with lunar calculations, and accurate solar computation was necessitated by the pegging of Easter to the vernal equinox, as dated at the time of the Council of Nicaea. Despite an elaborate apparatus of "epacts," "golden numbers," and "dominical letters," Christian scholars in the West from the eighth century onward noticed that observable astronomical events did not always square very well with their computations in the Easter tables. Calendar reform was proposed as early as the 13th century, and although the papacy began to take the problem seriously in the later Middle Ages, more astronomical data was needed. The calendar reform finally promulgated by Pope Gregory XIII on February 24, 1582, in the papal edict, or bull, known as *Inter Gravissimas* rested on Nicolaus Copernicus's new mathematical calculations of the motions of the heavenly bodies. The reform was the work of Aloysius Lilius, who had been a physician at the University of Perugia, and the German Jesuit mathematician Christopher Clavius.

As for the solar cycle, the new Gregorian calendar provided that three leap years should be suppressed in every 400 years to balance out the 11-minute, 14-second surplus per year caused by the Julian reckoning of the year at 365 ¼ days. Thus, the Gregorian solar rule is that century years shall be common years instead of leap years, except when the year number is divisible by 400. Therefore, in the Gregorian calendar 1700, 1800, and 1900 were not leap years, but the year 2000 constituted a leap year. In translating Julian (Old Style) dates to their Gregorian equivalents, the following table is useful. For dates:

from October 5, 1582, through February 28, 1700, add 10 days;
from February 29, 1700, through February 28, 1800, add 11 days;
from February 29, 1800, through February 28, 1900, add 12 days;
from February 29, 1900, through February 28, 2100, add 13 days.

In an effort to preserve the "Nicene" Easter rule intact, the Gregorian calendar reformers decided to restore the vernal equinox to March 21, its calendrical date at the time of the Council of Nicaea. To accomplish this, Pope Gregory XIII ordered that 10 days be omitted from the calendar in 1582. Thursday, October 4, was to be followed directly by Friday, October 15, in that year. The reformers also used January 1 as the beginning of the new year.

The new Gregorian calendar had to win acceptance in a Europe that was bitterly divided by the Protestant Reformation. It was accepted almost immediately in Catholic countries, and thenceforth the Julian calendar became known as the Old Style calendar and the Gregorian calendar as the New Style calendar. Spain, Portugal, and most Italian states put the reform into effect as specified, making the day after October 4, 1582, turn into October 15. France instituted the reform two months later by following December 9 directly with December 20. In the Catholic provinces of the Netherlands, the Gregorian calendar was instituted on or shortly before January 1, 1583. The Catholic cantons of Switzerland instituted the new calendar in 1583. Emperor Rudolph II proclaimed the reform for the Holy Roman Empire in September 1583, ordering that January 6, 1584, be followed at once by January 17; this was done in the Catholic states of the empire, but Protestant resistance meant that the imperial courts had to reckon by both Old and New Styles. The Gregorian reform became effective in Poland on January 1, 1586, and was adopted in Hungary in 1587.

Except for the Dutch principalities of Holland and Zealand, who instituted the New Style as of January 1, 1583, and Sweden for a brief time, Protestant peoples and rulers refused to recognize the papal calendar reform because of their conflict with Catholicism. The Eastern Orthodox churches charged the Roman Catholic church with heresy and with contravening the Council of Nicaea. In the Spanish Netherlands and Bohemia (now the Czech Republic), Protestants resisted the new calendar by force of arms. Thereafter the calendar change continued to be a cause of ill-feeling and even violence in lands with religiously mixed populations.

This period of strife did not end until the Lutheran German states met in 1699 at the urging of the theologian and mathematician Gottfried Wilhelm von Leibniz. At the Diet of Regensburg it was agreed that the solar aspects of the Gregorian calendar were to be accepted, and it was decreed that February 18, 1700, be followed immediately by March 1. The Diet also urged the United Netherlands to accept the Gregorian calendar, which the individual provinces did in 1700 and 1701. Denmark and Norway likewise instituted the New Style in 1700, and the Protestant cantons of Switzerland made it effective as of January 12, 1701. In 1700, however, the German and Swiss Protestants simultaneously adopted a distinctive Easter reckoning based on Johannes Kepler's astronomical tables, which they maintained until 1778, when Frederick II of Prussia used his royal power and influence to have Easter reckoned thenceforth by the Gregorian means.

Queen Elizabeth I of England, a Protestant, was not inclined to accept Pope Gregory XIII's new calendar. As a result, England and its dominions maintained the Julian calendar for 170 more years and continued the medieval practice of observing the new year in March. The Gregorian calendar was finally adopted by an act of Parliament in 1751 and took effect throughout Great Britain and its colonies, including her colonies in the Americas. This act provided that December 31, 1751, would be followed by January 1, 1752 (not 1751), and thus the dates from January 1 through March 24 never existed in the year 1751. By the 18th century, the Gregorian reform required the suppression of 11 days of the Julian calendar. Thus the above-mentioned act of Parliament also provided that September 2 be followed directly by September 14 in 1752.

In Sweden the Roman Catholic King John III's attempt to institute the Gregorian calendar soon after 1582 foundered because of Protestant resistance. After a second abortive attempt in the early 1700s, the New Style calendar was finally introduced into Sweden in 1753, as of March 1.

For nearly two centuries after the initial Gregorian reform, Europeans found it necessary to date letters with two sets of dates when corresponding with persons employing a different calendar style. Old Style dates were placed above a line and New Style below, for example:

25 May, 1660

---

4 June

In addition, for dates from January 1 through March 24, the American colonists and the British had to give double years as well, until the 1752 changeover to the Gregorian calendar. For example:

23 January, 1627

---

2 February, 1628

During the French Revolution, the French unsuccessfully attempted to overthrow the Gregorian calendar. To divorce Republican France dramatically from the old regime, and especially from the Catholic church, on October 5, 1793, a revolutionary convention approved what was known as the Revolutionary, or Republican, calendar. Its year contained 12 months of 30 days each, with months divided not into weeks but into three *décades* of ten days each. Five extra days were added at the end of the year for celebration as revolutionary national holidays, called *Sansculottides*, and every fourth year was to have a sixth extra day. The Republican new year began on September 22, the anniversary of the proclamation of the Republic, and the whole Republican calendar was made retroactive to September 22, 1792, with

1792–93 becoming the year "I" of the Republic (Republican year numbers being expressed in Roman numerals). Implicitly this new calendar entailed a rejection of the entire Christian era as well (see Appendix B: The Era). Napoleon Bonaparte abolished the calendar in the year XIV, returning France to the Gregorian calendar as of January 1, 1806.

With the ascendancy of Western Europe and the United States in the 19th and 20th centuries, the Gregorian calendar spread around the world, at least for official business. In 1873 the Meiji government of Japan instituted the Gregorian calendar as the official calendar, making January 1 of that year Japan's first Gregorian day. The traditional Japanese calendar was also maintained, however, and Japan is still one of the many two-calendar nations around the world today. On January 1, 1912, the new Republican government of China took the same step. Like Japan, however, China also kept its traditional calendar. On February 7, 1918, the Soviet revolutionary government adopted the New Style calendar for Russia. For example, the October Revolution in Russia that would lead to the creation of the Soviet Union began on the night of October 24 Old Style (November 6 New Style). During and after the First World War the Gregorian calendar was adopted by the Balkan states: Bulgaria (1916), Yugoslavia (1919), Romania and Greece (1924). In 1927 Turkey adopted the Gregorian calendar, leading the way for other Islamic countries in the years to follow.

APPENDIX B: THE ERA

Relatively late in the development of time reckoning, scholars in the Mediterranean world first conceived of "eras." An era is a lengthy period of time commencing from a fixed point (called its "epoch"), which serves to order all subsequent years in relation to one another. People slowly recognized the advantages both for historical writing and for celestial observation of numbering very long series of years sequentially according to an era, rather than in repetitive cycles. They even more slowly evolved a name for this chronological concept. The English word "era," dating from the early 17th century, comes from the late Latin *aera* or *era*, which apparently began to be used in the Renaissance to signify an entire system of chronology. In medieval Spain the word *aera* was prefixed to individual year numbers (as in *aera* 1072) to indicate that the year was reckoned according to the "Spanish Era" (see below)— i.e., the word *aera* functioned somewhat like the letters A.D. Earlier *aera* had probably meant "counters used in calculation" from the plural of the word *aes*, meaning "brass" or "money."

The era most commonly used in the Western world today is the Christian era. It became the dominant era throughout the world in the 20th century, even though a number of other era systems continue in use in certain nations. Years of the Christian era are typically designated either A.D. for the Latin *anno Domini* ("in the year of the Lord") or B.C. to signify time "before Christ." In recent years, to avoid the Christian bias of the A.D. and B.C. designations, usage of C.E. for "common era" and B.C.E. for "before the common era" has become more common.

In modern times, years of this era have started on January 1. By extrapolation it is often said that the "epoch," or starting point, of the era was January 1, A.D. 1, but this is anachronistic (see p. 1-2). For centuries in medieval Europe other days eclipsed January 1 as the beginning of the calendar year (see also January 1: New Year's Day and Appendix A: The Calendar).

There have been a wide variety of dating systems other than the Christian era. Most early chroniclers, like the keepers of the oral tradition among preliterate peoples, were content to suggest long spans of time by such vague phrases as "five generations" or to date events from some natural calamity. In kingdoms, the somewhat more sophisticated system developed of dating events by the year of the current ruler's reign, for example, "in the fourth year of King Alfred." These regnal or reign-year systems were very common throughout history and are still used in some countries as a complement to the Christian era dating system out of respect for tradition. The regnal method of dating is fraught with difficulties, however, particularly in deciding the day from which a monarch's regnal years should begin.

Very early in their history, the Chinese devised an ingenious and more regular system to record the years and to supplement imperial reign-years on official documents, even though the reign-years remained the most common form of dating in China until the 20th century. Under their lunar-solar calendar, which goes back to very ancient times, the Chinese came to mark the years by an astronomically calculated cycle of 60 years that was overlaid with metaphysical significance. This sexagenary cycle rests upon the combination of ten "celestial stems," based on the five "basic elements," with 12 "terrestrial branches" deriving from the Far Eastern signs of the zodiac. Each series constantly rotates in such a way as to make a total of 60 possible combinations. Eventually the 60-year cycle was adopted by the Koreans, Japanese, and Vietnamese as well. Instead of being numbered, each year in the cycle is named, being designated by two Chinese characters called its *E-to*, giving its branch and stem names. For serious chronological work, the Chinese sometimes employed a 180-year cycle combining three 60-year cycles and projected backwards in time to the reign of the legendary Emperor Huang-ti in the third millennium B.C. Since the seventh century B.C., shorter 12-year cycles called *Chi*, in which years are referred to simply by their branch names (as in "year of the hare"), became a popular means of avoiding the complexity of the 60-year cycle. Each sexagenary cycle embraces five *Chi*. Probably in the second century B.C., the Chinese introduced still another chronological system, based on periods of unequal length called *Nien-hao* that were named distinctively after some remarkable event. Under the first Ming emperor (A.D. 1368), however, it was decided that a new *Nien-hao* would henceforth be declared only at the start of a new emperor's reign. All of these year systems, with their various inconveniences, were officially set aside in 1912 when the newly founded Republic of China succeeded the last imperial dynasty (the Manchus) of the old Chinese empire.

For many centuries the ancient Greeks and Romans also designated the years in accordance with their political systems. Rather than being numbered, the years were named for the chief officers of the state at the time. For example, years were named for the magistrates known as *archons* in Athens and for the consuls in Rome. Early Greek scholars also calculated natural cycles by which dates were sometimes given. Most famous was Meton's highly accurate lunar cycle of 19 years, which would later be used by Christians to help calculate the date of Easter.

Not satisfied to name years after the consuls, Roman historians devised the "Era of Rome," in which years were dated from the semi-mythical founding of the city and styled A.U.C. for *ab urbe condita*, or "from the founding of the city." Although they agreed on April 21 as the starting day, educated Romans were not in agreement about which year to assign to the founding of Rome, and different years were used. As a result, this era remained a device of the intellectuals and was not adopted for general transactions, which continued to be dated by consulates well into the Christian period. In the 19th century, however, the era of Rome was revived by scholars of ancient civilizations and given the conventional starting point (or epoch) of 753 B.C. and so A.U.C. 1 would correspond to 753–752 B.C.

Since the time of Omar I, the second caliph, most Muslims have observed the "era of the Hegira" in commemoration of the Prophet Mohammed's flight from Mecca to Medina in 622 A.D., taking as its beginning the first day of the month of Muharram (July 16, 622 A.D.). According to this era, years are styled A.H. for *anno Hegirae*, "in the year of the Hegira." Since the year of the Islamic calendar is purely lunar, with a length of either 354 or 355 days, 33 years of the Muslim era are nearly equal to 32 years of the Christian era. The era of the Hegira has increasingly become secondary, however, to the Western calendar in the Islamic world ever since Turkey went over to the Western calendar in 1927.

At the end of the 18th century, the French Revolutionary government launched the only decisive departure from the Christian era that has been attempted in modern Western dating. Revolutionary France, in adopting a wholly new Republican calendar to replace the Gregorian calendar so closely associated with royal and ecclesiastical authority (see Appendix A: The Calendar), retroactively declared on October 5, 1793, that the "Republican era" had begun on September 22, 1792. Napoleon Bonaparte reinstituted the Christian era in French dating, along with the Gregorian calendar, on January 1, 1806, in the middle of the year XIV of the French Republic.

During the American Revolution, the alliance of the 13 former colonies abandoned the ancient British practice of dating official documents by the reign-years of the monarch and noted instead on its documents the "year of Independence" together with the year of the Christian era. Today, presidential proclamations still state that they have been signed at Washington, D.C., on a given day of the month and in a given year "and of the Independence of the United States the ____" (the blank being filled in with the number of years since the signing of the Declaration of Independence).

In the 19th century, when historians writing about ancient times began to systematically extend the Christian era back to the period before Christ, a difficulty inherent in the original dating system became apparent. Traditionally, the years had been expressed in Roman numerals, but there is no Roman numeral for zero. Thus, there is no year 0 between 1 A.D. and 1 B.C., which means that in order to compute the interval between a date that is A.D. and another that is B.C. a person must reduce the apparent sum by one. For example, the interval between January 1 in the year 2 B.C. and January 1 in the year A.D. 2 is three years rather than four years. The absence of a year 0 has given rise to the argument that the turn of the second millennium A.D. properly begins on January 1, 2001, rather than January 1, 2000, as only 1999 years will have passed by the latter date in the Christian era's A.D. styling. However, the symbolic significance of the year 2000, combined with centuries of habit in marking the turn of the century in years ending with two zeros—and by implication marking millennia with years ending in three zeros—seem to indicate that the new millennium will be calculated from January 1, 2000, by most systems of reckoning.

APPENDIX C: THE DAYS OF THE WEEK

The English word "week" is derived from the Anglo-Saxon word *wicu* and ultimately from the Germanic *wikon*, both words probably meaning "turn" or "change" and designating a period of time amounting to less than a month and now consisting of seven days.

The month has been divided in various ways throughout history. In ancient Egypt, for example, the phases of the moon resulted in a division of the month into fractional parts, such as decads or pentads known as "moon weeks." Other ancient peoples settled the length of the week arbitrarily without considering the length of the month and invented for their convenience the "market week," usually ranging from four to eight days. The early Romans used an eight-day market week.

The exact origin of the seven-day week has been lost in antiquity. Various theories have been proposed. One theory is that there were seven days for the seven known celestial bodies (excluding Earth) during ancient times, namely the sun, the moon, Mercury, Venus, Mars, Jupiter, and Saturn (the outer planets of Uranus, Neptune, and Pluto were not discovered until modern times). Another theory relies on the influence of the Old Testament, namely the account in Genesis of how God created the world in six days and rested on the seventh. This seventh and last day of the week, known as the Sabbath (Shabbat), was therefore set aside as the Hebrew holy day of rest and worship in keeping with Genesis 2:3, "And God blessed the seventh day, and sanctified it."

In the Roman calendar the first day of the week was Sunday, known as *dies solis*, or "sun's day." The second day (today's Monday) was *dies lunae*, for moon's day, the third day (today's Tuesday) was *dies Martis*, for Mars's day, after the god of war, the fourth day (today's Wednesday) was *dies Mercurii*, for Mercury's day, after the god of commerce and messenger of the gods, the fifth day (today's Thursday) was *dies Jovis*, or Jove's day, after Jupiter (the king of the gods), the sixth day (today's Friday) was *dies Veneris*, or Venus's day, after the goddess of love, and the seventh day (today's Saturday) was *dies Saturni*, or Saturn's day, after the god of agriculture.

The use of these pagan names for the days of the week remained an accepted practice even after the emperor Constantine made Christianity the official religion of the Roman Empire. The English names for the days of the week were heavily influenced by the Roman names.

Sunday, the first day of the week, gets its name from the Anglo-Saxon *sunnandaeg* from *sunnan* for sun and *daeg* for day. Like the equivalent Roman name of *dies solis*, Sunday is regarded as a name surviving from ancient sun worship. With the Christianization of the British Isles, Sunday became not only the day of worship but a day of rest. Legal measures were frequently used to enforce both obligations.

According to an English statute of 1558–59, any person who did not attend church services was subject to a penalty of 12 pence, as well as church censure. As the Puritan movement gained momentum in the 17th century, restrictive moral legislation became commonplace, and most secular activities were strictly forbidden on Sunday. The colony of Virginia passed such legislation as early as 1629. Practically every American colony enacted Sunday legislation, although Puritan New England outdid other regions. The term "blue laws" for this type of puritanical lawmaking was first coined by an Anglican clergyman, Samuel A. Peters of Hebron, Connecticut. After the American Revolution, various blue laws continued to exist in most states, but the bulk of them were repealed by the middle of the 20th century or were invalidated by the Supreme Court. Nonetheless, prohibitions on the sale of alcohol or even recorded music persist in many areas of the United States, especially where religious fundamentalism is deeply rooted, and many retail businesses remain closed on Sundays regardless of what they sell.

The name of Monday comes from the Anglo-Saxon *monandaeg*, or "moonday," which is a translation from the Roman name *dies lunae*, or "moon's day."

Tuesday comes from the Anglo-Saxon *Tiwesdaeg*, or *Tiw's day*. It is named for Tyr, the Norse god of war and battle, whom the Anglo-Saxons called Tiw. His identification with Mars, the Roman god of war, caused the Anglo-Saxons to translate the *dies Martis*, or "Mars's day," of the Romans as *Tiwesdaeg*. In the Germanic pantheon Tyr, or Tiw, was regarded as the bold wrestler among the gods. His cult seems to have been widespread, especially in England, Germany, and Iceland.

Wednesday is named after the Norse god Odin, also known as Woden or Wuotan. The name comes from the Anglo-Saxon word *Wodnesdaeg*, or "Woden's day." Odin, the father of Tyr and Thor, was considered the highest, oldest and wisest of the Germanic gods. The cult of Odin was followed primarily in Germany and England, but his exploits are also related in the Icelandic prose and poetic *Eddas*, which tell how Odin and his brothers slew the giant Ymir and from his body created the world. Ymir's flesh became the dry land; his bones, the mountains; his teeth and jaws, rocks and pebbles; and his blood the ocean. His skull became the vault of the heavens. Odin lived in the palace of Valhalla, a sort of martial paradise where the god welcomed brave warriors after death and treated them to an eternity of fighting and feasting. Probably because of his wisdom and skill in magic, Odin became identified with Mercury, the Roman god of commerce who was the fleet-footed messenger of the gods. Therefore, the Roman day of *dies Mercurii*, or "Mercury's day," became *Wodnesdaeg* or "Woden's day."

Thursday is named for Thor, the Norse god of thunder. His chariot, drawn by he-goats named Tooth-gnasher and Gap-tooth, was said to cause the thunder when it was drawn through the heavens. The eldest and strongest son of Odin, Thor was armed with a magical hammer named Mjollnir which returned when thrown. Thor used his hammer to kill his implacable enemies, the giants. In all northern countries, and especially in Iceland, the cult of Thor was highly developed, although few details about the worship are known today. For reasons that are unclear, Thor was identified with the chief Roman god Jupiter. The Anglo-Saxons thus termed the Roman *dies Jovis*, or "Jove's day," their *Thursdaeg*, or "Thor's day."

Friday is named for Frigg or Frigga, the wife of Odin in northern mythology. Her name became confused with that of Freya, the Scandinavian goddess of fertility, matrimony, light, and peace. Because of Frigg's identification with Freya and Freya's similarity to Venus, the Roman goddess of love, the Anglo-Saxons translated the Roman day of *dies Veneris*, or "Venus's day" as *Frigedaeg*, or "Frigg's day." Although pagans in northern countries regarded Friday as the luckiest day of the week, early Christians believed that it was unlucky since it was the day on which Christ had been crucified.

Saturday was the only day in the Anglo-Saxon week that continued to be named after one of the Roman gods. As the Romans called it *dies Saturni*, or "Saturn's day," the Anglo-Saxons called it *Saterdaeg*, after the Roman god of planting and agriculture. Saturn apparently became identified with the Greek deity Kronos or Cronus, the primeval Titan who ruled the world in the mythical Golden Age of peace and plenty. Defeated in battle by his son Zeus, Kronos supposedly went to Rome, where he was welcomed by Janus, the Roman god of doorways (see January). Saturn's festival, known as the *Saturnalia*, was celebrated in December (see December).

APPENDIX D: SIGNS OF THE ZODIAC

In both astronomy and astrology, the zodiac is the designation that the ancients gave to an imaginary band or zone of the heavens. It is about 16 degrees in width, extending eight degrees on each side of the ecliptic, the apparent annual path of the sun amongst the stars as seen from Earth. The zodiac includes the orbits of the sun and the moon, as well as of the five planets (Mercury, Venus, Mars, Jupiter, and Saturn) which were thought erroneously to revolve around the Earth. The other planets, namely Uranus, Neptune, and Pluto, were not discovered until modern times.

The zodiac is divided into 12 equal sections, the so-called signs of the zodiac, each named for a constellation located within these sections at the time of the ancients. The 12 constellations of the zodiac are Aries, Taurus, Gemini, Cancer, Leo, Virgo, Libra, Scorpio, Sagittarius, Capricorn, Aquarius, and Pisces. All but one of these constellations seemed to represent an animal or other living creature; hence the name *zodiac*, which is derived from the Greek, either from *zoon*, a "living thing," or *zoidion*, the diminutive of animal, and *kykios*, "circle." It is thus usually interpreted as a "circle of animals."

The zodiacal constellations were already known by the Greek equivalents of their present Latin names more than two thousand years ago. They were not invented by the Greeks, however. Interest in these constellations, which have been termed the "fossil remains of primitive stellar religion," extends back to the dawn of astronomy. The zodiac is believed to have originated with the early civilizations of Mesopotamia (roughly present-day Iraq) in the Middle East. The Akkadians, who created a flourishing civilization in the fourth millennium B.C., described the stars in detail. They passed on their star system to the Babylonians, whose cuneiform tablets, boundary stones, and works of art indicate the existence of a carefully thought out network of star names including the zodiac. The Babylonian system probably arose early in their history, before 2000 B.C. Cuneiform tablets recounting the Creation legend, which were compiled from more ancient records during the reign of King Assurbanipal of Assyria around 650 B.C., include a passage that appears to indicate the acceptance of 36 constellations: 12 northern, 12 southern, and 12 zodiacal. The zodiac system was most likely transmitted from Mesopotamia through the seafaring Phoenicians to the Greeks and from Greece to the Western world.

The fourth-century B.C. Greek astronomer Eudoxus of Cnidus was probably the author of the earliest Greek work that treated groups of stars as constellations. This early work did not survive to modern times, but a verification of it was made by Aratus, a third-century B.C. poet at the court of Antigonus II Gonatas, king of Macedonia, who was himself a patron of philosophy and poetry. In an astronomical treatise entitled *Phenomena*, Aratus gave the first systematic literary account of the stars. He listed 44 constellations, including 13 central or zodiacal ones: Aries, Taurus, Gemini, Cancer, Leo, Virgo, Libra, Scorpio, Sagittarius, Capricorn, Aquarius, Pisces, and the Pleiades.

The great second-century B.C. Greek astronomer Hipparchus wrote the first known comprehensive catalog of the heavens, listing at least 850 stars. This commentary was based on the works of Eudoxus and Aratus. Unlike Aratus, however, he did not keep the Pleiades separate from Taurus but combined them and thus enumerated 12 constellations rather than 13. Some 300 years after Hipparchus, in the second century A.D., the famous Greco-Egyptian scholar and mathematician Ptolemy set down a similar scheme in the *Almagest*. Islamic scholars later transmitted the work to Western Europe.

Since antiquity there have been no major alterations in the zodiacal system. In A.D. 1627 Julius Schiller tried in his *Coelum stellatum Christianum* to have the names denoting mythological pagan ideas replaced with the names of apostles, saints, and other renowned Christian figures. For example, Aries was to become St. Peter and Taurus would become St. Andrew. The innovation was short-lived, as was a similar attempt later made by E. Weigelius, who wished to have the constellations of the zodiac represent the symbolic arms of various European dynasties.

It should be noted in this discussion that other ancient civilizations defined and named the constellations of the zodiac in a different way from the Western world. For example, as expressed in the works of the Chinese astronomer Shih-Shen (c. 500 B.C.), the Chinese have their own distinctive signs of the zodiac and still assign them great weight in their culture.

In ancient times, the start of the year was reckoned from the beginning of spring, namely the vernal equinox (see March 21) which is the day on which the sun appears to pass through the intersection of the ecliptic and the celestial equator in what was perceived as its annual course. Day and night are of equal length at this time, and the ancients therefore chose the vernal equinox as the point from which to calculate the 12 zodiacal positions. At the time of Hipparchus, whose calculations (c. 120 B.C.) form the basis of the present zodiacal system, the sun was in Aries at the time of the vernal equinox. Thus the order of the 12 zodiacal constellations, going eastward, traditionally began with Aries.

There are various theories about the origins of the naming of each of the constellations in the zodiac.

Aries, the Ram (March 21–April 19), may have been named after the ram whose golden fleece was the goal of the Argonauts, the legendary band of Greek heroes led by Jason.

Taurus, the Bull (April 20–May 20), may have been named after an episode in Greek mythology where the chief god Zeus fell in love with the Phoenician princess Europa. Assuming the disguise of a great white bull, the god enticed the maiden to mount him, whereupon he swam to Crete and the princess became the mother of three of his children.

Gemini, the Twins (May 21–June 21), was associated with many mythical twins, among them Castor and Pollux of Greco-Roman legend. They were the twin sons of Zeus and Leda, the wife of King Tyndareus of Sparta.

Cancer, the Crab (June 22–July 22), may symbolize the claws of a crab. According to the Roman writer and philosopher Macrobius, the name "crab" arose from the ancient belief that the particular zodiacal constellation "walks backward" like a crab, as does the sun at the summer solstice when the day reaches its maximum length and then begins to retreat.

Leo, the Lion (July 23–August 22), derives its name from the ancient association of the lion with heat or fire, and thus the lion is an appropriate symbol for the hottest time of the year. Further, according to Greek mythology, the hero Hercules successfully slew an enormous beast known as the Nemean lion in fulfillment of one of his legendary 12 labors. Zeus then raised the lion to the heavens in tribute to Hercules.

Virgo, the Virgin (August 23–September 22), may be named after Ishtar, the Babylonian goddess of love and fertility. Ancient mythologies are replete with the veneration of virgins, however, so the origin of the name remains unclear.

Libra, the Scales (September 23–October 23), represents the only inanimate object in the zodiac. The scales refer to the balancing or equality of night and day at the season when the sun arrives at the autumnal equinox.

Scorpio (Scorpius), the Scorpion (October 24–November 21), may be named after a Greek fable in which the famous hunter Orion boasted to Artemis, the goddess of the moon and the hunt, and Leto, the mother of Apollo and Artemis, that he would slay all of the animals in the world. A scorpion, acting upon the orders of the two goddesses, thereupon stung him to death. Zeus raised the scorpion to heaven as a constellation.

Sagittarius, the Archer (November 22–December 21), was represented by the Greeks as a centaur, half-man and half-horse, in the act of shooting an arrow. The third-century B.C. astronomers termed Sagittarius a satyr. In remote antiquity, the constellation probably represented the Babylonian god of war, the equivalent of the Roman god Mars.

Capricorn (Capricornus), the Goat (December 22–January 19), is named after the Latin *caper*, for "goat" and *cornu*, for "horn." The ancients maintained that the sun of the winter solstice was like a child in infancy and therefore the name may also have been connected with the Caprine nurse of the young solar god mentioned in various Eastern legends.

Aquarius, the Water-Bearer (January 20–February 18), is probably named after the ancient Egyptian god of waters. This may well be the oldest of all the zodiacal signs.

Pisces, the Fishes (February 19–March 20), may represent the "wet month" of the Egyptians when the waters of the Nile began their annual flooding. There is also a Greek legend involving Aphrodite, the goddess of love, and Eros, the god of love who was also her son and companion. The two were supposedly surprised by the monster Typhon on the banks of the Euphrates River in Mesopotamia and sought safety by jumping into the water, where they were changed into the two fishes that have come to represent Pisces.

The signs of the zodiac still retain significance in astrology and, to a certain degree, in the popular culture. Even in modern times, astrologers still use birthdays to cast horoscopes and make prognostications based on the zodiacal sign in which those birthdays fall. Many newspapers publish horoscopes on a daily basis, although mostly for amusement. For astronomers, however, the zodiac represents a hopelessly antiquated means of charting the heavens. The movement of the stars, which, like the sun, slowly rotate around the center of the Milky Way galaxy, has caused such a shift over the intervening thousands of years that the constellations of the zodiac have actually moved an entire 30 degrees since the time of the ancient Greeks. Therefore, as a result of the precession of the equinoxes—the clockwise progression of the equinoctial points at which the sun crosses the celestial equator—the March equinox that occurred when the sun was in Aries at the time of Hipparchus (second century B.C.) now occurs when the sun is in the constellation of Pisces, which now occupies the sign of Aries. So although we still say the sun moves into Aries on March 21, the vernal equinox, it actually enters the constellation Pisces. Modern stellar cartography (star mapping with telescopes and various advanced devices) has long since made reliance upon the constellations obsolete.

APPENDIX E: UNITED STATES CONSTITUTION

[The Constitution established the modern federal system of government in the United States. In this system, various powers are delegated to the three branches of the federal government: executive, legislative, and judicial. Other powers are reserved for the states, and certain liberties enjoyed by the citizenry are protected. The Constitution was drafted during the Constitutional Convention that first met in Philadelphia, Pennsylvania, on May 25, 1787, and it was ratified by the required nine of the 13 states by June 21, 1788. Effective 1789, the Constitution superseded the Articles of Confederation (see Appendix G). Many of the essays in this book relate to the Constitution; consult the Index for further information.]

Preamble

We the People of the United States, in Order to form a more perfect Union, establish Justice, insure domestic Tranquility, provide for the common defence, promote the general Welfare, and secure the Blessings of Liberty to ourselves and our Posterity, do ordain and establish this Constitution for the United States of America.

Article I.

Section 1. All legislative Powers herein granted shall be vested in a Congress of the United States, which shall consist of a Senate and House of Representatives.

Section 2. The House of Representatives shall be composed of Members chosen every second Year by the People of the several States, and the Electors in each State shall have the Qualifications requisite for Electors of the most numerous Branch of the State Legislature.

No Person shall be a Representative who shall not have attained to the Age of twenty-five Years, and been seven Years a Citizen of the United States, and who shall not, when elected, be an Inhabitant of that State in which he shall be chosen.

Representatives and direct Taxes shall be apportioned among the several States which may be included within this Union, according to their respective Numbers, which shall be determined by adding to the whole Number of free Persons, including those bound to Service for a Term of Years, and excluding Indians not taxed, three fifths of all other Persons. The actual Enumeration shall be made within three Years after the first Meeting of the Congress of the United States, and within every subsequent Term of ten Years, in such Manner as they shall by Law direct. The Number of Representatives shall not exceed one for every thirty Thousand, but each State shall have at Least one Representative; and until such enumeration shall be made, the State of New Hampshire shall be entitled to chuse three, Massachusetts eight, Rhode-Island and Providence Plantations one, Connecticut five, New-York six, New Jersey four, Pennsylvania eight, Delaware one, Maryland six, Virginia ten, North Carolina five, South Carolina five, and Georgia three.

When vacancies happen in the Representation from any State, the Executive Authority thereof shall issue Writs of Election to fill such Vacancies.

The House of Representatives shall chuse their Speaker and other Officers; and shall have the sole Power of Impeachment.

Section 3. The Senate of the United States shall be composed of two Senators from each State, chosen by the Legislature thereof, for six Years; and each Senator shall have one Vote.

Immediately after they shall be assembled in Consequence of the first Election, they shall be divided as equally as may be into three Classes. The Seats of the Senators of the first Class shall be vacated at the Expiration of the second Year, of the second Class at the Expiration of the fourth Year, and of the third Class at the Expiration of the sixth Year, so that one third may be chosen every second Year; and if Vacancies happen by Resignation, or otherwise, during the Recess of the Legislature of any State, the Executive thereof may make temporary Appointments until the next Meeting of the Legislature, which shall then fill such Vacancies.

No Person shall be a Senator who shall not have attained to the Age of thirty Years, and been nine Years a Citizen of the United States, and who shall not, when elected, be an Inhabitant of that State for which he shall be chosen.

The Vice President of the United States shall be President of the Senate, but shall have no Vote, unless they be equally divided.

The Senate shall chuse their other Officers, and also a President pro tempore, in the Absence of the Vice President, or when he shall exercise the Office of President of the United States.

The Senate shall have the sole Power to try all Impeachments. When sitting for that Purpose, they shall be on Oath or Affirmation. When the President of the United States is tried the Chief Justice shall preside: And no Person shall be convicted without the Concurrence of two thirds of the Members present.

Judgment in Cases of Impeachment shall not extend further than to removal from Office, and disqualification to hold and enjoy any Office of honor, Trust or Profit under the United States: but the Party convicted shall nevertheless be liable and subject to Indictment, Trial, Judgment, and Punishment, according to Law.

Section 4. The Times, Places, and Manner of holding Elections for Senators and Representatives, shall be prescribed in each State by the Legislature thereof; but the Congress may at any time by Law make or alter such Regulations, except as to the Places of chusing Senators.

The Congress shall assemble at least once in every Year, and such Meeting shall be on the first Monday in December, unless they shall by Law appoint a different Day.

Section 5. Each House shall be the Judge of the Elections, Returns, and Qualifications of its own Members, and a Majority of each shall constitute a Quorum to do Business; but a smaller Number may adjourn from day to day, and may be authorized to compel the Attendance of absent Members, in such Manner, and under such Penalties as each House may provide.

Each House may determine the Rules of its Proceedings, punish its Members for disorderly Behaviour, and, with the Concurrence of two thirds, expel a Member.

Each House shall keep a Journal of its Proceedings, and from time to time publish the same, excepting such Parts as may in their Judgment require Secrecy; and the Yeas and Nays of the Members of either House on any question shall, at the Desire of one fifth of those Present, be entered on the Journal.

Neither House, during the Session of Congress, shall, without the Consent of the other, adjourn for more than three days, nor to any other Place than that in which the two Houses shall be sitting.

Section 6. The Senators and Representatives shall receive a Compensation for their Services, to be ascertained by Law, and paid out of the Treasury of the United States. They shall in all Cases, except Treason, Felony, and Breach of the Peace, be privileged from Arrest during their Attendance at the Session of their respective Houses, and in going to and returning from the same; and for any Speech or Debate in either House, they shall not be questioned in any other Place.

No Senator or Representative shall, during the Time for which he was elected, be appointed to any civil Office under the Authority of the United States, which shall have been created, or the Emoluments whereof shall have been encreased during such time; and no Person holding any Office under the United States, shall be a Member of either House during his Continuance in Office.

Section 7. All Bills for raising Revenue shall originate in the House of Representatives; but the Senate may propose or concur with Amendments as on other Bills. Every Bill which shall have passed the House of Representatives and the Senate, shall, before it become a Law, be presented to the President of the United States; If he approve he shall sign it, but if not he shall return it, with his Objections to that House in which it shall have originated, who shall enter the Objections at large on their Journal, and proceed to reconsider it. If after such Reconsideration two thirds of that House shall agree to pass the Bill, it shall be sent, together with the Objections, to the other House, by which it shall likewise be reconsidered, and if approved by two thirds of that House, it shall become a Law. But in all such Cases the Votes of both Houses shall be determined by Yeas and Nays, and the Names of the Persons voting for and against the Bill shall be entered on the Journal of each House respectively. If any Bill shall not be returned by the President within ten Days (Sundays excepted) after it shall have been presented to him, the Same shall be a Law, in like Manner as if he had signed it, unless the Congress by their Adjournment prevent its Return, in which Case it shall not be a Law.

Every Order, Resolution, or Vote to which the Concurrence of the Senate and House of Representatives may be necessary (except on a question of Adjournment) shall be presented to the President of the United States; and before the Same shall take Effect, shall be approved by him, or being disapproved by him, shall be repassed by two thirds of the Senate and House of Representatives, according to the Rules and Limitations prescribed in the Case of a Bill.

Section 8. The Congress shall have Power to lay and collect Taxes, Duties, Imposts, and Excises, to pay the Debts and provide for the common Defence and general Welfare of the United States; but all Duties, Imposts, and Excises shall be uniform throughout the United States;

To borrow Money on the credit of the United States;

To regulate Commerce with foreign Nations, and among the several States, and with the Indian Tribes;

To establish an uniform Rule of Naturalization, and uniform Laws on the subject of Bankruptcies throughout the United States;

To coin Money, regulate the Value thereof, and of foreign Coin, and fix the Standard of Weights and Measures;

To provide for the Punishment of counterfeiting the Securities and current Coin of the United States;

To establish Post Offices and post Roads;

To promote the Progress of Science and useful Arts, by securing for limited Times to Authors and Inventors the exclusive Right to their respective Writings and Discoveries;

To constitute Tribunals inferior to the Supreme Court;

To define and punish Piracies and Felonies committed on the high Seas, and Offences against the Law of Nations;

To declare War, grant Letters of Marque and Reprisal, and make Rules concerning Captures on Land and Water;

To raise and support Armies, but no Appropriation of Money to that Use shall be for a longer Term than two Years;

To provide and maintain a Navy;

To make Rules for the Government and Regulation of the land and naval Forces;

To provide for calling forth the Militia to execute the Laws of the Union, suppress Insurrections and repel Invasions;

To provide for organizing, arming, and disciplining, the Militia, and for governing such Part of them as may be employed in the Service of the United States, reserving to the States respectively, the Appointment of the Officers, and the Authority of training the Militia according to the discipline prescribed by Congress;

To exercise exclusive Legislation in all Cases whatsoever, over such District (not exceeding ten Miles square) as may, by Cession of particular States, and the Acceptance of Congress, become the Seat of the Government of the United States, and to exercise like Authority over all Places purchased by the Consent of the Legislature of the State in which the Same shall be, for the Erection of Forts, Magazines, Arsenals, dock-Yards, and other needful Buildings; And

To make all Laws which shall be necessary and proper for carrying into Execution the foregoing Powers, and all other Powers vested by this Constitution in the Government of the United States, or in any Department or Officer thereof.

Section 9. The Migration or Importation of such Persons as any of the States now existing shall think proper to admit, shall not be prohibited by the Congress prior to the Year one thousand eight hundred and eight, but a Tax or duty may be imposed on such Importation, not exceeding ten dollars for each Person.

The Privilege of the Writ of Habeas Corpus shall not be suspended, unless when in Cases of Rebellion or Invasion the public Safety may require it.

No Bill of Attainder or ex post facto Law shall be passed.

No Capitation, or other direct Tax shall be laid, unless in Proportion to the Census or Enumeration herein before directed to be taken.

No Tax or Duty shall be laid on Articles exported from any State.

No Preference shall be given by any Regulation of Commerce or Revenue to the Ports of one State over those of another: nor shall Vessels bound to, or from, one State, be obliged to enter, clear, or pay Duties in another.

No Money shall be drawn from the Treasury, but in Consequence of Appropriations made by Law; and a regular Statement and Account of the Receipts and Expenditures of all public Money shall be published from time to time.

No Title of Nobility shall be granted by the United States; And no Person holding any Office of Profit or Trust under them shall, without the Consent of the Congress, accept of any present, Emolument, Office, or Title of any kind whatever from any King, Prince, or foreign State.

Section 10. No State shall enter into any Treaty, Alliance, or Confederation; grant Letters of Marque and Reprisal; coin Money; emit Bills of Credit; make any Thing but gold and silver Coin a Tender in Payment of Debts; pass any Bill of Attainder, ex post facto Law, or Law impairing the Obligation of Contracts, or grant any Title of Nobility.

No State shall, without the Consent of the Congress, lay any Imposts or Duties on Imports or Exports, except what may be absolutely necessary for executing its inspection Laws: and the net Produce of all Duties and Imposts, laid by any State on Imports or Exports, shall be for the Use of the Treasury of the United States; and all such Laws shall be subject to the Revision and Control of the Congress.

No State shall, without the Consent of Congress, lay any Duty of Tonnage, keep Troops, or Ships of War in time of Peace, enter into any Agreement or Compact with another State or with a foreign Power, or engage in War, unless actually invaded or in such imminent Danger as will not admit of delay.

Article II.

Section 1. The executive Power shall be vested in a President of the United States of America. He shall hold his Office during the Term of four Years, and, together with the Vice President, chosen for the same Term, be elected, as follows:

Each State shall appoint, in such Manner as the Legislature thereof may direct, a Number of Electors, equal to the whole Number of Senators and Representatives to which the State may be entitled in the Congress: but no Senator or Representative, or Person holding an Office of Trust or Profit under the United States, shall be appointed an Elector.

The Electors shall meet in their respective States, and vote by Ballot for two Persons, of whom one at least shall not be an Inhabitant of the same State with themselves. And they shall make a List of all the Persons voted for, and of the Number of Votes for each; which List they shall sign and certify, and transmit sealed to the Seat of Government of the United States, directed to the President of the Senate. The President of the Senate shall, in the Presence of the Senate and House of Representatives, open all the Certificates, and the Votes shall then be counted. The Person having the greatest Number of Votes shall be the President, if such Number be a Majority of the whole Number of Electors appointed; and if there be more than one who have such Majority, and have an equal Number of Votes, then the House of Representatives shall immediately chuse by Ballot one of them for President; and if no Person have a Majority, then from the five highest on the List the said House shall in like Manner chuse the President. But in chusing the President, the Votes shall be taken by States, the Representation from each State having one Vote; A quorum for this Purpose shall consist of a Member or Members from two thirds of the States, and a Majority of all the States shall be necessary to a Choice. In every Case, after the Choice of the President, the Person having the greatest Number of Votes of the Electors shall be the Vice-President. But if there should remain two or more who have equal Votes, the Senate shall chuse from them by Ballot the Vice President.

The Congress may determine the Time of chusing the Electors, and the Day on which they shall give their Votes, which Day shall be the same throughout the United States.

No Person except a natural born Citizen, or a Citizen of the United States, at the time of the Adoption of this Constitution, shall be eligible to the Office of President; neither shall any Person be eligible to that Office who shall not have attained to the Age of thirty five Years, and been fourteen Years a Resident within the United States.

In Case of the Removal of the President from Office, or of his Death, Resignation, or Inability to discharge the Powers and Duties of the said Office, the Same shall devolve on the Vice-President, and the Congress may by Law provide for the Case of Removal, Death, Resignation, or Inability, both of the President and Vice President declaring what Officer shall then act as President, and such Officer shall act accordingly, until the Disability be removed, or a President shall be elected.

The President shall, at stated Times, receive for his Services, a Compensation, which shall neither be increased nor diminished during the Period for which he shall have been elected, and he shall not receive within that Period any other Emolument from the United States, or any of them.

Before he enter on the Execution of his Office, he shall take the following Oath or Affirmation: "I do solemnly swear (or affirm) that I will faithfully execute the Office of President of the United States, and will to the best of my Ability, preserve, protect and defend the Constitution of the United States."

Section 2. The President shall be Commander in Chief of the Army and Navy of the United States, and of the Militia of the several States, when called into the actual Service of the United States; he may require the Opinion, in writing, of the principal Officer in each of the executive Departments, upon any Subject relating to the Duties of their respective Offices, and he shall have Power to grant Reprieves and Pardons for Offences against the United States, except in Cases of Impeachment.

He shall have Power, by and with the Advice and Consent of the Senate, to make Treaties, provided two thirds of the Senators present concur; and he shall nominate, and by and with the Advice and Consent of the Senate, shall appoint Ambassadors, other public Ministers and Consuls, Judges of the supreme Court, and all other Officers of the United States, whose Appointments are not herein otherwise provided for, and which shall be established by Law; but the Congress may by Law vest the Appointment of such inferior Officers, as they think proper, in the President alone, in the Courts of Law, or in the Heads of Departments.

The President shall have Power to fill up all Vacancies that may happen during the Recess of the Senate, by granting Commissions which shall expire at the End of their next Session.

Section 3. He shall from time to time give to the Congress Information of the State of the Union, and recommend to their Consideration such Measures as he shall judge necessary and expedient; he may, on extraordinary Occasions, convene both Houses, or either of them, and in Case of Disagreement between them, with Respect to the Time of Adjournment, he may adjourn them to such Time as he shall think proper; he shall receive Ambassadors and other public Ministers; he shall take Care that the Laws be faithfully executed, and shall Commission all the Officers of the United States.

Section 4. The President, Vice President, and all civil Officers of the United States shall be removed from Office on Impeachment for, and Conviction of, Treason, Bribery, or other high Crimes and Misdemeanors.

Article III.

Section 1. The judicial Power of the United States shall be vested in one Supreme Court, and in such inferior Courts as the Congress may from time to time ordain and establish. The Judges, both of the supreme and inferior Courts, shall hold their Offices during good Behaviour, and shall, at stated Times, receive for their Services, a Compensation which shall not be diminished during their Continuance in Office.

Section 2. The judicial Power shall extend to all Cases, in Law and Equity, arising under this Constitution, the Laws of the United States, and Treaties made, or which shall be made, under their Authority; to all Cases affecting Ambassadors, other public Ministers and Consuls; to all Cases of admiralty and maritime Jurisdiction; to Controversies to which the United States shall be a Party; to Controversies between two or more States; between a State and Citizens of another State; between Citizens of different States, between Citizens of the same State claiming Lands under Grants of different States, and between a State, or the Citizens thereof, and foreign States, Citizens, or Subjects.

In all Cases affecting Ambassadors, other public Ministers and Consuls, and those in which a State shall be Party, the supreme Court shall have original Jurisdiction. In all the other Cases before mentioned, the supreme Court shall have appellate Jurisdiction, both as to Law and Fact, with such Exceptions, and under such Regulations as the Congress shall make.

The Trial of all Crimes, except in Cases of Impeachment, shall be by Jury; and such Trial shall be held in the State where the said Crimes shall have been committed; but when not committed within any State, the Trial shall be at such Place or Places as the Congress may by Law have directed.

Section 3. Treason against the United States, shall consist only in levying War against them, or in adhering to their Enemies, giving them Aid and Comfort. No Person shall be convicted of Treason unless on the Testimony of two Witnesses to the same overt Act, or on Confession in open Court.

The Congress shall have Power to declare the Punishment of Treason, but no Attainder of Treason shall work Corruption of Blood or Forfeiture except during the Life of the Person attainted.

Article IV.

Section 1. Full Faith and Credit shall be given in each State to the public Acts, Records, and judicial Proceedings of every other State. And the Congress may by general Laws prescribe the Manner in which such Acts, Records, and Proceedings shall be proved, and the Effect thereof.

Section 2. The Citizens of each State shall be entitled to all Privileges and Immunities of Citizens in the several States.

A Person charged in any State with Treason, Felony, or other Crime, who shall flee from Justice, and be found in another State, shall on Demand of the executive Authority of the State from which he fled, be delivered up, to be removed to the State having Jurisdiction of the Crime.

No Person held to Service or Labour in one State, under the Laws thereof, escaping into another, shall, in Consequence of any Law or Regulation therein, be discharged from such Service or Labour, but shall be delivered up on Claim of the Party to whom such Service or Labour may be due.

Section 3. New States may be admitted by the Congress into this Union; but no new State shall be formed or erected within the Jurisdiction of any other State; nor any State be formed by the Junction of two or more States, or Parts of States, without the Consent of the Legislatures of the States concerned as well as of the Congress.

The Congress shall have Power to dispose of and make all needful Rules and Regulations respecting the Territory or other Property belonging to the United States; and nothing in this Constitution shall be so construed as to Prejudice any Claims of the United States, or of any particular State.

Section 4. The United States shall guarantee to every State in this Union a Republican Form of Government, and shall protect each of them against Invasion; and on Application of the Legislature, or of the Executive (when the Legislature cannot be convened) against domestic Violence.

Article V.

The Congress, whenever two thirds of both Houses shall deem it necessary, shall propose Amendments to this Constitution, or, on the Application of the Legislatures of two thirds of the several States, shall call a Convention for proposing Amendments, which, in either Case, shall be valid to all Intents and Purposes, as Part of this Constitution, when ratified by the Legislatures of three fourths of the several States, or by Conventions in three fourths thereof, as the one or the other Mode of Ratification may be proposed by the Congress; Provided that no Amendment which may be made prior to the Year One thousand eight hundred and eight shall in any Manner affect the first and fourth Clauses in the Ninth Section of the first Article; and that no State, without its Consent, shall be deprived of its equal Suffrage in the Senate.

Article VI.

All Debts contracted and Engagements entered into, before the Adoption of this Constitution shall be as valid against the United States under this Constitution, as under the Confederation.

This Constitution, and the Laws of the United States which shall be made in Pursuance thereof, and all Treaties made or which shall be made, under the Authority of the United States, shall be the supreme Law of the Land; and the Judges in every State shall be bound thereby, anything in the Constitution or Laws of any State to the Contrary notwithstanding.

The Senators and Representatives before mentioned, and the Members of the several State Legislatures, and all executive and judicial Officers, both of the United States and of the several States, shall be bound by Oath or Affirmation, to support this Constitution; but no religious Test shall ever be required as a Qualification to any Office or public Trust under the United States.

Article VII.

The Ratification of the Conventions of nine States, shall be sufficient for the Establishment of this Constitution between the States so ratifying the Same.

Done in Convention by the Unanimous Consent of the States present the Seventeenth Day of September in the Year of our Lord one thousand seven hundred and Eighty seven and of the Independence of the United States of America the Twelfth IN WITNESS whereof We have hereunto subscribed our Names,

George Washington,
President and deputy from Virginia.

Connecticut:
William Samuel Johnson
Roger Sherman

Delaware:
George Read
Gunning Bedford Jr.
John Dickinson
Richard Bassett
Jacob Broom

Georgia:
William Few
Abraham Baldwin

Maryland:
James McHenry
Daniel of St. Thomas Jenifer
Daniel Carroll

Massachusetts:
Nathaniel Gorham
Rufus King

New Hampshire:
John Langdon
Nicholas Gilman

New Jersey:
William Livingston

David Brearley
William Paterson
Jonathan Dayton

New York:
Alexander Hamilton

North Carolina:
William Blount
Richard Dobbs Spaight
Hugh Williamson

Pennsylvania:
Benjamin Franklin
Thomas Mifflin
Robert Morris
George Clymer
Thomas FitzSimons
Jared Ingersoll
James Wilson
Gouverneur Morris

South Carolina:
John Rutledge
Charles Cotesworth Pinckney
Pierce Butler

Virginia:
John Blair
James Madison Jr.

AMENDMENT I

Congress shall make no law respecting an establishment of religion, or prohibiting the free exercise thereof; or abridging the freedom of speech, or of the press; or the right of the people peaceably to assemble, and to petition the Government for a redress of grievances.

AMENDMENT II

A well-regulated militia, being necessary to the security of a free State, the right of the people to keep and bear arms shall not be infringed.

AMENDMENT III

No soldier shall, in time of peace, be quartered in any house without the consent of the owner, nor in time of war, but in a manner to be prescribed by law.

AMENDMENT IV

The right of the people to be secure in their persons, houses, papers, and effects, against unreasonable searches and seizures, shall not be violated, and no warrants shall issue but upon probable cause, supported by oath or affirmation, and particularly describing the place to be searched, and the persons or things to be seized.

AMENDMENT V

No person shall be held to answer for a capital, or otherwise infamous crime, unless on a presentment or indictment of a Grand Jury, except in cases arising in the land or naval forces, or in the militia, when in actual service in time of war or public danger; nor shall any person be subject for the same offense to be twice put in jeopardy of life or limb; nor shall be compelled in any criminal case to be a witness against himself, nor be deprived of life, liberty, or property, without due process of law; nor shall private property be taken for public use without just compensation.

AMENDMENT VI

In all criminal prosecutions, the accused shall enjoy the right to a speedy and public trial, by an impartial jury of the State and district wherein the crime shall have been committed, which district shall have been previously ascertained by law, and to be informed of the nature and cause of the accusation; to be confronted with the witnesses against him; to have compulsory process for obtaining witnesses in his favor, and to have the assistance of counsel for his defense.

AMENDMENT VII

In suits at common law, where the value in controversy shall exceed twenty dollars, the right of trial by jury shall be preserved, and no fact tried by a jury shall be otherwise reexamined in any court of the United States, than according to the rules of the common law.

AMENDMENT VIII

Excessive bail shall not be required, nor excessive fines imposed, nor cruel and unusual punishments inflicted.

AMENDMENT IX

The enumeration in the Constitution of certain rights shall not be construed to deny or disparage others retained by the people.

AMENDMENT X

The powers not delegated to the United States by the Constitution, nor prohibited by it to the States, are reserved to the States respectively, or to the people.

AMENDMENT XI

The judicial power of the United States shall not be construed to extend to any suit in law or equity, commenced or prosecuted against one of the United States by citizens of another State, or by citizens or subjects of any foreign state.

AMENDMENT XII

The Electors shall meet in their respective States and vote by ballot for President and Vice President, one of whom, at least, shall not be an inhabitant of the same State with themselves; they shall name in their ballots the person voted for as President, and in distinct ballots the person voted for as Vice President, and of the number of votes for each, which lists they shall sign and certify, and transmit sealed to the seat of the Government of the United States, directed to the President of the Senate; the President of the Senate shall, in the presence of the Senate and House of Representatives, open all the certificates and the votes shall then be counted. The person having the greatest number of votes for President shall be the President, if such number be a majority of the whole number of Electors appointed; and if no person have such majority, then from the persons having the highest numbers not exceeding three on the list of those voted for as President, the House of Representatives shall choose immediately, by ballot, the President. But in choosing the President, the votes shall be taken by States, the representation from each State having one vote; a quorum for this purpose shall consist of a member or members from two-thirds of the States, and a majority of all the States shall be necessary to a choice. And if the House of Representatives shall not choose a President whenever the right of choice shall devolve upon them, before the fourth day of March next following, then the Vice President shall act as President, as in case of the death or other constitutional disability of the President. The person having the greatest number of votes as Vice President, shall be the Vice President, if such numbers be a majority of the whole number of electors appointed; and if no person have a majority, then from the two highest numbers on the list, the Senate shall choose the Vice President; a quorum for the purpose shall consist of two-thirds of the whole number of Senators, and a majority of the whole number shall be necessary to a choice. But no person constitutionally ineligible to the office of President shall be eligible to that of Vice President of the United States.

AMENDMENT XIII

Section 1. Neither slavery nor involuntary servitude, except as a punishment for crime whereof the party shall have been duly convicted, shall exist within the United States, or any place subject to their jurisdiction.
Section 2. Congress shall have power to enforce this article by appropriate legislation.

AMENDMENT XIV

Section 1. All persons born or naturalized in the United States, and subject to the jurisdiction thereof, are citizens of the United States and of the State wherein they reside. No State shall make or enforce any law which shall abridge the privileges or immunities of citizens of the United States; nor shall any State deprive any person of life, liberty, or property, without due process of law; nor to deny to any person within its jurisdiction the equal protection of the laws.
Section 2. Representatives shall be apportioned among the several States according to their respective numbers, counting the whole number of persons in each State, excluding Indians not taxed. But when the right to vote at any election for the choice of Electors for President and Vice President of the United States, Representatives in Congress, the executive and judicial officers of a State, or the members of the legislature thereof, is denied to any of the male inhabitants of such State, being twenty-one years of age, and citizens of the United States, or in any way abridged, except for participation in rebellion, or other crime, the basis of representation therein shall be reduced in the proportion which the

number of such male citizens shall bear to the whole number of male citizens twenty-one years of age in such State.

Section 3. No person shall be a Senator or Representative in Congress, or Elector of President and Vice President, or hold any office, civil or military, under the United States, or under any State, who, having previously taken an oath, as a member of Congress, or as an officer of the United States, or as a member of any State Legislature, or as an executive or judicial officer of any State, to support the Constitution of the United States, shall have engaged in insurrection or rebellion against the same, or given aid or comfort to the enemies thereof. But Congress may by a vote of two-thirds of each House, remove such disability.

Section 4. The validity of the public debt of the United States, authorized by law, including debts incurred for payment of pensions and bounties for services in suppressing insurrection or rebellion, shall not be questioned. But neither the United States nor any State shall assume or pay any debt or obligation incurred in aid of insurrection or rebellion against the United States, or any claim for the loss or emancipation of any slave; but all such debts, obligations and claims shall be held illegal and void.

Section 5. The Congress shall have the power to enforce, by appropriate legislation, the provisions of this article.

AMENDMENT XV

Section 1. The right of citizens of the United States to vote shall not be denied or abridged by the United States or by any State on account of race, color, or previous condition of servitude.

Section 2. The Congress shall have the power to enforce this article by appropriate legislation.

AMENDMENT XVI

The Congress shall have power to lay and collect taxes on incomes, from whatever sources derived, without apportionment among the several States, and without regard to any census or enumeration.

AMENDMENT XVII

Section 1. The Senate of the United States shall be composed of two Senators from each State, elected by the people thereof, for six years; and each Senator shall have one vote. The electors in each State shall have the qualifications requisite for electors of the most numerous branch of the State Legislatures.

Section 2. When vacancies happen in the representation of any State in the Senate, the executive authority of such State shall issue writs of election to fill such vacancies: Provided, That the Legislature of any State may empower the Executive thereof to make temporary appointments until the people fill the vacancies by election as the Legislature may direct.

Section 3. This amendment shall not be so construed as to affect the election or term of any Senator chosen before it becomes valid as part of the Constitution.

AMENDMENT XVIII

Section 1. After one year from the ratification of this article the manufacture, sale, or transportation of intoxicating liquors within, the importation thereof into, or the exportation thereof from the United States and all territory subject to the jurisdiction thereof for beverage purposes is hereby prohibited.

Section 2. The Congress and the several States shall have concurrent power to enforce this article by appropriate legislation.

Section 3. This article shall be inoperative unless it shall have been ratified as an amendment to the Constitution by the Legislatures of the several States, as provided in the Constitution, within seven years from the date of the submission hereof to the States by the Congress.

AMENDMENT XIX

Section 1. The right of citizens of the United States to vote shall not be denied or abridged by the United States or by any State on account of sex.

Section 2. Congress shall have power to enforce this article by appropriate legislation.

AMENDMENT XX

Section 1. The terms of the President and the Vice President shall end at noon on the 20th day of January, and the terms of Senators and Representatives at noon on the 3rd day of January, of the years in which such terms would have ended if this article had not been ratified; and the terms of their successors shall then begin.

Section 2. The Congress shall assemble at least once in every year, and such meeting shall begin at noon on the 3rd day of January, unless they shall by law appoint a different day.

Section 3. If, at the time fixed for the beginning of the term of the President, the President elect shall have died, the Vice President elect shall become President. If a President shall not have been chosen before the time fixed for the beginning of his term, or if the President elect shall have failed to qualify, then the Vice President elect shall act as President until a President shall have qualified; and the Congress may by law provide for the case wherein neither a President elect nor a Vice President shall have qualified, declaring who shall then act as President, or the manner in which one who is to act shall be selected, and such person shall act accordingly until a President or Vice President shall have qualified.

Section 4. The Congress may by law provide for the case of the death of any of the persons from whom the House of Representatives may choose a President whenever the right of choice shall have devolved upon them, and for the case of the death of any of the persons from whom the Senate may choose a Vice President whenever the right of choice shall have devolved upon them.

Section 5. Sections 1 and 2 shall take effect on the 15th day of October following the ratification of this article.

Section 6. This article shall be inoperative unless it shall have been ratified as an amendment to the Constitution by the Legislatures of three-fourths of the several States within seven years from the date of its submission.

AMENDMENT XXI

Section 1. The Eighteenth article of amendment to the Constitution of the United States is hereby repealed.

Section 2. The transportation or importation into any State, Territory, or Possession of the United States for delivery or use therein of intoxicating liquors, in violation of the laws thereof, is hereby prohibited.

Section 3. This article shall be inoperative unless it shall have been ratified as an amendment to the Constitution by conventions in the several States, as provided in the Constitution, within seven years from the date of the submission hereof to the States by the Congress.

AMENDMENT XXII

Section 1. No person shall be elected to the office of the President more than twice, and no person who has held the office of President, or acted as President, for more that two years of a term to which some other person was elected President shall be elected to the office of President more that once. But this Article shall not apply to any person holding the office of President when this Article was proposed by Congress, and shall not prevent any person who may be holding the office of President, or acting as President, during the term within which this Article becomes operative from holding the office of President or acting as President during the remainder of such term.

Section 2. This article shall be inoperative unless it shall have been ratified as an amendment to the Constitution by the Legislatures of three-fourths of the several States within seven years from the date of its submission to the States by the Congress.

AMENDMENT XXIII

Section 1. The District constituting the seat of Government of the United States shall appoint in such manner as Congress may direct: A number of electors of President and Vice-President equal to the whole number of Senators and Representatives in Congress to which the District would be entitled if it were a State, but in no event more than the least populous State; they shall be in addition to those appointed by the States, but they shall be considered, for the purposes of the election of President and Vice President, to be electors appointed by a State; and they shall meet in the District and perform such duties as provided by the twelfth article of amendment.

Section 2. The Congress shall have power to enforce this article by appropriate legislation.

AMENDMENT XXIV

Section 1. The right of citizens of the United States to vote in any primary or other election for President or Vice President, for electors for President or Vice President, or for Senator or Representative in Congress, shall not be denied or abridged by the United States or any State by reason of failure to pay poll tax or any other tax.

Section 2. Congress shall have power to enforce this article by appropriate legislation.

AMENDMENT XXV

Section 1. In case of the removal of the President from office or of his death or resignation, the Vice President shall become President.

Section 2. Whenever there is a vacancy in the office of the Vice President, the President shall nominate a Vice President who shall take the office upon confirmation by a majority vote of both houses of Congress

Section 3. Whenever the President transmits to the President Pro tempore of the Senate and the Speaker of the House of Representatives his written declaration that he is unable to discharge the powers and duties of his office, and until he transmits to them a written declaration to the contrary, such powers and duties shall be discharged by the Vice President as Acting President.

Section 4. Whenever the Vice President and a majority of either the principal officers of the executive departments or of such other body as Congress may by law provide, transmits to the President Pro tempore of the Senate and the Speaker of the House of Representatives their written declaration that the President is unable to discharge the powers and duties of his office, the Vice President shall immediately assume the powers and duties of the office as Acting President. Thereafter, when the President transmits to the President Pro tempore of the Senate and the Speaker of the House of Representatives his written declaration that no inability exists, he shall resume the powers and duties of his office unless the Vice President and a majority of either the principal officers of the executive departments or of such other body as Congress may by law provide, transmits within four days to the President Pro tempore of the Senate and the Speaker of the House of Representatives their written declaration that the President is unable to discharge the powers and duties of his office. Thereupon Congress shall decide the issue, assembling within forty-eight hours for that purpose if not in session. If the Congress, within twenty-one days after receipt of the latter written declaration, or, if Congress is not in session within twenty-one days after Congress is required to assemble, determines by two-thirds vote of both houses that the President is unable to discharge the powers and duties of his office, the Vice President shall continue to discharge the same as Acting President; otherwise, the President shall resume the powers and duties of his office.

AMENDMENT XXVI

Section 1. The right of citizens of the United States, who are eighteen years of age or older, to vote shall not be denied or abridged by the United States or any state on account of age.

Section 2. The Congress shall have power to enforce this article by appropriate legislation.

AMENDMENT XXVII

No law varying the compensation for services of the Senators and Representatives shall take effect, until an election of Representatives shall have intervened.

APPENDIX F: DECLARATION OF INDEPENDENCE

[The Declaration of Independence, America's historic assertion of freedom from the British Empire, was ratified by the Continental Congress on July 4, 1776, and signed on that same day. See the Independence Day essay at July 4 and the other relevant essays throughout this book.]

When in the Course of human events, it becomes necessary for one people to dissolve the political bands which have connected them with another, and to assume among the powers of the earth, the separate and equal station to which the Laws of Nature and of Nature's God entitle them, a decent respect to the opinions of mankind requires that they should declare the causes which impel them to the separation.

We hold these truths to be self-evident, that all men are created equal, that they are endowed by their Creator with certain unalienable Rights, that among these are Life, Liberty, and the pursuit of Happiness. That to secure these rights, Governments are instituted among Men, deriving their just powers from the consent of the governed. That whenever any Form of Government becomes destructive of these ends, it is the Right of the People to alter or to abolish it, and to institute new Government, laying its foundation on such principles, and organizing its powers in such form, as to them shall seem most likely to effect their Safety and Happiness.

Prudence, indeed, will dictate that Governments long established should not be changed for light and transient causes; and accordingly all experience hath shewn that mankind are more disposed to suffer, while evils are sufferable, than to right themselves by abolishing the forms to which they are accustomed.

But when a long train of abuses and usurpations, pursuing invariably the same object, evinces a design to reduce them under absolute Despotism, it is their right, it is their duty, to throw off such Government, and to provide new Guards for their future security.

Such has been the patient sufferance of these Colonies; and such is now the necessity which constrains them to alter their former Systems of Government. The history of the present King of Great Britain is a history of repeated injuries and usurpations, all having in direct object the establishment of an absolute Tyranny over these States. To prove this, let Facts be submitted to a candid world.

He has refused his Assent to Laws, the most wholesome and necessary for the public good.

He has forbidden his Governors to pass Laws of immediate and pressing importance, unless suspended in their operation till his Assent should be obtained, and when so suspended, he has utterly neglected to attend to them.

He has refused to pass other Laws for the accommodation of large districts of people, unless those people would relinquish the right of Representation in the Legislature, a right inestimable to them, and formidable to tyrants only.

He has called together legislative bodies at places unusual, uncomfortable, and distant from the depository of their public Records, for the sole purpose of fatiguing them into compliance with his measures.

He has dissolved Representative Houses repeatedly, for opposing, with manly firmness his invasions on the rights of the people.

He has refused for a long time, after such dissolutions, to cause others to be elected; whereby the Legislative powers, incapable of Annihilation, have returned to the People at large for their exercise; the State remaining, in the mean time, exposed to all the dangers of invasions from without and convulsions within.

He has endeavored to prevent the population of these States; for that purpose obstructing the Laws for Naturalization of Foreigners; refusing to pass others to encourage their migration hither, and raising the conditions of new Appropriations of lands.

He has obstructed the Administration of Justice, by refusing his Assent to Laws for establishing Judiciary powers.

He has made Judges dependent on his Will alone, for the tenure of their offices, and the amount and payment of their salaries.

He has erected a multitude of New Offices, and sent hither swarms of Officers to harass our people, and eat out their substance.

He has kept among us, in times of peace, Standing Armies, without the consent of our legislatures.

He has affected to render the Military independent of, and superior to, the Civil power.

He has combined with others to subject us to a jurisdiction foreign to our constitution and unacknowledged by our laws; giving his Assent to their Acts of pretended Legislation:

For quartering large bodies of armed troops among us;

For protecting them by a mock Trial from punishment for any Murders which they should commit on the inhabitants of these States;

For cutting off our Trade with all parts of the world;

For imposing Taxes on us without our Consent;

For depriving us, in many cases, of the benefits of Trial by Jury;

For transporting us beyond Seas to be tried for pretended offences;

For abolishing the free System of English Laws in a neighboring Province, establishing therein an Arbitrary government, and enlarging its Boundaries so as to render it at once an example and fit instrument for introducing the same absolute rule into these Colonies;

For taking away our Charters, abolishing our most valuable Laws, and altering fundamentally the Forms of our Governments;

For suspending our own Legislatures, and declaring themselves invested with power to legislate for us in all cases whatsoever.

He has abdicated Government here by declaring us out of his Protection and waging War against us.

He has plundered our seas, ravaged our Coasts, burned our towns, and destroyed the lives of our people.

He is at this time transporting large Armies of foreign Mercenaries to complete the works of death, desolation and tyranny already begun with circumstances of cruelty and perfidy scarcely paralleled in the most barbarous ages, and totally unworthy the Head of a civilized nation.

He has constrained our fellow Citizens taken Captive on the high Seas to bear Arms against their Country, to become the executioners of their friends and Brethren, or to fall themselves by their Hands.

He has excited domestic insurrection among us, and has endeavored to bring on the inhabitants of our frontiers the merciless Indian Savages, whose known rule of warfare is an undistinguished destruction of all ages, sexes and conditions.

In every stage of these Oppressions We have Petitioned for Redress in the most humble terms. Our repeated Petitions have been answered only by repeated injury. A Prince, whose character is thus marked by every act which may define a Tyrant, is unfit to be the ruler of a free people.

Nor have We been wanting in our attentions to our British brethren.

We have warned them, from time to time, of attempts by their legislature to extend an unwarrantable jurisdiction over us.

We have reminded them of the circumstances of our emigration and settlement here.

We have appealed to their native justice and magnanimity; and we have conjured them by the ties of our common kindred to disavow these usurpations, which would inevitably interrupt our connections and correspondence.

They too have been deaf to the voice of justice and of consanguinity. We must, therefore, acquiesce in the necessity, which denounces our Separation, and hold them, as we hold the rest of mankind, Enemies in War, in Peace Friends.

We, therefore, the Representatives of the United States of America, in General Congress, Assembled, appealing to the Supreme Judge of the world for the rectitude of our intentions, do, in the Name, and by the authority of the good People of these Colonies solemnly publish and declare, That these United Colonies are, and of Right ought to be, Free and Independent States; that they are Absolved from all Allegiance to the British Crown, and that all political connection between them and the State of Great Britain is, and ought to be, totally dissolved; and that, as Free and Independent States, they have full

Power to levy War, conclude Peace, contract Alliances, establish Commerce, and do all other Acts and Things which Independent States may of right do.

And for the support of this Declaration, with a firm reliance on the protection of Divine Providence, we mutually pledge to each other our Lives, our Fortunes, and our sacred Honor.

[Signed by] John Hancock [who presided over the assembly]

[Also signed by the following persons from the following colonies]

New Hampshire: Josiah Bartlett, William Whipple, Matthew Thornton

Massachusetts: John Hancock, Samual Adams, John Adams, Robert Treat Paine, Elbridge Gerry

Rhode Island: Stephen Hopkins, William Ellery

Connecticut: Roger Sherman, Samuel Huntington, William Williams, Oliver Wolcott

New York: William Floyd, Philip Livingston, Francis Lewis, Lewis Morris

New Jersey: Richard Stockton, John Witherspoon, Francis Hopkinson, John Hart, Abraham Clark

Pennsylvania: Robert Morris, Benjamin Rush, Benjamin Franklin, John Morton, George Clymer, James Smith, George Taylor, James Wilson, George Ross

Delaware: Caesar Rodney, George Read, Thomas McKean

Maryland: Samuel Chase, William Paca, Thomas Stone, Charles Carroll of Carrollton

Virginia: George Wythe, Richard Henry Lee, Thomas Jefferson, Benjamin Harrison, Thomas Nelson Jr., Francis Lightfoot Lee, Carter Braxton

North Carolina: William Hooper, Joseph Hewes, John Penn

South Carolina: Edward Rutledge, Thomas Heyward Jr., Thomas Lynch Jr., Arthur Middleton

Georgia: Button Gwinnett, Lyman Hall, George Walton

APPENDIX G: ARTICLES OF CONFEDERATION

[The Articles of Confederation preceded the United States Constitution and were in effect from the time of the American Revolution until June 21, 1788, when the Constitution was ratified by the required nine of the thirteen states. There are a wide variety of essays in this book concerning these events, especially the ratification of the Constitution. In summary, the Articles of Confederation provided for a loose alliance amongst the states that proved to be an ineffective form of national government, which is why the Articles were ultimately replaced by the Federal structure of the modern Constitutional system in 1788.]

To all to whom these Presents shall come, we the undersigned Delegates of the States affixed to our Names send greeting.

Articles of Confederation and perpetual Union between the states of New Hampshire, Massachusetts-Bay, Rhode Island and Providence Plantations, Connecticut, New York, New Jersey, Pennsylvania, Delaware, Maryland, Virginia, North Carolina, South Carolina, and Georgia.

Article I. The Stile of this Confederacy shall be "The United States of America."

Article II. Each state retains its sovereignty, freedom, and independence, and every power, jurisdiction, and right, which is not by this Confederation expressly delegated to the United States, in Congress assembled.

Article III. The said States hereby severally enter into a firm league of friendship with each other, for their common defense, the security of their liberties, and their mutual and general welfare, binding themselves to assist each other, against all force offered to, or attacks made upon them, or any of them, on account of religion, sovereignty, trade, or any other pretense whatever.

Article IV. The better to secure and perpetuate mutual friendship and intercourse among the people of the different States in this Union, the free inhabitants of each of these States, paupers, vagabonds, and fugitives from justice excepted, shall be entitled to all privileges and immunities of free citizens in the several States; and the people of each State shall free ingress and regress to and from any other State, and shall enjoy therein all the privileges of trade and commerce, subject to the same duties, impositions, and restrictions as the inhabitants thereof respectively, provided that such restrictions shall not extend so far as to prevent the removal of property imported into any State, to any other State, of which the owner is an inhabitant; provided also that no imposition, duties or restriction shall be laid by any State, on the property of the United States, or either of them.

If any person guilty of, or charged with, treason, felony, or other high misdemeanor in any State, shall flee from justice, and be found in any of the United States, he shall, upon demand of the Governor or executive power of the State from which he fled, be delivered up and removed to the State having jurisdiction of his offense.

Full faith and credit shall be given in each of these States to the records, acts, and judicial proceedings of the courts and magistrates of every other State.

Article V. For the most convenient management of the general interests of the United States, delegates shall be annually appointed in such manner as the legislatures of each State shall direct, to meet in Congress on the first Monday in November, in every year, with a power reserved to each State to recall its delegates, or any of them, at any time within the year, and to send others in their stead for the remainder of the year.

No State shall be represented in Congress by less than two, nor more than seven members; and no person shall be capable of being a delegate for more than three years in any term of six years; nor shall any person, being a delegate, be capable of holding any office under the United States, for which he, or another for his benefit, receives any salary, fees or emolument of any kind.

Each State shall maintain its own delegates in a meeting of the States, and while they act as members of the committee of the States.

In determining questions in the United States in Congress assembled, each State shall have one vote.

Freedom of speech and debate in Congress shall not be impeached or questioned in any court or place out of Congress, and the members of Congress shall be protected in their persons from arrests or imprisonments, during the time of their going to and from, and attendance on Congress, except for treason, felony, or breach of the peace.

Article VI. No State, without the consent of the United States in Congress assembled, shall send any embassy to, or receive any embassy from, or enter into any conference, agreement, alliance or treaty with any King, Prince or State; nor shall any person holding any office of profit or trust under the United States, or any of them, accept any present, emolument, office or title of any kind whatever from any King, Prince or foreign State; nor shall the United States in Congress assembled, or any of them, grant any title of nobility.

No two or more States shall enter into any treaty, confederation or alliance whatever between them, without the consent of the United States in Congress assembled, specifying accurately the purposes for which the same is to be entered into, and how long it shall continue.

No State shall lay any imposts or duties, which may interfere with any stipulations in treaties, entered into by the United States in Congress assembled, with any King, Prince or State, in pursuance of any treaties already proposed by Congress, to the courts of France and Spain.

No vessel of war shall be kept up in time of peace by any State, except such number only, as shall be deemed necessary by the United States in Congress assembled, for the defense of such State, or its trade; nor shall any body of forces be kept up by any State in time of peace, except such number only, as in the judgment of the United States in Congress assembled, shall be deemed requisite to garrison the forts necessary for the defense of such State; but every State shall always keep up a well-regulated and disciplined militia, sufficiently armed and accoutered, and shall provide and constantly have ready for use, in public stores, a due number of filed pieces and tents, and a proper quantity of arms, ammunition and camp equipage.

No State shall engage in any war without the consent of the United States in Congress assembled, unless such State be actually invaded by enemies, or shall have received certain advice of a resolution being formed by some nation of Indians to invade such State, and the danger is so imminent as not to admit of a delay till the United States in Congress assembled can be consulted; nor shall any State grant commissions to any ships or vessels of war, nor letters of marque or reprisal, except it be after a declaration of war by the United States in Congress assembled, and then only against the Kingdom or State and the subjects thereof, against which war has been so declared, and under such regulations as shall be established by the United States in Congress assembled, unless such State be infested by pirates, in which case vessels of war may be fitted out for that occasion, and kept so long as the danger shall continue, or until the United States in Congress assembled shall determine otherwise.

Article VII. When land forces are raised by any State for the common defense, all officers of or under the rank of colonel, shall be appointed by the legislature of each State respectively, by whom such forces shall be raised, or in such manner as such State shall direct, and all vacancies shall be filled up by the State which first made the appointment.

Article VIII. All charges of war, and all other expenses that shall be incurred for the common defense or general welfare, and allowed by the United States in Congress assembled, shall be defrayed out of a common treasury, which shall be supplied by the several States in proportion to the value of all land within each State, granted or surveyed for any person, as such land and the buildings and improvements thereon shall be estimated according to such mode as the United States in Congress assembled, shall from time to time direct and appoint.

The taxes for paying that proportion shall be laid and levied by the authority and direction of the legislatures of the several States within the time agreed upon by the United States in Congress assembled.

Article IX. The United States in Congress assembled, shall have the sole and exclusive right and power of determining on peace and war, except in the cases mentioned in the sixth article—of sending and receiving ambassadors—entering into treaties and alliances, provided that no treaty of commerce shall be made whereby the legislative power of the respective States shall be restrained from imposing such imposts and duties on foreigners, as their own people are subjected to, or from prohibiting the exportation or importation of any species of goods or commodities whatsoever—of establishing rules for deciding in all cases, what captures on land or water shall be legal, and in what manner prizes taken by land or naval forces in the service of the United States shall be divided or appropriated—of granting letters of marque and reprisal in times of peace—appointing courts for the trial of piracies and felonies committed on the high seas and establishing courts for receiving and determining finally appeals in all cases of captures, provided that no member of Congress shall be appointed a judge of any of the said courts.

The United States in Congress assembled shall also be the last resort on appeal in all disputes and differences now subsisting or that hereafter may arise between two or more States concerning boundary, jurisdiction or any other causes whatever; which authority shall always be exercised in the manner following. Whenever the legislative or executive authority or lawful agent of any State in controversy with another shall present a petition to Congress stating the matter in question and praying for a hearing, notice thereof shall be given by order of Congress to the legislative or executive authority of the other State in controversy, and a day assigned for the appearance of the parties by their lawful agents, who shall then be directed to appoint by joint consent, commissioners or judges to constitute a court for hearing and determining the matter in question: but if they cannot agree, Congress shall name three persons out of each of the United States, and from the list of such persons each party shall alternately strike out one, the petitioners beginning, until the number shall be reduced to thirteen; and from that number not less than seven, nor more than nine names as Congress shall direct, shall in the presence of Congress be drawn out by lot, and the persons whose names shall be so drawn or any five of them, shall be commissioners or judges, to hear and finally determine the controversy, so always as a major part of the judges who shall hear the cause shall agree in the determination: and if either party shall neglect to attend at the day appointed, without showing reasons, which Congress shall judge sufficient, or being present shall refuse to strike, the Congress shall proceed to nominate three persons out of each State, and the secretary of Congress shall strike in behalf of such party absent or refusing; and the judgment and sentence of the court to be appointed, in the manner before prescribed, shall be final and conclusive; and if any of the parties shall refuse to submit to the authority of such court, or to appear or defend their claim or cause, the court shall nevertheless proceed to pronounce sentence, or judgment, which shall in like manner be final and decisive, the judgment or sentence and other proceedings being in either case transmitted to Congress, and lodged among the acts of Congress for the security of the parties concerned: provided that every commissioner, before he sits in judgment, shall take an oath to be administered by one of the judges of the supreme or superior court of the State, where the cause shall be tried, "well and truly to hear and determine the matter in question, according to the best of his judgement, without favor, affection or hope of reward": provided also, that no State shall be deprived of territory for the benefit of the United States.

All controversies concerning the private right of soil claimed under different grants of two or more States, whose jurisdictions as they may respect such lands, and the States which passed such grants are adjusted, the said grants or either of them being at the same time claimed to have originated antecedent to such settlement of jurisdiction, shall on the petition of either party to the Congress of the United States, be finally determined as near as may be in the same manner as is before prescribed for deciding disputes respecting territorial jurisdiction between different States.

The United States in Congress assembled shall also have the sole and exclusive right and power of regulating the alloy and value of coin struck by their own authority, or by that of the respective States—fixing the standards of weights and measures throughout the United States—regulating the trade and managing all affairs with the Indians, not members of any of the States, provided that the legislative right of any State within its own limits be not infringed or violated—establishing or regulating post offices from one State to another, throughout all the United States, and exacting such postage on the papers passing through the same as may be requisite to defray the expenses of the said office—appointing all officers of the land forces, in the service of the United States, excepting regimental officers—appointing all the officers of the naval forces, and commissioning all officers whatever in the service of the United States—making rules for the government and regulation of the said land and naval forces, and directing their operations.

The United States in Congress assembled shall have authority to appoint a committee, to sit in the recess of Congress, to be denominated "A Committee of the States," and to consist of one delegate from each State; and to appoint such other committees and civil officers as may be necessary for managing the general affairs of the United States under their direction—to appoint one of their members to preside, provided that no person be allowed to serve in the office of president more than one year in any term of three years; to ascertain the necessary sums of money to be raised for the service of the United States, and to appropriate and apply the same for defraying the public expenses—to borrow money, or emit bills on the credit of the United States, transmitting every half-year to the respective States an account of the sums of money so borrowed or emitted—to build and equip a navy—to agree upon the number of land forces, and to make requisitions from each State for its quota, in proportion to the number of white inhabitants in such State; which requisition shall be binding, and thereupon the legislature of each State shall appoint the regimental officers, raise the men and clothe, arm, and equip them in a solid-like manner, at the expense of the United States; and the officers and men so clothed, armed, and equipped shall march to the place appointed, and within the time agreed on by the United States in Congress assembled. But if the United States in Congress assembled shall, on consideration of circumstances judge proper that any State should not raise men, or should raise a smaller number of men than the quota thereof, such extra number shall be raised, officered, clothed, armed, and equipped in the same manner as the quota of each State, unless the legislature of such State shall judge that such extra number cannot be safely spread out in the same, in which case they shall raise, officer, clothe, arm, and equip as many of such extra number as they judge can be safely spared. And the officers and men so clothed, armed, and equipped, shall march to the place appointed, and within the time agreed on by the United States in Congress assembled.

The United States in Congress assembled shall never engage in a war, nor grant letters of marque or reprisal in time of peace, nor enter into any treaties or alliances, nor coin money, nor regulate the value thereof, nor ascertain the sums and expenses necessary for the defense and welfare of the United States, or any of them, nor emit bills, nor borrow money on the credit of the United States, nor appropriate money, nor agree upon the number of vessels of war, to be built or purchased, or the number of land or sea forces to be raised, nor appoint a commander in chief of the army or navy, unless nine States assent to the same: nor shall a question on any other point, except for adjourning from day to day be determined, unless by the votes of the majority of the United States in Congress assembled.

The Congress of the United States shall have power to adjourn to any time within the year, and to any place within the United States, so that no period of adjournment be for a longer duration than the space of six months, and shall publish the journal of their proceedings monthly, except such parts thereof relating to treaties, alliances or military operations, as in their judgement require secrecy; and the yeas and nays of the delegates of each State on any question shall be entered on the journal, when it is desired by any delegates of a State, or any of them, at his or their request shall be furnished with a transcript of the said journal, except such parts as are above excepted, to lay before the legislatures of the several States.

Article X. The Committee of the States, or any nine of them, shall be authorized to execute, in the recess of Congress, such of the powers of Congress as the United States in Congress assembled, by the consent of the nine States, shall from time to time think expedient to vest them with; provided that no power be delegated to the said Committee, for the exercise of which, by the Articles of Confederation, the voice of nine States in the Congress of the United States assembled be requisite.

Article XI. Canada acceding to this confederation, and adjoining in the measures of the United States, shall be admitted into, and entitled to all the advantages of this Union; but no other colony shall be admitted into the same, unless such admission be agreed to by nine States.

Article XII. All bills of credit emitted, monies borrowed, and debts contracted by, or under the authority of Congress, before the assembling of the United States, in pursuance of the present confederation, shall be deemed and considered as a charge against the United States, for payment and satisfaction whereof the said United States and the public faith are hereby solemnly pledged.

Article XIII. Every State shall abide by the determination of the United States in Congress assembled, on all questions which by this confederation are submitted to them. And the Articles of this Confederation shall be inviolably observed by every State, and the Union shall be perpetual; nor shall any alteration at any time hereafter be made in any of them; unless such alteration be agreed to in a Congress of the United States, and be afterwards confirmed by the legislatures of every State.

And Whereas it hath pleased the Great Governor of the World to incline the hearts of the legislatures we respectively represent in Congress, to approve of, and to authorize us to ratify the said Articles of Confederation and perpetual Union. Know Ye that we the undersigned delegates, by virtue of the power and authority to us given for that purpose, do by these presents, in the name and in behalf of our respective constituents, fully and entirely ratify and confirm each and every of the said Articles of Confederation and perpetual Union, and all and singular the matters and things therein contained: And we do further solemnly plight and engage the faith of our respective constituents, that they shall abide by the determinations of the United States in Congress assembled, on all questions, which by the said Confederation are submitted to them. And that the Articles thereof shall be inviolably observed by the States we respectively represent, and that the Union shall be perpetual.

In Witness whereof we have hereunto set our hands in Congress. Done at Philadelphia in the State of Pennsylvania the ninth day of July in the Year of our Lord One Thousand Seven Hundred and Seventy-Eight, and in the Third Year of the independence of America.

APPENDIX H: MAYFLOWER COMPACT OF 1620

[Shortly after they arrived off the coast of modern-day Massachusetts, on November 21, 1620 (November 11, 1620 according to the old Julian calendar still being used by English at the time), the Pilgrims signed the famous Mayflower Compact. The Mayflower Compact was a historic precedent in that it established a colonial government that operated with the consent of the governed. See the Forefathers' Day essay at December 21 for further information.

The reader will note the reference to Virginia within the document. At the time, the English still broadly referred to the unexplored Atlantic seaboard as "Virginia," and had not yet named what would become the various American colonies. All of the signers were men, per contemporary custom. Also per contemporary custom, only some of the men were entitled to use the honorific "mister" or "Mr." before their full names.]

IN THE NAME OF GOD, AMEN. We, whose names are underwritten, the Loyal Subjects of our dread Sovereign Lord King James, by the Grace of God, of Great Britain, France, and Ireland, King, Defender of the Faith, &c. Having undertaken for the Glory of God, and Advancement of the Christian Faith, and the Honour of our King and Country, a Voyage to plant the first Colony in the northern Parts of Virginia; Do by these Presents, solemnly and mutually, in the Presence of God and one another, covenant and combine ourselves together into a civil Body Politick, for our better Ordering and Preservation, and Furtherance of the Ends aforesaid: And by Virtue hereof do enact, constitute, and frame, such just and equal Laws, Ordinances, Acts, Constitutions, and Officers, from time to time, as shall be thought most meet and convenient for the general Good of the Colony; unto which we promise all due Submission and Obedience.

IN WITNESS whereof we have hereunto subscribed our names at Cape-Cod the eleventh of November, in the Reign of our Sovereign Lord King James, of England, France, and Ireland, the eighteenth, and of Scotland the fifty-fourth, Anno Domini; 1620.

Mr. John Carver	Digery Priest
Mr. William Bradford	Thomas Williams
Mr Edward Winslow	Gilbert Winslow
Mr. William Brewster	Edmund Margesson
Isaac Allerton	Peter Brown
Myles Standish	Richard Britteridge
John Alden	George Soule
John Turner	Edward Tilly
Francis Eaton	John Tilly
James Chilton	Francis Cooke
John Craxton	Thomas Rogers
John Billington	Thomas Tinker
Joses Fletcher	John Ridgdale
John Goodman	Edward Fuller
Mr. Samuel Fuller	Richard Clark
Mr. Christopher Martin	Richard Gardiner
Mr. William Mullins	Mr. John Allerton
Mr. William White	Thomas English
Mr. Richard Warren	Edward Doten
John Howland	Edward Liester
Mr. Steven Hopkins	

APPENDIX I: IMPORTANT PUBLIC HOLIDAYS AND EVENTS

Here is a list of the most widely recognized public holidays and events. Many are officially recognized under federal and/or state law. See the index for specific references to the appropriate essays in this book.

Christmas
Christmas Eve
Columbus Day
Earth Day
Easter
Father's Day
Flag Day
Good Friday
Halloween
Hanukkah
Independence Day
Kwanzaa
Labor Day
Martin Luther King Day
Memorial Day
Mother's Day
New Year's Day
Passover
Presidents' Day
Rosh Hashanah
St. Patrick's Day
Thanksgiving
Valentine's Day
Veterans Day
Yom Kippur

INDEX

Harry S. Truman and, 350
U.S. uses first, against Japan, 564-65
Attucks, Crispus, 185
Auden, W.H., birthday, 112
Audubon, John James, birthday, 314-16
August, origin of name, 554
Augustine, St., feast of, 614-15
Augustus Caesar, 554-55
authors. *See* fiction and literature; poetry
Autumn, begins, 665
aviation
Air Force becomes equal branch of, 654-55
Lindbergh lands in Paris, 379-80
National Aviation Day, 598
Wright Brothers' first flight, 834-35

Baden-Powell, Robert, 126
Baez, Joan, birthday, 48
Balanchine, George, birthday, 49
Balboa, discovers Pacific Ocean, 670-71
Baldwin, James, birthday, 558
Balfour Declaration, Congress endorses, 665-66
ballet
Balanchine, George, birthday, 49
balloon flights, first successful, 40-41
Baltimore, Md., fire (1904), 125
Bancroft, George, birthday, 686-87
Bank of North America, 36
banks and banking
Federal Reserve System established, 849-50
first commercial bank established, 36
J.P. Morgan's birthday, 288-89
National Bank Act, 164
Franklin D. Roosevelt's Hundred Days, 452-53
Barnum, P.T., birthday, 506-7
Barry, John, death of, 642-43
Bartholomew, St., feast of, 606-7
Barton, Clara, birthday, 854-55
baseball
Jackie Robinson's birthday, 103-4
"Battle Hymn of the Republic" (song), 109-10
Battleship Maine Memorial Day, 144-45
Bay of Pigs invasion, 289
Bean, Alan L.
Apollo 12 mission is launched, 771
Beatles, arrive in the U.S., 124-25
Beecher, Henry Ward
Lyman Abbott's birthday, 838-39
birthday, 471-72
Bell, Alexander Graham, birthday, 180-81
Bennington, Battle of, 589-90
Bennington flag, 445

Bering, Vitus, 243
Berlin Airlift (1948), begins, 472-73
Bill of Rights, ratification, 831-32
birth control
Margaret Sanger's birthday, 645-46
Black Hills, S.D., 282, 283, 474, 750
Custer's Last Stand, 474-75
discovery of gold, 474, 750
Black Muslims
Malcolm X's birthday, 374-75
Elijah Muhammad's birthday, 696
"Black Tuesday," Crash of 1929, 737
Blackwell, Elizabeth, 83
Blaine, James G., birthday, 105
blind, education for
Helen Keller's birthday, 481-83
blizzard of 1888, 194-95
bombings
Haymarket Square, 290
Hiroshima and Nagasaki, official report, 486-88
Oklahoma City, 294-95
"Bonus Army," evicted from Washington, D.C., 549
Boone, Daniel, reaches Kentucky, 427-31
Booth, Catherine Mumford, 270, 271
Booth, Edwin, birthday, 768-69
Booth, John Wilkes
assassination of Abraham Lincoln, 283
Booth, William, birthday, 269-71
Boston, Mass., British troops evacuate, 211
Boston Massacre, 185-86
Boston Tea Party, 832-34
botany and horticulture
Luther Burbank's birthday, 189-90
Asa Gray's birthday, 777-78
bowl games, 12, 13
boxing
Muhammad Ali's birthday, 67-68
Boy Scouts of America, 125-26
Bradford, William, death of, 375-76
Branch Davidians
attack on compound in Waco, Texas, 293-94
Brandeis, Louis, birthday, 769
Brandywine, Battle of, 639-40
Breckinridge, John, birthday, 79
Bretton Woods Conference, begins, 493-94
Bridget, St., 171
broadcasting, commercial radio, begins, 614
Brook Farm
Charles A. Dana's birthday, 572-73
Brown v. *Board of Education* (court case), 368-70
Brown, Grace "Billie," murder of, 521-22

church history. *See* religion and church history

Churchill, Winston
 makes "Iron Curtain" speech in U.S., 186-87
 Teheran Conference, 798-99

cigarette smoking
 R.J. Reynolds abandons "smokeless"
  cigarette project, 170
 Surgeon General issues first report on
  dangers of, 54-55

Cinco de Mayo, 343

Circumcision, feast of, 3

Citizenship Day, 653-54

Civil Rights Act of 1957, 637-38

Civil Rights Act of 1960, 344

Civil Rights Act of 1964, 497-98

Civil Rights Act of 1968, 274
 Supreme Court expands fair housing rights,
  456

civil rights movement
 Fifteenth Amendment ratified, 244
 Marcus Garvey's birthday, 592-93
 Jesse Jackson's birthday, 697
 John F. Kennedy addresses nation, 436-38
 Martin Luther King Day, 72-76
  King is assassinated, 254-55
 Malcolm X's birthday, 374-75
 Thurgood Marshall's birthday, 494-95
 Supreme Court:
  expands fair housing rights, 456
  orders school desegregation, 368-70
 Frederick Moore Vinson's birthday, 82
 Voting Rights Act of 1965, 565-66

Civil War. *See* American Civil War

Civilian Conservation Corps, 452

Clark, George Rogers, 113, 228

Clarke, John, birthday, 696-97

Clay, Cassius. *See* Ali, Muhammad

Clay, Henry
 birthday, 278-80
 fights duel with John Randolph, 265
 Missouri admitted to Union, 579-81
 presidential elections of 1824 deadlocked,
  805-6

Clemens, Samuel Langhorne, birthday, 802-3

Cleveland, Grover, birthday, 215-17

Clinton, George
 New York ratifies U.S. Constitution, 545-46

Clinton, Hillary Rodham
 birthday, 732-33
 graduation address from Wellesley, 407-9

Clinton, William Jefferson
 administration announces new policy
  concerning gays in the military, 99

birthday, 595-97
 issues national apology for Tuskegee
  experiments, 368

Clinton, Fort
 British capture Forts Clinton and
  Montgomery, 693-94

Cobain, Kurt, death of, 265-66

Coburn, James, birthday, 618

Cody, William F. (Buffalo Bill), 165-66

coinage of money
 U.S. Mint established, 248-49

Cold War
 Bay of Pigs invasion, 289
 Berlin Airlift begins, 472-73
 Cuban Missile Crisis, 726
 Gorbachev resigns and Soviet Union
  dissolves, 855
 Harry S. Truman and, 350
 limited nuclear test ban treaty signed, 562-64
 Soviets launch *Sputnik I*, 689-90
 Truman Doctrine, 195-98
 Winston Churchill makes "Iron Curtain"
  speech in U.S., 186-87
  See also
  Korean War
  Vietnam War

college bowl games, 12
 Tournament of Roses, 12-13

colleges and universities
 Antioch College chartered, 364-65
 Columbia University opens, 532
 Dartmouth College case decided, 110-11
 Dickinson College chartered, 754
 first football game, 756
 first medical school in U.S., 339
 Georgetown established, 755-56
 Harvard established, 756-58
 Mark Hopkins's birthday, 116
 Mount Holyoke founded, 759-60
 Temple University founded, 146-47
 Tuskegee Institute founded, 257
 Whitman College chartered, 148
 Yale University established, 258

Collins, Michael (astronaut)
 first manned landing on moon, 536-538

Colorado, admitted to Union, 555-56

Columbia University, opens, 532

Columbus, Christopher, departs for New World,
 559

Columbus Day, 703-4

Common Sense, 51
 Thomas Paine's birthday, 98

composers. *See* music and musicians

Doolittle, "Jimmy"
    bombing raid on Japan, 291-92
Douglas, Stephen A., 275-76
Douglass, Frederick, birthday, 140
Dow, Neal, birthday, 221-22
Dred Scott decision, 213
dueling, 265
Dunmore, John Murray, Lord
    Battle of Great Bridge, Va., 819-20
Dylan, Bob, birthday, 385-86

Eakins, Thomas, birthday, 544-45
Earth Day, 223-24
earthquakes
    Alaska, 236-37
    Charleston, S.C., 618
    New Madrid, Mo., 834
    San Francisco earthquake and fire, 291
Easter, 238-40
    Ash Wednesday, 130-31
    egg-rolling contests, 242-43
    Good Friday, 237
    Holy or Maundy Thursday, 235-36
    Holy Saturday, 238
    Monday, 242-43
    Palm Sunday, 225-26
Eastern Orthodox churches
    Easter, 239
    Palm Sunday, 226
    Russian Orthodox Christmas, 35
economics
    Crash of 1929, 737
    Federal Reserve established, 849-50
    Milton Friedman's birthday, 553
    John Kenneth Galbraith's birthday, 711
    International Monetary Fund, 493
    Panic of 1873, 663-64
        See also
        bankers and banking
        gold standard
        Great Depression
Eddy, Mary Baker, birthday, 528-29
Edison, Thomas
    birthday, 131-32
    electric light bulb perfected, 724-25
education
    George Bancroft's birthday, 686-87
    Mark Hopkins's birthday, 115
    Horace Mann's birthday, 340-41
        See also
        colleges and universities
        deaf, education for
        women's education

Eells, Cushing, birthday, 147-48
egg-rolling contests, at Easter, 242-43
Eighteenth Amendment, ratified, 64-65
Einstein, Albert
    birthday, 199-200
    U.S. uses first atomic bomb against Japan,
      564-65
Eisenhower, Dwight D.
    birthday, 706-9
    D Day and, 423-24
    Adlai Stevenson and, 117-18
Election Day, 752
elections
    Twelfth Amendment proclaimed ratified,
      671-73
    Twenty-fourth Amendment ratified, 82-83
    presidential (1824), deadlocked, 805-6
Eleventh Amendment, declared ratified, 37-38
Eliot, John, baptized, 561-62
Ellsberg, Daniel, "Pentagon Papers" case
    decided, 489
Ellsworth, Oliver, birthday, 326-28
Emancipation Proclamation, 6-8
Emerson, Ralph Waldo, birthday, 387-89
environmental conservation
    Arbor Day, 303-4
    Rachel Carson's birthday, 392-93
    Earth Day, 223-24
    Grand Canyon National Park established,
      164-65
    John Muir's birthday, 302
    John Wesley Powell and, 230
    Rural Life Sunday (Soil Stewardship
      Sunday), 339-40
epidemics, influenza strikes U.S., 194
Epiphany, feast of, 28-29
Epiphany Eve, 23
Episcopalians
    Samuel Seabury appointed first Protestant
      bishop in U.S., 770-71
Erie Canal, opens, 731-32
Erikson, Leif, 698
evangelists
    St. John, feast of, 858-59
    St. Luke, feast of, 718
    St. Mark, feast of, 314
Everglades, becomes national park, 813-14
explorers and exploration.
    Balboa discovers the Pacific, 670-71
    Richard E. Byrd's birthday, 729-31
    Columbus Day, 703-4
    Columbus departs for New World, 559

flags and flag observances
> first national flag, 8, 445
> Flag Act of 1818, 256
> Flag Day, 444-47
> Pledge of Allegiance, first use, 704

Floralia, 247

Florida
> admitted to Union, 181-82
> ceded to U.S., 531
> Everglades becomes national park, 813-14
> Gasparilla Festival, 127-28
> Ponce de León claims, for Spain, 263-65
> Purchase Treaty, signed, 158
> Salvador Dali Museum opens in St. Petersburg, 189

flower festivals
> Lei Day, 337
> National Cherry Blossom Festival, 262
> Portland Rose festival, 421-22
> Puyallup Valley Daffodil Festival, 256
> Tournament of Roses, 12-13
> Tulip Time, 362-63
> *See also* apple blossom festivals

flu. *See* influenza

folk festivals
> Pennsylvania Dutch, 484

folk heroes
> Johnny Appleseed's birthday, 673

folk music
> Joan Baez's birthday, 48

football
> college bowl games, 12, 13
> first college game, 756
> Don Shula's birthday, 22-23
> Tournament of Roses, 12-13

Ford, Gerald R., birthday, 524-26

Ford, Henry
> birthday, 552-53
> institutes $5/day minimum wage, 25

Ford, John, birthday, 107

Fordicidia, 246

Forefathers' Day, 843-44

Forrest, Edwin, birthday, 193

Foster, Stephen, Memorial Day, 58-59

"Four Freedoms," enunciated, 30-31

Four Power Treaty, 768

Fourteen Points
> Woodrow Wilson's birthday, 865-66

Fourteenth Amendment, proclaimed ratified, 548-49

Fourth of July, 500-503

France
> adopts Declaration of the Rights of Man, 609

> recognizes the United States, 122-23

Francis Ferdinand, Archduke, assassinated, 484-85

Franklin, Benjamin
> Albany Congress convenes, 459-60
> birthday, 65-66
> Constitution ratified, 465-66

free speech, limited by "clear and present danger," 179-80

Freedmen's Bureau, 862-63

freedom of the press. *See* press, freedom of

Free-Soil Party, organized, 574-75

Frémont, John C., 33, 57, 95, 134, 307, 362, 508-10, 542, 555, 624, 636, 688, 743

French and Indian War
> Albany Congress convenes, 458-60
> Monongahela, Battle of, 513-15
> George Washington and, 155-56
> Pontiac, Ottawa chieftain, 298

Friedan, Betty, birthday, 115

Friedman, Milton, birthday, 553

Frost, Robert, birthday, 232-34

Fugitive Slave Laws, first, 138

Fuller, Melville W., birthday, 132-33

Fulton, Robert, steamboat sails, 591-92

Fundamentalism
> William Jennings Bryan and, 218, 515-16

fur trade
> John Jacob Astor's birthday, 529-30

Gable, Clark, birthday, 107-8

Gadsden Purchase, 867-68

Galbraith, John Kenneth, birthday, 711

Gallaudet, Thomas H., starts the first school for deaf, 285

Galveston hurricane of 1900, 634-35

Garfield, James A.
> assassinated, 495-97
> birthday, 780-81

Garnier, Charles, 718, 720-21

Garvey, Marcus, birthday, 592-93

Gasparilla Festival, 127-28

Gaspee (ship)
> Rhode Island Independence Day, 341

Gates, Bill, birthday, 736-37

George, St., feast of, 307-8

Georgia
> founding of the colony, 137
> James Oglethorpe's birthday, 845-46
> ratifies U.S. Constitution, 14-15

Gershwin, George, birthday, 674

Gettysburg, Battle of, 492-93

Gettyburg Address, 778-80

Mississippi River
La Salle reaches mouth of, 267-69
Jacques Marquette's birthday, 415-17
Missouri
admitted to Union, 579-82
New Madrid earthquake, 834
Missouri Compromise, 275
Henry Clay and, 279
mistletoe, 853
Moby-Dick (Herman Melville), 556-57
Mohawk Indians
North American Martyrs, 719-20
Mondale, Walter, birthday, 25-26
Monongahela, Battle of, 513-15
Monroe, James, birthday, 323-24
Monroe Doctrine, 324
promulgated, 806-7
Montana
admitted to Union, 762
becomes a territory, 390-91
Montgomery, Fort
British capture Forts Clinton and
Montgomery, 693-94
Montgomery bus boycott, 73, 806
month names, derivation, 2
Moody, Dwight L., birthday, 118
moon landings
Apollo 12 is launched, 771
first manned, 536-38
Morgan, J.P., birthday, 288-89
Mormon Church
formally organized, 260-61
Joseph Smith Jr.'s birthday, 847-49
Pioneer Day, 542-43
Mormon Tabernacle Choir, gives first
performance, 602
Morris, Esther Hobart
Wyoming passes first law giving women right
to vote, 824-25
Morrison, Jim, death of, 500
Morse, Samuel F. B., opens first U.S. telegraph
line, 386-87
Morton, Julius Sterling
Arbor Day, 303-4
Moscow Conference, 739-41
Mother's Day, 353-54
Mott, Lucretia Coffin
birthday, 17-18
First Women's Rights Convention, 534-35
Mound Builders, 460, 750, 822-23, 825, 829, 859
Mount Holyoke College, founding of, 759-60
movies. *See* actors and actresses; film directors
and producers

Muhammad, Elijah, birthday, 696
Muhlenberg, Frederick Augustus, 248
Muir, John, birthday, 302
Murrow, Edward R., birthday, 313-14
music and musicians
Joan Baez's birthday, 48
"Battle Hymn of the Republic" (song), 109-
10
Robert Burns's birthday, 86-87
Stephen Foster Memorial Day, 58-59
George Gershwin's birthday, 674
Victor Herbert's birthday, 108-9
Francis Scott Key's birthday, 557
Florence Mills's birthday, 88
See also rock-and-roll music
Muslim holidays
Ramadan, 870-71
My Lai massacre, 209

Nagasaki (Japan)
atomic bombing of, official report, 486-88
U.S. uses first atomic bomb against Japan,
565
NASA, 94, 690
Apollo 12 mission to the moon is launched,
771
Challenger explodes, 94
first evidence of extraterrestrial life
announced, 566-68
first Mars probe, 600
John Glenn orbits the Earth, 151-52
Pioneer 10 launched; first probe to leave the
solar system, 179
Nation of Islam
Malcolm X's birthday, 374-75
Elijah Muhammad's birthday, 696
national anthem
Francis Scott Key's birthday, 557
"Star Spangled Banner," 641-42
National Association for the Advancement for
Colored People (NAACP)
Thurgood Marshall's birthday, 494
National Aviation Day, 598
National Bank Act, 164
National Cherry Blossom Festival, 262
National Industrial Recovery Act (NIRA), 453
National Maritime Day, 380-81
national monuments and parks
Statue of Liberty dedicated, 736
Grand Canyon National Park, 164-65
See also historic sites and monuments
National Recovery Administration (NRA),
Clarence Darrow and, 290-91

Penn, William, 431
  birthday, 709-10
Pennsylvania
  Liberty Bell hung in Independence Hall, 431
  nuclear accident at Three Mile Island, 237-38
  ratifies U.S. Constitution, 827-28
Pennsylvania, University of
  first medical school in U.S., 339
Pennsylvania Dutch folk festival, 484
"Pentagon Papers" case, decided, 489
Pentecost, 370-72
Perot, H. Ross, birthday, 480-81
Perry, Oliver Hazard, birthday, 602-3
Pershing, John J., birthday, 643
Persian Gulf War
  Operation Desert Storm begins, 63-64
  U.N. approves international coalition for Operation Desert Storm, 801-2
Peter, St., and St. Paul, feasts of, 488-89
Petersburg, Va., siege of, 433-34
Philadelphia, Penn.
  Independence Day, 500-503
  Liberty Bell hung in Independence Hall, 431
Philadelphia, College of
  first medical school in U.S., 339
Philippine Independence Day, 441-43
Philippines
  Battle of Leyte Gulf, 163, 727
  Battle of Manila Bay, 336-37
  Douglas MacArthur returns to, 722-24
  Philippine Independence Day, 441-43
phonograph
  Thomas Alva Edison's birthday, 131-32
photography
  Robert Mapplethorpe's birthday, 753
Pierce, Franklin, birthday, 789-90
Pilgrims
  death of William Bradford, 375-76
  Forefathers' Day, 843-44
  John Alden Day, 557-58
  Thanksgiving Day, 795
Pioneer 10, launched, 179
Playboy magazine, Hugh Hefner's birthday, 269
Pledge of Allegiance, first use, 704
Plessy v. Ferguson (court case), 373
Pluto (planet), discovery announced, 199
Plymouth colony
  death of William Bradford, 375-76
  Forefathers' Day, 843-44
  formation of New England Confederation, 376-77
  John Alden Day, 557-58

  Thanksgiving Day, 795
Pocahontas,
  John Smith assumes Jamestown Council presidency, 638-39
Poe, Edgar Allan, birthday, 71-72
poetry
  American Poet Laureate established, 841-42
  W.H. Auden's birthday, 112
  Robert Burns's birthday, 86-87
  Emily Dickinson's birthday, 821
  Robert Frost's birthday, 232-34
  Oliver Wendell Holmes's birthday, 615-16
  Henry Wadsworth Longfellow's birthday, 166
  James Russell Lowell's birthday, 157-58
  Edgar Allan Poe's birthday, 71-72
  James Whitcomb Riley's birthday, 694-96
  Carl Sandburg's birthday, 27-28
  William Shakespeare's birthday, 308-9
  John Greenleaf Whittier's birthday, 836-37
  Walt Whitman's birthday, 406-7
Poland, 1939 invasion of, 620
political leaders and figures
  James G. Blaine's birthday, 105
  John Breckinridge's birthday, 79
  William Jennings Bryan:
    birthday, 217-18
    Scopes "Monkey Trial" and, 515-16
  Aaron Burr's birthday, 120-21
  John C. Calhoun's birthday, 214-15
  Simon Cameron's birthday, 190-91
  Henry Clay's birthday, 278-80
  Robert Dole's birthday, 540
  Stephen A. Douglas, 275-76
  Newt Gingrich's birthday, 453-54
  Barry Goldwater's birthday, 9-10
  Alexander Hamilton's birthday, 52-54
  Hubert Humphrey's birthday, 393-94
  Jesse Jackson's birthday, 697
  Robert F. Kennedy's birthday, 781
  Robert R. Livingston's birthday, 797-98
  George McGovern's birthday, 535-36
  Walter Mondale's birthday, 25-26
  Tip O'Neill's birthday, 820
  H. Ross Perot's birthday, 480-81
  John Randolph's birthday, 417-18
  Sam Rayburn's birthday, 26-27
  Thomas B. Reed's birthday, 717-18
  Elihu Root's birthday, 147
  John Rutledge's death, 532-33
  Adlai Stevenson's birthday, 117-18
  Charles Sumner's birthday, 31-32
  George C. Wallace's birthday, 607

Daniel Webster's birthday, 66-67
    See also
    Franklin, Benjamin
    Frémont, John C.
    presidents and presidency
Polk, James K.
    birthday, 748
    Oregon Treaty ratified, 451-52
Ponce de León, Juan, claims Florida for Spain, 263-65
Pontiac (Ottawa chieftain), death of, 298
pony penning, on Chincoteague Island, 550-51
Portland Rose Festival, 421-22
Potsdam Declaration
    U.S. uses first atomic bomb against Japan, 565
Powell, John Wesley, birthday, 229-30
power blackout, Great Northeast Power Failure, 762-63
Presentation of Our Lord, feast of, 111-12
Presidential Succession Act of 1947, 534
presidents and presidency
    birthdays:
        John Adams, 738-39
        John Quincy Adams, 520-21
        Chester A. Arthur, 690-91
        James Buchanan, 305-7
        George Bush, 439-41
        Jimmy Carter, 680-82
        Grover Cleveland, 215-17
        William Jefferson Clinton, 595-97
        Calvin Coolidge, 503-4
        Dwight David Eisenhower, 706-9
        Millard Fillmore, 32-33
        Gerald R. Ford, 524-26
        James A. Garfield, 780-81
        Ulysses S. Grant, 319-22
        Warren G. Harding, 746-47
        Benjamin Harrison, 598-600
        William Henry Harrison, 126-27
        Rutherford B. Hayes, 688-89
        Herbert Hoover, 576-78
        Andrew Jackson, 201-3
        Thomas Jefferson, 280-82
        Andrew Johnson, 860-64
        Lyndon B. Johnson, 610-13
        John F. Kennedy, 396-400
        Abraham Lincoln, 134-36
        James Madison, 206-7
        William McKinley, 97-98
        James Monroe, 323-24
        Richard M. Nixon, 42-48
        Franklin Pierce, 789-90

        James K. Polk, 748
        Ronald Reagan, 119-20
        Franklin D. Roosevelt, 100-103
        Theodore Roosevelt, 733-36
        William Howard Taft, 648-49
        Zachary Taylor, 790-92
        Harry S. Truman, 348-52
        John Tyler, 240-41
        Martin Van Buren, 812-13
        George Washington, 155-57
        Woodrow Wilson, 864-67
    First Ladies:
        Hillary Rodham Clinton, 407-9, 732-33
        Dolley Madison, 377-78
        Eleanor Roosevelt's birthday, 700-702
    first veto, 258
    Inauguration Day, 76-77
    presidential elections of 1824 deadlocked, 805-6
    Succession Act of 1947, 534
    Twenty-fifth Amendment ratified, 129-30
    Twenty-second Amendment ratified, 166-67
        See also names of individual presidents.
Presidents' Day, 149
Presley, Elvis, birthday, 38-39
press, freedom of
    John Peter Zenger acquitted, 560-61
    "Pentagon Papers" case decided, 489
    Supreme Court expands, 192-93
Prince Kuhio Day, 236
Princeton, Battle of, 17
Proclamation of Rebellion, Great Britain issues, 603-4
Prohibition
    Eighteenth Amendment ratified, 64-65
    Twenty-first Amendment ratified, 811-12
Prosser, Gabriel
    slave revolt, 617-18
psychology
    B.F. Skinner's birthday, 221
public education
    Horace Mann's birthday, 340-41
Puerto Rican Constitution Day, 543-44
Pulaski, Casimir, birthday, 184-85
Puritans
    John Winthrop's birthday, 56
    Roger Williams arrives in America, 116-17
        See also Pilgrims
Puyallup Valley Daffodil Festival, 256

Queenston Heights, Battle of, 706

race car events
  Indianapolis 500, 389-90
radio
  commercial broadcasting begins, 614
  Edward R. Murrow's birthday, 313-14
  Tokyo Rose is convicted of treason, 677-78
  Wolfman Jack's birthday, 79
railroads
  first transcontinental, 354-55
  Cornelius Vanderbilt's birthday, 391-92
Ramadan, 870-71
Randolph, John
  birthday, 417-18
  fights duel with Henry Clay, 265
Rauh, Joseph, birthday, 19
Rayburn, Sam, birthday, 26-27
Reagan, Ronald, birthday, 119-20
reaper
  Hussey's, first exhibited, 498
  Cyrus McCormick's birthday, 145-46
Reconstruction era
  Andrew Johnson's birthday, 861-63
Reed, Thomas B., birthday, 717-18
Rehnquist, William, birthday, 682-83
relativity, theory of
  Albert Einstein's birthday, 199-200
religion and church history
  Lyman Abbott's birthday, 838-39
  Henry Ward Beecher's birthday, 471-72
  John Carroll appointed first Roman Catholic
    bishop in U.S., 755-56
  Russell H. Conwell's birthday, 146-47
  Mary Baker Eddy's birthday, 528-29
  Cushing Eells's birthday, 147-48
  James Cardinal Gibbons's birthday, 541-42
  L. Ron Hubbard's birthday, 198
  Ann Lee's birthday, 171-72
  Lutheran Church in America:
    merger completed, 109
    organized, 485
  Methodist Church:
    merger becomes effective, 355-56
    United Methodist Church formed, 309
  Dwight L. Moody's birthday, 118
  Mormon Church:
    formally organized, 260-61
    Pioneer Day, 542-43
    Joseph Smith Jr.'s birthday, 847-49
  Salvation Army Founder's Day, 269-71
  Samuel Seabury appointed first Protestant
    bishop in U.S., 770-71
  United Church of Christ formed, 478
  United Presbyterian Church formed, 395-96

U.S. establishes diplomatic relations with
    Vatican, 51-52
  Roger Williams arrives in America, 116-17
  John Winthrop's birthday, 56
religious freedom
  Forefathers' Day, 843-44
religious holidays and holy days
  All Saints Day, 745-46
  Ascension Day, 346-47
  Ash Wednesday, 130-31
  Candlemas, or Feast of the Presentation of
    Our Lord, 111-12
  Christmas, 851-54
  Circumcision, Feast of, 3
  Easter, 238-40
  Epiphany Eve, 23
  Epiphany, 28-29
  Fast Day in New Hampshire, 322-23
  Hanukkah, 846-47
  Holy Innocents, Feast of, 860
  Immaculate Conception of Mary, 818
  Kwanzaa begins, 857
  Mardi Gras, or Shrove Tuesday, 128-29
  Passover (Pesach), 299-300
  Pentecost, 370-72
  Ramadan, 870-71
  Rosh Hashanah, 683
  Rural Life Sunday (Soil Stewardship
    Sunday), 339-40
  Russian Orthodox Christmas, 35
  Shavuot, 371, 435
  Sukkot, 710-11
  Tishah B'Av, 582
  Yom Kippur, 699
    See also names of individual saints
Republican Party, founded, 508-9
retailing
  Marshall Field's birthday, 594-95
Reuther, Walter, birthday, 620-21
Revere, Paul, birthday, 13-14
Reynolds (R.J.) Tobacco Company, abandons
  "smokeless" cigarette project, 170
Rhode Island
  John Clarke's birthday, 696-97
  Independence Day, 341-42
  ratifies U.S. Constitution, 401-3
  Roger Williams arrives in America, 116-17
Rhode Island colony
  acts to prohibit perpetual slavery, 373-74
right to counsel, Supreme Court expands, 217
Rights of Man (Thomas Paine), 98-99
Riley, James Whitcomb, birthday, 694-96
Robinson, Jackie, birthday, 103-4

Robinson, John
    Forefathers' Day, 843-44
rock-and-roll music
    Beatles arrive in the U.S., 124-25
    Kurt Cobain, death of, 265-66
    Bob Dylan's birthday, 385-86
    Buddy Holly killed in plane crash, 114
    Madonna's birthday, 590
    Jim Morrison, death of, 500
    Elvis Presley's birthday, 38-39
    Woodstock begins, 587-88
Rockefeller, John D., Sr., birthday, 510-11
rocket science
    Robert Goddard's birthday, 692-93
    Wernher Von Braun's birthday, 227
Roe v. *Wade* decision, 79-80
Rogation Sunday, 339
Rogers, Will, birthday, 752-53
Roman Catholic Church, in North America
    Frances Cabrini, St., birthday, 526-27
    John Carroll appointed first Roman Catholic
        bishop in U.S., 755-56
    James Cardinal Gibbons's birthday, 541-42
    Isaac Jogues, St., and companions, feast of,
        718-21
    Jacques Marquette's birthday, 415-17
    John Cardinal Neumann, St., feast of, 23-24
    Elizabeth Ann Seton, St., feast of, 19-21
    U.S. establishes relations with Vatican, 51-52
Roosevelt, Eleanor, birthday, 700-702
Roosevelt, Franklin D.
    birthday, 100-103
    "fireside chats," 614
    gold clause repealed, 421
    Hundred Days, 452-53
    Lend-Lease Agreement, 158-59, 587
    orders Japanese American internment, 150
    Eleanor Roosevelt's birthday, 700-2
    Teheran Conference, 798-99
    U.S. enters World War II, 818
Roosevelt, Theodore, 34, 165, 302
    birthday, 733-36
Root, Elihu, birthday, 147
Roots (Alex Haley), 582
Rose Bowl, 13
Rosh Hashanah, 683
Rough Riders, 301, 302, 734
Rural Life Sunday, 339-40
Russian Orthodox Christmas, 35
Rutledge, John, death of, 532-33

Sacagawea
    Lewis and Clark expedition completed, 668

Saigon, fall of, 328-29
saints. *See names of individual saints*
Salvador Dali Museum, opens in Florida, 189
Salvation Army Founder's Day, 269-71
San Francisco earthquake and fire (1906), 291
San Ildefonso, treaty of, 683-84
San Jacinto, Battle of, 300-1
San Juan Hill
    Theodore Roosevelt's birthday, 734
Sandburg, Carl, birthday, 27-28
Sanger, Margaret, birthday, 645-46
Santa Anna, Antonio López
    Battle of San Jacinto, 300-1
    fall of the Alamo, 188-89
Santa Claus, 815
    Christmas Eve, 850-51
Santa Fe Fiesta, 624-26
Saturnalia, 804-5
Savannah (ship)
    National Maritime Day, 380-81
Scandinavian holidays
    Leif Erikson Day, 698
    Norwegian Constitution Day, 372
    Walpurgis Night or Spring Festival, 332
school desegregation
    Civil Rights Act of 1964, 498
    Supreme Court orders, 368-70
science and scientists
    Louis Agassiz's birthday, 394-95
    Rachel Carson's birthday, 392-93
    Albert Einstein's birthday, 199-200
    Robert Goddard's birthday, 692-93
    Asa Gray's birthday, 777-78
    Linus Pauling's birthday, 169-70
    Pluto (planet) discovered, 199
    Scopes "Monkey Trial" begins, 515-16
    B. F. Skinner's birthday, 221
    Edward Teller's birthday, 60-61
        See also
        computers
        inventors and inventions
        medicine
        naturalists
Scientology, Church of
    L. Ron Hubbard's birthday, 198
Scopes "Monkey Trial"
    begins, 515-16
    William Jennings Bryan and, 218, 515-16
    Clarence Darrow and, 290, 515-16

Tokyo Rose is convicted of treason, 677-78
Harry S. Truman's birthday, 349-50
U.S. enters, 818
U.S. troops land in North Africa, 760-62
U.S. uses first atomic bomb against Japan,
  564-65
Victory in Europe (V-E) Day, 347
Victory over Japan (VJ) Day, 585-86
World's Championship Sled Dog Races, 138
Wounded Knee, massacre at, 867
Wright, Frank Lloyd, birthday, 431-33
Wright brothers, first flight, 834-35
writers. *See* fiction and literature; poetry
Wyoming
  admitted to Union, 519-20
  passes first law giving women right to vote,
    824-25

XYZ affair, 253

Yale, Elihu, birthday, 258
Yale University, 258
Yalta Conference, United Nations and, 728-29
Yeltsin, Boris, 855
YMCA, founded, 426-27
Yom Kippur, 699
Yorktown, Va., British surrender at, 722
Young, Brigham, 542-43, 849
YWCA, 427

Zenger, John Peter, acquitted, 560-61
Zimmerman Note, 260